W9-AHF-912

International Dictionary of
MODERN DANCE

International Dictionary of
MODERN DANCE

WITH A PREFACE BY
DON McDONAGH

EDITOR
TARYN BENBOW-PFALZGRAF

CONTRIBUTING EDITOR
GLYNIS BENBOW-NIEMIER

ST. JAMES PRESS

AN IMPRINT OF GALE

DETROIT • NEW YORK • LONDON

Taryn Benbow-Pfalzgraf, *Editor*
Glynis Benbow-Niemier, *Contributing Editor*

Joann Cerrito, *Project Coordinator*

Laura Standley Berger, Dave Collins, Nicolet V. Elert, Miranda Ferrara,
Kristin Hart, Margaret Mazurkiewicz, Michael J. Tyrkus,
St. James Press Staff

Peter M. Gareffa, *Managing Editor, St. James Press*

Mary Beth Trimper, *Production Director*
Deborah Milliken, *Production Assistant*

Cynthia Baldwin, *Product Design Manager*
Pamela A. E. Galbreath, *Art Director*
Pamela A. Reed, *Photography Coordinator*
Randy Bassett, *Image Database Supervisor*
Robert Duncan, Mike Logusz, *Imaging Specialists*

While every effort has been made to ensure the reliability of the information presented in this publication, St. James Press does not guarantee the accuracy of the data contained herein. St. James Press accepts no payment for listing; and inclusion of any organization, agency, institution, publication, service, or individual does not imply endorsement of the editors or publisher.

Errors brought to the attention of the publisher and verified to the satisfaction of the publisher will be corrected in future editions.

This publication is a creative work fully protected by all applicable copyright laws, as well as by misappropriation, trade secret, unfair competition, and other applicable laws. The authors and editors of this work have added value to the underlying factual material herein through one or more of the following: unique and original selection, coordination, expression, arrangement, and classification of the information.

All rights to this publication will be vigorously defended.

Copyright © 1998
St. James Press
835 Penobscot Building
Detroit, MI 48226

All rights reserved including the right of reproduction in whole or in part in any form.

Benbow-Pfalzgraf, Taryn.
    International dictionary of modern dance / Taryn Benbow-Pfalzgraf.
        p.   cm.
    Includes bibliographical references and index.
    ISBN 1-55862-359-0 (alk. paper)
    1. Modern dance--Dictionaries.   I. Title
GV1585.B46 1998
792.8′ 03--dc21   98-9853
                                                                        CIP

Printed in the United States of America

Cover photograph: Joyce Herring in *Lamentation*, © Johan Elbers.

St. James Press is an imprint of Gale

10 9 8 7 6 5 4 3 2

CONTENTS

PREFACE

Unlike the popular forms of social or folk dance and court-derived ballet, serious concert dance outside these traditions had no existence or identifying name prior to the last decades of 19th century. The works appeared in the popular theater as part of variety entertainment; though not sharing a common technique they were identifiable by their serious, artistic intent. They featured expressive movement tailored by and for performance by the individual artists according to their creative desires. A systematized theory of expressive, dramatic movement had been taught by François Delsarte in France and spread throughout Europe by Émile Jaques-Dalcroze in Switzerland and Genevieve Stebbins and Steele Mackaye in the United States. Because its principles applied equally to the different performing arts of opera, drama, mime, and dance it had significant influence among the nascent dancers and choreographers.

Toward the end of the 19th century dedicated individuals like Loie Fuller, Ruth St. Denis, Isadora Duncan, and Ted Shawn (all in the United States), Rudolf Laban (Hungary), Maud Allan (Canada), Margaret Morris (England), Aleksander Sakharoff (Russia), Grete Wiesenthal (Austria), and Sada Yacco (Japan) were performing regularly. For want of a better name, "classic" dance was affixed to the work of those artists who patterned their works on idealized Greek or Roman models. Others were simply called dance artists, displaying their own specialty acts.

St. Denis and Shawn came together professionally as the enthusiasm for solo female dancers waned with a public caught up in social dancing and its stellar exemplars, Irene and Vernon Castle. After participating in programs combining selected St. Denis solos and ballroom dancing by Shawn and a partner, the two were soon embarked on an ambitious project to create a large concert dance company. They first established a school in the Westlake district of Los Angeles that attracted students from around the country. St. Denis was the muse, role model, and sometime teacher of the students, while Shawn busied himself with the details of the school, teaching extensively, preparing publicity materials, and writing a book praising the artistry of St. Denis. Their company, named Denishawn, toured on the popular vaudeville circuits and was the most important serious dance company in the country. In addition to the staff in their own school, paid, licensed teachers instructed students throughout the United States in Denishawn techniques using lesson plans drawn up by Shawn.

By the second decade of the 20th century the name "modern dance" had begun to be used to describe the work of Denishawn successors, American choreographers Martha Graham, Doris Humphrey, Charles Weidman, Hanya Holm, Helen Tamiris, and Lester Horton. Central European or Expressionist dance (*Ausdruckstanz*) was the term applied to the contemporaneous creative work of choreographers in Austria, Germany, and the Scandinavian countries. These included Mary Wigman, Gret Palucca, Yvonne Georgi, Oskar Schlemmer, Kurt Jooss (all Germany), Rosalia Chladek (Austria), Harald Kreutzberg (Austria, Germany, Switzerland), and Ronny Johansson (Sweden). Nikolai Foregger (Russia) sought subject matter in the machine energy of the 20th century. In all cases schools of movement were being formed based on the individual choreographer's vocabulary of movement; these were derived from their own conception of where the movement impulse originated, and how it was to be developed logically.

In the United States, Graham, Humphrey, and Weidman rejected the aesthetic of Denishawn, terming it "Dancing Gods and Goddesses," and opted for personal or social themes of more immediate import to the individual, performed in costuming closer to contemporary dress than the exotic gowns worn by earlier performers. While differing greatly in the expression of their artistic convictions, the choreographers of this generation developed movement styles that were percussive, spare, and virtually devoid of the dramatic "silent movie" gesture that characterized the previous generation. Weighted movement was desired as they considered the floor on which they danced to be a source of strength to be courted rather than a support from which to be liberated. Their dances ordinarily retained a narrative, dramatic structure or developed the expression of a mood.

Dance composition became a standard part of dance training largely under the influence of composer, conductor, and accompanist Louis Horst, whose own musical studies had routinely included composition. He codified his method in the text *Pre-Classic Dance Forms,* while Doris Humphrey outlined her own keenly analytical approach to choreography in *The Art of Making Dances.* It was this generation of dancers who brought widespread public attention to this emerging form of serious concert level dance.

One of the chief publicizing efforts was mounted each summer under the direction of Martha Hill and Mary Josephine Shelley. Starting in 1934 the Bennington College Summer School of Dance offered students the opportunity to study with the "big four": Graham, Humphrey, Weidman, and Holm. The latter had emigrated from Germany and opened a studio in New York in 1933 founded on the principles developed by Mary Wigman. In addition to technique, classes in composition, stagecraft, and music history were offered. Festival performances at the end of the six-week course featured works by resident choreographers using members of their own companies as well as enrolled students. The student body drew heavily from teachers in physical education departments around the country, and established an informal network of local sponsors for the choreographers' own company tours. Public acceptance came slowly during the 1930s but increased in the 1940s when this generation of choreographers was invited to choreograph musicals for the popular theater and present their own company seasons in more popular theatrical venues. Among the most active in this area was Tamiris, who had begun her dance career in the ballet company of the Metropolitan Opera.

On the West Coast, Lester Horton, whose initial interest in Amerind culture brought him to modern dance, had established a company and a theater devoted entirely to dance presentation in Los Angeles. He also utilized his choreographic talents in a variety of movies. Colorblind in his training of dancers, Horton had the first integrated company in the United States. He encouraged the work of Alvin Ailey, Carmen de Lavallade and Janet Collins, among others. Ailey, like Pearl Primus and Katherine Dunham before him, addressed themes of racial equality, social injustice, and religious fervor that stemmed from the black experience after forcible transplantation to the Western hemisphere. Stylistically they found the narrative structure of the post-Denishawn period most useful for their work as did later choreographers like Talley Beatty, Donald McKayle, George Faison, Eleo Pomare, Garth Fagan and Bill T. Jones.

In Germany, just as their counterparts in the United States had done, choreographers sought contemporary thematic subjects and developed innovative vocabularies of movement. Technically they pursued the sculptural understanding and use of space molded by and molding the individual. Frequently, shaping of the body lent itself to pantomimic characterization of idealized types. At other times the body was abstracted by costume and mechanical gesture to a non-human form acting purposefully in space without any specifically human traits. At the opposite end of this presentational spectrum was a school of unclad dancers who drew inspiration from the "living statues," presentations inspired by the classic Greek nude.

Rhythmic self-accompaniment was employed with an emphasis on percussive structure in solos and group works. Building upon an interest in outdoor activity, large gymnastic spectacles were designed. In virtually all cases little or no attention was paid to ballet which had been the major form of theater dance prior to the 20th century. The one notable exception was Kurt Jooss, who developed a synthesis of ballet and contemporary dance technique while omitting pointe work for the female dancer.

The accession to power of the Nazi party brought an end to Expressionist dance as the major dance force in Germany. Ballet became mandatory in education and funds for Expressionist schools and performance were terminated. By the end of World War II, its existence was obliterated with the exception of a few small studios where survivors of the prewar generation still taught.

The postwar years in the United States saw a proliferation of new companies established by dancers who had been active with the major choreographers of the previous generation. They retained their theatricality in terms of stagecraft but modified the techniques in which they had been trained. Among the most radical innovations were the serious questioning of narrative structure and the deemphasis of human passion as a motivating force in the development of a work. The most extreme of this postwar group was Merce Cunningham, a former member of the Graham company. With stories no longer dominant, attention was focused upon dance gesture and movement for itself. Settings and costumes did not have to reflect a historical time or place nor did dancers have to shape their roles to conform to dramatic characterizations. What remained was the imaginative deployment of trained dancers performing the choreographer's designs in a nonrealistic space.

Working with his musical director, composer John Cage, Cunningham further unhitched the previously dominant team of interdependent composer, designer, and dancer under the control of the choreographer. The choreographer plotted the movement and duration of the dance first, then told the composer and artist of choice the length and "climate," to use Cunningham's own word, of the piece, upon which each then worked separately. Dancers relied on counts rather than rhythmic support from scores in performance. The results were exceptional. However, Cunningham clung to modern dance tradition by continuing to use the proscenium arch stage, by commissioning new music for each new dance, by forming his company from highly trained dancers, and by using theatrically designed costumes.

Sybil Shearer and Anna Halprin, choreographers from the Humphrey-Weidman tradition, also abandoned strict chronological narrative and found inspiration for many of their dances in natural rhythms and settings. Hanya Holm's pupil Alwin Nikolais was more interested in motion than emotion and eschewed personal dramatic encounters in favor of successive images. These sequential mosaics depicted beings moving in quaintly surreal settings created by lights, slide projections, costuming, and the physically disjunctive movements of an innocently mechanical character. His dances did not have a narrative structure either, but the resultant collection of incidents had thematic coherence. Paul Taylor, another former member of the Graham company, alternated between plotless works and charming fairytale presentations that blended humor and tragedy with a knowing quasi-innocent eye. The works of this generation departed from linear logic in structuring but maintained allegiance to sound theatrical practice.

In the 1960s, choreographers disassociated themselves from all of the theatrical conventions of their predecessors and concentrated primarily upon body movement, trained or untrained. They performed indoors or out, from rooftops to street locales, almost everywhere in fact except in proscenium arch theaters. Everyday clothing was often favored as costuming as well as nudity at times. Choreographic design could emerge from game situations in which rules directed the activities of performers without the intervening hand of the choreographer. Sources as diverse as ambient sound, taped collages of sports or news broadcasts, or snatches of popular or classical music provided the aural decor. The minimalist revolution at its most extreme sought to make dances out of any human movement taken alone without theatrical or technical embellishment. This movement had its roots in the early 1960s with a course in composition taught by pianist, accompanist and composer Robert Dunn at the Cunningham studio. Reacting against the formal composition structures taught in Louis Horst's classes, Dunn made time or space assignments and accepted any compositional solution offered without criticism. He simply tried to ascertain the intent of the piece presented, and by questioning attempted to stimulate further creative thought. It was non-judgmental teaching that encouraged those taking the course to understand the logic of their own choices and explore them fully.

Among those taking Dunn's course were Yvonne Rainer, Simone Forti, Trisha Brown, Deborah Hay, Steve Paxton, and Lucinda Childs. Looking for a venue to present their work, Rainer and Paxton auditioned for the Reverend Alva Carmines, assistant pastor of the Judson Memorial Church in New York's Greenwich Village. The church had earlier offered space to painters who presented "Happenings" and proved equally accepting of dancers and choreographers. The Judson Dance Theater became a performing component of the church's community outreach program and remained so for the next decade. The choreographers attracted to this group were equally accepting of artists such as Robert Rauschenberg, Robert Morris, Robert Huot, Alex Hay, and others who wished to explore performance as a vehicle for their ideas.

The severity of the minimalists was followed in the 1970s, 1980s, and 1990s by a return to theatricality and technical rigor. It was theatricality of a bizarre and at times cartoonish nature, outrageous in its disregard for past performance pieties, and eclectic in its combinations of formal dance and athletic movement. Sex graduated from hidden agenda to overt subject in many works including those of Stephen Petronio and Martha Clarke. The spoken word, which had been a side-occurrence in the 1960s, became text in dances by Jane Comfort, Doug Elkins, and Mark Dendy. Technique was restored to an honored though not totally dominant position, and the proscenium arch stage returned to favor as a performing venue.

Modern dance in Europe received a boost after World War II with the example of touring modern dance companies from the United States. Students from Europe began to enroll in the Martha Graham school in some numbers, appearing with her company and then returning to their own countries. American modern dancers were invited to teach and help establish performing ensembles abroad that would pass into the directorial hands of indigenous dancers. The work of these companies has differed from nation to nation. French companies stress logical exposition, those in Germany imaginative theatrical dance (*Tanztheater*), and England favors dramatic narrative presentation. Companies in South and Central America vary widely in their approaches, and have picked and chosen from a variety of sources. Japan, influenced early in the 1930s by German Expressionist dance, has combined that impulse with traditional dramatic forms to develop Butoh, the slow moving, imagistic, and intensely passionate form of modern dance ritual.

Modern dance has been and continues to be taken up as a liberated form of serious dance expression in each country that has been exposed to it. The influence of the vigorous creative life of American companies broadly stimulated modern dance development throughout the world in the second half of the 20th century. This influence has encouraged choreographers to develop the movement language that speaks most directly to their own audiences. They have been encouraged to adapt and build upon the style that originally caught their creative attention and not to slavishly imitate it. Modern dance from its inception has encouraged individual expression in choice of themes and means of performance.

—Don McDonagh

EDITOR'S NOTE

This first edition of the *International Dictionary of Modern Dance* comprises more than 400 entries on all aspects of modern dance, ranging from biographical entries on dancers to essays on major movements and styles to overviews of the development of modern dance in countries around the world. Entries were selected by a distinguished international board of advisers and compiled by dancers, dance scholars, and other dance professionals. A wide variety of sources have been used to help shape this work. Don McDonagh's two tomes, *The Rise and Fall and Rise of Modern Dance* (1970), and *The Complete Guide to Modern Dance* (1976) have been invaluable tools. Jack Anderson's books, including *Choreography Observed* (1987), *Ballet and Modern Dance: A Concise History* (1992), and especially *The World of Modern Dance: Art without Boundaries* (1997) have also helped shape the direction of this book, while the editor frequently consulted Leslie Getz's *Dancers and Choreographers: A Selected Bibliography* (1995) to find information on anyone and everyone associated with dance. In addition, researchers for this project spent many hours at the Dance Collection of the New York Public Library at Lincoln Center, which contains a wealth of information on dancers past and present. Of course, no single volume could possibly encompass all of modern dance, and exigencies of time, place, and access to information have resulted in some selectivity. Nevertheless, this volume contains an unprecedented amount of information on the people, events, and features of modern dance. A chronology of notable events in the development of modern dance and a bibliography of writings on the subject enhance the usefulness of this work.

The editor would like to thank first and foremost John, Jordyn, Wylie, Foley, and Hadley. Many thanks are due as well to Don McDonagh for his enduring patience and breadth of knowledge; to Norton Owen for his help and reliability; to Mary Strow and Paula Murphy for their early enthusiasm and contributions; to Glynis Benbow-Niemier, Jocelyn Prucha, Lori Prucha, and Jordyn Pfalzgraf for their editorial efforts; and last but by no means least to Joann Cerrito, who truly made this book possible with a wonderful sense of humor and always knowing the right thing to say.

CHRONOLOGY OF MODERN DANCE

1839
François Delsarte begins teaching his principles of movement and expression.

Steele MacKaye studies with Delsarte and brings "Harmonic Gymnastics" to the United States.

1892
Loie Fuller performs her famous *Serpent Dance* at the Folies-Bergère in Paris.

Ruth St. Denis sees Genevieve Stebbins perform her Delsarte-inspired poses and movements.

1900
St. Denis and Isadora Duncan see Sada Yacco (Japanese dancer and actress) and Loie Fuller perform at the Universal Exhibition in Paris.

Isadora Duncan's first public concert in London.

1906
Maud Allan performs her controversial *The Vision of Salomé* in Vienna.

St. Denis performs *Radha* in New York.

1910
Émile Jaques-Dalcroze opens his school of eurhythmics in Hellerau, Germany.

1911
Tórtola Valencia, after success in London, premieres in Madrid and is hailed as "the muse of the poets."

1913
Premiere of Stravinsky's *La Sacre du printemps* (*The Rite of Spring*), choreographed by Nijinsky for Diaghilev's Ballets Russes.

The Speyer School, part of Columbia Teachers College, begins offering dance classes taught by Gertrude Colby.

Ted Shawn and Norma Gould become partners, performing and teaching in Los Angeles.

Mary Wigman goes to Ascona for the summer to study with Rudolf Laban; she studies and works with Laban for the next seven years.

1914
St. Denis and Ted Shawn marry, then establish Denishawn the next year in Los Angeles.

Mary Wigman makes her first public performance with *Witch Dance* and *Lento*.

1915
Michio Ito debuts in London.

Neighborhood Playhouse opens in New York City.

1916
Valeska Gert gives an outrageous performance in one of Rita Sacchetto's productions and soon becomes known for her eccentric solos.

Martha Graham attends Denishawn school in Los Angeles, where she meets Louis Horst who is accompanist for the school and company.

Margaret H'Doubler goes to New York to study dance education with Gertrude Colby and Bird Larson; begins teaching dance at the University of Wisconsin the next year.

Ronny Johansson gives first solo of her own choreography.

1918
Doris Humphrey begins dancing with Denishawn.

1919
Mary Wigman opens her school in Dresden.

Gertrude Bodenwieser makes her first solo appearance.

1920
Laban forms Tanzbuhne Laban for creating and performing experimental and abstract dances.

1921
Isadora Duncan, amidst much controversy, begins a school in the new Soviet Union.

Angna Enters becomes Michio Ito's partner.

Charles Weidman joins Denishawn and partners Martha Graham in *Xochitl*, the dance Ted Shawn choreographs specifically for Graham.

1923
Bodenwieser choreographs *Demon Machine*.

Yvonne Georgi and Harald Kreutzberg leave Wigman's company to become soloists at the Hanover Opera under the direction of Max Terpis.

1925
Denishawn tours Asia.

Gret Palucca, after studying and dancing with Wigman, opens her own school in Dresden.

Jaques-Dalcroze's Hellerau-Laxenburg School opens outside of Vienna.

1926
Martha Graham debuts her first choreography in New York.

Angna Enters, known for her dramatic character sketches, performs her first solo program.

Georgi and Kreutzberg, dancing together, begin successful annual tours of Europe and the States.

1927

The first Dancers' Congress in Magdeburg, Germany.

Kurt Jooss is appointed dance director of the Folkwang in Essen, Germany, where he begins to build a dance company.

Isadora Duncan is tragically killed in an auto accident in Nice, France.

Helen Tamiris performs her first program of choreography, including a piece called *The Queen Walks in the Garden* performed in silence.

University of Wisconsin, Madison, offers its first dance degree program.

The *New York Herald* appoints its first dance critic, former music critic Mary Watkins, who stays on for seven years.

The *New York Times* appoints its first dance critic, John Martin, who will write for the paper until 1962.

1928

Second Dancers' Congress in Essen, Germany.

Doris Humphrey and Charles Weidman, upon leaving Denishawn, form their own company.

Humphrey choreographs two important works: *Air for the G String* and *Water Study*.

Kazuo Ohno sees La Argentina perform and decides to study dance.

Loie Fuller dies.

1929

Wigman choreographs and performs one of her most well-known cycles, *Shifting Landscapes*.

1930

Third Dancers' Congress in Munich, Germany.

Mary Wigman begins the first of three successful U.S. tours.

Uday Shankar forms a dance company; he tours and performs a mix of traditional Indian and modern dance until the 1960s.

Ted Shawn's first solo tour to Europe, where he dances in Margarete Wallmann's *Orpheus Dionysos* at the Munich Congress.

José Limón begins dancing with Humphrey/Weidman Dance Company.

Martha Graham choreographs and performs the groundbreaking *Lamentation*; during the whole dance she is seated on a bench, wrapped tightly in a tube-like dress.

Anna Sokolow joins Martha Graham's company.

Pauline Koner gives her first solo performance at the Guild Theater in New York.

1931

Hanya Holm establishes a Mary Wigman School in New York.

1932

Denishawn disbands, and Ted Shawn and St. Denis pursue separate careers.

Katherine Dunham establishes a school in Chicago.

Lester Horton forms the Lester Horton Dancers in Los Angeles.

Kurt Jooss choreographs *The Green Table,* which wins the first prize at the International Choreographers Competition in Paris.

Kurt and Grace Graff, who both trained with Laban in Germany, settle in Chicago and found the Little Concert House in Hyde Park.

Workers' Dance League is founded to support left-wing dance groups, including the New Dance Group (also founded in 1932).

1933

Ted Shawn establishes his all-male dance ensemble and they perform until 1940.

Ballets Jooss leaves Germany to avoid Nazi persecution and takes up residence at Dartington Hall in England in 1934.

Gertrud Kraus choreographs and stages *The City Waits.*

John Martin publishes *The Modern Dance.*

1934

Martha Hill, a former Graham dancer, establishes the Bennington Summer School with the help of Mary Josephine Shelley; it remains open until 1942.

Louis Horst founds and edits *Dance Observer.*

The 92nd Street YMHA begins offering dance classes and provides a performing space for modern dancers.

Bella Lewitzky begins working with Lester Horton, a collaboration that lasts the next 15 years producing the "Horton technique" for teaching.

Pauline Koner, a student of Fokine, begins two years of performing in the Soviet Union; her later dance compositions are influenced by her experiences in the U.S.S.R.

Katherine Dunham forms the Chicago Negro School of Ballet and Negro Dance Group. The next year, with the help of two fellowships, Dunham goes to the Caribbean to study indigenous dance.

1935

Shawn choreographs and his Men Dancers perform *Kinetic Molpai* with music by Jess Meeker.

Gertrud Kraus leaves Austria and settles in Palestine where she teaches dance and lays the groundwork for Israeli modern dance.

Isamu Noguchi designs the set for Martha Graham's *Frontier*, the first of many designs he will do for Graham and other choreographers.

1936
An International Dance Festival is held along with the Olympics in Berlin; many dancers from Europe and the U.S. boycott the festival.

The Dance Project, part of the WPA's Federal Theatre Project, is established.

Charles Weidman's *Lynchtown* premieres in New York, performed by the Humphrey/Weidman Dance Company.

1937
Hanya Holm choreographs and presents *Trend* at the Bennington Festival, then in New York.

1938
Rudolf Laban flees Germany and finds a home in England at Dartington Hall.He soon begins work on his notation system.

1939
Hanya Holm's *Tragic Exodus* becomes first dance production televised in the United States.

Gertrud Bodenwieser settles in Sydney, Australia, after her husband dies in a concentration camp; she founds a school and brings modern dance to Down Under.

Anna Sokolow is invited to Mexico City to perform and in 1940 is asked to establish a dance group.

Waldeen von Falkenstein is invited to Mexico to perform and is asked to stay and direct the Ballet of Fine Arts (directed briefly by Sokolow). Falkenstein stays in Mexico, eventually becoming a citizen, and dedicates herself to establishing and maintaining a national dance company.

Merce Cunningham joins Martha Graham's company.

1940
Ann Hutchison, Helen Priest Rogers, and Eve Gentry found the Dance Notation Bureau in New York City.

Mary Washington Ball organizes the first summer festival at Jacob's Pillow; the following summer Alicia Markova and Anton Dolin organize the festival.

1941
Michio Ito leaves the U.S. in response to Japanese Internment and never again contributes to dance in the United States.

Sybil Shearer makes her debut as a solo performer in New York City.

1942
Edwin Denby, former dancer, replaces Mary Watkins as dance critic at the *Herald Tribune*; he remains until the end of World War II.

William Bales, Jane Dudley, and Sophie Maslow perform together for the first time; they will choreograph socially conscious works and perform together well into the 1950s.

Ted Shawn takes over as director of Jacob's Pillow Dance Festival, serving for the next 30 years.

1943
Pearl Primus premieres *Strange Fruit*, based on Lewis Allen's poem of the same name, at the 92nd Street YMHA.

1944
Doris Humphrey ends her performing career.

Charles Weidman forms his own company.

Katherine Dunham forms a touring company.

Martha Graham's *Appalachian Spring* premieres at the Library of Congress, with set design by Isamu Noguchi and music by Aaron Copland.

Glen Tetley begins studying with Hanya Holm.

1945
Merce Cunningham leaves Graham to concentrate on his own choreography with John Cage as a collaborator and advisor.

1946
José Limón forms his own company with Doris Humphrey as artistic director.

1948
The New York Public Library Dance Collection is established.

Alwin Nikolais joins the Henry Street Settlement House (formerly the Neighborhood Playhouse).

Donald McKayle performs with Sophie Maslow and Jean Erdman; he goes on to choreograph dances like *Games* (1951) and *District Storyville* (1962) out of black urban experience.

American Dance Festival at Connecticut College is established.

1949
José Limón choreographs and premieres *The Moor's Pavane* at the American Dance Festival in Connecticut.

Pauline Koner performs in Limón's *The Moor's Pavane* and forms Pauline Koner Dance Consort.

1951
James Waring forms Dance Associates.

1952
Anna Halprin forms her experimental Dance Workshop on the grounds of her home in Mt. Tamalpais near San Francisco; many young choreographers attend these improvisational workshops including Kei Takei, Meredith Monk, and Trisha Brown.

1953
Lester Horton dies.

Merce Cunningham choreographs *Suite by Chance*, his first work incorporating chance in most of its choreographic design.

Alwin Nikolais choreographs *Masks, Props and Mobiles*, his first experiment with multimedia.

1954
Paul Taylor forms his first dance group.

José Limón's company tours South America under the auspices of the state department.

1956
Maud Allan dies.

1958
Alvin Ailey founds the Alvin Ailey American Dance Theatre.

Martha Graham choreographs and premieres *Clytemnestra* in New York.

Doris Humphrey dies.

Rudolf Laban dies.

1959
Tatsumi Hijikata, one of the founders of Butoh, choreographs and performs his controversial version of *Forbidden Colors*, Yukio Mishima's novel.

1960
Alvin Ailey choreographs *Revelations* inspired by African-American spirituals.

1962
The first performance is given by Robert Dunn's students at the Judson Memorial Church in Greenwich Village; Judson Dance Theater holds performances by experimental choreographers into the 1970s.

Glen Tetley choreographs *Pierrot Lunaire*.

1964
Paul Taylor Dance Company tours Europe.

Louis Horst dies.

1965
Twyla Tharp forms her own company.

Elizabeth Cameron Dalman founds Australia Dance Theatre.

Suzanne Musitz founds Dance Company of New South Wales.

Gus Solomons jr joins Merce Cunningham Dance Company.

1966
London School of Contemporary Dance opens, and the following year London Contemporary Dance Theatre gives its first performance under the artistic direction of Robert Cohan.

Association of Dance Companies is founded.

Helen Tamiris dies.

Tharp choreographs *Re-Moves*, a structurally intricate dance representative of her early choreographic work.

1968
Toronto Dance Theatre, founded by David Earle, Patricia Beatty, and Peter Randazzo, gives its first performance.

Ruth St. Denis dies.

Harald Kreutzberg dies.

1969
Martha Graham retires from performing.

1970
Joan Belle Meyers founds Philadelphia Dance Company (Philadanco) as an offshoot of the Philadelphia School of Dance Arts which she founded in 1960.

The dance collective Grand Union is formed by Becky Arnold, Douglas Dunn, David Gordon, Barbara Lloyd Dilley, Steve Paxton, and Yvonne Rainier.

1971
Jonathan Wolken, Moses Pendleton, and Steve Johnson found Pilobolus.

Alvin Ailey's *Cry*, choreographed for Judith Jamison, premieres.

Butoh company Dai Rakida Kan is founded by Akaji Maro with over 100 dancers.

1972
Pina Bausch becomes director of the Wuppertal Dance Theater.

Steve Paxton's piece *Magnesium* is performed by 11 male dancers at Oberlin College and is considered an important precurser to Paxton's development of contact improvisation.

José Limón dies.

Ted Shawn dies.

1973
Brooklyn Academy of Music opens Le Percq Space designed for experimental dance and theater productions.

1974
Canada's Dancemakers gives its first outdoor and theater performances.

Moming Dance and Arts Center is founded in Chicago and provides space and support for experimental dance for the next 15 years.

1975
Butoh company Sankai Juku is founded by Ushio Amagatsu.

Bill Evans forms his own dance company after spending seven years with Repertory Dance Theater, Salt Lake City.

Merce Cunningham choreographs *Westbeth*, the first of many pieces choreographed especially for and with video.

Charles Weidman dies.

Yvonne Georgi dies.

1976
Dance in America, the first-ever televised dance series, is broadcast on public television channel WNET-13.

Einstein on the Beach, a collaborative effort between Robert Wilson, Philip Glass, and Lucinda Childs premieres at Festival d'Avignon, France, and at the Metropolitan Opera in New York.

Oberlin Dance Collective (ODC), founded in 1971, moves to San Francisco to become ODC/San Francisco.

1978
Dance Umbrella annual dance festival is founded in London.

1979
Dance Company of New South Wales (Australia) is renamed Sydney Dance Company and makes its New York premiere two years later under the direction of Graeme Murphy.

1980
Momix is founded by Moses Pendleton of Pilobolus.

1981
Twyla Tharp choreographs *The Catherine Wheel*.

1983
Trisha Brown, with a score by Laurie Anderson and set designs by Robert Rauschenberg, choreographs *Set and Reset*.

1984
Jawole Willa Jo Zollar founds Urban Bush Women, the first modern dance company of African-American women.

1987
The first Canada Dance Festival is held in Ottawa.

1988
Mark Morris choreographs and premieres *L'Allegro, il pensoroso, ed il moderato* at the Royal Theatre in Brussels.

1989
Angna Enters dies.

1991
The first fringe Festival of Independent Dancers (fFIDA) is held in Toronto.

1993
Bill T. Jones choreographs and premieres the controversial *Still/Here,* a tribute to his partner, Arnie Zane, who died of AIDS, and to those who live with terminal illnesses.

Alwin Nikolais dies.

1997
Bessie Schönberg dies.

International Dictionary of
MODERN DANCE

ADVISERS

Clive Barnes
Ann Barzel
Peggy Berg
Don McDonagh
Paula Murphy
Norton Owen
Selma Odom
Mary Strow
Patricia Tarr

CONTRIBUTORS

Judith B. Alter
Andrea Amort
Carol Anderson

Jan Baart
Karen Barbour
Ann Barzel
Linda Belans
Glynis Benbow-Niemier
Sydonie Benet
Gigi Berardi
Peggy Berg
Amy Bowring
Stephen Bradshaw
Susan Broili
Diane Hubbard Burns
Ramsay Burt

Christopher Caines
Sharon Chaiklin
Sue Cheesman
Paula Citron
Kristen Thomas Clarke
Delfin Colomé
Lynne Conner
Elizabeth Cooper
Katherine Cornell
Nena Couch
Jenifer Craig
Marilyn Cristofori

Dena Davida
Thomas DeFrantz
Edwige Dioudonnat
Janette Goff Dixon
Melanye White Dixon
Anita Donaldson

Teren Damato Ellison
Joan L. Erdman

Rita Felciano

Iris Garland
Janine Gastineau
Judith Gelernter
Jens Giersdorf
RoseLee Goldberg

Bengt Häger
Sophie Hansen
Holly Parke Harris
Joanna G. Harris
Kristin M. Harris
Dawn Hathaway
Linde Howe-Beck
J. Hussie-Taylor
Donald Hutera

Judith Brin Ingber

George Jackson
Naomi Jackson
Chris Jones
Ragna Sara Jónsdóttir
Susan Jordan

Maura Keefe
Julie A. Kerr-Berry
Naseem Khan
Kim Kyoung-ae
Kim Tae-won
Kim Young-Tae
Helma Klooss
Judson Knight
Leslie Hansen Kopp

Gia Kourlas
Rebekah J. Kowal
Anthea Kraut
Laura Kumin
Sandra Kurtz

Lee Jong-ho
Lee Soon-yeol
Darcy Lewis
Julinda Lewis-Ferguson
Yatin C. Lin
Gregg Lizenbery
Sondra Lomax
Barbara Long

Daryl F. Mallett
Michelle Man
Lisa Anderson Mann
Giora Manor
Fiona Marcotty
Murielle Mathieu
Lodi McClellan
Donald McManus
Judi Miller
Christine Miner Minderovic
Marcelo Isse Moyano
Ann Murphy
Paula Murphy

Suzanne Neumayer

Kate O'Neill
Ou Jian-ping
Norton Owen

Kaija Pepper
Guillermo Perez
Wendy Perron
Dolores Ponce Gutiérrez
Barbejoy A. Ponzio
Jennifer Predock-Linnell
Valerie Preston-Dunlop
Stacey Prickett
Jane Pritchard

Karen Raugust
Carrie Rohman
Douglas Rosenberg
Cynthia Roses-Thema
Sanjoy Roy
Sarah Rubidge
Adriane Ruggiero

Lisa Jo Sagolla
Siobhán Scarry
Louis Scheeder
Katja Schneider
Norbert Servos
Rhonda Shary
Adrienne Sichel
Herbert M. Simpson
Michael Wade Simpson
Deborah Smith
Janet Mansfield Soares
Diana Stanton
Patricia Stöckemann
Mary Strow
Philip Szporer

Iro Valaskakis Tembeck
Kristen Thomas-Clarke
Karl Toepfer
Margarita Tortajada Quiroz

Sako Ueno

Ann Vachon
Valerie Vogrin

Larry Warren
Jill Waterman
Martha Ullman West
Raewyn White
Leland Windreich
Charles Humphrey Woodford
Lisa A. Wroble

Karen Zimmerman

LIST OF ENTRIES

Kenneth King
Demetrius Klein
Koldemama Dance Company
Chris Komar
Pauline Koner
Korea Overview
Gertrud Kraus
Harald Kreutzberg

La Malinche
Rudolf Laban
Lamentation
Phyllis Lamhut
Rachel Lampert
Pearl Lang
Josefina Lavalle
Sigurd Leeder
Leine & Roebana
Ralph Lemon
Liz Lerman
Bella Lewitzky
Li Chiao-Ping
Liat Dror & Nir Ben-Gal
Limbs Dance Company
José Limón
Lin Hwai-min
Susanne Linke
Gertrude Lippincott
Katherine Litz
Edouard Lock
London Contemporary Dance Theatre
Murray Louis
William Louther
Lar Lubovitch
Lynchtown

Iris Mabry
Terrill Maguire
Mal Pelo
Sara Shelton Mann
Vincent Sekwati Mantsoe
Judith Marcuse
Maguy Marin
Susan Marshall
Jennifer Mascall
Sophie Maslow
Helen McGehee
Donald McKayle
Nancy Meehan
Annelise Mertz
Meryl Tankard Australian Dance
 Theatre
Barbara Mettler
Mexico Overview
Bebe Miller
Modern Dance and Classical Ballet
MoMing Dance & Arts Center
Momix
Meredith Monk
Elisa Monte
Claudia Moore

Jack Moore
The Moor's Pavane
Mark Morris
Robert Morris
Moving into Dance Performance Company
Jennifer Muller
Barton Mumaw
Graeme Murphy
Music for Modern Dance

Josef Nadj
Daniel Nagrin
Nam Jeong-ho
Phoebe Neville
New Dance Group
New Dance Trilogy: Theatre Piece, With My Red Fires,
 and New Dance
New Zealand Overview
Lloyd Newson
Nightwandering
Alwin Nikolais
92nd Street YM-YWHA
Isamu Noguchi
Robert North
Cynthia Novack
Lisa Nowak

ODC/San Francisco
May O'Donnell
Ramón Oller

Ruth Page
Gret Palucca
Park Myung-sook
David Parsons
Steve Paxton
Moses Pendleton
Rudy Perez
Wendy Perron
Stephen Petronio
Philadanco
Photography and Modern Dance
Pilobolus Dance Theater
The Place
Eleo Pomare
Kathryn Posin
Postmodern Dance
Angelin Preljocaj
Preservation of Modern Dance
Primitive Mysteries
Pearl Primus
Provisional Danza
Peter Pucci
Neta Pulvermacher

Linda Rabin
Yvonne Rainer
Rambert Dance Company
Peter Randazzo
Robert Rauschenberg
Don Redlich

AHN Ae-soon

Korean dancer and choreographer

Born: 30 April 1960 in Seoul. **Education:** Graduated from the undergraduate and graduate dance departments at Ewha Women's University; studied dance with Yook Wan-soon. **Career:** Formed Modern Dance Group Nesaram, 1983; choreographed *Guys and Dolls,* the first musical ever to be produced in Korea; performed with Yook Wan-soon's company during an international tour, 1983; danced with the Korean Contemporary Dance Company; participated in Japan's International Dance Festival, 1984; performed solo works; choreographed for the Korean Modern Dance Company, 1985; studied at Alvin Ailey school, PERI Dance School, Dance Space, American Dance Festival, 1991; subsequently attempted to combine American modern dance with certain elements of Asian life; first Korean dance artist ever to perform in Rencontres Choreographiques Internationales de Seine-Denis with Ssit Kim, 1992. **Awards:** Grand Prize, Seoul International Dance Festival, for *Encounter,* 1991; Grand Prize, Korean Choreographer's Competition, for *Empty Space,*1994; Best Dancer Award at Recontres Choreographiques Internationales de Seine-Denis, 1994; selected as Artist of the Month sponsored by Munwha Broadcasting Coporation (MBC) and Samsung, 1997; best musical choreography award for *My Footprint Isn't Left Anywhere,* 1997.

Roles

1982   Spirit (cr) in *Ryu Kwan Soon* (Yook Wan-soon), Yook Wan-soon Dance Company, London

Past Person (cr) in *Legend* (Yook Wan-soon), Yook Wan-soon Dance Company, Seoul

1983   Person (cr) in *The Light* (Yook Wan-soon), Yook Wan-soon Dance Company, Seoul

Mary Magdalene (cr) in *Jesus Christ Superstar* (Yook Wan-soon), Yook Wan-soon Dance Company, Seoul

Shadow (cr) in *About the Things That Pass On* (Kim Kyoung-oak), Korea Contemporary Dance Company, Seoul

Blood (cr) in *The One Thing* (Kim Ki-in), Kim Ki-in Modern Dance Company, Seoul

1984   Crane (cr) in *The Crane* (Yook Wan-soon), Yook Wan-soon Dance Company, Seoul

Flower (cr) in *The Flower* (co-choreographed by Modern Dance Group Nesaram), Seoul

Transparent Light (cr) in *Purple Color* (Kim Ki-in), Korea Contemporary Dance Company, Seoul

1985   Woman (cr) in *The Village of Forsythia* (Orita Gatzuko), Korea Modern Dance Company, Seoul

Eve (cr) in *A Human Being of Eden* (Park Myung-sook), Korea Contemporary Dance Company, Seoul

Soul (cr) in *Salpuri V* (Lee Jung-hee), Korea Contemporary Dance Company, Seoul

Wind (cr) in *Nine Clouds and Nine Dreams* (Park Myung-sook), Korea Contemporary Dance Company, Seoul

1986   Crying person (cr) in *Negro Spiritual* (Yook Wan-soon), Yook Wan-soon Dance Company, Seoul

Light (cr) in *Seoul Light from the East* (Yook Wan-soon), Korea Modern Dance Company, Seoul

Grass Leaf (cr) in *Illusion of Leaves of Grass* (Park Myung-sook), Korea Contemporary Myung-sook Dance Company, Seoul

The Divided Man (cr) in *Han-Du-Re* (Yook Wan-soon), Korea Modern Dance Company, Seoul

1987   Soul (cr) in *Invocation for the Dead Spirit* (Park Myung-sook), Korea Contemporary Dance Company, Seoul

A Pattern (cr) in *Wheel* and *Inside the Rain* (Kim Ki-in), Modern Dance Group Nesaram, Seoul

A Traveler (cr) in *Silk Road* (Yook Wan-soon), Korea Contemporary Company, Seoul

Woman of Love (cr) in *A Picture Book of People* (Whang Moon-suk), Korea Contemporary Dance Company, Seoul

1988   Waterdrop (cr) in *Mul Ma Ru* (Yook Wan-soon), Korea Modern Dance Company, Seoul

1990   Exorcist (cr) in *Ecstasty* (Kook Soo-ho and Yook Wan-soon), Korea Contemporary Dance Company, Yugoslavia

1991   Sad man (cr) in *Encounter II* (Manga)(Yook Wan-soon), Korea Contemporary Dance Company, Moscow and Leningrad

Works

1983   *Root* (solo; mus. Ry Cooder), Seoul

Guys and Dolls (musical; mus. Frank Loss), Kwangjang Theatre Groupe, Munye Theatre, Seoul

Into the Space of Cosmos (mus. various, arranged Ahn Ae-soon), Modern Dance Group Nesaram, Sejong Cultural Center, Seoul

1984   *Eve* (solo; mus. Kitaro), Ahn Ae-soon Modern Dance Company, Space Theatre, Seoul

1985   *Obscure Dream* (mus. various, arranged Ahn Ae-soon), Ahn Ae-soon Modern Dance Company, Munye Theatre, Seoul

Energy (mus. various, arranged Ahn Ae-soon), Ahn Ae-soon Modern Dance Company, Munye Theatre, Seoul

Image of the Poor (mus. various, arranged Ahn Ae-soon), Ahn Ae-soon Modern Dance Company, Munye Theatre, Seoul

1987   *Root II* (solo; mus. Hans Otte), Munye Theatre, Seoul

Reflection (mus. Hans Otte), Ahn Ae-soon Modern Dance Company, Munye Theatre, Seoul

One of the Summits (mus. Hans Otte), Ahn Ae-soon Modern Dance Company, Munye Theatre, Seoul

Hansel and Gretel (for musical, mus. Chung Sung-jo), Hyundai Theatre Company, Munye Theatre, Seoul

1988   *Mysterious Balance* (solo; mus.various, arranged Ahn Ae-soon), Hyundai To-Art Hall, Seoul

Unknown (mus. Craig Peyton), Korea Contemporary Dance Company, Munye Theatre, Seoul

Cabaret (musical; mus. John Cander), Kwang Jang Theatre Company, Munye Theatre, Seoul

1989   *Water in Transparency* (mus. Kim Young-dong), Korea Contemporary Dance Company, Apple Corps Theater, New York

1990   *Burden* (mus. Hans Otte), Korea Modern Dance Company, National Theatre of Korea, Seoul

Encounter (mus. Kim Ji-yuk), Korea Contemporary Dance Company, Munye Theatre, Seoul

1992   *A Moving Panorama* (mus. Hans Otte), Ahn Ae-soon Modern Dance Company, Munye Theatre, Seoul

Washing-off (mus. Kim Ji-yuk), Korea Modern Dance Company, Munye Theatre, Seoul

A Chorus Line (musical; mus. Marvin Hamlisch), Korea Modern Dance Company, Munye Theatre, Seoul

Root III (solo; mus. various, arranged Ahn Ae-soon), Munye Theatre, Seoul

1993   *Reincarnation* (mus. Hans Otte), Ahn Ae-soon Modern Dance Company, Seoul

1994   *Burden II* (mus. Hans Otte), Jeune Ballet France Company, La Boule Theatre, France

Sun, Moon, Breath (mus. Michael Nyman), Korea Contemporary Dance Company, Munye Theatre, Seoul

Flower Carriage (musical; mus. Choi Jong-hyouk), Seoul Art Company, Seoul Arts Center, Seoul

Empty Space (mus. Kim Young-dong), Ahn Ae-soon Modern Dance Company, Baldwin Theater, North Carolina

1995   *Sun, Breath, Moon* (mus. Ravel), Korea Contemporary Dance Company, Munye Theatre, Seoul

1996   *Bright* (mus. Ravel), Ahn Ae-soon Modern Dance Company, Munye Theatre, Seoul

The Mother (musical; mus. Lee Seong-jae), Dongsung Theatre Company, Seoul

A Dream of Mansuek (solo; mus. Park Yong-ki), Munye Theatre, Seoul

Peter Pan (musical; mus. Ahn Gil-yung), Hyundai Theatre Company, Munye Theatre, Seoul

My Footprint Isn't Left Anywhere (musical), Metropolitan Musical Company, Sejong Cultural Center, Seoul

1997   *The Way* (mus. Jordi Savall), Korea Contemporary Dance Company, Munye Theatre, Seoul

Naked Monkey (musical; mus. Ma Dong-suk), Ahn Ae-soon Modern Dance Company, Seoul Art Center, Seoul

Donqihotea (musical; mus. Mitch Leigh), Aram Theatre Company, Munye Theatre, Seoul

Publications

By AHN: books—

Research about the Later Period of Modern Dance, Centering around the Judson Group, Ewha Press, Seoul, 1983.

By AHN: articles—

"Research on the Special Characteristics of Eating Disorders in Female Athletes," *Korean Jounal of Sports Science* (Seoul), March 1997.

On AHN: articles—

"Dances by Ahn Ae-soon," *The Great Advent of Dance Art* (Seoul), 1997.
Kim Tae-won, "Postmodernistic Change, Variation, and Spacial Dreams," *Performing Arts & Film Review* (Seoul), 1996.
Kim Young-tae, "A Hymn of Ahn Ae-soon's Life," *Auditorium* (Seoul), January 1987.
Lee Jong-ho, "Acheivement of Korean-Style Modern Dance," *SPACE* (Seoul), August 1997.
"The Popularization and Economic Aspects of Dance," *Performing Arts & Film Review* (Seoul), 1997.

*   *   *

Ahn Ae-soon is an independent choreographer whose works are remarkable in the Korean modern dance field of the 1990s. Unlike other Korean modern dance choreographers who often hold a position at a university or lead their own companies, she does neither. However, she is invited almost every year as a guest choreographer by representative modern dance companies in Korea such as Korea Contemporary Dance Company and Korea Modern Dance Company. And in order to maintain her status as an independent choreographer, she is actively involved in dance parts in musicals, which are enjoying a rising popularity in the Korean theatrical world. She also helps choreograph dance movements in plays, and helps to train actors.

Ahn's dance career started with her entry into the department of modern dance at Ewha Women's University, which forms the mainstream of today's Korean modern dance. There she met Yook Wan-soon, a representative teacher of Korean modern dance, and participated in Korea Contemporary Dance Company, which Professor Yook founded in 1975 with modern dance graduates of Ewha Women's University. After her graduation in 1983, she presented her first work, *Root,* at the Sejong Cultural Centre, but it didn't attract much attention. During her Master's degree course at Ewha Women's University, she came to recognize the fast-changing currents in the world of modern dance. Her thesis in 1985 was about Judson choreographers who had formed American postmodern dance in the 1960s. At that time, joining in Kim Ki-in's *Purple Color* (1984), she became interested in an aesthetics of dance which is passive and minimalist rather than functional or active.

After the mid-1980s, Ahn's choreography developed in two different technical directions. One was very intensely expressing functional and rhythmical movement, and the other was expressing the opposite, movement of certain silence, slowness, improvisation or an intentional lack of completion, emphasizing emptiness and the effect of space. Examples of the former direction are *Unkown* (1988) and *Mysterious Balance* (1988), in which she created the aesthetics of movement that could be called a depictional space transfer. In other words, in a space, a dancer's body appears abruptly just like a bright dot, and as it moves on it shows concentration, clarity, and an exquisite, cheerful movement like that of a waterdrop jumping and rolling on oil paper.

However, in the 1990s, with her interests shifted to Korean, or rather, oriental symbolism, Ahn shifted to a quality of movement which often "breaks off" that technical smoothness and continuity already acquired. This is sometimes abrupt and unexpected, and as the

Judson choreographers of the 1960s had done, intentionally eschews dance movements as the dance resolves itself into ordinary movements. In her pieces *Sun, Breath, Moon* (1995) and *A Dream of Mansuek* (1996), whose subject matter is taken from a Korean doll-play, she lets dancers such as Lee Yoon-kyung and Kim Hee-jin repeatedly run on the stage, or yawn slowly, and she shows actions crumbling down very weakly between paragraphs when a soloist tries to execute strenuous maneuvers, demonstrating that human life is controlled by a different and contrary power of relaxation, a strong inertia.

Besides these special features of movement, what makes her works valuable is that since 1989, as guest choreographer of the Korea Contemporary Dance Company, she tries to represent the mental symbolism latent in Korean culture and the typical Korean lifestyle, which lacks a clear distinction between concepts of life and death. Though not borrowing the story-telling form of dance drama, but rather applying a symbolic and intensive spacial sense, she tries to show not only blind motion but also aesthetic consciousness emphasizing silence and emptiness. Moreover, in her piece *Encounter* (1990), which gave Korea Contemporary Dance Company the grand prize, prize for best actor, and for best choreographer at the 12th Seoul International Dance Festival, she desired one world without the confrontation of different beliefs, and a kind of life without disruption, using effectively symbolic equipment and blue fabric.

It is surely an oriental world view to tie opposite things together, or to describe a world without distinction about life and death. But the power of her works is that this mental symbolism, concentrating movement without superfluity, an aesthetic of blank and intentional incompletion, forms a structure in which each tensely confronts the other, as they seem to interpenetrate, but do not do so. (I often call this type of dance "the embodiment of regional lyricism aesthetics.")

Through her piece *Encounter* she brought in as collaborators an artist, Sin Sun-hee, who was remarkable in flat decoration, and a composer, Kim Ji-wook, who lyrically unified clear and pastoral wind instruments and synthesizer. Her good relationship with professional dancers also allowed her to bring in excellent dancers such as Lee Yoon-kyung and Kim Hee-jin, members of the third generation of Korea Contemporary Dance Company. In her latest work, *The Way* (1997), she created a humorous dance mixing acrobatic feats and meditative poise for older dancers in their thirties and forties, the first and second generations of Korea Contemporary Dance Company.

Ahn Ae-soon was selected to participate in the 3rd and 4th Bagnolet festivals in France (Rencontres Choreographiques Internationales de Seine-Denis). At the American Dance Festival in 1996, she presented *Empty Space,* a re-choreographed piece, as a member of the International Choreographic Residency. She was also invited as a Korean delegate to La Boule Dance Festival in 1995, a culture exchange program between Korea and France, where she worked with Claude Brumachon. In 1997, she was appointed as Artist of the Month by Munwha Broadcasting Corporation (MBC) and choreographed dances for the award-winning play *My Footprint Isn't Left Anywhere*.

—Kim Tae-won

AILEY, Alvin

African-American dancer, choreographer and company director

Born: Alvin Ailey, Jr. 5 January 1931 in Rogers, Texas. **Education:** Studied tap dance briefly and "primitive dance" with Thelma Robinson; attended the University of California at Los Angeles, Los Angeles City College, and San Francisco State College; studied at Lester Horton studio sporadically, 1949-53; acting lessons with Stella Adler, 1960-62. **Career:** Joined Horton dance ensemble, 1953; first choreography in workshop, 1953; first professional choreography for Horton ensemble, 1954; danced in *Carmen Jones*; Horton Company performed Ailey's choreography on television programs *Party at Ciro's, The Red Skelton Show,* and *The Jack Benny Show;* moved to New York, fall 1954; studied with Hanya Holm, Anna Sokolow, Charles Weidman, and Karel Shook; performed with companies of Donald McKayle, Anna Sokolow, and Sophie Maslow; performed on and off- Broadway, in *The Carefree Tree* (1955), *Sing, Man, Sing* (1956), and *Show Boat* (1957); first concert for his own ensemble, 1958; acted in dramatic plays on and off Broadway, in *Tiger, Tiger Burning Bright, Call Me By My Rightful Name, Ding Dong Bell,* and *Two by Saroyan;* directed productions of *African Holiday* and Langston Hughes' *Jerico-Jim-Crow* ; toured with company for U.S. State Department to Far East, 1962; staged several works for Harkness and Joffrey Ballet companies, 1962-66; founded Dance Theater Foundation, 1967; staged Broadway musical *La Strada,* 1969. **Awards:** Honorary degrees from Princeton University, Bard College, Adelphi University, and Cedar Crest College; United Nations Peace Medal, and National Association for the Advancement of Colored People Springarn Medal, 1976; lifetime achievement, Kennedy Center Honors, 1988. **Died:** Due to complications from AIDS, 1 December 1989.

Works (all works premiered in New York unless otherwise noted)

1953   *Afternoon Blues* (mus. Bernstein), solo, Lester Horton
           Studio, Los Angeles
1954   *According to Saint Francis* (mus. Kingsley), Lester Horton
           Dancers, Los Angeles
        Creation of the World (*La Creation du Monde*) (mus.
           Milhaud), Lester Horton Dancers, San Diego
        Mourning Morning (mus. Robinson), Lester Horton Dancers, Los Angeles
1958   *Blues Suite* (mus. traditional Blues, arr. Anderson, Ricci),
           Alvin Ailey and Company
        Ode and Homage (mus. Glanville-Hicks), Alvin Ailey
           and Company
        Ariette Oubliée (mus. Debussy), Alvin Ailey and Company
        Redonda/Cinco Latinos (mus. Baxter, Fields, Prado, Black,
           Liter, Knudson-Black Gonzalez), Alvin Ailey and Company
1959   *Mistress and Manservant* (mus. Ravel), Shirley Broughton
           Dance Company
1960   *Sonera* (mus. Caturla), Alvin Ailey and Company
        Revelations (mus. traditional), Alvin Ailey Dance
           Theatre (AADT)
        Creation of the World (second version; mus. Milhaud),
           Ailey and Matt Tunney duet, AADT
        African Holiday (mus. various), theatrical revue
        Jamaica (mus. Arlen), Summer Stock Theater, Jones
           Beach, New York
        Knoxville: Summer of 1915 (mus. Samuel Barber), AADT
        Three for Now—Modern Jazz Suite (mus. Giuffre, Lewis),
           AADT
1961   *Roots of the Blues* (mus. traditional), Ailey and de Lavallade
           duet, AADT
        Gillespiana (mus. Shifrin), AADT

Hermit Songs (solo, mus. Barber), AADT
Been Here And Gone (mus. traditional folk), AADT

1962 *Creation of the World* (third version; mus. Barber), AADT
Feast Of Ashes (mus. Surinach), Robert Joffrey Ballet, Lisbon, Teatro San Carlos

1963 *Reflections in D* (mus. Ellington), AADT
Labyrinth (mus. Rosenthal), AADT
My People (First Negro Centennial), (mus. Ellington), theater, Chicago
Rivers, Streams, Doors (mus. traditional folk), AADT, Sao Paolo, Brazil

1964 *Jerico Jim Crow* (mus. traditional), theater
The Twelve Gates (mus. traditional Spirituals, arr. Sellars), de Lavallade and James Truitte duet, Jacob's Pillow, Beckett, Massachusetts

1965 *Ariadne* (mus. Jolivet), Harkness Ballet, Paris, France

1966 *Macumba* (mus. Harkness), Harkness Ballet, Gran Teatro del Liceo, Barcelona, Spain
El Amor Brujo (mus. de Falla), Harkness Ballet, Paris
Anthony and Cleopatra (mus. Barber), Metropolitan Opera

1967 *Riedaiglia* (mus. Riedel), AADT, Swedish Television Production

1968 *Quintet* (mus. Nyro), AADT, Edinburgh Festival, Scotland

1969 *Diversion No. 1* (mus. various), AADT, Los Angeles
Masekela Langage (mus. Masekela), AADT
La Strada (mus. Bart) Broadway musical

1970 *Streams* (mus. Kabelac), Alvin Ailey American Dance Theatre (AAADT)
Gymnopedies (mus. Satie), AAADT
The River (mus. Ellington), American Ballet Theatre

1971 *Archipelago* (mus. Boucourechliev), AAADT
Flowers w/Lynn Seymour (mus. Janis Joplin, Big Brother and the Holding Company, Pink Floyd, Blind Faith), AAADT
Choral Dances (mus. Britten), AAADT
Cry (mus. Coltrane, Nyro, Voices of East Harlem), solo for Judith Jamison, AAADT
Mass (mus. Bernstein), theater, opening of John F. Kennedy Center for the Performing Arts, Washington, D.C.
The Mingus Dances (mus. Mingus, arr. Raph), Joffrey Ballet, City Center
Mary Lou's Mass (mus. Williams), AAADT
Myth (mus. Stravinsky), AAADT

1972 *Lord Byron* (mus. Thompson), Juilliard American Opera Center
The Lark Ascending (mus. Williams), AAADT
Shaken Angels. (mus. various: Pink Floyd, Bill Withers, Alice Cooper), Dennis Wayne and Bonnie Mathis duet, New York Dance Festival, Delacorte Theater
Carmen (mus. Bizet), Metropolitan Opera
Sea Change (mus. Britten), American Ballet Theatre, Washington, D.C.
Love Songs (mus. Hathaway, Simone), Alvin Ailey City Center Dance Theatre (AACCDT)

1973 *Four Saints in Three Acts* (mus. Thompson), opera direction/staging by Alvin Ailey
Hidden Rites (mus. Sciortino), AACCDT

1974 *Ailey Celebrates Ellington* (mus. Ellington), Alvin Ailey Workshop, Television Special

1975 *Night Creature* (mus. Ellington), AACCDT
The Mooche (mus. Ellington), AACCDT

1976 *Black, Brown & Beige.* (mus. Ellington), AACCDT
Pas de 'Duke' (mus. Ellington and Ellington), Jamison and Baryshnikov duet, AACCDT
Three Black Kings (mus. Ellington and Ellington), AACCDT

1978 *Passage* (mus. Smith), solo for Jamison, AAADT
Shigaon! Children of the Diaspora (mus. various), Bat-Dor Company, Tel-Aviv, Israel

1979 *Solo for Mingus* (mus. Mingus), AAADT
Memoria (mus. Jarrett), AAADT
Phases (mus. Sanders, Byrd, Roach), AAADT

1981 *Spell* (mus. Jarrett), Jamison and Godunov duet, AAADT
Landscape (mus. Bartók), AAADT

1982 *Satyriade* (mus. Ravel), AAADT

1983 *Au Bord du Precipice* (mus. Metheny, Mays), Paris Opera Ballet, Paris
Escapades (mus. Roach), Aterbaletto Reggio Emilia Italy
Isba (mus. Winston), AAADT, Richmond, Virginia
Can't Slow Down (mus. Richie), AAADT

1984 *For Bird—With Love* (mus. Charlie Parker, Dizzy Gillespie, Count Basie, Jerome Kern, Coleridge-Taylor Perkinson), AAADT, Kansas City, Kansas

1986 *Caverna Magica* (mus. Vollenweider), Royal Danish Ballet, Copenhagen
Witness (mus. traditional gospel, as recorded by Jessye Norman), Royal Danish Ballet, Copenhagen
Survivors (mus. Roach), AAADT

1988 *La Dea della Acqua* (mus. Moore), La Scala Opera Ballet, Italy
Opus McShann (mus. McShann, Brown), AAADT, Kansas City, Kansas

Publications

By AILEY: book—

With A. Peter Bailey, *Revelations: The Autobiography of Alvin Ailey,* New York, Birch Lane Press, 1995.

On AILEY: books—

Dunning, Jennifer, *Alvin Ailey: A Life In Dance,* New York, 1996.
Jamison, Judith, with Howard Kaplan, *Dancing Spirit: An Autobiography,* New York, 1993.
Long, Richard, *The Black Tradition in American Dance,* New York, 1989.

On AILEY: articles—

DeFrantz, Thomas, in "Stoned Soul Picnic: Alvin Ailey and the Struggle to Define Official Black Culture," *Soul: Black Power, Politics and Pleasure,* New York: 1997.
Gruen, John, "Looking Ahead," *The Private World of Ballet,* New York, 1975.
Hodgson, Moira, and Thomas Victor, "Alvin Ailey City Center Dance Theatre," in *Quintet: Five American Dance Companies,* New York, 1976.

Alvin Ailey with Alexander Godunov and Judith Jamison. Photograph © Johan Elbers.

Moore, William, "Alvin Ailey (1931-1989)," *Ballet Review,* Winter 1990.

*   *   *

The broadly-based, international audience now so familiar with American modern dance honestly didn't exist before Alvin Ailey's dances and his company's operations reached out to claim it. In this, the impact of Alvin Ailey's efforts in contemporary dance are almost incalculable. Ailey nurtured a visceral, emotionally accessible style of performance that converted scores of neophytes into fans of the art.

Born in Rogers, Texas, Ailey was the only child of working-class parents who separated when he was an infant. In 1942 he and his mother moved to Los Angeles, where Ailey first saw the Ballet Russe de Monte Carlo and Katherine Dunham's company. The lasting impression that these two seemingly divergent companies made upon young Ailey became evidenced in the wide-ranging repertory that his namesake company later cultivated, and in Ailey's avid interest in varied forms of theatrical dance.

Ailey began dance study at Lester Horton's Hollywood studio in 1949, where he developed a weighty, smoldering performance style that suited his athletic body. When Horton died suddenly in 1954, Ailey offered three choreographic scenarios—his first, excepting a solo for a composition workshop—which the Horton ensemble performed to mixed reviews. Ailey moved to New York in 1954 to dance with partner Carmen de Lavallade in the Broadway production of Truman Capote's *House of Flowers.* Performing success in several Broadway shows and the companies of Donald McKayle, Anna Sokolow, and Sophie Maslow led Ailey to found his own dance theater company in 1958.

Successful from the start, the company's first concert premiered Ailey's *Blues Suite;* two years later Ailey's unequivocal masterpiece, *Revelations,* established his company, comprised mostly of African-American dancers, as the foremost dance interpreter of African-American experience. In total, however, Ailey's choreography resisted "ethnic" classification. His output includes pointe ballets, modern dance ballets, and staging for theater pieces. His dances privilege no form over another, stressing instead a facile interplay between genres. Ailey's theatrical tastes, combined with a variety of technique training undertaken at the Horton School, the Dunham School, and in classes taught by Hanya Holm, Anna Sokolow, and Charles Weidman, contributed to a playful sense of movement-style juxtaposition in several works. *Blues Suite,* for example, contains sections of early 20th-century social dances, Horton dance technique, Jack Cole-inspired jazz dance, and ballet partnering. Unifying the piece is an arching dramatic scenario and a blatant theatricality designed to galvanize its audience.

Ailey danced in his own works during the company's first years, and his performances in the solo *Hermit Songs* garnered praise equally for his choreography, his dramatic abilities, and the sensuous masculinity he exuded. His strength and charisma made him a formidable partner to Graham soloist Matt Turney in *Creation of the World* and Carmen de Lavallade in *Roots of the Blues.* His strongest interests lay in choreography, however, and he retired from his own dancing career when he was only 34, in 1965.

Several Ailey dances established precedents for American dance. *Feast of Ashes* created for the Robert Joffrey Ballet in 1962 and derived from Lorca's *The House of Bernarda Alba,* is among the first successful ballets choreographed by a modern dancer. In 1966 Ailey contributed dances for the New York Metropolitan Opera's inaugural production at Lincoln Center, Samuel Barber's *Antony and Cleopatra.* In 1970 he created *The River* for American Ballet Theatre. Set to an original score commissioned from Duke Ellington, this ballet convincingly fused pointe ballet technique with Ailey's hybrid modern vocabulary. *Night Creature* (1974), made for his school's student ensemble and also set to an Ellington score, extended the possibilities of theatrical jazz and ballet technique in sections of petite allegro juxtaposed to black social dance steps.

Several Ailey works examine the depths of sorrow lurking beneath a glamorous theatrical facade. *Quintet, Flowers, The Mooche, Au Bord du Precipice,* and *For Bird—With Love* each offers a dramatic portrait of celebrity gone awry. Framed by the trappings of extravagant costume, lighting, and implicit public adulation, the characters in these ballets reveal an intense private despair and loneliness in their offstage lives. The theme held special resonance for Ailey and other African-American artists of his generation who shouldered the responsibility of representing their race in terms of concert dance.

Ailey also made abstract works which investigated the qualities of movement, usually outfitted with a ritualistic narrative overlay. *Streams, Hidden Rites, The Lark Ascending, Landscape,* and *Isba* feature strong compositional designs and oblique dramatic narratives of transformation. Ailey seldom detailed the themes of these abstract works; he preferred to let their visceral impact speak for themselves.

In total, Ailey's choreography is concerned with the bases of humanity and the ability of people to collaborate through dance. As he told interviewer John Gruen in 1975, "I am trying to express something that I feel about people, life, the human spirit, the beauty of things. I'm trying to celebrate man's achievements—the beauty of music, of shapes, of form, of color, light, texture. The idea of a person doing this with his body—the idea of freedom through discipline—is beautiful to me."

Alvin Ailey understood that his contribution to American dance was necessarily linked to his experiences as a black man. He made enormous emotional sacrifices to shower the world with his visions of the powerful beauty of black dancers, and the ability of modern dance to bridge cultural and social differences. He worked continually to develop a vibrant African-American presence in concert dance; onstage, behind the scenes, and in the audience. As he settled into elder-statesman status, he spoke less and less about making art and more and more about the difficulties of maintaining a company. Business pressures mounted, and personal disappointments, combined with an untreated manic-depressive illness, led Ailey to a painful emotional breakdown in 1980. He recovered from this to choreograph more than a dozen works, several of which are among his finest. His legacy to the dance world was to foster a freedom of choice—from ballet, modern, and social dance movement—to best express humanity in movement terms suited to the theatrical moment. He was fond of saying, "The dance came from the people. It should always be given back to the people."

His works are to be found in the repertories of ballet and modern dance companies in Europe and the United States, including American Ballet Theatre, the Joffrey Ballet, Paris Opera Ballet, London Festival Ballet, Maryland Ballet, the Royal Danish Ballet, Batsheva Dance Company, Dayton Contemporary Dance Company, Philadelphia Dance Company, and the Alvin Ailey American Dance Theatre.

—Thomas DeFrantz

AIR FOR THE G STRING

Choreography: Doris Humphrey
Music: J. S. Bach
First Production: Little Theatre, Brooklyn, New York, 24 March 1928.

Publications

Books—

Cohen, S. J., *Doris Humphrey—An Artist First,* Middletown, Connecticut, 1972.
Humphrey, Doris, *The Art of Making Dances,* New York, 1959.
Marriett, Jane, *Air for the G String,* New York, 1975.
Siegel, M. B., *Shapes of Change: Images of American Dance,* New York, 1979.
———, *Days on Earth,* New Haven, 1993.

Articles—

Stodelle, Ernestine, "*Air for the G String,*" *Ballet Review,* 11(4), 1984.

*   *   *

First performed only four months before she left the Denishawn organisation, *Air for the G String* is a summation of what Doris Humphrey learned from and achieved while working with Ruth St. Denis. It is set to J. S. Bach's well known *Air for the G String* from the *Suite no. 3 in D for Orchestra.* Humphrey recalled in *The Art of Making Dances* that when, as a child, she heard her mother playing this on the piano, "[it] so struck me to the heart that it was almost the first dance I composed as an independent choreographer." It is one of several pieces which Humphrey choreographed to music by Bach, including *Bourée* (1920), *Passacaglia* (1938), and *Four Choral Preludes* and *Partita in G Major* (both 1942).

Air for the G String gives no hint of the modernist asceticism which characterises much of the work Humphrey would produce in the years immediately following her break from Denishawn. Instead it is arguably the finest example of the form which St. Denis called "music visualisation." While it was St. Denis who created music visualisation, it is generally acknowledged that Humphrey herself substantially contributed to it, sometimes in collaboration with her mentor. Humphrey had acquired a sophisticated understanding of music from her mother who had trained as a concert pianist. *Air for the G String* does not make the literal interpretations of musical scoring and melody that characterise St. Denis' pieces; nor, as M. B. Siegel pointed out in *Shapes of Change: Images of American Dance,* does it present a series of static tableaux. Instead the transitions between its momentarily suspended poses are as important as the groupings into which the dancers continually coalesce.

The five women dancers gracefully glide through intricately interwoven floor patterns while making shapes with the long, heavy drapery of their dresses. These patterns and shapes smoothly evolve one into another, complementing and counterpointing the developing discords and resolutions of the music. According to Ernestine Stodelle in *Ballet Review,* the pastel or gold coloured dresses, with their cape-like extensions, were inspired by the paintings of the Florentine Renaissance painter, Fra Angelico. Indeed the dancers'

gently arched upper backs and their hands, clasped as if in prayer, make them look like a group of Fra Angelico angels.

Some commentators have suggested that the dancers exude an air of calm placidity and spirituality. This quality indicates the extent to which Humphrey was still working within the conventions of Denishawn. Siegel observed that whereas Ruth St. Denis "could make an ordinary dance seem mysterious and seductive by the way she performed it," in *Air for the G String,* "Humphrey showed that the dance could create its own enigma." A key element that distinguishes this piece from St. Denis' work is the lack of hierarchy among the dancers. Even when Humphrey herself danced the central role for the first and only time when the piece was filmed in 1934, the five women seem a group of equals, the central figure merely playing a more important role within the composition of symmetrical and asymmetrical groupings. Not only was *Air for the G String* recorded on film, but it survived until the 1940s as one of the most popular pieces in the repertoire of the Humphrey-Weidman Dance Group. More recently it has been reconstructed by Ernestine Stodelle who danced it in the 1930s, and notated by Jane Marriett in 1975.

—Ramsay Burt

ALASKA DANCE THEATRE
American dance company

Founded 1981 in Anchorage; Alice Sullivan joined as artistic director and established a year-round school of dance, 1983; pianist program initiated, 1983; first annual Student Showcase, 1984; first Anchorage MOBIUS concert, 1985; first guest choreographers, 1987; began affiliation with Anchorage Symphony, 1989; studio moved to Grandview Gardens Cultural Center, 1991; toured Soviet Far East, 1992; moved to a permanent community dance facility, 1993; began Summer Dance Lab, 1994; began affiliation with Anchorage Opera, 1995.

Works (choreographer in parentheses)

1987	*No Flowers for the Clown* (Foreman)
1988	*Doin' Dorsey* (Freydont)
	Canaries for Two (Frey)
	Oblesquian Journey (Kautzky)
	Niagara Falls (Recktenwald)
1989	*Reflections* (Sullivan)
	Basambas (Crosby)
	Ballimp (Recktenwald)
	Im Chambre Separee (Recktenwald and Doyle)
	Spanish Waltzes (Sullivan)
1990	*Passing* (Brandstrom)
	Odyssey (O'Slynne)
	Baroque Tapestry (Sullivan)
	Kyrie (Recktenwald and Speir)
	Till the End of Time (Bradford)
	Vivaldi Con Brio (Speir)
	Motherless Child (Recktenwald with company)
	Sona Vita Mutallis (Kautzky)
	Mea Culpa (Recktenwald with company)
	Waiting. . . (Gabriel)

1991   *Street Dances* (O'Slynne)
        Illustrations (Perry)
        Bulgarian Women (Recktenwald with company)
        Sonny's Squall (Recktenwald)
        The Dreaming (Speir)
        Jade (T. Speir)
        Liposuction (Recktenwald and Tipton)
        Baroque Tapestry (Sullivan)
        Doom Tac a Doom (Cersosimo, Dezso, Speir, and Speir)
        Strange Cargo (O'Slynne)
1992   *Eidolon* (Gabriel)
        Beyond the Box (Tipton with Cersosimo)
        Exit (Speir)
        How the Army Broke Her Spirit (Heginbotham)
1993   *Six on the Avenue* (Austin)
        Ascending (Sullivan)
        Cry (Partusch)
        And Rachel Wept (Tipton)
        Womation (Recktenwald)
1994   *Plunge* (Moulton)
        Circle of Voices (Austin)
        100° C (Partusch)
        For Tony (Partusch and St. Thomass)
        Valses Poeticos (Sullivan)
        picture kept. will remind. me. (Tipton)
        Stabat Mater (Recktenwald)
1995   *Centone di Sonate* (Rockland)
        Miliki (Austin)
        Seagulls (Qi)
        Reely? (Partusch)
        Grand Tarentella (Perry)
1996   *Yours Anne* (Austin)
        Plumb Nuts (Partusch)
1997   *Shadowplay* (Austin)
        Core (L'Etoile)
        Swan Rink, Op. II (Partusch)
        Seascapes (Rockland)
        Why? (Staskiewicz)

Publications

Berardi, Gigi, "Season of Celebration in Store for the Alaska Dance
    Theatre," *Anchorage Daily News,* September 1992.
———, "Dance Theatre Undergoes a Metamorphosis in First Ten
    Years," *Anchorage Daily News,* February 1993.

                    *   *   *

Alaska Dance Theatre occupies a unique position in Anchorage
dance as the only dance company with a school and both city and
state funding. The school enrolls students from the south-central
Alaska region, including Seward and Wasilla, maintaining an enrollment of about 500 students each session. Over its 16-year history,
ADT has served more than 4,000 students, almost all from the
Anchorage area, where more than half the population of the state
resides. Dance companies in Alaska's two other major cities—
Fairbanks and Juneau—serve much smaller audiences.

Much of the credit for building the school, the dance company, and
repertory goes to artistic director Alice Sullivan. Sullivan was born in
Cape Yakataga, trained in Anchorage, and received her B.F.A. in ballet
from the University of Utah in 1975. Subsequently, she was a company apprentice with the First Chamber Dance Company in Seattle,
later joined the Minnesota Ballet, and was the founder of the ballet
program at the University of Minnesota in Duluth. She returned to
Alaska in November of 1983 to assume the directorship of ADT.

Alaska Dance Theatre has produced the annual MOBIUS concerts (a reference to the "mobius strip") since 1985, drawing guest
artists from such companies as American Ballet Theatre, Twyla
Tharp Dance Company, and the Martha Graham Dance Company.
For Sullivan, "MOBIUS" refers to the exploration of "the infinite
possibilities of movement" while "weaving contemporary ballet,
modern, and jazz dance to offer a full spectrum of mood and movement in each concert."

Sullivan has seen ADT develop into what she calls a "whole entity"—with a school, a company, community education programs,
scholarship programs, and year-round performances. The company
has come a long way, from its converted army barracks days (on the
Alaska Pacific University campus) to residing in a permanent dance
facility centrally located and well-suited to serving the community.
ADT's studios are situated in a building built specifically for dance,
formerly known as The Dance Center. With the purchase of the new
building in 1993, ADT expanded its dance class offerings and number
of company performances. Today, ADT presents close to 45 public
performances a year, most of them in Anchorage.

Prominent guest artists such as Donlin Foreman, Tomm Ruud, El
Gabriel, Judy Austin, Lisa Ford Moulton, Jiang Qi, Susan Perry,
Heather McEwen, and Jeffrey Rockland have set contemporary
works for the company. Resident choreographer C. Noelle Partusch
produces a wide range of works, many with a comic theme. One
sports parody, *Swan Rink, Op. II,* featured a stage set for ice hockey
with the dancers dressed in tulle and pointe shoes. Dance critic
Tracey Pilch (*Anchorage Daily News,* February 1997) referred to
the piece as "stealing the show. . . . Dancers mimicked the rather
unlikely relationship between ballet and ice hockey." The "dancers
appeared sure of their places and had fun. . .while being charmingly
appealing to its audience." Writer Anne Herman described
Partusch's *Plumb Nuts,* accompanied by Garrison Keillor's witty
commentary, as a "delightful release for those of us who have seen
too many versions of the perennial ballet chestnut *The Nutcracker.*"

The success of ADT in Alaska, where other dance companies
such as Alaska Contemporary Dance Company have not continued, can be attributed, in part, to effective fund raising efforts
combined with the artistic vision of Alice Sullivan. She considers
that these are "tough financial times for the arts. We're proud that
we're in the Season-Support category status with the Alaska State
Council on the Arts. We're getting money at a time [when] we were
told it was impossible."

Sullivan's direction is guided by important themes: continuity, ingenuity, survival, hard work, and cooperation. These themes help Sullivan
put her dance philosophy into practice: to educate the "whole" dancer,
that is, the person as well as the performer. Alaska Dance Theatre aims
to provide a nurturing environment for the young dancer. "I feel very
good about the training for the students. We give them a good foundation," says Sullivan. "We try to educate students in many different
styles, and encourage them to work with guest choreographers and
perform." In addition to the ability to work in many styles of dance,
the company is noted for its strong technique.

Judy Austin, formerly of Hubbard Street Dance Theatre and a
favorite choreographer of the troupe says, "ADT dancers are disciplined, eager, unafraid to approach all styles. . . . I always work off
dancers; my inspiration comes from [them]." Adds Sandra Baldwin,
Director of Outreach and Education, Oregon Ballet Theatre, "When

I think of my experience with ADT, the words commitment and integrity come to mind. With ADT, all my needs are anticipated in a cooperative, problem-solving manner." El Gabriel, Professor of Dance, University of California, Irvine, comments, "ADT is becoming one of the leading dance companies in the country."

—Gigi Berardi

ALLAN, Maud

American dancer and choreographer

Born: Maud Durrant in 1873 in Toronto, Canada. **Education:** Studied piano in the U.S. and Berlin. **Career:** Was a budding concert pianist, 1890s; inspired by a Botticelli painting, gave up piano and turned to dance; began performing solos, 1903; debuted *Vision of Salomé*, 1906; opened at the Palace Theatre in London, 1908; published her autobiography, *My Life and Dancing,* 1908; toured the world, 1910-15; returned to Los Angeles, 1940s. **Died:** 7 October 1956 in Los Angeles.

Works

1903	*Spring Song* (mus. Mendelssohn), Vienna
	Dances to the music of Bach, Beethoven, Schubert, Schumann
	Marche funebre (mus. Chopin)
	Ave Maria (mus. Schubert)
	Valse caprice (mus. Rubinstein)
1906	*Vision of Salomé* (mus. Remy)
1908	*Nair, the Slave*
	Melody in F (mus. Rubinstein)
1910	*Orfeo*

Other works include: *Valse in A Minor, Mazurka in G Sharp Major* (mus. Chopin), *Mazurka in B Flat* (mus. Chopin), *Peer Gynt Suite, Le Roi s'Amuse, Sarabande and Gavotte* (mus. Bach), *Beautiful Blue Danube Waltz* (mus. Strauss), *Eight Preludes* (mus. Chopin), *Moment Musical* (mus. Schubert), *Am Meer* (mus. Schubert), *Barcarolle* (from *Tales of Hoffman,* mus. Offenbach), *Dance of the Sugar Plum Fairy* (mus. Tchaikovsky), *Arabian Dance, L'Apres-midi d'une Faune, Pavanne, Reverie, Gopak,* and *Valse Triste.*

Publications

By ALLAN: books—

My Life and Dancing, London, 1908.

On ALLAN: books—

Caffin, Caroline, and Charles H. Caffin, *Dancing and Dancers of Today: The Modern Revival of Dancing as an Art,* New York, 1912, reprint, 1978.
Cherniavsky, Felix, *The Salome Dancer: The Life and Times of Maud Allan,* Toronto, 1991.
———, *Did She Dance: Maud Allan in Performance,* Toronto, 1992 (four computer disks including Allan's autobiography).

Cohen-Stratyner, Barbara Naomi, *Biographical Dictionary of Dance,* New York, 1982.
Kendall, Elizabeth, *Where She Danced,* New York, 1979.
McDonagh, Don, *The Complete Guide to Modern Dance,* Garden City, New York, 1976.
Sorell, Walter, *Dance In its Time,* Garden City, New York, 1981.

On ALLAN: articles—

Cherniavsky, Felix, "Maud Allan's Tour of India, the Far East, and Australia," in *Society of Dance History Scholars Proceedings,* Ninth Annual Conference, New York, 1986.
———, "Maud Allan," series of articles, all published in *Dance Chronicle,* 1983, 1984, 1985, 1986.
Koritz, Amy, "Dancing the Orient for England: Maud Allan's *The Vision of Salomé,*" *Theatre Journal,* March 1994.
McDearmon, Lacy, "Maud Allan: The Public Record," *Dance Chronicle,* 1978.
Weigand, Elizabeth, "Maud Allan and J. T. Grein," in *Society of Dance History Scholars Proceedings,* Sixth Annual Conference, Ohio, 1983.

*   *   *

Maud Allan was an interpretive dancer of the early 20th century who helped pioneer acceptance of dance as a way to express personal and emotional attitudes in movement. The popularity and seriousness of her work at the height of her career drew public and critical attention to this developing art form. Although she always considered herself to be an individual artist rather than part of a movement, her work introduced concepts that were later at the heart of the emerging modern dance movement.

Allan was born Maud Durrant in Toronto in 1873 and moved to San Francisco as a child. She had a great gift for music and moved to Berlin in 1895 to continue her studies as a concert pianist. Allan's great musical sensitivity and fertile imagination provided the foundations for her explorations in dance. In her autobiography *My Life and Dancing* (1908), Allan describes a moment during a 1900 museum visit when her ideas about a new form of dance began to crystallize. The rhythm and flowing lines of Botticelli's *The Return of Spring* inspired her to think of dance in a new way: "Art is a method of expression, the expression of feelings and thoughts through beautiful movements, shapes and sounds," she writes. "To try to express in movement the emotions and thoughts stirred by melody, beautiful pictures and sculpture had become my ambition."

Although such thoughts about the expressive, personal nature of dance are common today, they were radically different from those held during Allan's time. Common theatrical dancing, or show dancing, primarily consisted of groups of women doing like steps and kicks and an occasional "exotic" dancer. Ballet, the only serious theatrical dance, was concentrated in Europe, and Allan deplored its restricted movements and rigid training. Allan set about developing a way in which she could express herself through movement, often incorporating influences prominent at the turn of the century. Like many other interpretive dancers, Allan was intrigued with François Delsarte's teachings about the relationship between body and spirit, and a revival of interest in ancient Greece heavily influenced her desire to rediscover ancient Greek dances. Her friend, Marcel Remy, supported Allan's emerging interest and later composed and arranged music for her, including the score to her *Vision of Salomé.*

Allan's dances shared many characteristics with other interpretive dancers, like Loie Fuller, Ruth St. Denis, and Isadora Duncan. Costumes were usually simple Grecian tunics or draped fabrics which accentuated the body's movement, although exotic dresses were also used. The dancers used expressive arm and hand movements and danced barefoot. Allan's preference for performing to classic music, by composers like Mendelssohn, Bach, and Schubert, reflected her deep understanding of the music.

Allan eventually abandoned studying piano to devote herself to dance. She debuted in 1903 in Vienna as a dancer and began touring the continent. Allan's gracious, charming nature and press accounts of her risqué *Salomé* dance combined to create opportunities for her to become acquainted with influential people who helped advance her career. A performance for King Edward VII at Marienbad in 1907 led to an engagement at the Palace Theatre in London. On 6 March 1908 Allan opened at the Palace and began an unprecedented record of more than 250 performances. Her program included classic dances and her famous *Vision of Salomé*. The story of Salomé, Herod's stepdaughter who demanded John the Baptist's head on a platter as a reward for her dancing, was a popular subject at the time. Allan first performed *Vision of Salomé* in December 1906. She liked to describe the dance as the spiritual awakening of a young girl, but London audiences were enticed to the theater with advertisements emphasizing the erotic nature of the dance. In some respects, their perverse expectations were met; Allan's costume was exceedingly revealing for the times, consisting of a bejeweled bra, draping beads, and sheer fabric. Her kiss on the severed head shocked audiences.

Once in the theater, audiences also experienced Allan's dance visualizations of classic music. Critics praised her highly personal dances and recognized her aesthetic seriousness; interest in this new interpretive dance was growing. In the fall of 1908 Allan, St. Denis, and Duncan all were playing London theaters, with Allan reigning as London's favorite. Allan's *Salomé* dance was widely imitated on both sides of the Atlantic. An injury on stage later that year prevented Allan from performing for three months. She returned to the London stage, but her audiences had begun to dwindle. By 1910 Allan began touring, which took her to five continents by 1923. In her first tour to the United States, the enthusiasm for her *Salomé* dance was dampened by the many imitations which had preceded her performance—nevertheless, there was enough positive audience attention here, and elsewhere in her travels, for her to continue to tour. She visited North America in 1910 and 1916, toured India, Asia, and Australia, with the Cherniavsky Trio as accompanists, from 1913 to 1915, and also performed in Egypt, New Zealand, and South Africa.

The success of Allan's tours slowly declined. She started a dance school in London, but the highly personal nature of her dancing did not lend itself to establishing a lasting legacy. In the mid-1940s she returned to Los Angeles, California, where she died in 1956.

—Janette Goff Dixon

ALSTON, Richard

British dancer, choreographer, educator, and company director

Born: 1949 in England. **Education:** Eton College, 1961-65; Foundation Course in Fine Arts, Croydon College of Art, 1965-67; London Contemporary Dance School, 1967-70; studied with Merce Cunningham, 1975-77. **Career:** Independent choreographer, 1970-85 and 1992-94 (including commissions from English National Opera, Ballet Rambert, Royal Danish Ballet, the Royal Ballet, Second Stride Dance Company, and Extempory Dance Company); artistic director, Strider, 1972-75; artistic director, Richard Alston and Dancers, 1978-79; resident choreographer, Ballet Rambert, 1980-86; artistic director, Rambert Dance Company, 1986-92; artistic director, The Place, 1994-present; artistic director, Richard Alston Dance Company, 1994-present. **Awards:** Honorary Doctorate, University of Surrey, 1992; officer, Order of Arts and Letters, France, 1995.

Works (premiered in London unless otherwise noted)

1968   *Transit* (mus. Ronald Lopresti), London Contemporary Dance School (LCDS) Workshop
        Matrix (mus. Bahutu chant), student workshop, Acland Burghley School
1969   *Something To Do* (text Gertrude Stein), LCDS Workshop
        Still Moving Still (mus. Shakuhachi), LCDS Workshop
1970   *Cycladic Figure* (mus. John Cage) LCDS Workshop
        Winter Music (mus. Cage)
        Departing in Yellow (mus. Michael Finnissy), LCDS Workshop
        Pace (mus. Handel), LCDS Workshop
        Nowhere Slowly (mus. Stockhausen), LCDS lecture-demonstration
        Goldrush (mus. Neil Young), LCDS Workshop
1971   *End, which is never more than this instant, than you on this instant, figuring it out and acting so. If there is any absolute, it is never more than this one, you, this instant, in action, which ought to get us on* (mus. Finnissy), LSCD Workshop
        Shiftwork (mus. Rossini), LCDS Workshop
        Cold (mus. Adam), LCDS Workshop
        After Follows Before (mus. Wagner), LCDS
        Who Is Twyla Tharp? (text Peter and Alison Smithson), London Festival Ballet Workshop
1972   *Combines* (mus. Schubert, Bach, Chopin; songs by Ella Fitzgerald, Connie Boswell, Frances Langford, and Mildred Bailey; film by Sally Potter) London Contemporary Dance Theatre
        Balkan Sobranie (mus. Jean Françaix, Stravinsky, and Japanese flute music) Scottish Ballet, Glasgow
        Routine Couple (taped conversation of George Burns and Gracie Allen), Strider
        Thunder (mus. Arlen's *Stormy Weather*), Strider
        Tiger Balm (mus. Anna Lockwood), Strider
        Windhover (mus. Lockwood), Strider
        Headlong (mus. Lockwood), Strider
        Interior (mus. Scott Joplin, Bulgarian folk music), LCDS Workshop
        The Average Leap (mus. Majorca Orchestra), Strider
1973   *Lay-Out* (mus. Lockwood), London Contemporary Dance Theatre
1974   *Rainbow Bandit 1* (mus. Charles Amirkhanian), Strider
        Blue Schubert Fragments (mus. Schubert), London Contemporary Dance Theatre
        Soft Verges Hard Shoulder (mus. Lockwood), Strider, Bingley, Yorkshire

Split (mus. Philip Corner [after Chopin]), Strider, Paris

Slow Field (mus. Stephen Montague), Strider, Sheffield

1975 *Souvenir* (mus. Satie), Strider

Zero Through Nine (mus. Montague), Strider

Two Saints in Three Acts, Strider, Sheffield

Standard Steps (mus. Satie, voice of Marcel Duchamp), Strider, Oxford

Compass, Strider, Nottingham

Slight Adventure, Mirjam Berns/Albert Reid, New York

1976 *Solo Soft Verges,* Eva Karczag, New York

Edge, Christopher Banner/Siobhan Davies/Sally Hess, New York

UnAmerican Activities, Alston/Banner/Davies/Karczag, New York

1977 *Connecting Passages,* Alston/Ruth Barnes, New York

Blueprint, Extemporary Dance Theatre, Hornchurch, Essex

Home Ground (mus. Purcell), Maedée Duprés

1978 *Breaking Ground* (mus. Purcell), Richard Alston and Dancers

Doublework (originally in silence; later, mus. James Fulkerson), Richard Alston and Dancers

The Seven Deadly Sins (mus. Weill), English National Opera

Distant Rebound 2 (mus. Mumma), Richard Alston and Dancers

Unknown Banker Buys Atlantic (mus. Cole Porter), Richard Alston and Dancers

Behind the Piano (mus. Satie), Richard Alston and Dancers

1979 *Elegiac Blue* (mus. Constant Lambert), Richard Alston and Dancers

Dumka (mus. Dvorák), LCDS Workshop

1980 *Bell High* (mus. Maxwell Davies), Ballet Rambert, Manchester

Schubert Dance (mus. Schubert), Maedée Duprés, Bristol

The Field of Mustard (mus. Vaughan Williams), Siobhan Davies/Juliet Fisher

Landscape (mus. Vaughan Williams), Ballet Rambert, Bristol

Rainbow Ripples (mus. Amirkhanian), Ballet Rambert, Oxford

1981 *Sugar* (mus. Fats Waller), Belinda Neave, Derby Playhouse

The Rite of Spring (mus. Stravinsky), Ballet Rambert

Soda Lake, Michael Clark

Swedish Dances (mus. Swedish folk music), Richard Alston/Mary Fulkerson, Dartington Festival, Devon

Berceuse (mus. Chopin), Lucy Burge, Derby

Night Music (mus. Mozart), Ballet Rambert, Newcastle

1982 *Bellezza Flash* (mus. Monteverdi), Michael Clark/Siobhan Davies/Tom Jobe, for "The South Bank Show," London Weekend Television

Danse fra Pagodernes Rige (mus. Britten), Royal Danish Ballet, Copenhagen

Dutiful Ducks (mus. Amirkhanian), Michael Clark

Crown Diamonds (mus. Auber), Rambert Academy

Apollo Distraught (mus. Nigel Osborne), Ballet Rambert

Fantasie (mus. Mozart), Ballet Rambert

1983 *Chicago Brass* (mus. Hindemith), Ballet Rambert, Birmingham

Facing Out (mus. Lindsay Cooper), Maedée Duprés

Java (mus. Inkspots), Second Stride, Leeds

The Brilliant and the Dark (mus. Britten), Second Stride, Leeds

Midsummer (mus. Tippett), Royal Ballet

1984 *Voices and Light Footsteps* (mus. Monteverdi), Ballet Rambert

Wildlife (mus. Osborne), Ballet Rambert, Brighton

Coursing (mus. Oliver Knussen), Ashley Page/Bruce Sansom

1985 *Mythologies* (mus. Osborne), Ballet Rambert

Dangerous Liaisons (mus. Simon Waters), Ballet Rambert, Southampton

Cutter (mus. John Marc Gowans), Extemporary Dance Theatre, Epsom, Surrey

1986 *Zansa* (mus. Osborne), Ballet Rambert, Bradford

1987 *Pulcinella* (mus. Stravinsky), Ballet Rambert, Leeds

Strong Language (mus. John Marc Gowans), Ballet Rambert,

1988 *Rhapsody in Blue* (mus. Gershwin), Rambert Dance Company, Birmingham

Hymnos (mus. Maxwell Davies), Rambert Dance Company, Canterbury

1989 *Cinema* (mus. Satie), Rambert Dance Company, Birmingham

Pulau Dewata (mus. Claude Vivier), Rambert Dance Company

1990 *Dealing with Shadows* (mus. Mozart), Rambert Dance Company

Roughcut (mus. Steve Reich), Rambert Dance Company, Newcastle

1992 *Cat's Eye* (mus. David Sawer), Rambert Dance Company, Bristol

Le Marteau sans Maitre (mus. Boulez), Compagnie Chopinot, La Rochelle, France

1993 *Prelude and Fugue* (mus. Britten), Modern Dance Company of the State Opera, Ankara, Turkey

Sad Eyes (mus. Britten), Richard Alston Dance Company, Aldeburgh, Suffolk

Delicious Arbour (mus. Purcell), Shobana Jeyasingh Company, Nottingham

1994 *Movements from Petrushka* (mus. Stravinsky), London Contemporary Dance Theatre, Aldeburgh

Rumours, Visions (mus. Britten), London Contemporary Dance Theatre, Aldeburgh

Shadow Realm (mus. Simon Holt), Richard Alston Dance Company, Coventry

Something in the City (mus. Man Jumping), Richard Alston Dance Company, Coventry

1995 *Stardust* (original title, *Sometimes I Wonder;* mus. Hoagy Carmichael), Richard Alston Dance Company, Kuala Lumpar, Malaysia

1996 *Orpheus Singing and Dreaming* (mus. Birtwistle), Richard Alston Dance Company

Secret Theatre (mus. Birtwistle), Richard Alston Dance Company

Okho (mus. Xenakis), Richard Alston Dance Company

Beyond Measure (original title, *Bach Measures;* mus. Bach), Richard Alston Dance Company

1997 *Brisk Singing* (mus. Jean-Philippe Rameau), Richard Alston Dance Company, Brighton

Light Flooding into Darkened Rooms (mus. Denis Gaultier, Jo Kondo), Richard Alston Dance Company, Brighton

Publications

By ALSTON: articles—

"Movement and People First," *Dance and Dancers,* June 1978.

On ALSTON: books—

Jordan, Stephanie, *Striding Out: Aspects of Contemporary and New Dance in Britain.* London, 1992.

On ALSTON: articles—

Constanti, Sophie, "Richard Alston: The Humanist Approach," *Dance Theatre Journal,* 1989.
Jordan, Stephanie, "Second Stride: The First Six Years," *Dance Theatre Journal,* 1988.
———, "Interviews with Richard Alston and Nigel Osborne," *Choreography & Dance,* 1992.
Kane, Angela, "Richard Alston: Twenty-one Years of Choreography," *Dance Research,* Autumn, 1989.
Macauley, Alistair, "Notes on Dance Classicism," *Dance Theatre Journal,* 1987.
———, "Processes, Connections, Bloodlines; Ballet Rambert," *Dance Theatre Journal,* 1983.
———, "Second Stride Second Year," *Dance Theatre Journal,* 1983.
"Rambert at the Top: Special Rambert Issue," *Dance Theatre Journal,* 1987.
Robertson, Allen, "Full Circle," *Dance Now,* Spring 1995.

*   *   *

Richard Alston was one of the leading innovators in British dance in the 1970s (others being the X6 collective, Britain's Judson Church). At a time when the London Contemporary Dance Theatre and School and Ballet Rambert were developing a Graham-derived style of British modern dance, Alston was investigating the artistic approaches that had been developed as a challenge to this kind of work in America, first by Cunningham, then by the Judson Dance Theater. On leaving London Contemporary Dance School (LCDS) Alston formed Strider, the first experimental dance group to be recognised officially by funding bodies in Britain. (Among its members was Eva Karczag, later to dance with Trisha Brown.) Strider experimented with using everyday movement, assemblage and montage, and other nondance devices as elements of its works.

Alston first became interested in dance through ballet, in particular through the work of Frederick Ashton. (He also acknowledges a debt to Fred Astaire.) It is the work of Merce Cunningham, however, that has had the greatest influence on Alston throughout his career. Alston was introduced to Cunningham's work in the late 1960s when still an art student. Cunningham's approach to movement made a great impression on Alston and in 1975 he left London to study with Cunningham in New York. While there he saw the work of artists such as Trisha Brown, Lucinda Childs, and Douglas Dunn. This period of study and immersion in the New York dance scene proved to be a turning point in his career.

Returning to Britain with a deeper knowledge of the movement source of his work, Alston took Cunningham's movement and choreographic ideas and transformed them to suit his own artistic sensibility. He combined the detail and specificity of Cunningham's movement with the soft, released weightiness of the release tech-

niques he had learned under the guidance of Mary Fulkerson in the early 1970s. He drew on the results of Cunningham's chance procedures—the textural density of the stage picture, the unpredictability of spatial and rhythmic connections in the movement of dancers—but brought them under the control of his choreographic imagination. Unlike Cunningham he deliberately worked toward a closer connection between movement and music, while maintaining the excitement of unexpected connections between them. The choreographic style Alston developed as a result of his time in America has stayed with him throughout his career.

On his return to Britain in 1977 Alston formed a small ad hoc group, Richard Alston and Dancers. Among its members were Ian Spink and Siobhan Davies, later to become major choreographers in their own right. Richard Alston and Dancers, unlike Strider, performed only Alston's choreography. During this period Alston supplemented his income by teaching and in doing so performed a service of immense importance to British independent dance by introducing a whole generation of young British dance artists to Cunningham's dance technique and choreographic practices. The effects of this resonated through the independent dance scene in Britain for many years.

Although some of Alston's work at this time retained its earlier connections with the experimental dance work of the New Dance scene, by 1977 it was becoming increasingly more aligned with a more conventional theatre dance tradition. Finally, in 1980, having created *Bell High* for the company in the preceding year, Alston was invited to become Ballet Rambert's resident choreographer. In 1986 he was appointed the company's artistic director.

During his artistic directorship, which lasted until 1992, Alston introduced general dance audiences across Britain to a more rigorously formalist mode of modern dance than they had known previously. He changed the name of the company to Rambert Dance Company and invited Merce Cunningham, Trisha Brown, Lucinda Childs, and David Gordon to create works for its programmes.

While with Rambert Dance Company Alston began to commission contemporary British visual artists such as Richard Smith (*Wildlife*), Howard Hodgkin (*Night Music, Pulcinella*), and John Hoyland (*Zansa*) to create designs for his works. He also consistently used musical scores from late-20th-century contemporary composers, most notably Nigel Osborne (for *Apollo Distraught, Wildlife, Zansa, Mythologies*) and Peter Maxwell Davies (for *Bell High* and *Hymnos*). In doing so Alston aligned dance with other contemporary arts, making it evident that dance could have as much substance and conceptual complexity as contemporary literature, visual art, and music and that such work deserved as much interest in what lay beneath its surface as did the works of artists from other disciplines. Although Alston's artistic policy converted many audience members (many of whom would later become influential in the British dance scene), it seems that the road he was taking was too radical for many at a time when artistic conservatism was becoming dominant in Britain. In 1992 his period as artistic director of one of Britain's major modern dance companies came to an end.

In 1994, after a period as an independent choreographer, Alston became artistic director of The Place. At this same time he formed his own touring dance company, the Richard Alston Dance Company, and continued to create new work on a regular basis. Alston has maintained his interest in contemporary music, working to the music of composers such as Harrison Birtwistle (for *Orpheus Singing and Dreaming* and *Secret Theatre*) and Iannis Xenakis (for *Okho*), but he is also using more music from earlier times.

Alston's work, which has undergone many shifts in emphasis since 1969, has had a profound effect on developments in British dance, particularly during the late 1970s and the 1980s. In the late 1990s his work is less rigorously formalist than it was at the height of his time with Rambert Dance Company, as he returns to a more intimate investigation of the possibilities choreography can offer. The choreographic intelligence that has characterised his work throughout his career, however, remains.

—Sarah Rubidge

ALUM, Manuel

Puerto-Rican dancer, choreographer and company director

Born: 23 January 1943 in Arecibo, Puerto Rico. **Education:** Attended Wright Ammundson, 1959-61; studied in Chicago with Neville Black, 1958-59; ballet in New York with Mia Slavenska and Margaret Black; modern with Martha Graham, 1961; Paul Sanasardo, 1962. **Career:** Dancer, Paul Sanasardo Dance Company, 1963-73; assistant director, Saratoga Performing Arts Center, 1965-70; assistant artistic director, Sanasardo company, 1969-73; founder, Manuel Alum Dance Company, 1973; danced/choreographed King of Thailand's birthday celebration, 1987; choreographed for Asia Society, Folkwangschule (Essen, Germany), Ballet Rambert (London), Bat-Dor Dance Company (Israel), Ballet Hispanico, Dance Theatre of Harlem, Taller de Histriones, North-South Dance Festival, Washington Ballet, and others; taught at UCLA, Cal Arts, American Dance Festival, Pina Bausch's Wuppertal Dance Theatre, and others. **Awards:** National Endowment for the Arts (NEA) grants, beginning 1970; New York State Council for the Arts grants, beginning 1970; Dancer of the Year, Government of Puerto Rico, 1975; first Japan/U.S. Friendship Commission grant, 1979; Best Performer, Musical America, 1981. **Died:** 12 May 1993 in New York City.

Roles (performed with the Paul Sanasardo Dance Company and choreographed by Sanasardo)

1966   *Excursions*
        Cut Flowers
        An Earthly Distance
        The Animals Eye
1970   *Footnotes*

Works

1963   *Familiar Trio*
        Wings I Lack
1965   *Nightbloom* (mus. Serocki)
1966   *The Offering* (mus. Penderecki)
        Storm (mus. Luciuk)
1967   *Dream after Dream and After*
        The Cellar (mus. Kilar)
        Fantasia
1968   *Dream and Trail*
        Palomas (mus. Oliveros)
1969   *Overleaf* (mus. Messiaen)

1970   *Era* (mus. Penderecki)
        Roly-Poly (mus. Berio)
1971   *Terminal*
1972   *Sextetrahedron*
        Woman of Mystic Body, Prey for Us
1973   *Deadlines*
        East—To Nijinsky
        Juana for Bat-Dor Dance Company
        Moonscapes for Dance Theatre of Harlem
        Steps—a Construction
1974   *Escaras* for Ballet Rambert
        Ilanot (Young Trees) for Bat-Dor Dance Company
        Yemaya
1976   *B.B.B. (Bowery Bicentennial Celabration)*
        El Tango
        ToGetHer, (originaly a section of *Escarsas*)
        Dream Rem #51177
1978   *On the Double*
1979   *Untitled*
1981   *Made in Japan*
1991   *Made in Malaysia: A Shamanic Journey*

Publications

Baker, Bob, Review, *Dance Magazine,* August 1975.
Interview, *Dance and Dancers,* December 1974.
Goodman, S., "Manuel Alum," *Dance Magazine,* March 1969.
Jowitt, Deborah, Review, *Village Voice,* 12 July 1976.
Martin, John, "Dance Scrapbook," *New York Times,* 19 March 1961.
Maskey, Jacqueline, *Dance Magazine,* November 1963.
Reynolds, Nancy, *The Dance Catalogue,* New York, 1979.
Thom, RoseAnne, Reviews, *Dance Magazine,* October 1975.

*   *   *

Manuel Alum was born in Puerto Rico, and began dancing after he moved to the United States in the late 1950s. After studying dance with Neville Black in Chicago, Alum moved to New York City in the early 1960s where he studied ballet with Mia Slavenska and Margaret Black, as well as modern dance at Martha Graham's school in 1961, and with Paul Sanasardo in 1962. Alum was with Sanasardo for many years, first as a student, then as a dancer, and eventually acting as assistant artistic director for the Paul Sanasardo Dance Company.

Some of Sanasardo's creative influence was manifested in Alum's choreographic subject matter, which tended to the serious and issue-oriented (some might say depressing). Alum also modeled his own virtuosic movement after Sanasardo, who was known for his extraordinarily precise movement. Once Alum joined Sanasardo's company in 1963, he quickly rose to the rank of lead dancer. While still with Sanasardo, Alum began to choreograph his own pieces, setting some of them on the Sanasardo company. Soon afterward, he was ready to go out on his own. Following the example of numerous other dancers who were unquestionably talented and whose choreography was innovative and original, Alum formed the Manuel Alum Dance Company in 1973. His skills had already been recognized by Sanasardo and others within the dance community, but beginning in 1970 Alum was awarded the first of many grants from both the National Endowment for the Arts (NEA) and the New York State Council for the Arts.

As Alum's reputation grew, he became in high demand as a guest choreographer both domestically and abroad, and as an educator.

Manuel Alum (right) with Eleo Pomare, Robert Small and Clay Taliaferro. Photograph by Tom Caravaglia.

He served as the assistant director (summers) for the Saratoga Performing Arts Center, taught at UCLA, Cal Arts, the Folkwangschule in Essen, Germany, as well as both performing and teaching workshops at the American Dance Festival and the Lincoln Center's special programs and festival. Alum created choreography for a wide range of companies from Ballet Rambert in London and Bat-Dor Dance Company in Israel to Dance Theatre of Harlem and the Washington Ballet. Pina Bausch invited him to perform and teach at her Wuppertal Dance Theatre, and the Asia Society commissioned him to create *Made in Mayalsia: A Shamanic Journey,* modeled on Alum's 1981 *Made in Japan,* which developed from his sojourn in that country, as the first recipient of a Japan/ U.S. Friendship Commission grant.

   Although Alum became well-known during a time when many modern dancers were immersing themselves in experimental dance and choreography, his work is primarily remembered as deep and psychically painful, yet beautiful in its technical precision—a lesson learned through Sanasardo and in turn from Sokolow—often considered the "queen" of isolation and despair themes in modern dance. Alum's pieces

may have centered on emotional angst, yet his dancing rose above the inherent tragedy and was distinct and captivating. Anna Kisselgoff of the *New York Times* called his *Made in Japan* "mesmerizing," while Jennifer Dunning, writing for the same paper in 1993, called Alum a "performer of dark and powerful intensity."

   Alum's precise and subtle movements were very communicative, even within periods of stillness—much like a rest in a measure of music; he also incorporated seemingly random movement, which added interesting texture to his dances. *The Cellar* (1967), Alum's highly acclaimed solo, conveyed the loneliness of waiting; *East—to Nijinsky* (1973), another stunning solo, pulsed with a religious theme, movements suggesting the fervent prayer of a pious Jew. Many of Alum's pieces reflected the language, ethnic motifs, and religious symbols of his background; many cultures in the Caribbean had been influenced by various religions and rituals of West Africa, and in his work, *Yemaya* (1974), Alum draws from the Yoruban belief in *Orisa,* according to which divine beings are identified with oceans, forests, land formations, storms, and other natural phenomena. Each divinity has its own characteristic personality with symbolic garments, colors, and paraphernalia. *Yemaya* depicts the sea goddess of the same name, and in Alum's piece the seven dancers dressed in light blue and white perform "despojo," a ritual cleansing away of negative spirits.

Though many of Alum's pieces deal with tragic circumstances of one kind or another, some portray the ugly violence lurking in the human soul, such as *El Tango* (1976), a work in which two women dressed in evening gowns dance, stalking each other, until the dance ends with a stabbing. *ToGetHer*, also from 1976, portrays another couple, this one man and woman, who are in continual confrontation. The viewers sense the concealed, or barely contained violence between the two individuals. Alum's work *Era* (1970) juxtaposes the chaos of a violent society with a delicate and passionate pas de deux, yet the piece turns vicious, ending with a brutal rape.

Palomas (1968), too, revisited Alum's landscape of violence, only this time in the form of war. In the dance, Alum included images of peace, along with the agony, fear, and horrors of war. In contrast, Alum's *Ilanot* (1974; meaning "young trees") was created for the Bat-Dor Dance Company of Tel Aviv, featuring an ensemble of nine dancers with a pas de deux as well as a solo danced by Alum. The costumes are simple and earthy, the stage atmosphere dependent upon the woodsy lighting technique, and the rhythm and movement of the dancing seem perpetual.

Manuel Alum died at the very young age of 50, in May 1993, decades before his time. Though he accomplished much in his lifetime, whether portraying the darkest tendencies of the soul through searing solos or providing lighter entertainment for dance companies around the globe, there's no telling how much further he could have taken the art form. Fearless to present the ugliest side of human nature, Alums did so with compassion and peerless precision.

—Christine Miner Minderovic

ALVIN AILEY AMERICAN DANCE THEATRE
American repertory dance company

The Alvin Ailey American Dance Theatre (AAADT) began in 1958 as a repertory company of seven dancers devoted to both modern dance classics and new works created by founder Alvin Ailey and other young artists. Before this, modern companies typically presented work only by their founders. Ailey's repertory plan, modeled after ballet company practice, signaled a shift in the range of material available to dancers and audiences at a single performance. This policy held profound implications for all modern dance companies, as it predicted the ability of a company to outlive its founder and sustain a vibrant standard of performance across generations.

The eclectic repertory of AAADT has included work in a variety of idioms such as ballet, neo-African, jazz, Graham modern, Horton, and Dunham technique. Important pieces danced by the company include Ailey's *Blues Suite* (1958), Jerome Robbins' *New York Export, Opus Jazz* (1958), Donald McKayle's *Rainbow 'Round My Shoulder* (1959), Talley Beatty's *The Road of the Phoebe Snow* (1959), John Butler's *Carmina Burana* (1959), Ailey's *Revelations* (1960), Anna Sokolow's *Rooms* (1965), Louis Johnson's *Lament* (1965), Geoffrey Holder's *Prodigal Prince* (1967), Ulysses Dove's *Vespers* (1986), Judith Jamison's *Forgotten Time* (1989), and Donald

Byrd's *Dance at the Gym* (1991), as well as dances by venerable American choreographers Ted Shawn, Pearl Primus, Katherine Dunham, Lester Horton, and Joyce Trisler. In 1976 AAADT celebrated composer Duke Ellington with a festival featuring 15 new ballets set to his music, a project which brought new critical consideration of Ellington's musical achievement. The expansive range of works and dance idioms tests the mettle of Ailey dancers, who are known for their astounding strength, dramatic projection, and versatility.

Within a decade, AAADT also danced works by diverse choreographers including Garth Fagan, George Faison, Bill T. Jones, Lar Lubovitch, Elisa Monte, Jennifer Muller, Eleo Pomare, and Jawole Willa Jo Zollar. In its earliest years, AAADT toured extensively, bringing dance to a large audience that had never encountered concert performance. This young and largely African American audience provided the wellspring of support essential to the Ailey enterprise. The AAADT established its vast international reputation through a series of tours begun in 1962 by a five-month engagement in Southeast Asia and Australia. Sponsored by the International Exchange Program under the Kennedy Administration, this tour established a pattern of performance in foreign countries continued by journeys to Rio de Janeiro (1963); a European tour including London, Hamburg, and Paris (1964); an engagement at the World Festival of Negro Arts in Dakar, Senegal (1966); a 16-week European tour including the Holland Festival in Amsterdam (1967); and a U.S. State Department-sponsored nine-nation tour of Africa (1967). In 1969 the company completed a successful run on Broadway, thereby securing a committed American audience. In 1970 AAADT became the first American modern dance company to perform in the postwar Soviet Union. The company has retained peerless stature as a touring ambassador of goodwill since the 1970s, both domestically and abroad. By 1989, the AAADT counted over 30 dancers on its roster and had been seen by some 15,000,000 people worldwide.

Ailey encouraged his dancers to present highly emotional and dramatic performances, a strategy that created the first series of star personalities, who were not choreographers, in American modern dance. Judith Jamison's electrifying performance of Ailey's *Cry* presented a coherent relationship between the dancing body and the experience of living as a black woman in America. *Cry* has been successfully assumed by several Ailey dancers, most notably Donna Wood, Sara Yarborough, Nasha Thomas, and Renee Robinson. In 1972 Ailey created the elegiac tripartite solo *Love Songs* for Dudley Williams, revived in 1993 by dancer Michael Thomas. Gary DeLoatch, a longtime principal with the company, brought an eloquent intensity to his roles, especially as the pusher in Talley Beatty's *The Stack-Up* (1983) and as Charlie Parker in Ailey's *For Bird—With Love* (1984). Innumerable significant dance personalities have passed through AAADT, including Marilyn Banks, Hope Clarke, Carmen De Lavallade, George Faison, Miguel Godreau, Thelma Hill, Mari Kajiwara, Linda Kent, Desmond Richardson, Kelvin Rotardier, Elizabeth Roxas, Clive Thompson, Mel Tomlinson, James Truitte, and Sylvia Waters.

Building on his fond memories of the Horton studio, Ailey founded the Alvin Ailey American Dance Center in 1969 to educate dance students in the history and art of ballet and modern dance. Courses at the school include dance technique and history, music for dancers, dance composition, and theatrical design. Predicting the future of his school's needs, Ailey formed the Alvin Ailey Repertory Ensemble in 1974 as a bridge between study and membership in professional dance companies. This junior company flourished, maintained its own full touring schedule, and set a stan-

Alvin Ailey Dance Company: *The Mooch,* **1977. Photograph © Beatriz Schiller.**

dard for similar junior companies affiliated with Martha Graham, Paul Taylor, and the Joffrey Ballet. In 1984 the Alvin Ailey Student Performance Group was created under the direction of Kelvin Rotardier to offer lecture-demonstration programs to communities traditionally underserved by established arts institutions.

In 1989 Dance Theater Foundation Inc., the umbrella organization for AAADT and the Ailey School, initiated the Ailey Camps program, an outreach program designed to enhance the self-esteem, creative expression, and critical thinking skills of inner-city youth through dance. Success of the initial venture in Kansas City, Missouri, led to similar programs begun in New York City (1990) and Baltimore, Maryland (1992). Although Ailey created the AAADT to feature the talents of his African American colleagues, the company was never exclusively black. Determined to provide an interracial performance venue denied American audiences before the civil rights era, Ailey integrated his company to counter the chauvinism implicit in segregation.

Upon Ailey's death in 1989, Judith Jamison became artistic director of the company, to work closely with rehearsal director Masazumi Chaya. Under their tenure the company experienced extensive annual turnover; still the standard of performance remained admirably high. AAADT emerged from financial difficulties in 1992, when *Dance Magazine* proclaimed it "recession-proof"

due to powerful development efforts on the part of the Dance Theater Foundation Inc.'s board of directors. This financial accomplishment, derived from careful fiscal management, an extensive touring schedule, and sold-out seasons in nearly every conceivable venue, represented yet another first for an American modern dance company.

Publications

On AAADT: books—

Allen, Zita, *Alvin Ailey American Dance Theatre: 25 Years*, New York, 1983.

Hodgson and Victor, "Alvin Ailey City Center Dance Theater," in *Quintet: Five American Dance Companies,* New York, 1976.

Mitchell, Jack, *Alvin Ailey American Dance Theatre: Jack Mitchell Photographs.* Kansas City, 1993.

On AAADT: articles—

Bailey, A. Peter, "Alvin Ailey at the Met," *Ebony,* October 1984.

Hardy, Camille, "Recession-Proof Dance Leadership," *Dance Magazine,* October 1992.

Topaz, Muriel, editor, "Alvin Ailey: An American Visionary," *Choreography and Dance: An International Journal,* 4 (Part 1), 1996.

Washington, Ernest L., editor, "Alvin Ailey: The Man and His Contributions," *Talking Drums! The Journal of Black Dance,* May 1990.

—Thomas DeFrantz

AMERICAN DANCE FESTIVAL

Nonprofit organization that produces an annual six-week summer event of the same name featuring performances and a school on the Duke University campus in Durham, N.C.; year-round offices in Durham and New York; first operated as ADF in 1948 at Connecticut College in New London, Connecticut; moved to Durham in 1978; traces its roots to Bennington College in Vermont where a summer dance school was established in 1934; performances added, 1935; summer festival continuing until WWII intervened, 1942; current directors: Charles and Stephanie Reinhart; past directors: Mary Josephine Shelly, Martha Hill, Jeanette Schlottmann, and Theodora Wiesner.

Publications

On ADF: books—

Anderson, Jack *The American Dance Festival,* Durham, N.C., 1987.
Townes, Alta Lu, *The American Dance Festival: Dancing Across Cultures,* Durham, N.C., 1984.

*   *   *

The American Dance Festival (ADF) represents a major home for modern dance, as one of the largest, in number of performances, and one of the few summer modern dance festivals in the United States. For over half a century, the festival has and continues to nurture this indigenous American art form through classes, stage performances and by commissioning works from master, emerging and foreign modern dancemakers.

Through its Emerging Generations and Young Choreographers and Composers' programs, the festival has helped such dancemakers as Bill T. Jones, Mark Dendy, Mark Morris, and Molissa Fenley not only emerge, but become bright, shining stars in the dance firmament. Pilobolus, Twyla Tharp, and Laura Dean were also "graduates" of these programs in which the festival commissions new works to be created and presented during the six-week event. The 1981 Emerging Generations program included Johanna Boyce's dance in a swimming pool, with live harp accompaniment, as well as work by Bill T. Jones and Arnie Zane and Fenley. That same year, the ADF began to recognize lifetime contributions to American modern dance by establishing the annual Samuel H. Scripps American Dance Festival Award of $25,000, funded by Scripps. Martha Graham, one of the pioneers of modern dance, received the first award. Sitting regally in a tall, upholstered chair on stage, she told stories to a spellbound audience.

Over 200 dances have premiered at the festival, including such classics as Graham's *Diversion of Angels* (1949), José Limón's *The Moor's Pavane* (1949), Alwin Nikolais' *Kaleidoscope* (1956), Merce Cunningham's *Summerspace* (1958), and Paul Taylor's *Aureole* (1962). The festival has always honored its roots with periodic revivals, but in 1988, it began a project to pay homage to and preserve the modern dance works of black choreographers. That year, the festival commissioned Donald McKayle to set his *Games* on the Durham-based African American Dance Ensemble, directed by Chuck Davis. The ADF's Classic Revivals and Black Traditions in American Modern Dance projects went on to set other works by McKayle, as well as such choreographers as Pearl Primus, Eleo Pomare and Talley Beatty on such companies as Joel Hall Dancers, Philadanco, and the Dayton Contemporary Dance Company. "We're rewriting our own history in modern dance," Charles Reinhart told the *Durham Sun* that year. As a result of this "rewriting," audiences have been treated to the power, passion, and precision of such dances as Primus' *Strange Fruit,* McKayle's *Rainbow 'Round My Shoulder,* Pomare's *Blues for the Jungle* and Beatty's *Mourner's Bench.*

From the first season in Connecticut, foreign students have been drawn to the festival. But, since the 1980s, the ADF has taken a decidedly international turn. Charles Reinhart spoke of the rise, in the 1980s, of the level of creativity in modern dance on a worldwide bases, in part, encouraged by the fall of dictatorships. "We're going to go to wherever we feel the creative spark is, and geography isn't important," Reinhart said in his 1988 interview. The Reinharts found one such spark on a mountaintop in Kyoto, Japan, in 1979 where they saw the Butoh (dark soul) troupe Dai Rakuda Kan perform *Sea-Dappled Horse.* At the 1982 festival, ADF introduced the company and work to American audiences, who watched in shock and astonishment as dancers, faces contorted in silent screams, eyes rolled back so that only the whites showed, proceeded to present a cataclysmic, two-and-a-half-hour dance performed without intermission. Other foreign forays have resulted in the American debut, at the festival, of many other international companies.

The festival instigated the International Choreographers Workshop in 1984 and drew dancemakers from England, France, Indonesia, India, and the Philippines to immerse themselves in modern dance by attending performances and classes. Out of this workshop came the inclusion of an international modern dance program, beginning in 1987, as a regular part of the performance lineup. Also in the late 1980s, the ADF instigated the Institutional Linkages Program of exchanges through which it has already sent teachers to a number of countries, including China, Russia, Argentina, South Africa, Venezuela, Uruguay, Czechoslovakia, and Zaire. The Reinharts have also taken shortened versions of the festival abroad 10 times as of 1997, to Tokyo, Korea, India, and Russia, offering performances as well as classes taught by such master teachers as Betty Jones (former principal dancer with the José Limón Company).

Betty Jones has also been included among master teachers employed at the ADF's summer festivals in America, where it continues a long tradition dating back to the 1930s at Bennington where teachers for the summer festival included Martha Graham, Doris Humphrey, Charles Weidman and Hanya Holm. Other teachers have included Lucas Hoving, another former principal dance with the Limón Company, and Klarna Pinska, a former dancer who spent 50 years with American modern dance pioneer Ruth St. Denis. Teachers scheduled for the 1998 festival include Betty Jones, Donald McKayle and Carolyn Adams (former principal dancer with the Paul Taylor Dance Company), and Matt Mattox, recipient of the

1998 Balasaraswati/Joy Ann Dewey Beinecke Endowed Chair for Distinguished Teaching, established by the ADF in 1991.

Now famous festival students have included Meredith Monk, Madonna, and Paul Taylor. For almost two decades, the festival offered training for critics through its Dance Critics Conference. The ADF continues audience development through community classes, lectures and demonstrations to help people understand the nature of the art form. "We know what modern dance is not," co-director Charles Reinhart said. What it is can be just about anything—as ADF audiences have learned. In the first 20 years in Durham, audiences saw dances in a garden, creek, swimming pool, on the grass, and in trees as reminders of the pioneer spirit of modern dance as choreographers push into new frontiers. "We're always going to have the avant-garde," Deborah Jowitt, then critic at the *Village Voice,* stated in an ADF lecture in 1981, "The nature of modern dance has been revolutionary."

Others have offered tips on watching this ever-changing art form based on individual freedom of expression. "Don't worry about what it means," Charles Reinhart has said, "Modern dance is a visual art form. . .You might like the colors, the movement; you respond to the dance. . .It does something to you."

—Susan Broili

ANDERSON, Carol

Canadian dancer, choreographer, artistic director, educator, and writer

Born: 17 January 1951 in Regina, Saskatchewan. **Education:** B.F.A. in dance, York University, 1973; further training at London School of Contemporary Dance, Cunningham Studio, Guthrie-Rotante Company, José Limón Company, Manhattanville College, Jennifer Muller Summer Session, Naropa Institute Summer Session, accompanist's workshop with Gwendolyn Watson; studied Graham technique with David Earle, Ahuva Anbary, Robert Cohan, Helen McGehee, Jane Dudley, Flora Cushman, Clover Roope, and others; Limón technique with Carla Maxwell, Risa Steinberg, Doug Varone, and others; studied ballet with Nanette Charisse, Grant Strate, Yves Cousineau, and others; studied Wigman-based tanzgymnastik and improvisation with Frau Til Thiele and Judy Jarvis; Laban-inspired dance with Patricia Cannon; contact improvisation with Lisa Nelson; contemporary barre classes with Patricia Miner and Peggy Baker. **Career:** Founding member, Judy Jarvis Dance Company, 1968; founding member Dancemakers, 1973; associate director of Dancemakers, 1980-81; co-director, 1981-85; artistic director, 1985-88; resident choreographer, 1988-89; guest dancer for Rinmon, Toronto Independent Dance Enterprise, and Guthrie-Rotante Company; independent choreographer and writer, since 1988; taught at Centennial College, York University, George Brown College, Canadian Children's Dance Theatre, School of Toronto Dance Theatre, and Teachers Collective (all Toronto); Burnaby Arts Centre and Main Dance Place (Vancouver); Ottawa Dance Theatre and Le Groupe de la Place Royale (Ottawa); Les Ateliers de Danse Moderne de Montreal Inc.; and Dansens Hus (Copenhagen). **Awards:** Dora Mavor Moore Award nominations for new choreography for *Angel Food* (1986), *Time and Fevers* (1988), and *Bone House* (1993); Ontario Scholarship, 1967; Chalmers Scholarship, 1972, 1973; Andromeda Scholarship, 1980; Dance

Ontario Award, 1994; and numerous Canada Council and Ontario Arts Council grant awards for choreography and arts writing.

Works

1974	*Sarabande* (mus. Bach)
1976	*Lumen* (mus. R. Murray Schafer)
1977	*Schooner* (mus. Keith Jarrett)
1979	*Nereid* (mus. original vocal score)
	Slow Air (mus. Scots Celtic music) solo for Patricia Fraser
1980	*Quick Studies* (mus. Ravel) for Dancemakers
1981	*Decade* (mus. Steve Reich), solo
	Roja (mus. Gwendolyn Watson)
1982	*Intaglio* (mus. Thomas Tallis) for Dancemakers
	Keen (mus. traditional Celtic)
	Fledgling (mus. Satie)
	Shore/A Slow Dance (mus. traditional Celtic; text John Montague)
1983	*Windhover* (mus. Michael J. Baker) for Dancemakers
	Warsawa (mus. David Bowie)
	Allegro Mysterioso (mus. Scriabin), solo
	In Time of Waiting (mus. Pergolesi)
	Remembered Music (mus. Vivaldi) for Dancemakers
1984	*Under Stars* (mus. Brian Eno)
	Rain (mus. Meredith Monk) for Ottawa Dance Theatre
	Missing Persons (mus. Henry Kucharzyk) for Dancemakers
1985	*River* (mus. Gordon Phillips) for Dancemakers
	Invictus (mus. Brian Eno) for Dwight Shelton
	Curriculum Vitae (mus. Matthew Fleming) for Groupe de la Place Royale
	Matrix (mus. James Tenney) for INDE '85
1986	*Angel Food* (mus. Michael J. Baker) for Dancemakers
	Letter to Leonardo w/Philip Drube (mus. Giovanni da Palestrina)
	Those Damn AM Songs (mus. Barbra Streisand, Linda Ronstadt) for Julia Sasso
1987	*Broken Symmetry* (mus. Ann Southam) for Dancemakers
	Polyhymnia Muses (mus. Elliott), solo
1988	*Time and Fevers* (mus. Elliott; text W.H. Auden, Norman Armour)
	d'ark (mus. Elliott), solo
	Nowell Sing We (mus. Elliott) for Canadian Children's Dance Theatre (CCDT)
	Burning House (mus. Elliott) for Dancemakers
1989	*Garden* (mus. Claude Debussy) for CCDT
1990	*Haiku* (mus. Elliott) for CCDT
1991	*"London"* (mus. Elliott) for CCDT's *Songs of Innocence and of Experience*
1992	*Stones* (mus. traditional Bulgarian music) for York University Dance Ensemble
	Waulking Songs (mus. traditional/contemporary Celtic music), School of Toronto Dance Theatre
1993	*Flesh Dress* (mus. Chopin; text Anderson) for fFIDA
	Bone House (mus. traditional Australian Aboriginal music) for Matthias Sperling
	Sephardic Songs (mus. traditional Spanish Sephardic songs) for CCDT
1994	*Flying Dream* (mus. Loreena McKennitt) for Unionville High School Dance Program

Lady Be Good (mus. Gershwin) for Shaw Festival
Les Belles Heures (mus. Elliott) for CCDT
1995   *Memoir* (mus. Michael Nyman), Cawthra Park High
      School Dance Program
1997   *Lily* (mus. Elliott) for CCDT

Other works include: Collaborations with Toronto Independent Dance Enterprise: *Second Wind* (1981) and *Common Ground* (1979); *Cutting Losses* (1982-83), with Terrill Maguire; the original *Court of Miracles* (1983) with Toronto Dance Theatre.

Publications

By ANDERSON: books—

Judy Jarvis, Dance Artist: A Portrait, Toronto.
Editor, *This Passion: For the Love of Dance*, Toronto, 1998.

By ANDERSON: articles—

"Canadian Children's Dance Theatre," "Fusion: Cross-Cultural Dance," and "Judy Jarvis," in *The Canadian Encyclopaedia*, Toronto, 2nd edition, 1997.
"Rachel Browne: Dancing Toward the Light," in *Canadian Dance Studies 2*, Toronto, 1997.
Contributions to "Reader's Corner" in *Dance Umbrella of Ontario (DUO) Newsletters,* Fall 1995, Spring 1996, Winter 1996.

On ANDERSON: articles—

Crabb, Michael, "Carol Anderson," in *101 From The Encyclopaedia of Theatre Dance in Canada*, ed. Susan MacPherson, Toronto, 1997.

Films and Videotapes

Carnival of Shadows for the documentary *The Greatest Show* (chor. Anderson, dir. Barbara Willis-Sweete; mus. R. Murray Schafer), Rhombus Media, 1988.
Canadian Brass: A Christmas Experiment, Rhombus Media, 1997.

*   *   *

Carol Anderson can truly be called a citizen of Canadian dance. A generous dancer, prolific choreographer, nurturing teacher and outstanding writer, she has been giving to the Toronto dance community since the early 1970s. She has acted as an advisor to the various levels of government arts funding as well as foundations and awards committees, has donated choreography to companies such as the Canadian Children's Dance Theatre, and more recently has dedicated herself to preserving Canada's dance history through her writing. She was honored for her contributions to the dance community in 1994 with the Dance Ontario Award.

Born in Saskatchewan, Anderson began her training in Regina with Royal Academy of Dancing teacher Eileen Carnrike. Anderson's family then moved to Ottawa, where she studied with another ballet teacher, Ingrid Bolf. When her family moved to Montreal a few years later she was introduced to modern dance through Laban-trained teacher Patricia Cannon. This initial exposure was enhanced when her family moved to Toronto where she was able to see Toronto Dance Theatre perform.

After finishing high school, Anderson enrolled in literature courses at Queen's, University in Kingston; here she met Judy Jarvis. Jarvis taught dance in the physical education department at Queen's and also ran a modern dance club. The Wigman-trained dancer was an inspiring presence to her students. After two years at Queen's Anderson returned to Toronto to join Jarvis' company. For the 1969-70 season, Anderson led a rigorous schedule of traveling to the northernmost end of Toronto for morning classes at York University, traveling down to the southern end of the city for afternoon classes and then rehearsing with Jarvis in the evening. Jarvis' work was exciting and fresh and very appealing to the dancers, but after a year Anderson decided to enroll in York University's dance program full-time.

Having completed many of her credits at Queen's, Anderson was able to focus on dance courses at York. She was always creating dances; no doubt her creativity had been fostered by Jarvis' improvisation sessions. Upon graduation, Anderson received a Canada Council grant to study abroad and having been inspired by Robert Cohan she traveled to England. She studied at the London School of Contemporary Dance where she was deeply influenced by teacher Jane Dudley, however, Anderson soon felt impulses to pursue more professional activities and returned to Toronto at the time that fellow York graduate Andrea Ciel Smith was starting a company called Dancemakers. Dancemakers made its debut with an outdoor concert in July 1974. Anderson continued to work with Dancemakers while teaching at York University until 1978 when she decided to go to New York to experience the world's dance mecca and to perform with the Guthrie-Rotante Company. The experience finally gave her a sense that the path she had chosen was a legitimate and acceptable way to earn a living. After about 18 months she returned to Toronto where she began to work with Dancemakers again and collaborated occasionally with Toronto Independent Dance Enterprise.

Anderson was associate director of Dancemakers from 1980 to 1981, co-director with Patricia Fraser from 1981 to 1985, sole artistic director from 1985 to 1988, and then resident choreographer for the 1988-89 season. She had been contributing choreography regularly since the company began. She finds her earlier works particularly meaningful; *Sarabande*, set to a solo cello piece by Bach, was created at London Contemporary Dance Theatre and was a trio which summed up what she had learned about craft and beauty. *Lumen,* which became a mainstay in Dancemakers repertory, was Anderson's first entree into the symbolism of dance. *Schooner* was very work-intensive; she spent hours and hours just creating the movement. *Decade, Allegro Mysterioso, Polyhymnia Muses* and *d'ark* were a group of solos Anderson created for herself to which she felt a great connection. When setting work on other dancers there is a distance between the communication of the movement and what physically happens, having what she refers to as "a tendency towards abstraction"; Anderson feels that in these solos she can at least be specific to herself. *Angel Food*, a highly intricate dance, received a Dora Mavor Moore Award nomination for best new choreography in 1986.

By 1987 Anderson was beginning to feel burnt-out from the demands of artistic direction. Choreographically she felt restricted by schedules and by her knowledge of the existing repertory—she felt herself creating pieces to fit into that repertory. When she tried to resign at the end of the 1987-88 season, the board of directors convinced her to at least remain as resident choreographer. She stayed for one more season but it was a difficult time as the company struggled with its transition from being a repertory company.

Anderson was the last of the original Dancemakers and her leaving marked a significant change in the company: it ceased being a repertory company and began to perform solely the work of its artistic director.

Free to do whatever she wanted, Anderson worked on a few solo performances but, having spent years touring with Dancemakers, the idea of following the touring circuit in Canada wasn't very appealing. She began to work on collaborations and commissioned choreography. With the aid of a Canada Council grant, she traveled Europe, saw as much dance as she could, and investigated the art of combining video and dance. She collaborated with filmmaker Barbara Willis-Sweete and composer R. Murray Schafer on the film *The Greatest Show* by choreographing *Carnival of Shadows*. She and composer Kirk Elliott presented *Time and Fevers* at the INDE '88 festival of new music and choreography. This dance combined Elliott's score with W.H. Auden's text and used five dancers and an actor. The combination of literature, original music and dance was a rewarding and exciting experience for Anderson.

In 1988 she also choreographed her first dance for Canadian Children's Dance Theatre (CCDT). Over the next decade she choreographed six more pieces for CCDT, collaborating frequently with Elliott. Among her dances for CCDT are *Haiku* created for the company's tour to China in 1991; *Sephardic Songs* inspired by young girls dancing in the Jewish quarter of Seville, Spain, during Anderson's trip there in 1992 (exactly 500 years after the expulsion of the Jews from Spain); and *Lily*, an abstract look at the relationship between the Virgin Mary and the Angel of the Annunciation which focused on the particular movement qualities of two of the company's dancers.

Anderson's newly found freedom also enabled her to write about dance. Literature and writing had always been an interest but time restrictions didn't allow this aspect of her artistic talent to develop. Her first project was the monograph *Judy Jarvis, Dance Artist: A Portrait*, but while working on this massive project she also wrote smaller articles and continued to teach and choreograph. She has written articles for text books, encyclopaedias, and newsletters and is in the midst of compiling and editing *This Passion: For the Love of Dance*, an anthology of articles written by dancers and choreographers about the dancers, choreographers, or teachers who inspired them to dance. It includes the writing of notable Canadian choreographers such as Patricia Beatty, Anna Blewchamp, Terrill Maguire, and Conrad Alexandrowicz. Anderson has become very passionate about collecting and preserving Canada's dance history. *This Passion* will be published by the archive and publishing house Dance Collection Danse, with whom Anderson collaborates frequently.

Anderson is also recognized as an accomplished teacher. She has taught in the major dance centers of Canada and was a founding member of Toronto's Teachers Collective. Recently she has found herself questioning her role as a teacher as the prospects for Canada's young dancers are somewhat dismal; however, she continues to be an inspiring presence to members of the Canadian Children's Dance Theatre and enjoys working with this company because the dancers, although under age 18, are performing regularly.

Anderson sees her life in dance as a long apprenticeship, a steady progress to freedom of expression. She has a very deep connection to dance and sees it as a sensitive art form, mutable according to the time, and that is what continues to draw her to it. Her dedication to the art form, its continuance, its development and its preservation, is inspiring and is appreciated by the community of which she has for so long been an integral part.

—Amy Bowring

ANDERSON, Lea

British dancer, choreographer and company director

Born: 13 June 1959 in London. **Education:** Middlesex College, 1977; St Martin's School of Art, 1979-80; BA Honours Dance Course at Laban Centre for Movement and Dance, 1981-84. **Career:** Co-founded female trio the Cholmondeley Sisters (later the Cholmondeleys), also the name of her first dance, with Teresa Barker and Gaynor Coward, 1984; company became a quartet in 1986, and later acquired additional dancers; founded the all-male group the Featherstonehaughs, 1988; began making full-scale theatrical productions for both companies, either separately or combined, with *Flag*, 1989; choreographed the British section of the Bicentennial parade the Marseillaise, celebrating the French Revolution, Paris, 1989; first filmed performance *Flesh and Blood*, 1990, Arts Council of England; has made work for Transitions *(Les Six Belles, We Don't Know What We're Saying,* and *Factor Six)*, La Bouche, Opera North, and other companies as well as choreographing for Leicester Polytechnic third-year students; choreographed the National Theatre and NT studio productions *Bow Down, Down by the Greenwood Side, Showsongs,* and *Mask of Orpheus,* the National Theatre company in a series of Harrison Bertwistle operas and, for the Donmar Warehouse, *Cabaret;* choreographed *Opera Sportif* for Leicester International Dance Festival, 1991; choreographed both of her companies in *Cross Channel* for BBC televison, 1992; wrote and presented two series of *Tights, Camera, Action!* for Channel 4 television, 1992 and 1994, including choreographing three short films. **Awards:** Digital Dance Awards, 1987, 1988, 1989; GLA Dance Award, 1987; London Dance and Performance Award for Outstanding Achievement, 1988; National Organisation for Dance and Mime in association with Dance Umbrella and *Time Out* awards, 1988; *Time Out*/01 for London Award, 1990; Rencontres Choreographiques Internationales de Bagnolet, 1990; London Dance and Performance Award, 1991; *Time Out* Award for Special Achievement, 1992; *Time Out* Dance Award, 1992; Bonnie Bird Award; Barclays New Stages Award, 1992.

Works

1984	*The Cholmondeley Sisters* (mus. Madden), Cholmondeleys
	Pole Dance (mus. Dead Can Dance), Cholmondeleys
	Health and Efficiency (mus. Madden), Cholmondeleys
1985	*Dragon* (mus. Madden), Cholmondeleys
	Signals (mus. Goat), Cholmondeleys
	Kolo (no mus.), Cholmondeleys
	Cutty Sark (no mus.), Cholmondeleys
1986	*Baby, Baby, Baby* (mus. Donaldson/Kahn, sung by Nina Simone), Cholmondeleys with first appearance of two Featherstonehaughs
	La Paloma (mus. Mexican), Featherstonehaughs, later adapted for the Cholmondeleys
	The Cliches and the Holidays (mus. traditional Catalan), Cholmondeleys
	The Fly and the Crow (mus. D. Madden), Cholmondeleys
	Heel in the Earth (mus. Cocteau Twins), Cholmondeleys
	Renoir, Mon Tricot (no mus.), Cholmondeleys
1987	*Marina* (mus. Bizet, Rossini, Verdi), Cholmondeleys
	But We Don't Know What. . . (mus. Madden), Transitions Dance Company

No Joy (mus. Madden), Cholmondeleys
Fishwreck (mus. Madden), Cholmondeleys
Carriage of Arms (mus. traditional Bulgarian), Cholmondeleys
Clump (mus. Blake), Featherstonehaughs and Cholmondeleys

1988   *Wear 2 Next* (mus. Blake), Cholmondeleys and Leicester Polytechnic students
Big Dance Number (mus. Madden, Blake), Cholmondeleys
Pastorale (mus. Blake), Cholmondeleys
Venus in Mourning (mus. Madden), Cholmondeleys
Parfum de la Nuit (mus. Callas in Bellini's *Norma*, Cholmondeleys)
The Futurists (mus. Madden), Cholmondeleys
Flag (mus. Madden, Blake), Cholmondeleys and Featherstonehaughs
Slump (mus. Blake), Featherstonehaughs

1989   *Flesh and Blood* (mus. Blake), Cholmondeleys

1990   *Factor 6* (mus. Blake), Transitions Dance Company
The Show (mus. various, Blake, Madden), Featherstonehaughs
Marseillaise (mus. DJs Ben and Andy), Cholmondeleys and Featherstonehaughs, plus 100 dancers, site-specific
Cold Sweat (mus. Blake, Madden), Cholmondeleys
Le Jeu Interlour du Tennis (mus. Madden, Khader), Jeunes Ballet de France, site-specific
Sardinas (mus. Blake), Cholmondeleys and Featherstonehaughs

1991   *Big Feature* (mus. various w/Madden, Blake), Featherstonehaughs
Opera Sportif (mus. Blake), Cholmondeleys

1992   *Birthday* (mus. Blake), Cholmondeleys and Featherstonehaughs
Walky Talky (mus. Madden), Cholmondeleys
Immaculate Conception (mus. Blake), Featherstonehaughs
Cross Channel (dir. Margaret Williams; mus. Blake), Cholmondeleys and Featherstonehaughs
Perfect Moment (dir. Margaret Williams; mus. Blake), Cholmondeleys and Featherstonehaughs
Jesus Baby Heater (dir. Douglas Brothers; mus. Blake), Featherstonehaughs

1993   *Precious* (mus. Blake), Cholmondeleys and Featherstonehaughs

1994   *Metalcholica* (mus. Madden), Cholmondeleys
Waiting (dir. Anderson; mus. Blake), Cholmondeleys
Spectre de la Rose (dir. Margaret Williams; mus. Madden), Featherstonehaughs
Joan (dir. Williams; mus. Madden), solo
The Bends (mus. various), Featherstonehaughs

1995   *Featherstonehaughs Go Las Vegas* (mus. Blake, Madden), Featherstonehaughs
Car (mus. Madden), Cholmondeleys

1997   *Flesh & Blood* (mus. Blake, Victims of Death), Cholmondeleys

1998   *The Featherstonehaughs Draw on the Sketch Books of Egon Schiele* (mus. Madden), Featherstonehaughs
Beach Huts (mus. Blake) Cholmondeleys and Featherstonehaughs, site-specific

Publications

On ANDERSON: books—

Mackrell, Judith, *Out of Line: The Story of British New Dance,* London, 1992.
Robertson, Allen and Donald Hutera, *The Dance Handbook,* second edition, London, 1998.

Films and Videotapes

Cross Channel and *Perfect Moment,* both directed by Margaret Williams with music by Blake featuring the Cholmondeleys and Featherstonehaughs, 1992.
Jesus Baby Heater, dir. Douglas Brothers, Featherstonehaughs, 1992.
Waiting, dir. Anderson, Cholmondeleys, 1994.
Spectre de la Rose, dir. Margaret Williams, Featherstonehaughs, 1994.
Joan, dir. Williams, Anderson solo, 1994.
Velvet Goldmine, dir. Todd Haynes, choreography by Anderson, 1997.

*　　*　　*

Lea Anderson was one of the most delightful and original finds of British dance in the mid-1980s. Her gradual rise to the top rank of the country's dancemakers, despite what some observed as her limitations as a choreographer, was well-deserved.

Along with friends and fellow Laban Centre alumni Teresa Barker and Gaynor Coward, Anderson made her first splash with the all-female trio the Cholmondeleys. The name, derived from an anonymous Elizabethan portrait in London's Tate Gallery and pronounced 'chum-leez', is indicative of the quirky humor embedded in many of their early dances. These were short, witty and beguiling works marked by a mimetic, code-like movement vocabulary and a knowing sense of play. The basis of much of her choreographic invention is a kind of calligraphic and often deliberately awkward, minutely detailed minimalism, with intricate movements strung together in a framework of rigid counts and fiendishly precise geometric patterns.

Anderson's initial branding as a miniaturist was, in part, a stylistic consequence of her need to choreograph for such unconventional venues as small clubs, cabarets, and even above and below the River Thames (aboard a floating art gallery and inside the Greenwich Tunnel, respectively). As she became better established and moved into more traditional venues, the attempts she made to correspondingly expand the scope of her work were not always appreciated, let alone recognized.

She was also making dance that fit her and her cohorts' physiques and characters. The Cholmondeleys were never inexpressive, robotic super-technicians, delicate balletic sylphs or elongated muses a la George Balanchine. (Anderson's debut dance, a duet called *The Cholmondeley Sisters,* amusingly subverted and domesticated the classic ballerina image.) Instead they are sturdier women in whom rhythm and grace are at the service of a more telling idosyncrasy. As a result, gestures in Anderson's universe may carry dramatic impact but rarely in themselves speak of grandeur.

In the late 1980s Anderson consolidated her potential by founding a male group christened, with equal eccentricity, the Featherstonehaughs ("fan-shaws"). Even more than the Cholmondeleys, this male manifestation of her talent betrayed

Anderson's former, abortive ambitions as a rock singer/songwriter. After achieving initial success for them via small, tight ensemble pieces like *Clump,* a neat study in masculine conformity, she began devising productions (*The Show, Big Feature*) structured like a series of record album 'tracks'. It was a sure way to harness and enhance the men's friendly, off-beat cult-band energy.

Concurrently Anderson began combining both companies in ever more ambitious and popular performances that, among other things, juxtaposed the questioning of gender stereotypes implicit in her work for each group separately. The first of these efforts, the 1988 *Flag,* was rightly considered something of a breakthrough. Adopting as her theme the politics of nationalism, Anderson boldly extended the concentrated muscularity and unison strength of her 1985 Cholmondeleys' piece *Dragon.* In the party-like *Birthday* (1992), the mood shifted from the anarchic to the intimate in a full-length piece shot through with tenderness, humor, and a wistful, approachable glamor. Anderson toyed further with her troupes' commonalities and differences in *Precious* (1993). Here alchemy was used as a metaphor for the quest for fulfillment of desire, as she put her dancers through four sections identified by color (black, white, red and gold).

Religious art and iconography provided at least part of the creative impetus for both the Featherstonehaughs' *Immaculate Conception* (1992), staged outdoors, and the Cholmondeleys' *Flesh and Blood* (1989). The latter, one of Anderson's most celebrated and accomplished works, has the distinction of being the first British modern dance to be officially designated for study by the country's education system. It demonstrated that Anderson was certainly capable of more than just clever antics. Full of ritualistic, medieval overtones, this edgy, darkly lyrical piece cast the Cholmondeleys as alternately furious, mysterious and fetishistic saints and martyrs clad in long, rippling metallic gowns. The choreography included some recognizable movement that seemed to be extravagantly magnified.

By the mid-1990s Anderson's detractors were accusing her of having run out of ideas, of being unable to sustain and hold one idea, and of dipping into the same quirky, repetition-based bag of tricks with which she'd made her name. This was an underestimation of her creative resources and keen sense of self-challenge. As if to offset criticisms of predictability by steering clear of mid-scale proscenium theatres, Anderson conceived *Car.* Here was a dance—or, rather, three of them, each self-contained and lasting about fifteen minutes—that could be taken literally on the road. The ploy behind this truly mobile entertainment (which toured Britain, France and the Netherlands in 1995 and 1997) was that the setting for the trio of dances was a Saab 9000. The cast of six women, alternately portraying identically dressed Jackie Kennedys, members of the Dadaist movement in back-to-front clothing, and sexy spirits out for a joyride, conducted a not-always-scrutable series of fastidiously timed gyrations and curious acrobatics in, around and atop the vehicle. Anderson was asking audiences to consider the automobile as a symbol of fashion and worship, as she underlined its connections with assassinations, accidents and road rage.

In 1998 Anderson likewise maneuvered her men's group in a new direction. For *The Featherstonehaughs Draw on the Sketch Books of Egon Schiele* she imaginatively aligned herself with the raw and strikingly mannered work of Viennese artist Schiele. Her goal was not so much to replicate as to three-dimensionalize onstage the disturbing and vital spirit inside the physical shapes of his drawings and paintings. The piece was a canny and peculiar combination of the pictorial and the psychological. Anderson felt a special em-

pathy for Schiele since, like him, her working habits entail the keeping of notebooks in which to jot down ideas and drawings for new dances and collect pertinent media images as further inspiration. Her art background, plus her affinity for filmmaking, are additional boons for new pieces.

Throughout her career Anderson has benefited from regular collaborations with a handful of pals including Oscar-nominated costume designer Sandy Powell, progressive jazz composer/musician Steve Blake, and percussive sound-scorer/manipulator Drostan Madden.

—Donald Hutera

ANDREWS, Jerome
American dancer and choreographer

Born: 7 September 1908 in Plaistow, New Hampshire. **Education:** Studied ballet and ballroom dancing, Cornish School, Seattle; also studied with Ruth St. Denis, Martha Graham, Louis Horst; worked with Doris Humphrey, Hanya Holm, and Margarethe Wallmann; attended the Jooss-Leeder school (England); continued ballet training with Olga Preobrajenska and Léo Staats; also studied ethnic dancing and Eastern philosophy. **Career:** Cabaret acts, New York, until 1930; soloist, Radio City Music Hall, 1930-37; danced with Léonide Massine, Humphrey, and Graham; discovered Pilates to overcome an injury, 1940; taught at Pilates Studio, 1944-45; dancer, with Ruth Page, 1947-48; met Mary Wigman, 1951; founder, Dance Companions Company (later renamed Jerome Andrews Dance Company), Paris, 1953. **Died:** 25 October 1992 in Paris.

Roles

1936   *Prometheus* (Sigurd Leeder), Paris

Works (all works premiered in Paris, France)

1936   *Rhapsody in Blue*
1953   *Meeting*
1960   *Day of the Earthquake* (mus. Chávez)
1964   *A Dead Soul Dances with an Angel*
1967   *Fleeting Capture* (mus. Parmegiani)
1968   *Mask of a Double Star* (mus. Semprun)
1970   *Ode*

Other works include: *Macbeth, The Beggar, Pierrot, Japanese Sketches, The Actor,* and *Oedipus,* and various solos performed in Paris.

*   *   *

Despite his modest origins in the United States, Jerome Andrews had the luck to belong to a cultivated and very arts-inspired family; his mother convinced him to explore his artistic creativity, enrolling him at the Cornish School in Seattle, Washington, to study a variety of dance, including ballet, ballroom, and social or entertainment-inspired dancing. During his adolescence, as Andrews's talent and interest grew, he took courses in the technique and dance styles of

Ruth St. Denis, Martha Graham, and Louis Horst. His rather eclectic education went from an emphasis on ballet to modern dance, along with Japanese, Indian, and ethnic dances (African, Mexican, and others), no doubt inspired by St. Denis's amalgamation of Western and non-Western movement.

Andrews began his professional dance career with short solos performed in Los Angeles and New York cabarets and clubs. He also appeared in solos at Radio City Music Hall in New York from 1930 to 1937. Andrews proved himself to be a quick study, combining his excellent technical skill with a lithe, graceful expressiveness. Critics of the time applauded his virtuosity, innovation, and enjoyed his high jumps and risk-taking on stage. John Martin of the *New York Times* noticed Andrews during his Radio City Music Hall days and was impressed enough to include Andrews in his book, *America Dancing*, published in 1936, stating "He possesses a great technique [and] moves with an admirable fluidity. We don't have the opportunity to see such possibilities each day."

Although gaining recognition as a talented dancer, Andrews continued taking courses in the 1940s to improve his knowledge and technique, working with Ivan Tarasoff, Léonide Massine, Doris Humphrey, Martha Graham, and studying at the Jooss-Leeder school in England. After an injury sidelined him in 1940, Andrews discovered the "Pilates Method" for reconditioning and rebalancing the body, and he not only overcame his injury but taught at the Pilates studio from 1944 to 1945.

Long fascinated by Mary Wigman, whose works he'd seen during her American tours, Andrews finally met the dance legend in New York in 1951. The meeting shattered his life and understanding of dance—and Andrews began a new quest for dance by taking classes at Wigman's wokshops in the States and then at her studio in Berlin. Andrews became aware of dance in an entirely new manner, as much for the audience as for the human body, a dance that transcended time, style, and nationality. He shifted his focus to the "poetry" of the human mind and body, finding, as Wigman believed, that each human being possessed a kind of poetry inherent in each gesture.

The 1950s were years of fame for Andrews, as then-editor of *Dance Magazine* Helen Dzermolinska confirmed in 1951, calling his solos virtuosic and magnificent, and marvelling at his ability to communicate through dance so peerlessly. Critic Pierre Thiriot, writing in 1952, found Andrews an "extremely gifted artist" and very accessible to his audiences. During the 1950s, Andrews relocated to France, where in 1953 he founded his first company, Dance Companions, which was renamed the Jerome Andrews Dance Company in 1964. Many young dancers and choreographers who would go on to well-known careers in France were members of his troupe, including Jacqueline Robinson, Karin Waehner, Laura Sheleen, Noelle Janoli, and Françoise and Dominique Dupuy, whose performance in Andrews' *Mask of a Double Star* (1968), brought not only fame to its choreographer, but generated considerable acclaim for the Dupuys and set the stage for a new generation of French modern dance. Two other choreographic works, *Day of the Earthquake* and *Fleeting Capture*, cemented the stature of Andrews as major influence and innovator of France's struggling modern dance scene.

In addition to his dancing and choreographing, Andrews was also a great educator who tried to help his dancers find their own identities. In a conference in 1975, Andrews extolled the virtues of giving students the freedom to find their own way, to combine their intuition and experience into a workable dance style. Andrews' philosophy could be summed up by a simple statement uttered at another dance conference in 1969 in Paris: "Movement is something living in the heart," he said, "it's fleeting, you can't [name] it." For Andrews, movement may have been from deep within and fleeting, but he harnessed its power and was able to teach this to his students. By combining a knowledge of one's own body with intuitive experiment, and following Wigman's Expressionist style, Andrews was able to introduce the dialectic connection between dance and music and forge a new landscape of French dance.

—Murielle Mathieu

ANTHONY, Mary

American dancer, choreographer, and educator

Born: 11 November 1916 in Newport, Kentucky. **Education:** Took up dance after seeing Martha Graham perform in the 1930s; studied with Hanya Holm and became her assistant, 1940s; studied with Martha Graham and Louis Horst, early 1950s. **Career:** Founder, Mary Anthony Dance Studio, New York City, 1954; founder, Mary Anthony Dance Theatre, 1956; one of the first to introduce modern dance to American television audiences; performed on Broadway; choreographer for commercial theater in Rome; taught and choreographed in Italy, Taiwan, and Israel; taught at Tanglewood, Jacob's Pillow, and the American Dance Festival; was artist-in-residence at various universities. **Website:** www.assist-net.com/Mary_Anthony.

Roles

1943	*Orestes and the Furies* (Holm)
1954	*Lyric Suite* (Sokolow)
1955	*Three Promenades with the Lord*
	Frontier Ballad

Works

1949	*Chaconne* w/Joseph Gifford
	Genesis (XIX)
	Giga
1950	*Voltare pro Venere*
1953	*Barbanera*
1955	*Passa d'Oppo*
1956	*Threnody* (mus. Britten)
	Songs (mus. Debussy)
1957	*The Purification (of Ritual of Purification)*
1958	*Blood Wedding*
	The Catbird Seat
1963	*At the Hawk's Well*
1967	*Gloria*
1968	*Antiphon*
1969	*In the Beginning: Adam*
1970	*In the Beginning: Adam and Eve*
1971	*A Ceremony of Carols*
	Cain and Abel
1975	*Seascape*
1979	*Tryptich*
1980	*Lady of the Sea*
1996	*Tabula Rasa*

Other works include: *The Dialogue, Plaisanteries d'amour, The Wind, Aperitif,* and numerous works for the *Look up and Live* and *Lamp unto My Feet* television series.

Publications

On ANTHONY: articles—

Timm, Fred, "A Celebration of Life and Dance," *Dance Magazine,* December 1996.
Topaz, Muriel, "Mary Anthony Dance Theatre," *Dance Magazine,* March 1997.

*   *   *

Mary Anthony is an esteemed dance teacher and choreographer, who is still active in the field, even in her eighties. She has remained a traditionalist throughout her career, focusing on choreography that tells a story, often inspired by mythology, classic literature, or the Bible. Martha Graham, with whom she studied for a time, is among her major choreographic influences.

During her junior year of high school Anthony saw Martha Graham perform at Ohio Wesleyan University and promptly decided to become a dancer. She moved to New York in the 1940s and studied with Hanya Holm, subsequently joining her company and becoming her assistant. She later studied with Martha Graham in the 1950s, and was invited to become a member of Graham's troupe. She declined the offer, however, opting instead to found her own school and company. The New York City-based Mary Anthony Dance Studio was launched in 1954, followed by the Mary Anthony Dance Theatre in 1956; both are still active more than 40 years later and are currently overseen by the Mary Anthony Dance Theatre Foundation.

In the 1950s Anthony was one of the first people to introduce modern dance to American television audiences, choreographing *The Lord's Prayer* for a Sunday-morning religious program called *Look Up and Live.* Between 1957 and 1959, she choreographed for a total of 20 telecasts of *Look Up and Live* and *Lamp unto My Feet,* another religious program aired on CBS. One of her early works, *Threnody* (1956), is still considered her signature piece. Set to a Benjamin Britten score, the 20-minute, 10-dancer piece is typical of her narrative choreographic style. It is based on John Millington Synge's *Riders to the Sea,* a one-act play that tells the story of a grieving woman who has lost her sons to the sea (the word "threnody" means "lament"). Some observers have viewed the piece as depicting war and the suffering it causes. The aesthetic beauty of the piece, as noted by critics over the years, is typical of Anthony's work. Louis Horst said of *Threnody,* "Here is the most beautiful and complete dance composition this observer has seen.... This is something approaching perfection."

Another of Anthony's early pieces is entitled *Songs* (1957), and it is also characteristic in terms of its clear exposition, its lyrical style, and the sensitivity of the choreography to the music. It is inspired by William Blake poetry and set to music by Debussy. Like *Threnody, Songs* also garnered reviews that commented on Anthony's poetic style. Jennifer Dunning, writing in the *New York Times,* called *Songs* "hauntingly lyrical [with] the emphasis. . . on simplicity and an ageless craft."

Anthony's works are often cited for their well-crafted quality. Fred Timm, one of Anthony's students, describes her work as follows:

Her dances, often based in literary narrative, certainly on emotional truth, are always linked to the human tradition. There is nothing cryptic; Mary's intention is to communicate, to share with her audience the discoveries that she, as an artist and as a person, has dared to explore.

In the 1970s, Anthony choreographed a number of religious-themed pieces, including *In the Beginning,* about Adam and Eve, *A Ceremony of Carols,* and *Cain and Abel.* While some of her older works remain her most popular, she continues to choreograph new dances into her eighties; for example, *Tabula Rasa* was choreographed for her eightieth birthday celebration in 1996 at the Sylvia and Danny Kaye Playhouse at Hunter College in New York, and premiered there.

Anthony is credited with establishing many of the modern dance techniques that are part of the contemporary dance canon. Clive Barnes, writing in the *New York Times,* found that Anthony had "a notable role in establishing the technical and stylistic qualities to be found in modern dance today." The universal themes contained in her dances continue to create a connection with her audiences. As Walter Terry said of Anthony in the *New York Tribune,* "her dance springs from the pulse of the heart and courses outward into the drama of life."

While Anthony is a respected choreographer, she is probably even more renowned as a teacher of dance. In her more than 40 years as the director of the Mary Anthony Dance Studio, her students have included Rudy Perez, Ronald Brown, and Fred Timm, among many others, and her faculty has included Anna Sokolow, Bertram Ross, and other members of her company, including Gwendolyn Bye. Anthony has a reputation as a strict teacher, yet with the ability to make dance instruction fun. In addition to teaching at her eponymous school, Anthony has instructed professional dancers in other venues. Abroad, she has taught in Italy, Taiwan, and Israel, while in the U.S. she has served as a dance instructor at Tanglewood, Jacob's Pillow, and the American Dance Festival. She also has participated in artist-in-residence programs at universities, such as a two-week stint at the University of Kansas in 1996, when she was 80. Anthony has also brought her and her company's teaching skills into primary and secondary schools through a national tour.

—Karen Raugust

APPALACHIAN SPRING

Choreography: Martha Graham
Music: Aaron Copland
Set Design: Isamu Noguchi
First Production: Library of Congress, Washington, D.C., 30 October 1944
Original Dancers: Martha Graham (Bride), Erick Hawkins (Husbandman), May O'Donnell (Pioneering Woman), Merce Cunningham (Revivalist), Nina Fonaroff, Pearl Lang, Marjorie Mazia, and Yuriko (Followers)

Other productions include: Mikhail Baryshnikov (Husbandman) and Rudolf Nureyev (Preacher) as guests of the Martha Graham

A 1987 performance of *Appalachian Spring* featuring Mikhail Baryshnikov and Terese Capucilli. Photograph © Beatriz Schiller.

Dance Company, New York, 6 October 1987. *Appalachian Spring* has been standard in the Graham repertoire since its premiere.

Publications

Martin, John, "The Dance: Washington Festival," *New York Times,* 5 November 1944.
Mueller, John, "Martha Graham Then and Now," *Dance Magazine,* December, 1977.

Films and Videotapes

Martha Graham Dance Company, Dance in America, dir. Merrill Brockway, Indiana University Audiovisual Center, 1976.

*   *   *

Appalachian Spring, set to Aaron Copland's Pulitzer Prize-winning score, is easily one of Martha Graham's most popular and enduring works. The piece was a favorite with critics and audiences from its beginning. After seeing it performed for the first time in 1944, John Martin of the *New York Times* noted the unprecedented "joyousness" it represented in Graham's choreography. And in the 1940s *Appalachian Spring,* with its celebration of basic human

relations, stood in sharp contrast to the realities of World War II.

Noguchi's set provided a minimalist representation of the Bride and Husbandman's new farmhouse, including a rocking chair of nearly two-dimensional narrowness and a fence rail that marked the boundary of the couple's property. A slanted tree stump sat slightly upstage and furnished the Revivalist with a pulpit. Graham would later say of such Noguchi sets that, as a dancer, they left one alone.

Set in the early American settlement era, the central action of the piece is the couple's possession of their new home as a symbol of all that they had hoped for in their future. The Revivalist, his Followers, and the Pioneering Woman help to initiate the couple into a life of tradition, community, and marital love. The piece, initially considered an example of "early Americana," is highly allegorical. The Bride and Husbandman not only express their personal joys and reservations, but they also communicate the collective hopes and anxieties of America as a burgeoning nation. The roles of the preacher and his followers confirm the work's symbolism as these characters allow Puritan morality to shape the movements of their lives.

Graham's choreography in *Appalachian Spring,* while rich and variegated, is also structurally symbolic. The Revivalist, with cautionary and sometimes accusatory gestures, joins his fussy and restrained Followers in establishing the boundaries of morality that delineate the couple's new life. Occasionally, however, the pious group indulges in mutual lapses of restraint. The sagacious Pioneering Woman is more consistent; her sweeping movements are an attempt to teach the young Bride all that her elder has already experienced.

The newlyweds, of course, command most of the attention in the piece. When dancing alone, the Husbandman's movements are decisive and proud. His use of space suggests delight in his property and, more generally, the promise of expansion that was so integral to the American frontier experience. The Bride's dancing is primarily joyous, though some of her freer moments are cut short by remembered inhibition or fear of future struggles. In fact, she shares her anxieties about bearing children with the Pioneering Woman. When dancing together, the couple inhabits a delightful harmony and embraces the discipline that their peers enjoin. On a few occasions, the two find themselves pleasantly surprised as they connect while executing a movement that had been thought to be autonomous.

Appalachian Spring provided a somewhat early example of the inventive floor work that Graham would continue to develop in her choreography. The Bride and Husbandman, in particular, assume various contracted positions on the floor. Nevertheless, the piece is also filled with athletic jumps by the male dancers, energetic leaps by the Bride, and several stunning lifts of the Bride by her partner.

In restagings of the piece, the "dark moments" that the Bride experiences have caused choreographic disagreement. Some believe that the piece ends on a frightful note as the Bride looks out in fear at the vast unknown with her husband, unseen, behind her. Others have downplayed uncertainty in the piece and emphasized the primarily festive nature of the couple's youthful optimism. This point of contention probably reflects the fact that *Appalachian Spring* was somewhat anomalous in Graham's frequently grave repertoire.

—Carrie Rohman

ARRIAGA, Guillermo
Mexican dancer, choreographer, educator, and director

Born: 4 July 1926 in Mexico City. **Education:** Began dance studies at the National Ballet of Mexico, then Mexican Academy of Dance; studied modern dance with Waldeen, Ana Mérida, José Limón, Doris Humphrey, Merce Cunningham, Anna Sokolow, and Mira Kinch; studied ballet with Margaret Craske and Adolph Bolm; studied folkloric dance with Vicente T. Mendoza and Marcelo Torreblanca; studied Spanish dance with La Meri; studied at Jacob's Pillow, Massachusetts, 1952; studied music with Pedro Michaca; theater with José Ignacio Retes, Seki Sano and Fernando Wagner; art history with José Rojas Garciadueñas; scenic arts with José Rojas Garciadueñas and Antonio López Mancera; and archaeology with Diego Rivera and Miguel Covarrubias. **Career:** Member of the companies of Lettie Carroll and Enrique Vela Quintero; teacher and choreographer, Mexican Dance Academy, 1949-63; dancer, Fine Arts Ballet; founded with Alejandro Jorodowsky first Mexican mime group; founder and dancer, Contemporary Ballet, 1953; founder and dancer, Mexican Ballet, 1956; founder, director, and dancer, Popular Ballet of Mexico, 1958-64; teacher, director of scenery, Folkloric Ballet of Mexico, 1961-63; founded Mexican Folkloric Ensemble, 1964; toured the United States, Israel, Germany, Portugal, Philippines, and Hong Kong; director, office of foreign artistic programs, and choreographer, XIX Olympic Games Committee, Mexico City, 1968; director, Radio Department, Mussart record company, 1969-70; advertising and promotion manager, Mussart, 1970-73; promotion manager, Peerless record company, 1975-80; manager, Cultural and Educational Events, Social Activities National Fund, FONAPAS, 1979; created the National Dance Award (also known as the Continental Contemporary Dance Contest), 1980; host, television series, *Mexico in the Culture* with Margot Fonteyn, 1982; director, dance department, National Institute of Fine Arts (NIFA), 1983, where he founded the Dance Research, Documentation and Archives Center; director, National Dance Company, NIFA, 1985-87; festivals director and consultant, NIFA, 1994-97. **Awards:** Recipient of Latin American Dance Award, *Ballet de Chile* magazine, 1953; outstanding dancer and choreographer of the year, Venezuela, 1957; honorary citizen, Fort Worth, Texas, 1961; St. Louis, Missouri, trophy for cultural contributions, 1962; gold medal, president López Mateos, 1963; diploma, Radio and Television Journalists Association, 1964; first place, Music Festival, Israel, 1964; homage for life in dance, NIFA, 1990; homage in honor of 70th birthday, National Institute of Fine Arts, with restaging of *Zapata*, 1996. Member, National Creators System, 1994-.

Roles (performances with the Mexican Ballet, Mexican Dance Academy, Mexico City, unless otherwise noted)

1949	The deer, *La balada de la luna y el venado* (*The Moon and the Deer Ballad*) (Mérida)
	A horse, *El pájaro y las doncellas o Danza del amor y la muerte* (*The Bird and the Maidens or Dance of Love and Death*) (Mérida)
1951	*Tierra* (*Earth*) (Noriega)
	A man, *Redes* (*Nets*) (Limón)
1952	*La Valse* (Gutiérrez)
	Boyfriend of Lucero, *Sensemayá* (Bracho)
	Entre sombras anda el fuego (*Fire Moves Amongst Shadows*) (Jordán)
	The baker, *La madrugada del panadero* (*The Baker's Dawn*) (Sokolow)
	The poet, *Ermesinda* (Cardona)
1953	The angel, *La Anunciación* (*The Annunciation*) (Reyna)
	Sones jarochos (Beristáin)
	El peladito, *Titeresca* (*On Puppets*) (Beristáin)
	The husband, *La Manda* (Reyna)
1954	The deer, *La hija del Yori* (*The daughter of Yori*) (Reyna)
	Coro de primavera (*Spring Chorus*) (Waldeen), Contemporary Ballet, Mexico City
1956	Young quetzal, *Balada de los quetzales* (*Quetzals Ballad*) (Mérida), Fine Arts Ballet, Mexico City
1959	*La culebra* (*The Snake*) (Benavides), Fine Arts Ballet, Mexico City
	Christ, *El chueco* (Keys), Fine Arts Ballet, Mexico City

Works (performances with the Mexican Ballet, Mexican Dance Academy, Mexico City, unless otherwise noted)

1951	*El sueño y la presencia* (*The Dream and the Presence*) (mus. Galindo)
1952	*La balada mágica* (*The Magic Ballad*) (mus. Jiménez Mabarak)
	Antesala (*Antechamber*) (mus. Hernández Moncada)

1953   *Zapata* (mus. Moncayo), IV Youth Festival, Bucharest,
        Rumania
1954   *Huapango* (mus. Moncayo), Contemporary Ballet,
        Mexico City
        Romance (*Romance*) (mus. Pergolesi and Respighi), Con-
        temporary Ballet, Mexico City
1956   *Cuauhtémoc* (mus. Revueltas), Fine Arts Ballet, Mexico
        City
1963   *Fauno 63* (*Faun 63*) (mus. Burrel)
1968   Olympic Flame Reception (mass ballet), XIX Olympic
        Games, Teotihuacan, Mexico

Other works include: Has choreographed approximately 800 short works for film, television, theater, and opera in Mexico and other countries, and nearly 60 repertory works for various folkloric groups.

Publications

On ARRIAGA: books—

50 años de danza en el Palacio de Bellas Artes, Mexico, 1997.
Aulestia, Patricia, "Guillermo Arriaga," *Homenaje una vida en la danza 1990*, Mexico, 1990.
Tibol, Raquel, *Pasos en la danza mexicana*, Mexico, 1982.
Tortajada Quiroz, Margarita, *Danza y poder*, Mexico, 1995.

*   *   *

Guillermo Arriaga is one of the most prestigious performers and choreographers in Mexican dance. His name is closely associated with the nationalist modern dance movement, for he is the creator and original performer of the pinnacle work of the movement, *Zapata* (1953).

At age 23 Arriaga embarked on what would become a brilliant dance career. As a child he had studied music and developed later as an actor, participating in such works as *Mariano Pineda* (García Lorca), *Saint Joan* (Bernard Shaw), and *El tejedor de Segovia* (Juan Ruiz de Alarcón). Inspired by developments in modern dance at the time, he began his first formal studies in the National Ballet of Mexico and at the Mexican Dance Academy. In the latter, he was taught by Ana Mérida, and they subsequently worked together in several companies. Mérida launched him as a principal dancer in her work *The Ballad of the Deer and the Moon* (1949), for which he won wide acclaim as a brilliantly expressive deer. Many works followed in which Arriaga skillfully developed as a performer and faithfully expressed his choreographers' requirements.

In 1951 Arriaga was in Costa Rica, after having traveled to Europe, when Miguel Covarrubias, chief of the Dance Department of the National Institute of Fine Arts (NIFA), asked him to return to Mexico to participate in a work that the Mexican Ballet of the Mexican Dance Academy was mounting in collaboration with José Limón and Doris Humphrey. Limón was a seminal influence for the Mexican dancers and choreographers, especially for the male dancers who, like Arriaga, reaffirmed their vocation by seeing him dance and by working with him.

When Arriaga returned to Mexico, Covarrubias invited him to choreograph. Under Humphrey's supervision the first work emerged: *The Dream and the Presence* (1951). The work was a success and ranked among others of high quality, including *El Chueco* (Guillermo Keys). Like others created during this period in Mexican modern dance, *The Dream and the Presence* had populist con-

tent and a nationalist inclination. Blas Galindo composed the music, and José Chávez Morado designed the scenery and costumes. In this work Arriaga approached the subject of death, which he resolved with sensitivity, fantasy, and great originality.

After seeing Arriaga's work with the Mexican Ballet, kinesiology teacher Josefina García (who had traveled to Mexico with José Limón), offered him a grant to attend the summer courses at Jacob's Pillow, in Massachusetts. There, Arriaga had the opportunity to see Limón, Ted Shawn, and Ruth St. Denis dance, and to study ballet with Margaret Craske, Spanish dance with La Meri, and modern dance with Myra Kinch. He received offers to work in New York, but preferred to develop his artistry in his own country.

In 1952 Covarrubias left his position as dance director at NIFA, which meant a loss of support and cohesion for Mexican modern dance. However, Covarrubias continued helping a small group of dancers: Arriaga, Rocío Sagaón, Olga Cardona and Antonio de la Torre, who would later comprise the Contemporary Ballet group. Working under more difficult conditions than with the Mexican Ballet, Arriaga decided to create a work devoted to the national hero Emiliano Zapata. First he conceived the work as a great production; he actually wanted horses and rifles on the stage. Yet he soon reduced it to a duet created for himself and Rocío Sagaón. The result was a master work, recognized and applauded by leading international critics and world audiences. Without superfluous elements, he presented the leader's life, struggle, death, and heritage. Arriaga as Zapata and Sagaón as Mother Earth demonstrated a moving strength and intensity, not only for local, contemporary audiences but also for later viewers and those abroad. As it did in the 1950s, *Zapata* continues to symbolize a poetic and heroic spirit, which Arriaga summarized in an emotional artistic reality. It is the only work of the era that forms a part of the repertory of several companies; in 1997, at a celebration of Arriaga's 70th birthday, it was danced by five companies and confirmed as a masterpiece of the Mexican dance. In addition, it was produced for television by the Cultural and Educational Television Unit of the Public Education Secretary in 1984.

Zapata was the result of the cohesion of numerous elements: the work of Arriaga and Sagaón; the influence of Covarrubias, who designed the scenery and costumes; the selected music (José Pablo Moncayo's *Temporal Earth*), and Limón's influence over the creators. The work premiered on 18 August 1953, when the Contemporary Ballet performed at the National Study Theater during the Fourth Festival of Youth in Bucharest, Rumania. The Mexican debut was in November of the same year, a performance that comprises a seminal event in the history of Mexican modern dance.

From 1956 through 1958 Arriaga joined Ana Mérida and other artists in founding a new Mexican Ballet, with which they traveled to several cities of the country, besides successfully touring Venezuela, where they danced for 20,000 spectators in the inauguration of the Acoustic Shell, Bello Monte Hills. In 1958 Arriaga, together with Josefina Lavalle, founded the Popular Ballet of Mexico, which had a modern and folkloric dance repertory. With that company too, he toured the country and attended the Universal and International Exposition in Brussels, Belgium (1958). There, they enjoyed great success, especially with *Zapata*.

Gradually, the Popular Ballet turned away from modern dance and, like Arriaga, focused on folkloric dances. As an extension of this work, during 1961 and 1963 Arriaga joined the Folkloric Ballet of Mexico as a teacher and director. In 1963, for a short period, he and Mérida revived the Mexican Ballet, but again in 1964 he focused on folkloric dance. In the same year, José Ignacio Retes and

Julio Prieto invited him to establish the Mexican Folkloric Ensemble of the Social Security Mexican Institute, bringing together 125 dancers, musicians and singers to tour the United States, Israel, Germany, Portugal, the Philippines and Hong Kong.

In 1968 Arriaga joined the work team of the Cultural Olympic Games which took place in Mexico City. Then he acted as director of Foreign Artistic Programs and choreographed a mass ballet of 1,525 dancers for the reception of the Olympic flame in the archaeological ruins of Teotihuacan. For the following 10 years, Arriaga separated from dance and dedicated himself to music composition and the recording industry. However, in 1969, during the centennial of Emiliano Zapata, he was invited to stage *Zapata* in conjunction with festivities organized by the Mexican government and attended by the country's president. This production resulted in an offer to manage the Cultural and Educational Agreements of the Social Activities National Fund (FONAPAS). There, he undertook an intense support of dance, opening new theaters for this art, promoting several companies in every dance genre, creating seasons in popular spaces and founding, together with the Metropolitan Autonomous University, the National Dance Award. The latter has been essential for the development of new contemporary dance,

convoking every year since 1980 numerous groups and young choreographers who use the award as a showcase for their work. Thus, the award has become a catalyst of the independent contemporary dance movement in Mexico. Since 1994 the National Dance Award has extended to include a Continental Contemporary Dance Contest, with the participation of groups and choreographers from throughout the continent.

In 1983 Arriaga received another important appointment, as director of dance at NIFA, where he has continued his wide-ranging work, including founding the country's first research center devoted to dance, the Dance Research, Documentation and Information National Center "José Limón" (founded as Dance Research and Documentation Center). From 1985 through 1987 Arriaga served as director of the National Company of Dance at NIA, which, despite being the official ballet company, incorporated again within its repertoire the most significant nationalist modern dance works. Since 1994 Arriaga has been a member of the Creators National System, an institution comprising the most recognized artists of the country.

—Margarita Tortajada Quiroz;
translated by Dolores Ponce Gutiérrez

BAGOUET, Dominique

French dancer and choreographer

Born: 9 July 1951 in Angoulême, France. **Education:** Studied ballet, Rosella Hightower School (Cannes), 1965-69; modern with Carolyn Carlson and Peter Goss (Paris), 1974; went to the U.S., 1975; studied with Jennifer Muller, Lar Lubovitch, Maggie Black; Graham and Cunningham technique with May O'Donnell. **Career:** Dancer, Alfonso Cata Ballet, 1969; Felix Blaska Company, 1970; 20th Century Ballet (Maurice Béjart), 1971-73; Chandra Group (Maguy Marin), 1973-74; Joseph Russillo Company, 1974; founder, Bagouet Company (Paris), 1976; artist-in-residence, Montpellier (France), beginning 1980; director, Montpellier National Choreographic Center, 1980; founder, Montpellier Dance Festival, 1980; posthumous creation by his former dancers of *Bagouet Notebooks*, 1993. **Awards:** First Research Prize, Bagnolet Competition, 1976. **Died:** 9 December 1992 in Montpellier, of AIDS.

Works

1976	*Night Song*
1980	*Under the Waning Light*
1982	*Elusives*
1984	*Love Deserts* (mus. Mozart, Murail)
1985	*Lucien's Crawl*
1986	*Assaï* (mus. Dusapin)
1986	*Fantasia Semplice*
1987	*Angel Jump* (mus. Beethoven, Dusapin), set by Boltanski
1988	*Ten Angels* (video-dance, directed by Picq)
1989	*Basically Furnished*
1991	*Necessito* for the Seville Universal Exposition
1992	*So Schnell*

Publications

Aubry, Chantal, *Bagouet*, France, 1989.

*   *   *

From 1976 to 1979, Dominique Bagouet created more than 14 works for his fledgling dance troupe in a effort to finance its survival. Yet good fortune came his way in 1980 when he was offered an artist-in-residence position in the town of Montpellier, France, with a studio and interested dance fans.

Bagouet chose improvisation as a choreographic principle; his work shifted between a pure, formal style of dance and abstract choreography, while incorporating an inventive use of space and composition, and with a theatricality often focusing on strange, humorous, and timeless characters. Bagouet's personal style, sometimes described as neo-baroque, was always subtle, filled with micro-gestural movements of the hands and wrists, feet, and specific tilts of the chest. *Love Deserts*, a work from 1984, shows off Bagouet's rigorous choreographic style, with mathematically precise movement. His precision carried over to his use of space as well, maintaining very tight spacial restrictions, its sharpness reminiscent of the beautifully sculpted French gardens of the 18th century—artful, symmetrical, and gesturally pure.

Throughout his career, Bagouet worked with well-known artists, such as musician Pascal Dusapin and painter Christian Boltanski for 1987's *Angel Jump*. This work was composed from within Boltanski's unique and somewhat skewed vision of the dance world, full of provocation: "The interest of dance lies in the fact that it's against nature. If we enjoy seeing a ballet dancer, [it's] because it's a kind of physical torture." Boltanski's conception of dance raised questions in the relationship between choreographer and dancer: is a choreographer, when creating physically demanding movements and pushing his/her dancers to the limit, producing an artistic form of torture? Bagouet tried to answer some of these issues in *Angel Jump*, filled with small scenes and solos for each "angel." The dancers appeared like figurines, the stage set up with an "on-stage" area as well as an "off-stage" area. The performance was filled with duality, the opposition of sophisticated, poetical dancing vs. stilted movement, dancers appearing both "on" and "off" the stage, life vs. death, a connection between elements which seem to have no common link.

Bagouet also created additional studio and performance space, attached to his choreographic headquarters in Montpellier, for professional dance workshops to introduce his complex brand of dance education to the public. Recognition of Bagouet's work arrived in 1992, when he was hailed as a "national treasure," and Paris Opéra Ballet invited his company to present his 1992 piece, *So Schnell*. It was the first time that a choreographer of the "new" French dance was invited to share the limelight with the legendary Paris Opéra Ballet's. Unfortunately, Bagouet's career and life were cut short when he died of AIDS in December of 1992. Yet his gift was a fundamental contribution to choreography, through his carefully-articulated composition, technical precision, and the unerring expression of micro-gestures that defined a new theatricality in French modern dance. Both as a tribute and to keep his vision and works alive, in 1993 Bagouet's former dancers created the *Bagouet Notebooks* through reconstruction of his notes and videos and from their own personal experiences and recollections. Another memorial came during a 1994 Anna Halprin workshop in Montreal, Canada, when attendees were asked to dedicate a created dance to someone important in their life, and a well-known French dance critic dedicated her dance to the memory of Dominique Bagouet and his work. Lastly, Bagouet's 1986 work, *Assaï*, was also recreated in 1996 with young dancers.

—Murielle Mathieu

BAKER, Peggy
Canadian dancer, choreographer, artistic director, and educator

Born: Peggy Laurayne Smith, 22 October 1952 in Edmonton, Alberta. **Education:** Studied tap with Shirley Shroffel and Rean Smith (mother); ballet with Karen Barber; theatre at Alberta Provincial Drama Seminar (Drumheller, Alberta); attended University of Alberta (theatre major), Edmonton, 1970-71; trained in Graham-based technique at School of Toronto Dance Theatre with Patricia Beatty, David Earle, Peter Randazzo and Marie Marchowsky, 1971-74; studied modern dance at London Contemporary Dance Theatre with Kasuko Hirabayashi; in New York, studied at the Martha Graham School of Contemporary Dance, José Limón Dance Company, and Paul Taylor Studio; Jennifer Muller/The Works and Lar Lubovitch Dance Company (College Park, Maryland); Teachers' Collective with Patricia Miner, Toronto; acting at Herbert Berghof Studio, New York; ballet with Maggie Black, Jocelyn Lorenz and Christine Wright, and Zena Rommett, New York; studied neural-muscular training and anatomy with Irene Dowd, New York; solo exploration with Annabelle Gamson, New York; studied Pilates with Jean-Claude West, New York. **Family:** Married composer-musician Michael J. Baker, 1971; divorced, 1989; married composer-musician Ahmed Hassan, 1990. **Career:** Dancer (apprentice), Toronto Dance Theatre, 1973-74; co-founder, 1974, dancer, 1974-80, and artistic director, 1979-80, Dancemakers, Toronto; first independent choreography, 1978; dancer, Lar Lubovitch Dance Company, New York, 1981-88; rehearsal director, Lar Lubovitch Dance Company, New York, 1986-88; founder, Peggy Baker/Solo Dance, Montreal, 1990; first solo concert, 1990; dancer, Mikhail Baryshnikov's White Oak Dance Project, 1990; director, Contemporary Arts Summer Institute, Simon Fraser University, Burnaby, British Columbia, 1991-94; artist-in-residence, the National Ballet School of Canada, Toronto, 1993 to the present; founder, Peggy Baker Dance Projects, Toronto, 1996; taught at New York University, Laban Institute, Montréal Danse and LADMMI (Montreal), Le Groupe de la Place Royale (Ottawa, Ontario), Winnipeg Contemporary Dancers (Winnipeg, Manitoba), Dancers Studio West (Calgary, Alberta), EDAM (Vancouver), Dancemakers, Lois Smith School of Dance, School of Toronto Dance Theatre, Toronto Dance Theatre, York University, and National Ballet School of Canada (Toronto), Rosas, Brussels, Belgium. **Awards:** Funding grants from the Canada Council, Ontario Arts Council, Metro Toronto Cultural Affairs, and Laidlaw Foundation.

Roles (all original cast roles)

1972   *Los Sencillos* (Patricia Beatty), Toronto Dance Theatre
        Pocamania (Kathryn Brown), Toronto Dance Theatre Choreographic Workshop
        Baroque Suite (includes *Mirrors, Lyrical Solo, Duet, Lament, Finale,*) Toronto Dance Theatre
1973   *Atlantis* (David Earle), Toronto Dance Theatre
        Ray Charles Suite (Earle), Toronto Dance Theatre
        The Dybbuk (Donald Hines), Toronto
1974   *Wretched Ha! Ha!* (Odette Oliver), Toronto Dance Theatre Choreographic Workshop
        Garden of the Forking Paths (Anna Blewchamp), Toronto Dance Theatre Choreographic Workshop
        Bugs (Earle), Toronto Dance Theatre
        Parade (Earle), Toronto Dance Theatre

1975   *La Belle Époque* (includes *Waltz Suite, Deux Epigraphes Antiques, L'Hôtel Splendide,* and *Vignette*), Camerata Music Ensemble
        Field of Dreams (Earle), Toronto Dance Theatre
        Arrival of All Time (Blewchamp), Dancemakers, Toronto
        Terminal (Blewchamp), Dancemakers, Toronto
        Fools in the Palace (Norman Morrice), Dancemakers, Toronto
        Blue (Nomi Cohen), Dancemakers, Toronto
        Forest (Robert Cohan), Dancemakers, Toronto
1976   *Homage* (Blewchamp), Dancemakers, Toronto
        Just Passing Through (Nomi Cohen), Dancemakers, Toronto
1977   *Schooner* (Carol Anderson), Dancemakers, Toronto
        Chimera (Kyra Lober), Dancemakers, Toronto
        Was It in Her Blood? (Janice Hladki), Dancemakers, Toronto
        Bend Down Low (Blewchamp), Dancemakers, Toronto
        Sequenza and a Few Words (Nomi Cohen), Dancemakers, Toronto
1978   *Marathon* (Blewchamp), Dancemakers, Toronto
        Fading Fast (Janice Hladki), Dancemakers, Toronto
1979   *A.K.A.* (Blewchamp), Dancemakers, Toronto
        Variations on a Summer's Theme (Donald McKayle), Dancemakers, Toronto
        Spiral (Karen Jamieson), Dancemakers, Toronto
        Pole Fiction (Paula Ravitz), Dancemakers, Toronto
        Two Bits (Joan Phillips), Dancemakers, Toronto
        Bay Shimmers (Beth Harris), Dancemakers, Toronto
        The Daintiness Rag (Blewchamp), Dancemakers, Toronto
1980   *Quick Studies* (Anderson), Dancemakers, Toronto
        Mirrors, Masques and Transformations (Marcuse), Judith Marcuse Dance Projects Society, Shaw Festival, Niagara-on-the-Lake, Ontario
1981   *Playgrounds* (Marcuse), Judith Marcuse Dance Projects Society, Vancouver, British Columbia
1982   *Motor Party* (Moulton), Charles Moulton Dance Company, New York
1983   *Big Shoulders* (Lubovitch), Lar Lubovitch Dance Company, Ravinia Festival, Chicago, Illinois
        American Gesture (Lubovitch), Lar Lubovitch Dance Company, Jacob's Pillow Festival, Lee, Massachusetts
        Tabernacle (Lubovitch), Lar Lubovitch Dance Company, Taipei, Taiwan
        Gears Align (Charles Moulton), Lar Lubovitch Dance Company, Tokyo, Japan
        Adagio and Rondo for Glass Harmonica (Lubovitch), Lar Lubovitch Dance Company, San Diego, California
1984   *A Brahms Symphony* (Lubovitch), Lar Lubovitch Dance Company, San Francisco
1985   *Concerto 622* (Lubovitch), Lar Lubovitch Dance Company, Angers, France
1986   *The Organization of Sadness* (Tere O'Connor), New York
        Blood (Lubovitch), Lar Lubovitch Dance Company, Berlin, Germany
1987   *Of My Soul* (Lubovitch), Lar Lubovitch Dance Company, Edwardsville, Illinois
        Glossolalia (Moulton), Charles Moulton Dance Company, New York
        Dream Combine (Moulton), Charles Moulton Dance Company, New York

Cuban and Western (Moulton), Charles Moulton Dance Company, New York

1988 *Musette* (Lubovitch), Lar Lubovitch Dance Company, Champaign-Urbana, Illinois

The Windows (Christopher House), Path Dance Company, Baltimore, Maryland

1989 *Peggy Baker and Janie Brendel Solos and Duets* (includes *A Lost World* [Martita Goshen] duet, *The Volpe Sisters* [Doug Varone] duet, *Accident* [Annabelle Gamson] solo), New York

1990 *Continuum* (Stephanie Ballard), Winnipeg, Manitoba

Romeo and Juliet Before Parting (James Kudelka) duet, Canada Dance Festival, Ottawa, Ontario

Sand (Gamson), Dance in Canada Awards Gala, Calgary, Alberta

Motorcade (Mark Morris), White Oak Dance Project, Boston

1991 *Person Project* (Tere O'Connor), DanceWorks, Toronto

This Isn't the End (James Kudelka), Peggy Baker/Solo Dance, New York

Inner Enchantments (Molissa Fenley), DanceWorks, Toronto

1992 *Beautiful Day* (Mark Morris), Peggy Baker/Solo Dance, Ottawa, Ontario

1995 *Assara* (Patricia Beatty), from the film *Dancing the Goddess,* Toronto

Savanna (Fenley), New York

1996 *Les Parts des Anges* (Paul-André Fortier), Fortier Danse-Création, Montreal

1997 *One Voice* (Stephanie Ballard), Peggy Baker Dance Projects, Toronto

Pelléas et Mélisande (James Kudelka), Toronto Symphony Orchestra, Toronto

1998 *Cirrus* (Irene Dowd), Peggy Baker Dance Projects, Toronto

Works

1978 *Album* (mus. Beethoven, Clark Terry, popular American), Dancemakers, Toronto

Terrain (mus. Bach), York University Dance Department, Toronto

1979 *Disc* (mus. Michael J. Baker), York University Dance Department, Toronto

1980 *Valentine Brown, Live!* (mus. Susan Cox), Toronto Workshop Productions, Toronto

The Nightingale (mus. Michael J. Baker), Dancemakers/ Prologue to the Performing Arts, Toronto

1982 *Series* (mus. self-generated rhythmic score), MusicDanceOrchestra, Toronto

1990 *Le Charme de l'impossible* (mus. Mark Kolt) solo, Peggy Baker/Solo Dance, Winnipeg Dance Festival, Winnipeg, Manitoba

1991 *Sanctum* (mus. Ahmed Hassan), Winnipeg Dance Festival, Peggy Baker/Solo Dance, Winnipeg, Manitoba

1992 *Brahms Waltzes* (mus. Brahms), Peggy Baker/Solo Dance, Artspace Dance Series, Peterborough, Ontario

Le Charme de l'impossible (mus. Mark Kolt) trio, National Ballet School of Canada, Toronto

1993 *La vie de bohème* (mus. Michael J. Baker), Peggy Baker/ Solo Dance, Toronto

Geometry of the Circle (mus. Ahmed Hassan), Peggy Baker/Solo Dance, Quebec City, Quebec

Black Border with Moving Figures (mus. Chopin, Liszt), Peggy Baker/Solo Dance, Toronto

Three Intermezzi (mus. Brahms), Peggy Baker/Solo Dance, Quebec City, Quebec

Her Heart (mus. Brahms), Peggy Baker/Solo Dance, Toronto

1994 *Brute* (mus. Prokofiev), Peggy Baker/Solo Dance, Vancouver Recital Society, Vancouver

1995 *In a Landscape* (mus. Cage), fringe Festival of Independent Dance (fFIDA), Toronto

Alpine Holiday (mus. Christoph Dienz), National Ballet School of Canada, Toronto

1996 *Why the Brook Wept* (mus. Cage), Peggy Baker/Solo Dance, Toronto

1997 *Encoded Revision* (mus. Michael J. Baker), Peggy Baker Dance Projects, Chico, California

Garland (mus. Peter Garland) solo, Peggy Baker Dance Projects, Toronto

Strand (mus. Ann Southam), Peggy Baker Dance Projects, Toronto

1998 *Weskit, Hanky, Tinder Box* w/Richard Daniels (mus. Henry Crowell), New York

Sylvan Quartet (mus. Chan Ka Nin), Amici Chamber Ensemble, Toronto

Publications

On BAKER: books—

Macpherson, Susan, editor, *101 from the Encyclopedia of Theatre Dance in Canada,* Toronto, 1997.

On BAKER: articles—

Jung, Daryl, "Peggy Baker's Bravado," *NOW* (Toronto), 17 November 1994.

Lerner, Raissa, "Body Language: Art of Animation," *N.Y.C. Metro,* March 1988.

Films and Videotapes

Prokofiev by Two: Romeos and Juliets, film appearance; dir. Barbara Willis Sweete, 1990.

Mark Morris, Choreographer, for *Adrienne Clarkson Presents,* Canadian Broadcasting Corporation, 1992.

Peggy Baker for *Sunday Arts and Entertainment,* Canadian Broadcasting Corporation, 1992.

Zero Patience, film appearance; dir. John Greyson, 1992.

Sanctum, dir. Lisa Cochrane, Cine Qua Non/The Pulse Project, 1995.

No Guilt, dir. by John Faichney, 1996.

Originals in Art, Bravo! New Style Arts Channel, 1996.

Women: A True Story, dir. Rina Fratacelli, Baton Broadcasting, CTV, 1996.

Accident by Design: Creating and Discovering Beauty, dir. by Daniel Conrad, Rhodopsin, 1997.

Dancing the Goddess, dir. by Ariadne Ochrymovych, Isis Film Productions, 1997.

*   *   *

Peggy Baker. Photograph © Lois Greenfield.

Peggy Baker is one of the most respected modern dancers in Canada. Her lean, tight, athletic body has the brilliant control and fluidity of a gymnast, while her overlong arms in motion are pure lyrical grace. Baker's movements are clean, clear and crisp, but every step she takes is imbued with passion and meaning. She commands the stage with her strong attack and rivets the eye in her stillness.

Although Baker studied tap and ballet as a child, her main interest was acting. It was in 1968, at a theatre workshop in Drumheller, Alberta, that she first encountered Patricia Beatty, cofounder of Toronto Dance Theatre (TDT). Beatty, who was teaching creative dance and improvisation at the workshop, had a profound effect on the young Baker. "Until then," says Baker, "I had seen dance as play, never as a career. Watching a great artist like Trish, I realized the potency of movement because she was able to verbalize, through her body, images that were so deeply profound." Baker completed one year as an acting major at the University of Alberta in Edmonton before succumbing to the lure of Graham-based modern dance. In 1971, at age 19, she and her husband, musician Michael J. Baker, moved to Toronto where Baker attended the School of Toronto

Dance Theatre. Such was her raw talent and quick study that she was put almost immediately into the company class and, after just two years, was made an apprentice. In retrospect, Baker believes she was pushed too quickly, learning dance steps without having the technique to support them and being unprepared for the intensity of performance.

Feeling out of her depth at TDT, Baker joined with a group of York University dance graduates in 1974 to found Dancemakers, a company whose repertoire embraced a potpourri of styles including those of Limón and Cunningham. In 1976—which she calls her "learning her craft and growing up year"—Baker was given a Canada Council study grant and attended a wide variety of technique classes in New York. She came home with a new maturity and a different perspective on herself and dancing. Baker rejoined Dancemakers and developed a particular closeness with choreographer-artistic director Anna Blewchamp. The two women had an intense relationship that led Baker to a deeper understanding of what she could do inside a work. When Blewchamp left Dancemakers in 1979, Baker became artistic director, but as a dancer she had lost a close creative collaborator.

Throughout the 1970s, Baker took classes with American modern dance legends to broaden her technique base, including two summer sessions with Lar Lubovitch in 1979 and 1980. "Meeting Lar was like meeting Trish Beatty," says Baker. "I was blown away by his powerful aesthetic and what he expressed through dance." When Lubovitch asked Baker to join his company in 1980, she at first refused, but was lured to New York to see if his company felt right for her. She remained with Lubovitch for seven years, fulfilling her longing for an intense relationship with a creator. The New York sojourn, however, ended Baker's marriage. From the start, Baker distinguished herself in the company. She became rehearsal director in 1986, which allowed her love of teaching to flourish. She was also a creative muse to Lubovitch's protégé, Charles Moulton. Lubovitch cast Baker in great extant pieces such as *Marimba, North Star,* and *Cavalcade,* as well as in original works, including *Big Shoulders* (1983), *Concerto 622* (1985), and *Of My Soul* (1987). The dancer was the only woman in the company to perform choreography created for men, with Lubovitch using Baker's androgynous looks to convey ambiguous sexuality or a unisex expression of physicality. Over time, however, Baker became frustrated by the narrow focus of her roles and by Lubovitch's increasing penchant for more balletic works. Although their parting in 1989 was a bitter one, Baker credited Lubovitch with being the biggest influence on her artistic development. In fact, Baker based her own choreography on a Lubovitch principle—that the audience must read the dancer's body like poetry.

Feeling rootless in New York, Baker moved to Montreal where she had close friends. In 1990, a pivotal year for the dancer, Baker founded Peggy Baker/Solo Dance to pursue her own works; participated in the first tour of Mikhail Baryshnikov's White Oak Dance Project with choreographer Mark Morris; performed her own choreography to great acclaim at the Festival of Canadian Dance in Winnipeg, Manitoba; and married Toronto-based musician-composer, Ahmed Hassan, with whom she had become reacquainted while teaching and performing in Winnipeg. In 1993, Baker was appointed the first artist-in-residence at the National Ballet School of Canada where she taught modern dance and had a permanent rehearsal space for creation. A gifted teacher, Baker was sought after across Canada to conduct classes and workshops. She also became known for her lecture/demon-

strations that revealed the artist inside the art. Baker's solo repertoire includes her own works as well as those by important choreographers, many of them original creations with original scores. Americans Mark Morris, Molissa Fenley, and Annabelle Gamson, and Canadians James Kudelka, Christopher House, Patricia Beatty, and Paul-André Fortier have all contributed works. In 1996, she founded Peggy Baker Dance Projects to expand her choreographic interests beyond solo work.

Although Baker dabbled in choreography while at Dancemakers and with Lubovitch, only after becoming an independent artist did her dancesmith talents flower. Her style pares movement down to a clean, articulate starkness where nothing is extraneous. She also never gives in to abandon, preferring intensity to melodrama. Her works contain a deep, humane spirituality, and her themes are inspired from life, music, literature, and art. *Brahms Waltzes* (1992) is underscored by Brahms' unrequited love for Clara Schumann; *Her Heart* (1993) is a dance of reconciliation for Baker's mother; *Brute* (1994) is Baker's riveting portrayal of the horrors of war, fueled by images from Picasso's *Guernica;* and Baker's understanding of Ophelia in *Hamlet* produced *Why the Brook Wept* (1996). Baker has also developed a close collaborative relationship with concert pianist Andrew Burashko. In both *Brahms Waltzes* and *Her Heart,* for example, the piano is not mere accompaniment but contributes to a fascinating spatial and musical dynamic with the dancer. Baker credits her work with Burashko for instilling in her a greater understanding of the art of interpreting music, and their recitals have been well received across Canada. Baker has also created moving duets for herself and Hassan, who suffers from multiple sclerosis and is confined to a wheelchair. *Sanctum* (1990), for example, is about restriction. Hassan performs on a variety of primitive instruments, confined to his place by his disability. Baker, a shaman figure, is confined to hers by the boundaries of a square of light. "I'm eclectic in my points of departure," says Baker, "but each piece becomes an investigation. Because of my acting background in creating character, I keep working through different levels and strata to find deeper meanings. I also react viscerally to music. As the music begins to reveal itself, I gather stimulation for the dance."

—Paula Citron

BALDWIN, Mark

Fijian-born dancer, choreographer, and company director based in London

Born: Fiji. **Education:** B.F.A., Elam School of Fine Arts, University of Auckland. **Career:** Founding member of Limbs Dance Company; dancer, New Zealand Ballet, Australian Dance Theatre, and Rambert Dance Company (formerly Ballet Rambert), 1983-92; first independent choreography for Rambert Dance Company, 1991; founder Mark Baldwin Dance Company (MBDC), 1992; toured new work in Britain and abroad; commissioned for Rambert Dance Company, Modern Ballet of Argentina, Phoenix Dance Company, the Turkish State Opera House, 4D, and English National Ballet; resident choreographer, Scottish Ballet, 1995. **Awards:** Bonnie Bird Award, 1993; Ballroom Blitz Commission, 1993; *Time Out* Award, 1995.

Roles (for Ballet Rambert until 1987, when renamed Rambert Dance Company, unless otherwise noted)

1984	*Intimate Pages* (Bruce), Birmingham
	Wildlife (Alston), Brighton
	Sergeant Early's Dream (Bruce), Canterbury
1985	Pierrot, *Pierrot Lunaire* (Tetley), London
	Mythologies (Alston), London
	Java (Alston), London
	Dipping Wings (Evelyn), Glasgow
1986	*Soda Lake* (Alston), Manchester
	Swamp (Clark), London
	Night with Waning Moon (Bruce), London
1987	*Strong Language* (Alston), London
	Leopold, *Wolfi* (Seymour), London
	Septet (Cunningham), Glasgow
	Cinema (Alston), Birmingham
	Pulcinella (Alston), Leeds
	Rushes (Davies), Manchester
1988	*Rhapsody in Blue* (Alston), Birmingham
	Soldat (Page), Manchester
	Hymnos (Alston), Manchester
	Embarque (Davies), Manchester
1990	*Four Elements* (Childs), Oxford
	Roughcut (Alston), Newcastle
	Currulao (Page), London
	Embrace Tiger and Return to Mountain (Tetley), London
1993	*Escape at Sea* (Spink), Second Stride, London

Works

1983	*Herald* (mus. Bell), Ballet Rambert Workshop, Twickenham
1984	*Rose Headed Woman* (mus. Henderson), Ballet Rambert Workshop, London
1986	*Pussy Footing* (mus. Comfrey), Ballet Rambert Workshop
1987	*October Mountain* (mus. Hovhaness), Rambert Dance Company Collaboration V Workshop, London
1991	*Island to Island* (soundtrack Craft), Rambert Dance Company, Oxford
1992	*Gone* (mus. Grieg), Rambert Dance Company, Manchester
1993	*Spirit* (mus. Poulenc), Rambert Dance Company, Oxford
1994	*Banter Banter* (mus. Stravinsky), Rambert Dance Company
	Collection of Moving Parts
	Factual Nonsense (in silence) solo, Mark Baldwin Dance Company, London
	More Poulenc (mus. Poulenc), MBDC, London
1995	*Dances From Cyberspace* (mus. Handel), MBDC, London
	Samples (mus. Ravel), MBDC, London
	Out of Doors (mus. Bartók), MBDC, London
	Concerto Grosso (mus. Handel), MBDC, London
	Homage (in silence), MBDC, London
	Vespri (mus. Monteverdi), MBDC, London
	Even More solo: Antonia Franchesci, MBDC, London
1996	*Haydn Pieces* (mus. Haydn), Scottish Ballet, Glasgow
	Mirrors (mus. Ravel), MBDC, London
	Ae Fond Kiss (mus. Stravinsky), Scottish Ballet, Glasgow
	Lash, MBDC, London
	Confessions (mus. Macmillan), MBDC, London
	Sister (mus. Macmillan), MBDC, London
1997	*Labyrinth* w/Anish Kapoor (mus. Henze), MBDC, Berlin

Publications

On BALDWIN: book—

Pritchard, Jane, ed., *Rambert: A Celebration,* London, 1996.

On BALDWIN: articles—

Charman, Elizabeth, "Dances from Cyberspace," *Dance Now,* 1995.
Nugent, Ann, "Dancers of Ballet Rambert: Three Members of the Company in Its 60th Year," *Dance and Dancers,* June 1986.
Penman, Robert, "Dance on Television," *Dancing Times,* June 1994.

Films and Videotapes

Braun, Terry, dir., *The Net,* BBC, 1994.

*   *   *

Mark Baldwin has established himself as one of Britain's most prominent and successful choreographers, creating works for both European and British companies, in addition to choreographing for his own company. He first came to public attention in the 1980s as a dancer for the Ballet Rambert, specifically in his portrayal of Pierrot in Glen Tetley's *Pierrot Lunaire,* in which he revealed a strong sense of the dramatic and a facility for comic expression.

Raised in New Zealand, he moved to Australia, arriving eventually in Europe. His dancing career took an auspicious turn when he was engaged as a replacement for the role of Ferdinand in Glen Tetley's *The Tempest,* in Ballet Rambert's 1979-80 season. Officially joining the company as a dancer in 1983, Baldwin was given the opportunity to work with Christopher Bruce, Michael Clark, and Richard Alston; three of Britain's leading choreographers. It was primarily under Alston's guidance, however, that he developed his personal style, and began exploring choreographic possibilities.

Essentially a repertory company, Ballet Rambert underwent a decisive change in 1986 when Alston was appointed artistic director. Choreographers such as Siobhan Davies, Lucinda Childs, and Merce Cunningham were invited to make works for the company, committing the company to a more formal aesthetic. Baldwin featured prominently in Rambert's dance seasons, and the predominance of non-narrative dance, attending specifically to structural design, that characterized this period, is a stylistic element apparent in much of Baldwin's own work.

In developing company choreographic workshops, Alston provided in-house choreographers a space to flourish, and it is here that Baldwin had the opportunity to develop and hone his choreographic skills. His first major work for the company, *Island to Island,* originated from the company workshops and entered the main repertoire in 1991. Accompanied by a computer generated score, in this work Baldwin expressed an interest in the application of technology in dance, an issue which became increasingly prevalent in contemporary dance in the 1990s, and one which he was later to take up in producing work for his own company.

In 1992 Baldwin emerged as an independent choreographer, creating solos on colleagues and himself, whilst continuing to make work for Rambert Dance Company. He eventually formed his own company, and presented his first collection of work in 1994 during the Spring Loaded season at The Place in London. He performed a humorous, quirky solo, *Factual Nonsense,* and *More Poulenc,* an episodic dance set at a house party in which Baldwin cast himself as a screwball character, further indulging his sense of humour.

In the same year, he appeared in a television documentary, *The Net,* in which he explained and demonstrated the choreographic potential of *Lifeforms,* a computer software programme, famously employed in the work of Cunningham. Consisting of an infinitely malleable, three-dimensional figure in space, it is essentially an aid to choreography offering a practical and financially viable method of composing movement material. Baldwin devises movement initially on the computer, later transposing it onto his own body. The results are videotaped and, after incorporating his own improvisations, he creates phrases of movement to be edited together in varying formats, and, finally, to be undertaken by the dancers. In 1996 he decided to put *Mirrors* onto the Internet so that subscribers could contribute their ideas, thus creating and documenting new compositions.

Eclectic in both choice of music and movement, Baldwin shows a predilection for classical composers, enhancing a traditional relationship between music and dance; although he is just as likely to use music by the Beatles as by Handel. He incorporates movement from a wide range of styles, adding occasional gestural eccentricities to conventional ballet vocabulary and manipulating the movement in a way that allows him to deal with narrative. While he adheres to the compositional principles of formalist dance inherited from his experience with Rambert Dance Company, he nonetheless finds a very personal form of expression.

Dances From Cyberspace at the Riverside Studios, London, in 1995, was the umbrella heading for a collection of dance works that coherently expressed his personal strengths and influences, musicality, wit, and carefully structured, intricate design. The work displayed an aptitude for choreography but also expressed a regard for the identity of his dancers, as Elizabeth Charman explains in *Dance Now* (1995). Although *Lifeforms* generated much of the movement in these dances, Baldwin encouraged the performers to interpret the movement on their bodies, and in so doing invest it with a humanity that offered still further choreographic potential. He managed to suggest emotional undercurrents and a mutual sympathy between the dancers as people, yet a strict narrative or meaning remained understated and ambiguous.

Baldwin's versatility and broad taste won him the position of resident choreographer for the Scottish Ballet in 1995, confirming his status as one of Britain's foremost choreographers. Classical in style, *Haydn Pieces,* and the later *Ae Fond Kiss* set to Stravinsky, are plotless ballets, emphasising musicality rather than story, which enabled Baldwin to extend his range of movement and devise structural invention of greater complexity.

Baldwin continues to explore his particular creative inspiration, presenting dance that frequently reflects both classical and modern traits, a dual legacy that underpins and sustains his success. A diligent approach to his craft, coupled with his achievements so far, indicate that Baldwin will be ascribed a place in the history of British dance.

—Dawn Hathaway

BALES, William
American dancer, choreographer, and company director

Born: 1910 in Carnegie, Pennsylvania. **Education:** B.S., University of Pittsburgh; drama degree, Carnegie Institute of Technology; studied tap, and ballet with Frank Eckl in Pittsburgh; scholarship to train with Doris Humphrey and Charles Weidman in New York, 1935. **Family:** Married to actress Jo Van Fleet. **Military Service:** Served in World War II. **Career:** Taught dance, Irene Kaufmann Settlement; dancer, Humphrey-Weidman Company, 1936-40; also performed on Broadway, guested with Hanya Holm, and danced with the Radio City Music Hall Ballet; member, Eleanor King's Theater Dance Company; performer and teacher, New Dance Group; co-founder, Dudley-Maslow-Bales Trio, 1942; taught at Bennington College, 1940-67; also taught at Connecticut College, Juilliard, New York University, and UCLA; launched the dance department and served as dean, SUNY-Purchase until 1975; retired from teaching 1980. **Died:** 1990.

Roles

1935	Dancer (cr), *New Dance* (Humphrey)
1936	Dancer (cr), *With My Red Fires* (Humphrey)
	Dancer (cr), *Theatre Piece* (Humphrey, Weidman)
1937	*Icaro* (Eleanor King), Theater Dance Company
1938	Dancer (cr), *Passacaglia and Fugue in C Minor* (Humphrey)
1940	*Straw Hat Review,* Tamiment Encampment

Other roles include: Many performances for the New Dance Group in New York City.

Works

1940	*Black Tambourine,* solo, Tamiment Encampment, Pennsylvania
	Opus 0/1, Tamiment Encampment, Pennsylvania
1941	*Il Combattimento di Tancredi e Clorinda* w/Nona Schurman (mus. Monteverdi)
	Es Mujer (mus. Chavez), Bennington College, Vermont
1942	*To a Green Mountain*
	Bach Suite w/Dudley & Maslow
1943	*Peon Portraits: Adios*
	As Poor Richard Says. . .(A Colonial Charade) w/Dudley & Maslow (mus. Gregory Tucker), duet
	Peon Portraits: Field Hands
1945	*Three Dances in Romantic Style*
	Sea Bourne (mus. Gregory Tucker)
	Furlough: A Boardwalk Episode w/Dudley (mus. Robert McBride), duet
	A Winter's Tale
1947	*Soliloquy*

1949   *Judith*
       Rip Van Winkle
1950   *Impromptu*
1951   *The Haunted Ones*

Publications

On BALES: books—

De Mille, Agnes, *America Dances,* New York, 1980.
Lloyd, Margaret, *The Borzoi Book of Modern Dance,* New York,
       1949.
Taylor, Paul, *Private Domain,* New York, 1987.

*   *   *

William Bales was a dancer, choreographer, and educator. His
peak years as a dancer and choreographer occurred in the 1940s
during his membership in the New Dance Group and, especially, in
his more-than-a-decade-long tenure in the influential Dudley-
Maslow-Bales Trio. He is often cited for having an even greater
impact, however, as a teacher of dance.

Born in Carnegie, Pennsylvania, in 1910, Bales received his bachelors degree from the University of Pittsburgh and a drama degree
from the Carnegie Institute of Technology. Before moving to New
York in 1934, he studied ballet with Frank Eckl in Pittsburgh. His
modern dance studies began in New York with modern dance pioneers Doris Humphrey and Charles Weidman. He joined their group,
the Humphrey-Weidman Company, in 1935 and performed with it
as a featured member from 1936 to 1940. During his tenure there,
Bales originated roles in several of their most important works. The
two dancers' influence was noticeable in Bales' later choreographic
and teaching work, where he emphasized his own individual version of the Humphrey-Weidman technique.

Bales also performed in other venues during the late 1930s, in
addition to his work with Humphrey-Weidman. He accepted dance
roles on Broadway, performed with the Radio City Music Hall
Ballet, and was involved with the Tamiment Encampment, reaching
Broadway in 1940 with that company's *Straw Hat Revue.* In 1937
Bales performed in *Icaro,* the first major choreographic work of
Humphrey-Weidman member Eleanor King. With other members
of the cast, most of whom also performed with the Humphrey-
Weidman troupe, Bales joined the Theater Dance Company, an
organization founded by King. He was also a member of the progressive New Dance Group Studio in New York for many years,
where he taught and performed. Many of the New Dance Group's
members came from Graham's company, including Jane Dudley
and Sophie Maslow. Bales became one of the studio's most important figures, dancing in various group members' productions over
the years.

Bales joined with Dudley and Maslow for a concert sponsored
by *Dance Observer* in 1942. The performance marked the start of
a 12-year collaboration known as the Dudley-Maslow-Bales Trio,
which staged concerts in New York and elsewhere. The three performed both as a trio and in larger works with other members from
the New Dance Group, including Pearl Primus and Anne Sokolow.
They frequently staged concerts at universities and other low-cost
venues, intending to introduce dance to new audiences and, simultaneously, to spread the idea that dance did not require complicated
productions. They also performed at events such as the American
Dance Festival.

The three trio members had experienced a variety of training—all
had studied ballet and modern dance—which led them to incorporate a range of themes and styles into their works. They gained a
reputation as strong performers with an interest in theatrical works,
and became known for their humor and the harmonious way they
danced together in their pieces, some of which were collaboratively
choreographed. The three were interested in social themes and
American folklore, and their productions featured racially mixed
companies. Folk musician Woody Guthrie appeared with them as a
guest artist several times. Dance historian Don McDonogh wrote
of the Dudley-Maslow-Bales Trio:

> Besides creating an excellent small company the three rep-
> resented as many diverse strains of the modern dance world
> and expressed the freer and more tolerant attitude that be-
> gan to develop after the 1930s. . . . In their creative work
> they expressed a lively appreciation of theatrical values
> and toured very successfully for many years. The three
> were not afraid to include humorous pieces in repertory
> and rejected the somewhat somber face that modern dance
> presented to the world in the 1930s.

It was during the Dudley-Maslow-Bales years that Bales created
most of his choreography. His body of work is relatively small,
amounting to just 16 pieces through 1951. Many were solos, such
as *To a Green Mountain Boy* (1942), *Peon Portraits* (1943), and
Impromptu (1950), the latter set to Satie and incorporating spirals
as a movement motif. His works tended to be dramatic, and his
ability to mimic various character types was often highlighted in
his dances. *Es Mujer* (1942) is typical of Bales' work in that it tells
a story through the use of recognizable characters. It is about a
sailor and his relationships with the various women in his life, all of
whom pine for him while he is at sea. The sailor's demeanour
changes in his relationships with each: his mother, his sisters, two
prostitutes, and the woman he loves.

Bales' performances with the Dudley-Maslow-Bales trio ended
in 1954. From that point, he devoted himself primarily to dance
education. Since 1940, he had taught at Bennington College, which
he continued to do until 1967, becoming dance director (he gave
Paul Taylor a scholarship). He also conducted classes at Connecticut College, the New Dance Group Studio, New York University,
and the University of California at Los Angeles, as well as at Juilliard
for several years starting in 1962. He launched the dance program at
the Purchase campus of the State University of New York, and
became its first dean. He remained at SUNY-Purchase until 1975,
and continued to teach dance until 1980.

—Karen Raugust

BAT-DOR DANCE COMPANY
Israeli modern dance company

Bat-Dor Dance Company (Bat-Dor meaning "contemporary" in
Hebrew) was founded by Baroness Batsheva de Rothschild in 1967.
From its founding, Jeannette Ordman has been its artistic director
and guiding force. The name Bat-Dor not only stands for the dance
company, but adorns its studios and theatre in Tel-Aviv, as well as
a large school (for up to 400 students at a time), in which classical

Bat-Dor Dance Company: *Prism,* **1978. Photograph by Mula and Haramaty.**

ballet (with examinations from the Royal Academy of Dance in London) as well as modern dance is taught. The Bat-Dor school also operates a branch in Be'ersheba, the largest town in the southern part of Israel.

Baroness Batsheva (Bethsabee) de Rothschild was the scion of an old Jewish family of bankers famous for its philanthropic works in Israel and abroad. She was born in London in 1914, and grew up in Paris where she studied biology. When the Nazis conquered France, she escaped to New York. Interested in modern dance, she enrolled in Martha Graham's school. When Graham's annual season in New York was in danger of being canceled due to financial difficulties, Rothschild offered to provide the sum needed. This was the beginning of a deep friendship between Rothschild and Graham that lasted many years, and this special relationship made it possible for Rothschild to enlist Graham's help decades later when she founded her first Israeli dance company, eponymously named the Batsheva Dance Company, in 1964.

In 1949 Rothschild wrote a book about modern dance in America, *La danse artistique aux USA: tendences moderne.* The book was published in Paris in 1949, and was probably the first book written in French about modern dance. Two years later, in 1951, Rothschild

visited Israel for the first time and returned with the Graham company several years later in 1956. She decided to settle down in Israel and soon after her arrival began sponsoring young Israeli dancers and choreographers, by providing funding for productions or study abroad. Among these were Rena Gluck, Moshe Efrati, and Rena Schenfeld.

In 1963 Rothschild set out to organize a professional modern dance company in Israel with the help of Graham, who would become its first artistic advisor. The Batsheva Dance Company was the result and the company appeared publicly for the first time in December, 1964. In looking for a ballet teacher for her new company, Rothschild met Jeannette Ordman, a South African ballet dancer who had immigrated to Israel. After a short time Rothschild made it known that she intended to make Ordman a soloist of the company and its artistic director as well. The dancers vehemently opposed this appointment, as Ordman had no experience in modern dance whatsoever. Most of the founding members threatened to resign, should the proposed appointment of Ordman be realized. The solution was the founding of another dance company by Rothshild, Bat-Dor Dance Company, to provide Ordman with the opportunity to dance and choreograph.

In 1993 Rothschild announced she had to curtail the company's activities due to financial problems; the same year a fire gutted the Bat-Dor building. After a hiatus of two seasons the company started performing again, on a reduced basis, with about only 12 dancers, some of these recent immigrants from Russia.

Though Ordman herself no longer dances, she continues to direct the company and the school. To her credit, Bat-Dor was the first Israeli company to tour Poland and China and has had an eclectic repertory comprised of works by Lar Lubovitch, Paul Sanasardo, Robert Cohan, Gigi Caculeanu, Ed Wubbe, Nils Christe and many others, and Israeli choreographers Mirali Sharon and Domy Reiter-Soffer.

—Giora Manor

BATSHEVA DANCE COMPANY

Israeli dance company

Batsheva Dance Company was founded by Batsheva de Rothschild in 1964. Most of the founder-generation of dancers had studied in New York at the Juilliard School and the Martha Graham studio with the help of grants from the Rothschild Foundation. Graham herself and some of her dancers, such as Robert Cohan (who later became Batsheva's artistic advisor in 1980s) and Linda Hodes (who later married Israeli dancer Ehud Ben-David), came to Tel-Aviv to teach the Israeli dancers Graham's or their own works. Graham became the company's first artistic advisor.

Among the dancers of the original group were Rena Gluck, Moshe Efrati, Rina Schenfeld, Ehud Ben-David and Rahamim Ron. The young company excelled in Graham's works such as *Embattled Garden, Herodiad* or *Diversion of Angels*. Later works by José Limón, Jerome Robbins, John Butler, Anna Sokolow, Norman Morrice, Donald Mckayle, and John Cranko as well as by Moshe Efrati were added to the repertory. The Israeli dancers, especially the men, lent Batsheva performances vigor and vitality, compensating for the lack of polished technique with brilliant "chutzpa." When Batsheva toured Europe and the U.S. in 1970 and 1972, the critical reaction was ecstatic.

In 1974 Graham was in Israel to create her only work not choreographed especially for her own company, the biblical *The Dream,* with music by Mordecai Seter and set by Dani Karavan. Yet in the mid-1970s the performing rights and special relations between Batsheva and Martha Graham were withdrawn. This occurred after Linda Hodes, who had served as joint artistic director of Batsheva with Kai Lothman, left Israel and returned to New York to become

Batsheva Dance Company: *The Mythical Hunters,* 1965. Photograph by Mula and Haramaty.

a director of Graham's company. Hodes' and fellow director Ron Protas' policy was not to licence any company, apart of the Graham Company itself, to perform her works.

In 1973 Batsheva de Rothschild severed ties with the Batsheva company, devoting her attention and financial support to her other company, Bat-Dor—which threatened the very existence of Batsheva. Telegrams of protest from all over the dance world poured in. Batsheva then became a publicly supported company, subsidized mainly by the Israeli Ministry of Education and Culture.

Artistic directors (among then Brian MacDonald, William Louther, and Paul Sanasardo) came and went. Only in the 1980s when Shelley Sheer and David Dvir became joint artistic directors, were prominent choreogaphers such as Mark Morris, Daniel Ezralow and the Israeli Ohad Naharin invited to create for the company, which rejuvenated its repertory. Beginning in 1981 Ohad Naharin was invited by Batsheva nearly each season to create works. Being both an Israeli and a gifted innovative choreographer, Naharin's works (such as 1983's *Innostress*, which dealt in a personal way with the traumatic war in Lebanon the previous year) were what the company most needed, a direction and a purpose. After his long affiliation, Naharin was appointed artistic director in 1990, and his works brought Batsheva to the cutting edge of contemporary dance once more.

Apart from its primary company of about 20 dancers, the Batsheva Ensemble supplies the new young talent that is the life blood of any artistic group. Both groups have been performing such hits as Naharin's *Anaphasa or Mabul*. The Ensemble, lead by Naomi Perlow, also performed its own works, mainly for young audiences. Its dancers were chosen by audition, to join the company for one season; at the end of the year, the best were offered contracts with Batsheva proper.

Batsheva performed a repertory of 35 works in 1996, appearing in 189 performances attended by about 100,000 spectators. This popular acclaim has mostly been due to the work of Naharin, who has been known to use local popular rock musicians for accompaniment. Guest choreographers invited by Naharin have included Jiri Kylian, Wim Vandekeybus, Angelin Preljocaj and William Forsythe. Though in this year there was a general decline of about 23 percent in the attendance of dance performances in Israel, Batsheva is still the country's leading modern dance company.

Publications

Manor, Giora and Ruth Eshel, editors, "Thirty Years of Batsheva," Special Supplement in *Israel Dance Quarterly,* No. 4, Haifa 1994.

—Giora Manor

BAUMAN, Art
American dancer and choreographer

Born: 1939 in Washington, D.C. **Education:** Studied dance and drama, George Washington University; ballet, Washington School of Ballet, graduated 1959; student of composition at the Juilliard School of Music; studied modern dance at Martha Graham School; ballet at the Metropolitan School of Ballet; Broadway dance at June Taylor School and Herbert Berghof School; film production, New York University. **Career:** Co-founder, Contrasts Dance Group, 1962; began choreographing for summer stock and Dance Theatre Workshop, 1966. **Died:** 1993.

Works

1962	*Journal* (mus. Webern), Clark Center for the Performing Arts, New York
1963	*Desert Prayer* (mus. Janacek), Theater of Riverside Church, New York
	The Time of Singing (mus. Dewey Ownes), Theater of Riverside Church, New York
	Barrier (mus. Badings), Theater of the Riverside Church, New York
	Break Forth into Joy (mus. Robert Starer), Theater of Riverside Church, New York
	Nocturne (mus. Schuller, Hall), George Washington University, Washington, D.C.
1966	*Errands* (mus. The Ventures, Beethoven), Dance Theatre Workshop (DTW), New York
	Headquarters (mus. Barry), DTW, New York
	Periodic (mus. tape collage), DTW, New York
1967	*Burlesque/Black and White* (mus. tape collage), DTW, New York
	Dialog (mus. Michael Czajkowski), DTW, New York
	In the Back of the Closet (with narration from Wolfgang Kohler's *The Mentality of Apes*)
1968	*Relay* (mus. Michael Czajkowski), DTW, New York
	Chances (Improvisation), Minor Latham Playhouse, New York
1969	*Sketches for Nocturne*, (mus. Schuller, Hall), Minor Latham Playhouse, New York
1970	*Approximately 20 Minutes (Improvisation)*, (mus. Michael Czajkowski), Manhattan School of Music, New York
1971	*Dancing in Sheep Meadow*
	DTW Improvisation Group
	Materializations
1972	*Dancing in the Cathedral*
	A Dance Concert for Radio
	You Are Here
	A Movement Project
	Dances for Women
	A Piece about Pieces
	Mute Piece w/Anthony LaGiglia
1974	*Westbeth* (for video)
1975	*Exercise Piece*
	Changing Steps
	Rebus
	Solo
	Sounddance
	Blue Studio: Five Segments
1976	*Torse*
	Squaregame
	Videotriangle
1977	*Travelogue*
	Inlets
	Fractions
1978	*Exercise Piece I*
	Exercise Piece II
	Exchange
	Tango

1979	*Locale*
	Roadrunners
1980	*Exercise Piece III*
	Duets
	Fielding Sexes
1981	*Channels/Inserts*
	10's with Stones
	Gallopade
1982	*Trails*
	Quartet
1983	*Coast Zone*
	Inlets 2
	Roaralorio
1984	*Pictures*
	Doubles
	Phrases
1985	*Deli Commedia*
	Native Green
	Arcade
1986	*Grange Eve*
	Points in Space
1987	*Fabrications*
	Shards
	Carousal
1988	*Eleven*
	Five Stone
	Five Stone Wind
1989	*Cargo X*
	Field and Figures
	August Pace
	Inventions
1990	*Polarity*
1991	*Neighbors*
	Loosestrife
	Trackers
	Beach Birds
1992	*Beach Birds Forlamera*
	Change of Address
	Touchbase
	Enter
1993	*Doubletoss*
	CRWDSPCR
1994	*Breakers*
	Ocean
1995	*Ground Level Overlay*
	Windows
1996	*Tune In/Spin Out*
	Rondo

*   *   *

Art Bauman was born in 1939 and raised in Washington, D.C. He studied dance and drama at George Washington University and ballet at the Washington School of Ballet. After graduating in 1959, Bauman moved to New York and entered the Juilliard School of Music where he received attention from the composer Louis Horst, who encouraged Bauman to concentrate his efforts on choreography. After two years as a full-time student at Juilliard, Bauman dropped most of his courses and continued to take only composition classes. Bauman's dance background was broad and embraced many disciplines—in addition to studying composition at Juilliard,

he went on to study modern dance at the Martha Graham School, ballet at the Metropolitan School of Ballet, Broadway and musical-style dancing at the schools of June Taylor and Herbert Berghof, and film production at New York University.

Bauman is perhaps best-known for the painstaking and fastidious method by which he created a dance. While exploring an idea, Bauman experimented with movement, light, and sound, and created individual dance components. Rather than create a piece where one part flows or evolves into the next part, Bauman edited and perfected each component and then arranged them in a particular sequence or presented them simultaneously. He often paired components together because of their paradoxical relationship rather than their associative relationship. One of his choreographed segments could be altered, or they could be rearranged, without affecting the flow of the whole dance. The idea for one of his works of art, like a poem or book, could suddenly emerge but take a very long time to actually carry the idea through to the end product. Bauman once likened his rather tedious style of choreographing to a description that poet Robert Frost gave about writing one of his poems: the idea burst forth very quickly, and he wrote the poem in an afternoon—then spent six months editing it. Bauman's choreographic methods somewhat resemble the process by which a film is made, with the scenes shot out of sequence, edited, and joined together in a logical sequence to make a whole.

Bauman formed his first dance group, Contrasts, in 1962 along with several other Juilliard students. Contrasts played to a variety of community centers and colleges in the northeastern U.S. with modest success. This experience provided Bauman the opportunity to create and perform dances professionally but did not provide a steady income. While working on his own dances, Bauman worked at a number of odd jobs to support himself. For a time he worked as stage manager and production assistance in the theater, and did choreography for summer stock. Some of the pieces Bauman created during this time include a female solo entitled *Desert* (1963), *Prayer* (1963), and a duet choreographed for Bauman and a female dancer, entitled *Now Is the Time of Singing* (1963). More notable was *Nocturne*, an abstract dance he created for himself and three women. The piece, set to music by Gunther Schuler, was commissioned by George Washington University. Bauman, who was extremely proficient at sound editing, arranged Schuler's music to suit the dance and mixed guitar into it as well. *Nocturne* was the first dance with which Bauman experimented with his characteristic, modular style of choreography.

For many years, Bauman was closely associated with the Dance Theatre Workshop (DTW), during which time he created some of his most successful and innovative works. The DTW was established in 1966 for presenting experimental choreography and the work of new choreographers. Performances for the DTW were generally held in a small loft, and Bauman specifically choreographed his pieces to fit the space. Bauman expanded on his modular technique and created four progressive dances, *Errands* (1966), *Headquarters* (1966), *Burlesque/Black and White* (1967), and *Dialogue* (1967) which became the most successful of the four. With each piece, Bauman's technique and the movement of the dancers became more technologically precise. These pieces, often called his "photographic" pieces, received favorable attention and Bauman was invited to perform at The Place, a notorious center for modern dance London.

Bauman was one of the first choreographers to create mixed media presentations using photographic images and film projected onto a backdrop and spoken narration for the sound aspect. *Dia-*

logue melded film and dance, and Bauman made a series of films specifically for *Dialogue*—producing a surreal experience. Dancers seemed to appear out of the film and then disappear into it—a two-dimensional visual field shifting into the third dimension and back. Bauman's thought-provoking *In the Back of the Closet* (1967), included a narration of Wolfgang Köhlers's *The Mentality of Apes.*

In the late 1960s Bauman's choreographic process changed. While keeping a precise technological framework, Bauman had his dancers rely on improvisation to form a dance. For the piece *Approximately 20 Minutes (Improvisation)*, Bauman devised a series of specific cues that the dancers and/or musicians reacted to. While the cues were not improvisational, the order in which the cues were presented provided a surprise element to the performers. Bauman often designed dances for specific spaces (like the DTW loft) and choreographed this piece to be performed "in the round"—with the audience surrounding the dancers.

Bauman died in 1993. He is remembered as a modern dance innovator who helped to break down the barriers between the audience and performers—and as a modern choreographer who was very much concerned with the process of creating a dance as well as the finished product.

—Christine Miner Minderovic

BAUSCH, Pina

German dancer, choreographer, and company director

Born: Philippine B. Bausch, 27 July 1940 in Solingen. **Education:** Studied with Kurt Jooss at the Folkwangschule in Essen; scholarship to Juilliard (where she studied with Antony Tudor), 1958. **Career:** Performer, Paul Sansasardo and Donya Feuer Dance Company, New American Ballet, and Metropolitan Opera, 1958-62; returned to Germany and joined the Folkwang Ballet, 1962; began choreographing for Folkwang, 1968; founded Tanztheater Wuppertal, 1973; served as head of the dance department of Folkwang Hochschule, 1983-88; artistic director, Folkwang Tanzschule, 1993.

Works (performances in Wuppertal, Germany, unless otherwise noted)

1968	*Fragment* (mus. Bartók), Essen
1969	*Im Wind der Zeit* (mus. Dorner), Essen
1970	*Nachnull* (mus. Malec), Munich
1971	*Aktionen fuer Taenzer* (mus. Becker)
1972	*Bacchanal fuer "Tannhaeuser"* (mus. Wagner)
	Wiegenlied (mus. children's song)
	Solo Philipps 836885 D.S.Y. (mus. Henry)
1974	*Fritz* (mus. Mahler, Hufschmidt)
	Iphigenie auf Tauris (mus. Glück)
	Free Jazz Improvisation (mus. Schönberg, Christmann), Berlin
	Zwei Krawatten (text Kaiser)
	Ich bring Dich um die Ecke (mus. various)
	Adagio fuenf Lieder von Gustav Mahler (mus. Mahler, pop)
1975	*Fliegenflittchen* (mus. Offenbach)
	Orpheus und Eurydice (mus. Glück, pop)

	Fruehlingsopfer (mus. Stravinsky, pop)
	Die sieben Todsuenden (mus. Weill, pop)
1977	*Blaubart* (mus. Bartók, Borzik, Cito, pop)
	Komm, tanz mit mir (mus. various)
	Renate wandert aus (mus. various)
1978	*Er nimmt sie and der Hand und fuehrt sie in das Schloss, die andern folgen)* (mus. various), Bochum
	Café Müller (mus. Purcell)
	Kontakthof (mus. various)
1979	*Arien* (mus. various)
	Keuschheitslegende (mus. various)
1980	*1980—Ein Stueck von Pina Bausch* (mus. various)
	Bandoneón (mus. tangos)
1982	*Walzer* (mus. various), Amsterdam
1983	*Nelken* (mus. various)
1984	*Auf dem Gebirge hat man ein Geschrei gehoert* (mus. various)
1985	*Two Cigarettes in the Dark* (mus. various)
1986	*Viktor* (mus. various)
1987	*Ahnen* (mus. various)
1989	*Palermo, Palermo* (mus. various)
1991	*Tanzabend II* (mus. various)
1993	*Tanzabend I* (mus. various)
1994	*Ein Trauerspiel* (mus. various)
1995	*Danzón* (mus. Burkert)
1996	*Nur Du* (mus. various)
1997	*Der Fensterputzer* (mus. various)

Publications

On BAUSCH: books—

Abeele, Maarten Vanden, *Pina Bausch,* Edition Plume, 1996.
Birringer, Johannes, *Theatre, Theory, Postmodernism,* Bloomington & Indianapolis, 1991.
Schlicher, Susanne, *Tanztheater: Traditionen und Freiheiten,* Hamburg, 1987.
Schmidt, Jochen, *Tanztheater in Deutschland,* Frankfurt, 1992.
Servos, Norbert, *Pina Bausch Wuppertal Dance Theater: Or the Art of Training a Goldfish—Excursions into Dance* (translated by Patricia Stadié), Cologne, 1984.

On BAUSCH: articles—

Goldberg, Marianne, "Artifice and Authenticity: Gender Scenarios in Pina Bausch's Dance Theatre," *Women & Performance,* 1989.
Hoghe, Raimund, "The Theatre of Pina Bausch," *Drama Review,* March 1980.
Kaplan, Larry, "Pina Bausch: Dancing around the Issue," *Ballet Review,* Spring 1987.
Nugent, Ann, "*The Green Table* and *Café Müller,*" *Dance Now,* Autumn 1992.
Wehle, Philippa, "Pina Bausch's Tanztheater—A Place of Difficult Encounter," *Women & Performance,* Winter 1984.

Films and Videotapes

Die Klage der Kaiserin, film, chor. by Bausch, Berlin, 1990.

*   *   *

Pina Bausch: *Arien.* **Photograph © Beatriz Schiller.**

Pina Bausch is arguably the most important post-World War II German choreographer. Influenced by the surviving remnants of prewar German Expressionist dance, American modern dance, and the theatrical innovations of the 1960s, she and a group of other German choreographers (Gerhard Bohner, Reinhild Hoffmann, Hans Kresnik, and Susanne Linke among them) have created the genre now known as "Tanztheater" (dance theater). Heide-Marie Haertel, writing in *Tanztheater 1992* has positioned Tanztheater as a "theater of fragments." It is an accurate description of what Bausch does, both in terms of the collage-like results and the means of achieving them.

Born to innkeeper parents in Solingen one year after the outbreak of World War II, Bausch started to dance at age 14. Her prodigious qualities as a dancer gained her a scholarship to Juilliard in 1958 where she studied with Antony Tudor. Upon her return to Germany she soon assumed increasingly important roles with the new Folkwang Ensemble and began to choreograph her own work. Invited to the Wuppertal civic theaters in 1972, where she subsequently established her own Wuppertal Tanztheater, she started by choreographing such operas as Glück's *Iphigenia of Tauris* and *Orpheus and Eurydice* and the bacchanal of Wagner's *Tannhaeuser.* Her 1975 *Le Sacre du Printemps,* a no-holds-barred interpretation of Stravinksky's early-20th-century classic, scandalized and shocked her audiences, in part because the dancers performed on a peat-covered stage and danced themselves close to physical collapse. Yet in 1997 the work was accepted into the repertoire of the Paris Opera Ballet.

Starting with *Bluebeard, on listening to a recording of Béla Bartók's opera Duke Bluebeard's Castle,* in which the protagonist literally destroys the opera through interruptions and repetitions of the recorded score, she began to develop dance theater works which freely mix film, music, text, movement, stand-up comedy, and variety acts. The resulting collages are nonlinear, unfocused, and weighty with detail. Constructed out of individual episodes, mosaic-like coherent pictures emerge with distance. Just as her performers wend their way not only through emotional, but physical obstacle courses—she has filled the stage with chairs, water, peat moss, grass, carnations, and rubble—audiences are constantly confronted with contradictory images and emotions. Every issue, Bausch has said, can be looked at from two sides; this mindset is reflected in her œuvre.

As early as her best-known work *Cafe Müller* (1978), Bausch set out the themes which still haunt her: loneliness, alienation, humiliation, and cruelty—but also, though sometimes barely perceptible—tenacity, hope, humor, and tenderness. The works of the 1980s, *1980, Walzer, Nelken*, and *Ahnen* among them, are remarkable for the hostility expressed between men and women, and the rawness of emotions which they embody. Since the mid-1980s Bausch has created a series of site-specific works (*Viktor, Palermo, Palermo, Tanzabend II* and *Ein Trauerspiel, Nur Du,* and *Der Fensterputzer*) in which she incorporated her basic themes with information gathered in Lisbon, Palermo, Madrid, and Vienna, the American West and Hong Kong. Her usual procedure for these works has been to visit the locations and soak up as many impressions as possible which she then, with the help of her dancers, works into loosely constructed amalgams.

One reason why a Bausch work is sometimes difficult to watch is her use of repetition. Certain painful or banal episodes are performed over and over as if to hammer home a particular point. In later works these bludgeoning episodes have subsided—not that Bausch has changed her mind about the human animal, just that elements of compassion and a sense of humor at the absurdity of the *comédie humaine* have been allowed to surface more openly. Bausch maintains that she is "not interested in how people move, but in what moves them." Honesty for Bausch means that she has to ground her work in the life of real people. If that reality is ugly, so be it. Though her vision is dark, it is not hopeless. For one thing, the mixture of autobiography and fiction her dancers not so much *re*present, but present (they call each other, for instance, by their real names) is reassuring. The periodic addresses to the audience and the fact that the dancers often observe themselves in the act of performing also establishes a commonality of perception which seems to deny the impossibility of communication and intimacy.

Memories as encoded in the bodies of the dancers also speak to the possibility of intimacy. Sleepwalking, silly little rituals, and children's games play a prominent part in Bausch's work; they speak of a time, mostly half-forgotten, when existential loneliness had not yet constricted human vision. Bausch also puts much faith in the power of dance. Whether it is a mere physical jockeying for position, or one of many episodes of social dancing, the body in purposeful motion for Bausch is a sign of life and hope, a connection to something outside the individual. A key role here is played by Bausch's use of dance-hall music. Superficial and sentimental, it still speaks straight to the heart. The banality of most lives may not be inspiring, but these days Bausch seems to see contemporary men and women more as sad sacks than as depraved. She leaves the door open to other possibilities of being, even though she doesn't show her audiences how to walk through it.

—Rita Felciano

BEATTY, Patricia

Canadian dancer, choreographer, artistic director, educator, and writer

Born: 13 May 1936 in Toronto, Ontario. **Education:** Studied creative dance for children with Jean Macpherson, Heliconian Club, Toronto; studied ballet with Gladys Forrester and Gweneth Lloyd, Toronto; Bennington College, B.A. in dance 1959; studied modern dance, Connecticut College Summer School, José Limón School, Martha Graham School of Contemporary Dance with Bertram Ross and Helen McGehee. **Career:** Dancer, Mary Anthony Dance Com-

pany, 1959-60; Pearl Lang Dance Company, 1960-65; founder, New Dance Group of Canada, Toronto, 1967; first independent choreography, 1957; cofounder and co-artistic director, Toronto Dance Theatre (with David Earle and Peter Randazzo), Toronto, 1968; cofounder, the School of Toronto Dance Theatre, 1968; resident choreographer, Toronto Dance Theatre, 1987-93; teacher, creative dance for children at Scarborough Country Day School, Westchester, New York; New Dance Group and 92nd St. YMHA, New York; Graham technique (later Beatty/Graham-based technique) at Bloor St. YMHA, New Dance Group of Canada, and School of Toronto Dance Theatre, Toronto; first solo concert of works, 1979; producer, *Painters and the Dance,* collaboration between visual arts and choreography, 1983; *Dancing the Goddess,* 1993, 1995; lecturer, "The Process Revealed," Toronto Dance Theatre lecture series 1996, 1998. **Awards:** Dance Ontario Award (with David Earle and Peter Randazzo), 1982; Award of Merit, City of Toronto, 1984; Toronto Arts Award for the Performing Arts (with David Earle and Peter Randazzo), 1988; funding grants from the Ontario Arts Council, Toronto Arts Council, and Laidlaw Foundation.

Roles (original cast roles with the Toronto Dance Theatre, premiering in Toronto, unless otherwise noted)

1959	*Riders to the Sea* (later called *Threnody*) (Anthony), Mary Anthony Dance Company, Bennington College, Bennington, Vermont
1960	*Apasionada* (Lang), Pearl Lang Dance Company, Yale University, New Haven, Connecticut
1961	*Chanukah Festival* (Sophie Maslow), *Rite of Spring/ Dances for Israel,* New York
1963	*Broken Dialogues* (Lang), Pearl Lang Dance Company, New York
1964	*Persephone* (Lang), Pearl Lang Dance Company, New York
1965	*Shorebourne* (Lang), Pearl Lang Dance Company, New York
1967	*Fragments* (Peter Randazzo), New Dance Group of Canada, Toronto
1968	*Mirrors* (David Earle)
	The Recitation (Earle)
1969	*A Thread of Sand* (Earle)
	Lovers (Earle)
1970	*Portrait* (Earle)
1971	*The Silent Feast* (Earle)
	Baroque Suite (includes *Mirrors, Lyrical Solo, Duet, Lament, Finale*)
1973	*Atlantis* (Earle)
	Ray Charles Suite (Earle)
1974	*Bugs* (Earle)
	Parade (Earle)
1975	*La Belle Époque* (includes *Waltz Suite, Deux Epigraphes Antiques, L'Hôtel Splendide,* and *Vignette*), Camerata Music Ensemble, Toronto
	Field of Dreams (Earle)
1977	*A Simple Melody* (Randazzo)
1979	*The Light Brigade* (Randazzo)

Other roles include: Various roles in works by Lucas Hoving, Jeff Duncan, and Gloria Contreros, New York, 1963-64; solos in own works, 1967-83.

Works (performances with TDT, premiering in Toronto, unless otherwise noted)

1957	*Stripling* (mus. Jenny Paulson), Bennington College Dance Program, Bennington, Vermont
1958	*Rite* (mus. Milhaud), Bennington College Dance Program, Bennington, Vermont
1959	*The Scarlet Letter* w/Stanley Burke (mus. Lionel Nowak) duet, Bennington College Dance Program, Bennington, Vermont
1967	*Momentum* (mus. Couperin, Rameau, Ann Southam), New Dance Group of Canada, Toronto
	Flight Fantasy (mus. Musitonics—George Natchoff, Carol Rattray), New Dance Group of Canada, Toronto
1968	*Against Sleep* (mus. Southam)
1969	*Study for a Song in the Distance* (mus. Michael Craden, John Wyre)
1970	*First Music* (mus. Ives)
	Hot and Cold Heroes (mus. the Rolling Stones, Jimmy Hendrix, Ann Southam)
1971	*Rhapsody in the Late Afternoon* (mus. Milton Barnes)
1972	*Los Sencillos* (mus. Howard Marcus, Michael J. Baker)
1973	*Harold Morgan's Delicate Balance* (mus. Ann Southam)
1975	*The Reprieve* (mus. Southam)
1979	*Seastill* (mus. Southam)
1980	*Lessons in Another Language* (mus. Norman Symons)
	Skyling (mus. Michael J. Baker, Lawrence Shragge, Eric Harry)
1981	*Mas'harai* (mus. Michael J. Baker)
1983	*Rite for Future Time* (mus. Sharon Smith)
	Raptures and Ravings (mus. Robert Daigneault), part of *Painters and the Dance,* Toronto
	Emerging Ground (mus. Southam), part of *Painters and the Dance,* Toronto
1985	*Radical Light* (mus. Carlos Chavez), Ann Arbor, Michigan
1991	*Threshold* (mus. Copland)
1992	*Mandala* (mus. Alejandra Nuñez, Geoff Bennett, Mark Hand)
1993	*Garden of Origins* (mus. David Akal Jaggs), part of *Dancing the Goddess,* Toronto
	Gaia (mus. Sharon Smith), part of *Dancing the Goddess,* Toronto
1995	*Assara* (mus. Sharon Smith) solo for *Dancing the Goddess '95,* Toronto
1997	*Assara* (mus. traditional Greek and Arabic) solo for *Spring Rites,* Toronto
	Omega (mus. Jean Pitché), part of *Spring Rites,* Toronto

Publications

By BEATTY: books—

Form without Formula: A Concise Guide to the Choreographic Process, Toronto, 1985.

On BEATTY: articles—

Bernstein, Tamara, "Exploring Archetypal Themes," *Toronto Globe and Mail,* 16 September 1993.
Citron, Paula, "A Step Back to Move Forward: Transition at Toronto Dance Theatre," *Performing Arts* (Toronto), Summer 1983.
Littler, William, "Dancing a Hard Road," *Toronto Star,* 5 November 1988.

Films and Videotapes

Toronto Dance Theatre in England, CBC, 1973.
Music to See, CBC, 1977.
Risk Takers, Vision Television Network, 1991.
Originals in Art, dir. Dan Robinson, Bravo! New Style Arts Channel, 1995.
Sunday Arts and Entertainment, CBC, 1995, 1996 and 1997.
Dancing the Goddess, documentary, dir. Ariadne Ochrymovych, Isis Film Productions, 1997.

*   *   *

Of the three cofounders of Toronto Dance Theatre, Peter Randazzo is considered the most intellectual, David Earle the most passionate, and Patricia Beatty the most psychological. Inspired by Martha Graham, Beatty's works are intense, dense, mysterious, spiritual, and profound. Her themes are about the subconscious, sexuality, the eternal feminine, and the mysteries of nature. More akin to pieces of art than dance, her work is enhanced by collaboration with composers and designers. As Beatty says: "I don't want to entertain; I want to compel."

Beatty was born to privilege and attended a private girls' school. As an outlet for her high energy, she studied ballet, but felt hemmed in by both her conventional lifestyle and ballet's autocratic system. In a handbook of American universities, Beatty read about the liberal arts college in Bennington, Vermont, and was enthralled by a program description that stressed creativity. "I was alive but I felt incomplete," she says. "Bennington was my liberating experience. The school connected every intellectual pursuit to life. I was educated there, not trained." Although Beatty had never seen contemporary dance, she enrolled in the dance program, as a performance and choreography major under teacher William Bales, and immediately became enamoured with the principle of internal, organic movement. Beatty even pursued extra classes at the Connecticut College summer program. Her choreographic template was set from the very first piece she created as a sophomore—original music and a deep exploration of a theme. *Stripling* (1957) used a score by fellow student Jenny Paulson and focused on a newly born animal attempting to get up on its legs. She also discovered her modus operandi. "When I created *Rite* in my junior year, I realized it was a group piece with solos. I'm not an architect. I'm a painter; I move dancers across a canvas. I can't construct group pieces en masse because I get absorbed in detail."

After graduation Beatty joined Mary Anthony's company for a brief time, and then attended José Limón's school on scholarship. She switched her studies to Graham technique because she needed to be more grounded than was possible with the up-in-the-air Limón style. Her professional career resumed when she joined Graham disciple Pearl Lang in 1960. While working with Lang for the next five years, Beatty continued her Graham studies and also taught creative dance to children, propelled by a belief that stimulating creativity in students of any age is of paramount importance. "I was determined to give young people what I never got," she says. Working with Lang and other choreographers, such as Sophie Maslow and Lucas Hoving, Beatty discovered the wonderful mix of passion and artistry that choreography could have.

Beatty became increasingly dissatisfied with the circus lifestyle of New York, and, because the pioneering spirit had always appealed to her, Beatty returned to Toronto in 1965, a Graham missionary. "New York didn't need my work," she declares. "Canada did." Her goal was to show a new style of dance where women were elegant, dignified, and strong. When she opened her school, she found that her most creative students were ballet rejects. Beatty spent two years training their unformed bodies, and in December 1967 she felt ready to launch her company, New Dance Group of Canada, the name an homage to her mentor William Bales and his New Dance Group in New York. Beatty's flagship piece for the opening concert was *Momentum,* a complex psychological work based on Shakespeare's *Macbeth,* which mirrored Graham's archetypal works. Also participating were Peter Randazzo, a former Graham company member, and his friend, Toronto native and former Limón dancer, David Earle. Since Earle and Randazzo were also thinking of beginning a modern dance company in Toronto, Beatty joined forces with the men in 1968 to cofound the Toronto Dance Theatre (TDT) and the School of Toronto Dance Theatre. The elegant, stately Beatty continued to perform until she was 47, leaving the stage in 1983. In 1993 she gave up her position as resident choreographer at TDT to work independently. A supremely gifted teacher, she continued to give classes at the school in technique that was Graham based but fused with her own life experience.

Beatty was the least prolific of the TDT cofounders. Her slow creative process was motivated by a desire to make dances that were both beautiful and serious, and that dealt with issues of the human condition similar to the great works of literature and the theatre. The duet *Against Sleep* (1968) confronted primal fear, temptation, and suicide, with the male figure portraying the archetypal demon lover. The solo *First Music* (1970) was the last karmic journey to total serenity, the undertone of which was complete surrender to sexuality. The courageous *Seastill* (1979) used a front scrim to diffuse the portrait of beautiful, tranquil sea creatures in their underwater haven—a work without conflict, yet abandoning itself to complete sensuality. Beatty, an avid collector of contemporary art, has always had a strong visual component to her dances. Her exquisite 1983 program, *Painters and the Dance,* featured three works designed by prominent Canadian artists—*Raptures and Ravings* (Gordon Rayner), *Emerging Ground* (Graham Coughtry), and *Skyling* (Aiko Suzuki). As a champion of Canadian composers, Beatty has commissioned original scores for most of her works. She has had a particularly fruitful collaboration with artist Aiko Suzuki and composer Ann Southam.

At the beginning of the 1990s, Beatty turned her attention almost exclusively to creating choreography dedicated to the sacred feminine, many pieces of which were gathered into *Dancing the Goddess* concerts in 1993 and 1995. For Beatty, the goddess archetype represents balance, nurturing, healing, and reverence for the sanctity of the body and nature. Dances made in the name of the sacred feminine can be a positive force in the world. As she says, "I'm interested in what defines life, not what takes it away." *Mandala* (1992) is a magnificent coming of age ritual as older women prepare young girls for life. The solos *Gaia* (1993) and *Assara* (1997) are dedicated to goddess figures, while *Garden of Origins* (1993), with a set based on Persian miniature paintings, is an archetype of the sacredness of sexuality, as god/goddess parents teach their children the act of love—a work where women and men are equal, as opposed to the Eden myth where women are sinners created from men. In fact, Beatty equates Christianity and patriarchy with fas-

cism. Her dances are designed to confront our deepest, darkest emotions and liberate them from man-made restrictions.

Beatty has always felt that her career is one small cog in a cosmic wheel much bigger than herself, a universe where modern dance, the sacred feminine, and loving the planet are the most important things. Says Beatty: "In dance, both the dancer and the audience go through a transformation to a new level of awareness. There is no difference between the audience and me. We're in life together."

—Paula Citron

BEATTY, Talley

American dancer, choreographer, educator, and company director

Born: 1923 in Cedargrove, Louisiana. **Education:** Began studying dance with Katherine Dunham, 1934; later also studied with Martha Graham and Aubrey Hitchins. **Career:** Performance debut, Chicago Civic Opera, 1935; dancer, Katherine Dunham Company, 1940-46; solo dancer and co-choreographer, Maya Deren's *A Study in Choreography for Camera,* 1945; became freelance dancer in 1947 and created short-lived nightclub act with partner Janet Collins; first choreographed a suite of dances for recital, 1948; directed and appeared in own company, 1949-55; choreographed for numerous theatrical productions, 1960s-70s; created *The Black District* (1968) and *The Stack Up* (1982) for the Alvin Ailey American Dance Theatre; subject of video for American Dance Festival series, *Speaking of Dance,* 1993. **Awards:** Scripps/American Dance Festival Award, 1993. **Died:** 1995 in New York.

Roles

1937	Priest, *Yanvalou*
	Fugitive, *Tropic Death*
	Featured dancer, *Carnival Dances,* Katherine Dunham Company, YMCA's Negro Dance Evening, New York
1938	Original Cast, *La Guiablesse* (Ruth Page)
1941	*Cabin in the Sky* (Balanchine)
1946	Original cast, partnered w/Pearl Primus, *Showboat* revival (Tamiris)
	Original cast, *Spring Brazil* (Esther Junger)
	Original cast, *Blackface* (Lew Christiansen), Ballet Society production
1957	Original cast, *A Drum Is a Woman,* a Duke Ellington *U.S. Steel Hour* on CBS-TV
1958	Original cast, *Procession and Rite* (Syvilla Fort)
	Original cast, *Legend and Trajectories* (Emily Parham)

Works

1948	*Jim Crow*
	Blues
	Sonatina
1949	*Southern Landscape*
1950	*Dances of the Mulatress from the North*
	The Passionate Power St. Claire
	Region of the Sun

       Tone Poem
       Void
1951   *Fire on the Hill*
1958   *Hamsin*
       Introduction, Entrance and Dance of the Gloao
       The Way Out East St. Louis Toodleoo
1959   *Nobody Came*
       The Road of the Phoebe Snow
       Oh! Moonlight, Oh! Starlight
       Field Calls and Work Songs
1960   *Come and Get the Beauty of It Hot*
1962   *Come and Get the Beauty of It Hot* (revised)
       Look at All Those Lovely Red Roses
1963   *Danse au Nouveau Cirque Paris 1897*
1964   *The Migration*
       Powers of Six
1967   *Montgomery Variations*
1968   *The Black Belt*
       The Black District
       A Wilderness of Mirrors
1969   *Antigone*
       L'Histoire d'un Petit Voyage
1970   *Bring My Servant Home*
1972   *Poème de l'Extase*
1973   *Caravanserai*
       Cathedral of Heaven
1975   *Tres Cantos*
       The Nymphs Are Departed
1982   *The Stack Up*
1984   *Blueshift* (sequel to *The Stack Up*)
1993   *Ellingtonia*
1995   *Pretty Is Skin Deep Ugly Is to the Bone*

Other works include: *Paranoia-Afro-Cuban Dance,* 1954; *The Blacks,* 1961; *Ballad for Bimshire,* 1963; *House of Flowers* (revival), 1968; *But Never Jam Today* (Black Expo at New York City Center; choreographed segment), 1969; *Billy No Name,* 1970; *Don't Bother Me, I Can't Cope,* 1970; *Ari,* 1971; *Bury the Dead,* 1971; *Croesus and the Witch,* 1971; *Your Arms Too Short to Box with God,* 1977; *But Never Jam Today* (premiere of expanded version), 1979.

Publications

On BEATTY: books—

Clark, Veve A. and Margaret B. Wilkerson (eds.), *Kaiso! Katherine Dunham: An Anthology of Writings,* Berkeley, 1978.
Emery, Lynne Fauley, *Black Dance from 1619 to Today,* Princeton, 1988.
Giordano, Gus, *Anthology of American Jazz Dance,* Evanston, 1978.

On BEATTY: articles—

Barnes, Clive, "Dance: Broadway Touch," *New York Times,* 30 January 30 1969.
———, "Dance: The Wizardry of Talley Beatty," *New York Times,* 5 September 1967.
Dunning, Jennifer, obituary, *New York Times,* 1 May 1995.
Garafola, Lynn, "Dayton Contemporary Dance Company," *Dance Magazine,* February 1997.

Marks, Marcia, "The Alvin Ailey American Dance Theatre," *Dance Magazine,* March 1969.
Martin, John, "Negro Dance Art Shown in Recital," *New York Times,* 19 February 1940.
———, "The Dance: A Negro Art," *New York Times,* 25 February 1940
Murphy, Anthony C. "A Dance to Ellington," *American Visions,* June-July 1994.
Naude, Alice, "Sweet Silver," *Dance Magazine,* October 1995.

Films and Videotapes

On BEATTY—

A Study in Choreography for Camera, dir. Maya Deren, 1945.
Talley Beatty, American Dance Festival, 1993.

         *   *   *

    Talley Beatty's career as dancer, teacher, choreographer, and company director spanned six decades, from the mid-1930s to the 1990s. Born in Cedargrove, Louisiana, in 1923, he moved with his family to Chicago while still a young child. At the age of 11 he began studying dance with Katherine Dunham; he made his stage debut a year later with the Chicago Civic Opera, and by 16 he was a principal dancer in Dunham's company.

    Beatty's arrival into the dance world and the nurturing of his artistic talents were informed by the cultural phenomenon of Negro Dance, which burst upon the American scene in the 1930s. This popular term referred not only to the ancestry of the dancers involved, but to the African and African-American themes of choreographic works as well. Katherine Dunham was at the forefront of this cultural explosion. Under her tutelage Beatty learned her revolutionary technique, which was largely based upon African dance studies in the West Indies, in conjunction with classical technique. Beatty developed as a performer in such Dunham works as *Rites de Passage* (1941) and *Tropical Revue* (1943). He continued his studies while performing in New York, taking ballet class in a dressing room adjacent to the studio while class was being conducted, or alone at early morning or late night hours, because of the whites-only policy prevalent at the time. These instances of racism and those he encountered while touring with Dunham's company admittedly shocked him and contributed to defining the themes that would later dominate his choreography.

    Singled out by reviewers for both praise and criticism, Beatty was undeniably an exceptional dancer. *New York Times* reviewer John Martin is renowned for having difficulty with Beatty's unique talent. In his review of the Dunham company's New York City premiere, Martin found Beatty "to be a trifle difficult. His serious dallying ballet technique makes him stand out from the general style of the company most unfortunately." One week later, in a second review, Martin again referred to the distressing tendency to introduce the technique of the academic ballet and again made specific reference to Beatty. Others, however, found Beatty's dancing desirable. In the *Borzoi Book of Modern Dance,* Margaret Lloyd described him as an excellent dancer "[whose] leaps become phenomenal, a sort of universal wish fulfillment to navigate the air." And in Beatty's *New York Times* obituary (1 May 1995), Jennifer Dunning praised his dancing for the "exceptional physical control and intense emotion that later characterized his choreography." Even by today's more rigorous technical standards, a viewing of

Talley Beatty: Paul B. Sadler in Beatty's *Southern Landscape*, 1992. Photograph © Johan Elbers.

Beatty's solo performance in Maya Deren's experimental film, *A Study in Choreography for Camera* (1945), reveals a fluidity that is striking in its simultaneous grace and power. The controversy over Beatty's performances is most likely as revealing of the times as it is of Beatty himself, reflecting the ongoing social controversy surrounding the turbulent confluence of African-American and European-American aesthetic heritages.

Beatty left the Dunham company in 1946 and further diversified his performance experiences, appearing in nightclub acts, musical theater, and film, in addition to the concert stage. The list of choreographers for whom he worked includes Ruth Page, Lew Christiansen, Balanchine, and Syvilla Fort, among others.

Even with such an auspicious dancing career, Beatty is best known and revered as a brilliant choreographer who, along with Alvin Ailey, Donald McKayle, Eleo Pomare, and Louis Johnson, extended the vocabulary of concert dance considerably. Continuing along the path forged by Dunham, Beatty juxtaposed the shimmies and shakes of African dance, the struts and shuffles of ballroom, tap, disco, modern, and classical technique. He most frequently set universal themes within the wide variety of everyday life in the African-American experience. Similar to the varied nature of his

performing career, Beatty choreographed for numerous venues: the concert stage, nightclubs, Broadway, off-Broadway, and television.

Curiously, though many consider Beatty's work to be in the jazz genre, Beatty himself did not. In the 1993 American Dance Festival (ADF) video entitled *Talley Beatty,* he acknowledged Martha Graham as being most influential to his work as a choreographer and made it clear that he was totally unfettered by convention: "I don't speak to all those rules that Doris Humphrey and Louis Horst taught me. So if I see somebody and I like what they're doing I say, let's see if we can put that here." His self-described style is a mixture of Graham connective steps, Dunham technique, and a little ballet with Louisiana hot sauce on it. Beatty believed it was his combination of genres, high energy, and races that created the jazz energy and impression.

Beatty established his own company in 1949, which successfully toured the U.S. and Europe and disbanded in 1955. He went on to choreograph works for a wide variety of companies in America and abroad, including the Boston Ballet, Birgit Cullberg Ballet in Stockholm, Batsheva Dance Company in Israel, Inner City Dance Company of Watts, Los Angeles, Ballet Hispanico in New York, and the Alvin Ailey American Dance Theatre. His works continue to be included in the repertory of the Ailey company, as well as the Dayton Contemporary Dance Company, Philadanco, and the Cleo Parker Robinson Dance Ensemble.

Among his most celebrated works is *Southern Landscape* (1949), which was inspired by Howard Fast's published history of the post-Civil War Reconstruction period in the South, *Freedom Road.* The third section of this work, *Mourners' Bench,* was a signature solo piece for Beatty and has become part of the Alvin Ailey American Dance Theatre's repertory. *The Road of the Phoebe Snow* (1959), considered by many to be Beatty's best work, utilizes the setting along the tracks of the old Lackawanna railroad to explore adolescent life along the visible and invisible lines that divide and segment society. It has to do with alienation and how we mistreat each other, Beatty explained in the ADF video. The dance suite, *Come and Get the Beauty of It Hot* (1960), highly praised by both John Martin and Clive Barnes for its brilliance and beauty, has produced *Toccata* and *Congo Tango Palace* as independently popular excerpts. *The Stack Up,* created for the Ailey company in 1982, is a fast-paced, unflinching portrayal of the violence surrounding the drug culture in inner city life.

In addition to performing and choreographing, Beatty taught dance intermittently throughout his career. He was the recipient of the 1993 Scripps/American Dance Festival Award and continued to work until just before his death, of complications from diabetes, in 1995.

—Teren Damato Ellison

THE BELOVED

Choreography: Lester Horton
Music: Judith Hamilton
Costume Design: Lester Horton
First Production: Dance Theater, Los Angeles, 22 May 1948.
Original Dancers: Bella Lewitsky and Herman Boden
Other productions include: First performed by Alvin Ailey and company in 1964; performed by Dance Theatre of Harlem 11 December 1971 at Hunter College with Gayle McKinney and Walter Raines.

Publications

Warren, Larry, *Lester Horton: Modern Dance Pioneer,* Pennington, New Jersey.

*   *   *

The Beloved is a beautifully crafted, eight-minute work in the modern style noted for its innovative lifts and dramatic intensity. Horton found his inspiration for the dance in a newspaper article about a man in the Midwest who had beaten his wife to death with a Bible for suspected infidelity. In the work Horton clearly and succinctly presents a series of images based on this elemental plot, focusing on the woman's experience. When originally performed, Bella Lewitsky astounded critics with her electrifying performance of the wife's role.

The piece opens at the edge of the climactic situation. As the dance begins, a man and a woman sit at a table in high ladder-back chairs facing the audience, suggesting, as Don McDonagh observes, "probity of the most unyielding sort." A short poetic text is heard presenting an idealized image of woman as lovely, pure and unblemished. The statement "there is no spot on thee" is immediately followed by the man shifting his eyes toward the woman in distrust, and angrily slamming the Bible he is reading closed. He reaches out his hand for her, and the dance begins.

Through the first part of the piece a succession of discrete music and dance images show various facets of the woman's experience. One sees her reaching out to God asking why the tragic situation is happening, her arms and hands outstretched to the sky in several movements and lifts. One also sees her wanting the husband to trust her innocence and be close to her, as when she goes to him on her own initiative, putting his arms around her. Moving toward and away from him, she tries to assess the situation and find out what is wrong. In a particularly striking moment she circles him with little flicking arm gestures that imply questioning and imploring simultaneously. There are also jarring images of violence as when the husband throws her to the ground. Throughout, in contrast to her constant motion, the man remains rigid and self-contained, performing stiff stylized walks with a mesmerized focus that suggests a psychotic state.

At the end of the long first section the couple return to the table and chairs, both now with twitching neurotic gestures, the wife having exhausted all possible reactions to the situation, and the husband prepared to kill. This time when he reaches out to her, she retreats to the side of her chair. However, she has no choice and is forced to return to him. In this as well as other movements in the remaining part of the piece she constantly pulls away yet holds on to him at the same time, clearly afraid yet fulfilling her role as a loyal wife. This simultaneous pushing and pulling articulates a larger social and historical commentary on the subservient role of women in turn-of-the-century New England where bigotry and sexual chauvinism "held women subservient" (from Horton's program note). The work ends with a neck lift in which the man carries the woman back to the chair while strangling her.

The Beloved addresses similar themes concerning Puritan repression as explored by Martha Graham and Doris Humphrey in their Americana dances. While Horton remains a rather enigmatic figure in modern dance history, receiving criticism for erratic and insubstantial choreographic ability, this work remains exemplary in the economy of its expression, and the power of its choreographic images. The dance relies on dynamic extremes and dramatic gestures characteristic of much modern dance to convey its message. At the same time, lack of reliance on codified movements and the creation of original images make *The Beloved* a unique contribution to the modern style.

—Naomi Jackson

BENNATHAN, Serge

French-born Canadian dancer, choreographer, and artistic director

Born: Serge Jacques Léon Ben-Nathan, 14 August 1957 in L'Aigle (Orne), France; emigrated to Canada, 1985. **Education:** Studied ballet and gymnastics; trained in ballet, modern and folk dance with André Glegolsky and Hector Estrems at L'Académie internationale de danse, Paris, France, 1971-75. **Family:** Married dancer Carolyn Woods, 1993. **Career:** Dancer, Ballet National de Marseille Roland Petit, Marseilles, France, 1975-81; first choreography, 1980; first complete concert of works, 1980; resident choreographer, Centre de Danse International Rosella Hightower (Cannes, France), 1981; founder and artistic director, Compagnie Serge Bennathan (Cannes, France),1982-85; dancer, Ottawa Dance Theatre, 1985; dancer, Le Groupe de la Place Royale (Ottawa, Ontario), 1986-87; independent dancer and choreographer (Vancouver, British Columbia), 1987-90; artistic director, Dancemakers (Toronto, Ontario), 1990 to present; tours to Canada, U.S., France, Germany, Morocco, Montenegro, Greece and Austria; guest choreographer, Simon Fraser University Summer Institute (Burnaby, B.C.) 1991-92; resident choreographer, Grant MacEwan College (Edmonton, Alberta), 1995 and 1997; director, *Song of Songs* (mus. collage; chor. Julia Alpin, Marie-Josée Chartier, Shannon Cooney, Julia Sasso, and Hope Terry; coll. with Toronto Chamber Society, dir. David Fallis), Dancemakers, 1997; appeared in *Variations chromatiques,* (mus. Bizet, chor. Petit), Ballet National de Marseille Roland Petit (TV version, 1978), *The Magic of Dance*, documentary series, host Margot Fonteyn (chor. Petit, BBC), 1979, and *Bon baisers d'Amérique*, news magazine/ performing arts series, Television Cinq (TV5), 1996. **Awards:** Fondation de la Vocation (Paris, France), 1982; Choreography Award, Concorso Internazionale di Coreografia (Turin, Italy), 1983; Choreography Award, Le Conseil de Provence-Alpes-Côte d'Azur (France), 1984; and Dora Mavor Moore Award for New Choreography (Toronto Theatre Alliance), 1995; funding grants from the Canada Council.

Roles (original cast (cr) roles; performances with Ballet National de Marseille Roland Petit unless otherwise noted)

1975   Ensemble, *Coppélia* (new version; mus. Delibes; chor. Petit), Paris

        Soloist, *Variations chromatiques* (mus. Bizet; chor. Petit), Paris

1976   Soloist, *Casse-Noisette* (mus. Tchaikovsky; chor. Petit), Paris

1977   Ensemble, *Fascinating Rhythm* (mus. Gershwin; chor. Petit), Marseilles

1978   Soloist, *Ragtime* (mus. Stravinsky; chor. Petit), Marseilles

        Ensemble, *La Dame de pique* (mus. Tchaikovsky; chor. Petit), Marseilles

1979   Ensemble, *La Chauve-Souris* (mus. Strauss; chor. Petit), Monte Carlo, Monaco

        Soloist, *Parisiana 25* (mus. various), Marseilles

1980   Soloist, *Le Fantôme de L'Opéra* (mus. Landowski; chor. Petit), Paris

Other roles include: *Carmen, Le Loup, Cyrano de Bergerac, Notre-Dame de Paris, Les Intermittences du coeur* and other choreography by Roland Petit, Ballet National de Marseille Roland Petit, Marseilles, France, 1975-81; choreography by Dwight Shelton, Ottawa Dance Theatre, 1985; Jane Mappin, Davida Monk, Katherine Labelle and Tom Stroud, Le Groupe de la Place Royale, 1986-87; and solos (cr) in own works from 1980 to 1989.

Works

1980   *Heurteubise* (duet with Mireille Bourgeois; mus. Hindemith), Ecole de Danse de la Ville de Marseille Gala, Marseilles, France

        Roland Petit donne Carte blanche (includes *Heurteubise* [mus. Hindemith, 1980], *Le Départ* [mus. Gershwin], *La Quête* [mus. Jacques Brel], *Les Planetes* [mus. Holtz], and *Yiddish Lieder* [mus. Zupfgeigenhansel]), Théâtre du Merlan, Marseilles

1981   *Passing By* (mus. Keith Jarrett), Centre de Danse International Rosella Hightower, Cannes, France

        L'Imaginist (mus. Martinu), Centre de Danse International Rosella Hightower, Cannes

1982   *Les Heures frenetiques* (mus. Keith Jarrett), Jeune Ballet de France, Cannes

        Sul filo di Orfeo (mus. Ludovico Einaudi), Balletto Teatro Comunale di Firenze, Maggio Musicale Fiorentino, Florence, Italy

1983   *Contre la melancholie* (mus. Zupfgeigenhansel), Athens Ballet Theatre, Athens Festival, Athens, Greece

        Les Aventures de Tim Landers (mus. collage), Compagnie Serge Bennathan, Istres, France

        Le Départ (mus. popular Jewish), Compagnie Eddie Toussaint, Montreal, Quebec

1984   *We Go* (mus. Joe Jackson, Ultravox), Compagnie Serge Bennathan, Lyons, France

        Stravinsky (mus. Stravinsky), Compagnie Serge Bennathan, Cannes

        Le nain rouge (mus. Duncan Yougerman) Compagnie Serge Bennathan, Chateauvallon, France

1985   *The Story of the Ogre* (mus. collage), Ottawa Dance Theatre, Ottawa

1986   *White Vision* (mus. R. Strauss), Ottawa Dance Festival, Ottawa

1987   *The Boat* (mus. collage), Le Groupe de la Place Royale, Canada Dance Festival, Ottawa

1988   *The Hunt* (mus. Arne Eigenfeldt), Dancecorps, Vancouver

        And He Lies Himself Down as if to Sleep (mus. Eigenfeldt), Off-Centre Dance Company, Simon Fraser University, Burnaby, British Columbia

        Untitled (group piece for seven dancers, San Francisco Ballet; mus. collage), Théâtre du Pharo, Marseilles

        Small People behind the Big Red Suns (mus. Eigenfeldt), Judith Marcuse Dance Company, Vancouver

        The Fall (mus. Eigenfeldt), Ballet British Columbia, Vancouver

1989   *Heaven* (mus. collage), Calgary City Ballet, Calgary, Alberta

        Mirages (mus. Eigenfeldt), Ballet Jörgen, Toronto

        Le Voyage (mus. Eigenfeldt), Jeune Ballet International de Cannes

        The Desires of Merlin (mus. Pärt, Britten), Ballet British Columbia, Vancouver

        Arithmetic and Calculus (mus. Eigenfeldt), EDAM (Experimental Dance and Music), Vancouver

1990   *The Song of the Nightingale* (mus. Eigenfeldt), Vancouver

        La Beauté du Diable (mus. Russell Shumsky, Toni Stanick), Vancouver

1991   *Muses pastorales No. 1 et No. 2 et un Baigneur endormi*, Ottawa Ballet Theatre

        Muse No. 3 Running in Circles (solo for Katherine Labelle; mus. Russell Shumsky), Vancouver

        Sarah McLaughlin's *Path of Thorns* (chor. for music video)

Quand les Grands-mères s'envolent (work-in-progress; mus. Michael Nyman), Simon Fraser University Summer Institute, Burnaby, British Columbia

Quand les Grands-mères s'envolent (mus. Eigenfeldt; design Nancy Bryant), Dancemakers, Toronto

Little Boy Lost and Found (part of *Songs of Innocence and of Experience*; text William Blake; coll. with nine chor.; mus. Kirk Elliott), Canadian Children's Dance Theatre, Toronto

1992   *Miniature*, Canadian Children's Dance Theatre, Toronto

Chronicles of a Simple Life (work-in-progress; mus. Michael Nyman), Simon Fraser University Summer Institute, Burnaby, British Columbia

Chronicles of a Simple Life (mus. Eigenfeldt; design Nancy Bryant), Dancemakers, Toronto

Mario and the Magician (chor. for opera; mus. Harry Somers; dir. Robert Carsen), Canadian Opera Company, Toronto

Turandot (chor. for opera; mus. Puccini; dir. Robert Carsen), Flanders Opera, Antwerp, Belgium

1993   *Untitled Solo* (mus. Purcell; part of *Horse on the Moon* [four solos for Claudia Moore; mus. collage; chor. Ginette Laurin, Serge Bennathan, Lola McLaughlin, Tedd Robinson]), Toronto

The Strangeness of a Kiss (mus. Eigenfeldt; design Nancy Bryant), National Ballet of Canada, Toronto

Untitled Solos (mus. collage), Simon Fraser University Dance Department, Burnaby, British Columbia

Carmen (chor. for opera; mus. Bizet; dir. François Racine), Canadian Opera Company, Toronto

1994   *Les Vents tumultueux* (mus. Eigenfeldt; design Nancy Bryant), Dancemakers, Toronto

In and Around Kozla Street [Warsaw] (mus. Eigenfeldt; design Nancy Bryant), Ballet British Columbia, Vancouver

1995   *Sable/Sand* (mus. Ahmed Hassan; design Nancy Bryant), Dancemakers, Toronto

Faust (chor. for opera; mus. Gounod; dir. Robert Carsen), Le Grand-Théâtre de Genève, Geneva, Switzerland

Jenufa (chor. for opera; mus. Janáãek; dir. Nicholas Muni), Canadian Opera Company, Toronto

1996   *Les Arbres d'Or* (mus. Eigenfeldt; design Nancy Bryant), Dancemakers, Toronto

Salome (chor. for opera; mus. R. Strauss; dir. Atom Egoyan), Canadian Opera Company, Toronto

1997   *The Last I Saw...* (mus. Gavin Bryars), Alberta Ballet, Edmonton, Alberta

Trilogy of Sable/Sand—Like Dunes, Like Water, People (includes *Sable/Sand* [1995], now called *People*; mus. Ahmed Hassan), Dancemakers, Toronto

Boy Wonder Project (mus. Eigenfeldt; design Nancy Bryant), Ballet British Columbia, Vancouver

Les yeux fermés (solo for Katherine Labelle mus. Eigenfeldt), Vancouver

Eugene Onegin (chor. for opera; mus. Tchaikovsky; dir. Robert Carsen), Metropolitan Opera Company, New York City

1998   *Exile* (work-in-progress), School of Toronto Dance Theatre, Toronto

Exile (mus. Eigenfeldt; design Nancy Bryant), Les Ballets de Monte Carlo, Monaco

Publications

On BENNATHAN: articles—

Citron, Paula, "Spurned Dancer Back as Director," *Toronto Star,* 18 February 1991.

Collins, Daniel, "Dancemakers," *Dance International* (Vancouver), Spring 1994.

Liam, Lacey, "Show Some Emotion Choreographer's Motto," *Globe and Mail* (Toronto), 14 December 1990.

Littler, William, "How a Choreographer Found His Dream Home," *New York Times,* 31 March 1996.

Tenaglia, Susan, "A Different Vision: Toronto's Dancemakers," *The World and I* (Washington, DC), July 1997.

Walker, Susan, "Arts World Clamors for Serge Bennathan," *Toronto Star,* 20 February 1997.

Films and Videotapes

Appeared in *Variations chromatiques,* (mus. Bizet, chor. Petit) for the Ballet National de Marseille Roland Petit (TV version, 1978); *The Magic of Dance* documentary series, host Margot Fonteyn (chor. Petit, for the BBC, 1979); *Bon baisers d'Amérique*, news magazine/performing arts series, Television Cinq (TV5), 1996.

*   *   *

In 1990, when Serge Bennathan was appointed artistic director of Dancemakers, Toronto's second oldest professional contemporary dance company, he had already established himself as one of Vancouver's busiest independent choreographers. In Toronto, however, he was virtually unknown, a situation he soon remedied. Within the next few years, every work he created for Dancemakers was nominated for the prestigious Toronto Theatre Alliance's annual Dora Mavor Moore Award for New Choreography which Bennathan finally won for *Sable/Sand* in 1995. Under Bennathan, Dancemakers has also acquired both a national and international profile with performances across Canada and tours to Europe, North Africa, and the United States, the latter including a well-received visit to New York's Joyce Theater in 1996.

Bennathan's commitment to dance was late in coming. The child of a military family, Bennathan spent his early years in nine different cities in his native France, an upbringing which made him both self-reliant and rebellious. His disciplinarian father insisted he find an interest to keep him off the streets, and the youngster chose ballet because a friend was taking classes. By the time he was 11, Bennathan was living two separate lives—a dutiful school boy and a gang member sliding into petty crime. When a dance teacher in Rheims suggested he should do advanced studies in Paris, Bennathan saw dance as an escape, both from his own unhappy home life and a future as a career criminal. By 14, he was living on his own in Montmartre and training at L'Académie internationale de danse. Two 1974 events focused Bennathan's attention seriously on dance. The happy-go-lucky teenager arrived minutes before a student performance without any warmup and was slapped by a teacher for his lack of commitment. Shortly after, the Académie's artistic director, Nicole Chirpaz, took Bennathan to see Rudolf Nureyev perform at the Palais de Sport. The combination of the harsh reprimand and Nureyev's artistry produced a newfound dedication and passion in Bennathan for dance as his life's work.

At 17 Bennathan auditioned for Roland Petit and was devastated when he was not chosen. Almost as an afterthought Petit pointed to the dejected Bennathan and said, "I'll take him too." For the next five years Bennathan performed with Le Ballet National de Marseille Roland Petit, reveling in the exciting, creative atmosphere of Petit's new company. According to Bennathan, he was "a gutsy, physical, dramatic dancer with high jumps, but no sense of lines," and although he was an ensemble member, he was given soloist parts, even playing Dr. Coppélius in the new *Coppélia* which Petit had created for himself. It was the legendary choreographer who pushed the young dancer to create work when he realized that Bennathan hungered for a deeper relationship with dance. In 1980 Bennathan showed five pieces at Théâtre du Merlan in Marseilles which mirrored the narrative/neoclassical bent of his mentor, but the success of this concert also soured his relationship with Petit, and the following year he left the company.

Jean-Luc Barsotti, the administrator of Rosella Hightower's school in Cannes, had seen the Merlan show and offered Bennathan a choreographic residency. Bennathan founded his own company in Cannes in 1982, and despite the group's success throughout France, chronic underfunding led to his ending the venture in 1985. That year he emigrated to Canada, a country he had toured with Petit. "My choreographic walls needed to be broken open," he has said, "and I had to get away from the parochialism of France." Ottawa's Le Groupe de la Place Royale under Peter Boneham was Bennathan's "hammer." Boneham had given up public performances to create a choreographic lab that concentrated on the creative process—or as Bennathan says, "a perfect place to explore how to create movement and construct dances." Bennathan then established his freelance career in Vancouver in 1987 and in 1990 became artistic director of Dancemakers in Toronto, the latter to provide a stable environment for his own creation.

Bennathan sees his growth as a choreographer as evolutionary, with each work a building block to the next. He does not create steps; he explores themes. From story ballets, he has moved to works that portray the "poetic essence of emotions"—from ballet movement, he has developed a physicality that contains its own duality—the feet and torso grounded in the gravity of modern dance, but an upper body that conveys openness, particularly in the swinging use of arms—a style he calls "precision freedom." Bennathan's dancers create a strong presence on stage and their energetic bodies are given strong, bold movement to fill the space. His favourite tools of expression are stylized pedestrian, natural, organic movement, unpredictable dramatic pauses, and prolonged moments of stillness. Bennathan also plays with contrasts, a body in the foreground being intensely physical juxtaposed with another figure that is frozen. While he directs the audience to the essential stage picture, he also choreographs smaller details happening elsewhere on stage—the main image being enhanced by a subtext. His approach is unisexual, using the masculinity of the women and the femininity of the men with equal measure. Bennathan also prefers mature dancers in their late 20s or older to bring the maturity and intensity he needs to his pieces. "I push my dancers to project the humanity of the work. I don't want the audience to focus on what the dancers are doing but on what the work is saying. I'm always talking about relationships and I want the communication between the audience and the dancers to be as direct as possible. The audience should recognize themselves in what is happening on stage."

While his emotionally powerful works are not autobiographical per se, they are often triggered by personal events which Bennathan transforms into many-layered metaphors that resonate with uni-versal significance. *Quand les Grands-mères s'envolent,* his first work for Dancemakers, was inspired by the death of his grandmother, but dealt with the larger themes of isolation within the family and the struggle between youth and old age. The death of Barsotti in Cannes became the haunting, yet life-affirming, exploration of the many aspects of friendship in *Chronicles of a Simple Life. Les Arbres d'Or* followed a nostalgic visit to the Normandy of his childhood, and this reflective experience was transformed into a parade of images depicting how the events of youth inform the adult. *Sable/Sand* was a reconciliation with his Algerian-born father by paying homage to both his Sephardic-Jewish heritage and the North African/European collision of cultures Bennathan had encountered in Marseilles. Most of his mature pieces have involved close collaboration with two Vancouver colleagues—composer Arne Eigenfeldt and designer Nancy Bryant—whose contributions have helped shape both the look and feel of his work.

As well as creating dances for his own company, Bennathan has been commissioned by Ballet British Columbia, the National Ballet of Canada, Alberta Ballet and Les Ballets de Monte-Carlo, among others. Since 1992 he has also established a career as a choreographer and movement specialist for opera, particularly in collaboration with acclaimed director Robert Carsen and designer Michael Levine, which includes productions for Toronto's Canadian Opera Company, Antwerp's Flanders Opera, Geneva's Opéra du Grand-Théâtre and New York's Metropolitan Opera.

—Paula Citron

BENNINGTON SCHOOL OF DANCE

The Bennington School of the Dance began in 1934 as an experiment in dance education and continued for a total of nine summer sessions, eight on the Bennington College Campus and one session at Mills College in Oakland, California. Bennington's original mission was to be a center for the study of modern dance. In this, it was extraordinarily successful. The summer sessions rapidly became known as a sanctuary for the artists of this new dance form, for it provided a place to live and work, to choreograph and produce—in an exciting, collaborative, and supportive environment. Bennington was revolutionary both in the art created there and in its wide-reaching influence on American dance. It was largely instrumental in modern dance coming to be seen as a legitimate movement by critics and accepted by audiences that it helped create.

Bennington's presence on a college campus bestowed the academic seal of approval on its programs. The strong, new repertory created and produced there was later reproduced throughout the country and proved very influential. The summer sessions generated a huge amount of publicity; modern dance was an attractive subject, for very few people had seen or read about anything like it. Much of this publicity was in fact favorably biased because many of those who were writing about Bennington, such as *New York Times* critic John Martin and Louis Horst, were involved with the program.

Over 1,000 students, the majority of whom were dance teachers themselves, left Bennington prepared to promulgate a theory and a set of techniques in a new, cohesive form. Prior to Bennington there were no programs devoted solely to modern dance. Its success, however, inspired new programs at the Connecticut College School of the Dance and the Juilliard dance department. Other than the social and job-minded Federal Dance Project there had been no public support of modern dance prior to Bennington. Again, inspired by Bennington's success, new forms of support were established including the American Dance Festival and the dance residency programs of the National Endowment for the Arts and the Rockefeller Foundation.

The school's founders were director Martha Hill, administrative director Mary Josephine Shelly, and Bennington College president Robert Devore Leigh. The so-called "Big Four," Martha Graham, Doris Humphrey, Charles Weidman, and Hanya Holm, headed the original faculty. Sixteen of the 42 dances that premiered at Bennington over its duration were created by these four choreographers.

Humphrey was able to move into the creation of larger-scaled dances because of the number of dancers available at Bennington to perform. Works she created there, such as *New Dance, With My Red Fires, Passacaglia in C Minor* and *Decade* signaled the beginning of a new era of full-length theatrical dances. Hanya Holm's East Coast debut occurred at Bennington, creating an awareness of the German school of dance. She also composed her first work, the great *Trend* and began her collaboration with Arch Lauterer, with whom she would work for many years. The formation of associations such as this was just one more way that Bennington was significant. Charles Weidman created *Quest* and *Opus 51* there, but perhaps his largest contribution was simply as a male presence, helping to ensure that Bennington and the modern dance world would not be perceived as a strictly female domain.

Despite all the big names and rising stars who arrived at Bennington, Martha Graham was the dominant presence. She was already the best-known modern dance figure and she was a commanding, somewhat authoritarian, teacher. From the start she was favored by the administration and she alone was in residence each summer. After the school closed, it was Graham who was invited to return to Bennington as artist-in-residence for three years. During her long tenure, Graham premiered the most new pieces as well: *Panorama, Opening Dance, Immediate Tragedy, American Document, El Penitente, Letter to the World,* and *Punch and Judy.*

Although the dances created were often wildly different, there were similarities in themes. The artists at Bennington were aware of themselves as members of a fledgling artistic community and were concerned with both their place in society and the social issues of the time. Martha Graham's *Immediate Tragedy,* Anna Sokolow's *Facade-Episozione Italian,* and José Limón's *Danze de la Muerte* dealt with the rise of fascism, for example.

The original faculty was joined by Louis Horst, John Martin, Gregory Tucker, and Bessie Schönberg. Original music was an integral part of creation at Bennington. Only five of the dances premiered there relied on pre-composed scores. Many relationships were established between choreographers and the composers; in addition to Horst, the composers in residence were Vivian Fine, Ray Green, Hunter Johnson, Norman Lloyd, Harrison Kerr, Alex North, Robert McBride, Jerome Moross, Lionel Nowak, Harvey Pollins, Wallingford Riegger, Gregory Tucker, and Esther Williamson.

The student body and faculty rosters included most of the current generation of modern dancer professionals as well as the generation that would succeed them. Young choreographers such as Anna Sokolow, José Limón, Esther Junger, Eleanor King, Louise Kloepper, and Marian Van Tuyl received Bennington fellowships.

The curriculum focused on technique and the structure of dance; Louis Horst, for one, believed dancers had to understand choreography in order to dance most effectively. Over the years courses were added in drama, music, stagecraft, and stage design. Bennington-

trained dancers did not learn their craft in a vacuum but within the context of professional production. Students had a chance to see for themselves the proponents of a variety of dance expressions—the three major schools being those of Graham, Humphrey-Weidman, and Holm— and to choose with whom to work. Students also had the opportunity to create dances of their own, within formal boundaries set by the teachers. Experimentation abounded, with young dancers eager to fashion something new out of what they'd seen and learned.

Though this rich experiment lasted for less than 10 years, its legacy clearly lived on. Margaret Lloyd was not alone in her assessment that "in some ways the Bennington years were the most important years in the whole history of the American modern dance."

—Valerie Vogrin

BETTIS, Valerie

American dancer, choreographer, educator, and company director

Born: 20 December 1919 in Houston, Texas. **Education:** Studied one year at University of Texas, Austin; studied with Hanya Holm, New York; studied ballet with Carmelita Maracci. **Family:** Married Brazilian composer Bernardo Segall, 1943 (divorced 1955); married Arthur A. Schmidt, 1959. **Career:** Member, Hanya Holm's dance company 1937-40; solo performer and choreographer, 1941-48; teacher, Perry-Mansfield School of the Theater, Steamboat Springs, Colorado, 1942; founder, dancer/teacher, Dance Studio Foundation, 1964-73 and Valerie Bettis Dance/Theater Company, 1964. **Awards:** "Finest Young Dancer of the Year" and "Best Solo Composition" (*The Desperate Heart*), chosen by John Martin in the *New York Times,* 1943; Donaldson Awards for Best Debut and Best Dancing on Broadway, 1948; *Mademoiselle* Award for Outstanding Women, 1948; Critics Award for best TV dance of season, 1949. **Died:** New York City, 26 September 1982.

Roles

1937	*Trend* (Hanya Holm)
1938	*Metropolitan Daily* (Hanya Holm)
	Dance Sonata (Hanya Holm), duet with Holm
1948	*Inside USA* (theater)
1950	*Great to Be Alive!* (theater)
	Bless You All (theater)
1951	*The Dance of Life* (film)
1952	*The Time of the Cuckoo* (theater, Arthur Laurents; replaced Shirley Booth on tour)
1957	*Back to Methuselah* (theater)
1960	*Winesberg, Ohio* (Donald Saddler)
1961	*The Threepenny Opera* (replaced Lotte Lenya), Theater De Lys
1962	*Brecht on Brecht* (replaced Lotte Lenya on Broadway)

Works (most were solos for the Valerie Bettis Dance Company)

1941	*Theme and Variations*
	Triptych

	City Streets
	Country Lane
1942	Salute
	And the Earth Shall Bear Again
	Southern Impressions
1943	The Desperate Heart (revived 1979)
	Prairie Born
	Daisy Lee
1944	Caprice
	And Dreams Intrude
	Glad to See You (theater)
1945	Theatrics
	Facts and Figures
	Dramatic Incident
1946	Suite
	Rondel for a Young Girl
	Tocatta for Three
	Yerma
	Beggars Holiday (theater)
1947	Virginia Sampler, Ballet Russe, Monte Carlo
	Status Quo
	In Transit
	Figure '47
1948	As I Lay Dying
1949	Domino Furioso
	It Is Always Farewell
1951	Peer Gynt (theater)
	Two on the Aisle (theater)
1952	Affair in Trinidad (film)
	A Streetcar Named Desire, Slavenska-Franklin Ballet, Montreal
	The Golden Round (trio version, 1960)
1953	Let's Do It Again (film)
	Salomé (film)
1954	Athena (film)
1956	Circa '56
1958	The Past Perfect Hero
	Ulysses in Nighttown (theater)
1959	Closed Door (revised 1970)
1960	Early Voyagers
1962	If Five Years Pass (theater)
1963	Entirely Different Early Voyagers
1964	He Who Runs
	Inventions of Darkness
	Songs and Processions
1968	Arena For One
1970	On Ship
1974	Adam and Eve (opera)
1975	The Corner
	Poems
1976	Echoes of Spoonriver (theater)
1978	Randall Jarrell's Next Day (theater)

Publications

On BETTIS: articles—

Amer, Rita F., "The Desperate Heart: A Dance of Images," Dance Notation Journal, Spring 1986.

Lloyd, Margaret, "New Leaders: Valerie Bettis," in The Borzoi Book of Modern Dance, New York, 1949.

Simpson, Herbert M., "Valerie Bettis: Looking Back (a Dance Magazine portfolio, produced by William Como and Richard Philp, designed by Herbert Migdoll), originally in Dance Magazine, February 1977.

Films and Videotapes

A Steercar Named Desire, Dance Theater of Harlem, New York.

*   *   *

Valerie Bettis was an extraordinarily talented dancer/actress whose career as a significant modern dance choreographer was overshadowed, perhaps, by her innovations in combining dance, literature, and drama and by her own performing. Strikingly beautiful and a technically strong dancer, she was physically unforgettable, with a memorable, deep voice, which in later years resembled that of Tallulah Bankhead.

Born in 1919 in Houston, the tall, blonde Texan became a student of Hanya Holm in New York, making her professional dancing debut there in Holm's epic, Trend. She also studied ballet briefly on the West Coast with Carmelita Maracci. Bettis toured with Holm's company for two years, then began choreographing and dancing solo concerts in 1941 in New York. She toured South America in 1946 accompanied by her husband, pianist Bernardo Segall. For decades thereafter she ran her own company in New York, taught in her own studio there, and, until her death in 1982, regularly mounted experimental dance-theater performances with her students. At various times the Valerie Bettis Dance Company included such distinguished dancers as Duncan Noble, Lucas Hoving, and Kathryn Posin. Bettis also choreographed Broadway shows and ballets for major companies.

A pioneer in television dance, Bettis choreographed the first experimental concert dance on CBS television in 1946, produced by Tony Miner. In 1949 she choreographed a 16-week series of groundbreaking television dances for the Paul Whiteman TV show and later created original dances for TV specials and Omnibus, including Gershwin's 136th Street Blues. In the early 1950s Bettis went to Hollywood, where she appeared in several films, most notably as the villainess in Affair in Trinidad opposite Rita Hayworth whom she coached, for whom she choreographed several films, and with whom she acted occasionally. She also had a considerable stage career as actress and singer as well as dancer. In one capacity or another she worked with a who's who of modern American dance and theater.

Her most famous work was a solo dance, The Desperate Heart, accompanied by Bernard Segall's music and a recited poem by John Malcolm Brinin. Bettis first performed The Desperate Heart at the Humphrey-Weidman Studio in New York on 24 March 1943. Twisting, leaping, huddling, searching in obvious torment, the dancer eventually exits still seeming to reach desperately for some emotional resolution. Louis Horst called it "the finest modern dance solo of this decade" and ranked it with Martha Graham's Frontier. Major critics like John Martin and Edwin Denby commented admiringly on its inherent drama, not seeming like dance composition at all. Critic Walter Terry called Bettis modern dance's "prima ballerina." Such distinguished later dancers as Margaret Beals and Peggy Lyman have performed The Desperate Heart in concerts, none quite matching Bettis' intense involvement. This work and her As I Lay Dying (which somehow encapsulated William Faulkner's heavily developed narrative into 45 minutes of dance and spoken recitation) emphasize Bettis' enduring interest in spoken dramatic texts wedded to dance movement. They both also raise questions about the enduring viability of her choreography versus its supreme achievement in her own performing of her work.

Bettis was the first modern dance choreographer to contribute a work for a classical ballet company when she created *Virginia Sampler* for the Ballet Russe de Monte Carlo in 1947. Her most enduring ballet, *A Streetcar Named Desire* (based on Tennessee Williams' play and set to music by Alex North), was first performed by the Slavenska-Franklin Ballet in Montreal, 9 October 1952, then in New York in December. Slavenska and Franklin had the leading roles of Blanche DuBois and Stanley Kowalski, later played impressively by Bettis and Igor Youskevitch, Nora Kaye and John Kriza (Ballet Theater, 1954), and Virginia Williams and Lowell Smith (Dance Theatre of Harlem, 1986). Franklin's National Ballet of Washington, DC, also revived *A Streetcar Named Desire* in April 1974.

In her own works Bettis was as much actress as dancer: in *The Golden Round* she played Lady MacBeth; her *Early Voyages* was Bettis' treatment of Truman Capote's *Other Voices, Other Rooms;* her *Daisy Lee* was based on a radio play by Horton Foote; and *Closed Door* was Bettis' take on Sartre's *No Exit.* On television Bettis appeared in lead roles in a number of all-star "spectacular" drama specials: Claire Booth Luce's *The Women* on NBC; Candace in Faulkner's *The Sound and the Fury;* Linda in Philip Barry's *Holiday* on CBS; Strindberg's *The Stronger* on Philco TV Playhouse; Hedda in *Hedda Gabler.* On Broadway and in a few regional theaters Bettis played serious roles in such challenging plays as George Bernard Shaw's mammoth *Back to Methuselah.* She staged the movement for *Ulysses in Nighttown* in New York, and performed and directed it in Europe.

Her first choreography for a musical play was *Glad to See You* in 1944, but it "closed out of town," and Duke Ellington's *Beggars Holiday* (1946) was her first to get to Broadway. Afterward came others, but Bettis also won awards and made a Broadway reputation in starring roles as a dancer, notably in choreography by Helen Tamiris, such as her famous "Tiger Lily" and "Haunted Heart" solos in *Inside USA.* In *Bless You All* (1950) Bettis was one of four performers carrying a themeless Broadway revue based on their talents (Mary McCarthy, Jules Munshin, Pearl Bailey, and Bettis). Her solo works are still performed, as is her ballet, *A Streetcar Named Desire*, but she is best remembered as a teacher/director and performer.

—Herbert M. Simpson

BIRD, Bonnie

American dancer and educator

Born: 30 April 1915, in Seattle, Washington. **Education:** Attended the Cornish School, Seattle, 1920s. **Family:** Married; three children. **Career:** Principal demonstrator, teacher, and assistant, Martha Graham Dance Company, 1933-38; director of dance department, Cornish School, 1938-41; director of 92nd Street YM-YWHA's Children's Dance Program, 1951-64; staged first conference on the creative teaching of dance for children, 1952; founder, the Merry-Go-Rounders; director, the Laban Centre, 1974; taught at Smith College, Reed College, New York University. **Died:** 9 April 1995.

Roles (with Martha Graham Dance Company, New York City)

1934	*Celebration* (Graham)
	Integrales (Graham)
	American Provincials (Graham)
1935	*Course* (Graham)
	Panorama (Graham)
1936	*Horizons* (Graham)
	Chronicle (Graham)

Publications

On BIRD: articles—

Jowitt, Deborah, "In Memoriam, Bonnie Bird," *Village Voice,* 2 May 1995.
Ross, Janice,"Bonnie Bird: Balancing the Academic with the Practical," *Dance Teacher Now,* September 1988.

*   *   *

Bonnie Bird performed as part of Martha Graham's original dance troupe during her brief career as a dancer, appearing in the premieres of several of Graham's early works. She is best known for her 70-plus years as a dance educator, having taught at all the major summer schools of dance and at many universities, including Smith College, Reed College, and New York University.

A native of Seattle, Bird began her dance training there in the 1920s at the Cornish School. Beginning at age eight, Bird worked closely with Cornish School's founder and director, Nellie Cornish. In 1929 Martha Graham joined the Cornish faculty and made an immediate impression on Bird as well as the other young, ballet-trained students for whom modern dance was entirely new. Before she left Seattle, Graham invited Bird to join her in New York. Sensing in Bird the gifts of a natural teacher, Graham set her up as principal demonstrator, teacher, and assistant. The two worked together from 1933 to 1938, with Bird experiencing firsthand the genesis of Graham's classroom technique as well as performing in Graham's company. Bird thought of Graham's technique classes as a laboratory in which experiments with movement were conducted and Graham could clarifying her ideas about movement. Bird was impressed by how much of what the dancers did in class was reflected on stage.

By 1938 Bird was ready to move out on her own as an instructor. She left Graham's company and returned to Seattle to head the dance department of the Cornish School. Three months after her arrival an acting student named Merce Cunningham switched to a dance major and became Bird's most illustrious pupil. She worked with him for several years before she introduced him to Martha Graham, who immediately asked him to join her company.

In 1941 Bird left the Cornish School and went with her husband, a professor of psychology, to the University of California, Berkeley, where he joined the faculty. Over the course of raising their three young children she developed a life-long interest in children's dance and dance therapy. She was dissatisfied with the existing programs, which simply taught children as if they were miniature adults. She began studying the new research being done in how children learn and soon incorporated games and creative imagery into her work with kids. Bird was asked to head the 92nd Street YM-YWHA's Children's Dance Program in New York City in 1951. She reorganized a chaotic program and developed a systematic program that stressed consistency, as well as a curriculum that shepherded students along, developing their technical skills, creativity, and growth as dancers. As an outgrowth of the Y's program, Bird staged the first conference on the creative teaching of dance for children in 1952. For the next seven years this conference was a clearing house of ideas for dance teachers, and was a precursor of the American Dance Guild.

When Bird left the 92nd Street Y in 1964 its enrollment had risen to 300 students. More importantly, she had created a seminal curriculum and methodology for teaching children dance. She had also established a professional children's company, the Merry-Go-Rounders, with the aim of producing creative dance-theater performances for young audiences. In 1973, Bird's career took another turn when Marion North, British Laban Movement expert, lectured in New York. The two met, became friends, and a year later North invited Bird to join her in directing the Laban Centre in London.

At Laban, Bird was able to synthesize her experience as a professional dancer and her years as an educator to a new breed of dance students. Through her work, she had been instrumental in bridging the gap between the professional and pedagogic aspects of dance; she has always insisted on a balance between the theoretical and the practical. Bird began her career when modern dance itself was a new experiment and her involvement in dance has spanned most of its evolving history and acceptance. Likewise she has seen much change throughout her teaching career, from the days when modern dancers were mostly converts from ballet, to the more recent acceptance of university-trained dancers. The dancers she worked with in the 1980s (she retired in 1989) had to earn degrees before they were accepted into the Laban Centre's own young professional Transitions Dance Company, as well as dance companies throughout the United Kingdom, the United States, and Europe.

—Valerie Vogrin

BLEWCHAMP, Anna

British-born Canadian dancer, choreographer, educator, artistic director, and writer

Born: 1947 in London. **Education:** Completed academic and professional dance training at Ballet Rambert School, 1964; M.F.A., York University, 1992; studied dance at the Dance Centre and School of Contemporary Dance (London); American Dance Festival, Connecticut College; Alvin Ailey School, Martha Graham School (all New York); Lois Smith School of Ballet, Boris Volkoff School of Dance, School of Toronto Dance Theatre, Dancemakers, and Pavlychenko Studio (all Toronto). **Career:** Performed with Junction Dance Company, Gary Cockrell Dancers, Global Village Theatre, Festival of Underground Theatre, Judy Jarvis Dance Company, and Toronto Dance Theatre; has choreographed for Hamilton Opera Chorus, Winnipeg Contemporary Dancers, Ottawa Dance Theatre, Concert Dance Company, Aspace, Festival of Underground Theatre, Global Village Showcase, Ballet Ys, 15 Dance Lab, Ann Ditchburn Dances, Danceworks, Encore! Encore!, INDE '88 Festival of New Music and Dance, Dance Umbrella of Ontario, and Quantum Leap, for which she was also administrator writer and artistic director; member, Dancemakers, 1975-85; associate artistic director, teacher/resident choreographer, Dancemakers, 1977-78;

artistic director/resident choreographer, 1978-79; has taught at London School of Contemporary Dance, The Dance Centre, Hornsey College of Art, St. Martins School of Art; Le Groupe de la Place Royale (Ottawa); and the Hall Community Centre, Three Schools of Art, Global Village Theatre, Factory Theatre Lab, Toronto Dance Theatre, Equity Showcase, and has served as artistic director for the York University Dance Ensemble; assistant professor, York University, since 1989. **Awards**: Canada Council grants, 1975, 1976, 1983, 1984, 1991; Arts Council of Great Britain Choreography Award, 1977; Ontario Arts Council Choreography Award, 1978, 1981, 1984; Jean A. Chalmers Award for Choreography, 1979; Floyd Chalmers Award, Performing Arts Creation, 1981; Toronto Arts Council Choreography Award, 1985; Judy Jarvis Dance Foundation Award, 1992; Master's Thesis Prize at York University, 1993.

Works (set to sound collages created by Anna Blewchamp unless otherwise indicated)

1974	*Ahmal and the Night Visitors* (mus. Menotti), Hamilton Opera Chorus
	Who Is Near Me? (silence)
	Baggage
	Homage
	Garden of the Forking Paths (mus. Harry Partch), Toronto Dance Theatre
1975	*Terminal,* Dancemakers
	Arrival of All Time (mus. Ann Southam), Dancemakers
	Relics (mus. Milhaud), Ballet Ys
1976	*Bend Down Low* (mus. Bob Marley), Dancemakers
1977	*Fata Morgana* (mus. Hindemith), Ballet Ys
	Marathon (mus. Reich), Dancemakers
	They Can't Take That Away from Me, Dancemakers
1978	*Daintiness Rag,* Dancemakers
1979	*Solo #1,* Susan MacPherson
	Solo #2, Keith Urban
	Solo #3, Janice Hladki
	A.K.A. (#1), Dancemakers
1980	*Tyger-Tyger* (mus. Marjan Mozetich)
	Side Step (no mus.), Concert Dance Company of Boston
1981	*Shadows of Formal Selves* (mus. Marjan Mozetich, text Graham Jackson), Toronto Dance Theatre
	3 o'clock in the morning, Pavlychenko Studio
	A.K.A. (#2)
1983	*Party Piece,* York University Department of Dance
	Concerto (mus. Stanitc), York University Department of Dance
	Cast a Cold Eye (mus. Laurie Anderson), Ottawa Dance Theatre
1984	*East-Above* (mus. Laurie Anderson), Pavlychenko Studio
	Prevailing Winds (mus. Orchestral Maneuvers in the Dark), Pavlychenko Studio
	Giverny (mus. Marjan Mozetich), Ottawa Dance Theatre
	Lionheart (mus. Aaron Davis)
	Ariel (mus. Aaron Davis)
1985	*The Doppleganger Effect*
	After the Fire (mus. Marjan Mozetich)
1986	*Encore! Encore!* (mus. Harry Freedman; collaborative dance/theatre project produced by Dance Collection Danse), Expo '86, Vancouver

1988   *Evensong* (mus. Gordon Phillips), INDE '88 Festival of
        New Music and Dance
1989   *Last Rites: New Dawn* (mus. Gordon Phillips), York Dance
        Ensemble
        Mutable Signs (mus. Reich), York Dance Ensemble
1990   *Speaking in Tongues* (mus. Reich), York University De-
        partment of Dance
        Selected Studies
1995   *The WX Project* (mus. John Oswald)
1996   *Let X Equal X* (mus. Laurie Anderson), York Dance En-
        semble

Other works include: Various works produced by a collaborative group, 1968-69; invited performances at Hornsey College of Art, Royal College of Art, and St. Martin's School of Art; independent works in Toronto, 1970-74.

Publications

By BLEWCHAMP: articles—

"Gweneth Lloyd: Discovery of an Artist," *The Last/Lost Dance Symposium: Preserving the Legacy*, Toronto, 1992.
"Reconstruction: The Archeology of Dance—Lawrence Adams, Anna Blewchamp, Rhonda Ryman, Selma Odom and Deepti Gupta Discuss the Changing Field of Dance Reconstruction," *Dance Connection,* September/October 1992.
"The Wise Virgins Reconstructed," *Dance Connection*, September/October 1992.
"Gweneth Lloyd and The Wise Virgins: Arguments for the Reconstruction of a Canadian Ballet," in *Canadian Dance Studies 1,* edited by Selma Odom and Mary Jane Warner, Toronto, 1994, and in *IV International Conference on Dance Research Conference Proceedings*, 1996.
"Shadow on the Prairie, an Interactive CD-Rom," *Dance Collection Danse News*, No. 42, 1996.
"Technology in Scholarly Presentations: Navigation and Interaction," in *Society of Dance History Scholars Proceedings*, 1996.
Contributor, *Dictionary of Dance: Words, Terms and Phrases*, edited by Susan MacPherson, Toronto, 1997.
Various reviews and articles by Blewchamp in *Dance in Canada* and *Canadian Dance News* from 1974-76.

On BLEWCHAMP: articles—

Citron, Paula, "Blewchamp Roaring out of Choreographic Closet," *Toronto Star*, 8 November 1985.
Jackson, Graham, "Facades: The Work and Times of Miss Anna Blewchamp," *Dance in Canada*, Winter 1979.
Littler, William, "Sleuth Solves the Case of the Lost Lloyd Ballet," *Toronto Star*, 2 March 1992.
O'Toole, Lawrence, "Dancers Must Be People Too," *Globe and Mail*, 25 January 1978.

Films and Videotapes

3 o'clock in the morning, for *Dance for the Electronic Age*, broadcast by Rogers Television, 1983.
Baggage, documented by 15 Dance Lab, 1976.
Gweneth Lloyd: Discovery of an Artist, keynote address at The Last/Lost Dance Symposium: Preserving the Legacy, 1992.

Interpreting the Skies, Video-Dance Independent Research Project, Canada Council, 1991.

*   *   *

Anna Blewchamp has contributed to Toronto's dance community in diverse ways: as a dancer, choreographer, writer, advisor, educator, and scholar. She is often described as extremely private and has on occasion disappeared from the public eye, preferring to be involved in dance in a behind-the-scenes capacity. Yet in the studio or classroom she comes alive, bringing the knowledge and compassion necessary to nurture her students to new levels of achievement.

Blewchamp began her dance training in London as a child studying academics and dance first at the Corona Theatre Academy and then the Ballet Rambert School. She studied jazz with Gary Cockrell and danced for him before going to New York in 1966, where she continued her jazz studies with Luigi and Matt Mattox. She returned to England in 1967 and began saving money in order to settle in North America. The draft and the Vietnam war made returning to the U.S. difficult for Blewchamp and her husband. Encouraged by friends they decided to settle in Toronto in 1969.

Almost immediately she began teaching a combination of jazz and modern dance at a community center called The Hall and it was here that she made connections with a variety of Toronto artists. One was Elizabeth Swerdlow who, with her husband Robert, ran the Global Village Theatre. Blewchamp studied with them, performed in their productions and choreographed for their showcases. The Hall also connected Blewchamp with Factory Theatre founder Ken Gass who recruited her to teach movement classes to his company of actors.

Through the early part of the 1970s, Blewchamp taught on a freelance basis and did some choreography through Trinity College at the University of Toronto, where she was encouraged to form a small company. Through her freelance teaching she met students from the School of Toronto Dance Theatre who spoke highly of their teachers and the Martha Graham technique. Despite a less than satisfactory experience with Graham technique in England, Blewchamp enrolled in the School of TDT. Here she was profoundly inspired by the teachings of TDT founders Peter Randazzo, David Earle and Patricia Beatty. By 1973 she was a teacher in the school and a company apprentice/member performing roles and premiering as the "Lady in Red" in Randazzo's psychodrama *Nighthawks*.

While continuing her work as a teacher, choreographer and performer in Toronto, she would also make jaunts to New York to study at the Martha Graham School, Alvin Ailey School and American Ballet Theatre School. Blewchamp even returned to England, with the help of a Canada Council grant, and taught at London School of Contemporary Dance and choreographed and performed for Junction Dance Company.

By the mid-1970s she was choreographing regularly for the Toronto-based company Dancemakers. In 1977 Blewchamp was appointed associate artistic director, teacher and resident choreographer of Dancemakers. The following year Blewchamp was the company's artistic director. Many of her dances became mainstays of Dancemakers repertoire including *Arrival of All Time, A.K.A., Terminal* and *Homage*. In *Terminal* and *A.K.A.* Blewchamp creates a collage of 20th-century social dancing such as the charleston, jitterbug, 1940s ballroom, and disco. *Homage* is a satirical tribute to theatrical dance and looks at movement by Astaire, Petipa,

Balanchine, Humphrey, Graham and others. *Arrival of All Time*, inspired by Virginia Woolf's suicide note, is known as a modern dance classic in Canadian history and is in the repertoire of the Danny Grossman Dance Company.

Through the 1970s and 1980s Blewchamp choreographed for a variety of companies. Notable works include *Marathon,* which was a break from the usual for Blewchamp. Before *Marathon* much of her previous work was emotionally based, but *Marathon* is more movement driven and is closely related to the Steve Reich score. *Tyger-Tyger*, a collaboration with Canadian composer Marjan Mozetich, is about various aspects of relationships. The solo dance *Prevailing Winds* is meaningful to Blewchamp primarily due to the stunning way in which it was performed by dancer Patricia Miner. *Shadows of Formal Selves* was a large and rewarding project in which Blewchamp collaborated with writer Graham Jackson. The 50-minute piece was created for Toronto Dance Theatre and involved 22 dancers, actors and actresses. It looked at the way in which Western culture carelessly destroys its idols by appropriation and analysis and used the three Bronte sisters as an example; much to the chagrin of some viewers but to the delight of its creators, it was quite humorous.

Throughout her career, Blewchamp was encouraged by colleagues and the arts councils to form a company, but it was never something she really wanted to do. However, the encouragement she received did prompt her to produce *Quantum Leap* in 1985, a retrospective of her work which also featured a new choreography called *After the Fire*. The four-evening run presented some of Toronto's most distinguished dancers including Lois Smith, Randy Glynn, Suzette Sherman, Patricia Fraser, Michael Conway, Russell Kilde, Patricia Miner, and Gail Benn. The inspiration for *After the Fire* came from two books by Russell Hoban, *Riddley Walker,* which is set after a nuclear holocaust, and *Pilgermann,* which is about the first Crusade to the Holy Land. Blewchamp was drawn to these books for their mystical brilliance and through a lengthy correspondence with Hoban.

In 1986 Blewchamp was commissioned to choreograph a dance as part of Dance Collection Danse's Encore! Encore! presentation at Expo '86. This Canadian dance archive was only a few years old at the time and its founders, Miriam and Lawrence Adams, and a team of researchers had collected considerable information about Canada's dancing past. The entire project involved the reconstruction of twelve dance works created in the 1940s and 1950s by six Canadian choreographers, research into the dance works and their choreographers, video taping and notation of each dance, and a multi-media presentation at Expo '86 in Vancouver. The presentation, performed by actor/dancers Jackie Burroughs, Ricardo Keens-Douglas and Vanessa Harwood, used Blewchamp's choreography, a score by Harry Freedman, slides and film from the project's research and a script written by Jim Purdy to introduce characters from Canadian dance history such as Boris Volkoff, Gweneth Lloyd, Françoise Sullivan and Jeanne Renaud. This project prompted the ongoing existence of Dance Collection Danse which collects and preserves materials from Canadian dance history, and publishes and distributes books and educational resources.

York University has been an important part of Blewchamp's life in the last decade. In 1984 she did some guest teaching in the dance department and then began to teach on contract. In 1989 she was made an assistant professor and her course load included technique, composition and repertory. Soon after she began teaching full-time, Blewchamp was encouraged by the chair of the dance department, Mary Jane Warner, to pursue further academic studies through the

department's M.F.A. program. Blewchamp embarked on a project of mammoth proportions—she sought to reconstruct Gweneth Lloyd's lost dance *The Wise Virgins*. Lloyd, co-founder of the Royal Winnipeg Ballet, lost almost all of her choreographic notes in a fire at the ballet's home in 1954. However, Blewchamp came across a piece of National Film Board film that showed a section of *The Wise Virgins*. Blewchamp was intrigued by the choreography, noticing that it resembled movement created by pioneers such as Graham and Humphrey, and yet Lloyd had not studied American modern dance. With considerable research into Lloyd's life and choreography, and then by working with Sheila McKay and other original cast members including Arnold Spohr, and with the advice of Lloyd, Blewchamp was able to piece together this lost dance. It was then mounted on the York Dance Ensemble. This remarkable achievement earned Blewchamp a Master's Thesis Prize in 1993. Since the completion of her M.F.A., Blewchamp has added graduate and undergraduate dance theory courses to her list of teaching credits and has supervised numerous undergraduate independent studies and graduate research. She has also presented papers at several conferences.

Blewchamp has continued to serve the university in many ways, acting as artistic director for performances and the York Dance Ensemble, sitting on search, tenure and performance committees, and contributing choreography to the York Dance Ensemble's repertoire. Her choreographic contributions include *Last Rites: New Dawn, Mutable Signs,* and *Let X Equal X.*

Human relationships, the isolation of artistry, social concerns, people in the world, the joy of pure movement, these are all aspects of Blewchamp's choreography. However, her career as a whole cannot be summed up merely by her choreography, for her contributions as a teacher, advisor and scholar are part of the complexities that make up this "extremely private" artist. She feels she has always had a love/hate relationship with dance. She has been at times completely frustrated by it, other times uncontrollably drawn to it. Choreography is an agonizing endeavour, but for Blewchamp, "dance has true eloquence and speaks from the soul."

—Amy Bowring

BODENWIESER, Gertrud

Austrian-born dancer, choreographer, and educator based in Australia

Born: Gertrud Bondi, 1890 in Vienna. **Education:** Studied ballet as a child; proponent of Jaques-Dalcroze's *rhythmique* teachings. **Career:** Acquired stage name of "Bodenwieser" and gave her first solo, 1919; instructor, Vienna State Academy of Music and Dramatic Art, 1919-26; professor, 1926-38; founder/director, Tanzgruppe Bodenwieser; toured London, 1929; later toured South America; emigrated to Australia via New Zealand, 1939; major dance pioneer in Australia, forming school and dance troupe. **Died:** 1959 in Sydney, Australia.

Works

1923   *Damon Maschine* (*The Demon Machine*), (mus. Mayer)
1936   *Masks of Lucifer*

1945   *Waltzing Matilda*
1954   *Waltzing Matilda* (new version)
1956   *Aboriginal Spear Dance*

Other works include: *Angular Play of Lines, Arbeitstanz, Cart Drawn by Man, Errand into the Maze, Exchange of Vibrations, The Great Hours, The Inconstant Prince, Life of the Insects, Pilgrimage of Truth, The Rhythms of the Subconscious,* and *Swinging Bells.*

Publications

By BODENWIESER: books—

The New Dance, Vaucluse, Australia, c. 1960.

On BODENWIESER: books—

Anderson, Jack, *The World of Modern Dance: Art Without Boundaries,* Iowa City, Iowa, 1997.
Dunlop MacTavish, Shona, *An Ecstasy of Purpose: The Life and Art of Gertrud Bodenwieser,* Dunedin, New Zealand, 1987.
Grayburn, Patricia, editor, *Gertrud Bodenwieser: A Celebratory Monograph on the 100th Anniversary of Her Birth,* Surrey, England, 1990.

On BODENWEISER: articles—

Denton, Meg Abbie, and Genevieve Shaw, "Gertrud Bodenwieser: The Demon Machine," *Dance Notation Journal,* Spring 1986.
Forster, Marianne, "Reconstructing European Modern Dance: Bodenwieser, Chladek, Leeder, Kreutzberg, Hoyer," Proceedings of the Conference "Dance Reconstructed: Modern Dance Art Past, Present, Future," New Brunswick, New Jersey, 1992.
Richardson, Philip J. S., "The Sitter Out (column)," *Dancing Times,* June 1929 and July 1929.

*   *   *

Not much is written about Gertrud Bodenwieser and what little that has been published is difficult to obtain in the United States. Born in Vienna, Austria, in 1890, Bodenwieser started her life as Gertrud Bondi, the daughter of a stockbroker. She studied dance as a child, but when she later decided to become a professional dancer, her family frowned upon the endeavor, claiming the stage was not an acceptable medium for a proper young woman. To smooth ruffled feathers, Gertrud took the stage name of "Bodenwieser" to distance her unsavory career from the family name. Once Gertrud set her sights on dancing, she became a follower of movement theorist Émile Jaques-Dalcroze and his rhythmic training, later called "eurhythmics." According to Jack Anderson, Bodenwieser was so taken with Jaques-Dalcroze's work that she proclaimed, "Dalcroze may be likened to one of those great mariners who sailed out to discover another route to some land, and discovered a whole unknown continent."

In 1919, though Gertrud was nearly 30 years of age, she gave her first solo performance and was shortly thereafter hired as an instructor of dance at the Vienna State Academy of Music and Dramatic Art. She was eventually promoted to a full professorship in 1926. During this time, she formed and directed the Tanzgruppe Bodenwieser, a dance troupe that helped Bodenwieser develop her own unique style of modern dance in Central Europe. For some of her œuvre, her vision was to transmogrify mechanical movements into a form of dance. Productions such as *Arbeitstanz* and her most famous piece, *Damon Maschine* (*The Demon Machine*), illustrated this mechano-anthropomorphy, a major element in the arts of the 1920s and 1930s and evidenced in other works of the time, some glorifying the precision of a mechanized world, others, like Bodenwieser's *Damon Maschine* glimpsing a stark, precise society toppling into mechanical anarchy.

Another factor Bodenwieser worked into some of her dances was to take advantage of a very feminine trait—long, flowing hair. Though both men and women could qualify today, Bodenwieser found the swishing and sweeping arcs of long locks could add a sensual, almost pretty element to her works. Two of Bodenwieser's most notable students from Vienna gained prominence in their own right: Gertrud Kraus, who later created her own mechanized anti-utopia statement in *The City Waits* and produced an impressive body of work; and Hilde Holger, who went on sow the seeds of modern dance both in India in 1939 and later in England in the 1950s.

Touring Europe extensively, Bodenwieser's group garnered some attention, with London's *Dancing Times* editor Philip J. S. Richardson writing about the troupe twice in his "Sitter Out" column in June and July of 1929. According to Anderson, Richardson favored Bodenwieser's technique over that of Wigman, finding it a pleasant cross between ballet and the new "modern" dance, calling it "less iconoclastic and therefore more understandable" than Wigman's dancing. Most of Bodenwieser's work concentrated on fluidity of motion, sometimes concentrated on various components of a single theme, and she often employed improvisation in her classes. In 1932 Bodenwieser was nominated, along with a veritable who's-who of the time including Rosalia Chladek, Trudi Schoop, Oskar Schlemmer, Kurt Jooss, and others, for the International Choreographers' Competition in Paris. Though she was eclipsed by Jooss and his antiwar masterpiece, *The Green Table,* the competition helped bring her name ever more into the forefront.

In 1938, following Germany's annexation of Austria, Bodenwieser and her husband fled to Paris, where he worked in radio. While Bodenwieser had been on tour with her company to South American and picked up where she left off, when the Germans overran France, her husband was captured and sent to a concentration camp, where he perished. Bodenwieser kept busy to stem the grief—dancing, choreographing and touring—going from South America to New Zealand to Australia. Bodenwieser set up housekeeping in Sydney, and began a 20-year association with a country with little knowledge or appreciation of modern dance. Following the lead of another dance pioneer, Margaret Barr, Bodenwieser set up a school and touring company and began adopting Australian traditions into the work, such as choreographing two versions of the famed *Waltzing Matilda* (1945, 1954), as well as creating *The Pilgrimage of Truth, Life of the Insects,* and *Aboriginal Spear Dance* (1956).

Bodenwieser toured Australia extensively, teaching throughout the country and training scores of new teachers and dancers who have continued her legacy. Bodenwieser, who was considered a major proponent of modern dance in Australia, died in Sydney in 1959. As of 1977, her dance center was directed by Margaret Chapple and Keith Bain, two notable former students. In 1990, 100 years after Bodenwieser's birth, Patricia Grayburn edited a much-needed anthology of essays about the European dancer and choreographer published by the University of Surrey Press, in Surrey, England.

—Daryl F. Mallett and Sydonie Benet

BOHNER, Gerhard

German dancer and choreographer

Born: 19 June 1936, in Karlsruhe. **Education:** Karlsruhe (1954-56); thereafter at the Mary Wigman Studio in Berlin. **Career:** Dancer, Mannheim National Theater, 1958-60, Frankfurt am Main Municipal Stages, 1960-61); soloist, German Opera, Berlin, 1961-71; ballet director, Darmstadt State Theater, 1972-75, Bremen State Theater (together with Reinhild Hoffmann), 1975-81. Guest choreographer for ballet companies in Berlin, Cologne, Hamburg, Munich, the Wuppertal Dance Theater, the Berlin Academy of the Arts, Marseille, France, and the Netherlands Dance Theater. **Awards:** Second Prize, choreography competition in Cologne, 1969, for *Spannen-Abschlaffen.* **Died:** 13 July 1992, in Berlin.

Works

1969   *Spannen/Abschlaffen* (mus. Carlos Roqué Alsina), Schaubühne am Halleschen Ufer, Berlin
1971   *Die Folterungen der Beatrice Cenci* (mus. Gerald Humel), Akademie der Künste, Berlin
1972   *Lilith* (mus. Humel), Akademie der Künste, Berlin
        Présence (mus. Bernd Alois Zimmermann), Darmstadt State Theater
1974   *Der wundebare Mandarin* (mus. Bartók), Darmstadt State Theater
1977   *Das Triadische Ballet* (mus. Hans-Joachim Hespos), Akademie der Künste, Berlin
1980   *Zwei Giraffen tanzen Tango* (mus. Gerald Humel), Theater Bremen
1981   *Bilder einer Ausstellung* (mus. Mussorgsky), Theater Bremen
1983   *Schwarz Weiss zeigen* (mus. Handel, Branca), Akademie der Künste, Berlin
1986   *Abstrakte Tänze und Drei Bauhaustänze* (mus. Pfrengle, Hindemith), Kunsthalle Schirn, Frankfurt am Main
1989   *Im (Goldenen) Schnitt I und II* (mus. Bach), Akademie der Künste, Berlin

Publications

On BOHNER:

Gerhard Bohner: Tänzer und Choreograph, Berlin, 1991.

*   *   *

As early as the mid-1960s, Gerhard Bohner, still working as a dancer at the German Opera, began his first small choreographic works in Berlin. He won second prize at the choreography competition in Cologne (1969) for *Spannen—Abschlaffen (Contraction—Release),* and made his decisive breakthrough with *Die Folterungen der Beatrice Cenci (The Torture of Beatrice Cenci)* (1971), which critics enthusiastically dubbed "the first horror ballet." Already, the choreographer's personal signature could be seen: a finely calculated balance between severity of form and emotion, which set him apart from the other pioneers of Tanztheater.

When he was appointed ballet director in Darmstadt in 1972, his goals there were not limited to further developing his choreographic style. His programmatically named Darmstadt State Theater was to be a company independent of the opera and to eliminate the hierarchical differentiation between soloists and corps de ballet. After three years, however, the politically engaged, emancipatory program was cancelled by the authorities. Gerhard Bohner returned to independent work, giving an important part of its history back to dance repertoire, which previously had not been very tradition-conscious, as far as modernity was concerned. His reconstruction of Schlemmer's *Das Triadisches Ballet (Triadic Ballet)* on behalf of the Berlin Academy of the Arts would signal for Bohner the beginning of a lengthy examination of the Bauhaus stage, whose experiments fascinated him. For Bohner, this meant stepping through abstract formalities, finding a new way to reach people again. His position in space, the way he moved, hindered or free, developed into his essential theme.

Bohner made another attempt (1978-81) at establishing an unrestricted dance piece in a municipal theater, this time at the Bremen Theater. When he was unable to attain the conditions he had hoped for, Bohner decided once and for all to work independently, where his work, especially his solos, would set the framework for the development of contemporary dance. Dancing in his own pieces at an age when most dancers would have long since ended their careers, he portrayed the limits and possibilities of an aging dancer's body. In his works, he placed inner emotion above external agility, personality above dance technique. Choreography always speaks a clear, ascetically sobered language that is intimate but never private.

Bohner's solo, *Schwarz Weiss zeigen (Show Black and White),* counts as one of his outstanding later works. Two walls, one black, one white, positioned at an acute angle, cut a triangle out of the stage area, which is sparsely furnished with cubic objects. The two parts of the piece are equally clearly distinguished from one another. In the first, to Handel piano suites played on the harpsichord by Glenn Gould, the dancer uses his path of movement to trace circles, lanes, and tracks in the room: a choreographic statement in itself. In the second part, to soft jazz music, a "partner" in the form of a jointed wooden doll joins in. She can be molded, supported, stood up again, yet the doll is not human, it cannot react on its own. The jointed doll becomes a mirror of one's own movement potential.

Six years later, in a very similar spirit, Bohner created the double choreography *Im (Goldenen) Schnitt I und II (In the Golden Section I and II).* Here again, a precise identification of the dancer's own space is seen in the differing rooms created by the sculptors Vera Rohm and Christian Schad. The choreographer measures the movement radius of his aging body. He tests the movements—of the arms, the legs, the head; an investigation of anatomic possibilities carried out with great kinetic logic. Solemnly and clearly the dancer talks about aging: solemnly, almost meditatively in the first part, far-reaching in the second part. The final result is the image of a still, reclaimed disclosure of human animality. It was just this reduction that allowed Bohner to set the stage for associations. The room, which Vera Rohm surrounds with cracked wooden grave markers with Plexiglas attachments on the upper portions, resembles not only an archaic ritual site but also a concentration camp. The person inside is alone, but not necessarily lonely. He reassures himself of himself with simple movements and relates himself to the objects and to the world.

The examination of abstract objects and spatial design always serve as a medium through which human traits can at last be touched. Stemming from the choreographer's basic beliefs that everything is in motion, his pieces continually fight to maintain the delicate balance between man and objects which must be repeatedly re-established. Only when the material has been dealt with precisely can reassurance be attained, leading to the core of human existence.

The work of Gerhard Bohner represents an isolated phenomenon in the development of dance theater, but has been gaining in importance as the result of newer reconstructions, such as of *The (Golden) Section,* by the Spanish choreographer Cesc Gelabert in 1996 at the Berlin Art Academy.

—Norbert Servos

BOURNE, Matthew
British dancer, choreographer and company director

Born: 13 January 1960 in London. **Education:** Laban Centre for Movement and Dance, graduating in 1985 with a degree in dance/theatre. **Career:** Toured with Laban's Transitions Dance Company, 1985-86; danced with Opera Restor'd, Edgar Newman and Moving Mountains; co-founded Adventures in Motion Pictures (later known as AMP), and made first choreography for this company, 1987; founding member of Lea Anderson's all-male group the Featherstonehaughs, 1988; choreographed dramatic and musical productions at the Royal Shakespeare Company (*As You Like It,* 1989), National Youth Theatre (*The Tempest,* 1991, revived 1993) and in the West End (*Children of Eden,* 1990; *Oliver!,* 1994) as well as for other British and European youth, theatre and opera companies and European festivals. **Awards:** Bonnie Bird Award, 1989; Barclay's New Stages Award, 1991; for *Swan Lake:* Los Angeles Drama Critics Circle; Los Angeles Robby Awards; Los Angeles Drama-Logue Awards; Laurence Olivier Award for Outstanding Achievement in Dance, 1995; *Time Out* Dance Award, 1995, 1996; *Gay Times* Reader's Award; *Manchester Evening News* Award; South Bank Show Award for Outstanding Achievement in Dance.

Works

1987   *Overlap Lovers* (mus. Stravinsky, Man Jumping, Dos Filiberto), AMP, London
1988   *Spitfire* (mus. Glazunov, Minkus), AMP, London
         Buck and Wing (mus. Blake), AMP, London
1989   *The Infernal Galop* (mus. Boyer, Prud'homme, Offenbach, Les Compagnons de la Chanson), AMP, London (redesigned and revived, 1992)
1990   *Children of Eden* (mus. Schwartz), Prince Edward Theatre, London
         Show Boat (mus. Kern & Hammerstein), Malmo Stadteater, Sweden
1991   *Town & Country* (mus. Elgar, Coates, Stachey, Coward, Rachmaninov, Grainger, Bach), AMP, Bristol
         A Midsummer Night's Dream (mus. Britten), English National Opera, London
1992   *Deadly Serious* (mus. Gounod, Herrmann, Grofé, Porter, Rozsa, Sibelius, Waxman, Manners), AMP, Bristol
         The Nutcracker (mus. Tchaikovsky; co-director Martin Duncan), AMP, Edinburgh
         The Percys of Fitzrovia (mus. Strauss, Martinu, Liszt, Brahms, Tchaikovsky, Grainger, Ganne, Ries), AMP, London

1993   *Late Flowering Lust* (mus. Parker), AMP with Nigel Hawthorne, BBC2
         Drip: A Narcissistic Love Story (mus. Lee), AMP, BBC2
1994   *Highland Fling* (mus. Lovenskiold, Lerner & Loewe, *Auld Lang Syne*), AMP, Bristol
         Oliver! (mus. Bart), London Palladium
         Watch with Mother (mus. Grainger), National Youth Dance Company, London
1995   *Watch Your Step!* (mus. Berlin), Her Majesty's Theatre, London
         Roald Dahl's Little Red Riding Hood (mus. Patterson), AMP with Julie Walters, Ian Holm and Danny DeVito, BBC1
         Swan Lake (mus. Tchaikovsky), AMP, London
1997   *Cinderella* (mus. Prokofiev), AMP, London

*   *   *

For someone who received no formal dance or music training until he was in his early twenties, Matthew Bourne has done all right for himself. In 1996, his company's massively popular, male-dominated reinterpretation of *Swan Lake* became the longest-running dance production in the history of London's West End. In this, and the string of earlier movement-based performances he made for Adventures in Motion Pictures (AMP), Bourne's savvy as scenarist-director, rather than choreographer, places him closer to the realm of theatre than dance.

London-born, Bourne made his unofficial theatrical debut at the age of eight as the Sugar Plum Fairy in a boy scouts' performance. Bourne enjoyed movies and musicals (Fred Astaire remains an idol), but didn't see his first ballet until he was in his teens. (It was, almost prophetically, Scottish Ballet's *Swan Lake* at Sadler's Wells Theatre, where his own Swan Lake would premiere nearly 20 years later.) A star-struck autograph hound, he lurked on the fringes of the entertainment world via jobs in the BBC archives, a ticket agency, and the National Theatre's bookshop. The course of his life changed with his enrollment in the dance-theatre programme at the Laban Centre. He studied ballet and contemporary technique and joined Laban's Transitions Dance Company for the year following his 1985 graduation.

It was during a company tour on China Airways that someone spotted the phrase "Adventures in Motion Pictures" on a plastic headset bag. The words were appropriated as the name of the small-scale repertory company founded by Bourne and a handful of fellow Laban and Transitions graduates. They scored their first hit with Jacob Marley's *Does Your Crimplene Go All Crusty When You Rub?*, a peculiarly funny piece set in a sort of time-warp disco for deadbeat misfits. Gradually AMP (as they came to be known) acquired an administrator and, as word-of-mouth spread about the company's cleverness, vitality and style, it was awarded small project-funding grants.

Bourne's initial contribution consisted of performing as well as devising short works that formed part of an evening's repertoire. His early dances employed tango and tap as takeoff points. But it was the show-stopping *Spitfire*—Jules Perrot's *Pas de Quatre* transposed to the world of men's underwear advertising—that pointed him in a direction he would make his own. Of AMP's original founding members, only Bourne stayed the course. As head of the company and the brains behind its one-act and then full-length productions, he became recognized as a master of pastiche, the maker of suave, camp, impeccably timed light entertainments that used droll, highly stylised body language and affectionate, knowing cultural parody—often of dance—as tools for a (sometimes facile) social satire.

Bourne's is a singularly British, quite gay and uncannily commercial sensibility. Influenced by the energy of American musicals, his work is dance made accessible to a non-specialist audience. While he has a flair for maneuvering groups about a stage, his pieces are also littered with small, mimetic gestural details that suggest choreographer Frederick Ashton (another Bourne hero) and marked by an attention to facial expression and characterization that bespeak an almost old-fashioned theatricality. The cast's performances tend to be zestful, the designs usually evocative and witty. But for all their charm and vigorous imagination, Bourne's productions can lack a sufficient amount of good steps. As a choreographer, his limitations show. In Bourne's defense, he has professed greater comfortability with the director label, referring to AMP's output as "shows" rather than "ballets."

Bourne's *The Infernal Galop,* a gentle mockery of the foibles and pretensions of the French, is peppered with songs by the likes of Edith Piaf and features a running gag about two sailors whose mutual flirtation in a *pissoir* is continually interrupted. In *Town & Country* he cocked a dreamy yet sharp eye at the manners and mores of the English upper and lower classes. The opening act is set at a posh hotel full of imperious, wealthy tweed-wearing types, while the second half switches to the outdoors, where spring-footed locals indulge in clog dances and similar manifestations of rustic high spirits. Less amusing is *The Percys of Fitzrovia,* Bourne's trivial take on the Bloomsbury set. Subtitled *An Arty Farce,* it lacked both edge and appeal.

He made good on AMP's moniker via *Deadly Serious,* a ripe tribute to Alfred Hitchcock movies in both their black-and-white and technicolor guises. Bourne's first evening-length show, it demonstrated his skill at mining every absurdity buried in a strong concept. But it also pointed up his overreliance on nudge-nudge, wink-wink kitsch. Only near the climax did the spoofing tone start to drop and a straighter-faced acknowledgment of the dark forces at work in Hitchcock's cinema emerge.

While devising AMP's shows, Bourne also found time to stage movement for West End plays and musicals, opera, and some television. These projects were a valuable training ground as Bourne guided AMP from mid-scale troupe, touring the provinces, to internationalion acclaim with frequently tongue-in-cheek revisions of ballet classics. *Highland Fling* is *La Sylphide* transplanted to a contemporary Glasgow housing estate overrun with the beer-swilling, tartan-clad unemployed; the sylph herself is a mud-stained punk. Critical reaction was mixed, though some felt that Bourne legitimately reached the romance and underlying pathos of his source material. AMP's *Nutcracker,* unusual in that it was co-directed, starts out not in the plush digs of the privileged but rather in a miserable orphanage where it is filthy rich officials, not rodents, who must be overthrown. The titular hero comes on like Frankenstein, only later to reveal himself as either a gay pin-up, heterohunk, or both.

Disarming as these works were, no one was prepared for the rapturous reception accorded AMP's *Swan Lake.* Transcending the gender gags and parasitic in-jokes marring some of his earlier pieces, Bourne honored Tchaikovsky's score while brilliantly reinventing a familiar plot line. His Prince, a repressed, tormented neurotic from a dysfuntional House of Windsor, falls for a male swan—leader of a pack of equally feral, feathered males—who materializes just as he's about to drown himself in a city park. Whether the love the Prince feels is homoerotic or the projection of a seriously dam-

aged ego, Bourne creates an atmosphere of dangerous, forbidden passion that is the essence of Romantic ballet. The contemporized quality of Bourne's approach was underscored by such scenes as that set in a deliciously seedy, 1960s-style club, contrasted with an endearingly silly Victorian-era ballet-within-the-ballet.

Moving, magical, and meticulously thought-out, *Swan Lake* was Bourne's, and the company's, ticket to fame. Taking the show under his wing, megaproducer Cameron Mackintosh helped facilitate its move to the West End, where Lynn Seymour was granted her request to play the icy Queen mother. Mikhail Baryshnikov, once rumored to be interested in being part of the expected Broadway transfer, wondered if Bourne might consider conceiving a show for him? Critics, even ballet purists, were laudatory, and the public flocked to see it.

In 1998 as Bourne's Adventures in Motion Pictures was restructuring and readying an IPO (initial public offering) of its stock, *Swan Lake* was headed to Broadway, to be followed by two-year tours in the U.S. and throughout Europe (beginning in Spring 1999).

Lightning didn't strike quite as flashily with AMP's follow-up. Set during London's wartime Blitz, *Cinderella* premiered directly in the West End. Despite its astute (some said formulaic) packaging, it lacked the coherent emotional resonance and indefinable rightness of its immediate predecessor. Nor was it choreographically up to snuff. Nevertheless, Bourne's star remained high, and *Cinderella* was slated to open in Los Angeles, Washington, D.C., and New York in 1999.

—Donald Hutera

BOWMAN, Elaine

English-born Canadian dancer, choreographer, company director, and educator

Born: Mary Elaine Bowman, 24 January 1946 in Stow Longa, England. **Education:** Attended Leeds College of Art, 1966-67; Dartington College of Art, 1968-70; London School of Film Technique, 1970-71; London School of Contemporary Dance, 1970-71; emigrated to Canada, 1971; studied at Toronto Dance Theatre; major dance teachers include Helen McGehee, Robert Cohan, Jane Dudley, Patricia Beatty, David Earle, Peter Randazzo, Bertram Ross, Takako Asakawa, Milton Myers, Dana Reitz, Jean Asselin and Denise Boulanger (mime), and Irene Dowd (anatomy). **Family:** Married Peter Hoff. **Career:** Principal dancer, Marie Marchowsky Dance Theatre (Toronto), 1976-78; guest performer, Toronto; taught at Marchowsky School, School of the Toronto Dance Theatre, Toronto Dance Co-op, 1972-78; first independent concert, 1982; dance instructor, University of Calgary, 1979-81; founded with husband Hoff, Dancers' Studio West (Calgary); began Alberta Dance Explosions, 1983; lecturer, Alberta College of Art, 1990-97; consultant, Saskatchewan Arts Council, Grant MacEwan College (Edmonton); juror, Canada Council's Alternatives and Emergence Programs.

Roles

1974   Title role, *The Good Witch of Plum Hollow* (Donald Himes), Eaton Auditorium, Toronto

The Dance Creations of Kathryn Brown (Brown, Bowman), Toronto Workshop Productions Theatre

1979   *Along Dark Streets*, (Clark, Stott), Dance in Canada Association (DICA)conference, University of Waterloo, Ontario

1985   *Mainstage 85* (Donna Krasnow), University of Calgary Theatre

L'Histoire du Soldat (Dana Leubke), Calgary

1990   "Lucky," *After Godot* (Randy Glynn), Randy Glynn Dance Project, Max Bell Theatre, Calgary

Other roles include: Solos and roles in own works, beginning 1972; 18 performances (either as lead dancer or soloist) with the Marchowsky Company, 1976-78; *Prime Time Dreams*, 1985, and others.

Works

1972   *Out on a Limb,* Toronto
Resources, Central Library Theatre, Toronto

1973   *Steps and Ladders*; remounted 1982 for DICA Conference, Ottawa

1974   *Masque, an Evening of Dance* w/Kathryn Brown, Barry Smith, Toronto

1976   *Waiting* w/Brown, Toronto Dance Theatre

1979   *The Sirens of Pelorus*
I Believe in You

1980   *Chinook*

1981   *An Evening of Solos and Duets* for Dancers' Studio West (DSW) Company, University of Calgary Theatre

1982   *The Waterbrothers*
Plastic Genesis
An Introduction

1983   *A Kind of Killing*
Revolving Doors
Burning Times
Hay Una Mujer
Feast of Queens
12% Solution

1984   *Human Weather* w/Phyllis White and Gail Benn, Studio Theatre, Calgary
Off the Hook
The Fool Part 2 (Flash of the Silly Giddy)

1985   *Just Pulling Your Leg* w/Mitchell Rose, DSW, Calgary
Guilt
Age of 37
Working Class Hero

1986   *Dancer* (film collaboration w/Anisa Lalani)
Moon over Calgary w/Moon Joyce, Calgary
Lying in the Bed I Made
African Sanctus
Leaving it Behind

1988   *Someone*
Dancing Family
Desert Cactus
Mondrian (retitled *Imbalance*)

1989   *Tender Gestures*
Burning Issues
i & i

1990   *Point A to B*
Obedience

Soulitude
Two I Knew

1991   *Meadow*

1992   *Love Me*

1996   *The Field*

Publications

Flynn, Anne, "Elaine Bowman," in *101 from the Encyclopedia of Theatrical Dance*, Toronto, 1997.

Wyman, Max, *Dance Canada*, Vancouver, 1989.

*   *   *

After studies in fine arts, dance, and filmmaking, Elaine Bowman emigrated to Toronto in October 1971. She continued her Graham-based studies at the Toronto Dance Theatre (TDT), while acting as the company's photographer. She supported herself with a series of menial jobs, and attributes her interest in choreographing to her attempts to speed up the assembly line while on the midnight shift at a cosmetics factory. Bowman began to work with Marie Marchowsky, performing principal roles from 1976 to 1978 with the Toronto-based Marie Marchowsky Dance Theatre. Bowman worked as a teacher with Marchowsky's school, teaching in a pure, strong Graham style, and at the School of the TDT from 1972 to 1979. She also taught at the Toronto Dance Co-op, an entity started by two Alberta-born dancers. During her years in Toronto she was a founding member of Dance Ontario, and served as a board member of the Dance in Canada Association.

At the invitation of chairman Keith Burgess, an acquaintance from the Dartington College of Art, Bowman moved to Calgary to take a teaching position at the University of Calgary in 1979. Choreography and direction began to take precedence in her career. Dancer's Studio West (DSW) was the result, the company and theatre which Bowman and her husband Peter Hoff began in 1980. Bowman left the university in 1981 to concentrate her activities at Dancers' Studio West. As well as providing a home and focus for Bowman's work, Dancers' Studio West has been part of the CanDance Network since the early 1980s, and is a major presenter of dance in Calgary. As a result of Bowman and Hoff's efforts, dozens of companies and independent artists from North America have performed in Calgary, including (since 1980), Ankoko Butoh, the Martha Graham Company, Toronto Dance Theatre, the Danny Grossman Dance Company, Jennifer Muller, and Louis Falco.

Bowman sees herself as a "physical poet" and is a distinctive soloist. Over the course of creating many works for the ensemble and for herself, she has moved from abstract, formalistic interests to the pursuit of a more personal, autobiographical expression. She sees her artistic work as "functional," nourishing a very human need for group connections and experiences. Her interest in Graham's work, the strength of ritual, its archetypal, religious and spiritual import, is a base and nourishment for her own work. Dance artists, Bowman maintains, are communicators for a language of the soul. She speaks of the responsibility of the dancer to allow the truth to be seen, and ascribes importance to the power of parables. In her work as a lecturer she speaks about the creation of dance as a distillation of imagery, of spiritual and physical truth.

Bowman worked with company ensembles of dancers and trained in her daily classes, from 1980 to 1983 and from 1988 to 1991. She has continued to create and perform her solo repertory, touring her work for ensemble and as a soloist through western Canada and appearing at many festivals. She has been very involved with building a community for modern dance in Calgary—where without the presence of Bowman and DSW—contemporary dance would barely have had a toehold. The Springboard Dance Collective, another Calgary entity, came out of a DSW choreographic lab. Since 1983 Bowman has presented Alberta Dance Explosions, an annual showcase for Alberta choreographers.

Three years ago Bowman built a new space for Dancers' Studio West with her own hands. Committed to the ongoing work of teaching, creating, and building an audience for contemporary dance in Calgary, Bowman is a feisty, irrepressibly active lover of dance.

—Carol Anderson

BRAVO, Guillermina

Mexican dancer, choreographer, educator, and company director

Born: Guillermina Nicolasa Bravo Canales, 13 November 1920 in Chacaltianguis, Veracruz, Mexico. **Education:** Studied music at the National Conservatory of Music, 1936; studied dance at the National School of Dance; studied with Estrella Morales, 1938. **Career:** Member of the Fine Arts Ballet, 1939; first performance, 1940; joined Theater of the Arts Ballet, 1940; toured U.S. universities, 1941; taught dance at the Seki Sano theater study; first choreography, 1946; founder-director, Waldeen's Ballet, 1946; Mexican Dance Academy, National Institute of Fine Arts, 1947; National Ballet of Mexico, 1948; toured indigenous regions for research purposes; toured Mexico, Russia, China, Romania and Italy with National Ballet, 1957; Cuba, 1960, 1984; U.S. 1966, 1986; Puerto Rico, 1987; Europe, 1974, 1978, 1980, 1988, 1990; traveled to Africa, 1977; Greece, 1980; Germany, 1986; founded school within National Ballet; *The Drowned Paradise* included in television series, 1984. **Awards:** Cultural Olympic Games Award for 20 years of professional life, 1968; Dance Festival of Guadalajara, 1970; Cervantino International Festival, 1971, 1976; Folkloric Ballet of Mexico homage, 1976; Veracruz State, 1979; Oaxaca's House of Culture named after her, 1980; A Life in Dance homage, National Institute of Fine Arts, 1985; José Limón Award, National Institute of Fine Arts, 1989; Veracruz Institute of Culture homage, 1989; homage for 50 years of artistic life, 1990; Guillermina Bravo Award created, National and International Festival of Contemporary Dance, San Luis Potosí; national homage, 1996; best theater choreography (for *Matka*), Theater Critics and Chroniclers Association Award (subsequently named after Bravo), 1975; best theater choreography (for the *Threepenny Opera*), 1977; Arts National Award, 1979; named Emeritus Creator, National Creators System, 1994; Arts and Literature Commission member, Arts and Culture National Fund.

Roles

1936   *Ballet simbólico 30-30* (*30-30 Symbolic Ballet*) (G. and N. Campobello, Salas), National Dance School, Mexico City

1940   *Procesional* (*Processional*) (Waldeen), Fine Arts Ballet, Mexico City

        Seis danzas clásicas (*Six Classic Dances*) (Waldeen), Fine Arts Ballet, Mexico City

        La segunda damita, *La Coronela* (Waldeen), Fine Arts Ballet, Mexico City

1945   *Valses* (*Waltzes*) (Waldeen), Ballet of Waldeen, Mexico City

        Tres preludios (*Three Preludes*) (Waldeen), Ballet of Waldeen, Mexico City

        Sinfonía concertante (Waldeen), Ballet of Waldeen, Mexico City

        Sonatas españolas (*Spanish Sonatas*) (Waldeen), Ballet of Waldeen, Mexico City

        Una invitada, *En la boda* (*At the Wedding*) (Waldeen), Ballet of Waldeen, Mexico City

        La traicionera (*Elena the Traitor*) (Waldeen), Ballet of Waldeen, Mexico City

        Suite de danzas (*Dances Suite*) (Waldeen), Ballet of Waldeen, Mexico City

        Cinco danzas en ritmo búlgaro (*Five Dances in Bulgarian Rhythm*) (Waldeen), Ballet of Waldeen, Mexico City

        Allegretto de la quinta sinfonía (*Fifth Symphony Allegretto*) (Waldeen), Ballet of Waldeen, Mexico City

1946   *El cielo de los negros (Negro Heaven)* (Mérida), Ballet of Waldeen, Mexico City

1947   Un ángel, *Día de Difuntos o el triunfo del bien sobre el mal* (*All Souls' Day or the Triumph of Good from Evil*) (Mérida), Mexican Dance Academy, Mexico City

1949   *La doma de la fiera* (*The Taming of the Shrew*) (Waldeen), Mexico City

        La doncella del trigo (*The Wheat Maiden*) (Waldeen), National Ballet of Mexico, Mexico City

        Danzas románticas (*Romantic Dances*) (Waldeen), National Ballet of Mexico, Mexico City

        Tres ventanas a la vida patria (*Three Windows to the Patriotic Life*) (Waldeen), National Ballet of Mexico, Mexico City

        Estudio revolucionario (*Revolutionary Study*) (Waldeen), National Ballet of Mexico, Mexico City

        Cinco variaciones de Bach (*Five Variations of Bach*) (Waldeen), National Ballet of Mexico, Mexico City

1951   *Los cuatro soles* (*The Four Suns*) (Limón), Mexican Ballet of the Mexican Dance Academy, Mexico City

1952   *Concerto* (Lavalle), National Ballet of Mexico, Mexico City

1953   La maestra, *La maestra rural* (*The Rural Teacher*) (Lavalle), National Ballet of Mexico, Mexico City

        Emma Bovary, *Emma Bovary* (Lavalle), National Ballet of Mexico, Mexico City

1955   El diablo, *Juan Calavera* (Lavalle), National Ballet of Mexico, Mexico City

1956   *Las naderías* (*The Mere Nothings*) (Fealy), New Dance Theater, Mexico City

        Fantasía y fuga (*Fantasy and Fugue*) (Francis), New Dance Theater, Mexico City

        La señorita, *Canción de los buenos principios* (*Good Principles' Song*) (Gaona), National Ballet of Mexico, Mexico City

1958   *Corrido del sol* (*Sun's Ballad*) (Gaona), National Ballet of Mexico, Mexico City

        Fuegos artificiales (*Fireworks*) (Fealy), National Ballet of Mexico, Mexico City

1960　Mi nana, *Mi nana (My Nanny)* (De Bernal), National Ballet of Mexico, Mexico City

1967　*Danza para bailarines (Dance for Dancers)* (Yuriko), National Ballet of Mexico, Mexico City

Works (performances with the National Ballet of Mexico, premiering in Mexico City unless otherwise noted)

1946　*Cuarteto opus 59 número 3 (Quartet opus 59 number 3)* (mus. Beethoven), Ballet of Waldeen, Mexico City

　　　Sonata número 7 (Sonata number 7) (mus. Prokofiev), Ballet of Waldeen, Mexico City

1947　*El Zanate* (mus. Galindo), Mexican Dance Academy, Mexico City

　　　Preludios y fugas (Preludes and Fugues) (mus. Bach), Mexican Dance Academy, Mexico City

1949　*Fuerza motriz, ballet de masas (Motive Force, Mass Ballet)* (mus. Contreras, Jiménez Mabarak, Prokofiev)

1951　*Recuerdo a Zapata (Memories of Zapata)* (mus. Jiménez Mabarak)

　　　La conquista del agua (The Conquest of Water) (mus. Jiménez Mabarak), National Ballet of Mexico, Michoacán tour

　　　Alturas de Machu Pichu (Heights of Machu Pichu) (mus. Beethoven), National Ballet of Mexico, Michoacán tour

1952　*Guernica* (mus. Noriega)

1953　*La nube estéril (The Sterile Cloud)* (mus. Noriega)

1954　*Rescoldo (Embers)* w/Josefina Lavalle (mus. Noriega)

1955　*Danza sin turismo (Dance Without Tourism)* (mus. Revueltas)

1956　*El demagogo (The Demagogue)* (mus. Bartók)

1957　*Braceros (Labourers)* (mus. Elizondo)

1958　*Imágenes de un hombre (Images of a Man)* (mus. Revueltas)

1959　*Los danzantes (The Dancers)* (mus. indigenous)

1960　*El paradíso de los ahogados (The Drowned Paradise)* (mus. Jiménez Mabarak)

1961　*Danzas de hechicería (Sorcery Dances)* (mus. Elizondo)

1962　*El bautizo (The Baptism)* (mus. Moncayo)

1963　*Margarita* (mus. Elizondo)

　　　La resortera de oro (The Golden Catapult) (mus. Jiménez Mabarak)

1964　*La portentosa vida de la muerte (The Prodigious Life of the Death)* (mus. Jiménez Mabarak)

1965　*¡Viva la libertad! (Hurrah! to Freedom)* (mus. Honneger)

1966　*Pitágoras dijo... (Pythagoras said...)* (mus. Jiménez Mabarak)

1967　*Comentarios a la naturaleza (Comments to Nature)* (mus. Britten)

1968　*Amor por Vivaldi (Love for Vivaldi)* (mus. Vivaldi)

　　　Montaje (Staging) (mus. Penderecki)

　　　Apunte para una marcha fúnebre (Sketch for a Funeral March) (mus. Mahler)

　　　Juego de pelota (Ball Game) (mus. Elizondo)

1969　*Los magos (The Magicians)* (mus. Mahler)

　　　Acto de amor (Love Act) (mus. Vivaldi)

1970　*Melodrama para dos hombres y una mujer (Melodrama for Two Men and a Woman)* (mus. Penderecki)

1971　*Interacción y recomienzo (Interplay and Recommence)* (mus. Mahler)

1972　*Homenaje a Cervantes (Homage to Cervantes)* (mus. Bach and Foss), National Ballet of Mexico, International Cervantino Festival, Guanajuato City, Guanajuato

1973　*Estudio número 1. Danza para un muchacho muerto (Study no. 1, Dance for a Dead Boy)* (mus. Bach)

　　　Estudio número 2. Danza para un efebo (Study no. 2, Dance for an Ephebe) (mus. Bach)

　　　Estudio número 3. Danza para un bailarín que se transforma en águila (Study no. 3, Dance for a Dancer that Transforms into an Eagle) (mus. Bach)

1975　*Estudio número 4. Lamento por un suceso trágico (Study no. 4, Lament for a Tragic Event)* (mus. popular Andalusian)

1976　*Estudio número 5. Retrato de una mujer enajenada (Study no. 5, Portrait of an Intoxicated Woman)* (mus. Bach)

1977　*Epicentro (Epicentre)* (mus. Foss)

1978　*Reacción de duelo (Grief Reaction)* (mus. Villalobos)

1979　*Estudio número 6. Primer trazo sobre un toro (Study no. 6, First Sketch On a Bull)* (mus. Bach)

　　　Estudio número 8. Leona-cazadora (Study no. 8, Huntress Lioness) (mus. Bach)

1980　*Estudio número 7. Segundo trazo sobre un toro (Study no. 7, Second Sketch on a Bull)* (mus. Wagner)

　　　Visión de muerte (Death Vision) (mus. Varèse)

1981　*Los cómicos (The Comics)* (mus. anonymous 16th century)

　　　La vida es sueño (Life is a Dream) w/Federico Castro and Jaime Blancon (mus. Xenakis, Byrd, Cabanilles, baroque)

　　　Cuatro relieves (Four Reliefs) (mus. Schumann)

1982　*Estudio número 9. Una quimera (Study no. 9, A Chimera)* (mus. Enríquez)

1983　*El llamado (The Call)* (mus. water drum and buma of the Pygmies of Cameroon, Rivero)

1984　*Reportaje de la patria (Patriotic Report)* (mus. Stockhausen)

1985　*La batalla (The Battle)* (mus. Shostakovich, indigenous)

1987　*Constelaciones y danzantes. Homenaje a Rufino Tamayo (Constellations and Dancers. Homage to Rufino Tamayo)* (mus. Rivero, Sánchez)

1988　*Bastón de mando (Staff of Command)* (mus. Rivero, Sánchez)

1989　*Sobre la violencia. Homenaje a Alfonso Reyes (About Violence. Homage to Alfonso Reyes)* (mus. Glass, Rivero, Capetillo)

1990　*La tambora (The Drum)* (mus. Rivero, Capetillo, Sánchez), National Ballet of Mexico, International Cervantino Festival, Guanajuato City, Guanajuato

1991　*Entre dioses y hombres, Código Borgia (Among Gods and Men: Borgia's Code)* (mus. Rivero, Capetillo, Eidel, Devos)

Other works include: Choreographed dances for plays by Emilio Carballido *(Yo también hablo de la rosa; Silencio pollos pelones, ya les van a echar su máiz; Cantata a Hidalgo; Acapulco los lunes; Almanaque de Juárez; Tianguis)*, 1967; Eugene O'Neill (selected scenes), 1967; Shakespeare (selected scenes), 1967; Witkiewiez *(Matka)*, 1974; Maeterlinck *(The Blue Bird)*, 1975; Euripides *(Medea)*, 1975; Bertolt Brecht *(The Threepenny Opera)*, 1977; Oscar Wilde *(Salome)*, 1978; Rodolfo Usigli *(Los viejos)*, 1979; Alejandro Licona *(Huelum)*, 1980; Calderón de la Barca *(La vida es sueño)*,

1981; Lope de Vega *(Fuenteovejuna),* 1982; Igor Stravinski *(A Soldier's Tale),* 1982; Emilio Carballido *(Orinoco),* 1982; Shakespeare *(Hamlet),* 1990.

Publications

On BRAVO: books—

50 años de Danza en el Palacio de Bellas Artes, Mexico City, 1984.
Tibol, Raquel, *Pasos en la danza mexicana,* Mexico City, 1982.
Tortajada Quiroz, Margarita, *Danza y poder,* Mexico City, 1995.

On BRAVO: article—

Lynton, Anadel, "Guillermina Bravo," in *Homenaje Una Vida en la Danza 1985,* Mexico City, 1985.

*　　*　　*

Guillermina Bravo is considered Mexico's most important modern and contemporary dance artist. She has pursued her career for more than six decades, promoting Mexican dance and its creators and playing an essential role in Mexican dance history. The value of her work is enormous, especially considering its context in a country where support of the arts in general, and of dance in particular, has been minimal. Indeed, one of the essential virtues of Bravo's work has been perseverance.

Bravo was born in Chacaltianguis, a little town in the state of Veracruz, Mexico. After living in several cities in Mexico, in the late 1920s she moved with her family to Mexico City. In 1936 she began to study at the National Conservatory of Music, where her teachers included Manuel M. Ponce and Candelario Huízar, both of whom belonged to the first generation of Mexican nationalist music composers. In addition to studying music, Bravo enrolled in the only existing official dance school in Mexico at that time, the National Dance School (NDS), under the direction of Nellie Campobello. Her teachers included Nellie and Gloria Campobello, Xenia Zarina, Ernesto Agüero, and Tessy Marcué. The American dancer, Dora Duby, instructed students in modern dance. While at the NDS, Bravo participated in the *30-30 Symbolic Ballet,* a seminal work in the history of Mexican modern dance.

In 1938 Bravo left the NDS and enrolled in the school of Estrella Morales. In 1939 the American choreographer, Waldeen, began selecting dancers to form a Mexican modern dance company, the Fine Arts Ballet, with support from the Fine Arts Department of the government of Mexico. From Estrella Morales' school, Waldeen selected Bravo, among other dancers, to join the new company. Like the rest of her schoolmates, Bravo was profoundly impressed by Waldeen and her artistic proposal, fully supporting Waldeen's plans despite the prevailing social prejudices against professional dance.

Waldeen's group sought to create a national dance by restoring the popular and indigenous elements of Mexican culture. The company had a clear political agenda, leading Bravo to join the Mexican Communist Party. Bravo would later abandon this affiliation when the party failed to support her work.

In 1940 Bravo made her professional debut with the Fine Arts Ballet in a season of works which included *La Coronela* by Waldeen, a creation which marked the birth of the Mexican nationalist modern dance movement. Once the company disintegrated, Bravo, her teacher, and other artists joined the Theater of the Arts Ballet, with which they continued to work through the early 40s, touring the U.S. in 1941.

In 1946 Waldeen abandoned Mexico and her students, leading Bravo and Ana Mérida to found Waldeen's Ballet, for which they choreographed their first works. The following year, Carlos Chávez, then director of the National Institute of Fine Arts, invited Bravo (as director) and Mérida (as assistant manager) to found the Mexican Dance Academy. The group began intensive study and creative work, traveling to several indigenous zones to carry out research that would become the starting point of their dance creations. Bravo's *El Zanate* was the first of these ethnographically inspired works.

In 1948 Bravo had profound artistic and political differences with Mérida and Chávez, leading her to abandon the Mexican Dance Academy and to found her own company, the National Ballet of Mexico, to be codirected with Josefina Lavalle. This marked the beginning of an arduous enterprise which has sustained the National Ballet apart from official institutions. Although it has received some governmental support, the company has managed to dictate its own agenda throughout its 50-year history. The company toured all over the country, including small indigenous communities, performing in the open air in parks, markets, or other open spaces. The most important tours during the early years of the ballet were in the center of the country, as part of the Literacy Campaign (1949); in the Bajío with the Maize Commission and the Chopin Year celebration (1949); in Michoacán state with the Tepalcatepec Commission (1951); and in Veracruz state with the Papaloapan Commission (1952). This work reflected Bravo's political commitment, characterized by her solidarity with popular causes.

In 1957 Mexican dance underwent a very important change, which expressed itself through, and was headed by, Bravo and the National Ballet. That year, the company, as the Contemporary Ballet of the National Institute of Fine Arts, was invited to the Sixth World Festival of Democratic Youth in Moscow. Performing on several open-air stages, the company was successful with the Russian public but not with the country's governmental authorities, who saw modern dance as "anti-aesthetic." Nevertheless, under the name of the National Contemporary Ballet of Mexico, both Mexican companies were invited to perform in China, Romania and Italy, where they achieved ample critical and public acceptance.

The 1957 tour marked a shift in Bravo's work, as she put aside realism and nationalism, as well as dance inspired by literature, and initiated the creation of new works. In a development which she later referred to as her "nonrealist stage," Bravo sought to develop a new dance language. The company also became more consolidated technically as it began to count on better trained dancers. Then modern dance shifted to more contemporary dance in Mexico, with Bravo being one of the two choreographers from the 1940s and '50s who remained active.

Since its foundation, the National Ballet ran its own school to train company dancers. Despite the fact that in the early years the National Ballet refused to follow rigorous dance techniques, in 1956 the Graham technique was introduced in the company's school, and since 1963 the company has established contacts with the Graham School of New York. In 1970, with the support of the National University of Mexico, the Contemporary Dance and Experimental Choreographic Seminary was created. The seminary broke away from the National Ballet in 1980, becoming a contemporary dance company directed by Raquel Vázquez. In the same year, the National Ballet founded a new school called the National Ballet College.

In 1991 Bravo and her company founded, in the city of Querétaro, the National Center of Contemporary Dance, with the support of the National Institute of Fine Arts, the Culture and Arts National Council and the government of the state of Querétaro. The National Ballet College and the company take part in the National Center, and have initiated programs of study leading to a B.A. degree in contemporary dance, choreography, teaching, research and theatrical production, pioneering this kind of education in the state.

Bravo has been Mexico's most prolific modern and contemporary dance choreographer, thanks in large part to the stability that the National Ballet has given her. She has been the inspiration for many Mexican and foreign dancers, choreographers, composers, and designers. Over the course of some 50 years, and in spite of numerous changes in government policies, Bravo and the National Ballet have remained vital forces in the Mexican cultural community.

—Margarita Tortajada Quiroz
translated by Dolores Ponce Gutiérrez

BROMBERG, Ellen
American dancer and choreographer

Born: 1952, Roswell, New Mexico. **Education:** University of Arizona, B.F.A. 1975, M.F.A. 1998. **Family:** Married to Erich Hansen. **Career:** Dancer, Kadimah Dance Company, Tuscon, 1966-70; dancer, teacher, and choreographer, Utah Repertory Dance Theater (RDT), Salt Lake City, 1974-78; independent choreographer since 1981; artistic director, San Francisco Moving Company, 1983-86, and Ellen Bromberg Ensemble, 1987-89; assistant professor of dance, University of Arizona, 1990-93; numerous residencies, workshops, and lectures. **Awards:** National Endowment for the Arts choreography fellowships, 1975, 1996; Isadora Duncan Dance Award for *The Black Dress,* 1988, for *Singing Myself a Lullaby,* 1997; Bonnie Bird Choreography Award for North America, 1992.

Works

1975   *Getting Off* (no mus.), RDT
1976   *Triplet* (mus. Corea), RDT
1978   *Vestments of Visitors* (mus. McFerrin), Bromberg and McFerrin, Salt Lake City
        Museum Piece I (mus. by dancers), independent production, Salt Lake City
        Apres L'Entree (mus. Julian Bream), Dance Kaleidoscope, St. Louis
1979   *Museum Piece II* (mus. by dancers), independent production, Salt Lake City
        Mouthpiece (mus. McFerrin), Cathy Williams Solo Performance, New York
1980   *Portrait, Part I* (mus. Brian Bromberg), solo
        Corners Turned (mus. collage), Living Dance Theater, Tucson
1981   *Fragments* (mus. collage), solo, Sharon Jean Leeds, San Francisco Dance Theater

1982   *In Our Next Episode. . .* (mus. San Francisco Saxophone Quartet), trio
        Portrait, Part II (mus. Miles Davis and Earle Brown), solo
1983   *In the Same Breath* (mus. Victor Spiegel), duet, San Francisco Moving Company
        Still Moving (mus. Spiegel), for television broadcast, KQED-TV, San Francisco
1984   *Toonings* (mus. McFerrin), Pacific Dance Ensemble, Stockton, California
1985   *Dream and Variations* (mus. Carmen Borgia), solo, Deborah Slater Performance, San Francisco
1986   *Consonance* (no mus.), San Francisco Moving Company
        Journey (mus. Victor Spiegel), San Francisco Moving Company
1987   *Over the Rainbow* (mus. Willie Nelson), Ellen Bromberg Ensemble
1988   *Folk Dance* (mus. Spiegel), California State University—Hayward
        The Black Dress (mus. Paul Sturm), Indiana University, Bloomington
        Moon, Moon (mus. by dancers), Ellen Bromberg Ensemble
1989   *Listening to the Heart* (mus. Gregorian chants and medieval), Ellen Bromberg Ensemble
        The Other Wilderness (mus. Henry Gwaizda), American Dance Festival, Durham, North Carolina
1990   *Work from Emptiness* (no mus.), site-specific for Earthworks Performance Space, Yellow Springs Institute, Chester Springs, Pennsylvania
1992   *Homeland* (mus. David Bromberg), University of Arizona
        The Healing (mus. Spiegel), Transitions Dance Company, London
1993   *Dawn's Attic* (mus. Patrick Neher), University of Arizona
        A Sad Little Dance (mus. Bartók, Stravinsky, Shostakovich), University of Arizona
        Canopy (mus. Chuck Koesters), Orts Dance Theater, Tucson
1994   *Common Ground* (mus. David Bromberg), Ballet Arizona, Phoenix
        So Long Shangri-La (mus. Vic Damone), solo for Frank Shawl, Berkeley, California
        Home (mus. Glass), solo
        Quintetto Vivace (mus. Vivaldi), University of Arizona
1995   *Aria for an Endangered Species* (mus. Ono), Core Performance Company, Atlanta
        Singing Myself a Lullaby (mus. Spiegel), solo, John Henry Performance, San Francisco

Publications

On BROMBERG: articles—

Berson, Misha, "Swan Song for Dance Master," *San Francisco Chronicle,* 28 January 1990.
Graves, Barbara, "Respectable Repertory," *Studio Dance Revue,* January 1984.
Murphy, Ann, "John Henry and Ellen Bromberg," *Dance Magazine,* September 1995.
———, "Edge Festival," *Dance Magazine,* July 1996.
"Ellen Bromberg," *Studio Dance Revue,* October 1984.

Films and Videotapes

The Black Dress, for *Alive from Off-Center*, KQED-TV, San Francisco, 1989.

The Postman, film with choreography by Bromberg, Warner Brothers, 1997.

*   *   *

Born in New Mexico, Bromberg grew up in Tucson, Arizona. She studied dance with Frances Smith Cohen starting at age six, and performed with Cohen's Kadimah Dance Theater from 1966 to 1970. She continued her studies at the University of Arizona, earning her B.A. in dance in 1975. Even before graduating, however, Bromberg had joined the Repertory Dance Theater in Salt Lake City in 1974, performing as part of the ensemble until 1978. During her tenure there she created two works for the group, *Getting Off* (1975) and *Triplet* (1976).

In 1978, Bromberg returned to Tucson to teach at the University of Arizona and serve as a movement specialist for both the Arizona Commission on the Arts and the National Endowment for the Arts Artists in the Schools programs. In 1981, she relocated to the San Francisco Bay area, where she stayed for nearly a decade. After a one-year stint as guest artistic director at the Henry Harris Green Theater Dance Company in Berkeley, she was named artistic director of the San Francisco Moving Company, a repertory troupe, where she remained from 1983 to 1986. Meanwhile, she continued to teach, at the Shawl-Anderson Dance Center in Berkeley and at Mills College in Oakland. She developed a reputation as one of the finest movement teachers in the region.

In 1987, Bromberg formed the Ellen Bromberg Ensemble to stage her own works, beginning with what many consider her signature piece, *The Black Dress* (1988). Bromberg returned to Tucson in 1990 to take a teaching position at the University of Arizona and to continue her studies in dance, culminating with a master's degree. Meanwhile, she has continued as an independent choreographer; her works have been performed throughout the U.S. by both students and professional companies, as well as in the United Kingdom, Germany, China, Korea and Japan. She has also been an artist-in-residence and lecturer at numerous univerities and dance companies.

Bromberg's works often focus on social issues, usually from a feminist perspective, and on human relationships. Critics call her dances visceral, turbulent, athletic, sensuous and witty, and her choreography sharply honed. Her pieces run the emotional gamut from anger and fear to joy, and often contain humor. Each gesture has meaning and, while the works are abstract, audiences can usually discern a storyline. Her choreography builds upon the modern tradition created by the likes of Donald McKayle, Lar Lubovitch, and especially Anna Sokolow and José Limón. Bromberg was influenced by these choreographers through her years performing their works. Bromberg's concern with social issues is evident in works such as *Aria for an Endangered Species* (1995), set to music by Yoko Ono, whose sculpture *Endangered Species 2319-2322* inspired the piece. The abstract dance has been called a warning about the fragility of the human race. *Singing Myself a Lullaby* (1995) documents the impending AIDS-related death of its performer, John Henry, who commissioned the work in 1993. The piece combines Henry's live performance, which includes him drawing an outline of his body in red chalk and smearing it, with a video of previous performances of the work. As Henry's condition weak-

ens, the video takes over portions of the dance that he cannot perform, until at the end the video is all that will remain. Each performance is different: as the dancer's physical condition deteriorates, the video expands and the live portion is simplified. The piece will be in its finished form only at the end of Henry's life.

Social themes are also evident in *Homeland* (1992), which was inspired by Bromberg's reactions to the Gulf War. Set to music by Bromberg's brother David, the piece diverges from most of Bromberg's body of work by virtue of its epic scale. As she told the *Tucson Citizen,* "Usually I go inside the individual, into the inner psyche. This time I'm looking at all of society. It is the societal level of the inner psyche."

Bromberg's choreographic works often focus on relationships. For example, *The Other Wilderness* (1989), commissioned by the American Dance Festival as part of its Young Choreographers and Composers Project and set to music by Henry Gwiazda, is a duet for a man and woman whose attempts at communication fail, in part thwarted by environmental forces. Their lack of intimacy is demonstrated by the performers dancing back to back. One is illuminated by a circle and the other a square of light, which never quite fit. Relationships are also at the core of *Over the Rainbow* (1987), which humorously portrays the absurdity of relationships—between the sexes and between nations—to the accompaniment of a series of Willie Nelson songs. *The Black Dress* also centers on relationships and, typically, reflects feminist themes. Inspired by an Alex Katz painting, it features six women wearing the uniform of the "little black dress." Their passions are bared as the dance proceeds, depicting their struggle against confinement and offering a comment on women's social roles and society's expectations of them. The piece was reconceptualized for film in 1989, airing on PBS's Alive from Off-Center, and it earned Bromberg an Isadora Duncan Award. Feminist themes are also at the heart of *Moon, Moon* (1988), a provocative piece danced in silence by seven women. It reflects on women's communal experiences and recollections, depicting struggle, pain and oppression, as if seen through a dream.

Humor is central to much of Bromberg's work, although underlying themes and meanings are never obscured. For example, *Toonings* (1984) is composed of a series of fun "movement cartoons" set to a Bobby McFerrin mouth-organ accompaniment. Five dancers, dressed in bright colors, perform crazy lifts, run without going anywhere, carry each other around and joyously complete other movements. Despite this atmosphere of fun, critics note that the piece has substance as well. Similarly, the 10-minute solo *Portrait* (1982), set to the music of Miles Davis and Earle Brown, starts out as an amusing look at a businessman's world but later includes disturbing images, turning into a social commentary typical of Bromberg's work.

—Karen Raugust

BROWN, Carolyn

American dancer, choreographer, educator, filmmaker, and writer

Born: Fitchburg, Massachusetts. **Education:** Philosophy major, graduated *cum laude* from Wheaton College in Massachusetts, 1950; enrolled in the Juilliard School, 1952. **Family:** Married to composer Earle Brown. **Career:** Principal dancer, Merce Cunningham

Dance Company, 1953-72; Dean of Dance at State University of New York (SUNY) at Purchase, 1980-82. **Awards:** *Dance Magazine* award, 1970; honorary Doctor of Fine Arts, Wheaton College, 1974.

Roles (as a principal dancer for the Merce Cunningham Dance Company, with choreography by Cunningham, unless otherwise noted)

1953	*Exercise Piece* (Antony Tudor), Juilliard
	Suite by Chance, Urbana, Illinois
	Banjo, Black Mountain College, North Carolina
	Dime a Dance, Black Mountain College, North Carolina
	Septet, Black Mountain College, North Carolina
	Fragments, New York
1954	*Minutiae*, Brooklyn
1955	*Springweather and People*, Annandale-on-Hudson, New York
1956	*Galaxy*, South Bend, Indiana
	Suite for Five in Space and Time, South Bend, Indiana
	Nocturnes, Jacob's Pillow, Massachusetts
1957	*Labyrinthian Dances*, Brooklyn
	Picnic Polka, Brooklyn
1958	*Antic Meet*, New London, Connecticut
	Summerspace, New London, Connecticut
	Duet w/Cunningham, *Night Wandering*, Stockholm
1959	*From the Poems of White Stone*, Urbana, Illinois
	Gambit for Dancers and Orchestra, Urbana, Illinois
	Rune, New London, Connecticut
1960	Duet w/Cunningham, *Theatre Piece*, New York
	Crises, New London, Connecticut
	Solo, *Hands Birds*, Venice
	Solo, *Waka*, Venice
	Music Walk with Dancers, Venice
1961	*Suite de Danses* (for television), CBC-TV Montreal
	Aeon, Montreal
1963	*Field Dances*, Los Angeles
	Story, Los Angeles
1964	*Winterbranch*, Hartford, Connecticut
	Cross Currents, London
1965	*Variations V*, New York
	How to Pass, Kick, Fall and Run, Chicago
1966	*Place*, Saint-Paul de Vence
1967	*Scramble*, Chicago
1968	*RainForest*, Buffalo
	Walkaround Time, Buffalo
	Assemblage, KQED-TV, San Francisco
1969	*Canfield*, Rochester
1970	*Tread*, Brooklyn
	Second Hand, Brooklyn
	Signals, Paris
	Objects, Brooklyn
1972	*Landrover*, Brooklyn
	TV Rerun, Brooklyn
	Borst Park, Brooklyn

Works

1968	*Car Lot* (mus. Earle Brown), Manhattan Festival Ballet, New York
1970	*West Country* (mus. Edward Elgar), Juilliard Dance Ensemble, New York
1973	*Bunkered for a Bogey, or Steve Paxton Did It First* (chance composition), Among Company, New York
1974	*House Party*, Among Company, New York
1975	*Circles* (mus. Terry Riley), Maryland Dance Theatre Company, University of Maryland, College Park
1978	*Balloon* (mus. Earle Brown), Ballet Théatre Contemporain, London
1979	*Rhosymedre* (mus. Ralph Vaughan Williams), Margaret Jenkins Dance Company, San Francisco
	Child's Play (Homage à Denishawn II) (mus. Robert Schumann), Purchase Dance Corps, New York
1981	*Dune Dance* (film; mus. James Klosty)
	Port de Bras for Referees (mus. Earle Brown), Purchase Dance Corps, Purchase, New York

Publications

By BROWN: books—

Contributor, *Merce Cunningham*, edited by James Klosky, New York, 1975.

On BROWN: articles—

Goodman, Saul, "Carolyn Brown," *Dance Magazine*, May 1956.
Maynard, Olga, "In Celebration of Carolyn Brown," *Dance Magazine,* July 1971.
Mueller, John, "Carolyn Brown's *Dune Dance*," *Dance Magazine*, September 1981.
Percival, John. "American Recipe, French Cuisine," *Dance and Dancers,* February 1978.
Woodard, Stephanie, "Decision-Making Dancers," *Ballet Review*, Winter 1992.
Zimmer, Elizabeth, "Revamping Dance at Purchase," *Dance Magazine*, November 1981.

*   *   *

A principal dancer with the Merce Cunningham Dance Company for 20 years, Carolyn Brown has performed throughout the United States and around the world, winning worldwide acclaim as one of modern dance's greatest technicians.

Born in Fitchburg, Massachusetts, Brown began dancing at the age of three. Her mother, Marion Rice, had a school of Denishawn dance, and so Carolyn naturally danced as part of her daily activities, receiving training in the Denishawn technique until the age of 18. During high school, Brown accompanied her mother to a dance teachers' convention in Chicago, and received strong encouragement from teacher Gladys Hight, who was struck by Brown's natural ability.

But Brown was determined to make a career out of writing, and accordingly enrolled in Wheaton College in her home state. At Wheaton, Brown majored in philosophy and was elected to Phi Beta Kappa, all the while maintaining her dance activities—acting as president of the dance group there, as well as choreographing regularly for school musicals. Shortly after her graduation in 1950 she married composer Earle Brown, who later composed scores for many of Merce Cunningham's works and eventually for Carolyn's own choreographic pieces. The couple moved to Denver, where

Carolyn took a position teaching dance and drama at a private school. Although still intending to pursue a literary career, Brown became a performing member of Jane McLean's Dance Company, which toured in Colorado and Wyoming. It was in Denver that Brown first became acquainted with Cunningham, who urged her to continue to pursue dance, and in 1952 she moved to New York to study with him.

Although she had originally intended to enroll in graduate school at Columbia, Brown decided at the last minute to enroll in the Juilliard School. There she received training from Martha Hill, Martha Graham, Louis Horst, and Norman Lloyd, as well as ballet instruction from Antony Tudor and Margaret Craske, with whom she continued to study until 1976. After one year at Juilliard, Cunningham asked Brown, along with several other of his students, to join a newly formed company at Black Mountain College in North Carolina for the summer. Following that experience, Brown finally resolved to commit herself to dance and spent the next 20 years performing and touring the globe with the Merce Cunningham Dance Company.

Not only did Cunningham begin to create choreography suited specifically to Brown's controlled lyric style, but she danced as Merce's partner in many pieces during those years when crucial innovations were being made in American modern dance, including the incorporation of chance processes into the project of choreography. A 1971 *Dance Magazine* article by Olga Maynard entitled "In Celebration of Carolyn Brown," declared Brown "as much his collaborator as. . .his instrument." In that same article, Brown provided her impression of that first decade of work with Cunningham: "The 1950s were fantastic years. A new world opened up with the music of John Cage, Earle Brown and Morton Feldman, and the art of Bob Rauschenberg and Jasper Johns, to name a few. . . . At that time it seemed that everything was possible, because artists of whatever media were genuinely interested in one another." In May of 1970, her dancing earned her a *Dance Magazine* Award. Brown also appeared in several films featuring Cunningham's choreography, including the award-winning *Cage/Cunningham*.

In 1972 Brown left the Cunningham company, afraid that Cunningham might have grown bored with her. As she revealed in a winter of 1992 symposium entitled "Decision-Making Dancers," published in *Ballet Review*, "[Cunningham] knew what my body could do. And the me that I kept hoping he'd find—he never found it. Obviously I never showed it. I mean this passion, this yearning to be free." After 20 years of dancing Cunningham's evolving visions, Brown began a second career as a choreographer. Her work to date has been performed by a number of different groups, such as the Juilliard Dance Ensemble, Among Company, Ballet Théâtre Contemporain, the Maryland Dance Theatre Company, the Margaret Jenkins Dance Company, and the Purchase Dance Corps. Reviewers have commented on the precise movements and patterns, as well as the romanticism of Brown's choreography. In 1981 she also conceived and directed a film entitled *Dune Dance*, which blended dance and film techniques to capture the nature of movement performed on sand dunes.

In 1980 Brown was hired to run the dance division at the State University of New York's College at Purchase, and for two years she acted in the liaison post as dean. She continues to work on projects documenting her experiences as a dancer.

—Anthea Kraut

BROWN, Ronald K.
American dancer, choreographer, and company director

Born: 18 July 1966 in Brooklyn, New York. **Education:** Attended Edward R. Murrow High School of Communications; studied modern dance with Mary Anthony, 1983-85; Bessie Schönberg 1987-89; Jennifer Muller, 1986-90. **Career:** Founder, Ronald K. Brown/ Evidence 1985; dancer, Jennifer Muller/The Works 1986-90. **Awards:** American Dance Festival/Scripps Humphrey/Weidman/ Limón Award, 1991; Manhattan Community Arts Fund, 1994; Edward & Sally Van Lier Fund Fellowship, 1994; Artists' Projects: New York State Regional Initiatives, 1994; National Endowment for the Arts (NEA) choreographic fellowships, 1995, 1996.

Roles

1987	*Interrupted River*, Jennifer Muller/The Works, New York
1988	*Occasional Encounters*, Jennifer Muller/The Works, New York
	City, Jennifer Muller/The Works, New York

Works

1984	*Paean* (mus. Ahmad Jamal), New York
	Cold Obstacle (mus. Pat Metheny), New York
1985	*My Air Conditioner Is Broken* (mus. Aboriginal traditional), Brooklyn
	Tones (mus. Jeff Majors), Brooklyn
	Cooties: Don't Bug Me (mus. Byrne and Eno), Brooklyn
	Evidence (mus. John Lurie), Brooklyn
1986	*Feats & Therapy* (mus. Jeff Majors), Brooklyn
	One in No Strange Land (mus. Art of Noise), Brooklyn
	In No Strange Land Too (mus. Handel and Voodoo Ray), Brooklyn
	In No Strange Land III (mus. David Byrne), Brooklyn
	In No Strange Land 5 (mus. Art of Noise), Brooklyn
	Streaks (mus. Art of Noise), Brooklyn
	When I Grab the Chance (mus. Byrne & Eno), Brooklyn
1987	*The Heat* (mus. Peter Gabriel), Brooklyn
	Untitled Solo 21 (mus. Jean Luc-Ponty), New York
	Release the Blues (mus. Andy Monroe), New York
	A Bundle of Sticks Watching a Fire, New York
	Adjacent Only Once (mus. Oliver Lake), Brooklyn
1988	*A Pocketful of Waiting* (mus. Darby & Etheridge), New York
	Coming Up for Air (mus. Yello), New York
	Dive (mus. Wally Badarou), New York
	Next (mus. Bach, Wonder and Makeba), New York
	Never Alone Too, Brooklyn
	Tapestry (mus. Oliver Lake), Brooklyn
	On Making Noise (mus. Yanni), New York
1990	*The Gift* (mus. Kronos Quartet), New York
	Sockets (mus. John Hassell), New York
	Tendrils (mus. Pärt), New York
1991	*Conversations in a Whisper* (mus. Robert Een), New York
	The Core (mus. David Simons), Durham, North Carolina
1992	*No More Waiting* (mus. Sound Effects/Ronald K. Brown), New York
	A Shorter Walk, Quito, Ecuador

Folks (mus. traditional blues), Durham, North Carolina

What's Your Name Anyways? (mus. Willemon), New York

1993   *Combat Review/Witches in Response* (mus. Don Meissner), New York

      Guard Duty (mus. Don Meissner), New York

1994   *Dirt Road/Morticia Supreme's Revue* (mus./text Essex Hemphill, Donald Woods, Ronald K. Brown, Trevor Jones, Aretha Franklin, Labelle, Ellison, Edwards, Marvin Gaye, Billie Holiday, Adu, Hale, J. Whitehead, G. McFadden, and V. Carstarphen), Lee, Massachusetts

1996   *Lessons* (mus./text Sandye Wilson, Zap Mama, Dr. Martin Luther King, Jr., Bobby McFerrin, Gloria Gaynor, Mahalia Jackson, Gil Scott-Heron, Herbert Brewster, Wunmi Olaiya, Bucketheads and Curtis Mayfield), New York

      Ebony Magazine: To a Village (mus./text Wunmi Oliaya and Ronald K. Brown), commissioned and performed by Cleo Parker Robinson Dance Ensemble, Denver

1997   *Free* (mus. Fahall Igbo), Durham, North Carolina

1998   *Better Days* (mus./text J. Ellison & E. Batts, MKL, G. Winston James), New York

      Incidents (mus. Staple Singers, Herbert Brewster and Wunmi Oliaya), New York

      Journey (mus. Wunmi Oliaya), Philiadelphia, Pennsylvania

      Destiny (mus. Mohammed Kamara and Winmi Olaiya), New York

Publications

Dekle, Nicole, "Profile of an Upcoming Choreographer: Ronald K. Brown," *Dance Magazine*, July 1995.

Dunning, Jennifer, "A Storyteller with a Fresh Voice," *New York Times*, August 16, 1994.

———, "The Meaning of. . . ," *Village Voice*, 30 August 1994.

Jowitt, Deborah, "*Heat* Effect," *Village Voice*, 13 April 1993.

Kisselgoff, Anna, "Telling Stories of Love, Loss and Racism," *New York Times*, 15 January 1998.

Supee, Burt, "Prodigal Son," *Village Voice*, 6 March 1990.

Tobias, Tobi, "Battle Cries," *Village Voice*, 11 February 1992.

West, C. S'thembile, "*Combat Review/Witches in Response*," *Attitude*, Fall/Winter 1995.

Zimmer, Elizabeth, "Against All Odds," *Village Voice*, 18 April 1988.

*   *   *

Ronald K. Brown's politically and socially charged dances reflect his background and identity as a gay, African-American choreographer. Brown's career is still relatively young; most recently his company Evidence, which was launched in 1985, took part in the 1998 Joyce Theater's Altogether Different festival in New York City.

Born in the Bedford-Stuyvesant section of Brooklyn on 18 July 1966, Brown is a storyteller's choreographer. He began creative dance at the age of six at a Police Athletic League summer program, but when he turned 12, his plans changed. On the way to an audition for admission into the Dance Theatre of Harlem's summer program, which he regarded as his "destiny," his mother went into labor with Brown's younger brother. Despite his young age, he took this as a sign that he should focus his attention on writing and

Ronald K. Brown. Photograph © Johan Elbers.

become a journalist—his only other interest. At Edward R. Murrow High School of Communications, he wrote for the school newspaper and graduated in 1983 at the age of 16. During the summer vacation before he was to enter college, he started dancing again, studying ballet with Patty Donn in Brooklyn and modern dance, composition, and pedagogy with Mary Anthony and Anna Sokolow. At that time, Anthony's company was inactive; soon after Brown's arrival, however, Anthony revived it. Brown danced repertory pieces for a year and left Anthony's studio in 1985 to concentrate on creating his own work. "Her work was theatrical, and it was about people—both of which I connected to—but it wasn't contemporary."

An older, more experienced dancer, William Adair, who was dancing in Jennifer Muller's company, advised the 19-year-old Brown to continue his study of dance. For a year, Brown attended classes at the Muller studio, while supporting himself by working at the Silvercrest Bakery in Newark, New Jersey. Finally, Muller needed a male dancer; Brown quit his job and joined Muller's troupe, where he danced for two years officially and then two years as a guest artist. During this time, Brown began choreographing. Family members, including his grandmother and mother, donated $300 for Brown to form his troupe Evidence, which was also the title of his first dance in 1985. In the solo *Evidence*, Brown explored how individuals are the product of their ancestry; today, it's obvious that the piece was a launching pad for future choreographic examinations of race and class. For Brown, the name Evidence stands for what his dancers are all about: stripping away stereotypes to reveal the truth.

In response to his 1993 *Combat Review/Witches in Response*, an evening-length piece set to an ambient sound score by Don Meissner, Deborah Jowitt wrote, "the spat-out way they're performed and the more original slashing, stomping moves that surround them in the phrases give the work a consistent and gripping style." No matter the subject matter, Brown never neglects his lush, powerful movement. One of his most acclaimed pieces, the 1994 *Dirt Road/Morticia Supreme's Revue*, weaves sensual dancing with a loose, narrative look into the generational drama of a black family. Built around the themes of cultural assimilation and the loss of loved ones, *Dirt Road* is a series of vignettes set to a collage of pop and gospel music. Brown has said, "To be an African-American is to be always preparing for loss." In *Dirt Road*, it is a loss that propels a family to return home.

Burt Supee noted in a 1990 *Village Voice* review, "Brown is a young choreographer with breathtaking style. He has passion intelligence and a talent for devising dynamic movement. But his prodigal impulse is to say everything at once." It's obvious that he's still in the process of taming his creative flow of ideas. At his Joyce Theater debut in the Altogether Different Festival, Brown presented sections from two works, *Incidents: First Journey* and *Better Days: First Time Through*. Eventually, both will become evening-length works. *Incidents*, a dance for five women, started out with an image of a slave narrative; as the dancers spun and leapt in loose-fitting, white dresses, the work took on a painterly quality. *Better Days*, named after a former nightclub populated by gay black men, dizzingly captured the utter joy of movement.

But Brown's dances are more than pretty. He relies on the spoken word as well as music to get his messages across; text may seem like a background element but often serves as the inspiration for the choreography. He has used the writings and speeches of Allen Wright, Essex Hemphill, Donald W. Woods, Gil Scott-Heron and Dr. Martin Luther King, Jr., to give his lush movement context. He also writes poetry that centers around how spirituality connects to race and perseverance. Even so, he doesn't consider himself to be a political choreographer. "I want to make dances, I want to tell stories," he explained. "But I think because of my background, what I want to talk about has a political and social message. I have to claim, okay, there is a flavor of activism in the work. In the studio, I'm very sly about it. I say to myself, I'm just making dances. But I know that my work is about creative protest."

—Gia Kourlas

BROWN, Trisha

American postmodern dancer and choreographer

Born: Aberdeen, Washington, 1936. **Education:** Mills College, Oakland, B.A., dance, 1958; studied with Louis Horst, American Dance Festival, summers, 1955, 1959, 1961. **Career:** Dancer, Judson Dance Theater, beginning 1960; founded Trisha Brown Company, 1970; has received commissions from the National Gallery of Art, Lincoln Center for the Performing Arts, Berlin's Hebbel Theater, the Montepellier Festival de Danse, and others. **Awards:**

John Simon Guggenheim Memorial Foundation choreographic fellowship, 1975, 1984; honorary doctorate, Oberlin College, 1983; *Dance Magazine* award, 1987; Lawrence Olivier award, 1987; Officer, Order of Arts and Letters (France), 1988; MacArthur Foundation fellowship, 1991; Meyerhoff professorship, Goucher College, 1991; Samuel H. Scripps American Dance Festival Award, 1994; appointed by President Clinton, National Council of the Arts, 1994; Prix de la Danse Société des Auteurs et Compositeurs Dramatiques, 1996; honorary member, American Academy of Arts and Letters, 1997; honorary doctorate, Mills College, 1998.

Works (all works premiered in New York unless otherwise stated)

1961	*Structured Improvisations* w/Forti, Levine
1962	*Trillium*, Maidman Playhouse
1963	*Lightfall*, Judson Memorial Church
	2 Improvisations, YAM Festival
	Improvisation on Chicken Coop Roof, George Segal's Farm
	Falling Solo With Singing, Pocket Theater
1964	*Rulegame 5*, Humboldt State College, California
	Target, Humboldt State College
1965	*Motor*, Ann Arbor, Michigan
	Homemade, Broadway
1966	*String* (includes *Motor, Homemade,* and *Inside*), Judson Memorial Church
1967	*Shrunk Cabbage*, 222 Bowery
	Salt Grass, 222 Bowery
	Waders, 222 Bowery
	Medicine Dance, Sun Dance, Pennsylvania
1968	*Planes*, SUNY, New Paltz, New York
	Snapshots, SUNY, New Paltz
	Falling Duet, Riverside Church Theatre
	Ballet, Riverside Church Theatre
	Dance with the Duck's Head, Museum of Modern Art
1969	*Yellowberry*, Newark State College, Newark
	Skymap, Newark State College
1970	*Man Walking Down the Side of the Building*, Wooster Street
	Clothes Pipe, Wooster Street
	The Floor of the Forest, Wooster Street
	Other Miracles, etc., Wooster Street
	Leaning Duets, Wooster Street
	The Stream, Astro Festival
1971	*Walking on the Wall*, Whitney Museum of American Art
	Leaning Duets II, Whitney Museum of American Art
	Falling Duet II, Whitney Museum of American Art
	Accumulation 4½, New York University
	Rummage Sale, New York University
	The Floor of the Forest, New York University
	Roof Piece, Wooster & Lafayette
1972	*Accumulation 55'*, L'Attico Gallery, Rome
	Primary Accumulation, Wadsworth Atheneum, Hartford, Connecticut
	Theme and Variations, Wadsworth Atheneum, Hartford
1973	*Woman Walking Down A Ladder*, Wadsworth Atheneum, Hartford
	Group Accumulation, Sonnabend Gallery
	Group Primary Accumulation I, Spring Festival
	Roof Piece, Broadway & White streets

Trisha Brown Dance Company: *Group Primary Accumulation: Raft Piece.* **Photograph © Johan Elbers.**

Group Accumulation II, Festival d' Automne, Paris
Structured Pieces I, Festival d' Automne, Paris
Accumulation with Talking, American Center, Paris
1974 *Figure 8*, Contemporanea, Rome
Split Solo, Contemporanea, Rome
Drift, Kennedy Center, Washington, D.C.
Spiral, 383 West Broadway
Pamplona Stones, 383 West Broadway
Structured Pieces II, Walker Arts Center, Minneapolis
1975 *Locus (in progress)*, 541 Broadway
Structured Pieces III, American Dance Festival, New London, Connecticut
Pyramid, Seibu Theater, Tokyo, Japan
1976 *Solos Olos* (with reprise of *Locus* and *Pyramid*), BAM
Duetude, Lee, Massachusetts
Line Up 1976, Festival de la Sainte Baumé, Aix-en-Provence, France
Structured Pieces IV, Fort Worth, Texas
1977 *Line Up* (new version), BAM
1978 *Water Motor*, Public Theatre
Splang, Public Theatre
1979 *Accumulation with Talking Plus Water Motor*, Oberlin, Ohio
Glacial Decoy, Walker Arts Center, Minneapolis

1980 *Opal Loop/Cloud Installation*, 55 Crosby Street
1981 *Son of Gone Fishin'*, BAM
1982 *Set and Reset*, Festival of Montpellier, d'Avignon, France
1985 *Lateral Pass*, Walker Arts Center, Minneapolis
1986 *Carmen*, Teatro di San Carlo, Naples, Italy
1987 *Newark*, Centre Nationale de la Danse Contemporaine (CNDC), Théâtre d'Angers, France
Zummo, CNDC, Théâtre d'Angers
1989 *Astral Convertible*, City Center
1990 *Foray Forêt*, Lyon Biennale de la Danse, France
1991 *Astral Converted (50")* National Gallery of Art, Washington D.C.
For M.G.: The Movie, L'Hippodrome de Douai, France
1992 *One Story as in Falling*, Montpellier Danse Festival, France
1993 *Another Story as in Falling*, Zellerbach Playhouse, University of California, Berkeley
1994 *Yet Another Story*, Joyce Theater
If you couldn't see me, Joyce Theater
1995 *You can see us*, Montpellier Festival de Danse, France
"M.O.," La Monnaie, Brussels, Belgium
1996 *Twelve Ton Rose*, BAM
1998 *L'Orfeo*, La Monnaie, Brussels
Canto/Panto, Berlin, Germany

Trisha Brown performing *Water Motor,* 1978. Photograph © Lois Greenfield.

Publications

By BROWN: articles—

With others, "Conversation in Manhattan," *Impulse,* 1967.
"Three Pieces," *The Drama Review,* March 1975.
With Douglas Dunn, "Dialogue: On Dance," *Performing Arts Journal,* Fall 1976.

On BROWN: books—

Banes, Sally, *Terpsichore in Sneakers: Post-Modern Dance,* Boston, 1980.
Brown, Jean Morrison (ed.), *The Vision of Modern Dance,* Princeton, New Jersey, 1979.
Livet, Anne (ed.), *Contemporary Dance,* New York, 1978.
Wynne, Peter, *Judson Dance: An Annotated Bibliography of the Judson Dance Theater and of Five Major Choreographers—*

Trisha Brown, Lucinda Childs, Deborah Hay, Steve Paxton, and Yvonne Rainer. Englewood, New Jersey, 1978.

On BROWN: articles—

Goldberg, Marianne, "Trisha Brown: All of the Person's Person Arriving," *The Drama Review,* Spring 1986.
———, "Reconstructing Trisha Brown: Dances and Performance Pieces, 1960-75," copyright 1990.
Sears, David, "A Trisha Brown-Robert Rauschenberg Collage," *Ballet Review,* Fall 1982.
Siegel, Marcia B., "New Dance: Individuality, Image, and the Demise of the Coterie," *Dance Magazine,* 1974.
Sommer, Sally R., "Equipment Dances: Trisha Brown," *The Drama Review,* September 1972.
———, "Trisha Brown Making Dances," *Dance Scope*, Spring/Summer 1977.
Vail, June, "Moving Bodies, Moving Souls: Trisha Brown Company in Stockholm," in *Society of Dance History Scholars Proceedings,* University of California, Riverside, 1992.

*   *   *

Ordinary movement + extraordinary skill = Trisha Brown. This is the equation Trisha Brown has been manifesting into dance throughout her career. Initially as a founding member of the Judson Dance Theater in New York, Brown experimented with the structure and form of movement. She delved into modern dance to seek the new, the different, the untried and untested. Through dances composed of everyday movement her voyage necessitated a new vocabulary of dance. Her technique of no releve with much upper torso movement and fluid thrown-away steps has provoked critics to define her dances using the Brownian theory of motion—a ceaseless irregularity of movement of dust particles in liquids and gases.

Brown choreographs as a scientist in a laboratory, questioning all aspects of dance from the technical theories of kinesiology to the theatricalilty of a performance. With its lack of emotional encounters, some have classified Brown's work as unisex dance. However, while personality is not important in her work, her peices by no means lack emotion. Contained in her choreography is the beauty of looking at movement in as pure a form as possible. Brown's emotion lies in unfolding the natural awareness of movement in space and time. But having microscopically eyeballed the electrons and protons of individual dance movements, Brown then wanted to put the atoms of dance back together to explore sequences of movement. This she accomplished in her three pieces entitled *Accumulation, Primary Accumulation,* and *Group Accumulation,* developing sentences of movement by adding motions one to another until an entire sequence was established. This series is typical of Brown's creation of work in cycles, exploring movement ideas over the course of three dances.

Originally rejecting all traditional trappings of costumes, sets, and music Brown transported the theatricality of dance to a new level. She developed her sense of theater by providing challenges to her dancers, her audience and to dance itself. A good example of how all three are combined into one piece is *The Falling Duet* where she and another dancer took turns falling—trying to outdo each other. The dancers were prodded into creating ever new ways of doing the same move and the audience had to seek the thread of dance in this competition as the definition of dance itself was pushed to new limits.

Early in her career she defined the essence of a dancer in *Rulegame 5.* Performers followed along five paths marked out by masking tape and signifying five different levels; in each level, the performers followed an activity, their stance ranging from erect to prone, making necessary adjustments by talking to each other. In a pioneering site-specific work, aptly titled *Roof Piece,* Brown tested, among other things, the impact of the environment on dance. She scheduled a performance to take place on the rooftops over 12 blocks in New York City in 1971, with one dancer initiating movement and being followed by the dancer on the nearest rooftop with as little distortion as possible. In 1979 she began a series of large-scale theatrical productions, collaborating with prominent artists from the fields of visual arts and music. These dances, which transform the traditional stage space, were created with such artists as Robert Rauschenberg, Donald Judd, Laurie Anderson, Fujiko Nakaya, Robert Ashley, Alvin Curran, Nancy Graves, and John Cage. In 1994 Brown did the nearly unthinkable in her solo *If you couldn't see me*—instead of facing the audience, she performed the entire piece with her back to them. *M.O.,* the first work in Brown's Music Cycle, embraced the complex poly-rhythms of Bach's *Musical Offering* while developing an intricate structure of its own. It was followed by *Twelve Ton Rose,* with music from Anton Webern's *Opus Nos. 5,7, and 28,* and, in 1988, Brown's most ambitious endeavor in this cycle—choreographing and directing a new production of Monteverdi's *L'Orfeo.*

Choreographers usually reveal their individual likes and dislikes with bits and pieces of their personality strewn throughout their works of art. In looking at Trisha Brown's collection, there is a mind filled with insatiable curiosity, attempting to solve the riddle of the internal power of movement. Brown's work lets us peek at a soul of an adventurer motivated by a passion for logic and reason.

—Cynthia Roses-Thema

BROWNE, Rachel

American-born dancer, choreographer, company director, and educator based in Canada

Born: Ray Minkoff, 16 November 1934, in Philadelphia. **Education:** Girls' High School and Sholem Aleichem Folk Shul; studied piano at the Curtis Institute and Ballet; in New York, studied with Benjamin Harkavy, Alfredo Corvino, Robert Joffrey, and Antony Tudor in New York. **Family:** Married to Don Browne; three daughters. **Career:** Danced with Ryder-Frankel Dance Company, 1954-56, Royal Winnipeg Ballet, 1957-61; first choreography created 1964; founder, Contemporary Dancers, 1972; toured Canada and the United States extensively, including appearances at Jacob's Pillow, Delacorte Festival, and Wolf Trap; founder, School of Contemporary Dancers, 1964; National Choreographic Seminar, Banff School of Fine Arts, with Robert Cohan and Todd Bolander, 1980; resigned as artistic director Winnipeg Contemporary Dancers, 1983; artist-in-residence, York University, 1987-88; first full-evening work, *Toward Light,* 1994; adviser and assessor for Canada Council, Ontario Arts Council, Manitoba Arts Council, Chalmers Choreographic. **Awards:** Clifford E. Lee Choreographic Award; more than a dozen Canada Council Grants, 1967-90, including a 1989 Senior Arts Grant, and 1990 Media Projects in Dance Grant; awards from

Manitoba Arts Council beginning 1986; YWCA "Woman of the Year" for contribution to Winnipeg's cultural life, 1977; Jean A. Chalmers Award in Choreography, 1995; Order of Canada, 1997.

Works (with the Winnipeg Contemporary Dancers and premiered in Winnipeg unless otherwise noted)

1964	*Odetta's Songs and Dances* (mus. Odetta), remounted 1971
1967	*Anerca* (mus. Varèse, Webern, and Inuit chants, read by Renee Jamieson), remounted 1972
1968	*Where the Shining Trumpets Blow* (mus. Mahler)
1969	*Variations* (mus. Bach), solo
1970	*Rhythming* (mus. Billy Graham), solo
1972	*Blues & Highs* (mus. Laura Nyro), solo
1974	*Contrasts* (mus. Bartók)
1975	*The Woman I Am* (mus. Paul Horn, poetry by Dorothy Livesay, read by Renee Jamieson)
1976	*Interiors* (mus. Jim Donahue, lyrics after Dorothy Livesay), duet
1978	*The Other* (mus. Ravel, poetry by Dorothy Livesay and Adrienne Rich), solo
1979	*Solitude* (mus.Brahms), duet
1981	*Dreams* (text: dancer's dreams), from a sketch made at 1980 National Choreographic Seminar, Banff School of Fine Arts
	Haiku (mus. Owen Clarke), duet
1982	*M.L.W.* (mus. Mary Lou Williams), solo
1983	*Shalom* (mus. Bach), solo
1985	*Camping Out*, choreographed with Murray Darroch and Tedd Robinson (mus. Liszt), solo
1987	*Old Times Now* (mus. Almeta Speaks), solo
	In a Dark Time the Eye Begins to See (mus. Vangelis, Pachelbel)
1989	*Sunset Sentences* (mus. Barber, Diana McIntosh)
1990	*My Romance* (mus. Almeta Speaks), solo
	Continuum, (mus. Bach)
	Fine, Thank You! (mus. Odetta)
1991	*Freddy* (mus. Kurt Weill), solo, Founders Studio, Royal Winnipeg Ballet, Winnipeg
	Pat's Bach (mus. Bach), solo, Winchester Street Theatre, Toronto
1992	*Dream Rite* (mus. Diana McIntosh), INDE Festival, Toronto
	Sharonblue (mus. Cole Porter), solo, Toronto
	Mouvement (mus. Xolotol), solo
1993	*Three Haiku* (mus. Xolotol), solo
1994	*K.J.4* (mus. Keith Jarrett)
	Toward Light (mus. Bach, Ann Southam)
1995	*Re-tuning, or The Great Canadian Hoedown* (mus. Ann Southam)
1996	*Six Messages* (mus. Ann Southam), School of Contemporary Dancers, Winnipeg
	Edgelit (mus. Ann Southam), solo

Publications

On BROWNE: articles—

Anderson, Carol, "Rachel Browne: Dancing Toward the Light," *Canadian Dance Studies 2,* York University, Toronto, Ontario, 1997.

———, "Rachel Browne," *101 from the Encyclopedia of Theatre Dance in Canada,* Dance Collection Danse Press/es, Toronto, 1997.

Brownell, Kathryn, "Toronto Dance Festival," *Dance in Canada,* 1979.

Review of *Anerca, Dance in Canada* 4, 1975.

"Noticeboard," *Dance in Canada* 14, 1977-78.

Enright, Robert, "Contemporary Dancers: A Prairie Lament Becomes a Song of Hope," *Dance in Canada* 34, 1982.

Forzley, Richard, "Contemporary Dancers Canada: New Directions," *Dance in Canada* 44, 1985.

Good, Jacqui, "Contemporary Dancers," *Dance in Canada* 38, 1983-84.

———, "Dance-Maker: The Turbulent and Moving Times of Rachel Browne," *Border Crossings* 8, 1989.

McCracken, Melinda, "A 30th Anniversary in Winnipeg" in *Dance Collection Danse, The News* 36, 1994.

Singen, Kevin, "Contemporary Dancers," *Dance in Canada* 16, 1978.

Stringer, Muriel, "Contemporary Dancers," *Dance in Canada* 31, 1982.

*   *   *

Influential as a creator, teacher, and a singular moral force in Canadian dance, Rachel Browne has been a member of this country's dance community since coming to Canada to join the Royal Winnipeg Ballet. Honest, dogged, political, feminist, she forged Winnipeg's Contemporary Dancers, Canada's first modern dance company, out of the wintry Manitoba prairie. Along the difficult path she has followed as a director, choreographer, and dancer, Browne reinvented herself as a modern dancer and creator, and has evolved to be Canada's senior woman choreographer. She has honed her work to a spare, elemental eloquence which speaks of her feminist convictions and her passion for wonderful music and poetry.

Browne was born Ray Minkoff on 16 November 1934 in Philadelphia, the child of Russian emigre parents. She recalls an indulged childhood, being taken to music lessons and dancing after she saw a ballerina at the age of six and insisted on dancing that way. Formative influences included Antony Tudor, who came as a guest to Philadelphia. She recalled his direction as sophisticated and subtle, as he looked to draw out ethereal movement qualities from students on whom he was setting *La Sylphide.*

Fighting what, by her own definition, was a less than perfect physique for classical ballet, Browne determined to become a ballet dancer. The day she graduated from high school she moved to New York City, where she supported her studies with a series of typing jobs. She studied intensively with Benjamin Harkavy, to whose exquisite musical taste she attributes her own high standards of musicality in classes. She recalls his clarity of attention to organic alignment and the beautiful, unmannered movement phrases he invented. Browne was involved with a group of dancers calling themselves the New Century Dancers, who were committed to creating and to being politically enlightened. She performed with the Ryder-Frankel company, accompanying them on gruelling tours. Browne also studied at the New School for Social Research, where she met Don Browne, who would later become her husband. Despite her constant, obsessive practice, Browne realized finally that she was not going to achieve her ideal of dancing classical roles in New York City. At Harkavy's invitation, she accompanied her teacher to Winnipeg in 1957, where he directed the Royal Winnipeg Ballet for a year.

Browne left the ballet at the age of 26. She had married at 18, and her husband, and the prevailing social mores, said that a woman of her age should be home with children. Rachel and Don Browne adopted two daughters, and had one of their own. Browne put aside her beloved work and dutifully stayed home to be a mother. Before long, miserable, she was watching rehearsals at the Royal Winnipeg Ballet, and soon teaching for the Lhotka Ballet Studio.

She began to choreograph. Her first work, *Odetta's Songs and Dances* (1964), started as a solo. She realized that the movement coming out of her was fresh, earthy, modern dance. Suffering the loss of her identity as a ballet dancer had somehow broken her obsessive devotion to classical ballet. The *Odetta* dance expanded to become a simple, folk-like celebration. Its sunny harmony reflected an ideal of dance and an innocence which were to earn the young choreographer accolades with audiences, and cause her great grief in the development of her company.

Winnipeg Contemporary Dancers came into being easily. Performances were sought after. Browne was advised however, that Winnipeg, a middle-sized Prairie city which already had a ballet company could not sustain another dance company. She stayed, and the company has thrived in Winnipeg.

In the early years of the company Rachel Browne was the chief director, teacher, creator, booking agent, fund-raiser, and dancer. She was adamant that the company be a repertory company and was philosophically committed to presenting a varied and entertaining mix of styles on the company's programs. The company became an important commissioning vehicle, staging work by emergent Canadian choreographers including Karen Jamieson, Paula Ravitz, Judith Marcuse and Jennifer Mascall. The company mounted work by American choreographers including Cliff Keuter, José Limón, Lynn Taylor-Corbett, Dan Wagoner, Bill Evans and others. Browne made yearly trips to New York, studying Limón and Graham techniques, bringing home her new knowledge to expand and deepen the range of the company's dancers. Support for the company was based, in the early days, on her own qualities as a dancer.

As dance evolved in the country, the modern dance of Canada's earliest days began to pale beside the risky theatricality of new dance in Montreal. The feeling festered in Winnipeg's Contemporary Dancers that Rachel Browne's vision could not sustain her position as artistic director. Bitter disagreement with the board of directors and the dancers in her company eventually led Browne to step down as artistic director in 1983. Since that time she has maintained a shifting relationship with the company, where she is acknowledged a founding artistic director. At times she has conducted successful fundraising campaigns to support the company's ongoing vitality. The school she began in 1972 continues to be esteemed as one of a small number of excellent centres of contemporary dance training in Canada.

Leaving her administrative duties freed Browne to choreograph. Early on, her work was based in the structures and harmony of her training. She has always shown a fondness for passionate poetry, particularly that of Dorothy Livesay, and had a profound relationship with her great music. Her feminism too is a guiding force, evident in her works, notably *Haiku* and *The Woman I Am*.

After leving the Contemporary Dancers, Browne became interested in stripping everything non-essential from movement. She created and presented work in silence. Since 1987 she has presented evenings of her own choreography. Her works *Mouvement* and *Four Haiku* are very different from her earlier work. Instinctual, animal-like movement, images of reaching and grasping, breaking through, rough gestures, movement in its own time, still and spare,

characterize her new creation. She is interested in intangibles, in subtle nuances of emotion and meaning. Women's lives and expression are her subject, grounded in her own long path of motherhood, of lonely responsibility and rigourous artistic challenges, in her deeply held political convictions.

In 1995 Rachel Browne presented her first evening-length work, *Toward Light*. It was performed by eleven women of varying ages, including Browne herself. Recently she has been affected by the lambent clarity and probing curiosity of contemporary Canadian composer Ann Southam's music. *Toward Light* marked the beginning of their collaboration. Browne's newer works—*Six Messages* and *Edgelit*, both created in 1996, show a certain refinement, a movement toward a new phase following her intense preoccupation with paring away everything but the deep root of the urge to move.

Browne feels compelled to continue to create. Her long-enduring passion for dance has liberated her voice. Committed to her art, she is an important model to many young Canadian dancemakers. She has encouraged emerging creators. Among these are Ruth Cansfield, Tedd Senmon Robinson, who became a later artistic director of Winnipeg's Contemporary Dancers, and Gaile Peturrson-Hiley. She has inspired seasoned performers with the creation of roles which challenge their mature understanding. She continues to teach, choreograph and advise in the School of Contemporary Dancers, and has created works for the Canadian Children's Dance Theatre, for Patricia Fraser and Davida Monk.

—Carol Anderson

BRUMACHON, Claude

French dancer, choreographer, and company director

Born: 2 May 1959 in Rouen. **Education:** At 13 years, entered the Fine Arts school and studied dance for five years. **Career:** Dancer, Ballet de la Cité, 1978-80; worked with Christine Gérard (Arcor), 1980-81; founded choreographic research group with Benjamin Lamarche; first choreography was in Susan Buirge's workshops, *Biographie* with Marie-Pascal Lescaut; first independent choreography, national and international tour, 1981; danced in Karine Saporta's company and founded a second choreographic research group with Lamarche and Brigitte Farges, 1982; founder, Rixes company, 1984; first European tour, 1986; staged *Féline* (Feline), Paris Opéra, 1989; Asian tour, 1991; director, Centre Chorégraphique National de Nantes, officially opened 5 May 1992; African tour (Nigeria, Reunion Island, Namibia), 1994; Philippines, 1995. **Awards:** 16th Bagnolet International Dance Competition Award; Audience Award; Seine Saint Denis Award and Third Jury's Award for *Atterissage de Corneilles sur l'Autoroute du Sud*, 1984; Joinville-le-Pont "Forum de Danse" (Dance Forum) Competition Award for Best Contemporary Creation for *Oc le Narquois et Oriane l'Effraie*, 1984; Cointreau Award; J.B.F. Award for the Best Musical Creation; Bonnie Bird Award (London Laban Center); Villa Medicis Award for *Texane*, 1988; Ministry of Foreign Affairs grants to choreograph in Chile, South Africa, and Hungary.

Roles

From 1978-80, numerous roles for Ballet de la Cité, and *Hypnotic circus* for Karine Saporta, 1982.

Works

1981   *Duo* (Duo), duet Claude Brumachon/Benjamin Lamarche
1982   *Niverolles duo du col*, duet Brumachon/Lamarche, Paris
1983   *Il y a des engoulevents sur la branche d'à côté* (*There Are Some Nightjars on the Next Branch*), Paris
        Epervière (*Sparrowhawk*), solo for Frédérique André
1984   *Attérissage de corneilles sur l'Aatoroute du sud* (*The Landing of Crows on the Southern Motorway*) (mus. Christophe Zurfluh), Rixes, created for the 16th Bagnolet International Dance Competition
        Nyroca Furie (mus. Zurfluh), Rixes, Forts Aubervilliers
        La tristesse des pingouins dans l'Arctique (*The Sadness of the Penguins in the Arctic*) (mus. Zurfluh), duet, Brumachon and Véronique Dupont
        Le Sirli de Béjaïa (*Béjaïa's Sirli*), created for the Jeune Ballet de France, Paris
1985   *Oc le Narquois et Oriane l'Effraie* (*Oc the Sardonic and Oriane the Scared*), (mus. Zurfluh), Rixes, Abbaye des Prémontrés, Pont à Mousson
1986   *Le roncier où songe l'imante pie-grièche* (*The Brambles Where the Magpie Lover Daydreams*) (mus. Zurfluh), Rixes, Rennes
        La dérive des fous à pieds bleus (*The Drift of the Blue-Footed Fools*) (mus. Zurfluh), duet, Rixes, American Center, Paris
        Vagabond des bastides (*Vagabond of the Mansions*) (mus. Zurfluh, based on Vivaldi's *Nisi Dominus*), solo with Larmache, Rixes, New-Morning, Paris
1987   *Attila et Nana les moineaux friquets*, (*Attila and Nana of the Sparrows*) (mus. Zurfluh), M.A.C. Créteil
        Les Querelles de harfangs (*The Quarrels of Owls*), created for the Jeune Ballet de France, Paris
        Complainte du Gerfaut (*Gerfaut's Lament*), for students of the CNDC, Angers
1988   *Texane* (mus. Zurfluh), Rixes, Saint Quentin en Yvelines
        Bricolage Secret (*Secret Tinkering*), for school children, Evry
        Le piedestal des vierges (*The Virgins' Pedestal*) (mus. Zurfluh), Rixes, Lancelot du lac Festival
        Naufragé (*Shipwrecked*), for Laban Center students, London
1989   *Féline* (mus. Christine Groult), creation for the G.R.C.O.P., Centre Georges Pompidou, Paris
        Folie (*Madness*) (mus. Zurfluh), Rixes, Aubusson
        Le chapelier travaille du chapeau (*The Hatter is Going Mad*), for school children, Evry
1990   *L'enfant et les sortilèges* (*The Child and the Magic Spells*), created for the Ballet de l'Opéra de Nantes
1991   *Eclats d'Absinthe* (*Absinth's Slivers*) (mus. Zurfluh), Rixes, Chapelle des Capucins, Paris
        Fauves (*Wildcats*) (mus. Zurfluh), Rixes, Nantes Festival
        La Complainte du Gerfaut (*Gerfaut's Lament*), recreated for Ballet de l'Opéra du Rhin
1992   *Alice*, for school children, Nantes
        Lame de fond (*Groundswell*) (mus. Groult), Aix-en-Provence Dance Festival
        Les funambules du désir (*The Tightrope Walkers of Desire*), for Jeune Ballet de France and the Philippines Ballet, Manila
        Les Indomptés (*The Untamed*), duet for Jeune Ballet de France, Paris

Vertige, duet for the C.N.S.M. of Lyon
Les Déambulations de Lola (*Lola's Strolls*), duet, Brumachon and Valérie Soulard, Paris
Exceptional déambulatoire performance, C.C.N.N., in Rudas bath of Budapest and Municipal bath of Bratislava
1993   *Nina, ou la voleuse d'esprit*, "déambulatoire" (*Nina, or the Theft of Spirit, "Strolling"*) (mus. Bruno Billaudeau), C.C.N.N., Fine Arts Museum of Nantes
        Emigrants (mus. Zurfluh), C.C.N.N., Saint-Nazaire
        Les Amants gris (*The Grey Lovers*) (mus. Berlioz), for the C.N.S.M., Paris
1994   *Bohèmes-Hommes* (*Bohemian Men*), (mus. Billaudeau), C.C.N.N., Studio Jacques Garnier
        Les Avalanches (mus. Zurfluh), C.C.N.N., La Réunion
1996   *Les Larmes des dieux* (*The Cries of the Gods*), Franco-Nigerian creation (mus. Zurfluh), Lagos
        Una vita (*One Life*), (mus. Billaudeau), C.C.N.N., Couëron
        Icare (mus. Billaudeau), solo, C.C.N.N., Avignon's Festival
1997   *Bohèmes-Femmes* (*Bohemian Women*) (mus. Billaudeau), C.C.N.N., Théâtre des Abbesses, Paris
        Los ruegos (*The Prayers*) (mus. Billaudeau), for Chilean dancers, Santiago del Chili, La Florida Municipality
        Une Aventure extraordinaire (mus. Billaudeau), C.C.N.N. and Théâtre de l'Olivier, Istres
        Le Magicien d'Oz (mus. Billaudeau), C.C.N.N., Théâtre Graslin, Nantes
        La Blessure (*The Injury*) (mus. Billaudeau), duet for Marie-Claude Pietragalla and Lamarche, Festival de Sète
        Les Nuits perdues (*The Lost Nights*) (mus. Billaudeau), for the Raatikko Ballet of Helsinki, Finland
1998   *Dandy*, duet for Brumachon and Véronique Redoux, Théâtre des Abbesses, Paris
        Humains dîtes-vous! (*Human You Say!*) (mus. Billaudeau), C.C.N.N. and La Coursive, La Rochelle
        Déambulatoire autour de Kandinsky! (*Strolling around Kandinsky*) (mus. Billaudeau), C.C.N.N., Fine Arts Museum of Nantes
        Déambulatoire humains dîtes-vous! (*Strolling: Human You Say!*) (mus. Billaudeau), C.C.N.N., Anne de Bretagne de Nantes Castle

*   *   *

Born in Rouen in 1959, Claude Brumachon studied fine arts before starting a dance career in the Ballets de la Cité in 1979. In 1981 he founded a research group in choreography with Benjamin Lamarche; together they created their first duet *Niverolles duo du col* in 1982. Brumachon danced in the companies of Karine Saporta, Susan Buirge, and Christine Gérard, while Lamarche also danced with Saporta as well as in the companies of Philippe Decoufle and Daniel Larrieu.

Establishing his own company Les Rixes (The Fights) three years later, Brumachon was appointed as director of the Centre Chorégraphique National de Nantes in 1992. Since then he has been invited as an artist to the Philippines, La Réunion (Indian Ocean), South Africa, Hungary and Chili. From 1983 to 1987, Brumachon's company was in its "bird era." During this period, the names of works involved birds in a poetic or metaphorical fashion, i.e. 1983's

Epervières, 1984's *Atterrissage de corneilles sur l'autoroute,* an award-winner in the 16th Bagnolet International Dance Competition, *La tristesse des pingouins dans l'Arctique, Le roncier où songe l'aimante pie-grièche, Attila et Nana les moineaux friquets,* and *Les Querelles de harfangs,* both in 1987. This topic arose again in Benjamin Lamarche's solo choreography *Icare solo* in 1996.

Continuing with the series, some of Brumachon's works were created to be performed outside of theaters—like the *deambulatorie* (strolling) series which began with 1992's *Les déambulations de Lola,* followed by two pieces in 1993: *Nina ou la voleuse d'esprit,* performed in the Nantes Museum of Fine Arts, and *Emigrants,* performed at the Saint-Nazaire Submarine Base. *Una Vita* had to be performed in the street, while in 1998 *Déambulatoire autour de Kandinsky* was performed in the Nantes Museum of Fine Arts and *Déambulatoire humains dîtes-vous!* was performed in the Castle of Anne de Bretagne.

Human feelings, the complex universe of human behaviour and internal tensions, conflicts, and fragilities are the driving forces of Brumachon's choreography. The exaltation of his dancers' bodies is visible in a very athletic, energetic, and sometimes spectacular movement where dancers are manhandled to highlight their articulation and muscular definition. Bodies are drawn together and piled up throughout Brumachon's works.

Le piedestale des vierges, from 1988, evoked medieval sculpture and notions of romance in questioning modern male-female relationships. In the same year Brumachon created *Texane,* awarded the Bonnie Bird Prize from the Laban Center in London and as well as a prize from the 20th Bagnolet International Dance Competition, based on his childhood memories; he was the child who observed the proletarian world of adults. The first version of *Bohème* choreographed for a male quartet retraced the intimacy of men's private relationships with each other. The counterpart of this choreography, created in 1996, was for a female quartet. Inspired by the writings of the 18th-century libertines, Brumachon created *Les avalanches* in 1994, while *Lame de fond* from 1992 expressed the unspoken everyday feelings in the daily meeting of two couples.

The human condition was honored in works created during intercultural meetings; in *Les larmes des dieux,* a 1996 Franco-Nigerian creation, demigod dancers witnessed break-ups, contradictions, rituals, and love between France and Nigeria; *Los ruegos* in 1997, created for Chilean dancers, concerned a family's separation and feelings of helplessness; *Humains dites vous?* in 1998 was based on the religious wars of the 16th century. Brumachon not only choreographs for his own company but also for the Jeune Ballet de France, including *Le Sirli de Béjaïa, Les Querelles de harfangs, Les Funanbules du désir,* and *Les Indomptés.* For the students of the Centre National de Danse Contemporaine d'Angers he created *La Complainte du Gerfaut* in 1987, which was recreated in 1991 for the Ballet of the Rhin Opera.

—Edwige Dioudonnat

BUIRGE, Susan

American-born dancer, choreographer and company director based in France

Born: 1940 in Minneapolis. **Education:** Studied law and communications before dance; attended Connecticut College; graduated, Juilliard School of Music, 1963; studied with Alwin Nikolais and Murray Louis at the Henry Street Playhouse. **Career:** Dancer and soloist, Nikolais Dance Theater, 1963-68; dancer, Murray Louis Dance Company, 1963-68; relocated to France, 1970; created Dance-Theater-Experience, Paris; founder, Dance Theater Susan Buirge, 1975 (later changed to Susan Buirge Project); artistic consultant, Aix Dance Festival, 1980-86; retired as a dancer, 1990; first choreographer as a representative of S.A.C.D. (Society of Drama Authors and Composers), 1992-95; artist-in-residence, Japan, 1992-93; artist-in-residence, Arsenal Theater, Metz, France, beginning 1997.

Roles

1964	*Sanctum* (Nikolais)
	Junk Dances (Louis)
1965	*Tower* (Nikolais)

Other roles include: Further performances of works by both Nikolais and Louis from 1963-68 at the Henry Street Playhouse in New York.

Works

1962	*Trilogy*
1968	*Televanilla* (mus. Glass)
1976	*From West to East*
1977	*Imprints*
1978	*Lapse*
1982	*Charge allaire*
1983	*En Ac et en Ille*
1985	*Sky Fragment*
1987	*Suzanne in Bath*
1988	*Ephese's Travel*
1990	*Big Exile*
1994	*Kin-Iro no Kaze no Kanata,* with Ma to Ma Group
1996	*Ubusuna*
	Mizu Gaki

Publications

By BUIRGE—

From East to West—Memories 1989-1993, Bois d'Orion, 1996.

On BUIRGE—

Michel, Marcelle, *Dance of the 20th Century,* Paris, 1995.

*   *   *

Susan Buirge was born in Minneapolis in 1940. She discovered dance as a college student while taking classes in communications and law, and soon began to train in the technique of José Limón, Merce Cunningham, and Martha Graham.

Buirge created her first choreography, *Trilogy,* in 1962, while studying at the Juilliard School of Music, from which she graduated the next year, 1963. After graduation, Buirge joined the company of Alwin Nikolais, staying for five years. At the same time, she was also a member of the Murray Louis Dance Company, which shared the performance space at the Henry Street Playhouse. In 1970, thanks to her father's travels and the many tales he spun, Buirge set out for France, and later decided to settle there. She began teaching and founded her own company, Dance Theater Susan Buirge, in 1975 (later renamed Susan Buirge Project).

Buirge's early choreographic works were heavily influenced by her association with Nikolais, but she soon found her own style, while maintaining Nikolais' great fluidity of movement. Buirge also worked her way to a more abstract style, close to American minimalism in form and movement, and has been creating avant-garde dances for the French dance landscape.

Buirge began to influence future French choreographers through her knowledge and technique; her philosophy of movement became linked with the mind—as the mind created strong images, Buirge found that movement was automatically dictated and voluntarily reduced to the minimum. Each of her dances sought a personal truth, which were easily read in each of her works. She also tried to make her dancers respond to the intellectual side of dance in addition to its more obvious physical part. Many of France's next generation of choreographers followed Buirge's style of dance, which also included courses in improvisation, as the new and exciting approach to thinking and performing. Buirge had a profound impact on the latest wave of French modern dance that emerged at the beginning of the 1980s, including such artists as Christine Gèrard, Maite Fossen, Santiago Sempere, and François Raffinot, who were among her former dancers.

Buirge's choreography has two characteristic traits—first, she works with visual artists (like Jean-Luc Poivret) and videographers (like Serge Bourteline), and was among the earliest choreographers to introduce multimedia elements into her dances, as in *Televanilla*, in 1968. This solo, set to music by Philip Glass, added both film and video to choreography at a time when such combinations were unheard of in France. Secondly, Buirge also began to perform in unusual places, years before the term "site-specific" was coined or fashionable. Her *En Ac et en Ille* was produced in the ruins of an 18th-century "folie," a sort of romantic small castle; another work, *Charge allaire*, was produced in the Aix-en-Provence airport.

Buirge's *Sky Fragment* represented another significant change in her choreographic path when she collaborated with writer Marianne Alphant to produce an autobiographical text, on which the dance was based. As writer Marcelle Michel wrote in *Dance of the 20th Century* in 1995, *Sky Fragment* contained "a special characteristic of new French dance: an abstraction covering emotion, but nourished and tinted by this emotion." Another Buirge work, *Big Exile*, from 1990, marked her last performance as a dancer. This solo, symbolic of her decades in dance—50 years old, with 30 years as choreographer, and 20 years in France—was inspired by her travels in Syria, Ethiopia, Greece, and India.

In the 1990s, after her retirement from active performing, Buirge took another career turn and began to concentrate on dance research and composition based on non-Western traditions. She began to work with Asian companies, like the Ma to Ma Group, during several residences abroad, including one at the Kujiyama Villa of Kyoto, Japan, in 1992 and 1993, which greatly flavored her later creative endeavors. Later in the decade, Buirge's choreography became centered around the poetry and rituals associated with Oriental imagery, and her most recent works, *Ubusana* and *Mizu Gaki*, have portrayed a very specific Oriental tradition—the four seasons—with the former representing winter and the latter spring. *Matomanoma*, another piece from this era, has been described as a sort of battle of wills between Japanese and French cultures. In

1997 Buirge was the artist-in-residence at the Arsenal Theater of Metz, France, using her gifts to educate students, teachers, and others to her unique perceptions of dance, both Western and non-Western, with an emphasis on Oriental imagery and poetry.

—Murielle Mathieu

BULL, Richard
American dancer, choreographer, and company director

Born: c. 1930 in Detroit, Michigan. **Education:** Wayne State University, Detroit, B.A.; New York University, M.A. in dance and the related arts; studied dance at Bennington College with William Bales and Ruth Currier; studied with Alfred Brooks, Maxine Munt, Erick Hawkins, Alwin Nikolais, Mary Anthony, Martha Graham, Pearl Lang, and Merce Cunningham. **Career:** Worked as a jazz pianist, New York City, 1950s; accompanist for dance classes at the New Dance Group, Juilliard School, Connecticut College, New York University as well as for Daniel Nagrin, Mary Anthony, Lucas Hoving, Bob Hamilton, and Martha Graham, New York City, 1950s; member of Munt/Brooks Dance Company, New York City and on tour; choreographed and danced in improvisations, 1960s; formed the New York Chamber Dance Group, 1960s; taught at New York University, late 1960s; chairman of the dance department of the State University College at Brockport, New York, 1970-78; co-founded the Warren Street Performance Loft and the Improvisational Dance Ensemble with Peentz Dubble and Cynthia Novack, New York City, 1978; group renamed the Richard Bull Dance/Theatre, 1983; created works for the Concert Dance Group of Boston, the Off-Track Dancers of St. Louis, and Margaret Beals; collaborated with photographer Douglas Quackenbush, filmmaker Bill Rowley, and German cybernetic sculptor Peter Vogel; musical collaborators included Skip LaPlante, Daniel Epstein, Jay Clayton, Ratzo Harris, Elliott Sharp, Duvid Smering, Lou Grassi, Jane Ira Bloom, and Joel Chadabe; choreographic work includes American premiere of John Osborne's *The World of Paul Slickey*, numerous works for students at New York University, and the major part of the repertoire of the New York Chamber Dance Group and the Richard Bull Dance/Theatre; served on the New York State Council of the Arts dance panel, the board of directors of the American Dance Guild, the Committee on Research in Dance, and executive committee of the New York State Dance Association.

Works

1965	*Conversations*
	Three*Place*One
	Suite Teens
1966	*How to Solve It*
	Progress Report
1967	*Imitations I & II*
	Revelations
	Chiaroscuro
1968	*War Games: Strategies, Tactics, Diversions and Delights*
	Thirteen Ways of Looking at a Blackbird
	Phorion
	Sanctuaries

1969   Mr. Blue
        People/Places/Things
        Analogues I & II
        Action Music II (section of evening-length work by Tom
            Johnson)
        Body Count
1970   Gallery
        The Centering Dance
        Making and Doing
        Domus
        Sing-Along Sun King
1971   The Bacchae
        The Hartwell Building can Dance
        Cousin Caterpillar
1972   Bedtime Story
        L'Histoire du Soldat
        Octandre
        Armistice
        Cycles
        In a Plastic Garden
        Hartwell Dances Again
        Five Handball Court Dances
        Introductions are in Order
        The Haircut: A Documentary Dance
        Space Games
        Suite Teens (revised)
        One Hand, Two Hands, Mouth
1973   The Gentle Dance
        Command Performance
        The Dance that Describes Itself
        Celebration City w/Jonathan Atkin
1973   9.16666666666666666666
        Opera Scenes
        The Many Dances Once Dance Dance
1974   Medieval Dances w/Dianne Woodruff
        The Dance that Describes Itself
        Hamburger (American Ritual, Part I, Part I; dir. Duvid
            Smering)
        Bowling for Dollars (American Ritual, Part II; dir. Smering)
        The Centering Dance (revised)
        The Barn Dance at 20 Adams Street: A Utilitarian Dance
            Event
        Variations on "The Barn Dance at 20 Adams Street"
        The Walking Dance
        Small Step, Giant Leap
        Feedback
        Overload
1975   Eight Dorian Dances
        The Counting Dance
        Thank You, Masked Man
        Visions
        The Tourist
        Etudes
        It's Gonna Rain (later performed as The Cosmic Egg)
        Just Improvising
        Masked Music
1976   A Jazz Dance
        I'm On My Way I and II
        Jesus' Blood
        The Longest Dance w/Cynthia Novack
        Bicentennial Vaudeville

        The Greek Dances
        Five Variations on "Ten Cents a Dance"
1977   Ambience
        The Dance That Describes Itself
        The Dance That Explains Itself
        Loft Dance
        Local New
1978   Interactions
        The Smithsonian Dances
        The Conspirators
        Crossovers
        Story Dance
        Making Contact
1979   Trilogy
        Prologue
        Slow Blues
        Solo Set
        Telltale
        Cityscape
        In This Place
        Suite
        La Parole
        Groupdance
1980   Recursion
        Three Sets (Strolling, Monkey Dance, Didactic Dalliance,
            Water Wheel)
        Relay: An Environmental Dance Work
        Onagainoff
        Soundings
        My Story
        The Sounding Wall: Ten Etudes and Fantasia
        Touring Dance
        Relay

Publications

On BULL: articles—

Jowitt, Deborah, review of The Dummy Dances, performed by the
    Richard Bull Dance/Theatre, Village Voice, 17 November 1992.
———, review of War Games: Strategies, Tactics, Diversions, and
    Delights, performed by the New York Chamber Dance Group,
    Village Voice, 20 June 1968.
Shaw, Alan J., review of The Barn Dance, choreographed by Rich-
    ard Bull, Dance Magazine, May 1977.

*   *   *

Richard Bull made his mark as a dancer and stager of improvisational movement pieces. During a long career, Bull has worked as a
dancer, teacher, and choreographer of dance theatre works. His
Richard Bull Dance/Theatre, based in lower Manhattan, has developed a repertoire of dances that work from movement structures,
which are performed differently each time they are presented in
concert. Writing in the Village Voice (17 November 1992) dance
critic Deborah Jowitt noted that although Bull's work is improvised, its solid structure gives it the appearance of being choreographed, with dancers often reacting spontaneously within a structure. In his performance notes for The Centering Dance, Bull stated
his intention: "In this dance you are working as a choreographer as
well as a performer, and must make yourself aware of what the

Richard Bull in 1983. Photograph © Johan Elbers.

other dancers are doing. . . . Talk your way through the dance; let us know what's happening inside your head. Keep the movement simple: do not get into gesture or elaborate locomotor patterns. The dance is primarily a spatial experience which builds on an aesthetic of relationship between performers and the various spatial centers within the performing area."

Bull's dances have been performed in lofts, in art galleries, on college campuses (*Hartwell Is Dancing*), and in vast public spaces such as the Xerox Square in Rochester, New York (*Celebration City*). Bull's troupe has included student dancers and members of the public. *The Longest Dance,* a 12-hour dance, was performed in the spring of 1976. While teaching at Brockport, Bull had his students present dances at various places on the campus and in the community. They paraded in public places, staked out dancing ground for themselves, and danced. His dances often included dialogue. *Hartwell Dances* takes its name from an evening of dances staged by Bull in and around the Hartwell Building on the Brockport campus. In *Celebration City,* the public was invited to take part in a multimedia event in the center of Rochester. The dancers, both company members and the public, were illuminated by several World War II searchlights. Background music was live and recorded. Bull invited anyone to join in and to come and go as they pleased. His idea was to turn the city over to the people. He even choreographed a set of dances to a worship service with the theme "The Cycles of the Seasons."

One of his most famous pieces, *The Barn Dance at 20 Adams Street,* is a concert work based on a piece Bull set on his student-dancers in the summer of 1974. In that event, the barn in Bull's backyard was painted by a large cast of dancer-painters. The con-

cert version of *The Barn Dance* uses a videotape of the original event in counterpoint to a condensed reworking of the original movements. The audience watches as the on-screen dancers carry buckets and ladders, while dancers in the studio act out a ladder by forming ranks and crawling over each other. The dancers call out the tools of the trade: brush, sandpaper, etc. The dancers simulate the actual painting of the barn by painting the video screens. A score by Lou Grassi accompanied each dance. Critic Alan J. Shaw found the work was undermined by its pretentiousness and fascination with technological wizardry. "While it tries to establish a new relation between 'work' and 'artwork,'" Shaw wrote, the *Barn Dance* "gets trapped in the very dichotomies it seeks to transcend."

Other works such as *Jesus' Blood* and *The Cosmic Egg* explored strong spatial imagery to create their effects. Both dances used minimalistic structures as a setting for the movement. *The Cosmic Egg* had an original music score performed by Duvid Smering on horns and Richard Bull on piano.

Bull's improvisations included detailed instructions, or scenarios, for the dancers, as well as visual schematics on how he imagined the piece evolving. This is the way his written schematic opens for *Making and Doing*: "The basic idea. . .is to work with the repeats and false-starts which are built into the text and the choreography. . .and an actual rehearsal situation. All of the seemingly false starts and returns to the beginning which occur in Act I are seen, in Act II, to be part of a longer choreographic sequence. Act III is intended to frighten the audience into thinking we are beginning all over again, and that the piece will never end. Which, indeed, it may not." The dance was designed for an open-theatre presentation, using a cleared space surrounded by audience members. It has been performed many times by various groups. Don McDonagh noted that *Making and Doing* was "an imaginative blend of rehearsal dance materials."

While teaching at New York University, Bull devised one of his most potent improvisations, and his first major work. In *War Games: Strategies, Tactics, Diversions, and Delights* (1968), Bull used nine female students from the New York University High School Dance Workshop to supplement his own New York Chamber Dance Group dancers. Writing in the *Village Voice* (1968), critic Deborah Jowitt called the dance "astringent, vulgar, funny, and bursting with energy." This work presents the horrors of war as they might be described by the host of a television variety show. Speaking through a microphone, Bull sends bandaged dancers out into the audience, calls the audience's attention to the falls of a dancer on crutches, or assures the audience that dancers struck down by fake bullets are not really dead. The "carnage" is accompanied by a background of patriotic songs, nature sounds, and rifle fire. Some of the choreography was Bull's, some was devised by the students. Jack Anderson, writing in the August 1968 edition of *Dance Magazine,* found *War Games* to have more power than Bull's other works "perhaps because it was the only one whose theme seemed to engage him personally and passionately."

Some dance critics found Bull's work overly academic. Robert J. Pierce, writing in the *Soho Weekly News,* described Bull's works as "not too-demanding technically, they used large numbers of dancers. The movement stresses quality rather than actual steps. Structure tended to be clear, simple, and limited to a few compositional elements." In *Jesus' Blood* (1977), Bull had his dancers improvise a movement which begins in a cluster and slowly revolves. The dancers look at each member of the audience, which is seated in the round. The effect was like having the stage, rather than the dancers, revolve. *The Cosmic Egg* (1977) also featured a cluster of dancers. Each of 12 dancers devised three phrases of movement. Each of the movements has a different length. Each phrase was repeated a certain number of times. The cluster widened into a circle, revolved, then spiralled back into a cluster. *Visions* (1977) deals with the concept of different levels and is also about running and blocking movements. The final section explores the nature of empty space without dancers to fill it.

Writing in the 1978 issue of *American Dance Guild Newsletter,* Lillie F. Rosen found *Visions* had "some good ideas but was so brief that you gained little impression of the goings on." Rosen advised Bull to work his ideas through so as to extract all their potential. *Five Variations on "Ten Cents a Dance"* found Bull using the Rodgers and Hart song as sung by five different singers. Dancers in evening dress flirted with customers in what was supposed to be a cheap dance hall, while other dancers in a conga line repeated the same phrases. Rosen found the work poignant and nostalgic to a degree, but the attraction began to wane by the third repetition of the song.

Bull usually wrote the text for his improvisations. In *The Dance That Described Itself,* Bull had his dancers recite the following text as they performed the choreography: "I am the Dance. Hear me, gather round; I am the Dance. You will see me as I am, as I describe myself to you, as my dancers tell me through my movement."

Many of Richard Bull's improvisations are strange and disturbing. *The Dummy Dances* is one of these works. In it, Bull manipulates Cynthia Novack (his wife, also known as Cynthia Jean Cohen Bull) like a ventriloquist's dummy. The two exchange roles, however, as Cohen Bull urges Bull into *her* idea of his role. In her review of *The Dummy Dances* in the *Village Voice,* Deborah Jowitt (1992) noted that "the two wanted to explore every possible nuance of this troubling, unpleasant Pygmalion relationship . . . But the anger is redeemed by a real tenderness that makes the dance gripping and often very moving."

Over the years Bull has worked with a small group of dancers in carrying out his improvisations. The group included the late Cynthia Novack, Peentz Dubble, Vicki Kurtz, and David Brick. In 1995 Bull introduced dancers Kelly Donovan, Olasebikan Freeman, Meg Fry, and Aggie Postman. All had studied with Novack at Wesleyan University.

—Adriane Ruggiero

BURROWS, Jonathan

English dancer, choreographer, and company director

Education: Studied at the Royal Ballet School; attended the Gulbenkian International Choreographic Summer School. **Career:** Dancer, Royal Ballet in London, 1979-91; promoted to soloist, 1986; teacher of English folk dance (Royal Ballet School), 1979-84; dancer, Rosemary Butcher Dance Company on a project basis, from 1986; founded the Jonathan Burrows Group, (initially supported by the Royal Ballet), 1988; company independent since 1992. **Awards:** Ursula Moreton Choreographic Award, 1978; Frederick Ashton Choreographic Award and the Digital Dance Award, 1991; Prudential Award for Dance, 1995.

Roles

Royal Ballet: Magdaveya, Head Fakir in *La Bayedere* (Markarova/ Petipa); Ugly Sister in *Cinderella* (Ashton); Shy Boy in *The Con-* cert (Robbing); Capuchin (cr) and Ragenau in *Cyrano* (Bintley); the Doctor (cr) in *Different Drummer* (MacMillan); Alaskan Rag in *Elite Syncopations* (MacMillan); Stuart-Powell in *Enigma Variations* (Ashton); Widow Simone in *La Fille mal gardee* (Ashton); Elderly Client in *Manon* (MacMillan); Bratfisch in *Mayerling* (MacMillan); *Les Noces* (Nijinska); Nutcracker Prince and Herr Drosselmeyer in *The Nutcracker* (Petipa); Texan Kangaroo Rat in *'Still Life' at the Penguin Cafe* (Bintley); Wolf and Puss in Boots in *The Sleeping Beauty* (Petipa). Rosemary Butcher Dance Company: *After the Last Sky* (cr), *Flying Lines, Landings, Pause and Loss, Space Between, Traces,* and *Touch the Earth* (cr).

Works

1980	*With a Gaping Wide-Mouthed Waddling Frog* (mus. country dance tunes), solo, Riverside Studios, London
	Catch (mus. Douglas Gould), Sadler's Wells Royal Ballet, Exeter
	Listen (in silence), Extemporary Dance Company, Shaw Theatre, London
1981	*Just for Kicks,* London Contemporary Dance School, London
1982	*A Man at the Zoo,* Riverside Studios, London
	Cloister (mus. Edward Lambert), Spiral Dance Company
	Driving Rain, Riverside Studios, London
1983	*The Winter Play* (mus. Dudley Simpson), Sadler's Wells Royal Ballet, Birmingham
1986	*Hymns* (mus. traditional hymns), duet, Riverside Studios, London
	A Tremulous Heart Requires (mus. Nicholas Wilson), Riverside Studios, London
	Squash (mus. Nicholas Wilson), Riverside Studios, London
1988	*Hymns* (expanded version; mus. Wilson Simonal, traditional hymns, Bach, Chopin), Jonathan Burrows Group, The Place, London
1989	*dull morning* (originally *dull morning cloudy mild;* mus. Matteo Fargion), Jonathan Burrows Group, The Place, London
1990	*Stoics Part I* (mus. Johann Strauss Jr., Matteo Fargion, Mendelssohn), Jonathan Burrows Group, Riverside Studios, London
1991	*Stoics* (originally *Stoics 11;* mus. Mendelssohn, Bach, Curly Puttnam, Matteo Fargion, Johann Strauss Jr.), Jonathan Burrows Group, The Place, London
	Stoics Quartet (final quartet of *Stoics;* mus. Mendelssohn), Royal Ballet, Royal Opera House, London
1992	*Very* (mus. Matteo Fargion), Jonathan Burrows Group, The Place, London
1994	*Our* (mus. Matteo Fargion), Jonathan Burrows Group, The Place, London
1995	*Hands* (film; director, Adam Roberts; mus. Matteo Fargion), Jonathan Burrows, BBC/Arts Council Dance for the Camera series
	Blue Yellow (film; director, Adam Roberts; mus. Kevin Volans), Sylvie Guillem, BBC/RD Studio Productions/ France 2
1996	*The Stop Quartet* (mus. Matteo Fargion, Kevin Volans), Jonathan Burrows Group, Vooruit Arts Centre, Gent, Belgium

1997   *Walking/music* (mus. Kevin Volans), Frankfurt Ballet, Frankfurt

Publications

By BURROWS: articles—

With Chris de Marigny, "Burrows: Our Thoughts," *Dance Theatre Journal,* Spring/Summer, 1994.

On BURROWS: articles—

Hunt, Marilyn, "Jonathan Burrows: Laughter of Recognition," *Dance Magazine,* October 1993.

Levene, Louise, "By Royal Assent," *The Independent,* 13 April 1991.

Meisner, Nadine, "Closing in on Ballet?," *Dance Theatre Journal,* Autumn/Winter 1996.

Percival, John, "Moving Beyond Dance," *The Times,* 30 October 1992.

Sacks, Ann, "Adventures in Body Language," *The Independent on Sunday,* 18 October 1992.

Thorpe, Edward, "Talking to an Enigma," *Dance and Dancers,* June/July 1991.

Films and Videotapes

The Far End of the Garden (film), London, Beaulieu Films, BBC and Arts Council, 1991.

*   *   *

English choreographer Jonathan Burrows is not easily summed up. A product of the Royal Ballet School, he was a dancer with the Royal Ballet for 12 years; yet his choreography has rarely looked balletic. Taken into the company on the strength of his student pieces, during his tenure there he choreographed almost entirely for the modern dance arena. And yet his work is not neatly described in established modern or postmodern dance terms, perhaps because a strong initial influence on his style was English folk dance. In recent years, his work has shifted in tone and content, making it perhaps too soon to sum up his style at all. As he has from the start, Burrows continues to forge his own path.

Burrows began his ballet training with his mother in County Durham, in the north of England, before following his sister to the Royal Ballet School in 1970. There he studied English folk dance in addition to ballet and, in the Upper School, attended the composition class run by faculty member Richard Glasstone, and Kate Flatt, a modern dance choreographer who fueled his interest in modern and postmodern dance.

Burrows joined the Royal Ballet in 1979 as an "apprentice choreographer"—a vaguely defined, short-lived position—and as a member of the corps de ballet. (A noted character dancer, he became a soloist in 1986.) His works for the company number only two, however, both for the Sadler's Wells Royal Ballet. One of them, *The Winter Play* (1983), based on the traditional mummers play, featured reworkings of traditional morris and sword dances. Burrows taught English folk dance at the school in these early years, and the physicality of the technique—the stamping feet, the snapping movement phrases—has informed the movement style in much of his output.

From the beginning of his choreographic career, Burrows allied himself with the modern dance world, presenting work independently at Riverside Studios and choreographing for a few modern dance companies. In 1986 minimalist choreographer Rosemary Butcher asked him to dance in a retrospective of her works, and he has been a sometime member of her company since then. Butcher traces her lineage to the Judson Church movement, and Burrows also counts among his influences American postmoderns such as Trisha Brown and Steve Paxton, with whom he studied briefly.

After the initial flurry of activity in the early 1980s, Burrows took a hiatus from choreography, re-emerging with the duet *Hymns,* presented at the 1986 Dance Umbrella. An expanded version for five dancers was performed in 1988 by the newly formed Jonathan Burrows Group. The group operated under the auspices of the Royal Ballet, which provided financial and administrative support, although the dancers had to work in their spare time and the pieces were presented at The Place Theatre, a modern dance venue. In January 1992 Burrows and two regular dancers, Lynn Bristow and Deborah Jones, left the Royal, and the group became an independent company, funded by grants and awards. Having toured nationally while with the Royal, the group began to tour Europe as well.

Burrows' works since the company's formation fall roughly into two phases, although, on first encounter, each of the stage pieces seemed a departure from the last. Broadly speaking, the first four pieces can be said to deal with life outside the dance, the more recent pieces with its formal properties. The ambiguity of the former often made their meanings difficult to grasp. Movements could be read with either positive or negative attributes; the dancers' expressionless faces could make them seem detached from their actions. Burrows used this to effect in his most popular work, *Stoics* (1991), a look at the stoical English. The piece was both funny, as dancers remained unperturbed while manhandled and hoisted around in unbecoming positions, and unsettling, as their flailing limbs and stomping feet revealed the frustration and anger masked by the polite facades. Violence and humor ran in tandem in other pieces too. The wrestling holds and tackles of *Hymns* (1988) were part of its wry comments on the moralistic songs. The audience's laughter at the slapstick-like sequences in *Very* (1992) could also have been a nervous response to the piece's raw aggression.

Our (1994), the only work for his group in which Burrows has not danced, marked a transition toward abstraction although it too had emotional resonances, sometimes disturbing, sometimes luminous. In his current phase of work, Burrows seems primarily concerned with exploring structure, time, and space using a limited range of movement (which has moved away from his previous style). *The Stop Quartet* (1996) was a virtuosic display of rhythm and timing, with the dancers ceaselessly treading small, quick steps in counterpoint only to halt simultaneously. This contrast of movement and stillness was echoed by the music, which was interspersed with silence, and the design, with the criss-crossing lines on the floor leaving patches of darkness. *Blue Yellow* (1995), made for Sylvie Guillem's *Evidentia* film series, also had an intermittent format: the short segments of choreography, which the French ballet star danced in a room viewed from the doorway, were separated by blackouts, the music filtering in only occasionally. Reports from Germany indicate that this sparse, cerebral phase of work continues with *Walking/music* (1997) for the Frankfurt Ballet. Where Jonathan Burrows is heading, only time will tell. He undoubtedly will continue to defy summing up.

—Chris Jones

BUTCHER, Rosemary
British choreographer, company director, and educator

Born: 4 February 1947 in Bristol. **Education:** Dartington College of Arts, Devonshire, 1965-68; University of Maryland on a Whitney Foundation scholarship, 1968-69; studied in New York with Elaine Summers, Yvonne Rainer, and others, 1979-72. **Career:** Lecturer, Dartington College of Arts, Devonshire, 1969-70 and 1980-81, Dunfermline College, Scotland, 1973-74, Middlesex Polytechnic, 1974-76; founded the Rosemary Butcher Dance Company, 1976; company's first appearance at Dance Umbrella and the Dance at Dartington Festival, 1978; resident choreographer, Riverside Studios, London, 1977-78; dance advisory teacher for Camden and Westminster, London, 1990-93; lecturer, Kingsway College, London, 1993-94; lecturer, University of Surrey, 1994-97; visiting fellow of the Royal College of Art, London, 1995-97. **Awards:** Royal Society of Arts Award for *Landings,* 1977; GLAA Dance Award, 1985; *Time Out* Choreography Award, 1987.

Roles

1979	*Solo Duo*
1980	Solo, *Dance for Different Spaces*
1981	Solo, *Shell: Force Fields and Spaces*
1985	Solo, *Flying Lines*
1987	*Touch the Earth*
	Traces

Works

1974　*Uneven Time,* Scottish Ballet's Moveable Workshop, Edinburgh College of Art
　　　Multiple Event, Dance Theatre Commune, Stanhope Institute, London
1976　*Pause and Loss* (mus. Alan Lamb), Rosemary Butcher Dance Company (RBDC), Serpentine Gallery, London
　　　Landings (mus. Alan Lamb), RBDC, Serpentine Gallery, London
　　　Ground Line, solo for Maedee Dupres, Bermondsey Docklands, London
　　　Passage North East, RBDC, Arnolfini Gallery, Bristol
　　　Multiple Event, RBDC, Arnolfini Gallery, Bristol
1977　*Space Between,* RBDC, Riverside Studios, London
　　　White Field (mus. Colin Wood), RBDC, Riverside Studios, London
　　　Empty Signals (mus. Colin Wood), RBDC, Serpentine Gallery, London
　　　Anchor Relay, RBDC, Serpentine Gallery, London
1978　*Theme* (photography Darryl Williams), RBDC, Serpentine Gallery, London
　　　Suggestion and Action (spoken instructions Rosemary Butcher), RBDC, Acme Gallery, London
　　　Uneven Time, solo for Maedee Dupres, X6 Dance Space, London
　　　Touch and Go, RBDC, Middlesex Polytechnic
　　　Catch 5, Catch 6, RBDC, Battersea Arts Centre, London
1979　*Dances for Different Spaces* (mus. Jane Wells), RBDC, Riverside Studios, London

　　　Solo Duo, RBDC, Riverside Studios, London
　　　Landscape (mus. George Crumb), RBDC, Atlantic College, Glamorgan
1980　*Five-Sided Figure* (mus. Mark Turner, Jane Wells, Peter Wiegold; design Jon Groom), RBDC, Riverside Studios, London
　　　Six Tracks, RBDC, Dartington College of Art, Devon
1981　*Shell: Force Fields and Spaces* (mus. Jim Fulkerson; design Jon Groom), RBDC, Riverside Studios, London
　　　Spaces 4 (design Heinz-Dieter Pietsch), RBDC, ICA, London
1982　*Traces* (mus. Tom Dolby; design Heinz-Dieter Pietsch), RBDC, Riverside Studios, London
　　　Field Beyond the Maps (mus. Jim Fulkerson) solo for Sue MacLennan, Edinburgh Festival
1983　*The Site* (mus. Malcolm Clarke; design Heinz-Dieter Pietsch), RBDC, Riverside Studios, London
　　　Imprints (mus. Malcolm Clarke; design Heinz-Dieter Pietsch), RBDC, Riverside Studios, London
1984　*Night Mooring Stones* (mus. Max Easterly; film Jane Rigby), RBDC, Riverside Studios, London
1985　*Flying Lines* (mus. Michael Nyman; set Peter Noble), RBDC, Riverside Studios, London
1987　*Touch the Earth* (mus. Michael Nyman; design Heinz-Dieter Pietsch), RBDC, Whitechapel Art Gallery, London
1989　*After the Crying and the Shouting* (mus. Wim Mertens; design Ron Haselden), RBDC, ICA, London
　　　d1 (mus. Jim Fulkerson; design Zaha Hadid), RBDC, Royal Festival Hall, London
1990　*d2* (mus. Jim Fulkerson; design John Lyall), RBDC, Christ Church, Spitalfields, London
　　　3d (mus. Jim Fulkerson; design John Lyall), RBDC, Tramway Theatre, Glasgow
1992　*Of Shadows and Walls* (mus. Jim Fulkerson; film Nicola Baldwin), RBDC, Riverside Studios, London
1993　*Body as Site* (mus. Simon Fisher-Turner; design Paul Elliman, Anya Gallacio, Ron Haselden, John Lyall), RBDC, Centre for Contemporary Arts, Glasgow
1995　*After the Last Sky* (film installation; mus. Simon Fisher-Turner; video David Jackson), RBDC, Royal College of Art, London
　　　Unbroken View (mus. Simon Fisher-Turner, film Sigoune Hamann), RBDC, South Hill Park, Bracknell
1996　*Unbroken View-Extended Frame* (mus. Tom Murray; visual artist Su Grierson), Group N, Tramway Theatre, Glasgow
1997　*Fractured Landscape, Fragmented Narratives* (mus. Jonny Clark; film Noel Bramley), RBDC, Riverside Studios, London

Publications

By BUTCHER: articles—

"What Is Dance?," *Dance Now,* Summer 1992.

On BUTCHER: articles—

Burt, Ramsay, "Finding a Language," *New Dance,* June 1988.
Crickmay, Chris, "Dialogues with Rosemary Butcher," *New Dance,* Spring 1986.

Dodds, Sherril, "The Momentum Continues," *Dance Theatre Journal,* Spring 1977.

Meisner, Nadine, "An English Pioneer," *Dance and Dancers,* February 1987.

———, "Rosemary Butcher," *Dance Now,* Summer 1997.

On BUTCHER: books—

Jordan, Stephanie, *Striding Out,* London, 1992.
Mackrell, Judith. *Out of Line: The Story of British New Dance,* London, 1992.

*   *   *

English choreographer Rosemary Butcher has mined her narrow seam for more than 20 years, with ever more profound results. Her rigorous, minimalist aesthetic has set her apart from the rest of British dance, but she has uncompromisingly followed her vision, unswayed by current dance styles or funding trends. And, over the course of 40 works, she has acquired an audience and gradually gained critical recognition. Her cerebral, distilled work repays the viewer's engagement with a richness of texture, of atmosphere, of feeling, and of experience.

In 1965, Butcher was the only dance specialist in the first intake of students for Dartington College of Art's dance and drama course, where she was taught Graham technique and composition by Flora Cushman of the Graham school. After graduating from the three-year course with a teaching qualification, Butcher studied for a year at the University of Maryland, under Dorothy Madden, and then returned to Dartington to teach. But, feeling at odds with the Graham technique and uncertain of her future in dance, she left for New York in 1970. There she met choreographer and filmmaker Elaine Summers, who suggested she take workshops with Yvonne Rainer and other proponents of the Judson Church movement. Their ways of moving and their ideas on what could constitute dance were a revelation; Butcher had found her path.

Her sojourn in New York from 1970 to 1972 predated visits there by other British choreographers, such as Richard Alston and Siobhan Davies, as well as the arrival of Mary Fulkerson and Steve Paxton at Dartington College to teach release-based technique and contact improvisation. This may partly explain Butcher's singularity in the British dance scene. Certainly, when the Rosemary Butcher Dance Company made its debut in 1976 at the Serpentine Gallery, few in London could appreciate the new aesthetic.

Several hallmarks of her style were apparent from the start. The works are created through improvisation, with the dancers improvising around a given instruction, and Butcher calling out further instructions as they move. Several early pieces also used structured improvisation in performance. Butcher choreographs from a limited range of simple, clear movements, developing, repeating, layering. The movements happen in real time, performed without projection in an absorbed, focused manner. Her works have consistently been presented in unconventional spaces—outside, in churches, and, particularly, in art galleries. Indeed, with her concern for form, space, and structure, it is unsurprising that Butcher more readily aligns herself with the visual art rather than the dance world.

Collaborating with a visual artist—artist, architect, filmmaker—has been a mainstay of Butcher's work since 1980. The dance interacts with or responds to the visual environment, which structures the space. In the 1980s, Butcher's most important collaboration was with German artist Heinz-Dieter Pietsch, who provided the installations for five works. During this time, the feel of her work changed. From the energetic, broad sweep of movement pure and simple, prevalent in the 1970s pieces, the works became subdued and subtle, more sculptural, more atmospheric. After having dealt strictly with movement mechanics in the early pieces, Butcher allowed emotional resonances to emerge.

The Site (1983), which was inspired by a visit to an Iron Age fort, involved instructions based on archeological excavation terms, and its primordial atmosphere called to mind ancient peoples and their links with the land. This theme was revisited in *Touch the Earth* (1987), inspired by the Native Americans' loss of their territories and conveying a community's sadness and disquiet about their land.

Touch the Earth was Butcher's second collaboration with composer Michael Nyman, after *Flying Lines* (1985), and these two have probably been her most popular works. With instructions taken from a kite flying manual, *Flying Lines* had an exhilarating finale of running, forward and backward, arms outstretched, that evoked the freedom of flight. With this work, there was a brief increase in the number of dancers used as Butcher explored group energy and experimented with a systems-based approach to patterning movement. The "d" trilogy (1989-90) also involved an expansion of space, progressing from *d1's* installation of simply lines on the floor to *d2's* catwalks and projected slides of the bridge-like structure that was central to *3d.*

Since *Body as Site* (1993), Butcher has returned to individuals, form, and the state of the body, with a new interest in image. She sees her work as moving art installations, and this was taken to its logical conclusion in *After the Last Sky* (1995), an installation of four films, projected on the walls of a gallery, that interspersed rolling skyscapes with shots of a dancer doing a short, tight movement phrase.

Her stage pieces have not, however, translated well to film. Butcher's work has to be seen in performance to experience its texture and its absorbing atmosphere: *Body as Site* staged in a pewless Guildford Cathedral, light streaming in through the high windows, the dancers moving calmly between the columns and slowly traversing Anya Gallacio's gauzy white flooring before the altar; the flickering, washed out film of *Unbroken View* (1995) enclosing the dancers as they unravelled snatches of recovered movement. The economy of means belies the depth of the resonances.

The Rosemary Butcher Dance Company operates on a project basis, acquiring grants for the creation of each new piece. Butcher has always supported herself by teaching—initially technique and then choreography—in a variety of settings, from schools to universities. Many dancers who had their start with her company in the early years have gone on to become choreographers in their own right: Julyen Hamilton, Maedee Dupres, Sue MacLennan, Miranda Tufnell, Gaby Agis, and Dennis Greenwood (the company's longest serving member). Other dancers, such as Jonathan Burrows and Gill Clarke, have come with established careers. Butcher's movement may be non-technical, but it requires professional dancers to embody it with clarity and conviction.

—Chris Jones

BUTLER, John
American dancer and choreographer

Born: John Nielson Butler in Memphis, Tennessee, 19 September 1920. **Education:** Studied at the Graham School and American

School of Ballet, New York. **Career:** Dancer in Broadway musicals and with Martha Graham Company, 1942-55; choreographer for Broadway and off-Broadway shows, 1947-49; choreographer, New York City Opera, 1951-54; founder, director and choreographer, John Butler Dance Theatre, from 1953; performed at Festival of Two Worlds, Spoleto, Italy; company renamed American Dance Theatre, 1958; dance director, Spoleto Festival, 1958; has choreographed works for Alvin Ailey American Dance Theatre, Australian Ballet, American Ballet Theatre, Batsheva Dance Company, Harkness Ballet, Metropolitan Opera, New York City Ballet, New York City Opera Company, Nederlands Dans Theater, Paris Opera Ballet, and Pennsylvania Ballet as well choreography for television. **Awards:** *Dance Magazine* Award, 1964. **Died:** 1993.

Works

1953   *Masque of the Wild Man* (mus. Glanville-Hicks), John Butler Dance Theatre, Jacob's Pillow Dance Festival, Lee, Massachusetts

Malacchio (mus. Provenzano), John Butler Dance Theatre, American Dance Festival, New London, Connecticut

1954   *The Brass World* (mus. Jolivet), John Butler Dance Theatre, Brooklyn

Three Promenades with the Lord (mus. American folk), John Butler Dance Theatre, Jacob's Pillow Dance Festival

1955   *Frontier Ballad* (mus. traditional American folk), John Butler Dance Theatre, Brooklyn

The Letter and the Three (mus. jazz, arranged Shirley), Geoffrey Holder and Company, New York

1959   *Carmina Burana* (scenic cantata; mus. Orff), New York City Opera, New York

In the Beginning (mus. Barber), New York City Opera, New York

The Sybil (mus. Surinach), American Dance Theatre, Spoleto Festival

The Five Senses (mus. Schuller, Starer, Lees, Siday, traditional folk songs), American Dance Theatre, Spoleto Festival

Brief Encounter (mus. Bowles), American Dance Theatre, Spoleto Festival

Amusement Park (mus. Bowles), American Dance Theatre, Spoleto Festival

Album Leaves, John Butler Dance Theatre, Spoleto Festival

1960   *Turning Point* (mus. Evans, Lewis, Hopkins), Idlewild Festival of the Arts, California

Portrait of Billie (mus. Billie Holiday songs), Jacob's Pillow

1961   *Willie the Weeper in Ballet Ballads* w/Tetley, Ray (mus. Moross), East 47th Street Theatre, New York (originally part of *Nausicaa*, opera by Glanville-Hicks, Athens International Festival)

1962   *Alone*, Freda Miller Memorial Concert, New York

Hadrianas (mus. Starer), Nederlands Dans Theater, Rotterdam

1963   Dances in *Jeanne d'Arc au Bucher* (dramatic oratorio; mus. Honegger), Santa Fe Opera, Santa Fe

Sebastian (mus. Menotti), Nederlands Dans Theater, Amsterdam

1964   *Catulli Carmina* (mus. Orff), Caramoor Festival, Katonah, New York

Ceremonial (mus. Bartók), Caramoor Festival, Katonah, New York

1965   *Chansons de Bilitis* (mus. Debussy), Festival of Two Worlds, Spoleto

1966   *Villon* (mus. Starer), Pennsylvania Ballet Company, Second Harper Festival, Chicago

1967   *Aphrodite* (mus. Lees), Boston Ballet, Boston

After Eden (mus. Hoiby), Harkness Ballet, New York

A Season of Hell (mus. Glanville-Hicks), Harkness Ballet, New York

Landscape for Lovers (mus. Hoiby), Harkness Ballet, New York

The Captive Lark (mus. Starer), Village Theatre

1968   *Threshold* (mus. Durko, Bacewicz), Australian Ballet, Sydney

The Initiate (mus. Bacewicz, Durko), Repertory Dance Theater, Salt Lake City

Encounters (mus. Subotnick), Repertory Dance Theater

Labyrinth (mus. Somers), Royal Winnipeg Ballet, Winnipeg

1970   *The Minotaur* (mus. Carter), Boston Ballet, Boston

Journeys (mus. von Webern), Pennsylvania Ballet, Brooklyn

Itineraire (mus. Berio), Ballet-Theatre contemporaine, Paris

1971   *Hi-Kyo* (mus. Fukushima), Ballet-Theatre Contemporaine, London

1972   *Tragic Celebration* (*Hara-Kiri*; mus. Fukushima), Gala Benefit for the Dance Collection of the New York Public Library

According to Eve (mus. Crumb), Alvin Ailey Dance Theater, New York

La Voix (mus. Crumb), Ballet du Rhin

Moon Full (mus. Tzui Auni), Batsheva Dance Company

1973   *Black Angel* (mus. Crumb), Pennsylvania Ballet, Philadelphia

Trip (mus. Berio), Les Grands Ballets Canadiens, Montreal

Integrales (mus. Varese), Paris Opera Ballet, Paris

Ameriques (mus. Varese), Paris Opera Ballet, Paris

1974   *Cult of the Night* (mus. Schönberg), Frankfurt

Puppets of Death (after Shakespeare's *Othello*; mus. Schönberg), Batsheva Dance Company, Tel Aviv

1975   *Medea* (mus. Barber), Festival of Two Worlds, Spoleto

1976   *Les Noces* (mus. Stravinsky), The Dance Company (of New South Wales), Sydney

Facets (mus. various songs), solo for Judith Jamison, Alvin Ailey American Dance Theatre, New York

Othello (mus. Crumb), Pittsburgh Ballet Theatre, Pittsburgh

1977   *Icarus* (ice ballet; mus. Crosse), John Curry Theatre of Skating, Palladium, London

1978   *Les Doubles* (mus. Dutilleux), Bavarian State Opera Ballet, Munich

Othello (mus. Dvorak), Ballet of La Scala, Milan

1979   *The Commitment* (mus. Bernstein), solo for Judith Jamison, Kansas City Ballet, Kansas City

1980   *Dawns and Dusks* (mus. Hoddinott), Ballet of the German Opera on the Rhine, Duisburg

1981   *George Sand—A Landscape* (mus. Chopin), Bat-Dor Dance Company, Tel Aviv

1983   *Quest* (mus. Ruggieri), Les Grands Ballets Canadiens
1987   *Romeo and Juliet* ("chamber version"; mus. Prokofiev),
        Princeton Ballet, Princeton

Other works include: For New York City Opera—dances in operas *The Consul* (mus. Menotti; 1950), *Bluebeard's Castle* (mus. Bartók; 1952), *La Cenerentola* (mus. Rossini; 1953), *Die Fledermaus* (mus. Strauss; 1953), *La Traviata* (mus. Verdi: 1953), *The Tender Land* (mus. Copland; 1954), *The Marriage of Figaro* (mus. Mozart; 1959); also individual works *The Letter* (mus. Ravel), *The Old Woman Laments Her Youth* (mus. Starer), *Ritual* (mus. Starer), *Hypnos* (mus. Evans), *Shadow of Madness* (mus. Castellnuovo), *La Testament* (mus. Pound), *Tragic Celebration* (mus. Starer), *Alone* (mus. Guiffre), dances in *Amahl and the Night Visitors* (mus. Menotti). For the television program *Lamp Unto My Feet*, CBS-TV, 1960-64—*Saul and the Witch of Endor, David and Bathsheba, Psalms, Esther, Ballet of the Nativity, Brief Dynasty, Ceremony of Innocence.* Also for television—*The Mark of Cain,* CBS-TV, 1963; *The Adventure,* CBS-TV, 1954; *Creation and Fall,* for the program *Look Up and Live,* 1955; *L'Enfance du Christ,* CBS-TV, 1955; *Jepthah's Daughter,* CBS-TV, 1965; *Five Ballets of the Five Senses,* Lincoln Center/Stage 5 series, NET-TV, 1967.

Publications

By BUTLER: articles—

"Confessions of a Choreographer," in *The Dance Experience,* 1970.

On BUTLER: articles—

Barnes, Clive, "Dance: Its Lost Tradition," *Dance Magazine,* February 1994.
Caradente, G., "Ballet at the Spoleto Festival," *Dance Magazine,* October 1959
Hardy, Camille, "Have Dances, Will Travel," *Dance Magazine,* February 1994.
Hering, Doris, *"Carmina Burana,"* *Dance Magazine,* November 1959.
Loney, Glenn, "All the Strange Things: John Butler on Opera Choreography," *Dance Magazine,* August 1971.
———, "Busy John Butler Reports on Roving Choreography," *Dance Magazine,* January 1974.
Terry, Walter, "The Legacy of Isadora Duncan and Ruth St. Denis," *Dance Perspectives,* Winter, 1960.
———, "Erotic Dances in the Starlight," *Saturday Review,* 22 July 1967.
———, "Beautiful Bodies," *Saturday Review,* 24 February 1968.

*   *   *

John Butler, a dancer and choreographer in the tradition of Martha Graham, was among the first generation of men to succeed in American modern dance, a field where women had traditionally dominated. He choreographed for a wide variety of venues, including opera companies, television, and the Broadway stage.

Butler was born near Memphis, Tennessee, in 1920. He moved to New York City in 1942 to become a dancer, despite the fact that he and his father became permanently estranged because of his decision. He won a scholarship to study with Muriel Stuart at the School of American Ballet in New York, and one for the Dance

Players organization in Bucks County, Pennsylvania, where he took classes with Eugene Loring. To support himself financially, Butler taught ballroom dancing at the Donald Sawyer Dance Studios. He began studying with Martha Graham in 1944 and eventually became a long-term member of her company, dancing many key roles and partnering with her.

When Merce Cunningham left Graham's company in the 1940s, Butler, along with Mark Ryder, assumed many of his former roles. Butler was with the company during what many consider Graham's peak; his roles included the Revivalist in her *Appalachian Spring* and the Poetic Beloved in *Deaths and Entrances.* Among Butler's early choreographic works were *Malocchio* (1953), *Masque of the Wildman* (1953), *The Brass World* (1954), *Davy Crockett* and *Three Promenades with the Lord* (both 1955).

In 1958, Butler was appointed dance director for the Spoleto Festival in Italy, and for two years his company appeared there. (His work at Spoleto continued; he choreographed *Medea* for the Festival in 1969.) His company, the John Butler Dance Theatre, performed from 1955 to 1961, appearing at the American Dance Festival, Brooklyn Academy of Music, and Jacob's Pillow, among other venues. Dancers associated with his group included Carmen de Lavallade, Glen Tetley, Lar Lubovitch, Geoffrey Holder, Buzz Miller, Mary Hinkson, and Scott Douglas. During this period, Butler had been doing independent choreographic projects for other companies in addition to his work for his own troupe, and he disbanded the John Butler Dance Theatre in 1961 to focus on his freelance work.

As an independent choreographer, Butler was versatile, doing work for both classical ballet and modern dance companies. His choreography was known for its expressiveness, inventiveness, theatricality, and especially for its beauty. It was heavily influenced by his years with Martha Graham, incorporating her technique, her use of props, and her tendency toward allegorical and mythical themes. He often choreographed to classic composers such as Carl Orff, Gian Carlo Menotti, and Samuel Barber. Butler worked with ballet companies including the Joffrey Ballet, the American Ballet Theatre (where Baryshnikov danced in several roles), the Pennsylvania Ballet, Harkness Ballet, the Boston Ballet, and the Royal Winnipeg Ballet, as well as modern dance troupes such as Salt Lake City's Repertory Dance Theater. He worked frequently with the Alvin Ailey American Dance Theatre.

As with many literary-based choreographers, Butler worked extensively in Europe, and was better known there than in the United States for much of his career, particularly during the 1970s. His friendship with ballerina Carla Fracci, for whom he created *Medea, Othello* and *Phaedra,* resulted in many commissions in Italy, where he was highly acclaimed. In addition, he worked in Munich, Sydney, Montreal, Warsaw, and South America. He also had a long relationship with Nederlands Dans Theater.

Much of Butler's renowned work occurred through his associations with opera companies. He worked for the New York City Opera from 1951 to 1954, becoming dance director in 1952. He created dances for many productions there, including *Carmina Burana* in 1959. *Carmina* was his first popular success, becoming a milestone in Butler's career. During his lifetime, *Carmina* was presented by more than 30 companies, and it remains his most produced piece. In addition to *Carmina Burana,* Butler staged or re-staged dances for *Carmen, Aida, Catulli Carmina, Amahl and the Night Visitors* (first created for television), *La Cenerentola, Die Fledermaus, La Traviata, Rigoletto,* and *Love of Three Oranges* for the company. He also created dances for the Metropolitan Opera, the Boston Opera, and the Santa Fe Opera Company.

John Butler: Judith Jamison performing Butler's *Facets*. Photograph © Johan Elbers.

The versatile choreographer was involved with much more than modern dance and ballet concerts and staging dances for opera companies, however. In 1943, he made his first appearance in a Broadway musical, dancing the leading role of *Dream Curly* in Agnes de Mille's *Oklahoma* ballet. He continued performing on the stage, in *On The Town* (1944), *Hollywood Pinafore* (1945), and *Inside USA* (1948). His interest in the theater led him to choreograph for the off-Broadway play *The Consul* in 1947, which was significant because it was the first time he worked with composer Menotti, who became his lifelong friend and collaborator. Butler also choreographed *Livin' the Life* (1957) and *A Family Affair* (1962), both Jerome Robbins productions. He appeared in films as well, such as MGM's *Words in Music* in 1948, in which he performed with Allyn McLerie. (The two subsequently partnered in a nightclub act.)

Butler also worked extensively in television, creating many experimental programs during the late 1940s, 1950s, and 1960s, all performed by his company. One of his major works for television was *Amahl and the Night Visitors* for NBC Opera Theatre in 1951, which he later restaged elsewhere. His work on *Amahl* led to his engagement as choreographer by the New York City Opera. While his television projects were frowned upon by some of his dance colleagues, they allowed him to fund his other work.

Butler was one of the first choreographers to set pieces to jazz music. In 1960, he created *Portrait of Billie,* about the life of singer Billie Holiday, which Butler and de Lavallade performed at its premiere at the Newport Jazz Festival, marking the first appearance by a modern dance troupe there. Butler died of lung cancer in 1993 at age 73.

—Karen Raugust

BUTOH

Butoh has been called grotesque, shocking, poetic, humorous, and mesmerizing. This Japanese dance of darkness uses more mental than physical technique. "Bu" meaning dance and "toh" meaning step—Butoh is a dance-drama sculpting slow, controlled movement into contorted figures and meditative images. Performed initially with shaven heads and white painted bodies, it has been called by its founder, Tatsumi Hijikata, "the dance of the unmoveables."

Butoh is the cultural fallout of postwar Japan: Hijikata saw the aftermath of the A-bomb as a prime opportunity to do away with the rigid structures of the Japanese way of life. Hijikata met Kazuo Ohno in 1954 and the two formed a partnership creating Butoh dances that lasted many years.

Kinjiki in 1959 was the first performance of Butoh. In this short piece performed without music, Ohno enacted having sex with a live chicken and in the process strangled it between his legs. Out of the darkness Hijikata walked over to him. The images Hijikata and Ohno danced were so haunting and dark that Butoh was dubbed by writers, poets, and critics of the time as *Ankoku Butoh* or the "Dance of Darkness," "an" meaning dark and "koku" meaning black. This is the more correct name for Butoh dancing by the Japanese, as Butoh by itself can also mean social dancing. Buyo is also interchangeable with Butoh, but Hijikata simply preferred "Butoh."

Hijikata was the primary choreographer and used the short bowed legs and stooped back of the Japanese rural farmer to express and expose the irregularities and distortions of postwar life. In an effort to go back to their animal instincts Hijikata and Ohno shaved their heads, painted their bodies white, and danced naked. Kazuo Ohno contributed to their dance through his knowledge and admiration of German Expressionism, which he incorporated into exaggerated and fragmented body poses of emotional release.

With the use of the entire body Butoh cracked the mask of classical Japanese dancing in the Noh and Kabuki theatres. But while seeking to break new ground, Butoh did not abandon its Japanese roots. As in a Japanese tea ceremony reflecting the Eastern philosophy of timelessness, Butoh movements are slow and meditative as if to suspend time; transformation and metamorphosis are the foundation of Butoh technique. If you are to dance as a rooster, you do not portray the rooster—you lose yourself and become the rooster. The diminution of self to a greater whole is also an integral part of Eastern thought. The ability to relax is another skill needed to perform Butoh. Noguchi Taiso, a set of exercises originated by Noguchi Michizo, is often used by Butoh dancers to release bodily tension. Increasing the power of concentration and freeing the imagination are necessary to allow the energy to flow from the artist's soul to the stage. Improvisation is vital to learning these skills and to physically painting the mental pictures of the Butoh artist.

Butoh blossomed in the 1970s through the group of over 100 Butoh dancers called DaiRakidaKan. Founded by Akaji Maro in 1971, these Butoh dancers lived together in a commune and dedicated themselves to totally incorporating Butoh into their everyday lives. Akaji studied with Hijikata in the 1960s but his real contribution to Butoh is in enlarging its spectacle by adding dynamism and drama. The company eventually disbanded in 1986 but has given rise to many smaller performing groups.

The decade of the 1990s has seen an international interest in this avant-garde Japanese art form. Butoh workshops occur from Finland to Florida and Butoh artists have expounded on the dance's original elements and incorporated the theories of Zen, improvisational dance, and elements of choice. Like modern dance in the Western world, Butoh has been flavored by individual artists and choreographers as they chisel their interpretation of the body and reality into movement. Most Butoh performances range from 50-80 minutes as the artists need this time to bring about the building of the meditative state to an ecstatic level. Mustuko Tanaka in Buto-sha Tenkei's *Nocturne* (1995) can drip liquid from her eyes and ears on cue and become so entranced that the audience can see only the whites of her eyes as she plunges deeper and deeper into concentration.

Eiko and Koma, a group now situated in the U.S., began their study of Butoh from Hijikata in 1971. Their slow, deliberate movements are highly individualized and delicate. Another popular touring group, Sankai Juko (translated as "studio of mountain and sky"), was begun in 1975 by Amagatsu Ushio, Semimaru, and Iwashita, former members of DaiRakidaKan. This all-male group is said to combine illusionism mixed with Butoh. In 1985 the group was performing *The Hanging Piece,* in which the dancers suspended themselves upside-down tied to a rope, when tragically one of the dancers, Yoshiyuki Takada, fell and was fatally injured. Since then, to honor the fallen dancer, the group choreographed and performed a piece entitled *Kinkan Shonen* where one dancer hangs from a rope and the others perform around him. Poppo and the Gogo Boys is another example of a Butoh-based choreography infused with other elements. Poppo focuses mostly on the mental aspects of Butoh, but with a shamanistic style of dancing that melds punk, Pina Bausch, heavy metal and basically all that he has encountered in life into his choreography.

Butoh: Kazuo Ohno's *Ka Cho Fu Getsu*, 1993. Photograph © Johan Elbers.

Butoh was more of the counterculture in Japan until 1985 when a Butoh festival was held for the first time. Now that it has emerged as an accepted international art form, there is more tolerance in Japan and, for the most part, Butoh dancing has been tamed by time. But the need to display the images of the night, of our unconscious, to make the unseen visible is still the essence of Butoh. Butoh dances in search of the meaning—of the dance of life.

—Cynthia Roses-Thema

BYRD, Donald
American dancer, choreographer, and educator

Born: 21 July 1949 in New London, North Carolina. **Education:** Yale University, 1967-68; Tufts University, 1968-73; Cambridge School of Ballet, 1969-73; London School of Con-temporary Dance, 1972; Alvin Ailey American Dance Center, 1976. **Career:** Artistic director, Donald Byrd/The Group, beginning 1978; professor of dance, California Institute for the Arts, 1976-82; has also taught at Ohio University, University of California, Santa Cruz, and Harvard Summer Dance Center. **Awards:** Many grants, awards and fellowships from organizations and corporations, including AT&T Foundation, Ford Foundation/Pew Charitable Trust, Harkness Foundation for Dance, Jerome Foundation, Joyce Mertz Gilmore Foundation, Manhattan Community Arts Fund, Mary Flagler Cary Charitable Trust, Metropolitan Life Foundation, National Endowment for the Arts (NEA), New York Foundation for the Arts, New York State Council on the Arts, and Rockefeller Foundation; Third Grand Prix International Video Dance Festival, Special Mention for *Bolla Blue*, 1990; New York Dance and Performance award ("Bessie") for *The Minstrel Show*, 1992; First Prize (featured film) International Film Festival for *Unsettled Dreams*; Philip Morris New Works Grant, 1997.

Works (premiered in New York City and with Donald Byrd/The Group, unless otherwise noted)

1983	*P-HP (Post Holocaust Pop)*, Dance Theatre Workshop
	Low Down and Dirty Rag, Dance Theatre Workshop
1984	*Noh Help Wanted*, Zenon Dance Company, Minneapolis, Minnesota
1985	*Concerning Vices, Circumstances & Situations*, LaMama
1986	*Divertimento*, Theatre of the Open Eyes
1987	*Crumble*, Alvin Ailey Repertory Ensemble, Redbank, New Jersey
1988	*Enactments in Time of Plague*, Symphony Space
	Whoosh/Matts, Frankfurt, Germany
	Shards, Alvin Ailey Dance Theater, Kansas City, Missouri
1989	*Prince Ravaged*, Dance Place, Washington, D.C.
	Triptych, Triplex Theater
	Rend, Triplex Theater
	Chamber I, Dance Theater of Harlem Workshop
	A Seasonal Passion, Impulse Dance Company, Boston, Massachusetts
1990	*Surveillance*, Dance Theater Workshop
	Multi-Cultural Man
	What Makes Samantha Run?, Japan American Cultural Center, Los Angeles
	Jazz Dogs
1991	*Prodigal*, Aaron Davis Hall
	The Minstrel Show, Dance Theatre Workshop
1992	*Drastic Cuts*, Bryn Mawr College, Pennsylvania
1993	*Bristle*, Dance on the Edge, Towson, Maryland
	Juju, Aaron Davis Hall
	An Annotated Tale, Symphony Space
1994	*Juju 2*, Alice Tully Hall
	Meditations on Revelations, Central Park Summerstage
	Ni Centre, Ni Peripherie, Conservatoire de Paris, Paris
	The Communion, Lula Washington's LACDT, Los Angeles
1995	*Life Situations: Daydreams on Giselle*, Joyce Theater, Altogether Different Series
	I Was Looking at the Ceiling and Then I Saw the Sky (musical; dir. Peter Sellars, mus. John Adams and June Jordan)
	American Dream, Rheinland Pfolz Kultursommer, Germany
1996	*The Beast*, Meany Hall, University of Washington, Seattle
	Still at the *Arts Alive!* Festival, Johannesburg, South Africa
	The Harlem Nutcracker, Gammage Auditorium, Tucson
1997	*Carmina Burana*, New York City Opera, New York State Theatre
	Aida, San Francisco Opera, San Francisco
	Fin de Siecle, Alvin Ailey American Dance Theater, City Center

Other works include: Many works for both national and international companies including Alvin Ailey American Dance Theatre, Dance Theater of Harlem, Impulse Dance Company, New York City Opera, Conservatoire de Paris, San Francisco Opera, Zenon Dance Company, and others.

Films and Videotapes

A Formal Response, video, 1986.
The Rehearsal, video, 1987.
Speak Easy, video, 1988.
Bolla Blue, dance video, 1989.
Unsettled Dreams, film, choreographed and co-directed by Byrd, 1996.

Publications

Sommers, Pamela, "Donald Byrd: Thinking on his Feet," *Washington Post*, 9 May 1986.

*   *   *

Donald Byrd was born in New London, North Carolina, on 21 July 1949. He studied at Yale University from 1967 to 1968 and majored in philosophy at Tufts University from 1968 to 1973. While he was at Tufts, Byrd also studied at the Cambridge School of Ballet, from 1969 to 1973, while attending the London School of Contemporary Dance during 1972. In 1976 Byrd went to the Alvin Ailey American Dance Center, and danced with such greats as Mia Slavenska, followed by Twyla Tharp, Karole Armitage, and Gus Solomons Jr.

Following his education, Byrd went on to become professor of dance at the California Institute for the Arts from 1976 to 1982, and has also served as a faculty member of Ohio University (1980), the University of California, Santa Cruz (1980-81) and Harvard University's Summer Dance Center (1991), as well as the faculties of California State University, Long Beach, and Wesleyan University.

Byrd started his own group, Donald Byrd/The Group, in 1978 in Los Angeles and served as its artistic director, moving the group to New York in 1983. Since that time, he has choreographed over 100 works for his own group, as well as a number of other prestigious organizations such as the Alvin Ailey American Dance Theatre, New York City Opera, La Conservatoire de Paris, San Francisco Opera, Atlanta Ballet, Oregon Ballet Theater, Philadelphia Dance Company (a.k.a. Philadanco), the Pacific Northwest Ballet, and Butler Ballet, among others.

In the late 1980s, Byrd became involved in a project that would either make or break Donald Byrd/The Work—a new version of the *Nutcracker,* but from an African American perspective. The project started when David Berger approached Alvin Ailey in the late 1980s to do an Afrocentric reworking of E.T.A. Hoffmann's famous *Nutcracker Suite.* Ailey passed, but Byrd approached Berger in 1989 with the idea of performing it. After several years on hold, the project was given the green light. Berger, a former member of Duke Ellington's Orchestra, rearranged the 31-minute piece that Ellington and Billy Strayhorn had recomposed in 1962 from Tchaikovsky's famous *Nutcracker Suite* into a two-hour score, played by a 17-piece orchestra.

Byrd collaborated with a host of well-known artists to stage *The Harlem Nutcracker,* sparing no expense. Combining ballet with popular and modern dance forms, the production featured Elinor McCoy as Clara and Gus Solomons Jr. as her husband. Twenty-five other dancers, including Elizabeth Parkinson, performed along with the Lafayette Inspirational Ensemble with sets designed by Eduardo Sicangco, who was inspired by collages of the late Harlem artist Romare Bearden, as well as the original Cotton Club. Gabriel

Donald Byrd. Photograph © Johan Elbers.

Berry came on board to design the costumes, working with Rodney Gordon Studios, Donna Langman Studios, and Paula Buchert. Byrd received a great deal of notice and critical acclaim when he staged the finished production in Tucson, Arizona, in 1996, and it was the most costly production his 18-year-old company had undertaken, with a final price tag at just over $1 million. When the work debuted at the Brooklyn Academy of Music in December 1996, *New York Times* critic Anna Kisselgoff raved "Whatever you want to call it, Mr. Byrd and David Berger. . .have produced an exuberant, stylish entertainment." Further, Kisselgoff applauded Byrd's no-holds-barred style: "but when Mr. Byrd lets loose with his typical high-energy kinetic thrust, speed and eclectic flair, he transforms the usual candy kingdom. . .into a jiving floor show."

The year before *The Harlem Nutcracker* debuted, Byrd created the choreography for an unusual musical "fusion of contemporary politics, with contemporary romance," called *I Was Looking at the Ceiling and Then I Saw the Sky*. By taking actual words from a survivor of the 1994 Los Angeles earthquake and working with director Peter Sellars and composers John Adams and June Jordan, Byrd was able to combine jazz, rock, and gospel and his brand of dance into entertainment with a conscience. Another work from 1995, *Life Situations: Daydreams on Giselle*, which originally premiered at the Joyce Theater in New York, was taken to the Arts Alive! Festival in Johannesburg, South Africa, in 1996. Margaret

Jenkins, writing in *Citizen,* called Donald Byrd/The Group the "high-light" of the festival and urged readers to attend: "The last performance is tonight and anyone who enjoys witty, incisive and integrated choreography performed with tremendous flair and *brio,* should not miss it." She went on to find Byrd's choreography "remarkable but accessible. . .a mix of neoclassical ballet and Times Square modernism shot through with elements of mischievous fun and highly perceptive insight."

Another of Byrd's works, perhaps his darkest and most provocative, is 1996's *The Beast,* which is about domestic violence. Jack Anderson, writing for the *New York Times,* stated "Donald Byrd is not only choreographically intelligent and imaginative, but unpredictable as well." Though somewhat reminiscent of Lester Horton's *The Beloved,* Byrd's work delivered its punches with what Anderson characterized as "a slightly sardonic fashion" in parts while others "seethed with the turbulence of German Expressionism." Anderson further credited Byrd with a nod to Kurt Jooss' classic 1932 ballet, *The Green Table,* for *The Beast*'s "powerful conclusion."

Throughout the 1990s Byrd worked on an ongoing project called *JazzTrain,* utilizing the musical skills of such composers as Max Roach, Geri Allen, and Vernon Reid. The pieces, commissioned by nearly 20 disparate organizations (including the American Dance Festival, Jacob's Pillow, the Brooklyn Academy of Music, and others), began debuting in sections, with the latest in June 1998 at the Wolf Trap Farm Park for the Performing Arts outside Washington, D.C. In addition to his choreography, commissions, and teaching, Byrd sits on the board of both Dance/USA and the Dance Theatre Workshop, and has served a panelist for the Wisconsin Arts Board, the Western States Alliance of Arts Administrators, the Artists Foundation, and the New York Foundation for the Arts. After more than two decades of award-winning choreographing for ballet, theater, opera, and modern dance, Byrd continues not only to be a driving force in American dance but to fulfill his company's mission statement to "communicate the value of the performing arts to a broad audience and to educate this audience to the relevance of performance to daily life."

—Daryl F. Mallett and Sydonie Benet

CAGE, John (Milton, Jr.)
American composer

Born: 5 September 1912, in Los Angeles, California. **Education:** Los Angeles High School, graduated 1928; Pomona College, Claremont, California, 1928-30; study in Europe; private study with pianist Richard Buhlig, theory with Adolph Weiss, 1933, and under Henry Cowell at New School for Social Research, New York; studied counterpoint with Arnold Schönberg, and at University of California, Los Angeles. **Family:** Married Andreyevna (Xenia) Kashevaroff in 1935 (dissolved 1945). **Career:** Dance accompanist (and first meeting with Merce Cunningham), Cornish School, Seattle, Washington, 1938; taught course in new music, Chicago Institute of Design, 1941; moved to New York permanently, 1943; musical director for Cunningham's troupe; taught occasional courses, New School for Social Research, 1956-60; fellow, Center for Advanced Studies, Wesleyan University, Middletown, Connecticut, 1960-61, 1970; composer in residence, University of Cincinnati, 1967; associate, Center for Advanced Study, University of Illinois, Urbana, 1968-69; artist in residence, University of California, Davis, 1969; Charles Eliot Norton Professor of Poetry, Harvard University, 1988-89. **Awards:** Guggenheim Fellowship, 1949; American Academy of Arts and Letters award, 1949; membership, American Academy 1968; Thorne Music Scholarship, 1969; fellow, American Academy, 1978; Karl Sczuka Prize, 1979; Mayor's Award of Honor for Arts and Culture, New York City, 1981; Commandeur de l'Ordre des Arts et des Lettres, 1982; Notable Achievement Award, Brandeis University, 1983; member, Percussive Arts Hall of Fame, 1983; Doctor of All Arts *honoris causa,* California Institute of the Arts, 1986; Kyoto Prize, 1989. **Died:** 12 August 1992.

Works

For a listing of Cage's collaborations with Cunningham, see the Cunningham entry.

Publications

By CAGE: books—

Silence, Middletown, Connecticut, 1961.
A Year from Monday, Middletown, Connecticut, 1968.
To Describe the Process of Composition Used in Not Wanting to Say Anything about Marcel, Cincinnati, Ohio, 1969.
Notations, with Alison Knowles, New York, 1969
M, Middletown, Connecticut, 1973.
Writings through Finnegans Wake, New York, 1978.
Empty Words, Middletown, Connecticut, 1979.
Another Song (accompanying photographs by Susan Barron), New York, 1981.

For the Birds (conversations with Daniel Charles), Salem, Massachusetts, 1981.
Mud Book, New York, 1982.
Themes and Variations, Barrytown, New York, 1982.
X, Middletown, Connecticut, 1983, 1986.
I-VI (the Charles Eliot Norton Lectures, Harvard University, 1988-89), Cambridge, 1990.

On CAGE: books—

Dunn, R., editor, *John Cage,* New York, 1962.
Gena, Peter, and Jonathan Brent, *A John Cage Reader,* New York, 1982.
Griffiths, Paul, *Cage,* London, 1981.
Jubota, S., *Marcel Duchamp and John Cage,* New York, 1968.
Kostelanetz, Richard, editor, *John Cage,* New York, 1970.
———, *Conversing with Cage,* New York, 1988.
Nyman, Michael, *Experimental Music: Cage and Beyond,* New York, 1974.
Revill, David, *John Cage: A Biography,* London, 1992.
Sontag, Susan, *Styles of Radical Will,* New York, 1969.
Tomkins, Calvin, *The Bride and the Bachelors,* New York, 1965.

*   *   *

Born in Los Angeles in 1912, composer and philosopher of music John Cage is considered one of the most prominent avant-garde personalities. Cage's compositions have been deemed controversial, and some critics have ridiculed his work. Nevertheless, his ideas have influenced numerous musicians, dancers, artists, poets, and writers. Cage's ideas and compositions have also served as a catalyst for the development of new music. His fabrication and use of homemade instruments, "chance" sound, "happenings," and "musiciruses," have caused displeasure and hard criticism among some music circles, but Cage's work most certainly changed how people defined music.

Cage was one of the first composers to experiment with the electronic production of music. A Cage composition might include readings from a James Joyce novel (*Finnegan's Wake* was a favorite), contemporary prose, or the incorporation of 19th-century music, sounds from the city or the country, and computer-generated or moderated sounds. Composing music for dance was a significant aspect of Cage's career for more than 50 years, particularly in connection with Merce Cunningham, for whom he was musical director for several decades. Cage also was commissioned to write scores for many other choreographers as well.

Cage took piano lessons as a child and maintained a high scholastic average in high school. He attended college for two years, traveled extensively in Europe and North Africa, and began to compose music. He moved to New York City and supported himself by giving lectures on modern art and music. During this time, Cage

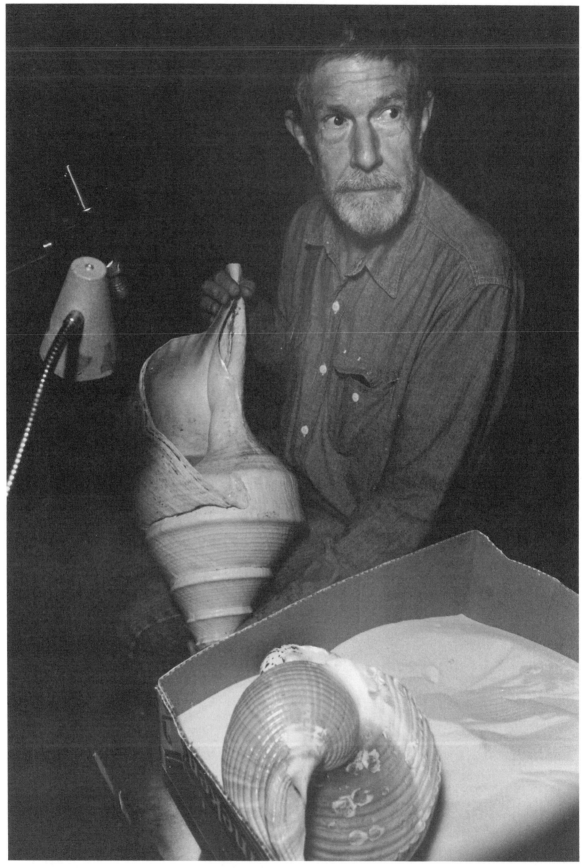

John Cage performing *Exchange* with the Martha Graham Dance Company. Photograph © Johan Elbers.

developed a mathematical system modeled after the style of Bach to compose his music. He became extremely interested in the music of Arnold Schönberg, and eventually studied with Schönberg, as well as with two of Schönberg's students, Richard Buhlig and Adolph Weiss. Cage also studied with composer Henry Cowell. Cage's early pieces were often based on experimentation with the chromatic scale or rhythm, and the sound possibilities of nontraditional instruments—with many compositions largely percussive. Cage often used traditional instruments, but in a nontraditional fashion such as the "prepared piano"—a piano with various objects placed on the strings, or stuffed with, for example, newspaper, to alter the pitch and tone when the keys are struck. In addition, piano strings were sometimes strummed, plucked, or hit directly by the musician or with an object. Compositions composed specifically for the prepared piano include *Bacchanale* (1940), which was written for dancer Sylvia Fort, and Cage's most well-known work for prepared piano, *Sonatas and Interludes* (1946).

His theory of "total soundspace," which gives equal importance to sound and nonsound (silence), and allowing chance sounds, like the rolling of dice, bird calls, traffic noise, etc. to be incorporated into a piece resulted in works like the well-known composition *4'33"* (1952). This piece was, in essence, four minutes and 33 seconds of silence and whatever chance or random sounds that occurred within that amount of time. Another unusual composition, *Imaginary Landscape No. 4* (1951), consisted of 12 radios, tuned at random.

Perhaps the fundamental idea that has defined Cage's work is the concept of chance. Cage was greatly influenced by Eastern thought, particularly Zen Buddhism and the ancient Chinese divination manual, *Book of Changes*, or the *I Ching*. His opus *Music of Changes* (1951) was inspired by the *I Ching*—to Cage, chance (which replaces destiny and fate) was a basic metaphysical principle determining our material being within the random events in our everyday lives. Chance allows a departure from convention, thus providing the freedom to form something new. Cage shared ideas about chance and the focus on process (as opposed to product) with many contemporary artists who have altogether made a significant impact on contemporary society. All artists—painters, choreographers, dancers, musicians, composers, etc.—are concerned primarily with form and content, but variations are created by a change in, for example, speed, duration, sequence, loudness, audibility, spatial orientation, and phrasing. In essence, chance creates the finished piece.

Cage's first composition using chance operations, *Sixteen Dances* (1950), was composed for Cunningham. Cage and Cunningham often worked together by composing and choreographing independently, agreeing only to the length of the finished piece. The only relation between the music (or sound accompaniment) and the movement of the dancers was that each happened to occur within the same time frame. Cage also performed in many of Cunningham's performances. In the dance *How to Pass, Kick, Fall, and Run* (1965), Cage would sit at a table to the side of the stage and provide the "chance" sound accompaniment—reading anecdotal stories from his book *Silence* or from *A Year From Monday*. The stories were told in one-minutes intervals, often letting several minutes pass before reading another. In addition, Cage would smoke cigarettes and sip champagne, often gulping and swallowing loudly into a microphone. Other well-known compositions for dance include *Concerto for Piano and Orchestra* for Cunningham's *Antic Meet* (1958), and an electronic version of *Atlas Eclipticals* (Cage used astrological charts for this piece) with *Winter Music* used for the piece *Aeon* (1961). Cage's later music, particularly pieces such

as *Europeras 1 & 2* (1987), was influenced by synergy concepts developed by Buckminster Fuller and Marshal McLuhan. Cage is also known for his multimedia events or "Happenings."

Other examples of Cage's work, like *Musicircus* (1967) consisted of a conglomeration of dancers, singers, musicians, and mimes performing simultaneously along with slide shows and light shows. Along with Lejaren Hiller, Cage composed HPSCHD (pronounced "harpsichord," 1967), a piece based on harpsichord-like sounds in which 51 tapes of computer-modified works by several composers were played at once or in any combination. Along with several real harpsichords on stage, the piece was played through 51 speakers directed at the audience. In 1994, two years after his death, Cage's *Rolywholyover* opened at the Museum of Contemporary Art in Los Angeles. *Rolywholyover* could be described as a museum circus or a composition for a museum; this unusual exhibit, perhaps a giant interactive memorial to John Cage, consisted of three exhibition spaces. Cage's visual works—etchings, watercolors, and drawings—along with his scores and writings were displayed along with the art and writings of approximately 50 of Cage's favorite artists including Marcel Duchamp and William Burroughs. The placement of the art and furniture and the choice of music played was chosen randomly by a computer, and changed daily.

In addition to becoming a respected artist, John Cage has become a pop culture icon. The term "clinamen," used by the Greek philosopher Epicurus, has been used to describe John Cage's impact on the Western world. Clinamen, in short, is the sudden, undetermined swerve of a atom, causing collisions and new forms.

—Christine Miner Minderovic

CAMPOBELLO, Nellie and Gloria
Mexican dancers, choreographers, educators, and researchers

Born: NELLIE—María Francisca Luna, 17 November 1900 in Villa Ocampo, Durango; GLORIA—María Soledad Luna, 21 October 1911 in Parral, Chihuahua. **Education:** Both sisters began their dancing studies with Adela, Amelia, and Linda Costa, Carmen Galé, Stanislava Mol Potapovich, Carol Adamchevsky, Eleanor Wallace and Lettie Carroll, 1925; Gloria studied with Vicenzo Celli, New York, 1946. **Career:** First public appearance in Carroll Ballet, touring several Mexican cities, 1927; appeared as a duet and toured Cuba, 1929; taught dance in the national music and dance section of the Fine Arts Department, (Mexico's Public Education sector), 1930-31; founders, teachers, and choreographers, Dynamic Plastic School, 1931; Dance School of the Fine Arts Department (later called National Dance School [NDS]), 1932; Nellie directed NDS, 1937; coauthored *Ritmos indígenas de México* (Indigenous Rhythms of Mexico), 1940; began the Dance Corps of the NDS, 1941; founded the Mexico City Ballet, 1942; Mexico City Ballet presented seasons in the Palace of Fine Arts, 1943, 1945 and 1947; Gloria was principal dancer for the company and danced with Anton Dolin, 1947; worked lifelong for the NDS; and was José Clemente Orozco's favorite model. **Awards:** Medal of Merit of the National Institute of Fine Arts, 1963; Life Dance Homage, National Institute of Fine Arts, (Nellie) 1985; (Gloria) 1996; three schools named after Gloria and one for both sisters; street Villa Ocampo, Durango named for Nellie. **Died:** GLORIA—4 November 1968; NELLIE—has been missing since 1985.

Roles (all performances with Carroll Ballet Classique, premiering in Mexico City, unless otherwise noted)

1927   El príncipe feliz (Nellie), *Una fantasía bucólica (A Bucolic Fantasy)* (Carroll)

El Favorito (Nellie) and Una joven que sufre de amor no correspondido (Gloria), *Fantasía oriental (Oriental Fantasy)* (Carroll)

Diamante (Nellie) and Perla (Gloria), *Ballet de las joyas (Jewel's Ballet)* (Carroll)

(Nellie) *Ballet ruso (Russian Ballet)* (Carroll)

(Gloria) *Polka clásica (Classical Polka)* (Carroll)

(Nellie and Gloria) *Ay qué normalistas!* (Carroll)

Boxeador (Nellie), *Knock Out* (Carroll)

(Nellie and Gloria) *Muñecas danzarinas (Dancing Dolls)* (Carroll)

1930   (Nellie and Gloria) *Ballet del árbol (The Tree Ballet)* (Zybin) Public Education Secretary, Mexico City

Other roles include: Performed solos and duets in own works, 1929, 1930, 1932.

Works (choreographed by Gloria and Nellie for the Public Education Secretary's Dance School in Mexico City unless otherwise noted)

1930   *Escena tarahumara (Tarahumara Scene)* (mus. Mendoza), duet

La Zandunga (Nellie) (mus. Mexican popular, arr. Chávez) solo

Jarabe tapatío (mus. Mexican popular) duet

Yucatán Fantasy (mus. Mexican popular) duet

1931   *Ballet yaqui El Venadito (Yaqui Ballet, The Little Deer)* (mus. Mexican popular, arr. Núñez)

Ballet simbólico 30-30 (30-30 Symbolic Ballet) w/Ángel Salas (mus. Domínguez), Dynamic Plastic School, Mexico City

1932   *Tehuana* (mus. Mexican popular)

Jarana (mus. Mexican popular)

Juanita (mus. Mexican popular)

Son de Jalisco (Jalisco's Son) (mus. Mexican popular)

Jarana 3 x 4 (mus. Mexican popular)

Son michoacano (Michoacan Son) (mus. Mexican popular)

El palomo (The Dove) (mus. Mexican popular)

1934   *Cinco pasos de danza (Five Dancing Steps)* (Gloria) (mus. Mexican popular, arr. Domínguez)

Bailes istmeños (Istmo's Dances) (Nellie) (mus. Mexican popular)

La danza de los Malinches (Malinches' Dance) (Gloria) (mus. Mexican popular, arr. Domínguez)

La virgen y las fieras (The Virgin and the Beasts) (Gloria) (mus. Mexican popular, arr. Domínguez)

Ballet simbólico Simiente (Seed Symbolic Ballet) (Nellie) (mus. Domínguez)

1935   *Barricada (Barricade)* w/Ángel Salas (mus. Kostakowsky)

Clarín (Cornet) w/Ángel Salas (mus. Kostakowsky)

Uchben C'Coholte (An Ancient Cemetery) (Gloria) (mus. Ayala)

Las biniguendas de plata (The Silver) (mus. Meza)

Ballet de masas tierra (Earth Mass Ballet) (mus. Domínguez)

El coconito (Gloria) (mus. Mexican popular)

1937   *La Zandunga* (Gloria) (mus. Mexican popular)

Ballet Mexicano (Nellie) (mus. Mexican popular)

Estampas románticas (Romantic Images) (Gloria) (mus. Chopin)

La casada infiel (The Unfaithful Wife) (Gloria)

Dos estampas o Ballet tarahumara (Two Images or Tarahumara Ballet) (Gloria) (mus. Díaz and Ríos)

En la escuela o Una clase de técnica clásica (At School or A Classical Technic Class) (Gloria)

Ballet simbólico español Bandera (Spanish Symbolic Ballet: Flag) (Nellie) w/Ernesgo Agüero (mus. Falla, Abéniz and Ravel)

Polka (Gloria) (mus. Drigo)

1938   *Evocación* (Gloria) (mus. Debussy)

Sobre el Danubio (Over the Danube) (Gloria) (mus. Strauss)

Amanecer (The Dawn) (Gloria) (mus. Beethoven)

Danza indígena (Indigenous Dance) (Gloria) (mus. Mexican popular)

Las Sílfides (The Sylphides) (Gloria) (mus. Chopin)

Danza de los Concheros (Concheros' Dance) (Gloria) (mus. indigenous)

Ritmos indígenas de México (Mexican Indigenous Rhythms) (Gloria) (mus. indigenous)

1941   *La siesta del fauno (L'après-midi d'un faune)* (Nellie) (mus. Debussy), Ballet Corps, NDS, Jalapa, Veracruz.

El espectro de la rosa (Spectre de la rose) (Nellie) (mus. Weber), Ballet Corps, NDS, Jalapa, Veracruz

Variaciones de otoño (Autumn Variations) (Nellie) w/Linda Costa, Ballet Corps, NDS, Jalapa, Veracruz

1943   *Umbral (Threshold)* (Gloria) (mus. Schubert), Mexico City Ballet, Mexico City

Alameda 1900 (Gloria) (mus. Hernández Moncada, Pacheco, Martínez, Morler, De la Peña, Espinosa, Lerdo de Tejada, Rosas and Waldteufel), Mexico City Ballet, Mexico City

Fuensanta (Gloria) (mus. Elorduy, Ponce, Villanueva, Domínguez, Martínez and Castro), Mexico City Ballet

Obertura republicana (Republican Overture) (Nellie) (mus. Chávez), Mexico City Ballet

1945   *Pausa (Pause)* (Gloria) (mus. Beethoven), Mexico City Ballet, Mexico City

Circo Orrín (Orrin Circus) (Gloria) (mus. various, arr. Hernández Moncada), Mexico City Ballet

Vespertina (Evening) (Nellie) (mus. Mozart), Mexico City Ballet

Ixtepec (Nellie) (mus. various, arr. Hernández Moncada), Mexico City Ballet

1946   *Aleluya* (Gloria) (mus. Strauss), Mexico City Ballet

1947   *Feria (Fair)* (Nellie) (mus. Galindo), Mexico City Ballet and Markova Dolin Ballet, Mexico City

1968   *Voces de la Revolución (Revolution's Voices)* (Gloria) (mus. various; script Nellie)

Publications

By NELLIE: books—

Apuntes sobre la vida militar de Franciso Villa, Mexico City, 1940.
Cartucho, Jalapa, 1931.
Las manos de mamá, Mexico City, 1937.

Mis libros, Mexico City, 1960.
Tres poemas, Mexico City, 1957.
¡Yo!, Mexico City, 1929.
with Gloria Campobello, *Ritmos indígenas de México,* Mexico City, 1940.

By NELLIE: article—

"Ocho poemas de mujer," *Revista de La Habana,* 1930.

On NELLIE & GLORIA: books—

50 años de Danza en el Palacio de Bellas Artes, Mexico City, 1984.
Aulestia, Patricia, *Nellie Campobello,* Mexico City, 1987.
Segura, Felipe, *Gloria Campobello. La primera ballerina de México,* Mexico City, 1991.
Tortajada Quiroz, Margarita, *Danza y Poder,* Mexico City, 1995.

*   *   *

Nellie and Gloria Campobello's lives were inseparable; they developed together as dancers, teachers, choreographers, and researchers. Only in the field of literature did Nellie Campobello distinguish herself apart from her sister. Both sisters were central figures in Mexican dance. They brought to Mexican dance the agenda of the Mexican nationalist post-revolutionary movement and developed it in grandiose mass ballets, similar to the German mass ballets created by Laban and Wigman. From their position in the National Dance School (NDS), they promoted the training of numerous male and female dancers who would eventually form the modern dance and ballet companies which emerged in the 1930s. In 1941 they made a new aesthetic statement, now based in classical ballet but retaining nationalist themes.

Born in the northern part of Mexico, where the armed movement had been very intense, the Campobello sisters moved to Mexico City in 1923. Two years later, Anna Pavlova and her ballet company performed in the city, stimulating both sisters to immerse themselves in the world of dance. They immediately began studying dance with the Italian Costa sisters (Adela, Amelia, and Linda), Mexican Carmen Galé; Polish artists Stanislava Mol Potapovich and Carol Adamchevsky, and Americans Eleanor Wallace and Lettie Carroll. In 1927 they made their debut in the Carroll Ballet, for which they adopted the name Campbell. With this company, which had a large commercial repertoire including ballet and music hall works, they performed in several theaters in Mexico City, as well as touring to other Mexican cities. In 1929 the sisters separated from Carroll and began performing as a duet in traditional Mexican dance works. They had considerable critical and popular success, and under the name of Campobello, toured Cuba.

Back in Mexico in 1930, the Campobellos joined the National Music and Dance departments of the Fine Arts Department, part of the Public Education system, as teachers. In addition to teaching, dancing in the Public Education group, and creating a new repertoire based in traditional dance, they participated in the Cultural Missions, founded in 1923 by José Vasconcelos. These missions took numerous teachers and artists to the most remote villages to recover indigenous art and customs. The Campobellos actively participated in this work as they traveled throughout the country, compiling indigenous dances and presenting their own dance works.

Contemporary critics considered their works to be "the first high-quality Mexican dance spectacle presented in Mexico." In 1931 they performed one of Mexican dance's fundamental works, the *30-30 Symbolic Ballet,* for the first time. A mass ballet which included more than 1,000 dancers and public school students, this spectacle was collectively conceived, with the Campobellos and Ángel Salas creating the choreography, Francisco Domínguez composing the music, and Carlos González as the artistic director. The *30-30 Ballet* was maintained within the dance repertoire and was presented in several cities and stadiums across the country until 1960. The work introduced a new concept of dance to the Mexican public; the spectacle's expressiveness and grandeur, its naturalistic movement, and its identification with workers and peasants (at the end of the work the *Internationale* was sung), were all central to the new dance form.

The work carried out by the Campobello sisters in the 1930s was politically and aesthetically committed to the nationalist cultural project and had as its objective the building of countrywide unity and the furthering of its values. The Campobellos maintained this with other mass ballets such as *Seed Symbolic Ballet* (1935), *Earth Mass Ballet* (1936), *Cornet* (1935), and *Barricade* (1935). Besides this choreographic work, the Campobellos participated in the creation of the Dynamic Plastic School (1931) and the Dance School (1932). The latter was the first official Mexican school dedicated to training professional dancers and had as its goal the creation of modernist dance, using innovative techniques to create a national, original dance language. It was proposed that the development of such a dance language would give a universal perspective to the newly created Mexican dance movement. In the Dance School (later called the National Dance School [NDS]) the Campobellos instructed several generations of Mexican male and female dancers, created a broad repertoire, and introduced new dance techniques. They became the country's most recognized dance specialists; when Martha Graham visited Mexico in 1932, she was told that she could consult Nellie Campobello about Mexican dance.

In addition to the innovative modern dance presented in their mass ballets, the Campobellos created several works based on traditional Mexican dances, reflecting the national debate between tradition and modernity in post-revolutionary Mexico. In 1937 Nellie became director of NDS, a post she occupied for nearly 50 years. The changes she introduced created a more formal program of study, emphasising technical training and countrywide performances. In 1940 the Campobello sisters published *Indigenous Rhythms of Mexico,* a pioneering work in Mexican dance anthropology which described the sisters' anthropological research among the indigenous cultures of Mexico. In this book they delineate the "sacred language" of the indigenous bodies and the ways of reading, understanding, and recreating it on the dance scene. For her part, Nellie Campobello published several books of poetry and novels which, beginning in the 1980s, have gained recognition as important works in the corpus of Latin American literature.

In 1941 the Campobellos modified the emphasis of their dance work and, with the government's support, formed the Ballet Corps of the NDS, founding the Mexico City Ballet in the following year. With the latter, the Campobellos' aesthetic and choreographic focus switched to classical dance. They restaged the traditional repertoire as well as the works of Diaghilev's Ballets Russes. In addition, the sisters created new works using Mexican themes, music, and design, but within the framework of classical ballet. The company performed three seasons in the Palace of Fine Arts (1943, 1945, and 1947) with Gloria as the principal dancer. In the 1947 season the Mexico City Ballet joined the Markova-Dolin Ballet, and Gloria Campobello had the opportunity of dancing with Dolin. The visiting artists also danced in Gloria's version of *The Sylphides,* as well as in Nellie's *Feria* and *Ixtepec.*

The Campobellos worked very closely with the artists and intellectuals of the period. Writer Martín Luis Guzmán and the muralist painter José Clemente Orozco were members of the Mexico City Ballet. In addition, the sisters gathered a large number of artists to participate in the company's productions including such Mexican art personalities as Carlos Mérida, Carlos Chávez, Julio Castellanos, Eduardo Hernández Moncada, Roberto Montenegro, Carlos Orozco Romero, Antonio Ruiz, José Pablo Moncayo, Federico Canessi, Blas Galindo, Germán Cueto, and Carlos Marichal.

The three Mexico City Ballet seasons were pivotal in the development of dance in Mexico. The company broadened the audience base for Mexican dance, encouraged the growth of a new generation of professional dancers, and prepared the ground for the acceptance of a new modern dance movement. After 1947, however, the Campobellos were abandoned by the official dance community and lost the support of the governmental agencies which had funded much of their work. They continued to work within the NDS, but never regained the influential position they'd previously enjoyed. They were, in part, displaced by a new, American-led modern dance movement which received substantial government support.

Gloria worked with the NDS until her death in 1968, and Nellie did too until 28 January 1985, when she disappeared, the victim of a kidnapping. Since her disappearance several committees of artists and intellectuals have been formed to seek government assistance in finding her, but without any success to date.

—Margarita Tortajada Quiroz;
translated by Dolores Ponce Gutiérrez

CANADA

From its beginnings as cuttings from American and European dance traditions, Canadian modern dance has grown to become a dynamic expression of contemporary Canadian culture. While the strength of individual creators is always borderless, various threads of identity can be traced. Its sources, Expressionist and Graham-based, provide one set of trails. Canadian contemporary dance can also be seen as part of the social, geographical, and even political traditions of disparate parts of this enormous, varied country— regional differences, the two founding cultures of the country, (British and French), and the present cultural diversity, are all reflected in dance creation. On the west coast, the Vancouver dance scene is currently influenced by indigenous and Asian culture; at the centre of the country, Toronto's spectrum of activity and its shifting identity as a "company town," attest to the city's strong entrepreneurial and financial focus; and the idiosyncratic, uniquely evolving dance scene in Montreal articulates the cultural ferment which stimulates the Quebec art world.

Many European and American companies came to Canada's urban centres—Toronto and Montreal, and less occasionally Vancouver. Isadora Duncan appeared in Toronto in 1909; the Toronto-born Maud Allan was another early influence, as was Mary Wigman, who appeared in Toronto in 1930 and 1931. Harald Kreutzberg came to Canada as well, as did Kurt Jooss' company, and the Swiss-based Trudi Schoop. Torontonian Saida Gerrard studied with Hanya Holm, danced with the Humphrey-Weidman company and came back to Canada to teach for two years.

During the 1930s an experimental dance group flourished at the Margaret Eaton Centre, headed by Mildred Halfend, a young woman who attended the Amy Sternberg school, an important dance centre of the day. Halfend aimed to make ideas she saw in on-tour performances by Duncan, Jooss, and Pavlova relevant to her own experience. In Montreal, Elsie Salomons was a pioneering modern dance teacher in the English-speaking educational system; Thelma Wagner, who taught at McGill University in the Wigman style, hosted the Humphrey-Weidman company; Norma Darling operated a Montreal company in the 1930s, creating in a style influenced by Jooss' work; and George Erskine-Jones was also a notable performer in Montreal at this time.

Englishwoman Ruby Ginner's revived Greek dances were the source of Hilda Davies' work in the 1920s in Halifax, Nova Scotia. Ginner's work may have also influenced early activity in Vancouver, where there were modern dance performances in the opera house. Denishawn toured in Canada in the decade from 1910 to 1920, and Edna Malone, from Nelson, British Columbia, who had attended the Denishawn school, toured with the company and later returned to British Columbia to teach. Josephine Slater, a Shawn disciple, published a modern dance magazine from her home in New Westminster, British Columbia.

After World War II Canada was enriched by a wave of European immigrants who brought their Expressionist dance to Toronto and Montreal. In Toronto, Lithuanian-born, Laban-trained Yone Kvietys, Willy Blok Hanson, and Wigman disciple Bianca Rogge were active through the 1940s and 1950s. Another key figure was Nancy Lima Dent, who brought her studies with Elizabeth Leese, Hanya Holm, and Doris Humphrey to the New Dance Theatre, a company she formed with Cynthia Barrett, and later the Nancy Lima Dent Dance Company. Cynthia Barrett became one of the first choreographers to work regularly in television, which was, in its early days, an important vehicle for the development of Canadian dance. Bianca Rogge, Lithuanian-born and Wigman-schooled, moved to Toronto in 1956. Styling themselves Contemporary Choreographers of Toronto, Rogge, Kvietys, Lima Dent, and Tutti Lau, another German immigrant, staged an evening of modern dance in February 1960, the first of its kind in Canada. Seeded by these women's creation and training, a tiny growth of modern dance began. David Earle, Susan Macpherson, and Judy Jarvis all crossed paths with these trailblazing women in the 1950s in Toronto.

In Montreal early activity was animated by Kvietys, Biroute Nagys, and Laban-trained Elizabeth Leese, who had studied at the Jooss-Leeder school before settling in Canada in 1939. Ruth Sorel, Polish-born and ballet-trained, was a noted theatrical dancer in Europe. By 1946 she had formed a performing ensemble in Montreal, dancing a dramatic brand of psychological social commentary in Wigman-influenced ballet style. In 1948 the first Canadian Ballet Festival welcomed Sorel as the first Canadian to excel at a new art— modern dance. Montreal was further home to two true luminaries of dance in Quebec, Françoise Sullivan and Jeanne Renaud. Sullivan was a signatory of the famous *Le Refus Global* (Total Refusal) artists' manifesto, in which Quebec artists declared their dissociation from the binding strictures of Quebec political and religious life. The "Automatistes" declared their intentions to follow the intuitive, rather than rational path of artistic discovery. Sullivan called dance "a reflex, a spontaneous expression of intense emotion" and went on to refine her talents as a visual artist, becoming a noted sculptor and painter. Jeanne Renaud had returned to Montreal after time in Paris and New York and began collaborating with Sullivan, who created sets and decor for Renaud's dances. She also worked with Françoise Riopelle, another Automatiste. In 1966 Renaud founded Montreal's Le Groupe de la Place Royale, an experimental company that became home to Peter Boneham and Jean-Pierre Perreault. After directing Le Groupe until 1972, Renaud became an officer of the Canada Council, director of the dance program at the Cultural Affairs Ministry of Quebec, and advisor to the Conservatoire d'Art Dramatique et de Musique of Quebec City and Montreal.

A wave of Canadian dance artists headed for the established modern dance scene of New York City and encountered the inspiration of Martha Graham's dance theatre and the sweeping humanism of Limón. As they trickled back to Canada, their influence began to shape modern dance. First among the modern dance companies in Canada were Winnipeg's Contemporary Dancers, founded by Rachel Browne, which gave its first performances in 1964. Browne, an American-born dancer formerly with the Royal Winnipeg Ballet, guided the new company from an amateur community-based group to fully professional stature. A further generation of choreographers, among them Ruth Cansfield, Tedd Senmon Robinson, and Tom Stroud headed the company after Browne's departure. Another early prairie company was Regina Modern Dance Works, founded by Marianne Livant in 1974, which toured widely under the direction of Maria Formolo and Susan Jane Arnold. In 1979 Formolo joined forces with Keith Urban, sharing the company's directorship, until they relocated in Edmonton, Alberta in 1982.

On Canada's west coast, developing dance included the companies of Anna Wyman, Paula Ross, Karen Rimmer (neé Jamieson), and Judith Marcuse, as well as Mountain Dance Theatre, operated by Mauryne Allen and Fredi Long, Prism Dance Theatre, headed by Gisa Cole and Jamie Zagoudakis, and Experimental Dance and Music (EDAM). EDAM's members, Barbara Bourget, Jay Hirabayashi, Lola Maclaughlin, and Jennifer Mascall have since gone in dissimilar directions.

In Toronto, Trish Beatty joined her New Dance Group of Canada with David Earle and Peter Randazzo in the early days of the Toronto Dance Theatre, which has become a powerful centre in Canada, with a stellar company of passionate dancers. The company is presently headed by Christopher House, and over TDT's 30-year history many seminal figures have emerged, from Peggy Baker and Susan Macpherson to Benoit Lachambre and Bill Coleman. The school of TDT is a magnet for aspiring dancers, who train in Graham-based technique.

Judy Jarvis was a force on the Toronto scene from the late 1960s through the early 1980s, as was Dancemakers, made up of graduates of York University's Dance Department in 1973. Its founder, Andrea Smith, later danced with Louis Falco and with Martha Graham's company. Other members, several of whom assumed the company's directorship, went on to notable careers, among them Anna Blewchamp, Carol Anderson, Patricia Fraser, Patricia Miner, William Douglas, Conrad Alexandrowicz, Susan McKenzie, Bill James, and Serge Bennathan (Dancemaker's current director).

Two other Toronto phenomena are Robert Desrosiers and Danny Grossman. Desrosiers, a wild child at the National Ballet School, later founded Desrosiers Dance Theatre; Grossman danced with Paul Taylor's company before coming to Canada and has created forceful works often with outspoken social criticism. Toronto Independent Dance Enterprise (TIDE), started in 1978 by York University graduates, was based in improvisational techniques; 15 Dance Lab gave Toronto independents a toehold in the community.

In Montreal, Martine Époque's Groupe Nouvelle Aire, founded in 1968, was a locus for many of the dance artists who have gone on to remarkable careers. Françoise Sullivan came out of choreographic retirement for Groupe Nouvelle Aire and her original approach to choreography had a profound effect on many creators of the next generation—Daniel Leveille, Ginette Laurin, Michele Febvre, Paul-André Fortier, Edouard Lock, and others. Linda Rabin, after training at the Juilliard School and working with a number of companies in Europe and Israel, returned to Montreal and founded Les Ateliers de Danse Moderne de Montréal Incorpores (LAADMI) with Candace Loubert. Another phenomenon of Canadian modern dance is Margie Gillis, whose ecstatic, free-spirited performances have earned her a stature akin to Isadora Duncan's.

Dance has been a flickering presence on Canada's East Coast. The Halifax Dance Co-op was set up as an informal company and umbrella organization in 1973; Island Dance Theatre in Prince Edward Island, and later Sekai and Company in Halifax were breaths of fresh talent. In 1981 Jeanne Robinson, a former dancer with Sekai, started Nova Dance Theatre in Halifax, where it continued until 1989.

The strength of individual creators has been boosted by opportunities for growth and challenge. Grant Strate, an early member of the National Ballet of Canada, has played a vital developmental role in the rise of modern dance creation in Canada. He was the first Chair of the dance department at York University, setting up a lively model of diversity and investigation into all aspects of dance which continues to deepen to this day. Strate organized a series of National Choreographic Seminars, the first in 1979, which were practical hothouses, and incubated many collaborative relationships among choreographers, composers and dancers. He has also organized catalytic dance writers' conferences.

As in early years, festivals play an important role in the visibility of dance in Canada. Toronto Workshop Productions Theatre was home to two festivals, held in 1976 and 1978. The first featured Toronto artists; the second had a more national focus. Currently, the Canada Dance Festival, held biannually at Ottawa's National Arts Centre, and Montreal's Festival Internationale de Nouvelle Danse, which started in 1985, are the focus of intense national and international attention. Toronto's annual fringe Festival of Independent Dance (fFIDA) began in 1992 and was preceded by four INDE Festivals. Instigated by maverick choreographer Terrill Maguire, these were staged in 1985, 1988, 1990 and 1992. Dancing on the Edge is a further nationally representative festival, staged in Vancouver.

The role of universities in the growth of dance in Canada has been significant. York University, the University of Waterloo (though the program is now closed), Simon Fraser University, the University of Alberta at Calgary, and Montreal's Concordia University and the Université de Québec à Montréal have all provided a focus for dance, a place where many dancers have trained, and found both a kind of creative ferment and a sense of evolving context for contemporary dance. As well as being a bridge in some ways between the professional and academic worlds, some schools have affiliations with Dance Collection Danse, a Toronto-based archive and publisher dedicated to the preservation of Canada's dance heritage. In 1985 Dance Collection Danse mounted Encore! Encore!, an ambitious project reconstructing dances from the 1940s and 1950s by Françoise Sullivan, Jeanne Renaud, Gweneth Lloyd, Boris Volkoff, Nesta Toumine and Nancy Lima Dent. Dance Collection Danse's work has been instrumental in ensuring that dance is no longer a throw-away art in Canada.

An upcoming generation of dancers and creators faces challenges of finance, venue, ways of using new technology artistically and in enticing new audiences. There are many avid creators on the scene, including a movement toward the integration, through the fusion of styles, of many influences, classical East Indian, Spanish, Japanese, Chinese. A distinctly Canadian feeling of space, rhythm, irony, and innocence often bubbles up, as contemporary dance mirrors the changes in the face of the nation for new times. Dance artists continue to push the borders of dance. There is tremendous energy in the desire to forge new ways of seeing, understanding, creating and performing dance. The common thread is diversity, and how dance lives through Canada's vast, dynamic mosaic.

Publications

101 from the Encyclopedia of Theatre Dance in Canada, Toronto, 1997.
Canadian Dance Studies, Volumes 1 & 2, Ontario, 1994, 1997.
Dance in Canada Index 1972-85, Toronto, 1995.
Tembeck, Iro, "Dancing in Montreal: Seeds of a Choreographic History," Studies in Dance History, Fall 1994.
Warner, Mary Jane, Toronto Dance Teachers 1825-1925, Toronto, 1995.
Wyman, Max, Dance Canada, Vancouver, 1989.

—Carol Anderson

CANADA DANCE FESTIVAL

The biennial Canada Dance Festival, held in Ottawa, is a place to risk and challenge and meet around the art. During the festival's 10-day run, it is both a showcase and partner in the creation of new Canadian choreography. At the 1996 edition of the festival, the lineup featured more than 50 paid and free performances throughout the city, including nine world premieres and seven commissioned works. Audiences had a chance to see over 450 of Canada's leading dancers and choreographers in their newest works. The raison d'être of the festival is to show contemporary expression, with a guaranteed strong slate of cross-cultural representation and regional diversity. The budget for the festival in 1996 was $850,000; it derives 45 percent from government, 25 percent from festival partners (the National Arts Centre in association with the National Gallery of Canada) and 15 percent from box office. The remaining support comes from foundations and corporate sponsors.

The Canada Dance Festival (CDF) is the nine-year-old offspring of the annual conference of the Dance in Canada Association (DCA), which for 14 years migrated from city to city. It was an organization aimed at bringing together modern dance and classical ballet practitioners, as well as university professors and professional dance teachers. The annual conference was a wide-ranging event with scholarly papers given alongside performances and master classes. The Chalmers choreographic prize, the country's top dance honour, was awarded at these conferences. When, in 1987, the DCF was created as a national festival, it became Canada's only all-Canadian "one-discipline, one country" festival, uncovering the state of dance in the country. Shortly afterward, the DCA ceased operation. The festival retained the objective of bringing Canadian choreographers and dancers together from across the country to support and foster the creation of new Canadian dance and artists and unveil the results to audiences. While it is the country's most representative and extensive dance event, curatorial prerogative is exercised, with an invitation-only policy; but it is an unjuried festival with no formal call for proposals.

The biennial nature of the festival suits it well, says its producer, Cathy Levy (also programmer of Toronto's Harbourfront dance season), because there's simply a greater concentration of creative and financial resources to be mustered up over a two-year period. Diminished resources at funding sources like the Canada Council, the federal arts funding body, and the inability of various agencies to respond to the community's needs, have ultimately dictated the overall focus of the festival. At the same time, Levy is involved in substantial maneuvering required to keep the festival afloat.

The survival of international, professionally placed festivals is a huge issue in Canada. Festivals are not just tourist attractions, but there's an investment, in both economic and social development terms; festivals are also key partners in leveraging long-term results for participants. Presenting a work at the CDF can catapault an artist into a presenter's registry or turn around a company's funding fortunes with a year-long tour. International presenters often attend because they know this is the place to see Canadian dance. Montreal's Festival International de Nouvelle Danse (FIND) attracts more buyers from abroad, but FIND generally does not commission as many works as CDF, nor do the Canadians appearing at FIND necessarily show their most recent creations.

To break through to uinitiated audiences, the popular "Max Chats," featuring veteran Vancouver-based dance critic Max Wyman, fill the breach, through a series of free, informal, pre-show discussions about the evening's choreographers. Free outdoor performances near the National Gallery provide another key to bringing dance to the public. Film screenings are an integral part of the festival package. Other activities during the CDF include morning master classes, open to local dancers and dance students.

—Philip Szporer

CANADIAN FESTIVALS, 1948-78

In a country as large and sparsely populated as Canada, festivals have been a necessary catalyst for the nation's dance booms. There have been two major booms: the late 1940s to early 1950s, and the 1970s, with small bursts in various cities in between. In both periods, festivals created an opportunity for the nation's dance companies to communicate and the necessary atmosphere to raise the profile of dance in the country.

The first of these festivals began at a cocktail party in Toronto in 1947. Russian immigrant Boris Volkoff (founder of the Volkoff Canadian Ballet) and David Yeddeau (manager of the Winnipeg Ballet) discovered over drinks that they had both been involved with ballet companies since the early 1930s and yet knew nothing of one another. They felt a festival was the only way to make Canadians realize that Canada had a dance community. Yeddeau reportedly sent out hundreds of letters to dance companies and schools across Canada, but only two replied: the Ruth Sorel Modern Dance Group in Montreal and Panto-Pacific Ballet in Vancouver.

The first festival was successful and disastrous at the same time. It was the spring of 1948 in Winnipeg and festival founders were preparing their gala performance for the Governor General of Canada. First the theatre flooded; then the replacement theatre (a converted Odeon movie house) was only free for two nights instead of three and had fewer seats, so about 1,000 tickets were returned to patrons. In addition, a new stage had to be built the night before the opening performance, then more rain flooded the railway and the Panto-Pacific Ballet from Vancouver was unable to reach Winnipeg—so the festival shrunk to three groups: The Winnipeg Ballet, Volkoff Canadian Ballet, and the Ruth Sorel Modern Dance Group. Finally, shortly after the performance began, Yeddeau learned that the Governor General planned to stay for only the first dance. To keep the vice-regal couple in the audience, Yeddeau ordered all of the dancers to directly follow the act in front of them so the entire performance ran without a single break or intermission. Despite its problems, this festival began an annual, national dance event that took place in various Canadian cities until 1954 and created the awareness and appreciation of dance that led to the present Canadian dance community.

After the 1948 festival, the Canadian Ballet Associates (CBA) was formed to organize future festivals, to maintain a noncompetitive, all-Canadian environment, along with the highest possible standard of performance. The festival of 1949, held in Toronto, attracted radio, film and print media and created such an interest from dance companies that the CBA appointed adjudicator Guy Glover to travel the country searching for the best companies to participate in the next festival. The 1950 festival was held in Montreal, the year 1951 was skipped, 1952 was in Toronto, 1953 in Ottawa and 1954 in Toronto again.

By 1954 the festivals were losing momentum. Money was more difficult to find and organizers of this year's festival attempted to get public funding from the municipal government but wound up in a battle with Toronto's city controllers, who didn't consider dance an art form. This created an uprising of local artists and arts organizations such as the Toronto Symphony Orchestra, who protested on behalf of the dance companies. It was a unifying event for Toronto artists as a whole, however, the CBA felt the festivals had run their course and disbanded.

While the festivals were called "Ballet Festivals," they provided a means for modern dance to make a grand entry into the Canadian dance scene. Key modern dance choreographers included Ruth Sorel, Elizabeth Leese and Nancy Lima Dent. Sorel and Leese, both immigrants, contributed the influences of European modern dancers such as Mary Wigman and Trudi Schoop. Although both preferred the expressive and organic qualities of modern dance, they felt ballet was an essential complement to training. Dent was a Toronto dancer who began ballet training at age 19 and traveled to New York City to train with Humphrey, Limón and Graham. She is noteworthy for creating dances to comment on serious social issues such as atomic weapons and violence in 1950s comic books.

In 1960, Dent, with three other modern dancers, Yone Kvietys, Ruth (Tutti) Lau and Bianca Rogge, organized a Modern Dance Festival held that February in Toronto. Evidence suggests these women, along with Biroute Nagys, organized a modern dance festival each year until 1963. While these festivals weren't noted for creating the dance awareness of their predecessors, they did foster the growth of modern dance in Canada and gave early performing opportunities to some of the key people in the modern dance boom of the 1970s including David Earle, Susan MacPherson and Judy Jarvis.

By the end of the 1960s three modern dance companies that would form the backbone of the 1990s modern dance community had been created: Winnipeg's Contemporary Dancers (1964), Le Groupe de la Place Royale (1966) and Toronto Dance Theatre (1968). The early 1970s saw a surge of creation in modern dance across the country but, as was seen in the 1950s, no one was very aware of what other artists were doing. The creation of the Dance in Canada Association in 1972 aided communication somewhat but companies still weren't fully aware of each other and audience awareness required a drastic increase. Again, festivals were the necessary catalyst.

While the 1976 Toronto Modern Dance Festival was not the first modern dance festival held in Toronto, it was significant because it occurred at a time when the modern dance community of the 1990s was just beginning. This festival increased the visibility of modern dance in Toronto, proved people would watch dance night after night and improved the communication and professional relationships among artists in the modern dance community.

The idea of creating a project with a group of dancers and companies was first discussed by David Earle and Judy Jarvis at the 1976 Dance in Canada Conference in Halifax. The following September Dancemakers and Toronto Dance Theatre tried to book space at Toronto Workshop Productions for the same time period; a collaboration was the simplest solution. Earle, Patricia Beatty, Peter Randazzo (the three founders of Toronto Dance Theatre), TDT's Managing Director Roger Jones, Danny Grossman, Jarvis, members of Dancemakers and Margaret Dragu held a meeting to discuss the possibility. These people, plus independent choreographer Kathryn Brown, participated in the five-week festival with the majority of administration and funds provided by TDT.

On opening night, all groups performed to give audiences a sampling of what the entire festival held in store. It was on this night that dancer Jean-Louis Morin and others were strategically placed in the audience to throw vegetables and yell, "Amateur!" just to liven things up. It was also the night Earle streaked across the stage in the largest presentation of his dance *Bugs* ever seen.

Coinciding with the modern dance festival was the National Ballet of Canada's 25th Anniversary and while the Ballet was attracting all of the press, it wasn't attracting all of the audiences. The festival box office remained steady, and the Ballet's anniversary seemed to help the festival because there was so much dance awareness at the time. Finally, modern dance was getting an audience beyond the choreographers' friends and families.

The 1976 festival led the way to a national modern dance festival held in Toronto in 1978. Presented again at Toronto Workshop Productions Theatre, the festival opened with a gala presentation of the National Ballet of Canada, the Royal Winnipeg Ballet, and Les Grands Ballets Canadiens. This was a rather significant event considering the rivalry that existed between Canada's three major ballet companies at the time. The next five weeks included two or three performances each by Toronto Dance Theatre, Danny Grossman, Les Ballets Jazz, Winnipeg's Contemporary Dancers, Le Groupe Nouvelle Aire, Paula Ross Dancers, Entre Six, Judy Jarvis, Dancemakers, Regina Modern Dance Works, Le Groupe de la Place Royale, Ballet Ys, Halifax Dance Coop and Anna Wyman Dance Theatre. There were also late night performances of the National Tap Dance Company, Paul Gaulin Mime Company, Fulcrum Contact Improvization, Margaret Dragu, Kathryn Brown and David Earle.

The 1980s saw the rise of the independent choreographer in Canada and with that the development of large, regional festivals to showcase the work of independents. Examples include Dancing on the Edge in Vancouver, Festival Internationale de Nouvelle Danse (FIND) in Montreal, the Canada Dance Festival in Ottawa and the fringe Festival of Independent Dance Artists (fFIDA) in Toronto. These annual festivals attract artists and audiences from all over the world. However, they owe their very existence to their predecessors—who created the necessary awareness and communication to bring Canada's dance community to the forefront.

Publications

Callwood, June, "Ballet Rally," *Maclean's Magazine,* 1 March 1949.
Glover, Guy, "The Canadian Ballet Festival," *Canadian Art*, Summer 1949.
Glover, Guy, "Reflections on Canadian Ballet," *Canadian Art,* Spring 1951.
Jackson, Graham, "The Toronto Dance Festival," *Dance in Canada,* Winter 1977.
Swoboda, Victor, "Third Canadian Ballet Festival," *Dance International,* Fall 1995.

—Amy Bowring

CAPUCILLI, Terese

American dancer

Born: 1956 in Syracuse, New York. **Education:** Studied in Syracuse with Miss Augustine and at Syracuse Ballet with Deborah Boughton; B.F.A., State University of New York (SUNY) at Purchase; granted a scholarship for study at the Jacob's Pillow School in Massachusetts and later studied with Maggie Black in New York City; after college, won a scholarship to the Martha Graham school. **Career:** Dancer, Kuzuko Hirabayashi Dance Theater and Marcus Skulkind Dance Company, New York; joined the Graham company, 1979; toured extensively with Graham company in the U.S., Europe, the Middle East, and Asia; took over many of Graham's leading roles.

Roles (performances with the Martha Graham Company, choreographed by Graham, unless otherwise noted)

1979   *Diversion of Angels*
1983   *Phaedra's Dream*
1984   The Chosen One, *The Rite of Spring*
         Radio On (Jean-Louis Morin)
         Gender (Morin; mus. David Byrne)
1988   The One Who Dances, *Letter to the World*
         Solo, *Deep Song*
1989   Jocasta, *Night Journey*
1990   Woman, *Maple Leaf Rag*
1992   Solo, *Salem Shore*
1994   Solo, *Sketches from Chronicle*

Other roles include: Lead roles in Graham's *Errand into the Maze, Clytemnestra, Herodiade, Appalachian Spring, Canticle for Innocent Comedians, The Heretic, Letter to the World* and *Temptations of the Moon, Serenata Morisca* (chor. Ted Shawn as a solo for Capucilli).

Publications

On CAPUCILLI: articles—

Dunning, Jennifer, "Young Dancer Takes on Martha Graham's Roles," *New York Times,* 4 April 1985.
Garafola, Lynn, *Dance Magazine,* January 1991.
New Times, 18 November 1981.
Smith, Amanda, "Review of *Radio On,*" *Dance Magazine,* November 1984.
Syracuse Herald-Journal, 17 November 1981.
Tobias, Tobi, "Terese Capucilli Carries on the Dramatic Tradition of Martha Graham," *New York,* 21 September 1987.

*   *   *

Terese Capucilli is a leading member of the Martha Graham Company. She is noted for her powerful, dramatic stage presence. During a 20-year career, Capucilli assumed many of Graham's most famous roles and, in effect, became "Martha"—so complete was her dedication to carrying on the fever-pitch performance style of her famed predecessor. Capucilli emulated Graham's hairstyle as well. With her small frame, dark hair and dark, luminous eyes, Capucilli appears girlish offstage. On stage, that impression disappears as delicacy is replaced by wiry strength and fierce attack. Critic Tobi Tobias called Terese Capucilli "the foremost contemporary interpreter of the impassioned, heroic women who stand at the center of Graham's classic works."

Not all critics were so appreciative of Capucilli's devotion, however. Some criticized her for the sameness of her performances and noted a lack of individuality that obscured her skills as a dancer. Writing in *Dance Magazine* in January 1991, Lynn Garafola noted that Capucilli "never played down an effect or fine-tuned a response or calibrated changes in dynamics. She approached her roles ... by impersonating Graham." Some critics doubted whether or not Graham's dancers could cope with the subtler effects of her melodramatic works. Joan Acocella, for example, found Capucilli's expressiveness too often blunted by lack of modulation. Acocella maintained that Capucilli had been taught to perform Graham's work at maximum intensity from start to finish. A 1989 performance of Jocasta (with Mikhail Baryshnikov as Oedipus) in *Night Journey* provoked praise from Tobias who singled out Capucilli's increased nuance and fire in the role. Capucilli's intensity and passionate near-abandon on stage mesmerize audiences. Never out of control, Capucilli just looks that way. Former teacher and mentor Carol Fried described Capucilli as "born to dance. She has the machinery for it. On top of that, she has a spirit and a drama that you can't teach."

A love of performance motivates Capucilli. She was born and raised in Syracuse, New York, one of seven siblings in an Italian-American family. As a child she studied with a local teacher, Miss Augustine, and learned ballet, tap, and jazz. While attending Westhill High School she added voice lessons. Terese made her musical theater debut with the Pompeian Players in Syracuse. Joan Consroe, Capucilli's teacher from the Syracuse Ballet Theater school, introduced Terese to the Graham method. Capucilli was attracted to the technique and its combination of drama and theatricality. Consroe suggested to Capucilli that she enroll at SUNY Purchase. That branch of the New York state university system combined a regular curriculum of liberal arts courses with a concentration in dance. While at Purchase, the young dancer attended a Graham-company performance and was deeply impressed by the combined emotive force and human drama being presented on stage. With the help of Fried, a teacher at Purchase, Capucilli was granted a scholarship to study at the Graham school for nine months after graduating from college. In addition to this early introduction to the Graham technique, Capucilli performed as a member of the Kuzuko Hirabayashi troupe. Hirabayashi was a graduate of the Graham school. During

Terese Capucilli performing Martha Graham's *Deep Song*, 1988. Photograph © Johan Elbers.

one summer break Capucilli won a scholarship to the Jacob's Pil-low School in Massachusetts.

Capucilli's talent and hard work garnered results soon after she joined the Martha Graham company in 1979. She got her first featured role in *Diversion of Angels* (1948) almost immediately after she joined the company. Capucilli recalled in the *Syracuse Herald-Journal* that the roles were parcelled out depending on whether or not Graham thought a dancer was ready. Graham saw a fearless spirit in Capucilli and rewarded her.

Capucilli began to dance many of Martha Graham's former roles in the mid-1980s. The woman in *Errand into the Maze* (1947) was the first major Graham role taken over by Capucilli. One of Capucilli's favorite roles is *Herodiade* (1944). The concept of a woman accepting her fate and coming to terms with inevitable death is a powerful one. She also had the opportunity of creating new roles with Graham. Her most famous created role is the "Chosen One" in *Rite of Spring.* Capucilli was the sacrificial girl who dances herself to death in this 1984 Graham work. Shuddering from deep within her body, Capucilli falls exhausted only to rise and dance again. Tobias, writing in *New York* magazine, noted the dancer's potential as a star. In 1988 Capucilli took on the Graham role in

Deep Song, a solo work first choreographed by Graham in 1937. Capucilli danced the role of a woman reacting in anguish and mourn-ing to the horrors of war.

In her 1991 piece *Maple Leaf Rag,* Graham created a role for Capucilli in which the young woman was given room to show off her sense of humor. Reclining on a balance beam-like structure, Capucilli (as Martha) watches her fellow dancers as they parody such earlier Graham works as *Night Journey* (1947) and *Letter to the World* (1940).

In 1992 Capucilli and Graham rehearsal director Carol Fried col-laborated on the reconstruction of *Salem Shore,* a nine-minute solo choreographed by Graham in 1943. It was shown at New York's City Center in October 1992. *Salem Shore* centers on the wife of a 19th-century sea captain. The woman recalls their courtship while awaiting her husband's return. Actress Claire Bloom spoke the text—a poem by Elinor Wylie—while Capucilli, costumed in a long, white dress, danced the lyrical steps. Capucilli—reaching out with extended arm and leg to a man seen only in memory—highlighted Graham's poignant storytelling while displaying a different side of her artistry.

In 1994 Capucilli gave an impressive performance of another early Graham work. *Chronicle,* a social protest piece, was first performed in 1936. In the 1994 performance, held at the Brooklyn Academy of Music, the work was called *Sketches from Chronicle.* It consisted of the sections from the 1936 work entitled "Spectre: 1914," "Steps in the Street," and "Prelude to Action." They used the photographs of Graham taken by Barbara Morgan, as well as other source materials, to reconstruct this work. In the "Spectre: 1914" section, Capucilli, dressed in a wide skirt with a red lining, remains stock-still on a platform. Her torso is tense but mobile and her fists are crossed. She rises on a two-tiered platform and manipulates the fabric of her skirt. The skirt becomes a red shroud, symbolic of the coming of war. The dancer sinks and beats her fists on the floor until she lies back on the platform. In the "Prelude to Action" sequence, Capucilli, now dressed all in white, performs a vibrant solo.

Capucilli has also performed outside the Martha Graham company on occasion. In May 1984, she appeared with then fellow Graham dancer Jean-Louis Morin in a performance of his choreography. Some of the energetic choreography (such as *Gender*), resembled Graham's work in that the woman was strong and dominant. In *Radio On,* Morin depicted Capucilli in a frenzied dance to music by David Byrne. Yet the dance left reviewer Amanda Smith of *Dance Magazine* wishing that someone would choreograph for Capucilli's delicacy as well as her intensity and strength.

Capucilli's respect, admiration, and affection for Martha Graham is profound. According to Capucilli, exposure to Graham has been the most important aspect of her dance career. When asked about Capucilli, Martha Graham said: "She has not disappointed me."

—Adriane Ruggiero

CARLSON, Ann

American dancer, choreographer, and performance artist

Born: 21 October 1954 in Park Ridge, Illinois. **Education:** University of Utah, B.F.A. in modern dance, magna cum laude, 1976; University of Arizona, M.S. in dance, 1983 (first graduate student in dance). **Career:** Dancer, Territory Dance Theater, Tucson, Arizona, 1979-82; with Meredith Monk, 1986. First solo concert, 1986; director and choreographer for *The Kabballah,* libretto by Michael Korie, composed by Stewart Wallace, 1989; and *Hydrogen Jukebox,* libretto by Allen Ginsberg, composed by Philip Glass, 1990; choreography presented throughout the U.S. including Los Angeles, New York, Durham, N.C., Boston, Milwaukee, Houston, Chicago, Washington, D.C., and Seattle, also West Germany, Austria, Prague, Mexico City, and Banff, Canada; has had artist-in-residence in Columbus (Ohio), Seattle, Minneapolis, Portland, Helena (Montana). **Awards:** New York Dance and Performance Award ("Bessie"), 1988; National Choreographer's Award, 1988; Metropolitan-Life Young Talent Award, 1988; American Dance Festival Award, 1988; Choreographic fellowship, National Endowment for the Arts (NEA), 1989-91; NEA Solo Performance Award, 1990; Wexner Center for the Arts Artist-in-Residence Award, 1992; CalArts Alpert Award in Dance, 1995.

Works

1986   *Balcony* (solo)
          Sloss, Kerr, Rosenberg & Moore (*Real People Series:* lawyers)

          Home Court Advantage (*RPS:* basketball players)
          Are You Home (*RPS:* mother and daughter)
          Mental Gymnastics
          Rings (*RPS:* security guards)
1987   *Middle Child* (solo)
          Lunch (*RPS:* Philip Morris executives)
          Catch and Release (*RPS:* fly-fishers and fiddlers)
          Scared Goats Faint (*Animal Series*)
          Visit Woman Move Story Cat Cat Cat (*Animal Series*)
1988   *Keeping Track* (solo)
          You Face Here
          Milk (*RPS:* dairy farmers)
          The Dog Inside the Man Inside (*Animal Series*)
          Sarah (*Animal Series*)
          Duck, Baby (*Animal Series*)
1989   *Teacher* (*RPS:* New York public school teachers)
          See (*RPS:* visually-impaired performers)
          Dead (*Animal Series*)
          See (*White Series*)
1990   *Sold* (*White Series*)
          Blanket (solo)
          Flag
          Ode
          Angels in Public Places
1991   *Untitled*
1992   *Chorus* (*White Series*)
          Walk (*White Series*)
          Walk (*RPS:* religious sisters)
          Angels, Part 1
          Sit Down Now (*RPS:* developmentally disabled adults)
          Zero Here (solo)
1993   *Pink*
1994   *Mirage*

Publications

On CARLSON: articles—

Aguilera-Hellweg, Max, "Ann Carlson: Dancing with Creatures Great and Small," *Mirabella*, January 1994.

Anderson, Jack, "The Magic of Dreams," *New York Times*, 13 September 1994.

———, "New York Newsletter," *Dancing Times* (London), April 1988.

———, "Some Choreographers Take to the Ice Rink," *New York Times*, 16 February 1991.

———, "When Cats, Teacups and Feathers Join the Cast," *New York Times*, 16 January 1994.

Armstrong, Gene, "Dancer's Real World," *Arizona Daily Star*, 14 July 1988.

Beers, Carole, "Carlson's Mixed-Media Version of *White* Certainly Isn't Vanilla," *Seattle Post-Intelligencer*, 27 March 1993.

Blake, Jon, "*White* Employs Mass Culture in Exploration of Everyday Life," *Seattle Post-Intelligencer,* 27 March 1993.

Breslauer, Jan, "Ann Carlson's Happy Moving Between Different Worlds," *Los Angeles Times*, 11 May 1995.

Cunningham, Carl, "Ann Carlson's *White*," *Houston Post*, 9 May 1993.

Dunning, Jennifer, "Dance in Review," *New York Times*, 28 June 1993.

———, "Walking Toward Death in Her Sensible Shoes," *New York Times,* 24 December 1990.

Eddings, Amy L., "A Thick Blanket of Years," *New York Native*, 31 December 1990.

Gladstone, Valerie. "Megadance Yields Mixed Results," *Daily News* (New York), 6 August 1991.

Holmes, Ann, "*White* a Joyful Collision of Dance and Real Life," *Houston Chronicle,* 17 May 1993.

Jowitt, Deborah, "Signs of Life," *Village Voice*, 1 October 1991.

Kisselgoff, Anna, "America: Love It, Leave It but Surely Perform to It," *New York Times,* 5 August 1991.

Kriegsman, Alan, "Ann Carlson, True to Life," *Washington Post*, 27 April 1995.

Kronen, H. B., "Ann Carlson Performance Speaks with Strong Voice," *Union-News*, 16 August 1991.

McDonald, D. J., "Haunting Images at Jacob's Pillow," *Berkshire Eagle*, 17 August 1991.

Mehalick, Susan, "Reflections of America," *Metroland,* 1991.

Rotenberk, Lori, "Attitude on Disability Makes *Animals* Special," *Chicago Sun Times*, 19 June 1993.

Smith, Sid, "*Animals* Includes Some Bite: Cuddly Work Still Has Issues," *Chicago Tribune*, 18 June 1993.

Strini, Tom, "Sublime Method Makes *Animals* Speak," *Milwaukee Journal*, 29 June 1990.

Supree, Burt, "All Too Human," *Village Voice*, 6 September 1986.

————, "Snows of Yesteryear," *Village Voice*, December 1991.

Temin, Christine, "Ann Carlson's *Animals* Not to Be Missed," *Boston Globe*, 8 April 1989.

Weiss, Hedy, "*Animals* Links Human, Four-Footed Creatures," *Chicago Sun Times*, 18 June 1993.

Yazigi, Monique P., "*Mirage* Beneath the Bridge," *New York Times*, 11 September 1994.

Zimmer, Elizabeth, "Catacomb Carnival," *Village Voice*, September 1994.

*   *   *

Ann Carlson says her aesthetic was formed by two distinct experiences, both in 1966. She had studied ballet since she was six years old, but it was a lecture and demonstration conducted by Murray Louis at the Chicago Museum of Contemporary Art that opened her eyes to the possibility of dance being "any conscious movement in time and space." The same year Carlson also saw a performance of the New York City Ballet. During George Balanchine's *Who Cares?* the orchestra made a mistake and for a brief moment, everything stopped. "The dancers just stood there," says Carlson, "their hyper-extended knees pushed back, their costumes hanging lifelessly at their sides. It was so awkward." With a

Ann Carlson: *Dancing in the Streets,* 1997. Photograph © Beatriz Schiller.

sudden clarity that changed her awareness forever, Carlson realized that ballet was fundamentally just a form. From that moment on, Carlson believed "that whatever was going to get across an idea, that's what needed to be used."

Accordingly, Carlson's work tends to be called "performance art" for lack of a more distinctive label. Years ago, Carlson told critic Nancy Dalva, "if there's a name to put on [my work], something's wrong." In recent years, she has softened on this issue and is now willing to identify her pieces as dances, or theatrical works, or performance pieces, depending on the work.

Carlson once told *Arizona Daily Star* critic Gene Armstrong, "I don't even consider my work singularly dance work. I'm much more interested in the art of performance and how it relates to our lives. I consider my movement only one element of the whole of what I do." She also said, "What I feel I need to investigate as a person I funnel through my work," further explaining, "I'm just trying to find new ways to work with people and address the world."

Though she has tried to "push the edges of who is usually on stage," and who an audience "usually expect[s] to be on stage," Carlson likes to "shake up some of those norms a bit. I ask people to ask themselves, 'who do I hold up as purveyors of information and wisdom and symbolism and metaphors?'" Carlson works project-by-project in what could be called a "cast-specific" process. So far, she has cast a child with Down Syndrome, basketball players, lawyers, nuns, goats, a kitten, a dog, a goldfish, visually-impaired children, a mother and daughter, fiddlers, fly fisherman, security officers, school teachers, cigarette company executives, a farmer and her dairy cow, 30 elementary school children, ballet dancers, and modern dancers in her eclectic work. All of her work is characterized by eloquence, egalitarianism, and strong vocal and visual components. As a choreographer, Carlson is widely recognized as an advocate for placing special-needs children and adults in the arts.

Carlson is perhaps best known for her groups of a half-dozen or so pieces that fall within such groupings as the "Real People Series" or the "Animal Series." The impetus for creating the Real People series, Carlson once told *Los Angeles Times* critic Jan Breslauer, "had to do with being starved for information about the outside world." The Animal series began as a choreographic challenge when Carlson wanted "to make works that could respond to a living being, that I couldn't choreograph in the way that I'd been taught to choreograph."*Chicago Sun Times* critic Hedy Weiss wrote that *"Animals* is as much a study in social anthropology and psychology as it is a work of dance theater." In response to *Animals,* Tom Strini of the *Milwaukee Journal* wrote that beneath the "quirky imagery and coy and fleeting relation to mundane reality lies a Classical sense of form, pulse, rhythm and cadence. The sensibility is Haydenesque."

As a performer, says *Chicago Tribune* critic Sid Smith, Carlson is "Winsome and droll, both jester and poet." Her works "combine two disparities of live performance: predetermined discipline and unpredictable improvisation." For one section of *Animal Series* called *Visit Woman Move Story Cat Cat Cat,* Carlson is nude, expertly tumbling and frolicking like a gorilla with her live kitten.

New York Times critic Jennifer Dunning observed that "Carlson is a major performance artist and choreographer with a gift for dryly suggestive evocation. Hers is an unsentimental eloquence, whether she is dealing with a goat in the *Animals* series, young lawyers in her *Real People* series, or death. She uses her compact body and clear, open looks to achieve a simplicity and directness

that are perfect foils for her considerable gifts as a vocal mimic and actress." Other critics, such as Alan Kriegsman, found that Carlson "follows in the tradition of Meredith Monk and Beverly Blossom—nothing the least bit artificial about her impersonations—it's as though she's naturally able to get under the skin of a plethora of human stereotypes, without reducing any of her subjects to caricature. She is, in short, a veritable original who has much to tell us about the varieties of human experience."

In the late 1990s Carlson described herself as in a transitional period and was choreographing several new solos, including one performed on horseback, called *West.*

—Lodi McClellan

THE CATHERINE WHEEL

Choreography: Twyla Tharp
Music: David Byrne
Set Design: Santo Loquasto
Lighting Design: Jennifer Tipton
Costume Design: Santo Loquasto
First Production: Twyla Tharp Dance Company, Winter Green Garden, New York, 22 September 1981
Original Dancers: Sara Rudner, Tom Rawe, Jennifer Way, Shelley Washington, Christine Uchida, Raymond Kurshals, Richard Colton, William Whitener, John Carrafa, Katie Glasner, John Malashock, Mary Ann Kellogg, Shelley Freydont, Keith Young, Barbara Hoon

Other productions include: Adaptation by Tharp of the original stage production for television, British Broadcasting Company (BBC), 1 March 1983; *Great Performances: Dance in America,* 28 March 1983. The final section, "The Golden Section," has been reset by Tharp for her own company and others.

Publications

Books—

Siegel, Marcia, *The Tail of the Dragon,* Durham, North Carolina, 1991.
Tharp, Twyla, *Push Comes to Shove,* New York, 1992.

Articles—

Barnes, Clive, "Twyla's Zone: A Touch of Punk," *New York Post,* 23 September 1981.
Crisp, Clement, "Television/The Catherine Wheel," *Financial Times,* 2 March 1983.
Croce, Arlene, "Oh, Tharp Pineapple Rag!" *New Yorker,* 12 October 1981.
Jowitt, Deborah, "Tharp Against the Whirlwind," *Village Voice,* 30 September/6 October 1981.
Kisselgoff, Anna, "Dance: Twyla Tharp's New 'Wheel'," *New York Times,* 23 September 1981.
———, "Twyla Tharp's Growing Pains," *New York Times,* 4 October 1981.
Tobias, Tobi, "The World According to Tharp," *New York,* 12 October 1981.

A Tharp company production of *The Catherine Wheel*. Photograph © Johan Elbers.

Films and Videotapes

The Catherine Wheel, BBC, London and New York, 1984.

*   *   *

Twyla Tharp's *The Catherine Wheel* incorporated her eclectic movement vocabulary, the rigorous choreographic techniques developed through her earlier work, her affinity to popular American culture, a narrative that could be understood and appreciated on one or many levels, and a section of breathtaking pure dance that remains in her repertory and continues to amaze audiences. In addition, it is an example of the artistically successful collaborations characteristic of her work.

While not Tharp's first venture in the use of plot or narrative (other works include *When We Were Very Young,* 1980, and *The Bix Pieces,* 1971), *The Catherine Wheel* is her most extended and complex narrative work, full-length without intermission. It examines Tharp's vision of the 1980s nuclear family (Father, Mother, Brother,

Sister, Maid, Pet joined by the Poet): full of aggression and anger finding release as sexual and physical violence. A pineapple, ever increasing in size, is used as the object of desire, lust and greed. Instead of its traditional role as a symbol of hospitality, Tharp's pineapple (the shape of atomic bombs dropped on Hiroshima and Nagasaki and of hand grenades) is a symbol of destruction. The Leader of the Chorus, commenting on the disintegration and degradation of the family, strives for perfection and suffers for it as did St. Catherine for whom the wheel of torture was named. The Father and Mother reach an uneasy reconciliation which leads toward the extended finale, "The Golden Section," a pure-dance section called "apotheosis" and "transfiguration" by the critics.

For the family in *The Catherine Wheel,* Tharp built on a base of heightened and extended pedestrian movement interspersed with tap dance, social dance, mime, facial and physical mugging, pratfalls and stage fighting. She has revisited partnering, the couple dance and social dance in many ways over the years (other explorations include *Nine Sinatra Songs* and *The Men's Piece*), and all three are important elements in *The Catherine Wheel.* The dance of reconciliation between the mother and father encapsulates some of the issues that Tharp addresses in the couple dance—control and who has it, strength, balance—and runs through an abbreviated history of American social dance of the last century.

Showcasing the ensemble nature, strength, and virtuosity of the Tharp dancers, Tharp explored innovative partnering throughout *The Catherine Wheel*. The movement in "The Golden Section," requiring total trust and reliability on the part of the dancers, is fast and dangerous with multiple difficult and unusual lifts, leaps, throws, and pirouettes performed without visible preparation by ever-changing combinations of dancers.

Throughout her career, Tharp has collaborated successfully with other artists, and *The Catherine Wheel* is an example of the high level of that work. Tharp commissioned the score to *The Catherine Wheel* from David Byrne, of the rock music group Talking Heads, who created an often hard-driving and rhythmic accompaniment. Longtime Tharp collaborators Santo Loquasto and Jennifer Tipton also made significant contributions to the production. Loquasto's sets for the narrative section included a metal structure of poles, cages, and wheels that loomed over the stage or were lowered as needed during the dance, changing the nature of the dance space, creating the family's home, or becoming instruments of torture. Tipton's lighting provided a range of light from full to closely focused, outlining dancers in silhouette, or creating shadow play. Loquasto's costumes of gold and the gold backdrop bathed in golden light provided a visual manifestation of the high level of dance energy required for the finale.

While Tharp herself wrote in *Push Comes to Shove* that *The Catherine Wheel*, with the exception of "The Golden Section," was not fully successful because of a lack of "coherence and cohesion," the critical response was generally quite enthusiastic: Arlene Croce called the work "a major event in our theatre," and Marcia Siegel felt it signaled a need for reconsideration of "our concept of avant-garde."

Tharp adapted *The Catherine Wheel* for television in 1983; the production was well-received and is available on videotape. Tharp also continues to set "The Golden Section" on her own company and others, keeping a part of the full-length *The Catherine Wheel* in repertory.

—Nena Couch

CERVERA, Alejandro

Argentine dancer and choreographer

Born: 11 December 1951 in Buenos Aires. **Education:** Studied sociology at University of Buenos Aires; Municipal School of Music; studied dance at Superior Institute of Art of the Colon Theater, Buenos Aires. **Career:** Dancer with various groups; associate director of Ballet Contemporáneo del Teatro Municipal General San Martín, 1985-87; director of Ballet del Sur, 1992-96; professor of music for dancers, Teatro Municipal General San Martín school.

Works (for the Ballet Contemporáneo del Teatro Municipal General San Martín, Buenos Aires, unless otherwise noted)

1978	*Seis veces Verdi* (mus. Verdi)
1979	*Coppelia* (mus. Delibes, Jose Maranzano)
1983	*Direccion obligatoria* (mus. Reich)
1986	*Tango vitriola* (mus. AAVV)
1987	*Azul 20* (mus. Pedro Aznar)
	Bach N. 3 (mus. Bach)
1988	*Danza para cinco percucionistas* (mus. Daniel Sais)
1989	*Solo para bailarina con viola obligada* (mus. Bach and others), Goethe Institute, Buenos Aires
1994	*Alicia en el pais de las maravillas* (mus. Jorge Agesta, Miguel Gomis), Ballet del Sur, Bahía Blanca, Argentina
1997	*Historia del soldado* (mus. Stravinsky), Fundación Astengo, Rosario, Argentina

Other works include: Numerous operas for the Colon Theater, Buenos Aires, and several films.

* * *

Cervera was born in a typical middle-class neighborhood of Buenos Aires. At the age of five, he became interested in music and began taking classes with a private tutor. He then enrolled in the Escuela Municipal de Música de Buenos Aires. In spite of his youth, he was awarded a scholarship at Teatro Colón, the country's most distinguished lyric theater. There he attended his first concerts, operas, and ballets. Attracted to modern dance from the beginning, he diligently followed the work of the Ballet del Teatro San Martín, the dance troupe which, 15 years later, he would direct. He studied piano and oboe, and taught high school and special education. Teaching music to physically disabled children introduced him to the different aspects of movement in space, lessons which would serve useful later in his career as a choreographer.

At the age of 19, Cervera auditioned, almost by accident, for an intensive dance course for young men given by the grand masters of modern dance in Argentina at the time. He passed the enrollment requirements and began to study. Classes were held in the same building where the Ballet del Teatro San Martín taught, directed by Oscar Araiz. There he became interested once again in modern dance. When the course ended, the Teatro San Martín had dissolved, so he enrolled in the Instituto del Teatro Colón, taking classes in ballet. At the same time, he continued with modern dance, taking private lessons with the best masters. By the mid 1970s, he was dancing professionally in music hall spectacles, musical theater, and on television.

In 1977, the Ballet Contemporáneo del Teatro Municipal General San Martín was resurrected, and its new director, Ana Maria Stekelman, invited Cervera to participate. There he began a long relationship with the company, where he stood out at first as a dancer, then a choreographer, and eventually as director. This encompassed the 10 years between 1977 and 1987, without a doubt the company's most creative and brilliant period.

Toward the end of the 1970s, Cervera began working as a choreographer in children's productions and for small independent groups. He choreographed his first work for the Ballet, *La Valse y Coppelia*, with Ana Maria Stekelman, in 1978. In 1983, during the war against England for possession of the Falkland Islands (Las Islas Malvinas), he created his first major work, *Dirrecion obligatorio*, which dealt with the themes of authoritarianism, dictatorship, and war.

In 1985 he was offered directorship of the Ballet, to be shared with two colleagues, Norma Binaghi and Lisu Brodsky. This lasted until 1987, the year he decided to leave his position in the Teatro and work freelance. He traveled to the United States, and while in residence with the American Dance Festival, created *East Gym*

Tango, which was later changed to *Tango Vitrola,* one of his most critically acclaimed works and one of his most famous. Between 1987 and 1989, he also created *Azul 20* and *Danza para cinco percusionistas,* works inspired by the abstraction of music and color. These last three works toured varied locations of Argentina and its environs.

In 1989, he was invited to direct the Ballet del Sur, a distinguished Argentine dance company. He worked there until 1996, creating a significant body of work that established the group among the best, as much for ballet as modern dance. Recently, Cervera has moved to operatic choreography, returning in this way to his origins in music, the starting point for all his choreographic work.

—Marcelo Isse Moyano; translated by Rita Velazquez

CHANDRALEKHA
Indian dancer and choreographer

Born: Chandralekha Patel, in Nadiad, Gujarat state, India. **Education:** College in Bombay; moved to Madras, 1949; first teacher Guru Ellappa Pillai; *arangetram* Madras, 1952. **Career:** First choreography, 1960.

Works

1960	*Devadasi,* Madras
1972	*Navagraha* (performed with Kamadev)
1984	*Primal Energy*
	Tillana w/Max Mueller Bhavan, East-West Dance Encounter, Bombay
1985	*Angika*
1986	*Angamandalam,* USSR-India Festival
1989	*Prana*
	Lilavati
1991	*Sri*
1994	*Yantra*

Publications

About CHANDRALEKHA: books—

Bharucha, Rustom, *Chandralekha: Women/Dance/Resistance,* Indus, 1995.

*   *   *

"The day I was born, I knew I was going to be a dancer," Chandralekha (as she is universally known) has asserted. The defiant certainty of the statement is typical of a woman who has resolutely paddled her own canoe, in dance and in life. A doctor's daughter from the state Gujarat, she had—as many Indian girls do—learned Bharat Natyam, the strong sculptural dance style from South India. She was fortunate in her major guru, Guru Ellappa Pillai, a denizen of one of the great teaching families of the south, and her connection with other great dancers, particularly the legendary Balaswaraswati and Rukmini Devi, founder of the school Kalakshetra. Later German dancer and choreographer Pina Bausch was to be recognized as a kindred spirit.

Chandra's formal debut, her *arangetram,* took place in Madras—the cradle of Bharat Natyam and home of the fiercest critics—in 1952. It was by all accounts a triumph. The dance world welcomed a future classical star, and official international tours followed. However, Chandra herself was never unreservedly happy. She later recounted a sudden revelation when she had been performing a complex expressive item in the Bharat Natyam vocabulary, a *varnam.* The item had been replete with images of water and fecundity: the performance had been in aid of drought relief. How could life and art be so separate, she had thought, and in that "split second, I was divided, fragmented into two people." The rest of her creative life can be reasonably argued to have been an attempt to integrate those two sides. While trying to winnow out the accretions that, in her view, had made Bharat Natyam decorative and marooned in a sterile religiosity, she paradoxically came up with a form that seems to many a radical break with tradition. Chandralekha herself would argue that she is returning dance to its original creative, life-connected function and principle, "It must go back to the people, to the body." But for many she is a dangerous maverick—a tiny woman with long white flowing hair and a distinctly unconventional lifestyle.

Chandra's first relatively mile assault on Bharat Natyam was based in narrative. *Devadasi* (1960) used the traditional temple-dancer or devadasi as its focus, and the classical structure to comment on her decline. The piece was given only four performances, but it contained a section, the *Tillana,* that was to surface in 1984 as an independent dance piece. The classical dance world, in the years in between, had seen little of Chandralekha beyond one piece, *Navagraha* (1972-73). The contradictions had become too great and the voices from the world of the street too compelling. Instead Chandra threw herself into feminism and radical politics. She designed, painted, wrote, organized, and deepened her friendships with key individuals who were important in her developing philosophy of life.

A focal year for modern dance in India was 1984—the year when the first East-West Dance Encounter occurred at the National Centre for Performing Arts in Bombay. Chandralekha had been induced to come out of dance retirement and to bring back her *Tillana.* The urgent debate that took place around the place of dance in society and its own ability to change propelled her back into choreography and dance. The first result was *Angika* (1985), described by her unofficial biographer, Rustom Bharucha, as "Chandra's manifesto of the body in dance." First choreographed for three women (including Chandralekha) and seven men, it changed over the years in subsequent showings at prestigious foreign festivals (e.g. West Germany's International Dance Festival 1988, Berlin and London 1992).

To the classical dance afficionado, *Angika* was a blow. It demanded equal athleticism from men and women (martial leaps and bold body swings); it abandoned the stylized male/female conventions of Bharat Natyam, the tradition-sanctioned jewelry and makeup. It looked austere, and its movement took control of the stage in direct contrast to the dynamic of Bharat Natyam. There were no stories of gods and goddesses, but the gods were there. The piece's exploration of primal energy embodied in its use of yoga, for example, took it into the realm of the mother goddess—an area near to Chandralekha's heart. The social comment of the earlier *Devadasi* was carried through: two male groups impassively watch the dancers performing, underlining the prurience to be found in the old dance practice of men watching women. The most lasting image provided an antithesis to that more common situation—Chandra bestriding a recumbent male, electric with energy. The production made a tremendous impact in India, and indeed abroad. However, Chandra did not build directly on it till *Sri* in 1991.

Before then, she created the less successful *Angamandalam* (1986), and the charming *Lilavati* (1989), a piece based on a 10th-century mathematical text in which the mathematician explains concepts to his young daughter with examples couched in terms of the natural world. *Prana* (1989) had counterpointed yoga *asanas* with Bharat Natyam dance units; Chandra had imposed a very slow rhythm on both, resulting in a slow and grave grandeur that mirrored the spaciousness of yogic breathing. *Sri* focused on the female principle—the movement took and extended elements used in earlier pieces, building up an articulate and moving picture of female strength, both when oppressed and when liberated. The slow crab-like movements of women across the stage contrasted with their whip-like kicks: individuality—they showed—could be isolation, the group could be both anonymous and sustaining. The journey tracked through the dance ended with Chandra alone center stage, flat on her back and facing away from the audience. Slowly her white legs rose and entwined themselves meditatively, giving rise to thoughts of birth and of Shakespeare's "naked unaccommodated man" from *King Lear*.

In the West, Chandralekha's company is viewed as modern or contemporary—yet she herself lays claim to a direct bloodline from Bharat Natyam. "You don't throw away your culture when you reject some of its taboos, codes, and cliches," she has said, suggesting that the boundaries drawn by the West between modern, classical, and contemporary dance might stand reexamination in the world of Indian dance.

—Naseem Khan

Remy Charlip performing *March Dance Umbrella*, 1978. Photograph © Johan Elbers.

CHARLIP, Remy

American dancer, choreographer, artist, designer, and writer

Born: 10 January 1929 in Brooklyn. **Education:** Cooper Union, B.A., 1949; dance at the New Dance Group Studio; Juilliard School with Antony Tudor and Margaret Craske; study with Mary Anthony, Jean Erdman, and others. **Career:** Dancer, Merce Cunningham Dance Company, 1950-61; dancer, Living Theater, 1950-62; co-founder, Paper Bag Players (children's theater), 1958; founder/director, member, Judson Dance Theater, 1964-70; founder/director, Remy Charlip Dance Company, 1977; artist-in-residence, Los Angeles Museum of Contemporary Art, late 1980s. Has taught at Bates College, Colorado Dance Festival, Harvard Summer Dance Program, Hofstra University, Mills College, Sarah Lawrence College, University of California at Santa Barbara, and others. **Awards:** Professional achievement award, Cooper Union, 1984; two Ingram Merrill awards; three Isadora Duncan awards; two OBIE awards, and numerous grants and fellowships including the National Endowment for the Arts (NEA), U.S./Japan Commission Arts fellowship and others; special exhibition, Library of Congress, 1997.

Works

1949	*Drama in Ex Libre* (theater)
1951	*Falling Dance*
	Dr. Faustus Lights the Lights (theater)
	Dialogue Between the Manikin and the Young Man (theater)
1952	*Crosswords for Cunningham Company*
1953	*Exquisite Corpse Number 1*
1954	*Exquisite Corpse Number 2*
1956	*Obertura Republicana* w/Paul Taylor, Marian Sarach, James Waring, David Vaughan
1959	*Cut-Ups* (theater)
1960	*Scraps* (theater)
	Tonight We Improvise (theater)
1961	*Group Soup* (theater)
1962	*Fortunately* (theater)
	Man is Man (theater)
1964	*December*
	April
	Patter for a Soft Shoe Dance (theater)
	Leonce & Lena (theater)
	Sing Ho! For a Bear (theater)
1965	*Dance for Boys*
	April and December
	A Beautiful Day (theater)
1966	*Meditation*
	Theater Songs of Al Carmines (theater)
	Jonah (theater)
	More, More, I Want More (theater)
1967	*Étude*
	Between the Black and the White There is a Rainbow
	Clearing
	An Evening of Dances, Plays, and Songs
	I Am My Beloved w/Aileen Passloff
	Concrete Rainbow

Celebration of Change
Variety Show (theater)
A Re-examination of Freedom (theater)
I Ching Poem for Johnny (theater)
Bertha (theater)
Well...Actually (with James Waring, John Herbert McDowell, theater)

1968   *Dr. Kheal*
        Differences
        Meditation (II)
        Green Power w/Ken Dewey
        Sneaker Players (II)
        Sayings of Mao Tse Tung (theater)
        Celebration (theater)
        Untitled Play (theater)

1969   *Hommage à Loie Fuller* for Osaka World Fair
        Dark Dance
        The Red Burning Light (theater)
        Yellow Umbrella Dance
        Spring Play (theater)

1970   *Under Milkwood* (theater)
        Biography, National Theater of the Deaf
        Faces (theater)

1971   *The Book is Dead* for Caen Bibliothèque
        Secrets, National Theater of the Deaf

1972   *Dance*
        Instructions from Paris for Nancy Lewis

1973   *Quick Change Artists* for Scottish Theatre Ballet
        The Moveable Workshop
        Mystery Play (theater)

1974   *Thinking of You Thinking of Me*
        Arc en Ciel
        Mad River

1976   *If I Were Freedom*
        Tiempo Azul for Taller de Danza Contemporanca, Caracas
        Faces and Figures Found on the Wall Below the Barre Made by the Students in Madame Franklin's Ballet Studio on the Top Floor of the Teatro Municipal in Caracas, Venezuela for Juan Monson
        The Woolloomooloo Cuddle
        Instructions from Guatamala for José Ledezma
        Part of a Larger Landscape
        Instructions to New York for Eva Karczag
        Danza por Correo for José Ledezma

1977   *Opening*
        A Week's Notice
        Art of the Dance
        Imaginary Dances
        Travel Sketches

1978   *Painting Flying*
        A Tree Blossoms at a Woman's Touch for Jeannette Lentvaar
        El Arte de la Danza for José Ledezma
        I Am My Beloved (II) for Ronald Dabney, Jeannette Lentvaar

1979   *Garden Lilacs* for Idella Packer, Karen Bean
        Six Mail Order Dances for Forty People in Six Open Spaces, Bates College Dance Company
        Dance in a Bed with a Pillow (filmed and broadcast by WGBH-TV)
        250 Dances on a Diagonal with 250 Guest Towels

1980   *Green Again*
        Alone Some, Twosome for Ronald Dabney, Sheila Kaminsky

Red Towel Dance for Barbara Roan
Foodoomyo for Richard Zelens
Los Palos Grandes for Abelardo Gameche, Eduardo Ramones
Twelve Contradances for Ronald Dabney, Lance Westergard
Happy, Happy, Happy We
Every Little Movement, A Homage to Delsarte for David Vaughan, Al *Carmines*
Waves w/Toby Armour
Dance on a Floor for Toby Armour
39 Chinese Attitudes for Nancy Lewis
Our Lady of the In Between for Toby Armour
Do You Love Me Still?. . .Or Do You Love Me Moving?

1984   *Growing Up in Public* w/Lucas Hoving
        Before Me Peaceful

1985   *Pillows and Comforter* for Tandy Beal and Dancers

1988   *Amaterasu*

1995   *Ludwig and Lou*

Other works include: *Glowworm, Meet, Dance in a Bed, Dance on a Floor, Nuit Blanche* for Sally Hess, *Flowering Trees, Ten Imaginary Dances, Everything Must Change* w/Ronald Dabney, *Every Little Movement,* and *Ten Men.*

Publications

By CHARLIP: books—

Arm in Arm (1967)
Handtalk: An ABC of Fingerspelling and Sign Language w/Mary Beth and George Ancona (1974)
Hooray for Me w/Lillian Moore and Vera B. Williams
I Love You (1998)
The First Remy Charlip Reader (1986)
Thirteen w/Jerry Joyner

On CHARLIP: articles—

Aloff, Mindy, Review, in *Dance Magazine,* April 1983.
Laine, Barry, "In Search of Judson," in *Dance Magazine,* September 1982.
Pierpont, Margaret, "A Conversation with Remy Charlip," in *Dance Magazine,* April 1980.
Ross, Janice, Review, in *Dance Magazine,* February 1995.
Vaughn, David, "Making Things Up: About Remy Charlip," in *On the Next Wave 2,* October 1984.

*   *   *

Remy Charlip's interests in modern dance are as boundless as his imagination. He has been a dancer of his own work and that of many others; he has choreographed works with intricate rhythms, precise movements, sign language, and nondance actions; and he has designed inventive costumes and sets. Charlip doesn't confine himself to dance, he also writes and directs for theater, and has published several books for children. Despite the great diversity, his flights of imagination are all suffused with his wit, warmth, attention to detail, and irrepressible optimism for the human condition.

Charlip was born in Brooklyn, New York, in January 1929. His early ambition was to be a painter, and he studied fine arts at the Cooper Union in New York, receiving a degree in 1949. Attracted

113

by the freedom in dance, Charlip expanded the scope of his creative energies and began studying dance at the New Dance Group Studio; at the Juilliard School with Antony Tudor and Margaret Craske; and with Mary Anthony, Irving Burton, and Jean Erdman.

While supporting himself by working as an artist and graphic designer, Charlip began studying and working with Merce Cunningham. As a member of Cunningham's company, from 1950 to 1961, Charlip created roles in many works, including *Suite for Five in Space and Time* (1956), *Antic Meet* (1958), and *Aeon* (1961). In the early 1960s Charlip began to focus on choreography. His work owes much to his training with Cunningham, but Charlip incorporates new sources of movement and perception to create wholly-original and imaginative works. Charlip's works rely on gesture and ordinary movements, but they also are graced by dance steps with great rhythmic sophistication. His pieces often feel like vignettes, a quick slice of a story rich in detail and precision.

Like many dancers and choreographers of the postmodern period of modern dance, Charlip worked with the avant-garde Judson Dance Theater in New York. Charlip presented his solo work *Meditation* (1966) at Judson and performed it again in 1982 in a program honoring the 20th anniversary of the first Judson concert. In this dramatic piece, a solitary man's conservative clothing give the impression of a well-ordered, controlled life, but his facial expressions and gestures reveal his inner torment. Charlip also choreographed works performed by others at Judson as well as dancers outside of the group—Aileen Passloff performed his sensitive *April* and *December* at Judson in 1964; six women danced to Eskimo and African music in *Clearing* (1967), one of many group works created by Charlip. In addition, Charlip designed exciting and innovative costumes for his own dancers and others and often performed as well. He has choreographed for Black Mountain College, Sarah Lawrence College, London Contemporary Dance Theatre, Scottish Theatre Ballet, Taller de Danza Contemporanea in Caracas, and for his own Remy Charlip Dance Company, founded in 1977.

From the 1950s to early 1970s, Charlip worked on many theater productions choreographing, designing sets and costumes, writing music and scripts, and directing. He worked with the Living Theater to create *Dr. Faustus Lights the Lights* (1951), *Man is Man* (1962), and other productions. He directed *A Beautiful Day* at Judson in 1965 for which he was received an OBIE award. Charlip has also worked with the National Theater of the Deaf, writing and directing productions, as well as authoring with Mary Beth and George Ancona the 1974 publication *Handtalk: An ABC of Fingerspelling and Sign Language.*

Charlip's fascination with the expressiveness of sign language has been incorporated into many of his works, including *Every Little Movement* in which a solo performer expands the gestures of sign language, in progressive steps, into a dance; and *Happy Happy Happy We* (1980), where dancers sign as they perform a dance of lively hops and shuffles.

Throughout his career, Charlip has tapped his early interest in visual arts. He is known for his highly imaginative costume designs and has also designed sets and produced dance posters and flyers. His sketches of dancers proved to be the springboard for a unique way to choreograph.

In 1972, Charlip produced the first in a series of dances which came to be known as "air mail dances." Nancy Lewis had contacted Charlip to commission a dance for an upcoming concert. Weeks later, remembering the commitment, Charlip sent her a picture postcard with a sketch of a woman lying on a couch and a note indicating that this would be the first position in the dance. With Lewis' consent,

Charlip then sent her a series of sketches of movements in the dance, inspiring Lewis to create the transitions from one to the next. This unusual choreographic effort became *Instructions from Paris.*

From this initial collaboration by mail, Charlip later developed dances for many choreographers and companies. He would send 20 to 40 sketches for each work, at times allowing the performer to order the movements. These dances proved a fascinating departure from the norm for choreography, with always intriguing results—for even the same notations, when developed by more than one choreographer, produced strikingly different dances. Nevertheless, Charlip's touch was evident in each dance.

Charlip has also been very active with children's theater and is a writer and illustrator of children's books. He is a founding member of the Paper Bag Players, a children's theater group based in New York that began in 1958, and was a writer, director, designer, and performer for the group until the early 1960s. Additionally, Charlip has written dance criticism in several leading publications, including *Ballet Review, Contact Quarterly, Movement Research Journal, Village Voice* and others.

More recently, the Oakland Ballet commissioned the premiere of Charlip's *Ludwig and Lou* in 1995, which uses primarily nondance actions accompanied by Beethoven's *Twelve Contredanses* and Lou Harrison's *Suite for Cello and Harp.* Throughout his long, varied, and distinguished career, Charlip has created works for and with a veritable who's-who of international dancers and companies including Carolyn Brown, Viola Farber, Annabelle Gamson, Lucas Hoving, Margaret Jenkins, the Joffrey Ballet, John Herbert McDowell, the New South Wales Dance Company (Australia), Opeleiding Moderne Dans (Amsterdam), Rudy Perez, Valda Setterfield, Dan Wagoner, James Waring, the Welsh Dance Theater, and scores of others.

—Janette Goff Dixon and Sydonie Benet

CHILDS, Lucinda

American dancer and choreographer

Born: 26 June 1940 in New York City. **Education:** Early training in ballet and piano; studied at the Hanya Holm school; with Helen Tamiris, Judith Dunn, Bessie Schönberg, and at the Merce Cunningham studio; B.A., Sarah Lawrence College, 1962. **Career:** Founding member, Judson Dance Theater, 1963-66; formed Lucinda Childs Dance Company, 1973; collaborated with Robert Wilson and Philip Glass on the opera, *Einstein on the Beach,* 1976; toured internationally with *Einstein;* choreographed *Dance* with music by Glass and film/decor by Sol LeWitt, 1979; company tours Europe, 1980s; begins collaborating with harpsichordist Elisabeth Chojnacka, 1990; has taught at Harvard Summer Dance Center and elsewhere. **Awards:** *Village Voice* Obie Award, 1977; John Simon Guggenheim Foundation Fellowship, 1979; officer, Order of Arts and Letters (France), 1996.

Works

1963   *Pastime*, Judson Memorial Church
        Three Pieces, Judson Memorial Church

Lucinda Childs performing in *Available Light,* 1983. Photograph © Beatriz Schiller.

Minus Auditorium Equipment and Furnishings, Gramercy Arts Theater

Egg Deal, Judson Memorial Church

1964   *Cancellation Sample*, Surplus Dance Theater, Stage 73

Carnation, Institute of Contemporary Arts, Philadelphia

Street Dance, Studio of Robert and Judith Dunn

Model, Washington Square Art Gallery

1965   *Geranium*, Alfred Leslie Studio

Museum Piece, Judson Memorial Church

Screen, Bridge Theater

Agriculture, Once Festival, Ann Arbor, Michigan

1966   *Vehicle*, 69th Regiment Armory, Nine Evenings of Theater and Engineering

1968   *Untitled Trio*, Judson Memorial Church

1973   *Particular Reel Checkered Drift Calico Mingling*, Whitney Museum of American Art

1975   *Duplicate Suite Reclining Rondo Congeries on Edges for 20 Obliques*, Y.M.C.A., Nyack

1976   *Radial Courses Mix Detail Transverse Exchanges*, Washington Square Methodist Church

Cross Words Figure Eights, Danspace at St. Marks Church

Einstein on the Beach, (solo, Act I, Scene ii), Theatre Municipal, Avignon, France

1977   *Plaza Melody Excerpt Interior Drama*, Brooklyn Academy of Music (BAM)

1978   *Katema*, Stedlijk Museum, Amsterdam

1979   *Dance* (concert version) (mus. Glass w/Philip Glass Ensemble), Stadsschouwburg, Eindhoven, Holland

Dance (mus. Glass), BAM

1981   *Mad Rush* (mus. Glass), for Le Groupe Recherche Choreographique de l'Opéra de Paris

Relative Calm (mus. Gibson), Theatre National de Strasbourg, France

1982   *Formal Abandon Part I*, solo (mus. Riesman), Tinel de la Chartreuse, France

Formal Abandon Part II, quartet (mus. Riesman), Harvard University, Cambridge, Massachusetts

1983   *Available Light* (mus. Adams), Festival de la Danse, Chateauvallon, France

Formal Abandon Part III (mus. Riesman), Theatre de la Ville, Paris

1984   *Cascade* (mus. Reich), Pacific Northwest Ballet, Seattle

Outline, solo (mus. Bryars), Whitney Museum of American Art

Premiere Orage (mus. Shostakovich), Paris Opera Ballet, Paris

Field Dances (mus. Glass, Wilson), BAM

1986   *Portraits in Reflection* (mus. Galasso, Nyman, Shawn, Swados), Joyce Theater

Clarion (mus. Chihara), Pacific Northwest Ballet, Seattle

Hungarian Rock, solo (mus. Ligeti), University of Nebraska, Lincoln

1987   *Calyx* (mus. de Wit), Joyce Theater

Lichtknall (mus. Grosskopf), Berlin Opera, Berlin

1989   *Mayday* w/ Sol Lewitt (mus. Wolff), Teatro Lirico, Milan

1990   *Perfect Stranger* (mus. Zappa), Lyon Opera Ballet, Lyon, France

Four Elements (mus. Bryars), Rambert Dance Company, Oxford, England

1991   *Rhythm Plus* (mus. Ligeti, Ferrari), Theatre de la Ville, Paris

1992   *Oophaa Naama* (mus. Xenakis), Charleroi/Danses, Palais des Beaux-Arts, Charleroi, Belgium

1993   *Concerto* (mus. Gorecki), Grande Auditorio Fundacao Calouste Gulbenkian, Lisbon, Portugal

One and One (mus. Xenakis), Theatre de la Ville, Paris

Impromptu (mus. Kurylewicz), Theatre Debussy, Cannes, France

1994   *Chamber Symphony* (mus. Adams), Bayerisches Staatsballett, Munich

Trilogies (mus. Schwartz), Ohio Ballet, Appalachian Summer Festival, Boone, North Carolina

1995   *Commencement* (mus. Krauze), Theatre Debussy, Cannes, France

Solstice (mus. Mache), Theatre Debussy, Cannes

Kengir (mus. Mache), Cour d'Honneur due Palais des Papes, Avignon, France

From the White Edge of Phrygia (mus. Montague), Theatre de la Ville, Paris

1996   *Hammerklavier* (mus. Eggert), Bayerisches Staatsballett, Munich

Other works include: Opera work, choreography for Luc Bondy's *Salomé* (1992), *Reigen* (1993), and *Don Carlos* (1996); Peter Stein's *Moïse und Aaron* for De Nederlands Opera; directing 1995's *Zaïde;* and reuniting with Robert Wilson for *La Maladie de la Mort* (1997).

Publications

By CHILDS—

"Notes, 1964-1974," *Drama Review,* March 1975.

On CHILDS: books—

Banes, Sally, *Terpsichore in Sneakers: Post-Modern Dance,* Boston, 1980.

Kreemer, Connie, *Further Steps: Fifteen Choreographers on Modern Dance,* New York, 1987.

Livet, Anne, *Contemporary Dance,* New York, 1978.

Wynne, Peter, *Judson Dance: An Annotated Bibliography of the Judson Dance Theater and of Five Major Choreographers— Trisha Brown, Lucinda Childs, Deborah Hay, Steve Paxton, and Yvonne Rainer,* Englewood, New Jersey, 1978.

On CHILDS: articles—

Berman, Janice, "Lucinda Childs Adds Fun to Lift the Spirit," *New York Newsday,* 10 February 1994.

Chin, Daryl, "Talking with Lucinda Childs," *Dance Scope,* Spring/Winter 1979.

Jowitt, Deborah, "Flying In," *Village Voice,* 22 February 1994.

Kisselgoff, Anna, "Trading the Cerebral for the Sensual," *New York Times,* 14 February 1994.

Mazo, Joseph, "Lucinda Childs Returns," *Dance Magazine,* February 1994.

Reardon, Christopher, "Performers Who Cast Tall Shadows," *Christian Science Monitor,* 1 March 1994.

Robertson, Allen, "Pristine Steps for the Patient," *The Times,* 18 October 1994.

*   *   *

Lucinda Childs Dance Company: *Relative Calm,* **1981. Photograph © Johan Elbers.**

The objectivity reflected in the perspective of minimalists and others in the visual arts world during the 1960s had parallel relationships in the development of dance during the same period. Members of the Judson Dance Theater, through their close associations and collaborations with visual artists and through their own explorations, spurred a range of discoveries of what movement could express on its own terms. Of these, Lucinda Childs mined a focus on low-contrast reductionism, repetition, and clarity to create a body of works that reflected a new symphonic radiance.

Growing up in New York City, Childs received early dance training, but didn't concentrate her ambitions on dance until an exposure to the work of Helen Tamiris. She attended Sarah Lawrence College as a dance major, studying with Judith Dunn and master teacher Bessie Schönberg. After graduation in 1962, Childs began to study at Merce Cunningham's school in Manhattan, where she was introduced to Yvonne Rainer, and was deeply affected by the simplicity and immediacy of Rainer's gesturally based performance work.

Childs joined the Judson Dance Theater soon afterwards, studying composition with Robert Dunn, and beginning her own choreographic explorations. In this first thread of inquiry, she was interested in using nondance material in a way that still carried the formal weight of theatrical dance work. Her solution to this creative problem was to generate movement through interacting with ob-

jects, often accompanied by spoken monologues that provided a floating context of commentary on her activities. While Childs and many of her peers were working with pedestrian sources of movement, her approach was anything but casual—these early pieces reflected careful construction and rigorous sensibility. Some of the works she created during the next few years were *Pastime* (1963), *Carnation* (1964), and *Geranium* (1965).

One of the pieces from this period, *Street Dance* (1964), proved pivotal in informing the trajectory of Childs' body of work in the years ahead. It situated the audience in the windows of a loft overlooking the street, where two performers, far enough away to be seen only indistinctly, pointed out some of the surrounding architectural features to the viewers above. Their activities were simultaneously and precisely narrated by an audiotape in the same room as the spectators. The underlying themes of variation in perspective and repetition of objective information from different standpoints were to be expressed in many of Childs' future works.

After spending several years choreographing and performing in the creative milieu of the Judson artists, Childs began to break away from their multiple influences. Between 1966 and 1973, she created very little new work, but continued studying (including ballet), researching, and developing her thoughts about dance. In her experimentation over these years, Childs dropped her incorporation of the objective use of referential elements such as props and text, and became interested in manipulating perception through the use of abstract movement as the main expressive element.

In 1973 she formed her dance company in order to fully construct this new direction in her work. Over the next five years she created pieces that included *Calico Mingling* (1973), *Particular Reel* (1973), *Congeries on Edges for 20 Obliques* (1975), *Radial Courses* (1976)—a total of 16 solo and small group works. Initially she focused on simple, nondance movement, such as walking, lunging, running, or rolling, framed within clearly wrought, highly structured scores; these involved spatial patterns and arrangement of the movement vocabulary into subtle relationships of counterpoint. The material in these pieces was presented factually, in silence, with a restricted palette of core phrases to explore variation through repetition, contrasting spatial orientation, and reorganizing their order. The precise execution was unencumbered by theatrical performance overlay, devoid of any expressionist emotive commentary by the dancers.

During this period, Childs first saw the work of theater director Robert Wilson, and was invited to collaborate with him and composer Philip Glass in Wilson's seminal five-hour opera *Einstein on the Beach*. She performed in the piece, as well as choreographing it; her leading role included an unforgettable solo in which she generated intense drama solely by walking back and forth repetitively with patterned directional changes for an extended period. Childs' now distinct sensibility was fully met by Glass' minimalist music, also based on cycles of repetition. This experience was the beginning of a collaborative way of working for the choreographer. In 1979 she made *Dance* for the Brooklyn Academy of Music (BAM), to a score by Glass, and with film/visual decor by Sol LeWitt. This work was followed by *Relative Calm*, in 1981, to the music of Jon Gibson; Wilson designed the lights and visual elements. In these two evening-length pieces, Childs continued her interest in repetitive structures and the use of pure movement. The dancers swept across the stage in cycling, tightly patterned fields of movement; when slight changes in the structure occurred, they stood in momentous relief to the dance's monochromatic scope. These low-contrast waves of activity focused the viewer's perception in specific yet prismatic ways, magnified and illuminated variations in detail, and provided subtle gradations of perspective. The concentration and structure that defined these dances revealed a meditative, trancelike quality, their purity pointing to a release into ecstasy.

These works were also marked by the evolution of the simplicity of her movement choices into more recognizable dance steps—walking, running, and skipping began to be colored by references to classical, technical dance steps akin to ballet or Merce Cunningham's vocabulary. While movement was clearly and precisely executed in the lower limbs of the body, each dancer's upper body was free to react in subtle individual ways, providing a variety of movement tones to the dances. This approach of allowing the torso to register the effects of weight and momentum through a responsive release offered a uniquely contemporary treatment of the classically chiseled steps at its base.

Childs also addressed different possibilities of perspective in these pieces through the use of split-level sets that arranged the dancers in a variety of viewpoints, and through film imagery repeating and multiplying the images of the dancers. These fully-realized works were followed by others of the same character, including *Available Light* (1983) with music by John Adams, and *Portraits in Reflection* (1986), which featured a score commissioned from four different composers. Besides creating a number of major new dance works in the 1990s with many different collaborators, Childs has also continued to work in theatrical projects with Robert

Wilson, and others including Luc Bondy and Peter Stein. The evolution of Childs' vocabulary into a more technical dance vocabulary, in addition to the purity of her focus, also led her into choreographic projects for ballet companies, including commissions from the Paris Opera Ballet and Pacific Northwest Ballet.

—Fiona Marcotty

CHISENHALE DANCE SPACE

From its 1976 origins as a collective of dance artists who dubbed themselves X6, through and beyond its 1981 relocation to its present home in East London, Chisenhale Dance Space has fulfilled its ambitions as one of the United Kingdom's leading centres for experimentation and research in dance and movement.

Founding members Fergus Early, Maedée Duprès and Emilyn Claid were soon joined by Mary Prestidge and Jacky Lansley, all of whom have since made significant contributions to British independent dance. Their motives were as much practical as artistic. Apart from desiring a place to discover and exchange creative ideas, they wanted an inexpensive, warm and sizable rehearsal space, teachers with whom to take regular classes, and a venue suitable for presenting their work.

The X6 gang settled on a disused building at Butler's Wharf in London's docklands, with a room that was spacious, well-lit, and had a wooden floor. Having their own space gave them the freedom to inaugurate a nurturing alternative to established dance institutions. The wide-ranging classes and workshops they introduced were easygoing and non-competitive, attracting students from The Place, the Laban Centre and Dartington College. X6 formed a fruitful association with Dartington and its influential head of dance, American-born Mary Fulkerson.

Rather than reach a wider, general dance audience, the work produced by X6—process-oriented, self-expressive, frequently politicized, and often marred by an unfinished quality—tended to serve friends and peers. X6 was nevertheless one of the important seedbeds for a later flowering of indigenous modern British dance. The magazine *New Dance* (1977-88), founded by X6 members, provides a lasting record of the collective's interests, methods and philosophy.

X6 folded in 1980 due to extensive property development in the docklands. But also, by then X6 may simply have run its course. Before the closure, however, steps were taken to found another artist-run space. An old warehouse on Chisenhale Road was converted into artists' studios, and the remains of the collective arranged to take over a top-floor room big enough to present performances.

Although the floor was laid in 1981, Chisenhale Dance Space did not officially open until December 1984. Since then it has maintained a larger membership than X6, as well as an administrator, higher-profile programming, and closer links with the local community. The expansion of the collective's creative horizons has also continued, especially after the appointment of the first artistic directorship in 1993. Chisenhale commissions new work, organizes summer schools and special workshop intensives, and provides for both resident choreographers and fully mentored choreographic development projects. The programming reflects an ongoing appreciation of innovation via cross-collaborations between dance and such art forms as design, photography, poetry and music. Additionally, there have been seasons composed around such styles and themes as butoh dance, physical theatre, contact improvisation, site-specific work, solo performance, and issues of cultural and personal identity.

Chisenhale's performance space is 30 feet wide by 40 feet long, and seating capacity is approximately seventy on five tiers of bleachers. While activities generated at Chisenhale have usually been more marginal and certainly less product-focused than those at The Place, among the many British-based artists who have benefited from association with this seminal organization are Yolande Snaith and Lea Anderson (alumnis of Dartington and Laban, respectively), Gaby Agis, Jamie Watton and Fiona Edwards, and Javier de Frutos.

Publications

Jordan, Stephanie, *Striding Out,* London, 1992.
Mackrell, Judith, *Out of Line: The Story of British New Dance,* London, 1992.

—Donald Hutera

CHLADEK, Rosalia
Austrian dancer, choreographer, and educator

Born: 21 May 1905, Brno, Austria-Hungary (now Czech Republic). **Education:** School for Rhythm, Music, and Physical Education in Hellerau, near Dresden, 1921 to 1924. **Career:** Taught at the Hellerau School near Dresden; and at the Hellerau-Laxenburg School near Vienna, 1924-28; taught at the Basel Conservatory, 1928-30; artistic director, Hellerau-Laxenburg dance ensemble and director of gymnastic and dance education, 1930-38; director of modern dance, German Master Centers for Dance in Berlin; education director for "Dance for the Stage and for the Studio" at the Vienna City Conservatory, 1942-52; head of the dance department at the Vienna Academy of Music and Drama, 1952-70; directed a special course, "Modern Dance Education and Pedagogy—The Rosalia Chladek Method," 1961-77; led master classes for professional dancers "Movement for Dancers—the Chladek Method," 1972-93 in Strasbourg, after 1994 in Vienna; since Chladek's death, her method has been taught in six European countries by the "International Chladek Society" (IGRC; Ingrid Giel, president). **Awards:** Second Prize at the First International Competition for Choreography in Paris, 1932; Second Prize at the First International Competition for Solo Dance in Warsaw, 1933; granted a professorship in 1936, as well as various other awards by the City of Vienna and the State of Austria. **Died:** 3 July 1995 in Vienna.

Roles

1923	*L'Homme et son désir* (Valeria Kratina), Hellerau Festival and the Vienna Modern Music Week
	The Wooden Prince (Valeria Kratina), Hellerau Festival and the Vienna Modern Music Week

Works (selected)

1923	*Slavonic Dance No. 8* (solo; mus. Dvorak), Hellerau near Dresden
1925	*A Suite in Ancient Style* (solo; mus. Corelli), Brno, Czechoslovakia
1928	*Rhythm Cycle* (solo; including *The Spinning Dance* by I. Albeniz), Brno
1929	*Histoire d'un soldat* (mus. Stravinsky), Basel
1930	*Elements Cycle* (solo; mus. A. Kleiner; partly without musical accompaniment), Vienna
	Don Juan (mus. Gluck), Basel
	Intrada (solo; mus. Liszt), Vienna
	Pulcinella (mus. Stravinsky), Basel
1931	*Figures from Petrouchka* (solo; mus. Stravinsky), Vienna
1932	*Alcina-Suite* (mus. Handel), Laxenburg near Vienna
1934	*Life of St. Mary* (solo; mus. traditional), Basel
	Joan of Arc (solo; mus. Kleiner; Neuber, second setting), Basel
1936	*Narcissus* (solo; mus. *Mythologische Suite* by Kleiner; Takacs, second setting)
1938	*Archangel Suite:* "Michael" (solo; mus. Kleiner; Karger, second setting), Stockholm, and "Lucifer" (without music), Stockholm
1943	*La Dame aux camélias* (solo; mus. Chopin), Dresden
1948	*Kleine Passion* (mus. Biber), Vienna
1949	*Peter and the Wolf* (mus. Prokofiev), Vienna
1951	*From Morning to Midnight* (mus. Gershwin, Copland, Berlin), Vienna
	Afro-American Poetry (solo; accompanied by recitation of folk song lyrics), Vienna
	An American in Paris (mus. Gershwin), Vienna
1952	*Afro-American Poetry* (poetry by McKay, Alexander, Hughes, Johnson), Vienna
1953	*Sappho Songs* (mus. Rühm), Vienna
1959	*The Demon* (mus. Hindemith), Vienna
1968	*Curriculum aeternum* (mus. electronic), Vienna

Other works include: Chladek was guest choreographer at Italy's "Classical Festivals" (at Syracuse, Paestum, Ostia, and Vicenza) from 1933 to 1952. In addition she choreographed plays for the Salzburg Festival (e.g. *Everyman,* 1947), as well as operas and operettas. She choreographed and directed Gluck's opera *Orpheus and Eurydice* for the Vienna State Opera, as well as G. F. Händel's opera *Julius Caesar* in Salzburg, in 1959. Chladek also did film and TV work.

Publications

By CHLADEK: articles—

"What Is Dance?," *tanz aktuell* (Berlin), May-June 1991.

On CHLADEK: books—

Alexander, Gerda, and Hans Groll, editors, *Tänzerin Choreographin Pädagogin Rosalia Chladek,* Vienna, first edition, 1965, fourth edition, 1995.
Oberzaucher-Schüller, Gunhild, *Ausdruckstanz,* Heinrichshofen, 1992.

Films and Videotapes

Rosalia Chladek Dancer Choreographer Pedagogue—Scenes from my Life, dir. Piotr Szalsza, Televisfilm, Vienna, 1996.

*   *   *

Rosalia Chladek's life work first became fully appreciated by dance experts only in 1985. That year, Chladek, at the age of 80, started restoring her old "solo designs" (the artist preferred not to use the term "choreography") and sharing them with young dancers. As a result, *Lucifer*, a 1938 piece without music, was performed in the 1980s by Harmen Tromp. Chladek created the Lucifer figure as a contrast to Michael, (both had solos in the *Archangel Suite*). Chladek imagined Michael as a repressed, malicious, and, above all, human figure, who had fallen away from God. This newly restaged dance finally enabled younger dancers to appreciate Chladek's ability to blend form and content in a manner that was non-classical, elegantly clear, and in harmony with the spirit of *Ausdruckstanz*, creating a unified work of art.

At the avant-garde Hellerau School, Chladek became acquainted, thanks to the efforts of her teachers Valeria Kratina and Jarmila Kröschlova, with Emile Jaques-Dalcroze's innovative pedagogical ideas; she learned about the newly discovered importance of rhythm, also appreciating the contemporary *Ausdruckstanz*. Having established herself in Vienna in 1925, Chladek set two goals for herself: first, she wanted to create a teaching method for dancers based on the natural capacities of the human body; second, she wanted to create numerous choreographies. In addition, she also gained great fame as a dancer. Even Mary Wigman was entranced by Chladek:

> The dancer. . . . I see her in front of me; she is small and slim: a perfectly trained, powerfully beautiful body straightened to its full height—an ideal vertical line—an aristocrat of dance. . . . In every detail, in every differentiated nuance, one sees the same clarity, the same transparency as in the large gestures. Heroism, pathos, playfulness, and lyrical feelings are balanced and expressed in the form of dance, creating an absolute unity of expression itself and the instrument of expression.

Chladek was, as recently discovered films from the 1920s to the 1940s show, a perfectly shaped dancer, who knew how to transmute her passion into elegance. She sought a perfect balance of form and content, striving to the use the body's full potential, without, at the same time, jeopardizing the naturalness and clarity of movement. In her spare time, she designed dance cycles, which, being devoid of any narrative content, remained completely subordinated to the music, particularly to its rhythmical form. Musical pieces, whether by the old masters (Corelli, Händel, etc.), or contemporary composers (Stravinsky, Hindemith, etc.) constituted the most important point of departure. As a choreographer, Chladek later became interested in presenting larger female figures. Her most important musical adviser and accompanist was the pianist and composer Arthur Kleiner, who emigrated during the reign of Nazism. There are some reconstructed portraits of Chladek, which only she denied were hers. *Joan of Arc* (1934) and *La Dame aux camélias* (1944), both restaged by Chladek, demonstrate both the artist's grasp of dramaturgy, as well as her interpretive method, strongly affected by a sort of excessive psychological realism. Half a century after their premiere, the restaged pieces strike the viewer as classics of modernism. They are free of any kitsch or pathos. Thanks to the efforts of Gerhard Brunner, former director of the Vienna Ballet, who in 1988 organized an evening of restaged Chladek dances, her works are now part of Austria's patrimony.

Emerging from the cultural context of Central European Expressionism, Chladek turned to an aesthetic of dignity, which prompted some of her contemporaries to criticize her as proud and cold. In fact, she was constantly plagued by self-doubt. This blend of introversion and reserve made her life difficult, despite her great success. In 1932, the 27-year-old choreographer was awarded the Second Prize in a competition in which Kurt Joos won the First. Decades later, Joos, Wigman, and Kreutzberg acknowledged her as a leading dance educator.

However, the method for teaching dance that she created between 1930 and 1938 and conveyed for decades to generations of dancers primarily at the Vienna Dance Education Centers, and elsewhere, repeatedly drew criticism. According to her critics, her method subordinated training to sheer technical virtuosity. True, as a dancer, Chladek was blessed by a remarkable physical aptitude (particularly her ability to execute enormous leaps), which caused widespread envy. Indeed, one could regard Chladek's method as an intellectual construct, since things were explained, not shown, to the student. In a certain way, her method constitutes a challenge for the educated, reflective person, who can adopt it in his or her own creative way. The method is based on the natural aptitudes of the body, and is still taught in Vienna; abroad, in several European cities, Chladek's method is disseminated by teachers through the International Rosalia Chladek Society.

Considering the public's increasing demand, in recent years, to learn more about such risky subjects as the everyday life of artists under Nazism, we must examine Chladek's career from that particular angle. She was neither an exile, like her Jewish colleagues Gertrud Kraus, Gertrud Bodenweiser, and Margarete Wallmann, nor a resolute resistance fighter, like Hanna Berger. However, she was among those artists, who, without swearing allegiance to any political party, decided to remain in Austria after Hitler's incorporation of their country into the "Reich." These artists continued working without having to betray their art, and lived in a sort of inner exile. However, in retrospect, it is natural to feel uncomfortable her decision to work in Berlin, where she taught modern dance at the "Master Centers for German Dance" from 1940 to 1941. Upon her request, however, she returned to Vienna. It was not until 1950 that she first performed in New York, as part of an artistic exchange program.

The life work of this important choreographer, who in the 1940s and 1950s contributed to numerous theater and opera productions, devoting, as time went on, increasing attention to the relationship of dance and the spoken word, constitutes Austria's most significant contribution to this century's modern dance movement.

—Andrea Amort; translated by Zoran Minderovic

CHOI Chung-ja

Korean dancer, choreographer, and company director

Born: 5 April 1945 in Mokp'o, Chollanamdo. **Education:** Entered Soodo Women's Teachers College 1964, undergraduate and graduate programs for ballet and modern dance; studied modern dance and choreography at Goldsmith Laban Center in England, 1978. **Career:** Became professor at King Sejong University, 1978; performed opening concert for the Choi Chung-ja Dance Company at the Laban Theatre, 1980; returned to Korea, 1982; became chairperson of the Modern Dance Association of Korea and choreographed *Sandy Hill* for the 1988 Seoul Olympics; helped host World Dance Festival which helped to internationalize the Korean dance community by inviting many foreign performers, 1988; held over 100 tours in the Americas, Southeast Asia, Europe; turned her dance group into municipal dance company, 1995; performed at 1996 Olympic Games in Atlanta; hosted Seoul Future Dance Biennial Contest, 1997; art director of Tatmaroo Modern Dance Company; vice-president of the Korean Dance Society for the Future; president of the division of dance of the Korean Physical Education Society. **Awards:** Special Prize in Creative Dance, International Choreography Competition, Japan, 1984; Prize of Cultural Merits in appreciation of choreographing a modern dance for Seoul Art Company's performance (*Ardent Wishes of the People*) in Pyungyang, North Korea, 1985; prize from the Minister of Physical Education in appreciation of choreographing a dance for the Seoul Olympics, 1988; Corpanas Prize, 1988; Grand Prize at the Dance Festival of Korea, 1989; Grand Prix, Song-ok Cultural Foundation, 1989; Choreography Prize in 40th Seminar of ICHPER, 1997.

Roles

1979   Pupa (cr) in *Butterfly* (Kim Jeong-wook), Kim Jeong-wook Dance Group, Seoul

1981   *Song of the West* (Mary Wigman), Laban Center faculties and graduate school students performance, Laban Theatre, London

Works

1980   *Point* (solo; mus. various, arranged Choi Chung-ja), London
        Something Lost (solo; mus. Holst), Choi Chung-ja Modern Dance, Laban Theatre, London

1981   *Old and New* (solo; mus. various, arranged Choi Chung-ja), Choi Chung-ja Modern Dance, Laban Theatre, London

1982   *Revelation* (solo; mus. various, arranged Choi Chung-ja), Choi Chung-ja Tatmaroo Modern Dance Company, Sejong Cultural Center, Seoul
        Thirst (solo; mus. Samulori & Kim So-hee Pansori), Choi Chung-ja Tatmaroo Modern Dance Company, Sejong Cultural Center, Seoul
        Basketball (solo; mus. Bony M.), Choi Chung-ja Tatmaroo Modern Dance Company, Sejong Cultural Center, Seoul

1983   *Flowing Sands* (solo; mus. Tomita), Korean & Japanese Creative Dance Association Performance, Choi Chung-ja Tatmaroo Modern Dance Company, Munye Theatre, Seoul
        Everlasting Life (solo; mus. Kim Jung-gil), Choi Chung-ja Tatmaroo Modern Dance Company, Sejong Cultural Center, Seoul

1984   *The Land* (solo; mus. Motita), Choi Chung-ja Tatmaroo Modern Dance Company, Munye Theatre, Seoul
        It Comes Flowing Out (solo; mus. Tomita), Choi Chung-ja Tatmaroo Modern Dance Company, Munye Theatre, Seoul
        Everlasting Life (solo; mus. various, arranged Choi Chung-ja), Choi Chung-Ja Tatmaroo Modern Dance Company

1985   *Invocation* (solo; mus. Hwang Byoung-ki), Choi Chung-ja Tatmaroo Modern Dance Company, Hoam Art Hall, Seoul
        Ardent Wishes of the People (solo; mus. Kim Jung-gil), Choi Chung-ja Tatmaroo Dance Company, National Theatre of Korea, South & North Korea Culture Exchange Special Program, Seoul and Pyungyang Grand Theatre, Pyungyang

Choyong (solo; mus. Kim Jung-gil), Choi Chung-ja Tatmaroo Modern Dance Company, Munye Theatre, Seoul
Fiddler on the Roof (musical; mus. Jerry Burk), Seoul Metropolitan Musical Company, Sejong Cultural Center, Seoul

1986   *Mirror* (mus. Philip Glass), Choi Chung-ja Tatmaroo Modern Dance Company, Munye Theatre, Seoul

1987   *At the Cross Road* (mus. various, arranged Choi Chung-ja), Choi Chung-ja Tatmaroo Dance Company, National Theatre of Korea, Seoul
        Sunlight into my Heart! (solo; mus. Vangelis), Choi Chung-ja Tatmaroo Dance Company, Munye Theatre, Seoul

1988   *Changwha and Hongryun* (solo; mus. Kim Soo-chul), Choi Chung-ja Tatmaroo Dance Company, Munye Theatre, Seoul
        A Drop of Water (solo for Kim Hyung-nam, mus. Kim Young-dong), Dong-a Dance Competition Grand Prix, Sejong Cultural Center, Seoul
        Sandy Hill (co-choreographed, mus. Choi Dong-sun), Choi Chung-ja Tatmaroo Modern Dance Company, Olympic Opening Ceremony, Chamsil Olympic Stadium, Seoul
        Journey of Butterfly (mus. Francisco Semprun), Choi Chung-ja Tatmaroo Modern Dance Company, National Theatre of Korea, Seoul
        Genesis (co-choreographed, mus. Choi Dong-sun), Choi Chung-ja Tatmaroo Modern Dance Company, Handicapped Olympic Opening Ceremony, Chamsil Olympic Stadium, Seoul

1989   *One, Two. . .* (mus. Melita), Choi Chung-ja Tatmaroo Dance Company, National Theatre of Korea, Seoul
        Giselle-White Pavilion (mus. Adolf Adan, Vangelis), Choi Chung-ja Tatmaroo Dance Company, Hoam Art Hall, Seoul
        Bullimsori (mus. Kim Soo-chul), Choi Chung-ja Tatmaroo Modern Dance Company, Dance Festival of Korea Grand Prix, Munye Theatre, Seoul, Chungju, Taegu, P'ohang, Jaechun, Mokp'o, Kumi

1990   *Flower Festival* (solo; mus. Samulnori), Choi Chung-ja Tatmaroo Modern Dance Company, Bulgaria Varan Open Opera Theatre Sofia, National Palace of Culture, Sofia
        Autumn (solo; mus. Hwang Byoung-ki), Choi Chung-ja Tatmaroo Modern Dance Company, Bulgaria Varan Open Opera Theatre Sofia, National Palace of Culture, Sofia
        The Sound of Drum (mus. Samulnori), Choi Chung-ja Tatmaroo Modern Dance Company, Bulgaria Varan Open Opera Theatre Sofia, National Palace of Culture, Sofia

1991   *Young People's Parade* (mus. Bill Withers), Choi Chung-ja Tatmaroo Modern Dance Company, Hoam Art Hall, Seoul

1992   *Wandering Youngsters* (mus. Bill Withers), Choi Chung-ja Tatmaroo Modern Dance Company, Hoam Art Hall, Seoul
        Into the Spring (mus. Stephan Micus), Choi Chung-ja Tatmaroo Modern Dance Company, Hoam Art Hall, Seoul
        Something Lost (mus. Jean Pierre), Choi Chung-ja Tatmaroo Modern Dance Company, National Museum of Contemporary Sculpture Park, Seoul
        Where the Time Rests (mus. Maurice Jarre), Choi Chung-ja Tatmaroo Dance Company, National Museum of Contemporary Sculpture Park, Seoul
        Grey of Morning (mus. Andrew Lloyd Webber), Choi Chung-ja Tatmaroo Dance Company, National Mueum of Contemporary Sculpture Park, Seoul

1993   *Light* (mus. Kim Jung-gil), Choi Chung-ja Tatmaroo Dance
        Company, Celebration Performance for Presidential
        Inaugural, Little Angels Art Center, Seoul
        Standing Woman (mus. various, arranged Choi Chung-ja),
        Choi Chung-ja Tatmaroo Dance Company, Seoul
        Winter Tango (mus. Loreena McKennitt), Choi Chung-ja
        Tatmaroo Dance Company, Munye Theatre, Seoul
1994   *Purple Potato, White Potato* (dir.; choreographer Lee Eun-
        sun), Choi Chung-ja Tatmaroo Modern Dance Com-
        pany, Munye Theatre, Seoul
1995   *Beach Man* (mus. Sarah Vaughan & Bruce Kurnow), Choi
        Chung-ja Tatmaroo Modern Dance Company, Sejong
        Cultural Center, Seoul
        The Boom of Buk (solo; mus. Samulnori), Choi Chung-ja
        Tatmaroo Modern Dance Company, North Miami
        Beach Cultural Center, Miami
        Toward the 20th Century (mus. Vladmir Spivakov), Choi
        Chung-ja Tatmaroo Modern Dance Company,
        Chongmyo Park, Seoul
        Desire of Nation (mus. Kim Jung-gil), Choi Chung-ja
        Tatmaroo Modern Dance Company, Chongmyo Park,
        Seoul
        Summer (mus. Sarah Vaughan & Bruce Kurnow), Choi
        Chung-ja Tatmaroo Modern Dance Company, Taegu
        Culture Center, Taegu
        Festival of Light (mus. Hwang Byoung-ki), Choi Chung-
        ja Tatmaroo Modern Dance Company, Kwangju
        Great Joy (mus. Hwang Byoung-ki), Choi Chung-ja
        Tatmaroo Modern Dance Company, Children's Park
        Open Stage, Seoul
1996   *A Special Tune of Arirang* (mus. Kim Soo-chul), Choi
        Chung-ja Tatmaroo Modern Dance Company, Atlanta
        Olympic Art and Culture Festival
        Flying Wings (mus. Kim Jung-gil), Choi Chung-ja Tatmaroo
        Modern Dance Company, Seoul
        The Street Man (mus. various, arranged Choi Chung-ja),
        Choi Chung-ja Tatmaroo Modern Dance Company,
        Hoam Art Hall, Seoul
        The Woman in the Fall (Mus. Hwang Byoung-ki), for
        Korea-China Culture Exchange, Choi Chung-ja
        Tatmaroo Modern Dance Company, Beijing Century
        Theatre
        Newcomer (mus. Sarah Vaughan & Bruce Kuonow), for
        Korea-China Culture Exchange, Choi Chung-ja Tatmaroo
        Modern Dance Company, Beijing Century Theatre
1997   *Swan Song* (mus. Kronos Quartet), Choi Chung-ja
        Tatmaroo Modern Dance Company, Seoul Education
        Culture Center
        We Are the World (mus. Hwang Byoung-ki), Choi Chung-
        ja Tatmaroo Modern Dance Company, ITI Congress &
        Theatre of Nations Opening Ceremony, National The-
        atre of Korea, Seoul

Publications

By CHOI: books—

Theories on Dance Movement and Dancing, Seoul, 1985.
Choreography and Movement, Seoul, 1988.
Understanding Dance Education and Choreography, Seoul, 1993.
Dance Science, co-author, Seoul, 1995.

On CHOI: articles—

Kim Tae-won, "Choi Chung-ja's Dance: The Socialization and Glo-
    balization of Korea's Common Feelings," *Performing Arts & Film
    Review* (Seoul), Summer 1995.
Konstantionove, Peter, and Peye Gergova, "Choi Chung-ja Perfor-
    mance Makes the Audience Rejoice with the Sounds of Life,"
    CHOOM (Seoul), September 1991.

*   *   *

When Korean modern dance was rapidly growing in the 1980s,
developing a kind of modern dance renaissance, Choi Chung-ja took
a different path from the mainstream, forming a group of rather
instinctive and heathy dance with unique artistic characteristics.
What we call the mainstream refers to the Korea Contemporary
Dance Company, which consisted of Ewha Women's University
graduates of contemporary dance and used Martha Graham's techniques as a creative and educative system. However, Choi Chung-ja
was not influenced by American modern dance; she was, rather,
strongly influenced by Rudolf Laban's creativity concept and theory
of movement, to which she was exposed while studying at the
Laban Centre of Goldsmith College at London University.

Prior to her studying in London in the early 1980s, Choi received
intensive ballet training from a strict ballet professor, Kim Jung-
wook, at King Sejong University, which is now one of Korea's best-
known professional dance institutions. However, she was more
interested in modern dance, in which she could more freely utilize
her creativity. After graduating from King Sejong University with a
M.A. in 1977, she studied at the Laban Center of London, where in
June of 1981 she presented her *Old and New* and thus began a career
in creative choreography. A year later, in October of 1982, she
presented four pieces at Sejong Cultural Center in Seoul. Among
those four, in *Thirst* and *Revelation,* she was able to successfully
apply many abstract movements in portraying the internal agonies
of the Korean people. In *Thirst* she used traditional Korean music
and instrumentation, combined with Pansori (the Korean traditional way of singing) performed by Kim So-hee, to create an appropriate emotional effect for the dance. On the other hand, another
piece called *Basketball* was noted for its postmodern experimental
characteristics, freely utilizing modern dance techniques to express
the world of sports. Clearly, Choi Chung-ja was developing two types
of dance: one which expresses a combination of agony and pain with a
longing for a religious salvation, the other type witty and playful.

Trying to solve this question of the salvation of human kind from
pain and agony in a greater scale, using the idea of religious symbolism (in her case, Christianity), marked the performance *Bullimsori.*
The main character of the piece, Choi Byung-hee, is a person in
darkness and despair, who gets lifted up by a giant hand-like sculpture at the end. This symbolizes his freedom from pain. The scene
symbolizes the agony of Korean society in the 1980s, with its
military regime and anti-democratic suppression. It also represents
the primary question of all human beings: the question of its original existence and salvation. She made use of Kim soo-chuol music,
which is strongly emotional in a typical Korean way, and she sets
the tone for the dance by using music to precede the actual movements of the dance. At the same time, she utilized an almost-naked
group. This represented the collective nature of primitive society—human life before civilization. Therefore, in Choi Chung-ja's
choreography, music and dance arouse the audience's emotions by
using two different waves or rather, two different channels. This

method is successfully sublimated and thus creates a noticeable artistic effect. In 1991, she began a dance cycle based on the four seasons; the first piece, *Autumn,* a trio, depicted sharp, shivering stimulation.

The characteristics of her choreography, producing sensuous expression but at the same time portraying the pain of human existence, can be considered as a discordance. This sometimes causes an unexpected structure of performance. Another part of her seasons dance cycle, *Winter Tango* (1993), is a good example of such discordance. This piece shows slow dance movements that represent the coming spring and fast dance movements that symbolize a celebration of spring. These two movements are contrary to each other, but together they create a colorful fantasy.

Like her work *Basketball,* the last piece in her seasons cycle, *Beach Man* (1995), used acrobatic movements similar to those of Philobolus, the American modern dance group, and with its cheerful swing jazz accompaniment is reminiscent of the wildness of the summer season.

Choi Chung-ja has a tendency to prefer spectacle rather than finely structured movement. Therefore, her choreography is very sensual, primitive and honest. But also, it carries a discordance between internal emotions and external expressions, producing unexpected about-faces, something like postmodern disorganization. For the best conveyance of performance, she trains her dancers very strictly, taking into consideration each dancer's physical characteristics and their ability, and she requires them to use all parts of their body in a three-dimensional sense and urges them to think of themselves as sculptures. She also emphasizes the application of Korean traditional dance techniques to movement of arms and feet, as other second generation Korean choreographers often do.

Her passion for creation and education of dance is noticeable in Korean modern dance history. From 1988 to 1991, which was the most important period in the development of Korean modern dance, she served as the president of the Modern Dance Association of Korea and while in that position invited dance companies and choreographers from around the world to perform in Korea. She was also invited to Japan and was able to show Japanese audiences that Korean modern dance had developed and matured artistically. In 1985 she enabled the cultural exchange between South and North Korea through Seoul Art Company's performance in North Korea. In the 1990s, when Cold War tensions were breaking down, she began to tour the former communist countries in eastern Europe. She continues to make contact with Laban Center in London to root down Laban's education method in the Korean contemporary dance. Today, Choi Chung-ja's dance company is extremely popular with the Korean public, and it is not surprising to find that many excellent Korean modern dancers like Choi Myung-hee, Choi Il-kyu, Kim Tae-hoon, Kim Hyung-nam, Ahn Chu-kyung, Choi Sung-sook, Oh Buyng-ae, and Chung Myung-ji, are from her dance company.

—Kim Tae-won

CHONG, Ping

Asian-American theater director, choreographer, video and installation artist

Born: 2 October 1946 in Toronto, Canada. **Education:** Attended Pratt Institute, 1964-66; School of the Visual Arts, 1967-69; stud-

ied dance with Meredith Monk, 1969-72; formed Ping Chong and Company, 1972; curator/designer, 10th Anniversary Exhibition, Department of Cultural Affairs, 1986. **Awards:** CAPS Fellowship 1974, 1975; Obie Award for *Humboldt's Current,* 1977; National Endowment for the Arts (NEA) New Genre fellowship, 1981; Villager Award for *A.M./A.M.-The Articulated Man,* 1982; Grand Prize, Toronto Video Festival, 1983; NEA Arts Visual Arts Fellowship 1984; Guggenheim fellowship, Maharam Design Award 1985; NYFA Choreographers Fellowship 1987; McKnight Fellow 1988, 1992; NEA choreographic fellowship, 1989, 1990, 1991; Bronze Star, Sacramento International Film and Video Festival, 1990; New York Dance and Performance Award ("Bessie") for Sustained Achievement in the Performing Arts, 1992; National Artist Residency Grant Award, 1993; Silver Award, Dance on Camera Festival, 1993; Winton Fellow, University of Minnesota, 1994.

Roles

1971	Dancer, *Vessel* (Meredith Monk), Meredith Monk/The House, New York
1975	Dancer, *Small Scroll* (Meredith Monk), Meredith Monk/The House, New York
1976	Dancer, *Quarry* (Meredith Monk), Meredith Monk/The House, New York

Works

1972	*Lazarus,* New York
1973	*I Flew to Fiji, You Went South,* New York
1974	*Chacon* w/Monk (mus. Monk), New London, Connecticut
	Paris w/Monk (mus. Monk), Paris
1975	*Fear and Loathing in Gotham,* New York
1976	*Venice/Milan* w/Monk (mus. Monk), George Washington University, Washington, D.C.
1977	*Humboldt's Current,* New York
1981	*Nuit Blanche,* New York
	Rainer and the Knife, Chicago
1982	*A.M./A.M.—The Articulated Man,* New York
	Anna into Nightlight, New York
1983	*A Race,* Seattle, Washington
	The Games w/Monk (mus. Monk), Berlin
1984	*Angels of Swedenborg,* Chicago
	Astonishment and the Twins, Lexington, New York
1985	*Nosferatu: A Symphony of Darkness,* New York
1986	*Kind Ness,* Boston
1987	*Without Law, without Heaven* (mus. Norman Durkee), Seattle
1988	*Maraya—Acts of Nature in Geological Time,* Montclair, New Jersey
	Quartetto (mus. Henk van der Meulen), Rotterdam
	Snow, Minneapolis
1989	*Skin—A State of Being,* New York
	Noiresque—The Fallen Angel, New York
	Brightness, New York
1990	*Deshima,* Utrecht
	Elephant Memories, Chester Springs, Pennsylvania
	4AM America, Milwaukee
1991	*I Will Not Be Sad in this World,* College Park, Maryland
1992	*Undesirable Elements/New York,* New York
	American Gothic, New York

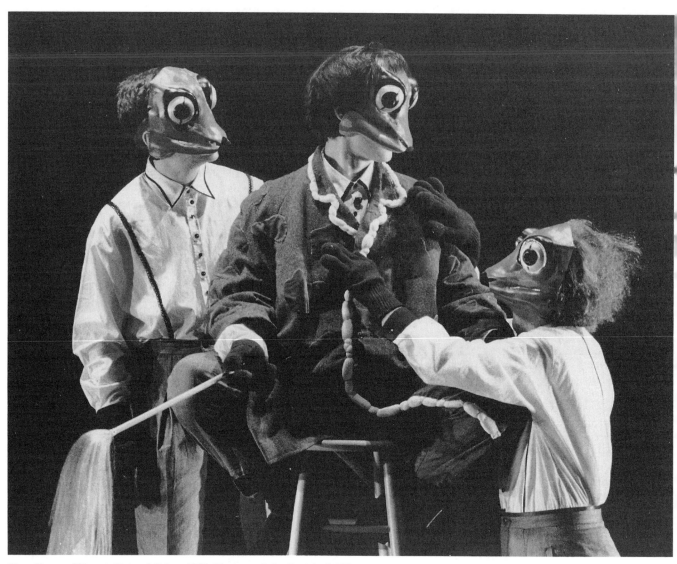

Ping Chong: *Skin—A State of Being,* 1989. Photograph by Beatriz Schiller.

1993   *Undesirable Elements/Cleveland,* Cleveland
1994   *Persuasion,* University of Minnesota, Minneapolis
        Undesirable Elements/Twin Cities, Minneapolis
1995   *Undesirable Elements/Seattle,* Seattle
        Gaijin (Undesirable Elements/Tokyo), Tokyo
        Chinoiserie w/Michael Matthews and Guy Klucevsek
            (mus. Klucevsek), Buffalo, New York
1996   *Interfacing Joan* w/Louise Smith, New York
        98.6: A Convergence in 15 Minutes w/Muna Tseng, New
            York
1997   *After Sorrow* (Vietnam) w/Muna Tseng and Josef Fung
            (mus. Fung), New York

Publications

Bromberg, Craig, "Ping Chong (review)," *Dance Magazine,* May
    1985.
Carroll, Noel, "A Select View of Earthlings: Ping Chong (United
    States)," *Drama Review,* Spring 1983.

Dillon, John, "Three Places in Asia," *American Theatre,* March
    1996.
Evett, Marianne, "Cultural Diversity Dissected," *Plain Dealer*
    (Cleveland), 5 March 1993.
Freligh, Rebecca, "Weaving Multicultural Tapestry," *Plain Dealer,*
    5 March 1993.
Holden, Stephen, "Collisions of East and West," *New York Times,*
    16 November 1995.
Osborn, M. Elizabeth, "The Divine Comedy of Ping Chong," *Next
    Wave Magazine,* October 1986.
Petrie, Carolyn, "True Stories," *City Pages,* 25 January 1995.
Simon, Jordan, "The Gentrification of Avant-Garde Theater," *Taxi,*
    April 1987.
Simons, Tad, "All Together Now," *Twin Cities Reader,* 19-25 Octo-
    ber 1994.
Steinman, Louise, "Ping Chong Diplomacy: World Theater," *Fresh
    Weekly,* January 11-17 1983.
Sterritt, David, "The Fascinating Theater Art of Ping Chong," *Chris-
    tian Science Monitor,* 29 May 1984.

Films and Videotapes

Education of the Girl Child, director with Meredith Monk, 1973.

* * *

Over the years, the nucleus of Ping Chong's work has shifted from allegorical tales to history, whether it be of the world or his own. Just as with his mentor and former collaborator Meredith Monk, his work has become less avant-garde and more accessible to a varied audience. But as he explained in *American Theatre* magazine, "Accessibility is about communication, not compromise."

The native New Yorker and first-generation Asian-American still creates works that explore the outsider and the unfamiliar in uncompromising terms. But with his focus on stories rather than mystical tales, he has opened his wry theatrical observations on racial prejudices to a wider audience. Like Monk, Chong's work incorporates the complexity of several disciplines: theater, dance, ritualized gesture, slides, film, spoken text, music, and immaculately designed sets. Chong was born in 1946 in Toronto, Canada. His parents, who were performers with the Peking Opera during the 1930s, arrived in San Francisco on a North American tour and decided to stay. From the Bay area, they moved to Vancouver and Toronto, finally settling into New York's Chinatown, where they ran a Chinese restaurant-coffeeshop. Chong's first language was Chinese; his days at public school were always followed by Chinese school. It wasn't until high school in midtown Manhattan that he became exposed to teenagers of other nationalities. At that time, he aspired to become a filmmaker, studying both film and visual art at the School of Visual Arts and Pratt Institute.

After film school, Chong's focus changed. Instead of concentrating on the specialized, "aggressive" world of filmmaking, he decided he would like to try merging several art forms.

Chong always had an interest in dance; during the late 1960s and early 1970s, he began to study with Monk. *Paris, Venice/Milan,* and *Chacon,* created by Chong and Meredith Monk over four years during the 1970s, is dubbed the "travelogue series." Like Monk, with whom he collaborated for eight years, Chong's work is difficult to classify. His themes of loneliness and alienation are driven by moments of awkward, erratic movement or sustained stillness. His first independent theater work, the melancholy *Lazarus,* was presented in 1972 and opened with slides of a street and stairwell of a tenement building. After the set was arranged (a table, tablecloth, coffee pot, and flower), Lazarus arrived, his head wrapped like a mummy's. A letter from a woman is read while he eats. Like all of Chong's work, it is still voyeuristic, somehow eerie, and unnerving to watch.

His painterly sets and stage images are also perfectly arranged—not an element is out of place. "The traditional Japanese household is neat, but the traditional Chinese one is messy—and our household was working class and chaotic. There were six kids in the house, and the place was a real mess! And that's why I live alone today in a very orderly apartment." In 1985, Chong's *Nosferatu: A Symphony of Darkness,* an updated version of *Dracula,* was set in the immaculate but suffocating apartment of a couple, Jonathan and Nina Harker. Though the names were the same as the Bram Stoker book and F.W. Murnau's silent film, *Nosferatu,* in Chong's piece, the couple was a pair of vapid yuppies. Oblivious to all that surrounds them they talk frantically about job obsessions and sex (it was reported that 50 to 60 percent of the *Nosferatu* text was taken from published interviews with yuppies) and wait for guests to arrive at a dinner party. When Dracula arrives, Jonathan is still conducting business over the telephone. Questions are posed on a big screen: "What is darkness? And in this room, can anyone determine the whereabouts of darkness?" In *Dance Magazine,* Craig

Ping Chong: *Skin—A State of Being,* 1989. Photograph by Beatriz Schiller.

Bromberg concluded that "Chong locates the darkness in Western culture with startling theatrical clarity without ever imputing the West itself."

Since 1992, Chong has directed versions of *Undesirable Elements,* an ongoing series of community-specific works (thus far, the following cities have participated: New York City, Cleveland, Minneapolis, Seattle, and Tokyo). Each production explores the effects of history, culture, and ethnicity on the lives of individuals in a community and is a collaboration with eight individuals of varying backgrounds who represent a spectrum of cultures. It is staged in a circle, which, according to Chong, means that "nobody is better than anybody else." One reviewer in Minneapolis wrote, "The cumulative power of these shared stories is nothing short of astonishing."

Part of Chong's Asian trilogy, *Chinoiserie* (which he describes as a "docu-concert-theater-lecture"), refers to the 18th-century fixation with decorative Chinese and faux-Chinese designs. At the beginning of the piece, the director stands at a podium recalling an evening at a Chinese restaurant when a woman remarked, "Why don't they use knives and forks?" He delves into history, describing the story of an early Chinese immigrant's contribution to the railroad system, the British colonization of China, and the brutal 1982 murder of Vincent Chin in Detroit as well as his own experiences with racism. Thus far, it is his most personal work. Interestingly, but not surprisingly, Chong's intent to dissect cultures hasn't wavered. In 1982, his introduction to *Nuit Blanches* read, "As a young adult I felt like I was sitting on a fence staring at two cultures. You go out into the bigger world and start looking at it with the kind of objectivity an anthropologist has." And even though his work is clearer to audiences, he hopes that they leave with more of a sensory awareness than an intellectual one. "I want the audience to understand the other side of the fence, what it feels like not to comprehend." Chong is successful in his art because—unlike many in the dance-theater world—he has the gift of storytelling. His current project, *Kwaidan,* is an ambitious puppet-theater work based on the Japanese ghost stories of Lafcadio Hearn, premiering in mid-1998 at the Center for Puppetry Arts in Atlanta.

—Gia Kourlas

CHOREOLOGICAL STUDIES

The term choreology was first used in the 1920s by Rudolf Laban to encompass knowledge of the structure of spatial forms of dance (choreutics) and of its rhythmic and dynamic content (eukinetics) together with dance notation (Labanotation) and the cultural content of dances (choreosophy). Ethnochoreology was established in 1960 for the study of folk dance as a sister discipline to ethnomusicology. Comparable progress towards an adequate "-ology" for dance as a theatre art has followed but the centres of choreological activity are not yet coordinated. Practical scholarship is a concept promoted among those involved in choreology, dance people equally at home with theoretical discourse and practice who can bridge the gap between academic and performer, researcher and artist.

Choreologist is a title used by the Benesh notators for people who write scores and rehearse ballets from the score. While both of these functions are part of the choreological domain a choreologist may not be a notator at all, but use the associated skills necessary for analysis and/or synthesis of the several perspectives required for adequate scholarly practice and theory in dance.

Choreological studies centre on the morphology of dance material. Dance specific methods have had to be devised which enable the ephemeral material of dance to be held in some permanent way so that a relatively objective analysis of it can be made. For much mainstream work the notation systems of Laban and of Benesh are used as a way of recording on paper the movement of the body in space and time. In association with this record analysis is then possible of the bodily coordination, the movement's rhythmic and dynamic organisation and its spatial patterning. A variety of methods are used; some for rhythm are based on musicological analysis, some arising from Labananalysis and Effort/Shape. Concepts of time, energy, space, and kinetic flow appear in dance in greater variety than that offered in Effort/Shape. For example, a choreographer may be interested in time as duration, time as metre, time as pace and tempo, time as past, present and future, time as sudden and sustained qualities, time as breath rhythm, or psychological time. A broad cognizance of choreographic practice has enabled methods to be constructed to allow data to be collected about a work appropriate to its content rather than to any one analytic perspective.

Analyses are undertaken of the choreographic structure, the identification of formal elements, their clustering and their manipulation in single bodies and in ensembles. Some of the practical work undertaken as a way of understanding structure is useful for both composing new work and appreciating existing works. Research in ethnochoreology on the form of folk dances provided the first structural methods from which the identification of the complex structuring of theatre works has developed.

The use of notation may be unsatisfactory for some dance since choreographers' ideosyncratic use of rhythm or of space results in their work being incompatible with the grammars of notation systems just as some contemporary music is incompatible with traditional music script. Action rhythm rather than metric rhythm (Merce Cunningham), indeterminacy rather than fixed form (Rosemary Butcher), virtual spatial forms to be registered rather than actual spatial pathways to be made (William Forsythe) are three examples of incompatibility. Video recordings are used instead of notation but these constitute one performance of a work by one group of dancers, often taken from one perspective. Style one, that of the choreographer's movement material, and style two, the personal style of the dancer dancing it has to be distinguished. Ideally both a score and a video are required for micro-morphological research of dance style.

Since morphology is concerned with both the form and its function the dance specific methods interface with those from extrinsic disciplines such as semiotics. Dance forms signal meaning within cultures and subcultures. Semiological analysis identifies codes, rules and norms within a style, it identifies intentional and unintentional references in narrative works and hidden signs in abstract works. Semiotic analysis overlaps with reception theories which juxtapose the signs put in the dance material by the choreographer, signs added by the performers and the signs imagined to be in the dance by each spectator.

Aesthetic theory interfaces with morphology by looking at the movement forms as art, distinguishing between aesthetic and mundane content as well as aesthetic awareness and evaluative criticism of the work. Some choreographers use unaltered mundane material as art while others manipulate mundane material structurally and others create illusions by subsuming the mundane into established dance vocabularies. How this is achieved is looked at through structural methods.

Politics of dance interfaces with dance material by looking at the dance work and the performers as political objects, especially the dancer's body as a subversive element. The performative perspective appreciates the performer not as a body but as an individual personality with power to engage with the material and alter its impact through micro-adjustments to the material's form. Starting from Laban's effort theory choreological methods can identify or engender such micro differences of intention. Performers' experience of their own movement is approached through a phenomenological perspective in which the dancer as object and as subject are contrasted. The politics of performing as a manipulated object or an intentional subject is an issue approached within choreology. Gender and feminist issues as they affect the form or influence its function are of interest.

What the medium of a dance work might be is a choreological concern. The role of music or sound in a work is crucial to its identity. So too is the space in which the dance is presented or with which the dance is made. The various strands of the dance medium may integrate, or co-exist, or be juxtaposed, or contracontextual or interdependent according to the stylistic decisions of the creative team. Choreological analysis therefore takes into account the movement, the performers, the sound, the space and their nexus or web of interrelationship. Because contemporary choreographers cross traditional borders between dance and neighbouring arts such as physical theatre, performance art, using speaking dancers, dancing musicians, tumblers, jugglers, audience participation, site specific dances, and so on, choreological perspectives have to take account of much more than the form of the movement. The form of the whole event can only be addressed by including all strands of the dance medium.

Processes in choreographic art-making form a part of choreological research. What is looked at is formulation rather than form. Many perspectives are used—how choreographers interact with their dancers, how they create alone or co-create the work, how they rehearse, how they edit, how they cast, what they regard as the essentials and the inessentials of the work, what their attitude to sound and space are, how they cooperate with composers and designers, how they recast and remount their work.

Because dance is now literate and many works are remounted from the score and others from the video, questions on the identity of a work are prevalent. Materialist and idealist concepts are considered, that is, does the identity of the work lie in the material of the work itself or in the ideas behind the material? A dance that was shocking in 1912 will almost certainly not shock today. When remounting the work should you concentrate on its material and so miss its original impact or do you regard its injunctive qualities as part of its identity and so look for ways of addressing the shock element? Remounting, recreating, reproducing are all ways in which a repertory art deals with the form and function of its heritage and choreologists engage with the issues that have to be considered.

The advent of video dance and digital dance, the use of computer graphics and computer systems for notated scores has opened up areas for the development of choreology far beyond the parameters of Laban's original foundations as well as choreography beyond the original parameters of modern dance.

A piece of research in dance may rely entirely on extrinsic methodologies but currently research at doctoral level may include practice for which choreological methods are helpful. The fact that choreology uses graphic systems which cope with the continuous nature of motion and the concurrency of several lines of activity in a work alongside the written word makes it more amenable to the rigorous demands for objectivity in the most subjective of arts.

Publications

Books—

Adshead, J., ed., *Dance Analysis: Theory and Practice,* London, 1988.
Benesh, R. and J., *Reading Dance: The Birth of Choreology,* London 1983.
Eco, Umberto, *The Open Work,* New York, 1989.
Fiske, J., *Introduction to Communication Studies,* London, 1990.
Foster, S. L. *Reading Dance: Bodies and Subjects in Contemporary American Dance,* Berkeley, 1986.
Fraleigh, S., *Dance and the Lived Body,* Pittsburgh, 1987.
Guiraud, P., *Semiology,* London, 1975.
Hutchinson Guest, A., *Labanotation,* New York, 1977.
Laban, Rudolf, *Mastery of Movement,* 4th edition, London, 1980.
Longstaff, J., A. Sanchez-Colberg, and V. Dunlop- Preston, eds., *A Guide to Dance Analysis Methodologies from a Choreological Perspective,* London, 1998.
Pavis, P. *Languages of the Stage: Essays in the Semiology of the Theatre,* New York, 1982.
Preston-Dunlop, Valerie, *Dance Words,* London, 1995.
———, *Looking at Dances: A Choreological Perspective on Choreography,* London, 1998.

Articles—

Armelagos, A. and Sirridge, M., "The Identity Crisis in Dance," *Journal of Aesthetics and Art Criticism,* 1978.
Genova, J., "The Significance of Style," *Journal of Aesthetics and Art Criticism,* 1979.
Lange, R., "Dance Notation and the Development of Choreology," *Musica Antiqua VIII,* Polska, 1988.
Marion, S., "Authorship and Intention in Re-Created or Notated Dances," *5th Hong Kong International Dance Conference/Notation Papers,* 1990.

—Valerie Preston-Dunlop

CHOUINARD, Marie

Canadian dancer, performance artist, choreographer, and company director

Born: 14 May 1955 in Quebec City. **Career:** First solo piece perfomed with composer Rober Racine, 1979; founder, general and artistic director, La Compagnie Marie Chouinard, 1990; participated in *Performance,* an Austrian television series examining music, dance and ritual, and featuring Laurie Anderson, Robert Wilson, and Trisha Brown, 1982. **Awards:** Jacqueline-Lemieux Award, 1986; Chalmers Award, 1987; Lifetime Achievement Award, 1993; Paper Boat Award (Glasgow), for *Le Sacre du printemps,* 1994.

Works

1979	*Cristallisation* (mus. Rober Racine), solo
	Dimanche matin, mai 1955, solo

Danse pour un homme habillé de noir et qui porte un revolver, solo

Déjeuner sur l'herbe, solo

Divertissement génométrique, un trio

1980   *Mimas, lune de Saturne*, solo

La Leçon, solo

Dislocations, solo

Chanson de gestes, solo

Quelques façons d'avancer tranquillement vers toi, solo

Jaune, solo

Récréation, solo

Dimanche matin, mai 2005, solo

Conversations, solo

Voyages vers les milbes, duo with Claude Vivier

Auto-portrait no. 1, performance piece

Auto-portrait no. 2, performance piece

Petite danse sans nom, performance piece

Les Grenouillées, performance piece with the Music Dance Orchestra

Les oeufs, ou Autrefois il y avait, il y a longtemps, au temps où. . ., performance piece

Cinq danses pour le public, performance piece

1981   *Danseuse-performeuse cherche amoureux ou amoureuse pour la nuit du Ier juin*, performance piece

1982   *Meat meets Meat*, duo with Claude-Marie Caron

Marie chien noir, solo

1984   *Table of Contents 1*, solo

1985   *Chebre*, performance piece with Claude-Marie Caron

Earthquake in the Heartchakra, solo

Table of Contents II, solo

1986   *Drive in the Dragon*, solo

Crue, solo

STAB (Space, Time and Beyond), solo

1987   *L'Après-midi d'une faune*, solo

1988   *Biophilia*, solo

1989   *Poèmes d'atmosphères*, solo

1991   *Les Trous du ciel*, Compagnie Marie Chouinard

1993   *Le Sacre du printemps*, Compagnie Marie Chouinard

1994   *Prélude à l'après-midi d'un faune*, Compagnie Marie Chouinard

1996   *L'Amande et le diamant*, Compagnie Marie Chouinard

Publications

On CHOUINARD: books—

Tembeck, Iro, "Dancing in Montreal: Seeds of a Choreographic History," *Journal of the Society of Dance History Scholars*, Vol. V, Number 2, Fall 1994.

Films and Videotapes (by Chouinard)

J'aurais aimé vous voir danser, madame Akarova, RBTF Brussels, 1990.

Marie chien noir, Western Front, 1982.

Performance, in collaboration with ORF-Austria; with Laurie Anderson, Robert Wilson, Trisha Brown, Simone Forti, and Marina Abramovic, 1982.

Les Trous du ciel, Raymond St-Jean, dir., 1992.

Le Sacre du printemps, Isabelle Hayeur, dir., 1995.

*   *   *

It's been almost 20 years since Montreal-based Marie Chouinard has risen to become one of Quebec's most provocative and exported dance talents. She took up dance after she applied, and wasn't accepted, into theatre school. She wasn't thinking about dance as an art form, or even a chosen profession. She was dancing in the broader sense "as a joy for my soul, for my body."

Her individualistic style was evident early on, when she was expelled from her classical dance classes at Studio d'expression corporelle by her master teacher, former New York City Ballet dancer Tom Scott. She had refused to be part of his recital. Chouinard persisted on her own, training in a rented studio. One day, Dena Davida—head of the now defunct Qui Danse? showcase which brought together a number of upcoming, independent Montreal dancers and choreographers—stopped by and asked Chouinard to present something. Chouinard accepted the invitation and, in 1979, her first creation *Cristallisation*, a solo piece performed with composer Rober Racine, premiered at Montreal's prime alternative visual and performing arts venue, Galerie Vehicule Art.

The successful response to the show propelled Chouinard into the ranks of Quebec's burgeoning group postmodern of dancers and choreographers, many of whom were exploring dance on personal terms. She characterized her dance process as "choosing gestures and sound to just show the essentials," and she delved deeply into the sensual and sexual sides of life.

Initially, Chouinard's ritualistic performances shocked some, but drew many others to her work. Her national status grew when she performed a conceptual short piece, *La petite danse sans nom* (1980), at Toronto's Art Gallery of Ontario. She entered with a pail, paced around the floor, placed the pail in the middle, pliéd in a second position over it, then urinated and carried the bucket off-stage. People hadn't seen anything like it on stage. Some were rattled, some protested, while others smiled. The piece was banned in Montreal for a time.

Dancing, per se, seemed a minor part of her performance. She took chances and pushed boundaries—for the audience and for herself—with her primitivist aesthetic. In subsequent work, like *Mimas, lune de Saturne* (1980), *Plaisirs de tous les sens dans tous les sens* (1981), and *Marie chien noir* (1982), Chouinard drooled, rang bells, chanted, soaked her hair in a tub of water, masturbated. The work was sanctified and compelling. The acts weren't reckless; in retrospect, her self-absorbed experimentation, her mundane perfunctory way of doing things, cast a spell, leading audiences into what she calls "awakening the soul, the mind, and the spirit."

Trips abroad, living in New York, Berlin, Bali and Nepal, enlarged her perspective of dance and the possible vocabulary of the body. She studied Buddhism in Tibet, and dance in Burma and Bali. Chouinard continued to incorporate voice, sound, body language, and eroticism in an authentic, grounded style that set her apart from the rest of Montreal's creative, but more gymnastic, theatrical dance community. In her futuristic-looking *STAB (Space, Time and Beyond)* (1986), she painted her G-stringed body crimson red, capped her head with a long tail-like antenna, and accompanied her gestures with amplified breathing and guttural sounds.

STAB seemed a precursor for her re-reading of Vaslav Nijinsky's *Après-midi d'un faune* (1987), with the Faun, an androgynous creature, standing tall with goat horns on her head, and needles jutting from her shoulder, breast and padded thigh. Her contemporary allusions to sexuality and AIDS took Nijinsky's work one step further. In one dramtic act, she breaks off the horn and places it over her groin, and sheathes it with a red condom.

Chouinard continued as a solo artist until 1990. She then retreated from the stage and began to create group works as director of her own company, La Compagnie Marie Chouinard. Works include *Les Trous du ciel* (1991), inspired by Inuit culture, and *The Rite of Spring* (1993), set to Stravinsky's music. Her most recent work, *L'Amande et le diamant (The Almond and the Diamond)* (1996), reflects her interest in Tantric tradition. "The diamond is the symbol of the male sex, and the almond is more like the vulva," she commented. Before this, Chouinard had never choreographed any male-female connection in dance, or included any erotic duet in her work.

Over the years, Chouinard has been investigating and increasing her awareness, stimulated by Eastern thought and art. Chouinard is passionate about creating dance; but, she also declares, unapologetically, that "life is possible without dance." What she celebrates in her work, she says, is "an amazement or an awe in front of the phenomena of life—this biological event—a mixture of blood and flesh and soul—that is temporary and total and immense."

For Chouinard, the spine organizes all the movement of the body through space. The grey material in the brain, she says, goes into the spine; so, the spine is the "receptacle of the mind of the dancer."

Beyond these perceptions, a central concern is how the movement manifests itself in her dancers. There's a decisiveness in the smallest gesture. She's looking for "luminescence from the inside." There are many variables, but no shortcuts. It is her wish that dancers assimilate the vocabulary, use it, go with it, play with it, and master the work. Chouinard never has her dancers improvise on stage.

The constraints of what she calls "integrating approaches" are immense—often ten things to do in one minute—but the result is fluid. Movement is organic and harmonious, a fine tuning of the soul and the system, leading to alignment.

Marie Chouinard's repertoire includes more than 30 creations ranging from 90 seconds to 90 minutes. Since its foundation, La Compagnie Marie Chouinard has performed regularly at some of the world's most prestigious international festivals.

—Philip Szporer

CLARK, Michael

British dancer, choreographer, and company director

Born: 2 June 1962 in Aberdeen, Scotland. **Education:** Traditional Scottish dance training from age four; won numerous awards and trophies at Highland gatherings; educated in ballet at the Seivwrig School of Dance, where he starred in their annual Spice of Life revues; studied Cecchetti under Richard Glasstone at the Royal Ballet School, London, 1975-79. **Career:** Joined Ballet Rambert, 1979-81, working primarily with Richard Alston; worked as freelance dancer in Britain with Mary Fulkerson and Ian Spink, and in New York with Karole Armitage; appeared in Armitage dances *Parafango* and *Romance,* filmed by Charles Atlas; attended the International Summer School for Choreographers and Composers led by Merce Cunningham, 1981; first public concert at London's Riverside Studios, 1982, where he became resident choreographer in 1983 and from which he toured reduced-scale versions of his work; launched Michael Clark and Company, 1984, touring worldwide; formed the Michael Clark Foundation, a fund-raising and educational body, 1986; directed the foundation's first summer school in Glasgow, 1987.

Roles

1978	*Odd One In* (Glasstone), Royal Ballet School
	Bell High (Alston), Ballet Rambert
1980	*Landscape* (Alston), Ballet Rambert
	Rainbow Ripples (Alston), Ballet Rambert
1981	*Soda Lake* (Alston)
	Drastic Classicism (Armitage)
1982	*Dutiful Ducks* (Alston)
1990	*MiddleSex Gorge* (Petronio)

Works

1980	*Surface Values,* Ballet Rambert Workshop season
1981	*Untitled Duet,* Ballet Rambert Workshop season
1982	*Of a Feather, Flock,* Karole Armitage and dancers
	A Wish Sandwich
	Rush
1983	*Parts I-IV* (mus. Branca, Griffiths, Rental, Gowans, Rowlatt)
	12XU, Extemporary Dance Theatre
	1st Orange Segment, Stephanie Jordan
1984	*Morag's Wedding,* English Dance Theatre
	Flippin Eck/O Thweet Myth-tery of Life, Mantis Dance Company
	New Puritans (mus. The Fall), duet version, London
	New Puritans (mus. The Fall) Michael Clark and Company, London
	Do You Me? I Did (mus. Gilbert), Michael Clark and Company, London
	Le French Revolting, Paris Opera Ballet G.R.C.O.P.
1985	*Angel Food,* Paris Opera Ballet
	Not H.AIR, Michael Clark and Company
	HAIL the classical (mus. Ravel), Scottish Ballet
	our caca phoney H. our caca phoney H. (mus. Hinton, The Fall), Michael Clark and Company, Edinburgh
1986	*No Fire Escape in Hell* (mus. The Fall, Gilbert, Hinton, Laibach, Madden, Rogers), Michael Clark and Company, London
	Drop Your Pearls and Hog It, Girl, London Festival Ballet
1987	*Pure Pre-Scenes* (mus. Chopin, traditional pub songs, Madden), Michael Clark and Company
	Swamp (mus. Gilbert), Ballet Rambert
	Because We Must (mus. pipes and ear trumpet, Lewis, Gilbert, traditional Scottish), Michael Clark and Company, Sadler's Wells Theatre, London
1988	*I Am Curious Orange* (mus. The Fall), Michael Clark and Company, Amsterdam
1989	*Rights,* Phoenix Dance
	Hetrospective: Bed Peace, w/Stephen Petronio, London
1992	*Wrong Wrong* w/Stephen Petronio (mus. Stravinsky)
	Mmm. . . or Michael's Modern Masterpiece (mus. Stravinsky, The Sex Pistols, T Rex, Public Image Limited, Sondheim), Michael Clark and Company, Nottingham
1994	*O* (mus. Stravinsky, Public Image Limited), Michael Clark and Company, Newcastle

129

Publications

On CLARK: books—

Mackrell, Judith, *Out of Line: The Story of British New Dance,* London, 1992.
Robertson, Allen and Donald Hutera, *The Dance Handbook,* second edition, London, 1988.

Films and Videotapes

Bellezza Flash, performance by Clark, for *South Bank Show,* London Weekend Television, 1982.
Hail the New Puritan, fantasy-documentary directed by Charles Atlas, 1985.
No Fire Escape in Hell, BBC, 1986.
Because We Must, BBC, 1989.
Comrades, film directed by Bill Douglas featuring Clark, 1987.
Prospero's Books, film directed by Peter Greenaway and featuring Clark as Caliban, 1991.

*   *   *

Michael Clark's meteoric impact on British dance in the mid-1980s made him something of a household name, even amongst those who never saw him. The notoriety was based heavily on his witty, outrageous deployment of bottom-baring costumes and the use of such props as chainsaws, giant teapots and strap-on phalluses. With their camped-up, clubland energy, Clark and his free-floating "family" of dancers (notably Ellen Van Schuylenburch, Julie Hood and Matthew Hawkins), collaborator-friends (like designer Leigh Bowery, design team BodyMap and filmmaker/lighting specialist Charles Atlas) and groupies giddily flouted standard notions of good taste. But while Clark courted controversy, his theatrical shock tactics, bad-boy image and rock-star following never obscured the fact that he was a remarkable dancer with a considerable talent for making steps.

For a so-called "punk prince of ballet," Clark's origins were modest, even sheltered. The son of Presbyterian farm folk, he began his career in boyhood, dancing in the tradition of his native Scotland. It seemed likely he'd succeed his teacher as a local celebrity performing in area holiday shows and ceilidhs. But at thirteen, having already been co-opted into a Scottish Ballet production of *The Nutcracker,* Clark was accepted into the well-regimented Royal Ballet School. There he began to hone his natural kinetic gift while astonishing his instructors as both star pupil and problem child. During this time he also discovered contemporary dance and the rebellion of punk, aesthetics that jointly appealed to his developing identity.

Clark dropped out of the Royal when offered a job at Ballet Rambert. Still in his teens, he garnered raves as the centerpiece of work by choreographer Richard Alston. A visit to New York City and exposure to experimental dance guru Merce Cunningham fired up Clark's innate iconoclasm. It was time for him to cut loose as a free-lancer. He left Rambert in 1981, having already begun to work with modern choreographers like one-time Cunningham principal Karole Armitage and to create pieces for himself and small-scale British companies. His appointment as resident choreographer at London's trendy Riverside Studios paved the way for Clark's next logical step: the founding of his own, eponymous troupe. Clark, a divinely built, androgynous gay man with the face of a naughty cherub and a sharply irreverent, exhibitionistic sensibility, had arrived.

It was somewhat of a case of Nijinsky crossed with Boy George. Clark's impudent, charismatic blending of formal proficiency with a jokey, nose-thumbing, do-your-own-thing attitude branded him the decade's No. 1 rising star and enfant terrible. His string of early dance extravaganzas were whirlygigs of provocation and subverted classicism, wherein swatches of cool, beautiful movement might be deliberately broken up with neofascist gestures or disco-influenced pelvic thrusts. The ironically named *New Puritans* featured rampant transvestism and bravura dancing in platform shoes. *I Am Curious Orange* (the title a pun on an arty Swedish skin-flick from the 1960s) was a smart farrago of history, politics and football with a raucous original score, played live, by regular Clark associates, the cult rock band The Fall.

London's sterner, more hide-bound critics lambasted the rude, helter-skelter enthusiams of *our caca phoney H., our caca phoney H.,* a slapstick-psychedelic send-up of 1960s-style "happenings" and the rock musical *Hair* (one of Clark's favorite cultural references). Perhaps they missed the confrontation underpinning Clark and company's sexually ambiguous, tongue-in-chic, lampshade-on-the-head party turns. The young choreographer's implied message seemed to be a that art is less a matter of imposing order upon chaos than of mining the chaos surging beneath a veneer of order. Rather than wishing to trash classical dance, Clark was targeting its sacred-cow cliches and gender stereotyping and, in the process, setting social norms aspin.

Throughout the 1980s Clark was British dance's much-hyped man-of-the-moment. Besides creating and globally touring his own performances, he kept his profile high by accepting numerous commissions at home and on the continent. Risk remained an important factor. Aspects of Clark's personal life had always spilled into his work. This was never more evident than during his relationship with American dancer-choreographer Stephen Petronio. The lovers' most infamous appearance found them in bed in a posh London art gallery, perfoming a fifteen-minute duet that essentially amounted to public sex. There was even talk of merging their separate companies into a single, Manhattan-based entity.

The end of this intense, tumultuous union, plus Clark's excess of activity and some debilitating bouts of substance abuse, sapped some of his creativity. Nevertheless, in the first half of the new decade he emerged from a necessary period of self-assessment with two of his best, most sophisticated dances to date. The companion pieces *Mmm. . . ,* also known as *Michael's Modern Masterpiece,* and *O* were both inspired by Stravinsky scores (*The Rite of Spring* and *Apollo,* respectively). In the first it was clear that Clark's spirit of assaulting, madcap mischief hadn't deserted him. *Mmm. . .* was shot through with zany gimmicks (a bare-breasted cameo for Clark's 68-year-old mother Bessie, a retired nurse, and Bowery's toilet-bowl costumes), and the opening section featured an ear-splitting rock soundtrack. But the piece, seriously grounded in themes of life, death and rebirth, also contained potent, lyrical, prodigiously inventive dance passages like a breathtaking, climactic "sacrificial" dance for the American Joanne Barrett, clad only in a pair of white underpants.

O continued Clark's development as a disciplined dancemaker ready to shed the buoyant, anarchic baggage of his youth and rediscover dance's primitive power. From the ritualistically slow pacing and weighty, angled voluptuousness of the first act ensemble, through to a second-act reinterpretation of Apollo's birth commencing in a mirror-walled cubicle (Clark's own design), he came up with his most sober, spellbinding piece of choreography yet. It appeared as if the brilliant but self-indulgent, eternally reckless Peter Pan of dance had grown up.

However, not all of Clark's demons were vanquished by this brace of successes. Through a perverse coupling of perfectionism and unreliability, he blew his chance at creating a new work for his alma mater, the Royal Ballet. The commission was cancelled two weeks prior to its scheduled 1994 premiere, Clark having completed only a few minutes of choreograhy. He went into another artistic seclusion underscored by rumors of a difficult physical injury.

Given Clark's unpredictable past, there's no telling when and in what manner the once-wild *wunderkind* will again materialize. With his penchant for reworking old material, and the tendency his dances have to evolve even after their premieres, it might be apt to regard his entire oeuvre as a single, semi-autobiographical statement. The next chapter may be delayed, but it's bound to be worth the wait.

—Donald Hutera

CLARKE, Martha
American dancer and choreographer

Born: 3 June 1944 in Baltimore, Maryland. **Education:** Began dance training at the Peabody Conservatory with Carolyn Lynn; attended summer sessions at the Perry-Mansfield School of Theatre and Dance, Connecticut School of Dance, and American Dance Festival; attended Juilliard, New York. **Family:** Married Philip Grausman, 1966 (divorced 1980); one son. **Career:** Dancer, Anna Sokolow's company; dancer, Pilobolus Dance Theatre, 1971-79; co-founder, Crowsnest Dance Company, 1978. **Awards:** Obie Award for best new American play, *A Metamorphosis in Miniature,* 1982; Obie Award for playwriting, *Vienna: Lusthaus,* 1986; grants from the Guggenheim and Rockefeller foundations and National Endowment for the Arts; MacArthur Foundation fellowship, 1990.

Roles

Various roles from 1960-66 while dancing for Sokolow, including the original productions of *Rooms* and *Lyric Suite;* various roles from 1971-79 in premiere productions while with Pilobolus Dance Theatre.

Works

1977	*Portraits* w/Linda Hunt, New York
	Nocturne (mus. Felix Mendelssohn), solo
	Fallen Angel, solo
	Vagabond, solo
	Grey Room, solo
	Paglioccio, solo
	Wakefield, solo
1979	*La Marquise de Solana,* Crowsnest, New York
1980	*The Garden of Villaindry* w/Félix Blaska and Robert Barnett (mus. Noa Ain), Crowsnest, New York
1981	*Haiku* w/Félix Blaska and Robert Barnett, Crowsnest, New York
1982	*A Metamorphosis in Miniature* w/Linda Hunt (mus. Noa Ain), New York
1983	*Fromage dangereux* (later became *Gibbous Moon,* mus. Noa Ain), Crowsnest, New York
1984	*The Garden of Earthly Delights* (mus. Peaslee), Crowsnest, New York
1986	*Vienna: Lusthaus* (mus. Peaslee), Crowsnest, New York
1987	*The Hunger Artist* (mus. Peaslee), Crowsnest, New York
1988	*Miracolo d'Amore* (mus. Peaslee), Spoleto Festival U.S.A., Charleston, South Carolina
1990	*Endangered Species* (mus. Peaslee and Stanley Walden), Brooklyn
1993	*Dammerung* w/Gary Chryst and Jeanne Solan, Durham, North Carolina
1995	*An Uncertain Hour* (lieder music by Berg, Wolf, Schumann, Webern), Nederlands Dans Theater III, New York

Publications

On CLARKE: articles—

Belans, Linda, "Dance Review: Martha Clarke at ADF," pele.nando.net/ events/dance/ c_review.html.

———, "Intuition Inspires This Choreographer," pele.nando.net/ events/m_clarke.html.

———, "The Hunger Artist," *New Republic,* 9 March 1987.

Brustein, Robert, "*Miracolo d'Amore,*" *New Republic,* 22 August 1988.

Goldberg, RoseLee, "An Uncertain Hour," *Artforum,* November 1995.

Jacobs, Laura, "*Miracolo d'Amore,*" *New Leader,* 8 August 1988.

Jacobson, Daniel, "Martha Clarke's Imaginary Gardens," *Ballet Review,* Winter 1985.

Kendall, Elizabeth and Daniels, Don, "A Conversation with Martha Clarke," *Ballet Review,* Winter 1985.

Ostlere, Hilary, "Alas, No Giraffe," *Dance Magazine,* October 1990.

Renikova, Eva, "The Chic of the New," *National Review,* 3 December 1990.

Small, Michael, "Stripping Old Vienna Down to Its Bare Essentials, Martha Clarke Scores a Theatrical Triumph," *People Weekly,* 1 September 1986.

Films and Videotapes

Martha Clarke, Light and Dark: A Dancer's Journey, Joyce Chopra, dir., WNET-TV, New York, 1981.

*   *   *

Martha Clarke, choreographer, dancer, and theater director, occupies an important place as an innovator in the field of modern dance. She is best known for her evening-length, often controversial avant-garde works that effectively blur the divisions between dance and theater.

Clarke was born in Baltimore, Maryland, in 1944 to a musical household: her father was a jazz musician turned lawyer and her mother was an amateur pianist and chamber musician. Growing up in the suburb of Pikesville, Clarke was sent to small private schools and began studying dance at the Peabody Conservatory at the age of six. As a teenager she attended a summer session at the Perry-

Mansfield School of Theatre and Dance in Steamboat Springs, Colorado, and it was there that she committed herself to dance upon being cast in the role of a child in choreographer Helen Tamiris' *Ode to Walt Whitman.*

Spending subsequent summers at the American Dance Festival and the Connecticut College School of Dance, Clarke received instruction from many of America's modern dance pioneers, including Louis Horst, Martha Graham, Merce Cunningham, Charles Weidman, José Limón, and Alvin Ailey. After her junior year of high school Clarke decided to enroll in a two-year dance program at New York's Juilliard School. At Juilliard she trained primarily in Graham technique, but also studied with ballet master Antony Tudor.

Upon leaving Juilliard, Clarke joined Anna Sokolow's modern dance company, and this choreographer would make a lasting impression on her. As Hilary Ostlere reported in *Dance Magazine* in 1990, Clarke declared "Sokolow's emotional expressionism" to be "at the root" of all she has done. Clarke performed with Sokolow's company for several years, even following Anna to Israel and living with her there. But Clarke's ensuing marriage to sculptor Philip Grausman resulted in a five-year hiatus from the dance world. During that period Clarke and her husband moved to Rome and she gave birth to a son, David. Returning to the United States, the family settled in rural Connecticut. In 1971 her husband accepted a position as artist-in-residence at Dartmouth College and Clarke soon resumed her dance career. It was at Dartmouth that Clarke encountered Pilobolus Dance Theatre, first working evenings with Alison Chase, the young group's teacher, and eventually performing, touring, and choreographing with the company. Known for its unusual gymnastic style, the troupe performed works such as *Untitled,* which featured Clarke and Chase as nine-foot-tall Victorian women concealing two naked men beneath their long skirts.

Eager to conceptualize her own work, Clarke left Pilobolus after seven years and in 1978 formed Crowsnest with French dancer/choreographer Félix Blaska, and Robby Barnett, a fellow founding member of Pilobolus. The group debuted at the American Dance Festival in July of 1979 and exhibited a series of solos Clarke had created, including *Fallen Angel* and *Nocturne.* Also in the original Crowsnest company was actress Linda Hunt, with whom she collaborated on a number of performances. In 1977 the two women produced *Portraits,* which brought together Hunt's monologues and Clarke's dance solos. In 1982 the two also collaborated on *A Metamorphosis in Miniature,* a reworking of Kafka's *Metamorphosis* set to music, which won an Obie Award as the best new American play for the 1981-82 season. It was during these years that Clarke made the transition from strictly dancer and choreographer to performance artist and director.

Late in 1983, Lyn Austin, who had produced *A Metamorphosis in Miniature,* called Clarke to ask for ideas for a new theatrical piece. The eventual result was *The Garden of Earthly Delights,* which premiered at St. Clement's Church in November of 1984. Inspired by the paintings of Flemish master Hieronymus Bosch, Clarke's theatrical interpretation was a large-scale collaboration between all who were involved in the production, from composer Richard Peaslee, to light designer Paul Gallo, to costume designer Jane Greenwood, to writer Peter Beagle, to the seven dancers and three musicians themselves. Decidedly a mixed-genre piece, *Garden* combined dance, acrobatics, props, and lighting to create a series of images simultaneously grotesque and beautiful. Received with wild enthusiasm by New York critics, *The Garden of Earthly Delights* essentially erased all disciplinary boundaries, existing instead *"between* dance and theater," as Clarke herself proclaimed in a 1985 interview with *Ballet Review*'s Elizabeth Kendall and Don Daniels.

Following her first major success, Clarke turned to turn-of-the-century Vienna for inspiration for her next full-length work. With *Vienna: Lusthaus,* Clarke was "catapulted. . .into the 'theatrical genius' category," according to a 1995 column by Linda Belans in the *Raleigh News and Observer.* Recreating the atmosphere of the 16th-century pleasure pavilion to which its title refers, *Vienna: Lusthaus* opened at St. Clement's Church in the spring of 1986 and moved to the Public Theater a few weeks later. Although some audiences were puzzled by the piece, critics generally applauded it and Clarke earned an Obie Award for her work on the production.

Clarke's next few collaborative efforts, which continued to take inspiration from various works of art, were not as enthusiastically received. Based on a group of Kafka stories, *The Hunger Artist* debuted at St. Clement's in February of 1987 as a work in progress, but never managed to reopen as a completed work. *Miracolo d'Amore,* which drew on drawings by Tiepolo, first appeared in the spring of 1988 at the Spoleto Festival U.S.A. in Charleston, South Carolina, and then opened at New York's Public Theater, but failed to garner critical acclaim. Clarke followed with the ambitious *Endangered Species,* which put cast-trained animals into the dance-theater mix, but the piece was canceled only two weeks after its October 1990 premiere at the Brooklyn Academy of Music's (BAM) Next Wave Festival.

Despite these setbacks, Clarke continues to create evocative and visually arresting performance art pieces. In 1995 she premiered *An Uncertain Hour* as part of Lincoln Center's "Serious Fun!" summer series. This work was expanded from a 1993 duet entitled *Dammerung* and was created for and with Nederlands Dans Theater III, a company for dancers over age 40. The piece, dedicated to Clarke's mother, who died earlier in 1995, took the 1920s as its setting, interspersing violent images with extended moments of quiet foreboding. Clarke also continues to choreograph and direct other theatrical productions, such as the opera *Marco Polo* at the Munich Biennale in 1996.

—Anthea Kraut

CLYTEMNESTRA

Choreography: Martha Graham
Music: Halim El-Dabh
Set Design: Isamu Noguchi
First Production: Adelphi Theatre, New York, 1 April 1958
Dancers: Martha Graham (Clytemnestra), Paul Taylor (Aegisthus), Yuriko (Iphigenia), Helen McGehee (Electra), Matt Turney (Cassandra), Ethel Winter (Helen of Troy), Bertram Ross (Agamemnon and Orestes), Gene McDonald (Hades, Paris, the Watchman, and the Ghost of Agamemnon), David Wood (Messenger of Death), Ellen Siegel, Richard Kuch, Akiko Kanda, Carol Payne, Ellen Graff, Bette Shaller, Lois Schlossberg, Dan Wagoner, and George Nabors (Chorus)

Publications

Articles—

Hering, Doris, "St. Joan, Clytemnestra and Martha Graham," *Dance Magazine,* June 1958.
Martin, John, "Dance: Graham," *New York Times,* 6 April 1958.

———, "Dance: Miss Graham's 'Clytemnestra,'" *New York Times,* 2 April 1958.

Oleaga, Milton, "The Solitary Athlete," *Dance Magazine,* December 1963.

*　*　*

Clytemnestra is usually considered to be Martha Graham's most ambitious choreographic undertaking, and many critics recognize it as the high point of her career. Graham was in her sixties when the piece was premiered, so she brought years of experience with movement and staging to its creation. Fittingly, *Clytemnestra* takes on an epic quality as it requires more than two hours to perform its rendering of Aeschylus' entire *Oresteia.* In many ways, the work stands as the pinnacle of Graham's so-called Greek cycle, which includes *Cave of the Heart, Errand into the Maze,* and *Night Journey* (with subjects of Medea, the Minotaur, and Jocasta, respectively).

Audiences and critics have sometimes been overwhelmed by the stature of *Clytemnestra,* which was called staggering, esoteric, indirect, and difficult when it first appeared in 1958. But the critical consensus confirmed Doris Hering's early estimation that the work was a masterpiece "of such boldness that it far exceeds the wildest imaginings of that visionary. . .Isadora Duncan, who reaffirmed the role of dance in relation to Greek tragedy." John Martin of the *New York Times* also recognized this masterly culmination in his first review, in which he called *Clytemnestra* "a kind of summation of all [Graham's] delvings into psychological archaism."

The work is set as a four-part retrospective in which all of the events and reconsiderations are filtered through Clytemnestra's perceptions. The prologue finds Clytemnestra in the underworld, scorned by Hades himself. It introduces all the characters and major events that will comprise the remaining drama. The action of the second section takes place in the world of the living as Clytemnestra remembers and relives her past. It follows a primarily narrative order and dramatizes the Fall of Troy, the return of Agamemnon to Clytemnestra, and their vexed household. The third section is dominated by Orestes' and Electra's revenge against their mother and Aegisthus, her lover. And the fourth part, or epilogue, returns to the underworld where Clytemnestra acknowledges her deeds and so proffers a kind of reconciliation.

When *Clytemnestra* premiered, its set was considered unusual for Isamu Noguchi, whose work was often spare. This stage design, on the contrary, was remarkable for the richness of color used in its golden net, scarlet drapes, and sky-blue platform. A number of spears also served multiple purposes in the work, sometimes standing in as a funeral bier or the spoils of war. The use of two singers at the beginning of the work sparked some critical disagreement. Bethany Beardslee and Robert Goss, seated at either side of the stage in contemporary dress, began to sing as a kind of Chorus, but their role was assumed by dancers for the remainder of the work.

Like the work itself, the choreography in *Clytemnestra* was vast and forceful. As Martin noted at its opening performance, the piece attempted to communicate "a vivid psychological experience" through blunt yet sometimes "lumbering" qualities. The movement was deliberate and demanded much of its audience to communicate its deeply humanist struggle. But most critics accepted the heaviness of the piece as part of its ritualistic genius. Graham herself danced several moments with her signature intensity, but she sometimes sat watching as younger dancers performed Clytemnestra's memories. Of particular stylistic note were David Wood's initial procession as the Messenger of Death, Gene McDonald's diverse abilities as King Hades, Paris, and Agamemnon's ghost, and Yuriko's delicate rendering of Iphigenia's fate. Beyond these individual scenes, Clytemnestra's seduction of Agamemnon and her duet with Aegisthus provided classic Graham performance.

Clytemnestra enjoyed its greatest success in the decade following its first production. Indeed, in 1963 *Dance Magazine* stated, "*Clytemnestra!* What more can one say about this evening-long masterpiece that has for the past five years soared above virtually the entire output of the New York stage?" These remarks would become one of Graham's last garnerings of unqualified praise.

—Carrie Rohman

COHAN, Robert

American dancer, choreographer, educator, and company director based in London

Born: 1925 in New York City. **Education:** Studied dance with Martha Graham, 1946. **Military:** Served in the Navy during World War II. **Career:** Dancer, Martha Graham company, 1946-56 and 1962-69; began teaching at Graham school, 1948; co-director of company, 1966; danced in Broadway musicals (*Shangri-La, Can-Can*) and in the film *A Dancer's World,* 1956; founder/director, own group (known as the Robert Cohan Dance Company for 1962), 1958-62; choreographed for Batsheva Dance Company, 1964-65; artistic director, London Contemporary Trust, 1967-83; triumvirate of directors, London Contemporary Dance Theatre (LCDT), 1983-88; appointed to Dance Panel of the Arts Council of Great Britain, 1984; *Configurations,* an exhibition of his photographs, toured Britain, 1984; artistic advisor, LCDT, 1992-94; has taught at the New England Conservatory of Music (Boston), Juilliard School, Connecticut College, and New York University; director, Gulbenkian National Choreographic Summer School (Guildford, England), 1977-78. **Awards:** *Evening Standard* Award for the Most Outstanding Achievement in Ballet, 1975; Society of West End Theatres Award, 1978; honorary Commander of the British Empire, 1988; honorary degrees from University of Exeter, 1993; Middlesex University, 1994; Kent University, 1996.

Roles (all roles choreographed by Graham and performed by the Martha Graham Dance Company)

1948	*Diversion of Angels*
1950	Fool, *Eye of Anguish*
1962	Theseus, *Phaedra*
1965	*Part Real—Part Dream*
	David, *The Witch of Endor*
1967	Hector, *Cortege of Eagles*

Other roles include: Aegisthus in *Clytemnestra,* the Stranger in *Embattled Garden,* Jason in *Cave of the Heart,* in *Night Journey, Acrobats of God,* the Revivalist and the Husbandman in *Appalachian Spring,* and others in the Graham company repertoire.

Works (after 1969, performed by London Contemporary Dance Theatre unless otherwise noted)

1954	*Perchance to Dream* (mus. Debussy), Robert Cohan Company, American Dance Festival, New London
1958	*Streams* (mus. Hovhaness), University of Rochester
1959	*Seabourne*, Eastman School of Music
	The Pass (mus. Lester), University of Rochester
	Eclipse (mus. Lester), Festival of Contemporary Arts
	Ceremony for Serpents (mus. Lester), Newton High School
	Hunter of Angels (mus. Maderna), University of Rochester
1960	*Veiled Woman*, Robert Cohan Dance Company, Jacob's Pillow
	Vestige (mus. Lester), RCDC, Jacob's Pillow
	Praises (mus. Hovahanes), RCDC, Jacob's Pillow
	The Tomb (mus. Lester), RCDC, Jacob's Pillow
1963	*Luna Park* (mus. Lester), RCDC
	Celebrants (mus. Surinach), RCDC
1965	*Hall of Mirrors* (mus. Shariff), Batsheva Dance Company
1967	*Tzaikerk* (mus. Hovhanes), London Contemporary Dance Group, East Grinstead
	Sky (mus. Lester), London Contemporary Dance Group, East Grinstead
1969	*Shanta Quintet* (mus. Meyer), London Contemporary Dance Group, London
	Side Scene (mus. pre-classic), London
	Cell (mus. Lloyd), London
1970	*X* (later developed into *Mass*), (mus. Kafel), Oxford
1971	*Consolation of the Rising Moon* (mus. Williams), London
	Stages (mus. Nordheim, Downes), London
	Lifelines (mus. BBC Radiophonic Workshop), BBC-TV
	People Alone (mus. Downes), London
1973	*People Together* (mus. Downes), London
	Mass (mus.weir), Oxford
1974	*Waterless Method of Swimming Instruction* (mus. Downes), Lausanne
	No Man's Land (mus. Barry Guy), London
	Men Seen Afar (mus. Tangerine Dream), BBC-TV
	Salomé, Intel (Austro-German TV)
1975	*Class* (mus. Keliehor), London
	Mask of Separation (Myth), (mus. Alcantra), London
	Place of Change (mus. Schönberg), London
	Stabat Mater (mus. Vivaldi), Stirling
	Khamsin (mus. Downes), Leeds
	Nympheas (mus. Debussy), York
1977	*Nightwatch* w/ Davies, Bergese and North (mus. Downes), London
	Forest (mus. Hodgson), London
	Genesis Reconsidered, Batsheva Dance Company
1978	*Eos* (mus. Barry Guy), Bournemouth
	Falling Man (mus. Pheloung)
	Ice (mus. Subotmik), London
1979	*Songs, Lamentations and Praises* (mus. Burgon), Jerusalem
	Rondo (mus. McDowell), London
1980	*Field* (mus. Hodgson), Horsham
1981	*Dance of Love and Death* (mus. Davis, Nancarrow), Edinburgh
1982	*Chamber Dances* (mus. Burgon), Southhampton
	Journal, Batsheva Dance Company, Tel Aviv
1984	*Agora (Common Land)*, (mus. Bach), Leeds
	Sinfonia Sacra (mus. Panufnik), Batsheva Dance Company, Tel Aviv
	Skyward (Skylark) (mus. Alberga), Northampton
1986	*Ceremony (Slow Dance On A Burial Ground)*, (mus. Montague), Eastbourne
	Mass for Man (mus. Burgon), BBC-TV
	Interrogations (mus. Pheloung), Edinburgh
	Video Life (mus. Barry Guy), Rimini
1987	*The Phantasmagoria* w/Jobe, Singh Bhuller, (mus. Pheloung), Birmingham
1989	*Crescendo* (mus. Bedford), London
	In Memory (mus. Henze), London
	Metamorphosis (mus. Britten), London
	Stone Garden (mus. Osbourne), London
1993	*A Midsummer Night's Dream* (mus. Pheloung, Mendelssohn), Scottish Ballet, Glasgow

Publications

By COHAN: articles—

"Contemporary Dance Survival: Robert Cohan Talks to *Dance and Dancers*," *Dance and Dancers*, February 1972.
"Getting to Know You: Robert Cohan Talks to *Dance and Dancers* about London Contemporary Dance Theatre's Residencies in the Regional Colleges," *Dance and Dancers*, April 1976.
"Robert Cohan," in *The Dance Workshop*, Allen & Unwin, 1986.

On COHAN: books—

Clark, Mary, and Crisp, Clement, *London Contemporary Dance Theatre*, Dance Books, London, 1989.
Drummond, John, "A Golden Stage," *Dance Theatre Journal*, Autumn/Winter 1996.
Goodwin, Noel, "Based on Love," *Ballet News*, April 1983.
Monohan, James, "The Place—Robin Howard's Triumph," *Dancing Times*, October 1979.

Films and Videotapes

Lifelines (mus. BBC Radiophonic Workshop), BBC-TV, 1971.
No Man's Land (mus. Barry Guy), London, 1974.
Men Seen Afar (mus. Tangerine Dream), for BBC-TV, 1974.
Salome, Intel (Austro-German TV), 1974.
The Story of Job (mus. Vaughan Williams), for Thames Television, 1977.
Mass for Man (mus. Burgon), BBC-TV, 1986.

* * *

Although Robert Cohan's career falls into two phases, the first in the United States where he was a valued member of Martha Graham's company and one of Graham's partners from 1950; and the second phase, beginning in 1967, in Britain where he was artistic director of the London Contemporary Dance Trust and a key figure in the establishment of contemporary dance (specifically that based on Graham technique) in the United Kingdom. He is also significant as a choreographer, educator, designer, photographer, and author.

Cohan was inspired to take up a career in dance after seeing Robert Helpmann's dramatic and symbolic ballet, *Miracle in the Gorbals*, during his posting to Britain during World War II. Within four months of joining the Graham School of Contemporary Dance in New York in 1946, he graduated into the company where he remained until 1956 when he left to perform in Broadway musicals and films to fund his own choreographic ventures and, briefly, his own company. He returned to the Graham Company in the 1960s (performing with them until 1969) as well as dancing with colleagues. He continued to dance until 1972, performing in the early days of London Contemporary Dance Theatre when the novice company needed the weight of a seasoned artist.

As a choreographer he was in some respects an heir of Graham both in style and subject matter reinterpreting myths for a contemporary audience and for their universal relevance. In *No Man's Land* he precisely analyzed the Orpheus story. He has presented immediately recognisable situations on stage such as in the powerful *Cell*, portraying six individuals trapped in an enclosed space, a work that quickly marked London Contemporary Dance Theatre (LCDT) as an important force in the British dance scene. Other memorable works include the witty *Waterless Method of Swimming Instruction* with its comic elements; the fluid impressionistic *Nympheas* which combined fragments of Monet's *Waterlilies* with selected music by Debussy while the dancers performed, often flat, against a two-leveled white wall; *Forest* with its soundscape score suggestive of images drawn from nature; and the masterwork, *Stabat Mater*, for an all-female cast representing facets of Mary, the Mother of Christ, grieving at the foot of the Cross.

Appreciating the trend for large-scale in Britain and realizing it was a way to enhance bookings for his company, Cohan created a succession of full-evening works. The first, the multimedia *Stages*, followed a hero's spiritual journey to self-awareness; *Dances of Love and Death* (commissioned through the 1981 Tenant Caledonian Award for the Edinburgh Festival) portrayed impressions of mythological, fictional, and real-life lovers; and a third, *The Phantasmagoria*, co-choreographed with Tom Jobe and Darshan Singh Bhuller, was inspired by 18th and 19th-century popular entertainment. Cohan's most recent full-evening presentation was a new departure in working with classically-trained dancers, a version of *A Midsummer Night's Dream* for the Scottish Ballet with his long-term collaborators Barrington Pheloung (composer) and Noberto Chiesa (designer).

As a designer (under the name of Charter) Cohan introduced Britain to the use of side-lighting (pioneered in the U.S. by Jean Rosenthal) when he lit the LCDT's first performance at East Grinstead. This gave a sculptural quality to dancers' bodies and Cohan maintained a successful parallel career as a lighting designer. *Khamsin* with its shiny floor, use of fabrics, and impressive lighting focused as much on design as movement.

Cohan's importance as a pedagogue, both in teaching dancers and in educating the public to appreciate new styles of movement, should not be underestimated. He began teaching in the Graham School in 1948 and had an impressive list of teaching credits before Robin Howard invited him to London. There he taught in the School and gave frequent classes to the dancers of London Contemporary Dance Theatre. Although these drew on 1960s Graham technique, Cohan appreciated that British dancers were temperamentally different from Americans— thus the technique evolved somewhat differently. The British-style Graham was given a choreographed showcase in Cohan's *Class*.

For the Contemporary Dance Trust, Cohan was a significant mentor for aspiring choreographers, giving them the encouragement and opportunities they needed and sharing Howard's belief that the company should have an individual repertory. Through the introduction in 1976 of American-style dance residencies in colleges and schools, Cohan gave those involved in dance education the opportunity to appreciate the developments in Britain since the mid-1960s. Cohan is an articulate speaker and presenter both live— delivering lectures and master classes—and on television. A substantial body of his work has been televised, mainly by Bob Lockyer

for the BBC, which preserved productions that are longer performed (since the company he developed has ceased to exist).

Cohan was the man who gave form to Robin Howard's vision that contemporary dance could take root in Britain. As the dancers of his company recorded at the end of their company's life, "Bob has molded, inspired, and guided generations of dancers and is the person above all others responsible for the legacy of excellence long-associated with this company. Few men can command such respect so effortlessly, and indeed if there is a testimonial to his achievement it's in the enormous commitment he engendered from his dancers." In a tribute written for the "Britain Salutes New York" Festival in which London Contemporary Dance Theatre took part, Robin Howard credited Cohan with being responsible for no less than the "transformation of the dance scene in England."

—Jane Pritchard

COHEN, Ze'eva
Israeli dancer, choreographer, and educator

Born: 15 August 1940, in Tel Aviv, Israel. **Education:** Educated in public school; first studied dance with Gertrud Kraus in *Ausdruckstanz* Expressionist modern style and improvisation from ages 5-16 years, followed by Graham technique with Rena Gluck; Juilliard School, diploma in dance, 1966; Fordham University, B.A. cum laude, 1974; New York University, M.F.A. in dance, 1981. **Military Service:** Israeli army, 1958-60. **Family:** Married singer Peter Ludwig; one daughter, Keren. **Career:** Dancer, Rena Gluck Dance Company, 1956-58, Bemat Machol, 1958-60, Anna Sokolow's Lyric Theater, Tel Aviv, 1962-63, Anna Sokolow Dance Company, 1963-69, American Dance Theater, 1964, Juilliard Dance Ensemble, 1963-66, Pearl Lang Dance Company, 1967; founding member and dancer, Dance Theatre Workshop, 1968-71; dancer, Ze'eva Cohen Solo Repertory Company, 1971-86; started solo program at the Cubiculo, 1971, touring extensively throughout the U.S., to many European festivals, and also in Israel until 1983; formed Ze'eva and Dancers as a company and made *Wilderness, Swamps and Forest;* freelance choreographer, working with large companies and in other styles such as the Boston Ballet and Alvin Ailey Repertory Company, 1983; created the dance studies program at Princeton University, 1969, which she still directs and which became part of the Theatre and Dance Program, 1972; full professor, Princeton University (received tenure in 1995). **Awards:** Kinor David prize for best choreography in Israel for *Wilderness, Swamps and Forest* for the Batsheva Company, 1979; National Foundation for Jewish Culture Award 1986, 1995; Swarthmore College Choreographer Residency, 1995; National Endowment for the Arts (NEA) awards 1973, 1974, 1975, 1984, 1986, 1987, 1988, 1991; New York State Council on the Arts, 14 grants since 1971; Institute for Art and Urban Resources, Inc., 1986; New Jersey State Council on the Arts, 1989, 1990; Con Edison and Edith C. Blum Foundation.

Roles

1963	*The End?* from *Rooms* (Sokolow), Tel Aviv
	Opening figure in *Dreams* (Sokolow), Tel Aviv
1966	Opening figure in *Dreams* (Sokolow), American Dance Festival, Connecticut College

Ze'eva Cohen performing *Dances for Isadora*. Photograph © Johan Elbers.

1967	Princess in *L'Histoire du Soldat* (Sokolow), Carnegie Hall
	Duet with Jeff Duncan from *Lyric Suite* (Sokolow), 92nd St. YW-YMHA, New York
	Yael in Lang's *Song of Deborah* (Lang), City Center, New York
1968	*Escape,* from *Rooms* (Sokolow) on CBS
1971	*Three Excerpts/Resonances* (J.Duncan), Cubiculo Theatre, New York
	Dances for Isadora (Limón), Delacourt Theatre, Central Park, New York
1972	*Tempo* (Keen), Dance Theatre Workshop, New York
	Dance Hole (Lamhut), Dance Theatre Workshop, New York
	Talking Desert Blues (Tekei), Dance Theatre Workshop, New York
1973	*32 Variations in C-Minor* (Waring), Dance Theatre Workshop, New York
1975	*Mothers of Israel,* (Oved), Dance Theatre Workshop, New York
1976	*Countdown* (Perez), Dance Theatre Workshop, New York
1979	*Clearing* (Farber), Riverside Church, New York
1980	*Someone* (Nagrin), NYU Tisch School of the Arts

Works

1976	*Goat Dance* (mus. Crumb), Boston Ballet members, Boston
1977	*Rainwood* (mus. Crumb and Iranian classical music and environmental sounds), University of California at Santa Cruz, California
1979	*Wilderness, Swamps and Forest* (mus. Crumb, Iranian classical music, and environmental sounds), Batsheva Dance Company, Tel Aviv
1985	*Ode* (for Chicago Repertory Dance Ensemble, mus. Vangelis), Emerson Theatre, Chicago
1992	*Circles II* (mus. Chambers, Ellington, Roach), Seattle
1993	*Suppliant Women* by Euripides (dir. Rehm; mus. Keck), Washington, D.C.
	Mountains of Myrrh (solo), New York
1986	*Sephardic Songs* (mus. traditional Sephardic songs; perf. and arr. by Waverly Consort), Joyce Theater, New York
1995	*Women and Veils* (mus. Keck), New York
1996	*Mother's Tongue/I Love You* (with Jill Sigman; mus. traditional Yiddish songs and Klezmer music), Amsterdam, the Netherlands
	Negotiations (with Aleta Hayes; mus. Jones), New York
1997	*From Sand to Water* and *Habachor (The First Born)* (mus. Keck, Michael), Inbal Dance Theater, Suzane Delal Theatre, Tel Aviv

Other works include: Choreography for the following dance companies: Alvin Ailey Repertory Company, Ballet Omaha, Batsheva Dance Company, Boston Ballet (first and second companies), Chamber Dance, Chiang Ching Dance Co., Chicago Repertory Dance Ensemble, Ze'eva Cohen and Dancers, Ze'eva Cohen Solo Dance, Colloquium Contemporary Dance Exchange, Contemporary Dance Theater, Dance Kaleidoscope, Dance Odyssey, Detroit Dance Collective, Forces of Nature, Fusion Works, Inbal Dance Theater, Kibbutz Contemporary Dance Company, Jimena Lasonsky Dance Company, Daniel Lewis Dance Company, North Carolina Dance Theater, Pennsylvania Dance Theater, Shakespeare Festival Theater, Spectrum Dance Theater, Tamar: Israel Chamber Dance Theater, Tanzprojekt, and The Yard, in addition to many educational institutions, such as University of California at Santa Cruz.

Publications

By COHEN: articles—

"Two Life Stories," *Movement Research Performance Journal,* August 1996.
"Two Life Stories" (in Hebrew), *Israel Dance Quarterly,* December 1996.

On COHEN: books—

Katz, Jane, *Artists in Exile: American Odyssey.* New York, 1983.
Warren, Larry, and Sokolow, Anna, *The Rebellious Spirit.* Princeton, 1991.

On COHEN: articles—

Fanger, Iris M., "Ze'eva!—A Close Up," *Dance Magazine,* March 1976.
Princeton Times, 5 November 1995.

*   *   *

Ze'eva Cohen's childhood was influenced by the political climate in the land on the Eastern coast of the Mediterranean. Her parents were politically active working for an independent Israel, her father absent for several years of her early childhood, jailed by the British for his clandestine activities against the British Empire. Her own family's ethnic and traditional culture as Yemenite-Jews was placed aside in favor of a new Israeli society combining Jewish refugees from Nazi Europe, other Arab lands besides Yemen, and immigrants from countries such as Russia and the Americas. Her parents wanted her to receive a modern education. Likewise, when their daughter was given dance lessons, it was logical for them to enroll her in Gertrud Kraus's modern dance studio. Kraus was the premiere modern dancer in Tel Aviv, famous for her Gertrud Kraus Dance Troupe, for her work choreographing at Habimah, the National Jewish Theatre, and for her work at the Palestine Folk Opera and, occasionally, with the Palestine Orchestra. Later when independence came, Kraus created the Israel Ballet Theatre. Working with the Vienna-trained Kraus proved to be a formidable choice for Ze'eva. She was trained in improvisation and in the European expressionist *Ausdruckstanz* style modified through Kraus' artistry and imagination. The dramatic formative years of Israel matched Ze'eva's childhood. Through Kraus, Ze'eva found effective ways to draw out potent expression in her dancing; it was this feature, as she matured, that made her attractive to Sokolow and, later, other choreographers in America. Sokolow, who had come to Israel to help train the Inbal Yemenite Dance Theatre, became so enamored with the new Israel that she formed her own modern dance company there, inviting Cohen to join.

She also helped Cohen to venture to America, where she enhanced her dance technique and earned her dance degrees. Her searing interpretations, especially as a favorite interpreter of Sokolow's dances, became well known. Cohen's Israeli background, incongruously steeped with European modern dance training through Kraus, gave her a power and depth to her interpretive work rather unfamiliar in America. She became a sought after choreographer and teacher, her images and her supportive manner especially beloved. For example, in her classes she has told her students to think of their body as a wind instrument.

The list where she has given master classes and return engagements for her teaching is extensive and includes Harvard University Summer Dance Program (1975-77, 1992, and 1993), Swarthmore College Dance Program, Alvin Ailey American Dance Center (1982-90 in choreography), Boston Ballet Summer Dance Program (1980-90), American Dance Festival, Colorado College (1982 and 1984), and Yale Drama School, among others. When Princeton added women students in September 1969, the university decided to expand their arts offerings; Cohen came to teach dance. It was there that she built a new place for dance and a stable teaching situation for herself. In a Princeton newspaper story (from the *Princeton Times,* 5 November 1995, p. DD 1) she said she really understood how it was possible to make professional modern dance suited to a general liberal arts context, by making a creative component, a technical and an academic component woven into one course. She has been able to enhance the program until it has blossomed to the point where some students, including David Rousseve, Carter MacAdams, Juilio Rivera, June Balish, and Jose Mateo, have become professional dancers.

Cohen's creativity and sense of the importance of constructive cooperation also can be seen in her work at the Dance Theatre Workshop (DTW) in 1969 where she was a founding member. Simultaneously with her Princeton teaching, she was involved with the programs at DTW, which were run cooperatively for about 10 years under Jeff Duncan. The idea was to develop a collective of artists, sharing the expenses, office work, publicity, and the performances. "We were influencing each other's works by dancing with each other," Cohen has said about being in dances by Linda Tarnay, Elizabeth Keen, Jeff Moore, Art Bauman, Jeff Duncan, Kenneth King, Jamie Cunningham, Deborah Jowitt, Rudy Perez, Francis Alenikoff, and Kathy Posin. Dance Theatre Workshop became one of the essential forces in New York modern dance.

Cohen presaged the whole phenomenon of dancers returning to the solo concert format in the late 1970s. Her performances were drawn from 28 solos by 23 choreographers, many commissioned under Dance Foundation Ze'eva Cohen. These concerts, seen in European dance festivals, in Israel, and throughout the United States, were so successful and she was perceived as so popular that she was shown on the cover of *Dance Magazine* in 1976. By the 1990s, though she had withdrawn from active performance in favor of her Princeton teaching, she had lost none of her powers as a performer and as a choreographer, as described by Jennifer Dunning in the *New York Times.* In the 1996 review, it was reported that Cohen chose the potent subject of African American and Jewish relations for her work *Negotiations,* and that Cohen tested the changing temperature of an encounter between two women in which the balance of power shifted continuously and subtly. "One woman was Jewish, the other black ... blessedly, Ms. Cohen offered no overt political or social message ... the dance suggested much through purely physical terms, making its last gesture even more emotionally stunning than it would otherwise have been." A new facet in Cohen's work for the Inbal Dance Theatre in Israel in the spring of 1996 is her exploration of her Yemenite background in ways she has not acknowledged before, seen in the inclusion of syncopated rhythms, simultaneously moving body parts, and desert images.

—Judith Brin Ingber

COMFORT, Jane
American dancer, choreographer, and company director

Born: 15 October 1945. **Education:** Degree in painting, University of North Carolina, Chapel Hill, 1967; studied in New York with Merce Cunningham. **Career:** Danced with James Cunningham, 1976-78; began choreographing, 1978; founded her own troupe, Jane Comfort and Company. **Awards:** Numerous grants and fellowships from the National Endowment for the Arts (NEA), New York State Council on the Arts, New York Foundation for the Arts, Harkness Foundation, Joyce Mertz-Gilmore Foundation, *Dance Magazine* Foundation, and others.

Works

1978	*Steady Shift*
1982	*Incorrect Translations*
1983	*Artificial Horizon*
1985	*TV Love*
1986	*Cliffs Notes: Macbeth*
1989	*Portrait*
1990	*Deportment: South*
1991	*Deportment: North*
1993	*Faith Healing*
1995	*S/he*
1996	*Three Bagatelles for the Righteous*

Other works include: Choreography for the Tony award-winning Broadway musical *Passion* (Stephen Sondheim and James Lapine), and for the film *Francesca Page,* shown at the Sundance Film Festival and Cannes Film Festival, 1997.

*   *   *

Jane Comfort is an artist whose interests and work span the white trash and debutante's world of the American south, the gender and race wars of contemporary America, and the political implications of living in a world where images and sound bites have created their own reality—a world of multiple, meaningless meanings. Somehow, Comfort strives to confront preconceptions and ignorance with all the humor, grace, and power that a fine artist possesses.

Comfort began her career as a visual artist at the University of North Carolina, in Chapel Hill. Her interests quickly turned to dance, and she moved to New York where she began to train at the Merce Cunningham studio, and soon after, to perform with Jamie Cunningham. Comfort is extremely comfortable in all artistic venues, including the visual, the kinetic, the musical, and the theatrical. One of the first modern choreographers to fully integrate text and movement in the past two decades, Comfort concerned herself first with the musicality of words and phrases, studying how they could be combined with abstract movement without jarring the audience as they shifted from the nonliteral to the literal forms.

Comfort felt that working with text was natural to her, explaining, "(W)hen I started talking [in dance performances] in 1979, almost no one was, but I knew [it] was the right path for me." In addition, Comfort commented, "Most choreographers, it seems, hire writers to create texts in collaborations. I have always written my own, or 'co-existed' with the masters," as in such works as

Jane Comfort: *Deportment North.* **Photograph © Johan Elbers.**

1986's *Cliff Notes: Macbeth* and 1990's *Faith Healing.* "I think by writing my own texts, I have been more in touch with the rhythms that entered our bodies," Comfort says, intending to "create theater in which movement and language exist in a non-hierarchical relationship, each deepening the meaning of the other until the truest story emerges." Gradually, Comfort built upon this skill and has now developed a seamless, choreographic style which easily bridges the integration of text with movement, acting, and song. She is without equal in this area, and this has given her work an unusual degree of accessibility while allowing her to develop content that is difficult to sustain in most abstract genres. Her dancers are as much singers and actors as they are dancers—ultimately, they are consummate performers who are as generous and willing with audiences as any company performing today. The *Washington Post* describes Comfort's work as "a truly new form," as it weaves, in Wagnerian fashion, a *gesamkunstwerk* of modern proportions.

Comfort's movement style is difficult to describe, and, in some ways, is often lost in the context of the works she creates. With so much going on visually, musically, theatrically, and choreographically, it is sometimes difficult to appreciate the subtlety of dancing which is so fully integrated into the content of the piece. With her work, it would perhaps be more accurate to say that the movement is always supportive of the message, and that by this very virtue, it seems to disappear into the meaning of the dance. Still, Comfort can be credited with creating some breathless moments of pure dance in her choreography, as in the final movement of 1996's *Three Bagatelles for the Righteous*, a departure from Balinese fan dances, and the exquisite duet for two men in *S/he* from 1995. A *Village Voice* review commented that "Comfort, having bravely spoken out from both heart and enraged intelligence, now shows the heart of dancing itself."

Comfort has a unique capacity to see the underbelly of human life in compassionate terms, which delineates both the humor and pathos of much of her work. Her skill as an artist is strongly linked to her way of noticing the banal details that structure human life. For most of us, these details dominate our lives, forming a kind of imprisonment of ignorance. Comfort ranks as a first-rate artist who takes it upon herself to wake us from our sleepwalking—allowing us to participate in the weird richness of a life which rejects nothing.

—Peggy Berg

COMMOTION COMPANY

New Zealand dance company directed by Michael Parmenter

Works by Michael Parmenter

1979   *Blues in Twos* (mus. Williams, Washington), Dance Arts, Dunedin
        Miserere (solo; mus. Bach), Dance Arts, Dunedin
1981   *8 O'Clock Express* (mus. The Misfits), National School of Ballet, Wellington
        Bamboo (mus. Harris), On the Move, Wellington
        Syndrum (mus. Harris), On the Move, Wellington
        Kyrie (mus. Macahut), On the Move, Wellington
1982   *Cellobration* (mus. Mountfort), On the Move, Wellington
        Curl (mus. Nock), On the Move, Wellington
        Colour Cry (mus. Reich), On the Move, Wellington
        Jubilus (mus. Bach), National School of Ballet, Wellington

1983   *Speaking Frankly* (mus. Sinatra), Joint Concern, Wellington
        Dances on Glass (mus. Glass), Joint Concern, Wellington
        A Night in the Tropics (mus. Gottschalk), Joint Concern, Wellington
        La Creation du Monde (mus. Milhaud), New Zealand School of Dance, Wellington
        Between Two Fires (solo; mus. Body, Tyler-Wright; film Watson), Wellington
1984   *For Marie from Mike* (solo for Marie Gray), Footnote Dance Company, Wellington
1985   *Insolent River: A Tango* (with Marie Gray; mus. Four Volts and Jonathon Besser), Wellington
        Recollections of a Journey (mus. Body), One Extra Dance Company, Sydney
        Or in Graves Alone (with Frank van de Ven), London
1988   *Fields of Jeopardy* (mus. Downes), IndepenDance, Auckland
        GO (with Lyne Pringle; mus. Downes, Psathas, Shanly), Wellington
        Insolent River: A Romance (with Lyne Pringle; mus. Downes), Wellington
1990   *Intimate Constellations* (mus. Bach), Commotion Company, New Zealand International Festival, Wellington
        Tantra (mus. Downes, Psathas, Shanly), Commotion Company, New Zealand International Festival, Wellington
        Listeners at the Breathing Place (mus. Messiaen), Commotion Company, New Zealand International Festival, Wellington
        Venture (mus. Downes, Psathas, Shanly), Footnote Dance Company, Wellington
        Wilderness (solo; mus. Satoh), Wellington
        Blood Wedding (dir. Beaumont; mus. Downes), New Zealand Drama School, Wellington
1991   *Weathers from a Spark* (mus. Bach), Commotion Company, Wellington
        Bhakti (mus. Parsons), Footnote Dance Company, Wellington
1992   *Tide* (mus. Psathas), Hono Tai, Wellington
        Genetrix (solo; mus. Downes), Suzanne Renner, Dunedin
        Elegies (mus. Body), Royal New Zealand Ballet, Wellington
        The Race (mus. Downes), Commotion Company, Wellington; adapted for Television New Zealand, Dir. Taylor
        Equatorial (mus. Sakamoto), Commotion Company, Wellington
        Satellite Glances (mus. Ishikawa), Commotion Company, Wellington
        Sweetheart Rising to Celestial 100% (mus. Yoshimatsu), Commotion Company, Wellington
1993   *The Dark Forest* (mus. Watson), Commotion Company, Wellington
        Aphrodisia (mus. Ichikawa, Queen, Vangelis, Morricone), Hero Festival, Auckland
1994   *Vinyl Oven* (mus.various), Footnote Dance Company, Wellington
        Etruscan Elegies (mus. Glanville-Hicks), Royal New Zealand Ballet, Wellington
1995   *A Long Undressing* (solo theatre work, dir. C. Downes, mus. D. Downes), Wellington
1998   *Satellite Glances* (new version, mus. Downes), Footnote Dance Company, Adelaide
        Jerusalem (mus. Downes), Commotion Company, Wellington

Commotion Company: *The Dark Forest.*

Publications

Avery, Michael, "Sounds and Movement: The Vision of Michael
   Parmenter," *Music in New Zealand,* Spring 1992.
Whyte, Raewyn, "Causing a Commotion," *Dance Australia* June/July 1993.
————, "Dance Works of 1993: A Review Article," *Illusions* (New
   Zealand), Winter 1994.

Films and Videotapes

Tide, dir. Oomen for *Dance and the Camera,* Television New
   Zealand, 1994.
Weightless, dir. Oomen for *Dance and the Camera,* Television New
   Zealand, 1994.
The Dark Forest, dir. Stitt, Television New Zealand, 1995.

*   *   *

Commotion Company was initiated and formed by dancer/
choreographer Michael Parmenter in 1989. The company made
its debut during the 1990 New Zealand International Festival
with the production *Gravity and Grace,* followed later that year
with a retrospective season of Parmenter choreography, *Re-Works
1980-1990.* Major seasons of new works followed in each of the
next four years. *Weathers from a Spark* toured nationally in
1991; *Inside Now,* a programme of eight shorter works including
works commissioned from Ann Dewey and Charles Neho, toured
regionally in 1992; the dance-theatre epic *The Race* was seen in
two centers in 1992 and 1993; and *The Dark Forest* premiered in
1993, accompanied by two shorter works from the company's
repertory.

The company was in recess 1994 through 1997 while Parmenter
pursued other projects, including performing with Compagnie Ljada
in Switzerland; studying and traveling in New York, Greece and the
American southwest; creating commissioned works for Footnote
Dance Company and the Royal New Zealand Ballet; touring his
solo show *A Long Undressing,* and writing a book about his life in
dance. During this time Commotion members continued to perform
in projects with other choreographers, such as Douglas Wright,
Mary-Jane O'Reilly, and Susan Jordan.

The dancers came together again in 1995 to make a film of *The Dark Forest* which was broadcast on national television in 1996 and went on to win a Certificate for Creative Excellence at the 1997 US International Film and Video Festival. In 1998, a dance-opera, *Jerusalem,* completed a trilogy comprising *Go* (1988) and *The Race* (1992).

Parmenter formed Commotion Company after a decade of professional performance experience in New Zealand (with Val Deakin in 1977-78, Limbs Dance Company in 1980), in Australia (with Human Veins in 1982, One Extra in 1985-86) and in the United States (with Erick Hawkins Dance Company in 1984, 1986, Stephen Petronio and Dancers in 1984, Mai Juku in 1984-86). Behind him also was a decade of creating solo, duet and trio choreographic projects with a number of continuing collaborators—dancers Marie Gray (1981-82, 1984-85), Michelle Richecoeur (1981-82); composer Jack Body (1983, 1985); dancer Lyne Pringle (1987-89); composer David Downes and designer Andrew Thomas (both 1988-90). He wanted to work in an ongoing way with a group of dancers with whom he could develop a distinctive movement vocabulary and way of working. The goal for the company was to extend Parmenter's choreography in new ways, and create a repertory with a distinctive aesthetic that would have an ongoing life and be widely seen.

At the time of establishing the company, Parmenter had recently recovered from major surgery for life-threatening cancer, and had received an HIV+ diagnosis. He wanted two things: to choreograph to the music of the great composers Bach, Stravinsky, and Messiaen, whose works had long inspired him—music he describes as sustaining him through his illness; and to continue his collaboration with New Zealand composers Jack Body and, particularly, David Downes, with whom he had already created several major works.

Parmenter's own choreographic aesthetic and approach to training dancers for his new company was strongly influenced by Erick Hawkins, Min Tanaka, and Stephen Petronio, through his experience of studying with them and dancing in their companies. His distinctive partnering style was developed out of several years training and performing with fellow New Zealand dancer Lyne Pringle. By the end of its second year, Commotion Company had become a tight-knit ensemble of seven dancers with a shared aesthetic developed through Parmenter's teaching and from developing his new choreographies together. The company quickly developed a loyal and growing audience, achieving popular acclaim for the densely packed, high-energy, high-risk *Fields of Jeopardy* which became a signature work, and for the more contemplative *Sweetheart Rising to Celestial 100%,* which honored the memory of local performer Leigh Ransfield who had died from AIDS. The company was acclaimed for the vitality, musicality and sensuousness of the dancing, for the disciplined physicality of the dancers, and for their ability to be fully present in every moment of the performance.

The company received project funding from the Arts Council for the creation of new choreographies, and their commitment to working with New Zealand music, performed live where possible, also attracted support from the Douglas Lilburn Foundation. However, no funding was available for the maintenance and performance of an ongoing repertoire, and the company's goal for such development was not realised. Perhaps ironically, several works originally made on Commotion Company are currently in the repertoire of Footnote Dance Company, and are regularly performed by them along with other works that company has commissioned from Parmenter.

Given the lack of funding to sustain a continuing repertory and meet the costs of ongoing administration, Commotion Company could not exist as a full-time modern dance company. It became instead a projects-based company with core dancers who were available for most projects, supplemented with other independent dancers when required. Over the company's first decade, more than 25 dancers performed under its auspices, developing and honing skills and knowledge essential to their survival as independent dance artists who move from project to project.

Commotion Company's core members, all exceptional dancers, have developed ongoing dance careers. Lisa Densem has performed regularly with the Douglas Wright Dance Company over a series of projects, and with Jordan & Present Company. She is drawing attention as an emerging choreographer, and has received commissions from Isadora's Tribe and the New Zealand International Festival of the Arts. Claire O'Neill has performed regularly with the Douglas Wright Dance Company over a series of projects, and with other New Zealand choreographers on a projects basis. She co-directs and choreographs for Company Blue Vault with Nicole Bishop. Taane Mete has performed regularly with Taiao, Douglas Wright Company, and is a founding member of Black Grace Dance Company. He is a regular performer at the drag nightclub the Staircase, and performs internationally as a cabaret singer with Mika and the Uhuras. Helaina Keeley has performed with the Douglas Wright Dance Company and with Auckland Ballet, and was a founding member of Retina Dance. Helen Winchester has danced with the Douglas Wright Dance Company and has for a number of years taught modern dance and the Parmenter repertory at the New Zealand School of Dance. Peter Sears has continued dancing in New Zealand and Australia, most recently with Meryl Tankard's Australian Dance Theatre.

—Raewyn Whyte

COMPAGNIE BEAU-GESTE
French dance company

Founded 1980 by Dominique Boivin, Christine Erbe, Christine Gaz, Isabelle Job, and Philippe Priasso; directed by Dominique Boivin since 1981; in residence in Moulin du Robec, 1981-83; at the Art Center, Mont St. Aignan, 1983-88; Ville Nouvelle de Val de Reuil, since 1989; won a "Humor" award for *Quelle fut ta soif?* (*What Did You Thirst For?*), 1976.

Works

1976	*Quelle fut ta soif? (What Did You Thirst For?)* (mus. Boivin), Bagnolet
1978	*Vol d'oiseaux (Flight of the Birds)* (mus. Peyron, Gautier), Angers
1979	*Crouche hue Dada* (mus. Peyron), solo, Avignon
1981	*Solo (Solo 2)* (mus. Peyron), Paris
	Ex-Libris (mus. Garnier), for Centre Nationale de la Danse Contemporaine (CNDC), Angers
	Météo marine (Marine Meteorology) (mus. Garnier), for CNDC, Montpellier
	Welcome (mus. Elvis Costello), duet, Montpellier
	Solo (Solo 4) (mus. collage), solo, Darnétal
	Blème aurore (Pale Daybreak) (mus. Peyron, Chancerel)

Supermarché (Supermarket) (mus. Purcel), duet

Lasada Illuminations, Rouen

1982 *Grege Aria* w/David, Lawton (mus. Biscuit), Dardénal

Janvier (January) (mus. *Carmina Burana,* Clementic Consort), solo, Dardénal

Bye-Bye (mus. Biscuit), solo, Dardénal

Chut (Shhh!) w/Lawton (mus. Meredith Monk), trio, Dardénal

Brise-lames (Breakwater), Louis Ziegler (mus. Ziegler), Strasbourg

Nuit blanche (Sleepless Night) (mus. Boivin), solo

Parcours (Journey) (mus. Boivin, Berlinguen), Avignon's Festival

Zig zag (mus. collage), Mont St. Aignan

Oncle Raoul, chor. A. David, (mus. Biscuit), Avignon

Duo w/Hifler (mus. silence, mechanical birds), Mont St. Aignan

1983 *Veuve Cliquot (The Widow Cliquot)* (mus. Léandre), Rotterdam Werkcentrum Dans, the Netherlands

Venus et les toutous (Venus and the dogs) (mus. collage), Mont St. Aignan

Désir désir (Desire, Desire) (mus. company), Heurteauville

1984 *Strada fox* (mus. Biscuit), Maison de la Danse, Lyon

Histoires lamentables (Pitiful Stories) (mus. Mussorgsky), solo, Darnétal

Exo-Serre (mus. Strauss), Rouen

Encore lui (Him Again!) (mus. according to performance), solo, Seine Maritime

Art y show (mus. Tanietz), Lyon

Tiré à 4 épingles (Dressed up) (mus. Biscuit)

Evènement Beau-Geste (included *La chambre séparée, Péripéties, Bouledouge,* and *Imposture;* mus. varied), Mont St. Aignan

1985 *Papiers peints (Wallpaper)* (mus. Azam), Le Havre

Princes de Paris (mus. collage), Le Havre

Strip-Tease w/Grand Magasin, Paris

L'école des hommes oiseaux (The School of the Bird-Men), chor. Nikolais (mus. Nikolais), Aix-en-Provence

Les petites fournis respirent encore (The Little Ants Are Still Breathing) w/Grand Magasin, (mus. Grand Magasin), Paris

1986 *Le tombeau de Joseph M.* (mus. Biscuit), Paris

Dis, la St Valentin, c'est quoi? (Tell Me, What Is Valentine's Day?) (mus. collage, Pavie), Mont St. Aignan

"Zoopsie Comedie" Grande Revue Moderne w/Lolita (mus. Azam, Michon, Melody Four, Biscuit), International Theatre and Tanz Festival, Salzburg

La machine célibataire (The Celibacy Machine) (mus. Court Circuit), Mont St. Aignan

1987 *Vulgo le cafard (Vulgo the Cockroach)* (mus. Mozart), solo, St. Étienne

Dedicacé à Marie de France (mus. Pavie, Clanet), trio, St. Étienne

Danses Singulières (mus. Satie, Parvie), Andé

1988 *Les jardins de bagatelle (Gardens of Trivialities)* (mus. CBG), Mont St. Aignan

Climat d'amour (Climate of Love) (mus. CBG), Bouxwiller and Mulhouse

Le piège de Meduse (Medusa's Trap) (mus. Satie, Parvie, Le Nouvel Ensemble Contemporain), Mont St. Aignan

1989 *Baïonnette (Bayonet)* (mus. CBG, Spot), St. Étienne

Des fleurs, des fleurs, des fleurs. . . w/Gréau, Noisette (mus. Court Circuit, Noisette), Mont St. Aignan

Noir destin blanc mouton (Black Destiny, White Sheep) (mus. Lyon), Paris

Follis (Bellows) (mus. Pavie, Clanet), Reims

Le cabinet des curiosités (included *Grrr coeur noir, Têtes d'épingles,* and *Baisers hâtifs*), Châlon-sur-Saône

Qu'a bu l'âne au lac? (What Did the Donkey Drink at the Lake?), chor. Ziegler, (mus. de Chenerilles), Mulhouse

Aqua ça rime? (What Does Water Mean?) (mus. CBG, Michon), Val de Reuil

La grande piste (The Huge Floor) (mus. varied), Val de Reuil

Romantic monstre (mus. CBG), Val de Reuil

Tutu Noël panpan l'année (Tutu Christmas Smack-Smack the Year) (mus. CBG), Mont St. Aignan

1991 *Nuit en fourure (Night in a Fur Coat)* (mus. CBG), Rouen

Belles de nuit (Ladies of the Night) (mus. CBG, Kramer), Caluire

Le ruisseau et l'océan (The Brook and the Ocean) (mus. Casays), Mont St. Aignan

Les amours de Monsieur Vieux Bois (The Love Stories of Mr. Old Wood) (from Rodolphe Toepffer), (mus. Pesson, Queyras, Robault, Marin), Geneva

La cour de marbre (The Marble Court) w/others, Paris

1992 *Nuit du fantastique* (mus. *Rocky Horror Picture Show*), Val de Reuil

Le chat et la souris (The Cat and the Mouse) w/Lelièvre (mus. Payen), St. Étienne

Carmen (mus. Erbé, Michon), Geneva

1993 *La belle étoile, cabaret pataphysique* (mus. collage), Tulle

Récital (mus. Satie, CBG), Tulle

Hommage à Nikolais (mus. Nikolais), Malakoff

1994 *La danse une histoire à ma façon, (The Dance, a Story in My Way)* (mus. CBG), solo, Vénissieux

Aux champs d'amour (mus. *Carmina Burana,* Clementic Consort), Vénissieux

Les sept dernières paroles du Christ (The Seven Last Words of Christ) (mus. Haydn), solo for Jean Guizerix, Aix-en-Provence Dance Festival

1996 *Petites histoires au-dessus du ciel (Small Stories above the Sky)* (mus. Chevalier, live, and CBG), Valence

1997 *Les belles (The Beauties)* w/Chevalier (mus. CBG), Moscow

Orphée aux enfers (Orpheus in the Underworld) w/Ros de la Grange (mus. Offenbach), Geneva

Mécaniques (Mechanics) (mus. CBG), St. Marcel

*   *   *

Dominique Boivin, Christine Erbe, Philippe Priasso, Christine Graz, and Isabelle Job met in 1979 at the Centre National de Danse Contemporaine d'Angers (CNDC, the Angers National Center for Contemporary Dance), which was managed by Alwin Nikolais. One year later, in 1980, they decided to create their own dance troupe called the Compagnie Beau-Geste (Beautiful Gesture) in which they would be both dancers and choreographers.

Born in 1952, Dominique Boivin started his dance career through the circus. He studied mime with Daniel Stein, classical dance with Béatrice Mosera, and contemporary dance with Catherine Altalani, Merce Cunningham, and Douglas Dunn in the United States. His contributions to the CBG have been many; he has choreographed dozens of works including *Blème aurore* in 1981, *Parcours* the next year, and a fable in 1987 where an insect called *Vulgo le cafard* wants to fly. Through humor and fantasy, Boivin traces a ludicrous and emotional portrait of the culpability and weakness of this allegorical insect who dances in Mozart's *Requiem*. With 1989's *Baïonnette*, he attempted to find, on the fringe of history, the roots of the popular perception of the French Revolution. To serve this purpose, he used the dancers' movements to create legible traces of their physical and emotional differences, favoring fragility rather than certitude.

Isabelle Job composed *Bouledogue* and *Baisers hâtif*, and perfomed in *Le cabinet des curiosités* in 1990, while Isabelle Erbé choreographed *Piège de Méduse* and *Tête d'épingles*, and also performed in *Le cabinet des curiosités*.

Philippe Priasso started dancing in Lyon with Anne-Marie Lemaître, trained at the CNDC in 1978 and 1979, and danced in Nikolais' company from 1979 to 1981. Lured by Nikolais personally, he collaborated with him on several projects, including the creation of a small stage set for the Festival d'Aix in 1985, and was Nikolais' assistant while he taught a master class in January 1989 in Paris. Priasso has choreographed several acclaimed works for Compagnie Beau-Geste (CBG), among them the solo *Danses singulières* and *Dédicace à Marie de France*, both in 1987. In collaboration with a circus, he created *Follis* in 1989, a dreamlike carnival of animals reflecting shared cultural memories and of European folklore.

Since 1982 Christine Graz has developed, in parallel with her collaboration with Beau-Geste, a series of events called *Lasada*, consisting of dances in windows, with painting and musical stories. She also choreographed *Grr...coeur noir*, and performed in *Le cabinet des curiosités* and *Art y show* in 1984, a fashion parade parody where Boivin was magically cut into small pieces, and also performed levitation.

Many choreographies have been authored by the entire company, such as *Désir désir* in 1983 or the very futurist cabaret *Zoopsie comédie* in 1986, created for more than 20 dancers in concert with the Company Lolita, and with the participation of fashion designer Christian Lacroix. Performed in the Parisian cabaret *Le Bataclan*, this comedy mixes legend with science fiction. With *Princes de Paris*, the company unpredictably cut between a series of contrasting Parisian images.

Strada Fox (1984), based on the music of Karl Biscuit, is also a group creation, and illustrates through the saga of human behavior from mastery to madness, while the mock artistic "happening" *Nuit en fourrure* from 1991, performed without a stage in a castle courtyard, was a farcical open-air cabaret in three acts. Music halls and cabarets were also the topic of *Cabaret Pataphysique* and *La belle étoile* in 1994, inspired by Alfred Jarry's sense of the absurd.

Comic strips were also honored in a comedy ballet composed in two parts: *Les amours de Mr. Vieux Bois* in 1991 by Rodolph Toepffer. Conceived as a suite about impulsive amorous aberrations, the first part presents Monsieur Vieux Bois hounding his beloved, while the second shows his beloved harassing a Monsieur Cryptogame.

Another innovative work, where the dancers wear kitsch costumes, *Petites histoires au dessus du ciel* cuts between the many trivialities and futilities that crowd our existence as we wait for the arrival of our Prince Charming. A similar topic was presented in *Carmen* (1995), where in a more theatrical dance, Carmen becomes a City Hall heroine—a pretext to show the huge differences between our dreams and the reality of everyday life. Everyday life

was also covered in *Belles de nuit* from 1991, where through the eyes of a dog called Rita, we see the sadness and nostalgia of poor and lonely people. Rita was also the heroine of *Récital* in 1993, a suite of short pieces for three dancers, pianist, and dog, revisiting classical choreography. One year later the company also created *Paroles du Christ*, where Christ's message is questioned, and *La danse, une histoire à ma façon*, a performance built around an author's knowledge and memories of dance.

Common to the works of the Compagnie Beau-Geste are a sensitivity to the nuances of our lives, the use of dream sequences, absurdity, and burlesque humor. The company has also produced educational dance performances, such as *Mécaniques*, a performance for schools which clearly demonstrates the creative choreographic process. Educational works on dance for the general public include *Vénus et les toutous*, *Les jardins de bagatelle*, or *Tutu Noël Panpan l'année*, which is about Christmas Eve.

—Edwige Dioudonnat

COMPAÑIA NACIONAL DE DANZA
Spanish dance company

After the death of Franco in 1975 ended 40 years of dictatorship in Spain, Spanish society experienced a dynamic development in all fields: political, economic, social and, of course, cultural. This development demanded the creation of certain cultural institutions, like a national ballet, sponsored by the public budget. Up until this time only private companies, more related to traditional Spanish dance (flamenco and "escuela bolera") had assumed this role. However, in 1979, when the young dancer and choreographer Víctor Ullate decided to return to Spain, after having worked for an extended time with Maurice Béjart, the ministry of culture asked him to create a national classical-based ballet company, to be called the Ballet Nacional de España—Clásico, to coexist with a twin company—also state-sponsored—called the Ballet Nacional de Danza Española. In spite of the governmental support, Ullate had to fight against the very practical questions of building up a new company in a country that had a very short tradition in classical dancing. He tried to set up a repertoire with contemporary leanings while based on rigorous classical training—as a kind of epigonic tribute to Béjart's views.

Ullate was replaced in 1983 by María de Avila, who assumed the direction of both the state-run companies (classical and Spanish dance). She succeeded in attracting the interest of Spanish audiences, through the restagings of great neoclassical choreography like that of Balanchine, Tudor, and others, and managed to develop both the skills and potential of her dancers and the company. Three years later, in 1986, the twin companies were separated and a new directorship was initiated. The Ballet Lírico Nacional was born—with what many considered a peculiar name—and Ray Barra was designated as its artistic director. Barra and the company's dancers reached an understanding of what was needed to survive, and the company started touring abroad. The socialist government of Felipe Gonzalez began, at that time, to dedicate more finds and attention to dance and in 1987 adopted a program of positive measures for to further the development of contemporary dance, but then made a bizarre move by putting Maya Plisetskaya at the head of the company. The Russian ballerina—who would later receive Spanish citizenship—was full of good intentions, but placed an excessively narrow and personal focus on the company's repertoire by selecting choreography for which she alone had an affinity or fondness (such as *La fille mal gardée*, for example).

The true renewal came in 1990, when Nacho Duato returned to Spain and was offered the directorship of the state-run company, under the new name of Compañía Nacional de Danza (CND). Duato submitted a three-year plan to the Ministry of Culture, which was fully accepted. He subjected himself and the entire company to a huge renovation of both style and administration. After many problems, Duato was able to clean up the situation and, little by little, gained the full confidence of his dancers, the critics and audiences as well. Duato has given the CND its own distinctive style—one that is homogeneous, compact, unified, and which defines its artistic personality—a style which goes very well with the postmodernity that invaded all the cultural sectors in Spain in the early 1990s. Its connection with the Spanish audiences is almost complete, and its success on foreign stages (the company has been touring worldwide since 1992) have given Compañía Nacional de Danza, a healthy reputation in the international dance landscape. Three examples of the high praise received by CND came from noted critics Horst Koegler, Anna Kisselgoff, and John Percival. Koegler stated in *Stuttgarter Zeitung* that the company's dancers were not only "highly motivated and better trained," than most but that the company was impressive because of its "vitality, its evident and strong energy and its passion, sometimes completely animal." Kisselgoff, writing for the *New York Times* in 1994, also commented on the troupe's strength, stating that its "energy comes from the earth, it's even elementary, getting its strength from the sand, the fire and the air, which are never far away from the images of Nacho Duato's choreographies." Lastly, Britain's Percival wrote in the *Times* of CND's ever-evolving personality, "It's a dance company from Spain, and not at all a company of Spanish dance."

Publications

Kisselgoff, Anna, review, *New York Times,* 13 May 1994.
Koegler, Horst, review, *Stuttgarter Zeitung,* 13 May 1994.
Percival, John, review, *The Times* (London), 17 March 1994.

—Delfín Colomé

CONGO TANGO PALACE

Choreography: Talley Beatty
Music: Miles Davis, Gil Evans; "Soleo" from *Sketches of Spain*
Costume Design: Georgia Collins
First Production: YM-YWHA, New York, 29 October 1960
Original Dancers: Georgia Collins, Mini Marshall, Altovise Gore, Joan Peters, Mabel Robinson, Herman Howell, Jerome Jeffrey, Tommy Johnson, Ronald Platt, Dudley Williams, Albert Popwell

Other productions include: Alvin Ailey American Dance Theatre, Dayton Contemporary Dance Company, Philadanco

Publications

Barnes, Clive, "Dance: The Wizardry of Talley Beatty," *New York Times,* 5 September 1967.

————, "Dance: The Broadway Touch," *New York Times,* 30 January 1969.
Marks, Marcia, "The Alvin Ailey American Dance Theatre," *Dance Magazine,* March 1969.
Nash, Joe, "Talley Beatty," *African American Genius in Modern Dance,* American Dance Festival, 1994.

*   *   *

Congo Tango Palace was originally the finale of *Come and Get the Beauty of it Hot,* a suite of six dances which loosely follows a group of urban dwellers throughout the day. Since the debut of the suite, both the opening dance, *Toccata,* and *Congo Tango Palace* have frequently been presented as independent works with great success. *Congo Tango Palace* has been hailed for its thrilling vitality, subtly stylized movement, and deceptively skillful choreography.

The setting of *Congo Tango Palace* is a nightclub in a Hispanic ghetto. The lights are dim, the musical rhythm is dominant and driving, the restless men and women are on the prowl. The stage is statically charged with barely contained violence as all seem to challenge the very air they breathe. Men and women enter separately. As the stage fills with bodies, lines begin to form only to dissolve, couples coalesce and then fly apart, an individual dashes offstage alone while a newly formed group momentarily dominates, slashing a diagonal path across the stage. From the moment it begins, *Congo Tango Palace* is a relentless onslaught of movement and raw, seething vitality with which Beatty creates a montage of pain and mistrust masquerading as bravado.

Don McDonagh pays eloquent tribute to Beatty's achievement in this work in his book *The Complete Guide to Modern Dance*:

> Beatty's evocation of life in a ghetto area, hardened to disappointment and mistrustful of easy happiness, is masterly. One has the continual sense of time being the enemy. One has to take what one can now and not wait for tomorrow, and taking involves a certain roughness. There is no time for polite exchange. The emotions are raw and the dancing gives them full vent.

Jeraldyn Blunden, founder and director of the Dayton Contemporary Dance Company, describes the tone of the work and the technical demands of the choreography as inseparable:

> It's savagery! . . . . And it's just the movement [creating this tone], because the movement is very hard. We're talking about high arabesques and slow spins on the floor, and all this is done as percussively as you can possibly get it out—as well as the syncopation [of the movement] being off the syncopation of the music.

Congo Tango Palace is quintessntial Beatty in every respect, from the dominance of rhythm to the contemporary American theme. The highly stylized movement—pulled-up torso, high arms and long lines—gives the impression of Spain to Beatty's signature mix of dance genres, while remaining completely American.

The original ending was considered too dangerous to cast and crew, and has since been changed. In the original production, Georgia Collins was flown upside-down on a rope tied to her feet while her partner pushed and twirled her about the stage. Reconstructions have frequently replaced flying from the rope with partnered lifts and spins which continue as the stage goes dark, shortly before a splintering crash abruptly halts the music. Either ending is uncomfortable: a disturbing non-ending to pain.

Perhaps more dramatically than most Beatty works, *Congo Tango Palace* does not draw any conclusions or moralize. Beatty merely presents a picture of the world of the young and disenfranchised as he sees it.

—Teren Damato Ellison

CONTACT IMPROVISATION

In the midst of an improvisation, a man might lean on a woman who would cradle him descending slowly, then drop: both partners entwined on a mat before rolling—torsos over sides, legs, arms, scissoring out—away from each other until a brush of the ankles prompts retrogression into a new embrace. From the vertical to the horizontal, accelerating and slowing down, through tension and surrender, the path these dancers take will remain unpredictable but precisely right. They'll show aplomb in the interplay of weight and nerve impulses, bone structure and muscle strength: supporting, rotating, slipping through each other and pulling back up. Their impetus draws from some deep personal well and this intimacy spreads to the periphery, creating a communal feel that erases boundaries between individual and companion, performers and the audience. Viewers could recall athletic displays while valuing the artistry of expression; enjoy the sociability while recognizing the fine-tuning of each individual. Such is the impact of contact improvisation.

A dance form that may be likened to sports, contact improvisation took shape and grew throughout the 1970s and 1980s, often documented on video. It still thrives on egalitarian sentiments and physical experimentation, availing itself of cyberspace in listings of international events, organizations, and dedicated individuals.

Following the social upheavals that shook the late 1960s and the coeval unrest in dance, theater, and music, contact improvisation shared the spirit of those times. "The people creating contact improvisation . . . were for the most part young, college-educated, white, middle-class Americans living in transient, communal settings . . . [who] began to see [this] dancing as an expression of a way of life with certain values . . . [and] the body as a sensuous, intelligent, natural part of each person, requiring acknowledgment and promising insight," Cynthia Novack pointed out in her essential study, *Sharing the Dance,* which analyzes the context and nature of contact improvisation.

Antecedents in dance also informed the development of contact improvisation, and Novack identified three key figures: Merce Cunningham, with his chance, non-narrative, non-symbolic presentations; Anna Halprin, an improviser and explorer of "natural" physical idioms; and Erick Hawkins, seeker of movement efficiency and sensuousness from a scientific, philosophical base. The inherent rebelliousness of postmodernism also came into play as seen in the work of the Judson Dance Theater, a hotbed of collective innovation.

These cultural trends encouraged the participation of many individuals such as Nancy Stark Smith, Daniel Lepkoff, and Dena Davida, who gained a high profile performing and teaching groups in contact improvisation. Yet one figure emerged as central to its creation and development: Steve Paxton, who named this way of moving and shaped it through his continuing explorations.

Paxton profited from an eclectic background in gymnastics and aikido, experimental theatre and composition. His curriculum has included performing with the Cunningham company, collaborations with Yvonne Rainer and work with the improvisational collective, the Grand Union. Personal affinities and communal experiences, shaped by a reaction to the dance heritage, bore upon a type of movement he elaborated, energized by the physiological and emotional impulses of immediate human interaction and perpetuated in non-hierarchical contexts.

A significant event in Paxton's career occurred with the presentation of *Magnesium,* a piece that grew out of his improvisations and was passed on to a group of 11 male performers at Oberlin College in 1972. Many of its characteristics became representative of the look and attitude of contact improvisation: the plain, comfortable outfits, the transformation of energy from the vigorous to the meditative, task-like actions exploring support and yielding, personal focus and connection with a partner. The closing section, sometimes known as "The Stand," took participants through subtle shifts in weight, balance, and alignment from a vertical position and turned into a common exercise for contact improvisors.

In contrast to other currents in modern dance, contact improvisation has resisted strict codification and identification with one personality. Still, a desire to promote safety in teaching and to share information gave birth to *Contact Quarterly,* begun as a newsletter in 1975 and currently published as a biannual magazine under Nancy Stark Smith's editorship.

Contact improvisation has found venues from college gyms to art galleries, maintaining a welcoming attitude while extending possibilities for its approach, often in gatherings called "jams." Events can come off as demonstrations, presented without the structuring—in direction or performance—of traditional dance. Yet this expression has also gained amplitude and daring, with the development of more technically challenging sequences and thematic veins. Interviewed after her participation at the 25th anniversary celebration of contact improvisation at Oberlin College, South Florida choreographer Karen Peterson noted, "Some of the tightly knit performances there superceded any set choreographies I've seen in trust, honesty, and sensitivity." Her excitement, both as a viewer and practitioner who works with a group of mixed-ability dancers, represents a sensibility that has kept contact improvisation flourishing in regional nuclei. As she explained, "Not going through specified shapes but listening to an inner rhythm suits a range of abilities. People in wheelchairs, so attuned to impulses, to moving from sensation, understand and take to contact improvisation confidently."

Peterson's work constitutes a fruitful application of contact skills further witnessed in groups such as California's Touchdown Dance USA, which trains blind and deaf people, even promoting this movement base as a "healing art." Similarly, the ideals of contact improvisation flourish in such retreat centers as Earthdance in New England, with roots in communal living and sights on spiritual awareness. Workshops in contact improvisation are valued for their body-mind integration and facilitation of sharp physical response. The influence of this movement can be seen in a range of choreographies by artistic directors such as Bill T. Jones, and Randy Warshaw, who keeps contact as part of company training, stamping his repertory with free-flowing energy and mental acuity. As dance educator Martha Myers has asserted, "It's difficult to imagine today's dance without CI. Its concepts and practice have permeated our dance training, performance and choreography. On its own, it's a major technical development in late-20th century dance. As one of several ingredients comprising the loosely defined 'new dance' or 'release technique,' it's seen across forms and throughout the country."

Publications

Books—

Bainbridge Cohen, Bonnie, *Sensing, Feeling, and Action,* Northampton, 1993.
Hanlon Johnson, Don, *Body, Spirit, and Democracy,* Berkeley, 1994.
Novack, Cynthia J., *Sharing the Dance,* Madison, Wisconsin, 1990.

Articles—

Crolius, Ali, "Earthdance Survives Changing Vision, Changing Times," *Daily Hampshire Gazette,* 4 September 1996.
Hougee, Aat, "Paths of Change," *Contact Quarterly,* Summer/Fall 1992.
Novack, Cynthia J. and Anne Kilcoyne, "On the Braille in the Body: An Account of Touchdown Dance Integrated Workshops with the Visually Impaired and the Sighted," *Dance Research,* Spring 1993.

—Guillermo Perez

COSTUME DESIGN

Costume designers have always been the silent but potent collaborators of modern dance choreographers. The work of the costumer is fraught with paradox: while the designer may regard himself or herself as an artist, he or she must subjugate his/her art to fulfilling the vision of the choreographer. Many times in the history of modern dance, a choreographer's work has been deepened immeasurably by the costume designer's creations.

At first, many of the innovators of modern dance eschewed costumes (and scenery) as a reaction to classical ballet in general and to Diaghilev's stagings for his Ballets Russes in particular. Modern dance would never have the equivalent of artists such as Roerich, Golovine, Goncharova, Tchelitchev, Benois, Bakst, de Chirico, Picasso, and Laurencin—all of whom transformed ballet by treating the stage as one huge canvas. These designers allowed their imaginations to bring orientalism, cubism, and folk art to the stage. Their designs often encompassed both scenery and costumes. Modern dance choreographers rebelled against the strictures of classical ballet by liberating the body from stiff tutus, bejeweled and restrictive bodices, elaborate headdresses, tights, and satin toe shoes. These costume elements were discarded in favor of loose-fitting, flowing dresses of diaphanous silk, bare legs, and bare feet. However, this is not to say that the makers of modern dance were in rebellion against theatricality. Some choreographers at the dawn of modern dance saw another way to "dress" the dance. Loie Fuller embraced costuming as a way to revolutionize dance. The American-born Fuller created a unique art form by intermingling masses of silk cloth, music, and lighting to spectacular theatrical effect. Her fellow American, Isadora Duncan, was deeply impressed by Fuller and adopted her use of drapery in extending the gesture. Duncan, the mother of barefoot dancing, designed and sewed (with her mother and brother Raymond to help) Grecian-inspired dresses to create an ambience for her "free" dance. Her costumes were inspired by

the classical sculptures and vase paintings she had viewed in the British Museum, at the Louvre, and during her first visit to Greece in 1903. Duncan's filmy outfits fell in gentle curves and folds around her—they also barely disguised her body. But they were essential to the image she wanted to create. All those who saw Duncan dance noted her costumes and how they billowed behind her as she skipped, ran, and jumped. Other costumes, while revealing less of Duncan, had equal impact. Duncan danced to the French national anthem, the *Marseillaise*, in Paris in 1916. It was the depths of World War I and Duncan's costume was a blood-red robe. Her performance created a sensation—for the French, Duncan embodied the ultimate triumph of the human spirit.

In the 1920s another American, Ruth St. Denis, used carefully researched and elaborately constructed costumes to recreate ethnic dances or dance-dramas for Denishawn, the company she founded with her husband Ted Shawn in 1914. The ethnic dances devised by St. Denis included the Hindu-inspired work, *Radha*, and famous solos such as *The Incense, Nautch,* and *Yogi*. Her choreography involved the manipulation of saris, wide skirts, and trains. In *The Spirit of the Sea*, St. Denis' costume covered the entire stage with yards of green silk falling down her shoulders in every direction. For St. Denis, the voluminous material represented an extension of the movements of her body.

The chief costume designer for Denishawn was Pearl Wheeler. Despite Wheeler's efforts, St. Denis always wanted more theatricality in the costumes her dancers wore and required them to sew on additional sequins, appliques, and paillettes. *Xochitl,* choreographed by Ted Shawn, was an example of the elaborately costumed Denishawn dance-dramas. It was based on Shawn's studies of Mayan, Aztec, and Toltec legends and featured a young Denishawn dancer, Martha Graham. Graham, feeling stifled creatively, broke away from Denishawn in 1923 to create her own dances on her own body. She also left behind Denishawn's veils and exoticism. However, Graham's experience with Denishawn left her with a genuine feeling for what costumes could do for her evolving dance style. Graham also had the skills to create and sew her own costumes. She also knew (from the years at Denishawn) how to instruct her dancers on the way to drape and fold fabric on the body.

Economy was a major concern in Graham's early years as a choreographer. She operated on a strict budget and was forced to buy the least expensive fabrics. Economic concerns forced Graham to explore fabrics such as tricot, jersey, and stretchy synthetics. Her costumes were models of their kind in that they sought to give dancers additional fluidity and a sense of drama. With Graham, the costume became an intrinsic part of the dance. In *Heretic* (1929) she created designs out of wool jersey which she bought for 18 cents per yard. Graham and her dancers sewed up the costumes just before the performance. She was dressed in white, the company in black. Graham's costumes evolved along with her choreography. In the solo *Lamentation* (1930), she wore a long tube of tricot, tied at the middle with a string. Inside her costume, Graham stretched her body in an attempt to express the boundaries of grief. According to Agnes de Mille in *Martha: The Life and Work of Martha Graham*, "the material clung to her body and made every position look as though it was carved in stone." In *Ekstatis* (1933), Graham wore another tube dress. As she noted in her autobiography, the jersey fabric allowed her to explore the relationship between the hip and the shoulder. With each stretch she became more aware of the articulation of her body.

One of Graham's most beautiful costumes was the one she designed for herself for *Primitive Mysteries* (1931). In this study of the Virgin Mary as a young girl, Graham created a white cotton dress with large, loose sleeves. It was a communion dress and wedding dress in one. She wore her dark hair loose down her back. The group wore simply cut dresses of dark-blue jersey which they sewed themselves. Graham was rarely satisfied with her work, however, and was known to rip up costumes just before the premiere of a new piece. She would then rework the costumes piece by piece; her dancers learned to pin and sew with lightning speed.

Edythe Gilfond began to design costumes for Graham and her company in the late 1930s with *Deep Song* (1937), *American Lyric* (1937), *American Document* (1938), and *Every Soul Is a Circus* (1939). In the next decade, Gilfond provided Graham with some of her most legendary looks: the wide-sweeping skirt of the One Who Danced in *Letter to the World* (1940), the dark dress for *Death and Entrances* (1943), the Bride costume for *Appalachian Spring* (1944), and the Medea costume for *Cave of the Heart* (1946). In *Dark Meadow* (1946), Gilfond's costumes referred to the primitive and nonhuman quality of the dance. While not rooted in a particular time, the costumes—midriff-baring dark tops with sashed, two-tone skirts for the women and dark pants for the men—evoked Mexico's ancient past. Graham (as the One Who Seeks) wore a flame red dress.

When Graham's hands became too crippled by arthritis to construct her own costumes she turned to some new talents for creative input. Halston, the American fashion designer of the 1970s and 1980s noted for his use of luxurious, drapable fabrics, reworked the costumes for *Episodes* in 1979 and created the costumes for such late Graham works as *Acts of Light* (1981) and *The Rite of Spring* (1984).

The 1930s and 1940s were heady times for costume designers in modern dance. They were inventing a new art form as they went along. Pauline Lawrence (later Limón) was one of the chief costume designers of this period. Lawrence studied to be a pianist and joined the Denishawn company as a pianist in 1917. There she trained under Pearl Wheeler's direction and helped create the elaborate costumes so beloved by Ruth St. Denis. Lawrence then played piano for Martha Graham, the Doris Humphrey-Charles Weidman group, and eventually, for José Limón's company. Lawrence's most famous costumes were created for Limón, whom she married, and his dancers. Pauline Lawrence Limón designed and made the costumes for Limón's masterpiece, *The Moor's Pavane* (1949), using one or two elements such as a collar, sleeve, or belt to create a time frame for the work with simplicity and directness. Lawrence's costumes had no linings or hems in order to avoid restricting the movement of the dance. The torso of a dress was one piece of material and the fabric over the thigh was almost always flat. The movement of the dance and the idea behind it always suggested the material to be used and the color. Lawrence favored fabrics such as jersey (in wool, silk, cotton, or rayon) because of its ability to cling to the body, and crepes, muslin, and cotton.

Muslin, easily dyed or painted, was perfect for period costumes because it could be pleated, crinkled, or baked. Satin was avoided for almost all costumes by Lawrence except period costumes as it hampered the movement of the body. Metallic cloths were to be avoided at all cost because they distracted the attention of the audience. Lawrence bought the material for her costumes, dyed it if necessary, and cut and sewed the material into finished works. In dying costumes for a group dance, Lawrence varied each one slightly. The same dress would be the same color but with variations in shade. Lighting was always a consideration in the creation of costumes. According to Lawrence, the best results could be achieved only if lighting and color were considered together. She knew how lights and fabric could give depth to the stage. Lawrence's other designs included the costumes for *La Malinche* (1949) and *There Is a Time* (1956).

Betty Joiner's costumes for Hanya Holm's multisectioned *Trend* (1937) were models of simplicity and expressiveness. Joiner took into consideration how skipping and rocking steps as well as runs and leg swings would influence the flow of fabric. Joiner, a former dancer, sketched numerous dancers of the 1930s and 1940s while studying at the Bennington School of the Dance at Bennington College in Vermont. Her subjects included Martha Graham, Doris Humphrey, Charles Weidman, and Hanya Holm. Joiner created charts noting the movement of the dance and the expected response of fabric to the movement. For *Trend* Joiner dressed the all-female cast in rough fabric. The long dresses had fitted midriffs and tops with cap sleeves. The front of the skirts were deeply split for freedom of movement. Joiner varied the costumes for each section of the work: "Our Daily Bread" was costumed in monochromatic color, while "The Gates Are Desolate" section showed slightly more color and a slightly different look—skirts wrapped around to the side and light-colored blouses revealed dark fabric exposed at the midriff. "The Effete" had more elaborate dresses with vertical bands across the bodice. As the lead dancer in *Trend*, Holm wore a simple, long-sleeved, jersey dress and one with a short, elbow-length cape.

Pared-down costumes in jersey or silk did produce a purity of style in many choreographers. However, this design approach did not work for all. In the 1960s many modern dance choreographers looked to artists to help them form their vision of a dance piece. In 1954 painter Robert Rauschenberg became the resident costume and scenic designer for the Merce Cunningham Dance Group. There, he began to use people for his medium. For his early stage designs he posed dancers as part of the set and called them "live decor." Rauschenberg's designs for *Summerspace* (1958) consisted of a backdrop of pointillistic dots which were repeated on the unitard costumes of the dancers. He also designed for *Field Dances* (1963) and *Winterbranch* (1964) among others.

Rauschenberg's residency with Cunningham ended in 1964 but he has designed works for other choreographers since then. In 1979 he designed the sets and costumes for Trisha Brown's *Glacial Decoy;* this was followed by *Set & Reset* in 1985. For this work, Rauschenberg created sheer, square-cut tops and boxy, calf-length pants for the dancers. The fabric was covered with checkerboard designs, swirls, and latticework in white and charcoal gray.

Remy Charlip has had a varied career as a dancer, choreographer, designer, director, author, and illustrator. While a dancer with the Merce Cunningham company from 1951 to 1961 Charlip also designed costumes. Charlip is also a founding member of the Paper Bag Players. His costume designs include *Meditation* (1966) for which he also choreographed and danced. By the 1970s, costume designers such as Santo Loquasto were placing their stamp on modern dance. Loquasto first came to prominence as the costume designer for Twyla Tharp. He copied the practice garb of Tharp's dancers—unraveling sweaters, torn sweatpants, ripped T-shirts—and created a whole new, dance look. For *Sue's Leg* (1975), Loquasto created beige satin pants cropped off at the calf, short, boxy tops fitted at the wrists with contrasting material, and leg warmers. Tharp's dancers performed the work twice in the same evening, the first time wearing Loquasto's costumes, the second time wearing the practice clothes the dancers had rehearsed in. According to Tharp, the audience got to see the sweaty, gritty work behind the virtuosity. Loquasto was Tharp's costume designer for numerous works including *Push Comes to Shove* (1976), *Baker's Dozen* (1979), and *The Catherine Wheel* (1981). His costumes perfectly captured and enhanced the floppy and catch-it-if-you-can movements of Tharp's early works.

In recent years Loquasto designed costumes for Mark Morris' *Drink to Me Only with Thine Eyes* (1988), Dana Reitz's *Private Collection* (1995), *Unspoken Territory* (1995), a solo Reitz made for Mikhail Baryshnikov, and *Necessary Weather* (1993), a collaborative work with Reitz, lighting designer Jennifer Tipton and dancer Sara Rudner. In this last work, Loquasto's white costumes effectively caught and reflected Tipton's ever-changing light.

Publications

Books—

Blair, Fredrika, *Isadora: Portrait of the Artist as a Woman,* New York, 1986.
De Mille, Agnes, *Martha: The Life and Work of Martha Graham,* New York, 1991.
Graham, Martha, *Blood Memory: An Autobiography,* New York, 1991.
Joiner, Betty, *Costumes for the Dance,* New York, 1937.
Terry, Walter, *Miss Ruth,* New York, 1969.
Tharp, Twyla, *Push Comes to Shove: An Autobiography,* New York, 1992.

—Adriane Ruggiero

CRITICISM, AMERICAN

Written evaluation of American modern dance began appearing on the heels of the art form, and the earliest years of modern dance criticism in the United States are marked by the struggle to define the role and function of both the emerging art form and its critical discourse. The most celebrated artists of the solo dance movement caught the attention of American newspapers before and shortly after the turn-of-the-century: Loie Fuller's *Serpentine Dance* was singled out by mesmerized vaudeville critics in 1892; Isadora Duncan's early "dance illustrations" first made the society pages of the New York dailies in 1898; and Ruth St. Denis' "Temple Dances" were extensively covered by the *New York Times'* Sunday arts section in 1906. By the decade of the 1900s, reviews of the solo dance movement began appearing in ladies magazines and arts journals ranging in tone from *Cosmopolitan* ("Dancing and Pantomime," 1904) to *Theatre Arts Magazine* ("Note on the Isadora Duncan Dancers," 1917). In addition, two distinguished music critics, H.T. Parker (*Boston Evening-Transcript*) and Carl Van Vechten (*New York Times*) began contributing insightful and intelligent reviews of the emerging modern dance field.

It wasn't until the fall of 1927, however, that dance criticism emerged as a bona fide field of independent journalistic writing. As noted in *Spreading the Gospel of the Modern Dance: Newspaper Dance Criticism in the United States, 1850-1934:*

> Between September and November 1927, New York City's three leading dailies—the *New York World,* the *New York Herald Tribune,* and the *New York Times*—all hired full-time dance writers. In this brief space of two months, dance criticism in the American press was transformed from a haphazard and largely throwaway subspecies of music criticism to a specialized field of arts reporting and commentary.

In these early years of newspaper dance criticism, the three pioneer dance critics, Lucile Marsh, Mary F. Watkins, and John Martin, struggled collectively with several issues integral to the development and codification of a new art form: a) identifying the ontological status of modern dance; b) inventing a useful vocabulary to describe a purely visual form; and c) agreeing about the proper function of dance criticism: that is, should its style be primarily descriptive, evaluative, or prescriptive?

Of these struggles, the problem of identifying the ontological status of the modern dance has proven to be the most difficult for dance critics over the course of the 20th century. Tension over defining what the modern dance "is" probably started as soon as Isadora Duncan began making substantial philosophic and cultural claims for her "dance of the future," but it reached a crisis point with the controversy surrounding Duncan's use of Beethoven's *Seventh Symphony* in her American concert tours of 1908 and 1909. Male music critics of the period found Duncan's physical interpretation of Beethoven's masterpiece to be blasphemous and—in the words of the music critic for the *New York Post*—"too absurd for serious consideration." This tension between critics and creators over defining what is appropriate material for modern dance has continued. In 1957, *Dance Observer* critic Louis Horst responded to the debut of a minimalist work by Paul Taylor with a blank column, thus signaling his disapproval of Taylor's then-startling experimentations with form and content in the modern dance.

Since 1927 the extent to which one style of dance criticism is emphasized over another has often signaled important changes in the evolution of the discourse. By 1930 the three pioneer newspaper dance critics had largely settled into a uniquely prescriptive style of writing in which advocacy for modern dance artists and for acceptance of the form were foremost considerations. These critics wrote their reviews *to* and *for* the dance artists and were only peripherally concerned with the newspaper reader. By the mid-1930s, however, as the modern dance became more familiar (and thus acceptable) to the larger culture, this heavily prescriptive style was replaced with more traditional modes of arts reporting and reviewing. Critics offered evaluations of dance performances that were unquestionably written for a mainstream newspaper readership rather than for dance artists. Around this time, a wide range of dance journals began publication, including those devoted exclusively to the modern dance (*Dance Observer*) or to extensive coverage of politically motivated dance forms (*New Theatre*). In addition, by 1934 the *New York Times'* John Martin was the only full-time dance critic left on a New York daily, thus firmly establishing him as the most authoritative and influential dance critic in the U.S. and earning him the title "father of dance criticism." Other important critical voices from the prewar period include Margaret Lloyd (*Christian Science Monitor*), Walter Terry (*Boston Herald* and *New York Herald Tribune*) and Claudia Cassidy (*Chicago Sun*).

The World War II and postwar eras mark a significant dip in newspaper coverage of the modern dance, perhaps a reflection of more conservative tastes in the dance-going public and a loss of energy among modern dance artists. This period saw a clear divergence in career tracks between critics specializing in the modern dance versus those specializing in ballet. Among the latter, Edwin

Denby still managed to make significant contributions to the discourse surrounding the modern dance, especially in his writings for *Modern Music* and the *New York Herald Tribune.*

In the late 1950s and early 1960s, an avant-garde performance and visual arts culture emerged out of Greenwich Village that included a number of innovative dance artists working to expand the modern idiom. The most exciting critical response to this wave of postmodern dance activity was provided by Jill Johnston, dance critic for the *Village Voice.* Banes writes that Johnston, in pioneering a form later identified as "New Criticism," made several key contributions to the critical discourse, including the creation of a "personalized, descriptive criticism" that explored writing forms and strategies "analogous to those she wrote about: the found phrase paralleled the found objects of pop art and neodada, or the found movements of postmodern dance; stream-of-consciousness correlated to assemblage and improvisatory dance composition." Johnston's work as an art critic for *Art News* and her interest in a variety of performance art forms also encouraged a broader view of dance as a co-mingling art form influenced by and influencing of other avant-garde activity during the period.

The dance boom of the 1970s broadened the scope of dance awareness nationally and engendered the appointments of bona fide dance critics (as opposed to music critics assigned to cover dance concerts) on many regional newspapers. In New York, Deborah Jowitt's work at the *Village Voice* emphasized a highly literate and readable style of analysis, while a new generation of dance critics at the *New York Times* took the place of John Martin, who had retired in 1962 after more than 30 years as the paper of record's chief dance critic. During the 1980s a number of strong critical voices in a variety of publications began actively challenging the hegemony of the *Times,* including among others Jowitt, Arlene Croce, Burt Supree, Nancy Goldner and Marcia B. Siegel. This flurry of dance writing activity also included the formation of the Dance Critics Association, a member organization representing critics from all over the country and internationally. In addition, scores of dance specialty publications appeared ranging from the academic (*Dance Research*), to the practical (*Dance Teacher Now*), to the esoteric (*Contact Quarterly*).

Modern dance criticism at the end of the 20th century continues to struggle with the issues that confronted the pioneers of the form in 1927. In 1994, *New Yorker* dance critic Arlene Croce attacked a dance by Bill T. Jones on the grounds that it was "unreviewable" because of its subject matter. In *Still/Here,* Jones made a dance piece based on video tapes of terminally ill people discussing their situations. Responding to the extremely raw nature of the dance's content, Croce began her article by stating: "I have not seen Bill T. Jones's *Still/Here* and have no plans to review it" and went on to argue that because of its confessional/real-life nature, a work of this sort is "unintelligible as theatre" and thus not a work of art. The publicity and discussion generated by this statement once again brought to the surface fundamental questions for modern dance critics and artists alike: what is modern dance, and what is the role and function of the critic in interpreting this evolving form?

Publications

Books—

Conner, Lynne, *Spreading the Gospel of the Modern Dance: Newspaper Dance Criticism in the United States, 1850-1934,* Pittsburgh, 1997.

Croce, Arlene, *Afterimages,* New York, 1977.
Holmes, Olive, *Motion Arrested: Dance Reviews of H.T. Parker,* Middletown, CT, 1982.
Johnston, Jill, *Marmalade Me,* New York, 1971.
Jowitt, Deborah, *The Dance in Mind: Profiles and Reviews, 1976-1983,* Boston, 1985.
Siegel, Marcia B., *The Shapes of Change: Images of American Dance,* Boston, 1979.
Theodores, Diana, *First We Take Manhattan: Four American Women and the New York School of Dance Criticism,* Amsterdam, 1996.
Van Vechten, Carl, *The Dance Writings of Carl Van Vechten,* edited and with an introduction by Paul Padgette, New York, 1974.

Articles—

Croce, Arlene, "Discussing the Undiscussable," *New Yorker,* 26 December 1994.
Marsh, Lucille, "Criticizing the Critics," *American Dancer,* January 1934.

—Lynne Conner

CRY

Choreography: Alvin Ailey
Music: "Something about John Coltrane" (Alice Coltrane); "Been on a Train" (Laura Nyro); "Right On, Be Free" (Voices of East Harlem)
Lighting Design: Chenault Spence
First Production: City Center, New York, 4 May 1971
Original Dancer: Judith Jamison
Other performances include: Consuelo Atlas, Deborah Chase, Danielle Gee, Deborah Manning, Renee Robinson, Dwana Smallwood, Nasha Thomas-Schmitt, Donna Wood

Publications

Articles—

Barnes, Clive, "Judith Jamison's Triumph: Ailey's *Cry* Depicts the Black Woman's Ordeal," *New York Times,* 5 May 1971.
Finkel, Anita, "The Road and the River," *New Dance Review,* Winter 1994.

*   *   *

"If I have 20 yards of fabric, I love it. I don't like something on me that doesn't have a life of its own, that could say what it has to say even if I stand still," dancer Judith Jamison confessed in her autobiography, *Dancing Spirit.* She could have been talking about the costume for *Cry,* Alvin Ailey's 1971 solo for her, which she performed in a voluminous white skirt improvised at the last minute from the "Wading in the Water" section of *Revelations.* Even audiences who have never seen a production of Ailey's celebrated piece will recognize its original interpreter in her most famous role. The innumerable photographs of the regal dancer in *Cry,* her yards-wide ruffled skirt swirling, dipping and extending her magnificent body, have become among the most famous in modern dance. The piece has since been successfully interpreted by other women from the Alvin Ailey company.

Judith Jamison performing *Cry*, 1979. Photograph © Johan Elbers.

According to Jamison, *Cry* had its origins in "Bo Masekela," her solo for *Masekela Language,* a work Ailey had premiered two years earlier, in 1969. The description of "Masekela" as one of "mounting tension and then release" certainly can be applied to *Cry*'s figure of a woman whose indomitable spirit cannot be quenched. The piece is unsparing in its depiction of dejection, pain, and despair but also buoyant in its belief in the power of the human spirit. The choreographer had dedicated *Cry* to "Black women everywhere—especially our mothers," a dedication whose emotional weight was so intimidating to Jamison that, had she known about it, she "would have dropped the cloth [a prop] and left the stage *immediately*."

Cry became not only a personal triumph for Jamison but has remained one of the company's most requested pieces. It was an immediate success; at its premiere it garnered a 10-minute ovation. Clive Barnes described it as having crystallized "the story of black woman in America told with an elliptic and cryptic poetry and a passionate economy of feeling." Barnes saw in *Cry*'s three sections "African roots, urban despair and finally black freedom." Marcia Siegel described them as moving "from oppression through sorrow and pain to a kind of anguished liberation." Jamison herself thought of *Cry* as celebrating life and beauty, being beset by "the devastations of what's going on in the world" and finally tuning in to "the strengths of women who have endured since the beginning of time." Like every superior work of art, *Cry* transcends the immediacy of its circumstances to reveal something universal about the human condition.

One of Ailey's most tightly organized works, *Cry* also beautifully illustrates the fusion of modern, African-derived jazz and ballet styles toward which he had been striving since his days with Lester Horton. Sky-high extensions and deep arabesques are as much at home in *Cry* as head rolls, whipping hips, and oscillations. Particularly noteworthy is Ailey's expressive use of the arms and the torso. *Cry* derives its emotional force, however, from the intensity and clarity of its movement language with which Ailey created a complex picture of a woman on her journey through life.

Cry starts with the presentation of a simple prop. Priestess-like, the dancer approaches the audience with a white cloth, draped over her arms, which she deposits at the edge of the stage. It becomes a bed to be straightened, a rag to use scrubbing floors, a turban to be flung on impetuously, and constraints from which to escape. Every subsequent movement, whether it be ground-hugging plies, arms that strain out of their sockets with clenched fists or fluttering hands, legs defiantly planting themselves or kicking the sky, tells of another step taken toward some kind of liberation. Physically the piece also gradually expands to conclude with a series of triumphant leaps and space-eating turns. At the end the dancer quietly walks off, her head held higher than we have ever seen it before.

—Rita Felciano

CUMMINGS, Blondell

American modern dancer, choreographer, and educator

Born: 1949 in South Carolina. **Education:** Graduated from New York University. **Career:** Performed with the New York Chamber Group, Meredith Monk, Liz Keen, and Repertory Dances; was an original member of Meredith Monk/The House; appeared in *The Photographer Far From the Truth* by Philip Glass; debut as a choreographer with *Point of Reference*, 1971; founded Cycle Arts Foundation, a multidisciplinary arts collaborative that incorporates dance, theater, and visual, media, and literary arts into workshops, media, and performance, 1978; her work *Commitment—Two Portraits* (consisting of *Chicken Soup* and *Nun)* premiered on PBS' *Alive from Off-Center*, 1988; profiled in Michael Blackwood's *Dancing on the Edge;* taught at the City College of New York, Lincoln Center Institute, Cornell University, New York University, Wesleyan College, and Hofstra College; toured throughout the U.S., Europe, and Asia; appeared at the Festival Mondial du Theatre, the Vienna Festival, Paranarrative Series at P.S. 1 (New York City), Dance Theatre Workshop, Art on the Beach, Danspace, Black Dance America (at BAM), Hong Kong Arts Center, and Shanghai Ballet Academy. **Awards:** Fellowships from the National Endowment for the Arts and the New York State Council on the Arts; her video *A Visual Diary* won the Ithaca Video Festival Award.

Works

1971	*Point of Reference*
1980	*The Ladies and Me (A Visual Diary)*
	A Friend w/Frank Bantle, Caridad Garcia, and Ronn Pratt
	A Friend II
1983	*Food for Thought* w/Trinket Monsod
1984	*The Art of War/Nine Situations*
1986	*A Nun Story*
1987	*To Colette, Too*, Blondell Cummings and Performers
1991	*Omedele and Guiseppe* (part of *Relationships: Intimate and Not so Intimate*)
1995	*Women in the Dunes* w/Junko Kikuchi (based on the Kobo Abe novel)

Other works include: *The Relationship Series, Basic Strategies I through V, Cycle, He Searched from Wall to Wall, Passing Images,* and *3B49.*

Publications

On CUMMINGS: articles—

Dixon, Brenda, "Blondell Cummings: *The Ladies and Me,*" *The Drama Review*, December 1980.

Dunning, Jennifer, Review of *The Art of War, New York Times*, 15 November 1984.

———, Review of *Omadele and Guiseppe, New York Times*, 9 December 1991.

Goler, Veta, "Living with the Doors Open: An Interview with Blondell Cummings," *High Performance*, Spring/Summer 1995.

Films and Videotapes

A Visual Diary, 1980.
Commitment—Two Portraits (consisting of *Chicken Soup* and *Nun*), for PBS' *Alive from Off-Center,* 1988.
Dancing on the Edge, film, dir. Michael Blackwood.

*   *   *

Blondell Cummings is noted for choreography that blends dialogue, mime, and video, as well as personal reflections into unique, often virtuosic pieces. Cummings does not isolate her experiences as a black woman from other cultures; rather, she chooses to explore the similarities and differences between her culture and others to arrive at some universal truth. A gifted actor and forceful personality, the compact and strong Cummings has a sure theatrical sense. She often collaborates with other performers including Gregory Tate, Carole Bovoso, George Lewis, Patricia Jones, and Shirley Clark. She has choreographed both solo and group works.

In 1983 she premiered one of her most vivid and well-known theater pieces, *Food for Thought*, at the Bessie Schönberg Theater in New York City. *Food* consists of six performance pieces united, unsurprisingly, by the theme of food. Each one is separated by a brief blackout. In *Chicken Soup*, Cummings wields a frying pan while she chats, howls, and laughs to herself in a display of astuteness, timing, and power. Her articulate hands and torso combined with an expressive face enable her to impart nuance to practically every movement. In *Meat and Potatoes* Cummings, dressed as a construction worker, chews on a sandwich and drinks from a thermos. Reviewing the work in the *Village Voice* in 1983, critic Deborah Jowitt noted that although Cummings' dances often seemed profound, other times, Jowitt couldn't pick up on anything but "carefully wrought surface." Other critics found Cummings' *Food* a confirmation of her outstanding talent for characterization. Writing in *Saturday Review*, Nancy Goldner stated that "Cummings's opaque declarations add up to a shimmering summation of a life."

Emotional states interest Cummings and inform her work. So do the ways relationships join people together. In December 1991, Cummings performed her piece *Omadele and Guiseppe* at the Danspace Project of St. Mark's Church in New York City. This work, part of a program titled *Relationships: Intimate and Not So Intimate*, explored the subject of interracial marriage. Cummings danced the role of Omadele to Tom Thayer's Guiseppe. The couple carries out their combative relationship against a backdrop of dialogue, music, slide projections, and a fold-out house. The work incorporates pointed anecdotes in its presentation of two people who bring the baggage of their own backgrounds to their married life. The two dancers look back upon their own childhoods with unsentimental eyes and are able to suggest the uneasiness that often rests in marriages—interracial and otherwise—despite the love, intelligence, and sensitivity of the partners.

In May 1980 Cummings performed several dances including *The Ladies and Me (A Visual Diary)* and *A Friend*. In *Ladies*, Cummings found a nearly ideal outlet for her emotive powers. This piece evokes the feelings expressed by several famous black female singers from the 1930s to the 1970s. Cummings used several props to suggest a woman recollecting her past life. Dressed in a robe, she yawns, stretches, and moves from a chair to a table. Gradually working the kinks out, she starts to shake and jerk and then, as the music plays, sways from side to side. This movement gives way to jumps for joy as she transforms herself from middle-age to youth and back. Her deep contractions, undulations, and vibrations reflect the moodiness of the music. Cummings' movement combined facial expressions, mime, and naturalistic acting techniques with rhythmic dance impulses that, according to dance critic Marcia B. Siegel, "seem to be large abstractions of physical feeling-states, like blown-up photographs." Critics praised Cummings' ability to execute each movement with great care and her chameleon-like quality for changing character.

In *A Friend* Cummings employs several dancers—Frank Bantle, Amy Berkman, Caridad Garcia, and Ronn Pratt—to explore male-female friendships. The dancers use video, live and taped dialogue, dance, and mime. Critic Robert Greskovic, writing in *Dance Magazine* in September 1980, noted that "Cummings has managed to reveal personal, self-analytic perceptions in a way that does not embarrass her or her audience." Later that year, Cummings presented excerpts from *A Friend II* at the Black Theatre Alliance. This was indeed a reworking of *A Friend,* but displayed Cummings in another mood. She moved around her imagined apartment and seemed to be cleaning up after a party. As she tossed out the remnants of the festivities she seemed to recall the friends she had just entertained. Slides showed the faces of her friends and a shadow-play amusingly explored the intimacies that exist between friends. Reviewer Burt Supree of the *Village Voice* noted the "secure feeling of connectedness and warmth welling out of these images."

One to find inspiration in everyday activities as well the unusual, for another work, Cummings used Chinese general Sun-tzu's ancient treatise on the proper techniques for making war to create a new theater/dance piece in 1984. Titled *The Art of War/Nine Situations*, Cummings and collaborator Jessica Hagedorn, explored in particular, Sun-tzu's theme to "Make your everyday stance your combat stance." Cummings understood the wide-ranging applications of this statement. She then applied it to everyday life in several vignettes. A cast of characters including Laurie Carlos, Jessica Hagedorn, Evangeline Johns, Miny Levine, Trinket Monsod, John Rusk, Leslie Yancy, and Ralph Lemon appeared as soldiers, spies, businessmen, a wife, a child, and a missionary nun. In one

Blondell Cummings with Tom Thayer in *3B49,* 1988. Photograph © Beatriz Schiller.

section, Cummings performed a bouncing solo to a tarantella while in another she used her arms to convey a sense of rage and doom.

In December 1995 Cummings collaborated with Japanese dancer and choreographer Junko Kikuchi for *Women in the Dunes* a so-called "visual novel" inspired by the Kobo Abe novel of the same name. In this work, the text of the Abe novel is projected onto the arch of the Japan Center's stage. Mounds of rice, dry reeds, hats, bowls, and small tables cover the stage. The primary set decoration is a straw-roofed hut. The music was provided by jazz cellist Diedre L. Murray and a sextet of musicians playing traditional African and Japanese instruments. Tapes of nature sounds were also used to set the mood. Cummings and Kikuchi devised a work divided into 12 individual chapters each with its own moments of visual poetry. In one chapter, Cummings and Kikuchi eat together in the styles of their own cultures: Cummings from a bowl in the style of Africans, Kikuchi using chopsticks as in the style of her native Japan. In another section, Cummings danced a bold and joyous dance with raffia fans while Kikuchi danced a more sedate, measured dance while holding a folded paper fan. Sometimes the text of the Abe novel was read on tape. While some critics seem puzzled about what to call Cummings' work—"Is it dance?" being the most common question asked—most find her work thrillingly theatrical and often moving.

—Adriane Ruggiero

CUNNINGHAM, James

Canadian dancer, choreographer, and educator

Born: Toronto, Canada. **Education:** Studied drama and dance with Dorothy Goulding; graduated from the University of Toronto; graduated from the London Academy of Dramatic Arts; worked in theater in England. **Career:** Created first dances while in England, then returned to North America, 1965; went to the Martha Graham School in New York City before joining the Dance Theatre Workshop; founded James Cunningham's Acme Dance Company, 1969; company-in-residence as part of the Artists-in-Schools Program of the National Endowment of the Arts (NEA); has taught at Pratt Institute, Brooklyn, New York. **Awards:** Received a John Simon Guggenheim fellowship, 1971.

Works

1968	*Father Comes Grandly Down and Eats Baby*
1969	*Lauren's Dream* w/Lauren Persichetti
1970	*The Junior Birdsmen,* Connecticut College Summer Festival
	Lions and Roaring Tigers
	Evelyn the Elevator
	Mr. Fox's Garden
1971	*The Clue in the Hidden Staircase*
1972	*Treasures from the Donald Duck Collection*
1973	*Everybody in Bed*
1974	*Apollo and Dionysus: Cheek to Cheek*
	Dancing with Maisie Paradocks
1975	*The Ham Show: Isis and Osiris* w/Lauren Persichetti
1979	*The Attic Window*
1986	*The Road to the Bay*

Other works include: *Rainbow Bridge, Mr. Fox Asleep,* and others.

Publications

On CUNNINGHAM: articles—

Dunning, Jennifer, "A Blithe Spirit With Sober Credits," *New York Times*, 22 January 1978.
Onodo, Karen, Review, *Dance Magazine*, April 1986.
Robertson, Michael, Review, *Dance Magazine*, January 1980.
Smith, Amanda, Review, *Dance Magazine*, June 1978.

* * *

Dance observers who saw James Cunningham as the "Spectre of the Rose" in *Dancing with Maisie Paradocks* (1974) can never forget the sight: the elastic-bodied Cunningham dressed in large cabbage roses and leaves with a big bow-like flower on the top of his head, flower clenched in one hand and in full leap towards who knows where. The image both echoed Nijinsky's famous leap and parodied it, but with gentle good humor. Such is the essence of much of Cunningham's work. His dances are highly theatrical mixes of music, dance, and the spoken word as in *Rainbow Bridge*. This work opens with Cunningham recollecting his youth in Canada during World War II and then moves into a fantasyland inhabited by animals and fairytale characters. Some reviewers have used the term "collage-like" to describe Cunningham's style. Others have called him a comic dancer and choreographer who tacks on jokes and allusions to a core of dance. His dances are by all means dreamlike, whimsical, and comical. In fact, Cunningham has often used dreams uncovered in therapy sessions as material for his work. He also invites his audiences to join in the dance. Growing up in straight-laced Toronto in the 1940s made the young Cunningham want to explore a world of fantasy in which he could act out flowers, animals, spirits, men, and women. As the head of his own Acme Dance Company, Cunningham is its best dancer. He alone seems completely at home in the wide-eyed, child-like humor which epitomizes his work. Although he describes his work as improvisational, Cunningham does give it structure through a careful editing process.

Cunningham will often make references to famous ballets such as the Dying Swan or *Afternoon of a Faun* and parody them. In *Dancing with Maisie Paradocks*, Cunningham finds ample food for his special brand of humor. The work begins simply enough—six dancers in white sheets chant and dance in a circle. They quickly give way to dancers in animal masks and a woman manipulating a parasol. Cowboys, businessmen, a man dressed as a bride, a woman dressed as a dog, and a manic soldier performing a drill routine make appearances in various vignettes. The hilarious goings-on reach a climax when the "Spectre" (inspired by the *Spectre of the Rose*) enters and comes face to face with the slumbering soldier. They dance together for a while and the flower-creature leaps into the soldier's arms before leaping off. The rest of the cast enter and dance various confrontational encounters. The work concludes with the entire cast clad in their white sheets doing a step in unison. *Maisie* explores the concept of opposites, in gender, for example, and in issues of strength and weakness. Writer Don McDonagh called the mood of *Maisie Paradocks* "manic," but also found it a brilliant mixture of recitation, dance, song, and mime.

In a work from 1979, *The Attic Window*, Cunningham continued to receive inspiration from the *Spectre of the Rose*. Here, the Spectre visits a general in a nightmare, and they dance together. In the same work, Cunningham acts out the role of a professor who meets a faun and falls in love. Other absurdity mixed with satire is in *Mr. Fox Asleep*, where

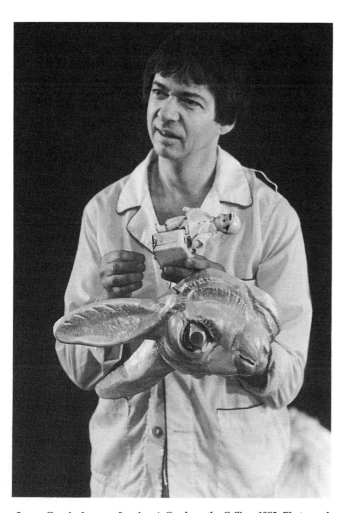

James Cunningham performing *A Crack on the Ceiling,* 1982. Photograph © Johan Elbers.

Cunningham provides a wicked interpretation of a Martha Graham dancer using his cupped hands to walk across the floor like dainty feet.

James Cunningham was born in Toronto, Canada. He studied acting and dancing from the age of eight with Dorothy Goulding and began to appear on Canadian television while still in his early teens. He received degrees in literature and drama from the University of Toronto and later moved to England where he studied at the London Academy of Dramatic Arts. After graduation from drama school, Cunningham toured England with an improvisational group whose mission was to bring dance and improvisational theater into British schools. He also worked as an assistant director with BBC television. Modern dance interested Cunningham and after five years in London, he moved to New York City to study at the Martha Graham School. After a year and a half of studies with Graham, Cunningham left to work with Art Bauman of the Dance Theatre Workshop. Cunningham also spent a year in Stratford, Ontario, where he took part in the Shakespeare Festival. It was an excellent grounding for an aspiring choreographer in that Cunningham taught, set dances, directed, and acted. The experience made it clear that these were all activities he wanted to combine in his own work.

Upon his return to Dance Theatre Workshop, Cunningham started to work on his own dances. The first major showing of his choreography took place in 1970. A chance encounter with the head of the dance department at Connecticut College led to the debut of his first major work, *The Junior Birdsmen,* at Connecticut College's summer festival. In this highly eclectic work, Cunningham mixes verbal jokes and steps from *Swan Lake* and references to Egyptian and Hindu myths.

Cunningham has taught at Pratt Institute in Brooklyn, New York, and has been involved in promoting arts in schools. To that end, he served as a member of the artists' advisory board of the federally funded Artists-in-Schools Program. His Acme Dance Company was in residence in upstate New York in the late 1970s presenting lecture demonstrations using movement as a means of teaching general curriculum. Cunningham has also been involved in training teachers to use movement as a teaching tool, as well as rehearsing works and performing with children in school settings. His ability to inspire children is one of his most important accomplishments.

Cunningham explained his choreographic drive in a 1978 interview with Jennifer Dunning: "I've wanted to do pieces that would be available to people as people, not just to dance audiences." As a result, Cunningham often invites nondancers to take part in his works; it's his way of making people feel attached to art. Cunningham started out improvising steps and movements in a free-associative style and from within this free-form atmosphere he was able to conjure up images from many sources. In his work from 1986—*The Road to the Bay*—Cunningham devised a duet for two dancers dressed in pajamas, for example. Nothing seems too remote as inspiration for James Cunningham's unique brand of comic dance theater.

—Adriane Ruggiero

CUNNINGHAM, Merce

American dancer, choreographer, company director, and video/filmmaker

Born: Mercier Philip Cunningham, 16 April 1919 in Centralia, Washington. **Education:** Centralia High School; studied tap and ballroom dancing with Maude M. Barrett; also attended George Washington University, Washington, D.C.; Cornish School, Seattle; Bennington College School of Dance summer sessions, and Mills College, Oakland, California. **Career:** Dancer, Martha Graham Dance Company, 1939-45; first independent choreography (with Jean Erdman and Nina Fonaroff), 1942; first solo concert with composer John Cage, 1944; founder, Merce Cunningham Dance Company, Black Mountain College, North Carolina, 1953; first tour of U.S., 1955; first world tour, 1964; began annual seasons at City Center Theater, New York, 1973; collaborated on dance videos from 1974, first with Charles Atlas, later with Elliot Caplan; appeared on PBS' *Dance in America* series, 1977; directed *Points in Space* (with Elliot Caplan) for the BBC, 1986; subject of *Cage/Cunningham,* film portrait (dir. Caplan, 1991). **Awards:** John Simon Guggenheim Foundation fellowships, 1954 and 1959; *Dance Magazine* Award, 1960; honorary D. Litt., University of Illinois, 1972; Samuel H. Scripps/American Dance Festival Award for lifetime achievement, 1982; Commander of the Order, French Ministry of Culture, 1982; Award of Honor, Mayor of New York, 1983; honorary member of American Academy and Institute of Arts and Letters, 1984; MacArthur Foundation fellowship, 1985; Kennedy Center Honors, 1985; Laurence Olivier Award for *Pictures,* London, 1985; Prague D'Or, Prague International Television Festival award for *Points in Space,* 1986; New York Dance and Performance Award ("Bessie"), 1986 (with Cage), 1993; Algur H. Meadows Award, Southern

Methodist University, Dallas, Texas, 1987; Legion d'honneur, 1989; National Medal of Arts, Washington, D.C., 1990; Digital Dance Premier Award, London, 1990; Award of Merit, Association of Performing Arts, New York, 1990; Wexner Prize with John Cage, Wexner Center for the Arts, Ohio State University, 1993; Medal of Honor, Universidad Complutense of Madrid, 1993; Dance and Performance Award for *Events*, London, 1993; ISPAA/Tiffany Award for Outstanding Contribution to Dance, New York, 1993; "Best of Show" award, Dance on Camera Festival, New York, for *Beach Birds for Camera*, 1993; Grand Prize IMZ Dance Screen Fesitval, Frankfurt, for *Beach Birds for Camera*, 1993; Académie des Beaux-Arts/Studio Adaptation for *Beach Birds for Camera*, 1994; Grand Prix International Vidéo Danse award, for *Beach Birds for Camera,* Stockholm, 1994; Honorary D.F.A., Wesleyan University, Middletown, Connecticut, 1995; Lion d'Or, Venice Biennale, 1995.

Roles

1939   Acrobat (cr) in *Every Soul Is a Circus* (Graham), Martha Graham Company, New York

1940   Christ Figure (cr) in *El Penitente* (Graham), Martha Graham Company, New York

          March (cr) in *Letter to the World* (Graham), Martha Graham Company, New York

1941   Pegasus (cr) in *Punch and Judy* (Graham), Martha Graham Company, New York

1943   Poetic Beloved (cr) in *Deaths and Entrances* (Graham), Martha Graham Company, New York

1944   Revivalist (cr) in *Appalachian Spring* (Graham), Martha Graham Company, New York

1948   Jonas, a Mechanical Monkey in *The Ruse of Medusa*, Black Mountain College, North Carolina

Works (all works premiered in New York, and, from 1953 onward, for the Merce Cunningham Dance Company unless otherwise noted)

1942   *Seeds of Brightness* w/Jean Erdman (mus. Lloyd), Bennington, Vermont

          Credo in Us w/Jean Erdman (mus. Cage), Bennington, Vermont

          Ad Lib w/Jean Erdman (mus. Tucker; then Cage from 1946), Bennington, Vermont

Merce Cunningham with dancers in *Trackers,* 1991. Photograph © Johan Elbers.

Renaissance Testimonials (mus. Powers), solo, Bennington, Vermont

Totem Ancestor (mus. Cage), solo, Humphrey-Weidman Studio

1943   *In the Name of Holocaust* (mus. Cage), solo, Chicago

Shimmera (mus. Cage), solo, Chicago

The Wind Remains (mus. Bowles), Zarzuela after Garcia Lorca, Cunningham, Erdman and others

1944   *Triple-Paced* (mus. Cage), solo

Root of an Unfocus (mus. Cage), solo

Tossed as It Is Untroubled (mus. Cage), solo

The Unavailable Memory of (mus. Cage), solo

Spontaneous Earth (mus. Cage), solo

Four Walls (mus. Cage), dance-play, Perry-Mansfield Workshop, Steamboat Springs, Colorado

Idyllic Song (mus. Satie, arranged Cage), solo, Richmond, Virginia

1945   *Mysterious Adventure* (mus. Cage), solo

Experiences (mus. Cage, Gearhart), solo

1946   *The Encounter* (mus. Cage), solo

Invocation to Vahakn (mus. Hovhaness), solo

Fast Blues (mus. Baby Dodds), solo

The Princess Zondilda and Her Entourage (mus. Haieff)

1947   *The Seasons* (mus. Cage), Ballet Society

The Open Road (mus. Harrison), solo

Dromenon (mus. Cage)

1948   *Dream* (mus. Cage), solo

Dances in *The Ruse of Medusa* (mus. and libretto Satie), Black Mountain College, North Carolina

A Diversion (mus. Cage), Black Mountain College, North Carolina

Orestes (mus. Cage), solo, Black Mountain College, North Carolina

1949   *Effusions avant l'heure* (later called *Games*, also *Trio*) (mus. Cage), Paris

Amores (mus. Cage), duet, Cunningham and LeClerc, Paris

Duet (for Betty Nichols and Milorad Miskovitch), Garden Fête, Paris

Two Step (mus. Satie), solo, New York City Dance Theatre

1950   *Pool of Darkness* (mus. Weber)

Before Dawn, solo

Waltz (mus. Satie), Louisiana State University student group, Baton Rouge

Rag-Time Parade (mus. Satie), Louisiana State University, Baton Rouge

Waltz (mus. Satie), solo

1951   *Sixteen Dances for Soloist and Company of Three* (mus. Cage), Millbrook, New Jersey

Variation (mus. Feldman), solo, Seattle, Washington

Boy Who Wanted to Be a Bird, solo, Martha's Vineyard, Massachusetts

1952   *Suite of Six Short Dances* (mus. various, arranged Jennerjahn), solo, Black Mountain College, North Carolina

Excerpts from Symphonie pour un homme seul (later called *Collage*) (mus. Schaeffer, Henry), Creative Arts Festival of Brandeis University, Waltham, Massachusetts

Les Noces (mus. Stravinsky), Creative Arts Festival of Brandeis University, Waltham, Massachusetts

Theater Piece (by John Cage; mus. Tudor), Black Mountain College, North Carolina

Suite by Chance (mus. Wolff), Urbana, Illinois

Solo Suite in Space and Time (mus. Cage), solo, Baton Rouge, Louisiana

Demonstration Piece, Louisiana State University student group, Baton Rouge

Epilogue (mus. Satie), Louisiana State University, Baton Rouge

Banjo (mus. Gottschalk), Black Mountain College, North Carolina

Dime a Dance (mus. various, arranged Tudor), Black Mountain College, North Carolina

Septet (mus. Satie), Black Mountain College, North Carolina

Untitled Solo (mus. Wolff), Black Mountain College, North Carolina

Fragments (mus. Boulez)

1954   *Minutiae* (mus. Cage), Brooklyn

1955   *Springweather and People* (mus. Brown), Annandale-on-Hudson, New York

1956   *Lavish Escapade* (mus. Wolff), solo, South Bend, Indiana

Galaxy (mus. Brown), South Bend, Indiana

Suite for Five in Space and Time (later called *Suite for Five*) (mus. Cage), South Bend, Indiana

Nocturnes (mus. Satie), Jacob's Pillow Dance Festival, Massachusetts

1957   *Changeling* (mus. Wolff), solo, Brooklyn

Labyrinthian Dances (mus. Hauer), Brooklyn

Picnic Polka (mus. Gottschalk), Brooklyn

1958   *Collage III* (mus. Schaeffer, Henry), solo, Pittsburgh

Antic Meet (mus. Cage), New London, Connecticut

Summerspace (mus. Feldman), New London, Connecticut

Night Wandering (mus. Nilsson), duet, Royal Opera House, Stockholm

1959   *From the Poems of the White Stone* (mus. Chou Wen-Chung), Urbana, Illinois

Gambit for Dancers and Orchestra (mus. Johnston), Urbana, Illinois

Rune (mus. Wolff), New London, Connecticut

1960   *Theater Piece* (mus. Cage), duet, Composers' Showcase

Crises (mus. Nancarrow), New London, Connecticut

Hands Birds (mus. Brown), Carolyn Brown solo, Venice

Waka (mus. Ichiyanagi), Carolyn Brown solo, Venice

Music Walk with Dancers (mus. Cage), duet, Venice

1961   *Suite de Danses*, Canadian Broadcasting Corporation (CBC), Montreal

Aeon (mus. Cage), Montreal

1963   *Field Dances* (mus. Cage), Los Angeles

Story (mus. Ichiyanagi), Los Angeles

1964   *Open Session*, solo, Hartford, Connecticut

Paired (mus. Cage), duet, Hartford, Connecticut

Winterbranch (mus. Young), Hartford, Connecticut

Cross Currents (mus. Nancarrow, arranged Cage), London

Museum Event no. 1, Vienna

1965   *Variations V* (mus. Cage)

How to Pass, Kick, Fall and Run (mus. Cage), Chicago

1966   *Place* (mus. Mumma), Saint-Paul de Vence

1967   *Scramble* (mus. Ichiyanagi), Chicago

1968   *Rainforest* (mus. Tudor), Buffalo

Walkaround Time (mus. Behrman), Buffalo

1969   *Canfield* (mus. Oliveros), Rochester

1970   *Tread* (mus. Wolff), Brooklyn

Second Hand (mus. Cage), Brooklyn

Signals (mus. Tudor, Mumma, Cage), Paris

Objects (mus. Lucier), Brooklyn

1971   *Loops* (mus. Mumma), solo, Museum of Modern Art
1972   *Landrover* (mus. Cage, Mumma, Tudor), Brooklyn
       TV Rerun (mus. Mumma), Brooklyn
       Borst Park (mus. Wolff), Brooklyn
1973   *Un jour ou deux* (mus. Cage), Paris Opera Ballet
1975   *Exercise Piece*
       Changing Steps (mus. Cage), Detroit
       Rebus (mus. Behrman), Detroit
       Solo (mus. Cage), Detroit
       Sounddance (mus. Tudor), Detroit
1976   *Torse* (mus. Amacher), Princeton, New Jersey
       Squaregame (mus. Kosugi), Adelaide, Australia
1977   *Travelogue* (mus. Cage)
       Inlets (mus. Cage), Seattle
1978   *Exercise Piece I*
       Exercise Piece II (mus. Cage), Toronto
       Exchange (mus. Tudor)
       Tango (mus. Cage), solo
1979   *Roadrunners* (mus. Tone), Durham, North Carolina
1980   *Exercise Piece III* (mus. Cage)
       Duets (mus. Cage)
       Fielding Sixes (mus. Cage), London
1981   *10's with Shoes* (mus. Kalve)
       Gallopade (mus. Kosugi), London
1982   *Trails* (mus. Cage)
       Quartet (mus. Tudor), Paris
1983   *Inlets 2* (mus. Cage), Lille-Roubaix
       Roaratorio (mus. Cage), Lille-Roubaix
1984   *Pictures* (mus. Behrman)
       Doubles (mus. Kosugi), Durham, North Carolina
       Phrases (mus. Tudor), Angers
       Native Green (mus. King)
       Arcade (mus. Cage), Pennsylvania Ballet, Philadelphia
1986   *Grange Eve* (mus. Kosugi)
1987   *Fabrications* (mus. Pimenta), Minneapolis
       Shards (mus. Tudor)
       Carousel (mus. Kosugi), Jacob's Pillow, Massachusetts
1988   *Eleven* (mus. Ashley)
       Five Stone (mus. Cage, Tudor), Berlin
       Five Stone Wind (mus. Cage, Kosugi, Tudor), Avignon
1989   *Cargo X* (mus. Kosugi), Austin, Texas
       Field and Figures (mus. Tcherepnin), Minneapolis
       August Pace (mus. Pugliese), Berkeley, California
       Inventions (mus. Cage), Berkeley, California
1990   *Polarity* (mus. Tudor)
1991   *Neighbors* (mus. Kosugi)
       Trackers (mus. Pimenta)
       Beach Birds (mus. Cage), Zurich
       Loosestrife (mus. Pugliese), Paris
1992   *Change of Address* (mus. Zimmerman), Austin, Texas

Publications

By CUNNINGHAM: books—

Changes: Notes on Choreography, edited by Frances Starr, New York, 1968.
Le danseur et la danse, entretiens avec Jacqueline Lesschaeve, Paris, 1980; as *The Dancer and the Dance,* Merce Cunningham in conversation with J. Lesschaeve, London and New York, 1985.

By CUNNINGHAM: articles—

"Space, Time and Dance," *trans/formation,* 1952.
"The Impermanent Art," *7 Arts,* 1955.
"A Collaborative Process between Music and Dance," *TriQuarterly 54,* Spring, 1982.

On CUNNINGHAM: books— (See also General Bibliography)

Adam, Judy (ed.), *Dancers on a Plane: Cage/Cunningham/Johns,* London, 1989.
Croce, Arlene, *Going to the Dance,* New York, 1982.
———, *Sight Lines,* New York, 1987.
De Gubernatis, Raphael, *Cunningham,* Paris, 1990.
Denby, Edwin, *Looking at the Dance,* New York, 1949.
Klosty, James (ed.), *Merce Cunningham,* New York, 1975.
Tomkins, Calvin, *The Bride and the Bachelors,* New York, 1968.

On CUNNINGHAM: articles—

Acocella, Joan, "The Quality of Merce," *Harper's Bazaar,* March 1994.
Cohen, Selma Jeanne, ed., "Time to Walk in Space," *Dance Perspectives 34,* Summer, 1968.
"High-Wired Act," *Inc.,* 17 September 1996.

Films and Videotapes

Choreographed by Cunningham—

Story (dir. Seppala), Finnish Broadcasting Company, 1964.
Variations V (dir. Arnbom), Studio Hamburg, Nordeutscher Rundfunk, 1966.
Assemblage, KQED-TV, San Francisco, 1968.
Walkaround Time (dir. Atlas), 1973.
Westbeth (dir. Atlas), 1975.
Video Triangle (part of event for television, dir. Brockway), WNET-TV, 1976.
Squaregame Video (dir. Atlas), 1976.
Blue Studio: Five Segments (dir. Atlas & Cunningham), WNET-TV lab, 1976.
Event for Television (dir. Merrill Brockway), PBS' *Dance in America* series, 1977.
Fractions I (dir. Atlas), 1978.
Torse (dir. Atlas), New York Public Library for the Performing Arts at Lincoln Center, 1978.
Locale (dir. Atlas), 1980.
Channels/Inserts (dir. Atlas), 1982.
Coast Zone (dir. Atlas), 1983.
Della Commedia (dir. Caplan and Cunningham), 1985.
Points in Space (dir. Caplan and Cunningham), 1986.
Changing Steps (dir. Caplan and Cunningham), 1989.
Beach Birds for the Camera (dir. Caplan), 1993.

*   *   *

Mercier Philip Cunningham is considered to be the grand old man of modern dance. He is also considered to be the leader of avant-garde dance, a revolutionary, an innovator and perhaps, the antithesis of traditional modern dance. Modern dance grew out of a reaction to classical ballet, and Merce's style of modern dance was

Merce Cunningham: *Phrases,* **1982. Photograph © Beatriz Schiller.**

formed in response to traditional modern dance. Yet, ironically, many ballet companies have incorporated dances choreographed by Cunningham into their repertories. Of the dozens of dances he has choreographed, some of Cunningham's best known include, *Suite for Five in Space and Time* (1956), *Summerspace* (1958), *Winterbranch* (1964), and *How to Pass, Kick, Fall and Run* (1965).

Cunningham grew up in Centralia, a small town in Washington where he studied several forms of dance. In 1937 Cunningham became a dance student at the Cornish School of Fine and Applied Arts in Seattle, where he first met composer and faculty member John Cage, who later became his collaborator and close companion. During the summers, Cunningham took dance courses offered at Mills College in Oakland, California. The first summer he danced with Lester Horton, and the following summer, when the Bennington Dance department was in residence at Mills College, Cunningham took classes with Martha Graham and the Humphrey-Weidman company. Consequently, he was invited to join both dance companies, and chose to dance with Martha Graham in New York. Cunningham became a principal dancer with Martha Graham's com-

pany and remained with her for five years. He also studied ballet with George Balanchine at the American School of Ballet.

Even while dancing with Graham's company, Cunningham was developing his own distinct choreography and technique. During the mid-1940s Cunningham started collaborating with John Cage and began to assemble his own dance company. In 1953, Cunningham was invited to teach a dance course at Black Mountain College in North Carolina. Several dancers with whom Cunningham was working, including Paul Taylor, Viola Farber, Remy Charlip, and Carolyn Brown accompanied him to Black Mountain College. After the summer, Cunningham kept the group together, thus forming the Merce Cunningham Dance Company. In its earliest years, the dance company had John Cage as music director, set designer, agent, accompanist, cook, and mentor—in short, Cage performed any feat necessary to keep the company going.

Cunningham shared, along with Cage, an attraction to and fascination with the *Chinese Book of Changes,* or *I Ching,* which introduced the concept of chance into their artistic processes. Also adopting a Zen perspective, Cunningham altered the typical approach to creating and producing a dance. The "dance" or the movement was no longer dependent on the rhythm of music. Each element of a choreographed piece—lighting, costumes, sound accompaniment, and movement—were equally dependent on each other, or, independent. A particular section of choreography wasn't any more important than another section; they could be interchangeable. Another concept Cunningham applied to his choreography was "open form music," conceived by musicians Morton Feldman and Earle Brown, which meant that "music is indeterminate of its performance." Once the choreography was set, the performance of a piece would change from performance to performance depending on which sections of the dance were used, in what order they were performed, and in which combination; furthermore, dancers could alter the form of the dance by changing the duration of a section. Think of a piece of music by Eric Satie with no measure bars or time signatures, or visualize a Calder mobile where an element itself does not change, only its position within the whole. Cunningham typically choreographs a dance in silence and his dancers rehearse in silence. His performances generally include live accompaniment, rather than recorded sound. Most of the time, Cunningham would choreograph a dance without ever hearing the composed music—choreographer and musician would create their pieces independently, subsequently conjoining the two art forms. The only determined factor, naturally, would be the length of the respective pieces. Cunningham trains his dancers to perform independently, completely disregarding costumes, lighting, music, or stage sets.

Cunningham's pieces were a clear departure from the traditional conflict and resolution, or cause and effect structure of dance. *Suite by Chance* (1953) was Cunningham's first dance where most of the elements of the dance were chosen with the aid of chance methods. Many of Cunningham's pieces such as, *Dime a Dance* (1953), *Galaxy* (1956), *Scramble* (1967), and *Landrover* (1972), consist of several sections that could be rearranged or performed in varying order, or created by an open form method. His choreography was like an abstract painting; during his early years in the 1950s—the age of Abstract Expressionism—Cunningham found that he fit into an evolving group of abstract artists and musicians such as Jasper Johns, Andy Warhol, Robert Rauschenberg, Gordon Mumma, Christian Wolff, and of course, John Cage. Cunningham also collaborated with many other contemporary artists and musicians who composed music for or designed sets and costumes for his company. For these modern artists, to have such a strong peer group was not only a luxury but constituted a cultural force strong enough to radically change the way Americans viewed art, dance, and music.

Cunningham's company struggled for many years, and performances were not plentiful. In 1964 he and his dancers embarked on a world tour and were so well-received that some engagements were extended by several weeks. Upon their return to the U.S. the company toured the country with the aid of grants from the National Endowment for the Arts (NEA) and the New York State Council on the Arts.

Significantly, Cunningham's work reflects change as well as chance. In the early 1970s Cunningham began performing "Events," which were excerpts from his repertory arranged into various sequences. Always open to new ideas and technology, Cunningham began to use the unlikely medium of television to show his work. Along with Charles Atlas, he produced films and videos of dances created specifically for television. *Westbeth* (1975) was his first dance made for video. The video *Points in Space* (1986) won the highest award at the Prague International Television Festival, and was a finalist in the American Film Festival. *Beach Birds for Cam-*

era (1993), which also won several prizes, was the last Cunningham dance that John Cage composed for his very close friend before his death in 1992. Currently, Cunningham is using computers to choreograph new pieces. With a software program called *Life Forms* that has three windows, a space grid, a timeline, and a sequence editor, he is discovering new movement possibilities. To Cunningham, a computer is a tool of discovery.

Although his dancers are not particularly emotive, his dances are not without emotion. Cunningham's dances evoke a number of moods and reactions from an audience. His dances affect us because, in their abstract way, they reflect life. The fact his dances can be performed in unlikely places (for example, Grand Central Station or a gym), performed with or without music, lights, or props is, in a sense, a reassurance that a random arrangement of movement or "life" can continue no matter what. According to Cunningham's perspective, dance should not reflect life but is life.

—Christine Miner Minderovic

CURRIER, Ruth
American dancer, choreographer, and educator

Born: Ruth Miller 1926. **Education:** Attended Black Mountain College; studied with José Limón and Doris Humphrey. **Career:** Joined José Limón Dance Company, 1949; Humphrey's assistant, 1952-58; began choreographing, 1955; formed Ruth Currier and Dancers, 1961; became artistic director, Limón company, 1972; courses and workshops, Ruth Currier Studio, 1981-91; has been an artist-in-residence and taught at numerous colleges and universities worldwide, including Bennington College, Juilliard, New York University, Ohio State University, Sarah Lawrence College, and others; retired in 1991.

Roles (all performances with the José Limón Dance Company)

1949	*Invention* (Humphrey)
	La Malinche (Limón)
1950	*Day on Earth* (Humphrey)
	Concert (Limón)
1951	*Night Spell* (Humphrey)
1952	*The Visitation* (Limón)
1953	*Ruins and Visions* (Humphrey)
1954	*Felipe el Loco* (Humphrey)
1956	*There is a Time* (Limón)
1958	*Missa Brevis* (Limón)

Other roles include: *Lament for Ignacio Sánchez Mejías* (Humphrey) and others in the Limón repertory.

Works

1955	*The Antagonists*
	Idyl
1956	*Becoming*
	Resurgence
	Triplicity
1958	*To Lean, to Spring, to Reach, to Fly*
	Dangerous World

1959	*Brandenburg Concerto No. 4* w/Doris Humphrey
1960	*Transfigured Season*
	Toccanta
1961	*Places*
	Quartet
	Resonances
	A Tender Portrait
1963	*Diva Divested*
1965	*To wish ... together ... fearsomely*
1966	*Triangle of Strangers*
	Night Before Tomorrow
1967	*Fantasies and Façades*
	Arena
	Some Idols
1975	*Phantasmagoria*
1976	*Storm Warning*

Publications

Clarke, Mary, and David Vaughan (eds.), *The Encyclopedia of Dance & Ballet*, New York, 1977.

Mazo, Joseph H., *Prime Movers: The Makers of Modern Dance in America*, New York, 1977.

McDonagh, Don, Review, *New York Times*, 6 June 1967.

Skrzesz, Kenneth, "Ruth Currier: Translating Humphrey," *Dance Magazine*, August 1990.

*   *   *

Owing much to the creative influence of Doris Humphrey, Ruth Currier helped carry on the rich tradition of Humphrey and José Limón with her work as a dancer, creative assistant, company artistic director, and teacher. Currier was Doris Humphrey's creative assistant during the 1950s and enabled Humphrey to create memorable works with the José Limón Dance Company even though Humphrey was no longer able to demonstrate the movements. After Limón's death, Currier's artistic direction helped enable his company to continue to prosper. Currier also has shared her knowledge of dance with others through her extensive teaching.

Currier was born Ruth Miller in 1926. She was raised in Durham, North Carolina, and attended Black Mountain College. She moved to New York to study dance with Humphrey and Limón, joining Limón's company in 1949. José Limón Dance Company had been formed in the mid-1940s following Limón's return from service in World War II. Doris Humphrey had retired from performing in the mid-1940s because of an arthritic hip, and she became the artistic director for Limón's company.

Currier was Humphrey's creative assistant from 1952 to 1958. Currier excelled at translating Humphrey's verbal images into physical movements which embodied Humphrey's vision and met with Humphrey's approval. She worked with Humphrey on *Brandenburg Concerto No. 4* and completed the work following Humphrey's death in 1958. Currier also assisted Humphrey in staging work for the American Dance Festival in New London, Connecticut, and helped her in teaching choreography.

Currier performed in many of the works created by Humphrey, including *Invention* (1949), *Lament for Ignacio Sánchez Mejías*, *Day on Earth* (1950), *Night Spell* (1951), *Ruins and Visions* (1953), and *Felipe el Loco* (1955). She appeared in works by Limón as well, among them *La Malinche* (1949), *Concert* (1950), *There is a Time* (1956) and *The Visitation* (1952). In 1955 Currier began to choreograph her own work. Her choreography was heavily influenced by her experience with Humphrey; in both her choreography and teaching, Currier employs Humphrey's concept of fall from and recovery of balance. In a 1990 article in *Dance Magazine* by Kenneth Skrzesz, Currier describes what she believes the basic concept of dance to be: "One must find a stable center in order to lose it. One has to learn to lose that center and recover it. One must isolate body parts to find the richness of movement within each part. And, finally, one must be able to make coordinations of these isolations while falling, recovering, and thrusting through space."

While acknowledging her belief in Humphrey's dance theories, Currier was not restricted to specific movements or techniques. In fact, such restrictions would have been opposed to the Humphrey tradition as she knew it. In 1955 Currier choreographed *The Antagonists*, her first work. In this duet with Betty Jones, Currier created a fence in a triangular configuration which separates two women. The timid woman on the inside resists the efforts of the other woman to free her from the enclosure. Currier used this dramatic episode to explore interaction between opposing forces which can never be reconciled. Currier also developed this work to demonstrate her abilities beyond those as a lyrical dancer; the success of this work resulted in her later being cast as a street urchin in Humphrey's *Ruins and Visions* and performing the Crucifixus solo in Limón's seminal *Missa Brevis*.

Currier presented *The Antagonists* (1955) and *Becoming* (1956) with José Limón's company. In 1961, she created her own company, Ruth Currier and Dancers. Other of her works include *Toccanta* (1960) and *Quartet* (1961), and she created work for her company and for her students at Bennington College and Sarah Lawrence College. Following Limón's death in 1972, Currier became artistic director of the company for five years. Under her leadership, the company continued to create new works and to revive works from the Limón and Humphrey repertory, including Humphrey's *The Shakers*. The José Limón Dance Company became the first major company to remain active after the death of its founding choreographer.

After resigning as artistic director for the Limón company, Currier expanded her teaching career. Her teaching philosophy carries on the essence of what she had learned from Humphrey; she encouraged her students to avoid being restricted to any one specific technique and prodded them to explore movement through imagination, experience, and a knowledge of composition. She believed in working with a dancer's individual physical and emotional abilities to reach each dancer's potential. Beginning in the late 1970s, Currier became an artist-in-residence at schools in Europe and South America. Later she returned to the United States to teach in New York City and elsewhere at such schools as Juilliard, Bennington College, Sarah Lawrence College, Ohio State University, and New York University. From 1981 to 1991, Currier taught technique and workshops in composition and repertory at her own studio in lower Manhattan, the Ruth Currier Dance Studio, until she retired.

—Janette Goff Dixon

DAI Ai-lian

Chinese dancer, choreographer, educator and company director

Born: Wu Ai-lian in Trinidad, 10 May 1916; family originated from Xinhui County, Guangdong Province of Mainland China. **Education:** Local primary school; started dance training at 5 in 1921 with her cousin; studied piano and music theory, 1923; began fundamental ballet training with a local English teacher named Nell Walton, 1928; passed the medium courses in piano and music theory organized by the London-based Trinity Academy of Music, 1929; arrived in London, 1931, started formal ballet training successively with Anton Dolin, Marie Rambert and Margaret Craske alongside Alicia Markova, Frederick Ashton, Antony Tudor, and Vera Zorina, among others, and appeared in a children's role in the musical version of *Hiawatha.* **Family:** Married 1) the painter Ye Qian-yu, 1940 (divorced 1956); 2) Ding Ning (divorced). **Career:** Began to choreograph and dance her own works, 1933; often took part in patriotic activities organized by the London-based Chinese Movement Committee, including fund-raisers for Madam Sun Yat-sen's China Defense League; began modern dance training with Leslie Borrows-Goosens and Earnest Berke, and danced in the latter's company for two years, meanwhile studying German Expressionistic Dance with Kurt Jooss, Sigurd Leeder, Lisa Ullmann and Rudolf von Laban at the Experimental Arts Centre in Dartington Hall, as well as Labanotation with Ann Hutchinson in the Jooss-Leeder School, 1939; back to China via Hong Kong, 1940; went to Guangxi, Xikang and Guizhou to study and collect local minorities dances; taught ballet and modern dance, Chinese minorities dances, and introduced Labanotation to China for the first time at Chongqing National Opera School and National Academy of Social Education; invited to teach, choreograph and dance in the newly established Dance Section at Yucai School with Wu Xiao-bang at Yucai, 1943-44; together with Ye Qian-yu, went to collect Tibetan dances in Xikang and other remote areas, 1945; lectured on Chinese folk dances at La Meri's Ethnic Dance Center in New York City and participated in the performances at the Brooklyn Academy of Music at the invitation of the U.S. State Department; founded the Chinese Music & Dance Academy, where she taught ballet, modern, folk dances and Chinese dance drama; taught dance at the music department of Beijing National Fine Arts Academy and the physical education department of the National Teachers College, as well as in the summer dance school jointly organized by all the local universities and colleges, 1948; attended the first conference of All-China Literary & Arts Workers' Representatives, and was elected Chairperson of China National Dance Artists Association (CNDAA) in 1949; attended the First Chinese People's Political Consultative Conference (CPPCC); appointed deputy director of dance company attached to the Central Academy of Drama; attended Paris-Prague World Peace Conference as one of the official representatives of the Central Government of the People's Republic of China; appointed deputy director of the Central Song & Dance Ensemble, appointed principal of the newly established Beijing Dance School and attended the first Chinese National People's Congress (CNPC), and elected vice-chairperson of the Chinese Dance Art Research Society, 1953; elected vice-chairperson of the CNDAA, 1960; appointed director of the Attached Ballet of the Central Opera & Ballet Theatre and deputy director of the theatre, 1963; during the Cultural Revolution, 1966-76, was divorced by Ding Ning and did all kinds of manual labor in the countryside-based "Red Art May 7th Cadres School"; returned to work as artistic adviser to the Attached Ballet to the Central Opera & Ballet Theatre, 1978; lectured at the CNDAA-held Dance Notation Seminar and taught the first course in Labanotation in Beijing; joined the leadership and the jury of the First All-China Dance Competition in August; founded the Chinese Labanotation Society, 1985; started the "Dances for Everyone" Campaign among children and old people as well as others to popularize dance as a life-art form for everyone, 1987; has alternately lived in Beijing and London, where she restaged some of her representative dances on the local overseas Chinese non-professional dance companies from 1988. **Awards:** *Lotus Flower Dance* and *The Flying Apsaras* were awarded the "Masterpiece of Chinese Dance in the 20th Century," 1994; honored with the title of Fellow of the Hong Kong Academy for Performing Arts, 1996.

Roles

1921   Children's solos in *Bluebells in Fairyland,* Xilan Chen Troupe, Trinidad

        Children's solo in *Happy Foot* (Xilan Chen), Xilan Chen Troupe, Trinidad

1931   Role in *Hiawatha* at the Royal Albert Hall, London

1943   Sister in *Brother & Sister Opening Up Wasteland* (Yangge Opera), Dance Section of Yucai School, Chongqing

Works

1933   *Queen's Floral Handkerchief,* London

        Yang Gui-Fei, solo, BBC, London

        At the Persian Fair, solo, BBC, London

        Black Doll, solo, BBC, London

        Marching Forward, solo, BBC, London

        The Weeping Willow, solo, BBC, London

        Beggar, solo, BBC, London

        The Thai Dance, solo, BBC, London

1941   *The Eastern River,* solo, Chongqing

        Homesick, solo, Chongquing

        Youth Dance, solo, Chonquing

        A Story of a Guerilla, solo, Chongquing

A Sold Daughter, solo, Chongquing

Dream, solo, Chongquing

Air Raid, solo, Chongquin

The Dumb Husband Carrying His Paralytic Wife on His Back, solo, Chongquing

The Miao Nationality's Moon, solo, Chongquing

Sister Zhu Sending Eggs, solo, Chongqing

1942   *Vigilance,* solo, Chongqing, Guilin and Kangding

A Goddess in the Forest, solo, Chongqing, Guilin and Kangding

Gypsy Dance, solo, Chongqing, Guilin and Kangding

A Girl Picking an Ear of Grain, Chongqing, Guilin and Kangding

1943   *Xinjiang Folk Dance,* solo, Yucai School, Chongqing

1946   *Russian Dance, The Yao Nationality's Drum Dance,* solos, fund-raising concert for Zhixin English & German Languages School, Chongqing

Luo Luo Love Songs, Lucky Fairy & Heavenly Pearl, Ba-Aa Xuan-Zi, Happy Maitreya, Lhasa Tap Dance, Hanbarhan, solos, Border Region Music & Dance Festival, Chongqing

Tibetan Dance, solo, Brooklyn Academy of Music, New York

1949   *Long Live the People's Victory, Grand Yangge Dance: Reconstructing Our Motherland, The Great Unity of All the Chinese Nationalities,* w/others, Dance Company Attached to the Central Academy of Drama, Beijing

1950   *The Pigeon of Peace* w/Ouyang Yu-qian, Ding Ning, Wang Ping, Gao Di-an and Zhao Yun-ge, Dance Company Attached to the Central Academy of Drama, Beijing

1951   *Spring Outing,* Chinese Youth Cultural Troupe, Third World Youth Festival, Berlin

1953   *Lotus Flower Dance,* Chinese Youth Art Troupe, Fourth World Youth Festival, Prague

1955   *The Flying Apsaras,* Chinese Youth Art Troupe, Fifth World Youth Festival, Warsaw

1958   *Anhui Floral Lantern Dance* and *Consoling Dance,* solos, Capital's Art Circle Consoling Delegation, Fujian Border Region

Socialism Is Good, the Beijing masses

1960   *Eight Little Heroes,* Xiamen Municipal Dance Company, Fujian Province

Publications

On DAI: articles—

Kisselgoff, Anna, "China's Dance Doynne Brings Troupe to U.S.", *New York Times,* 4 March 1986.

Ou, Jian-ping, "Ensemble in Beijing Is Cradle of Chinese Song and Dance," *Dance Magazine,* August 1988.

———, "From 'Beasts' to 'Flowers': Modern Dance in China," in *East Meets West in Dance: Voices in the Cross Cultural Dialogues, Choreography and Dance Studies,* edited by Ruth Solomon and John Solomon, Chur, Switzerland, 1995.

Ou, Jian-ping, translator in *Brief Biographies of Contemporary Chinese Dance Celebrities,* China National Dance Artists Association, Beijing, 1995.

                         *   *   *

Dai Ai-lian is one of the two great giants (the other is Wu Xiao-bang) in Chinese contemporary dance history. Like Wu, she started with ballet and later turned to modern dance abroad and came back to China to develop her own way. To be precise, the creative dance activities in the Chinese major cities in the 1930s and 1940s and before New China was born in 1949 were almost all conducted and later led by or at least connected with these two pioneers. Dai, however, differs from Wu (who started to learn dance in Japan at 23 after his college education and quite some life experiences in China) in being much purer and simpler; she started to dance at the age of five in 1921 out of her sheer love for music and movement, out of her dancing or moving nature, and in fact she has been doing everything out of her sheer love all her life time.

From the very beginning of her dancing career in that remote island country of Trinidad, it was her fiery love for dance that urged her to be so bold as to write for autographed photos from the London-based ballet superstars like Anton Dolin and Alicia Markova; yet she was lucky and got what she wanted. Following this lucky thread, she went to London and began her formal ballet training with the ballet masters like Dolin, Marie Rambert and Margaret Craske. However, no professional ballet companies would hire her due to her Chinese origins. Out of her love for dance, she began to study modern dance with Leslie Borrows-Goosens, Ernest Berke, Kurt Jooss, Sigurd Leeder and Rudolf von Laban, and found more of herself in this milieu, and even a position in Berke's company for two years. Yet her good wishes for and experiments in combining the beauty of ballet and the creativeness of modern, which were unacceptable to both sides at that time, brought an end to this precious job.

During the Japanese occupation of China and World War II, Dai's love for her motherland prompted her to become involved in fund-raising performances in London to support China and finally brought her back to China in 1940, despite the fact that she knew little about it and indeed did not even speak the language. However, she returned home nevertheless, to the place where her family originated, where she belonged, and most excitingly, where she was badly needed. There she married one of the most famous Chinese painters, Ye Qian-yu, who helped organize her first fund-raising concerts in Hong Kong for the good of her motherland, after only a few months' contacts; and love gave this delicate young lady enough heroism to travel to remote and dangerous areas to learn the folk dances of the Chinese minorities, which she re-choreographed and staged in theatres for the first time in China's history.

When New China was born in 1949, Dai's deep love for her motherland and her great contributions to the Chinese dance development naturally aroused a profound love and respect for her in return, and she was elected the first chair of China National Dance Artists Association, given the honor of attending the first Chinese People's Political Consultative Conference, the first Chinese National People's Congress, and the Paris-Prague World Peace Conference, as well as the responsibility for founding positions of all the major Chinese dance institutions.

In 1956, when Dai divorced her husband to marry a much-younger man, her career suffered a severe downturn. This, at least, is the natural conclusion drawn from the biographical facts. On the other hand, I would also like to add, she is lucky to have had such a loving heart and always got what she wanted, while we who are too practical might never reach her spiritual ecstasy of love.

Certainly, the causes for her declining creativity in choreography also should include the extremely tense political situation in China after 1957, which obviously excited her in a profound way, which can be seen from her 1958 dance *Socialism Is Good,* choreographed for the masses, but soon puzzled and even annoyed her, as she, like many other talented artists such as Wu Xiao-bang, was asked to do all kinds of manual labor instead of being assigned to choreograph and dance. Nevertheless, she survived the next 20 years with nothing left (even her second and much younger husband left her during the "Cultural Revolution") but her loving heart, and became extremely active again—not as a dancer or choreographer, but as a Chinese ambassadress of dance. Her extraordinary contributions to international dance exchanges and friendship between the dance artists of China and foreign countries have been fully recognized and cherished both nationally and internationally, the best examples of which are her vice-chairwomanship of the Conseil International de la Dance under UNESCO since 1982, and the placement of her bust in the hall of the Royal Academy in London in 1981.

In short, Dai's great contributions to the development of Chinese dance have already become an integral part of world dance history; but do remember that it is her love which has successfully taken her through all the hardships and up-and-downs, and finally to her glorious present!

—Ou Jian-ping

DAKIN, Christine
American dancer, educator, and choreographer

Born: Christine Whitney Irving, 25 August 1949 in New Haven, Connecticut. **Education:** University of Michigan, 1967-71; studied with Vera Embree, Elizabeth Bergman, Gay Delanghe, Pearl Lang, Kazuko Hirabayashi, Igor Schwezov, Nina Stroganova and Vladimir Dokoudovsky; at the Martha Graham School, New York, 1971. **Family:** Married Robert Ford Dakin 1969 (divorced 1982); married Stephen J. Mauer 1985. **Career:** Taught at Ann Arbor Dance Theater (Michigan), 1965-71; teacher/choreographer, Fairleigh Dickinson University, (New Jersey), 1971-73; dancer/rehearsal director, Pearl Lang Dance Company, 1971-79; dancer, Kazuko Hirabayashi Dance Company, 1974-76; began teaching at the Martha Graham School of Contemporary Dance, 1972; principal dancer, Martha Graham Dance Company, beginning 1976; dancer/helped found Buglisi/Foreman Dance Ensemble, 1991; taught at Guanajuato University (Mexico), 1982; visiting instructor, Ballet Nacional in Mexico and Ballet Contemporaneo in Buenos Aires, 1993; currently teaches at Graham, Juilliard, and Alvin Ailey American Dance Center; appointed associate artistic director, Martha Graham Dance Company, 1997. **Awards:** *Dance Magazine* Award, 1994; ArtsLink Grant to return to Russia, 1996; Honorary Doctor of Arts Shenandoah University; Rockefeller U.S. Mexico Fund for Culture Grant for teaching and choreography, 1998.

Roles (choreography by Martha Graham, performed with the Martha Graham Dance Company, New York, unless otherwise noted)

1972   *Shirah* (Lang), Pearl Lang Dance Company, Hunter Playhouse

1974   *Watergate* (Lang), Pearl Lang Dance Company, Jacob's Pillow

1975   *Plain Song* (Lang), Pearl Lang Dance Company, Aaron Copland 75th Birthday Celebration

           Night of 4 Moons and Lone Shadow (Kazuko Hirabayashi), Kazuko Hirabayashi Dance Theater, Hunter Playhouse

1978   *Dybbuk* (Lang), Pearl Lang Dance Company, 92d Street YM/YWCA

           Frescoes, Sackler Gallery Metropolitan Museum of Art

1979   *O Thou Desire Who Art about to Sing,* Jerusalem, Israel

1980   *Carmina Burana* (Elizabeth Bergmann), University of Michigan

           Diversion of Angels, Metropolitan Opera

1981   *Acts of Light,* Kennedy Center, Washington, D.C.

           Jocasta, *Night Journey,* City Center Theater

           Bride, *Appalachian Spring,* Kennedy Center, Washington, D.C.

           Seraphic Dialogue, Alte Oper, Frankfurt

1982   Ariadne, *Errand into the Maze,* Alte Oper, Frankfurt

           A Woman, *Herodiade,* Tivoli Theater, Copenhagen

           Graham Repertory, the White House, Washington, D.C.

1983   Phaedra, *Phaedra's Dream,* Herod Atticus Theater, Athens, Greece

           Medea, *Cave of the Heart,* Pitti Palace, Florence, Italy

1984   *Rite of Spring,* New York State Theater

           Clytemnestra, Paris Opera House

           Phaedra, *Phaedra's Dream,* Paris Opera House

1986   *Tangled Night,* Royal Theater, Copenhagen

1987   Hecuba, *Cortege of Eagles,* City Center Theater

1988   Phaedra, *Phaedra,* Teatro Communale, Florence

           Circe, City Center Theater

1989   *Letter to the World,* Grand Theater de Québec, Canada

           She Who Seeks, *Dark Meadow,* Bienalle de la Danse, Lyon, France

1991   *Maple Leaf Rag,* Ravinia Festival, Illinois

1992   *Clytemnestra* (title role), City Center Theater

           Deep Song, City Center Theater

           Hard to Be a Jew (Pearl Lang), Yiddish Theater w/Zvee Scooler and Joseph Buloff

1993   *Demeter and Persephone* (Twyla Tharp), City Center Theater

1994   *Runes of the Heart* (Buglisi/Foreman), Buglisi/Foreman Dance Ensemble, Clark Studio Theater

           Clytemnestra (title role), Brooklyn Academy of Music (BAM) Opera House

           Death and Entrances, BAM

1996   *Bare to the Wall* (Buglisi/Foreman), Buglisi/Foreman Dance Ensemble, Joyce Theater

           Molting (Buglisi), guest solo with Bavdilovich Dance Theater, Vladivostok

           Snow on the Mesa (Robert Wilson), Kennedy Center, Washington, D.C.

           Chronicle, Rome

Works

1997   *Waywards,* University of Shenandoah Dancers, Kennedy Center, Washington, D.C.

           A Trio, Ballet Nacional de Mexico

Publications

On DAKIN: articles—

Hardy, Camille, "Martha Graham Dance Company," *Dance Magazine,* January 1995.

Horosko, Marian, "Graham Moves: Offstage, Onstage," *Dance Magazine,* July 1991.

Solomons, Gus Jr., "Dark Emotions, Blazing Fire: Christine Dakin," *Dance Magazine,* October 1993.

Film and Videotapes

Le Sacre du Printemps, documentary film featuring Dakin.

Courage, documentary film featuring Dakin, Buglisi/Foreman Dance Troupe.

*   *   *

Though Christine Dakin began studying dance at the age of 21, she has shown exceptional talent as a performer, masterfully dancing the part of Graham's Clytemnestra with the Martha Graham Dance Company in 1992, and she continues to be a dedicated and inspirational teacher. Though Dakin has been slowly delving into choreography, collaborating on her first piece in 1991 with Terese Capucilli for the Buglisi/Foreman Dance ensemble, her enthusiasm for modern dance expression is evident in the energy and emotion of her performances for which she received the 1994 *Dance Magazine* Award. Commenting on this special intensity, Gus Solomons Jr. has said: "Dakin brings to her interpretations a fire similar to that which ignited Graham's own performances."

Christine Dakin was born in New Haven, Connecticut in 1949. She attended the University of Michigan in 1967 to study French and Russian with a goal of teaching. While there she began taking dance classes, discovering the emotional and dramatic language of dance. She studied with Vera Embree, Elizabeth Bergman, and Gay Delanghe. After seeing performances of the José Limón, Paul Taylor, and Martha Graham dance companies, she decided to pursue dance with the intent of teaching, since she felt she was too old to pursue a performance career.

In 1971 she went to New York to study at the Martha Graham School of Contemporary Dance. After a short time she was awarded a scholarship and on a whim auditioned for an apprentice group being formed by Bertram Ross and Mary Hinkson for the purpose of teaching Graham's existing repertoire. "Of course I wasn't nervous," Dakin told Solomons in a *Dance Magazine* interview. "I had no illusions of anything happening." She made the cut to finalist and eventually into the group.

Exhilarated by the excitement of learning the Graham technique from Graham Company veterans, her skills improved at an accelerated pace. She began thinking a performing career was indeed a possibility, though it took her several auditions before she succeeded in becoming part of the ensemble. Her determination has been well rewarded. In 1976 she graduated to participation in the actual Martha Graham Dance Company. She worked her way through the ranks, becoming a major soloist with the company, dancing both new roles as well as recreating many of Graham's original signature roles. One of her first principal roles for the Graham company was as the Bride in *Appalachian Spring.* Dakin says it remains one of her favorites because of the elegance and formality of the choreography and the darker emotion beneath the surface, which she believes becomes richer each time she explores it. Dakin approaches her roles as if an actress, exploring the inner being of the character to determine the emotion and motivation behind each movement of the choreography. Within this approach is the basis of the Graham technique—a means to show the soul of the charac-

ter. "She [Graham] drew movement out of herself to portray characters and emotions," Dakin has said.

For the original roles Dakin has spent hours watching films of Graham performing her own choreography, looking for the nuances that capture the drama and emotion, learning the tilt of the head or the arch of the back or neck, small details that authenticate the pieces. She also turned to these films to restore parts of the original choreography for Graham's *Clytemnestra* which Dakin performed during the October 1992 season, less than a year after Graham's death. The sixth dancer ever to execute Graham's epic role, Dakin succeeded in achieving her own high expectations as well as delighting the audience with the clarity of her dancing. Joseph Mazo said of the performance, "Dakin has demonstrated that a style as distinctive and personal as that of Martha Graham can be continued, and, indeed, revitalized, even after the passing of its creator."

Though an exceptional soloist, Dakin remains a team player. She admits that her own performance is only as good as the ensemble as a whole for touching the emotions of the audience. For this reason, and the inherent teacher within, she coaches other members, inspiring them with her passion and energy for the dance. Dakin has also studied with and performed in the companies of Pearl Lang and Kazuko Hirabayashi. Together with other principal dancers of the Martha Graham Dance Company, Dakin and Jacqulyn Buglisi, Terese Capucilli, and Donlin Foreman formed the Buglisi/Foreman Dance Ensemble in 1991. Known for their theatrical appeal and dramatic intensity, they have been invited to perform at prestigious theaters from Taipei to Stuttgart to Milan. Buglisi/Foreman Dance was also invited to both the 1993 and 1994 International Dance Week programs in Prague. The ensemble is expected to be responsible for launching a new vision of Graham's "dance as theater" into the 21st century.

Through her vocation as a teacher, Dakin will also undoubtedly influence the dancers and the technique of modern dance for the 21st century. She has been on the faculty at the Martha Graham School of Contemporary Dance since 1972 and at the Julliard School since 1989. She has taught through guest instructorships at the University of Michigan, the Lincoln Center Institute, Duke University, and the Alvin Ailey American Dance Center. Her teaching has also taken her around the world. In 1992 her original desire to teach the Russian language was exercised when she visited Vladivastok, Russia, to teach dance. In 1982 she guest taught at the Guanajuato University in Mexico and during the summer of 1993 she was visiting instructor at Ballet Nacional in Mexico and Ballet Contemporaneo in Buenos Aires.

As part of her work with her students, Dakin has choreographed short pieces for them to perform. She says she continues to explore choreography slowly, waiting until she has a need and desire to create before pursuing it. Though she has collaborated with members of the Buglisi/Foreman Dance and their work has received standing ovations, Dakin remains modest. Of the short pieces created for her students, she told Solomons, "The dance turned out well; it had a beginning, a middle, and an end, and it was in my own style."

She continues to create, to study modern dance, to perform, and most importantly for the future of the dance, to teach. Her exuberance for the Graham technique remains high as does her desire to preserve the Graham aesthetic. Says Dakin, "Martha's theater, her dance, is really a ritual on many levels, one we all share in some way, and which we carry within us always."

—Lisa A. Wroble

DALMAN, Elizabeth Cameron

Australian dancer, choreographer, educator, and company director

Born: Elizabeth Cameron Wilson, 23 January 1933 in Adelaide, South Australia. **Education:** Presbyterian Ladies College; Wollongong University, Master of Creative Arts, 1994. Studied classical ballet and Margaret Morris technique with Nora Stewart, Adelaide; studied ballet with Maria Fay, Kathleen Crofton and Audrey de Vos, London, 1957; studied with Kurt Jooss, Folkwangschule, Essen. **Career:** Early performances with Ballet der Landen, Holland, 1958-59; *My Fair Lady*, Holland, 1959-61; Eleo Pomare Dance Company, Germany and Holland, 1961-63; founded Elizabeth Dalman School of Modern Dance, 1964; founder, and resident choreographer of the Australian Dance Theatre (ADT), Adelaide, South Australia, 1965; artistic director of ADT 1965-75, with first tour to Europe and New York, 1968; then to Asia-Pacific, 1970-75; solo programs, Papua New Guinea, 1973; founded Ventimiglia School of Dance and Ventimiglia Youth Dance Theatre, 1977; guest artist, Academie de Danse, Menton, France, 1984-85; Danskern, Holland, 1985 and 1987; co-founded community dance company, Dance Excentrix, Adelaide, 1987; the Mirramu Creative Arts Centre, Canberra, Australia, 1990. **Awards:** Agosto Medioevale Festival Award, Italy, 1984 and 1985; Canberra Critics' Circle Award, 1990; Ausdance International Day Award for contribution to dance in Australia, 1991; Australian Artists Creative Fellowship Award, 1994; Order of Australia Medal for contributions to contemporary dance in Australia, 1995.

Elizabeth Dalman performing *This Train*, 1965. Photograph by Jan Dalman.

Works (solo programs)

1986	*Together We Are Alone*
1988	*Sciangiarusca*
1992	*Mother, Madre, Daughter, Girl-Child*
1996	*Bella Donna*
1997	*Singing the Silence*

Other works include: Following is a selection of Dalman's 30 works for the Australian Dance Theatre from 1965 to 1975—*This Train* (mus. Peter, Paul and Mary), *Bushfire* (mus. Ravi Shankar), *Primitive Rituals* (mus. Olatunji), *Collage* (mus. George Michell), *Three Songs* (mus. Manuel de Falla), *Blues for Two* (mus. Ron Carter), *Creation* (mus. Don Ellis), *The Sun and Moon* (mus. Peter Sculthorpe), *Rondel* (mus. Peter Sculthorpe), *Corroboree* (mus. John Antill), *Leaving* (mus. Bach), *Children of Time* (mus. George Dreyfus, Jack Body).

*   *   *

While Elizabeth Cameron Dalman's name may not be all that well-known internationally, Australian dance owes much to this modern dance pioneer. As a company founder, dancer, choreographer, and teacher, Dalman has personified a passionate belief in dance that not only set the blueprint for a uniquely Australian dance heritage but remains an active force in Australian dance more than 30 years later. Yet a lifelong commitment to modern dance could hardly have been anticipated from someone of Dalman's background. She was born in 1933 into a wealthy, "old-establishment" family in the small southern city of Adelaide, and her formative dance experience was directed in the main to classical ballet—in those days considered an acceptable pastime for a young woman of her social status, but certainly not a serious career choice. However, not one to adhere strictly to convention, Dalman set her heart on being a ballet teacher, and to this end traveled to London in 1957 to study with various teachers, Audrey de Vos among them. She gained a deeper appreciation of modern dance after her time at the Folkwangschule in Essen, then under Kurt Jooss' directorship, and her work with American dancer Eleo Pomare. Both experiences left her convinced that modern dance was the only way for Australian dance to go (notwithstanding the fact that the Australian Ballet had just begun its life as the country's national dance company).

Driven by this conviction, Dalman committed herself to the establishment of a modern dance company: founded in 1965 and still in existence today, the Australian Dance Theatre (ADT), remains her greatest legacy to Australian dance—and to international dance, since the company has been an integral part of the international dance dialogue since its inception. During her 10 years as artistic director, Dalman choreographed approximately 30 works, among the most notable being *This Train* (created in the early 1960s to the popular "freedom" songs of Peter, Paul and Mary), one of the few of her early works to survive today. Through the auspices of the company Dalman was also instrumental in the development of a generation of dancers and choreographers, many of whom have contributed significantly to the Australian or international dance scene in their own right.

While Dalman fully recognised the value of a school to underpin her company, it was primarily her love of teaching and her desire to bring dance to the wider community that led her to establish the Australian Dance Theatre School at the same time the company was founded. In a small city studio, many of Adelaide's more radical university students were introduced to what was at the time a new and exciting dance form that reflected the antiauthoritarian, antiwar sentiment just beginning to stir the quiet and rather staid city.

Dalman's time with ADT ended abruptly in 1975 after a bitter struggle with its Board of Management over the company's artistic direction. Bewildered and hurt that her life's work had come to such an end, Dalman took herself back to Europe—this time to Italy, where many years earlier she had found what she sensed was her "tribal home." Despite her initial intention to do entirely without dance, Dalman found it impossible to resist what was for her a way of life. So eventuated the rather unusual outcome of an Australian modern dance pioneer contributing to the development of the art form in Italy, through the founding of the Ventimiglia School of Dance and the Ventimiglia Youth Dance Theatre.

Dalman occasionally returned to Adelaide for family visits, but it was only in 1987 that she felt she could comfortably move home, where she immediately turned her attention to another of her passions—that regardless of age or circumstance, every person should have the opportunity to dance. The result was the founding of Dance Excentrix, a thriving community dance company, its major work—*Sciangiarusca*—performed as part of the international Adelaide Festival Fringe (1988). At the same time Dalman continued her involvement with young people, working as an artist-in-residence in several of the country's fledgling tertiary dance programs.

In 1990 Dalman's life entered what she regards as her "second major vision"—the founding of the Mirramu Creative Arts Centre in Canberra, the nation's capital. As her publicity brochure explains, at Mirramu "artists and members of the community can explore and extend their creativity in a harmonious, powerful and nurturing environment. It is a place of dreams, inspiration, creativity and well-being." The programs offered at Mirramu reflect Dalman's dance and life philosophy: a children's creative dance camp, a three-day self-discovery journey for women, a summer solstice celebration—all of which involve dance in combination with the other arts, and all of which take advantage of the beautiful surrounding bushland environment.

In concert with her directorship of Mirramu, Dalman continues to extend her own work as a dancer and choreographer. Created in 1990, her best-known program—the full-length *Bella Donna*—is an autobiographical work in which the artist pays tribute to the many women who have influenced her life through dance. Her solo, *Singing in Silence*—an homage to St. Cecilia, patron saint of music—was premiered in Taiwan in late 1997.

Despite Dalman's seminal contribution to Australian contemporary dance, public recognition of her achievements has been slow in coming. The mid-1990s, however, brought some redress with the conferral of two particularly significant awards: the Order of Australia Medal in 1995 and a five-year Australian Artists Creative Fellowship in 1994, which has given Dalman the opportunity to move into yet another creative sphere—writing her autobiography and putting on record the early years of the Australian Dance Theatre.

—Anita Donaldson

DANCE THEATRE WORKSHOP

The United States experienced an explosion in modern dance during the 1950s and 1960s. Unless a dance ensemble was well-known or had a large budget, performance space was hard to come by. Dance groups performed in unlikely places—usually places that tolerated or supported the out-of-the-ordinary and the experimental. In 1964 Jeff Duncan, having received a Rockefeller grant, transformed the loft where he lived on West 20th Street in New York City into a dance performance area. Duncan, along with Jack Moore and Art Bauman, shared an interest in alternative, experimental performance and sought to provide a space for modern dance performances. In 1965 the three choreographers founded the Dance Theatre Workshop (DTW). In addition to having a performance space to show their own work, other choreographers could show their work as well.

The Workshop was small and cramped, but was an ideal place for dancers and choreographers to show new pieces. Dance groups received free publicity and inexpensive rehearsal space; performers and ensembles had the opportunity to present their pieces more than once, often for several weekends, and also received audience feedback—an essential element of performance. In such an atmosphere, performers and choreographers were able to "perfect" works in progress. Although the Workshop was utilized by many performers, a core group of regular participants eventually formed. Among the regulars were Martha Clarke, Judith Dunn, Rudy Perez, Wendy Perron, Kei Takei, and John Wilson. Most of the time, the various performers and dance groups would share the evening's performance time as well as the production costs.

After 10 years, Dance Theatre Workshop outgrew the loft space. So in 1975 DTW moved from Duncan's small loft into the premises of Jerome Robbins' American Theater Laboratory, located above the Economy Tires factory on West 19th Street. David White, dancer and modern dance aficionado, became the full-time manager and artistic director of the Dance Theatre Workshop. White formed a strong, structured organization and was able to acquire public and private funding. In 1976 DTW opened its first season with three, four-week series of performances. In the 20 years since the Workshop moved into its new space, the annual budget has grown from $80,000 to more than $3,000,000. The Workshop has also become internationally known and is looked to as a model for the presentation of dance and off-beat theater and music performances.

In the early 1980s, DTW, along with the Morgan Guaranty Trust Company, established the New York Dance and Performance Award—known as the "Bessie." Bessies, so named for choreographer, teacher, and chairman emeritus at Sarah Lawrence College, Bessie Schönberg, have been awarded annually to those whose works are outside the mainstream and deemed innovative. While the principal focus of the Bessie award is choreographers, awards are also given to those who have contributed to the dance world in other ways such as designers, dancers, composers, filmmakers, and producers. Some of the awards bear cash, while others bestow only honor. Like other performance awards, it was hoped that the Bessie would serve as a stimulus for the art world and the general public to pay more attention to this particular sector of performance art.

Even though the space and the organization were larger, Dance Theatre Workshop kept its intimate atmosphere and was still thought to be the place to try out new ideas. Many well-known performers, dancers, and choreographers, such as Bebe Miller, Bill T. Jones, Mark Morris, Susan Marshall, Bill Irwin, and Whoopi Goldberg were frequent performers, and received early recognition while affiliated with the DTW. In the mid-1990s, the Workshop purchased the building it currently inhabits, and has made plans to create a larger performance space, offices, and dressing rooms. Despite government funding cutbacks to the arts, this organization has managed to remain active. Dance Theatre Workshop is considered to be one of the central establishments in the modern dance world.

Publications

Acocella, Joan, "Programming the Revolution," *Dance Magazine,* February 1987.
Back Stage, 18 January 1991.
Solomons, Gus Jr., "DTW Passes Three Milestones," *Dance Magazine,* January 1995.
Vreeland, Nancy, "Dance Theater Workshop to Award 'Bessies' for Non-Mainstream Work," *Dance Magazine*, May 1984.

—Christine Miner Minderovic

DANCEMAKERS
Canadian dance company

Founded by York University graduates Andrea Ciel Smith and Marcy Radler with dancers Carol Anderson, Noelyn George, David Langer, Kevin Peterman, Peggy Baker and Grant McDaniels; first outdoor performance in July 1974; first theatre performance in September 1974. Separated itself from other modern dance companies of the time by performing a repertory consisting of work by many different choreographers in a variety of styles, and operated in a very democratic fashion for the first three years as no artistic director was appointed. In 1977 Peggy Baker and Patricia Miner became co-directors with Anna Blewchamp as associate director; Blewchamp was director from 1979-80, Baker from 1980-81 with Carol Anderson and Patricia Fraser as associate directors; Anderson and Fraser co-directed from 1981-85; Anderson assumed sole charge in 1985 and then remained as resident choreographer when Bill James became artistic director in 1988; Serge Bennathan has been artistic director since 1990; now largely performs Bennathan's choreography.

Publications

Books—

Crabb, Michael, "Carol Anderson," in *101 from the Encyclopaedia of Theatre Dance in Canada,* Susan Macpherson, ed., Toronto, 1997.
———, "Peggy Baker," in *101 from The Encyclopaedia of Theatre Dance in Canada*, Susan Macpherson, ed., Toronto, 1997.
———, "Serge Bennathan," in *101 from The Encyclopaedia of Theatre Dance in Canada*, Susan Macpherson ed., Toronto, 1997.
———, "Patricia Fraser," in *101 from The Encyclopaedia of Theatre Dance in Canada*, Susan Macpherson, ed., Toronto, 1997.
Wyman, Max, *Dance Canada*, Vancouver, 1989.

Articles—

Ciel Smith, Andrea, "Diary of a Prison Tour," *Dance in Canada,* Spring 1977.
Collins, Daniel, "Serge Bennathan," *Dance International*, Spring 1994.
Hickman, Susan, "Dancemakers Score with Haunting Trilogy of Movement," *Ottawa Citizen,* 21 February 1997.
Jackson, Graham, "Dancemakers Find Stability in a Flow of Changes," *Performing Arts Magazine,* Spring 1978.
Jackson, Graham, "Dance Profile: Peggy Baker," *Performing Arts Magazine*, Spring 1979.
Kelly, Deirdre, "Storefront Dance: It's All a Matter of Streetscape," *Globe and Mail*, 8 November 1989.
O'Toole, Lawrence, "Dancemakers: Democratic Scavengers Become a Full-Fledged Company," *Globe and Mail*, 10 April 1976.
Smith, Kathleen, "Dancemakers, Hart House Theatre, Toronto, 22-25 April 1981," *Dance in Canada*, Fall 1981.

*   *   *

Author Max Wyman writes in his book *Dance Canada* (1989) that people joked in the mid-1970s that every time a York University dance department class graduated, five new dance companies were formed. However, it wasn't the forming that was difficult, it was the surviving, and Dancemakers is one of those companies born out of York that did survive. It was created by York dance department graduates Andrea Ciel Smith and Marcy Radler with a handful of strong, idealistic dancers.

Dancemakers debuted in July 1974 by dancing on Toronto's Markham Street in front of the David Mirvish Gallery. The company developed a relationship with Mirvish, performing in his gallery several times. Mirvish and his father Ed, owners of the famed Royal Alexandra Theatre and the new Princess of Wales Theatre, are two of Toronto's biggest presenters of commercial theatre.

In September 1974, Dancemakers presented its first theater performance. With the help of an Ontario Arts Council grant they were able to present a program that featured the work of Kelly Hogan and Mitchell Rose, both New York choreographers; founding member and York graduate Carol Anderson; William Holahan, another York graduate, collaborated with Smith and Anderson; and Grant Strate, the founding chair of the dance department at York. Strate not only choreographed for the company but also coached the dancers and supplied them with rehearsal space at York. In their first press release they wrote, "the impetus for the formation of the Dancemakers arose out of the needs of several young choreographer-dancers to give significant expression to their concepts of the making of dance works" or more simply put, dancers who needed to dance. Another release to the press states that "Dancemakers hopes to widen the modern dance audience by performing their dances beyond the confines of the conventional theater. Plans include performance in shopping centers and on the street itself." They felt they could offer Toronto audiences a different kind of dance experience from the National Ballet, Toronto Dance Theatre or 15 Dance Laboratorium.

Originally, they were only going to perform work created by company members, but even before their first performance they realized how naive that was and decided to have an open door policy. A year later, this is what set them apart from other budding modern dance companies; they were a repertory group open to collaborative association with any number of choreographers using any number of styles. They eventually built a repertoire composed of dances by Robert Cohan, Norman Morrice, Nina Wiener, Paul Taylor, Donald McKayle, Lar Lubovitch, Grant Strate, Anna Blewchamp, Judith Marcuse, Janice Hladki, Paula Ravitz, Mitchell Rose, Kelly Hogan, Jennifer Mascall, Karen Jamieson, and company members Carol Anderson, Peggy Baker, Patricia Fraser and Conrad Alexandrowicz.

Part of the original mandate was to widen the modern dance audience by performing their dances in places other than conventional theaters. They did this by performing in schools, rehab centers, recreation centers and even prisons. At one Toronto school, kids were enthralled as the dancers demonstrated the dance meanings of speed, level, space and dynamics, and showed them how to create a movement phrase and demonstrated improvisational dance-making.

The interesting thing about Dancemakers' early years is that there was no artistic director. Smith had planned to disband the company after one season but the response was so positive that they kept producing shows. However, no one was ready to take on the responsibility of artistic direction, therefore, decisions were made democratically. It wasn't until 1977, when three of the founding members left Canada, that some kind of leadership had to be established in order to keep the company going. Thus, Peggy Baker and Patricia Miner assumed the roles of co-directors.

When the company first formed the dancers were paid $5 per week, while choreographers were paid whatever was available. In one case, Noelyn George crocheted an afghan as payment for the choreographer. In the early years the dancer turnover was frequent mainly because of the money. In 1978, Graham Jackson wrote that "Dancemakers is about as far from stable as you can be and still exist as a performing group." For him, stability meant having a solid corps of dancers, a permanent repertoire, a definite look and maybe an operating grant from one of the arts councils, and yet in its four years of existence Dancemakers didn't have any of these things. However, there was consistency in a handful of individuals important to the company's history.

Carol Anderson had a fifteen-year association with Dancemakers as a dancer, choreographer, and director. Anderson brought influences from studies with London School of Contemporary Dance, José Limón, Merce Cunningham and Judy Jarvis. By the company's second season, Anderson was contributing work regularly. Among these is *Windhover* (1983) which became a signature piece for Dancemakers. Other notable dances are: *Those Damn AM Songs, Decade, Lumen* and *Quick Studies.*

Peggy Baker, whose leadership led to a coherent and powerful performance group, also contributed original choreography and stellar dancing. While studying at the School of Toronto Dance Theatre, Baker performed in the Dancemakers debut concert and occasionally contributed choreography such as *Album*—a dance of four "snapshot" vignettes inspired by her family photo album—and *Disc-a pop-star*, a disco lament. Baker's strength and versatility as a dancer is legendary as she has gained an international reputation as a highly acclaimed solo dancer and choreographer.

While the list of dancers for each performance was slightly different, by 1976 the company did have a choreographic constant in Anna Blewchamp. She created many significant pieces for Dancemakers including *Arrival of All time, A.K.A., Terminal* and *Homage.* In works such as *Terminal* and *A.K.A.,* Blewchamp brings in pieces of 20th-century social dancing such as the charleston, jitterbug, 1940s ballroom and disco. *Homage* is a satirical tribute to theatrical dance, everything from Fred Astaire to Petipa and Balanchine to Humphrey and Graham. *Arrival of All Time* is known as a modern dance classic in Canadian history and was inspired by Virginia Woolf's suicide note.

Both Patricia Fraser and Patricia Miner joined Dancemakers in 1975, Fraser coming from York University and Miner from Toronto Dance Theatre. Both contributed to Dancemaker's survival through leadership and their extraordinary abilities as dancers. Fraser began her movement training in Scottish Highland dance but easily made the transition to more serious ballet and modern training at York University. Fraser became Dancemakers' associate director in 1980 and then co-director with Anderson from 1981-85. Never wanting to perform just one kind of movement, Fraser worked well performing the diverse choreography of the Dancemakers repertoire from Paul Taylor's *Aureole* to Conrad Alexandrowicz's comic solo *Mump,* created specially for Fraser. After leaving Dancemakers in 1985, Fraser continued to perform independently, commissioning work from choreographers such as Rachel Browne, Christopher House and Paul-André Fortier. Fraser has also established herself as a teacher, founding the Teachers Collective with Miner and Sylvain Brochu in 1991. Since June 1994 she has been principal of the School of Toronto Dance Theatre and was acting principal since the previous September.

Miner received her training from the National Ballet School, the School of Toronto Dance Theatre, London School of Contemporary Dance and the José Limón Company, with whom she performed in the summer of 1977. She toured Europe with Toronto Dance Theatre before joining Dancemakers. From 1977 to 1979 she co-directed the company with Baker bringing stability to the company after many of the founding members left Toronto to pursue other interests. Versatility was a must for any Dancemakers dancer and Miner had this in spades. She moved easily from the Twyla Tharpish movement of Nina Wiener's *A Friend Is Better Than a Dollar* to the modern classicism of Barry Smith's *Galliard* to the leggy awkwardness of her preadolescent character in *Baker's Album.* Miner has distinguished herself as a teacher and administrator with Toronto's Teachers Collective and she has become a mentor for many of Toronto's rising independent dancers. In 1997, Miner, with Baker and Fraser, founded the Contemporary Dance Summer School for professional dancers.

After Anderson resigned as artistic director in 1988, Dancemakers took a major turn moving from a repertory company to one that performed mainly the work of its artistic director. From 1988 to 1990 that position was held by choreographer Bill James. James cut his teeth as a dancer with Le Groupe de la Place Royale and then eventually choreographed for Le Groupe, O'Vertigo and Danse-Partout before coming to Toronto. James had studied architecture before turning to dance but had difficulty handling the mathematical side of it. However, his fascination with space and form have stayed with him. He is interested in formalism but his dances are often gritty and raw looking. When he came to work for Dancemakers, he had been living in rural Quebec, so his move to Toronto set him to experimenting with dance in an urban environment. An example is *Atlas Moves Watching* which took place in a storefront on Toronto's busy Queen St. West. The dancers performed with their backs to the store window so that whatever happened on the street was a part of the dance.

James brought innovative choreography to the company, but Dancemakers struggled with the transition from being a repertory company and James resigned as artistic director in 1990. He has continued his innovative, site-specific work as an independent choreographer in Toronto.

French-born Serge Bennathan, Dancemakers' current artistic director, assumed the position in 1990. Bennathan studied ballet in Paris and at age 17 joined Roland Petit's Ballet de Marseilles for which he began choreographing two years later. He emigrated to Canada in 1985 and danced with Le Groupe de la Place Royale, Experimental Dance and Music (EDAM), Dancecorps, the Judith Marcuse Dance Company and Ballet British Columbia before coming to Dancemakers. Under his direction, Dancemakers has moved away completely from its eclectic repertory tradition, but has gained a stylistic homogeneity as well as wider international acclaim. Among the works Bennathan has contributed are: *Quands les grands meres s'envolent* (1992), which explores his emotional experience after the death of his grandmother; *Les vents tumulteux* (1993), which mixes text and movement and explores the creative passion of artists and won a Dora Mavor Moore Award nomination for best new choreography; his haunting *Sable/Sand* (1995) won a Dora Mavor Moore Award for new choreography. In 1997, *Sable/Sand* was expanded into a trilogy with the sections "Like Dunes," "Like Water," and "People," and was set to the Arabic-inspired score of Ahmed Hassan. Although Bennathan describes his work as simply "contemporary" and "organic," critics have claimed that he has brought the only authentic exponent of "new dance" to Toronto.

For a company that was to present just one season of work and then disband, Dancemakers has become a mainstay of Toronto's dance community. Its studios have become a performance venue and rehearsal space for the independent community; past and present dancers such as Julia Sasso, Philip Drube and Sylvie Bouchard contribute choreography to Toronto's dance scene regularly, and under Bennathan's guidance the Dancemakers continue to present innovative and challenging choreography.

—Amy Bowring

DANIEL, Nora

American dancer, choreographer, and educator

Born: Nora Reynolds in Los Angeles, 24 October 1955. **Education:** Began dancing as a child under the guidance of her mother and mentor, Bella Lewitzky; North Carolina School of the Arts, graduated 1973; also studied ballet with Jocelyn Lorenz and Maggie Black; studied Rommett technique with Zena Rommett, 1978-80; trained in Pilates at the Physicalmind Institute in Santa Fe, New Mexico, from 1994. **Career:** Dancer, Bella Lewitzky Dance Company, 1973-78, Lar Lubovitch Dance Company, 1978-82; performed three seasons with the Mark Morris Dance Group, the Merce Cunningham Dance Company, and Dance Theatre Workshop, 1980-82; first independent choreography, 1979; founder, Nora Reynolds Dance, 1986, Nora Daniel and Dancers, 1995; faculty associate, University of New Mexico, 1983-95; has also traveled throughout the U.S, Europe, and Canada as guest artist; currently an integrative conditioning/movement reeducation instructor and practicing Reiki master, Nora Daniel Studio, Albuquerque, Mew Mexico.

Roles

1969   *Orrenda* (Lewitzky), Bella Lewitzky Dance Company, Idyllwild, California

1970   *Kineasonata* (Lewitzky), Bella Lewitzky Dance Company, Idyllwild, California

1971   *Pietas* (Lewitzky), Bella Lewitzky Dance Company, Florida State University, Tallahassee

1972   *Scintilla* (Lewitzky), Bella Lewitzky Dance Company, University of California at Berkeley

1973   *Game Plan* (Lewitzky), Bella Lewitzky Dance Company, Los Angeles

1974   *Spaces Between* (Lewitzky), Bella Lewitzky Dance Company, Colorado State University, Denver
          Five (Lewitzky), Bella Lewitzky Dance Company, American Dance Festival, New London, Connecticut

1975   *V.C.O.* (Voltage Controlled Oscillator) (Lewitzky), Bella Lewitzky Dance Company, Los Angeles

1976   *Greening* (Lewitzky), Bella Lewitzky Dance Company, American Dance Festival, New London
          Inscape (Lewitzky), Bella Lewitzky Dance Company, Los Angeles

1977   *Pas de Bach* (Lewitzky), Bella Lewitzky Dance Company, Los Angeles
          Trio for Saki (Lewitzky), Bella Lewitzky Dance Company, Los Angeles
          Jigsaw (Susan Rose), Bella Lewitzky Dance Company, Los Angeles

1978   The Bride in *Les Noces* (Lubovitch), Lar Lubovitch Dance Company
          Exsultate Jubilate (Lubovitch), Lar Lubovitch Dance Company
          North Star (Lubovitch), Lar Lubovitch Dance Company
          Marimba (Lubovitch), Lar Lubovitch Dance Company

1979   *Up Jump* (Lubovitch), Lar Lubovitch Dance Company

1980   *Cavalcade* (Lubovitch), Lar Lubovitch Dance Company
          Castor and Pollux (Morris), Mark Morris Dance Group, New York

1981   *Gloria* (Morris), Mark Morris Dance Group, New York
          I Love You Dearly (Morris), Mark Morris Dance Group, New York

1982   *Big Shoulders* (Lubovitch), Lar Lubovitch Dance Company
          Tehelim (Lubovitch), Lar Lubovitch Dance Company
          Avalanche (Lubovitch), Lar Lubovitch Dance Company
          Blue Danube (Lubovitch), Lar Lubovitch Dance Company
          Eight Person Precision Ball Passing (Charles Moulton), Lar Lubovitch Dance Company
          Gears Align (Charles Moulton), Lar Lubovitch Dance Company
          Celestial Greetings (Morris), Mark Morris Dance Group, New York
          Songs That Tell a Story (Morris), Mark Morris Dance Group, New York
          New Love Song Waltzes (Morris), Mark Morris Dance Group, New York
          Etudes Modernes/Jr. High (Morris), Mark Morris Dance Group, New York

1983   *Tamil Film Songs* (Morris), Mark Morris Dance Group, New York
          Song of the Woman (Lewitzky), Bella Lewitzky Dance Company, Los Angeles

Works

1979   *Axis* (solo; mus. Cluster), Choreoground Theatre, New York

1983   *Cross Current* (solo; mus. Saint Saëns), University of
        New Mexico, Albuquerque
        Freeze Frame (solo; mus. Eno, Van Tieghem), Contem-
        porary Dance Alliance

1984   *Solo in Four Parts* (solo; mus. Bach), University of New
        Mexico, Albuquerque

1985   *Insitu* (mus. Vivaldi), University of New Mexico Dance
        Ensemble, Albuquerque
        Voices Passing w/ Lee Connor (mus. Leoninus), Univer-
        sity of New Mexico, Albuquerque

1986   *Gravity's Web* (mus. Steve Roach), Carolina dancers, South
        Carolina
        Jardin Au Fou (collaboration; mus. Rodelius), South Caro-
        lina Governor's School students

1987   *Terrain* (mus. Cluster), University of New Mexico Dance
        Ensemble, Albuquerque
        New York Counterpoint (mus. Steve Reich), University
        of New Mexico Dance Ensemble, Albuquerque
        Passenger (mus. Jon Hassell), Akasha, Chicago
        And He Was (solo; mus. collage), California State Univer-
        sity, Long Beach
        Social Dances (mus. Mozart), Danzantes

1989   *Center's Edge* (mus. Sydney Davis), Nora Reynolds
        Dance, Santa Fe

1990   *Duet* (mus. Voix Bulgares), Nora Reynolds Dance, Santa
        Fe
        Irish Songs (mus. Beethoven), Nora Reynolds Dance,
        Santa Fe
        Oracle (mus. Istvan Marta), University of New Mexico
        Contemporary Dance Ensemble, Albuquerque

1991   *Different Drumming* (mus. Doug Nottingham), Univer-
        sity of New Mexico Contemporary Dance Ensemble,
        Albuquerque
        In My Soul (mus. EmmyLou Harris), Nora Reynolds
        Dance, Santa Fe
        Walking/Falling (mus. Laurie Anderson), Bella Lewitzky
        Dance Company, Los Angeles

1992   *With and Without* (mus. Planxty), Aspen Dance Connec-
        tion, Colorado
        Any Emotion (mus. Test Dept.), Aspen Dance Connec-
        tion, Colorado

1993   *Solitaire* (mus. Larry Attaway), California Arts Dance
        Ensemble
        Mercy (mus. Anonymous 4), Nora Reynolds Dance, Al-
        buquerque
        Sextet (mus. Dave Bryant), Nora Reynolds Dance, Albu-
        querque
        Travellers (mus. John Bartlit), Nora Reynolds Dance,
        Albuquerque
        Brand New Dance (mus. EmmyLou Harris), Nora
        Reynolds Dance, Albuquerque
        A Map of Time (mus. Vito Ricci, J. Siberry), Webster
        Dance Theater

1994   *Mysterious Adventure* (mus. Cage), Nora Reynolds Dance,
        Albuquerque
        Forest Scenes (mus. Schumann), Nora Reynolds Dance,
        Albuquerque
        Erzatska! (mus. 3 Mustaphas 3), Nora Reynolds Dance,
        Albuquerque

1995   *Strange but True* (mus. Evan Ziporyn), Main Dance/Nora
        Daniel and Dancers, Albuquerque

1996   *Planctus* w/ Bill Evans (mus. Steve Peters), Daniel and
        Evans, Albuquerque

Publications

On DANIEL: articles—

Banes, Sally, review of Mark Morris Dance Group, *Dance Maga-
zine,* April 1982.
Robertson, Michael, review of Lar Lubovitch Dance Company,
Dance Magazine, August 1978.
Rosen, Lillie, "A Conversation with Bella Lewitzky," *Ballet Review,*
Fall 1982.

*   *   *

Nora Daniel's business card announces "Dance, Reiki, and Integrative Conditioning." On one level, it's just another calling card; on
another, it's indicative of the various paths this modern dancer,
choreographer, and teacher has taken.

Referring to herself as an "addictive improvisor," Daniel has
been inventing movement since she was three years old. In a 1991
interview with David Steinberg of the *Albuquerque Journal,* her
mother, Bella Lewitzky, commented: "At the age of three, Nora
was creating her own movements to the music of Carl Orff's
Carmina Burana, and then two years later dancing the whole choral
work." It was evident that Daniel had inherited her mother's gift of
movement.

Daniel studied dance throughout her childhood and continued to
study ballet and modern dance while attending the North Carolina
School of the Arts, where she worked with Agnes de Mille. After
graduating in 1973, she returned to Los Angeles to perform with her
mother's company. Sensing a need to venture out on her own, she
moved to New York five years later to dance with the Lar Lubovitch
company. While with Lubovitch, she also performed in concerts
choreographed by Mark Morris. Then in 1984, she moved to New
Mexico to establish herself as an independent choreographer and
teacher.

Participating in the creative process with Agnes de Mille, Bella
Lewitzky, Lar Lubovitch, and Mark Morris contributed significantly to Daniel's movement and creative repertoire. From each of
these unique individuals she drew a different vision: DeMille's mix
of drama and dance, Lewitzky's shape-oriented movement,
Lubovitch's chaotic momentum and loose, flowing movement, and
Morris' visual description of music through dance.

Order, structure, and form are the building blocks of Daniel's
style; she likes movement and considers herself a purist in that
sense. Referring to her choreographic process as mathematical, she
takes a phrase, disassembles, and rearranges it. Then, she looks at it
in a different order or applies the same operational equation to the
transformed product to reorder it again.

Daniel's fascination with weight and gravity is exemplified in her
work *Walking and Falling,* which is part of the Lewitzky company's
repertoire. Performed to Laurie Anderson's lyrics, the constant
expression of earth-boundness, use of momentum, and directional
changes occurs in a witty exploration of off-balance movement. As
the dancers express a variety of humorous interpretations of walking and falling, their bodies are subject to the difficult task of maintaining a pose while trying to contain the stored energy of momentum absorbed between each walk and fall. With each step-oriented
pose, the increased frustration to conserve suspended energy be-

comes more visible. Incapable of conserving their momentum any longer, the dreidel-like bodies release the chaotic forceful energy in rebellion.

Visual art, especially film, has also been an inspiration for Daniel's work, because films can be viewed repeatedly and still provide revelations for the viewer. She enjoys creating pieces which hold a wealth of thematic material: "Looking at it over and over again, there are always hidden messages. I like to have things that might seem ornate to people, but I like the density of relativity going on."

Daniel defines her work as abstract because it travels between the surreal and literal worlds. *Sextet* (1993), also included in the Lewitzky repertoire, masterfully typifies Daniel's talent for creating work rich in abstraction. Three couples represent a cross-section of society through the physically expressive vignettes of relationships in space. Constructed in six sections, the dance presents contrasting interpretations of human relationships, creating the layers of meaning Daniel always seeks.

Having arrived at a transitional point in her career, Daniel feels she has not moved away from dance but only from the structure in which it has been confined for many years. Referring to her healing work as "integrative conditioning," Daniel utilizes her eye for movement to to assess the flow of energy through the human body. A breath constriction problem, for example, may be due to an impediment of the flow, an energy "cyst." Daniel works toward keeping energy flowing in a balanced way through the use of Reiki.

For Daniel, dance is an intelligence that resides in the body, a form of creative intelligence that doesn't have to be confined to an art form. Her goal as a teacher and as a healer has always been the same: "to help people be more genuine in terms of being themselves," to discover the natural intelligence of their bodies. Daniel thinks that discovery can be made equally well by watching great choreography or through experiencing the natural forces of one's own body: "I realized that any imitation of anything isn't worth much. Anything that pursues the core can be very valuable. Pursuing the core of healing you get back to the same information that you would find if you were someone like Mark Morris pursuing the core of structure in choreography and music. They are not dissimilar at all."

Wondering if her work is going to continue on stage or in the healing arts, she comments, "I am very real in what I am doing, but I am also inventing what I am doing as I do it, which is what I love. It couldn't get any better than that for me."

—Barbejoy A. Ponzio

DAVIES, Siobhan

British dancer, choreographer, and company director

Born: Susan Davies, 18 September 1950, in London. **Education:** Studied art at the Hammersmith College of Art & Design; enrolled at the newly founded London School of Contemporary Dance, 1967. **Career:** Apprentice dancer with London Contemporary Dance Theatre (LCDT) during its first London season, 1969; became a full member, 1971; first professional choreography, 1972; appointed associate choreographer of LCDT, 1974; resident choreographer, 1983; founded Siobhan Davies and Dancers, 1981; co-founded Second Stride with Richard Alston and Ian Spink, 1982; founded Siobhan Davies Dance Company, 1988; associate choreog-

rapher for Rambert Dance Company, 1989-91. Television broadcasts include *Silent Partners,* London Weekend TV; *South Bank Show,* 1985; *White Man Sleeps,* 1989 (IMZ Dance Screens Best Studio Adaptation, 1991); *Wyoming,* 1989; *White Bird Featherless,* 1995. **Awards:** Fulbright Fellowship in Choreography, 1987; Digital Dance awards, 1988-90; Laurence Olivier Award, 1993; Member of the British Empire, 1995; Prudential Award for the Arts 1996; honorary fellowship, Trinity College of Music, 1996.

Roles

Numerous roles for London Contemporary Dance Theatre, choreographed by Robert Cohan, including *Nympheas, Waterless Method of Swimming Instruction, Stabat Mater;* also created roles for Richard Alston and Dancers, and the Ian Spink Group; created the role of Anna in the English National Opera's production of *The Seven Deadly Sins* (Alston; 1978).

Works (premiered in London, unless otherwise noted)

1972	*Relay* (mus. Colin Wood, Bernard Watson), LCDT
1974	*Pilot* (mus. Igg Welthy, Stephen Barker), LCDT, Southampton
	The Calm (mus. Geoffrey Burgon), LCDT, Manchester
1975	*Diary* (mus. Gregory Rose), LCDT, Liverpool
1976	*Step at a Time* (mus. Geoffrey Burgon), LCDT, Manchester
1977	*Nightwatch,* w/Micha Bergese, Robert Cohan, Robert North (mus. Bob Downes), LCDT
	Sphinx (mus. Barrington Pheloung), LCDT, Manchester
1978	*Then You Can Only Sing* (composed and sung by Judyth Knight), LCDT, Manchester
1979	*Celebration* (10th and 15th century music, arr. Nicholas Carr), Ballet Rambert, Horsham
	Ley Line (mus. Vincent Brown), LCDT
1980	*Something to Ten* (mus. Benjamin Britten), LCDT, Mold
	Recall (mus. Vincent Brown), LCDT
	If My Complaints Could Passions Move (mus. Benjamin Britten), London School of Contemporary Dance
1981	*Plain Song* (mus. Erik Satie), Siobhan Davies and Dancers
	Standing Waves (mus. Stuart Dempster), Siobhan Davies and Dancers
	Free Setting (mus. Michael Finnissy), LCDT, Coventry
1982	*Mazurka Elegiaca* (solo for Linda Gibbs, mus. Benjamin Britten), King's Lynn
	Rushes (mus. Michael Finnissy), Second Stride, Oxford
	Carnival (mus. Camille Saint-Saëns), Second Stride, Coventry
1983	*The Dancing Department* (mus. Bach), LCDT, Oxford
	Minor Characters (text Barbara McLauren), Second Stride, Edinburgh
1984	*New Galileo* (mus. John Adams), LCDT, Leeds
	Silent Partners (mus. Orlando Gough), Second Stride, Brighton
1985	*Bridge the Distance* (mus. Benjamin Britten), LCDT, Oxford
	The School for Lovers Danced (mus. Mozart), Second Stride, Hexham
1986	*The Run to Earth* (mus. Brian Eno), LCDT, Eastbourne
	and do they do (mus. Michael Nyman), LCDT

1987   *Red Steps* (mus. John Adams), LCDT, Canterbury
        Three untitled pieces for television (mus. David Owen; text, Susan Sontag), LCDT, Channel 4 TV
1988   Play within a play for Ron Daniels' production of *Hamlet,* Royal Shakespeare Company
        Embarque (mus. Steve Reich), Rambert Dance Company, Manchester
        White Man Sleeps (mus. Kevin Volans), Siobhan Davies Dance Company
        Wyoming (mus. John Marc Gowans), Siobhan Davies Dance Company
1989   *Sounding* (mus. Giacinto Scelsi), Rambert Dance Company, Nottingham
        Cover Him with Grass (mus. Kevin Volans), Siobhan Davies Dance Company
        Drawn Breath (mus. Andrew Poppy), Siobhan Davies Dance Company
1990   *Signature* (mus. Kevin Volans), Rambert Dance Company, Brighton
        Dancing Ledge (mus. John Adams), English National Ballet
        Different Trains (mus. Steve Reich), Siobhan Davies Dance Company
1991   *Arctic Heart* (text, Gretel Ehrlich; mus. John Marc Gowans), Siobhan Davies Dance Company
1992   *Winnsboro Cotton Mill Blues* (mus. Frederic Rzewski, with tape by Mark Underwood, Roger Heaton), Rambert Dance Company
        White Bird Featherless (mus. Gerald Barry), Siobhan Davies Dance Company, Mold
        Make-Make (tape compiled by David Buckland), Siobhan Davies Dance Company
1993   *Wanting to Tell Stories* (mus. Kevin Volans), Siobhan Davies Dance Company, Brighton
1994   *Between the National and the Bristol* (mus. Gavin Bryars), CandoCo
        The Glass Blew In (mus. Gavin Bryars), Siobhan Davies Dance Company, Bracknell
1995   *Wild Translations* (mus. Kevin Volans), Siobhan Davies Dance Company, Sheffield
        The Art of Touch (mus. Domenico Scarlatti, Matteo Fargion), Siobhan Davies Dance Company, Manchester
1996   *Trespass* (mus. Gerald Barry), Siobhan Davies Dance Company, Blackpool
        Affections (mus. Handel, arr. Gerald Barry), Siobhan Davies Dance Company, Oxford
1997   *Bank* (mus. Matteo Fargion), Siobhan Davies Dance Company, Blackpool

Publications

On DAVIES: articles—

Dance Now, special Siobhan Davies issue, Spring 1997.
Dance Theatre Journal, special Siobhan Davies issue, Spring 1996.

On DAVIES: books—

Jordan, Stephanie, *Striding Out,* London, 1992.

Films and Videotapes

White Man Sleeps, PAL, 1997.
Wyoming, PAL, 1997.

*   *   *

Siobhan Davies is a long-standing, influential figure in British contemporary dance, and one of its most important choreographers. Like her contemporary Richard Alston, she came from an art college background before enrolling in the first full-time course at the newly founded London School of Contemporary Dance in 1967. After joining the London Contemporary Dance Theatre in 1969, she became a prominent dancer in the company, noted for the passion she invested in her performances. In 1970 she performed with Ballet for All, the Royal Ballet's choreographic workshop; she subsequently became a member of Richard Alston and Dancers alongside her career with LCDT. She stopped dancing in 1983.

Davies also showed a precocious choreographic talent, encouraged by LCDT's artistic director, Robert Cohan. Reacting against the Graham technique of her training (Cunningham was an important early influence, as was Alston), she initially experimented with improvisations to jazz as a way of exploring new movement possibilities. For her first professional piece, *Relay* (1972), she was inspired by sports movement, admiring its directness of action and ease of execution. The piece won critical favour, and Davies soon established a reputation as a major British choreographer.

Davies' early pieces tended to stress shape, line, and design in body movement. *Sphinx,* made in 1977, marked a significant development. Here she explored animal-like movements, consciously trying to avoid the habitual associations of the human body (legs for walking, arms for gesturing, head for orienting) as a way of organically expanding the body's movement potential. The resultant articulacy of the torso, the fluent, dynamic interaction of body parts, and the weighted facility of movement have since become hallmarks of her choreographic style.

This organic structuring of the body is only one aspect of choreography; equally important is the structuring of the dance—how groups work together, placement, and timing on stage. In *Plain Song,* made for her Siobhan Davies and Dancers in 1981, she wove together deliberately complex phrases for seven dancers, aiming for both intricacy of detail and clarity of form. She has since developed this tension between complexity and legibility to a considerable degree of sophistication, notably in *Embarque* (1988) and *Bank* (1997).

Davies formed Siobhan Davies and Dancers in 1981 alongside her commitments at LCDT in order to experiment on a more personal plane. She followed this up in 1982 by co-founding the influential Second Stride, with Richard Alston and Ian Spink. With this company she made several character-based pieces, such as *Minor Characters* and *Silent Partners,* continuing an interest that had appeared in *Then You Can Only Sing* (1978) and *Something to Ted* (1980). Typically, the drama in these pieces is on an intimate, introspective scale. With these works Davies also began experimenting with small gestural movements, a vein she has continued to mine, for example in *Wyoming* (1988) and *Different Trains* (1990).

A turning point for Davies came in 1987. She took a break from choreographing, embarking on a nine-month study trip to America on a Fulbright Fellowship, and she left both LCDT and Second Stride. On her return in 1988 she formed the Siobhan Davies Dance Company, and also began choreographing for Rambert Dance Company, where she was associate choreographer from 1989 to 1991.

Once again choreographing simultaneously for a large repertory company and her own independent group, she now seemed to have found a new vigour. With Rambert she made the dazzling *Embarque,* a large-scale abstract work to music by Steve Reich; while with her own company she produced *White Man Sleeps* and *Wyoming*—intimate, contemplative pieces in which she used release techniques and image-based work for the first time. After *Winnsboro Cotton Mill Blues,* made for Rambert Dance Company in 1992, Davies has worked solely with her own company, producing such finely crafted works as the elegiac *The Glass Blew In* (1994), the poignant *Wild Translations* (1995), and the contrasting companion pieces *Trespass* and *Affections* (both 1996).

Davies tends to use contemporary music (often commissioned), which seems to give her a greater freedom to shape the dance from a movement basis. Recently she has also used Baroque music: Scarlatti for *The Art of Touch* (1995) and Handel for *Affections.* Significantly, however, in both these pieces she also worked with contemporary scores to allow more play between movement and music: the second half of *The Art of Touch* used a score for harpsichord by Matteo Fargion, echoing Scarlatti's music, while the movement in *Affections* drew on her previous piece, *Trespass,* which was set to a score by Gerald Barry.

Davies has occasionally used spoken text in her work, though rarely literally. Sometimes it becomes a source of rhythmic interest, as in *Then You Can Only Sing* (1978); elsewhere, for example in *Minor Characters* or *Arctic Heart* (1991), it provides a backdrop for the choreography, resonating with the dance rather than mirroring it. The same is true for the designs she uses, as important for Davies as the music. Most frequently she has worked with her photographer partner David Buckland, whose designs range from photo images echoing the dancers in *Free Setting, Rushes* and *Silent Partners,* the moving metal grilles of *Wanting to Tell Stories,* to the huge rotating fan-blade of light in *Wild Translations.* Other striking sets included the top-lit chequered floor in *White Bird Featherless* (by Peter Mumford and Antony McDonald), and Hugh O'Donnell's vivid abstract backcloth for *Red Steps* (1987). Designs for her dances tend to be clear and boldly imagined, adding their own layer to the choreography while allowing space for the dance.

Davies is a modernist choreographer, with a deeply felt commitment to finding out what dance can communicate on its own movement-based terms. Like Cunningham, she believes that movement has its own inherent expressive power. Unlike Cunningham, however, she integrates her movement with the music and design, sometimes closely, but more usually allowing considerable play, finding moments of contact, counterpoint and separation. And unlike "pure dance" choreographers, her works are often suffused with sensuality and humane passion, and an interior emotional landscape often seems submerged just beneath the surface. Hovering between the abstract and the figurative, her work is never solely formal, yet never straightforwardly narrative. This point was made most directly in *Wanting to Tell Stories* (1993), where, using movement as a starting point rather than narrative or character, she nevertheless constructed a dramatic, richly expressive piece whose "story," as she put it, "couldn't be told in any other way except through dance."

—Sanjoy Roy

DAVIS, Chuck
American dancer, choreographer, and company director

Born: 1 January 1937 in Raleigh, North Carolina. **Education:** Attended Howard University, 1966-68; studied with Owen Dodson. **Military:** U.S. Navy, special high school program, 1953-57. **Career:** Dancer, Klara Harrington Dance Company, beginning 1959; Olatunji Dance Company, 1962-66; Eleo Pomare Dance Company, 1966-68; Bernice Johnson Dance Company, beginning 1966; began teaching, South Bronx Community Theatre, c. 1966 (has also taught college and universities nationwide); founder/director, Chuck Davis Dance Company, 1967-83; artist-in-residence, American Dance Festival, summers beginning 1974; founder, DanceAfrica annual festival, 1977; founder, African-American Dance Ensemble, 1994; founder, Alayanfe (children's dance company), 1985. **Awards:** New York Dance and Performance Award ("Bessie"), 1992.

Works

1969	*Isicathulo I* (mus. Khalid Saleem)
1970	*Lamban Guinee* (mus. Saleem)
1983	*Mandiana* (mus. Saleem)
	Fanga (mus. Saleem)
1984	*Dundunba* (mus. Saleem)
1985	*Drought* (mus. Saleem)
1986	*Isicathulo II* (mus. Saleem)
	Peace Rally (mus. Saleem)
	Odun De (mus. Saleem)
	Boks N'Daye II (mus. Saleem)
1990	*Yette Sorte* (mus. Saleem)
	Simple Prayer
	Healing Forces (mus. Saleem)
	Odyssey (mus. Spies)
1991	*Dance Styles* (mus. Saleem, Kelte)
1992	*Powerful Long Ladder* (mus. African-American women)
1994	*Vanishing Runner*
	Koo Koo
1995	*Waterwheel*

Other works include: *Ritual of Awareness, Martyrs, Dance Forever Ya'll, Rites of Passage, Namaniyo, Gboi,* and *Power Source I-II-III.*

Publications

On DAVIS: articles—

Anderson, Jack, "An Evening of Getting Together," *New York Times,* 27 June 1997.
————, "Dance: Chuck Davis," *New York Times,* 11 February 1986.
————, "Heritage of Black Dance Gets a Boost in Durham," *New York Times,* 6 July 1986.
Conrad, Willa, "Energy Bursts through Ensemble's Interpretation of African Dance," *Charlotte Observer,* 8 November 1995.
Dunning, Jennifer, "A Celebration of Africa in Ritual and Spectacle," *New York Times,* 11 May 1997.
————, "A Continent's Rich Rhythms Resound Anew," *New York Times,* 23 May 1993.

Fortson, Olivia, "African-American Festival," *Charlotte Observer*, 26 May 1996.

Haithman, Diane, "Peace, Love—and Dance," *Los Angeles Times*, 29 October 1995.

Jackson, Bob, "African Dancer Chuck Davis Returns to Denver, Boulder," *Rocky Mountain News*, 7 April 1997.

Lewis, Junlinda, "DanceAfrica America," *Dance Magazine*, September 1995.

Reinhardt, Carol, "Troupe Offers More Than Great Dance," *Charlotte Observer*, 11 November 1992.

Shulgold, Marc, "Company Preserves—and Shares—African Dance," *Rocky Mountain News*, 17 July 1997.

Sommers, Pamela, "A Continental Drift of Dancers," *Washington Post*, 6 June 1997.

*   *   *

Chuck Davis is a leading force in African-American dance. Through his Durham, North Carolina-based African-American Dance Ensemble, his community-outreach work in association with the American Dance Festival, and his role as founder of DanceAfrica, an annual festival of dance and culture, he has raised the profile of African-inspired dance in the United States.

Born on 1 January 1937 in Raleigh, North Carolina, Davis spent time in the U.S. Navy before attending Howard University from 1966 to 1968. There, he studied under poet and critic Owen Dodson, a leader in African-American theater. Davis then moved to New York in 1963, where he immersed himself in modern, jazz, and African dance. He joined the Klara Harrington Dance Company in 1959, his first professional dance job, and from then until 1968 was associated with a number of troupes, including the Olatunji Dance Company, the Eleo Pomare Dance Company (including in the premiere of *Blues Jungle* in 1966) and the Bernice Johnson Dance Company, as well as with Raymond Sawyer and Joan Miller. During this time, Davis also began teaching dance at the South Bronx Community Theatre.

In 1967 Davis decided to form his own ensemble, the Chuck Davis Dance Company, which specialized in presenting traditional African-American dance in the U.S. and around the world. Eventually, it became one of the most well-known troupes of its kind. In 1977, the Chuck Davis Dance Company participated in FESTAC, an international exposition and celebration of African culture, held in Lagos, Nigeria. Davis has returned to the continent every year since then, often bringing students, to study traditional dance styles and music. Visiting Africa had been a dream of his since 1964, when he saw a performance of the Sierra Leone National Dance Company at the New York World's Fair.

In 1974 Davis joined the dance faculty of the American Dance Festival in Durham, North Carolina, where he remains a summer artist-in-residence. The Chuck Davis Dance Company relocated to Durham in 1980, at the invitation of ADF, and was in residence there from 1980 to 1984, launching ADF's Community Services Program, which taught dance to members of the community. As a result of this community outreach, Davis began to realize, in 1983, that the level of dance proficiency in the community at large was approaching that of a professional dance troupe, so he formed the African-American Dance Ensemble (AADE), a professional company composed of community members and focusing on African-inspired dances. Its premiere was in February 1994, and it continues to perform in the U.S. and in Europe.

The African-American Dance Ensemble's mission includes research, education, and performance. It revives and stages African, Afro-Caribbean and African-American dances, particularly those in danger of being lost. The troupe performs authentic reconstructions of dances such as the Nigerian *Nataka Tow*; the *Ntore*, the dance of the Royal Watusi Warriors; *Bamaya* from Northern Ghana; and *Lenjen Celebration* from Gambia. The pieces are choreographed by Davis or guest choreographers such as Obo Addy and Abdou Kounta. The company also performs new pieces inspired by African or African-American themes, such as Davis' *Forget Not the Seed*, to poetry by Mel Tomlinson; Kariamu Welsh Asante's *Wait for Me Son*, based on a Zimbabwean legend; Donald McKayle's *Distant Drums*; and Ronald K. Brown's *Free*, to a text about slavery. It also revives dances by premiere black choreographers, such as McKayle's 1951 *Games*, the first traditional modern dance work performed by the Ensemble, staged in 1986 by McKayle himself.

AADE's performances are called "sharings," rather than concerts, and reflect the group's motto, "peace, love, respect for everybody." Audience participation is stressed, including hugging, greeting the dancers and each other, clapping, playing instruments, and dancing. The message is that African dance is a community gathering; demonstrations by dancers and percussionists are intended to add an educational element to the entertainment, and Davis ties the whole thing together by acting as "griot," or storyteller.

Embracing the community has always been an important facet of AADE. Their community dance project, "Sankofa," allows them to bring dance into the neighborhoods of the cities where they perform. Workshops, classes, and lecture-demonstrations for adults and, especially children, are the major tools used to make dance relevant to the area. For example, Davis might lecture on "From Africa to Hip-Hop: Contemporary Urban Dance." As Davis explained to the *Los Angeles Times*, "We are about more than dance, we are about living. We are about culture, we are about sharing and respect and learning more about our heritage."

In addition to his work with his own company, Davis is renowned as the founder of the DanceAfrica dance festival. The annual celebration began when Davis' original troupe, the Chuck Davis Dance Company, was invited to perform at the Brooklyn Academy of Music in 1977. Davis suggested a festival of African dance instead. In 20 years, the event has expanded to more than a week of master classes, symposia, performances, and an African bazaar offering traditional foods and crafts. It has also spread to seven cities, in addition to Brooklyn.

DanceAfrica performances are similar to those of the African American Dance Ensemble (which participates in the festival), with Davis acting as griot. Concerts/sharings always pay tribute to mentors of African-American dance and music, such as Pearl Primus, Katherine Dunham, and Syvilla Fort, and end with all the companies on stage at once for the finale. Participating troupes are diverse, and have included Memory of African Culture, headed by Djimo Kouyate of Senegal, Rennie Harris' PureMovement, a hip-hop group, and Lygya Barreto and his Roots of Brazil. Each festival has a central theme, and all the groups comprise one part of a continuing storyline.

Davis has also directed and choreographed for the stage, with major works including *Babu's Magic (An African Folk Tale)*, *Babu's Juju*, *Lion and the Jewel* and *Medea*. As part of his interest in teaching dance to children, Davis founded Alayanfe (Children's Dance Company) in Durham in 1985. He is also a much-in-demand guest artist-in-residence with dance ensembles across the country, and is a popular teacher of master classes at universities and school programs, and at other institutions ranging from Brooklyn's John F. Kennedy Center to the Black Theatre Alliance. Davis won a "Bessie" award for his contributions to dance in 1992.

Davis's outgoing and joyous personality is one of the driving forces behind the popularity of both the African-American Dance Ensemble and DanceAfrica. Jennifer Dunning of the *New York Times* describes Davis as "larger than life and full of boisterous good cheer."

—Karen Raugust

DEAN, Laura

American dancer, choreographer, and company director

Born: 3 December 1945 on Staten Island, New York. **Education:** Studied with Lucas Hoving, Third Street Settlement, New York; with Muriel Stuart, School of American Ballet; attended New York's High School of the Performing Arts. **Career:** Dancer, Paul Taylor Dance Company, 1965-66; founder, Laura Dean Dancers and Musicians, 1976; choreographed for skater John Curry.

Works (created for and performed by the Laura Dean Dancers and Musicians unless otherwise noted)

1966	*3 Minutes and 10 Seconds*
1967	*Christmas Piece*
1968	*Theater Piece*
	Life Is All Around You
	Red-White-Black
	No Title
1970	*At Alan Saret's*
	An Hour in Silence
1971	*Bach Preludes*
	A Dance Concert
	Stamping Dance
1972	*Quartet Squared*
	Trio
	Circle Dance
	Square Dance
1973	*Walking Dance*
	Jumping Dance
	Changing Pattern Steady Pulse
	Spinning Dance
1974	*Response Dance*
	Changing
1975	*Drumming* (mus. Steve Reich)
1976	*Song* (mus. Dean)
	Dance
1977	*Spiral*
1979	*Music*
1980	*Night* (mus. Dean), Joffrey Ballet
	Tympani
1982	*Fire* (mus. Steve Reich), Joffrey Ballet
	Sky Light
	Solo in Red
1983	*Inner Circle*
	Enochian

1985	*Impact*, Brooklyn Academy of Music
1986	*Forcefield* (mus. Steve Reich), Joffrey Ballet
1988	*Space*, New York City Ballet
1993	*Billboards* (mus. Prince), Joffrey Ballet
	Arrow of Time, Albany Berkshire Ballet
	Ecstasy (mus. Dean)
	Infinity (mus. Dean)
1994	*Light*, Aman World Music and Dance Troupe
	Night Wind

Publications

By DEAN: articles—

"Notes on Choreography," *Dance Scope*, Fall/Winter 1974-75.
"Seven Dances by Laura Dean and Company," *Drama Review*, March 1975.

On DEAN: books—

Anderson, Jack, *Ballet and Modern Dance: A Concise History*, Pennington, New Jersey, 1992.
———, *Choreography Observed*, Iowa City, 1987.
Au, Susan, *Ballet and Modern Dance*, London, 1988.
Blom, Lynne Anne, and L. Tarin Chaplin, *The Intimate Act of Choreography*, Pittsburgh, 1982.
Coe, Robert, *Dance in America*, New York, 1985.
Cohen, Selma Jeanne, *Next Week, Swan Lake: Reflections on Dance and Dances*, Middletown, Connecticut, 1982.
Croce, Arlene, *Going to the Dance*, New York, 1982.
Jowitt, Deborah, *Time and the Dancing Image*, New York, 1988.
Robertson, Allen, and Donald Hutera, *The Dance Handbook*, Boston, 1988.
Taylor, Paul, *Private Domain*, New York, 1987.

On DEAN: articles—

"Laura Dean," in *Current Biography Yearbook 1988*.
Duffy, Martha, "*Billboards*," *Time*, 1 November 1993.
Hardy, Camille, "*Billboards*," *Dance Magazine*, March 1994.
Hunt, Marilyn, "Laura Dean Musicians and Dancers," *Dance Magazine*, September 1994.
Jacobs, Laura A., "*Forcefield*," *The New Leader*, 16 June 1986.

*   *   *

Laura Dean is a leading New York postmodern dancer and choreographer. She is known for her minimalist, mesmerizing folk-dance-style works, in which simple motifs, notably spinning, are repeated for long periods of time as the dancers form geometric patterns, such as circles within circles.

Born in 1945 on Staten Island, Dean attended New York's High School of the Performing Arts. She then spent one year in Paul Taylor's New Dance troupe (replacing Twyla Tharp), where she danced in the premiere of Taylor's *From Sea to Shining Sea*. She left the Taylor group to become a choreographer and raise a family. Despite her short tenure with Taylor, he, along with Merce Cunningham and Alwin Nikolais, is often cited as one of her major influences.

Laura Dean performing *Spiral,* 1977. Photograph © Lois Greenfield.

In 1968 Dean went to San Francisco for two years, after which she returned to New York and, from 1971 to 1974, performed the first of several minimalist works based on repetitions of simple patterns. Pieces premiering during these three years include *Stamping Dance, Square Dance, Jumping Dance,* and *Spinning Dance.* In the latter, Dean and two other female dancers spun silently for an hour. Audiences responded to the women's strength and awareness of each other more than to the aesthetics of the dance, a situation that would persist for many of Dean's minimalist works. She continued to create repetitive, geometric dances, including the follow-the-leader *Response Dance* (1974) and the 90-minute *Drumming* (1975). The latter marked the first time Dean accompanied a piece with a full score, provided by Steve Reich. He would become a frequent collaborator in her future endeavors.

In 1976 Dean formed her own company, Laura Dean Dancers and Musicians—and well-known dancers Mark Morris and Dana Reitz are among those who have been members of the group. *Song,* the troupe's debut piece, was accompanied by a score created by Dean, slight music in which some sections were vocalized by the dancers. This was the first time Dean choreographed to her own composition, a practice she repeated often during the rest of her career with growing success.

The act of spinning while creating shifting circles within circles became a trademark of Dean's dances, especially throughout the 1970s, as is evident in works *Spiral* (1977) and *Dance* (1978). Purely abstract without any narrative thread, her dances consisted of solos and unison sections (with movements performed simultaneously or in cannon), but never included segments featuring partners. The focus of Dean's choreography is on the dancers' hands and feet, with torsos kept immobile. The pieces are concerned with the process of dancing, or the act of doing the steps, rather than with their effect on the audience; it often seems as if the dancers are having fun performing the works and are oblivious to those watching. The long periods of repetitive movement make any small change, whether in geometric pattern or in the steps used, important.

Dean's dances have often been described as ritualistic, cozy, and communal. Critics frequently comment upon her works' association with folklore, especially the "whirling dervishes of the Middle East," as well as an eclectic collection of influences from the East Indies, Russia, and early American history, not to mention tap and disco. Dean herself, however, rarely aligns or associates herself publicly with a particular philosophy.

In 1980 Dean choreographed the first of many pieces for the Joffrey Ballet, entitled *Night,* which was accompanied by her own two-piano score. Spinning and other motifs typical of her work translated well to ballet, and her works appealed to the youth market, an audience the Joffrey was trying to attract. Dean's style also translated well to into figure skating, and she choreographed for skater John Curry. Other pieces for the Joffrey included *Fire* (1982) and *Forcefield* (1986), to a Steve Reich score. In addition, Dean was one of four choreographers who contributed to a full-length ballet for the Joffrey, *Billboards* (1993), which was set to the music of the artist then known as Prince. Hers was the first of the four parts, and was called *Sometimes it Snows in April*.

In the 1980s, Dean began to explore the possibilities of solos and duets, and was also interested in the interaction between soloists and groups. Rather than choreographing a series of different solos within one piece, many of her solos were broken into parts, whereby it seemed as if several dancers shared one solo. Among the Dean works created during this period were *Sky Light* and *Solo in Red* (both 1982), *Inner Circle* and *Enochian* (both 1983). Other significant pieces during the 1980s include *Tympani* (1981), *Music* (1980), *Impact* (1985) for the Brooklyn Academy of Music, and *Space* (1988) for the New York City Ballet.

Over the years, her dances have become increasingly complicated and grander, with motifs expanding to include aerobic activities such as high kicks and split jumps (as in *Billboards*), as well as simpler more familiar motifs of spinning. Many of her dances remain meditative in nature; her music is sometimes referred to as "trance music." Dean's versatility in adapting her motifs to different styles of dance is noticeable from her work in the 1990s. Among other pieces, she choreographed *Light* (1994) for Aman World Music and Dance, a folk dance troupe; *Night Wind* (1994), a reworking of her *Arrow of Time* (1993), for the Albany Berkshire Ballet; and *Ecstasy* (1993) and *Infinity* (1990) for her own troupe.

Throughout her career, Dean has been concerned with innovation, always adding new motifs or patterns to her works while building upon movements established in earlier pieces. A review by Marilyn Hunt of the premieres of *Ecstasy* and *Infinity* suggests how Dean's work has changed over time, while still retaining her core motifs. Hunt writes: "Laura Dean's choreography for her own company continues to look like no one else's and, at the same time, like the dance equivalent of world music, because it works with the universal, basic building blocks of dance." *Ecstasy* and *Infinity* look "very '90s, with their rising volume, excitement, and frantic speed, all based on Dean's own percussive scores. Yet the usual folklike quality of Dean's work is still present in the simple repeated steps, geometric floor patterns, and sense of community."

—Karen Raugust

DEATHS AND ENTRANCES

Choreography: Martha Graham
Music: Hunter Johnson
Set Design: Arch Lauterer
Costume Design: Edythe Gilfond
First Production: Bennington College, Vermont, 18 July 1943
Principal Dancers: Martha Graham, Jane Dudley, Sophie Maslow (The Three Sisters); Merce Cunningham (The Poetic Beloved); Erick Hawkins (The Dark Beloved)
Other productions include: Ziegfeld Theatre, 1947; Martha Gra-

ham Dance Company, Lunt-Fontaine Theatre, New York, May 1977; City Center, New York, October 1993; Brooklyn Academy of Music (BAM), September 1994.

Publications

Books—

Graham, Martha, *The Notebooks of Martha Graham*, New York, 1973.

Magriel, Paul David, ed., *Chronicles of the American Dance*, New York, 1978.

McDonagh, Don, *Martha Graham: A Biography*, New York, 1973.

Thomas, Dylan, *Deaths and Entrances; Poems*, London, 1955.

Trowbridge, Charlotte, *Dance Drawings of Martha Graham*, New York, 1945.

Articles—

Baker, Rob, "Ancestral Footsteps: Martha Graham Dance Company, Lunt-Fontaine Theatre, May 16-June 11, 1977," *Dance Magazine,* September 1977.

Beiswanger, George W., "Lobby Thoughts and Jottings," *Dance Observer,* February 1944.

Croce, Arlene, "Graham without Graham," *Dancing Times*, November 1970.

Cunningham, Katharine, "Martha Graham Dance Company at Brooklyn Academy," *Dance and Dancers* (London), January 1971.

Denby, Edwin, "Martha Graham's New *Deaths and Entrances*," *New York Herald Tribune*, 16 January 1944.

Graham, Martha, "Martha Graham Speaks," *Dance Observer,* April 1963.

Hering, Doris, "St. Joan, Clytemnestra and Martha Graham; A Review: Martha Graham and Her Dance Co., April 1-13, Adelphi Theatre, NYC," *Dance Magazine*, June 1958.

———, "And Tomorrow? What Did the Martha Graham Dance Company—Without Miss Graham—Tell Us about Her Art and Its Future?," *Dance Magazine,* December 1970.

Krokover, Rosalyn, "The Dance: Two New Works by Graham; La Meri Pupil offers Novelty," *Musical Courier,* 5 January 1944.

Martin, John Joseph, "Second View: On Re-Seeing Martha Graham's Recent *Deaths and Entrances*," *New York Times*, 16 January 1944.

Orthwine, Rudolf, "Martha Graham," *Dance Magazine*, January 1944.

Sloat, Susanna, "Radical Graham," *Attitude* (Brooklyn, NY), Fall 1994/Winter 1995.

Sorell, Walter, "The Martha Graham Dance Company; Brooklyn Academy of Music, October 2-8," *Dance News,* November 1970.

Stodelle, Ernestine, "Midstream; The Second Decade of Modern Dance: Martha Graham," *Dance Observer,* October 1962.

Tobias, Tobi, "A Shot in the Dark," *New York*, 25 October 1993.

*   *   *

In his biography of Martha Graham, Don McDonagh describes the conditions surrounding the debut of Graham's *Deaths and Entrances* on 18 July 1943: it was quite literally a dark and stormy night, shaken by a summer thunderstorm which knocked out the electricity in the rooftop theatre of the Bennington College Commons Building. Absorbed in her playing, the pianist seemed unable to stop, but the dancers waited for the storm to pass. It seemed a fitting backdrop for the composition which inspired Graham herself, reacting to hearing it years later, with words such as "witchcraft," "creative energy," and "the wine of blood and death."

The work itself, drawn loosely from a Dylan Thomas poem of the same name, is elusive. Ostensibly the story of three sisters dwelling with their memories of past loves and lost opportunities—symbolized by the male dancers designated as the "Dark Beloved" and the "Poetic Beloved"—it is on another level a psychodrama featuring the three Brontë sisters under the spell created by Charlotte Brontë's *Wuthering Heights*. And of course there are elements of autobiography on Graham's part.

In line with the experimental fiction of such writers as James Joyce and Marcel Proust, which held considerable sway among the literati of wartime America, there is no plot as such in *Deaths*. Rather, it is a psychological struggle between the principal sister, played in the original by Graham herself, and her two siblings (Jane Dudley and Sophie Maslow). In fairy-tale fashion, one of these is her protector while the other seeks to undermine her—again, on a psychological rather than an explicit level. Dancing in and out of the main character's consciousness are the Dark Beloved and the Poetic Beloved (Erick Hawkins and Merce Cunningham respectively), who disappear and reappear like memories that are repeatedly picked up and put down, recalled and forgotten.

Memory is the centerpoint of the composition, in which time flows not on a linear path, but back and forth in an associative hopscotch that offers no real resolution at the end. All the viewer knows is that whatever struggle has engaged the sisters' consciousness for the duration of the work, it is over now. The rest is all memory, which Graham evokes through what was then a novel use of props on the modern dance stage. A vase, a goblet, a shell, and two phallic chess pieces, one red and one white, all make their appearance, and all have been assigned meanings by scholars of Graham's work. The blue glass goblet, for instance, has been identified by Margaret Lloyd as "the cup of happiness in love." However, some symbols defy attempts at identification: "What precisely is the significance of the large conch shell and the white vases," Lloyd wrote, "I have yet, after repeated viewings, to learn."

The significance of *Deaths and Entrances* itself, on the other hand, is not nearly so elusive. Not only does it show Graham at the height of her powers in creative experimentation, its inaugural production featured some of the greatest names of modern dance on a tiny, intimate stage. Like many great events, it began small, on a shoestring, and it very nearly did not happen at all. Given the conditions of rationing in 1943, Graham had to improvise props and costumes. The latter she and Arch Lauterer created, in a fitting wartime touch, by altering clothes from an Army-Navy store, turning sailors' black trousers into dresses. Graham also had to schedule the performance around Hawkins, who had to leave for New York, where he had a steady job as understudy to Curly and Judd in *Oklahoma*.

Hawkins and Graham were the only two performers to appear in the 1947 revival at the Ziegfeld. Since that time, the show has run several other times, to varying degrees of success. Writing in *New York* magazine half a century later, Tobi Tobias savaged a 1993 revival performance by the Martha Graham Company: "[*Deaths*] steadfastly refuses to explain what's going on—beyond the rampaging of a bunch of dark, churning emotions, rivalry and thwarted desire being prominent." Generally, as time has gone on and audiences stand at a further remove from Graham and the excitement of the moment, critics are less patient with the inaccessibility of this

particular production. Yet on that "dark and stormy night" in the summer of 1943, it was possible to believe that Graham and her companions on stage were exploring the frontiers of modern dance—which they were.

—Judson Knight

de CHÂTEL, Krisztina

Hungarian-born dancer, choreographer, and company director based in the Netherlands

Born: 3 August 1943 in Budapest, Hungary. **Education:** Began dance studies with Kurt Jooss and Hans Züllig at Folkwang Hochschule, Essen (Germany), 1963; moved to Amsterdam, 1969; studied with Koert Stuyf and Ellen Edinoff (who had been influenced by Merce Cunningham and Martha Graham). **Career:** Dancer, BEWTH and Stichting Eigentijds Dans; first choreography, *Voltage Control 1*, 1976; founder/director, Dansgroep Krisztina de Châtel, 1978; successfully toured Europe, Canada, the U.S., Latin America, and Asia; created her 31st choreographic work, 1997. **Awards:** Two choreographic prizes, 1987; long-term grant from the Netherland's Ministry of Culture.

Works

1977	*Voltage Control I* (mus. Glass)
1978	*Voltage Control II* (mus. Glass)
1979	*Lines* (mus. Glass)
	Variaties op een thema (mus. Glass)
	Afwijkend (mus. Xenakis)
	Aan jou (mus. Zamfir)
1980	*Light* (mus. Willems, van Es)
1982	*Forgó* (mus. Van Es)
1983	*Wiederkehr* (mus. Vogels)
	per aspera (mus. Bartók)
1984	*Thron* (mus. Wang)
1985	*Solos* (mus. Bartók, van Es, Nasaka)
	Ritornel (mus. Eno, Budd, Vangelis)
	Föld (mus. Glass)
	Trio (mus. van Es)
1986	*Typhoon* (mus. ten Holt)
	Nummer Achtenveertig (mus. Rosendaal, Cage, Ashley)
1987	*Staunch* (mus. McDowell)
1988	*Change* (mus. Borden)
	Shower Power (mus. Rzewski)
	Vortex (mus. Poppy)
	Heaven Can Wait (mus. Stoljikovic)
	Blue Pacifica (mus. King)
1989	*Dualis* (mus. Hagen)
1990	*Imperium* (mus. Purcell)
1991	*Sequence* (mus. Glass, Wang)
1992	*Weep, Cry and Tangle* (mus. Shostakovitch)
	Paletta (mus. Reich)
1993	*Concave* (mus. collage)
1994	*Facetten* (mus. Beethoven)
	Muralis (mus. Schubert)
1995	*Stalen Neuzen, een dansfilm* (film)
	Solo IV (mus. Bach)
	In het voorbijgaan (mus. Vivaldi)

Krisztina de Châtel: *Typhoon*, **1992. Photograph © Johan Elbers.**

1996   *Vanitas* (mus. Bach)
1997   *Solo V* (mus. Reich)
        Vide (mus. Volans)
        Kindred Doppelgängers (mus. Frith)
        Ló (mus. Ensemble Muzikás, The Orb, Chemical Brothers)

Other works include: *Studiovoorstelling, Studiovoorstelling II,* and *Studiovoorstelling III.*

Publications

Van Schaik, Eva, *Krisztina de Châtel: Balancing Between Brains and Buttocks,* Ons Erfdeel, 1990.
————, "Tearing Down the Walls, *Muralis* by Dansgroep Krisztina de Châtel," *Ballet International,* February 1995.

*   *   *

To have a dance group bearing your name is an honour reserved for choreographers with their own exclusive style. Hungarian Krisztina de Châtel is such a choreographer. In 1963 she left Budapest, Hungary, to study with Kurt Jooss at the Folkwang Hochschule in Essen, Germany.

Under the leadership of Jooss and Hans Züllig, she was introduced to neoexpressionistic dance, which de Châtel did not feel was her way to compose dance. In 1969 de Châtel arrived in Amsterdam, where she took classes from Koert Stuyf and Ellen Edinoff who had just returned from the U.S. and were influenced by Merce Cunningham. Cunningham's style and manner of choreographing was more appealing to the Châtel, as were the technical aspects of Martha Graham's dancing. De Châtel has longed for strict ordering principles, as a controlled and carefully arranged outlet for her thoughts and emotions.

Though she started her dance career in the late 1960s, de Châtel began drawing attention as a choreographer in the late 1970s. She founded her eponymous company in 1978, a structurally subsidized modern dance company of seven dancers, which became one of the most important representatives of Dutch modern dance. She has been regarded as a prominent modern choreographer, distinguishing herself with a unique œuvre of a consistent, high quality. Under her leadership, Dansgroep Krisztina de Châtel has developed into a modern dance group with an exquisite dancers' tableau.

Most of de Châtel's choreography consists of full-length productions bringing together dance, music, and art in a striking fashion. While de Châtel's point of departure is and remains minimal dance, her productions can differ greatly in character. Her work can be very sober and compelling, but also dramatic. Her œuvre actually forms one grand statement about how this artist experiences life: her work reveals themes such as struggle, isolation, anger, and sexual relations, even though the choreographer puts them into an abstract form. Yet this form is always clear, controlled à la Mondrian. This evokes friction with her Hungarian temperament, her expressionism, with which she tries to break through the strict form. This dualism makes her productions very formal, dramatic, but always in balance, somewhere on this scale of extremes.

In one of her early productions, *Lines*, she make references to Oskar Schlemmer's lecture "Mensch und Kunstfigur." His 'metaphysical mathematics' were closely followed de Châtel. In *Lines* the square dance floor is demarcated by 16 pillars of light and the space becomes very tight. Four females shift in ever changing patterns: severe and strict they create circles, triangles, rectangular figures, diagonals, which according to Eva van Schaik, who wrote a biography of de Châtel, submit the dancers' motoric movements to the laws of stereology, in an effort to release the historical and psychological limitations of life. Van Schaik believes de Chatel's approach to choreography is dialectical: she tries to find a balance to control unreconcilable extremities, like Dionysiac and Apollonian, chaos and harmony, love and hate. She wants controllable restrictions to expose an identical passion—however much anyone can be victimized by the nature of technique, ever-present energy will keep him/her alive—this minimal force within each one of us, making us walk, breathe, persevere. In this trust she explores the extreme borders of human exhaustion, searching for a synthesis of antipoles. Her musical preference is minimal, with its repetitive series and shifting rhythmic patterns. She drives her dancers to the brink of exhaustion in arithmetically repetitive patterns that redetermine the parameters of space, time, and physical attack.

In *Staunch*, five male dancers dance for an hour to strong African rhythmic music, within a space between four walls, that slowly draw together. *Föld* was created to be danced against and on a high circular wall of earth, where her six dancers fight an exhaustive battle during which the wall is trodden down. In *Typhoon* there is a battle of wills against four wind ventilators. De Chatel isn't trying to dehumanize her dancers but to exploit their instinctual movements; to this end she has created a myriad of solo performances, of which the most striking are *Vortex,* danced by Oerm Matern, *Solo IV* by Ann van der Broek and *Solo V* by Massimo Malinari. In the latter, de Châtel accentuates Malinari's wide upper torso through arm movements that stay at shoulder height with the same rhythmical movements, while Malinari turns and jumps around the stage.

Ann van der Broek was given a solo because her dancing was so expressive, with rounded body movements filled with energy and power and flashy arm movements that spoke of passion.

In 1987 de Châtel was awarded two important choreography prizes in the Netherlands, which fully marked her emergence as a choreographer of merit. Her work has been performed in small auditoria and on large stages, depending on the type of production, and she has devised works for Het Muziektheater Amsterdam, for the Holland Festival and for Springdance in Utrecht. Dansgroep Krisztina de Châtel's expenses have been helped through a long-term grant from the Netherland's Ministry of Culture, and through this support has come increasing interest in the company abroad. It has already toured in Europe, Canada, the United States, Latin America and Asia.

One of de Chatel's few evening-length pieces is *Muralis,* a work that opened a festival in Montreal in 1995, and was de Châtel's symbolization of modern Europe. For *Muralis,* Judith Lansink designed a long wall, placed diagonally deep into the stage to leave only half of the space for the dancers. The wall's only decoration is a Renaissance-styled balcony. The first part of the performance is danced to Shubert's *String Quartet in C Major,* performed live onstage. Five male dancers move graciously with long steps, their arms swinging. Covering the space in strict lines and fluidly changing positions, their bodies touch each other gently, building up and releasing tension. Two women at the balcony embrace, climb down and mingle with the men. The ensemble dancing is intense, but sober. In the second half of the piece, the wall is stripped away until only the framework and the balcony are left. The dance steps are repeated exactly the same, only now without music. For de Châtel, the piece is representative of the Berlin Wall, and her spare, stripped down choreography expressed what she characterized as the emptiness and ugliness that followed its fall. "Life," de Châtel has commented, "where the (Berlin) wall was torn down, is now empty and without beauty."

De Châtel has also choreographed for film and video as well as the stage; she has worked on two films, and the same qualities that emerge on the stage are present in the films. In the summer 1997 de Châtel created her 31st choreography; she remains faithful to her principles.

—Helma Klooss

de JONG, Bettie
Dutch-born dancer

Born: 1 May 1933 in Sumatra, Indonesia. **Education:** Studied dance from the age of seven; moved to Holland, 1946; high school education, Wageningen, 1946-52; studied dance with Theo Branzs, 1948-52; history major, University of Amsterdam, 1953-54; studied with Max Doyes, a founder and choreographer of the Ballet of the Lowlands, 1955-58; moved to New York in 1958 to study the Martha Graham technique and became an apprentice in the Martha Graham Dance Company, 1960-61. **Career:** Dancer, Netherlands Pantomime Theatre, 1955-58; understudy, Pearl Lang's company, 1960; assisted Dutch modern dancer and choreographer Lucas Hoving in class demonstrations, Connecticut College, 1959-60; dancer, Paul Taylor Dance Company, 1962; official rehearsal mistress, Paul Taylor Dance Company, from 1984; retired from the stage, 1985.

Roles (original cast roles with the Paul Taylor Dance Company, unless otherwise noted)

1961	A Fury, *Clytemnestra,* Martha Graham Dance Company, New York
1962	One of three Las Entrometidas, *Apasionada,* Pearl Lang Dance Company, New York
	Shira, Pearl Lang Dance Company, New York
	Tracer, Paris
1963	*La Negra,* Mexico City
	Party Mix, New York
	II (Dos), *Piece Period,* New York
	Scudorama, Connecticut College, New London, Connecticut
1964	*Red Room,* Spoleto, Italy

Bettie de Jong (center) in *Sacre du Printemps*, 1980. Photograph © Johan Elbers.

1965	Plymouth Rock in *From Sea to Shining Sea*, New York
	Nine Dances with Music, New York
	Part Three in *Post Meridian*, New York
1966	A Planet in *Orbs*, the Hague, Holland
1967	*Lento*, Connecticut College, New London
1968	*Public Domain*, Geneseo
1969	*Churchyard*, New York
1970	*Big Bertha*, Detroit
	Foreign Exchange, Washington, D.C.
1971	Duet with Rudolph Nureyev, *Big Bertha*, CBS-TV, New York
	The Text in *Book of Beasts*, Washington Monument, Washington, D.C.
	Fetes, British Columbia, Canada
1972	Looking Forward in *Guests of May*, Worchester, Massachusetts
1973	Mrs. Noah in *Noah's Minstrels*, Middleton, New York
	Michael, the Defending Angel in *American Genesis*, Boston
1975	*Esplanade*, Washington, D.C.
1976	*Cloven Kingdom*, New York
1980	Rehearsal Mistress in *Le Sacre du Printemps*, Washington, D.C.

1981   *House of Cards*, New York

Publications

On de JONG: books—

Taylor, Paul, *Private Domain*, New York, 1987.

On de JONG: articles—

Barnes, Clive, "Dance: Joyous Hymn to God and Life," *New York Times*, 7 July 1966.
———, "Paul Taylor's *Lento* Given its Premiere, *New York Times*, 26 December 1967.
Goodman, Saul, "Bettie de Jong, *Dance Magazine*, November 1964.
Harriton, Maria, "Dance News," *Dance Magazine*, May 1971.
Taub, Eric, "Footnotes," *Ballet News*, April 1985.
Williams, Peter, "Monsters and Minstrels," *Dance and Dancers*, September 1973.

*   *   *

Bettie de Jong's long career as a dancer has proved that she was more than just a magnificent muse for Paul Taylor, but that she was the most loyal of friends as well. De Jong danced in the Paul Taylor Dance Company for 23 years and has been its rehearsal mistress since the 1970s, although the title did not become official until 1984.

Bettie de Jong was born in Sumatra, Indonesia. Her father was an agricultural engineer working in rubber research in Malang and her mother was a nurse. She started dancing at the age of seven, the earliest her mother could get her accepted into a class. During the World War II Japanese occupation of Indonesia, her family was interned in a concentration camp for three years. As soon as the war ended, they moved to Holland, where de Jong and her older sister could attend high school in Wageningen. She studied dance with Theo Branzs and was a history major for two years at the University of Amsterdam. She didn't make up her mind to forge a career in dance until she was 22. At 5 feet, 10 inches, however, de Jong was much too tall to be a ballet dancer; at that time, especially, the men in Europe were too short for partnering. In 1954 the Martha Graham Company performed in Amsterdam and de Jong immediately knew that she wanted to focus her attention on modern dance.

She stayed in Holland for three years and studied with Max Doyes, a founder and choreographer of the Ballet of the Lowlands. When he formed the Netherlands Pantomime Theatre, de Jong became a member. In 1958 she acquired a student visa and moved to New York to study the Graham technique. She was granted a scholarship; in addition, she worked part-time in the school's office, taught classes, and served as Ethel Winters' au pair for a year. She became an apprentice in the Martha Graham Dance Company and performed as a Fury in *Clytemnestra*. De Jong also served as an understudy in Pearl Lang's company, dancing in the premieres of *Shira* and *Apasionada* as well as in John Butler's *Carmina Burana* with the New York City Opera. During the summers she assisted Dutch modern dancer and choreographer Lucas Hoving during class demonstrations at Connecticut College.

While still teaching at the Graham school, de Jong found out from a student that Paul Taylor was looking for dancers. She ran into him by accident one day and asked, "Is it true that you're giving an audition?" He replied, "It's a closed audition, but you're welcome to come." Not only did she secure a spot in his company, she became Taylor's most frequent and favorite partner. In his autobiography, *Private Domain,* Taylor describes de Jong as thus: "Her eyes are gray blue, except for the left one, which is half brown. Straight ash-blond hair is skinned back in a tight knot. Cheekbones and other facial features are spaced exactly the right distance apart to project well from a stage. Picture a lovely reed dancing."

Agile despite her height, de Jong is remembered for her adeptness at playing humor with a straight face (as required by Taylor on many occasions) as well as evoking raw emotion. Her dozens of roles ranged from the snooty hostess in the spoof *Party Mix* to a lonely, distraught young woman in *Scudorama* and Plymouth Rock in *From Sea to Shining Sea*. After the premiere of Taylor's *Lento,* a piece choreographed in three parts and set to Haydn, Clive Barnes wrote in the *New York Times,* "The first has the solitary, stately figure of Bettie de Jong—wearing a long robe and looking like a dignified yet desolate Hecuba—surrounded by five other girls, like a wailing Greek chorus."

Taylor always took advantage of de Jong's long, elegant line. Her most famous character, ironically so because she spent much of the time standing still, is as Big Bertha, watching over a family in which the seemingly all-American father (originally danced by Taylor)

rapes his daughter. In the September 1973 issue of *Dance and Dancers,* Peter Williams wrote, "[Taylor] veers from one extremity of mood to another under the influence of Bettie de Jong's baleful glare. And how she dominates the ballet, even when just standing there; at one point (when the mother refuses to put another coin in the machine) her eyes suddenly enlarge and glitter, and it is then that you know her victims don't stand a chance."

The season de Jong retired from the stage in 1985, Taylor formally rested Big Bertha. Now, as rehearsal mistress for the Taylor Company, de Jong is responsible for fine-tuning the repertory and, when there's a new piece, making sure that the details are clear. She travels with the company and when on tour de Jong is also responsible for the look of the stage, the lighting, and the music. She occasionally gives pre- and post-performance lectures.

De Jong never had choreographic aspirations. "I'm really a reproductive artist, and have been really lucky that I came into modern dance at a time when you could do that," she says. "Most modern dancers have to make a vehicle for themselves; I didn't." Taylor, in his book, concurs, "Probably no one has ever had a muse like dear Bet."

—Gia Kourlas

de KEERSMAEKER, Anne Teresa

Belgian postmodern dancer, choreographer, and company director

Born: 1960 in Wemmel, Belgium. **Education:** Studied at Mudra, Maurice Béjart's school in Brussels, 1978-80; attended New York University's School of the Arts, 1981. **Career:** First choreography, *Asch*, 1980; founder, Rosas, 1983; became resident company of Belgium's national opera company, La Monnaie; founder/director, PARTS (Performing Arts Research and Training Studios), Brussels, 1996. **Awards:** New York Dance and Performance Award ("Bessie"), 1988; Eve du Spectacle, (Belgium), 1989; Best Foreign Choreography Award (Japan), 1989; Solo d'Oro Award (Italy), 1989; Grand Prix Vidéo Dance (France), 1989; London Dance and Performance Award, 1989; two Dance Screen Awards (Vienna), 1992; Dance Screen Award and Prize for Best Adaptation, Festival du Film sur L'Art (Montreal), 1994.

Works

1980	*Asch* (mus. Biran, Coppin), Brussels
1982	*Fase: Four Movements to the Music of Steve Reich* (mus. Reich), Brussels
1983	*Rosas danst Rosas* (mus. De Mey, Vermeersch), Brussels
1984	*Elena's Aria* (mus. Mozart), Brussels
1986	*Bartók/Aantekeningen* (mus. Bartók), Brussels
1987	*Verkommenes Ufer/Medeamaterial/Landschft mit Argonauten* (text Müller), Utrecht
	Mikrokosmos—Monument/Selbstportraet mit Reich and Riley (und Chopin is auch dabei)/In zart fliessender Bewegung (mus. Bartók, Ligeti), Hallen van Schaarbeek
1988	*Ottone, Ottone* (mus. Monteverdi), Brussels; video version Verdin and De Keersmaeker, 1991
1989	*Hoppla* (film by Kolb, mus. Bartók), Brussels

Anne Teresa de Keersmaeker: *Rosas danst Rosas,* 1987. Photograph by Beatriz Schiller.

1990	*Stella* (mus. Ligeti), Haarlem
	Achterland (mus. Ligeti, Ysaye), Brussels; film version by De Keersmaeker, 1994
1992	*Erts* (mus. Beethoven, Webern, Schnittke, Berio), Brussels
	Rosa (film by Peter Greenaway, mus. Bartók), Brussels
	Mozart/Concert Arias-un moto di gioia (mus. Mozart), Avignon
1993	*Toccata* (mus. Bach), Amsterdam
	Mozart Materiaal (film by Torfs and Persijn)
1994	*Kinok* (mus. De Mey, Bartók, Beethoven), Brussels
	Amor constante más allá de la muerte (mus. de Mey), Brussels
1995	*Erwartung/Verklaerte Nacht* (mus. Schoenberg), Brussels
1996	*Rosas danst Rosas* (film by De Mey), Brussels
	Tippeke (film by De Mey)
	Woud (mus. Berg, Schönberg, Wagner), Brussels
1997	*Percussion Evening* (mus. De Mey, Reich, Lindberg), Brussels

Publications

On DE KEERSMAEKER: articles—

Felciano, Rita, "A Love-Hate Affair with Dance," *Dance Magazine,* March 1998.

Hughes, David, "Making Legs Stop," *Dance Theatre Journal,* Summer 1991.

Mallems, Alex, "The Belgian Dance Explosion of the Eighties," *Ballet International/tanz aktuell,* February 1991.

Roy, Sanjoy, "Toccata," *Dance Now,* Summer 1994.

Spangberg, Marten, "Organising Time and Space," *Ballet International/tanz aktuell,* June 1995.

Van Kerkhoven, Marianne, "The Dance of Anne Teresa De Keersmaeker," *The Drama Review,* 1984.

*   *   *

In 1981, 21-year-old Anne Teresa de Keersmaeker received a scholarship to study in New York. After enrolling at New York University's School for the Arts, the young Belgian artist left after barely a year because, as she has said, she was anxious to do her own work. She produced her first choreography, the site-specific *Asch* while still a student at Maurice Béjart's training center, Mudra, a school whose open spirit she tried to recreate in her own Performing Arts Research and Training Studio (PARTS); the school enrolled its first students in 1996.

Though influenced in its vigorous theatricality by her older colleague Pina Bausch and the German Tanztheater, de Keersmaeker's work combines fierce physicality and abandonment with rigorously-structured formality. She herself has described her approach as one of great economy, one in which she tries to get the maximum out of the minimum. Her language may be restricted, often minimal and repetitive, but the energy which propels the movement is as high-octane as anything seen on contemporary dance stages. It makes for choreography that is at once raw and assaultive but also intellectually challenging and elegant. Many of her works have also been translated into award-winning films and videos by other artists and by de Keersmaeker herself.

De Keersmaeker develops her work in tandem with the musical compositions that are an integral part of her dances. Not visualizations in the sense that the movement mimics the score, her dances, nevertheless are intricately intertwined with the music which resides at their core. She and her dancers—they collaborate very closely—create counterpoints, mirror images or parallel tracks. They dance inside, around, and with the musical lines. This is especially true with the complex musical compositions with which she has begun to work since the early 1990s, but it was already evident in *Fase: Four Movements to the Music of Steve Reich*, a work she began while a student in New York.

Fase, a duet for de Keersmaeker and Michèle Ann De Mey, was inspired by the almost imperceptible changes and asymmetric periodicity of Steve Reich's music. The duet follows Reich's approach in the way its spinning moves, raised arm gestures, and ambling walking patterns go in and out of phase with each other and the music. She elaborated on this approach in *Rosas danst Rosas*, the first piece for her four-woman company, Rosas. In it she imbues a tough dancerly vocabulary and ordinary gestures—running a hand through the hair, touching a breast, examining of the fingernails—with a physical fierceness that leaves the performers exhausted to the point of collapse. The power expended is like that of high-impact sports, but the spirit is nonaggressive and vulnerable. In de Keersmaeker's work, fragility and strength, chaos and order—coexist, however uneasily.

De Keersmaeker followed these stringently constructed, quasi-mathematical games with works which gave the dancers more individual room, fewer unison repetitions and which introduced text—used both for its phonic quality and its verbal content—and other theatrical elements. *Elena's Aria*, for instance, incorporated excerpts from a speech by Fidel Castro as well as quotes from Tolstoy's *War and Peace*; *Bartók/Aantekeningen* used fragments from Georg Büchner's *Lenz* and Peter Weiss' *Marat/Sade*; and *Stella* got its name from Goethe's *Stella* as well as the character from Tennessee Williams' *A Streetcar Named Desire*. The thrust towards dance theater culminated in de Keersmaeker's setting of Heinrich Müller's play *Verkommenes Ufer. . . .* Belgian critic Alex Mallems has called Müller the playwright who "best expresses the feeling of being torn apart," which is a central concern of de Keersmaeker's work.

With the introduction of men into her company in the late 1980s, hostile gender relationships, which were implied only in the loneliness and constriction of the early works, rose more openly to the forefront. Men and women confront each other, their paths intersect, they may interact, but at best they come to an uneasy understanding of each other. But de Keersmaker also uses these tensions as challenges to work out opposing and complementary formal relationships, such as those created by presenting her dancers as grounded in the reality of their humanity; the literal and metaphorical meanings of gestures and texts; and her use of the same material in different contextual relationships. The sheer richness of detail—gestures, steps, patterns, actions, film, music, words—which she layers into these multi-hued textures give her works a sense of

baroque architecture in which the sensuous details, however, are held in place by an iron-clad overall structure.

One somewhat unusual characteristic of de Keersmaeker's choreography is her frank recycling of material from one work to another. She either directly quotes it or reshapes it into a different context. But a sense of déjà vu sometimes cannot be avoided. *Mikrokosmos* (1987), for instance, incorporates a section from the previous year's *Bartók/Aantekeningen; Achterland* owes much to *Stella* (both from 1990); *Stella*, on the other hand, has its seeds in the sleeping scene between the men and a woman in 1988's *Ottone/ Ottone.* For *Kinok* she reworked Beethoven's *Grosse Fuge, Op. 133*, which she already had used in *Erts*, in addition to material from the filmed version of *Rosas danst Rosas.* Her pieces almost linearly evolve out of each other.

Since the early 1990s a new fluidity, a gentleness, expressed in a kind of yearning has entered de Keersmaeker's work. She is much too thoughtful and intelligent an artist to become Pollyana-ish or sentimental. Nevertheless, the newer pieces are more optimistic in the sense that they at least allow for the possibility of bridging the chasm between people, between men and women, between life and art. There is sheer joy in the way the dancers intertwine with the unfolding lines of *Toccata.* Both *Amor Constante* and *Woud*, are affirmative of man's capacity for love. Or may be de Keersmaeker's newly found serenity simply has something to do with the fact that, as she increasingly enters deeper into the spirit of the major scores she has chosen to work with—Berg, Mozart, Bach, Beethoven, Schönberg, they have made a greater impact on her. Or maybe as she has matured as an artist the simple process of working, or "playing" with music, space and time, has become more joyful and, therefore, more life-affirming in itself.

—Rita Felciano

de LAVALLADE, Carmen
American dancer, choreographer, and educator

Born: 6 March 1931 in Los Angeles. **Education:** Began dance lessons while in her teens and auditioned for the Lester Horton Dance Theater while still in high school; studied with Martha Graham, Margaret Craske, and Carmelita Maracci; took courses at Los Angeles City College; studied acting with Stella Adler during the late 1950s and early 1960s. **Family:** Married actor, dancer, painter, and writer Geoffrey Holder, 1955; son, Leo Antony Holder, born 1957. **Career:** Professional debut with Lester Horton Dance Theater, 1950; moved to New York City to star in the Broadway musical *House of Flowers*, 1954; appeared with Geoffrey Holder's company in *Banda* and on television in John Butler's *Flight* and Duke Ellington's special *A Drum Is a Woman*, 1956; appeared in Gian-Carlo Menotti's opera *Amahl and the Night Visitors*, 1957; prima ballerina, Metropolitan Opera Ballet, 1956 and 1958; danced in Butler's *Carmina Burana* for New York City Opera, 1959; appeared at Jacob's Pillow Dance Festival with Butler, 1960; danced with James Truitte in Horton's *The Beloved*, 1960; danced for Butler and Glen Tetley, 1961; began dancing with Alvin Ailey, 1961; toured the Far East with the de Lavallade-Ailey Dance Company, 1962; danced in Butler's *Catulli Carmina*, Caramoor Festival (Katonah, New York), 1964; debuted with American Ballet Theatre in Agnes de Mille's *The Four Marys* and *The Frail Quarry*, 1965; danced in Tetley's *Pierrot Lunaire* and *The Mythical Hunters*, Hunter

College (New York), 1966; danced title role in Butler's *Aphrodite,* Boston Ballet, 1967; formed the Carmen de Lavallade Theater of Dance, late 1960s; choreographer/artist-in-residence at Yale School of Drama; board of directors, Association of American Dance Companies, 1967-68. **Awards:** Numerous honors and awards including honorary doctorate in fine arts, Boston Conservatory of Music, 1994; an Obie Award for Broadway, 1966; *Dance Magazine* Award, 1966.

Roles

1950	Salomé, *The Face of Violence* (Lester Horton)
1951	*Another Touch of Klee* (Horton)
	Medea (Horton)
1952	*Liberian Suite* (Horton)
	Dedication in Our Time (Horton)
1954	*House of Flowers* (Herbert Ross), Broadway
1956	*Banda* (Holder)
	Flight (Butler), for television
	Madame Zzaj, *A Drum Is a Woman,* for television
1957	Lead dancer, *Amahl and the Night Visitors* (Butler)
1959	*Carmina Burana* (Butler)
1960	Billie Holiday, *Portrait of Billie* (Butler)
	The Beloved (Horton)
1961	Cocaine Lil, *Willie the Weeper* (Butler)
	The Comet, *The Eccentricities of Davy Crockett* (Glen Tetley)
	Bess, *Porgy and Bess* (Joe Layton), part of *The Gershwin Years,* TV special
	Roots of the Blues (Ailey)
	Letter to a Beloved (Butler)
	Dedication to José Clemente Orozco (Horton)
1963	*Blood of the Lamb* (Donald McKayle)
	Three Songs for One (Holder)
1964	*Reflections in the Park* (McKayle)
	Catulli Carmina (Butler)
1965	*The Four Marys* (Agnes de Mille)
	The Frail Quarry (de Mille)
1966	Columbine, *Pierrot Lunaire* (Tetley)
	The Mythical Hunters (Tetley)
	Chronochromie (Tetley)
1967	*Aphrodite* (Butler)
	Suite and Light (Holder and Ailey)
	The Captive Lark (Butler)
	Bilitis, *Chanson de Bilitis* (Butler)
	Dithyramb (Tetley)
	Come Sunday (Holder)
	Five Ballets of the Five Senses (Butler)

Works

1974	*Nightscape,* solo
1979	*Sensemaya,* for Dance Theatre of Harlem
	Allegro
	A Midsummer Night's Dream (for Yale Repertory Theatre)
1992	*Lucia di Lammermoor* (for the Metropolitan Opera)
	Rusalka (for the Metropolitan Opera)
1993	*Die Meistersinger von Nurnberg* (for the Metropolitan Opera)

Publications

"Carmen de Lavallade," in *Current Biography,* 1967.
Clippings file of Carmen de Lavallade in the Dance Research Collection of the New York Public Library at Lincoln Center for the Performing Arts, Lincoln Center.

Films and Videotapes

Film appearances in the early 1950s included *Lydia Bailey, Demetrius and the Gladiators, The Egyptian, Carmen Jones* (starring Dorothy Dandridge), and *Odds Against Tomorrow* (starring Harry Belafonte); acting/dancing debut in John Butler's *Flight,* Duke Ellington's *A Drum Is a Woman* (television, 1956), "Bess" in a televised ballet sequence of Joe Layton's *Porgy and Bess* (1961), John Sayles' film *Lone Star* (1996).

* * *

Carmen de Lavallade has been one of the shining lights of the American dance scene for nearly three generations. Whether appearing in a ballet, in the West Indian dances and African-American spirituals choreographed by her husband Geoffrey Holder, or in the works of neomodernists John Butler, Glen Tetley, or Alvin Ailey, de Lavallade has always been the epitome of the total dancer. She brings physical beauty, a strong technique, and a sure sense of theater to every role she assumes. More importantly, she has the ability to melt into a role completely and unforgettably. Like so many of her contemporaries, Carmen de Lavallade has personality. As a result of her commitment to the totality of her art, de Lavallade's appearances on stage, in film, and on television have imprinted themselves on the memories of viewers. Tall and slender, with large, brown eyes, and long, expressive hands she has moved audiences and critics alike. Such words as "sinuous," "soft," "liquid," "lavishly endowed," and "endlessly graceful" have been used to describe her performances. Once her dancing career subsided, de Lavallade focused her attention on acting, appearing in numerous productions of the classics. In 1986, she played the role of Astarte in Robert Schumann's *Manfred* (with text by Byron) at the New England Conservatory's Festival of Music.

Yet always, the exploration of movement continued to hold an interest for her. In 1993 she danced *Ain't No Way,* a solo by Milton Myers to music by Aretha Franklin. Writing in the *New York Times,* Jennifer Dunning remarked that de Lavallade's performance, "measured yet harrowing in its rawness, ought to be required viewing for today's young dancers." In 1996 de Lavallade appeared with Gus Solomons Jr. and Dudley Williams in "Masters in Performance," dancing *Thin Frost* with Solomons and as well her own *Willie's Ladies Sing the Blues,* choreographed with Geoffrey Holder. The same year she acted as producing director for the Joyce Trisler Danscompany's performances at St. Mark's Church in New York City, while also teaching as a professor of dance at Adelphi University in the late 1990s.

Carmen Paula de Lavallade was born in Los Angeles, California, in 1931. Her parents, Leo Paul and Grace, had two other daughters, Yvonne and Elaine. Carmen's father worked as a bricklayer and postman to support his family during the Depression years. The de Lavallades were of Creole ancestry with French, African, and German forebears. As Carmen recalled in a newspaper interview, racial background was not a major issue in her family. When de Lavallade's two sisters had asked their father about the family's racial background, he responded that he didn't think it was important. The family was theater-minded but in the 1930s "theater was not a thing someone could do," Carmen recalled, because the chances of making a living from it were just too remote. A cousin of Carmen's, Janet Collins, was a noted dancer and choreographer who had studied ballet and modern dance and had performed concert works with Lester Horton. Collins went on to become a leading dancer at the Metropolitan Opera in New York City. It was partly Collins' experiences that broke the ground for young Carmen's entrance into a performing arts career. Carmen's participation in dance began in her teens when she went to live with an aunt after her mother's death.

Her dancing began in earnest while she was a student at Thomas Jefferson High School in Los Angeles. She auditioned for the Lester Horton Dance Theater while still in high school and was taken on as an apprentice when she was 16. Her sponsor was none other than Lena Horne. Horton's choreography consisted of short concert works with national and/or ethnic influences. He was able to simplify and popularize ethnic dance forms in such works as *Voo-doo Ceremonial* (1932) and *Aztec Ballet* (1934). Horton was hired by several Hollywood film studios to stage musical segments of such 1940s films as *Rhythm of the Island* and *Tangier*. His students included Joyce Trisler, Bella Lewitzky, James Truitte, and Alvin Ailey. While studying with Horton, Carmen danced, made costumes, and even played in the orchestra. De Lavallade regards Horton as a wonderful, generous teacher whose ideas long influenced her artistic life. It was Horton who steered the young dancer to Los Angeles-based ballerina Carmelita Maracci when she asked for additional training. De Lavallade also appreciated the discipline of training, performing, and taking care of herself during tours with the company. While she was studying dance she also took courses in physical education at Los Angeles City College.

Carmen de Lavallade made her professional debut in 1950 in the role of Salomé in Horton's ballet, *The Face of Violence*. This role impressed many reviewers who singled out the young dancer for her physical beauty and the dramatic impact of her dancing. Lena Horne brought de Lavallade to the attention of producers at Twentieth Century-Fox studios; and thus began her foray into films. In the early 1950s she appeared in small but distinctive roles in *Lydia Bailey, Demetrius and the Gladiators, The Egyptian, Carmen Jones* (starring Dorothy Dandridge), and *Odds Against Tomorrow* (starring Harry Belafonte). While filming *Carmen Jones,* de Lavallade came to the attention of the film's choreographer, Herbert Ross, who chose the young woman to star in a Broadway show entitled *House of Flowers*, a production based on a story by Truman Capote with Harold Arlen music co-starring Alvin Ailey. While in the show she met another dancer, the Trinidad-born Geoffrey Holder, whom she married in 1955. As de Lavallade recalled, Holder came into her life "like a dozen steel bands,"—she had found her partner on stage and in life.

After *House of Flowers* completed its run, de Lavallade was engaged by the Metropolitan Opera. De Lavallade was featured in many ballets staged for the opera and also appeared with the American Ballet Theatre as a guest artist for two seasons. She appeared in *The Four Marys* as Mary Hamilton, a role created especially for de Lavallade by Agnes de Mille. The 1950s and 1960s were periods of intense work for the young dancer as she appeared on television in numerous works choreographed by John Butler. She also danced in works by her husband Holder for his dance company and in concert performances of the choreography of Butler, Ailey, and Glen Tetley. In the midst of this activity she also managed to find the time to take acting lessons. De Lavallade's artistic life began to assume its

unique, eclectic nature. As she once stated in an interview, "I've touched on all the arts. . . . I've never had a scheduled life. Most of my career has been roundabout. In fact, I've had a very peculiar career." De Lavallade was a muse to many who came in contact with her.

In *Portrait of Billie*, John Butler choreographed one of her most famous roles: that of Billie Holiday. In this role she created a restless and vulnerable portrayal of the tragic singer; her interpretation has never been equaled. Whether snapping her fingers tartly, caressing her thighs, or matching her movements to the recorded music of Holiday's singing, de Lavallade was in full command of her art. In 1954, Butler choreographed a role for her in his *Carmina Burana* for the Caramoor Festival in Katonah, New York. This work combined oratorio, opera, and dance. De Lavallade was one of the four soloists who created a sensation with Butler's sensual movements. In 1961, she danced in another Butler work, *Letter to a Beloved*, with a solo consisting of spiral turns, runs, and falls which were extended by de Lavallade's manipulation of the long train of her velvet dress.

In addition to roles for Butler and others, de Lavallade was also a major force in the dance of Alvin Ailey. She was one of his first dancers and appeared with him in a duet from 1961, *The Roots of the Blues,* in which she appeared sullen, sultry, provocative, sensuous, willful, and intense. It was a riveting performance and helped cement the association between the two dancers. The two joined forces and formed the de Lavallade-Ailey Dance Company—and their performances were highlights of the dance season. Ailey was the choreographer and de Lavallade the associate artistic director and assistant choreographer; the group went on a tour of the Far East a year later.

In the late 1960s de Lavallade formed her own company, the Carmen De Lavallade Theatre of Dance. It appeared in concert programs in New York City performing works by Holder and Butler. But it was always as a performer that de Lavallade made her mark. One of her signature works was a piece choreographed for her by Holder, called *Come Sunday,* filled with African-American spirituals sung by Odetta with de Lavallade dancing with all the emotion contained in such songs as "Deep River." In another solo, *Three Songs for One* (1963, choreography by Holder), de Lavallade seemed, in the words of Walter Terry, "to transcend mere form as she gives up the very radiance. . .of dance itself." She used her slender arms and hands to create flowing gestures that matched the music—"Songs of the Auvergne"—or cut through space with joyous leaps. Costumed in a airy white dress, she seemed to take a delicate delight in nature. Historical reconstruction has also interested de Lavallade as shown in her 1973 performances at Jacob's Pillow. Here, she danced two early-20th-century works by Ruth St. Denis: *Incense* and *The Yogi*.

In the 1970s, de Lavallade began to choreograph and stage a variety of works. In 1975 she choreographed the movement for Alvin Epstein's production of *A Midsummer Night's Dream* at the Yale Repertory Theatre in addition to acting the role of Titania. It was a sterling success for de Lavallade the choreographer and dancer. As Jack Kroll noted in his review in *Newsweek,* "It would take a Shakespeare himself to describe Miss de Lavallade, whose supernal beauty embodies not only the physical but. . .the moral power of her presence." De Lavallade devised witty movements for the human characters and lofty, otherworldy moves for Titania and Oberon. As Titania, clad in a flesh-colored-bodystocking and wearing a silver wig, de Lavallade seemed to inhabit another, supernatural realm. In *Sensemaya,* choreographed for Dance Theater of Harlem, de

Carmen de Lavallade performing with the Alvin Ailey American Dance Theatre, 1970. Photograph © Johan Elbers.

Lavallade reached back into her Horton days to devise a dance based on the Mayan legend of creation. The music was by Silvestre Revueltas and de Lavallade's choreography tells the story of creation briefly but directly. Two women, whose arms and legs are intercoiled, represent a shapeless earth monster, Eddie Shelman and Lowell Smith enact two Mayan gods; they separate the two figures until one is placed above the other to signify the creation of heaven and earth. The steady pulse and repetition of the piece heighten the feeling of ritual.

De Lavallade also extended her acting during the late 1960s and 1970s. She was intent to learn a new artistic vocabulary. As a result, she appeared in more than 19 roles—from Doña Anna in *Don Juan* to Anna II in the *Seven Deadly Sins*—with the Yale Repertory Theatre and other groups. De Lavallade credited Robert Brustein, dean of the Yale School of Drama, with "pushing" her into acting. He hired her to teach movement to the actors at Yale Repertory Theatre and she went on to appear in the classics and modern works both at Yale and with the Roundabout Theater in New York City. As she stated in a 1979 interview, "You can take a lifetime to discover what you want to say in your art." In the late 1990s Carmen de Lavallade is imparting her knowledge to dance students while also exploring and expanding her art with friends, colleagues, and husband Geoffrey Holder.

—Adriane Ruggiero

DELSARTE & JAQUES-DALCROZE

FRANÇOIS DELSARTE—**Born:** 1811 in Solesmes, France. **Education**: Studied singing and music at the Conservatory of Paris where he lost his voice due to poor training and resolved to universalize and better music training. **Career:** Spent years observing gesture and voice, developing his own system of training called "Cours d'Esthetique Applique." **Died:** 1871.

EMILE JAQUES-DALCROZE—**Born:** 1865 in Vienna. **Education:** Studied music in Vienna and Paris. **Career**: Professor of harmony, Geneva Conservatory; developed a system of rhythmic training to help students kinesthetically understand musical rhythm, known as "Eurythmics," which became popular all over Europe; opened his own school, Hellerau (Germany), 1910; school closed during WWI; later reopened under direction of a former student. **Died:** 1950, in Geneva.

Publications

By JAQUES-DALCROZE: books—

Eurythmics, Art and Education (translated by Frederick Rothwell), New York, 1930.
Rhythm, Music and Education (trans. Harold F. Rubenstein), London, 1967.

On DELSARTE & DALCROZE: books—

Bachmann, Marie-Laure, *Dalcroze Today: An Education Through and Into Music* (trans. David Parlett), Oxford, 1991.

Morgan, Anna, *An Hour with Delsarte: A Study of Expression,* Boston, 1892.
Shawn, Ted, *Every Little Movement*, Pittsfield, MA, 1963.
Spector, Irwin, *Rhythm and Life: The Work of Emile Jaques-Dalcroze*, New York, 1990.

On DELSARTE & DALCROZE: articles—

Balance, John, "Jaques-Dalcroze and his School," in *Gordon Craig on Movement and Dance*, ed. New York, 1977.
Dasgupta, Gautam, "Commedia Delsarte," *Performing Arts Journal*, September, 1993.
Ruyter, Nancy Lee Chalfa, "American Deslartians Abroad," in *Society of Dance History Scholars Proceedings*, Riverside, CA, February 1992.
———, "Appendix 1: Dalcroze Eurythmics," in her *Reformers and Visionaries: The Americanization of the Art of Dance*, New York, 1979.
———, "Appendix 2: A Tentative List of Delsartian Books in English in Chronological Order," in her *Reformers and Visionaries: The Americanization of the Art of Dance*, New York, 1979.
———, "A Sampling of Exercise Materials from American Delsarte Manuals," in *Society of Dance History Scholars Proceedings*, Ohio, February 1983.
Zoete, Beryl de, "A Tribute to My Master, Jaques-Dalcroze," in her *Thunder and the Freshness*, London and New York, 1963.

*   *   *

While not dancers, Delsarte and Dalcroze both had an important influence on the beginnings of modern dance. Delsarte was born in Solesmes, France, in 1811 and studied music at the conservatory in Paris. Through bad training, his singing voice was ruined and, according to Ted Shawn in *Every Little Move* (1954) Delsarte "dedicated his life to the task of discovering great general laws and principles of art and expression" in order to save future students from the same fate. Delsarte spent years observing people and accumulating material for a taxonomy of expressive gesture which, sometime around 1839, he began teaching as "Cours d'Esthetique Applique" or applied aesthetics. His taxonomy-making put Delsarte squarely in the Victorian era's predilection for collecting and ordering in the name of science. His system was elaborate, focusing more on declamation and oration than movement, and as Walter Sorrel points out in *Dance In Its Time* (1981), was largely responsible for "elocution. . .finally [being] given a foundation and philosophy."

Delsarte was a deeply religious man and his beliefs were reflected in his system's trinitarian design: he divided the body into three zones (head/torso/limbs); identified three great orders of movement (oppositions/parallelisms/successions), nine laws of motion, and so on. According to Shawn, Delsarte believed that "the three principles of our being, life, mind, and soul, form a trinity" and "God is triune in nature and essence, so is Man." Delsarte's categories, subcategories, and cross-categories could lead to innumerable combinations to interpret human expression, but more importantly he believed the learning of his system (which he felt he had "discovered" as inherent in all humanity) would lead to a perfect alignment of expression and meaning, or unity between the triune parts of human nature.

Steele Mackaye, an innovator in American theater, studied with Delsarte in 1869 for eight months and brought what he learned back to the U.S. in addition to working out, with Delsarte's approval, his own "Harmonic Gymnastics" to help students prepare to use Delsarte's system. Mackaye's version of Delsartian principles became very popular in the states, and as its popularity increased, others cashed in by copying and simplifying (sometimes beyond recognition) the teaching of the system. "Delsarte" (as it was called in the U.S.) was largely reduced to statue-posing and drawing room entertainment. The Delsarte craze almost went the way of all crazes, except that a few nascent American dancers had either seen Delsarte inspired performances (a young Ruth St. Denis saw Genevieve Stebbins perform, which opened a whole new world of movement for her) or studied with Delsarte-trained teachers (Ted Shawn, early in his career, studied with Mrs. Perry King and later with Mrs. Richard Hovey). Deborah Jowitt in *Time and the Dancing Image* (1988) points out Delsarte helped prepare the way for modern dance because, through the popularity of his system, he made "thinking about the body not only advisable but fashionable" and although his theory "dealt primarily with 'attitudes' and gestures, performed while standing in place, it was full of spatial implications." Dancers St. Denis and Shawn, in particular, took these spatial implications and ran with them.

In Europe not long after Delsarte's death in 1871, another musician was concerned with his students' lack of rhythmic sensibilities and began work on his own system of movement to enhance their kinesthetic sense of music. Emile Jaques-Dalcroze was a professor of music at the Geneva Conservatory when he developed his "eurythmics" to teach the rhythmic structures of music, believing what could be felt and understood through the body would result in a better intellectual grasp and performance of music. It is possible he knew of Delsarte's work; his division of the body into three zones echoes the earlier system. Eurythmics became hugely popular with the wider public and had a lasting cultural impact largely because, as Sorell has said "Dalcroze came at the right moment in history when motion was of prime interest; when dancers emerged who wanted to reveal inmost experiences. . .unhampered by century old rules; when Pathe created its first moving pictures in Paris."

In 1910, in Hellerau (outside Dresden), two German manufacturers (Wolf and Harald Dohrn) built Dalcroze a school and in 1912, an auditorium for performances. The auditorium had no proscenium stage, but an experimental "open" stage, and there, in 1913, Dalcroze in collaboration with the stage and light designer Adolphe Appia produced Glück's *Orfeo ed Euricide*. While Dalcroze did not consider his school a dancing school, or eurythmics dance training, Jack Anderson has noted, "exercises for his advanced students were often kinetically demanding and the rhythmic training they provided was valuable for dancers, as well as musicians." The young Marie Rambert studied and taught with Dalcroze in Hellerau, where she worked with many dancers including Nijinsky and the Ballets Russes. Diaghilev thought the rhythmic training of Dalcroze's method would help Nijinsky choreograph and the corp dance the complex musical score for Stravinsky's *Le Sacre du printemps*.

Dalcroze also knew Isadora Duncan and "admired her freedom and plasticity while deploring her musical inexactness" according to Jowitt. Ruth St. Denis knew of his work from her own studies as well as from Doris Humphrey who had studied Dalcroze techniques in Chicago with Mary Wood Hinman, and according to critics like Sorell, Dalcroze's "handwriting can be detected" in a few of St. Denis' music studies and especially in *An Unfinished Symphony* of 1931.

Dalcroze worked with other dancers and choreographers, including Michio Ito, Hanya Holm, and Kurt Jooss. Perhaps one of his most well known students, who turned down her opportunity to

direct one his schools in Berlin in 1913, was Mary Wigman. She had taken a summer off to study with Rudolf von Laban and felt she had "moved beyond" Dalcroze's confining gymnastics into a greater adventure of improvisation and sought to explore her own dance impulses.

Dalcroze's school in Hellerau closed at the outset of World War I when he protested German militarism and left for Geneva where he remained. A former student, Christine Baer-Frissel, reopened the Hellerau school in 1919, and a second school, called Hellerau-Laxenburg, opened outside Vienna in 1925. Dalcroze was largely forgotten after World War II, though he continued to teach until his death in 1950. Of his influence on modern dance, Walter Sorell says: "He helped prepare the ground for many creative minds and bodies to explore artistic possibilities beyond his method."

—G. Benbow-Niemier

DENDY, Mark
American dancer, choreographer, playwright, and actor

Born: 29 May 1961, Weaverville, North Carolina, as Mark Brown Dendy. **Education:** North Carolina School of the Arts, B.F.A., 1983; American Dance Festival, summers, 1981-83. **Career:** Founder and artistic director, Mark Dendy Dance and Theater, 1983-present; performed with the Martha Graham Dance Ensemble, 1983-84; and companies of Pearl Lang, 1983-85; Ruby Shang, 1983-86; Pooh Kaye's Eccentric Motions, 1984-89; guest artist with Jane Comfort and Company, 1990-94. **Awards:** National Endowment for the Arts (NEA) grants, 1986, 1987, 1988, 1995, 1996; New York State Council on the Arts award, 1986; Massachusetts Arts Council award, 1987; National Society of Arts and Letters Sustained Achievement Award, 1990; Philip Morris award, 1990, 1992; Joyce Mertz Gilmore Foundation award, 1990, 1992, 1993; Harkness Foundation award, 1992; North Carolina Arts Council award, 1992; American Dance Festival/Scripps Humphrey Weidman Limón Fellowship for Choreography, 1995; New York Dance and Performance Award ("Bessie"), 1997; Choo San Goh award, 1997; Tennessee's Outstanding Achievement Award, 1997; Jerome Foundation award, 1998.

Works (selected repertory; created by Dendy for his company unless otherwise noted)

1982	*Solo* (danced by Dendy, changing music), North Carolina School of the Arts
1985	*Beat* (live spoken score), American Dance Festival
1986	*Garden,* Heineman American Dance Festival's Young Choreographers and Composers Project, North Carolina
1987	*Torn,* Mortilla, Dancin' in the Streets, New York
1988	*The White Week,* Mortilla, Jacob's Pillow, Massachusetts
1991	*Bugs of Durham, Are We Going Somewhere?* (original score by Carman Moore), American Dance Festival, North Carolina
	Ballet One, Wall Matthews (commissioned by and for Pacific Northwest Ballet), Seattle
	Lore, Nitty Gritty Dirt Band, Will the Circle Be Unbroken, Volume one, Raleigh, North Carolina

Mark Dendy in 1986. Photograph © Johan Elbers.

Back Back (spoken text, commissioned by the Joyce Theater's Altogether Different Series), New York

1993   *Busride to Heaven* (theater piece written and performed by Dendy, commissioned by Bates Dance Festival), Maine

Fire (dance/theater piece Jerry Lee Lewis, commissioned by P.S. 122), New York

1994   *Bardo, Tibetan Chants and Rituals* (commissioned by American Dance Festival), Durham, North Carolina

1995   *Symmetries* (John Adams, commissioned by and for the Pacific Northwest Ballet)

1996   *Ritual* (Andres Gribou, commissioned by American Dance Festival)

Fauns (mus. Debussy, commissioned by American Dance Festival)

Aria (Tibaldi singing Catalani's *La Wally*, commissioned by and for Li Chiao-ping), American Dance Festival

1997   *First Chair* (mus. Shubert, commissioned by and for Mary Cochran)

Dream Analysis (dance/theater, mus. Stravinsky, Webern, and songs made popular by Judy Garland with script by Dendy), Joyce Theater, New York

Les Biches (mus. Poulanc, commissioned by and for Pacific Northwest Ballet)

Augury, Kennedy Center, Washington, D.C.

Publications

"A Conversation with Mark Dendy," *Ballet Review,* Fall 1990.

*   *   *

Mark Dendy's education began as a young blonde-haired, blue-eyed boy, raised in the mountains of North Carolina in a home he shared with his mother, daddy, brother Ben, his twin sisters Nelljean and Mary Madelyn, Aunt Jessie, and his maternal grandmother. Religion (his grandfather was the town's Presbyterian minister), the family, and his southern heritage became the palette for his multidimensional life as a choreographer, dancer, playwright, and actor.

Dendy received his B.F.A. from the North Carolina School of the Arts in modern dance in 1983 and formed his company, Mark Dendy Dance and Theater, that same year. He has performed with the Martha Graham Dance Ensemble, as well as with Pearl Lang, Ruby Shang, Pooh Kaye's Eccentric Motions, and as a guest artist with Jane Comfort and Company.

Between 1987 and 1995 he received five grants from the National Endowment for the Arts and support from the Jerome Foundation and the New York State Council on the Arts. He was the recipient of the American Dance Festival's Scripps Humphrey Weidman Limón Fellowship for choreography, and he was involved in the Emmy award-winning television program *Smithsonian World.*

With *Beat* in 1985, Dendy established himself as a choreographer and dancer who could make and perform high-speed, witty, "dancey" dances. The following year he exhibited this side with *Garden* at the American Dance Festival (ADF); since then, his career has been formed by a trinity of art forms among which he crisscrosses—dance, theater, and site-specific works. His dance work can be spiritual and meditative, as in the mesmerizing pure dance *Bardo,* inspired by the Tibetan *Book of the Dead.* It can be Grahamesque dramatic as in *Aria,* the riveting solo he made for Li Chiao Ping, which premiered at ADF in 1996. And he successfully tackled his first chair dance with *First Chair,* which he created for former Paul Taylor soloist Mary Cochran.

Dendy's site-specific works are always ambitious productions, such as the section he choreographed in Ruby Shang's *The Small Wall Project* in 1984; Dendy created a rap song-driven, modern dance history lesson on Duke University's campus (ADF's home). *Bugs of Durham, Are We Going Somewhere?,* seven years later, starred Volkswagen Beetles. And in *Ritual,* the work he set on about 50 ADF students in 1996, he transformed Reynolds Industries Theatre (Duke), from the lobby to the rafters, into a sacred meeting ground where the audience and performers merged as equal participants in the rites they created.

Dendy created *Dream Analysis,* a work that merges dance, theater, and musical genres, for his 1997 Joyce Season. His dance/theater work is rooted in social issues with pieces like *Back Back,* an over-the-top statement against political, religious, and social reactions to the AIDS epidemic, and with *Fire,* a look at abuse and homophobia played against the backdrop of the 1950s.

In the years between, Dendy became a "G.I.," or Gender Illusionist, as he pegs it. He developed his women characters well before the drag craze hit the mainstream. In 1985 he created Meemaw, the old Southern mountain woman with a bible in one hand and a TV remote in the other. He received critical acclaim for his powerful performance as Amanda in Jane Comfort's 1992 *Faith Healing,* an adaptation of Tennessee Williams's *Glass Menagerie.*

His theatrical tour de force, *Busride to Heaven,* established Dendy as an accomplished playwright and actor. The one-person show reaches back to his roots, reclaiming his spirituality and his life through drama. *Busride* is a brilliant one-person theater piece that Dendy penned and in which he played all four parts, including three women, all drawn from real life. Dendy also appeared in the musical film spoof *Francesca Page* in 1996, in a big blonde wig, royal blue taffeta dress, and pumps.

He has also crossed over into choreographing for ballet companies including the Pacific Northwest Ballet, Charleston Ballet, and Nashville Ballet. Dendy's recent virtuosic duet, *Fauns,* inspired by the life of Nijinsky, might just be the best dance work he's done to date. The running motif that leaves Dendy breathless serves as metaphor for his own life, one that finds him accruing experiences and creating art with a vengeance. To date, he has lived a life that could easily be one of his own theater pieces.

—Linda Belans

DESROSIERS, Robert

Canadian dancer, choreographer, designer, and artistic director

Born: 10 October 1953 in Montreal, Quebec. **Education:** Studied ballet with Aline Legris, Montreal; educated and trained at the National Ballet School of Canada, Toronto, with Carole Chadwick and Daniel Sellier, 1965-71; studied ballet with Maggie Black and Stanley Williams, New York; Raymond Franchetti, Paris; studied theatre and movement with Lindsay Kemp, London; studied Limón and Falco technique with Hugo Romero, Montreal; studied tai chi with Master Moy, Toronto; studied modern dance with David Earle and Peter Randazzo at School of Toronto Dance Theatre, Toronto. **Family:** Married dancer Claudia Moore, 1979 (divorced, 1985). **Career:** Dancer, the National Ballet of Canada, Toronto, 1971-72; Les Ballets Felix Blaska, Grenoble, France, 1973-74; Les Grands Ballets Canadiens and Contemporary Dance Theatre, Montreal, 1975; Ballet Ys, Toronto, 1975-76; Dancemakers, Toronto, 1976-77; Lindsay Kemp and Company, London, 1978; Toronto Dance Theatre (TDT), Toronto, 1979-80; first independent choreography, 1975; first solo concert of own works, 1977; founder, Desrosiers Dance Theatre (DDT), Toronto, 1980; first tour of Canada, 1982; Canadian festivals include Québec Été Danse, Lennoxville, Quebec, 1982-84; Expo '86, Vancouver; Calgary Olympics Cultural Festival, Calgary, Alberta, 1988; first tour abroad, Hong Kong Festival, 1984; foreign appearances include Hong Kong Arts Festival; Centre Georges Pompidou (Paris), American Dance Festival, Jacob's Pillow Festival, Brooklyn Academy of Music (BAM) Center; Singapore Arts Festival; Caracas International Festival (Venezuela); STEPS '90—Festival international suisse de danse (Switzerland), Festival of Two Worlds (Spoleto, Italy). **Awards:** Jacqueline Lemieux Prize, 1981; Jean A. Chalmers Award for choreography, 1985; funding grants from Canada Council, Ontario Arts Council, Metro Toronto Arts Council, Toronto Arts Council, Laidlaw Foundation and du Maurier Arts Council.

Roles

1975   *Nelligan* (Ann Ditchburn) duet, Ballet Ys, Toronto
1977   *Fauré's Requiem* (David Earle), Toronto Dance Theatre (TDT), Toronto
1979   *Re'em* (Karen duPlessis), TDT Choreographic Workshop, Toronto
        The Light Brigade (Peter Randazzo), TDT, Toronto
        Rejoice in the Lamb (David Earle, Nancy Ferguson), TDT
1980   *Ice Age* (Mitchell Kirsch), TDT
        Stolen Thunder (Nancy Ferguson), TDT Choreographic Workshop
        Courtyard (David Earle), TDT
        Smenkhkare, *Akhenaten* (David Earle), TDT
1984   Nelligan, *Émile Nelligan, Elusive Players* (Ann Ditchburn), Harbourfront, Toronto

Other roles include: Various roles with Les Ballets Felix Blaska, Grenoble, France; Contemporary Dance Theatre, Montreal; Ballet Ys, Toronto; solos in own works, 1975 to present.

Works

1975   *Désert* (mus. Chilliwack, John McLaughlin), Contemporary Dance Theatre, Montreal
1976   *It's Krime* (mus. Couperin, Ego), Toronto
        The Hunt w/percussionist Ricardo Abreut, solo, Toronto
1977   *Take the Subway to the Moon* w/poet-visual artist Albert Gedraitis (mus. Gordon Phillips, Mississippi John Hurt) solo, Toronto

1979   *Dream in a Dream* (mus. Bill Grove, Geordie McDonald, Derek Partling), TDT Choreographic Workshop, Toronto

1980   *Visions of Death as a Clown* (later called *Night Clown*) (mus. Gordon Phillips, Michael Brook), Desrosiers Dance Theatre (DDT), Toronto
        The Fisherman's Carnival (mus. Pat Metheny), Masha Stone Summer Dance School, Niagara-on-the-Lake, Ontario
        Picasso Phase One (mus. Bill Grove), (DDT), Toronto
        Brass Fountain (mus. Bill Grove; rescored, John Lang, 1984), DDT, Toronto

1981   *Plutonium Jungle* (mus. Ahmed Hassan, Bill Grove), DDT, Dance in Canada Conference, Montreal

1982   *Bad Weather* (mus. Gordon Phillips, Sara Dalton Phillips), DDT, Québec Été Danse, Lennoxville, Quebec

1983   *The Fool's Table* (mus. Gordon Phillips, Sara Dalton Phillips), DDT, Toronto
        Ciel Rouge (mus. Ahmed Hassan, John Lang), DDT, Toronto
        L'Hôtel Perdu (mus. Jean Dorais, Ahmed Hassan, and John Lang), DDT, Québec Été Danse, Lennoxville, Quebec

1984   *Ultracity* (mus. Jean Dorais, Ahmed Hassan, John Lang), DDT, Toronto
        Rendez-vous Lunaire (mus. Ahmed Hassan, John Lang) duet, National Ballet School of Canada's 25th Anniversary Gala, Toronto
        Sardonicus (mus. UB40) solo, Toronto Independent Dance Enterprise (T.I.D.E.) Birthday Celebration, Toronto

1985   *Blue Snake* (mus. John Lang, Ahmed Hassan), National Ballet of Canada, Toronto

1986   *Mirrors* (mus. Ahmed Hassan, John Lang), DDT, Toronto
        Lumière (mus. Ron Allen, Ahmed Hassan, John Lang, Gordon Phillips), DDT, Toronto

1987   *Concerto in Earth Major* (mus. Ron Allen, John Lang), DDT, Toronto
        Laundry Days (mus. John Lang), Winnipeg Contemporary Dancers, Winnipeg, Manitoba

1988   *Incognito* (mus. Eric Cadesky, John Lang), DDT, Calgary Olympics Cultural Festival, Calgary, Alberta

1989   *First Year* (mus. Eric Cadesky, John Lang), National Ballet School of Canada, Betty Oliphant Theatre Opening Gala, Toronto
        Arc en Ciel (mus. Eric Cadesky, John Lang), Lyon Opera Ballet, Lyon, France

1990   *Jeux* (mus. Eric Cadesky, John Lang), DDT, Toronto

1991   *Full Moon* (mus. Mozart, Eric Cadesky), DDT, Glory of Mozart Festival, Toronto
        Black & White (mus. Eric Cadesky, John Lang; additional music Alfred Schnittke, Peter Sculthorpe), DDT, Toronto

1992   *Moons of Morning* w/Menaka Thakkar (mus. Ron Allen), DDT and Menaka Thakkar Dance Company, Toronto

1993   *Black & White in Colour* (mus. Eric Cadesky, Anne Bourne, John Lang), DDT, Toronto

1994   *White Clouds* (mus. Eric Cadesky), DDT, Toronto

1995   *Musical Chairs* (mus. Eric Cadesky), DDT, Toronto
        Pinocchio (mus. Eric Cadesky), Hamilton Ballet Youth Ensemble, Hamilton, Ontario

1996   *Corridors* (mus. Eric Cadesky, John Lang), DDT, Toronto

1997   *Pierrot* (mus. Eric Cadesky, John Lang, Thomas Tallis, Istvan Marta), DDT, Toronto
        Vivaldi Sacred Songs (mus. Vivaldi), DDT, Toronto

Publications

On DESROSIERS: books—

Macpherson, Susan, ed., *101 From the Encyclopedia of Theatre Dance in Canada,* Toronto, 1997.
Wyman, Max, *Dance Canada: An Illustrated History,* Vancouver, 1989.

On DESROSIERS: articles—

Citron, Paula, "He Pleased Everyone but Himself, So Desrosiers Built a New *Incognito,*" *Toronto Star,* 3 February 1989.
Crabb, Michael, "Robert Desrosiers," *Dance in Canada,* Fall 1979.
Doob, Penelope, "Robert Desrosiers: Magician of Dance," *Performing Arts* (Toronto), March 1988.
Kelly, Deirdre, "Stepping into Magic and Light," *Financial Post* (Toronto), 13 February 1993.
Littler, William, "Stepping into a Mystical Realm," *New York Times,* 27 January 1991.
Rudakoff, Judith, "Robert Desrosiers: Breaking Boundaries, Shaking Foundations," *Canadian Theatre Review,* Winter 1990.
Rudnicki, Elaine, "More Than an Ocean Apart/Robert Desrosiers: Canada's Modern Dance Ambassador," *Dance in Canada,* Summer 1989.
Smith, Gary, "The Puppet Master," *Hamilton Spectator,* 8 April 1995.

Films and Videotapes

All That Bach, dir. Larry Weinstein, Rhombus Media, 1984.
Le Circle du silence, La chaîne française [TFO], 1987.
I am a Hotel, mus. Leonard Cohen, chor. Ann Ditchburn, "C" Channel, 1983.
Lovers in a Dangerous Time, music video by Bruce Cockburn, 1984.
The Making of the Music for Blue Snake, dir. Niv Fischman, Rhombus Media, 1985.
A Moving Picture, Rhombus Media, 1987.
Nelligan, mus. André Gagnon, chor. Ann Ditchburn, 1984.
Not by the Book (documentary on schizophrenia), dir. Kari Skogland, TV Ontario, 1994.
The Originals (dir. Dan Robinson, City TV, Toronto, 1991).
A Salute to "Dancers for Life," CBC, 1995.

*   *   *

Robert Desrosiers is a rugged individualist who flies in the face of conventional dance icons. For him, inspiration is more truthful than rules. His international fame is based on provocative works that blend high-energy, physically demanding, intensely athletic movement with an audacious theatricality. As much spectacle as dance, Desrosiers' stage creations are filled with outrageous props, highly imaginative costumes, and startling sets. His characters have cryptic names like "Mermaid of Wisdom" or "Soulcatchers," and each episode of the work is given a fanciful title. While his eye-catching dance theatre can be enjoyed on the visual level alone, his wild imaginings are the tip of the iceberg concealing profound meta-

Robert Desrosiers: *Incognito,* **1991. Photograph © Johan Elbers.**

physical concepts. Desrosiers is a philosopher of dance, much influenced by Eastern thought, yoga, and tai chi. In his world, tormented man, plagued by past and present follies, is in search of harmony. His choreography is almost autobiographical, mirroring his own self-growth as he strives for higher levels of consciousness. The corollary is the hope that his works will reach out to others "on some kind of path of self-search." Sadly, Desrosiers was drawn to his mysticism by the suicide of an older schizophrenic brother. This family tragedy was the wellspring for the choreographer, then only 19 years old, to begin his journey in search of cosmic understanding.

Desrosiers was sent to dance school when he was five because his body was always in motion. When the Kirov Ballet toured to Montreal in 1964, Desrosiers was one of the local children used for *Cinderella* and *Raymonda.* He auditioned for the National Ballet School of Canada and, at age 12, arrived in Toronto, a Québecois boy who spoke no English. At the school he discovered two wonderful worlds, dance and visual arts. All of his time outside dance class was spent in the art room. After graduating he became a member of the National Ballet of Canada (NBC) but lasted only one year, finding the company stifling. The next phase of his life was exploration, or as he says, "finding out what I wanted from dance and what I didn't." After further ballet studies in France, he was joined by fellow NBC dropout Claudia Moore, and the couple

danced with Felix Blaska in Grenoble for a year. Finding France too traditional, they moved to London to attend the classes of the *enfant terrible* visionary of theatre, Lindsay Kemp. Kemp taught movement through imagery in order to stimulate truthful motivation, an important principle which Desrosiers absorbed. Returning to North America, the couple settled in Montreal where they took up with another "madman," Mexican-born choreographer Hugo Romero. Romero had himself been trained by teachers, such as Limón and Falco, who were heavily influenced by German Expressionism. Dancing in Romero's Contemporary Dance Theatre introduced Desrosiers to speed of movement. "Hugo's dances were frantic," he recalled in an interview with this author.

Desrosiers eventually returned to Toronto to perform with various modern and ballet companies, but after a short time he returned to London and joined Lindsay Kemp's company in search of an elusive sense of freedom. When he rejoined Moore in Toronto in 1979, he danced with Toronto Dance Theatre for a year. With the realization that there would never be any company he could call home except his own, Desrosiers Dance Theatre was born in 1980. "I had to put aside my fear of what was acceptable and follow my own creativity," he says. His company has toured his unique vision of dance all over the world.

Desrosiers' creativity demands originality of visual concepts and music. While often he is his own designer, he has also worked with artists who are able to carry out his far-fetched ideas; hats that carry an urban jungle of skyscrapers, a papier-mâché cow that can be swung in the air by the tail, a giant tsunami tidal wave that engulfs the stage, a grand piano that chases after its pianist, or a double-sided man. His choice of composers runs to avant-garde creators of both melody and soundscape like John Lang and Eric Cadesky. Desrosiers' metaphysical-theatrical approach is a form of self-expression that goes beyond the rational. The choreographer feels a kinship to the French-Canadian *patenteux*, artisans who are motivated by an inescapable creative drive to produce extravagantly original and imaginative folk art. "*Les patenteux* are part of my heritage," he says, and like them, he works by intuition. His ideas spring from the subconscious, and the meaning behind his work is not revealed to him until after all the components are brought together.

Aspects of his philosophy of life anchor all his works. His earlier pieces centred on disorderly man in a disordered world, yearning for something better. In *Plutonium Jungle* (1981), Desrosiers explored the primal curse of conflict, with his dancers divided into two sets of elemental characters, one futuristic, one primitive, both fighting for dominance. The banquet of *The Fool's Table* (1983) represents different facets of ego, with the Fool as the supreme self surrounded by ancient karma of medieval danse macabre and plague symbolism. When the table, spinning madly, closes on the Fool, it is the beginning of his transformation and his journey to the light. *Blue Snake* (1985), created for the NBC, is dominated by a huge head with arms, which fills the cyclorama. After chaotic comings and goings, the piece ends with dancers joyfully being lifted by the hands and fed into the giant mouth, the pathway to a higher state of being. With *Blue Snake* Desrosiers' focus subtly shifted from the madness of the world to the search for the harmony for the soul. *Incognito* (1988) is about insanity and presents a parade of images from the darkest nightmares, but the work ends in hope. *Black & White* (1991) and *In Colour* (1993) form a complete work; the first half highlights the contrasts that exist in human nature, while the second is an ebullient riot of colourful costumes that alludes to a higher, more unified existence. *Corridors* (1996) is a journey of self-discovery as Mr. Key tries to find his place in the universe. It is a work of juxtaposition, swinging wildly between images of frenzied buffoonery and serene cosmic awareness.

In his prime, Desrosiers was a magnificent dancer, and his solos were the centrepieces of his works. Latterly, he has taken on more character roles. Occasionally, he has dropped all trappings of theatricality to fine-tune his choreographic language and bring it more in balance with the visual elements. *Jeux* (1990) may have disappointed die-hard fans, but the work was crucial to his development as a dancesmith. After *Jeux,* Desrosiers emerged as a choreographer of risky, acrobatic floorwork, difficult and intricate partnering, and dense, rapid movement. A Desrosiers signature is "horizontal dancing," which uses momentum to fly parallel to the floor. His original company members were dancing actors, but as his movement vocabulary evolved, Desrosiers gravitated to fluid, flexible, gymnastic dancers of considerable technical ability. Nowhere was this more evident than in *Vivaldi Sacred Songs* (1997), a pure dance celebration of spirituality, manifested in a joyous kaleidoscope of movement executed at breathtaking speed. The stage is completely draped in white and there are no shadows; it is a triumph of light.

—Paula Citron

DIETRICH, Urs
Swiss-born dancer and choreographer

Born: 1958 in Visp, Switzerland. **Education:** Studied dance at the Folkwang College in Essen, 1981-85; scholarship for New York study from the Cultural Ministry of North Rhine, Westfalia. **Career:** First choreographic work *Job (Hiob)* (solo, 1984); dancer at the Folkwang Dance Studio, 1986-87; first group choreography, 1988; collaborated with Susanne Linke on choreographic and dance projects, 1988-90; member of Susanne Linke's company for Ruhr-Ort, 1991; choreographed for the Folkwang Dance Studio; co-director of the Bremen Dance Theater with Susanne Linke from 1994. **Awards:** Kurt Jooss Prize from the city of Essen, 1985.

Works

1984	*Hiob* (solo; mus. bach), Folkwang-Hochschule, Essen
1988	*Das kalte Gloria* (mus. collage), Folkwang Tanzstudio, Essen
	Affekte (mus. collage), duet w/Susanne Linke, Paris
1990	*Effekte* (mus. collage), duet w/Susanne Linke, Velbert, Germany
1991	*Sanguis* (mus. Bach, Bowie), Folkwang Tanzstudio, Recklinghausen
1992	*Onno* (mus. collage), Folkwang Tanzstudio, Essen
1993	*...Und der Sommer zog gen Süden* (mus. Vogelstimmen), duet w/Thomas Stich, Munich
1994	*Einmal Elysium—Einfach* (mus. collage), Folkwang Tanzstudio, Recklinghausen
1995	*Das kalte Gloria II* (mus. Vivaldi, Mendelssohn-Bartholdy), Bremer Tanztheater, Bremen
	Echo: Die Freundlichkeit des Hundes (mus. Sibelius, Bach, Vivaldi), Bremer Tanztheater, Bremen
	Da war plötzlich: Herzkammern (mus. Tom Korr), solo, Bremen
1996	*Die Langsamkeit des Augenblicks* (mus. Adams, Kuhn, Bley-Borkowski), Bremer Tanztheater, Bremen
1997	*DO RE MI FA SO LATITOD* (mus. Beethoven), Bremer Tanztheater, Bremen

*   *   *

Behind each and every movement lies the conviction never to allow movement for movement's sake alone. Not the dancer, rather, the dancing human being is the bearer and mediator of his choreography. With this philosophy, Urs Dietrich represents the tradition of the Folkwang College. There the trained textile print designer, who came to dance late in life, studied from 1981 until 1985. His most significant teachers and supporters were Hans Züllig, Jean Cébron and Susanne Linke, three personalities who have shaped the image of this school in their roles as educators, choreographers and individuals.

From the onset of his training, Urs Dietrich was given the opportunity to work with the school's affiliated dance troupe, the Folkwang Tanz Studio (FTS). Susanne Linke, director of the FTS at the time, immediately integrated him as a permanent dance troupe member. For Urs Dietrich, this was an unexpected opportunity and challenge. He gained his first stage experience and, more importantly, was confronted with Susanne Linke's working methods, her scorn for artistic compromise, and the radical nature of her language of movement. Her work fascinated him and inspired the young dancer to conduct his own choreographic experiments. In his fourth year of study he staged his first solo, *Job,* which was awarded the Kurt Jooss Prize by the city of Essen. After receiving a graduate grant from the Folkwang School, he produced his first group choreography in 1987, *Das kalte Gloria (Cold Gloria)*. In this piece, the Folkwang pupil devotes himself with playful pleasure to his own métier, movement. Analyzing each movement, he demonstrates the endless diversity of the vocabulary he derived from the traditions of von Laban and Jooss. In 1987, he ceased dancing at FTS, but continued to choreograph, creating among other pieces *Sanguis* and *Onno,* whose objective and content were human emotion, predicaments, rivalries, addictions and longings, cooperation, and the individual's fight for survival. Again and again, Dietrich's choreography combines clearly structured dance sequences with passages that appear to be improvised, procuring a bit of hope, in spite of the harsh reality of his images, through humorous and comedic moments and by hinting at another dimension that lies hidden within the material. Urs Dietrich draws inspiration for his works from the observance of everyday occurrences, from situations and images that create parallels for him and converge to make a statement. He continued his career as dancer/choreographer with his collaborative

choreographic and dance work with Susanne Linke, as well as his solo works. At the beginning of the 1994-95 season, he and Susanne Linke took over the direction of the Bremen Dance Theater. For this ensemble he created *Die Langsamkeit des Augenblicks (The Slowness of the Moment* (1996) and *DO RE MI FA SO LATITOD (Do Re Mi Fa So LaTiDeath)* (1997), two group pieces in which the dynamic of movement and the message it conveys have gained even more precision and density.

—Patricia Stöckemann
translated by Joyce Han-Voth

DORFMAN, David

American dancer, choreographer, and company director

Born: 7 November 1955 in Chicago. **Education:** B.S., Washington University in St. Louis, 1977; M.F.A. in dance, Connecticut College, 1981. **Career:** Dancer, with the companies of Susan Marshall and Kei Takei, 1982-86; founder/director, David Dorfman Dance

David Dorfman (standing right) performing *Sleep Story,* **1988. Photograph © Beatriz Schiller.**

Company, 1985. **Awards:** Four National Endowment for the Arts (NEA) fellowships; New York Dance and Performance Award ("Bessie"), for *Familiar Movements*, 1996.

Works

1987	*Sleep Story*
1990	*Horn* w/Dan Froot
1993	*Out of Season* (part of the Athlete's Project)
1994	*Hey*
	Bull w/Froot
1995	*approaching no calm counting laughter*
1996	*Sky Down*
	Familiar Movements (part of the Family Project)
	Job w/Froot

*   *   *

David Dorfman stands as one of the truly "nice guys" of modern dance, an unusual star without the ego to match. He risked his first dance class while studying business at Washington University in St. Louis, Missouri, after playing football and baseball as a youth. His range as a choreographer reflects the various worlds he has been a part of—he dons a business suit as easily as the paraphernalia of team sports, and grants a degree of respect and curiosity to these "other" worlds that greatly enlarges his appeal as a choreographer and as a human being.

Dorfman's work is often a mix of abstract phrases of movement—slippery structures that threaten to fall apart or disappear—and content-flooded relationships with humor and pathos receiving equal attention. He initiates deep collaborations with dancers and with nondancers, arriving at movement works that finally realize the dream of the postmodern aesthetic—that is, to diminish the felt distance between audience and performers. The work remains dancerly enough to sustain the audience's desire to be engaged at the theatrical level, but simultaneously creates a bridge between audience and performers that anyone could ostensibly pass over. Perhaps as a result of coming to dance at a relatively late age, he has a rare and genuine appreciation of the movement of nondancers, saying that he "finds a rawness and innocence in nondancers that is wonderful and truly difficult to bring out in trained dancers." His own body has more of the stocky muscularity of an athlete than a trained dancer, which gives his dancing an unusual weightedness—not unlike a large bear, he can be fluid and surprisingly quick, with all the deftness it takes to rob honey from a hive.

Dorfman welcomes the opportunity to develop a level of engagement with his community that will support a renewed understanding of what the very word "culture" means. "It is my view that in our American culture specifically, we are taught that we need to be exceptionally good at an art form in order to practice it," he explains. "I think this mode of thinking is what prevents us all from taking ownership of our culture and re-weaving it in ways we desire so that culture can be an active part of the fabric of everyday life." In addition, Dorfman believes "We are our culture, and I think it's our responsibility and right to share all kinds of art with all kinds of people." An example of Dorfman's cultural responsibility are the Athlete's Project and the Family Project, both long-term efforts to build communities of both dancers and nondancers. Of the former, Dorfman said ". . .you always have athletes calling dancers fairies and dancers calling athletes Neanderthals. I'm trying to bring the two camps together." In each of these projects, Dorfman has initiated residencies where the life experiences and performances of volunteers from each community are integral to the development of the work over time.

Dorfman is an artist who works hard to create community awareness, and this is evident in his choreography and in the teaching residencies and workshops he has created. One of his latest works, *The Family Project*, brings together a mix of ages and races to dance about blood bonds common to all.

Dorfman's personal involvement as a musician (he played a number of instruments as a child) has also had a strong influence on his work. Many of his works are performed to live music, and his choices are an eclectic mix of many different styles and genres. His classic duet with Dan Froot called *Horn*, remains the standard for musicians who dance while playing. The dance presents the two men in kilts, practically wrestling the sound out of one another as each man in turn is lifted by the other, forcing each to blow powerfully into their respective horns.

There is something vaguely Chaplinesque about the funny and sad mixture in Dorfman's work, a quality that reveals a deep understanding of human nature. His compassion marks him as an extraordinary artist of our time.

—Peggy Berg

DOUGLAS, William

Canadian dancer, choreographer, company director, and educator

Born: 25 September 1953 in Amherst, Nova Scotia. **Education:** Studied vocal and instrumental music and music theory, Toronto Conservatory of Music; University of Waterloo, Ontario, B.S. in environmental studies, 1974; Carleton University, Ottawa, B.A. in architecture, 1978; studied dance with Toronto Dance Theatre, 1978-80, Merce Cunningham Studio, Maggie Black, and others, 1981-91. **Career:** Worked in the fields of architectural design, interior design, and drafting in Ottawa and Toronto, 1969-79 and New York, 1984-90; dancer, Ottawa Dance Centre Workshop Company, 1975-78; apprentice, understudy, and student choreographer, School of the Toronto Dance Theatre, 1978-80; company member, Dancemakers, Toronto, 1980-83; also danced in companies for choreographers Judy Jarvis, David Earle, and Graham Jackson, 1980, Paula Ravitz, 1982, Patricia Beatty and Jennifer Mascall, 1983, all in Toronto; danced with Douglas Dunn and Dancers, 1983-85, choreographers Susan Osberg, Bill Young, Brenda Daniels, and Shelly Lee, in New York City, 1985-91; first choreographic compositions, School of the Toronto Dance Theatre and Dancemakers, 1982-83; founder, William Douglas Dance, Montreal, 1986; founder, William Douglas Dance, New York, 1991. **Awards:** National Arts Centre Award, 1992; Grand Prize for Professional Choreographers at the *Rencontres choregraphiques internationals de Seine Saint-Denis*, Bagnolet, France, 1994; New York Dance and Performance Award ("Bessie") for choreography, New York, 1995; Prix d'auteur at the *Rencontres choregraphiques internationales de Seine Saint-Denis*, Bagnolet, France, 1996. **Died:** Montreal, 10 March 1996.

Roles (selected)

1979	*The Eye of the Beholder* (opera), Toronto
1980	*Time in a Dark Room* (David Earle and Graham Jackson), Toronto Dance Theatre

William Douglas in *Anima*. Photograph by Cylla von Tiedemann.

1982   *Second Wind* (Paula Ravitz), Toronto Independent Dance Enterprise

1983   *True Lies* (Jennifer Mascall), Vancouver

1991   *Sous les paupières closes* (Hélène Leclair), Montreal

1992   *Katabasis* (Linda Rabin), Montréal Danse, Montreal

1993   *Dream Report* (José Navas), Montreal

Works (performances by William Douglas and Dancers unless otherwise noted)

1983   *Sunday Afternoon* (mus. Ann Southam), Dancemakers, Toronto

1985   *Field Point* (mus. Charles Davis Jr.), New York

1986   *Blind Mice: The Trio* (w/flutist Craig Goodman, painter Ross Lewis), New York

       Archipelago (five dancers and live jazz quintet), New York

1987   *Travelling in Darkness, Herons, Hands, Girls and Dogs, . . . and the Air* (mus. Daron Hagen), suite of five dances, New York, Montreal, Nova Scotia tour

       Son of Archipelago (mus. Thomaz Ostergren, Sue Terry), New York

1988   *E/motional/ogic* (mus. Jalalu-Kalvert Nelson), New York

1989   *His Three Beautiful Daughters: Desire, Despair, Delight* (mus. Jalalu-Kalvert Nelson), New York

1990   *Carved in Flesh,* group of five solos and duets: *Roam* (mus. Jonathan Larson), *Anima* (mus. John Oswald), *Duets from Delight* (mus. Miles Green), *T.V. Dance #1* (mus. Norman Slant), *Carved in Flesh* (Mary Kelley), Toronto and New York

1992   *T.V. Dance #2* (mus. Norman Slant), Ateliers de Danse Moderne, Montreal

       We Were Warned (trio with Douglas, Navas, Porte; mus. Reid Robbins), Toronto

1993   *Saffron, Thorn and Echo* (mus. Timothy Sullivan), solo, Montreal

       Entretemps (mus. Laurent Maslé), Dance Deparment of the University of Quebec, Montreal

       Autograph (mus. Timothy Sullivan), cross-Canada tour

       Apollo (mus. Timothy Smith), Montreal, Toronto, Regina, Edmonton

       The Golden Zone (mus. Timothy Sullivan), Montreal

1995   *Lighthouse* (mus. Laurent Maslé), New York

       Unforseen Departure (mus. Robert Lepage), New York

       While Waiting (mus. Mary Kelly), New York

       Interrogation (mus. Reid Robins), Montreal

       At Nightfall (mus. Kathy Kennedy), Montreal

       Love Is a Stranger (mus. Frédéric Le Junter and Pierre Berthet, Charleroi, Belgium

       In Lavender (mus. Timothy Sullivan), Longueuil, Quebec

       WX Project (mus. John Oswald), Toronto

1996   *Heros* (collage of solos with seven dancers and composers), Montreal

Films and Videotapes

Adrienne Clarkson Presents: William Douglas, CBC, Toronto, 1993.
E/motional/ogic, dir. Lisa Cochrane, chor. Douglas, Toronto, 1994.

*　　*　　*

Canadian contemporary choreographer William Douglas will long be remembered in North Amercia and Europe for the elegant, intelligent and sensual formality of his dancing and choreography. His deep humanistic regard for the resources of each dancer, and his seminal collaborations with numerous contemporary dancers, composers and designers also mark his distinct approach within the postmodern dance landscape. Throughout his short and prolific career, he defined a style reflecting his cartesian fascination with randomness and collage (although unlike the Cage-Cunningham paradigm, set inside a unified environment), views which stem from early studies and work in architectural design and drafting as well as Cunningham technique and philosophy. Perhaps his most enduring contribution to the dance milieu may be the serene and dignified manner in which he died, working passionately on new choreography even while spending nights in a hospital bed.

Graduating in 1978 from the Carleton University School of Architecture, he worked in the field of achitecture and interior design while dancing with the Ottawa Dance Centre Workshop Company in student productions. He continued to develop his career as a professional dancer in Canada with the Judy Jarvis Dance Company and Toronto Dance Theatre, TIDE, Dancemakers, and EDAM.

In 1981 Douglas went to New York City, where he began a decade-long study of technique and composition at the Merce Cunningham Studio, supported by numerous study and project grants from Canada Council and the Ontario Arts Council. He soon became a familiar dancer in the downtown New York dance scene of the 1980s, dancing in works by veteran postmodernist Douglas Dunn as well as Bill Young, Susan Osberg, Linda Daniels, and Shelly Lee.

Returning to Montreal, Canada in 1991, he founded William Douglas Danse. Also upon his arrival in Montreal, he was offered a permanent guest teaching position in modern dance technique and composition classes of the dance department of the University of Quebec in Montreal, where his rigorous and yet sensual approach to Cunnigham-inspired pedagogy profoundly influenced his students.

Early choreographies developed during his New York sojourn were often short abstract studies of human nature, performed with live music. It was with the bold, high-energy trio *We Were Warned* (1992), created with new music composer Reid Robins and commissioned for the Canadian INDE Festival in Toronto, that Douglas later won the choreography prize from the *Rencontres choregraphiques internationales de Seine Saint-Denis* in France. He went on to receive international acclaim and toured numerous Canadian and European dance festivals and venues, as well as staging annual New York presentations. *We Were Warned* was followed by an accumulation cycle in which each work contained increasingly more dense layers of media and meaning: the quartet *Apollo* (1993), quintet *The Golden Zone* (1994), sextet *Love Is a Stranger* (1995), and finally a septet, *Heroes* (1996).

Douglas continuously drew inspiration from the kinetic and human qualities of particular dancers, who remained close artistic collaborators: Daniel Firth, Bill Coleman, Laurence Lemieux, Francine Liboiron, and others. Two of these dancer-collaborators remained central to Douglas' creative process and emerging aesthetic throughout his career: José Navas, a vibrant, intense Venezuelan dancer he met while immersed in the New York City dance milieu, and French-born-and-trained Dominque Porte, a charismatic dancer with virtuousic technical abilities. Navas eventually became his companion and closest artistic associate, and soon after Douglas' serene and courageous death from AIDS in 1996, Navas was appointed artistic director of William Douglas Danse.

—Dena Davida

DOUGLAS WRIGHT DANCE COMPANY
New Zealand dance company

Works (choreographed by Wright)

1981   *Back Street Primary* (poetry, J. Frame; mus. Talking Heads), Limbs Dance Company, Auckland

1982   *Late Afternoon of a Faun or Thrilled to Bits* (solo, after Nijinsky; mus. Debussy), Limbs Dance Company, Auckland

Baby Go Boom (mus. Holiday, Armstrong, Farnell), Limbs Dance Company, Auckland

Kneedance (mus. Anderson), Limbs Dance Company, Auckland

Walking on Thin Ice (mus. Ono), Limbs Dance Company, Auckland

Aurora Borealis (mus. Ono, Anderson, Hagen), Limbs Dance Company, Auckland

1983   *Land of 1000 Dances* (mus. Small, Pickett), Limbs Dance Company, Auckland

Sorry to Have Missed You (mus. Tartini), Royal New Zealand Ballet, New Moves, Wellington

Rantrstantrum (mus. Branca), Limbs Dance Company, Auckland

Dog Dance (solo; mus. Cage), Douglas Wright, New York

1984   *Threnody* (solo; mus. Penderecki), Douglas Wright, Auckland

It's Not Unusual (mus. Tom Jones), Douglas Wright and Brian Carbee, Auckland

Cubist Cowboy Shootout (with Brian Carbee; mus. various), Auckland

1985   *Halcyon* (mus. Vivaldi), Limbs Dance Company, Whangarei

1986   *Parallel* (mus. Busby), for two gymnasts, New York

1987   *Hey Paris* (mus. Ayler, Hirt, Nancarrow), Douglas Wright and Dancers, New York

Quartet (mus. Vivaldi), Douglas Wright and Dancers, New York

Faun Variations (solo; mus. Ravel), Paul Taylor Company, City Centre, New York

1988   *Now Is the Hour* (mus. McGlashan and various), Limbs Dance Company, New Zealand International Festival of the Arts, Wellington

Aria (solo, text Dostoevsky), M. J. O'Reilly, Auckland

1989   *How On Earth* (mus. various), Douglas Wright Dance Company, Auckland

A Far Cry (mus. Bartók), Australian Dance Theatre, Adelaide

1990   *Passion Play: A New Dance* w/Kilda Northcott, Wellington

Gloria (mus. Vivaldi), Douglas Wright Dance Company, Wellington

1991   *As It Is* (mus. Bartók, Laird), Douglas Wright Dance Company, Auckland

1992   *Beethoven* (mus. Beethoven and the Shangri-Las), graduating students of the Performing Arts School, Auckland

The Decay of Lying (text, Wilde; mus. Lully), Royal New Zealand Ballet, Wellington

Elegy for Jim, Leigh and Bayly (solo, mus. Wilson), Artzaid Benefit, Wellington

1993   *Forever* (mus. various), Douglas Wright Dance Company, Auckland

1996   *Ore* (solo), Next Wave Festival, Auckland

Buried Venus (mus. Farr and various), Douglas Wright Dance Company, New Zealand International Festival of the Arts, Wellington

Aida (directed by Wright), Victorian State Opera, Melbourne

1997   *Forbidden Memories* (a work for theatre based on a novel by James Purdy), Auckland

Cunning Little Vixen (directed by Wright), Opera Australia, Sydney

Rose and Fell (mus. Pärt, Gubaidulina, Mussorgsky), Royal New Zealand Ballet, Wellington

Publications

McNaughton, Howard, "Performing on the Faultlines: Douglas Wright's *Forever*," in *(Post)Colonial Stages: Critical and Creative Views on Drama, Theatre and Performance in Colonised Cultures,* edited by Helen Gilbert, Hebden Bridge, England, 1998.

Whyte, Raewyn, "Dance Works of 1993: A Review Article," *Illusions* (New Zealand), Winter 1994.

———, "Buried Venus: An Interview with Douglas Wright," *Landfall* (New Zealand), Autumn 1996.

Films and Videotapes

I Am a Dancer/Gloria, documentary film, dir. Bollinger/Oomen, Top Shelf Productions, TV1 national television broadcast, Sunday Arts, 1990.

Elegy for Jim, Leigh and Bayly, dance film; dir. Chris Graves, New Zealand International Film Festival, Wellington, 1992.

As It Is: A Fragment, for television broadcast, dir. Graves, *Dance and the Camera,* Television New Zealand national broadcast, 1994.

Forever, dance film co-directed with Graves, TV1 national television broadcast, 1995.

Ore, dance film co-directed with Graves, Wellington, 1996.

*   *   *

The Douglas Wright Dance Company was established in New York in 1984 as Douglas Wright and Dancers. At the time dancer/choreographer Wright was a member of the Paul Taylor Company, with whom he danced from 1983 to 1987. His dancers included members from the Taylor company, from Mark Dendy & Dancers, and from Limbs Dance Company, with whom Wright had danced from 1980-83. The New Zealand dancers traveled from New Zealand to New York to perform with him in 1984 (at Dance Theatre Workshop), in 1985 (at Field Pineapple in Chicago), and in 1987 (at the 14th Street Y in New York City). The company's repertoire included works originally made for Limbs—*Ranterstantrum* (1983) and *Halcyon* (1985); Wright's solos *Dog Dance* (1983), and *Faun*

Douglas Wright Dance Company performing *Forever*. Photograph © Peter Molloy.

Variations for the Paul Taylor Company (1987); plus premiere works *Quartet* (1987) and *Hey Paris* (1987).

The company was re-established in New Zealand during 1989 as the Douglas Wright Dance Company and made their New Zealand debut with a national tour of the evening-length *How on Earth*. Major new works followed on an 18-month development cycle, with national tours, *Gloria* in 1990; *As It Is* in 1991; *Forever* in 1993, *How on Earth* (reworked) in 1994; and *Buried Venus* in 1996. Shorter works such as *Ranterstantrum*, *Quartet* and *Hey Paris* were also maintained within the company repertoire, and were shown again in the company's 1997 retrospective season along with *Kneedance* (originally for Limbs Dance Company in 1982), Wright's solo *Elegy* (1992), and *Gloria*. International tours were made to London and Holland in 1993 with *Gloria* and *A Far Cry*; to Australia and to Switzerland in 1994 with *Forever*, and to Australia in 1996 with *Buried Venus*. Wright's works have also been mounted on Australian companies, and he has collaborated on several dance films.

Between company projects, the dancers worked on other projects with New Zealand choreographers and explored other pursuits, while Wright worked on his film projects with director Chris Graves. Wright also took up creative projects with DV8 Physical Theatre in 1988/89, and directed operas in Australia—*Aida* in 1996 and *Cunning Little Vixen* in 1997.

Wright had specific objectives when he re-established his dance company in New Zealand. He wanted to pursue his choreographic development wherever it would lead him, to work with dancers who could creatively engage in the process of developing new work, and he hoped that eventually the company would be able to live and work in New Zealand while regularly performing elsewhere in the world. Keeping in mind the need for new works to be developed over a period of 18 months, and the realities of arts funding, the company was project-based. Dancers with the ability to meet the technical and expressive demands of Wright's distinctive style of dance, and who would be available in an ongoing way, were taken on to meet the requirements of each project, ensuring the development by company members of a shared aesthetic and working process. Apprentice dancers were also included as understudies in each season.

The company has always been built around technically strong dancers who have an understanding of Wright's aesthetic and can contribute creatively to the development of new works. The initial ensemble comprised former Limbs dancers Shona McCullagh, Glenn Mayo, Debra McCulloch, Marianne Schultz and Kilda Northcott, who returned from Australia to join them. Recent New Zealand

School of Dance graduate Mia Mason replaced the injured Debra McCulloch during the rehearsal process.

The process of developing new work has remained consistent. Wright chooses his theme and researches it over a period of a year, creates some material then conducts an intensive workshop with the dancers for the project, working through improvisation and a journal process with contributions from company members. Several months later the work is shaped through an intensive rehearsal period prior to premiere and touring.

Diagnosed HIV-positive in 1990, Wright celebrates the life force, while exploring its darker aspects. His evening length works focus on questions of fundamental importance drawn from his own life experiences and those of his dancers: Why do people treat themesleves and one another so badly? Why is it so hard to find love? What happens after death? What is it that moves us and gives us joy? He sees artistic form as a means to challenge things taken for granted, and creates disturbing, provocative images, as well as beautiful images, to achieve this end.

Internationally recognised as a choreographer of great power, Wright is lauded for the intensity and passion of his work, for his choreographic wit, for his ability to speak clearly to others through dance despite the intensely personal nature of much of the material. In presenting his choreography, his New Zealand company has also gained international recognition. Wright is internationally recognised also as a brilliant performer, passionately lyrical and intensely expressive, a performer of gravity-defying moves which seem to exceed the known limits of human movement. Similar qualities are evident, though in a less developed way, in members of his ensemble, and are influential in their continuing development as dancers and choreographers.

—Raewyn Whyte

DOVE, Ulysses
American dancer and choreographer

Born: 1945 in Columbia, South Carolina. **Education:** Studied at Harvard University; B.A. in dance, Bennington College; moved to New York and studied with Mary Anthony and Pearl Lang; won a scholarship to study with Merce Cunningham, 1970. **Career:** Dancer, Merce Cunningham Dance Company, until 1973; performed in Sokolow's *Rooms,* 1973; principal dancer, Alvin Ailey American Dance Theatre, 1973-80; first choreography, 1979; assistant director, Groupe de Recherche Choreographique de l'Opéra de Paris, 1980-83; freelance choreographer, 1983-1996. **Awards:** New York Dance and Performance Award ("Bessie"), 1989 for *Episodes;* Emmy award for choreography, PBS' *Dance in America* series, for *Two by Dove.* **Died:** June 1996, of AIDS.

Works

1979	*I see the Moon . . . And the Moon Sees Me*
1980	*Inside*
1984	*Bad Blood* (mus. Laurie Anderson)
	Red Angels (mus. Richard Einhorn), New York City Ballet's Diamond Project II
1986	*Civil Wars* (mus. Phillip Glass), (opera)
1989	*Vespers* (mus. Mikel Rouse), Dayton Contemporary Dance Company
1990	*Urban Folk Dance* (mus. Michael Torke)
1992	*Serious Pleasures* (mus. Robert Ruggieri), American Ballet Theatre
	Dancing on the Front Porch of Heaven, Royal Swedish Ballet
1996	*Twilight* (mus. Michael Torke), New York City Ballet

Other works include: *Pieces of Dreams* and *Nightshade,* for the Groupe de Recherche Choreographique de l'Opéra de Paris, in the early 1980s; director for *Br'er Rabbit Whole* (Freedom Theater, 1989) and Adrienne Kennedy's *Black Children's Day* (Brown University).

Publications

On DOVE: articles—

Obituary, *Boston Globe*, 12 June 1996.
Obituary, *Dance Magazine*, August 1996.
Dalva, Nancy, "New York City Ballet," *Dance Magazine*, September 1996.
Gladstone, Valerie, "Dove's Odyssey," *Town & Country Monthly*, June 1995.
Goldstein, Nancy, "Fiery Tribute to a Master," *Newsday*, 19 June 1996.
Jacobs, Laura, Review, *Serious Pleasures, The New Leader*, June 29, 1992.
Kriegsman, Alan M., "On PBS, Dove Takes Flight," *Washington Post*, 25 March 1995.
Levy, Suzanne, "Dove's Vibrant *Vespers*," *Washington Post*, 16 May 1988.
Obituary, *Newsday*, 13 June 1996.
Segal, Lewis, "Visual Elements Leap to the Fore in *Dove*," *Los Angeles Times*, 22 March 1995.
Southgate, Martha, "Ulysses Dove: Communicative Choreography," *Essence*, March 1992.
Thom, Rose Anne, "Two by Dove," *Dance Magazine*, March 1995.
Topaz, Muriel, "Ulysses Dove: The Actors' Fund Loves Dove," *Dance Magazine*, June 1996.
Trucco, Terry, "The Diamond Project II: A New Tradition at New York City Ballet," *Dance Magazine*, May 1994.

Films and Videotapes

Episodes (performed by the Ailey troupe), for *Dance in America*, 1991.
Two by Dove, consisting of *Vespers* (performed by the Alvin Ailey American Dance Theatre) and *Dancing on the Front Porch of Heaven* (performed by the Royal Swedish Ballet), *Dance in America* series, PBS, 1995.

*   *   *

Ulysses Dove was an acclaimed dancer and choreographer whose career ended prematurely in 1996 when he died of AIDS at age 49. His African-American roots led him to focus on urban themes in many of his dances, which were characterized by intense emotion and athletic power.

Born in Columbia, South Carolina, Dove received his BA in dance from Bennington College after spending time at Howard University and other institutions. Shortly after earning his degree, he moved to

Ulysses Dove with Sara Yarbrough in *Portrait of Billy*. **Photograph © Johan Elbers.**

New York City and spent time with the companies of Mary Anthony and Pearl Lang. In 1970, he received a scholarship to the Merce Cunningham School, and subsequently joined Cunningham's dance troupe, where he remained until 1973. A turning point occurred in his career that year, when choreographer Anna Sokolow asked him to perform her classic *Rooms*. Alvin Ailey took note of his performance, and invited Dove to join his company, where he soon became a principal dancer. He remained with the Alvin Ailey American Dance Theatre from 1973 until 1980, and his association with the troupe remained strong throughout his career. Ailey gave Dove his first chance as a choreographer in 1979, when his *I See the Moon. . .And the Moon Sees Me* debuted.

The fact that he was a member of both Cunningham's and Ailey's companies is a testament to Dove's versatility as a dancer. In fact, he is the only person to perform with both groups. Cunningham's and Ailey's styles are very different, and only a very versatile performer could succeed in the two companies. After leaving Ailey, Dove served as the assistant director of the Groupe de Recherche Choreographique de l'Opéra de Paris, the experimental arm of the Paris Opera, from 1980 to 1983. During that time, he choreographed *Pieces of Dreams* and *Night Shade*, and became a respected choreographic presence in Europe. After leaving Paris, Dove became a freelance choreographer, rather than forming his own troupe. As a freelancer, he created works for modern dance and ballet companies worldwide, especially in Europe, where companies including the Royal Swedish Ballet, Ballet France de Nancy, Basel Ballet, Cullberg Ballet of Sweden, and the London Festival Ballet commissioned works from him.

He also choreographed pieces for numerous North American companies, including the New York City Ballet, the Dayton Contemporary Dance Company, Les Ballets Jazz de Montreal and the American Ballet Theater. The Alvin Ailey American Dance Theatre gave many of his works premieres, including *Inside* (1980), *Bad Blood* (1984) to a Laurie Anderson score, and *Episodes* (1989), which won him a New York Dance and Performance Award ("Bessie") for Achievement in Dance.

Dove's choreography is permeated with energy, force, athleticism, and abstract emotion, and often takes place within an environment that evokes modern urban life. Just such a work is his 1990 *Urban Folk Dance*, set to music by Michael Torke, which portrays two pairs of dancers in adjacent spaces that represent neighboring apartments. Dove's dances are also known for their inventiveness, including angular, fast-paced choreography that combines techniques from ballet and modern dance. One of Dove's best-known works, *Vespers*, is a good example. It is performed by six women who leap on and off of six chairs. Set to a percussion score by Mikel Rouse, the piece was created for the Dayton Contemporary Dance Company in 1986 and performed frequently by the Ailey troupe.

Dove's *Red Angels*, which was created for the New York City Ballet's Diamond Project II in 1984, features four dancers dressed in red against a black backdrop, moving in and out of shafts of white or red light to an electric violin score by Richard Einhorn. *Serious Pleasures*, set to music by Robert Ruggieri, features doors through which dancers are hidden and revealed under yellow lights. They slam the doors as they enter and exit throughout the piece. *Serious Pleasures* was premiered by the American Ballet Theater in Chicago in 1992, marking Dove's first piece for the ABT, and is subtitled "The Merciless Battle Between Spirit and Flesh." Other significant works include *Dancing on the Front Porch of Heaven*, which was commissioned by the Royal Swedish Ballet in 1992, and his last piece, the ballet *Twilight*, to a score by Michael Torke, which was created for the New York City Ballet in 1996, and premiered less than a month before Dove's death.

As suggested from the descriptions above, Dove often made props central to the dance, whether it be chairs, women's flowing hair, or, as in *Night Shade*, water being splashed from a big wooden tub. Dove's work was featured on PBS's *Dance in America* series in 1995, in an episode entitled *Two by Dove*. The program featured *Vespers*, performed by the Alvin Ailey American Dance Theatre, and *Dancing on the Front Porch of Heaven*, by the Royal Swedish Ballet, and won Dove a primetime Emmy for best choreography. (*Dance in America* also featured Alvin Ailey in a 1991 program, in which Dove's *Episodes* was one of the featured works.)

In addition to modern dance and ballet, Dove also choreographed the opera *Civil Wars* (1986), collaborating with director Robert Wilson and composer Philip Glass. He was also a theater director in his own right, helming the Freedom Theater's 1989 production of *Br'er Rabbit Whole*, and, prior to that, Adrienne Kennedy's *Black Children's Day* at Brown University.

As a freelance choreographer, Dove was never able to witness a program composed entirely of his own works. Six days after his death in 1996, however, a memorial and Actors Fund benefit called *For the Love of Dove* featured six of his dances, including *Urban Folk Dance*, part of *Serious Pleasures, Vespers, Red Angels,* and *Dancing on the Front Porch of Heaven*. The pieces were performed by members of several companies that worked with Dove throughout his career, including the New York City Ballet, the Dayton Contemporary Dance Company, the Alvin Ailey American Dance Theatre, the American Ballet Theater, and the Royal Swedish Ballet.

—Karen Raugust

DRAPER, Paul
American dancer and choregrapher

Born: 25 October 1909 in Florence, Italy. **Education:** Attended Lincoln School, New York, Loomis Institute, Windsor, Connecticut, and Polytechnic Institute, Brooklyn; studied tap dancing briefly in New York; later studied with Anatole Vilzak and Anatole Oboukhoff at the School of American Ballet. **Family:** Married Heidi Vosseler, 1941. **Career:** Assistant music critic, New York *World;* instructor, Arthur Murray School of Dance, 1930; dancer, Plaza Theatre, London; danced in a variety of musical productions and venues, 1932-36; appeared in the film *Colleen,* 1936; began creating his own dances in 1939; career waned in the 1950s after he was blacklisted; professor of theater, Carnegie-Mellon Institute, 1967-78. **Died:** 1996.

Works

1939	*Ad Lib Duet*
	Bye-Bye Blues
1941	*Gavotte, Minuet, Tocatta in A Major*
	Fantasia in C Minor
	Golliwog's Cake Walk
	The Blue Danube Waltz
	Rondo Opus 49, No. 2

	Clair de Lune
	It Ain't Necessarily So
	Intermezzo Opus 47, No. 7
	Malagueña
1942	*Capriccio*
	Astunaz
	Dance without Music
	Blues in the Night
1943	*Organ Grinder Swing*
	Bagatelle
1945	*Tocatta in E Flat Minor*
	Partitia in B Flat
1946	*Cancion triste y danza allegro*
1947	*Political Speech*
1953	*Alcina Suite*
	On the Beat
	A Sharp Character
	On the Avenue
	The Assassin
	To His Coy Mistress
	St. James Infirmary
	French Folk Songs
	Irish Jig
1954	*New Dance*
1955	*Sonata for Tap Dancers*
	Classical Blues
	Stay with It
	Greensleeves
1958	*Prelude in C Sharp*
	Prelude in E
	Jazz Adversary
	Two Afternoons
1959	*Allegro*
1962	*Gigue*
	Solfegietto
	Tea for Two
1963	*Chorale and Choral Prelude*
1965	*Il Combattimento di Tancredi e Clorinda*
1966	*Name-Who?, Number-What?, (Other)-(You), Address-Where?*
1977	*Untitled Solo*
1980	*Tap in Three Movements for Ten Dancers*

Publications

On DRAPER: books—

Ames, Jerry, and Jim Segelman, *The Book of Tap: Recovering America's Long Lost Dance,* New York, 1977.
Croce, Arlene, *Afterimages,* New York, 1977.
Frank, Rusty E. *TAP!: The Greatest Tap Dance Stars and Their Stories,1900-1955,* New York, 1990, 1994.

On DRAPER: articles—

"A Conversation with Paul Draper, *Ballet Review,* vol. 5, no. 1.
"Paul Draper," *Dance Magazine,* December 1996.

*   *   *

Paul Draper was a popular tap dancer in the 1940s, until his career was effectively cut short when he was blacklisted. His technique of combining tap with classical music and ballet technique led him to be accepted as a member of the modern dance community, despite the differences between the disciplines of tap and modern dance. He performed in concerts with well-known modern dancers, as well as in more traditional tap venues such as vaudeville and on Broadway.

Draper was born in Florence, Italy, in 1909, the son of American parents. He was primarily self-taught as a tap dancer, although he studied briefly with Tommy Nip and with Buddy Bradley, a black choreographer, in the early 1920s and 1930s. He worked for a time at Arthur Murray Studios as a ballroom dancing instructor to support himself. Early in his career, Draper traveled to Europe, stopping first in London. He became a last-minute replacement in a traveling vaudeville show, *Sensations of 1932,* partnering with a woman whose male counterpart had unexpectedly left the tour. After performing throughout England with the review, Draper went to Paris and got hired at a night club, Le Boeuf sur le Toit. He was in Europe for a total of two and a half years, returning to the United States in 1932.

In 1933, Draper joined with soft-shoe dancer Jack Albertson to form Paul Draper and Company. The two men, along with a group of female dancers, performed in vaudeville theaters throughout Long Island and the boroughs of New York City. After the company disbanded, Draper continued on the vaudeville circuit as a soloist, putting on four to five shows a day. It was about this time that Draper began experimenting with a combination of tap and classical music to create a new form of entertainment, the concert tap performance. He wanted to raise tap to a classical art form, while at the same time making the works of classical composers accessible to mass audiences by tapping to them. Draper began to create dances to Handel and Bach, and incorporated the works into his solo concerts. In an article in *TAP! The Greatest Tap Dance Stars and Their Stories,* Draper wrote:

> I was a dancer trying to make a difference as an artist, trying to make something that hadn't existed before, and trying to change the lives of whoever saw it. . . . I was never, ever going to become a ballet dancer, but I started to learn how to move around so that I was able to do the things I had wanted to do: make sounds which were rhythmically appropriate and sensible, and imaginative and inventive, and still look something like a dancer.

Draper was hired to perform at the Hotel Pierre, which was experimenting with nightclub entertainment. He was also booked at the Persian Room in the Plaza Hotel for three years, where he experimented further with classical music in conjunction with Eddy Duchin and his orchestra. Draper also appeared as a soloist at the Waldorf and the Rainbow Room in New York, the Coconut Grove in Los Angeles, and Chez Paree in Chicago. At the same time, Draper's innovations were also being acknowledged by the modern dance community: in 1938, he was invited to participate in a concert in Washington, D.C., with the dance companies of Martha Graham, Hanya Holm, and Anna Sokolow.

In 1940, Draper met Larry Adler, a concert harmonica player with an interest in classical music, after they were both hired by Radio City Music Hall. The two agreed to give a joint concert in Santa Barbara, California, which was successful enough for them to continue performing together from 1941 to 1949. They staged sellout concerts in large halls across the country, their repertoire including dances tapped to Scarlatti, Scriabin, Debussy, Ravel, Mozart, and Tchaikovsky, as well as jazz numbers. In one of his best-known works, *Sonata for Tap Dancer,* Draper danced without musical accompaniment. He also created satirical pieces, such as *Dance Hall* and *A Sharp Character.*

Draper's and Adler's careers suffered drastically when both were blacklisted in 1948. Draper moved to Geneva, Switzerland, in 1950, but returned to the United States in 1954. He remained active in the dance community, although his career never came close to the levels of popularity he had achieved in the 1940s. He performed on the Broadway stage and with various opera companies throughout the 1950s, including with his aunt, the monologist Ruth Draper, on Broadway in 1954. He danced the title role in an off-Broadway production of Stravinsky's *Histoire du soldat* (1955), and later danced in *Gentleman, Be Seated!* at the New York City Opera and in the Broadway musical *Come Summer.* He worked as a choreographer, creating the dances for *Archy and Mehitabel* at the Goodspeed Opera and a piece for American Dance Machine, and was a professor of theater at the Carnegie-Mellon Institute from 1967 to 1978. Draper also performed as a modern dancer, appearing at the American Dance Festival annually from 1962 to 1967. During this time, he entered a period of experimentation. In 1965, he premiered *Il Combattimento di Tancredi e Clorinda* at the festival. It was a dramatic piece inspired by Monteverdi's madrigal opera, based on Tasso's *Jerusalem Delivered.* It was far outside his field, containing no tapping, and was recognized as an ambitious effort but overall was not well-received. At the 1966 Festival, he premiered a solo called *Name-Who?, Number-What?, (Other)-(You), Address-Where?* This unaccompanied experimental piece involved tapping, but was characterized by somber emotional content.

—Karen Raugust

DREAMS

Choreography: Anna Sokolow
Music: Teo Macero
First Production: Anna Sokolow Dance Company, Theresa L. Kaufmann Concert Hall, YM/YWHA, New York, 8 May 1961
Original Dancers: Julie Arenal, Juki Arkin, Buck Heller, Nancy Lewis, and Jack Moore
Other productions include: One of eight sections of The Way (choreography by Mary Wigman), Symphony Hall, Boston, 1933; *Sueños* (Sokolow's revision of *Dreams*; music by Anton Webern; scenery and costumes by Antonio Lopez Mancera; with original dancers Aurora Agüeria, Miguel Araiza, Amparo Bonett, Rafael Carapia, Juan Casados, Beatriz Flores, Josefina Lavalle, Sergio Lezama, Roseyra Marenco, Francisco Martinez, Carlo McNielli, Rosalío Ortega, Rosa Reyna, José Rosas, Rocio Sagaón, Adriana Siqueiros), Ballet de Bellas Artes, Palace of Fine Arts, Mexico City, 1961.

Publications

Siegel, Marcia B., *The Shapes of Change: Images of Modern Dance,* Los Angeles, 1979.

———, *Watching the Dance Go By,* Boston, 1977.

Warren, Larry, *Anna Sokolow: The Rebellious Spirit,* Princeton, NJ, 1991.

*   *   *

As a teenager, Israeli-born dancer/choreographer Anna Sokolow performed with the Martha Graham Dance Company until 1938. In the 1930s Sokolow and her generation (including Sophie Maslow, Jane Dudley, and Helen Tamiris) were among the first choreographers to envision modern dance as potential protest against social injustice, fascism, and the evils of war. Yet it is the mood rather than the subject matter that people tend to remember about Sokolow's work. Sokolow's dances tap into the American 20th-century psyche by addressing despair, loneliness, sexual repression, alienation, depression, violence, anger, and fear as fodder for artistic expression. The psychological mood, more than any other aspect within Sokolow's dances, is the driving impulse.

In the spring of 1961 Sokolow decided to use her troubled dreams as a basis for a new work. She told an interviewer that she had always had bad dreams, but that she had no idea what they meant or how they might develop in her choreography. Over the next several months Sokolow presented drafts of *Dreams,* not as premieres but as informal showings of a work-in-progress at the Herbert Berghof Studio, where she also taught Sunday morning classes for actors, at the "Y" in the Freda Miller Memorial Concert (both in New York), and at the American Dance Festival in Connecticut.

Dreams was divided into nine scenes. In her book *Watching the Dance Go By* critic Marcia B. Siegel described and interpreted two of the scenes: "A man and woman embrace. The tighter they hold each other, the less they seem to feel, until they are frantically clutching at the flesh next to theirs, as if trying to make sure it's there. A man runs in place, bent over, his arms hanging down. He looks over his shoulder from time to time, expecting to see someone watching him. Atonal music of brasses and percussion drives him more and more frenetically until he falls, one hand to his face, as if he had pushed himself down." In another section, a woman runs past a group of blank-faced men in black, who surround her, hoist her up, and, as she walks forward on their shoulders groping for their hands, continually replace each other like a precipitous, endless escalator. Sokolow biographer Larry Warren observed that, "The characters in *Dreams* crush us with their helplessness, desperation, remembered nobility, irretrievable relationships, and lost selves"—like strange visions from nightmares, more felt than analytically understood.

For at least three years after the first performance of *Dreams* Sokolow labored to reveal the underlying meaning and context of the dance. In the fall of 1961 she presented *Dreams* in Mexico City, with a much larger cast, different music, and a Spanish title. She later added and subtracted dancers, finally settling on a cast of eight. She eventually pieced together a musical score that included Macero, Webern, and Bach. Most significantly, over time she began to associate images of the dance to her reading of Andre Schwartz-Bart's *The Last of the Just,* about the Nazi concentration camps. When Sokolow vividly remembered the experience of staring at a death-camp number tatooed on a man's arm in Israel, *Dreams* finally came into focus. Although Sokolow altered the choreography very little, her directions to the dancers assumed greater specificity. As reported by Warren, in one rehearsal for *Dreams* Sokolow told the dancers, "When we see your face, we know your name. They may have given you a number, but we know your name."

Although *Dreams* was not widely recognized as a dance about the Holocaust until the 1970s, Sokolow's personal epiphany resonated within the work. In 1966, after a performance of *Dreams* at the American Dance Festival, critic Doris Hering observed: "*Dreams* gave one the sensation of being in the presence of a special kind of bravery. It has the effect of Käthe Kollwitz's "Old Woman Greeting Death"; of all of Kokoschka; of Aushwitz, Dachau; of the faces of soldiers in the grip of battle fatigue."

Sokolow eventually dedicated *Dreams* to Holocaust victim Anne Frank, yet the dance has remained universally abstract. Warren observes that, even today, "It is still possible to see *[Dreams]* as a timeless allegory of terror and hopelessness."

—Lodi McClellan

DRIVER, Senta

American dancer and choreographer

Born: 5 September 1942 in Greenwich, Connecticut. **Education:** Attended Ohio State University. **Career:** Dancer, Paul Taylor Company, 1967-73; founder and director, Harry, 1974-91; has written on dance, held various other roles (including caring for premature babies) since 1991.

Roles (with the Paul Taylor Dance Company)

1967	*Lento* (Taylor), New London, Connecticut
	From Sea to Shining Sea (revised), (Taylor), New York
1968	*Private Domain* (Taylor), New York

Other roles include: Repertory versions of *Aureole, Piece Period,* other works by Taylor for the troupe.

Works

1966	*Collection*
	Dances to This Music
1975	*Board Fade Excerpt* ("music" was taped light cues made during a rehearsal of *Missa Brevis* by José Límon)
	Two Dances from Dead Storage
	The Star Game
	Anniversary
	Melodrama
1976	*The Kschessinska Variations*
	Gallery
	Second Generation
	Matters of Fact
	Since You Asked
	Converging Lines
	Pièce d'Occasion
	In Which a Position Is Taken, and Some Dances
1977	*Running the Course*
	Sudden Death
1978	*Exam*
	On Doing w/Tom Johnson, American Dance Festival, Durham, North Carolina
1979	*Simulcast* w/Peter Anastos, Brooklyn Academy of Music (BAM)
	Theory and Practice
	Crowd w/Carol Palmer
	Primer, BAM
1980	*Reaches,* The Kitchen, New York
1981	*Missing Persons,* New York
1984	*Survivors (The Black Trio)*
1987	*Avner, Rena, Bud and Roxie, Lilian and Sam*
1989	*The Grand Duchesses Laughing* (mus. Ben Hazard, Robert Kaplan), American Dance Festival
	Show, Joyce Theater, New York
	Video 5000, Joyce Theater, New York

Publications

By DRIVER: articles—

"Passion Is Also Important: Anna Sokolow at Ohio State," *Dance Scope*, Fall 1966.
"Dancers and Dancing," *Dance Chronicle*, 1983.
With Harris Green and Ruthanna Boris, "Three Views of Kirkland's Grave," *Ballet Review*, Winter 1987.
"Two or Three Things That Might Be Considered Primary," *Ballet Review*, Spring 1990.
"Board Spotlight," *Dance/USA Journal,* March/April 1991.
"Edward Stierle (1968-1991)," *Ballet Review*, Fall 1991.
"Frankfurt," *Ballet Review*, Fall 1994.
"Montreal," *Ballet Review*, Spring 1996.

On DRIVER: books—

Anderson, Jack, *Choreography Observed*, Iowa City, 1987.
Myers, Gerald, ed., *Philosophical Essays on Dance,* Brooklyn, 1981.

On DRIVER: articles—

Brown, Alan M., "Interview: Senta Driver," *New Performance*, 1980.
Daly, Ann, "Interview with Senta Driver," *Women & Performance*, 1987/1988.
Eginton, Meg, "Senta Driver Takes the Plunge," *Dance Ink* (New York), July/August 1991.
Jowitt, Deborah, "Strong Medicine: Senta Driver Seeks Ways to be of Use," *Village Voice,* 30 April 1996.
———, "Senta Driver: Stomping out a Niche for Herself," *Village Voice*, 22 October 1979.
Lewis, Julinda, "Senta Driver and the Erotic Potential," *Dance Magazine*, May 1982
Martin, Claire, "Harry," *Dance Magazine*, February 1981.
Nuchtern, Jean, "Three Women: Sara Rudner, Senta Driver, Wendy Rogers," *Dance Magazine*, May 1976.
Reiter, Susan, "Harry, The Kitchen," *Dance News*, March 1981.
Robertson, Michael, "Harry," *Ballet News*, January-February 1980.
Smith, Amanda, "From Classical to Modern," *Dance Magazine*, December 1976.
Tobias, Tobi, "Dance: Senta Driver," *New York*, 27 November 1989.
Vaughan, David, "What's in a Name?" *Dance Magazine*, June 1977.
Zimmer, Elizabeth, "New York City: Harry, Dance and Other Works by Senta Driver," *Dance Magazine*, October 1986.

*   *   *

Senta Driver (right) with Amy Tinkham and Larry Hahn in *Survivors: The Black Trio,* 1986. Photograph © Johan Elbers.

When critics write about Senta Driver, they almost invariably refer to her "intelligence," "wit," "intellectualism," or some variation thereof. She grew up planning to be a medieval scholar, after all, and not only has she written extensively on dance, her work as a choreographer shows that she closely studied the history that preceded her. Almost as quickly, suggestions of quirkiness or unconventionality arise when describing this choreographer who gave her dance company the bizarre name of "Harry" and composed pieces such as *Board Fade Excerpt*, whose only "music" comes from the lighting directions for the production of an entirely unrelated work.

Rarely, however, do writers mention the quality of heroism in relation to Senta Driver, yet it is a theme throughout her life and work. After seven years with Paul Taylor's dance company, she found herself out of a job in 1974, laid up with tendonitis in both Achilles tendons. It was then that she formed her dance company, and a major theme of the work that followed in her most richly creative years of the middle 1970s revolved around an exploration of physical power. And later, in the twilight of her work as a choreographer during the early 1990s, Driver showed perhaps the greatest heroism of her career.

Driver at her best always caused people to talk and speculate. There was, for instance, the question of where she got the name "Harry." Calling her "one of the most exasperating choreographers at work today," Jack Anderson wrote, "Take the name of her company. What does she call it? The Senta Driver Dance Company? The Senta Driver Dance Ensemble? Senta Driver and Dancers? None of the above. . . . And ask her what that name means and she may ask you why a name has to mean anything." In a 1982 interview with Julinda Lewis, Driver herself offered the explanation that it was the nickname of a tomboyish Queen of Norway from the early 20th century. But, said Driver, "You don't have to believe this if you don't want to."

And certainly the work itself caused speculation. There was for instance the solo *Memorandum* from *The Kschessinska Variations* (1976), in which Driver walked around the stage calling out the names of famous ballerinas in a measured cadence. Or there was the "music" to *The Grand Duchesses Laughing* in 1989, which Camille Hardy described as "a recorded orchestration of chirps, gurgles, and moans by the dancers." Or there was her inclusion of the sounds made by dancers' feet on the floor, at that time a highly unusual touch: "It's amazing," she said in 1982, "that in the middle of a tap dance revival a dancer feels hesitant about making a sound against the floor. That's been one of the most controversial things we've done. I think of it as a movement you can hear." She would take this to an extreme in 1984 with *Survivors (The Black Trio)*, in which the dancers' muttered incidental phrases made the only additional soundtrack.

And there were her experiments with weight and mass, which had in their subtext a sense of experimentation with gender roles themselves. Driver's directions often required women to catch other women, men to catch other men—and women to catch men. In choosing dancers, therefore, she looked for smaller men and larger women to compensate for the difference in size. Audiences were stunned when in *Missing Persons* (1981), for instance, they saw Nicole Riché lift a male partner and spin him.

With characteristic heroism, Driver's goals for her experiments with weight and mass were far from modest: "I want to expand the limits of human physical achievement." There was nothing of the braggart in this; rather, she genuinely saw herself as advancing the realms of possibility. In another statement from the 1982 Lewis interview, Driver said, "I've been influenced by a friend of mine who is a scientist. She has made me feel that the sense in which I use the word 'experiment' is more like hers than the traditional art use. . . . An experiment is an act of proof, an act of penetrating falsehood." At the other end of the decade, however, Driver appeared physically weary, and much of her experimentation seemed to fall flat. Tobi Tobias in *New York*, for instance, dismissed the use of video and music by the Roches in her 1989 composition *Show* as "another sorry example of contemporary dance, once starkly self-sufficient, succumbing to the multimedia trappings that might make it more popular." And Camille Hardy in *Dance Magazine* referred drily to the anticlimactic *Duchesses Laughing* as being "interrupted, at one point, by bringing down the curtain."

This was not exactly accessible stuff, and it led to smaller audiences and decreased funding. Finally, in January 1991, Driver announced that she was closing Harry. Two months later, with characteristic bravado, she *premiered* two works as the company's final performance. So what does a legend of modern choreography do when she finds herself unemployed at 49 years old? If she is Senta Driver, she takes up nursing—specifically, caring for babies born prematurely. In words both touching and inspiring, she told Deborah Jowitt in 1996: "a preemie. . .is not plump and smooth and inert. . .You can feel the physical energy. . . They're *working* at breathing, they're *working* at living," she said, "I didn't find it pathetic. I found it thrilling."

Again, Driver the heroine was not focusing on herself—in fact, Jowitt described her behavior with doctors and nurses as "an almost aggressive humility"—but on human potential. Thus she was able to overcome the sorrow of leaving choreography, which pained her so much that she had to go to bed for three days after giving her first post-retirement interview. In the years since closing Harry, when she is not holding babies or helping a friend run a doomed campaign for New York attorney general, Driver has spent her time in a role she described as "gentleman scholar." A thoughtful student of dance, she has written a number of articles and reviews, and will probably write many more in the future. She suggested in 1982 that she wanted to be remembered as someone who "change[d] the tenor of everything after them," and it seems that she has achieved that goal.

—Judson Knight

DUATO, Nacho
Spanish dancer, choreographer, and company director

Born: Ignacio Duato Barcia 8 January 1957 in Valencia. **Education:** Dance studies at Rambert School (London), Mudra School (Brussels),and Alvin Ailey American Dance Center (New York). **Career:** Joined Cullberg Ballet (Stockholm), 1980; brought to Nederlands Dans Theater by Jirí Kylián, 1981; first choreography, 1983; worked in close collaboration with painter and designer Walter Nobbe; appointed resident choreographer with Kylián and Hans van Manen, Nederlands Dans Theater, 1988; appointed director, Compañia Nacional de Danza by the Ministry of Culture of Spain 1990; toured the world with Compañía, where he danced until 1996; currently freelance choreographer for different companies. **Awards:** First Prize Internationaler Choreographischer Wettbewerb Köln (Germany), 1983; VSCD Gouden Dansprijs (Netherlands),

1987; Chevalier de l'Ordre des Arts et des Lettres (France), 1995; Medal of Valencia University (Spain) 1997.

Roles (with the Nederlands Dans Theater)

1980	*Soldatenmis* (cr), (Kylián)
1981	*Four Sea Interludes* (cr), (Christie)
	Lieder eines fahrenden Gesellen (cr), (Kylián),
	Nomaden (cr), (Kylián)
	Village Songs (cr), (Bruce)
1982	*Curses and Blessings* (cr), (Kylián & Bruce)
	Dreamtime (cr), (Kylián)
	Footnotes (cr), (Warren)
	Ghost Dances (cr), (Bruce)
1983	*Mada* (cr), (Vincent)
	Stamping Ground (cr), (Kylián)
	L'Enfant et les Sortileges (cr), (Kylián)
1984	*Wiegelied* (cr), (Kylián)
	Balletscenes (cr), (vanManen)
1985	*Heart's Labyrinth II* (cr), (Kylián)
1986	*L'Histoire du Soldat* (cr), (Kylián)
1987	*Sechs Tänze* (cr), (Kylián)
	Chamelcon Dances (cr), (Naharin)
	Kaguyahime (cr), (Kylián)
	Songs of the Night (cr), (Murphy)
1988	*Sint Joris Rijdt Uit* (cr), (Kylián)
	Tabula Rasa (cr), (Naharin)
1989	*Black Cake* (cr), (van Manen)
	Tanz-Schul (cr), (Kylián)

Other roles include: Performances in his own choreography for Compañía Nacional de Danza, 1990-96.

Works

1983	*Jardí Tancat* (mus. Bonet), Netherlands Dans Theater (NDT), Hoorn
1984	*Danza y Rito* (also called *Sinfonía India*; mus. Chávez), NDT
1985	*Ucelli* (mus. Respighi), NDT
1986	*Synaphai* (mus. Xenakis & Vangelis), NDT, Secheveningen
1987	*Bolero* (mus. Ravel), NDT
1988	*Arenal* (mus. Bonet), NDT, Amsterdam
	Raptus (mus. Wagner), NDT
	Chansons Madecasses (mus. Ravel), NDT
1989	*Cor Perdut* (mus. Bonet), NDT, Den Haag
1990	*Concierto Madrigal* (mus. Rodrigo), Compañía Nacional de Danza (CND)
	Opus Piat (mus. Beethoven), CND, Madrid
	Rassemblement (mus. Bissainthe), Cullberg Ballet, Örebro, Sweden
1991	*Empty* (mus. collage), CND, Madrid
	Aj Ondas que Eu Vin Ver (mus. Codax), CND
	Kaburías (mus. Brower), CND
	Coming Together (mus. Rzewski), Madrid
1992	*Mediterrània* (mus. collage), CND, Valencia (Spain)
	Duende (mus. Debussy), Netherlands D. T., Den Haag
1993	*Cautiva* (mus. Iglesias), CND, Madrid
	Na Floresta (mus. Villalobos), CND, Madrid
	Alone for a Second (mus. Satie), CND, Madrid

1994	*Tabulae* (mus. Iglesias), CND, Madrid
	Ecos (mus. Micus), CND, Madrid
1995	*Cero sobre Cero* (mus. Iglesias), CND, Madrid
1996	*Por vos muero* w/Miguel Bosé (mus. ancient Spanish) CND, Madrid
	Again and Again and Again, CND, Madrid
1997	*Self* (mus. Iglesias), CND, Madrid
	Romeo y Julieta, (mus. Prokofiev) CND, Madrid
	Remanso (mus. Granados), CND, Madrid

Publications

By DUATO: articles—

"Dance Expresses. . .," in *Moviments* (Generalitat Valenciana, ed.), Valencia, Spain, 1997.

On DUATO: articles—

Siegmund, Gerald, review, *Frankfurter Allgemeine Sonntagszeitung*, 5 May 1996.

*   *   *

The attractive plunge of Spain into modernity, through its transition into democracy after the death in 1975 of the Dictator Franco, has mirrored concrete milestones in almost every social field. In dance, a very significative role has been played by Nacho Duato, who at the head of the Compañía Nacional de Danza (National Dance Company, financed by the state budget) has cooperated, firmly and decisively, to build up choreographic modernity in Spain.

Duato was very young when he left Spain to be trained in several schools as diverse as Rambert, Mudra, and Alvin Ailey. This diversity gave him a useful versatility, and a good capacity for synthesis. His excellent training, together with his well-formed body, led him to succeed as a dancer, under the expert hands of Jirí Kylián, who sheltered him as a truly intellectual and artistic father. Kylián molded Duato's sensitivity and not only converted him into an international star, but instilled in him a deep sense of choreographic composition. Kylián's influence is very evident in Duato's choreographic language; yet Duato has also been able to contribute a number of personal features to build up his own choreographic language.

Duato's choreography shows a special lyricism that corresponds well with the postmodern aesthetics of his time, which in turn have provoked a good connection with audiences. His works are of great diversity due to his fertile inspiration, full of fantasy and passionate energy. René Sirvin, in his column in *Le Figaro* has written that "with Nacho Duato the Spanish Dance has found a new style, original and powerful."

Duato has frequently broken the limits of musical Eurocentrism with large spectacles using non-European music (as in *Cor Pedut, Rassemblement* or *Mediterrània*); he is a universal choreographer. Using his Mediterranean roots, he is sensual and luminous and frequently acts as a shaman of powerful ancestral rites, translated into a modern language. Gerald Siegmund, writing in *Frankfurter Allgemeine Sonntagszeitung* in 1996 has commented that "the taste for symmetry, the excellent ornamental postures of arms and legs, belong also to Duato's vocabulary, as well as his capacity to built up scenes." After heading the Compañía Nacional de Danza for many years, he has consolidated his choreographic formulas—very well received all over the world—into a coherent and conceptual rigor.

Duato is especially demanding with the expressive capacity of his creations. Writing about his choreographic aspirations, he wrote in an article entitled "Dance Expresses. . ." in 1997,

> I like the audience to receive energy through the body of the dancer. I try to abstain from using any kind of superficial adornments in the costumes and the sets. I feel the need to express sensations with body movements, without the help of ostentatious set designs. When the company comes out on stage, I like the audience to receive a considerable charge of energy and sensitivity through the dancer's body. Dance must incorporate a bit of joint celebration and participation; it's not something that leaves the audience out, but permits it to take part in what is happening.

Such commitment to pure entertainment has been one of the most important keys to the success of Duato as a choreographer. His aesthetic behavior is complemented by a strong personal commitment of both time and its circumstances, and he frequently incorporates political statements into his dance, as a member of a cultural, global "polis," in which values require a solid presentation and defense.

—Delfin Colomé

DUDLEY, Jane

American dancer, choreographer, educator, and company director

Born: 3 April 1912 in New York City. **Education:** Began studying with Martha Graham, 1935; also studied with Louis Horst. **Career:** Member, Hanya Holm's troupe, 1931-35; joined New Dance Group, 1934; dancer, Martha Graham Dance Company, 1938-44, later as guest performer; taught at Neighborhood Playhouse, 1938-58; co-founder, Dudley-Maslow-Bales Trio, 1942; director, New Dance Group, 1950-66; taught at Bennington College, Connecticut College (1948-53), Teacher's College, Columbia University (1956-64); artistic director, Batsheva Dance Company (Israel), 1967-70; director, London School of Contemporary Dance, 1970-90; still teaching in the late 1990s.

Works

1934 *The Dream Ends,* New Dance Group
      In the Life of a Worker, New Dance Group
      Time Is Money (poem by Sol Funaroff), New Dance Group
      Death of Tradition w/Sophie Maslow, Anna Sokolow
1935 *Call*
      Middle-Class Portraits (Swivel Chair Hero, Dream World Hero, Aesthete, Liberal) (mus. Estelle Parnas), New Dance Group
1937 *Song for Soviet Youth Day* (mus. Borislav Martinu), New Dance Group
      Under the Swastika (mus. Alex North), New Dance Group
      Satiric Suite w/Maslow, William Matons, Sokolow
      My Body, My Carcass
      Songs of Protest (mus. Lawrence Gellert), New Dance Group

      Fantasy
      Evacuation w/Maslow
1938 *Cult of Blood*
      Jazz Lyric (mus. Earl Robinson)
      Nursery Rhymes for Grownups
      Women of Spain w/Maslow (mus. Joaquin Turina, flamenco)
1939 *The Ballad of Molly Pitcher* (mus. Earl Robinson, text Edwin Rolfe), solo
1940 *Harmonica Breakdown*
1941 *Pavanne*
      Skatter-brain
      Dissonance
      Gymnopedie w/Maslow
      The Kiss of Judas
1942 *Bach Suite* w/Maslow and William Bales
      Caprichos (from *Women of Spain* w/Maslow
1943 *As Poor Richard Says. . .* (with Sophie Maslow and William Bales)
      American Morning (mus. Marc Blitzstein, text David Wolff)
1944 *Songs for a Child*
      Spanish Suite w/Maslow (mus. traditional Spanish)
      Swing Your Lady (mus. Kraber), solo, on CBS-TV
1945 *Furlough: A Boardwalk Episode* w/Bales
      New World A-Comin' (mus. Sonny Terry)
1946 *The Lonely Ones* (sound effects by Zoe Williams)
      Ballads for Dancers
1949 *Out of the Cradle Endlessly Rocking*
      Vagary
1950 *Passional*
1953 *Reel*
      Family Portrait
1979 *Several Brahms Waltzes*
      Five Characters and Conclusion
      The Green Branch
1980 *Suite of Four Dances*
1982 *Paying My Dues*
1988 *Island; I See My City Again*
      Proverbs

Other works include: *The Betrayed, Short Story* (mus. Paul Creston), and *Adolescence* (mus. Earl Robinson).

Publications

By DUDLEY—

"The Early Life of an American Dancer," *Dance Research,* Spring 1992.

On DUDLEY: books—

Denby, Edwin, *Dance Writings,* New York, 1986.
McDonagh, Don, *The Complete Guide to Modern Dance,* Garden City, New York, 1976.

On DUDLEY: articles—

In *Biographical Dictionary of Dance,* edited by Barbara Naomi Cohen-Stratyner, New York, 1982.

Dunning, Jennifer, "Martha in Present Tense," *New York Times,* 25
    September 1994.
Garafola, Lynn, Review, *Dance Magazine,* October 1988.
Gladstone, Valerie, "Where Even the Ghosts Give Encouragement,"
    New York Times, 2 February 1997.
Hunt, Marilyn, "Graham Dancers Bring Jewish Lore to London,"
    Dance Magazine, April 1991.
Sears, David, "Breaking Down *Harmonica Breakdown*," *Ballet
    Review,* Winter 1989.
Tobias, Anne, "Jane Dudley Retrospective," *Ballet Review,* Winter 1989.
Tobias, Tobi, Review, *New York Times,* 13 June 1988.

*   *   *

Jane Dudley is a dynamic force in modern dance performance,
choreography, and instruction. She worked closely with Martha
Graham as a student, dancer, and teacher. Later, her choreography
retained characteristic Graham movements while also incorporating
dance sequences which were more easily accessible to audiences.
Dudley has extended Graham's influence through her guidance at
dance schools and companies worldwide.

Dudley was born in New York City in 1912. The daughter of a
dance instructor, she studied with Hanya Holm at the Wigman
School in New York in the early 1930s before leaving to attend the
1935 workshop at Bennington College in Vermont led by Martha
Graham. Even though Dudley had been warned years earlier by
Ruth St. Denis to stay away from "ugly" modern dance, especially
Graham's style, Dudley sought extra classes with Graham and soon
joined her company.

Graham's revolutionary dance technique had a profound influence on Dudley. Whether as a participant or an observer, Dudley
relished her time with Graham. Graham wanted movement to be
expressive, powerful, and disciplined—dancers were trained to reach
for the sensation of the movement, or, as Dudley once described it,
for "what went on, what the feel of it was inside the body."
Throughout her life, Dudley has remained true to her mentor;
Graham's legacy is reflected in Dudley's choreography and over the
years she has been devoted to sharing her understanding of Graham's
vision with others.

Dudley was a member of Graham's company for more than a
decade and later returned as a guest artist. As a member of Graham's
all-female group, and often a soloist, Dudley helped introduce
Graham's stylistic dance to the world. Graham's early works em-
phasized dancing as a group with simple, percussive movements.
"Contraction" and "release" became common terms to describe
Graham's technique of muscular movements and Dudley's choreography retains these characteristics. One of Dudley's most memorable performances was as the stern Ancestress in *Letter to the
World* (1940). In this dance, inspired by the life of poet Emily
Dickinson, Dudley's character confronts Graham's, the One Who
Dances, to force her to abandon love and desire. Dudley also danced
with Graham as one of the three sisters in *Deaths and Entrances*
(1943), based on the lives of the Brontë sisters.

Dudley has long been associated with the New Dance Group in
New York, which she joined in the early 1930s. She later became
director from 1950 to 1966. Born in the politically turbulent Depression era, the New Dance Group encouraged its members to
address social problems faced by people at that time. Dudley met
this challenge in her own choreography with such works as *In the
Life of a Worker* and *Time Is Money* (both 1934), *Middle-Class
Portraits* (1935), *Songs of Protest* (1936) and *Under the Swastika*

(1937). By the 1940s the New Dance Group's reputation as a
source of fine dancers began to overshadow its social activism and
Dudley began a new troupe called the Dudley-Maslow-Bales Trio
with fellow New Dance Group members Sophie Maslow and William Bales in 1942.

This highly trained company was well-received by critics and audiences. Maslow and Dudley, both from Graham's company, and the
Humphrey-Weidman-trained Bales created dances which were friendly
and more easily accessible to audiences than much of earlier modern
dance. The humor and exuberant joy of their dances stood in sharp
contrast to the solemn, at times grim dances, then associated with
modern dance. The trio toured the country successfully and performed
together until the mid-1950s when Dudley was forced to retire from
performing because of an arthritic hip. Dudley choreographed one of
the trio's most popular dances, *Harmonica Breakdown* (1940), a comic
dance about pushing on, come what may. It shifts from slow shuffles to
energetic bursts and back again, inspired by Sonny Terry's *Harmonica
and Washboard Breakdown.* This dance delighted audiences in the
1940s and continues to be enjoyed today. Dudley also created the trio's
As Poor Richard Says. . . (1943, with Maslow and Bales) and *The
Lonely Ones* (1946), based on the drawings of William Steig. Other
important choreography by Dudley includes *Family Portrait* (1953)
and *Passional* (1950).

In addition to dancing and choreography, Dudley's influence on
modern dance is felt through her extensive teaching in schools and
companies worldwide. Dudley began teaching the Graham technique,
often alongside Graham, beginning in the 1930s at the Neighborhood
Playhouse in New York and in Graham's School of Contemporary
Dance. She has also taught summer school courses at Connecticut
College in New London, Teacher's College at Columbia University, and
Bennington College, Vermont. Dudley has expanded Martha Graham's
legacy worldwide through her artistic direction outside the United
States. Graham gave the Batsheva Dance Company in Israel her full
support during its inception by working with its dancers both in the
U.S. and Israel and by the late 1960s the company was well-established within Israel but not elsewhere. Graham turned to Dudley to
continue working with the company while Graham honored other
commitments. As its artistic director, Dudley shaped the company for
its first successful European tours. Dudley then carried Graham's influence to Great Britain at the London School of Contemporary Dance.
This school introduced the Graham technique to Britain and continues
to train outstanding modern dancers. Dudley served as director of
contemporary dance until 1990, then continued to choreograph and
teach there and elsewhere.

Dudley's ongoing interest in social issues, first evidenced in her
early dancing and choreographing with the New Dance Group, and
later during her years as the group's director, surfaced again in the
late 1980s with the debut of *Island; I See My City Again* (1988) in
response to the faceless violence plaguing Manhattan in these years.
Another work, *Proverbs,* also premiered in 1988.

—Janette Goff Dixon

DUNCAN, Isadora
American pioneering dancer, choreographer, and teacher

Born: 26 May 1877 in San Francisco. **Education:** Largely self-
taught; her mother brought home music and books and the family,

though poor, all read voraciously, sang, and danced. **Career:** Began teaching neighborhood friends as a teenager; first dancing engagement as one of Titania's fairies for Augustin Daly's *A Midsummer Night's Dream,* 1896; musician Ethelbert Nevin arranged concert performances for her in New York; traveled to London and performed in private homes of the wealthy; toured Europe performing barefoot, free interpretations of classical Greek dance; returned to the United States a success; opened a school and adopted several of her dancers; **Died:** 14 September 1927.

Works

1902	*Orpheus*
1904	*Beethoven Programs—Sonate quasifantasia, Op. 27, No. 2*; *Studien zur siebenten Symphonie, Op. 92*; *Presto aus der Sonate, Op. 10, No. 1*; *Menuet,* and *Sonate Pathétique, Op. 13*
1905	*Brahms Waltzes*
	Chopin Waltzes
	Chopin Mazurkas
	Introduktion und sieben deutsche Tänze
	An der schone blaue Donau
	Iphigenia in Aulis
	Orpheus
1908	*Seventh Symphony* (mus. Beethoven)
	Three National Dances—Norwegian, Slavonic, Spanish
1909	*Marche Militaire*
	Six German Dances
1911	*Gigue*
	Two Gavottes
	Bacchanale, from *Tannhäuser*
	Dance of the Flower Maidens, from *Parsifal,* Act III
	Dance of the Apprentices, from *Die Meistersinger,* Act III
	Orpheus (23 vignettes)
1914	*Ave Maria*
	Marche héroïque
	King Stephen
	Unfinished Symphony
	Waltzs (Reflet d'Allemagne)
1915	*Chopin Program*
	Oedipus
	Fifth Symphony (mus. Beethoven)
	Marseillaise
1916	*Iphigenia in Tauris*
	Morceau symphonique de la rédemption
	Sixth Symphony (mus. Tchaikovsky)
1917	*Marche Lorraine*
	Marche Slave
	Marche funèbre
	Sonate
	Trois poèmes
1920	*Prelude to Parsifal*
	Régéneration de Kundry, from *Parsifal*
1921	*Seventh Symphony* (mus. Schubert)
1922	*Internationale*
	Bénédiction de Dieu
	Funérailles
	Scriabin Program
	Funeral March, from *Götterdammerung*
	Prelude and Death of Isolde, from *Tristan und Isolde*
1923	*Une Nuit sur le Mont Chauve*
	Southern Roses Waltz
	Entrance of the Gods into Valhalla, from *Das Rheingold*
1928	*Mazurka*
	Slow March
	The Three Graces

Other works include: *Dance Idylls* (including *Bacchus et Ariadne, Primavera, Pan et Echo, Musette, Tambourin, Ange avec violon, Das Mädchen und der Tod, Orpheus, Menuet, Romanesca* (for children), *Entre acte* (for children), *Rondo* (for children), and *Impressions of Revolutionary Russia* (included *Marche Slave*).

Publications

By DUNCAN: books—

Isadora Duncan—My Life, London, 1927.
The Art of the Dance, New York, 1928 (reprinted 1970).

On DUNCAN: books—

Desti, Mary, *The Untold Story: The Life of Isadora Duncan 1921-1927,* New York, 1929.
Duncan, Irma, *Duncan Dancer,* Middletown, Connecticut, 1966.
———, *Isadora Duncan: Pioneer in the Art of Dance,* New York, 1958.
———, *The Technique of Isadora Duncan,* New York, 1937 (reprinted Brooklyn, 1970).
MacDougall, Allan Ross, *Isadora: A Revolutionary in Art and Love,* New York, 1960.
Magriel, Paul David, *Isadora Duncan,* New York, 1947.
Miller, Judi, *Women Who Changed America,* Manor Books, 1976.
Schneider, Ilya Ilyich, *Isadora Duncan: The Russian Years,* Translated by David Magershack, London, 1968.
Seroff, Victor, *The Real Isadora,* London, 1972.
Sorell, Walter (ed.), *The Dance Has Many Faces,* (Revised second edition) New York, 1966.
Steegmuller, Francis (ed.), *Your Isadora: The Love Story of Isadora Duncan and Gordon Craig,* New York, 1974.
Terry, Walter, *Isadora Duncan—Her Life, Her Art, Her Legacy,* Dodd, Mead & Company, 1963.

On DUNCAN: articles—

Maria-Theresa, "The Spirit of Isadora Duncan," in Myron Howard Nadel and Constance Gwen Nadel (eds.), *The Dance Experience: Readings in Dance Appreciation,* New York, 1970.
Roslavleva, Natalia, "Prechistenka 20: The Isadora Duncan School in Moscow," *Dance Perspectives,* 1975.
Terry, Walter, "The Legacy of Isadora Duncan and Ruth St. Denis." *Dance Perspectives 5,* 1960.

*   *   *

It is commonly believed that Isadora Duncan was just a spiritual entity floating around in gausy tunics, dancing barefoot, living her life like her art, and leaving no dance vocabulary as a legacy for her followers—this is not true. Lori Bevilove, of the Isadora Duncan Foundation for Contemporary Dance, Inc. has been a performer and teacher of the Duncan technique for over 20 years. She, like many other aspiring dancers, received private coaching from some of the original Isadora Duncan dancers, known as "the Isadorables," who carried on Isadora's style of dancing.

Isadora Duncan was born in San Francisco in 1878. Her whole family was artistic, bohemian, and temperamental. Her mother divorced her father, a poet, after she was born. The young Dora Angela, always known as Isadora, never knew him. Her early life was rich in spirit but one of material poverty; in general, she ran free. Her first ideas of movement came from watching waves roll in and out to sea, and at the age of six, she founded the first Duncan School of Dance. Her dance theory was based on emotion.

The family soon established an "act." Mrs. Duncan played the piano and booked them into local well-to-do society homes. When the Duncans moved to New York, the powerful theatrical producer, Augustin Daly, gave Isadora an interview and cast her in a touring company of Shakespeare's *A Midsummer Night's Dream*. Convinced her style of dance didn't fit, Isadora soon quit. When she returned, the family rented a studio in Carnegie Hall. Close to the Metropolitan Opera House, in its full glory in the 1890s, Isadora watched the operatic stars come and go. Before long, with a young composer named Ethelbert Nevin, she prepared a series of concerts for the salons of Mrs. Astor, Mrs. Styuvesant Fish, and Mrs. Belmont. This was an audience bred on Russian ballet, and as they watched her sudden runs and quick leaps followed by slow, interpretive movements, her body draped only in gauzy tunics, they applauded politely. Isadora felt she could cut the chill in the air with a knife; she did, however, cause a mild sensation in 1899 when she danced her interpretation of *The Rubaiyat* at the Lyceum Theater.

Isadora, her brother Raymond, and Mrs. Duncan went to London. One of Isadora's patrons was there and Isadora asked for an advance. She was a smash success and doors began to open. The *London Times* covered her dancing and deemed her "Bottecelli-like." Experimenting with body movements, she discovered the point were her spiritual and technical approach to the dance intertwined. She decided all motion originated in the solar plexus and not, as previously believed, in the spine. On this principle, together with the emotional force of gravity, she built her system, her school, and her legacy to modern dance.

Joining Raymond, an individualist even on the Left Bank of Paris, she studied the little figures on the Greek vases he was sketching in the Louvre. Though greatly influenced by the French scientist of movement expression, Francoise Delsarte, she expanded on his theories. In the early 1900s Isadora and Raymond went to Greece where she began her "Hellenic period." Isadora would dance as the spirit moved her and was named the "maid of Athens." About this time, she discovered she had another talent, that of making headlines.

Isadora only married once, but the two men in her life who gave her the most support were Edward Gordon Craig, son of British actress Ellen Terry, and Eugene Singer of the Singer sewing machine fortune. All her life her fight between her work and her loves waged, but what was scandalous back then wouldn't even make headlines today. The greatest tragedy of Isadora's life was when her two young children, Patrick and Deirdra, were drowned in the Seine. Isadora was desolate.

Leonid Krassin, who had seen Isadora dance the *March Slav*, convinced her to go to Russia and found a school of the dance. The Isadora Duncan State School opened in 1921, but again, she couldn't compete with ballet. Her little pupils were so cold in the barn-like school, they couldn't move. Worse, she had fallen in love again with a Russian. They talked in sign language and she married him

because that was the only way he could be admitted to the United States. Though she admitted to being a "revolutionary," Isadora was branded as a Bolshevik and an anarchist. Her concerts were flops, and her dancing was misunderstood. Singer, ever loyal to Isadora, paid for she and her husband, Sergei, to go to France. She never again returned to the United States; the country, from where her dance had sprung, didn't want her.

Her marriage was a failure and when Sergei left, Isadora absorbed herself in her work. She toured Russia but the very people she wanted to dance for couldn't afford a ticket to see her. She, too, was broke and appealed to family and friends. She had never been in more trouble even in her early days, and worse, she was haunted by her brilliant past and an appetite for beauty and luxury.

In 1925 she returned to Paris and moved to Nice where in between performances, she wrote her autobiography, *My Life*.

On 14 September 1927 Isadora was in exceptionally high spirits. Having just returned from the hairdresser, and finally with some funds, even enough money to buy a car, she was wearing a spectacular Chinese-red shawl around her neck and shoulders to ward off the chill as the Riviera dusk turned to evening. The heavy fringe hung down and caught in the rear wheel of the low two-seated car. The car stopped immediately, but it was too late. The first turn of the wheel had broken Isadora's neck. She was dead, at age 49. It was unbelievable; 10,000 people thronged the streets of Paris to attend her funeral. She left behind film clips and a nation who rejected her dancing but could identify her name.

Along with other pioneers of modern dance, Isadora influenced generations of modern dancers around the world. There are many "mothers" of modern dance, including Ruth St. Denis and Martha Graham, but many consider Isadora Duncan as an irresistible, irrepressible, and important guiding spirit that brought modern dance to the forefront of the dance world.

—Judi Miller

DUNCAN, Jeff
American dancer and choreographer

Born: Thomas Jefferson Duncan, Jr., 4 February 1930, in Cisco, Texas. **Education:** Attended North Texas University and Denver University; studied dance with Hanya Holm, Colorado Springs, 1949, and with Alwin Nikolais and Doris Humphrey in New York. **Career:** Debut, Henry Street Playhouse, 1952; served as assistant to Doris Humphrey, Juilliard Dance Ensemble; assistant to Anna Sokolow, from 1954; dancer with the New Dance Group, and with Doris Humphrey at the 92nd St. YMHA; first independent choreography, 1957; founded his own company, 1960; founder, with Jack Moore and Art Bauman, Dance Theatre Workshop, 1965; instructor and company director, University of Maryland, from 1977. **Died:** 26 May 1989, in Baltimore.

Roles (selected)

1953	*Poor Eddy* (Humphrey)	
1954	*Lyric Suite* (Sokolow)	
1955	*Plain and Fancy* (Tamiris)	
	Red Roses for Me (Sokolow)	
	Rooms (Sokolow)	

| 1958 | *Session 58* (Sokolow) |
| 1959 | *Destry Rides Again* (Kidd) |

Works

1954	*Image*
1957	*Antique Epigrams*, solo
	Three Fictitious Games
1958	*Frames*
1959	*Terrestrial Figure*
1960	*Opus 1, No. 1*
	Outdoors Suite
1961	*Il Combattimento*
1962	*Rite of Source*
	Quartet
1963	*Duet*
	Trio
	Winesburg Portraits
1964	*Revelation*
	Six Bagatelles
	Diversions for Five
1965	*Glimpse*
	Summer Trio
1966	*Canticles*
	Statement
	Studies for an Ominous Age
	Preludes
	Diminishing Landscape
1967	*Three Studies*
	View (part 1)
1969	*Body Parts*
	Vinculum
	Les Sirènes
	Resonances
1970	*The Glade*
1971	*Douprelude*
	Lenten Suite
	Space Test
1972	*Shore Song*
1973	*Canticles No. 2 for Three*
	View (completion)
	Cantique de Cantique
1974	*Pieces in May*
	Phases of the Oracle
1975	*Bach Fifth Clavier Concerto*
1976	*Contrast Suite*
1977	*Sky Paths/Places*
	Quartet for Women
1979	*The Heptasoph Pieces*
1980	*La Mesa del Brujo*

Publications

On DUNCAN: articles—

Cameron, Zelda, "Review," *Dance Magazine,* February 1980.

Jowitt, Deborah, "Remembering Jeff Duncan," *Dance Magazine,* November 1989.

Kisselgoff, Anna, "Duncan Obituary," *New York Times,* 29 May 1989.

Merry, Suzanne, "Review," *Dance Magazine,* May 1980.

Films and Videotapes

The Joy of Bach, PBS, New York, 1978.

*   *   *

Jeff Duncan was a an influential promoter of modern dance through his efforts as a dancer, choreographer, teacher, and organizer. He began his career as a gifted dancer with Doris Humphrey and Anna Sokolow, among others. While choreographing his own work, he collaborated with others to found the Dance Theatre Workshop, an important showcase for modern dance in New York.

Thomas Jefferson Duncan Jr. was born in Texas in 1930. While a college student in Texas, he saw a performance by the Martha Graham Company and decided to pursue dancing. He transferred to Denver University to study dance and worked with Hanya Holm, a European Expressionist dancer, in her summer school of dance. Moving to New York City, Duncan trained with Alwin Nikolais and Betty Jones of the José Limón Company. He performed in Nikolais' company and in the New Dance Group. Doris Humphrey saw Duncan perform and asked him to be her assistant at the Juilliard Dance Ensemble, where he performed in Humphrey premieres for the company and in other works. Humphrey chose Duncan to dance the Young Lover in the 1953 revival of *With My Red Fires.* He also performed for her in *Poor Eddy* (1953).

Duncan's abilities as a gifted, intense dancer also led to his working with Anna Sokolow. He was principal dancer in her company for 12 years and became her assistant in 1954. Duncan created the leading male role in Sokolow's *Lyric Suite* (1954); the emotive but nonnarrative choreography in *Lyric Suite* made it a landmark for many in modern dance. In Sokolow's *Rooms* (1955), Duncan first performed the "Panic" solo and later added "Dreams" to his repertoire. His performance in *Session* (1958) was another highlight in his affiliation with Sokolow.

Duncan also appeared in opera, regional theater, and television. During the 1950s, he danced on Broadway in Sokolow's *Red Roses for Me*, Michael Kidds' *Destry Rides Again*, and Helen Tamiris' *Plain and Fancy.* Duncan made his debut as a choreographer in 1957 to favorable reviews of his solo work *Antique Epigram* and *Three Fictitious Games* and went on to form his own company in 1960. Duncan's choreography reflects the influence of his mentor Sokolow in its themes of solitude and dreams. Originally trained as a musician, Duncan had a refined sense of timing and flow which he harnessed to reveal interior drama in his dances. His gift for characterization was displayed in his classic *Winesburg Portraits* (1963). Based on Sherwood Anderson's novel *Winesburg, Ohio*, this dance creates characters the audience can understand even when the characters lack a knowledge of themselves. Other important works created by Duncan in the 1960s include *Resonances, Diminishing Landscape*, and *Canticles*.

Duncan's accomplishments as a brilliant organizer and untiring promoter of modern dance equal those of him as dancer and choreographer. In 1963 Duncan rented a small loft at 215 West 20th Street in New York, and with his funds depleted from recently producing two concerts, he was looking for a way to escape the common necessity of saving great sums to be able to produce one show. His goal was to create work in the loft and invite others in to see it, in much the same way Humphrey and Charles Weidman once did.

Soon other dancers and choreographers were asking to use the space and Duncan recognized the need for a studio-theater with low

Jeff Duncan. Photograph © Johan Elbers.

overhead where dancers could present their work. The studio would be offered for several weekends, rather than the usual one performance, thus giving choreographers the opportunity to better gauge how the work is received by audiences.

In 1965 Duncan joined with Jack Moore and Art Bauman to organize the Dance Theatre Workshop (DTW) as a non-profit organization dedicated to supporting choreography and its theatrical and musical elements. Duncan had worked with Moore to found Contemporary Dance Production in the late 1950s, which had been the proving ground for Duncan as a choreographer. During his decade as the Workshop's director, Duncan doggedly worked in all facets of the company. He handled advertising, publicity, and grant-writing; he created settings and music on a limited budget but with unlimited imagination. Often dances developed at DTW were later performed elsewhere in theaters, concert halls, or on tours organized by Duncan. Choreographers who showed dances at the Workshop include Art Bauman, Rudy Perez, Kathryn Posin, Cliff Keuter, James Cunningham, Meredith Monk, and Kenneth King.

The Workshop helped start *Eddy*, a dance publication, in 1974 and the next year relocated to a larger space at 219 West 19th Street.

Duncan moved to Baltimore in 1977 to accept a teaching position at the University of Maryland, and became an influential figure in the Baltimore dance community. He was the founder and director of the university's resident company Impetus. He also founded and

was artistic director of the Jeff Duncan Dance Repertory Company and supported PATH, a company associated with the Theater Project, an experimental group in Baltimore. Duncan died in Baltimore in 1989.

—Janette Goff Dixon

DUNHAM, Katherine

American dancer, choreographer, company director, and educator

Born: 22 June 1909 in Joliet, Illinois. **Education:** Studied dance as a child; studied anthropology at Northwestern University; travelled to the West Indies to study dance, 1936; University of Chicago, Ph.D. in anthropology. **Family:** Married John Pratt, 1941 (died); one daughter. **Career:** Founded her own company, Ballets Nègres, in 1931; danced with Chicago Opera Company, 1935-36; dance director, Negro Unit of the Federal Theater project, Chicago, 1938; dance director, New York Labor Stage, 1939; choreographer for Broadway productions and later for films in Hollywood; founder, Dunham School of Arts and Research, New York, 1945 (closed 1954), and Katherine Dunham Dance Company; director, Performing Arts Training Center, Southern Illinois University, from 1967; founder, Katherine Dunham Center for the Arts and Humanities, East St. Louis, Illinois. **Awards:** *Dance Magazine* Award, 1968; Samuel Scripps American Dance Festival Award, 1968; American Dance Guild Award, 1975; Great Cross of Honor and Merit, government of Haiti, 1983; National Museum of Dance Hall of Fame, 1987; Order of the Southern Cross, Brazil; Albert Schweitzer Award.

Works (selected; Dunham has choreographed over 150 ballets, plays, films, and concert works)

1937	*L'Ag'Ya*
1938	*Barrelhouse*
1940	*Cabin in the Sky* (film)
	Tropics
	Le Jazz Hot
	Pins and Needles (revue)
	Bre'er Rabbit an' de Tah baby
	Plantation Dances
1941	*Carnival of Rhythm* (musical)
	Rites de Passage
	Star Spangled Rhythm (musical)
	Stormy Weather (musical; film, 1943)
1942	*Rara Tonga*
1943	*Choros*
	Tropical revue
	Bahiana
	Island Songs
	Mexican Rumba
	Peruvienne
	Rumba, Santiago de Chile
	Tableaux of Spanish Earth
	Ti' cocomacaque
	Woman with a Cigar
	Florida Swamp Shimmy

	Callata
	Plantation Dances
1944	*Flaming Youth*
	Havana Promenade
1945	*Carib Song* (musical)
	Shango
1947	*La Comparasa*
	Bal Nègre
1948	*The Octoroon Ball*
	Casbah (musical)
1950	*Brazilian Suite*

Publications

By DUNHAM: books—

Journey to Accompong, New York, 1946.
The Dances of Haiti, Mexico, 1947, Los Angeles, 1983.
A Touch of Innocence, New York, 1959, reprinted, Chicago, 1994.
Island Possessed, New York, 1970, reprinted, Chicago, 1994.

On DUNHAM: books—

Aschenbrenner, Joyce, *Katherine Dunham,* New York, 1981.
Beckford, Ruth. *Katherine Dunham,* New York, 1979.
Siegel, Marcia B. *The Shapes of Change.* Boston, 1979.
Sorell, Walter, *The Dance through the Ages,* New York, 1967.

*   *   *

Katherine Dunham is considered to be one of the most prominent figures in American modern dance. During her career as a dancer and choreographer, Dunham formed her own dance troupe and developed her own technique of dance, which has been taught in studios throughout the United States. Dunham is given credit for breaking down racial barriers in the dance world and has been deemed a pioneer and a revolutionary. She was among the first African-Americans to study indigenous, Afro-centered dances and present them as an art form. She has been the subject of several books, has authored several of her own, and is working on her second autobiography. Dunham has received numerous awards, honorary degrees, and commendations from the United States and several Caribbean countries. Dunham lived in both the United States and Haiti for many years but returned to her home in East St. Louis, Illinois, after the overthrow of Aristide in 1991.

Dunham studied anthropology and earned a doctorate from the University of Chicago, where noted anthropologists Margaret Meade, Franz Boas, Robert Redfield, and Melville Herskovits were active. While compiling material for her masters thesis, Dunham studied the dances of several Caribbean countries, which manifest an unusual and interesting conglomeration of cultures. All that Dunham has taught and created proceeds from her efforts to combine anthropology and dance. Although Dunham drew much of her material from the various Caribbean cultures, she felt most drawn to and inspired by Haiti because its culture and dances were the most representational of those in Africa. During her time in Haiti, Dunham closely observed and studied the dance forms associated with social occasions and religious rituals, particularly Vodun (voodoo). Dunham became ordained in Haitian Vodun's most powerful order called the serpent cult of Daballa, and in so doing went through several initiation rituals, including walking on a bed of hot coals.

She later explained, "To really know Haiti, I had to belong and be formally initiated into the religion."

After her time spent in the Caribbean, Dunham developed her own dance form, which could be described as a blend of ballet, American folk dance, and moves borrowed from various African and South American cultures. The distinguishing features of Dunham's technique include the isolation and movement of a particular anatomical area—for example, obvious hip and pelvic movement or shoulder movement, and many of her barre exercises are performed in parallel position.

As a child growing up in Joliet, Illinois, Dunham took ballet lessons for many years, but later found there was virtually no place for her as a classically trained dancer. African-Americans were accepted as entertainers on the stage in the form of minstrel-type shows, vaudeville acts, revues, and in nightclubs. Dancers such as Josephine Baker and Bill "Bojangles" Robinson were among the widely accepted African-American dancers. The American folk opera, *Porgy and Bess* (George Gershwin), helped to portray African-Americans as serious stage performers, but it was the work of artists such as Katherine Dunham who helped bring both the African-American dancer and culture into the mainstream American dance scene. In 1940 Dunham brought her revue called *Tropics and Le Jazz Hot* to New York City. The show was intended as a one-night show, but played to full houses on Broadway for two weeks. Soon after, Dunham choreographed several movies, including *Stormy Weather* and *Pardon My Sarong.* Along with George Balanchine, Dunham choreographed the stage show *Cabin in the Sky.* Later Dunham choreographed a 1963 production of Verdi's *Aida.* In all, Dunham has choreographed over 150 ballets, half a dozen stage shows, 13 films, and three operas.

Dunham is also a political activist and many of her dances have reflected her political and social views. While touring South America during the 1950s, Dunham created *Southland,* a dance which portrayed the true story of the lynching of an African-American male falsely accused of raping a white woman. The music composed for the dance was a combination of jazz and blues, and included a requiem mass. The dance premiered in Santiago, Chile, over the objections of U.S. officials. Dunham has also been very outspoken about segregation. During one performance in Lexington, Kentucky, in 1944 Dunham taped a sign from a bus on her back which stated "For Blacks Only." At the end of the performance, she announced to the audience that her troupe would never perform there again. In 1952, while performing in Sao Paulo, Brazil, Dunham was prevented from joining her husband, who was white, in their hotel room. As a result, Dunham filed a lawsuit which eventually led to a bill passed by the Brazilian legislature that made discrimination in public places illegal. As an octogenarian, she made world headlines not as a dancer, but because of her 47-day hunger strike to protest the U.S. government's treatment of Haitian refugees.

Many of Dunham's dances are based upon people she has met, places she has visited, or a particular piece of music. For example, *Woman with A Cigar* is a dance about a woman Dunham met while traveling around the Caribbean Islands who carried along a parrot in a cage and smoked cigars. One of her first major ballets, which tells the story of a fatal love triangle, *L'Ag'Ya* (1938), was funded by the Works Project Administration (WPA). Dunham used the West African martial art form ag'ya as the basis for the dance. *L'Ag'Ya* went on to become a featured dance in Alvin Ailey's three-hour program, *The Magic of Katherine Dunham.* Another dance in Ailey's program is *Choros,* a lively dance featuring two couples and a solo female. *Choros* was inspired by the music of Vadico Gagliano and

19th-century Brazilian architecture. The dance *Rites de Passage* was originally developed to enhance and illustrate a lecture entitled "An Anthropological Approach to Theater" that Dunham delivered at Yale University.

Dunham was the director and leading performer in her dance group, the Dunham Company. Many of her dance students, such as Talley Beatty, went on to form their own dance companies. There is a dance group sponsored by Southern Illinois University and a performing arts center named after Katherine Dunham, but with no connection to Dunham whatsoever; she neither sponsors these groups nor receives any money from them. Dunham lives in her house which contains all her costumes, stage props, instruments, and archival materials—all of which are in danger of being ruined. There is no film or video recording of Dunham's technique or dances. Since the mid-1960s, after retiring from the stage, Dunham has devoted her time and effort to various community causes both in Haiti and in her hometown of East St. Louis, where she has put her efforts into her training center for nearly 30 years. As the 1990s draw to a close, Dunham is confined to a wheelchair in which she still dances.

—Christine Miner Minderovic

DUNLOP (MacTAVISH), Shona
New Zealand dancer, choreographer, educator, and writer

Born: Dunedin, 20 April 1920. **Education:** Studied dance from 1935 at the Vienna State Academy for Music and Dramatic Art under Gertrud Bodenwieser. **Family:** Married missionary Donald MacTavish in 1948 (died, 1955); two daughters and one son. **Career:** Dancer with Bodenwieser Gruppe in Vienna and Sydney 1938-48; toured South America in 1938; taught for 8 years in Sydney; operated her own Dunedin studio 1958-91; founded Dunedin Dance Theatre, 1963; dance critic for Otago Daily Times, 1958-90; New Zealand correspondent for Dance Magazine 1970 to the present; continues to teach and take workshops. **Awards:** MBE for Service to the Arts, 1985.

Roles (for Bodenwieser Viennese Ballet, Sydney; choreographed by Bodenwieser)

1939	*El Fauno*, solo
1940	*Snake Charmer*, solo
1941	Terror (cr) in *The Mask of Lucifer*
	Cain (cr) in *Cain and Abel*
1945	Glorious Prince (cr) in *O World*
	Solo in *Trilogy of Joan of Arc*
1946	Individual (cr) in *The One and the Many*

Works

1965	*Hunger* (mus. Dvorak), Dunedin Dance Theatre, Dunedin
1966	*Encounter* (mus. Holst and Southgate), Ecumenical Conference, Hamilton NZ, and Australian Broadcasting Co. Television
1970	*Easter Canticles* (mus. Britten, Messian, Bartók), Cape Town

	Orlando w/ L. Petherbridge (mus. J. Drummond), Dunedin Dance Theatre, Dunedin
1973	*Pania of the Reef* (mus. W. Southgate), New Zealand Ballet, Dunedin, filmed by Television New Zealand
1980	*Requiem for the Living* (mus. Penderecki, words Kirkup), Dunedin Dance Theatre, Dunedin
	Danced Eucharist (mus. J. M. Talbot), Dunedin Dance Theatre, St. Paul's Anglican Cathedral, Dunedin
	Death of a Bullfighter w/ L. Petherbridge (words Garcia Lorca), Dunedin Dance Theatre, Dunedin, filmed by Television New Zealand
1981	*While Grandmother Played Bridge* w/ L. Petherbridge (mus. John Drummond)
	Transfigured Night (mus. Schönberg, words R. Dehmel), solo for Bronwyn Judge, Wellington
1983	*Bars* (mus. C. Cress Brown), Dunedin
1988	*Jepthah's Daughter* (mus. Bernstein), solo for Bronwyn Judge, Dunedin
1991	*Coup de Folie* w/ L. Petherbridge (mus. E. Carr), Dunedin Dance Theatre, Dunedin
	The Call (mus. Villa Lobos), solo for Susan Simpson, Dunedin
1993	*Joan of Arc* (mus. Lober), reconstruction of Bodenwieser 1945 *Trilogy*, Carol Brown
1994	*Two Inches behind the Eye* (mus. A. Ritchie), from writings of Janet Frame, Footnote Dance Company, Oamaru
	Wellspring to Isadora (mus. various), solo for Bronwyn Judge, Dunedin
	The Magnificat (mus. Bach), Christian Dance Fellowship of NZ, Christchurch
1996	*A Question of Love* (mus. Anthony Ritchie), Dunedin
	My End Is the Beginning (mus. Anthony Ritchie), solo for Bronwyn Judge, Dunedin

Publications

By DUNLOP: books—

Lord of the Dance, Christchurch, 1967.
Be Jubilant My Feet, Melbourne, 1975.
An Ecstasy of Purpose: The Life and Art of Gertrud Bodenwieser, Dunedin, 1987.
Leap of Faith: My Dance through Life, Dunedin, 1997.

Films and Videotapes

Pania of the Reef, New Zealand Ballet, Dunedin, filmed by Television New Zealand.
Out into the Blue, documentary, dir. H. Ogonowska-Coates, Fraser-Tilly Productions, Oamaru, 1997.

*   *   *

Shona Dunlop was born in Dunedin, New Zealand, in 1920. At the age of fifteen, and after the death of her father some three years before, Dunlop, her mother and older brother, embarked on a trip to Europe where she ventured into her first dance classes with Gertrud Bodenwieser at the Vienna State Academy for Music and Dramatic Art. She also had further training in Paris under Ellen Tels. Dunlop's training under Bodenwieser was the start of a long association that eventually saw her become a principal dancer with the Bodenwieser

Shona Dunlop (MacTavish) in *Cain and Abel*.

Gruppe. In 1938 the Bodenwieser Gruppe undertook a nine-month tour of South America. Germany had by then invaded Austria and because Bodenwieser and many of her dancers were Jewish this tour was a means of escape. Although very inexperienced and young, Dunlop went along on the tour, and she quickly became noted for her dramatic interpretations of roles. She later won critical acclaim for her role as Cain in *Cain and Abel* (1941).

In 1939, after the South American tour finished, Bodenwieser was forced to relocate in order to escape the Nazi regime. Due to Bodenwieser's connections with the Dunlop family, she initially chose New Zealand, but when some of her dancers toured to Australia she took the opportunity to reform her company in Sydney. Dunlop became an assistant to Bodenwieser, which gave her experience and exposure to ideas from which her own teaching would spring in the succeeding years.

As a critic, and with firm beliefs and opinions steeped in the central European traditions of dance, Dunlop has used her own experience as a yardstick for all contemporary dances. This has previously caused some tensions within the New Zealand dance scene, as the majority of dancers have absorbed the standards of American modern and postmodern dance approaches.

The first modern dance professional group to tour New Zealand was the Bodenwieser Viennese Ballet in 1947. As pointed out by Dunlop in her autobiography, *Leap of Faith* (1997), only two Viennese trained dancers remained in the company (she being one of them) at this time. This tour visited large and small centres with several reviewers commenting on Dunlop's versatility as a soloist. She had by now attained principal status. In 1948 Dunlop suddenly left the company, married missionary Donald MacTavish and went to live in China, all within a three-week time span.

Dunlop is a very direct and forthright personality and has been able to surmount great personal tragedy. Following the death of her husband in 1955, she returned to Dunedin with three small children after an absence of twenty years. In 1958 she opened her own studio of dance and subsequently started Dunedin Dance Theatre (1963). The influence of Bodenwieser was very apparent in her ideas concerning both technique and composition. However, as time has passed, these ideas have filtered through "a Shona lens," inflected by ideas which have impacted on her life in very different cultures: China (1948-50), South Africa (1950-55), and in the Philippines (1981). Here Dunlop spent a year as a professor of dance at the Silliman University in Dumaguete city on the Philippine Island of Negros, teaching and choreographing. These experiences provided a wealth of material and inspiration for her classes, which always included improvisation and a variety of music in keeping with her acute sense of musicality.

Dunlop's work as a teacher is of primary importance to her contribution to dance in New Zealand. In her teaching she attracted and nurtured women of strong independent mien.

Dunlop has always been determined to provide the opportunity for dissemination and preservation of Bodenwieser's contribution to the world of dance, particularly Ausdruckstanz, and was pivotal in the publication of Bodenwieser's book *An Ecstasy of Purpose* in both English (1987) and German (1992). Her interests include reconstruction of Bodenwieser's choreography, with the remounting of several works including the germinal work *Demon Machine* (1924) and *Trilogy of Joan of Arc* (1947), a solo choreographed on Dunlop which has been videoed to provide a permanent visual record. Of importance is that this solo has been reconstructed on a former student, Carol Brown, who continues the lineage with her Ph.D. solo performance *The Mechanics of Fluids* (1995). The last section of Brown's choreography has direct references to the ideas and techniques she gained in her formative years of study with Dunlop in Dunedin.

Geographical isolation has meant that recognition for the contribution Dunlop has made to dance has only recently spread to the wider dance community. Former students including Bronwyn Judge have funded a documentary *Out Into the Blue* (1997) in which Judge becomes the vehicle by which Dunlop's dance self is relived. Her role in this film is pivotal, capturing the spirit of Dunlop's dance philosophy, style and passion. Trained under Dunlop and associated with her for many years, Judge is known for her powerful expressive presence as a dancer. She has gone on to carve out her own career living in a very isolated community near Oamaru in the South Island. She has collaborated with poets, designers, writers and a video artist.

Dunlop has long had a commitment to liturgical dance, developed in China and South Africa while working with her missionary husband. This commitment was celebrated in 1975 when she was appointed as the first adviser in dance to the 5th Assembly of the World Council of Churches in Nairobi. Much of her work has been choreographed specifically for various churches but her close association with the church has not led her to shy away from controversial subjects, as is evidenced in her recent work *A Question of Love* (1996), which deals with a lesbian relationship. This dance was her response to the Presbyterian General Assembly of New Zealand's refusal to ordain gay men and women.

Dunlop is always searching for new ideas and inspiration for her choreography and teaching. She draws from many different sources including art, music, drama, mythology, social concerns and topical issues. The rich tapestry of her life has shaped her character and greatly influenced her work. Her strengths and fortitude have been illustrated in her philosophy and commitment to dance. Dunlop, although in her seventies, is still extremely active and continues to teach, choreograph, write and reconstruct, cementing a central European dance strand to a contemporary dance lineage in New Zealand.

—Sue Cheesman

DUNN, Douglas
American dancer, choreographer, and company director

Born: 19 October 1942 in Palo Alto, California. **Education:** B.A. in art history, Princeton University, 1964; studied with Audreé Estey, Princeton Ballet Society, 1962; trained at Jacob's Pillow Dance Festival school with Margaret Craske, Ted Shawn, Matteo, and Gus Solomons Jr., 1963; Joffrey Ballet School, 1964-65; schools of Merce Cunningham, Margaret Jenkins, 1968. **Career:** Dancer, Yvonne Rainer and Group, 1968-70; Merce Cunningham Dance Company, 1969-73, Grand Union collective, 1970-76; founder/artistic director, Douglas Dunn and Dancers, beginning 1976; commissions include Paris Opera Ballet, Groupe de Recherche Choreographique de l'Opéra de Paris, Grande Ballet de Bordeaux, New Dance Ensemble of Minneapolis, Walker Arts Center (Minneapolis), Repertory Dance Theater (Salt Lake City), Ballet Théâtre Francais de Nancy, Institute for Contemporary Art (Boston), Perth Institute of Contemporary Art (Australia), and Portland State University (Oregon). **Awards:** Fellowships and awards include Cowles Chair, University of Minnesota, the National Endowment for the Arts, New York State Council on the Arts, John Simon Guggenheim Memorial Foundation, New York Foundation for the Arts, Lila Wallace-Reader's Digest Fund, Foundation for Contemporary Performance Arts, and Creative Arts Public Service Program.

Roles

1960	*Tread* (Merce Cunningham)
1969	*Continuous Project—Altered Daily* (Rainer)
1970	*Second Hand* (Cunninghan)
	Signals (Cunningham)
	Objects (Cunningham)
	The One Hundreds (Twyla Tharp)
1971	*Roof Piece* (Trisha Brown)
1972	*Landrover* (Cunningham)
	TV Rerun (Cunningham)
1973	*Changing Steps* (Cunningham)

Works (premiered in New York City unless otherwise noted)

1971	*Dancing Here* w/Pat Catterson, Merce Cunningham Studio
	One Thing Leads to Another w/Sara Rudner
1972	*Pas du Two* w/Sheela Raj, American Center, Paris
	Eight Lanes, Four Approaches w/Rudner, Barnard College
	Co-Incidents w/David Gordon, Cunningham Studio
1973	*Orange My Darling Lime*, Theater at Saint Clements
	Nevada, solo, New School
1974	*101* (silence), Douglas Dunn Studio
	Four for Nothing, Dunn Studio
1975	*Part I Part II* w/David Woodberry, Dunn Studio
1978	*Lazy Madge II*, Zellerbach Playhouse, Berkeley, California
	Coquina (mus. Ashley), Zellerbach Playhouse, Berkeley
	Relief (mus. John Driscoll), Pioneer Memorial Theater, Salt Lake City
1979	*Foot Rules* (mus. Driscoll), Akademie der Kunste, Berlin
	Echo (mus. Driscoll), Summergarden, Museum of Modern Art

1980   *Suite de Suite* (mus. Radigué), Grand Théâtre de Nancy, France
1981   *Skid* (mus. Driscoll), Festival d'Automne, Paris
        View (mus. Driscoll), Festival d'Automne, Paris
        Hitch (mus. Fisher), Festival d'Automne, Paris
        Cycles (mus. Lacy), Soissons
        Terri's Dance, Théâtre Femina, Bordeaux, France
        Chateauvallonesque (mus. Driscoll), Chateauvallon Festival, southern France
        Holds (mus. Driscoll), Harvard University, Cambridge
        Walking Back (mus. John Driscoll), 14th Street "Y"
1982   *Game Tree* (mus. Fisher)
1983   *Second Mesa* (mus. Driscoll, Lerman), Institute of Contemporary Art, Boston
        Secret of the Waterfall (mus. Waldman; poetry Bye)
1984   *1st Rotation* w/Linda Shapiro, Leigh Dillard (mus. Steve Kramer), Jewish Community Center, Minneapolis
        Elbow Room (mus. Fisher), Théâtre Municipal de Nimes, France
        2nd Rotation (mus. Fisher), Maison de la Culture, Grenoble, France
        Futurities (mus. Lacy), Grand Théâtre, Lille, France
        Pulcinella (reset; mus. Stravinsky), Joyce Theater
        Naropa East, Naropa East Benefit
1985   *Jig Jag* (mus. Kuivila), 14th Street "Y"
        3rd Rotation (mus. Fisher), 14th Street "Y"
        Lift for Alice Kaltman, La Jolla Art Museum
        Pacific Shores, Geneva, Switzerland
1986   *Dances for Men, Women & Moving Door* (mus. Lucier), Marymount Manhattan College
1987   *Peepstone* (mus. Debussy, Dylan, Arbeau, Bartlet, Mozart, Glück), Capitol Theater, Salt Lake City
        The Perfect Summer Dress w/Anne Waldman (mus. Budd, Fahey, Mozart, Garland), Naropa Institute
        Operia (mus. Verdi, Wagner, Varèse, Mozart)
1988   *November Duet* (mus. Little Sonny), Douglas Dunn Studio
        Haole (mus. Eno; text Eldredge, Tattersall), Whitney Museum's Equitable Center Theater
        Gondolages (mus. Strauss) for Jean Guizerix/Wilfride Piollet, France
        Matches (sound Burckhardt), The Kitchen
1989   *Wildwood* (reset; mus. Bryars), Dunn Studio
        Peepstone (reset; mus. Debussy, Dylan, Arbeau, Bartlet, Mozart, Glück)
        Ahoy (mus. selection by Dunn), Staten Island Ferry
        The Great Dinosaur Rescue (mus. Cimino, Albagli, Klibonoff), Imagination Celebration and New York State Museum, Albany
        Sky Eye (mus. Campra), St. Mark's Church
1990   *Unrest* (mus. Cole), St. Mark's Church
        Blocs (mus. Waits, Temptations, Mahler), University of Minnesota, Minneapolis
        Don't Cry Now (mus. Gaye, Chiffons, Wood, Shirelles), University of Montana, Missoula
        Roses (mus. Rachmaninov) for Linda Shapiro, New Dance, Minneapolis
1991   *Double Bond* (mus. Elam), Rhode Island College, Providence
        Rubble Variations (mus. Soviet Army Chorus and Band, conducted by Colonel Alexandrov), solo, Bates Summer Dance Festival, Lewiston, Maine

Hurry Up, University of Minnesota, Minneapolis
Let's Get Busy (mus. Adams), American University, Washington, D.C.
1992   *Rubble Dance* (mus. Cole, Smith, Black), Dance Theatre Workshop
        Landing (mus. Lacy), Dance Theatre Workshop
        Skid (mus. Driscoll), Dance Theatre Workshop
        The Star Thrower (mus. Cimino), Greensboro, North Carolina
        Octopus (reset), Lincoln Center's Serious Fun
        Stucco Moon (mus. Ireland) for Shapiro, New Dance, Minneapolis
1993   *Rock Walk* (mus. Shehab), Urbana, Illinois
        Dance for a Past Time (mus. Vickery, Mustard, playing live) for Perth Institute of Contemporary Arts, Perth, Western Australia
        Tangling (mus. Pye), Edith Cowan University, Perth, Western Australia
        Pulcinella (reset; Stravinsky), Grand Théâtre de Bordeaux, France
        Empty Reel (mus. traditional Scottish) for Renée Wadleigh, Urbana, Illinois
1994   *Disappearances*, next to Marine Midland Bank, Broadway, Cedar & Liberty
        Dance for New Dances (video dance; mus. Quinlan), Minneapolis
1995   *Roses* (reset; mus. Rachmaninov)
        Lost in Light (mus. Fleming) for Dance Department, Denison University, Granville, Ohio
        Caracole (mus. Walton, Lawson), Dunn Studio
1996   *Spell for Opening the Mouth of N* w/Joshua Fried (mus. Fried; text Margraff), The Kitchen
        Return Dance (mus. Fried), trio, Princeton University Alumni Concert, New Jersey
1997   *Familial Fetches' Usufructuary Footfalls* (mus. collage by Dunn), solo, DixonPlace
        Riddance (mus. collage by Burckhardt), Taipei Theater

Publications

By DUNN: articles—

"Not Bad, Not Bad," *Eddy 3*, April 1974.
"Notes on Playing Myself," *Eddy 4*, Summer 1974.
"Words," [Fanny Logos], *Eddy 4*, Summer 1974.
"Talking Dancing," in *Merce Cunningham* by James Klosty, New York, 1975, 1986 also in Banes, Sally, *Terpischore in Sneakers: Post-Modern Dance*, Boston, 1980.
"Thirteen Replies for a Video Editorial," *Dance Scope 9*, Spring/ Summer 1975.
"Hide & Seek," [Fanny Logos], *Eddy 7*, Winter 1975-76.
"Interview," *Semiotext(e)*, vol III, no. 2, 1978.
"Dunn on Dancing," *Live Performance Art 4*, 1980.
"No Such Thing," and "The Heart of the Artist," *Dance Ink*, 1990.
"Sneakers," *Dance Ink*, 1993/4.
"Fearing," *Contact Quarterly,* 1994.
"Dear Friends," *Contact Quarterly*, 1995.
"Going Bird Meets Cougar-Asleep-on-Tree-Branch," *New Literary History*, 1995.
"I'm Dancing," in *Parallel Stances*, edited by Elena Alexander as part of the Critical Voices in Art series, 1998.

Douglas Dunn (lower left) and dancers, 1991. Photograph © Beatriz Schiller.

On DUNN: books—

Franko, Mark, *Dancing Modernism/Performing Politics*, Bloomington and Indianapolis, 1995.
Kostelanetz, Richard, *Merce Cunningham—Dancing in Space and Time, Essays 1944-1992*, Pennington, New Jersey, 1992.
Kreemer, Connie, *Further Steps: Fifteen Choreographers on Modern Dance*, New York, 1987.

On DUNN: articles—

Banes, Sally, "Review of *Gestures in Red*," *Chicago Reader*, 6 June 1975.
Calvetti, Paola, "Douglas Dunn," *Evidentidanza '81, Quaderni della Rassegna*, 1981.
Dunning, Jennifer, "His 'Conventional' Is Different," *New York Times*, 16 September 1979.
Draegin, Lois, "Face the Music and Dance," *Soho News*, 3 December 1980.
Goldner, Nancy, "Upstage and Downstage," *Soho News*, 30 April 1980.
Jowitt, Deborah, "Gestures Printed on Space," *Village Voice*, 26 May 1975.
———, "Douglas Dunn Makes Dance about Making up his Mind," *Village Voice*, 14 June 1976.

Siegel, Marcia, "Dunn Reposing," *Soho Weekly News*, 24 October 1974.
———, "Postmodern Patriarchs," *Hudson Review*, Autumn 1984.
———, "Free Standing Structures," *Hudson Review*, Summer 1988.
"Work-in-Progress Interview with Douglas Dunn, Jeffrey Schiff and John Driscoll," *Art & Dance*, Boston, 1982.

Films and Videotapes

Mayonnaise—Part I, film with Charles Atlas, 1972.
101, film by Amy Greenfield, 1974.
Solo Film & Dance, incorporated *Mayonnaise—Part I* and *101*, Oberlin Dance Collective, San Francisco, 1977.
Secret of the Waterfall, originally commissioned by Susan Dowling for New Television Workshop, WGBH-TV Boston, shot on Martha's Vineyard, 1982.
The Myth of Modern Dance, video-dance, PBS' *Alive from Off-Center*, 1990
Rubble Dance, Long Island City (mus. Bill Cole), directed/edited by Rudy Burckhardt, Long Island City, 1991.

*   *   *

In a 1997 letter to friends, Douglas Dunn offered a key to his choreography, writing that his "dancing can be looked at on a continuum with other, non-theatrical things. It has rhythm, texture, variations in tempo, and is suggestive, both by intent and by the near impossibility of doing anything with the body that doesn't provoke an association, of the sights and scenes of everyday life." Clearly "suggestive" of the world around them, Dunn's dances draw on familiar experience, physical and emotional. Quoting again from the letter, "the difference between what's on stage and what's not is the former's higher degree of concentration of the elements, their arrangement, providing opportunity for attentive meditation and response." His works are composed of "concentrated" morsels of experience, collected, collaged, juxtaposed, or strung together, but inevitably performed with uninhibited ease. For his company, Dunn seeks out dancers who look natural in almost any context, from the most formal and stylized, to the most casual and mundane. In fact, in any Dunn dance, the performers assume a variety of personas, from "people on the street" to radiant, graceful, and technically articulate dancers. This is how Dunn himself appears in his work: a mutable being aware of and adapting to new circumstances. For him, choreographing is a process of noticing the new in the familiar, and of recognizing a fresh coherence among experiences.

Perpetually drawn to the physical and the intellectual, in his work Dunn attempts to balance these aspects of himself and to explore his relationship to dance, as a dancer and as a mover. These themes resonate in his life as well. For example, tennis and basketball were Dunn's first physical outlets; he did not begin dancing until his junior year at Princeton University, when he was convinced by a professor to take classes at the nearby Princeton Ballet Society. After graduating from Princeton in 1964, he moved to New York City intending to dance and earn a master's degree from the New School in the psychology of art. To support himself, he worked full-time as a welfare caseworker in the Bronx, while he studied ballet at the Joffrey School. Tiring of this hectic city life, and unsure about his future as a professional dancer, Dunn took a job at the Gunnery School in Connecticut, where he taught English and Spanish and coached sports— occasionally performing in ballets presented in Hartford, Connecticut.

After three years at the Gunnery, Dunn moved back to New York City in the summer of 1968. He began studying Merce Cunningham technique with Margaret Jenkins and at the Cunningham School. In a September 1979 *New York Times* article Dunn revealed that this introduction to the ideas of Merce Cunningham "immediately changed [his] life." Dunn was impressed with Cunningham's straightforward approach to dance training—"with the lack of. . .irrelevant talking in class"—and his workmanlike attitude toward the creative process. Cunningham established for Dunn that dancing could be about itself, not the embodiment of a narrative subtext, but about the body moving in time and space. In 1969, after approximately a year at the studio, he joined the Merce Cunningham Dance Company.

Dunn's new consciousness about dance coincided with the experimentation of a generation of performers who, in the 1960s, had taken inspiration from Cunningham and John Cage, and were push-

ing beyond even their pragmatic notions of dance and composition. Many of them studied composition with iconoclast Robert Dunn. In 1969, Yvonne Rainer, an artist on the vanguard of this trend, asked Dunn to participate in her *Continuous Project—Altered Daily*, an improvisatory piece which evolved between 1969 and 1970. Collaboration on Rainer's project spawned a collective of choreographer/performers who called themselves "the Grand Union," including Dunn, Becky Arnold, David Gordon, Barbara Lloyd (Dilley), Steve Paxton, Trisha Brown, and Rainer. The participants in Grand Union were most interested in investigating artistic choices made in the moment of performance; they performed without rehearsals.

Traces of Dunn's experiences with Cunningham, and with Grand Union, appear in his choreography; nevertheless, it does not look derivative. Like Cunningham, he is interested in line, shape, movement quality, dimensionality in space, attention to time—all concerns which are particular to the dance medium. However, unlike Cunningham, he does not consistently impose chance procedures on the choreographic process. Instead, the forms of his dances evolve through attempting each time to vary the choreographic process. Often, Dunn collects material for choreography by observing actual human behavior. The form and content of his work evolve as he discovers new constellations of these everyday experiences. Thus the spontaneity which characterizes Dunn's work is an effect of this impromptu creative process, which eventually leads to set material. Although Dunn does not collaborate with the members of his company on the invention of movement, he draws ideas from the potential of his dancers, especially those with whom he has had a long working relationship. He often collaborates with other artists including: musicians Robert Ashley, Bill Cole, John Driscoll, Linda Fisher, Joshua Fried, Steve Lacy, and Alvin Lucier; poets Anne Waldman and Reed Bye; designer and composer David Ireland; lighting designer Carol Mullins; designer Mimi Gross; and film- and videomakers Charles Atlas and Rudy Burckhardt.

An adventurous and inexhaustible master of movement and situation invention, Dunn makes dances which consistently evade those who wish to define their style or method. In fact, his work is best known for its plain challenge to audience expectations. However, his work can be seen in terms of phases, which sometimes overlap, each defined by a central artistic inquiry. In his early work, he examined thematic extremes such as movement and stillness, and the social situation of the performance. Dunn's formal concerns appear in *Foot Rules* (1979) and *Skid* (1981), and were combined with poetry in *Secret of the Waterfall* (1983). Persona is investigated in *Matches* (1988) and *Unrest* (1990). Premodern Western and ethnic/tribal music influenced Dunn's conception of *Gondolages* (1988), *Haole* (1988), *Sky Eye* (1989), and *Roses* (1990). He experimented with a large scale in *Rubble Dance, Long Island* City (1991), *Stucco Moon* (1992) and *Spell for Opening the Mouth of N* (1996), and cultivated the potential of individual performers in more intimate works such as *Caracole* (1995) and *Haole* (1988), a solo.

—Rebekah J. Kowal

EARLE, David

Canadian dancer, choreographer, artistic director, and educator

Born: Charles David Ronald Earle, 17 September 1939 in Toronto, Ontario. **Education:** Studied ballet with Fanny Birdsall and Beth Weyms; studied acting/performance at Toronto Children's Players with Dorothy Goulding, Toronto; attended Ryerson Institute of Technology, radio and television arts major, Toronto, 1957-59; trained at the National Ballet School of Canada Professional Program, 1959-63; trained with Nancy Schwenker, Shirley Cash, and Donald Himes; studied modern dance with Yoné Kvietys, Toronto, 1960-63; Martha Graham, José Limón, Louis Horst, and Donald McKayle, New York; Betty Jones at Connecticut College, New London, 1963; Bertram Ross, Yuriko, Helen McGehee, and Gene MacDonald at Martha Graham School of Contemporary Dance, New York, 1963-65. **Career:** First choreography, 1963; dancer, José Limón Dance Company, New York, 1965-66; dancer, choreographer, and assistant artistic director to Robert Cohan, London Contemporary Dance Theatre, London, 1966-68; cofounder with Patricia Beatty and Peter Randazzo, Toronto Dance Theatre (TDT) and School of Toronto Dance Theatre, Toronto, 1968; first solo concert of works, 1975; founder, School of Toronto Dance Theatre Professional Training Program, 1979; artistic director, TDT, 1987-94; resident choreographer, 1994-95; artist-in-residence, 1996; founder, Dance Foundation David Earle and Dancetheatre David Earle, Elora, Ontario, 1997; taught at Ballet Rambert, London School of Contemporary Dance, Canadian Children's Dance Theatre Summer School, fringe Festival of Independent Dance, Université du Québec à Montréal and L'École superieure de danse du Québec, Danse Partout, Banff School of the Arts, Main Dance Place Professional Program, Victoria Arts Collaborative, Stages Performing Arts School, Suddenly Dance Theatre, Southern Methodist University, (Dallas), New York University. **Awards:** Dance Ontario Award (with Patricia Beatty and Peter Randazzo), 1982; Clifford E. Lee Award (Banff Festival of the Arts), 1987; Dora Mavor Moore Award for new choreography (Toronto Theatre Alliance), 1987; Toronto Arts Award for performing arts (with Patricia Beatty and Peter Randazzo), 1988; Grand Prix International de Video-danse de Sete Press Award (France), 1990; Gemini Award, 1990; Jean A. Chalmers Award for distinction in choreography, 1994; the Order of Canada, 1997; funding grants from Canada Council, Ontario Arts Council and Toronto Arts Council.

Roles (original cast roles with Toronto Dance Theatre unless otherwise noted)

1963	*Evolutions* (Yoné Kvietys), Canadian Modern Dance Festival, Toronto

	City's Stroke (Yoné Kvietys), Canadian Modern Dance Festival, Toronto
1965	Ensemble, *My Son, My Enemy* (José Limón), José Limón Dance Company, New York
1967	*Sky* (Robert Cohan), London Contemporary Dance Theatre, London
	Fragments (Peter Randazzo), New Dance Group of Canada, Toronto
	Head Witch, *Momentum* (Patricia Beatty), New Dance Group of Canada, Toronto
	Heritage (Cynthia Barrett Newman), New Dance Group of Canada, Toronto
1968	*Against Sleep* (Beatty)
1969	*Continuum* (Randazzo)
	I Had Two Sons (Randazzo)
1970	*Voyage for Four Male Dancers* (Randazzo)
	Hot and Cold Heroes (Beatty)
1972	*The Amber Garden* (Randazzo)
	Los Sencillos (Beatty)
1974	*The Letter* (Randazzo)
1975	*The Reprieve* (Beatty)
1977	*A Simple Melody* (Randazzo)
1979	*The Light Brigade* (Randazzo)
1980	*Lessons in Another Language* (Beatty)
	Skyling (Beatty)

Other roles include: Performed roles in *Missa Brevis* and *A Choreographic Offering* (chor. Limón), José Limón Dance Company, New York, 1965-56; and solos (cr) in own works from 1963.

Works (for Toronto Dance Theatre, premiering in Toronto, unless otherwise noted)

1963	*Recitative and Aria* (mus. Michael Kearns), Contemporary Dance Yoné Kvietys, Toronto
1967	*Witness of Innocence* (mus. Grazyna Vacewicz), London Contemporary Dance Theatre, London
	Angelic Visitation #1 (mus. Frank Martin), New Dance Group of Canada, Toronto
1968	*The Recitation* (mus. Ann Southam), *Dance Concert,* Toronto
	Angelic Visitation #2 (mus. Ned Rorem, Donald Himes), *Dance Concert,* Toronto
	Mirrors (mus. Bach)
1969	*Lovers* (mus. Ned Rorem)
	Fire in the Eye of God (mus. Dudley James)
	A Thread of Sand (mus. Southam)
1970	*Operetta* (mus. Beethoven), Guelph, Ontario
	Portrait (mus. baroque arr. by Southam)
1971	*Balleto al Mio Bel Suon* (mus. Monteverdi), Guelph Spring Festival, Guelph, Ontario

Legend (mus. Southam)

The Silent Feast (mus. Robert Daigneault)

1972   *Boat, River, Moon* (mus. Southam)

Baroque Suite (includes *Mirrors* [mus. Bach, 1968], *Lyrical Solo* [mus. Pachelbel], *Duet* [mus. Corelli], *Lament* [mus. Pachelbel], *Finale* [mus. Vivaldi])

1973   *Christmas Concerto* (ensemble reworking of *Baroque Suite Duet* [1972]; mus. Corelli)

Ray Charles Suite (mus. Ray Charles)

Atlantis (mus. Robert Daigneault,)

1974   *Bugs* (mus. Robert Daigneault), Guelph Spring Festival, Guelph, Ontario

Parade (mus. Satie), Camerata Music Ensemble, Toronto

1975   *La Belle Époque* (includes *Waltz Suite* [mus. Schubert], *Deux Epigraphes Antiques* [mus. Debussy], *L'Hôtel Splendide* [mus. Fauré], and *Vignette* [mus. Satie]), Camerata Music Ensemble, Toronto

Field of Dreams (mus. Robert Daigneault), Ottawa, Ontario

1976   *Quartet* (mus. Michael Conway Baker), London, Ontario

1977   *Fauré's Requiem* (mus. Fauré), Festival Singers of Canada, Toronto

Mythos (mus. David Akal Jaggs)

1978   *Courances* (mus. Michael Conway Baker)

Raven (mus. Michael J. Baker)

1979   *Sweet and Low Down* (mus. Gershwin)

The Wedding Duet (mus. Bach)

Coronation of a Boy King (mus. David Akal Jaggs), Opening of Tutankhamen Exhibition, Art Gallery of Ontario, Toronto

1980   *Courtyard* (mus. Ravel)

Akhenaten (reworking of *Coronation of a Boy King*, mus. David Akal Jaggs)

Chiaroscuro w/Graham Jackson (includes *La Bilancia* [mus. David Passmore], *Frost Watch* [misc. spoken text], and *Emozioni* [mus. Mina arr. by Michael J. Baker]), *An Evening of Dance the Word*, Toronto

Moonchase (mus. Debussy)

Exit, Nightfall (mus. Bach, Iannis Xenakis, Gregorio Allegri, Kirk Elliott)

Journey (mus. Marsha Coffey), Bloor St. United Church for Amnesty International, Toronto

Baroque Suite (includes *Duet* [mus. Corelli], *Mirrors* [mus. Bach], and a reworked *Finale* [mus. Vivaldi])

1981   *All the Books in Heaven* w/Graham Jackson (mus. Finzi)

1982   *Ormai* w/Graham Jackson (mus. Mina), *A Moveable Feast*

Dido and Aeneas w/James Kudelka, Christopher House, Phyllis Whyte, Kenny Pearl (mus. Purcell), Stratford Summer Music Festival, Stratford, Ontario

1983   *Realm* (mus. Kirk Elliott, David Akal Jaggs, traditional international folk music), the National Ballet of Canada, Toronto

Court of Miracles w/Carol Anderson, James Kudelka, Peter Randazzo and Christopher House (mus. medieval and Renaissance)

1984   *Cape Eternity* (mus. Milton Barnes), Toronto International Festival, Toronto

Sacra Conversazione (mus. Mozart), Banff Festival of the Arts, Banff, Alberta

Orpheus and Eurydice (mus. Glück), Guelph Spring Festival, Guelph, Ontario

1985   *Emotional Geography* (mus. Bach)

1986   *Sacred Garden* (mus. Pergolesi)

Studies in a Southern Light (mus. Ibert), School of TDT

1987   *Sunrise* (mus. Brahms)

Cloud Garden (mus. trad. Japanese), Banff Festival of the Arts, Banff, Alberta

1988   *Palace of Pleasure* (mus. baroque collage)

Chichester Psalms (mus. Bernstein), Canadian Children's Dance Theatre, Toronto

1989   *El Amor Brujo* (mus. de Falla), Music at Sharon Festival, Sharon, Ontario

Scheherazade w/James Kudelka (mus. Rimsky-Korsakov), Les Grands Ballets Canadiens, Montreal

1990   *Quodlibet* w/David Earle and Christopher House (*Romance* [mus. Bach], *Autumn Leaves* [mus. Ellington], *Capriccio* [mus. Bach], *Scherzo* [mus. Schumann], *Debate* [mus. Cage])

Openings and Inventions (mus. Bach), School of TDT

Dreamsend (mus. Webern)

Triumph of Love (mus. Bach)

Two Renaissance Songs w/Christopher House (*Sacred Garden* [mus. Pergolesi] *Zefiro Torna* [mus. Monteverdi])

1991   *Ancient Voices of Children* (mus. George Crumb), Chamber Concerts Canada, Buffalo, New York

"The Voice of the Ancient Bard" (mus. Kirk Elliott) in *Songs of Innocence and of Experience*, Canadian Children's Dance Theatre, Toronto

1992   *Diving for the Moon* (mus. Rodney Sharman)

Untitled Monument (mus. Toru Takemitsu)

Rosa's Song (mus. Eleni Karaindrou), School of TDT

Visible Distance: A Bach Suite (mus. Bach), Ottawa

Architecture for the Poor (mus. Marjan Mozetich), Ballet British Columbia, Vancouver

Angels and Victories (mus. Valerie Ross), Polish Dance Theatre, Warsaw, Poland

"Undetermined Landscape" (mus. Pärt) duet, in *The Dance Goes On*, Benefit for Dancer Transition Resource Centre, Toronto

1993   *Clay Forest* (mus. Pärt), Ballet Creole, Toronto

The Painter's Dream (mus. Peter Landry), 25th Anniversary Celebration, Brock University, St. Catharines, Ontario

Between the Shadows and Light (mus. Rodney Sharman), Ontario Ballet Theatre, Toronto

Pillow of Grass (mus. Rodney Sharman), Suddenly Dance Theatre, Victoria, British Columbia

Errata w/D.A. Hoskins (mus. David Darling), Suddenly Dance Theatre, Victoria, British Columbia

Duet from the Bach B Minor Mass (mus. Bach), School of TDT

In November w/D.A. Hoskins (mus. William Burkhard, David Darling, Bach), School of TDT

1994   *Three Bach Solos* (mus. Bach) solo, Halifax, Nova Scotia

1995   *Furniture* (mus. Canadian composer miniatures), TDT and Arraymusic, Toronto

El Cachondeo (mus. David Keane), School of TDT

1996   *Elsewhere* (mus. Gyorgy Kurtag, Pärt), the Kiss Project, Vancouver

Maelstrom (mus. Arvo Pärt, Gyorgy Kurtag, Michael Thomas, Dmitri Yanov-Yanovsky, Zygmunt Krauze), Spring Rites, Toronto

Sang w/Sean Marye (mus. Bach)

1997   *Passions* w/Sean Marye, reworking of *Sang* (mus. Bach),
        Dance And Desire, Vancouver

        Walking in Venice I (mus. Schnittke), the Kiss Project,
        Vancouver, British Columbia

        Walking in Venice II (mus. Schnittke, Gavin Bryars,
        Damian le Gassick), Spring Rites, Toronto

        Last Hour of Light (Aleksander Lasson), Dancetheatre
        David Earle, Elora Festival, Elora, Ontario

        Danny Boy w/Sean Marye (mus. trad. Irish), Dancetheatre
        David Earle, Elora, Ontario

        Une Cantate de Noël (mus. Honegger), Canadian Children's
        Dance Theatre, Waterloo, Ontario

Publications

On EARLE: books—

Macpherson, Susan, editor, *101 From the Encyclopedia of Theatre
    Dance in Canada,* Toronto, 1997.

Wyman, Max, *Dance Canada: An Illustrated History,* Vancouver,
    1989.

On EARLE: articles—

Citron, Paula, "A Step Back to Move Forward: Transition at Toronto
    Dance Theatre," *Performing Arts* (Toronto), Summer 1983.

Jung, Daryl, "Songs of *Sang* Unleash Passions of David Earle," *NOW*
    (Toronto), 12 December 1996.

Littler, William, "Dancing a Hard Road," *Toronto Star,* 5 November
    1988.

Walker, Susan, "TDT Founder David Earle Steps Toward New
    Future," *Toronto Star,* 5 December 1996.

Films and Videotapes

Dance Class, dir. Joan Hansen, National Film Board of Canada, 1971.

Dance for Modern Times (film), dir. Moze Mossanen, CBC, 1988.

The Dancemakers, dir. Moze Mossanen, TV Ontario, 1988.

Dance Makes Wave (TV special), CBC, 1985.

The Day It Is, CBLT-TV, Toronto, 1969.

Gala (film), dir. John N. Smith, National Film Board of Canada, 1982.

Music to See (performing arts series), Canadian Broadcasting Cor-
    poration, 1977.

Original in Art, dir. Dan Robinson, Bravo! Network, 1995.

Performance, CBMT-TV, Ottawa, 1984.

A Personal Understanding of Death (educational documentary se-
    ries), dir. Daniel Berman, prod. Christa Singer, Sleeping Giant
    Productions, 1998.

Prokofiev by Two: Romeos and Juliets, dir. Barbara Willis Sweete,
    Rhombus Media, 1990.

Ravel (film), dir. Larry Weinstein, Rhombus Media, 1987.

Toronto Dance Theatre in England, CBC, 1973.

Toronto International Festival Opening Concert (TV special), CBC,
    1984.

*   *   *

David Earle is one of the most prolific, beloved, and honoured
choreographers in Canada, with works in the repertoire of contemporary dance and ballet companies across the country. The attraction of Earle's choreography is his compassion and humanity. He is
a true Renaissance man, blessed with a great intellect and spirituality. He is tremendously well-read and extremely knowledgeable
about art. Although commissioning original scores has played an
important part in his career, he has also used great works from the
classical music repertoire to inspire many of his choreographies.
His natural curiosity has also led him to collaborate with music
ensembles, poets, and actors, as well as opera and theatre companies. "An important influence has been Jean Cocteau and his belief
that art eludes definition and should be recognized as a pure experience," Earle told this author in an interview.

Earle studied radio and television arts in college, but he dropped
out after seeing a performance in Toronto of the Bolshoi Ballet in
1959; at age 19 he was determined to become a dancer. "The spiri-
tual-sexual-sensual connection is important to me," Earle explained,
"and dance is the medium of their fusion. Dance can't be repressed;
you must surrender to it because it is greater than the dancer. It is
the pure expression of truth." Earle became a scholarship student at
the professional program of the National Ballet School of Canada
(NBS) and, during the next four years, found a mentor in NBS
eurhythmics teacher Donald Himes who introduced him to the music
of great composers as well as modern dance. Himes performed in
the company of Yoné Kvietys, a Laban-based pioneer of contemporary dance in Toronto, and along with his ballet studies, Earle
took classes with Kvietys. "From the start," he says, "I had one
bare foot in modern and the other in ballet." In 1963 Earle danced
with Kvietys' company at the Canadian Festival of Modern Dance
in Toronto, which inspired him to take a summer course in modern
dance at Connecticut College.

While in Connecticut Earle fell under the spell of Martha Graham. That fall he moved to New York and enrolled at the Graham
School, pushing his ballet body through two years of transition to
become a modern dancer. At the school he met Peter Randazzo, a
company member who become his close companion, and Patricia
Beatty, a fellow student from Toronto. After a year dancing with
the Limón company, Earle went to London in 1966, where he assisted Robert Cohan at the London Contemporary Dance Theatre
and appeared in the company's first season as both a dancer and
choreographer. On a visit back to Toronto in 1967, he danced in the
first concert of Beatty's New Dance Group of Canada. The following year, the trio cofounded the Toronto Dance Theatre (TDT) and
its Graham-based school. In 1987 Earle became the sole artistic
director of the company, and in 1994 he assumed the position of
resident choreographer. In 1996 Earle left the company to pursue
freelance projects, and in 1997 he founded Dancetheatre David
Earle in Elora, Ontario, a quaint rural village an hour from Toronto
with a strong artistic community. He continues to criss-cross the
country giving classes and is considered one of the most inspirational modern dance teachers in Canada.

Earle claims that elements of fairy tales and the influence of
Martha Graham are in all his work. Fairy tales became ingrained in
his thought process when, as a child, he performed them as plays
with Toronto Children's Players in a repertoire that also included
legends and Greek myths. Graham's melding of myth and sexuality
has remained a lifelong influence. "Graham's technique was created
for the recovery of instinct," he says. "I chose instinctual nature
over conscious nature as the basis for my choreography." A significant number of Earle's works deal with themes of death. Earle
believes the roots of this darkness grew out of an incident that
happened during the war years. Because he was an impressionable
child with an with an active, sensual imagination, the terrifying

spectacle of Mussolini being burned in effigy in a public park has remained an engraved image in his mind. This morbid streak is manifested by a collection of pictures and photographs depicting the dark side of human nature that Earle, a self-declared "image addict," keeps in notebooks. In fact, when he is rehearsing a work, he collects images to illustrate his themes, which he shows to the dancers as a stimulant to emotion. He is also inspired by the dancers he works with, using their unique forms of expression as choreographic tools.

To try to pigeonhole Earle's themes is impossible because his interests range far and wide, making him an eclectic and versatile choreographer. Among the scores of works he has choreographed, several characteristic types can be discerned. He has created dances of shimmering beauty inspired by Japanese and Eastern cultures (*Boat, River, Moon,* 1972); intense works about archetypes, ritual, and mythology (*Atlantis,* 1973); whimsically humorous pieces (*Bugs,* 1974); pure dance works inspired by music (*Baroque Suite,* 1980); magnificent choral movement symphonies which are overtly emotional and profoundly spiritual (*Sacra Conversazione,* 1984); works that focus on the dark bond between death and sexuality (*Dreamsend,* 1990); and vivid narrative portrayals of the human condition (*Maelstrom,* 1996). The one constant, whether in solo or group work, is his beautifully crafted choreography, impeccable in design and structure. He is considered an architect of dance whose vision encompasses the broadest horizon of what is possible on a stage, and he is much admired for his finesse at moving large numbers of dancers through space. A particular signature of Earle's choreography, which became the basic building tool of his ensemble pieces, emerged after reworking *Baroque Suite Duet* (1972) into the larger ensemble piece *Christmas Concerto* (1973). In this work his out-of-phase, random canon has all the dancers performing the same movement patterns, but not in unison.

In the late 1990s subtle shifts occurred in Earle's choreography. He began to be less conscious of having themes and more prone to view dance as a visual art form. Earle, a photographer of note whose laminated-on-wood photographs have been exhibited in galleries, has been particularly influenced by the photographic medium. "Photography has infused my choreography," he says. "Cropping and framing a picture has taught me different ways of using my eye." In this latter phase of his career, Earle was also increasingly drawn to more modern, discordant, 20th-century music, and his dance vocabulary was modified. *Walking in Venice* (1997), for example, is radically different from Earle's previous works because it is extremely physical, a result of his experimenting with producing original sculptural forms. Whether this trend will take Earle away from his theatrical, lyrical, and emotional trademark dances remains to be seen. "I have always been in fashion because I made a choice to remain out of fashion," he says. "I never succumbed to postmodernisms. Dance for me will always be three-dimensional architecture. I will always preserve the ideals of dance."

—Paula Citron

EDAM PERFORMING ARTS SOCIETY

Canadian dance company

EDAM stands for Experimental Dance and Music; collective formed in Vancouver, British Columbia, 1982; founding members were six

independent dancer/choreographers and one musician: Peter Bingham, Barbara Bourget, Ahmed Hassan (the sole musician), Jay Hirabayashi, Lola MacLaughlin, Jennifer Mascall, and Peter Ryan; had four artistic directors by 1987; Bingham became sole artistic director in 1989; based at the Western Front Lodge since its origination.

*   *   *

From its formation, EDAM has been an adventurous company committed to experimentation, collaboration, and presenting improvisation as an art form. The casual evenings of dance at their studio at the Western Front Lodge continue to be an important testing ground for the community's dance ideas, as do the more polished shows at several small theaters around town. Even in the latter case, however, it would not be unusual to find company members warming up on stage as the audience is seated.

A spirit of adventure was perhaps the cohesive force for the disparate founding group of independent creators, whose variety of dance backgrounds included ballet, modern, and contact improvisation. At that time, with funding for independents still in its early days, banding together was also one way to survive. Certainly, the company's early mandate to provide a flexible structure to support and promote individual and group projects reflected a need for both individual expression and group support.

Programs in the first years, with all seven members jostling for space, were made up of individual choreographies and structured improvisations by various members of the group, with the occasional guest artist; these were usually danced by the company with musicians and other dancers brought in as needed. An example of a typical mixed bill was offered at the Firehall Theater in 1984. Bingham and Mascall contributed a playful improvisation and Mascall remounted *True Lies* (1983), while Bourget premiered *Four Women,* Ryan contributed *Scripts* (1978), and frequent guest artist and contact improvisation's founder, Steve Paxton, contributed *Jag Ville Görna Telefonera* (1964).

Under a sole directorship, EDAM has continued to offer truly mixed evenings of dance by encouraging the participation of local choreographers. *Forced Issues,* begun in the late 1980s, was a series of informal evenings held at the Western Front that included works in progress and pieces by experienced as well as novice choreographers. This evolved in 1994 to *Other Issues,* a showcase for finished works, performed over three weekends.

Collaboration has always been at the core of EDAM's creativity, both within the company and with a variety of guest artists. Their first major collaboration as a group, *Run Raw: Theme and Variations,* at the Western Front in 1983, was an attempt to capture the excitement of competitive sports in dance. To prepare for the physical extreme they wanted to show, the company alternated dance class with circuit training, weight lifting, high jumping, and gymnastics. The result was an interweaving dance of colliding, dashing, sliding, and panting, pushed to such an extreme that in performance one dancer ended up with a broken arm and another with an injured ankle.

Some of the major collaborative works initiated and choreographed by present artistic director Bingham are *Critical Mass* (1989), with poet Gerry Gilbert and musician Jeff Corness; *Dreamtigers* (1992), with artist Mona Hamill, photographer Chris Randle, and a trio of jazz musicians; *Remember Me from Then* (1996), co-choreographed with Ballet British Columbia's artistic director, John Alleyne; and *Born Naked, Died Blonde: Our Roots Exposed* (1996), a culmination of eight years of collaboration between Bingham and jazz composer/musicians Coat Cooke and Ron Samworth, with five dancers and the live 10-piece NOW** Orchestra.

The company under Bingham has a changing roster of dancers, who usually have backgrounds in modern dance and ballet, though they train together in contact improvisation, which forms the distinctive basis for much of their work. The touch and tumble of contact has always been the core of Bingham's work, although modern and ballet techniques were added under the influence of EDAM's cofounders and can be evidenced in the choreographed pieces Bingham began creating in 1983.

EDAM's influence on the Vancouver dance scene is significant. Aside from its work as a presenter, the style and dynamics of contact improvisation—the part of EDAM's aesthetic that has consistently impressed critics and audiences from the beginning—can be seen in much local work. Founding members who have gone on to form their own Vancouver-based companies are Bourget and Hirabayashi (Kokoro Dance), MacLaughlin (Lola MacLaughlin Dance), and Mascall (Mascall Dance).

EDAM has toured Canada four times and performs regularly at the Canada Dance Festival in Ottawa. Since its inception, the company has received municipal, provincial, and federal funding.

—Kaija Pepper

EIKO & KOMA
Japanese-born American dancers and choreographers

Born: Eiko Otake, 14 February 1952 in Tokyo, Japan; Koma Takashi Yamada, 27 September 1948 in Niigita, Japan. **Family:** Married to each other; two sons. **Education:** Studied Butoh with Tatsumi Hijikata, Tokyo, 1971, with Kazuo Ohno, 1972; studied with Manja Chmiel, Germany, 1972. **Career:** Danced and choreographed together since 1971; moved from Tokyo to Amsterdam, 1973; toured Europe and Africa; first appeared in New York in 1976 and have since settled there. **Awards:** John Simon Guggenheim Fellowship, 1984; New York Dance and Performance Awards ("Bessies") for *Grain* and *Night Tide*, 1984, for *Passage*, 1990; MacArthur Fellowship, 1996.

Works (performed by Eiko & Koma unless otherwise noted)

1976	*White Dance* (mus. medieval, Bach), Japan Society, New York
1977	*Fur Seal* (mus. Schubert, Hovhannes, Beatles), Riverside Dance Festival, New York
1978	*Before the Cock Crows* (mus. Near Eastern), Dance Theatre Workshop, New York
1979	*Fluttering Black* (mus. Glenn Branca), Performing Garage, New York
	Trilogy: Fission (mus. Andean folk), Dance Umbrella Festival, New York
1980	*Trilogy: Cell* (mus. Andean folk), Oberlin College
1981	*Trilogy: Entropy* (mus. Andean folk), Los Angeles Institute of Contemporary Art

	Nurse's Song (mus. Allen Ginsberg, poem by William Blake), The Kitchen, New York
1983	*Beam* (mus. Asian folk; harmonium played by Eiko), American Dance Festival, Durham, North Carolina
	Grain (mus. Japanese, Tibetan, and Indonesian folk), Kampo Cultural Center, New York
1984	*Night Tide*, Dance Theatre Workshop, New York
	Elegy, American Dance Festival, Durham, North Carolina
1985	*Thirst* (no mus.), Dance Theatre Workshop, New York
1986	*By the River*, Massachusetts College of Art, Boston
	Broken Pieces (mus. Sarangi), CoDanceCo, Dance Theatre Workshop, New York
	Shadows (performed with *Beam*, *Night Tide*, and *Elegy* as *New Moon Stories*), Next Wave Festival, Brooklyn Academy of Music
1988	*Tree*, Next Wave Festival, Brookly Academy of Music
1989	*Canal* (mus. Los Jaivas), Southern Theatre, Minneapolis
	Rust, American Dance Festival, Durham, North Carolina
	Memory (mus. Deuter), New Lex Theatre, Lexington, New York
	Passage, Painted Bride Art Center, Philadelphia
1991	*Land* (mus. Robert Mirabal), Next Wave Festival, Brooklyn Academy of Music
1993	*Wind* (mus. Mirabal and Eiko & Koma), performed with Yuta Otake, Hennepin Center for the Performing Arts, Minneapolis
1994	*Dream* (mus. John Gibson), Dance Alloy Company, Pittsburgh
	Distant (mus. Ushio Tomikai), solo for Koma, New Lex Theatre, New Lexington, New York
1995	*River* (outdoor version; mus. Japanese traditional), w/ Judd Weisberg, Art Awareness, Lexington, New York
	Echo (mus. Japanese traditional), Japan Society, New York
1997	*River* (proscenium version; mus. Somei Satoh), Lafayette College, Easton, Pennsylvania
1998	*Breath*, Whitney Museum of American Art, New York

Publications

On EIKO & KOMA: articles—

Aloff, Mindy, "Eiko & Koma," *The Nation*, 14 June 1986.

Horn, Laurie, "*Grain* Deeply Felt, Hauntingly Beautiful," *Miami Herald*, 13 December 1986.

———, "Profound Minimalism from Koma & Eiko," *Miami Herald*, 5 March 1990.

Howell, John, "The Slow Beauty of Eiko & Koma," *Newsday*, 5 April 1990.

Hunter, Susan, "Eiko & Koma Personify Anguish in *By the River*," *Atlanta Constitution*, 20 March 1989.

Kaliss, Jeff, "Japanese Body English," *San Francisco Chronicle*, 16 June 1991.

Kriegsman, Alan, "The Clinging Creations of Eiko & Koma," *Washington Post*, 20 November 1989.

Segal, Lewis, "*Dance Park* Series," *Los Angeles Times*, 31 July 1985.

Smith, Helen, "Eiko & Koma Will Splash around at Dance Festival," *Atlanta Constitution*, 27 May 1989.

Sommers, Pamela, "Dance Place: Eiko & Koma," *Washington Post*, 23 October 1987.

———, "Eiko & Koma: Dynamic Duo," *The Washington Post*, 6 March 1992.

Eiko and Koma: *Tree,* 1988. Photograph © Johan Elbers.

Temin, Christine, "New Eiko & Koma Work Tedious Yet Enthralling," *Boston Globe,* 14 June 1986.

Films and Videotapes

Tentacle, ARC Videodance, New York, 1983.
Wallow, ARC Videodance, New York, 1984.
Bone Dream, ARC Videodance, New York, 1985.
Lament, with filmmaker James Byrne, Walker Art Center, 1986.
Husk, 1987.
Undertow, with filmmaker James Byrne, 1988.

*   *   *

Eiko and Koma are co-choreographers and performers of minimalist duets, influenced both by the Japanese avant-garde dance form Butoh and the German Expressionist dance of Mary Wigman. Their works are characterized by ultra-slow movements and focus on humanity's universal struggle to survive.

Eiko Otake was born in Tokyo in 1952 and her husband, Koma Takashi Yamada, was born in 1948 in Niigita, Japan. They met in 1971, while they were both studying with the founders of Butoh, Kazuo Ohno and Tatsumi Hijikata. Eiko and Koma spent the next five years traveling through the Soviet Union and living in the Netherlands and in Germany, where they studied with Wigman disciple Manja Chmiel. In 1976 the couple moved to New York, staging their U.S. premiere, *White Dance,* three months later. They have remained in New York ever since, performing there and touring throughout the U.S., including Chicago, Atlanta, Los Angeles, and the Jacob's Pillow Dance Festival, with which they have a long relationship.

Eiko and Koma's performances, which are often categorized as performance art or dance-theater rather than modern dance, are rooted in the traditions of German Expressionism as well as in Butoh. The latter, a Japanese art form that originated after World War II as a response to Hiroshima, is anti-Western and thoroughly pessimistic. The couple's work differs somewhat from Butoh in that it incorporates some Western themes and contains an optimistic outlook, although it is still very dark. In fact, Eiko and Koma separate themselves from Butoh, and refer to their technique, which they teach in New York studios and at universities, as "Delicious Movement."

The most obvious characteristic of their choreography, which it has in common with Butoh, is the excruciatingly slow movement,

Eiko and Koma: *By the River,* **1987. Photograph © Beatriz Schiller.**

performed with precision, tension, control, concentration, devotion, and sustained energy, sometimes for more than an hour at a time. It can take several minutes to move an inch or two. The technique has been described as hypnotic or mesmerizing, allowing the mind to empty and receive disparate images. While many audiences and critics appreciate this Zen-like quality, others find the pieces tedious.

Eiko and Koma manipulate the sense of time during the course of their works, making some long pieces, such as the 50-minute *Fur Seal*, seem to speed by, while shorter pieces, such as the 15-minute *Beam*, seem epic. Jack Anderson, writing about their performance at the 1983 American Dance Festival, said, "Usually, the two dancers slow time down; but even when they moved quickly during their performance, they moved in a time scheme different from that of everyday reality. They rearranged time to suit their own creative purposes."

The duo's work is often described as primal, natural, and organic, and the movement frequently takes place in an environment that represents the natural world. Fabric backdrops resembling landscapes, pools of water (or in one case, an actual river), and sand or rice grains on stage support this natural atmosphere, as do the performers' long, unruly hair and frequent habit of performing in the nude. There is a sexual element to many of their works, usually depicted as a separation followed by a brief coming together, bringing relief and then further separation.

Within each piece, their bodies can seem to represent shapes within the landscape, humanoid figures, or animals. They can assume grotesque shapes, or can accentuate the beauty of the body within its natural environment. The shape of the body is highlighted dramatically through the use of film-noir style lighting that sculpts the muscles. Their works are generally performed to minimalist music. Native American flute and drums, sound effects, or grunting noises made by the duo are all used as accompaniment. Early in their careers, Eiko and Koma tended to work with classical or folk music, but, increasingly, segments of pieces or entire works are performed in silence.

Their work is meant to be ambiguous, resulting in different meanings for each individual watching a performance. The pieces lack a climax and it can be difficult to discern their meaning. Critics find Eiko and Koma's work enigmatic, describing it as tedious yet enthralling, minimalist yet profound, horrifying yet beautiful, specific yet universal, neutral yet expressive, and detached yet personal.

Eiko and Koma have collaborated almost exclusively on duets for themselves (with occasional appearances by their two young sons) since 1972. Infrequently, another group, such as New York's CoDanceCo, may perform their works, or they may collaborate with another group, as they did with the Chanticleer choir of San Francisco in 1991. The couple has created more than 20 works in two decades of performing. The titles of their works are in keeping with their minimalist outlook: *Tentacle, Bone Dream, Lament, Thirst, Memory, Wind*, and *Grain*.

Some of their pieces have been filmed, such as *Lament*, an eight-minute collaboration with filmmaker James Byrne, and some of their on-stage performances contain filmed elements, such as flickering objects projected onto a fabric backdrop in *By the River*, and a film by Dave Geary showing the couple dancing which is interwoven into *Passage*.

Eiko and Koma's works focus on the human soul and how it endures, survives, and even prevails in the face of a hostile environment. "The world of Eiko & Koma is a pitiless one, but it's never stagey or contrived," writes critic Alan Kriegsman. "The power of their work derives, aside from the prodigious muscular and rhythmic control of the performances, from the uncompromising purity of their vision." Dance reviewer Susan Hunter adds, "It's hard to know what all this means, and the metaphysical theater of Eiko and Koma can be tedious and painful. Yet, for all its anguish, there's a serenity to the vision, a completeness, that is satisfying and unexpectedly beautiful."

—Karen Raugust

EILBER, Janet

American dancer, choreographer, company director, and actress

Born: 27 July 1952 in Detroit. **Education:** Interlochen Center for the Arts, graduated 1969; Juilliard School of Music, B.F.A. in dance 1973; apprentice, Martha Graham school and studio. **Family:** Married to screenwriter John Warren; children: two daughters. **Career:** Principal soloist, Martha Graham Dance Company, 1972-80, 1985, 1993-94; co-founder and co-director, American Repertory Dance Theater, from 1994; guest appearances, American Dance Machine, Joffrey Ballet, and on Broadway; has also appeared on television and in films, including roles in the television series *This Is Kate Bennett, Two Marriages,* and *The Best Times;* has taught at Paris Opera Ballet, American Dance Festival, Interlochen Arts Academy, Los Angeles High School for the Performing Arts, California State University, Martha Graham School for Contemporary Dance. **Awards:** Two Lester Horton Awards for production and performing for the reconstruction *The Weeping Women in Dance,* 1995.

Roles (choreographed by Martha Graham for the Martha Graham Dance Company unless otherwise noted)

1971	*Revel* (Limón)
1974	*Holy Jungle*
1975	*Point of Crossing*
	Adorations
	The Scarlet Letter
	Partner, *Lamentation*
	Point of Crossing
1977	*Shadows*
1978	*Flute of Pan*
1980	Lead dancer, *Dancin'* (Broadway)
	Lead dancer, *Swing* (Broadway)
1981	Lead dancer, *The Little Prince* (Broadway)
1987	Lead dancer, *Stepping Out* (Broadway)
1986	*The Stab* (Susana Tambutti)

Other roles include: Pioneer Woman, *Appalachian Spring, Day on Earth, Deaths and Entrances, Deep Song, Diversion of Angels, Frontier, Lucifer, Plain of Prayer* and *Seraphic Dialogues* for the Graham company; *Wing* (Limón), *Little Me* and *Cabaret* for Broadway; *Saturday's Child* (Donald McKayle), *Debut at the Opera* (Agnes de Mille), *Satyric Festival Song*, a solo performance at BAM's Next Wave Festival.

Janet Eilber in Martha Graham's *Satyric Festival Song.* **Photograph © Nan Melville, 1998.**

Works

1979   *Through the Looking Glass* (mus. Deems Taylor), Eilber
        w/Midland Symphony
1984   *Stalkings* (mus. tape collage of sexist commercials), Peggy
        Lyman Dance Company
1990   *Gift Rap* (mus. Michael Silversher), Encino Players
1991   *The Point* (mus. Nilsson), Los Angeles
1992   *Feiffer's Dancer* (no mus.), solo
        Just So (mus. Bobby McFerrin), Los Angeles Chamber
        Ballet
1993   *anyone lived in a pretty how town* (mus. Allen Krantz),
        Mount Gretna Festival
1994   *Face 2 Face* (mus. Silversher), Los Angeles Repertory
        Company
        Now I Become Myself (mus. Allen Krantz), Mount Gretna
        Festival
1995   *Advice to the Players* (mus. Allen Krantz), Mount Gretna
        Festival

Publications

On EILBER: books—

Coe, Robert, *Dance in America*, New York, 1985.
Croce, Arlene, *Afterimages*, New York, 1977.
McNeil, Alex, *Total Television*, New York, 1996.
Willis, J., ed., *Dance World*, New York, 1966-79.

On EILBER: articles—

O'Neill, Kate, "Interlochen Center for the Arts," *Dance Magazine*,
    January 1997.
Perlmutter, Donna, "Los Angeles Dance Theatre," *Dance Magazine*,
    July 1995.

Films and Videotapes (featuring Eilber)

Antigone: Rights of Passion, video written, produced and directed
    by Amy Greenfield, 1992.
Appalachian Spring, *Great Performances: Dance in America*, PBS,
    1975.
Hard to Hold, MCA, 1984.
Mighty Joe Young, 1997.
Romantic Comedy, MGM/Fox, 1983.
Whose Life Is It Anyway?, MGM, 1981.
The Craft, Tristar, 1996.

*   *   *

Janet Eilber has had a diverse career encompassing dance, musical theater, film, and television. As a performer, she is primarily known for her years as a lead dancer with the Martha Graham Dance Company during the 1970s and, more recently, as the co-director of the American Repertory Dance Theatre.

Born in Detroit, Michigan, in 1952, Eilber was trained in both ballet and in the Graham technique of modern dance. She trained early at the Interlochen Center for the Arts, where both her parents taught, and then studied at the Juilliard School of Music with Helen McGehee, Mary Hinkson, and Ethel Winter, all Graham dancers.

In 1972 Eilber joined the Martha Graham Dance Company, eventually assuming leading roles. Known for her lyrical style, Eilber performed in many Graham revivals and in new works by Graham and other choreographers. Some of her important performances with the Graham company included the Pioneer Woman in Graham's *Appalachian Spring*, in a concert recorded for PBS's *Dance in America* series in 1975, and as one of the two partners in *Lamentation*, which Graham revived for her and Peggy Lymon in 1975. Eilber danced in the world premieres of Graham's *The Scarlet Letter* (1975), *Shadows* (1977), and *Flute of Pan* (1979), and in the premiere of José Limón's *Revel* (1971). She also had roles in Graham's *Seraphic Dialogue*, *Diversion of Angels*, *Day on Earth*, *Plain of Prayer*, *Point of Crossing*, *Frontier*, *Deaths and Entrances*, *Holy Jungle*, *Adorations*, and *Lucifer*, and in Limon's *Wing*, among others, and performed them both in repertory and in recitals.

In addition to Lyman, Eilber danced with many other notable performers during her tenure with Graham's company, including Margot Fonteyn, Yuriko, Pearl Lang, Lucinda Mitchell, Elisa Monte, and Peter Sparling, among many others. While with Graham, Eilber danced occasionally with other companies, including in concerts staged by other members of the Graham troupe, such as Sparling, another Interlochen alumnus. She also frequently made guest appearances with the American Dance Machine, a group that performed dance segments from Broadway musical theater productions. Her work with American Dance Machine in the 1970s led to leading dance roles in several major Broadway shows.

Eilber's theater work, which combined dance and acting, in turn led her to pursue a career in television and films. She moved to Los Angeles and began to accept acting roles in the 1980s, and continues to act occasionally in the 1990s. She was featured in two short-lived television series, the hour-long dramas *Two Marriages* (1983) and *The Best Times* (1985). She continues to make guest appearances on television.

Eilber has maintained her dance career as well, being particularly active in the 1990s, primarily in Los Angeles. In 1991, she created the choreography for a Los Angeles revival of *The Point*, a 1971 animated children's video and television special created by musician Harry Nilsson, which had been staged in 1975 by the Boston Repertory Theatre. In 1992, she performed in a made-for-video film written, produced, and directed by Amy Greenfield, which also starred former Graham dancer Bertram Ross, called *Antigone: Rights of Passion*. The 85-minute Mystic Fire Video release combined dramatic dance and "radical" music, with very little narration.

Eilber has also collaborated with composer-guitarist Allen Krantz on a number of works commissioned by the Music at Gretna Festival. The three works, for which Eilber choreographed and performed the dance parts, are for chamber ensemble featuring guitar and dancer. They include *anyone lived in a pretty how town* (1993), *Now I Become Myself* (1994), and *Advice to the Players* (1995). Eilber is currently co-director, with Bonnie Oda Ramsey (another former Graham lead dancer) of the American Repertory Dance Theatre. The company's mission is to support and produce reconstructions of important dance works, primarily solos, by men and women choreographers, as well as newer pieces by international choreographers.

The company's roster includes works by Sophie Maslow, Martha Graham, Mary Wigman, and Jane Dudley. It produces themed programs of dance reconstructions in the L.A. area, including *Weeping Women in Dance* (1994), *Trailblazers* (1995), and *The Indomitable Spirit of Woman* (1995). Homsey and Eilber both won a 1995 Lester Horton Award for the reconstructions of *Weeping Women*.

In addition to staging the reconstructions, Eilber and Ramsey also perform in the works, and Eilber received a second Horton award for her performances in *Weeping Women*. She has danced in solos such as Graham's *Deep Song* and Donald McKayle's *Saturday's Child*, as well as in group works, such as excerpts from Agnes de Mille's *Debut at the Opera*. Eilber also performs newer pieces, such as *The Stab* (1986), choreographed by Susana Tambutti of Argentina, in which her performance has been described as a "tour de force." The company, which includes Nancy Colahan and Risa Steinberg in addition to Eilber and Ramsey, performs at its own events and elsewhere, such as at the American Dance Festival in 1996 and at the Japan American Cultural & Community Center's "Celebrate California Series" in 1997, where their concert was called "Eyes Wide/Dancing Forward."

Eilber has also performed reconstructions of Graham works at other venues, such as at the Brooklyn Academy of Music's Next Wave Festival, in a series called "Radical Graham," part of New York's Martha Graham centennial celebration. There Eilber danced Graham's 1932 solo *Satyric Festival Song*. She also lectures on dance, and was a featured speaker at the 1996 American Dance Festival.

—Karen Raugust

EINSTEIN ON THE BEACH

Choreography: Andrew de Groat
Direction: Robert Wilson
Music and vocal text: Phillip Glass
Set Design: Robert Wilson, with Christina Gianini assisted by James Finguera
Costume Design: Robert Wilson
Lighting Design: Beverly Emmons
First production: Festival d' Avignon, France, Summer 1976; first U.S. production, Metropolitan Opera House, 21 November 1976.
Principal performers: Lucinda Childs, Samuel M. Johnson, Sheryl Sutton
Other productions include: Next Wave Festival, Brooklyn Academy of Music (BAM), 11 December 1984 and 19 November 1992; Stuttgart State Opera/Stuttgart Opera Ballet, Ludwigsburg Castle Festival, 8 October 1988.

Publications

Alliata, Vicky, ed. *Einstein on the Beach; an opera in four acts by Robert Wilson and Phillip Glass, with choreography by Andrew de Groat.* New York, 1976. [Includes essays in English, Italian, and French, by the editor and Richard Foreman; with examples from the musical scores, dance notation score, script, and stage design.]
Baker, Rob, *"Einstein on the Beach*; Waves of Power," *Soho Weekly News,* 12 August 1976.
Bromberg, Craig, "The 'Next' Thing," *1992 Next Wave Journal,* BAM, Brooklyn, New York.
Croce, Arlene, "Slowly Then the History of Them Comes Out," *Going to the Dance,* New York, 1982.
"Einstein on the Beach" in *On the Next Wave* (BAM, Brooklyn, New York), December 1984.

Glass, Phillip, "Notes on *Einstein on the Beach,"Performing Arts Journal*, Winter 1978.
Hughes, David, "Screams in Hyperspace," *Dance Theatre Journal*, Winter 1992.
Koegler, Horst, "Reviews/Eye on Performance...International," *Dance Magazine*, March 1989.
Koegler, Horst, "Continuing the Bauhaus tradition," *Dance and Dancers*, April 1989.
Kriegsman, Alan M. *"Einstein* in Music and Dance: Wilson's Theory of Relativity," *Washington Post*, 28 Novemer 1976.
Tobias, Tobi, "Out of This World," *New York*, 14 December 1992.
Vaughan, David, "A Place Where They Are," *Dance Magazine*, August 1976.

Films and Videotapes

Dance Brew, dir. Mark Montellese; produced by Montellese and Debra Sosa, 1986.
Einstein on the Beach (documentary of 1984 BAM revival), for *Great Performances*, WNET-TV, 1986.
Einstein on the Beach, (videotape performance at BAM Opera House, 20 December 1984).

*   *   *

Robert Wilson and Philip Glass decided to collaborate in 1974 with no specific project in mind; once they had agreed on Albert Einstein as a theme, they conceived the opera's structure and key imagery jointly. Though he had labeled many of his earlier theatrical spectacles "operas," *Einstein on the Beach* was Wilson's first work to use a commissioned score (he had previously relied on silence or *bricolages* of recorded music), and represented to many the first effective integration of music in his work. The work was also Wilson's first to connect its theme organically to his theatrical method and manner; Wilson's emphasis on the viewer's self-awareness of point of view and frame of reference resonates with Einstein's relativistic theories of time and space.

Einstein premiered at the Festival d'Avignon in summer 1976, and was then produced by the Byrd Hoffman Foundation, Wilson's not-for-profit organization at Metropolitan Opera for two Sunday nights the following November. The production featured dancer-choreographer Lucinda Childs, and actors Sheryl Sutton and Samuel M. Johnson. Choreography was by Andrew de Groat; five members of de Groat's eight-member company doubled as singers. Though both performances were sold out, large numbers walked out on the four-and-a-half-hour, intermission-less evening, and *Einstein* left Glass and Wilson in debt—Glass was driving his cab the night after the premiere.

In 1976 *Einstein* was seen as a theatrical work by noted (or notorious) director-designer Wilson, with a score by a young composer whose music was admired only by a cult-like following. *Einstein* soon acquired a legendary aura however, and rocketed Glass to fame, while Wilson departed to work in Europe's state-supported theaters and opera houses. For the 1984 revival professional singers were hired for the chorus, and the scoring and text somewhat revised. With the revival a critical consensus emerged, which saw the work as Wilson's most influential and artistically successful piece, and as the best of Glass' theatrical scores. Wilson's subsequent creations, often spectacular to the point of decadent *luxe*, were derided by some critics as "corporate modernism," while Glass' 1980s music often strayed into bombast. By the 1992 re-

Einstein on the Beach. **Photograph © Beatriz Schiller.**

vival, for which the sets were entirely rebuilt, *Einstein* was considered an opera by Glass, as staged by Wilson, and had become an icon of late 20th-century culture. Both revivals involved extensive international tours.

Although it corresponds somewhat to Wagner's concept of the *Gesamtkunstwerk*, a "total art work" integrating music, scenery, text, and action, *Einstein* is not a conventional opera. It presents no linear narrative of Einstein's life and work, but instead offers a poetic meditation of the figure of Einstein shared in collective memory, treating the great physicist less as a historical person than as a mythic character. The performers are almost all dressed as Einstein, in baggy grey slacks with suspenders, short-sleeve dress shirts, and sneakers.

Wilson structured the opera visually with three leitmotifs deployed in a rigorously symmetrical framework through the nine scenes of the opera's four acts: a train (which later metamorphoses into a building based on New York's Holland Tunnel air shaft), a trial/prison setting with an enormous bed, and a "field" (empty stage) over which hovers a toy-like flying saucer. The acts are bracketed by five "knee plays" (Wilson's idiosyncratic term for prelude, postlude, and entr'acte), which take place downstage right of the proscenium curtain, performed by Childs and Sutton. Wilson filled his predetermined structure with largely arbitrary action generated in a collective rehearsal process. Among *Einstein*'s famous images are Child's slow transformation from socialite Patty Hearst into a machine-gun-wielding revolutionary; the illuminated

bed slowly ascending into the flies over a soaring violin ostinato; and the dazzling interior of the "space machine" revealed in the penultimate scene. *Einstein* distills in its imagery and sound some of the central terrors and thrills of the 20th century—speed, noise, space travel, nuclear war, humanity's shrinking before an expanding conception of the universe, the exhilarating and awful power of technology—and makes them tangible as no conventionally discursive treatment of Einstein's life and work ever could.

Glass' musical structure exactly parallels the sequence of images and their transformations. *Einstein*'s idiom is the familiar sound of Glass' mature style, and closely related to the big concert scores that immediately preceded the opera's composition, "Music in Twelve Parts" and "Another Look at Harmony." Consonant harmonies evolve slowly beneath a churning surface of polymetric figuration, with swirling arpeggios in fast, strict pulse (this relation of harmony to rhythm has been interpreted as a musical evocation of Einstein's relativity theory). The music's foundation is rhythm: the harmonies and in turn, melodies, are essentially functions of Glass' cyclic structures and additive rhythmic processes. The sung text consists of numbers and solfeggio syllables—one of the many self-referential elements that in the 1970s made the opera's own structure appear to be its true subject. The musical ensemble includes electric keyboards, winds, chorus with soprano and tenor soloists, and a violinist place between the stage and pit wearing exaggerated Einstein make-up and a white wig.

Einstein has monologues corresponding to arias (Childs and Johnson wrote parts of their own texts), but no dialogue, and almost no interaction among the performers. Most of the text was written by Christopher Knowles, a 13-year-old autistic boy befriended by Wilson, in response to the question, "Who is Einstein?" Fragmented, stuttering and obsessive, the text incorporates such ephemera of mid-1970s New York radio stations as song lyrics, call numbers, disc jockey schedules and advertisements. The title, found in Knowles' libretto, echoes that of Nevil Shute's apocalyptic, postnuclear 1956 novel *On the Beach*, and the 1959 film version of it, both popular in the 1960s.

Einstein includes three dances: in the first scene Childs does a restless 40-minute striding dance back and forth on a diagonal downstage, gradually adding hops and skips. In one hand she holds a pipe; with the other, she writes equations in the air, as if on a blackboard (a key recurrent motif). For the opera's two "field" scenes—which function to cleanse the visual palette, like a shot of ice vodka between courses of a rich meal—de Groat's choreography used the dervish-like spinning of his early style, enriched with gestures and jumps (the dances were praised by critic David Vaughan, who nonetheless thought them more effective when performed outside the opera). For the 1984 revival, Childs made new dances, performed by her company, in her signature style: elementary ballet steps arranged in symmetrical linear patters, structured without progression or climax, and executed with serene, buoyant, unisex athleticism. Childs' dances seem to manifest some timeless energy, as though human motion were itself a fundamental constituent force of the universe. The entire opera, however, may be considered as dance, because of Wilson's meticulous staging, which transcends "blocking" to approach choreography.

Both Childs' and de Groat's companies performed their versions of the group dances as concert works, under the respective titles *Field Dances* and *Red Notes* (the latter premiered in its final form, with text from Gertrude Stein, on 11 April 1979 at the Brooklyn Academy). Katherine Posin also choreographed her *Later That Day* to the field scenes' music, premiered by the Alvin Ailey American Dance Theatre on 8 February 1980 in Washington, D.C. The complete opera was also staged in neo-Bauhaus style in Stuttgart in 1988, as a collaboration between the Ludwigsburg Castle Festival and the Stuttgart State Opera/Stuttgart Opera Ballet, produced by Glass and directed by Achim Freyer.

The opera's success made it extremely influential on European *Tanztheater* and on American theater, dance, and performance art. As Roger Copeland has said, *Einstein* signified an unashamed return to theatrical spectacle, and the end of "the poor theater" that had dominated American stages through the 1960s. For Alan Kriegsman, *Einstein's* appearance at the Met was a sign that mainstream culture had co-opted an avant-garde previously committed to attacking it, while Craig Bromberg noted that *Einstein* more than any other work proved the commercial viability of Downtown art in the 1970s, and transformed a coterie audience into a mass audience for experimental theater in the 1980s. *Einstein* was the quintessential "crossover" oeuvre, the first to move Soho artists from their lofts to opera houses. It was also exemplary collaborative work, anticipating the obsession with collaboration among BAM's programmers and publicists in the 1980s. Indeed, although *Einstein* did not appear in BAM's Next Wave festival until 1984, it is the paradigmatic Next Wave event, as much for its outsize ambition and the hype of its marketing as for its artistic style.

Einstein was perhaps most influential in the new attitude toward the audience that it embodied. The opera challenged its audience in ways familiar in the avant-garde tradition since dada and the Bauhaus: the music's unrelenting amplified onslaught, and the agonizing *largissimo* of Wilson's dissociated staging of a bizarre and fragmentary text, tested the viewer/auditor's capacity to sustain boredom and bafflement, or to find boredom and bafflement somehow interesting. At the same time, the opera presciently infused the didactic spirit of Judson-era dance-theater with the pleasure principle that became de rigueur in the 1980s' circus of conspicuous cultural consumption: the music casts a mesmeric spell, and the immaculate beauty of the evolving stage picture ravishes the eyes—a calculated amalgam of estrangement and enchantment.

—Christopher Caines

ENTERS, Angna
American dancer and choreographer

Born: Anita Irene Enters, 28 April 1907, in New York. **Education:** Educated privately in the U.S., Europe, and Asia; studied ballet in Milwaukee and dancing with Michio Itow; studied painting at the Art Students' League in New York. **Family:** Married Louis Kalonyme. **Career:** Founder and director, Theatre of Angna Enters, 1926-60; also designed costumes and sets and composed music for dance; painter with works exhibited throughout the U.S. and England and in the permanent collection of the Metropolitan Museum of Art; lecturer; artist in residence, Dallas Theater Center and Baylor Univeristy, during the early 1960s. Created Commedia dell'Arte sequence for the film *Scaramouche,* 1952. **Awards:** Guggenheim fellowships, 1934, 1935. **Died:** 25 February 1989, in Tenafly, New Jersey.

Works (for the Theater of Angna Enters from 1926)

1923	*Moyen Age (originally Ecclésiastique)*
1926	*Cakewalk: Charleston Blues*
	Contre Danse
	Dance of Death
	Tales of the Vienna Waltzes
	Promenade
	Les Sons et Les Parfums Tournent dans l'Air du Soir
	A Spanish Dancer
	Columbine
	Cakewalk: 1897
	Cardinal
	Habenera
	Piano Music: A Dance of Adolescence
	Polonaise: Dance of Death #2
	Sapphic
	Man His Origin Is Dust
	Odalisque
	Der Rosenkevalier (Waltz)
	Second Empire
	Entr'acte 1860
	Rendezvous
1927	*Entr'acte 1927*
	A Merry Widow
	Bar Maid
	In Pursuit of Art: Piano Music No. 2

Bourée
Antique á la Française
Dancing School Accompanist: Piano Music No. 3
Entr'acte 1920
Heptameron
Queen of Heaven: French Gothic
1928   *Aphrodisiac: Green Hour*
Black Magic, Blue Hour: Park Avenue
Field Day
La Sauvage Elegante
The Yellow Peril
Saturnalia: Pagan Rites
Tristan
1929   *Commencement: Piano Music No. 4*
Delsarte, With a Not Too Classic Nod to the Greeks
En Garde or the Red Heart
Inquisition Virgin: Spain 16th-Century
Pavana: Spain 16th Century
*'Tis Pity She's a ***
Carneval: Lorette
High Life
Odalisque: Haremlik
Antique in the English Manner: Rosetti, Ltd.
1930   *Daunce We Praunce We*
Oh the Pain of It
Shaking or the Sheets: A Dance of Death
Contre Danse No. 2: Invention
Romance Country: Olivette
Court of Love: 18th-Century France
Pique-Nique 1860: Déjeuner au Bois
Webs
Narcissism
1931   *American Ballet 1914-1916*
Art d'Amour
Ikon-Byzantine
Medieval Night's Dream, Spain
Piano Music No. 5: Hurry Up It's Time!
Prelude to Dementia: Narcissism No. 2
Societe Anonyme
Stars and Stripes Forever
Auto da Fe: Spain 15th-Century
Farmer in the Dell
Flemish Saint
1932   *Boy Cardinal: Spain 15th-Century*
German Angel: Reformation
Life Is a Dream: Remembered Things
Peon's Heavenly Robe
Vienna Provincian, 1910s
Virgin of the Fields: Mexican Cycle
1933   *Pagan Greece*
Effeminate Young Man: Amour Malade
Holy Virgin Pursued by Satan
Santa Espana del Cruz, 16th Century
1934   *Back to "Childhood"*
Danse Macabre: Vodvil, Let's Go to Town
David Dances before the Ark
Sevillano: Boroque Interlude
1935   *Dama del Moche: Malaga Night, 1820*
Figures in Moonlight: Danse Macabre No. 2
Ishtar
Isis-Mary

Red Hot Mamma
Little Sally Water
1936   *American Ballet No. 2, 1908-1912*
Deutchland Über Alles: German Tripper
Flesh Possessed Saint: Red Malaga, 1936
Mme. Pompadour: Solitude, 1900
Time on My Hands: Two Modern City Women
Spain Says "Salud"
1937   *End of the World: Paris August 1914*
Japan "Defends" Itself
A Modern Totalitarian Hero
T'ang: Chinese Dynastic
Venus Americana, 1937
London Bridge Is Falling Down
1938   *Balletomane: Connoisseur, Riviera Stay Away from My Door*
La Cuisine Française
Impertinente-Habanera
Mr. Mozart Has Breakfast
Artist's Life
Grand Inquisitor: Spain, 15th-Century
1939   *Crackpot Americana*
Weiner Blut: Vienna 1939
Homage to Isadora
1942   *Dilly Dally: Ah Sweet Mystery of Life*
My First Dance: Hungarian Routine
Hollywood Horror Story
She Loves Me, She Loves Me Not
1950   *Dilly Dally No. 2: American Primitive*
1952   *Dilly Dally No. 3*
Fleur du Mal: Tango Dancer, Paris 1900
Flowering Bud
Moyen Age No. 2
Pierrot: Figures in Moonlight
1955   *French Provincial: Chagrin d'Amour*
Les Sons et les Parfums tournent dans l'Air du Soir no. 2
1959   *Figures in Moonlight No. 2: Harlequin*
1960   *Bird in Net*
Dama del Noche: Homage to Goya
Overture

Publications

By ENTERS: books—

First Person Plural, New York, 1937.
Silly Girl, Cambridge, Mass. 1944.
Among the Daughters (novel), New York, 1955.
Artist's Life, New York, 1958.
On Mime, Middletown, Conn., 1965.

On ENTERS: books—

Mandel, Dorothy, *Uncommon Eloquence: A Biography of Angna Enters*, Denver, 1986.

*   *   *

Talented and versatile, Angna Enters was an accomplished performer, artist, and writer. She stands alone as the creator of an original and distinctive dance style which brought her international acclaim.

Several seemingly straightforward facts about Enters' life are not without some question. Born Anita Irene Enters, she later changed her name to Angna, but conflicting reports circulated as to the origin of the new name. Most biographical reference works give her date of birth as 28 April 1907, yet in *Uncommon Eloquence* (1986), Enters' biographer, Dorothy Mandel, points out there is evidence she was born before this date, especially because she appears to have graduated from Milwaukee's North Division High School in 1915. Also unclear during much of Enters' lifetime was her relationship with Louis Kalonyme, her devoted companion of more than 40 years. While several sources note that she married him in 1936, none of Enters' contemporaries knew when or even if they had married.

Enters was born to Edward and Henriette (Gasseur-Styleau) in New York City, where she lived until her family moved to Milwaukee, Wisconsin, in 1914. Both of her parents had come from Europe, and she spent much of her time as a young child with her mother's family in the south of France. Enters did not attend school regularly but received her education privately both in the United States and Europe. She had some training in music and art as well as instruction in dance from a ballet master in Milwaukee. It is interesting that this would be almost the only formal dance training she would receive.

Around 1920, Enters moved to New York City, where she enrolled in American genre painter John Sloan's class at the Art Students League. Shortly thereafter she received an introduction to Michio Ito, the Japanese dancer who had developed a system of 10 basic gestures to express all the meanings of life. In her autobiographical work *First Person Plural*, Enters writes of working at Ito's studio: "It was not the dance that had lured me there, but a dissatisfaction with my painting, and a simultaneous hunch about the value of a study of movement to help my painting." Later, however, dance performance would become the central focus of her career.

Ito recognized Enters' talent and told her she could be a professional dancer, but Enters had no desire to learn conventional dance routine or to work under someone else's system. For financial reasons, she did agree to be Ito's partner for a short time, but not long after she stopped dancing with him and later denied that his work in any way influenced hers. Both while she was working with Ito and after she left him, Enters developed her own distinctive form of dance and pantomime outside the prescribed rules of theater and dance. Mandel writes, "her idea was to experiment with joining the fluidity of dance to the gestures and facial expressions of acting, in theatrical settings, using musical accompaniment but without speech—and to go beyond the confinement of traditional mime costumes." Enters would originate the term "dance-mime" to describe her performances, and she developed what would become a repertory of nearly 300 character vignettes. Among her most famous creations was *Moyen Age* (1926), an attempt to convey the spirit of a gothic Virgin carved in stone.

In 1924 Enters shared her first public performance with three musicians; her solo debut was 17 October 1926 in New York City's *Little Theater*. For these early performances, Enters did everything herself, including designing and distributing her own handbills and window cards.

From the start and throughout her career, critics were appreciative of her talent but puzzled by her medium. Dancer Jean Erdman called Enters "an unclassifiable and unique artist." Stark Young wrote of Enters in the 26 May 1926 issue of the *New Republic*, "At bottom she is indefinable, remote, almost macabre, and blessed with style as painters use the word—in her case a kind of tragic style." In the *Nation* (5 December 1928) Louis Untermeyer called her "a dancer who does not dance; an actress who does not speak; a dramatist who makes the audience supply the drama." Perhaps Enters did not mind that her work defied strict categorization. Writing of the early modern dancers Mandel notes that, "[Enters] would always remain on the fringe of that dance world, never acknowledged as a true dancer by its members. But then [she] did not attempt to ally herself with any group within the dance, preferring to stand apart and go her own distinctive way in the theatre."

In 1927 Enters first engaged a manager and in February of 1928 held her London debut at St. Martin's Theater. She was well-received and returned later in the same year and during subsequent years for many more performances. In fact, from 1928 to 1960, Enters toured Europe, the U.S., and Canada extensively, performing her "Theater of Angna Enters." Her travels enriched her work; in particular, five summers spent in Spain from 1931 to 1936 gave rise to a series of Spanish mimes, several of which dealt with the Spanish Inquisition.

For all her performances, Enters designed her own costumes, choreographed her own work and sometimes composed her own music. In a 1934 letter Enters wrote, "as to the mime, it is more rounded and with the music I have composed, it is the first modern attempt I know of to offer a dramatic presentation in which the performer is the author of everything presented."

Even as Enters perfected her dance performances, she did not forget her earlier artistic pursuits. In 1933 she first exhibited paintings of some costume sketches she made while crossing the Atlantic from Europe, and after that she held exhibitions of her own paintings and sculptures at galleries in the U.S., Canada, and London. The Metropolitan Museum of Art still displays in its permanent collection Enters' *Spain Says Salud*. In 1934 and 1935, Enters received Guggenheim awards to study mime, art, and music forms in Greece and Egypt.

Starting in 1938, Enters was a screenwriter under contract to MGM. She also wrote several plays, three volumes of autobiographical works, the novel *Among the Daughters* (1956), and an analysis of her work, *On Mime* (1966). Later in her career, she taught classes in mime for actors as artist-in-residence at the Dallas Theater Center and Baylor University and as a fellow at the Center for Advanced Studies at Wesleyan University.

As Enters was the only one ever to perform her works, the only surviving record of her performances may be a 1959 *Camera Three* television production of four of her most popular compositions.

—Karen Zimmerman

ERDMAN, Jean

American dancer, choreographer, educator, and company director

Born: 20 February 1917 in Honolulu, Hawaii. **Education:** Attended Sarah Lawrence College, New York; studied with Martha Graham at Bennington Summer School and at the School of American Ballet, New York City; tutored by several teachers in the dance styles of the Far East. **Family:** Married Joseph Campbell, 1938 (died 1987). **Career:** Dancer, Martha Graham company, 1938-43; guest-performed with the same company after 1943; collaborated with Merce Cunningham on several works, 1940s; founded Jean

Erdman Dance Group, 1950; toured with Dance Group around the world, 1940-60; choreographed her most famous work, *The Coach with the Six Insides,* 1962; directed the dance theater program of the New York University School of the Arts, until 1972; founded Theater of the Open Eye, mid-1970s. **Awards:** Vernon Rice and Obie Award for *The Coach with the Six Insides,* 1963; Drama Desk Award for *Two Gentlemen of Verona.*

Roles

1938   *American Document* (Graham)
1940   One Who Speaks, *Letter to the World* (Graham)
1941   Ideal Spectator, *Every Soul is a Circus* (Graham)
1949   *Punch and the Judy* (Graham)

Works

1940   *Departure*
1941   *Rigaudon*
        Baby Ben Says Dada
1942   *Seeds of Brightness* w/Merce Cunningham (mus. Lloyd), Bennington, Vermont
        Credo in Us w/Merce Cunningham (mus. Cage), Bennington, Vermont
        Ad Lib w/Merce Cunningham (mus. Tucker; Cage from 1946), Bennington, Vermont
        The Transformation of Medusa
        Forever and Sunsmell
1943   *The Wind Remains* w/Merce Cunningham and others, New York City
        Creature on a Journey
1945   *Dawn Song*
        Daughters of the Lonesome Isle
        Changing Moment
1946   *Ophelia*
        Passage
        People and Ghosts
1947   *Sea Deep*
1948   *Hamadryad*
        En Peregrinage
        Jazz Maze
        Four-Four Time
1949   *The Perilous Chapel*
        Festival
        And a Gigue
1950   *The Solstice*
        The Fair Eccentric
1951   *Changingwoman*
        Upon Enchanted Ground
        Io and Prometheus
        Sailor in the Louvre
1952   *The Blessed Damozel*
        The Burning Thirst
1953   *Song of the Turning World*
        Broken City
1954   *Pierrot the Moon*
        Bagatelle
        Salutation
        Weather of the Heart
        Strange Hunt

1955   *Spring Rhythms*
1956   *Duet for Flute and Dancer*
1957   *Fearful Symmetry*
        Harlequinade
1958   *Elegy*
        Moments Free and Engaged
        Four Portraits
1959   *The Road of No Return*
        Now and Zen—Remembering
        Solos and Chorale
1960   *Twenty Poems from e.e. cummings*
1961   *Dance in Five-Eight Time*
1962   *The Coach with the Six Insides* (based on Joyce's *Finnegan's Wake*)
1964   *Partridge in the Jungle Gym*
1967   *The Castle* w/Jimmy Guiffre
        Encounter in the Grove
1968   *Llove Ssong Ddance*
1969   *Ensembles*
        Safari
        Excursion
        Voracious
        Venerable as an Island is Paradise
1970   *Twilight Wind*
1972   *The Marathon*
        Moon Mysteries
1974   *The Silken Tent*
        Rapid Transits
1976   *Gauguin in Tahiti*
1977   *Such Sweet Thunder*
1980   *The Shining Hour*

Other works include: Choreographed works for theater including *Les Mouches,* 1948; *The Enchanted,* 1950; *Otherman—Or the Beginning of a New Nation,* 1954; *Hamlet,* 1964; *Yerma,* 1964; *Marriage on the Eiffel Tower,* 1967; *The Municipal Water System Is Not Trustworthy,* 1968; *The King of the Schnorrers,* 1970; *Two Gentlemen of Verona* (Delacorte Theatre production only), 1971; *The Making of the King,* 1972; *Moon Mysteries* (three plays by William Butler Yeats), 1972; *The Only Jealousy of Emer,* 1973.

Publications

By ERDMAN: articles—

"A Contemporary Dancer Looks at Her Heritage," *Dance Magazine,* November 1960.
"The Dance as Non-Verbal Poetical Image," *Dance Observer,* April 1949.
"On the Teaching of Choreography: Interview with Jean Erdman by Martha Coleman," *Dance Observer,* April 1952.

On EDRMAN: articles—

"Jean Erdman," in *Current Biography,* 1971.

Films and Videotapes

The World of Jean Erdman, 1997.

*   *   *

Jean Erdman, modern dancer, choreographer, and teacher was a member of the Martha Graham company in the late 1930s and early 1940s. Like her Graham colleague and early collaborator, Merce Cunningham, Erdman went on to found her own dance company. The broader arena of avant-garde theater soon beckoned Erdman, however, and she used her talents to blend dance, theater, and the spoken word in numerous theater productions. As a choreographer, Erdman worked with actors who could move like dancers and with dancers who could act. She formulated dances from what she referred to as "an uncommitted void," in which the dance movement emanates from a natural or artless body stance.

Erdman believed strongly that every gesture expresses something from life. In an article in *Dance Observer* (1949), Erdman suggested that rhythm and "movement texture" form the main tools of the dancer. Erdman's goal, both as a dancer and choreographer, was to treat the stage as a magical or spiritual place which the dancer transforms into a real or imagined place. A committed internationalist, Erdman employed concepts and movement styles from many different dance and theater traditions. She was especially interested in the Japanese Noh play and its use of space, drama, music, and movement. The dances of India, Indonesia, and Polynesia also influenced Erdman's work as dancer, choreographer, and director. Her marriage to the well-known scholar Joseph Campbell, from 1938 until his death in 1987, undoubtedly influenced her intellectual approach to the dance. She shared Campbell's interest in universal myths and legends and has incorporated many mythological themes into her work. In *Daughters of the Lonesome Isle* (1945), Erdman was inspired by Celtic tales about the Isle of Women. Erdman used three female dancers and dressed them in a classic, timeless fashion. The women dance in a circle in twilight. They represent different female archetypes: the nourishing, creative mother; the youthful woman, full of vigor; and the searching, yearning woman. Each moves in a distinct style. The distinctive movement texture of each dancer, and the way each movement plays off the other, comprises the action of the piece.

Erdman proposed that artists make fresh statements for each creative work and mold something new out of chaos. She tried to do this in her work by searching for the telling gesture that sprang from the subject. She praised the U.S. for being unencumbered by the past and thus free to take the creative lead in the arts.

Erdman's work as a choreographer has been both criticized and praised for stressing the intellectual and physical elements of dance to the detriment of the emotional. The most striking element of her work is her exploration of the relationship between music and dance. Her dances counterpoint the music rather than merely accompanying it. Erdman was an early proponent of nontraditional music, and her collaborations with musicians John Cage, Louis Horst, Lou Harrison, Ezra Laderman, Milton Babbitt, and Luciano Berio were notable.

Jean Erdman was born in Honolulu, Hawaii in 1917. Her great-grandparents had migrated to the islands from New England to perform missionary work among the islanders. As a child growing up in Hawaii, Erdman learned the hula and was exposed to the music and dance of Polynesia. She was struck from an early age by the ease with which the islanders incorporated dance into their everyday lives. Her family supported her youthful interest in the arts. In the early 1930s Erdman moved to the mainland to attend Miss Hall's School in Pittsfield, Massachusetts, from which she graduated in 1934. She then attended Sarah Lawrence College in Bronxville, New York. She had planned to prepare for a career in the theater but discovered dance instead. Sarah Lawrence was also im-

portant to Erdman because it was at the college that she met Joseph Campbell, then a professor of literature, whom she later married. Upon leaving school Erdman toured Bali, Java, Cambodia, India, and Spain. In each country she was impressed and inspired by the ethnic dances of the people. In 1938 she joined the Martha Graham company as a dancer. She performed with the Graham troupe for four and a half years, becoming a leading dancer. Like other dancers in the Graham troupe, Erdman wanted to try her own approach to dance. After leaving Graham, Erdman choreographed her first dance—a solo called *The Transformation of Medusa*—at Bennington College in 1942. Her movements were based on the positions of ancient Greek bas-reliefs.

Following World War II, Erdman toured the Far East as a soloist, the first dancer to take part in a U.S. cultural exchange program. In 1950 she founded her own dance company, the Jean Erdman Dance Group, and made her first tour of the U.S. She also presented annual concerts in New York city of her solo and group work. Donald McKayle was a featured soloist in Erdman's company during the 1950s. In addition to setting dances on her own group, Erdman also taught and danced with the New Dance Group in New York.

As a dancer Erdman was praised for her womanly charm and warmth. Tall and dark-haired, she typified a Mother Goddess figure. She was especially interested in collaboration. Her most famous collaborators were Merce Cunningham, with whom she danced in the Martha Graham company in the late 1930s and early 1940s; Carlus Dyer, a sculptor and scenic designer; composer Lou Harrison; and choreographer and former Erdman student, Donald McKayle.

In 1962, Jean Erdman debuted and performed in her most famous work, *The Coach with the Six Insides. Coach,* as it came to be known, transformed James Joyce's stream-of-consciousness masterpiece, *Finnegan's Wake,* into a three-act comedy piece. Erdman combined dance, song, the spoken word, pantomime, and dramatic scenes. Teiji Ito wrote the mock folk tunes, jigs, and reels for the brief vignettes in which company members Anita Dangler, Van Dexter, Erdman, Leonard Frey, and Gail Ryan spoke Joyce's puns, jokes, and mispronunciations with rich inflection and musicality. Erdman had studied *Finnegan's Wake* for years and was entranced by Joyce's work. She received a grant from the Ingram Merrill Foundation to complete the work. In addition to setting the work, Erdman danced the role of Anna Livia Plurabelle. She employed a multitude of visual elements to convey the witticisms of Joyce's world: red scarves streamed forth to indicate anger, and dancers used their bodies to create a motorcar. *The Coach with the Six Insides* ran for 16 weeks in New York and was performed to theater audiences around the world including the Theatre des Nations in Paris, the Dublin Theatre Festival, and the Festival of the Two Worlds in Spoleto, Italy.

Teaching provided Jean Erdman with another avenue for presenting her ideas about dance and theater. She was an artist-in-residence at the University of Colorado, the University of British Columbia, and the University of Hawaii. For three years she headed the dance department at Bard College in New York. In 1967 she established a dance program at New York University's School of the Arts. A gifted speaker and writer, Erdman has lectured widely on the elements and structure of the dance. As a teacher of dance composition, she urged her students to translate their ideas, no matter what the source, into rhythmic terms. She taught recognition of meter and rhythmic patterns, as well as counterpoint of rhythms, in her classes. Erdman encouraged her students to use costumes, paintings, proverbs, and poetry as sources of inspiration for composition. In 1989, the Jean Erdman Video Project was unveiled. The three-phase project, sponsored by the Foundation for the Open Eye, was begun in 1988 and captured Erdman's work from 1942 to 1957. In 1997, *The World of Jean Erdman* was released on video-cassette. Part One—the Early Dances—contains memorable dances from the 1940s including *Passage* and *Daughters of the Lonesome Isle;* Part Two—the Group Dances—contains works from the late-1940s and early 1950s.

—Adriane Ruggiero

ERKERT, Jan

American dancer, choreographer, and company director

Born: 7 April 1951 in West Bloomfield, Michigan. **Education:** University of Utah, Salt Lake City, B.F.A. in dance 1973. **Career:** Dancer, assistant director, Mordine & Company, 1974-79; founder, Jan Erkert and Dancers, 1979; taught at the University of Chicago, 1980-90. **Awards:** Fulbright Scholar, 1988; five Artistic Achievement Ruth Page Awards; numerous choreographic awards from the National Endowment for the Arts and the Illinois Arts Council.

Works (for Jan Erkert & Dancers, premiering in Chicago, unless otherwise noted)

1978	*Blue Doll*
1979	*Sonata for Violins & Horns* (mus. Reiser)
	Sculpt (mus. Reiser)
	Trappings (mus. Correlli)
	Uccello (mus. Reiser)
1981	*Spinning Round* (mus. Beatles)
1982	*Mountain of Needles* (mus. Byrne and Eno)
1983	*Bill & Coo* (mus. George Shearing)
	The Wedding Anthem
1984	*The Dancing Wu Li Masters* (mus. Claudia Howard Queen), Champaign, Illinois
1986	*Teleos*
	Strayaway (mus. Kirkpatrick)
	Regarding, Waves (mus. Simon/Onderdonk)
	Broken Wings (mus. Shiflett)
	Perseverance of a Mare (mus. Bach)
1987	*Right Now* (mus. Brahms, Adams, Beastie Boys)
	Circuit (mus. Le Mystère de voix Bulgares)
	How To Be an Other Woman (mus. Beethoven)
	Conversations at a Dinner Table
	Fame & Fortune (mus. Twinning, text Erkert), Champaign, Illinois
1988	*Untitled Until Further Notice*
	A Dance for Five Men (mus. Russian traditional), Champaign, Illinois
	Floating Mind (text Erkert), Champaign, Illinois
	Antigamente (mus. Volans), Champaign, Illinois
1989	*Journal Entry #1, Chicago 1989*
	Tocatta & Fugue (mus. Bach), Taiwan
	Journal Entry #2, Taipei 1989 (mus. Chen), Taiwan
1990	*Making a Bed for a Dead Cow* (mus. Pennington McGee)

	Sensual Spaces III (mus. des Pres and de Victoria), Colorado
1991	*Sensual Spaces IV* (mus. des Pres and de Victoria)
	Minutes Hours Days Decades (text Shineflug, Mordine, Kast)
	Untitled in White with TV (mus. Schubert)
	Forgotten Sensations (mus. Codax)
1992	*About Men ... About Women*
	Ways of my Fathers (from 1987, mus. Ba-Benzele Pygmies)
	Between Men (mus. Manitas de Platas and Jose Reyes)
	Glass Ceilings (mus. Peter Gabriel)
	Portrait of 5 Men (text Erkert)
	Sensual Spaces V (mus. Victoria)
1993	*Sensual Spaces* (mus. Victoria), Japan
	Six Short Solos in White with Audience (mus. eclectic)
	Two Lives of Women (mus. Glenda Baker, text Baker/Erkert)
	The Creation of the World (mus. Milhaud), Evanston, Illinois
	Kisses Blown Down Thru the Ages (mus. collage, text Erkert), Ft. Worth, Texas
	Turn Her White with Stones (mus. Weinger)
1994	*Scene 1, Take 3* (mus. Baker/Lemper)
1995	*Whole Fragments* (mus. John Adams)
1996	*Gaps* (mus. Cameron Pfiffner)
	Puerta del Alma (Doorway to the Soul) (text Octavio Paz)
1997	*UnWeavings* (mus. Gustavo Leone)

Publications

Barzel, Ann, "Jan Erkert & Dancers," *Dance Magazine,* October 1986.

Bradford, Judy, "Back Injury Leads to 'Healing' Dance," *South Bend Tribune,* 6 November 1995.

Delacoma, Wynne, "Jan Erkert & Dancers," *Dance Magazine,* August 1987.

Mark, Bing J., "Jan Erkert Troupe Performs in NextMove Festival," *Philadelphia Inquirer,* 15 March 1997.

Molzahn, Laura, "Jan Erkert & Dancers," *Reader,* Chicago, 28 March 1997.

Putnam, Margaret, "Moments of Magic,"*Dallas Morning News,* 12 September 1993.

Survant, Cerinda, "Two Women's Tales," *Dance Magazine,* October 1991.

Wiltz, Teresa, "Ageless Artistry," *Chicago Tribune,* 6 April 1997.

*   *   *

Jan Erkert is a Chicago-based dancer and choreographer whose company, Jan Erkert & Dancers, has established itself as a major force on the Chicago dance scene, touring both nationally and internationally. Erkert's company has garnered critical acclaim for performing carefully crafted works that, typically, display a commitment to social issues.

Born outside Detroit on 7 April 1951, Erkert graduated cum laude from the University of Utah at Salt Lake City in 1973 with a B.F.A. in dance. Upon moving to Chicago, she joined Mordine & Company—the professional dance group supported by Columbia College—with whom she performed until 1979, also acting as as-

Jan Erkert. Photograph by William Frederking.

sistant director to Shirley Mordine. In Chicago she received training from artists such as Ralph Lemon, Bebe Miller, Joe Goode, Trisha Brown, Bill T. Jones, Viola Farber, and Doug Varone. In addition to her affiliation with Columbia College, Erkert was on the faculty at the University of Chicago from 1980 to 1990, taught at MoMing Dance & Arts Center, and completed guest artist residencies at numerous universities throughout the United States.

In 1979 Erkert created a space for her own choreographic conceptions by founding Jan Erkert & Dancers. Since then she has created more than 50 works and her company has performed throughout the Chicagoland area, as well as nationally and in such countries as Germany, Israel, Japan, Mexico, Nicaragua, and Taiwan.

Departing from the more traditional pick-up company model, Erkert made a conscious choice in 1991 to concentrate on building a tight ensemble of experienced dancers. In a 1996 artist's statement Erkert expressed her intent to make "a commitment to developing a particular stylistic point of reference that both honors the individual voice, yet provides a commonality of focus." Indeed, critics agree that Jan Erkert & Dancers is a mature, technically strong company, and they frequently comment on the group's athleticism, in addition to its rapid fluidity and clarity of movement. Teresa Wiltz of the *Chicago Tribune,* for example, remarked in a review of a 1997 performance entitled *Ageless Artistry* that "when. . .former Hubbard Street dancer [Ginger] Farley lifts her leg, it's because she really means it, rather than indulging in a Look-Ma-I've-Got-Legs! display of grand battements."

Erkert's choreography, which draws on a modern dance vocabulary of falls, lifts, and twists, and frequently makes use of text, evocative music, and everyday gestures, tends to alternate between tension and relaxation. Regularly addressing important social issues such as the relationship between gender and culture, Erkert's work offers, as she states, "a woman's perspective, weaving movement, film, images and light to provoke visceral responses and create opportunities to rethink ideas about the world." But although her choreography tends to provoke emotional responses, dance reviewers note that it manages to do so without resorting to pure sentimentality. *Tribune* critic Wiltz maintains that "the grace of Erkert's choreography lies in its understatement."

In 1994 Erkert sustained a serious injury to her back and had to undergo a lengthy rehabilitation process, relearning to walk as well as to dance. Out of this grueling ordeal emerged *Whole Fragments,* which premiered in Chicago in 1995. Curious about the relationship between patient and health-care provider, Erkert began a discussion between doctors and dancers, which eventually took form in this explorative work about the nature of therapy, healing, and dancing itself.

Over the years Jan Erkert & Dancers has demonstrated its dedication to community involvement, consistently creating opportunities for both interacting with and exploring issues of various communities. In 1992, for example, Erkert began volunteer work at the Marjorie Kovler Center for the Treatment of Survivors of Torture in Chicago. There she conducted movement and memory workshops with a group of Cambodian women suffering from posttraumatic stress syndrome stemming from the terror of the Cambodian killing fields. In the process of giving voice to their experiences these women collaborated with Erkert in the creation of poetry and images that eventually took choreographic shape in *Turn Her White with Stones,* a solo for company member Suet May Ho, which premiered in 1994. In a 1997 review for the Chicago *Reader* Laura Molzahn declared this piece her "paradigm for the dry, hard dance that wrings the heart." A documentary by videographer Sara

Livingston, entitled *Turn Her White with Stones: The Journey,* traces how this dance was constructed.

Likewise in 1995 and 1996 Jan Erkert & Dancers participated in two community outreach programs, the "Border Project: Crossing Cultural/Gender Lines," which evolved into an afterschool dance program at the Northwestern University Settlement House in Chicago's West Town neighborhood, and a similar program at the José de Diego Community Academy in the same area. Both programs helped young students explore creative movement and, ultimately, to perform their own choreographic works.

Erkert continues to teach in the Dance Department at Columbia College and to tour with her company.

—Anthea Kraut

ESPLANADE

Choreography: Paul Taylor
Music: Bach's *Violin Concerto No. 2 in E Major, Double Concerto (Two Violins) in D Minor, Largo,* and *Allegro*
First Production: Paul Taylor Dance Company, 1 March 1975 at Lisner Auditorium in Washington, D.C.; first New York performance 11 June 1975 at the Lyceum Theater
Original Dancers: Bettie de Jong, Carolyn Adams, Nicholas Gunn, Eileen Cropley, Elie Chaib, Monica Morris, Greg Reynolds, and Ruth Andrien.

Publications

Anderson, Jack, *Ballet Review,* 1977.
Baker, Robb, *Dance Magazine,* August 1975.
Gillespie, Noel, *Dance Magazine,* May 1975.
Reiter, Susan, *Ballet Review,* Fall 1986.
Taylor, Paul, *Private Domain: An Autobiography,* New York, 1987.
Vaughan, David, *Dancing Times,* August 1975.

*   *   *

Esplanade is one of Paul Taylor's most glorious creations. In this landmark work from 1975, Taylor's sense of gracious and generous neoclassicism is firmly joined to his signature rounded athleticism. Five female and three male dancers bob along on the long, unbroken wave of Bach's music (the second and third movements of the *Double Concerto* were used by George Balanchine in *Concerto Barocco*). They begin with ordinary walking, hopping, and skipping steps that escalate along with the musical impulse. As the speed in the score mounts, the easy-going, nondance steps give way to faster jumps, rapid crossings of the stage, vigorous slides, and falls to the floor. The high energy of the work is counterbalanced by moments of tender partnering and others that evoke suffering or pain. As Jack Anderson noted in *Ballet Review* (1977), "the pedestrian movements are done with extraordinary vivacity and are movements only virtuosos can perform."

It is important to note that there is no storyline in *Esplanade.* Taylor's use of an open space for leisurely walking and strolling alludes to an esplanade, a country dance popular in the late 1700s. There are five sections in *Esplanade,* with each one aligning perfectly to a movement of Bach's score. In the first movement, three men and three women enter walking. They alternate their walk with a gentle hop and skip. They change directions and often hold hands. In time, one woman emerges as a kind of ringleader or mistress of the dance. In Taylor's egalitarian world, everyone gets a chance to lead and follow. A man emerges to lead the group. This moment is soon punctuated by rapid runs across the diagonal of the stage. In one of the most memorable sections of *Esplanade,* the dancers recline on a diagonal as a fleet female leaps between their bodies. All then rise and intertwine in a ring, which gives way to a square dance. The couples of the square dance then break off. This is followed by a full-tilt run by the cast, broken by several sudden, dead stops. Although momentarily frozen, the dancers are ever alert to the music. After a few beats they are off again.

The second section begins slowly and with stately movements. Three dancers open this movement. They are followed by a woman who moves like quicksilver. A tall, physically imposing woman (first danced by Bettie de Jong) beckons to another woman and a man. The tall woman evokes a gentle, maternal figure. Taylor sets her apart from the other women dancers by costuming her differently. The other members of the cast dance near her or with each other in unison with her; yet they never actually dance with her. She remains mysterious and remote. A series of skimming steps performed by another woman counterpoints the steady, almost mournful walk of the "mother" figure. Soon several women enter in a frieze-like motion that suggests grieving. They could be ancient Roman funerary figures. One woman is convulsed by grief as other dancers walk on their hands and knees, heads hanging downward.

The third section is initiated by a young woman who leads the other dancers in rapid runs across the stage. The runs give way as the dancers form a circle. Most of the dancers cluster in a pose as if they were having their photograph taken. The young woman gently tugs each couple on the shoulder as if suggesting a time to play. This female has an ebullient, allegro solo noted for its runs, turns, and quicksilver changes of direction. She ends her dance by jumping into the arms of one of the men.

The fourth movement is andante in tempo. Couples enter to stately strings. They kneel, clasp each other, walk, and run. A man cradles a woman in his arms and the other couples echo this moment of gentle support. The mood is one of easy give-and-take. A sense of courtliness emerges as women kneel and present their hands to their male partners. A man drapes his partner sideways alongside his body. A couple reclines almost like Etruscan tomb figures. Another couple engages in playfulness as the man swings his partner around his neck as her legs fly out into space. Yet another couple rolls along the floor. At one point the man supports the woman's upright body as she slowly stands on his middle. Risk is taken and shared.

The fifth and concluding movement involves the dancers in daring slides and falls to the floor. Up to this point in *Esplanade,* there has been no time to rest for the dancers. Now, in the final section, Taylor asks the dancers to pull out all the stops and push the motion to the extreme. Slides into the floor follow fast, one upon the other. One woman vigorously and viciously throws herself to the floor as she tries to maintain her balance. A man spins like a top and leaps backward. The women match the men in daring as they leap like cannonballs into their partners' waiting arms. Finally, a lone woman signals the end of the dance as she extends her arms solemnly to the left and right.

Esplanade shows off Paul Taylor's delight in surprising the eye. The sleek lines of some of his movement are frank borrowings from

ballet. These are refreshingly contrasted with little jolts, such as a jutting pelvis, an angled wrist, and a tipped head. Bodies are bounced off the floor or suspended in the air. Dancers curl and uncurl themselves into unique shapes and make swift, startling changes of direction. Above all, there is the illusion of simplicity. A walk is more than just a walk. Straight lines turn into circle dances. The dancers' faces are in "neutral" but their bodies are in "overdrive" as they respond to the constant, driving energy of Bach's music.

—Adriane Ruggiero

EVANS, Bill

American dancer, choreographer, educator, and company director

Born: James William Evans, 11 April 1946, in Lehi, Utah. **Education:** University of Utah, B.A. in English 1963, M.F.A. in dance 1970, certified Laban/Bartenieff Movement Analyst, 1997; apprenticed at Harkness Ballet. **Military Service:** U.S. Army, 1963-65. **Career:** Dancer, Chicago Opera Ballet, 1965-70; dancer and artistic coordinator, Repertory Dance Theatre, Salt Lake City, 1968-74; founded Bill Evans Solo Dance Repertory, 1974, and Bill Evans Dance Company, 1975; founder and artistic director, Bill Evans Summer Institute of Dance, from 1976. University of Utah, Salt Lake City, creative associate 1967-74, assistant professor 1974-76; associate professor, University of Indiana, 1986-88; University of New Mexico, Albuquerque, assistant professor 1988-89; associate professor 1989-92, full professor 1992 to present; numerous workshops, visiting professorships, and teaching residencies; founder, Dance Across the Borders, Master Artist Concert Series, National Dance Association Annual Conference. **Awards:** Guggenheim Fellowship, 1976; Albuquerque Arts Alliance Bravo! Award for dance event of the year, 1997; National Dance Association Scholar/Artist, 1997.

Works

1967	*Dance for Three People* (mus. Satie), Department of Modern Dance, University of Utah
	Lute Suite (mus. Bach), Department of Modern Dance, University of Utah
1968	*Interim* (mus. Henk Badings), Repertory Dance Theatre, Salt Lake City
	Bach to Bach (mus. Norma Dalby), RDT, Salt Lake City
	Chairs, American Dance Symposium, Wichita, Kansas
	Facets (mus. Prokofiev), Children's Dance Theatre, Salt Lake City
1969	*When Summoned* (mus. Subotnick), Deutsche Opr Ballet, Berlin
	Tropic Passion (mus. Milhaud), RDT, Salt Lake City
1970	*For Betty* (mus. Vivaldi), RDT, Salt Lake City
	Sea Children, Chidren's Dance Theatre, Salt Lake City
1971	*Tin-Tal* (mus. Mahapurush Misra), RDT, Salt Lake City
	Malcomb (mus. Zarek), Iowa Dance Councils Summer Workshop
	Old American Songs (mus. Copland), Alexandra Ballet Company, St. Louis

1972   *Five Songs in August* (mus. Sussman), RDT, Salt Lake
       City
       Piano Rags (mus. Joplin), RDT, Salt Lake City
       The Legacy (mus. Shapero), RDT, Salt Lake City
       Gospel Songs (mus. Mormon hymns), RDT Summer
       Workshop, Salt Lake City
1973   *Hard Times* (mus. Deseret String Band), RDT, Salt Lake
       City
       Three Bach Dances (mus. Bach), Jacob's Pillow Dance
       Festival
       Cambridge Dances (mus. Bach), Harvard Summer Dance
       Center Company
       Within Bounds (mus. Riley), RDT, Salt Lake City
       Solstice (mus. Subotnick), Giordano Dance Company,
       Evanston, Illinois
       Dances for King Chapel (mus. Jensen), Iowa Dance Coun-
       cils, Cornell
       Harold (mus. Joplin), Bill Evans Solo Dance, Edmondton
1974   *Juke Box* (mus. Glen Miller), RDT, Moorhead, Minne-
       sota
       As Quiet As (mus. Colgrass), Virginia Tanner's Children's
       Dance Theater, Salt Lake City
       Iris and Emily, RDT, Salt Lake City
       Meditation (mus. Bernstein), Fairmount Contemporary
       Ballet Company, Cleveland
       Bernstein's Mass, Utah Symphony Orchestra, Salt Lake
       City
1975   *Concerto for Diverse Dancers* (mus. Vivaldi), Depart-
       ment of Modern Dance, University of Utah
       Companion Pieces (mus. Evans), RDT, Salt Lake City
       Echoes of Autumn (mus. Pafunik), Ballet West, Salt Lake
       City
       Summerdance (mus. Evans), Choreo 18, Washington, D.C.
       End of the Trail (mus. Bill Monroe and Montana Slim),
       Dance Montana, Missoula
       Salt Lake City Rag (mus. Jensen), Iowa State University
       Dancers, Ames
1976   *Bach Dances* (mus. Bach), Bill Evans Dance Company,
       Salt Lake City
       I've Got a Gal in Kalamazoo (mus. Miller), Bill Evans
       Solo Dance, American Dance Festival
       The Dallas Blues (mus. Smith), BEDCO, American Dance
       Festival
       Mack and Mabel, Pioneer Memorial Theatre, Salt Lake
       City
1977   *Conjurations* (mus. David Sannella), BEDCO, Seattle
       Barefoot Boy with Marbles in His Toes, BEDCO, Seattle
       Ashtabula Rag (mus. Brian Dykstra), BEDCO,
       Ashtabula, Ohio
1978   *Impressions of Willow Bay* (mus. Sannella), BEDCO, Se-
       attle
       The New London Quadrille (mus. traditional marches),
       BEDCO, New London, Connecticut
       Double Bill (mus. Bill Evans Trio), BEDCO, Seattle
1979   *Craps* (first and third movements) (mus. Mark Johnson,
       Joe LaBarbera), BEDCO, Seattle
       Captive Voyage (mus. George Crum), Atlanta Contem-
       porary Dance Company
       Mixin' it Up (mus. Bill Evans Trio), BEDCO, Seattle
       The Field of Blue Children (mus. mus. Sannella), Cynthia
       Gregory and Bill Evans, Seattle

1980   *Huntsville City Limits* (mus. Kim and Sannella), Christine
       Sarry and Gregg Lizenberry, Seattle
       Restless Bond (mus. Linda Dowdell), Lee Connor and
       Lorn MacDougal/Dances of the High Desert, Santa
       Fe
       Making the Magic (mus. Sannella), BEDCO, Seattle
       Concerto for Tap Dancer and Orchestra (mus. Morton
       Gould), Bill Evans Solo Dance, Seattle
       The Rhode Island Rag (mus. Eubie Blake), collaboration
       of four different Rhode Island companies, Providence
1981   *Index* (mus. Robert Fripp, Brian Eno), BEDCO, Dallas
       Diverse Concerto (mus. Vivaldi), BEDCO, Chico, Cali-
       fornia
       Sweet and Lovely (mus. Evans), Bill Evans Solo Dance,
       Seattle
       Waltz for Debby (mus. Evans), Bill Evans Solo Dance,
       Seattle
       Le Jazz (mus. Bohuslav Martinu), Pacific Northwest
       Ballet Company, Seattle
       Restless, Linda McAndrew, Chicago and New York
1982   *Chartered Flight* (mus. Simon Jeffes), North Carolina
       Dance Theatre, Winston-Salem
       Cakewalkin' Babies (mus. Bessie Smith), BEDCO, Se-
       attle
       Alternating Current (mus. Jeffes and Sannella), Jim
       Coleman and Terese Freedman Duet Company, Port
       Townsend, Washington
       Doin' M' Best (mus. Jeffes), Easy Moving Company,
       Raleigh
       Keep on Tryin' (mus. Jeffes), Dancers Unlimited Reper-
       tory Company, Dallas
       Episodes (mus. Sannella), Fusion dance Company, Mi-
       ami
       Storm Warnings (mus. Jeffes), Harbinger Dance Com-
       pany, Detroit
       Homecoming (mus. Andrej Panufnik), BEDCO, Seattle
       This Way and That (mus. Lucinda Lawrence), University
       of Illinois Dance Company, Urbana
1983   *Origins and Impulses* (later *For Anna*) (mus.
       Shostakovich), BEDCO, Seattle
       The New People Too (text traditional Native American
       poetry), Contemporary Dance Theatre, Cincinnati
       To Be Continued (mus. Jeffes), Dancers Company of
       Brigham Young University, Provo
       Out of Sorts (mus. Jeffes), Territory Dance Theatre, Tuc-
       son
       Tuesday Morning (mus. Evans and Yoken), Dance Art/
       San Antonio
       Calabash Boom (mus. Floyd Williams), Pittsburgh Dance
       Alloy
       Thoughts on Parting (mus. Scott Cossu), Bill Evans Solo
       Dance, Seattle
1984   *Prairie Fever* (mus. Jeffes), Contemporary Dancers
       Canada, Winnipeg
       Umbre Solstice, Interlochen Arts Academy Dancers,
       Interlochen, Michigan
       Emily's Dilemma (mus. Gale Ormiston), Dance Art/San
       Antonio
       From Here to Eternity, Bill Evans Solo Dance, Winnipeg
       Grounded Assent (mus Pärt), Dance Company of
       Middlebury, Vermont

Bill Evans. Photograph © Jack Mitchell.

1985 *Weathered Wall,* Five College Dance Department Dancers, South Hadley, Massachusetts

Side Orders (mus. Jeffes), Thomson/Trammel Duet Company, Harrisonburg, Virginia

Dream Tigers (mus. Villa Lobos), BEDCO, Meadville, Pennsylvania

Craps (with second movement; mus. Steve Kim), Ririe-Woodbury Dance Company, Salt Lake City

In a Former Life (mus. Evans), Chrysalis Repertory Dance Company, Houston

Soliloquy (mus. Evans), Bill Evans Solo Dance, Salt Lake City

Dances for My Father (mus. Basie), Bill Evans Solo Dance, Salt Lake City

In the Nick of Time (mus. Monk), Bill Evans Solo Dance, Salt Lake City

1986 *In the Beginning* (mus. Jeffes), RDT, Salt Lake City

Comes Winter (mus. Evelyn Jensen), Iowa State University Dancers, Ames

Plainsong (mus. Jeffes), Wichita State Unversity Dancers, Kansas

No Laughing Matter (mus. Jeffes), Meredith College Dancers, Raleigh, North Carolina

Tide Pool (mus. Jeffes), University of Hawaii Dancers, Honolulu

Three Tangos (mus. Valeria Munnariz), Co-Motion Dance Company, Seattle

Shattered Butterflies (mus. Munnariz), Mills College Repertory Dance Company, Oakland

Nostalgias (mus. Munariz), Santa Fe Dance Foundation

And That's Final (mus. Jeffes), Denton Women's University Dance Faculty, Texas

The Fundamental Things Apply (mus. Jeffes), Bill Evans Summer Institute of Dance, Colorado Springs

1987 *Suite Summer* (mus. Gregory Ballard), BESID, Colorado Springs

Summer Songs (mus. Sweet Honey in the Rock), BESID, Bloomington, Indiana

Take One-Take Two (mus. Eno and Bach), Indiana University Dance Theatre, Bloomington

Heartwind (mus. Jeffes), Towson State University Dancers, Baltimore

Suite Benny (mus. Goodman), RDT, Salt Lake City

1988 *Flip Side at the Savoy* (mus. Ellington), Penelope Hanstein and Gail Zaks, Denton, Texas

Suite Duke (mus. Ellington), Co-Motion Dance Company, Seattle

BLT Blues, BESD, Bloomington, Indiana

1989 *Round Seven* (mus. Jesse Mano), Colorado Repertory Dance Company, Boulder

SunRiseDanSet (mus. Jeffes), Star Dance Swan Contemporary Dance Theatre, Edmond, Oklahoma

Hallowed Halls (mus. Carl Landa), Emma Willard School Dancers, Troy, New York

The Skin Drum, University of New Mexico Opera Workshop, Albuquerque

The Rocky Horror Show (and director), New Mexico Repertory Theatre Company, Santa Fe

1990 *Summer's Night Dance,* (mus. Evans), Star Dance Swan Contemporary Dance Theatre, Edmond, Oklahoma

There Was a Boy (mus. Nat "King" Cole), BESD, Albuquerque

Fable (mus. Chris Shultis), UNM Contemporary Dance Ensemble, Albuquerque

Cuttin'a Rug, UNM Contemporary Dance Ensemble, Albuquerque

1991 *Uncoiled Heart* (mus. Mozart), BEDCO, Magnifico Festival of the Arts, Albuquerque

Chantdance (mus. Evans), Albuquerque Youth Dance Group

Danza (mus. Inti-Illimani), UNM Contemporary Dance Ensemble, Albuquerque

Bob's Blues (mus. Robert Tate), UNM Contemporary Dance Ensemble, Albuquerque

Jumpin' with Jefferson (mus. Jefferson Vorhees), UNM Contemporary Dance Ensemble, Albuquerque

Velorio (mus. Faure), El Paso International Dance Theatre

1992 *Velorio II* (mus. Faure), UNM Contemporary Dance Ensemble, Albuquerque

Velorio III (mus. Faure), Strong Wind Wild Horses, Seattle

Monk Dances (mus. Monk), Evans and Jenkins, Seattle

Holiday Sweet (mus. Oscar Peterson), Evans and Jenkins, Seattle

Sentinels (mus. Eno), BEDCO, Magnifico Festival of the Arts, Albuquerque

Espiritus de la Tierra (mus. Inti-Illimani, Evans), Albuquerque Youth Dance Troupe

1993 *Back at You* (text and music with Kestutis Nakas and John Bartlit), BEDCO, Albuquerque

Incantations for Elizabeth (mus. Evans), University of New Mexico Dance Comany, Albuquerque

Rhythm on Tap (mus. Artie Shaw), Albuquerque Youth Dance Troupe

Mingus Amongus (mus. Mingus), Strong Wind Wild Horses, Seattle

No Mean Feet (mus. Evans), UNM Contemporary Dance Ensemble, Kobe, Japan

Circular Reverie (mus. Faure), Ballett Impulso de Monterrey, Mexico

1994 *Pilgrimage* (mus. David Yoken, Mikko Mikkla), Contemporary Dance School, London

Winterdance (mus. Yoken), TUTVO Dance Compnay, Turku, Finland

Los Perdidos (mus. Bach), BEDCO, San Luis Potosi, Mexico

Mingus Amongus II (mus. Mingus), BEDCO, Albuquerque

Velorio IV (mus. Faure), Velorio Project Company, Seattle

Rhythms of the Soul w/ Shirley Jenkins and Johnson and Peters (mus. Jim Knapp), Evans/Jenkins/Johnson/Peters, Seattle

How to Name It (mus. Ilaiyaraaja), BESD, Albuquerque

Dance Begun on Christmas Day (mus. Chopin), BESD, Pune, India

1995 *Suite Christmas* (mus. Berlin), BESD, Albuquerque

Vigil (mus. Faure), Montclair State University Dance Company, New Jersey

Rhythms of the Heart (mus. Jerry Mulligan), BEDCO, Albuquerque

Suite Rhythm (mus. Shaw), Wisconsin Dance Ensemble, Madison

Celebration for Paquita (mus. Evans), Celebrate Youth Dancers, Albuquerque

Velorio V (mus. Faure), Ball State University Dance Theatre, Muncie, and Anderson Young Ballet Theatre, Anderson, Indiana

1996 *Saintly Passion* (mus. Bach), BEDCO, Seattle

Naturescape Unfolding (mus. Eno), BEDCO, Albuquerque

Revisitations (mus. Perschetti), BDCO, Albuquerque

Ritmos Calientes (mus. Cal Tjader), BESD, Kuopio, Finland

Planctus w/ Nora Reynolds Daniel (mus. Steve Peters), Magnifiso Festival of the Arts, Albuquerque

Cellular Breathing (mus. Taj Mahal), BESID, Seattle

Tribute (mus. Cirque du Soleil), Jackson High School Dancers, Everett, Washington

Incantations II (mus. Warlen Bassham), Dance Kaleidoscope, Seattle

Incantations III (mus. Evans), Desert Dance Theatre, Rock Springs, Wyoming

Ceremony of the Springtime Moon (mus. Evans), Magnifco Youth Dance troupe, Albuquerque

Spirit Walk (mus. Quantum Dreaming), Dance Theatre El Paso

1997 *Albuquerque Love Song* (mus. Michael Cava), BEDCO, Albuquerque

Los Ritmos Calientes w/ Sara Hutchinson, Skip Randall, Mark Yonally (mus. Brubeck, Fernandez, Silver), BEDCO, Deming, New Mexico

Climbing to the Moon (mus. Cava), Cava-Parker Dance Company, Seattle

Isle of View (mus. Jeffes), Peninsula Dance Theatre, Bremerton, Washington

Celtic Odyssey (mus. Altan), Jackson High School Dancers, Everett, Washington

Spirit Walk II (mus. Quantum Dreaming), University of New Mexico Dance Company, Albuquerque

The Nutcracker, act I (mus. Tchaikovsky), New Mexico Ballet Company, Albuquerque

Publications

On EVANS: articles—

Fruits, Liz Winslow, "Spotlight on Bill Evans," *Dance Teacher Now,* May/June 1993.

Smith, Amanda, "Bill Evans: A Modern Day Dance Frontiersman," *Dance Magazine,* February 1977.

*   *   *

Bill Evans was born in Lehi, Utah, an isolated Mormon town of five thousand. He discovered music on the radio and tap dance through Hollywood musicals, and he was creating his own dances by the time he was five. He took his first dance lessons in the third grade from Charles Purrington, a tap teacher in Salt Lake City. He continued tap and ballet classes with Purrington's daughter, June Park. He also studied ballet for a time in high school with Willam Christensen.

Evans went to college at the University of Utah, earning his degree in English but only two courses shy of a ballet major. He was a principal dancer with the school's Utah Ballet, the company that later became Ballet West. He also studied briefly with Helen Tamiris and Daniel Nagrin and performed extensively with the university's modern dance department.

Evans' dance career was interrupted in 1963 by a two-year army stint. During a tank training maneuver he suffered multiple fractures of his ankle; he was unable to walk without crutches for a year. Following his discharge he went to New York City, determined to pursue a career in dance. He danced as an apprentice at the Harkness House, where he studied 11 hours a day, including classes in jazz, Graham technique, music for dance, Labanotation, and gymnastics. The day ended with a two-hour ballet session with Jack Cole. Rebecca Harkness was grooming him to be a member of her company, but at 26, Evans was impatient to begin his career as a professional dancer.

He was accepted as a principal in Ruth Page's Chicago Opera Ballet. The company did an autumn season with the Chicago Opera and a six-week winter season in Chicago, followed by a three-month bus tour. The performance experience was invaluable but the touring pace was not for Evans. He returned to Salt Lake City in 1967, where he was invited to join the newly established Repertory Dance Theater (RDT) and where he had plentiful opportunities to choreograph. He worked concurrently on an MFA at the University of Utah. In 1969 critic Walter Terry was impressed by Evans' work and recommended him to the West Berlin Opera Ballet, which was looking for young American choreographers. He spent a month in Berlin, creating *When Summoned,* a work about the pull between East and West.

Back in Utah, he created several works a year for RDT. In 1975, after seven years with RDT, Evans formed his own dance company, along with Gregg Lizenbery, Kathleen McClintock, Ann Asnes, and Shirley Jenkins. The new company toured the U.S. extensively in an attempt to establish itself. The strategy worked; the company received enthusiastic reviews, including a triumph at the American Dance Festival in New London, Connecticut. Soon thereafter, Evans was contacted by the president of the board for Seattle's Dance Theater and asked to take the company over. It was a fortuitous match, for the company was able to establish itself very quickly in Seattle with a strong board, a building, a school, and funding from regional sources, as well as the National Endowment for the Arts. Renamed the Bill Evans Dance Company, it became the major company in Seattle and its continued extensive touring established it and Evans as major players in modern dance outside New York City.

During the seven years in Seattle Evans created 39 dances, including *Barefoot Boy with Marbles in His Toes* (1977), a piece named after his childhood practice of stamping around the room with the marbles acting as tap shoes and *Double Bill* (1978), a collaboration with jazz pianist Bill Evans, his first such collaboration. Certain sections of the dance called for improvisation from both dancers and musicians, with each discipline cuing the other through rhythmic motifs. In 1986 he established a new home for his company at the University of Indiana at Bloomington, where he took the position of coordinator of dance. Evans formed the new core of his company from some of his dancers from Seattle, such as Shirley Jenkins and Rip Parker, as well as newcomers, such as Debra Knapp, who was already teaching there.

In November 1987 the Bill Evans Dance Company and the David Baker Jazz Ensemble unveiled 13 largely improvisational works to newly composed music. This program, with some variation, was performed as *Fascinatin' Rhythms* in New Mexico in 1989. At least 20 dances flowed together in a commingling of tap, jazz, and modern dance, heavy on the percussion. *Round Seven, One and Two*, a trip-up, fall-and-catch-me dance blended into *Movement Game*, with crazy, innovative manipulations and witty plays on such basic gestures as lifting a cigarette and blowing a kiss. This keen eye for the details of body language which betray human frailty and absurdity, combined with Evans' his ability to communicate and entertain with humor, are predominant characteristics of his dance.

In 1988 the University of New Mexico hired him to be the dance head of the department of theatre and dance. Once again Evans brought together a core of dancers from throughout the country to study and work with him in New Mexico. University dance ensembles were formed using the best of the undergraduate and graduate students, and toured with the Evans company throughout New Mexico, in large and small communities, from Taos to Silver City. The highly accessible material, combining tap, jazz and modern styles, was enthusiastically welcomed, and again resulted in a broad touring agenda. Always working to expand the audience for modern dance, Evans often choreographed dance education right into the program.

Bill Evans is a well-known figure abroad. Throughout the 1980s and 1990s Evans fit summer gigs of teaching and performing in France, New Zealand, Australia, India, Japan, and Mexico into his schedule. His travels are a frequent source of inspiration, drawn from a specific location's topography or quality of life. *How to Name It,* for example, was his artistic response to India. Drawing on the sinuous upper torso movement of India's Kathak dance, Evans created a hybrid form using tap and Indian rhythms, as well as jazz variations, accompanied by a fusion of Eastern and Western-style music.

Now in his fifties, Evans is still an energetic performer, appearing in solos and with his current tap partner, Sara Hutchinson. Evans' career as a choreographer has increasingly focused on social issues, such as the AIDS epidemic, even as he continues to concentrate on the local community in New Mexico and its unique ethnic mix. He organized several Festivals of Percussive Dance, for example, in which area dancers gather to celebrate the folk origins of flamenco and tap dance.

Considered one of the best dance teachers in America, Evans continues to work hard in dance education for children as well as professionals; he's kept the Bill Evans Summer Institute going since 1976 and he has started two youth dance projects in Albuquerque.

—Valerie Vogrin

EZRALOW, Daniel
American dancer and choreographer

Born: c. 1957 in Los Angeles, California. **Education:** Attended University of California, Berkeley, 1974-76, medical studies; began taking dance classes, and performed with UCB resident company under the direction of David and Marni Wood; moved to New York, 1976; studied with Alvin Ailey, Joffrey Ballet, at Juilliard. **Career:** Dancer, 5 x 2 Plus Dance Company, 1976-79 (leaving for several months in 1978); Lar Lubovitch Dance Company, 1978;

Paul Taylor Dance Company, 1979-83; Pilobolus Dance Theater; co-founder/choreographer, Momix Dance Theater, 1983-87; founder, ISO Dance, 1987-94; choreography for Opening Ceremonies, Winter Paralympique Games, Albertville; 1990 World Cup Soccer Championships in Italy; created ballets for Paris Opera Ballet, Hubbard Street Dance Company, Batsheva Dance Company (Israel), London Contemporary Dance Company and others. **Awards:** Bob Fosse Award for Alternative Choreography, 1996; Emmy, *Episodes*, Los Angeles; Premio Positano Individual Achievement award, Italy.

Works

1979	*Parson Nibs and Rude Beggars* w/Moses Pendleton, Pilobolus Dance Theater
1981	*Day Two* w/Pendleton, Pilobolus Dance Theater
	Apotheoses Picasso w/Pendleton, La Fête du L'Humanité, Paris
1982	*Brothers* w/David Parsons
1984	*Dogfish*, Batsheva Dance Company, Israel
1985	*SVSPLKT*, Batsheva Dance Company
1986	*The Great Pretender/Extasis*, Batsheva Dance Company
1987	*Irma Vep*, London Contemporary Dance Theatre
	Soon, Paris Opera Ballet
1988	*Eight Heads for Ori*, Batsheva Dance Company
1989	*Super Straight Is Coming Down*, Hubbard Street Dance Chicago
1990	*Read My Hips*, Hubbard Street Dance Company
1991	*White Man Sleeps*, Maggio Danza, Florence, Italy
1992	*Nutcracker*, City Children's Nutcracker, Minneapolis
	Scapino Meets Dap, Scapino Ballet Rotterdam, Holland
1993	*In Praise of Shadows*, Hubbard Street Dance Chicago
1994	*Tour D'Olandia*, Ballet di Arena di Verona
	Mandala, Ballet di Arena di Verona
1997	*Mandala*, Raw Zeal Productions
	Lady Lost Found, Hubbard Street Dance Chicago
	Metal Spring, American Repertory Ballet

Other works inlcude: Choreography for Wagner's *The Flying Dutchman* (Los Angeles Opera, directed by Julie Taymor); *Aida* (Maggio Musicale production, music directed by Zubin Mehta); Dana Broccoli's musical, *Florinda;* director/choreographer, *Salgari* (Arena di Verona, Italy); *Parade* (with Harold Prince); and with Vittorio Gassman in *Ulysses and the White Whale*.

Films and Videotapes

Films—Lina Wertmuller's *Camorra; Ulysses and the White Whale;* Julian Temple's *Earth Girls are Easy;* Marco Bellocchio's *The Vision of the Sabbath Witches; The Last Concert;* and Mauro Bolognini's *Casa Riccordi;* television—*A Tribute to Sarajevo* (New Year's Eve live Eurovision TV broadcast); *Beatles Songbook* (PBS); *Windows* for Danish television (Bravo); "Tears," for *Red Shoes Diaries* (Showtime); *Episodes*, ISO Dance (PBS, KCET-TV in Los Angeles); *Fiori Di Pietra* (RAI Eurovision Special); *St. Asera Lino, Finalmente Venerdi* (RAI Television Special); and *San Remo Music Festival* (RAI Television Special); music videos—U2, *Even Better Than the Real Thing*; David Bowie's *Glass Spider* tour; Sting, *They Dance Alone*; Pat Metheny, *Japan Program*, and others; commer-

Daniel Ezralow with Ashley Roland. Photograph © Johan Elbers.

cials—Coca-Cola, BMW Italia, The Gap, Sapporo Beer (Japan), Noritake Chinaware (Japan), Raymond-Weil watches, and Xerox-Fuji; specials: *Gold at the Guggenheim* (Benefit for AMFAR); *Winter Paralympiques* (Opening Ceremonies, Albertville); *Mens' and Womens' Spectacles* (Fashion, Issey Miyake); *Dancers and Friends* (Friends Indeed Benefit, New York City).

Publications

On EZRALOW: articles—

Bleiberg, Laura, "Running Wild," *Ballet News*, April 1983.
Connors, Thomas, "Hubbard Street Dance Chicago," *Dance Magazine*, August 1994.
Eichenbaum, Rose, "Ezralow Premiere of One-Man Show in L.A.," *Dance Magazine*, March 1998.
Ezralow, Orrin, "Dance Is Life!—Daniel Ezralow."
Farnham, Lloyd, "Imagining Eighth-Century Showtunes: New Musical *Florinda* Puts Twists on Spanish Legend," *Back Stage West*, 29 June 1995.
Feingold, Danny, "Daniel Ezralow Returns to the Home Front," *Village View*, 9-15 February 1990.
Hardy, Camille, "Hubbard Street Dance Chicago," *Dance Magazine*, February 1995.
Hering, Doris, "American Repertory Ballet," *Dance Magazine*, May 1997.
Stenn, Rebecca, "Ezralow's Lady Found in Chi.," *Dance Magazine*, April 1997.
Stuart, O., "The Powers of Optimism," *Dance Magazine*, August 1988.
Tobias, Tobi, "American Repertory Ballet," *New York*, 3 March 1997.

*   *   *

Daniel Ezralow was born and raised in an affluent section of Los Angeles. While in high school, he ran on the track and field team and his specialty was the hurdles; he also played basketball and enjoyed skiing. After graduation in 1974, he left Los Angeles to attend college at the University of California at Berkeley, with the intent of becoming a doctor.

While a freshman at UC Berkeley, Ezralow began taking dancing classes and, as he later put it, "went head over heels for it." The following year, he was performing with the school's resident company, and by 1976, he had given up his pursuit of a medical degree to see if he could make it in dancing. Ezralow moved to New York City, where he studied with the Alvin Ailey and Joffrey Ballet companies, as well as the Juilliard school. Several months later, he was working as a professional with 5 x 2 Plus Dance Company under the direction of Bruce Becker and Jane Kosminski. He describes himself in *Ballet News* as "kind of crazy," telling Becker and Kosminski he wasn't sure about becoming a company dancer "because I still wanted to train." They assured him that if he took the job he could still continue to take classes.

While at 5 x 2, Ezralow met Moses Pendleton, a founding member of Pilobolus Dance Theater. One day, Ezralow blew up at Pendleton because he felt Pendleton wasn't giving him enough direction in choreography. Ezralow claims the incident changed his insight into choreographing—and was the beginning of a long-lasting friendship with Pendleton. Ezralow remained with 5 x 2 for

two years before leaving to join the Lar Lubovitch Company in 1978. After a brief stay there, he returned to 5 x 2 for another year, where he planned his next move: joining the Paul Taylor Dance Company. The brash young Ezralow told Taylor one day that he wanted very much to dance with the company; out of a field of 90 aspiring male dancers at an audition soon thereafter, Ezralow was asked to joined the company.

Ezralow danced with the Taylor company from 1979 to 1983. While there, Ezralow also worked with Pendleton on several projects for Pilobolus, including *Parson Nibs and the Rude Beggars* (1981), *Apotheoses Picasso* (1981) and *Day Two* (1979), which started out one day when Ezralow and Pendleton were caught in a sudden rainstorm, stripped off their clothes and "proceeded to create a scene straight out of a caveman film." Also in 1981, Ezralow worked with fellow Taylor dancer David Parsons to create *Brothers*, a duet which they began composing "amid snowdrifts in a hotel parking lot in Cleveland, Ohio, at ten o'clock at night."

In 1983 Ezralow and Pendleton co-founded Momix Dance Theater, a spinoff of Pilobolus-styled dancing, where Ezralow continued to perform and choreograph until 1987. While at Momix, Ezralow began forays into the worlds of high fashion, co-choreographing and directing with Issey Miyake fashion/dance extravaganzas in New York, Paris, and Tokyo. He also entered the television and film industry, where he choreographed and performed in music videos for John Fogerty, U2, Julian Lennon, and The Lover Speaks, as well as working on Julian Temple's film *Earth Girls Are Easy*. Also during his tenure at Momix, Ezralow independently created works for the Paris Opera Ballet, the Batsheva Dance Company of Israel, Der Deutsche Oper Berlin and the London Contemporary Dance Theatre. He also appeared in the lead role in a film called *Camorra*, by Lina Wertmuller.

In 1987 Ezralow left Momix with fellow dancers Jamey Hampton, Ashley Roland, and Morleigh Steinberg to co-found ISO (I'm So Optimistic) Dance Theatre, where he performed and choreographed until 1994. He continued with his independent work, choreographing work for David Bowie's *Glass Spider* tour as well as a music video, *They Dance Alone*, for Sting. He also worked with the a cappella group The Bobs, both on their U.S. tour and on a PBS special, as well as with Batsheva Dance Company, Chicago's Hubbard Street Dance Company, and television and film work in Italy, including the 1990 World Cup Soccer Championship commercials.

In 1995 Ezralow choreographed author Dana Broccoli's musical *Florinda*, set in eighth-century Spain, incorporating Spanish and Moorish style music composed by John Claflin and Laurence O'Keefe. He received the Bob Fosse Dance Award for Alternative Choreography in 1996. Other awards won include an Emmy for the television series he co-created, called *Episodes*, and the Italian Premio Positano for Individual Achievement. In 1997 the American Repertory Ballet performed Ezralow's *Metal Springs*, with music composed by Yuvol Ron. The next year, 1998, Ezralow's multimedia event *Mandela* had its U.S. debut, and Ezralow choreographed for his largest audience ever—the 70th Annual Academy Awards at the Dorothy Chandler Pavilion. He danced in several creative sketches for films nominated in the choreography category including *Men in Black, The Full Monty,* and *Titanic* (*The Full Monty* won). The sky is the limit—Ezralow continues to create spectacles of sight and sound for delighted audiences around the world.

—Daryl F. Mallett

FABLES FOR OUR TIME

Choreography: Charles Weidman
Music: Freda Miller
Set & Costume Design: Charles Weidman, A. Spolidore
Lighing Design: Jack Ferris
First Production: Charles Weidman and Company, Jacob's Pillow Dance Festival, 11 July 1947
Original Dancers: Charles Weidman, Felisa Conde, Betty Osgood, Carl Morris, Betts Lee, Emily Frankel, Sharry Traver; narrator—Jack Ferris

Publications

Hering, Doris, "*Fables for Our Time,*" *Dance Magazine,* September 1947.
Martin, John, "Weidman Ballet Opens its Season," *New York Times,* 19 April 1948.
Terry, Walter, "Moderns in Review," *Dance News,* September 1947.
Reproduction of composer's holograph of the piano part, with manuscript notes on the narration and choreography, a sound recording of a 1967 interview of Weidman by Marian Horosko, excerpts recorded in two films (1964 and 1972) of Weidman's company, a 1980 videotape of Repertory Dance Theatre, and a large collection of performance photographs are available at the Dance Collection of the New York Public Library for the Performing Arts.

*   *   *

Charles Weidman used funds from a Guggenheim fellowship to create *Fables for Our Time,* one of his most enduring works. He initially staged four of Thurber's classic tales: "The Unicorn in the Garden," about a henpecked husband's revenge; "The Shrike and the Chipmunks," about an artistic chipmunk and his nagging, materialistic wife; "The Little Girl and the Wolf," an updated Red Riding Hood story; and "The Owl Who was God," in which an owl inadvertently becomes an oracular demagogue worshiped by a mob of forest animals. For the New York premiere, at the Mansfield Theater on 18 April 1948, Weidman replaced the third section with "The Courtship of Arthur and Al," in which a ne'er-do-well young beaver courts a girl who turns him down to marry a workaholic older beaver, only too see the latter gnaw his way to an early grave.

A narrator (originally the work's lighting designer, Jack Ferris) strolls through the action, sometimes helping between the fables to rearrange the brightly painted plywood boxes—an old Humphrey-Weidman standby—that comprise the set. He recites Thurber's texts, almost verbatim, in short sections, who action and dialogue the dancers enact in representational pantomime (Weidman used his trademark "kinetic pantomime"—a dancerly expansion of natu-

ralistic gesture—in only a few passages). Freda Miller's clattery piano score supports the action in the melodramatic style of silent-movie accompaniment, underscoring the work's slapstick element. The wolf and the shrike (a malevolent chipmunk-eating bird) were originally rendered as surreal marionettes on long poles, after Thurber's drawings, by Spolidore. The narrator sums up each fable with a punning moral, such as (for the beavers) "Better to have loafed and lost than never to have loafed at all."

Weidman made no attempt to mimic the loopy style of Thurber's original cartoon illustrations, but he perfectly captured the writer's irony and *faux-naif* wit. Except for the slightly tatterdemalion costumes (by Weidman), *Fables* received rave reviews; Weidman's subtle comic timing and characterization earned special praise. Remarking on the almost inevitable convergence of Thurber's and Weidman's senses of humor, Don McDonagh, writing in *The Complete Guide to Modern Dance,* called the work "a marriage of sensibilities that were made for one another."

Fables became a minor modern dance classic, and remained in Weidman's repertory until his death in 1975. In the 1960s he choreographed three more tales from Thurber's collection, usually selecting a set of three or four for a given performance. The new stories were "Tigress and Her Mate," in which a tigress kills her grumpy husband, turning him into a rug for her children (another marionette) to play on; "The Clothes Moth and the Luna Moth," about the doomed love of an old gray cloth-muncher (Weidman) for a glamorous, light-obsessed female; and "The Moth and the Star," a poignant story performed in silence, in which a young moth grows old and dies in a lifelong attempt to fly to a distant star.

Weidman also mounted *Fables* on companies other than his own, including the New Dance Group in the late 1950s, and Salt Lake City's Repertory Dance Theater in the 1970s. Shortly before he died, Weidman set the work on the Mary Anthony Dance Theatre (Anthony had appeared in the New Dance Group version). Anthony acquired the original props and costumes, toured her version ("Unicorn," "Chipmunks," "The Moth and the Star," and the beavers) widely, and maintained it in her company's repertory through the 1990s.

—Christopher Caines

FAGAN, Garth

Jamaican-born American dancer, choreographer, and company director

Born: 3 May 1940 in Kingston, Jamaica. **Education:** Studied in Jamaica with Ivy Baxter; early influences included Pearl Primus and Lavinia Williams; graduate of Wayne State University, Detroit, Michigan; studied dance with Martha Graham, José Limón, Alvin

Ailey, and Mary Hinkson. **Career:** Performed with Jamaica National Dance Company; soloist, Wayne State University Dance Group, 1961-66; choreographer and principal soloist, Detroit Contemporary Dance Company, 1965-67; director, All-City High School Dance Company, Detroit, 1967-70; director/instructor of dance, Eastman School of Music, Rochester, New York, 1970-87; director/instructor of dance, State University of New York (SUNY) at Brockport, New York, 1970—; founded Garth Fagan Dance in Rochester, New York, 1970 (originally known as Bottom of the Bucket But . . . Dance Company, later renamed The Bucket Dance Theater and then Garth Fagan Dance); first en pointe work, *Footprints Dressed in Red* created for Dance Theatre of Harlem, 1986; solo for Judith Jamison, *Scene Seen,* 1988; *Jukebox for Alvin* for Alvin Ailey American Dance Theatre, 1994; *Never No Lament* for José Limón Company, 1994; directed and choreographed first fully-staged production of Duke Ellington's street opera *Queenie Pie* at the Kennedy Center; opening production of Joseph Papp's New York Shakespeare Festival's "Shakespeare Marathon: *A Midsummer Night's Dream,*" and Walt Disney Production of *The Lion King* for Broadway, 1997; Garth Fagan Dance has performed throughout the U.S. in major cities, on college campuses, and in Europe, Africa, Asia, the Near and Middle East, South America, and the Netherlands, for France's Chateauvallon Festival, Turkey's Istanbul Festival, in the West Indies, and in such venues as the International Arts Festival (New Zealand), Internationales Tanzfest N.R.W. (Germany), Basel Tanz (Switzerland), the Israel Festival in Jerusalem, the Vienna Festival-Tanz, the Festival of Two Worlds (Italy), Jacob's Pillow, Spoleto USA, Dance/Aspen, and the first National Black Arts Festival. **Awards:** Distinguished University Professor of the State University of New York; three-year choreography fellowship from the National Endowment for the Arts, 1983-85; New York State Governor's Arts Award, 1986; Arts for Greater Rochester Cultural Award, 1986; National Council for Culture and Art Monarch Award, 1987; John Simon Guggenheim fellowship, 1989; Lillian Fairchild Award for Meritorious Production in the Creative Arts, 1982, 1993; *Dance Magazine* Award, 1990; four New York Dance and Performance Award ("Bessie"); Learning Through Art/ Guggenheim Museum Children's Program Role Model Award, 1992; Musgrave Medal, Jamaica Institute of Art, 1995; Detroit All-City School Award, 1995; Fulbright 50th Anniversary Distinguished Fellow, 1996; honorary doctorates from the Juilliard School, the University of Rochester, Nazareth College (Rochester, New York), and Hobart and William Smith Colleges (Geneva, New York).

Works (all performances by Garth Fagan Dance unless otherwise noted)

1967	*Life Forms/Death Shapes* (mus. Surinach), revised 1973
1970	*Roots* (mus. Olatunji)
1971	*Four Women* (mus. Simone)
	Yesternow (mus. Davis)
	Liberation Suite (mus. Shirley, Mingus, and the Last Poets)
1973	*Polk Street Carnival* (mus. Mandrill)
	Thank You Jesus (mus. Shirley, traditional)
	Grits Soufflé (mus. Mahavishnu Orchestra)
1974	*Duets* (mus. Brahms)
	4 + 1 (Rehearsing Around) (mus. live improvisation)
1976	*Salon for Fashionable Five-Toed Dragons* (mus. Moore)
1977	*Untitled* (mus. Jarrett)

1978	*From Before* (mus. MacDonald)
1979	*Oatka Trail* (mus. Dvorak)
1981	*Of Night, Light & Melanin* (mus. Jarrett)
	Prelude (mus. Ibrahim and Roach), revised 1983
1982	*Touring Jubilee 1924 (Professional)* (mus. Preservation Hall Jazz Band)
	Daylight Savings Time (mus. Pastorious, Alias)
1983	*Proscript Posthumous: Ellington* (mus. Ellington)
	Sonata and the Afternoon (mus. Brahms)
	Easter Freeway Processional (mus. Glass)
1984	*Sojourn* (revival) (mus. Greene)
1985	*Never Top 40 (Jukebox)* (mus. Puccini, Arlen, Dowe, McNaughton, Viadana, Art Ensemble of Chicago)
1986	*Mask Mix Masque* (mus. Jones, Horn)
1987	*Footprints Dressed in Red* (mus. Adams), Dance Theatre of Harlem
	Passion Distanced (revival) (mus. Pärt)
	Traipsing through the May (mus. Vivaldi)
1988	*Time After Before Place* (mus. Art Ensemble of Chicago)
	Scene Seen (solo) for Judith Jamison, The Jamison Project
	A Midsummer Night's Dream, produced by Joseph Papp, Public Theater, New York
	Landscape for 10 (mus. Brahms)
1989	*Telling a Story* (mus. Davis)
1990	*Until, By & If, I & II* (mus. Pullen)
1991	*Griot New York* (mus. Marsalis)
	Mozhop's Mall (mus. Mozart)
1992	*Moth Dreams* (mus. Jolivet, Monk, Marsalis)
1993	*Draft of Shadows* (mus. Diamond)
	Jukebox for Alvin (mus. Dvorak, Mahal, Jarrett, Dunbar/ Shakespeare), Alvin Ailey American Dance Theatre
1994	*Postcards: Pressures & Possibilities* (mus. Baker)
	Never No Lament (mus. Kronos Quartet), José Limón Dance Company
1995	*Earth Eagle First Circle* (mus. Pullen, African Brazilian Connection, Chief Cliff Singers)
1996	*Mix 25* (mus. Marsalis, Brahms, Cage, Suso)
1997	*Nkanyit* (mus. Carter/Lundy, National Percussion Group of Kenya)
	The Lion King on Broadway for Walt Disney Productions

Publications

On FAGAN: articles—

Belans, Linda, "Garth Fagan: A Man with Stories to Weave Sets up His Loom at ADF," http://www2.nando.net.events.dance/ garth.html (originally published in the *Raleigh News & Observer,* Durham, North Carolina).

Greskovic, Robert, "Review," *Dance Magazine,* April 1994.

Hunt, Marilyn, "Review," *Dance Magazine,* March 1994.

Simpson, Herbert M., "Review," *Dance Magazine,* December 1994.

Thom, Rose Anne, "New York *Griot,*" *Dance Magazine,* February 1995.

Films and Videotapes

Griot New York, Great Performances—Dance in America series, PBS, 1995.

*   *   *

Garth Fagan Dance Company: *Until, By, and If,* 1990. Photograph © Beatriz Schiller.

To say that Garth Fagan's works are as original as they are universal is merely to give substance to a cliché; yet like many stereotypes, even some clichés have their origins in fact. Fagan's body of work, created mostly for his own company, Garth Fagan Dance, is as diverse and eclectic as the music he chooses: Duke Ellington, Miles Davis, Antonin Dvoák, Keith Jarrett, Max Roach, Wynton Marsalis, Vivaldi, John Cage, Brahms. His singular technique blends the best of modern dance, ballet, postmodern dance, and the weighted movements of African, Afro-Brazilian, and Caribbean dance forms in a way that sculpts dancers into lean-torsoed, strong performance athletes who defy gravity as easily as one would walk across a stage. The dancers he has trained leap into jumps without bending their knees (witness the midair split from a standing position in *Griot New York*), turn in midair, balance and lean on space, not unlike the way Michael Jordan defies the laws of physics on the basketball court (and don't think Fagan doesn't look to the NBA for inspiration). The limbs are elongated. The feet are as tightly and carefully positioned as in ballet. The backs are supple, as flexible as fingers. The ensemble work is searingly strong, filled with complex spatial relationships and polyrhythms, yet individual dancers stand out: Steve Humphrey, Norwood Pennewell, Bit Knighton, Valentina Alexander, among others. They are fast, very fast, and can stop on a dime only to flow effortlessly into—or out of—a sustained adagio. They are superb technicians, yet they re-

tain their individuality. Fagan's dancers are real people with real smiles.

When asked who or what influenced this distinctive choreographic vision, Fagan surprisingly attributes his success to his parents. His mother, a supportive and nurturing woman, was devoted to the arts, and his father taught him always to analyze, objectify, and strive for perfection. In his native Jamaica, he studied dance with Ivy Baxter and Lavinia Williams, and as a teenager he toured Latin America with Baxter's National Dance Company of Jamaica. In the U.S., he studied dance with Martha Graham, José Limón, Alvin Ailey, Pearl Primus, and with Pat Welling at his alma mater, Wayne State University. Prior to starting his own company, Fagan went to "every dance festival in the country I could possibly go to, just to experience what everyone was doing. After I saw everything that I could in dance, I decided that I needed to develop a different format to present dance from my cultural perspective, still bearing in mind the standards and values of the dance of the day." After rehearsing an African dance with Pearl Primus, Fagan sought her advice on ways to meld the African and American cultural experiences to expand the dance vocabulary "the way French court dances stretched ballet." In other words, he wanted to use tradition as a building block to create something new; a feat many have attempted. Fagan succeeded where most others failed. Upstate Rochester, New York, in 1970 was not exactly the center of the dance world. Fagan decided to start a predominantly black company, not because he is a black choreographer, a label he despises, but because he saw that opportunities for black dancers were limited as compared to opportunities for white dancers. As his company grew in size and stature, the dancers became multicultural as well.

But most daring of all, Fagan started with untrained dancers, many of whom would have been considered too old to begin dance training by accepted standards. The Bessie award-winning Steve Humphrey, for whom Fagan has created numerous dances over more than two decades (notably, one of the two male roles in the 1979 duet *Oatka Trail*), may be the quintessential Fagan dancer, for he began his training as an adult, and Fagan has been his only teacher. When asked by Alvin Ailey about doing "things the hard way" with untrained dancers, Fagan explained that there was a distinct advantage to doing things his way: he would not have to break his dancers of what he considered the bad habits and artifice picked up in dance class. Reminiscent of and undoubtedly influenced by the holistic training that Katherine Dunham required of her dancers decades earlier, Fagan's dancers not only take dance classes and rehearse, but also attend, discuss, and critique dance performances, art exhibits, concerts, and films. They must be able to compare and contrast movement in painting, sculpture, and architecture, as well as in dance.

Perhaps the most successful example of Fagan's vision, as well as his most critically acclaimed work to date, is *Griot New York*, a full evening-length collaboration with composer/trumpeter Wynton Marsalis and sculptor Martin Puryear. Woven through the eight sections of the work, which has been recorded for PBS' *Great Performances—Dance in America* series, one can find the rhythms and weighted influence of African roots, the line and placement of ballet, the dynamics of American modern dance, and the pedestrian sensibilities of postmodern dance. One of the most memorable sections, the "Spring Yaoundé" duet, as performed by Norwood Pennewell and Valentina Alexander, is simple, elegant, and luxurious, as the two manipulate each other's bodies, echoing and reforming the shape, movement, and dynamics of the sculptor's giant garden hoe that rests on the stage.

Black dance; modern dance with a postmodern sensibility—these and other labels have been bandied about in an attempt to categorize Garth Fagan. Perhaps Fagan sums himself up most succinctly in an interview for the second edition of *Dance as Theatre Art*, "Time After Before Place," when he says, "Use of space and movement invention, redefining space and form—that's what I . . . do." Without a doubt, Garth Fagan Dance, with its daring sense of time and energy, spatial and rhythmic complexity, and memorable visual imagery, holds a special place in the history of American modern dance.

—Julinda Lewis-Ferguson

FAISON, George

American dancer, choreographer, and theater director

Born: 21 December 1945 in Washington, D.C. **Education:** Attended Howard University, 1964-66; studied dance with the American Light Opera Company, the Capitol Ballet, and with Owen Dodson at Howard University. **Career:** Dancer, Elizabeth Hodes' Harlem Dance Company; principal dancer, Alvin Ailey American Dance Theatre, 1967-69; founder, artistic director, choreographer, and dancer, George Faison Universal Dance Experience, 1971-75; founder Fais One Productions; choreographer for Ballet Hispanico, Afro-American Total Theater, Lincoln Center Repertory Company, Negro Ensemble Company, Capitol Ballet Company, and the Alvin Ailey American Dance Theatre; choreographer for concerts of Stevie Wonder, Roberta Flack, Earth, Wind & Fire, Dionne Warwick, Sister Sledge, the Supremes, Melba Moore, and Gladys Knight and the Pips, and for television and film productions; director of stage productions and music videos, including a 1993 revival of *The Wiz*, Noa Nin's 1994 opera *The Outcast,* and Arthur Kopit's play *Indians*; composer; costume designer; founder, American Performing Arts Collaborative. **Awards:** Antoinette Perry Award, Best Choreographer, and Drama Desk Award, for *The Wiz,* 1975.

Roles

1969   *Masakela Language,* Alvin Ailey American Dance Theatre, New York
1968   *Purlie* (musical), Broadway Theater, New York

Other roles include: *Quintet, Blues Suite, Congo Tango Palace,* and *The Black Belt* with the Alvin Ailey American Dance Theatre.

Works (as choreographer unless otherwise noted)

1971   *Nigger Nightmare* (play), New York Shakespeare Festival, Public Theater
        The Dolls (play)
        The Gazelle, Alvin Ailey American Dance Theatre, New York
        Poppy, George Faison Universal Dance Experience (GFUDE), New York
        Slaves, GFUDE, New York
        Suite Otis, Alvin Ailey American Dance Theatre, New York
1972   *Don't Bother Me, I Can't Cope* (musical comedy), Playhouse Theater, New York
        The Coloureds, GFUDE, New York
        Black Angels, GFUDE, New York
        We Regret to Inform You, GFUDE, New York
        Ti-Jean and His Brothers (play; also assistant director), New York Shakespeare Festival, Delacorte Theater
        Everyman and Roach (play), Everyman Theater Company, New York
1973   *Tilt* (and composer), GFUDE, New York
1974   *Boedromion,* GFUDE, New York
        In the Sweet Now and Now, GFUDE, New York
        Reflections of a Lady, GFUDE, New York
        The Wiz (musical comedy; also composer with others), Majestic Theater, New York
1976   *1600 Pennsylvania Avenue* (play; also director), Mark Hellinger Theater, New York
        Inner City (play; and director), New Theater of Washington, Washington, D.C.
        Hobo Sapiens, Alvin Ailey American Dance Theatre, New York
1980   *Up on the Mountain* (and director), Kennedy Center Musical Theater Lab, Washington, D.C.
1981   *Apollo, Just Like Magic* (and director, composer with Timothy Graphenreed)
        The Moony Shapiro Songbook (musical comedy), Morosco Theater, New York

1982   *Rhinestone,* Richard Allen Center, New York

1983   *Porgy and Bess* (opera by George and Ira Gershwin), Radio City Music Hall, New York

1984   *The Cotton Club* (film)

1985   *Sing, Mahalia, Sing* (musical; and composer with others), Arie Crown Theater, Chicago

1990   *American Jam Session* (musical; and composer with Timothy Graphenreed), Aix en Provence Jazz Festival, France

1991   *Betsey Brown* (musical), McCarter Theater, Princeton, New Jersey

         The Josephine Baker Story (film)

1992   *Golden Gate* (musical), Theater Toursky, Marseilles, France

         Cafe America, GFUDE

         C'mon and Hear (musical; mus. Irving Berlin), McCarter Theater, Princeton, New Jersey

1995   *Mad Pain,* GFUDE

1996   *Idol Obsession,* Ballet Hispanico, Joyce Theater, New York

1997   *Heaven and the Homeboy* (musical; and composer with others), Theaterfest, Montclair State University, New Jersey

         King (and director), Clinton Inaugural, Washington, D.C.

Publications

On FAISON: articles—

Allen, Zita D., "Black Dance Doesn't Exist," *Dance Magazine,* May 1976.

Dunning, Jennifer, "For George Faison, Life Has Been a Series of Happy Accidents," *New York Times,* 27 November 1977.

Peterson, Maurice, "Spotlight on George Faison," *Essence,* January 1975.

Southgate, Martha, "George Faison, All the Right Moves," *Essence,* February 1991.

*   *   *

For more than 20 years, George Faison has been a force in concert dance and theater. A dancer and modern dance choreographer, he has also had success in film, video, and television.

While in high school, Faison received training in theater with the American Light Opera Company and studied dance with the Jones Haywood Capitol Ballet and Carolyn Tate of Howard University. In 1964 he entered Howard University to study dentistry but also spent much time in the theater department, where he received more dance training. However, a 1966 performance by the Alvin Ailey American Dance Theatre inspired him to leave college for New York City to pursue a career in dance. In New York, he studied with Elizabeth Hodes, Thelma Hill, James Truitte, Louis Johnson, and Dudley Williams.

Faison became an immediate success in the New York dance scene. He spent a season in Hodes' Dance Theatre of Harlem and was chosen as Lauren Bacall's dance partner in a segment of ABC-TV's *Stage 67.* In 1967 he became a principal dancer with the Alvin Ailey Company, a position he would hold for three years. During this time he created a major role in Ailey's *Masakela Language* (1969) and performed in his *Quintet* and *Blues Suite* as well as in Talley Beatty's *Congo Tango Palace* and *The Black Belt.*

After leaving Alvin Ailey, Faison danced in the Broadway musical, *Purlie,* but considered it artistically stifling. As a result, he used his savings for a hall, publicity, and costumes and founded the George Faison Universal Dance Experience in 1971. As choreographer and artistic director, Faison created original work for the company as well as designing costumes and dancing. Speaking in 1974 of the vision underlying the Universal Dance Experience Faison remarked: "All kinds and classes of people will embrace dance when they see it in a context that relates to their own experience. Dance is not just for the elite, it is universal." The company's first modern dance concert incorporated original music by Miles Davis and was well-received. Among those who danced for the company were Debbie Allen, Renee Rose, Gary DeLoatch, and Al Perryman. The company disbanded in 1975.

Suite Otis (1971) is among the best-known works choreographed by Faison for his own company. Set to the music of Otis Redding, the dance is for five couples and typifies Faison's blending of traditional ethnic dance and ballet. *Gazelle* (1971) was inspired by Faison's observations of gazelles in a Kenya game reserve and deals with tribal hunters taken into slavery. Originally choreographed for his own company, Faison then reconceived its costuming in 1988 with masks that enhanced the work's African flavor.

Faison also created pieces with an historical and political bent as well as several confronting social problems. *Poppy* (1971), for example, explores drug abuse, while *Mad Pain* (1995) treats disaffected urban youth. Faison frequently incorporates popular music into his pieces. As Maurice Peterson wrote of Faison in *Essence* (January 1975): "Foremost is his objective to make the dance medium a more widely accepted and commercially viable form of entertainment. That is why he would much rather choreograph to Otis Redding than Tchaikovsky, and his pieces are much closer in style to *Soul Train* than *Swan Lake.*" *Hobo Sapiens* (1977), a solo Faison choreographed for the Alvin Ailey Company, was set to the music of Stevie Wonder; *Mad Pain* included rap music and street and club dancing. Faison said in 1977: "I was interested in pop music. That may have turned some people off, but I found beauty in the ordinary and everyday."

Faison's choreographic debut on Broadway came in 1972 with the show *Don't Bother Me, I Can't Cope.* Since that time, he has worked extensively in musical theater, choreographing more than 30 plays and musicals including *The Wiz* (1975), for which he was the first African American to receive a Tony Award, and a Radio City Music Hall production of *Porgy and Bess* (1983), which earned him Tony nomination.

To finance his dance pursuits, Faison began to choreograph concerts for such artists as Stevie Wonder; Earth, Wind, & Fire; and Gladys Knight and the Pips. He has also worked in television and in 1989 conceived and produced the special, *Cosby Salutes Ailey* for the 30th anniversary of the Alvin Ailey American Dance Theatre. He was also nominated for and won an Emmy Award for his choreography of the HBO special *The Josephine Baker Story,* which aired in 1991.

Recently, he founded APAC (American Performing Arts Collaborative), an organization which will develop and present theatrical, educational, and entertainment events. He adapted, directed, and choreographed *King* for President Clinton's 1997 inauguration and directed and choreographed its American production. He is considered an "elder statesman" among Ailey's choreographers and in 1997, the Alvin Ailey American Dance Theatre performed his ballet, *Slaves.*

—Karen Zimmerman

FALCO, Louis
American dancer and choreographer

Born: 1943 in New York. **Education:** Studied acting and dancing at
Henry Street Playhouse with Alwin Nikolais and Murray Louis;
studied dance at the New York School of Performing Arts. **Career:**
Joined Charles Weidman's company, late 1950s; danced with José
Limón Dance Company, 1960s; founder, Louis Falco and Featured
Dancers (later renamed Louis Falco Dance Company), 1967; cho-
reographed for Alvin Ailey American Dance Theatre, Ballet Rambert,
Boston Ballet, Nederlands Dans Theater, LaScala Opera Ballet and
others; then moved to television and film choreography. **Died:** 26
March 1993 of AIDS.

Works

1967	Argot
	The Gods Descend
	Translucens
1968	Huescape
1969	Timewright
1970	Caviar
1971	Ibid
	Journal
	The Sleepers
	The Gamete Garden
1972	Soap Opera
1973	Avenue
	Tutti-frutti
	Twopenny Portrait
1974	Storeroom
	Eclipse
1975	Caterpillar
	Pulp
1976	Champagne
1977	Hero
	Tiger Rag
1978	Escargot
1979	Saltimbocca
	Early Sunday Morning
1980	Kate's Rag
	Service Compris
	The Eagle's Nest

Publications

On FALCO: books—

McDonagh, Don, *The Complete Guide to Modern Dance*, Garden
City, New York, 1976.
Seigel, Marcia B., *Watching the Dance Go By*, Boston, 1977.

On FALCO: articles—

Borek, Tom, "Louis Falco & Company of Featured Dancers," *Dance
Magazine*, June 1969.
Dunning, Jennifer, "Louis Falco, a Creator of Chic Dances, Dies at
50," *New York Times,* March 1993.
Goodman, Saul, "Brief Biography: Louis Falco," *Dance Magazine*,
July 1963.

Kisselgoff, "Interview: I Would Love to Create Earthquakes
Onstage," *New York Times*, April 1977.
Saal, Herbert with Abigail Kiflik, "Footloose and Fancy-Free,"
Newsweek, 23 April 1979.
Terry, Walter, "Veteran, Taylor: Newcomer, Falco," *Saturday Review*,
13 January 1968.
Thom, Rose Ann, Reviews, *Dance Magazine*, June 1979.

Film and Videotapes

The Moor's Pavane (with Rudolf Nureyev, filmed for European
television, 1984); choreography for the hit movie *Fame* (1980),
music videos for the artist formerly known as Prince, films including *Angel Heart* (with Robert De Niro and Mickey Rourke),
Leonard Part VI, and *Off and Running.*

*   *   *

By all accounts an extraordinarily gifted dancer and charismatic
performer, as a choreographer Louis Falco captured a moment in
time—but never escaped it. His dances of the late 1960s and 1970s—
Argot, The Sleepers, Caviar, and *Journal*—exhibited the casual
intimacy and self-exploratory zeal that was emblematic of the 1960s
social revolution. Combined with an easy virtuosity, an often-play-
ful attitude, commissioned rock scores and frequent vocalization
among the dancers, his dances had an engaging and easily accessible
theatricality. Of his *Early Sunday Morning* (1979), Rose Anne
Thom wrote *Dance Magazine* that "images. . .evolved out of the
familiar Falco vocabulary of innumerable combinations of loose,
flinging limbs that suddenly crystallized in spectacular poses or
balances." Critic Marcia B. Siegel wrote that Falco, "one of José
Limón's heirs, has allowed his mentor's strong, successive movement to become more lush and round. Falco's dancers have a sexy
indulgent way of moving that turns people on."

Falco was born to Italian parents on Manhattan's Lower East
Side. As a teenager he returned there from Queens, where his
family had moved, to take acting and dancing lessons at the Henry
Street Playhouse, studying briefly with Alwin Nikolais and Murray
Louis. He enrolled in a vocational high school with the intent of
becoming a photographer, but auditioned a year later for the New
York School of Performing Arts and was accepted. It was there that
Charles Weidman saw him and took him into his company, cementing Falco's career in dance. He performed with Weidman's company for two years while finishing high school. "Charles Weidman
kept me in dance more than anyone else," Falco told an interviewer
in 1977. "I wouldn't have stayed in it without that excitement from
him as an artist." After high school he joined the company of
Weidman disciple José Limón. He danced for 10 years in Limón's
company, eventually taking on many of the roles Limón had made
for himself. In 1968, Walter Terry writing in *Saturday Review*, called
Falco "one of the finest young modern dancers in the world."

Falco gave the first formal concert of his own works as Louis
Falco and Featured Dancers in 1967 at New York's 92nd Street
YMHA, a showplace for up-and-coming young modern dance artists. His duet *Argot*, for himself and Sally Stackhouse, became a
signature piece for several seasons. His other inaugural works,
Translucens and *The Gods Descend*, were deemed immature by
critics and quickly succeeded by *Huescape*, a striking trio for himself, Jennifer Muller and Juan Antonio, and other dances, many
concerning the dynamics of personal relationships. In its early years
the company appeared at both Jacob's Pillow and the Spoleto

Louis Falco. Photograph © Jack Mitchell.

festivals. Renamed the Louis Falco Dance Company, it moved from the 92nd street location into regular New York theaters and wide-ranging touring. The company was well-received abroad and was popular on American college campuses, where the dancers combined performing with teaching residencies. Falco's dances were stylishly turned out; he frequently collaborated with well-known designers of the day such as William Katz (*Huescape*) and Marisol (*Caviar*).

During the prolific 1970s, Falco also created dances and/or set his choreography for Alvin Ailey American Dance Theatre, the Nederlands Dans Theater, Ballet Rambert, La Scala Opera Ballet, the Boston Ballet and others. In 1974 he joined Rudolf Nureyev to perform in a revival of Limón's *The Moor's Pavane* presented in New York and filmed for European television. Even before he made the leap to films and TV with his choreography in 1980 for *Fame*, the feature film about his high school alma mater, critics questioned whether Falco's sensual, easy-to-digest style was helping to popularize modern dance or contributing to its dilution into a pop idiom. Anna Kisselgoff, writing in the *New York Times* in 1977, called Falco's company "the ultimate in disheveled chic" and, describing its early-1970s popularity, added, "the Falco company was tuned in to its generation. It was concerned with 'lifestyles'—a word that came into fashion at the same time the company became fashionable itself. Some people, not entirely approvingly, called the group popular. Some called it pop."

Falco's explosive dances for *Fame* helped energize a meandering movie and launched him on a new career in the mass media. He choreographed several lesser-known films and did work in television series and commercials. His company disbanded in the early 1980s as he pursued his media interests, including choreographing music videos for Prince and other musical artists.

Falco died 26 March 1993 at the very young age of 50, a victim of AIDS. It's unlikely that Falco will be remembered as a groundbreaker in modern dance or one who moved it to a new level. Rather, he was a follower who took the principles of weighted movement he learned from Limón and Weidman and applied them in a style that captured the turbulent, youthful spirit of his times.

—Karen Raugust

FANDIÑO, Luis
Mexican dancer, choreographer, educator, and director

Born: Luis Fandiño Gómez Lamadrid, 22 March 1931 in Mexico City. **Education:** Studied graphic design, 1946-51; initiated dance studies at Mexican Dance Academy (MDA) with Antonio de la Torre, Guillermo Keys, and Elena Noriega. **Career:** First appearance, Mexican Ballet, MDA, 1951; founder and dancer, New Dance Theater, 1953; taught from 1953-60; principal dancer, New Dance Theater, until 1963; dancer, Folkloric Ballet of Mexico, 1962-63; guest dancer, National Ballet of Mexico, 1960-64; dancer, teacher/choreographer, 1964-75; manager and artistic co-director, 1970-75; participated in National Ballet of Mexico tours to Los Angeles and San Francisco, California, 1967-68; to cities in England, Spain, Poland, Rumania, Czechoslovakia, Yugoslavia, France, Italy and Holland, 1974; taught and coordinated the Contemporary Ballet of Xalapa, Veracruz University, and directed the Dance Institute, 1976; taught and directed Alternative Contemporary Ballet, 1978-88; jury

of the II (1981) and XIII (1992) National Dance Award, National Institute of Fine Arts (NIFA), and Metropolitan University; member, advisory board, National Dance Coordination, NIFA, 1992-93; jury, Cultural Projects Promotion, National Fund for Culture and Arts, 1992-93; has taught at Folkloric Ballet of Mexico, Independent Ballet, Scenic Arts School, Space of the Dawn dance school, Geodesic Tent dance school, Red Earth contemporary dance group, Contemporary Dance National School, and NIFA. **Awards:** NIFA award for contributions to contemporary dance, celebrating 35 years of professional activity, 1986; homage "A Life in Dance," NIFA, 1991; appreciation as Mexican dance teacher, 1991; National "José Limón" Dance Award, NIFA and government of state of Sinaloa, 1993.

Roles (all performances in Mexico City unless otherwise noted)

1951   The acrobat and a penitent, *El Chueco* (Keys), Mexican Ballet of the MDA

1952   *Antesala (Antechamber)* (Arriaga), Mexican Ballet
        La balada mágica (The Magic Ballad) (Arriaga), Mexican Ballet
        El invisible (The Invisible) (Noriega), Mexican Ballet
        A married man, *Sensemayá* (Bracho), Mexican Ballet
        Ermesinda (Cardona), Mexican Ballet
        La Valse (Gutiérrez), Mexican Ballet
        La madrugada del panadero (The Baker's Daybreak) (Sokolow), Mexican Ballet
        An old man, *La hija del Yori (Yori's Daughter)* (Reyna), Mexican Ballet

1953   A warrior, *Uirapurú* (Gutiérrez), Mexican Ballet
        A pachuco and a character in the courting, *El sueño y la presencia (The Dream and the Presence)* (Arriaga), Mexican Ballet
        A peasant, *El extraño (The Stranger)* (Jordán), Mexican Ballet
        A shepherd, *La Anunciación (The Annunciation)* (Reyna), Mexican Ballet
        Suite lírica (Lyric Suite) (Sokolow), New Dance Theater

1954   The young man who doesn't dream, *Tienda de sueños (Dreams Shop)* (Keys), Mexican Ballet
        A godfather, *El maleficio (The Curse)* (Noriega), Mexican Ballet
        In the cake walk, *El rincón de los niños (Children's Corner)* (Peñalosa), Mexican Ballet
        He, *Metamorfosis (Metamorphosis)* (Genkel), New Dance Theater
        A military man, *El muñeco y los hombrecillos (The Doll and the Little Men)* (Francis), New Dance Theater
        Rebozos (Wraps) (Flores), Mexican Ballet, Monterrey, Nuevo León

1955   Guillermo of Flavy, *Juana de Arco en la hoguera (Joan of Arc at the Stake)* (Francis), New Dance Theater

1956   *Fantasía y fuga (Fantasy and Fugue)* (Francis), New Dance Theater
        The poet, *Las naderías (The Trifles)* (Fealy), New Dance Theater

1957   *El mensajero del sol (The Sun's Messenger)* (Peñalosa), Mexican Ballet
        The bridegroom, *Los contrastes (The Contrasts)* (Francis), New Dance Theater

Caricaturas (Caricatures) (Genkel), New Dance Theater

An arguer, *El debate (The Debate)* (Francis), New Dance Theater

Procesiones (Processions) (Francis), New Dance Theater

The man, *El rostro del hambre (The Hunger Face)* (Fealy), New Dance Theater

Octeto (Octet) (Fealy), New Dance Theater

1959   *Tiempo de mar (Sea Time)* (Francis), New Dance Theater

Sara-Shi, danza de las telas (Sara-Shi, the Clothes Dance) (Hanayagui), Hidemi Hanayagui Company

1960   *Pastorela (Pastourelle)* (Flores Canelo), National Ballet of Mexico, Havana, Cuba

El demagogo (The Demagogue) (Bravo), National Ballet of Mexico, Havana

En la boda (At the Wedding) (Waldeen), National Ballet of Mexico, Havana

La iniciada (The Initiate) (Wood), National Ballet of Mexico

Braceros (Labourers) (Bravo), National Ballet of Mexico

1961   *Danzas de hechicería (Sorcery Dances)* (Bravo), National Ballet of Mexico

1962   *La danza del venado (The Deer Dance)* (Hernández), Folkloric Ballet of Mexico

1963   *Enlaces (Linkings)* (Francis), New Dance Theater

Crisis en blanco y negro (Black and White Crisis) (Francis), New Dance Theater

1964   The old man and the life, *La portentosa vida de la muerte (The Prodigious Life of Death)* (Bravo), National Ballet of Mexico

Los bailarines de la legua (The Roaming Dancers) (Genkel), National Ballet of Mexico

The sorcerer and a fire-worshipper, *Danzas primitivas (Primitive Dances)* (Gaona), National Ballet of Mexico

1965   *Viva la libertad (Hurrah! to Freedom)* (Bravo), National Ballet of Mexico

Ronda (Circle) (Fandiño, Flores Canelo, Romero, Bravo), National Ballet of Mexico

Amarga presencia (Bitter Presence) (Bravo), National Ballet of Mexico

1966   The poet, *Pitágoras dijo (Pythagoras Said)* (Bravo), National Ballet of Mexico

A triangle's member, *El tramoyista (The Stagehand)* (Flores Canelo), National Ballet of Mexico

Los elementos del desorden (The Disorder's Elements) (Castro), National Ballet of Mexico

A boy in a plastic suit, *El volantín del mago (The Magician's Kite)* (Gaona), National Ballet of Mexico

A dreamer, *Refrán del soñador (The Dreamer's Proverb)* (Filomarino), National Ballet of Mexico

1967   The wind, *Comentarios a la naturaleza (Comments to Nature)* (Bravo), National Ballet of Mexico

Ludio (Contreras), National Ballet of Mexico

Silencio en voz alta (Loud Voice Silence) (Filomarino), National Ballet of Mexico

1968   *Amor para Vivaldi (Love for Vivaldi)* (Bravo), National Ballet of Mexico

A Man in Montaje (Assembly) (Bravo), National Ballet of Mexico

Apunte para una marcha fúnebre (Sketch of a Funeral March) (Bravo), National Ballet of Mexico

A captain, *Juego de pelota (Ball's Game)* (Bravo), National Ballet of Mexico

1969   *Los magos (The Magicians)* (Bravo), National Ballet of Mexico

The general, *Daguerrotipos (Daguerreotypes)* (Castro), National Ballet of Mexico

Iokamaam, *Salomé* (Filomarino), National Ballet of Mexico

1970   *Melodrama para dos hombres y una mujer (Two Men and a Woman's Melodrama)* (Bravo), National Ballet of Mexico

Serpentina (Serpentine) (Fandiño), National Ballet of Mexico

1971   A horse-man, *Interacción y recomienzo (Interaction and Recommence)* (Bravo), National Ballet of Mexico

Solo, *Danza para bailarines (Dance for Dancers)* (Yuriko), National Ballet of Mexico

1972   *La manda* (Reyna), Mexican Ballet

Juan Calavera (Lavalle), National Ballet of Mexico

Al aire libre (In the Open Air) (Mérida), National Ballet of Mexico

Protagonist, *Homenaje a Cervantes (Homage to Cervantes)* (Bravo), National Ballet of Mexico

1973   *Estudio número 3. Danza para un bailarín que se convierte en águila (Study No. 3: Dance for a Dancer That Transforms into an Eagle)* (solo, Bravo), National Ballet of Mexico

Kms. p/h. (Kilometers per Hour) (Filomarino), National Ballet of Mexico

Espacios trazados (Traced Spaces) (Castro), National Ballet of Mexico

Trío '67 ('67 Trio) (Vázquez), National Ballet of Mexico

Investigación coreográfica sobre la histeria (Choreographic Research on Hysteria) (Vázquez), National Ballet of Mexico

Inmemorial (Immemorial) (Vázquez), National Ballet of Mexico

Works (all performances in Mexico City unless otherwise noted)

1965   *Ronda (Circle)* (w/Guillermina Bravo, Raúl Flores Canelo, Freddy Romero; mus. Velázquez and sound effects), National Ballet of Mexico

1966   *Dulcinea* (chor. and designs; mus. Foss), National Ballet of Mexico

Tenía que ocurrir, menos por menos da más (It Had to Happen, Minus by Minus Equals Plus) (mus. Homilius, Satie, Vivaldi), Chamber Dance of National Ballet of Mexico

1967   *Caleidoscopio (Kaleidoscope)* (mus. Brazilian popular), National Ballet of Mexico

Homenaje a Hidalgo (Homage to Hidalgo) (w/Gaona, Castro), National Ballet of Mexico, Guanajuato, Guanajuato

1968   *Tianguis (Market)* (w/Bravo, Castro), National Ballet of Mexico

1969   *Metrópoli (Metropolis)* (mus. Strouse), National Ballet of Mexico

1970   *Serpentina (Serpentine)* (mus. Fandiño), National Ballet of Mexico

261

1972   *Operacional I (Operational I)* (mus. Vivaldi), National
        Ballet of Mexico

1973   *Operacional II (Operational II)* (mus. Bedfor, Bodinus,
        Kabuki, Fandiño), National Ballet of Mexico

1976   *Diálogo (Dialogue)* (duet, mus. Fandiño), Contempo-
        rary Ballet of Xalapa, Veracruz University, Xalapa,
        Veracruz

1979   *Canto primero, de la soledad (First Chant, on Loneliness)*
        (mus. Mozart), Alternative Contemporary Ballet

1980   *Suceso, crónica, nacerá y crecerá libre (Event, Chronicle,
        It Will Be Born and Grow Free)* (mus. Oldfield), Alter-
        native Contemporary Ballet

1981   *En tres tiempos (In Three Times)* (mus. Strauss), Alterna-
        tive Contemporary Ballet

        Dos (Two) (mus. Vivaldi), Alternative Contemporary
        Ballet

        Anécdota (Anecdote) (mus. Wonder), Alternative Con-
        temporary Ballet

1982   *Memorias (Memories)* (mus. Oldfield), Alternative Con-
        temporary Ballet, San Luis Potosí, San Luis Potosí

1983   *Canto tercero, de la libertad (Third Chant, On Freedom)*
        (mus. Fandiño), Alternative Contemporary Ballet

        *Segundo canto, de la enajenación (Second Chant, On Alien-
        ation)* (mus. Eliovson, Walcott), Alternative Contem-
        porary Ballet

1984   *Vitral, del amor (Stained-Glass Window, On Love)* (mus.
        Bach), Alternative Contemporary Ballet

        Reflejos (Reflections) (mus. Bloch), Alternative Contem-
        porary Ballet

1985   *Ceremonial, de la vida y de la muerte (Ceremonial, On
        Life and Death)* (mus. Oldfield, Vincent, Libert,
        Meakin), Alternative Contemporary Ballet

1987   *Episodios (Episodes)* (mus. Chopin, Bach, Handel,
        Robinson, Moore), Alternative Contemporary Ballet

1993   *Por Vivaldi (To Vivaldi)* (mus. Vivaldi), National Contem-
        porary Dance School, National Professional Teaching
        of the Dance System, NIFA

        Historia con dos mujeres (Story with Two Women) (mus.
        Vivaldi, Bach, Orff, Chopin, Mozart), National Con-
        temporary Dance School

1994   *Puertas y susurros (Doors and Whispers)* (mus. Davis)
        National Contemporary Dance School

1995   *Vive Bach (Bach Lives)* (mus. Bach), National Contem-
        porary Dance School

1996   *Suertes (Lots)* (mus. Brazilian popular), Contemporary
        Dance Specialty, National Classic and Contemporary
        Dance School, NIFAs

Publications

On FANDIÑO: books—

50 años de Danza en el Palacio de Bellas Artes, Mexico City, 1984.
Tibol, Raquel, *Pasos en la danza mexicana*, Mexico City, 1982.
Tortajada Quiroz, Margarita, *Danza y poder*, Mexico City, 1995.
———, *Luis Fandiño: danza generosa y perfecta*, unpublished.

*   *   *

Luis Fandiño is one of the most important dancers and choreographers in Mexican modern and contemporary dance. His peers

have acknowledged his work, and the critics have praised him as a
sensitive, expressive, and virtuous dancer and choreographer of rare
talent. Since the 1950s Fandiño has actively participated in the
Mexican modern-contemporary dance movement as a dancer,
teacher, choreographer, and director, and he has exerted an important influence over the many male dancers with whom he has worked.

Fandiño made his first contact with the dance through the cinema
and theater, but in 1951 he decided his vocation when he saw a
performance by José Limón. He enrolled in the Mexican Dance
Academy, and shortly after he was part of the company's cast,
dancing in works by such choreographers as Guillermo Keys and
Elena Noriega. Fandiño had a fundamental contact with Xavier
Francis at the Mexican Dance Academy (MDA); he acknowledges
him as his teacher, and in 1953 he left the Academy to form the
New Dance Theater headed by Francis and the Danish dancer Bodil
Genkel. This company stood out for offering an alternative to the
dominant modern dance conventions of the moment: it was an independent testing space, where the work followed a technical and
compositional rigorousness. The nationalist dance was then hegemonic and was the only one which was acknowledged by the public
and the critics. However, the New Dance Theater brought forth a
different style which incorporated more universal subject matter
and compositional forms. Their radical efforts resulted at first in
criticism but also the recognition of being the most technically
rigorous company.

Fandiño's great artistic sensitivity and technical strictness gained
him invitations to several festivals. He excelled in those features
expressed by him in every New Dance Theater work, and was
invited to work with other companies, including the National Ballet
of Mexico and the Folkloric Ballet of Mexico. He also participated
in some musical comedies, choreographed by Guillermo Keys, which
offered him a new dance panorama, because until that moment and
even today, the concert dance has occupied an elitist position in
relation to other commercial dance expressions. Nevertheless,
Fandiño has known how to use elements of musical comedy, as well
as dance for cabarets and night clubs.

In the 1960s Fandiño joined the National Ballet of Mexico, and
until 1975 he danced in works choreographed by Guillermina Bravo
(its director), Raúl Flores Canelo, Gloria Contreras, Yuriko, and
David Wood, among others. In the National Ballet, Fandiño made
his debut as a choreographer and achieved great successes, including
Caleidoscopio (Kaleidoscope), *Serpentina (Serpentine)*, *Operacional
I (Operational I)*, and *Operacional II (Operational II)*. Due to a
streak of rebelliousness, Fandiño refused to undertake training of
the Graham technique, which prevailed in Mexico after the 1960s,
especially through the National Ballet of Mexico. Several Graham
company teachers had come from New York to Mexico to teach it,
but Fandiño refused to attend their courses. Instead, he stated the
necessity of developing his own technique, evolved out of the needs
of the Mexican dancers and not determined by a fixed creative form,
but capable of developing the whole capacities of the dancers. In
spite of it, when the Japanese Yuriko joined the National Ballet of
Mexico as a teacher and guest choreographer in 1951, she selected
Fandiño to execute the main character of her work *Dance for Dancers*. Fandiño made his debut as artistic co-director and manager
with the National Ballet, which permitted him to channel the
company's work toward a more universal vision. He emphasized
technique and the need of developing a nonliteral dance.

Fandiño was the first dancer in many new works performed by
the National Ballet, especially those by Guillermina Bravo, during
the 15 years which he spent with that company. Moreover, he won

great acceptance as a choreographer; he initiated innovations in composition, space and use of music (he composed many of the scores for his choreographic pieces), improvisation and other elements, including the introduction of musical comedy and night club forms. He was also acknowledged during the tours he made in the United States and several European countries, always standing out from the rest of the dancers.

After leaving the National Ballet, in 1976 he worked in the Dance Department of the University of Veracruz, the sole Mexican university with a dance faculty. Together with a team of collaborators, he inspired advanced studies in contemporary dance, founded a company and established work forms and organizations which in many senses still exist today. In 1979 Fandiño took control of the Alternative Contemporary Ballet, a group with which he participated in several events and for which he created a new choreographic repertory. This was very important work because Fandiño participated in the new independent contemporary dance movement, working closely with the emerging generation of dancers and choreographers who altered the country's scenic dance. Fully mature, Fandiño embarked upon the independent dance adventure, experimenting with it as he had in the 1950s.

Under the direction of Fandiño, Alternative assembled an important number of dancers who executed their director's choreographic works. These included: Isabel Hernández, Klever Vieira, Soledad Ortiz, Ricardo González, and Roberto Hernández. Fandiño did not only work with mature dancers, but he developed his own, consolidating a cohesive team in spite of the many dancers who would later defect to other national and international companies. When Alternative disintegrated in 1988, Fandiño dedicated himself exclusively to teaching; he had taught since the beginning of his dance career, but for the first time it became his main activity. Since then, he has remained closely involved with young students, contributing to their training as artists and dancers in several dance groups and at the National Classic and Contemporary Dance School of the National Institute of Fine Arts. Fandiño has developed his own methods of dance training, deriving from the knowledge he has gathered throughout his multifaceted career. In the late 1990s his technique gained consideration in diverse professional dance schools of the National Institute of Fine Arts as a "neutral technique" and was imparted, with some modifications, at various training levels.

—Margarita Tortajada Quiroz
translated by Dolores Ponce Gutiérrez

FARBER, Viola

German-born American dancer and choreographer

Born: 25 February 1931 in Heidelberg; came to U.S. in 1938; naturalized 1944. **Education:** American University, Washington, D.C., 1949-51; Black Mountain College, North Carolina, 1951-52. Studied dance with Margaret Craske, Alfredo Corvino, Katherine Litz, and Merce Cuningham. **Family:** Married Jeffrey Clarke Slayton, 1971. **Career:** Dancer, Merce Cunningham Dance Company, 1953-65, Katherine Litz Dance Company, 1959, and Paul Taylor Dance Company; formed her own company in 1968; instructor of dance, Merce Cunningham School, 1961-69, Adelphia University, New York, 1959-67, Bennington College, Vermont, 1967-68, New York University, 1971-73; chair of dance department, Sarah

Lawrence College, 1988—; choreographer, Viola Farber Dance Company, Théâtre Contemporain d'Angers, Ballet Théâtre Français, Repertory Dance Theater, Manhattan Festival Ballet, Nancy Hauser Dance Company. **Awards:** Gold Medal, Ninth International Dance Festival, Paris, 1971; Guggenheim Fellowship, 1981; also grants from the New York Council on the Arts and New York Department of Cultural Afairs.

Roles

1953   *Suite for Five in Space and Time* (Cunningham), Merce Cunningham Dance Company

1956   *Galaxy* (Cunningham), Merce Cunningham Dance Company

1957   *Picnic Polka* (Cunningham), Merce Cunningham Dance Company

1959   *Dracula* (Litz), Katherine Litz Dance Company
        From the Poems of White Stone (Cunningham), Merce Cunningham Dance Company
        Rune (Cunningham), Merce Cunningham Dance Company

1960   *Crises* (Cunningham), Merce Cunningham Dance Company

Other roles include: *Antic Meet, Suite by Chance Minutiae,* and *Rag-Time Parade,* all for Merce Cunningham Dance Company.

Works (for Viola Farber dance Company unless otherwise indicated)

1965   *Seconds*
1966   *Surf Zone,* Manhattan Festival Ballet
1968   *Excerpt*
        Legacy
        Notebook (mus. Farber), Judson Memorial Church, New York
        Time Out
        Turf
1969   *Duet for Mirium and Jeff*
        The Music of Conlon Nancarrow
        Passage
        Pop. 11
        Pop. 18
        Quota
        Standby
        Three Duets
        Tristan and Iseult
1970   *Area Code*
        Co-Op
        Curriculum
        Passengers, Repertory Dance Theater, Salt Lake City, Utah
        Tendency
        Window
1971   *Mildred* (mus. Carl Czerny)
        Patience
        Survey (mus. David Tudor)
1972   *Default*
        Dune (mus. Alvin Lucier)
        Five in the Morning, Repertory Dance Theater, Salt Lake City Utah

Poor Eddie
Pure Patience
Route Six (mus. Longines Radio Favorites transcript),
   Brooklyn Academy of Music, New York
1973   East 84th Street Block Party (outdoor performance)
      Soup
      Spare Change
1974   Defendant
      Dinosaur Parts
      House Guest
      No Super, No Boiler
      Willi I
1975   Bronx Botanical Garden (outdoor performance)
      Brooklyn Museum
      Duet for Susan and Willie
      Five Works for Sneakers
      McGraw-Hill Building (outdoor performance)
      Motorcycle/Boat
      Night Shade
      Rainforest
      Some Things I Can Remember
1976   Sunday Afternoon
1977   Lead Us Not into Penn Station
1978   Dandelion
1979   Local
      Doublewalk
      Private Relations

Publications

On FARBER: articles—

"Dancers in Cap and Gown: Northeast College Dance Festival,"
   Dance Magazine, December 1995.
Deresiewicz, Bill, "Ralph Lemon Company," Dance Magazine,
   January 1996.
Jowitt, Deborah, "Out of Bounds," Village Voice, 3 October 1995.
Topaz, Muriel, "Dancers in Cap and Gown," Dance Magazine,
   September 1993.

*   *   *

Dynamic performer, choreographer, and teacher Viola Farber has been called the "Matriarch of the Avant-Garde." As a student and then a member of Merce Cunningham's dance company, Farber was liberated from the strict formalism of traditional modern dance to express internal energies in relation to everyday movements. To Cunningham's razor sharp, precise movements, Farber's own choreography adds a spirit of humor in unexpected twists and quirks, and an amusing use of props and costumes. Her dances are usually abstract, percussive, and with an energy level reaching toward the excessive.

Farber was born in Heidelberg, Germany, on 25 February 1931. She came to the United States with her parents, Eduard and Dora Farber, at the age of seven. Raised in the U.S., she became a naturalized citizen in 1944. In 1949, at the age of 18, she attended American University in Washington, D.C., to study music, and to study ballet with Alfredo Corvino and Margaret Craske. She attended Black Mountain College in North Carolina in 1953, studying modern dance with Katherine Litz, John Cage, and Merce Cunningham.

Viola Farber performing *Dinosaur Parts*, 1978. Photograph © Johan Elbers.

When Merce Cunningham founded his dance company in 1953, Farber was one of its original members. Cunningham's approach to modern dance, considered extremely radical at the time, was to have great influence on Farber. No one, other than Martha Graham, with whom Cunningham studied, had such a profound effect on the modern dance inspired by Isadora Duncan. Duncan's revolt against the light, ethereal, and effortless style of ballet emphasized the strength and effort of the dance focusing on the downward movement. Every movement became individual, coming from within the mind and body of the dancer. The Graham technique expanded on Duncan's to become an exploration of the inner state of the dancer and was characterized by movements of contraction and release. Cunningham's dance was balanced, strong, and rhythmic; with quick shifts of weight and frequent, rapid changes in direction to cover a wide area of the dance floor. Movements of the arms, legs, and torso were isolated, to flow in sequence, one gesture following another.

Farber's performances with Merce Cunningham Dance Company during this period were dynamic and unforgettable. She also performed in works by other choreographers, including Paul Taylor in 1953, as his mother in *Jack and the Beanstalk*, and with Katherine Litz in 1959 as a vampire in *Dracula*. While with Cunningham's company until 1965, Farber created solos for many of his pieces, including *Picnic Polka* (1957), *From the Poems of White Stone* (1959), and *Crises* (1960). She also performed featured roles in his choreographed suites including *Antic Meet, Suite by Chance Minutiae*, and *Rag-Time Parade*. Farber began choreographing complete pieces in 1965.

After forming the Viola Farber Dance Company in 1968, she concentrated on choreography for her own repertoire. Her works have been performed by the Repertory Dance Theatre of Utah and the Nancy Hauser Dance Company. She has also created works for specific companies, such as the Manhattan Festival Ballet, and one piece choreographed specifically for television in 1976 called *Brazos River* aired on PBS.

To the Cunningham technique Farber added rapid turns, twists, and jumps of intense energy and emotion. According to Don McDonagh in *The Rise and Fall and Rise of Modern Dance,* Farber brought "a humorous, bounding enthusiasm that is definitely a personal contribution of human warmth" to the Cunningham style. *Notebook,* created in 1968 and first performed at the Judson Memorial Church in New York, is an example of chance order, fragmented movement, and the humor associated with Farber choreography. Three women and one man find themselves in a desperate situation as a police whistle sounds and the four converge and diverge in a series of actions expressing agitation and worry. A reader heralds clichés throughout, such as "birds of a feather," "a stitch in time," and ending with "if the shoe fits, wear it," as relationships are acted out among the three women and one man befitting the clichés. "In effect," McDonagh explains, "they have one another for good or ill and they may as well try to make the best of it."

Farber married Jeffrey Clarke Slayton in June of 1971. Together they won a gold medal for expression and creativity at the Ninth International Dance Festival in Paris in 1971. Farber has received several fellowships and grants from the National Endowment for the Arts, the New York State Council on the Arts, and the New York Department of Cultural Affairs.

When the Viola Farber Dance Company disbanded in 1986, Farber joined the faculty of Sarah Lawrence College where she is now dance department chair. She has also guest taught in London and served as the artistic director for the Centre National de Danse Contemporaine in Angers, France from 1981 to 1983.

In October 1995, about a year after having hip replacement surgery at the age of 64, Farber danced with former student Ralph Lemon. Collaboration on the duet *Threestep (Shipwreck),* was performed at an event marking the final season of the Ralph Lemon Dance Company after 10 years of existence. Said Bill Deresiewicz in a review of the performance for *Dance Magazine,* "Austere and indomitable, Farber was as compelling a presence as her lush and youthful partner. But for the most part, the two didn't so much dance together as dance at the same time." In an article in *Village Voice,* Deborah Jowitt quotes Lemon explaining how Farber changed his whole understanding of modern dance—he was practicing a phrase of Farber's when "She walked over, very kindly, and asked me to do it as fast as I could. And I did. She continued to say that. I got to the point beyond just doing it fast, where I experienced something I'd never experienced before: the dancing phrase disappeared, and it was just this emotional experience of movement."

Farber has projected her life philosophy through her teaching of modern dance. "One of the wonderful elements in the study of dance is that it teaches realism," she said in a December 1995 *Dance Magazine* interview. "We have to accept the fact that there are things that we cannot verbalize and that reach us in a place where words cannot. . . . [Dance] reaches us differently, we process it differently."

—Lisa A. Wroble

FEDERAL DANCE THEATRE

The Federal Dance Theatre (also referred to as the Federal Dance Project) was established in 1936 as a distinct entity within the Works Progress Administration (WPA) relief organization. It employed professional dancers, choreographers, musicians, designers, and technicians who had been receiving relief payments, assigning them the mission of producing socially relevent dance pieces for the American people, in particular audiences that had not previously had access to the theater. WPA director Harry Hopkins firmly believed that artists should be able to pursue their professions and were as entitled to federal support as were workers with other skills. In the spring of 1935 he supervised the creation of a Federal Art Project, Federal Music Project, and Federal Writers Project. In August of that year he added the Federal Theatre Project to this white-collar division of the WPA and appointed Hallie Flanagan as its national director.

It was proposed initially that dancers would be employed by three units within the Federal Theatre Project rather than have autonomy within the WPA, but this arrangement was considered by many to be inadequate to meet the needs of so many unemployed dancers. Helen Tamiris, an extremely active and vocal member of the New York dance community, was most persuasive in arguing that dancers merited their own unit within the WPA. Tamiris traveled to Washington to meet directly with Flanagan and Hopkins, and was instrumental in convincing them that modern dance could not only address relevent social issues but also that the WPA needed to provide many more jobs for dancers if it was going to help them through the crisis of the Great Depression. With the support of Flanagan, Congress established an independent Federal Dance Theatre (FDT) in January of 1936.

Major units of the FDT operated in New York City, Chicago, and Los Angeles, although the organization also mounted a few limited engagements in Philadelphia, Tampa, Dallas, and Oregon. The New York City unit had an executive committee that included choreographers Tamiris, Doris Humphrey, Charles Weidman, Felicia Sorel, and Glück-Sandor, with Don Oscar Becque serving as project director. Given an operating budget of $155,000 and a hiring quota of 185 dancers, the committee was slated to mount eight productions within the first six months of operation. By June of 1936, however, the employment quota had not been reached and only a few performances had been given. The obstacles that arose in trying to produce dances of high artistic merit and social significance within the framework of a federal bureaucracy led to mounting frustrations among the dancers and choreographers. In November of 1936 a public meeting was held to address issues of mismanagement. Numerous accusations were launched against director Becque, who was thought by many to be an ineffectual leader, with the result that Becque resigned in December and was succeeded by Lincoln Kirstein. When Kirstein resigned only a month later, Stephen Karnot of the Theatre Project was made supervisor.

Despite the problems caused by red tape, production delays, and changes in personnel, the FDT in New York served as a choreographic showcase for modern dance luminaries Tamiris, Humphrey, and Weidman. Tamiris, in particular, devoted herself to fulfilling the mission of the project. She choreographed four major productions for the FDT, including *How Long, Brethren?,* a suite of dances based on African American protest songs, and *Adelante,* a dance-drama set against the background of the Spanish Civil War. Other

Ruth Page and Bentley Stone in the Federal Dance Theatre production of *Guns and Castanets*, 1939. Photograph by Maurice Seymour; courtesy National Archives.

noteworthy productions included Weidman's *Candide* and Humphrey's revival of *With My Red Fires*.

The dance unit in Chicago produced an eclectic array of works by noted choreographers Katherine Dunham, Grace and Kurt Graff, Berta Ochsner, Ruth Page, and Bentley Stone. *L'Ag Ya*, Dunham's portrayal of love and festival in Martinique, and the Page/Stone production of *Frankie and Johnny* were both highly successful in using folk themes to popularize modern dance.

In Los Angeles, dancer/choreographer Myra Kinch directed a group of approximately 25 young dancers, among them Bella Lewitsky. In such works as *An American Exodus* and *Let My People Go*, Kinch focused on the American experience as well as gripping social problems. Although modern dance was rarely seen in Los Angeles, Kinch's works were extremely well received.

Just as the FDT was gaining momentum and building new audiences for modern dance, it was subjected to congressional budget cuts which called for reducing personnel by one-third. In New York, this news provoked angry demonstrations and work stoppages. The proposed budget cuts spurred dancers to stage the first sit-in strike in the history of American theater: led by Weidman, the protest took place on 17 May 1937 and attracted 500 sympathizers. Unfortunately, neither political agitation nor the box-office success of its productions could dissuade Congress; budget cuts were enacted in October of 1937, and the resulting reduction in personnel necessitated that the FDT lose its autonomy and merge with the Federal Theatre Project.

The death knell for the FDT came in the summer of 1938 when conservative opponents of the Roosevelt administration, led by Republican congressman Martin Dies and J. Parnell Thomas of the House Un-American Activities Committee, launched accusations of communist infiltration and subversive activity against the FTP as a way of discrediting Roosevelt and his New Deal policies. The FTP and the FDT were sacrificed for political expedience and were disbanded in June of 1939 when President Roosevelt signed a new relief bill which officially ended funding for the Federal Theatre Project.

Publications

Books—

Brown, Lorraine, and John O'Connor, editors, *Free, Adult, Uncensored: The Living History of the Federal Theatre Project*, Washington, D.C., 1978.
Flanagan, Hallie, *Arena*, New York, 1940.

Articles—

Cooper, Elizabeth, "Tamiris and the Federal Dance Theatre, 1936-39," *Dance Research Journal*, Winter 1997.
Gilfond, Henry, "Public Hearing: Federal Dance Theatre," *Dance Observer* 3, no. 9, 1936.
Heymann, Jeane Lunin, "Dance in the Depression," *Dance Scope*, Summer 1975.
Schlundt, Christena, "Tamiris: A Chronicle of Her Dance Career 1927-1955," *Studies in Dance History*, Fall/Winter 1989.
Tish, Pauline, "Remembering Helen Tamiris," *Dance Chronicle* 17, no. 3, 1994.

—Elizabeth Coooper

FENLEY, Molissa

American performance artist, choreographer, and artistic director

Born: 15 November 1954 in Las Vegas, Nevada. **Education:** B.A. in dance, Mills College, Oakland, California, 1975. **Career:** Artistic director, Molissa Fenley & Dancers, 1977-88; artistic director, Momenta Foundation, Inc., 1985—. **Awards:** Beard's Fund Fellowship, 1980; National Endowment for the Arts (NEA) choreographic fellowships, 1981-85, 1989, 1991-95; Jerome Foundation grant, 1983-85, 1987; NEA Dance Company grant, 1986; New York Dance and Performance Award ("Bessie") for *Cenotaph*, 1986 and for *State of Darkness*, 1988; Harkness Foundation grants, 1987, 1989, 1992-96; Philip Morris Companies, Inc. grant, 1987-97; New York Foundation for the Arts choreography fellowship, 1989; Foundation for Contemporary Performance Arts grants, 1989, 1992, 1994; Joyce Mertz-Gilmore Foundation grants, 1990-92, 1995; Arts International Fund for U.S. Artists at Foreign Festivals grant, 1990, 1994; Mary Flagler Cary Charitable Trust grants, 1991, 1992, 1996; Fan Fox & Leslie R. Samuels Foundation grant, 1992; Heathcote Art Foundation grant, 1996; Suitcase Fund grant, 1997.

Works

1977	*Planets* (mus./costumes Fenley), Merce Cunningham Studio, New York
1978	*The Willies* (mus./costumes Fenley), duet, Dance Theater Workshop
1979	*The Cats* (mus./costumes Fenley), trio, Merce Cunningham Dance Studio
	Video Clones (mus./costumes Fenley; visual elements Haring), duet, School of the Visual Arts, New York
	Red Art Screen (mus./costumes Fenley), duet, School of Visual Arts
	Mix for The Kitchen, New York
1980	*Boca Raton* (mus. dance mix of Talking Heads), duet, Grey Art Gallery, New York
	Energizer (mus. Freedman), for Dance Theater Workshop, New York
	Praxis (mus. Freedman), trio, CAPC in Bordeaux, France
	Between Heartbeats, solo version of *Praxis*, Institute of Contemporary Art, London
1981	*Peripheral Vision* (mus. Freedman), solo, Washington, D.C.
	Gentle Desire (mus. Freedman), for American Dance Festival, Durham, North Carolina
1982	*Eureka* (mus. Gordon), solo, for Dance Theater Workshop
1983	*Hemispheres* (mus. Davis/visual elements Clemente), for BAM's Next Wave Festival
1985	*Esperanto* (mus. Sakamoto), Joyce Theater, New York
	Cenotaph (mus. Tacuma/text Bogosian), for Jacob's Pillow Dance Festival, Lee, Massachusetts
1986	*A Descent into the Maelstrom* (mus. Glass), for Australian Dance Theatre, Adelaide Festival, Australia
	Feral (mus. Lloyd), for Ohio Ballet repertoire
	Geologic Moments (mus. Glass, Eastman), for BAM's Next Wave Festival
1987	*Separate Voices*, a group work performed in silence

Molissa Fenley performing *Geologic Moments,* **1986. Photograph © Johan Elbers.**

1988   *In Recognition,* dedicated to Arnie Zane (mus. Glass),
       solo, for Serious Fun Festival at Lincoln Center
       State of Darkness (mus. Stravinsky), solo, for American
       Dance Festival
1989   *Provenance Unknown* (mus. Glass), solo, for The Kitchen
       Augury w/ Doug Varone (mus. Hyams-Hart), for Ameri-
       can Dance Festival
1990   *The Floor Dances (Requiem for the Living)* (mus.
       Mikolaj Gorecki), solo, for Dia Center for the Arts,
       New York
       Bardo (mus. Satoh), solo, for Jacob's Pillow
1991   *Inner Enchantments* (mus. Glass), solo, for Peggy Baker,
       Toronto
1992   *Threshold* (mus. Satoh), solo, for Joyce Theater
       Place (mus. Part), solo, for Foundation for Contempo-
       rary Performance Arts and William Hale Harkness
       Foundation
1993   *Channel* (mus. Satoh), solo, Joyce Theater
       Nullarbor (mus. Lloyd), solo, Joyce Theater
       Sightings (mus. Oliveros), solo, Joyce Theater
       Witches' Float (mus. Lucier), solo, Krannert Arts Center,
       University of Illinois, Urbana
       Escalay (mus. El Din), duet, The Kitchen
       Tilliboyo (mus. Musa Suso), solo, The Kitchen
1994   *Bridge of Dreams* (mus. Anderson), solo, originally as a
       group work for Deutsche Oper Ballet, Berlin
       Jalan Jalan (mus. Harrison), solo, Joyce Theater
1995   *Sita* (mus. Glass), solo, Joyce Theater
       Savanna (mus. Garland), solo, for Peggy Baker, 92nd
       Street "Y" Playhouse 91 Series, New York
       REGIONS: Chair, Ocean Walk & Mesa (mus. Payne),
       solo, 92nd Street Y Playhouse 91 Series
1996   *Pola'a* (mus. Harrison), solo, Jacob's Pillow
1997   *Trace* (mus. Hart Makwaia; text Jesurun), w/Hart
       Makwaia, Jesurun, Fowler, Joyce Theater
       On the Other Ocean (mus. Behrman), solo, Sonoma State
       College, California

Films and Videotapes

Alive from Off-Center, collaboration with video artists John Sanborn
& Mary Perillo, PBS, 1987.
Metamorphosis, music video with Philip Glass, VH-1, 1989.
Molissa Fenley at the Blackie, produced by Lyn Webster, Granada
TV's Celebration, 1989.

Publications

By FENLEY: article—

"Engram," *Drama Review,* Winter 1983.

On FENLEY: articles—

Banes, Sally, "'Drive,' She Said: The Dance of Molissa Fenley,"
Drama Review, December 1980.
Kreemer, Connie, *Further Steps: Fifteen Choreographers on Mod-
ern Dance,* New York, 1987.

*   *   *

Choreographer and performer Molissa Fenley burst upon the downtown New York dance world in 1980, with a fast-paced and dazzling work entitled *Energizer,* which instantly marked a shift in direction from the highly conceptual dance experimentation domi-nating new dance throughout the 1960s and 1970s, to the newly aggressive and dramatic mood of the 1980s.

Fenley was born in Las Vegas in 1954, spent her teens in Nigeria and Spain (both countries deeply affect her dance sensibilities) and returned to the United States to study at Mills College, California, from which she received a degree in dance in 1975. Two years later, she moved to New York City and formed Molissa Fenley and Dancers, a small group of dedicated dancers with whom she worked for several years before concentrating on solo performances. Richly eclectic—Fenley selectively appropriated gestures from dance his-tory—and selective in her training methods—she worked out in a gym for four hours a day to build the necessary stamina for her breakneck speed choreography—Fenley's early reputation was built on works such as *Hemispheres* (1983), *Cenotaph* (1985) and *Espe-ranto* (1985), each of which added visually startling dance imagery to her vocabulary. She developed an unusual upper body language (so often neglected in Western dance) suggesting Balinese finger narratives or pictures from ancient hieroglyphs and, at the same, showed an acute understanding of the work of the era's fine artists (such as Francesco Clemente, Richard Long, Richard Serra, or Tatsuo Miyaajima, among others), in utilizing contributed objects or back-drops to particular dance pieces.

Fenley's broad cultural interests have resulted in works that are both visceral and intellectual, highly sculptural and visual on the one hand, and complex in their references to dance discourse on the other. From 1988 she concentrated on choreographing and per-forming solo works starting with *State of Darkness* (1988), a haunt-ing interpretation of Stravinsky's *Rite of Spring,* followed by *Bardo* (1990), commissioned by Jacob's Pillow Dance Festival, *Place* (1992), *Nullarbor* (1993) and *Sita* (1995), all commissioned by the Joyce Theater in New York. With each new work, her passion for unusual musical composition became more evident; composers whose work has been incorporated into her choreography include Anthony Davis, Philip Glass, the Kronos Quartet, Henryk Mikolaj Gorecki, Årvo Pärt, Pauline Oliveros, and Raiuchi Sakamoto.

Other than choreography for herself, Fenley has created works for a variety of other companies, including the Ohio Ballet (*Feral,* 1986), the Australian Dance Theatre (*A Descent into the Mael-strom,* 1986), the Deutsche Oper Ballet of Berlin (*Bridge of Dreams,* 1994) and the National Ballet School of Canada (*Inner Enchant-ments,* 1996). Her work has been performed by the Bill T. Jones/ Arnie Zane Company, Elisa Monte and David Brown, Dance Al-loy, and Peggy Baker. Fenley has also experimented in other media; television credits include a commissioned collaborative work with John Sanborn and Mary Perillo for PBS' *Alive from Off-Center,* *Molissa Fenley at the Blackie* for Granada TV's "Celebration," and a music video for VH-1 of *Metamorphosis* by Philip Glass, directed by Scott B. Fenley's unique talent has also been recognized with numerous grants and awards, including eight NEA choreographic fellowships, a Beard's Fund Fellowship, a CAPS grant, and a New York Foundation for the Arts fellowship. In addition, she has re-ceived two New York Dance and Performance awards for her cho-reography. From 1984 through 1986, Fenley was an artist-in-resi-dence at the Harkness Ballet Foundation and since 1986, has been an artist-in-residence at Dia Center for the Arts.

—RoseLee Goldberg

15 DANCE LABORATORIUM

Experimental modern dance was virtually nonexistent in Toronto by the early 1970s. However, in 1972, two iconoclast ex-National Ballet of Canada dancers named Miriam and Lawrence Adams would change the way audiences and critics viewed dance. By the early 1970s there were basically two dance companies in Toronto: the National Ballet of Canada (since 1951) and the Toronto Dance Theatre (since 1968). Yet the formation of 15 Dance Laboratorium would reject the institutionalism of Toronto's ballet company and the seriousness of modern dance at that time.

Miriam Adams had been a corps de ballet dancer in the 1960s but had become very unhappy with her career as a swan or a flower. She realized that she didn't want to be a more important swan, she didn't want to be a swan at all. And Lawrence, who was a dynamic soloist, best known for his role as Mercutio in *Romeo and Juliet*, was feeling like his life was taking on an uncomfortable sameness. Consequently, they left the National Ballet in 1969 feeling, according to Lawrence, like "small cogs in an institutional wheel that increasingly turned, they felt, just to crank out money." They also felt as if they were just employees of some company and what they did didn't really contribute to the Canadian experience.

After leaving the National Ballet, Lawrence and Miriam taught ballet at the studio of Lois Smith, Canada's first prima ballerina. Miriam conducted fairly conventional classes but Lawrence would often tell his students to warm up by lying in the sun. He was a cynic, often asking his dancers why they worked so hard when they could never really make a living as dancers. One day he finally got fed up with hearing how no one could get a job and he told his students, "We're going to do a show and everybody's going to be equal, and you're all going to make your own dances, and you're all going to dance in each others' dances, and no, I'm not in charge—you're in charge."

The philosophy of 15 Dancers was to create pieces that contained meaningful ideas; keep costs low and have control over space and repertoire; and to become generalists, who not only danced but took on all other production duties. The name "15 Dancers" came from the original number of dancers. After Lawrence's announcement, the 15 dancers each donated $15 and Lawrence booked Toronto's Poor Alex Theatre for one evening. Smith loaned her studios for rehearsals and the dancers worked intensely.

Their debut performance was 13 June 1972; admission was $1 and the program consisted of a brown piece of paper listing five works named only with a number starting at 10 and ending at 15 with intermission as "12." Only the first names of the choreographers were listed. All of the 15 dancers came from a ballet background so it wasn't unusual that the program opened with some ballet pieces; yet Lawrence and Miriam created some very interesting, ground-breaking dances. The first dance was a *pas de trois* called *Ten* by Donna Nickeloff. *Thirteen* was a duet about an engaged couple by Clyde (nobody remembers his last name) who was apparently good at combining conventional ballet with mime in a schmaltzy way. Clyde also performed *Eleven,* which was the only piece on the program that was improvised; it was performed in silence and Clyde was dressed in brief trunks and ankle bells. The piece has been described as interesting or insufferably long and it used a lot of free-flowing stamping, clapping, bouncing, and nonballetic movement. The most popular work was *Fourteen* by Miriam Adams. It was an ode to yogurt, only a few minutes long

and involved a lot of jumping and tumbling to a score made up of a poem of chanted fruit flavours and some orchestrated Beatles music. Lawrence's piece was *Fifteen* and consisted of a solo to a speech by Richard Nixon about Vietnam and the movement involved a lot of kicking and stamping at an exposed brick wall.

There was no media coverage of this performance by request of the Adamses. They were more interested in the accomplishment than any critical reaction to it. The collective made a profit of $136 which Lawrence used to book the theatre for two more nights the following July. Not all 15 were up to the challenge in July and eventually the group narrowed down to four or five. The group continued to perform over the next couple years and did some touring in 1974 to Oshawa, Hamilton, Ottawa, and Montreal.

A notable piece is their version of the *Nutcracker* presented at the same time as the National Ballet's annual Christmas show. This version had a cast of four with Lawrence as the Prince, Diane Drum as the Sugar Plum Fairy, Cynthia Mantel as Clara, and Miriam as the entire corps de ballet. The dance included a pas de deux in which the Sugar Plum Fairy fights the Prince in a boxing ring. Another dance, which proved unsuccessful with critics and audiences but a legendary dance no less, consisted of Lawrence building a brick wall.

In the fall of 1974, 15 Dancers became 15 Dance Laboratorium and was a performance space instead of a collective. Lawrence and Miriam rented a space on George Street in Toronto and created a forum for experimental dance. Everyone from Anna Blewchamp to Margie Gillis to Jean-Pierre Perreault performed at 15 Dance Laboratorium. Participants who became well-known for their performance art are Margaret Dragu, Elizabeth Chitty, and Lily Eng. The space existed for choreographers and performers to try out new works, learn the practical side of dance production, or simply exchange ideas about dance. There was no censorship as to what went on stage. Each troupe or choreographer received a $250 fee as well as 80 percent of the box office and less experienced artists received no payment except the box office. The theatre seated 52 people and only about six dancers could move comfortably on stage at a time. At this juncture, Lawrence and Miriam were known as the poorest impresarios in history and supported themselves with a picture-framing business that shared space with the studio. Lawrence described his and Miriam's role at 15 Dance Lab as "janitors who sweep the floor and clean the john, both integral parts of dance production."

Critics accused the Adamses of promoting a "nihilist philosophy" toward conventional dance forms without contributing anything of lasting artistic value, and yet they were praised for liberating dance and the dance audience. On 30 June 1980, 15 Dance Laboratorium closed its doors when the Adamses felt the need to move on. They turned their focus to publishing, creating a tabloid titled *Canadian Dance News* featuring news, opinions, and reviews. While *Canadian Dance News* no longer exists, they have continued in publishing and are also notable for preserving Canada's dance history. In 1986 they began a reconstruction project called Encore! Encore! which recreated six original Canadian dances all choreographed before 1952. During the project they discovered what a vast dance history Canada had and founded Dance Collection Danse (DCD) to promote and preserve Canadian dance through publishing and an electronic archiving system. DCD publishes an historical newsletter called *The News*, a tabloid titled *The Dance News* covering current dance news and issues, and books by Canadian historians about Canadian dance.

Publications

Fisher, Jennifer, "From Post-Ballet to Post-Modern: Revisiting the Debut Concert of Toronto's Fifteen Dance Collective," *Canadian Dance Studies,* 13 June 1972.

Jackson, Graham, "The Avant-Garde Kaleidoscope Which Is 15 Dance Laboratorium," *Performing Arts in Canada,* Winter 1976.

———, "15 Dance Lab Doors Close," *Performing Arts in Canada,* Summer 1980.

—Amy Bowring

FILM, VIDEO, AND DANCE

The history of dance for the camera is rich and varied and intersects the history of a number of other disciplines as well. While Hollywood has produced some of the most well-known dance films, it's the independent filmmakers and videomakers who have collectively created a body of work noteworthy for redefining the relationship of the choreographer and the camera.

Dance for the camera occupies a wholly different space than dance for the theater; one could say it's a hybrid form, existing in a virtual space contextualized by the medium and method of recording. It's not a substitute for, or in conflict with, the live theatrical performance of a dance, but rather a wholly separate yet equally powerful way of creating danceworks. From Eadward Muybridge, an English-born photographer working in Pennsylvania in the 1870s, who invented a system of placing numerous cameras in a line and snapping photographs in rapid succession, to Maya Deren, whose work with dance and the camera is a benchmark of the genre, and beyond into the contemporary era, imagemakers have rigorously explored dance and the camera in all of its permutations. Since the earliest days of photography, artists working with optical mediums have been fascinated by the possibility of recording human movement, and in particular, dance.

It's important to make a distinction between the documentation of a dance, dance for television, and dance created specifically for the camera. Dance documentation is generally done to preserve a choreography or a performance in its totality; all entrances and exits should be included and the choreography should be seen as an unbroken whole, with no editing from beginning to end. This requires a very wide shot and much of the energy of the performance is lost. Television dance is generally shot with multiple cameras placed in strategic locations including one wide or master shot; the resulting footage is then edited together in post-production to give multiple viewpoints of the dance while still preserving the choreography. Dance for the camera is something entirely different: a hybrid combining the technology and techniques of film or video with dance to create a work that can only exist as film or video. It's not a documentation or a record of a choreography, but an entirely autonomous work of art.

Since its early days, video has come to serve two distinct and singular functions in regard to dance: the first and still most commonly used, is as a tool for documenting and archiving dance; the second is as a site for the creation of unique and singular works of art. If one considers the theater with its proscenium arch as a *site* for the performance of dance, then one might also consider video, with its specific frame size as a sort of architectural space as well. Just as the theater has an architectural specificity, the same can be said

of video. Yet the theater offers no permanent storage for dance, after a performance one is left with the lingering yet ephemeral image of the dance as it was in the theater; within the technology of video, the storage is actual and allows the audience to view it repeatedly.

All works of art, including video dance, reflect something of the culture from which they came; no artwork can be created in a vacuum and dance for the camera is no different. As technology has advanced over the past 100 years, the works reflect those advances: Amy Greenfield's *Earth Trilogy* (1971) and Carolyn Brown's *Dune Dance* (1978) are works immediately recognizable as products of the 1970s, reflecting the attitudes and concerns of the era. We can read both works by the signifiers evident in the structural language, film stock, and movement quality, even the duration of the pieces, all of which gives us clues to its era of creation. Maya Deren's *A Study in Choreography for Camera* (1945) with Talley Beatty finds the filmmaker breaking taboos, transgressing stereotypes and making a distinctly political statement by featuring an African-American not as a servant or a butler as Hollywood did at the time, but rather as a fully formed human being, an elegant and talented dancer. Deren uses the dancer as the constant in a shifting landscape of place and time, the flow of movement unbroken as location changes from scene to scene, questioning our relationship to the logic of chronology. At moments in Deren's silent film, Beatty seems suspended in mid-air for an impossible length of time; at others, an unfolding of the dancer's arm begins in one location and seamlessly ends in another, the choreography literally "moving" the viewer into another place.

Dance for the camera has mirrored the upheaval in our culture and served as a site for the discussion of issues of gender, race, disability, and the very nature of dance itself, even while leaving us with a palimpsest of the concerns of the makers in their time. In choreographer Victoria Marks' video dance work, *Outside In*, directed by Margaret Williams in 1995, the choreographer uses video to explore gender identity and issues of ability/disability. The work was created with dancers from CandoCo, an English dance company featuring differently abled dancers and performers. Marks uses video to explore physical identity to discover a new understanding of dance, empowering and humanizing dancers of differing abilities, presenting them as sensuous and playful human beings.

Merce Cunningham, a pioneer in the field of video dance (who has worked extensively in film as well) explored this site concept directly in his 1979 Cine Dance *Locale*, directed by Charles Atlas. The title of the piece refers specifically to the fact that this was *not* a work for the theater and exists entirely within the purview of the camera. Earlier Cunningham and Atlas had relied on a stationary camera, but with *Locale* the camera moves at breakneck speed, dancers randomly appearing and disappearing from the frame. The effect is quite the opposite of the entrances and exits in the theater—the camera is in a sense discovering the movement, already in progress.

In the videotape *Blue Studio,* directed by Atlas, Cunningham is in the studio, or on the road; the point of view constantly shifting as Cunningham "dances" with dancers videotaped in black and white in earlier period of time. It is the collision of images and score (by John Cage) existing in a contingent electronic space that gives the piece both its form and content. The site of video dance allows the maker to project the dancer into the landscape by providing a foreground and as figurative or as a Renaissance painting might. In Zbigniew Rybczynski's 1990 videotape, *The Orchestra*, the dancers are literally placed into the architecture and landscape of France using digital editing technologies. The director inserts dancers into locations including the Louvre, a Paris opera house, and the Chartres Cathedral, using sophisticated matting and post-production techniques. This serves not merely a kitschy "we can do this so we did" purpose, but layers the choreography in a way not possible on a proscenium stage and visually reinforces the classical music chosen for the score. Additionally, using digital techniques, Rybczynski is able to multiply the number of dancers on screen and to create scenarios of repetition and movement that never existed.

Singing Myself a Lullaby, a theater piece involving video as a scenic element was produced in 1993 through a collaboration between choreographer Ellen Bromberg, dancer/choreographer John Henry, and the author of this essay. Henry, HIV-positive for some time, had begun to address his illness in his work and asked Bromberg and myself to create a piece that would ultimately last beyond his death. As with the work *Still/Here*, choreographed by Bill T. Jones, with video by Gretchen Bender, *Singing Myself a Lullaby* was a work for the theater using video to track the changes in Henry's body as AIDS took hold, but also provided imagery on stage through which he could confront his personal history and find a resolution to his life as a gay man, a dancer, and a teacher in the process of dying. While *Still/Here* spoke in the voices of numerous people facing terminal illness, *Singing Myself a Lullaby* focused only on Henry, and as the illness progressed over three years, Bromberg's choreography for the stage was also set for the camera and combined in post-production with resonant images of Henry's life, both metaphorical and literal.

Singing Myself a Lullaby was presented a number of times over these three years, each performance different from the previous as Henry's body became ravaged by AIDS. As his illness progressed, the projected video images also changed and were remade to include images of the previous performances and to replace the choreography Henry was unable to perform. The use of video as a central element allowed us to create a work that was constantly in flux; changing as its subject changed. In the final performance at San Francisco's Edge Festival in 1996, Henry, only minimally able to appear on stage was, along with the dance community, able to examine the arc of his life through movement, text, and projected images.

Another approach to video dance in works choreographed by Molissa Fenley (*Bardo in Extremis*, directed by Douglas Rosenberg, 1996) and Eiko & Koma, (*Wind*, directed by Rosenberg, 1996) is one in which the camera acts as interpreter or observer. In this instance, elements of the choreography not perceived in the theater version become the focus of the wandering lens of the camera. By working in the very intimate space between the performer and the audience, it becomes possible to uncover the minutae of gesture. In both works, movement is framed in extreme close-up and the camera wanders "upstage" of the performers to expose a view of the dance unavailable to a theater audience. The articulation of Fenley's hands, for instance, becomes epic as it fills the screen—the broad image of Fenley experienced on stage is reduced to its essence as the intensity of her gaze or the position of a hand are metaphorically transformed into a subtext of the dance itself.

Yellow River (Hwang Ho) with choreographer Li Chiao-Ping began in 1990 with the adaptation of a piece originally choreographed for the stage. As a video dance, *Yellow River (Hwang Ho)* took the form of a non-linear narrative combining movement with text and landscape to create a personal history of Li's experience as a first generation Chinese-American. Stories and superstitions told to Li by her mother are woven into and layered over the choreography as the piece unfolds and moves between the imagistic and the narra-

tive. Using video as the site, *Yellow River (Hwang Ho)* parallels the history and struggles of China and Chinese people with Li's childhood in San Francisco. In the tape, Li's dancing is placed in locations that support the narrative and provide additional context for the work. Speaking directly to the camera/audience, Li personally engages the viewer in a discourse about the creation of her own identity.

Athletic movement is layered throughout the piece with ritual gesture and scrolling text reinforcing and articulating the narrative. The theater version of *Yellow River (Hwang Ho)* was subsequently altered to include projected video images from the tape, replacing the text originally spoken on stage with a videotaped Li. This layering of movement and video allowed the choreographer to tell her story in both dance and image simultaneously and cradled the choreography within a visual landscape.

The task of articulating choreography within the site of video is a collaborative process—unlike cinema, there is often no script as the tendency in contemporary choreography is toward the nonnarrative or abstract. Consequently, fixing an ephemeral art form within the structure of video requires not only intimate knowledge of the choreography but a high degree of trust as well. The camera can be an intrusive presence as it not only records but influences the dance and the dancer as well. When creating dance for the camera, collaborators have a tendency to assume a relationship based in a sort of hierarchy that places the camera in service of the choreography and is at odds with the very nature of collaboration.

The camera tends to exert a sort of authority that shapes a situation it is intended to simply reveal or fix—this reinforces a sort of hierarchy that early media artists sought to destroy. By allowing the camera to completely dictate form one compromises the choreography; by ignoring the presence of the camera, one may compromise the video dance. In both situations, the video dance is destined to feel lifeless or empty, occupying a site that is satisfying neither as documentation or video dance. This paradox has occupied the thinking of a number of theorists and critics including Walter Benjamin, who in his seminal essay, "The Work of Art in The Age of Mechanical Reproduction," written in 1936 said, "Even the most perfect reproduction of a work of art is lacking in one element: its presence in time and space, its unique existence at the place where it happens to be." Benjamin explains this presence as the "aura" of a work of art, in a sense the spirit or texture that is lacking in its mechanical representation. Video dance can never be the dance itself, only the *other*. However, to accept Benjamin's paradigm would be to deny that the power of such mechanically reproduced works as Cunningham's *Beach Birds for Camera* or numerous others that have successfully challenged Benjamin's assertions within the site of video dance. As a successful model of both collaboration and mechanical reproduction, one must only think of Barbara Morgan's photographs of Martha Graham. When we conjure Martha, the image that comes to one's mind may well be a Morgan photograph. Again, the mechanically reproduced image becomes a marker or signifier for the original. The photograph is not the dancer, nor the dance, but is a hybrid of technology and dance resulting in a unique and autonomous object. The idea that a videotape can accurately represent or re-create a live performance is at best, myth. However, when approached as a hybrid form, a collaboration between choreographer and camera within the site of video can transcend the method of reproduction and succeed on its own terms.

—Douglas Rosenberg

FIND

The Festivale internationale de nouvelle danse (FIND) was conceived during the early 1980s by three arts specialists: Diane Boucher, Dena Davida, and Chantal Pontbriand. Their association began during a two-year contemporary dance presentation series (1978-81), which they organized at the Montreal Museum of Fine Arts. At the time, Pontbriand was in charge of lecture and performance activities at the museum, and she hired Davida as dance curator. All three shared a vivid interest in postmodern dance as one of the most vital artistic forms of the contemporary arts scene, and continue to work together in the programming and organizing of the festival.

They developed the concept of the festival within a period of rapid development in Quebec experimental contemporary dance and the simultaneous establishment of numerous other arts festivals in the city of Montreal. This major Canadian city had become renowned as the French-culture capital of North America, with strong ties to Europe, and as an increasingly internationalist, intercultural urban center. Ever since the artist-led revolution The Global Refusal in 1948 catapulted Quebec society into a frenzy of modernism, the artistic milieu has continued to provide vibrant leadership in defining the emerging Québécois culture through the creation of a body of artworks in theater, dance, literature, music, visual arts, and architecture.

Into this artistic ferment and after several years of discussion and fundraising, the first FIND was launched. Programming priorities sought a balance between established Canadian choreographers and a selection of the most influential and visionary contemporary choreographers from other countries, seminal historical references with more recent developments, and carefully included artists from different choreographic generations and aesthetic outlooks.

Although the heart of the festival programming would always be the mainstage presentations in numerous theaters ranging from the opera house to the experimental lab, a cluster of supporting activities was established with other organizations around town by Boucher and Davida: gallery exhibitions, video and cinema showings, workshops and master classes, a free public noontime performance series, and morning audience talks with choreographers. Also adjunct to the festival, and a natural outgrowth, is a marketplace for scores of visiting critics and reporters, programmers, and artists from around the world. A lively group of off-festival presentations in several dance studios and the city network of Maisons de Culture also sprang up to provide showcasing opportunities for local choreographers.

The first festival presented, in close succession, three of the most important figures of the day: Pina Bausch, Trisha Brown, and Merce Cunningham. Also on the programme were Japanese Butoh choreographer Muteki Sha and several Canadians, including the burgeoning La La La Human Steps Company of Montrealer Edouard Lock. The second festival nearly doubled the number of invited companies to 17, and introduced the concept of a thematic focus on a specific country each time: France (1987), Japan (1989), Montreal (1991, the city's 350th birthday), Britain (1993), the Netherlands (1995), Spain and Portugal (1997). Although several American and English Canadian choreographers and the occasional Japanese artist are included in each festival, the FIND's programming remains a reflection of the intense interest in Quebec with European culture.

Today the biannual festival has carved out a privileged niche in the international dance community. The 12-day celebration of experimental dance functions as a crucial gathering place, trend-setter, and political forum to advance the field.

—Dena Davida

FLORES CANELO, Raúl

Mexican dancer, educator, choreographer, set and costume designer, and director

Born: Raúl Flores González, 19 April 1929 in Monclova, Coahuila. **Education:** Studied plastic arts at the University of Arizona and Academy of San Carlos in Mexico City, 1949; initiated dance studies at the Mexican Dance Academy (MDA) with Ana Mérida, 1949; at the National Ballet of Mexico, 1951; also studied music, dramatic composition and analysis, and choreography. **Career:** Joined Fine Arts Ballet as dancer and designer, 1959; traveled and studied in several U.S. cities, with Limón, Sokolow, Nikolais, Holm, and others, 1965-66; founder/director and choreographer, Independent Ballet of Mexico, 1966; toured the U.S. (1968), Central America and Cuba (1969), and cities of France and Holland (1975); established Choreography Internal Contest, 1982; created works for National Ballet of Mexico, Independent Ballet of Mexico, the Fine Arts Ballet, Dance Company of the Veracruz University, National Dance of Cuba, and Contempodance. **Awards:** Ford Foundation fellowship, 1965; International Choreographers Colloquy of Angers, guest, 1974; Mexican Theater and Music Chroniclers Union Award, 1980; A Life in Dance Homage, National Institute of Fine Arts (NIFA), 1989; Iberoamerican Choreography Oscar López Contest, jury (Quito, Ecuador), 1990; José Limón Award, National Institute of Fine Arts and government of Sinaloa, 1990; homage in Viena, 25th International Dance and Ballet Film Week, 1992; homage at the National and International Contemporary Dance Festival, San Luis Potosí, 1992; creation of the Raúl Flores Canelo Award within the same festival, 1992; inauguration of the Raúl Flores Canelo Theater at the National Center of the Arts, Mexico City, 1995. **Died:** 3 February 1992 in Mexico City.

Roles (all performances in Mexico City unless otherwise noted)

1949	*Norte* (*North*) (Mérida), Mexican Dance Academy (MDA)
	Sinfonía India (*Indian Symphony*) (Hernández), MDA
1951	*Recuerdo a Zapata* (*Memories of Zapata*) (Bravo), National Ballet of Mexico
	Los cuatro soles (*The Four Suns*) (Limón), Mexican Ballet, MDA
1952	*Guernica* (Bravo), National Ballet of Mexico
	Concerto (Lavalle), National Ballet of Mexico
1953	*La nube estéril* (*The Sterile Cloud*) (Bravo), National Ballet of Mexico
1955	*Danza sin turismo* (*Dance Without Tourism*) (Bravo), National Ballet of Mexico
	El gendarme (The policeman), *Juan Calavera* (Lavalle), National Ballet of Mexico
1956	*El demagogo* (*The Demagogue*) (Bravo), National Ballet of Mexico
1958	*Imágenes de un hombre* (*Images of a Man*) (Bravo), National Ballet of Mexico

1959   *Tierra* (*Earth*) (Noriega), National Ballet of Mexico
      La culebra (*The Snake*) (Benavides), Fine Arts Ballet

1960   *Opus 1960* (Sokolow), Fine Arts Ballet
      Un cirquero (A circus man), *Juguetes mexicanos* (*Mexican Toys*) (Noriega), Fine Arts Ballet
      Santa María 2 A.M. (*Saint Mary 2 a.m.*) (De Bernal), Fine Arts Ballet
      Interludio (*Interlude*) (Lavalle), Official Ballet of Fine Arts
      El médico (The physician), *Complejo de Electra* (*Electra Complex*), Fine Arts Ballet

1962   *Danzas de hechicería* (*Sorcery Dances*) (Bravo), National Ballet of Mexico
      Triángulo de silencios (*Triangle of Silence*) (Mérida), Fine Arts Ballet
      La visita (*The Visit*) (Bracho), Fine Arts Ballet
      El cazador (The hunter), *La balada del venado y la luna* (*The Deer and Moon Ballad*) (Mérida), Fine Arts Ballet

1964   *La portentosa vida de la muerte* (*The Prodigious Life of Death*) (Bravo), National Ballet of Mexico
      Los bailarines de la Legua (*The Roaming Dancers*) (Genkel), National Ballet of Mexico

1965   *Cinco por cinco* (*Five Times Five*) (Castro), National Ballet of Mexico

1967   *Canciones* (*Songs*) (Fealy), Independent Ballet of Mexico
      You Bastard (Gurrola), Independent Ballet of Mexico

1969   *Bulcanin* (Fealy), Independent Ballet of Mexico
      El idealista (The idealist), *Retratos agónicos y vivientes* (*Dead and Living Portraits*) (Castro), Independent Ballet of Mexico
      Desiertos (*Deserts*) (Sokolow), Independent Ballet of Mexico

1970   *A* (Fealy), Independent Ballet of Mexico
      Gimnopedia (*Gymnospaedics*) (Henríquez), Independent Ballet of Mexico
      Invenciones (*Inventions*) (Henríquez), Independent Ballet of Mexico

1971   *Cambios* (*Shifts*) (Fealy), Independent Ballet of Mexico
      Espacio (*Space*) (Henríquez), Independent Ballet of Mexico
      Antígona (*Antigone*) (Fealy), Independent Ballet of Mexico

Works (as choreographer and costume and set designer; all performances in Mexico City unless otherwise noted).

1958   *Pastorela* (*Pastourelle*) (mus. percussions played by dancers), National Ballet of Mexico, Monclova, Coahuila
      Un buen partido (*A Good Match*) (mus. Elizondo), National Ballet of Mexico
      La Anunciación (*The Annunciation*) (mus. Elizondo), National Ballet of Mexico

1960   *La boda de Pancha* (*The Wedding of Pancha*) (mus. Elizondo), National Ballet of Mexico

1961   *La balada de los amantes* (*The Lovers' Ballad*) (mus. Vivaldi), National Ballet of Mexico

1964   *Epitafio para un muchacho sin destino* (*Epitaph for a Boy Without Destiny*) (mus. Lewis, Brown), National Ballet of Mexico
      Luzbel (*Lucifer*) (mus. Elizondo), National Ballet of Mexico

Adán y Eva (*Adam and Eve*) w/Valentina Castro (mus. Elizondo), National Ballet of Mexico

1965   *Ronda* (*Circle*) w/Luis Fandiño, Freddy Romero, and Guillermina Bravo (mus. Velázquez and sound effects), National Ballet of Mexico

1966   *El tramoyista* (*The Stagehand*) (mus. Lopresti, Vivaldi, and the Beach Boys), National Ballet of Mexico

1967   *Juegos de playa* (*Beach Games*) (mus. Benichou), Independent Ballet of Mexico
      Librium (mus. Parker, Albinoni), Independent Ballet of Mexico

1968   *Plagios* (*Plagiarism*) (mus. Villarreal, Brown, Indian popular, and Mexican folk), Independent Ballet of Mexico

1969   *El fin* (*The End*) (mus. Lewi and Morrison), Independent Ballet of Mexico

1970   *Elegía* (*Elegy*) (mus. Rumanian popular), Independent Ballet of Mexico

1972   *Ceremonias* (*Ceremonies*) (mus. Italian popular), Independent Ballet of Mexico
      Ciclo (*Cycle*) (mus. Chávez), Independent Ballet of Mexico
      Tema y evasiones (*Theme and Evasions*) (mus. Brown, Caballero, Villanueva, Elizondo, Jaramillo, Schatner, and Brazilian popular), Independent Ballet of Mexico

1973   *La espera* (*The Wait*) (mus. Revueltas), Independent Ballet of Mexico
      Vespertina (*Vespertine*) (mus. Revueltas), Independent Ballet of Mexico

1975   *Presagio* (*The Omen*) (mus. Carrillo), Independent Ballet of Mexico

1976   *El hombre y la danza* (*Man and the Dance*) (mus. various), Independent Ballet of Mexico

1977   *Solo, La autodestrucción es la consecuencia de la vida no vivida* (*Solo. Self-Destruction Is a Consequence of an Unlived Life*) (mus. Revueltas), Independent Ballet of Mexico
      Numerito (*Little Number*), Independent Ballet of Mexico

1979   *Jaculatoria* (*Ejaculation*) (mus. Ponce, Mancini, Froberger, Chopin, and Wagner), Independent Ballet of Mexico

1981   *De jaulas y mariposas* (*On Cages and Butterflies*) (mus. Crumb), Independent Ballet of Mexico
      De aquí, de allá y acullá (*From Here and There*) (mus. Mozart, Verdi, Pérez Prado, and Moré), Independent Ballet of Mexico
      Queda el viento (*The Wind Remains*) (based on the novel *The Human Mourning* by Revueltas; mus. Carrillo, Sánchez, Revueltas, Chávez, Bernal Jiménez, and Elizondo), Independent Ballet of Mexico
      Tres fantasías sexuales y un prólogo (*Three Sexual Fantasies and a Prologue*) (mus. Hadjidakis, Wolf, Winteer, Darling, Mancini, Egyptian popular, Revueltas, Aguilar, Flores, Barry, and Pardomo), Independent Ballet of Mexico
      Soliloquio (*Soliloquy*) (mus. Schubert), Independent Ballet of Mexico

1982   *Bagatelas* (*Trifles*) (mus. Velázquez), Independent Ballet of Mexico

1985   *Danzas de primavera* (*Spring Dances*) (mus. Sarden, Portal, Munron, and traditional), Independent Ballet of Mexico

1987   *Terpsícore en México* (*Terpsichore in Mexico*) (mus. various authors, selection Rafael Castanedo), Independent Ballet of Mexico

   Auras (mus. Bach, Ligeti, Hadjidakis, Nazaret, Rossini, Devrese, Kapainapoi, and Japanese popular), Independent Ballet of Mexico

   Huapango por la paz (*Peace Huapango*) (mus. Moncayo), Independent Ballet of Mexico

   Homenaje a Enrique Ruelas (*Homage to Enrique Ruelas*) (mus. Schubert), Independent Ballet of Mexico

1988   *Poeta* (*Poet*) (mus. Schubert, Villanueva, Thompson, Brahms, Schumann, Hadjidakis, and Alcalá), Independent Ballet of Mexico

   El bailarín (*The Dancer*) (mus. Karaindrou), Independent Ballet of Mexico

1989   *Preguntas nocturnas* (*Nocturnal Questions*) (mus. Branca, Mertens, Jurgens, Kneiper, and Karaindrou), Independent Ballet of Mexico

   Las fodongas (mus. Joplin), Contempodance

1990   *Pervertida* (*The Pervert*) (mus. Lara, Revueltas, Sarde, Addison, and Juan Gabriel), Independent Ballet of Mexico

1991   *Divertimento para caballos* (*Horse Divertissement*) (mus. Pérez Prado), Independent Ballet of Mexico

Publications

On FLORES CANELO: books—

50 años de Danza en el Palacio de Bellas Artes, Mexico City, 1984.
Lynton Anadel, "Raúl Flores Canelo," *Homenaje Una vida en la danza 1989*, Mexico City, 1989.
Tortajada Quiroz, Margarita, *Danza y poder*, Mexico City, 1995.

Films and Videotapes

The Wait (choreography by Flores Canelo), Cultural and Educational Television Unit of the Public Education Secretary, 1984.

*   *   *

Raúl Flores Canelo was a versatile and innovative choreographer and designer in the second generation of Mexican modern dance. His eclectic and vital works are chiefly characterized by humor, irreverence, irony, genuineness, and popular appeal.

Born Raúl Flores González in the northern mining city of Monclova, Coahuila, Flores Canelo was in early contact with diverse artistic expressions: his first dance teachers were his aunts, who taught him ballroom dancing, a genre in which he excelled throughout his life. The son of a traditional family, he had to overcome several obstacles to study art, and especially, dance. Flores Canelo completed his secondary education at a U.S. military academy in Missouri. He then entered the art department at the University of Arizona, where he studied painting. In Phoenix, Arizona, he attended his first professional dance performance, the Ballets Russes. In 1949 he moved to Mexico City and entered the San Carlos Academy to study painting. As a part of his work, he visited the Mexican Dance Academy (MDA) to make dance drawings and decided instead to study there. His first teacher was Ana Mérida, and he was immediately incorporated into the company's performances. He abandoned his painting and dance studies due to family pres-

sure, but in 1951 returned to Mexico City and joined the National Ballet. In this company he studied dance with Guillermina Bravo and Xavier Francis, in addition to music with Guillermo Noriega, dramatic analysis and composition with Luisa Josefina Hernández, and choreography with Bodil Genkel.

In the National Ballet he changed his name from Raúl Flores González to Flores Canelo. His skin was so white and his hair so blond that he was forced to wear brick red body makeup in order to perform the nationalist ballets of the epoch. As a male, he confronted his family's and society's incomprehension as he dedicated his life to dance. He participated in numerous tours and popular performances that the National Ballet held in the country, and in 1955 he began to integrate dance, theater, plastic arts, and craft elements to design elaborate costumes, sets, props, and lighting for several works.

Simultaneous with his work at the National Ballet, in 1959 he joined the Fine Arts Ballet, where he worked with Anna Sokolow, who had a definite impact on his development, particularly in releasing him from formalism. For the next several years, Flores Canelo taught dance teachers in diverse artistic and cultural institutions of the country, including the Mexican Institute of Social Security and the Lake's House of the National University of Mexico. In 1965 he received a fellowship from the Ford Foundation and visited several U.S. cities, including San Francisco, Los Angeles, Salt Lake City, and Washington. He studied in New York at Juilliard, and the schools and studios of Merce Cunningham, Martha Graham, and Hanya Holm, and had teachers that included José Limón, Anna Sokolow, Alwin Nikolais, Helen Tamiris, and Lucas Hoving. He saw numerous contemporary dance and ballet companies and assisted in theatrical productions for concerts, films, museums, and operas. He also confirmed his conception of socially relevant dance and an interplay between dance and the popular classes, all of which he found absent from the work of the Mexican National Ballet. For this reason, on his return to Mexico he separated from this company and founded the Independent Ballet, with many of the National Ballet's dancers who followed him.

This new company defined itself as an artistic community without dogma—and expressed the independent feeling sought by its members in its heterogeneity (it was formed by two Venezuelans and two North Americans), its wide technical work (Graham, Francis, classical, theater, and others) and its choreographic style. Beginning with its first performance at the Fine Arts Palace (1967), the company showed its eclectic proposal, including works by Flores Canelo, John Fealy, and the theatrical director Juan José Gurrola. The company then drew the attention of a new kind of dance public: university students and intellectuals, as their productions vouched the new needs of the epoch, mingling, for example, classic and rock-and-roll music with rural and urban popular music.

Contributing to this innovative line, such choreographers as Graciela Henríquez and John Fealy worked with the Independent Ballet, and the company always counted on the support and works of Anna Sokolow, who personally came to stage them. From its inception through 1970, the Independent Ballet performed twice a week on a variety of Mexican stages, as well as in the U.S., Central American countries, and Cuba; they were partially funded by the Organization for the International Promotion of the Culture and performed in the Fine Arts Palace. In 1975 the Independent Ballet toured France and Holland. In Paris, they performed at the Theater of the Ville, on television and throughout the country; in Holland they performed in several cities while participating in a national dance festival. The Europeans gave a favorable reception to the presented works and considered the company daring with their profound works; Flores Canelo was compared to Béjart. In 1976, due to their European success, the Independent Ballet received a NIFA subsidy, which gave it more stability and possibilities for creating new works.

The company's French tour also brought it to the attention of Maurice Descombey. Former director of the Paris Opera Ballet, he came to Mexico and staged several works including *Year Zero* (1976) and *Loneliness Zarabanda* (1977). Artistic differences caused a break-up between the members of the company, some of whom remained loyal to Flores Canelo, while the others sided with Descombey and Gladiola Orozco (co-director of the company since 1974), who ultimately kept the company's subsidy, studio, productions and name. Again, the followers of Flores Canelo, now under the name of Raúl Flores Canelo Dance Company, succeeded in the recovery (in 1980) of the name Independent Ballet and obtained a new NIFA subsidy. Meanwhile, Descombey and Orozco changed their company's name to Space Theater Ballet.

The breakup did not weaken the Independent Ballet but gave it greater focus. It was then that Flores Canelo created his work *Man and the Dance* (1978), which has been performed more than 500 times in Mexico City and has been seen by some 8,000,000 people throughout Mexico. Moreover, in 1981 they again toured Cuba, and Flores Canelo showed, for the first time, some important contemporary Mexican dances, including *Three Sexual Fantasies and a Prologue, Soliloquy* and *The Wind Remains*, which have been maintained within the repertory and which, together with *The Wait* (1973) are recognized as some of the most transcendent works by Flores Canelo.

Flores Canelo's success was in part due to the stability offered to him, first, by the National Ballet, and later, by the Independent Ballet, from which many important dancers and choreographers have emerged. Since 1982 the Independent Ballet has carried on its Internal Choreography Contest, which has inspired younger dancers to initiate creations of their own.

After the death of Flores Canelo in 1992, his wife Magnolia Orozco, along with Manuel Hiram, assumed the direction of the company. They have maintained its founder's work, again staging such classics as the work of Anna Sokolow (like *Rooms*, 1996) and promoting the works of a new generation of choreographers.

—Margarita Tortajada Quiroz
translated by Dolores Ponce Gutiérrez

FOLKWANG HOCHSCHULE

German dance school

Founded as Folkwangschule, 1927; Kurt Jooss, co-founder, serves as director, Sigurd Leeder his closest associate. In 1928, formed the experimental group "Folkwang Dance Theater Studio," which has existed continuously under various names until today; fusion of Rudolf von Laban's Central School of Berlin with the Folkwang School of Essen in 1929; Kurt Jooss' *Der grüne Tisch* (*The Green Table*) wins first prize at the international choreography competition in Paris, 1932; in 1933, Jooss and his ensemble, Ballets Jooss, leave National Socialist Germany and establish the Jooss-Leeder School of Dance in Dartington Hall in southern England (until 1940);

directors, dance department of the Folkwang School: Albrecht Knust, 1934; Trude Pohl, 1935-49; Kurt Jooss, 1949-68; significant instructors are Hans Züllig and Jean Cébron; organized international dance courses with visiting lecturers, 1959-61; granted college status, 1963; Hans Züllig directs the dance department, 1968-83, followed by Pina Bausch, 1983-88; democratic reorganization of the departments following the University Reform of 1987; Lutz Förster has been the dance department representative, 1991—.

* * *

The Folkwang School (today Folkwang Hochschule, or College) is the only professional school of modern dance in Germany that can look back on an uninterrupted tradition. As the birthplace of German dance theater, the school wrote dance history. Even today, Folkwang generates choreographers who influence and diversify the dance scene in Germany.

When the Folkwang School of "Music, Dance and Speaking" opened its doors in 1927, co-founder Kurt Jooss assumed the position of dance department director. One of his initial goals was to create a solid base for modern dance through systematic training. Such a foundation did not exist in Germany for the personality-oriented modern dance called expressive dance. What counted was individual expression, which was raised to an aesthetic standard, opening doors for dilettantism. Many novices frequently replaced technical and artistic quality with misinterpreted individualism and personal feelings were often mistaken for artistically formed expressive gestures.

Jooss, together with his closest associate Sigurd Leeder, sought to combat this trend. His teacher, Rudolf von Laban, had already laid the foundation for a modern dance training program. Laban's theories of movement and space became the basis for the curriculum developed by Jooss and Leeder. Laban had not designed a new codex of movement, rather, he identified the principles of movement: with choreutics defining the spatial components and eukinetics those of dynamic expression. Both choreutics and eukinetics constituted major fields of study at the Folkwang School. They were to avoid teaching the students a fixed vocabulary of movement, unthinkingly training their bodies. Choreutics and eukinetics demanded a conscious, inquisitive exploratory approach to movement and stimulated creativity. Other basic courses included dance technique (body control with the help of études in the sense of modern dance), general movement training, dance improvisation composition, dance notation (kinetography/Labanotation) and a modified classical training.

In 1929, Rudolf von Laban's Central School of Berlin fused with the Folkwang School in Essen. Kurt Jooss had founded the Folkwang Dance Theater Studio a year previously as an experimental stage. It served as a platform for his own choreographic work and gave his students a forum for their first stage experience. The affiliation of school and dance group were important to Jooss, seen as a way of further developing the new dance technique into a newly formulated dance theater.

With the Folkwang Dance Theater Studio, which under his direction became an integral part of the Essen Opera House and went on tour as the Folkwang Dance Stage, Jooss created his prize-winning piece *Der Grüne Tisch (The Green Table)* for the international Choreography Competition (Concours de Chorégraphie) in Paris in 1932. This work represented the international breakthrough for Jooss and his ensemble, which thereafter performed as a private venture under the name "Balletts Jooss." *The Green Table,* performed to the music of Fritz Cohen, with the stage design of Hein Heckroth, is considered one of the masterpieces of modern dance choreography. It is an anti-war piece, portraying in eight scenes the senselessness and neverending misery of war in archetypal images. Each scene is basically a variation of the same theme, death. With this piece, Jooss formulated a modern plea for more humanity, which remains relevent even today. Just a few months later, Jooss would prove that he understood this as more than just an artistic statement. When the National Socialists under Adolf Hitler came into power in 1933 and demanded that Jooss part with his Jewish composer Fritz Cohen as well as his Jewish dancers, Jooss refused. He left Germany with his ensemble and in 1934 found asylum in Dartington Hall in southern England.

Sigurd Leeder and students from the Folkwang School followed to continue their work in Dartington Hall. There Jooss and Leeder established the Jooss-Leeder School of Dance, which followed the curriculum of the Folkwang School of Essen and existed until 1940. Direction of the Folkwang School, now led by Albrecht Knust (1934) and Trude Pohl (1935-1949), had to succumb to the aesthetic and ideological guidelines of the NSDAP. A studio group, which also performed at political functions, was able to survive. During the twelve years of NS domination, the German dance movement was isolated from international development, which not only led to artistic stagnation, but also degraded it to a form of amusement and entertainment.

When Jooss returned from English exile in 1949 and again took over the direction of the Folkwang School, he began to rebuild modern dance training in Germany. Here, his international experience was an asset. He placed modern dance technique as an equal next to classical ballet and introduced European folklore as a subject. Eukinetics, choreutics, improvisation, composition and dance notation remained established components of the curriculum. This combination of courses reflected Jooss' desire to ensure an education that was encompassing and up-to-date. He also managed to keep modern dance alive, even though it had been declared dead after World War II. To expand the offerings of the Folkwang School, Jooss introduced summer courses from 1959 to 1961, featuring American instructors teaching modern American techniques (Graham, Limón), jazz or ballet (among others Antony Tudor, Lucas Hoving, Alfredo Corvino). In 1961, Jooss created master classes, which promoted young dancers and choreographers. The new Folkwang ensemble, the Folkwang ballet, then emerged from these master classes. Jooss succeeded not only in continuing the tradition of the Folkwang School, but also in once again securing it a respectable place in the (German) dance landscape normally obsessed with ballet.

His associates Hans Züllig and Jean Cébron played a role as well. Züllig was Jooss' premier dancer and helped develop and shape many roles in the Jooss repertoire. When Jooss retired in 1968, Züllig replaced him as director of the dance department of the Folkwang School and held that position until 1983. Jean Cébron, a Jooss-Leeder pupil who mastered classical dance technique as well as modern forms, was one of the internationally sought-after soloists and instructors of the post World War II era. He has been teaching at the Folkwang College since 1961 (with interruptions) and was conferred the title of Professor of Modern Dance in 1976. Entire generations of dancers and choreographers were inspired by Züllig and Cébron, among many others Pina Bausch, Reinhild Hoffmann and Susanne Linke, the founder of German dance theater, as well as Joachim Schlömer, Urs Dietrich and Daniel Goldin, whose individual styles add new facets to today's dance landscape.

Several students remained true to the Folkwang School even after graduation.

Pina Bausch created her first choreographic works for the Folkwang Ballet, which was under her artistic direction from 1969 to 1973 and was renamed the Folkwang Dance Studio [Folkwang Tanzstudio (FTS)]. She also functioned as director of the dance department from 1983 to 1988. Susanne Linke was in charge of the FTS from 1975 until 1985 (until 1977 together with Reinhild Hoffmann) and even today is an active guest choreographer at Folkwang.

Since the university reform of 1988, the departments at Folkwang are democratically organized. An exception was made for the dance department, where Lutz Förster has been the representative for the study of dance since 1991. Förster also received his education at the Folkwang School, was a member of the Limón Dance Company and their associate artistic director, and has been one of the protagonists of Pina Bausch's Wuppertal Dance Theater since 1975. He taught contemporary dance at Folkwang. As a member of an instructor team, he marked a generational change, never ceasing to adhere to the pedagogical maxims of Jooss, which state that it is not dancers that we wish train, but dancing human beings.

—Patricia Stöckemann
translated by Joyce Han-Voth

FONAROFF, Nina
American dancer and choreographer

Born: 1914. **Education:** Lincoln School of Teachers College, Columbia University; trained with Michel Fokine, and the School of American Ballet; also studied painting, costume and stage design, and acting; studied composition with Louis Horst. **Career:** Dancer, Martha Graham Dance Company, 1937-46; assistant to Horst and Graham; first choreography, 1941; formed own company, 1945; retired from choreographing, 1954; director of choreography, London Contemporary Dance Theatre, 1971-1980s; has taught at Adelphi University, Bennington College, Lincoln School, Martha Graham Studio, and University of Baltimore.

Roles (choreographed by Graham for the Martha Graham Dance Company)

1938	*American Document*
1940	*Letter to the World*
1941	*Punch and The Judy*
1943	*Deaths and Entrances*
1944	*Appalachian Spring*

Other roles include: Many Graham productions from 1938 through 1946.

Works

1941	*Yankee Doodle, American Prodigy: An American Fantasy* (mus. Louis Horst)
	Hoofer on a Fiver (mus. Tcherepnine)
1942	*Cafe Chantant, 5 am* (mus. Larmanjat)

> *Little Theodolina, Queen of the Amazons Fantasy of a
>   Little Creature* (mus. Horst)
> *Yankee Doodle Greets Columbus, 1492* (mus. Horst)

1945   *Feast* (mus. John Cage)

1946   *Of Sundry Wimmen* (mus. medieval; text Chaucer)
> *Dance of Languor* (mus. Darius Milhaud)
> *Born to Weep* (mus. Horst)
> *Of Tragic Gesture* (mus. Ralph Gilbert)
> *Lazarus* (mus. John Stewart McLennan; story Leonid
>   Andreyev)

1947   *Recitative and Aria* (silence)
> *Mr. Puppet, a Monody* (text Fonaroff)

1950   *Masque* (mus. John Stewart McLennan)

1953   *Requiem* (mus. McLennan)

Publications

By FONAROFF: articles—

"Louis Horst," *Journal of the Society for Dance Research,* Summer 1984.

Sketches in *The Dance Observer,* 1938-53 (reproduced in Dorothy Madden's *You Call Me Louis, Not Mr. Horst,* the Netherlands, 1996).

On FONAROFF: articles—

Balcom, L., "Nina Fonaroff," *Dance Observer,* August-September 1942.

———, "Nina Fonaroff and Company," *Dance Observer,* 1953.

Clippings files from the Dance Collection of the New York Public Library for the Performing Arts at Lincoln Center.

Martin, John, "The Dance: A Debut," *New York Times,* 10 November 1946.

Terry, Walter, review, *New York Herald Tribune,* 24 December 1950.

*　　*　　*

Born in 1914, the daughter of concert violinists, Nina Fonaroff was raised in New York City, and noted primarily as a dancer who performed supporting roles in Martha Graham's company from 1938 to 1946. In addition, Fonaroff was respected for her individuality as a choreographer, with her talent as a visual artist contributing to the multiplicity of her work. As a teacher of dance technique in the United States and later dance composition in Great Britain Fonaroff encouraged many students who appreciated her critical eye and sensitive teaching style.

Fonaroff received her early education at the Lincoln School of Teachers College, Columbia, and trained in dance under Michel Fokine, and at the School of American Ballet in New York City. She then studied painting with George Grosz, and drawing, costume and stage design in Zurich and Berlin before enrolling in the acting program at the Cornish School in Seattle, Washington. After a single day in a dance class for actors taught by visiting artist, Martha Graham, she deserted the drama for dance, and returned to New York City for further professional study. She joined Graham's concert group in 1937, while studying dance composition with Louis Horst, (Martha Graham's mentor, musical director, and intimate partner until 1938). Fonaroff soon was indispensable as an assistant to both Graham and Horst in courses they taught at Teachers College, Columbia, Sarah Lawrence College and the Neighborhood Playhouse.

As a dancer, Fonaroff's physical qualities (blond and diminutive) contrasted the dark, dramatic Martha Graham on stage. From 1937 to 1946, Graham created various roles for Fonaroff such as a child as in *Letter to the World,* 1940, and the "pert brat" in *Punch and The Judy* (1941), group works choreographed during summer residencies at the Bennington School of the Dance. During this period, Fonaroff choreographed studies under Horst's guidance, performing regularly in his lecture-demonstrations at Bennington College and the YW-YMHA's Kaufman Auditorium in New York City.

Horst encouraged Fonaroff's choreographic work (as he had for Graham), writing scores for her first pieces created as special projects at Bennington, *Yankee Doodle, American Prodigy: An American Fantasy* (1941) and *Little Theodolina, Queen of the Amazons* (1942) and reviewed in *Dance Observer* as "hilarious and delightful." Nina became Horst's confidante and partner (replacing Graham after 1938), and they remained companions throughout the 1940s. Fonaroff formed her own company in 1945, and for the next eight years continued to present her choreography in concert primarily at Bennington, and at Choreographer's Workshop at the Studio Theatre on West 16th Street and the YM-YWHA in New York City with works praised in *Dance Observer* as "unique and poignant" with "rare tenderness and excellence." After leaving the Graham company in 1946 she gave her first full-length concert at the YM-YWHA winning acclaim from *New York Times* critic John Martin who stated, "Here is a distinguished talent, highly individual in character, with something to say, and certainly with the means to get it said with taste, imagination and authority."

Fonaroff's choreography often combined dance with drama, using text as in 1946's *Lazarus,* (based on a short story of Leonid Andreyev) and in her work, *Feast* (1945). In 1950 critic Walter Terry described her group work *Masque* in the *New York Herald Tribune,* as "a piece about a marionette who unties his strings only to discover that life on his own is disappointing, empty and tragic." Among the dancers for whom she choreographed were Helen McGehee, Jack Moore, and Natanya Neumann, Bertram Ross, and Doris Rudko, who appreciated her meticulous crafting, and attention to detail. But, self-critical and dissatisfied with the concert scene, Fonaroff stopped choreographing abruptly by 1954. Although she continued to assist Horst at the Neighborhood Playhouse for several years longer, Nina's interest in dance waned in favor of the theater.

Fonaroff had taught dance technique at Lincoln School, Adelphi College, the YW-YMHA, the Martha Graham Studio, the University of Baltimore, and at Bennington College while a company member. However, after leaving Graham and throughout the 1950s, Fonaroff's teaching favored the placement and vocabulary of ballet and her work with actors rather than the rigors of Graham technique. When Fonaroff was asked to join the faculty of the London Contemporary Dance School as director of choreography in 1971 after a long hiatus from the creation and teaching of dancemaking, she began anew, moving to London to begin another phase of her dance career. With misgivings at first, she sought her own methods for teaching dance composition, and over the next years evolved methodologies totally different from her earlier work with Horst. Rather than teach Horst's formal approach, Fonaroff stressed sensory and emotional aspects in motivating choreography from a kinetic point of view, asking students to draw imaginative movement materials from their personal experiences. Often in her classes only a few students would take the lead as choreographers, with others working creatively as dancers. Fonaroff continued to serve as a mentor to her students at the London Contemporary Dance School throughout the 1980s, also giving special choreographic workshops throughout Europe, specifically for the choreography department of Danshoskolan in Stockholm, Sweden.

—Janet Mansfield Soares

FOOTNOTE DANCE COMPANY
New Zealand dance company

Works

1983   *Peter and the Cat-burglar* (chor. D. Tarrant; mus. Prokofiev, Lancaster, Lumley)
Encounter (chor. D. Tarrant; mus. Poulenc, Shostakovich)
Da Da Da (chor. M. Owen)
Challenge (chor. B. Carbee; mus. D. Ellington, B. Goodman)
Looking for Clues (chor. L. Fuller; mus. Pabner)
Kicking Stones (chor. D. Tarrant; mus. T. James)
Tribute (chor. Footnote; mus. Rimsky-Korsakov)

1984   *Eat to the Beat* (chor. G. Mayo; mus. Blondie)
Glove Box (chor. L. Davey; mus. Crusaders)
For Marie from Mike (chor. M. Parmenter; mus. K. Jarrett)
Three by Two for You (chor. S. Jordan; mus. L. Jordan)
Waits in Black (chor. Footnote; mus. The Stranglers)
Twist and Shout (chor. T. Verhoeven; mus. The Beatles)
Into White (chor. Footnote; mus. C. Stevens, K. Urban)
Toys from the Boys (chor. Lyne Pringle)
Reincarnation (chor. G. Mayo; mus. F. Santana)
Whip It (chor. G. Mayo; mus. Devo)

1985   *Sidewinder* (chor. S. Stopforth; mus. L Donaldson)
Three Little Pigs (chor. S. Stopforth)
Circles (chor. D. Tarrant; mus. Vangelis)
Night Children (chor. B. Doherty; mus. A. Davis)
Blue for Two (chor. D. Tarrant; mus. E. Klugh)
Darktown Strut (chor. S. Stopforth; mus. A. Hunter)
Stamp out Quicksand (chor. G. Mayo; mus. R. Lewis)
Been There, Done That (chor. S. Jordan; mus. various)
Silks (chor. D. Tarrant; mus. M. Nock)

1986   *Flight-Path* (chor. M. Nepia; mus. M. Fisher)
Keep It Cool (chor. T. Verhoeven; mus. G. Howard),
The Empty Beach (chor. G. Sporton; mus. Vollenweider)
Double Take (chor. G. Sporton; mus. G. Moncrieff)
Pi R squared (chor. G. Sporton; mus. A. Sonderlager)
Awa (chor. C. Jannides; mus. Talking Heads)
Passing James Haze (chor. F. Molloy; mus. Cadona)
Body Jungle & Tunnels (chor. C. Jannides; mus. E. Grismonti & N. Vasconcelos)
Combined Operations (chor. B. Carbee; mus. The Staple Singers)
The Dynamic Duo (chor. G. Sporton; mus. A. Nettleback & G. Badger)
An Enchanted Evening (chor. G. Sporton; mus. Rogers & Hammerstein)
The Home Danger (chor. D. Tarrant; mus. N. Palmer)
On the Beat (chor. P. Spooner; mus. G. Jones)

1987   *Work Work Work* (chor. M. J. O'Reilly)
Peace de Resistance (chor. S. McCullagh; mus. various)
From behind the Green (chor. L. Davey; mus. P. Metheny)
Just Looking (chor. J. Bull; mus. D. Buchanan)
Family Reunion (chor. R. Schwabl)
Little Red Riding Hood (chor. The Company)

1988   *Taniwha* (chor. D. Tarrant; mus. various, from a story by R.Kahukiwa)
Sun Sea and Sandwiches (chor. C. Stock; mus. B. Greenberg)
Venture (chor. M. Parmenter; mus. D. Downes, J. Psathas, D. Shanly)

1989   *Water* (chor. D. Macfarland; mus. Handel)
Bach Variations (chor. D. Macfarland; mus. Bach)
Whisp (chor. D. Macfarland; mus. S. Denheim, R. Horowitz)
Marshmallows and Mustard (chor. M. White; mus. Upper Hutt Posse)
Bakugeki (chor. P. Edwards)

1990   *Just Out of Reach* (chor. A. Dewey; mus. P. Cline, S. Prentice)
Carnivale Animale (chor. D. Tarrant; mus. Saint-Saens)
The Man Whose Mother was a Pirate (chor. D. Tarrant; story M. Mahy)
Pipers Galliard (chor. A. Dewey; mus. trad)
Everyday (chor. C. Isaac & A. Baird; mus. The Jam Machine)
Weighting Game (chor. S. Major; mus. David Downes)
Zebra Crossing (chor. D. Belton; mus. M. Avery)

1991   *Tantra* (chor. M. Parmenter; mus. D. Parsons)
Here Today... (chor. D. Tarrant; mus. Six Volts, Schtung, Shine)
Fields of Jeopardy (chor. M. Parmenter; mus. D. Downes)
Meeting Places (chor. B. Carbee; mus. I. Zagni)
Fresh in Exposed Places (chor. M.J. O'Reilly; mus. D. Buchanan, D. McGlashan)
Bhakti (chor. M. Parmenter; mus. D. Parsons)

1993   *Anything Goes* (chor. D. Tarrant; mus. Blue Samanthas)
Letter Home (chor. S. Jordan; mus. J. McLeod)
What's That? (chor. A. Dewey; mus. N. Palmer)
Cry Baby Moon/Marama Tangiweto (chor. P. Jenden; mus. J. Bolton, story K. Mataira and T. Kemp)
Mary Mary (chor. S. McCullagh; mus. M.E. Bossi, Ravel)
Poutokomanawa (chor. M. Gray; mus. C. Sengelow & K. Gournov)

1994   *Kneedance* (chor. D. Wright; mus. L. Anderson)
Two Inches Behind the Eye (chor. S. Dunlop; mus. A. Ritchie)
Pick-up-Sticks (chor. D. Tarrant; mus. Blue Samanthas)
Spirit Winged (chor. L. Davey; mus. Neville Brothers)
Why? (chor. W. Jarman; mus. Wairere Iti)

1995   *Hello Goodbye* (chor. D. Tarrant; mus. I. Patterson & Blue Samanthas)
New Kids on the Block (chor. S. Stopforth; mus. Bad Creation)
Bodylaugh (chor. A. Capper-Starr)
Bodyschlock 5,6,13 (chor. H. Cooper; mus. G. Armstrong)
Vinyl Oven (chor. M. Parmenter; mus. various)

1996   *Tell Me a Story* (chor. D. Tarrant; mus. D. Downes & Battlecat)
Tidal Journey (chor. S. Fraser; mus. S. Reich)

1997 *The Pelt, the Pork and the Princess* (chor. S. McCullagh; mus. J.Gibson & various)

Rough Fusion (chor. M. Gray; mus. D. J. Mu)

Fish In Chips (chor. N. Bishop; mus. Prince Tui Teka, Lag and Breath, Tall Dwarfs)

Safe Landings (chor. D. Tarrant; mus. various)

Dress Me In Boots (chor. S. Milham; mus. S. Milham)

(to)instigorate (chor. J. Duncan; mus. Ludvigson, Shihad & Chopin)

Whil'igig (chor. C. Gardner; mus. D. Leahy)

Mechano (chor. M. Harvey; mus. S. Gallagher)

1998 *Satellite Glances* (chor. M Parmenter; mus. D. Downes)

Nineteen Seventeen (chor. J. Nelson; mus. S. Gubaidulina)

The Brain (chor. S. Stopforth; mus. E. Ranglin)

Link with Me (chor. J. Duncan; mus. D. Leahy)

Fast Forward (chor. D. Tarrant; mus. K. Young)

One More Than Two (chor. C. Gardner; mus. From Stratch)

*   *   *

Footnote Dance Company was established during 1983 as a dance-in-education company to bring workshop and performance programmes to schools throughout New Zealand. The company developed out of a summer project in which senior dancers of the Deirdre Tarrant Dance Studio presented workshop and performance programmes for Wellington Summer City Festivals in 1981 and 1982. Public response to these activities was highly enthusiastic, and a six month pilot project followed in 1983, taking the workshop and performance programmes into primary schools with funding from a government work scheme. On the successful conclusion of the project, the company was formally established under the direction of Deirdre Tarrant.

In 1985 the company began working in secondary schools, and added a theatrical performance season to their activities, with new works commissioned for this event to supplement the repertoire of existing works choreographed by Deirdre Tarrant. In 1986 a community performance series was also added, and a policy of commissioning new work from New Zealand choreographers, composers, and designers was formalised.

This combination of dance-in-education supplemented by community performances and an annual theatre season of new works commissioned from New Zealand choreographers, has continued to the present. Footnote is the second-longest running professional dance company in New Zealand, with only the Royal New Zealand Ballet surviving longer. It is a client of the Arts Council and receives annual funding for its programmes.

Over the years Footnote has maintained a company size of five dancers plus an artistic director and administrator, and an apprentice dancer is often included in the company. In line with current business philosophy, it is a lean and mean company, balancing the achievement of artistic objectives against the achievement of business and financial objectives.

The dancers who become members of Footnote tend to be recent graduates of tertiary level dance training programmes in New Zealand and Australia, without specific knowledge of dance-in-education approaches. Introductory dance-in-education training is provided at the beginning of each nine-month season, and is continued on-the-job. The company's schedule is demanding, with intensive touring to primary and secondary schools throughout the country for six months, and three months in the studio preparing the year's

programmes, learning the repertory, and working with choreographers on new works commissioned for theatrical performance. Dancers on average stay one or two years with the company, although there have been exceptions—founding member Tanya Verhoeven was in the company for four years, while Bill Jarman was a member for eight years before moving to Australia to continue his dance career. More than 52 dancers have passed through Footnote's ranks, gaining valuable experience in teaching, performance and choreography, and learning to survive the pressures of intensive touring. A significant roster of New Zealand dance professionals received their first employment contracts from the company—among them Shona McCullagh, Helen Winchester, Lisa Densem, Taane Mete, Glenn Mayo, and Raewyn Hill.

The company's contribution to the development of New Zealand choreography is particularly significant as it acts as a repository of New Zealand's recent choreographic history. Choreographers Michael Parmenter, Shona McCullagh, Sally Stopforth, Ann Dewey and Merenia Gray maintain a continuing relationship with the company, making new works specifically for it, and from time to time reconstructing or restaging previously choreographed works. Long-established New Zealand choreographers such as Shona Dunlop, Mary-Jane O'Reilly, Douglas Wright and Susan Jordan have also provided works for the repertory. American choreographer Duncan Macfarland, a dance-in-education specialist, was in residence with the company during 1989, providing both new works and a professional development programme for them.

The company's commitment to developing New Zealand choreography extends to company members, and a number of dancers have received choreographic commissions while in its ranks, providing a foundation for future development. The company achieves high standards of excellence in its dance-in-education programmes, and they have become regular return visitors at a number of schools throughout New Zealand. Since 1994 they have also been making regular forays to Australia to work with both schools, attend conferences and ensure that the company is seen as an employment opportunity for Australian dancers.

—Susan Jordan and Raewyn Whyte

FOREMAN, Laura

American dancer, choreographer, company director, and artist

Born: c.1945 in Los Angeles. **Education:** Graduated from the University of Wisconsin. **Family:** Married John Everett Watts. **Career:** Dancer, Tamiris-Nagrin Dance Company; founder, Laura Foreman Dance Theatre; founder, Choreoconcerts, 1964; founded the dance department at the New School for Social Research, 1971, where she is still on the faculty.

Works

1961 *Evocations*

New Dance

Divided

Lyric Dances

1962 *Last*

Sound Piece

1963	*Improvisation Suite*
	Seasonals
1964	*Memorials*
	Expiations
	Freedom Suite
1966	*Study I*
	Study II
	Film Dances
1967	*Solo Suite*
	Study
	Experimentals
	Media Piece
1968	*A Time*
	Events
	Group Dances
	Pulses
	Media Dances I
	Games
1969	*Study*
	Perimeters
1970	*Signals*
	Epicycles
	untitled
	Events II
1971	*glass and shadows*
	Laura's Dance
	Commercials
	Signals II
1972	*Environments I*
	Environments II
	Skydance
	Margins
	Spaces (Collage I)
	Spaces (Collage II)
1973	*Performance*
	Locrian
	Spaces (Collage III)
	Spaces (Collage IV)
	songandance (still life, lecture-dem, songandance)
1974	*Postludes*
	à deux
	city of angels
1975	*Monopoly*
1976	*Program*
1977	*Heirlooms*
1978	*Entries*
1979	*Time-Coded Woman*

Publications

By FOREMAN: books—

Close Encounters, New York, 1997.

On FOREMAN: articles—

Anderson, Jack, "ChoreoConcerts and Critiques," *Dance Magazine,* January 1973.
———, "Sold Out: Performances That Never Actually Took Place," *New York Times,* 12 July 1981.
Baker, Rob, "Liberated Dance: Out of the Concert Hall and into the Streets," *Dance Magazine,* August 1972.
———, "New Dance," *Dance Magazine,* September 1972.
Dunning, Jennifer, "Pick a Dance," *Dance Magazine,* July 1977.
Kendall, Elizabeth, "Dog Days of Summer," *Dance Magazine,* September 1974.
Marks, Marcia, "ChoreoConcerts and Critiques," *Dance Magazine,* December 1971.
Maskey, Jacqueline, "Dance at the Bridge," *Dance Magazine,* February 1966.
Mason, Nancy, "ChoreoConcerts," *Dance Magazine,* January 1971.
Rosen, Lillie F., "Pongsan Masked Dancers and Foreman," *Dance News,* September 1977.
Stern-Obstfeld, Sam, "ChoreoConcerts Workshop," *Dance Magazine,* August 1973.
Stodelle, Ernestine, "Contemporary Dance Productions," *Dance Observer,* August-September 1961.
Stodolsky, Ellen, "Laura Foreman Dance Company," *Dance Magazine,* June 1973.
Thorn, Rose Ann, "Three Events," *Dance Magazine,* December 1974.

*   *   *

Laura Foreman is a postmodern dancer, avant-garde performance artist, conceptual visual artist, and writer. She is also a long-time dance educator and a sponsor of opportunities for young choreographers to present new works.

Born in Los Angeles, Foreman graduated from the University of Wisconsin. During the 1960s and early 1970s, she danced with the Tamiris-Nagrin Dance Company, where she performed in works including Helen Tamiris' *Versus.* She also danced in the company of her Tamiris-Nagrin colleague, Marion Scott, including in works such as *The Tenderling* and *Going.* Others with whom Foreman performed include Harriet Anne Gray and Anna Halprin.

Foreman began choreographing her own works in 1961. Many of them were presented at the 92nd Street YM/YWHA in New York under the auspices of Scott's Contemporary Dance Productions, an organization that featured new works by young modern dance choreographers. However, from the 1960s to the 1980s, Foreman stopped performing to focus on her own choreography, presented by her troupe, the Laura Foreman Dance Company, later known as the Laura Foreman Dance Theatre. Her pieces are described as dancetheater events that focus both on humor and anxiety, and incorporate dramatic themes or incidents, as well as movement, singing and speaking. They feature everyday activities such as hairbrushing and eating, and often rely on props. For example, *Heirlooms* (1977) featured a knitting bag, an apple, and reels of film. Despite the pedestrian nature of Foreman's work, the movement she employs is often described by critics as balletic. Her choreography is set to eclectic taped collages combining music, sounds, speeches and media clips. Many of the soundtracks were composed by her husband, John Watts, with whom she collaborated until 1982.

Many of her dances involve the idea of the passage of time. In *A Time* (1968), she used radio and video clips to conjure up various eras. She oftenjuxtaposes images in an unconventional way. For example, *Signals II* (1972) contains a pregnant woman performing ballet moves and a vocalist singing about an incinerated paint can. "What fascinates me is not so much the separate ingredients of my works, but the way in which they fit together," Foreman told *Dance*

The Laura Foreman Dance Company performing at the Ward-Nasse Gallery, 1976. Photograph © Johan Elbers.

Magazine in 1972. "I work a lot with chance technique, but that doesn't mean things are thrown together at random. You still have to select and order your material."

Foreman is known for the way she tailors her dances to their performance spaces. For example, in one of the *Spaces* series (1973), she used the studio's interior and exterior spaces, including the elevator, the balcony and a rooftop visible through a window. Similarly, in *Skydance* (1972), which was performed in New York's Central Park, skywriters traced "sky ballets" and wrote choreography instructions in the sky during the piece.

Foreman frequently incorporates mixed media in her works, as in the *Study* pieces. An untitled 1970 piece integrated live video, performers, and the audience. *Timecoded Woman* (1979) was a performance/installation piece involving the use of video.

Many of Foreman's dances demand a high degree of athleticism from the performers. For example, in *à deux* (1974), a duet for a large and a small man, one supported the other horizontally as they both walked in unison, one on the floor and one on the wall.

From 1980 to 1982, Foreman focused on solo performance art works, which were collaborations with Watts containing video, text, live music and/or orchestra. In 1981, Foreman and Watts stretched the definition of dance/performance with a piece called *Wallwork,* two performances of which were advertised on posters throughout New York City. The performances appeared in dance

calendars in local newspapers, and an informational phone number was set up. Some of the posters acquired sold-out stickers after a time, and callers to the ticket number were informed that the work was sold out. In fact, no performance was ever planned. The piece in its entirety consisted of the posters and publicity, as critics were informed through confidential statements explaining the project.

Her works during this period were largely improvised, and were untitled or titled at the moment of creation. The same is true of her work with the Richard Keene Quintet, with which she has performed from 1983 to the present. The group creates improvisational works in alternative spaces, clubs, and coffee houses around New York. Foreman has also choreographed for television, including commercials for ABC Television in 1971. She created dances for *City Junket,* a play by poet Kenward Elmslie, in 1980, also serving as the production's assistant director.

Foreman is known for her strong support of other choreographers. She founded the Choreographers Theatre in 1964 as a place for choreographers to present single works as part of a larger program. Her series of ChoreoConcerts and Critiques, jointly presented by the New School for Social Research in New York and the Choreographers Theatre, featured the premieres of four choreographers per show, followed by a presentation by each choreographer and a question-and-answer period. Foreman presented works in the ChoreoConcerts (in addition to serving as director), as have choreographers ranging from Stuart Hodes to Gus Solomons, Jr., as well as young, relatively unknown creators.

A long-time dance educator, Foreman relaunched the dance department at the New School (which had been a center of modern dance in the 1930s), where she has served as director of dance, as well as the physical fitness and recreation departments and the movement specialist certification program, since 1971. She teaches frequently, both at the New School and at other venues, including Parsons, the Art Students League, the Metropolitan Museum of Art, and the Chapin School.

In addition to her work in dance and performance art, Foreman is a published writer and visual artist. Her short stories have appeared in publications including *Confrontation* and *The Santa Clara Review.* Her first short-story collection, *Close Encounters,* was published in 1997. Her conceptual art works, which range from large-scale installations to small sculptures, have been shown in numerous galleries and museums.

—Karen Raugust

FORTI, Simone

Italian-born American dancer and choreographer

Born: 1935 in Florence, Italy; moved to the United States in the early 1940s. **Education:** Attended Reed College, Portland, Oregon; studied dance with Anna Halprin, 1956-59; studied briefly with Merce Cunningham and Martha Graham. **Family:** Married artist Robert Morris (divorced); married Robert Whitman, 1962 (divorced 1966). **Career:** Worked at a nursery school in New York City; first independent choreography, 1959; participated in Happenings with Morris and Whitman in the early 1960s; subsequently performed in her own works.

Works

1959	*Green Space*
1960	*See-Saw*
	Rollers
1961	*Slant Board*
	Huddle
	Hangers
	Platforms
	Accompaniment for La Monte's "2 Sounds"...
	From Instructions
	Censor
	Herding
1967	*Face Tunes*
	Cloths
	Elevation Tune No. 2
	Song
1968	*Book*
	Bottom
	Fallers
	Sleepwalkers
	Throat Dance
1971	*Buzzing*
	Illuminations; performed with Charlemagne Palestine
1974	*The Zero*
	Crawling
1975	*Big Room*
	Red Green
1976	*Planet*
1978	*Fan Dance*
1979	*Estuary*
	Home Base
1981	*Jackdaw Songs*
1989	*Touch*
1991	*Animations*
	Collaboration
	To Be Continued
	Still Life

Publications

By FORTI: book and articles—

"Theater and Engineering—An Experiment," *Artforum 5,* February 1967.

Handbook in Motion, Halifax, Nova Scotia: Press of the Nova Scotia College of Art and Design, and New York: New York University, 1974.

"Dancing at the Fence," *Avalanche,* December 1974.

"Bicycles," *Dance Scope,* Fall 1978.

On FORTI: articles—

Cash, Debra, "Forti: Emissary from the Woods," *Boston Globe,* 26 April 1988.

Sommers, Pamela, "Simone Forti's *Jackdaw Songs,*" *Drama Review,* Summer 1981.

*   *   *

American postmodernist choreographer and dancer Simone Forti was born in 1935 in Florence, Italy. Forti and her Italian-Jewish parents escaped first to Switzerland in 1939, then emigrated to the United States in the early 1940s. She spent her childhood in Los Angeles, and attended Reed College in Portland, Oregon. She and her then-husband, artist Robert Morris, dropped out of college and moved to San Francisco in 1956. There, Forti began her dance training at the age of 21 with Ann (later Anna) Halprin. For four years, she danced with Halprin's school and performance group, the Dancer's Workshop, which was known for drawing on nature for inspiration, and substituting improvisation and free association for specialized and more formal movements (Halprin had broken with conventional modern dance just the year before). Halprin's emphasis on "natural movements" influenced Forti's later work.

When Forti and Morris moved to New York City in 1959, Forti studied briefly at the Martha Graham School and the Merce Cummingham Studio. During this period, Forti taught at a nursery school and became fascinated by the movement of children. She felt that Cunningham, though a brilliant dancer, articulated an adult condition of movement—isolated, fragmented, and artificial—while what she herself offered was "still very close to the holistic and generalized response of infants." And as far as the Graham classes were concerned, Forti's refusal to hold her stomach in was a bit of a problem.

Forti had been fascinated with unusual contrasts dating to her discovery of surrealistic films during high school. In 1960, she saw

Simone Forti: *On a Revolving Stage,* 1976. Photograph © Beatriz Schiller.

one of Robert Whitman's early "Happenings," *E.G.,* which struck her as reflecting the surreal juxtapositions she had envisioned in dance. Later that year, she participated in another Whitman Happening, *The American Moon.* In December of 1960, she created two pieces, *See-Saw* and *Rollers,* both based on adult bodies using children's playground equipment. *See-Saw* began with a man and a woman (Robert Morris and Yvonne Ranier) on a see-saw. Yvonne Ranier, quoted in *Avalanche 5* (Summer 1972), later said that *See-Saw* had a profound influence on her work: "One thing followed another. Whenever I am in doubt I think of that."

In *Rollers,* a singing performer stood in each of two shallow boxes on wheels. The boxes could be made to career wildly by the audience pulling on the three ropes attached to the boxes and stretched through the loft. Forti explains in *Handbook in Motion* that this was meant to produce "an excitement bordering on fear, which automatically becomes an element in the performance."

Forti's next performance, a collection of pieces called *Five Dance Constructions and Some Other Things,* created in the spring of 1961 for a series at Yoko Ono's loft on Chambers Street, included *Slant Board, Huddle, Hangers, Accompaniment for La Monte's "2 Sounds" and La Monte's "2 Sounds," from Instructions, Censor,* and *Herding. Huddle* is now considered a seminal work, and a precursor to the improvisational genre of the 1970s. *Huddle* was later performed by Fluxus (a neodadaist group that included George Maciunas, Alison Knowles, George Brecht, and Dick Higgins) in Paris, Copenhagen, and Düsseldorf, as a classic example of noninstrumental action music.

During 1961 Forti worked with Trisha Brown and Dick Levine to create improvisations using rule games. One such game that became a mainstay of her improvisations and workshops—*Over, Under, and Around*—incorporated two sets of rules: one known to all parties, and one set secret, creating a piece full of the juxtapositions she loved, some movements seeming harmonious and fluid (three soon-anticipated actions, going over, under, and around the other performers) and other movements full of tension and chaos (performers trying to simultaneously go over each other).

In 1962 Forti married Robert Whitman, and during their marriage (from 1962 to 1966) she helped him with many of his Happenings, including *Hole, Flower, Night Time Sky, Water,* and *Prune/Flat.* She did not choreograph any of her own pieces again until after her divorce from Whitman. By 1967 Forti was again choreographing and presented three new pieces—*Cloths, Song,* and *Face Tunes*—at the School of Visual Arts. These pieces began a period focused more on sound than movement. In *Cloths,* performers behind screens, flipped cloths over the screen, and sang songs, overlapping taped songs, and interspersed with moments of silence. In *Face Tunes,* Forti devised a machine that rolled a long scroll painted with seven faces in profile. As the faces scrolled by, Forti played a slide whistle. In *Song,* Forti sang a Tuscan folk song in counterpoint to a recording of the Beatles' "Fool on the Hill." In 1968 she created three pieces for a concert at the Cornell School of Architecture, *Book,* which added pairs of slides projected on a screen to *Song,* and *Bottom*—in which drumming, a single chord (sung by Forti, LaMonte Young, and Marian Zazeela), a vacuum cleaner, and a whistled tune accompanied slides. *Fallers* surprised the audience with the sight of free-falling bodies (performers leapt from the roof of the penthouse where the performance was held to the terrace).

Late in 1968, Forti gave a concert in Rome, where she began to explore animals and their movements, a study that occupied her for the next 10 years. Her fascination with polar bears swinging their heads back and forth and flamingoes sleeping while standing on one foot were both incorporated into her piece *Sleepwalkers,* which she termed a "zoo mantra." In *Crawling,* Forti explores the movements of bees, rabbits, elephants, crows, snakes, and bears. *Planet,* a group piece with almost 40 performers, involves moving from crawling to walking and back to crawling and a number of animal movements, including the lion (performed by Forti), an elephant, bird, monkey, lizards, and three young bears, using large circular motions and incorporating *Huddle.* Forti's observations on the animal's "dance behavior" echo her concept of a human dancer's "dance state," an almost meditative state of deep concentration that Forti first recognized during her time studying with Halprin.

Forti went to Turin in 1969 to work with an experimental theatre group, The Zoo, and to Rome to participate in the Festival of Music, Dance, Explosions, and Flight. She also attended the Woodstock Festival, which led to a year of traveling, communal living, and drug experimentation. Even during this year of "trying to be me," she found herself examining movement—balance, weight, momentum, and other classic elements of dance. She returned to New York, briefly studied singing with Pandit Praith Nath, who had taught LaMonte Young. Forti then returned to California, where she occasionally substituted for Allen Kaprow at the California Institute of the Arts, leading open dance sessions called "Open Gardenia."

Forti experimented constantly with three concepts: crawling (reflecting both her interest in the movements of children and animal dance behavior); animal movements; and circling (which has roots in both the kinesthetic boundaries of form—such as in her rules games—and her belief in numerology). Forti's mid-1970s works, *Red Green, Big Room, Planet,* and *Fan Dance,* revolve around these three themes, but particularly focus on circling and banking.

—Lisa Anderson Mann

FORTIER, Paul-André

Canadian dancer, choreographer, educator, and company director

Born: Waterville, Quebec, 30 April 1948. **Education:** Seminaire de Sherbrooke, Université de Sherbrooke, B.A. 1968, diploma in Arts 1971, M.A. 1972. **Career:** First independent choreography, 1979. Founder, Fortier Danse-Creation, 1981; co-director (with Daniel Jackson) of Montreal Danse, 1986-89; faculty member, dance department, Université du Quebec, Montreal, 1989; resumed performing career, 1987; subject of television documentary, *Adrienne Clarkson Presents,* CBC-TV, 1995. **Awards:** Jean A. Chalmers Prize for choreography, 1983; Dora Mavor Moore Award for Outstanding Choreography, 1992-93.

Works

1978	*Derrière la porte un mur* (mus. Kodaly), Groupe Nouvelle Aire
	Images noires (mus. Cage), Groupe Nouvelle Aire
1979	*Reve 1* (mus. Cage), Groupe Nouvelle Aire
	Parlez-moi donc du cul de mon enfance, for three dancers and one actor
1980	*Violence* (mus. Muzak)

1981   *Bande dansinée,* Giard-Soulières
       Fin (mus. military marches)
1982   *Pow!... t'es mort* (mus. mix)
       Création (mus. Dionne)
       Lavabos (mus. Miller), Québec Été Danse
       Moi, King Kong (mus. Mingus), solo, commission for
           Margie Gillis
       Non coupable (mus. Kucharczyk), solo, commission for
           Susan Macpherson
1983   *Ca ne saigne jamais...* (mus. Dionne)
       Gravitation (mus. Werren)
1984   *Assis soient-ils* (mus. mix)
       Venus 84 (mus. Werren), solo for female dancer
1985   *Chaleur* (mus. Boudreau)
1986   *Brûler* (mus. Boudreau)
1987   *Tell* (mus. Liszt), Montreal Danse
       Le Mythe décisif, Les Grands Ballets Canadiens
       Sans titre et qui le restera (mus. Lamandier), solo
       O-Pé-Ra Savon
1989   *Désert* (mus. Ravel), Montreal Danse
       Les Males heures (mus. Leboeuf), solo
       L'Été latent (mus. Leboeuf)
1991   *Plein le coeur* (mus. Leboeuf), Danse-Partout
       Lost (mus. Fleming), solo, commission for Patricia Fraser
       La Tentation de la transparence (mus. Leboeuf), solo,
           Canada Dance Festival
1993   *Bras de plomb* (mus. Leboeuf), solo
       Double Silence, duo
1995   *Novembre* (mus. Bryars), solo, Les Grands Ballets
           Canadiens
1996   *Tête d'Ange* (mus. Leboeuf), solo, commission for An-
           drew de Lotbinière Harwood
       Entre la memoire et l'oubli (mus. Marcel), Montréal Danse
       La part des anges (mus. Leboeuf)

Publications

On FORTIER: books—

Tembeck, Iro, *Dancing in Montreal: Seeds of a Choreographic History,* Journal of the Society of Dance History Scholars Studies in Dance History, Vol. V, Number 2, Fall 1994.

*   *   *

Through his diverse talents as choreographer, dancer and teacher, Paul-André Fortier has established himself as one of the key figures who helped shape the Montreal dance scene over the last 20 years. Imposing labels trail him, such as "eminence grise" or "spearhead of a movement," and for good reason. During the early 1980s, Fortier woke people up with a series of confrontational choreographies. The work was categorized variously as strong, grotesque, explicit, violent, sexual and shocking, but also remarkably clear, theatrical and original. The "theatre in revolt" offerings made audiences reconsider just what can happen when an artist grabs hold of an audience's imagination and doesn't let go.

Before the Quiet Revolution in the 1960s, a pivotal time in the province's political and social evolution, the Catholic Church in Quebec restrained and dictated life in the province for decades. For anyone who grew up Catholic in Quebec in those years, Fortier's work rang true as an expression and a challenge to the philosophical

and social status quo in the province. The intensity of his performance exploded traditional categories of dance, embracing the visual arts, philosophy, and religion. His radical, totally innovative, intellectually stimulating choreographies offered a true psychological landscape.

Fortier came to dance by chance, at the ripe age of 21. He taught college-level literature and theatre from 1971 to 1975. At the same time, beginning in 1973, he started dancing with the (now defunct) contemporary Groupe Nouvelle Aire, home to many of Montreal's most innovative and experimental dancemakers. And for a year, he pursued intensive study in classical ballet at Les Grands Ballets Canadiens. In 1975, with Le Groupe Nouvelle Aire, dance became his full-time professional endeavour.

Fortier's career took a different path in 1979, when he left the Nouvelle Aire company to become an independent dancer and choreographer. He used his background in theatre and literature as a defining marker of his creative output. His first independent full-length piece, *Parlez-moi donc du cul de mon enface (Speak to Me of My Childhood's Arse),* laid the foundation for his dance-theatre approach. It included edgy spoken text and a powerful use of space and decor as counterpoints to the choreography. His original style, seen in subsequent work, continued to involve the participation of artists from various disciplines, and depended on a heavy use of symbolism rarely seen in Quebec dance—a defining element shared among other local choreographers of the time, such as Jean-Pierre Perreault.

Fortier formed his own group, Fortier Danse-Creation, in 1981. That same year, he won the country's most prestigious choreographic prize, the Jean A. Chalmers Award. In June 1983, he took part in a workshop for television choreographers and directors, "Dance for an Electronic Age," directed by Edward Villella and Pierre Morin. Also that year, he was the sole Canadian choreographer to take part in Alwin Nikolais' international workshop for professional choreographers and composers in London.

From the start, classical dance and its soft, beautiful fairy tales bored him silly. He didn't reject the form, he just wouldn't do it. Moreover, he never understood why dance never addressed the prime issues of film and literature: sex, violence, and death. So he did.

Fortier is passionate about his profession, and wants to turn people on, not turn them away. His stature is such that he sees himself as an elder in the contemporary dance community. He's at an age where identity is no longer defined by physical feats. But, he admits, learning never stops. His rapport with his students keeps him fresh, and he says, "sends me back to how I do things." An articulate, powerful force, Fortier has a fierce desire to provoke an unsettling response. If in the past his vision of humanity was violent and disturbing, he seems to have cleared out those concerns, now interested in exploring the experience of facing "the things in life we don't understand." Dance, for him, is a tool for vision and insight. It's Fortier's sincere belief that in the intimacy of the theatre, peoples' senses can be altered. For Fortier, as a performer, when the magic of theatre happens, he disappears, and "it's the body in movement that lives."

In 1986 he teamed with Daniel Jackson and founded the production and touring company Montreal Danse, conceived of as a springboard for local and international choreographers and focused on building a repertory of new works. He co-directed the company until 1989, when he joined the faculty of the Dance Department of the Université du Quebec in Montreal. In 1987, he also returned to performing with *Fortier en solo.* Two years later, Montreal Danse paid tribute to Fortier's ten-year career. The evening's program showcased his works, including *Tell, Le Mythe decisif, Brûler,* and *Désert.*

Notable collaborations with renowned Canadian visual artist Betty Goodwin brought new acclaim in *La Tentation de la transparence* and *Bras de plomb* (inspired by her painting, *Black Arms*). The four solos in the latter work are not marked by a narrative, nor by pyrotechnics, but by a simplicity, and Goodwin's expressive lead arm extensions. The work is a haunting metaphor on liberty and an expose on the ensuing constraints of life. In the fall of 1996, Fortier presented the quartet *La Part des anges,* a subtle, refined and contemplative ensemble work.

Fortier's ardent exploration is matched by the fearless creative approach he's pursued. His vivid stage presence combines grace and intensity, concentration, not to mention stamina. Remarking on his performance, he says, the possibility of failure before an audience is both frightening and gratifying. "I feel remorse when I'm not delivering. Like love, you cannot cheat. The other person will feel it."

—Philip Szporer

FRANCO, Sergio

Mexican dancer, choreographer, and company director

Born: Juan Emilio Franco, 16 March 1906 in Oaxaca, Mexico. **Education:** Studied declamation with Manuel Bernal, Mexico City; dance with Nina Shestakova, 1930s; with Serge Oukransky, Los Angeles, 1935. **Career:** Member of several theater companies and dancer with the Shestakova company, 1930s; soloist, touring the country, 1934; member, Helvi Andreeva ballet company, 1935; debut with Azteca and Maya Representations, 1935; member, Oukransky dance company, Los Angeles, 1935; created his "prehispanic" dance spectacle, presented in California, other U.S. cities, and Mexico City's Palace of Fine Arts; worked with Mexican dancer Magda Montoya, 1937; danced in the Fine Arts Ballet with works by Waldeen, 1940; worked with Xenia Zarina, 1941; opened a dance school and company in the Athenaeum of Science and Art of Tlaxcala, 1944; in the Roses Conservatory of Morelia, Michoacán, 1945; and in the city of Chihuahua, 1954; toured as a soloist and with diverse groups in Mexico, the U.S., Guatemala, Honduras, Costa Rica, El Salvador, and Spain; created works with composer Miguel Bernal Jiménez including the opera *Tata Vasco* and *Los tres galanes de Juana.* **Died:** 25 March 1968 in Guadalajara, Mexico.

Roles

1934 *Danza oriental (Oriental Dance)* (Shestakova), Concert Ballet of Nina Shestakova, Oaxaca, Oaxaca

 Danza húngara (Hungarian Dance) (Shestakova), Concert Ballet of Nina Shestakova, Oaxaca

 Pierrot y Colombina (Pierrot and Columbine) (Shestakova), Concert Ballet of Nina Shestakova, Oaxaca

 Danza gitana (Gypsy Dance) (Shestakova), Concert Ballet of Nina Shestakova, Oaxaca

1935 *Baile holandés (Dutch Dance)* (Shestakova), Helvi Andreeva Group, Monterrey, Nuevo León

 Muñeca elástica (Elastic Doll) (Shestakova), Helvi Andreeva Group, Monterrey, Nuevo León

 Fantasía gitana (Gypsy Fantasy) (Shestakova), Helvi Andreeva Group, Monterrey, Nuevo León

 Fiesta rusa (Russian Feast) (Shestakova), Helvi Andreeva Group, Monterrey, Nuevo León

 Danza del pozole (Pozole Dance) (Detru), Azteca and Maya Representations, Mexico City

 Los negritos (The Little Negroes) (Detru), Azteca and Maya Representations, Mexico City

 Caballeros tigre y águila (Tiger and Eagle Knights) (Detru), Azteca and Maya Representations, Mexico City

 K'at o la bruja (K'at or The Witch) (Detru), Azteca and Maya Representations, Mexico City

 Quetzalcóatl (Detru), Azteca and Maya Representations, Mexico City

 Cemetéotl (Detru), Azteca and Maya Representations, Mexico City

 Chicén Itzá (Detru), Azteca and Maya Representations, Mexico City

 Tláloc (Detru), Azteca and Maya Representations, Mexico City

 Cenzontli (Detru), Azteca and Maya Representations, Mexico City

1936 *La princesa cautiva (The Captive Princess)* (Detru), Azteca and Maya Representations, Mexico City

 Suite gitana (Gypsy Suite) (Detru), Azteca and Maya Representations, Mexico City

1940 *Procesional* (Waldeen), Fine Arts Ballet, Mexico City

 Seis danzas clásicas (Six Classical Dances) (Waldeen), Fine Arts Ballet, Mexico City

 Danza de las fuerzas nuevas (New Forces Dances) (Waldeen), Fine Arts Ballet, Mexico City

 Peón (Man), *La Coronela* (Waldeen), Fine Arts Ballet, Mexico City

Works

1936 *K'at* (mus. Joseph), Azteca and Maya Representations, San Francisco

 Xochiquétzal (mus. indigenous), Azteca and Maya Representations, San Francisco.

 Tláloc (mus. Joseph), Azteca and Maya Representations, San Francisco

 Xtabay (mus. indigenous), Azteca and Maya Representations, San Francisco

 Nacon (mus. Joseph) solo, Azteca and Maya Representations, San Francisco

 Cambodian (mus. Strickland), Azteca and Maya Representations, San Francisco

 Marioneta or Pantomima (mus. Drigo), Azteca and Maya Representations, San Francisco

 Danza rusa (Russian Dance) (mus. popular), Azteca and Maya Representations, San Francisco

 Tehuana (mus. popular), Azteca and Maya Representations, San Francisco

 Ritual azteca (mus. indigenous), Azteca and Maya Representations, San Francisco

Chiapaneco (mus. popular), Azteca and Maya Representations, San Francisco

Guacamaya de fuego (Fire Macaw) (mus. indigenous) solo, Azteca and Maya Representations, San Francisco

Xipetotec (mus. indigenous), Azteca and Maya Representations, San Francisco

1937 *Canción guerrera (Warrior Song)* (mus. indigenous), Azteca and Maya Representations, San Francisco

Tigre y águila (Tiger and Eagle) (mus. indigenous), Azteca and Maya Representations, Mexico City

Kinich-Kakmó (mus. indigenous), Azteca and Maya Representations, Mexico City

1938 *Danza de la doble espada (The Double Sword Dance)* Sergio Franco, Mexico City

Visión de fuego (Fire Vision) (mus. De Falla) solo, Sergio Franco, Mexico City

Dios de la felicidad (Happiness God) (mus. indigenous, arr. Joseph) solo, Sergio Franco, Mexico City

Jarana or Jarana Yucateca (mus. popular) solo, Sergio Franco, Mexico City

Hopoc (mus. Mussorgsky) solo, Sergio Franco, Mexico City

Yayax can (Blue Snake) w/Magda Montoya (mus. indigenous, arr. Joseph) duet, Sergio Franco and Magda Montoya, Mexico City

Príncipe de Itzá (Itza Prince) w/Magda Montoya (mus. indigenous, arr. Joseph) duet, Sergio Franco and Magda Montoya, Mexico City

Jugador de pelota (Ball Player) w/Magda Montoya (mus. indigenous, arr. Joseph) duet, Sergio Franco and Magda Montoya, Mexico City

Xipetotec (Golden God) w/Magda Montoya (mus. indigenous, arr. Joseph) duet, Sergio Franco and Magda Montoya, Mexico City

La pluma (The Feather) w/Magda Montoya (mus. Mexican popular, arr. Joseph) duet, Sergio Franco and Magda Montoya, Mexico City

Los moros (The Moorish) w/Magda Montoya (mus. popular, arr. Joseph) duet, Sergio Franco and Magda Montoya, Mexico City

Itzel and Nazul w/Magda Montoya (mus. indigenous, arr. Joseph) duet, Sergio Franco and Magda Montoya, Mexico City

Esclavos (Slaves) (mus. Chopin and Tcherepine) solo, Sergio Franco and Magda Montoya, Mexico City

Chiapanecas w/Magda Montoya (mus. indigenous, arr. Joseph) duet, Sergio Franco and Magda Montoya, Mexico City

Luz y sombra (Light and Shadow) w/Magda Montoya (mus. Scribiane) duet, Sergio Franco and Magda Montoya, Mexico City

1939 *Javanés* (mus. Strickland) solo, Sergio Franco with Josefina Luna, Mexico City

La ofrenda in Bangkok (The Offering in Bangkok) (mus. arr. Joseph and Cárdenas), Sergio Franco with Josefina Luna, Mexico City

Knich Kak Moo (mus. indigenous, arr. Joseph and Cárdenas), Sergio Franco with Josefina Luna, Mexico City

Suite (mus. Schumann and Bach), Sergio Franco and Magda Montoya, Mexico City

Gavota (mus. Beethoven), Sergio Franco and Magda Montoya, Mexico City

Máscaras (Masks) (mus. Debussy), Sergio Franco and Magda Montoya, Mexico City

Pájaros tristes (Sad Birds) (mus. Ravel) duet, Sergio Franco and Magda Montoya, Mexico City

Danza del fuego (Fire Dance) (mus. De Falla) solo, Sergio Franco and Magda Montoya, Mexico City

Fantasía griega (Greek Fantasy) w/Magda Montoya (mus. Schubert) duet, Sergio Franco and Magda Montoya, Mexico City

Prelude (mus. Scribiane) solo, Sergio Franco and Magda Montoya, Mexico City

1940 *Aida* (mus. Verdi), Opera Company, Mexico City

Carmen (mus. Bizet), Opera Company, Mexico City

Mazurka (mus. Spanish popular), Sergio Franco and Magda Montoya, Mexico City

Dos aspectos (mus. Scott) solo, Sergio Franco and Magda Montoya, Mexico City

Esquema para un ballet moderno. Estudio de la línea recta (Sketch for a Modern Ballet. Straight Line Study) (mus. Jiménez Mabarak), Sergio Franco and Magda Montoya, Mexico City

Tango español (mus. Albéniz) duet, Sergio Franco and Magda Montoya, Mexico City

Kochi (mus. arr. Montiel) solo, Sergio Franco and Magda Montoya, Mexico City

Semblanza morisca (Moorish Portrait) (mus. Montiel), Sergio Franco and Magda Montoya, Mexico City

Allegro bárbaro (mus. Bartók) solo, Sergio Franco and Magda Montoya, Mexico City

Momentos psicológicos (Psychological Moments) (mus. Moussorgsky) duet, Sergio Franco and Magda Montoya, Mexico City

Merlitones (Nutcracker) (mus. Tchaikovsky and Bach), Sregio Franco and Magda Montoya, Mexico City

Pas de cinq (mus. Tchaikovsky), Sergio Franco and Magda Montoya, Mexico City

1944 *Krishna* (mus. Indian), Dance Academy of Athenaeum of Science and Art of Tlaxcala, Tlaxcala City

Exaltación (mus. Prokofiev), Dance Academy of Athenaeum of Science and Art of Tlaxcala, Tlaxcala City

Eagle (mus. Becker), Dance Academy of Athenaeum of Science and Art of Tlaxcala, Tlaxcala City

Espectáculo de masas: Sacrificio, Muerte de Xicoténcatl, Danza de la muerte, Danza del fuego sagrado (Mass Spectacle: Sacrifice, Death of Xicoténcatl, Death Dance, Sacred Fire Dance) Dance Academy of Athenaeum of Science and Art of Tlaxcala, Tlaxcala City

1947 *Djoged* w/Xenia Zarina (mus. popular Bali), Xenia Zarina and Sergio Franco, Mexico City

1948 *Tata Vasco* (mus. Jiménez Bernal), Morelia Ballet, Madrid, Spain

1950 *Javanesa* (mus. Javanese), Sergio Franco Mexican Ballet, Santa Ana, El Salvador

Espectáculo de masas Día de Tezcatlipoca (Mass Spectacle: Tezcatlipoca Day) Sergio Franco Mexican Ballet, San Salvador, El Salvador

1951 *Las canacuas de los guares* (mus. popular), Sergio Franco's Mexican Ballet, New York City

La Bamba (mus. popular), Sergio Franco's Mexican Ballet, New York City

1952	*Alborada and Zapateado* (mus. Bernal Jiménez), Sergio Franco's Mexican Ballet, New York City
	Los tres galanes de Juana (mus. Bernal Jiménez), Sergio Franco's Mexican Ballet, Mexico City
	Posada (mus. popular), Sergio Franco's Mexican Ballet, Mexico City
1955	*Ritmos tarahumaras (Tarahumara Rhythms)* (mus. indigenous), Dance School of Chihuahua, Chihuahua City
1957	*Huapango* (mus. Hernández Moncada), Chihuahua Ballet, Chihuahua City
1958	*Sensemayá* (mus. Revueltas), Chihuahua Ballet, Chihuahua City
1959	*Norte* (mus. Revueltas and Chávez), Chihuahua Ballet, Chihuahua City
1960	*El duelo (The Duel)* (mus. Revueltas), Chihuahua Ballet, Chihuahua City
1961	*Ensayo geométrico (Geometrical Essay)* (mus. Phillipot), Chihuahua Ballet, Chihuahua City
	Shotis (mus. popular), Chihuahua Ballet, Chihuahua City
	Esquema para un ballet moderno (Sketch for a Modern Ballet) (mus.Chávez), Chihuahua Ballet, Chihuahua City
1962	*Tehuantepec* (mus. popular), Chihuahua Ballet, Chihuahua City

Publications

On FRANCO: books—

50 años de Danza en el Palacio de Bellas Artes, Mexico, 1984.
Segura, Felipe, *Sergio Franco. México en el ritmo del universo,* Chihuahua, Mexico, 1995.
Tortajada Quiroz, Margarita, *Danza y poder,* Mexico, 1995.

*   *   *

Sergio Franco was a very important artist in the history of Mexican dance, but he has unfortunately fallen into oblivion. He was born in the city of Oaxaca, but the Mexican revolution forced his family to move to Mexico City. Franco joined a number of Mexican theatre companies as an actor, sharing the stage with some of the great personalities of Mexican theatre such as Virginia Fábregas and Maria Tereza Montoya. He began his formal studies in declamation at Manuel Bernal's private school, presenting recitals in Veracruz and other cities. He would later incorporate that knowledge into the dance.

At the beginning of the 1930s, he began his dance studies with Russian dancer and teacher Nina Shestakova (who had formed part of the Opera Privée of Paris) and later joined her company as a dancer. The number of male dancers in the company was very large, which was unusual for that time. In 1934 he appeared as Juan Sergio Franco in solo roles, and the company toured Mexico as Nina Shestakova's Ballet Concierto, with a traditional classic ballet repertoire as well as original works by Shestakova. In 1935 Franco participated in another ballet group organized by a Shestakova student, Helvi Andreeva, with which he toured northern Mexico.

Throughout the early years of his career, Sergio Franco maintained a traditional approach to classic ballet, but on 22 June 1935 he made his debut with Azteca and Maya Representations, a dance troupe formed by four soloists: Gertrude Knowlton (a student of Shestakova and Lettie Carroll), Joseph Broun (former dancer of the Michio Ito company), Enrique Uranga (from Shestakova's Mexican troupe), and Franco. The four of them adopted new names for their spectacle, appearing as Dzul (Broun), Detru (Knowlton), Kin (Uranga), and Yoal or Yoali (Franco). This was the first company to recreate prehispanic dances, and their work enjoyed considerable success. The significance of this work lay in the company's archaeological reconstructions of ancient patterns of movement based on prehispanic codes; their arrangement of original music based on surviving indigenous instruments; and their incorporation of masks, costumes and props that were inspired by archaeological artifacts. They counted on the advice and contribution of the most important Mexican archaeologists and anthropologists, who became directly involved with the dance work, recovering basic elements from prehispanic cultures that had been abandoned but that were re-emerging with the nationalist trends of the period. This company toured the country, marking a very important moment in Mexican dance. Other Mexican and foreign artists also participated in this trend, but Franco and his partners had a larger audience and achieved greater recognition due to their work's high quality and accuracy. The company's fame even reached the U.S. with an article about them appearing in the *Christian Science Monitor* (1935).

In 1936 Azteca and Maya Representations traveled to the U.S. Their tour of California included a performance at the Norma Gould Auditorium in Los Angeles, where Martha Graham had performed earlier that year. When he arrived in Los Angeles, Franco resumed his ballet training, enrolling in the school of Serge Oukransky, whose company he later joined as a dancer. Franco stayed in Los Angeles and put together a show with dancer Jaime Goodmon and singer Suzanne Torres; the trio performed in several forums, including the Corona Club, the Taft Auditorium, International House, and the Palace Hotel's Palm Court. Franco returned to Mexico in 1937, where he performed with Enrique Uranga and Soledad Ponce, incorporating the prehispanic dances of Nina Shestakova into his repertoire.

In 1937 Franco joined Mexican dancer Magda Montoya, and together they presented new works. Montoya was exceptional because of her use of free expression and the natural movements of the body, and with her Franco added a new dimension to his work. His partnership with Montoya brought him closer to modern dance and gave him an opportunity to find his own means of dance expression. Besides being a formidable acrobat, Franco possessed impressive technical skills, great expressiveness, and a beautiful physique.

Using these elements and his choreographic creativity, Franco produced a wide repertoire for himself and Montoya, garnering public and critical acclaim in their countrywide tours. In addition to dealing with prehispanic subjects, he borrowed themes from foreign countries, such as the work of Ruth St. Denis and Ted Shawn in the U.S., which had greatly influenced the members of the Azteca and Maya Representations. Also from the Americans, Franco adopted an almost religious attitude towards his dance, as each one of his works became a mystical experience.

In 1939, with the Mexican government's support, the American dancer and choreographer, Waldeen, organized the Fine Arts Ballet. In 1940 this company premiered some of the works that would come to be considered icons of modern dance in Mexico. Franco participated in the Fine Arts Ballet as the most important male dancer, performing the main role, Peón, in *La Coronela,* which is considered a turning point in the nationalist Mexican modern dance movement.

In 1941 the government of the state of Tlaxcala invited Franco to perform and create a mass ballet, and to found a dance school within

289

the Athenaeum of Science and Art. Franco's work in Tlaxcala was the first step in a concerted effort to educate the public about dance in general, and modern dance in particular, through the opening of dance schools and the founding of local companies in cities across the country. To achieve this, Franco had to confront the country's prejudices against dance. His work as a choreographer was very extensive and included opera, modern dance, and ballet stylizations, which were widely disseminated throughout Mexico, Central America, the U.S., and Spain.

In 1945 Franco began a joint project with Mexican composer Miguel Bernal Jiménez, who would play an important role in the production of new works. Bernal invited him to participate in the Roses Conservatory in the city of Morelia, Michoacán, and to collaborate in the foundation of a dance company and school. Before undertaking these projects, Franco embarked on a tour of the U.S., traveling to Arizona, Texas, and California. On his return to Mexico, Franco settled down in Morelia where he founded the Ballet of Morelia, with which he toured the country. His company then traveled to Spain, where they achieved wide success with their performance of the opera *Tata Vasco* by Bernal Jiménez. This success was repeated in 1952 with the company's mounting of *Los tres galanes de Juana*. In 1949 the governor of Michoacán resigned, and Franco, whose school was set on fire by the governor's opponents, had to abandon Morelia.

In 1949 Franco reorganized the Ballet of Morelia under a new name, Sergio Franco's Mexican Ballet, embarking on an extensive tour of Mexico, El Salvador, Costa Rica, Guatemala, and Honduras. In 1951 he was invited to the American Natural History Museum of New York, where he performed several times with a small group of dancers. In 1954 Franco was invited by the government of the state of Chihuahua to form a dance company and school, in which he laboured until his death in 1968.

—Margarita Tortajada Quiroz
translated by Dolores Ponce Gutiérrez

FRASER, Patricia

Canadian dancer, choreographer, educator, and company director

Born: Patricia Pritchard 12 November 1952 in Toronto, Ontario. **Education:** Competed as a Scottish Highland dancer as a child; received B.F.A. with honors from York University, Toronto; studied with Ahuva Anbary, Ethel Winter, Robert Cohan, Gus Solomons Jr., Grant Strate, Yves Cousineau, and Norman Morrice; studied in New York at the schools of Martha Graham, Merce Cunningham, and José Limón; in London, Robert Cohan's School of the London Contemporary Dance Theatre; neuromuscular training with Irene Dowd in New York and Toronto, 1988-90; training in Pilates in Toronto, Stott Studios, and in Vancouver with Dianne Miller. **Career:** Taught at Dumferline College in Edinburgh, Scotland, Jordanhill College, Glasgow, and the Renfrewshire Dance Project, 1976-77; dancer, Dancemakers, Toronto, 1977-79; associate director, 1979-80; co-artistic director with Carol Anderson, 1980-85; teaching credits include lecturer, Dancemakers, 1978-90; lecturer and course director, 1985-87, and visiting assistant lecturer, 1987-88, both York University; guest teacher, Ottawa Dance Theatre, 1981-84; Simon Fraser University, Vancouver, 1983, 1990; Banff

School of Fine Arts, 1985; Le Groupe de la Place Royale, 1988; School of Contemporary Dancers, Winnipeg, 1990-93; Montréal Danse, 1990; Les Ateliers de Danse Moderne de Montréal, 1990, 1991; Victoria Arts Collaborative 1992, 1993; School of the Toronto Dance Theatre (TDT), 1990, 1991; with Patricia Miner and Sylvain Brochu, founded the Teacher's Collective, Toronto, 1991; faculty, School of TDT, 1993; principal, School of TDT, 1994; soloist and guest artist in choreography from 1985 to present. **Awards:** York University Fine Arts Scholarship, 1975; Ontario Arts Council, Creative Artists in the Schools, 1977; Canada Council grant, 1978, 1982; Chalmers Performing Arts Training Award, 1988; Ontario Arts Council choreographic award, 1989; Canada Council Arts Grant "A," 1990; Chalmers Performing Arts Training Grant, 1993.

Roles (all performances premiered in Toronto unless otherwise noted)

1974	*Forest* (cr) (Robert Cohan)
	Terminal (cr) (Anna Blewchamp)
	Fools in the Palace (cr) (Norman Morrice)
	Following Station Identification (Mitchell Rose)
1977	*Album* (cr) (Peggy Baker)
	A Friend Is Better Than a Dollar (Nina Weiner)
	Marathon (cr) (Anna Blewchamp)
	Bend Down Low (cr) (Blewchamp)
	Schooner (Carol Anderson)
	Lumen (Carol Anderson)
	Galliard (Barry Smith)
	Arrival of All Time (Blewchamp)
1978	*a.k.a.* (cr) (Blewchamp)
	Spiral (cr) (Karen Jamieson)
	Pole Fiction (cr) (Paula Ravitz)
	Variations on a Summer's Theme (cr) (Donald McKayle)
1979	*Quick Studies* (cr) (Anderson)
	The Nightingale (cr) (Peggy Baker)
	Sandsteps (cr) (Grant Strate)
	Dark of the Moon (Beth Harris)
	Disc (cr) (Baker)
1980	*Aureole* (Paul Taylor)
	Gleanings of Natural History (Martha Bowers)
1981	*Cuts* (cr) (Judith Marcuse)
	When Evening Spreads Itself Against the Sky (cr)(Robert Cohan)
1982	*Windhover* (cr) (Anderson)
	Walking the Line (cr) (Jamieson)
	Three Epitaphs (Paul Taylor)
1983	*Despair Comics* (cr) (Jamieson)
	The Pond (Conrad Alexandrowicz)
1984	*River* (cr) (Anderson)
	Auto-da-Fe (cr) (Alexandrowicz)
	Knot a Couple (Linda Rabin)
	Mansion (cr) (Alexandrowicz)
	unfinished business (cr) (James Kudelka)
1985	*After the Fire* (cr) (Blewchamp)
	East Above (Blewchamp)
	Lionheart (Blewchamp)
1986	*Broken Symmetry* (Anderson)
	Romeo (Tom Stroud)
	Fountain Dance (cr) (Terrill Maguire), Canada Dance Festival, Ottawa

1988   *Full Circle* (cr) (Paula Ravitz)
1989   *In the Belly of the Whale* (cr) (Darcey Callison)
        Don't Make Fun (cr) (Phillip Drube), DanceWorks,
           Toronto
1991   *The Kiss of Death* (cr) (James Kudelka)
        Uplands (cr) Christopher House)
        Lost (cr) (Paul-André Fortier)
        Pat's Bach (cr) Rachel Browne)
        Canadian Short Stories, duMaurier Theatre, Toronto
        Letters on Dancing and Ballet: Part III (Alexandrowicz)
        Sandboxes (Darcey Callison), DanceWorks, Toronto
1992   *Odeum* (cr) (Judith Miller)
        Letters on Dancing and Ballet: Part IV (Conrad
           Alexandrowicz)
        Shalom (Rachel Browne)
1993   *Four Haiku* (cr) (Browne)
1994   *Toward Light* (cr) (Browne)

Works

1977   *The Road Not Taken* (mus. Robert Lacey), Eastwood
           Theatre, Glasgow, Scotland
1982   *Marital Blister 1* (mus. country and western collage),
           Dancemakers Workshop
1983   *Marital Blister 2* (mus. country and western collage),
           Dancemakers Workshop
1984   *When the Bough Breaks* (mus. George Axon, text by Rob-
           ert Morgan), children's production
        Happy Families (mus. Disney collage), Dancemakers
1985   *Last Walk* (mus. Gustav Holst), Banff Festival of the
           Arts
1988   *Sonnet* (mus. Joe Jackson), Premiere Dance Theatre, York
           University
1991   *Homefront* (mus. Kirk Elliott), School of Winnipeg Con-
           temporary Dancers
1992   *Florence: The Lady with the Lamp* (opera), Elora Festi-
           val, Ontario
1993   *Upstream,* Victoria Arts Collaborative and School of Con-
           temporary Dancers, Winnipeg

Publications

By FRASER: articles—

"The Medical Aspects of Dance," edited by Donna Peterson, Garry
   Lapenskie, and Albert W. Taylor for *Headlines,* 1987.
"Dance and the Artist in the School," *Journal of the Canadian As-
   sociation for Health, Physical Education and Recreation,* 1988.

On FRASER: articles—

Crabb, Michael, "Patricia Fraser," in *101 from The Encyclopedia of
   Theatre Dance in Canada,* Toronto, 1997.
Profiles in *Dance in Canada,* Fall 1981, Summer 1982, Spring 1984,
   and Winter 1985.
Wyman, Max, *Dance Canada,* Vancouver, 1989.

                    *   *   *

Patricia Fraser began her dance training at the age of eight, soon
becoming a champion Highland dancer. Early in her career her unique

performing presence distinguished her. Perhaps her amazing ability
as an interpreter to make lightning switches in style, mood, and
rhythm stem from her early experience, in which seamless transitions from one traditional dance to another seem to travel telepathi-
cally from musician to dancer. Fraser's extraordinary jump and
musicality seem bred in the bone.

Although she had originally intended to become a physical edu-
cation teacher, Fraser auditioned for the Dance Department at York
University, Toronto, in its early days. She holds a B.F.A. from
York, and while there studied Graham technique with Ahuva Anbary,
Moss Cohen, and many stellar guests, among them Helen McGehee,
Ethel Winter, Noemi Lapsezon, and Robert Cohan. She also studied ballet with Grant Strate, Angela Leigh, Yves Cousineau, and
Norman Morrice, and studies with Gus Solomons Jr. and Al Huang
furthered her technical base. A belief in the value of diversity has
become a hallmark of Fraser's own approach to training. During the
1974 season, while still a student, Fraser began to perform with
Toronto's Dancemakers. On graduation from York University, Fraser
moved to Scotland, her husband's homeland. While there she taught
in primary and secondary schools for the Renfrewshire Dance
Project, and was a guest teacher at Dunfermline College of Education in Edinburgh, and at Jordanhill College of Education in Glasgow.
Returning to Canada in 1977, Fraser rejoined Dancemakers; she
became associate director in 1979 and co-artistic director in 1980,
sharing these directorial roles with Carol Anderson. She resigned
from Dancemakers in 1985, following internal disagreement about
the company's direction and leadership.

While a member of Dancemakers, Fraser met the challenges of
the varied repertory and the climate of creativity with a seemingly
endless appetite for new styles of movement. She danced everything from Paul Taylor's *Aureole* to Karen Jamieson's plangent
Despair Comics; many new roles were created for her. Since leaving
Dancemakers has Fraser continued to pursue her performing career
as a soloist and guest artist, appearing in work by Rachel Browne,
Judith Miller, Conrad Alexandrowicz, and Darcey Callison. In 1990
Fraser was awarded a Senior Arts Grant from the Canada Council
to mount a solo show *Canadian Short Stories*. She commissioned
and staged solos from a bouquet of well-known Canadian choreographers, Paul-André Fortier, James Kudelka, Browne, Christopher
House, and Alexandrowicz. As always, she met the dramatic and
dancerly challenges of this range of works, from witty to bleak,
with great skill and depth. As a performer she continues to mature,
and has cultivated an ongoing connection with the creations of
Rachel Browne, whose work is grounded in the expression of women
of all ages.

Fraser has a strong identity in Canada as a teacher. She was on the
faculty at York University from 1985 until 1988 and guest taught at
many Canadian schools, including the Banff School of Fine Arts, Simon
Fraser University, Halifax Dance Association, School of Contemporary Dancers, Winnipeg, and Les Ateliers de Danse Moderne de
Montréal. She has also taught the companies at Montréal Danse and
Winnipeg's Contemporary Dancers. Fraser joined the faculty of the
School of the Toronto Dance Theatre in 1993 and the next year became
its principal. The school offers Graham-based technique, barre work,
and guest teachers in Limón technique; studies include anatomy, body
work, dance composition, improvisation, partnering, and history. Students grow dramatically through workshops and repertory classes,
and many performance opportunities. Recent graduates of the school
are meticulously-trained, beautiful movers.

In 1991 Fraser began the Teacher's Collective, with Pat Miner
and Sylvain Brochu, which offers a daily technique class to Toronto's

independent professional community. In 1997 she instigated a summer intensive, "Strictly Modern," taught by herself, Paticia Miner, and Peggy Baker. In addition, Fraser is a thoughtful proponent for the art of dance, and is sought after as a consultant. She has been involved with the liaison of professional artists in the schools, was a member of the Canada Council's Modern Dance Training Committee and served as a member of Canada Council's Assessment Review Committee. She is a charter member of the Canadian Alliance of Dance Artists, which seeks to promote standards of remuneration and work conditions for independent dance artists. She acts as a juror, assessor, and teacher for the Canada Council, Ontario Arts Council and Toronto Arts Council.

Patricia Fraser values diversity—her own talents as a dancer and administrator, planner and instigator, are all in play. A generous and singular dancer, she has given her energies to creating roles in works by many important Canadian choreographic voices. Fraser embodies creative choices, a dedication to pursuing both developed talent and new directions, starting new initiatives, and embracing change. She is both a distinctive artist in her own right, and a pragmatic and artistic role model for the many students she encounters.

—Carol Anderson

FRINGE FESTIVAL OF INDEPENDENT DANCE (fFIDA)
Canadian dance festival

When the first fringe Festival of Independent Dance was held in Toronto in August 1991, it was not imagined by co-founders Allan Kaeja and Michael Menegon that the event would become one of the most important dance gatherings in Canada, nor that it would attract international attention. A "one of a kind," fFIDA is the only entirely noncurated dance festival in the world. fFIDA grew out of a real need. Both Kaeja and Menegon were independent choreographers frustrated by the lack of performance opportunities given the rising cost of production, the cutbacks in government funding, and the paucity of dance presenters. Inspired by the success of fringe theatre festivals, the duo decided a dance fringe was an idea whose time had come. The festival was designed to be a one-time event that would give "indies" an inexpensive shared showcase. The men obtained a small grant from the Ontario Arts Council, and under the auspices of the Dance Umbrella of Ontario, a Toronto-based service organization, put out a call to the dance community. Their mandate was simple—a non-curated event where participants were chosen on a first-come, first-served basis. The small "f" in "fringe" was meant to denote their populist aims.

The first year fFIDA presented 34 choreographers, mostly Toronto-based, in a six-day festival at the Winchester Street Theatre. Each day featured five hour-long programs, each hour shared by three choreographers/collectives who had 20 minutes each to show their work. Programs were repeated three times each, giving the participants a daytime, evening and weekend showing. The artists paid an entrance fee, and fFIDA provided the professional support and technical staff. Artists shared the box office receipts and were responsible for their own marketing and publicity, helped by a fFIDA package on how to write press releases and design programs. The first festival was a runaway success attracting huge

lineups and sold out houses. Part of the freshness of fFIDA was the "strange bedfellows" programming. Choreographers were put together in a helter-skelter fashion which meant that a potpourri of styles and dance forms could end up in one time slot. A modern dancer might be the sandwich between a belly dancer and a flamenco artist. As Menegon said, "If you don't like what someone's doing, you just have to wait 20 minutes for the next performance." Another attraction was the populist ticket price—$7 for each show.

In the first year, Kaeja and Menegon had to beat the bushes to find participants; by the second year, artists were clamoring to get in. The men increased the festival to 10 days and put a cap on 48 "Mainstage" choreographers/collectives. They also introduced the "Late Nite" series in 1992, which was held at the Bloor Street YMHA. Each Late Nite program, which begins at 11:00 p.m. features five choreographers who are given 10 minutes each to perform. The Late Nite events get two showings and are open to any choreographer with or without experience. In order to make sure that fFIDA Mainstage became a performance opportunity for bona fide independent choreographers, each participant in the first festival had to have two years professional experience in the dance field. This was raised to three years in 1993 and five years in 1995 as the pool of artists widened. "We are not curated," Kaeja has said, "but we have to have criteria. We're interested in dedicated, serious dance artists." In 1995, the festival relocated both the Mainstage and Late Nite events to the more state-of-the-art Buddies in Bad Times Theatre.

So popular has the festival become, that all participants are now chosen by lottery with the rest put on a waiting list. Half the spaces are reserved for Toronto and Ontario residents, while the other half is given over to choreographers from the rest of Canada and abroad. The first fFIDA had six non-Ontario choreographers; in 1997 there were 30. Over 100 choreographers/collectives participated in the 1997 festival, which also featured 600 dancers. Canadians were represented from coast to coast, from St. John's, Newfoundland, to Victoria, British Columbia. Americans came from seven states (New York, New Jersey, Michigan, Illinois, Florida, Georgia and California). There were also performers from Sweden, Venezuela, Italy, Austria, Mexico, Belgium and Japan. In fact, the Japanese are the single largest international component outside the Americans. The fascinating aspect is that fFIDA has become known mostly by word of mouth. In 1997, the festival launched its own web site (http://ffida@ican.ca) as a way of reaching a larger community of dancers.

The festival has always encouraged off-site events, either site-specific or venue-based. In 1997, Dusk Dances, a site-specific regular, became a permanent part of fFIDA curated by Sylvie Bouchard and David Danzon. Twelve choreographers are invited to create work that is presented in two different programs in Trinity-Bellwoods Park in Toronto's west end. Dusk Dances begins at twilight and has attracted huge crowds who come to see the highly imaginative outdoor work that uses the topography of the park as its scenic design. Another 1997 innovation was the linking of fFIDA to dance training. Breaking Ground, under the directorship of Toronto Dance Theatre company member Sean Marye, held open classes for 70 students and proved to be extremely successful. Never wanting to be entirely predictable, fFIDA has tried new programming. In 1997, two Mainstage shows were given over to "No Tech" performances to encourage spontaneity. There were no technical rehearsals and the lighting crew improvised on the spot. Each No Tech program featured five choreographers who had 10 minutes of presentation time. A particularly successful No Tech artist was Toronto-based Ethel Maud. In each of her three showings, she brought in a different musician with whom to improvise. One even played an electrified trumpet! Unfortunately, most of the other No Tech performers brought extant works. To correct this problem, the 1998 No Tech was limited to improvisational artists only, with a shared program of four participants, each performing for 13 minutes. Another 1998 innovation was the introduction of the Senior Artist Mainstage Show, a shared hour for two choreographers with over 10 years of experience each. There is also discussion about having some themed programs and a dance film component in the future.

Over the years, the dynamic of fFIDA has changed. In the early days, the work was more experimental with many choreographers using the showcase to test new ideas. When it became known that fFIDA performances were being reviewed by the mainline Toronto media, and that the festival was being attended by presenters from across the country, the U.S., and Europe, choreographers began to bring more polished work. One of the great successes of fFIDA is that it has served as a launching pad to a career as presenters take up an artist. In 1991, Lynda Gaudreau was a little-known Montreal choreographer. Her success at fFIDA was the beginning of an international career. As well, participating international artists have invited Canadian choreographers to perform in their countries. While modern and contemporary dance has dominated the event, ballet dancers have brought work as well. The fFIDA success of the National Ballet of Canada's Dominique Dumais was a contributing factor in her being invited to create a production for her own company in 1998. Sadly, Quebec has been under-represented at fFIDA given the size of its dance community, a problem Kaeja and Menegon are working to correct. Ironically, important presenters from Quebec attend the festival.

Since 1995, fFIDA has been an independent organization with its own board of directors. The festival operates on a minuscule budget of $92,000 a year and is supported by the Department of Canadian Heritage, the Ontario, Metro Toronto and Toronto Arts Councils, and the Ontario Ministry of Culture, Citizenship and Recreation. Government funding covers only 53 percent of the budget. The rest is supplied by the participation fees, sale of T–shirts and corporate and private donations. Mainstage artists pay a $321 application fee, while No Tech/Improv artists pay $175 and Late Nite $125. The festival also gets a grant from the provincial Summer Career Placement Program to train five students for the technical crew. In 1997, Menegon and Kaeja began to alternate years as artistic director to allow them to pursue their own independent work.

—Paula Citron

FRONTIER

Choreography: Martha Graham
Music: Louis Horst
Set Design: Isamu Noguchi
Lighting and Costume Design: Martha Graham
First Production: Martha Graham Dance Company, 28 April 1935, part of *Perspectives* performance at the Guild Theatre in New York City
Dancer: Martha Graham

Other productions include: Film by Julien Bryan of Graham (in her early 40s) dancing the piece in full costume

Publications

Barnes, Clive, "Martha's Dance Immortal," *Dance Magazine,* July 1991.
Brooks, Virginia, "Martha on Film," *Dance Magazine,* July 1991.
De Mille, Agnes, *Martha: The Life and Work of Martha Graham,* New York, 1991.
"Martha's Dances," *Dance Magazine,* July 1991.
Mazo, Joseph, "Martha Remembered," *Dance Magazine,* July 1991.
McDonagh, Don, *Martha Graham: A Biography,* New York, 1973.

* * *

Frontier was one of Martha Graham's early solo dances. It was originally performed as the first part of a performance entitled *Perspectives,* in conjunction with the piece *Marching Song.* The latter was soon dropped from her repertoire, thus leaving *Frontier* to exist on its own. The success of *Frontier* proved that it certainly would survive as a production in its own right, and it was kept as part of Graham's repertoire for a number of years. It also marked a significant first for Martha Graham in terms of her creative development as a dancer and artistic visionary. Until this time, Graham had simply used black drapes as her sole stage adornment. *Frontier* was Graham's first use of a set in her work and the beginning of a longtime collaboration with sculptor Isamu Noguchi.

As is evident by its title, *Frontier,* like other pieces such as *Appalachian Spring, American Document,* and *Panorama,* was a foray into the American physical and psychological landscape. In the words of Agnes de Mille, "*Frontier* was a dance essentially about space." This is evidenced in the music, set, theme, and choreography of the piece. As McDonagh stated in his biography, "Graham celebrated the vigor, the tenacity, and the character of the settlers of the West who conquered an area of wilderness." The piece revolved around the initial conquering of the wilderness and the beginnings of the taming and civilizing of the American frontier landscape.

Noguchi's set design revealed his penchant for the sculpturesque and minimalist approach to creating a visual metaphor on the stage. His creations reflected Graham's desire to use three-dimensional objects almost as another character in the dance piece, rather than using a flat, painted backdrop. The set of *Frontier* consisted of a length of fence post located at the rear of the stage. A V-shape was created by extending ropes from the fence upward to the portals of the theatre, allowing the eye to travel toward the seemingly endless horizon of the implied terrain. This single piece on the stage effectively conveyed the emotions and the sense of space that Graham's choreography embodied. Furthermore, the prop itself was not necessarily the intended sculpture. In Noguchi's eyes, it was the space itself that was the set construction, with the rope merely bisecting the space, thus creating the appropriate illusion. The costume was simple, reminiscent of the clothing that a woman at that time and place might have worn. Graham was dressed in a modest long-sleeved white blouse and a long, dark-colored skirt. Her hair was held back by a matching hair band. It was stern and simple, alluding to a Quaker or Amish style of dress. The effectiveness of the costume was apparent, as her loose, flowing skirt billowed and swirled around her as she jumped and turned.

The accompanying choreography allowed the dancer to claim her own territory in this vast landscape. Various descriptions of the movement can be found, but several themes emerge in identifying specific choreographic elements. The steps performed suggested the creation of a personal space within the frontier, of regaining control of her environment and possessing her space. Her steps and jumps connoted the marking of territory both in a horizontal/vertical shape and then more directly forward on the stage. Her square floor patterns suggested the shape of pasture land and a way of dividing a vast piece of land into more manageable spaces. What began as a division of territory ended as a more relaxed, confident exploration of what she knew was her own.

Frontier is considered one of Graham's first heritage dance successes. In 1937 Lincoln Kirstein compared Graham's efforts to those of Whitman and Hawthorne, saying, "She has created a kind of candid, sweeping and wind-worn liberty for her individual expression." It is because of Graham's ability to evoke such a sense of the feeling of the frontier through her beautiful and emotional movements that revivals of the piece were often ubsatisfying to watch and sometimes even considered failures. After Graham departed from the stage, other dancers, including Peggy Lyman and Carol Langly, performed the role. Although it may not have been the same as Graham herself, each dancer brought new life to the role in a piece of choreography that allowed the personality of each dancer to shine through. A noteworthy rendition of the piece is one that was performed by Graham herself, preserved on film. Sometime between 1936 and 1939, Graham performed the piece for film-maker Julien Bryan. It was made on a small budget and consequently was not edited for a number of years. It exists, however, so that future generations of dancers and dance scholars can see Graham herself dance one of her best known solo pieces, an important part of her impressive repertoire.

—Kristin M. Harris

FULLER, Loie

American dancer, choreographer, company director, and lighting designer

Born: Louie Fuller, 22 January 1862, in Fullersburg, Illinois, daughter of free-thinkers Delilah and Reuben Fuller; began performing at about age two when she recited "Mary Had a Little Lamb" before an audience of adults. **Education:** Attended school sporadically from age five to 15; taught dancing by her father (who ran a dance academy), won her first prize at 13, 1876. **Career:** Began singing and performing, 1875; went on a nine-month tour with Chicago's Felix A. Vincent Comedy Company, 1878; went to London, then toured U.S. East Coast with several theatrical companies, gaining a modest reputation, 1878-89; developed *Serpentine*, a skirt dance in which varicolored lights were projected on filmy robe, 1891; performed at Folies Bèrgére (Paris), 1892; was a major player in Paris influencing painters, glass artists, and sculptors as well as composers, poets and clothing designers by 1893; began traveling extensively from 1893, but always returned to Paris; produced her version of Oscar Wilde's *Salomé*, personally overseeing painters, carpenters and electricians, 1895; achieved top billing at Folies Bèrgére, 1898; had own building at the Universal Exposition in Paris and presented a Japanese theatrical troupe, 1900; performed in South America, 1904; presented her own performances as well as those of Japanese actress Madame Hanako, Colonial Exposition in Marseille, 1906; performed new work with magic-lantern scenery, her largest-scale dance spectacle in London and Paris, 1907; published memoir, *Fifteen Years of a Dancer's Life,* France, 1908; founded school of "natural dancing" and presented pupils in *Ballet of Light,* London Hippodrome, 1908; memoir published in London and Boston, 1913; appeared at an Athens gala sponsored by the King of Greece to benefit victims of Balkan Wars, 1914; joined sugar heiress Alma Spreckels in establishing two museums, San Francisco Palace of the Legion of Honor and Maryhill in Washington State, during World War I; mounted successful stage version of *Lily of Life* at the Paris Opera, 1920; film version made 1920-21; began three-season run of "fantastic ballets" Théâtres des Champs Elyseés, 1922; spectacular *Sur la Mer* show for International Decorative Arts Exposition in Paris, 1925; performed in San Francisco and New York, 1925. **Died:** 1 January 1928; buried in Père Lachaise Cemetery in Paris.

Works

1891	*Serpentine*
1892	*Violet*
	Butterfly
	Danse blanche
1893	*Widow*
	Mirror
	Good Night Dances
	La Danse des nuages
	The Flower
	The Rainbow
1895	*Salomé* (*Salute of the Sun, Les Éclairs, L'Orage*)
	La Nuit
	Le Firmament
	The Lily Dance
	Fire Dance (Flame)
1898	*The Bird*
	Une Pluie de Fleurs
1899	*Les Sylphes*
	Lumière et ténèbrè
	Danse de l'or L'Archange
1901	*Danse fluorescent la Tempête*
1902	*La Danse funèbre*
	La Danse religion
	La Danse de peur
	La Danse d'aveugle
	La Danse inspirée par le nocturne de Chopin
1903	*The Grottoes*
	Danse mystérieuses
	Les Petites femmes
	Chez les papillons
	L'Eau
	Danse l'espèce
1904	*Radium Dance*
1905	*Flight of the Butterflies*
	Dance of 1000 Veils (includes *Storm at Sea* and other dances)
1906	*Bottom of the Sea*
	Egyptian Dance from *The Huguenots*
	Spanish Dance from Carmen
1907	*India Pantomime* (*Les Ames errantes, Les Nuages qui passent, Les Feux de l'enfer*)

Salomé (includes *Danse des perles* and other dances)
   (mus. d'Humieres-Schmitt)
1908 Ballet of Light (*Open Sea, Snowstorm, Unfolding Spirit*)
1909 Butterflies (mus. Massenet)
   Marche Turque
   Elfin Dance
   Spring Song
   Ophelia
   Tragedy Dance
   Diana the Huntress
   Dance des sylphes
   Dance of The Hands
   Peer Gynt (*Ase's Death, Dance of Anitra, The Arab Dance,*
      Solveig's Song and *Mourning*)
   Ave Maria
   Prelude No. 4 (mus. Chopin)
   Valse, Rosen aus Dem Suden
   Chaconne (mus. Durand)
   Bacchanal
   Tarantella
   Scherzo (mus. Schumann)
   Das Mädchen und der Tod Suite (mus. Rameau)
   Studies, Op. 25 (mus. Chopin)
   Serenade (mus. Schubert)
   Shadow Dance (mus. Meyerbeer)
   Midsummer Night's Dream
   Lied
   Intermezzo
   Nocturne (mus. Griffin)
   Finale
   Wedding March
1910 Volcanic Eruptions
   Sweeping Fires
1911 Dance of Miriam
   Danse Macabre
   Le Danse de martyrs
   Danse de l'offrande
   Danse de coquetterie
   Dance of the Eyes
   Numéro fantastique (*Un Grand voile*)
   L'Oiseau noir
   Danse ultra violette
1912 Cycle de danses
   Les Petits riens (mus. Mozart)
   Water Music (mus. Handel)
   Points of Light
   Nell Gwyn Dance
   Dance for Music from Diocletian
   Danse des Sylphes (from *The Damnation of Faust*)
1913 Mille et une nuits (*Fêtes, Sirènes, Pelleas et Mélisande,*
      Dans l'oasis, Orgie de lumière)
   Children's Corner (*Dr. Gradus ad Parnassum* and other dances)
1914 Hall of the Mountain King (mus. Peer Gynt)
   Orchestration de Coulerus sur deux préludes
   Prométhée
   Pastorale
   La Forêt Hantée
   La Feu d'artifice
   Egyptian Sun Dance
1915 Ballet of Serpents
   Ballet d'opal noire

Black Flame
Marche militaire
School of Imagination Dances (*The crowd in succession:*
   Hatred, Joy, Sorrow, and other dances)
Clown Dance
Battle of the Flowers
Emptying the Bobbin of Its Thread
The Wind
Thunder
Water
The Grinding Mill
Tearing of the Rose
Till She Falls
Butterfly and Birds
St. Jean Preaching to the Birds
St. Jean Walking on the Water
Little Witches
1920 Le Lys de la vie
1921 Chimères
   Chant de Nigamon
   Saudades de Brazil
1922 Ballet fantastique
   Les Ombres
   Sorcières gigantiques
   Ombres partes (*Gennes Feériques, Point, Feu, Lys*)
   Bal de neige
1924 Temptation du feu
   Le Deluge
1925 L'Escalier monumental

Publications

By FULLER:

Fifteen Years of a Dancer's Life, Boston, 1913 (reprint New York,
   1975).

On FULLER: books—

Current, Richard Nelson and Marcia Ewing Current, *Loie Fuller:
   Goddess of Light,* Boston, 1997.
Duncan, Isadora, *My Life,* New York, 1927.
Garafola, Lynn, *Diaghilev's Ballets Russes,* New York, 1989.
Harris, Margaret Haile, *Loie Fuller: Magician of Light,* Richmond,
   Virginia, 1979.

On FULLER: articles—

Kermode, Frank, "Loie Fuller and the Dance Before Diaghilev,"
   Partisan Review 28, January-February 1961.
Sommer, Sally R., "Loie Fuller," *Drama Review,* March 1975.
———, "Loie Fuller's Art of Music and Light," *Dance Chronicle* 4.
———, "The Soul of Art Nouveau," *Women's Review of Books,* No-
   vember, 1997.

Films and Videotapes

Lily of Life, based on a fairytale by Queen Marie of Romania,
   1920-21; two other short films (one incomplete at her death).

*   *   *

295

Loie Fuller was a dancer who denied that she was really a dancer. She was a choreographer who, according to Sally Sommer, created abstract dances before almost anyone else, but agreed with her critics that she wasn't really a choreographer, either. What she never denied was that she took maximum advantage of the invention of incandescent light and other technology and was a lighting designer for dance and theatrical spectacle of considerable achievement. This was her principal contribution to modern dance, although as Sommer points out, "she was the first of the American modern dancers to forge the path that other modern dance pioneers, such as Isadora Duncan and Ruth St. Denis would follow. . . She directed and choreographed her own dance company, as well as managing other performers." In addition, she was "an avid amateur scientist, discovering new methods and dyes to color her silks and extracted phosphorescence from strontium salts in order to paint her. . .costumes with cool light." She also invented a number of devices for stage illumination and was one of the first to perform in what is today the common theatrical space known as a "black box."

She made other contributions to the arts as well—she was an impresario who presented Isadora Duncan in her first European tour and at the turn of the 20th century developed a strong interest in what we now call multiculturalism. Her dances served as an inspiration for a great many visual artists and designers and, at one time, no woman's face or figure was more represented on posters, lamps, or in glass art. Her interest in science led to strong friendships with Pierre and Marie Curie, the discoverers of radium, and Claude Flammarian, one of the most distinguished French astronomers of his day. Fuller was a precursor of the Futurists, who admired her for her use of the technological advances of her time to create stage spectacles.

She was also a collector of art who helped to build the reputation of Auguste Rodin in the U.S., and was a co-founder of two American art museums, Maryhill in Washington State and the Palace of the Legion of Honor in San Francisco. Fuller, who can also be considered part of the earliest wave of American expatriates in Paris, along with painter Mary Cassatt, was a social catalyst who introduced important people to one another for their mutual benefit.

The most important contribution made by Fuller was as a modernist. Born in Chicago in 1862, she was undereducated, even for a woman of her day, but had the inquiring, experimental mind of today's dance artists who try anything to see if it works. Her manipulation of light to create images of a blooming lily or burning fire was not unlike the manipulation of video images to abstract the disintegration of the body in Bill T. Jones' 1994 piece *Still/Here*. The French, who adored her, called her "La Loie" and deeply appreciated her work. Following a 1907 performance, one critic stated: "This is not a dance but a witchery, almost a religion. [La Loie] has reminded us that the dance is not an exercise in acrobatics; she has inspired us to disdain pointes and ballerinas in pink tights and gauze skirts. She has restored our admiration for simple and harmonious poses, and her gestures have often made us think of ancient statuettes. She has prepared us to appreciate the art of Isadora Duncan."

Hard working, even when ill, which she was a great deal of the time, Fuller was an artist for whom everything she saw or read or heard was grist for the mill: as an actress, performing in plays with elaborate stage effects, she saw the possibilities and created colored gels to go over lights, all of far greater subtlety than those being used by others. By the time she wrote her 1908 memoir, *Fifteen Years of a Dancer's Life,* she had developed a theory of dance and its accompanying music and lights: "In the quiet atmosphere of a conservatory with green glass," she wrote, "our actions are different from those in a compartment with red or blue glass. But usually we pay no attention to this relationship of actions and their causes. These are, however, things that must be observed when one dances to an accompaniment of light and music properly harmonized." Like Isadora Duncan, who was slightly younger and much more beautiful than she (some critics late in Fuller's performing career pointed out that she was more than pleasingly plump), Fuller rebelled against the strictures of classical ballet, thought dancing was for the purpose of expressing emotions rather than telling a story, and was interested in presenting visualizations of music. The most spectacular example of the latter came late in her career, when with her students she presented a spectacle accompanied by Claude Debussy's *La Mer*. Premiering at the 1925 Decorative Arts Exhibition in Paris, *Sur la mer immense* (*On the Mighty Sea*) was presented on "a monumental staircase in the Grand Palais," where as described by Richard Nelson Current and Marcia Ewing Current "[s]tretched over the stairs was a tremendous expanse of silk cloth, hundreds of square feet of it. Underneath, invisible, the girls held up the cloth and manipulated it while projectors threw light of varying color and intensity upon it. The effect was fluid drapery, a silken sea that rose and fell, rolled and ran, seethed and foamed." Underrated by many dance historians and critics, and even herself, Fuller was truly a pioneer in the visual art of marrying light and movement to make dances. The actual work has not endured; her approach and her interest in merging art and technology have. She was not just a pioneer in dance, however; the moving image fascinated her so much that she made a film as early as 1918, one of few women working in the new form at the time. She was working on her third film at the time of her death on New Year's Day, 1928.

—Martha Ullman West

FUSION IN MODERN DANCE

Reflecting aspects of the current world picture, dancers of the past and present are products of their age. The manifesto of modern dancers during the 1930s and 1940s was the expression of self; today, in the 1990s, the manifesto of postmodern dancers is expression of multiculturalism. In her book *Writing Dance in the Age of Postmodernism,* Sally Banes states that postmodern dance "has become multicultural in every sense. . . . It is multi-ethnic; it advocates diversity of gender, sexual choice, age, and physical ability; and it includes within its vocabulary every available genre of dance, gleaned for the entire hierarchy of cultural levels."

"What if you put Irish step dance and certain Balinese dance gestures together in the context of a Handel sonata?," Doug Elkins quips in Nicole Dekle's *Dance Magazine* article "More Than a Series of Cool Things Strung Together." Doug Elkins, known for combining hip-hop with modern dance, typifies one of the many new generation of choreographers fusing various styles of postmodern dance with a flagrant content of all sorts. His dances are eclectic; they are modern dance phrases infused with popular dance movements that are sporadically out of context.

In addition to style, fusion exists especially in terms of ethnic influences—African-American choreographers such as Urban Bush Women meld African Dance with modern. Jewish choreographer

David Dorfman draws inspirations for his work from his own life growing up in a Jewish working-class family in Chicago. The title of his 1991 performance, *Dayenu* ("Enough"), which refers to the song sung in Hebrew at Passover that expresses gratitude for all that God has given, reflects his own cultural traditions. Also, Dorfman's performers come in every age, shape and size, which communicates to the viewer that there are only ascending boundaries in movement performance.

Members of other ethnic groups—such as the Latina choreographers Viveca Vasquez and Merian Soto and the Japanese choreographers Eiko and Koma and Yoshiko Chuma—have influenced multicultural expression in postmodern dance. Identifying themselves as both black and postmodern, a group of choreographers— Blondell Cummings, Bill T. Jones, Bebe Miller, Ishmael Houston-Jones, and Fred Holland—integrated and introduced political themes of black identity in their dances. Other choreographers enhance balletic virtuosity with the expression of modern and ethnic dance such as Jiri Kylian's *Stomping Ground,* which blends the principles of aboriginal dance with those of classical ballet.

Furthermore, there are choreographers who interlink "high" and "low" dance culture—the avant-garde, the popular, the commercial, and the vernacular—in their pieces. Twyla Tharp's exploration of mixing the popular and the vernacular with ballet began in the 1970s in *Eight Jelly Rolls* (1971) and *Deuce Coupe* (1973). Drawing ideas from cartoons, television comedies, and pop songs, Jim Self infuses his choreography with the popular and the commercial. Others follow suit; Barbara Allen's dances resemble Harlequin romances and Martha Renzi's work imitates an MTV music-video structure.

Contemporary choreographers' proclivity for appropriating techniques from salsa and hiphop dancing, roller skating, and juggling, and fusing them with other styles, did not begin with the postmodern era. Fusion in dance has existed historically even though it was never recognized or politically viewed as such. With the beginning of court ballet, which really has its origins in folk dance, from romanticism to postmodernism, incorporating mystical themes and exotic movements of other cultures into Western dance forms has been happening for centuries. Consequently, fusion was a choreographical method passed down from one generation of dance artists to the next. From the Diaghilev and Denishawn threads of Orientalism to the Balanchian themes of African-American jazz, the tradition of fusion is a long one.

Along with the tradition of fusion, it is necessary to stress there are changes in the form and presentation of dance movements to accommodate the contemporary trends of the day. Postmodernism, an intellectual convention of our times, is the trend of the 1990s. In her 1993 article, *Postmodernity, Architecture and Critical Practice,* Micha Bandini maintains that "postmodernism has become a construct built on images and words in such a manner that it perpetuates its own cultural legitimacy. Its status makes it compulsory."

In keeping up with status, contemporary dance has become less concerned with formalism and more concerned with the politics of identity—a characteristic of the postmodern phase. Because there is a resurgence of essentialist cultural nationalism, postmodern techniques has been adapted to create that political identity. In direct response to the populist imperative, choreographers and dance scholars alike consciously ring their work in line with the term "multiculturalism."

Perhaps, this tendency is a response to the current stresses and restrictions put upon those participants to connect with the current trend toward content in postmodern dance rather than interest in a particular community. Dance anthropologist Joanne Kealiinohomoku asserts that "restless dancers, always searching for new dance materials, are discovering and experiencing the dance of Others." New interest in diversity and pluralism warranted the appropriation of various techniques and traditions for other cultures, and American subcultures, once rejected or ignored, are now being politically recognized and represented.

In *The Tale of the Dragon,* Marcia Siegel articulates that "from one movement to the next, from one era to the next, dance itself is always a kind of transition, an arena where ideas appear, collide, contend, accommodate, and evolve into new ideas." Dance reflects its society. The history of modern dance is really each artist striving to define how the mind and body work in the contemporary world of that time. Their mosaic of movement today is represented and determined by the contemporaneity of their world. Thus dancers and their work are subjected to the tapestry that weaves together politics, the arts, and everyday life.

Publications

Bandini, Micha, "Postmodernity, Architecture and Critical Practice," *Mapping the Futures: Local Cultures, Global Change,* edited by Jon Bird, Barry Curtis, Tim Putnam, George Robertson, and Lisa Tickner, London and New York, 1993.

Barnes, Sally, *Writing Dance in the Age of Postmodernism,* Hanover, 1994.

Dekle, Nicole, "More Than a Series of Cool Things Strung Together," *Dance Magazine,* February 1991.

Kealiinohomoku, Joanne, "Angst over Ethnic Dance," in *Cross-Cultural Dance Resources Newsletter,* Summer 1990.

Siegel, Marcia, *The Tale of the Dragon,* Durham and London, 1991.

—Barbejoy A. Ponzio

FUTURISM

There is a certain irony in the fact that in the early part of the 20th century the Futurists, who were against classical art in all forms, including ballet, and somewhat illogically favored the glorification of contempt for women and the destruction of feminism, should have addressed their attention to the art of the dance and utimately exerted an extremely strong influence on it. Most of the pioneers in modern dance, from Loie Fuller to Isadora Duncan, Ruth St. Denis, and Mary Wigman, were in fact women.

The Futurist movement began in 1909 when the Paris newspaper *Le Figaro* published the "Futurist Manifesto," a document of far-reaching impact on a number of the arts, which was written by Filippo Tomasso Marinetti, an Italian playwright. Its goal was an aesthetic revolution, to overthrow the prevailing literary and artistic conceptions in favor of a new aesthetic of the future. The main themes of the Futurist movement were, according to James Joll in *Intellectuals in Politics,* "violence, destruction, hatred of the past and its values, and at the same time intense excitement about the prospects of the new century. . .[with] an awareness of the beauty of machines which could replace the more traditional objects of aesthetic satisfaction, and a realization of the heightening of experience which new sensations of speed and mechanical power could give."

While the 1909 Manifesto addressed issues of energy, rashness, speed and "the perilous leap," dance was not specifically addressed until 1917, when Marinetti, an admirer of Loie Fuller, issued a second Manifesto, this one of the Futurist Dance: "We Futurists prefer Louie (sic) Fuller and the 'cakewalk' of the Negroes (utilization of electric light and mechanisms)," he wrote, after lambasting classical ballet, Isadora Duncan (for sloppy emotionalism), and Emil Jacques Dalcroze for emphasis on muscularism. "One must go beyond muscular possibilities," he wrote, "and aim in the dance for that ideal multiplied body of the motor that we have so long dreamed of. One must imitate the movements of machines with gestures; pay assiduous court to steering wheels, ordinary wheels, pistons, thereby preparing the fusion of man with the machine, to achieve the metallicity of the Futurist dance." Moreover, Futurist Dance was to be accompanied not by musical compositions by Debussy or Mozart, but by "organized noises," such as the *musique concrete* created by such composers as Edgard Varese as early as 1920, and poetry. Moreover, Marinetti wrote, "the Futurist dance can have no other purpose than to immensify heroism, master of metals, and to fuse with the divine machines of speed and war."

In his Manifesto for Dance, Marinetti proposed three different scenarios for dances complete with choreographic directions, including one called the Dance of the Aviatrix; none of them were ever produced. In fact, little futurist choreography ever made it to the stage, and the movement left behind no new technique or school of movement, but did leave an approach to conceptual art, an ideological attitude of mind, and an emphasis on stage effects, particularly lighting design, which had important ramifications for mid- and late-20th century dance—ballet as well as modern—and, as the first iconoclastic, avant-garde movement of the 20th century, performance art.

"Futurist performance," writes historian Lynn Garafola, "extended the limits of traditional forms in unusual and often extreme ways." Sergei Diaghilev became intrigued, as did Igor Stravinsky, by the Futurists as early as 1914. That year the great impresario considered producing a ballet created by Italian designer Giacomo Ballo called *Printing Press,* which featured a dozen "robot-actors" impersonating parts of the machine. Instead, Diaghilev commissioned the designer to create the production for Stravinsky's *Fireworks,* but the Futurist influence was there.

It was in the second decade of the century and in Diaghilev's company in particular, in part thanks to the Futurists, the lines began to be blurred between classical ballet and the new modern dance as practiced by Isadora Duncan (who wrote an essay on dance of the future), Loie Fuller, Mary Wigman, Kurt Jooss, and Vaslav Nijinsky. For both camps, Garafola noted, "the triumph of mechanistic concepts in movement, design, and characterization called for a new performance style, one that conveyed emotion by abstracting, concentrating, and projecting it from behind a mask of eloquent impassivity."

Diaghilev was very much part of a movement in which modern performance developed in association with visual arts. In the 1920s,

the Bauhaus artists, Oskar Schlemmer in particular, created dances based on geometric principals which like the Futurists rejected past traditions. Surrealists, like Jean Cocteau, created scenarios for dance; Fernand Leger made sets for the Paris- based Ballets Suedois.

The trend continued to the end of the 20th century. Merce Cunningham, who often uses a computer to choreograph, has collaborated with a number of visual artists, including Robert Rauschenburg and uses the I Ching to choreograph by chance. Alwin Nikolais incorporated many Futurist and Bauhaus concepts into his work in the 1950s; and German choreographer Pina Bausch uses dramatic visuals in her work and has the confrontational Futurist style eschewed by Diaghilev. In Bausch's performance pieces there is the same kind of interaction with members of the audience that were a feature of Futurist theater performances. And in her work, as well as that of many other dance artists of the late-20th century, spoken text is used as well as sound collage to accompany the dances. Trisha Brown, Robert Wilson, and Yvonne Rainier, who issued a manifesto of her own in the 1960s, are all heirs of the Futurists, bending their concepts to their own artistic vision.

As RoseLee Goldberg points out in her essay on "Performance Art from Futurism to the Present," in almost every case, avant-garde visual artists in the 20th century first tested their ideas in performance, then made the paintings, sculptures and so on. "Despite the fact that most of what is written today about the work of the Futurists, Constructivists, Dadaists and Surrealists concentrates on the art objects produced by each period, it was more often than not the case that these movements found their roots and attempted to resolve problematic issues in performance." In other words, images had to move before they could be fixed in paint, stone, or other media—and dance became inextricably bound to visual art.

Publications

Books—

Flint, R.W., ed., *Marinetti: Selected Writings,* New York, 1972.
Garafola, Lynn, *Diaghilev's Ballets Russes,* New York, 1989.
Huxley, Michael and Noel Witt, editors, *The Twentieth Century Performance Reader,* London, 1996.
Joll, James, *Intellectuals in Politics,* New York, 1960.

Articles—

Berghaus, Gunter, "Giannina Censi's Influence on Futurism, *Dance Theatre Journal,* 1990.
Sowell, Deborah Hickenlooper, "Marinetti's Manifesto of Futurist Dance," *Society of Dance History Scholars Proceedings,* 1985.
Takvorkian, Rick, "The Line, the Curve and the Border, Fragments of a Performance Definition," *Ballet International*, April 1990.

—Martha Ullman West

GALILI, Itzik

Israeli dancer, choreographer, and company director

Born: 1962 in Tel Aviv. **Career:** Dancer, Bat-Dor Dance Company and then Batsheva Dance Company; also worked with Choo-San Goh, Mark Morris, David Parsons, Ohad Naharin, Elisa Monte, Daniel Ezralow, and Robert North; first choreography, *Double Time,* 1990; has created works for Scapino Rotterdam, Het Nationale Ballet, Reflex, Nederlands Dans Theater II (all Netherlands); Gulbenkian Ballet Portugal, Les Grands Ballets Canadiens, Ballet du Grand Théâtre de Genève, Batsheva Dance Company, Tac Company Aachen, and Nye Carte Blanche Norway; founded Galili Dance, 1992. **Awards:** First prize, Gvanim International Choreographers Competition (Israel) for *The Old Cartoon,* 1990; Public's prize, International Choreographers Competition (Groningen) for *The Butterfly Effect,* 1992; Philip Morris Final Selection Award, 1994; nominated for Lucas Hoving Prize, 1995; Galili Dance awarded a national subsidy, 1996.

Works

1990   *Double Time* (mus. William Scheller), Batsheva Dance Company, Tel Aviv
       Old Cartoon (mus. collage), Batsheva Dance Company, Tel Aviv
       My Little Garden Party (mus. Peter Gabriel, Yens & Yens), Galili Dance, Tel Aviv
1991   *Cage* (mus. Yens & Yens), freelance dancers, Amsterdam
       Trekidos (mus. Yens & Yens), Reflex Danscompany, Stadsschouwburg Assen
       Black Donut (mus. Motel Bokassa), Pforzheim Staatsteater Dance Company, Germany
       Gloves (mus. collage), Luc Buoyer, Amsterdam
       The Butterfly Effect (no music), Batsheva Dance Company, Tel Aviv
       For Tsouklamia, Just That (mus. Motel Bokassa), Batsheva Dance Company
1992   *Facing,* Batsheva Dance Company,
       Earth Apples (mus. Mercedes Sosa), Galili Dance, Amsterdam
       Blind Kingdom (mus. Jon Hassel), Nederlands Dans Theater II, the Hague
1993   *Cinderello* (mus. Sergei Prokofiev), Ballet du Grand Théâtre de Genève, Switzerland
       Duet (mus. Henryk Gorecki), Dutch National Ballet, Amsterdam
       Her Light Made of Sand (mus. Curt Steinzor), Galili Dance, World Olympic University Games, U.S.A.
       Peruriem (mus. Michael Nyman), Scapino Rotterdam, Rotterdamse Schouwburg

       To Topography Too (mus. Yens & Yens), Galili Dance, Amsterdam
       When You See God Tell Him (mus. Scott Johnson), Galili Dance, Amsterdam
1994   *The Irony of Antimatter* (mus. Justin Billinger), Dutch National Ballet w/Holland Dance Festival, Stadsschouwburg Amsterdam
       Ma's Bandage (mus. Yens & Yens), Scapino Rotterdam, the Hague
       If (mus. Bach), Szeged Ballet, Hungary
1995   *Through Nana's Eyes* (mus. Tom Waits), Gulbenkian Ballet, Lisbon
       Between L. . . (text Galili), Stichting Doublet w/Holland Dance Festival, the Hague
       Uhlai (mus. Årvo Pärt, Bart Visman, Scott Johnson), Galili Dance, Heerlen
1996   *Chronocratie* (mus. Gene Carl), Galili Dance, Amsterdam and Heerlen
1997   *Fragile* (mus. Gavin Bryars), Galili Dance, Heerlen
       Below Paradise (mus. Gene Carl Band), Scapino Rotterdam, Rotterdamse Schouwburg
       Blink (mus. Gavin Bryars), Nye Carte Blanche, Norway

Films and Videotapes

Come Across, film directed by Wolke Kluppel with choreography by Galili.

*   *   *

Itzik Galili is a versatile choreographer. Though Galili never had a proper dance education, he practiced martial arts and folk dance, and adapted classical technique by watching. He started dancing at the Bat-Dor Dance Company, after which he joined Batsheva Dance Company until he left Israel for the Netherlands at the beginning of the Gulf War in 1990. Since his arrival in Amsterdam, he has created many choreographic works and has danced in some of them. His tempo in creating is amazingly high and his works are multifaceted; the success of his work has resulted in invitations from many major companies worldwide to choreograph, as well as awards, and success for his project-based company, Galili Dance (formed in 1992).

One cannot easily link Galili to one certain style of dance. His dances are based on modern dance, are often abstract, and closely linked to his selection of music. They are frequently poetic and lyrical, as well as colorful and exciting in their expression. Galili visualizes feelings of tenderness, distress, and relief in a compelling way—often representational and inspired by experiences from his difficult youth. About these emotional memories, Galili has said he often wants "to scream it out," but instead channels this energy into his choreography. Emotions, intuition, and intellectual thought have become the primary seeds for a new dancework.

Itzik Galili: *Uhlai, 1995.* **Photograph by Oliver Schutt.**

Galili's way of working is constantly different, which keeps his work interesting and fresh. He often departs from restrictions imposed on dancers or introduces text and props on stage. The duets Galili created for himself and his dance partner and wife, the fascinating ex-Netherlands Dans Theater dancer Jennifer Hannah, are extremely moving. In *Uhlai,* two individuals try to escape their own limitations and discover the magic in life neither had seen before. Another duet, *When You See God Tell Him*, set to the music of Scott Johnson, is a series of vignettes about a Jewish-American journalist and a society full of hate.

The energy level in Galili's work is reminiscent of Ohad Naharin, his fellow countryman and choreographer. Both have a strong instinct for survival and embody a *joie de vivre* from their creative efforts. Galili prefers to collaborate with live musicians. He's choreographed several works to the music of composer Gene Carl, including *Chronocratie,* an absolute highlight of their collaboration, and comparable to Cunningham and Cage's *Ocean.* The dancers, one after the other, moved behind seven pianos placed around the stage and play minimal scores composed by Carl composed. Within the 16 dancers there are not only seven pianists, but also a dancing countertenor Joachim Sabate. A huge mattress is part of the performance space and the dancers play with gravity by jumping high and moving in slow motion. Time, the constant changing sequences of the piano themes, and space, are used ingeniously in this earthbound work. The fluid movements are breathtaking and beautiful, contrasting nicely with the ever-changing tempo and sound of the piano. Jennifer Hannah's solo expressed a very feminine sexuality, choreographed with both sensitivity and intensity by Galili, and leads to her questions of "How is life created?" and "Where does it come from?" in the end sequence.

Questions are a recurring theme in Galili's work, supported by a romantic atmosphere and strengthened by appropriate costuming and sets; he is also a passionate explorer of women's feelings in *Ma's Bandage.* This work was an inquiry into domestic violence, representational, Galili says, of "a woman trying to understand the past's influences upon her life and future. The fears that accompany her do not influence her opinions or her will to be detached from norms and habits."

Galili also likes to experiment with film and video. His first choreography for film, *Come Across,* in collaboration with film director Wolke Kluppel, was a resounding and immediate success. Galili also created *Patato* in the same vein, and has had two of his performances televised (*When You See God Tell Him* and *Between L. . . for An Evening of Dutch Dance*).

In 1998, Galili Dance premiered its new version of Galili's first choreography, *Double Bill* along with *Through Nana's Eyes,* a work set to the music of Tom Waits, and *Conscious Dreams,* a collaboration with the Gertrude Figuren Theater.

—Helma Klooss

GAMES

Choreography: Donald McKayle
Music: Traditional
Set Design: Paul Bertelson
Lighting Design: Pamela Judson-Stiles
Costume Design: Remy Charlip

First Production: Hunter Playhouse, New York City, 25 May 1951
Original Dancers: Esta Beck, Eve Beck, Louanna Gardner, Remy Charlip, John Fealy, George Liker, John Nola
Original Singers: Shawneequa Baker, Donald McKayle

Other productions include: African American Dance Ensemble, Alvin Ailey American Dance Theatre, Alvin Ailey Repertory Dance Ensemble, Ballet Hispanico, Cleveland/San Jose Ballet Company, Dallas Black Dance Theatre, Dayton Contemporary Dance Company, Donald McKayle and Company, Eliot Feld Ballet Company, Inner City Repertory Dance Company, Juilliard Dance Theatre, Lula Washington Los Angeles Contemporary Dance Theatre, New Dance Group, Repertory Dance Theatre.

Publications

Books—

Cohen, Selma Jeanne, *The Modern Dance: Seven Statements of Belief,* Middletown, Connecticut, 1966.
Long, Richard A., "Decades of Achievement," in *The Black Tradition in Modern Dance,* New York, 1989.

Articles—

Hering, Doris, "The Concert Season in Review," *Dance Magazine,* July 1951.
Manchester, P. W., Review, *Dance News,* April 1953.
Marks, Marcia, "The Subject Is People," *Dance Magazine,* February 1963.

*   *   *

Games is recognized as one of Donald McKayle's most enduring works, and the reasons for its appeal are readily apparent. In this, his first piece of choreography, McKayle succeeded in telling a story and creating an ambiance that remains as poignant and universally communicative as when it premiered on a double bill with a work by fellow choreographer Daniel Nagrin. Doris Hering in her review of the first performance perceptively described the work as having captured with "uncanny perception the shadowed happiness of little city children."

More than 10 years later, in a conversation with *Dance Magazine*'s Marcia Marks, McKayle explained the genesis of *Games.* While observing children in a playground, where he served as volunteer play director, he recalled a frightening incident in his own childhood. While engaged with some buddies in a friendly street game in the Bronx, one of the children was accosted by a police officer, who for no apparent reason beat the child. Recalling fear as a constant companion of his childhood, McKayle began to wonder whether this was a universal childhood experience; it also inspired him to explore the role of play in a child's life. He began to research traditional games and songs, from which he eventually fashioned the 1951 *Games.* To this writer McKayle has explained that an earlier, quite different version was performed by the short-lived Contemporary Dance Group (with Helen Tamiris as artistic director) at the Charles Weidman Studio Theater in 1950.

The narrative aspect of *Games* is quite simple. Under the watchful eyes of two adults, four boys and three girls play such street games as stick ball, hopscotch, jump rope, and hide-and-seek. They challenge each other, play-act, show off, and revel in the sense of freedom and security offered by physical activity and playing with others. The adults are watching them from a street-level window on one side of the stage. A lamp post upstage center and the suggestion of another house, replete with stoop, completes the setting.

The apparently fun activities, however, carry with them a pervading sense of unease. Shoving matches result in two boys falling and not rebounding right away. One of them, who seems out of place in the group, cringes and curls into a fetal position. One of the girls repeatedly suffers humiliation. In addition, there is the invisible threat embodied in "Chickee, the cop." Eventually the policeman's offstage act of violence against one of the girls shatters everyone's fragile sense of security, turning their lives from play into tragedy.

P. W. Manchester has noted that *Games*, in addition to the terror of an unseen but ever-present oppression, illustrates two additional childhood realities: "the callousness, even brutality, of all children in their attitude toward each other as well as their close-knit unity with each other against the grown-up world."

Games is divided into three continuous sections: Play, Hunger and Terror—the elements which McKayle most often found represented in traditional folk material. He gave most of the accompanying songs and nursery rhymes to the two adult singers but included sometimes competitive interchanges between them and the dancers. Some of the work's most dramatic scenes are performed to the sounds of only the dancers' bodies.

Single-sex groupings, most notably a shadowboxing quartet for the men and a trio of double-dutch jump-ropers and a mother-child playing game for the women, alternate with ensemble sections. A high point is a fantasizing solo for the "outsider" in which McKayle hints at the reason for the boy's not fitting in. The dancer picks up two cans and uses them as binoculars, a bull's horns, guns, and—earrings. The choreographer's movement language is solidly based in modern dance's simple clarity and groundedness. A swinging lower right arm gesture, combined with a jaunty walk, introduced at the very beginning of *Games,* can be seen as a key to the work's double-edgedness. It is at once a cocky gesture of defiance and a conventional movement signifying a cop walking down the street swinging his billy club. As the work progresses, McKayle gradually widens the discrepancy between the surface texture of make-believe and the undercurrent of reality. It reaches a climax in the tightly structured compactness of the scenes choreographed to songs going back to slavery. That the songs have become identified merely with "games" can not obscure the fact that they are based on the horrors of a childhood existence marked by cotton picking, cabbage planting, slavery, and orphanhood, so when tragedy strikes in the end, the viewer is horrified but not surprised.

—Rita Felciano

GAMSON, Annabelle

American dancer and choreographer

Born: 6 August 1928 in New York City. **Education:** Studied with Julia Levien, Irma and Anna Duncan, Anita Zahn at the King-Coit School, and Katherine Dunham. **Family:** Married, two children, two grandchildren. **Career:** Dancer, Katherine Dunham's troupe; appeared on Broadway, 1940s and 1950s; lived in Venice and Rome,

1950-53; held a lecture/demonstration program with Levien on reconstructing works of Isadora Duncan, 1972; first solo concert of reconstructed Duncan works, 1974; began reconstructing works of Eleanor King and produced Eleanor King Retrospective Project (with King lecturing), 1988; founder, Annabelle Gamson Dance Solos. **Awards:** Guggenheim fellowship; Jack I. and Lillian L. Poses Outstanding Artistic Achievement, Brandeis University, 1990; New York Dance and Performance Award ("Bessie"), Special Citation, 1990.

Roles

1947	*Finian's Rainbow* (Michael Kidd), Broadway
1948	*Make Mine Manhattan* (Michael Kidd), Broadwau
1950	*Arms and the Girl* (Kidd), Broadway
1954	*L'Histoire du Soldat* (Anna Sokolow)
1955	*Pipe Dream,* Broadway
1957	*La Muerte Enamorado* (Enriqué Martinez), American Ballet Theatre Workshop

Other roles include: The Cowgirl in Agnes de Mille's *Rodeo* for American Ballet Theatre.

Works

1973	*True Spirits* w/Irene Feigenheimer, Barbara Roan, and Anthony LaGiglia
1976	*First Movement*
	Five Easy Pieces
	Portrait of Rose
1978	*Dances of Death*
1979	*Two Dances*

Other works include: *Pentimento, Marin Marais, Waiting, Tanzlieder,* and *William and Mary and John;* reconstructions of many Duncan works, including *Brahms Waltzes, Étude No. 2, Opus 1, Little Prelude, Mother, Revolutionary Étude, Sonata Pathetique, Valse Brilliante,* and *Water Study;* as well as Wigman's *Pastoral* and *Dance of Summer.*

Publications

On GAMSON: books—

Anderson, Jack, *The American Dance Festival,* Durham, North Carolina, 1987.
———, *Choreography Observed,* Iowa City, Iowa, 1987.
Coe, Robert, *Dance in America,* New York, 1985.
Croce, Arlene, *Afterimages,* New York, 1977.
Plett, Nicole, editor, *Eleanor King: Sixty Years in American Dance,* Santa Cruz, New Mexico, 1988.
Robertson, Allen, and Donald Hutera, *The Dance Handbook*, Boston, 1990.
Willis, J., editor, *Dance World,* New York, 1966, 1979.

On GAMSON: articles—

Aloff, Mindy, "Annabelle Gamson," *The Nation,* 22 February 1996.
Berman, Janice, "Summer Arts Preview: Dance," *Newsday,* 27 May 1990.

Buell, Richard, "Happy Union of Two Forms," *Boston Globe*, 13 April 1983.

"Drop, Rise, Breathe: Elizabeth Kendall talks to Annabelle Gamson," website: ⟨http://www.webcom.com⟩.

Horn, Laurie, "Troupe Preserves Vintage Moderns," *Miami Herald*, 19 October 1984.

Kaplan, Renee, "New York Tonight," *Newsday*, 22 January 1987.

Rivchun, Barbi Leifert, "A Stage Sampler Stitched by Women," *Newsday*, 8 January 1989.

Thom, Rose Anne, "Isadora Duncan: The Dances," *Dance Magazine*, November 1996.

Films and Videotapes

Étude No. 2, Opus 1, reconstruction of Duncan's dance, for PBS' *Dance in America*, 1976.

*   *   *

Annabelle Gamson is a dancer and choreographer, but is primarily known for her reconstructions of the works of other well-known female dancers, most notably Isadora Duncan.

Gamson was born in New York City in 1928, one year after Duncan's death in 1927. She studied first, as a child, with Julia Levien, who danced with the companies of Irma and Anna Duncan, students of Isadora Duncan who took her name. She also took classes with Anita Zahn, at the King-Coit School, and at the Katherine Dunham studio. She made her first professional dance appearance with Dunham's company at the Café Society Uptown, which specialized in presenting jazz and Afro-Haitian dance programs.

Before her concert dance career began in earnest, Gamson appeared in a number of theatrical productions. By the time she was 18, she had earned an understudy role in the road company of Jerome Robbins' *On the Town*, and she appeared in Michael Kidd's *Finian's Rainbow* in 1947. She was also featured in Kidd's *Make Mine Manhattan* (1948) and *Arms and the Girl* (1950).

After a respite of several years in Paris, Gamson returned to the U.S. in 1955, and to Broadway, where she had a role in *Pipe Dream* that year. She also danced for television audiences, including on *The Ed Sullivan Show* and the religious program *Lamp Unto My Feet*. She occasionally danced for Anna Sokolow, including as the Princess in Sokolow's staging of the opera *L'Histoire du soldat*, and with Agnes de Mille as the Cowgirl in de Mille's *Rodeo* for the American Ballet Theatre (ABT). She also danced in a premiere for the ABT's Ballet Theatre Workshop, *La Muerte Enamorado* (1957), choreographed by Enrique Martinez. Gamson took a hiatus from performing during the 1960s, concentrating instead on working with opera companies and teaching dance.

The 1970s began her period of greatest renown, thanks to her decision to reconstruct Isadora Duncan's work. She studied Duncan's choreography with Levien, and the two held a lecture-demonstration in 1972. She presented her first solo concert containing Duncan works in 1974 at the Dance Theatre Workshop, combining the Duncan pieces with some of her own. (Meanwhile, she also participated in other performances—like collaboratively creating and dancing in *True Spirits* in 1973 with Continuing Dance Exchange members Irene Feigenheimer, Barbara Roan, and Anthony LaGiglia.)

Gamson's Duncan work was viewed by some critics as "naive" at first, given the drastic changes in dance during the 1960s, particularly those forwarded by postmodern dancers such as the members of the Judson Dance Theater. Still, most observers have come to believe that she is the preeminent Duncan reconstructionist—several others appeared in the 1970s, including Maria-Theresa, Levien, Kay Beardsley, and Jeanne Bresciani, some inspired by Gamson's work—and have given her mostly positive reviews throughout the 1970s and beyond. Some of the Duncan works she has reconceived include *Mother, Sonata Pathetique*, and Scriabin's *Etude No. 2, Opus 1* (which dealt with the loss of Duncan's children and was performed by Gamson on the PBS series *Dance in America* in 1976), as well as *Valse Brilliante* to Chopin, *Brahms Waltzes, Revolutionary Étude, Little Prelude* and *Water Study*.

While Gamson was true to Duncan's actual choreography (in fact, it was her work that made audiences realize that Duncan had choreographed reproducible pieces, rather than primarily improvising, as was thought), she differed from other Duncan reconstructionists in that she did not mimic Duncan's style, but rather infused the pieces with her own individuality and force. She interprets Duncan's work, adding her own expressiveness. Her work has highlighted some of the nuances in Duncan's pieces that most viewers had not noticed before, and revived Duncan's reputation as a noted choreographer—as she had often been remembered more as a larger-than-life personality than for her achievements in dance.

Gamson has frequently performed Duncan works, sometimes in full concerts, sometimes in combination with her reconstructions of other dancers' work, and sometimes in combination with her own choreography. She appeared at the American Dance Festival several times in the 1970s, as well as at Carnegie Hall, the 92nd Street Y in New York, Dance Theatre Workshop, the Joyce Theater Dance Festival, the Lyon Festival, and Jacob's Pillow. In addition to her reconstructions of Duncan's dances, Gamson also reconstructed some of the work of German dancer Mary Wigman in the 1970s, including *Pastoral* and *Dance of Summer*, both originally created in 1929. She continued to work with Wigman pieces into the 1980s, but has been quoted as saying she ultimately decided that Wigman's cooperation with the Nazis during World Ward II was offensive to her as a Jewish-American.

In the 1980s, Gamson began reconstructing some of the works of Eleanor King, many of which had been virtually forgotten. In May 1988, Gamson produced the Eleanor King Retrospective Project, in which members of her company performed the King reconstructions. King was in attendance and gave lectures in conjunction with the event.

Gamson's own choreography is less well-known than her reconstructions, but she has produced several of her own works. They include *First Movement* (1976), *Five Easy Pieces* (1976), *Portrait of Rose* (1976), *Dances of Death* (1978) and *Two Dances* (1979), as well as *Pentimento, Marin Marais*, and *Waiting*. Her musical accompaniment includes Mozart, Stravinsky, Steve Reich, Elliott Carter, Shostakovich, and Mongolian folk music.

She often stages both her reconstructions and her own work with her company, Annabelle Gamson Dance Solos, members of which have included Sarah Stackhouse, Risa Steinberg, Sylvia Martins, and Sue Bernhard. Gamson also appears in solo concerts, and in some cases, other companies perform her work as well. For example, the Denishawn Repertory Dancers and the Repertory Dance Theatre in Salt Lake City have staged some of her Duncan reconstructions; Musica Viva and Concert Dance Company in Boston performed her *William and Mary and John*, which was originally conceived as a solo, and the Limón Dance Company has performed her *Tanzlieder*. Gamson also performs as a guest artist with groups such as the Bill Evans Dance Company in Seattle.

Gamson won a Jack I. and Lillian L. Poses Creative Arts Award from Brandeis University in 1990 and a Special Citation at the 1990 New York Dance and Performance Awards ("Bessies"). Pianist Garrick Ohlsson, who frequently accompanies Gamson, says "She is uncannily sensitive to music, and working with her is like a strenuous chamber-music rehearsal. She is demonic, powerful, sensuous and extravagant."

—Karen Raugust

GARTH, Midi

American dancer and choreographer

Born: 28 June 1920 in New York City. **Education:** Attended Chicago Musical College and Roosevelt University, Chicago; studied with Francesca de Cotelet, Nanette Charisse, Louis Horst, Sybil Shearer, Elsa Fried, at the New Dance Group studio, and others. **Career:** Danced with Sybil Shearer, Chicago; began solo works, performing at the 92nd Street Y, Henry Street Playhouse, Hunter College, and other venues; taught at Hull House Settlement. **Awards:** Audition winner, YMHA, 1949; Ingram Merrill choreography award, 1961; Yaddo Fellowship, 1962.

Works

1949	*No Refuge*
	Times Cast a Shadow
	Dreams
	Exile
	Predatory Figure
1951	*No Refuge II*
	Waking
	Dreaming
	Decisive Moment
	Ode for the Morrow
	Worship of a Flower
	Prelude to Flight
1952	*Pastoral*
	Allegro
	Hither Thither
1954	*Tides*
	Voices
	Anonymous
	Two People
1956	*Time and Memory*
	Penalty
	City Square
1958	*A Suite of Dances*
	Scerzando
	Double Image
1959	*Sea Change*
	Juke Box Pieces
	Ricardanza
	Three Tragic Figures
	Retrospect
1961	*This Day's Madness*
	Voyages

1963	*Versus*
	Night
	Imaginary City
1965	*Day and Night*
1966	*Other Voices*
	Four Elements
	Summer
1967	*Three Solos (Summer, Winter, Night)*
1969	*Warm Up*
	Impressions of Our Time
1970	*Workout*
1973	*Solo for Three*
	Hommage
	Solo
	Images of Our Time
1975	*Workout for Six*
	Chorale Song
1976	*Open Space*
	Trio
1978	*Koto Song*
1979	*Images and Reflections*

Publications

Hering, Doris, "*Prelude:* Midi Garth," *Dance Magazine*, May 1966.

Hering, Doris, and Walter Sorrell, "Season in Review," *Dance Magazine*, July 1956.

Marks, Marcia, "Midi Garth 92nd Street Y," *Dance Magazine,* June 1966.

Nutchtern, Jean, "Perspectives," *Dance Magazine,* July 1973.

*   *   *

Midi Garth emerged onto the modern dance scene in the United States during the mid-1950s, and at the time her style and approach to choreography was considered unusual. Garth, who was a native New Yorker, had studied with a myriad of educators including ballet with Nanette Charisse, composition with Louis Horst, technique with Else Fried and Sybil Shearer, as well as at the New Dance Group studio. For several years, Garth lived in Chicago, where she studied acting, music, and dance at Roosevelt University and music at the Chicago Musical College. She also studied ballet with John Petri and Berenice Holmes, but one of her earliest mentors and influences was Shearer, with whom she later danced at the Chicago's famous Goodman Theatre. Garth has pointed out, however, that her primary source of inspiration was Francesca de Cotelet, who was her first dance teacher when Garth was a young girl living in New York. It was de Cotelet who helped Garth realize that she was not an "ungainly" youngster and encouraged Garth to pursue a career in dance.

After her studies in Chicago, Garth returned to New York. There, she took classes with Louis Horst in composition—which Horst typically divided into three main types: primitive, archaic, and medieval; but for Garth and a few of her contemporaries such as Merle Marsicano, Horst invented a new category of dance composition—impressionistic. To Horst, "impressionistic" was a term he used to include dancers whose work didn't fall within the bounds of the melodramatic, socially relevant themes of traditional modern dance. Garth rejected the logical, cause-and-effect style of choreography and didn't depend on a literal theme or piece of music to serve as the focal point of her dances.

Garth belonged to a generation of dancers trained by those modern dancers who were, essentially, effecting a major shift in modern dance performances—from the literal to the conceptual. Some dance writers describe this era as representing the shift from a Freudian to a Jungian perspective in dance expression. Garth's dances often depended on her mood, consecutive performances of a particular dance often appearing as different dances. Her choreography was extremely personal and perhaps worked best when she performed it—perhaps the reason for her modest success as a soloist.

Though some critics have deemed Garth's choreography repetitive—her movements limited to floor contractions, flailing arms, and parallel plies in profile—others have called her work uniquely satisfying. Garth's work was essentially abstract, evoking a variety of emotional reactions from her audiences. Meaning was implied, rather than explained by a direct image or bold dance "statement." Garth, whose movements and gestures were performed with extreme precision, was fascinated by moving body parts in counterpoint; consequently, she often built an entire dance on a particular movement or quality of movement. Her style cannot be associated with any particular dance school or identifiable dance philosophy, and she has typically been defined by critics as a dance individualist.

Anonymous (1954), set to the monotonous sound of a metronome, is perhaps Garth's best-known work. Performing on a bare stage, Garth wore a black-hooded costume, moving in an abrupt, percussive manner to the repetitive ticking. The piece had no clear beginning, middle, or end—instead Garth's rhythmic movements were periodically interrupted by random languorous swaying. Other well-known works include *This Day's Madness* (1961), which portrays the frenzied atmosphere of the everyday rat race. For this piece, Garth dressed in a business suit and moved around two madly typing "secretaries," displacing her body from its usual balance. Garth's well-known solo, *Prelude to Flight* (1951) suggested the preparatory movements of birds about to take to flight.

Garth's performing ensemble fluctuated: sometimes there were several members, other times she was the sole performer. Garth drew from Albert Camus' tenet that while everything is hopeless or seems hopeless, one must behave as if it is not. So Garth has performed whichever pieces fit the particular ensemble she is working with—group pieces, duets, and when necessary, solos. Garth's work has been described as sparse, elusive, and ruminative, and while her work may not be exceptionally popular, she has been a maverick of modern dance.

—Christine Miner Minderovic

GENDAI BUYO KYOKAI

Gendai Buyo Kyokai [Contemporary Dance Association of Japan], founded in 1972, is the largest and most influential modern dance affiliation in Japan, to which private teachers and their students, choreographers, studio directors, and such register. As of 1997, this organization consolidates over 2,300 members, which constitutes a large majority of modern dance practitioners. The association has helped the advancement and diffusion of modern dance in Japan, with regular activities including the organization of joint concerts, workshops, research projects, the publication of printed and visual materials, awarding honors to its members, and

coordinating competitions (usually with a newspaper, prefectural government, or arts-related organization, with the association's senior members occupying a majority of jury positions) to judge dancers' techniques or choreographic skills.

On the other hand, despite the Gendai Buyo Kyokai's support for dance, it has been directed by mostly elderly members and is considered conservative, and run in a hierarchal fashion. The association's earliest predecessor, Nihon Geijutsu Buyoka Kyokai [Japan Artistic Dance Association], founded in 1948, three years after World War II ended, facilitated the revival of the modern dance community from the wartime decline. During the war, creative activities ceased, for dancers were only allowed to perform in sympathy to the war effort. Additionally, many dance studios, especially those in Tokyo, were destroyed by air raids. So after the war, both modern dance and ballet exponents came together and organized a series of joint *yoh-bu* [Occidental dance] concerts. Although these programs were artistically inconsistent, dozens of small works by individual studios were presented, and served to revitalize interest in dance.

The association was expanded into a nationwide organization called Zen Nihon Geijutu Buyo Kyokai [All-Japan Art Dance Association] in 1956. Principal members included Baku Ishii, Seiko Takata, Takaya Eguchi, Nobutoshi Tsuda, Kenji Hinoki, and Tonao Hiraoka among others. As the ballet branch independently founded the Japan Ballet Association in 1972, the modern dance branch was reorganized and assumed the present name of Gendai Buyo Kyokai at the same time. Seiko Takata (1895-1977), the most senior pioneer figure in the modern dance community assumed the post of chairman. Appointments for directors were handed down mostly to Takata disciples. The current chairman is Midori Ishii (b. 1913), former student of another pioneer, Baku Ishii (1886-1962).

The association supports several annual concerts each organized separately in accordance with the participants' level of experience, i.e. newcomers, junior members, mature members, or veterans. Concerts for newcomers and junior members consist of many short pieces or vignettes presented one after the other; one-act works are reserved for either mature members or veterans. The association's eight branches also organize independent concerts to present works choreographed and danced by branch members. These performances rarely attract large numbers of the general public; the association sells tickets to its members or performers are required to buy (and resell if possible) tickets of their own performances. As the association doesn't have an official, affiliated dance company, each work is performed by a member choreographer and his/her studio dancers.

An annual domestic tour is held and sponsored by Japan's Ministry of Cultural Affairs. The average length of a tour is about one week, stopping at several cities. Three or four one-act works choreographed by senior members usually make up the program. Honors are also presented annually and include Best Dancer, Best Ensemble, and the Newcomer's award. The Takaya Eguchi Achievement Award is awarded to a senior member. The association also co-organizes the annual All-Japan Dance Competition, judged mostly by the association's senior members.

To date, modern dance has never received sufficient nor consistent governmental subsidies nor corporate funding to build up a solid financial foundation. There have been no legitimate professional dance companies established; any troupes organized have enjoyed little popular acclaim. The association's activities supplement the lapse in funds and popularity by maintaining a self-sufficient structure to produce performances, provides opportunities for its dancers and chorepgraphers, assembles audiences, and awards honors. Thus the association has contributed to the diffusion of modern dance, while its insular hierarchy has been criticized for its antiquated notion of modern dance and reliance upon the style of dance initiated by the early pioneers. Many of the fledgling dancers and choreographers, though trained under senior members of the association, very often choose to work outside the association's scope.

—Sako Ueno

GEORGI, Yvonne

German dancer and choreographer

Born: 29 October 1903 in Leipzig. **Education:** Studied at Dalcroze Institute, Hellerau, 1920, and at the Wigman school in Dresden from 1921. **Family:** Married Louis Arntzenius, 1932. **Career:** Debut as a concert dancer, Leipzig, 1923; dancer, Kurt Jooss' company and Munster Stadteater, 1924-25; choreographer, Reussisches Theater, Gera, 1925-26, and Theater of the City of Hanover, 1926-31; formed her own company, 1931; performed with Wigman group, with Harald Kreutzberg, and in solo concerts to 1939; choreographer, Board of City Theaters, Amsterdam, during World War II, Dusseldorf Opera House, 1951-54; ballet director, Hanover State Theater, 1954-70. **Died:** 25 January 1975 in Hanover.

Works

1924   *Persisches Ballet*
1925   *Der Dämon* (mus. Hindemith), Reussisches Theater, Gera
1926   *Barabau* (mus. Rieti), Reussisches Theater, Gera
       Pulcinella (mus. Stravinsky), Reussisches Theater, Gera
       Petrouchka
       Arabische Suite
       Saudades do Brazil (mus. Milhaud), Reussisches Theater, Gera
1927   *Rococoscenes*
       Deutsche Danz
       De Puppernfée
1928   *Tanzsuite* (mus. Wellesz), Hanover Opera House
       Don Morte (mus. Wilckens), Hanover Opera House
       Baby in Der Bar (mus. Grosz), Hanover Opera House
       Prince Igor
       Remembrances of Spain
       Robes, Pierre and Co. (mus. Wilckens), Hanover Opera House
       Das Seltsame Haus (mus. Hindemith), Hanover Opera House
       Kassandra
1929   *Joseph's Legend*
       Orpheus and Euridyce
       Der Fächer
       Eine Kleine Nachtmusik
1930   *Pavane* w/Harald Kreutzberg
1931   *Le Train Bleu* (mus. Milhaud), Berlin State Opera House
1933   *Acis et Galathée* (mus. Lully), Amsterdam Wagner Society
1935   *Goyescas* (mus. Granados), Hanover Opera House
1936   *Diana* (mus. Voormolen), Amsterdam

1939   *Prometheus* (mus. Beethoven), Ballets Yvonne Georgi, Amsterdam
       Old Dutch Dances
       Symphonie Fantastique (mus. Berlioz), City Theatre, Amsterdam
       Festive Dances
       Souvenir
1951   *Apollon Musagète* (mus. Stravinsky), Düsseldorf Opera Ballet
       Das Feuervogel (mus. Stravinsky), Düsseldorf Opera Ballet
       Les Animaux modèles (mus. Poulenc), Düsseldorf Opera Ballet
1952   *Die Geschöpfe des Prometheus* (mus. Beethoven), Düsseldorf Opera Ballet
       Das Goldfischglas (mus. Andreissen), Düsseldorf Opera Ballet
       Die vier Temperamente (mus. Hindemith), Düsseldorf Opera Ballet
       El Amor Brujo (mus. de Falla), Düsseldorf Opera Ballet
       Coppélia (mus. Delibes), Düsseldorf Opera Ballet
1953   *Herzog Blaubarts Burg*
       Wendungen, Düsseldorf Opera Ballet
       Pas de coeur (mus. von Einem), Düsseldorf Opera Ballet
       Le Sacre du printemps (mus. Stravinsky), Düsseldorf Opera Ballet
1955   *Orpheus*
       Human Variations (mus. Gould), Hanover State Opera Ballet
       Les Biches (mus. Poulenc), Hanover State Opera Ballet
1956   *Glück, Tod, und Traum*
       Der Mohr von Venedig (mus. Blacher), Hanover State Opera Ballet
1957   *Le Loup* (mus. Dutilleux), Hanover State Opera Ballet
       Elektronisches Ballett (mus. Badings), Hanover State Opera Ballet
1958   *Der Schatten*
       Evolutionen (mus. Badings), Vienna State Opera Ballet
       Bacchus et Ariadne
       Agon (mus. Stravinsky), Vienna State Opera Ballet
1959   *Die Ballade*
       Das Einhorn, der drache und der Tigerman (mus. Menotti), Hanover State Opera Ballet
       Ruth (mus. Erbse), Vienna State Opera Ballet
       Königliche Spiele
1960   *Die Frau aus Andros* (mus. Badings), Hanover State Opera Ballet
1961   *Angst* (mus. Constant), Hanover State Opera Ballet
       Bluebeard's Nightmare
       Hamlet
       Passacaglia No.1
1962   *Metamorphosen* (mus. R. Strauss), Hanover State Opera Ballet
       The Miraculous Mandarin
1963   *Suite in Four Movements*
1964   *Demeter* (mus. Blacher), Schwetzingen
1965   *Der Golem* (mus. Burt), Hanover State Opera Ballet
1968   *Paradis perdu* (mus. Constant), Hanover State Opera House
1970   *Jeux vénitiens* (mus. Lutoslawski), Hanover State Opera House

1971   *Trionfi* (mus. Orff), Teatro Colón, Buenos Aires
1973   *Skorpion* (mus. Gould), Hanover Ballet

Publications

On GEORGI: books—

Gruen, John, *The Private World of Ballet,* New York, 1975.
Isa Partsch-Bergsohn, *Modern Dance in Germany and the United States,* Chur, Switzerland, 1994.
Martin, John, *Ruth Page: An Intimate Biography*, New York, 1977.
Preston-Dunlop, Valerie, and Susanne Lahusen, eds. *Schrifttanz,* London, 1990.

*   *   *

German dancer, choreographer, teacher, and ballet mistress Yvonne Georgi was a student in the first class of modern dance pioneer Mary Wigman. Along with several other members of that group, she went on to become one of the leaders of the German Expressionist period in dance, known as the *Ausdruckstanz.* In addition to performing as a soloist, she had a long career staging dances for opera and theater companies in Europe, and was a prolific choreographer. She is probably best known, however, especially in the United States, as the longtime and highly acclaimed duet partner of Harald Kreutzberg.

Georgi was born in 1903. Along with Max Terpis, Hanya Holm, and Gret Palucca, as well as Kreutzberg, Georgi studied with Wigman early in her career, soon joining Wigman's company. (Georgi also spent time training in ballet and modern dance with Dalcroize, Hellerau, Viktor Gsovsky, Sigurd Leeder, and Kurt Jooss.) In 1923 Georgi and Kreutzberg left Wigman's troupe, relocating to Hanover and becoming dance soloists at the State Theater there. Former classmate Terpis, who had directed the State Theater since leaving Wigman the previous year, had extended them an invitation to join him.

Georgi performed as a dance soloist in the theater (in Hanover and elsewhere) and in concert for more than 15 years, from her debut in 1923 until 1939. She gave solo concerts in Europe, including in Poland, Germany, Austria, and Holland, as well as in the U.S. In addition to her solo work, she also performed duets with Kreutzberg. From 1926 to 1932, Kreutzberg and Georgi partnered on successful annual tours throughout much of the world. They co-choreographed many of their pieces together, and also performed in duets created by Kreutzberg, such as *Angel of Annunciation*, and in their own solos. Kreutzberg was an exceptionally strong stage presence, and Georgi was one of the rare dancers whose style complemented his, and who was able to perform with him without being overwhelmed.

Georgi and Kreutzberg, through their tours of the U.S., played a great role in introducing German modern dance to American audiences and performances. Their concerts were among the first opportunities Americans had to see German dance, which had evolved further than American modern dance as of the 1920s and 1930s. Their influence encouraged the exchange of ideas between U.S. and European modern dance performers, as well as helping to create an increased number of visits to Europe by American dancers to study and perform.

Georgi and Kreutzberg were among the few German dancers who were allowed to continue touring abroad as the National Socialists began to gain power in their homeland. This was because their performances were primarily entertaining rather than ideological, and thus fit into the Nazis' dictates that all art appeal to mass audiences. As the National Socialists became stronger, however, Georgi decided to emigrate to the Netherlands in 1938, where she formed a dance company that performed throughout Holland and abroad. She also taught dance.

Georgi's role as Kreutzberg's duet partner and co-choreographer garnered her most of her acclaim outside Europe, but she probably had a greater impact overall in forwarding modern dance as an element within German theater and opera. Prior to the war, Georgi had served as ballet mistress at the Münster Stadteater from 1924 to 1925, at the Gera Opera House from 1925 to 1926, at the State Theater of Hanover from 1926 to 1931 (which became a leading venue for modern dance under her direction), and with the Amsterdam Opera from 1932 to 1934. (She continued to perform as a soloist and with her own company as well as maintaining her positions with these companies.)

After World War II Georgi began to focus less on performing and concentrate more on her work as ballet mistress and choreographer. She returned to Germany after the war, assuming the position of ballet mistress at the Düsseldorf Opera in 1951 and stayed until 1954. Subsequently, she returned to Hanover, becoming ballet mistress and director of the dance training program at the Landestheater in 1954, and remaining there for more than two decades until the year of her death, 1975. Georgi also frequently served as a guest choreographer for various opera and theatrical companies in Europe, especially in the 1930s through the 1950s, including the Berlin State Opera, the Vienna State Opera, and the Salzburg Festival.

Along with Kreutzberg, Gret Palucca, Rosalia Chladek, Edgar Frank, and Vera Skoronel, Georgi was one of the most prolific choreographers of solos in Germany. Naturally, through her long work as a ballet mistress, she also created numerous pieces for the theater and opera as well as solos and duets. All told, Georgi choreographed more than 70 works in her 50 years as a choreographer. She also choreographed the dances for a French film, *Dream Ballerina* (1950), as well as doing work for German and Austrian television.

Georgi's choice of composers was diverse; she created dances to electronic scores by Henk Badings, as well as works to Beethoven, Hector Berlioz, Boris Blacher, Gottfried von Einem, Ravel, Strauss, Stravinsky, Jacques Ibert, Albert Roussel, Arnold Schönberg, Jurriaan Andriessen, and Carl Orff, among others.

Georgi had a great impact on the younger generations of modern dancers, both European and American. Her performances (especially her duets with Kreutzberg) inspired the likes of José Limón and Erick Hawkins, and her work as a teacher forwarded the careers of students such as Lucas Hoving, who studied with her in his native Holland.

—Karen Raugust

GERMANY

Germany was the vortex of modern dance currents which spread throughout Europe in the early decades of the 20th century. Dance was an expression of modernity or modern identity to the extent that it heightened awareness of the body as a historical force capable of expanding the power and freedom of individuals within an increasingly complex and systemized social reality. In its formative years, German modern dance culture sought generally to integrate the individual body into a large concept of social and even national identity. For this reason, dance pervasively aligned itself with a range of other artistic and social activities, such as gymnastics, theatre, educational reform, hygienic reform, nudism, ecological education, and utopian social planning. Women assumed an overwhelming share of responsibility for the development of the dance culture. Indeed, the origins of modern dance in Germany in the early years of the 20th century may be located in the desire of women to redefine female identity according to emancipating ideals.

The history of early German modern dance is in large part a struggle against the excessively confined image of female desirability projected by ballet culture. But foreign thinking was important in stimulating the emancipatory impulse. Francois Delsarte's (1811-71) system for coding bodily expression had a powerful disciple in the American Genevieve Stebbins (1857-1915), whose student, Hedwig Kallmeyer, introduced the concept of "harmonic gymnastics" to female students in Berlin around 1904. Another American, physician Bess Mensendieck (1864-1957), settled in Vienna, where she oversaw a network of schools throughout Germany which adopted her system for creating efficient and beautiful performances of ordinary actions. Swiss educator Émile Jaques-Dalcroze (1869-1950) exerted great influence on dance thinking through his doctrine of "rhythmic gymnastics," which proposed that the health and expressive authority of the body (at any age and from any social class) depended above all on intensely sensitive responses to music, particularly the rhythmic element. Dance was, from the Dalcrozian perspective, entirely a response to a highly rationalized external stimulus. The Dalcroze school established at Hellerau, in 1914, created a luminous, temple-like atmosphere that imbued the study of bodily movement with an imperturbable Gallic-Grecian rationalism. A further influence on the German scene was Isadora Duncan, whose daring, free-spirited personality was a more successful model for releasing creative energies than anything in her dance technique or aesthetic, and even the schools run by her sister, Elizabeth Duncan, in Darmstadt and Salzburg, cautiously attempted to go beyond Duncan's notion that dance is mostly just a "picture" of what music "inspired" in the dancer.

With the advent of World War I, Germans moved confidently away from foreign models and toward the formation of a distinctly Germanic identity for modern dance. Dance absorbed much of the irrationalism and emotional turbulence of German Expressionism, with its focus on internal rather than external sources of energy, and the term *Ausdruckstanz*, or Expressive dance, became a widely accepted appellation for modernist currents in dance culture. The period between 1914 and 1935 was exceptionally rich and perhaps unsurpassed in German contributions to the art of dance. But in spite of the communal and nationalistic rhetoric used everywhere to justify enthusiasm for dance, the vast historical evidence of the time suggests that the chief value for dance lay in its power to differentiate bodies rather than unify them, to reveal highly distinct personalities, to promote individual rather social identity. From 1914 until around 1925, the professional dance world heavily favored concerts featuring programs of solo dances performed by a single dancer.

An astonishingly large number of women embarked upon careers as solo dancers, including, to name only some of the most prominent, Niddy Impekoven, Edith von Schrenck, Sent M'ahesa, Gertrud Leistikow, Rosalia Chladek, Grit Hegesa, Julia Marcus, Charlotte Bara, Gret Palucca, Lucy Kieselhausen, Tatiana Barbakoff, Mila Cirul, Grete Wiesenthal, Gertrud Kraus, Laura Oesterreich, and Leni Riefenstahl. Solo dancers shaped personal aesthetic styles that vastly expanded and complicated the expressive range of modern dance, from the tragic (Schrenck) to the grotesque (Valeska Gert), the morbid and perverse (Anita Berber), the decorative (Rita Sacchetto), the aristocratically suave (Clothilde von Derp), the fanatically abstract (Hilda Strinz), the bizarrely primordial (Lavinia Schulz), and the religiously mystical (Bara).

Probably the most powerful personality to emerge was Mary Wigman (1886-1973), who more than anyone showed the capacity of dance to achieve the tragic and heroic identity that encouraged audiences to view dance very seriously. She greatly enlarged the bodily vocabulary of modern dance so that the body became a site of intense dramatic conflict, released from the Dalcrozian and Duncanesque obligation of dance to express joy or genial modes of optimism. And she further freed the body from the "tyranny" of music, of the synchronicity advocated by Dalcroze, under whom she had studied; the percussion orchestras she favored invariably followed cues given by the dancer. Wigman's school in Dresden, founded in 1919, produced many distinguished students who established Wigman schools elsewhere in Germany, and by 1928 she was perhaps the most famous dancer in Europe.

By 1925, however, interest in group dancing escalated rapidly, due in large part to the mesmeric personality of Rudolf Laban (1879-1958), one of Wigman's teachers, who in 1914 established himself as the leader of a fantastically seductive movement cult which spread well beyond Germany. Laban emphasized the concept of "movement choirs," complex and often convoluted interactions between bodies which urged dance to move outside the concert hall and appropriate new spaces for performance. He wrote abundantly on dance in a cryptic, mystical style which had extraordinary inspirational power, and he devised the now standard Labanotation system for notating dance, but his choreographic work itself actually left less of an imprint than that of those who were his students.

German group choreography was as rich in innovation and diversity of expression as the solo mode. Vera Skoronel (1906-1932) aggressively pursued a geometric formalism while Hertha Feist (1896-1990) specialized in large-scale allegorical pieces. Wigman showed a strong inclination to dramatize tensions between leaders and followers. Lola Rogge favored ambitious theatrical productions based on themes from classical mythology, but Hans Weidt (1904-1988), sympathetic to Communism, created dances which advocated the triumph of oppressed masses over capitalist exploitation. Kurt Jooss (1901-1979) developed a satiric, critical perspective on contemporary society through a movement style derived from the observation of movements performed within social reality itself. This approached achieved international recognition in *The Big City* (1929) and *The Green Table* (1932). Meanwhile, the Bauhaus theatre laboratory, under the direction of Lothar Schreyer and then Oskar Schlemmer, performed a variety of daring group choreographic experiments in which extremely modernistic design and costume elements allowed even the most elemental movements to appear profoundly strange.

By the early 1930s modern dance culture appeared to have reached a saturation point. Schools of dance proliferated throughout Germany and enrollments continued to surge, but the audience for dance did not expand enough to accommodate the professional aspirations of so many dancers, over 90 percent of whom were women. The solution for many leaders of modern dance lay in a reconciliation with ballet, in the hope that the state-subsidized theatre system, which inexplicably continued to finance a large and largely undistinguished ballet apparatus, might expand opportunities for modern dancers. Laban and Wigman students succeeded in gaining control of ballet appointments to the majority of German opera companies, although Wigman herself remained staunchly opposed to any affiliation with ballet. As a result, modern dance became much more suffused with theatrical values and attention to narrative coherence, with a corresponding diminishment of movement innovation and taste for audacious experimentation of relations between sound and movement or movement and space. Some Wigman students, like Margarethe Wallmann, Claire Eckstein, and especially Yvonne Georgi, thrived in the theatrical milieu, but by 1935 it was clear that modern dance would not survive by appropriating the official theatre apparatus; it would maintain its waning appeal mostly through private schools governed by strong personalities.

The Nazi regime directed a skeptical and sometimes downright hostile attitude toward modern dance. From the Nazi perspective, modern dance, with its focus on ecstatic experience and expressionistic disturbance of perception, had contributed to the fragmentation of German society and lacked credibility as a force for national unity. Culture Minister Joseph Goebbels advocated the development of a distinctly "German" idea of ballet, somehow derived from folk-dance motifs, but this direction led nowhere in a nation whose appetite for ballet was never as strong as its hunger for modern dance. Yet in an atmosphere intolerant of artistic modernism, modern dance could only languish and assume an increasingly marginal relation to German culture as a whole. Nevertheless, the Third Reich was not altogether destitute of memorable and exciting dance talents, including Ilse Meudtner, Maja Lex, Oda Schottmüller, Lola Rogge, and Helge Peters-Pawlinin. The all-female school of Dorothee Günther, active since the early 1920s, perfected a unique Expressionist aesthetic in which dancers made their own music and musicians and dancers exchanged roles in an effort to grasp repressed, "elementary" principles of movement and sophisticated group expressivity. The greatest of the male solo dancers from the expressionist era, Harald Kreutzberg, achieved the peak of his fame during the 1930s. Marianne Vogelsang and Dore Hoyer, whose artistry reached maturity after the war, began their careers during the Third Reich with an undisguised attachment to Expressionist values. The regime itself claimed ardent sympathizers from the Expressionist era: Jutta Klamt in Berlin promoted a sort of Aryanized modern dance which glorified a mystical, feminine relation between "blood and movement"; Heide Woog, Hanns Niedecken-Gebhard, and Lotte Wernike applied modern dance principles to the production of spectacular Nazi propaganda rallies.

But it was not a healthy period for German modern dance. Wigman retreated into melancholy, mythic images of a remote female heroic identity. Seeing that the regime would offer him no serious opportunities to develop his career, Laban emigrated to England in 1937, where he focused on movement education with practical applications to industry. But many others had already preceded him into exile, carrying the legacy of Expressionist dance to South America (Jooss, Wallmann), the United States (Hanya Holm, Lotte Goslar), and Australia (Gertrud Bodenwieser).

The immediate postwar era, however, was not especially congenial to German modern dance either. Older dancers, such as Wigman, Kreutzberg, and Palucca, managed to find audiences and students who remembered their earlier achievements, but the society which sought to build a "new" Germany nevertheless tended to adopt a deeply ambivalent attitude toward any modernist cultural impulses that might be held responsible for the Nazi catastrophe. Through-

out the late 1940s and the 1950s, ballet prospered in Germany to a greater degree than at any other time. In the schools, the prestige of American modern dance thinking reached its apogee. A genius of ecstatic and emotionally explosive Expressionist dancing like Dore Hoyer could find herself, in both Germany and America, so isolated and estranged from the cultural reality that she committed suicide in 1967. And yet the German ballet seemed unable to develop a distinctive or "Germanic" identity independently of Expressionist influences. In a sense, Expressionist values became institutionalized within an elaborate theatre system (rather than within an educational system) in which they became subordinate to the politically acceptable demands and authority of ballet technique and respect for narrative coherence.

The situation changed dramatically in the 1960s. When Jooss returned from England, he experienced considerable difficulty in re-establishing (1951) in Essen the Folkwang Dance School he had led so successfully in the years before the Third Reich. But by the 1960s, his notion of a dance technique based on the social-critical observation of movement in life had gained enough disciples who defined the identity of German modern dance for the rest of the century. With "Tanztheater," as articulated by Jooss, ballet and modern dance were not opposing forces but synthesized approaches to movement which dramatized the ways in which bodies encode socially determined power relations. Perhaps Jooss's most important student was Pina Bausch (b. 1940), who also studied briefly at Juilliard. As ballet director of the Wupperthal theatre, Bausch achieved huge international acclaim in the 1970s and 1980s for her flamboyantly ambitious productions. She expanded the scale of modern dance pieces to monumental dimensions and introduced an often intimidating and self-consciously controversial seriousness of purpose. Her works included spectacular stunts, complex gender reversals, "undanceable" musical accompaniments, convoluted variations within repetitions, extravagant theatrical devices, and cluttered stages which revealed the precarious conditions under which modern bodies moved skillfully and tragically through the obstacles, the debris, the "messes" created by history and contemporary environments.

Other major figures within the Tanztheater aesthetic included Susanne Linke, Gerhard Bochner, Reinhild Hoffmann, and Johan Kresnik, all favoring grandiose dramatic moods requiring the resources of large-scale, state-subsidized theatres. Tanztheater allowed Germany to become once again the dominant source of energy for European modern dance and to challenge even the authority of American modern dance. But this aesthetic was actually the apotheosis of the original aim of German modern dance—to use dance and "expressive movement" to define modern identity in terms of the body's power to impose itself on an "integrated" range contexts for describing reality: theatre, physical education, public space, collective action, psychological analysis, social reform, sexual reform, and cognitive evolution. Yet unlike American dance, with its center of gravity in New York, the vortex of German modern dance had no geographical specificity. It was never a unifying force within European dance culture because its lack of a central point of emanation implied that the chief value for modern dance lay in its power to amplify difference and free the body from pervasive, constraining pressures for unity of identity and a common destiny.

Publications

Bach, Rudolf, *Das Mary Wigman-Werk*, Dresden, 1933.
Brandenburg, Hans, *Der moderne Tanz*, Munich, 1921.

Laban, Rudolf, *Gymnastik und Tanz*, Oldenburg, 1926.

Lämmel, Rudolf, *Der moderne Tanz*, Berlin, 1928.

Manning, Susan A., *Ecstasy and the Demon: Feminism and Nationalism in the Dances of Mary Wigman*, Berkeley, 1993.

Mueller, Hedwig, *Mary Wigman. Leben und Werk der grossen Tänzerin*, Berlin, 1986.

Oberzaucher-Schüller, Gunhild, editor, *Ausdruckstanz*, Wilhelmshaven, 1992.

Scheper, Dirk, *Oskar Schlemmer. Das Triadischeballett und die Bauhausbühne*, Berlin, 1988.

Schlicher, Susanne, *TanzTheater*, Reinbek bei Hamburg, 1987.

Schmidt, Jochen, *Tanztheater in Deutschland*, Berlin, 1992.

Toepfer, Karl, *Empire of Ecstasy: Nudity, Movement, and German Body Culture, 1910-1935*, Berkeley, 1997.

Vietta, Egon, *Stage-Dancing in Germany*, Darmstadt, 1956.

—Karl Toepfer

GILLIS, Margie

Canadian dancer, choreographer, and company director

Born: Margaret Rose Gillis, 9 July 1953 in Montreal, Quebec. **Education**: Studied gymnastics, ballet, and adagio (with brother Christopher) with Mabel Bowlus; also studied with Eleanor Moore Ashton, Linda Sky Raine, and Linda Rabin (all Montreal), and May O'Donnell, Allen Wayne, and others in New York. **Career:** Began performing her own dances, gaining immediate popular acclaim; guest artist, Les Grands Ballets Canadiens, Paul Taylor Dance Company, Momix, Stephanie Ballard and Dancers, and in Martha Clarke's Off-Broadway production, *The Garden of Earthly Delights;* social, political and AIDS activist through performances in Germany, Hungary, Canada, and New York; taught self-developed kinesthetics and choreography, Jacob's Pillow, Oakland (California), Japan, the Philippines. **Awards:** Named Canadian Cultural Ambassador, 1981; Quebec Cultural Ambassador, 1986, touring France, Germany, Spain, Italy, Greece, New Zealand, Hong Kong, Malasia, India, Japan, the U.S.; Order of Canada, 1988.

Roles (commissioned by Gillis from other choreographers)

1978	*Estuaries* (John Goodwin), New York
1979	*Premonition* (Linda Rabin), Montreal
1982	*Duet* (Paul Taylor), Montreal
	Moi, King Kong (Paul-André Fortier), Montreal
	Thin Ice (C. Gillis), Montreal
1984	*Nocturne* (Martha Clarke), Toronto
	Lithium for Medea (Stephanie Ballard), Montreal
1986	*The Habit* (John Butler), Montreal
1987	*Prayer* (Ballard), New York
1988	*Spell It Out* (C. Gillis), Montreal
1989	*Luv's Alphabet* (C. Gillis), Montreal
	Mara (Ballard), Winnipeg
	Time Out (Ballard), Montreal
1992	*A Gathering* (Ballard), Montreal
1993	*Landscape* (C. Gillis), New York
1995	*The Farewell* (Pauline Koner), New York
1996	*Behind the Window, Inside the Courtyard, Where There's a Fountain* (Robert Wood), New York

	Los Hilos de Mi Sangre (Wood), Montreal
1997	*Helix* (Irene Dowd), New York

Other roles include: Group work and guest dancing in *Overspill* (Martha Karess), New York, 1976; *The White Goddess* (Linda Rabin), Montreal, 1976; *Hear After* (Leslie Dillingham), New York, 1976; *The Garden of Earthly Delights* (Martha Clarke), New York, 1984; *Dracula* (James Kudelka), Montreal, 1985; *Anna* (Stephanie Ballard), Winnipeg, 1987; *Continuum* (Stephanie Ballard), Winnipeg, 1990; *Andalusian Green* (C. Gillis), New York, 1992; *Icarus at Night* (C. Gillis), New York, 1994; *The Unveiling* (Robert Wood), New York, 1995; *Ascencion* (Wood), New York, 1996; *Momix* (Moses Pendelton), Princeton, 1996.

Works

1972	*Love Song* (mus. popular) Montreal
1973	*Willie* (mus. Joni Mitchell), Shango, Winnipeg
1974	*Words* (poetry and songs by Gillis), Vancouver
	Reflections (mus. Chard), Vancouver
	Entrance (mus. Chard), Vancouver
	Meditation (in silence), Vancouver
	Going Back (mus. Chard), Vancouver
1975	*Prison Blues* (mus.Chard) Vancouver
	Sombrero Sunday (mus. Chris Cherlock), Victoria
	The Dream (in silence), Vancouver
	Woman La Lune (mus. John Renbourn), Vancouver
	6 Songs (mus. Chris and Tommy Sherlock), Victoria
1976	*Sisters of Mercy* (mus. Leonard Cohen), Wyoming
1977	*Mercy (*mus. Loggins & Messina, Leonard Cohen), Winnipeg
1978	*Glacier* (poem, Jack Udashkin), New York
	Learning How to Die (mus. Louis Furey), Montreal
	Waltzing Matilda (mus. Tom Waits), Edmonton
	Clown (mus. Miriam Charney), New York
1979	*Lullaby* (mus. Bach), Montreal
	One (in silence), Montreal
1980	*On the Nickel* (mus. Tom Waits), Montreal
	Broken English (mus. Marianne Faithful), Toronto
	Once Upon a Time Right Now (mus. John Menegon), Montreal
	The Window (mus. Leonard Cohen), Montreal
	Untitled (in silence), Nancy, France
1981	*Jersey Girl* (mus. Tom Waits), Montreal
	Lush Life (mus. Michel Therrien), Montreal
1982	*Le X sur l'Endroit* w/Louis Guillemette and Jack Udashkin (mus. popular), Montreal
	Secrets (mus. Michel Therrien), Montreal
1983	*Give Me Your Heart Tonight* (mus. Shakin' Stevens), Montreal
	How the Rosehips Quiver (mus. Dalglish & Larsen), Montreal
	Third World Dream (mus. Talking Heads), Montreal
	Who Gets to Fly Anymore Anyway (mus. Talking Heads), Montreal
1984	*Untitled* (mus. Pachebel, Quebec City Orchestra), Montreal
1985	*Slipstream* (mus. Bach), Montreal
	Someone Missing (mus. Eugene Friesen), Montreal
1986	*Magritte* (mus. Paul Simon), Montreal
	The Little Animal (mus. Eugene Friesen), Montreal

Margie Gillis performing *Torn Roots, Broken Branches*. **Photograph © 1997 by Annie Leibovitz.**

Vers la Glace w/C. Gillis, James Kudelka (mus. Eugene Friesen and David Rothenberg), Montreal

1987   *Testimony of the Rose* (mus. Friesen), Montreal

1988   *From Grace's Garden* (mus. English madrigals), Montreal

Like the Moon Pulls the Tide (mus. Fabiano), Calgary

Roots of the Rhythm Remain (mus. Fabiano), Calgary

1989   *Bloom* (narrated by Siobhan McKenna), Montreal

1990   *Milkmaid* w/Paolo Styron, Marie Gourcault (mus. collage), never performed

Variations (mus. Bach), Prague

With Earth (mus. Bulgarian SR&T Female Choir), Montreal

1991   *Desert* (mus. Sinead O'Connor), Montreal

Je t'en prie (mus. Jean Lenoir), Montreal

Margret of Roseland w/Ballard (mus. various), Montreal

1992   *Bloom Two* (narrated by E.G. Marshall), Quebec

Hommage (mus. André Gagnon), Quebec

1993   *Ne me quitte pas* w/C. Gillis and Joao Mauricio (mus. Jacques Brel), Quebec

Torn Roots, Broken Branches (mus. Sinead O'Connor), New York

1994   *Empty Light* w/Ballard (mus. Akikazu Nakamura), Tokyo

Certains Cris (poem by Lise Vézina-Prévost; mus. André Prévost), Montreal

Untitled w/Danny Ezralow (mus. Aijub Ogada), New York

1995   *The Heaven I Cannot See* w/Paola Styron (mus. Purcell & Mahler), Toronto

The Stolen Child w/Brent Carver (mus. Jacques Brel, Evelyn Danzig), Montreal

Fallen Angels w/Robert LaFosse (mus. Steve Martnland), Columbus, Ohio

Dusk w/Joao Mauricio (mus. Bach, Vivaldi), Montreal

Seul le Désir w/Robert Wood (mus. Arvo Part), Lennoxville, Quebec

1996   *The Waltz* w/Rex Harrington (mus. Leonard Cohen), Toronto

I'm a Stranger Here Myself w/James Kudelka (mus. Kurt Weil), Toronto

Window of Loss w/Joao Mauricio (mus. Jacques Brel), Lake Placid, New York

Comme un pierre sur le ciel w/Mauricio (mus. Akikazu Nakamura), St-Florent le Vieil, France

Slipstream II (mus. Bach), Toronto

Miss Spider's Wedding (mus. Eugene Friesen, Steve Silverstein, Glen Velez), New York

Come by the Hills (mus. traditional), London, Ontario

1997   *The Dream* w/Rina Schenfeld (mus. John Oswald, Pie Liew, Eleni Kiandrow), Tel Aviv, Israel

Nothing Clings to You w/Paola Styron (mus. Friesen, Oswald), New York

Improv (mus. Ashley McIsaac), Vancouver

Lily of the Lamplight (mus. Carly Simon), New York

1998   *The Voyage* (mus. Gilles Vigneault, Gaetan Leboeuf), Ottawa

Publications

On GILLIS: books—

Alonzo, Anne-Marie, *La Danse des Marches,* Montreal, 1993.

Films and Videotapes

Body Emotions/Margie Gillis, prod./dir. Bernard Picard for CBC-TV, Montreal, 1981.

L'Univers de Margie Gillis, prod. Jean-Gaetan Seguin for Radio Quebec television, Montreal, 1985.

Eye on Dance, prod. Celia Ipiotis for Arc Videodance, documentary and interviews with Christopher and Margie Gillis, New York, 1990.

Certains Cris/En Avant la Musique, prod. James Dormier for Radio Canada television, Montreal, 1994.

Salute to Dancers for Life, prod. Veronica Tennant, CBC-TV, Toronto, 1994.

Celebrate the Earth, prod. Judith Murray/Donna Roberts, New Vue Productions, CBC-TV and YTV Canada Inc., 1995.

Wild Hearts in Strange Times, prod. Veronica Tennant, CBC-TV, Toronto, 1997.

*   *   *

Although Margie Gillis occasionally performs with other dancers and companies, she is known as a soloist of exceptional stage presence whose dances express an emotional reaction to internal forces. By dancing, as she says, "from the inside out," she combines physicality and spirituality in cathartic, highly personal moments.

Gillis came to the stage from outside mainstream dance. As a child she studied gymnastics, ballet and adagio, performing her first recital with her older brother Chris at the age of three. One of four children of an athletic family where both parents were Olympic skiers, Gillis as a teenager studied with several prominent teachers in New York and Montreal, began choreographing for herself, and briefly joined a short-lived company, Shango. Her first solo performances occurred in Vancouver in 1975. Two years later in Winnipeg she was received with amazement and wild enthusiasm at the Dance in Canada Conference, an annual gathering of dancers from across the country. Her stocky, sturdy body, so unlike those of most dancers, shuddered with passion, giving birth to her trademark jump

for joy during curtain calls. This was frequently followed by a flood of tears, as if there was no other way to release seething emotions triggered by dancing.

She quickly became a popular success, crisscrossing first Canada and later the world with programs that most always included *Mercy,* the Winnipeg showstopper. With her meter-length chestnut hair and her loose-fitting dresses, she raced and whirled about the stage, shifting directions suddenly as if she'd crashed into an invisible barrier, rolling and diving in huge arcs and flips to the strains of popular music and the feelings bubbling up from within her. *Mercy* became her signature piece along with the descriptive *Waltzing Mathilda* (1978), about a frowsy woman in a tattered flower dress whose pain and confusion was evidenced in stop-start staggerings and twistings on turned-in feet that culminated in wide embraces, falls and slides.

Gillis became a cult figure in her home city of Montreal. Her reputation as a folk heroine spread across the country and her concerts were generally sold out despite the fact that the Canadian modern dance movement was still in its infancy. Her popular success and personal charisma lead to comparisons with Isadora Duncan although the two had little in common except an overwhelming need to perform. Gillis' exceptional expressiveness and her gift for emotional nuance won further acclaim in China where in 1979 she became the first modern dancer to appear since the Cultural Revolution. Extensive touring in Asia, Europe, and New Zealand as well as North America followed. Canada's Prime Minister Pierre Trudeau named her a Canadian cultural ambassador in 1981. She received a similar honor five years later from her native Quebec. The Order of Canada was bestowed on her in 1988.

Unwilling to set boundaries for herself in her early days, Gillis danced whenever the mood struck—in parks, on streets, on concrete floors as well as in small theatres, huge halls and stadiums. Her spontaneity endeared her to her public but raised concern—and jealousy—among her peers who never took her seriously. She is not known to Canadians as a teacher, although she has taught her self-developed method of active kinesthesis throughout the U.S. and in Asia. This process of manifesting thought, emotion, imagination and spirituality through muscle action is the basis of all her choreography.

Gillis choreographed a large body of works for herself dealing mainly with her response to themes dictated by music or personal and social concerns. She was one of the first Canadian dancers to take up social causes, becoming a presence at many international concerts, particularly AIDS' benefits. Her brother Christopher's death in 1993 left its mark on her dancing. Her solos became much more somber and introspective, riskiness and daring were restrained, the curtain of hair that had swung loose and wild in hair shows that often drew more attention than her dancing, was braided or bound. But the dances were as impassioned and evocative as ever as she used her grief to help her explore deeper ways of expressing herself.

Gillis began commissioning occasional works in 1979. Paul Tayor, with whose company Christopher danced for 17 years and with which she would later guest, made *Duet* for the brother and sister in 1982. Christopher choreographed his first works for Margie and himself and appeared with her regularly in Montreal and New York. As her career progressed, Margie commissioned dances from choreographer-friends, a couple of whom gave her rights to perform their own solos. Martha Clarke offered *Nocturne* in 1984. In 1995, Pauline Koner, then 82, whose career with the Limón Dance Company spanned 43 years, made Gillis the only dancer besides herself to perform *The Farewell* (1962) which was dedicated to Doris Humphrey.

—Linde Howe-Beck

GLASSER, Sylvia

South African dancer, choreographer, educator, and company director

Born: Sylvia Rhoda Brenner, 1 December 1940 in Pietersburg, South Africa. **Education:** Diploma, London College of Dance and Drama, 1963; studied at the schools of Martha Graham, Erick Hawkins, and Merce Cunningham, New York, 1970; Witwatersrand University (Johannesburg), B.A. 1973; University of Houston, M.A. 1977; studied with Alwin Nikolais and Murray Louis, New York, 1984. **Career:** Founder/director, Experimental Dance Theatre, 1967-76; taught workshops, beginning 1976; taught in the U.S. (Texas, Illinois, New York), 1977; founder/artistic director, Moving Into Dance Performing Company (MID), 1978; formed Community Dance Teacher's Training Course, 1992; has taught, lectured, and toured with MID in Australia, Canada, Spain, the U.S.A and Holland **Awards:** David Webster Memorial Award, 1990; nominated for AA Vita Award for choreography, 1992; FNB Vita Choreographer of the Year award, South Africa, 1994.

Works

1967	*The Book of the Dead* (mus. Liszt)
1968	*Pavane* (mus. Ravel)
	The Bond (mus. Stravinsky)
1969	*Time Out* (mus. Brubeck)
1971	*Threnody to the Victims of Hiroshima* (mus. Penderecki)
	Mikrokosmos (mus. Bartók)
1972	*The Hollow Men* (mus. Kabelac)
	Bach '72 (mus. Bach)
1973	*Uirapuru* (mus. Villa-Lobos)
	Anatomy of a Dance (mus. Newcater)
	Spirals (mus. Earl Brown)
1974	*Collage on Time—T.S. Eliot* (mus. Stockhausen, Wells, Kagel, Ohana, Brubeck)
1975	*Just for Fun* (mus. Stravinsky)
	Woman (mus. Hindemith)
1976	*Constructures* (mus. Partch)
1977	*Primal Pulse* (mus. traditional)
	Monody (mus. Penderecki, Gregorian Chant)
1978	*Flow-By Fly-High* (mus. Santa Esmeralda)
	Vortex of Fear (mus. collage)
1979	*Die Lied van die Reen* (mus. traditional)
1980	*Creation of Death* (mus. Milhaud)
1981	*Icarus* (mus. Pousseur)
	Dreamdance (mus. Glass)
	Die Vaal Kostertjie (mus. traditional)
1982	*Black Orpheus* (mus. Jobin & Bonfa)
	Not for Squares (mus. 16th-century court dances, St. Marie, Blood, Sweat & Tears)
	Take 5 (mus. Brubeck)
	Rebecca (mus. Villa-Lobos)
	Glasser on Glass (mus. Glass)
1983	*Die Siel van die Mier* (mus. Partch)
	Signs of the Zodiac (mus. Stockhausen)
	Turn Back my Daughters (mus. Bartók)
	Net 'n Bietjie Bach (mus. Bach)
1984	*There Is a Dream Dreaming Us* (mus. traditional African)
	Raindance (mus. Phillips)
	African Litany (mus. Juluka)
1985	*Show Orff* (mus. Orff)
1986	*For Whom the Bell Tolls* (mus. Penderecki, Queen, Beethoven, Sibelius)
	Sounds Great (mus. Kinsey)
	Press Freedom (mus. Weather Report)
	The Flaming Terrapin (mus. Malan)
1987	*The Mind Also Moves* (mus. collage)
	Rattle Dance (mus. ankle-rattles and drums)
1988	*There Is Only the Dance* (mus. Vollenweider)
	Man Is an Island (mus. African drums, Glass; 16th-century court dances)
1989	*African Cassandra* (mus. Naidoo)
	Dansynergy (mus. Naidoo)
1990	*Signals Signs & Whatnots* (mus. Mapfumo)
	African Evocation (mus. Azumah)
1991	*Tranceformations* (mus. Naidoo)
	Paths of Sound (mus. Mbuli)
1992	*Midnight of the Soul* (mus. James)
1993	*African Spring* (mus. Vivaldi)
	Zimbili—They Are Two (mus. Roth)
1994	*Stone Cast Ritual* (mus. Roth)

Publications

By GLASSER: articles—

"Encounter with Nikolais/Louis," *Arabesque*, February 1984.
"Dance in Canada Conference," *Arabesque*, November 1984.
"An Interview with Alwin Nikolais," *Arabesque*, February 1986.
"An Interview with Billyan Billay," *Arabesque*, March 1986.
"Is Dance Political Movement?," *Dance Journal*, 1990.
"Fusing the Divided," AADE Conference Perth, Australia, January 1991.
"Appropriation and Appreciation," Joint Conference of the Society of Dance History Scholars and the Congress on Research in Dance (CORD), New York, June 1993.
"The Notion of Primitive Dance," *Journal for the Anthropological Study of Human Movement*, 1993.
"Turning Disadvantage into Advantage through Dance in South Africa," 12th IAPESGW Congress, Melbourne, Australia, July/August, 1993.
"Transcultural Trans(ce)formation," CORD Conference, Miami, November 1995.
"Transcultural Trans(ce)formation," *Journal of Visual Anthropology*, 1996.

Films and Videotapes

Performances televised on SABC-TV: *Just for Fun, Spirals, Whirlygigs* (children), *Dies Lied van die Reen* and *Die Vaal Koestertjie* (both based on stories by Eugene Marais), *Net 'n Bietjie Bach,*

Anatomy of Dance, and *Tranceformations;* also choreographed for SABC-TV programs *Kraaines* and *Met Trompet en Tambour.*

*   *   *

South African choreographer and educator Sylvia Glasser first taught classical ballet and modern dance in the early 1960s. She formed the Experimental Dance Theater performance group in 1967 and working in her garage studio began developing and teaching her unique movement style. She stopped teaching ballet and modern and from 1971 concentrated on a movement voice of her own. In 1978 Glasser founded the Moving Into Dance Performing Company and School, and by 1987 the fledgling organization was able to move to the more accessible Braamfontein Recreation Center. Ten years later, MID took up residence in its own building "Mophatong wa Thabo" in the inner city development of the Newtown Cultural Precinct of Johannesburg; it has won several awards, toured all over the world, had its performances telecast on SABC-TV, performed at the inauguration of President Mandela in May of 1994, and for Queen Beatrix of the Netherlands in 1996.

Early influences in Glasser's dance career include Martha Graham, Erick Hawkins, Merce Cunningham, and Alwin Nikolais, as well as classical ballet. The turning point in her life came from her growing interest in African music and dance, through her contact with father and son enthnomusicologists Andrew and Hugh Tracey. Glasser began to channel a specifically African influence into the content of her work; her first choreography on this journey was *Primal Pulse* in 1977, performed by an all-white American cast in Houston. This work was later performed in 1978 in the Box Theater at the University of the Witwatersrand in South Africa, but ironically, though all the dancers were South African, they too were also all white. Glasser's response was to found the Moving Into Dance Performance Company in 1978, as a nonracial dance group. Apartheid issues were still law in South Africa at this time, so the startup of this racially integrated dance company was a great challenge to the government.

Glasser's interest in understanding African culture had grown through her studies in anthropology at the University of the Witwatersrand. She completed three years of study and was awarded the David Webster Memorial Award for academic excellence. She also worked closely with Professor David Lewis-Williams, the curator of the Rock Art Research Unit at the University of the Witwatersrand. This connection would have a great impact on the creation of the award-winning *Tranceformations* (1991). Some of Glasser's other pieces for MID exploring Afro-fusion identity include earlier works *Raindance* and *There's a Dream Dreaming Us* from 1984, *Dansynergy* from 1989, *African Spring* (1993), *Stone Cast Ritual* (1994), and her 1997 work *Passage of Rites.* As artistic and executive director of MID, Glasser has influenced and taught a new generation of dancers and choreographers who have formed new community dance groups in South Africa, like the Soweto Dance Theatre, Border Youth, the Creators, and the Soweto Community Dance Project.

As a dance educator, academic, and author Glasser has addressed many international conferences. In 1995 she presented a lecture demonstration on the topic of "Transcultural Transformations" at the CORD (Congress on Research in Dance) Conference in Miami, Florida, and in 1997 was a keynote speaker at the daCi Conference presenting a paper on "Dancing to the Dynamics of Cultural Diversity." The same year, she presented a paper on "Appropriation and Appreciation" of South African dance at the International Conference for Dance and Music at the University of Cape Town. The work of Sylvia Glasser as an educator and choreographer has been disseminated throughout Africa and South Africa, as well as in Europe, Australia and the United States. MID's Afro-fusion dance technique and choreographic style is an original and unusual trademark of South African dance heritage, especially from 1978 to today. Glasser has been the primary initiator and collaborator who has nurtured and strengthened this new modern dance experience.

—Jill Waterman

GOLDIN, Daniel
Argentine dancer, choreographer, and company director

Born: 14 July 1958 in Buenos Aires. **Education:** Studied contemporary dance at the Teatro Municipal General San Martín with, among others, Renate Schottelius and Cristina Barniels, 1980-86. **Career:** Dancer, Ballet Contemporanéo of the Teatro Municipal General San Martín; went to Germany to attend the Folkwang-Hochschule in Essen, 1987; studied with Hans Züllig, Jean Cébron, and Lutz Förster; member of the Folkwang Tanzstudio and guest dancer in Pina Bausch's company in Wuppertal; director, Tanztheater at the Städtische Bühnen, Münster from 1996.

Works

1986	*La peregrinación* (mus. Cao), 7th Concurso de las Artes y las Ciencas de Argentina, Buenos Aires
1992	*La sombra y la luna* (mus. Cao, Seoane, and traditional music of Connemara), Cagliari, Italy
1993	*A la deriva* (mus. Borodin, traditional music of Galicia), Teatro delle Saline, Cagliari, Italy
1994	*Alborada* (mus. Cao), Theater im Pumpenhaus, Münster
	Cuentos del camino: Wegerzählungen (consisting of *La peregrinación, La sombra y la luna, A la deriva, Alborada*), Théâtre Toursky, Marseille
	Finisterre (mus. Cao, Seoane, and traditional music), Theater Satiricon, Essen; revised 1997, Städtische Bühnen, Münster
1995	*Papirene Kinder* (mus. Smetana, Mendelssohn, Bartholdy, Bruch, et al), Stadttheater, Krefeld
1996	*Esperas* (mus. Shostakovitch), Ruhrfestspielhaus, Recklinghausen
1997	*Cancionero: Liederbuch* (mus. Barrios and traditional Latin American), Städtische Bühnen, Münster
	Labyrinth w/Daniel Condamines (mus. Bach et al, and traditional Japanese, Korean, and Greek), Städtische Bühnen, Münster

*   *   *

Daniel Goldin's works are about the recollections and the emotions generated by his interest in individual past and collective experience. The choreographer himself, son of Ukranian Jewish immigrants and born in Buenos Aires in 1958, walks along the borders: educated in Buenos Aires at the Teatro Municipal General San Martín and by Renate Schottelius (a former pupil of Mary

Wigman who emigrated to Argentina during the Third Reich and who exerted the strongest influence on Goldin), he went to Germany in 1986, having seen performances of Pina Bausch's and Susanne Linke's companies in Argentina. At the Folkwang-Hochschule in Essen he deepened his knowledge of German dance and continued with his series of duets which he had started with *La peregrinación.* The following pieces, *La sombra y la luna, A la deriva,* and *Alborada,* all deal with the world of Galician farmers, and later Goldin put all four into an evening-length production. The four duets exemplify Goldin's ability to find suitable movements in a well-structured and concentrated form. The pilgrim routes to Santiago de Compostela and their myths are the subject of *Finisterre.* Goldin picked up a different theme in *Papirene Kinder:* how to live as a Jew after the Third Reich. In this piece, he created intense images ranging from Jews freed from a concentration camp to their finding a new beginning. With *Cancionero: Liederbuch,* Goldin's first evening-length work as director of the Tanztheater company attached to the Städtische Bühnen in Münster, he returned to the continent of his childhood, bringing to the stage a pastiche of daily life in Latin America at the edge of nature's and society's destructive forces.

Goldin often uses traditional music, not unusual for choreographers in the Tanztheater tradition, though not in an arbitrary postmodern way. For Goldin, music is important in that it creates an atmosphere in which his choreographic "narrations" unfold. Goldin's use of traditional music shows a significant difference from most Tanztheater choreographers; unlike Bausch, for example, in whose pieces traditional music serves as mere background to the presentation of universal patterns of human behavior, Goldin chooses his music in accordance with the overall topic. The result is always a very coherent work. However, *Esperas* and *Labyrinth* are more than other pieces reflections of humankind's contemporary state.

Goldin's choreographic oeuvre is distinguished by a highly poetic quality, whereas his movement vocabulary seems rather purist, cleverly making use of recurrent motifs. It is a contemporary adaptation of the expressive Folkwang tradition to a personal modern dance idiom.

—Katja Schneider

GOODE, Joe

American and dancer, choreographer, actor, director, writer, and company director

Born: 1950 in Presque Isle, Maine. **Education:** Studied ballet, tap, hula, and baton; B.A. in theater arts, Virginia Commonwealth University, 1973; actor and budding writer/director, the Performing Garage; studied with Merce Cunningham, Viola Farber, Finis Jhung; performed in chorus lines in Yiddish theatre and with Sophie Maslow, Twyla Tharp, 1973-77; member, Margaret Jenkins Dance Company, 1979-81; first independent choreography, 1982; first solo concert, American Inroads Series, San Francisco, 1983; founder and artistic director, Joe Goode Performance Group, beginning 1986; appeared on *Alive from Off-Center* by KQED-TV with *29 Effeminate Gestures,* 1989; Dance on Camera Festival, New York, *Goode Travels,* feature documentary (Julie Miller Productions), 1995. **Awards:** National Endowment for the Arts choreographic fellowships, 1985-88; Wallace Alexander Gerbode Foundation Interdisci-

plinary Arts Award, 1989; Dance Bay Area Isadora Duncan Dance Award for Outstanding Achievement in Performance and in Choreography, 1987, 1990; California Arts Council Artist Fellowship, 1991; American Council for the Arts Dewar's Profiles Performance Art Award in Choreography, 1991, 1992; film and video *Without a Place* (produced by Julie Miller Productions), 1992, San Francisco Business Arts Council Artistic Excellence Award, 1994; Pew Charitable Trusts/New York Foundation for the Arts National Dance Residency Program Grant, 1995; Isadora Duncan Dance Award, 1997.

Works

1984	*I'm Sorry*
1987	*29 Effeminate Gestures,* Bay Area Dance Series, Oakland
1988	*The Ascension of Big Linda into the Skies of Montana* w/ artist James Morris, San Francisco
1989	*The Disaster Series* w/artist James Morris, San Francisco
1990	*Remembering the Pool at the Best Western* w/artist and architect Stanley Saitowitz, Zellerbach Playhouse, Berkeley
	The Reconditioning Room for Capp Street Project/AVT, San Francisco
1991	*Their Names Must Be Spoken,* in commemoration of World Aids Day 1991, San Francisco
1992	*Seven Meditations on Murder in the Family,* for the Pennsylvania Ballet, Philadelphia
	Down a Small Path, Zenon Dance Company, Minneapolis
	Without a Place, for Theater Artaud, San Francisco
1993	*Convenience Boy* for NEA Presenting and Commissioning Program, Columbia College, Chicago
1994	*Whisper It to Me in My Ear,* Joyce Theater, New York
1995	*In This Dream I Had,* for Mills College, Oakland
	Take/Place w/Beth Custer, San Francisco
1996	*The Maverick Strain* w/Nayland Blake (mus. Beth Custer, Club Foot Orchestra Quintet), San Francisco
1997	*Four Feelings,* San Francisco

Publications

Adams, K. B., "Artist Brings Life Experience to Performance Art," *Cincinnati Enquirer,* 25 September 1989.

Felciano, Rita, "Anything Can Happen: Joe Goode's Impressive *Disaster,*" *San Francisco Bay Guardian,* 5 July 1989.

———, "Goode on Their Feet," *San Francisco Bay Guardian,* 1 May 1991.

———, "Goode Thing: Joe Goode Uses Movement to Highlight Finely Drawn *Monologues,*" *San Francisco Bay Guardian,* 18 May 1994.

Kisselgoff, Anna, "Goode Group Offers Irony and Wit in New York Debut," *New York Times,* 21 January 1994.

Ross, J., "Working Hard to be the Bad Boy of Modern Dance," *Dance Magazine,* January 1989.

Segal, Lewis, "Enter a Troublemaker with a Watering Can," *Los Angeles Times,* 20 May 1989.

Shank, T., "Joe Goode's Performance Lifestyle: An Interview with Theodore Shank," *Theatre Forum: International Theatre Journal,* September/Fall 1994.

Tucker, M., "Joe Goode Troupe's Provocative *Big Linda,*" *San Francisco Chronicle,* 6 September 1986.

Joe Goode (standing) performing *Convenience Boy* with Wayne Harrand. Photograph © Johan Elbers.

Tucker, M., "Joe Goode's *Disaster*—It's Anything But," *San Francisco Chronicle,* 8 July 1989.

Ulrich, A., "Voyage of Self-Discovery in a Motel Swimming Pool," *San Francisco Examiner,* 2 June 1990.

Zimmer, E., "Joe Goode's Wild Ride," *San Francisco Sentinel, Inside Arts,* 2 June 1991.

Films and Videotapes

29 Effeminate Gestures, for *Alive from Off-Center*, KQED-TV, 1989.

Without a Place, Julie Miller Productions, 1992.

Stareways w/filmmaker Tim Boxell, San Francisco, 1994.

Goode Travels, documentary, Julie Miller Productions, 1995.

*   *   *

Little in Joe Goode's early years would seem to have prepared him for life as a champion postmodern raconteur. Choreographer/dancer, director/actor, writer/satirist, Goode knew he was a performer at eight years of age. Since childhood, his passionate love affair with language and writing has inspired investigations of fantasies, daydreams, memories and inner drives.

Goode was born in 1950 in Presque Isle, Maine, 40 miles south of Canada. He moved to Virginia early in his life where his father, a journalist, bought a newspaper. His mother had been a dancer of sorts, performing in swing-era nightclubs in New York City. What led Goode to his first ballet lesson was the proverbial follow-your-sister-to-dance-class route. By high school he was performing with a local civic ballet company. He began to feel dissatisfied that there was no place in his dancing for his love of language. Goode decided to redirect himself in the theatre because he felt it was a more literate form of expression.

After studying acting and earning his B.F.A. in drama from Virginia Commonwealth in 1973, Goode left for New York and for the next five years became a regular on the off-Broadway circuit, dancing in chorus lines in Yiddish theatre, performing in avant-garde plays and taking classes from Merce Cunningham, Viola Farber, and Finis Jhung. He danced with Sophie Maslow on Broadway and briefly performed with Twyla Tharp's dance company. At the Performing Garage, he worked in experimental plays by Richard Scheckner and Joseph Chakin and wrote and directed his own plays. His work as an actor/director in New York's experimental theatre movement brought depth and focus into his soon-to-be created theatrical/dance works.

In the fall of 1977 at the age of 26, Goode moved to San Francisco. In 1979 he joined Margaret Jenkins' dance company and performed with the group for three years. In the early 1980s, Goode began to create dances for himself. His first were born of a time when the impersonal legacy of postmodern dance was being challenged by an international outburst of theatrical Expressionistic stagings. Pina Bausch's Germanic ballets of interpersonal conflict and Japan's "dance of the dark soul" Butoh movement used the threads of Expressionism to move dance into a new phase. For the zeitgeist of the time, the human soul was back on stage. Like his artistic predecessors, e.g., Fokine, Cecchetti, and Jaques-Dalcroze, Goode's theatrical dances sought to reflect naturalism.

At the beginning of 1981, Goode's tragic love affair with a cowboy from Yukon, Oklahoma, was a logical place for him to begin as a young choreographer/writer. But Goode's dance—designed as an important and serious piece—elicited the opposite response from the audience; they thought it was hilarious. "The piece," said Goode, "was a rather bizarre arrangement of sound and movement." His use of sexually explicit language in *Yukon, Oklahoma,* earned him the nickname of "the Sam Shepard of dance."

Many of his early solo dances are essays about male and female loneliness, narcissism, and the frustrations and crossed communications of couples. He made a duet, *Her Song,* in the mid-1980s for himself and his actress-sister. The dance is filled with the anger of nasty bickering that results when social pressures trickle down into the intimate moments of family life.

His other dances were concerned with making private histories ring with some kind of universal truth. In 1989 Goode created the *Disaster Series* which was influenced by playwright Samuel Beckett, who wrote a one-act play about a private disaster called *Catastrophe,* and by visual artist Andy Warhol, who invoked tabloid disasters by incorporating newspaper images in his early paintings. In one section of Goode's *Disaster Series,* a woman begins to speak with a whisper that quickly builds to a scream, while quietly stepping into the performance space, wedging herself up into one corner of the room like a moth climbing to a window sill.

The 1980s found the new American dance taking on a more confessional perspective. American choreography had two uniquely human signatures: humor and hope. Goode has taken humor as his cathartic signature; it resonates in all of his danceworks from his early days as a choreographer. Maintaining a knack for self-deprecating humor, Goode believes that people need to keep laughing at themselves and especially at life's tragedies.

Many of his dances provoke social and political concerns and explore taboos and fears we supress. *Remembering the Pool at the Best Western* (1990) is a conversation with a dying man about what dying might be like. Like other Goode pieces it deals with events that are puzzling, accidental, unexpected, often out of control. He specifically dares to be open and celebratory about his sexuality. Goode's solo *29 Effeminate Gestures* is structurally pure classicism with its theme and variations; it's about tolerance and society's homophobic fear and disapproval. Goode states, "I am interested in what it means for someone who is gay to make art that is informed by his sensibility as a gay person; by his mandatory suffering, which I feel is a large part of being gay; by his mandatory alienation; by his inclusion of a feminine sensibility. That's who I am, and all those things come into play every time I walk into a studio."

In a 1984 solo Goode capitalized on the phrase, *"I'm Sorry"* (using Brenda Lee's popular 1950s song with the same title), by creating a character of a "former Catholic boy's apology for what he has become." *I'm Sorry* was a liturgical lament "for being a homosexual man in a culture that wants macho heroes, for being an artist in a society that wants steady wage-earners, and for being a dancer who, instead of offering complacent viewing, puts these issues before audiences."

Goode formed his group, the Joe Goode Performing Dance Company, in 1986. His dancers are expected to be strong actors as well as trained movers, and they must have the ability to speak text while executing difficult sequences of movements. His company's working process involves the collision of sound and movement into surprising sequences that scramble the familiar. "It's like dealing with two sides of your personality at the same time," Goode has reflected. He will start a new dancework with what he calls " a superimage." For instance, *Whisper It to Me in My Ear* (1994) grew out of a dialogue between person and place: "Can we be together? Can I possess you? Can you possess me?"

His trademark in his earlier choreography was one of pairing "pruned, controlled dancing with wild, screaming vocals" and "all-too-human gestures next to crisp poetic imagery." Recent danceworks have evolved from "performance art to performance architecture." In *Markers* (1992) Goode changed the focus from breaking boundaries to connecting them. His cross-genre performances brought content to the fore. His recent pieces speak more clearly about real life as he designs structures of formal theatre. For example, *Remembering the Pool at the Best Western,* (1990) explores moments of grief and loss, *Without a Place* (1992) examines the relationship between two women, and *Convenience Boy* (1993) probes emotional themes of cultural disposability.

Through the end of the 1980s and into the 1990s, Joe Goode's Performance Group has gained a commanding reputation in the international and national dance community. Goode's danceworks are now in the repertoires of prestigious modern and ballet companies in the United States. He remains focused on the human condition and its innermost mysteries.

—Jennifer Predock-Linnell

GORDON, David
American dancer and choreographer

Born: New York City, 14 July 1936. **Education:** Degree in fine arts from Brooklyn College; studied dance with Merce Cunningham. **Family:** Married Valda Setterfield; one child. **Career:** Performed in the companies of James Waring and Yvonne Rainer in the 1960s; founding member of the improvisational group, The Grand Union; founder, Pick Up Performance Company, 1971; director of plays for the stage. Panelist and chairman of the dance program panel of the NEA. **Awards:** Guggenheim Fellowships, 1981, 1987; New York Dance and Performance Award ("Bessie") and Obie award for the play *The Mysteries and What's So Funny?*; Obie award for *The Family Business,* 1994; National Theatre Artist Residency Grant, Pew Charitable Trusts, 1995.

Works

1962	*Mama Goes Where Papa Goes*
	Mannequin Dance
	Helen's Dance
1963	*Random Breakfast*
	Honey Sweetie Dust Dance
1964	*Silver Pieces (Fragments)*
1966	*Walks and Digressions*
1971	*Sleepwalking*

1972   *Liberty*
      The Matter (I)
      The Matter (II)
      One Part of the Matter
      Oh Yes
      6-Incidents (with Douglas Dunn)
      David Gordon Doing Windows
1974   *Spilled Milk Variations*
      One Act Play
      Chair, Alternatives 1 through 5
1975   *Chair (plus Symmetrical Form 1975)*
1976   *Times Four*
      Personal Inventory
      Times Four
1977   *Wordsworth and the Motor*
1978   *Not Necessarily Recognizable Objectives (or Wordsworth Rides Again)*
      What Happened
      Mixed Solo
1979   *An Audience with the Pope, or This Is Where I Came In*
      The Matter (Plus and Minus)
      Close Up
      Song and Dance
      Solo Score
      Lifting Duet
1980   *By Two*
      Untitled Solo (as a trio)
      Dorothy and Eileen
      Untitled solo with unlimited backup group
      Double Identity Part One
      Soft Broil
1981   *Pas et Par*, Theatre du Silence, Lyons, France
      Big Eyes (Grote Ogen), Werkcentrum Dans, the Netherlands
      Phone Call
      Double Identity Part Two
      Profile
      Counter Revolution, Extemporary Dance Theatre, London
1982   *T.V. Reel*
      10 Minute T.V.
      Trying Times
      Big Eyes II
1983   *Passing Through*, Sharir Dance Company, Texas
      Limited Partnership, New Dance Ensemble, Minnesota
      The Photographer, Brooklyn Academy of Music Next Wave Festival
      Framework
      Short Order, Ohad Naharin Dance Company
      Passing Sentence, Concert Dance Company, Boston
1984   *Negotiable Bonds*, Stuart Pimsler Dance Theater
      Field Study, Extemporary Dance Theatre, London
      Piano Movers, Dance Theatre of Harlem
      My Folks
      A Plain Romance Explained
1985   *Field, Chair and Mountain*, American Ballet Theatre
      Beethoven and Boothe, Group Recherche Choregraphique de l'Opéra de Paris
      Four Cornered Moon, Clive Thompson Dance Company
      Offenbach Suite
      Nine Lives

      Four Man Nine Lives
      Eleven Women in Reduced Circumstances, New York University
1986   *Panel* (television work; produced by KTCA/*Alive from Off-Center*)
      Renard (director), Spoleto USA Festival
      Transparent Means for Travelling Light
      The Seasons
      Murder, American Ballet Theatre
      Bach and Offenbach, Extemporary Dance Theatre, London
1987   *David Gordon's Made in U.S.A.* (television work; PBS/*Great Performances*)
      Minnesota
      The Seasons
1988   *Pounding the Beat, and Slaughter*
      My Folks (television work; co-production with BBC)
      Mates, Rambert Dance Company, London
      Sang and Sang
      Four Stories, New York University
1989   *United States*
      Birds, Trees and the Birthday of Congress
      Weather
1991   *The Mysteries and What's So Funny?* (musical drama; also writer and director)
1992   *Punch and Judy Get Divorced* (television work: KTCA/ALIVE TV)
      Punch and Judy (Dance for White Oak Dance Project)
1994   *The Family Business* w/Ain Gordon (musical drama), Dance Theater Workshop, New York
1995   *The Firebugs* (musical drama; also director), Guthrie Theater, Minneapolis
1996   *Punch and Judy Get Divorced* (musical drama; also director; with Ain Gordon), American Music Theater Festival
1997   *Silent Movie* w/Ain Gordon

Publications

On GORDON: books—

Banes, Sally, *Terpsichore in Sneakers*, Boston, 1980.
Croce, Arlene, *Sight Lines*, New York, 1987.

Films and Videotapes

Dance in America: Beyond the Mainstream, directed by Merrill Brockway for WNET-TV, 1980; *Dance in America*, directed by Don Mischer, WNET-TV for *Great Performances*, 1987.

*   *   *

David Gordon was a witness to and co-creator of postmodern dance. Gordon started performing professionally with James Waring's Company in 1956, while he was earning a degree in fine arts at Brooklyn College. In the early 1960s he choreographed works that flouted many of the conventions of modern dance: the literal, the narrative, formalized choreography, and physical virtuosity. In the mid-1960s he and many of his peers became disenchanted with choreography. Gordon, Yvonne Rainer, Barbara Dilley, Steve Paxton, Douglas Dunn, Trisha Brown, Becky Arnold, and

Nancy Lewis formed The Grand Union, an improvisational group that performed from 1970 until its demise in 1976. Gordon emerged from Grand Union a more refined and competent choreographer. He has since choreographed for such companies as the American Ballet Theater and Dance Theatre of Harlem. In 1971 Gordon formed the still-active Pick Up Performance Company.

Gordon's work is humorous and subtly iconoclastic. The movements are easy, appearing effortless in execution with repetition as an essential device. Also predominant in Gordon's work is his use of wordplay that is rife with puns and double entendres; sentences that double back upon themselves and spin off into new dimensions. He constantly reframes the habitual into something the viewer might forever miss were it not for Gordon's restructuring focus. Arlene Croce in *Sight Lines* (1987) refers to Gordon as a "collagist" because many of his themes, motifs, and ideas frequently show up reconfigured in later works. Gordon defines himself as a "reinventor," stating in 1980's *Dance in America*, "I don't think there is anything left to invent, I think there are only new combinations of things and a new way of looking at something and a new way of showing somebody else to look at something and that's a kind of reinvention." Gordon's predilection to reinvent and his collagist tendencies are most graphically evident in his consistent use of the common folding chair.

Gordon's first work using the chair in 1974 was *Chair, Alternatives 1 through 5*. In *Excerpt from Chair*, filmed in 1980 for *Dance in America*, Gordon and wife Valda Setterfield stand facing the audience several feet in front of two blue-enamel folding chairs. They look at each other and take an arcing clockwise path to the chairs, they sit and cross one leg over the other. So far nothing unusual has occurred, but hereafter everything is out of the ordinary. They fall off the chair. Catching the momentum with both hands they recover to stand with backs to the audience, turn and step on and over the chair. The chair now evolves before the viewer's eyes into a toy, then a bed. Next it is slipped on as a long garment pulled along the length of the prone body, then wiggled through as a snake would shed its skin. Stepped onto, into, around, under and through, the chair becomes a metaphor for the breaking of everyday rote behavior. Chairs will never seem the same to the viewer. In Gordon's mode the movements are easy and unhurried; although he and Setterfield perform the same pattern clearly they are unconcerned with staying in unison. The viewer is confronted by the limitlessness of the chair's use and by the ways life becomes restricted by the maintenance of such things as the acceptable way to use a chair.

The chair returns again in Gordon's *Made in the U.S.A.* (for WNET-TV's *Great Performances,* 1987) near the end of a duet with Setterfield and Mikhail Baryshnikov. He shoves the chair across the stage toward Setterfield; she sits, crosses her legs, stands, and Baryshnikov sits. They engage in a rather polite encounter filled with a dialogue that two people might have during a walk in the park; the chair's presence does nothing to shatter their gentle repartee. They take turns sitting upon the chair and each other; when Setterfield admonishes Baryshnikov to "go west" he takes the chair and pushes it like a baby carriage across the stage and into its next reincarnation: *TV Nine Lives* (1987).

Performed with six dancers and one chair this episode of the chair's evolution often resorts to slapstick. Dancers are costumed in plaids, stripes, baggy pants, vests, ties, and fedoras. Behind them, a cartoon-like backdrop of mountains is colored by similar plaid patterns with chairs piled on top in random disarray. The musical score is a medley of old time western tunes, each of which

includes lyrics that mention different states and towns across the United States. With more bodies have come more possibilities with which to explore the myriad ways a chair can be danced. Despite so many dancers the chair remains the focal point; the bodies move with typical Gordon ease. However, pantomime, not seen in the earlier works, is rampant here as is greater physicality and dynamic changes. The chair becomes a literal object: a scooter, a lookout point, a weapon. Its presence (in earlier works) as a metaphorical object has given way to the literal; here the imagination of the viewer is entertained rather than invoked. The work ends with a barroom shootout as now the chair, banged on the floor, replicates gunshots as Baryshnikov twitches and writhes to the floor in death.

—Holly Parke Harris

GOSLAR, Lotte

German-American dancer, clown, choreographer, and company director

Born: 1907 in Dresden, Germany. **Education:** Studied at Mary Wigman's school, and with Gret Palucca, 1920s. **Career:** Joined Gret Palucca's company; cabaret performer, combining mime, clown, and dance; joined the Peppermill Revue, directed by Erika and Klaus Mann, Prague, 1933; worked with George Voskovec and Jan Werich, Prague, mid-1930s; toured to U.S. with Peppermill Revue, 1937; performed at Turnabout Theatre in Los Angeles, 1943-53; ran a studio in Los Angeles and tutored film actors in movement and acting; founded Pantomime Circus, 1954. **Died:** 16 October 1997 in Barrington, Massachusetts.

Works

1930	*The Disgruntled,* Cabaret, Dresden
1933	*Fairy Tales,* Peppermill Revue, Zurich
1938	*Liebestraum* (mus. Liszt), Peppermill Revue, Prague
1939	*The Artist in Person* (mus. Eilenberg), YMHA, New York
1947	*Galileo* (mus. Eisler; text, Brecht), Coronet Theatre, Los Angeles
1954	*Life of a Flower,* Pantomime Circus, New York
1956	*Grandma Always Danced,* Pantomime Circus, New York
1957	*Clowns and Other Fools,* Pantomime Circus, New York
1963	*All in Fun,* Pantomime Circus, Los Angeles
1965	*Charivari* (mus. Varèse and Colgrass), Joffrey Ballet, New York
1968	*Greetings,* Delacorte Theatre, New York
	Diabelli Variations, Pantomime Circus, New York
1969	*Talent Show,* Pantomime Circus, New York
	Collector's Items, Pantomime Circus, New York
1972	*Circus Scene* (mus. Mache), Pantomime Circus, ANTA Marathon Dance Festival, New York
	All's Well That End. . ., Pantomime Circus, ANTA Marathon Dance Festival, New York
	Ends and Odds (mus. Schubert), London Contemporary Dance Theatre, London
1975	*Conversation with an Ant,* Pantomime Circus, New York
	Leggieros (mus. Beethoven), Hartford Ballet, New York

1976   *For Feet Only,* Pantomime Circus, London
1979   *Him,* Pantomime Circus, New York

Publications

By GOSLAR: books—

What's So Funny? London, 1998.

By GOSLAR: articles—

"From Dresden to Hollywood," *Dance Magazine,* February 1998.

On GOSLAR: articles—

Koegler, Horst, "Lotte Goslar 1907-97," *Dance Magazine,* January 1998.
Robertson, Michael, "Lotte Goslar, Choreographer and Clown," *Dance Magazine,* December 1980.
Schechter, Joel, "Lotte Goslar's *Circus Scene,*" in *Durov's Pig: Clowns, Politics and Theatre,* New York, 1985.

*   *   *

Lotte Goslar was the first performer to successfully bridge modern dance and cabaret clowning, a combination she spent most of her life refining and perfecting through her performances, choreography, and teaching. As the clown princess of modern dance, she influenced both dancers who wished to explore clowning and clowns who wished to explore dance. In this way she helped to broaden the expressive language of two important 20th-century performance traditions.

Looking back in her memoirs to her childhood in Dresden, Goslar said that she "was always in motion," and that her mother always claimed that she had danced in her cradle. Although Goslar had always danced, she had almost no formal dance training. She was exposed to modern dance for the first time in her teens, when she witnessed a performance by students of Gret Palucca. After this experience she became obsessed with the idea of meeting Palucca and studying modern dance. Her first formal lessons, however, were at the school of Mary Wigman, where Goslar did not flourish, rarely saw the great teacher, and left after a couple of months. Disillusioned with the Wigman school, she auditioned for Palucca, who appreciated the raw, untutored quality of Goslar's performance and soon gave her a chance to dance in her company.

Although Goslar worshiped Palucca and tried to learn from her, she realized that her own style must lead in an entirely different direction. With a short, squat figure and a face like pudding, Goslar was never going to create the same emotional response as Palucca herself. The more she tried to imitate her mentor, the more she found herself turning away from Palucca's abstract poetic movement. She began to develop her own physical language, rooted in the same simplicity and honesty that she admired in Palucca, yet more character driven, comic, and theatrical. Goslar's clowning manifested itself in the portrayal of comic characters, frequently of the opposite sex or of indeterminate gender. The first clown performance she ever created was *The Disgruntled,* presented as a solo at cabaret theatres in her native Dresden rather than with Palucca and her company. In this dance, or clown show, Goslar played a male character who was full of "nonsense anger," according to Goslar.

Goslar joined the Peppermill Revue in 1933, a cabaret-style theatre troupe dedicated to new forms and social commentary, under the direction of Erika Mann, daughter of novelist Thomas Mann. With Peppermill, Goslar began to apply her comic talent and idiosyncratic dance style to political satire for the first time. The nonsense anger of *The Disgruntled* became focused against the threat of fascism. During a performance in Switzerland of *Fairy Tales,* choreographed by Goslar, Erika Mann played a combination fairy-godmother/Nazi storm trooper. The police used tear gas to stop rioting in the audience between socialists and fascists. Other cabaret artists had developed social commentary in their comic routines, especially in Germany where the clown Karl Valentin and playwright Bertolt Brecht had collaborated on farcical revues with a political edge, but Goslar was the first to combine clown and modern dance. She retained the aesthetic principles of modern dance even though the content of her pieces was often political in nature.

Goslar toured Europe with Peppermill and was performing in Prague when the Nazis came to power in Germany. She stayed in Prague rather than return to her homeland under Hitler's rule. Goslar toured to the U.S. with Peppermill, where she attracted attention despite a mediocre response by the American press. Goslar felt an instant kinship with the U.S., where she felt free from the political tensions of Europe. Although her work had become increasingly political in nature, Goslar always insisted that she was essentially an apolitical person, though a committed anti-fascist. She jumped at the opportunity of escaping the stifling atmosphere of war-torn Europe and moved permanently to the U.S. in the early 1940s.

Goslar settled first in Los Angeles where she performed at the Turnabout Theatre for 10 years. During this period, which she was later to refer to as the happiest and busiest of her life, she also gave lessons at a private studio where many film actors came to study acting and movement with her. She became an active member of the émigré community of Hollywood, developing friendships with Charles Chaplin, Charles Laughton and Elsa Lanchester, and later with Bertolt Brecht and Hans Eisler.

Goslar collaborated with Laughton, Brecht, and Eisler, providing choreography for the English language premiere of Brecht's *Galileo,* in which Laughton played the title role and Eisler composed the music. Brecht was so impressed with the diminutive, dancing clown that he wrote a performance piece especially for her entitled *Circus Scene.* Although Goslar did not produce *Circus Scene* until 1972, it has become synonymous with the Goslar approach. In *Circus Scene,* Goslar played a circus clown trying to subdue a lion. With whip in hand she set out to confront two male dancers who portrayed the beast. By the end of *Circus Scene,* the lion transformed into the human, and the clown transformed into the lion. Goslar's comedy was tempered in this dance by a frightening sense that the audience was committing a sinful act through their enjoyment of the clown's and lion's suffering. Indeed, Goslar insisted that she saw nothing funny in the situation itself. Her object in performing *Circus Scene,* and many of her other dances, was a contradictory impulse to make the audience laugh on the one hand, and make them aware that they shouldn't be laughing on the other. Attempting to explain her position as social satirist, Goslar told Joel Schechter: "I am very much interested in human relations, what people do to each other, good or bad."

Goslar's life reached another turning point in 1954 when she formed her own company, The Pantomime Circus, and moved from the West Coast to Connecticut. Primarily a solo performer up until the founding of the Pantomime Circus, Goslar began to nurture an ensemble of younger performers who could dance and clown to her choreography. To provide a repertoire for her new company, she recycled some of her earlier productions, some of which had their genesis as solo works in the late 1930s, restaging them for ensemble performance. Goslar kept the Pantomime Circus going for 40 years, touring widely in America and Europe and appearing regularly in New York.

With Pantomime Circus as her showpiece, Goslar enjoyed an even wider acclaim and sphere of influence than she had during her success in Los Angeles. As modern dance became increasingly influenced by postmodern aesthetics, Goslar's influence increased. She provided a precedent for an entire generation of young dancers who ventured into clown territory, most notably Bill T. Jones, whose *Secret Pastures* (1984) was built around the Goslaresque concept of a puppet-like clown and his manipulator. The remarkable success of clown Bill Irwin owes even more to Goslar, with such works as *Largely New York* (1989) in which his antic, physical clowning provided a counterpoint to the disciplined movement of a chorus of modern dancers in a postmodern environment. By the time of her death in 1997, Goslar was no longer viewed as a comic performer on the fringe of modern dance. Rather, her combination of the comic and serious modes, and her use of a variety of styles, from mime and circus clowning to ballet and modern dance, placed her work as an important precursor to the postmodern aesthetic so prevalent in contemporary dance.

—Donald McManus

GOTTSCHILD, Hellmut

German-American dancer, choreographer, and performance artist

Born: 30 July 1936 in Berlin. **Education:** Studied visual arts while growing up; then trained with Mary Wigman through 1961; teaching assistant for Wigman, Berlin, 1961-67. **Family:** Married Brenda Dixon, 1991. **Career:** Founded/directed with Brigitta Herrmann and Inge Sehnert, Gruppe Motion Berlin, 1962-68; emigrated to U.S., 1968; professor of dance, Temple University, 1968-96; founder/director with Herrman and Manfred Fischbeck, Group Motion Media Theater, 1968-71; founder/artistic director, ZeroMoving Dance Company, 1972-93; soloist and independent performance artist, beginning 1993. Professor Emeritus, Temple University, beginning 1996. **Awards:** Hazlett Award for Excellence in the Arts, 1984; Temple University's Creative Achievement Award, 1986; Pew Fellowship in the Arts, 1992-93; Philadelphia city paper's "Most Astonishing Dancer," 1994; Philadelphia Repertory Development Initiative grant, 1995; Pennsylvania Council on the Arts Fellowship, 1995; Dance Advance grant, 1997; numerous federal, state, and private grants for ZeroMoving Dance Company, 1972-93; Jefferson Bank's Declaration Award, 1989; Philadelphia Dance Alliance's Stella Moore Award, 1992.

Works

1959   *Veraenderungen (Changes),* (mus. Gottschild), solo
        Hahnentanz (Rooster Dance), (mus. Kessler)
1960   *Vegetative* (mus. Gottschild), solo
        Duo I w/Brigitta Herrmann (no music)
        Ein Kleines Spiel (A Little Play), (scored w/metronome)
        Bemuehtes Flattern (Exerted Flutter), (mus. Gottschild), solo

1961   *Duo II* w/Herrmann (no music)
        Habanera w/Herrmann (mus. Ravel), duet
        Sechs Kleine Stuecke (Six Little Pieces), (mus. Schönberg), duet for Herrmann and Inge Sehnert
        Umhoehlt (Hollow Surroundings), (no music), solo
1963   *Toccata* (mus. Hindemith), trio, Gruppe Motion Berlin (GMB)
        Zweiklang (Twotone), (mus. Hindemith), duet, GMB
        Aur I (originally Aurus), (mus. Ferrari), solo
        Aur II (mus. Warren), solo
1964   *Indian Summer* (mus. Curran), duet, GMB
        Samur (no music), solo
        Modulation V (mus. Dockstader), quintet, GMB
        Yuma (mus. Raaijmakers), solo
        Glockenduo (Duet with Bells), (mus. Chavez), duet, GMB
        Whirls (mus. Badings), trio, GMB
        Sarabande (mus. Heinz Stockhausen), trio, GMB
1965   *Singende Boegen (Singing Arcs,* revised version of Indian Summer), (mus.Curran), duet, GMB
        Mavena (mus. Malec), for Music Biennale, Zagreb, Yugoslavia
        Duo in Weiss (Duet in White), (mus. Badings), duet, GMB
1966   *Ornamente (Ornaments),* (mus. Staempfli), trio, GMB
        (Untitled), (mus. Borden), quartet, GMB
        Stadion (Stadium), (mus. Curran), quartet, GMB
1967   *Countdown fuer Orpheus* w/Herrmann (multimedia), GMB
1968   *Soufflé* w/Herrmann (mus. Malec), GMB
        Talk (mus. Rolling Stones), Group Motion Media Theatre (GMMT)
        Countdown fuer Orpheus (revised), (multimedia; mus. Musica Electronica Viva Roma, Kessler), GMMT
1969   *The Great Theater of Oklahoma Calls You* (based on Kafka; multimedia), GMMT
1970   *Before and There and Here and Now and Then* (mus. Rzewski), GMMT
1972   *Dogs Are Faithful* (multimedia; mus. Porett), ZeroMoving Dance Company (ZM)
1973   *The Time within the Time within the Time* (multimedia; mus. Porett), ZM
1974   *How to Survive without Candy* (mus. improvised by dancers), ZM
        Suite for Radio and Eardrums (mus. transistor radio, dancers), ZM
1975   *Four Movements for Moving Voices Moving* (mus. vocals, Epstein; text Gertrude Stein), ZM
        We All Live on a White, ZM
1976   *Riverways* (mus. Epstein, dancers), ZM
1977   *Night Tales* (mus. Epstein), ZM
1978   *Solo and Duet,* ZM
1979   *Vindauga* (tribute to Wigman), (mus. Epstein), ZM
1981   *Software* (mus. Debussy), ZM
1982   *The Yellow Sound,* solo, commissioned by the Guggenheim Museum, New York and Frankfurt, ZM
1983   *Music Piece* (mus. Epstein), ZM
        Looking at the Wolf (solo) and *Meet the Pigs* (trio), (mus. Epstein; text Gottschild), ZM
1984   *Wolf Dances* (later called *Beginning with Wolves*), (mus. Gottschild, Epstein), ZM
1985   *Waiting Room,* ZM
        Light Scape (mus. Epstein), duet, collaboration with Relache, Ensemble for New Music, ZM

Hellmut Gottschild, 1989. Photograph © Beatriz Schiller.

1986   *Modulations of Silence,* ZM
        Quartet with Onlookers (mus. Meneely-Kyder) for Part-
            ners Dancing, Hartford, ZM
1987   *Where Do People Gather* (mus. Makihara), ZM
1988   *Scratch Marks* w/Karen Barnonte (mus. Ravel), ZM
1989   *Ash and Flowers* (mus. Kluscevec, Makihara), ZM
        We Liked Your Coat and Undressed You (mus. Taylor), ZM
1990   *The Late, Late Afternoon of the Faun* (mus. Taylor), ZM
1991   *Mary's Ark, Blue Eyes, and the Inability to Dissolve* (text
            Gottschild) for Olympia Werkstatt Berlin, solo
        Don't Cry Wolf, solo
1992   *Onlookers* (mus. Kluscevec), ZM
1993   *Meet Mr. R.* (mus. Seidman)
1994   *Weavings* (mus. Epstein), solo
        Stick It Out w/Brenda Dixon Gottschild
1995   *Tongue Smell Color* w/Dixon Gottschild
1996   *Frogs* w/Dixon Gottschild (mus. Goode)

*   *   *

German-American dancer, choreographer and performance artist
Hellmut Gottschild was born in Berlin in 1936. In his early years,

Gottschild studied visual arts; he went on to study dancing under
the direction of Mary Wigman, and later, in 1961, became her teaching assistant, serving with her until 1967. In 1962, Gottschild co-
founded the dance company Gruppe Motion Berlin with Brigitta
Herrmann and Inge Sehnert, serving as its co-director until 1968.

Gottschild emigrated to the United States in 1968 and began
teaching dance at Temple University. Upon his arrival, he co-founded
another dance company, called Group Motion Media Theater, again
with Brigitta Herrmann, now joined by Manfred Fischbeck.
Gottschild served as Group Motion's co-director until 1971, during which time he danced and choreographed the troupe's increasingly multimedia performances. In 1972, Gottschild left Group
Motion, which still is performing today, to found ZeroMoving
Dance Company. Like his previous dance company affiliations,
Gottschild served as ZeroMoving's artistic director, choreographer,
and a performer until 1993. In the later years, Gottschild served as
co-director with Karen Bamonte, to whom he left the organization,
which she reformed into a new ensemble.

Gottschild himself has received many awards and grants through
the years, including the Hazlett Award for Excellence in the Arts
(1984), Temple University's Creative Achievement Award (1986),
and a Pew Fellowship in the Arts (1992-93). ZeroMoving Dance

Company has also been similarly celebrated and awarded, as a recipient of Jefferson Bank's Declaration Award (1989), the Philadelphia Dance Alliance's Stella Moore Award (1992), and others.

In 1982 Gottschild was commissioned by the Guggenheim Museum to choreograph a piece of history—for the world premiere performance of *The Yellow Sound*, a stage composition by painter Wasily Kandinsky. The production, which was subsequently performed in New York and Frankfurt, was originally supposed to debut early in the 20th century, but was prevented from doing so by the outbreak of World War I. Another commission of historical note came Gottschild's way in 1991 when he was asked to choreograph a full-length work for Olympia Werkstatt Berlin as part of Berlin's bid for the 2000 Olympic Games. The resulting performance, *Mary's Ark, Blue Eyes, and the Inability to Dissolve*, a solo, was Gottschild's personal account of his years with Mary Wigman in postwar Berlin, with reflections of the nationalism/socialism of the time as well as the 1936 Olympiad. The work included text by Gottschild and was later performed in several cities in Germany.

This same year, 1991, also marked the marriage of Gottschild to performance studies researcher Brenda Dixon, whom he met as a colleague in the dance department at Temple University. The two began performing together in the late 1990s, including duet theater/movement performances like *Stick it Out* (1994) and *Tongue Smell Color* (1995), and *Frogs* (1996).

In 1993 Gottschild embarked upon a new direction in his career, trading in the security of organization and company for the flexibility and directness of being a solo artist. He has performed both domestically and internationally, including in New York (Judson Church); Philadelphia (Drake Theater, Conwell Dance Theater, Painted Bride Art Center); Berlin (Akademie der Kuenste, Der Komische Oper, Tanz Tangente, State Ballet School); Munich (Hasting Studio); Frankfurt (Tanz- und Theaterwerkstaetten); Dresden (Mary Wigman Tage), and others. Gottschild conversion to solo act has been successful; he continues to receive recognition from critics—especially from the folks in the city where he makes his home—he was named the "Most Astonishing Dancer" by Philadelphia's city newspaper in 1994 and went on to receive a Philadelphia Repertory Development Initiative grant, a Pennsylvania Council on the Arts fellowship the following year, and a Dance Advance grant in 1997.

In 1996 Gottschild retired from his full-time position as professor of dance at Temple University to devote more attention to his artistic work, although he continues to teach the occasional class. His performance work in the 1990s embodies a multifaceted blend of styles, featuring movement theater pieces in which he employs a wide range of theatrical means, pure movement works, improvisational events, and collaborations of varying nature. The juxtaposition of complex postmodern ideas and approaches with the simple, sensual movement of German modern dance accounts for a dramatic and ironic body of work that makes Gottschild profoundly different from other American choreographers of his generation, or before or after.

—Daryl F. Mallett

GRAFF, Grace (Cornell) & Kurt

Dance and choreography team

Education: GRACE—Studied ballet with Adolph Bolm, Enrico Cecchetti, and Lubov Egorova; modern with Rudolf Laban and Martha Graham, 1930s. KURT—Studied and danced with Kurt Jooss. **Career:** Began dancing together, 1930s; appointed directors of the Federal Theater, c. 1935; founded the Graff Ballet and toured the United States; company disbanded, 1947; taught summer workshops, then created light comic operas, late 1940s and 1950s; moved to Austria, 1960s.

Works

O, Say Can You Sing; Ode to Living; Renaissance, duet; *Behind the Mask* (included *Dance of Discontent, Rise of the Inciter, Fall of the Inciter,* and *The Garden Party*); *Con Vivo* (mus. Scarlatti); *Romance* (mus. Satie); *Viennese Trilogy* (included *Cabaret, Fantasia,* and *Night in the Street*); *Vintage 1912* (included the solo *Girl in the Wind, Harvest, Morning, Rain, Ripening Fields* and the duet *Two Without Care*).

* * *

Grace Cornell was born in Chicago, to a family prominent in the history of the city. She studied with Adolph Bolm in Chicago in the 1920s, and then with Enrico Cecchetti in Milan and Lubov Egorova in Paris. In 1929 she gave a concert of solo dances choreographed by Petipa, Bolm, and Egorova in Chicago's Blackstone Theater—and later repeated this well-received performance in the Théâtre des Champs Elysées in Paris. In 1930, she studied with Rudolph Laban and various German modern dance teachers in Germany. On her return to the United States, she studied for a short time with Martha Graham, and in 1932, danced for many weeks with José Limón at the Roxy Theater.

At the Laban school, Grace Cornell met Kurt Graff, an Austrian who had studied and danced with Kurt Jooss. They began dancing together, married, and settled in Chicago. They co-choreographed a repertoire of lyrical dances to light classical and popular music and appeared in high-class venues such as the Drake Hotel and the Palmer House's Empire Room. The Graffs acquired a studio and stage for intimate performances, calling it the "Little Concert House," in reality the former coach house of the large Cornell mansion on Chicago's south side. In the mid-1930s, the couple presented a well-received program of solos and duos of modern dance in the Goodman Theater, and were appointed directors of the dance unit of the Federal Theater.

The major accomplishment of the Graffs during this time was the creation of dances for a musical titled *O, Say Can You Sing*. The unemployed dancers with whom they worked were of every persuasion—ballet, modern, jazz, etc. Serving as the directors, Grace and Kurt were also the principal dancers in a large-scale ballet they choreographed, entitled *Viennese Trilogy,* to music of Castelnuova-Tedesco. The three sections of the piece were *Cabaret, Night in the Street,* and *Fantasia*. The Graffs also danced a powerful duet titled *Renaissance,* in which they moved romantically on and around a huge table, costumed in the style of the Borgias. This tantalizing number became their signature dance.

In 1938, the dance unit of Chicago's Federal Theater, now with Ruth Page and Bentley Stone as its directors and under the title of Ballet Fedré, presented an all-dance program. The Graffs and their group presented *Behind this Mask,* a large-scale piece with political implications. The listed cast of characters included Proletariat, Sentries, King, Queen, Royal Guards, The Decrepit, and Slum Women. Kurt Graff played the role of the Inciter who performed the *Dance* of Discontent; he also danced the Rise of the Inciter and the Fall of the Inciter. The most colorful scene was The Garden Party, danced by the group.

After the demise of the Federal Theater, the Graffs and the group of 18 dancers now known as the Graff Ballet presented a program at the Goodman Theater. The program included Con Vivo (music by Scarlatti) danced by the group, Romance (music by Satie) danced by Grace and Kurt, and their Borgia mood piece, Renaissance. In Ode to the Living, Kurt's role was Death, and Grace was Daughter of the Streets. In a livelier mood was Vintage 1912, danced by the Graffs and the group. The program included the four-part Singing Earth in which the corps de ballet danced the first section Morning; Grace danced the solo Girl in the Wind, and Kurt romped in Two without Care. The group danced Rain, Ripening Fields, and Harvest. After a short tour, the company—now known widely as the Graff Ballet—spent the summer of 1940 rehearsing and preparing repertoire in a lovely old estate in Vermont. To polish the technical abilities of a troupe of many backgrounds, the Graffs secured Elizabetta Kovriguine, a former Diaghilev Ballet dancer, who had been active in theater presentations in Paris.

Through 1945, the Graff Ballet toured America with the above mentioned repertoire, plus new works added from time to time. In 1947 the company was disbanded and Grace and Kurt Graff settled in Meadow Hearth, a country estate near Hopkinton, New Hampshire. For several years they conducted summer courses in modern dance, then gave up teaching and produced light and comic operas. In the 1960s the Graffs left America and lived in Austria in an old castle outside the city of Graz.

The Graffs were excellent performers—they were both highly attractive personally—Grace tall, slim and blonde; Kurt well-formed and darkly handsome. Both were well-trained in several techniques of dance, and moved especially well. Their style was lyric and accessible in the manner of Kurt Jooss' works.

—Ann Barzel

GRAHAM, Martha

American dancer, choreographer, and company director

Born: 1894 in Allegheny, Pennsylvania. **Education:** Graduated from Cumnock School of Expression, 1916; began classes at Denishawn, 1916. **Family:** Married dancer Erick Hawkins, 1948; divorced 1954. **Career:** Teacher, Denishawn, beginning 1918; dancer, Denishawn, 1919-23; dancer, John Murray Anderson's Greenwich Village Follies, 1923-25; teacher, Eastman School for Dance and Dramatic Action, 1925; founded her first company, the Group, 1926; taught summers at Bennington College (Vermont), 1938-42. **Awards:** First dancer to receive a Guggenheim Foundation fellowship, 1931; Capezio Award, 1960; Aspen Award in Humanities, 1966; Brandeis University Creative Arts Award, 1968; Family of Man Award, 1968; Distinguished Service to Arts Award, National Institute of Arts and Letters, 1970; Handel Medallion, City of New York, 1970; Handel Medallion, City of New York, 1973; proclaimed a "National Treasure," and given the Medal of Freedom by President Ford, 1976; Kennedy Center Honors Award, Washington, D.C., 1979; Royal Medal of Jordan, 1979; Samuel H. Scripps American Dance Festival Award, 1981; Bryn Mawr College M. Carey Tomas Prize, 1983; Artpark Award, 1983; Golden

Florin Award (Italy), 1984; Knight of the French Legion of Honor, 1984; Carina Ari Medal, presented by Princess Christina of Sweden, 1985; Grand Vermeil Medal (France), 1985; President Reagan's National Medal of Arts, 1985; Honorary Citizen of Tennessee Award, Chattanooga, 1986; Premio Porselli Award (Italy), 1987; Certificate of Appreciation (Tucson), 1988; City of Bari Award (Italy), 1989; Seal of the City of Pittsburgh, 1989; City of Boston Award, 1989; Order of the Precious Butterfly with Diamond, Emperor Akihito (Japan), 1990; Lifetime Achievement Award, Council of Fashion Designers of America, 1991; honorary doctorates from Harvard University, Wayne State University, Wesleyan University, and Yale University. **Died:** 1991.

Works (premiered in New York City unless otherwise noted)

1926   Chorale (mus. Franck)
        Novelette (mus. Schumann)
        Tanze (mus. Schubert)
        Intermezzo (mus. Brahms)
        Maid with the Flaxen Hair (mus. Debussy)
        Arabesque No. 1 (mus. Debussy)
        Clair de Lune (mus. Debussy)
        Danse Languide (mus. Scriabin)
        Désir (mus. Scriabin)
        Deux Valses Sentimentales (mus. Ravel)
        Masques (mus. Horst)
        Trois Gnossiennes: Gnossiennne, Frieze, Tanagra (mus. Satie)
        From a XIIth-Century Tapestry, later retitled A Florentine Madonna (mus. Rachmaninoff)
        A Study in Lacquer (mus. Bernheim)
        The Three Gopi Maidens (mus. Scott)
        Danse Rococo (mus. Ravel)
        The Marionette Show (mus. Goossens)
        Portrait—After Beltram—Masses (retitled Gypsy Portrait) (mus. de Falla)
        The Flute of Krishna (dance and film; mus. Scott), Rochester
        Prelude from "Alceste" (mus. Glück), Rochester
        Scene Javanaise (mus. Horst), Rochester
        Danza Degli Angeli (mus. Wolf-Ferrari), Rochester
        Bas Relief (mus. Scott), Rochester
        Ribands (mus. Chopin), Peterboro, New Hampshire
        Scherzo (mus. Mendelssohn)
        Baal Shem (mus. Bloch)
        La Soirée dans Grenade (mus. Debussy)
        Alt-Wien (mus. Godowsky, arr. Horst)
        Three Poems of the East (mus. Horst)
1927   Peasant Sketches (mus. Rebikov, Tansman, Tchaikovsky)
        Tunisia (mus. Poldini)
        Lucrezia (mus. Debussy)
        La Canción (mus. Defossez)
        Arabesque No. 1, revised (mus. Debussy)
        Valse Caprice (mus. Scott)
        Spires (mus. Bach)
        Adagio (mus. Handel)
        Fragilité (mus. Scriabin)
        Lugubre (mus. Scriabin)
        Poème Ailé (mus. Scriabin)
        Tanzstück (mus. Hindemith)

Revolt (mus. Honegger)

Esquisse Antique (mus. Inghelbrecht)

Ronde (mus. Rhené-Baton)

Scherza (mus. Schumann), Ithaca, New York

1928 *Chinese Poem* (mus. Horst)

Trouvères (mus. Koechlin)

Immigrant: Steerage, Strike (mus. Slavenski)

Poems of 1917: Song Behind the Lines, Dance of Death (mus. Ornstein)

Fragments: Tragedy, Comedy (mus. Horst)

Resonances: Matins, Gamelin, Tocsin (mus. Malipiero)

1929 *Danse* (mus. Honegger)

Three Florentine Verses (mus. Zipoli)

Four Insincerities: Petulance, Remorse, Politeness, Vivacity (mus. Prokofiev)

Cants Magics: Farewell, Greeting (mus. Mompou)

Two Variations: Country Lane, City Street (mus. Gretchanioff)

Figure of a Saint (mus. Handel), Millbrook, New York

Resurrection (mus. Harsányi)

Adolescence (mus. Hindemith)

Danza (mus. Milhaud)

Vision of the Apocalypse: Theme and Variations (mus. Reutter)

Moment Rustica (mus. Poulenc)

Sketches from the People: Monotony, Supplication, Requiem (mus. Krein)

Heretic (mus. old Bréton song—de Sivry)

1930 *Prelude to a Dance*, retitled *Salutation* (mus. Honegger)

Two Chants: Futility, Ecstatic Song (mus. Krenek)

Lamentation (mus. Kodály)

Project in Movement for a Divine Comedy (in silence)

Harlequinade (mus. Toch)

1931 *Two Primitive Canticles* (mus. Villa-Lobos)

Primitive Mysteries: Hymn to the Virgin, Crucifixus, Hosanna (mus. Horst)

Rhapsodics: Song, Interlude, Dance (mus. Bartók)

Bacchanale (mus. Riegger)

Dolorosa (mus. Villa-Lobos)

Dithyrambic (mus. Copland)

Serenade (mus. Schönberg)

Incantation (mus. Villa-Lobos)

1932 *Ceremonials* (mus. Engel)

Offering (mus. Villa-Lobos), Ann Arbor, Michigan

Ecstatic Dance (solo; mus. Harsányi), Ann Arbor

Bacchanale No. 2 (mus. Riegger), Ann Arbor

Prelude (mus. Chavez)

Dance Songs (mus. Weisshaus)

Chorus of Youth—Companions (mus. Horst)

1933 *Tragic Patterns* (mus. Horst), Newark, New Jersey

Elegiac (mus. Hindemith)

Ekstasis (mus. Engel)

Dance Prelude (mus. Lopatnikoff)

Frenetic Rythms (mus. Riegger)

1934 *Transitions* (mus. Engel)

Phantasy: Prelude, Musette, Gavotte (mus. Schönberg)

Celebration (mus. Horst)

Four Casual Developments (mus. Cowell)

Integrales (mus. Varèse)

Dance in Four Parts: Quest, Derision, Dream, Sportive Tragedy (mus. Antheil)

American Provincials: Act of Piety, Act of Judgement (mus. Horst)

1935 *Praeludium* (mus. Nordoff)

Course (mus. Antheil)

Perspectives: Frontier and *Marching Song* (mus. Horst)

Panorama (mus. Lloyd), Bennington, Vermont

Formal Dance, later retitled *Praeludium No. 2* (mus. Diamond)

Imperial Gesture (mus. Engel)

1936 *Horizons* (mus. Horst)

Salutation (mus. Engel), Los Angeles, California

Chronicle (mus. Riegger)

1937 *Opening Dance* (mus. Lloyd), Bennington, Vermont

Immediate Tragedy (mus. Cowell), Bennington, Vermont

Deep Song (mus. Cowell)

American Lyric (mus. North)

1938 *American Document* (mus. Green), Bennington

1939 *Columbiad* (mus. Horst)

Every Soul Is a Circus (mus. Nordoff)

1940 *El Penitente* (mus. Horst), Bennington

Letter to the World (mus. Johnson), Bennington

1941 *Punch and the Judy* (mus. McBride), Bennington

1942 *Land Be Bright* (mus. Kreutz), Chicago

1943 *Salem Shore* (mus. Nordoff)

Deaths and Entrances (mus. Johnson)

1944 *Imagined Wing* (mus. Milhaud), Washington, D.C.

Herodiade (mus. Hindemith), Washington, D.C.

Appalachian Spring (mus. Copland), Washington, D.C.

1946 *Dark Meadow* (mus. Chavez)

Cave of the Heart, originally titled *Serpent Heart* (mus. Barber)

1947 *Errand into the Maze* (mus. Menotti)

Night Journey (mus. Schuman), Cambridge, Massachusetts

1948 *Diversion of Angels*, title at first performance *Wilderness Stair* (mus. Dello Joio), New London, Connecticut

1950 *Judith* (mus. Schuman), Louisville, Kentucky

Eye of Anguish (mus. Persichetti), Erick Hawkins and Company

Gospel of Eve (mus. Nordoff)

1951 *The Triumph of St. Joan* (mus. Dello Joio), Louisville, Kentucky

1952 *Canticle for Innocent Comedians* (mus. Ribbink)

1953 *Voyage* (mus. Schuman)

1954 *Ardent Song* (mus. Hovhaness), London

1955 *Seraphic Dialogue* (mus. Dello Joio)

1958 *Clytemnestra* (mus. El-Dabh)

Embattled Garden (mus. Surinach)

1959 *Episodes: Part I* (mus. Webern)

1960 *Acrobats of God* (mus. Surinach)

Alcestis (mus. Fine)

1961 *Visionary Recital* (mus. Starer)

One More Gaudy Night (mus. El-Dabh)

1962 *Phaedra* (mus. Starer)

A Look at Lightning (mus. El-Dabh)

Secular Games (mus. Starer), New London, Connecticut

Legend of Judith (mus. Seter), Tel Aviv, Israel

1963 *Circe* (mus. Hovhaness), London

1965 *The Witch of Endor* (mus. Schuman)

Part Real—Part Dream (mus. Seter)

1967 *Cortege of Eagles* (mus. Lester)

1968	*Dancing—Ground* (mus. Rorem)
	A Time of Snow (mus. Dello Joio)
	The Plain of Prayer (mus. Lester)
	The Lady of the House of Sleep (mus. Starer)
1969	*The Archaic Hours* (mus. Lester)
1973	*Mendicants of Evening* (mus. Walker)
	Myth of a Voyage (mus. Hovhaness)
1974	*Holy Jungle* (mus. Starer)
	Jacob's Dream (mus. Seter), Jerusalem, Israel
1975	*Lucifer* (mus. El-Dabh), Fonteyn, Nureyev, and company
	Adorations (mus. Frost)
	Point of Crossing (mus. Seter)
	The Scarlet Letter (mus. Johnson)
1977	*O Thou Desire Who Art about to Sing* (mus. Kupferman)
	Shadows (mus. Menotti)
1978	*The Owl and the Pussycat* (mus. Surinach)
	Ecuatorial (mus. Varèse)
	Flute of Pan (mus. traditional)
1979	*Frescoes* (mus. Barber)
	Episodes, reconstructed, reworked (mus. Webern), London
1980	*Judith*, reworked (mus. Varèse)
1981	*"Acts of Light"* (mus. Nielsen)
1982	*Dances of the Golden Hall* (mus. Panufnik)
	Andromache's Lament (mus. Barber)
1983	*Phaedra's Dream* (mus. Crumb), Athens, Greece
1984	*The Rite of Spring* (mus. Stravinsky)
	Song (mus. traditional)
1986	*Temptations of the Moon* (mus. Bartók)
	Tangled Night (mus. Egge)
1987	*Untitled* (mus. Stravinsky)
	Celebration, reconstruction (mus. Horst)
	Persephone (mus. Stravinsky)
1988	*Letter to the World*, reconstruction (mus. Johnson)
	Night Chant (mus. Nakai)
	Deep Song, reconstruction (mus. Cowell)
1989	*American Document* (mus. Corigliano)
	Steps in the Street, reconstruction (mus. Riegger)
1990	*Maple Leaf Rag* (mus. Joplin)

Films and Videotapes

A Dancer's World, film, dir. Nathan Kroll, *1957.*
Appalachian Spring, film, dir. Nathan Kroll, 1959.
Night Journey, film, dir. Alexander Hammid, 1960.

Publications

By GRAHAM: books—

The Notebooks of Martha Graham, edited and with an introduction
  by Nancy Ross Wilson, New York, 1973.
Blood Memory, New York, 1991.

By GRAHAM: articles—

"The American Dance," in Virginia Stewart and Merle Armitage, eds.,
  The Modern Dance, New York, 1935.
"A Modern Dancer's Primer for Action," edited by Frederick R.
  Rogers, in *Dance: A Basic Educational Technique,* New York,
  1941.

"A Dancer's World," *Dance Observer,* 1958.
"Martha Graham Speaks," *Dance Observer,* 1963.
"How I Became a Dancer," in Myron Howard Nadel and Constance
  Gwen Nadel, eds., *The Dance Experience: Readings in Dance
  Appreciation,* New York, 1970.

On GRAHAM: books—

Armitage, Merle, ed., *Martha Graham,* New York, Dance Horizons,
  1966.
De Mille, Agnes, *Martha, the Life and Work of Martha Graham,*
  New York: Random House, 1991.
Hanna, Judith Lynne, *Dance, Sex, and Gender,* Chicago, 1988.
Leatherman, Leroy, *Martha Graham: Portrait of the Lady as an
  Artist,* New York, 1966.
McDonagh, Don, *Martha Graham,* New York, 1974.
Morgan, Barbara, *Martha Graham: Sixteen Dances in Photographs,*
  New York, 1941.
Stodelle, Ernestine, *Deep Song: The Dance Story of Martha Graham,*
  New York, 1984.
Terry, Walter, *Frontiers of Life: The Life of Martha Graham,* New
  York, 1975.
Trowbridge, Charlotte, *Dance Drawings of Martha Graham,* New
  York, 1945.

*   *   *

In a career that spanned the course of over six decades, dancer
and choreographer Martha Graham has contributed more to dance,
theater, and the modernist movement than any other artist of our
time. She not only created a revolutionary technique which has
come to be part of the permanent dance vocabulary, but has left in
her wake a rich legacy of choreographic work. Her contributions
continue to affect and shape the work of artists today, reaffirming
Graham's much deserved place in history as a pioneer of modern
dance.

Martha Graham was born in Allegheny, Pennsylvania, in 1894 to
Dr. George and Jenny Graham. Hers was a strict Presbyterian upbringing. In 1908 the family moved to Santa Barbara where Graham
attended high school. When Martha was 17, she went with her
father to a concert given by Ruth St. Denis which irrevocably altered the course of her life. Determined to perform, she enrolled in
the Cumnock School of Expression in Los Angeles where she had
regular lessons in dramatics, dance, and speech. It wasn't until
1916, at the age of 19, that Graham enrolled in Denishawn to begin
her first serious dance training.

The years at Denishawn were formative for Graham, though she
eventually shed their aesthetics to find her own. Upon first entering the school, her dancing abilities were so limited that Miss Ruth
thought her totally hopeless. Within two years, however, Graham
was established with Denishawn as a teacher and from 1919 to
1923 became a member of the company, appearing in such title
roles as *Xochitl* and meeting with success as a magnetic performer.
Graham left Denishawn, and after performing for two years in the
Greenwich Village Follies, she took a leap of faith and began her
lifelong career as an independent artist.

In developing her own technique, Graham strove to strip away
the sentimental elaborations of ballet as well as the careful aesthetics of Denishawn that was her training. Graham was interested in
expressing pure emotion, a concept more closely linked with the
aims of Native American dance than of our Western culture. What

developed out of Graham's introspection was a revolutionary technique and movement style uniquely her own, undergirded by her philosophy that "out of emotion comes form." She pioneered this bare bones approach to dance, removing the arms, face, and even hands to concentrate on the torso and spine as the wellspring of pure expression. Graham's technique used a contraction and release of the body's center as a way of initiating movement, mirroring the rhythm of breathing. She explored the relationship to the floor with her innovative falls and floorwork, and made use of pelvic tension, the flexed foot, body opposition, inwardly rotated leg positions, and a freer torso, all of which dancers today take for granted as simply part of the vernacular. Her technique has become so inextricably woven into the fabric of dance vocabulary that the enormity of Graham's impact is difficult to grasp.

Graham's approach to the dance is a unique contribution in and of itself. As her *Notebooks* testify, words were always a root source for Graham. She was not only an avid reader with enduring interests in literature, poetry, and psychology, but as her longtime friend Rachel Yocum recalls, "Martha loved language and used it beautifully, even magically." Finding creative stimulus in such diverse sources as Nietzche, T.S. Eliot, and James Joyce, and infusing her movement ideas with imagery and metaphor, Graham's dance had a vitality, a deep impulse that gave a verity to her movement, something her audiences and critics found hard to ignore. In the words of Pearl Lang, "[Graham] has given the dancing body an additional concept: that of inner space." Here was an artist who would use dancers in her work as much more than tensile instruments; Graham wanted thinking dancers who were willing to read in their spare time, delve into the depths of the characters she created, and use introspection as she did, as a pathway to the "inner landscape." The importance of this contribution should not be underestimated as Graham's approach proved instrumental in recharting dance on the map as a form of high art and communication. Agnes de Mille, in *Martha, the Life and Work of Martha Graham*, confirms that Graham had in fact, "re-establish[ed] dancing among the major arts, as the servitor of religious and intellectual purpose, and, as a corollary, establish[ed] its practitioners as serious artists."

The dancers with whom Graham worked form an impressive list; many went on to acclaimed careers not only as dancers, but as some of the most important dance educators and choreographers of the century. Among Graham's early recruits were Martha Hill, Gertrude Shurr, Dorothy Bird, Anna Sokolow, Sophie Maslow, May O'Donnell, and Pearl Lang. Later groups enjoyed such talents as Jean Erdman, Ethel Winter, Yuriko, Nina Fonaroff, and Mary Hinkson. Graham's company also had an outstanding group of men: Erick Hawkins, Merce Cunningham, Stuart Hodes, Glen Tetley, Paul Taylor, Dan Wagoner, Bertram Ross, and Mark Ryder.

One of Graham's immeasurable contributions is her legacy of choreographic work. She produced pieces at an almost feverish pace, the scope of the work reflecting her constant evolution as an artist. Graham's company, known at first simply as "the Group," made its New York debut in 1926. By 1929 the company had grown to 16, and audiences were surprised to find Graham and her cadre of female dancers dressed in plain, dark costumes, using angular gestures and percussive movement, and relating to the floor in unconventional ways. Graham's early compositions reveal her interest in the primitive and the struggle of the individual, as in the first great ensemble works, *Heretic* (1929) and *Primitive Mysteries* (1931). In 1930, Graham presented *Lamentation*, a solo in which she placed herself in a tubing of tricot, and stretching her body into sculpted forms created an outer landscape which spoke powerfully of the distended emotional terrain of grief. This solo remains Graham's most vivid representation of her philosophy "out of emotion comes form."

During the 1930s, Graham established herself in America's mind as an important artistic voice. She gained wide recognition for her role as the "Chosen One" in Massine's acclaimed 1930 version of *Le Sacre du Printemps* and in 1931 became the first dancer to receive a Guggenheim Fellowship. In 1937, President and Mrs. Roosevelt invited Graham to perform at the White House, the first such invitation ever extended to a dancer. Throughout the decade, Graham's style became less rigid and formalized and her work turned to themes that were often American, with *Frontier* (1935) the signature piece of the 1930s. Graham danced this solo in a manner so forthright, free, and with such clarity of purpose that she seemed to carve out her territory from sheer will alone. In Merle Armitage's 1937 collection of essays on Graham, Lincoln Kirstein, who had criticized the artist's earlier works as depicting a kind of "stark hysteria" wrote that Graham "has in *Frontier* much of the courage of Whitman's unachieved dream, but she also has a more realistic and present spirit. . . . She has created a kind of candid, sweeping and wind-worn liberty for her individual expression."

In 1938 Graham was brought on staff at Bennington College in Vermont, where she taught each summer until 1942. It was here that she met Erick Hawkins, who was to become her lover and later her husband. With the inclusion of men into the company, Erick the first to join in 1938, Graham's choreographic work began to travel along a rich new vein, her work finding its impulse in the complex entanglements of human relationships, Jungian psychology, and stories from the Greek and Hebrew mythic traditions. What emerged was a rich collaboration of dance and theater where great figures from literature and myth were explored at the most basic psychological level. This genre of the psychological dance-drama was a unique Graham invention.

As early as 1940, Graham had used introspection as a choreographic device when she examined the inner world of Emily Dickinson in *Letter to the World*. Now her explorations deepened into the basics of human emotion—rage, jealousy, fear, desire—with introspection as the choreographic touchstone from which to explore the inner drama of her characters. Among the many subjects of her explorations were Medea in *Cave of the Heart* (1946), Ariadne in *Errand into the Maze* (1947), Jocasta in *Night Journey* (1947), *Judith* (1950), Joan of Arc in *Seraphic Dialogue* (1955), and *Clytemnestra* (1958). With women as the protagonists in many of these classic stories, Graham created an entire repertoire of works recast from a woman's perspective, a point not lost on feminist theorists; though Graham never considered herself a feminist, we find in her work some of the most bold and multifaceted representations of female identity.

Graham's effect on the theater and on all art forms has been tremendous, not only because of her contributions to dance, but due to her revolutionary collaborations. Of particular importance is her work with sculptor Isamu Noguchi, who added a unique dimension to Graham's theater with over 35 designs; her long association with lighting designer Jean Rosenthal; and her work in costume design. Graham not only worked with such distinguished designers as Halston, but was herself enormously inventive in the use of fabrics. Of seminal importance was her connection with Louis Horst, her accompanist and musical director from 1926 to 1948. Horst not only composed scores for some of Graham's most successful works but was also her sage and friend, lending invaluable criticism and encouragement to her creative endeavors. It was Horst who stimulated her interest in modern music, introducing her, and subsequently the public, to composers such as Prokofiev and Bartók, then not widely known. Graham gradually came to use the American composers, enjoying rich collaborations with such artists as Edgard Varèse, Norman Dello Joio, and Aaron Copland, the result of this last venture the unforgettable *Appalachian Spring* (1959). The greatest testament to her far-reaching influence is the Aspen Award in Humanities which Graham received in 1966, naming her the "individual anywhere in the world who has made the greatest contribution to the advancement of the humanities."

From the beginning, Graham administered a needed dose of intellect to dance, and as she continued to produce works of substance, the literature surrounding the dance hurried to keep pace. Agnes de Mille, in her biography of the artist, goes so far as to say that Graham "gave rise to a body of critical thinking merely by producing works of sufficient stature. . .to compel judgement of serious quality and merit." That Graham gave birth to a higher level of critical thinking around the dance is not inconceivable, as her work not only revolutionized dance form and subject matter, but her collaborations with musicians, set designers, and other artists simply gave critics more to consider. She further provoked her audiences with such radical innovations as incorporating text into her pieces and experimenting with narrative structure. As early as 1929, *New York Times* dance critic John Martin said of her work: "It burns with the slow and deadly fire of the intellect. She does the unforgivable thing for a dancer to do—she makes you think."

Batsheva de Rothschild began making considerable financial contributions to Graham's company in the 1950s. Her patronage made possible the commission of sets and musical scores, the establishment of the Martha Graham School of Contemporary Dance, and worldwide tours which brought the company as far east as Burma and Thailand. The focus in Graham's later career turned, in part, to preserving her life's work, and it was during this time that Graham revived some of her classics, as in the 1987 landmark revival of *Appalachian Spring* with Nureyev and Baryshnikov in leading roles. Today the Graham company enjoys its sole position as the oldest continuously performing modern troupe in the world; and each year the School, which has grown steadily since its inception over 40 years ago, trains scores of dancers from all over the world.

Graham continued to choreograph up until her death in 1991. She had stubbornly refused to retire from the stage until her mid-70s, often performing under considerable duress as she was, by that time, acutely arthritic. After one such performance, Graham's friend and analyst Frances Wickes told her, "Martha. . .you are not immortal." Yet Graham has become just that. She has left behind her body of work, a new dance vocabulary, and scores of dancers steeped in her technique, philosophy, and approach. She has left an indelible mark upon the bodies and minds of dancers and artists alike, affecting us in our daily practices, in the way we think about and approach movement. She has, in fact, stayed her mortality with the permanence of her art.

—Siobhán Scarry

THE GRAND UNION

American performance group

The Grand Union (sometimes referred to by its corporate name, Rio Grande Union) was a collective of postmodern choreographers/

performers who created collaborative, improvisational dance. Their intent was to use their performances as an opportunity to ask questions about the nature of dance and of performance.

Nine members made up the Grand Union over the course of its six-year lifespan, beginning in 1970. The original group consisted of Becky Arnold, Douglas Dunn, David Gordon, Barbara Lloyd Dilley, Steve Paxton, and Yvonne Rainer; Trisha Brown, Nancy Green Lewis, and Lincoln Scott (known as Dong) joined soon thereafter. (Arnold left the group in 1972, and Rainer left in 1973 to become a filmmaker.) All nine had worked together frequently for the previous decade, dancing in and observing the works of the others.

Most were members of the Judson Dance Theater and had previously studied with Merce Cunningham.

The six original Grand Union members were all in the Yvonne Rainer Company and, in fact, it was their participation in one of Rainer's works, *Continuous Project-Altered Daily,* that provided the impetus for the formation of the Grand Union.

In *Continuous Project,* Rainer's intent was to create an ever-evolving piece that would change between and during performances. She also wanted to blur the line between the creation and performance of dance, by introducing new movement sequences that could be learned or rehearsed during the performance. Rainer wanted to delve into the relationships between dance and everyday behaviors, between the performers and the audience, and between the dancers and the material. Like much of Rainer's work, and that of the other members of the Judson group, the piece focused on activities from daily life, such as walking, jumping, and falling, rather than traditional dance movements.

Significantly, as far as Grand Union was concerned, *Continuous Project* also experimented with choreographic democracy and improvisation. The dancers were given the power to create new sequences during the performance. They could initiate predetermined movements (consisting of solos, duets, and group steps) at any time during the performance by bringing out a prop, calling out a direction, or playing appropriate music. The dancers had the option to repeat movements, change the progression of the dance, stop a sequence, or insert their own improvisation. (After a while, each performer was limited to one chance per performance to improvise on their own.) The atmosphere was casual, and performers would discuss what they were doing with each other as they were doing it.

The Grand Union was created to further explore the questions raised in *Continuous Project.* The piece laid the foundation for Grand Union's style, as well as its themes. In particular, the Union's work furthered the notion of a democratic process of performance and choreography. While Rainer was the "boss-lady," as she called it, in *Continuous Project,* in Grand Union there were no leaders or followers. The choreographic process involved all nine dancers, each of whom brought their own varied experiences and personal styles into the mix. Each also had their own theories about how the group should operate, and their disagreements and antagonisms added to the dynamic of the collective as much as their collaborative efforts did.

At the beginning of the Grand Union, the process was similar to that of *Continuous Project.* Performances incorporated predetermined elements, which were performed in a different order each night. For example, Rainer conceived of a new work, *Grand Union Dreams* in 1971. She created the initial movements, then handed the work over to the dancers, who finished the piece collaboratively. Within performances, members took turns as temporary leaders

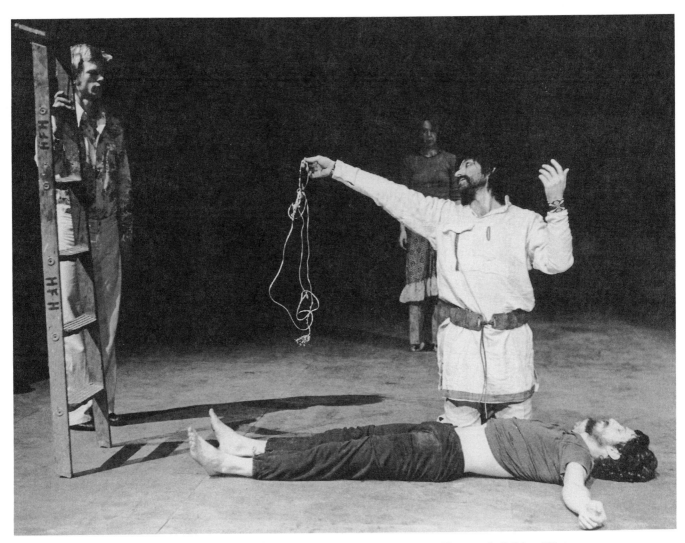

Grand Union: From left, Douglas Dunn, Nancy Lewis, David Godon, and Steve Paxton. Photograph © Johan Elbers.

and choreographers. (Some critics and audiences continued to regard Grand Union as Rainer's group in its early years, despite her efforts to be perceived as an equal.) By 1972 the group's efforts had evolved into a more democratic method of improvisation that was always open to suggestions from any of the members and did not rely on preconceived movements. Any individual could control aspects of the performance at any time if he or she wanted to and the others could follow, or continue to work separately; each dancer could introduce new material or expand on the material of others if they so desired. Some dancers kept to themselves, while some temporarily formed duets or groups. As the process developed, individual personas and styles became evident. Personas might change radically from one night to the next, or from moment to moment within each performance. The diverse styles and concerns of the individual members, and the resulting disagreements, continued to play a role in the creative process. The interaction between the performers and their changing relationships with one another over the course of the performance were of great significance.

Dialogues and monologues were as much a part of the performance as movement, and large doses of humor and sexual innuendo were evident in each performance. Free associations prompted by props, music, or conversations would spur new movements. There

were no goals or expectations for any performance; the purpose was to explore ideas, not to come up with definitive solutions. Some performances had interesting moments from a viewing perspective, while others did not; the purpose was not to create a beautiful finished work, but rather to explore the process that contributes to a final performance.

The Grand Union's evenings of dance were never predictable, but as time went on, they began to become more consistent. In the beginning, there had been no process, and that added to the interest of the experiment. After several years, a process inevitably became established, and this ultimately subtracted some of the interest, for both the audience and the performers. In 1975 critic Arlene Croce, writing for the *New Yorker,* described the group's performances as "free for alls of improvised dialogue, schticks, and stunts, much of it purposely funny, all of it inconsequential, none of it more than incidentally concerned with dancing." This evolution contributed, in part, to the group's eventual demise.

Another factor was that each performer was involved simultaneously with his or her own choreography, and increasingly wanted to focus on this independent work. After some unsuccessful early attempts at integrating members' individual work with the Union's, the two worlds were kept completely separate. (The group occasionally tried to integrate guest performers such as Simone Forti, Carmen Beuchat, Lisa Nelson, and Rainer into the process, but this was also unsuccessful.) Another reason for the eventual dissolution of the group was the inevitable result of what they were trying to achieve. The process, as it developed, naturally caused conflicts. In the interest of furthering cooperation, these conflicts were not discussed openly, but ultimately caused friction. Individual styles of each performer also began to annoy some of the others, and the respective dancers' commitment to Union performances varied. Finally, the end came in 1976, and the Grand Union gave its final performance in Missoula, Montana, that year.

The Grand Union's performances were typical of postmodern dance in their abstract nature, lack of extraneous theatrical elements, and in the way they used the stage and its accoutrements as a way to reveal the essential character of dance and performance, rather than to create an illusion. Their experiments in the group dynamics of improvisation and in a democratic choreographic process influenced many dancers who followed, such as Bill T. Jones and Arnie Zane. The Union's work also affected later performers, such as Twyla Tharp, Lucinda Childs, and the group's own Trisha Brown, who consciously took the opposite approach, focusing specifically on the geometric and precise structure of dance.

Publications

Banes, Sally, *Terpsichore in Sneakers: Post-Modern Dance,* Boston, 1980.
————, *Writing Dancing in the Age of Post-Modernism.* Miami, OH, 1994.
Croce, Arlene, *Afterimages.* New York, 1977.
Robertson, Allen and Donald Hutera, *The Dance Handbook,* Boston, 1988.

—Karen Raugust

GRAY, Harriette Ann
American dancer, choreographer, and educator

Born: 1913 in Kansas City, Missouri. **Education:** Graduate of Lindenwood College, Missouri; studied at Humphrey-Weidman studio, New York. **Family:** Married Barney Brown, 1939; daughter born in 1942. **Career:** Dancer, Humphrey-Weidman Dance Company, 1933-40; assistant to choreographer Jack Cole, Hollywood, 1940-51; co-founder/director, Dance at New Studio for Actors and Dancers in Los Angeles; founder, Harriette Ann Gray Dance Company, 1947; premiered many pieces at 92nd St. YM/YWHA in New York City; director, dance program at Perry-Mansfield Summer School of Theatre and Dance (Colorado), 1950-79; teacher/head of dance department, Stephens College (Missouri), 1955-78; director, Mid-America Dance Company, 1968-73. **Died:** 20 April 1987 in Columbia, Missouri.

Roles (with Humphrey-Weidman Dance Company, premiering in New York, unless otherwise noted)

1936   *Quest* (Weidman)
1937   *To The Dance* (Humphrey)
1938   *Passacaglia and Fugue in C Minor* (Humphrey)
        Opus 51 (Weidman)
1939   *New Dance* (Humphrey)
1940   *On My Mother's Side* (Weidman)

Works

1946   *Spring Fever*
        A Lantern to See By
1947   *When Satan Hops Out*
        Dance for Two
        Folk Suite
        Taken with Tongues
        Grooved
1948   *Dance Cartoons*
        The Ballad of the Little Square
1949   *Subject for a Short History*
1950   *Footnote to History*
1951   *A Woman of No Importance*
1952   *Saturday Night*
1953   *The Albatross*
1954   *Broken Flight*
        To Be
        The Barrel
1957   *Debussy Petite Suite*
1965   *Alone in a Crowd*
1966   *Minoan Suite*
1967   *Trojan Suite*
1968   *Five Short Pieces*
        Heads or Tails

Publications

On GRAY: books—

Bonali, Gloria Ann, *Harriette Ann Gray: Her Life and Her Career, 1913-1968*, Ph.D. dissertation, Texas Woman's University, 1970.

On GRAY: articles—

Obituary, *Dance Magazine*, October 1987.
Review, "Harriette Ann Gray and Company," *Dance Observer*, June-July 1953.
Obituary, *New York Times*, 12 May 1987.

Films and Videotapes

Lady in the Dark, 1947.
Amahl and the Night Visitor, 1956.
Orpheus and Euridice, 1957.
Kismet, 1957.
Carousel, 1957.
The King and I, 1958.
Kiss Me Kate, 1963.
My Fair Lady, 1964.
The Soldier's Tale, 1968.

*   *   *

Harriette Ann Gray made a significant contribution to American modern dance throughout several decades, beginning as a performer, and later becoming a choreographer, teacher, and administrator. Having attended summer dance classes at the Perry-Mansfield Camp and School in Steamboat Springs, Colorado, and Bennington College, in Bennington, Vermont, she moved to New York in 1936 to become a member of the Student Workshop at the Humphrey-Weidman School. Soon she became a member of the Humphrey-Weidman Dance Company and performed with exceptional technical skill and athleticism. As one of the leading members of the company, Gray was described by Charles Weidman as having "a phenomenal body, a wonderful extension and tremendous elevation." Her interpretation of major roles in classic Humphrey and Weidman pieces was unparalleled.

In 1940 Gray moved to Los Angeles, where she taught dance at the Extension School of UCLA, and movement for actors at various motion picture studios. She performed in several films and became an assistant to choreographer Jack Cole, working with stars such as Rita Hayworth and Ann Miller. Each summer during the 1940s, she returned to Perry-Mansfield to teach and choreograph. While in southern California, Gray co-founded the New Studio Workshop for Actors and Dancers.

In 1951 Gray formed the Harriette Ann Gray Dance Company, consisting of many former Perry-Mansfield students and based in Los Angeles. After a year of touring, the company moved to New York. Gray continued to perform with what Louis Horst called "that fabulous technique," and her choreography was distinctively honest and direct. Gray also found time to establish the Theater Studio for Actors and Dancers. The company performed throughout the U.S. until 1955, when it disbanded, and Gray accepted a position as dance instructor at Stephens College in Columbia, Missouri.

At Stephens, Gray expanded the dance curriculum and, over the span of several years, transformed the fledgling associate of arts dance program housed in the department of physical education to a comprehensive dance department within the division of arts, offering a B.F.A. degree. Gray continued to teach during summers at the Perry-Mansfield School of Theatre and Dance and by 1963 the school merged with Stephens college to become Stephens/Perry-Mansfield. The merger resulted in a rigorous, year-round course of study for dance majors, and produced many dancers who went on to professional acclaim. The curriculum reflected not only offerings in modern dance technique and choreography, but courses in ballet, jazz, and ethnic dance—a breadth unique in the early days of dance in higher education. Gray remained at the core of the Stephens and Perry-Mansfield programs until her retirement in 1978; her legacy as an exuberant, inspiring dancer and teacher lives on in the Harriette Ann Gray Dance Studio at Stephens.

—Mary Strow

GREENBERG, Neil

American dancer, choreographer, company director, and educator

Born: 17 April 1959 in Minneapolis. **Education:** Began tap at age four, Nancy Raddatz Dance School; attended Minnesota Dance Theater and School, 1970-76; studied modern and ballet at Juilliard, 1976-77; began studying at Merce Cunningham Dance Studio, 1978; Cecchetti method of ballet, 1977-90; studied anatomy and kinesiol-

ogy with Irene Dowd, 1986-87; at Susan Klein School of Dance, from 1989; attended Klein Stretch and Placement workshops, 1989-95; Klein Teacher's workshops, 1994-98; Zero Balancing workshops, 1995-97. **Career:** Dancer, Merce Cunningham Dance Company, 1979-86; also danced with the companies of Manuel Alum, Molissa Fenley, Kazuko Hirabayashi, Rachel Lampert, and others; founder, Dance by Neil Greenberg, 1986; teacher, SUNY, Purchase, 1987 to present; artist-in-residence programs include Studio Jan Luijkenstraat (Amsterdam), 1981, 1985; Dancemakers Studio (Toronto), 1989; Portland Summer Dance Center (Maine), 1990; Harvard University Summer Dance Center, 1991; Budapest (Hungary), 1992; Cornell University, 1992; Taiwan, 1993; Teatro Alla Scala (Milan), 1994; Danscentrum (Stockholm), 1992, 1996; University of Minnesota, Cowles Chair, 1998; dance curator of The Kitchen, 1995 to present. **Awards:** Harkness Foundation Space Grant, 1988; NEA choreographic fellowships, 1988, 1989, 1990, 1991, 1995; New York State Council on the Arts Grants, 1990-97; New York Foundation for the Arts fellowships, 1990, 1996; Metropolitan Life Foundation *Emerging Dance Program* Award, 1991; John Simon Guggenheim Memorial Foundation Fellowship, 1992; Joyce Mertz-Gilmore Foundation grant, 1992; Harkness Foundation dance grants, 1992-97; New York Dance and Performance Award ("Bessie") for *Not-about-AIDS-Dance*, 1995; Foundation for Contemporary Performance Arts Grant, 1997.

Roles (for the Merce Cunningham Dance Company with choreography by Cunningham unless otherwise noted)

1980	*Exercise Piece III*, New York
	Fielding Sixes, London
1981	*Channels/Inserts*, New York
	10's with Shoes, New York
1982	*Trails*, New York
	Numbers, New York
1983	*Coast Zone*, New York
	Roaratorio, Lille-Roubaix, France
1984	*Pictures*, New York
	Doubles, Durham, North Carolina
	Phrases, Angers, France
1985	*Arcade*, Pennsylvania Ballet

Other roles include: Performed in *A Soldier's Tale*, the Eliot Feld Ballet, and guest appearances with other companies.

Works

1983	*Hero*
1985	*Amnesty*
1986	*Morphine*
1987	*MacGuffin or How Meanings Get Lost*
1988	*Stage-Gun-Dance*
1989	*Stage-Gun-Solos*
1990	*Branches, Swords, Flowers, Spears, Ribbons*
1991	*Crux Eruption*
	The Pursuit of Certainty
	Destiny Dance
1992	*I Am a Miserable and Selfish Person (Kick Me Dance)*
1993	*A Truth Dance*
1994	*Not-about-AIDS-Dance*
1995	*The Disco Project*

Neil Greenberg performing *A Truth Dance*. Photograph © Johan Elbers.

1997   *Part Three (Judy Garland)*
         Part Three (My Fair Lady)

Publications

By GREENBERG: Articles—

"I'm Living with AIDS and So Are You," *Purchase College Free Press*, 1994.
"Review of Lucy Guerin's *Incarnadine*," *Ballet Review*, Spring 1995.
"Unbearable and Inescapable," *Movement Research Performance Journal #10*, 1995.
"Neil Greenberg Talks to Elizabeth Streb about Subjectivity and Objectivity in Art but Discussion Turns to Life and Death," *Movement Research Performance Journal #11*, 1995.

On GREENBERG: articles—

Anderson, Jack, "Writing a Diary with Choreography," *New York Times*, 7 January 1996.

Daniels, Don, "Three New Choreographers Alone Together," *Ballet Review*, Winter 1988.
——, "Keeping Up with the Times," *Ballet Review*, Spring 1992.
——, "Music at the Close," *Ballet Review*, Summer 1996.
——, "Urban Renewal," *Ballet Review*, Spring 1997.
Harris, William, "A Dance that Both Is and Isn't," *New York Times*, 1 May 1994.
Jowitt, Deborah, "Sunny Steps," *Village Voice*, 8 November 1988.
——, "Alive and Kicking," *Village Voice*, 16 January 1996.
Kaplan, Larry, "My Brother, My Self," *POZ*, April-May 1995.
Kelly, Patrick, and Otis Stuart, "Neoromanticism, Men, and the Eighties: Dancing the Difference," *Dance Magazine*, January 1989.
Kourias, Gia, "Burn, Baby, Burn," *Time Out New York*, 13-20 December 1995.
Whitaker, Rick, "Ins and Outs," *Ballet Review*, Spring 1996.
——, and Don Daniels, "A Conversation with Neil Greenberg," *Ballet Review*, Spring 1997.

*   *   *

Over the course of his career as a dancer and choreographer, Neil Greenberg has developed a choreographic lexicon that integrates kinesthetic, emotional, and cognitive ways of knowing and representing the world and the self. Beginning tap dance at age four, he enrolled as a teenager in the Minnesota Dance Theater and School and was especially drawn to modern dance as an expressive language. Greenberg experimented with different idioms of movement and performing situations between the fall of 1976, when he moved to New York City to attend the Juilliard School's Dance Division, and the summer of 1979, when he was asked by Merce Cunningham to join his company. During his first year at Juilliard, he auditioned for Twyla Tharp, one of his earliest influences, and the Eliot Feld Ballet.

Hired by Feld to perform in *A Soldier's Tale*, the company's summer production, Greenberg left Juilliard to pursue a professional career in March, 1977. The year after, he performed with a variety of choreographers on a freelance basis, and began studying Cecchetti ballet with Janet Panetta. During this year Greenberg decided not to pursue the more "classical"style of modern dance and as an alternative was drawn to the Merce Cunningham studio, where dancing was a physical and aesthetic experience. After one year at the school, he was asked to join the company to replace Jim Self. Greenberg's experiences in the Cunningham company influenced the formation of his own dance philosophy. From Cunningham, Greenberg borrowed the idea that a dancer must balance the need for self-expression with a devotion to the precision of movement. Dancing in Cunningham's *Events*, unique performances in which dancers perform randomly assembled movement phrases from the repertory, piqued his interest in the effect of reviving and re-performing fragments of choreographic material, outside of their original context. Moreover, the protean composition of the *Events* spurred him to think about dance as being analogous to verbal language, whose meaning depends not only on vocabulary, but on syntax. Thus, elements of a dance, such as steps and movement phrases, are like words whose meanings vary depending on their relation to each other, and their position within a composition.

Unlike Cunningham, who determines his choreographic structures by chance to challenge the logic of syntax and elude interpretation, Greenberg uses syntactical choices to creates layers of interpretive possibilities. His choreography illustrates the principle that meaning in the world is multifaceted and interpretation is context-dependent. Greenberg creates choreographic collages of compositional elements: abstract movement, mimetic gestures, text written on placards or projected onto the set, silence, sound, and props. His dances are marked by equivocal signs: gestures that could have several meanings at once, or juxtapositions of movement, text, and sound, that undercut each other through irony. His movement style is characterized by a vigorous and coordinated physicality that reflects a deep anatomical understanding of how the body moves. Action is often initiated distally, by fingers, hands, and feet, or from a mid-limb joint, like a wrist, elbow, or knee. Limbs jet or stretch into planes in space, or cause a spiral sequencing through the body, as a turn. Dancers do not make shapes in space, as destinations in themselves; shapes are created as the body moves.

In his work, Greenberg acts both as company member and soloist—his solos are usually idiosyncratic, marked by more personal, mimetic gestures and varied facial expression. Partnering is conspicuously absent from his work. Greenberg has said that its absence is both an expression of his own feelings of isolation and an aesthetically conveyed social protest against dances that represent the world as heterosexual.

Greenberg's choreographic aesthetic has developed over time. Early works, such as *Amnesty* (1985) and *Morphine* (1986), were concept-driven. Formed by a subtle intention to represent the significance of syntax to a dance's interpretation, these works were generally misunderstood by audiences and the critics alike. Greenberg took a different tack with *MacGuffin or How Meanings Get Lost* (1987). The title was drawn from filmmaker Alfred Hitchcock's term for a narrative red herring—appropriate for a dance which explicitly tackles the problem of choreographic meaning. Here, Greenberg's sensibility crystallized into a dance-collage of compositional elements: formal movement, cheeky gestures, placards with Delsartean witticisms, character costumes, which all converged in silence. Dances made between 1988 and 1992 resembled *MacGuffin* as poignant melanges of irony and pathos.

Greenberg's prior choreographic ideas culminated in *Not-about-AIDS-Dance* (1994), his self-proclaimed "latest immortality project." It illuminated a deepening and refinement of his aesthetic philosophy, and marked a turning point in his personal life. The period in which he made the dance coincided with the AIDS-related deaths of seven significant people in Greenberg's life, including his older brother, Jon. The dance opened with a solo performed by Greenberg under a projected caption, "This is the first material I made after my brother died." This solo set the scene for the rest of the dance, which acts as a combination scrapbook, diary, and memorial. Captions, telling us about the lives of the performers, the origin of recycled movement phrases, and Greenberg himself, were projected above the action. They added conceptual and emotional dimension to the movement phrases that "deaccumulate," according to Greenberg: "Instead of structures accumulating, they disintegrate over and over."

Amidst information offered about the other dancers' personal lives, family deaths, considerations of mortality, and professional disappointments, Greenberg confessed his own preoccupation, his HIV-positive status. During an exuberant solo a caption read, "I've known I was HIV+ since 1987. I don't know now why I am revealing it publicly. I don't know what made it 'private' in the first place. I'm asymtomatic today." *The Disco Project* (1995) revisited moments of its predecesor, *Not-about-AIDS-Dance* intimating the resonance of the past in the present, in memory, and in the body's movement. The dance posed more questions than it gave answers— including "How does one survive AIDS?" Greenberg's latest dances are homages to icons of (gay) popular culture; they are peppered with physicalized vitality and luscious abandon.

—Rebekah J. Kowal

GRIOT NEW YORK

Choreography: Garth Fagan
Music: Wynton Marsalis
Set Design: Martin Puryear
First Performance: 1991, Brooklyn Academy of Music, New York.
Original Dancers: Valentina Alexander, Norwood Pennewell, and Natalie Rogers.

Other productions include: PBS' *Great Performances*, 20 February 1995.

Publications

Anderson, Jack, "A Vision of Steps That Often Clash," *New York Times*, 2 May 1996.

———, "Beauty and Heroism Emerge from Snarls and Tangles," *New York Times*, 25 November 1994.

Charles, Eleanor, "The Guide," *New York Times*, 20 February 1994.

Hunt, Marilyn, "Garth Fagan Dance," *Dance Magazine*, March 1994.

Jackson, George, "An African Odyssey, " *Dance Magazine*, September 1997.

Kisselgoff, Anna, "A Master of the Dynamic Image with an Unexpected Guise," *New York Times*, 17 November 1994.

———, "Neighbors on 42nd Street, but a World Apart," *New York Times*, 1 February 1998.

Mandel, Howard, "Don Pullen's African Brazilian Connection, Chief Cliff Singers, Garth Fagan Dance," *Down Beat*, November 1995.

Mason, Francis, "A Conversation with Garth Fagan," *Ballet Review*, Spring 1995.

O'Connor, John J., "A Dance Tells the Tale of Urban Vicissitudes," *New York Times*, 20 February 1995.

Simpson, Herbert M., "Draft of Shadows," *Dance Magazine*, December 1994.

Thom, Rose Anne, "Griot New York," *Dance Magazine*, February 1995.

Tobias, Tobi, "Garth Fagan Dance," *New York*, 5 December 1994.

*   *   *

"Griot" is a West African word that means "storyteller," and thus, *Griot New York* is a collection of stories about life in the Big Apple. The performance, which takes up a full evening, is made up of a number of music-and-dance vignettes which tell stories about New York City. The work is a collaboration between Garth Fagan, world-famous trumpeter Wynton Marsalis, and sculptor Martin Puryear.

Fagan's distinctive style, which blends modern dance, classical ballet, jazz, and African and Caribbean dance, lends all of its parts to this performance. One vignette, "Bayou Baroque," is a love story duet danced by Norwood Pennewell and Natalie Rogers, two of the principal dancers in Fagan's 23-year-old dance company; a second vignette, "High-Rise Riff," satirizes the lifestyles of Yuppies; and a third, "The Disenfranchised," brings to light the plight of the homeless in large urban areas. Fifteen dancers and seven musicians make up the cast of the entire performance.

The musical score for *Griot New York* was created and written by Wynton Marsalis and encompasses a variety of musical styles, ranging from calypso to waltzes, and features some solos played by Marsalis himself on a heavy, gold-crusted horn given to him by the Bird himself, Charlie Parker. This marked Marsalis' first ballet score; there's also a "Musical Interlude" with the work that allows the seven-piece Wynton Marsalis Septet a chance to play for the audience without the "distraction" of the dancers on stage.

Griot New York debuted at the Brooklyn Academy of Music (BAM) in 1991. Since then, it has been performed throughout the United States and in Vienna, as well as appearing on the Public Broadcasting System's (PBS) *Great Performances* series in 1995. Fagan, described by Anna Kisselgoff in the *New York Times* as "a master of the dynamic image in its unexpected guise," also sometimes stages one or more of the vignettes in medley performances throughout the world, such as in the November 1994 performance

of *Never Top 40* at the Joyce Theater in New York, which featured "Bayou Baroque" and "Spring Yaounde."

—Daryl F. Mallett

GROSSMAN, Danny

American dancer, choreographer, and artistic director based in Canada

Born: 13 September 1942, in San Francisco, California. **Education:** George Washington High School; studied modern dance with Gloria Unti in San Francisco, Gertrude Shurr and May O'Donnell in New York City; studied ballet with Wishmary Hunt and Don Farnworth in New York City; attended Connecticut College summer course, 1963. **Career:** Dancer, Paul Taylor Dance Company, 1963-73; guest artist, Toronto Dance Theatre (Toronto), 1973; artist-in-residence, York University (Toronto), 1974; taught part-time until 1977; founder, Danny Grossman Dance Company, 1978. **Awards:** Chalmers Award for choreography, 1978.

Works

1975	*Higher* (mus. Ray Charles)
1976	*National Spirit* (mus. Medley of Marches)
	Fratelli (mus. Darius Milhaud)
	Couples Suite: Couples/Inching (mus. Terry Riley/music of Zimbabwe by Maraire)
	Triptych (mus. Darius Milhaud)
1977	*Curious Schools of Theatrical Dancing* (mus. François Couperin)
	Ecce Homo (mus. Bach)
	Bella w/Judy Jarvis (mus. Puccini)
1979	*Flurry + Bebop Meet Sideslip & the Muse* (mus. T. Monk, A. Tatum, C. Taylor)
1981	*Endangered Species* (mus. Krzysztof Penderecki)
	Nobody's Business (mus. Jelly Roll Morton, Joe Turner)
1982	*Portrait* (mus. Murray Geddes)
1983	*Shaman* (mus. Murray Geddes)
1984	*Genus* (mus. Karl Stockhaussen)
1985	*Scherzi* (mus. J.B. Arban)
	Ces Plaisirs (mus. Ann Southam)
	Magneto Dynamo (mus. Charles Mingus)
	Divine Air (mus. Gordon Phillips)
1986	*Hot House: Thriving on a Riff* (mus. Charlie Parker)
1987	*La Valse* (mus. Ravel)
1988	*Memento Mori* (mus. Bach)
1989	*Twisted* (mus. Lamber, Hendricks, Ross)
	The Equilibrist (mus. John Coltrane)
1990	*Ground Zero* (Shostakovich)
1991	*Carnival* (mus. music of Martinique)
	Rite Time (mus. Ray Charles)
1992	*Blessed the Beasts* w/Lawrence Gradus (mus. Bach)
	human form divine (mus. Kirk Elliott)
1993	*Rat Race* (mus. Kirk Elliott)
1995	*It shall come to pass* w/Rina Singha (mus. Bob Becker)
1996	*Visionary Realm* (mus. Kirk Elliott)
1997	*Spiritus* (mus. Schubert)
	Hear the Lambs A Cryin' (mus. Paul Robeson)

Publications

On GROSSMAN: book—

Wyman, Max, *Dance Canada*, Vancouver, 1989.

*   *   *

As the son of a Polish-Hungarian Jewish father and an Irish Catholic mother, Daniel William Grossman grew up in a highly politicized household. He walked his first picket line when he was 10 and as a student participated in the historic Berkeley demonstrations. When one considers this background, it's not surprising that his work is full of social commentary, awareness, and humanistic concerns. Major themes include racism, sexuality, war and human conflict, poverty, nationalism, shamanism, respect for nature, and personal spiritual growth. His work is not restricted to serious social commentary, however; the influences of folk dance, mime, the circus, visual art, and music are evident in his humorous, athletic, and frequently satirical choreography.

Always athletic, Grossman began folk dancing in grade school and by 1960 was studying and performing modern dance with Gloria Unti. In 1963, at a summer course at Connecticut College, he met Paul Taylor, who invited him to join his company in New York City. Grossman danced with Taylor for the next 10 years and toured throughout the world with the company. During this decade, Grossman performed 17 roles, many of which were created specifically for him. Taylor was a major influence in Grossman's life and his dance *Aureole* is included in the Danny Grossman Dance Company repertoire.

While studying in New York Grossman made what would become a life-changing connection with Canadian dancer David Earle. Earle and Grossman met in 1962 and were roommates during their New York days. They maintained their friendship and Earle invited Grossman to be a guest artist with Toronto Dance Theatre (TDT). What began as two weeks became a season and more than 20 years later Grossman is still an integral part of the Toronto dance community.

In 1974 Grossman joined the faculty at York University while he continued to work with TDT. It was essentially a single work, *Higher,* made at York University in 1975 that ultimately led to the Danny Grossman Dance Company (DGDC). It was after the success of this piece about a man and a woman dancing with two chairs and a ladder to the music of Ray Charles, that Grossman created his own company. For the first couple years the company's performances were somewhat sporadic because Grossman was still creating choreography for TDT and other companies in North America. But in 1978 the company was established on a full-time basis. During their first summer DGDC did a three-week tour of Massachusetts, appearing at Jacob's Pillow, Harvard Summer Dance Centre, and Boston's Summerthing festival. Upon their return to Toronto they were the first modern dance company to perform at the Ontario Place Forum.

In the summer of 1978 the Canadian Broadcasting Corporation (CDC) taped a half-hour television special on the company that aired nationally that fall. At the same time the Dance in Canada Association announced that Grossman was the recipient of the 1978 Chalmer Award for choreography. Following these events the company did a nine-week tour of western Canada. This tour was financially successful because of the dancers' ability to do double duties. In addition to performing, teaching, and rehearsing, the dancers drove the truck, managed the tour, did technical set-up, wardrobe, and most of the publicity.

Grossman is a prolific choreographer, having created a repertoire of more than 30 works. Of his work he says: "My concerns are personal and human, and the work I do is a mirror of all of us, what we've done and where we're going. The artist asks questions, because he really feels that we have to evolve as a species. What it boils down to then is a simple matter of wanting to communicate." His work is influenced somewhat by his years with Paul Taylor, but he doesn't fit into any particular school of modern dance such as Graham or Limon. His way of moving is unique; it continues to be physically demanding and very athletic. His choreography has many nondance influences, the first being his parents' political beliefs and their taste in art and music. Grossman remembers growing up listening to everything from folk to Bach to Arabic music. The music of Grossman's teenage years, such as Ray Charles, has also played a part. Even films have contributed. Grossman says his solos were psychological journeys but also theatrical like Charlie Chaplin.

The mid-1970s were a prolific period for Grossman. He says he didn't have the confidence or the discipline to choreograph when he was in Taylor's company so it was as if the choreography had been building inside him, just waiting to come out. The company continues to perform his early works because they are as important to his life and the repertoire as his most recent work. In 1976 alone he created four new pieces: *Couples Suite, National Spirit, Fratelli* and *Triptych.* These four dances and *Higher* were performed at the 1976 Toronto Modern Dance Festival (see Canadian Dance Festivals, 1948-78). *National Spirit,* about American patriotism, was his first political satire. *Triptych* is a haunting and powerful dance about personal physical abuse. Three more works emerged from Grossman in 1977. *Curious Schools of Theatrical Dancing* was his first solo about a paranoiac, physically dangerous dance to the death. *Ecce Homo* is based on religious paintings and drawings of ecstasy and sin. *Bella* was a collaboration with colleague Judy Jarvis, inspired by the creators' love of Puccini and Chagall's paintings of lovers. Other notable pieces include the apocalyptic *Endangered Species;* the tongue in cheek *Nobody's Business,* playing with our perceptions of sexuality and gender; the very dark *Ces Plaisirs,* after Collette's book *The Pure and the Impure; La Valse,* a sarcastic look at poverty and wealth; as well as other collaborative works such as *Blessed the Beasts* with Lawrence Gradus and *It shall come to pass* with Rina Singha.

The preservation of dance is important to Grossman and his company has remounted works by Patricia Beatty, Anna Blewchamp, Paula Ross, Judy Jarvis, Lawrence Gradus, Charles Weidman, and Paul Taylor. Grossman's own history is being preserved in the archives at York University and through software created by Eddie Kastrau. A DGDC dancer since 1986, Kastrau created Performance History Database in 1995. It is used by several dance companies to record information about performances, repertoire, dancers, presenters, venues, and other archival information. Another dancer, Trish Armstrong, is working toward codifying a Grossman technique.

Residencies and outreach are an important part of DGDC. By using the varying backgrounds of the dancers, DGDC offers a variety of workshops and lecture/demonstrations, such as workshops in Grossman Technique, Graham Technique, Afro-Caribbean and Modern Dance, Ukrainian and Modern Dance, Choreographic Process, Dance for Drama Students, Dance for Physical Education Students, and Setting Group Works and lectures on Dance in Canada,

Visual Arts, Musical, and Social and Political Influences in Grossman's work, Archiving Dance, Dance and Body Image, Designing for Dance, Stage Management, and Arts Administration. Grossman has also taught extensively at the Juilliard School of Music and Drama, Brown University, Simon Fraser University, the Performing Arts Workshop in San Francisco, Paul Taylor Studio, Harlem Dance Foundation, and Toronto's Ryerson Polytechnic and York Universities. His works have been performed by Theatre Ballet of Canada, Judith Marcuse Dance Company, Citidance Company of the City College of New York, Paris Opera Ballet, Les Grands Ballets Canadiens, the National Ballet of Canada, DancEast, and Canadian Children's Dance Theatre.

Grossman has continued in the footsteps of his parents as a political activist. He is on the board of the Toronto Arts Council; in 1993 he participated in the Dance/USA National Task Force on Dance Education; he was a driving force behind Dance 2020, a forum discussing the future of dance in Ontario; he has been involved in Artsvote, a campaign to educate local voters and politicians about issues in the cultural sector; and he holds the position of Adjunct Professor in the Department of Dance at York University.

—Amy Bowring

LE GROUPE DE LA PLACE ROYALE

Canadian dance company

Le Groupe de la Place Royale (GPR) was incorporated in 1966 and became the first official contemporary dance company of Quebec. Its director, a major figure in Quebec contemporary dance, was Jeanne Renaud (b. 1928) acknowledged as one of the founding mothers of an indigenous modern dance, together with her contemporaries Françoise Riopelle (b. 1927) and Françoise Sullivan (b. 1925). These three women were closely associated with a group of rebel artists of Montreal who published in 1948 an artistic manifesto known as *Le Refus global*. This notorious manifesto proclaimed the birth of Automatisme, a primarily visual art movement which went beyond Surrealism and relied on spontaneity and the unconscious for its creative inspiration. In its wish to break with tradition and the past it favored an individualistic, uncensored art work that was abstract and nonfigurative. The Automatiste art movement, spurred by Paul-Emile Borduas, was a liberating influence advocating full artistic freedom and the rejection of clergy-dominated traditional Quebec society. It contributed to Quebec's cultural awakening even though the publication of *Le Refus global* resulted in many of the signatories losing their jobs. Others went into self-imposed exile towards greener artistic pastures such as New York and Paris for creative inspiration.

After an initial training in ballet with Montreal pioneer Gerald Crevier and in modern dance with Elizabeth Leese, Renaud studied with Hanya Holm, Mary Anthony, and Merce Cunningham in New York. In 1949 she went to join some of the exiled Automatistes in Paris, and performed concerts together with Françoise Riopelle who was also based in Paris at that time.

Renaud returned to Montreal in 1959 and was urged to join Riopelle's newly created dance school, Ecole de Danse Moderne de Montreal, as both teacher and dancer/choreographer. Renaud collaborated with Riopelle until 1965 at which point she decided to branch out on her own. The result was *Expression 65,* a concert featuring Renaud's works which ran for several weeks in the pocket theatre of Place Ville Marie. Encouraged by the success of this solo venture Renaud decided a year later to found Le Groupe de la Place Royale taking the name of the small square in old Montreal where the studios were located.

The new company recruited dancers from Les Grands Ballets Canadiens, which might seem odd at first glance. Yet the group's aesthetics favoured purity of line, and formalism, which was in keeping with classical training. Peter Boneham, another charter member, soon became her assistant and partner, choreographing and teaching for the company and for the school which they had also opened.

Under Renaud's tutelage the group was committed to encouraging artistic expression of all types. Its vision was to expand the boundaries of dance via experimentation, research, and innovation. Renaud choreographed over 40 works, mostly for the company. Her pieces rejected narrative structures and favoured multidisciplinary collaboration between the visual and performing arts. Examples of this kind of work are found in *Sur un poème de St Denis Garneau* (1969), a plastique rendering of the mood poem of the Québécois poet, and in *Karanas I and II* (1968) a stage duet emphasizing linear purity with a filmed version being shown simultaneously but with the dancers in the nude. Far from being sensual, this piece was intentionally Apollonian.

Boneham, meanwhile, had trained as a ballet dancer in his native Rochester, New York, before studying modern dance with James Waring and performing as a soloist for the Metropolitan Opera Ballet, the William Dollar Concert Ballet, on Broadway, in summer stock productions, and at Radio City Music Hall. He arrived in 1965 in time to take part in *Expression 65*.

Renaud headed the troupe for six years, juggling her tight schedule of teaching at the school and giving company class while serving as an administrator, artistic director, fundraiser, dancer, and choreographer. By 1972 she had withdrawn mainly because of burn-out, and the artistic directorship went to Boneham, who quickly sought the collaboration of Jean-Pierre Perreault, a dancer with the company.

The Boneham/Perreault duo experimented with voice, creating joint choreographies that included spoken text. This exploration was best seen in *Danse pour sept voix* and *Les nouveaux espaces,* both created in 1976. As they incorporated voice to movement these works became more theatrical and less abstract. Perreault remained co-artistic director of the company until 1981 during which time he choreographed 20 works, some of them in collaboration with Boneham.

In 1977 Le Groupe de la Place Royale relocated to the Canadian capital of Ottawa, which had no resident dance company at that time, in the hope that this move would help build a bigger audience and also bring in more financial backing. In Montreal critical and audience reaction to their experimental works was mixed, the pieces often seeming too hermetic for the public. The move to Ottawa did in fact give the group greater visibility and backing. Stylistically the company's works showed some recurring characteristics that were mainly Cunningham inspired: several simultaneous actions occurring in different spaces; movement phrases with quick-changing spatial orientation; choreography seen as a series of interchangeable independent sections; music and dance moving separately in the work.

By 1981 Perreault chose to sever ties with the company that had nurtured him and to explore a career as an independent dancemaker.

He soon became one of the leading figures of Canadian dance earning an international reputation as innovative choreographer and craftsman of monumental group works. Meanwhile Boneham remained the sole artistic director and continued to create pieces until 1988. In fact this was his most prolific choreographic period and he created theatrical pieces such as *The Collector of Cold Weather* (1981), *Faustus* (1983), *The Living Room* (1985), and *Trio* (1987); in these pieces, dancers often sang, spoke, acted and provided their own musical accompaniment.

The company stopped touring in 1988 and developed a new vision: the concept of Dance Lab emerged with the mandate of helping the research phase in the creative process. Le Groupe Dance Lab offers a rehearsal work venue and permanent dancers to Canadian choreographers during a limited residency with the aim of helping discover new ways of dancemaking. It is also an opportunity to take risks without worrying about audience attendance and reception. Peter Boneham often acts as mentor to this dance equivalent of a playwrights' workshop. Dance Lab's formula is a unique opportunity for artistic soul-searching in Canada and is well appreciated by the Canadian dance community. Generally speaking Boneham's artistic vision looks to enlighten and teach, to challenge and move the audience, and to show dancemakers how to accept failure and learn from this valuable experience.

Publications

Elton, Heather, "Welcome to My Laboratory," *Dance Connection,* June/July/August 1991.

MacGillivray, Jean, "Le Groupe de la Place Royale: Twenty Years of Dance Innovation," *Performing Arts in Canada,* September 1986.

McLaughlin, Hillary, "The 20th Anniversary of Le Groupe de la Place Royale: A Celebration and a Legacy for Canadian Modern Dance," *Dance in Canada,* Spring 1986.

—Iro Valaskakis Tembeck

LE GROUPE NOUVELLE AIRE

Québécois dance company

Founded in 1968 by Rose-Marie Lèbe and Martine Epoque; originally named Groupe Nouvel'aire but eventually took the more correct spelling of Nouvelle Aire. Main imagemaker and choreographer was Martine Epoque; artistic mandate was to promote new choreography using contemporary musicians whether Québécois or international. Other choreographers included Paul Lapointe, Philippe Vita, Edouard Lock, Iro Tembeck, Christina Coleman, Paul-André Fortier. Ecole Nouvelle Aire was the school attached to the company where classes in their idiosyncratic technique were being taught along with improvisation and other dance styles. The company toured Canada and the United States and Europe until it disbanded in 1982. Featured in Canadian television productions.

*   *   *

In the late 1960s, Le Groupe Nouvelle Aire and its rival company Le Groupe de la Place Royale emerged in the choreographic landscape and would prove to be the strongest breeding grounds for indigenous modern dance in Quebec. Dancemakers such as Jean-Pierre Perreault, Edouard Lock, Paul-André Fortier, and Ginette Laurin were nurtured within these two experimental dance troupes. They then branched out independently and fashioned in the 1980s what would become known as Montreal's particular style of movement.

Prior to that, several important modern dance pioneers hailing from European modern dance had settled in Montreal during the war years. Unfortunately these early dancemakers did not find the support structure and financial backing necessary to create permanent companies since the Canada Council was yet to be created, while Canadian television started in 1952 and the Quebec Cultural Affairs Ministry only came into existence in 1960. The most well-known European arrival was Ruth Abramowitz Sorel (1907-74), a noted dancer with Mary Wigman from 1923 to 1928 who, after an international career, lived in Montreal for a decade, during which time she ran a school and had a troupe that toured Canada. There was also Elizabeth Leese, (1916-1962) of German-Danish origin, a former dancer with Trudi Schoop and a student of Laban and Jooss. She worked in Montreal from 1944 to her death in 1962. Finally there was Biroute Nagys, (b. 1920) a Lithuanian who had graduated from Rosalia Chladek dance academy and who opened schools and gave concerts in Montreal from 1948 right through to the 1970s. Though their works received both critical and public acclaim, these pioneers lacked the proper means to foster the next generation of dancemakers.

Meanwhile a parallel strand of dance experimentation grew out of three native Montrealers: Françoise Sullivan (b. 1925), Françoise Riopelle (b. 1927), and Jeanne Renaud (b. 1928), who went to study with Hanya Holm in New York and returned regularly to Montreal to present dance concerts. This threesome paved the way for a more lasting modern sensibility and were to become the founding mothers of indigenous Quebec modern dance. Renaud went further and incorporated the first official modern dance troupe: Le Groupe de la Place Royale (GPR).

Two years after Place Royale's founding a new troupe came into existence. Le Groupe Nouvelle Aire (GNA) was a dance collective founded in 1968 by teachers and students of the physical education department of the Université de Montréal. In the early days two French-born women, Rose-Marie Lèbe and Martine Epoque, headed the company which went through three distinct stages in its evolution. Quite quickly Martine Epoque became its main imagemaker and the person responsible for giving the group its specific signature style. Born in Southern France, Epoque had come to Quebec in 1967 to teach Dalcroze eurhythmics at the Université de Montréal and with Lèbe had rallied their respective students and trained them and presented performances right away. These culminated two years later with dance productions at the prestigious Place des Arts.

From its outset Le Groupe Nouvelle Aire wished to promote choreographic experimentation and to create a new technique that would identify the company as having a "Québécois" style of movement. Epoque's aesthetics was influenced by Béjart's neoclassical lines, and by her Dalcroze training. Pieces like *De Profundis* (1971), *Evanescence* (1972), and *Amiboisme* (1970) were particularly representative of her work. The movements were rhythmically complex and the technique she developed was originally difficult to master. With time it became more fluid and versatile but maintained its characteristic irregular rhythms, its marked contrast in dynamics and shapes and its frequent use of body isolations. Ecole Nouvelle Aire opened in 1969 and in its heyday in the 1970s boasted some 450 students. The GNA technique was developed and taught there along with improvisation and occasional classes in other styles.

By 1972 the second stage of development occurred in the company as it shed its P.E. beginnings. Few of the original 25 student enthusiasts were left and the newcomers hailed from different artistic backgrounds: some came from mime, others from theatre, yet others were classically trained. Though technically stronger and more individualistic than the initial dancers they could never however fit in a corps de ballet mould. An unusual fact for the time was that many of these dancers held univerisity degrees in literature, theatre, sports or fields other than dance since that was not then available in Canada. The working atmosphere in the studio was always one of questioning the creative process. Aside from Epoque's choreography there were new exciting works being created by dancer Paul Lapointe. These were overtly theatrical and sought to craft a new movement language with each piece reflecting the particular chosen theme.

Experimentation and originality were the guiding principles of Le Groupe Nouvelle Aire. The invention was mostly focused on the training and in the movement phrases. Financially, the company was subsidised by different level government grants but did not have an operating grant till its third stage of development. As such, the dancers would clock in a five-hour day and use the rest of the time to teach dance in the various colleges and universities. In so doing they helped build quite a following among the diverse student bodies with which they came into contact. Modern dance however, still remained a hermetic art form for Montrealers who were not sufficiently exposed to this type of experimentation.

In 1975 a major turning point occurred. Epoque went on sabbatical in the United States and new choreographers sprang from within the group. The shift was also aesthetic as more theatricality appeared and emotion was reinstated in the choreographies. There was less emphasis on forging a new movement language, the tendency being to create mood pieces such as Edouard Lock's first choreography, *Temps Volé* or in *Howl* by Iro Tembeck. The Limón techinque was now taught in company class by Linda Rabin, a Montrealer who was back in her home town for a year, and by other members of the Limón company in intensive clinics. Accordingly, the group's danceworks started showing breath in the phrasing and also incorporated the fall and recovery technique.

Part of the troupe's new image incuded the Choréchanges, or choreographic exchanges which basically were studio performances aimed at helping budding choreographers hone their craft and receive immediate feedback from the invited audience. The public was thus being demystified as to experimental dance while dancers were at the same time able to learn how to scale their performances for more intimate setting.

By 1977 Le Groupe de la Place Royale moved to Ottawa and left the coast clear for Le Groupe Nouvelle Aire, by then the only established modern dance troupe remaining in the city. At this point it started receiving operating grants which required a new rescheduling of the work week leaving no possibility for outside work or teaching. The company had now become established and sported a traditional format. Many of the dancers of the second generation such as Paul-André Fortier, Iro Tembeck, and Edouard Lock decided to leave preferring to create their own mini-troupes and to pursue their own personal experimentation. They were soon to be joined by Ginette Laurin.

As the company's third and final stage of development came into being the new dancers were more homogenous, better trained, and ready to accept full time jobs and a repertory format. There were however no choreographers among them. Even Epoque had loosened her ties having accepted a position at the dance department of Université du Québec a Montreal. Martine Haug, a former dancer and rehearsal mistress with the company then took over the artistic helm. She commissioned new pieces from the very dancemakers who had left the group thus creating an unnecessary redundancy in the choreographic landscape. One of the structures was superfluous and had to go. Curiously it turned out that it was the more established one that buckled under so that Le Groupe Nouvelle Aire was forced to disband in 1982.

The move towards independent dancemaking prospered in Montreal during the 1980s and was responsible for the burgeoning of several small troupes that negated contemporary modern dance vocabulary and leaned towards Bauschian type dance-theatre. Quite quickly a curious role reversal occurred in Montreal. With neither Le Groupe Nouvelle Aire nor Le Groupe de la Place Royale remaining in the choreographic landscape, independent dancemakers took on the role of the establishment rather than the avant-garde. And the real establishment—or more conventional modern dance—was in effect erased from the picture.

—Iro Valaskakis Tembeck

GUANGDONG MODERN DANCE COMPANY
Chinese modern dance company

Started in 1987 as a modern dance training program in Guangzhou (formerly Canton), the capital city of Guangdong Province, Mainland China, by Yang Mei-qi, the former principal of Guangdong Dance School, with funding from the Asian Cultural Council (ACC); renamed Modern Dance Practice Company of Guangdong Dance School in 1990; officially established in 1992 as the first full time professional modern dance company in Mainland China, with the formal approval from Guangdong Provincial Cultural Bureau and funding from the bureau and the private donation of Willy Tsao, pioneer of Hong Kong modern dance and its first artistic director; has toured extensively inside and outside China, including India, Korea, Singapore, France, Germany, Switzerland and United States, as well as Hong Kong and Macao; has won three gold and one silver medal at the Paris International Dance Competition.

Publications

Ballet International/Tanz Aktuell (Berlin), no. 1, 1998, special China issue.

Belans, Linda, "Bright Moments in Early Stages of Guangdong's Development, *News & Observer* (Durham, North Carolina), 22 July 1991.

Chin, Gwin, "New Movement in China," *New York Times,* 19 May 1991.

Dunning, Jennifer, "A Learning Experience for the Teachers, Too," *New York Times,* 14 July 1991.

Kisselgoff, Anna, "A Troupe from China Masters the New," *New York Times,* 22 July 1991.

————, "The Person, the Group: Reflections from China," *New York Times,* 1 November 1997.

Ou Jian-ping, "From "Beasts" to "Flowers": Modern Dance in China, in *East Meets West in Dance: Voices in the Cross-Cultural Dialogue,* edited by Ruth Solomon and John Solomon, Choreography and Dance Studies Series No. 9, Chur, Switzerland, 1995.

Ries, Daryl, "Guangdong Modern Dance Company," *Dance Magazine,* June 1992.

Supree, Burt, "China Hybrid," *Village Voice,* 6 August 1991.

*   *   *

In the autumn of 1987, a group of 20 dancers gathered at Guangdong Dance School after tough auditions all over China, and became the first group of Chinese students to receive Western modern dance training. Ten years later, a second group of students has grown up and danced triumphantly both nationally and internationally.

Yang Mei-qi is the principal of Guangdong Dance School and a charming lady famous for her ability to teach Chinese folk dance and well-known for her determination to get what she wants. Without her there certainly would not have been this very first modern dance company in China, and all the favorable conditions of this contemporary world, such as increasing world peace and cooperation and easier global communications, would not have benefitted the Mainland Chinese dance circle. And the newly adopted modern dance in this country, as imported from the West and inspired by Guangdong Modern Dance Company, has carried Chinese culture from traditionalism to modernism on the international stage and served both Chinese modern dance and Chinese modern culture well in setting up an attractive and exciting image much more easily and smoothly than Chinese traditional dances or Western ballet, both of which have naturally paid more attention to the strict maintenance of their historic forms. In this sense, one could never overestimate the significance of Yang Mei-qi's historical contributions as the founder of the company.

Obviously, without Guangdong Modern Dance Company, the first international harbor for both importing Western modern dance and exporting Chinese modern dance, the many richly talented dancers and administrators connected with the company would not have been able to find the right place to help China with their precious suggestions; they would not have been able to share their profound expertise in technique, improvisation, composition, choreography, production, injury prevention, history and aesthetics, concepts, and philosophy; moreover hundreds of thousands of people outside Mainland China would not have been able to know more about China than that world-famous Great Wall. And all this generous support has constituted the decisive element of a "harmonious human relationship."

In addition, without the reform policies adopted by the Chinese government, and without the in-depth understanding of the central government's policy by sympathetic officials, it would have been totally impossible for the birth of this company, to say nothing of allowing this government-run company to constantly accept the large amount of regular funding from Willy Tsao, a Hong Kong artist.

Distant water could never immediately quench one's deadly thirst, as well said by our Chinese ancestor, and this maxim describes the great contributions of Willy Tsao as a teacher, choreographer, artistic director, donor, and friend of the company. For the past ten years, he is the only person either inside or outside China who has been constantly ready to help at all times; whenever Yang Mei-qi phoned him to say that she had no teacher at hand, he put aside his own company in Hong Kong and went to Guangzhou. Since the company was set up formally in 1992, when he was officially appointed artistic director, he has worked for the company on a more regular basis, spending half of every month in Guangzhou. He has also donated one million Chinese yuan out of his own pocket every year to pay the dancers, which has successfully kept them from dancing in night clubs, a common trick for survival for many Chinese dancers in other companies, and enabled them to concentrate on their modern dance careers. He has also given separate funds for converting the company's old studio into a well-equipped public theater, paid for travel, and financed healthcare for dancers.

However, the most touching story about his whole-hearted devotion to the company and to the newly prosperous Chinese modern dance after its long struggle under political pressure is not that he has always been willing to provide free and first-class service as an eloquent performance presenter, interpreter, and even a porter whenever he was needed, nor that he has given all his creative ideas to the company, but that in 1995 when he was unexpectedly removed from the post of artistic director and lost a voice in making artistic decisions, he still gave 600,000 Chinese yuan that year in order to save the company from bankruptcy. Luckily, this situation, miserable for him and disastrous for the young dancers, only lasted for a year, and he resumed the post in 1996.

Tsao's genius is manifest in his works, which include four award-winning short works, *Ancestors* (1990), *Banished from Heaven* (1994), *Shadow of Light* and *My Rhythm* (both 1996), choreographed expressly for Guangdong, two full-length modern jazz ballets, *City Romance* (1989) and *Young Sky* (1991), which became some of the best loved works in the repertoire and extremely popular with younger audiences, and his latest full-length modern dance drama *Sailing Across the Sea of Life.*

Excitingly, the birth and growth of Guangdong Modern Dance Company in 10 years has signifcance reaching far beyond the company itself; it has become both a flagship for the promotion of Chinese modern dance movement and, to a larger extent, of modernism in Chinese culture. In addition, it has become a cradle for the further development of modern dance in the country: Wang Mei, one of the major faculty members of the first two-year modern dance program at Beijing Dance Academy since 1991, and Jin Xing, the first artistic director of Beijing Modern Dance Company (the second professional modern dance company in this country), have all studied with Guangdong.

—Ou Jian-ping

HALPRIN, Anna
American dancer, choreographer, and educator

Born: Anna Schuman, 13 July 1920, in Wilmette, Illinois. **Education:** Bennington Summer School of Dance, 1938-39; University of Wisconsin, B.S. in dance 1943, Ph.D. with honors, 1994. **Family:** Married Lawrence Halprin, 1940; two children. **Career:** Dancer and choreographer; founder, Impulse Magazine, 1948; founder, San Francisco Dancers' Workshop, 1955, Tamalpa Institute, 1978; Distinguished Teaching Chair, American Dance Festival, 1996. **Awards:** Guggenheim Fellowship, 1970-71; American Dance Guild Award, 1980; named to Isadora Duncan Hall of Fame, 1986; Teacher of the Year Award, California Teacher's Association, 1988; Lifetime Achievement Award in visual and performing arts, *San Francisco Bay Guardian* newspaper, 1990; Vision and Excellence Award, Women of Achievement, 1992; Samuel H. Scripps Award for Lifetime Achievement in Modern Dance, American Dance Festival, 1997; honorary doctorate, Sierra University, 1987.

Works (for the San Francisco Dancers' Workshop to 1980; then for Tamalpa Institute)

1959   *Flowerburger,* Jay Marks Contemporary Dance Theater, San Francisco
        Rites of Women, San Francisco Playhouse
1960   *Birds of America or Gardens without Walls,* International Avant-Garde Arts Festival, Vancouver
1962   *Four-Legged Stool* (mus. Terry Riley), San Francisco Playhouse
        Five-Legged Stool (mus. Morton Subotnik, David Tudor), San Francisco Playhouse
        April 1962 Event (mus. Riley, LaMonte Young), University of California, Los Angeles
1963   *Exposizione* (mus. Berio), International Festival of Contemporary Music, Venice
        Visage (mus. Berio), Music Biennial, Zagreb, Yugoslavia, and Rome
1964   *Procession* (mus. Subotnik), University of California, Los Angeles
1965   *Parades and Changes* (mus. Subotnik, Folke Rabe), 12 versions between 1965 and 1967, performed in Stockholm, Poland, Los Angeles, San Francisco, Berkeley, and New York
1965   *Apartment 6,* Helsinki and San Francisco
1967   *The Bath* (mus. Pauline Oliveros), Atheneum Museum, Hartford, Connecticut
        Myths (mus. Casey Sonabend), series of 10 performances at the San Francisco Dancers' Workshop Studio

1968   *Ome* (mus. Sonabend), University of Oregon, Portland
        Lunch (mus. Charles Amirkhanian), Hilton Hotel, San Francisco
        San Francisco State University C10 (mus. Sonabend), San Francisco State University
1969   *Ceremony of Us,* San Francisco Dancers' Workshop with Studio Watts, Mark Taper Forum, Los Angeles
        Look (mus. performers), Museum of Art, San Francisco
        Event in a Chapel (mus. Sonabend), Pacific University, Stockton, California
1970   *New Time Shuffle* (mus. Richard Friedman, Bo Conley), Soledad Prison
        Kadosh, with Rabbi Samuel Brodie, Beth Sinai Temple
1971   *Initiations and Transformations* (mus. James Fletcher Hall), University Art Museum, Berkeley
        Animal Ritual (mus. James Fletcher Hall), University Art Museum, Berkeley
1976   *Citydance,* audience participation pieces in the streets of San Francisco continuing through 1977
1977   *Ritual and Celebration,* audience participation piece, Berkeley
1978   *Male and Female Rituals* (mus. Kirk Nurock and natural sounds), City Center Theater, New York
        Arcosanti Alive, with Paolo Soleri, Arcosanti, Arizona
1979   *Celebration of Life/Cycle of Ages* (mus. Rod Marymor, Sandy Hershman), Hilton Hotel, San Francisco
1980   *Search for Living Myths and Rituals through Dance and the Environment,* with Lawrence Halprin, public dance event, College of Marin Fine Arts Theater and sites in Marin county
1981   *In and On the Mountain* (mus. Kirk Norwick), Mt. Tamalpais and College of Marin Theater
1982   *Thanksgiving* (poetry and narration by Kush), public dance event, Mt. Tamalpais
1983   *Return to the Mountain* (mus. Weldon McCarty, Shakti, Bo Conley), Mt. Tamalpais and Redwood High School Gym, Larkspur, California
1984   *Run to the Mountain* (poetry and narration by Kush), Mt. Tamalpais and Redwood High School Gym, Larkspur, California
1985   *Circle the Mountain* (mus. Brian Hand, Suru), Mt. Tamalpais and Redwood High School Gym, Larkspur, California
        Earth Run, public dance event, United Nations Plaza, New York, and Big Sur, California
1986   *Circle the Earth: A Dance in the Spirit of Peace* (mus. John Gruntfest, Grand Rudolph, Weldon McCarty, Terry Riley, with poetry and narration by Kush), public dance event, Redwood High School Gym, Larkspur, California

1987   *Circle the Earth: A Peace Dance with the Planet* (mus. Brian Hand, singer: Susan Osborn), public dance event, Redwood High School Gym, Larkspur, California
        The Planetary Dance, public dance event performed in 63 cities around the world

1988   *Circle the Earth: Dancing Our Peaceful Nature,* public dance event, Marin Headlands

1989   *Circle the Earth: Dancing with Life on the Line,* Mt. Tamalpais and Redwood High School Gym, Larkspur, California

1990   *Carry Me Home* (mus. Jules Beckman and Norman Rutherford), Positive Motion dancers, Theatre Artaud, San Francisco

Publications

By HALPRIN: books—

Circle the Earth Manual: A Guide for Dancing Peace with the Planet, with Allan Stinson, Kentfield, California, 1984.
Citydance 77, with James Nixon and James T. Burns, San Francisco, 1978.
Collected Writings, 3 vols., San Francisco, 1973-86.
Movement Ritual I, Kentfield, California, 1979.
Moving Toward Life, Hanover, 1995.
A School Comes Home, with Jim Burns, San Francisco, 1973.

On HALPRIN: books—

Broughton, James, *She Is a Moving One,* San Francisco, 1988.
Hindman, James, *Happening Theory and Methodology: Allan Kaprow, Claes Oldenburg, Ann Halprin 1959-1967,* Ann Arbor, 1976.
Homan, Dianne Christine, *Ritualistic Interpretations in the Works of Halprin, Hay, Dean, and Takei,* University of Oregon, 1985.
Roose-Evans, James, *Experimental Theatre from Stanislavsky to Peter Brook,* New York, 1984.
———, *Passages of the Soul: Ritual Today,* Dorset, England, 1994.
Turner, Diane Mary, *Bay Area Modern Dance: the Influence of Anna Halprin and the Development of Unique Trends,* Ann Arbor, 1985.

On HALPRIN: articles—

Daly, Ann (ed.), "What Has Become of Postmodern Dance?," *The Drama Review,* 1992.
Egan, Carol, "Honors for West Coast Innovator Anna Halprin," *Dance Magazine,* July 1980.
Hartman, Rose, "Talking with Anna Halprin," *Dance Scope,* Fall 1977.
Jean, Norma, and Deak Frantisek, "Anna Halprin's Theatre and Therapy Workshop," *Tulane Drama Review,* March 1976.
Luger, Eleanor R., and Barry Lane, "When Choreography Becomes Female," *Christopher Street,* December 1978.
Monk, Meredith, et al., "Ages of the Avant-Garde," *Performing Arts Journal,* XVI, 1994.
Moore, Dick, "Dance Journal," *City Arts Monthly,* April 1981.
Murphy, Ann, "Edge Festival," *Dance Magazine,* July 1996.
Pierce, Robert, "The Ann Halprin Story," *Village Voice,* 10 March 1975.
Rainer, Yvonne, "Yvonne Rainer Interviews Ann Halprin," *Drama Review* 2, 1965.
Serlin, Ilene A., "Interview with Anna Halprin," *American Journal of Dance Therapy,* 1996.

Films and Videotapes

Beeson, Coni, dir., *Ann: A Portrait,* American Film Institute, 1971.
Circle the Earth: Dancing with Life on the Line, Media Arts West, 1989.
Halprin, Anna, dir., *Embracing Earth,* Abrahams-Wilson Productions.
Positive Motion, Abrahams-Wilson Productions, 1991.
Ritual of Life and Death and Dance for Your Life, filmed by Ellison Horne, 1989.
Safer, Joan, dir., *Inner Landscapes,* KQED-TV, 1992.

*   *   *

For more than four decades, pioneer Anna Halprin has been a seminal figure in modern dance. During her long career, the work of this "distinguished rebel" has evolved from a search for new forms of dance to a belief that dance can have a profound effect on the individual, society, and even the planet.

Though Halprin would ultimately challenge both the form and function of modern dance, it was in this tradition that she began her career. Having studied under Margaret H'Doubler at the University of Wisconsin-Madison in the late 1930s, Halprin later danced in New York in Broadway musicals and with the Humphrey-Weidman Company. After moving to California in 1945 with her husband, Lawrence Halprin, she formed a modern dance studio with Welland Lathrop and by the 1950s, as modern dance reached its pinnacle, Halprin was well-established in the field. However, she soon began to distance herself from the mainstream of modern dance. In Halprin's book *Moving Toward Life* (1995), Sally Banes writes, "to Halprin and many of her peers, what had once been a dramatically new and eloquent art form now seemed hidebound." Halprin left the studio she had formed with Lathrop and temporarily retired.

In 1955, hoping to reinvest modern dance with freshness and vitality, Halprin founded the San Francisco Dancer's Workshop, which met on the outdoor dance deck at her home in Kentfield, California. In its modest beginnings, the workshop was an experimental laboratory including among its members dancers, musicians, architects, poets, and psychologists. Later the company attracted the attention of the avant-garde art world, and was invited to perform around the country as well as at major international art festivals.

It is generally agreed that the evolution of Halprin's ideas can be seen in four overlapping phases, with the formation of the Dancer's Workshop and its early experiments marking the first phase. Using improvisation, Halprin concentrated on shedding the stylized movements and techniques of modern dance. This early work shows H'Doubler's influence in its emphasis on personal creativity and movement studies over dance as a perfect art form. In her dances, Halprin discarded the predictability of cause and effect, created sensory experiences without continuity or meaning, and formed dances from ordinary tasks such as pouring water, throwing colorful objects in the air, and changing clothes.

Halprin also eschewed the technical apparatus and production system of modern dance. *Five-Legged Stool* (1962) broke from the proscenium arch paradigm and expanded performance space to include aisles, ceilings, and even the outside sidewalks. In another departure from the mainstream, Halprin incorporated vocalizations, music, and props into her performances. In all these endeavors, she began her life-long interest in process over product, always searching for new ideas rather than perfecting a repertory of dance pieces.

It is no doubt because of this early experimental period that in a 1981 piece in *Dance Journal,* Dick Moore called Anna Halprin "the mother of post-modern dance." Indeed, some of the most influential figures in dance experimentation in New York during the 1960s—Simone Forti, Yvonne Ranier, Trisha Brown, and Meredith Monk—were products of Halprin's workshops in the 1950s.

Parades and Changes (1965) ushered in a new phase of Halprin's work. In her early experiments, she used improvisation to develop the content of a work, but in performance its final form was fixed. In *Parades and Changes* however, Halprin departed from this practice and began to use what she called "scores"—preplanned designs or sets of instructions for a process, allowing for individual input during the performance itself. The intense and sometimes hostile audience response to works such as *Parades and Changes* caused Halprin to consider how she might include the audience in the creative process. As a result, in this second phase of her work Halprin created "audience participation events," most notably *Myths* (1967), a year-long series in which the audience were instructed to complete certain tasks thus becoming an integral part of the performances.

During this period, Halprin was influenced by several noted psychologists, among them Fritz Perls and John Rinn (Gestalt Therapy), who affirmed her vision of breaking down the barrier between art and life. This vision gave birth to more innovations: increasingly, she worked with non-professional dancers and continued to expand her use of space, performing dances at bus stops, beaches, churches, and museums. The next period of Halprin's work grew out of her belief that dance had the potential to effect social change. In preparing *Ceremony of Us* (1969), Halprin conducted workshops with an all-black group in Watts and an all-white group in San Francisco. The two groups then came together for the 10 days and nights preceding their public performance, the goal of which was to challenge both the performers and the audience to reconsider their ideas about race. In Halprin's view, dance could transform and heal.

Halprin's struggle with cancer in 1972 led her to further explore the therapeutic possibilities of dance and inaugurated the present phase of her work. Because dance aided her own healing process, she began to create healing rituals for other cancer patients and those afflicted with AIDS. In particular, *Circle the Earth—Dancing with Life on the Line* (1989) dealt directly with the AIDS epidemic.

Halprin's ideas evolved to the extent that she saw the need to replace her workshop with a formal training program and in 1978 founded the Tamalpa Institute with her daughter, Daria Halprin-Khalighi. Tamalpa serves as a center for the study of movement, dance, the healing-arts, the creative process, myths, rituals, and community art; its aim is to practice the Halprin Life/Art process whereby real-life issues are translated into original dance art. Halprin's statement that "the natural process of the artist is from concern about the self to concern for the community to concern for the globe," mirrors the progression of her own work. During the 1980s and 1990s, she devoted her efforts to large group dances for the environment and world peace. Out of this work has grown the *Planetary Dance*, a prayer of healing for others and the Earth, which is performed each spring in 36 countries around the globe.

In 1997 Halprin received the Samuel H. Scripps Award for Lifetime Achievement in Modern Dance, a testimony to her stature and enduring influence. Her work has touched many disciplines and to this day remains vital.

—Karen Zimmerman

HARPER, Meg

American dancer and choreographer

Born: 1944 in Evanston, Illinois. **Education:** B.F.A. in dance (honors), University of Illinois, 1966; studied with Joan Skinner, Merce Cunningham. **Career:** Dancer, Merce Cunningham Dance Company, 1967-77; taught at Merce Cunningham Studio, 1968-91; faculty chair, Cunningham Studio, 1991-96; dancer and assistant rehearsal director, Lucinda Childs Company, 1979-90; assistant to Robert Wilson's production of *The Meek Girl,* 1994-95; has taught at American University, Atlantic Center for the Arts, California State University (Long Beach), Centre de la Danse, Cornish School for the Arts, Florida State University, Harvard Summer Dance Center, International Ballet Seminar (Copenhagen), Jacob's Pillow Dance Festival, La Danse à Aix, New Performance Gallery (San Francisco), Paris Opera, Pratt Institute, Théâtre du Silence, Théâtre Contemporain de la Danse, University of California-Santa Cruz, University of Illinois, University of Minnesota, University of Texas, University of Washington, Virginia Commonwealth University, and White Oak Dance Project. **Awards:** National Endowment for the Arts Choreography fellowships, 1979, 1984, 1985.

Roles (with the Merce Cunningham Dance Company unless otherwise noted)

1968	*Walkaround Time* (Cunningham), Buffalo, New York
	Rainforest (Cunningham), New York
1970	*Tread* (Cunningham), Brooklyn
1972	*Landrover* (Cunningham), Brooklyn
	Borst Park (Cunningham), Brooklyn
1976	*Squaregame Video* (Cunningham), Adelaide, Australia
	Torse (Cunningham), Princeton, New Jersey
	Melody Excerpt (Lucinda Childs), Lucinda Childs Dance Company, Brooklyn Academy of Music (BAM)
	Interior Drama (Lucinda Childs), Lucinda Childs Dance Company, BAM
1979	*Dance* (Childs), Lucinda Childs Dance Company, BAM
1980	*Wonder, Try (Sketchy Version)* (Charles Atlas)
1981	*Relative Calm* (Childs), Théâtre National de Strasbourg, France
1995	*Tides of Time* (Emma Diamond)

Works

1978	*Long-Distance,* trio w/Andrew de Groat and Garry Reigenborn (mus. Eleanor Hovda), Cunningham Dance Studio, New York
1982	*Women of Iron,* duet w/Elizabeth Streb, Harvard Summer Dance School, Cambridge
1984	*Upon Dreaming of the Death of a White Buffalo* w/composer Eleanor Hovda), commissioned by Concert Dance Company of Boston
	Wolf Moon Waltz w/Eeanor Hovda, Merce Cunningham Dance Studio, New York
1985	*Romp* w/Garry Reigenborn

1986   *Old, Old Story* w/Reigenborn (mus. Charles Ives)
1988   *Gobe Gobang* w/Reigenborn (mus. Stephen Solum)
1989   *Upon Dreaming...*
        Ritual Tasks, Rhode Island College Dance Group, Providence
1997   *Round Two Dance* w/Reigenborn, Cunningham Dance Studio, Riverside Church, New York

Publications

Anderson, Jack, "The Dance: Meg Harper," *New York Times,* 27 October 1982.

Films and Videotapes

1975   *Westbeth* (for video, dir. Cunningham and Charles Atlas), New York
1977   *Event for Television* (for video), aired on PBS' *Dance in America* series

*   *   *

Meg Harper is a postmodern dancer and choreographer. She is most often remembered for her association with the Merce Cunningham Dance Company, where she performed in most of Cunningham's repertory and in his *Events.* She has also been a long-time teacher at his studio and has restaged several Cunningham works. She was a member of the Lucinda Childs Company for more than a decade, and has choreographed her own works and participated in those of other dancers.

Harper was born in 1944 in Evanston, Illinois. After graduating from the University of Illinois in 1966, where she trained with former Cunningham dancer Joan Skinner, she moved to New York and began studying with Cunningham. She joined the Merce Cunningham Dance Company in 1968, and remained there until 1977. While with Cunningham's troupe, Harper's co-members included several notable modern dancers, including Carolyn Brown, Douglas Dunn, Ulysses Dove, Jim Self, and Gus Solomons, Jr., among many others. She was a featured performer in several works on the Cunningham roster, and, over the years, she performed in virtually all of his repertoire. She was known as a virtuosic performer with the ability to project a strong individual personality, a reputation she has maintained throughout her career.

Cunningham developed an interest in producing dance for video, and Harper performed in many of these projects, both in archival footage and in new dances created for the video medium. They include *Westbeth* (1975), which was Cunningham's first use of video and was produced in collaboration with filmmaker Charles Atlas; *Squaregame Video* (1976), which was, like several of his video projects, originally conceived for adaption to video; *Event for Television* (1977), which took its title from the "Events" Cunningham's company presented in unconventional spaces; and *Torse* (1978), which was designed as a pair of films to be projected simultaneously on adjacent screens. *Event for Television* was aired on an episode of PBS's Dance in America series that highlighted selections from Cunningham's repertoire.

In 1979, Harper joined the Lucinda Childs Company, where she remained until 1990, serving as assistant rehearsal director for the last two of those years. She danced in a number of Childs' works during this period, including *Dance, Melody Excerpt, Relative Calm,* and *Interior Drama.* Like other dancers in Childs' troupe, Harper was able to maintain her strong individual personality on stage, while performing exacting ensemble works. As Childs noted in a 1981 interview in the *New York Times,* "I look for very individual dancers who are still in some way comfortable with this kind of dynamics and able both to be articulate and to sustain the movement in these long pieces, clearly and cleanly."

In addition to her long tenures with Cunngham and Childs, Harper has also appeared in works by other choreographers. For example, she danced in Charles Atlas's live performance piece, *Wonder, Try (Sketchy Version)* (1980), and in Emma Diamond's *Tides of Time* (1995). In addition, she has collaborated with other choreographers, including Gary Riegenborn on *Old, Old Story* (1986) and *Gobe Gobang* (1988), and Elizabeth Streb on *Women of Iron* (1982). Her own works include *Upon Dreaming of the Death of the White Buffalo* (1984), a collaboration with composer Eleanor Hovda commissioned by the Concert Dance Company of Boston. Harper has collaborated with Hovda on other pieces as well, including *Long-Distance* (1978) and *Wolf Moon Waltz* (1984). Although Harper has created large works, such as *Upon Dreaming...* and *Ritual Tasks* (1989), for eight women and eight seven-foot poles, most of her works are solos or small ensemble pieces. From 1994 to 1995, Harper was the assistant to theater director Robert Wilson for his production of *The Meek Girl.* Harper has remained connected with Cunningham's work since leaving his company. She has restaged and taught his work for troupes such as Mikhail Baryshnikov's White Oak Project, which added *Signals* to its repertory. In 1994, Harper and Cunningham assistant artistic director Chris Komar revived Cunningham's 1974 work, *Sounddance.* Harper has been a long-time teacher of Cunningham technique, both at the Merce Cunningham Studio and in residencies in the U.S. and abroad. She has been an instructor at the Cunningham Studio since 1968, becoming faculty chair in 1991. She has traveled extensively as an artist in residence both in the U.S.and abroad. She currently splits her time each year between the Cunningham Studio and freelance performing and teaching. In 1997, Harper appeared in the premiere of the Round Two Dance company, with Maria D'Avila, Keith Sabado, Andrew Boynton and Garry Reigenborn, in a Reigenborn piece.

—Karen Raugust

HAUSER, Nancy

American dancer, choreographer, educator, and company director

Born: Nancy McKnight, 20 November 1909 in Great Neck, New York. **Education:** Studied with Louise Revere Morris, Doris Humphrey, Charles Weidman, and Hanya Holm, 1926-36. **Family:** Married to artist Alonzo Hauser; children: two sons, one daughter. **Career:** Member, Hanya Holm Dance Company, 1932-36; instructor, Finch Junior College, 1933-37; Milwaukee Department of Recreation, 1938-43; Carleton College, Northfield, Minnesota, 1944-47; assistant professor, 1950-60; instructor, Macalester College, St. Paul, 1946-49; artistic director, Dance Guild Theatre and School, 1961-68; artistic director, Guild of Performing Arts, Minneapolis, 1968-81; artistic director, Nancy Hauser Dance Company, Minneapolis, 1968-90; instructor, Hanya Holm School of Dance, Colorado College, Colorado Springs, Colorado, 1984; instructor, University of Minnesota, 1981-90. **Awards:** Outstanding Achievement in Arts Award, YWCA; Minnesota State Arts Board grants, 1976, 1977, 1980; numerous other corporate and government grants, including a 1975 National Endowment for the Arts grant. **Died:** 17 January 1990.

Works (selected)

1966	*Visions*
	Everyman Sonata
1967	*Saeta*
1970	*Counterpoint*
	Lyric Suite
	Parta Partita (mus. Bach)
1971	*No Comment*
1972	*Abstracts*
1975	*Beginnings*
1976	*Recherche*
1977	*Dream Cycle*
1978	*Everness*
	Getting Along, Getting Together
1979	*Back to Bank*
1980	*Circle of the Sun*
	Trio, Minneapolis
1981	*U.S., Inc.*
	Wheeling
	Romanza
1983	*Requiem*
	Fragments, Shirley Mordine Dance Company, Chicago

Publications

On HAUSER: articles—

Anderson, Jack, "Dancing in General," *Dance Magazine*, December 1975.

Hering, Doris, "The Dancers from Dinkytown: Charting the Most by Sturdy First Steps of the Minnesota Dance Theatre," *Dance Magazine*, December 1969.

Ingber, Judith Brin, "The Dancing Playground," *Dance Magazine*, July 1972.

Kendall, Elizabeth et al., "Perspectives," *Dance Magazine*, June 1974.

Rosenwald, Peter J., "Nancy Hauser, Linda Tarnay," *Dance News*, December 1975.

Timmis, Joan, "Reviews National: St. Paul, Minnesota," *Dance Magazine*, November 1987.

——, "At 77, Nancy Hauser Plans a Partial Retirement," *Dance Magazine*, July 1987.

"Voices: Interview with Nancy Hauser," *Contact Quarterly* (Northampton), Winter 1989.

*   *   *

When Nancy McKnight Hauser died in early 1990, she left an enormous human legacy. There were first of all her three children: sons Anthony and Michael, classical and flamenco guitarists respectively, and daughter Heidi Jasmin, who in 1987 replaced her mother as director of the Nancy Hauser Dance Company (NHDC).

But her influence extended far beyond her family. The Nancy Hauser Dance School (NHDS) trained hundreds of students, among whom were future members of the Alwin Nikolais, Murray Louis, Don Redlich, Paul Taylor, Tricia Brown, and Meredith Monk dance companies. Others, such as Ralph Lemon, Charlie Moulton, Sara and Jerry Pearson, Maria Cheng, and Gary Lund, formed companies of their own. Fully one-third of the Minnesota Dance Alliance members in the 1990s had received some degree of training at the NHDS, and the strong arts presence in that state owed much to Hauser.

In the end, it was a legacy that spread far and wide; and in her beginnings, as a biographical brochure produced by the dance company in the 1980s stated, Hauser was "a direct link to the deepest roots of modern dance in America." When Nancy McKnight, who grew up on Long Island, first started to study her art, modern dance still went under the name of "natural interpretive dance." But big changes were afoot in the 1920s, when she saw a performance by Mary Wigman at Carnegie Hall and decided she wanted to become a dancer. Studying with the German-based Wigman was impossible, but in 1931 the young dancer began working with Wigman's protegee, Hanya Holm. Thus commenced a relationship that would continue for the next six decades, during which time Hauser would progress from being Holm's student to being her colleague to being her close friend.

As Holm's assistant in 1934 she attended the first summer dance institute at Bennington College, and gained exposure to works by Martha Graham, Doris Humphrey, Charles Weidman, and other greats of modern dance when those talents were in full bloom. A few years later, having married sculptor Alonzo Hauser, she moved to Milwaukee. The Hausers stayed there just long enough for Nancy to launch one of the first major citywide dance programs outside of New York City; then in 1944, they moved to Minnesota, where she would live for the rest of her life.

During the 1950s, while she was raising her family on a farm in Eagan, Minnesota—a home where artists and intellectuals, including Buckminster Fuller, often gathered—Hauser taught at Carleton and Macalester colleges. Then in 1961 she founded the Dance Guild Theatre in a St. Paul studio; seven years later, in alliance with her son Michael and several others, this became the Guild School of Performing Arts. The next 13 years, from 1968 to 1981, were something of a golden age, as the Guild—by then based in a former knitting mill near the University of Minnesota—commissioned numerous works by dancers and musicians. The Guild also offered training, and a range of students from children to professional artists studied dance, music, theatre, and mime there.

Out of the Guild grew the NHDC and the NHDS in 1981. The latter taught some 400 students a year, and the former became a touring group that in the 1990s would travel to the Far East. By the 1980s Hauser, in her seventies, was starting to vary her heavy schedule of teaching, choreography, and the demands of an artistic directorship. In 1983 she served as artist-in-residence at the University of Wisconsin in Madison, and in 1984 she taught alongside her mentor and friend Hanya Holm in Colorado. By 1987, three years before her death, she was ready to pass on the artistic director position to her daughter Heidi Hauser Jasmin.

In recalling her mother's style as a choreographer and instructor, Jasmin has said, "She never believed in fad and fashion influencing the arts. She wanted her dancers to have a strong sense of rhythm, suspension, and a three-dimensional sense of space in their work..." Though she obviously possessed a strong will, as a teacher Hauser was far from dogmatic, educating her students in principles of movement rather than specific styles. More remarkably, as an artistic director she actually encouraged her dancers to choreograph their own pieces, certainly a generous practice.

Perhaps due to her concentration on motion rather than particular styles, her choreography tended toward abstraction, and in fact she used the word "abstract" in the title of one composition. Yet this did not make NHDC performances somber ones: Jack Anderson, following their New York debut in 1975 complained that he didn't see *enough* seriousness. Allen Robertson, reviewing a number of performances by Minneapolis companies five years later, suggested that the combination of *Everness* and its companion piece *Trio* seemed incomplete. The first work displayed flowing movements, danced by women, which contrasted with the hard, sharp motions of the men dancing in the second piece. To Robertson, this contrast was "perhaps more academic than need be."

Robinson may have had that impression because Hauser was always at heart a teacher, teaching even in her choreographic work. The NHDC has had a firm philosophy, carried on under the administration of Jasmin, which holds that "dance is a visual medium that first comes from the creative source within the artist, and then must find a universal language of movement that others can understand." To this end, the Hauser school seeks to give students a full and well-rounded education that brings in improvisation, composition, rhythmic training, dance production, and performance. Thus through the NHDC and NHDS, still a force in the 1990s, Nancy Hauser's legacy—begun when modern dance was in its nascent years—continues to grow long after her passing.

—Judson Knight

HAWKINS, Erick

American dancer, choreographer, and company director

Born: Frederick Hawkins, 1909 in Trinidad, Colorado. **Education:** Harvard University, B.A. in Greek Antiquity, 1930; studied dance with Harald Kreutzberg and later at George Balanchine's School of American Ballet. **Family:** Married Martha Graham, 1948 (separated, 1950; divorced 1954). **Career:** Dancer, American Ballet Company, 1935-37, Ballet Caravan, 1936-39; guest dancer, 1938, and lead dancer, 1939-51, Martha Graham Dance Company; formed his own company and school in 1951. **Awards:** Mellon Foundation Award, 1975; Guggenheim Fellowship, 1978; Dance Magazine Award, 1979; Samuel H. Scripps American Dance Festival Award for lifetime achievement, 1988; National Medal of Arts, 1994; honorary doctorate, Western Michigan University, 1983. **Died:** 23 November 1994.

Works (as choreographer for his own company unless otherwise indicated)

1937	*Showpiece,* Ballet Caravan, New York
1940	*Insubstantial Pageant*
1941	*In Time of Armament*
	Liberty Tree
1942	*Curtain Raiser*
	Primer for Action
	Yankee Bluebritches
	Trickster Coyote (revised 1965)
1943	*The Parting*
	Saturday Night

1944	*The Pilgrim's Progress*
1945	*John Brown,* Martha Graham Dance Company, New York
1947	*God's Angry Men*
1947	*Stephen Acrobat,* Martha Graham Dance Company, New York
1948	*The Strangler*
1952	*The Lives of Five or Six Swords*
1957	*Here and Now with Watchers*
1960	*Eight Clear Patches*
1961	*Early Floating*
	Sudden Snake Bird
1963	*Spring Azure*
	Cantilever
1964	*To Everyone Out There*
	Geography of Noon, Connecticut College Dance Festival
1965	*Lords of Persia,* Connecticut College Dance Festival
	Naked Leopard (solo; mus. Kodály)
1966	*Dazzle on a Knife's Edge*
1968	*Tightrope,* Brooklyn Academy of Music
1969	*Black Lake,* Riverside Church, New York
	Of Love, ANTA Theater, New York
1972	*Angels of the Inmost Heaven,* ANTA Theater, New York
	Classic Kite Tails (mus. David Diamond), ANTA Theater, New York
	Dawn Dazzled Doors, ANTA Theater, New York
1973	*Greek Dreams, with Flute*
1974	*Meditations on Orpheus*
1975	*Death Is the Hunter*
	Hurrah!
	Parson Weems and the Cherry Tree, etc.
1979	*Agathlon*
1981	*Heyoka*
1983	*Plains Daybreak*
	Summer-Clouds People
1984	*The Joshua Tree*
	Avanti
1986	*Today with Dragom*
	Ahab
1987	*God, the Reveller*
1988	*Cantilever II*
1989	*New Moon*
1991	*Killer of Enemies*
	Intensities of Wind and Space
1993	*Each Time You Carry Me This Way*
1994	*Many Thanks*

Publications

By HAWKINS: books—

The Body Is a Clear Place, Princeton Books, 1992.

On HAWKINS: books—

de Mille, Agnes, *Martha,* New York, 1991.

On HAWKINS: articles—

Acocella, Joan, "Dance: Classically Modern Mischa," *Wall Street Journal,* 1 April 1997.

Erick Hawkins performing _Ahab,_ 1986. Photograph © Beatriz Schiller.

Grausam, A. B., "Erick Hawkins: Choreographer as Sculptor," _Dance Magazine,_ November 1974.

Jowitt, Deborah, "Dual Nature," _Village Voice,_ 27 February 1996.

——, "Call if Found," _Village Voice,_ 18 March 1997.

Kisselgoff, Anna, "Erick Hawkins, Lover of Beauty," _New York Times,_ 4 December 1994.

Films and Videotapes

Erick Hawkins's America, video, PBS/Dance Horizons, n.d.

*   *   *

In a career that spanned 60 years, choreographer Erick Hawkins introduced a fresh perspective to modern dance—one colored by Zen philosophy, Eastern ideals of beauty, and a belief that dancers' motions should be free of strain. His metaphoric dances celebrated the processes of nature rather than the workings of the human psyche—a sharp departure from the established modern dance of the 1950s, when Hawkins began formulating his style.

Hawkins' unique approach, devoid of theatrical drama and permeated with an easygoing serenity, was slow to win converts. Many found it tedious. Allen Hughes of the _New York Times_ considered Hawkins' 70-minute pas de deux, _Here and Now with Watchers_ (1957), "one of the most trying theatrical experiences of our time." Yet by the late 1960s and early 1970s, Hawkins was acknowledged by many as a visionary for such spare, meditative works as the aforementioned _Here and Now, Eight Clear Places_ (1960), _Early Floating_ (1962), and _Classic Kite Tails_ (1972). Walter Sorell wrote that "Hawkins and his company move with utter tranquility, seeking an expression of purity, the feeling of movement rather than the movement itself. His technique produces a quality of almost meditative effortless and poetic sensuousness."

It was not only as a choreographer that Hawkins earned a place in modern dance history. Arguably, his role as a dancer in Martha Graham's company was as important an influence on the future of the art form. From 1938 to 1950, his presence as the first male dancer with Graham's company (and, for a time, her husband) profoundly affected her work and shaped a number of her seminal dances. She created key roles for him in _Every Soul Is a Circus_ (1939), _El Penitente_ (1940), _Letter to the World_ (1940), _Deaths and Entrances_ (1943), and _Appalachian Spring_ (1944), among others. Agnes de Mille, in her biography, _Martha,_ wrote that what Hawkins gave Graham was "imponderable." "He got her thinking in terms of relationship to men, in terms of their way of moving, their bodies, their dynamics, their presence. He paved the way for work with other men. He immensely broadened her canvas." In short, he helped to mature her art.

Hawkins was also instrumental in helping Graham operate the company during the 1940s; he raised funds, formulated business plans and arranged musical commissions—notably Aaron Copland's score for *Appalachian Spring*. But serving as Graham's partner and muse was not what the Harvard-educated, independent-minded Hawkins intended for his career.

Born Frederick Hawkins in Trinidad, Colorado, in 1909, Hawkins often spoke of his roots in the American Southwest. One summer early in his dance career, he took a car trip around the area in order to observe the various American Indian celebrations. He later told Eleanor Rogosin: "It was important because I wanted to see a place where dance was used, not as entertainment or show business, not as virtuosity, but as one aspect of an expression of the total outer and inner world of a people." He added that it was also important for him to see grown men dancing in a serious way, "not as though they were some sort of trained poodle."

While a student at Harvard, where he majored in Greek civilization, he attended a concert in New York City by the German modern dancer Harald Kreutzberg and was inspired to become a dancer. After college he studied briefly with Kreutzberg in Salzburg, Austria. In 1934 he began studying at George Balanchine's School of American Ballet in New York. He danced with the American Ballet and Ballet Caravan, both precursors of the New York City Ballet, in the mid-1930s before joining Graham's company in 1938.

Although Graham encouraged Hawkins' choreographic efforts and produced some of his early pieces (*John Brown,* 1945; *Stephen Acrobat,* 1947), he could not escape her shadow. He left the company abruptly in 1950, while on a European tour, to pursue his own vision.

The aesthetic that evolved in Hawkins' work hardly could have been more different from Graham's if he had been aiming for antithesis. Like his contemporary and fellow Graham alumnus Merce Cunningham, Hawkins eschewed the psychological drama that pervaded Graham's ballets. He also rejected the contraction-based technique she developed, as well as all other dance techniques that imposed artificial notions of what shape the dancing form should take. He sought his subjects in the metaphorical representation of nature and strove to develop a system of dance that was tension-free and kinesthetically correct. His dances, often revealingly costumed, displayed an appreciation for the beauty of the human body as one of nature's perfect forms, and a belief that the body reflected the spirit.

From the beginning of his career, Hawkins was adamant that his dances be presented to live music, and many of the scores were created by his wife and longtime collaborator, contemporary composer Lucia Dlugoszewski. Other composers whose music Hawkins has used include Virgil Thompson, Alan Hovhaness, David Diamond and Zoltán Kodály. Hawkins commissioned sets from Helen Frankenthaler, Isamu Noguchi, Stanley Boxer, and others.

Hawkins' company toured widely and successfully during the 1960s, 1970s, and 1980s, finding more acceptance, especially in its early years, in the provinces and on college campuses than it did in New York. In June of 1967 *Dance Magazine* reported that the Erick Hawkins Dance Company's 70-performance tour to 60 U.S. and Canadian cities was among the most extensive made by a modern dance company.

Hawkins performed up until a decade before his death in 1994, at the age of 85. His company has continued to perform his work posthumously.

In the months before he died, Hawkins composed a last dance, *Journey of a Poet,* for Mikhail Baryshnikov, an admirer of Hawkins who had aided the company financially. Though the piece was created as a 25-minute solo, Baryshnikov converted some sections to ensemble dances and performed it with his White Oak Dance Project in 1997. Some critics were unmoved by this gesture and remained skeptical of Hawkins' overall aesthetic. Reviewing *Journey of a Poet,* Joan Acocella wrote in the *Wall Street Journal:* "Mr. Hawkins was into Eastern religions and therefore showed a certain aggressive naivety, whereby, for example, we were supposed to stare in holy awe if he raised his arm and held it there.... Like much of Mr. Hawkins' work, the piece is thin," she concluded, " and it would have looked thinner if Mr. Baryshnikov hadn't added the ensemble."

Over the course of his lengthy career, however, Hawkins won over many of his initial detractors. In a 1997 review of his company, *Village Voice* critic Deborah Jowitt confessed:

> When I first saw *Early Floating* in the 1960s, it didn't mean much to me. I found it drifty, lacking the muscle I expected from modern dance. . . . Now I see *Early Floating* as the expression of an idyllic sensuality. Hawkins was an immensely cultivated man who saw nothing naive in enjoying, and stressing, the brush of a foot against the floor. [I] realize that what he wanted us to perceive was the is-ness of each spare move.

—Diane Hubbard Burns

HAY, Deborah
American dancer and choreographer

Born: 18 December 1941 in Brooklyn, New York. **Education:** Trained by her mother in children's tap; studied dance at the Henry Street Settlement House and American Dance Festival summer schools; studied at the Merce Cunningham studio. **Career:** Original member, Judson Dance Theater, 1961-65; dancer, Merce Cunningham Dance Company, 1964; begins choreographing for large groups of untrained dancers, 1965; annual workshops in Austin, Texas, 1980-95; founder, Deborah Hay Dance Company, 1980; focused on solo work, 1995 to present. **Awards:** Numerous grants and awards from the National Endowment for the Arts, Texas Commission on the Arts, and the City of Austin; John Simon Guggenheim Foundation Fellowship, 1983; McKnight National Fellowship, 1995; Rockefeller Foundation's Belagio Fellowship with artist Tres Arenz, 1997.

Works

1962   *Rain Fur* (no music), Judson Dance Theater, New York City

    5 Things (no music), Judson Dance Theater

    Rafladan w/Alex Hay, Charles Rotmil (no music), Judson Dance Theater

1963   *City Dance* (mus. Richard Andrews), Judson Dance Theater

    All Day Dance (no music), Judson Dance Theater

    Elephant Footprints in the Cheesecake w/Fred Herko (mus. Edward V. Boagni), Judson Dance Theater

	Would They or Wouldn't They? w/Fred Herko (no music, renamed *They Will*, 1964), Judson Dance Theater
1964	*All Day Dance for Two* (no music), Judson Dance Theater
	Three Here (no music), Moderna Museet, Stockholm
	Victory 14 (mus. 8 radios), TV Studio, 81st & Broadway, New York
1965	*Hill* (no music), Kurher's Country Club, New York
1966	*No. 3* (no music), Judson Dance Theater
	Serious Duet (no music), Judson Dance Theater
	Rise (no music), Judson Dance Theater
	Solo
1967	*Flyer* (no music), Artist's Lofe, New York
	Group I (no music), School of Visual Arts, New York
1968	*Group II* (no music), Anderson Theater, New York
	Ten (no music), Anderson Theater
1969	*Half-Time*
	20 Permutations of 2 Sets of 3 Equal Parts in a Linear Pattern (no music), Whitney Museum of American Art, New York
	Deborah Hay with a Large Group Outdoors (no music), Damrosch Park, Lincoln Center, New York
	26 Variations on 8 Activities for 13 People Plus Beginning and Ending
1970	*Deborah Hay and a Large Group of People from Hartford* (no music), Wadsworth Atheneum, Harford, Connecticut
	20-Minute Dance (no music), Emanu-El Midtown TM & YWHA, New York
1971	*Deborah Hay and "The Farm"*
1972	*Wedding Dance for Sandy and Greg*
1976	*Solo Dances* (ongoing from 1976)
1977	*The Grand Dance* (ongoing from 1977 to 1979)
1980	*Leaving the House*
	The Genius of the Heart
	HEAVEN/below

Other works include: *Moving through the Universe in Bare Feet, My Heart, Viola,* and *Lamb, lamb, lamb, lamb, lamb. . .,* 1992.

Publications

By HAY: books—

Moving through the Universe in Bare Feet: Ten Circle Dances for Everybody, with drawings by Donna Jean Rogers, Chicago, 1975.
Lamb at the Altar: The Story of a Dance, Durham, North Carolina, 1994.

By HAY: articles—

"Dance Talks," *Dance Scope,* Fall/Winter 1977-78.
"Playing Awake: Letters to My Daughter," *Drama Review,* Winter 1989.
"*Lamb, lamb, lamb, lamb, lamb. . .*: A Movement Libretto for 42 Individuals," *Drama Review,* Winter 1992.
"Ages of the Avant-Garde," *Performing Arts Journal,* January 1994.

On HAY: books—

Anderson, Jack, *Ballet & Modern Dance: A Concise History,* Princeton, New Jersey, 1986.

Banes, Sally, *Terpsichore in Sneakers: Post-Modern Dance,* Boston, 1980.
———, *Democracy's Body: Judson Dance Theater 1962-1964,* Ann Arbor, Michigan, 1983.
Foster, Susan Leigh, *Reading Dancing: Bodies and Subjects in Contemporary American Dance,* Berkeley, Los Angeles, London, 1986.
Livet, Anne, editor, *Contemporary Dance,* New York, 1978.
McDonagh, Don, *The Complete Guide to Modern Dance,* Garden City, New York, 1976.
Wynne, Peter, *Judson Dance: An Annotated Bibliography of the Judson Dance Theater and of Five Major Choreographers—Trisha Brown, Lucinda Childs, Deborah Hay, Steve Paxton, and Yvonne Rainer,* Englewood, New Jersey, 1978.

On HAY: articles—

Anderson, Jack, "In a Church, Lamb Images," *New York Times,* 26 October 1994.
Chin, Daryl, "Deborah Hay: A Brief Introduction," *Dance Scope,* Fall/winter 1977-78.
Daly, Ann, "An Experimentalist in Soul and Body," *New York Times,* 30 March 1997.
———, "The Play of Dance: An Introduction to *Lamb, lamb, lamb, lamb, lamb...,*" *Drama Review,* Winter 1992.
Jeffers, Bill, "Leaving the House: The Solo Performance of Deborah Hay," *Drama Review,* March 1979.

*   *   *

From the Judson Dance Theater to her own dance company in Austin, Texas, Deborah Hay has been at the forefront of postmodern dance as both a performer and choreographer. Since the 1960s, Hay has helped develop a new form of modern dance that encompasses not only the physical aspects of the art, but also its social dynamics.

Hay was born 18 December 1941 in Brooklyn, New York. She began dancing early, taking dance lessons from her mother. Her professional training in modern dance began at the Henry Street Settlement House, which was home to the dance companies of Alwin Nikolais and Murray Louis. She also studied summers at the American Dance Festival and in the early 1960s, Hay became a student at the Merce Cunningham studio in New York City. She took part in a dance workshop run by Robert Dunn that allowed her and the other students to choreograph a set of concert works. In 1962, the group staged a performance of these dances at the Judson Memorial Church in New York City's Greenwich Village, a liberal Protestant church that was a well-known venue for political and artistic expression. These performances gave rise to the Judson Dance Theater, a company that pioneered a new form of avant-garde art.

The Judson Dance Theater challenged the conventions and traditions of artistic dance. In addition to Hay, this group also included dancers and budding choreographers such as Trisha Brown, Yvonne Rainer, Judith Dunn, Steve Paxton, and James Waring. The group did not seek the approval of their contemporaries in dance, which allowed them the freedom to experiment with both dance and its presentation. The focus moved from the individual dancer or choreographer to the community, emphasizing a collective process in developing dance performances. The result was theater, and the effect on modern dance was profound. The company extended the boundaries of what was acceptable on the dance floor, opening the floodgates of experimentation and creativity. Their challenge to convention continues today, raising fundamental questions about the definition of dance, and as Jack Anderson writes "the answers to those questions have often been stimulating and provocative."

While the Judson Dance Theater folded in the mid-1960s, the dancers and choreographers who had been a part of it continued to promote their new views of modern dance. Like many of her colleagues, Hay believed that dance should reflect her perceptions of life. In the late 1960s and into the 1970s, she began to delve into the importance of community and communal living as a way for personal growth and began to express this idea through her choreography of group dances that often included untrained performers. In the 1960s, Hay remained in New York City; her dances were performed at such venues as the Anderson Theater and the Whitney Museum of American Art. In 1971, she moved to a commune in Vermont, where she continued to work with untrained dancers. During these years, Hay created a series of 10 circle dances which were collected in a book entitled *Moving through the Universe in Bare Feet: Ten Circle Dances for Everybody,* accompanied with illustrations by Donna Jean Rogers.

In 1976 Hay relocated to Austin, Texas, and continued to work with groups of dancers. It was here, in Austin, that she began an annual workshop, running from 1980 to 1995. Each workshop lasted four months and included both trained and untrained performers. It was during this time that Hay moved away from her earlier group dances and began to concentrate on solo work; from her workshop, where she created group dances, Hay would whittle and reshape the choreography into a solo work for herself. One workshop, for instance created a group dance entitled *My Heart,* from which Hay developed her solo work, *Voila.* Hay has called her workshops a form of meditation, "imagining every cell in my body," she mentioned in a 1994 interview, "has the potential to dialogue with all that there is."

From another of her workshops in the early 1990s emerged one of her most well-known works, the group dance *Lamb, lamb, lamb, lamb, lamb. . .,* which inspired Hay's second book, *Lamb at the Altar: The Story of a Dance* published by Duke University Press in 1994. In the introduction, Hay explains that besides including the movement libretto for *Lamb, lamb, lamb, lamb, lamb. . .,* her book (as well as the dance itself) is an exploration of dying. "I understand dance to include the action of dying, whether I choose to realize it," she said, "I am making an effort to come to terms with dying as an experimental process of which I posses negotiable comprehension." While Hay may have been exploring death, reviews of the performance suggest the performance's meaning was obscure. Though reviewers were impressed with the effect created by the dancers, and several articles appeared in such publications as *Drama Review* (including one by Hay herself in 1992), few seemed to grasp the symbolic purpose of the lamb.

Although it has not always been understood, Hay's work has received acclaim from important voices in the artistic community. She has won several fellowships from organizations such as the Guggenheim Foundation and the National Endowment for the Arts. Hay has also spread her innovations in dance throughout the world, performing and teaching workshops in such places as Canada, Mexico, and Australia. Her writings on dance, which have appeared in the journals *The Drama Review* and *Contact Quarterly,* have also extended Hay's influence.

Since 1995, Hay has put her workshops on hold to dig deeper into the possibilities of choreography. She's working with trained dancers and creating expanded versions of her previous dances. Her aim is to learn more about the material she has already created from new perspectives. Hay also continues to develop her eponymous dance company which she started in 1992. Whether in a group or as a solo dancer, Hay has been an important influence in modern dance. Like many of those who started the Judson Dance Theater, Hay's work challenges the conventions and traditions of dance, expanding its expressive vocabulary and creating new definitions of this art form.

—Kristen Thomas Clarke

H'DOUBLER, Margaret
American dance educator and author

Born: Margaret Newell Hougen Doubler in 1889 in Beloit, Kansas. **Education:** Madison High School, Madison, Wisconsin; University of Wisconsin, majored in biology and minored in philosophy, 1906-10; Teachers College of Columbia University, New York City, 1916-17. **Career:** Taught physical education and later "natural" or creative dance, Columbia Teachers College, 1911-16 and 1917-54; founded the extracurricular dance group, *Orchesis,* which spread to colleges and universities throughout the U.S.; guest teacher at various universities; author of several books on dance in education for teachers and students, including *A Manual for Dancing* (1921), *The Dance and Its Place in Education* (1925), *Dance: A Creative Art Experience* (1940), *and Movement and Its Rhythmic Structure* (1946). **Awards:** Outstanding Woman of the Community Award, University League of Wisconsin, 1945; American Association of Health, Physical Education, and Recreations Honorary Award, 1953; American Association of Health, Physical Education, and Recreation Gulick award, 1973.

Publications

By H'DOUBLER: books—

Dance: A Creative Art Experience, Madison, 1940.
Dance and Its Place in Education, New York, 1925.
A Guide for the Analysis of Movement, Madison, 1950.
A Manual for Dancing, Madison, 1921.
Movement and Its Rhythmic Structure, Madison, 1946.
Rhythmic Form and Analysis, Madison, 1932.

On H'DOUBLER: books—

Alter, Judith B., *Dance-Based Dance Theory: From Borrowed Models to Dance-Based Experience,* New York, 1990.
———, *Dancing and Mixed Media: Early Twentieth-Century Modern Dance Theory in Text and Photography,* New York, 1994.

On H'DOUBLER: articles—

Alter, Judith B., "Music and Rhythm in Dance: H'Doubler's Views in Retrospect," *Society for Dance History Scholars: Conference Proceedings, 1984.*
Moore, Ellen A., "A Recollection of Margaret H'Doubler's Class Procedure: An Environment for the Learning of Dance," *Dance Research Journal,* Fall/Winter, 1975-76.

Remley, Mary Lou, "The Wisconsin Idea of Dance: A Decade of Progress, 1917-1926," *Wisconsin Magazine of History*, Spring 1975.

*   *   *

Margaret H'Doubler, a pioneer of modern dance in higher education, influenced the field by the curriculum she evolved, the teaching method she developed, the students she taught, and the books she wrote. Some of her most famous students are Martha Hill, who along with Mary Josephine Shelly established and directed the Bennington Summer School of Dance; Elizabeth Hayes, dancer and author, who established the Dance Department of the University of Utah in Salt Lake City; Betty Toman, dancer and author who directed the Dance Department at the University of Iowa; and Anna Halprin, dancer, author, and teacher of most of the dancers who developed postmodern Dance at the Judson Church in the late 1960s and early 1970s.

H'Doubler's work in dance began in the context of pageantry which was taught by Mary Beegle, Gertrude Colby, and Bird Larson at Barnard College and Columbia Teacher's College; and continued with music visualization based on Dalcroze rhythmic techniques which she learned and adapted from the teaching method of Miss Alys Bentley, music teacher, whom she observed while in New York City in 1917. Courses in pageantry were taught at the University of Wisconsin as early as 1914 but were no longer offered by the time H'Doubler succeeded in establishing in 1926 and 1927 the first university-level dance major in the United States.

Dance for H'Doubler was an educational activity to develop students' intellectual, emotional, and physical capabilities. The influence of H'Doubler's initial college major in biology and family background in music continued throughout the development of the program. The curriculum eventually included anatomy and physiology with the nursing students, philosophy of art, rhythmic studies, creative technique and composition classes, and an emotions seminar as well as courses in liberal arts and education; the program's focus remained on teacher preparation. While traveling in Germany in 1929, she became acquainted with Mary Wigman-protégé and contemporary, solo-dancer Harald Kreutzberg. He became a frequent guest teacher at U.W. in the years before World War II. Kreutzberg was the only professional modern dancer whose work H'Doubler supported. When Louise Kloepper, a former dancer with Mary Wigman came to study and then remained to teach, H'Doubler's respect for Kreutzberg's artistry influenced her decision to employ the former professional dancer.

The teaching method H'Doubler developed over the 44 years of instructing beginning dancers combined the anatomical function of the human body, demonstrated on the skeleton she had in class, with creative discovery utilizing the specific action chosen that day. Students explored this action first on the floor, then standing and finally traveling across the floor. While rarely demonstrating she guided the students from wide-ranging exploration to specific motor skills and rhythmic combinations evolved from their most basic components. This method emphasized improvisation, kinesthetic understanding, and individual development; it was rarely competitive. Intellectual grasp of movement was basic, followed by students' emotional expression in the combinations done by the entire class and the individual's variations of them which followed.

The evolution of H'Doubler's theoretical understanding of dance is evident in a close study of her books *A Manual for Dancing* (1921), *Dance and Its Place in Education* (1925), and *Dance: A Creative Art Experience* (1940). For instance, dance in the first two books was primarily musical visualization; by 1940 she recognized dance as autonomous and separate from music. In these early books she emphasized dancing, the *activity*; by 1940 she discussed the field of dance and described a dance as an *entity*. This change is evident even in the titles of these books. Though she did not believe dances could be notated, she evolved, with Mary Fee, a rhythmic notation for dance which all the students continued to study until the late 1970s. Her emphasis on the physiological functioning of the body in dance increased over the years, and she offered numerous examples focusing on kinesiological principles in *Dance: A Creative Art Experience*. These principles replace descriptions and drawings of specific exercises or detailed lists of songs and appropriate subjects to interpret which are found in her earlier two books.

H'Doubler's vision of some dance activities remained unchanged during her tenure at the University of Wisconsin. In her writing, performance was de-emphasized although students performed annually to popular acclaim. She continued to separate professional and educational dance. Because of her viewpoint and the fact that most of the dance faculty trained under H'Doubler, more than 20 years passed after she retired (in 1954) before an M.F.A. degree was established at the University of Wisconsin. The central role of rhythm in life and art increased; she paraphrased ideas from philosophers John Dewey and Yrjo Hirn to buttress her Jacques-Dalcroze–derived understanding and practices. Finally her stance that participation in the arts improves the lives of everyone and that all citizens in a democracy are entitled to creative arts experiences aligns her with the radical utopians and progressive educators with whom she shared this idealistic vision. This message along with her emphasis on developing each student's creativity continues through each book and remains inspirational to most students who read especially *Dance: A Creative Art Experience*.

In 1940, like such other dance educators and professionals as Doris Humphrey and Mary Wigman, H'Doubler offered a theoretical, systematic, and schematic method to guide students in composing dances and to augment their creative expression. She identified eight tools to help students structure movement patterns into a unified form: variety, contrast, climax, transition, balance, sequence, repetition, and harmony. To illustrate the interconnectedness of these tools, she offered the image of a spider web, thus, showing them to be coequal. These "Form Factors" interweave (she uses the image of a weaving) with "Techniques"—strength, flexibility, quality coordination, and specific skills; "Rhythmic Factors"—pulse, intervals, duration, stress, speed, meter complex combinations, syncopation; and "Space Factors"—direction, focus, line of motion: direct or deviating; distance or range, planes: horizontal, vertical, diagonal; levels: high, low, medium; body facing: forward, sideward, backward. H'Doubler's guide for analysis of movement reflects the Laban and Wigman concepts which H'Doubler learned from her work with Kreutzberg and Louise Kloepper. They also illustrate her teaching goal of combining intellectual and expressive with physical and creative experience. Because many of the graduates from her dance program took positions in schools, colleges, and universities throughout the United States, her influence continues today. Orchesis groups continue to meet and perform, and in dance programs students continue to take courses in rhythmic analysis of movement. Most significant is the continuing emphasis on the centrality of the creative process in the study of dance in high schools and institutions of higher education.

—Judith B. Alter

HILL, Martha

American modern dance educator

Born: 1900 in East Palestine, Ohio. **Family:** Married Thurston Davies, 1952. **Education:** Student of piano and voice; Teachers' College, Columbia University, B.S. 1929; New York University, M.A. in dance, 1941; studied ballet with Anna Duncan; Dalcroze eurhythmics; modern dance with Martha Graham, 1926. **Career:** Dancer, Martha Graham's Dance Company, 1929-31; director of dance, New York University, 1930-51; University of Oregon, beginning 1931; co-founder and director, Bennington School of the Dance (later Bennington School of the Arts), 1934-41; chairman of dance department and choreographer, Bennington College, 1932-51; co-founder and director, American Dance Festival, Connecticut College (later at Duke University, Durham, North Carolina), 1948; co-founder and director, Juilliard School of Dance, 1951-85; artistic director emeritus, Juilliard School of Dance, 1985; faculty, Kansas State Teachers' College and University of Chicago. **Awards:** New York City Mayor's Award of Honor for Arts and Culture; American Academy of Physical Education Award for services in dance education; honorary degrees from Adelphi University, Bennington College, Juilliard School of Dance, Mount Holyoke College, and Towson State University. **Died:** 19 November 1995 in Brooklyn, New York.

Publications

By HILL: articles—

"Antony Tudor: The Juilliard Years," *Choreography & Dance,* 1989.
"José Limón and his Biblical Themes," *Choreography & Dance,* 1992.

On HILL: books—

Anderson, Jack, *Ballet & Modern Dance: A Concise History,* Princeton, New Jersey, 1986.
Chujoy, Anatole, and P.N. Manchester, *The Dance Encyclopedia,* New York, 1967.
Kriegsman, Sali Ann, *Modern Dance in America: The Bennington Years,* Boston, 1981.

On HILL: articles—

Belitt, Ben, "Words for Dancers, Perhaps: An Interview/Memoir on the Bennington School of the Dance," *Ballet Review,* 1980.
"Juilliard Head Changes Hats," *Dance Magazine,* April 1985.
Dunning, Jennifer, "Martha Hill, Dance Educator, Is Dead at 94," *New York Times,* 21 November 1995.
Kisselgoff, Anna, "The Innovations of Martha Hill," *New York Times,* 28 March 1982.
Topaz, M., "Martha Hill, 1900-1995," *Dance Magazine,* February 1996.

*   *   *

More educator than dancer, Martha Hill was a pioneer in the development of modern dance. As a co-founder of three prominent dance schools—the Bennington Dance Program, the American Dance Festival, and the Juilliard School of Dance—Hill helped cultivate the talents of young artists such as Doris Humphrey and Hanya Holm, who would later rise to prominence in modern dance. As well as an educator, Hill was a dancer, studying with such greats as Martha Graham. At the start of Hill's career, modern dance was little more than physical education elective. In the course of her career, however, she established modern dance as a highly regarded performance art.

Martha Hill was born in 1900 in East Palestine, Ohio, an area she called the "Bible Belt." Little dancing took place in East Palestine. Instead, Hill spent her youth studying piano and voice. She circuitously entered the dance world as a physical education student at Columbia's Teachers' College in New York City. She began studying dance during her summers in New York, where she took ballet with Anna Duncan and also pursued Dalcroze eurythmics. In 1926, when she saw Martha Graham dance for the first time, Hill was extremely impressed and decided that she needed to study with Graham. After completing her bachelor's degree at Columbia in 1929, Hill became a member of Graham's dance company from 1929 to 1931. In 1931 Hill began her career as an educator, training dancers and arranging festivals for Kansas State Teachers' College, the University of Chicago, the University of Oregon, as well as other colleges and universities.

In 1934, while teaching at New York University's fledgling dance school, Hill co-founded the Bennington School of Dance with Mary Josephine Shelly and Robert Devore Leigh. The program was initially criticized as a mere training ground for physical education teachers. In defense of her students and the program, according to Anna Kisselgoff's 1982 article for the *New York Times,* Hill responded that "I have always said that dance is an art. Dance in education and dance in theater are not different things. The degree of proficiency may vary but the aim is to do dance as dancing, and to teach it as dance." Despite the early criticism, the Bennington School of Dance eventually helped establish modern dance as a separate art form, launching the careers of dancers and choreographers such as Charles Weidman and Alwin Nikolais. As director of this program, which ran for nine summers, Hill created, in Sali Ann Kriegsman's words, a "haven for the leading artists of the day; a laboratory for experienced and neophyte choreographers; a major production center that drew informed audiences and critics to programs of new works. . . and an arena for experiment in which the sister acts of music, drama, design, and poetry were assembled in the service of the dance." The Bennington program ended as World War II brought much United States' arts activity to a temporary standstill, but the school's work ensured the development of modern dance would soon resume.

After Bennington folded, Hill continued to develop influential programs in the dance world. In 1948, she became the founding director of Bennington's successor, the American Dance Festival, which took place at Connecticut Collegebut later moved to Duke University in Durham, North Carolina. Like Bennington, the American Dance Festival was a training ground for both new and experienced dancers. As its director, Hill taught and influenced many of the leaders in the field. She believed that through such festivals, students could experience three crucial elements of dance education: learning dance techniques, watching the great dancers perform, and communication with fellow dancers. She once wrote that she hoped new students would come through this process "with an informed attitude toward dance where they no longer secretly use the 19th-century classification of dance that is 'graceful, ungraceful, or disgraceful,' nor yet again fall victim to the old fundamentalist quarrel between the traditional ballet and the experimental modern dance, which is now only a tale with which the elders sometimes divert the young."

In 1951, Hill furthered dance education with the establishment of the first dance department at the Juilliard School in New York City. The school of dance was to parallel the school of music, with dance students learning the two major forms of Western dance, ballet and modern dance. Hill believed that both should be taught to prepare young dancers for a performance career. To bring home a steady paycheck in the unpredictable world of dance, Hill believed dancers needed to be versatile. Although teaching both styles of dance was considered experimental at the time, the Juilliard School of Dance, under Hill's directorship, produced such dance luminaries as Paul Taylor, Martha Clarke, and Dudley Williams.

Hill stepped down as director from Juilliard in 1985, taking on the role of artistic director emeritus. During her tenure, she received the New York City Mayor's Award of Honor for Arts and Culture. Hill was also a member of the dance advisory panels for both the School of Performing Arts in New York and the Cultural Exchange Program. Among her other honors were the American Academy of Physical Education Award for her work in dance education and honorary degrees from Adelphi University, Bennington College, the Juilliard School, Mount Holyoke College, and Towson State University. She also received a master of arts in dance from New York University in 1941.

Outside of the public sphere, Hill married her lifelong partner Thurston Davies in 1952; he died in 1961. Hill passed away at her home in Brooklyn, New York, on 19 November 1995 at the age of 94. Her impact on modern dance was phenomenal; through her development of three of the major dance centers in the U.S., she not only influenced many of the world's premiere modern dancers, she also helped define the aesthetics of modern dance, as well as the path that modern dance continues to take today.

—Kristen Thomas-Clarke

HINKSON, Mary

American dancer and choreographer

Born: 1930 in Philadelphia, Pennsylvania. **Education:** Bachelor's degree, University of Wisconsin; studied with Louis Horst and Martha Graham. **Family:** Married to Julian Johnson. **Career:** Dancer and teacher, Martha Graham Dance Company, 1951; toured Europe with Graham's troupe, 1954; guest appearances with companies of Pearl Lang, John Butler, Glen Tetley, George Balanchine, Anna Sokolow, and American Ballet Theatre; soloist, New York City Opera Ballet, 1952, 1955; taught at Juilliard School, 1952; Dance Theatre of Harlem, 1955.

Roles (all roles performed with the Martha Graham Dance Company and choreographed by Graham unless otherwise noted)

1952   *Chosen One* (Pearl Lang)
        Canticle for Innocent Comedians, New York
1954   *Ardent Song*, London
        The Warrior, *Seraphic Dialogue* (evolved from solo created by Graham, *Triumph of St. Joan*), ANTA Theatre, New York

1959   *Rainbow 'Round My Shoulder* (Donald McKayle), 92nd Street YM-YWHA
1960   *Acrobats of God*, New York
        Figure in the Carpet (George Balanchine), New York City Ballet
1961   *Visionary Recital*, New York
1962   *Phaedra*, New York
1963   Circe, *Circe*, London
1965   *Part Real Part Dream*, 54th Street Theatre, New York
1966   *Carmina Burana* (John Butler)
        Ricercare (Glen Tetley)
1973   Clytemnestra, *Clytemnestra*
1975   Dancer Anna, *Seven Deadly Sins* (Anna Sokolow)

Other roles include: *Deaths and Entrances, El Penitente,* the Awakener in *Samson Agonistes.*

Works

1951   *Make the Heart Show*

Publications

On HINKSON: books—

McDonagh, Don, *Martha Graham: A Biography.* New York, 1973.

On HINKSON: articles—

Hering, Doris, "Reviews," *Dance Magazine,* May 1962.
Kisselgoff, Anna, "Dance: Martha Graham Brings Back *Clytemnestra,*" *New York Times,* 2 May 1973.

*   *   *

American modern dancer and choreographer Mary Hinkson was a member of the Martha Graham Dance Company. She took over Graham's role as The Awakener in *Samson Agonistes* and was the first dancer other than Graham herself to dance the part of Clytemnestra in Graham's piece of the same title.

Hinkson was born in Philadelphia in 1930. After earning her bachelor's degree from the University of Wisconsin, she went to New York and studied modern dance with Louis Horst and Graham. At 21 years of age, Hinkson was privileged to be accepted as a member not only of the Martha Graham Dance Company but as faculty at the school as well. "At one time in the intensely competitive world of modern dance, class at the Graham studio was considered a requisite for membership in the Company. It was a form of paying one's dues to a private and very exclusive club," writes Don McDonagh.

Hinkson appeared on the scene at a time of growing turmoil. Graham, close to 60 at this time, would soon begin relinquishing the reins of many of her dancing roles, yet cling to others or refuse to allow them to be performed, such as Clytemnestra. At the same time, the world of modern dance was changing and to continue to allow the Graham Company a strong presence, older dances in the repertoire would need to be performed again, which meant piecing them together from odd notes, movie clips, and the memories of aging dancers. Tension between the younger members of the company and older ones would take its toll, causing some of the older members to leave and create their own companies.

Hinkson was intensely dedicated to the company and to the Graham technique. Her strength, together with Bertram Ross, a fellow principal dancer, under the administration of Leroy Leatherman, would bring new vitality to the faltering company during Graham's extended illness in the early 1970s. They would see Graham through difficult press conferences, dissuade her from canceling performances, and renew her interest in the progress and forward movement of the Graham influence on modern dance.

As early as 1954, a short three years after joining the company, Hinkson was selected to be one of 14 in the company to tour Europe. The trip, however, got off to a rough start. Graham had had a bad reception in Europe years earlier and it was with some apprehension that she accepted the honor of representing the United States abroad. The Graham Company's tour was to serve as ambassadors of dance in an American effort to counter Russian cultural influence of foreign governments. London audiences were uncomprehending and critics were still insisting on referring to modern dance as "barefoot" and "free" dance. To top it off Graham had not completed choreography on *Ardent Song,* which was to premiere the second week. She met with resistance from the company when she tried to cancel the piece and Hinkson, along with Linda Margolies and Matt Turney, had to improvise a gap in the choreography during each performance of *Ardent* for the entire tour. *Ardent Song* did meet with favorable reviews in London and continued to be performed in Holland, Sweden, and Denmark. During each performance, the improvised part did not meet with Graham's approval for scripting the steps and the three dancers were exhausted and frustrated by the end of the tour.

Graham continued to create new pieces and Hinkson appeared in featured roles in *Canticle for Innocent Comedians, Acrobats of God, Part Real—Part Dream*, and *Seraphic Dialogue.* The latter had evolved from a solo Graham created called *Triumph of St. Joan* (1951). In *Seraphic Dialogue*, four dancers portray Joan of Arc, in roles representing different aspects of her life, and allowing a play between past and present, between memory and future as Joan interacts with St. Michael. Hinkson danced the role of the Warrior.

Part Real—Part Dream was a piece that caused contention between the older and newer dancers in the company. It was one of two new pieces performed for a three-week fall season at the 54th Street Theater in 1965. The other pieces included a revival of *Appalachian Spring*, a reconstructed *Primitive Mysteries* and *The Witch of Endor.* Most of the creative effort went into *Dream* which McDonagh regards in *Complete Guide to Modern Dance* as "a frolic in an exotic garden." Graham played the part of the witch in *The Witch of Endor* and scripted herself as aloof to the other dancers. The rift deepened with the new *Primitive Mysteries,* which the younger generation liked but the older generation, having something to compare it to, did not.

In the early 1960s, Graham relinquished roles to Hinkson, as well as other members of the company. The first for Hinkson was Graham's role in *Visionary Recital.* Later she would take over the role of the Awakener in *Samson Agonistes.* But the culmination would be the extraordinary role of Clytemnestra in 1973. It had not been performed since 1967 and Hinkson would alternate the title role during the season with Pearl Lang. Hinkson was said to dance the part to "savage perfection" and though critics said Graham herself was irreplaceable, Hinkson was splendid.

Hinkson's best-known role in the repertoire was the title role in *Circe*, which premiered in London and New York in 1963. She also found time for guest appearances with the companies of many choreographers, including Pearl Lang, John Butler, Glen Tetley, George Balanchine, and Anna Sokolow, in addition to dancing as

soloist for the New York City Opera Ballet. She also created the only female role in Donald McKayle's *Rainbow 'Round My Shoulder.* She expanded her teaching to the Juilliard School in 1952 and the Dance Theatre of Harlem in 1955.

Besides her capable strength as a dancer, she helped breathe fresh life into the Graham Company. Though Graham had slowly stopped performing, in 1969 she retired, fully intending to see to the management of her studio and company until a series of illnesses kept her out of contact for a year and a half. The company was in serious trouble, having taken a huge step backward. With the company not at full strength, principal dancers were leaving to start their own companies and very few loyal and capable dancers remained. Hinkson, Ross, and Leatherman, for the first time in the company's history, held auditions for dancers to join the Graham Company. Dancers who weren't quite good enough were coming from the ranks of the studio, so something had to be done. The three also instigated a new format using the strongest repertory in the field of modern dance in a series of studio performances. Graham had not done this since the beginning of the company in the 1920s and for her it was a giant step into the past.

Without Hinkson's dedication and that of the other loyal members, the Graham Company would have disbanded. Their actions succeeded in renewing Graham's interest in the forward movement of her company, and securing a place for it in the years to come.

—Lisa A. Wroble

HODES, Linda

American dancer, choreographer, and educator

Born: Linda Margolies, 3 June 1933 in New York City. **Education:** Began studying at the Martha Graham school, 1942. **Family:** Married fellow Graham dancer, Stuart Hodes, 1954 (divorced, 1963); married Israeli dancer Ehud Ben-David, 1968 (died 1977). **Career:** Dancer, Martha Graham Dance Company, 1952-69; dancer, Paul Taylor Dance Company, 1961-68; founding member, Batsheva Dance Company, 1964; rehearsal director, Nederlands Dans Theater, 1970-71; co-artistic director, Batsheva Dance Company, 1972-75; returned to Graham Company, 1977; associate artistic director, 1979-91; director, Paul Taylor School and Taylor 2, 1992-98; Taylor Foundation preservation project, from 1998. **Awards:** Emmy award, *Speaking in Tongues*, associate producer, 1991.

Roles

1952	*Canticle for Innocent Comedians* (Graham), New York
1954	*Ardent Song* (Graham), New York
1955	Joan/Joan the Martyr, *Seraphic Dialogue* (Graham), New York
	La Lupa (with Stuart Hodes)
1958	Cassandra, *Clytemnestra* (Graham), New York
	Deaths and Entrances (Graham), New York
1960	*Acrobats of God* (Graham), New York
	Diversion of Angels (Graham), New York
1961	*Visionary Recital* (Graham), New York
	Junction (Paul Taylor), New York
	Insects and Heroes (Paul Taylor), New York

1962   Young Judith, *Legend of Judith* (Graham), London
        Pasiphae, *Phaedra* (Graham), New York
        Pierrot Lunaire (Tetley), New York
1963   *Embattled Garden* (Graham), New York

Works

1952   *Demonium*
1953   *World on a String*
1955   *Reap the Whirlwind*
1959   *Curley's Wife*
        Sphingi
1967   *The Act,* for Batsheva Dance Company, Tel Aviv

Publications

On HODES: books—

de Mille, Agnes, *Martha: The Life and Work Martha Graham.* New
    York, 1991.

On HODES: articles—

"Hotline. . .People," *Dance Magazine*, October 1992.
Horosko, M., "Graham Moves: Offstage, Onstage," *Dance Maga-
    zine,* July 1991.
"Linda Hodes," in *Biographical Dictionary of Dance* by Barbara
    Naomi Cohen-Stratyner, New York, 1982.
Shaphiro, L., "The Ball is Over," *Newsweek,* 15 October 1990.

*   *   *

Linda Hodes (neé Margolies) has long been associated with two
of the leading modern dance companies of our time, those of Martha
Graham and Paul Taylor, as well as playing a pivotal role in the
development of Batsheva de Rothschild's Batsheva Dance Company based in Israel. Born in New York City in 1933, Hodes began
her dance training at the Martha Graham School at age nine, joining
the Graham Company in 1952 at the age of 20. She performed
under the name Margolies until her marriage to Stuart Hodes (another dancer with the Martha Graham Company), then performed
under the name Linda Hodes.

Hodes danced with the Graham Company from 1952 to 1969,
and again from 1977 to 1992. In addition to dancing with the Graham Company, she danced with the companies of Paul Taylor,
Glen Tetley, Norman Walker, and Stuart Hodes. She was a founding
member and teacher of the Batsheva Dance Company in Tel Aviv,
Israel, in 1964, and later choreographed her popular work, *The Act,*
for the company. Batsheva, a Graham-inspired company, was sponsored by Graham's frequent benefactor, Batsheva de Rothschild,
and through this association with the company, Hodes met her
second husband, Ehud Ben-David, also a dancer with Batsheva.
Hodes left Israel and in 1970 began working as ballet master and
rehearsal director for the Nederlands Dans Theater, staying until
the following year. In 1972, she returned to Batsheva to work as
artistic co-director.

After leaving Batsheva the second time, Hodes came back to the
United States and in 1977 returned to the Martha Graham Company. Graham, at age 75, had been hospitalized during a period of
ill-health, and on her return to the company, she relied more and
more heavily on Ron Protas, a photographer who befriended her

while she was hospitalized. This was the beginning of a turbulent
time in the history of the Martha Graham Company. When Graham
resumed her leadership of the company, she turned against many of
the longtime dancers, including Bertram Ross and Mary Hinkson,
who had been associate directors since 1971. She involved Protas in
the management of the company in spite of the fact that he was
considered inexperienced, arrogant, and difficult by many of the
dancers. Subsequently, many dancers left the company.

Hodes seemed to weather this difficult time better than many of
the other longtime members of the Graham Company; Graham's
faith appeared unwavering when Hodes was put in charge of repertory dances. Hodes' longevity at the Martha Graham Company
may reflect her philosophy about dance, as quoted in a *Dance
Magazine* issue dedicated to Graham after her death (October
1991): "I think that dancers who go from company to company,
changing their movement and vocabulary, eventually wash out.
That's not a commitment to anything." Thoroughly committed
to the Graham technique, Hodes is considered an excellent teacher,
and has worked not only with the Graham Company and School
and the Graham-inspired Batsheva, but also with Paul Taylor's
school, Juilliard, the American Dance Festival, and the Rubin
Academy. During the 1980s, Hodes and Protas began the
Herculean task of archiving the history of Graham's work; a
project that proved nearly impossible though they managed to
preserve several dances, including *Cave of the Heart*, and *Errand into the Maze*, along with others. Graham went along with
the project, though without enthusiasm; she herself had little
interest, according to Agnes de Mille's *The Life and Work of
Martha Graham,* stating "I am more interested in achievement
than archives." Today these films and interviews are considered
invaluable resources for those studying Graham's work.

Hodes was an associate artistic director of the Graham Company
from 1977 to 1991. By 1988, Martha Graham had signed a document (distributed in 1990 by Ron Protas), designating Protas and
Hodes as her successors. The document reserved "final artistic
decision" for Protas, but it nonetheless signified that Hodes had
remained in the good graces of Graham at the time the document
was written. After Graham's death in April of 1991, Hodes resigned following disagreements with Protas.

In addition to her long history with Graham, Hodes had also
worked with Paul Taylor, first dancing together in the Martha Graham Company, then dancing for him at the Paul Taylor Company
from 1961 to 1968. She served as his consultant on his *Esplanade/
Runes* project for PBS' *Dance in America* series in 1978 and was
associate producer of the Emmy-award winning production, *Speaking in Tongues*. In 1992 Hodes joined the Paul Taylor staff as
director of the Paul Taylor School and Taylor 2, the second company sponsored by Taylor's Dance Foundation, a position she held
until mid-1998, when she began editing the foundation's mammoth
Repertory Preservation Project.

—Lisa Anderson Mann

HOLM, Hanya

German choreographer, dancer, educator, stage director, and
company director

Born: Johanna Eckert, 3 March 1893 in Worms-am-Rhein, Germany. **Education:** Konvent der Englischen Fraulein, the Hoch

Conservatory of Music in Frankfort, and the Dalcroze Institute. **Career:** Principal dancer, Mary Wigman Dance Company in Germany, 1921-31; chief instructor at the Wigman Central Institute in Dresden; changed name to Hanya Holm, 1923; relocated to New York City to open a Wigman Institute, 1931; renamed the Hanya Holm School of Dance, 1936; became U.S. citizen and debuted the Hanya Holm Dance Company with its first national tour, 1936; served on summer faculty, Mills College, California, 1932; served on faculty at Perry-Mansfield, Colorado, 1933; invited to teach at the Bennington College School of Dance's summer sessions, 1934-41; founded summer program at Colorado College, Colorado Springs, 1941; taught summer classes at Colorado College, 1941-84; premiered *Trend* at Bennington in 1937, *Work and Play* in 1938, *Tragic Exodus* and *They Too Are Exiles* in 1939; *Metropolitan Daily* chosen by NBC-TV as first live telecast of American modern dance, 1939; Broadway choreography began with *Ballet Ballads* and *Kiss Me Kate,* 1948; noted for original choreography for *My Fair Lady,* 1956; *Camelot,* 1960; first Labanotation score to copyright choreography (*Kiss Me Kate*) registered with the Library of Congress, 1952. **Awards:** *New York Times* Award for Best Choreography for *Trend,* 1937; *Dance Magazine* Award for Best Group Choreography for *Tragic Exodus,* 1938; Duke University Centennial "Women in Art," 1939; New York Drama Critics' Award for Best Choreographer for *Kiss Me Kate,* 1948; Critics' Circle Citation for Best Musical, *The Golden Apple,* 1954; nominated for a Tony Award for *My Fair Lady,* 1957; Federation of Jewish Philanthropies for "Outstanding Contribution to Modern Dance Movement in America," 1959; Honorary Doctor of Fine Arts, Colorado College, Colorado Springs, 1960; Capezio Dance Award, 1978; Samuel H. Scripps/American Dance Festival for lifetime achievement, 1984; *Dance Magazine* Award for lifetime contributions, 1990; Fred Astaire Award, 1991. **Died:** 3 November 1992 in New York City.

Roles

1929	Princess (cr) in *L'Histoire du Soldat,* Schauspielhaus, Dresden, Germany
	Original Cast in *Das Totenmal* (cr), Mary Wigman Company, Munich, Germany

Works

1928	Euripedes' *Bacchae*
1929	*Plato's Farewell to His Friends,* Open-Air Theater in Ommen, Holland
	L'Histoire du Soldat (mus. Stravinsky), Dresden
1930	*Das Totenmal* w/Mary Wigman (based on poem and music by Albert Talhoff), Munich
1936	*Salutation* (mus. Henry Cowell), Bennington Festival, Vermont
	Drive (mus. Harvey Pollins), Bennington Festival, Vermont
	Dance in Two Parts (mus. Wallingford Riegger), Bennington Festival, Vermont
	Sarabande (mus. Harvey Pollins), Bennington Festival, Vermont
	In Quiet Space (mus. Franziska Boas), Bennington Festival, Vermont
	City Nocturne (mus. Riegger), Bennington Festival, Vermont

	Four Chromatic Eccentricities (mus. Riegger), Bennington Festival, Vermont
	Primitive Rhythm (mus. Lucretia Barzun Wilson), Bennington Festival, Vermont
	Festive Rhythm (mus. Riegger), Bennington Festival, Vermont
1937	*Trend* (mus. Riegger and Edgard Varèse; sets Lauterer), Bennington Festival, Vermont
1938	*Dance of Introduction* (mus. Henry Cowell and Freda Miller), Y.M.H.A., New York
	Etudes (mus. Harvey Pollins, Franziska Boas, Margaret Dudley) Bennington Festival, Vermont
	Dance Sonata (mus. Harrison Kerr), Bennington Festival, Vermont
	Dance of Work and Play (mus. Norman Lloyd), Bennington Festival, Vermont
	Metropolitan Daily (mus. Gregory Tucker), Bennington Festival, Vermont
1939	*Metropolitan Daily* (rewritten for television; mus. Gregory Tucker), NBC-TV
	Tragic Exodus (mus. Vivian Fine), Bennington Festival, Vermont
	They Too Are Exiles (mus. Vivian Fine), Bennington Festival, Vermont
1941	*Dance of Introduction* (mus. Henry Cowell), Mansfield Theatre, New York
	The Golden Fleece (mus. Alex North; theme and costumes Kurt Seligmann), Mansfield Theatre, New York
	From This Earth (mus. Roy Harris) Fine Arts Center Theatre, Colorado Springs, Colorado
1942	*What So Proudly We Hail* (mus. American folk songs arranged by Roy Harris), Fine Arts Center Theatre, Colorado Springs
	Namesake (mus. Roy Harris; sets Lauterer), Fine Arts Center Theatre, Colorado Springs
1942	*Parable* (mus. Couperin arranged by Paul Aaron), Fine Arts Center Theatre, Colorado Springs
1943	*Suite of Four Dances* (mus. Cage), Central High School of Needle Trades, New York
	Orestes and the Furies (mus. John Coleman), Fine Arts Center Theatre, Colorado Springs
1944	*What Dreams May Come* (mus. Alex North), Fine Arts Center Theatre, Colorado Springs
1945	*Walt Whitman Suite* (mus. Roy Harris), Fine Arts Center Theatre, Colorado Springs
	The Gardens of Eden (mus. Darius Milhaud), Fine Arts Center Theatre, Colorado Springs
1946	*Dance for Four* (mus. Riegger), Fine Arts Center Theatre, Colorado Springs
	Windows (mus. Freda Miller), Fine Arts Center Theatre, Colorado Springs
1947	*And So Ad Infinitum (The Insect Comedy),* Fine Arts Center Theatre, Colorado Springs
1948	*The Eccentricities of Davey Crockett Ballet Ballads* (mus. Jerome Moross; book John Latouche), Maxine Elliott's Theatre
	The Insect Comedy (play by Karel and Josef Capek; co-directed with José Ferrer), New York City Center
	$E = MC^2$ (nonmusical play by Hallie Flanagan Davis), Brander Matthews Hall, Columbia University

Xochipili (mus. Carlos Chávez; sets Ricardo Martinez), Fine Arts Center Theatre, Colorado Springs

Kiss Me Kate (mus. Cole Porter; book Bella and Samuel Spewack), Century Theatre, New York

1949   *Blood Wedding* (nonmusical play by Federico García Lorca), New Stages

Ionization (mus. Edgard Varese), Fine Arts CenterTheatre, Colorado Springs

Ozark Suite (mus. Elie Siegmeister), New York City Center

1950   *The Liar* (mus. John Mundy; book Alfred Drake), Broadhurst Theatre, New York

Five Old French Dances, Fine Arts Center Theatre, Colorado Springs

Out of This World (mus. Cole Porter; book Dwight Taylor and Reginald Lawrence), Century Theatre, New York

1951   *Kiss Me Kate* (mus. Cole Porter; book Bella and Samuel Spewack), Coliseum, London

Prelude, Fine Arts Center Theatre, Colorado Springs

Quiet City, Fine Arts Center Theatre, Colorado Springs

1952   *Kindertotenlieder* (mus. Mahler), Fine Arts Center Theatre, Colorado Springs

Concertino da Camera, Fine Arts Center Theatre, Colorado Springs

My Darlin' Aida (mus.Verdi; book Charles Friedman), Winter Garden Theatre, New York

1953   *Ritual,* Fine Arts Center Theatre, Colorado Springs

Temperament and Behavior, Fine Arts Center Theatre, Colorado Springs

1954   *The Golden Apple* (mus. Jerome Moross; book John Latouche), Phoenix Theatre, New York

Presages (mus. Herbert Elwell), Fine Arts Center Theatre, Colorado Springs

L'Histoire du Soldat (mus. Stravinsky), Wheeler Opera House, Aspen Festival, Colorado

1955   *Desert Drone,* Fine Arts Center Theatre, Colorado Springs

Pavane (from Gian Carlo Menotti's St. Sebastian Ballet), Fine Arts Center Theatre, Colorado Springs

Sousa March, Perkins Hall Auditorium, Colorado Springs

Reuben, Reuben (mus. and book Marc Blitzstein), Shubert Theatre, Boston

1956   *My Fair Lady* (mus. and book Lerner and Loewe) Mark Hellinger Theatre, New York

The Ballad of Baby Doe (mus. Douglas Moore; book John Latouche) Opera House, Central City, Colorado

Preludio and Loure (mus. Bach), Fine Arts Center Theatre, Colorado Springs

The Vagabond King, Paramount movie

1957   *Chanson Triste,* Fine Arts Center Theatre, Colorado Springs

You Can't Go Home Again, Fine Arts Center Theatre, Colorado Springs

Pinocchio (mus. Alec Wilder; book Yasha Frank after C. Collodi classic), NBC-TV

Ozark Suite (mus. Elie Siegmeister), Brooklyn Institute of Arts and Sciences

Where's Charley? (mus. Frank Loesser), Opera House, Manchester

The Dance and the Drama, "Folio" Program, Canadian Broadcasting Company

1958   *Where's Charley?* (mus. Frank Loesser), Palace Theatre, London

My Fair Lady (mus. and book Lerner and Loewe), Drury Lane Theatre, London

1959   *Orpheus and Euridice* (mus. Glück), Queen Elizabeth Theatre, Vancouver

1960   *Christine* (mus. Sammy Fain; book Pearl S. Buck), 46th Street Theatre, New York

Camelot (mus. and book Lerner and Loewe), Majestic Theatre, New York

1961   *Music for an Imaginary Ballet,* Broadmoor International Theatre, Colorado Springs

1962   *Orpheus and Euridice* (mus. Glück), O'Keefe Centre, Toronto

1963   *Figure of Predestination,* Fine Arts Center Theatre, Colorado Springs

Toward the Unknown Region, Fine Arts Center Theatre, Colorado Springs

Dinner with the President, CBS-TV Special from Washington, D.C.

1964   *My Fair Lady* (mus. and book Lerner and Loewe), Habimah National Theatre, Tel Aviv

Theatrics, Fine Arts Center Theatre, Colorado Springs

1965   *Anya* (mus. Rachmaninoff; book Guy Bolton and George Abbott) Ziegfeld Theatre, New York

1967   *Spooks,* Armstrong Theatre, Colorado Springs

1975   *Rota* (mus. George Crumb [from *Makrokosmos* series]), Don Redlich Dance Company, New York

1977   *Homage to Mahler,* Riverside Church, New York

1980   *Four Nocturnes* (mus. George Crumb), Armstrong Theatre, Colorado Springs

Perpetuum Mobile, Blues, Continuum (mus. Ravel), Don Redlich Dance Company, Armstrong Theatre, Colorado Springs

1981   *Cantanta Profana* (mus. Bartók), Don Redlich Dance Company and students in the Colorado College Summer Festival of the Arts, Armstrong Theater, Colorado Springs

Jocose (mus. Ravel, *Sonata for Piano and Violin*), Don Redlich Dance Company, Riverside Dance Festival, New York

1982   *Ratatat* (mus. Baby Dods), Don Redlich Dance Company, New York

1983   *Jocose* (mus. Ravel, *Sonata for Piano and Violin*), Armstrong Theater, Colorado Springs

1985   *Capers* (mus. Henry Brandt), Don Redlich Dance Company, Joyce Theater, New York

Publications

By HOLM: articles—

"The Dance, the Artist-Teacher, and the Child," *Progressive Education,* 1935.

"The German Dance in the American Scene," *Modern Dance,* edited by Virginia Stewart, New York, 1935.

"Mary Wigman," *Dance Observer,* November 1935.

"Dance on the Campus—Athletics of Art?," *Dance Magazine,* February 1937.

"The Mary Wigman I Know," *The Dance Has Many Faces,* edited by Walter Sorell, 1951, revised edition, 1966.

"Mary Wigman Celebrates 80 Years This Month," *Dance News,* November 1966.

"Pioneer of the New Dance," *The American Dancer,* Los Angeles, April 1933.

"Trend Grew upon Me," *Magazine of Art,* March 1938.

"To Be With It," *Focus on Dance,* 1977.

"Who Is Mary Wigman?," *Dance Magazine,* November 1956.

On HOLM: books—

Sorell, Walter, *Hanya Holm, The Biography of an Artist,* Connecticut, 1962.

On HOLM: articles—

Bassor, Henriette, "Flights Beyond the Horizon with Hanya Holm," *The American Dancer,* Los Angeles, May 1941.

Butler, Gervaise, "Hanya Holm," *Dance Observer,* February 1938.

Cristofori, Marilyn, "Spotlight on Hanya Holm: Portrait of a Pioneer," *Dance Teacher Now,* May 1990.

Martin, John, "Hanya Holm in 'Fair Lady' Helps Make a Masterpiece," *New York Times,* 29 April 1956.

Martin, John, "Hanya Holm: *Trend* Blazes a Trail toward Theatre Forms," *New York Times,* 2 January 1938.

Siegel, Marcia B., "A Conversation with Hanya Holm," *Ballet Review,* Spring 1981.

Sferes, Andrea, "Bibliography & Research Sources," in "HANYA HOLM, The Life and Legacy," *The Journal for Stage Directors & Choreographers,* Spring 1993.

Terry, Walter, "The Holm Dances for a New Musical," *New York Herald Tribune,* 25 March 1956.

Tobias, Tobi, "Hanya Holm: A Young Octogenarian," *Dance News,* March 1979.

Todd, Arthur, "Camelot: Choreography by Hanya Holm," *Dance Observer,* January 1961.

Films and Videotapes

Hanya: Portrait of a Pioneer, produced by Marilyn Cristofori, Dance Horizons Video, 1985.

*   *   *

Hanya Holm, one of the 20th century's major choreographers of American modern dance and Broadway musicals, was highly regarded and sought after as an innovative master educator. Holm is credited with introducing Labanotation, theories of spatial dynamics, and rigorous improvisation to the American dance scene.

Born near the Rhine River in Germany, she was baptized Johanna Eckert. She received extensive music education at the Hoch Conservatory of Music (alongside Paul Hindemith) as well as four years at the Dalcroze Institute. In 1921 she joined Mary Wigman and became part of the development of "German Expressionist Dance." For 10 years she toured Europe as a principal dancer and was chief instructor at Wigman's Central Institute in Dresden. During that time she changed her name to Hanya Holm.

When impresario Sol Hurok offered to finance a Wigman school in America, Holm, nervous about the political undercurrents of Hitler's rise, volunteered to relocate. Hurok arranged everything: her travel, the studio, her housing. The day after arriving, in Sep-

tember 1931, Holm began teaching. Hurok, a businessman and producer, was not interested in waiting the five years Hanya needed to train a company, so in 1932 he turned the school over to her. As promised, she debuted her trained company in 1936!

Finding that Wigman's mysticism and Germanic themes had little to do with American temperaments, environments, or rhythms, she developed her own theories and created a modern style that emphasized freedom and a flowing quality for the torso and back, yet remained firmly based on universal principles of motion and the laws of physics. Her natural sense of humor blossomed and, although her choreography was still concerned with visionary messages about humanity's relation to the universe, the dancing was lyrical, witty, and open. In summer 1932 Hanya taught at Mills College in California and in 1933 at Perry-Mansfield, Colorado. Invited to teach at the famous Bennington Summer School of the Dance from 1934 to 1941, she was regarded as one of the "Four Pioneers" of American modern dance. In 1941 Holm founded the influential summer program at Colorado College, Colorado Springs, where she taught for 43 years.

Her New York school and the summer program became meccas for dancers of all disciplines. Critic Walter Terry commented that any dancer, whether East Indian, tap, ballet, or any other style, could become a better dancer because Holm's theories could be applied to all. Her three-year program offered technique, anatomy, theory, dance history, pedagogy, composition, improvisation, and Labanotation. A few famous students include Alwin Nikolais, Valerie Bettis, Glen Tetley, Mary Anthony, Louise Kloepper, Nancy Hauser, Elisabeth Waters, Don Redlich, Anabelle Lyon, Bambi Lynn, and Murray Louis.

Holm's masterwork, *Trend,* commissioned by the Bennington Festival in 1937, had as its central theme the survival of society. Stunning for its architectural form, symphonic development, and emotional intensity, *Trend* received the *New York Times Award* for Best Dance. In 1939 *Dance Magazine* awarded Holm's *Tragic Exodus* Best Group Choreography. Also in 1939, *Metropolitan Daily* was selected by the National Broadcasting Company (NBC) for the first live telecast of modern dance. Viewers within a 50-mile radius of New York City were treated to Holm's witty and satiric views of newspapers.

The Holm company was admired for its kinesthetic accessibility. Critic Walter Terry wrote in February 1941: "Hanya Holm and her girls were always the most lyric of the moderns. While the feminine contingent of other modern dance companies usually resembled a gang of sexless automatons, Miss Holm's company inevitably danced with feminine grace and charm."

Hanya gained distinction as a choreographer/director for opera, theatre, and Broadway. After her success with *Ballet Ballads* (1948) she was invited to choreograph a new Cole Porter musical. *Kiss Me Kate* (1948) was enthusiastically greeted as a milestone in the development of the American musical and Holm was recognized with a New York Drama Critics Award as Best Choreographer that year. At Hanya's request, the Labanotation score was registered with the Library of Congress in 1952, the first complete choreography to be so copyrighted.

Holm choreographed for musicals throughout the 1950s and 1960s, earning special accolades for *The Golden Apple* (1954) and great acclaim for *My Fair Lady* (1956). For her work on this smash hit, she was nominated for a Tony Award. In his *New York Times* review John Martin summed up her influence: "Hanya Holm should get some sort of specially designed gold medal for what she has done with *My Fair Lady,* and Moss Hart deserves at least a silver one for grasping the necessity of having her do it." Further Martin commented that Holm's "Choreographic phrasing emerges time and time again through the dramatic action" and was "just about as ideal a fusion of the literary-dramatic element of the theatre with the choreo-musical element as has been seen in our time."

Other of Holm's Broadway musicals included *My Darlin' Aida* (1952), *Camelot* (1960), and *Anya* (1965), and among her film/ television creations were *The Vagabond King* (Paramount, 1956), *The Dance and the Drama* (CBC, 1957), and *Dinner with the President* (CBS 1963). During the 1970s and 1980s the Don Redlich Dance Company became the chief repository for Hanya's concert dances. For its 1985 New York season the company presented *Ratatat* (1982), *Jocose* (1983), and *Capers* (1985). These dances revealed that the Holm wry sense of humor, wit, poignancy, and keen intelligence were as sharp and vital as during their original pioneering decade.

Holm remained essentially unimpressed with her greatness as an artist and ever committed to generously sharing all she knew. Her teaching at Juilliard, the Nikolais-Louis studio, and Colorado College extended until she was well past age 90. As an Honored Guest at the American Film Institute at the Kennedy Center in Washington, D.C. for the 1985 Women in Film and Video Festival, she repeated one of her famous remarks, "You will find out that one life is not enough. You will want to have several lives in which to discover what there is to be discovered."

—Marilyn Cristofori

HORST, Louis

American composer

Born: 12 January 1884, in Kansas City, Missouri. **Education:** Studied violin and piano at Adams Cosmopolitan School, San Francisco; studied composition in Vienna, 1925. **Family:** Married Betty Cunningham, 1909 (subsequently separated; never divorced); also had long-term relationship with Martha Graham. **Career:** Accompanist for theater companies and silent films in California, 1902-15; accompanist and music director for Denishawn, 1915-25; music director, Martha Graham Company, 1926-48, Helen Tamiris, 1927-30, and Doris Humphrey and Charles Weidman, 1927-32; also served as composer and accompanist for numerous other dancers, including Harald Kreutzberg, Yvonne Georgi, and Ruth Page; teacher of dance composition at the Neighborhood Playhouse School of Theatre, 1928-64; also taught at Sarah Lawrence College, 1932-40, Bennington Summer School of Dance, 1935-45, American Dance Festival, 1948-63, and Juilliard Schools, 1958-63; founder and editor, *Dance Observer* magazine, 1934-64. **Awards:** Capezio Award, 1955; honorary doctorate, Wayne State University, Detroit, 1963; Creative Award of the American Academy of Physical Education, 1964. **Died:** 23 January 1964, in New York.

Works (compositions for dance; choreographer in parentheses)

1919	*Japanese Spear Dance* (Shawn)
1925	*Byzantine Dance* (St. Denis)
1926	*Three Poems of the East* (Graham)
	Two Balinese Rhapsodies (Page)
1928	*Fragments* (Graham)
1931	*Primitive Mysteries* (Graham)
1932	*Chorus of Youth* (Graham)
1933	*Three Tragic Patterns* (Graham)
1934	*American-Provincials* (Graham)
	Celebration (Graham)
	Pleasures of Counterpoint No. 2 (Humphrey)
1935	*Frontier* (Graham)
1936	*Horizons* (Graham)
1937	*Graduation Piece* (Lang)
1939	*Columbiad* (Graham)
1940	*Little Theodolina* (Fonaroff)
	El Penitente (Graham)
1941	*Transformations of Medusa* (Erdman)
	Mountain White (de Mille)
1942	*Yankee Doodle* (Fonaroff)
1946	*Born to Weep* (Fonaroff)
1948	*Tale of Seizure* (Yuriko)

Publications

By HORST: books—

Modern Dance Forms, New York, 1960.
Modern Dance Forms in Relation to the Other Modern Arts, with Carroll Russell, San Francisco, 1961.
Pre-Classic Dance Forms, first published 1937, reprinted, Princeton, NJ, 1987.

On HORST: books—

Soares, Janet Mansfield, *Louis Horst: Musician in a Dancer's World,* Durham, NC, 1992.
Stodelle, Ernestine, *The Story of Louis Horst and the American Dance,* Cheshire, CT, 1964.

On HORST: articles—

Hughes, Allen, "Illustrious Dean of American Dance Celebrates His Eightieth Birthday," *New York Times,* 12 January 1964.
Sabin Robert, "Louis Horst and Modern Dance in America," *Dance Observer,* February 1953, March 1953, April 1953.
Sorell, Walter, "Louis Horst: The Music Man of Modern Dance," *Dance Magazine,* December 1984.

*   *   *

Of Louis Horst and modern dance it can be said without hyperbole that he was present at the creation. He worked closely with and encouraged many of the early seminal figures, helped forge a new role for music in dance, was the first serious student, critic, and scholar of the emerging form, and had an enduring influence on dancers and choreographers during his long career as teacher and coach.

Horst was born in 1884 in Kansas City, Missouri. When he was a teenager, his family moved to San Francisco, where he studied violin and piano. He began his musical career in northern California as an accompanist for vaudeville and silent film. His long association with dance began in 1915 when he came to the attention of the Denishawn Dance Company when they needed a conductor for about 10 days. Horst agreed to step in, and he stayed for 10 years, playing and arranging music for Ruth St. Denis and Ted Shawn.

Martha Graham left Denishawn in 1923; in 1925 Horst also left for New York to join her. They worked together very closely; he remained her musical director until 1948. Observers credited Horst with being a calming influence on Graham, contributing poise to balance her headstrong, mercurial genius. Graham herself wrote in *Dance Perspectives 16*, that "his sympathy, and understanding, but primarily his faith, gave me a landscape to move in. Without it, I should have certainly been lost."

Horst was a very popular accompanist in New York at recitals and Broadway rehearsals. A congenial man, he was a welcome asset on grueling company tours. In addition to Graham he played for Humphrey and Weidman (who he encouraged to break off on their own), Helen Tamiris, Agnes de Mille, Ruth Page, Adolf Bolm and Harald Kreutzberg. He was one of the first composers to work beside a choreographer in the creation of a dance. Horst composed many scores for Graham, including several of her landmark dances. This role of composer/accompanist was quite new, and although Horst believed that music was secondary to dance in this collaboration, his contribution was not. If *Primitive Mysteries* is Graham mysticism, her creative response to an ancient rite, the dance also reflects Horst's appreciation of primitive art.

The dance is elegant and formal; the action follows the course of a Spanish Christian passion play, with the Virgin Mary as the central character. However, the movement of the dancers and the music (Indian, with flute, oboe, piano and percussion added) summoned the sound and feel of an American Indian ritual. This perfect integration of music and movement amounted to something altogether unique—part ritual, part miracle play.

Horst also composed scores for Doris Humphrey, Agnes de Mille, Nina Fonaroff, and Jean Erdman, among others. Horst was obviously well-placed to be an informed observer of modern dance. He was determined to bring informed, methodical thinking to it as well. In 1934, while other dance publications ignored or derided modern dance, Horst founded the monthly *Dance Observer*, assembling a group of talented young writers such as Winthrop Sargent, Robert Sabin, and Arthur Todd. Contributors shared his enthusiasm and dedication; the magazine was non-profit and non-paying. The magazine carried reviews as well as longer, analytical pieces; significantly, one could read in its pages about what was being done at colleges and universities. Though Horst and the publication he ran until his death were always friends of dance, firm critical standards were the rule, with the possible exception of Martha Graham; to some it seemed she alone could do no wrong in Horst's eyes.

Notwithstanding these accomplishments, he is best known for his workshops and classes in formal dance composition. As in his other capacities, his reputation as a teacher and coach was that of a supremely knowledgeable, unforgiving critic, and deflator of egos. He was not a dictator however; he persuaded through the force of his beliefs and the power of persuasion, for he was known equally as a beloved, encouraging mentor and passionate lover of dance. His influence during his long tenure as a teacher cannot be overestimated. Horst trained an enormous number of choreographers, dancers, musicians, and actors during his years at the Neighborhood Playhouse (1928-64), the Bennington Summer Schools of Dance (1934-45), American Dance Festivals (1948-1963), and the Juilliard School (1958-64) as well as stints at the Teachers College at Columbia University, Sarah Lawrence College, Barnard College, and the Connecticut College Summer School of Dance.

Form was Horst's byword. Thus a key aspect of his teaching was the study of preclassical musical forms, such as the minuet or the pavane, and contemporary music in those forms. Much like a teacher of poetry would instruct students to write a sonnet before they move on to free verse, Horst had his students invent movements that corresponded to these classical musical forms and organize them into dances before they began creating subjectively. He was interested in true composition—creating original movement in the service of a theme. Moving, not stepping, he said, contrasting modern dance with ballet.

He was highly disdainful of undisciplined expressionism and bluntly discouraged any sort of improvisational approach; many young choreographers he worked with struggled against this constraint. He insisted that each dance should have a recognizable form of its own. As Don McDonagh observed in *The Rise and Fall and Rise of Modern Dance*, if Horst believed that music was a useful frame for dance, much as a frame was useful to a painting, "he was no more able to conceive of a painting without a frame than of dance without similarly structured limits."

Horst was an educator of audiences as well as dancers and choreographers. He served on the Dance Committee at the New School for Social Research, where he helped initiate the lecture-demonstration series to assist laypeople in understanding modern dance. He also held a seminal series of lecture-demonstrations in dance composition at the YM/YWHA in New York, another spawning ground for dance and choreographic talent.

The last years of Horst's life closely resembled previous years. On Mondays he taught at the Neighborhood Playhouse; on Tuesdays, the Martha Graham School; and on Wednesdays at Juilliard. He spent much of the rest of his energies on *Dance Observer* and attending as many dance events as possible. Representative of the admiration felt for Horst, in 1955 he received the Capezio Dance Award, which cited his contribution to the modern dance as a composer, accompanist, teacher, critic, and general force for progress. And the *New York Times* celebrated his 80th birthday with this sentiment: "Because he has always cared unselfishly, the American dance world is deeply in his debt and privileged to wish him well on this special day."

—Valerie Vogrin

HORTA, Rui
Portuguese/German dancer and choreographer

Born: c. 1957, in Portugal. **Education:** Studied with the Gulbenkian Ballet in Europe; studied with Alvin Ailey American Dance Theatre, late 1970s. **Career:** Artistic director, S.O.A.P. Dance Theatre, Mousonturm, Frankfurt, 1991-present.

Works (selected; for the S.O.A.P. Dance Theatre in Frankfurt unless otherwise noted)

1991	*Wolfgang, Bitte,* Dance Workshop Europe, London
	Long Time Before the End
1992	*Domestic Arrangements*
	Made to Measure
1993	*Ordinary Events*
	Standby, Transitions Dance Company, London

1994   *Object Constant*
        A necessidade de se estar onde se este (*The Necessity of Being Where One Is*), S.O.A.P./En Danca (Brazil), Tanz und Theatre International, Hanover
1995   *Glass*
1996   *Khôra*

Publications

On HORTA: articles—

Boxberger, Edith, "The Sufferings of the Times," *Ballett International/Tanz Aktuell*, July 1994.

Bramley, Ian, "Don't Look Now!," *Dance Theatre Journal*, Summer 1995.

————, "Rui Horta," *Dance Theatre Journal*, Autumn 1993.

Constanti, Sophie, "Reviews: The Turning World," *Dance and Dancers*, August 1993.

————, "*The Turning World*," *Dancing Times*, August 1993.

David, Simone, "Making Room for Current Developments," *Ballett International/Tanz Aktuell*, November 1994.

Garcia, Sylvia, "Tanz- und Badefreuden im Kurtheater," *Tanz und Gymnastik*, 1993.

Gradinger, Malve, "Innovation Out of the Tradition," *Ballett International/Tanz Aktuell*, April 1995.

Henss, Rita, "Geschicktes Arrangement," *Ballett International*, October 1992.

Jowitt, Deborah, "Uncommon Market," *Village Voice*, 7 October 1997.

Marigny, Chris de, "Bagnolet 1992," *Dancing Times*, October 1992.

Milz, Bettina, "Beyond the Silences," *Ballett International/Tanz Aktuell*, October 1995.

Odenthal, Johannes, "Movement-Energy-Perception," *Ballett International/Tanz Aktuell*, January 1996.

Percival, John, "Dance Workshop Europe," *Dance and Dancers*, October 1991.

Percival, John, "Review, *Long Time Before the End*," *Dance and Dancers*, August 1992.

————, "Review, *The Turning World*," *Dance and Dancers*, July 1993.

Siegmund, Gerald, "In the Coldness of This World," *Ballett International/Tanz Aktuell*, December 1996.

Wesemann, Arnd, "Broadway Hoofing," *Ballett International/Tanz Aktuell*, June 1995.

*   *   *

Choreographer Rui Horta, artistic director of S.O.A.P. Dance Company based in Frankfurt's Mousonturm, has called himself a member of "the first post-revolutionary generation" of modern dance. As such, he has suggested choreographers need a new vocabulary, a new language.

A member of an aristocratic family in Portugal, Horta came of age in the midst of the pro-democracy revolution that rocked his homeland in 1974. In that year, Horta turned 17 and discovered dance. He studied first with the Gulbenkian Ballet, then headed for America and the Alvin Ailey school. In New York he learned the techniques of Graham, Horton, Cunningham, and others, and though he originally planned only to study for a few months, he ended up staying for years. Yet in spite of his extensive training by others, he has said that he still views himself as largely self-taught. Perhaps the choreographer meant that his career has been marked by a constant striving to develop a new voice, to invent or reinvent. His quests sometimes lead him into contradiction, "We live in a society that's dominated by intellectual understanding," he has said, urging discovery of "other levels of perception," such as those offered by the body. To an American, at least, the notion that society is dominated by the intellect rather than the body would come as a surprise, since popular culture extols physical beauty and power and holds the pursuits of the mind in contempt; but Horta is speaking from a European perspective—and, ironically, from the perspective of an intellectual.

But then, self-consciousness is never far from Horta's work, and he has embraced postmodernism with self-referential compositions such as *Object Constant*. It is a dance within a dance, watched by a comically brutal artistic director-type who snarls witticisms such as, "I hate being angry; it pisses me off." He watches the other dancers dancing and makes comments to the audience, telling them what to think, "We know this is very beautiful, isn't it?," he demands. Sometimes he places himself impishly within the thoughts of his viewers, as when a group of women partially remove their dresses, covering their breasts with them, "Are they going to drop their tops?" he asks lasciviously.

Horta's compositions bring in elements other than dance: there is speech, as in *Object Constant*, but also a heavy use of lighting and props. As for the themes, they usually carry a powerful dose of negativity, as in *Diving*. The latter focuses on the familiar image of a frightened would-be diver hesitating to make the big leap from the board while others in the pool cavort with abandon; the difference here, though, is that everyone including the diver is a grownup, and the diving board is clearly something metaphorical, murky, and ultimately quite ominous. In this composition blue plastic bowls and skillful use of lighting greatly enhance the presentation by creating the sense of a pool filled with shimmering blue water. *Domestic Arrangements*, built around the theme of a male-female struggle, is rife with props, including a group of shapes that alternately become walls, a bed, a stage.

Another distinguishing feature of Horta's work is its circularity. Often a piece ends where it began, and that is usually not a good place to be—another modern touch. *Standby*, for instance, starts with an apparently happy individual emerging on stage with words that identify him as a man marked for doom, "I feel great today!" It ends with the first man having left the stage a crumpled heap, his inner turmoil illustrated by the twisting movements of those around him, while a hapless woman comes on and utters the fateful words: "I feel great today!" The music starts again, the stage fades to black, and the audience knows where this is all going.

Reflecting on this thematic circularity in other works as well as in *Standby*, Ian Bramley in *Dance Theatre Journal* wrote: "Horta is forceful, but his power is a kind of centrifugal force, only coming from repeatedly going round in circles covering and redeveloping familiar material. But what now?... I for one will be waiting to see where he goes next."

Horta has certainly had no shortage of ideas, as he showed in a January 1996 interview in the English-language edition of *Tanz Aktuell*. (Very little has been written about him on the west side of the Atlantic; of the limited English literature on Horta, virtually all of it is in British publications such as *Dance and Dancers, Dancing Times,* and *Dance Theatre Journal*.) He was working on several productions, he said, including a five-year retrospective called *Letters from Under the Skin.* Also in the works was a collaborative interpretation of Hermann Hesse's brooding novel *Steppenwolf.*

As for what he would *not* be doing in the future, Horta said he would not be moving to any large-scale civic theatres or opera houses. The scale of his work, he says "places it on the independent scene: working with eight-to-10 dancers," using and maintaining the "intimacy" of smaller performance places. As for the larger theatres, he admitted to having had one tempting offer, from the London Contemporary Dance Theatre, but that was just before he'd taken the S.O.A.P. job instead. "I can't see myself in that world with all its compromises," he commented of this different style of dance and theatre.

Critics have found the self-conscious postmodernism of his work by turns fascinating, amusing, and grating. Horta, meanwhile, has continued to grow, rooted in a supreme self-confidence that may be a byproduct of his upper-class background. The title of one 1994 work says it all: composed when he was in the middle of dividing his energies between S.O.A.P. and En Danca, a company halfway across the world in Brazil, it was called *A necessidade de se estar onde se este—The Necessity of Being Where One Is*. Once again, the language is self-referential and postmodern—quintessential Horta.

—Judson Knight

HORTON, Lester

American choreographer, educator, and company director

Born: 23 January 1906 in Indianapolis, Indiana. **Education:** Studied ballet in Indianapolis with Theo Hughes; also studied ballet and Hindu dance in Chicago. **Career:** First choreography, Indianapolis Little Theater, where he learned the basic crafts of theater; moved to Los Angeles, 1930; studied and performed with Michio Ito; started teaching, 1932; formed Lester Horton Dancers (the first interracial dance company in the U.S.) with Bella Lewitzky as lead dancer, 1932; choreographed *Sacre du printemps* for the Hollywood Bowl, 1937; began choreographing for Hollywood films (19 in all), 1939; opened first theater/academy for dance in the U.S. offering classes in technique, performance, and theater arts and crafts, 1946; classroom space convertible into a fully professional theater for weekend concerts, 1948; first New York appearance, 1953; won high praise for his choreography's unique theatricality, dynamic contrasts and high caliber of dancers. **Died:** 2 November 1953, in Los Angeles.

Works (premiered in Los Angeles unless otherwise noted)

1928	*Song of Hiawatha* (mus. various composers), Horton and group
1929	*Siva-Siva* w/Katherine Stubergh (mus. Sol Cohen)
1931	*Kootenai War Dance* (mus. percussion), solo
1932	*Voodoo Ceremonial* (mus. percussion), Horton and group
	Takwish, The Star Maker (mus. Roland Klump), group
1933	*Oriental Motifs* (mus. percussion), Horton and group
1934	*Allegro Barbaro* w/Dorothy Wagner (mus. Bartók)
	May Night w/Wagner (mus. Selim Palmgren)
	Hand Dance (mus. Polynesian percussion), group
	Lament (Braham van den Berg; mus. Hebrew melody)
	Incantation from Aboriginal Suite (T. Masarachia; mus. percussion)

	Two Arabesques (mus. Satie), group
	Dances of the Night (mus. percussion), group
	Salomé (mus. Constance Boynton), Horton and group
	Aztec Ballet (mus. percussion), group
	Second Gnossienne (Elizabeth Talbot-Martin; mus. Erik Satie)
	Concerto Grosso (Thelma Babitz; mus. Ernest Bloch)
	Painted Desert Ballet (mus. Homer Grunn) group
	Chinese fantasy (mus. percussion), group
	Bolero (mus. Ravel), group
	Ave (Patty-Max Green; mus. Kodály)
	Maidens (mus. Federico Mompou) group
	Salutation (mus. Dane Rudhyar), solo
	Gnossienne # 3 (Elizabeth Talbot-Martin; mus. Satie)
	Vale (Patti-Max Green; mus. Kodály)
1935	*Mound Builders* (mus. Sidney Cutner) Horton and group
	Antique Suite (Ana Kurgans; mus. Molinaro—arranged by Respighi)
	Pentacost (mus. Dane Rudhyar), solo
	Dictator (mus. Sidney Cutner), Bruce Burroughs and group
	Dance of Parting (Mary Meyer; mus. Vicenzo Davico)
	Rain Quest (mus. Bertha Miller English), group
	Conflict w/Mary Meyer (mus. percussion)
	Ritual at Midnight (mus. Constance Boynton), group
	Tendresse w/Mary Meyer (mus. Alexander Krien)
	Sun Ritual (mus. Miller English), group
	Rhythmic Dance w/Meyer (mus. Alexandre Tansman)
	Salutation to the Depths (Talbot-Martin; mus. Dane Rudhyar)
	The Mine (mus. Cutner), group
	The Art Patrons (mus. Cutner), group
1936	*Growth of Action* (mus. Dane Rudhyar), group
	Two Dances for a Leader (mus. Cutner), group
	Flight From Reality (mus. Rudhyar), solo
	Lysistrata (mus. Cutner), group
	Ceremony (mus. Miller English), group
1937	*Prelude to Militancy* (Bella Lewitzky; mus. Gian Francesco Malipiero)
	Chronicle (mus. Cutner) group
	Salomé (revison; mus. Miller English) Horton and group
	Le Sacre du printemps (mus. Stravinsky), group
	Prologue to an Earth Celebration (mus. Villa Lobos), group
	Pasaremos (Bella Lewitzky; mus. Miller English)
	Haven (Charles Pressey and group; mus. Miller English)
	Conquest (mus. Lou Harrison), group
1939	*Departure From the Land* (mus. Gerhardt Dorn), group
	Something to Please Everybody (mus. Lou Harrison), group
	Five Women (mus. Gerhardt Dorn), group
1940	*Sixteen to Twenty-Four* (mus. Harrison), group
	A Noble Comedy—revision of *Lysistrata* (mus. Simon Abel), group
1941	*Pavanne* (Sonia Shaw; mus. William Byrd)
1946	*Shootin' Star* (Sol Kaplan musical)
1947	*Barrel House* (mus. Anita Short Metz), group
1948	*Totem Incantation* (mus. Judith Hamilton), Lester Horton Dancers
	The Beloved (Bella Lewitzky, Herman Boden; mus. Judith Hamilton)

Salomé—revision (mus. percussion), Lester Horton Dancers

Warsaw Ghetto (Bella Lewitzky, Sondra Owens; mus. Kaplan)

The Park (dialogue by Sonia Brown), Lester Horton Dancers

The Bench of the Lamb (mus. Mary Hoover), Lester Horton Dancers

Tongue in Cheek (musical review staged by Horton and Lewitzky)

1950 *Estilo de Tu* (mus. Copland), Lester Horton Dancers

A Bouquet for Molly (mus. Earl Robinson), Lester Horton Dancers

El Rebozo (mus. Mary Hoover), Lester Horton Dancers

Salomé (revision; mus. percussion), Lester Horton Dancers

Brown County, Indiana (mus. Kenneth Klaus), Lester Horton Dancers

1951 *Tropic Trio* (mus. Audree Covington), Lester Horton Dancers

On the Upbeat (mus. Audree Covington), Lester Horton Dancers

Another Touch of Klee (Stan Kenton), Lester Horton Dancers

Medea (mus. Covington), Lester Horton Dancers

Girl Crazy (revival; mus. George Gershwin)

Annie Get Your Gun (revival; mus. Berlin)

1952 *Seven Scenes with Ballaballi* (mus. Gertrude Rivers Robinson), Lester Horton Dancers

Liberian Suite (mus. Duke Ellington), Lester Horton Dancers

Prado de Pena (mus. Gertrude Rivers Robinson), Lester Horton Dancers

1953 *Dedications in Our Time* (mus. Rivers Robinson, Kenneth Kraus), Lester Horton Dancers

Salomé (final revision; mus. percussion), Lester Horton Dancers

Publications

By HORTON: articles—

"An Outline Approach to Choreography," *Educational Dance,* August-September 1940.

"American Indian Dance," *Educational Dance,* October 1941.

On HORTON: books—

Lloyd, Margaret, *The Borzoi Book of Modern Dance,* New York, 1949.

Warren, Larry, *Lester Horton: Modern Dance Pioneer,* New York, 1977 (reprinted New Jersey, 1991).

On HORTON: articles—

Barnes, Clive, "Genius on Wrong Coast," *Los Angeles Herald-Examiner,* 3 December 1967.

Cohen, Selma Jeanne, editor, "The Dance Theater of Lester Horton," *Dance Perspectives,* Autumn 1967.

Terry, Walter, "Lester Horton Wins at the "Y," *New York Herald Tribune,* 5 April 1953.

Films and Videotapes

Choreographed by Horton—

Moonlight in Havana, 1942.
White Savage, 1943.
Phantom of the Opera, 1944.
Climax, 1944.
Ali Baba and the Forty Thieves, 1945.
Salomé, Where She Danced, 1945.
Frisco Sal, 1945.
Tangier, 1946.
Tarzan and the Leopard Woman, 1946.
Siren of Atlantis, 1948.
Bagdad, 1949.
Golden Hawk, 1952.
3-D Follies, 1953.
South Sea Woman, 1953.

On Horton—

Genius on Wrong Coast, documentary by Lelia Goldoni, Philadelphia, Star Steps, 1994.

* * *

In the richly creative period between World Wars I and II, when modern dance was coming into its own as an art form in the United States, it was widely believed that all of the creative activity of any significance was centered in New York City. Yet in Los Angeles, Lester Horton was making similar and no less important strides in building a body of work that was to be one of the cornerstones of American modern dance.

Horton's interest in dance was triggered at the age of 16, after seeing authentic Indian dancing in a touring Wild West show. A few years later, he attended a performance of the Denishawn Dancers, and was overcome—overcome not only by the beauty of the Denishawn repertoire, but by the newness of the music, the splendid costumes, and the dancers as well. Touring with Denishawn at that time were Martha Graham, Doris Humphrey, and Charles Weidman who were, with Horton, to become pioneers of American modern dance.

Horton's first dance training at a local Indianapolis dance studio included ballet, some aesthetic dance, and a version of Denishawn training. At the age of 20, seeking to broaden his horizons, he moved to Chicago where he studied ballet and Hindu dance. His next step was to study authentic American Indian dance with master teachers in Santa Fe, New Mexico. Soon after his return to Indianapolis he accepted an offer from the Indianapolis Little Theater to participate in the creation of a pageant, *The Song of Hiawatha.* Within a short time, he was asked to do the part of Hiawatha and both art and dance direction. The pageant was successful enough to be performed throughout Indiana, and in major cities in Ohio as well. *Hiawatha* toured California the next summer.

In 1930 Horton decided to make Los Angeles his home, and within months he was studying with and dancing for Michio Ito, who had a background of Japanese theater and training at the Dalcroze School. From Ito he learned what he later called "organic use of props," and Ito's concept of "Plays for Dancers" later served as a model for Horton's "choreodramas." Soon after moving to Los Angeles, Horton started teaching. His classes were designed for the rapid growth of untrained dance students who had public performance as their goal; they wanted to perform, and he wanted a dance company. His teaching techniques developed rapidly in both depth and specificity to achieve these goals. Students were challenged not only to grow quickly in their dancing skills, but also to make individual statements when they danced. "Be yourself," he often said to his dancers. Horton continued to develop and refine his approach to teaching until his death in 1953, and his training technique is now considered one of the finest in the modern dance idiom.

Not long after he started teaching Horton attracted a devoted following of gifted and hard-working students who became the nucleus of the first group of Lester Horton Dancers—including Bella Lewitzky, who would become his leading dancer. Their association was to last 15 years. For the Olympic Festival of the Dance in Los Angeles in 1932, Horton choreographed *Voodoo Ceremonial*, a work full of frank eroticism and images of pagan ritual, unusual for the time. The earthy beauty of young women dancing bare-legged, in full swinging skirts of crisp white, was an image that Horton frequently used, and one that Alvin Ailey, trained by Horton 20 years later, used in his first masterwork, *Revelations*.

Working with Horton was like attending an academy for dance and theater. From the earliest years, Horton's company members learned to work with him in the creation of his beautiful and ingenious props and costumes, and to build and paint sets. Horton also gave them individual research assignments covering a wide variety of subjects related to the arts. Through the years it was this kind of group learning experience, beyond technique, that was unique to his training.

Public interest in the company grew rapidly, and the Lester Horton Dancers appeared several times in the city's largest theaters, Philharmonic Hall and the Shrine Auditorium, and in other theaters throughout the state. Horton's name was becoming synonymous with modern dance on the West Coast. During the years of the Great Depression, many writers, visual artists, and dancers, created "agit-prop" [agitation-propaganda] works based on Marxist principles. Horton had no desire to proselytize, believing that the only people who would come to such performances were those "already convinced." He did, however, join in the battles of his time, choreographing several powerful dances decrying the rise of Nazism both in Germany and in the U. S., with titles such as *Dictator* (1935), and *Prelude to Militancy* (1936).

Sprinkled into his repertoire during this same period was a group of lyrical dances with such titles as *May Night* (1934), *Dance of Parting* (1935), and *Romantic Duo* (1935), the latter an exquisite version of boy tenderly meeting girl. In 1936 he choreographed *Lysistrata*, the ancient Greek comedy, in which he developed the antiwar theme entertainingly. A program of antiwar pieces, lyric works, and substantial dramatic works on a single program might seem like an odd combination, but not for Horton. He had had a wide range of interests ever since childhood, and throughout his career that range was reflected in the variety of the works he choreographed.

Two highlights for the company came in the late 1930s when Horton was invited to choreograph *Sacre du printemps* at the enormous Hollywood Bowl (the first time *Sacre* was staged by an American choreographer), and that same year a performance at the beautiful and prestigious Greek Theater. Both were performances "under starry skies," as *Song of Hiawatha* had been. By the end of the decade, Horton's work began to reflect his interest in how the individual is affected by his immediate environment, and his concern for a generation that had been tortured by a Depression and was now facing the inevitability of a great war. Sections from his

1939 work, *Sixteen to Twenty-Four* were titled: "Birthright," "Problems—Men and Women Without Work," "Deferred Marriage," and "Threat of War."

In the early 1940s, Horton began to accept Hollywood film assignments, ranging from the romantic *Moonlight in Havana* to the exotic *White Savage* with some serious works in between (*Phantom of the Opera*). Most of the income from the 19 films he choreographed between 1942 and 1953 went towards the opening of a theater/academy of dance. In 1946 Horton and three close associates pooled their resources, found a building at 7566 Melrose Avenue in West Los Angeles, and, after a few months of renovation, opened the school. It took two years of design and construction work (mostly done by the new owners), to make the classroom space convertible into a fully functioning theater for weekend performances; the first of its kind in the United States. Opening night for Dance Theater was 22 May 1948, and the new theater, its performing artists, and Horton's choreography all won high praise both from critics and modern dance enthusiasts. One of the three dances premiered on the program was *The Beloved,* inspired by a newspaper article about a man who had beaten his wife to death with a Bible because he suspected her of infidelity. This timeless work earned a place in the modern dance repertoire.

In the next two years, Horton created eight new dances, ranging in subject matter from the Warsaw Ghetto to the paintings of Paul Klee. His company would become highly regarded not only for the breadth of its repertoire but for its interracial makeup—it was the first interracial dance company in the United States. In 1950, after two very successful years of operation, the Dance Theater partnership was dissolved. To worsen matters, Bella Lewitzky and a few other leading dancers in the company had decided to go off and develop their own work. Now, full responsibility for the school and theater rested in Horton's hands, and, in addition, he had the challenge of preparing exceptional students at the school to dance leading roles in the upcoming season. There was very little time to accomplish this. Two of the dancers chosen, Carmen de Lavallade and James Truitte, would prove just how exceptional they were, and within a short time, the newly rebuilt company was ready for the new season. For that season, and two more to come, Horton choreographed nine new concert works as well revivals of *Annie Get Your Gun* and *Girl Crazy*. Among the new concert works was a choreodrama based on a contemporary version of the Greek tragedy, *Medea* (1951), a stunningly theatrical realization of Duke Ellington's *Liberian Suite* (1952), and in 1953, the last year of his life, the memorable *Dedications in Our Time*. One of these dedications, "To Jose Clemente Orozco," is now, like *The Beloved,* considered a modern dance classic.

On 29 March 1953, Lester Horton's choreography was shown for the first time in New York City. The enthusiastic audience reaction was seconded a few days later by *Herald Tribune* critic Walter Terry: "The Lester Horton Dancers brought freshness of ideas, new faces, fine dancing, theatrical verve and even, perhaps, a healthy dash of envy to New Yorkers who attended." Ted Shawn was in the audience and was pleased enough with what he saw to invite the company to open the next summer season at the famed Jacob's Pillow. The Lester Horton Dancers had been "discovered" on the East Coast. A few months after the company's New York debut, Lester Horton's many years of overwork, privation, and neglect of his health took their toll, and he died of heart failure. He was 47.

Several modern dance companies influenced by Horton and his technique still perform in the U.S.; one of these, the Alvin Ailey

American Dance Theatre, which has toured internationally for many years, may well be the best-known modern dance company in the world. Ailey once declared: "Lester Horton was the greatest influence of my career. He is the reason I do all this." Thousands of dance students have studied and are now studying Horton's strong, clean, sensuous technique throughout the U.S. and abroad. Lester Horton was one of the most powerful and innovative choreographers and teachers of this century and should be considered one of the significant pioneers of American modern dance.

—Larry Warren

HOUSE, Christopher

Canadian dancer, choreographer, and educator

Born: 30 May 1955 in St. John's, Newfoundland. **Education:** Attended Prince of Wales Collegiate; Memorial University of Newfoundland for two years; University of Ottawa, B.S. in science 1976; B.F.A., York University, 1979; studied ballet with Joyce Schietze in Ottawa, Sandra Caverley and Grant Strate in Toronto, Zena Rommett, Alfredo Corvino, and Lawrence Rhodes in New York City; studied modern dance with Elizabeth Langley in Ottawa, Norrey Drummond in Toronto, and Nikki Cole in New York City. **Career:** Joined Toronto Dance Theatre as a dancer, 1979; appointed resident choreographer, 1981; appointed associate artistic director, 1993; appointed artistic director, 1994. **Awards:** Chalmers Choreographic Award, 1983; Dora Mavor Moore Award for *Green Evening, Clear and Warm*, 1985; Clifford E. Lee Award, 1986; Royal Bank Choreographic Commission for Expo '86, 1986; Dora Mavor Moore Award for *Artemis Madrigals*, 1988; Toronto International Music/Dance Award, 1992; inducted into the Hall of Honour of Newfoundland and Labrador, 1996.

Works

1978	*Gambado* (mus. medieval composition)
	Nemesis (mus. Gordon Phillips)
	Enhanced Radiation (mus. John Sidall, Miguel Frasconi)
1979	*Timpan Reel* (mus. Chieftains)
	Page of Swords (mus. Miguel Frasconi)
	Mantis (mus. Varèse)
1980	*Toss Quintet* (mus. Reich)
1981	*Schola Cantorum* (mus. Satie)
	Orphic Construction (mus. Miguel Frasconi)
	Sports et Divertissements (mus. Satie)
	Conjugation (mus. Cage)
1982	*Boulevard* (mus. Satie)
	The Excitable Gift (mus. Bach)
	Fleet (mus. Cage)
1983	*Glass Houses* (mus. Southam)
	Landscape with Figures (silence)
	Court of Miracles Act II Dances
1984	*Untitled Quartet* (mus. Southam)
	Animated Shorts (mus. Michael Baker)
1985	*Indagine Classica* (mus. Vivaldi)
	Schubert Dances (mus. Schubert)
	green evening, clear and warm (mus. Mozart)

1986	*Crossfade Miniatures* (mus. Stravinsky)
	Goblin Market (mus. Southam)
	Go Yet Turning Stay (mus. Stravinsky)
1987	*Handel Variations* (mus. Brahms)
	Off the Floor (mus. Henry Kucharzyk)
1988	*Jeux Forains* (mus. Stravinsky)
	Delphic Shards (mus. Greek)
	Artemis Madrigals (mus. Stravinsky)
	The Windows (mus. Glass)
1989	*Island* (mus. Reich)
	Scherzo (mus. Schumann)
	Distant City (mus. Claude Vivier)
	Serifos (mus. Vivier)
1990	*Debate* (mus. Cage)
	Fjeld (mus. Pärt)
	The Court of Lions (mus. Nas Kotter, Francis Pilkington, Josquin des Pres)
	Zefiro Torna (mus. Monteverdi)
1991	*Noli Me Tangere* (mus. Henry Kucharzyk)
	Cafe Dances (mus. salon music, various composers)
	Uplands (mus. Agnes Buen Garnak)
1992	*Early Departures* (mus. John Rea)
	Agitato (mus. Roger Sessions)
	Amor's Gavottes (mus. Mozart)
1993	*Evensong* (mus. Kevin Volans)
	Barnyard (mus. Jimmey Dorsey, Babe Wagner, Frankie Yan)
	Encarnado (mus. Viver, orchestrated by John Rea)
	Four Towers (mus. Robert Moran)
1994	*Colder Ink* (mus. Tim Brady)
	Delicate Pleasures (mus. Graham Fitkin)
1995	*Cactus Rosary* (mus. Terry Riley)
	Columbus (mus. Michael Baker)
	Book of Hours (mus. Bruno Degazio)
1996	*Pingo Slink* (mus. Robert Moran)
	Metamorfoses Nocturnas (mus. Legeti)
1997	*Paladin Vespers* (mus. Vivier)
	Apollo's Touch (mus. Rodney Sharman)
	Bottari (mus. Kung Chi Shing)
	Crptoversa (mus. Robert Moran)

Publications

On HOUSE: articles—

Kaiser, Pat, "Christopher House: Capturing the Magic," *Performing Arts,* Fall 1984.

Kaiser, Pat, "Christopher House: A Choreographer Fascinated with Structure and Form," *Dance in Canada,* Summer 1986.

Kelly, Deirdre, "Variety Adds Spice to TDT Menu," *Globe and Mail,* 19 March 1986.

Smith, Sid, "Toronto Dancers Strike Lightning," *Chicago Tribune,* 1 April 1985.

Mason, Francis, "A Conversation with Christopher House," in *Canadian Dance Studies 2,* edited by Selma Odom and Mary Jane Warner, Toronto, 1997.

*   *   *

Christopher House, who had been heading in the direction of political science, suddenly found himself in his mid-20s turning towards an interest in the arts. The interest had always been a part of him, but growing up in St. John's, Newfoundland, in the 1960s didn't offer him an atmosphere where artistic endeavours, particularly in boys, were encouraged. He had dabbled in community theatre as an adolescent but his participation was discouraged by his father. Music had always been a part of his and his brother's lives as their mother taught them how to play the piano. Dance wasn't even an art form he ventured into—St. John's boys did not dance. He even recalls seeing ballet on television and thinking it was such a silly way for adults to behave.

By the start of his fourth year at the University of Ottawa, House had completed most of his degree requirements which allowed him to take several theatre courses. "Movement for Actors" was among them and teacher Elizabeth Langley exposed him to something that would change his life forever. Langley taught a modern dance and improvisation class, but more importantly, she exposed House to teachers such as Nikki Cole who inspired him to expand his studies. Cole had a great impact on House and he soon realized he needed to move outside Ottawa to study dance seriously.

House spent six months in New York City where he continued to study modern with Cole as well as ballet with Alfredo Corvino. It was an exciting time in New York; dance was going through a boom period. He recalls participating in classes with massive numbers of people and being very happy despite living in a loft that had once been a slaughterhouse and not always having enough food to eat. Realizing this was more than a passing fancy, House's father suggested he study dance at the university level and made a deal with his son that would make this possible. In 1977 House enrolled in the dance program at York University. There he received his first serious exposure to Graham-based technique with Norrey Drummond. In 1978 House danced in David Earle's *Atlantis* for Toronto Dance Theatre's 10th Anniversary season. He was asked to join as an apprentice as they were short men but decided he needed more training so he continued his studies at York for another year. He joined TDT as a dancer in 1979.

TDT was both stimulating and intriguing; there was a tremendous mythology at the time surrounding the founders (Earle, Patricia Beatty, and Peter Randazzo). House took Earle's classes first and thoroughly enjoyed them. He loved Earle's movement and teaching manner and over the next several years he learned much from Earle about art and life. Randazzo was also a mentor; he was a great dancer and gave dynamic classes. House began to take over Randazzo's roles as Randazzo gradually lessened the amount of performing he did. House had already choreographed six works before joining TDT and he continued to choreograph after joining the company by participating in TDT's Choreographic Workshops. He was recognized early as being a gifted choreographer and by 1981 was appointed resident choreographer—the first time such a position had been created since the company's founding in 1968.

Pat Kaiser wrote that House's "knack of blending complex movement with a good-natured throwaway approachability sets him apart from his peers as an adept explorer of his craft." Critics have credited him with creating shifting patterns, pauses, and accelerations. Significant works include his early solos *Nemesis* and *Timpan Reel*. While the movement in *Nemesis* is quite raw, *Timpan Reel* uses more academic, technical movement. *Toss Quintet*, created at a TDT choreographic workshop and set to the music of Steve Reich, includes many patterns and reflects studies House had done in composition. When it was brought into the TDT repertoire it was quite a contrast to the existing dances by the company's founders. Also created for a workshop was *Schola Cantorum*. House feels it is one of his most consciously created

pieces as he set up rules for himself in making it—which meant spending hours deliberating over very tiny choices. For him, the process was "like solving a puzzle in the most complex way."

A breakthrough piece which audiences and critics raved about is *Glass Houses.* Described by Sid Smith in the *Chicago Tribune* as "lightning fast and delightfully joyous," this virtuosic dance takes root in an idea from Doris Humphrey that symmetry was death in modern dance. This idea set House on an exploration to create a symmetrical dance which turned out to be the farthest thing from deathly. *Schubert Dances* and *green evening, clear and warm*, both created in 1985, are part of what House describes as his "Balanchine period" during which he repeatedly traveled to New York to see the ballet master's choreography. Deirdre Kelly of the *Globe and Mail* wrote that *Schubert Dances* revealed House's "brilliance and intellectual depth" as a choreographer. *Green evening, clear and warm*, a Dora Award winner, is a social satire about the hypocrisy of courtship. House considers it a feminist piece in which women are made fools of by men who are more stupid than they are. This dance indicates a change in House's work in the mid-1980s to include more emotion and characterization in his choreography. House won his second Dora Award in 1988 for one of his personal favourites, *Artemis Madrigals*, which is set to Stravinsky's *Duo Concertant*—music once used by Balanchine.

House entered a new choreographic phase in the 1990s. His dances became longer, more ambitious, and more challenging for the audience. *Early Departures* was a part of this next breakthrough. A highly acclaimed piece, it became a dance about AIDS despite having a very different beginning. House described its beginning as being more about "guilt and uncertainty in relationships in 1991, and having lost so many friends and surviving."

House's choreographic endeavours have not been limited to TDT. Early in his career he choreographed *They Pitched Camp* and *Page of Swords* for performances at 15 Dance Lab, a 1970s performance venue for experimental choreography in Toronto. He has also created work for Ottawa Dance Theatre, Les Grands Ballet Canadiens, Banff Festival Ballet, Dancemakers, soloists Peggy Baker and Patricia Fraser, Judith Marcuse Dance Company, National Ballet of Canada, Ballet British Columbia and Ballet Gulbenkian. He has brought in the influences of choreographers such as Peggy Baker and James Kudelka to work with TDT and has worked on collaborations with Toronto's Arraymusic and Korean artist Kim Soo-ja.

House has a fascination with structure and form. His choreographic interests include texture, speed, weight and balance but he approaches these with the elements of surprise and thrill. He is extremely musical and composers enjoy working with him. He describes his prolific list of works as schizophrenic because of his fear of repetition; however, this fear has created a body of work unlike anyone else's and, individually, the works are unlike each other. It has made for an exciting addition to a vast body of work in the history of Canada's third-oldest modern dance company.

—Amy Bowring

HOVING, Lucas
Dutch dancer, choreographer, and educator

Born: Lucas Hovinga, 5 September 1912, Groningen, the Netherlands. **Education:** Studied tap dance with Frida von Brueggen;

studied expressive dance with Florrie Rodrigo in Amsterdam; piano accompanist from childhood to Wigman-trained teacher Neel Kuiper. **Military Service:** Dutch Armed Forces in exile, World War II. **Family:** Married American Lavina Nielsen (former Jooss Ballet dancer), 1943. **Career:** Choreographed and performed vaudeville dance routines with Henny Vles, 1931; joined the Florrie Rodrigo company, 1936; performed in premieres of Yvonne Georgi's *Hungarian Dances, Le Tricorne, Die Geschoepfe des Prometheus,* and *Schaduwen,* 1938; left for Dartington Hall with scholarship to Folkwang Hochschule in exile, September 1938; joined Jooss Ballet and began tour of the Americas; danced in Martha Graham's *Letter to the World* as well as in commercial theater in New York during World War II; joined José Limón's company, 1948, and originated roles in *The Moor's Pavane, Emperor Jones, The Traitor,* and others; Nielsen joined Limón's company, 1952, and husband and wife toured in duet program, from 1950; director, Lucas Hoving Dance Company, 1961-71; director, Rotterdam Dans Academie, 1971-78; coach and artistic advisor, José Limón Company; director, Dancelab and Lucas Hoving Performance Group, San Francisco; premiered monologue, *Growing Up in Public,* created with Remy Charlip at Next Wave Festival, Brooklyn Academy of Music, 1984. **Awards:** NEA Choreographer's Fellowship; Stanford University's Heritage Award; Sustained Achievement Award from San Francisco Bay Area's Isadora Duncan Awards; tribute at American Dance Festival, 1992.

Roles

1938	The Miller, *LeTricorne* (Georgi)
	Zeus, *Die Geschoepfe des Prometheus* (Georgi)
1939	Politician, *The Green Table* (Jooss)
1941	Lead, *Drums Sound in Hackensack* (de Mille)
1942	Member of quartet, *Letter to the World* (Graham)
1948	El Conquistador, *La Malinche* (Limón), José Limón Company, New York
1949	Iago, *The Moor's Pavane* (Limón), José Limón Company, New York
1951	Tezcatlipoca, *The Four Suns* (Limón)
	Cortez and Maximillian, *Dialogues* (Limón), Mexico
1952	The Angel, *The Visitation* (Limón), American Dance Festival
1953	The Son, *Ruins and Visions* (Humphrey), American Dance Festival
1954	The Leader, *The Traitor* (Limón), American Dance Festival
1956	The White Man, *The Emperor* (Limón), Empire State Music Festival

Works

1941	*Newsreel* (for the Jooss Ballet), New York
1949	*Dawn in New York* (solo), New York
1950	*The Battle* (mus. Ada Reif; text Gertrude Stein), solo, New York
1951	*La Tertula* w/Lupe Serrano, Mexico City
1953	*Electra* w/Nielsen
	The Perilous Flight (mus. Bartók, Hoving and Nielsen), Connecticut College
	Satyros (Spring) (mus. Poulenc; Hoving and Nielsen), Connecticut College
1955	*Time of Innocence*
	Ballad, Connecticut College
	Satyros (Summer and Autumn) (mus. Poulenc; Hoving and Nielsen), Connecticut College
	Love for Three Oranges (mus. Prokoviev), New York
1958	*Ommegang* (mus. Wolfram Fuerstenau), Ballet der Lage Landen, Netherlands
	Suite of Negro Spirituals, Scapino Ballet, Netherlands
1960	*Wall of Silence* (mus. Florence Schmitt), Connecticut College
1961	*Encounters*
1962	*Divertimento*
	Strange to Wish Wishes No Longer (mus. Webern)
	Parades and Other Fancies (mus. Armin Schibler), New York
	Has the Last Train Left? (mus. Henk Badings), New York
	Suite for a Summer Day (mus. Peter Schickele), New York
1963	*Aubade* (mus. Birger, Karl Bloomdahl), Connecticut College
1964	*Incidental Passage* (mus. Czerny), New York
	Icarus (mus. Chin-Ichi Matushita), New York
1965	*St. Patrick*
	The Tenants (mus. George Riedel), Connecticut College
	Satiana (mus. and text Erik Satie), Connecticut College
1966	*Variation on the Theme of Electra* (mus. Varèse), New York
1967	*Rough-In* (mus. Hank Johnson), Connecticut College
1968	*She's Leaving Home* (mus. collage), New York
1969	*Wall,* New York
	Uppercase (mus. Gay DeLanghe, Charles Phipps)
	Opus '69 (mus. Pierre Henry), New York
	Home (theatrical public TV production), New York
1970	*Aubade II* (mus. Pierre Henry), Connecticut College
	Kaleidoscope, Bat-Dor Dance Company, Israel
	Reflections (mus. Watson), Connecticut College
1971	*Collega,* Rotterdam Danscentrum, Netherlands
	Zipcode (mus. collage; with additional choreography by Pina Bausch)
	Assemblage, Lucas Hoving Dance Company plus 30 additional dancers, Connecticut College
1974	*Songs for Chile,* Rotterdam, Netherlands
1982	*Collage,* San Francisco
1983	*Sion*
1984	*Vacillating Blues* (mus. Gregory Ballard), Lucas Hoving Performance Group, San Francisco
	Six Short Dances (mus. Renaissance era), Lucas Hoving Performance Group, San Francisco
	Opus '84 (mus. Yello), Lucas Hoving Performance Group, San Francisco
	Pits and Thumbs (mus. Xenakis), portion of Lucas Hoving Performance Group, San Francisco
	Songs for a Distant Land (mus. Gregory Ballard), Lucas Hoving Performance Group, San Francisco
1985	*Celebration* (mus. Jerry Gerber), Lucas Hoving Performance Group, San Francisco
1986	*Requiem Suite, Part One, The Land Was Dying,* Michael Kelly Bruce
	Piaf (mus. Piaf), Alice Condodina, Santa Barbara
1987	*Episode* (mus. John Toenjes), San Francisco

1988   *Search* (mus. Pierre Henry)
         A Day in Your Life, José Limón Dance Company
1990   *Rush Hour,* Dance Company Reflex, Netherlands

Other works include: *The House of Bernardo Alba* (mus. Albeniz Iberian Suite); *A Hunting We Will Go* (mus. Strauss waltzes from *Der Fledermaus*); *View from a Mountain,* Salt Lake City, Utah; *Variations on a Dramatic Theme.*

Publications

On HOVING: book—

Siegel, Marcia, *Days on Earth, The Dance of Doris Humphrey,* Yale University Press, 1987.

On HOVING: article—

Burgering, Jacques, "Lucas Hoving: The Circle That Goes Around," unpublished MA thesis, Washington, D.C.: American University, 1995.

* * *

Lucas Hoving is one of the second generation of modern dance performers, choreographers, and teachers in the United States who may be best remembered as a master teacher, but whose seminal 14-year partnership with José Limón radically expanded and deepened the scope of modern dance expression for men in the second-half of the 20th century.

Hoving was a musical prodigy born into a petit-bourgeois family in northern Holland near the German border, where his father ran a butcher shop in the storefront of the family boarding house. When he was about 12 years old he became the accompanist at the Eclecta club of rhythmic gymnastic. A year later Wigman protege Neel Kuiper took over the establishment and taught classes derived from her studies with Wigman, Kurt Jooss, and Rudolf Laban. From school productions to paid performances for town events, Hoving began hammering out an adolescent career as an untrained dancer and cafe musician until, at 18, he moved to Amsterdam to study dance.

In time he joined the company as well as the collective household of political choreographer Florrie Rodrigo, where he was surrounded by prominent members of the Dutch left and received his first strong taste of politics and humanism, which was to shape all of his subsequent artistic choices. As fascism marched through Europe and prevented radical artists like Rodrigo from practicing, Hoving found work with the European dance sensation Yvonne Georgi and then, in 1938, received a scholarship to study at the exiled Folkwang Hochschule at Dartington Hall, England, where Kurt Jooss and the Jooss Ballet had taken refuge. There Hoving had his first serious technical training and learned from such illustrious teachers as Jooss, Gertrude Heller, and Sigurd Leeder, studying everything from choreutics, kinetics, and ballet to meditation, all of which were to become the foundation of his teaching.

Due to the outbreak of world war, Hoving found himself thrust suddenly into the Jooss Ballet and just as precipitously on tour to the Americas. The company toured for nearly two years and during this period, with Jooss interned by the British, new choreography came from the company ranks, with Hoving, the youngest company member, winning the first assignment. His *Newsreel,* choreographed with the help of the company members, shared the New York bill for its premiere at the Maxine Elliot Theatre with such Jooss dances as *Prodigal Son, Chronica,* and *Spring Tale.*

Europe was cut off to dancers from the continent and many, like Hoving, were marooned in the United States. For Hoving this tragedy forced him onto the American dance scene, to which, despite a stint in the army and forays to Europe, he was to transfer his artistic allegiance.

In 1941 the Jooss Ballet disbanded, and Hoving, along with many company members, joined the circus of Dutchman and exiled steel magnate Bernard van Leer, who asked Hoving to form a ballet within the circus and become the troupe's choreographer. Among his dances was *Rhapsody in White,* in which dancers in white tutus rode the backs of white Lippizaner horses.

In 1942 he joined the Royal Dutch Army in exile and was sent to New York to await orders. There he began studying with Martha Graham, dancing in the quartet in her *Letter to the World.* He also performed on Broadway in Catherine Littlefield's *Kiss for Cinderella* at the Roxy Theatre, and with the road company of *Hellzapoppin.* With Graham, whom he esteemed highly but whose technique he found overly percussive and posed, he began to define for himself his preferred dance style. With José Limón he was to find it.

Limón and Hoving met in Nanette Charisse's ballet class after the war, each man recognizing in the other a complementary nature. In 1948, shortly after Limón launched his own troupe, Hoving joined the group, after which time Limón began making dances of moral and humanistic complexity in which ethical struggles were often enacted by two men as alter-egos. Works such as *The Moor's Pavane, The Traitor,* and *The Emperor Jones* featured his partnership with Hoving and explored the nuances of repressed emotion between men and the consequences of power. Although their explicit object was not to create dances about men, they nevertheless shaped charismatic, ambiguously erotic duets that, in their passion, echoed lovers' duets of traditional ballet.

Hoving's wife, Lavina Nielsen, joined the company in 1952 and performed with Hoving in such dances as *There Is a Time* and *Blue Roses.* After 10 years of constant company touring and residencies Hoving began increasing his commitment to the duet program that he and Nielsen shared, which was a vaudeville-like sampler of dances.

During this period Hoving also built an important career as a teacher, holding positions at Juilliard and the New York High School of Performing Arts, and directing the Silvermine School in Connecticut. From 1948 to 1958 he assisted Louis Horst at the American Dance Festival, again performed on Broadway in such productions as the original *Sound of Music,* and directed operas for the Peabody Art Theater in Baltimore.

By 1960 Hoving wanted to move out on his own. Although he had never felt a great compulsion to choreograph even as he created work, he was weary of the growing trend in modern dance away from expressivity toward spiritless technical proficiency. Hoping to find a new freedom and independence, in 1961 he formed his own troupe, the Lucas Hoving Dance Company. Although the company produced few masterworks, *Icarus* among them, Hoving was part of the experimental movement in modern dance that, for him, began with Rodrigo in Amsterdam but was ignited anew by Anna Halprin's avant-garde performances. His aim became to form a band of performers who would create dances together.

By 1970 the political turmoil in the U.S. drove Hoving to disband the troupe and return to Europe, and he was invited by Jooss to Stockholm, Sweden to develop a dance program. In 1971 he moved to the Rotterdamse Dans Academie, where he became director for seven years, overhauling the staid establishment and giving the Dutch a vehicle to develop their own voice in modern dance.

In 1981 Hoving, who had returned to teach in New York, took a workshop with Halprin at Esalen in California. The experience convinced him to move to the San Francisco Bay area, where he and Nielsen initially joined a Sufi household in Marin. Once in the Bay area, Hoving resumed teaching and instituted Dancelab in San Francisco, which, in 1985, became the Lucas Hoving Performance Group, comprising local dancers who ranged from the amateur to the professional. In 1984 Hoving premiered a dance monologue created with actor, dancer, and writer Remy Charlip, drawn from Hoving's *Random Notes of a Contemporary Romantic*. The work premiered a month after Hoving's 72nd birthday at the Brooklyn Academy of Music's Second Next Wave Festival. Hoving began a new career that lasted almost a decade in which he took the monologue to universities and colleges around the country as part of a residency program. In 1991, in a birthday tribute to him, *The Moor's Pavane* was reconstructed with Betty Jones in her historic role as Desdemona, Carla Maxwell as Emilia, Clay Taliafero as Othello, and Lutz Foster as Iago.

—Ann Murphy

HOYER, Dore

German choreographer, dancer, and educator

Born: 12 December 1911 in Dresden, Germany. **Education:** In Jaques-Dalcroze-influenced rhythmic education schools, Dresden; also attended the Gret Palucca school. **Career:** Choreographed and danced performances with solo pieces throughout her entire life; danced and choreographed at theaters in Plauen, 1931-32, and Oldenburg, 1933-34; member, Mary Wigman's dance group, 1935-36; danced at the Deutsche Tanzbühne, 1940-41, the Theater des Volkes in Dresden, 1941-43, and the theater Graz, 1943-44; opened her own school in Dresden, 1946-48; leader of the ballet company, Hamburger Staatsoper, 1949-51; danced in Harald Kreutzberg's *Moira von Mykene*, and Wigman's *Le Sacre du Printemps;* toured throughout Latin America, mostly Argentina, from 1952. **Awards:** German Critic Award, 1951. **Died:** 1 January 1968, in Berlin.

Roles

1935	*Tanzgesänge (Dance Songs)* (Wigman)
1938	*Orpheus und Eurydike*
1940	*Apollon und die Amazone*
	Goyescas
1943	*Tanzendes Barock (Dancing Baroque)*
	Kirmes von Delft (Fair of Delft) (Bergeest)
	Der Zauberladen (The Magic Shop) (Bergeest)
1950	*Anfang und Ende (Beginning and End)*
1956	*Moira ton Mykene*
1957	*Le Sacre du Printemps* (Wigman)

Works

1933	*Afrikanisches Kriegerlied (African War Song)* (mus. Colaridge, Taylor), solo, Dresden
	Allegro ritmico (mus. Engel), solo, Dresden
	Ballade, solo, Dresden
	Drei Gesichter (Three Faces) (mus. Finke), solo, Dresden
	Gotisches Lied (Gothic Song) (mus. Satie), solo, Dresden
	Stiller Tanz (Quiet Dance) (mus. Satie), solo, Dresden
	Tanz in schwarz (Dance in Black), (mus. Cieslak), solo, Dresden
	Tanz in weiß (Dance in White) (mus. Cieslak), solo, Dresden
	Vierteilige Studie (Study in Four Parts), solo, Dresden
	Zwei ernste Gesänge, I-II (Two Serious Songs) (mus. Cieslak), solo, Dresden
1934	*Allegro ritmico*, second version (mus. Engel), solo, Dresden
	Barlumi, I-V
	Drei stille Tänze, I-III (Three Quiet Dances) (mus. Satie), Dresden
	Flackernd (Flickering) (mus. Cieslak), Dresden
	Fragment (mus. Cieslak), Dresden
	Maken, I-V (Masks) (mus. Malipiero), Dresden
1935	*Drei Tänze für eine kleine Gruppe (Three Dances for a Small Group)*
	Fünf namenlose Tänze, I-V (Five Unnamed Dances)
	Sieben Gesichte (Seven Faces)
	Wechselnde Lichter (Changing Lights)
	Zweite stille Suite, I-III (Second Quiet Suite)
1936	*Schrei (Cry)* (no mus.)
1938	*Allegro barbaro*
	Enge der Großstadt (Confinement of the City) (mus. folk songs)
	Weite des Landes (Wilderness of the Country) (mus. folk songs)
1944	*Amazone*
	Brotbacken (Baking Bread)
	Der Geliebte (The Lover)
	Potiphars Weib (Potiphar's Wife)
	Signale (Signals)
	Stille (Silence)
	Vibrato
1946	*Tänze für Käthe Kollwitz (Dance for Käthe Kollwitz)*
1947	*Gesichte (Faces)*
	Mütter (Mothers)
	Rebellion
	Schießbude (Rifle Range)
1948	*Antigone*
	Der große Gesang (The Great Song)
	Erinnerung an einen Garten (Remembering a Garden)
	Es war ein Bursche und sein Mädchen (There Was a Young Man and His Girl)
	Gesichte unserer Zeit (Faces of Our Time)
1949	*Lyrik*
1950	*Anfang und Ende (Beginning and End)* (mus. Ravel), Hamburger Staatsoper, Hamburg
	Der Fremde (The Stranger) (mus. Wiatowitsch), Hamburger Staatsoper, Hamburg
	Junger Tag (Beginning Day)
	Vision (mus. Stravinsky), Hamburger Staatsoper, Hamburg
	Zigeuner (Gypsy) (mus. Bartók), Hamburger Staatsoper, Hamburg
1951	*Der Holzgeschnitzte Prinz (The Wooden Prince)* (mus. Bartók), Hamburger Staatsoper, Hamburg
	Kontraste (Contrasts)

Sarabande: "Ich gehe zu Dir" (I'm Walking Towards You)
Sonate für 2 Klaviere und Schlagzeug (Sonata for Two Pianos and Percussion) (mus. Bartók), Hamburger Staatsoper, Hamburg

1952 Judith
Maria Magdalena (mus. Bach)
Mit Trommel und Gong (With Drum and Gong)

1953 Ohne Gnade (Without Mercy)
Scherzo
Südliche Impressionen (Impressions from the South)

1954 Monologe
Südamerikanische Reise (South American Journey) (mus. Ravel, Wiatowitsch, Albeniz, Kenton, Finke, Montiyn, Bach)

1955 Amahl und die nächtlichen Besucher (Amahl and the Night Visitors) (mus. Menotti), Städtische Bühnen, Ulm
Die Geschichte vom Soldaten (The Soldier's Tale) (mus. Stravinsky), Städtische Bühnen, Ulm
Zwischen Gestern und Morgen (Between Yesterday and Tomorrow)

1956 Akzente
Auf schwarzem Grund (On Black Surface) (mus. Wiatowitsch, Klebe, Ohana)
Finale (Final)
Tanzlied (Dance Song)
Totenwiegenlied (Lullaby for the Dead)
Zu Ehren der Dichterin (In Honor of the Woman Poet)

1957 Jephta
Tänze nach Scarlatti (Dances on Scarlatti)
Kinder der Erde (Children of the Earth)

1958 Cantata Romantia
Mosaico

1959 Die Frauen von Trachis (The Women of Trachis)
Moses und Aron (mus. Schönberg)

1961 La Idea
Cadena de Fugas

1962 Affectos Humanos (mus. Wiatowitsch), Folkwangschule, Essen
Bach-Präludien
Orpheus
Ostinato
Tragödie (Tragedy)

1963 Elektra
Faust I
Faust II

1964 Androclus und der Löwe (Androcles and the Lion)
Die Sanfte (The Gentle Woman)

1956 Notturno

1966 Aus dem Wohltemperierten (Excerpts from the Well-Tempered)
Grosstadt (City)

1967 Asien Suite

Publications

On HOYER: books—

Müller, Hedwig, Frank-Manuel Peter, and Garnet Schuldt, *Dore Hoyer: Tänzerin*, Cologne, 1992.

*   *   *

Dore Hoyer is one of the main figures that linked the German *Ausdruckstanz* (German modern dance) of the 1920s and contemporary German Tanztheater (dance theater). She shares this position with such important German dancers and choreographers as Mary Wigman, Gret Palucca, Marianne Vogelsang, Kurt Jooss, and Jean Weidt. Unlike her contemporaries, Hoyer vanished from German dance history because she was not affiliated with a school or theater at the time of her death. This is unfortunate because Hoyer was the most important solo dancer from the 1930s through the 1960s.

Hoyer was born to a working class family and raised in Dresden. Her childhood was determined by World War I and the postwar situation of the Weimar Republic. Dresden became the center of *Ausdruckstanz*, when Emile Jaques-Dalcroze founded his school for rhythmic education in Hellerau, a village near Dresden, before World War I. Mary Wigman studied in Hellerau for three years and returned to Dresden after the war, founding her own dance school in 1920, as did Gret Palucca in 1924. Hoyer attended rhythmic movement classes for four years, as well as studying with a Jaques-Dalcroze disciple for two years before she enrolled at the Palucca school in 1930.

After she finished her exams at the Palucca school, Hoyer danced for one season as a soloist at a theater in Plauen. In Germany almost every town has its own theater, which usually houses a drama department, opera, and a ballet company. These multipurpose theaters require their dancers to perform in many different genres of performance; thus Hoyer mostly danced in musicals as well as operatic productions, often not very demanding tasks for a dancer. Not surprisingly, Hoyer lasted only one season and returned to Dresden, where she met the musician and composer Peter Cieslak. Although their tumultuous three-year relationship terminated with Cieslak's suicide in April 1935, the composer was highly influential on Hoyer's career. Cieslak composed most of the accompanying music for Hoyer's first three successful solo performances in Dresden.

Hoyer, who had choreographed several dances and operas during a one-season engagement at the Oldenburger theater, asked Mary Wigman in 1935 if she could join her dance group. Though Wigman was aware of what some termed Hoyer's "difficult personality," she valued her abilities as a performer and her promising choreographic talents. Wigman agreed to an engagement though it was a difficult time for modern dancers in Germany, as the fascist government cut most financial support for modern dance. Only a few famous choreographers were able to continue their work, and even they were forced by fascist officials either to discontinue working by the beginning of World War II or to cooperate with the fascists' ideas of entertainment.

Mary Wigman was among the few choreographers that still received support when the fascists were beginning to gain political power. Her *Tanzgesänge* (dance songs) premiered successfully on 9 November 1935 in Berlin at the Deutschen Tanzfestspiele and toured for one year throughout Germany, the Netherlands, Denmark, and Sweden. Hoyer performed several solo dances in Wigman's choreography during this tour, but she hardly adjusted to the concept of a group choreography. This short engagement was followed by four years without regular income.

The devastating financial situation forced Hoyer to apply for a position at the newly-founded national dance company, the Deutsche Tanzbühne. Although this company was established by the German propaganda ministry to create a German national dance form, it soon became obvious that modern dance was incompatible with the fascist ideology. The *Deutsche Tanzbühne* was disbanded in 1941 and Hoyer danced in several operas for two seasons at the

Theater des Volkes in Dresden. Yet she had never stopped choreographing her own solo programs, and even toured through the war-destroyed Germany in 1943. The same year, Hoyer accepted an offer to dance as a soloist at the theater in Graz.

All theaters in Germany were closed in 1944. Hoyer worked at an optical factory and desperately longed for the Allies to conquer Germany. Soon after the end of the war, Hoyer opened her own school in same building where Wigman had taught in the now-devastated Dresden. The same year she created a major group choreography about one of the most influential German painters and sculptresses: *Tänze für Käthe Kollwitz*. Although Hoyer enthusiastically supported the socialist development in East Germany, she soon got in conflict with the communist ideology. Her solo dances were too individual for the Soviet-occupied zone of Germany. Hoyer left East Germany in 1948 and was invited to lead the ballet company at the Hamburger Staatsoper in 1949. Her hope to reach a broader audience with her modern dance choreography at this famous opera house was not fulfilled. The audience and the critics valued Hoyer's work highly, but she did not succeed in transforming the company into a modern dance group. Hoyer resigned, disappointed in 1951. She never agreed again to any lasting commitment with a theater, and participated only in projects that were interesting to her. In 1956, Hoyer danced in Harald Kreutzberg's production *Moira von Mykene* in Athens. One year later, she created with her own interpretation of sacrifice in a remake of Wigman's choreography for *Le sacre du printemps* in Berlin, one of Hoyer's most important roles. Arranged by Wigman, Hoyer successfully performed the same year in New York and New London.

Still, Hoyer was only satisfied with her solo choreographies, especially after she received standing ovations during a tour throughout Argentina and Brazil in 1952. In the following years she repeatedly returned to South America to perform her solo work as she had finally found the affirmation she so desperately desired and had received in Germany. German dance in East Germany was focused on tradition with folk dance and Soviet-styled ballet, while in West Germany the focus was still on ballet, though in varied styles and both excluded any development or preservation of modern dance. Hoyer realized the repetition of the situation from the fascist era. She was decreasingly provided with possibilities to perform her own work. Even her important choreography *Affectos Humanos* in 1962 did not receive the necessary attention. As a result of this vanishing appreciation of her work, Hoyer became increasingly depressed and committed suicide in her apartment in 1968. It took nearly 20 years for the German dance scene to rediscover Hoyer's choreography when two contemporary modern dancers, Suanne Linke and Arila Siegert independently reconstructed Hoyer's *Affectos Humanos*.

—Jens Giersdorf

HUBBARD STREET DANCE CHICAGO
American dance company

Founded 1977 in Chicago by artistic director Lou Conte; Gail Kalver joined as executive director, 1984; first public performance, 1978; first television special featuring the company, WTTW/Channel 11 (Chicago), 1981; received Governor's Award from the state of Illinois, 1986; began collaboration with Twyla Tharp, 1990.

Works (choreographer in parentheses)

1978	*Chickenscratch* (Conte)
	Bill Robinson Tribute (Conte)
	The 40s (Conte)
1979	*Party Music* (Conte)
	Odyssey (Bataille)
	New Country (Conte)
1980	*Gershwin Dances* (Conte)
	Hurry Up and Wait (Conte and Bataille)
	At the Rosebud (Conte)
1981	*Three Part Invention* (Bataille)
	Rodin Impressions (Conte)
1982	*The Entertainers* (Anderson)
	Line Drive (Conte and Bataille)
	Diary (Taylor-Corbett)
1983	*Tiempo* (McFall)
	"Go!" Said Max (Taylor-Corbett)
	Full Moon (Bataille)
1984	*Bonnie & Clyde* (McFall)
	Appearances (Taylor-Corbett)
1985	*It's Your Move* (Bataille)
	First Turn (Hilsabeck)
1986	*Cobras in the Moonlight* (Sappington)
1987	*Case Closed* (Taylor-Corbett)
	Rose From the Blues (Conte, Hilsabeck, Levi)
	The Envelope (Parsons)
1988	*And Now This* (Sappington)
	Step Out of Love (Sappington)
	The Kitchen Table (Cratty)
1989	*Champagne* (Ward)
	SUPER STRAIGHT is coming down (Ezralow)
1990	*Mirage* (Sappington)
	READ MY HIPS (Ezralow)
	Sue's Leg (Tharp)
1991	*Baker's Dozen* (Tharp)
	Percussion Four (Fosse)
	The Golden Section (Tharp)
1992	*Nine Sinatra Songs* (Tharp)
1993	*The Forging Ground* (Sappington)
	In Praise of Shadows (Ezralow)
1994	*Perpetuum Mobile (Perpetual Motion)* (Wainrot)
	Heroes (Kudelka)
1995	*Quartet for IV (and sometimes one, two or three...)* (O'Day)
	I Remember Clifford (Tharp)
	Fait Accompli (Tharp)
1996	*HELLBLONDEGROOVE* (O'Day)
1997	*Lady Lost Found* (Ezralow)
	Na Floresta (Duato)
	Jardi Tancat (Duato)

Publications

Articles—

Berman, Janice, "The Tharp Magic Takes Over," *New York Newsday*, 20 October 1994.

Connors, Thomas, "Hubbard Street Dance Chicago," *Dance Magazine*, August 1994.

Hubbard Street Dance Chicago: Ron De Jesus (left) and Krista Ledden in Twyla Tharp's *I Remember Clifford.* **Photograph by Ruedi Hofmann.**

Dunning, Jennifer, "New Tharp Work Is Set to Jazz Classics of the 50's," *New York Times*, 11 August 1995.

Ostlere, Hilary, "Hubbard Street on the Move," *Dance Magazine*, June 1996.

Survant, Cerinda, "Hubbard Street Dance Chicago," *Dance Magazine*, September 1993.

Weiss, Hedy, "Hubbard Street Dance Chicago Wins New Admirers in Berlin," *Chicago Sun-Times*, 9 December 1996.

*   *   *

Hubbard Street Dance Chicago (HSDC) is internationally recognized as Chicago's leading dance company. Celebrating its 20th anniversary season in 1997-98, HSDC today consists of 20 culturally diverse, acclaimed dancers and maintains a distinctive and highly energized artistic style that fuses theatrical jazz, modern dance, and classical ballet technique. In contrast to many modern dance companies which showcase the work of a single artist, HSDC continually exhibits a wide range of choreographic styles; the troupe's repertoire includes works by such renowned choreographers as Twyla Tharp, Daniel Ezralow, Nacho Duato, Kevin O'Day, Margo Sappington, David Parsons, and Bob Fosse. Over the years HSDC has performed for worldwide audiences, appearing at dance venues including the American Dance Festival, the Joyce Theater, the Holland Dance Festival, and the Singapore Festival of the Arts.

Much of the company's success derives from its founder and artistic director, Lou Conte. Raised in Du Quion, Illinois, Conte began tap lessons at the young age of seven and attended Southern Illinois University as a zoology major. He continued to study dance both with Marie Hale, current artistic director of Ballet Florida, and at the Ellis-Du Boulay School in Chicago, and at the age of 22 landed a chorus role in Bob Fosse's *How to Succeed in Business without Really Trying*. From the mid-1960s to the early 1970s, Conte appeared in and choreographed over 30 musicals, touring both nationally and internationally. In the mid-1970s he returned to Chicago and opened a studio; in 1977, he founded what began as a modest company of four women. Initially performing in schools and nursing homes for senior citizens, this small group soon gave a concert at Chicago Public Library's Cultural Center, which proved a success. Since then Conte has received numerous awards, including the inaugural Urban Gateways Jessie Woods Award and the Sidney R. Yates Arts Advocacy Award in 1995. Conte's *The 40s*, a playful piece that celebrates the Big Band Era, has become the company's signature work and an audience favorite worldwide.

From the beginning, HSDC has captured public attention, appearing in numerous U.S. and Canadian programs. After viewing the company's first television special, aired on Chicago's public TV station in 1981, Fred Astaire characterized the performance as "some of the greatest dancing I've seen in years." The company's other television appearances include a national PBS special entitled *A Grand Night—The Performing Arts Salute to Public Television* in 1988, NBC's *Today Show* also in 1988, and CBS's *Crown Jewel* in 1989.

In 1990 HSDC commenced the Tharp Project, an ongoing relationship with world-renowned choreographer Twyla Tharp. As part of this arrangement, the company acquired several of her works, including *The Fugue*, *Baker's Dozen*, and *Sue's Leg*, thereby becoming a major repository for her work. In addition, in 1995, Tharp specifically created *I Remember Clifford* for HSDC dancers. This piece, set to 1950s jazz classics, tells the story of a loner who experiences alienation, rebellion, and finally redemption. The work

provided a special break for Ron De Jesus, one of the troupe's prominent dancers, whom Jennifer Dunning of the *New York Times* described in August of 1995 as "a commanding presence of affecting modesty, performing this star turn with impressive subtlety." *Dance Magazine*'s Cerinda Survant found that Tharp's witty, elastic choreographic style challenged the dancers in the company "to develop a performance style that married their hallmark virtuosity to clarity, subtlety, and ease" and various other reviewers have confirmed that HSDC rose to the occasion. Without question, the Tharp Project proved a significant marker in the company's history, diversifying their repertoire and sparking substantial growth.

In particular, the company has experienced significant financial growth over the years. Hubbard Street's budget has grown from $8,000 in 1978 to over $3.2 million in 1998. A not-for-profit organization, the troupe annually raises over $1.6 million from individual, corporate, foundation, and government contributions, making it, in the words of writer Hilary Ostlere "one of the most vital success stories in today's dance world." Outreach programs also constitute a vital portion of HSDC's work. Annually serving more than 17,000 students, the company offers a variety of school activities, which simultaneously build new audiences and attract young people to dance while serving the Chicago community.

In recent years HSDC has also begun to secure a name for itself in several European countries. On a 1996 tour, for example, the company proved to be wildly popular in Berlin, where it sold out at most performances during its run at the 1,100-seat Schiller Theatre. Local German critics raved about the technical skill and energy of the dancers. Likewise, the company continues to receive exuberant praise from American critics for its electric performance style and its rich repertoire. "Hubbard Street Dance Chicago," reviewer Jennifer Dunning wrote in 1995, "should bottle itself. . .as a cure for the ills of the era."

—Anthea Kraut

HUMPHREY, Doris

American dancer, choreographer, educator, and company director

Born: 17 October 1895 in Oak Park, Illinois. **Education:** Completed 13 grades at the Francis W. Parker School, Chicago; trained with Mary Wood Hinman in ballroom, clog, folk, and aesthetic dancing; studied ballet with Josephine Hatlanek, Andreas Pavley, and Serge Oukrainsky. **Family:** Married Charles Francis Woodford 7 June 1932; son Charles Humphrey Woodford born 8 July 1933. **Career:** Founded her own school of dance in Oak Park, 1913; attended Denishawn School, 1917; became its featured performer and teacher; first choreography, *Valse Caprice,* 1919; toured the Orient with Denishawn, 1925-26; left Denishawn with Charles Weidman and Pauline Lawrence to form the Humphrey-Weidman School and Company, 1928; toured nationally and taught at Bennington College Summer School, Teachers College, and Perry-Mansfield Camp, 1930s; opened Studio Theatre in New York City, 1940; last performance, *Inquest,* at Swarthmore College, Pennsylvania, 1944; became artistic director, José Limón Dance Company, 1945; appointed head of the Dance Center, 92nd Street YMHA, 1947; faculty member, Connecticut College School of Dance, 1948-58; Juilliard School of Music, 1951-58; director, Juilliard Dance

Doris Humphrey performing *To the Dance*. Photograph by Bois; courtesy of Charles Humphrey Woodford.

Theatre, 1954-58. **Awards:** Received *Dance Magazine* prize, 1938; John Simon Guggenheim fellowship, 1949; Capezio Award, 1954. **Died:** 29 December 1958.

Works

1920   *Valse Caprice (Scarf Dance)* (mus. Chaminade), Egan Little Theater, Los Angeles
     Bourrée (mus. Bach), Potter Theater, Santa Barbara
     Soaring, w/Ruth St. Denis (mus. Schumann), Spreckles Theater, San Diego
     Sonata Pathetique w/Ruth St. Denis (mus. Beethoven), Spreckles Theater, San Diego

1923   *Sonata Tragica* (mus. MacDowell), Apollo Theater, Atlantic City

1924   *Scherzo Waltz (Hoop Dance)* (mus. Ilgenfritz) Academy of Music, Newburgh, New York

1926   *A Burmese Yein Pwe,* with Ruth St. Denis (mus. Vaughan), Victoria Theater, Singapore
     At the Spring (mus. Liszt), Shuraka-Kan Theater, Kobe, Japan
     Whims (mus. Schumann), Philharmonic Auditorium, Los Angeles

1928   *Air for the G String* (mus. Bach), Little Theater, Brooklyn
     Gigue (mus. Bach), Little Theater, Brooklyn
     Concerto in A Minor (mus. Grieg), Little Theater, Brooklyn
     Waltz (mus. Debussy), Little Theater, Brooklyn
     Papillon (mus. Rosenthal), Little Theater, Brooklyn
     Color Harmony (mus. Vaughan), Little Theater, Brooklyn
     Pavane of the Sleeping Beauty (mus. Ravel), Little Theater, Brooklyn
     The Fairy Garden (mus. Ravel), Little Theater, Brooklyn
     Bagatelle (mus. Beethoven), Little Theater, Brooklyn
     Pathetic Study (mus. Scriabin), Little Theater, Brooklyn
     The Banshee (mus. Cowell), John Golden Theater, New York
     Rigaudon (mus. MacDowell), solo concert, St. Stephens College, Annandale, New York
     Sarabande (mus. Rameau-Godowsky), Civic Repertory Theater, New York
     Water Study (no music), Civic Repertory Theater, New York

1929   *Air on a Ground Bass* (mus. Purcell), Guild Theater, New York
     Gigue (mus. Bach), Guild Theater, New York
     Concerto in A Minor (mus. Grieg), Guild Theater, New York
     Speed, Guild Theater, New York
     Life of the Bee (mus. Pauline Lawrence), Guild Theater, New York
     The Call (mus. Rudhyar), Agora, Lake Placid
     Quasi-Waltz (mus. Scriabin), Agora, Lake Placid
     Courante (mus. Green), Agora, Lake Placid
     Mazurka to Imaginary Music (no music), Agora, Lake Placid

1930   *A Salutation to the Depths* w/Charles Weidman (mus. Rudhyar), Maxine Elliott's Theater, New York

Breath of Fire (mus. Rudhyar), Maxine Elliott's Theater, New York
Drama of Motion (no music), Maxine Elliott's Theater, New York
La Valse (mus. Ravel), Maxine Elliott's Theater, New York

1930   *Descent (Into a Dangerous Place)* (mus. Weiss), Maxine Elliott's Theater, New York
     March (mus. Tcherepnine), HW, Opera House, Boston
     Salutation (no music), Prentiss Auditorium, Cleveland
     Etude No. 1 (mus. Scriabin), Robin Hood Dell, Cleveland
     La Valse (mus. Ravel), Philadelphia

1931   *The Shakers (Dance of the Chosen)* (mus. Lawrence), Craig Theater, New York
     Dances of Women (mus. Rudhyar), Craig Theater, New York
     Burlesca (mus. Bossi), Craig Theater, New York
     Lake at Evening (mus. Griffes), Craig Theater, New York
     Night Winds (mus. Griffes), Craig Theater, New York
     Tambourin (mus. Rameau), Robin Hood Dell, Philadelphia
     Three Mazurkas (mus. Tansman), Washington Irving High School, New York
     Variation on a Theme of Handel (mus. Brahms), Washington Irving High School, New York
     Two Ecstatic Themes (mus. Medtner, Malipiero), Washington Irving High School, New York

1932   *The Pleasures of Counterpoint* (mus. Achron), Guild Theater, New York
     Dionysiaques (mus. Schmitt), Guild Theater, New York

1933   *Suite in E,* with Charles Weidman (mus. Roussel), Lewisohn Stadium, New York

1934   *Rudepoema (Sacred Dance)* (mus. Villa-Lobos), Guild Theater, New York
     Pleasures of Counterpoint No. 2 (mus. Pollins), Guild Theater, New York
     Pleasures of Counterpoint No. 3 (mus. Horst), Guild Theater, New York
     Exhibition Piece (mus. Slonimsky), Guild Theater, New York
     Theme and Variations (mus. Brahms), Severance Hall, Cleveland
     Credo (mus. Chavez), Dance Theater, Baltimore

1935   *Duo-Drama* (mus. Harris), Guild Theater, New York
     New Dance (mus. Reigger), Bennington College Theater, Bennington, Vermont
     New Dance, Variations and Conclusions (mus. Reigger), Guild Theater, New York

1936   *Theatre Piece* (mus. Reigger), Guild Theater, New York
     With My Red Fires (mus. Riegger), Armory, Bennington, Vermont

1937   *To the Dance* w/Weidman (mus. Leonard), Alumni Hall, Bloomington, Indiana

1938   *American Holiday* (mus. Mamorsky), Guild Theater, New York
     Race of Life (mus. Fine), Guild Theater, New York
     Passacaglia in C Minor (mus. Bach), Armory, Bennington, Vermont

1939   *Square Dances* (mus. Nowak), Washington Irving High School, New York

1940   *Variations* (mus. Lloyd), Vassar College, Poughkeepsie, New York

Song of the West (mus. Nowak, Harris), Madison College, Harrisonburg, Virginia

1941   *Dance"ings"* (mus. Nowak), H-W Studio, New York

Decade, w/Weidman (mus. Bach, Copland, others), Bennington, Vermont

1942   *Song of the West Rivers* (mus. Harris), H-W Studio, New York

Four Chorale Preludes (mus. Bach), H-W Studio, New York

Partita in G Major (mus. Bach), H-W Studio, New York

1943   *El Salon Mexico* (mus. Copland), HW Studio, New York

1944   *Inquest* (mus. Lloyd), H-W Studio, New York

Canonade (mus. Nordoff), H-W Studio, New York

1946   *The Story of Mankind* (mus. Nowak), Bennington College Theater, Bennington, Vermont

Lament for Ignacio Sánchez Mejías (mus. Lloyd), Bennington College Theater, Bennington, Vermont

1947   *Day on Earth* (mus. Copland), Beaver County Day School, Brookline, Massachusetts

1948   *Corybantic* (mus. Bartók), Palmer Auditorium, New London, Connecticut

1949   *Invention* (mus. Lloyd), Palmer Auditorium, New London, Connecticut

1951   *Quartet No. 1 (Night Spell)* (mus. Rainier), Palmer Auditorium, New London, Connecticut

1952   *Fantasy, Fugue in C Major, Fugue in C Minor* (mus. Mozart), Palmer Auditorium, New London, Connecticut

1953   *Deep Rhythm (Ritmo Jondo)* (mus. Surinach), Alvin Theater, New York

Ruins and Visions (mus. Britten), Palmer Auditorium, New London, Connecticut

1954   *Felipe el Loco* (mus. Gomez, Montoya, Segovia), Palmer Auditorium, New London, Connecticut

1955   *The Rock and the Spring* (mus. Martin), Juilliard Concert Hall, New York

Airs and Graces (mus. Locatelli), Palmer Auditorium, New London, Connecticut

1956   *Theatre Piece No. 2* (mus. Luening), Juilliard Concert Hall, New York

Dawn in New York (mus. Johnson), Juilliard Concert Hall, New York

1957   *Descent into the Dream* (mus. Petrassi), Juilliard Concert Hall, New York

Dance Overture (mus. Creston), Palmer Auditorium, New London, Connecticut

Brandenburg Concerto No. 4 in G Minor w/Ruth Currier (mus. Bach), Juilliard Concert Hall, New York

Publications

By HUMPHREY: books—

The Art of Making Dances, New York, 1959.

By HUMPHREY: articles—

"New Dance: An Unfinished Autobiography," *Dance Perspectives,* Spring 1966.

On HUMPHREY: books—

For a listing of books on Doris Humphrey, see General Bibliography.

Films and Videotapes

Air for the G String, Westinghouse; *Brandenberg Concerto No. 4,* Ohio State University and University of Oregon; *Day on Earth,* Dance Film Archive, University of Rochester; *Doris Humphrey Technique,* Princeton Book Company; five coaching videos with Ernestine Stodelle: *Water Study, The Call/Breath of Fire, The Shakers, Two Ecstatic Themes, Air for the G String,* Princeton Book Company; *Lament for Ignacio Sánchez Mejías,* Walter Strate; *New Dance,* Connecticut College American Dance Festival; *The Shakers,* Thomas Bouchard; *Water Study,* Dance Film Archive, University of Rochester; *With My Red Fires,* Connecticut College American Dance Festival; *With My Red Fires* and *New Dance,* Princeton Book Company.

*   *   *

Doris Humphrey is one of the founders of American modern dance. She began her professional performing and choreographic career at Denishawn, eventually leaving to follow her own quest to make dances that would express an American spirit. Through performing, teaching, lecturing, writing, and the "missionary work " (her own term) of touring, she helped to establish the fledgling new art from its outset.

The complex influences of family, history, education, and circumstance propelled Humphrey from a young age. In the 1930s while promoting the Humphrey-Weidman Company, she wrote: "My dance comes from the people who had to subdue a continent, to make a thousand paths through forest and plain, to conquer mountains, and eventually to raise up towns of steel and glass." A further, simpler explanation appeared in the June-July-August 1932 issue of *Trend, Quarterly of the Seven Arts,* as "There is only one thing to dance about: the meaning of one's personal experience."

Humphrey's ancestors were people who had, in fact, arrived in New England when it was a wilderness and through successive generations had become religious and educational leaders. She was a direct descendent of Elder William Brewster of the *Mayflower.* Both her maternal and paternal grandfathers were ordained ministers in the Congregational Church. Her parents, however, were not particularly religious, and as a child she grew up in the hotel they managed in Chicago amid the excitement of what was then the fastest growing city in the world—a city rebuilding itself with skyscrapers after the disastrous fire. Both her parents were musical—her father an amateur singer, and her mother a trained pianist. It was from them that she derived the sense of musicality that was to distinguish her choreography.

Humphrey's parents placed great value on education, enrolling her in the Francis Parker School, founded by a colleague of John Dewey and based on Dewey's principles of progressive education. The emphasis there was on experimental and experiential learning. Its innovative curriculum included dance classes in which Humphrey immediately shone. Her dance teacher, Mary Wood Hinman, became her mentor and lifelong friend. Humphrey was the first student to have completed all 13 grades of the Francis Parker School, and carried throughout her life its educational philosophy based on democratic principles, inquiry, and individualism. After graduating from Francis Parker, Humphrey composed several dances for children that were published in Mary Wood Hinman's *Gymnastic and Folk Dances* (1914).

Her senior year was a watershed in several ways. As a "senior project" she and another girl, traveling with Humphrey's mother as accompanist, were engaged to perform in men's clubs of the Sante Fe Railroad. Often the performances were in saloons, but when they were in church halls, dance was not allowed. This encounter with religious prejudice against dance led to a lifelong break with formal religion. Years later, in 1930, Humphrey would compose *The Shakers*, based on Shaker ritual, as a tribute to the sect that incorporated dance into its religious services, and espoused the philosophy of Friedrich Nietzsche who proclaimed that he could only believe in a God who danced. In Nietzsche's book, *The Birth of Tragedy*, she also found expression of the duality in the contrasting experiences of her childhood in his ideas of the Apollonian and Dionysian. Humphrey used these opposing forces to dramatic effect in her choreography.

Shortly after graduation, while attending a ballroom workshop with Irene and Vernon Castle in New York, she received a telegram telling her that the hotel in which her parents had worked had been sold and to return at once to the home of friends in the Chicago suburb of Oak Park. Her father was out of a job and it was up to the 18-year-old Humphrey, with her mother as accompanist, to become the support of the family by teaching dance.

Oak Park, her birthplace, with its quiet, tree-shaded streets, numerous churches, and "blue laws," was quite a departure from the raucous, noisy street and theatrical clientele of her home in the hotel. Some of her first classes were at Unity Temple, the Unitarian church designed by Frank Lloyd Wright. The village of Oak Park boasted 24 other buildings designed by Wright; it is conceivable Humphrey absorbed some of her sense of architecture through her daily exposure to Wright's work. She developed her skills as a teacher and learned, of necessity, to be self-reliant, in the four years she spent in Oak Park. In this crucial period, Humphrey seems to have gained the self-confidence and inner strength that would later emerge in her image as a spiritual leader—a role she cast for herself in her choreography for *Air for the G String, Concerto in A Minor, Life of the Bee, The Shakers, New Dance,* and *Passacaglia.* At the same time she grew increasingly restless and longed for the opportunity to perform rather than to teach.

At the suggestion of Mary Wood Hinman, Humphrey enrolled at the Los Angeles-based Denishawn School's summer session in 1917, a step that would change her life forever. After auditioning for Ruth St. Denis, she heard the words from Miss Ruth that she had longed for, "You shouldn't be teaching, you should be dancing." With Miss Ruth as her guiding spirit, Humphrey remained at Denishawn for 10 years, becoming its leading dancer and teacher. Encouraged by Miss Ruth to choreograph, Humphrey's *Valse Caprice* (*The Scarf Dance*), *Hoop Dance,* and *Soaring* became hits both on the concert and vaudeville stages. Miss Ruth's idea of music visualization and her theatrical sense contributed greatly to Humphrey's development during the Denishawn years.

Ultimately, Humphrey outgrew Denishawn, finding its authoritarian direction unsympathetic to new ideas, its reliance on non-American dance imitative, and its artistry compromised by appearing in Ziegfield Follies. In 1928 she and co-Denishawners Charles Weidman and Pauline Lawrence (later Mrs. José Limón) left to form the Humphrey-Weidman School and Company in New York City, which remained in existence until 1945. The themes of her solo *The Call/Breath of Fire* and the group work *Life of the Bee* relate to her departure from Denishawn. *Water Study*, composed in 1928, embodies Humphrey's discoveries of "fall and recovery" (the process of falling away from and returning to equilibrium), breath rhythm (phrasing and dynamics associated with breathing), and natural movement (movement derived from a natural source). The reduction of dance to basic elements became the basis for her technique and *Water Study*, her much-performed, landmark piece has become a part of the training of modern dancers in colleges and universities.

During the 1930s, as social and political issues predominated, Humphrey's work turned toward the examination of human relationships, both interpersonal and societal, in such compositions as *New Dance, With My Red Fires, The Race of Life, Passacaglia,* and *Theatre Piece.* As an idealist, she came to view the dance group as capable of showing human perfectibility and harmony—and this in an age of growing violence, cynicism, and despair. Her vision of the ideal society is expressed in the "Variations and Conclusion" from *New Dance* in which unity of purpose allows for individual diversity. Alternatively, the dance group could hold a mirror up to society as it really is—competitive, discordant, and susceptible to mobism. Her last performance as a dancer was in *Inquest* (1944), an examination of public indifference to poverty.

Her performing career cut short by arthritis, Humphrey turned her attention to composition and teaching choreography. She became artistic director of the José Limón Company and head of the Dance Department of New York's 92nd Street YMHA, where she innovated the first course in choreography. She also served on the faculties of the Juilliard School and the Connecticut College Dance Festival. Her choreography for the Limón Company included *Day on Earth, Lament for Ignacio Sánchez Mejías, The Story of Mankind,* and *Ritmo Jondo,* works that embodied universal themes: the life cycle, death and immortality, the foibles of human history, and relations between the sexes.

Humphrey was an early believer in the value of Labanotation. The scores of many of her works are available through the Dance Notation Bureau for the purpose of reconstruction, and they are the most performed of any notated choreographer. At the end of her life, Humphrey completed the manuscript for *The Art of Making Dances*, published posthumously in 1959, articulating her principles of choreography. It has remained in print ever since, influencing generations of students in all areas of dance. At the time of her death in 1958, she began working on her autobiography, which was later completed by Selma Jeanne Cohen and published in 1972 as *Doris Humphrey: An Artist First.*

Summing up her importance to modern dance, *New York Times* critic John Martin wrote: "Doris Humphrey is an enduring part of the dance in America, as the granite under the soil is enduring. We can turn nowhere in the art without finding her."

—Charles Humphrey Woodford

I

ICELAND

The pioneers of modern dance affected a broad range of people in different corners of the world. In Iceland, their ideas about movement flourished for awhile though they did not take a firm hold. Iceland was, until the beginning of the 20th century, a peaceful peasant and fishing society with the population evenly dispersed on the coasts of the island. Only in the late 19th century did a major population centre appear in the capital Reykjavík, due to industrial development in both the fishing industry and farm management. Service and commerce increased quickly. In 1900 the population of Reykjavík was 6,000 inhabitants (three percent of the whole population) but only 10 years later it had reached 12,000 or 14 percent of the whole population.

Since 1900, then, the capital has been the major cultural centre of the country and today over 150,000 people live in Reykjavík. People who were educated abroad came back to Iceland more aware of the cultural changes in the surrounding world. They therefore strained towards a higher level of education and arts in Reykjavík to be comparative to the neighbouring countries. Theatres, galleries, and educational institutions grew quickly and so did the education of dance. Although the tradition of classical ballet theatre did not reach Iceland until the 1920s, the tradition of modern dance did rather quickly after it emerged on both sides of the Atlantic.

In 1947 modern dance technique was incorporated in the gymnastic classes at the Icelandic College of Physical Education and Sport. The initiative came from Sigríður Valgeirsdóttir, a young Icelandic woman, who had recently returned to Iceland after a six-year period of dance studies in Berkeley, California. She had studied with Martha Graham, Doris Humphrey, Charles Weidman, and many more, so with her the newly emerged discipline came straight to Iceland. Enthusiastic to spread her knowledge, Valgeirsdóttir tried to establish a school and company in Reykjavík. Since the Icelanders had only recently become familiar with classical training, the new style of modern dance confused them and for the first class most of the girls showed up thinking they were to dance in tutus and pointe shoes. After an honest attempt to spread modern dance around the country, Valgeirsdóttir found a new path and trained a group of dancer-gymnastics at the Icelandic College of Physical Education and Sport. It was a modern gymnastic troupe that traveled in Iceland and its neighbouring countries, using Valgeirsdóttir's choreography and music by various Icelandic composers. Although the troupe's style was based on modern dance, they attended festivals with other gymnastic groups in Scandinavia, since modern dance wasn't known there either at that time.

In 1952 the National Theatre of Iceland opened a ballet school, the first and only school with public support. Although the school has always been strictly classical it has from time to time included modern training, depending on the range of guest teachers. Other dance schools (Jassballettskóli Báru, Dansstúdíó Sóleyjar,

Kramhúsið) have also occasionally taught modern technique since the 1960s. The techniques of Graham, Cunningham, Limón and Horton have all been taught for a few years at a time, coming and going with different teachers. A few times modern jazz companies have been established, but none have persisted for more than two or three years at a time.

In 1973 the Icelandic Ballet was established, the first company (and still the only one) to receive governmental support. The company has always been rather small, ranging from 10-20 dancers, and can mostly be defined as neo-classical. It plays the key role in dance events in Iceland and is the only company that has maintained itself for more than a couple of years. In the late 1990s it was lead by a young Icelander, a former dancer with the Icelandic Ballet and Tanz-Forum Köln, named Katrín Hall. She took over the artistic direction in the fall of 1996 and decided to change the company into a modern one—which was quite an attestation to the modern tradition, to finally receive attention and governmental support.

Modern dance has been taught for many years in various places but has never gotten a firm hold in Icelandic culture. One could blame the small population of the country for the difficulties of establishing a solid modern tradition, or the negligence of governmental support for education in dance. But now, with the Icelandic ballet recognising the tradition, one hopes modern dance has found a permanent home in Iceland where it has been coming and going for 70 years.

—Ragna Sara Jónsdóttir

IMPULSE DANCE THEATRE
New Zealand Dance Company

Works

1976	*Prelude* (chor. J. Bull; mus. D. Brubeck)
	Collage I (chors J. Bull, P. Jenden, M. Clyaton; mus. various)
	To P. J. (chor. G. Sciascia; mus. R. Flack)
	Scrum (chor. J. Bull)
	Henry (chor. B. Robinson; mus. R. Wakeman)
	O.K. Eliot, so let's go (chor. J. Bull; words T. S. Eliot)
	Inverted Personages (chor. J. Bull; mus. B. Childs)
	Continuum (chor. J. Bull)
	Untitled Work I (chor. J. Bull)
	Schmultz (chor. P. Robinson; mus. Nilsson)
	Glop (chor. J. Bull)
	Nocturne (chor. P. Jenden; mus. Albinoni)
	Whispers (chor. J. Bull; mus. MCDonald Sinfield)
	Dolls (chors A. Gray, P. Jenden; mus. A. Kostenlanetz)
	Mal-Doom (chor. G. Sciascia; mus. E. Varese)

Bathers (chor. P. Jenden; mus. W. Herman)
Solitude (chor. S. Cheesman; mus. D. Crosby)
Suite for Five (chor. J. Bull; mus. B. Hansson)

1977   *Blute* (chor. L. Davey; mus. The Commodores)
Of a Feather (chor. P. Jenden; mus. Boccherini)
Windscape (chor. M. Clayton; mus. W. Carlos)
Triangle (chor. J. Bull; mus. Weatherreport)
Room 47 (chor. P. Jenden; mus. Pergolesi)
Dunedin: Weather or Not (chor. H. Oldfield; mus. D. Farquhar)
Life-Flow (chor. B. Robinson; mus. The Beetles)
Intrusion (chor. D. Groves; mus. J. Nitzche)
Membrum (chor. L. Davey; mus. T. Van Leer)
Windscape (chor. M. Clayton; mus. W. Carlos)
Thoughts Passing (chor. J. Bull; mus. E. Weber)
Five Minutes Flat (chor. The Company)
Dominion (chor. S. Jordan; mus. various; words A.R.D. Fairburn)
The Emperor's Nightingale (chor. P. Jenden; mus. Stravinsky)
Credits (chor. J. Bull)
Sportsplay (chor. J. Bull; mus. D. Graham)
Credits (chor. J. Bull; mus. M. Oldfield)
Mobile (chor. L. Davey; mus. R. Argent)
Somebody (chor. D. Goves; mus. J. Armatrading)
Timepiece (chor. S. Jordan; mus. P. Patterson)
A Wedding Album (chor. P. Jenden; mus. Poulenc)

1978   *Siblings* (chor. S. McEntree; mus. C. Riley, P. Rutter)
Five N' Counting (chor. R. Stratful; mus. D. Brubeck)
Labyrinth (chor. N. Carroll; mus. V. Kucera)
Blue Dedications (chor. P. Jenden; mus. various)
Ponty Pieces (chor. J. Bull; mus. J. L. Ponty)
Block One (chor. L. Davey)
Dancers at a Funeral (chor. P. Jenden; mus. D. Lilburn)

1979   *Theatre Piece* (chor. J. Bull; mus. J. Pastorius) w/New Zealand Ballet, Nelson
Fanfare (chor. J. De Leon; mus. A. Copland), w/New Zealand Ballet, Nelson

1980   *Signals* (chor. J. Bull; mus. T. Rypdal)
A Solo for Four (chor. H. Busfield)
Donnelly's Wig (chor. H. Busfield; mus. L. Schifrin)
Predilection (chor. M. Dickinson; mus. Tangerine Dream)
Get Set (chor. L. Davey; mus. Weatherreport)
Touch Tone (chor. G. Sciascia; mus. E. Varese)
Lifeline (chor. D. Sanders; mus. Preux)
Tease for Two (chor. J. Bull; mus. E. Weber)
The End Is Just Another Beginning (chor. J. Laage; mus. R. Kvistad)
Spin It (improvised work by the Company; mus. Dooby Brothers)
Wanangai-I-Te-Rangi (chor. G. Sciascia; mus. R. Harris and J. Body)
Timepiece 80 (chor. D. Tarrant; mus. R. Fox)
Songs of Emancipation (chor. B. Robinson; mus. V. Murphy)
Nockabout (chor. S. Jordan; mus. M. Nock)
John Wilson's Playground (chor. H. Busfield; mus. A. Lithgow)
Pierced (chor. M. Dickinson; mus. A. Heenan)
Open Sandwich (chor. J. Bull; mus. O. Cheesman0
Friends (chor. D. Sanders; mus. W. Southgate)

Front, Back and Side On (chor. H. Busfield; mus. C. Cree Brown)
Carousel (chor. J. Bull; mus. D. Lilburn)

1981   *Equinox* (chor. J. Carrol)
Window (chor. P. Buchman)
Two Sides of Us (chor. J. Scoglio)
At the Park (chor. P. Buchman)
Faces (chor. P. Buchman)

*   *   *

By the mid-1970s, the need to establish a professional full time modern dance company in New Zealand had become urgent. Impulse Dance Theatre was initiated and formed by Jamie Bull in 1976. She was well supported by some senior members of a Wellington dance group, the remnants of the New Dance Group of the 1940s. Many of these older women were financially comfortable and still retained a passion for dance.

Bull invited Liz Davey, Paul Jenden, Debbie Groves and Alison Grey to be the dancers, and Impulse Dance Theatre started rehearsing on 6 February 1976. They gave themselves six months to survive and all were salaried the same on a minimum wage. They aimed to be a national company based in Wellington (the capital city), taking dance to the people, with two national tours each year including workshops, schools performances, and public performances. They wanted to be a distinctively New Zealand repertory modern dance company, promoting New Zealand choreographers and giving opportunities to dancers to work professionally.

Impulse did indeed prove the need for professional modern dance in this country and in 1977 Impulse became an incorporated society with a board ultimately responsible for the company's survival. They survived far longer than the initial six months, lasting until April 1982. Bull was the artistic director until late 1981 when Pamela Buchman, from Australian Dance Theatre, was employed. During its six years of existence, 19 dancers sharpened their craft both as performers and as choreographers, and many alumni are still professionally involved in dance either in New Zealand or internationally. The intention of the fledgling company was to break down barriers of ignorance in the community that usually assumed classical ballet to be the only valid form of professional dance. Of necessity the style was eclectic, although it can be argued that an Impulse style did eventually emerge. Guest choreographers were employed, but company members had many opportunities to choreograph.

Bull's background had been in sports and physical education. She had trained at the University of Otago's School of Physical Education, which was enjoying a time of strong dance emphasis in the curriculum under the auspices of John Casserley. She brought to Impulse astute business skills and a passion for dance, rather than dance technique and professional experience.

Impulse had enjoyed Arts Council support from the outset but in the end its popularity was outstripped by Limbs Dance Company, an Auckland-based company which attracted a huge student audience. Eventually the government arts funding body commissioned Peter Brinson from England to review the structure of the dance profession in this country. He concluded that our population base could only support one professional modern dance company and consequently funding was withdrawn from Impulse and invested in Limbs.

Jamie Bull herself went on to freelance choreography, dance therapy and arts administration. She has mounted and toured many

Impulse Dance Theater: *Collage I.*

projects that have received Arts Council funding, her most experimental piece being *Back Beach Time* (1982) and *End of Times Chimes* (1984) in collaboration with visual artist Michael Smither. In the 1970s Smither developed an audio-visual harmonic scale using slides and sound. In these two works Bull added movement to complete the effect of total immersion in light and sound. Bull also worked in collaboration with Lyne Pringle in touring performances and workshops; and has had extensive experience as artist-in-residence for mental health programmes.

Liz Davey has had a profound influence as a teacher, especially during her time at NZ School of Dance where she has trained many of the professional performers active today. She is herself a graduate of the NZ School of Dance, when it was the National Ballet School, but has had intensive periods of training in America, especially with Bella Lewitzky. Her association with Impulse covered the period from its inception to its demise. Davey is currently teaching at Whitireia Community College Performing Arts School where she heads the Pakeha (European) dance programme.

Lyne Pringle, part of Impulse from 1979-81, has now carved out a dance career in her own right. Her initial dance training was at University of Otago School of Physical Education under Alison East, but she has also had intensive periods of training at the Hawkins studio in New York. She had a collaborative and creative partnership with Jamie Bull from 1987 to 1990 and was intensely involved with Michael Parmenter as performer in *Go, Insolent River, A Romance,* and *Gravity and Grace.* As a performer she has also danced for Susan Jordan in *Carillon Dance* (1991) and *Bone of Contention* (1993), Jan Bolwell in *Takitoru* (1995), and *Warwick Broadhead* (1997). Her own works include many short works com-

missioned for other companies as well as two evening length productions of her own, *She* (1992) and *Kilt* (1995). Pringle, resident in Wellington, is a regular guest teacher and choreographer for UNITEC dance programme in Auckland, and also teaches at Toi Whakaari (NZ Drama School) and NZ School of Dance. She is also involved in the Isadora's Tribe seasons, which is a platform for emerging and established choreographers.

Paul Jenden is perhaps the choreographer who has emerged from Impulse Dance Theatre the most strongly in his own right. He was with Impulse from its foundation up until the end of 1978, when he branched out as a freelance artist. He came to dance through puppetry, drama and stage design and today he is as well known for his screen and stage designs as he is for his choreography. He creates all his own costumes, which are an integral part of the choreography. He spent three years abroad dancing in America, Europe, Asia and Australia before deciding to base himself in his home country with his partner, Louis Solino, who danced in the José Limón Company from 1968 to 1979. Jenden has continued to produce a major show each year for himself and Solino, as well as freelance choreography for the Royal New Zealand Ballet, New Zealand School of Dance, and Footnote Dance Company. In 1993 he formalised his company as the Fandango Company and explicitly choreographed works with gay and lesbian themes, such as *Dancing the Gay Fandango* (1993), *Fairy Stories* (1994 and 1997), and *Fruitful Gestures* (1994) all of which use an extended company of dancers. Jenden has also been very successful with three children's shows in the *Hairy McClary* series based on the best-selling children's books series written and illustrated by New Zealand author Lynley Dodd, with music by Wellington composer Jan Bolton. Jenden has choreographed and designed these shows, which have played to thousands of children in New Zealand and Australia.

Although Impulse Dance Theatre is not in existence today, its groundbreaking work has produced numerous dance artists who still continue to practice their craft today as performers, choreographers and teachers. Its model was the modern dance practiced in America, especially that of college departments. It was an earnest company, which laid a foundation for others to build on.

—Susan Jordan

INBAL DANCE THEATRE
Israeli modern dance company

Inbal Dance Theatre (renamed Inbal Multicultural Arts Center in 1996) was founded in 1949 by Sara Levi-Tanai. Of Yemenite extraction, she was born at the beginning of the century in Jerusalem and raised in orphanages run by pedagogues from Russia and Central Europe. She encountered her own Jewish-Yemenite culture only when she came to Tel-Aviv to become a kindergarden teacher at the Levinsky Teachers Seminar.

Levi-Tanai wished to become an actress but instead started to compose songs, often set to her own poems, and dances for her young students. During World War II she joined a kibbutz and staged large-scale pageants primarily on biblical themes, using people of all ages and combining dance, singing, and spoken texts, in a manner later termed "multimedia."

She returned to Tel-Aviv, where in 1948 she encountered a group of Yemenite youngsters who had recently immigrated to Israel. She

Inbal Dance Theatre: *The Story of Ruth.*

realized that the cultural traditions, the special dance steps, the melodies, the ancient texts, dress, and ornaments were a unique source of inspiration. She began choreographing her own compositions with these youngsters and after a year the group began to perform with growing success all over Israel.

When in 1952 Jerome Robbins arrived to report on the dance scene in Israel, he became enthusiastic, calling the mainly vertical dance movement of the Yemenite men, who always danced in a semi-plie, *Yemenite Gothic.* His report recommended supporting a fledgling company called Inbal (a Hebrew term meaning "the tongue of a bell") and bringing technique teachers from abroad to instruct its dancers, whom he found fascinating but untrained (Anna Sokolow was to become the first of these.) He found Sara Levi-Tanai's choreography brilliant, original, and unique. In 1956 the American impresario Sol Hurok invited Inbal to tour the United States.

Critics and the audiences in the U.S. and Western Europe were enthusiastic, captivated by the bearded men and lithe women, who accompanied dance with singing and the playing of drums. John Martin of the *New York Times* found Inbal "irresistible" and remarked that its "biblical dramas remind one of Greek tragedy."

Levi-Tanai had taken the cultural heritage of the Yemenite Jews and from these materials forged a modern dance idiom all her own. The basic Yemenite step, the Da'asa, which she often used, was for her the quintessence of walking barefoot in the desert. Her sources of inspiration have been the Bible, the lansdcape of Israel, the desert, and poetry, such as that of the Yemenite poet Shalom Shabazi who lived in Yemen in the 17th century. Out of these Yemenite ethnic materials, Levi-Tanai forged her unique modern dance language. Some of Levi-Tanai's major works for Inbal include 1955's *Song of Debora,* the following year's *Yemenite Wedding,* both the original *Story of Ruth* from 1961 and its revival in 1996, *Carry Us to the Desert* (1964), *Jacob in Horan* (1973) and *Song of Songs,* from 1982, which was remounted along with the *Story of Ruth* in 1996.

Margalit Oved had been the star of Inbal from 1948 into the 1960s when she left for California, where she taught and directed her own company. But in 1993 Oved returned to Israel and for two seasons became Inbal's artistic director after Levi-Tanai was unceremoniously retired in 1992. Levi-Tanai's dethroning as matriarch and leading spirit of the company was not due only to her advancing age. Her anarchic methods of working often disrupted rehearsal schedules, and premiere dates were postponed again and again. Her reluctance to let other, younger choreographers develop their own works made life for the management of Inbal unbearable. But the crucial point the would-be reformers overlooked was that the canon of Sara Levi-Tanai's works was the true *raison d'être* of the company.

Like many great artists, Levi-Tanai for many years tenaciously resisted any attempt to recreate or reconstruct her great choreography. Only in 1996 were her *Story of Ruth* and *Song of Songs* were

Inbal Dance Theatre: *Ode to Shabbazi.*

successfully restaged by veteran Inbal dancers, headed by Ilana Cohen, who had choreographed several successful works of her own for Inbal in past years. In 1997 Cohen was appointed pro-tem artistic director. And so, Inbal, Israel's oldest professional dance company, has known many difficult periods—artistically, financially, and from diminished public acclaim. But it has struggled on and in 1996 became a full-fledged arts center, renamed the Inbal Multicultural Arts Center.

Publications

Bahat, N. & A, "Some Notes on Traditional Scriptual Hand Movements [...] of the Yemenite Jews, *The World of Music,* Berlin, 1981.
Manor, Giora, *Inbal: Quest for a Movement Language,* Tel-Aviv, 1975.

—Giora Manor

INDIA

Modern dance in India is an indigenous creative form, originating in the 1930s, and preceding the rediscovery and renaissance of Indian classical dance forms in the 20th century. While India's classical dance stems from antiquity, the impetus for India's modern dance came from the demands of European orientalism rather than a rebellion against classicism. In fact, the oriental dance, perceived in the West as ethnically authentic, was the beginning of India's modern dance history.

The creative or modern dance of India began with Uday Shankar, who established the first Indian company to tour outside of the country, which debuted at the Théâtre des Champs Elysées in Paris on 3 March 1931. Until that time only a few Western exponents of Indian dance (including Ruth St. Denis), mostly untrained in its disciplines and techniques, had presented Indian-themed dances in Western stagings. Shankar created a dance form which later became known as "Shankarstyle," using linear counts to coordinate movements based on Indian sculpture and paintings, everyday life in India, and ideas from dances seen during his 1930 tour of India with his co-producer, Alice Boner. He taught this style of creative dance to students and troupe members at his Uday Shankar India Culture Centre at Almora, in the foothills of the Himalayas, from 1939 until its closing in 1943.

Some disciples of Shankar became the next generation of India's modern dancers, including Sachin Shankar and his Ballet Unit, Narendra Sharma at the Modern School and with his company Bhoomika, and Shanti Bardhan and his Little Ballet Company, later directed by Gul Bardhan and Shankar disciple Prabhat Ganguli. Others, imbued with the creative spirit of Almora, founded schools and theatres, including Triveni Kala Sangam and Bharatiya Kala Kendra, with its Kamani Auditorium, both in New Delhi. Modern dance was brought into film through other students of Shankar, including Guru Dutt, Mohan Segal, and Sardar Mallik, as well as Zohra Segal and her husband Kameshwar.

Shankarstyle-inspired modern ballets in India such as the Indian National Theatre (later India Renaissance Artists) production of *Discovery of India*, and the New Delhi production of *Ramayana*, originally conceived by Narendra Sharma for Bharatiya Kala Kendra, and with continued choreography by Debendra Shankar and others. Productions such as kathak dance-dramas, and bharata natyam ballets adapted ideas from the creative dance schools of India, moving from solo dance performances to ensemble performances. This shift was both aesthetically and pragmatically induced by a combination of the interest of Indian audiences in traditional stories of Hindu culture, and the burgeoning schools of dance after independence, which trained "proper" young women in the arts of India's classical heritage. Only a few of these productions could be characterized as modern, since they usually alternated pantomime and classical dance in creating a narrative.

Modern or creative dance was submerged after Indian independence when the new state gave its major support and recognition to classical and folk dances of India. While Shankar settled in Calcutta and opened his Uday Shankar India Culture Centre there in the 1960s, training students in Shankarstyle mainly under the guidance of Amala Shankar, his wife and partner, most young girls and a few boys chose to learn kathak or bharatanatyam, or the local classical form of kathakali in Kerala or Manipuri in Manipur. Later Odissi and Chhau, as well as Kuchipudi, Mohini Attam, and kalaripayyat, a martial art of Kerala, were added to the dance classes available to children. Most of these students were learning dance as a cultural heritage, and left the dance when they entered higher studies or were married.

Only in 1984, during and after the Bombay "East-West Dance Encounter," sponsored by the National Centre for the Performing Arts and Germany's Max Mueller Bhavan, was the new direction of India's modern dance given wide notice and support. Chandralekha, trained in bharatanatyam at Kalakshetra in Madras, who had left the dance for social causes some years earlier, offered a stunning program at the Dance Encounter, reviving her *Tillana* (from *Devadasi*) and *Surya Namaskar* (from *Navagraha*). In the second East-West Encounter the following year, she offered her first major new production in years, *Angika*, inspiring others to bring forward their modern and creative dance choreography, and fostering a revolution of Indian dance in the modern era. Chandralekha's productions used students trained at Kalakshetra, but in completely nontraditional choreography, costume, staging and juxtapositions. Incorporating bharatanatyam, yoga, and kalaripayyatt in her choreographic vocabulary, Chandralekha stunned the dance world of India, and later audiences abroad, with her precisely timed images and choreographic inventiveness.

Kumudini Lakhia, whose school in Ahmedabad trained kathak dancers in traditional technique, has become a creative and innovative choreographer, using these techniques in modern productions for many years with music by her partner Atul Desai. Birju Maharaj, the leading exponent of Lucknow gharana kathak, based at Kathak Kendra in Delhi, has produced new choreography for kathak, as has Keshav Kothari. But it is in Calcutta that modern dance has two primary exponents who are developing, each in their own direction, dance which is Indian and yet irretrievably modern. One is the company of Ananda and Tanusree Shankar, who are a music-and-dance choreography team, with Ananda composing and Tanusree working with him on choreography and costumes. Their school, which has about 800 students, trains Bengali youngsters in a series of leveled classes, in techniques adapted from the Shankarstyle training Tanusree had from Amala Shankar. Their company, of about 25 dancers, performs as Ananda Shankar Dance Company in India and abroad, in both original works and dances commissioned by various organizations and industries. Shankar has also with Chandralekha and others choreographed huge national and sports productions using thousands of children as dancers.

Also in Calcutta, modern dancer Manjusri Chaki-Sircar and her daughter and disciple Ranjabati have created for their Dance Guild a grammar of movements which are both new and based on ethnographic study of India's multiple dance forms, including tribal and folk dance as well as classical styles. This grammar is the basis for dance productions and solo choreography.

Two dancers, soloists, who have been engaged in both dance and choreography of modern Indian dance for many years, are Uttara Asha Coorlawala and Astad Deboo. Coorlawala, based in New York, was trained in bharata natyam, jazz, and modern dance including Martha Graham style. She choreographs her own dances and occasionally does so for other groups. She studied Graham style, and danced with Matteo for some years before moving in her own directions. Astad Deboo, born and raised in Bombay, was trained in Kathakali, and has had an international career in modern dance, only in recent years receiving recognition in India for his works. His ultramodern movement, based sometimes on indigenous classical and folk forms, is choreographed in solo dances which challenge and satirize these forms, while demonstrating his engagement with them.

Daksha Sheth, trained by Kumudini Lakhia in traditional kathak in Ahmedabad, and later in Delhi, has moved to incorporate the grammar of several dance forms into modern choreographies with new music, produced by her husband Devissaro, an Australian trained in north Indian dhrupad and khyal styles. She based her company, AARTI, first in Mathura, near Delhi, but is now near Tiruvananthapuram, in Kerala in south India. There she is experimenting with kalaripayyat, adding it to her repertoire which also includes chhau. Also in the south, in Bangalore, Bharat Sharma, trained by his father Narendra Sharma as well as others in Shankarstyle, Chhau and Western modern dance at the Murray Louis studio in New York, has been working with dancers to found a new company for modern dance. Some former company members of Chandralekha have begun their own choregraphic works, have been well received in Bangalore, New Delhi, Bombay, and Madras.

Anita Ratnam, trained in classical bharata natyam, is producing new choreographic fusions of styles, using the spoken poetry of A.K. Ramanujan, a series of male dancers in her Purusha, and other experimental combinations. Malika Sarabhai, who began her career as a classical dancer trained by her mother, the classical dance doyen Mrinilini Sarabhai, has moved into modern choreography with various groups, and has also developed solo shows with modern themes and choreography, in collaboration with John Martin.

Thus the modern dance of India is accelerating in its acceptance, and in the interests of companies presenting new productions to wider audiences in India and abroad. Often the outcome of dancers trained in classical styles is to move to new choreography and themes in their repertoire.

This shift is characterized by current themes, with a shift from traditional movement to new kinetic grammars, the substitution of linear for traditional cyclical rhythms, collaboration with new music and spoken poetry, and replacement of elaborate costumes based on ancient sculpture to simple saris and leotards with indigenous materials predominating. The perpetual smile of the classical dancer has been replaced by a serious demeanor reflective of inner concentration, and the productions are mainly duets and ensembles, rather than soloists. This modern dance is avowedly Indian in its elements, yet intended to engage contemporary audiences in themes and values relevant to their lives, in India and abroad.

Publications

Banerjee, Projesh, *Indian Ballet Dancing*, New Delhi, 1983.

Bharucha, Rustom, *Chandralekha: Woman, Dance, Resistance*, New Delhi, 1995.

Bhavnani, Enakshi, *The Dance in India: The Origin and History, Foundations, the Art and Sciences of the Dance in India—Classical, Folk and Tribal*, Bombay, 1965.

Erdman, Joan L., "Dance Discourses: Rethinking the History of the 'Oriental Dance', in *Rethinking Dance: Criticism in Transition*, edited by Gay Morris, London, 1996.

Khokar, Mohan, "The Free Dance," in *Traditions of Indian Classical Dance*, New Delhi, 1979.

—Joan L. Erdman

ISRAEL

Modern dance in Israel began in 1919 when Russian-born dancer and choreographer Baruch Agadati (born 1895 in Odessa; died 1976 in Tel-Aviv) arrived as an immigrant and performed his expressionistic-cubist solos in Tel-Aviv and Jaffa. Indeed, until the end of World War I, when Israel (Palestine) became a British mandate, there was no stage dancing of any kind.

Agadati created and performed Hassidic portraits from the Ukraine and Belarus, later adding such figures as a Yemenite-Jewish farm worker and an effeminate Arab dandy from Jaffa to his portrait gallery. His style was expressionistic, influenced by the Russian cubist and constructivist painters and stage designers of the period. Agadati also successfully toured in Europe; he experimented with dance unaccompanied by music—an innovation received by his home audience with animosity—which made him abandon dancing altogether in 1930.

The first modern dance studio was founded by Margalit Orenstein (born 1888 in Vienna; died 1973 in Tel-Aviv), a trained physical education teacher, soon after her arrival with her husband in 1922. She choreographed dances for her twin daughters, Yehudit and Shoshana, who performed together until the 1940s. Her granddaughter, Gabi Eldor, became a choreographer and dance critic.

Israel is a land where modern dance has been dominant right from the beginning and classical ballet played a minor role. The Russian-trained ballerina Rina Nikova (born 1898 in Russia; died 1974 in Jerusalem) opened a ballet studio in Tel-Aviv in 1924. With her students—mostly young girls of Yemenite extraction—she founded her Biblical Ballet company. She was a very perceptive artist and soon realized that to choreograph on biblical themes the traditional *danse d'école* steps were much less appropriate than the traditional Yemenite-Jewish steps her pupils showed and taught her. In later

years, Jewish-Yemenite dance and music were to play an important role in modern dance in Israel.

Yardena Cohen (born 1910, Haifa) went to study modern dance with Gret Palucca and Mary Wigman in Germany in the 1920s. Returning to Haifa in the mid-1930s, she began choreographing solos for herself. A native artist, she was constantly looking for authentic Middle-Eastern rhythms and steps. She engaged Oriental musicians, who accompanied her with the Arab tabla (drum) and the oud (plectrum string instrument). Her style was a vigorous synthesis of Central European and Oriental *Ausduckstanz*. She was also instrumental in the unique phenomenon of Israeli folk dance being created by professional, modern choreographers in the 1930s and 1940s.

The most influential dancer and choreographer in Israel from the first day of her a triumphal solo tour in 1931 (and again in 1933) was the Viennese-born Gertrud Kraus. She settled in Tel-Aviv in 1935 and soon began to appear with her students as the Gertrud Kraus Group, sometimes in joint concerts with the Palestine Orchestra, known today as the Israel Philharmonic, and later as the resident dance company of the Folk Opera during World War II.

Among the new immigrants fleeing Europe after the Nazis gained power in 1933 were several professional modern dancers, such as Lea Bergstein (born 1902, Poland; died 1989, Kibbutz Ramat Jochanan), Rivka Sturman (born 1905, Leipzig, Germany) and Tille Roessler (born 1907, Poland; died 1959, Tel-Aviv).

In order to earn a modest income they became school teachers and as such were charged with staging end-of-term performances as well as public festivities celebrating the Jewish holy days. Those who joined kibbutzim (collective agricultural settlements) felt the need for original movement material for the festive outdoor performances they choreographed. Using European social dances such as the waltz or the polka in their new homeland seemed absurd. So they began creating a new kind of Israeli folk dance, based on their knowledge of modern dance and indigenous Oriental movement elements, which soon became popular in spite of their quasi-artificial origin. The first large gathering of these new folk dance groups took place at Kibbutz Dalia in 1944. For it, Yardena Cohen, Rivka Sturman, Gertrud Kraus and others staged a pageant of their works with amateur groups. This marked the beginning of a folk dance movement, lead by Gurit Kadman (Gert Kaufmann, born 1897; died 1989, Tel-Aviv), another Central European movement and gymnastics teacher, which still flourishes to this day.

An annual folk dance festival has taken place since 1987 at the town of Karmiel, in which Israeli stage dance companies, such as the Kibbutz Contemporary Dance Company, Koldemama, Bat-Dor, and the Israel Ballet, as well as guest companies from abroad (including the Nederlands Dans Theater, the National Dance Company of Spain, and the Ballet Contemporaneo of Caracas) have performed. This festival has become a unique meeting point for folk dancing and artistic modern dance, and lasts for three days each July, attracting about 120,000 dancers and spectators.

Soon after Israel became an independent state, a large wave of immigrants from Europe (mostly survivors of the Holocaust) and the Arab countries arrived in Israel. Among these were many Yemenite Jews. With a group of Yemenite youngsters Sara Levi-Tanai founded her Inbal Dance Theatre in 1949, which later toured the world with great success.

In 1951 Gertrud Kraus established a professional modern dance group, the Israel Ballet Theatre, for which American choreographer Talley Beatty created *Fire in the Hills*, a work about a settlement being attacked by Arabs. Due to financial difficulties this venture lasted for only about 18 months. Also during the 1950s several dancers born and educated in the United States, such as Rena Gluck, Rina Shacham and Rachel Emanuel, as well as Israeli artists who studied modern dance abroad, mainly at the Juilliard School in New York, began to work and create in Israel. Among these were native-born dancers Moshe Efrati (of the Koldemama Company) and Rina Schenfeld who went on very successful solo careers. Beginning in the mid-1950s, American choreographer Anna Sokolow came to Tel-Aviv each year to teach technique to Inbal dancers, and she soon gathered a group of young dancers who would perform her works (such as *Rooms, Dreams,* and *Lyric Suite*) for her Lyric Theatre. Some of her dancers, such as Rina Schenfeld, Ehud Ben-David and others joined the Batsheva Dance Company, founded by Batsheva de Rothschild in 1964. Martha Graham's company toured Israel in 1956 and this visit enhanced the growing influence of American modern dance, which replaced the Central European *Ausdruckstanz*-style that had been dominant in Israeli modern dance since the 1930s. Graham became the first artistic advisor of the Batsheva company. She also sent several of her dancers, including Robert Cohan, Linda Hodes, Jane Dudley and others to teach the new company many well-known Graham works.

When its founder and producer, Batsheva de Rothschild wished to appoint the South African ballet dancer Jeannette Ordman as the artistic director of Batsheva, the leading dancers refused to accept this decision and threatened to resign. As a result Rothschild founded another company in 1967 to provide a framework for Ordman to dance and create, namely the Bat-Dor Dance Company. Moshe Efrati, one of the original Batsheva dancers, began choreographing for the company in 1969. He also began experimenting with deaf dancers. After leaving Batsheva he started his own company, Koldemama, and has remained until the present day its sole choreographer and artistic director.

Another of Israel's well-known dance companies, the Kibbutz Contemporary Dance Company, was founded in 1970 by several dance artists who were members of kibbutzim. In 1974 Yehudit Arnon became its artistic director, a post she held until 1997. She was replaced by the company's house choreographer, Rami Be'er. During the 1980s a new generation of dance artists became prominent. The influence of postmodern American dance and even more so of European choreographers such as Pina Bausch and Jiri Kylian became evident. Innovative experimental work was carried out by Ruth Ziv-Eyal, former Batsheva soloist Rina Schenfeld, Yaron Margolin, Oshra Elkayam, Ruth Eshel and others. In the mid-1980s an attempt was made to start a new young company, TAMAR, by

Meira Eliash-Chain (as general manager), Zvi Gotheiner, Amir Kolben and others. The original TAMAR group lasted just two seasons, was reassembled in Jerusalem in '88, and disbanded again after just three seasons. In spite of its short lifespan, TAMAR was influential among the younger generation of dancers and choreographers. Amir Kolben, its last artistic director, became the chief exponent of politically oriented postmodern dance in Israel.

In 1990 Ohad Naharin was appointed artistic director of Batsheva. Due to his innovative, vigorous and idiosyncratic choreographic style the company regained its international status. At the same time, a new trend has been evident in modern dance; instead of waiting on the sidelines for commissions to create for the well-known companies, young choreographers and dancers are running their own small companies and groups—mostly on minimal government subsidies. Prominent among these choreographers are Liat Dror and Nir Ben-Gal, Ido Tadmor's group, and those of Noa Dar, Anat Danieli, and more. Vertigo is a small but vigorous company performing the works of Noa Wertheim and Adi Sha'al, which has been touring abroad as well as performing in Israel. Also based in Jerusalem is Yaron Margolin's dance group, which has recently been experimenting with the integration of oriental dance and music into modern choreography.

According to a survey by the National Council for Culture and the Arts, there were seven professional companies active in Israel in 1995: they gave 621 performances for adult and young audiences, attended by 340,000 spectators, 67 percent of their budgets came from public (mainly governmental) subsidies, and 33 percent from the sale of tickets and their own income.

Publications

Books—

Eshel, Ruth, *Dancing with the Dream,* Tel-Aviv, 1991.
Manor, Giora, *Baruch Agadati, the Pioneer of Modern Dance in Israel,* Tel-Aviv, 1986.
———, *The Gospel According to Dance (The Bible as Dance),* New York, 1980.
———, *The Life and Dance of Gertrud Kraus,* Tel-Aviv, 1978.

Articles—

Ingber, Judith Brin, "Shorashim," *Dance Perspectives,* No. 59, 1974.

—Giora Manor

JACOB'S PILLOW DANCE FESTIVAL

Jacob's Pillow Dance Festival is recognized as one of America's most hallowed sites for dance activity of all kinds, having served as a center for performances, classes, and creative residencies since 1933. It is located on 150 wooded acres in the Berkshire Hills of western Massachusetts, on a remote country road in the Township of Becket. Its facilities include 18th-century barns as well as more recent structures constructed to blend with the rustic wood-frame buildings that give the site its unique character.

Although now considered a crossroads of the dance world, Jacob's Pillow began its life as a retreat. In 1931, Ted Shawn was separated from his wife Ruth St. Denis, and the Denishawn era was coming to a close. Shawn owned a Japanese-style estate in Westport, Connecticut, where he conducted summer training programs, but he was increasingly frustrated by the lack of space and steady stream of New York City visitors. When he learned of an abandoned farm in rural Massachusetts, he jumped at the chance to buy it. From an old letterhead he found in the house, he learned that the property had been known as "Jacob's Pillow—A Mountain Farm." It apparently took this unusual name from a large pillow-shaped boulder in back of the farmhouse. The Book of Genesis tells the story of Jacob laying his head upon a rock and dreaming of a ladder to heaven, and the nearby stagecoach road had long been known as Jacob's Ladder.

Shawn converted one of the old barns into a studio and used it during the summers of 1931 and 1932 to rehearse his touring programs with a small group of Denishawn dancers, including Jack Cole and Barton Mumaw. It was this group that first presented a program in Boston devoted entirely to men's dances, an experiment which led to the establishment of Ted Shawn's Men Dancers and signaled a new era for Shawn and for Jacob's Pillow. The Pillow served as headquarters for the Men Dancers from 1933 until its last cross-country tour in 1940, and for seven seasons all Pillow performances were presented by Shawn's company. It was also during this time that classes were first offered, originally under the banner of the Shawn School of Dance for Men.

When the Men Dancers disbanded in 1940, Shawn leased the Pillow to dance educator Mary Washington Ball, who initiated the Berkshire Hills Dance Festival with nine performances of ballet, modern, oriental, and Spanish dance. This was the first time a full range of dance had been presented at the Pillow, a practice which would become a Pillow tradition. Shawn again leased the property in 1941, this time to Alicia Markova and Anton Dolin, who presented a stellar list of artists in the barn studio including the young Ballet Theatre with such dancers as Lucia Chase, Nora Kaye, and Anthony Tudor, who spent his free time in a nearby barn creating his masterpiece, *Pillar of Fire*.

A group of local supporters banded together in the fall of 1941 to formally incorporate Jacob's Pillow Dance Festival, buying the property from Shawn and then installing him as director. A new theater was built adjacent to the barn studio, the 530-seat Ted Shawn Theatre (later enlarged to 618 seats), still in use today. Meanwhile, the newly expanded school became known as the University of the Dance, with a faculty that included Bronislava Nijinska and Joseph Pilates. A hallmark of Pillow performances for the next 35 years was the three-part program mixing ballet stars, modern companies, and "ethnic" groups performing in every imaginable style. Among the mixed programs were Alicia Alonso and Erik Bruhn, grouped with the Merce Cunningham Company and the Spanish dancer La Mariquita; a choreographer's workshop program featuring new works (including Robert Joffrey's first major ballet); and a combination of Melissa Hayden and Michael Maule, a rare East Coast appearance by the Lester Horton Dance Theater (with a young Alvin Ailey and Carmen de Lavallade), and La Meri in dances of India, Burma, Java, and Japan.

Beginning in the 1950s, Jacob's Pillow became known as a major importer of international dance attractions, offering U.S. audiences their first look at Balasaraswati, the National Ballet of Canada, the Royal Danish Ballet, Les Grands Ballets Canadiens and the Nederlands Dans Theater. The San Francisco Ballet made its East Coast debut at the Pillow, and Shawn was also actively involved in the regional ballet movement, promoting it by offering the first national exposure to companies from Miami, Atlanta, Washington and Boston.

Shawn's failing health in the 1960s and shifting currents in the dance world inevitably diminished the Pillow's preeminence. After Shawn's death in 1972, the Pillow's very existence was in peril, until a series of one-year directors (John Christian, Walter Terry, and Charles Reinhart) was followed with a solid five-year tenure by Norman Walker, proving that the Pillow could continue without its founder.

Liz Thompson's decade-long directorship in the 1980s reclaimed worldwide attention with an ambitious combination of artistic residencies, commissions, collaborations, and new initiatives. Thompson began a program of structural refurbishment and expansion which was continued by her successor, Sam Miller: a new 180-seat Studio/Theatre, an outdoor performing space, an expanded stage and entrance for the Ted Shawn Theatre, a visitors' center, renovated housing and other improvements. Miller, who directed the festival from 1990 to 1994, also spearheaded a number of alliances with other institutions such as the Massachusetts Museum of Contemporary Art and winter programs with various sponsors in Philadelphia. This expansionist phase, while crucial to the Pillow's physical health, took a toll on the organization's financial stability. At its lowest point in early 1995, the festival was in debt totaling more than $5,000,000 and there was a serious possibility that bankruptcy would be declared.

The 1995 crisis was the last of a long series of financial difficulties that had plagued the festival since its inception. Under Sali Ann Kriegsman's leadership from 1995 through 1997, the Pillow's entire accumulated debt was eliminated and its future was secured.

Kriegsman developed a long-range plan for the institution which organizes its ongoing mission into four interrelated program areas: presentation, creative development, education, and preservation. In late 1997, Ella Baff was named executive director.

The Pillow's summer seasons, lasting from late June to late August each year, continue to comprise the widest possible range of dance disciplines and artists along with student workshops, professional conferences, humanities programs, and a host of other activities. More information on Jacob's Pillow and its programs may be found on its Website: www.jacobspillow.org.

—Norton Owen

JAMES, Bill

American-born dancer, choreographer, and artistic director

Born: William Henry James, 25 November 1951 in Cleveland, Ohio. **Education:** Attended University of North Dakota, Grand Forks, North Dakota, Fine Arts Major, 1969-70; University of Portland, Portland, Oregon, Fine Arts Major/Pre-Architecture, 1970-71; studied modern dance and Wigman technique with Frances Allis; studied ballet with Larry Long at the Ruth Page Foundation and with Ed Parrish, Chicago; attended Ballet Horizons Summer Course (Victoria, British Columbia), the Royal Winnipeg Ballet Professional Program (Winnipeg, Manitoba), Banff School of Fine Arts (Banff, Alberta), attended classes with Sandra Neels, Merce Cunningham, Risa Steinberg, Carla Maxwell, José Limón, and Maggie Black, New York; trained in piano and French horn; studied voice with John Devers, New York, and Pauline Vaillancourt, Montreal. **Career:** Dancer, Le Groupe de la Place Royale, Montreal and Ottawa (Ontario), 1975-85; first independent choreography, 1976; artistic director, Dancemakers, Toronto, 1988-90; artistic director-producer, opening and closing events, Singapore Festival of Arts, 1990; *In Red Night,* First Night Celebrations, Toronto, 1991; *The 365 Day Garden,* Toronto, 1993-94; founder (with composer Chiyoko Szlavnics), Art in Open Spaces, Toronto, 1995; director, developmental choreographic lab, National Ballet of Canada, Toronto, 1996 to present; founder, Atlas Moves Watching Productions, Toronto, 1997; teacher, York University (Toronto); Canterbury School for the Arts (Ottawa, Ontario), Université du Québec à Montréal, Ministry of Community Development, Singapore; National Ballet of Canada's Creating Dances in the Schools Program; editor, *The Creative Process—Dance,* CD-ROM, produced by Le Groupe de la Place Royal and Animatics Multimedia, 1995. **Awards:** Funding grants from the Canada Council, Ontario Arts Council, Toronto Arts Council, Laidlaw Foundation, and Japan-Canada Fund Award.

Roles (original cast roles with Le Groupe de la Place Royale unless otherwise noted)

1975   *A Thin Dance for Three Thieves* (Peter Boneham), Montreal
        Les Bessons (Jean-Pierre Perreault), Montreal
        13 Choreographies (collective), Montreal
1976   *A Studebaker for Jimmy* (Boneham), Montreal
        Les Nouveaux Espaces (Boneham and Perreault), Montreal

1977   *Love Songs* (Boneham), Montreal
        Parallèle (Perreault and Sandra Neels), Montreal
        Malarn (Perreault), Ottawa, Ontario
1978   *What Happened* (Boneham), Ottawa
        Signs (Perreault), Ottawa
        Runaway (Michael Montanaro), Ottawa
        Dilos (Boneham), Ottawa
1979   *Dernière Paille* (Perreault), Ottawa
1980   *Short Distance Dance, Vacation on Venus* (Suzanne McCarrey), Ottawa
        Shooter Shute (Tassy Teekman), Ottawa
        Solo (Perreault), Ottawa
        Permanent Wave (Boneham), Ottawa
        Collector of Cold Weather (Boneham), Ottawa
1981   *Calliope* (Perreault), Ottawa
1982   *Sprung Wooden Answer Period with a Latin American Beat* (Michael Montanaro), Ottawa
        Call at All (Tassy Teekman), Ottawa
        But I Love You (Daniel Léveillé),Compagnie Daniel Léveillé, Montreal
1983   *Faustus* (Boneham), Ottawa
1985   *The Living Room* (Boneham), Ottawa
        Looking from Inside Out (Tassy Teekman), Ottawa

Works

1976   *Sietes Fleches,* Galerie Vehicule, Montreal
1977   *Interventions,* Ottawa
1978   *Postcard* (mus. Claude Vivier) solo, Le Groupe de la Place Royale, Ottawa
1979   *Trio* (mus. Bill James), Le Groupe de la Place Royale, Ottawa
1980   *Prophecy* w/Richard Purdy (text Peter Handke), Le Groupe de la Place Royale, Ottawa
1981   *Zeno* (mus. Janet Henshaw-Danielson), Le Groupe de la Place Royale, Ottawa
1983   *Cables to the Ace* (mus. John Cage, text Thomas Merton), Le Groupe de la Place Royale, Ottawa
1984   *Egypt* w/Tassy Teekman and Janet Oxley (mus. Matthew Fleming), York University, Toronto
        Mutual Aid (mus. Fleming) duet, Le Groupe de la Place Royale, Ottawa
1985   *crete beat* (mus. Johnny B.), S.A.W. Gallery, Ottawa
        Monica Unanswered (mus. Fleming), Le Groupe de la Place Royale, Ottawa
        Atlas Moves Watching (mus. Fleming), Inde' 85 Festival, Toronto
1986   *Nuit Rouge* (mus. Pierre Tanguay), O Vertigo, Festival d'Été, Quebec City
        Amorosa (mus. Fleming), Danse Partout, Quebec City
        Geography (mus. Fleming), Toronto
1988   *Cable* (mus. Roch Tremblay), Le Musée de la Civilisation, Hull, Quebec
        Creuser jusqu'en Chine (mus. Fleming) Université de Québec à Montréal
1989   *Predators of Light* (mus. Rodney Sharman), Dancemakers, Toronto
1990   *In the Trees* (mus. Michael J. Baker), Dancemakers, Toronto
        The Curse of the Witch Queen (mus. Bruce Robertson), Singapore Festival, Singapore

The Floating Forest w/Meenakshy Baskar and Hansel Aung (mus. Iskandar Ismail), The Singapore Fringe Festival, Singapore

1991   *Ice and Fire* (mus. Fleming), Le Groupe de la Place Royale, Ottawa

In Red Night w/Peter Chin, Toronto

1992   *D'Helice* (mus. Moebius & Rodelius), Danse Partout, Le Musée du Québec, Quebec City, Quebec

Big Pictures (mus. Michael J. Baker), Arraymusic Ensemble, Canada Dance Festival, Ottawa

Seven Mountains (mus. Ron Allen), Toronto

1993   *Deluge* (mus. Robert W. Stevenson), Toronto

Water trio, Le Groupe de la Place Royale, Ottawa

1994   *Flux* (mus. Robert W. Stevenson), Toronto

The Nomad Project trio, Arcosanti, Arizona

Lines (mus. Richard Sacks), Toronto

1995   *Inferno* (mus. Chiyoko Szlavnics), Toronto

1996   *Wind* (mus. Luc Marcel), Buddies in Bad Times Theatre, Toronto

1997   *Dances on a Plane* (mus. Kevin Volans), Ottawa School of Dance, Ottawa

Publications

On JAMES: articles—

Bush, Catherine, "*Red Night* Will Lead First Night a Fiery Dance," *eye* (Toronto), 12 December 1991.

Citron, Paula, "Dancemakers to Change Direction with Arrival of New Artistic Director," *Toronto Star,* 18 March 1988.

Cochrane, Lisa, "The Spirit of the Garden," *stepTEXT* (Toronto), fall 1973.

Gunter, Kirsten, "Bill James Creates Atlas of Our Times," *Metropolis,* 9 November 1989.

Hunt, Nigel, "Bill James: Playing with Space or the Intimacy of Extremes," *Canadian Theatre Review,* Winter 1990.

Jung, Daryl, "Bill James Stimulated by Environment," *NOW* (Toronto), 2 June 1994.

Kelly, Deirdre, "*Inferno* Borne of Myth and Dance," *Toronto Globe and Mail,* 25 July 1995.

Sasitharan, T., "Drums and Dance on Fort Canning," *Straits Times* (Singapore), 17 January 1990.

Smith, Kathleen, "Dancemakers: A View from the Treetop," *Toronto Sunday Sun,* 15 April 1980.

Films and Videotapes

Revolution Resolution, University of North Dakota, Grand Forks, 1970.

Flux, directed by Nick De Pencier, Pipe Dream Communications, 1995.

*   *   *

In Canada, Bill James reigns supreme as the choreographer of site-specific works. A dropout architectural student, James switched his interest from designing buildings to creating environments for dance that also convey a political or social subtext. Beginning in 1993 he headed a collective of choreographers, visual artists, and musicians in *The 365 Day Garden,* a series of performances celebrating the changing seasons in a downtown Toronto vacant lot.

The following year, James co-founded *Art in Open Spaces* for which teams of choreographers and composers produced original site-specific works at public sculptures (1995) and public fountains (1997). For James, these events are important because dance is placed into everyday life where it becomes populist, accessible art. During extensive travels from 1975 to 1995, James observed various cultural traditions, rituals, and mythologies which have informed his visionary works, particularly the Asian belief in art as a community event.

The roots of James' fascination with created environments can be traced back to a student assignment at the University of North Dakota, a Super-8 film installation entitled *Revolution Resolution* (1970). Amid a forest of Coca-Cola cans hanging on wires, two films were shown simultaneously, one of formal gardens, the second, of scenes of protest. "The piece was partly political, and partly abstract," says James. "I was justifying the belief that you can still view the world aesthetically while horrible things are going on around you. Life is a hard reality, but it doesn't have to be without beauty." James switched to a pre-architecture course at the University of Portland in Oregon, and took dance classes at neighbouring Reed College because he had always been fascinated by the structure of choreography. He became so dance-crazed that he dropped out of college and moved to Chicago, where he studied ballet as a scholarship student at the Ruth Page Foundation as well as modern dance with Wigman-protégé Frances Allis.

Because James was a school dropout, and therefore eligible for the draft in the midst of an escalating Vietnam War, his family immigrated to Canada in 1972, settling in Saskatchewan. James continued his dance training in Vancouver followed by two years in the Royal Winnipeg Ballet Professional Program. With the realization he would never be a ballet dancer because he started too late, James decided to return to architecture. On the way to the Pratt Institute in New York in 1975, he made a side trip to visit friends in Montreal and found his calling. He saw a performance of Le Groupe de la Place Royale, and says James, "It was a Boneham 'event,' modeled after Cunningham, where all kinds of ideas are gathered together in one big experiment. I auditioned the next day and stayed 10 years." James was entranced by the creative exploration of artistic directors Peter Boneham and Jean-Pierre Perreault who believed both in the formal tenets of dance as well as in breaking the rules. Because every company member had to "create," James began to choreograph. His first piece, *Sietes Fleches* (1976), was a series of Native American rituals constructed around an installation of sticks and rocks. Later pieces worked with a mix of live dancers and video cameras. Le Groupe instilled in James a postmodernist ethic—that anything, no matter how pedestrian, could be included in dance; that dance did not adhere to one technique; and that playing with ideas was an evolutionary theory. "I don't have a specific choreographic language," James has said, "I have ideas. Each piece becomes a new world. I don't want Bill Jamesisms. I'm influenced by performance art where you use your body as necessary, and not from a dancer's training."

James left Le Groupe in 1985 when he was no longer able to dance. His startling first piece as an independent choreographer would make his name. Created for Toronto's Inde Festival, *Atlas Moves Watching* (1985), a work about class structure and urban decay, was set in an inner city empty storefront, with the audience inside looking out. Dances took place both inside the store and out on the street where spontaneous interaction between the cast and passersby became part of the show because James likes the "juxtaposition of extremes." The text was by Thomas Merton who has been a big influence on James. In fact, James has created four works inspired by the writings of the American philosopher monk. Encouraged by the success of *Atlas Moves Watching,* James made Toronto his home base and embarked on a pan-world career as a site- specific choreographer.

When working in theatres, James has either stripped the audience area of all traditional trappings or created new walls to transform the space. In *Creuser jusqu'en Chine* (1988), he built a divider down the middle of the audience, and spectators chose the performance they would see by their decision as to which side of the divider to sit on. James also experiments in manipulating his audiences with a desire to make them less passive. In *Geography* (1986), spectators went on a walking tour of 100 years of history, a moving exposé of colonialism that was spaced out over the huge floor space of an abandoned plant. In *Flux* (1994), audience members were given folding camp stools and allowed to choose their own vantage point in an empty World War I munitions dump, thus becoming part of the installation itself. The choreographer is also an painter and sculptor, and while earlier works have used his own designs, latterly he has turned to architects and visual artists to help create environments, beginning with *Predators of Light* (1989), a work about obsession that used variously shaped movable sculptures designed by Dereck Revington to create the set.

Lit from within, the sculptures filled the audience-in-the-round seating with an eerie, four-dimensional light. Another important device for James is the use of original scores, with the musicians and their instruments becoming fixtures in the design. An ongoing project is the exploration of the four elements. Mary Lou Lobsinger's installation for *Flux* (1994) involved a huge wading pool, enormous vertical slabs of ice, and rain running down plastic sheets. *Serpent Lines* (1994) paid homage to the earth with a mountain range of sand created by Dereck Revington and John McMinn. *Inferno* (1995) used Cylla von Tiedemann's visuals of fire along with atmospheric lighting and spectacular pyrotechnics. Still to come is *Wind* which is in development. In all James' works, the dancers are the instruments of his political or social protest, whether the fat cat city slickers pouring out of a limousine in *Atlas Moves Watching,* the caged specimens in *Geography*'s human zoo, or the 1960s protesters in *Seven Mountains* (1992).

James briefly became artistic director of Dancemakers (1988-90) to find a stable base for his work, but the structured organization of a company was antithetical to his method of creation. He prefers experimentation, such as found in the National Ballet of Canada's choreographic lab, a program headed by James since 1996 which helps dancers to become creators. He also is in the forefront of transferring dance to the medium of CD-ROM. "I represent contemporary expression," says James, "I want the audience to be confronted with dance in new ways."

—Paula Citron

JAMIESON, Karen

Canadian dancer, choreographer, educator, and company director

Born: 1947. **Education:** University of British Columbia, Canada, B.A. in anthropology; studied dance in New York City. **Career:** Member, Alwin Nikolais Dance Company, c. 1970; teacher of dance,

Simon Fraser University, Burnaby, British Columbia, mid-1970s; co-founder, dancer/choreographer, Terminal City Dance Company, Vancouver, 1976-82; founder/director, dancer/choreographer, Karen Jamieson Dance Company, Vancouver, 1983-present. **Awards:** Chalmers Dance Award, 1980.

Works (premiered in Vancouver, unless otherwise noted)

1969	*Medium,* created at Intermedia workshop at Simon Fraser University, Burnaby, British Columbia
1977	*Tales from the Terminal City*
1978	*Snakes and Ladders,* Winnipeg, Manitoba
1980	*Cantus*
1981	*Coming Out of Chaos* (mus. Hassen), solo
1982	*Red Madonna*
1983	*Sisyphus* (mus. MacIntyre)
1985	*Road Show*
	Hoofers (mus. Ferreras)
1986	*Altamira* (mus. Ruddell and Ferreras)
1987	*Rainforest* (mus. Ruddell and Ferreras)
1988	*Vessel* (solo, mus. Ferreras)
	Bateau (mus. Bach)
1989	*Danceland* (mus. Corness)
	Vessel (new version with design by Itter)
	Drive (mus. Elliott), Winnipeg, Manitoba
	The Man Within (mus. Corness), Winnipeg, Manitoba
1990	*Mudwoman* (solo)
	Rock of Ages (mus. Corness)
	Passage (mus. Corness), Ottawa, Ontario
1991	*MixK'aax* (mus. Corness)
	Gawa Gyani (mus. Corness)
1992	*Faust* (opera with Tamahnous Theatre, mus. Corness)
1993	*Tales of Descent* (mus. Corness)
1994	*Counterplay* (mus. Corness)
1995	*Redemption* (mus. Corness)
	Mask (solo, mus. Corness)
	Snake (mus. Corness)
	Homeland (mus. Hurst)
1996	*Shattered Space* (mus. Hurst)
1997	*Stone Soup* (mus. Hurst and Kendall)

Publications

On JAMIESON: book—

Wyman, Max, *Dance Canada,* Toronto, 1989.

On JAMIESON: articles—

Lacey, Liam, "Dancing in the Dark," *Globe and Mail,* 6 June 1991.
Rupp, Shannon, "Making a Bridge with Stones," *Globe and Mail,* 10 May 1997.

*   *   *

Karen Jamieson and her work are uniquely Canadian. She has been dancing, teaching, directing, and creating in the Vancouver area since 1969, focusing her energies on her dance company since 1983. There is no other artist in Canada who fuses as many dance styles and cultures as Jamieson.

Like many, Jamieson began her serious dance training in New York City. She studied both ballet and modern dance intensively for a four-year period during the early 1970s, and during that time she performed with the Alwin Nikolais Dance Company. When she returned to Canada, performing became secondary to her choreography. Jamieson (who at that time was known by her married name, Rimmer) first worked as a director and choreographer with Savannah Walling at the Terminal City Dance Company in Vancouver in 1976. Jamieson and Walling created the company to explore the boundaries of dance, music, and theatre, something both had begun during workshops at Simon Fraser University. The title of the company indicated their reverence for Vancouver and its isolated position relative to the rest of Canada. Jamieson, through her choreography, often enlightened the rest of the country about issues important to British Columbia, the terminus of the Trans-Canadian railroad, and home to many bands of Native groups. Terminal City Dance Company closed its doors in 1983 because the founders wanted to explore new initiatives. The Karen Jamieson Dance Company opened its doors that same year.

Throughout her choreographic works, Jamieson maintained her link with anthropology, the discipline she studied at university, and incorporated her love of dance with the study of cultures and peoples. Her small yet potent company quickly gained international recognition performing her dance, which has often been described as primal and shamanistic. The troupe performed at various festivals including Dancefest in Baltimore, Festival of Canadian Modern Dance in Winnipeg, Canadian Dance Festival in Ottawa, Le Festival International de Nouvelle Danse in Montreal, and the Holland Festival in Amsterdam. Her company and choreography is recognized as uniquely Canadian and representative of the West Coast. Native culture definitely influenced and impacted Jamieson's choreography, although, as she noted in an interview with the *Globe and Mail* in June of 1991: "A lot has been written about my work and native culture, but the actual truth was the only piece I ever did that was influenced by native culture was *Rainforest* (1988). I've been fascinated by native culture since childhood, but it's only been a direct influence on [*Gawa Gyani*] and *Rainforest.*"

Gawa Gyani, Jamieson's monumental cross-cultural piece based on the Gitksan creation myth, debuted at the Museum of Anthropology at her alma mater, the University of British Columbia, in 1991. The piece explores the relationship of Gitskan creation legends to the creation story Jamieson was most familiar with from the Old Testament. She worked closely with Gitksan artists and expanded her company to include Native dancers alongside professional modern dancers. The fact that the company toured the work throughout British Columbia, in villages where the story originated, certainly proved that the Gitksan did not feel the choreography patronized their culture. *Gawa Gyani* was not the first or the last of Jamieson's choreography that presented the ritual of dance.

Another piece of choreography that gained a lot of media attention for Jamieson was her site-specific work of 1990 entitled *Passage.* This piece captured the imagination of her audience, especially the critics, because it electrified such a voluminous and solemn space. Her dancers performed in the halls of Canada's National Gallery in Ottawa (Ontario) alongside an exhibit of the British Columbia painter, Emily Carr. Carr, like Jamieson, was fascinated with Native themes, many of her canvases included the overwhelming image of totem poles set in the wilderness. Jamieson's unique interpretation and residency at the National Gallery brought attention to the often neglected works of Carr and, correspondingly, to Jamieson herself.

The foundation of many of Jamieson's productions are collaborations, between cultures and artists. Since 1988 she has collaborated with composer Jeff Corness. His creations cannot be classified into one genre; like Jamieson's dance, he adapted his musical style to the project at hand. This creative relationship has been a pivotal catalyst for Jamieson's work. Most recently their cooperative efforts were halted when both the choreographer and composer were involved in a serious car accident where Corness sustained head injuries from which he is still recovering. Since that time the choreographer has revisited her association with composer Peter Hurst. Jamieson's connection to her co-creators remains an essential element of her dance.

In May of 1997 Jamieson summarized her feelings on the purpose of dance to the *Globe and Mail*: "I have this conviction that the primary function of dance is to connect us to that spirit of place. Dancers have their feet on the ground, so they have the potential to connect with earth and embody the spirit." Jamieson's remarkable choreography embodied both the spirit and soul of Vancouver and Canada.

—Katherine Cornell

JAMISON, Judith

American dancer, choreographer, and company director

Born: 10 May 1944 in Philadelphia. **Education:** Attended Fisk University, Nashville. Studied dance at Marion Cuyjet's Judimar School of Dance; with Anthony Tudor, Maria Swoboda; Philadelphia Dance Academy with James Jamieson, Nadia Chilkovsky, Yuri Gottschalk; later studied with Patricia Wilde, Dudley Williams, and Paul Sarasardo in New York City. **Career:** Principal dancer, Alvin Ailey American Dance Theatre, New York, 1965-80; guest artist with Swedish Royal Ballet, 1972, American Ballet Theatre, 1976, Vienna State Opera, 1977, Béjart's Ballet of the 20th Century, 1979; has also appeared on television including *Dance in America* (PBS); as dancer for television film, *Memories and Visions,* 1973; *Ailey Celebrates Ellington,* CBS, 1974; *The Cosby Show,* NBC, 1986; *Alvin Ailey Televison Special,* NBC, 1988; *The Dancemaker: Judith Jamison,* PBS, 1988; founder of Jamison Project, 1988; artistic director, Alvin Ailey American Dance Theatre, since 1989. **Awards:** *Dance Magazine* Award, 1972; Candace Award, 1990; Frontrunner Award, 1992; Women of the Arts Award, 1992; honorary doctorate degrees from numerous universities; board member, National Endowment for the Arts, 1972-76.

Roles

1965	Mary Seaton, *The Four Marys* (de Mille), American Ballet Theatre, New York
	Congo Tango Palace (Beatty), Alvin Ailey American Dance Theatre (AAADT), national tour
	"Drag" trio in *Toccata* (Beatty), AAADT, national tour
	Rooms (Sokolow), AAADT, national tour
	Revelations (Ailey), AAADT, national tour
	Blues Suite (Ailey), AAADT, national tour
	Road of Phoebe Snow (Beatty), AAADT, national tour
1966	Pasiphae in *Ariadne* (Ailey), Harkness Ballet, New York
	Josephine in *Yemanja* (Ailey), Harkness Ballet, New York

Judith Jamison in John Butler's *Blood Memories*, 1976. Photograph © Johan Elbers.

1967   The mother in *Knoxville: Summer of 1915* (Ailey), AAADT, African and European tours

       Erzulie in *The Prodigal Prince* (Holder), AAADT, African and European tours

       Black Belt (Beatty), Ailey American Dance Theater, African and European tours

1969   *Reflections in D* (Ailey), AAADT, New York

       The Sun in *Icarus* (Hoving), AAADT

       Bo Masekela in *Masekela Language* (Ailey), AAADT, New London, Connecticut

1970   *Dance for Six* (Trisler), AAADT, Russian tour

       Poeme (Koner), Alvin Ailey American Theater, Russian tour

1971   Solo, *Cry* (Ailey), AAADT, New York

       Choral Dances (Ailey), AAADT, New York

       Mary Lou's Mass (Ailey), AAADT, New York

1972   *Lark Ascending* (Ailey), AAADT, New York

       Carmina Burana (Butler), AAADT, New York

       Eve in *According to Eve* (Butler), AAADT, New York

1973   *Hidden Rites* (Ailey), AAADT, New York

       Missa Brevis (Limón), AAADT

1974   Solo, *Spirituals* (Collins), AAADT, New York

1975   Bessie Smith in *The Mooch* (Ailey), AAADT, New York

1976   Female lead with Mikhail Baryshnikov in *Pas de "Duke"* (Ailey), AAADT and American Ballet Theater

       Liberian Suite (Horton), AAADT, New York

       Solo, *Facets* (Butler), AAADT, New York

       Fecundity in *Blood Memories* (McKayle) AAADT, New York

       Caravan (Falco), AAADT, New York

1977   Potophar's wife in *Josephlegende* (Neumeier), Vienna State Opera House, Hamburg, and Munich

1978   Marie Laveau in *Passage* (Ailey), AAADT, New York

1979   *Le Spectre de la Rose* (Béjart), Maurice Béjart's Ballet of the 20th Century, Brussels, Paris, and New York

       The madam in *District Storyville* (McKayle), AAADT, New York

1980   Solo, *Inside* (Dove), AAADT, New York

       Pas de deux with Alexander Godunov, *Spell* (Ailey) AAADT, New York

1981   *Sophisticated Ladies,* Broadway musical, New York

Works

1984   *Divining* (mus. Dinizulu and Ellison), AAADT, New York

       Just Call Me Dance (mus. Hartfield), Maurice Béjart's Ballet of the 20th Century, Brussels

1986   *Time Out* (mus. Hartfield), Mary Day's Washington Ballet

       Time In (mus. various contemporary), Ballet Nuevo Mundo de Caracas

1987   *Into the Life* (mus. various contemporary), Jennifer Muller/ The Works, New York

1988   *Tease* (mus. various contemporary), Alvin Ailey Repertory, New York

1989   *Forgotten Time* (mus. "Le Mystère des Voix Bulgares"), Jamison Project, New York

1991   *Rift* (mus. Hendryx), AAADT

1993   *Hymn* (mus. Ruggieri), AAADT

1995   *Riverside* (mus. Dinizulu), Alvin Ailey American Dance Theater, New York

1996   *Sweet Release* (mus. Wynton Marsalis), AAADT, New York

Publications

By JAMISON: articles—

Interview with John Gruen, *Sound of Dance*, November 1975.

"Alvin Ailey," *Alvin Ailey: An American Visionary,* edited by Muriel Topaz, New York, 1996.

By JAMISON: books—

Dancing Spirit: An Autobiography, New York, 1993.

On JAMISON: articles—

Gladstone, Valerie, "Judith Jamison Leaps Forward," *Ms. Magazine*, November/December 1991.

Hunter-Gault, Charlayne, "An African Goddess from Philly," *New York Times,* 19 November 1972.

Jowitt, Deborah, "Call Me a Dancer," *New York Times Magazine,* 5 December 1976.

Reiter, Susan, "Ailey Women!!," *Dance Magazine,* November 1993.

Simpson, Janice C., "Carrying On the Legacy," *Time Magazine,* 15 July 1991.

On JAMISON: books—

Haskins, James, *Black Dance in America,* New York, 1990.

Hodgson, Victor, *Quintet: Five American Dance Companies,* New York, 1976.

Long, Richard, *The Black Tradition in American Dance,* New York, 1989.

Maynard, Olga, *Judith Jamison: Aspects of a Dance,* New York, 1982.

*   *   *

Judith Jamison's accomplishments and contributions as a dancer have made her one of the most well-known performing artists of the 20th century. She danced with the Alvin Ailey American Dance Theatre for 15 years and during that time she emerged as an international dance star. Her exquisite dancing and elegant persona transformed the stage into a landscape filled with magic, power, and spirit. Her career has encompassed the modern dance and ballet worlds, musical theater, choreography, and the founding of her own dance company. In 1989, after the death of Alvin Ailey, Jamison was selected as the artistic director of the AAADT and her charge was to lead the world's most widely seen dance company into its fourth decade and the 21st century.

Jamison's journey to the helm of one of America's premiere dance companies began in Philadelphia, Pennsylvania, a vibrant center of African-American culture for much of this century. Jamison's mother was an arts enthusiast and her father was an accomplished musician. With their encouragement, Jamison began studying dance at the age of six. According to Marion Cuyjet, her first ballet teacher, Jamison displayed natural dance ability from the start of her studies and was viewed as a prodigy. Although Jamison's primary training was in ballet, she also studied tap, Afro-Caribbean, jazz, modern and acrobatics. Her teachers at Cuyjet's

Judimar School of Dance included Delores Brown Abelson, John Jones, John Hines, Ann Bernadino Hughes, and Ernest Parham.

Jamison's formal debut was in 1959, at the age of 15, when she danced the role Myrtha in *Giselle*. After graduating from high school, Jamison briefly entertained the idea of a career in psychology and entered Fisk University. However, she left the school after her freshman year to enroll at the Philadelphia Dance Academy. In 1964 Agnes de Mille discovered Jamison in a master class at the school and invited her to come to New York to perform in American Ballet Theatre's (ABT) production of the *Four Marys*.

When her work with ABT was over, Jamison stayed in New York, hoping to find work in a professional dance company. She worked at the World's Fair temporarily and then auditioned for choreographer Donald McKayle for a Harry Belafonte television special. She was not chosen during the audition, but this experience was a turning point in her quest for a dance career. Alvin Ailey, a friend and colleague of McKayle's, watched the audition and was quite impressed with Jamison. Three days later Ailey called Jamison and invited her to join his dance company. According to Jamison, her performance at the audition was dreadful, but Ailey apparently saw something extraordinary in her that was waiting to be nourished. He was also quite taken with her statuesque beauty.

Jamison danced with the Ailey Ailey American Dance Theater from 1965 to 1980. She came into prominence as a principal dancer during the dance boom of the 1970s. As a performer she was known for her expressive yet subtle movement delivery that was grounded in complete emotional, intellectual, and physical commitment. Ailey created many roles for Jamison; the most notable was *Cry* (dedicated to all black women, especially our mothers). Her majestic and powerful performance of the work moved dance critic Clive Barnes to describe her as an "African queen." *Cry* was one of the landmark modern dance works of the 20th century and established Jamison as an international star.

Jamison was uneasy with being referred to as a star. She often stated: "Don't call me a star. Call me a dancer." She believed her talent was a God-given gift and that it was her responsibility to use it. Jamison felt strongly that her colleagues should also be recognized for their proficiency.

During Jamison's tenure with AAADT, she and Ailey grew to be close friends and she maintained an abiding faith in his mission to entertain and to educate. She appreciated the opportunity to perform Ailey works in addition to a diverse repertory which included choreography by Donald McKayle, Talley Beatty, Janet Collins, John Butler, Anna Sokolow, Louis Falco, and Ulysses Dove. Her travels with AAADT took her throughout the United States and abroad and she appeared as a guest artist with ballet companies worldwide.

In 1980 Jamison left AAADT and assumed a starring role in the Broadway musical *Sophisticated Ladies*. In the mid-1980s she began to develop her skills as a teacher and choreographer. In 1984 the Ailey company premiered her first dance work, *Divining*, and four years later in 1988 she formed her own dance company, the Jamison Project. Her choreography, like Ailey's, is rooted in an African-American aesthetic, and uses a dance language that speaks to the universality of the human spirit.

Shortly before his death in 1989, Alvin Ailey asked Jamison to take over his duties as artistic director of AAADT, and she accepted without hesitation. She inherited a company with tremendous financial debt but with help from a new board of directors and a progressive fiscal plan, stability was established. Although challenged with the demands of an artistic director, she continued to

coach dancers and choreograph. In 1997 her dream of taking the company to South Africa became a reality. Under her leadership, the company and affiliate programs have flourished with the assistance of Masazumi Chaya (associate artistic director), Sylvia Waters (director, Alvin Ailey Repertory Ensemble) and Denise Jefferson (director, Alvin Ailey American Dance Center). Jamison has also created a national outreach dance camp program for children ages 11 to 14. Summer camps have been established in Kansas City, Baltimore, and New York City.

Under Jamison's direction, AAADT's repertory continues to present dance classics such as Ailey's *Revelations*, in addition to the work of contemporary choreographers such as Garth Fagan, Donald Byrd, Brenda Way, Billy Wilson, Shapiro and Smith, Lar Lubovitch, and Jawole Willa Jo Zollar. Jamison is adamant about honoring Ailey's vision of creating a company dedicated to the preservation and enrichment of the American modern dance heritage and the uniqueness of black cultural expression.

—Melanye White Dixon

JAPAN

When modern dance germinated in Japan in the 1910s, a variety of time-honored dances ranging from academic, theatrical, and folkloric to popular were thriving. Modern dance, however, was not what evolved from or against this heritage—it was considered one of the Occidental dances, called *yoh-bu*, introduced from overseas after the seclusion policy (enforced in 1639) came to end in 1854. The term "yoh" meaning Occidental, was more or less synonymous with "modern" in those days.

The institution that cradled pioneers such as Baku Ishii (1886-1962), Masao Takata (1895-1929) and Seiko Takata (1895-1977), was Teikoku Gekijo [Imperial Theater], which opened in Tokyo in 1911. The theater had an opera department, whose resident artists were trained in classical ballet, Occidental music and Japanese dancing. Giovanni Vittorio Rosi, the former mime-dancer at Teatro alla Scala Ballet in Milan and dancer-choreographer at the Alhambra Theatre in London, taught ballet, and staged both operas and ballets for the Imperial Theater. Rosi is considered the first ballet instructor to teach in Japan. Contrary to its name, Imperial Theater was a private venture initiated by enlightened businessmen, who intended to build the Japanese equivalent of European opera houses. The Occidental programs, however, did not earn popular acclaim, and the opera department closed in 1916.

Although the Imperial Theater's venture to nurture opera and ballet did not come to fruition, and its members were only given sporadic exposure to yoh-bu, these dancers and choreographers formed the nucleus of what would later become modern dance in Japan. Many well-known dancers of the 1910s and 1920s performed at the Imperial, including Boris Romanov and Yelena Smirnova, Anna Pavlova, the Denishawn company, and Ruth Page. For Japan, the Imperial Theater offered the first legitimate opportunities for dancers to learn "modern" technique as well as traditional Japanese dancing.

Baku Ishii, one of the resident artists who had resigned before the closure of the Imperial Theater's opera division, premiered a series of works dubbed *buyo shi* [dance poem] in a 1916 concert, co-organized with composer Kosaku Yamada (1886-1965) who had been inspired by Isadora Duncan and Émile Jaques-Dalcroze during his music study in Europe in the early 1910s. This performance marked the first modern dance concert in Japan. Many of the other former Imperial member artists took part in another program, called the "Asakusa Opera," a hodgepodge of song, dance, and farce presented in popular theaters in Asakusa, a downtown suburb of Tokyo. Such programs enjoyed immense popularity until Tokyo was hit by a devastating earthquake 1923. Just before the Asakusa Opera performances came to end, Baku Ishii, and Masao and Seiko Takata traveled to the United States and Europe for a few years. They gained firsthand knowledge of the trends of overseas modern dance, and visited the schools of Mary Wigman, Denishawn and others, attending concerts, and presenting their own programs as well. Visiting foreign countries was yet a rarity in the 1920s, and the overseas experiences of these dancers proved invaluable in terms of modern dance exposure, and gave them an experience few could imagine in this day and time. Upon their return to Japan, Ishii and Takatas opened private *kenkyujo* [studios] in Tokyo, and became major exponents of modern dance in Japan.

Those who followed the course of Ishii and Takatas in the 1920s and 1930s, becoming influential figures in Japanese modern dance include Toshi Komori (1887-1951), Michio Ito (1893-1961), Takaya Eguchi (1900-77), Kenji Hinoki (1908-83), Masatoshi Shigyo (1908-83), and Nobutoshi Tsuda (1910-84). They formulated the Japanese variant of modern dance, heavily influenced by German pioneers Wigman and Dalcroze. Subsequently, many of their disciples have taken over the styles molded by these pioneer figures—yet with an emphasis to today's inclination toward narrative work or depicting certain themes through nonballetic movements.

Unlike the Imperial Theater and Asakusa Opera companies, these modern dance pioneers did not have corporate sponsorship nor immense popularity. The season of each studio was short and infrequent, yet quite a number of studios evolved and were supported primarily by the tuition of students as well as the dancer/choreographers themselves. It has become an accepted practice in Japan that performers bear financial responsibility, paying certain fees for their stage appearances and are often responsible for buying a certain number of tickets for performances. Such a financial exploitation of students/dancers is consistent with those of Japan's other traditional performing arts. Another common characteristic is a hierarchal structure going back to the original pioneers, with each faction (such as the Ishii-faction or the Takata-faction) developing seniority based upon one's position within the faction. Like other traditional performing arts, disciples mostly study and perform within one's own faction—ironic since modern dance evolved through the modernization of Japan's cultural arts—only to adopt conventions enhanced by traditional arts. Unfortunately, such a mentality still exists today.

Private dance studios number in the hundreds today and have formed a solid base for Japan's modern dance community. They are the most common vehicle to train dancers, for institutions equivalent to legitimate public dance schools or conservatories haven't developed to date. Elementary modern dance is sometimes incorporated in general school education as part of physical education, but not in arts education.

During the 1930s and the first half of the 1940s, modern dance under the military government was aesthetically curtailed as were virtually all aspects of the arts. Once World War II broke out, dancing was in demand only for "comfort" or "entertainment" performances to whip up war sentiment. Freedom of expression was restored when World War II terminated in 1945, and modern dance re-emerged out of ruins of war. Within a few years, major studios began joint concerts and by the 1950s individual studios flourished again.

The postwar period proceeded under the strong influence of American modern dance. The first American company to reach Japan was Martha Graham's in 1955, followed by many others including Alvin Ailey, José Limón, Merce Cunningham, Paul Taylor, and Alwin Nikolais. Postmodern dancers were seen, too, although on an ad hoc basis. Ignited by the American dancers, many Japanese dancers went to study in New York, most frequently at Graham's school. Kaoru Ishii, Kei Takei, and Bonjin Atsugi studied at the Juilliard School in the 1960s, and others also joined major companies: Akiko Kanda, Takako Asakawa, and Yuriko Kimura danced with Graham; Miki Orihara and Rika Okamoto are currently with the Graham troupe; and Masazumi Chaya and late Michihiko Oka are former Ailey dancers.

While many Japanese dancers and choreographers leaned towards American-styled modern dance, Tatsumi Hijikata (1928-86), who trained with disciples of Takaya Eguchi and Seiko Takata, in the 1960s originated an avant-garde dance that would later become known "butoh." Butoh dancers tended to be estranged in Japan; however, when their appearances at European and American dance festivals from the 1970s onward earned critical acclaim, their domestic recognition improved.

During the 1980s, new stimulus came from European choreographers such as Maguy Marin, Pina Bausch, William Forsythe, and Jiri Kylian whose companies debuted in Japan one after another. Inspired by these European exponents, the younger generations of Japanese choreographers have formulated more diverse styles. The rise of an independent younger generation has been facilitated by the gradual increase in subsidies and corporate sponsorships available to dancers in the late 1980s.

Over the years, modern dance enhanced by the Wigman-inspired pioneers and their followers has come to be considered an antiquated dance form. The younger generation's style emerged as an artistic objection to such conventionality as well as the older generation's hierarchal factions. Today the term "contemporary dance" is frequently used to identify the style of the younger generation, while "modern dance" signifies the archaic. The first of the newer generation to emerge was Saburo Teshigawara, whose unorthodox integration of dancing and scenography has been highly acclaimed on the international dance festival circuit. Also worth noting are Dumb Type, a Kyoto-based group founded in 1984 by then-art college students, including the late Teiji Furuhash; Sakiko Oshima and Naoko Shirakawa of H Art Chaos; Kota Yamazaki; Chie Ito, Yoko Koyama, and Mimiko Yamashita of Strange Kinoko Company; Akiko Kitamura; Kenshi Noumi; Kazuyuki Futami, and Shinji Nakamura.

In addition, another notable occurrence in Japanese dance is the 1997 inauguration of SPAC Dance, a resident company of the Shizuoka Performing Arts Center theatre complex in Shizuoka Prefecture. This marks the first dance company fully subsidized by a state or municipal government. For modern dance, a risky private venture since its inception, to be made a public venture for the first time is a major step in the evolution of this art form.

Publications (in Japanese)

Kusaka, Shiro, *Gendai Buyo ga Mietekuru* [Comprehending Modern Dance], Tokyo, 1997.

Muramatsu, Michiya, *Watashi no Buyo Shi; Janarisuto no Kaiso, Jo-kan* [Personal Dance History, Memoir of a Journalist, No. 1]. Tokyo, 1985.

———, *Watashi no Buyo Shi; Janarisuto no Kaiso, Chu-kan* [Personal Dance History, Memoir of a Journalist, No. 2]. Tokyo, 1992.

———, *Watashi no Buyo Shi; Janarisuto no Kaiso, Ge-kan* [Personal Dance History, Memoir of a Journalist, No. 3]. Tokyo, 1992.

Miura, Masashi, editor, "Ima Dansu no Jidai" ["Now, the Age of Dance"], *Dance Magazine*, August 1994 (special issue).

—Sako Ueno

JARVIS, Judy

Canadian dancer, educator, choreographer and company director

Born: Ottawa, Ontario, 6 May 1942. **Education:** Havergal College, Toronto; University of Toronto 1962-65. Studied dance with Wigman-trained Bianca Rogge; studied at Mary Wigman School, Berlin, 1965-67, also Laban Centre, London; studied yoga, ballet, contemporary dance in New York 1971-73; attended McArthur College of Education, Kingston, Ontario, 1983. **Career:** Choreographer beginning in 1965; founded her own company, 1970; later companies toured Canada, to New York's Riverside Dance Festival (1977), Edinburgh Fringe Festival (1980); taught at numerous schools and colleges throughout Canada. **Awards:** Canada Council study grant, 1964; Jean A. Chalmers Award in Choreography, 1974; Judy Jarvis Foundation started 1987. **Died:** 1 November 1986, in Toronto.

Works

1965	*The Way of the Cross* (text, Henri Ghéon, mus. Tchaikovsky, Beethoven), St. Michael's School, Toronto
1966	*Prophet* (solo; unaccompanied), Berlin
	Ophelia/Water (solo; mus. Erik Satie), Berlin
1967	*And Death Shall Have No Dominion* (solo; text, Dylan Thomas), Berlin
	Prayer for Peace (solo; mus. Toshiro Mayuzumi), Berlin
	Bird/Flight (solo; mus. Henry Jacobs), Berlin
	If I Were a Carpenter (solo; mus. Joan Baez), Berlin
	Trance (solo; mus. Ethiopian traditional), Kingston, Ontario
1968	*Viet Rock* (mus. Megan Terry), Queen's University Drama Department, Kingston, Ontario
	Woman Who Looks Back (solo; unaccompanied), Kingston, Ontario
	Missa Luba (mus. African Mass), Kingston, Ontario
1969	*Marriage Song* (solo, mus. Miriam Makeba), Kingston, Ontario
	Allegro (solo; mus. Vivaldi), Kingston, Ontario
	Blake Piece (solo; text, William Blake), Kingston, Ontario
	Reflections (solo), Kingston
1970	*Love Cycle* (duet; mus. Gregorian chant), Toronto
	Breath (dancers vocalizing),Toronto
	Tribal (mus. percussion, Efrem, flute, Heineman), Toronto
	Offering, Toronto
	Ceremony (mus. Bach), Toronto
	Genesis (mus. Penderecki), Toronto
	Castle (mus. Tony Scott, Shinichi Yuize, Hozan Yamamato; text, Denise Levertov), Toronto

1971	*Circus* (duet; vocalization), Toronto
	Changes (duet; vocalization), Toronto
	Circle Game (voices of students), University of Waterloo
1972	*Earth Move* (duet; voices of students), Toronto
	Space Game (duet; squash court sounds), Toronto
	And So On (duet; vocalization), Toronto
	Clouds (duet; dancers vocalizing), Toronto
	Street (solo; Integral Yoga Chant), Toronto
1973	*Rain Flow* (solo; rainfall), Toronto
	Sun (solo; Tibetan bells), Toronto
	Tapestries (trio; mus. New Group), Toronto
1974	*The Red Hat* (solo), Toronto
	Totem, Toronto
	Nora, Blacklack and B. (text by Jarvis and dancers)
	In Transit (mus. Pierre Ouellette), Toronto
	Just Before and In Between (trio; mus. Janko Jezovsek, sound Frank Canino), Toronto
	People. . . People
	Song of the Wine (solo; mus. Boisville)
	The Watcher (duet; mus. Cimarosa)
	Three Women (trio; mus. Steve Miller Band)
	Chaos (solo; mus. Albinoni, Jesovsek, voice of Mary Wigman)
	I Sold You & You Sold Me (duet; mus. Jesovsek)
	Interlude (mus. Jesovsek)
	Dares to Go First (mus. Jesovsek)
	Crowd (voices)
1975	*Anatomies* (duet; text, organ donor's guide, read by Frank Canino), Toronto
	Metalways (solo; mus. Pierre Ouellette), Toronto
	Marat (solo), Toronto
	Exit (solo), Toronto
1976	*In the Long Ago Land* (trio; text, Dylan Thomas), Toronto
	Apartments, Toronto
1977	*Bella* (duet, created with Danny Grossman; mus. Puccini), Winnipeg, Manitoba
	Fiasko (trio; mus. collage), Toronto
	The River (mus. Alan Booth), Toronto
1977	*Wall* (solo; natural sound), Toronto
1978	*Anchorman* (solo), Toronto
	Dark Animal (duet; vocalization), Toronto
	The Hairy Edge (duet; dancers' text), Toronto
	The Little Potentate, Toronto
	Chester (dancers'text), Toronto
	Dream Snaps (dancers'text), Toronto
	Peer Gynt (mus. Greig), Toronto
1979	*Shell* (trio; text by dancers), Toronto
	Nuntius (mus. 13th century/disco collage), Toronto
	Wings (text), Toronto
1980	*Cosmos* (mus. Vangelis), Toronto
1982	*Catherine the Great* (solo; historic text and dancer's script), Toronto
1986	*Remembrance Day* (mus. soundtrack from *Hair*), Madonna High School, Toronto

Publications

By JARVIS: articles—

"Artist in the Schools," *Spill*, 1978.

On JARVIS: articles—

Kimmerle, Marliesse, "Judy Jarvis—A Remembrance," *Ontario CAPHER Dance News,* January 1987.
Manley, Mary Elizabeth, "Profile of Judy Jarvis," *Dance in Canada,* 1975.

On JARVIS: books—

Anderson, Carol, *Judy Jarvis, Dance Artist: A Portrait,* Toronto, 1993.

*   *   *

Judith Anne Jarvis was a maverick on the Canadian dance scene. A proponent of Expressionist modern dance at a formative time in the emergent dance scene of Toronto, she was a strong presence in Canadian dance from the late 1960s through the early 1980s.

As a child, Jarvis was encouraged to take up athletic activity to counter an asthmatic condition. She figure-skated through her childhood and later took up badminton, winning, among many other distinctions, the 1961 Canadian Junior Open championship. She spent her unhappy, fiercely competitive, sporting girlhood at Havergal College, an exclusive Toronto girls' school. While she was a student of modern languages and history at the University of Toronto, Jarvis came to dance. She took classes with Bianca Rogge, one of Toronto's earliest modern dance teachers, herself a former student at the Mary Wigman School. It was evident from the beginning that Jarvis had a vocation to create—Rogge's Sunday evening studio concerts featured some of Jarvis' early choreographic efforts, mostly solos.

Estranged from her family by her determination to dance, Jarvis followed an intuitive compulsion, traveling to Berlin in 1965 to study at the Mary Wigman School. She became one of Wigman's last protégés. Cold, poor and isolated in Cold War Berlin, Jarvis was determined to reconfigure herself physically and psychically, to transfigure herself from athlete to dancer. During her two years in Europe Jarvis also traveled, taking courses at the Laban Centre in Paris, studying mime in Paris and painting in Switzerland. While studying in Europe, she developed a number of the tiny, jewel-like solos which were the hallmark of her solo repertoire. *Bird* was a particularly significant dance, succinct, poignant, the movement at once austere and fastidiously detailed.

On her return to Canada Jarvis took a job at Queens University in Kingston, Ontario, beginning a long phase of her career. It was through her tireless teaching that she inspired many young students from 1969 through the mid-1970s in the burgeoning dance programs at the University of Waterloo, University of Windsor, University of Toronto, St. Frances Xavier University, as well as at University of Montreal, Hockley Valley School of Fine Arts, University of Alberta, National Arts Centre, and at Queens. This was one of Jarvis' great gifts. She had a power to inspire through her teaching. Her principles were simple. She based movement in the rhythms of breath. Students were guided toward finding their own expression through improvisation. Her classes were charged with a genuine sense of discovery, a fresh connection of body and mind, an exciting engagement for aspiring dancers, a special experience of meshing spirit and physical expression.

Concurrent with her peripatetic teaching, Jarvis was pursuing her solo career, building a reputation for her dances, perfect miniatures, and for her impassioned, charismatic performance. Jarvis returned to Berlin to present a solo concert at the Schaubühne

Theatre in 1968. Her concert, presented in the shadow of the death of the great Expressionist Dore Hoyer, earned her attention in the German press. Some declared her a successor to Hoyer. Her themes were many, from universal to literary to girlish, often archetypal and mythic. She chose recorded music from eclectic sources: concrete music, Penderecki, Vivaldi, koto music, Miriam Makeba. Jarvis made elegant use of space, occasional masks and props, dancing in costumes of her own invention. In *Prophet* she was wrapped mummy-like in a long silver shimmer of velvet, the fabric a gift from Mary Wigman, seen as a shining arc in one of the photographs of Wigman's *The Language of Dance.* For *Bird* Jarvis wore black tights, a long-sleeved white leotard, white gloves, and a birdlike hood she fashioned from plum-coloured velvet.

Jarvis was ambitious, dreaming of a flourishing dance troupe. As her creative career unfolded she had a series of companies; many young dancers spent impressionable times performing her work. Jarvis lived an ongoing struggle to balance the claims of creativity, her solo aspirations and her companies' needs. A first company ended when a fire burned down her Toronto studio in March 1971. She then spent two years in New York City, studying ballet, yoga and contemporary dance technique, performing with the Cunningham repertory performance group in 1972. She was associated with the Dance Theatre Workshop from 1970 to 1972.

During Jarvis's long teaching association with the University of Waterloo, students Gina Lori Riley and Pam Grundy became the core of her company. Committed to her increasingly spare vision of dance, they were part of the creation of *Three Women,* one of Jarvis' most memorable works, remarkable for its simplicity, the acuity of the characters' movement and Jarvis' characteristic black humour. *Just Before and In Between* was notable for its minimal, hallucinogenic images of death and dying.

In 1974 Jarvis was the first modern dance choreographer to be awarded the prestigious Jean A. Chalmers Award in Choreography. She traveled to New York's Riverside Dance Festival in 1977 and to the Edinburgh Fringe Festival in 1980. Deborah Jowitt called her "brave and original," and remarked on her extraordinary powers of observation, her sensitivity to how people move. Jarvis toured her companies widely in Canada, giving concert performances and workshops, and performing in many schools.

Occasionally she undertook creative collaboration. In one such she created *Bella* with Danny Grossman, a whimsically lyric trio for a man and a woman and a beautiful painted wooden horse, inspired by the paintings of Marc Chagall. The work remains active in Grossman's repertoire. Another fruitful collaboration was with Larry McCullough, resulting in *Clouds* and *Changes.*

Always an outsider, pursuing a lonely and often visionary path, Jarvis worked in theatrical dance before it was widely practiced. Through the 1970s her movement work grew leaner and more difficult to categorize. Meanwhile, the dance scene in Toronto was blossoming, bursting with the lush physicality of Toronto Dance Theatre, the athletic comedy and tragedy of Danny Grossman's work, the growth of Robert Desrosiers' madcap physical fantasy and Dancemakers' wide-ranging explorations. Though Jarvis' work was always refined, deeply considered, honest and compassionate, realized through improvisation and meticulous polishing, her work and company fell out of favour with the cultural agencies. In 1981 the Canada Council, which had supported her activites since 1974, stopped funding her activites. In 1982 Jarvis created a solo for herself, *Catherine the Great,* a hybrid of dance, theatre and history, but it was not well received. The Ontario Arts Council stopped funding the company in 1983.

Jarvis went back to school, gaining her teacher's certificate in the Artist in the Community Program at McArthur College of Education in Kingston, Ontario. Long an advocate of dance in the educational system, she was a consultant when curriculum was being developed for introducing dance into the high school system of Ontario. Jarvis became a teacher of Dramatic Arts at Madonna High School, Toronto, where she directed several school productions. She had a show of drawings and paintings at Toronto's Mitchell Gallery in 1983. She died in a fire in 1986.

Jarvis is remembered in the repertory of the Danny Grossman Dance Company and Gina Lori Riley Dance Enterprises which have remounted *Three Women, Just Before and In Between, Prophet, Clouds,* and other works. Jarvis' legacy lives as well through people who worked with her. Frau Til Thiele, whom Jarvis assisted in emigrating to Canada, was a teacher of mime and *tanz gymnastik* in Mary Wigman's school for three decades. Through her teaching, Frau Thiele's influence became in turn part of the fabric of Canadian dance. Gina Lori Riley went on to become a modern dance pioneer in Windsor, Ontario, founding her own company, creating work based in strong physical imagery, touring and doing educational work in schools. Pamela Grundy is a featured performer and associate director with the Danny Grossman Dance Company. In 1987 the Judy Jarvis Dance Foundation was established to promote and protect the memory of her work. At the members' discretion the Judy Jarvis Pop-Up Award is awarded intermittently to artists who are irrepressibly creative and unquenchably devoted to dance, as was Jarvis herself.

—Carol Anderson

JAZZART DANCE THEATRE

South African dance company

Pioneering South African dance company based in Cape Town with origins in the Jazzart jazz studio founded by Sonje Mayo in 1975; directed by Sue Parker, 1978-82 who established the Sue Parker Jazzart Contemporary Dance Company; directed by Val Steyn, 1982-86 when she formed Pace Dance Company; as Jazzart Dance Theater, became Jazzart dance Theatre under the direction of Alfred Hinkel and has functioned as a collective taking a political stance in pursuit of democratic dance; backed by its record of innovative dance in education work, Jazzart became the modern dance company of the Cape Performing Arts Board (dance company of the Cape Performing Arts Board), 1992.

*   *   *

From the 1980s into the early 1990s Jazzart Dance Theater became synonymous with cutting-edge politcally provocative dance. Writer Njabulo Ndebele, at the time vice rector of the University of the Western Cape, stated: "The future of our culture in our country lies virtually in the ability to take full advantage of the untapped talents of the individual South African as well as the wealth of artistic traditions available to us. I was able to recognise in [Jazzart] a committed attempt to take full advantage of these traditions. . . . You have been able to do through dance, what our politicians have thus far found elusive. You have affirmed the power of art." This observation was made in 1992 two years prior to South Africa's first democratic elections at a time when bombings and atrocities occurred nationwide on a daily basis.

Jazzart, South Africa's longest surviving modern dance company started out as a jazz studio founded by Sonje Mayo in Cape Town in 1975 after her return from studying dance in Britain, Canada, and New York. Flouting the race laws, dancers took class and performed together. When Mayo moved up to Johannesburg, where she started her Mayo Modern Dance Ensemble, Sue Parker ran the Jazzart Contemporary Dance Company from 1978 until 1982. Upon Parker's departure to London, Val Steyn directed the company until 1986 when Alfred Hinkel took over. Jazzart Dance Theatre then became a socio-political hot potato. Hinkel, Dawn Langdown, John Linden, Jay Pather, and the rest of the collective refused to perform in apartheid structures. They isolated themselves from the rest of South Africa's dancemakers and began creating a new technique and a vocabulary reflective of the rhythms, rituals, body shapes, and weight of South African dancers.

Jazzart publicly challenged Eurocentric training methods and aesthetics. These viewpoints created much acrimony but their practical training and vision were impossible to ignore. Jazzart's motto "Everyone can dance," anchored in Hinkel's pathways of natural movement technique began to make an impact. In addition Jazzart's technical approach was all-inclusive; while incorporating imported modern and postmodern ways of teaching and moving, the teachers and choreographers incorporated indigenous urban dance forms like gumboot dancing (a workers' dance) and regional variations of mapantsula (township jive) and Zulu indlamu (traditional dance). When text was used it embraced Xhosa, Zulu, Tamil and Afrikaans—the languages of the multicultural company. In its use of heritage, a political buzzword in democratic South Africa, Jazzart again proved to be a creative step ahead for it was one of the first South African companies to produce work which dealt with gender (women lifting men), sexuality, and race. Through their experimentation and dance-in-education programmes throughout the townships surrounding Cape Town and nationally, technique suffered. The hand-to-mouth existence, because the company refused to accept politically tainted government money, took its toll. Jazzart flummoxed everyone in 1992 when they announced they would become the state-funded Capab Performing Arts Board's modern dance company. As it turned out, the timing was perfect.

At Capab Hinkel was able to strengthen technique and the now-salaried company began to tour Africa. In March 1997 it represented the country at an African arts market in Abidjan, Ivory Coast, and then later in the year became the first South African dance company to perform in Morocco. Also in 1997, Hinkel received a special Standard Bank National Arts Festival award for his "vision, commitment and contribution" to South African dance. Another Jazzart award, was the 1990 AA Vita Award for choreography of the year for an untitled work (later named *Bolero*), which juxtaposed Ravel's score with gumboot and traditional African rhythms. It has become a signature work in the South African repertory with two distinctive versions performed by Jazzart and Pace Dance Company (which was renamed State Theatre Dance Company in October 1997). Jazzart also received a 1995 FNB Vita production of the year for its inventive postmodern *Medea* created in collaboration with Cape Town's Magnet Theatre.

In the late 1990s this core collective of dancers, teachers, and choreographers left Cape Town spreading their influence to other provinces of the country. In a sense the Jazzart pioneers went home: director/choreographer/teacher/performer Jay Pather returned to KwaZulu Natal and became artistic director of the Playhouse Dance Company's multicultural Siwela Sonke Dance Theater, which was formally launched in April 1997. Siwela Sonke (Zulu for "crossing over to a new place altogether") grew out of a community training project piloted by Hinkel who also directed the short-lived, independent Phenduka Dance Company (1990) which preceded Siwela Sonke. As a performer and choreographer Pather helped pave the way for gay rights, later enshrined in South Africa's new constitution, in collaborative theatre works like *The Homosexuals* (out in Africa) for the Hearts and Eyes Theatre Collective (1992) and *The Stories I Could Tell. . .,* four solos devised and performed dealing with the diverse black gay experience. This dance theatre work, directed by Peter Hayes, was performed at the 1995 ArtRage festival in Perth, Australia, in 1995 and at the Out of Afrika Festival in Munich, Germany, in 1997. As a political activist Pather taught the African National Congress' Amandla Cultural Group while it was in political exile in Angola in 1990. In 1995 he directed and choreographed *Ahimsa-Ubuntu* which traced, through dance and text by sociologist Fatima Meer, the history of South Africa's disenfranchised people dating from the activism of Mahatma Gandi and the rise of the African National Congress. This multimedia history lesson, using classical ballet, kathak, bharata natyam, Zulu dance, gumboots, and fusions of these forms, toured India and Sri Lanka (another first for cross-cultural South African dance) in November 1996, performed by the fledgling Siwela Sonke and dancers from the Playhouse Dance Company.

Dawn Langdown went back to the semi-desert countryside of the Northern Cape, to her copper mining hometown town of O'Kiep where she originally met Hinkel in 1978 and danced in his Namakwalandse Dans Geselskap. Still retaining her connections with Hinkel and Jazzart, Langdown started a dance development project in the country's largest and most neglected province. In between setting up this project in 1997, Langdown taught a street dance workshop in Florida for Urban Bush Women and Jawole Willa Jo Zollar, whom she met while attending the Bates Dance Festival in 1996.

This Afrikaans-speaking artist (classified "coloured" by apartheid law) brought her language, when it was still branded the language of the oppressor, onto the stage in works like the politically confrontational *Ekanievatie* (1991), the feminist *Unclenching the Fist* (1994) and *Medea* (1994), her solo show *Soe Leop Ons ... Nou Nog* (1996) and *The Sun, the Moon and the Knife* (1995) exploring San (bushman) history. Among the Jazzart alumni who have made a considerable mark on South African dance are Debbie Goodman and Jacqui Job, who formed Jagged Dance; dancer/teacher/choreographer Susan Abraham; teacher/dancer/ administrator Jennifer van Papendorp; Siwela Sonke teacher/dancer Simpiwe Magazi; dancer/choreographer Geli Schubert; dance critic Roslyn Sulcas; and drama and dance lecturer Clare Dembovsky. Dembrovsky's M.A. thesis *Jazzart Dance Theatre: Dance, Identity, and Empowerment in a Changing South Africa* was awarded a distinction at the University of Surrey in 1997.

—Adrienne Sichel

JENKINS, Margaret

American dancer and choreographer

Born: c. 1944 in San Francisco, California. **Education:** Trained at Welland Lathrop; attended Juilliard, studying with Martha Graham and José Limón; attended UCLA, dancing with Al Huang. **Career:**

Taught at the Merce Cunningham Studio and helped restage works for European companies, 1964-70; dancer, with companies of Gus Solomons, Jr., James Cunningham, Twyla Tharp, and Viola Farber; began choreographing, 1969; founder, Margaret Jenkins Dance Company, 1973. **Awards:** Isadora Duncan Award for *Age of Unrest* (1991).

Roles

1965	*Cede Blue Lake* (cr) (Twyla Tharp)
	Unprocessed (cr) (Tharp)
1966	*Re-Moves* (cr) (Tharp), Judson Memorial Church
1968	*Notebook* (Viola Farber), Judson Memorial Church
	Excerpt (Farber)
1969	*Quota* (Farber)
	Passage (Farber)

Works

1969	*Leeway*
1970	*Running with the Land*
1976	*Equal Time*
	Lapinsky
	Story
1977	*About the Space in Between*
	Video Songs
1978	*Copy*
	Interferences II for Seven
	Into Three
	Red, Yellow, Blue
1979	*Segue* (mus. Aquis-Sinerco), Summer Festival Palace of Fine Arts
1980	*Invisible Frames* (mus. Rova Saxaphone Quartet)
	Straight Words (mus. Gans), 15th St. Studio
	Versions By Turns (words/sound Palmer), 15th St. Studio
	Duets (mus. Braxton, Cage, Palmer and others), 15th St. Studio, for *Images of Modern Dance*, KQED-TV
1981	*Harp* (mus. Terry and McGhee), Zellerbach Playhouse
1982	*Cortland Set* (word/sound Palmer), 15th St. Studio
	What Ever Happened to Tina Croll (mus. Glass, Harrison) originally for the opening of New Performance Gallery, Herbst Theater, San Francisco
	In The Round II, New Performance Gallery
1984	*First Figure* (mus. Deane), Stanford
	Max's Dream (originally performed live w/Kronos Quartet, commissioned score by Jon Geist and San Francisco Community Chorus), Zellerbach, Playhouse, Berkeley
1985	*Inside Outside/Stages of Light* (mus. Fontana), Herbst Theater
	Pedal Steal (mus. Allen) for Brooklyn Academy of Music (BAM)
1986	*Home Part I* (mus. Amache), solo, Theater Artaud
	Home Part II (mus. Dresher), Theater Artaud
1987	*Shelf Life* (mus. Dresher, text/narration Eckert), Theater Artaud
	Georgia Stone (mus. Ono), Zellerbach Hall
1988	*Rollback* (mus. Allen) for KIMO Theater, Albuquerque
	Shorebirds (mus./text Eckert), Zellerbach Playhouse
	Steps Midway (mus. Eckert), solo, Zellerbach Playhouse

1989	*And So They* (text Eckert), duet, Zellerbach Playhouse
1989	*Light Fall* (mus. Cloidt), Theater Artaud
	Miss Jacobi Weeps (mus. Frasconi), Theater Artaud
1990	*Woman Window Square* (mus. and text Eckert), Krannert Center for the Performing Arts, Urbana, Illinois
1991	*Age of Unrest* (mus. Dresher), Laney College, Oakland
	Sightings w/Ellie Klopp for Oakland Ballet (mus. Sculthorpe), Paramount Theater, Oakland
1992	*Strange Attractors* (mus. Volans, *white man sleeps*), Columbia College, Chicago
	Wasn't It This (mus./text Eckert), solo, Jacob's Pillow
1993	*The Gates (Far Away Near)* w/Ellie Klopp (mus. Dresher), Columbia College, Chicago
	A Site-Specific Work For the Opening Festival of the Center for the Arts at Yerba Buena Gardens w/Klopp and Remy Charlip (mus. Ostertag)
1995	*Liquid Interior* w/Klopp (mus. Bimstein) for Repertory Dance Theater, Salt Lake City
1997	*Fault* w/Klopp (mus. Lang and Curran) for Center for Theater Arts, University of California, Zellerbach Playhouse, Berkeley

Publications

On JENKINS: books—

Croce, Arlene, *Going to the Dance*, New York, 1982.

Cunningham, Merce, and Jacqueline Lesschaeve, *The Dancer and the Dance*, New York and London, 1980, 1985.

Richard Kostelanetz, editor, *Merce Cunningham: Dancing in Space and Time: Essays 1944-1992,* Pennington, New Jersey, 1992.

Robertson, Allen, and Donald Hutera, *The Dance Handbook*, Boston, 1988.

On JENKINS: articles—

David, Martin A., "Margaret Jenkins Plays It on the Edge," *Los Angeles Times*, 6 March 1988.

Kaufman, Sarah, "Jenkins Looks Back, Forges Ahead," *Washington Post*, 5 May 1995.

Kriegsman, Alan M., "Jenkins: Dance Disjunct," *Washington Post*, 19 September 1986.

Roca, Octavio, "Jenkins' *Fault* Shakes Things Up," *San Francisco Chronicle*, 27 October 1996.

Ross, Janice, "The End of the Beginning: the Margaret Jenkins Company at Twenty," *Dance Magazine*, June 1994.

Smith, Sid, "Jenkins, Eckert put Distinctly Personal Touches on Works," *Chicago Tribune*, 24 March 1991.

Stowe, Dorothy, "Great Things Are Done When Men and Mountains Meet," *Dance Magazine*, March 1997.

Tucker, Marilyn, "It's Home Sweet Home for Jenkins Troupe New Seven-Week Baywide Tour," *San Francisco Chronicle*, 3 May 1992.

———, "Jenkins Dancers Back Home," *San Francisco Chronicle*, 8 June 1990.

———, "Jenkins' *Sightings* A Sight to Behold in Oakland," *San Francisco Chronicle*, 18 November 1991.

———, "Jenkins' Evolving Dances," *San Francisco Chronicle*, 17 March 1989.

———, "Many Paths in New Jenkins Dance," *San Francisco Chronicle*, 11 May 1992.

———, "Time Improves Some of Jenkins' Dances," *San Francisco Chronicle*, 10 March 1989.

Films and Videotapes

Duets, for *Images of Modern Dance,* KQED-TV, 1980.

*   *   *

Margaret Jenkins is considered the leading modern dancer and choreographer on the West Coast. Her work is influenced by years with Merce Cunningham, but she has remained focused on introducing new innovations into her dances. Many of her works have been premiered by her San Francisco-based troupe, the Margaret Jenkins Dance Company.

Jenkins began her training in San Francisco before moving to New York to study at Juilliard for a year, where her instructors included Martha Graham, José Limón, and Antony Tudor. She returned to California to study at the University of California in Los Angeles, where she first saw a performance of Cunningham's troupe. The following year, without finishing her degree, she went back to New York, becoming a member of Twyla Tharp's original company. She performed as one of the principals in Tharp's 1966 *Re-Moves*, which premiered at Judson Memorial Church. Jenkins also danced with Viola Farber's company, where she starred in Farber's 1968 *Notebook* opposite Dan Wagoner, and also performed with the companies of Gus Solomons, Jr., and James Cunningham.

Jenkins' greatest influence, it appeared, was Merce Cunningham. She studied with him in New York, and taught for years at the Merce Cunningham Studio where she was responsible for the first staging of Cunningham pieces for the ballet, and led the company on a trip to Stockholm to work with the Cullberg Ballet. She also recorded *Summerspace*, one of Cunningham's well-known works, in Labanotation, and taught it to the Boston Ballet and the Theatre du Silence in New York. Jenkins left the Company in 1970, but her ties remain; in fact, many of her students ultimately join the Cunningham troupe.

After moving back to San Francisco in 1970, she began teaching "Cunningham-plus" technique to full classes; the students were attracted by her established reputation as a good teacher. In 1973 she formed the Margaret Jenkins Dance Company, which is the oldest modern dance group in San Francisco. The company gave its first performance in 1974. (Jenkins' personal San Francisco debut, *Running with the Land*, premiered in 1970.)

Since her return to San Francisco, she has created ballets for companies ranging from Sweden's Cullberg Ballet to the Oakland Ballet, as well as modern dance pieces, many for the Margaret Jenkins Dance Company. Among her many longtime collaborators have been composers Paul Dresher and Alvin Curran, poet Michael Palmer, performance artist Rinde Eckert, stage director Carey Perloff, set and lighting designer Alex Nichols, and costume designer Sandra Woodall. The importance of collaboration is, in fact, one of the driving forces behind all of Jenkins' work. Her dances are often created with the full participation of her dancers, who are given due credit. Her choreographic method, unlike Cunningham's, is a democratic one; she believes that the creative process should be a social activity. She often develops dances by creating movement challenges for her dancers, then selecting results she likes. This collaborative process has led at least two dozen of her dancers—numbering more than 75 over the first 20 years of her company—to become renowned choreographers in their own right. They include

Margaret Jenkins Dance Company: *The Gates*. **Photograph © Johan Elbers.**

Bill Young, Joe Goode, and Lisa Fox, as well as her longtime troupe member and associate director, Ellie Klopp.

Whereas Cunningham was interested in pure movement, Jenkins is interested in abstracting emotional, political, and social themes, as well as in movement. For example, *Fault* (1996) contains earthquake imagery but is really about political and social disintegration. *Woman Window Square* (1990) was inspired by a tour of the Soviet Union that year. *All The Rage* (1994), performed to a Bob Ostertag score written for the Kronos Quartet, is accompanied by a tape collage and is about discrimination against gays and lesbians. *The Gates (Far Away Near),* a 90-minute work created in 1993, was intended as an artistic response to political attacks on the National Endowment for the Arts (NEA).

Many of Jenkins' choreographic works evoke western Americana themes. For example, *Liquid Interior* (1994), set to a score by Utah musician Phillip Birnstein, is about the short lives of desert creatures. The 35-minute *Pedal Steal* (1989) combines 1950s retro and western themes; it was commissioned for the 1985 New Wave Festival at the Brooklyn Academy of Music (BAM). *Rollback* (1988) is another example of a western-themed work. Some of Jenkins' pieces can be categorized more as performance art rather than modern dance, particularly those on which she collaborated with Eckert. These include *And So They Say* and *Shorebirds Atlantic*, done to a spoken voiceover, both of which were created in 1991 with Eckert. Her own *Miss Jacobi Weeps* (1989) and *Steps Midway*,

a nude solo before a set of funhouse mirrors, also border on performance art.

Other significant Jenkins works include *Strange Attractors* (1992) to a score by Kevin Voland; *Age of Unrest* (1991) with music by the Paul Drescher ensemble, which won her an Isadora Duncan Award; and the Peter Sculthorpe-scored *Sightings* (1991), choreographed for the Oakland Ballet, which features 13 dancers and is about angels. No matter what their themes, all of Jenkins' works—she created 60 dances with her company in its first 20 years—are known for being intellectually challenging. The Margaret Jenkins Dance Company performed at the prestigious Lyon Festival in France in 1990, and has toured the Soviet Union, France, Belgium, and England, as well as venues around the U.S., particularly in the Bay Area. In the early 1990s, its busy performance schedule included 45 concerts a year.

In 1983, Jenkins partnered with dancer Brenda Way and her ODC/San Francisco group. The two companies jointly purchased the New Performance Gallery in San Francisco's Mission District, which served as an office-studio complex for both. Performance space there was limited, however, and the Margaret Jenkins Dance Company often performed at San Francisco's Theatre Artaud when in town. In early 1995, due to the financial strain of sustaining an on-going dance concern, Jenkins disbanded her full-time company and sold her interest in the New Performance Gallery building. Since then, her company has been composed of a small staff and a changing group of dancers, who are hired on a project-by-project rather than repertory basis.

Jenkins has been actively involved in dance-related concerns and in promoting the advancement of dance as a career. In 1981, she, along with other dance leaders, started the professional association Dance/USA. She has also served on the dance panel of the NEA. Although she maintains a clear connection to modern dance tradition, Jenkins is concerned with innovation in each new piece. Her works are created for athletic dancers, with an emphasis on strong lower bodies, legs and feet. Her dances focus on the entire ensemble; each dancer exhibits his or her own individual style but is part of the group rather than being a star.

—Karen Raugust

JEON Mi-sook
Korean dancer, choreographer, and educator

Born: 3 September 1958 in Soonchun, Korea. **Education:** Studied dance at Jinmyoung High School; B.A. and M.A. in dance, Ewha Women's University; studied at the London Contemporary of School of Dance on scholarship, 1990-91; attended Martha Graham School, and workshops at the American Dance Festival and Bates Dance Festival. **Career:** Dancer, TAM Modern Dance Company, 1981 to present; has taught at Seoul Arts High School since 1984; member, education curriculum committee of Dance in Education Ministry. **Awards:** Awarded Best Individual Performance for Claiming Your Own Identity, Dance Festival of Korea, 1987; numerous awards for production, choreography, and individual performances at other festivals; First Young Artists of Today Award, Ministry of Culture and Sports of Korea, 1993; Critics Award, Dance Critics Association of Korea, 1996.

Roles

1981	*The Pattern of Clouds* (Cho Eun-mi), Cho Eun-mi & TAM Dance Company, Seoul
	Word (Park In-sook), Korea Contemporary Dance Company, Seoul
	A Journey of the 13th Month (Kim Ki-in), Korea Contemporary Dance Company, Seoul
1982	*Four Moons* (Chun Hye-ri), TAM Dance Company, Seoul
	Ryu Kwan-soon (Yook Wan-soon), Yook Wan-soon Dance Company, Seoul
	Salpuri I (Lee Jung-hee), Korea Contemporary Dance Company, Hawaii
	The Pattern of the Bronze Pottery (Cho Eun-mi), TAM Dance Company, Seoul
1983	*Jesus Christ Superstar* (Yook Wan-soon), Yook Wan-soon Dance Company, Rome
	Panorama (Kim Hae-kyung), TAM Dance Company, Seoul
	Island (Ahn Sin-hee), TAM Dance Company, Seoul
1985	*Blue Papers Floating in the Air* (Kim Hae-young), TAM Dance Company, Seoul
	Sam-Si-Rang (total art, dir. Kim Dong-hoon), TAM Dance Company, Experimental Theatre, Seoul

	No Such Soul Hasn't Flaw (Cho Eun-mi), TAM Dance Company, Seoul
1986	*Face* (Cho Eun-mi), TAM Dance Company, Seoul
	Sonata (Cho Eun-mi), TAM Dance Company, Seoul
	The Envelope Containing Time (Cho Eun-mi), TAM Dance Company, Seoul
1987	*Silk Road* (Yook Wan-soon), Korea Contemporary Dance Company, Vancouver
1989	*Mesia* (Chun Hye-ri), TAM Dance Company, Seoul
	The Tinkle of a Bell (Kim Hae-kyung), TAM Dance Company, Seoul
1993	The Door of Sea (Kim Hae-kyung), TAM Dance Company, Seoul
1995	Conversation (Cho Eun-mi), TAM Dance Company, Seoul

Works

1982	*Creation of Your Own Gesture with Your Own Sound* (mus. various, arranged Joen Mi-sook), trio, Jeon Mi-sook, Jung Do-young and Park Kyung-ae, Space Theatre, Seoul
	Tranquil Sight (mus. various, arranged Joen Mi-sook), Jeon Mi-sook and Jung Do-young, Space Theatre, Seoul
	Dream without Sleep (mus. various, arranged Joen Mi-sook), solo, Munye Theatre, Seoul
1984	*Farewell* (mus. Michell Colombie), Jeon Mi-sook and Kim Ji-hyung, Munye Theatre, Seoul
1987	*Claiming Your Own Identity* (mus. Kim Hyun), Jeon Mi-sook and TAM Dance Company, Munye Theatre, Seoul
	Blossom of Tears (mus. Philip Glass), Seoul Arts High School Students, Ryu Kwan-soon Memorial Center, Seoul
1988	*Variation for Three Different Scents* (mus. Vivaldi), Seoul Arts High School Students, National Theatre of Korea, Seoul
1989	*De-ja Vu* (mus. Michael Portal), Munye Theatre, Seoul
	Deca Voice-Floating Song (mus. Park Il-kyu), Jeon Mi-sook and other dancers, Munye Theatre, Seoul
	Crystal Ball Like Amusement (mus. Albinoni), Seoul Arts High School Students, National Theatre of Korea, Seoul
1991	*A Vagabond* (mus. Ren Aubry), Jeon Mi-sook and TAM Dance Company, Munye Theatre, Seoul
	Wedding Tango (mus. Michael Nyman), Jeon Mi-sook and Park Yong-ok, Munye Theatre, Seoul
	A Brief Rest, Then a Long Voyage (mus. Enya), Seoul Arts High School Students, National Theatre of Korea, Seoul
1992	*A Station* (mus. Peter Gabriel), for Kang Kyung-mo and Kim Sung-whan, Munye Theatre, Seoul
	Juvenile March (mus. Gershwin) Seoul Arts High School Students, National Theatre of Korea, Seoul
1993	*Chinese Zodiac Sign-Year of Dog, 1958* (mus. Chang Young-kyu), Munye Theatre, Seoul
	Winter, Spring, Summer, Autumn (mus.Vivaldi), Seoul Arts High School Students, National Theatre of Korea, Seoul
1994	*Senseless* (mus. Chang Young-kyu), TAM Dance Company, Munye Theatre, Seoul
1995	*Soaking into Your Heaven* (mus. Philip Glass), Seoul Arts High School Students, National Theatre of Korea, Seoul
1996	*A Dog, Dream and a Chrysanthemum* (mus. Michael Nyman), TAM Dance Company, Munye Theatre, Seoul

An Oneiric Tale (mus. Chang Young-kyu), Seoul Arts High School Students, National Theatre of Korea, Seoul

1997 *Shangri-La* (mus. Les Dancseuses D'izu), Seoul Arts High School Students, National Theatre of Korea, Seoul

Butterfly...Rain (mus. Jean-Jacques Schmidely), Munye Theatre, Seoul

Publications

By JEON: articles—

"The Moonlight Which Is Still Ringing in My Ears," *CHOOM,* July 1983.

"What's the Problem with Our Dance Education?" *Magazine Auditorium,* 26 April 1986.

"Wedding Tango-Choreography Episode," *Korean Modern Dance,* 1992.

"Good-bye Yellow Road," *Korean Modern Dance,* 1992.

On JEON: articles—

Chang Kwang-ryul, "The Talk of the World Hidden in Jump Roping," *Magazine Auditorium,* April 1993.

Kim Kyoung-ae, "The Example That Abstract Dance Will Succeed," *Literature & Arts Review,* April 1989.

Kim Song-bae, "Letter to a Dancer-We Who Were Found Amidst Chaos," *CHOOM,* March 1989.

Kim Tae-won, "Fairy Tale-Like, Rural Power of the Imagination of Dance," *Magazine Auditorium,* March 1989.

————, "The Small Appearance of One Modern Dancer:Jeon Mi-sook's Dances," in *The Vision of Culture and Dance,* Seoul, 1991.

Moon Ae-ryung, "The World of Jeon Mi-sook's Works," *Monthly Essay,* June 1997.

Lee Jong-ho, "Jeon Mi-sook: Ironical Relation Between Disposition and Work," *SPACE,* January 1997.

* * *

Jeon Mi-sook, together with the Korea Contemporary Dance Company, has led the field from the beginning of Korea's short modern dance history. She has also worked as a dancer and choreographer for TAM Dance Company, another of the country's leading dance troupes.

In her dances of the 1980s, Jeon Mi-sook attempted to ascertain an inner self and a rapport with nature based on lyricism in such works as *Claiming Your Own Identity, Deca Voice-Floating Song,* and *Vega Bond.* At the end of the decade and into the early 1990s, however, she poured her efforts into fierce criticism of society. Often, her criticism went too far and was seen as subversive. In the dance *Deja Vu,* she criticized civilization by looking at environmental problems. In her production of *Wedding Tango,* the focus shifted, for the first time, from the artist's ego to the problems of family, society, and organized groups. This tendency is very apparent in her works *Chinese Zodiac Sign-Year of Dog, 1958* and *Dog, Dream, and Chrysanthemums.* In *Chinese Zodiac Sign-Year of Dog, 1958,* the year 1958 points not only to the year of the choreographer's birth, but serves as a collective portrayal of the generation born in 1950s who had to forgo their individual identities and natural desires for the sake of economic development—endlessly producing goods to meet the export drive. In the dance, Jeon Mi-sook performs a single, meaningless movement, caged in a doghouse while in the background men continuously and mechanically jump rope. These men symbolize the baseless collective domestication of people who must always be doing something to alleviate their anxiety and uneasiness. They forget or stop trying to find the real meaning of their existence, while they are tamed for the uses of society.

Her production *Dog, Dream, and Chrysanthemums* (1996) consists of three acts: "A lousy dog-like world," "Dreaming men in such a world," and finally "the ending of all through death." The final act occurs in the mists of a chaotic atmosphere and with outraged and dramatic movements. A woman wearing a huge Korean folk skirt with chrysanthemums (which symbolize death), comes out of the orchestra pit slowly, giggling insanely. The laughter seems to ridicule a humanity that has lost its self-consciousness and only dreams—thriving unconsciously and breathlessly. Kim Tae-won appropriately described it as "the most horrifying, grotesque, and sarcastic piece of work that Korea's theater art produced in 1996."

Jeon Mi-sook's dance seems to point to a world dominated by lunacy and coincidence. Her view of humanity's real nature is sardonic and ironic, and her world view nihilistic. This worldly view appeared as early as 1982 in *Tranquil Sight. Tranquil Sight,* or a "tranquil angle of view" implies the angle of comfort that death brings and which the choreographer suggests is the most comfortable angle that humanity can take. The concept of death often appears in her works, but death characterized by Jeon Mi-suk assimilates tranquillity, unlike the expressionistic approach to death expressed by her predecessor, the choreographer Lee Jung-hee.

Despite Jeon Mi-sook's particular dance style that values genuine dancing above all else, some critics have noted that her movements have an abundance of mimetic elements and hence have dramatic aspects. This may not come out of an intended dramatic expression but more an earnestness in dealing with her inner self, which in turn leads to spontaneous dramatic expressions. If one describes her works chronologically, they have evolved from pieces focused on individuals toward collective groups. Yet the fundamental orientation of her dances still comes out of the real existence of a single person. Looking over her works, the early lyricism and naturalism tended to fall short of idealism because of human limitations. Some try to categorize her tendency as ontological, but she is clearly existentialist.

If Korea's modern dancing actively began to develop with Yook Wan-soon, dancers like Kim Bok-hee, Kim Wha-suk, Lee Jung-hee, Choi Chung-ja, Nam Jeong-ho and others can be described as followers, though they worked to establish their own styles. Jeon Mi-sook has taken a more independent path than these predecessors. She has a unique, versatile methodology and art and has established herself as among the leading second-generation choreographers.

—Lee Jong-ho

JEYASINGH, Shobana

Indian-born British choreographer and company director

Born: 1952 in Madras; lived in India and Malaysia before settling in London. **Education:** University of Sussex, M.A. in Renaissance studies; initially trained as a Bharata Natyam dancer and trained in Britain as a soloist, 1980-87. **Career:** Formed the Shobana Jeyasingh

Dance Company in 1988; television appearances include (for Channel 4) *Map of Dreams,* and *Dancing by Numbers*; (for BBC2) *Late, Duets with Automobiles* (1994), *Network East* Dance Special, and *Away Game* (1997). **Awards:** London Dance and Performance Award, 1988; Digital Dance Award 1988, 1990, 1992; Arts Council Women in the Arts Project Award, 1993; *Time Out* Dance Award (Best Choreography), 1993, 1996; Prudential Award for the Arts, 1993; member of the British Empire, 1995. honorary master's degree, University of Surrey; honorary doctorate, De Montfort University.

Works

1988   *Configurations* (mus. Michael Nyman), Shobana Jeyasingh Dance Company, London

1989   *Defile* (mus. Club Mix from Jamestown Studios), Shobana Jeyasingh Dance Company, London
       Janpath (mus. Charlie Moriano and the Karnatica College of Percussion), National Youth Dance Company

1990   *Correspondences* (mus. Kevin Volans), Shobana Jeyasingh Dance Company, London

1991   *Late* (mus. Michael Nyman), Shobana Jeyasingh Dance Company, London
       Byzantium (mus. Christos Hatzis), Shobana Jeyasingh Dance Company, London

1992   *Making of Maps* (mus. Alistair McDonald), Shobana Jeyasingh Dance Company, London

Shobana Jeyasingh: *Palimpsest,* **1996-97. Photograph by Hugo Glendinning.**

1993   *Romance*. . . with Footnotes* (mus. Glyn Perrin, Karaikudi Krishnamurthy), Shobana Jeyasingh Dance Company, London

1994   *Duets with Automobiles* (for television; directed by Terry Braun; mus. Orlando Gough), Shobana Jeyasingh Dance Company

1995   *Raid* (mus. Glyn Perrin, Ilaiyaraaja), Shobana Jeyasingh Dance Company, London

1996   *The Bird and the Wind* (mus. Eero Hameenniemi), Shobana Jeyasingh Dance Company, Joensuu, Finland
       Palimpsest (mus. Graham Fitkin), Shobana Jeyasingh Dance Company, London

Publications

By JEYASINGH: articles—

"Getting Off the Orient Express," *Dance Theatre Journal,* Summer 1990.
"Imaginary Homelands: Creating a New Dance Language," *Border Tensions: Proceedings of the Fifth Study of Dance Conference,* edited by Janet Lansdale & Chris Jones, Guildford, 1995.
"Text, Context, Dance," *South Asian Dance: The British Experience,* edited by Alessandra Iyer, *Choreography and Dance,* 1997.

On JEYASINGH: articles—

Briginshaw, Valerie, "'Making a Bedroom Out of a Public Building': Hybridity and Nomadic Subjectivity in Shobana Jeyasingh's *Duets with Automobiles,*" *Confluences,* Cape Town, 1997.
Jordan, Stephanie, "Networking Dances: *Home and Away* in the Choreography of Shobana Jeyasingh," *New Dance from Old Cultures,* edited by Crusader Hillis and Urzsula Dawkins, Australia, 1997.
———, "*Palimpsest* as Creative Practice and Analytical Technique: Secret Complexities in the Work of Shobana Jeyasingh," in *Confluences,* Cape Town, 1997.
Roy, Sanjoy, "Dirt, Noise, Traffic: Contemporary Indian Dance in the Western City," *Dance in the City,* edited by Helen Thomas, London, 1997.
———, "Multiple Choice," *Dance Theatre Journal,* Summer 1997.
Rubidge, Sarah, *Romance* . . . with Footnotes,* (book and video), London, 1995.

Films and Videotapes

By Jeyasingh—

Making of Maps, video and education pack, London.

*   *   *

Shobana Jeyasingh is a pioneering modernist British choreographer and company director. Born in Madras, India, she trained in the classical Indian dance Bharata Natyam, and after arriving in Britain she toured for several years as a solo performer in this style. She formed her own company in 1988, and stopped dancing in 1991 to focus on her choreography. To date, the company has been all-female, partly, Jeyasingh says, because of the difficulty of finding suitable male dancers trained in Bharata Natyam, and partly because she has not yet wished to address gender difference on stage.

While touring as a classical dancer, Jeyasingh grew dissatisfied with the strictures of Bharata Natyam. She began experimenting with the style, and produced her first piece, *Configurations*, in 1988. Jeyasingh had always preferred the *nritta*, or pure dance aspect of Bharata Natyam, and in *Configurations* she dissected *nritta* into its elemental components—clean lines, clear spatial directions, sharply defined body shapes and rhythmically articulate footwork—and reconfigured the traditionally solo form into an ensemble piece, using formal devices of repetition and variation in time and space. A sparkling, abstract geometry of movement, the piece broke new ground on a number of counts: for stripping away the embellishments of *nritta* to get at its skeletal framework; for composing a group dance from a traditionally solo style; and for setting Bharata Natyam to a (commissioned) score by minimalist composer Michael Nyman, whose analytical compositional methods echoed her own.

Making of Maps was a significant development from this "analytical" mode, Jeyasingh varying Bharata Natyam-derived movement much more widely. One moment in the piece summarises her intent: one dancer adopts a classical pose while another pulls her gently off centre until she overbalances. Both *Making of Maps* and *Romance*... *with Footnotes* explore this tension between classical and personal style, alternating between the precision of Bharata Natyam and more waywardly idiosyncratic movement.

Raid marked a further development. Taking inspiration from the team sport *kabbadi*, Jeyasingh set two types of movement against each other, dance and sport, the two teams edgily making forays into each others' territories. It was a liberating piece: using sports movement freed Jeyasingh from the constraints of classical dance, hitherto the central reference point of her choreography, and opened up a greater spatial and dynamic range.

Palimpsest, Jeyasingh's finest work to date, shows her savouring this newfound freedom. More intriguingly complex than previous works, with a wider dynamic range and more sophisticated use of stage space, it is nevertheless, characteristically, a tightly structured piece, its phrases repeated and varied in a sequence of abstract episodes. It draws on diverse movement sources, including *nritta*, *abhinaya* (the dramatic, expressive aspect of Bharata Natyam), the martial arts *chhau* and *kalari*, naturalistic gesture, and idiosyncratic movement invention as well as a tongue-in-cheek reference to "Western contemporary dance." Unlike in *Raid*, where contrasting styles appear as distinctive blocks of movement, here they are interwoven in variegated, overlapping phrases. *Palimpsest* stands as a testament to the ground that Jeyasingh has covered since she first embarked on her own determinedly individual choreographic path.

Jeyasingh commissions contemporary scores for her work, notably from Michael Nyman, Glynn Perrin, and Graham Fitkin. Several times she has used scores which mix together an Indian and a Western composition, for example *Making of Maps* (Alistair Macdonald with R. A. Ramamani), *Raid* (Perrin with Ilayaraaja) and *Romance*. . . *with Footnotes* (Perrin, with Karaikudi Krishnamurthy).

The designs she uses tend to be bold and simple, based on shape and colour and leaving ample space for the dance. Notable designs include Belinda Ackerman's starkly effective set for *Romance*...*with Footnotes*, and Keith Khan's strikingly inventive sets and costumes for *Raid*, and especially *Palimpsest*.

Jeyasingh has occasionally commissioned other choreographers for her company. Her earliest commission was *Speaking of Sakti* (1991) by modern Indian choreographer Chandralekha. Then came

Richard Alston's *Delicious Arbour* (1993), set to music by Purcell, an experiment in how another modernist choreographer would work with dancers trained in a different movement style. Laurie Booth's *Astral Shadows* (1997) was another experiment, Jeyasingh this time finding her concern with *chhau* and *kalari* echoed in Booth's interest in *capoeira*, a Brazilian martial art.

A choreographer of keen intellect, Jeyasingh is a modernist in outlook, interested in the form and framework of movement, and where narrative and emotion do enter her work, they are generally couched in abstract terms. Yet as a modernist Indian artist in Britain, she often finds herself caught in an impossibly contradictory position arising from dominant ideas about tradition, race, and modernity in a culture that associates modernity with the West, and the West with the white. So although her choreography is above all concerned with shaping and composing movement, it is often received in simplistic cultural terms that attempt to define and categorise Indian and Western heritages—most frequently by citing her use of Bharata Natyam-derived movements with Western music, or by attributing any "non-traditional" movement to the influence of Western contemporary dance.

Jeyasingh's choreography can certainly be seen to evoke questions of culture and identity, but never literally. Rather, it does so at the level of form. By experimenting with forms of movement rather than simply stating cultural ideas, Jeyasingh expands their possibilities, moving beyond East/West dichotomies towards looser, more open configurations of the aesthetic and the cultural. Rather than aiming for a unifying fusion of cultures or of movement styles, she allows herself to range freely between them. As such, she finds a formal analogue for the complex experiences of multicultural urban life, particularly the experience of diaspora, inventing paths that wander between past and present, tradition and modernity, the personal and the cultural, the rooted and the free.

—Sanjoy Roy

JOHANSSON, Ronny

Swedish choreographer, dancer, and educator

Born: 26 July 1891 in Riga, Latvia. **Education:** Various early studies in ballroom and character dance; serious study with Heinrich Kröller (a pupil of Staats and Zambelli, the latter a dancer/ choreographer who became one of the most influential classical dance personalities in his time), 1913-16; influenced by von Derp and the Wiesenthal sisters; choreographed and danced first solo, 1916; traveled to the U.S. to dance, choreograph, and lecture, 1924-31, 1938, 1939; continued to dance and choreograph throughout central Europe until 1940s; developed pedagogic exercises and innovations (floor schooling) admired by Ted Shawn, Martha Graham, and John Martin; head teacher at the Royal Dramatic Theatre (Stockholm) in movement for actors, 1942-62. **Awards:** Swedish government bestowed a lifetime salary from 1964-79. **Died:** 1979 in Stockholm.

Works

1916   *Menuette* (mus. Paderewski)
        Valse Caprice (mus. Rubinstein)

Other works include: *Gavotte Joyeuse* (mus. Mozart), *Polka* (mus. Glazunov), *Machine Dance, Bauerntanz* (mus. Grieg), and *Mazurka* (mus. Chopin).

Publications

Junk, Victor, *Handbuch des Tanzes Stuttgart*, 1930.
Svedin, Lulli, *Memoirs*, Stockholm, 1986.

*   *   *

Ronny Johansson was an early exponent of modern dance whose intelligence and innovative influence was probably even more important than her mastery as a performer and choreographer. She happened to be born in Riga of a Swedish father who did business there, and an English mother. When she was a student at the university, her family was transferred to Sweden and she followed them in 1913, giving up her academic studies. With an inborn passion for performing, she hesitated between becoming a dancer or an actress. At 22 years of age her experience of dance was limited to the ballroom (quite choreographically precise at that epoch), as well as style and character dances such as mazurka, krakoviak, etc., which belonged to an upper-class girl's basic education.

She sought advice of Clotilde von Derp, the Countess von der Planitz, and thanks to von Derp's influence, Johansson was accepted as a pupil by Heinrich Kröller, a noted classical dancer and leading classical master in central Europe who later went on to have a great career as choreographer and maitre de ballet in opera theaters in Vienna, Berlin, and other cities. Johansson followed Kröller and his ballerina wife, Clara Gabler, for nearly four years during their consecutive engagements, learning from them both. In 1916 Johansson was ready for her debut, a full evening of solos performed by herself, mostly in her own choreography (some by Kröller), with the shortest possible time for costume changing in between (a common pattern for most important dancers of that time). Among the items on the debut program, several she would perform for years afterward, was a *Menuette* to music by Paderevski and *Valse Caprice* to Arthur Rubenstein. In the beginning she resembled the sisters Wiesenthal in beautiful, charming dances derived from the ballroom. Johansson's sense of humor was remarkable—a witty aloofness, bordering on satire, that quite often glinted forth and obliterated all things pathetic. Such lightness coupled with elegance was rare. Johansson never became overly expressionistic—she shunned ugliness—her appearance was of refinement and superiority, somewhat lighthearted, perhaps, but superbly performed. Only later in her long career did she turn to complicated creations and technical feats, like her *Machine Dance*, where parts of her body simultaneously represented a wheel, a piston, a lever, and so forth, each with its own rhythm independently of the others, even in counterpoint—a technical proficiency which foreshadowed the brilliance of Murray Louis. Stark, tragic moods were not in Johansson's nature, nor did she let herself be influenced by anyone once she had established her personal art. Her recitals she never shared with any partner—when she did share a performance, such as with Sent M'Ahesa, they appeared in layers, taking every other performance (in part to help with such quick costume changes, the eternal problem for dancers of this time).

After her extremely well-received debut, Johansson performed the same program in Stockholm in 1916 and began touring central Europe. In Vienna, she appeared almost yearly from 1919, the same year she had great success in London at the Coliseum. Though she never danced in Paris, she was a favorite in the mixed vaudeville programs of the huge variety theaters, which provided early modern dancers with long series of appearances, often twice a night for a month in each town. Feeling the strain of heavy work, Ronny Johansson experimented with different ways of keeping up her technical skill by without overdoing the leg muscles. She borrowed elements from sports and athletes teachers and out of this she created a floor exercise, while lying or sitting down. When she went to New York in 1925, it was the novelty of this training system, her own innovation, that first attracted her colleagues at the Denishawn School. Invited to demonstrate her training exercises, the demonstration was attended by Martha Graham and many others. It proved to be the first of innumerable classes in America.

Long afterwards, Graham confirmed that she'd been quite influenced by Johansson, and had incorporated these floor exercises in her technical system. An American critic wrote, "after Duncan's and Pavlova's deaths, and since Ruth St. Denis has withdrawn, Ronny Johansson is now indisputably the foremost of dancers." Johansson gave two recitals in New York and five in Chicago, and was engaged as a soloist with Adolf Bolm's Company (partly doing her own choreography). She then taught at the Denishawn School, and in 1926 she succeeded Graham as choreographer at the Eastman School in Rochester, New York. She was regularly employed in the "live" artistic interludes between films in movie theaters and also traveled throughout the U.S. giving lectures at universities and recitals. She had a deep commitment to pedagogy and she was unremittingly active in promoting it.

In 1929, the Great Depression in U.S. deprived her of her working permit and Johansson returned to Stockholm. She was able to come to the States again in 1931, engaged by Elsa Findlay at the Booth Theatre, New York, and toured the country intermittently with her lecture-performances until 1939. Back in Stockholm, she had opened her own school in 1933, and kept it as her primary working site until 1942 when the Royal Swedish Dramatic Theatre engaged her as teacher and coach of movement for the actors, as well as style and character dances. She developed systems for these, and contributed much to the standard of acting in Sweden. She withdrew from the Royal Swedish Dramatic Theatre in 1962 and the government awarded her with a yearly salary for life for her contributions. She died in Stockholm in 1978.

—Bengt Häger

JONES, Betty
American dancer and educator

Born: 1926 in Meadville, Pennsylvania. **Education:** Studied with Evelyn Blevins; studied at Jacob's Pillow working with Ted Shawn and Alicia Markova, 1941-46; studied ballet technique with Maggie Black, Margaret Craske, Antony Tudor, Anatole Vilzak, and Aubrey Hitchins, New York; modern dance with Hanya Holm, Louis Horst, Doris Humphrey, José Limón, Alwin Nikolais, Ted Shawn, and Dan Wagoner. **Career:** Professional debut in the musical *Oklahoma,* USO tour to the Philippines and New Guinea, 1945; toured the U.S. in Agnes De Mille's *Bloomer Girl,* 1946-47; member of José Limón Dance Company, 1947-72; created Desdemona in *The Moor's Pavane,* José Limón Dance Company, 1949; founded Dances We Dance with partner Fritz Ludin, 1964; toured with Ludin throughout U.S. and Europe with a repertoire of varied works by choreographers such as Murray Louis, Dan Wagoner, Martha Wittman, and Twyla Tharp; assisted José Limón in mounting *Missa Brevis* for the University of Utah; taught at Connecticut College Summer School, Juilliard School, Internationale Sommerakademie of Cologne (Germany), Centre International de la Danse (Paris), and American Dance Festival; moved to Honolulu, Hawaii, 1976; choreographed works for the Hawaii Dance Theater of the University of Hawaii; appeared on WNET-TV's *An Hour with José Limón* and in the film version of *The Moor's Pavane*. **Awards:** Named to the Balasaraswati/Joy Ann Dewey Chair for Distinguished Teaching by the American Dance Festival, 1993.

Roles

1948	*Concerto* in D Minor
1949	His Wife (Desdemona), *The Moor's Pavane*
	Soprano soloist, *Malinche*
1951	A Night Figure, *Night Spell* (Humphrey)
1952	Fantasy figure, *Fantasy and Fugue* (Humphrey)
1953	*Ritmo Jondo* (Humphrey)
	A girl, *Visions* (Humphrey)
1955	One of the Three Graces, *Airs and Graces* (Humphrey)
	Symphony for Strings
1958	*The Antagonist* (Ruth Currier)
1959	*Concerto Grosso*
1961	*A Tender Portrait* (Currier)

Works

1972	*Of Heads, Hands and Other Things*

Publications

On JONES: articles—

Christian Science Monitor, 20 April 1973.
Interview, *Honolulu Advertiser,* 2 February 1993.
Betty Jones Clippings File, Dance Research Collection of the New York Public Library at Lincoln Center, New York.

*   *   *

Betty Jones was a major modern dancer of the post-World War II era. As a core member of José Limón's dance company from 1949 to 1972, she created many celebrated roles. Critics hailed her talent as "monumental" and "incredible." Of all the roles created on her, the Desdemona character in *The Moor's Pavane* (1949) is the most famous.

Betty Jones was born in Meadville, Pennsylvania in 1926. While still quite young, she moved with her family to Albany, New York, where her father was New York State director of health and physical education. Both her dance-loving mother and her father encouraged their daughter's interest in dance. Jones began her formal dance training at the age of four under Vivian Milstein, studying tap and ballet. When her family moved to a suburb of Albany, Betty concentrated on ballet with a new teacher, Evelyn Blevins. Determined to become a ballet dancer, the teenaged Jones auditioned for the famed British ballet dancers Alicia Markova and Anton Dolin, who, in 1941, were directing the season of dance events at Jacob's Pillow

in Massachusetts. Despite her youth, Jones was accepted and took classes with Markova. Jones returned to the Pillow for several summers as a scholarship student. While there, she began to study modern dance with Ted Shawn.

Upon graduation from high school, Jones moved to New York City to pursue her goal of a dancing career. She studied at the ballet studios of Igor Schwezoff, Anatole Vilzak, and Aubrey Hitchins. She also took classes in Spanish dance with Arthur Mahoney. When the USO mounted a tour of the Broadway hit musical *Oklahoma* (with choreography by Agnes De Mille), Jones was hired as a singer and dancer. In 1947 Jones was in the cast of another musical, *Bloomer Girl,* by Agnes De Mille. After her engagement with that show ended, Jones joined the José Limón Dance Company.

Jones created many famous roles as a member of the Limón company. Her first important vehicle was *Concerto Grosso.* In addition to her dancing, she used her fine singing voice in *La Malinche* and in *The Queen's Epicedium* (a dance set to a funeral ode for a 17th-century English queen). But it was her role in *The Moor's Pavane* that brought the most critical acclaim. In retelling Shakespeare's *Othello,* José Limón used the framing device of a formal court dance, the pavane, to establish the story of four characters—The Moor, His Wife, His Friend, and His Friend's Wife. The dancers establish their roles by means of stately, highly charged, but intensely controlled gestures. These are interrupted by private asides which reveal the characters' conflicts and passions. Betty Jones' gentle and poignant portrayal of the innocent wife established her as a leading modern dancer.

The Limón company was small, and its members were like a family. At first, Jones' technique—mainly ballet based—was a bit strait-laced for Limón. As Jones recalled in a piece about Limón in the *Christian Science Monitor,* she and Limón had an ongoing debate about how a dancer should behave. They amused rather than convinced each other, but their mutual respect grew firmer and deeper.

Critics were unanimous in their praise for Betty Jones' dancing. They noted her fair, good looks, and her exquisite movement sense. As Walter Terry pointed out in his review of Dances We Dance at Jacob's Pillow, Jones could be tender or heroic, lyrical or sharp, slow or fast, but she was always radiant. Doris Hering called her dancing "crystalline" with a synthesis of drive and delicacy that was a joy to see. Her ballet technique enabled her to execute lightly poised balances and her modern dance background gave her a sculptor's ability to model herself in space. Elizabeth Kendall found her total presence deeply moving.

In 1964 Betty Jones and Swiss-born dancer Fritz Ludin, a member of the Limón troupe from 1963 to 1968, joined forces to perform a program of modern dance pieces by various choreographers. They danced such works as *Facets* by Murray Louis, *The Warrior and the Widow* by Carl Wolz, *Duet* by Dan Wagoner, *Journey # 2: For an Angel and a Clown* by Martha Wittman, and *Improv to Haydn* by Fritz Ludin. They were invited by Ted Shawn to appear at Jacob's Pillow and also appeared at the Centre International de la Danse in Paris. During the 1973 Avignon Festival in France they were invited to perform and teach under the aegis of the Rencontres Internationales de Danse Contemporaine. Both Jones and Ludin were on the faculties of the Juilliard School in New York City; the Connecticut College School of Dance in New London, Connecticut; the Long Beach Summer School of Dance in Long Beach, California; and, most recently, as artists-in-residence at the University of Hawaii in Honolulu. Jones also appeared as a soloist with the Libby Nye Dance Company at the Entermedia theater complex in New York City.

Jones continues to codirect Dances We Dance and teach at various dance festivals and schools in the U.S. and abroad. Noting that age is irrelevant, she told the *Honolulu Advertiser* in 1993: "If dance is a passion for you, you just keep going. Dancing is my life. Everything I do is around dancing."

—Adriane Ruggiero

JONES, Bill T. and ZANE, Arnie
American dancers, choreographers, and company directors

Born: JONES—William Tass Jones, 1952; ZANE—1948 in the Bronx. **Education:** Both attended the State University of New York (SUNY) at Binghamton. **Career:** Formed American Dance Asylum with Lois Welk, 1973; founded Bill T. Jones/Arnie Zane Company, 1982; commissioned by the Alvin Ailey American Dance Theatre to create *How to Walk an Elephant,* 1985; JONES—named resident choreographer, Lyon Opera Ballet, 1994; has received commissions from modern dance, ballet, and opera companies including the Berkshire Ballet, Berlin Opera Ballet, Boston Academy of Music's Next Wave Festival, Boston Ballet, Boston Lyric Opera, Diversions Dance Company, Glyndebourne Festival Opera, Houston Grand Opera, Lyon Opera Ballet, New York City Opera, and St. Luke's Chamber Orchestra. **Awards:** JONES—Creative Artists Public Service (CAPS) fellowship for choreography, 1979; choreographic fellowships, National Endowment for the Arts, 1980, 1981, and 1982; New York Dance and Performance Award ("Bessie"), 1989; "Izzy" award for *Perfect Courage,* 1990; Dorothy B. Chandler Performing Arts Award, 1991; *Dance Magazine* award, 1993; MacArthur fellowship, 1994. ZANE—Creative Artists Public Service (CAPS) fellowship for photography, 1973; second CAPS fellowship, for choreography, 1981; choreographic fellowships from the NEA, 1983 and 1984. TOGETHER—German Critics Award for *Blauvelt Mountain,* 1980; New York Dance and Performance Award ("Bessie") for choreographer/creators, 1986. **Died:** ZANE—1988 of AIDS.

Works

1973   *Pas de Deux for Two* (mus. Benny Goodman), 137 Washington Street, Binghamton, New York
1974   *A Dance with Durga Devi* (mus. Tibetan temple chants, Bessie Smith), American Dance Asylum, Binghamton, New York
        Negroes for Sale (mus. collage by Jones), Collective for Living Cinema, New York
        Entrances, American Dance Asylum, Binghamton, New York
        Track Dance, State University of New York, Binghamton
1975   *Could Be Dance,* American Dance Asylum, Binghamton
        Dancing and Video in Motion (with American Dance asylum, Peer Bode, Meryl Blackman), Experimantal Television Center, Binghamton
        Women in Drought, American Dance Asylum, Binghamton
        Acrosss the Street (spoken text by Jones, film by Arnie Zane), American Dance Asylum, Binghamton

Impersonations, American Dance Asylum, Binghamton
Everybody Works/All Beasts Count (mus. Jesse Fuller), American Dance Asylum, Binghamton
1977   *For You,* Daniel Nagrin Theater, New York
        Walk, Daniel Nagrin Theater, New York
        A Man, Daniel Nagrin Theater
        Asymmetry: Every Which Way (mus. Lou Grassi), Roberson Art Center, Binghamton
        Da Sweet Streak Ta Love Land (mus. Otis Redding), Clark Center, New York City
1978   *Whosedebabedoll? Baby Doll* (spoken text by Jones and Zane), American Dance Asylum
        Floating the Tongue, Kent School for Boys
        Naming Things Is Only the Intention to Make Things (vocal mus. Jeanne Lee), The Kitchen, New York
        Progresso (with Sheryl Sutton, text by Jones and Sutton), American Dance Asylum, Binghamton
1979   *Monkey Run Road* (mus. Helen Thorington), American Dance Asylum, Binghamton
        Echo (mus. Helen Thorington), The Kitchen, New York
        Addition, Washington Square Church, New York
        Circle in the Distance (with Sheryl Sutton, text by Jones and Sutton), Washington Square Church, New York
1980   *Dance in the Trees* (mus. Jeff Cohan and Pete Simonson), Hartman Land Reserve, Cedar Falls, Iowa
        Open Spaces: A Dance in June (mus. Dan Hummel, Mark Gaurmond, Thomas Berry), Waterloo, Iowa
        Untitled Duet (with Sherry Satenstrom; mus. Dan Hummel, Marcia Midget, Dartanyan Brown), Recreation Center, Waterloo, Iowa
        Balancing the World, University of Northern Iowa, Cedar Falls
        Sweeps (with Arnie Zane; video by Meryl Blackman), Zurich, Switzerland
        Blauvelt Mountain (mus. Helen Thorington), Dance Theatre Workshop, New York
        Sisyphus (mus. Helen Thorington; spoken text by Jones), Kennedy Center, Washington, D.C.
        Social Intercourse: Pilgrim's Progress (text and lyrics by Jones; music arranged by Joe Hannon), American Dance Festival, Raleigh, North Carolina
        Break (mus. George Lewis), Nicollete Island Amphitheater, Minneapolis
        Valley Cottage (mus. Helen Thorington, text by Jones and Zane), Dance Theatre Workshop, New York
        10: First Part (spoken text by Jones), performance for bicycle, voice, slide, and dress, Dance Theatre Workshop, New York
        10: Second Part, Dance Theatre Workshop, New York
        Ah! Break It! (mus. Jalalu Calvert Nelson), Werkcentrum Dans, Rotterdam
1982   *Three Dances* (mus. Mozart and Peter Gordon; spoken text by Jones), Harvard University
        Rotary Action (mus. Peter Gordon), New dance, New York
        Dance for the Convergence of Three Rivers (mus. George Lewis), Three Rivers Arts Festival, Pittsburgh
        Shared Distance, duet with Julie West, The Kitchen, New York
        Duet x 2 (mus. Bach), duets with Robe Besserer and Brian Arsenault, The Kitchen, New York City

1983　*Intuitive Monentum* (mus. Max Roach and Connie Crothers), Brooklyn Academy of Music

Fever Swamp (mus. Peter Gordon), comissioned by Alvin Ailey American Dance Theatre, performed Santa Monica

Naming Things (with Philip Mallory Jones and David Hammons; mus. Miles Davis, traditional), performed with Rhonda Moore and Poonie Dodson, Just Above Midtown Gallery, New York

21, solo, Recreation Center, Waterloo, Iowa

Corporate Whimsy (mus. Bryon Rulon), New York University

Casino (mus. Peter Gordon), Ohio State University, Athens

1984　*Dances with Brahms* (mus. Brahms), Paula Cooper Gallery, New York

1985　*1, 2, 3* (mus. Carl Stone), Joyce Theater, New York

Holzer Duet. . .Truisms (text by Jenny Holzer), duet with Lawrence Goldhuber, Joyce Theater, New York

M.A.K.E (spoken text by Jones and Zane), Joyce Theater, New York

Pastiche (mus. James Brown, Eric Dolphy), Joyce Theater, New York

Freedom of Information (mus. David Cunningham, spoken text by Jones), Theatre de la Ville, Paris

Secret Pastures (mus. Peter Gordon), Brooklyn Academy of Music

1986　*Virgil Thompson Etudes* (mus. Virgil Thompson), commissioned for Thompson's birthday, performed at Chanterelle, New York

Animal Trilogy (mus. Conlon Nancarrow), Biennale Internationale de la Danse, Lyons, France

1987　*Where the Queen Stands Guard* (mus. by Vittorio Rieti), Manhattan Community College, New York

Red Room (mus. Stuart Argabright, Robert Longo), Buffalo, New York

1988　*The History of Collage* (mus. Charles R. Amirkhanian, "Blue" Gene Tyranny), Cleveland

Chatter (mus. Paul Lansky), American Dance Festival, Durham, North Carolina

Soon (mus. Weill, Bessie Smith), Celebrate Brooklyn Festival

1989　*Don't Lose Your Eye* (mus. Sonny Boy Williamson, Paul Lansky), Path Dance Company, Baltimore

Forsythia (mus. Dufay, text by Zane), duet with Arthur Aviles, Joyce Theater, New York

La Grande Fete (mus. Paul Lansky), Joyce Theater, New York

It Takes Two (mus. Ray Charles, Betty Carter), commissioned by Terry Creach and Stephen Koester, Dance Theatre Workshop, New York

Absence (mus. Penderecki, Berlioz), Joyce Theater, New York

D-Man in the Waters (mus. Mendelssohn), commissioned in part by St. Luke's Chamber Orchestra, New York

1990　*Last Supper at Uncle Tom's Cabin/The Promised Land* (mus. Jules Hemphill), Next Wave Festival, Brooklyn Academy of Music

History of Collage Revisited (mus. Charles R. Amirkhanian and "Blue" Gene Tyranny), Divions Dance Company, Cardiff, Wales

1991　*Havoc in Heaven* (mus. John Bergamo), Berkshire Ballet, Albany

1992　*Broken Wedding* (mus. Klezmer Conservatory Band), commissioned by Boston Ballet

Die Offnung (mus. John Oswald), commissioned by Berlin Opera Ballet

Love Defined (mus. Daniel Johnston), commissioned by Lyon Opera Ballet

Our Respected Dead (mus. Daniel Johnston), Joyce Theater, New York

Fete (mus. Paul Lansky), Joyce Theater, New York

Last Night on Earth (mus. Kurt Weill, Bessie Smith, traditional), Joyce Theater, New York

1993　*Achilles Loved Patroclus* (mus. John Oswald), Joyce Theater, New York

War Between the States (mus. Ives), Joyce Theater, New York

There Were So Many. . . (mus. Cage), Joyce Theater, New York

And the Maiden (mus. Bessie Jones and group), Joyce Theater, New York

Just You (mus. Frank Loesser, Harry Woods, Coslow Johnston, Klages-Greer, Cole Porter, Hoffman-Manning), Joyce Theater, New York

1994　*Still/Here* (mus. Kenneth Fragelle, traditional, Vernon Reid), Biennale Internationale de la Danse, Lyon

1995　*New Duet* (mus. John Oswald, Laurel McDonald), RomaEuropa Festival, Rome

Deggs w/Toni Morrison and Max Roach, Lincoln Center, New York

24 Images per Second, Lyon Opera Ballet

1996　*Bill and Laurie: About Five Rounds* w/Laurie Anderson, Joyce Theater, New York

Ballad (poems written and read by Dylan Thomas), Joyce Theater, New York

Blue Phrase (mus. Dolphy), Joyce Theater, New York

Love Re-Defined (mus. Daniel Johnston), Joyce Theater, New York

Sur la Place (mus. Brel), Cour d'Honneur, Festival D'Avignon, France

1997　*Lisbon* (mus. collage by Gregory Bain), Emerson Majestic Theater, Boston

We Set Out Early. . .Visibility Was Poor (mus. Stravinsky, Cage, Vasks), Kennedy Center, Washington, DC

Publications

By JONES: books—

Jones, Bill T., with Peggy Gillespie, *Last Night on Earth,* New York, 1995.

On JONES & ZANE: books—

Zimmer, Elizabeth, "Bill T. Jones: Preparing *The Last Summer at Uncle Tom's Cabin*," in *Breakthroughs: Avant-Garde Artists in Europe and America, 1950-1990,* New York, 1991.

Zimmer, Elizabeth, and Susan Quasha, editors, *Body against Body: The Dance and Other Collaborations of Bill T. Jones & Arnie Zane,* Barrytown, New York, 1989.

Bill T. Jones performing *Ballad*, 1996. Photograph © Johan Elbers.

On JONES & ZANE: articles—

Dunning, Jennifer, "Living, Dying and Restorative Anger," *New York Times,* 16 October 1992.

Gates, Henry Louis, Jr., "The Body Politic," *The New Yorker,* 29 November 1994.

Gillespie, Peggy, "Disciple of Dance," *Boston Globe Magazine,* 14 March 1993.

Jowitt, Deborah, "Bill as Bill," *Village Voice,* 20 October 1992.

Kaye, Elizabeth, "Bill T. Jones," *New York Times Magazine,* 6 March 1994.

Tracy, Robert, "Full Circle," *Dance Magazine,* October 1992.

Wallach, Maya, "A Conversation with Bill T. Jones," *Ballet Review,* Winter 1990-91.

Zimmer, Elizabeth, "Sex and the Dead," *Village Voice,* 27 October 1992.

Films and Videotapes

Rotary Action, duet performed by Jones and Zane, coproduced with WGBH-TV Boston and Channel 4 in London.

Fever Swamp, choreographed by Jones for *Great Performances,* WNET, New York, 1983.

Untitled, choreographed by Jones for *Alive from Off-Center,* PBS, 1988.

Last Supper at Uncle Tom's Cabin/The Promised Land, documentary aired on *Dance in America,* PBS, 1992.

Still/Here, segment on Bill Moyer's *Healing and the Arts* series, 1994.

*   *   *

Denounced by the Vatican, listed as one of *People Magazine*'s "Most Beautiful People in the World," and venturing with his dance company into thematic hotbeds like homosexuality, racism, and fatal illness, Bill T. Jones is to late-20th-century dance a superbly rebellious while politically correct representative. A black gay man with a body that was photographed by Robert Mapplethorpe, Jones is part showman, part philosopher. He is openly HIV-positive, and the world watches him with a ticking clock always in the background. As a choreographer, his work ranges from erotic to neoclassic, political to drippingly romantic, raw and gestural to cool and poetic. Jones chose dance; it was a way to be seen, a way to say something important, and it was cheap. In this era of $38-million-dollar-movies, it is important to remember that dance is, still, simply, bodies moving through space. It is an art everyone can afford to do.

Jones maintains Arnie Zane's name on the company masthead years after his partner and former lover died of AIDS. Jones understands image and publicity and has managed to be the rare artist who is both cool and hot, acceptable to the critics and dance elite, and popular with the general public. Bill T. Jones/Arnie Zane Dance Company concerts are events blending high art and spectacle, are often sold out, and always well-covered (with pictures) by the press. The company has positioned itself in a way to escape the veil of obscurity which has befallen modern dance in general.

The dance company began as a student collaboration between two men who, from the first, shared a bed along with their idealism. What grew out of their combination was dance that dealt in opposites, as the dissimilar Jones and Zane did in their life together. "In Your Face" politics were countered, if not in the same dance, perhaps in the next, with Balanchinian formalism. Hatred and love, words and dance, family and lust, humor and grief, ecstatic life and hideous death—Jones and Zane borrowed postmodern styles and infused them with passion. When Zane died of AIDS in 1988, Jones grieved choreographically, and it may have been his willingness, from that point on, to deal with big issues and nonsubtle emotions that struck a chord with audiences, grant-makers and theatrical presenters. A dance company with one dead artistic director grew and thrived. It was a way for audiences to survive also.

Jones and Zane met at the State University of New York at Binghamton in the early 1970s, where Jones' background as an athlete and Zane's interest in photography and cinema lead them into as many experimental endeavors as they could find around them. The political era of the 1960s was over, but the idealism and hippie lifestyle still flourished in places like Binghamton. In dance, contact improvisation grew out of that culture, and Jones/Zane's first artistic efforts came out of a collaboration with their contact improvisation teacher, with whom they formed American Dance Asylum in 1973. Subsequently, Jones and Zane worked for years as a solo and duet company, winning New York appearances at venues such as Dance Theatre Workshop, and backing from grant-makers such as Creative Artists Public Service and the National Endowment for the Arts (NEA). They formed Bill T. Jones/Arnie Zane Company in 1982 and went on to create over 45 works for their own group, as well as commissioned works for the Alvin Ailey American Dance Theatre, Boston Ballet, Lyon Opera Ballet, Berlin Opera Ballet and others.

The repertoire was as deliberately diverse as the dancers of all sizes, shapes, and colors they took into their company. In 1982 their evening-length piece, *Intuitive Momentum,* premiered at the Brooklyn Academy of Music (BAM) with the live accompaniment of jazz drummer Max Roach. The reviews were ecstatic. The company subsequently toured internationally, appearing at prestigious venues such as Sadler's Wells in London, Theatre de La Ville in Paris and the Kennedy Center in Washington, and also was booked by the United States Information Agency on a tour of Asia in 1986.

In 1984 *Secret Pastures* and *The Animal Trilogy* appeared in New York at the Joyce Theater and BAM's Next Wave Festival, involving collaborations by Peter Gordon, Keith Haring, and Willi Smith. *Last Supper at Uncle Tom's Cabin/The Promised Land* premiered, again, as part of the Next Wave Festival in 1990. Combining narrative, jazz, a revision of a famous dance from a Rogers and Hammerstein movie, and a cast including a 100 "real people" who appear naked in the last section, *Last Supper* was a controversial hit. The company embarked with this piece on a 22-city domestic tour, which was followed by appearances in Berlin, Amsterdam, Madrid and Montpellier, France.

In 1992 the company celebrated its 10th anniversary. *Still/Here,* the next evening-length work, which developed out of workshops Jones held with terminally-ill cancer and AIDS patients, was less successful artistically, although a furor arose when eminent dance critic Arlene Croce railed in the *New Yorker* against the "victim art" of the current period, refusing to review the piece. Jones' health remains stable and bookings, grants, and tours continue to be lined up into the next century. Jones' company has new members and new choreography every season, although the formula of diversity and contrast seems to be set. It remains to be seen, at the turn of the century, as Jones turns 50, whether the transition will be successfully made, as Graham, Cunningham, and other long-lived performers and choreographers were able to—into a Bill T. Jones/Arnie Zane Dance Company without a Bill T. Jones onstage, minimally clad, demanding our attention.

—Michael Wade Simpson

JOOSS, Kurt

German dancer, choreographer, and educator

Born: 12 January 1901 in Wasseralfingen. **Education:** Studied photography, piano, singing, composition, acting, and speech at various schools in Germany, 1919-21; studied dance with Rudolf Laban, 1920-24. **Family:** Married Aion Siimola, 1921; two daughters. **Career:** Began collaborating with Laban, 1922; co-founder, Neue Tanzbühne; began choreographing, 1924; appointed director, Folkwangschule, 1927; founder/director, Folkwang Tanztheater (later became Folkwang Tanzbühne), 1928-47; antiwar classic *The Green Table* debuts, 1932; fled Nazis to England, 1933; co-founder, Jooss-Leeder School of Dance (Devon, England), 1934-40; Ballets Jooss established in Cambridge, 1941-47; returned to Essen, Germany, and reestablished Folkwang school and company, 1949; ballet master, Düsseldorf Opera House, 1954-56; retired, 1968. **Awards:** Medaille d'Or for *The Green Table*, Concours Internationale de Choreographie, Paris, 1932. **Died:** 22 May 1979 in Heilbronn, Germany.

Selected Works

1924   *Ein persisches Märchen* (mus. Wellesz)
        Persisches Ballett (mus. Wellesc)
1925   *Der Dämon* (mus. Hindemith)
        Die Braufahrt (mus. Rameau, Couperin)
1926   *Larven* (mus. Cohen)
        Tragödie (mus. Cohen)
1929   *Drosselbart* (mus. Mozart)
        Pavane (mus. Ravel)
1930   *Petrushka* (mus. Stravinsky)
        Gaukelei (mus. Cohen)
        Le Bal (mus. Rieti)
1931   *Coppélia*
        Prodigal Son (mus. Prokofiev)
        Pulcinella (mus. Stravinsky)
1932   *The Green Table* (mus. Cohen)
        The Big City (mus. Tansman)
        A Ball in Old Vienna (mus. Lanner)
1933   *Seven Heroes* (mus. Purcell, Cohen)
1935   *The Mirror* (mus. Cohen)
        Johann Strauss, Tonight! (mus. Strauss)
1943   *Company at the Manor* (mus. Beethoven, Cook)
1944   *Pandora* (mus. Gerhard)
1948   *Juventud* (mus. Handel)
1951   *Colombinade* (mus. Strauss, Montijn)
1959   *Fairie Queen* (mus. Purcell)
1962   *Castor and Pollux* (mus. Rameau)
1966   *Dido and Aeneas* (mus. Purcell)

Publications

On JOOSS: books—

Anderson, Jack, *Ballet and Modern Dance: A Concise History*, Pennington, NJ, 1992.
———, *Choreography Observed*, Iowa City, IA, 1987.
———, *The World of Modern Dance: Art without Boundaries*, Iowa City, 1997.

Au, Susan, *Ballet and Modern Dance*, London, 1988.
Blom, Lynne Anne, and L. Tarin Chaplin, *The Intimate Act of Choreography*, Pittsburgh, 1982.
Coe, Robert, *Dance in America*, New York, 1985.
Cohen, Selma Jeanne, *Next Week, Swan Lake: Reflections on Dance and Dances*, Middletown, Connecticut, 1982.
Croce, Arlene, *Going to the Dance*, New York, 1982.
Hodgson, John, and Valerie Preston-Dunlop, *Rudolf Laban: An Introduction to his Work and Influence*, Plymouth, England, 1990.
Partsch-Bergsohn, Isa, *Modern Dance in Germany and the United States: Cross Currents and Differences*, Tucson, 1994.
Reynolds, Nancy, and Susan Reimer-Torn, *Dance Classics: A Viewer's Guide to the Best-Loved Ballets and Modern Dances*, Pennington, New Jersey, 1980, 1991.
Robertson, Allen, and Donald Hutera, *The Dance Handbook*, Boston, 1988.

*   *   *

Kurt Jooss was a leading figure in the second generation of European modern dance, working in the period following the height of European Expressionism and in the footsteps of Mary Wigman and Rudolf Laban. His politically themed works led to persecution by the Nazi regime and exile from Germany, but his troubles did not prevent him from creating new works or gaining an international following.

Jooss was born in 1901 near Stuttgart. After spending time at the Württembergische Hochschule für Musik in 1920, Jooss began studying with Laban later that year and soon became his star pupil, a lead dancer in his troupe, and his assistant for four years. Jooss danced the male lead in *Die Geblendeten (The Deluded)*, which was the first production of Laban's dance company, the Tanzbühne Laban. Jooss also helped develop Labanotation (or *tanzschrift*), a method of dance notation still used today.

Jooss went with Laban to Hamburg in 1922, along with another dancer, Aino Siimola, who became Jooss's wife and life-long collaborator in 1929. While in Hamburg, Jooss also met Sigurd Leeder, who would become a close colleague. They performed a joint program, *Two Male Dancers*, in 1924. The same year, Jooss left Laban to become ballet master in Münster, though Jooss' association with Laban would continue throughout his career, and Laban's influence was evident in Jooss' choreographic style for years to come. In Münster, Jooss founded the Neue Tanzbühne (New Dance Stage) and became the dance department head at the new Westphalian Academy of Movement, Speech, and Music. Between 1924 and 1926, Jooss created five major works, including *Persisches Ballett*, set to music by Wellesc (1924); *Der Dämon*, to a Hindemith accompaniment (1925); *Die Brautfahrt* to music by Rameau and Couperin (1925); and *Larven* and *Tragödie*, to scores by Fritz Cohen (1926).

In 1927 Jooss was appointed the director of the Folkwangschule in Essen and launched the Folkwang Tanzbühne the following year, and became the ballet master at the Essen Opera House in 1930. While in Essen, he also organized the Second Dancer's Congress, which was intended to promote dance as a profession in Europe. (Laban had organized the first Congress in 1927.) Jooss considered himself a ballet choreographer throughout his career. He believed modern dance was an extension of ballet, rather than its antithesis, and that modern dance could be enhanced by ballet technique. This was a unique perspective at the time—and his modern dances incorporated simplified classical ballet movement, but in a more natural, freer, less complicated style than typical for ballet—even dropping some of the hardcore elements of ballet such as pointe shoes and pirouettes.

Jooss' works are theatrical, narrative, and representational rather than abstract, and incorporate political and social themes. This was true beginning with his first major works, created in Essen, including *Pavane* (1929) and *The Green Table* (1932), for which he is best remembered today. *The Green Table* is an antiwar piece based on the medieval Dance of Death and set to music by Fritz Cohen. Death, portrayed by Jooss in the premiere, is a key figure in the work; other characters include Diplomats, the Profiteer, the Old Woman, the Standard Bearer, and the Guerrilla Woman. Although the piece was inspired by World War I, it is relevant to modern audiences and is still performed today, under the watchful eye of Jooss's daughter, Anna Markard Jooss. Other Jooss works from this period include the light *A Ball in Old Vienna* (1932) and *The Big City* (1932). *The Green Table* won first prize (Medaille d'Or) in a prestigious choreography competition, the Concours Internationale de Choreographie, in Paris in 1932, and remained Jooss' most popular piece.

Because of the political nature of his work, as well as his association with Cohen, a Jewish composer, Jooss was forced to leave Germany under pressure from the Nazis in 1933. He took his company on tour for a year, finally settling at Dartington Hall in Devon, England in 1934. There he founded the Jooss-Leeder School with Sigurd Leeder. In the 1930s and 1940s, Jooss and his company (Ballets Jooss) toured annually throughout Europe, the United States, and South America, gaining an international reputation. His time in England was productive choreographically as well.

Jooss' years in Devon were ended by World War II. The school closed and Jooss, without British citizenship, was imprisoned for six months. He had earlier disbanded his company for a time in 1942, and created a temporary troupe of a dozen members including himself. In 1947, Jooss was granted citizenship and his company performed in Europe on behalf of the British Occupation Army. Financial difficulties forced Ballets Jooss to be disbanded again in 1947, so Jooss accepted an offer to become guest choreographer for the Chilean National Ballet in 1948, during which time he created *Juventud* and *Dithyrambus*. He returned to Europe in 1949, when he received an invitation to teach a summer course at the Folkwangschule back in Essen, and one from the Swiss Association of Professionals in Dance and Gymnastics for their summer school in Zurich. He again became the director of the dance department at the Folkwangschule, and formed the Folkwang Tanztheater der Stadt Essen, which made its debut performance in 1951 at the Essen Opera House. During this period, Jooss created *Colombinade* (1951), a humorous piece, *The Night Train* (1951), which was set in a railway compartment with two passengers, and *Journey in the Fog* (1952), which Jooss considered on a level with *The Green Table*. It was performed in four movements, representing Exile, Barbed Wire, Shadows, and Journey.

In 1953 Jooss lost the support of the Essen government and disbanded the company. He became the chief choreographer with the Düsseldorf Opera for two years beginning in 1954, and continued teaching at the Folkwangschule. He choreographed an opera production of *The Fairie Queen* in 1959. Jooss retired in 1968, but continued to restage his ballets around the world. He also revised the Labanotated scores of his dances with the help of his daughter Anna.

In 1976 the Joffrey Ballet performed an entire Jooss program, which he attended, in honor of his 75th birthday. The performance

included *The Big City*, *Pavane on the Death of an Infanta* (formerly *Pavane*), *A Ball in Old Vienna*, and *The Green Table*. A Joffrey production of *The Green Table* was filmed for the first episode of PBS's *Dance in America* series in 1976, which also featured an interview with Jooss. In May of 1979 Jooss died in a car accident near Stuttgart.

While Jooss is best known as a prolific ballet and modern dance choreographer, he is also remembered as a respected educator—among his students were Pina Bausch, Birgit Cullberg, Dai Ailian, Lucas Hoving, and Ann Hutchinson.

—Karen Raugust

JORDAN & PRESENT COMPANY
New Zealand dance company

Works (choreographed by Susan Jordan)

1975	*Brandenburg VI* (mus. J. S Bach), Auckland University Dancers
1976	*Dominion* (mus. A. Watson), Movement Theatre, Auckland
	Time Piece (mus. King's Singers), Movement Theatre, Auckland
	Maiden Over (devised sound score), Movement Theatre, Auckland
	Two into One Won't Go (mus. M. De Falla), Movement Theatre, Auckland
	Colour Spot (mus. G. Zamfir), Movement Theatre, Auckland
	Varia Three (mus. Bach), Movement Theatre, Auckland
	Nockabout (mus. M. Nock), Impulse Dance Theatre, Wellington
	Opening (mus. C. Hemmingsen), Wellington City Art Gallery official opening
1982	*Satin Pattern* (mus. Haydn), MA Thesis Concert, Washington, D.C.
	In Passing Go (mus. Authentic French folk tunes), MA Thesis Concert, Washington, D.C.
	The Guy, Fawkes (mus. H. Lazarof), MA Thesis Concert, Washington, D.C.
1983	*Three By Two For You* (mus. L. Jordan), Footnote Dance Co., Wellington
1984	*Cry Peace* (mus. N. Fitzgerald), Jordan & Present Co., Wellington
	Pacifist Piece (mus. N. Fitzgerald), Royal NZ Ballet, Wellington
	Walks of Life (mus. New Order), Royal NZ Ballet, Wellington
	Sea Fall (mus. N. Fitzgerald), NZ School of Dance, Wellington
1985	*Unknowing Steps* (mus. M. Scullion and various, text S. Beckett), Jordan & Present Co., Wellington
	Been There, Dance That (mus. various), Footnote Dance Co., Wellington
	Country Club (mus. various), Fusion Dance Co, Napier
1986	*Against the Grain* (mus. various), Jordan & Present Co., Wellington

Jordan & Present Company: *Bone of Contention.*

Holy Women (mus. various), IndepenDance, Auckland

1987 *Holy Women* (mus. various), new staging in 1993. Jordan & Present Co., Wellington

Bags of Tricks (mus. J. S. Bach), Southern Ballet, Christchurch

East, West (mus. R. Shankar), NZ School of Dance, Wellington

1988 *Stone the Crow* (mus. various), Jordan & Present Co., Wellington

Face Value (mus. S. Alexander), Jordan & Present Co., Wellington

Letter Home (mus. J. McLeod), Mary-Jane O'Reilly solo show, Auckland

1990 *Harambee! Harambee!* (mus. various), World Vision Commonwealth Tour of NZ

1991 *Carillon Dance* (mus. T. Hurd), outdoor work, Jordan & Present Co., Wellington

Still (mus. S. Alexander), Jordan & Present Co., Wellington

1992 *The Rest Is Silence* (mus. G. Smith and various, text Shakespeare), Court Theatre, Christchurch

Capital Discovery Place Opening (mus. various), outdoor work, Wellington

1993 *Bone of Contention* (des. C. Bagnall, mus. H. Fisher), Jordan & Present Co., Wellington

Hagar's Lament (mus. J. Johnson), solo for Debbie Bright, Wellington

1994 *Crossings* (mus. various big band jazz), outdoor work, Christian Dance Fellowship of NZ, Christchurch

Blinding Light (mus. various), Wellington College of Education, Civic Square Pageant, Wellington

Face Value, new version for camera (mus. S. Alexander), Jordan & Present Co., Wellington

1996 *Car Ballet* (mus. J. Roddick), outdoor work, Jordan & Present Co., Wellington

Publications

By JORDAN: articles—

"Postmodern Dance: on the Fringe of the Dance Mat," *Dance News* 29, 1984.

"Fool's Paradise: Clowning Today," *Central* 1, 1986.

"A Residency Examined," *Tirairaka Dance in New Zealand* 14, 1995.

"Parallel Lines: The Projected Image of Dance Versus the Live Encounter," in *Is Technology the Future for Dance? The Green Mill Dance Project Papers 1995,* edited by Hilary Trotter, Canberra, 1996.

"Dancing On: A Profile of Tairoa Royal," *DANZ* 3, 1997.

On JORDAN: books—

Bolwell, Jan, *Susan Jordan: The Making of a New Zealand Chore-ographer,* Wellington, 1992.

On JORDAN: articles—

"Creativity in Christian Dance," *Accent,* October 1987.
Gaitanos, Sarah, "Dancing Trio in Full Swing," *Sunday Star,* 20 November 1988.
Van Helden-Stevens, Karel, "Perspectives on Dance: An Interview with Susan Jordan," *Sound and Vision,* September 1995.
Whyte, Raewyn, "Dancing at the Edge," *Dance News,* August 1987.
———, "Dance Works of 1993: A Review Article," *Illusions: NZ Moving Image and Performing Arts Criticism,* Winter 1994.

*   *   *

Jordan & Present Company was established during 1984 by choreographer Susan Jordan. She had recently returned to New Zealand with a Master's degree in choreography from the American University in Washington D.C., and she had a clear mission: to expand the boundaries of modern dance in New Zealand in distinctly postmodern directions.

The modern dance presented in New Zealand in 1984 by companies such as Limbs, Footnote, Jenden and Solino, and Fusion Dance Theatre placed its emphasis on formal stylistic qualities, technically correct movement, a close relationship between movement and music, with the rhythm and mood and structure of movement relating closely to musical structure, with movement generated and directed by the choreographer, and with few references to the real world beyond the dance.

By contrast, the approach taken by Jordan, strongly influenced by the dance-theatre works of Meredith Monk, Pina Bausch and Sankai Juku, involve a performance vocabulary based in everyday movement performed in real time in a theatrical setting. Works are often performed in silence or with non-musical accompaniment; are episodic, multi-narrative structures in which images and sequences of movement recur or repeat, often commenting on some earlier appearance of the same sequence; and make symbolic use of everyday objects such as coins, rocks, pyjamas, teacups. Jordan's intention was to address real issues in people's lives—her own life, the dancers' lives, the lives of New Zealanders—with the invitation to audience members to examine issues in their own lives in response.

Knowing her work would be considered experimental, and would therefore be unlikely to attract significant box office support in its initial season, Jordan established a project-based, pick-up company, aiming to make one new project each year during a concentrated rehearsal period. The dancers are chosen for their willingness to collaborate in the exploration of new choreographic directions, rather than for their technical expertise, although all have full-time dance training and professional experience.

The collaborative working process of the company has changed very little over the years. It is designed to maintain individuality in the performers: each dancer researches their particular sections of the dance and contributes movement, images and text to the work as a whole, retaining their own way of moving and their own identity. Jordan selects from the material each dancer creates, and works with them to structure it into the dance.

The works presented by Jordan & Present Company, more-or-less annually since their debut in 1984, have always contained social commentary, focussed around issues of personal importance to Jordan, who describes herself as a Christian feminist. The experiences shown in the works are drawn from the dancers; the personal blended with the political to show that each person makes choices, which have implications for society as a whole. By this means, the attitudes of New Zealand society are examined, and encouragement is offered to individuals to take responsibility for their own actions and choices. *Cry Peace* (1984) explored New Zealand attitudes to war and peace throughout the twentieth century; *Carillon Dance* (1991) reconsidered them during the Gulf War. *Unknowing Steps* (1985) examined personal responsibility for the choices we make in the context of family life. *Against the Grain* (1986) examined these choices in relation to social issues, at the same time reinterpreting Biblical parables in the light of late-20th-century moralities. *Holy Women* (1988) critically questioned the treatment of women by the Church through the ages, while celebrating the achievements of women. *Stone the Crow* (1989) explored shifting relationships of younger members to the oldest woman of the family, and reflected on New Zealand attitudes to the elderly. *Bone of Contention* (1992) saluted the suffragists who achieved the vote for women in New Zealand, and *Face Value* (1995) considered the institution of marriage from a feminist perspective.

Since 1988, Jordan's work has moved out of the theatre into public, civic spaces, commenting with irony on the history and politics of the performance site. *Carillon Dance* (1991) was performed at the foot of the National War Memorial and Carillon during the Gulf War, honouring those whose lives have been lost in wars, pointing up the monumental stupidity of going to war, affirming efforts for peace and celebrating life, while drawing attention to the often overlooked music produced within the carillon. *Tiramarama/Blinding Light* (1994) brought people from normally invisible groups to perform in Civic Square—intellectually handicapped adolescents, women in their seventies and eighties, mothers with babies in strollers, men with motor-mowers. *Car Ballet* (1996) also in Civic Square, made ironic comment on the male love affair with the automobile and used eight cars and dancers.

Jordan's work has contributed significantly to the continuing development of modern dance in New Zealand. She has introduced postmodern structures and strategies into dance making in this country, and has shown what can be achieved when dancers are actively involved in the creative development of dance theatre projects. She has also provided an ethical model of artistic contracting, by creating employment contracts in which full respect and protection is given to the dancers' rights as performers and creative contributors. Through her work with members of Jordan & Present, she has fostered the creative development of 27 dancers, many of whom have continued to contribute to the development of dance in New Zealand, as dancers and in other ways.

—Raewyn White

JOSA-JONES, Paula

American dancer, choreographer, educator, and company director

Education: B.A., Lawrence University, 1968; M.A., Tufts University, 1971; Certified Movement Analyst certification, Laban/

Bartenieff Institute, 1982. **Career:** Founder/director, Jones/Performance Works, beginning 1985; has taught at Tufts University, 1977-88; Boston University, 1987-90; Jung Institute summer intensive, 1990; co-director, Green Street Studios, Cambridge (Massachusetts), 1991 to present; Bates Summer Dance Festival, 1993-97; has published several articles in *Contact Quarterly*. **Awards:** Several grants, fellowships, and awards from Massachusetts Cultural Council, New England Foundation for the Arts, U.S./Mexico Fund for Culture, Interarts Fellowship award, and others.

Works

1986	*Tremble* (video-dance w/Grabill)
	Epiphanies (video-dance w/Grabill)
	Frogs in a Well
1987	*Bone Field*
	Auf Dein Eigenes Wohl
	In Visible Light
1988	*Anima Motrix*
	At the Edge of the Garden
	Les Petits Morts
1989	*Branch*
	Until We Are Bone, Jacob's Pillow Festival
1990	*White Dreams, Wild Moon*
1991	*The Messenger*
	Flesh
	Skin w/Pauline Oliveros, Yellow Springs Institute
1992	*Eine kleine Nachtmusik,* Jacob's Pillow
	Masque, The Yard
1993	*Ofrenda (sin ti/contigo)*
	The Yellow Wallpaper, for Northeastern University
1994	*Kin*
	Branch (video-dance collaboration w/Sebring)
1995	*Wonderland,* Jacob's Pillow
	El Fantasma del Rio w/Oliveros
	Ghost Factory w/Ballantyne, Deuhr, Goss
	Skin, Meat, and Bone, George Washington University
	Ghost Dance w/Oliveros
1996	*Raving in the Wind* for the Joyce Theater
	Ashes, Ashes for Rhode Island College Dance Company
1997	*Tongue*
	Light and Bone w/poet Dine, photographer Xenios, Cervantino Festival, Mexico

Films and Videotapes

Tremble and *Epiphanies,* video-dances with Vin Grabill, both 1986. *Branch,* video-dance collaboration with Ellen Sebring, 1994.

*   *   *

Paula Josa-Jones' work grows out of a strong interest in dramatic form combined with a choreographic process which merges improvisational and authentic movement practices. She earned degrees in English and drama from Lawrence University, an M.A. in drama from Tufts University, and received Movement Analyst certification from the Laban/Bartenieff Institute in 1982.

Josa-Jones' work includes numerous collaborations with poets, musicians, video and visual artists, including the seminal work *Ghost Dance,* commissioned by the U.S./Mexico Fund for Culture and created in Monterrey, Mexico, in 1995 with composer Pauline Oliveros. The work takes place in a wooded area, with masked dancers moving through the trees and areas occupied by audience members. The performers exist as specters, playing off of the Mexican Day of the Dead festival, constantly appearing and disappearing depending on one's vantage point. Josa-Jones also collaborated with Oliveros on another work in 1995, *El Fantasma del Rio,* and had previously worked with Oliveros for 1991's *Skin,* which premiered at the Yellow Springs Institute.

Josa-Jones' work has similarities to the deeply psychological and often dark world presented by the Tanztheater of Pina Bausch; yet Josa-Jones doesn't concern herself exclusively with the male/female relationships always at the center of Bausch's work.

The nonlinear, dramatic vignettes presented by Josa-Jones are deeply personal, while charged with the archetypal energy of a Jungian shadow world. A movement vocabulary at once consistent with Josa-Jones' choreographic vision and with each of her dancers' personal eccentricities marks her collaborative process as especially curious. "The dancers, actors, and I enter the world of each piece through deep-diving vocal and movement improvisation," Josa-Jones explains. "Bodies, habits, and expectations are slowly broken down, decomposed, to reach the point where the performer is 'naked,' working from a place of emptiness and receptivity." In addition, Josa-Jones says, "Often work that is exhilarating one day may be discarded the next, or reappear as a fragmentary root of another scene or movement later. Images cluster, shifting their shapes and relationships during the rehearsal process. In this way the layers of the dance grow. It's like wandering in a dark cave: harrowing and breathtaking."

Josa-Jones is able to preserve the odd moments that evolve through improvisation—like the occasional awkwardness of a fine dancer revealing the most human and poignant qualities within—and weave them into an integrated triangle of dancer/choreographer/dance. As a result, her dances have a spontaneous quality—as though the dancers were making them up as they went along—even as it is clear that each dance is fully choreographed. Josa-Jones can also be credited with enhancing the possibilities of dance video, since her work lends itself to the imagistic world of cross-fades, a kind of supernatural visual exposure, with dancers moving across frames as if entering alternate worlds or states of consciousness. Her work with video artists defies the axiom that dance does not translate into two-dimensional media. "My passion is for work that contains both the fantastic and the mundane," Josa-Jones says. "I seek to create dance theater in which all of the elements (visual, aural, emotional) come into a balanced and surprising play, in which images are not simply illustrative or theatrical, but compelling and revealing. I want to make work which is transformative at the deepest level."

Her work as both a choreographer and an educator is informed by her integration of Peter Sellars' statement, "Being awake in the theater is good practice for being awake in the world," to which she replies, "I think we also have to dream to awaken fully." Josa-Jones invites her audience, her students, and her dancers to master the skill of being "in the body," which she says means "discover[ing] movement from a place of attention, stillness, and active listening ... experiencing fully the web of movement and choreographic choices as they are being performed." There's a deep humanity at the core of Josa-Jones' work that can be at once edifying and terrifying; Deborah Jowitt of the *Village Voice* called the group a "commedia dell'arte troupe from hell. . .that has toppled over the edge into nightmare," yet Josa-Jones' work ultimately rescues us as well.

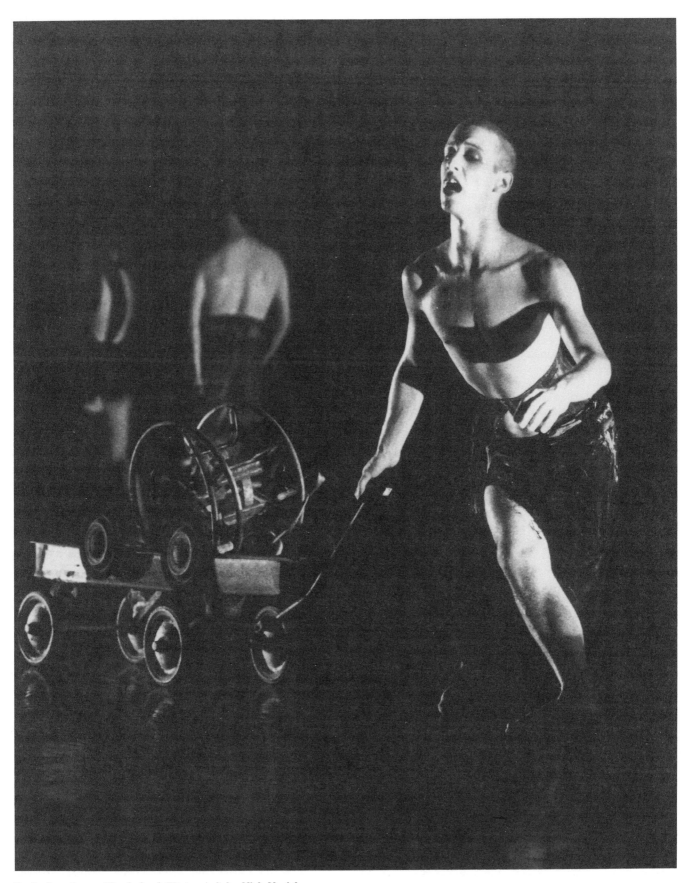

Paula Josa-Jones: *Wonderland.* **Photograph by Nick Novick.**

Her excavation of the human spirit allows us to emerge on the other side of our own nightmares with images that leave us both stunned and energized.

—Peggy Berg

JOSÉ LIMÓN DANCE FOUNDATION

The José Limón Dance Foundation, officially incorporated in 1968, is the parent organization for three entities which perpetuate the legacy of José Limón: the Limón Dance Company, the Limón Institute and Limón West Dance Project. The Limón Foundation has the distinction of being the first major American modern dance institution to survive the death of its founder.

The Limón Dance Company is the oldest of the foundation's three components, having begun its life as the José Limón Dance Company with performances at Bennington College in the summer of 1946. In a departure from the general practice of choreographers heading their own companies, Doris Humphrey was named as artistic director of Limón's group, serving in that capacity from 1946 until her death in 1958. During this period, the company served as the artistic home for new works by both Humphrey and Limón, as well as showcase for works by company members such as Ruth Currier, Lucas Hoving, and Pauline Koner. After Humphrey's death, José Limón assumed the title of director, which he would hold until his own death in 1972.

During Limón's lifetime, his company achieved many distinctions. It was the first American modern dance company to perform in Europe (1950), the first performing arts group to tour under the auspices of the American Cultural Exchange Program (1954), the first dance company to appear in Central Park's Delacorte Theater (1962) and the first dance troupe to perform at Lincoln Center (1963). The company performed in every American Dance Festival season from 1948 to 1973, and appeared at the White House (with Limón in 1967 and again in 1995 after his death). Immediately following Limón's death in 1972, company member Daniel Lewis was named acting artistic director, and he led the group on an extensive tour to the Soviet Union in 1973. Ruth Currier was then appointed as the permanent artistic director, serving until 1977 and establishing the company's identity as a repertory ensemble devoted to reviving the dance of Limón and Humphrey and commissioning new works. The company's very survival was at stake during this time and for many years thereafter, as many people questioned the need for it to continue functioning without José Limón at the helm.

In 1977, another of the company's leading dancers, Carla Maxwell, became the acting artistic director, a post she assumed permanently the following year and retains to this day. Under Maxwell's direction, the Limón Dance Company has become known for its diversity and its versatility, presenting dances by Garth Fagan, Kurt Jooss, Jirí Kylián, Phyllis Lamhut, Murray Louis, Daniel Nagrin, Anna Sokolow, Doug Varone and many others. Over the years, Maxwell has brought in a number of different artists to work with her in overseeing the company. Among them have been former company members (such as Jennifer Scanlon and Lucas Hoving) as well as those from outside the Limón tradition (Lutz Forster and Ian Horvath). In 1995 Donald McKayle was named as the company's resident choreographer and artistic mentor. At the present time, Sarah Stackhouse serves as rehearsal director and longtime company dancer Nina Watt is billed as artistic associate.

In 1985 the name was officially changed to the Limón Dance Company (from the José Limón Dance Company) in order to differentiate the company's image from the personal legacy of José Limón. It continues as the main repository of his dances as well as a champion of the unique theatrical style established by Humphrey and Limón, touring around the world and presenting home seasons on a regular basis in New York City. Other well-known dancers not already mentioned who have spent significant portions of their career in the company are Betty Jones, Louis Falco, and Jennifer Muller.

The Limón Institute has been formally constituted since 1986 to handle the educational and archival aspects of the foundation, as well as the licensing of Limón's dances to other companies. Among its projects has been the publishing of an illustrated catalogue of Limón's dances and *The Limón Journal*, a periodical which disseminates information on the Limón repertory. The Institute also organized a comprehensive exhibition in collaboration with the New York Public Library for the Performing Arts, *The Dance Heroes of José Limón*, on view in 1996 and 1997.

The Limón West Dance Project was organized by company member Gary Masters in 1992 to broaden the Foundation's reach onto the West Coast and to solidify its position as a national institution. Based in San Jose, California, this venture has initiated major residencies and performing seasons for the Limón Dance Company and nurtured a chamber ensemble to conduct residency activities, school programs, and performances throughout the region. The ensemble occasionally performs jointly with the Limón Dance Company and includes several of Limón's chamber works in its repertory.

All of the foundation's activities are generated from its home base in New York City's Soho district. A large studio fulfills most of the company's rehearsal needs and houses classes in Limón Technique. Under the same roof are the foundation's archives and an administrative staff. More information on the foundation's activities may be found on its website: www.limon.org

—Norton Owen

JUDSON DANCE THEATER

Judson Dance Theater was a collective of dancers, composers, and visual artists in the early 1960s whose experimentation is widely recognized as the beginning of postmodern dance. Initially a group of students studying composition at the Merce Cunningham studio, the participants produced concerts of their work at the Judson Memorial Church in New York City. Breaking with the thematic presentation of early modern dance, they forged a new aesthetic of elemental formal concerns, unadorned experiment and democratic methods, all infused with a heady, lids-off sense of play.

In 1960 John Cage asked Robert Dunn, who played piano for classes at the Cunningham studio (and other studios including Martha Graham's), and who was studying experimental music with him at the New School for Social Research, to teach composition. Influenced by Cage, Cunningham, and their embrace of Eastern philosophies, Dunn began teaching the new class that at first consisted of five students: Yvonne Rainer, Steve Paxton, Simone Forti, Paulus Berensohn, and Marni Mahaffay. "My general attitude in teaching," Dunn wrote in a 1989 *Contact Quarterly*, "was influenced by several somewhat disparate factions. I was impressed by what I had come to know of Bauhaus education in the arts, particularly from the writings of Moholy-Nagy, in its emphasis on the nature of the materials and on basic structural elements." In addition, Dunn's association with John Cage "had led to the project of constantly extending perceptive boundaries and contexts. From Heidegger, Sartre, Far Eastern buddhism, and taoism, in some personal amalgam, I had the notion in teaching of making a 'clearing,' a sort of 'space of nothing,' in which things could appear and grow in their own nature." Dunn's philosophy brought him a long distance from the approach of Louis Horst, then presiding guru of modern dance composition, whose insistence on a theme-and-variations format had become formulaic by that time. Taking the lead from Cage's methods in experimental music, Dunn introduced chance procedures. Sometimes his assignments were wide open, bound only by the merest structure, e.g. "make a three-minute dance." The students felt freed and challenged by Dunn's teaching and excited by each other. In 1961, the students organized an informal showing at the Living Theater, but in 1962, they searched for a place to perform their work publicly. Rainer and Paxton auditioned their dances at the 92nd Street "Y" and were turned down. Judson Memorial Church on West 4th Street in Greenwich Village had already exhibited works by pop artists, including "Happenings" by Claes Oldenburg, Jim Dine, Red Grooms, and Allan Kaprow, and film and poetry. Al Carmines, then the new minister, welcomed the young dancers. The first performance, entitled *A Concert of Dance*, was given 6 July 1962 and lasted over three hours. It presented works by Judith Dunn (who assisted her husband Robert in teaching some of the sessions), Ruth Emerson, Deborah Hay, Fred Herko, Steve Paxton, David Gordon, Gretchen MacLane, John Herbert McDowell, Rudy Perez, Yvonne Rainer, Carol Scothorn, Elaine Summers, Jennifer Tipton and others. Later concerts were numbered, reaching number 16 in April 1964, and included works by Trisha Brown, Remy Charlip, Lucinda Childs, David Gordon, Sally Gross, Elizabeth Keen, Aileen Passloff, Albert Reid, and Arlene Rothlein, among others.

One of the hallmarks of Judson Dance Theater was the cross-pollination of ideas of artists of different disciplines. Visual artists Robert Rauschenberg, Robert Morris, Alex Hay, and Robert Huot made dances; so did composers Philip Corner, John Herbert McDowell, James Tenney, and Malcolm Goldstein; writer Jackson Mac Low contributed material and ideas. Collage, fragmentation, loosely-structured scores, radical juxtaposition, and chance were shared methods; pedestrian movement and spontaneity were shared values. The following descriptions give a glimpse of the type of actions seen at Judson Church and other places where the group performed: in *Mannequin Dance* (1962), David Gordon slowly turned and descended to the ground wearing a bloodied lab coat and singing Broadway tunes while James Waring passed out balloons and asked the audience to let the air out slowly; in *Witness II* (1964), Judith Dunn danced a solo during Robert Dunn's *Doubles for 4,* in which four performers played with cards to indicate patterns of clapping; in Trisha Brown's *Lightfall* (1963), she and Paxton perched on each other's backs, fell, and ran to a tape of Forti whistling; in *Carnation* (1964), Lucinda Childs jabbed sponges in her mouth and later did a handstand while kicking off a huge sock; in *Flat* (1963), Steve Paxton walked around while removing pieces of clothing and hanging them on hooks pasted to his skin; in *Prairie* (1963), Alex Hay strapped himself to the top of a metal structure designed by sculptor Charles Ross, with a pillow for padding, and answered his own voice on tape asking him how he felt; in *Pelican* (1963), Rauschenberg and a fellow artist glided on roller skates, parachutes aloft, occasionally lifting Carolyn Brown, who wore sweat pants and pointe shoes; in Yvonne Rainer's *Terrain* (1963), slats of wood were hurled down from the balcony while dancers performed disjunctive movements; Philip Corner followed a score in *Keyboard* (1964) by playing the piano with his heel and other body parts; and in Carolee Schneemann's *Lateral Splay* (1963), 12 performers ran at top speed until they collided with an object or another runner.

Carmines, Judson's minister, wrote in the 1967-68 issue of *Dance Scope* that "My sensation from the first concerts was one of awe at the stinging vitality of the work, and fear and anxiety that the traditional ground rules of all art seemed to be obliterated by the work. . .One quality which seemed to pervade most of the early Judson dance pieces (though not all, one could never be absolute about such extraordinary diversity) was a kind of serene, powerful attention to the movement—or lack of movement—happening at the exact [same] time."

Among the dancers' primary influences were Merce Cunningham, James Waring, Anna Halprin, and the Living Theater. Some of the dancers, like Steve Paxton and Judith Dunn, were members of Cunningham's company. Aileen Passloff, David Gordon, and Yvonne Rainer had worked with Waring, a ballet teacher and choreographer known for his wit and camp. Gordon writes in *Movement Research Performance Journal* (no. 14) that he was already familiar with chance procedures through Waring's classes, while some of the other dancers had studied with Anna (then Ann) Halprin in California. Forti had danced with her from 1956, Gross in 1957, and in the summer workshop of 1960 Forti met Rainer, Brown, Emerson, and June Ekman there. The Halprin emphasis on improvisation and task dances fostered a relish for game structures, spontaneity, and a workmanlike demeanor. Steve Paxton attributes some of his sense of the new permissiveness to seeing the anarchic, on-the-edge Living Theater, which was upstairs in the same building. In Banes' *Democracy's Body: Judson Dance Theater 1962-1964,* Paxton says, "The work I did there was first of all to flush out my 'why-nots'. . . .'Why not?' was a catch-word at that time. It was a very permissive time."

Though we tend to remember only the most formal and rebellious aspects, Judson involved dance artists of many different styles. Some of the dancers were inclined to the lyrical and romantic, e.g. Fred Herko, Arlene Rothlein and Aileen Passloff, but all the individual styles fed into the makings of postmodern dance. As Rainer said in a Bennington College Judson Project interview, "There was new ground to be broken, and we were standing on that ground." Writer Jill Johnston reveled in the breakthroughs, serving as advocate and news bearer as passionately as John Martin had spread the word about Martha Graham decades earlier.

Like the Bauhaus and Diaghilev eras in Europe, Judson Dance Theater was a period of innovation and crossover influences that changed the arts. Like Bauhaus, Judson rejected the grandiosity of its forbears and searched instead for beauty in the ordinary. Other lasting achievements of Judson were the breakdown of the choreographer vs. dancer hierarchy; extending the Cagean dictum that "any sound can be music" to "any movement can be dance"; a new approach to phrasing that shunned "climax" and treated each movement democratically; a rejection of the "heroic" presentation of ballet and early modern dance in favor of ordinary, human-scale figures; the validity of choices being made in performance; and a conviction that dance could stem from curiosity rather than agonizing. All of these contributed to a new sense of engagement for the performer and a greater alertness for the audience.

The directions that Judson artists took their work in the 1970s to the 1990s are numerous. In Trisha Brown the Judson minimalism has blossomed into a full-bodied, articulate, elusive style of movement; Deborah Hay has built an ethic around dance in communities; David Gordon has incorporated word and movement in his theater works with the anti-hero aesthetic of Judson; Steve Paxton developed contact improvisation and sustained a solo career as a dancemaker who improvises; the improvisation group the Grand Union, initiated by Yvonne Rainer, continues to serve as the elusive model for young improvisers while Rainer herself became an experimental narrative filmmaker; Elaine Summers pioneered kinetic awareness, one of the first release techniques; Carolee Schneemann developed movement assemblages and became part of the feminist performance art movement; and Brown and Lucinda Childs pioneered full-blown interdisciplinary collaborations with visual artists such as Robert Rauschenberg and Sol LeWitt. These examples had a tremendous influence on the next generation of choreographers as well as on the artists who developed performance art in the 1970s. One could say that the legacy of Judson Dance Theater is the challenge to navigate between two seemingly opposite values: total permissiveness and freedom on the one hand, and the minimalist aesthetic—the wish to pare down to essentials—on the other.

Publications

Books—

Banes, Sally, *Democracy's Body: Judson Dance Theater 1962-64*, Durham, North Carolina, 1995.

———, *Writing Dancing in the Age of Postmodernism*, Hanover, New Jersey, 1994.

———, *Greenwich Village 1963: Avant-Garde Performance and the Effervescent Body*, Hanover, 1993.

———, *Terpsichore in Sneakers: Post-Modern Dance*, Hanover, 1987.

Halprin, Anna, *Moving Toward Life: Five Decades of Transformational Dance,* Hanover, 1995.

Johnston, Jill, *Marmalade Me* (expanded), Hanover, 1997.

Jowitt, Deborah, *Time and the Dancing Image,* New York, 1988.

Livet, Anne, editor, *Contemporary Dance,* New York, 1978.

McDonagh, Don, *The Rise & Fall & Rise of Modern Dance,* New York, 1971.

Rainer, Yvonne, *Work: 1961-1973,* New York, 1974.

Wynne, Peter, *Judson Dance: An Annotated Bibliography of the Judson Dance Theater and of Five Major Choreographers— Trisha Brown, Lucinda Childs, Deborah Hay, Steve Paxton, and Yvonne Rainer,* Englewood, New Jersey, 1978.

Articles—

Dunn, Robert, "Judson Dance Theater," *Contact Quarterly*, Winter, 1989.

"Judson Dance Theater," *Ballet Review*, Vol. 1, 1967.

"Judson Dance Theater," *Dance Scope*, Fall-Winter 1967-68.

Perron, Wendy (guest editor), "The Legacy of Robert Dunn," *Movement Research Performance Journal #14.*

Perron, Wendy, editor, *Judson Dance Theater: 1962-1966*, Bennington College Judson Project catalogue, 1981.

Bennington College Judson Project interviews and video reconstructions are available at the Dance Research Collection of the New York Public Library at Lincoln Center, and at The Kitchen Center in New York City.

—Wendy Perron

KAST, Maggie

American dancer and choreographer

Born: Maggie Nash, 7 March 1938 in Toronto. **Education:** Studied with Ethel Butler; University of Chicago, B.A. 1958; Catholic Theological Union, M.T.S. 1987. **Family:** Married Eric C. Kast, 1960 (died 1988); children: three sons and one daughter. **Career:** Danced with Ethel Butler, Washington, D.C.; first choreography, 1961; co-founder/director with Neville Black, Chicago Contemporary Dance Theater (CCDT), 1963-65; sole director, beginning 1965; CCDT disbanded 1980s; began liturgical dancing through the Catholic Theological Union.

Works

Facade; My House: The Place and Body; A Mother Remembers; Children's Crusade; Crossings; Dies Irae: Days of Anger; Dithyramb; Embodied Prayer; Fairy Tale; Four Encounters; Fresh Footprints; Hop, Skip, Run and Dance; Infidelities; Jamboree; Medieval Pilgrimage; Never Gonna Dance; Nothing Is the Thing to Fear; Particles; Purification for Sylvia Plath; Roman Circus; Silence for the Living; Sinister Adventure; So to Speak; Spy Counter Spy; The Vietnam Story; Travels and Farewells; and *Tropical Juice.*

* * *

Maggie Kast has had a long career in Chicago as a dancer, choreographer, and director of the Chicago Contemporary Dance Theater. She studied modern dance with Ethel Butler, a veteran of the Martha Graham Dance Company, and danced with Butler's Washington, D.C., group in the 1950s. Kast came to Chicago circa 1960 to attend the University of Chicago, and has lived there ever since, centering her career in and around the city.

Kast's first choreography was *Facade* performed in 1961 at Northwestern University's Thorne Hall under the auspices of the Chicago Dance Council. After graduation from the University of Chicago, with a bachelor's degree, she lived in the intellectually lively Hyde Park area. In 1963, together with dancer Neville Black, she founded the Chicago Contemporary Dance Theater, a modern dance performance ensemble collaborating with Chicago composers, musicians, and designers. When Black moved to the West Indies in 1965, Kast became the company's sole director for the following years.

The first performances of the CCDT were held in The Last Stage, a venue for avant-garde theatricals in the University of Chicago area. Later the group performed in various Chicago modern dance sites—Synthetic Theater (a store front), MoMing (a converted Church), and the Dance Center of Columbia College (a rehabilitated cinema theater). In the 1970s CCDT became the resident dance company of the Body Politic, an enclave of several theater spaces and a dance studio. There Kast conducted a dance school and presented the company for several years.

Trained in the Martha Graham technique and some classical ballet, Kast had an eclectic dance vocabulary. She was not interested in abstract dance; in her works there was always a strong message—humanistic, political, feminist, religious. A protester of the Vietnam War, in the 1970s she choreographed *The Vietnam Story,* an explicit picture of life in a south Vietnam village portraying the wrongfulness and cruelty of the war. Before family values became politically correct, Kast translated her own domestic experiences into dance. There was her solo *A Mother Remembers* to Bartók music, and *Tropical Juice* to music by Douglas Ewart, called a "celebration of primal womanhood." The tragedy of the accidental death of one of Kast's young children was the basis of a heartbreaking dance, and there was more than domesticity in 1979's *My House: The Place and Body* with the subtitle *I've Come in Mourning to be Born In.*

Maggie Kast was particularly successful in presenting dances for children, whose ways she was acutely aware of in her charming *Hop, Skip, Run and Dance* and *Never Gonna Dance.* Kast's dances were innovative and years ahead of their time—the frequent murky symbolism was explained by verbal elements; she encouraged audience involvement; invented new types of movement; and used vocal sounds other than verbal. With the closing of the Body Politic premises in the 1980s, the Chicago Contemporary Dance Theater and school ceased to exist, and Kast turned her dancing and choreography to a longtime interest—liturgical dance, sponsored by the Catholic Theological Union. With the collaboration of a like-minded group, she explored movement as prayer, patterning the choreography to the unique church space.

—Ann Barzel

KEEN, Elizabeth

American dancer, choreographer, company director, and educator

Born: 1938 in Huntington, New York. **Education:** Studied with Hanya Holm at the Adelphi University Children's Theater program; attended prep classes at Juilliard; attended Radcliffe College then Barnard College, trained at the School of American Ballet. **Career:** Danced and toured with Tamiris-Nagrin Dance Company, 1960-62; dancer, Paul Taylor Dance Company, 1961-62; co-founder, Studio Nine; founder/artistic director, Elizabeth Keen Dance Company, 1970; faculty, Juilliard, from 1989; has also taught at Sarah Lawrence College, New York University, Pratt Institute, and Princeton University. **Awards:** Several National Endowment for the Arts (NEA) choreographic fellowships.

Roles

1960   *Womansong* (Tamiris)
1961   *Junction* (Taylor), Hunter College Playhouse
          Insects & Heroes (Taylor), Connecticut College

Other roles include: Revivals of *Three Epitaphs, Rebus,* and others by Taylor.

Works (performed at the Judson Memorial Church in New York City unless otherwise noted)

1962   *Dawning* (mus. Friedman), Woodstock, New York
          Sea Tangle (mus, Friedman), Woodstock, New York
          The Perhapsy (e.e. cummings poetry), Woodstock, New York
          Match (with Gus Solomons, Jr.), Woodstock, New York
1963   *Bird Poem* (mus. Friedman)
          Blinkers (mus. Tristano)
          Reins
          Formalities (mus. Stravinsky)
1965   *Suite in C Minor* (mus. Bach)
          Red Sweater Dance
          One X Four
1967   *Scanning* (mus. Giuffre)
          Short Circuit
          Stop Gap (mus. Tatum)
          Rushes
          Attics
          Recipe
1968   *Sub-Sun*
          Everyman, city streets in Brooklyn
1969   *Point*
          Mime Hamlet (theater), Stratford, Connecticut
          West Side Story (theater, mus. Bernstein), city streets in Brooklyn
          Mr. Estaban (theater)
1970   *Poison Variations* (mus. Watson, Press), Manhattan School of Music
          The Train
          On Edge
          Quilt
1971   *Parentheses*
          Quilt (revised), (mus. traditional), Judson Dance Theater
1972   *Amalgamated Brass*
          Tempo
          The Unravish'd Bride
          The Mother of Us All (theater)
          Anna K (theater)
          Act Without Words, No. 2
1973   *Onyx*
          Dancing to Records
          Enclosure Acts
1974   *Seasoning*
          The Freedom of the City (theater)
1975   *A Polite Entertainment for Ladies and Gentlemen* (mus. Foster), City Center
          Line Drawing
          Polly (theater)
          Open Parenthesis
          Close Parenthesis
          Dancing to Records
1976   *Rainbow Tonight*
          The Kitchen (theater)
1977   *A Fair Greeting*
          The Last Snack
          Carmina Burana
          U.S.A. (theater)
1978   *Continuum*
          The Forget-Me-Not
          Garlic and Sapphires
          My Mother Was a Fortune Teller (theater)
          Swamp (theater)
1979   *Slash*
          Ruins
1980   *Quadrille*
          King David
          Jane Avril (theater)
1982   *Taking the Air*

Other works include: *Mini-Quilt, Pale-Cool, Pale-Warm;* several operas including *Carmen, Falstaff, La Traviata, Polly, Salomé, The Beggar's Opera, The Fiery Angel,* and *The Mother of Us All; A Comedy of Errors* for Joseph Papp's New York Shakespeare Festival; other productions for the American Shakespeare Theatre, Goodman Theatre (Chicago), McCarter Theatre (Princeton), ArtPark, Long Wharf (New Haven), and others.

Publications

On KEEN: books—

Clarke, Mary, and David Vaughan, editors, *The Encyclopedia of Dance & Ballet,* New York, 1977.
McDonagh, Don, *The Complete Guide to Modern Dance,* Garden City, New York, 1976.
———, *The Rise and Fall and Rise of Modern Dance,* New York, 1970.

On KEEN: articles—

Barnes, Clive, review, *New York Times,* 8 February 1967.
"Elizabeth Keen," in *Biographical Dictionary of Dance* by Barbara Naomi Cohen-Stratyner, New York, 1982.
Zimmerman, Elizabeth, review, *Dance Magazine,* November 1982.

*   *   *

Elizabeth Keen's diverse interest in movement, be it modern dance, ballet, mime, or a combination of several forms, is revealed in the variety of her work. She has demonstrated a knack for experimentation, including multimedia approaches with the use of projected images and the spoken word. Her work often is dramatic without being forced into rigid characterization or stories, and generally infused with what Don McDonagh, writing in *The Complete Guide to Modern Dance,* characterized as "a wickedly deft sense of humor."

Born in Huntington, New York, in 1938 Keen was interested in dance and drama from an early age. She participated in the Adelphi University Children's Theater program, under the direction of Hanya Holm, and attended the Preparatory Division of the Juilliard School. During her second year at Radcliffe, Keen decided to pursue dance training more seriously and transferred to Barnard College in Manhattan where she could study dance at one of the area's well-known dance schools. She studied ballet at the School of American Ballet and modern dance at the Tamiris-Nagrin studio; later study included composition with Robert Dunn and mime. Her choreography reflects her ever-widening interests in dance by incorporating ballet, modern dance, mime, natural gesture and movement, and even European court dancing.

Keen was a member of the Tamiris-Nagrin Dance Company from 1960 to 1962. She performed in Helen Tamiris' *Womansong* (1960), among others. During this time, she also joined the Paul Taylor Dance Company with which she toured for a year, appearing in *Insects & Heroes*, *Junction*, *Rebus*, and *Three Epitaphs*. Keen left the Paul Taylor company in 1962 to pursue her own choreography. She joined with other young choreographers, including Gus Solomons Jr., to rent a loft where each could choreograph. The resulting cooperative was named Studio Nine. Another collective, formed in 1962, was the Judson Dance Theater, which proved to be an important showcase for Keen's work. Although she was not one of the founding members of Judson, she showed her own work and participated in the work of others at this focal point for avant-garde performance in the 1960s. Keen eventually formed her own company, Elizabeth Keen Dance Company, in 1970.

Keen's early works were mostly solos to jazz scores, including *Dawning* and *Sea Tangle*, both performed at the second Judson Dance Concert in Woodstock, New York, in 1962. In *Sea Tangle*, Keen explores being able to move easily in all directions by simulating the weightlessness of space or floating in water. Experimentation has become a sort of hallmark of Keen's choreography; she has used unconventional space—such as a rooftop—with as much as ease as a more traditional venue. Works now deemed "site-specific" were attempted by Keen long before the term emerged, and as McDonagh puts it, "There seems to be no space too difficult for her to consider as suitable for dance." Another facet of Keen's adventurous tinkering is with music. While most of her work is performed to music, the movement does not always imitate the structure of the musical piece; at times Keen will even choreograph a work to one score but select a different, yet complementary piece, to be used in the finished performance.

In *Perhapsy* (1962), an early work without a jazz-based score, Keen experiments with the spoken word. Based on a poem by e.e. cummings, *Perhapsy* was Keen's first attempt to weave words into dance movements, an interest she developed in greater depth in her later work. The themes of Keen's work often take the form of dramatic nonlinear vignettes that don't adhere strictly or otherwise to a story or characterization. In *A Polite Entertainment for Ladies and Gentlemen* (1975), six couples dressed in 19th-century clothes perform to the music of Stephen Foster. They engage each other in glimpses of life which reveal the competition, jealousy, awkwardness, and infatuation found in relationships between men and women throughout time, although here veiled by social manners of the past.

Poison Variations (1970) grew from Keen's musings about Hamlet's mother, conjuring a series of "what ifs" about her complicity in the death of her husband. These episodes, along with others, illustrate the interconnection of relationships and their ultimate unreliability. Connecting the vignettes are displays of cooperation and indifference; the piece ends with a dancer's leap sending him crashing to the floor when another steps away from making the catch. Other works by Keen deal with human frustration. In *Scanning* (1967) a dancer performs movements demanding great technical ability with a joyousness that is tempered by frustration at not being able to quite reach the ultimate goal. *Short Circuit* and *Stop Gap*, both in 1967, also explore the frustration on expending energy with only limited results.

Keen has used film projections to heighten the effect of her choreography. In *Quilt* (1971), projected images of quilts join actual quilts to create a vibrant background which reinforces the image of the colorfully-costumed dancers swirling on stage. In *Rushes* (1967), images of three women dancing, abstract patterns, smoke, the sea, and other natural objects are projected while the same three women perform on stage. In *Taking the Air* (1982), Keen uses slides of turn-of-the-century beach scenes and dresses her dancers in period bathing suits.

Keen has been active in staging and choreographing for theater companies, street theater, and off-Broadway musicals. She has worked with the American Shakespeare Festival, the Williamstown Playhouse, the Lenox Arts Center, and the Kennedy Center. In the early 1980s, she was a resident choreographer with Daniel Lewis Dance, a repertory company. She has also taught in the drama division at the Juilliard School of Music since 1989.

—Janette Goff Dixon

KEUTER, Cliff

American dancer, choreographer, company director, and educator

Born: 1940 in Idaho. **Education:** Studied with Welland Lathrop; attended San Francisco State College; moved to New York to pursue dance studies. **Career:** Danced with several companies, including those of Anna Sokolow, John Herbert McDowell, Lucas Hoving, and Paul Sanasardo; joined Tamiris-Nagrin Dance Company, 1962; joined Paul Taylor Dance Company, 1967; co-founder, Studio Nine, 1963; formed his own company, 1969; co-director, Palo Alto Dance Theater; founder, New Dance Company; teacher, C.W. Post College (Long Island).

Roles

1963	*Rituals* (Tamiris), Tamiris-Nagrin Dance Company
	Versus (Tamiris), Tamiris-Nagrin Dance Company
	The Man Who Did Not Care (Nagrin), Tamiris-Nagrin Dance Company
1967	*Agathe's Tale* (Taylor), Paul Taylor Dance Company
	Lento (Taylor), Paul Taylor Dance Company
	Public Domain (Taylor), Paul Taylor Dance Company
1969	*Private Domain* (Taylor), Paul Taylor Dance Company
1970	*Dance in Two Rows (Version III)* (John Herbert McDowell), Judson Memorial Church, New York

Other roles include: *The American Journey* (Nagrin) and others for the Tamiris-Nagrin Dance Company; *Scudorama* (Taylor) and others for the Paul Taylor Dance Company, as well as works by Sokolow, Sanasardo, and Hoving.

Works

1963	*Collapse of Tall Towers*
	Entrances
1964	*Atsumori*

1965   *As It Was, Love*
        After a While, Love
1966   *A Cold Sunday Afternoon, A Little Later,* duet, Dance
            Theatre Workshop
        The Orange Dance
        Now What, Love
        White Shirt
        Cross-Play
        Hold
1967   *Beyond Night*
        Eight
1968   *Small Room*
        Dangling Man
        *Three-sided Peach Viewed Variously Three Hours of the
            Day of the Plastic Garment Bag*
1969   *The Game Man and the Ladies* (mus. Sims; costumes by
            Keuter), Minor Latham
        Playhouse, New York
        Letter to Paul
        Dream a Little Dream of Me, Sweetheart
1970   *Sunday Papers*
        Three for Four Plus One
        Twice
        Now Is the Hour in the Wild Garden
        Crown Blessed
        Bread, And the Proudest Man Around
        A Snake in Uncle Sammy's Garden
1971   *Amazing Grace*
        Gargoyles
        Wood
        Old Harry
        Poem in October
        If You Want Meditation, You Have to Work for It
        Fall Gently on Thy Head
1972   *New Baroque*
        I Want Somebody, Yes I Do
        Match
        Hold III
        Poles
        Passage
        Cui Bono
        A Christmas Story for Nederlands Dans Theater
1973   *Unusual in Our Time*
        Musete di Taverni
        Plaisirs d'Amour
        Visit
1974   *Restatement of Romance*
1975   *The Murder of George Keuter*
        Voice
        Burden of Vision
        Station
        Field
        Of Us Two
        Table
1976   *Tetrad*
        Interlude
1978   *Third Crossing*
        Catulli Carmina
        Day Before Easter
1980   *Women Song,* dedicated to Helen Tamiris, Palo Alto Dance
            Theater

1981   *Figures of Wind* for Ballet Rambert
1984   *Portal*

Publications

On KEUTER: articles—

Baker, Robb, "Cliff Keuter: Making Somethings Out of
    Everythings," *Dance Magazine,* December 1973.
"Cliff Keuter," in *Biographical Dictionary of Dance* by Barbara
    Naomi Cohen-Stratyner, New York, 1982.
Percival, John, review, *Dance Magazine,* July 1981.
Ross, Janice, review, *Dance Magazine,* September 1980.
———, review, *Dance Magazine,* June 1984.
Simpson, Herbert M., "Cliff Keuter: Reaching for the Human Re-
    sponse" *Dance Magazine* August 1979.

*   *   *

The imaginative dances of modern dancer and choreographer Cliff
Keuter have often been described as "surreal." His love of movement and his drive to convey a vision or his perception of reality,
are displayed in his energetic dances filled with unusual props and
stage settings.

Keuter was born in Idaho in 1940. He started dance lessons when
he was young, but started serious dance training with Welland
Lathrop in San Francisco when his family moved to California.
Keuter continued to study composition and technique with Welland
while he attended San Francisco State College as a creative writing
major and drama minor. Keuter met Daniel Nagrin at the college and
attended summer workshops with him in Maine. Keuter then moved
to New York where he studied dance and performed with various
dance companies. In 1962 he joined the Tamiris-Nagrin Dance Company and performed in Helen Tamiris's *Rituals* and *Versus* and
Nagrin's *The Man Who Did Not Care* and *American Journey.* He
joined the Paul Taylor company in 1967, with which he toured and
performed in *Agathe's Tale, Lento, Scudorama, Public Domain,* and
Private Domain. Other companies for which he performed include
those of Anna Sokolow, John Herbert McDowell, Lucas Hoving,
and Paul Sanasardo.

Even as a dancer, Keuter was more interested in choreography;
while in others' companies, he studied how dances were constructed.
In 1963 Keuter joined nine other young choreographers to share the
expenses of a loft in which they could work on their own dances.
They named their cooperative venture Studio Nine. Keuter performed his first duet, *Cold Sunday Afternoon, A Little Later* at the
Dance Theatre Workshop in 1966 with Elina Mooney, a Studio
Nine partner. Keuter formed his own company in 1969, after which
he largely only performed in his own works, except for some works
by Paul Sanasardo and members of Keuter's own company.

Keuter's choreography is designed to stimulate the imagination.
It's energetic and filled with changes in tempo and direction. He
makes wide use of props, everything from long styrofoam snakes
in *Old Harry* (1971) to collections of plastic helmet liners used as
cushioning in a soldier's steel helmet. Human relationships and the
matter of choice and indecision are frequent themes which Keuter
has explored with both seriousness and humor. His first dance for
his own company in 1969 took a humorous look at the relationships between men and women. In *The Game Man and the Ladies,*
Keuter is the lone man among three women vying for his affection.
As attentions shift among the dancers, the man struts his masculin-

Cliff Keuter with Karla Wolfangle performing *Table,* **1976. Photograph © Johan Elbers.**

ity while apparently enjoying the pursuit as much as the women enjoy the contest. Crumpled wads of newspaper, some stuffed into costumes and pulled out, others gathered from the floor, join a broom, a basketball, an umbrella, and helmet liners in the cast of props.

Keuter has often used a stream-of-consciousness approach in creating his dances. As both a poet and a painter, Keuter has a rich source of images from which to draw. After gathering the images, he edits and rearranges them to shape the work's dramatic tension. Keuter's works vary in the degree to which he distills the images. In discussing *The Murder of George Keuter* (1975), Keuter explains that in this dance "even though there is a randomness about it and a kind of cataclysmic tumult of violent activity which is juxtaposed with a certain poetic reverie and quietness and humor between these four rough and tough guys, there is at the core a central thread of urgency, which is 'Someone's gonna get killed!'"

Herbert M. Simpson, in his August 1979 article for *Dance Magazine*, describes Keuter's gift for stagecraft, stating that Keuter "seems to 'block' his dancers with a theatrical sureness that at all times presents a stage-picture which 'reads' clearly: primary and secondary focus, mood, character, dramatic thrust, and telling image are all correctly and vividly pictured." Although many of Keuter's dances tell stories, his focus is less on the narration and more on his perception of the issues creating the situation. At times his dances are energetic compilations of images and at other times they build in strength through joining dance and musical structures.

In the winter of 1972, Keuter created *A Christmas Story* for the Nederlands Dans Theater which used a 74-piece orchestra, a 60-foot-by-40-foot backdrop, and a large cast. The mammoth work also included three monsters slouching toward Bethlehem. He has set other works for the Nederlands Dans Theater and for the Bat-Dor Dance Company in Israel. Also in 1981, he created *Figures of Wind* for the Ballet Rambert.

Keuter was co-director of the Palo Alto Dance Theater, which was founded in 1978 by Richard Gibson, to be a launching pad for Gibson's students who want to join a professional dance company. Keuter premiered his *Women Song*, dedicated to Helen Tamiris, there in 1980. In addition, Keuter formed another troupe, the New Dance Company, based in San Jose. He has also taught for nine years at C.W. Post College on Long Island.

—Janette Goff Dixon

KIBBUTZ CONTEMPORARY DANCE COMPANY
Israeli modern dance company

There are about 230 kibbutzim (collective settlements) in Israel; the entire kibbutz population of today, however, is less than three percent of the country. Nevertheless, since the 1930s, artists belonging to the kibbutz movement have played a considerable role in the performing arts in Israel's general population.

In the late 1960s several dancers and choreographers—members of kibbutzim—decided to start a semiprofessional dance company as a framework for themselves and their works. They all were former students of many artists belonging to the generation of Gertrud Kraus, who worked in the central European Ausdruckstanz style of the 1930s. One of them, Oshar Elkayam, had formerly danced with the Batsheva Dance Company. In the beginning, the company worked and performed just two days a week because it was all the kibbutz organization could afford.

In 1973 Yehudit Arnon (born in Slovakia in 1926), a member of this aspiring group, became the artistic director of the fledgling Kibbutz Dance Company (the word "Contemporary" was later added to the company's name in order to preclude the possibility of audiences outside Israel erroneously thinking the group was a folkdance ensemble). Arnon held the post of artistic director until 1997 when Rami Be'er, the company's resident choreographer since 1990, took over. Arnon, along with Gene Hill-Sagan, who began choreographing for the KDC in 1977, became the group's mentors and ushered in the transition from a semiamateur group to a full-fledged professional modern dance company. Hill-Sagan had originally come to Israel with Flora Cushman at the invitation of the Jerusalem Rubin Dance Academy and the Bat-Dor Dance Company. Once in Israel, Cushman noticed that some of the students in her summer course were, as she put it, "connected to themselves"—meaning that they showed a certain honesty in their work and refrained from the usual show-offish quality so many dance students tended to exhibit. She soon realized that all of these students had come from training at the Regional Dance Studio at Ga'aton, directed by Yehudit Arnon. In 1975, Arnon invited Cushman to come work with the KCDC (where she remained until her death, devoted to the studio and its students; in tribute her ashes were buried in front of the KCDC studios).

The special atmosphere of the kibbutz company soon attracted well-known choreographers, who came to visit Ga'aton, in the northern part of Israel where the company worked, or saw performances during tours abroad; among these were Jiri Kylian, Anna Sokolow, Nils Christe, Mats Ek and Christopher Bruce, whose works became part of the KCDC's repertory. Suzanne Linke and Daniel Ezralow have also repeatedly worked for the KCDC. Among the Israeli choreographers who have created for the company are Hedda Oren, Ohad Naharin, Ruth Ziv-Eyal, Amir Kolben and others. When Rami Be'er rejoined the company after completing his compulsory military service in 1984, his share as a choreographer increased until he became house-choreographer and was later appointed artistic director in 1997.

Be'er's choreographic style is based on spatial movement design. He uses ramps, ladders and other elevations to achieve different levels from which the dancers perform. He has created several works, from 70 to 80 minutes in length, dealing with topical social or political phenomena; the lynchpins of his group works are emo-

Kibbutz Contemporary Dance Company: *Minuit.* **Dancer: Uri Ivgy. Photograph by Uri Nevo-Romano.**

tionally charged duets and solos. Among his important works are 1986's *Los Atados* with music by Oded Zehavi, and 1989's *Reservist's Diary*, dealing with his own experiences as a soldier during the Palestinian intifada [uprising]. Two years later came *Real Time*, about kibbutz education, followed by *Naked Town* in 1993, *Aide-memoire* in 1994, and *Someplace* from 1996. The company has 15 to 20 dancers and has toured extensively in Europe, America and the Far East.

Publications

Manor, Giora, editor, "Twenty-five Years of the KCDC," *Israel Dance Quarterly,* No. 9, 1996.

—Giora Manor

KIM Wha-suk
Korean dancer, choreographer, artistic director, and educator

Born: 2 December 1949, in Kwangju, southern Korea. **Education:** Studied ballet at Kwangju Girls High School, modern dance at Ewha

Women's University; Ewha Women's University, M.A. in dance education 1976; Hanyang University, Ph.D. 1986; learned "San-jo" from Kim Jin-gul, Korean traditional martial arts from Yook Tae-hwan. **Career:** Member of Yook Wan-soon Dance Company, 1969-76; founded Kim Bock-hee and Kim Wha-suk Modern Dance company, 1971; produced 36 works over the next 20 years, co-choreographed with Kim Bock-hee; first Korea tour, 1978, and annually thereafter; faculty at Kumran Girl's High School, 1972-78; first overseas performance with *Tale of Chun-hyang,* at Paris Cité Universaire, 1977; participated in 1st, 3rd, 7th, and 11th Dance Festival of Korea 1979-89; founded Kim Wha-suk SAPPHO Modern Dance Company, 1985, and became its company artistic director and choreographer; participated in the 23rd Paris International Dance Festival with *A Letter from Jinggangman,* 1985; performed *A Visit from Yosuk, The Princess of Shilla* at the 18th Cervantino International Festival, 1990; performed at the Asian Games Celebration Performance, 1986, and Seoul Olympic Celebration Performance, 1988; performed at 1994 Shanghai Arts Festival. President, Korean Contemporary Dance Academy, 1991-94; president, Korea Dance Education Society, from 1989; professor, Wonkwang University. **Awards:** *For My Friend in the Sky* was selected as one of the best modern dances by Munwha Broadcasting Corporation (MBC), 1984; awarded top honors at the 1st Dance Festival of Korea, 1979; prize in acting category, The Dance Festival of Korea, 1985; prize for artistic merit by the Korean Arts Critics Association, 1987; best choreography, the 11th Dance Festival of Korea, 1989.

Roles

1975   Mary Magdalene (cr) in *Jesus Christ Superstar* (Yook Wan-soon), Yook Wan-soon Dance Company, Seoul, Los Angeles, San Francisco

Works

1971   *The Design of Four Figures* (with Kim Bock-hee; mus. Arnold Shapero), Kim Bock-hee & Kim Wha-suk Dance Company, Seoul

Duet One Afternoon (with Kim Bock-hee, solo; mus. Rodrigo), Kim Wha-suk, Kim Bock-hee, Seoul

A Line in Flight (with Kim Bock-hee, mus. List, Schubert), Kim Wha-suk, Kim Bock-hee, Seoul

Duet Ah! Here's a Man Pursuing a Dream... (with Kim Bock-hee, solo; mus. Chopin), Kim Wha-suk, Kim Bock-hee, Seoul

The Light of Consciousness (with Kim Bock-hee, mus. An Ick-tae), Kim Bock-hee & Kim Wha-suk Dance Company, Seoul

Duet We Must Go Together (solo; mus. various, arranged Kim Wha-suk, Kim Bock-hee), Kim Wha-suk, Kim Bock-hee, Seoul

The Instant of Nirvana (with Kim Bock-hee, solo; mus. Raga), Kim Bock-hee & Kim Wha-suk Dance Company, Seoul

1975   *Tale of Chun-hyang* (with Kim Bock-hee, solo; mus. Jang Doug-sahn), Kim Bock-hee & Kim Wha-suk Dance Company, Seoul

The Wall (with Kim Bock-hee, solo; mus. Bartók, Milhaud), Kim Bock-hee & Kim Wha-suk Dance Company, Seoul

She Was a Visitor (solo; mus. various, arranged Kim Wha-suk), Seoul

1977   *Three Dance Movement* (with Kim Bock-hee, mus. Russell), Kim Bock-hee & Kim Wha-suk Dance Company, Seoul

In the Café (with Kim Bock-hee, solo; mus. Cho Hyan-gi), Kim Bock-hee & Kim Wha-suk Dance Company, Seoul

Light and Shade (with Kim Bock-hee, mus.various, arranged Kim Wha-suk), Kim Bock-hee & Kim Wha-suk Dance Company, Seoul

1978   *The Snare* (solo; with Kim Bock-hee, mus. Paik Byoung-dong), Kim Bock-hee & Kim Wha-suk Dance Company, Seoul

Come Out (with Kim Bock-hee, mus. Steve Reich), Kim Bock-hee & Kim Wha-suk Dance Company, Seoul

1979   *The Branch in Winter* (with Kim Bock-hee, mus. Frank), Kim Bock-hee & Kim Wha-suk Dance Company, Seoul

Three Scenes Reflected on the Window (with Kim Bock-hee, solo; mus. Paik Byoung-dong), Kim Bock-hee & Kim Wha-suk Dance Company, First Dance Festival of Korea, Sejong Cultural Center, Seoul

1980   *Morning Rain* (solo; mus. Kim Gi-jin), Seoul

Man's Life Running in Circle I (with Kim Bock-hee, mus. Kim Gi-jin), Kim Bock-hee & Kim Wha-suk Dance Company, Seoul

Gate (with Kim Bock-hee, mus. Kim Du-won, Takemitsu), Kim Bock-hee & Kim Wha-suk Dance Company, Seoul

1981   *The Letter from Jinggangman* (with Kim Bock-hee, solo; mus. Paik Byoung-dong), Kim Bock-hee & Kim Wha-suk Dance Company, Third Dance Festival of Korea, Munye Theatre, Seoul

1982   *Ensemble* (with Kim Bock-hee, solo; mus. Lee Don-eong), Kim Bock-hee & Kim Wha-suk Dance Company, Munye Theatre, Seoul

Father, Father (with Kim Bock-hee, solo; mus. Kim Young-dong), Kim Bock-hee & Kim Wha-suk Dance Company, Los Angeles

Duet Elegy (with Kim Bock-hee, solo; mus. Kim Youn-joòn), Kim Wha-suk, Kim Bock-hee, Los Angeles

Wailing (with Kim Bock-hee, solo; mus. Kang Jun-il), Kim Bock-hee & Kim Wha-suk Dance Company, Munye Theatre, Seoul

1983   *Oriental Zodiac I* (with Kim Bock-hee, solo; mus. Kang Joon-il), Kim Bock-hee & Kim Wha-suk Dance Company, Seoul

1984   *For My Friend in the Sky* (with Kim Bock-hee, mus. Milhaud), Kim Bock-hee & Kim Wha-suk Dance Company, Munwha Broadcasting Corporation Invitation Performance, Seoul

Oriental Zodiac II (with Kim Bock-hee, solo; mus. Kang Jun-ill), Kim Bock-hee & Kim Wha-suk Dance Company, MBC Invitation Performance, Seoul

1985   *Fantasy* (with Kim Bock-hee, solo; mus. Hwang Byoung-ki & Kim Su-ack), Kim Bock-hee & Kim Wha-suk Dance Company, 23rd Paris International Dance Festival, Paris

Binari (Prayer) (with Kim Bock-hee, solo; mus. Kang Joon-il), Kim Bock-hee & Kim Wha-suk Dance Company, Seventh Dance Festival of Korea, Seoul

1987   *An Outing of Sahri, Made of Mud* (with Kim Bock-hee,
       mus. Kang Joon-il), Kim Bock-hee & Kim Wha-suk
       Dance Company, Seoul
       Traces 878 (with Kim Bock-hee, mus. Bach), Kim Bock-
       hee & Kim Wha-suk Dance Company, Seoul
1988   *Dry Grass* (solo; mus. Debussy), Modern Dance of 12
       Choreographers Show, Seoul
       Man's Life Running in Circle II (with Kim Bock-hee,
       mus. Kim Gi-jin), Kim Bock-hee & Kim Wha-suk Dance
       Company, Seoul
       A Visit of Yosuk, the Princess of Shilla (with Kim Bock-
       hee, solo; mus. Kang Joon-il), Seoul Olympic Interna-
       tional Arts Festival, Seoul
1989   *Look Back and Hear This Sound* (with Kim Bock-
       hee, mus. Kang Joon-il), Kim Bock-hee & Kim
       Wha-suk Dance Company, 11th Dance Festival
       of Korea, Seoul
1991   *A Midsummer Night's Dream* (mus. Mendelssohn),
       SAPPHO Dance Company, Pusan
       Carman in the Mirror (with Han Hae-lee, Kang Hyung-
       sook, Shin Yong-sook; mus. Bizet, Handel), SAPPHO
       Dance Company, Seoul
1992   *A Woman with a Hat* (as dir. with Han Hae-lee, Kang
       Hyung-sook; mus. Bolling), SAPPHO Dance Com-
       pany, Icksan
1993   *Le bateau Ivre* (as dir. with Han Hae-lee, Shin Yong-
       sook; mus. Bach), SAPPHO Dance Company, Seoul
       The Fragrance of Orange Blossom Blows in the Wind
       (mus. Paganini, Bolling, Chopin, Kreisler), SAPPHO
       Dance Company, Kwangju
       When They Were Dreaming (as dir. with Han Hae-lee,
       Shin Yong-sook; mus. Shostakovich), Second National
       Dance Festival, Taejon
1994   *We Could Hear It Now and Then* (mus. Glass), Wonkwang
       University Dance Company, Chounju
       Requiem for the Things That Fade Away (as dir. with
       Kang Hyung-sook; mus. arranged Kim Wha-suk),
       SAPPHO Dance Company, Chounju
1995   *Zen Dance* (mus. Michael Vetter), SAPPHO Dance Com-
       pany, Iksan
       May, the Year 1980 (with Han Hae-lee, solo; mus. Youn
       Mung-oh), Kwangju
       September Bride (with Han Hae-lee; mus. Vivaldi, Bolling,
       Gounod, Puccini, Handel), Kwangju Biennale Dance
       Festival, Kwangju
       A Room without a Mirror II (as dir. with Han Hea-lee,
       Kang Hyung-sook; mus. Arvo Pärt, Donizetti),
       SAPPHO Dance Company, Seoul
1996   *To You Revived in Our Heart* (mus. Mozart), SAPPHO
       Dance Company, Chounju
       The Summer Moon (with Han Hea-lee; mus. Greek
       Contempory songs), Pusan Summer Dance Festival,
       Pusan
       The Winter Sun (as dir. with Han Hae-lee, Shin Yong-
       sook; mus. Chuck Mangione), SAPPHO Dance Com-
       pany, Pusan
       A Chair Someone Sat On (as dir. with Han Hae-lee, Shin
       Yong-sook; mus. Barber, Rachmaninov, Shostakovich),
       SAPPHO Dance Company, Seoul
1997   *Fire Dance* (mus. Hwang Sung-ho), Wonkwang Univer-
       sity Dance Company, Muju

The Land of Predilection (with Han Hae-lee, solo; mus.
   Shostakovich, Górecki, Schnittke, Vivaldi, Grieg),
   SAPPHO Dance Company, Seoul
Give Me Hands (with Han Hea-lee; mus. Mozart, Vivaldi,
   Offenbach, Fauré), Second Kwangju Biennale Dance
   Festival, SAPPHO Dance Company, Kwangju

Publications

By KIM: books (in Korean)—

Modern Dance Technique, with Kim Bock-hee), Seoul, 1981.
Dance Creation, with Kim Bock-hee, Seoul, 1983.
Dance Theory, with Kim Bock-hee, Seoul, 1983.
What Is Dance Education?, with others, Seoul, 1996.
A Collection of Dances; When They Were Dreaming, with Han Hae-
   lee, Seoul, 1996.

Editor, *Kim Bock-hee, Kim Wha-suk: 20 Years of Dance,* Seoul, 1990.
Editor, *Kim Wha-suk: SAPPHO 1985-1996,* Seoul, 1997.

*   *   *

Presently, Kim Wha-suk is the artistic director of SAPPHO
Modern Dance Company, which works in Chollabuk-do's Iksan, a
western province in Korea. It is a group which she founded herself,
and she acts as choreographer, dancer, and educator. Kim Wha-suk
has contributed to developing Korean modern dance in two very
significant ways. In 1971 she co-founded the Kim Bock-hee & Kim
Wha-suk Dance Company, which continued to 1990. The group
had a unique and individual style, striving to introduce deeper ideas
to Korean modern dance and rid it of monotony. Kim Wha-suk's
second major contribution to Korean modern dance started in 1985
when she started to work independently of Kim Bock-hee. She
formed her own group in a remote area far apart from Seoul and
from anything closely resembling a cultural center. There, she desperately desired to bring modern dance to a wider audience; her aim
was the diffusion of modern dance's artistic and educational values
to a wider audience. These efforts were crucial to the development
of Korean modern dance.

Kim Wha-suk studied modern dance at Ewha Women's University, which is considered to be the Korean mecca of modern dance.
Previously, she had studied ballet with Um Young-ja in Kwangju,
which is known in Korea as an artistic as well as political center.
This was during the later part of the 1960s. Having established this
foundation on which she could build, Kim Wha-suk entered the
modern dance department at Ewha University. There she was guided
by the passionate and strict hand of Korean modern dance's godmother, Yook Wan-soon. It was at Ewha that she met Kim Bock-
hee, the woman who would accompany her in her artistic endeavor
over the next twenty years. Professor Yook was committed to
Graham technique, to its rigid demand and to its emphasis in strict
physical training. Kim Wha-suk and Kim Bock-hee felt that Yook,
in her pursuit of well-trained dancers, had forgotten the importance
of dance being inspired through content or subject matter. It is for
this reason that, upon graduating from Ewha, they formed their
own dance group. Among their most basic artistic principles was
that, as they were Korean artists, their art should reflect elements
of Korean culture. As such, their dances contain many elements of
Buddhism as well as particular aspects which have a completely
Korean aesthetic sense.

In 1971, Kim Wha-suk, along with Kim Bock-hee, had the first dance concert staged at the National Theatre of Korea in Myongdong, Seoul, where she presented seven dances. Among them was *The Instant of Nirvana*, a 30-minute performance inspired by Indian Raga music and Buddhist ritual. In 1979 she and Kim Bock-hee won a prize for artistic brilliance at the Dance Festival of Korea for their *Three Scenes Reflected in the Window*. In 1987 Kim Wha-suk choreographed *An Outing of Sahri, Made of Mud*, an epical dance work which reflected the hard times Korea was experiencing at the end of the 1980s and also incorporating the Buddhist themes of suffering and the idea of reincarnation. In the 1980s Kim Wha-suk and Kim Bock-hee tried to free themselves from modern dance's blind worship of technique and overly abstract esthetics.

At the end of the 1980s Kim Wha-suk started to work out an outdoor dance performance at the National Museum of Contemporary Art which was then newly opened. Working in the outdoor space of the facility she created *Traces 878*. At this time, she and Kim Bock-hee were interested in women's role in Korean history and in mythology, in their hidden desires. It was on this theme that they closely collaborated with composer Kang Joon-il, whose music is very flowing, calm, and melodic, and with Jung Jin-duk, whose colorful and esoteric lighting design completes their unique ensemble. As a result they took a prize for choreographic brilliance at the 1989 Dance Festival of Korea for *Look Back and Hear This Sound*.

After turning 40, Kim Wha-suk redirected her energies toward her teaching career, becoming more deeply involved with SAPPHO, a dance company she had founded while serving as a professor at a university in Chollabuk-do. Kim Wha-suk took responsibility for all of the company's works, sometimes choreographing them herself and sometimes commissioning her peers or students to choreograph them. As artistic director, she programmed three kinds of dances: those for big theaters which incorporated many dancers and lavish costumes, dances for smaller theaters which allowed one to see the dancers' experimentation and individuality, and outdoor dance, which allowed the dancer and audience to interact more freely. With these three emphases SAPPHO has created some 18 works since 1991. With the help of her partner and one-time student Han Hae-lee, Kim Wha-suk produced five outdoor works. Unlike many large, outdoor works which are improvisational, Kim Wha-suk's works are firmly based on Han Hae-lee's scripts and show an attempt to intermingle with nature, so that three elements—dance, humanity, and environment—are brought together in a natural way. Korea has experienced much economic and industrial growth in the past few decades, resulting in a gulf between the rich and poor, and it has been Kim's goal to bridge this gulf by performing in outdoor, accessible sites: on campuses, parks, in front of museums, and even bus terminals.

Since 1995, Kim has used the energy and strength built up by her group over ten years to produce a series of dance works based on contemporary Korean history. In 1995, she choreographed *May, the Year 1980*, and in 1997 she choreographed *The Land of Predilection*. These works recreated the political events of the democratic movement in Kwangju in 1980, which is regarded wrongly as an anti-democratic demonstration due to military oppression. The pieces are requiems and are reminiscent of Isadora Duncan and Mary Wigman's serious concern about political and historical subjects. In addition, Kim combines various multimedia elements in those works. Han Hae-lee was responsible for the script, Lee Sang-il for slides, Yoon Myung-oh for musical composition and arrangement.

Futhermore, in the 1990s Kim's most important endeavor began. In 1989 she formed the body of dance educators. She became president of the Korean Dance Education Society for three successive generations. From an academic standpoint, one can say that she has enhanced the quality of dance education. If you consider that Korea is second in dance education in the world, right behind the United States in terms of the numbers of dance departments in universities, this came, actually, quite late. Kim is continuing with this idea in mind, striving to enhance Korean modern dance. In addition, she, like Doris Humphrey, has also written books and articles about modern dance composition. At present the dance company which she formed, SAPPHO, has many performers in their thirties; Kang Hyoung-suk, Shin Yong-sook, Choi Byoung-yong are distinguished among them, and they are producing many notable works. And so it is that Kim's students will be at least partly responsible for the next phase of Korean modern dance.

—Kim Tae-won

KING, Eleanor

American dancer, choreographer, company director, and educator

Born: 8 February 1906, Middletown, Pennsylvania. **Education:** Studied dance at Clare Tree Major's School of the Theatre, 1924; Theatre Guild School, 1926; studied dance with Doris Humphrey and Charles Weidman at Denishawn, 1927-28; studied mime with Etienne Decroux; also studied Oriental dance. **Career:** Dancer with the Humphrey/Weidman Concert Group, 1928-35; danced in *Le sacre du printemps* at the New York Metropolitan Opera House, 1930; founder, with José Limón, Ernestine Stodelle, and Charles Laskey, The Little Group, 1931; founder, Theatre Dance Company, 1937; first solo concert, 1941; founder, Eleanor King Dance Repertory Company and the Eleanor King Creative Dance Studio in Seattle, 1944; teacher, University of Arkansas, 1952-71; founder, Theater of the Imagination, 1957; retired to Santa Fe, New Mexico, in 1971. **Awards:** Named Santa Fe Living Treasure, 1986; New Mexico Governor's Award for Excellence in the Arts, 1987; NEA Fellowship, 1988. **Died:** 27 February 1991, in Haddonfield, New Jersey.

Works

1931	*B Minor Suite* w/ Limón (mus. Bach), duet
	Study (mus. Brahms), solo, Contemporary Arts Studio, Westport, Connecticut
	Mazurka w/ Limón (mus. Scriabin), duet, Brooklyn Ethical Culture School
1932	*Notturno* (mus. percussion accompaniment by Pauline Lawrence)
	Mazurka II w/ Limón (mus. Scriabin), duet
1934	*Antique Suite* (mus. Stravinsky, Ignoto, Respighi), solo, Montclair State Teachers College, New Jersey
	Andalouse w/ Limón (mus. Bizet), duet with Jack Cole
1935	*Song of Earth*, (mus. Goossens), solo, New School for Social Research, New York
	Mother of Tears (mus. Reutter), solo, Montclair State Teachers College, New Jersey
	Summer Song (mus. de Falla), solo

Festivals (mus. Debussy), solo, New London, New Hampshire

1936   *Summons to Sabbath* (mus. Diamond), solo, Waldorf Astoria Hotel, New York

Peace, An Allegory (mus. Scarlatti), solo, Henry Street Settlement Playhouse, New York

Prelude to Adventure (mus. Lissow), solo, University of Colorado, Boulder

1937   *Icaro* (mus. Diamond, text Lauro de Bosis, percussion Franziska Boas), Brooklyn Museum

American Folk Suite (mus. American traditional), solo, Theater Dance Company, New York

Warning, March, Lament (mus. Reutter), solo

1938   *Parodisms* w/ Elizabeth Colman (mus. Walton), Theater Dance Company, New York

Ode to Freedom (mus. "Bunker Hill Hymn"), Bennington School of the Dance, Vermont

American Folk Suite (mus. American traditional), group version, Bennington School of Dance, Vermont

1941   *Characters of the Annunciation* (mus. Hindemith), solo, Humphrey-Weidman Studio, New York

Roads to Hell (mus. Pitot), solo, Humphrey-Weidman Studio, New York

A Saint and a Devil (mo mus.), solo

Song for Heaven (mus. Bach), solo

Novella (mus. Purcell, Scarlatti), solo

1942   *Brandenburg Concerto No. 2* (mus. Bach), quintet

Beasts and Saints (text *Tales of the Desert Fathers*, arr. by Dora Richman for recitative and piano)

1943   *To the West* (mus. Harris), solo, Oregon State College

Dance for the Sun (mus. Chavez)

1944   *Ascendence; Agonistae* (mus. Lattimer)

Moon Dances (mus. Schönberg), solo, Portland Civic Theater, Oregon

1945   *Partita No. 6 in E Minor* (mus. Bach), solo, Bellingham, Washington

Who Walk Alone (mus. Berg), solo, Bellingham, Washington

Northwest Indian Spirit Dance (mus. percussion), solo, Mills College, California

1947   *Soliloquy in the Morning; Dance in the Afternoon* (mus. Harris), solo

She (mus. Johnson)

Tempest on Olympus (mus. Purcell)

1949   *Triumph of Man* (mus. Ralph Vaughan Williams), Repertory Playhouse, Seattle

Dance for the Spring (mus. Vivaldi)

Elegy and Toccata (mus. Arthur Benjamin)

1950   *Transformations* (no mus.), solo, Cirque Playhouse, Seattle

Concerto for Harpsichord (mus. Vivaldi), solo

Celestial Suite (mus. Corelli)

1951   *The Libation Bearers* (mus. Milhaud)

Invocation (mus. Bartók), solo, Reed College, Oregon

Choreography '51 (mus. Schumann)

1952   *Praeludium* (mus. Couperin), solo

Four Visions (mus. Hindemith), solo

1953   *The Ondt and the Grasshopper* (text *Finnegan's Wake*)

Testament (no mus.), solo, University of Arkansas, Fayetteville

Ceremony of Carols (mus. Britten)

1954   *Odyssey* (mus. Bartók), solo

Il Combattimento di Tancredi e Clorinda (mus. Monteverdi)

I Trionfi di Petrarch (mus. Bach, Vivaldi; text Petrarch)

1955   *Six Metamorphoses after Ovid* (mus. Britten)

Dialogue for Piano, Oboe and Bassoon (mus. Bruce Benward)

Three Ritual Figures from Hellas (mus. Bartók), solo, University of Arkansas, Fayetteville

Characters of the Annunciation (mus. Hindemith)

The Temptation of St. Anthony

1956   *Toccato* (mus. Bach), solo

Energico (mus. Robert Palmer)

1957   *Hagoromo* (mus. Alvin King)

Americana (mus. Randall Thompson)

Rhapsodic Suite (mus. Hovhaness), solo

1958   *The Unicorn, the Gorgon, and the Manticore* (mus. Menotti)

1959   *Vivace* (mus. Haydn)

Miracles (mus. Norman de Marco; text Walt Whitman)

Anna Livia Plurabelle (text Joyce)

Duet for Dancer and Piano (mus. Frank Lynn Payne), solo

Images Japonaises

1960   *Gilgamesh* (mus. Graeffe)

1962   *The Box* (mus. von Gluck), Theatre of the Imagination

Three Poems (text e.e. cummings)

Passacaglia (mus. Bach), solo

Burleskaniana (mus. Bartók), solo

1963   *Salutation: A Meditation on the East* (mus. Hovhaness)

Haniwa (mus. Kan Ishii), University of Arkansas, Fayetteville

For Americans (mus. Wydeveld), solo

1966   *Nuna Da Ut Sun Yi (Trail of Tears)* (mus. Roy Harris), Theatre of the Imagination

Light-Sound-Motion (mus. de Marco, Cage, Varese, Partusch)

1967   *Synthesis: The Well Tempered Dancer* (mus. Bach), International Cultural Festival, Kyoto

1968   *Circus Minimus* (mus. Prokofiev)

1969   *Symphonic Etudes* (mus. Schumann)

The Temptation of St. Anthony (mus. Gregory Clough)

Transformations

Noyes Fludde (mus. Britten)

1970   *Jesu, Joy of Man's Desiring* (mus. Bach)

The Eighth Psalm; The 137th Psalm (mus. Gregory Clough)

The Medium Addresses the Kami (mus. traditional Japanese), solo for male

Three Lamentations of Jeremiah (mus. plain song)

1971   *Night Song/Day Cry* (mus. Messiaen), solo

Five Dancers in Eight Acts (mus. Walworth)

Greening (mus. Paul Chihara)

1975   *A Fantasy on Tai Chi* (mus. Karel Husa)

1976   *Mater Dolorosa* (mus. Scarlatti), solo

Publications

By KING: books—

The Way of Japanese Dance, 1970.

Transformations: A Memoir by Eleanor King/The Humphrey-Weidman Era, Brooklyn, 1978.

Eleanor King. Photograph by Jane Grossenbacher.

On KING: books—

Cass, Joan, *Dancing through History,* Englewood Cliffs, NJ, 1993.
Plett, Nicole, ed., *Eleanor King, Sixty Years in American Dance*, Santa
    Cruz, NM, 1988.

On KING: articles—

Anderson, Jack, "Eleanor King Retrospective," *New York Times,* 12
    June 1988.

*   *   *

Eleanor King was a dancer and choreographer for more than 60
years. She was strongly influenced by Doris Humphrey, and was
known for her interest in Asian and other ethnic dance forms, as
well as her interest in themes of the western United States, where
she spent much of her career.

King was born in 1906, in Middletown, Pennsylvania, and grew
up in New York, graduating from high school in Brooklyn. She was
interested in theater before she became a dancer, and looked upon
dance as a form of theater. In 1927 she became a student of Doris
Humphrey at the Denishawn School though the encouragement of
her first dance instructor, Priscilla Robineau. She stayed at
Denishawn for a year, leaving to join Humphrey and Charles
Weidman when they departed to form their own troupe, the
Humphrey-Weidman Company. King danced in the first Humphrey-
Weidman performance, and took part in the creation of many of
their works, including *Color Harmony*, considered the first abstract
ballet in the United States, which was King's professional debut as
a performer in 1928; *Water Study*, the first music-less dance; the
Grieg Piano Concerto; *Life of the Bee*; *The Shakers*; *La Valse*; *Dances
for Woman*; and *Dionysiacs*. She danced in many other Humphrey
and Weidman works, including *School for Husbands, Gagliarda,
Danse, March Funebra,* and *Dances for Saturday, Sunday, Monday*. When Humphrey married and had a child, King assumed many
of her solos and leading roles, such as Elektra in Humphrey's
Oresteia and Cunegonde in Weidman's *Candide*.

Among the other members of Humphrey-Weidman at this time
were Ernestine Stodelle, Letitia Ide, and José Limón. With Stodelle,
Limón, and Charles Laskey, King formed the Little Group, composed of members of Humphrey-Weidman. They put on several
performances of their own works, including King's *Bacchanale* in
1932. In 1935, King left Humphrey-Weidman and did her last performances with the Little Group, in order to concentrate on her
work as an independent soloist and choreographer. Her first solos,
in 1935, were *Mother of Tears* and *Song of Earth*.

In 1938, her first major composition, *Icaro*, set to a Lauro de
Bosis verse, premiered at the Brooklyn Museum of Art. This performance gave her a reputation as a leading choreographer. The
piece was performed by members of the Theater Dance Company,
which King and others founded in New York in 1937, including Jack
Cole, Alice Dudley, Katherine Litz, Ada Korvin, William Bales,
Kenneth Bostock, William Miller, and George Bockman. The acclaim for *Icaro* resulted in King being named a Bennington Fellow in
1938. There she composed *Ode to Freedom* for 10 dancers and a
soloist, which was performed at the Bennington Festival that year.
She also performed *American Folk Suite* (1937) set to traditional
music.

The Theater Dance Company disbanded at the start of World
War II. King spent a few seasons with Cole's Ballet Intime and

made some night club and vaudeville appearances on the East Coast.
She then went out on her own for a year in 1941, producing her first
solo concert, which included the premieres of her *Roads to Hell* and
Characters of the Annunciation. In 1942 King left New York City.
While she returned many times for residencies and performances,
she was never again considered part of the New York dance establishment. After teaching briefly at Carleton College in Minnesota
and the Cornish School in Seattle, King established the Eleanor
King Dance Repertory Company and the Eleanor King Creative
Dance Studio in Seattle in 1945. She remained in Seattle from 1943
to 1952, and then moved to the University of Arkansas until 1971,
where she taught and staged ensemble programs under the Theater
of the Imagination name starting in 1957. (King taught at other
venues throughout her career, including at Bennington, UCLA, and
the Perry-Mansfield School, as well as in London and Holland.)

Starting in the late 1950s and early 1960s, King traveled extensively in Japan, where she studied Noh dances, and in other parts of
Asia; her first performance in Tokyo occurred in 1958. Her travels
in Asia heavily influenced many of her works. She often based her
choreography on Noh and Kabuki themes, and, like those dance
forms, used humor as well as makeup, masks, and costumes, to
develop character. *Salutation* (1963), often considered her signature
work, came out of this period of Asian travel.

In addition to Asian influences, many of her works are inspired
by American Indian themes and the geography of the American
West. Some pieces that incorporate these influences include *To the
West* (1943), *Who Walk Alone* (1945), and *Spirit Dance* (1945).
Many of her works also touch upon female interests and themes,
such as *She* (1946) and *Moon Dances* (1944). Classical subjects
infuse much of her work, including *Tempest on Olympus* (1947) and
Ritual Figures from Hellas (1955, 1970). She was especially interested in the dichotomy between Apollo and Dionysus, as outlined
by Nietzsche, with her sensibility leaning toward the Dionysian
side. King based dances on a wide variety of literary sources, ranging from James Joyce to Petrarch, and was often inspired by paintings. *Song of Earth* (1935) was based on a Breugel painting, and
Beasts and Saints (1942) on work by Rousseau.

Her choreography incorporates a wide range of styles, from
minimalism to folk dance. Her choice of music also reflects her
eclectic range. For example, *American Folk Suite* is set to traditional
tunes, *Transformations* (1950) to silence and *The Well-Tempered
Dancer* (1967, 1975) to Bach. As quoted in the *Borzoi Book of
Modern Dance*, King says: "There are no barriers between types of
dance. Any style, any period, any idea can be used, if used with
taste and imagination." Her interest in various styles of dance led
her to host a "One World in Dance" series for a few seasons in
Seattle in the 1940s, where she brought in American Indian, South
American, Scottish, Swedish, Hawaiian, Philippine, Japanese, black
American and Palestinian ethnic dance groups.

In 1971 she became professor emeritus at the University of Arkansas, retiring to Santa Fe, New Mexico, where in 1986, at age 80,
she was recognized as a Santa Fe Living Treasure. King was awarded
the National Endowment for the Arts' Choreographer's Fellowship in 1988. While much of her work had become unfamiliar to
modern dance audiences, reconstructions of her work by Annabelle
Gamson in the 1980s changed that. In May 1988 Gamson produced the Eleanor King Retrospective Project in New York, featuring King's works from 1937 to 1971 with King lecturing as part of
the series.

King's writings include *The Way of Japanese Dance* (1970), a
scholarly study, and *Transformations* (1978), her memoir of the

Humphrey-Weidman years. At the time of her death in 1991 at age 85, she was a director of Mino Nicholas's American Dance Repertory Theater in New York.

—Karen Raugust

KING, Kenneth

American dancer and choreographer

Born: 1 April 1948, in Freeport, New York. **Education:** Antioch College, degree in philosophy, 1966; studied dance with various teachers in New York in the early 1960s.

Works

1964	cup/saucer/two dancers/radio
1965	Spectacular
	Self-Portrait: Dedicated to the Memory of John Fitzgerald Kennedy
1966	m-o-o-n-b-r-a-i-nwithSuperLecture
	Blow-Out
	Camouflage
1967	Print-Out: (CELE((CERE))-BRATIONS: PROBElems & SOULutions for the dyEYEing: KING)
1968	A Show
	Being in Perpetual Motion
1969	exTRAVEL(ala)ganza
	Conundrum
	Phenomenology of Movement
1970	Secret Cellar
	Carrier Pigeon
	Christmas Celebration (I)
1971	INADMISSLEABLE EVIDENTDANCE
	Perpetual Motion for the Great Lady
	Christmas Celebration (II)
1972	Simultimeless Action (The Dansing Jewel, The Great Void)
	Solstice Event
	Christmas Celebration (III)
1973	Metagexis
	Patrick's Dansing Dances
	Mr. Pontease Tyak
	INADMISSLEABLE EVIDENTDANCE (II)
1974	Praxiomatics (The Practice Room)
	Time Capsule
	High Noon (A Portrait-Play of Friedrich Nietzsche)
	The Telaxic Synapsulator
1975	The Ultimate Expose
	Battery
1976	Battery (Part 3)
	RAdeoA.C.tiv(ID)ity
1977	Video Dances
	Labyrinth
1978	Dance S(p)ell
	Wor(l)d (T)raid
	The Run-In Dance
	Word Raid
1980	Space City
	Blue Mountain Pass
	Currency
1983	Lucy Alliteration
	Scream at Me Tomorrow
1984	Moose on the Loose
	Complete Electric Discharge II
	Countdown the Countdowns w/ poet Bob Holman
1985	Critical Path
1987	How to Write (Digital Picnic)
	Sooner or Later . . .
1989	Correlations
1990	The Tahlula Deconstruction
	Patrick's Second Dansing Dance
1992	Patrick's Fourth Dansing Dance (Orestes' Spell)

Publications

By KING: articles—

"On The Move: A Polemic on Dancing," *Dance Magazine,* June 1967.
In *Further Steps: 15 Choreographers on Modern Dance,* edited by Connie Kreemer, New York, 1987.

On KING: books—

Anderson, Jack, *Choreography Observed,* Iowa City, 1987.
Banes, Sally, *Terpsichore in Sneakers: Post-Modern Dance,* Boston, 1980.

On KING: articles—

Foster, Constance, "Making It New: Meredith Monk and Kenneth King," *Ballet Review,* June 1967.
Moore, Nancy, "New Dance/Criticism. Is It Whatever You Say it Is?" *Dance Magazine,* April 1974.

*   *   *

Kenneth King was an experimental postmodernist who developed an academically based multimedia approach to dance, combining film, words, machines and technology, characters, lighting, and costumes to create symbolic meaning.

King aspired to be an actor while in high school and during his early college days, acting in summer stock productions for three years starting in 1959. That year, as an apprentice actor at Adelphi College, he saw a lecture by Ruth St. Denis, which helped inspire him to try dance. His early theatrical experience manifested itself in his early works, which often combined dance with speaking characters and props. During his time at Antioch College in Ohio, he traveled often to New York as part of a work-study program. In the early 1960s, he studied dance with Syvilla Fort, the New Dance Group, Ballet Arts, and Paul Sanasardo. He also attended the Martha Graham School and took ballet with Mia Slavenska. In the summer of 1966 he studied with Merce Cunningham and Carolyn Brown briefly on a scholarship.

While still a student at Antioch in 1964, King began performing in New York. He presented theatre-dance and mixed-media works at the Bridge Theatre, Judson Memorial Church (as part of the second generation of the Judson group), the Gate Theatre, Clark

Kenneth King (second from left) performing *RAdeoA.C.tiv(ID)ity,* 1976. Photograph © Johan Elbers.

Center for the Performing Arts, the New School and Washington Square Galleries. Throughout the 1960s and 1970s, he and colleagues such as Phoebe Neville, Meredith Monk, Gus Solomons, Jr., Elizabeth Keen, Cliff Keuter, Steve Paxton, Laura Dean, Yvonne Rainer, and Twyla Tharp created experimental dances, often appearing in each others' works. Some of his notable early works include *cup/saucer/two dancers/radio* (1964), in which two dancers performed in their underwear; *Self-Portrait: Dedicated to the Memory of John Fitzgerald Kennedy* (1965), which included fragments of Kennedy speeches and props such as a watch and newspaper; *Blow-Out* (1966), in which he and Laura Dean, while seated in chairs, were attached to a wall by rubber bands; *Camouflage* (1966), which was set to readings from Alain Robbe-Grillet's static novel *In the Labyrinth* and featured King in a green helmet, toe shoes, and leotard, as he fell, jumped, screamed, and talked on the telephone; and *m-o-o-n-b-r-a-i-nwithSuperLecture* (1966), in which King's voice on tape talked about the birth and death of choreography, while a film showed a flower growing out of a dead rat, among other images. These pieces are typical of this period of King's work in terms of their use of the spoken word, film, props, and movements consisting of everyday actions, and in their incorporation of cultural and social concerns.

King believed that dance did not necessarily have to include traditional dance steps, and he sometimes appeared in disguises and used personae, even denying it was him dancing. One of his best-known works is *INADMISSLEABLE EVIDENTDANCE* (1971), which was about government coverups. The piece includes a recorded message in which King predicts the greatest scandal of the 20th century. In a reworking of the dance in 1973, King claimed he had predicted Watergate in the 1971 version.

King's work changed somewhat in the mid-1970s, when he began to rely less on characters and overt controversy, and more on dance, music (he began to collaborate with composers such as William Tudor beginning in 1976), and, as he termed it, "transmedia" exploration. He became very interested in the role of technology, including computers, in society and in dance. Some of his works from this period include *Time Capsule* (1974), which featured him reading from his own time capsule, then watering a pot of flowers; *High Noon* (1974), inspired by Nietzsche and particularly *Thus Spake Zarathustra* (King once wrote that "Nietzsche has a master key to the dance"); *Praxiomatics (The Practice Room)* (1974); the three-part *Battery* (1975-76); *RAdeoA.C.tiv(ID)ty* (1976-78), a project dedicated to Marie Curie; and *Dance S(p)ell* (1978). Many of these were created or evolved over a period of time. King considers himself a writer as well as a dancer/choreographer, and he often writes about his own dances and those of others, frequently in somewhat abstract language, analogous to the construction of his dances. He has contributed articles to the journal *Film Culture* and to the book

The New Art, among other publications. Like his dances, King's written pieces illustrate his fascination with technology and its associated language, but also a certain cryptic style and a sense of humor. In a piece called "Transmedia," included in Sally Banes' *Terpsichore in Sneakers: Post-Modern Dance,* King wrote:

> Ever since I began making dances in the early sixties, I've programmed movement—I like that word—meaning, constantly breaking down, repeating movement with an eye to the variations matrix of possibilities, recombining in any way steps, changes, rhythms, textures, etc., as well as their density of relay and delay so that any and all elements, components, and permutable options can be called up, assembled, or juxtaposed at any moment, or between and with any dancing body.

Marcia Siegel, writing in *eddy,* describes King's dancing as "a kind that more and more dancers are using: not concerned so much with 'choreography,' with steps, placement, design, structure, but with flow, rhythm, energy and inner experience." Many critics, however, have focused on trying to understand the verbal messages of King's pieces, rather than on aspects of movement within the dance. For example, Robb Baker, writing in *Dance Magazine,* described King's word games in the 1973 version of *INADMISSLEABLE EVIDENTDANCE* as "sort of Gertrude Stein Meets Higher Mathmatics and the New Technology, Revealing All About Nixon Double-Talk and Double-Think."

As artistic director of Kenneth King & Dancers/Company, King continues to choreograph and perform. He has a powerful stage presence, often utilizing a deadpan demeanour. His work tends to be intellectual, thought-provoking, and a challenge to understand. At the same time, the dances are expressive, often containing a feeling of anxiety. In addition to performing on stage and writing extensively, King also appeared in experimental films, including those of Andy Warhol.

—Karen Raugust

KLEIN, Demetrius

American dancer, choreographer, and artistic director

Born: 3 July 1962 in Ohio. **Education:** Attended Ohio State University, 1981-83; Wright State University, 1980-81; full scholarship to study with Dayton Ballet (Ohio); also studied at Ballet Metropolitan and Cincinnati Conservatory of Music, with James Truitte (both Ohio). **Family:** Married to Kathleen Johnson-Klein. **Career:** Assistant artistic director, Modern Dance Kentucky, 1983-85; guest artist and resident modern instructor/choreographer, Lexington Ballet, 1984-85; dancer/instructor, Buffalo Ballet Theatre (New York), 1986; dancer/choreographer, Dayton Contemporary Dance Company, 1985-86; artistic director, Demetrius Klein Dance Company, from 1986; featured dancer for Mary Luft, Stephen Koester, Talley Beatty, Alvin Ailey, James Truitte, Vera Blaine, and Kevin Ward; teacher, Very Special Arts (Florida), 1988-91; guest artist, University of Alabama (Tuscaloosa), 1992-93; Florida International University (Miami), 1990-94; University of Florida (Gainesville), 1992-94; taught at Harid Conservatory (Boca Raton,

Florida), 1991-95; Florida Atlantic University (Boca Raton), 1993-94; Harvard Summer Dance School, (Cambridge), 1993, 1994; Neighborhood Artists-in-Residency (NARP) Fellowship (Riviera Beach, Florida), 1993-95; Cowles Chair, University of Minnesota, Minneapolis, 1995; Master Artist-in-Residence, Atlantic Center for the Arts (New Smyrna Beach, Florida), 1996. **Awards:** Hector Ubertalli Award, 1991; Individual Artist Fellowship, 1991, 1995; National Endowment for the Arts (NEA) choreographic fellowship, 1995, 1996.

Works

1986	*Prelude*, West Palm Beach, Florida
1987	*Pas de Deux—20 Gestures* (*mean something*) (mus. Tom Waits), West Palm Beach
	The Issue of Twilight (mus. John Carlisle), West Palm Beach
	Excursion into White Lily (mus. Laurie Anderson), West Palm Beach
	Virus, West Palm Beach
	Tanecour, West Palm Beach
	Manual Transmissions (mus. Brian Eno), West Palm Beach
	Crumbling Beauty (mus. Tom Waits), West Palm Beach
	New Romantics (mus. Bruce Springsteen), excerpts commissioned for Miami Waves Experimental Media Festival
	"*Less Than Kinds/Shreds,*" West Palm Beach
1988	*Opus 1* (mus. Tom Waits), Miami Waves Experimental Media Festival
	Lovin' Feelin', Lake Worth, Florida
	Before I Wake (mus. Chameleon circus), Eden's Expressway, New York
	Reap the Whirlwind, commissioned by Airport Opening '88, Flights of Fantasy, Palm Beach International Airport
1989	*The Garden/Alone* (mus. traditional), Lake Worth
	Love or Perish (mus. Brahms), Lake Worth
1990	*Le Sacre du printemps*, commissioned and performed by Southern Ballet Theatre, Orlando
	Dream (mus. the Chieftains), Lake Worth
	Wilderness (mus. Ralph Vaughn Williams), Lake Worth
	L'Apres-midi d'un faune (mus. Claude Debussy), Lake Worth
	Sermon (mus. Steve Keller), Lake Worth
	Blue (mus. Hank Williams), Tampa
1991	*Foreigner* (mus. Le Mystere des Voix Bulgares), New York
	Patenteux (The Time Before the Fall) (mus. John and Bill Storch), Lake Worth
	Aria (a work in progress) (mus. Glück and Mozart), performed by Florida International University Dance Ensemble, Miami
1992	*Quartet*, Movement Research, New York
	La Valse (mus. Ravel), Movement Research, New York
	Brahms Waltzes, Watson B. Duncan Theatre, Lake Worth
1993	*Jeux* (mus. Claude Debussy, Bill and John Storch) Watson B. Duncan Theater, Lake Worth
	Le Sacre du printemps (revised) (mus. Igor Stravinsky), Watson B. Duncan Theatre, Lake Worth

Demetrius Klein performing *HOWL*, 1996. Photograph by John R. Lawrence.

I am Building You a Requiem Ten Miles High (mus. Puccini, Supremes, Jerry Butler), New York

Halos in Reverse (mus. Bill and John Storch, live percussion by Steve Keller), Watson B. Duncan Theatre, Lake Worth

1994   *Elemental* (A Forgotten Spaces Project) (mus. John and Bill Storch), Prince Theatre, Pahokee, Florida

A Crash Somewhere in the Middle (mus. John and Bill Storch), Crest Theatre, Delray Beach, Florida

Untitled (mus. John and Bill Storch), University of Minnesota

1995   *Hopeful Romantic Gentle* (mus. Chopin), Dayton Contemporary Dance Company

Sokol/Falcon

1996   *HOWL,* Miami

Giselle (mus. Adolphe Adam, Janis Joplin, Percy Sledge, Otis Redding, Aretha Franklin), Miami

Beat/Re-Mix (mus. John Coltrane)

1997   *Investigating the Opposites*, New York

Publications

By KLEIN: book—

Forgotten Places, 1995.

On KLEIN: articles—

Jowitt, Deborah, "Dance: Demetrius Klein Dance Company," *Village Voice*, 22 April 1997.

Passy, Charles, "Klein's *Messiah* Combines Classical, Modern," *Palm Beach Post,* 13 December 1993.

*   *   *

Lauded for his lyrical, elastic performing style and the originality of his choreography, Demetrius Klein began following the beat of a different drum at the age of 12 when, growing up in Hamilton, Ohio, he saw Gene Kelly in *An American in Paris* on television and declared his intention to dance.

He is still stepping to a different beat as he choreographs and runs his Demetrius Klein Dance Company from the unlikely outpost of Lake Worth, a West Palm Beach suburb on the southeast coast of Florida. His remoteness from any urban dance center helps shape his dances and the attitude with which he and his company perform them. One of the major changes in American dance over the past decade or two has been the blooming of so-called regional dance, which, according to Jennifer Dunning of the *New York Times*, was epitomized by the Demetrius Klein Dance Company. In her review of the company's engagement in Manhattan's Performance

Space 122 (P.S. 122), Dunning stated, "Gutsily athletic and angelic, the dancers share a bold but unself-conscious approach to movement that in part gives Mr. Klein's choreography its look of dewy freshness." Similarly, the *Village Voice's* Deborah Jowitt, reviewing a 1992 New York engagement, commented on "the curious freshness of Klein's work," adding, "It has Not-Made-in-New-York written all over it."

Born 3 July 1962, the son of a truck driver and an accountant, Klein began his dance training at 12, soon after his television encounter with Gene Kelly. At 15 his mother began taking him for lessons to the Cincinnati Conservatory of Music, where he came under the tutelage of Lester Horton disciple and Alvin Ailey alumnus James Truitte. Truitte steered the compact, 5-foot-6-inch dancer toward modern dance. He continued his dance training with a year at Wright State University followed by two at Ohio State University (OSU), where he studied the basics of dance composition with Vera Blaine. Blaine, then a professor at OSU, had studied with Martha Graham, Merce Cunningham, and Louis Horst, and had been Horst's sometime-assistant at the Graham school in New York in the early 1960s.

Klein left college in his junior year to perform, teach, and choreograph for a string of dance companies including the now-defunct Modern Dance Lexington, the Lexington Ballet, Buffalo Ballet Theatre and Dayton Contemporary Dance Company. He and his wife, dancer Kathleen Johnson-Klein, established their company in her hometown of Lake Worth in 1986. The company performs there regularly, sponsors an annual fall performing arts festival, offers a modern dance version of *Messiah* at Christmastime and, since the late 1980s, has made annual or biannual forays to New York City.

Klein's work often exhibits the athletic physicality, abstraction, and "undancerly" movements characteristic of postmodernism, with an infusion of physical contact and rough-hewn partnering displaying the influence of Klein's childhood sport, wrestling. Jowitt, in a 1992 review, observed that his dancing style "is often simple, but it's not pedestrian in terms of dynamics: it demands a sense of impetus, of flow. It may surprise you with neat if unballetic little cabrioles that erupt from a texture that's often largely made up of embracing, falling, pushing, rebounding off one another."

Thematically, Klein is concerned with a sense of community, humanity, and egalitarianism within his dances as well as within the community his dance company inhabits. In his novel 1995 piece, *Forgotten Places,* he built dances around historic locales in four cities, from Winston-Salem, North Carolina, to Minneapolis-St. Paul, utilizing local dancers in these site-specific performances. In his company, he has used dancers of varying skill levels, body types and ages. The idea, he told the *Palm Beach Post* in a 1994 interview, is to mirror the community for all the lumbering beauty that's there without trying to gussy it up. Klein has received two choreographic fellowships from the State of Florida and, in 1995 his first two-year choreographer's fellowship from the National Endowment for the Arts (NEA). In addition to his own company, his work has been danced by the Jacob's Pillow Men Dancer's Project, the Dayton Contemporary Dance Company, and the Southern Ballet Theatre of Orlando, Florida, as well as the dance departments of several universities and conservatories.

—Diane Hubbard Burns

KOLDEMAMA DANCE COMPANY
Israeli modern dance company

Koldemama ("Voice of Silence") is one of the few Israeli dance companies that perform only works by its artistic director, Moshe Efrati. The company's name derives from his work with deaf dancers in the late 1960s.

Born in Jerusalem in 1934, Efrati studied dance with Hassia Levi-Agron and later in New York with Martha Graham, Paul Taylor, and Louis Horst. He was one of the original Batsheva dancers, excelling in roles from works by Graham, Glen Tetley and Norman Morrice. In 1969 Efrati began choreographing his own works for the company with *Sin Lieth at the Door,* featuring music by Noam Sheriff and set design by Dani Karavan, followed in 1970 by *Ein Dor* with music by Zvi Avni and set design again by Karavan. Both works were performed repeatedly and well-received by critics and audiences.

Efrati, being an individualist, soon found out he wasn't really suited to be a company dancer. He became a freelance choreographer, but had a hard time finding work. He then began working with a group of youngsters with impaired hearing, accidentally discovering a method of letting them feel rhythm with their bare feet, by sensing vibrations. When trying to get the young students to pay attention, Efrait struck the wooden floorboards of the studio with a stick. The dancers all turned around to him, as if they had heard the noise. Upon this discovery, he built his "vibration-method" of teaching, which he and the company have demonstrated at many international congresses for the education of hearing-impaired people.

Among his deaf students he discovered several talented dancers, for whom he choreographed ballets concerning their disability. He also began using sign-language gestures as movement material. Later, with his mixed company (composed of hearing and nonhearing dancers) Efrati even recorded sounds made by his deaf artists and used them as a soundtrack for his choreography.

Although Efrati left Batsheva in 1969, he continued to choreograph for the company from time to time including 1976's *Until That I Arose.* The year before, in 1975, he had started his own company (whose name changed during the years from "Kol Demama" to Efrati Dance Company to today's Koldemama, for no apparent reason). Among his dancers were former Batsheva artists such as Esther Nadler and Gaby Barr. At first there were several deaf dancers, the most prominent among them Amnon Damti. By the late 1980s Efrati had lost interest in this aspect of his work. There was no lack of hearing-impaired dancers, but felt he had exhausted the possibilities of the approach. Since the early 1990s there was but one hearing-impaired dancer left in Koldemama. However, in later works, Efrati sometimes used sign language as a source for gestures and moves.

Efrati's wife, the former distinguished Batsheva soloist Esther Nadler, has since stopped dancing but works for Koldemama as teacher and rehearsal director. Over the years Efrati has been invited to create choreography for companies in Belgium, France, Germany, and others, and Koldemama has toured in Europe and America. In recent years Efrati turned his attention to Jewish subject matter, as in his 1982 *Psalms of Jerusalem,* and to Sephardic topics (*La Folia,* 1988; *Camina-y-torna,* 1990). *Psalms of Jerusalem* premiered at the annual Israel Festival, was set to specially composed music by Noam Sherif, a leading Israeli musician, and was based on religious motives, such as the blowing of the shofar (ram's horn) on the High Jewish Holidays, the sound of Christian

Koldemama Dance Company: *Textures*, **1978. Photograph by Yoram Rubin.**

church-bells and the call of the muezzin from the mosque minarette to gather together Moslems to prayer. This medley of symbols was a true portrait of the city of Jerusalem, where the ancient and the modern, and Moslem, Jewish and Christian faith and heritage mix.

Efrati's *Camina-y-torna,* premiered at the festivities held in Israel commemorating the five centuries that passed since the Jews were expelled from Spain (coincidentally the same year Christopher Colombus discovered America). As the name of the work implied, it used a recurring procession of movement to depict the wandering of the Jewish people from place to place throughout the Diaspora.

Efrati's movement style is very forceful and what it may lack in subtlety it gains in a very "Israeli" energetic directness. Koldemama continues performing Efrati's new works, and remains the only stable Israeli dance company devoted to a single choreographer's creations.

Publications

Books—

Efrati, Moshe, *Koldemama u'Mahol,* Tel-Aviv, 1981.

Articles—

Manor, Giora and Ruth Eshel, editors, "Twenty Years of Koldemama," Special Supplement, *Israel Dance Quarterly,* No. 6, 1995.

—Giora Manor

KOMAR, Chris
American dancer, choreographer, and educator

Born: 30 October 1947 in Milwaukee, Wisconsin. **Education:** University of Wisconsin-Milwaukee, B.F.A. in dance, 1970. **Career:** Founding member, Milwaukee Ballet Company, 1969; member, Merce Cunningham Dance Company, 1972-96; teacher, Merce Cunningham Studio, 1973-96; assisted and taught repertory workshops in the U.S. and Europe, including Théâtre du Silence in France, the Ohio Ballet, U.S. Terpsichore of New York, American Ballet Theatre, Rambert Dance Company of London, the Choreographic Research Group of the Paris Opéra, Werkcentrum Dans in Rotterdam, Pennsylvania Ballet, Paris Opéra Ballet, Pacific Northwest Ballet, Repertory Dance Theatre, New Dance Ensemble, Concert Dance Company, Charleroi-Danses, Boston Ballet, and Mikhail Baryshnikov's White Oak Dance Project; directed the activities of the Cunningham Dance Foundation's Repertory Understudy Group (RUG), including staging Cunningham dances such as *Septet* (1953), *Rune* (1958), *Summerspace* (1959), *Exchange* (1978), and *Fielding Sixes* (1980) for revival in the Cunningham Company repertory and for material used in Cunningham's Events; produced and served as host for *Rhythms in Space,* a cable TV program, 1982; named assistant artistic director of Cunningham Company, 1992; retired from the stage, 1993. **Awards:** New York Dance and Performance Award (*Bessie*), 1991. **Died:** 17 July 1996 in New York City.

Roles (as a principal dancer with the Merce Cunningham Dance Company)

1972	*Landrover,* Brooklyn
	TV Rerun, Brooklyn
	Borst Park, Brooklyn
1973	*Changing Steps,* Detroit
1974	*Westbeth* (made for video), New York
1975	*Exercise Piece,* New York
	Rebus, Detroit
	Sounddance, Detroit
1976	*Torse,* Princeton, New Jersey
	Squaregame, Adelaide, Australia
	Video Triangle (made for *Dance in America*), Nashville
1977	*Travelogue,* New York
	Inlets, Seattle
	Fractions I (made for video), Boston
1978	*Exercise Piece II,* New York
	Exchange, New York
1979	*Locale,* New York
	Road Runners, New York
1980	*Duets,* New York
	Fielding Sixes, New York
1981	*Channels/Inserts,* New York
	10's with Shoes, New York
1982	*Trails,* New York
1983	*Inlets 2,* New York
	Roaratoria, Roubaix, France
1984	*Pictures,* New York
	Phrases, New York
1985	*Native Green,* New York
1986	*Grange Eve,* New York
	Points in Space (made for video), San Francisco
1987	*Fabrications,* Minneapolis
	Carousel, Jacob's Pillow, Lee, Massachusetts
1988	*Eleven,* New York
	Five Stone, Berlin
	Five Stone Wind, New York
1989	*Field and Figure,* Minneapolis
	Inventions, Arles, France
	August Pace, Berkeley, California
1990	*Polarity,* New York
1991	*Trackers,* New York
	Loosestrife, Paris
1992	*Change of Address,* Austin, Texas
	Enter, Paris
1993	*Doubletoss,* Minneapolis
	CRWDSPCR, Durham, North Carolina

Publications

On KOMAR: books—

Vaughn, David, *Merce Cunningham: Fifty Years,* New Jersey: Aperture, 1997.

On KOMAR: articles—

"Chris Komar," obituary, *The Times* (London), 29 July 1996.
Clarke, Mary, and David Vaughn, "Chris Komar: Heir to a Master," obituary, *The Guardian,* 22 July 1996.

Dunning, Jennifer, "Chris Komar, 48, Dancer for Cunningham Company," obituary, *New York Times,* 19 July 1996.
Hunt, Marilyn, "Chris Komar," obituary, *The Independent,* 23 July 1996.

*　　*　　*

Dancer Chris Komar used to say that he became interested in dancing through rock 'n roll. By the time he reached college age, however, Komar was technically advanced enough to become a charter member of the Milwaukee Ballet Company. After graduating from the University of Wisconsin with a B.F.A. in dance, Komar joined his alma mater's faculty for two years. While still a student, Komar had been profoundly affected by a performance of Merce Cunningham's dance *Second Hand* (1970). In 1980 Komar reflected on the experience by saying, "When it was over, it was as if no time had elapsed, but I had an incredible sense of experience, almost like meditating, or dreaming while you're asleep. It was like all the disparate elements of a Rauschenberg collage, or a quilt made up of time."

In 1971 Komar left Milwaukee to study dance on a summer scholarship at Jacob's Pillow in Lee, Massachusetts, and then moved to New York City to study at the Cunningham Dance Studio, where his talent and dedication were quickly recognized. Cunningham later said of Komar, "He has an astonishing memory about details or shapes, how it felt, the proportion, the look of it, the transitions." After working as an apprentice for one year, in 1972 at age 23 Komar was accepted into the Merce Cunningham Dance Company as a full-fledged member. The Cunningham company, founded in 1955, was, and is, the foremost avant-garde dance company in the world.

In 1973 Komar began teaching at the Cunningham Dance Studio; the same year he was named assistant to the choreographer, a job that entailed helping Cunningham with repertory workshops throughout the United States and Europe. In addition, Komar became the director of the Repertory Understudy Group (RUG), a training ensemble for potential company members and a laboratory for revivals of Cunningham dances. In 1986 Komar began working on a book of Cunningham's vocabulary of classroom steps and their combinations, transcribed into dance notation. Although he worked primarily as a dancer and not as a choreographer, in 1992 Komar created *Inlets 3* for RUG using Cunningham's choreographic notes for *Inlets* (1977) and *Inlets 2* (1983) and by applying chance procedures explained to him by Cunningham. According to Cunningham company archivist David Vaughn, Cunningham began grooming Komar almost immediately to take over the artistic directorship of the Cunningham company upon the choreographer's retirement. Vaughn remembered, "It wasn't long after [Komar] joined the Cunningham company that it became clear that he was the heir apparent."

Between 1972 and 1993, when he retired from the stage, Komar created roles in more than 45 Cunningham dances, which he performed in stage premieres, as excerpts in Cunningham's "Events," and on film and video. Komar's physique was small, yet strong and resilient. He was not a flashy or unusually flexible dancer (leg extensions up to his ear or hypermobile joints) as were some of Cunningham's company members. Rather, Komar's appeal as a performer arose from his lucid execution, consistency, buoyancy in jumps, and thoughtful, elegant approach to Cunningham's dances. He knew how to attack movement with an arresting authority. In an obituary for the *New York Times,* Jennifer Dunning described Komar as a "slightly-built dancer with a big jump and unfailingly serious demeanor. He stood out for his terse way of moving and the clarity of thought and physical attack that he brought to Mr. Cunningham's choreography." Writing for the *New Yorker,* Arlene Croce described Komar as "dancing with that fanatical precision which makes us instinctively trust his every move." According to Vaughn, "the most memorable of the roles [Komar] created during the 20 years that he danced with the company were his solos in *Changing Steps* (1972), *Travelogue* (1977), *Channel/Inserts* (1981) and the passage in *Points in Space,* commissioned by the BBC in 1986, in which he danced Apollo-like with three or four 'muses.'"

Early in his career Komar was entrusted with roles Cunningham had created for himself in *Summerspace* (1958), *Rune* (1959), and *Winterbranch* (1964). Choreographer Kenneth King told writer Mary Clarke that he remembered Komar in *Torse* (1977), dancing "with Merce's mercurial, faun-like awareness amplifying his incredibly articulate performance of precise jumps, sharp, immaculate phrasing and delivery." Komar's devotion throughout the remainder of his 25-year career with the Merce Cunningham Dance Company to the performance, preservation, and articulation of Cunningham's vision was remarkable and, for a dancer in the Cunningham company, not to mention most modern dance companies, without precedent. Komar once said in reference to Cunningham, "His work is now my work." Working with the choreographer, said Komar, "keeps adding to my life—and not just to my life as a dancer but to my whole life."

—Lodi McClellan

KONER, Pauline
American dancer, choreographer, and educator

Born: 26 June 1912, the daughter of Russian-Jewish immigrants. **Education:** Studied with Michel Fokine, Michio Ito, Yeichi Nimura, and Angel Cansino; first stage appearance, in the children's corps of the Fokine Ballet, 1926; toured with Ito as a guest artist, 1928-29. **Family:** Married conductor Fritz Mahler, 1939. **Career:** Solo concerts, 1930-45; appeared in Near East, 1932; appeared at Radio City Music Hall, 1933; first American dancer invited to perform in the Soviet Union, 1935-36; staged works for Roxy Theater, 1945; choreographed for CBS-TV, 1945; guest artist with José Limón Dance Company, 1946-60; founder/choreographer, Pauline Koner Dance Company, 1949-60; performed and taught at Jacob's Pillow, American Dance Festival, in Mexico, Europe, South America; staged her works for Alvin Ailey, Batsheva Dance Company, Atlanta Ballet Company, Dayton Civic Ballet, and in Santiago and Italy; artist-in-residence, North Carolina School of Arts, 1965-76; performed at the White House, 1967; faculty, Brooklyn College, 1969-75; director, Pauline Koner Dance Consort, 1976-82; faculty, Juilliard, beginning 1986 (as well as guest lecturer at many colleges and universities); restaged *Poeme* for the North Carolina School of Arts, 1990; and *Concertino* for Dance Fusion, Philadelphia, 1990; guest teacher, Jacob's Pillow, Massachusetts, 1990; guest lecturer, University of the Arts, Philadelphia, 1991-92; staged *The Farewell* for Margie Gillis, 1995; restaged *Concertino* for Marymount College, 1998. **Awards:** *Dance Magazine* Award, 1963; conducted choreography/technique workshop in Tokyo by invitation of the Fulbright Commission, 1965; honorary doctorate of Fine Arts, Rhode Island College, 1985.

Works

1953   *Cassandra* (mus. Copland), solo
1955   *Concertino* (mus. Pergolesi)
1958   *The Shining Dark* (mus. Kirchner)
1962   *The Farewell* (mus. Mahler), solo
1963   *Solitary Songs Opus I* (mus. Valen), solo
1966   *Solitary Songs Opus II* (mus. Foss)
1968   *Poeme* (mus. Barber)
1975   *Solitary Songs Opus III & IV* (mus. Berio)
1976   *A Time of Crickets* (mus. Colina)
1977   *Mozaic* (mus. Bach)
1978   *Cantigas* (mus. Crumb, Medieval)
1980   *Flight* (mus. Rodrigo)

Other works include: *Three Funeral Marches, Suite of Soviet Impressions, Tragic Fiesta, Song of the Slums,* and other solos.

Publications

By KONER: books—

Solitary Song (autobiography), Durham, North Carolina, 1989.
Elements of Performance: A Guide for Performance in the Dance, Theater and Opera, Choreography and Dance Studies. Chur, Switzerland, 1993.

On KONER: books—

Cohen, Selma Jeanne, editor, *The Modern Dance: Seven Statements of Belief,* Middletown, Connecticut, 1965.
Chujoy, Anatole, and P.W. Manchester, *Dance Encyclopedia,* New York, 1967.
Lloyd, Margaret, *The Borzoi Book of Modern Dance,* New York, 1949.
McDonagh, Don, *The Complete Guide to Modern Dance,* Garden City, New York, 1970.
Sorrell, Walter, *The Dance Has Many Faces,* second edition, New York and London, 1966.

On KONER: articles—

Anderson, Jack, "Pauline Koner: An American Original," *Dance Magazine,* January 1998.
Kreigsman, Sali Ann, "Interview with a Maverick Modern: Pauline Koner," *Dance Scope,* Summer 1979.
Maynard, Olga, "Pauline Koner: A Cyclic Force," *Dance Magazine,* April 1973.
"Pauline Koner," in *Current Biography Yearbook 1964.*

*   *   *

The work of Pauline Koner is exceptionally original. Whether as a solo performer, guest artist with the José Limón Company or director of her own company, she created and maintained an individual approach to movement.

Koner never took a modern dance class nor did she pursue modern dance in rebellion against ballet. She began her dance studies with Michel Fokine only to discover for herself that she didn't like ballet dancing and pointe work. But rather than forfeit her studies, she used her ballet technique as a springboard into movement that

suited her talent. As a result she was a modern dancer with an incredible technique. From her ballet training came speed, elevation, precision, and turns. Her Oriental dance studies with Michio Ito and Yeichi Nimura gave her the fluidity of covering space and the importance of using her hands; Spanish dance technique from Angel Cansino gave Koner dynamics and rhythm. She developed spiral movement, contrast of sharp and lyrical movements, range, dimension, and the quality of suspension into her art form. In 1930 Koner broke from all attachments and gave her first solo performance at the Guild Theater in New York. Critic John Martin of the *New York Times* was immediately smitten, and convinced of her "unquestionable right to stand alone" as a performer. She continued to tour as a solo artist, both in the U.S. and abroad, including performances in Egypt, Palestine, and the Soviet Union, where she was the first American dancer ever to be invited to perform. In the mid-1940s, Koner was staging works for the Roxy Theater and even choreographing for television until she joined the José Limón Dance Company in 1946. There she remained until 1960 as a "permanent guest artist," working with Limón and his artistic director, the renowned Doris Humphrey, with whom Koner had a very special relationship. Koner called Humphrey her "outside eye" or choreographic advisor, and Koner sought Humphrey's opinion and advice on her new works. In an interview with Jack Anderson, Koner explained an "outside eye" as "someone you respect and someone who is sympathetic to you. But it also has to be someone who can shock you into new awareness."

Both her earlier association with Fokine and her new one with Doris Humphrey were major influences on Koner's philosophy of dance, and their ideas helped her to develop her own. From Fokine, Koner learned the total awareness of the body and that the spirit of movement was as important as the mechanics. Doris Humphrey taught Koner in their 13 years of working together how to look for different ways of expressing yourself so as to avoid getting into a rut. Humphrey's dictums—of going back to your original motivation; thinking of your ending before you're half-finished; looking for new arm shapes and body shapes; asymmetry as challenge and symmetry as security; and cutting a just finished dance by one-third—made a deep impression on her. Koner relied on Humphrey's acuity until Humphrey's death in 1958, telling Anderson that "our work together was a continuous revelation." *The Farewell,* Koner's solo dedicated to the memory of Humphrey, is perhaps her most precious choreographic gift to the history of modern dance. Performed to Mahler's last movement of *Das Lied von der Erde,* she developed her movements from the actual poetry used in the *Lied* with arm patterns from the shapes of branches and tree limbs. Koner continued to perform the tribute until 1982, then restaged it for Margie Gillis in 1995.

Koner's choreography originated in finding her motivation—an inward search prompted by words from a play, patterns of behavior from the person she was portraying, or exploration into emotions she wanted to suggest. The piece would be somewhat outlined in her head and then the details worked out through experimentation with gesture. To achieve her artistic goal as a catalyst in society providing hope in times of despair, Koner used her compassion to communicate with the audience in her portrayals. Her dances showed her need to search and reflect on the times she lived in and the people to whom she was exposed.

In *Cassandra,* the story of the prophetess of Troy foreseeing total destruction but frustrated that no one believes her, Koner created a universal character of a woman lamenting for a nation, for wars, and for the world. *Solitary Songs,* a group of solos created from 1962 through 1975, represented Koner's life leitmotif—being alone. Another important aspect of the creative process for Koner was spatial relations. Space to Koner was alive and she sought to interact with it and pierce it with her emotions, for example, she gave the impression of an emotionally closed-off individual by tilting her head and framing it with closed arms. She also used costumes, such as flowing skirts, as a major component of her choreography. The flowing skirts from *Cassandra* and *The Farewell* not only emphasized movement but created a stunning and lasting image.

In *The Shining Dark*, which was based on the life story of Helen Keller, Koner derived everything from factual images. By simulating the touching of objects and sensing the geometrical aspects of the objects around her, Koner created a pattern of movements becoming integral to the dance.

Another of Koner's most well-known performances came from her stay with the José Limón company. Koner created "Emilia" in Limón's masterpiece, *The Moor's Pavane,* for which she received much critical acclaim. This role allowed Koner to do what she does best—create a niche for herself through original movement. Her motivation for this came from her own interpretation of Shakespeare's words in *Othello,* upon which *The Moor's Pavane* is based. Though the choreography of this stunning work is credited to Limón, Koner created her own solo parts and also did so in other works, like *Ruins and Visions.*

Koner created her second dance company, Pauline Koner Dance Consort, in 1976 and toured with it until the company disbanded in 1982 due to lack of funds. During this time she began writing and has contributed to many dance publications; she also began teaching as a guest lecturer and artist-in-residence to pass on her knowledge both in the States and around the world in Italy, Holland, Chile, Brazil, and Japan. Her "Elements of Performance" course, to teach students the actual process of dancing and how to command stage presence, has become a signature program for Koner, and she has even produced a book series (with the same name).

Through the years, Koner has staged works in Rome, Amsterdam, the Hague, Santiago de Chile, and Buenos Aires, as well as made many television appearances. Several years before she published her *Elements of Performance* book, Koner wrote her autobiography, aptly titled *Solitary Song,* published by Duke University Press in 1989.

Koner seems to have been a romantic using movement to portray her psyche; while many other modern dancers used their imaginations to delve into the geometry of movement and develop patterns from outside, Koner used her muse to enhance the patterns of creativity inside her. For Koner choreography had to have a viewpoint. Romanticism allowed her to portray her individuality and surpass it through connecting to a universality that communicated her emotions to all. As her dancing and choreography were unique so is her place in the history of modern dance—her incredible technique gave her the freedom to develop her artistry to its fullest potential. Koner's work is a statement that artistry comes from inside and must be brought out of the individual through experimentation and improvisation. As she told Jack Anderson, to be a dancer one must be fated to do so, "Dance is so hard, physically and emotionally demanding, it has to be an obsession." The world is better place for Koner's obsession.

—Cynthia Roses-Thema and Sydonie Benet

KOREA

The history of change in Korean dance is one and the same with the history of change in the language used to describe Korean dance. Though dance critic Cho Dong-wha designates Korean "New Dance" as that emerging from the 1960s, its roots go back much further into history. Dance came to be known as a "cultural activity" in Korean society after Park Sae-moen, a former student of the Peoples' Music Company in Russia, came to Korea and performed the *Kopak* dance in 1921. The form of dance, much faster than any previously practiced, was further popularized by a student named Cho Tack-won. Additionally, performances by the Russian Hellen Group in 1924 introduced further forms of modern dance, which helped set the stage for a new understanding of Western movement styles and culture.

Ishihi Baku, Japan's first contemporary dancer, is considered as the beginning of dance as a contemporary art form. The advertisements for Baku's appearance heralded his performances as "New Dance" and the term soon applied to any and all dance that differed from Korea's traditional dances. Newspapers and other mass media of the time chose this dancing as the cornerstone to spawn a new cultural movement in Korean society, and when Cho Tack-won and Choi Seung-hee saw Ishihi's performance, both decided to follow him to Japan for training.

In 1929 Bae Ku-ja was the first Korean to open a dance research center and hold a concert; the next year, Choi Seung-hee held her first performance recital, went to Japan, and became a huge success by blending traditional Korean dance with modern. Cho Tack-won, meanwhile, after his first performance in 1934, was the one praised as giving shape to the so-called "New Dance" in Korea. Park Young-in, who later switched his citizenship from Korea to Japan, and was known as the leader of Japanese dance education, was the only Korean person to be taught by Mary Wigman.

In 1945, with Korea's independence from Japan at the end of World War II, Choi Seung-hee took many of her performers and went north. Later, as a result of the Korean War, dance in Korea became almost nonexistent. At this point Ham Kwi-bong, Moon Chul-min, and Jang Choo-wha became important figures in the dance world. Ham Kwi-bong's research center became the birthplace for many of Korea's exceptional future performers. While Ham Kwi-bong concentrated on technique, Moon Chul-min held forth on theory. In 1950, under the direction of Kim Kyoung-ok and Cho Dong-wha, the New Korean Dance Company was formed. Even during the Korean War they staged performances and became the centerpiece of Korean dance of the times. Ham Kwi-bong employed Mary Wigman's pedantic aesthetics in dance, introduced the dancing practices of pioneers such as Isadora Duncan, and created surprisingly new dance terminologies.

The founding of the dance department at Ewha Women's University in 1962 was the most important event in Korean dance history. The program was the first of its kind in Korea, and continues to turn out top dancers. Park Woe-sun, who studied Graham technique in Japan under Takada Seiko, persuaded the school to establish such a program, which set the foundation for modern dance to be accepted in the country. Her student, Yook Wan-soon, is considered as the progenitor of Korean modern dance; she was the first Korean woman ever to study with Martha Graham in America. In 1963 she took the name of an earlier collaboration and called her group "Orchesis." The style of this group was very different from that of the so-called New Dance of the time, and caused a great stir.

The appearance of Hong Sin-cha in 1973 was another pivotal event, even more shocking than Yook Wan-soon's systematic and socially conscious modern dance. Hong, who had been working in the dance field for 10 years, centering around the LaMaMa Theatre in New York, showcased herself as an example of overseas activities. Yook's dance group, consisting mainly of Ewha Women's University graduates, and another group, from the Modern Dance Association (founded in 1987), were polar opposite in the new era of Korean dance—each bringing collaboration with other artistic fields, introducing new dancers, academics, opening doors to overseas activities. Among those involved in the new era of Kroean dance were Ha Jung-ae, Lee Jung-hee, Kim Bock-hee, Kim Wha-suk, Park Myung-sook, Cho Eun-mi, Lee Sook-jae, Kim Yang-kun, Ahn Shinhee, and Chung Kui-in.

Choi Chung-ja, who was trained at London's Laban school, and Nam Jeong-ho who studied in France, helped to bring a surge of flavor to the modern dance. Festivals such as International Modern Dance festival, the Dance Festival of Korea, and others, along with the Korea Contemporary Dance Company's small theater dance movement started in the 1980s, worked to diversify and spread the dance activities in Korea. In 1975 the monthly dance magazine *CHOOM* was founded. Choom, a traditional Korean word meaning dance, meant more than "new dance," and the magazine played a vital role in establishing a dance culture in Korean society. It produced such famous dance critics as Lee Soon-yeol, Kim Young-tae, Chae Hee-wan, Lee Jong-ho, Kim Tchae-hyeon, and Kim Kyoungae, who established the Korean Dance Critics Society.

In 1975 there was a drive to produce new works based on traditional Korean dance, beginning with Yook Wan-soon. The Changmu Dance Company, under the direction of Kook Soo-ho, produced a work based on Stravinsky's *Le Sacre du Printemps*. World-famous video artist Paik Nam-jun collaborated with Kim Hyoen-ja and Bae Jeong-hae, artistic director of Seoul Metropolitan Dance Company. The visits of many foreign dance groups, the American Dance Festival, annual participation at the Rencontres International Choreographiques de Seine-St. Denis in France, and the introduction of foreign trends and co-productions have also helped Korean modern dance take hold and gain prominence. Presently, there are dance departments in about 45 universities and colleges and around 100 dance groups in Korea; dancers are often college professors who create dance companies from their students. Yet funding is still very tight for modern dance—those receiving funds are traditional dance companies and the only modern company established by the government is the Taegu Municipal Dance Group, led by Koo Bonsook in Taegu.

—Kim Kyoung-ae

Gertrud Kraus: *The Poet's Dream.*

founded Gertrud Kraus Dance Group, 1935; troupe becomes resident dance company of the Folk Opera in Tel-Aviv; head of dance department at Jerusalem Rubin Academy, 1954. **Awards:** Government of Israel's Israel Prize, 1963. **Died:** 23 November 1977 in Tel-Aviv.

Publications

On KRAUS: books—

Manor, Giora, *The Life and Dance of Gertrud Kraus,* Tel-Aviv, 1978.

On KRAUS: articles—

Ingber, Judith Brin, "The Gamin Speaks—An Interview with Gertrud Kraus," *Dance Magazine,* March 1976.
"Gertrud Kraus—20 Years after Her Demise," Special Supplement, *Israel Dance Quarterly,* No. 12, 1997.

*　　*　　*

KRAUS, Gertrud

Austrian dancer, choreographer, and educator

Born: 6 May 1903 in Vienna, Austria. **Education:** Studied piano, State Academy of Music, Vienna, then studied modern dance with Gertrud Bodenwieser, 1923. **Career:** Member, Gertrud Bodenwieser's dance company, 1924; quit to concentrate on her own choreography and gave first solo in Vienna, 1925; founded her own company and toured Europe, 1930; moved to Tel-Aviv and

To become a professional musician, Gertud Kraus studied piano at the State Academy of Music in Vienna from 190 to 1923. To earn a living, she accompanied modern dance classes taught by Ellinor Tordis. Teacher and students were astounded at an improvisation class when Kraus got up from the piano stool, kicked off her shoes, and danced a brilliant solo she had prepared. After receiving her diploma from the Piano Department, she again enrolled at the State Academy in the modern dance courses of Gertrud Bodenwieser in 1923. There being a modern dance course available in these years was unusual and progressive. A year later, in 1924, Gertrud joined Bodenwieser's dance company for a few months. But Kraus, being very creative and an independent spirit, found it impossible to be just a disciplined dancer in a group.

Kraus began rehearsing an entire solo program, the primary form of modern expressionistic dance at the time. She hired a large concert hall in Vienna, and in 1925 gave her first performance, becoming an acclaimed artist overnight. Kraus then opened her own studio, formed a company, and began traveling and touring Europe. The climax of her European activities came in 1930, when she and her group performed her *Songs of the Ghetto,* with music by Joseph Achron, at the International Dance Congress in Munich. A year later she toured Israel (then Palestine) and would return again in 1933 for another solo tour.

In 1933 Kraus staged a large-scale dance drama called *Eine Stadt Wartet (A City Waits)* on the open-air stage in the park next to the Burgtheater. The performance was based on a short story by Maxim Gorki, and set to original music by Marcel Rubin. The premiere was on the very day Hitler was elected Kanzler (Prime Minister) of Germany.

When the situation of Jews and left-wingers in central Europe deteriorated and Nazi influence grew, Kraus decided to emigrate. In 1935 she settled in Tel-Aviv, opened a new studio and founded the Gertrud Kraus Dance Group, which over next several years, from 1937 to 1940, frequently performed with the Palestine Orchestra (founded by Huberman and Toscanini in 1937). The Gertrud Kraus Dance Group also became the resident dance company of the Folk Opera in Tel-Aviv during World War II. Among the leading dancers of her group were Paula Padani, Naomi Aleskovsky, Hilde Kesten, and Vera Goldmann. Since there were no male dancers in the group, the taller women sometimes had to dance dressed as men. The Gertrud Kraus Dance Company ceased performing in the late 1940s.

In addition to choreographing for the group, Kraus often staged large pageants, as she had previously done in Vienna when she was an assistant of Rudolf von Laban, the legendary choreographer who had staged the annual dance procession of the trade unions.

In 1950 and 1951, after the establishment of the State of Israel, Kraus made an attempt to found a professional modern dance company, the Israel Ballet Theatre, which lasted for just 18 months and was disbanded because of the lack of funds. In 1954 Kraus stopped dancing and became the first head of the dance department of the Jerusalem Rubin Academy. She taught in her studio in Tel-Aviv until 1973, becoming a mentor for three generations of Israeli dancers and choreographers.

In 1963 Kraus was awarded the prestigious Israel Prize for her life achievement by the Government of Israel. She died in November 1977 after an illness and was buried in Tel-Aviv. In her memory, there is an annual choreography competition, held at the Rubin Academy in Jerusalem.

—Giora Manor

KREUTZBERG, Harald
German dancer and choreographer

Born: Reichenberg, Austria (now Liberec, Czech Republic), 11 December 1902. **Education:** Studied with Mary Wigman in Dresden. **Career:** Dancer, Hanover Ballet, 1922-25, Berlin Staatsoper, 1925-27; subsequently performed throughout Europe and the U.S. in solo performances and with Yvonne Georgi. **Died:** 25 April 1968 in Muri, Switzerland.

Works (partial listing)

1927	*Kuyawiak*
	March
	Gothic Dance
1928	*Revolt*
	Three Mad Figures
	Four Little Figures
1929	*Spanish Impressions*
	The Angel of Last Judgement
	The Spirit of Evil
	Romantic Dance Scene
	Flag Dance
1930	*The Jubilate*
	King's Dance
	Polonaise
	In the Twilight
	Variations
	Persian Song (with Georgi)
	Angel of the Annunciation
1932	*Waltz*
	The Hangman's Dance
	Gloria in Excelsis Deo
	The Cripples
	Petrouchka
	Three Miniatures in the Spanish Style
1933	*Dance of the Moon*
1936	*Pièta*
	Soldier of Fortune
1937	*Barcarole*
	The Romantic
	Dance through the Streets
	Orpheus' Lament for Euridyce
	Vagabond's Song
	Greek Theater: Scenes from the Oresteia of Aeschelus
	Tango at Midnight
	The Merry Pranks of Tyl Eulenspeigel
1939	*Choral*
	Night Song
	Hungarian Dances
1947	*Four Little Etudes*
	Evocation of the Evil One
	Li-Tai-Po
	Night Terror
1948	*In 3/4 Time*
	The End of Don Juan
	Trois Morceaux Caracteresque
	Song of the Stars
	From an Old Calendar

Variations on "Ah Du Lieber Augustin"
Notturno
Job Expostulateth with God
Jolly Trifles
1953 *The Guardian of the Realm of Shades*
1956 *Moira Ton Mykenon*
1960 *The Angel Lucifer*

* * *

Harald Kreutzberg was the leading male figure in the Expressionist period of Central European modern dance, known as the *Ausdruckstanz*. He was a forceful performer of solos and duets, and a prolific choreographer. Born in Reichenberg, Austria, (now Czechoslovakia) in 1902, Kreutzberg began his career as a graphic artist, attending the Academy for Applied Art in Dresden. He studied dance for three years, starting in 1920, with German modernist Mary Wigman, taking classes with her in Leipzig and Dresden; as a result, he decided to make dance his career. Wigman's first class consisted of a number of students who would go on to become modern dance pioneers, including Kreutzberg's future duet partner Yvonne Georgi, as well as Hanya Holm, Max Terpis, Gret Palucca, and Margarethe Wallmann. Kreutzberg went on to dance with Wigman's troupe for a time, as did the other class members.

Max Terpis left the group in fall 1922 to become the ballet master at the Hanover Opera. Kreutzberg and Georgi followed him there the next year, where they both became soloists. In 1924 Terpis left Hanover for the Berlin State Opera, where Kreutzberg joined him as a dance soloist. Kreutzberg came to the United States for the first time as part of the Berlin ensemble, where stage director Max Reinhardt noticed him in *Don Morte* (for which Kreutzberg shaved his head, a distinctive look he kept for the rest of his life). Reinhardt hired him to play the Master of Ceremonies in *Turandot* at the Salzburg Festival in 1926, and engaged him in the role of Puck in *A Midsummer's Night Dream* in 1927. Kreutzberg also danced in Reinhardt's *The Miracle* and *Jedermann* that year—and in 1928 went along when *Midsummer* toured the U.S., where his performance was critically acclaimed.

Kreutzberg also gave his first American recital in 1928, performing with dancer Tilly Loesch to the accompaniment of Louis Horst. In 1929 he and Georgi toured the U.S. in a concert of solos and duets, accompanied by Friederich Wilckens, who would become Kreutzberg's longtime collaborator. Their success led the two dancers to tour annually from 1930 to 1939. In addition, Kreutzberg joined Georgi at Hanover, where she had taken over from Terpis as ballet mistress, and it was there that they created many of their duets.

In 1929 Kreutzberg became acquainted with American dancer Ruth Page, who was greatly influenced by him and who described his performances as "elfin, yet spiritual." She studied with him in Salzburg in 1932, and they ultimately staged joint recitals in the U.S. and Asia from 1934 to 1936. Kreutzberg, who was already at his creative peak, performed at the Berlin Olympics in 1936, and continued touring in solo and duet concerts in Europe and America.

Both Wigman and Terpis had a great impact on Kreutzberg: Wigman for her technique and Terpis for adding a theatrical dimension to his performances. Kreutzberg continued to specialize in solos and duets throughout his career, focusing on dramatic pieces with recognizable characters. Some were based on literature, religious stories, ethnic folk dances, or mythology, and some were portraits of invented personalities. All of his dances were characterized by emotion, clearly demonstrated through movement. His pieces were also known for their humor, which was unusual in modern dance at the time, particularly in the U.S. Kreutzberg had a reputation for technical facility and craftsmanship (he designed his own costumes, stage designs, and props). He loved to perform, and his works were visual entertainment rather than profoundly meaningful, dramatic rather than abstract.

At the beginning of his first American tour, Kreutzberg was quoted as saying: "I am not a leader nor a creator of any school of dancing. I dance to express myself. I dance from my heart, blood and imagination. . . .I do not believe that dancing should tell a story or have a meaning; nor do I feel that a dancer must draw upon his experiences to express fully dances of great joy or great sorrow." In his *Introduction to the Dance*, critic John Martin added, "Self-expression, however, is far from the complete story, for besides that inner exuberance that moves [Kreutzberg] to action, there is a superb craftsmanship to hold him within bounds. It is compounded of several things in addition to mere bodily technic—a gift for the theatrical and a phenomenal instinct that tells him how things will look to an audience, a highly developed visual sense, and an innate talent for design."

During the Nazi regime, German dance stagnated, especially in comparison to the innovations occurring at that time in the United States. German dancers who wanted to continue performing, including Kreutzberg, had to follow the rules of the Nazi party—which meant dances had to appeal to mass audiences, and lack ideology. Kreutzberg, whose performances had always been more about entertainment than profound meaning, was allowed to continue touring after the Nazis came into power. In fact, he was one of the only well-known German dancers who maintained a good relationship with the Ministry of Propaganda during this period (others emigrated or were detained). He knew what his role had to be in order to continue dancing.

Yet, since he could not innovate, his dances began to look old when he started touring again after a hiatus during the war. He was still technically superior and a strong performer, but his pieces were perceived as shallow and decorative, and his repertoires consisted mainly of works he had choreographed in the 1930s. Still, he continued to perform until 1959, when he made his farewell appearance in Frankfurt. He also came out of retirement to dance the role of Death in Ruth Page's production of *Carmina Burana* in Chicago in 1965, three years before his death.

While Kreutzberg made his mark primarily as a performing artist, he was also a teacher. He opened a school in Bern, Switzerland, in 1955, and worked there until the end of his life. Among his students were Erick Hawkins and Muriel Stuart. He also influenced several dancers who saw his performances, notably Doris Humphrey and José Limón. In Selma Jeanne Cohen's *The Modern Dance: Seven Statements of Belief*, Limón wrote of Kreutzberg: "I saw that a man could, with dignity and towering majesty, dance. Not mince, prance, cavort, do 'fancy dancing' or 'show-off' steps. No. Dance as Michelangelo's visions dance and as the music of Bach dances."

—Karen Raugust

LA MALINCHE

Choreography: José Limón
Music: Norman Lloyd, with trumpeter, percussionist, pianist, female soprano (Betty Jones)
Costumes: Pauline Lawrence Limón
First Production: Ziegfield Theatre, 31 March 1949
Dancers: Pauline Koner (La Malinche), Lucas Hoving (El Conquistador), and José Limón (El Indio).

Publications

Krevitsky, Nik, *Dance Observer,* May 1949.
————, *Dance Observer,* August-September 1949.
McDonagh, Don, review, *New York Times,* 3 April 1976.

*   *   *

La Malinche is a dance for a woman and two men. Its subject is the conquest of Mexico by the Spanish conquistador Hernán Cortés. The main character of *La Malinche* is an Indian woman who lived in Mexico in the 1500s, the time of the Spanish conquest. Her real name was Malinalli Tenepal (ca. 1505-1530). Malinalli (also called Malintzin, Malinche, and Marina) was forced to serve with Cortés; she acted as his interpreter and also became his mistress.

Limón's work distills the epic story of Mexico's fatal contact with the Spanish. The dance is based on the following legend: upon Cortés' arrival in Mexico, he was presented with Malinche, an Indian princess, who acted as an the interpreter between the Aztecs and the Spanish. Malinche made it possible for Cortés to subdue the Aztecs and conquer Mexico. Malinche was baptized and given the name Doña Marina. After her death, a popular belief arose that her spirit returned to the Mexican people to lament her deeds and wash away her ancient treachery. As long as her people were ensalved, Malinche could never rest in peace, so returned to lead the Mexicans in their fight for freedom from Spain.

Limón's *La Malinche* unfolds to the sound of drums and cymbals. Two men and a woman enter marching to jaunty trumpet music. Their arms and hands are extended in front of their bodies, much like the figures of *santos,* the carved wooden statues of saints so popular in Mexican culture. One man holds a sword; the woman holds a flower. They act out the roles of Cortés and Malinche, while the second man, who carries nothing, acts out the role of El Indio, the Indian. The dancers form a circle and perform a round dance. The two men hoist the woman aloft between them and she then dances with Cortés. Then there's a solo for El Indio. Cortés stands with legs spread wide as Malinche kneels in front of him. He straddles her body and uses his sword to lift her. She then takes the sword in her hands while falling into a deep backbend, accepting Cortés' rule over her. The sword of the conquistador is also the cross of Christianity, which the Spaniards imposed on the Indians of Mexico. Malinche thus accepts the religion of the conquerors, then beckons Cortés forward and he marches boldly with the sword. He brandishes it in a triumphant display of power and might. Malinche rolls on the floor as Cortés continues his dance of conquest. Again, he uses his sword to lift her and move her along. In a formal pose, she receives the sword and also a great black skirt; her transformation into the helper of the Spaniards is completed.

In the next section, Cortés and Malinche walk hand in hand in a stately and dignified manner. Malinche tries to protect the crouching figure of El Indio from Cortés' wrath, yet El Indio points an accusing finger at Malinche. Her body takes on a new, less grand posture as she staggers forward, head lowered, grief-stricken. In her upright hand she displays a large scarf. As El Indio rests on his knees, his arms crossed in front of his hunched-over body, Malinche stands behind him and slowly envelops his figure with her large skirt. He throws it off violently and Malinche retreats, lurching to the insistent beat of drums and the keening of a female singer.

Then El Indio rises from his dejected and defeated pose, flexing his arms to the music of a trumpet and a piano as he raises them to heaven. He rises on his feet, leaps up, and dances in increasingly bolder movements. He punctuates his jumps and balances with vigorous foot stamping and raps on his thigh. El Indio and Malinche do a dance of buoyant jumps and hand-clapping in the style of traditional Mexican folk-dancing. The figure of Cortés collapses; Malinche presents El Indio with a flower, and they hold hands and lean sideways in a balanced pose. Their story ended, the three players march off to the same jaunty music that opened the dance.

The costumes by Pauline Lawrence Limón were simple but evocative of Mexico's past. La Malinche (Pauline Koner) was costumed in a long, broad skirt with a modified train and a jagged line of metallic fabric rimmed the lower part of the skirt. A blouse with a deeply scooped neckline and short cap sleeves completed the costume. Koner wore her dark hair parted down the center and pulled back tight around her head into two long braids intertwined with metallic ribbon that covered her breasts and reached to her waist. Limón ("El Indio") wore the loose-fitting white shirt and pants of the Mexican peon with modified dance sandals on his feet. Hoving ("El Conquistador") wore white pants and a white shirt decorated with ruffs gathered around a high collar and a medallion sewn onto the front of the shirt. In his hands, he carried the large cross that doubled as his sword to conquer and destroy the Aztecs.

Writing in the August-September 1949 issue of *Dance Observer,* Nik Krevitsky called *La Malinche* "a brilliant naive theatre piece in the spirit of the Mexican festival mystery plays." The same writer compared *La Malinche* to *El Penitente,* Martha Graham's work that also featured three peasants retelling a legend. But he was quick to point out that, while sharing many similarities, the two had very little in common as *La Malinche* was more lighthearted and sweeter in tone. John Martin of the *New York Times* (1949) stated that *La Malinche's* "earthy humor only half masks the traditional tribal passion in which the legend is based."

La Malinche quickly became recognized as one of Limón's major works and premiered the same year as his other masterpiece, *The Moor's Pavane*. Limón the dancer was at the height of his expressive powers; his powerful but supple physique was disciplined in every move. His strong hands and feet gave his gestures great weight with grandeur and elegance—as evidenced by his humble bend at the beginning of the dance that is transformed into his assertion of dignity at the end.

—Adriane Ruggiero

LABAN, Rudolf (Jean Baptiste Attila de Varalja)

Hungarian performer, choreographer, company director, writer, and theorist

Born: 15 December 1879 in Poszony (Bratislava). **Education:** Architecture School of the Ecoles des Beaux Arts, Paris. **Died:** 1 July 1958 in Weybridge, England.

Works

1916	*Der Spielmann (The Fiddler)*, Kaufleuten, Zurich
1917	*Die Sang an Die Sonne (Song to the Sun)*, Monte Verità hillside
1921	Bacchanale in Wagner's *Tannhäuser*, Nationaltheater, Mannheim
	Die Geblendeten (The Blinded Ones), Nationaltheater, Mannheim
1922	*Oben und Unten (Above and Below)*, Würtemburgisches Landestheater, Stuttgart
	Fausts Erlösung (Faust's Release), Ernst Merck Halle, Hamburg
	Der Schwingender Tempel (The Swinging Cathedral), Convent Garten, Hamburg
1923	*Kammertänze (Chamber Dances)*, Theater am Zoo, Hamburg
	Lichtwende (Dawning Light), Convent Garten, Hamburg
	Gaukelei (Illusions), Convent Garten, Hamburg
	Komödie (Comedy), Sagebiel, Hamburg
	Prometheus (Prometheus), Ernst Merck Halle, Hamburg
1924	*Agamemnons Tot (Death of Agamemnon)*, Sagebiel, Hamburg
	Dances for *Sommernachtstraum (A Midsummer Night's Dream)*, Deutsche Schauspielhaus, Hamburg
1925	*Tersichore*, Schauspielhaus, Hamburg
	Don Juan, Schauspielhaus, Hamburg
	Dämmende Rhythmen (Dawning Rhythms), Thalia Theater, Hamburg
1926	*Narrenspiel (The Fool's Mirror)*, Neues Theater am Zoo, Berlin
	Choreographische Tänze aus Wagner (Choreographic Dances on Wagner), touring

1927	*Ritterballett (Ballet of the Knights)*, Kurhalle, Bad Mergentheim
	Titan (The Titan), Stadthalle, Magdeburg
	Nacht (Night), Stadthalle, Magdeburg
1928	*Der Grünen Clowns (Green Clowns)*, Stadttheater, Essen
1929	*Festzug des Handwerkes und der Gewerbe (Pageant of Crafts and Trades)*, Ringstrasse, Vienna
	Alltag und Fest (Everyday and Festival), Sportstadion, Mannheim
1930	*Bacchanale* in Wagner's *Tannhäuser*, Wagner Festtheater, Bayreuth
	Polowetzer Tänze (Polovtsian Dances) in Borodin's *Furst Igor*, Staatsoper Unter den Linden, Berlin
	Dances for Rossato's *Zierpuppe (The Decorated Doll)*, Staatsoper
	Walpurgisnacht in Gounod's *Margarete*, Staatsoper
	Der Tanz der Siebenschleier (Dance of the Seven Veils) in R. Strauss's *Salomé*, Staatsoper
1931	Dances for Strauss' *Eine Nacht in Venedig (A Night in Venice)*, Staatsoper
	Dances Strauss' *Zigeunerbaron (The Gipsy Baron)*, Staatsoper
	Dances for Weber's *Oberon*, Staatsoper
	Operetta Jones' *Die Geisha (The Geisha Girl)*, Staatsoper
	Dances in Wolf Ferrari's *Die Schalkhafte Witwe (The Cunning Widow)*, Staatsoper
	Tänze (Dances), Schillertheater, Berlin
1932	Dances for Bizet's *Carmen*, Staatsoper
	Dances for Verdi's *Sizilianische Vesper (Sicilian Vespers)*, Staatsoper
	Dances for Mozart's *Idomeneo*, Staatsoper
1933	Dances for Wagner's *Rienzi*, Staatsoper
	Dances for Reznicek's *Donna Diana*, Staatsoper
1934	Dances for Bizet's *Die Perlenfischer (The Pearl Fishers)*, Staatsoper
	Dornröschen (Sleeping Beauty), Staatsoper
1936	*Tauwind in den Neuen Freude (The Warm Wind and New Joy)*, Dietrich Eckartbühne, Berlin

Publications

By LABAN: books—

Die Welt des Tänzers, Stuttgart, 1920.
Choreographie, Jena, 1926.
Gymnastik und Tanz, Oldenburg, 1926.
Kindes Gymnastik und Tanz, Oldenburg, 1926.
Schrifttanz, Vienna, 1928.
Editor, *Tanzfestspiele 1934*, Dresden, 1934.
Ein Leben für den Tanz, Dresden, 1935; as *A Life for Dance*, London, 1975.
With F.C. Lawrence, *Laban/Lawrence Industrial Rhythm and Lilt in Labour*, Manchester, 1942.
With F.C. Lawrence, *Effort*, London, 1947.
Modern Educational Dance, London, 1948.
Mastery of Movement on the Stage, London, 1950.
Principles of Dance and Movement Notation, Macdonald and Evans, London, 1956.
Choreutics, edited by Ullmann, London, 1966.
A Vision of Dynamic Space, compiled by Ullmann, London, 1984.

On LABAN: books—

Bartenieff, Irmgard, *Body Movement*, New York, 1980.
Dell, Cecily, *A Primer for Movement Description*, New York, 1970.
Foster, John, *The Infuence of Rudolph Laban*, London, 1977.
Green, Martin, *Mountain of Truth: The Counterculture Begins 1900-1920*, Hanover, New Hampshire, 1986.
Maletic, Vera, *Body, Space, Expression*, Berlin, 1987.
Preston-Dunlop, Valerie, *Rudolf Laban: An Extra-Ordinary Life*, London, 1998.

* * *

Laban's extraordinary career can be divided into three distinct episodes: from 1912 to 1919 as "Finding a Basis," from 1920 to 1936 as "Leading the Struggle for German Dance," and from 1938 through 1957 as "Researching Movement in Human Behaviour." From 1912 Laban grappled with the problem of how to safeguard the place of dance in the lives of ordinary people at a time when (1) their indigenous culture was in grave jeopardy through the disruption of rural community life and mass emigration to towns for work, and (2) theatre dance in the form of ballet was stagnant, music dependent, and offered no way forward for an art form of dance appropriate for the industrial culture of the 20th century. When he was 33 and living in Munich, he shifted emphasis from earning a living as an illustrator and graphic artist to regarding the renewal of dance as his life's work. With an acceleration of conceptual endeavour accompanied by rigorous and fundamental experimentation with an ad hoc group of dancers, including the young Mary Wigman, he laid down the basis for the development of European modern dance.

During this time Laban addressed the essential issues. If dance is to become a force in people's lives it must become independent of music visualisation, it must reject the limitation of the received movement vocabularies of ballet, folk dance, and social dance, and it must free itself from reliance on a story. The medium of dance—that is, the dancer's body and personality, the dancer's movement, the spatial forms and rhythmic patterns in which and with which the dance is made—become the content of dance. Laban was addressing the same issues as Wassily Kandinsky which led a way for the painter away from the portrait, the still life, and the landscape towards abstract art, colour, and form. Stravinsky and Schönberg were engaged in comparable rejections of the norms in music's past to work with irregular rhythms and atonal harmonic structures. Laban paralleled their innovations in his medium.

For dance to stand as an equal with the visual and sonic arts in their struggle for renewal, it had to become a literate art. To this end Laban accelerated his research into dance notation forms vowing to create a viable system for written dance, so enabling dance to free itself from dependence on oral tradition. He opened a school for Dance, Sound, Word and the Plastic Arts, or all arts that are movement-based, operating in the summer months at Monte Verità, the open air commune experimenting with alternative lifestyles arising from spiritual values. World War I forced him to continue his research and practice in Zurich by which time he had established Choreutics and Eukinetics as the practical and theoretical study of the dancer's space and the dancer's dynamics and rhythm, and he had become known through his lectures on the essential role of dance in all eastern and western cultures to the human being's expressive life.

In 1920 he commenced a period of experimental dance-making, establishing himself in Germany. He worked both in the mainstream theatres and, whenever possible, independently. He astounded audiences with abstract ensemble works, dances without music, dances with speech/choir accompaniment, group improvisations, dances with political themes, comic and satirical programmes, dances with percussion, dances with nudity. Each new work addressed a separate artistic problem so that his output was and is fundamentally valuable for its rich processes rather than its products. He promoted the male dancer and valued each dancer's personal movement style and physique as well as creative contribution. He established his company, the Tanzbühne Laban, with sponsorship in dollars which enabled him to create and tour until 1924 despite the hyperinflation that decimated the German economy. He and Dussia Bereska toured with the smaller Kammertanzbühne Laban until 1926 when an accident on stage ended his performing career.

Laban created celebratory choric works for amateurs, successfully setting up city Movement Choirs eventually throughout central Europe, convinced that everyone should have the opportunity for artistic bodily expression. He worked in contrast to and conflict with the popular Körperkultur (body culture) schools who promoted healthy bodily activity. Over 20 Laban Schools were set up, most with their own choir. From 1928 his notation was invaluable for writing these works so that they could be rehearsed in separate towns, the choirs coming together for the performances. Alongside presenting dance as theatre he developed principles to underlie a dancer's education, both as creative development for a child and as a professional dance artist's training. To this end he published books, on dance philosophy (1920), on movement analysis and writing (1926), on a rationale and curriculum for children's dance (1926), adult dance (1926), and on notation (1928). He set up the Choreographisches Institut as a revolutionary training place for professional dance people; today it would be regarded as a postgraduate centre for dance study. He promoted cooperative action by people from all kinds of dance to establish unions to protect jobs and conditions. This he did through initiating three Dancers' Congresses in 1927, 1928 and 1930.

Parallel with Laban, Mary Wigman (his erstwhile pupil), established herself as the leading German modern dancer of immense uncompromising talent and following. Kurt Jooss, also a pupil, established himself as a leading choreographer by amalgamating ballet's formal discipline with Laban's dynamic and dramatic vocabulary. Surprisingly neither of these two was offered the prize appointment of choreographer and director of movement to the Prussian State Theatres at the Berlin Opera House which, in 1930, went to Laban. At this point critical opinion on German dance had polarised into passionate defense of Laban's experimental ensemble choreography against a view that only star-studded virtuosity had value. The world financial slump of 1929 precipitated the rise to power of the National Socialist political party so that while creating the incidental dances for the Berlin Opera repertoire to mixed reception, Laban found himself to be a Nazi employee. In 1934 he was appointed as director of movement for the whole of Germany working uncomfortably under the Nazi Ministry of Propaganda. In 1936 he created a choric work for 2,000 dancers to open the cultural programme alongside the Berlin Olympic Games, dubbed "Hitler's Games." Supposed to be a work glorifying National Socialism, instead it promoted his own philosophy of mutuality and individual expressiveness. Laban was dismissed, denied a means to live, and nearly died of destitution before finding refuge in Great Britain in 1938.

Laban found employment in wartime Britain through F. C. Lawrence assisting workers in heavy industries. He developed his analysis of the "job Effort" allied to the "personal Effort" profile of the worker, a method diametrically opposed to that of "Time and Motion Study" experts. He recommended harmonic use of time, weight, space, and flow instead of shorter, faster movement calculated by a stopwatch count. His humane methods led to decreased stress and increased output. His effort observation of an individual's behaviour patterns, of immediate interest to art therapists especially at the Withymead Centre for psychotherapy, led to the foundation of Movement and Dance Therapy, since developed as an accredited profession. Actors found his effort and space theories invaluable. Drama schools such as the Royal Academy of Dramatic Art and Theatre Workshop incorporated his work into the actors' training. Laban's own artistic creativity shifted from dance to movement-based drama.

British movement teachers and the Ministry of Education wholeheartedly welcomed Laban's ideas and methods for dance for children. Creative movement as a means to education, rather than dance as a skill to be learned, took root in the state school curriculum by 1950 as Modern Educational Dance. Creative dance as a recreative art form for men and women was successfully introduced into Britain.

Laban worked all his life with apprentices whom he trained to develop the aspects of dance and movement theory and practice that he'd initiated. Hence with the breakup of his influence in Germany by the Third Reich, the emigration of German dancers in the 1930s, and on his death in 1958, his leading apprentices continued his work in their own specialties. The foundations he laid for modern dance and expressive movement transcend his personal style and can be found reappearing in avant-garde dance. Pina Bausch's Tanztheater and William Forsythe's use of Laban's choreutics are just two examples.

—Valerie Preston-Dunlop

LAMENTATION

Choreography: Martha Graham
Music: Zoltán Kodály (Piano Piece Op. 3 No. 2)
Costume Design: Martha Graham
First Production: For the Dance Repertory Theatre, New York, 8 January 1930
Dancer: Martha Graham

Publications (see also General Bibliography)

Armitage, Merle, ed., *Martha Graham,* New York, 1966.
De Mille, Agnes, *Martha: The Life and Work of Martha Graham,* New York, 1991.
Martha Graham Archive, San Francisco Performing Arts Library.
McDonagh, Don, *Martha Graham,* New York, 1974.
Stodelle, Ernestine, *Deep Song: The Dance Story of Martha Graham,* New York, 1984.

*   *   *

On 8 January 1930, Martha Graham premiered a solo that would come to be recognized as her first masterpiece. Graham had already produced four years' worth of independent concerts by this time, but it was not until this first production with the Dance Repertory Theatre and the magnetic performance of her solo *Lamentation* that Graham came into her own as an artist of significant merit, ability, and maturity. In *Lamentation*, Graham reveals to us the seed of genius that would come to bear on the next 60 years of her creative achievements.

When the curtain rose the night of the premiere, the audience found Graham seated on a long low platform enveloped in a tubing of tricot, only her narrow length of face visible under the cover of a hood. To a haunting score by Zoldan Kodaly, Graham danced her solo entirely from a seated position, stretching the material into distended and jagged forms that paralleled the dancer's interior landscape of anguish and grief. Through twistings of her torso and by extending parts of her body in sharp diagonals, Graham created tension lines in the fabric reminiscent of a face lined with sorrow. The slow stretching of the tricot further illustrated the interminable and aching feeling.

Her hands and feet emerged occasionally from the sculpture of fabric to grope the air or pull at the cloth, portraying the same tension and distortion. The gestures of *Lamentation* felt almost Greek in their tragedy as when the dancer grasped at her head with her hands in the beginning of the piece. Other gestures of mourning seemed to stem from the Hebraic tradition. Regardless of their origins, the movements and sculpted forms of *Lamentation* spoke the universal language of human suffering. When Graham drew her instep to her center, it was an expression of a primordial sadness.

Everything about this solo was shocking to her 1930 audience. The costuming, the subject matter, the movement itself, even the fact that the piece was performed while sitting, were all revolutionary to the dance. The late 1920s and early 1930s marked a period of experimentation for Graham; she stripped away the surface theatricalities she had learned in her years of study with Denishawn and searched for a way to express pure emotion. What emerged from this introspection was Graham's development of her own technique based on pelvic tension and release, and her philosophy that "out of emotion comes form."

In her early movement studies such as *Revolt* (1927) and *Immigrant* (1928), we see Graham's movement vocabulary begin to develop—the subtle articulation of the spine, the bold, assertive execution of movement, the angular possibilities of the shoulder and elbow. In *Lamentation* her developing technique found a mature artistic expression. The asymmetrical forms and tension-filled postures of this solo were not elaborations placed on the choreography but rather shapes emanating from the internal anguish of the dancer. It is, perhaps, Graham's quintessential representation of her choreographic philosophy.

Lamentation was, in fact, more sculptural than kinesthetic. Graham's innovative use of the newly developed stretch jersey along with the fact that the piece was performed in a seated position worked to create a moving sculpture on stage. It was as if Graham had loosened the being from inside a Henry Moore sculpture and then watched as the form moved from one grief-stricken pose to another. Agnes DeMille, in her biography of the artist, asserts that Graham's work not only stands apart from other abstract moderns but is "never wholly abstract," because of the emotionalism and vision that marks her creations.

Initial response to the work was mixed. For many, the emotionalism of *Lamentation* was viewed as overly dark or simply irrelevant. Dance critic John Martin observed in a 1931 article in the *New York Times*, "Miss Graham's dancing seems obscure and ludicrous to those who use dance recitals as a substitute for bridge

Joyce Herring in *Lamentation,* 1989. Photograph by Beatriz Schiller.

parties and backgammon." Graham's introspective studies of solitary figures (of which *Lamentation* was one), did in fact come years before this kind of artistic exploration was in vogue. When Graham explored these themes, she did so at the end of the jazz age, an era known more for its diversions than for its soul searching.

For others, *Lamentation* was an effrontery to the senses and was too much to bear. Not only was the movement—the contractions of the pelvis, the flexed feet and angular gestures—a direct challenge to long-established rules about aesthetics and movement; the composition was heavy with emotional intensity and Graham left the audience no route of escape. In bringing the inner world of grief into the public space of theatre, Graham challenged her audience to not only think but to feel.

Today *Lamentation* is recognized as Graham's first masterpiece and as a landmark in the history of modern dance. Like all of Graham's early works, *Lamentation* initially received a mixed bag of critical reviews. But Graham astutely retained *Lamentation* as part of her repertory long after the other compositions from that period faded into memory. The solo enjoyed many revivals in the Graham Company throughout the years as well, including in 1944

and 1994. *Lamentation* remains an important historical document of the revolutionary technique that changed modern dance. But it also endures as an emotionally powerful composition, with as much resonance today as it had 30 years ago when it was first created. It stands as a testament to the craftsmanship and artistic integrity of one of the great artists of our time.

—Siobhán Scarry

LAMHUT, Phyllis
American dancer and choreographer

Born: 14 November 1933 in New York City. **Education:** Studied with Alwin Nikolais and Murray Louis, Henry Street Playhouse. **Career:** Dancer, Alwin Nikolais Dance Company and Murray Louis Dance Company; choreographer for Henry Street recitals;

choreographer, Limón Dance Company; founder, Phyllis Lamhut Dance Company, 1970; taught at Swarthmore College, 1983; American College Dance Festival Association's National College Dance Festival, 1986; associated with Tisch School of the Arts at New York University's Dance International Choreography Project, 1990s.

Roles

1963	*Imago* (Alwin Nikolais)
	Interims (Murray Louis)
1964	*Sanctum* (Nikolais)
	Junk Dances (Louis)
1965	*Tower* (Nikolais)
1968	*Tent* (Nikolais)
1969	*Proximities* (Louis)

Other roles include: Many additional performances with both the Nikolais Dance Company and the Murray Louis Dance Company in the 1960s.

Works

1950	*Nostalgia*
1951	*Incantation of Greed*
1952	*Annoyous Insectator*
1953	*Theme and Variations*
	Periphery of Armor
	Cameo
1954	*Lady of Aviary*
	Interlude
1955	*Hex*
	Clock
	Gemini
	Loreli
	2 Dances
1956	*Stick Figure*
	Sleep
	Lament
	Tragedienne
	Ritual
1957	*Reverie*
	Excursion
	Coif
	Suite
	Willow
	Trifoliate
1958	*Unmirrored*
1959	*Hands*
	Lavella
	Cebrina
	Ceremonial
1960	*Pastel*
1961	*Herald*
	Fanfare
	Portrait
	March
1962	*Trilogy*
	Tocsin
	Puppet
1963	*Group*
	Shift

	Recession
	Touch Dance
1964	*Computer Piece*
1965	*3 Dance Movements*
	Ostinato
	Fickle Idol
1966	*Viods*
	Monody
	Incidentals
1967	*Come on and Trip*
1969	*Space Time Code*
1970	*Big Feature*
	Extended Voices
1971	*House*
	Area I
	Field of View
	Act I
1972	*Congeries*
	Scene Shift
	Two Planes
	Dance Hole
1973	*Terra Angelica*
	Z Twiddle
	OTD (Off Track Dancing)
1974	*Medium Coeli*
	Late Show
	Country Mozart
1975	*Theatre Piece (Untitled)*
	Solo with Company (Work in Progress)
	Hearts of Palm
	Conclave
1976	*A Bicentennial Celebration*
	Brainwaves
1978	*Disclinations*
	Dryad Essence
1979	*Mirage Blanc*
	Guerrero
	Musical Suite
1980	*Passing*
1983	*Disinclinations*
1987	*Junk Dances* (restaged)
1991	*Cleave*
1993	*Sacred Conversations*
1994	*Fantomes* (mus. Jalalu-Kalvert Nelson)
1995	*Deadly Sins* (collaboration with composer Andy Teirstein)

Publications

On LAMHUT: books—

Jowitt, Deborah, *Time and the Dancing Image*, New York, 1988.
McDonagh, Don, *The Rise & Fall & Rise of Modern Dance*, Pennington, New Jersey, 1970.
Partsch-Bergsohn, Isa, *Modern Dance in Germany and the United States: Cross Currents and Differences*, Tucson, 1994.

On LAMHUT: articles—

Deresiewicz, Bill, "Limón Dance Company," *Dance Magazine*, July 1994.

Phyllis Lamhut Dance Company: *Deadly Sins.* **Photograph by Tom Caravaglia.**

Draegin, Lois, "Two Troupes for the Price of One," *Newsday*, 13 December 1987.

Garafola, Lynn, "Limón Dance Company," *Dance Magazine*, Feb 1996.

Hering, Doris, "Deadly Sins," *Dance Magazine*, July 1995.

Jackson, George, "*Showcase*: Emerging Aesthetic," *Washington Post*, 19 February 1990.

Mazo, Joseph H., "A Limón Homage to Poland," *Newsday*, 24 March 1994.

Scher, Valerie, "City Choreographer Has Country Roots," *Philadelphia Inquirer*, 15 June 1983.

Seidel, Miriam, "Limón Troupe Performing Old and New," *Philadelphia Inquirer*, 24 October 1994.

Sommers, Pamela, "National College Dance Festival," *Washington Post*, 23 May 1986.

Temin, Christine, "A Dazzling Level of Energy," *Boston Globe*, 29 January 1983.

Tobias, Anne, "Subtle Tributes to the Master," *Newsday*, 25 April 1991.

*   *   *

Phyllis Lamhut is a contemporary experimental dancer and choreographer trained and influenced largely by Alwin Nikolais. She also has strong ties to the Limón Dance Company, for which she has choreographed several works.

Lamhut received much of her early training in a children's performing group formed by Nikolais at the Henry Street Playhouse, where she danced in the late 1940s and early 1950s. She later joined Nikolais' company, which was also based at the Henry Street Settlement on the Lower East Side of New York. She become one of his leading dancers, gaining a reputation for her superior flexibility, and performing in pieces choreographed by Nikolais and his close associate and longtime partner, Murray Louis. She ultimately left Nikolais to form her own New York-based company.

Her choreography, which is staged by her own troupe, the Phyllis Lamhut Dance Company, as well as the Limón Dance Company and others, is often is described as postmodern. Many pieces contain violence, and human beings are depicted as trapped by powerful modern forces that they do not necessarily recognize. It is somewhat surprising that her work has become so closely associated with José Limón's eponymous troupe since his death, since her choreographic sensibility is very different from his. In any event, several of her works are in the Limón repertoire. For example, Lamhut created *Sacred Conversations* in 1993 as a solo for Limón artistic director Carla Maxwell. In *Sacred Conversations*, Maxwell is costumed as a "barbarian priestess" surrounded by what seem to be boulders made of taffeta. The piece has been described as both humorous and edgy.

Lamhut's 1994 *Fantomes* is about urban fear, and its movements, costumes, and music all contribute to an environment fraught with violence. The score, by Jalalu-Kalvert Nelson, consists of synthesizer music accompanied by screams. The 10 dancers travel in posse-like packs, dressed in baggy shirts and wool caps. The overall shape and movement of the piece, and the emotions they create, are more important than the dancers' steps. As the performers violently tug at one another and crash into each other, with the men particularly aggressive toward women; by the end of the piece the dancers' shirts are ominously transformed into hanging nooses.

Many of Lamhut's other works are similarly provocative, such as the hour-long *Deadly Sins*, premiered by the Phyllis Lamhut Dance Company in 1995. She collaborated on the piece with composer Andy Teirstein, costume designer Lois Bewley, and lighting designer Phil Sandstrom.

Another of Lamhut's dances, *Cleave* (1991), is typical in that it incorporates her concern with contemporary social and political issues. The piece was described in a program note as "a contemporary folk dance inspired by the dismantling of the Berlin Wall." In it she employs movements such as steps, shuffles, hops, and skips in geometric patterns, which are performed by two divided groups that are ultimately united, although a single sad figure is seen among the celebrants.

Some of her choreographic works, such as *Disinclinations* (1983), are strongly reminiscent of her mentors, Alwin Nikolais and Murray Louis. The latter choreographed *Junk Dances,* first performed in 1964, with Lamhut in mind for a main role. *Junk Dances* was restaged in 1987 in a Nikolais/Louis joint season, with Lamhut reprising her original part. While the Limón Dance Company and her own troupe perform many of her works, several of her pieces are found in the repertoires of a wide range of other dance companies, from New Orleans Dance, a modern dance repertory company, to the York University Dance Ensemble of Canada.

In addition to her choreographic work, Lamhut teaches dance in New York and has taught at various schools and universities around the United States. Some of her notable students have included Kent Baker, Donald Blumenfeld-Jones, and Chantal Cadieux. She frequently teaches master classes, such as at Swarthmore College's Music and Dance Festival in 1983 and at the American College Dance Festival Association's (ACDFA) national festival held at the University of the District of Columbia Auditorium in 1986. In the 1990s, she has been associated with the Tisch School of the Arts at New York University, where she is involved in the TSOA Dance International Choreography Project. Lamhut also appears at various festivals and performances as a panelist or judge. For example, in 1990, she served on the panel that chose the program for the Choreographers Showcase at Prince George's Public Playhouse in Washington. Similarly, she was a panelist at the National Dance Residency Program in 1994.

In all of her choreographic works, Lamhut requires two major contributions from her dancers. First, she demands the constant intensity that give her works the emotional impact she intends; second, she wants the dancers to be sincere as they portray the feelings showcased in her works.

Lamhut's dances are often described as intelligent and well-crafted, and many tend toward the ritualistic with their changing geometric patterns and pedestrian steps. Yet, as an experimental choreographer, Lamhut's work is not always well-received or understood by audiences or critics. In a review of *Deadly Sins*, Doris Hering questioned much of the performance, including "Who were those motley creatures?" and "Why did they tug at one another? How was sin woven into their jagged conga line? Why did one woman retch and stick out her tongue? Why did three people grasp their shoes and furiously bang them on the floor? Why did a man stagger and stare? What did these actions have to do with sin, and where were they taking place? These were some of the questions suggested by Phyllis Lamhut's hourlong premiere, *Deadly Sins.*" Hering, however, went to conclude: "Perhaps she intended an ambivalent effect, telling us that human actions are often construed as sinful when in reality they are not. Perhaps she had an entirely different association. Either way, *Deadly Sins* was a provocative work."

—Karen Raugust

LAMPERT, Rachel
American dancer, choreographer, and company director

Born: 4 December 1948 in Morristown, New Jersey. **Education:** Mt. Holyoke College, 1965-66; New York University, studied ballet with Nanette Charisse, modern with Jean Erdman, Gladys Bailin, and Stuart Hodes, 1965-72. **Career:** Founded Rachel Lampert & Dancers, 1975.

Works

1971	*Going Nowhere*
	Divertimento
1974	*Oval*
1975	*Issue*
	Edge
1976	*The Frog Princess*
	Home
	Odyssey before Brunch
	Bloody Mary Sunday
	Turn
	Brahms Variations on a Theme by Handel
	Daguerrotype
1977	*Coasting*
	Doing the Dance
1978	*In Memory of the Lonesome Pine*
	Traffic
	Dark Dreams and Endings
	The Misanthrope (theater)
1979	*Now That We're Rolling* (theater)
	Solo Suite
	Prelude at the End of a Day
1980	*The Vagabond Stars* (theater)
	Cliff Walking
	Mirror
	After the Fact
	Me and Beethoven

1985   *What's Remembered*

Publications

On LAMPERT: articles—

Beck, Jill, "Rachel Lampert's *What's Remembered?*: A Critical Analysis," *Dance Notation Journal,* Spring 1985.
Vaughan, David, "Do You See What I Mean?," *Dance Magazine,* October 1977.

*   *   *

American modern dancer and choreographer Rachel Lampert formed her own company, Rachel Lampert & Dancers, in 1975. Her dances are often humorous and autobiographical in nature; their simplicity and linear storylines make them accessible to an audience of prosaic people.

Lampert was born in 1948 in Morristown, New Jersey, and raised in Brooklyn, New York. She took ballet classes as a child, showing a penchant for choreography by directing neighborhood children in dance routines on the front lawn. She wasn't introduced to modern dance until attending Mt. Holyoke College. Lampert continued her training in both modern dance and ballet at New York University's School of Arts. She studied ballet with Nanette Charisse and modern dance with Jean Erdman, Gladys Bailin, and Stuart Hodes. For many years she worked as Hodes' assistant.

When she formed her own company, Clarice Marshall and Holly Harbringer, whom she met while attending New York University, joined her as dancer-choreographers. In the *Biographical Dictionary of Dance*, Barbara Naomi Cohen-Stratyner describes Lampert's pieces as "very funny, using images of childhood and games in the perception of a fairly egocentric youngster." One such performance was *The Frog Princess,* first performed in 1976, which uses actual home movies of Lampert and friends playing and dancing to set the scene for the piece. The audience is to make the connection that the tiny, tutu-clad child is now the adolescent wallflower at a high school dance.

Many of Lampert's themes deal with relationships, between family and otherwise, as well as motifs of childhood memories. *Issue,* a trio of performances debuting in 1975, deals with a child's observances as her parents separate for divorce, while the following year's *Home* imaginatively used a baseball game as its framework. Other works include *Odyssey Before Brunch, Bloody Mary Sunday,* and *Turn* also in 1976, *Coasting* and *Doing the Dance* in 1977, and 1978's *In Memory of the Lonesome Pine* and *Traffic.* Though most of her pieces were created for her own dance company, Lampert's work has also been performed by the Connecticut Ballet, the San Antonio Ballet, and in solo concerts by Naomi Sorkin. In addition to concert works, Lampert created several dances for theater including *The Misanthrope* in 1978, *Now That We're Rolling* (1979) and an original musical for the Berkshire Theatre Festival in 1980 entitled *The Vagabond Stars.*

Writing in 1977, David Vaughan described Lampert's works as falling into two categories: biographical illustration, and what he characterized as "fast-moving, fluent, dancey group works." Several of Lampert's works fit into the former, like the successful *Issue,* as well as *Daguerrotype, The Frog Princess,* and *Edge;* while larger-scale pieces like *Brahms Variations on a Theme by Handel* fit the latter. Vaughn compared Lampert's *Edge* (1975) a

solo created for Alyce Bochette, to James Waring's *Feathers,* a solo he created for Raymond Johnson. Both pieces used the same Mozart music, and though the movements were different, Vaughn found Lampert's work "even made the same kind of contrast between the serenity of the music and the tension of the movement—the edge in question might have been the edge of a breakdown."

Twyla Tharp appears to have been an influence on Lampert, at least in her choice of music, especially composers like Mozart and Haydn, and her mixing of elements from jazz, tap, and ballet with modern dance. Yet unlike Tharp, according to Vaughn, Lampert "tends to skim over the surface of the music rather than digging deep into it. Even in *Brahms Variations on a Theme by Handel,* a large-scale work originally made for the Connecticut Ballet, the mixture of jazz, tap, modern, and ballet doesn't seem very audacious since Lampert stays so close to the meter of the music." Vaughan further states that Lampert "is a real talent" and considers her a choreographer with much potential still to be realized. He praised *Issue* as having form perfectly suited to content, though he was less glowing about *The Frog Princess,* considering it a bit superficial in its cataloguing of teen dance moves. Yet perhaps Lampert was content with the dancing itself, the expression of relationships, and the memories of childhood in a way that even audiences not conscripted into the world of modern dance would enjoy and understand. Few of her early performances were reviewed and there is seemingly little information available on this dancer and choreographer; yet her dancing appears to speak plainly in a language the average person will both understand and remember.

—Lisa A. Wroble and Sydonie Benet

LANG, Pearl

American dancer, choreographer, company director, and educator

Born: Pearl Lack, 29 May 1922 in Chicago, Illinois. **Education:** Attended Chicago City Junior College of the University of Chicago, 1938-41; studied with Nicholas Tsoukalas and Ruth Page. **Family:** Married to the actor Joseph Wiseman. **Career:** Danced with Ruth Page's Dance Theater; dancer, including many leading roles, the Martha Graham Company, New York, 1941-55; first dancer to assume two famous Graham roles: Three Marys in *El Penitente,* 1947; the Bride in *Appalachian Spring,* 1953; danced on Broadway, 1943-47; formed her own company, Pearl Lang and Company, 1952; choreographed for young dancers at the American Dance Festival and at Jacob's Pillow; choreographed several solo works for herself including *Windsung* and *Moonsung;* appeared at the Brooklyn Academy of Music (BAM), Fashion Institute of Technology, Brooklyn College, and Hunter College, New York; worked with the Batsheva Dance Company of Israel; set her work *Shirah* on the Dutch National Ballet, 1962; appeared with the Graham company as a soloist; appeared on television performing her own works, late 1950s and 1960s; danced Graham solos in concert, 1970s; taught at the Yale University School of Drama, the Juilliard School, the Neighborhood Playhouse, and the American Dance Center. **Awards:** Guggenheim Fellowships for choreography, 1960 and 1969.

Roles (all performances with the Martha Graham Company, premiering in New York)

1941	Pretty Polly, *Punch and the Judy*
1943	One of the Brontë sisters, *Deaths and Entrances*
1944	The Bride, *Appalachian Spring*
1946	*Dark Meadow*
1948	The Girl in Red, *Diversion of Angels*
1952	Death, *Canticle for Innocent Comedians*
1954	*Ardent Song*
1975	*Adorations*

Other roles include: Danced on Broadway in Agnes De Mille's *One Touch of Venus,* 1943; *Carousel,* 1945; and *Allegro,* 1947; Michael Kidd's *Finian's Rainbow*; Helen Tamiris' *Touch and Go.*

Works

1949	*Song of Deborah*
1951	*Legend*
1952	*Moonsung*
	Ironic Rite
	Windsung
1953	*Rites*
1955	*And Joy Is My Witness*
1956	*Juvenescence*
	Three at a Phantasy
1957	*Persephone*
1958	*Nightflight*
1960	*Black Marigolds*
	Shirah
	Sky Chant
1962	*Appassionada*
1963	*Broken Dialogues*
1964	*Shore Bourne*
1965	*Remembered Fable*
1969	*Piece for Brass*
	Tongues of Fire
1971	*Sharjuhm*
1972	*The Encounter*
	Two Passover Celebrations
	Moonways and Dark Tides
1974	*At This Point in Time ...*
1975	*The Possessed*
	Prairie Steps
	Plain Song
1977	*Kaddish*
	I Never Saw Another Butterfly
	Roundelays
1978	*Icarus*
	Cantigas Ladino
1979	*Noches Noches*

Other works include: Choreographed works for theatre and pageants including *Judith,* 1956; *Miriam's Song* and *Sabbath Song,* 1959; *Chassidic Dances,* 1962; *Murder in the Cathedral,* 1966; *Song of Deborah,* 1968; *Had Gadyo* and *Prayers at Midnight,* 1973. Also choreographed these works for television: *And Joy Is My Witness* for *Frontiers of Faith* (CBS-TV, 1960), *Black Marigolds* (1962), *Parable for Lovers* for *Look Up and Live* (CBS, 1956), *Persephone* (1958), *Prayer to the Dark Bird* for *Directions* (ABC-TV, 1966), *Rites* for *Look Up and Live* (CBS, 1956), *Trio, or Once Upon a Wish* (1958), and *Two Songs in Dance* for *Directions* (ABC, 1970).

Publications

By LANG: article—

Interview with Barbara Trecker, *New York Post,* 23 December 1974.

On LANG: articles—

Barnes, Clive, review of *The Possessed, New York Times,* 20 October 1977.
Sorell, Walter, review of *Nightflight,* performed by Pearl Lang, *Dance Magazine,* July 1958.
Tobias, Tobi, review of *The Possessed,* performed by Pearl Lang, *Dance Magazine,* March 1975.
Clippings file of Pearl Lang from the Dance Research Collection of the New York Public Library at Lincoln Center.

*   *   *

Pearl Lang's contributions to the world of dance as a performer would be enough to gain her a place in dance history. One of the leading interpreters of roles created for her by Martha Graham, and a riveting dancer of her own choreography, Lang was an eloquent choreographer of power and poetry whose works celebrate the human spirit. She found in the ritual and conflict of theater and dance a perfect outlet for her gifts, both as a dancer and as a maker of dances. Lang was drawn to biblical and Jewish-Hasidic themes, and her most riveting work reflects this interest. In 1975 she unveiled her first large group work, *The Possessed,* a three-act dance based on the legend of the Dybbuk. Lang turned Ansky's classic tale of Yiddish theater into what Clive Barnes of the *New York Times* called a "choreo-play of grave beauty."

Lang's interest in Jewish themes stems from her background. She was born to Russian Jewish immigrants who had settled in Chicago. Her father, Jacob Lack, was a tailor, and her mother, Frieda, was a dress designer. Like many immigrants, the Lacks struggled to grind out a living in their new land. Yet, as Lang recalled in a *New York Post* (1974) interview with Barbara Trecker, "there was a hunger for cultural things." Pearl was taken to poetry readings and lectures by her mother and enjoyed performances by the Chicago Symphony. Music, in the form of a large gramophone, was also in the Lack home. Lang recalled listening to records and acting out the role of the conductor. At the age of six she saw her first dance performance by the Irma Duncan dancers and knew what her career would be. She studied Greek folk dancing with Nicholas Tsoukalos and, at age 12, won a scholarship to the Frances Allis Studio in Chicago. There she studied ballet and modern dance. In 1939 she appeared with the Ruth Page Dance Theatre Company. A year later, a short course of study with Martha Graham in New York City inspired her to move to New York to study with Graham full-time.

The years spent with Graham were extremely productive and creatively satisfying for Lang. Graham featured her in many works including *Deaths and Entrances, Night Journey, Ardent Song, Letter to the World,* and *Diversion of Angels.* So valuable was her contribution to the company that Graham allowed her to be the first dancer to perform roles once reserved for Graham herself in *El Penitente* and *Appalachian Spring.* Lang supplemented her work with Gra-

Pearl Lang performing *The Song of Deborah.*

ham by appearing as a dancer in Broadway musicals including *Carousel* and *One Touch of Venus.*

When Lang left the Graham troupe in 1952, she continued to dance with the company as a guest artist. In 1974 Lang returned to the Martha Graham company to dance the role of Clytemnestra. It was the masterful performance of a mature artist who, according to *New York Times* dance reviewer Anna Kisselgoff, "came closest to Graham's own conception of the role. Here was a dancer who made the audience suffer along with Clytemnestra." Lang's technique was noted for its secure balances, quick turns, and easy shifts of direction. Yet Lang was more than a technical wizard. As dance critic Walter Terry pointed out, "a quality of luminosity always colored her movements."

Lang's devotion to the Martha Graham school and company was profound. Lang believed that Graham succeeded in establishing a basic technique for disciplined learning, teaching, performing, and choreographing. She used Graham technique in her work but expanded upon it for her own creative and teaching purposes. Lang's work as a choreographer is notable for its daring physicality and the demands it places on dancers' technique. In fact, some reviewers commented on the punishing quality of her choreography and its restlessness. Other critics pointed out what they perceived to be Lang's reliance on Graham mannerisms. But Lang remained true to Graham's teaching and influence. She also never asked of her dancers what she could not do herself.

Lang proved comfortable composing solos, duets, and large pieces and was drawn to composing story-dances. Plotted or plotless, Lang's dances seemed to emanate from the force of movement itself, and movement for Lang always reflected deeply held emotions. Outside of solos devised for herself, her first work as a choreographer was the duet *Song of Deborah.* It was commissioned by the Juilliard School of Music and performed there in 1949. This was followed by her other major work, *Rites* (1953), set to quartets of Béla Bartók. This work focused on the cycle of love, birth, and death, and on ceremonies of growth. Her choice of movement stresses daring, lyricism, and unison work. A sense of theatricality was never out of sight. As John Martin noted in his *New York Times* review of Lang's work, "Lang has had the good fortune to work in show business . . . and knows how to meet an audience both as choreographer and as a performer." Her work never seemed to leave the viewer unmoved; Walter Sorell commented in *Dance Magazine* (1958) on seeing her piece *Nightflight*: "Pearl Lang is an extraordinary dancer whose sense of drama complements her lyrical quality. She knows how to create an atmosphere of urgency about her as a performer as well as a choreographer."

The mystical *Shirah* (1960) is probably her most famous Hebrew piece and is clearly based on the dance vocabulary of Martha Graham. In it, Lang reestablishes the Jewish belief in the immortality of the soul. Its strong lyrical sweep reflects Lang's own qualities as a dancer. Her choice of music has always been interesting, too. In *Shirah,* Lang used Alan Hovhaness' concerto for viola.

The Possessed (1975) was the high point of Lang's choreographic creativity. As Tobi Tobias pointed out in *Dance Magazine* (1975), Lang succeeds due to her ability "to move back and forth fluently between the play's literal and its abstract manifestations." But it is as a choreographer and dancer of pure abstract movement that Lang triumphs. Many critics have wondered if her dance for the possessed Leye would have been as strong if performed by another dancer.

If Lang had drawbacks as a choreographer it was that she tried to pour too many ideas into her work. Reviewers were taken with her

intellect and willpower but some yearned for a little more stillness in her dances. They had to concede, however, that very few dancers were able to make unforgettable images with their bodies the way Pearl Lang could.

Pearl Lang is married to the stage and screen actor Joseph Wiseman and lives in New York City. She admits that being a dancer takes a toll on an individual's personal life. The physical, financial, and emotional drains are great. However, as Lang stated so aptly in the 1974 *New York Post* interview with Barbara Trecker, "you dance because you love to dance . . . dance is a glorification of the living moment . . . and people's lives are larger when they see it." Anyone who saw Pearl Lang dance or witnessed her dances was enriched and glorified.

—Adriane Ruggiero

LAVALLE, Josefina

Mexican dancer, educator, choreographer, company director, promoter, and researcher

Born: Josefina Martínez Lavalle, 29 January 1926 in Mexico City. **Education:** Studied at the National Dance School with Linda Costa, Ernesto Agüero, Luis Felipe Obregón, Francisco Domínguez, and Nellie Campobello, 1937-38; at Estrella Morales' Dance School, 1938-39; at the Grisha Navibach Dance School, 1938-39; at Fine Arts Ballet and Waldeen Ballet with Waldeen, 1940-46; at the Mexican Dance Academy with José Limón and Lucas Hoving, 1950; at the National Ballet of Mexico (BNM) with Xavier Francis, 1950-56; at the Fine Arts Ballet with Eugene McDonald, Merce Cunningham, Mary Anthony, Sonia Castañeda, Nellie Happee, Anna Sokolow, Yuriko, David Wood, 1957-62; and at the Nelsy Dambre's Academy, 1962-64; studied drama with Seki Sano and Alejandro Jorodowsky; studied law at National University of Mexico, piano studies at Academy of Antonio Gómezanda; dance and teaching dance at Fine Arts Ballet, 1939; B.A. artistic education; M.A. in artistic education/research. **Career:** Appeared with the Fine Arts Ballet, 1940-41; with the Arts Theater Ballet, 1941-42; with the Waldeen Ballet, 1946-47; with the Mexican Dance Academy (MDA), 1947-48; cofounder of the National Ballet of Mexico (NBM), 1948-56; founder, Dance School of Oaxaca, 1950; principal dancer of MDA, 1951; cofounder of Popular Ballet of Mexico, 1958; principal dancer/choreographer for Fine Arts Ballet, 1957-62; dancer/choreographer for Contemporary Mexico Ballet, 1963-66; toured Oaxaca and Istmo of Tehuantepec researching indigenous dances and music, 1947; toured with NBM as part of Literacy Campaign, 1949; with Amalia Hernández's Modern Ballet, to Havana, Cuba; with Popular Ballet of Mexico to Europe, officially representing the country in the cultural festival held during the world fair in Brussels, Belgium, 1958; toured England, Hungary, Poland, Czechoslovakia, Yugoslavia, China, and U.S.S.R.; Cuba with the Fine Arts Ballet, 1960; U.S. universities with Contemporary Mexico Ballet, 1964; taught for the MDA, 1947-69; directed MDA, 1959-69 and 1972-77; directed the Arts' Secondary Education Center, Public Education system, 1972-77; executive delegate, Dance National Fund (FONADAN), 1973-85; Latin American vice-president, International Dance Congress, 1974-78; founded the

Mexican Dance Association, 1975-76; dance consultant, Artistic Education Coordination, National Institute of Fine Arts (NIFA), 1978-83; dance consultant, Cultural Promotion, Public Education Secretary, 1984-88; researcher, CENIDI-Danza José Limón, NIFA, 1985 to present; published several works on dance research and a dance notation system. **Awards:** Music and Theater Chroniclers Union Award, 1976; Rafael Ramírez Medal, for 30 years of teaching, 1979; A Life in Dance Homage, NIFA, 1985; four Medals of Merit of Public Education Secretary and NIFA, 1995; Guillermina Bravo Award, 1996; member of the National System of Creators, 1994.

Roles (premiered in Mexico City unless otherwise noted)

1940   Una figura española, *Procesional (Processional)* (Waldeen), Fine Arts Ballet
        Seis danzas clásicas (Six Classic Dances) (Waldeen), Fine Arts Ballet
        Danzas de las fuerzas nuevas (New Forces Dances) (Waldeen), Fine Arts Ballet
        A woman and Kitty, *La Coronela* (Waldeen), Fine Arts Ballet

1947   *Sonata número 7 (Number 7 Sonata)* (Bravo), Mexican Dance Academy
        El cielo de los negros (Negro Heaven) (Mérida), Mexican Dance Academy
        Día de difuntos o el triunfo del bien sobre el mal (All Souls' Day or the Triumph of Good from Evil) (Mérida), Mexican Dance Academy
        Preludios y fugas (Preludes and Fugues) (Bravo), Mexican Dance Academy
        A maiden, *La balada del pájaro y las doncellas o danza del amor y de la muerte (The Bird and Maidens Ballad or Dance of Love and Death)* (Mérida), Mexican Dance Academy
        The kidnapped bride, *El Zanate* (Bravo), Mexican Dance Academy

1949   *La doma de la fiera (The Taming of the Shrew)* (Waldeen)
        Allegretto de la quina sinfonía (Fifth Symphony Allegretto) (Waldeen), National Ballet of Mexico
        La doncella de trigo (The Wheat Maiden) (Waldeen), National Ballet of Mexico
        Danzas románticas (Romantic Dances) (Waldeen), National Ballet of Mexico
        Tres ventanas a la vida patria (Three Windows to the Patriotic Life) (Waldeen), National Ballet of Mexico
        En la boda (At the Wedding) (Waldeen), National Ballet of Mexico
        Estudio revolucionario (Revolutionary Study) (Waldeen), National Ballet of Mexico
        Cinco variaciones de Bach (Five Variations of Bach) (Waldeen), National Ballet of Mexico
        Fuerza motriz, ballet de masas (Motive Force, Mass Ballet) (Bravo), National Ballet of Mexico

1951   The mother, *Recuerdo a Zapata (Memories of Zapata)* (Bravo), National Ballet of Mexico
        Alturas de Machu Pichu (Heights of Machu Pichu) (Bravo), National Ballet of Mexico

1953   *Al aire libre (At the Open Air)* (Mérida), Mexican Ballet, Mexican Dance Academy

La nube estéril (The Sterile Cloud) (Bravo), National Ballet of Mexico

1955   *Danza sin turismo (Dance without Tourism)* (Bravo), National Ballet of Mexico

1958   *Cuauhtémoc* (Arriaga), Popular Ballet of Mexico
        Zapata (Arriaga), Popular Ballet of Mexico

1960   *Orfeo (Orpheus)* (Sokolow), Fine Arts Ballet
        The shadow, *El hombre de barro (The Earth Man)* (Sakmari), Fine Arts Ballet
        Visiones fugitivas (Fugitive Sights) (Reyna), Fine Arts Ballet
        La Manda (Reyna), Fine Arts Ballet
        Opus 1960 (Sokolow), Fine Arts Ballet
        The doll, *Juguetes mexicanos (Mexican Toys)* (Noriega), Fine Arts Ballet
        Tierra (Earth) (Noriega), Fine Arts Ballet

1961   *Missa Brevis* (Limón), Fine Arts Ballet
        Ofrenda musical (Musical Offering) (Sokolow), Fine Arts Ballet
        Sueños (Dreams) (Sokolow), Fine Arts Ballet

1962   *Homenaje a Revueltas (Homage to Revueltas)* (Contreras), Fine Arts Ballet
        Piezas y bagatelas (Pieces and Trinkets) (Contreras), Fine Arts Ballet
        Presagios (Omens) (Reyna), Fine Arts Ballet
        The moon, *La balada de la luna y el venado (Moon and Deer Ballad)* (Mérida), Fine Arts Ballet
        Norte (North) (Mérida), Fine Arts Ballet
        Suite (Mérida), Fine Arts Ballet
        A girl, *La visita (The Visit)* (Bracho), Fine Arts Ballet
        Intramuros (Intramurally) (Ortega), Fine Arts Ballet, Mexico City
        Variaciones barrocas (Baroque Variations) (Ortega), Fine Arts Ballet
        Guide butterfly, *Fantasía (Fantasy)* (Sakmari), Fine Arts Ballet
        Triángulo de silencio (Silence Triangle) (Mérida), Fine Arts Ballet

Works (premiered in Mexico City unless otherwise noted)

1947   *Suite Provencale* (mus. Milhaud), Mexican Dance Academy
1949   *Carta a las madres del mundo (Letter to the World's Mothers)* (mus. Shostakovich), National Ballet of Mexico
1950   *El niño y la paloma (The Child and the Dove)* (mus. Contreras), National Ballet of Mexico
        Colorines (mus. Revueltas), National Ballet of Mexico
        Suite mexicana (Mexican Suite) (mus. Durán), National Ballet of Mexico
        Fuerzas nuevas (New Forces), Dance School of Oaxaca, Oaxaca
        Madres (Mothers), Dance School of Oaxaca, Oaxaca
        Juan al mar (John to the Sea), Dance School of Oaxaca, Oaxaca
1952   *Concerto* (mus. Vivaldi), National Ballet of Mexico
1953   *La maestra rural (The Rural Teacher)* (mus. Jiménez Mabarak), National Ballet of Mexico
        Danza de las fuerzas nuevas (New Forces Dance) (mus. Galindo), National Ballet of Mexico
        Emma Bovary (mus. Vivaldi, Bach and Tambourini), National Ballet of Mexico

15 de septiembre. Homenaje a Hidalgo (September 15th Homage to Hidalgo) (mus. Ximénez), National Ballet of Mexico

1954   *Variaciones sobre la alegría (Variations on Joy)* (mus. Jiménez Mabarak), National Ballet of Mexico

1955   *Juan Calavera* (mus. Revueltas and Elizondo), National Ballet of Mexico

1956   *Rescoldo (Embers)* w/Guillermina Bravo (suspended by the authorities of the National Institute of Fine Arts) (mus. Noriega), National Ballet of Mexico

1959   *Preludio y fuga de Santana (Santana's Prelude and Fugue)* (mus. Bach), Fine Arts Ballet

1960   *Interludio (Interlude)* (mus. Britten), Fine Arts Ballet
      Del sol (Sun) (mus. Salas) Masses Ballet

1961   *Informe ... a una Academia (Report. . .to an Academy)* (mus. Berg), Fine Arts Ballet

1962   *Danza para cinco palabras (Dance for Five Words)* (mus. Gassman), Fine Arts Ballet
      Ferial (mus. Ponce), Fine Arts Ballet

1968   *El dorado (The Golden One)* (mus. Elizondo and Piñeiros), Folkloric Ballet of Mexico

1974   *Danza para una muchacha muerta (Dance for a Dead Girl)* (mus. Kuri), Mexican Dance Academy

1975   *Retablo (Frieze)* (mus. Kuri) Mexican Dance Academy

1979   *A Nicolás* (To Nicolás. Homage to Nicolás Guillén)

1987   *Sueño de un domingo por la tarde en la Alameda (Sunday's Afternoon Dream in La Alameda)* (mus. Kuri), Mexican Dance Academy

1990   *El cantar de los vencidos (Conquered Song)* (mus. Kuri) Mexican Dance Academy

1993   *Nueva España (New Spain)* (mus. Purcell, Kuri and popular) Mexican Dance Academy

1994   *Cambio de tiempo (Change of Time)* (mus. Lavista and Kuri), Mexican Dance Academy
      En la florida estera de las águilas (mus. various authors) Mexican Dance Academy

1996   *A zarandearnos tiranita* w/Guillermo González (mus. various), Folkloric Ballet

Other works include: *Juan Calavera* (1955) was included in a television series by the Educational Television Unit of the Public Education Secretary, 1984.

Publications

On LAVALLE: books—

50 años de danza en el Palacio de Bellas Artes, Mexico, 1984.
Tortajada, Margarita, *Danza y poder,* Mexico, 1995.
———, *Mujeres de danza combativa,* Mexico, 1997.

On LAVALLE: articles—

Segura, Felipe, "Josefina Lavalle," in *Homenaje una vida en la danza 1985,* Mexico, 1985.

*　　*　　*

Josefina Lavalle is an essential element of Mexican dance because of her long, varied career and ongoing, active participation in the dance world. She is considered to be one of the primary authorities in the Mexican dance field. Besides being an accomplished dancer and choreographer, she has become a respected teacher, company director, dance researcher, and the head of independent and official institutions.

In 1937 Lavalle entered the National Dance School (NDS), where her teachers included Linda Costa, Ernesto Agüero, Luis Felipe Obregón, Francisco Domínguez and Nellie Campobello. She left this school and entered the Estrella Morales and Grisha Navibach school in 1938. Lavalle was one of the dancers chosen by Waldeen to form the Fine Arts Ballet (FAB), with which she performed in 1940 in the first Mexican nationalist modern dance work. With this work, Lavalle, along with a whole generation of young dancers, strengthened their resolution of fully dedicating themselves to modern, professional dance, having as their aim to examine its roots to define its unique identity. Lavalle faithfully undertook these goals, convinced, as she is today, after more than 60 years of dance work, of the validity of this enterprise.

After her stay in the FAB, Lavalle pursued work with the Arts Theater Ballet and, following the departure of Waldeen to the U.S., with the Waldeen Ballet, where the students adopted her teachings. In 1947 Lavalle participated in the formation of the professional modern dance company and creative workshop, the Mexican Dance Academy (MDA), undertaking research tours in indigenous areas, which became the basis for the creation of her first works.

Due to the emergence of artistic and political disagreements, in 1948 Lavalle abandoned the MDA and, accompanied by a group of dancers headed by Guillermina Bravo, founded the National Ballet of Mexico (NBM). Until 1956 Lavalle shared that vital company's direction, creating works which enriched the dance panorama and confirmed her talents as a gifted choreographer. During the same period she also studied with Xavier Francis. Her works *The Rural Teacher* (1953) and *Emma Bovary* (1953) won her acclaim as the creator of a new choreographic style in which poetry and dynamism were merged.

In 1955 she created one of the most representative works of the Mexican nationalist dance movement, *Juan Calavera,* in which she explored the Mexican concept of death with great originality and skill, accompanied by the music of Silvestre Revueltas and Rafael Elizondo, and the design of Raúl Flores Canelo. This is one of the few works by Lavalle still known today, thanks to the television series produced by the Cultural and Educational Television Unit of the Public Education Secretary in 1984.

Lavalle's belief that rigorous training was indispensable to a dancer's development created a rift within the NBM, which at that time favoured expressiveness over technique. Lavalle, who felt dance should combine both elements, broke away and embarked upon a lengthy tour of Europe and Asia, where in addition to working as a dancer and choreographer, she studied the different trends and techniques being used in the major dance capitals. She returned to Mexico in 1958 and immediately was invited by Guillermo Arriaga to co-direct a new company, the Popular Ballet of Mexico. In the same year, the company participated in the Brussels Universal and International Exhibition where their success garnered them several invitations to perform elsewhere. The company suffered a split, however, with one group remaining with Lavalle on a tour of London, Hungary, Poland, Czechoslovakia, and Yugoslavia. They were then invited to perform in China and the U.S.S.R., where they stayed for six months. During this time, Lavalle had the opportunity of furthering her studies of methods for teaching dance.

On her return to Mexico in 1959, Ana Mérida, chief of the dance department of the National Institute of Fine Arts (NIFA), invited

Lavalle to direct the Mexican Dance Academy, giving Lavalle an opportunity to apply her concepts about dance training. She introduced strict standards, rigorous programmes of study, and a skilled staff of teachers, thus earning the official acknowledgment of the Mexican government. Despite such enormous work heading the academy, Lavalle continued to work with the FAB as a dancer and choreographer. In addition, she studied with José Limón and Lucas Hoving in 1950 and with Eugene McDonald, Merce Cunningham, Mary Anthony, Sonia Castañeda, Nellie Happee, Anna Sokolow, Yuriko, and David Wood from 1957 to 1962. She also continued to create new works during this period, including *Report to an Academy* (1961), a work that revealed her as an innovative and polemical choreographer, while provoking a great deal of public debate.

Lavalle's artistic and academic background was very broad. In addition to her dance studies, she studied dramatic art with Seki Sano and Alejandro Jorodowsky; law, diplomacy, and concert piano. She also received degrees (B.A. and M.A.) in artistic education and research which enabled her to have a broad view of dance and its needs, and allowed her to offer new approaches to dance education. From 1947 to 1969 Lavalle taught at the Mexican Dance Academy, serving as director from 1959 to 1969, and again from 1972 to 1977. In 1961 she founded an experimental group within the academy, in which several choreographers worked with students until 1969. In 1977 Lavalle headed the academy's struggle to defend its academic mission, which was under fire from authorities seeking to dissolve the institution. Thanks in large part to Lavalle's efforts, the academy was able to survive.

In addition to her important educational role with the academy, Lavalle participated in the creation and direction of many other institutions that served different levels of dance, as the Artistic Education Center. In 1973 she created and directed a 13-year project, the Dance National Fund, which undertook research on, and the rescue of, Mexican traditional dance. In addition to analysing the nature of this kind of dance and its staging, the project created a dance notation system to record its traditional forms. In 1985 Lavalle joined a group of researchers who founded the present José Limón National Research, Documentation, and Information Center of the National Institute of Fine Arts. She has carried out several research projects within this organization, contributing to the history and understanding of Mexican dance. Since 1994 Lavalle has been a member of the National Creators System, is a dance consultant for several institutions, and actively participates in staging works of the Mexican nationalist modern dance movement.

—Margarita Tortajada Quiroz
translated by Dolores Ponce Gutiérrez

LEEDER, Sigurd

German dancer, choreographer, and educator

Born: 14 August 1902 in Hamburg, Germany. **Education:** Studied art before turning to dance. **Career:** First performance in Hamburg, 1921; was engaged by the Hamburger Kammerspiele soon thereafter; also danced in Munich; came to the attention of Rudolf Laban and soon danced in Laban's choreographic works, 1923; met Kurt Jooss, 1924; appeared with Jooss in dance evenings entitled *Zwei Mannliche Tanzer* (*Two Male Dancers*) in many German cities and in Vienna, Austria;

studied classical ballet with M. Thoma in Vienna; engaged by the Staatstheater Munster as a soloist while Jooss acted as ballet coach; became director of the dance department at the school of music, language, and movement in Munster, 1926; went to Essen and taught in Jooss' dance department at the Folkwangschule, 1927; performed in first performance of Jooss' *The Green Table* at the Choregraphic Competition in Paris, 1932; taught at the Ida Rubinstein school in Paris, and worked with Jooss on *Persephone* at the Paris Opera, 1933; toured with Jooss' company, Ballets Jooss, 1933-34; established the Jooss-Leeder School in Devon, England, 1934; briefly imprisoned during World War II; ballet master of the Ballets Jooss, 1942-47; ran his own London school, 1947-59; ballet master for Festival Year of Great Britain, 1951; director of dance studies and teacher at the University of Chile, Santiago, 1960-64; moved his school from London to Herisau, Switzerland, 1965. **Died:** 1981.

Roles

1923   The beggar, *Gaukelei* (Laban)
1924   *Two Male Dancers* (concert program with Jooss)
1932   *The Green Table* (Jooss)

Works

1926   *Nachtstuck,* solo
1939   *Danse Macabre*
        Dona Clara
1943   *Sailor's Fancy*
1952   *Nocturne*
1959   *Allegro Maestoso*

Publications

On LEEDER: articles—

Müller, Grete, "Sigurd Leeder School of Dance," *Tanz International,* February 1993.

*   *   *

Sigurd Leeder was a leading figure in modern dance in Germany in the 1930s, renowned for his collaboration with Kurt Jooss and for his contributions to the Ballets Jooss, as well as his role as a co-founder of the Jooss-Leeder School of Dance, one of the most important and innovative organizations in the dance firmament of wartime England. Leeder's impact on modern dance in England cannot be overstated. His school, located in London, was the first to offer a full-time, three-year professional modern dance education in England after World War II; it attracted students from all over the world. Leeder's genius as a teacher, both in England and later in Switzerland, touched many lives. His completeness as an artist was amazing: he painted, designed sets, choreographed ballets, staged operas, translated Rudolf Laban's movement theories into dance, and instructed scores of actors in how to move on stage. His vision of dance as a unity of body and soul has been preserved by his successor Grete Muller at his school in Hersinau, Switzerland.

Sigurd Leeder was born in the north German port city of Hamburg at the beginning of the 20th century. His artistic talents were evident from an early age and prompted his parents—owners of a printing business—to send him to art school. Leeder studied graphic design for two years in his native city but was soon attracted to dance. His attraction was influenced in part by one of his art teachers who integrated rhythm, form, and expression of line and color in his drawing lessons. By the early 1920s Leeder was improvising dances in performances with a youth dance group he had founded. These early experiments in dance led to Leeder's engagement by the Hamburger Kammerspiele, the classical theatre in Hamburg.

Leeder's reputation spread and he was engaged to dance in Munich as the partner of Jutta von Collande. The early 1920s were a dynamic time in Germany as artists, writers, and musicians explored new forms of expression. Leeder met Rudolf Laban in 1923 and was deeply impressed by Laban's theories of eukinetics, choreutics, and improvisation. One year later, Leeder met another individual who was to have a major role in his life. Kurt Jooss was a disciple of Laban when he and Leeder met in 1924. Jooss had worked with Laban at the National Theatre in Mannheim as an assistant and later, as a principal dancer. Jooss and Leeder became collaborators and remained so for 23 years. Their work together survived exile from their homeland, a world war, and wartime deprivation.

In 1924 Leeder and Jooss joined forces as a dance team. They performed throughout Germany in a concert program entitled *Two Male Dancers*. But both were still learning their art; Leeder expanded his dance training in Vienna, studying classical ballet with M. Thoma, while becoming a member of the avant-garde Munster Neue Tanzbuhne (Munster New Dance Stage) under Jooss' direction. The other members of the company included Aino Siimola and musician Fritz Cohen. The company gave ballet performances in Munster and toured Germany. In 1926 Leeder became director of the dance department at the school of music, language, and movement in Munster. But his and Jooss' careers were destined to flourish elsewhere. By the next year Leeder followed Jooss to the industrial city of Essen. There, Jooss founded the Folkwangschule with Leeder; Jooss directed the dance department and Leeder became the head teacher.

Jooss and Leeder aimed to synthesize contemporary and classical dance techniques with the goal of achieving the widest range of expression. Leeder's importance as a teacher of modern dance is great—he was a much-loved pedagogue whose creative energy, love for perfection, and great patience, combined with honesty, openness, and an ability to communicate, has been fondly remembered by former students. In Essen, Leeder developed his own style of teaching, placing great emphasis on allowing students to grow and mature within the context of the classroom. Improvisations in the classroom were more important than rehearsals and Leeder maintained a lively, spontaneous atmosphere in which students were free to demonstrate the emotional truth of the dance. They were criticized only when the criticism led to greater productivity. Leeder composed dance études for his students' development. These simple exercises, which followed a specific theme, combined dance technique, choreography, and Laban's theories of dance movement. Leeder notated his études in the system Laban devised and thus preserved them for future teachers and students. Leeder's vision of art and his way of training students was also shared by colleague Jooss.

Leeder's career continued to evolve in tandem with that of Jooss. In 1932, when Jooss choreographed *The Green Table*, Leeder was in the original cast. The work affirmed Jooss' reputation as one of the leading lights of European modern dance and brought even greater attention to his troupe. With the success of *The Green Table,* Jooss was able to achieve independence for his company and Ballets Jooss was born. When the rise of Nazism led to Jooss' decision to emigrate in 1934, Leeder followed. The two set up their school in Dartington Hall in Devon, England. The country estate contained workshops, a library, a theater, and a school. Students from all over

came to study dance, scenic and costume design, Laban notation, and choreography at the Jooss-Leeder School. The School produced numerous dancers including Hans Züllig, Ann Hutchinson, and others. Ballets and solo dances were given in the Barn Theatre at Dartington Hall.

Leeder's role as a teacher involved his choreograping works for his students. *Danse Macabre* (1939) was set to the music of Camille Saint-Saëns. In this work, dancers emerged from a mound of inert bodies. Two women provoked uneasy reactions from among the other dancers. Leeder costumed the dancers in black and had them wear tightly-drawn veils over their faces. In *Doña Clara* (1939), Leeder took the role of a rejected lover who haunted the wedding of his beloved. In a sinister ballroom scene, Don Ramiro (Leeder) danced the bride to death. A sense of foreboding was conveyed by Leeder's ghostly but intense dance.

During the war years, Jooss and Leeder remained in England while the Ballets Jooss toured the United States and South America. Leeder continued teaching in England at a studio in Cambridge. When the war ended, the company and their director and master teacher were reunited. Touring resumed until the late 1940s when Jooss decided to relocate his company in Germany. Leeder stayed in England and opened his own school, the Sigurd Leeder School of Dance, in London in 1947. His first studio was on Drury Lane in the heart of London's theatre district. Leeder was successful in this enterprise and soon founded his own dance group: the Sigurd Leeder Studio Group. Actors and movie stars were among his students. Today, former students of Leeder often work as movement teachers in acting schools in London and abroad.

Leeder's work in England in the late 1940s and early 1950s saw him involved in the world of British theatre. He was hired by the Old Vic Theatre to work as the movement director for their production of *Doctor Faustus* with Sir Cedric Hardwick. Leeder was ballet master for the Festival Year of Great Britain held in 1951 at the Glyndbourne Opera. He also created the dances for Verdi's *La Forza del Destino* for the Edinburgh Festival. Teaching remained paramount in Leeder's life, however, and he continued to be in demand as a guest instructor at summer seminars in Europe. In 1960 he received an invitation to take up a new assignment: director of studies and teacher in the school of dance at the University of Chile in Santiago, Chile. His former Jooss colleague, Ernst Uthoff, had been instrumental in transferring the Jooss-Leeder technique to Chile. Leeder remained there until 1964 when he decided to move back to Europe. He settled in Switzerland and opened a school in Herisau with Grete Müller. Although Leeder died in 1981, his school continues to operate under the directorship of Müller. In 1992—the 90th anniversary of Leeder's birth—the school held a special symposium. Teachers such as June Kemp, Bryan Payne, and David McKitterick were invited to give classes in Leeder-Jooss technique, eukinetics, choreutics, improvisation, dance composition and masks. Some of Leeder's dances were even reconstructed from Labanotation by Müller.

—Adriane Ruggiero

LEINE & ROEBANA

Netherlands-based dancing and choreographing duo

Harijono Roebana, born in 1955, studied philosophy and performance studies at the University of Amsterdam and modern dance at

Leine & Roebana: *Tales of Eversion.* **Photograph by Leoni Ravestein.**

the Theaterschool in Amsterdam, and has a background in music as well. Early in his career, Roebana danced in performances by choreographers Svea Staltmann, Arthur Rosenfeld, José Besprosvany and for Studio Onafhankelijk Toneel. He performs in most Leine & Roebana works.

Andrea Leine, born in 1966, studied ballet and modern dance at the Scapino Dansacademie and the Rotterdam Dansacademie. She worked with Studio Onafhankelijk Toneel and danced among others with Donald Flemming and also dances in most of Leine & Roebana's performances.

Since 1989 Andrea Leine and Harijono Roebana have worked together successfully, winning various awards at international choreography festivals and touring extensively with their dance productions. They have created works for Springdance, the Holland Festival and Korzo Theater. Their international breakthrough came in 1995 with *Glottisdans-If we could only even if we could* during the Festival de la Nouvelle Danse (FIND) in Montreal. In their work they question the dynamics of a society where individuals are increasingly part of a complex structure, while their autonomy, free will, integrity, and wholeness are at stake. There is an ever-increasing threat of disorientation in a world full of mass media and manipulated reality; with Leine & Roebana posing the question "Are we still able to distinguish between fact and fiction, between good and evil?"

Leine & Roebana have developed a unique dance idiom based on a novel approach to symmetry, rhythm and composition. Their quest to express the complexity of reality and the interference of its constituent parts has led to the creation of a highly original language of movement. Previous works by Leine & Roebana have been considerably more theatrical; more recently, however, they have reduced the dramatic elements in their performances in order to explore the possibilities of pure movement. In the late 1990s, they were scrutinizing the development of movement in individual parts of the body, the juxtaposition of rapid dynamics, and stillness and irony. Over the years, their work has been highly praised and rewarded, they've received awards from the Amsterdam Fund for the Art, the Lucas Hoving prize and a Philip Morris Finest Selection Award. They were also awarded for their work on behalf of the international concourse of Cagliari, Italy, and Bagnolet, France.

Though Leine and Roebana come from different backgrounds, with Leine's classical training and Roebana's studies in philosophy as well as performance, they form inspired team. Since their first piece, *Waldo,* in 1990, there have been several sustained characteristics in their work. The necessity of adaptation, first to one another, became characteristic for their way of working and a requirement for recruiting their dancers. They reveal little to their dancers about stage setting, content, or form during the process of creation, because they want to work from intuition, which has its own dynamics as well as restrictions.

Their search for their own dance language resulted in a technique that permits them to move one side of their bodies in a controlled manner, while moving the other in a casual, even careless fashion. Working at the extreme, they perform intriguing movements while striving for beauty, which appears at unexpected moments. Leine & Roebana do, however, create some rules to give the dancers something to hold on to; yet these restrictions leave space for something new. For example, instead of working with a left/right symmetry, they work with big/small symmetry; or they turn a series of movements backwards—arm movements are made by the legs and vice-versa. In this way a certain order comes into play, though order can be changed up until the last minute. Leine & Roebana's choice of music can also change the order of movement. For *Suites,* the

Beethoven score began later than the choreography, causing friction between the two worlds.

Leine & Roebana isolate movement in a way that causes capriciousness. The body falls apart, and the result is what they call "physical schizophrenia," which happens in *The Circle Effect.* To the electronic compositions of their work *Sound Palette* individuals and groups portray a world of high energy and restless movements. Outstretched arms cut the air like knives and initiate a seemingly spineless body posture; such immediate changes from high energy to "spineless" and clumsy are quite difficult for the dancers. In *Gottisdans/If we could only even if we could,* a quintet danced by Leine, Roebana, Tim Percent, Mischa van Dullemen, and Ederson Rodiques Xavier, the dancers' bodies seem to move on their own. According to Jolien Verwei, the choreography portrays the body as a decentralized entity, in which each part is the center of movement. Solos, duets, and group works alternate, and the decentralization of the body leads to extraordinary movements. "It's as if the head goes its own way while the body follows or goes in a different direction; then the head hangs loose, as if it was a separate element. The search for beauty is ever-present in these distorted body movements. The five dancers form a diverse unity: Andrea, strong and determined; Ernesto, firm and quiet; Tim, concentrated, smooth, and undulating; Mischa, alienated, thin, and nutty; Harijono, loose and casual."

It is fascinating what Leine & Roebana have achieved in such a short time; they are unique in the Dutch dance world. For their efforts, Andrea Leine and Harijono Roebana received a subsidy for a few years, but unfortunately, it wasn't enough to pay a group of dancers for longer than a few months. Yet the future is more than bright for Leine & Roebana, as they are clearly still on the rise.

Publications

van Veggel, G. J., "De ideale choreografie," *Dans 6,* 1994.
Verweij, Jolien, "Vormen van Taal," *Notes 11,* 1995.

—Helma Klooss

LEMON, Ralph

American dancer, choreographer, company director, writer, and visual artist

Education: University of Minnesota, B.A. 1975; studied with Zvi Gotheiner, Cindi Green, Zena Rommet, Ping Chong, Meredith Monk, Viola Farber, Nancy Hauser. **Career:** Founding member, Mixed Blood Theatre Company (Minneapolis); dancer, Nancy Hauser Dance Company; dancer, Meredith Monk/The House, 1979-81; also performed with Dana Reitz, Blondell Cummings and Bebe Miller; produced first evening-length concert, 1981; founder, Ralph Lemon Dance Company, 1985; conducts master classes, composition workshops and participates in artistic residencies in throughout the U.S., Mexico and Europe; associate artist, Yale Repertory Theatre (New Haven, Connecticut); collaborator (text), *Persephone,* Wesleyan University Press; *Konbit,* a video documentary collage; and in progress, a film project with choreographer Bebe Miller and filmmaker Isaac Julien. **Awards:** Eight National Endowment for the Arts choreographic fellowships; two New York Foundation for the Arts fellowships; American Choreographers Award, 1987; Gold Medal, Boston International Choreography Competition, 1988; New York Dance and Performance ("Bessie") Award, 1987; board member, Danspace Project at St. Marks Church; Dance/USA, 1989-91.

Works

1984   *Ant's Burden* (mus. Bob Roman), solo
     Romance (mus. Tom Waites)
     Folktales and Romance 4, evening-length performance produced by Dance Theatre Workshop, New York
     Boundary Water (mus. Beethoven), New Dance Ensemble of Minnesota
     Folktales with Men and Oranges, for Dance on the Lower East Side Festival, New York
     The Last Nights of Paris and Georgette, Dance Theatre Workshop

1985   *Plan de Liebe,* CoDanceCo
     Forest (mus. Linda Bouchard), duet, American Dance Festival
     And the Jungle Will Obliterate the Shrine/Seasons, RLC
     Scarecrow (mus. Hart)

1986   *Flock* (mus. Sibelius), Jacob's Pillow Dance Ensemble
     En Su Llama Mortal, Ballet Hispanico of New York
     Two w/Bebe Miller (mus. Hyams Hart)

1987   *Nightingales and Fishermen* (mus. Bach)
     Les Noces (mus. Ravel, Debussy), RLC
     Waiting for Carnival, New Dance Ensemble

1988   *Happy Trails* (mus. country and western collage), RLC
     Cherubino and the Nightingale (mus. Mozart), RLC
     Folkdance Duet (mus. traditional Norwegian folk), RLC
     Folkdance, Alvin Ailey Repertory Ensemble
     Punchinello, Boston Ballet

1989   *Joy* (mus. Cale), RLC
     Sleep (mus. Faure), RLC

1990   *Joy (Solo),* (mus. Satie), RLC
     Bogus Pomp, Lyons Opera Ballet
     Civilian, solo

1991   *Persephone* (mus. Davis), RLC
     Folkdance Sextet (mus. Beethoven), RLC
     Folkdance Solo (mus. taped conversation), RLC
     Don Juan, Graz Opera Ballet

1992   *Their Eyes Rolled Back in Ecstasy* (mus. Hyams Hart, Barrett, chants), RLC
     Their Eyes Rolled Back in Ecstasy/Solo (mus. Hyams Hart), RLC
     Phrases Almost Biblical, RLC
     My Tears Have Been My Meat Night and Day, Lyon Opera Ballet
     Folkdance (with songs), Batsheva Dance Company

1993   *Folkdance Sextet,* The Metropolitan Ballet of Michigan

Other works include: *Wanda in the Awkward Age* (mus. Hector Berlioz), and new works for the Joffrey Ballet, Limón Dance Company, Geneva Opera Ballet, and others.

Publications

By LEMON: books—

With Eavan Boland, Rita Dove, and Phillip Trager, *Persephone,* Middletown, Connecticut, 1996.

On LEMON: articles—

Bromberg, Craig, Review, *Dance Ink,* Fall 1994.
Fanger, Iris M., "Ralph Lemon: Private Man in the Public Arena," *Dance Magazine,* August 1991.

*   *   *

"Hopefully, my conscious concerns and intuition will come together to make work that even in its abstraction creates an art that speaks to many levels of the human condition." So sayeth Ralph Lemon, considered the contemporary dance world's "mythmaker." Lemon is a choreographer whose unique blend of choreographic craftsmanship with emotionally charged subtext has placed him in the historical ranks of contemporary dance vanguards. Powerfully philosophical, Lemon's artistic interests have guided him to change and evolve the form in which he works. With interests in multiple art forms, Lemon's work encompasses more than choreography; his expressive statements manifest themselves in movement, text, visual art, and film. Although the intersection of these venues in Lemon's work defies the boundaries of categorization, Ralph Lemon the choreographer/creator remains a strong link in the continuing legacy of modern dance.

Growing up in Minnesota in a stiflingly religious family environment, Lemon was a private child who brewed artistic creativity early on. Painting was an early venue for expression, and he went on to study literature and theater arts at the University of Minnesota. Lemon discovered dance at the suggestion of a drama teacher, and in movement Lemon found a physical outlet for artistic expression.

Lemon studied with Wigman-based choreographer Nancy Hauser in Minnesota and went on to dance in her company for two years. Lemon describes Hauser as a theorist who inspired in her students a holistic value for "art" rather than emphasizing strictly regimented, technical dance training. Thus, early in his dance career, Lemon thought of himself more as a creative artist than simply a dancer/performer, and his early efforts in choreography reflected an interest in collaboration between dance and other art forms.

In 1977 Lemon saw Meredith Monk's *Quarry;* he subsequently studied with Monk at the Naropa Institute in Boulder, Colorado, and went on to dance in her company after moving to New York in 1979. New York provided Lemon with a richly inspiring dance environment. After seeing the work of artists such as Merce Cunningham, Pina Bauch, and Trisha Brown, and being influenced by artists representing other expressive venues such as film, music, and visual art, Lemon began to embrace the idea of becoming a choreographer. In 1981 Lemon premiered his own work at the Cunningham Studio. At this time, modern dance was "at the height of the party," Lemon says. Dance was vital with a renewed interest in form and craft while sustaining the experimental attitude of the postmodernist era. Collaborations between dance and other art forms were beginning to be fruitful, and physicality came back to dance after the earlier inclinations of minimalism in movement.

Lemon choreographed with a "pick-up" group of dancers from 1981 to 1984, and officially formed his own company in 1985. The dance company model was vital at this time with many dance companies presenting seasons in New York and touring abroad. Lemon's success within this model came due to his evocative, mysterious, and likeably enigmatic choreography. Narrative in choreography was an early interest for Lemon as he felt that a story provided a universal, commonly understood language. Yet formal, classical craftsmanship in his work carried narrative subject matter to other layers of communication. Without burdening his work with a dra-

Ralph Lemon with Kelly McDonald in *Joy*, 1990. Photograph © Beatriz Schiller.

matic story, Lemon's choreography often suggests dramatic or emotional subject matter within the movement invention and craftsmanship of the dance.

Lemon has used a wide range of music in his performances, collaborating with composers such as John Cale, Rhys Chatham, Anthony Davis, Chris Hyams Hart, Francisco Lopez, Vernon Ried and Frank Zappa. The company toured worldwide and presented annual New York seasons from its debut in 1985 though 1995 in such venues as the Joyce Theater in New York, Jacob's Pillow Dance Festival, the Kennedy Center in Washington D.C., the American Dance Festival, Spoleto Festival/USA, DanceAspen and Colorado Dance Festival, the Center for Contemporary Art in New Mexico, the Cannes Festival in France, Mayfest Festival in Scotland, The Place Theatre in England, Linz and Vienna Festivals in Austria, Teatro San Martin in Argentina, and the 25th Annual Festival International de Teatro in Manizales, Columbia.

Lemon's philosophies guide him toward connections between his life and art; his innate impulses inform what he creates. He feels that as an artist, just as in life, he must work himself to a point and then allow the work to change, to explore what might exist beyond what he already knows. Change in 1995 meant branching out beyond the dance company model. He disbanded his group in order to explore his broadening interests in other art forms. Without the responsibilities of directing a dance company, Lemon has had the freedom to explore and develop his talents in writing and visual art, while dancing remains his sanctuary. He uses these other artistic venues intersected with choreography to present social and political issues in a variety of collaborative projects.

One of these projects, *Persephone*, published by Wesleyan University Press, includes photographs, poetry, and text written by Lemon and other artists. *Konbit* is a video documentary about the Haitian community in Miami. Lemon also collaborated with choreographer Bebe Miller and filmmaker Issac Julien for the dance/theatre film, *Two*. Another work, *Geography*, is a piece that combines artistic forms, crosses boundaries of culture and geography, and intersects postmodernist formal dance with traditional West African dance and theatre. Using the talents of composers, writers, and visual artists, Lemon, according to publicity for the project, "explores perceptions of racial and cultural identities, and how identity is translated, divided, subsumed and empowered by another, culturally foreign aesthetic." This project not only manifests itself as live, concert performance, but also includes a published catalogue, a video documentary focusing on the process of creating *Geography*, and a gallery exhibition. This interdisciplinary project exemplifies Lemon's broad, diverse interests and talents.

A driving force for Lemon's choreography and in workshops is his quest for balance between freedom and form. Though recognized for clever craftsmanship, Lemon's work is also intimately connected to the sacredness of the "human condition." His work has been commissioned by several leading dance companies but now also reaches beyond the realm of concert modern dance.

—Diana Stanton

LERMAN, Liz

American dancer, choreographer, and company director

Born: 25 December 1947, Los Angeles. **Education:** University of Maryland, College Park, B.A. (with honors in dance) 1970; George Washington University, Washington, D.C., M.F.A. in dance 1982. **Family:** Married to storyteller Jon Spelman; children: Anna Clare. **Career:** Artistic director/founder, Liz Lerman Dance Exchange, Washington, D.C., from 1976. **Awards:** Washington, D.C., Commission on the Arts and Humanities (five fellowships); National Endowment for the Arts (eight choreography fellowships); *Washingtonian Magazine* Mayor's Art Award; Excellence in an Artistic Discipline, 1988; National Corporate Fund for Dance, Washingtonian of the Year Award, 1988; *Washingtonian Magazine* American Choreographer Award, 1989; Washington's 25 Most Talented People, 1993.

Works (all works after 1976 were for the Liz Lerman Dance Exchange and premiered in Washington, D.C., unless otherwise noted)

1974	*New York City Winter,* St. Marks Church, New York City
1975	*Woman of the Clear Vision,* Mt. Vernon College
1976	*Memory Garden,* Washington Projects for the Arts
1977	*Ms. Galaxy and Her Three Raps with God,* Baltimore Theater Project, Baltimore
1978	*Elevator Operators and Other Strangers*
	Still Life with Cat and Fingers
	Bonsai, The National Arboretum, Washington, D.C.
1979	*RSVP,* O'Neill Choreographer's Conference, Waterford, Connecticut
	Who's on First?, City Dance, Warner Theater
1980	*Fanfare for the Common Man,* City Dance, The National Mall, Washington, D.C.
	Journey 1-4, Washington Project for the Arts
1981	*Current Events,* Dance Place
	Songs and Poems of the Body: In the Gallery, Kennedy Center, Washington, D.C.
	Docudance: Reaganomics, Dance Place
1982	*Songs and Poems of the Body: In the Text,* Dance Place
1983	*Docudance: Nine Short Dances about the Defense Budget and Other Military Matters,* Marvin Center
	Variation on a Window
	Pavanne for Two Older Women, New Music America, Old Post Office
1984	*Second Variation on a Window,* E. Hopper Dance Place
	Ives & Company, National Portrait Gallery, Washington, D.C.
	Space Cadet, Washington Project for the Arts
1985	*The Transparent Apple and the Silver Saucer,* Sidwell Auditorium
1986	*Russia: Footnotes to a History,* Museum of Contemporary Art
	Still Crossing, Liberty Dances, Battery Park, New York City
	Black Sea Follies, Lenox Arts Center, Lenox, Massachusetts
1987	*Atomic Priests: Coming Attractions*
	Sketches from Memory, DAMA Theater
	Atomic Priests: The Feature, Dance Theatre Workshop, New York City
1988	*Ms. Appropriate Goes to the Theater,* Dance Place
1989	*Reenactments,* The Kennedy Center, Washington, D.C.
	Floating Hand, Dance Place
	Five Days in Maine, Maine Festival, Portland, Maine

Liz Lerman (left) performing *Flying into the Middle,* 1995. Photograph © Beatriz Schiller.

1990   *May I Have Your Attention, Please,* Union Station
        Docudance 1990: Dark Interlude, 14th Street
            Dancecenter, New York City
        The Perfect Ten, Serious Fun! at Lincoln Center, New
            York City
        A Life in the Nation's Capitol
        Anatomy of an Inside Story, Dance Place
1991   *Short Stories (version 1),* The Barns of Wolf Trap, Vienna,
            Virginia
        Short Stories (version 2), American Dance Festival,
            Durham, North Carolina
        untitled, Meredith College, Raleigh, North Carolina
        The Good Jew? (mus. A. Tierstein), Israeli/Jewish Ameri-
            can Dance Festival, Boston
        untitled site-specific work, Kennedy Center
1992   *The Awakening,* McKinley High School
1993   *Incidents in the Life of an Ohio Youth,* BalletMet, Ohio
            Theater, Columbus, Ohio
        This Is Who We Are (mus. Wayne Horvitz), George Wash-
            ington University
        Spelunking the Center, Kennedy Center

1994   *Safe House: Still Looking,* (mus. Ysaye Barnwell), Cowell
            Theater, San Francisco
1995   *Flying into the Middle* (mus. Tchaikovsky, *Piano Trio in
            E*), Joyce Theater, New York
        Faith and Science on the Midway (Shehechianu Phase 2),
            Lansburgh Theatre, Washington, D.C.
        Portsmouth Pages, The Music Hall, Portsmouth, New
            Hampshire
1996   *Bench Marks (Shehechianu Phase 1) Nocturnes* (mus.
            Willie Nelson), Lisner Auditorium
        Light Years, INTELSAT Headquarters
        Fresh Blood (mus. Steve Elson), Queens Theater in the
            Park, Queens, New York
1997   *Shehechianu (complete)* (mus. Wayne Horvitz), Lansburgh
            Theater, Washington, D.C.

Publications

By LERMAN: books—

Teaching Dance to Senior Adults, Charles C. Thomas, 1984.

By LERMAN: articles—

"Are Miracles Enough?," *Dance/USA Journal,* Spring 1993; re-
    printed in *Grantmakers in the Arts,* Fall 1994.
"By All Possible Means," *Movement Research,* Fall/Winter 1994.
"The Jew, the Madonna and the Meaning of Art," *New Menorah,* Fall
    1994.
"Talking Dance," *Poor Dancer's Almanac,* Duke University Press,
    1993.
"Toward a Process for Critical Response," *Alternate Roots,* Fall
    1993; reprinted in *High Performance,* Winter 1993.

On LERMAN: articles—

Harding, C., "Liz Lerman: Wider Spectrum," *Dance Magazine,*
    January 1996.
Solari, Rose, "Standard of Beauty," *Common Boundary,* November/
    December 1996.

*   *   *

During the 1960s dancers were searching for pure movement and
minimalist structures were the forms that emerged. It was almost
enough to dissuade Liz Lerman from going into dance. After years
of childhood dance, first in California and then in Milwaukee, she
began as a dance major at Bennington College. She left because the
rigidity of thinking about dance at the time would not include her
innate sense of dance as storytelling. From early childhood Liz
Lerman had been influenced by her activist family to recognize the
importance of community and the interdependence of humans.

When she realized that institutions were interfering with the
essence of what art and dance were about for her, she was able to
return to school and develop her unique philosophy and choreographic skills. She recognized that dance was not only a performance art but that it connected to the creative needs of all people.
Dance is a shared communal experience.

She finished her degree at the University of Maryland. Over the
years she studied modern dance and ballet with Meriem Rosen,
Ethel Butler, Viola Farber, Peter Saul, Jan Van Dyke, Don Redlich,
Maida Withers, and Twyla Tharp and mime with Jan Kessler. In
Washington, D.C., she taught for several years in a private high
school that allowed her to experiment with choreograpy and working with a wide range of individuals. She went on to graduate school
to further develop her ideas that dance was about people dancing.

The death of her mother became a catalyst for the work that
followed. Lerman wanted to choreograph a dance that included the
stories her mother had told her and she needed older people to take
these roles. This was the beginning of her interest in intergenerational
dance. Her dance *Woman of the Clear Vision* (1975) incorporated
dancers of all ages. Working with the elderly in a variety of centers
reenforced her vision of dance as part of life for people in any
setting. Out of these experiences she created a performing company
called Dancers of the Third Age, who were primarily adults from 55
years of age. She went on tour with them to Scandinavia in 1985.
This company has since disbanded as it became too difficult to tour
with two companies.

In 1976 Lerman had created a nonprofit organization that became
known as the Liz Lerman Dance Exchange. Through this structure
she was able to procure and continues to receive funding from
government and private organizations to support her many endeavors. Her performing company is composed of nine to 12 dancers

from their 20s to late 70s in age and of varied racial backgrounds,
body types, and gender differences. Lerman believes that art has a
large spectrum of functions and she draws on all of them at different times: the spiritual, learning, healing, and the power of being an
individual within a group. They are all artistic processes, however,
and the aesthetics of the art is never sacrificed to any of these
functions.

Choreography has been a focal point. Lerman continues to produce several pieces each year based on humanism, humor, and delight in movement. These works tend to be lyrical and theatrical.
Whereas they may begin with improvisation they grow into highly
formalized structures. Her choreography covers a wide range of
topics and settings and she will add community dancers as needed.
She choreographed a piece for 800 performers on the steps of the
Lincoln Memorial in 1980 and was commissioned to perform the
dance *Still Crossing* in 1986 during the centennial celebration of the
Statue of Liberty in New York City. The Kennedy Center was the
focus of two site-specific pieces commissioned in 1991. Her desire
to bring dance closer to people has the company performing in
many venues in addition to the stage. Lerman has created and presented more than 55 pieces at this time (1997). The company has
toured throughout the United States and in Europe.

Dance technique, improvisation, and choreography is the craft
she teaches. Since 1976 she has participated as part of Dance Exchange residencies locally, nationally, and internationally. She taught
for seven years at Jacob's Pillow beginning in 1985. Her teaching
emphasizes how to relate to and develop what each dancer uniquely
has to offer. Lerman's philosophy is based on her social awareness
and deep respect for the differences among individuals. All of her
projects are experienced as a collaborative effort. Company members are encouraged to add ideas and create and perform their own
dances. To support choreographic learning, she has evolved a process of positive criticism entitled "Critical Response," which is
useful in many learning situations. Although movement is the medium of creation and expression, Lerman makes great use of language and narrative during performance, interweaving images from
both modalities to create integration of the visual and auditory.

Lerman makes use of the special skills company members bring.
They team teach both professional dancers and those in the community in places such as public schools, clinics for HIV-positive
adults, universities, and with other special groups. A two-year
examination of the role of the shipyard in the history, economy,
politics, and community of Portsmouth, New Hampshire culminated in a community-involved performance there in 1996.

In 1997 the Liz Lerman Dance Exchange found a home base for
the first time in Takoma Park, Maryland. The company immediately reached out to local schools and other community-based groups
to invite them to be part of the Dance Exchange. It is her hope that
the art of dance will help overcome the fragmentation that society
has developed to get back to the basic core of human understanding.

—Sharon Chaiklin

LEWITZKY, Bella

American dancer, choreographer, and educator

Born: 13 January 1916 in Los Angeles. **Education:** Began studying with Lester Horton, 1934. **Family:** Married architect Newell

Taylor Reynolds, 1940; daughter, Nora, born 1955. **Career:** Dancer, Horton Dance Group, 1936-47; co-founder with Horton, Dance Theater, 1946; founder/artistic director, Dance Associates, 1951-55; founder/artistic director, Bella Lewitzky Dance, 1966-97; first dean of dance, California Institute for the Arts, 1969-72; retired from dancing, 1978. **Awards:** John Simon Guggenheim Memorial Foundation fellowship, 1977; *Dance Magazine* award, 1978; National Dance Association award, 1979; American Dance Guild Annual Award, 1989; First California Governor's Award/Individual Artist, Lifetime Achievement, 1989; National Dance Association Heritage Honoree, 1991; Vaslav Nijinsky Award, 1991; University of Judaism Burning Bush Award, 1991; UCLA Center for the Performing Arts Excellence Award, 1992; Dance Resource Center of Los Angeles Lester Horton Lifetime Achievement Award, 1992; Dance/USA Honor, 1992; Andy Warhol Foundation for the Visual Arts Free of Expression Honor, 1993; Dance Resource Center of Los Angeles Lester Horton Sustained Achievement Award, 1995; Dance Resource Center of Los Angeles Lester Horton Award for Restaging or Revival, 1996; Bill of Rights Award, American Civil Liberties Union of Southern California, 1996; National Medal of Arts, 1997; honorary doctorates: California Institute of the Arts (1981), Occidental College (1984), Otis/Parsons School of Design (1989), Juilliard School (1993), Santa Clara University (1995).

Roles (choreographed by Lester Horton unless otherwise noted)

1937	*Prelude to Militancy*
	Chronicle
	Salomé (revision)
	Exhibition Dance No.1
	Le Sacre de Printemps
1938	*Pasaremos*
	Conquest
1939	*Something to Please Everybody*
	Tierra y Libertad!
1940	*A Noble Comedy*
	Sixteen to Twenty-Four
1947	*Barrel House*
1948	*The Beloved* (cr)
1949	*Warsaw Ghetto* (cr)
	The Park
1950	*Estilo de Tú* (cr)

Other roles include: Various performances (both solos and as a principal dancer) with the Horton Dance Group, 1934-50.

Works (beginning in 1966, all works premiered by the Lewitzky Dance Company)

1952	*¡Viviran! (They Shall Live)*
1953	*Leyendas De Mexico*
1954	*Women of Innisfree*
1958	*Elegy and Remembrance*
1966	*C-Saw*
	Trio for Saki
	Heritage
	Geodite
	Invisible Kingdom

1968	*Partite*
1969	*Orrenda*
	Sound Set
	On the Brink of Time
1970	*Kinaesonata*
1971	*Pietas*
1972	*Ceremony for Three*
	Scintilla
1973	*Bella and Brindle*
	Game Plan
1974	*Five*
1975	*Spaces Between*
	V.C.O. (Voltage Controlled Oscillator)
1976	*Greening*
	Inscape
1977	*Pas de Bach*
1979	*Recesses*
	Rituals
1980	*Suite Satie*
1981	*Changes & Choices*
1982	*Confines*
	Continuum
1983	*The Song of the Woman*
1984	*Nos Duraturi (We Who Shall Survive)*
1985	*8 dancers/8 lights*
1986	*Facets*
1987	*Impressions #1 (Henry Moore)*
1988	*Impressions #2 (Vincent Van Gogh)*
1989	*Impressions #3 (Paul Klee)*
	Agitime
1990	*Episode #1 (Recuerdo)*
1991	*Glass Canyons*
1992	*Episode #2*
	Episode #3 (The Outsider)
1993	*Episode #4 (Turf)*
1994	*Meta 4*
1996	*Four Women in Time*

Publications

On LEWITZKY: books—

Schiff, Benett, *Artists in Schools,* Washington D.C., 1979.
Warren, Larry, *Lester Horton: Modern Dance Pioneer,* Princeton, New Jersey, 1977.

By LEWITZKY: articles—

"A Vision of Total Theater," *Dance Perspectives,* 1967.
"Why the Arts Should be Cherished," *Town Hall Reporter,* January-February 1987.

On LEWITZKY: articles—

Barnes, Clive, "Lewitzky: A Legend Turned Real," *New York Times,* 24 October 1971.
Craig, Jenifer, "Lewitzky, Bella," in *Jewish Women in America: An Historical Encyclopedia,* New York, 1997.
Kline, Betsy, "Lewitzky Dancers Share Compelling Vision," *Pittsburgh Press,* 26 January 1987.

Lewitzky Dance Company: *Turf,* 1994. Photograph © Johan Elbers.

Marks, Marica, "Bella Lewitzky Dance Company," *Dance Magazine,* December 1971.

Mason, Nancy, "Bella Lewitzky Dance Company," *Dance Magazine,* November 1971.

Moore, Elvi, "The Performer-Teacher: An Interview with Bella Lewitzky," *Dance Scope,* Fall/Winter 1973/74.

Perlmutter, Donna, "Bella Lewitzky—A Tribute to Teachers Who Have Produced Outstanding Results,." *Dance Magazine,* January 1997.

Rosen, Lillie F., "A Conversation with Bella Lewitsky," *Ballet Review,* Fall 1982.

Segal, Lewis, "Lewitzky's Feminist Statement," *Los Angeles Times,* 23 September 1996.

Siegel, Marcia, "Hunting a Dinosaur," *Boston Herald Traveler,* 1 August 1971.

Sorell, Walter, "Reviews: Bella Lewitzky," *Dance News,* November 1971.

Swisher, Viola Hegi. "Bella Lewitzky: Dance is My Window of Life, Part I" *Dance Magazine,* April 1967.

———, "Bella Lewitzky: Dance is My Window of Life, Part II," *Dance Magazine,* May 1967.

*   *   *

Bella Lewitzky is a Los Angeles-based modern dancer, choreographer, and educator who retired in May 1997 at the close of her 31st season as artistic director of the Lewitzky Dance Company. In 63 years as a concert dance artist, the Lewitzky name became synonymous with West Coast modern dance, beginning as the brilliant interpreter of Lester Horton's spectacular dance dramas, and concluding with 30-week seasons of touring to international acclaim taking her repertoire of 51 major works to 43 states and 19 countries.

Born in Los Angeles, 13 January 1916, Lewitzky spent her childhood with her Russian immigrant parents and older sister in a socialist utopian colony in the Mojave Desert and on a chicken ranch in San Bernardino. In 1934 she moved to Los Angeles where she was introduced to Horton's brand of modern dance. She progressed from novice student to lead dancer of the Horton Dance Group in less than three years.

Horton's unorthodox kinetic vocabulary and eclectic subject matter, and Lewitzky's near perfect physical expressiveness, resulted in critical and popular success during their 15-year relationship. Growing aesthetic differences and divergent lifestyle preferences eventually ended in a permanent rift, but not before they created another bold experiment as partners. With William Bowne and Newell Taylor Reynolds, Horton and Lewitzky opened Dance Theater in 1946. Designed as what might be described a full-purpose dance enterprise, its services ranged from classes for all ages to development and presentation of performance seasons of the Horton Dance Group. It was the venue of the premiere of the last, and arguably greatest Horton-Lewitzky collaborations, *The Beloved* (1948) and *Warsaw Ghetto* (1949).

From 1951 to 1955, Lewitzky operated her second school and company, Dance Associates. During this period, she focused on pedagogical philosophy and choreographed her first independent, but admittedly Hortonesque, works. Lewitzky's family life and strongly held personal convictions affected her artistic and career choices. On 22 June 1940, she married architect Newell Taylor Reynolds. A fellow member of the Horton Dance Group, he was Lewitzky's partner, designer, consultant and companion. Lewitzky left Dance Associates and the pursuit of concert performance upon the birth of her daughter Nora, in 1955. She chose instead to work as a self-described itinerant studio teacher. She began to focus on integrating dance into the education of young children, developing programs as a teacher in her daughter Nora's progressive school. These ideas were later refined and disseminated during Lewitzky's participation in Arts IMPACT (Interdisciplinary Model Program in the Arts for Children and Teachers program) from 1970 to 1972, during the her tenure as the first dean of the School of Dance at California Institute for the Arts.

With the inception of her third company in 1966, Lewitzky earned a national reputation based on her own extraordinary performance abilities and an emerging oeuvre that adapted, but was not limited by, the style she had helped Horton to develop. Lewitzky, by this time in her fifties, drew nearly universal praise for her dancing. She retired as a performer at the age of 62.

Lewitzky's 46-year span of choreography and touring has led to mixed reviews. Positive reviews tend to praise the obvious strength of the training of her dancers, as evidenced by their individual and ensemble clarity. She is credited for creating dances with meticulous craftsmanship. Awe-inspiring physical command is often noted in association with a powerful abstract social message. Detractors have criticized her for not adhering more closely to her Horton roots, or for lack of emotional core because of an apparent intellectualized pursuit of space, energy and body confluences. A lifetime of works, including *On the Brink of Time* (1969), *Kinaesonata* (1971), *Spaces Between* (1975), *Nos Duraturi* (1984) and *Four Women in Time* (1996), stand as evidence that she has contributed mightily to the canon of modern dance, exposing many facets of life's prism, acknowledging a developing movement glossary, but unwilling to be tied to repeatable topics or approaches.

Lewitzky followed her father's lead in politics and committed early to socialist activism for political causes, on behalf of legal organizations and for civil liberties. Her uncompromising public positions affirming constitutional rights have put her at risk, in the center of national controversies, as well as led to her achievement of high honors. Lewitsky was subpoenaed as an unwilling witness before the House UnAmerican Activities Committee in 1951. Recent release of her FBI file through the Freedom of Information Act reveals that she was under surveillance until 1960. In 1991, she successfully sued the National Endowment for the Arts (NEA) objecting to constitutional infringements in an antiobscenity clause written into grant contracts.

Lewitzky worked for over a decade to create a new theater for dance in Los Angeles. Plans included a library, studios, and performance venues designed specifically for concert dance. After years marked by donations, city endorsements and groundbreakings, the project was still not adequately funded, and, unfortunately The Dance Gallery was not built.

Lewitzky has received over 50 awards, including five honorary doctorate degrees, the *Dance Magazine* award (1979), the first California Governor's Award for Lifetime Achievement (1989), and the National Medal of Arts (1997).

—Jenifer Craig

LI Chiao-Ping
American dancer and choreographer

Born: Nancy Lee in 1963, in San Francisco. **Education:** B.A. in theatre arts, University of California, Santa Cruz; M.A. in dance, University of California, Los Angeles; studied at the American Dance Festival. **Career:** Academic dance positions held at Hollins College and University of Wisconsin, Madison; co-director, Dziga Vertov Performance Group since 1991, Laughing Bodies Dance Theater, 1985-90; first appearance in the Inside/Out series at Jacob's Pillow, 1997; selected to participate in the Choreographer's Session at The Yard in Chilmark, 1997. **Awards:** Asian Pacific Women's Network Scholarship, 1987; UCLA Outstanding Achievement Award, 1989; nominated for a Bonnie Bird Choreography Fund North American Award, 1994, 1997; Scripps/ADF Humphrey-Weidman-Limón Fellowship for Choreography, 1996; Cross-Cultural Choreography Commissioning Project (or Men's Project), 1996.

Works

1985	*Echoes* (mus. Tangerine Dream, Stearns, Pink Floyd), University of California at Santa Cruz students, Santa Cruz
	Unleashed (solo; mus. de Machaut), University of California, Santa Cruz
	I Can Feel the Rings (solo; mus. Chinese gypsy women), University of California, Santa Cruz
1987	*Gallery Dances* (with Dayna Beilenson), Li with others, L.A. Photography Center, Los Angeles
	Last Game: The Children of Enola Gay (trio; mus. The Beatles), L.A. Photography Center, Los Angeles
	Galatea (solo; mus. Rodriguez), L.A. Photography Center, Los Angeles
1988	*Galapagos Olympiad* (quartet; mus. Haydn, Eno, sound effects), Li with others, L.A. Photography Center, Los Angeles
	The Ol' Ball 'N Chain (solo; mus. Williams), UCLA Dance Building, Los Angeles
1989	*Home on the Range* (duet; mus. Williams), Real and Wolf, UCLA Lab Theater, Los Angeles
	From Grace (quartet; mus. Picken), LACE, Los Angeles
	Urban Madness (mus. Byrne), Hamilton High School students, Norman J. Pattiz Concert Hall, Los Angeles
1990	*Silken* (mus. Hwong), Hollins College Theater, Roanoke

Passacaglia (solo; mus. Biber), Ron Brown, Westside Academy, Los Angeles

Points of Departure (sextet; mus. Reich), Hollins College Theater, Roanoke

La Mer (with Douglas Rosenberg; mus. Mozart), Li and Rosenberg, UMBC Dance Department, Baltimore

1991　*Yellow River* (solo; mus. Mozart and Chinese gypsy women), Theater Artaud, San Francisco

Chi (solo; mus. Branca), Hollins College Theater, Roanoke

Rapture (mus. Barber), Hollins College Theater, Roanoke

1992　*e* (trio), Hollins College Theater, Roanoke

Don Giovanni (for Opera Roanoke production with five dancers; mus. Mozart), Li with others, Mill Mountain Theater, Roanoke

Le Train du Memoir (with Rosenberg; mus. Rota, Alpert, Brandwayn, Scotto/Decaye, Verdi, Wayne-Beekman), Li with others, Theater Artaud, San Francisco

Yellow River (Hwang Ho) (solo; mus. Mozart and Chinese gypsy women), Reynolds Theater, Duke University, Durham, North Carolina

1993　*Collection of Battered Homes and Gardens* (suite of three pieces including the premiere of *Along at Last;* mus. Williams), Li, Pepper-Venzant, and Willis, Hollins College Theater, Roanoke

Entombed Warrior (solo; mus. Fang, Skeaping, Vitiello), Highways Performance Space, Santa Monica

Hyperopic Romances (quintet; mus. horse race, Chaplin, Sherman and Sherman, Mills brothers, Gane/Ladley/Weelkes), Lathrop Performance Space, Madison

Remembering Stories of Dragon Princess (with Dana Tai Soon Burgess; duet), Li and Burgess, Marvin Center, Washington, DC

Joong (Center) (with Rosenberg; solo), Page Auditorium, American Dance Festival, Durham

1994　*L'Annee du Chien* (trio; mus. LaBarbara), Lathrop Performance Space, Madison

Romeo and Juliet/Adam and Eve (with Rosenberg; mus. Tchaikovsky, Lynch, Bearbeitung, Doe and Exene, Chaplin, Brahms, Prokofiev, Stanislawski Brothers Band, Leoncavallo, Puccini, Bimstein), Dziga Vertov Performance Group, Theater Artaud, San Francisco

Tome (solo), University of Alaska Anchorage Studio Theater, Anchorage

afTErAte (mus. Crispell), Lathrop Performance Space, Madison

1995　*Pas un Faun* (solo), Kanopy Performing Arts Center, Madison

(T)Raveling (solo; mus. Ravel), Kanopy Performing Arts Center, Madison

Sen (solo; mus. Vitiello), Lathrop Performance Space, Madison

Untitled (mus. Fang), Li and others, Lathrop Performance Space, Madison

The Land Within (with Rosenberg; solo; mus. Sephardic songs, radio broadcasts)

Go (mus. Gorecki), Walker's Point Center for the Arts, Milwaukee

Dispossessed (trio; mus. Adams), Stiemke Theater, Milwaukee

1996　*Fin de Siècle* (solo; mus. Byrne), Grace Street Theater, Richmond

Li Chiao-Ping performing *Fin de Siècle,* 1997. Photograph by Jay Daniel.

Lattice Cuts (with Sally Silvers), Li and Silvers, P.S. 122, New York

Corpus Callosum (solo; mus. Branca), Cynthia Lay, Lathrop Performance Space, Madison

Go (for twelve dancers) (mus. Gorecki), ADF students, Baldwin Auditorium, American Dance Festival, Durham

Curling Feet/Stirring Air or I Barely Know Her (with Barbara Grubel; duet), Li and Grubel, The Ark, American Dance Festival, Durham

But Wait ... There's More (sextet; mus. Shostakovich and Waits), American Dance Festival students, The Ark, American Dance Festival, Durham

Odyssey (with Rosenberg; trio), Li, Rosenberg, and Bisogno, Ricardo Rojas Cultural Center, Buenos Aires

Lunar Ellipses, students at University of Wisconsin, Lathrop Performance Space, Madison

Tiny Fish (solo; mus. Levin), Tania Isaac, Lathrop Performance Space, Madison

1997　*RE:Joyce* (solo; mus. Vitiello), Spotlight Room, Madison Civic Center, Madison

Other works include: (solos created for Li as part of the Cross-Cultural Choreography Commissioning Project/"Men's Project,"

1996) *Aria* (Dendy; solo; mus. Catalani); *Judgment* (Wong; solo; mus. Cage); *Cross Cut* (Nagrin; solo,; mus. Ulstvolskaya); *Fall* (Dorfman; solo; mus. Dorfman); *Periphery* (Solomons; solo; mus. Terricciano); *I Dreamt I Should Not Reach Higher Than This* (Goode; solo; mus. Bernstein, Ducasse, Kudo, Nakanishi, Sanders).

Publications

By LI: articles—

"Text from 'Yellow River,'" Asian American Empowerment program organized by Dana Tai Soon Burgess, Washington, D.C., 1993.
"Yellow River (Hwang Ho): An Autobiographical Dance/Theater Journey in Search of Identity," *Proceedings,* Dance and Technology III Conference, Toronto, 1995.

On LI: articles—

Atkinson, Viki, "Sculptural Dance and Dendy Daring: ADF Update," *Spectator,* 18(33), 11 July 1996.
Harding, Cathryn, "Li Chiao-Ping: One Woman, Six Singular Works," *Inside Arts,* 8(4), September 1996.

*   *   *

Li Chiao-Ping is best known for her wildly inventive and athletic work. Since 1985, she has choreographed and collaborated on more than 50 pieces. Some of these pieces have been commissioned (Milwaukee Dance Theater, Symphony Space, Opera Roanoke, Southwest Virginia Ballet, Mulberry Street Theater); many of her works are collaborations, most often with videographer/artist Douglas Rosenberg. Li has received numerous honors and grants for her work, including the Scripps/American Dance Festival (ADF) Humphrey-Weidman-Limón Fellowship for Choreography in 1996.

Her style of dance is unique, a blend of gymnastics and Chinese martial arts, folk dance, jazz, ballet, and modern dance. It is a reflection of her eclectic training in the styles of Martha Graham, Eric Hawkins, José Limón, Merce Cunningham, Lester Horton, and Nina Wiener. Cathryn Harding [*Inside Arts* (1996)] described her as possessing "a fierce physicality and a determination to use her body to break down boundaries." Critics have described her works as "focused," "intense," "gripping," "articulate," "powerful and mysterious," and "full of conviction and understated humor."

In an interview with Harding, Li said "I felt growing up that I should have been a boy. I was always trying to be a son, because males are more valued in Chinese families. . . I always wanted to fight stereotypes of what girls can't do." Throughout her career, Li has made a reputation for her fierce and strong presence on stage, her brilliant technique, and her consummate execution of theme and movement. This approach has won her both gymnastic city championships as well as numerous dance awards and choreographic grants.

In 1991 Li created *Yellow River,* a piece combining movement, gesture, text, and landscape imagery to tell the story of growing up as a Chinese woman in America. The piece relied heavily on the stories, superstitions, and fables her mother told her when she was a child. The following year Li created her first video-dance, a version of *Yellow River (Hwang Ho),* with ADF Video Director Douglas Rosenberg.

Chi, choreographed in 1991, is Li's signature piece. This nine-minute solo, in contrast to the epic quality of the 40-minute-long *Yellow River,* is an abstract work with no props. It is based on the concept of life force or inner energy and is characterized by quick, explosive movements. *Chi* is representative of the overarching issues of culture and identity that have permeated her work.

Li's works explore the theme of place and culture with abstract characters—cultural composites—that inhabit unique worlds. A powerful, fighting heroine, a "warrior woman," was the focus of her 1993 work, *Entombed Warrior,* referring to the thousands of terra cotta soldiers discovered by archeologists near the site of the seat of the Q'in dynasty in China. Each of the "entombed warriors" was reported to have distinct and unique uniforms and facial characteristics. Li used the same image in her work, a woman warrior with different forms and faces, enduring, nurturing, fighting. Both sound and stage denoted a theatrical and ritual space in which the performance, as ceremony, took place.

In another work, *Untitled* (1995), inspired by a Forrest Fang story, "The Bridge of Chuan-Chou," Li depicted the different shapes and qualities of a body of water as it was shaped by the forces of nature and mythical spirits. *Go,* also choreographed in 1995, was based on a Chinese board game of strategy in war. In effect, the five dancers in the piece performed a kind of contemporary war dance. It was performed at the Kennedy Center in Washington, D.C. in the 1996 National American College Dance Festival.

Li also is interested in the interaction between dance and contemporary technology such as monitors and projection screens on stage. These pieces are emotional in tone and are set in visually and aurally dynamic environments. In an "Artist Statement" [Madison (1996)], Li wrote:

> My interest in the hybrid form of Video Dance or Dance for the Camera is in the medium's ability to be free of the body and live separately from it, unlike dance; in direct contrast to the risk involved with live performance, which depends almost entirely on the individual's presence, fitness, and artistry, the videotape can exist and travel alone. . .video. . .offers challenges generally not found within the scope of live performance, challenges which include maintaining a sense of intimacy, emotionalism, and physicality.

In 1991 Li became co-director of the San Francisco-based Dziga Vertov Performance Group and has been a prime collaborator in creating multimedia pieces for the company. Li created *Joong (Center)* with Douglas Rosenberg in 1993, using six monitors and two VCRs for video projection. The piece was funded by the New Forms Regional Grant Program administered by the Painted Bride Art Center in Philadelphia.

Li combines gesture and movements, music, visual imagery, sculptures, other props, and costumes to explore her athleticism. *Fin de Siècle* (1996), for example, was an athletic gauntlet of tests and tasks containing sports-derived gestural language.

Her recent Cross-Cultural Choreography Commissioning Project or "Men's Project" has received national recognition. The program premiered in March of 1997 at the Union Theater in Madison, Wisconsin. Li worked with six different male choreographers—Mark Dendy, David Dorfman, Joe Goode, Daniel Nagrin, Gus Solomons, Jr., and Mel Wong—each of whom created a solo for her. The project was a response, basically, to a question Li asked of each artist, "What happens when six choreographers, all American men of different ages, ethnic/ cultural/socioeconomic backgrounds, dance training, and life experiences, each make a work for the same female solo dancer?"

Mark Dendy's contribution to the project, *Aria,* was first performed at the American Dance Festival. *Dance Magazine* hailed it as "a study in steadfast devotion" and the *New York Times* considered it as "deeply personal responses to the aria's emotional intensity." This attention reflected Li's growing national stature as an innovative choreographer and daring performer.

—Gigi Berardi

LIAT DROR & NIR BEN-GAL DANCE COMPANY
Israeli modern dance company

The Liat Dror—Nir Ben-Gal Dance Company, in residence in Tel-Aviv, has performed works by its two joint choreographers, Liat Dror and her husband Nir Ben-Gal, since 1992. Both were born in kibbutzim in the northern part of Israel. The kibbutz has traditionally been known as a haven of the arts with artistic self-expression an integral part of

Liat Dror and Nir Ben Gal: *Into Oumry,* 1995.

475

kibbutz education. For Liat Dror and Nir Ben Gal, there was nothing unusual in their studying dance as teenagers.

Liar Dror was born in July of 1960 and Nir Ben-Gal was born in the same month a year earlier. After they finished their compulsory military service, they met in Jerusalem when they enrolled in the Rubin Academy Dance Department in Jerusalem. Being rather disappointed, after their first year there they decided to apply for an internship at the Ga'aton regional studios of the Kibbutz Contemporary Dance Company (KCDC). To be able to afford their tuition, they jointly became caretakers and cleaners of the studio. Yehudit Arnon, head of the studio and artistic director of the KCDC encouraged them in their experiments in choreography and in 1986 they began to choreograph both separately and together for the Batsheva Dance Company, the KCDC, and the Jerusalem Ensemble.

Since 1987 the couple has created and performed as a duo, and their hour-long *Two Room Apartment* received first prize from the showcase performances organized by the dance department of the Ministry of Education and Culture at the Suzanne Dellal Center in Tel-Aviv.

Their style may be described as poetic realism in terms of dance-theatre. Their *Equus Asinus,* performed in 1988, dealt with hard work and sweat, hence the "donkey" of the title. In Liat Dror and Nir Ben-Gal's early works, a pronounced stylistic influence of German "Tanztheater" and especially Pina Bausch's work was evident. A relentless use of repetitive movement-sequences, and a certain ruthlessness—almost bordering on cruelty and a total disregard of pain—is one of the components of their style.

They formed their own eponymous company, which premiered *Circles of Lust* with music by Ori Vidislavski, in 1992. *Anta Oumri,* which came in 1994, was based on the song of the famous Arab singer Aum Kaltsoum and depicted ablutions, therefore included nudity in the performance. The critical reaction as well as that of audiences was enthusiastic.

In 1996, the duo debuted *The Enquiry* which featured a political background and managed to deal with the interrogation of suspects—political, Palestinian, prisoners—without becoming cheap political propaganda, a danger always lurking behind dance with political messages.

Though Liar Dror and Nir Ben-Gal had received project-funding from the Ministry of Education and Culture early in their careers, when they became more successful they were able to partially finance their work by touring abroad. For example, in 1996, the Liat Dror & Nir Ben-Gal Company gave 49 performances. Earnings from ticket sales made up about half of the company's budget while the remainder was supplied by public subsidies.

As a married couple, their private lives and their work were often hard to separate as the couple's two small children accompanied them to rehearsals, performances and had toured with the company practically from their births. And although they choreograph together, Liat Dror is perhaps the more creative half of the partnership. As they are growing older, both have performed less in recent years, though both are still brilliant dancers, and have been leaving the actual dancing to the members of their company.

Publications

Articles—

Eshel, Ruth, "To Dance with the Times," *Israel Dance Quarterly,* No. 10, 1997.

Manor, Giora, "Alone and Together," *Israel Dance Quarterly,* No. 6, 1995.

—Giora Manor

LIMBS DANCE COMPANY

New Zealand Dance Company

Works

1978	*Bamboo* (chor. M. J. O'Reilly; mus. Mann)
	New Wave Goodbye (chor. C Jannides; mus. Spats)
	Scooby Doo (chor. M. J. O'Reilly; mus. Mahal)
	Sellotape I (chor. M. Baldwin; mus. Limbs)
	Flight One (chor. C. Jannides)
	Poems (chor. C. Jannides)
	Cajun Moon (chor. C. Jannides; mus. Mann & Houston)
	Satie (chor. C. Jannides; mus. Satie)
	Little Piano (chor. M.J. O'Reilly; mus. Bach)
	Backyard Frolics (chor. C. Jannides; mus. Limbs)
	Apart (chor. C. Jannides; mus. Hanssen)
	Funtime (chor. C. Jannides; mus. Cocker)
	Moth (chor. M. J. O'Reilly; mus. Kraftwerk)
	Watch it Buddy (chor. C. Jannides; mus. Limbs)
	After the Rain (chor. A. Batchelor; mus. Rypdal)
	Eno (chor. C. Jannides; mus. Eno)
	The Sculptor (chor. C. Jannides; mus. Philips)
	Reptile (chor. M.J. O'Reilly; mus. Burrell)
	TV Dance (chor. M. J. O'Reilly; mus. Gunn)
	Satisfaction (chor. C Jannides; mus. Devo)
	It Walks (chor. M.J. O'Reilly, poem Wein)
	Broken Lines (chor. K Northcott; mus. Ponty)
	Complicated Legs Dance (chor. C Jannides; mus. Swarbrick)
	Perhaps Can (chor. M.J. O'Reilly, mus.Davis)
	Red Riding Hood (chor. M.J. O'Reilly; mus. Coryrll & Corea)
	Ponsonby Hat Dance (chor. M.J.O'Reilly; mus. Limbs)
	Morphus (chor. C. Jannides; mus. Led Zepplin)
	Silence (chor. C Jannides; mus. Ultravox)
	Screen Piece (chor. C Jannides, theatre P. Ruter)
	Lucky Number One (chor. C Jannides; mus. Lovich)
	Russell's Dance (chor. R Kerr; mus. Saens)
	Games (chor. M.J. O'Reilly; mus. Oregon)
	Busy (chor. C. Jannides; mus. Jarre)
	Cocaine Bill & Morphine Sue (chor. C Jannides; mus. Pauline)
	Vertigo (chor. M. J. O'Reilly; mus. Jarret)
	Heart (chor. C Jannides)
1980	*Lumpy Porridge* (chor. M. J. O'Reilly; mus.Weber)
	Hot Fun (chor. P George; mus. Clark)
	Hendrix (chor. C. Jannides; mus. Hendrix)
	The Unicorn, the Gorgon and the Manticore (chor. M. J. O'Reilly; mus. Menotti)
	Shark Attack (chor. M. J. O'Reilly; mus. Split Enz)
	Brunswick Flats (chor. M.J. O'Reilly; mus. Limbs)
	Partners (chor. A. Batchelor; mus. Tcherepnin)
	I Got You (chor. M.J. O'Reilly; mus. Split Enz)

Bamiyon (chor. M.J. O'Reilly; mus. Towner)

Liebling (chor. M.J. O'Reilly; mus. Strauss)

Pyramid (chor. M.J. O'Reilly; mus. Laird)

On the Fiddle (chor. M.J. O'Reilly; mus. Grappelli)

Girl You Want (chor. M. Baldwin; mus. Devo)

Madness (chor. M.J. O'Reilly; mus. Madness)

Entering a Shell (chor. M. Baldwin; mus. McGlashan)

Saga or *Cargo* (chor. M.J. O'Reilly; mus. Preston & Hannan)

Negaton (chor. C.Jannides; mus. Faithful)

Melting Moments (chor. M. Baldwin; mus. Dvorak)

1981 *Talking Heads* (chor. M.J. O'Reilly; mus. Talking Heads)

Outside the Fight (chor. M. Baldwin; mus. Limbs)

Quiet Please (chor. M.J. O'Reilly)

Swingers (chor. M.J. O'Reilly; mus. Swingers)

Commute (chor. M.J. O'Reilly; mus. Riley)

Arcade (chor. M.J. O'Reilly; mus. McGlashan)

Suspicion (chor. C. Jannides; mus. Brown)

Backstreet Primary (chor. D. Wright; poem Frame; mus. Talking Heads)

Pink Slip (chor. A Batechelor; mus. Shostakovitch)

Soft Corps (chor. M.J. O'Reilly; mus. Davis)

Why Does the Chicken? (chor. M.J. O'Reilly; mus. Stravinsky)

1982 *Shadow of the Warrior* (chor. M.J. O'Reilly; mus. Laird)

Late Afternoon of a Faun or *Thrilled to Bits* (chor. D. Wright; mus. Debussy)

Baby Go Boom (Chor. D. Wright; mus. Holiday, Armstrong, Farnell) Limbs Dance Company, Auckland

Walking on Thin Ice (chor. D. Wright; mus. Ono)

Aurora Borealis (chor. D. Wright; mus. Ono, Hagen, Anderson)

Dracula (chor. M.J. O'Reilly; mus. McCurdy)

Purped Lives (chor. A. Batchelor; mus. Monk, Glass)

Kneedance (D. Wright; mus. Anderson)

1983 *Journey* (chor. M. J. O'Reilly; mus. Preston)

A Man with Two Devils Courts a Woman with an Angel (chor. C. Jannides; mus. Orchestral Manoeuvres in the Dark)

Poi (chor. M. J. O'Reilly; mus. Body)

Land of a 1000 Dances (chor. D. Wright; mus. Small, Pickett)

Tango 1&2 (chor. M. J. O'Reilly; mus. Stravinsky)

This Is a Love Song (chor. M. J. O'Reilly; mus. McGlashan)

Grace (chor. M. J. O'Reilly; mus. Jones)

Les Enfants de la Realite (chor. R. Kerr; mus. Schoenburg)

Sierra (chor. M. J. O'Reilly; mus. Manzanera)

I Dig That Movie Too (chor. M. J. O'Reilly; mus. Coconut Roughs)

3 Boxes (chor. R. Shang)

Domino (chor. G. Cash; mus. Shang)

Ranterstantrum (chor. D. Wright; mus. Branca)

Stilldance (chor. M. J. O'Reilly; mus. Beirach)

1984 *Study for 2 Dancers* (chor. C. Jannides; mus. Philips, Reichman)

Ngahere (chor. F. Molloy; mus. Easterbrook)

Nina (chor. M. J. O'Reilly; mus. Nina Hagen)

Overall Ease (chor. G. Lester; mus. Waller)

Contact (chor. G. Watson; mus. Presley, Powers, Cale)

Pinprick (chor. G. Watson; mus. Alvarez)

Decoy (chor. G. Lester; mus. McGlashan)

Bon Voyage (chor. P. Jenden; mus. Ravel)

Souvenirs (chor. M. J. O'Reilly; mus. D McGlashan)

Two Women (chor. K. T. Chan; mus. Chinese Peasants)

Scarf Dance (chor. K. T. Chan; mus. Vangelis)

Flying Ears Long Eyes (chor. M. J. O'Reilly; mus. Anderson)

1985 *Swing* (chor. S. McCullagh; mus. Yello)

Cool Bananas (chor. G. Mayo; mus. The Beat)

Sunday Horrors (chor. M. J. O'Reilly; mus. Zagni & Garden)

Brian Tries (chor. M. J. O'Reilly; mus. various)

Lift Music (chor. M. J. O'Reilly; mus. Broadhurst)

Swamp (chor. P. Jenden; mus. Sinclair)

Vigil Switch (chor. J. McLaughlin; mus. Takahashi, McGlashan)

Halcyon (chor. D. Wright; mus. Vivaldi) Limbs Dance Company, Whangarei

Concussion (chor. B. Carbee; mus. G Ludvigson, G Gash)

Tap Interlude (chor. M. J. O'Reilly)

1986 *Carnival of the Animals* (mus. Saint-Saens) w/Auckland Philharmonia

Tarawera (chor. M. J. O'Reilly; mus. Zagni)

Drum Sing (chor. S. McCullagh; mus. From Scratch)

Party Politics (chor. B. Carbee; mus. Gordon & Tieghem)

Its Not Unusual (chor. B. Carbee; mus. Jones)

Tell Me Why (chor. B. Carbee; mus. Bronski Beat)

Ballroom Dances (chor. S. McCullagh), video

1987 *Hey Paris* (chor. D. Wright; dir. G Nicholas) dance film, Wellington International Film Festival

Ego, Ergo (chor. R. Schwabl; mus. Riley)

When it Comes to Leaving (chor. D. Tanner; mus. Brahms, Eurythmics)

Hello Earth (chor. G. Mayo; mus. Bingen, Bartók, Bush)

Around and Back (chor. C Chappell; mus. Sky)

Soul Shoe (chor. L. Plunkett; mus. Newhook & Wilson)

Tricolore (chor. C. Cardiff; mus. Beethoven)

1988 *Now Is the Hour* (chor. D. Wright; mus. D McGlashan and various)

Pu Yi (chor. M. White)

Griselda's Dream (chor. D. McCulloch; mus. G. Brice)

Oppressed Laughter (chor. D. Tanner mus. Katchachurian)

Helga und Heinz (chor. S. McCullagh)

Seven-a-Side (chor. C. Cardiff; mus. A Green)

*   *   *

Limbs Dance Company was established in Auckland, New Zealand's largest and most multicultural city, in 1978. Founding directors Mary Jane O'Reilly and Chris Jannides, together with dancers Adrian Batchelor, Mark Baldwin, Kilda Northcott, Shona Wilson and Lynda Amos, intended to develop new choreographies which incorporated the talents of other artists, such as costume and set designers, musicians and composers. Their goal was to communicate, entertain and share their love of dancing, to show that modern dance could be enjoyable and exciting. They hoped to attract a wider audience for their particular brand of modern dance, which they saw as being quite different from that offered by their Wellington counterpart, Impulse Dance Theatre.

The Limbs company began as a group of friends working together in 1977 while most were receiving unemployment benefits.

Limbs Dance Company: *Drumsing.*

They made their debut performance in August to a student audience with a series of short, succinct dances, which made use of humour, choreographed by Jannides and O'Reilly. They received a standing ovation and went on to perform in parks and fashion parades, schools and rock music festivals, nightclubs and on television, all the while gathering an ever-increasing local following.

Heartened by their reception, the company was formally established, with dancers Mark Baldwin and Adrian Batchelor also contributing dances to the repertoire created by Jannides and O'Reilly, and with evening classes and weekend workshops helping to subsidise company costs. In 1978 they took their programme of performances and workshops out on the road, travelling to small towns and isolated settlements as well as cities, dancing in wool sheds and school halls. They were enthusiastically received everywhere they went, and they were a huge hit at the national Student's Arts Festival, resulting in a 1979 national tour on university campuses funded by the New Zealand Students Arts Council.

The popularity of Limbs performances led to an increase in Arts Council funding for the group, and they moved from project funding to annual funding in 1980, going on to represent the country at the South Pacific Arts Festival in Papua New Guinea, that year. They subsequently toured the United States in 1981, with performances in New York, Washington and Los Angeles. *New York Times* reviewer Jennifer Dunning described Limbs' performance as witty, refreshing and stylish. "May they return to New York soon" she wrote. Over the next seven years, they made tours to Australia, Japan, Hong Kong and returned to the United States, always receiving compliments and praise for their distinctive style and high-energy performances.

Mary Jane O'Reilly assumed the role of artistic director of Limbs in late 1979, when founding co-director Jannides left to establish his own company, D'Arc Swan. O'Reilly's training had been in ballet, at the National Ballet School in New Zealand and the Royal Ballet School in London. She also had some experience of American modern dance, and after dancing in Europe in a ballet company had resolved to pursue modern dance. At the time Limbs was formed she was teaching modern dance classes in Auckland.

Rather than adopt an established style such as Hawkins or Cunningham, Limbs developed their own distinctive style which incorporated the articulation, precision, and musicality of ballet and jazz, elements of Maori and Polynesian performance styles, aspects from theatre, gymnastics and acrobatics, and reflecting trends in local popular culture. The company was always exciting to watch.

Under O'Reilly's direction, Limbs steadily matured, artistically and technically. The repertoire began to change, with dances becoming longer and choreographically more complex, and increasingly set to New Zealand music. With the closure of Impulse Dance Theatre in 1982, Limbs became the national modern dance company. With increasing support from the Arts Council, and from a government employment initiative, and with increasing demand from the public for performances, classes and workshops, Limbs grew rapidly in size. By 1983, there were 10 dancers, 7 full time staff, plus a tour director, rehearsal director, studio manager and regular guest choreographers. With their Arts Council funding and significant corporate sponsorship arrangements, Limbs soon had an annual turnover of close to $1.5 million New Zealand dollars.

In the eleven years of Limbs' existence, almost 200 dances were made; some of them still performed as classic New Zealand choreography. Though O'Reilly choreographed a large proportion of the repertoire for Limbs, company members were encouraged to contribute new dances, and company members including Douglas Wright, Brian Carbee, Garry Lester, Shona McCullagh and Dale Tanner received company commissions. From 1983, works were also commissioned from choreographers outside the company. Russell Kerr and Paul Jenden form New Zealand, Ruby Shang and John McLaughlin from the United States, and Graeme Watson and Kai Tai Chan of Australia made works which extended the range of the dancers. The best-known and most highly regarded Limbs works, nevertheless, are those made by Mary Jane O'Reilly (*Reptile, Scooby Doo, Poi* and *Saga*) and by Douglas Wright *(Kneedance, Ranterstantrum, Halcyon, How On Earth* and *Quartet).*

O'Reilly remained artistic director until 1986, when in the aftermath of a devastating fire which destroyed the company's studio and accumulated sets, costumes, audio and video records, she found it impossible to continue. Cath Cardiff, rehearsal director at the time of the fire, managed and directed Limbs until 1989, when changes in government arts funding policy combined with the company's accumulated deficit forced them to cease operation. After this, key Limbs dancers continued to dance and make new works together on a project basis, and also formed the core of the Douglas Wright Dance Company from 1989. Following the demise of the Limbs school, a number of the Limbs dancers and teachers supported the establishment of the tertiary level Performing Arts School, offering full-time modern dance training. Now part of UNITEC Institute of Technology, the School of Performing and Screen Arts offers a bachelor's degree with a major in contemporary dance, and includes former Limbs alumni among the faculty.

A decade after they ceased operation, Limbs is remembered by many as New Zealand's most successful modern dance company. They achieved their goal to develop a wide audience for dance, and their example incited greatly increased participation in dance classes. Limbs tours overseas put New Zealand on the world dance map. Thirty-two dancers were members of the Limbs company during its existence, most of them going on to other companies or retraining in dance-related fields following their performance careers. Mary Jane O'Reilly has continued to work as teacher and choreographer since she left Limbs, and is perhaps best known for her choreography of the 1990 Commonwealth Games Opening Ceremony in Auckland, and her ballet *Jean* (1992) for the Royal New Zealand Ballet. In 1995, she established Auckland Ballet, a projects-based ballet company which creates and performs contemporary works, to date all choreographed by O'Reilly.

—Karen Barbour and Raewyn Whyte

LIMÓN, José Arcadio

Mexican-American dancer, choreographer, and educator

Born: 12 January 1908 in Culiacán, Mexico; became U.S. citizen in 1946. **Education:** Studied painting at the University of California in Los Angeles, and Art Students League, New York City; studied at the Humphrey-Weidman School, New York, 1929-40; attended summer programs at Bennington School of Dance and Mills College. **Family:** Married Pauline Lawrence, 1941 (died 1971). **Military:** Drafted, U.S. Armed Forces, choreographed and performed in several musicals, as a member of the Special Services, 1943. **Career:** Dancer, Humphrey-Weidman Company, 1930-40; began to choreograph, and formed The Little Group with Ernestine Henoch and Eleanor King, 1930; appeared on Broadway, including *Lysistrata* (1930), *Americana* (1932), and *As Thousands Cheer* (1933); choreographed Jerome Kern's *Roberta*, 1933; created a touring company in California with May O'Donnell and her husband, composer Ray Green, 1940; formed the José Limón Dance Company, with Doris Humphrey as artistic director, 1946; faculty, American Dance Festival at Connecticut College, summers of 1948-72; faculty, Juilliard School of Music, 1951-72; guest choreographer, Instituto Nacional de Bellas Artes, Mexico City, 1951; artistic director, José Limón Dance Company, after Humphrey's death, 1958; appointed artistic director, American Dance Theatre at Lincoln Center, 1964; toured with his company under the auspices of U.S. State Department to South America, 1954, 1960; Europe, 1957; Far East, 1963; final appearance as a dancer, 1969. **Awards:** Bennington College Choreography Fellow, 1937; winning audition, 92nd Street YMHA; *Dance Magazine* awards, 1950, 1957; honorary doctorate degree, Wesleyan University, 1960; Colby College, 1967; University of North Carolina, 1958; Oberlin College, 1971; Capezio Award, 1964; first grant from the National Endowment for the Arts (NEA), 1966; performed *The Moor's Pavane* at the White House, 1967; Samuel S. Scripps/American Dance Festival Award, 1989; inducted into the National Museum of Dance Hall of Fame, 1997. **Died:** 2 December 1972.

Roles

Various roles with the Humphrey-Weidman Company from 1930 to 1940; later created roles in many Humphrey works for the Limón Company, including *Lament for Ignacio Sánchez Mejías* (1946), *Day on Earth* (1947), *Night Spell* (1951), and *Ruins and Visions* (1953); also danced leading roles in most of his own works created before 1967.

Works

1930	*Étude in D-flat Major* (mus. Scriabin), New York
	Bacchanale w/Eleanor King and Ernestine Henoch (mus. percussion), New York
1931	*Petite Suite* (mus. Debussy), New York
	Tango (mus. Limón), New York
	B Minor Suite (mus. Bach), New York
	Mazurka w/Eleanor King (mus. Scriabin), New York
	Two Preludes (mus. Reginald de Koven), Westport, Connecticut
	Danza (mus. Sergei Prokofiev), Sharon, Connecticut
1932	*Bach Suite* w/Eleanor King (mus. Bach), New York
1933	*Canción y Danza* (mus. Federico Mompou), New York
	Pièces Froides (mus. Satie), New York
	Roberta (mus. Jerome Kern), Broadway, New York
1935	*1935*, Steamboat Springs, Colorado
	Three Studies (mus. Engel), New York
	Nostalgic Fragments (mus. Stravinsky), New York
	Prelude (mus. Poulenc), New York
1936	*Satiric Lament* (mus. Poulenc), New York
	Hymn (mus. percussion), New York
1937	*Danza de la Muerte* (mus. Henry Clark, Norman Lloyd), Bennington, Vermont
	Opus for Three and Props (mus. Dmitri Shostakovitch), Bennington, Vermont
1939	*Danzas Mexicanas* (mus. Lionel Nowak), Oakland, California

1940	*Three Preludes* (mus. Chopin), Pittsburgh
	War Lyrics (mus. Esther Williamson), Oakland
1941	*Curtain Raiser* w/May O'Donnell (mus. Ray Green), Fresno
	This Story is Legend w/May O'Donnell (mus. Ray Green), Fresno
	Praeludium: Theme and Variations w/O'Donnell (mus. Green), Fresno
	Three Inventories on Casey Jones w/O'Donnell (mus. Green), Fresno
1942	*Alley Tune* w/Helen Ellis (mus. David Guion), Colorado Springs
	Turkey in the Straw (mus. traditional), Colorado Springs
	Mazurka (mus. Chopin), Colorado Springs
	Chaconne (mus. Bach), New York
1943	*Western Folk Suite* (mus. Norman Cazden), New York
	Fun for the Birds (mus. Arthur Schwartz, Don Stevens), Richmond, Virginia
1944	Spanish Dance (mus. de Falla), Richmond
	Rosenkavalier Waltz (mus. R. Strauss), Richmond
	Mexilinda (mus. Rachmaninoff, Rimsky-Korsakov, Cazden, Infante, Milhaud, de Falla, Brahms, J. Strauss), Camp Lee, Virginia
	Deliver the Goods (mus. Frank Hundertmark), Camp Lee
	Song of the Medics (book, music, lyrics: Philip Freedman, Charles Broffman), Fort Dix, New Jersey
	Hi, Yank!, Fort Dix, New Jersey
1945	*Concerto Grosso* (mus. Vivaldi), East Orange, New Jersey
	Eden Tree (mus. Carl Engel, Limón), East Orange
	Three Ballads (mus. traditional, Charles Ives), New York
1946	*Danza* (mus. J. Arcadio), Becket, Massachusetts
	Masquerade (mus. Sergei Prokofiev), St. Louis
1947	*Song of Songs* (mus. Lukas Foss), Boston
	Sonata Opus 4 (mus. Bach), Boston
1949	*La Malinche* (mus. Lloyd), Boston
	The Moor's Pavane (mus. Purcell), New London
1950	*The Exiles* (mus. Schönberg), New London
	Concert (mus. Bach), New London
1951	*Los cuatro soles* (mus. Carlos Chávez), Mexico City
	Tonantzintla (mus. Antonio Soler), Mexico City
	Di logos (mus. Lloyd), Mexico City
	Antígona (mus. Miguel Covarrubias), Mexico City
	Redes (mus. Silvestre Revueltas), Mexico City
1952	*The Queen's Epicedium* (mus. Purcell), New London
	The Visitation (mus. Schönberg), New London
	El Grito (mus. Revueltas), New York
1953	*Don Juan Fantasia* (mus. Liszt), New London
1954	*Ode to the Dance* (mus. Samuel Barber), New York
	The Traitor (mus. Gunther Schuller), New London
1955	*Scherzo* (mus. Hazel Johnson), New London
	Symphony for Strings (mus. William Schuman), New London
1956	*There Is a Time* (mus. Norman Dello Joio), New York
	King's Heart (mus. Stanley Wolfe), New York
	The Emperor Jones (mus. Heitor Villa-Lobos), Ellenville, New York
1957	*Missa Brevis* (mus. Kodály), New York
1958	*Serenata* (mus. Paul Bowles), New London
	Mazurkas [originally titled *Dances* (in honor of Poznan, Wraclaw, Katowice, and Warszawa)] (mus. Chopin), New London

1959	*Tenebrae, 1914* (mus. John Wilson), New London
	The Apostate (mus. Ernst Krenek), New London
1960	*Barren Sceptre* w/Pauline Koner (mus. Schuller), New York
1961	*Performance* (mus. Hugh Aitken, William Bergsma, Jacob Druckman, Vittorio Giannini, Norman Lloyd, Vincent Persichetti, Robert Starer, and Hugo Weisgal), New York
	The Moirai (mus. Aitken), New London
	Sonata for Two Cellos (mus. Meyer Kupferman), New London
1962	*I, Odysseus* (mus. Aitken), New London
1963	*The Demon* (mus. Hindemith), New York
	Concerto in D Minor after Vivaldi (mus. Bach), New York
1964	*A Choreographic Offering* (mus. Bach), New York
1965	*Variations on a Theme of Paganini* (mus. Brahms), New York
	Dance Suite (mus. Prokofiev), Brooklyn
	My Son, My Enemy (mus. Vivan Fine), New London
1966	*The Winged* (mus. Hank Johnson), New London
1967	*MacAber's Dance* (mus. Jacob Druckman), New York
	Psalm (mus. Eugene Lester), New London
1968	*Comedy* (mus. Josef Wittman), New London
	Legend (mus. Simon Sadoff), New London
1969	*La Piñata* (mus. Burrill Phillips), New York
1971	*The Unsung* (in silence), Philadelphia
	Revel (mus. Elizabeth Sawyer), New York
	Dances for Isadora (mus. Chopin), Cleveland
	The Wind (mus. Joseph Castaldo), Philadelphia
1972	*Orfeo* (mus. Beethoven), New York
	Carlota (in silence), New York

Publications

BY LIMÓN: book—

José Limón: An Unfinished Memoir, edited by Lynn Garafola, Middletown, Connecticut, 1998.

By LIMÓN: articles—

"An American Accent," in *The Modern Dance: Seven Statements of Belief*, edited by Selma Jeanne Cohen, Middletown, Connecticut, 1966.

"American Dance on Tour," *Juilliard Review*, Spring 1958.

"Composing a Dance," *Juilliard Review*, Winter 1955.

"Dance in Education—Four Statements: Jean Erdman, Alwin Nikolais, Patricia Wilde, José Limón," *Impulse* 1968.

"Dancers are Musicians are Dancers," *Juilliard Review Annual*, 1966-67.

"The Dancers' Status Here and Abroad: Comparisons and Observations," *Dance Observer*, March 1958.

"Music Is the Strongest Ally to a Dancer's Way of Life," in *The Dance Experience*, edited by Myron Howard Nadel and Constance Gwen Nadel, New York, 1970.

"The Universities and the Arts," *Dance Scope*, Spring 1965.

"The Virile Dance," in *The Dance Has Many Faces*, edited by Walter Sorell, New York, 1966.

On LIMÓN: books—

Cohen, Selma Jeanne, *Doris Humphrey: An Artist First*, Middletown, Connecticut, 1972.

"José Limón," in *Current Biography 1968*, 1968.

Jowitt, Deborah, *Time and the Dancing Image*, New York, 1988.

Koner, Pauline, *Solitary Song*, Durham, 1986.

Kriegsman, Sali Ann, *Modern Dance in America: The Bennington Years*, Boston, 1981.

Lewis, Daniel, *The Illustrated Dance Technique of José Limón*, New York, 1984.

Lloyd, Margaret, "José Limón," in *The Borzoi Book of Modern Dance*, New York, 1949.

McDonagh, Don, "José Limón," in *The Complete Guide to Modern Dance*, Garden City, New York, 1976.

Pollack, Barbara, and Charles Humphrey Woodford, *Dance Is a Moment: A Portrait of José Limón in Words and Pictures*, Pennington, New Jersey, 1993.

Siegel, Marcia B., *Days on Earth: The Dance of Doris Humphrey*, New Haven, 1987.

————. *The Shapes of Change: Images of American Dance*, Berkeley, 1979.

On LIMÓN: articles—

Becker, Seva, "From Humphrey to Limón: A Modern Dance Tradition," *Dance Notation Journal*, Spring 1984.

Cunningham, Katherine, "The Legacy of José Limón," *Dance Scope*, Spring/Summer 1973.

Hill, Martha, "José Limón and his Biblical Themes," *Choreography & Dance*, 1992.

Martin, John, Review of *The Moor's Pavane*, *New York Times*, 16 December 1949.

————, article, *New York Times*, 12 April 1953.

Siegel, Marcia B., "José Limón (1908-1972)," *Ballet Review*, 1973.

Films and Videotapes

A Dance Is Never Finished, WETA, 1968

The Dance Theater of José Limón, WNET-TV, 1965

Three Contemporary Classics: The Moor's Pavane, The Emperor Jones, The Traitor, video release of three works filmed by the Canadian Broadcasting Company in 1955-56, Video Arts International, 1998.

The Moor's Pavane, filmed in an abridged version by Walter Strate, 1950.

*   *   *

José Limón was a dancer first. He firmly established the importance of the male dancer in American modern dance through the heroes he created and the masculine movement style of his choreography for men. John Martin of the *New York Times* wrote "His dance is that of a strong and mature man in command of all his powers, and it gives a completely new range and meaning to male dancing." With his startling good looks, above average height, and physical strength, he commanded a powerful stage presence, which Doris Humphrey used to good advantage in many works she created for him. His roles in his own choreography were more complex, and frequently based on literary or biblical figures, including Othello, Adam, Judas Iscariot, and Brutus Jones. These larger-than-life characters were engaged in an intense struggle with morality or fate. Limón's gestures were eloquent, his passions monumental. His movement style grew out of his own physicality, his breath, and weight. In his choreography the men moved with raw intensity,

José Limón Dance Company: *Missa Brevis,* 1990. Photograph © Beatriz Schiller.

while the women were often pliant, supple, and exquisite. Limón made a number of works for all male casts, in which the men often appeared bare-chested, focusing attention on their muscular torsos, the unrefined effort of their movement, and the expansive use of breathing.

Limón was born in Culiacán, Sinaloa, Mexico. His father, a musician, conductor, and pedagogue, was a widower and father of three when he married 16-year-old Francisca Traslaviña. She bore him 11 children (and another three who died at birth), of which José was the eldest. His mother was a devout Catholic, and raised the children accordingly.

The Mexican revolution wreaked havoc in José's young life; at the age of five he witnessed the death by gunshot of a young uncle. His father directed various military bands during this period, and the family had to move frequently, to Cananea, Hermosilla, Nogales, and finally across the border to Tucson, Arizona, when José was seven. His father worked in various Arizona cities as a musician and conductor, and finally settled his family in Los Angeles, California, when José was 12. Due to an early humiliation with English, young José resolved to master the language, and he continued to develop his prodigious vocabulary throughout his life. He exhibited early talent as both a musician and a visual artist. In high school he was

introduced to the glories of Western art, and at about the same time began to study piano.

When Limón was 18, his mother died in childbirth, a tragedy that drove him away from the Catholic Church and his father, both of which he blamed for this devastating loss. After high school he studied painting briefly at the University of California, and then, at the urging of three "bohemian" friends, he moved to New York City in 1928 to study at the Art Students League. There he soon became disillusioned by the painting classes, believing that his classmates and teachers were merely imitating the French moderns. His vision was more influenced by El Greco, but he despaired of ever equaling his idol. By chance he attended a dance performance by German Expressionist Harald Kreutzberg and Yvonne Georgi, and knew immediately that he had to dance. He enrolled in classes at the Humphrey-Weidman School, where Doris Humphrey and Charles Weidman became his artistic mentors. Pauline Lawrence, who had left Denishawn at the same time as Doris and Charles, served as school registrar, tour manager, costume designer, stage manager, and accompanist for Humphrey-Weidman. These four lived communally for several years. Limón had become an earnest disciple of a revolutionary new art form, American modern dance. After very little training, he became a member of the company, performed in Broadway shows they choreographed, and began his own early choreographic efforts.

Limón's apprenticeship with Humphrey-Weidman lasted over 10 years, during which time he was increasingly featured in their concert work. His first choreographic efforts began early, and in 1930 he formed "The Little Group" with two women from the company, Eleanor King and Ernestine Henoch. The Humphrey-Weidman Company spent several summers at Bennington College, where Limón was named a Choreography Fellow in 1937. The following year he choreographed his first major work, *Danzas Mexicanas*, one of several dances he made that explored Mexican themes.

In 1940, disgusted with the triviality of commercialized Broadway dance, Limón left for the West Coast to form a duet company with former Graham dancer May O'Donnell, and her husband, composer Ray Green. They developed a repertory with a commitment to contemporary American music and themes. World War II had begun in Europe, and Limón suspected he would soon be drafted. In 1941 he married Pauline Lawrence, and the following year returned to New York, disappointed with what he considered the provincialism of the San Francisco public.

In New York he resumed his association with Doris Humphrey, and created *Chaconne in D Minor*, a solo set to music by Johann Sebastian Bach, to be performed on an all-Bach program that Humphrey was producing. In April 1943, he was drafted. While in the army he was able to continue choreographing and performing, in shows for the Special Services. On weekend leaves he began choreographing for a small company under Humphrey's artistic direction, which was a precursor of the José Limón Dance Company. With dancers Dorothy Bird and Beatrice Seckler, he created *Vivaldi Concerto in D Minor*, which premiered in 1945.

Doris Humphrey had retired from dance due to a hip injury and ended her long association with Charles Weidman; now she began to choreograph for the new company, with works that took advantage of her former protégé's exotic good looks and compelling stage presence. Among these works were *Lament for Ignacio Sánchez Mejías, Story of Mankind, Day on Earth, Night Spell, Ritmo Jondo*, and *Ruins and Visions*.

Limón invited Pauline Koner and Lucas Hoving to work with him, and returning to his Mexican heritage for inspiration, made *La Malinche* in 1949, with an original score by Norman Lloyd. The same year, with Hoving, Koner and Betty Jones, he created *The Moor's Pavane*, which John Martin, writing in the *New York Times*, called "a magnificent piece of dance theater. . .one of the major works in contemporary dance repertory." Based on the tragic story of Othello, and set to music by Henry Purcell, this choreographic masterpiece has been continuously performed by ballet and modern dance companies worldwide.

In 1950 the Limón company performed in Mexico City, prompting an invitation to Limón to establish a school and company there. He created several new works for the Ballet Mexicano including *El Grito, Quatros Soles*, and *Tonantzintla* in 1951, but returned to his company in New York, and a faculty position at the new Dance Department at the Juilliard School of Music, where he taught for the rest of his life.

The Limón company had been a chamber ensemble until this time, consisting of individual soloists, including Ruth Currier and Letitia Ide. His choreographic experience in Mexico, and his work with Juilliard students, now motivated him to explore the use of an ensemble. Working with a group of all male dancers, he created *The*

Traitor (1954), *Scherzo* (1955) and *The Emperor Jones* (1956). He worked with a mixed ensemble in *Symphony for Strings* (1955), *There Is a Time* (1956), *Missa Brevis* (1958), *A Choreographic Offering* (1964), *The Winged* (1966) and *Psalm* (1967). In addition to these company works, he was creating dances almost every year for the student ensemble at Juilliard.

Limón was best known as a choreographer who made dance dramas, often based on literary or biblical themes. Lucas Hoving, lanky, blond and suave, was a striking contrast to Limón, who used him as a dramatic counterpart, particularly in *The Moor's Pavane, Dialogues, The Traitor*, and *Emperor Jones*. Tiny, quick, and dramatic, Pauline Koner was his partner in many works, and in others he used the sweetly lyric dancing of Betty Jones and Ruth Currier to represent feminine attributes. The womanly Letitia Ide had a weighted power that complemented his size. In later years he began to value greater technical virtuosity, in dancers such as Sarah Stackhouse, Jennifer Muller, Louis Falco, and Carla Maxwell, creating dances that challenged their skills while maintaining the breadth and weight of his original movement style.

Mexican themes recur throughout his work, from *Danzas Mexicanas, La Malinche, Dialogues, Tonantzintla*, and *Los Quatros Soles* to later works, *The Unsung* (1970) and *Carlota* (1972). Among his literary influences were William Shakespeare and Eugene O'Neill; religious themes appear in *The Exiles, The Visitation, The Traitor, There Is a Time* and *Missa Brevis*, in which Limón's figure is set apart from the group, alternately appearing as a leader and a doubter.

Another important source of inspiration was the music of his favorite composers, resulting in pure movement pieces. These celebrations of the human spirit were made manifest through exultant dancing, intricate spatial designs, and sensitive musical phrasing. *A Choreographic Offering* (1964) is an outstanding example—dedicated to Doris Humphrey, its vocabulary is entirely derived from her choreography, and Limón crafted this material into a glorious tribute to his mentor. Other notable works that were musically inspired include *Chaconne in D Minor, Vivaldi Concerto in D Minor, Mazurkas* (Chopin, 1958), and the unfinished *Beethoven Sonatas*, a full-evening work he began in 1970. He was also intrigued with silence, which he incorporated into *There Is a Time* and *The Winged* (1966), and then used in three of his last four pieces, *The Unsung*, the final section of *Dances for Isadora* (1971) and *Carlota*.

Limón became a U.S. citizen in 1946, and a cultural ambassador for the government in 1954, when his company inaugurated the first State Department's Cultural Exchange Program with a tour of four South American cities. In 1957 the company was sent by the State Department on a five month tour of Europe, including "Iron Curtain" countries Poland and Yugoslavia, which were overwhelmingly receptive. The company returned to South America in 1960, to the Far East in 1963, and to the Soviet Union in 1973 several months after Limón's death, all under State Department sponsorship. Limón was a guest at the Kennedy White House in 1962, and performed *The Moor's Pavane* at a White House state dinner in 1967 for Lyndon Johnson and his guest, King Hassan II of Morocco.

Limón was diagnosed with prostate cancer in 1967. Pauline Lawrence Limón died of cancer in 1971, and Limón died a year later, on 2 December 1972. His company became the first to survive the death of its founder, and celebrated its 50th anniversary in 1997.

—Ann Vachon

LIN Hwai-min

Taiwanese choreographer, company director, writer, and dancer

Born: 19 February 1947 in Chiayi, Taiwan. **Education:** Participated in Chinese folk dance competitions in elementary school; ballet lessons with Ku Ya-shin, Taichung; attended modern dance classes with Al Chung-liang Huang, Chinese Dance Institute, Taipai, (founded by Tsai Rey-yueh), 1967; B.A. in journalism, National Cheng-chi University, Taipei, 1965-69; attended University of Missouri's graduate school of journalism; M.F.A., University of Iowa Writer's Workshop, 1970-72; dance classes with Marcia Thayer and Linda Lee, University of Iowa: studied at Martha Graham and Merce Cunningham dance schools, 1971-72; student of Chinese Opera with Yu ta-kang, and of Japanese and Korean classical dance forms. **Career:** Began publishing fiction works at 14; toured with University of Iowa's dance ensemble, and with Chinese choreographer Chiang Ching, early 1970s; taught English and Journalism, Cheng-chi University, 1972; taught dance, Chinese Culture University; founder/director, Cloud Gate Dance Theater, 1973-88; interpretor for Graham's Taiwan visit, 1974; founded dance department, and first chairperson, National Institute of the Arts (NIA), Taipei, 1983; co-founded Taipei Modern Dance Company, 1984; *Fifteen Year Retrospective*, held in Taipei, 1987; choreographed solo for dancer Lo Man-fei titled *Requiem*, in honor of the Tiananmen Incident student Chai Ling, 1989; Cloud Gate Dance Theater regrouped with performances at the National Theatre, Taipei, 1991; directed the world premiere of opera *Roshomon*, Graz Opera, Austria, 1996. **Awards:** National Arts Award for the choreography of *Legacy*, 1980; one of the 10 outstanding young persons in the world, Jaycees International, 1983; Wu Sanlien Arts Award for *Tale of the White Serpent*; Fulbright Scholar, 1990; Lifetime Achievement Award, New York City and Chinese American Council, 1996; fellowship, Hong Kong Academy of Performing Arts, 1997.

Works (performed by Cloud Gate Dance Theatre in Taipei unless otherwise noted)

1970   *Butterfly Dream* (mus. Chou Wen-chung), solo, Iowa
1971   *Landscape* (mus. Chou Wen-chung), Iowa
1973   *Autumn Melancholy* (mus. Shen Chin-tung)
      Summer Night (mus. Shih Wei-liang), Taichung, Taiwan
      Leisure (mus. Lai Te-ho), Taichung
      Blind (mus. Hsu Chang-hui), Taichung
      Wu Lung Yuan (mus. Hsu Po-yun), Taichung
      Mien [Sleep] (mus. Wen Lung-hsin), Taichung
      Movement (mus. Lee Tai-hsiang), Taichung
      Revenge of the Lonely Ghost (mus. Shih Wei-liang), Taichung
1974   *Han Shih* (mus. Hsu Po-yun)
      No Cha (mus. Hsu Po-yun)
1975   *Tale of the White Serpent* (mus. Lai Te-ho), Singapore
      Phenomenon (mus. Wen Lung-hsin)
      The Hair Tree (mus. Fan Man-nung, Tsai Su-yu, Lin Hwai-min)
      One More Clear Night (mus. Ma Shui-long)
1976   *Wu Sung Kills the Tiger* (no music)
      Little Drummer (mus. Shih-Wei-liang)
      Two Slaps (no music)
      Vivaldi (mus. Vivaldi)
      Looking Forward (mus. traditional Nan-kuan)
      Wu Feng (mus. Lee Tai-hsiang)

1977   *The Red Twine* (mus. Doming Lam)
      Love Poem (mus. Kau Chin)
      Sun Pursuer (mus. Hsu Po-yun)
      Days by the Sea (mus. Wen Lung-hsin)
1978   *Legacy* (mus. Chen Da, Chen Yang, Lee Tai-hsiang), Chiayi, Taiwan
1979   *Liao tien-ting* (mus. Ma Shui-long)
      Nu Wa (mus. Lee Tai-hsiang)
1980   *After Paul Taylor* (mus. Handel), Taichung
1981   *Pas de Deux* (mus. Lai Te-ho)
      Milky Way (mus. Wang Chen-ping)
      Song of the Earth (mus. Lai Te-ho)
1982   *Prelude* (mus. Scriabin), solo
      Souvenir Photo (voices of Taiwanese aborigines and friends), solo
      Smoke (no. mus.), solo
      Solo x3 (mus. Glass), solo
      I am a Man (mus. Taiwanese pop), solo
      To Wei Chingsen (mus. Lizst), solo
      Street Game (mus. traditional Sri Lankan), City Contemporary Dance Company, Hong Kong
      Nirvana (mus. T. Mayuzumi), Paris
      Sheng Ming (mus. Lee Tai-hsiang)
1983   *Dream of the Red Chamber* (mus. Lai Te-ho)
1984   *Aspirin Fantasy*, Taipei Modern Dance Company
      The Scrapbook, Taipei Modern Dance Company
      Who Truly Understands Me?, Taipei Modern Dance Company
      Mama, why can't I dance Swan Lake?, Taipei Modern Dance Company
      The Last Waltz, Taipei Modern Dance Company
      Rite of Spring (mus. Stravinvsky), Tainan
      Bamboo Concerto (mus. Ma Shui-long)
      Adagietto (mus. Mahler), Tainan
      Summer 1984, Taipei (mus. Keith Jarrett), Kaoshiung, Taiwan
1985   *Dreamscape* (mus. Hsu Po-yun)
1986   *My Nostalgia, My Songs* (mus. arr. by Chang Chao-tang)
      Peacock Variation (mus. Ko Ta-yi)
1987   *Four Seasons* (mus. Vivaldi)
1989   *Requiem* (mus. Liszt)
1991   *Fortune Number Cards and Change of Costumes* (mus. Joseph Reiser)
      The River (mus. Hung Chien-Hui)
1992   *Shooting the Sun* (mus. Lee Tai-hsiang)
1993   *Nine Songs* (mus. Ju Percussion Group and various indigenous)
1994   *Fragrance of the Rice*
      Songs of the Wanderers (mus. Georgian folk)
1995   *Symphony of Lament*
1997   *Portrait of the Families* (mus. traditional Taiwanese, storytelling)
1998   *White* (mus. Stephen Scott), Taipei Crossover Dance Company

Publications

By LIN: book—

Translation of Jean-Claude Carriere's *Mahabarata*—the script (after the English translation by Peter Brook), Taipei, 1990.

By LIN: articles—

"Ch'an," *Cicada*, Taipei, 1974.
"Shuo wu," *On Dance*, Taipei, 1989.
"Tsa chien er kuo," *Brief Encounters*, Taipei, 1989.
"Tsuan chuan nao ho shuo gio go," *About Nine Songs*, co-authored with Hsu Kai-chen and Chi Hui-ling, Taipei, 1993.

On LIN: articles—

Cloud Gate Dance Foundation, "Yun-men kuai-men er-shi," *Cloud Gate at Twenty Photo Album*, Taipei, 1993.
Yu Kuang-chung et al., "Yun-men wu hua," *Cloud Dance Commentaries*, 3rd edition, Taipei, 1993.

* * *

Founded in 1973, Cloud Gate Dance Theatre is the oldest and most well-known professional dance company from Taiwan. Named after one of the earliest dances recorded in Chinese history, it's the first modern dance company to be founded among the whole pan-Chinese community. Its artistic director, Lin Hwai-min, is the leading force behind this company. At a time when dance as an artistic profession was still nonexistent in Taiwan, through his tireless efforts in professionalizing dance, developing audiences, and revolutionizing its related environment including stage management, arts administration, music commissioning, stage and costume design, etc. with a core group of people such as impresario and composer Hsu Po-yun, arts policy maker and theatre director Wu Ching-jye, Lin created a tremendous impact on the majority of choreographers, dancers, and performing artists active in Taiwan today. Functioning under the Cloud Gate Dance Foundation, the company also holds dance classes and is expanding to establish a second company to help foster young choreographic talents. Through their extensive tours of Taiwan, as well as the international tours to North America, Europe, Asia, and Australia, Cloud Gate made Taiwan visible in nations where its official status was no longer recognized. In other words, the ambassadorial contributions of this company cannot be overestimated.

Cloud Gate's influence on the dance scene in Taiwan today is also insurmountable; one could easily trace the roots of Taiwan's current leading dance companies back to this patriarchal one. For example, first generation Cloud Gate founding dancer Liou Shaw-lu left in 1984 to form Taipei Dance Circle with his wife, Yang Wan-rung, also a former Cloud Gate dancer for a brief period of time. Principal dancer Lin Hsiu-wei also founded Tai Gu Tales Dance Theatre in 1989. Other founding members Cheng Shu-gi, Wu Shu-jun, and Yeh Tai-chu, along with another Cloud Gate principal dancer Lo Man-fei have formed their own company, the Taipei Crossover Dance Company in 1994. Furthermore, through founding the Dance Department of the National Institute of the Arts in 1983, and later the first graduate program in dance in Taiwan in 1993, many established dancers of the younger generation also came under Lin Hwai-min's tutelage.

In terms of the choreography presented by Cloud Gate, although the majority have mainly consisted of Lin Hwai-min's own works, other artists' pieces have also been showcased. Earlier in the 1970s, many of the dancers would present their own works alongside, or even create a full evening of their own when Lin was engaged with other appointments abroad. Gradually, other local and international artists were also invited to collaborate, including Lin Li-jen, Chen Wei-chen, and Ku Ming-shen of Taiwan, Helen Lai of Hong Kong, as well as reconstructions of Doris Humphrey, Paul Taylor, and other contemporary Western artists. Regarding Lin's personal style, his œuvre of over 60 dances has also undergone significant changes through the decades. The first stage of Lin's work consisted of blending Graham technique, Peking opera-style movement, with Chinese myths and narratives, best represented by *Tale of a White Serpent* (1975). His next stage is evident in his signature piece, *Legacy* (1979), an epic dance-drama depicting the immigration history and hardship of the pioneers from the mainland China to Taiwan roughly 300 years ago, with dance vocabulary, music, and visual design based on Taiwanese aesthetics. The third stage consisted of works reflecting cosmopolitan settings, such as an adaption of *The Rite of Spring* danced to the Stravinsky score, but with the dancers portraying frantic youths of urban Taipei, the capital of Taiwan.

Between 1988 to 1991, Cloud Gate underwent a hiatus for nearly three years. During this period, many members went to the U.S. to either obtain graduate degrees or simply to get "re-charged." Lin Hwai-min for example, took up a Fulbright scholarship to New York University's department of performance studies in 1990, and also traveled extensively in India and Bali. After the regrouping of Cloud Gate, Lin's choreographic style again shifted, vastly shaped by his search for a spiritual belief in Buddhism and his travels in Asia. *Nine Songs* (1993) can be seen as a confluence of Tibetan, Indian, Indonesian, Japanese, Chinese and the indigenous cultures of Taiwan in terms of movement, music, and the visual design of the work. Advertised as the company's 20th anniversary commemoration, it marked a successful collaboration with well-known Chinese-American stage designer Ming-cho Lee, who also partnered with Lin for Cloud Gate's 10th anniversary evening-length program, *Dream of the Red Chamber* (1983). The following year, Lin presented *Songs of the Wanderers* (1994), with the theme focusing on religious pilgrimages and quests for spiritual gratification. In general, his movement vocabulary softened and the tempo slowed, a sharp contrast to the tensely bound and energetic segments of "Crossing the Black Water" from *Legacy*, the most frequently performed excerpt by Lin, Labanotated by Ray Cook, and reconstructed by dance departments of SUNY—Purchase in the States and Hong Kong's Academy of Performing Arts. In *Portraits of the Families* (1997), innumerable recently unearthed family portraits of various ethnic groups of Taiwan were projected gigantically on stage. Dancing bodies moved to the recorded interviews of people speaking of personal histories in their various dialects. Lin's background in journalism and fiction writing, as well as his long-term concern for the people of Taiwan and their fate under the tumultuous political and social upheavals through history, moves to the foreground, reflecting the deeply felt responsibility of this artist.

—Yatin C. Lin

LINKE, Susanne

German dancer, choreographer, educator, and company director

Born: 1944 in Lueneburg, Germany. **Education:** Studied with Mary Wigman, Berlin, 1964-67; attended Folkwangschule, Essen, 1967-70. **Career:** First choreography, 1970; dancer, Folkwang

Susanne Linke: *Jardincour,* **1988. Photograph © Beatriz Schiller.**

Tanzstudio, until 1973; co-director with Reinhild Hoffman, Folkwang Tanzstudio, 1975-77; sole director, 1977-85; director, Bremer Tanztheater, from 1994; choreographer-in-residence, Hebbel Theater, Berlin, 1994; artistic director, Choreographic Center NRW, Essen, 1996.

Works

1970	*Mono* (mus. Buring-Kakatus), Essen
1971	*Trio* (mus. Man), Essen
1973	*Habe die Ehre. . .zum Ball* (mus. Carlos), Essen
1975	*Danse funèbre* (mus. Mahler), Essen
	Puppe (mus. Mozart), Essen
	Trop tard (mus. Bosseur), Essen
1976	*Der Tod und das Maedchen* (mus. Schubert), Essen
	De la nuit à l'aube (mus. Brahms), Pont-à-Mousson
1977	*Warten Sie auch?* (mus. environmental), Essen
	Ach Unsinn (mus. various), Essen
	Satie (mus. Satie), Essen

1978	*Wandlung* (mus. Schubert), Heidelberg
	L'Histoire obscure (mus. Carlos), Essen
	Die Naechste bitte (mus. popular), Essen
	Ballade (mus. Modern Jazz Quartet), Essen
1980	*Im Bade wannen* (mus. Satie), Essen
	Wowerwiewas (mus. various), Essen
1981	*Frauenballett* (mus. Penderecki), Essen
	Flut (mus. Fauré), Essen
1982	*Es schwant . . .*(mus. Tchaikovsky), Essen
	Wir koennen nicht alle nur Schwaene sein (mus. Tchaikovsky), Essen
1983	*Am Reigenplatz* (mus. Ligeti), Muenchen
1984	*Orient-Okzident* (mus. Xenakis), Essen
1985	*Schritte verfolgen* (mus. Behne), Berlin
1986	*Also Egmont, bitte* (mus. Beethoven), New York
1987	*Affectos humanos* (mus. Wiatowisch, Mahler), Berlin
	Dolor, Hommage à Dore Hoyer (mus. Mahler), Berlin
1988	*Jardin Cour* (mus. various), Paris
	Affekte (mus. various), Paris

1990	*Effekte* (mus. various), Velbert
1991	*Ruhr-Ort* (mus. Bruemmer), Leverkusen
1992	*Tristan und Isolde* (mus. Wagner, Bruemmer), Den Haag
1993	*Dialog mit G.B.* (mus. Cage, Dietrich), Berlin
	Tu-Wa-Ga (mus. rock), Essen
1994	*Amasti Mai?* (mus. Bellini), Amsterdam
	Dialog I + II (mus. Cage, Pärt), Ferrara
	MaerkischeLandschaft (mus. Hollinger), Berlin
	Da war ploetzlich ... - Herzkammern (mus. Korr), Berlin
1996	*Hamletszenen* (mus. Steckel), Bremen
	Heisse Luft (mus. Bley-Borkowski), Bremen
1997	*Verstrickungen*, Bremen

Publications

Schlicher, Susanne, *Tanztheater: Traditionen und Freiheiten*, Hamburg, 1987.

Schmidt, Jochen, *Tanztheater in Deutschland,* Frankfurt am Main, 1992.

Sieben Irene, "I Don't Know if I Am Controllable," *Ballet International/tanz aktuell*, March 1994.

Films and Videotapes

Susanne Linke, Internationes 2710 and 2714, Charles Picq, L'Ina/Agat Films, 1991 and 1992 respectively.

*　　*　　*

As a small child Susanne Linke suffered from meningitis which resulted in brain damage, leaving her unable to speak until she was six years old. It's an experience that was profoundly isolating but also encouraged Linke to express herself nonverbally, through gesture and dance. A chance encounter at the age of 16 with the Expressionist dancer Dore Hoyer, inspired her to pursue dance professionally and to study with Mary Wigman in Berlin, and she was in the last group of students who graduated from the Wigman school. Linke can be considered a direct descendant of the prewar German *Ausdruckstanz* which strongly emphasized the development of an authentic vocabulary by searching for the motivation behind movement. "Dance," Linke has said, "is the expression in movement of what moves us inside." While her dances may have their genesis in personal experience or observation, she always pushes them into broadly human concerns.

Both Wigman and Hoyer embraced solo dances, and Linke has become best known in this dance form as well. Before starting a career as an independent choreographer in 1985, she produced a series of smaller works for the Folkwang Tanzstudio of which she had become director, after having graduated from the Folkwang school. In addition to crediting Pina Bausch for having encouraged her to choreograph, Linke says that Wigman showed her the "why" of dancing and the Folkwang training gave her the "how."

Linke made her first impact with a series of solos with strongly feminist overtones. While these works are imagistic in a way similar to other artists of the postwar Tanztheater, of which she is considered a leading practitioner, her work is also more rhythmically supple and more solidly grounded in movement. Linke often explores the loneliness, frustration, and sense of emptiness inherent in some women's lives. While many of these pieces are emotionally wrenching, Linke's touch can also be ironic and light as in one of her later works, *Heisse Luft* (1996), in which she skewers the power of arbitrary fashion ideals to which women submit themselves.

A Linke piece often starts out with Sisyphusian task gestures that then open, flower-like, into expansive dance sequences. Props whose meaning can change from one move to the next are used as conduits for change. Fabric, for instance, as a tactile, malleable material plays an important role metaphorically and in set design. In 1981's *Frauenballett*, three women, and one man dressed as a woman, measure and stretch seemingly unending lengths of fabric; in *Flut* Linke rolls and unrolls a bolt of blue cloth; in *Heisse Luft* personalities are created with yard goods. But ordinary household objects also hold untold attraction: in *Im Bade wannen* a woman obsessively scrubs a bathtub which becomes both a refuge and a prison, an object of beauty and one of disdain; in *Schritte verfolgen* she moves a table inch-by-inch by beating her body against it; the table is at any one time needed support, an enemy, a coffin, and an agent of liberation. *Schritte verfolgen*, her first full-evening solo, is a strongly autobiographical piece in which Linke traces her evolution from an imprisoned child into a dancer through the metaphor of learning to walk. From halting, unbalanced steps in a nightgown and felt boots, dragging herself along a barre, attempting tiptoes and timid arabesques (while a snow of white feathers wafts down on her), she gradually metamorphoses into an open-bodied swanlike modern woman.

Susanne Linke, 1989. Photograph © Beatriz Schiller.

Affectos humanos is a reconstruction of parts of Hoyer's 1962 eponymous piece in which the older dancer had explored vanity, greed, fear, love, and pain as basic human emotions. It's a piece of sharply chiseled and finely detailed vignettes, each with its own gestural vocabulary. Linke chose to reconstruct the first four sections only, re-choreographing the last, "Dolor" in which she appears as an aged but proud and undefeated Hoyer. It is a direct homage to her mentor and friend. A year later Linke created *Affekte* in which she set the same five emotions as a duet, for herself and partner Urs Dietrich. In this work, though nominally a duo, the two dancers only come in contact with each other through a violent confrontation (in "Fear") which turns the subsequent section ("Love") into "erotic gymnastics." As Schmidt describes the work in his comprehensive *Tanztheater in Deutschland*, both partners attempt to find comfort with each other but at the same time want to remain responsive to the externally imposed requirements for virtuosic movement.

Linke's full-length *Ruhr-Ort* is a consummately successful homage to the blue collar workers in Germany's aging steel industry and is her strongest piece of group choreography yet. Set on three dancers and three actors, *Ruhr-Ort* realistically depicts the physically grueling, and at times demeaning lives of working men (three dancers and three actors) whose days are controlled by the clock and the lunch bucket. If in the solo works she explored the world of women, often housewives, *Ruhr-Ort* is male with a vengeance, but also compassion. Linke created repetitive machinelike movements in which the performers swing real 35-pound sledgehammers (turning into fishing rods or male accouterments); lug 80-pound blocks of steel (to metamorphose into tombstones); run in place, going nowhere while beating out interlocking rhythms with their steel-clad boots; a shower and a set of clean clothes is about as close to transcendence as these men ever get. *Ruhr-Ort* is a mature, complex piece of craftsmanship that resonates with truth and poetry on an unlikely subject.

Maerkische Landschaft, inspired by the conflict between East and West Germans, is another all-male, strongly percussive work in which through the male psyche Linke explores human complexity and power relationships. People, she seems to say, on one hand want to be whole and integrated and yet they have an equally strong propensity toward disunity, even fratricide. Linke's complex vision of internal and external power relationships at its best, makes hers an eloquent commentary on warring forces within the individual and within society.

—Rita Felciano

LIPPINCOTT, Gertrude

American dancer, choreographer, educator, and writer

Born: 29 June 1913, St. Paul, Minnesota. **Education:** Attended University of Chicago, one year; studied dance with Marion Van Tuyl; graduated with a B.A. from University of Minnesota, magna cum laude and Phi Beta Kappa, 1935; student, Bennington School of the Dance, summers 1937-38; student, Martha Graham studio in New York, 1939; earned M.A. in Dance from New York University, 1943. **Family:** Married Benjamin Evans Lippincott, 1934. **Career:** Debut in Young Dancers Audition series, New York, 1944; assistant professor of dance, Mt. Holyoke College, 1943-46;

ran the dance center at the Minneapolis YWCA, 1949-57; assistant dance professor, Mills College, while her husband was at Stanford University, 1953; founder, Committee on Research in Dance, 1965 (later Congress on Research in Dance); adjunct professor of theatre, University of Minnesota, 1965-72. **Awards:** Auditions Award from the 92nd Street YWHA, New York City, 1944; choreographic awards from the Choreographers' Workshop (92nd Street YM-YWHA), 1948, 1949; Copper Foot Award, Wayne State University, 1964; Heritage Award from AAPHERD National Conference in Minneapolis, 1973; Distinguished Teachers Award, American Dance Guild in 1974; Founding Fellow Award from the National Council for the Arts in Education; National Retired Teachers Award, American Dance Guild; citation, Distinguished Service to Dance in the Twin Cities, Minneapolis Jewish Community Center, 1979; Outstanding Achievement Award from the University of Minnesota, 1982. **Died:** 2 June 1996.

Roles

1937   *Experiment in Dance with Choral Accompaniment* w/Jean Erdman and Barabara Mettler, Bennington Summer School, Vermont
1938   Dancer, *Ode to Freedom* (Eleanor King), Bennington College, Vemront
1941   The ballet girl, *Jim Dandy* (William Saroyan), University of Minnesota (UM)

Works (all works premiered in Minneapolis, unless otherwise noted)

1937   *Circular Motion* w/Ruth Hatfield and Lillian Zaret
1938   *Negro Lament* (included song *I Ain't Gonna Study War No More*), Walker Art Gallery
        Musica (mus. Cowell), Bennington, Vermont
        That Spanish Children May Not Die, Walker Art Gallery
        Dance of the Dictator
1939   *A Minnesota Saga: To Minnesota, Dance of the Indian Women and the French Voyageurs, Dance of the Immigrants, Dance of the Workers* w/Ruth Hatfield, (mus. M. Roberts, text by Meridel Le Sueur), St. Paul, Minnesota
        The Negro in American Life: And We Came to American Soil, We Gave Our Labor, We Worshipped God with our Songs and We Played, We Are Americans, Too) performed for St. Paul International Institute Folk Festival, St. Paul
        Anti-Fascist Chant (text by Meridel Le Sueur)
1940   *Five Negro Women in Nostalgia or History,* St. Paul
        Diary from Europe, St. Paul
        American Scenes (text by Meridel Le Sueur; mus. by M. Robertson)
1941   *The City* w/Ruth Hatfield
        Kentucky Mountains (with six company members)
        Lament from the South (for her African-American dancers)
        Song of the Range (solo)
        Diary from Europe, Episodes in the Lives of Those Who Live Under the Shadow of the Ever-Spreading Conflict
        Premonition of Disaster
        Panic-1941
        Oppression

Pavane for Our Time (mus. M. Roberts)

Deep River

Working Girls: Good Morning America, Noon Hour, Shovel Man, Fish Crier, I am the Negro, I Shall Look for You, I am the People, Good Night America w/ Althea Berglin, Natalie Goldner, Sophie Zwiaska, Rosie Edman, Betty Rohling, Edith Sonnenschein, and Catherine Johnson (poetry by Carl Sandburg), program for the International Ladies Garment Workers Union

NBC Calling Europe

Goddess of the Moon (commissioned score by Louis Horst)

The People Is Everyman, Everybody (poetry by Carl Sandburg)

Lament from the South

1942 *Pierrot Lunaire* (mus. Schönberg)

1944 *Burdensome Blues* (mus. Norman Lloyd)

1945 *Proverbs of a People* (text Carl Sandburg), Mt. Holyoke College, Massachusetts

1946 *Hot Sunday* (mus. Horst), 92nd Street YM-YWHA, New York

Invitacion (commissioned, Horst), Cornell, New York

The Devil Is Loneliness (mus. Nowack), Colorado State College, Fort Collins, Colorado

A Time for Tears (mus. Freda Miller), Cornell, New York

1947 *Dance of Dedication* (mus. Nowack), 92nd Street YM-YWHA, New York

La Danse des Mortes (commissioned, Horst)

Ki Yipee Yay (commissioned, Horst), Superior State College, Wisconsin

1948 *Deidre of the Sorrows* (commissioned, Henry Cowell, text John M. Synge), University of North Dakota

Summer Reveille, Baton Rouge, Louisiana

1949 *Madman's Wisp—An Ancient Irish Curse* (commissioned, Cowell)

La Danse Des Morts (included *Death and the Abbess*), (mus. Horst), 92nd Street YM-YWHA, New York

1950 *A Full Moon In March* (mus. Cowell), North Dakota Agricultural College

Love-Quickened Heart (commissioned, Horst)

1951 *Just We Two* (text Wiliam Steig)

Nightpiece (mus. P. Hindemith), YWCA in Minneapolis

Ruth (mus. Frederick Jacobi)

If Love Were Love (mus. Horst), 92nd Street YM-YWHA, New York

1952 *Goddess of the Moon* (mus. Horst), Oberlin College, Ohio

If Love Were Love (mus. Horst), 92nd Street YM-YWHA, New York

Proverbs of a People (text Sandburg)

L'Histoire du Soldat (mus. Tchaikovsky), sponsored by International Society for Contemporary Music, University of Minnesota

1953 *The Wild, Wild Woman* (text by Virgil Partch), Mills College, California

Three Excursions for Dancer and Pianist (mus. S. Barber), Mills College

Fantasque (choreographed with Eleanor Lauer; mus. B. Bartók), Mills College

Duo w/Eleanor Lauer (mus. F. Miller), Mills College

Nightpiece w/Lauer (mus. P. Hindemith), Mills College

1954 *Madonna della Rosa* (mus. Molinaro)

1955 *Echoes of Erin* (mus. Cowell)

Madonna Della Rosa

Will You Won't You Join the Dance: A Parable of Death (mus. Lucas Foss), Muncie, Indiana

1956 *Lost Love* (mus. Klein)

1957 *Wanderers on the Earth, Lost in a Past Life* (mus. Schönberg, Russell Walsch, text from James Joyce's *Ulysses*)

Mater Dolorosa: In Honor of Doris Humphrey (mus. Villa Lobos)

1958 *Tree of Sins* (mus. Esther Ballou)

Something Lies Beyond the Scene (text from Edith Sitwell's *Facade*)

Three Rituals (mus. Chavey), St. Paul

1959 *Requiem: In Memory of Doris Humphrey* (mus. R. Walsh), Women's Club

1960 *Excursions for Dancers and Pianist* (mus. Samuel Barber), Northern State Teacher's College, Aberdeen, South Dakota

Faces of Women (mus. Cowell), University of Oregon

Capriccio (mus. Darius Milhaud), Memphis State University, Louisiana

Tragic Lullaby

Dance of the Quick and Dead (mus. Schönberg)

1961 *Hymn of Praise* (originally titled *Tuesday's Child Is Full of Grace*), (mus. Cowell), Ball State University, Muncie, Indiana

Decoration Day (mus. Charles Ives), Town Hall, Provincetown, Massachusetts

Sea Drift (mus. D. Jahn), Town Hall, Provincetown

1962 *Creatures of Night* (mus. Bartók), Wisconsin State College, River Falls, Wisconsin

Sweet Spring (mus. A. Vivaldi), River Falls, Wisconsin

1963 *In a Salem Graveyard*

1964 *Portraits From Facade* (mus. P. Spong), Rackham Auditorium, Detroit

Homage to Horst (mus. C. Ives), Rackham Auditorium, Detroit

Publications

By LIPPINCOTT: books—

Aesthetics and the Dance, New York, 1943.

Editor, Dance Production, Washington, D.C., 1956.

By LIPPINCOTT: articles—a selection from over 100 published articles.

Journal of Health, Physical Education, Recreation and Dance: "The Function of the Teacher in Modern Dance Composition" (1945), "An Open Letter to Dance Educators" (1947), "Choreography for the Non-Professional Dance Group" (1948), "Improvisation in Techniques and Composition" (1958), "The Theory of Making Dances" (1960), "When Culture Goes to College" (1967).

Dance Observer: August-September 1946, "Pilgrim's Way," April 1947, "Some Problems in the Education of Dance Teachers," May 1947, "Book Review of Dance Memoranda by Merle Armitage," May 1947, "The Commonwealth of Art," January 1946, "An Experiment in Negro Modern Dance," 1947, "The Question of

College Dance Performances," March 1954, "Dance in the Round, Report of an Experiment in Spectator Participation," 1957, "The Use of Space in Dance and Architecture," 1959, "A Tribute to Louis Horst," 1963, "Alice in Wonderland: on Avant-Garde Dance."

Dance Magazine: 1947, "Will Modern Dance Become a Legend?," 1948, "Some Reflections on the Use of the Middle Body," 1948, "An Open Letter to Dance Educators," 1949, "The Relentless Road."

Focus on Dance: 1960, "A Conversation with Margaret H'Doubler," *Focus on Dance VIII,* "A Vocabulary for Modern Dance?," *Focus on Dance X,* "Louis Horst, a Quiet Genius Himself."

Dance Scope: 1965, "A Bright Future for the Dance," 1970, "Out of Old Contexts into New."

Impulse: 1952, "Economic Dilemma of a Concert Dancer," 1953, "The Case for a Master Lesson," 1957, "Contemporary Dance for the Young," 1965, "Report on Arts in Education and Government."

On LIPPINCOTT: articles—

Ingber, Judith Brin, "Gertrude Lippincott and the Development of Dance in Minneapolis," *Proceedings Society of Dance History Scholars, Joint Conference with the CORD,* New York Public Library for the Performing Arts, June 1993.

*   *   *

Lippincott grew up in Minnesota and made her name as the first modern dancer of note there. Her curiosity to study dance led her far from Minnesota and because of the places and people she chose to study and work with, and her artistry, her influence became national in scope. Her father, professor of dentistry at the university, and her sculptor mother urged her to artistic and academic excellence—she graduated magna cum laude from the University of Minnesota, studied one year at the University of Chicago under noted dance educator Marion van Tuyl and eventually went on for a masters in dance, an unusual degree at the time. While still an undergraduate, she married Benjamin Evans Lippincott, professor of political science at the University of Minnesota. His liberal, democratic political ideas influenced her and he was an unflagging moral and financial supporter of her art. His teaching stints at Oxford University in England, and at Stanford in California afforded her many new experiences to enhance her dance. In 1936 she was able to attend the International Dance Congress in Germany and the Olympics, where she saw Laban's dance exhibitions for the Third Reich. Professor Lippincott urged her to study at the now celebrated Bennington School of Dance in the summers of 1937 and 1938, where she met artists, writers, and photographers who proved to be lifelong associates.

She created the first modern dance group and school in Minneapolis, called the Modern Dance Center, in 1937. In her unpublished memoirs and scrapbooks housed at the Minnesota Historical Society one can see the 4 June 1939 column by John Martin for the *New York Times* called "The Dance Roots Afield." He summarized the sum total of American modern dance activity including events in Philadelphia, Chicago, Detroit, Boston, Baltimore, and New England as well as Minneapolis. "The Modern Dance group has just completed its second season ... gave a score of performances, lectures and demonstrations. The group has a lay guild besides its professional company and has sponsored exhibitions of dance pho-

tographs, drawings and books and percussion instruments. That is as far west as the record extends at the moment."

The Modern Dance Center and its company became one of the very first racially integrated performing groups in the country. Lippincott spoke of the difficulty of booking hotels on tour and described her system of going into hotels to register and prepay, and only then bringing in her dancers of color. By 1941, Lippincott's audiences of mainly Scandinavian and German ethnic Minnesotans were looking at an unusual group: Jewish and African American dancers, plus Italian Tony Charmoli and several others including the striking political writer Meridel Le Sueur, whose dramatic appearance was enhanced by traces of her American Indian heritage in her features.

Le Sueur's frankly communist views and the fact that she was the best known of the porlitariat protest women writers caused some controversy, but Lippincott was stimulated by working with her; Le Sueur's written texts in several of the pieces were significant; they helped to shape Lippincott's dances and the writer herself added considerably to the drama during the performance because of Le Sueur's own style and remarkable stage presence. *A Minnesota Saga* was her first serious project with a script by Le Sueur, to honor 100 years of the city of Minneapolis. Le Sueur and Lippincott shared concerns for the working women and minorities and in efforts to spread an interest in modern dance, their goals were united as performers and creators. In the winter of 1937 they set out in three cars to perform in Virginia, Minnesota, and Lippincott wrote that "it was so cold, we had to wrap our legs in newspapers, but Meridel kept up our spirits."

Lippincott spent the years during World War II in New York and Massachusetts, while her professor husband was stationed in the Far East. Her favorite teacher from Bennington was Doris Humphrey, and Lippincott studied choreography with Humphrey and also worked in her Choreography Group. Three times she performed in New York's prestigious modern dance venue of the 92nd Street YM-YWHA as an audition winner in their acclaimed series. She also completed her master's degree at New York University under Martha Hill (whom she had also known at Bennington). She also deepened her rapport with Louis Horst, studying with him and then commissioning him to compose several works for her choreography. She ran the dance program at Mount Holyoke College during this period.

Even after her return to Minnesota, she continued her national connections. Her interest in her Irish background saw her commissioning music by Henry Cowell which resulted in four dances: *Echoes of Erin, Deirdre of the Sorrows, Madman's Wisp* and *Full Moon in March.* By January 1951 she was listed as one of Louis Horst's *Dance Observer* magazine editors. She remained on the masthead of that important dance publication through 1960.

In different dance seasons from the late 1930s to the 1960 she created Minnesota companies such as the Modern Dance Group, the Studio Dance Group, the Dance Trio (Lippincott, Eunice Cain and Robert Moulton), the Dance Repertory Group (1957-62), and the Dance Duo. According to her unpublished memoirs she gave 107 concerts in 21 states plus Washington D.C., 72 master classes in 22 states crisscrossing America to over 250 colleges and universities. Oftentimes she drew on her connections to colleagues from Bennington and her New York years as well as colleagues in national dance organizations. She established a very special performing partnership with Robert Moulton for some 15 years; they toured as a duo and he was also part of her groups. In addition to performing with her, he created many of her unusual costumes

including a hand painted black suit on white for himself with matching skirt with blouse, also black on white, with matching miniature
hats. Their programs were known for their contemporary American music, their well honed, crafted and original pieces with humor
and a wide range of subject matter. (Her dance speeches were also
articulate and witty; one of her favorite stories of her travels retold
her performance at the Provincetown, Massachusetts, Town Hall
which was interrupted when a convict from the basement jail escaped and zigzagged through the dancers trying to avoid the police
running across the stage). Moulton brought her to the University of
Minnesota Theater Department, where he had become a full professor, arranging for her to teach from 1965-72 as an adjunct professor.

In addition to choreographing, teaching and performing, Lippincott
became a writer and editor of dance articles. She also helped to
develop many of the national dance organizations and firmly believed in the importance of united action to further dance in America.
which she served as board member, founder, editor or director, as
well as financial supporter. She remarked in her article "History or
Nostalgia?" that as a young faculty wife some relatives and friends
disapproved of her, but teachers and loyal colleagues and "the
moral and financial support of my husband kept me going at a time
when there was no Women's Liberation Movement, few dance organizations, no national Endowment of the Arts, no state and local
umbrella arts groups and very little overt support for dance." She
obviously wanted to change the climate, was a national adjudicator
for the American College Dance Festival, a founder of the Congress
on Research in Dance (CORD), board member of the American
Dance Guild, the AAPHPERD organization and the Soceity of
Dance History Scholars.

She remained loyal to the University of Minnesota, and directed her estate, after her death, to give the Department of
Theater Arts and Dance a gift in excess of $500,000. She also
funded the completion of the Louis Horst and Felix Fibich components of the Oral History Project at the Dance Collection of
the Performing Arts Library at the New York Public Library,
and made significant contributions to the Society of Dance History Scholars, creating the annual Gertrude Lippincott Award
for the best English language article on dance history or theory.
She also underwrote their monograph, "Studies in Dance History." Her ongoing interest in supporting modern dance and enhancing it for audiences also resulted in her funding a lecture
series on contemporary dance at Walker Art Center in Minneapolis, following her death, called the Gertrude Lippincott Talking Dancing Series.

—Judith Brin Ingber

LITZ, Katherine
American dancer, choreographer, and actress

Born: c. 1912 in Denver, Colorado. **Education:** Studied dance in
Denver with Martha Wilcox and later, in New York, with Doris
Humphrey and Charles Weidman. **Family:** Married American
painter Charles Oscar, c. 1947. **Career:** Created roles in Humphrey's
New Dance (1935), *Theatre Piece* (1936), *With My Red Fires* (1936),
and *Song of the West* (1940); also created roles in Weidman's *Opus
51* (1938) and *Flickers* (1941); danced on Broadway in Agnes de

Mille's groundbreaking *Oklahoma!* (1943) and *Carousel* (1945);
contributed *Susannah and the Elders* to *Ballet Ballads,* 1948; choreographic debut, 92nd Street YMHA, 1948. **Died:** 19 December
1978 in New York City.

Works

1948	*Impressions of Things Past*
	How I Wasted Time and Now Time Doth Waste Me
1949	*Four Studies*
	Daughter of Virtue
	Suite for a Woman
1950	*Blood of the Lamb*
1951	*All Desire Is Sad*
	Songs of Joy
	That's Out of Season
	Three Women
	Celebrations
	Pastorale
	One Death to a Customer
	The Glyph
1952	*Chorales for Spring*
	Twilight of a Flower
	Bound by House and Kin
1953	*Super Duper Jet Girl*
1954	*Madame Bender's Dancing School*
	Excursion
	The Lure
	Summer Cloud
	The Story of Love from Fear to Flight
1956	*The Enchanted*
	Summer Idyl w/Ray Harrison
	Intrigue w/Ray Harrison
	Archie and Mehitabel w/Harrison
1958	*Courting the Spell* w/Harrison
	In Terms of Time w/Harrison
	Prologue w/Harrison
	The Last Gasp of Love's Latest Breath w/Harrison
1959	*Dracula*
	The Fall of the Leaf
	And No Bird's Sing
1961	*Transitions*
1963	*Poetry in Motion* w/Paul Taylor
1964	*What's the Big Idea 321*
	Sell Out
	To Be Continued
1965	*Fatima*
	Continuum
	Solo with People
1968	*Stop, Look and Listen I'm Not Just a Number*
	Sermon
1969	*Harangue and Inner Thoughts*
	Adaptations V
	Fandango
	Big Sister
	Evolutions
1970	*Adaptations XI*
1971	*The Dress*
	Accumulations
	The Vision

1972	*Score*
	Mabel's Dress
	Marathon
1973	*In the Park*
	Echo
1974	*Territory*
	They All Came Home Save One Because She Never Left
1975	*Baroque Suite*
	Straining at the Leash
1976	*Women*
	Plane of Tolerance
1977	*Homage to Lillian Gish*
1978	*The Car that Went with Motor 88 Miles*

Other works include: The theater work *Susannah and the Elders* (comprises a section of *Ballet Ballads*), 1948.

Publications

On LITZ: articles—

Barnes, Clive, Review of *Continuum, New York Times,* 28 February 1967.
Champaign-Urbana Courier, 31 January 1965.
Martin, John, *New York Times,* 13 August 1950.
Maynard, Olga, "Katherine Litz Talks to Olga Maynard," *Dance Magazine,* January 1967.
Sargent, David, *Village Voice,* 2 February 1976.
Clippings file on Katherine Litz, Dance Collection of the Performing Arts Research Center at the New York Public Library at Lincoln Center.

*   *   *

Katherine Litz was a prominent dancer and choreographer of the 1940s, 1950s and 1960s. Her specialty was the intriguing solo vignette for a ladylike eccentric. She was sensitive and funny in her richly nuanced portraits. As Litz commented in an interview in *Dance Magazine* (May 1977), "I love the irreverent. I love it when people laugh." Some of Litz's portraits are vivid: a woman dancing in an old black chiffon dress, or the lady in the broad-brimmed hat, or the circus fortuneteller. One reviewer found in Litz a performer in the tradition of Isadora Duncan. She was the consummate solo dancer: fascinating, funny, and disturbing. Litz's personal brilliance did not transfer easily, and some of her dancers had trouble taking her movements onto their own bodies. David Sargent writing in the *Village Voice* found Litz's dances "like dreams about dances instead of finished works; images slide away before you can grasp them ... yet, like some dreams, her dances have undefinably alluring atmospheres. You can't shake them off."

Don McDonagh wrote of Litz's style: "She is fond of paradox and will allow a tragic gesture to become humorous simply by following the trajectory of the gesture. She might bend back with her hand pressed over her eyes in anguish only to continue to bend and end up inelegantly in a pile on the floor." During a long, fruitful career Litz performed throughout New York City and at such venues as Jacob's Pillow and the American Dance Festival. She gave her last performance with her company at Cornell University just three weeks before her death. She continued to teach and choreograph at her studio in Brooklyn Heights until her final hospitalization—she died of cancer on 19 December 1978; she was 66.

A native of Denver, Colorado, Litz first saw modern dance in her hometown, where for a time she took modern and ballet lessons with Martha Wilcox. Louis Horst was an early teacher, too. Horst taught music appreciation at the Perry-Mansfield Camp in Steamboat Springs, Colorado, which Litz attended as a young girl. She also read *Dance Magazine,* which her mother brought home. In this way Litz became acquainted with Ruth St. Denis, Ted Shawn, Doris Humphrey, and Charles Weidman. What motivated the young dancer was not so much other dancers but music. She had a record player at home and listened to her favorite recording, Grieg's *The Shepherd's Dance.* The swinging lilt of the Grieg music appealed to Litz. She also studied piano in addition to her dance lessons. She decided to become a modern dancer while still in high school; as she noted in a 1965 interview with the *Champaign-Urbana Courier* (Illinois), "When dance gets hold of you, you don't choose—it does!"

Despite her father's disapproval, Litz left Denver at age 17 and headed for New York at a time when modern dance was still a new art. She studied with Humphrey and Weidman in New York and became a soloist with their company. Litz lived the life of the poor but dedicated artist. She shared an apartment with several other dancers and took whatever part-time jobs came her way. In the summer of 1940 Litz went to Bennington College to study with Hanya Holm and returned in 1941 to study with Martha Graham. She also studied with Agnes de Mille and Mary Wigman. Litz studied ballet, too, during these formative years, under such teachers as Barbara Fallis and Richard Thomas.

Litz danced with the Humphrey-Weidman company from 1936 to 1942 and also danced with de Mille's concert company from 1940 to 1942. Weidman's gift for comedy had a special attraction for Litz, she credited him with the comic spirit that filtered into her work. Her first important role was the young girl in Humphrey's *With My Red Fires.* Another early influence was Sybil Shearer who invited Litz to travel to Chicago and work with her there. It was through Shearer that Litz met Agnes de Mille, who gave the young Litz her first Broadway roles in the musicals, *Oklahoma!* from 1943 to 1945, and *Carousel* from 1945 to 1947. Both musicals were revolutionary for dancers. It was the first time professional dancers were on stage for any significant length of time. When *Carousel* went on the road, Litz stayed in New York and married the American painter Charles Oscar. He encouraged Litz to begin her own work, yet their marriage later ended tragically when Oscar died in 1961, the victim of a mugging.

After 1948, Litz continued to present new solos every year. Her desire to set out on her own led to her break with Doris Humphrey who had invited Litz to join the José Limón Company, when she was its artistic director. Instead, Litz studied with Youri Bilsten, a Russian cellist recommended to her by Shearer. Bilsten's theories influenced Litz's movement. He urged her to "divide the muscle attention using theme and variations, making up a scale for yourself."

Litz's first solo concert was at the 92nd Street YMHA in New York City in April 1948. Litz's dance-making developed in the 1950s when she presented evenings of choreography at the Y. These performances were followed by national tours, appearances at dance festivals, and teaching engagements. She subsequently choreographed many solo dances for herself as well as group works. Some of the most memorable of the group dances are *Madame Bender's Dancing School* (1953), *The Enchanted* (1956; for an ABT workshop), three versions of *Dracula* (1959, 1960, and 1969), *Marathon* (1972), and *They All Came Home Save One Because She Never Left* (1974). Litz formed her own dance company in 1967 and taught and choreographed as artist-in-residence at many American universities. Litz defied age and continued performing well into middle age.

Litz has been long overlooked as a choreographer. Her dances are small and understated rather than big and boldly passionate. Her sense of the absurd and her ability to note small telling details about people and turn these observations into dances that are both pathetic and funny set her apart from her dance contemporaries. In *Fall of the Leaf,* Litz's zany sense of humor was unleashed—she appeared as if in some *belle époque* autumnal light wearing a wide-brimmed, gauzy hat. The image evoked romance and its possibilities; yet Litz exploded expectations as she removed the hat and solemnly placed it on her bosom. She then pushed it down to her hips and sent it on a journey all over her body. Audiences started to laugh gently, and their laughs soon turned to howls of delight.

With pithy movements and savage irony Litz's dances isolate the essence of a character or situation. In *The Lure,* Litz satirized the circus. She created a series of scenes which suggest a half-formed dream of a tawdry circus. Her humor and insights mainly relied on gesture and timing. A barker attracts people to a round-cheeked lady in a green robe (Litz) who flips her hands into little offering gestures. Perhaps she is a life-size fortune-telling machine; people come and go. Dancers depict trapeze artists and suggest space and motion with a minimum of motion while others act out lions and trained poodles. And through it all, the mechanical lady has everyone under her spell. *They All Came Home Save One Because She Never Left* is filled with atmosphere. Several relationships are made clear and others are left vague. Dancers move in dark ways to 19th-century waltz music. Such roles as mother, child, and seductress are hinted at mysteriously. Is this a portrait of a family? If so, then it is a deranged, disjointed unit.

Litz explored vampires and vampirism in her ballet *Dracula.* It was first danced in 1959 with Charles Weidman in the leading role. Revived briefly in 1960, Litz brought it back in 1970 at the Judson Poet's Theater in New York City. It was danced by a company of 11 dancers, including Litz as Mina Harker, to a score made up of various compositions of Charles Ives. Litz's work combines tongue-in-cheek drollery with a sense of the bizarre and macabre. At one point, the count dances on giant stilts while his vampire wives swirl about him.

Litz's approach to music has, according to John Martin in the *New York Times,* "always been off the beaten track." Often the music represents a dancer's actual antagonism to the expression of forces against which she is contending. Martin praised Litz for dealing with the serious and idiotic and for the deliberate disregard of the emotional intent of the music. Litz's movement quality was often spasmodic. It was as if she mirrored in her muscles what her nerve ends were doing. The most eloquent part of Litz's anatomy was her beautiful hands which darted, stabbed, clenched, reached, trembled, wandered, and queried. Likewise, she used her feet to define the deepest lines of her danced portraits. As a dancer, Litz moved with ease and naturalness. A sense of earthiness colored her movements and simple walks and dodges revealed a grandeur and largeness that might be associated with Litz's career as a Doris Humphrey dancer.

Fire in the Snow was another brilliant piece of Litzomania. In this bitterly funny work from 1950, a dignified woman (Litz) is trapped in long, tight white garments. She tries with futile gestures and constricted actions to release the emotional fire which neither her costume nor her personality will permit her to liberate. Not all watchers of the dance were taken with Litz's choreographic style. Clive Barnes, writing in the *New York Times* after a performance of Litz's *Continuum,* commented "the work had a strange quality of instant-forgetfulness. Miss Litz's humor is camp. She idles on the fringes of parody, she is mediocrely [sic] outrageous and moderately shocking. *Continuum* was about nothing." Litz once remarked that many of her dances were about decay—decay of a human being at sometime in his/her life, decay of a society. In *Twilight of a Flower* Litz was at her most poignant: an old woman relived the days of her youth in a dream.

Throughout her career, Litz was also a noted teacher of dance and taught courses at University of Illinois, the University of California at Los Angeles, Sarah Lawrence College, Bennington College, and University of Wisconsin.

—Adriane Ruggiero

LOCK, Edouard

Moroccan-born Canadian dancer, choreographer, and company director

Born: 3 March 1954 in Casablanca. **Education:** Studied literature and film at Concordia University, Montreal; studied with then joined Le Groupe Nouvelle Aire in his late teens. **Career:** Dancer, Le Groupe Nouvelle Aire; invited by Les Grands Ballets Canadiens to choreograph workshop production, *Solos pour quatre femmes (Solos for Four Women),* 1979; established independent company Lock Danseurs, 1980; choreographed *Lili Marlene in the Jungle* for Montreal and New York, 1980; changed company name to La La La Human Steps, 1985; toured Europe and North America, 1987; appeared with the Bolshoi Ballet, 1987; collaborated with rockers David Bowie (*Sound and Vision* world tour), Frank Zappa and the Ensemble Modern of Germany (Yellow Shark concert), 1992; choreographed film *Le Petit musé de Vélasquez* (dir. Bernar Hébert), 1993; *Bread Dances* (1988) set on Het Nationale Ballet of Holland, 1993; participated in international panel on culture and creation organized by France in Caen, 1994; choreographed *Étude* for Les Grands Ballets Canadiens, 1996; appeared in Michael Apted's film *Inspirations,* 1997. **Awards:** Jean A. Chalmers Award, 1981; Chalmers Award for choreography for *Oranges (Ou la Recherche du Paradis),* commissioned by Montreal's Musée d'Art Contemporain, 1981; New York Dance and Performance Award ("Bessie") for *Human Sex,* 1985; selected Personality of the Year in dance by Montreal newspaper *La Presse,* 1989; MVPA award for best choreography, 1993.

Works (all premieres in Montreal unless otherwise noted)

1975	*Temps Volé* (mus. Harry Somers)
1977	*La Maison de ma Mére* (mus. Henry Cowell)
	Remous (mus. Samuel Barber)
1978	*Solo for Danielle Tardif* (commissioned by Montreal Museum of Fine Art)
	Le Nageur (mus. John Steele)
	Solos pour Quatre Femmes (mus. John Cage)
1980	*Lili Marlene in the Jungle* (mus. Robert Racine)
1981	*Oranges (Ou la Recherche du Paradis)* (mus. Michel Lemieux)
1983	*Businessman in the Process of Becoming an Angel* (mus. Michel Lemieux), Toronto

Edouard Lock: *Lily Marlene in the Jungle.* Photograph © Johan Elbers.

1985   *Human Sex* (mus. Louise Seize, Randall Kay), Vancouver
1987   *New Demons* (mus. West India Company, René Despars, Olle Romo, Janitors Animated)
1988   *Bread Dances* (mus. Tchaikovsky) for Het Nationale Ballet, Amsterdam
1991   *Infante, C'est Destroy* (mus. Einsturzende Neubauten, David Van Tieghem, Skinny Puppy, Janitors Animated; arr. Yves Chamberland), Paris
1995   *"2"* (mus. Jean-Baptiste Forqueray, J. D'Angelbert, Jean-Philippe Rameau, Gavin Bryars, Shellac of North America, Kevin Shields, Iggy Pop, Jérô Charles), Paris
1996   *Étude* (mus. Gavin Bryars), St. Louis, Missouri

Films and Videotapes

Le Petit musé de Vélasquez, dir. Bernar Hébert, choreography by Lock, 1993.
Inspirations, dir. Michael Apted, appearance by Lock, 1997.

*   *   *

Just as George Balanchine gave serious music human form, so Edouard Lock makes visualizations of rock rhythms and social tensions. Wild, rebellious, energetic, and extreme, his reckless-look-ing, spasmodic choreography measures the pulse rate of urban stress at the end of the millennium.

It was apparent in 1975 when Lock created his first choreography, *Temps Volé* for three dancers at Montreal's Le Groupe Nouvelle Aire, that at 21 he knew how to make movement serve his ideas. With the three strong cinematographic works that followed—*La Maison de ma mère, Remous,* and *Le Nageur*—he took giant strides toward developing a personal style that nonetheless seemed rooted in the conservative contemporary dance espoused by the company with which he was connected. None of these early works exposed the radical direction he would take abruptly with *Lili Marlene in the Jungle* (1980), his first work as an independent choreographer and made for his own newly formed company, Lock Danseurs.

Looking like raw, edgy performance art, *Lili Marlene* challenged established ballet and modern dance, particularly the trend to minimalism in vogue at the time. It also demonstrated Lock's need to work closely with inspiring dancers. *Lili*'s star was classically trained Miryam Moutillet, who represented the daring innocence required for Lock's rabid urban jungle of a landscape that set the tone for his later works. The hour-long piece was a small-scale promise of the mega-productions, with their accompanying flirta-tions with ever-increasing extremes, that Lock would soon be tour-ing. With sprayed graffitti and electronic new sounds, *Lili* empha-sized risk and high energy in which performers slid bare-breasted across the floor as well as abstract hand and finger dances that would mark Lock's choreography for years to come.

His next work *Oranges (Ou la Recherche du Paradis),* commissioned by Montreal's Musée d'Art Contemporain, pushed surrealism further with dancers daringly balanced on paths of old glass milk bottles to raucous waves of electronic sound. In contrast to the off-the-wall dynamics, Lock performed soft, boneless-looking slithers, twitching and melting into the ground. For the next few productions, he made cameo appearances in his works, providing moments of limpid calm. He continued expanding his vision with free, explosive, gravity-defying movement that incorporated elements from other disciplines. Fascinated with extremes in keeping with the punk and new wave aesthetic, he used increasingly outrageous original electronic music (live, taped, or both and played at annihilating volume) and huge self-made photos and videos enlarged to proscenium arch dimensions with the effect that their weight—singly or combined—threatened to obliterate the tiny figures on stage.

Businessman in the Process of Becoming an Angel (1983) established a formula to be repeated in successive productions. Borrowing the principles of framing and montage from film, Lock deconstructed sequences, reassembling and repeating them in a multiple of combinations without any apparent connection. Avoiding coils of wiring snaking over the stage and used for sound and light equipment, black-clad dancers would march to the centre and take turns flinging themselves into demonic unisex twists and tosses culminating with horizontal rolls and torpedo dives. Unresolved, action would stop as suddenly as it had begun. The stop-start technique was reminiscent of video clips or musicians' behavior at rock concerts.

Louise Lecavalier, who was to symbolize La La La Human Steps for her seemingly inexhaustible energy and fierce-but-fragile stage persona, won a New York Dance and Performance Award ("Bessie") for *Businessman.* Lock got his own Bessie for *Human Sex* (1985), which took his love for technology to new heights with the addition of specially built dancer-activated devices that magnified shapes and sounds. In keeping with its rock connections, the company changed its name to La La La Human Steps in 1985. In *Human Sex,* Lock's habitual androgynous preferences shifted into role reversal with Lecavalier wearing a mustache and her partner in heavy eyebrow pencil, lipstick, and blush. By the time *New Demons* came along (1987), Lock's dancers—especially Lecavalier—had changed their body shapes and increased their strength with weights. *New Demons* took full advantage of their new abilities with pumped up virtuosity and fast, flashy bursts of energy. Bodies whizzed through the air and crash landed in a cross-cultural morass to traditional Indian music and high-tech Western rock.

In *Infante, C'est Destroy,* performance physicality reached its zenith and Lock acknowledged his debt to Lecavalier by projecting films of her on giant screens. Below the videos, the actual Lecavalier was one tough chick, throwing her partners and being thrown. On the screen she was both warrior goddess and victim, a heroine who survived bloody attacks by swords and Doberman dogs in a coat of 16th century armour and the magic of her tiny, fragile face.

By 1985 Lock was an international hot property. The mention of La La La Human Steps guaranteed sold-out houses on long tours. *Human Sex* played 117 times in two years. *New Demons* (1987) survived three years, giving 130 shows worldwide. These were unprecedented numbers by international dance standards.

A softening and maturation was heralded by *"2."* After Lecavalier suffered a serious accident (on her chiropractor's table), Lock examined human vulnerability instead of human strength and recklessness. Investigating maturation/disintegration and life/death, he filmed two Lecavaliers—one aged 30 years—and projected them side by side so that she appeared to be interacting with herself across the years. The slow, intense searches questioned the reckless performances of the real dancers below. The work's thoughtful, gentle films suggested that there might be something else beyond duck-and-dive urban reality. Lock has not clearly indicated that he's developing a spiritual dimension, however; La La La's world is still flailing with sexual equality, interdependence and independence, risk, and even violence. Lock's choreography speaks powerfully to the end of the millenium and Generation Xers raised in the quicksands of social, cultural, and economic instability and fast-changing technology.

—Linde Howe-Beck

LONDON CONTEMPORARY DANCE THEATER

For 27 years, from 1967 to 1994, London Contemporary Dance Theatre (LCDT) was a major force on the British dance scene. Its role was central to the establishment of American modern dance in Britain and indeed Europe and, as the critic Clement Crisp acknowledged, "Few enterprises in the arts during the past two decades have been so productive or so excellent. Nothing I suspect has been so fundamentally valuable to society in communicating the joys and rewards of an art form which has become so truly and splendidly national."

London Contemporary Dance Theatre was the result of one individual's vision and passion for the work of Martha Graham. Robin Howard (1924-1989), a lover of dance who had tired of the repetition of the classical ballet repertory, was won over by the dramatic richness of Martha Graham's performances and was prepared to plough his personal fortune into his love of dance. He also had the ability to secure a team led by artistic director Robert Cohan and administrator Janet Eager to guide its development.

After sponsoring Graham's 1963 visit to London, Howard established a trust for educational purposes, giving students scholarships to train in the United States. But he quickly learnt this took significant talent away from Britain and recognised the need to import teachers from America. For its first three years, LCDT fulfilled a largely educational role presenting lecture demonstrations modeled on "Ballet for All," but after the success of its first season in its own home theatre in the newly leased The Place (formerly Drill Hall of Artists' Rifles at Euston), for which Cohan created his powerful *Cell,* the group transformed itself into a significant performing company.

In the early years the company benefitted from its close relationship with Martha Graham. The 1969 Place season company included six dancers who were also members of Graham's company and the early repertory included several of her creations, *El Penitente* (1969) and *Diversion of Angels* (1974), but it quickly developed its own works and, most importantly, a host of new choreographers. After the first seasons the majority of the dancers were trained primarily at the London Contemporary Dance School and at all times it included an impressive array of technically secure dancers, having a particularly strong, athletic male contingent.

From the start European touring was important. In 1969 LCDT was first seen in France and the following year (when the dancers received year-round contracts) in Eastern Europe including Yugoslavia and Czechoslovakia. In 1977 the company first danced—to a standing ovation—in the U.S. where the *New York Times* described it as "an interesting, well-trained company." During its existence, LCDT performed in more than 50 countries worldwide including participating in the arts festivals linked to the Los Angeles and the Seoul Olympic Games. Most years the company would average two overseas tours and appear in Britain for around 16 weeks. The audiences they reached were further extended by periodically splitting the company for two parallel tours to smaller venues and, from 1976, residencies enabled them to educate their audience and build up a large youth following. From 1973 LCDT's main London seasons were held at Sadler's Wells Theatre but the Place was used for workshops and more experimental occasions.

The range of choreographers whose careers were launched (or substantially boosted) by creating works for LCDT is impressive, including Richard Alston, who was the first to break away and establish his own company, Strider, in 1973; Robert North whose popular successes included *Troy Game*—originally for six men—and *Death and the Maiden*; Siobhan Davies recognised as early as 1977 as "a beautiful dancer and a great choreographer"; and Micha Bergese, Anthony van Laast, Tom Jobe, Jonathan Lunn, Aletta Collins, and Darshan Singh Bhuller. Kim Brandstrup who, unlike the others, did not also dance with the company, created the Olivier Award-winning *Orfeo* for the dancers. Indeed, at the end of the company's existence, more works were being created by outside choreographers. Works that made the greatest impression were *Rikud* by Liat Dror and Nir Ben-Gal from Israel and *Rooster* acquired by Christopher Bruce.

Links with America were always important. It was thanks to LCDT that in the 1970s and 1980s British audiences saw choreography by Paul Taylor (another artist Howard had launched in Britain) as their repertory included *Three Epitaphs, Cloven Kingdom, Esplanade,* and *Arden Court.* Artistic directors in succession to Cohan came from the United States but neither Dan Wagoner (1989-91) nor Nancy Duncan (1991-92) were able to give the company their undivided attention.

London Contemporary Dance Theatre was quick to respond to trends; several of the early works were multimedia shows and design, particularly lighting design, was an important element in many productions. Much of the music used for productions was specially commissioned for dance. In the 1970s full-evening productions were gaining popularity on the ballet stage, and Cohan choreographed his own large-scale contemporary dance works to take to major theatres. These works, on immediately recognisable themes, even if not presented as linear narratives, made the company easier to market to British dance public.

London Contemporary Dance Theatre was always skilled in is approach to marketing. Indeed its honest naiveté in its early years, when Howard went out of his way to consult and woo critics, led to their genuine concern that the company would succeed and, with the excitement of its first decade, there was every reason it should. The company also developed a strong visual image encapsulated in photographs by Anthony Crickmay. The organization won enthusiastic young audiences through its extensive and continuing outreach programs and it developed a high profile from the start by showing a substantial amount of its work on television. In all educational fields, Cohan proved himself an able ambassador.

At the outset of the collaboration between Howard and Cohan, Howard assured Cohan of his support for all that "was created with love." He believed dance was a force for improving society by enhancing the quality of life for both performer and spectator. It was appropriate, therefore, that among the company's last performances was a "Gala Tribute" to Howard including a preview of a new work by Alston as well as revivals of Cohan's *Stabat Mater* and *Cell* (which would be the very last work danced by the company on 25 June 1994. LCDT's dancers arrived for the tribute straight from the Society of West End Theatres' awards ceremony, where they had received a final Olivier Award. If the company had lost some of its sense of purpose, it always maintained its quality.

It is significant that London Contemporary Dance Company folded only when the art flourished in Europe and its own pioneering work was complete. The Trust's other work—the theatre, school, promotional and educational activities—continue. In some senses the company was the victim of its own success for it closed when the competition for bookings was intense from the myriad of single-choreographer groups, many of which led by artists who had developed under the umbrella of the Contemporary Dance Trust.

Publications

Books—

Adshead, Janet and Richard Mansfield, *Company Resource Pack 1: London Contemporary Dance Theatre 1967-1975*, University of Surrey, 1985.
Clarke, Mary and Clement Crisp, *London Contemporary Dance Theatre: The First 21 Years*, London, 1989.
Mansfield, Richard, "London Contemporary Dance Theatre" in *20th Century Dance in Britain,* edited by Joan White, London, 1985.

Articles—

Goodwin, Noel, "Based on Love," *Ballet News*, April 1983.
Percival, John, "London Contemporary Dance Theatre," *Dance Magazine*, November 1975.

—Jane Pritchard

LOUIS, Murray

American dancer, choreographer, and artistic director

Born: 1926 in Brooklyn, New York. **Education:** Grew up in Manhattan with a sister who studied dance and introduced him to early modern dancers; attended Colorado College's summer session, conducted by Hanya Holm, and met Alwin Nikolais; B.A. in dramatic arts from New York University; started classes at the Henry Street Playhouse, where Nikolais was teaching. debuted in Nikolais' Playhouse Dance Company (later called the Nikolais Dance Theater). **Military Service:** U.S. Navy, discharged in 1946. **Career:** Debuted in Nikolais' Playhouse Dance Company (later called the Nikolais Dance Theater), 1949; headed new children's dance department at Playhouse Dance Company, 1951; founded Murray Louis Dance Company, 1953; toured India as a representative of the U.S. State Department, 1968; created two works for Rudolph Nureyev on Broadway, 1978; received commissions from the Ameri-

can Dance Festival, 16th International Festival of Dance at the Théâtre Champs-Elysées (Paris), Taorimina Art Festival (Sicily), and choreographed for Josesh Papp's New York Shakespeare Festival, Batsheva Dance Company (Israel), Placido Domingo's *The Tales of Cri-Cri*, began collaboration with the Dave Brubeck Quartet for the New York City Center, 1984; performed at Carnegie Hall for 10,000 children, 1995; choreographed for the Guggenheim Museum's "Works and Process" project; has published two books of essays; and worked extensively in film, video, and television.
Awards: First National Endowment of the Arts (NEA) grant, 1969; special citation by the mayor of New York City to Louis and Nikolais, 1989.

Works

1953	*Opening Dance*
	Little Man
	Antechamber
	Star Crossed
1954	*Affirmation*
	For Remembrance
	Courtesan
	Family Album
	Martyr
	Triptych
1955	*Piper*
	Court
	Dark Corner
	Monarch
	Night
	Polychrome
	Man in Chair
	Figure in Grey
	As the Day Darkens
	Small Illusions
	Frenetic Dances
	Belonging to the Moon
1956	*Bach Suite* (mus. Bach)
	Incredible Garden
	Corrida
	Harmonica Suite (Reflections)
1957	*Journal*
1959	*Entré-Acte*
1960	*Odyssey*
1961	*Calligraph for Martyrs*
1962	*Facets*
1963	*Interims*
	Suite for Diverse Performers
1964	*Transcendencies*
	Landscapes
	Junk Dances (mus. popular/opera collage)
	A Gothic Tale
1966	*Charade (Chimera)* (mus. Nikolais)
	Choros I
	Concerto
	Illume
1967	*Go 6*
1969	*Proximities* (mus. Brahms)
	Intersection
1971	*Personnae*
	Continuum

	Disguise
1972	*Hoopla* (mus. Lisbon State Police Band)
	Dance as an Art Form
1973	*Index ... (to necessary neuroses)*
1974	*Porcelain Dialogues* (mus. Tchaikovsky)
	Geometrics (mus. Nikolais)
	Scheherezade, a Dream
1975	*Moments*
1976	*Glances* (mus. Dave Brubeck)
1977	*Schubert* (mus. Schubert)
1978	*Figura* (mus. Paul Winter Consort)
1982	*A Stravinsky Montage* (mus. Stravinsky)
1984	*Four Brubeck Pieces* (mus. Brubeck)
1987	*Dramatis Personnae* (mus. Pia Gilbert)

Publications

By LOUIS: books—

Inside Dance, New York, 1980.
On Dance, Chicago, 1992.

By LOUIS: article—

"The Contemporary Dance Theatre of Alwin Nikolais," *Dance Scope,* 1973-74.

On LOUIS: books—

Lyle, Cynthia, *Dancers on Dancing,* New York & London, 1977.
Gruen, John, *People Who Dance: 22 Dancers Tell Their Own Stories,* Princeton, New Jersey, 1988.

On LOUIS: articles—

Barnes, Clive, "A Different Old Modern Dance," *Dance Magazine,* February 1997.
"Murray Louis," *Current Biography Yearbook 1968,* 1968.
Siegel, Marcia B., ed., "Dancer's Notes," *Dance Persepectives,* Summer 1969.
Zupp, Nancy Thornhill, "An Analysis and Comparison of the Choreographic Process of Alwin Nikolais, Murray Louis, and Phyllis Lamhut," unpublished dissertation, University of North Carolina at Greensboro, 1978.

Films and Videotapes

Nik and Murray, dir. Christian Blackwood, documentary, PBS *American Masters* series, 1987.
Murray Louis in Concert, video, Princeton Book Publishing, 1989.
Dance as an Art Form educational film series, produced by Louis.
The World of Alwin Nikolais, video series, 1996.

*   *   *

Murray Louis, who grew up in New York, loved the what he called the "Three Ms"—Macy's, the Metropolitan Opera, and the movies. His sister, who took dance classes, introduced him to early modern dancers and he saw his first modern dance concert at the age of 14. At 16, Louis was turning pages for Genevieve Pitot, accompanist for Helen Tamiris. Louis' introduction to modern dance came

Louis and Nikolais Dance Foundation: *Temple,* **1992. Photograph © Johan Elbers.**

of 14. At 16, Louis was turning pages for Genevieve Pitot, accompanist for Helen Tamiris. Louis' introduction to modern dance came during the days of the W.P.A., a time when many new and dynamic dancers and choreographers were receiving grants to work. Though any dance inclinations were interrupted when he was 18 and drafted into the Navy during World War II, upon his discharge he went to San Francisco where he studied acting, writing, and dance with Ann (later Anna) Halprin. He also worked in road company musicals and performed in a few night clubs. Once, during his time in San Francisco, Louis drove all the way to Connecticut to see Martha Graham perform. By the age of 22, during the summer of 1949, he began studying with Alwin Nikolais at Colorado College. In another 10 years, Louis would feel as if he had arrived as an "artist," and has been internationally known and considered to be among the greatest male dancer/choreographers ever since. For many, Murray Louis is the epitomé of a dancer.

In his early 20s, Louis intended to work in Broadway musicals. Broadway dance, which blended classical ballet, modern, and folk dance, offered variety and kept dancers employed. But, after studying with Nikolais at Colorado College, Louis accompanied him back to New York where Nikolais was the director of the Henry Street Playhouse. While earning his degree at New York Unviersity, Louis also took classes at the Henry Street Playhouse. He was soon teaching dance at Henry Street, and headed up a newly created children's dance department and serving as Nikolais' associate director. The children's performances were very popular and at one time the ensemble was giving 150 performances per year. During

his early years at the Henry Street Playhouse, Louis matured as a dancer and started to choreograph his own pieces. He had not only become the principal male dancer in the Nikolais Dance Theater, but had helped Nikolais perfect what is known today as the Nikolais/Louis technique. John Martin, the respected and knowledgeable *New York Times* dance critic, raved about Louis' talents on many occasions.

Louis was the perfect vehicle to perform Nikolais' choreography, so it was natural that Nikolais often created dances with Louis in mind. Louis had a charismatic demeanor, possessed an incredible sense of timing, had a lithe, androgynous appearance, and ear-to-ear grin—for which Nikolais described him as a sort of "pied-piper." Louis also possessed extraordinary muscle control and had the ability to isolate and move any part of his body—a body that moved as if controlled by some magical force. *Charade,* choreographed by Louis (1966) is a piece which demonstrates these unique physical abilities. Louis performs this piece from behind a hanging cloth that has three differently shaped and sized openings through which the audience watches him move from the largest to smallest. Enveloped in a stretch jersey suit, Louis is moving his hands to make his body appear oddly-shaped. He then appears in front of the hanging cloth in another costume, disappears, and reappears, moving with fluid grace. Throughout the dance, Louis mimes various activities and uses a theme and variation-style of movement.

Some of Louis' most well-known and popular pieces include the marital parody, *Junk Dances* (1964), which makes use of props such as a fire hydrant and a trash can, and has a urban tenement setting. *Hoopla* (1972), set to Portuguese music, uses widely imaginative costumes. The look for the performance is vast and one of a large company work—yet surprisingly requires only seven dancers. Dance, and all of its aspects became of tantamount importance to Louis. To him, dance is a complete language—a way and means to communicate and learn. Louis has shown a total commitment to the art of dance by dancing, choreographing, teaching, and even publishing two books of essays (*Inside Dance*, 1980; *On Dance*, 1992) about this art form. He teaches dance because, he says, teaching helps him to learn more about his art. Louis has also produced a series of films demonstrating his technique, and has served as an advisor to Dance Makers, a Boston-based modern dance company. He is supportive of others' talents and played an instrumental role in helping the dance group Pilobolus make its New York debut.

Like Nikolais, Louis' choreography has German Expressionist roots—most likely due to the influence of Hanya Holm, and his dances cannot be described as those having typical dance steps. He has choreographed pieces for the Royal Danish Ballet, the Berlin Opera Ballet, the Scottish Ballet, the José Limón Dance Company, and ballet's Rudolph Nureyev. All artists are inspired by an idea, a social or pastoral scene, a painting, or a particular piece of music. Essentially, movement serves as the seed for the creation of a dance. Louis first choreographs a piece and then finds appropriate accompaniment for it, although occasionally he has a piece of music in mind while developing a dance. He has used a wide variety of accompaniment and his choreography reflects diversity—his pieces do not display a single, identifiable style. Louis seeks to evoke the senses and to create images to provide the viewer with a path which connects their material, physical world to the spiritual world.

When talking about Murray Louis, it is impossible to discount the influence of Alwin Nikolais and their decades-long collaboration. Louis was a dancer with the Alwin Nikolais Dance Company for 20 years before forming his own dance ensemble, the Murray Louis Dance Company. In 1989, Nikolais and Louis combined their names and companies under the aegis of Murray Louis and Nikolais Dance—though each company remained a separate entity. Upon Nikolais' death in 1993, Louis became the sole director of Murray Louis and Nikolais Dance, which continued to have an active repertory of both its founders works and remains a well-respected bastion of the dance community.

—Christine Miner Minderovic

LOUTHER, William
American dancer, choreographer, and company director

Born: 22 January 1942 in Brooklyn, New York. **Education:** Studied tap at the school of Kitty Carson; attended New York's High School of Performing Arts for acting but switched to dance; went to Juilliard. **Career:** Dancer, May O'Donnell's company; dancer, New American Ballet Company, 1960; performed in Broadway musicals; joined Alvin Ailey American Dance Theater, 1963-64; Martha Graham Company, 1964-68; began teaching at the School of Contemporary Dance in London, 1969; first choreography, 1969; joined London Contemporary Dance Theatre, 1969; director of Batsheva Dance Company, 1972-74; director of Welsh Dance Theatre 1975-76; founded Dance and Theatre Corporation, 1976; guest appearances with the Royal Ballet, Royal Opera, Paul Taylor Dance Com-

pany, Merce Cunningham Dance Company, Anna Sokolow Dance Company, Hamburg Ballet Company, and Toronto Dance Theatre.

Publications

By LOUTHER: articles—

"Breath and form," *Dance and Dancers*, October 1977.

On LOUTHER: articles—

Armory, Mark, "Dancer's Tale," *London Sunday Times Magazine*, 9 March 1975.
Goodman, Saul, "William Louther: Brief Biography," *Dance Magazine*, June 1968.
Gow, Gordon, "Beyond the Mirror Image: An Interview with William Louther," *The Dancing Times* London, October 1970.
Williams, Peter, and Noel Goodwin, "*Vesalii Icones*, Queen Elizabeth Hall, London," *Dance and Dancers*, February 1970.

Roles

1962	*District Storyville* (Donald McKayle), New York
1963	*Panther* (cr), *Circe* (Martha Graham)
1965	*Part Real—Part Dream* (Graham)
1967	*Black New World* (McKayle)
1969	*Side Scene* (Robert Cohan), London
	Cell (Cohan), London
1971	*Stages* (Cohan), London
1972	*Kontakion: A Song of Praise* (cr), (Barry Moreland), London

Other roles include: *Diversion of Angels* (Graham), *Poem* (Anna Sokolow), *Hermit Songs* (Alvin Ailey), *The Road of the Phoebe Snow* (Talley Beatty), *Lament* (Louis Johnson), *Here's Love* (Michael Kidd), *Fade Out, Fade In* (McKayle) and others.

Works

1968	*Mantle*
1970	*Vesalii Icones* (mus. Peter Maxwell Davies), solo
1972	*Divertissement in the Playground of the Zodiac* (mus. George Quincy; costumes Louther), Welsh Dance Theatre.
	Inventions Part II (mus. Bach)
1975	*The Soldier's Tale* (mus. Stravinsky)
1976	*Me Duele* (poems by Jean Brierre)
	Prologos (mus. Peter Maxwell-Davies, others), Welsh Dance Theatre
	Plaintive Events (mus. Scott Joplin)
1980	*Voices*, Dance and Theatre Corporation
	Mirror
	Lyric Fantasies: I Am Woman (mus. George Quincy, Dolores Scott-Smith), Dance and Theatre Corporation, revised as *Woman* in 1987 for the Alvin Ailey Repertory Ensemble
1990	*Murder at the Town Hall* (mus. Quincy, Neal Tate)
1994	*Elijah* (mus. Roland Segun)
1995	*Lilith*
1996	*Obsession*
	Sacred Ground (mus. Zairian drumming)
	The Bride's Dance (mus. Aaron Copeland)

1997   *Stone Soul Picnic* (mus. Laura Nyro)
         Destiny Dances (mus. various), duet with Galina Panova

*   *   *

Before the era of American civil rights, many African-American dancers pursued rewarding careers in Europe. Eager to escape constrictions of racial stereotyping in the theater, and weary of harshly segregated and unequal conditions in their everyday lives in the United States, black performers took comfort in the hearty reception often accorded the most talented of their number abroad. William Louther is among the most distinguished of African-American artists whose career has achieved distinction as a dancer, teacher, choreographer, and company director in London and Tel Aviv.

Early in his career, Louther attracted attention as a dancer in work with Donald McKayle, Herbert Ross, Sophie Maslow, Norman Walker, and Hava Kohav. He danced on Broadway in several musicals, including *Here's Love* choreographed by Michael Kidd, and *Fade Out, Fade In*, choreographed by Donald McKayle. He continued a profitable association with McKayle and created a role in the premiere of *District Storyville* (1962), and performed the leading role in McKayle's panoramic chronicle of African-American experience, *Black New World* (1967).

Louther joined the Alvin Ailey American Dance Theater for its 1963-64 season, where he proved his remarkable versatility as a modern dancer in Ailey's *Hermit Songs, The Road of the Phoebe Snow* by Talley Beatty, and *Lament* by Louis Johnson. He caused a sensation in London dancing Ailey's long solo *Hermit Songs*. His slight build, strong technique, and intense sincerity produced a stirring portrayal of a devout monk on a mystical pilgrimage.

Louther joined the Martha Graham Company in fall of 1964 where he created the role of the Panther in *Circe* (1964). He became a soloist with Graham by the fall of 1966, and performed leading roles in *Diversion of Angels, Acrobats of God*, and *Secular Games*. His strong understanding of the Graham technique allowed him to develop into an excellent teacher of the idiom. After several tours through London with Ailey, Graham, and McKayle, Louther joined the London Contemporary Dance Theatre to dance leading roles during its inaugural 1969 season. He created roles in *Side Scene* (1969) and *Stages* (1971), both by Robert Cohan, and Barry Moreland's *Kontakion* (1972). He became a principal in the burgeoning contemporary dance scene in London, and spent the bulk of his subsequent career there.

Louther created his first choreography, *Mantle*, in 1968, based on the shapes of porcelain figurines he remembered from his grandmother's fireplace mantle. His first great success as a choreographer, however, came with the *Vesalii Icones*, a long solo set to music by Peter Maxwell-Davies. The dance drew parallels between the drawings of Andeas Vesalius and the Stations of the Cross. Critics lauded Louther for his impeccable musicality and ability to make the Graham technique speak clearly to the theme of man's anatomical destiny. Critics also noted the vivid theatricality of the staging, and of Davies' score, which at one point included Louther playing an out-of-tune hymn on a piano.

Louther's interest in religious themes continued throughout his career as a choreographer. He often appeared as an actor in his own works, and included singing and text in his ballets. On occasion, Louther's work took a political slant, as in the *Murder at the Town Hall* (1990), based on T.S. Eliot's play, *Murder in the Cathedral*, with additional interpolated texts by Malcolm X and Martin Luther King, Jr. Louther performed the title role in his two-act ballet *Elijah*

(1994), a demanding and theatrical work which required singing of its dancers.

Louther learned Hebrew as a boy in New York, and this skill served him well when he directed the Batsheva Dance Company from 1972 to 1974 in Tel Aviv, Israel. His tenure as a director was marked by his willingness to restructure the company from the ground up, and a strong commitment to perpetuating the Graham technique. He also directed the Welsh Dance Theatre from 1975 to 1976. He founded the Dance and Theatre Corporation in London in 1976; this company soon disbanded but was revived in 1980.

Louther retired from dancing because of health problems in the 1980s, then returned to the stage in the 1990s. He remained a well-respected and highly sought Graham teacher in London and throughout Europe. He continues to choreograph and appear in his own choreography.

—Thomas DeFrantz

LUBOVITCH, Lar
American dancer, choreographer, and company director

Born: 9 April 1943 in Chicago. **Education:** Attended University of Iowa; studied dance with Alvin Ailey and José Limón at Connecticut College, and with Lucas Hoving, Anna Sokolow, and Antony Tudor at the Juilliard School; Martha Graham School; Joffrey Ballet School. **Career:** Dancer with companies of Pearl Lang, Donald McKayle, John Butler, Glen Tetley, the Manhattan Festival Ballet, and the Harkness Ballet, 1963-67; founder, Lar Lubovitch Dance Company, 1968. **Awards:** Astaire Award, Theater Development Fund, for *The Red Shoes,* 1994.

Works (for Lar Lubovitch Dance Company, New York, unless otherwise noted)

1968   *Blue* (mus. ancient Eastern)
         Freddie's Bag (mus. collage)
         Journey Back (mus. Akira Miyoshi)
1969   *Unremembered Time/Forgotten Place* (mus. collage by Tony Scott, Kimio Eto)
         Greeting Sampler (mus. Toru Takemitsu)
         Incident at Lee (mus. tape collage)
         Transcendent Passage (mus. Pierre Henry, Morton Subotnik)
         Whirligogs (mus. Luciano Berio), Bat-Dor Company, Israel
1970   *Ecstasy* (mus. Oliver Messaien)
         Variations and Fugue on a Theme of a Dream (mus. Ramayana Monkey Chant)
         Sam Nearlydeadman (mus. collage by Lubovitch)
         The Teaching, for NBC Television broadcast
         Some of the Reactions of Some of the People of the Time Upon Hearing the Reports of the Coming of the Messiah (mus. Handel's *Messiah*), Gulbenkian Ballet, Lisbon
1971   *Social* (mus. Bach)
         Clear Lake (mus. Mendelssohn)
         The Time Before the Time After (After the Time Before) (mus. Stravinsky), Ballet Théâtre Contemporain
         In the Clearing (mus. Bach), Bat-Dor Dance Company

1972 *Joy* (mus. Bach), Ballet Rambert
      Air (mus. Bach)
1973 *Scherzo for Massa Jack* (mus. Ives), American Ballet Theater, New York
      Chariot Light Night (mus. Bach), video for Granada Television, London
1974 *Three Essays* (mus. Ives), American Ballet Theater
      Eight Easy Pieces (mus. Stravinsky), UCLA Dance Company, Los Angeles
      Zig-Zag (mus. Stravinsky), Pennsylvania Ballet
1975 *Avalanche* (mus. Bach)
      Rapid Transit (mus. Stravinsky)
      Girl on Fire (mus. Britten)
      Session (no mus.), Repertory Dance Theater, Salt Lake City
1976 *Les Noces* (mus. Stravinsky), Meadowbrook Music Festival, Rochester, Michigan
      Marimba (mus. Steve Reich), Maurice Béjart's Ballet of the Twentieth Century
1977 *Exultate, Jubilate* (mus. Mozart; soloist, Judith Raskin)
      Scriabin Dances (mus. Scriabin), Spoleto Festival, Charleston, South Carolina
1978 *North Star* (mus. Philip Glass)
      Valley (mus. Beethoven)
1979 *Tiltawhirl* (mus. Glass), ice-dance for skaters John Curry and Peggy Fleming
      Up Jump (mus. Duke Ellington, Charles Mingus, Max Roach)
1980 *Mistral* (mus. Glass, Brian Eno), for PBS *Dance in America* series
      Cavalcade (mus. Reich)
1981 *American Gesture* (mus. Ives)
      Beau Danube (mus. Strauss)
1983 *Big Shoulders* (no mus.)
      Tabernacle (mus. Reich)
1984 *Court of Ice* (mus. Bach), ice-dance for John Curry
      Adagio and Rondo for Glass Harmonica (mus. Mozart)
1985 *A Brahms Symphony* (mus. Brahms)
1986 *Concerto Six Twenty-Two* (mus. Mozart), Centre National de Danse, Angers, France
      Blood (mus. Geoge Antheil)
1987 *Of My Soul* (mus. Bach)
      Sleeping Beauty (mus. Tchaikovsky), ice-skating version for Anglia TV, England, and WGBH, Boston
      Into the Woods (Broadway musical; mus. Sondheim)
1988 *Musette* (mus. Poulenc)
      Rhapsody in Blue (mus. Gershwin), New York City Ballet
1989 *Fandango* (mus. Ravel)
1990 *From Paris to Jupiter* (mus. Mozart)
      Hautbois (mus. Mozart), Paris Opera Ballet
1991 *Sinfonia Concertante* (mus. Mozart), Pacific Northwest Ballet
      Waiting for the Sunrise (mus. Les Paul, Mary Ford), commissioned by Mikhail Baryshnikov for the White Oak Dance Project
1992 *American Gesture* (mus. Ives), Pacific Northwest Ballet
1993 *The Red Shoes* (Broadway musical; mus. Jule Styne)
1994 *So in Love* (mus. Cole Porter)
      The Planets (mus. Gustav Holst), ice-skating version for A&E Network and Rhombus Media

      Oklahoma! (London production of musical; mus. Rodgers and Hammerstein)
1996 *The King and I* (two dances; mus. Rodgers and Hammerstein)
      Touch Me (mus. The Doors), ice-dance for Paul Wylie
      Adagio (mus. Bach), ice-dance for Paul Wylie
      I'll Be Seeing You (mus. Kahal and Fain, performed by Mel Torme), ice-dance for Roca & Sur
      Gershwin Variations (mus. Gershwin), ice-dance for Ice Theater of New York
1997 *Othello* (mus. Goldenthal), Lar Lubovitch Dance Company, American Ballet Theater, San Francisco Ballet

Publications

On LUBOVITCH: books—

Gruen, John, *People Who Dance,* Princeton, 1988.

On LUBOVITCH: articles—

Croce, Arlene "Dancing," *The New Yorker,* 11 April 1988.
Gruen, John, "Lar Lubovitch, Lyricism & Craft," *Dance Magazine,* February 1990.
———, "Dance Return to Broadway: Lar Lubovitch, onto the Stage," *Dance Magazine,* April 1996.
Kisselgoff, Anna, "The Wider Dimensions of Lubovitch," *New York Times,* 31 October 1993.
———, "A Man of Movement Right at Home with Music," *New York Times,* 3 November 1994.
———, "Minimalism, Out; Romanticism, In," *New York Times,* 11 June 1995.
———, "Downtown Team's Uptown Premiere," *New York Times,* 26 May 1997.
Pall, Ellen, "Modern Romantic," *New York Times Magazine,* 11 May 1997.
Solomons, Gus, Jr., "So In Love," *Dance Magazine,* 1995.

*   *   *

One of modern dance's most eclectic emissaries, Lar Lubovitch has created dances in a variety of arenas, earning both kudos and criticism for his work. Choreographing prolifically for his own company and others since 1968, Lubovitch has gained a reputation for a free-flowing, music-driven style that has made his work popular with audiences and has polarized critics. He has produced more than 50 dances for his New York-based Lar Lubovitch Dance Company, which celebrated its 30th anniversary season in 1998. In addition, almost since the outset of his career, Lubovitch has created dances for other companies, often ballet companies seeking to update their repertories. His works have been performed by the New York City Ballet, American Ballet Theater, Paris Opera Ballet, Royal Danish Ballet, Stuttgart Ballet, Alvin Ailey American Dance Theatre, Mikhail Baryshnikov's White Oak Dance Project and others.

Since the mid-1980s, Lubovitch has further diversified, creating ice dances for Olympic champion skaters and providing choreography for Broadway musicals. He received a Tony Award nomination for his Broadway debut in 1987 with the musical staging of the Stephen Sondheim/James Lapine show *Into the Woods.* And in 1994, his ballet for the short-lived Broadway musical version of *The Red*

Lar Lubovitch Dance Company performing *A Brahms Symphony.* **Photograph © Lois Greenfield.**

Shoes was judged the only redeemable part of that show. The 18-minute ballet survives in the repertory of American Ballet Theatre.

"The popularity of Lubovitch's choreography—as well as much criticism of it—stems from its easy accessibility," wrote Gus Solomons Jr. in a 1995 *Dance Magazine* review. "It is feel-good, gracious, and unabashedly entertaining dancing, but it sometimes lacks the emotionally nutritional substance of a completely balanced artistic meal." Yet, in what has developed into a long-running print debate between New York critics, others differ. John Gruen, an ardent advocate, wrote in the February 1990 *Dance Magazine* that Lubovitch "continues to be among the world's most musical makers of dance, investing his work with a compelling lyricism and an almost breathless attempt to make every last . . . musical nuance inhabit his movements."

Lubovitch was born in Chicago in 1943, the second of four children. His father, the son of Russian immigrants, ran a small department store. As a boy, Lubovitch danced for fun and occasionally invented dances for makeshift shows he put on with his siblings. "I choreographed not knowing I was choreographing," he told Norma

McLain Stoop for a 1972 *Dance Magazine* profile. "I had no steps, no vocabulary, but it had great meaning to me—these shiftings of bodies through space."

Lubovitch had already taken some courses at the Art Institute of Chicago when he enrolled at the University of Iowa as an art major. But as a freshman in 1960 he attended a campus performance of the José Limón Dance Company—the first professional dance he had seen —and was immediately won over. The following summer he enrolled in dance classes at Connecticut College in New London, where his instructors included Limón and Alvin Ailey. From there he entered the Juilliard School in New York on full scholarship. His teachers included Louis Horst, Lucas Hoving, Anna Sokolow and Antony Tudor. While at Juilliard he began sporadically dancing with troupes headed by Pearl Lang, Donald McKayle, John Butler, Glen Tetley, and with the Manhattan Festival Ballet.

"I came to dancing very late," Lubovitch says in Gruen's 1988 book, *People Who Dance.* "But I had a ferocious determination to achieve certain abilities that the dancers around me already possessed." After Juilliard he studied at the Martha Graham School

502

and the Joffrey Ballet school, supporting himself with carpentry work and a night job as a go-go dancer at a Greenwich Village nightclub. In the mid-1960s he joined the Harkness Ballet, where he danced for two years. It was there that his desire to be a choreographer jelled.

"My idea was to choreograph for the Harkness, because they had many fine dancers and many bad works," he told Gruen. But the Harkness was not receptive. Lubovitch took a leave of absence to do a concert of his own works at the YMHA in New York City in October, 1968. The following year, with support of the Paul LePercq Foundation, he assembled a troupe of 20 dancers for two concerts at the YMHA that were enthusiastically received, and he was on his way as a choreographer.

Some of his noteworthy early efforts included *Ecstasy,* a plotless, lyrical piece to music of Olivier Messiaen; *Some of the Reactions of Some of the People Some of the Time Upon Hearing the Reports of the Coming of the Messiah,* to excerpts from George Fredric Handel's *Messiah; The Time Before the Time After (After the Time Before),* set to music of Igor Stravinsky; and *Whirligogs,* a study of alienation set to Luciano Berio's *Sinfonia.* The latter was originally commissioned for Israel's Bat-Dor Company, for which Lubovitch was visiting choreographer in 1971.

Lubovitch's career has been marked with intermissions during which he withdrew from dance to examine and refocus his art. He did this in the early 1970s and again in the early 1980s, dissolving and then reforming his company. Re-emerging in 1975, his choreography took a turn toward formalist structure reflected in his pieces to the minimalist composers Steve Reich *(Marimba,* 1976, and *Cavalcade,* 1980) and Philip Glass *(North Star,* 1978). Fueled in part by popularity of these dances and by the excellence of his dancers, his company was among the busiest attractions on the international touring circuit in the early 1980s.

After his early 1980s sabbatical, when he retired to upstate New York with self-described "choreographer's block," he seemed to have displaced his formal, minimalist period with a more romantic approach closer akin to his earlier works. In a 1995 review of the company's 25th anniversary season, Anna Kisselgoff wrote in *New York Times* that Lubovitch's *Brahms Symphony* (1985) "signaled Mr. Lubovitch's move away from Minimalist music and a return to the Romantic and Classical scores that led to the outpouring of emotional power in his finest works."

Another significant work of the 1980s—and one that brought him a great deal of publicity — was *Concerto Six Twenty-Two,* to Mozart's *Concerto for Clarinet and Orchestra, K. 622.* A hit at its American premiere at Carnegie Hall in 1986 (it had been created for the Centre National de Danse Contemporain in Angers, France, a year earlier), its chivalrous central duet for two men became a regular feature at AIDS benefits after it was performed at the Dancing for Life benefit at Lincoln Center in 1987. Mikhail Baryshnikov with his White Oak Dance Project also toured with it.

Concerto Six Twenty-Two provides just one example of the divided press Lubovitch has received. Kisselgoff extolled it for suggesting "depth of feeling through spatial design and subtle timing," and declared, "That *Concerto Six Twenty-Two* is a major work is not in doubt." Meanwhile, the *New Yorker's* Arlene Croce argued that "Lubovitch's images develop no cohesive meaning . . . *Concerto Six Twenty-Two* does not add up to the work it has been acclaimed as being."

Lubovitch continued to choreograph for his company and others in the 1990s, with notable commissions from the Paris Opera Ballet, Pacific Northwest Ballet, White Oak Dance Project, and the Kennedy Center in Washington, D.C. In 1993 he joined the creative team revamping the classic 1948 movie *The Red Shoes* for the stage. While the show was a flop (folding after 51 previews and five performances), critics lauded Lubovitch's choreography for the culminating ballet. Vincent Canby wrote in the *New York Times,* "With astonishing grace and wit, the ballet dramatized just about all that needs to be said about the sometimes obsessive nature of artists and the bargains they make with life."

For the next several years Lubovitch's energies were increasingly tapped for the commercial theater and ice dancing ventures. In 1994 he choreographed a new version of *Oklahoma!* for the London stage. In 1996 he choreographed two new dances and oversaw the recreation of Jerome Robbins' original choreography for the Broadway revival of *The King and I.*

He'd begun working on the ice in 1984 with John Curry: Dance on Ice and continued that interest with a full-length *Sleeping Beauty* on ice for television in 1987. In 1994 he choreographed Gustav Holst's *The Planets* for a television production featuring French skaters Isabelle and Paul Duchesnay that was nominated for an International Emmy Award and a Grammy Award.

Not until 1997 did he again focus his attention completely on the concert stage, this time for a joint commission by American Ballet Theatre and the San Francisco Ballet for his first full-evening ballet, a dance version of *Othello.* Lubovitch commissioned an original score from Elliot Goldenthal, best known for film scores. ABT premiered *Othello* in May of 1997. The press, as usual, was divided on the New York premiere, with Kisselgoff declaring it a success and Joan Acocella, in the *Wall Street Journal,* exclaiming "What a dud!"

In a 1997 article for the *New York Times Magazine,* Ellen Pall observed that stylistically Lubovitch's choreography falls outside the prominent movements in late 20th-century modern dance:

> While many of his colleagues soberly explore social ills or, fascinated by formal concerns, coolly toy with the limits of dance itself, much of his work is lushly romantic, passionate, tender, full of dazzling, ribbonlike curves, eye-confounding lifts and spins. . . . In a time when beauty is deeply suspect in all the arts, Lubovitch's work is frankly, shamelessly beautiful.

—Diane Hubbard Burns

LYNCHTOWN

Choreography: Charles Weidman
Music: Lehman Engel
Design: Charles Weidman
First Production: Guild Theatre, New York City, 26 January 1936
Original Dancers: Charles Weidman, members of the Humphrey-Weidman Dance Company
Other productions include: Charles Weidman Theatre Dance Company, with Janet Towner (inciter), Myra Hushansky and Barry Barychko (first duet), Janet Towner and Paul Wilson (second duet), and Selby Beebe and Barry Barychko (third duet), filmed for the Jerome Robbins Film Archive at the 92nd St. YM-YMHA, 23 May 1972; Xoregos Performing Company, with Paula Clare (inciter), Gregory Alexander (victim), Veronique Cimpson, Holly

San Francisco Museum of Modern Art, November 1977; Charles Weidman Dance Foundation, with Kara Vernarec (first inciter), Gayle Gibbons and Theodore Thomas (first duet), Vernarec and Raymond Sullivan (second duet), Krisha Marcano and Matthew Mohr (third duet), and Margaret Godwin, Juliet Harvey, Laurie Hershberger, Rosalynde Leblanc, Cynthia Schilb, Graham Smith, Tamara Tossey, and Kevin Verecke (victim), Dia Center for the Arts, New York City, 10 May 1992.

Publications

Hering, Doris, "The Season in Review," *Dance Magazine,* June 1948.
Kahn, Judy, "The Repertory Dancers of New Jersey, the Cubiculo, New York City, 3 April 1972," *Dance Magazine,* June 1972.
Ross, Janice, "Oakland: Oakland Ballet," *Dance Magazine,* April 1986.
Stevens, Larry, "All Weidman Program: Deborah Carr's Theatre Dance Ensemble," *Attitude,* January-April 1984.

*   *   *

Charles Weidman premiered his *Lynchtown* in 1936, exactly in the middle of his 18-year partnership with Doris Humphrey in the Humphrey-Weidman studio and company, which lasted from 1927 to 1945. It was an era distinguished by serious social commentary, perhaps more so than any subsequent epochs in modern dance history. Weidman, by contrast, seemed to stand outside this tendency; his works were characterized by lightheartedness, warmth, and spontaneity, and one of his hallmarks was the comical movement style called "kinetic pantomime."

The latter, used in works such as *Opus 51* (which premiered two years after *Lynchtown*) and—fittingly enough—*Kinetic Pantomime,* two years before *Lynchtown,* contrasted sharply with traditional representational pantomime. Don McDonagh, in his *Complete Guide to Modern Dance,* described it thus, "a blizzard of movement that did not attempt to tell a story but just to present kinetically related gestures no matter how incongruous their juxtaposition." Thus in *Opus 51* a woman "telling her beads like a pious nun" would push an imaginary bead to the bottom of the string and a man next to her fishing with an invisible pole would tug upward as though catching the bead, now transformed into a fish. There was no relation between the two acts, and that was precisely what made their linkage so amusing.

In *Atavisms,* a three-part suite of which *Lynchtown* was the most memorable and the most enduring, Weidman capitalized on back-and-forth interplay which, in the first two parts at least, was comical. *Bargain Counter* focused on a store's floorwalker battling a tide of bargain hunters; in the more biting *Stock Exchange,* a tycoon took center stage, literally pulling others down with him as his fortunes took a dive. Humor aside, there was obvious social commentary nonetheless in these two, particularly the latter. But *Lynchtown* seemed to be all commentary and no humor—unusual ground for Weidman, though he would later make a notable display of his somber side in *A House Divided* (1945).

As its name suggests, *Lynchtown* (sometimes rendered as *Lynch Town*) is about a lynching. Who is being lynched, or why, is not important; the key element is the crowd's frenzy, the hysteria that takes hold in the interplay of the figures inciting one another toward the culminating act of hatred. Here the central figure is not necessarily the victim, whose position is understandably passive, but the "inciter," the one who motivates the others to do the deed. It was fitting that this work should come out when it did, in 1936, a time when the Nazis' grip on Germany was tightening, when Stalin was turning from his slaughter of the peasantry to a bloodletting among the party ranks, when weird manifestations of mass paranoia were rocking America, incited by figures as diverse as Father Coughlin and Huey Long. No wonder *Lynchtown* has had such staying power. The dance, which runs to eight or nine minutes, has been filmed numerous times, perhaps most notably in May 1972 for the Jerome Robbins Film Archive at the 92nd Street YM-YWHA in New York, performed by members of Weidman's Theatre Dance Company. Even in the 1990s, six decades after its original presentation, *Lynchtown* continues to see revivals.

—Judson Knight

MABRY, Iris

American dancer, choreographer, and educator

Born: c. 1920 in Clarksville, Tennessee. **Education:** B.A., Smith College; trained in dance at the Neighborhood Playhouse in New York City; studied with Louis Horst, Martha Graham, and Elsa Fried; summer sessions at Bennington College School of the Dance, Bennington, Vermont. **Family:** Married Ralph Gilbert. **Career:** Acted in various stock companies; won an audition at the YMHA dance series, 1943; solo debut, Times Hall, New York City, 1946; appeared in Ballet Society programs, 1947; presented solo programs of her own choreography, often to music composed by her husband, Ralph Gilbert; concert works produced by the Choreographers Workshop, a nonprofit cooperative founded by Trudy Goth, New York, 1946; director of dance, Theater Department, Smith College, early 1950s; taught at Jacob's Pillow and the Perry-Mansfield School of Theatre.

Works (music composed by Ralph Gilbert for all works)

1946	*Litany*
	Witch Dance
	Dreams
	Sarabande
	Scherzo
	Bird Spell
	Rally
	Cycle
	Blues
1947	*Rhapsody*
	Allemande
	Doomsday
1948	*Counterpoint*
1948	*Lamb of God*
1953	*The Magic Cauldron*
1954	*Appassionata*
	Entr-acte
1955	*Cabaret*

Publications

On MABRY: article—

Terry, Walter, Review of *Sarabande* and *Witch Dance,* performed by Iris Mabry, New York, *New York Herald Tribune,* 8 May 1946.

* * *

Iris Mabry, a modern dancer of the 1940s and 1950s, specialized in choreographing solos for herself with piano accompaniment. Her preference was for mood pieces whose movements were small in dimension but burning in intensity. Long, lean, and dark-haired, Mabry exuded an air of glamorous mystery. Critics lauded her physical suppleness and expressiveness in dance pieces that were both startlingly intellectual and intense. John Martin of the *New York Times* noted Mabry's economy of movement and her way of clearing her dances of anything nonessential. Her forte was focusing on the smallest of gestures and giving them importance. The dancer explained her motivation in a program note to one of her performances (the Ballet Society, 1947): "The kind of dancing in which I am most interested is not concerned with narrative, nor with pantomime or symbolism.... I believe that movement *in itself* is an exciting and rich medium." Doris Hering commented on the almost deceptive naturalness that pervaded everything Mabry danced. Lincoln Kirstein, editor of *Dance Index,* noted Mabry's elegance and choreography which was, in Kirstein's view, "always rational and often brilliant." Other critics found Mabry to be an outstanding dancer but limited in choreographic talent, complaining that her choreography was overly cerebral and too often lacked organic clarity.

Mabry was born in Tennessee and grew up in an intellectual circle in Nashville. She graduated with a B.A. in philosophy from Smith College. In 1943 she married pianist-composer Ralph Gilbert, a native of Seattle. At first, she considered a career in academia but dance soon prevailed as a goal. Her 1946 debut in Times Hall in New York City was the first solo recital in modern dance Broadway had witnessed. That recital brought her instant recognition as a major talent. Mabry was also the first American modern dancer of her generation to appear in Paris as she and husband Ralph Gilbert spent seven months in France and received critical acclaim.

The lyrical *Litany* (music composed by Gilbert in 1943) was one of the earliest pieces performed by Mabry. Press photographs show the dancer dressed in a two-toned, long-sleeved costume, her long hair arranged around her head. She revealed a long and lean torso, thin arms, and poetically slender hands. Her elasticity and muscular control attracted viewers immediately as something very special. She used her entire body when dancing. Her fingers could tremble heavenward with joy, as Mabry showed to dramatic effect in *Lamb of God* (1955), a work inspired by certain passages from the Psalms and from a line of William Blake poetry, "And round the tent of God like lambs we joy." Her feet could beat the ground with urgency. Critics were deeply impressed with the way Mabry used her lean, flexible physique in creating the distorted shapes of devils, imps, and animals as in her piece *Witch Dance*. While beholden to modern dance geniuses Martha Graham and Doris Humphrey for some of her movement qualities, Mabry was no mere imitator of either.

Mabry's husband, Ralph Gilbert, was her regular collaborator. He composed the music for all of Mabry's dances and served as her accompanist. His style ventured through music as varied as classical and jazz, with the same introspection, wit, and intelligence as Mabry exhibited in her dancing. Mabry's choreographic output was small but distinctive. *Allemande* (1947) was done in jazz style to a trumpet solo; *Doomsday* (1947) dealt with the psychology of despair. In her program notes to this piece, Mabry wrote, "This is the moment after the final catastrophe, beyond the edge of terror: a moment without point of reference, or center of gravity, or sense of time." *Rhapsody* (1947) saw Mabry manipulating a scarf. Mabry's dancing in *Sarabande* (1946) and *Witch Dance* (1946) was hailed by *New York Herald Tribune* critic Walter Terry as "compelling." *Sarabande* suggested venom and hate within the formalism of a court dance while *Witch Dance* had moments of frenzy and malevolence. In *Dreams,* (1946) Mabry, costumed in a long, shoulder-baring dress with her hair arranged in a low chignon, used simple walking patterns that turned nightmarish as actions from everyday life invaded the dancer's dreams. Sheer hysteria has probably never been more relentlessly portrayed on our stage, one critic noted. To Gilbert's insistent, driving rhythm Mabry crossed over the stage in walks, runs, and poses, all the while remaining neurotically removed from the dance movements themselves. The movements hint at exasperation in a satiric and sometimes bitter way. Don McDonagh, writing in *The Complete Guide to Modern Dance,* said about *Dreams*: "Mabry made a case history dance for herself that was rich but allusive in psychological hints and touches. She dipped into the unconscious and came up with a character who was bombarded by the flux of popular culture and social inconsequentialities and in dreams, driven to play them out, to exorcise them by ironically imitating them."

In 1950 Mabry performed at Choreographers' Workshop with her own company, Iris Mabry and Company. She danced *The Box,* a dance for herself and three male dancers. In 1954 she performed *Appassionata,* a solo version of this work and presented it at the Brooklyn Academy of Music. *Appassionata* takes place in and around a dark red box-like structure. Mabry, costumed in white silk jersey, hung, clung, or crouched around this structure.

For many years Mabry maintained a home in the Berkshires in Massachusetts and a studio in Greenwich Village in New York City where she continued to dance.

—Adriane Ruggiero

MAGUIRE, Terrill

American-born dancer, choreographer, and educator based in Canada

Born: 2 May 1947 in Pasadena, California. **Education**: Attended University of California, Northridge and Los Angeles branches, B.F.A. in dance, 1969; studied modern improvisation with Gertrude Knight and ballet with Joan Cantrell in Pasadena; studied modern in Los Angeles and New York, with William Bales, Gus Solomons Jr., Bella Lewitsky, Betty Jones, Robert Rosselot, Donald McKayle, Robert Dunn, Viola Farber, Mel Wong, Ruth Currier and others; with Robert Cohan, Helen McGehee, David Earle, Sandra Neels, Patricia Beatty (all Toronto), Peter Boneham (Ottawa); studied ballet in Los Angeles and with Earl Kraul and Grant Strate (Toronto), Frank Augustyn and David Le Hay (Ottawa); also studied ethnic dance with Elsie Dunin and Hazel Chong Hood among others. **Career**: Performed with for Valentina Oumansky, Richard Oliver, Marie Marchowsky, the Mystic Knights of the Oingo Boingo (Los Angeles), Charles Weidman, Mel Wong, Martha Bowers, Elizabeth

Keen (New York), Grant Strate, Sandra Neels, Norman Morrice, Miriam Adams, Patricia Beatty, and Menaka Thakkar (Toronto); assistant professor and head of composition division, York University (Toronto), 1974-79; guest teacher, 1984; artist-in-residence, Randolph-Macon University (Lynchberg, Virginia), 1980-81; also taught at School of Toronto Dance Theatre and Ottawa Dance Centre; founder/artistic director, INDE Festivals of New Music and Dance and INDE Multidisciplinary Arts Projects, since 1985. **Awards**: York University Faculty Merit Award, 1978; Jean A. Chalmers Choreography Award, 1988; Dora Mavor Moore Award nomination for choreography, 1988; choreography awards from Canada Council, Ontario Arts Council, Toronto Arts Council.

Works

1976	*Chrysalis*
1979	*19 Minutes Etc.* (mus. Cage)
	Terradactyl (mus. Michael Byron)
1980	*Domaines* (mus. Boulez)
	Raining Heart (mus. Sharon Smith) for Toronto Dance Theatre
1981	*Fountain* (mus. Richard Cohen)
	Restless Rags (mus. James Tenney), Randolph-Macon College Dance Deptartment
1982	*Amaranthea* (mus. Gayle Young)
	River (mus. David Behrman)
1983	*Iolanthe* (Gilbert and Sullivan opera)
	Cutting Losses #1 (mus. Harry Mann and John Lang; text Maguire)
1984	*Califia* (mus. Simon Jacobs) for Theatre Ballet of Canada
	Cutting Losses #2 (mus. Robert Stevenson)
1985	*Molly* (mus. Alexina Louie; text: James Joyce)
	Hold Me (mus. Lawrence Schragge)
	Ivory (mus. Aaron Davis)
1986	*Confessions of a Romance Junkie* (mus. Miguel Frasconi; text Maguire)
	Celestial Navigations (mus. David Behrman) for Canada Pavillion, Expo '86
1987	*Fountain Dance: An Homage to Circe, Lorelei, and Esther Williams* (mus. Andrew Timar)
1988	*Only Time To/No Time Not To* (mus. Michele George and Wende Bartley)
1989	*Mingle*
	Hyacinth (mus. Ann Southam)
	Re-Birthing the Earth (mus. The Glass Orchestra)
	Arbor (mus. Evergreen Gamelan and The Glass Orchestra), Ryerson Theatre School Dance Deptartment
1990	*River of Fire* (mus. Brian Cherney), Jewish Music Society
	Daddy (mus. Elizabeth Swados)
	Aquapella (mus. Don Wherry) for the Newfoundland Sound Symposium
1991	*Rituals of Desire* (mus. Iva Bitova)
1992	*Points of Honour* (mus. Bach, Ann Southam and Gossens)
	Ceremony of Language (mus. Steve Gorn; poetry Richard Lewis)
	Cinq Sirens (mus. James Stephens with Voodoo Angelfish)
	At the Edge of Eden (mus. Debussy), Ottawa Ballet choreographic workshop

1993   *Crazy To Be Born* (mus. Alejandra Nunez)
1995   *Wavelengths* (mus. Dario Domingues)
       Bloodsongs (mus. collective creation with Richard Sacks)
1996   *Heart/Bones* (mus. Geoff Bennett; storytelling: Jan
       Andrews)
       Elective Affinities (mus. Mark Sepic)
1997   *Sanctuary* (mus. Kirk Elliott), site-specific for Art in Open
       Spaces, Trinity Bell Plaza, Toronto

Publications

On MAGUIRE: articles—

"First, Nature," *Musicworks,* Spring 1990.
Odom, Selma, "15 Dance Laboratorium: Toronto, Terrill Maguire, March 2-5, 1977," *Dance In Canada,* Spring 1977.
Oughton, John, "Terrill Maguire, University College Playhouse, Toronto, 12-14 December 1978," *Dance in Canada*, Spring 1979.
Small, Holly, and Susan Cash, "Terrill Maguire: Choreographer and Instigator," in *Canadian Dance Studies 2,* Selma Odom and Mary Jane Warner, editors, Toronto, 1997.

Films and Videotapes

Dear Bruce Springsteen, choreographed by Maguire for CBC-TV, 1987.

*   *   *

Since the 1970s, Terrill Maguire has carved a niche for herself as an extraordinary choreographer and solo dancer. Her work has explored environmental themes, the relationships between spirituality and sexuality, and personal trauma. She is also known for her innovations with site-specific choreography and the initiation of large-scale collaborative projects integrating dancers, artists and musicians.

Maguire grew up in Pasadena, California, and her childhood influences are a part of her work. While poor materially, her home was rich culturally and she was exposed to books, music, and her parents' artistic friends. Later, at UCLA, she interacted with a variety of artists, film and music students, and studied an array of cultural music and dance forms; the barriers between the art forms were broken down for her and this experience led to the variety of collaborative projects she has worked on throughout her life. One of Maguire's earliest teachers was Gertrude Knight, who taught modern dance and improvisational dance, fostering Maguire's creativity at a young age. Maguire had a natural affinity for dance which drew her to more formal training including classes with ballet teacher Adele Charaska De Angelo, who had danced with the Ballet Russe de Monte Carlo and the Ballet Company of Radio City Music Hall. But De Angelo's teachings did not end at ballet technique; she introduced Maguire to the spiritual and metaphysical writing of Gurdieff, Ouspensky, Buber and others. De Angelo even took the young dancer to hear Krishnamurti speak under an ancient oak tree in Ojai, California, when Maguire was just 16. Having broken from the Catholic Church at a young age, Maguire was open to different forms of spirituality and these spiritual influences would later manifest themselves in her work.

Maguire continued her training in the dance program at UCLA but was dancing professionally with Valentina Oumansky and Richard Oliver even before finishing her degree. After UCLA, she joined Marie Marchowsky's company. Marchowsky, a charter member of the Martha Graham Company, was set on bringing the discipline of Graham technique to California. It was a grueling life with long hours and little reward. The company often rehearsed for a full year before performing. While in Marchowsky's company, Maguire moved to rustic Topango Canyon and soon left the company, preferring the mountains to a freeway commute.

Maguire then taught and joined a performance group of musicians, actors and dancers called the Mystic Knights of the Oingo Boingo. This company's mandate was a 180-degree turn from that of Marchowsky's company. The group performed frequently and rehearsed little. They performed in the street, night clubs, parties and galleries and later at major fashion events in New York. After a couple years, the Mystic Knights were becoming increasingly commercial and Maguire decided to leave. Through fellow Mystic Knight Michael Byron, Maguire met and began to collaborate with an innovative group of musicians at the California Institute of the Arts, among them James Tenney and Richard Tietelbaum. She was also involved in spontaneous arts events called "Happenings" which were very much like events at New York's Judson Church.

In 1973, Maguire left for Toronto with Byron, who was heading to York University to begin graduate studies and work as a teacher in the music department. Maguire began teaching movement classes in the music department and soon made connections in the dance department. Within a year she was teaching modern and composition for the dance department and eventually became head of composition. York was pulsating with dance activity at the time and gave Maguire a rewarding choreographic outlet. As there were less than a handful of composition teachers in Canada at the time, Maguire had quite an influence on her students. She encouraged them to work from internal impulses and had them perform improvisations exploring body isolation, stillness, ritual and rhythm. Like De Angelo, she exposed her students to spiritual readings and books on music, art and theatre.

Maguire left York University in 1979 and lived in New York for three years, dancing for different choreographers, among them Mel Wong and Martha Bowers. She choreographed work at venues such as P.S. (Performance Space) 122, as well as site-specific pieces culminating in the Lincoln Center Out of Doors Festival. On a tour of the Atlantic provinces with Canadian musician Gayle Young, she met Don Wherry, founder of the Newfoundland Sound Symposium. For the first Symposium in July 1986, Wherry used Maguire, composer R. Murray Schaefer, and artist Michael Snow as facilitators to present workshops and performances.

Through the 1980s, Maguire was instrumental in giving new life to the independent dance community particularly with the creation of the INDE Festivals of New Music and Dance. The INDE Festivals, which were held in 1985, 1988, 1990 and 1992, were one of the first projects Maguire organized after returning to Toronto in 1982. She arrived to see her former students struggling to present their choreography because there were few opportunities for independent choreographers to show their work. Maguire came up with a festival format that would pair up Canadian choreographers and composers. The 1980s saw the rise of the independent choreographer in Canada and the creation of several regional festivals held annually to showcase the work of independents as well as special dance series such as Dance Ontario's Danceworks.

In the 1990s, Maguire has been active with outreach projects bringing dance into Ontario's art-starved schools. In the Ottawa region she has been performing in schools since 1993 collaborating with award-winning author Jan Andrews in a project titled *Telling the Old Stories*. She was also on the Arts Advisory Committee for the Ottawa Board of Education and has done professional development workshops for teachers in that Board. Maguire has done numerous residencies in schools throughout southern and eastern Ontario and participated in the National Ballet of Canada's "Dances in the Schools" projects.

In the early part of Maguire's career she experimented, quite successfully, with site-specific and environmental dances. An example is *Chrysalis* which originally took place high in the trees near her home in Maple, Ontario. Visual artist Jacqueline Humbert designed a hammock-like cocoon to hang in the trees from which Maguire emerged wearing a costume with secret zippers to allow beautifully painted silk butterfly wings to spread themselves. Maguire eventually dropped to the ground and fluttered into the woods. She has performed her renowned fountain dances in New York's Isamu Noguchi Fountain at the Chase Manhattan Bank Plaza, a Victorian fountain in Ottawa's Confederation Park and Toronto's Trinity Bell Plaza. At a retreat called the Yard on Martha's Vineyard, Maguire created *Terradactyl* which was performed in an open-sided barn set against a backdrop of the stars and the moon.

During Maguire's time at York she further developed her work as a solo dancer and choreographer. Dances created in this time include *Kali* about the Hindu goddess who is a force of both creation and destruction; *Run Ragged*, a high-velocity, step-packed solo to James Tenney's piano rag; *Marrow* which initiated movement from the deepest part of the body; and *Sea Changes* in which Maguire is bathed in blue light, and rises out of the floor like a sea creature subject to the ebb and flow of the sea. Another significant work that emerged in the 1980s was *Cutting Losses*. The dance deals with a personal trauma in Maguire's life and, while much like a solo, the work does include a second dancer who is somewhat of an alter ego and shifts from being compassionate to aggressive to burdensome. The dance mixes with a composition by Harry Mann and John Lang and spoken text by Maguire.

In the 1990s Maguire continued to explore spiritual themes including the relationship between sexuality and spirituality. Inspired by *The Song of Songs*, Maguire based *Bloodsongs* on this sensual passage from the bible. The dance takes root in the courtship of the Sumerian goddess Inanna—a story which predates *The Song of Songs*. A related work is *Crazy to Be Born* created with singer Alejandra Nunez and based on the creation myth of the Makiritare Indians of the Amazon.

Maguire continues to find ways of aiding struggling young artists to show their work and her contributions to independent dance in Toronto are immeasurable. She has also added substantially to the Toronto dance scene overall, not only through her own inspirational choreography, but through her impact as a teacher and the way in which she fostered choreographers such as Holly Small, Susan Cash, Maxine Heppner and Christopher House—artists who have all now made formidable contributions of their own.

—Amy Bowring

MAL PELO
Spanish dance company

Works

1989   *Quarere*
1990   *Cantal*
        Lucas

1991   *Principi de Memòria (The Beginning of Memory)*
        Mont-art
1992   *Sur, Perros del Sur (South, Dogs of the South)*
1993   *Canción para los pájaros*
        La otra mirada (The Other Look)
        Rhythm Method
        La mirada de Búbal
1994   *Recuerdos de Chera (Memories of Chera)*
        Dol
        Aral
1995   *Mundana*
1996   *La Calle del imaginero (Dream-maker's street)*

*   *   *

Mal Pelo, meaning "tousle-headed," is Spanish slang for "street urchin" and is the appropriately suggestive name of this Barcelona-based contemporary dance company that came into being in 1989. Co-creators María Muñoz (born in Valencia, 1963) and Pep Ramis (born in Majorca, 1962) met at the Institut de Teatre de Barcelona where Muñoz was specializing in contemporary dance and Ramis in puppetry and voice. On graduating, they furthered their training in Amsterdam and France and worked with different small independent dance companies before coming together again in Barcelona to form their own company with Catalan Jordi Teixidó.

Their success was immediate. Mal Pelo's *Quarere,* their full-length first production in collaboration with the Teatre Obert in Barcelona and the Klapstuk Festival of 1989 in Leaven, Belgium, was premiered at the festival before touring extensively throughout Europe, Canada, and United States. The idiosyncrasies of Mal Pelo's work have been clearly set out from the beginning, owing to the intrinsic understanding between Muñoz and Ramis, and their ability to transmit the company's own poetic view of the world with intrigue and honesty. Each of their productions combines a wide spectrum of artistic skills encompassing contact improvisation, postmodern or minimalist dance, acting, and mime. Their costume aesthetic of chunkily cut clothing, and a pseudo-chic rusticity implies their closeness to nature.

After *Quarere*, Mal Pelo was then offered various co-productions and short specially commissioned pieces for dance festivals throughout Europe, such as *Lucas* for the Festival Danse à Aix, Aix-en-Provence, France, and *Canción para los pájaros* for the South Bank Centre in London. These open-space dance pieces not only broadened the scope of the public's perception of modern and contemporary dance, but gave Spanish dance in particular a fresh, new identity beyond its own frontier.

Sur, perros del sur, the company's second full-length production in 1992, is one of the best examples of what has come to be recognized as Mediterranean art. Moving between reality and oneiric ambience, the characters are portrayed with a poignant sensibility without becoming overtly sentimental. Ramis' texts in Mallorquin enhance the often surreal landscapes. In 1996 Arts Ministry-funding allowed the company to expand from three dancers to five, and they created *La calle del imaginero*. It was to be a challenge for this tightly knit trio; nevertheless, the intimacy and essence of the core members' work was further enriched by the full embodiment of concepts, if not in movement, of the new members of the company.

When not performing, founders Muñoz and Ramis work independently and also give dance and choreographic workshops.

—Michelle Man

MANN, Sara Shelton

American dancer, choreographer, and educator

Born: 17 December 1943 in Nashville. **Education:** Studied dance with Franziskas Boas, Shorter College, Georgia; with Martha Graham, Erick Hawkins, Phyllis Lamhut, and Merce Cunningham in New York; later studied body awareness systems with Bonnie Cohen, Bill Weintraub, Hameed Ali, and Faisal Muquddam. **Career:** Taught at the New School for Social Research, the Henry Street Playhouse, the Stella Adler Acting School, and for the Murray Louis Company; dancer, Alwin Nikolais Dance Theatre, 1968-72; first independent choreography, 1967; artistic director, Halifax Dance Co-op, 1975-78; created Contraband with then-husband Byron Brown, 1979; second phase of Contraband in San Francisco Bay area, 1980; company developed cult status in San Francisco with production of *Evol,* 1985; appointed to the California Arts Council dance panel, 1985; began a seven-year project, *The Mira Trilogy,* 1990; artist-in-residence, Djerassi Foundation, Esalen Institute, Moving Arts, 1995. **Awards:** Isadora Duncan Awards, 1987 (best choreography); 1991 (outstanding company performance); 1993 (outstanding choreography and outstanding company performance).

Works

1967-72	*Camelot,* Trinity University, San Antonio, Texas
	Solo, Expo '67
	40 Minutes, solos for Michael Ballard, Emery Hermans, Mann
	Untitled, New York
	Catalogue 5, Portland, Oregon
	Duet for One, for Emery Hermans
	Trio for Dummy, for Hermans, Caroline Carlson, Mann
	Construction #1, for Hermans, Portland
	Falling, Fort Collins, Colorado
	Silence, San Francisco
1973	*American Dance Booth* (mus. improvised w/wire, cart, dog), Northampton, Massachusetts
	Crazy Dog Events, Hermans, Raymond Johnson, Jeanette Stoner, Mann, New York
	For Bo Jangles
1974	*Sarcophogus,* New York
	Gathering Shells, Cleveland, Ohio
	Precipice, Cleveland
	Yoke, Brooklyn
1975	*The Rosenfelds,* Maryland
	Stone
	Kiss My Nose I'm Angry, Cleveland
	Magic Words, Cleveland
1976	*Tender Moments,* St. Louis
	I Hate to Go to Bed at Night; I Hate to Get Up in the Morning, St. Louis
	Flying Solo, St. Louis
	Geode, New York
	Traffic, St. Louis
	String
1977	*R/RSVP*
	Phrase, Halifax, Nova Scotia

	Coats, Nova Scotia
	Goat Lake in Winter/or The Way It Should Be in Our Minds (Canadian Broadcasting dance series)
	Kata
	Golf
1978	*Chappo/Chapeau,* Halifax, Nova Scotia
	Doge, Vancouver
	Ku
	Labyrinth, Halifax, Nova Scotia
	Waltz, Halifax, Nova Scotia
	Odds, Halifax/Montreal/Toronto
	Torque, Halifax, Nova Scotia
	Limit, Nova Scotia
1979	*Smashed Carapace,* cross-Canada tour
	Performance, Halifax, Nova Scotia
	Left-Over Jam, San Francisco
	Squashed and Tormented Retina, Waterloo, Canada
	Smoke, Halifax, Nova Scotia
	Light
	Les Canadiens, Halifax, Nova Scotia
1980	*Gee Whiz, Mom, Would You Hold My Heart a Minute?,* San Francisco
	The Float, eastern Canada and New York
	Hit & Run Slide
1981	*Ace,* Northampton, Massachusetts
	Affluence, Nova Scotia, Maine, Massachusetts
	The Child, California and eastern Canada
	Ah Toe Nails/A Heart Graft, San Francisco
	Solo
	Thelma, San Francisco
	Oxbow, San Francisco
1982	*In Harold's Garden,* San Francisco
	Breath Strokes
	Apparition Lullaby, San Francisco
	Placemats and Paper Plates, San Francisco
1983	*KE and the Walking Girl*
	Walking in the Backfield, San Francisco
	Genau, Freiburg and Berlin, Germany
	Tote am langen Samstag, Freiburg, Germany
	WolfsTauben, Freiburg, Germany
	Circe, San Francisco
	The Hero, Oakland
	Aspirin Soliloquy, Los Angeles
	Pots Passage, Calgary, Alberta
1984	*Several Small Towns,* San Francisco
	Untitled
	Singing My Mother to Sleep, San Francisco
	Raskifely Sum, San Francisco
1985	*Isthmus,* San Francisco
	Evol, San Francisco
1986	*Religare—hope of the impossible,* San Francisco
1987	*The Invisible War,* San Francisco
1988	*Oracle,* San Francisco
1989	*Mandala,* Contraband men, San Francisco
1991	*Mira, Cycle I,* San Francisco
1992	*Mira, Cycle II,* San Francisco
1993	*Mira, Cycle III,* San Francisco
	Sketches for the Ancestors, Kirstie Simpson, Contraband women, San Francisco
1994	*Mira, Cycle III,* San Francisco
1996	*Return to Ordinary Life,* San Francisco

Publications

Harvey, Dennis, Review, *San Francisco Weekly,* December 1990.

*   *   *

Sara Shelton Mann, protégé of Alwin Nikolais and Murray Louis, is a rebel and iconoclast, leery of conventional structures. In San Francisco, where she has mothered an entire movement of guerilla-style, New Age rebel dance that throws together elegant Cunninghamisms with raw and muddied contact improvisation, caterwauling with throbbing African rhythms—Mann has strived for more than two decades to give rebellion a voice and a beat. At times, her company, Contraband, has seemed more a threaticalization of 1960s-style Happenings than a dance company, but always it maintains its spirit of freewheeling experimentation and play.

Mann was born and raised on a farm in the white segregated society of Nashville, Tennessee, on 17 December 1943. She attended Shorter College in Rome, Georgia, where she studied biology until she discovered pictures of the college's only dance teacher, Franziskas Boas (dancer and daughter of famed anthropologist Franz Boas) and her dog, on KKK leaflets. Mann sought out Boas, made her her mentor, and changed her focus from science to fine arts. When she became pregnant and was kicked out of college, she went to live with Boas and others on a farm. It was a household deeply active in the Civil Rights movement.

At Boas' prodding, Mann went north to New York in 1964 and entered an intensive 15-year period of dance training and exploration. She studied with Martha Graham, José Limón, Phyllis Lamhut, and Merce Cunningham, as well as Brynar Mehl, Cliff Keuter, Erick Hawkins, and Andrew Harwood. Later she learned a variety of forms of body awareness with Hameed Ali and Faisal Muquddam, Bonnie Cohen, Bill Weintraub, Ellen Fishburn, and Gen Togden. But seminal to her identity as a dancemaker was the period from 1968 to 1972 in which she studied and danced with Alwin Nikolais and Murray Louis. Nikolais' own freewheeling method of making "Shaman dances for our time" as a New York critic called them—discussing the nature and material of dance and of collaborating extensively with his dancers—became Mann's own approach to her work and teaching. She taught at the New School for Social Research, the Henry Street Playhouse, the Stella Adler Acting School, and for the Murray Louis Dance Company.

Mann began making her own work in 1967. Throughout the earliest period her dances had titles like *Silence, Duet for One,* and *Catalogue 5.* By 1973 Mann was creating pieces like *Crazy Dog Events,* made up of four solos based on American Indian ritual, and *For Bo Jangles,* a dance for six dancers on pistachio shells danced in a circle with the audience inside the ring. The wackiness of pistachio shells in concert with sacred ritual eventually became the signature of the company she founded, Contraband, whose holy sensualism and scruffily romantic and sometimes incomprehensible outrage seized the Bay Area in 1985 with its first large-scale work, *Evol.* Quickly the group became the barometer against which all other local performers were measured; for many years, few were regarded as so hip or so primally honest. They alone seemed to combine the Beat generation's belief in transcendence through exile from the status quo with the counterculture's trust in apotheosis through sexuality. As critic Dennis Harvey wrote in the *San Francisco Weekly* in 1990, Contraband has ruled the "world of archetypical, Californian self-exploration through dance, text and radical polemic."

The epic work *The Mira Trilogy,* begun in 1990, is effectively Mann's summation of her group style. Inspiration for the work was the life chronicle of the 16th-century Indian mystic, poet, politician, and saint Mirabai. Mirabai rejected life as a Brahmin and cast off the traditional role assigned her as a woman to devote herself through a combination of passive resistance and active alliances to religion and social justice. For Mann, Mirabai is a metaphor for her own plight as an "abandoned girl-child from Tennessee" and her struggle for spiritual wholeness.

Her process is collaborative, and the company has from the beginning strived for the social character of a collective, with each performer serving multiple roles and no role necessarily being taboo for any one performer. The imagistic nature of her style draws from the new German Expressionists such as Pina Bausch and Anna Teresa de Keersmaeker, with great value placed on social and mystical content. But the enactment relies far more on contact improvisation, martial arts, gymnastics, and body work than on recognizable dance vocabulary and its technical expression.

When Mann finally left New York, she took up the post of artistic director of the Halifax Dance Co-op in Nova Scotia from 1975 to 1978, and from 1977 to 1978 her work premiered at Dance in Canada. In 1979 she created the first incarnation of Contraband with her then-husband Byron Brown. After a year of research Mann produced and toured a full-length piece each year for three years—*The Float, The Child,* and *The Breath. The Child* was featured at the Toronto Theatre Festival in 1981. Mann arrived in the Bay Area in 1979 to work with a group called Mangrove that used contact improvisation for performance. Contraband continued to exist on the side and materialized and disbanded with every project. From 1982 to 1983 Mann also toured Germany and Switzerland. But then Mangrove dissolved. As an antidote, some of the members, along with Mann and Freddie Long, refashioned themselves into Mixed Bag Productions. When that collaboration ended, Contraband again rose up to take its place.

Contraband's 1985 performance of *Evol,* a ritual in which Rinde Eckert, Lauren Elder, Jim Cabe, and Benjamin Young collaborated, marked the beginning of nearly 10 years of company growth. Jess Curtis and Keith Hennessey became central figures in the evolution of the Contraband style, in which men could be loving and women ferociously strong. *Religare—hope of the impossible,* performed in the pit of a demolished low-income hotel in the Mission District of San Francisco, followed in 1986 and was among the most political of the dance events. The seven-year *Mira* cycle culminated with *Return to Ordinary Life* in 1996.

In 1985 Mann was appointed to the California Arts Council dance panel and in 1986 served as a judge for the Isadora Duncan Dance Awards. In 1987 she won an Isadora Duncan award for best choreography for *Religare.* In 1991 she won another award for outstanding company performance. In 1993 she was awarded two more accolades by the Isadora Duncan awards committee, one for outstanding choreography and another, again, for outstanding company performance. In 1995 she was artist-in-residence at the Djerassi Foundation and the Esalen Institute, both in California, and at Moving Arts in Cologne, Germany. The company has received numerous grants from local, state, and national funding agencies.

—Ann Murphy

MANTSOE, Vincent Sekwati

South African dancer, choreographer, and educator

Born: 26 April 1971, in Soweto. **Education:** Bona Secondary School in Diepkloof; scholarship, Moving into Dance (MID) school, 1970; diploma, MID Community Dance Teacher's Training program, 1992. **Career:** Dancer, Street Dance and Rathabile Youth Club; dancer, choreographer, and now associate director, Moving Into Dance Performance Company. **Awards:** Solo *African Soul* chosen Pick of the Fringe, Johannesburg Dance Umbrella, 1992; Most Promising Male Dancer Award, IGI Vita, 1993; Young Choreographer Award, FNB VITA, 1994; special scholarship award, Victorian College for the Arts, 1994; *Hanano, Blessing of the Earth* chosen as Best of the Fest, Arts Alive Dance Festival, 1995; *Gula Matari* awarded first prize, First Contemporary African Dance Competition, 1995; Young Artist of the Year, Standard Bank National Arts Festival, 1996; Choreographer of the Year, FNB VITA, 1996; Independent Choreographers Young Writers Award, Fifth Recontres Choreographiques Internationales des Bagnolet Seine-St. Denis (France), 1996; reworked version of *Speaking in Tongues and Ngoma*, Contemporary African Choreographic Award, 1996.

Roles (choreographed by Sylvia Glasser for the Moving into Dance Performance Company)

1991	*Tranceformations*
	Paths of Sound
1992	*Midnight of the Soul*
1993	*African Spring*
	Zimbili—They Are Two
1994	*Stone Cast Ritual*

Other roles include: Many performances with Moving into Dance, and as a guest artist for PACT Dance Company in South Africa.

Works

1992	*African Soul*, solo
1993	*Gula*, solo
	Gula Matari (mus. Gabrielle Roth), for group
	Sunduza, trio
	Anazasi (dedicated to Glasser)
1994	*Speaking with Tongues and Ngoma* (mus. Eric Van der Westen, Jeroen Van Vliet), Johannesburg Dance Umbrella
	Voice from the Seas for Pretoria Technikon
1995	*Hanano, Blessing of the Earth* (mus. Leonard Eto by Kodo) for Johannesburg Dance Umbrella
1996	*Men-jaro* (mus. Pan African Orchestra of Ghana), for Standard Bank National Arts Festival
	Speaking in Tongues and Ngoma (reworked)
1997	*Sasanka* for Dance Theatre of Harlem
	Mpheyane (mus. James Wood, Randy Crafton) for Johannesburg Dance Umbrella
	Tlotlo (mus. Mamady Keitha)

Films and Videotapes

Tranceformations, with performance by Mantsoe, SABC-TV, 1992.

Plane Song, choreography and performance by Mantsoe, BBC, 1993.

*   *   *

Vincent Sekwati Mantsoe was born and grew up in Soweto. Though he had a natural aptitude for dance, there were very few formal or vocational dance training opportunities in his township. His early dance experience was gained mostly through involvement with two energetic youth groups, called Street Dance and the Rathabile Youth Club. An important turning point came for the young Mantsoe in 1990, as he auditioned and received a scholarship to study dance at the Moving into Dance (MID) school. There he studied Afro-fusion and choreography with Sylvia Glasser, and was also exposed to contemporary dance and jazz. Another major influence on his career development was his anthropological study of African and Western dance, for which he received a diploma from the MID Community Dance Teacher's Training program in 1992.

Tranceformations, choreographed by Sylvia Glasser in 1991, was Mantsoe's first major public performance with MID; it also marked a television appearance as the performance was broadcast by SABC-TV. Mantsoe's debut showed him to be a noticeably different and gifted performer. He not only demonstrated his physical skills, but an intense spiritual understanding of the *San* (Bushmen) "Trance Dances," that were the inspiration for Glasser's work. Mantsoe's dancing revealed a much deeper connection in his interpretation of *Tranceformations*, as he drew on his own heritage and would later use these themes as a stimulus for many of his own choreographic works. Mantsoe is also a skilled African drummer, and his mother and grandmother are sources of inspiration and guidance in developing his sense of African ritual.

The fusion of different cultural identities within dance is a major theme Mantsoe explores within his work. He incorporates a variety of cultural influences into his movement vocabulary from the many people he has met on his travels while performing, teaching and choreographing, in Europe, Australia, the United States, and Africa. Mantsoe's choreographic skills and potential became eminently clear with the debut of *Gula Matari*, which he choreographed for MID to perform at the Dance Umbrella festival in Johannnesburg in 1993. Two years later, in 1995, *Gula Matari* won first prize at the First Contemporary African Dance Competition in Angola. The award included a tour for Mantsoe and MID to Kenya, Nigeria, Togo, Ghana, Gabon, the Ivory Coast, Congo, and Angola.

A highlight in Mantsoe's career was his collaboration with the Dance Theatre of Harlem in 1997, setting the newly created work *Sasanka* on the company for a performance in Washington, D.C. at the Kennedy Center, and then in New York. Other well-received danceworks by Mantsoe include 1993's *Sunduza,* and *Anazasi* (dedicated to Glasser), *Speaking with Tongues Ngoma* (1994), *Men-jaro* (1996) and 1997's *Mpheyane*, and *Tlotlo*, a recent work first performed at the Dance Factory Arts Alive Festival and then taken on tour to Germany.

Vincent Sekwati Mantsoe is currently the resident choreographer of MID and was appointed associate director in 1997.

—Jill Waterman

511

MARCUSE, Judith

Canadian dancer, choreographer, educator, and company director

---

Born: Judith Rose Margolick, 13 March 1947 in Montreal. **Education:** Studied modern dance with her aunt, Elsie Salomons, ballet with Séda Zaré (Vaganova method), Sonia Chamberlain (R.A.D.) and later at the Banff School with Brian Macdonald; attended the Royal Ballet School in London, with classes under Barbara Fewster, Maria Fay, Pamela May, Eileen Ward and others; additional study in New York with Benjamin Harkarvy, Antony Tudor, Hector Zaraspe, and at the school of American Ballet; classes in Banff, Alberta, with Vera Volkova. **Family:** Married Richard Frederick Marcuse in 1972; one daughter. **Career:** Dancer, Les Grands Ballets Canadiens in Montreal, 1965-68; Sadler's Wells Ballet, London, 1968; Ballet de Gèneve, Geneva, Switzerland, 1969; Bat-Dor Dance Company, Tel-Aviv, Israel, 1970-72; Classical Ballet of Israel, Tel-Aviv, 1972; Oakland Ballet, Oakland, California, 1972-74; Festival Ballet of Canada, Ottawa, 1973; Ballet Rambert, London, 1974-76; first choreographies for the Oakland Ballet, 1974, and for Ballet Rambert, 1975-76; toured Canada as a soloist, dancing in her own creations and in the works of other choreographers, and in lecture demonstrations, 1976-80; developed the Judith Marcuse Dance Projects Society in 1980 (later called Repertory Dance Company of Canada, Judith Marcuse Dance Company and Dance Arts Vancouver Society); has taught extensively, in both academic dance programs and for professional companies and community programs in Canada and the United States. **Awards:** Koerner Foundation Award, 1960; Chalmers Award for Choreogaphy, 1976; Clifford E. Lee Award for Choreography, 1979; Vancouver YWCA Woman of Distinction Award, 1985; Vancouver Award for Excellence in Theatre, 1986; West Vancouver 75th Anniversary Achievement Award, 1987; Canada 125 Medal, 1991; Silver Juried Award, New York City International Dance Film and Video Festival, 1994 and 1995.

Roles

1967   Primavera, *Carmina Burana* (Nault), Les Grands Ballets Canadiens, Montreal

1970   Principal dancer, *Whirligogs* (Lubovich), Bat-Dor Dance Company, Tel-Aviv

1972   Grisi, *Pas de Quatre* (Dolin), Classical Ballet of Israel, Tel-Aviv

1973   Snow Queen, *The Nutcracker* (Guidi after Ivanov), Oakland Ballet
        Angel, *Hansel and Gretel* (Guidi/Pause), Oakland Ballet

1974   First Song, *Dark Elegies* (Tudor), Ballet Rambert, London
        Polka, *Façade* (Ashton), Ballet Rambert, London
        Minerva, *Judgment of Paris* (Tudor), Ballet Rambert

1976   Principal dancer, *Ziggurat* (Tetley), Ballet Rambert
        Soloist, *Embrace Tiger* (Tetley), Ballet Rambert

Works

1974   *Fusion* (mus. Pachelbel), Oakland Ballet, California

1975   *baby* (mus. Lambert), Ballet Rambert, London

1976   *Four Working Songs* (mus. Miranda), Ballet Rambert, London; remounted for Les Grands Ballets Canadiens, Montreal

        Session (mus. African traditional), Dancemakers, Toronto, Ontario

1977   *Apart* (mus. Keeble), Entre-Six Dance Company, Montreal
        Re-Entry (mus. various), Winnipeg Contemporary Dancers
        Exit (mus. various), Mountain Dance Theatre, Vancouver

1978   *SpeakEasy* (mus. Keeble, G. Marcuse et al), Dennis Wayne and Company, New York
        Folk Song (mus. trad. Bulgarian), Judith Marcuse Dance Company

1979   *Celebration* (mus. Bach), Winnipeg Contemporary Dancers
        Noodlin' (mus. Diddly), Judith Marcuse Dance Company
        Sadhana Dhoti (mus. Jagg), Banff Festival, Banff, Alberta

1980   *Good Clean Fun* (mus. Beatles), Pacific Ballet Theatre, Vancouver
        Mirrors, Masques, and Transformations (mus. M. J. Baker, G. Marcuse and Keeble), Shaw Festival, Niagara-on-the-Lake, Ontario

1981   *Spring Dances* (mus. Schumann), Les Grands Ballets Canadiens, Montreal
        Cuts (mus. Nurock, Gesualdo), Dancemakers, Toronto
        Playgrounds (mus. Nurock), J. M. Dance Projects, Vancouver
        Transfer (mus. Nurock, Pergolesi), Nederlands Dans Theater, the Hague

1982   *Elegy* (mus. Monteverdi), Three's Company, San Diego
        We Can Dance: A Look at Dance and Dance-Making (mus. various), J. M. Dance Projects, Vancouver

1983   *Seascape* (mus. Bach), Les Grands Ballets Canadiens, Montreal
        Hors d'oeuvre (mus. Johnson), Les Ballets Jazz de Montreal
        Currents (mus. Nurock), Harbourfront Corporation, Toronto
        Aiby-Aicy-Aidi-Ai (mus. MacIntosh), J. M. Dance Projects, Vancouver

1984   *Bartók Sonata* (mus. Bartók), J. M. Dance Projects, Vancouver

1985   *Blue Skies* (mus. various), J. M. Dance Projects, Vancouver
        Traces (mus. Part), J. M. Dance Projects, Vancouver
        Closed Circuit (mus. Andreissen), J. M. Dance Projects, Vancouver

1986   *Cortège* (mus. Monteverdi), J. M. Dance Projects, Vancouver
        Time Out (mus. Touré), J. M. Dance Projects, Vancouver

1987   *Playing without Fire* (mus. Nurock), J. M. Dance Projects, Vancouver

1988   *Moving Past Neutral* (mus. Foss), Calgary Winter Olympics Arts Festival
        Threnody (mus. Monteverdi), Royal Winnipeg Ballet
        Purple Haze (mus. Hendrix), J. M. Dance Projects, Vancouver

1989   *Bach and Blue* (mus. Bach), J. M. Dance Projects, Vancouver

1990   *Madrugada* (mus. various), J. M. Dance Projects, Vancouver

1991   *Tales from the Vaudeville Stage* (mus. various), J. M. Dance Projects

1992   *Room* (mus. traditional African), Royal Winnipeg Ballet
1994   *States of Grace* (mus. Ferreras), J. M. Dance Projects

Other works include: Solos and duets for *In Concert: Judith Marcuse and Sacha Belinsky Dance,* first performed at the World's Fair, Knoxville, Tennnesse, 1982; dances in *Puttin' on the Ritz,* Belfry Theatre, Victoria, B.C., 1977, and Shaw Festival, Niagara-on-the Lake, Ontario, l980; dances for Vancouver Opera productions of *The Bartered Bride* (mus. Smetana), 1982; *Romeo et Juliette* (mus. Gounod), 1982; *Alcina* (mus. Handel), l990.

Publications

By MARCUSE: articles—

Interview with Paula Citron in *Dance Magazine,* April 1981.

On MARCUSE: articles—

"A Plea for Play: People," *Maclean's Magazine,* 14 September 1981.
Preston, Brian, "Dancing for Joy," *Imperial Oil Review,* Fall 1995.
Stein, Lynn A., "Connecting Dance and the Community with a Kiss,"
    Arts Alive, January/February 1996.
Tembeck, Iro, "Dancing in Montreal: Seeds of a Choreographic
    History," *Studies in Dance History,* Fall 1994.
Wachtel, Eleanor, "Moving Force," *Flare,* September 1980.
Zimmer, Elizabeth, "Choreographers in Process: Two Chalmers
    Winners, 1976," *Dance in Canada,* Winter 1977.

*   *   *

Judith Marcuse's diversified career encompasses performing, directing and choreographing dances in all the theatrical and commercial media. Her early training in Montreal crossed many boundaries and included both folk and traditional dance. From the Armenian, London-trained Legat disciple Séda Zaré she gained a solid base in classical ballet technique, augmented with additional studies with Sonia Chamberlain and Brian Macdonald. But it was Marcuse's aunt, Elsie Salomons, who had the most powerful influence on the development of a young dancer who would break through the confines of the ballet. Herself a ballet trainee under the emigré Ezzak Ruvenoff, Salomons, a graduate of McGill University in 1937, moved to London to work with Kurt Jooss and Rudolf von Laban. There she discovered the importance of integrating classical and modern dance techniques. Returning to Montreal, she offered eclectic training to her students and introduced social and political concerns into her creations. She also instilled in Marcuse a strong sense of obilgation to one's community and a need for social responsibility, both of which governed the dancer's creative life as an independent dancer and later as choreographer.

But the lure of classical ballet was strong. Marcuse spent three years at the Royal Ballet School in London, where prize pupils were given walk-on roles in the classics. The effect of watching such extraordinary dancers as Margot Fonteyn perform in *Sleeping Beauty* from a position on stage made an indelible impression. On returning to Canada, Marcuse joined the ensemble of Les Grands Ballets Canadiens, experiencing the trials of an organization which toured extensively. During her three-year tenure she performed in theatres throughout Canada and in 48 American states. Opportunities overseas took her to appearances with major companies in

London, Geneva, and Tel-Aviv and the chance for extensive touring abroad. Work with the Bat-Dor Dance Company of Israel and at London's Ballet Rambert gave her inspiration to achieve a unique personal signature which drew from elements of both classical and modern dance in a synthesis yet to be widely accepted in the dance world.

Marcuse's early solos and duets had a strong erotic component, a bold statement of gender, and what Max Wyman in *Dance Canada* has noted as "a kind of fluid anger, a compacted aggression, emotionally loaded."

A Canada Council grant in 1980 enabled Marcuse to create her first evening-length production, *Mirrors, Masques, and Transformations,* co-produced with the Shaw Festival. The doubling of the grant the following year allowed the production of *Playgrounds,* a work which involved a spoken text and the participation of both ballet-trained and contemporary dancers, along with actors, onstage musicians, and singers. These works were a point of departure for later activities of the Judith Marcuse Dance Projects Society with a similar collborative approach. In 1984 with a change of company title to Repertory Dance Company of Canada and the installation of a permanent ensemble, Marcuse saw the need to bring in emerging young choreographers from Canada and abroad, and new works were commissioned from Ginette Laurin, Danny Grossman, Christopher House, Grant Strate, Mark Morris, Ohad Naharin and Lar Lubovitch, the latter three thus makinq impressive debuts in Canada's dance scene. At that time the troupe began touring extensively and its educational functions expanded to include special youth projects and residency programs.

Marcuse's work as a choreographer for ensembles is well structured and logically conceived. She deals with both serious and comic materials, never resorting to a straight narrative form but preferring to empower her dances with the control of the mood and issue of the piece. Always accessible, never puzzling, Marcuse has never aspired to achieve the cutting edge that characterizes the work of many of her contemporaries. Relating to, informing and entertaining her audiences remain her objective. In an interview with Brian Preston, Grant Strate characterized her work as "contemporary ballet rather than modern dance.... It's rooted in a ballet technique. Her choreography has evolved ... becoming more inventive in terms of movement—she doesn't just arrange what she already knows. She's digging deeper into the emotional content." In *Dance Canada,* Max Wyman observed that her choreography, "a securely structured language of ballet-tinged modern movement," manifests itself in "a devotion to dancing that is done full-out, with a flung and sometimes angry passion; a determination never merely to doodle in space; a celebration of the sexuality of movement."

ln 1995, Marcuse initiated The Kiss Project, an ambitious community-centered offering in which over 200 dancers, choreographers, playwrights, actors, musicians, and visual artists in the Vancouver area are brought together for a winter festival, the heart of the event being the presentation of commissioned five-minute performance sketches involving the exchange of a kiss. A variety of workshops in the performing arts for adults and children link the artist with the community in general. The project has become an annual event in Vancouver. With it Marcuse follows in the footsteps of Elsie Salomons, who led the way a half century earlier in showing the interdependence of the dance arts and the community in which they flourish.

—Leland Windreich

513

MARIN, Maguy

French dancer, choreographer, and company director

Born: 1951 in Toulouse to Spanish immigrant parents. **Education:** Studied ballet, Toulouse Conservatory; enrolled at Mudra, Maurice Béjart's school (Brussels), 1970. **Career:** Dancer, Ballet de l' Opéra de Strasbourg; founding member, experimental group Chandra (Brussels); dancer, Béjart's Ballets du 20ième Siècle, 1974-77; first choreography, 1976; formed her own company (with Daniel Ambash), Théatre de l'Arche, 1978; renamed Compagnie Maguy Marin, 1984; company is based at the Maison des Arts et de la Culture in Créteil, on the outskirts of Paris; resident choreographer, Lyon Opéra Ballet, 1991-94; has also choreographed for Paris Opéra Ballet, Nancy Opéra Ballet, Compagnie Michel Nourkil, Dutch National Ballet Company, and Netherlands Dans Theatre III. **Awards:** Frst prize, Lyon and Bagnolet International Choreography Competition, 1977, 1978; France's Ministry of Culture Grand Prix for choreography, 1983.

Works

1976	*Yu Ku Ri* (mus. Louafi), Brussels
1977	*Evocation* (mus. Brahms), Lyon
1978	*Nieblas de nino* (mus. popular), Paris
	L'Adieu (mus. Dosse), Paris
	Dernier geste (mus. Bach), Aix-en-Provence
	Puzzle (mus. Reich), Manosque
1979	*Zoo* (mus. Stravinsky), Arles
	La jeune fille et la mort (mus. Schubert), Sabionetta
1980	*Canté* (mus. popular), Haden
	Réveillon (mus. Marini), Royan
	Contrastes (mus. Bartók), Lyon
1981	*May B* (mus. Schubert, Bryars), Angers
1982	*Babel Babel* (mus. Mahler, others), Paris
1983	*Jaleo,* Paris
1984	*Hymen* (mus. various), Avignon
1985	*Calambre* (mus. Rayon), Paris
	Cendrillon (mus. Prokofiev, Schwartz), Lyon
1986	*Eden* (mus. various), Angers
1987	*Leçons de ténèbres* (mus. Couperin), Paris
	Otello (mus. Verdi), Nancy
	. . .Des petits bourgeois les sept pèchés capitaux (mus. Will, Barras), Lyon
1988	*Coups d'états* (mus. Barras), Montpellier
1989	*Groosland* (mus. Bach), Amsterdam
	Eh, qu'est-ce que ça m'fait à moi? (mus. various), Avignon
1991	*Cortex* (mus. Mariotte), Paris
1992	*Ay dios* (mus. Mariotte), Lyon
	Made in France (mus. Mariotte), the Hague
1993	*Coppélia* (mus. Delibes), Lyon
	Waterzooi (mus. Mariotte), Reggio-Emilia
1995	*RamDam* (mus. Mariotte), Cannes and Val de Marne
1996	*Aujourd'hui peut-être* (mus. VolPuek), Paris

Publications

On MARIN: articles—

Danto, Ginger, "Marinade" *Village Voice*, 19 September 1995.
———, "Stirring Up an Emotional Stew," *New York Times*, 17 July 1994.

Ginot, Isabelle, "Back to a Clarity of Forms," *Ballet International/ tanz aktuell,* March 1997.
Gradinger, Malve, "Punk Counterworlds," *Ballet International,* April 1986.
Merril, Bruce, "France's Marin: I Have Found Myself," *Dance Magazine,* March 1986.
van Schaik, Eva, "Marin's *Groosland* and New Easter Programs," *Ballet International,* May 1989.

*   *   *

Born the youngest of four children to Spanish parents who had moved to southwestern France after the Spanish Civil war, Maguy Marin received her early dance training at the ballet conservatory in her native Toulouse. Later she studied in Paris with Nina Vyroubova. An engagement as soloist at the Ballet de l'Opéra de Strasbourg convinced her that she wanted to go beyond the confines of ballet. Enrollment in Maurice Béjart's free-spirited and multidiscipled school of the arts, Mudra, in Brussels, opened a new world performance possibilities for the young artist. It was an experience Marin has described as changing her life, "All my points of reference, simply melted away." In addition, "three years at the heart of Maurice Béjart's Ballet du 20ième Siècle gave me the opportunity to learn from a choreographer, to try out first choreographic attempts, and above all to dance out my soul."

Marin's choreography, from the early image-driven pieces to more recent movement-based work, is informed by a passion to explore human behavior. She wants us to look at our foibles and delusions, our vanities and pretenses, but also at our capacity for joy, change, and the life of the mind. Her perspective is sometimes satirical, often whimsical; somber, but never despairing. She has a finely tuned eye for the ridiculous modulated by an embracing sense of compassion. While she exposes false dreams, she embraces the act of dreaming.

Marin often experiments with masks, unison and pedestrian movements, small ordinary gestures, incomprehensible as well as very articulated spoken words, and drab uniform-like costumes—all to create textures which she hopes will reveal essence behind surface perception. Like her colleagues in the German dance theater, Marin is not interested in movement for its own sake but because it reveals of the human spirit. The tiny, almost imperceptible steps and gestures in 1981's *May B*, (a seminal work that has been performed over 300 times all over the world), for instance, reveal an incredible will to survive by its ghostlike characters. The heroine of *Calambre* (1985), a hard-edged mixture of flamenco dancer and rock idol, on the other hand, becomes vulnerable and human when she collapses and her mask of pretense is shattered.

In the 1980s Marin created some visually provocative, rather punkish works whose blatant theatricality, in the eyes of many critics, courted the banal. As she matured as an artist, she let go of the cruder aspects of her political imagery and developed a style at once more personal and less simplistic. Her later works are measurably more subtle. These days, at her best, she creates humane, serene dance theater with a delicious sense of the absurd. She has consciously reduced theatrical trappings in order to focus on the interaction of words, movements, and sound to create works with a definite philosophical bent. Marin has observed that the primary influence on her work comes from its subject matter. The themes out of which she spins her fables are drawn from the lives of ordinary folks. In 1989's *Groosland* she fights the "battle of the bulge" by putting a dozen grotesquely overweight (carefully padded) danc-

Maguy Marin: *Aujourd'hui peut-être*, 1996. Photograph by Dominique Lorieux.

ers onto the stage. Her working man's spot of paradise in *Babel Babel* (1982) is a grungy camping ground. While it was Samuel Beckett who godfathered the characters in *May B*, it's Marin's quasi-catatonic dancers that evoke a visceral response of familiarity. The emotions embodied in the vignettes of the masterful *Waterzooi* from 1993 are immediately recognizable as is the sense of overload by her information-bombarded office workers in *Ram* (the first section of 1995's *RamDam*).

Internationally Marin has become best known for her work with the Lyon Opèra Ballet. *Contrastes*, her first work for the company in 1980, explored class-consciousness in a very theatrical manner. The piece paired a group of downtrodden, shuffling workers with an upper-class couple indifferent to anything but their own self-importance. But Marin's breakthrough came with 1985's *Cendrillon*, her radical reworking of the Cinderella tale. Setting it in a dollhouse, integrating electronic sounds into the Prokofiev score, and cladding her dancers into foam-padded clothing and masks, the work's mixture of innocence (loss of innocence is a frequent concern of Marin's) and grotesquerie proved an immediate hit. More convincing was a refashioning of *Coppélia* in 1993, which has also been made into a film. Marin moved the story to an anonymous housing tract with a bunch of ball-kicking youth with too much time on their hands. The doll has been replaced by a movie image, replicable at will, but the longings of the heart, the capacity for cruelty, as well as the flights

of fancy and the vagaries of love, so much part of this 19th-century classic, clearly inspired Marin. They are themes which no doubt she will continue exploring.

—Rita Felciano

MARSHALL, Susan

American dancer, choreographer, and artistic director

Born: October 1958 in Pensacola, Florida; raised in Florida and Pennsylvania. **Education:** Studied ballet and gymnastics as a child; studied ballet and modern at the Pennsylvania Governor's School for the Arts; attended Juilliard School of Music, 1976-78. **Career:** First independent choreography, 1982; founder/artistic director, Susan Marshall & Company, since 1983; has commissioned works for the Boston Ballet, Dallas Ballet, Frankfurt Ballet, Montreal Danse, Brooklyn Academy of Music (BAM), and the University of Texas, Ohio State University, and others. **Awards:** New York Foundation for the Arts fellowship, 1985; New York Dance and Performance Award ("Bessie"), 1985; National Endowment for the Arts fellowships, 1986-91; Brandeis University Creative Arts Citation, 1988; American Choreographer Award, 1988; Guggenheim fellowship, 1990; *Dance Magazine* award, 1994.

Works

1982	*Fault Line*, The Yard, Martha's Vineyard
1983	*Trio in Four Parts*, Emanu-El Midtown YM-YWHA, New York
	Ward, CODANCECO, New York
1984	*Routine and Variations*, Performance Space 122, New York
	Arms, Performance Space 122, New York
1985	*Kin*, Brooklyn Anchorage, New York
	Opening Gambits, Dance Theatre Workshop, New York
	Common Run, CODANCECO, New York
1986	*Arena*, Dance Theatre Workshop, New York
	Gifts, for Le Groupe de Recherche Choreographique de l'Opera de Paris
	The Refrain, Dallas Ballet
1987	*Overture*, Boston Ballet
	The Aerialist, Dance Theatre Workshop, New York
	Kiss, Dance Theatre Workshop, New York
	Companion Pieces, Dance Theatre Workshop, New York
1988	*Interior with Seven Figures,* for BAM, New York
1989	*In Medias Res*, for Frankfurt Ballet, Frankfurt, Germany
	Figures In Opposition, Dancing in the Streets, New York
1990	*Contenders,* BAM, New York
	Articles of Faith, World Financial Center, New York
1992	*Standing Duet*, The Kitchen, New York
	Untitled (Detail), Ohio State University, Wexner Center
1993	*Entr'Acte I,* Serious Fun, Lincoln Center, New York
	Entr'Acte II, Serious Fun, Lincoln Center, New York
	Walter's Finest Hour, for Downtown Art Company, New York.
	Solo, Ballet Hispanico, New York
1994	*Fields of View*, University of Texas (Austin) and Brooklyn Academy of Music (BAM), New York
	Spectators at an Event, University of Texas & BAM, New York
	Private Worlds in Public View, Whitney Museum at Philip Morris
	Central Figure, Lyon Opera Ballet
1995	*Lines from Memory*, Montreal Danse
1996	*Les Enfants Terribles* (mus. Philip Glass), (commission), Zug, Switzerland
1998	*Run Toward the Noise* (mus. David Lang, performed by Bang On a Can All-Star Band; text Christopher Renino), Dartmouth College

Other works include: additional opera choreography for the Los Angeles Opera (*Les Troyens*), 1991; and *Midsummer Marriage* for the New York City Opera, 1993.

Publications

On MARSHALL: articles—

Acocella, Joan, "Desire under the Palms," *Dance,* 21 March 1990.
Anderson, Jack, "Choreography in the Pursuit of Happiness," *New York Times*, 6 January 1991.
———, "For Susan Marshall, Eloquence Is Movement," *New York Times*, 22 August 1993.
Banes, Sally, "American Postmodern Choreography," *Choreography & Dance,* 1992.
Berman, J., "Marshall's *Contenders* Becomes Champs," *New York Newsday*, 29 November 1990.
Brandenberg, H., "Dance Company's Fine Performance Kicks Off Spoleto," *Evening Post*, 23 May 1986.
Bromberg, C., "Movement But Less Metaphor," *Los Angeles Times*, 8 September 1987.
Campbell, R.M., "Susan Marshall's Dances Rise from the Streets of New York," *Seattle Post-Intelligence*, 24 April 1987.
Deresiewicz, B., "Susan Marshall's *Small Pleasures*," *Dance View*, Summer 1993.
Dunning, Jennifer, "Rituals of Complex Relations," *New York Times*, 8 December 1988.
Hardy, C., "Susan Marshall and Company," *Dance Magazine*, March 1989.
Hering, Doris, "Susan Marshall and Company," *Dance Magazine*, March 1993.
Jowitt, Deborah, "Susan Marshall and Company," *Village Voice*, 18 January 1986.
———, "Susan Marshall and Company," *Village Voice*, 22 December 1987.
Kisselgoff, Anna, "Dance: Susan Marshall and Troupe," *New York Times*, 7 December 1987.
———, "An Explorer Traverses Some Emotional Terrain," *New York Times*, 21 December 1992.
Predock-Linnell, Jennifer, "An Interview with Susan Marshall," The Kreisberg Group, Ltd., 1 June 1994.
Segal, Lewis, "A Raw Power in Marshall's Bleak Vision," *Los Angeles Times*, 12 April 1990.
Stuart, O., "Marshalling the Next Wave," *Dance Magazine*, December 1988.
Temin, C., "Choreographer Marshall Tops Dance Season," *Boston Globe*, 14 March 1987.
———, "Marshall Has a Winner in Contenders," *Boston Globe*, 8 March 1991.
Ulrich, A., "From Intimate to Epic," *San Francisco Examiner*, 7 April 1990.
West, Martha Ullman, "Choreographer Changes Stride Again," *Oregonian,* 31 March 1990.
Wiersbicki, J., "Marshall's Choreography Transforms The Ordinary," *St. Louis Dispatch*, 29 April 1990.

Films and Videotapes

Arms, for Lincoln Center's *Alive from Off-Center,* 1989.
Contenders, for *Alive from Off-Center,* 1991.

*   *   *

Exploring and creating visual metaphors that bare the truth about the human condition and the ways people surmount and survive it: this is Susan Marshall's art. Her work shows us how powerfully modern dance can express human reality. Marshall formally constructs time, movement, and focus to expose human intent. Her danceworks are about interaction, relation and response, and the people in them can be likened to magnets and their mysterious power to attract and repel. One magnet is inert and isolated, its forces invisible. Add another magnet and both immediately assert

Susan Marshall: *Untitled.* **Dancers: Eileen Thomas and Andrew Boynton. Photograph © Lois Greenfield.**

their forces setting the stage in motion and transforming the movement into sequences of interior states.

Marshall's artistic gift lies in her ability to create danceworks that elevate everyday action into theatrically expressive gesture while retaining a formal sense of architecture and emotional edge. One dance implies that although a heroic act, life is full of painful struggle and while success at some level is always attainable, it may not be what the person expected (*Contenders*, 1990); yet another suggests people striving for success are genuinely supportive of one another (*Untitled [Detail]*, 1992). These dances are commentar-

ies on American life: *Contenders,* with its drive for individual position and achievement; and *Untitled (Detail)* a viewing of a woman's struggle to reconcile parts of her life. *Contenders* and *Untitled (Detail)* are icons of our ravenous need to be loved and our undeniable fear of loneliness. In these pieces we see lovers who cannot quite live together; nor can they bear to be separate. We experience friends simultaneously trying to ignore and impress each other. Marshall creates archetypal characters whose helplessness is expressed through arm movements that embrace, fondle, and support while gripping, manipulating, and repelling space or each other.

Discreet gestures register alternately as lethal blows and tender caresses. She fashions choreography that is a conscious stream of metaphors for intimate human situations.

Born in 1958 and raised in Florida, Marshall was the daughter of political activists in the Civil Rights Movement. Her mother was also a recognized feminist writer and her father, a behavioral science scholar. Marshall's parents and their views were a strong force in her life and helped influence her working aesthetic. Her childhood training was in ballet, even though she knew she wanted to be a modern dancer and choreographer. Early on, Marshall was a maverick, choreographing dances in high school using wrestlers, gymnasts, and artists.

After attending the Juilliard School of Music for two years in the late 1970s, Marshall decided to strike out on her own to explore the craft of choreography. Two years later, she began to present her works in small New York dance venues. Her early works were meticulously formal dance studies. In the mid-1980s violence became a common theme, threading through many of her danceworks as she investigated and explored the psyche of human emotions and relationships. In 1983 Susan Marshall & Company was formed; in 1985 she presented her first concert at the Emanu-El Midtown YM-YWHA with *Eighteen Marbles, Fault Line*, and *Trio in Four Parts*.

Marshall uses a recognizable language of movement which threads itself through many pieces. For instance, the ending segment of *Trio in Four Parts* (1983) becomes the thematic motif of *Arms* (1984), a signature work of Susan Marshall & Company. Marshall's repeated use of arm gestures takes on different intentions when placed in different contexts. The gesturing arms symbolically reinvent new and complex dramatic moments in the lives of her characters. They exemplify Marshall's talent for creating exquisitely crafted multilayered, multidimensional images of emotional states and universal themes. Her attention to gestural detail allows us to "read" the emotion in her works. "My works chronicle a series of interior states,"declares Marshall. Dances like *Arms* (1984), *Kiss* (1987), and *Standing Duet* (1992) become visual movement conversations.

Marshall transforms everyday movement into semiabstract forms. She is taken by all kinds of simple movements, by the way someone might leave or enter a room, or the way two people walk toward each other in a corridor. Choreographers often use embraces, kisses, or touches as punctuation or as meaningful signifiers. Marshall might use an embrace, over and over and over again with subtle variations as it is repeated. The embrace becomes recognizable as a gesture with depth and possibilities. Beginnings of Marshall's danceworks like *Arms, Untitled (Detail),* and *Standing Duet* often find a couple quietly lingering in one spot, canonically repeating only a movement or two. For her, the repetition is a tool to present in familiar gestures more shades of meaning than if it were used only as a theatrical punctuation.

Often the same character types continue through different dances; both role reversal and mutual dependency may occur. Examples of both may be seen in *Ward* (1983), *Standing Duet, Untitled (Detail),* and *Interior With Seven Figures* (1988). In the opening image of *Standing Duet*, two performers appear, standing close to each other, rooted to the spot. Through a series of repetitive gestures, one dancer falters and sinks, the other, quickly responding, tries to support him. The dancer showing weakness simultaneously seeks assistance while trying to push his friend away, fearing to acknowledge his vulnerability. As the duet progresses, the roles become reversed and the previously strong dancer now needs help.

Marshall's work evokes emotions like discomfort, dysfunction, ecstasy, machismo, abandonment, and competitiveness. Her choreographic process reflects the methods of the choreographers of the 1960s whose styles were informed and inspired by unstylized, everyday movement. Through the development of her own working methods, Marshall has devised an "action and response" process to describe the way in which narrative works in her dances. According to Marshall, "one character responds to another's actions, and in so doing, each character becomes more defined." Her collaborative volleying is a process she "uses to create and sculpt the movement." Marshall works with a deliberately limited movement vocabulary; she wants to know the why and what of her characters. She describes herself as wanting the audience to think about the dancers as characters, asking "what's happening here?" Her danceworks are microcosms of people's inevitable struggle with emotional and situational conflict. She is interested in how humans accept, yet are afraid to acknowledge, their own vulnerability; striving to be self-sufficient, yet craving companionship.

During the mid-1990s, Marshall has begun to move from the narrative structure to include works that journey into text for performance. Her 1993 play *Walter's Finest Hour* was a new jump into scriptwriting. For Marshall, text "provides a framework, a locality, facts that educate about a particular situation." In 1996 Marshall collaborated with composer Philip Glass to create a dance-opera, *Les Enfants Terribles: Children of the Game*, "retelling Cocteau's tale of a quasi-incestuous brother and sister whose emotional games end in self-destruction."

In creating recent works such as *Spectators at an Event* (1994) Marshall catches the way in which complex occurrences can be frozen to float in our minds as a solitary memory. *Spectators* draws its inspiration from the 1940s journalistic photographer, Weegee (Arthur Fellig), whose stark realism captured the reactions of individuals and groups at the exact moment of witnessing images of murder, disorder, and other dramatic events in New York City during the 1930s and 1940s.

At times Marshall will create new choreographic projects that are "more dance-based, and less gestural." In *Fields of View* (1994) she challenged herself with "how to work with more pure dance materials," while maintaining an emotional content. At the center of *Fields of View* is what Marshall termed the "tangled relationship between experience and time." To this end, she describes that "our interior lives move fluidly through time. We revisit and rethink the past (uninterrupted by barriers even as we live in the present). We dream and rearrange the future." In an interview in 1994, Marshall stated that she envisioned *Fields of View* unfurling "like a scroll containing many smaller dances that recur, advance, recede and coexist." Her choreographic style shows a continuity of focus on examining our human condition through gestural landscapes and poetic dreams.

—Jennifer Predock-Linnell

MASCALL, Jennifer
Canadian dancer and choreographer

Born: Jennifer Wootton Mascall, 11 December 1952 in Winnipeg, Manitoba. **Education:** York University, Toronto, B.F.A., 1974. **Family:** Married John Macfarlane; children: Nicholas, Matthew, and Tobias. **Career:** Co-founder and co-artistic director, EDAM,

1982-89; artistic director, Mascall Dance, since 1989. **Awards:** Three-time recipient of External Affairs Grants to support tours of Scandinavia, Britain, Germany, and the Netherlands; Clifford E. Lee Award, 1981; Ann O'Connor Award, Edinburgh Fringe Festival, 1982; Dora Mavor Moore Award, 1983; Jacqueline Lemieux Award, 1983; Jesse Award, 1988; Commemorative Medal for 125th Anniversary of Canadian Confederation, 1992.

Works (selected)

1974	*Cassandra* (no mus.), with Greek text by Euripides spoken by Mascall, 15 Dance Laboratorium, Toronto
	Attica (mus. Frederic Rzewski), York University, Toronto
1975	*Conduction,* first solo concert, including *Sleeping Giant, Envoi* and *Gertrude Stein* (mus. Christopher Crawford and Andrew Timar), 15 Dance Laboratorium, Toronto
1977	*Homily Possum: A Space, Fall* (no mus.), for one dancer and three video monitors, 15 Dance Laboratorium, Toronto
	Fatty Acids (no mus.), Canada Dance Festival, Winnipeg
1978	*Swank(olors)* (mus. Saint-Saëns), Theatre Passe Muraille, Toronto
	Unicycle Blues (no mus.), 15 Dance Laboratorium, Toronto
	Q/O (no mus.), Dance in Canada Conference, Vancouver
1979	*Swan Nine to Five* (no mus.), Ontario Art Gallery, Toronto
	All Flames Are Waiting to Kill All Moths (no mus.), TIDE, Toronto
	Smashed Carapace (no mus.), Halifax, Nova Scotia
	From a Squashed and Tormented Retina (no mus.), Dance in Canada Conference, Waterloo
	Trifle (no mus.), 15 Dance Laboratorium, Toronto
1981	*Acoustic Noose* (mus. Bach), Banff Festival of the Arts
	No Picnic (no mus.), Toronto
	Broken Up (no mus.), Vancouver
1982	*No Picnic . . . A Study in Martyrs* (mus. Ernst Reyseger), Edinburgh Fringe Festival
	Sid's Kids, a punk musical, Autumn Angel Company, Toronto
	1947 Rambler Sedan Opaque (no mus.), EDAM, Vancouver
1983	*Offspring* (mus. various), evening of solos, Vancouver
	Silence, Deep Forest, My Life (mus. Debussy), Vancouver
	True Lies (mus. John Oswald), EDAM, Vancouver
	House Pets (no mus.), Nova Dance Theatre, Halifax, Nova Scotia
	A Strange Manuscript Found in a Copper Cylinder (mus. various), Autumn Angel Company, Toronto
1984	*The Light at the End of the Tunnel May Be the Other Train Coming Towards You* (mus. Brian Eno, later Chris Butterfield), Contemporary Dancers, Winnipeg
	Turbo Pascal (mus. Tom Hajdu), EDAM, Vancouver
	Hurry Blurry, See Dot Quick (mus. Tom Hadju), EDAM, Vancouver
1985	*If the Right Hand Only Knew* (no mus.), seven-set video construction, EDAM, Vancouver
1986	*Parade* (mus. John Oswald), EDAM, for Expo '86
	Gotta Go Now, Love Always (mus. Ahmed Hassan), Dancemakers, Toronto
1987	*The Table* (mus. Jack Velker), EDAM, Vancouver
	The Back Solo (no mus.), EDAM, Vancouver
1989	*Quelle Elle (Until I Arrive)* (mus. John Oswald), Montreal
	The Dumbfounding (mus. Christopher Butterfield), EDAM, Vancouver
1990	*Cathedral* (mus. Debussy), improvisation, talking about perceptions of dance, Toronto
	Spine Lines (mus. Michele George), Mascall Dance, Vancouver
	Story, First Hand (no mus.), Mascall Dance, Vancouver
	Story, Second Hand (live vocal accompaniment by Michele George; later, no mus.), Mascall Dance, Vancouver
	Ave Maria (live vocal accompaniment by Michele George), Ottawa
	New Material Only (duet; mus. Ahmed Hassan), National Arts Centre, Ottawa
	Carnival of the Animals (mus. Saint-Saëns), Arts Umbrella Youth Dance Company, Vancouver
1991	*Within These Four Walls* (mus. Sofia Gubaidulina), Mascall Dance, Vancouver
	Make a DANCE! (mus. various), a lecture demonstration, Mascall Dance, Vancouver
1992	*I'll Leave the Back Door Open* (mus. various), Mascall Dance, Vancouver
	The Lesson (duet; no mus.), Mascall Dance, Vancouver
1993	*The Shostakovich* (mus. Shostakovich), Mascall Dance, Vancouver
1996	*Not Only, but Also* (mus. Christos Hatzis), Mascall Dance, Vancouver
	Callasthenics (mus. Bellini, Verdi, Puccini, sung by Maria Callas), solo for Olivia Thorvaldson, Winnipeg

Publications

By MASCALL: books—

Editor and publisher, *Footnotes,* a collection of dance notes from 60 North American choreographers, 1978.

On MASCALL: articles—

Ryan, Peter, "Mascall on Mascall: Conversations with Peter Ryan," *Vandance,* Summer 1981.

Films and Videotapes

The Lesson, dir. Daniel Conrad, 1996.

*   *   *

After graduating from York University's new dance department in 1974, Jennifer Mascall quickly made a name for herself as one of the first of an explosion of independent choreographers across Canada, known both for her prolific output and the experimental nature of her work. Funding from the Ontario Arts Council assisted in her development as a solo dancer in Canada and Europe.

Rather than being concerned with narrative or plot, Mascall's choreography follows the demands of an idea, whether it is a physical or an emotional one. She believes in constantly refining her work, sometimes through performance. Thus her own solos were continually deepened and extended on stage; in fact, Mascall often used the intensely focused state of a performance to finalize a choreography. The line between improvisation and choreography

Jennifer Mascall: *The Shostakovich,* **1993. Photograph by David Cooper.**

is a porous one for Mascall, and improvisational skills form a great part of her aesthetic. Merce Cunningham, ballet, and contact improvisation have also influenced her uniquely expressive style, and her group choreography is notable for its virtuosic physical and emotional drive.

Incorporating other disciplines contributes to the fertile playground of Mascall's work. For instance, poet Gerry Gilbert accompanied her on stage in *What Touches Me When I See the Paint Is the Painting;* another piece, *The Dumbfounding,* involved a choir that followed a group of dancers around the Vancouver Art Gallery; in her solo *Cathedral,* Mascall spoke to the audience in her choreographer's persona. Critic Max Wyman drove home the variety and explosive effect of much of Mascall's choreography: "Absurdist one minute, minimalist the next, radically revisionist the one after that, her work assaults you from all sides with the uncomfortable, the unexpected, and the bizarrely theatrical."

In 1982, Mascall was one of seven founding co-directors of EDAM (Experimental Dance and Music), an adventurous collective in Vancouver, B.C. Contact improvisers Peter Bingham and

Peter Ryan were among the disparate group of founding members; others had backgrounds in ballet and modern dance. Mascall continued to explore improvisation with the group, particularly with Bingham. During this period, she created *The Table,* a group work which while choreographed nonetheless left open certain possibilities for change. The outstanding *Parade* was a choreographed piece for four dancers, three gymnasts, and one magician, with two of the dancers improvising.

In 1989 Mascall left EDAM to found her own company, Mascall Dance, which is usually composed of about a half-dozen dancers and can still be found at its original location at St. Paul's Anglican Church in Vancouver's West End. The company has received Canada Council funding since its inception. In its first year, Mascall Dance toured across Canada, presenting several remounts, including *The Light at the End of the Tunnel May Be the Other Train Coming Towards You* and a version of *Parade.* In addition, Mascall appeared in her solos, *Story, First and Second Hand,* performed in silence, and *Spine Lines,* with live accompaniment by singer Michele George. Also in 1989, Mascall formed the Nijinsky Gibber Jazz

Club, an in-studio event that has become an ongoing, if occasional project, to research and extend the possibilities of improvisation with dancers and other artists invited to participate.

—Kaija Pepper

MASLOW, Sophie

American dancer, choreographer, and educator

Born: New York City, 1912. **Education:** Studied composition with Louis Horst and dance with Blanche Talmud and Martha Graham at the Neighborhood Playhouse; attended Bennington College Summer School of Dance. **Career:** Dancer, Martha Graham Compnay, 1931-42, creating roles in most of Graham's productions; choreographed for the New Dance League; formed dance trio with Jane Dudley and William Bales, 1942-54; founded Sophie Maslow Dance Company, 1954; teacher and choreographer, New Dance Group; founding member of the American Dance Festival, Connecticut College, 1948.

Works

1934	*Themes for a Slavic People* (mus. Bartók), solo, New Dance Group
	Two Songs about Lenin
	Death of Tradition
	Challenge w/ Lily Mehlman and Anna Sokolow
1935	*Prelude to a May First Song*
1936	*May Day March*
1937	*Ragged Hungry Blues*
	Runaway Rag
	Satiric Suite w/ Jane Dudley, William Matons, and Sokolow
	Women of Spain w/ Dudley
	Evacuation w/ Dudley
1939	*Silicosis Blues*
1941	*Americana*
	Mountain Shout
	Sarabande
	Gigue
	Bourée
	Exhortation
	Melancholia
	Gymnopédie w/ Dudley
1942	*Dust Bowl Ballads,* solo
	Bach Suite w/ Dudley and William Bales
	Folksay (mus. American ballads; text Carl Sandburg), Maslow and others, Humphrey/Weidman Studio, New York
1943	*As Poor Richard says. . .* w/ Dudley and Bales
1944	*Llanto*
	Spanish Suite w/ Dudley
1945	*Fragments of a Shattered Land*
	Suite (Scherzo, Loure, Gigue) w/ Dudley and Bales
	Partisan Journey
	Inheritance
1948	*Champion,* New Dance Group
1949	*The Village I Knew,* New Dance Group
1951	*Four Sonnets*
	The Dybbuk (opera), New York City Opera
1953	*Israel in Dance and Song*
	Prologue
	The Snow Queen
	Three Sonnets
1954	*Celebration*
	The Sand Hog (play)
	Suite: Manhattan Transfer
1955	*The Gentleman from Cracow*
1956	*Anniversary*
	Three Wishes for Jamie (play)
1958	*The Diamond Backs*
	Three Sonatas
	Rain Check
1960	*The Machinal* (play)
1962	*The Golem* (opera), New York City Opera
1963	*Poem*
1964	*From the Book of Ruth*
1965	*In the Beginning*
	Dance of the Sabras
1966	*Collage '66*
	Invocation of David
1968	*Neither Rest nor Harbor*
1969	*Episodia*
	Ladino Suite
1971	*Country Music*
1973	*Touch the Earth*
1974	*The Big Winner*
1975	*Such Sweet Thunder*
	Songs for Women, Songs for Men
1976	*The Fifth Season*
	Decathalon Etudes
1979	*Theme and Variations*
1980	*Voices*

Publications

On MASLOW: articles—

Denby, Edwin, "Sophie Maslow,"in *Dance Writings*, New York: Knopf, 1986.

Dunning, Jennifer, "Martha in Present Tense," *New York Times,* 25 September 1994.

Gladstone, Valerie, "Where Even the Ghosts Give Encouragement," *New York Times,* 2 February 1997.

Harris, Joanna Gervertz, "From Tenement to Theater: Jewish Women as Dance Pioneers—Helen Becker (Tamiris), Anna Sokolow, Sophie Maslow," *Judaism: A Quarterly Journal of Jewish Life and Thought,* Summer 1996.

Martin, Claire, review, *Dance Magazine,* February 1981.

Tobias, Tobi, review, *New York,* 13 October 1986.

Vaughan, David, review, *Dance Magazine,* April 1985.

*   *   *

Sophie Maslow's contribution to modern dance began when she was a dancer in the 1930s and continues through her work as a choreographer and teacher. As a member of Martha Graham's early

Sophie Maslow and William Bales performing *Folksay*. **Photograph by David Linton.**

dance company, Maslow played an integral role in establishing modern dance as a serious, expressive art form. Later as a choreographer, she extended her training to bring a lightness and freedom to her dances which explore American themes and her own heritage.

A child of Russian immigrants, Maslow grew up in Brooklyn and studied dance at the Neighborhood Playhouse School of Theater in New York City as a teenager. There she studied composition with Louis Horst and dance with Blanche Talmud and Martha Graham. She joined Graham's all-female dance company in 1931. As an early member of the group, Maslow played an important role in introducing the world to the lean, percussive movements of Graham's work which sought to shake dance free of lyrical, decorative movements. Graham's dancers were expected to create a look, not simply follow dance steps. Maslow's talent and perseverance earned for her Graham's trust. *Primitive Mysteries* (1931) was the first dance Maslow performed with the group. She performed many other important Graham works, including *American Document* (1938) and *Letter to the World* (1940).

Maslow left Graham's company in 1940, but continued her association with Graham. In 1943 Graham, inspired by the writings of the Brontë sisters, choreographed *Deaths and Entrances* and cast herself, Maslow, and Jane Dudley as the three sisters. As a testament to Maslow's abilities, Graham trusted her to develop the details of the dance following Graham's general pattern. Well-trained in Graham's vision, Maslow also was instrumental in recreating *Primitive Mysteries* in 1964. When limited notes and the memories of the gathered dancers could not recall specific steps of the original performance, Maslow created new movements in the spirit of the original which met with Graham's approval.

Not wholly content with serving the revolution created by Martha Graham, Maslow sought the opportunity to create her own dances. The short-lived Studio Series of Graham's company offered Maslow an introductory showcase for her own choreography. In 1934 she celebrated the folk dances of the small villages of her Russian ancestry in her first piece, *Themes for a Slavic People* with music by Béla Bartók. Other early dances by Maslow reflect her concern with social issues. She shared the popular 1930s notion that dance can be an instrument of social change while also believing that dance, in itself, could enrich people's lives. Maslow was a member of the New Dance Group, founded in 1932 in New York, which sought, as one of its purposed, to address the issues of the Depression through dance.

Maslow also taught children and adult choreography and performance. During the mid-1930s, she produced *Two Songs About Lenin* and *May Day March* among others. With encouragement from the New Dance Group, she also pursued her interest in Israeli folk dances. Though the New Dance Group's reputation for social activism has dimmed and been replaced by one of dancing excellence, it continues to serve dancers to this day.

In 1942 Maslow joined with Jane Dudley and Humphrey-Weidman-trained William Bales to form the Dudley-Maslow-Bales Trio. Expressing the less solemn, freer attitude then evolving in modern dance, these well-trained dancers combined gestures of earlier modern dance, albeit now more relaxed, with more dance sequences. The trio's popular dances introduced modern dance to a wider audience. *As Poor Richard Says. . .* spun the sayings of Benjamin Franklin into one of the trio's biggest audience favorites. The popular trio, which grew out of the New Dance Group, toured the country successfully until Jane Dudley was forced to retire because of an arthritic hip in the mid-1950s.

Maslow created and performed many of her Americana dances during the 1950s and onward. The exuberance expressed in these dances is a testament to her strong feelings for people and their lives. *Dust Bowl Ballads* (1941) is the first of her signature works celebrating the American experience, including music from folk balladeer Woody Guthrie's "Dusty Old Dust" and "I Ain't Got No Home in This World No More." Maslow again turned to Guthrie for music and witticism in *Folksay* (1942). In this popular work, which has been cited as establishing her as a leading modern dance choreographer, Maslow weaves American ballads, verses by Carl Sandburg, mime, large patterns, barn dance steps, singing, and guitar playing into a series of vignettes which celebrates the spirit and pride of rural America following the Depression. Maslow later dedicated a work, *Woody Sez* (1980), to Guthrie.

Maslow's early interest in folk music included Israeli folk songs and expanded into other works on Jewish themes. One of her best known dances is *The Village I Knew* (1950). In highly stylized pantomime, Maslow illustrates the Sholom Aleichem tales of Russian Jewish village life. Israeli songs are also the foundation for *Celebration* (1954). Many of the works she choreographed for the New Dance Group and her own dance company, the Sophie Maslow Dance Company, continued her exploration of Jewish themes.

In addition to dance performances, Maslow has choreographed for the New York City Opera, including *The Dybbuk*, on and off-Broadway theater, television, summer theaters, and Hanukkah Festivals for Israel beginning in 1952 and continuing to 1967.

Maslow is a founding member of the American Dance Festival at Connecticut College in New London, where she has taught and performed. She also taught at Bennington summer residencies, and has been head of the dance department of Hebrew Arts School for Music and Dance in New York. She currently is on the board of directors and teaching staff of the New Dance Group Studio in New York.

—Janette Goff Dixon

McGEHEE, Helen

American dancer, choreographer, and educator

Born: 10 May 1921 in Lynchburg, Virginia. **Education:** Graduated from Randolph-Macon Women's College, 1942. **Career:** Dancer, Martha Graham Dance Company, 1940s; promoted to lead dancer, 1954; guest dancer with the companies of Robert Cohan, Erick Hawkins, Mary Hinkson, Pearl Lang, Bertram Ross, Paul Taylor, Yuriko, and others; founder, Helen McGehee & Dancers; has taught at the Graham Studio, Juilliard, and summers at Connecticut College, New London, Connecticut.

Roles (choreographed by Martha Graham and performed with the Martha Graham Dance Company)

1946	*Cave of the Heart*, New York
1947	Leader of the chorus, *Night Journey*, Cambridge, Massachusetts
	Errand into the Maze, New York
1948	*Wilderness Stair* (subsequently known as *Diversion of Angels*), Connecticut College, New London
1950	*Eye of Anguish* (for Erick Hawkins and Company) New York

1952	Mermaid, *Canticle for Innocent Comedians*, New York
1958	Electra, *Clytemnestra* (collaborated on costumes w/Graham), New York
1960	*Acrobats of God*, New York
1961	*One More Gaudy Night* (helped create costumes w/Graham), New York
1967	*Phaedra*, New York
	Cortege of Eagles, New York
1969	*The Archaic Hours*, New York

Other roles include: A myriad of Graham works for the Martha Graham Dance Company.

Works

1951	*The Pit* (mus. Hallstrom)
	Man with a Load of Mischief (mus. Horst)
1952	*La Intrusa* (mus. Calabro)
1957	*"I Am the Gate"* (mus. Hindemith)
1963	*Nightmare* (mus. Messiaen)
1967	*"The Only Jealousy of Emer"* (mus. Britten)
1969	*El Retablo de Maese Pedro* (mus. de Falla)
1978	*Changes* (mus. Britten)

Other works include: *After Possession, Ceremonies of Remembrance, First Light, Incursion, La Dame à la Licorne, Metamorposis, Outside, Passage to Freshness, Someone to Play With, Suspended Path, Undine,* and *Yarn.*

Publications

By McGEHEE: books—

To Be a Dancer, edited by A. Umaña, Lynchburg, Virginia, 1990.

On McGEHEE: books—

De Mille, Agnes, *Martha: The Life and Work of Martha Graham,* New York, 1992.
Jowitt, Deborah, *Time and the Dancing Image,* New York, 1988.
McDonagh, Don, *Martha Graham,* New York, 1973.
Taylor, Paul, *Private Domain,* New York, 1987.
Umaña, Alfonso, *Helen McGehee: Dancer,* New York, 1974.

*   *   *

Helen McGehee is best-known as a longtime lead dancer for the Martha Graham Dance Company, performing in many of Graham's major works from the 1940s through the 1960s. She also choreographed and performed her own dances, and was a respected teacher at Juilliard and elsewhere. She is known for her expressive, lyrical performances in roles ranging from Electra in *Clytemnestra* to a mermaid in *Canticle for Innocent Comedians*, as well as for her ability to express intense emotions in dramatic roles.

McGehee was born in 1921 in Lynchburg, Virginia. She entered the Martha Graham Studio school soon after graduating from Randolph-Macon Women's College in 1942, subsequently becoming a member of the Martha Graham Dance Company; she remained for more than 30 years, becoming a lead dancer in 1954. She performed in several Graham premieres, creating roles in works including *Night Journey* (1947), as the leader of the chorus; *Diver-*

sion of Angels, then called *Wilderness Stair* (1948); the full-evening *Clytemnestra* (1958); *Acrobats of God* (1960); *Phaedra* (1967); and *Cortege of Eagles* (1967). As a member of the company for so long, McGehee performed in nearly all of Graham's dances, from *The Archaic Hours* and *Errand into the Maze* to *Cave of the Heart*. In fact, she took over many of Graham's leading and solo roles as Graham aged. McGehee was with Graham during what was considered her creative peak, resulting in leading roles in many of Graham's most highly acclaimed classical works, including the characters of Medea and Ariadne.

McGehee danced with many of the premiere modern dancers of the time during her tenure with the Martha Graham Dance Company, including Pearl Lang, Bertram Ross, Robert Cohan, Mary Hinkson, Yuriko Kimura, Gus Solomons, Jr., Erick Hawkins, Paul Taylor, and many others. Her performances often garnered favorable reviews from the critics. For example, as Erick Hawkins' partner in *Diversions of Angels* (1947), she was termed "brilliant" by *Dance Magazine*. Yet, while McGehee's dancing frequently met with critical acclaim, she never achieved the high profile that many observers thought she deserved, since she remained with Graham's company—even while creating her own choreography and performing it—allowing Graham's forceful personality and presence to overshadow many of her accomplishments.

In fact, McGehee remains known primarily as a Graham dancer, in spite of her own body of choreographic work, which she composed for herself and her students. She won an audition at New York's 92nd Street Y in 1951, and shared a recital with Ronne Aul that season. Subsequently, she performed her pieces in concert at Kaufmann Concert Hall and other venues, as a soloist and with small ad-hoc companies largely composed of other Graham dancers. Among those who performed in her concerts were Jack Moore, Ross Parkes, Diana Gray, Lar Roberson and many others.

One of her best known works is *The Only Jealousy of Emer* (1967), which is based on a Yeats play and set to music by Benjamin Britten. Many of her works are based on literature, such as *The Oresteia*, commissioned by the Greek Theatre in Ypsilanti, Michigan, but other themes form the basis of her work as well. Some her choreography was inspired by Mexican folklore, such as such as *La Intrusia* (1952) and *El Retablo de Maese Pedro* (1969). She set her dance pieces to music by a diverse roster of composers, including Louis Horst, Paul Hindemith, Ada Reif, and Oliver Messiaen. Music was written especially for eight of her dances; her total body of choreography includes less than two dozen works, five of them commissioned. Notable works include *The Pit* (1951), *Man with a Load of Mischief* (1951), *I Am the Gate* (1957), *Nightmare* (1963), *Men with the Blue Guitar* (1966), and *Changes* (1978). Other pieces choreographed by McGehee include *Someone To Play With, Suspended Path, Outside, Undine, La Dame à la Licorne, Metamorposis, First Light, Incursion, After Possession, Yarn, Ceremonies of Remembrance,* and *Passage to Freshness.*

Along with other members of the Graham company, McGehee often performed in recitals of her own work or pieces by Graham at the Juilliard Theatre and elsewhere. She also contributed her own choreographic pieces, which were performed by her students during ensemble concerts. McGehee designed the costumes for her own performances, and collaborated with Graham on the costumes for some of her works, including *One More Gaudy Night* and evening-length *Clytemnestra*, for which she received some acclaim. Set designs for her own performances were created by her long-time collaborator, Alfonso Umaña, who later wrote a book about McGehee, aptly titled *Helen McGehee: Dancer* in 1974, published by Editions Heraclita, the same company that would later publish McGehee's own endeavor. In addition to performing and choreographing, McGehee devoted a significant amount of time to teaching, and was a respected dance instructor. Along with other Graham dancers, she taught technique classes at the New York-based Martha Graham School, at Juilliard, and at summer sessions at Connecticut College. She also taught in her home state of Virginia, and gave lectures and lecture-demonstrations throughout her career at universities and other settings, including the Interlochen Arts Academy, the University of Iowa, Syracuse University, and the Centre Americain in Paris. Her students included Paul Taylor, Jack Moore, and choreographer Francis Patrelle.

McGehee was known primarily as a lyric dancer, excelling at roles featuring beauty of movement and expressive storytelling. Yet she could show a surprising intensity in her roles when allowed to do so. Graham company member Paul Taylor, in his memoir *Private Domain*, wrote that while McGehee was usually cast in "ingenue" roles, she was "wonderfully wiry and vengeful as Electra." He noted that when she was cast in dramatic roles, she could turn into "a spark-ejecting demonette."

—Karen Raugust

McKAYLE, Donald

American dancer, choreographer, educator, and writer

Born: 6 July 1930 in Harlem, New York. **Education:** Attended New Dance Group on scholarship; studied modern dance, ballet, Haitian, Hindu, and tap. **Career:** Dancer, companies of Mary Anthony, 1948-52; Jean Erdman, 1948-53; Dudley-Maslow-Bales Trio and New Dance Group, 1948-55; Daniel Nagrin, 1951; Merce Cunningham, 1952; New York City Opera Ballet, 1952-54; Anna Sokolow, 1952-55; Martha Graham, 1955-56; founder/director, Donald McKayle and Dancers, 1952-69; artistic director, Inner City Repertory Dance Company, 1971-74; resident choreographer/artistic mentor, José Limón Dance Company, since 1995; full professor of dance, University of California, Irvine; artistic director, UCI Dance company. **Awards:** Capezio Award, 1963; Fellow, Black Academy of Arts and Letters, 1969; Emmy, *Free to Be You and Me,* 1974; NAACP Image Award, 1981; honored as part of Black Visions: Movements of the Black Masters, New York Public Library, 1989; Lauds and Laurels Award, University of California, Irvine, 1992; Samuel H. Scripps American Dance Festival Award, 1992; *Ebony*'s American Black Arts Award, 1992; American Dance Guild Outstanding Lifetime Achievement Award, 1994; Lehman Dance Award, 1994; Living Legend Award for Distinguished Achievement in Dance, 1994; Heritage Award, 1995; National Endowment for the Arts choreographic fellowship, 1995; Dance/USA Honors, 1996; Balasaraswati/Joy Ann Dewey Beinecke Endowed Chair for Distinguished Teaching, 1997; Distinguished Faculty Lectureship Award for Research, University of California, 1997.

Roles

1951	*Bless You All* (Broadway)
1952	*Just a Little Simple* (Off-Broadway)
1953	*Cain's Keep* (Off-Broadway)
1954	*House of Flowers* (Broadway)
	Lyric Suite (Sokolow)
1955	*Rooms* (Sokolow)
1957	*West Side Story* (Broadway)
	Copper and Brass (Broadway)
1961	*Free and Easy* (Blues opera), Europe

Works

1948	*Saturday's Child* (poem Cullen)
1950	*Creole Afternoon* (mus. traditional)
	Songs of the Forest (mus. Harrison)
	Exodus (mus. traditional)
1951	*Games* (mus. traditional)
1952	*Her Name was Harriet* (mus. traditional)
	Nocturne (mus. Hardin)
1953	*Four Excursions* (mus. Barber)
1954	*The Street* (mus. Levister)
	Prelude to Action (mus. Levister)
1956	*Her Name was Harriet* (new version; mus. arranged by Roberts)
1957	*Muse in the Mews* (mus. Giuffre)
1958	*Out of the Chrysalis* (mus. Bloch)
1959	*Rainbow 'Round My Shoulder* (mus. Lomax brothers, arranged by Decormier, Okun)
1960	*One-Two-Three, Follow Me* (mus. arranged by McKayle)
1962	*District Storyville* (mus. Freitag)
1963	*Legendary Landscape* (mus. Harrison)
	Arena (mus. Jackson)
	Blood of the Lamb (mus. Jackson)
1964	*Reflections in the Park* (mus. McFarland)
	Daughters of the Garden (mus. Bloch)
	Crosstown (mus. Richardson)
1965	*Incantation* (mus. Rodrigo, arranged by Davis)
	Wildneress (mus. Copland)
1966	*Burst of Fists* (mus. Roberts)
1967	*Black New World* (mus. Freitag, Roberts, Harris)
1971	*Sojourn* (mus. Jolivet)
1972	*Migrations* (mus. Weber, Kramer)
	Songs of the Disinherited (includes *I'm on My Way, Upon the Mountain, Angelitos Negros,* and *Shaker Life*)
1974	*Barrio* (mus. Davis)
1976	*Album Leaves* (mus. Morton)
	Recuerdos (mus. Villa-Lobos)
	Blood Memories (mus. Roberts, Malloy)
1977	*Mountain of Spices* (mus. Moondog)
	Argot
1982	*Ricochet* (mus. Bolling)
1983	*Solaris* (mus. Subramaniam)
	Collage
1984	*Avatar* (mus. Subramaniam)
1985	*Vever* (mus. Colleridge-Taylor Perkinson)
	Looking for Jerusalem (mus. Gronig, Manor)
1986	*Beneath the Baobab* (mus. Gronig)
	Apsaras (mus. Subramaniam)
1987	*Twilight* (mus. Villa-Lobos)
1990	*Rigalevio* (mus. Piazzolla)
	Distant Drum (mus. Piazzolla)
1991	*Sombra y Sol* (Images of Frida Kahlo), (mus. Copland)
	Infinite Journey (mus. Bruch)
1992	*House of Tears* (mus. Piazzolla)

1993   *Mysteries and Raptures* (mus. Subramaniam)
        Ring-a-Levio (mus. Piazzolla)
1994   *Vigils* (mus. Rzewski)
        Gumbo Ya-Ya, ballet commission (mus. Newton)
1995   *When I Grow Up. . .When I Was A Child* (mus. Terricciano)
1996   *Rainbow Étude* for the American Dance Legacy Institute
        (mus. arranged by McKayle, Terricciano)
1997   *Heartbeats* (mus. Roberts)
        The Seven Deadly Sins (mus. Terriacciano), includes *Lust,*
        Envy, Anger, Sloth, Pride, Gluttony, Greed with guest
        choreographers
        In the Deep Dreaming of My Hands (mus. Haza, Aloni,
        Tadros, DuPéré, Gagnon)
1998   *Delicious Obsession/Sweet Bondage* (mus. Ali Kahn)

Other works include: Writing, directing, and choreographing for a
myriad of theatrical productions: *Free and Easy, Trumpets of the
Lord, The Tempest, Golden Boy, As You Like It, Antony and Cleopatra,
The Four Musketeers, Raisin, Dr. Jazz, Sophisticated Ladies, The
Emperor Jones, South Pacific, Stardust, Rockin' with Rachmaninov,*
and others.

Publications

On McKAYLE: books—

Cohen, Selma Jeanne, editor, *The Modern Dance: Seven Statements
of Belief,* Middletown, Connecticut, 1996.
Sorrell, Walter, *The Dance Has Many Faces,* revised second edition,
New York & London, 1966.

Films and Videotapes

Film credits include *The Great White Hope* (1969), *Bedknobs and
Broomsticks* (1970), *Charlie and the Angel* (1972), and *The Jazz
Singer* (1980); television choreography: *Rainbow 'Round My Shoul-
der,* 1959; *The Called Her Moses,* 1960; *The 43rd Annual Academy
Awards,* 1970; *The Grammy Awards,* 1973; *Free to Be You and Me,*
children's special, 1974; *The Minstrel Man,* 1976; *The 49th Annual
Academy Awards,* 1977; *The Annual Emmy Awards,* 1979; *Dance
in America, 3 x 3,* 1985; and others.

*   *   *

Donald McKayle, born in Harlem, New York, struggled from
humble roots to become an eminent and distinguished American
choreographer, performer, director, writer, and educator, in dance,
theater, film, recordings, and television. As a child raised during the
Depression and World War II, possessing an active intelligence and
a myriad of talents and possibilities, he hoped to meet parental
expectations by seeking a career in a reliable, secure profession.
However, as a teenager, when he saw a performance by the legendary Pearl Primus, McKayle unexpectedly encountered what would
become his lifetime pursuit and passion.

Soon after seeing Primus, McKayle eagerly but awkwardly auditioned for the New Dance Group and, to his surprise, was awarded
a scholarship. This fortuitous occurrence helped seed and shape
what would become McKayle's burgeoning career. His voracious
appetite for movement led him to take advantage of the multitude
of dance offerings available—modern dance, ballet, Haitian, Hindu,
and tap. The prestigious faculty included Sophie Maslow, Jane

Dudley, William Bales, Mary Anthony, Pearl Primus, Jean-Leon
Destiné, Hadassah, and Paul Draper. There were few role models to
guide his youthful aspirations, and he primarily had to rely on his
own personal courage and persistence to pursue his dreams in the
face of the social restrictions and racial prejudices of the era. When
he appeared for auditions during the late 1940s and early 1950s and
was told, "Sorry, we are not using any Negroes," he responded, "I
am here, and I would like you to see me dance. . .maybe you'll
change your mind."

Minds were changed, slowly, but they changed. In 1951 McKayle
choreographed what would become an American classic, *Games,*
based on childhood play, rhymes, and chants. Exploring the light,
carefree innocence of youth and the darker social stigmas associated
with racial and social divisions, *Games* brought to the concert stage
an exquisite cameo about a century-and-three-quarters of inequities
and prejudice. This early work was called vibrant, vital, and visceral, and these characteristics have consistently infused his works.
The year 1951 was also the first time Broadway audiences became
aware of Donald McKayle, when he appeared in *Bless You All.* His
Broadway performing career continued through 1957 with appearances in *House of Flowers* (1954), *Copper and Brass* (1957), and
West Side Story (1957).

During the 1950s he danced in the companies of such innovators
as Jean Erdman, Mary Anthony, Merce Cunningham, Anna
Sokolow, and Martha Graham. He was also artistic director and
resident choreographer of Donald McKayle and Company, from
1951 through 1969. His company featured artists who would eventually become prominent outstanding leaders and performers in the
world dance scene, including Carmen de Lavallade, Arthur Mitchell,
Alvin Ailey, Mary Hinkson, Eliot Feld, and many others.

Early in his career, McKayle's choreographic talents were recognized not only within the concert dance world, but also by the
commercial and entertainment industries. Harry Belafonte, Rita
Moreno, Helen Gallagher, Diana Ross and the Supremes engaged
him to create choreography for their successful acts and reviews.
Fred Waring, Ed Sullivan, Bill Cosby, Mary Tyler Moore, and Dick
Van Dyke knew of McKayle's versatility and repeatedly called on
him to stylize dances for television that captured the essence of
their imaginative, trendsetting specials and shows. From 1951
through 1985 his work appeared on every major network and national public television in the United States. In 1974, McKayle was
awarded an Emmy for his work on *Free to Be You and Me.* He also
provided choreography for major film studios: Walt Disney's
Bedknobs and Broomsticks (1970); Paramount's *Cindy* (1977);
Samuel Goldwyn's *The Jazz Singer* (1980); and Tomorrow
Entertainment's *The Minstrel Man* (1976) which received an Emmy
nomination for best choreography.

The Broadway stage benefitted from McKayle's talent as both a
choreographer and director. His first Broadway production, *Golden
Boy* (1964), received a Tony nomination for best choreography. In
addition, McKayle was responsible for the concept, musical staging, and choreography for *Sophisticated Ladies* (1981), which was
honored with numerous awards. In 1975 he directed and created
choreography for *Raisin* (1974), winning a Tony award for best
musical plus nominations for best direction and best choreography.
The following year, he again was nominated for a Tony award for
best choreography for his work in *Dr. Jazz* (1975).

McKayle's diverse grounding at the New Dance Group prepared
him to work with a variety of dancers and companies. Throughout
his professional life, he has remained consistent with the tenet that
"dance has its own validity when its practitioners are able to make

their audiences respond with the very fibre of their own musculatures." He strives to establish just such an excitement in each dance he creates and charges every dancer with whom he works with the responsibility of meeting that goal. As Sasha Anawalt stated in the *New York Times* in 1991, McKayle translates "the black experience into easily understood dance—sensual, dramatic and unmistakably human." He has choreographed over 50 works for companies in the U.S., Canada, Europe, and South America. Many are being performed anew by dance companies around the States as part of the American Dance Festival's prestigious program, "The Black Tradition in American Modern Dance." Donald McKayle maintains an ongoing relationship with several dance companies that serve as repositories for his works: the Alvin Ailey American Dance Theatre, the Cleo Parker Robinson Dance Ensemble, the Cleveland San Jose Ballet, the Dayton Contemporary Dance Company, and the Los Angeles Contemporary Dance Theatre. Since 1995 he served as resident choreographer and artistic mentor for the Limón Dance Company.

In 1963 Mr. McKayle received the Capezio Award and in 1992, the Samuel H. Scripps/American Dance Festival Award for lifetime achievement in modern dance. McKayle received numerous awards in 1994 and 1995, from the American Dance Guild, the Lehman Dance Award, a Living Legend award from the National Black Arts Festival, the Heritage Award from the California Dance Educators Association, a choreographic fellowship from the National Endowment for the Arts (NEA), and he was honored in a retrospective program, "Trailblazers: Dancers of Change," saluting him and Agnes de Mille. Further awards arrived in 1996, and 1997, with Dance/USA honoring him for "outstanding accomplishments and contributions to dance" and the Balasaraswati/Joy Ann Dewey Beinecke Endowed Chair for Distinguished Teaching from the American Dance Festival. McKayle is the first creative artist to receive the Distinguished Faculty Lectureship Award for Research from the Academic Senate of the University of California, Irvine, and he was honored in a choreographic retrospective at the Auditorium Theater in Denver where he received a proclamation from Mayor William Webb.

Donald McKayle has served on the faculties of many prestigious institutions including the American Dance Festival, the Juilliard School, Bennington College, Bard College, Sarah Lawrence College, and was dean of the School of Dance at the California Institute of the Arts. He is a full professor of dance at the University of California, Irvine, in charge of graduate choreographic theses projects and is the artistic director of UCI's dance troupe.

—Gregg Lizenbery

MEEHAN, Nancy

American dancer, choreographer, and educator

Born: c. 1940 in San Francisco, California. **Education:** University of California, Berkeley, B.A.; studied dance with Ann Halprin, Welland Lathrop, Erick Hawkins, and Martha Graham. **Career:** Professional debut with the Halprin-Lathrop Dance Company, San Francisco, 1953; moved to New York City and joined the Erick Hawkins Dance Company in the early 1960s; toured with Hawkins as his partner; appeared with him at the Theatre des Nations in Paris, 1963; at the Brooklyn Academy of Music (BAM), 1968;

created roles in Hawkins' *Geography of Noon* (1964), *Black Lake* (1968), and *8 Clear Pieces* (1969), among others; taught at Hunter College while dancing with Hawkins; left the Hawkins Company in 1970; founded her own school and dance group, 1970; served on summer faculty, American Dance Festival in New London, Connecticut; her company has had annual New York seasons at the New York Dance Festival at the Delacorte Theatre, New York University, the Theatre of the Riverside Church, and the 92nd Street YM-YWHA. **Awards:** Guggenheim Fellowship for Choreography, 1976.

Works

1970	*Hudson River Seasons*
1971	*Whitip*
1972	*Live Dragon*
1973	*Bones, Cascades, Scapes*
1974	*Split Rock*
	Yellow Point
1975	*Grapes and Stones*
1976	*Threading the Wave*
1977	*Ptarmigan Wall*
1978	*White Wave*
1979	*How Near*
	One's Eye's Higher Than the Other
1980	*Seven Women*

Publications

On MEEHAN: articles—

Anderson, Jack, *Dance Magazine,* December 1969.
Duncan, Kathy, *Soho Weekly News,* 4 April 1974.
Jowitt, Deborah, *Village Voice,* 12 May 1975.
Pierce, Robert, *Village Voice,* 18 April 1974.
Rosen, Lillie, *Dance News,* October 1977.
Sorell, Walter, *Dance News,* May 1971.
———, *Dance News,* September 1975.

Clippings file on Nancy Meehan from the Dance Collection in the Performing Arts Research Center of the New York Public Library at Lincoln Center.

*   *   *

Nancy Meehan is a choreographer of highly intellectual modern dances. Dance critic Deborah Jowitt, writing in the *Village Voice,* noted that Meehan's dances seemed to her to be "a series of small, definite utterances—each on a single subject." Trained in the rigorous dance idiom of Martha Graham, Meehan danced with Graham alumnus and noted choreographer Erick Hawkins during the 1960s and 1970s. She and Hawkins were often featured together during this time. One of their most interesting dances was *8 Clear Pieces* (1969), a dance piece in which eight dances or tableaux named after such natural phenomena as star, night, and rain, became ceremonies of attention. According to Hawkins, this work was "an inquiry into new directions of seeing and hearing at the same time." The movements of Hawkins and Meehan appeared deceptively simple but were, in the words of *New York Times* dance critic Anna Kisselgoff, feats of virtuosity.

Nancy Meehan performing *Ptarmigan Wall*, 1980. Photograph © Lois Greenfield.

During her years with Hawkins, Meehan became imbued with his dance aesthetic and movement style. Hawkins' interest in Eastern theater and nature subjects as well as his use of lateral spatial patterns, fluid movements, and a nonliteral but strongly imaged structure influenced Meehan tremendously. She adopted his curving, gentle movements and melting jumps for her own. Hawkins (and Meehan) believed that life should always have room for childlike, innocent wonder. They also shared the same taste in music. However, Meehan left the Erick Hawkins troupe in 1970 to launch her own dance company and choreographed for it over the next 11 years.

Meehan organizes her work by a rhythm of images—like a painter or filmmaker. Meehan's choice of images is unique—they are animal, vegetable, and mineral even though the forms may not always be identifiable. Her dances present interesting shapes that connect with other shapes to form what feels like a whole. She does seem to establish theme ideas, however. These themes are usually hinted at by her titles: *Grapes and Stones*, and *Bones, Cascades, Scapes*, for example.

There is also a strong oriental feeling in Meehan's approach to nature and in her handling of materials; this may be an outgrowth of her San Francisco background or perhaps due to a time when she lived in Japan.

Meehan's dances are, in the words of one watcher of the dance, "pristine and succinct." Her best-known work, *Whitip* (pronounced "white tip"), is a plotless dance for six girls in white. It is performed without music. Meehan's motifs are based on bird movements: preening arms, a leg shooting out like a wing and then tucking back, a body poised vertically with arms stretched into a V-shape, and many others. She combines these motifs on her six dancers. The patterns appear to happen through chance but there is order to it all. Sometimes each dancer performs a different movement, and clarity emerges from the disarray when the viewer recognizes the motifs. Her control of materials combined with inventiveness of movement and structure makes *Whitip* a great work, according to Kathy Duncan of the *Soho Weekly News*.

Meehan likes to flatten the stage picture by always presenting her dancers facing front or facing back—often while they are moving sideways. In *Yellow Point* (1974), she explored the possibilities of human weight by having the dancers form themselves into ball shapes and then vigorously explode into sudden stamping movements. In *Grapes and Stones* (1975) she explored brief, strong movements to the music of Jon Deak.

Meehan did away with the kind of sculptural sets and costumes favored by Hawkins. Her dances are formal in their structure with a clean, uncluttered quality about them. It can also be said that she has a special sense of time—she likes to slow down time and many of her dances have, in the words of the *Village Voice*'s Robert Pierce, "an atmosphere of detached purposefulness." She's also not afraid to leave a stage empty for a few moments or to just leave one dancer on stage, immobile. Her choreographic profile seems to be a placidity even when the dances radiate energy. *Split Rock* (1974) consists of simple phrases in which dancers cluster together and then separate. They run in large circles and also walk. Individual phrases are separated from each other by stillnesses, some of which occur abruptly. More prominent stillnesses divide the entire work into sections. Meehan based her dance on the preparation and recovery positions of oriental martial arts. In one section, Meehan squats in a martial arts position turning her body into a triangular wedge while her company inclines forward from their heels like so many slabs of rock. Yet the reference to game-playing in the choreography left some reviewers unmoved. Meehan struck some as being cute when she floated up and down a line of dancers pulling on a leg here or playing peek-a-boo there.

Although Meehan got a late start in choreography, she has seemed content to take her time. She has been in no hurry to present her company until she thinks they are ready. In *Threading the Wave* (1976), Meehan entered new territory. A piano score by Eleanor Hovda suggests mysterious rites and slight turbulence. The dancers often quiver slightly and shake their hands like those in a trance. A line of dancers seems to pull in a soloist the way people in a boat would haul in a swimmer. Threading images—reclining figures reach delicately into the air beside them and pull something past them to the other side—please the eye. More important, they become a metaphor in which a concrete experience is summed up nonliterally through its essence.

According to Meehan, Japanese Noh drama is an Asian art that epitomizes content in this way.

White Wave (1978) is Meehan's most complex work. She uses a nature image as a metaphor for an aspect of human existence. A group of dancers propel another member outside their own line. This movement suggests a wave washing up objects on the beach. The same dancer who was washed up is later carried back by the ebbing patterns of the line. In her review of *White Wave*, *New York Times* dance critic Anna Kisselgoff saw the individual in the line as a metaphor for an individual reflecting upon himself or herself—of being able momentarily to step outside everyday existence.

Some critics found a number of Meehan's dances too long for one who edits her material so carefully. Those that tended to be 30 to 40 minutes each proved to be a long haul for audiences, but her dances have provided rewards for patient viewers. They often make the viewer think of sculptures; the more you walk around them, the more exciting facets and amazing angles you'll see. In addition to choreographing, Meehan also dances with her company. In *Threading the Wave*, she burst forth in red Chinese pajamas and performed an intense solo. In *Ptarmigan Wall* (1977) her long solo combined phrases from the actions of two groups of dancers. Lillie Rosen writing in *Dance News*, described Meehan's dancing as "fluidly nuanced and lacily delicate." In *Cloud...Roots* (1984), Meehan appeared briefly but powerfully at the end as "cloud" to frothing, squatting, tilting roots.

In the words of Walter Sorell: "Nancy Meehan is one of those rare dancer-choreographers who is truly avant-garde without ever testing the endurance of her audience. She is. . .exploring her own way of expressing her sensuous perceptions and her imagery moves and expands from the firm bridgehead of the past—as she experienced it."

—Adriane Ruggiero

MERTZ, Annelise

German-American dancer, artistic director, educator, and choreographer

Born: In Germany. **Education:** Studied modern (Wigman, Laban, Jooss), ballet (Vaganowa, Cechetti), and ethnic dance in Germany, 1940s; three years of graduate work, Folkwangschule, Essen; studied in New York with Alwin Nikolais and José Limón. **Career:** Performer, Berlin State Opera, Düsseldorf Opera, and Municipal

Theater Darmstadt; joined Jooss Tanz Theatre after World War II; teacher, Washington University, St. Louis, 1957-88; founder and director, Dance Concert Society (later renamed Dance St. Louis), 1966; Mark Twain Institute Dance Program, Washington University Summer Dance Institute, St. Louis Repertory Dancers (later renamed St. Louis Dancers); retired from Washington University, 1988. **Awards:** YWCA Leadership Award for outstanding contributions to the arts in St. Louis, 1983; St. Louis Art and Education Award for Excellence in the Arts, 1998.

Works

1962	*Facade* (mus. Sir William Walton; poems by Edith Sitwell), Washington University, St. Louis
1979	*Seaside Rag*, Washington University, St. Louis
1980	*Charleston Rag*, Washington University, St. Louis
1983	*Mertz Tango* (mus. Erik Satie), Riverside Theatre, New York
1984	*Facade I* (new production, same format: mus. Walton; poems Sitwell)
1985	*Facade II* (a very short piece added as complement to *Facade I*)
1986	*Ceremonial Rites*, Washington University, St. Louis

Other works include: Choreographed from 1958 to 1994 for the Washington University Dance Theater, St. Louis Repertory Dancers, and St. Louis Dancers—*Romantic Journeys* (mus. Erik Satie); *In a Courtly Manner* (mus. Scarlatti); *Suite* (mus. Bach, Tabauret, Hassler); *Festive Joy* (mus. Scarlatti); *Iphigenia of Tauris* (mus. Glück); *Images* (mus. Kurtz); *Coronation of Poppea* (mus. Monteverdi); *Tangent* (mus. Power); *Whimsey* (mus. Lecaine); *Suite by Chance* (mus. arranged); *Ceremonia de Jubilio (Suite); Jeu Vulgaire, Suite de Danse* (mus. Attaignant); *Triad* (mus. Bach); *Bach Switched On & Off (Suite), Fanfaronade* (mus. C.P.E. Bach); *Perihelion and Perigee, The Wonderful Widow of 18 Springs* (mus. collage); *I Recall* (mus. Satie); *Ragtime (Suite)* (mus. Joplin); *The Quiet Death of Annie's Comet* (mus. Steven Radeek); *Slavic Rag* (mus. Cobb); *La Femme d'Erte* (mus. arrangements); *Continuum (Suite)* (mus. Bach); *States of Being* (mus. Robert Ashley, Pauline Oliveros, Henry Cowell); *Ceremonial Rites* (mus. Phillip Glass); *Youkali* (mus. Satie); *Charleston Rag, Places; Gladly, sadly, madly and sometimes...* (mus. Wolfgang Thierfeldt); *A Day in My Life* (mus. Wolfgang Thierfeldt).

Publications

By MERTZ: articles—

"St. Louis Needs a Cultural Center," *St. Louis Post-Dispatch*, 1 October 1997.

On MERTZ: articles—

Fitterman, Stefan, "Counter Pointe: Annelise Mertz Dances to the Beat of a Different Drummer," *Riverfront Times*, 18-24 March 1987.
Louis, Murray, "The Seminal Influence of Annelise Mertz in Positioning Modern Dance," *Washington University*, Fall 1990.
Rohde, Hedwig, "Review: Landscapes, Plays, and Rituals," *Tagesspiele*, 22 July 1988.
Wierzbicki, James, "Choreographer Dances in Surprise Performance for Theater Anniversary," *St. Louis Globe-Democrat*, 17 April 1984.
Ziony, Ruth Kramer, "Turned On; Annelise Mertz at Washington University," *Dance Magazine,* September 1968.

*   *   *

Alwin Nikolais called Annelise Mertz "the Carrie Nation of dance in the Midwest, the St. Joan of St. Louis." One of her students at Washington University in St. Louis during the 1960s recalled: "She was by turns hilarious and bleak, historical and futuristic. She mirrored our American naivete with a vision that was at once brighter and darker than we could imagine." Murray Louis summed up her career with economy of expression, in a letter that consisted of just two sentences: "There are many people who talk about the arts and so few who do anything about it. You, Annelise, have done a great deal for the dance in America."

Their estimations are no exaggeration, especially when one considers that at the time she arrived in St. Louis in 1957, the city at the gateway to the West was virtually bereft of any dance culture. Certainly there was no modern dance culture of any kind, and beyond a Yuletide presentation of *The Nutcracker*, St. Louis was a stranger to dance. Annelise Mertz changed all that.

Born and raised in Berlin, Mertz came of age in a world torn apart on a public level by the Nazis and the devastation they wrought, and on a private level by her parents' divorce. Like many dancers, she did not set out to become one: in fact, she hoped to become an architect, but girls were not encouraged in such pursuits. By ultimately becoming a choreographer, she got to fulfill her dream of working in design—only her designs were living, rather than fixed in stone.

She became involved in dance first as a child, simply because she was frail and the family doctor recommended it for exercise. But as a young woman, she continued in the serious pursuit of her art, studying with a Russian dancer who had performed in Anna Pavlova's company. Later she earned her state certificate for dance, and won a coveted place with the State Opera in Berlin. There she performed under the baton of a number of famous conductors, including Herbert von Karajanl; later she moved to the Dusseldorf Opera, where she danced solo. But Germany in the 1940s was not exactly a place in which to nurture a healthy young career, and Mertz's ambitions quite nearly ran aground until she joined the Kurt Jooss Tanz Theatre. Jooss had fled the Nazis to England, but returned after the war, bringing with him his celebrated antiwar production, *The Green Table*. Mertz joined his company, and toured Europe with him for three years.

Upon leaving the Jooss Tanz Theatre, Mertz began a period of searching. She was engaged as a solo dancer in the Municipal Theater in Darmstadt, Germany, but left after a year when asked to perform more balletic dances on pointe. But postwar Germany, still reeling from the shocks of the past decades, was not a fertile ground for creative work and experimentation. If Mertz wanted to seriously practice modern dance, she would have to cross the Atlantic.

So she did in 1955, on what she intended as a mere exploratory trip to the U.S.—though as it turned out, she would never go back to Germany except as a visitor. Her first engagement was with the University of Illinois in Chicago to replace a teacher for one semester. She was then offered a full-time teaching position at Washington University in St. Louis. Dance at that time was a mere adjunct to the physical education program, something to keep young women busy and out of trouble—and it was funded with the same degree of seriousness. But Mertz had a vision, and within half a decade, she was able to put on a performance called *Facade,* a choreography to the music of William Walton and poetry of Edith Sitwell. Collages by Ernst Trova, entitled *The Falling Men* (now in the Museum of Modern Art) provided the backdrop for the dances. It proved to be very successful thought the odds were against it—an old worn-out theater, lights burnt out, and malfunctioning microphones (a new theater was built in 1973). Nevertheless, on that night in 1962, not only was modern dance born in St. Louis, but Mertz founded the Washington University Dance Theater.

In 1967 Mertz persuaded the Washington University administration to take dance out of the Physical Education department and to create a separate dance division. Together with the drama division, a Performing Arts department was developed. But her crusade for dance as an art form—initially a one-woman crusade—was not to be fought only on the battlefield of the university. For dance to be a vital part of the community, it had to touch the lives of the public at large, and that was why in 1966—quite literally in her living room—she and several others founded the Dance Concert Society, a non-profit organization to present professional dance companies. Over the following years, the Dance Concert Society (later renamed Dance St. Louis), along with Mertz's department at Washington University, created a flourishing environment for dance in the Midwest. "Those were the days when dancers were literally starving," she later recalled. "I can remember Merce Cunningham coming here and being put up in a friend's home. The artists loved it, and we loved it." Cunningham was not the only great who made the trek to the Show Me State on Mertz's invitation: the charismatic "dance missionary," as she was sometimes called, brought the companies of José Limón, Daniel Nagrin, Murray Louis, Alwin Nikolais, and Katherine Litz to St. Louis, while Dance St. Louis and the Edison Theater at Washington University have continued to attract dance artists and their troupes from all over the world.

The city saw many more performances of Mertz's work over the following decades performed by the Washington University Dance Theater and the St. Louis Dancers. The latter performed in Ireland and Berlin, but their touring was restricted since members of the company were part of Washington University's teaching faculty. Mertz danced from time to time, but teaching, choreographing, directing, and administrative duties allowed little time for performing. Yet in the mid-1980s, Mertz and fellow faculty member Gale Ormiston (a former dancer with the Nikolais Dance Theater in New York) performed in Mertz's *Facade I* and *Facade II* featuring new choreography of 12 short dances by Mertz and nine by Ormiston to the same music and poetry from the original *Facade* in 1962. In 1990, the St. Louis Dancers, the professional company Mertz had founded and headed, gave their last performance with a "Gala Farewell" at the Edison Theater on the Washington University campus.

Mertz has been far from inactive in the years following her retirement from teaching in 1988. She continued to teach and choreograph on a freelance basis and served on committee for the renewal of downtown St. Louis, pushing for the construction of a new cultural center for the performing and visual arts. She is also working on a book about creative movement education through dance and drama. Nikolai's observations remained as accurate as when he wrote them in 1979: "Heaven help you who hinder the process of her vision of dance in St. Louis. But bless her and all of you, indeed, who have so selflessly made such a healthy dance oasis in the depths of the country."

—Judson Knight and Sydonie Benet

MERYL TANKARD AUSTRALIAN DANCE THEATRE

Australian dance company

Founded as Australian Dance Theatre by Elizabeth Cameron Dalman, Adelaide, South Australia, 1965; artistic directors included: Elizabeth Cameron Dalman, 1965-75; Jonathan Taylor, 1976-85; Leigh Warren, 1987-92; renamed Meryl Tankard Australian Dance Theatre, 1993; artistic director, Meryl Tankard, and associate artist, Régis Lansac, from 1993.

Works (a selection of works choreographed by the above artistic directors for the Australian Dance Theatre, 1965-97)

1969-75 *Generation Gap, This Train, Bushfire, Creation, Landscape, Rondel, Corroboree, Children of Time, Opal, Lemon Piece Sky* (Dalman)

1976-85 *'Tis Goodly Sport, Stars End, Incident at Bull Creek, Flibbertigibbet, Midsummer Marriage, Wild Stars, The Wedding, Transfigured Night, Stripsody, Broken Head, While We Watch, High Flyers* (Taylor)

1987-92 *Verandah, Quirkshuffle, The Golden Slave, Never Mind the Bindies, Transient Pleasures, Let's Do It, Adieu, Beyond the Flesh, Tu Tu Wha, Petrouchka, Softly, Softly* (Warren)

1993-97 *Court of Flora, Nuti, Kikimora, Songs with Mara, Aurora, O Let Me Weep, Furioso, Possessed, Rasa, Inuk, Fortuna* (Tankard)

*   *   *

Capital of the state of South Australia, the small city of Adelaide boasts a dance company that ranks not only among the country's finest but is also the country's oldest in terms of modern dance. Established in 1965, the Australian Dance Theatre remains in essence very much as its founder Elizabeth Cameron Dalman intended: a company with a defined Australian focus; one which capitalises on the talents of Australian artists; one where the emphasis is on dance theatre; and one which is an active participant in the international dance dialogue.

Discounting a temporary interregnum in 1986 and 1987 by well-known festival director Anthony Steele, the company has seen four artistic directors in its 33-year history. While each has brought about a decisive change in artistic direction, there are nonetheless discernible (if not always immediately apparent) links between all four. Thus some general sense of continuity has been maintained, despite quite different approaches to the company in terms of both process and product.

Battling against the prevailing conservatism of the day, the locally-born Dalman was determined to establish the country's first professional modern dance company. Influenced by her time at the Folkwangschule in Essen (then under Kurt Jooss' directorship), and her work with the American dancer Eleo Pomare, Dalman nevertheless saw the company in distinctly Australian terms: Australian dancers, choreographers, composers, and visual artists, working on contemporary Australian themes and issues—including those concerned with the *Dreaming*—the creation myths and legends of Australia's indigenous people (with works such as *Creation, Opal,* and *Corroboree* reflecting that source). While Dalman's commitment to things Australian was paramount, she also understood the importance of exposing the company (and its audiences) to the work of international choreographers, which included her mentor Pomare (*Gin Woman Distress* and *Limousine for Janis*), Cliff Keuter (*Sunday Papers* and *Second Sight*) and Jaap Flier (former artistic director of the Nederlands Dans Theater, who became Dalman's co-artistic director in 1973). A notable Australian first was the performance by the company of Doris Humphrey's *The Shakers*, reconstructed by Ray Cook from the notated score in 1972.

With the appointment in 1976 of Jonathan Taylor as artistic director, the company took a somewhat more sophisticated English turn. A former dancer and choreographer with Ballet Rambert, Taylor brought with him not only a dance style that owed much to the English company, but some of its dancers and repertory as well. Of particular importance was the introduction of Australian audiences to the work of Christopher Bruce, with *Ghost Dances, Black Angels*, and *Holiday Sketches*, among those taken into the repertoire. Other well-known choreographers whose works were performed included Norman Morrice, Yuriko, Sara Sugihara, and Cliff Keuter.

In line with the Dalman company, both artistic director and company dancers contributed significantly to the repertory. Among Taylor's most successful works were the irrepressible *Flibbertigibbet, Quicksilver* (his tribute to Marie Rambert), and the Diaghilev-inspired *High Flyers*. Company choreographers included Joe Scoglio, Julia Blaikie (both former Rambert dancers) and Margaret Wilson.

The company's international reputation also increased during this time, with Taylor being invited to take the theatrical extravaganza *Wildstars* to the Edinburgh Festival in 1980. Developed in collaboration with designer Nigel Triffitt, the work was one of the few dance theatre pieces created on the company during Taylor's directorship. A further mark of ADT's international standing was Glen Tetley's creation on the company of his dramatic *Revelation and Fall* in 1984.

The 1987 appointment of Australian-born Leigh Warren saw the company return more specifically to the fundamentals of Dalman's philosophy: Australian dancers and choreographers (including Nanette Hassall and Graeme Watson), supported by Australia musicians (composer Carl Vine, for example) and designers (such as Mary Moore). Financial constraints also meant that Warren was unable to venture too far afield in his use of outside choreographers, and much of the company's repertoire during this period is local—either his or that of his dancers. Among the best of Warren's works are *Never Mind the Bindies, Transient Pleasures,* and the elegiac *Adieu,* although the high point of this 1987 to 1992 period would undoubtedly be the company's performance of William Forsythe's stunning *Enemy in the Field* in 1992. The focus on Warren's choreography inevitably meant that much of the repertoire reflected his dance heritage: work in a "mainstream modern" style with a touch of both Christopher Bruce (Ballet Rambert) and Jiří Kylián (Nederlands Dans Theater). At the same time the company began to venture into the realm of dance theatre, with such works as *Tu Tu Wha* and *Metro* (the latter created by theatre director Simon Phillips). Neither, however, was particularly successful.

It is in the current company (renamed the Meryl Tankard Australian Dance Theatre in recognition of the achievements of its latest artistic director, Meryl Tankard) that the dance theatre tradition has taken firm hold. Tankard spent several years with the Pina Bausch Wuppertal Tanztheater, and while the Bausch influence is evident, it is revealed more in the way that Tankard challenges convention (both cultural and dance-specific) and integrates multiple levels of meaning, than in any specific movement sense. By comparison to that of her three predecessors, Tankard's work is highly innovative and adventurous, with a greater emphasis on the theatrical: movement from a wide variety of sources, including ballet, tap, ballroom, circus, acrobatics, and sport; the use of voice in both song and text; and the strong emphasis on visual design through the work of Régis Lansac, the company's associate artistic director. In *Furioso,* for example, the dancers are suspended in midair, attached to ropes by harnesses, while the more gentle *Songs with Mara* has them singing Bulgarian folk songs.

Dalman had always envisaged ADT as a company with an international standing. While the hope has not fully been realised as yet, the present company is fast establishing a strong reputation abroad. Since its 1993 inception it has toured extensively, primarily to Europe (Germany in particular) and the United States, with its 1997 tour including performances at the Brooklyn Academy of Music, and has appeared at both international arts festivals held in Adelaide—the Barossa International Music Festival and the biannual Adelaide Festival of Arts.

—Anita Donaldson

METTLER, Barbara

American dancer, educator, film and video producer, and author

Born: 12 March 1907 in Chicago, Illinois. **Education:** Attended private school, Roycemore, Evanston, Illinois, and Smith College, Northampton, Massachusetts; trained at the Mary Wigman Central Institute of Dance in Dresden, Germany, 1931-33; Bennington Summer School of Dance, 1936. **Career:** Dancer of her own solos and group works until 1954; toured the East Coast and Midwest, 1953-54; taught in her own studio in the old Carnegie Hall, New York City, 1934-40; summer school classes in dance barns in Sanbornton and then Meredith, New Hampshire, 1940-53; in the Department of Expressive Movement, which she established, at Keuka College in Keuka, New York, 1943-46; in the Modern Dance Department of the Boston YWCA, 1949-53; at St. Paul's Rehabilitation Center of Newly Blinded Adults in Newton, Massachusetts, 1956-58; summer programs at Northern Arizona University (then Arizona State College) in Flagstaff and Arizona State University Art Department, 1961; Tucson Art Center, the Workshop Center for the Arts, and the Tucson Community School, 1961-63; School of Sciences of Sport at the National University in San Jose, Costa Rica, September 1979; her own Tucson Creative Dance Center, 1963-96; author of many articles, books, and producer and director of several films on the teaching of the arts of dance and improvisation. **Awards:** Arizona Arts Council Award, 1995.

Publications

By METTLER: books—

This Is Creative Dance! A Picture Book, Tucson, 1962.
Basic Dance on a College Level: Workshop at Goddard College, Boston, 1956.

Children's Creative Dance Book, Tucson, 1970.
Basic Movement Exercises, Tucson, 1973.
Group Dance Improvisations, Tucson, 1975.
Materials of Dance as a Creative Art Activity, Tucson, 1979.
The Nature of Dance as a Creative Art Activity, Tucson, 1980.
Dance as an Element of Life, Tucson, 1983.

By METTLER: articles—

"Relaxation: A Creative Element of Body Movement," *Dance Observer*, June-July 1943.
"The Relation of Dance to the Visual Arts," *Journal of Aesthetics and Art Criticism* 1946-47.
"What Is Dance?" *Dance Observer*, March 1949.
"Modern Dance: Art or Show Business," *Dance Observer*, May 1952.
"Manifesto for Modern Dance," *Dance Observer*, October 1953.
"Improvisation: The Most Creative Approach to Dance," *Dance Magazine*, July 1966.
"Group Movement Expression," *Dance Research Monograph One: 1971-1972*, edited by Patricia A. Rowe, New York, 1973.
"The Language of Dance," *Proceedings of the International Conference on Dance Research, 1985*, 1987.
"Creative Dance: Art or Therapy?" *American Journal of Dance Therapy*, 1990.

On METTLER: articles—

Paxton, Steve, "Book Review: *Materials of Dance as a Creative Art Activity*," *Contact Quarterly*, Summer 1977.
Stodelle, Ernestine, "Book Review: *Materials of Dance as a Creative Art Activity*," *Dance Observer*, December 1961.

Films and Videotapes (produced and distributed by Mettler Studios, Inc., unless otherwise noted)

Creative Dance for Children, four films, 1966-67.
Art of Body Movement, 11 videos, 1970.
Group Dance Improvisation, 1978.
A New Direction in Dance, 1978.
Pure Dance, 1980.
The Language of Movement, 1985.
Baby Dance, 1989.
Movimiento Creativo en Costa Rica, in Spanish, 1989.
The Faces of Wisdom: Stories of Elder Women, produced and directed by Catherine A. Busch-Johnston, Rough and Ready, 1993.

*   *   *

Barbara Mettler's work has contributed to the development of the most creative part of modern dance, the process of finding new movement through improvisation. For Mettler the improvised is the purest form of dance; anyone at any age is capable of dancing; and everyone is entitled to this creative art experience. Mettler's primary themes: beauty, freedom, and democracy, underlie her 60 years of work. Because she remained autonomous and taught primarily in recreational, not educational, institutions, she is among the few early modern dancers, like Anna Halprin in San Francisco and Georgette Schneer in New York, who have focused primarily on teaching laypeople rather than professional dancers.

The influence of Mary Wigman's and Rudolf Laban's work is evident in all Mettler's writings on dance. She emphasized pure dance, that is, body movement as the central source of dance; it need not serve any other purpose or art and is the basis of all the arts. Exploring the basic components of movement—time, space, and force—enables dancers to develop their movement range. The power and importance of group improvisation, as developed by Laban in movement choirs, remains a force in her work. She identified this as the "group body." And like her teachers, Mettler believed that all people can dance and are entitled to experience the joy and beauty of engaging in creative movement.

Mettler weaned herself from some of the practices she learned in her Wigman Institute training: the use of predesigned exercises given to students by the teacher at the beginning of class, the idea that improvisation serves only as a source for dance composition, that dancing requires an audience, and that dance is dependent on composed music. Like many other early modern dancers, Mettler used a wide variety of percussion instruments, standard and invented, and voice sounds, words, and body percussion as ways of sound-making for dance. She took this idea further where sound is improvised at the same time as the improvised dances and, like the dances, is not preplanned or rehearsed.

In the following paragraph from *Dance as an Element of Life*, Mettler's basic values in her teachings emerge:

> To liberate the dance artist which is in all of us, we each improvise our own body movements. Improvisation is the most accessible and the freest of all dance experiences. It means making up the movements of the dance while you are dancing. Anyone can do it, because we adjust our movements to our individual capabilities. At the same time it is the greatest challenge for even the most experienced dancer because, while improvising, we use all available skill in both the creation and execution of meaningful movement forms.

In simple jargon-free language, she defined improvisation, dancers, and the challenge of fully engaging in this creative art. Art, for Mettler, is beauty: "order, wholeness, truth, expression of an inner vision of perfection" which human beings need to make their lives complete. And any movement becomes dance-art when the feeling for its aesthetic form is the focus of the experience. The body, for Mettler, is the instrument and movement is the material of dance. "Movement feeling" in the body starts with the muscles where the kinesthetic sense gives sensations to the nervous system. These sensations arouse emotions which the mind registers; thus, one's entire being is concentrated in dancing. The more one practices improvising, the more skillful the dancer becomes. This skill leads first to freedom then to awareness and control.

Throughout her books, for each of her teaching guidelines, students first explore each movement theme as individuals, then work in duos, trios, small groups, and finally in large groups. In her books Mettler addressed teachers and commented on the needs of children, the shynesses of beginners, and the challenges for advanced students as she gives simple and clear instructions which can be used directly with classes.

Over the years Mettler devised a system to develop dancers' improvisational abilities. She began with the body and its separate parts and examined movement characteristics of tension and relaxation (a basic Laban/Wigman concept) and then opening and closing (a variation of the Laban "gathering and scattering"). Following this general introduction to movement, she considered the features of force: moving and not moving, moving and being moved, forceful and forceless movement, interrupted and sustained movement, and then interacting forces. Her introduction to "interacting forces" shows the thoroughness of her understanding of movement in *Dance as an Element of Life* (1985): "Tension and relaxation are conditions of muscles and nerves. Forcefulness and forcelessness are qualities of movement. Activity and passivity are a relationship between two or more moving bodies." She included the body instrument, the material of movement, and the interaction of dancers in her concept of force.

Mettler's conceptualization of "time" is also thorough, elegant, and clear. The exploration begins with pace, moves to duration, pulse, measure, then to metric patterns and finally rhythm. Rhythm, for Mettler is the most central yet abstract of the features of time. It must not be confused with metric pattern since this measures a time pattern. "Rhythm is the very life of movement. It can be perceived through the senses and felt intuitively, but never measured. Rhythm is integration of impulse, the creative principle of movement." Regular and irregular patterns can be rhythmic or not; in all her improvisations, she intended students to develop their feeling for rhythm.

Space, as Mettler presented it, proceeds from the simple and basic to the complex, like her other logically developed concepts. The space concepts emphasize the visible aspect of movement patterns: position, direction, size, and shape. For Mettler shape is in motion, such as straight or curving movements, whereas position is held. She clarified that both the body-instrument and movement-material can be curved or straight or the body can be in a curved position making straight movements and visa versa. Children can understand this idea by walking in curved or straight pathways.

After exploring force, time, and space, Mettler tied dance-movement to the other arts: music, the visual arts, and drama. In all she differentiated these from dance and urged her students to dance their responses. Her discussion of movement and sound includes sound and silence, voice sounds, speech, song (original and composed), sounds of hands and feet and other body parts, and instruments, both ordinary objects such as nails and spoons and traditional ones. Here, too, she followed the pattern of self-accompaniment, then students work in pairs, trios, quartets, and larger groups with sound accompanying dance and dance accompanying music.

When discussing movement and sight, Mettler emphasized how seeing can be external through the eyes and internal in the visual imagination. Connecting this area to the concepts of space, she included such contrasting kinds of line drawing as rough and smooth; such visual designs as plane—a flat surface; volume—an empty enclosed space; and mass—a filled space having thickness and weight; and finally existing environments beginning with clothing, indoor and outdoor spaces and objects, and then created environments.

In Mettler's final category for exploration, representational movement she differentiated movement with qualities abstracted from or representing specific life experiences. When dancing these derived qualities, students express the feelings stimulated by common animate and inanimate objects, machines, creatures, and finally specific emotions. In movements which express mood or emotion, she separated acting from pure dancing urging dancers to respond in dance movement, not specific actions of an actor.

As a master teacher, author, and film and video producer, Barbara Mettler contributed substantially to the development of teaching creative movement, and her work continues to reach children, their teachers, parents, laypeople, dancers, and artists worldwide.

—Judy Alter

MEXICO

Modern dance arrived in Mexico in 1939, during a moment of flourishing culture and passionate politics, through two North American choreographers: Waldeen (von Falkenstein) and Anna Sokolow. Out of their teachings a dance movement was born that revolutionized the country's prevailing dance in its form, technique, and creative conception. Their style developed into a movement in part because of the work at the National Dance School, under the direction of sisters Nellie and Gloria Campobello, and because the cultural and political atmosphere under President Cárdenas was conducive to this new art form.

The general history of Mexican dance, including modern dance, relates to the state government, for it has been a primary sponsor. The development impulse and support given to the dance by each of the Mexican administrations has been directly linked to their interest in it. In addition, the centralism that has characterized the country's political, economic, and cultural life must be taken into account, for it has fostered the concentration of dance activity almost exclusively in Mexico City. Since the end of the 19th century, Mexico had been visited by several of the world's emerging dance companies and soloists. One of these was Loie Fuller, who performed in Mexico in 1897, as well as others whose works showcased the styles of Isadora Duncan, Ruth St. Denis, Maud Allan, Fuller, and other dance pioneers.

After the Mexican Revolution had ended in 1920, a nationalist trend in cultural projects emerged, headed by the Public Education Secretary José Vasconcelos, which included dance. One of its measures was the incorporation of the teachings of Émile Jaques-Dalcroze and of dance and physical education into the public schools. Some foreign teachers were also working at private schools, mainly teaching classical dance and other genres, who sensitized the population and critics toward dance. Moreover, the visits of Anna Pavlova and her ballet company to Mexico in 1919 and 1925 gave a fresh impulse to the professionalization of dance and the emergence of an official school, the Dynamic Plastics School, in 1931. This academy was replaced in 1932 by the Dance School of the Fine Arts Department under the Public Education Secretary, where modern dance was incorporated and taught by the North American Dora Duby.

The Mexicans who adopted the modern style of dance were led by sisters Nellie and Gloria Campobello, whose huge and expressive mass ballets evoked those produced in Germany by Rudolf Laban and Mary Wigman; and Sergio Franco, who created many pre-Hispanic and Asian dance stylizations along the lines of Denishawn in the United States. Nevertheless, the work that can be properly considered as modern dance arrived in Mexico by means of Waldeen and Sokolow who surrounded themselves with artists, musicians, writers, and theater artists, and gave impulse to the new dance trends. The dancers who worked with each of them, "Waldeens" and "Sokolovas," constituted the first generation of Mexican modern dance artists and established a fierce rivalry. It's worthwhile to mention the special strength this generation—formed almost completely by women—to defend the dance profession during a time when dance was considered an exclusively ornamental activity. The fact that these women opted to dance professionally and, moreover, to pursue modern dance, meant to face the prejudices of the era.

The premiere of *La Coronela* by Waldeen (1940) marked the inception of the nationalist modern dance and its first crystallization. From this point on, choreography sought not only to reflect Mexican reality, but to rescue indigenous art and to recoup the nation's roots. The nationalist modern dance reflected developments in modern art, especially mural painting, and undertook the task of creating a unique art form with a universal mode of expression. Having this in mind, the Fine Arts Ballet was founded in 1940. Although Sokolow did not fully agree with such ideas, she directed the Mexican Classic and Modern Dance Group, then a troupe known as The Blue Dove, until a lack of support impelled her to abandon the country the same year. The Sokolovas united and continued dancing, and Sokolow periodically returned to the country to work with them.

The most important representatives of the first generation of Mexican dancers included Waldeen's group—Guillermina Bravo, Josefina Lavalle, Ana Mérida, and others; Sokolow's group was comprised of several talented dancers including Rosa Reyna, Carmen Gutiérrez, Ana Mérida (yes, she danced with both) and Josefina Luna. After some years in which modern dance lost its power due to a change in government, in 1947 the Mexican Dance Academy was formed, dependent on the recently created National Institute of Fine Arts, (NIFA) directed by musician Carlos Chávez. The Academy was founded as a professional dance company for the creation of works to project the national identity and roots using a modern language with universal appeal. Early on, the members of the Academy conducted research tours to several indigenous areas, where they picked dances and melodies to serve as the backbone for modern dance.

In 1948 the modern dance movement suffered a split out of which the National Ballet of Mexico was born, with an independent attitude that has been maintained for five decades. Guillermina Bravo and Josefina Lavalle were among its founders, and directed the company until 1956, when Bravo carried on alone. Bravo and the National Ballet have inspired the emergence of many dancers, choreographers, composers and designers, and influenced almost every modern dance professional in the country. In 1950, while Bravo and Lavalle commandeered the National Ballet, Miguel Covarrubias took charge of the Dance Department of the NIFA and stimulated nationalist modern dance, which reached its culmination with the Mexican Ballet of the Mexican Dance Academy. Thanks to the invitation of Covarrubias, several foreign artists arrived in Mexico in 1950 and inspired others through their teachings. The most important of them included Xavier Francis, a dancer, teacher and choreographer who gave solid technical basis to the dancers of the epoch; and José Limón, who in 1951 worked as a guest dancer, teacher, and choreographer with Doris Humphrey (as his artistic director) and the members of José Limón Dance Company.

In the 1950s it was held that nationalism afforded the most significant direction for Mexican arts, including dance. The language required by this nationalism should be expressive and full, intense, committed, and capable of revolutionizing form and content—namely modern dance.

The peak of the nationalist modern dance saw the appearance and development of several offerings. One of these emerged in the Experimental Group (1949) founded by Ana Mérida which, in spite of belonging to the Mexican Dance Academy, maintained a creative and organizational independence. Amalia Hernández founded the Modern Ballet of Mexico in 1949, with repertory by Waldeen and some folkloric dance works. Step by step this group modified its artistic proposal until becoming the Folkloric Ballet of Mexico, which is still directed by Hernández (the only other dance artist, along with Guillermina Bravo, who has received the National Arts Award).

From 1953 on, governmental change and the absence of a cohesive element (like Covarrubias), saw the emergence of new dance groups in several parts of the country, among them the New Dance Theater, established Xavier Francis, Luis Fandiño, and others to promote experimentation in fields detached from nationalism; the Contemporary Ballet, founded in 1954; and the change of the NIFA's resident company, the Mexican Ballet, to the Fine Arts Ballet in 1955, directed for a short time by Waldeen, who brought several leading dancers from North America, such as Merce Cunningham, Mary Anthony, Anna Sokolow, and David Campbell to Mexico.

In 1957 two companies, the Contemporary Ballet and the National Ballet, enjoyed a successful and inspirational tour of Europe and China and returned to Mexico with several new works in development. In 1958 another company emerged within NIFA—the Popular Ballet, co-directed by Guillermo Arriaga and Josefina Lavalle. Its repertory was formed by modern dance and folkloric works, the latter beginning to receive greater official support. In 1959 there were changes at NIFA, which strongly affected dance: Ana Mérida took charge of the Dance Department and attempted to unify all the modern dancers within a single company, the Fine Arts Ballet. In addition, Lavalle, directing the Mexican Dance Academy, promoted the legitimization of dance instruction and succeeded in obtaining professional titles for the dancers.

In 1961 the Fine Arts Ballet had Anna Sokolow and José Limón as its guest choreographers; Sokolow staged *Musical Offering* and Limón *Missa Brevis*; in 1962 the Fine Arts Ballet, National Ballet, Popular Ballet, and Chamber Ballet all participated in the First Mexican Dance Festival.

While the National Ballet strengthened and began its transition to contemporary dance, the New Dance Theater and the Fine Arts Ballet disappeared in 1963. The former lacked support, the latter was disbanded by NIFA to make room for the Classical Ballet of Mexico. The dismissed dancers were invited to join the National Ballet, the independent Contemporary Mexico Ballet, the Folkloric Ballet of Mexico, or to form new groups.

The 1960s marked a very difficult epoch for Mexican dance as "modern" dance became synonymous with "contemporary" dance, which meant the loss of its connections with other creative arts and challenged the dance to rely more on technical training than storyline. The National Ballet solved this problem by acquiring the Graham technique, which strengthened the company and placed more emphasis on the bodies of its dancers. In 1966 another company, the Independent Ballet, emerged from the National Ballet, directed by Raúl Flores Canelo, created as a reaction against the excess of technique. The Independent Ballet earned great public and critical acceptance by maintaining a direction considered "eclectic and against the orthodoxy."

The 19th Olympic Games held in Mexico in 1968 drew the companies of Martha Graham, Merce Cunningham, and Paul Taylor to perform along with several of Mexico's own dance troupes. The next decade brought the creation of several cultural agencies, including the Social Activities National Fund (FONAPAS); the Federal District Department, the Metropolitan Autonomous University, and the National Autonomous University of Mexico (UNAM). Three dance departments were also created at the University of Veracruz in Xalapa, the Autonomous University of Puebla, and at UNAM (which in 1981 created an enormous Cultural Center with a venue suited to dance theater). Two electronic media dance programs were initiated: *Dance Time*, on University Radio in 1973 and *Teledance,* on Channel 4 of Mexican television, and afterwards on Channel 11 in 1974, both directed by Colombia Moya. Next came the first magazine devoted solely to dance in 1977. Nevertheless, the government also interfered, resulting in the disappearance of the National Dance Board and the Mexican Dance Association, supported by the previous government, but dismantled by the new one which began in 1976. The latter also tried to break up the Mexican Dance Academy, founding in its place the National Professional Dance Teaching System in 1978, formed by three schools, the Classic Dance National School, the Contemporary Dance National School (including the Higher Choreography Center) and the Folkloric Dance National School.

In 1978 came another fracturing, this one in the Independent Ballet as the co-directors went their separate ways. Gladiola Orozco and Maurice Descombey directed one group later called the Space Theater Ballet, while Raúl Flores Canelo headed his own group, retaining the "Independent Ballet" name. Another milestone came in the form of two International Festivals of Contemporary Dance (in 1978 and 1979), with the participation of Ballet Theatre Contemporain, Alvin Ailey American Dance Theatre, National Ballet, Independent Ballet, 20th Century Ballet, and Louis Falco Dance Company. Before the advent of the 1980s, several contemporary dance venues appeared in Mexico including Contemporary Music and Dance Workshop of the Folkloric Ballet of Mexico (1974, with teachings of Alvin Nikolais and Louis Murray, among others); Mórula Group (emerged from the National Ballet, 1975); Expansion 7 (1973-77); Modern Dance Company of the Mexican Dance Academy (1976-78); Arsaedis (1979); and University Free Dance (1979).

The so-called "lost decade" of the 1980s began with three prominent companies subsidized by NIFA: the National Ballet, the Independent Ballet, and the Space Theater Ballet, which continue today. Yet numerous independent groups thrived as well with the birth of the new Mexican theater-dance and postmodernism. The first took great strength, due in large part to the presence of Pina Bausch and her Wuppertal Dance Theatre in Mexico (1980), who counteracted Cunningham's and Nikolais' influence over Mexican dance and rendered it more expressive. Many foreign companies toured Mexico in the 1980s, but the Germans had the greatest impact. As the independents took their dance to higher emotional levels, street dance also emerged and played an important part. The 1985 Mexico City earthquakes acted as a catalyst for the dancers' entrance to streets—as a human response to an injured population.

Mexican independent contemporary dance emerged from several factors including a more open conception of dance and the body, the fall of the world's hegemonic discourses, the search for new forms of expression in response to the economic crisis that shook the country, and as an answer to changing values of the era. Among these new groups were Tropicana's Holiday, Red Earth, Contradance, Utopia, Body Theater, In Movement, Purple, UX Onodance, Daily Assault, and many more. All have been supported with seasons organized by NIFA, UNAM, and some governmental agencies.

In 1983 the Dance Research and Documentation Center was formed within NIFA; in 1988 it took the name of Dance Research, Documentation, and Information National Center "José Limón," playing an outstanding role in the reflection of dance and the organization of national events.

Another important moment came in 1984, when the Public Education Secretary initiated a program for recovering the most important works of nationalist dance. Thanks to this, it was possible to restage such works as *Zapata* (Arriaga), *At the Wedding* (Waldeen), *La Coronela* (Waldeen), *The Meandering Tadpole* (Sokolow), *The*

Moon and the Deer Ballad (Mérida), *The Drowned Paradise* (Bravo), *La Manda* (Reyna), *The Roosters* (De Bernal), *Juan Calavera* (Lavalle), *Provincial* (Beristáin), and *The Wait* (Flores Canelo).

Awards and acknowledgments to dance personalities have also been forthcoming, including the NIFA's "A Life in Dance" award (since 1985), the Dance National Award "José Limón" of the same Institute and the government of Sinaloa; and several awards within the National and International Contemporary Dance Festival of San Luis Potosí. The neoliberalism of president Salinas modified the cultural and dance policies, creating the Culture and Arts National Board, the National Fund for Culture and Arts, and the Creators' National System, which have established a system of grants and financial support favoring several groups, choreographers, and dancers. Despite this, the independent groups have lost cohesion and only the most prominent dancers or choreographers have survived.

Yet numerous groups are working in the 1990s, and their number grows day by day. The country's professional dance schools also consolidated. The young choreographers emerging during this decade develop their own paths. A large number of seasons are held in many dance forums, as well as at dance festivals throughout the country, with the participation of new and experimental groups. Many new names appear in the Mexican contemporary dance, all searching for a unique and genuine form of expression which can reaffirm them as artists and win social acknowledgment for their work.

Publications

Baud, Pierre-Alain, *Una danza tan ansiada*, Mexico City, 1992.
Cardona, Patricia, *La danza en México en los años setenta*, Mexico City, 1980.
———, *La nueva cara del bailarín mexicano*, Mexico City, 1990.
Durán, Lin, *La danza mexicana en los setenta*, Mexico City, 1990.
Tibol, Raquel, *Pasos en la danza mexicana*, Mexico City, 1982.
Tortajada Quiroz, Margarita, *Danza y poder*, Mexico City, 1995.
———, *Mujeres de danza combativa*, Mexico City, 1997.
50 años de Danza en el Palacio de Bellas Artes, Mexico City, 1984.

—Margarita Tortajada Quiroz
translated by Dolores Ponce Gutiérrez

MILLER, Bebe

American dancer, choreographer, and company director

Born: 20 September 1950 in New York City. **Education:** Earlham College, Richmond, Indiana, B.A. in fine arts 1971; Ohio State University, M.A. in dance 1975. **Career:** Studied dance with Ruth Grauert, Murray Louis, Fran Reid, Phyllis Lamhut, and Nina Wiener, 1976 to 1982; performed with Dana Reitz in New York and Europe, 1983; first independent choreography, 1978; founder and artistic director, Bebe Miller Company, 1985; has taught at the University of Illinois at Champaign/Urbana, UCLA, New York University, Mt. Holyoke College, Movement Research in New York City, Sarah Lawrence College, University of Minnesota, Mills College, Middlebury College, Virginia Commonwealth University, Texas Women's University, Cal Arts and Stanford University, with residencies at Ohio State University in Columbus, Portland State

University in Oregon, Bates Dance Festival, SUNY/Purchase, NYU, and the Colorado Dance Festival. International teaching included The Dance Factory in Johannesburg, 1994; Thamesdown Dance in Swindon, England; T Junction in Vienna, 1995; and Lasica Associates in Melbourne, 1995. **Awards:** Creative Artists Public Service Fellowship, 1984; National Foundation for the Arts Choreographer's Fellowship, 1984, 1991; National Endowment for the Arts Choreographer's fellowships, 1985-88; New York Dance and Performance Award ("Bessie") for Choreography, 1986, 1987; American Choreographer Award, 1988; Guggenheim Fellowship, 1988; Outstanding Young Alumna, Earlham College, 1988; Dewar's Young Artists Recognition Award, 1990; National Dance Residency Program, 1996.

Works

1978	*Tune* (mus. Van Morrison), New York
1981	*Square Business* (mus. "M,"), New York
	Task/Force (mus. David Bowie, Brian Eno), New York
	Jammin' (mus. reggae, Sweet Honey in the Rock), New York
	Task Force (solo), New York
1982	*Vespers* (original mus. Linda Gibbs), New York
1983	*Story Beach* (original mus. Hearn Gadboia), New York
	Gotham (original mus. Hearn Gadboia), New York
	Guardian Angels (mus. Gregorian Chants), commissioned by CoDance Co, Pace University, New York
1984	*Trapped in Queens* (original mus. Scott Killian, Jonathan Kane), New York
	Reet City (mus. Hearn Gadbois), Brooklyn
1985	*Spending Time Doing Things* (mus. Duke Ellington), New York
	Gypsy Pie (original mus. Mike Vargas), New York
	No Evidence (original mus. Lenny Pickett), Seattle
1986	*A Haven for Restless Angels of Mercy* (original mus. Saqqara Dogs and George Sempepos), New York
	Working Order (original mus. Hearn Gadbois, Jonathan Kane; text by Holly Anderson, other music by Bach), Boston
	Heart, Heart (mus. Ladysmith Black Mombazo; text John Cheever), New York
	Two (collaboration with Ralph Lemon; original mus. Christopher Hyams-Hart), New York
	Walt's (original mus. by Scott Killian), commissioned by CoDanceCo, New York
1987	*The Habit of Attraction* (original mus. Christopher Hyams-Hart), Richmond
	This Room Has No Windows and I Can't Find You Anywhere (original mus. Christopher Hyams-Hart), commissioned by Zenon Dance Company, Minneapolis
	Butte (mus. Bach), commissioned by Creach/Koester, New York
1988	*Simple Tales* (original mus. Christopher Hyams-Hart, Jay Bolotin; text by Holly Anderson), New York
	Cracklin' Blue (mus. Patsy Cline), commissioned by Alvin Ailey Repertory Ensemble, New York
1989	*Thick Sleep* (original mus. Lenny Picket), Philadelphia
	Allies (mus. Fred Frith), Keene, New Hampshire
	Rain (original mus. Hearn Gadbois, other mus. Heitor Villa-Lobos), Brooklyn
	Vital Boulevard of Love (mus. Lou Reed), commissioned by Concert Dance Company, Boston
1990	*The Hidden Boy: Incidents from a Stressed Memory* (mus. Jay Bolotin), Louisville
1991	*The Hendrix Project* (mus. Jimi Hendrix Experience), Minneapolis
	Sanctuary (mus. Marianne Faithfull, Gospel at Colonus, traditional), commissioned by Zenon Dance Company, Minneapolis
1992	*Spartan Reels* (mus. Jonathan Kane, George Sampapos), commissioned by Phoenix Dance Company, Leeds, England
	Paisley Sky (mus. Jimi Hendrix Experience) commissioned by Boston Ballet
1993	*Nothing Can Happen Only Once* (original music by Christian Marclay; text by Ain Gordon), Columbus, Ohio
	Things I Have Not Forgotten (mus. Fred Frith), commissioned by Dayton Contemporary Dance Company
1994	*Cantos Gordos* (original mus. Don Byron), New York
	Daughter (mus. Robin Holcomb), commissioned by Pennsylvania Dance Theatre, State College, Pennsylvania
	Heaven + Earth (solo; mus. Ellen Fullman), New York
	Heaven + Earth (mus. The Five Blind Boys), Gabriel Faure, New York
	A Certain Depth of Heart, Also Love (mus. Robert Schumann, Led Zeppelin, The Pogues, Bill Frisell, Verdi), commissioned by Oregon Ballet Theatre, Portland
	Arena (mus. Led Zeppelin, Bill Frisell, Jimi Hendrix Experience), commissioned by PACT Dance Company, Johannesburg
1995	*Tiny Sisters in the Enormous Land* (original music by Robin Holcomb, text by Holly Anderson, video Kit Fitzgerald), Lewiston, Maine
1996	*Blessed* (mus. Cafe of the Gate of Salvation), New York
	Yard Dance (mus. Vusi Mahlassala, James Brown), New York
1997	*Voyages Plein d'Espoir* (mus. Richard Strauss, Cafe of the Gate of Salvation, Fred Frith, Bob Dylan), commissioned by Groupe Experimental Danse Compagnie, Fort de France, Martinique
	Roses in a Righteous Garden (mus. Cafe of the Gate of Salvation, Jim Morrison, the Holmes Brothers), commissioned by Oregon Ballet Theatre, Portland

Publications

By MILLER: articles—

"Statement," *Ms.* Magazine, January/February 1995.

On MILLER: books—

Banes, Sally, *Writing Dancing in the Age of Postmodernism,* Hanover, NH, 1994.
Long, Richard A., *The Black Tradition in American Dance,* New York, 1989.

*   *   *

Bebe Miller is a dancer and choreographer whose highly idiosyncratic and visionary work is informed, more than most, by her

Bebe Miller: *Tiny Sisters in the Enormous Land.* Photograph © Johan Elbers.

personal history as well as her training in dance. She was born in New York City in 1950 and grew up in the housing projects in the Red Hook section of Brooklyn. It was an unlikely spot for a career in theatrical dance to take root, but Miller's mother was determined that both her daughters would have dance and music lessons and see every free performance of music and dance available to them in New York City.

Miller began her dance training at age four, in the same year the U.S. Supreme Court ruled to desegregate public school education, studying with Alwin Nikolais and Murray Louis at the Henry Street Settlement Play House. These masters of theatrical wizardry had a profound influence on Miller's aesthetic vision, one that is nearly as important as her experience as an urban African American coming of age in an era of enormous social change in America, particularly in the relationships between races and the sexes.

"Just being out there as a black choreographer is a political statement," Miller said in a statement in *Ms.* magazine in 1995, after 17 years of making dances and 10 of running her own company. "The

work deals in human terms. I'll dissect things down to the level of the individual and relationships, rather than present them on a systematic political level." A graduate of Earlham College and Ohio State University, from which she received a Master of Fine Arts in dance in 1975, Miller performed from 1976 to 1982 with Nina Wiener and Dancers, and with Dana Reitz, in New York City and Europe in 1983. In 1985, Miller formed the Bebe Miller Company; she remains the eight-member troupe's artistic director as well as one of its dancers.

Since its founding, the company has toured extensively throughout the U.S. and Europe and has a repertoire of over 30 works, over half of them with originally commissioned music. Miller is a collaborative artist who has choreographed for many dance companies, including two classical companies—Boston Ballet in 1992 and Oregon Ballet Theatre in 1994 and 1997.

In nearly two decades of making dances—her first piece, *Tune,* was created in 1978—she has worked with composers, videographers, lighting designers, and writers to create the highly theatrical but abstract pieces that are her trademark. Like the previous generation of postmodern choreographers, Twyla Tharp among them, Miller has returned to such theatrical devices as costumes, lighting design, and set pieces to embellish what in recent years she calls "the telling of stories." In a magazine interview following a trip to South Africa in 1995, she discussed an improvisational performance in which she created with movement a series of South African pictures: "I needed to tell those stories— [there's] the feeling that it doesn't live unless it's communicated."

The emphasis on relationships and their stories started early on. Writing of a performance by the company at New York's Public School 122 in 1985, *New York Times* critic Jennifer Dunning said "The overall impression. . .was of nonstop dancing by five exceptional performers. Yet by the end of the program, one had the sense of witnessing quite complex emotions and relationships as well as being invited to share in the delight of purely physical wit." Of Miller's own dancing, Dunning wrote, "[she] is a thoughtful and intense performer with a neat, compact body that moves with utter economy and a distinctive blend of fluidity and deftness. She offered a quiet tour de force here, starting in silence with quirky, hermetic gestures that flew away from a corkscrewing center, and subsiding into soft leg swings that seemed to ease the music into being."

That corkscrewing, spiraling, swivelling center has remained a constant in Miller's anatomically based movement vocabulary, in which fluid dancing is often contrapuntal to angular gestures of the limbs or a rapid jerk of the pelvis. She has even managed to overlay the vocabulary of classical ballet with this idiosyncratic style, especially in her 1997 piece commissioned by Oregon Ballet Theatre, *Roses in a Righteous Garden*. In 1994's *A Certain Depth of Heart, Also Love,* her first piece for that company, and arguably a masterpiece, Miller, using such imaginative and visually stunning theatrical devices as a cascade of feathers falling from the flies above the stage onto a male soloist, and a sweep of rich red velvet cloth, created a commentary on classical ballet that was operatic in scale. Some dancers were on pointe; others in jazz or athletic shoes and far less classical technique was visible than in the later piece.

These pieces are not as well known as *The Hendrix Project* (1991), created in response to presidential candidate Michael Dukakis' repudiation of liberalism in the 1990 campaign. Writing for *High Performance*, San Francisco critic Rita Felciano described both the flavor of the choreography and Miller's dancing in this piece: "Stabbing and slashing the space around her with airborne splits and slicing arm thrusts, she established a circular movement rhythm that acquired the force of a hellish wheel. Danced entirely on the multicolored square that was both game board and mandala, Miller ended each of these sequences at the square's edge, piercing into the dark."

Miller continues to pursue her interest in basic human rights as communicated through dance, deeply influenced by time spent in South Africa where she feels greater progress is being made than in the United States. As critic Deborah Jowitt posed the question in a review of a 1996 performance in the *Village Voice*, "Is she the sensitive black American abroad, observing the postapartheid climate? Or—although race is something she's seldom dealt with directly—is she also the black woman with responses different from those of her four white cohorts? Her dances don't answer questions; they pose them."

—Martha Ullman West

MODERN DANCE AND CLASSICAL BALLET

There has been discussion about the influence of modern dance on ballet since modern dance began developing at the last turn of the century. Over time, the point of view has changed from the perspective that ballet is the primary concert dance form, able to "borrow" material from other forms and styles without experiencing any modification itself, to a more egalitarian position, holding ballet as one of several dance styles, continuing to evolve in response to changes in the larger dance community. And as modern dance established its own legitimacy (moving further away from defining itself by what it was not—ballet and theatrical dance) there was less concern about holding itself apart from other forms.

While the reforms of ballet choreographer Mikhail Fokine seen in works like *Les Sylphides* (1907) and *Firebird* (1910) were accompanied by speculation about the influence of Isadora Duncan and her new, "free" style of dancing, Fokine himself denied any causal affect. This attitude would be mirrored by modern dancers eager to put aesthetic space between their work and what they often considered to be the artistically bankrupt world of ballet. Although many of the works in the Ballet Russes and Denishawn repertories (operating simultaneously) shared a common thread of fascination with exotic plots and locale, any choreographic cross-fertilization was less openly acknowledged.

With the establishment of ballet in the U.S. in the 1930s and 1940s, modern choreographers were sometimes commissioned to stage works for ballet companies (e.g. Valerie Bettis' *Virginia Sampler* for the Ballet Russes de Monte Carlo, 1947) but the work is usually considered tangential to the companies' main purpose. More frequent were works by choreographers like Agnes deMille (especially *Rodeo*, 1942) who identified themselves as working within the ballet tradition while drawing source material from other areas, including modern dance. After World War II, the number of dancers training in both forms increased and the practice became more public. At this point, modern dance was often seen as bringing a more dramatic capacity to ballet technique, particularly through an enhanced use of the torso. Artists like Glen Tetley and John Butler, whose performing resumes include credits in both ballet and modern dance, went on to incorporate elements from both as choreographers. This trend gained momentum in the 1960s as more companies premiered works drawing on movement vocabularies outside of ballet as well as commissioning works from modern choreographers. The Joffrey Ballet was probably the most visible of these organizations, with dances like Robert Joffrey's *Astarte* (1967) and Gerald Arpino's *Trinity* (1971). Twyla Tharp's *Deuce Coupe* (1973) was one of the most successful of these works, bringing members of her own company together with the Joffrey dancers to a pop music score by the Beach Boys and scenery by graffiti artists. *Deuce Coupe* was a critical and financial success, and has served as a model for many other attempts to combine styles under the banner of a ballet company. It also saw a number of Joffrey dancers leave the company to join Tharp's ensemble, foreshadowing an emphasis on ballet training for modern dancers that would be developed later. The "dance boom" of the 1970s brought an expanded audience to the theater, many of whom were not interested in the distinctions between dance forms that had been nurtured previously. Changes in funding, especially the creation of government programs to support touring and the commissioning of new dances, allowed more companies to work year-round and gave choreographers the opportunity to think "larger." The Dance Touring Program of the National Endowment for the Arts (NEA) was especially influential in the development of dance outside the locus of New York City—it brought a wide variety of dance events to a far wider audience than was possible before. The ad hoc cross-pollination that works like *Deuce Coupe* created became institutionalized in funding policies from national to local levels in the 1980s. With grants like the NEA's program to bring together "unlikely partners," ballet companies in particular were encouraged to hire choreographers they wouldn't have considered otherwise. Many of these were postmodern choreographers who were not necessarily accustomed to working with professional ballet dancers (e.g. David Gordon with the Dance Theatre of Harlem, Lucinda Childs with Pacific Northwest Ballet). Rather than creating a hybrid technique, the dances coming from these commissions often utilized the choreographers' signature structural components and key elements of their movement style alongside standard ballet technique.

These new partnerships were occurring at the same time several influential ballet choreographers were dying (George Balanchine in 1983, Antony Tudor, 1987, and Robert Joffrey in 1988). There was a great deal of speculation about potential sources of new ballet choreography and a number of programs were started to develop ballet choreographers. The Carlisle Project and the Pacific Northwest Ballet's Off Stage Program were two such endeavors that offered modern choreographers the chance to work with ballet dancers. The long-standing tradition of including composition instruction in modern dance training was seen as a model for developing new ballet choreographers.

While more modern-trained choreographers were working in ballet companies, modern dancers started looking towards ballet training as a kind of "style-less" technique for themselves. Modern dancers incorporated the strength and facility of ballet (especially in the legs and lower body) but tended to leave out the complex countertensions of epaulment. This style was then brought back to ballet dancers through new choreography, so that some of the key differences between forms have been softened with time. This is exemplified in works like Tharp's *In the Upper Room* (1986, for her own company), where the "ballet" dancers (in pointe shoes) and the "modern" dancers (in sneakers) perform virtually identical material. When Tharp became an artistic associate of American Ballet Theater in 1988 she brought *Upper Room* with her, taking the process full circle.

As this century closes there is still speculation about the cross-influences of ballet and modern dance, and some express concern about ballet losing its essential nature in the development of this new material. With choreographers like Mark Morris, moving easily between ballet and modern dance assignments, it is unlikely that the changes of the last 100-some years will be erased.

Publications

Anawalt, Sasha, *The Joffrey Ballet,* New York, 1996.
Beaumont, Cyril W., *Michel Fokine and His Ballets,* New York, 1935, 1981.
De Mille, Agnes, *Dance to the Piper,* 1952.
———, *Martha,* New York, 1956, 1991.
Tharp, Twyla, *Push Comes to Shove,* New York, 1992.
Victor, Thomas, ed., *The Making of a Dance,* New York, 1976.
Wells, Bruce, interviewed by Alexandra Tomalonis, "The King of Crossover Crosses Back," *Ballet Alert,* October/November 1997.

—Sandra Kurtz

MOMING DANCE & ARTS CENTER

MoMing Dance and Arts Center was the primary venue for experimental modern dance in Chicago from 1974 to 1990. Prior to shutting its doors in December of 1990 due to severe financial stress, MoMing served as a performance space for avant-garde dancers, musicians, and other performers in Chicago, as well as for those visiting from New York and elsewhere. It possessed studio space for choreographers to use, held classes, and sponsored an eponymous performing group that staged dances in Chicago and around the country.

The center was founded in 1974 by a collective that included Jackie Radis, who ran the center for much of its history, Eric Trules, Jim Self, Kasia Mintch, Sally Banes, and Susan Kimmelman. Many of the original members had been in Shirley Modine's Chicago-based modern dance company, and wanted to continue working together after leaving the troupe. Their intent with MoMing was to create a larger audience for experimental dance and music in Chicago, and to provide a space for such performers to study and stage events. They rented a building owned by the Resurrection Lutheran Church, located on Barry Avenue outside the Chicago Loop on the city's North Side. (The center was credited in part with helping to gentrify the surrounding neighborhood.) The members of the collective performed at the center, as well as conducting classes and workshops. For example, Self presented a 12-week series called "Self Studies" at MoMing, and also taught classes there.

Eventually, the original collective disbanded, as its members left one by one. But others, many with administrative experience, replaced them over the years including Kay Wendt LaSota, Bill Dietz, Susan Bradford, Stan Trecker, Alida Caster, and Mary Trimball, among many others. Thus despite the departure of the original partners, MoMing survived as an independent arts organization. This type of structure, which didn't rely on funding from a university or other permanent organization, was rare, especially in Chicago at that time.

Although MoMing survived for 16 years, its financial stablility was never assured and its problems continued and worsened throughout its lifespan. In fact, it lost money consistently for the last half of its existence. MoMing's audiences declined (the opening night of its 15th anniversary season in 1988 attracted fewer than 30 attendees), it lacked the money to market its activities, its roster was composed largely of noncommercial work, and many of those involved with the organization were artists rather than administrators. All of these factors contributed to MoMing's eventual demise.

In 1985 MoMing's board of directors decided to close the center, but ultimately agreed to allow it to remain open under the direction of co-founder Jackie Radis. Three years later, Peter Thumbelston took over and made extensive efforts to save the center. He got MoMing involved in the National Performance Network, which provides funding to dance presentation venues, and worked to bring more well-known, audience-attracting companies from other cities to Chicago. In the end, however, his efforts were unsuccessful, and the center closed in 1990 after its landlord, having not been paid rent for some time, decided to sell the building in which MoMing was housed. The center tried to raise funds to buy the building, through benefit performances by Mikhail Baryshnikov's White Oak Project and the Doug Varone Dancers, among others, but was unsuccessful. MoMing's last performance was by long-time supporter Lauri Macklin and the Red Moon Theatre, who performed *Trouble Sleeping.*

During its life, MoMing hosted performance artists, improvisation groups, theater works, and avant-garde films, as well as experimental art and music. The center's dual mission was both to support local artists, and, increasingly over its lifetime, to bring in well-known performers to Chicago from other parts of the country and abroad. Among the many artists who choreographed for or performed at MoMing were Jan Bartoszek, Keiko Fuji, Michael McStraw, Jan Erkert, Suzanne Grace, Lauri Macklin, David Mamula, the Sunday Morning Improv Group, Bob Eisen, Donna Mandel, Kathy Maltese, Laurie Moses, Meredith Monk, Akasha and Company, Concert Dance Company, the David Puszh Dance Company, Jane Siarny, Susan Bradford, Susan Strong-Dowd, Judith Mikita, Desperate Measures, the Sock Monkeys, Ralph Lemon, Ping Chong, David Gordon, Bob Eisen, Trisha Brown, Laura Dean, Bill T. Jones, Robert Rauschenberg, Eiko and Koma, and Mark Morris.

MoMing presented many leading postmodern dancers, artists, musicians, writers, and poets before they were recognized, helping launch the careers of local performers and furthering the national reputations of guest artists from other cities. Trisha Brown was the center's first guest artist, in November of 1974. In 1975 Kenneth King was brought in as an artist-in-residence, beginning a long history of artist-in-residence programs featuring out-of-town performers with established reputations. (Performers associated with MoMing also occasionally toured the country under the MoMing name; for example, Trules and Radis performed under the MoMing banner at the Construction Company Dance Studio in New York in 1976.)

The center often grouped performances under themed series banners, such as "Dance Expo '90," "Dance and More for $1.98," and "German Dance: Living Memories with a Future." Its roster frequently featured interdisciplinary collaborations and theatrical productions, particularly around the mid-1980s, some highlighted in series such as "Making Collaborations." During Thumbleston's tenure, a Choreographers Showcase was developed. Postperformance discussions and wine-and-cheese receptions—a MoMing tradition from the beginning—enhanced the center's roster of performances.

While MoMing is probably best-known as a performance venue, it also acted as a vibrant center for students and working choreographers. The organization's classes and studios attracted more than 200 dancers, both professional and amateur, each week. The MoMing School of Dance was the site of classes in modern dance, ballet, jazz, improvisation, and tap for children and adults. MoMing also hosted workshops, at which local choreographer/performers were able to create their own pieces.

When MoMing closed in 1990, it left a large gap in Chicago's modern dance and experimental music community. While venues such as the Dance Center of Columbia College and Link's Hall tried to take its place to as great an extent possible, there remained a dearth of funding, performance and studio space, and support for avant-garde performing artists in Chicago. It took several years before the city's dance community was able to fully recover.

Publications

Christiansen, Richard, "MoMing Center's 'Dance Expo '90' Is Bursting with Life," *Chicago Tribune,* 3 August 1990.
———, "MoMing Dance Center Director Taking a Break," *Chicago Tribune*, 30 June 1988.
———, "MoMing Gives German Series a Sensational Start," *Chicago Tribune*, 1 November 1989.
———, "MoMing Takes Surrealistic Road into New Year," *Chicago Tribune*, 19 October 1987. ·
Heise, Kenan, "Peter Tumbelston, Dance Producer," *Chicago Tribune*, 28 January 1992.
Kappe, Gale, "MoMing Dance and Arts Center: Celebrating Ten Years of the Avant-Garde," *Chicago*, September 1984.
Maes, Nancy, "Chicago Modern Dance Takes a 'Giant' Step," *Chicago Tribune*, 17 February 1995.
McCracken, David, "Dance—Up and Away," *Chicago Tribune*, 23 April 1992.
"MoMing Birthday Cake Lacks Spice, Falls Flat," *Chicago Tribune*, 1 October 1988.
Smith, Sid, "Chicago Moving Company Celebrates and Reminisces," *Chicago Tribune*, 18 February 1992.
———, "Finding Its Niche, Unsung Link's Hall Studio Survives as a Small but Vital Performance Space," *Chicago Tribune*, 28 August 1994.
———, "MoMing's Variety Show of New Dance Hints at the Future," *Chicago Tribune*, 17 January 1990.
———, "Stepping In: Columbia College Taking Over MoMing Dance Projects," *Chicago Tribune*, 31 January 1991.

—Karen Raugust

MOMIX
American dance company

Momix was founded in 1980 by Moses Pendleton, co-founder of Pilobolus, and Alison Chase, a Pilobolus dancer. The troupe, named after a brand of cattle feed, refers to itself as a company of "dancer-illusionists."

The similarities between Momix and Pilobolus are many. Like Pilobolus, Momix is known for its abstract, muscular, acrobatic choreography, and for pieces that are more a series of tableaux than a flow of movement. The work of both companies combines gymnastics, theater, and modern dance to create unique and memorable visual effects. Both troupes' works are infused with humor and popular with dance audiences; both emphasize collaborative choreography, although the collective creative atmosphere and communal spirit are found to a lesser degree with Momix than Pilobolus.

Momix also diverges from its progenitor in several ways. One notable difference is Momix's extensive use of props. Pendleton once told the *New York Times* that Pilobolus uses bodies as props, while Momix uses props as extra bodies. In addition, Momix is known for employing lighting and mixed media such as slides projected onto a scrim in front of the dancers to add another visual layer to its pieces. Momix is further unlike Pilobolus in that it has always emphasized solo and duet performances, while the latter has focused on group works in which the dancers were symbiotic. Momix's works are generally choreographed by one or two people

Momix: *Venus Envy.* **Photograph © Johan Elbers.**

(one of whom is often Pendleton, the company's artistic director and primary creative force); in Pilobolus, collaboration is the norm. Input from the company remains important to Momix, but collaboration is not the primary focus. Its efforts to avoid anything "too Pilobolus" are conscious; still, the company's lineage is clear. As Anne Raver writes in the *New York Times*, "You can see the face of Pilobolus in a Momix dance exploded."

Momix grew out of Pendleton's initial forays as a performer and choreographer outside Pilobolus. The first was his participation in an Erik Satie celebration at the Paris Opera in 1978, after which Pendleton and Chase toured Europe as part of a mixed bill of modern dance and ballet works. When the ballet dancers on the program went on to other things, Chase and Pendleton continued to tour Europe with a roster of short pieces. In 1980, Pendleton choreographed the closing ceremonies of the 1980 Olympics. It was there that he performed a piece titled *Momix*, from which the company, founded officially that year, took its name. By 1984, Momix had five members and was performing in the U.S. and abroad, without Chase, as she had stopped performing after becoming pregnant.

The troupe performs works choreographed and co-choreographed by its members, particularly those of Pendleton. In general, Momix's choreography revolves around perpetually shifting, surrealistic imagery, and is known for its constantly changing identity. Its works invariably reflect this sensibility; for example, in *Brainwaving*, two

huge loops move across the stage and interact, set in motion by a pair of invisible dancers, while *Skiva*, created collaboratively by the company, is set to music by King Sunny Ade and His African Beats and performed by two dancers on pliable skis, which allow them to move their bodies forward and backward in an impossible-looking manner. Pendleton's *Venus Envy* features two dancers in a giant oyster shell; Alan Boeding's *Circle Walker* incorporates a giant gyroscopic wheel; and *Jonas et Latude* is a prison-themed piece set to a Vivaldi score.

Many of Momix's works are positive and upbeat, even when they focus on serious issues. Pendleton's 21-segment *Passion* (1991) is a 75-minute piece containing spiritual (yet not literally theological) themes. It is set to music by Peter Gabriel from the controversial Martin Scorcese film *The Last Temptation of Christ*. While it is a symbolic, emotional piece, it is also infused with humor, seductive imagery, and contemporary references. Beth Starosta, Owen Taylor, and other cast members assisted Pendleton on the choreography.

Pendleton's *Baseball* (1994) is one of Momix's best-known works. In typical Momix style, the 17-segment piece combines multimedia techniques, imagination, humor, joy, athleticism, skill, and excellent timing. With a cast of seven, it follows the development of the game from the days of cave people to the present. It appeals to adults with its sexiness and sophistication, while its protagonist, a giant baseball on roller skates, makes the piece fun for children as well. References range from cereal boxes to Botticelli.

Other pieces performed by Momix include Pendleton's *Kiss of the Spider Woman, Spawning, Medusa, Preface to Preview, Gifts from the Sea* and *Sputnik*; *Natural Endowment for the Arts*, a solo to Madonna's hit *Lucky Star* created by Pendleton, his wife Cynthia Quinn, and Beth Starosta; *Orbit*, a solo for a woman with a Hula Hoop, choreographed by Erin Elliott and Pendleton; and Pendleton and Quinn's *White Widow*, to music by Julie Cruise, which is a solo for a woman dangling from a string.

Momix tours frequently, and is especially popular in Italy, France, and the rest of Europe where the company has been featured in several television specials, including five Italian RAI features broadcast to 55 countries, and a performance on France's Antenne II. The troupe has also staged programs in South America, Russia, Asia, and Australia, as well as throughout the United States.

Several recordings feature the group—Momix performed in David Byrne's film *True Stories* (1986), and members Quinn and Karl Baumann played the role of the mechanical clown "Bluey" (under Pendleton's direction) in the movie *FX II*. In 1989 they appeared in the *Batdance* music video by the artist then known as Prince, and in 1991 on a laser disc with Charles Dutoit and the Montreal Symphony performing Mussorgsky's *Pictures at an Exhibition*. The latter earned an international Emmy award. Momix also appeared on PBS' *Dance in America* series, and in the first three-dimensional IMAX film, choreographed by Pendleton. The company was also awarded the Festival Choice Award at the Irish Life Dublin Theatre Festival in 1992 and the gold medal at the Verona Festival in 1994.

Among the dancers who have been associated with Momix are Daniel Ezralow, Sandy Chase, Celina Chaulvin, Kevin Kimple, Suzanne Lampl, Brian Simerson, Steve Gonzales, Solveig Olsen, Terry Pexton, Brian Sanders, Neil Peter Jampolis, Mitchell S. Levine, Kelly Holcombe and Owen Taylor. In 1987 a spinoff group, ISO, was formed by Ezralow, James Hampton, Ashley Roland and Morleigh Steinberg, all of whom are former members of Pilobolus and/or Momix. ISO has several traits in common with its forerunners, including its optimism, sense of fun, collaborative method, theatricality, and focus on creating unique shapes from human bodies.

Publications

Books—

Jowitt, Deborah, *Time and the Dancing Image*, New York, 1988.
Moritz, Charles, editor, *Current Biography Yearbook*, New York, 1989.
Robertson, Allen, and Donald Hutera, *The Dance Handbook*, Boston, 1988.

Articles—

Anderson, Jack, "Momix Merges Flesh and Spirit," *New York Times*, December 19, 1991.
———, "Whimsical Works by an Optimistic Troupe," *New York Times*, May 10, 1990.
Dunning, Jennifer, "Moses Pendleton, Choreographer and Product of His Time," *New York Times*, December 27, 1989.
———, "The Body, the Spirit and Momix," *New York Times*, December 22, 1991.
Kisselgoff, Anna, "The Boys and Girls of Summer in Another Field of Dreams," *New York Times*, December 20, 1994.

Kleiman, Dena, "Momix Dance Troupe: Surrealistic Images,"*New York Times*, January 2, 1987.
Looseleaf, Victoria, "Momix Dazzles in Top Athletic Style," *Los Angeles Times*, May 26, 1997.
Raver, Anne, "On Fertile Ground with the Master of Momix," *New York Times*, December 22, 1996.
Sulcas, Roslyn, "Momix," *Dance Magazine*, April 1997.

Films and Videotapes

Four Italian RAI features, directed by Pendleton; troupe appeared in David Byrne's film *True Stories* (1986); Pendleton directed and members Quinn and Baumann appeared as the robot "Bluey" in the movie *FX II*; danced in the *Batdance* music video by the artist formerly known as Prince (1989); performed with Charles Dutoit and the Montreal Symphony in Mussorgsky's *Pictures at an Exhibition* (1991); featured on PBS' *Dance in America* series; appeared in the first three-dimensional IMAX film, with segment choreographed by Pendleton.

—Karen Raugust

MONK, Meredith
American dancer, choreographer, composer, and company director

Born: Lima, Peru, 20 November 1942. **Education:** Took piano lessons from age 3 under Gershon Konikow and Marcia Polis Kosinsky; Sarah Lawrence College, Bronxville, New York (under Meyer Kupferman, Pal Ukena and Bessie Schönberg), B.A., 1964; studied voice under Vicki Starr, William Horn, John Devers, Jeanette Lovetri, Roland Wyatt, Ethel Raim and Gerald Siena; composition under Ruth Lloyd, Richard Averre and Glenn Mack; piano under Gershon Konikow. **Career:** Composer, dancer, singer, performer, filmmaker, stage director; performing debut New York City, 1964; formed interdisciplinary performance group the House, 1968; teacher Goddard College, Plainfield, Vermont, and New York University, 1970-72; formed Meredith Monk Vocal Ensemble, 1978. **Awards:** Obie Awards, 1971 (for *Vessel)*, 1976 (for *Quarry)*, 1985 (for "sustained achievement"); Guggenheim fellowships, 1972, 1982; Brandeis University Creative Arts Award in dance, 1974; First Prize (for *Education of the Girlchild)*, Venice Biennale, 1975; Creative Artist Program Service Awards, 1977, 1982; Villager Award for Outstanding Production of the Year (for *Recent Ruins)*, 1980, and 1983 (for *Turtle Dreams)*; New York Dance Film Festival Merit Award (for *Sixteen Millimetre Earrings)*, 1980; German Critics Prize, 1981 (for *Dolmen Music)*, 1986 (for *Our Lady of Late: Vanguard Tapes*; Atlanta Film Festival Special Jury Prize (for *Ellis Island)*, 1981; CINE Golden Eagle Award (for Ellis Island, 1981; Grand prize (for *Turtle Dreams [Waltz])*, Video Culture/Canada Festival, Toronto, 1983; New York Dance and Performance Award ("Bessie") for Sustained Creative Achievement, 1985; New York Foundation for the Arts fellowship Award in music composition, 1985, in choreography, 1996; National Music Theater Award, 1986; Sigma Iota fellowship, MacDowell Colony, 1987; Rockefeller Foundation Distinguished Choreographer Award, 1987; MacDowell Colony fellow, 1988, 1993, 1996; Doctor of Arts, Bard College, 1988; Doctor of Fine Arts, University of the Arts, Philadelphia, 1989;

Dance Magazine Award, 1992; Conlon Nancarrow and Yoko Sigiura fellowship, 1994; Norton Stevens fellow, 1994; MacArthur Foundation fellowship, 1995; Scripps American Dance Festival Award, 1996. **Address:** c/o the House Foundation for the Arts Inc., 131 Varick Street, Room 901, New York, New York 10013, U.S.A.

Works

1963	*Me*
	Timestop
1964	*Break*
	Diploid
1965	*The Beach*
	Cartoon
	Radar
	Relache
	Blackboard
1966	*16 Millimeter Earrings,* Judson Memorial Church
	Duet with Cat's Scream and Locomotive, Gate Theater, New York
	Portable
1967	*Blueprint,* outdoors, Woodstock, New York
	Excerpt from Work in Progress
	Goodbye/St. Mark/Windows
	Overload
1968	*Blueprints 3, 4, and 5*
	Co-op
1969	*Juice: A Theater Cantata,* Guggenheim Museum, Minor Latham Playhouse, and The Loft, New York
	Title: Title
	Tour: Dedicated to Dinosaurs
	Untidal: Movement Period
	Tour 2: Barbershop
	Tour 4: Lounge
1970	*Needle-Brain Lloyd and the Systems Kid: A Live Movie,* American Dance Festival
	Tour 5: Glass
	Tour 6: Organ
	Tour 7: Factory
	Voice Recital
1971	*Tour 8: Castle*
	Vessel: An Opera Epic, The House Gallery/Performing Garage/Wooster Parking Lot, New York
1972	*The Travelogue Series: Paris/Venice-Milan/Chacon* w/ Ping Chong, Roundabout Theater, New York
1973	*Education of the Girlchild: An Opera,* Common Ground Theater, New York
1974	*Anthology and Small Scroll,* Mickery Theater, Amsterdam
1976	*Quarry,* La Mama Annex, New York City
1978	*The Plateau Series,* St. Mark's Church, New York
1979	*Recent Ruins,* La Mama Annex, New York
1981	*Music Concert with Film,* The Space at City Center, New York
	Specimen Days: A Civil War Opera, Public Theater, New York
1983	*Turtle Dreams,* Plexus, New York
	The Games w/Ping Chong, Berlin
1987	*The Ringing Place,* Next Wave Festival, Brooklyn Academy of Music
1990	*Facing North,* The House Loft, New York
1991	*Atlas: An Opera in Three Parts,* Wexner Center for the Performing Arts, Columbus, Ohio
1994	*Volcano Songs,* Walker Art Center, Minneapolis
	American Archaeology #1, Roosevelt Island, New York
1996	*The Politics of Quiet,* PS 122, New York
	A Celebration Service, Union Theological Seminary, New York

Publications

On MONK: articles—

Belans, Linda, "Where Has Meredith Monk Been?," Nando.net, 27 June 1996.

Johnson, Jeff, "Celebration Enthralls Audience," *Spoleto Today/Post & Courier,* 6 June 1997.

Jowitt, Deborah, "Ice Demons, Clicks and Whispers," *New York Times Magazine,* 30 June 1991.

Laskin, Tom, "A Primordial Language," *The Progressive,* August 1997.

Films and Videotapes

By MONK—

Children, 1967.
Ballbearing, 1968.
Mountain, 1971.
Quarry, part of performance piece, 1975.
Paris, with Ping Chong, KTCA-TV, 1982.
Mermaid Adventures, part of performance piece *Turtle Dreams,* 1983.
Turtle Dreams (Waltz), WGBH, Boston, 1983.
Book of Days, Tatge/Lasseur Productions with The House Foundation for the Arts, 1988.

On MONK—

Meredith Monk, Mystic Hire Video, 1991

*   *   *

Meredith Monk is an acclaimed composer, singer, filmmaker, choreographer, and director. She is a pioneer in musical theater and the prolific creator of more than 100 works ranging from the intimate to the spectacular. Vocal recitals, films, videos, dances, cabaret acts, and various combinations thereof—her work defies classification, though she and others who have tried have called it theater cantata, live movie, and opera epic.

Quarry, Monk's 1976 masterpiece, is a collage of music, monologue, dramatic tableaux, solo and group chorale, dance, and film. Throughout, a private history is laid against the larger one of the Holocaust; a sick child stranded in bed is juxtaposed with an Old Testament couple in flight, who are mirrored in turn by these same actors in a later act, this time in the form of bedraggled European refugees. A child's dreams shift shape into monstrous visions of the modern age—images of World War II, dictators, a field of fallen bodies. Small, specific actions (a maid sweeping the floor) are set beside ritualistic ones (a milling throng of chanters, a procession of people carrying mushroom clouds or B-17s on the ends of sticks). Monk believes that art can restore a sense of community and common memory to the human race.

Meredith Monk: *The Politics of Quiet.* **Photograph by Virgile Bertrand.**

As a performing arts major at Sarah Lawrence College, Monk studied composition, voice, vocal and chamber music, and opera. She received a strong background in Merce Cunningham technique from Judith Dunn and Beverly Schmidt, who taught there. From the start, she was driven to figure out how to integrate music, movement and theater. Her first important solo, *Break* (1964) indicated some of her spatial concerns and revealed her as an innovator. Her soundtrack, a series of automobile noises, corresponded with moments in her dance (i.e. a starter turning over at the beginning of a movement), but overall the sound was not used as a rhythmic accompaniment. As she worked around the stage area she exclaimed "Oh!" whenever she confronted the limits of the proscenium arch. In this piece as well as other early works such as *Me* (1963), *Cartoon* (1965), and *The Beach* (1965) she used autobiography as subject matter; history, her own and in general, has remained central to her work.

In 1968 Monk founded The House, a company dedicated to an interdisciplinary approach to performance. Her antipathy for genre categories stems in part from her desire to create without restriction. She wants her audience to be equally unrestricted, to have the chance to experience and participate in a performance without having it pre-labeled. In 1971 Monk received an Obie Award for Outstanding Production for *Vessel,* a work memorable for her moving the cast and furniture from the first act from her loft to the parking lot, where Part III took place. This movement was entertaining, drew the audience into the work, and created the odd juxtaposition of a complete little living room within the larger space.

Indeed, Monk is a pioneer of such site-specific performance, creating works such as *Juice: A Theater Cantata in Three Installments* (1969) for the Guggenheim Museum, Barnard College's Minor Latham Playhouse, and the House Loft. The first installment made full use of the Guggenheim's six-story spiral, with 85 performers ascending and descending, moving toward and away from the railings. Next, the audience walked up the ramp, viewing miniature scenes of dancing or dancers caught in frozen poses (as well as the Roy Lichtenstein exhibit in the background). At the finale, all the performers rushed past the audience, down the spiral, and clustered in the main floor space which had been occupied by the audience at the beginning. In the second installment the work contracted, became more intimate, with four performers revealing themselves in personal situtations. Other elements such as a horse (appearing now as a child's rocking horse) were also rearranged and shrunk. The final installment (held at the loft) had no live performers. The costumes and stage props used in the previous installments were displayed, along with a videotape monologue of the four main performers discussing their roles. In this installment all the performing material from which the piece had developed was completely compressed.

Another such piece is *American Archeology #1: Roosevelt Island* (1994) in which Monk artfully manipulates the existing geography and history of Roosevelt Island. The idyllic afternoon setting of Lighthouse Park is juxtaposed with the nighttime ruins of a former smallpox hospital. The performance is punctuated by the noise of the boats on the river and automobile and airplane traffic, creating another intersection of past and present, real versus created.

Monk's works, composed as they are of small pieces, depend on tempo, repetition, exaggeration and context regardless of whether the emphasis of the performance is music or dance. *Atlas: An Opera in Three Parts* from 1991, commissioned by the Houston Grand Opera, The Walker Arts Center and the American Music Theater Festival, centers on one woman's life. Aspects of the vignettes depicting the heroine, Alexandra, and her traveling companions—a comic airport scenario, an arctic meditation on nature—are distorted, repeated, and embellished upon to form the arc of a spiritual quest. The music too depends on variation and repetition; units of sound are altered and developed harmonically on different instruments.

Typical of Monk's vocal works, *Atlas* has almost no text; the vocalists use sounds rather than words, delving down to basic human utterance. Works such as *Atlas* are an apparent natural extension of her career-long obsession with voice and body as vessels of expression. In light of Monk's ecumenicalism and spiritual concerns it is fitting that she would be commissioned by the American Guild of Organists to create *A Celebration Service*, a nonsectarian worship service. Once again, music, text, and movement are melded, here in an inspired celebration of the universal quest for spirituality. The piece is also a celebration of Monk's career, including works drawn from thirty years of her music. Monk's wordless melodies and folk-like choreography are interspersed with sacred readings from the past 2000 years, including an ancient Ethiopian work song, an 8th-century Buddhist text, and a 13th-century Sufi poem. Originally performed at the Union Theological Seminary in New York, the service was presented at Charleston's Spoleto Festival 1997.

Monk's innovations in interdisciplinary performance culture were recognized in 1995 with a prestigious John D. and Catherine T. MacArthur fellowship and in 1996 with the Samuel H. Scripps American Dance Festival Award. She and her ensembles continue to tour throughout the U.S. and internationally.

—Valerie Vogrin

MONTE, Elisa

American dancer and choreographer

Born: 1949 in Brooklyn, New York. **Education:** Attended Professional Children's School, New York City; studied with Martha Graham and others. **Career:** Debuted in Agnes De Mille's *Carousel;* joined Martha Graham Dance Company, 1974; danced with the companies of Mary Anthony, Ballet Études, Morse Donaldson, Pearl Lang, Lar Lubovitch, Pilobolus, and Marcus Schulkind; first performance of Elisa Monte Dance Company, 1981.

Roles

1977	*O Thou Desire Who Art About to Sing* (Graham)
1978	*Molly's Not Dead* (Pendleton/Pilobolus)

Other roles include: Agnes de Mille's *Carousel;* revivals of Graham's *Seraphic Dialogue, Clytemnestra,* and *Appalachian Spring; Dragon Lady* (Morse Donaldson), and *The Fred and Barbara Section, Ladies' Night Out, Circular Ruins,* and *Affetuoso* (Marcus Schulkind).

Works

1979	*Treading*
1980	*Pell Mell*
1987	*Audentity*
1993	*Diamond Song* (mus. Henryk Gorecki)
1994	*Vejle/Border Crossing* w/David Brown (mus. Puccini), duet
1995	*Mnemonic Verses*
	Feu Follet w/Brown (mus. Richard Peaslee)

Publicatons

On MONTE: books—

Anderson, Jack, *The American Dance Festival,* Durham, North Carolina, 1987.
Cohen-Stratyner, Barbara Naomi, editor, *Biographical Dictionary of Dance,* New York, 1982.
Mitchell, Jack, *Alvin Ailey American Dance Theatre: Jack Mitchell Photographs,* Kansas City, 1993.
Willis, J., editor, *Dance World,* New York, 1966, 1979.

On MONTE: articles—

Goldman, Phyllis, "Elisa Monte Dance," *Back Stage,* 12 July 1996.
———, "Elisa Monte Dance," *Back Stage,* 5 May 1995.
Hedgepeth, Timothy, "*Feu Follet,*" *Dance Magazine,* December 1995.
McQuade, Molly, "Elisa Monte Dance Company," *Dance Magazine,* May 1994.

*   *   *

Dancer and choreographer Elisa Monte's diverse training—she has studied and/or performed with companies ranging from the Martha Graham Dance Company and Lar Lubovitch to Pilobolus—has contributed to her reputation for eclectic performances and choreography. Concerts by her troupe, the Elisa Monte Dance Company, are renowned for their embrace of a wide variety of themes, genres, and styles of dance.

Born in 1949 in Brooklyn, New York, Monte attended the Professional Children's School in New York City, which educates young people who have professional careers in dance and other performing arts. Her dance studies, which incorporated both classical ballet and modern dance, included stints with Vladimir Dokoudovsky, Maggie Black, and Martha Graham. Monte made her professional dance debut in a revival of Agnes de Mille's *Carousel* and continued to work with de Mille on subsequent productions. She is probably best remembered early in her career for dancing with the Martha Graham Dance Company during the 1970s, where she had roles in revivals of many of Graham's best-known works, including *Seraphic Dialogues, Clytemnestra,* and *Appalachian Spring,* starting in 1974. She also performed in the world premieres of later Graham works, such as *O Thou Desire Who Art About to Sing* (1977). While

Elisa Monte: *Feu Follet.* **Photograph by Roy Volkman.**

with Graham's company, she danced with a variety of noted performers, including Janet Eilber, Margot Fonteyn, Turiko Kimura, Pearl Lang, Lucinda Mitchell, Rudolf Nureyev, and Peter Sparling.

Monte performed with several other choreographers, either as a guest artist or as a member of their dance companies. In the late 1960s and throughout the 1970s, she danced with the Mary Anthony Dance Theatre, Pilobolus (in *Molly's Dead*), and the Pearl Lang Dance Company, which she joined in 1968. She performed with Baku beginning in 1971 and Lar Lubovitch starting in 1972. She was also a member of Ballet Études and the Morse Donaldson

Dance Company, where she performed in his *Dragon Lady.* In 1981, Monte danced reconstructions of solos by Ruth St. Denis at the American Dance Festival, at which she appeared several other times.

In 1975, Monte joined the Marcus Schulkind Dance Company, where she held the positions of assistant artistic director, co-artistic director, and co-director. She danced in works by Schulkind, such as *The Fred and Barbara Section, Ladies' Night Out, Circular Ruins,* and *Affetuoso,* and in pieces by other choreographers. She also created the costumes for several of the group's productions. The company took the stage frequently at venues including the American Theatre Laboratory, Entermedia Theatre, St. Clement's Theatre, and Playwrights Horizons, as well as in Dance Umbrella events.

The Elisa Monte Dance Company, launched by Monte and her partner and artistic director David Brown, gave its first performance in 1981. The group has toured the U.S. and internationally in more than 30 countries, including in Russia and European nations, as well as performing at the Jacob's Pillow and Spoleto USA festivals. The dancers stage works created by Monte and Brown, including several co-choreographed by the two, as well as pieces by outside contemporary choreographers, including Schulkind, Cliff Keuter, and Sara Rudner. In keeping with Monte's tendency toward thematic and stylistic diversity, the company consists of eight soloists from different schools and styles, who hail from Tokyo, Trinidad and Tobago, Cuba, Tunis, and the United States.

All of the Monte dancers are trained in ballet, and her works combine ballet technique with themes more common to modern dance. The troupe is composed of intense, sensual dancers, who are technically proficient. Monte and Brown create works to both classical and modern composers, combining orchestral pieces with jazz, spiritual music, rock, and ethnic folk music from Africa and Asia, as well as America. Monte's work is rooted in tradition, although it takes its inspiration from numerous diverse forerunners and combines their influences in eclectic ways. Her pieces can be reminiscent of the work of other companies, ranging from Alvin Ailey and Pilobolus to the Joffrey Ballet. Some of Monte's choreographic works include *Treading* (1979), a duet about sea creatures; *Pell Mell* (1980); *Audentity* (1987), which incorporates asymetric, athletic movements; *Diamond Song* (1993), to a score by Henryk Gorecki; and *Mnemonic Verses* (1995), which combines Eastern sensual themes with an undercurrent of slavery. Women are often the focus of Monte's dances, and members of Monte's troupe have included Jane Blount, Nadine Mose, Martine Van Hamel, Malek Segai, and Marden Ramos, as well as men dancers such as Christian Canciani.

Monte has co-created several works with Brown, including *Vejle/ Border Crossing* (1994), a duet for two men set to Puccini; and *Feu Follet* (1995), one of the company's best-known works. *Feu Follet* is a two-act production that celebrates the culture of the Cajun people, outlining their history from France, through Nova Scotia, and on to Louisiana. To a score by Richard Peaslee that draws on Cajun musical history, the piece requires virtuosic performances from the company and draws on literary sources, including Henry Wadsworth Longfellow's poem *Evangeline*. It is typical of Monte/ Brown works in its extreme energy and sensuality, as well as its technical difficulty.

Monte's works have been performed by other ballet and modern dance companies as well as by the Elisa Monte Dance Company. They include the Boston Ballet, the African-American troupe Philadanco, and the Alvin Ailey American Dance Theatre. In addition to its combination of diverse genres, styles, and themes, Monte's company is also known for its attention to detail when it comes to the elements outside of dance that make up a whole production. Critic Phyllis Goldman, writing in *Back Stage* in a review of *Feu Follet*, says of the Elisa Monte Dance Company: "All the components that make a class-act theatrical dance production—lighting, music, costumes, exceptional dancers and inventive movement— click into place with the team's smooth professional touch, making their programs extremely likable in spite of some creative choices that may not totally succeed."

—Karen Raugust

MOORE, Claudia
American-born Canadian dancer, choreographer, and educator

Born: 14 April 1953 in Buffalo, New York. **Education:** Studied ballet with Stella Applebaum; educated and trained at the National Ballet School of Canada; studied Graham-based technique with Kazuko Hirabayashi at School of Toronto Dance Theatre and The Place, London; theatre with Lindsay Kemp and jazz dance with Matt Maddox, London; Limón and Falco technique with Hugo Romero, Montreal; Cunningham technique with Mel Wong and Douglas Neilson, New York; theatre with Yoshida Oida, Philippe Gaulier, and Monica Pagneaux, Paris; voice training for theatre with David Smukler and Loy Coutts and singing with Helga Tucker and Shanti Chakravorti, Toronto; video production with Pooh Kaye, Trinity Square Video, Toronto; dancefilm with Bernar Hébert (Cine Qua Non), Robert Lockyer (BBC) and Barbara Willis Sweete (Rhombus Media); directing, World Stage Festival, Toronto. **Family:** Married choreographer Robert Desrosiers, 1979; divorced 1985; married electronic media designer Laurie-Shawn Borzovoy 1987; children: Zoë, Zachary. **Career:** Dancer, the National Ballet of Canada, Toronto, 1971-73; Les Ballets Felix Blaska, Grenoble, 1973-74; Contemporary Dance Theatre, Montreal, 1975; Ballet Ys, Toronto, 1975-76; Toronto Dance Theatre, 1976-80; Desrosiers Dance Theatre, Toronto, 1980-87; first independent choreography, 1977; first full-length work, 1989; artistic director and co-producer, Physical Feast festival of theatrical dance, Buddies in Bad Times Theatre, 1995; founder, MOonhORsE dance theatre, Toronto, 1997; taught at Mercury Studio of Movement, Mascha Stom Centre, Toronto Dance Theatre, Desrosiers Dance Theatre, York University, Ryerson Polytechnic University Dance Program, Pavlychenko Studio, the National Ballet School of Canada, and Teachers' Collective, and Maguy Marin Company, Paris. **Awards:** Jacqueline Lemieux Award, 1991; funding grants from the Canada Council, Ontario Arts Council, and Toronto Arts Council.

Roles (all original cast roles)

1975   *Nelligan* (Ann Ditchburn) duet, Ballet Ys, Toronto
1976   *Couples Suite* (Danny Grossman), Toronto Dance Theatre (TDT)
1977   Pavane, *A Simple Melody* (Peter Randazzo), TDT
        Woman in white, *Recital* (Peter Randazzo), TDT
        Phaedra, *Mythos* (David Earle), TDT
        Fauré's Requiem (David Earle), TDT
1978   *Courances* (David Earle), TDT
1979   *Seastill* (Patricia Beatty), TDT
        Rejoice in the Lamb (David Earle, Nancy Ferguson), TDT
        Sweet and Low Down (David Earle), TDT
        Mantis (Christopher House), TDT Choreographic Workshop
1980   *Toss Quintet* (Christopher House), TDT
        Courtyard (David Earle), TDT
        Mirrors, Masques and Transformations (Marcuse), Judith Marcuse Dance Projects Society, Shaw Festival, Niagara-on-the-Lake, Ontario
        Ophelia and Dragonfly, *Visions of Death as a Clown,* later called *Night Clown* (Desrosiers), Desrosiers Dance Theatre, Toronto

Woman in Black, *Brass Fountain* (Desrosiers), Desrosiers Dance Theatre, Toronto

1981   Red Creature, *Plutonium Jungle* (Desrosiers), Desrosiers Dance Theatre, Montreal

Lavabo (Paul-André Fortier), Québec Été Danse, Lennoxville, Quebec

1982   Hoop Girl, *Bad Weather* (Desrosiers), Desrosiers Dance Theatre, Lennoxville, Quebec

1983   The Red Queen, *The Fool's Table* (Desrosiers), Desrosiers Dance Theatre, Toronto

Ciel Rouge, Desrosiers Dance Theatre, Toronto

Tango, *L'Hôtel Perdu* (Desrosiers), Desrosiers Dance Theatre, Lennoxville, Quebec

1984   Moon Duet, *Ultracity* (Desrosiers), Desrosiers Dance Theatre, Toronto

Rendez-vous Lunaire (Desrosiers), The National Ballet School of Canada's 25th Anniversary Gala, Toronto

Émile Nelligan, Elusive Players (Ditchburn), Harbourfront, Toronto

1986   The actress, *Lumière* (Desrosiers), Desrosiers Dance Theatre, Toronto

1987   Double Man Duet, *Concerto in Earth Major* (Desrosiers), Desrosiers Dance Theatre, Toronto

1988   *Terpsichore* (Carol Anderson), Toronto

1989   *Signatures* (James Kudelka), Betty Oliphant Theatre Opening Gala, Toronto

LaVoixLeCorps (Peter Chin), Toronto

Opium (dir. Lorne Brass), Festival of the Americas, Montreal

1993   *Horse on the Moon* (Ginette Laurin, Serge Bennathan, Lola McLaughlin, Tedd Robinson), Toronto

1997   *NorthEastSouthWest* (Peter Chin), Toronto

Freak Show (Bill Coleman), Toronto

Other roles include: Performed various roles with Les Ballets Felix Blaska (Grenoble, France); Contemporary Dance Theatre (Montreal); Ballet Ys (Toronto); solos in own works, 1977 to present; appeared in "Death and the Maiden" (chor. Véronique Bélliveau), *Beaux dimanches,* Société Radio-Canada (SRC), 1975; "Canticum Canticorum" (chor. Hugo Romero), *Beaux dimanches,* SRC, 1977; "L'Oiseau de feu" (chor. Hugo Romero), *Beaux dimanches,* SRC.

Works

1977   *Crysalis* (mus. collage), TDT Choreographic Workshop

1978   *Isis and Nefurtari* (mus. Gordon Phillips) TDT Choreographic Workshop

1980   *Les Orphélines* (mus. collage), TDT Choreographic Workshop

1981   *Broken Sky* (mus. collage), Pavlychenko Choreographic Workshop, Toronto

1982   *Steal Threads* (mus. Miguel Frasconi), Pavlychenko Choreographic Workshop, Toronto

Night Shift (mus. collage) George Brown College Dance Program, Toronto

1983   *Escape and the Lights of Macao* w/Miguel Frasconi and Albert Gedraitis (mus. Miguel Frasconi), Toronto

1984   *Where Did You Find Those Strange Glasses?* (mus. collage), Toronto International Festival, Toronto

Up Is the Only Direction I Understand (mus. collage), Pavlychenko Choreographic Workshop, Toronto

1986   *Oh No! Not You Shipwreck* (mus. Linda B. Smith), Pavlychenko Choreographic Workshop, Toronto

Rock-a-bye (mus. John Lang), Expo '86, Vancouver

1987   *Ma Poubelle* (mus. Eric Cadesky), Pavlychenko Choreographic Workshop, Toronto

Hors de Champs w/Marvin Green and Matthew Jocelyn (mus. Marvin Green), Café de la danse, Paris

1988   *Twister* (mus. collage) Canada Dance Festival, Ottawa, Ontario

Heartwings (mus. Marvin Green), Toronto

Animal Crackers (mus. John Lang), Toronto

Dove Lorenzo (mus. collage), Artspace Dance Series, Peterborough, Ontario

Home At' las (mus. collage), Ryerson University Dance Program, Toronto

1989   *The Fatal Entrance/the Wound/the Dark* (mus. Jan Kudelka), Toronto

Beauty and the Beast w/Carol Anderson and Laurie-Shawn Borzovoy (mus. Ian Mackie), La Groupe de la Place Royale, Ottawa, Ontario

D'Arc and Light (mus. collage), Toronto Fringe Festival, Toronto

Kleinzeit (mus. Rob Carroll, Ahmed Hassan), Toronto

A Mad Tea Party (mus. collage), Ontario Ballet Theatre, Toronto

1990   *Not a Holiday* (text original, Sir Francis Bacon), Dancemakers Choreographic Workshop, Toronto

Oh Zo (mus. Miguel Frasconi), Toronto

Zitti (mus. John Lang), Inde '90 Festival, Toronto

Fossil (mus. Eric Cadesky, John Lang), Toronto

1991   *Crow Sisters* (mus. Bill Grove), fringe Festival of Independent Dance (fFIDA), Toronto

A Day in the Life (mus. collage), Ontario Ballet Theatre, Toronto

Debris (mus. collage), Toronto

Crystal Palaces w/the Glass Orchestra and Vid Ingelvics (mus. the Glass Orchestra), Toronto

1992   *The Alchemical Theatre of Hermes Trismegistos* (mus. R. Murray Schafer), Theatre Autumn Leaf, Toronto

On the Town (mus. Leonard Bernstein), Shaw Festival, Niagara-on-the-Lake, Ontario

1993   *The Cook's Tale* (mus. John Lang) DanceWorks, Toronto

Gentlemen Prefer Blondes (mus. Jule Styne), Shaw Festival, Niagara-on-the-Lake, Ontario

Departure (mus. collage), Ontario Ballet Theatre, Toronto

Requiems for the Party Girl (mus. R. Murray Schafer), Theatre Autumn Leaf, Toronto

Box Pieces (mus. Eric Cadesky), Toronto

1995   *Dragon singing in my belly leads me to the darkest night* (mus. John Lang), Toronto

Splendor (mus. collage), Ontario Ballet Theatre, Toronto

1997   *Duality* w/Menaka Thakkar (mus. Ron Allen), Toronto

1998   *wishes* (mus. John Lang), Toronto

Other works include: Choreographed works for theatre including, *The Lorca Play* (dir. Daniel Brooks and Daniel McIvor), Augusta Company, Toronto, 1994; *A Chocolate Bath* (dir. Mark Christmann), Toronto, 1995; *Romeo and Juliet* (dir. Diana Leblanc), Stratford Festival, Stratford, Ontario, 1997; *Les Mots et Les Choses* (dir. Mark Christmann), Toronto, 1997; *Building Jerusalem* (dir. Ross Manson), Volcano Theatre, Toronto, 1997.

Publications

On MOORE: articles—

Kelly, Deirdre, "Moore Answers Call to Adventure," *Toronto Globe and Mail,* 30 November 1995.
Smith, Kathleen, "Living in a Box," *eye* (Toronto), 16 December 1993.
Tembeck, Iro, "Dancing in Montreal: Seeds of a Choreographic History," *Studies in Dance History,* Fall 1994.

Films and Videotapes

I Am a Hotel, TV special, chor. Ann Ditchburn, "C" Channel, Toronto, 1983.
All That Bach, chor. Robert Desrosiers, dir. Larry Weinstein, Rhombus Media, 1984.
Listen to the Radio, music video by Pukka Orchestra, chor. Moore, 1984.
Lovers in a Dangerous Time, music video by Bruce Cockburn, chor. Robert Desrosiers, 1984.
Top of His Head, dir. Peter Mettler, 1987.
I Vant to Be Alone, dir. Margaret Dragu, 1987.
Originals in Art, dir. Dan Robinson, Bravo! New Style Arts Channel, 1996.
Box Pieces, dir. Paul Carrière, Bravo! New Style Arts Channel, 1997.
Exotica, dir. Atom Egoyan, 1994.

*   *   *

Claudia Moore, an instinctive interpreter who could mold herself to any style, has always been an inspirational muse to choreographers. She was considered among the finest modern dancers in Canada, known for her beautiful, expressive lyricism, and an ability to make technique look easy. In her years at Toronto Dance Theatre (TDT) and Desrosiers Dance Theatre, she was the centrepiece of many important choreographic creations. "The roots of my own choreography can be traced back to all the juicy roles I was given when I was with those companies," she says. Not surprisingly, Moore's choreographic bent is for dance theatre. Most of her works contain movement and text inspired by provocative themes or narratives, and supported by strong visual elements. She has frequently collaborated with writers, directors, composers, and visual artists throughout her choreographic career. Says Moore: "I'm interested in the human condition and character behaviour. I'm always looking for ways to understand a human emotion or action. Even when I'm watching abstract dance, I'm looking for a story. For me, dance and theatre cannot be separated." While many of her works exhibit a droll, even quirky, sense of humour, Moore is also capable of producing works of deep poignancy and compassion.

Born in Buffalo, New York, Moore came to Toronto when she was 13 to attend the National Ballet School, and became a member of the National Ballet of Canada after graduation. When she found the corps de ballet held no personal challenge for her, she left the company after two years to join former colleague, Robert Desrosiers, in Europe. After dancing with Les Ballets Felix Blaska in Grenoble, France, the couple went to London and came under the spell of dance-mime-theatre artist Lindsay Kemp. From then on, finding "the place where dance and theatre meet" would become Moore's lifelong passion.

Returning to Canada, the couple settled in Montreal, where Moore had her first experience with modern dance performing with Hugo Romero's Contemporary Dance Theatre. "For a ballet-based person," she says, "it was exciting doing floor work to the rhythm of the drum. I kept discovering new meaning for movement and gesture, and a sense of power in using the torso. Modern dance became the obvious path of exploration for my own personal expression." Enticed by the possibilities of modern dance, Moore joined TDT in 1976 and immersed herself in the company's Graham-based dramatic, theatrical repertoire, performing in the works of all three co-artistic directors—Patricia Beatty, David Earle, and Peter Randazzo. When Desrosiers began his own company in 1980, Moore became the leading exponent of his fantasy-based, imaginative physicalization and strong emphasis on visual spectacle. Another important influence on Moore was Pina Bausch whose company toured to Toronto in 1984. Bausch's presentation of performers as human beings, her introduction of theatrical moments from the simplest of human traits, and the impact of her dramatic use of gesture were a revelation. "She gave me the courage to become more personal in my choreography," says Moore.

Moore and Desrosiers divorced in 1985, and Moore left the company in 1987. That year she married electronic media designer Laurie-Shawn Borzovoy who has become a frequent collaborator. Launching her career as an independent dancer-choreographer was a liberating experience for Moore. She had been choreographing for a decade but, in retrospect, realized her pieces were very introverted, even repressed. Says Moore: "When I was dancing with Robert, I had to explore what I wanted to say about his work. Now I was able to find out what I wanted to say in my own choreography and come to terms with my own vision." Her breakthrough piece was the delightful *Animal Crackers* (1988). Using a voice-over that quoted dreary passages about human behaviour from anthropology texts, Moore and her dancers portrayed human-animal fusion characters who performed cheeky choreography in direct contrast to what was being stated, creating a triumph of individualism and unpredictability.

In 1989 Moore created her first full-length work, *Kleinzeit,* based on Russell Hoban's cult novel. To portray the character of Kleinzeit, an Everyman in the throes of a midlife crisis, Moore used both an actor, Daniel Brooks, and a dancer, Tom Brouillette, cleverly weaving the verbal and physical together into an integrated unit. Moore's chief accomplishment was the presentation of well-developed characters epitomized by individualized, naturalistic choreography that translated personality into movement. *Debris* (1990) was another important piece in her development. The work explored aspects of love, primarily through the emotional tangle of romantic relationships, and was Moore's most personal statement to date. It was also the beginning of a Moore trademark—a close collaboration with dancers in which the dancers' and Moore's experiences are woven together to create the tapestry of the dance. "My performers interest me as people," she says. "I work with mature artists who are highly creative in their own right. What they bring to the work is very important." *Debris* was a choreographic landmark for Moore and a fine example of her growing sophistication in expressing thought through movement. The work also helped define her dance vocabulary which is anchored in strong, total physicality and fast, detailed movement, with much emphasis placed on arm gestures and facial expression. After *Crow Sisters* (1991), Moore stopped performing in her own work, feeling she could better function as an outside eye. After a long hiatus, she put herself back in her choreography with *wishes* (1998), a dark/light piece about desire and longing. Her work in other collaborations had made her feel comfortable enough to both explore and orchestrate the collective creative process from within. She did, however, invite actor-director Daniel Brooks to function as artistic advisor for the piece.

In the 1990s Moore dealt with a multitude of themes, both light and dark, with each work attempting to create new ways for movement to intensify the emotional journey. She moved away from text-based pieces to more abstract presentations in which text is just one of the elements. "I want to stage something in a way that is a discovery for the audience," she said. Her choreography was densely metaphoric and presented a cascade of shifting imagery. *Box Pieces* (1993), for example, was set amid the physicality of variously shaped boxes painted with windows and cityscapes designed by artist Joy Walker. Into this obvious man-made constraint—the boxes that house us—Moore introduced smaller, handheld boxes. She then maneuvered her dancers up, over, in, through, between, and under the boxes in an in-depth investigation of emotional and physical confinement. She created a parade of boxes that touch our lives including coffins, tool kits, radios, closets, televisions, suitcases, drums, cages, bedrooms, and even voice boxes. Pandora's Box was a leitmotif throughout and a key element in the cataclysmic ending.

It takes Moore upwards of two years to develop a piece, propelled by her desire to be exhaustive in her research. While she readies her own work, she choreographs for theatre, opera, and musicals, in addition to dancing for other choreographers.

—Paula Citron

MOORE, Jack

American dancer and choreographer

Born: 18 March 1926 in Monticello, Virginia. **Education:** Art major, University of Iowa; studied with Doris Humphrey, Louis Horst, Anna Sokolow, Merce Cunningham, Hanya Holm, and Martha Graham; attended Holm's summer dance course at Colorado College; studied at the School of American Ballet, and Connecticut College with Nina Fonaroff and Doris Humphrey. **Military Service:** Served in World War II. **Career:** Assistant/teacher, Neighborhood Playhouse; collaborations with Sokolow, and Katherine Litz; member/choreographer, Contemporary Dance Production concerts, 1961; dancer, Merce Cunningham Dance Company; dancer, Martha Graham Dance Company, 1953; dancer, Sokolow's Theatre Dance Company, 1955-66; co-founder, Dance Theatre Workshop, 1965; taught at Juilliard School of Music, Bennington College, Adelphi University, UCLA, and Connecticut College; advisor, The Yard, 1985; judge, Third Annual Choreographer's Showcase, Washington, D.C., 1986; participated in Tribute to Doris Jones, 1987. **Awards:** First Doris Humphrey Memorial Fellowship to the American Dance Festival, 1960. **Died:** June 1988.

Roles (choreographed by Anna Sokolow, unless otherwise noted)

1953	*City of the Ages*
1954	*Summer Cloud*
	Excursion
1955	*Red Roses for Me,* Broadway
	Rooms
1956	*Mignon*
	Poem
	La Traviata
	Orpheus of the Underworld
	The Tempest
	Susannah
1957	*Le Grand Spectacle*
	Copper and Brass
1958	*Session for Eight*
1961	*Dreams*
1963	*Suite No. 5 in C Minor*
1964	*Forms*

Works

1951	*Esprit de Corps*
	Clown '51
1957	*Somewhere to Nowhere,* 92nd Street YMHA, New York City
	The Act, 92nd Street YMHA, New York City
1958	*The Geek,* American Dance Festival, Connecticut College
	Cry of the Phoenix, American Dance Festival, Connecticut College
1959	*Area Disabled*
	Figure '59
1960	*Songs Remembered*
	Intaglios
1961	*Target*
1962	*Opticon—A Vaudeville of the Mind*
	Excursions
	Erasure
1963	*Chambers and Corridors*
1965	*Vintage Riff*
	Assays (nine short works created from 1963-65)
1966	*Parsley All Over the World*
	Four Elements in Five Movements
	Figure '66
1967	*Vintage Riff No. 2*
	Brew
	Rocks
1968	*Five Scenes in the Shape of an Autopsy*
1969	*Puzzle*
	Tracks
	Tracings
	Residue—Variants 1, 2, 3,4
1970	*Rocks* (revival)
1971	*Fantaisie pour deux*
	Ode
1972	*Blueprint: Gardenstrip*
	Three Odes
1973	*Ghost Horse Rocker*
	Tracks and Side Tracks
1974	*Nightshade*
	Garden of Delights
	Landscape for a Theater
1975	*Resume*
	Love Songs for Jason Mayhew
	Six Easy Pieces for Anna (for television)
1976	*Four Netsukes*
1985	*Three Tangos*

Publications

By MOORE: article—

"Dancer's Notes," *Dance Perspectives*, Summer 1969.

On MOORE: books—

Anderson, Jack, *The American Dance Festival,* Durham, North Carolina, 1987.
McDonagh, Don, *The Complete Guide to Modern Dance*, New York, 1976.
———, *The Rise and Fall and Rise of Modern Dance,* Pennington, New Jersey, 1970.
Warren, Larry, *Anna Sokolow: The Rebellious Spirit*, Princeton, New Jersey, 1991.
Willis, J., editor, *Dance World*, New York, 1966.

On MOORE: articles—

Obituary, *Newsday*, 30 June 1988.
"Jack Moore," in *Biographical Dictionary of Dance,* edited by Barbara Naomi Cohen-Stratyner, New York, 1982.
Sondak, Eileen, "Three's Company Lo-Tech Dance Series Is Off to a Fast-Paced Start," *Los Angeles Times*, 9 July 1990.
Temin, Christine, "Dancing by the Yard," *Boston Globe*, 13 June 1985.
Tomalonisz, Alexandra, "Battle of the Dance Makers," *Washington Post*, 17 February 1986.
"Washington's Ballet Bonanza. . .A Sudden Glut of Dancers and Choreographers," *Washington Post*, 19 April 1987.

*   *   *

Jack Moore was traditionally trained in modern dance, by virtue of his studying and dancing with such leaders as Merce Cunningham, Hanya Holm, Martha Graham, and especially, Anna Sokolow. Ultimately, however, he used his training to move in experimental directions. He co-founded the Dance Theatre Workshop, the leading experimental venue of its era.

Moore was born in Monticello, Indiana, in 1926 and, after service in World War II, became an art major at the University of Iowa. He participated in some amateur theatrical productions, and found that he liked performing on the stage. After attending Hanya Holm's summer dance course at Colorado College on a scholarship, he decided to pursue a career in dance and moved to New York in 1949.

Moore studied at the School of American Ballet and the Connecticut College School of Dance, as well as with Nina Fonaroff and Doris Humphrey. He also studied with Merce Cunningham for a summer, and performed with his company briefly. He took classes with musician Louis Horst, becoming an assistant in his composition course, as well as at the Martha Graham School. He went on to become a member of Graham's company for a season in 1953.

Anna Sokolow and Moore met that same year, and he began to study with her in 1954, beginning a long collaboration and friendship. He danced with her company, the Theatre Dance Company, from 1955 to 1966 in the U.S. and abroad, and worked with her on special projects afterwards. Along with other company members such as Alvin Ailey, Moore danced in many premieres of Sokolow's pieces, including in modern dance concerts, musicals, Broadway shows, and operas.

Moore became the most important male dancer to work with Sokolow. While he was with Sokolow, Moore also worked with other choreographers, many of them from the Graham company, including Nina Fonaroff, Helen McGehee, Pearl Lang, and Katherine Litz, and appeared with the City Center Opera Company. He also began producing his own dances in 1951. Sokolow encouraged him and other company members to experiment with their own choreography, assisting them as much or as little as they desired, and sharing programs with them at New York's 92nd Street YM-YWHA and elsewhere. Though Moore didn't want to form his own company, he did begin performing his solos in 1957, when he appeared at the 92nd Street Y as part of a program sponsored by Contemporary Dance Productions, of which he was a member. His program included the mood studies *The Act* and *Somewhere to Nowhere* (both 1957). The next year, he performed *The Geek* (1958), a mood study about a circus sideshow performer, and *The Cry of the Phoenix* (1958) at Connecticut College's American Dance Festival, where he was the first Doris Humphrey Fellow to have a summer residency and where he continued to participate for many years. He taught at the Juilliard School of Music in the early 1960s, where he created his first group works, including *Intaglios* (1960). He also created an emotional duet about relationships, *Songs Remembered,* that year, and the following year created *Target* for four dancers, which was inspired in part by Jasper Johns' series of paintings depicting targets. Throughout the years, Moore frequently performed his works in concerts presented by Contemporary Dance Productions.

Songs Remembered and *Target* were typical of Moore's style during his career, in that they were spare, understated, and contained a sense of uneasiness. His work was heavily influenced by Sokolow, but with an infusion of puns and humor. These two pieces also marked a turning point, however, as Moore moved away from the technique of characterization and thematic development in which he had been trained (and that characterized his early works), and toward a more abstract, experimental style. He continued this evolution at Bennington, where he accepted a teaching post and worked with students including Kathryn Posin, Wendy Summit, and Linda Tarnay. (In addition to Bennington and Juilliard, Moore taught at Adelphi University, the Neighborhood Playhouse, UCLA, and Connecticut College.) He began to focus on pure movement, creating a series of nine short experimental pieces over three years from 1963 to 1965 that he called *Assays*. They included both solos and works for four to five dancers; each was based on abstract movements without plot, theme, or characterization.

In 1964 Moore stopped performing at the 92nd Street Y and along with former Sokolow dancer Jeff Duncan and Art Bauman, co-founded the Dance Theatre Workshop as a venue for low-cost experimental modern dance work. The organization was launched in 1965. Moore considered DTW an outgrowth of his and Duncan's work with Sokolow. It became the main source of experimental dance after the Judson Church had peaked in this role, and launched the careers of many choreographers over the years, including Kenneth King, Bebe Miller, Susan Marshall, Mark Morris, and Bill T. Jones.

In the late 1960s, Moore continued to create small works for DTW and larger works for his students. Some of his notable dances from the late 1960s and early 1970s include *Five Scenes in the Shape of an Autopsy* (1968), *Rocks* (1970), and *Six Easy Pieces for Anna* (1975), which was created for television. He performed in concert recitals of his works through the 1970s, including classics such as *Songs Remembered* and newer works such as *Love Songs for Jason Mayhew* (1975). He sometimes gave recitals with other choreographers, such as Erin Martin and Marion Scott.

Moore, who died of lung cancer in 1988 at age 62, was active in the dance community to the end of his life. For example, he choreographed *Three Tangos* in 1985, was an advisor to New England's

The Yard artist colony that same year, judged the third annual Choreographer's Showcase in Washington, D.C. in 1986, and contributed to a Washington-based tribute to Doris Jones in 1987. Moore's style is sometimes referred to as "neo-dada," especially when props such as plants or an automobile tire were incorporated absurdly into the works. His work is also characterized as humorous even while containing elements of life's darker side, and as calm even when highly energetic.

—Karen Raugust

THE MOOR'S PAVANE
(Variations on the Theme of Othello)

Choreography: José Limón
Music: Henry Purcell, arranged by Simon Sadoff

Costumes: Pauline Lawrence
First Production: American Dance Festival, New London, Connecticut, 17 August 1949.
Principal Dancers: José Limón (The Moor), Lucas Hoving (The Moor's Friend), Betty Jones (The Moor's Wife), Pauline Koner (His Friend's Wife).

Publications

Articles—

Koner, Pauline, "The Truth about *The Moor's Pavane*," *Ballet Review* 8 (4), 1980.
Limón, José, "Composing a Dance," *The Juilliard Review*, Winter 1955.
Mindlin, Naomi, "José Limón's *The Moor's Pavane*: An Interview with Lucas Hoving," *Dance Research Journal*, Spring 1992.

*   *   *

The Moor's Pavane **performed by the José Limón Dance Company. Photograph © Beatriz Schiller.**

The Moor's Pavane was Limón's most popular and successful work and the work which firmly established his reputation as a choreographer. It was first performed in August 1949 at the American Dance Festival when the José Limón Dance Company was only two years old. Limón won the 1950 Dance Magazine award for The Moor's Pavane, and the piece introduced two linked preoccupations which recur in later pieces such as The Exiles (1951), The Traitor (1954), and The Emperor Jones (1956): a conflict and struggle between two men; and the great man brought down not only by those around him but also because of his own tragic flaw.

The Moor's Pavane consists of a suite of courtly dances loosely based on the idea of the pavane. Interspersed between these are scenes in which the four characters—The Moor, His Friend, The Moor's Wife, and His Friend's Wife—act out their tragic sequence of events. The plot of Shakespeare's Othello is reduced to a simple narrative involving the handkerchief which The Moor gives to his wife (Desdemona). In one duet His Friend (Iago) makes His Friend's Wife (Emilia) aware that he wants her to get the handkerchief for him, and she achieves this when Desdemona drops it during a court dance. Emilia then teases Iago with it, playing hard to get. Iago then, in turn, taunts The Moor with the handkerchief provoking him into killing Desdemona. The murder takes place on stage hidden behind Emilia's voluminous velvet skirts which her husband has spread out like a curtain. This is followed by a dénouement.

The creation of such powerfully dramatic roles was clearly a consequence of the age of the dancers who created the original roles in 1949. While Betty Jones (The Moor's Wife) was 23, Pauline Koner (His Friend's Wife) and Lucas Hoving (The Moor's Friend) were both 37, while Limón (The Moor) was 41. The Moor is proud and strong, with weighty steps and clenched fists. When the emotional pressure on him builds, he suffers his agonies nobly. Desdemona is virginally pure in a dress of white organdy, though she, like her husband, has a capacity for noble suffering. Iago is light on his feet, and uses his hands and arms precisely extended to make obsequious gestures. He whispers tauntingly in The Moor's ear, then steps back, smiling, to watch the result, but he grovels and cowers when The Moor's anger is turned against him. Emilia, Iago's wife, is voluptuous and sensual. Her obsession with her husband blinds her to his motives until the moment when she sees Desdemona's corpse and the Moor shows her the handkerchief.

The "pavanes" start with the dancers facing each other in a star formation, touching hands. The Moor initiates the dance and they separate into two pairs—by gender, then by marriage—forming lines and then reforming in a circle. Even during the "pavane" differences in characters begin to emerge, through characteristic gestures, and in the relative weight or lightness of their steps. The first "pavane" is formal and stately, the second more grandiose, while in subsequent ones the star becomes increasingly stretched and distorted, and partners often no longer face one another. Thus while the characters gradually disintegrate, so does the "pavane."

The overall structure of The Moor's Pavane was devised by Limón who also set the "pavane" sections. Hoving and Koner both maintained that they created much of their own movement material which Limón then edited and transformed. Doris Humphrey, who was artistic director of the company, gave suggestions when the piece was near completion, as she apparently and invariably did for Limón, as well as making two significant contributions during the production process. Initially, a new score, which was being composed for the piece, proved unsatisfactory and, halfway through the rehearsal period, Humphrey found some pieces by Purcell which were then adopted. Just before the premiere, Humphrey substan-

tially changed the ending of the piece by suggesting the use of the skirt as a curtain.

The José Limón Dance Company performed The Moor's Pavane more frequently than any other piece and it became their signature work. It has subsequently been produced by many other companies. The role of The Moor has been danced by ballet dancers including Bruce Marks and Rudolph Nureyev.

—Ramsay Burt

MORRIS, Mark
American dancer, choreographer, and company director

Born: 29 August 1956 in Seattle. **Education:** Franklin High School, Seattle; studied flamenco, ballet, European folk dance at Verla Flowers Dance Arts; attended José Greco summer school, Indiana, 1967; First Chamber Dance Company summer school, 1972-74; also studied ballet with Perry Brunson; studied flamenco in Madrid, dancing briefly with Royal Chamber Ballet of Madrid, 1974. **Career:** Dancer, Russian Balalaika Ensemble, Seattle, 1967-70; Koleda Folk Ensemble, Seattle, 1970-73; Eliot Feld Ballet, 1976-77; Lar Lubovitch Dance Company, 1977-78, 1983; Hannah Kahn and dancers, 1979-82; Laura Dean and Dancers, 1981-82; founder, Mark Morris Dance Group, 1980; first major New York performance at Brooklyn Academy of Music (BAM) Next Wave Festival, 1984 (also 1986, 1988); first U.S. tour 1985; first European tour 1986; artistic director, Monnaie Dance Group/Mark Morris, Brussels, 1988-91; founding choreographer, White Oak Dance Project, 1991; television appearances include Public Broadcasting Service (PBS) "Dance in America" specials, 1986, 1992. **Awards:** New York Dance and Performance Award ("Bessie") 1984, 1994; John Simon Guggenheim Memorial Foundation fellowship, 1986; MacArthur Foundation fellowship, 1991; Hamada Prize, Edinburgh Festival, 1995; Capezio Lifetime Achievement Award, 1997.

Roles

1985 Vampire, *One Charming Night* (Morris), Mark Morris Dance Group, New York

1989 Dido and the Sorceress, *Dido and Aeneas* (Morris), Monnaie Dance Group/Mark Morris, Brussels

1991 Party Guest and Arabian, *The Hard Nut* (Morris), Monnaie Dance Group/Mark Morris, Brussels

Other roles include: Solo and ensemble roles in works by Eliot Feld, Lar Lubovitch, Hannah Kahn, and Laura Dean; also performed solos in his own ensemble works, including *Dad's Charts* (1980), *Ten Suggestions* (1981), *O Rangasayee* (1984), *The Vacant Chair* (1984), *Jealousy* (1985), and *Offertorium* (1988).

Works (performances by the Mark Morris Dance Group unless otherwise noted)

1971 *Boxcar Boogie (Piece by Piece)* (mus. Lasry, Nancarrow, Partch, Reich), Verla Flowers Dance Arts, Seattle
   Cape dance (mus. traditional Spanish) Verla Flowers Dance Arts, Seattle

Dances for *The Wizard's Gift* (mus. Field, Kiesel, Lanz), Seattle Youth Theatre

1972   *Renaissance* (mus. 16th-century traditional French), Northwest Ballet Ensemble, Dance Theatre, Seattle

Mourning without Clouds (mus. Morris), Verla Flowers Dance Arts, Seattle

"Tango," "Charleston" for *U.S.A.* (musical theater work), Franklin High School, Seattle

1973   "Dances for Non-Nutritive Foods," in *It's Almost Like Being Alive* (mus. Shallat), Seattle

Dances for Celebration (mus. Schmidt), Franklin High School, Seattle

Rain in Spain, Jota, Spain (mus. traditional Spanish), Verla Flowers Dance Arts, Seattle

Barstow (mus. Partch), Summer Dance Laboratory, Port Townsend, Washington; staged First Chamber Junior Company, Seattle, 1974; Mark Morris Dance Group, 1980

1974   *In Pruning My Roses* w/Linda Mietzner (mus. Morris, Shostakovitch), Verla Flowers Dance Arts, Seattle

Jota de Alcañiz (mus. traditional Spanish), Verla Flowers Dance Arts, Seattle

Zenska (mus. Bartók), First Chamber Junior Company, Seattle; revised for Mark Morris Dance Group, 1980

1975   *Farruca Jerezana* (mus. traditional Spanish), Verla Flowers Dance Arts, Seattle

Spanish (mus. traditional Spanish), Verla Flowers Dance Arts, Seattle

"Dragon's solo" in *Saint George and the Dragon* (mus. Lamb), Northwest Chamber Orchestra Young People's Concerts, Seattle

1978   *Brummagem* (mus. Beethoven), Pacific Northwest Ballet, Seattle; revised and staged Mark Morris Dance Group, 1980; Spokane Ballet, 1981

1980   *Rattlesnake Song* (mus. Driftwood), Steffi Nossen Dance Company, Scarsdale, New York

Castor and Pollux (mus. Partch), New York

Dad's Charts (mus. Thompson, Jacquet), New York

1981   *Études Modernes* (mus. Nancarrow), Jersey City, New Jersey

Ten Suggestions (mus. Tcherepnin), Jersey City, New Jersey; revised and staged White Oak Dance Project, New York, 1990; Peggy Baker/Solo Dance, Toronto, 1991

Schön Rosmarin (mus. Kreisler), Mark Morris and dancers, Seattle

I Love You Dearly (mus. traditional Romanian), Kinetics Company, Seattle; restaged Mark Morris Dance Group, 1982; Greg Lizenberry, 1982

Gloria (mus. Vivaldi), New York; revised 1984

1982   *Canonic 3/4 Studies;* originally *Canonic Waltz Studies* (mus. Czerny, others), Mark Morris and dancers, Seattle

Jr High (mus. Nancarrow), Mark Morris and dancers, Seattle; revised, incorporating sections of *Études Modernes*, for Mark Morris Dance Group, 1982

Songs That Tell a Story (mus. I. and C. Louvin, Hill, Bain), Kinetics Company, Seattle; staged Mark Morris Dance Group, 1982

New Love Song Waltzes (mus. Brahms), New York

Not Goodbye (mus. traditional Tahitian), New York

1983   *Ponchielliana* (mus. Ponchielli), Jacob's Pillow summer student group

Caryatids (mus. Budd), Mark Morris and dancers, Seattle; staged Jacob's Pillow Jazz Workshop, Beckett, Massachusetts, 1984

Celestial Greetings (mus. popular Thai), Mark Morris and dancers, Seattle

Deck of Cards (mus. Logsden/Campbell, Frazier, Tyler), Mark Morris and dancers, Seattle

Dogtown (mus. Ono), Mark Morris and dancers, Seattle; revised for Mark Morris Dance Group, 1983

Bijoux (mus. Satie), New York

The Death of Socrates (mus. Satie), New York

Minuet and Allegro in G (mus. Beethoven), New York

The "Tamil Film Songs in Stereo" Pas de Deux (mus. contemporary Tamil film music), New York

1984   *Vestige* (mus. Shostakovich), Spokane Ballet, Spokane; staged Mark Morris Dance Group, 1985

O Rangasayee (mus. Tyagaraja), Mark Morris, Montreal; staged Mark Morris Dance Group, New York, 1984

Love, You Have Won (mus. Vivaldi), Seattle

My Party (mus. Françaix), Seattle; staged Second Avenue Dance Company, New York University, 1988

Prelude and Prelude (mus. Cowell), Seattle; revised 1985

She Came from There (mus. Dohnányi), Seattle

Forty Arms, Twenty Necks, One Wreathing (mus. Garfein), American Dance Festival Choreographers and Composers in Residence Program, Durham; staged Mark Morris Dance Group, 1986

Come on Home (mus. various), Jacob's Pillow summer students, Becket, Massachusetts

Slugfest, London

The Vacant Chair (mus. Root/Washburn, Rasbach/Kilmer, Jacobs-Bond), London

Championship Westling after Roland Barthes (mus. Garfein), New York

1985   *Marble Halls* (mus. Bach), Batsheva Dance Company, Jerusalem

Lovey (mus. Gano), Seattle

Jealousy (mus. Handel), Pittsburgh

Retreat from Madrid (mus. Boccherini), Paris

Handel Choruses (incorporating *Jealousy*; mus. Handel), New York

Frisson (mus. Stravinsky), New York

One Charming Night (mus. Purcell), New York

1986   *Mort Subite* (mus. Poulenc), Boston Ballet, Boston

Mythologies: Dances Based on the Essays of Roland Barthes (incorporating *Championship Westling, Soap Powders and Detergents*, and *Striptease*; mus. Garfein), Boston

"Salomé's dance" (for *Salomé*; Strauss), Seattle Opera

Ballabili (mus. Verdi), Seattle

The Shepherd on the Rock (mus. Schubert), Seattle

Esteemed Guests (mus. C.P.E. Bach), Joffrey Ballet, Los Angeles

Pièces en Concert (mus. Couperin), New York

Stabat Mater (mus. Pergolesi), New York

1987   *Sonata for Clarinet and Piano* (mus. Poulenc), Univeristy of Washington School of Music and Division of Dance, Seattle; staged Mark Morris Dance Group, 1987

Strict Songs (mus. Harrison), Seattle

La Folia (mus. Vivaldi), Cornish Dance Theater, Seattle
The Fantasy (mus. Mozart), Seattle
Nixon in China (mus. Adams), Houston Grand Opera, Houston (two dances: "The Red Detachment of Women" and "Dream Ballet")
Scarlatti Solos (mus. Scarlatti), Santa Barbara (improvised solo titled differently at every performance: *Lies, More Lies, Big Lies*, etc.)

1988   "Seven dances" *Orphée et Eurydice* (mus. Gluck), Seattle Opera, Seattle
Offertorium (mus. Schubert), 1988
Die Fledermaus (mus. Strauss), Seattle Opera, Seattle
Fugue and Fantasy (mus. Mozart), New York
Drink to Me Only with Thine Eyes (mus. Thomson), American Ballet Theatre, New York
"Fandango" in *Le Nozze di Figaro* (mus. Mozart), PepsiCo Summerfare Opera, Purchase
L'Allegro, il penseroso ed il moderato (mus. Handel), Monnaie Dance Group/Mark Morris, Brussels

1989   *Dido and Aeneas* (mus. Purcell), Monnaie Dance Group/Mark Morris, Brussels
Love Song Waltzes (mus. Brahms), Monnaie Dance Group/Mark Morris, Brussels
Wonderland (mus. Schönberg), Monnaie Dance Group/Mark Morris, Brussels

1990   *Behemoth* (danced in silence), Monnaie Dance Group/Mark Morris, Brussels
Going Away Party (mus. various country-western, performed by Bob Wills and his Texas Playboys), Monnaie Dance Group/Mark Morris, Brussels
Ein Herz (mus. Bach), Paris Opera Ballet, Paris
Pas de Poisson (mus. Satie), Monnaie Dance Group/Mark Morris, Brussels; staged White Oak Dance Project, 1990
Motorcade (mus. Saint-Saëns), White Oak Dance Project, Boston; staged London Contemporary Dance Theatre, 1992

1991   *The Hard Nut* (mus. Tchaikovsky), Monnaie Dance Group/Mark Morris, Brussels
The Death of Klinghoffer (mus. Adams), Monnaie Symphony Orchestra and Chorus, Brussels
A Lake (mus. Haydn), White Oak Dance Project, Vienna, Virginia; staged Mark Morris Dance Group, 1992
Le Nozze di Figaro (mus. Mozart), Monnaie Symphony Orchestra and Chorus, Brussels

1992   *Paukenschlag* (mus. Haydn), Les Grands Ballets Canadiens, Toronto
Beautiful Day (mus. Bach), New York
Polka (mus. Harrison), New York; incorporated into *Grand Duo*
Bedtime (mus. Schubert), Boston
Three Preludes (mus. Gershwin), Boston; staged White Oak Dance Project, 1992
Excursion to Granada: A Calypso Ballet (mus. various), Becket, Massachusetts

1993   *Grand Duo* (mus. Harrison), Amherst, Massachusetts
Mosaic and United (mus. Cowell) and White Oak Dance Project, New York
Home (mus. Shocked, Wasserman), New York
Jesu, Meine Freude (mus. Bach), Mark Morris Dance Group, Boston

1994   *Lucky Charms* (mus. Ibert), Boston
Maelstrom (mus. Beethoven), San Francisco Ballet, San Fransisco
The Office (mus. Dvorák), Irvine, California; staged Zivili (mus. Slavic traditional dance group), 1994
Rondo (mus. Mozart), Durham, North Carolina

1995   *World Power* (mus. Harrison), Berkeley, California
Three Russian Preludes (mus. Shostakovich), White Oak Dance Project, Becket, Massachusetts
Somebody's Coming to See Me Tonight (mus. Foster), Boston
Quincunx (mus. Donizetti), Les Grands Ballets Canadiens, Montreal
Pacific (mus. Harrison), San Fransisco Ballet, San Fransisco
Dido and Aeneas (film; dir. Barbara Willis Sweete; mus. Purcell), Canada

1996   *I Don't Want to Love* (mus. Monteverdi), Edinburgh
Orfeo ed Euridice (mus. Gluck), The Handel and Haydn Society/Mark Morris Dance Group, Iowa City

1997   *Rhymes with Silver* (mus. Harrison), Berkeley, California
Platée (mus. Rameau), Royal Opera, Covent Garden/Mark Morris Dance Group, Edinburgh

Publications

On MORRIS: books—

Acocella, Joan, *Mark Morris,* New York, 1993.
Brazil, Tom, *Dances by Mark Morris,* New York, 1992.
Croce, Arlene, *Sight Lines,* New York, 1987.

On MORRIS: articles—

Keefe, Maura and Marc Woodworth, "An Interview with Mark Morris," *Salmagundi* (Fall 1994-Winter 1995).
Vaughan, David, "A Conversation with Mark Morris," *Ballet Review* (Summer 1986).

Films and Videotapes

Falling Down Stairs, film, dir. Barbara Willis Sweete, Canada, 1994.

*   *   *

Mark Morris was born into a middle-class family that included no professional artists, but many amateur performers and dedicated social dancers. According to his family, he tried to dance before he could walk. Dancing remained a form of play until he saw José Greco's flamenco company at age eight, which inspired him to become a Spanish dancer. Morris studied with a local children's teacher, Verla Flowers, who recognized his unusual talent and became his mentor. At her school, in addition to flamenco, he studied ballet, fencing, and many forms of folk dance (surprisingly, he became a modern dance choreographer with little modern dance training). Morris first performed professionally at 11 with a local Russian troupe, and joined a large semiprofessional Balkan group, the Koleda Folk Ensemble, at 13. He began to teach and choreograph a year later. Morris also sang in high school choruses, and made a devoted self-study of the piano and an eclectic range of vocal music. Still determined

Mark Morris (center): *Pièces en Concert,* **1987. Photograph © Beatriz Schiller.**

to dance flamenco professionally, he traveled to Spain, but was dismayed by the repression, homophobia, and the poverty of dancers under Franco.

Morris moved to New York City in 1976 and danced for Eliot Fled, Lar Lubovitch, Laura Dean, and Hannah Kahn, learning from all, he has said, the value of naturalness in performance, and structural clarity in composition. Critics noted his singular musicality. In his prime (before a foot injury in 1986) Morris had a complete technique: both abandoned and refined, he projected his immersion in music through extraordinary rhythmic nuance. As Joan Acocella wrote in her elegant, insightful study of his life and work, Morris could "paint in the same phrase with a mop and a three-hair brush."

Morris' rise as a choreographer was meteoric. His breakthrough came with his company's appearance in the Next Wave Festival at the Brooklyn Academy of Music (BAM), only four years after a self-produced debut concert in 1980. Two of the works for the 1984 BAM concert, a revised version of *Gloria* and a 23-minute solo, *O Rangasayee*, made his reputation. *New Yorker* critic Arlene Croce, since 1983 Morris' most eloquent and polemical champion,

hailed him as the worthiest heir to the legacy of the modern pioneers. By 1986, at age 30, Morris had won a Guggenheim fellowship, been profiled in an hour-long public television program, begun to tour in the U.S. and Europe, and accepted his first major ballet commissions.

In 1988 Morris succeeded Maurice Béjart as resident choreographer at the Théâtre Royal de la Monnaie in Brussels, expanding his company from 12 to 27 dancers and renaming it the Monnaie Dance Group/Mark Morris. Morris never found a public in Brussels, and was dismissed by most Belgian critics, whose taste had been formed by Béjart's grandiose pop spectacles. With the resources of the Monnaie at his disposal, however, Morris created his largest-scale works to date: the two-hour *L'Allegro, il penseroso ed il moderato,* to Handel's oratorio; *Dido and Aeneas,* a danced rendering of Purcell's opera in which Morris, with no trace of camp, plays both Queen Dido and the Sorceress; and his version of *The Nutcracker,* titled *The Hard Nut* after the embedded story in E.T.A. Hoffmann's "Nutcracker and Mouse King." These first two works are widely regarded as masterpieces. The last is Morris' most extensive essay in irony; he updates the story to a nightmare vision of the 1960s, with designs after macabre comic-book artist Charles Busch and many male travesty roles—some on pointe.

Morris' presence in the U.S. was maintained during his years in Belgium by Mikhail Baryshnikov's White Oak Dance Project, which performed Morris' work exclusively for its first three tours in 1990 and 1991. Morris returned to the States in 1991 with a new repertory and his company transformed from a small troupe of peers and friends to a younger, more uniform group of 17 dancers. By 1997 Morris had one of the largest modern dance companies in the U.S., and was without question one of the country's leading artists.

Morris has called himself a traditional choreographer; his tradition is both modern dance, extending back to Duncan and Nijinsky, and the centuries-old inheritance of European folk dance. Morris' lush, visceral idiom draws richly on the styles of other choreographers; embedded in his dances are homages to, and loving parodies of, all the modern greats. His use of simple steps in intricate contrapuntal rhythms with lavish syncopation reveals his inheritance from Balkan and Spanish dance. He is noted for his ironic wit and ribald humor. An outspoken gay artist, he explored same-sex partnering in his early work for both its poetic and political resonance. He stands alone in his generation for his utopianism, and his unself-conscious reclamation of the great themes of early and middle modern dance: the relations of men and women to each other, to their community, and to the divine. He is fluent and protean, having created nearly 100 works between 1980 and 1997. His music (performed live if possible) is as varied as his themes, with an emphasis on the baroque, country-western and other American popular forms, and fiercely rhythmic American composers such as Harry Partch, Conlan Nancarrow, and Lou Harrison.

Though Morris devises a new vocabulary for every work, his presentation of the body is consistent. His dancers move characteristically with heels down, weight carried low. They stress unity of impulse over unison of line. Morris pushes them beyond conventional images of grace to reveal effort and risk. His dancers come in all colors, and many shapes and sizes; many are 30 or older. Despite a new emphasis on gestural detail and geometry since his Belgium years, his dancers always look earthy, not exotic or superhuman.

Asked at his first Brussels press conference for a philosophy of dance, Morris replied: "I make it up, and you watch it. End of philosophy." His dances themselves reveal the principles that underlie them. Morris roots his work in intuitive and analytic response to music. He consults a printed score whenever he can, and binds his dances intimately to the music at every metric and structural level. When the music has words (about half his works use vocal music), Morris represents the text using a full range of evocative gesture, from literal pantomime to abstract symbol. Though few of his pieces are explicitly narrative, all bear a narrative pressure; like the polyphonic music he favors, his dances seem not to suspend time, but to drive or sweep through it. Each dance grows around a core of gestures, postures, phrases, and ways of traveling, and Morris uses intrinsically musical procedures—exposition, rhythmic augmentation and diminution, variation in scale and dynamics, recapitulation—to develop his material. In the *World Book of Modern Ballet* (1952) John Martin described Balanchine's relationship to music in the following way:

Musically he has a tendency to literal rhythmic transcription which gives the effect almost of Dalcroze exercises to some of his compositions. . . . If his formal subservience to his music, and his apparent choice, indeed, of only that music to which he can be subservient, are weaknesses, his great strength lies in his fundamental musicality. This consists primarily of a subcutaneous recognition of the fact that the movement phrase and pulse of the dancer are elements as absolute and innate as the breath phrase and pulse of the singer upon which the art of music has been evolved. In his practice the intuitive correlation between the motor phrase and the musical phrase transform his choreography into a species of visible music.

Martin's analysis of Balanchine might apply unchanged to Morris. The invocation of the physical act of singing as the foundation of music is especially apt. Music is the heart of Morris' work: for his detractors, he merely illustrates or visualizes his scores; for his admirers, he always illuminates them.

—Christopher Caines

MORRIS, Robert

American sculptor, dancer, and choreographer

Born: 9 February 1931, in Kansas City, Missouri. **Education:** Studied engineering, University of Kansas City; art, Kansas City Art Institute, 1948-50; California School of Fine Arts, San Francisco, 1951; Reed College, Portland, Oregon, 1953-55; art history, Hunter College, New York, 1961-62, M.A. 1962; studied with Anna Halprin and Robert Dunn. **Military Service:** Army Corps of Engineers, Arizona and Korea, 1951-52. **Family:** Married Simone Forti (divorced). **Career:** Worked in theater improvisation, San Francisco, 1955-60; joined the Judson Dance Theater; collaborated in performance works, New York, 1963; contributor, *Artforum*, New York, since 1966; assistant professor, Hunter College, New York, 1967-69, full professor from 1969. **Awards:** Prize, Walker of Art Center, Minneapolis, 1966; First Prize, International Institute, Torcuato di Tella, Buenos Aires, 1967; Guggenheim International Award, 1967; Guggenheim Fellowship, 1969; Watson F. Blair Prize, 1972; Sculpture Award, Society Four Arts, 1975; Skowhegan Medal for Progress and Environment, Maine, 1978. D.F.A.: Williams College, Williamstown, Massachusetts, 1986.

Roles

1961	*See Saw* (Forti)
1963	*We Shall Run* (Rainer)
1964	*Part of a Sextet* (Rainer)

Works

1962	*War* w/Robert Huot, Judson Memorial Church, New York
	New Poses Plasticues w/Jill Johnston, Washington, DC
1963	*Arizona,* solo, Judson Memorial Church, New York
	21.3, Judson Memorial Church, New York
	Site w/Carolee Schneeman, Judson Memorial Church, New York
1965	*Waterman Switch,* Buffalo, New York
	Check, Judson Memorial Church, New York

Publications

By MORRIS: articles—

"Notes on Dance," *Tulane Drama Review,* Winter 1965.

On MORRIS: books—

Anderson, Jack, *Choreography Observed,* Iowa City, 1987.
Coe, Robert, *Dance in America,* New York, 1985.
Croce, Arleln, *Afterimages,* New York, 1977.
Current Biography Yearbook, New York, 1971.
Jowitt, Deborah, *Time and the Dancing Image,* New York, 1988.
McDonagh, Don, *The Rise and Fall and Rise of Modern Dance,* New York, 1970.
———, *The Complete Guide to Modern Dance,* Garden City, NY, 1976.
Tucker, Marcia, *Robert Morris,* New York, 1970.

*   *   *

Robert Morris is best known as a sculptor. During the 1960s, however, he spent three years studying, performing and choreographing dance works. Although he created just five pieces, they are considered significant contributions to the postmodern movement.

Morris was born in Kansas City, Missouri, on February 9, 1931. From 1948 to 1950, he studied at the University of Kansas City and the Kansas City Art Institute, before moving to San Francisco to attend the California School of Fine Arts from 1950 to 1951. He joined the U.S. Army Corps of Engineers in 1951, and after his service there attended Reed College from 1953 to 1955. He then returned to San Francisco, spending his time painting (he later switched to sculpture) and studying theater improvisation until 1959. He devoted the next two years to exploring film and theater, participating in theatrical events and "happenings" in California and New York. In 1961, he relocated to New York and began graduate studies in art history at Hunter College, where he subsequently taught. He has also conducted seminars, including at Yale and the University of Wisconsin.

Morris' minimalist sculptures include large-scale felt pieces, earthworks, and scatter pieces, where objects are randomly scattered around the exhibition space. Many of his works are temporary. He has been the subject of numerous exhibitions, including at the Whitney Museum, the Detroit Institute of Art, the Corcoran Gallery, the Museum of Modern Art, and the Tate Gallery. His awards include a Guggenhim Fellowship and a Chicago Art Institute prize.

Morris' exploration of dance occurred between 1963 and 1965. Like his sculptures, Morris' films, videos, and dances reflect the process of creation, as did those of the other postmodern dancers of the Judson Dance Theater, with whom Morris was associated. Although he had no formal dance training, Morris studied improvisational dance with Anna Halprin and composition with Douglas Dunn, along with many of the other members of the Judson group. He danced in works by several Judson dancers, including in Yvonne Rainer's *Part of a Sextette* and *We Shall Run.* Simone Forti created a work for him and Rainer, *See Saw,* in 1961. Critics noted the strength of his performances, calling them focused and direct. Morris also collaborated on two dance works prior to choreographing his own. They included *War with Robert Huot,* which was performed at Judson Memorial Church, and *New Poses Plastiques* with Jill Johnston, which debuted in Washington D.C.

Morris' own works were presented in New York, Ann Arbor, Buffalo, Stockholm and Düsseldorf. Movement was minimized, highlighting his interest in the relationship between bodies, mass, and scale. His dance works were often perceived as an extension of his art. For example, his sculpture *I-Box* (1962) featured a nude photograph of him, which foreshadowed his interest in the human body within his dances. Morris' first work was *Arizona,* a solo presented in 1963. It consisted of a series of demonstrations, such as a presentation of lights swinging in ever-smaller circles, and a section in which he continuously and almost imperceptibly changed his position 180 degrees. Critics noted that each movement was "concise and purposeful."

In his second work, *21.3,* Morris was accompanied by a tape of himself reading from an art history book, while he stood at a lectern and gestured soundlessly. Morris' best-known work is *Waterman Switch* (1965), first performed in Buffalo, New York, by him, Rainer and Lucinda Childs. It was one of the first Judson works to gain recognition among a wide audience. Its importance in terms of celebrating the body as an artistic subject and in reversing male and female roles, as well as its economy and its place as a preeminent example of the tenets of postmodern dance, were virtually ignored, however. What gained notoriety was the fact that he and Rainer ended the piece in a nude embrace, which was captured in a *Life* magazine photograph.

Site was another acclaimed Morris work. In it, he moved a group of large white panels around the stage to an accompaniment of hammering and sawing broadcast from a white box on stage. One panel is removed to reveal a nearly nude woman (posed as in Edouard Manet's painting, *Olympia*), whom Morris treated as just another object on the stage. Presented prior to *Waterman Switch, Site* was one of the first uses of near nudity in dance.

Morris' largest and final piece, *Check,* received little attention, overshadowed by *Waterman Switch. Check* was typical of Morris' work in that it was contructed as a series of situations rather than as a flow of movement, and was purposeful and direct. Its scale was much greater than previous pieces, however. It featured a cast of 40 divided into two teams with identifying ribbons. Dancers mingled with the audience until they heard a whistle, upon which they marched to their side of the space with the rest of their team and participated in movement drills in accordance with the team leader. When the drills were finished, they went back to wandering among the audience until the next whistle. Morris wrote several articles explaining the philosophy behind his dance works (he also wrote extensively in reference to his art). In the *Tulane Drama Review,* he explains his theories on movement, space and the use of objects indance, all of which he views as methods of solving choreographic problems:

> From the beginning I wanted to avoid the pulled-up, turned-out, anti-gravitational qualities that not only give a body definition and role as "dancer" but qualify and delimit the movement available to it. The challenge was to find alternative movement.... By the uses of objects which could be manipulated I found a situation which did not dominate my actions nor subvert my performance. In fact the decision to employ objects came out of considerations of specific problems involving space and time.... The objects I used held no inherent interest for me but were means for dealing with specific problems.

Morris often used objects to highlight the "coexistence of the static and the mobile."

After 1965, Morris created no further dance works, but became interested in the "performance" quality of materials, such as felt, used in his sculptures. He also remained connected to the dance world in other ways. For example, he created stage and costume designs for the Merce Cunningham Dance Company, notably for Cunningham's *Canfield* (1969). The set consisted of a dark vertical column mounted with a white light that moved slowly across the downstage area, casting shadows from the dancers' bodies. His sculptures also have been credited with influencing minimalist dancers such as Childs and Laura Dean, whose works incorporate repetitive patterns.

—Karen Raugust

MOVING INTO DANCE PERFORMANCE COMPANY
South African dance company

The Moving into Dance Performance Company (MID) is based in Johannesburg, South Africa, and was founded in 1978 by choreographer and teacher Sylvia Glasser, its current artistic and executive director. Since its inception it has been a racially integrated theater dance company of 12 dancers ranging in age from 20 to 35. MID is a non-profit organization working to create a new dance vocabulary in a South African context.

South Africa has been trapped in a culturally destructive apartheid political system, and during the 1970s choreographer and educator Sylvia Glasser began to see the great opportunity dance offered in bringing people of different cultural backgrounds together. The response to these initiatives provided opportunities for black South Africans to gain access to formal dance training and to create a chance for South Africans from all cultural backgrounds to share experiences through dance.

Glasser used the formation of her school and company as a point of protest against the apartheid regime. It also gave her the time and space to explore her commitment to researching South African indigenous dance. Combining her research with academic inquiry into dance anthropology, MID began to establish the new Afro-fusion dance technique and choreographic style which is their trademark today. This Afro-fusion vision has moved South African dance into a postapartheid era, giving a voice to the many South African cultural traditions that were undervalued and suppressed over the past 40 years.

Moving into Dance Company: *Tranceformations*, 1992. Dancer: Themba Nkabinde.

Since the 1960s, modern dance in South Africa has looked to the traditions of Europe and North America as a way of creating dance work. The South African dance content and structure was mostly informed by issues outside of the country and many dance companies based their technique on either Martha Graham or Alvin Ailey. The Afro-fusion of MID is different—it's directly concerned with forming new dance imagery and vocabulary out of the South African context and identity.

Tranceformations, choreographed by Sylvia Glasser in 1992 and *Gula Matari,* choreographed by Vincent Sekwati Mantsoe in 1995 are two landmark, award-winning works in MID's repertoire. The former focuses on the relationship between *San* (Bushmen) rock art, trance dance, and belief systems of the original hunter-gatherer peoples of Southern Africa. The dance work uses Western choreographic forms in synthesis with the San cultural content. It is a dance piece which pays tribute to a dispossessed people, shifting the hierarchical concepts of a Western-dominated theater tradition. *Gula Matari* was inspired by Vincent Sekwati Mantsoe's respect for his ancestors; he explores the relationship between the spirit of a bird seen through the dancing spirit of the performers. Mantsoe works with indigenous South African dance forms to build his own special Afro-fusion movement voice.

The first democratic election for South Africa in 1994 brought the country into world focus. South African dance culture, hidden for so many years, was suddenly in demand. From 1993 through 1997, MID performed outside the country more than within; requests from the around the world for the company's unique style of dance have soared. Mantsoe, who had been working as MID's resident choreographer, was appointed associate director to the company in 1997, the same year he set a work on New York City's renowned Dance Theatre of Harlem. This piece, called *Sasanka,* premiered at the Kennedy Center in Washington D.C. in April of 1997, defying the long-held belief that classical ballet and African dance were incompatible. For many, ballet carried an elitist status while African dance constantly struggling to be valued as a professional art form. Through collaborations with African artists like Mantsoe, African culturalism is now serving as a new texture and inspiration in closing the gap between modern dance and classical ballet.

For its 20th anniversary in 1998, MID lined up many performances in Europe, and ironically this South African dance group will be seen more by foreigners than by their own country's citizens. The company has won many prestigious dance and choreographic awards, including the South African FNB Vita Special Award for Contemporary Choreography and Dance. Mantsoe also won a prize the Fifth Recontres Choreographique Internationale in France.

Sadly, the status quo in government funding in South Africa still exists with the majority of state funds going to the classical ballet and Western-based modern dance companies. Cultural policy from the new 1994 government promises change to support previously devalued cultural forms. The future of this exciting and innovative South African dance company as a vehicle for the aspirations and expression of South African people lies in the practical application of the new government's legislation; until such time as a company like Moving Into Dance can be shared and appreciated both culturally and financially by its own people, the cultural dance struggle in South Africa will still be raging.

—Jill Waterman

MULLER, Jennifer
American dancer, choreographer, educator, and company director

Born: 16 October 1944 in Yonkers, New York. **Education:** Halstead School; studied dance at the Juilliard School. **Career:** Dancer, Pearl Lang Dance Company, 1960-63; principal dancer and assistant to José Limón, Limón Dance Company, 1963-71; artistic director, Lecture-Concert Trio, 1964-68; associate artistic director and principal dancer, Louis Falco Dance Company, 1968-74; artistic director, Jennifer Muller/The Works, 1974 to present; has created choreography for films and stage productions, including *Fame,* 1982; has taught Muller technique at the Juilliard School, Sarah Lawrence College, High School of Performing Arts, and Metrpolitan Museum of Art, among others, and has taught as a guest instructor throughout Europe and South America. **Awards:** Carbonell Award for best choreography for a musical, 1989.

Works

1969	*Elements*
1970	*More than Sixty Places*
1971	*Nostalgia*
	Cantata
	Rust
	Sweet Milkwood and Blackberry Bloom
1973	*Tub*
1974	*Biography*
	Four Chairs
	Clown
	Wyeth
	Winter Pieces
	Speeds
	An American Beauty Rose
1975	*Strangers*
	White
1976	*Crossword*
	Beach (in three acts)
1977	*Mondiaan*
	Predicaments for Five
1978	*Lovers*
1979	*Converstions*
	Solo
1980	*Chant*
1981	*Terrain*
1983	*Shed*
	Kite
1984	*Souls*
1986	*Darkness and Light*
	Fields
	The Enigma
	Couches
	Life/Times (Mathematics, In Tandem)
	For Burt
1987	*Interrupted River*
1988	*Occasional Encounters*
	City
1989	*The Flight of a Predatory Bird*
1990	*RIGHTeous About Passing (on the LEFT)*
	Refracted Light

1991   *Glass Houses*
        2-1=1/Regards
        arm in arm in arm. . .
        Woman with Visitors at 3am
1992   *Thesaurus*
        Momentary Gathering
1993   *Pierrot*
        HUMAN/NATURE: A Response to the Longhouse Gardens
        Orbs, Spheres, and Other Circular Bodies
        The Politician/Peeling the Onion
        The Waiting Room
        2-1=1/Attic
1994   *Desire: That DNA Urge*
        Point of View: A Case of Persimmons and Picasso
1995   *The Spotted Owl*
1996   *Promontory*
        Fruit
        The Dinner Party
        A Broken Wing

Publications

On MULLER: articles—

Deresiewicz, Bill, "Reviews," *Dance Magazine,* March 1992.
Hardy, Camille, "Jennifer Muller," *Dance Magazine,* January 1997.
Hering, Doris, "Reviews," *Dance Magazine*, September 1995.
Jowitt, Deborah, "In Air," *Village Voice,* 9 March 1993.
———, "Visionary Revisited," *Village Voice,* 7 November 1995.
Mazo, Joseph H., "Body Language," *Daily News,* 15 February 1993.
Supree, Burt, "Taking Off," *Village Voice,* 10 December 1991.
Whitaker, Rick, "Jennifer Muller," *Dance Magazine*, June 1993.
Zimmer, Elizabeth, "Dance: JM/The Works," *Village Voice,* 6 June 1995.
———, "Endangered Species," *Village Voice*, 13 June 1995.

*   *   *

Born in Yonkers, New York, in 1944, Jennifer Muller claims to have been a shy child who used dance to "stretch out emotionally," according to Joseph H. Mazo. Although her mother was an actress, Muller elected to study dance at Juilliard, rather than acting or directing. Muller began dancing professionally at age 15, as a member of the Pearl Lang Dance Company then went on to become a principal dancer with the José Limón Dance Company for nine years, and associate artistic director of the Louis Falco Dance Company for seven years. It was with this last company that Muller was "discovered" in 1974. Her *Tub,* meant to show the pleasure of the body in contact with water, was performed at the Thèâtre des Champs-Elysées in Paris, France. *Tub* displayed a full and generous quality of movement as it explored the touch of a fluid element.

Muller has been the artistic director of the contemporary dance company Jennifer Muller/The Works since its inception in 1974. The Works is a multiethnic creative company with a humanistic outlook; it has been committed to the belief that its passion for dance can be meaningfully shared with people of all ages, cultures, and walks of life. This tenet has taken the company on tours through 36 countries, four continents, and 29 states in the U.S., in performances at major theaters and festivals worldwide. Throughout its history, the company has played a crucial role in American communities. The Works has initiated and participated in numerous outreach programs in association with Hospital Audiences, Arts Connection, Lincoln Center, the Henry

Jennifer Muller: *The Spotted Owl.* **Photograph by Tom Caravaglia.**

Street Settlement, the Door, the HSPA, the High School for Fashion Industries and City as Schools. In addition, The Works' annual self-initiated educational outreach program has established direct relationships with individual schools in the New York public school system and a partnership with Hostos Center for Arts and Culture in the Bronx. The Works' extended residencies include California State and New York University Summer Arts Programs, Webster and Point Park Colleges, Artemis in Amsterdam, CNSMDP in Paris, and the American Dance Center in New York City. The company has held annual multiweek sessions that have included workshops at Perry Dance II in New York City, SUNY/Oswego, and The Dance Loft in Switzerland.

Since founding her company, Muller has often employed dialogue as an important element in her dances. She believes that although dance expresses emotions it does not express specifics. Thus, to Muller, words can bring another level of reality to a piece. *The Waiting Room,* which included dialogue, premiered in 1993 at the Joyce Theater in New York. Muller said the dance dealt "with issues of responsibility and involvement" and went on to explain to Mazo: "Are you going to let the mysteries happen? Are you going to take responsibility for your life? We're in an era when people are getting over the appeal of isolation—*The Waiting Room* shows people who are thrown together, and explores the inner dynamics that emerge."

The 1995 season marked the company's 30th anniversary, which was celebrated with two programs running for a week at the Joyce Theater. One program included excerpts of Muller's dances choreographed between 1975 and 1988, and *Speeds,* a signature Muller work created in 1974. This work featured a score by Burt Alcantara, white costumes and hats, and frequent changes of direction and velocities punctuated by the English word *change*. The other program opened with *Retroduets*, danced by an accomplished group of soloists, and featured the premiere of *The Spotted Owl* with music by Marty Beller. This latter work highlighted Muller's gift for sleekly dramatic staging; in it Muller attacks contemporary society through dance and dialogue. In her view, artists are too often victims of the world that surrounds them, since they are at odds with the key values of society (i.e., power and greed).

Muller's commissions have included creations and reconstructions for companies in the Netherlands (Nederlands Dans Theater, NDT 3, and Dansgroep Krisztina de Chatel); France (Ballet du Nord, the Lyon Opera Ballet, the Festival d'Avignon and CNSMDP); Germany (Sachsische Staatsoper Dresden and Tanz-Forum Koln); Italy (Aterballetto); Brazil (Ballet Stagium); Argentina (Ballet Contemporaneo; Israel (Bat-Dor Dance Company); Canada (Les Ballets Jazz de Montreal); as well as in the U.S. (Alvin Ailey American Dance Theatre, Hartford Ballet, Ballet Manhattan, the Ballet Theater of Annapolis, Utah Repertory Dance Theater, White Wave Rising, and the Verdehr Trio/Michigan State University commission for a PBS series on new music). The artists with whom Muller has worked with include Sandro Chia, Keith Haring, Yoko Ono, Tom Slaughter, Richard Smith, David Van Tieghem, and Nana Vasconcelos. During the past 25 years Muller has had a long-standing collaborative relationship with composers Keith Jarrett, Burt Alcantara, and Marty Beller as well as designers Karen Small, William Katz, and Richard Nelson. Muller has also created the design designation, Stageworks.

In the past 22 years, Muller has created over 50 works, including the full-evening works *Beach* (in three acts), *Strangers, Darkness and Light, Point of View, A Case of Persimmons and Picasso,* and the site-specific *HUMAN/NATURE, a Response to the Longhouse Garden,* yet Muller's greatest legacy may be as the consummate teacher.

Muller is one of the only choreographers of her generation to have developed a personalized teaching technique. Her Creative Mind/Whole Body Workshops, which are informed by principles adapted from Eastern philosophy, are open to dancers and nondancers alike. Muller and her company members and alumni teach these workshops worldwide. The program has produced 10 premieres and more than 30 student workshop projects. Muller has also directed courses in choreography and collaboration for the Artists' Trust in England, the Baltimore Mayor's Council in Maryland, and for Danswerksplaats in Amsterdam.

Muller's works have always dealt with emotional and societal issues. She believes that an artist's output usually has a thread, or theme, running through it, "Nobody comes up with anything new in life: nothing is discovered—what happens is that things are uncovered." The dance world has greatly benefitted from Muller's "uncovering," and more importantly, from her efforts to uncover dance for diverse populations.

—Barbara Long

MUMAW, Barton

American dancer, choreographer, and educator

Born: 1912 in Eustis, Florida. **Education:** Took ballet and modern dance classes when available, even correspondence courses; attended Rollins College, Orlando, Florida. **Military:** Served in the armed forces as an "Entertainment Specialist," to boost troops' morale, 1942-46. **Career:** Became Ted Shawn's chauffeur, dresser, and an ensemble dancer for Denishawn, 1931; went with Shawn to Becket, Massachusetts (the farm later called Jacob's Pillow), after the breakup of Denishawn, 1932; lead dancer, Ted Shawn's Men Dancers, 1933-48; Broadway and theatre performer, 1948-58; began reconstructions of Shawn's works with *Kinetic Molpai*, 1973; has been a major presence at Jacob's Pillow from 1932 to the present.

Works

1933	*Fetish,* Ted Shawn's Men Dancers
	Dyak Spear Dance, Men Dancers
1936	*The Banner Bearer,* Men Dancers
1938	*Spirits of the Earth,* Men Dancers
	High Priest and the Initiate, Men Dancers
1940	*Bourrée,* Men Dancers
	The God of Lightening, Men Dancers
1941	*Sonata,* solo
	Funerailles (War and the Artist), solo
1942	*Holy Rollers,* solo
	Two Spirituals: Get on Board L'il Children and *Sometimes I Feel Like a Motherless Child,* solo
	Lover, solo
	Alborado del Gracioso, solo
1946	*La Puerta del Vino,* solo
	La Cathédrale Engoutie, solo
1953	*Florida Aflame,* solo
1963	*Lady in the Dark,* solo
1967	*When Johnny Comes Marching Home,* solo
1973	reconstruction of *Kinetic Molpai* (Shawn, though some parts by Mumaw and others) for Alvin Ailey
1975	*I'll Make Me a World,* solo
1977	*Royal Hunt of the Sun,* solo
1992	*Men Dancers* (reconstruction of several of Shawn's works, with others)

Publications

By MUMAW: books—

With Jane Sherman, *Barton Mumaw, Dancer: From Denishawn to Jacob's Pillow and Beyond,* New York, 1986.

*   *   *

While Barton Mumaw is best known for his work as a leading dancer with Ted Shawn's Men Dancers, he is also a choreographer in his own right, as well as performer of musical theatre, and an eminent teacher. From the last days of Denishawn to the beginnings of Jacob's Pillow through a continuing presence at the Pillow today, Mumaw's life has touched many people. He came to modern dance in an era when dancing men were considered effeminate, and worked to transform that stereotype. The archives of Jacob's Pillow provide evidence that Mumaw's dancing was eloquent and exquisite, acclaimed by critics at a time when modern dance was only grudgingly accepted. To this day, Mumaw continues to have a powerful presence at Jacob's Pillow. As a teacher, lecturer, and reconstructor, Mumaw not only preserves but keeps alive the legacy of Ted Shawn and the early days of modern dance.

Mumaw's early training as a dancer started in his hometown of Eustis, Florida, with his participation in infrequently offered ballet and modern dance classes, as well dance correspondence classes through the mail. A dedicated student, he rehearsed daily in his backyard. After seeing a performance by the Denishawn group when they toured through Florida in 1930, Mumaw was determined to go to New York to study at the Denishawn School for the summer. He left New York to begin studying music at Rollins College in Orlando, Florida, where not long after Denishawn arrived to perform. In 1931, Mumaw left Rollins to become Ted Shawn's chauffeur and dresser and a Denishawn ensemble dancer, in exchange for tuition, housing, and meals. When Denishawn disbanded in 1932, Mumaw followed Shawn to Becket, Massachusetts, to the farm that was to become Jacob's Pillow. As a co-teacher with Shawn at Springfield College in Springfield, Massachusetts, Mumaw was instrumental in helping Shawn develop an approach to dancing that male students would find athletic and not "effeminate." Their movement vocabulary and style of teaching stressed the discipline of dance as an asset for the physique of athlete.

Stemming from this experience, in 1933 Shawn assembled a new company including Mumaw and others, a small touring group of men called Ted Shawn's Men Dancers, based out of Jacob's Pillow. For the next seven years, the Men Dancers toured the U.S., returning each summer to Jacob's Pillow. Mumaw was Shawn's constant companion: lover, confidante, as well as continuing his early responsibilities as dresser and chauffeur. Shawn choreographed many solos for Mumaw, as well as presented Mumaw's choreography on the Men Dancers programs. During these years, Mumaw and Shawn were careful to conceal the sexual side of their relationship, feeling it would detract from the masculine image for dance they were working to develop. With the onset of World War II, Shawn disbanded the troupe of men dancers, although he vowed to continue with summer performances at Jacob's Pillow.

Mumaw served in the armed forces from 1942 to 1946. When he was drafted, Mumaw declared himself a conscientious objector, which he later found out meant he was under surveillance for the duration of his tour of duty. At first, Mumaw was stationed in Biloxi, Mississippi, where Special Services headquarters assigned him the task of entertaining squadrons of soldiers who maintained B-24 bombers. Daniel Nagrin, fellow modern dancer, was also charged with morale boosting for the troops in the same company. Occasionally teaching physical education, but primarily performing for the troops, Mumaw brought modern dance to a new audience. In 1943, Mumaw was shipped overseas to England. For the duration of the war, his classification as an Entertainment Specialist kept him in England and allowed him to continue performing.

Returning to the States in 1946, Mumaw resumed his life as if he had never left, in both his professional and personal life with Shawn. It would not last. In an attempt to free himself from the dominant presence of Shawn in his life as a dancer and choreographer, Mumaw felt he needed to separate from him personally as well. He performed a series of solo concerts and, like many of his contemporaries from the modern dance world, Mumaw had an extensive career as a musical theatre dancer. From 1948 to 1958, he danced both on Broadway and in touring companies in musicals such as *Oklahoma* (Agnes de Mille), *The Golden Apple* (Hanya Holm), and *My Fair Lady* (Holm). Although he and Shawn both moved on to other partners, Mumaw continued to be deeply committed to Shawn and Jacob's Pillow. While Shawn was alive, he often invited Mumaw back to the Pillow to perform, featuring his solo works for Mumaw, as well as Mumaw's own choreography. In 1973, Mumaw reconstructed Shawn's *Kinetic Molpai* for the Alvin Ailey Dance Company. Further reconstructions included a production of *Men Dancers* in 1992, which combined reconstructions of Ted Shawn's dances with other important works for men.

In 1986, Mumaw published a book written with former Denishawn dancer Jane Sherman, *Barton Mumaw, Dancer: From Denishawn to Jacob's Pillow and Beyond,* which vividly illustrates Mumaw's years as a dancer and recounts his complicated relationship with Shawn. In 1988, Pillow archivists worked with Mumaw and long-time Pillow accompanist, Jess Meeker, to add music to silent films from early performances of the Men Dancers as the films were transferred to videotape. Mumaw is still ever-present at Jacob's Pillow. The weathervane that sits on top of the Ted Shawn Theatre is a cast-iron silhouette of him dancing. With his leg lifted, arm raised, head tilted back, Mumaw is perpetually moving forward, while remaining firmly attached to his roots.

—Maura Keefe

MURPHY, Graeme

Australian dancer, choreographer, and company director

Born: 2 November 1950 in Melbourne, Australia. **Education:** Educated in Launceston, Tasmania; studied ballet with Kenneth Gillespie; attended the Australian Ballet School, Melbourne, 1966-68. **Career:** Dancer, Australian Ballet, 1969; first independent choreography, 1971; Sadlers Wells Royal Ballet, London, 1972; Ballet Felix Blaska, Grenoble, France, 1972; International Ballet Caravan, 1974-75; rejoined Australian Ballet as dancer and resident choreographer, 1976; artistic director, the Dance Company (renamed Sydney Dance Company [SDC], 1979), 1976; first full-length work, 1978; toured Italy, 1980; New York, London, and Hong Kong, 1981; commissioned works for SDC from Barry Moreland, 1982; toured New York, Beijing, and Shanghai, 1985; U.S. and Europe, 1988; commissions for Ohad Naharin, Ralph Lemon, and Paul Mercurio, 1989; further foreign tours, most recently to New York, 1997. **Awards:** Australia Council Grant, 1971; Canberra Times Award for best new work, 1976; Sydney Critics Circle Award, 1978; member of the Order of Australia (AM) for services to dance, 1982; ADAMS—Dance Australia Award for best choreography, 1984; Australian of the Year, 1987; Honorary Doctor of Letters, University of Tasmania, 1992; Honorary Doctor of Philosophy, University of Queensland, 1992; Inaugural Sydney Opera House Honours, 1993.

Works

1971	*Ecco Le Diavole*
1976	*Glimpses*
1977	*Sequenza VII*
	Tip
	Fire Earth Air Water
	Scintillation
1978	*Poppy*
	Tekton
	Rumours (part)

1979	*Rumours* (complete)
	Signatures
	Sheherazade
1980	*Daphnis and Chloë*
	Viridian
	Beyond Twelve
1981	*An Evening*
1982	*Hate*
	Homelands
	Wilderness
1983	*The Selfish Giant*
	Flashbacks
	Some Rooms
1984	*Meander*
	Deadly Sins
	Old Friends
	After Venice
1985	*Boxes*
1986	*Sirens*
	Nearly Beloved
	New Friends
	Shining
	Fire and Ice, for skaters Jayne Torvill and Christopher Dean
1987	*Late Afternoon of a Faun*
	Song of the Night
	Gallery
1988	*VAST*
	Kraanerg
1989	*Evening Suite*
1990	*soft bruising*
	In the Company of Women
	King Roger
1991	*Bard Bits*
1992	*Nutcracker*
	Piano Sonata
	Synergy with Synergy w/percussion ensemble Synergy
1993	*Beauty and the Beast*
	The Protecting Veil
1995	*Fornicon*
	Berlin
1996	*Free Radicals*
	Embodied (for Mikhail Baryshnikov)

Other works include: Directed the Australian Opera production of *Metamorphosis,* 1985; *Turandot,* 1990; *Salomé,* 1993; created new production of *Les Troyens,* 1994.

Films and Videotapes

Astonish Me!, documentary, 1989.
Sensing, dance film, ABC-TV, 1993.

*   *   *

In many ways Graeme Murphy—choreographer, dancer, and artistic director—can be regarded as the personification of Australian contemporary dance. Australian born, his commitment to Australian dance and dancers, and to other Australian artists—choreographers, composers, musicians, and designers—is without equal. At the same time, by way of the Sydney Dance Company which he

has directed since 1976, he has been instrumental in bringing Australian dance to the wider international stage. Thus, not only dance but the performing arts as a whole in Australia, owe much to this highly innovative, and at times rather iconoclastic, artist.

If the chief characteristics of Murphy's dance were to be pinpointed, then "eclectic" and "theatrical" are the two words that would come to mind immediately. For, whether in the choice of movement, thematic content, or music, Murphy ranges far and wide, drawing on whatever he considers appropriate to realise his creative vision. That vision is, however, firmly anchored in the belief that dance should be theatre that excites, stimulates, provokes, and entertains.

Murphy's movement style is a case in point. A relatively conventional blend of ballet and modern lies at its heart, yet any number of movement sources—both dance and non-dance—are called on when it suits his purpose. *Daphnis and Chloë* (1980), for example, moves freely across time periods and movement sources: Greek shepherds and shepherdesses step out an elegant English country dance; Cupid zooms around on a skateboard; and Bryaxis (who has now become a punk-rocker) takes to the floor with gymnastic rolls and handstands.

Another dimension of Murphy's eclecticism is the frequent interplay between fact and fantasy, past and present, age and youth. While *Poppy* (1978), *After Venice* (1984), and *Beauty and the Beast* (1993) reflect this mix, it is in his highly innovative *Nutcracker* (created for the Australian Ballet in 1992) that these dynamic shifts reach their peak. Here the essence of Ivanov's ballet is woven in and around a contemporary storyline that not only has a specifically Australian context, but at the same time draws on both Russian ballet and its sociopolitical history.

As the above titles might suggest, the reinterpretation of classics—whether dance, text, or film—is also a common feature of Murphy's work. The full length *Poppy* (1978), for example, takes the life and art of Jean Cocteau as its theme. Part biography, part journey into the fantasy world of Cocteau's opium-charged imagination, the work includes not only a larger-than-life Diaghilev, but also alludes to some of the Ballets Russes masterpieces including *Le Spectre de la rose* and *Le Sacre du printemps.* In the high-tech *Beauty and the Beast,* elements from both the gothic tale and Cocteau's film version are reworked into a contemporary moral fable. Although serious messages (including sex, drugs, and the soulless passion for things technological) are embedded in the work, they are offset by a sharp and irreverent sense of humour—yet another Murphy trademark.

Diaghilev's aphoristic "astonish me" is one of Murphy's fundamental artistic credos; he firmly believes that dance should surprise rather than politely lead its audience along a well-trodden path. He is therefore an inveterate risk taker, prepared to challenge orthodox perceptions of, and expectations about, the art form. Again, his *Nutcracker* is a case in point. The work takes the question "What happened to Clara?" as its starting point and develops it into a penetrating commentary, not only on the original ballet, but also on the Russian roots of ballet in Australia and on the pain of loss and dispossession of country, culture, and identity.

Yet another aspect of Murphy's challenge to orthodoxy is the fact that he does not shy away from nudity and sexuality in his works. Bare flesh abounds, but there is rarely the sense that its use is merely gratuitous. Murphy simply revels in the body and its physicality, and, as he points out in the 1989 video documentary *Astonish Me!,* has "never looked at dance removed from sensuality and sexuality." The nudity ranges from the humorous (Cupid displays a wonderful pair of bare buttocks in *Daphnis and Chloë*, 1980), through the lusciously sensual (*Sensing*, 1993), to the more overtly sexual (*Fornicon*, 1995).

Any commentary on Graeme Murphy would be incomplete without mention of the close relationship between him, his longtime partner and muse, Janet Vernon, and the Sydney Dance Company. The relationship is essentially symbiotic, but one which has been of mutual benefit not only to those immediately concerned, but also to Australian dance as a whole. Yet for all that, Murphy and the SDC are regarded by many as synonymous; he has never been precious about exerting exclusive ownership over "his" company. He has ensured, instead, that its dancers are consistently exposed to the influences of other choreographers and other companies. Thus, Louis Falco's feisty *Black and Blue*, Ohad Naharin's *Arbos*, and Douglas Wright's *Gloria*, for example, have either been set on, or created for, the company. Importantly, Murphy has also encouraged company dancers to test their choreographic wings: Paul Mercurio and Gideon Obarzanek are among those who have successfully taken up the challenge.

Given that Murphy is still relatively young (he was born in 1950), there is little doubt that he will continue to make his mark on Australian dance and theatre arts. But given his penchant for the unusual and the untried, exactly what direction that contribution will take is less easy to identify. In this regard his own rather whimsical proposition in *Astonish Me!* is worth noting: "O.K. I'm brave enough. Are you going to come with me [for] the next ten years? I don't know where we're going yet, but let's find out together."

—Anita Donaldson

MUSIC FOR MODERN DANCE

Music is integral to dance not simply as a support for dancers, but as an art form in its own right. Modern music, however, left its solitary realm and began to have a more direct influence on, and to be influenced more directly by, other art forms of the time. With the advent and development of modern dance came a revision in the place of the composer in the creation of dance, as well as a difference in the role that music played in the creation and performance of a dance piece. Musicians and choreographers increasingly collaborated, thus creating productions that were truly integrated in style and underlying philosophy. Ideas such as kinetic links between dance and music came to the forefront, and experimentation with instruments, unconventional sounds and rhythms, improvisation, and silence became more common. Innovation was at its peak.

The name of Louis Horst is integral with the idea of modern dance composers. During his career, Horst acted as accompanyist, conductor, and composer for renowned modern dance artists such as Ruth St. Denis, Ted Shawn, Agnes de Mille, Doris Humphrey, and Martha Graham. Not only was he a musician, but his interest in the relationship between music and dance led to his work as collaborator with many of these choreographers. He first entered the Denishawn company at the age of 31, with no experience in working with dancers. Gradually, he began to notice the link between the kinetic response of dancers and the rhythmic impulse of musicians, thereby leading to his working with Miss Ruth in conceptualizing the music on the stage. Furthermore, Horst's interest in German

philosophers Schopenhauer and Nietzsche began to influence his work as well. Horst's first composition for the stage is recorded as 1919, for Shawn's solo piece, *Japanese Spear Dance*. Horst and Graham met when Graham was a dancer in the Denishawn company, at which time they began a passionate relationship that would inform their working relationship in the years to come. Horst left Denishawn and spent some time in Vienna, only to return to Graham in 1926. Their first collaboration, with Horst at the keyboard, included two Graham solos, *Masques* and *Alt Wein*. Some of their more well-known collaborative efforts include *Heretic* and *Primitive Mysteries*. Horst also worked with the Humphrey-Weidman Dance Company, walking the delicate balance between the contrasting choreographic styles of that company and Graham's. Perhaps Horst will be most remembered for his use of music to invigorate the movement, rather than act as a melodic support for the dancers.

Philip Glass, who has worked with artists such as Twyla Tharp, Martin Scorsese, Jean Cocteau, Jerome Robbins, and Samuel Beckett, is renowned as a composer at the forefront of the minimalist movement. His conventional training began as a child and continued until his discovery of composers such as Copland, Ives, and Schuman left him dissatisfied. It was his discovery of Indian music through working with Ravi Shankar that the direction of his music began to shift. His music can be characterized by the minimalist style, at the heart of which is a steady pulse, and a slowly changing harmonic rhythm. In 1971 Glass helped form a multidisciplinary artist collective called The Kitchen, which included such visionaries as Bill T. Jones and Arnie Zane, as well as Meredith Monk and Robert Mapplethorpe. Glass has worked in opera, film, and theatre and has composed music for dance pieces such as *A Descent into the Maelstrom* and *In the Upper Room*.

John Cage, revolutionary musician, is perhaps best known for his collaboration with Merce Cunningham. By the late 1930s, Cage was experimenting with what he called the prepared piano, a grand piano with strings that were adorned with different objects, including wood, rubber, metal, and felt. The insertion of these objects altered the sound of the piano, emphasizing its percussive sound and changing or eliminating each note's pitch and timbre. Furthermore, his interest in Eastern philosophy affected his attitude toward music; he believed that music was contemplative, divinely influenced, and naturalistic. Cunningham and Cage's collaborative efforts would leave audience and critics both stunned and enraptured. As Sam Richards states in 1996's *John Cage As. . .*, they disregarded conventional elements in music and dance, such as "narrative structure, timelessness, simultaneity, the idea that sounds and movements are inherently expressive without artists adding to them." The integration of silence as a sound in its own right, as well as Cage's systems of chance music, also infiltrated the performances. This helped to form a style of performance and a relationship between dance and music that had hitherto been unheard of and would influence many subsequent composers and choreographers.

Wallingford Riegger considered himself a radical composer, chiefly associated with the group of composers known as the "American Five." His Marxist philosophy indirectly influenced his musical creation and, perhaps, reinforced his self-image as a revolutionary rather than associating him with a particular ideology. His influence has been felt in the dance world as well, however. Riegger differed from many of his contemporaries in that, during the 1930s and 1940s, he collaborated with a number of the modern dance pioneers of the time. He began by composing what are considered minor musical pieces for choreographers such as Martha Graham, Helen

Tamaris, Anna Sokolow, and Erik Hawkins, establishing himself as an aspiring modern dance composer. Furthermore, he composed major pieces for Doris Humphrey's trilogy entitled *New Dance, Theatre Piece,* and *With My Red Fires.* These scores are considered the longest and most narratively complex pieces for which Riegger created. Finally, his compositions for Graham's *Chronicle* and Hanya Holm's *Tread* also helped place his name among those major modern dance composers.

Publications

Duckworth, William, *Talking Music,* New York, 1995.
Mertens, Wim, *American Minimal Music,* London, 1983.
Richards, Sam, *John Cage As. . .,* Oxford, 1996.
Soares, Janet Mansfield, *Louis Horst: Musician in a Dancer's World,* Ann Arbor, 1987.
Spackman, Stephen, *Wallingford Riegger: Two Essays in Musical Biography,* New York, 1982.

—Kristin M. Harris

NADJ, Josef

Slavic dancer, choreographer, and company director based in France

Born: 13 December 1957 in Kanijiza, in former Yugosalvia. **Education:** Showed early artistic talent, first painting exposition at 11; studied fine arts, Budapest; took course in theater and mime; arrived in Paris, 1980; studied mime with Marcel Marceau and Étienne Decroux; ballet with Yves Cassati; modern with Lari Leong, from 1980. **Career:** Dancer, Josiane Rivoire Company and Sidonie Rochon Company; dancer, Catherine Diverres, François Verret, and Mark Tompkins, 1980s; founder, Jel Theater, 1986; director, National Choreographic Center of Orléans, since 1995.

Works

1987	*Pekinese Duck*
1988	*Seven Rhinoceros Skins*
1989	*The Emperor's Death*
1990	*Comedia Tempio*
1992	*The Ladders of Orpheus*
1994	*Woyzeck*
	Anatomy of a Faun
1995	*Cry of the Chameleon*
1996	*Habacuc's Comments* (mus. Tickmayer)

* * *

Director of the National Choreographic Center of Orléans since 1995, Josef Nadj was born in a small town is what was Yugoslavia, and showed great artistic promise as a child. He studied fine arts in Budapest, Hungary, but found courses in theater and mime especially stimulating. Nadj ventured to Paris in 1980 and discovered a whole new world of creative arts—including mime studies with the well-known Marcel Marceau, ballet with Yves Cassati, and modern dance with Lari Leong. Taking his modern classes further, Nadj trained with several of France's new generation including Catherine Diverres, François Verret, and Mark Tompkins.

Nadj founded his own company, called Jel Theater, in 1986 and the company's first creation, *Pekinese Duck* was a tremendous and unexpected hit. Nadj credits his success with *Pekinese Duck* as partially being in the right place at the right time. The "new" French dance was indeed being recognized by the country, though Nadj's choreography brought something a bit different into the mix, an Eastern/Asian-tinged coloring to his movements that seems to have propelled *Pekinese Duck* to its instant fame, and opened the doors of many well-known Parisian theaters to the young dancer/choreographer.

Nadj's Eastern influences included writers Franz Kafka and Bruno Schulz, art director Jerzy Grotowski and mime Tomaszewski. His work is often compared to that of Polish director Tadeusz Kantor because of its theatricality. In Nadj's work, threaticality was focused on the premise that subject prevails over technique and movement; his dancers are not simply dancing on the stage but become theatrical characters. Men wearing black suits and bowler hats are frequently seen in his works, a nod to Charlie Chaplin's early screen antics.

In preparation for composing a new choreography, Nadj follows a simple pattern—once he begins to design and sculpt the movement, he asks each of his dancers for a personal commitment and contribution to the evolving performance. Since Jel Theater's corps is a mix of both Hungarian and French dancers, their rich cultural backgrounds add a further dimension to the choreography. For Nadj and Jel Theater, drama is put before formal dance research; the history of the story often takes precedence over the choreography. Nadj offers an imaginative vision of the world in drawing from legends, mythology, and varied traditions of his Eastern childhood. His past represents a treasure trove of memories and stories— *Pekinese Duck* was inspired by an amateur threatrical company from Kanijiza that dreamed of journeying to China to perform; the deathbed reminiscences of Nadj's grandfather, about war, served as the impetus behind 1988's *Seven Rhinceros Skins;* and Kanijiza's benevolent firemen with their brass band were the inspiration for 1992's *The Ladders of Orpheus.*

Nadj's dance vocabulary plays with fantasy, humor, derision, and the absurdity of the world. Yet is not overly nostalgic, often quite the contrary, trying to depict the modernity of Middle Europe at the beginning of this century. Though Nadj much of Nadj's work seems lighthearted, he also concerned with real issues, those that plagued mankind in the not-so-distant past as well as the future. He believes in being open-minded, and in building bridges between the past and present and from one nation to another.

Nadj's scenographic excess, with moving sets and a eclectic mix of dance, theater, mime, and illusion provide an inimitable spectacle. He has collaborated with set designer Goury for years, and together they have created stunning works. Goury's designs have ranged from simple to miraculous, sets and props appear and reappear during performances, wooden boards topple here and there, partitions contain a multitude of hiding places from which the dancers vanish or emerge. One of Goury's masterpieces was the set for *The Ladders of Orpheus,* where the stage appeared to be an infinitely moving labyrinth.

In 1995, Nadj was offered a new experience, to create a work for the national circus school. The commission meant a great deal to Nadj both personally and professionally, the inquiry was more than a confirmation of Nadj's talent—it meant his creativity was recognized beyond the dance world. The resulting work, *The Cry of the Chameleon* was another success, garnering him wide acclaim from the general public as well as in the dance community.

—Murielle Mathieu

NAGRIN, Daniel

American dancer, choreographer, educator, and writer

Born: 22 May 1917 in New York City. **Education:** B.S. in education, City College of New York, 1940; studied dance with Martha Graham, Anna Sokolow, Helen Tamiris, Mme. Anderson-Ivantzova, Nenette Charisse, and Edward Caton, 1936-56; studied acting under Miriam Goldina, Sanford Meisner, and Stella Adler, 1936-56. **Military:** Air Force during World War II, 1942-43. **Career:** Began choreographing, 1948; featured dance soloist on Broadway and in film, 1954-79; teacher, various institutions, summer sessions, etc., 1957-92; teacher, Silvermine Guild Art, New Canaan, Connecticut, 1957-66; teacher, SUNY Brockport, 1967-71; video director, 1972-85; teacher, Arizona State University, Tempe, AZ, 1982-92; author, 1988 to present; professor emeritus, 1992 to present. **Awards:** Doctorate of Fine Arts, SUNY, Brockport, 1991; LHD, Arizona State University, 1992; Balasaraswati/Joy Ann Dewey Beineke Chair for Distinguished Teaching, 1992; numerous arts grants.

Roles

1938	*Façade—Expositione Italiana* (Anna Sokolow)
1942	*Liberty Song* (Tamiris)
1945	*Up In Central Park*, Broadway
1946	*Annie Get Your Gun*, Broadway
1948	*Inside U.S.A.*
	Lend an Ear, Broadway
1949	*Touch and Go*, Broadway
1950	*Bless You All*
1952	*Just For You* (film)
1955	*Plain and Fancy*, Broadway
1977	*The Fall* (theatre)

Works

1942	*Private Johnny Jukebox*
1943	*"Landscape with Three Figures, 1859"*
1948	*Spanish Dance* (mus. Genevieve Pitot)
	Man of Action
	Strange Hero (mus. Stan Kenton and Pete Rugolo), New York
1950	*Dance In the Sun*
	The Ballad of John Henry
	Faces With Walt Whitman
1954	*His Majesty O'Keefe* (chor. for the film, by Warner Brothers)
	Man Dancing
	Tom O'Bedlam
1957	*Indeterminate Figure*
	Progress
1958	*Jazz: Three Ways* (mus. Nat King Cole), 92nd Street YM-YWHA, New York City
	Three Happy Men, 92nd Street YM-YWHA, New York City
	The Boss Man and the Snake Lady
	With My Eye and With My Hand, 92nd Street YM-YWHA
	A Dancer Prepares 92nd Street YM-YWHA
	For a Young Person, 92nd Street YM-YWHA
1959	*Dance In the Sun*

1960	*An Entertainment*
	An American Journey
1962	*Two Improvisations*
1963	*The Man Who Did Not Care*
1965	*Path*, 92nd Street YM-YWHA
	Not Me, But Him, 92nd Street YM-YWHA
	In the Dusk
	A Gratitude
	In Defense of the City
	Why Not
1968	*The Peloponnesian War*, Cubiculo Theatre, New York
1971	*The Image*
	Duet
	The Ritual
	Polythemes
	Wind I
	Rondo
	Mary Annie's Dance
	Rituals of Power
1972	*Songs of the Times*
	Fragment: Rondo I and II
	Ritual for Two
	Ritual for Eight
	Quiet Dance I, II
	Wounded Knee
	Sea Anemone Suite
1973	*Hello-Farewell-Hello*
	Steps
1974	*Untitled*
	Jazz Changes
	Sweet Woman
1975	*Nineteen Upbeats*
	The Edge Is Also a Center
1976	*Ruminations*
1977	*Someone*
	Untitled (II)
1978	*Getting Well*, American Dance Festival, Durham, NC
	The Fall
	Time Writes Notes on Us
	Silence is Golden
1979	*Jacaranda* (lib. Sam Shepard), Playhouse 46, New York
1981	*Poems Off the Wall*, 550 Broadway, New York
1993	*Apartment 18C*
1997	*Croissant*

Other works include: Nagrin has also choreographed for others, including an off-Broadway production of *Volpone* in 1957, and for *The Emperor Jones* at the Boston Arts Festival in 1964.

Publications

By NAGRIN: books—

How to Dance Forever: Surviving Against the Odds, New York, 1988.

Editor, *Helen Tamiris, Selections from the First Draft of an Uncompleted Autobiography,* Tempe, Arizona, 1989.

Dance and the Specific Image: Improvisation, Pittsburgh and London, 1994.

The Six Questions: Acting Technique for Dance Performance, Pittsburgh, 1997.

By NAGRIN: articles—

"In Quest of a Dance," *Dance Magazine* (New York), September 1951.
"American in the Fiji Islands; Half-way Around the World to Choreograph Dances for a Film [*His Majesty O'Keefe*]," *Dance Magazine* (New York), February 1954.
"The High Fidelity of Vision," *Impulse*, 1960.
Contributor, "Dancer's Notes," *Dance Perspectives*, Summer 1969.
Contributor, "Thirteen Replies For a Video Editorial," *Dance Scope* (New York), Spring/Summer 1975.
"Effective Videotaping of Dance," *Update Dance/USA*, November 1987.
"Dance Video," *Dance Magazine*, March 1988.
"Nine Points on Making Your Own Dance Video," *Dance Theatre Journal* (London), Summer 1988.
"Helen Tamiris and the Dance Historians," *Dance History Scholar*, 1989.
"Opinion: Artists Help Humanity Confront Its Own Image, World's Mysteries," *ASU Insight* (Tempe, Arizona), 1 October 1990.

On NAGRIN: books—

Gruen, John, *People Who Dance: 22 Dancers Tell Their Own Stories,* Princeton, New Jersey, 1988.
McDonagh, Don, *The Complete Guide to Modern Dance*, Garden City, New York, 1976.
Schlundt, Christena L., *Daniel Nagrin: A Chronicle of His Professional Career*, Berkeley, 1997.

On NAGRIN: articles—

Hering, Doris, "Daniel Nagrin and Donald McKayle with Guest Artists," *Dance Magazine*, July 1951.
Todd, Arthur, "*Volpone*, Movement By Daniel Nagrin,"*Dance Observer*, February 1957.
Horst, Louis, "Daniel Nagrin. . .," *Dance Observer*, December 1957.
———, "Daniel Nagrin," *Dance Observer*, April 1958.
Manchester, P. W., "Sophie Maslow and Company, Daniel Nagrin, Anna Sokolow Dance Company," *Dance News*, May 1959.
Marks, Marcia, "Daniel Nagrin, 92nd Street Y," *Dance Magazine*, June 1965.
Jackson, Harriet, "Daniel Nagrin," *Dance News*, June 1965.
Guest, Ann Hutchinson, "Daniel Nagrin, LAMDA Theatre (London)," *Dancing Times*, July 1967.
Fortney, Alan Jon, "Daniel Nagrin, an Evening of Dance and Cinema,"*Dance Magazine,* August 1968.
Fortney, Alan Jon, "Daniel Nagrin, *The Peloponnesian War*," *Dance Magazine*, January 1969.
Gruen, John, "Spotlight On: Daniel Nagrin," *Dance Magazine* (New York), June 1976.
Jowitt, Deborah, "The Dance Writes," *Village Voice*, 16 August 1988.
Loney, Glenn Meredith, "Daniel Nagrin's Magnet: *The Peloponnesian War*," *Dance Magazine,* August 1970.
Merry, Suzanne, "Daniel Nagrin," *Dance Magazine*, March 1979.
Pastore, Louise, "Daniel Nagrin," *Dance Magazine*, March 1975.
Robertson, Allen, "Daniel Nagrin in Sam Shepard's *Jacaranda*, " *Dance Magazine*, September 1979.
Schlundt, Christena L, "Daniel Nagrin: A Sketch for a Dance Portrait," *Dance History Scholar*, 1983.

Daniel Nagrin performing *Ruminations*, 1976. Photograph © Johan Elbers.

Tobias, Tobi, "Grace Despite Everything," *New York*, 18 April 1994.
Vaughan, David, "This, That, Is and Isn't. . .Daniel Nagrin," *Dance Magazine*, May 1975.

*   *   *

Two things strike a person who sees the studio photos of Daniel Nagrin that accompanied a June 1976 *Dance Magazine* profile by John Gruen. Nagrin is captured in movement, and he appears slender, muscular, powerful, moving like a soldier or—in a shot by Beverly Owen—a martial arts fighter. Thus one is moved to wonder, can this really be a man nearly 60 years old? And yet he was that old then. He had, after all, known Martha Graham and studied with her and other greats mid-century, not least among them Helen Tamiris, with whom he shared a brief and tempestuous marriage.

The other quality of Nagrin's appearance, in those 1976 photos at least, was the resemblance of his own ruggedly handsome features to those of the older Al Pacino of the 1990s. There is a certain poetic symmetry in that, because both men in their ways helped shape the image of the gangster in American art. But whereas Pacino's much more well-known portrayal of Michael Corleone in the *Godfather* movies helped perpetuate a mythic ideal conspicuously removed from the lives of real gangsters, Nagrin's haunted solo in *Strange Hero* fits the decidedly unromantic reality of a man always looking over his shoulder.

Strange Hero, which Nagrin first performed in a hotel ballroom on Eighth Avenue and 51st Street in New York in the spring of

1948, showcased many of the elements by which Nagrin's work would become characterized in his long and varied career. There was the sense of the doomed man struggling with his world; there was the powerful, unmistakably masculine sense of movement; and there was the solitude of Nagrin by himself on the stage—"the great loner of American dance," as Gruen called him. Twenty-eight years after its debut, when Nagrin put on a solo performance for Gruen during the course of the interview, the work had not lost any of its unsettling power—any more than its composer, seemingly frozen in his prime, had lost his.

Indicative of that power is the enormous width, breadth, and depth of Nagrin's career, any one element of which could have constituted an entire life's work for some. He danced on Broadway in the 1940s, and Oscar Hammerstein himself picked him to play the chief Indian in *Annie Get Your Gun*. (Audiences remembered the impact of his performance; Nagrin remembered the "slightly indecent little flap" that constituted his entire costume.) He served in the Army Air Force during World War II, though poor eyesight gained him an early discharge. He studied and/or worked with Graham, Anna Sokolow, Hanya Holm, and many others—including Helen Tamiris.

When he first auditioned for Tamiris in 1941, she rejected him. So Nagrin went away and studied with two other dancers, Sue Remos and Fanya Chochem, for a year. He might never have approached Tamiris again, but one of his partners wanted to get into Tamiris's Unity House organization. So he auditioned again, and this time, he said, "Helen Tamiris, toward whom I felt rather hostile, liked what she saw."

It was the beginning of a stormy relationship that would last for the next 25 years, but long before their personal involvement began was their professional interaction. Tamiris inspired him with her instinctive, nonverbal, impulsive style, though it would be a long time before they ever joined forces in the Tamiris-Nagrin Dance Company in 1960. In the meantime, Nagrin had his stint on Broadway, and very nearly gave up dancing.

Nagrin hadn't really meant to become a dancer; he had intended to be a psychiatrist—and of course, he did become one of sorts in the end, though he explored the psyche from the stage, not the couch. On Broadway he has said he felt "like a trained monkey," but then dancer Paul Draper inspired him toward what would become his trademark, solo dance shows. "Why aren't you doing solo concerts?" Draper demanded of him one day in 1955, after a performance of his own. Nagrin had no answer, though he didn't believe his body could stand the beating it would take in an entire 45- or 60-minute performance. Initially he suffered back pains—he was, after all, 40 years old when he began putting on these shows in 1957—but he soon developed a workable solo-concert formula.

Nagrin and Tamiris married in 1946. They formed their dance company three years later, but in Nagrin's words, "It turned out not to be an ideal way of working for me." The company lasted until 1963, the marriage not much longer. Tamiris died in 1966 of cancer, and Nagrin maintained a respect for her memory that promised to last longer than their partnership. Half a lifetime later, in 1989, he worked on editing her unfinished autobiography in Tempe, where he had moved in order to teach at the University of Arizona.

Teaching and writing constituted yet further avenues in which the mercurial Nagrin exercised his talent. Not only did he write numerous magazine pieces, he published several books, including 1997's *The Six Questions*. As for teaching, he did that quite literally all over the U.S. and Europe, from Connecticut to Hawaii at different points in his career. He also made several videos, and wrote on the making of videos under the tight budgetary constraints to which most dancers are subject.

At the conclusion of the 1976 interview, Nagrin had said, "The point is, rather than defining myself, I'd rather keep on working. Finally, work and more work is what it's all about!" His resume for the 20 years that followed seemed consistent with that earlier definition, and even as he approached his ninth decade, Nagrin remained a powerful and dynamic figure. In the midst of all this other activity, he managed to get married a second time in 1992, a few months short of his seventy-fifth birthday. By any measure, Daniel Nagrin's life has cut a deep swath in the world of modern dance and far beyond it.

—Judson Knight

NAM Jeong-ho
Korean dancer, choreographer, and educator

Born: 31 December 1952, in Kim'chon, South Korea, 31 December 1952. **Education:** Studied ballet from age 10; Ewha Women's University, B.A. 1975, M.A. 1978; Universtaire Haute Bretagne Rennes II, DEA 1979; University of Paris (Sorbonne), diplome de danse, 1981. **Career:** Instructor at IPAC, 1979-81; member of Jean Gaudin Dance Company, 1980-81; returned to Korea 1982; started career as dancer and choreographer; currently professor of dance, Korean National University of Arts. **Awards:** Copernas Award, Modern Dance Association of Korea, 1990; special award from Saitama International Dance Competition in Japan, 1990; Kim Su-gun Award of Culture and Art, 1993.

Roles

1980	Solist in *Voyage au bout du monde* (Gaudin), Jean-Gaudin Dance Company, Paris
1992	Solist in *Wither* (Kaoru), Tokyo Modern Dance Company, Tokyo

Works

1982	*Bonjour* (solo; mus. Bach), Space Theatre, Seoul
	Diagonal (solo; no mus.), Catholic Center, Space Theatre, Seoul
	Continuity (solo; mus. Kang Tae-whan), National Theatre of Korea, Seoul
1983	*Quartet* (mus. Pierre Henri), Nam Jeong-ho and others, Munye Theatre, Seoul
	Secret Garden (mus. Choi In-sik), Nam Jeong-ho and dancers, Munye Theatre, Seoul
1984	*Five Episodes* (mus. Keith Jarreth), Lee Eun-Kyu and others, National Theatre of Korea, Seoul
	Play I (mus. Ren Aubry), Nam Jeong-ho and dancers, Munye Theatre, Seoul
1985	*Play II* (mus. Ren Aubry), Korea Modern Dance Company, National Theatre of Korea, Seoul
1986	*Balloon Heart* (mus. John Surman), Nam Jeong-ho and others, Changmuchoomter, Seoul

1987	*Let's Go Out to Take the Moon* (mus. Korea Children Folksong), Nam Jeong-ho and others, Saitama Art Center, Japan
1988	*Self-Portrait* (solo; mus. Etienne Swartz), Munye Theatre, Seoul
	Les enfants terribles (mus. various, arranged Nam Jeong-ho), Modern Dance Group Zoom, Kyoungsung University, Pusan
1989	*Waiting for Somebody* (mus. Eric Serra), Hoam Art Hall, Seoul
	A Child Who Caught the Moon (solo; mus. Korea Children Folks song), Munye Theatre, Seoul
1990	*Kasiri* (solo; mus. Park Byoung-chun), Munye Theatre, Seoul
	L'après midi d'un faune (mus. Ren Aubry), Pusan Municipal Dance Company, Pusan Culture Center, Pusan
	Duet Dialogue (mus. Michelle Portal), Nam Jeong-ho and Lee Eun-kye, Kyoungsung University, Pusan
	Hey, What's Going on Over There? (mus. Jang Doug-sahn), Nam Jeong and others, Munye Theatre and Hackjun Theatre, Seoul
1991	*Like a Rolling Stone* (mus. Steve Reich), Modern Dance Group Zoom, Kyoungsung University, Pusan, and Actor Theatre, Tokyo
1993	*Les Lavageuses* (mus. Saitoh Tetsu), Seoul Art Center Opening Festival, Modern Dance Group Zoom, Seoul Arts Center, Seoul
	Les Lavageuses II (mus. Saitoh Tetsu), Ch'angwon City Dance Company, Ch'angwon Citizen Hall, Ch'angwon
1994	*Wanderers* (mus. Meredith Monk), Modern Dance Group Zoom, Pusan Cultural Center, Pusan
1995	*Bride* (solo; mus. Lee Geu-yong), Hong Kong Culture Center, Hong Kong
1996	*Go Out* (solo; mus. Park Byoung-chon), Munye Theatre, Seoul
1997	*I Danced in the Dream* (solo; mus. Ma Da-won), Seoul Arts Center, Seoul

Nam Jeong-ho performing *Kasiri*, 1990. Photograph © Choi Young-mo.

Publications

By NAM: books—

New Dance, translated by Margery J. Turner, Seoul, 1988.
Introduction to Modern Dance, Seoul, 1995.

On NAM: articles—

Lee Soon-yeol, "Overveiw of Nam Jeong-ho Works," *Magazine Space* (Seoul), 1993.

*   *   *

Nam Jeong-ho's freshness has grown since her first encounter with audiences with *Bonjour,* after her return from France in 1982. She was actively involved in dancing while educating herself in France—a last period of apprenticeship. She made a dramatic impression on European audiences as a nymph from the orient while performing as a member of Jean Gaudin Dance Company of Paris.

But, her intention wasn't to remain as a "nymph" or a dancer. Nam Jeong-ho turned to choreography from her first performance after returning home, and audiences welcomed her innovative style.

Several factors contributed to this success. It wasn't just because it was new to Korea's modern dance circles, which had mainly practiced the dancing style of Martha Graham. Korean audiences had been accustomed to somewhat somber, rigid forms of dance. The fresh impression of her dance no doubt resulted from the brilliance and vitality of her spirit as well as from the elasticity of her body. She is a stranger everytime we meet her and that is another factor of her freshness.

Like most other Korean professional dance artists, Nam Jeong-ho became a college professor and worked at Kyoungsung University's Department of Dance and Performing Arts in Pusan, the second largest city in Korea. While in Pusan, she introduced a variety of innovations.

In 1988, Nam Jeong-ho created Zoom Dance Company to further dance experimentation in Korea, taking the position of art director. The Zoom Dance Company grew to be one of Korea's foremost dance groups, performing frequently not only in Pusan but also in Seoul. The company has been acknowledged as "the most revitalizing dance group" in Korea.

In the same year, Nam Jeong-ho successfully planned the Beach Festival at Kwang-alli beach, inviting renowned guests from all over the world and providing young dancers with opportunities to practice and challenge their skills through performances and workshops. Subsequently, the Beach Festival has firmly established itself as an annual event.

Professor Nam Jeong-ho moved from her teaching position at Kyoungsung University to the Korean National University of Arts in 1996, but still leads the Beach Festival in Pusan. Among her various activities, the one that draws the most attention is her dance style. And despite the wide variety of her subject matter, in essence all these works constitute with a series of self-portraits. The most prominent manifestations of this self-portraiture are the subjects of children and play. Chae Hee-wan correctly refers to Nam Jeong-ho's dance as "an adult-produced children's world."

Despite her age, Nam Jeong-ho has retained a penchant for children's housekeeping play. Maybe she had no intention of getting out of infancy. Indeed, she may have rejected the idea of growing up all together, like the lad in Gunter Grass' Tin Drum. Despite the innocence and naivete that dominate her dance, it retains urban characteristics and the sophistication of modernism, which undercuts the essential innocence. Her dance numbers do not have the pure tranquility that Keats found in his Grecian Urn when he wrote, "Thou still unravished bride of quietness."

"Revealing of concealment, making a caricature of quotidian gestures, feline playfulness mixed with elegance, seriousness under the mark of comical expression;" such have been, as Chae Hee-wan rightly commented, the outstanding features of her dance. Everything is mixed and double layered and ambivalence presents itself in all of her works.

My Heart Laid Bare is ostensibly a self-portrait of French poet Charles Baudelaire. Yet this self-portrait, seemingly exposing all, is covered with villainous mask. Nam Jeong-ho often goes on stage wearing more than necessary layers of costumes, removing them one by one as her characters reveal themselves.

Some may consider Nam's dancing a bit light and depthless. As a matter of fact, her dances are light and cheerful. Her most light-hearted work is L'après midi d'un faune. The nymph always struggles to escape. A yearning for freedom and fear of capture are the innate characteristics of the nymph. These characteristics appear consistently in her works as an endless pursuit of change. Her continual search for the true portrayal of her own image through transformation will guide her performances and productions in the days ahead.

—Lee Soon-yeol

NEVILLE, Phoebe

American dancer, choreographer, and company director

Born: 28 September 1941, Swarthmore, Pennsylvania. **Education:** Wilson College, 1959-61; studied modern dance with Joyce Trisler, Daniel Nagrin and Helen Tamiris, Judith Dunn, Merce Cunningham, Nancy Meehan, Ruth Currier; studied ballet with Sonia Woichikowska, Aubrey Hitchens, Mia Slavenska, Peter Saul, Zena Rommett, Maggie Black; studied middle-eastern dance with Dunya, Anahid Sofian, Shamira. **Family:** Married 1) Philip Hipwell, 1969, 2) Philip Corner, 1996. **Career:** Dancer with Tamiris-Nagrin company, 1961-62, Judith Dunn, 1964, Elaine Summers, 1965, 1971, Carolee Schneemann, 1966, 1967, Meredith Monk, 1965, 1967-68, Elina Mooney, 1971-76; choreography presented at Clark Center

for the Performing Arts, 1962, 1963, Judson Memorial Church, 1966-70, Cubicolo, 1969-75, New York School for the Performing Arts, 1974-75; founded Phoebe Neville Dance Company, 1975; instructor, the Barlow School, 1968-71, Fieldston School, 1971-74; New York School for the the Performing Arts, 1974-76; Bennington College, 1981-83, 1987-88, Teavhers College of Columbia University, 1984; visiting lecturer, UCLA, 1984-86. **Awards:** Creative Artists Public Service Award, 1975; NEA fellowships 1975, 1979, 1980, 1985-87, 1992-94; Choreographic Fellow, New York Foundation for the Arts, 1989.

Works

1962	*Of the dark Air* (mus. Henry Cowell), solo, Clark Center for the Performing Arts, New York
1963	*Remnant* (mus. Alan Hovhaness), solo, Clark Center for the Performing Arts, New York
1966	*Terrible* (mus. Joe Jones; amplification of performers' breath), Neville with Judith Kuemmerle, Judson Memorial Church, New York
	Move (mus. Buddhist chants), Neville with Kenneth King and Meredith Monk, Judson Memorial Church, New York
	Ragaroni (mus. The Little Flowers), solo, Judson Memorial Church, New York
	Dance for Mandolins (mus. Prokofiev), Neville with Kenneth King and Meredith Monk, Judson Memorial Church, New York
1967	*Mask Dance,* solo, Judson Memorial Church, New York
	Eowyn's Dance, solo, Judson Memorial Church, New York
1968	*Nova* (mus. Messiaen), Neville with Sally Bowden, Toni Lacativa, and Micki Goodman, Judson Memorial Church, New York
	Light Rain w/Philip Hipwell (accompaniment Bob Dylan poetry), Judson Memorial Church, New York
1969	*Edo Wrap* w/Philip Hipwell (mus. Gagaku), Judson Memorial Church, New York
	Ninja (green), solo, Judson Memorial Church, New York
	Caryatid (mus. Alan Lloyd), solo, Judson Memorial Church, New York
	Termination (mus. Monteverdi), solo, Cubicolo, New York
1970	*Terminal* w/Micki Goodman, Cubicolo, New York
	Untitled Duet w/Philip Hipwell (mus. Messiaen), Judson Memorial Church, New York
1972	*Memory* (mus. Neville and Hipwell), Neville with Hipwell and Christopher Beck, Cubicolo, New York
	Night Garden (mus. Gagaku), Neville with Hipwell and Christopher Beck, Cubicolo, New York
	Triptych, Panels I and II (mus. Meredith Monk), solo, Cubicolo, New York
1973	*Triptych* (complete; mus. Meredith Monk), solo, Cubicolo, New York
	Passage in Silence, Neville with Christopher Beck, Cubicolo, New York
	Solo (mus. Hovda), Anthony LaGiglia, Cubicolo, New York
1974	*Cartouche* (mus. Purcell, arranged for tape), Neville with Christopher Beck, Cubicolo, New York
	Ladydance (mus. Hovhaness, arranged for tape), solo

1975   *Oracles* (mus. Hovda), Neville with Ellen Likvornik, Susan Okuhara, and Marleen Pennison, Washington Square Methodist Church, New York

1976   *Mosaic* (mus. M. Monk), Neville with Tryntje Shapli, Kathy Dumesnil, and Marleen Pennison, Riverside Dance Festival

    Tigris (mus. Carole Weber), Neville with Tryntje Shapli and Marleen Pennison

    Oran (mus. traditional bagpipes), Neville with John Dayger, TEARS, New York

1978   *Unnamed,* Neville with John Dayger, Riverside Dance Festival

    Passage, solo, Harvard Summer Dance Festival

    Dodona (solo version; mus. Skip LaPlante), Annabelle Gamson, SUNY at Purchase

1979   *Sandweaving* (mus. Hovhaness), Sheila Kaminsky, Washington Square Methodist Church, New York

    Overcast (mus. Chopin), Neville with John Dayger and Tryntje Shapli, Washington Square Methodist Church, New York

1980   *Dodona* (trio version; mus. LaPLante), Neville with Sheila Kaminsky and Tryntje Shapli, Washington Square Methodist Church, New York

    Nightfield (mus. traditional Irish), Sheila Kaminsky with Peter Davis, Dance Theatre Workshop, New York

1981   *Voyage* (mus. Rachmaninov), Neville with Jessica Fogel, Vic Stornant, Sheila Kaminsky, and Tryntje Shapli, Theater 46, New York

1982   *Nana por Nada* (mus. de Falla), Barbara Roan, Dance Theatre Workshop, New York

    Dolmen (mus. M. Monk), Neville with John Dayger, Sheila Kaminsky, Tryntje Shapli, Peter Bass and Peter Davis, Larry Richardson's Dance Gallery, New York

1983   *Anitergium* (mus. tarantella), solo, Larry Richardson's Dance Gallery, New York

1984   *Palantir* (mus. Hovda), Tryntje Shapli, Danspace Saint Mark's, New York

    5 Movements, Movements 2 & 3 (mus. Scott Johnson), Neville with Tryntje Shapli, Peter Davis, Vicki Lloid, Ted Marks, Chris Burnside, and Carol McDowell, Danspace Saint Mark's, New York

    Asteriana (mus. deFalla), Neville with Christopher Beck

1985   *Night Ride from Vaucouleurs* (mus. Stravinsky), Tryntje Shapli, California State University, Long Beach

1987   *5 Movements, Movements 1 & 4* (mus. Scott Johnson), Nikolais/Louis Dance Lab, New York

1988   *Watch This Space,* solo

    Anitergium II (Hohodowndownho) (mus. Josef Wittman), Neville with Tryntje Shapli

    5 Movements (complete; mus. Scott Johnson), Neville with others, Dance Theatre Workshop, New York

1990   *Sounding,* solo, Nikolais/Louis Dance lab, New York

1991   *Elegy* (mus. Faruk Tekbilek), solo, Warren St. Performance Loft, New York

1992   *Amazon Songs* (mus. Buen Garnas, Garborek), Warren St. Performance Loft, New York

1993   *Prelude/Phoebessence* (mus. Messiaen, Susu and the Cairo Cats), solo, Danspace St. Marks, New York

1995   *Presence* (mus. Philip Corner), Neville with Trish Doherty and Katherine Howard, Danspace Project

1996   *Mad Joan* (mus. La Nef), Neville with Katherine Howard, Edens Expressway

Publications

On NEVILLE: books—

Anderson, Jack, *Choreography Observed*, Iowa City, 1987.

Jacob, Ellen and Christopher Jonas, *Dance in New York*, New York, 1980.

Seigel, Marcia, *Watching the Dance Go By,* Boston, 1977.

On NEVILLE: articles—

Anderson, Jack, "Phoebe Neville: Going Her Own Way," *Dance Magazine*, February 1977.

Kronen, H. B., "Phoebe Neville: Images and Ideas," *Danscope,* 1977.

*　　*　　*

Phoebe Neville was born on 28 September 1941 in Swarthmore, Pennsylvania. Interested in art and music from a young age, she was sent by her parents to a summer arts camp in the Adirondacks to study cello; it was there that she was introduced to modern dance by Joyce Trisler, a teacher at the camp. Almost immediately after taking up serious study, she pushed herself too hard, resulting in a serious knee injury requiring several surgeries. Upon her recovery the following summer, she went to Jacob's Pillow, where she studied ballet with Margaret Craske and was enthralled by a solo dance concert given by Daniel Nagrin.

Neville subsequently studied dance for one year at Wilson College in Pennsylvania and was a member of the school's Orchesis group. Nagrin's path crossed Neville's again when he visited campus. As a result of working with her in his master class, she was invited to apprentice with the Tamiris-Nagrin Company. Daniel Nagrin and Helen Tamiris were ideal mentors for Neville.

Tamiris did not believe in dancers having to wait until later in their careers to choreograph, and she got Neville started almost at once. This was important because Neville felt she was getting a late start in the world of dance to begin with; additionally, she knew that due to her injuries she could never be a certain kind of professional dancer, for example, a member in a company with a rigorous performance schedule. Tamiris influenced Neville's composition method as well. Neville describes Tamiris' approach as one primarily concerned with internal motivation, an acting approach. She stressed how characterization and dramatic situation influenced movement.

In 1962 Neville debuted as a choreographer in New York. Her first dance, *Of the Dark Air*, appeared on a Clark Center Young Choreographers program. Neville enrolled in several workshops at the Judson Church and also helped establish Studio Nine, named after the space on the Lower East Side she shared with dancer/choreographers such as Meredith Monk and Kenneth King. Though she was involved throughout the 1960s with some of the most important dance production organizations of the time, her work has not received the attention of some of her contemporaries and early collaborators. She has had a singular career, one in which her creations didn't much correspond with major trends. While other postmodern American choreographers began working in mixed media and produced large, theatrical pieces, Neville was an Expressionist, following more along the lines of the Duncan-Wigman tradition.

Neville has relied on movement alone for the creation of effects. The influence of her study of T'ai Chi is evident; each motion is

Phoebe Neville in *Elegy*, 1991. Photograph © Jim Moore.

calculated and precise and the arms are often the focus of attention. Her works are small in scale, with a minimalist attention to detail. They are most often solos or duets, and rarely require more than three or four dancers. They are also notably dark and brief. Mystery and enigma are words often associated with Neville's work. *Cartouche* (1974) is a signature piece. As in other dances of this period, Neville took inspiration for her poses from paintings, in this case those of Michelangelo and Goya. The dance begins with Neville sprawled face down on the floor; a man crouches nearby, watching. The man leaps onto her, balances himself on her back, and makes the big emphatic gestures of an enthused rhetorician. Abruptly, Neville comes to life, grabs his ankles and eventually succeeds in toppling him. In the final pose, the two have traded places, with Neville standing on the back of the man. She stares out at the audience with her face contorted in a silent scream. As the dance was originally staged, this grappling of man and woman was readily interpreted as a feminist study. She later reset *Cartouche* to Bob Dylan's *Masters of War*. In this version the woman is wearing jeans and the man wears a business suit and carries a briefcase; the dance was now open to interpretation as a social commentary. Neville herself has repeatedly asserted that she does not create political dances, although her denials have been called disingenuous. She would have *Cartouche* seen as simply a meditation on power.

Neville's work is difficult to separate from her own performance in it. She inhabits her dances with intense concentration and clarity, with no gesture wasted or incidental. In the works considered Neville's best, the particular gestures, motions and images she chooses give expression to her inner experience in a way that is accessible to the audience. In *Memory* (1972) for example, the lighting is ingeniously manipulated by the dancers themselves, carrying lamps, candles or matches. In the most powerful scene, Neville appears on stage wearing asbestos gloves and a mask. She holds a burning fire before her and pours it from hand to hand.

Her work has been viewed as less successful when its Expressionism crosses over into to self-indulgence and pretentiousness; the self-generative 1993 work *Phoebessence* has been noted in this regard. Critics have often found her relentless enigmatic qualities have a tendency to give way to the gothic or surreal; their strangeness repels.

Neville has worked steadily since the early 1960s and has continued to work with other key dance figures. She has created a dance to Meredith Monk's score in *To Dolman Music* (1982) and was commissioned by Barbara Roan to create *Nana for Nada* (1982). Her new work premieres almost yearly in New York venues such as St. Mark's Danspace. Her work in the early 1990s was marked by langor as she turned to the music of North Africa and the Near East, with works such as *Elegy* (1991) and *Amazon Songs* (1992) set to the work of composers such as Faruk Tekbilek, Jan Garbarek, and Susa and the Cairo Cats.

—Valerie Vogrin

NEW DANCE GROUP

American dance company and school

Founded in 1932 in New York City by Miriam Blecher (and others); joined Worker's Dance League to bring "dance to the masses"

and soon established an outstanding school in all forms of dance (modern, ballet, ethnic, social/recreational) to train professional dancers, opening doors to students of all races and creeds; supported the Dudley-Maslow-Bales trio from 1942-54; incorporated as a non-profit organization with officers Jane Dudley, Nona Schurmann, and Judith Delman, 1944; after many moves, school was established at its present location, 254 West 47th Street, 1954; still serves hundreds of students, including Broadway dancers; present artistic director, Rick Schussel; Suzy Zimmerman, administrative director. In its six-decade history, over 1300 dancers have served as faculty, performers, staff. Outstanding dancers and dancer-choreographers include: Ronnie Aul, William Bales, Talley Beatty, Jane Dudley, Jean Erdman, Eve Gentry, Joseph Gifford, Hadassah, Sophie Maslow, Donald McKayle, Pearl Primus, and Charles Weidman.

Publications

Jacob, Ellen and Christopher Jones, *Dance in New York,* New York, 1980.
The New Dance Group Gala Concert: An Historic Retrospective of NDG Presentations, 1930s-1970s, American Dance Guild, 1993.

*   *   *

The New Dance Group, (NDG) a unique institution in the history of American dance training and social commitment, was founded in February 1932 by a group of second generation American dancers from Hanya Holm's Wigman School: Nell Anyon, Miriam Blecher, Fanya Geltman, Edith Langbert, Pauline Shrifman, and Grace Wylie. The New Dance Group's original aim was to make "dance a viable weapon for the struggles of the working class, " and "to reach people who had never had an opportunity either to dance or to attend recitals." Theirs was social and political agenda—to dance on personal subjects in a clear, almost simplistic manner, in order to reach a mass audience. The curriculum originally included courses on dance theory, technique at several levels (Dalcroze, Duncan, Graham, Humphrey-Weidman), folk, Hindu, various ethnic forms, teacher training, choreography, children's classes, and recreation/social dance—as well as Marxist theory!

With the advent of Roosevelt's Works Project Administration in 1935, the Worker's Dance League changed its name to the American Dance Association, and became the booking agent for unemployed dancers, while NDG flourished as a school and performing organization, evolving from revolutionary to more subtle artistic endeavors. In 1944, led by a faculty board of directors, NDG became a non-profit organization, maintaining studios with low tuition rates, serving 1000 adults and 300 children taking 1,800 classes weekly. Its articles of incorporation state its goal as "to foster the art of dancing and particularly the art of modern dance technique" and "to maintain and operate a school for training and instruction in modern dance technique and other forms of dancing," as well as "to financially aid and assist in the development of the literature, history and technique of various forms of dancing" and "promote a more general appreciation and comprehension of the cultural significance and value of the art of dancing."

The original Holm dancers, Miriam Blecher, Jane Dudley, and Eve Gentry were soon joined by Graham dancers Sophie Maslow and Jean Erdman, and Nona Schurman who taught Humphrey-Weidman technique. Masculine participation was evident by the work of Charles Weidman and José Limón and especially William

Bales. In 1942 Dudley, Maslow, and Bales united to form the Dudley-Maslow-Bales trio that is remembered fondly for such works as *Short Story* (Dudley, 1940), *Folksay* (Maslow, 1942) and *Es Mujer* (Bales, 1942) and well as the delightful *Lonely Ones* (Dudley, 1946) based on Steig cartoons, and *Bach Suite* (1942) and *As Poor Richard Says* (1943) both of which were done as "collective choreography." The trio toured extensively during and after World War II and made the NDG name known throughout the United States.

From the beginning NDG choreographers drew upon traditional sources, endlessly defining and extending the American dance experience. Jazz, square dance, ballroom and folk patterns from the "melting pot" of dance characterized such choreography as *Four Wall Blues* (Eve Gentry, 1941), *Jazz Trio* (Lee Sherman, 1941), *Dustbowl Ballads* (Maslow, 1941) and *Harmonica Breakdown* (Dudley, 1943). A noteworthy part of the NDG philosophy was the early inclusion of peoples representing the diversity of American life. Pearl Primus (*The Negro Speaks of Rivers*, 1943; *Strange Fruit*, 1943) and Donald McKayle (*Games*, 1951; *Rainbow Round My Shoulders,* 1959) are two of the many outstanding professionals who trained as scholarship students and went on the champion black dance. To the list add choreographer Talley Beatty whose *Danse au Noveau Cirque Paris* was premiered by the NDG in 1963. Jean Erdman taught Hawaiian dance in the early days and Hadassah (Hadassah Spira) performed not only dances with Hebraic themes, (*Shuvi Nafshi*, 1947), but also Hindu dance, particularly *Broadway Hindu* (1942) under the influence of Denishawn and jazz dancer Jack Cole.

Barbara Lloyd, writing in the *Borzoi Book of Modern Dance* in 1949, gives this perspective on NDG: "The story of the NDG is one of constant experiment, of continual branching out, of conceiving new ideas and coming to new conclusions. With its constantly changing personnel and headquarters, [and] its multitudinous performances, its growth has been bumpy, its life haphazard. That it has had so much influence while growing, that it has reorganized and stabilized itself into a thriving dance center and is still growing, is one of the modern miracles." Rick Schussel, NDG's current artistic director, boasts six studios, 29 dance instructors teaching 10 styles, and nine musicians—and is planning an expansion to include an additional midtown location. In its 66th year, NDG still sponsors Choreographers' Showcases, that are, according to its commemorative anniversary program, "encouraging the exploration of choreography as an art form to the cutting edge—and beyond."

—Joanna G. Harris

NEW DANCE TRILOGY

Theatre Piece

Choreography: Doris Humphrey with Charles Weidman
Music: Wallingford Reigger
Set Design: Erika Klein
Costume Design: Pauline Lawrence
First Performance: Guild Theatre, New York, 19 January 1936
Original Dancers: Doris Humphrey, Charles Weidman, José Limón, William Bales, Katherine Litz, Sybil Shearer, Louise Allen, Joseph Belsky, George Bockman, Kenneth Bostock, Jerry Davidson, Leticia Ide, Miriam Kradovsky, Ada Korvin, Joan Levy, Katherine Manning, Edith Orcutt, Beatrice Seckler, and Lily Verne

With My Red Fires

Choreography: Doris Humphrey
Music: Wallingford Reigger
Set Design: Gerard Gentile
Costume Design: Pauline Lawrence
First Performance: The Armory, Bennington School of the Dance, 13 August 1936; reconstructed in 1972 at the American Dance Festival
Original Dancers: Charles Weidman (Young Man), Katherine Litz (Young Woman), Doris Humphrey (Matriarch), Lillian Burgess and Maxine Cushing (Choric Figures), and Louise Allen, William Bales, William Canton, Philip Gordon, Ada Korvin, Miriam Kradovsky, Paul Leon, Joan Levy, José Limón, William Matons, Edith Orcutt, Beatrice Seckler, Sybil Shearer, Lily Verne and members of the Bennington College Workshop

New Dance

Choreography: Doris Humphrey with Charles Weidman
Music: Wallingford Reigger
Costume Design: Pauline Lawrence
First Performance: The Armory, Bennington School of the Dance, 3 August 1935; reconstructed in 1972 at the American Dance Festival
Original Dancers: Doris Humphrey, Charles Weidman, Beatrice Seckler, Sybil Shearer, Katherine Litz, Morris Bakst, William Bales, George Bockman, Kenneth Bostock, Noel Charise, Jerry Davidson, Ezra Friedman, Maurice Gilbert, Ada Korvin, Miriam Kradovsky, Joan Levy, Katherine Manning, William Matons, Edith Orcutt, Harris Poble, and Lee Sherman

Publications

Articles—

Humphrey, D., "New Dance," in *Modern Dance in America: The Bennington Years,* ed. S. A. Kriegsman, Boston, 1981.

*   *   *

Writing about Doris Humphrey's *New Dance Trilogy* in his 1936 book, *America Dancing*, critic John Martin pronounced: "The three sections which are on related themes constitute a single work of epic proportions, and though the perspective of time may alter the first estimate of its value, it looks at this close range very like the most important composition yet produced in the American Dance." *Theatre Piece*, *With My Red Fires*, and *New Dance*, too long to present in a single evening's performance, constituted an ambitious summary of what Humphrey believed modern dance could achieve. The three works encompassed a range of theatrical styles: the satirical mode in *Theatre Piece*, choral drama in *With My Red Fires*, and abstract, pure dance in *New Dance*. As she wrote in 1981, in the final piece of the trilogy, *New Dance,* Humphrey presented a utopian vision "of the world as it could be and should be: a modern brotherhood of mankind" whose seed developed out of her critique of modern life presented in the first two pieces.

While *New Dance* was intended to be the last section of the trilogy, it was the first to be choreographed. Lasting 40 minutes, it was the longest piece to develop from a single movement idea (rather than a suite of separate pieces) that any American modern dancer had up until then attempted. The dance vocabulary itself develops throughout the piece from simple leg and foot movements in simple floor patterns to movements of the whole body along increasingly dynamic circular pathways around the stage. Two leaders, danced by Humphrey and Charles Weidman, started by performing a duet then gradually led their dancers (who were seated at the side of the stage on boxes), into the middle to dance. First Humphrey brought on the women, then Weidman brought on the men, then all danced together. After a pause there followed the "Variations and Conclusion." Using the now familiar vocabulary of dynamic and exuberant movement—with its sweeping, off-centre turns that use the body's momentum—and creating complex centrifugal series of floor patterns for the group, all the dancers took it in turns to perform some solo material before gradually taking their place on the cubes that had been moved from the wings to a stepped tower centre stage. This high energy finale left many critics with a feeling of radiance and optimism. It demonstrated Humphrey's positivist, humanistic belief that the individual could achieve more through involvement with the group than he or she could do on their own.

The rectangular stage boxes and some of the movement motifs also appeared in the other two parts of the trilogy. *Theatre Piece*, which only now exists in photographs and descriptions, satirised the competitiveness of the modern world with sections showing office work, sports, and a madcap race, while a detached "Protestant," danced by Humphrey, deplores the cruelty that surrounds her. *With My Red Fires* is a narrative piece which explores the conflict between a powerful matriarch (initially danced by Humphrey) who uses her charismatic appeal to arouse and manipulate the community, and her daughter (initially Katherine Litz) who, against her mother's wishes, falls in love with a man (initially Weidman). It contains spectacular sections for a large chorus of dancers. Like Weidman's *Lynchtown* (1935) with which it has been compared, the piece is an indictment of small town intolerance and lack of ethical values.

New Dance was premiered at the Bennington College summer school in 1935, without the "Variations and Conclusions," which were finished in time for the New York premiere of *Theatre Piece* in January 1936. *With My Red Fires* was created during the 1936 summer school at Bennington and first performed with a cast of 45, when it was presented on alternate nights with *New Dance* and *Theatre Piece*. All three pieces remained in the company's repertory until 1942. "Variations and Conclusions" was notated in 1949, and during the 1950s Humphrey taught it, together with parts of *With My Red Fires,* during repertory classes at the Juilliard School in New York. Weidman oversaw reconstructions of *New Dance* and *With My Red Fires* at the American Dance Festival in 1972 where they were filmed.

—Ramsay Burt

NEW ZEALAND (AOTEAROA)

Modern dance in Aotearoa (the indigenous name for New Zealand) has been strongly influenced by American models, both modern and postmodern. It is also inflected by dance developments from Europe but has a local flavour and eclecticism that make it distinctive. New Zealand was once a colony of the British Empire and although small in both landmass and population it has produced an extraordinary amount of dance activity.

Maud Allan was the first professional modern dancer to tour and perform here in 1914, and there is evidence that teachers trained under Margaret Morris in England began teaching in this country in the early 1920s. Morris herself had been taught by Raymond Duncan, brother to the more famous Isadora, but went on to develop her own highly systematised dance pedagogy. Others relocated to Aotearoa in the face of European world wars. Gisa Taglicht arrived from Vienna in 1939 and taught movement and rhythmical gymnastics at the Wellington YWCA for 20 years. She also taught dance to a variety of trainee teachers and nurses and was tutor in movement for NZ Players and NZ Opera Company. The Austrian choreographer/director Gertrude Bodenweiser briefly settled in Wellington in 1939, but moved on to Australia where she re-established her dance company and school. Her Sydney-based company toured New Zealand most successfully in 1947 and 1949.

New Zealander Shona Dunlop MacTavish was one of Bodenweiser's lead dancers. In 1958 she established a school in Dunedin and has for 40 years kept alive the Bodenweiser legacy. Her students Bronwyn Judge, Carol Brown and Jan Bolwell are now established choreographers and educators whose work is shaping yet another generation of dance professionals.

Rona Bailey, who had trained in physical education and recreation, majoring in dance, in California and New York, introduced the American approach to modern dance during the 1940s. Bailey combined with physical educators Philip and Olive Smithells, and Edith Sipos, a Czechoslovakian refugee with European dance training, in establishing the Wellington New Dance Group (1945-47). The goal of this amateur group was to enjoy the pleasure of moving well and to develop dance that could be used in school and community recreation. There was strong social realism in the content of the choreography especially with anti-war sentiments. The group disbanded when Smithells relocated to Dunedin in 1948 to direct the School of Physical Education at the University of Otago. His passion for dance was reflected in their curriculum and it has been a compulsory core subject ever since.

American modern dance approaches were introduced in Auckland from 1941 to 1949 by Margaret Barr, an alumnus of Cornish College who had worked with the Martha Graham Company before establishing dance at Dartington Hall in England. When her position at Dartington was given to Kurt Joos, she came to New Zealand, and taught dance and drama under the auspices of the Auckland University College and the Workers' Educational Association. A controversial figure, her emphasis as a choreographer was strongly socialist and her uncompromising dedication to dance and socialism challenged colleagues, students and audiences alike. She eventually relocated to Australia to establish herself there.

Harold Robinson, a pupil of Barr's, received a bursary in 1947 to study ballet at Sadler's Wells, London. When he finally returned home to Auckland in the 1950s he continued a form of Barr's work highly influenced by classical ballet. His classes were a catalyst for many dancers and teachers still working today.

Boujke van Zon arrived from Holland via Indonesia in 1948 and brought with her Central European creative dance ideals grounded in Laban's theories. She taught hundreds of dancers to appreciate dance, and offered classes in choreography. Her eldest daughter, Carla van Zon, who taught in the Van Zon School, and in the Limbs School, also established the annual IndepenDance dance platform in Auckland (1985-89), and managed both Taiao and the Douglas

Wright Dance Company before becoming executive director of the New Zealand International Festival of Arts in 1994.

Professional modern dance was established in New Zealand during the late-1970s, riding on the back of a dance boom. The New Zealand Students Arts Council had established thriving arts festivals and university touring circuits. Dance at Otago University continued to grow and was nourished by students who undertook graduate study in America and returned to teach on staff. One such person was John Casserley who with Gaylene Sciascia formed a short-term touring company in 1973 called New Dance '73. Sciascia now heads the dance programme at Whitireia Community Polytechnic. Two other New Zealanders in that company were Sue Renner, now dance lecturer at Dunedin College of Education, and Jennifer Shennan who is a dance critic, writer and teacher. The group never intended to be ongoing and disbanded after the tour was over, leaving a vacuum and many would-be dancers in its wake.

Dance-Arts helped fill that gap in Otago (from 1975) and although never fully professional, has received choreographic funding. In 1976 there were two attempts to form professional groups; Susan Jordan with Movement Theatre based in Auckland and Jamie Bull with Impulse Dance Theatre in Wellington. Although Auckland has the larger population base, Bull chose wisely to be near the centre of government funding in Wellington and secured a grant from the Arts Council at the outset. Thanks to her management, Impulse existed for six years as a professional company.

A second Auckland company, Limbs Dance Company, started in 1977 under the joint direction of Mary-Jane O'Reilly and Chris Jannides. Many of the company's dancers received their initial professional experience with Movement Theatre, which had become a dance-in-education company under the direction of Raewyn Schwabl (now Thorburn).

Both Impulse and Limbs were repertory companies, but they adopted divergent approaches to training, choreography and presentation. While Impulse was seen as highly professional, the less formal style of Limbs held greater popular appeal and established an audience who developed along with them over the next decade until a growing deficit forced Limbs to cease operation in 1989.

Alison East, a graduate from Otago's School of Physical Education who trained in America then returned to the teaching staff, was the first independent choreographer to establish her own company, Origins Dance Theatre (1980). Her emphasis was on environmental dance accompanied by live music in collaboration with visual artists. East went on to establish the Performing Arts School (now part of UNITEC), offering the first full-time modern dance training in the country.

The fortunes of modern dance in this country have risen and fallen with the availability of funding schemes. Several small dance companies, for example, were established under work scheme funding during the 1980s, later to be abandoned when government policy changed. Fusion Dance Theatre lasted in Napier from 1985 to 1989. Taiao (1985-1992) in Auckland had a longer life and its focus was on generating dance by and for Maori youth. Footnote Dance Company, established in 1983, continues today as a dance-in-education company. The Arts Council, while continuing to fund Limbs as the national modern dance company, in the late 1980s also established the Choreographic Commission to fund projects by independent choreographers working as solo artists or with pick-up dance companies. Benefitting from this scheme, independent choreographers Susan Jordan, Michael Parmenter and Douglas Wright established project-based companies to present their distinctive works. Despite New Zealand's location at the bottom of the world, Wright

has achieved international acclaim for his choreography, and Parmenter has also received a number of commissions from Australian dance companies.

In the 1990s, a host of freelance dancer/choreographers live a precarious existence, making new work with the support of grants and commissions, and performing with projects-based companies. Several platforms assist emerging and established choreographers in continuing their development. In Wellington since the mid 1980s, the annual Fringe Festival and Isadora's Tribe projects offer low risk opportunities. In Auckland the 1995 and 1996 Next Wave Dance Festivals has been a drawcard for many and have encouraged the formation of local projects-based companies such as Black Grace Dance Company. The increasing representation and involvement of Maori and Pacific dancers working in both indigenous and European modern dance is challenging mono-cultural ideas and structures and is an exciting development for this country. There is diversity in approach and choreography, especially with Catherine Chappell and Dancers, which is a mixed-ability group using contact improvisation.

Choreography in New Zealand has tended to be issue-based and to require the collaborative input of all participants. Although haphazardly funded, modern dance in Aotearoa continues as a vibrant art form despite the small total population of 3.5 million and the tyranny of distance from other centres of modern dance.

—Susan Jordan

NEWSON, Lloyd

Australian dancer, choreographer, and company director based in London

Born: 2 March 1957. **Education:** Postgraduate degree in psychology, Melbourne; educated at London Conmtemporay Dance School, 1979-81. **Career:** Dancer and choreographer with Extemporary Dance Theatre, 1981-85; founded DV8 Physical Theatre, 1986; reworked many DV8 productions for filming. **Awards:** Digital Dance Production Award, 1987, 1988; Manchester Evening News Theatre Award for Dance, 1987; London Dance and Performance Award for Choreography, 1988; *Time Out* Dance Award, 1989; Evening Standard Ballet Award, 1989; Digital Dance Premier Award, 1990; Golden Pegasus Award, Melbourne International Festival, 1990; London Dance and Performance Award, 1990; IMZ Dance Screen for Dead Dreams of Monochrome Men, 1990; Prudential Award for Dance, 1991; SADAC Award (France), 1992; Prudential Award to commission new work, 1992; London Dance and Performance Award, 1992; Festival International du Film sur l'Art for *Dead Dreams of Monochrome Men,* 1992; Grand Prix International Video-Danse/Pierre Cardin Award, 1993; IMZ Dance Screen (best camera rework) for *Strange Fish,* 1993; TZ Rose (Germany), 1993; Prix Italia (Special Prize, Music and Arts) for *Strange Fish,* 1994; Festival International Dance Visions for best choreography, 1994; Prix Italia (Special Prize, Music and Arts) for *Enter Achilles,* 1996; IMZ Dance Screen (best camera rework) for *Enter Achilles,* 1996; San Francisco International Film Festival, Golden Spire Award for *Enter Achilles,* 1997; Prix du Ministre-President du gouvernment de la region Bruxelles—Capitale Charles Pique for *Enter Achilles,* 1997; International Emmy Award for *Enter Achilles,* 1997. **Website:** http://www.dv8.co.uk.

Works

1982 *Breaking Images* (mus. Berio, Jones), Extemporary Dance
   Theatre, London
1983 *One Woman, One Woman* (mus. Satie, Throbbing Gristle),
   Extemporary Dance Theatre, London
1984 *Space Invaders,* Extemporary Dance Theatre, London
   The Cheapest Things in Life (mus. Summer, Presley),
   Extemporary Dance Theatre, London
   Beauty, Art, and the Kitchen Sink (mus. Delibes, Lai and
   Arthurs), Extemporary Dance Theatre, Epsom
1985 *Bein' a Part, Lonely Art,* DV8
1986 *My Sex, Our Dance,* DV8
1987 *Elemen Three Sex,* DV8
   Deep End, DV8
   My Body, Your Body, DV8
1988 *Dead Dreams of Monochrome Men,* DV8
1990 *"if only . . . ,"* DV8
1992 *Strange Fish,* DV8
1993 *MSM,* DV8
1995 *Enter Achilles,* DV8
1996 *Bound to Please,* DV8

Films and Videotapes

Dead Dreams of Monochrome Men, for the *South Bank* show, Bravo!
 Network, 1989.
Strange Fish, filmed for the BBC, 1992.
Enter Achilles, filmed for the BBC, 1995.

* * *

Lloyd Newson's work for DV8 Physical Theatre has never made for easy viewing. But since the company's inception in 1986, Newson has acquired a rock-solid reputation as the deviser of bracingly intelligent, challenging, uncompromising productions that speak in strong physical (but also, upon occasion, verbal) language about the way human beings live today. Those who know the work keep returning to DV8 in hope of seeing something more real and raw than is normally encountered within the dance arena. Newson, one of the most iconclastic members of the British dance-theatre community, usually does not disappoint. Much of the attraction of his work is how direct and strong it is, yet how open to interpretation.

Newson didn't discover dance until college. His first professional job was the result of his being the sole body to show up at an audition for a New Zealand touring troupe. Before that, his postgraduate degree in psychology led to a year's work in a Melbourne child psychiatric clinic, an early school at which to sharpen his gift as an observer of human nature. Eventually Newson migrated to London, existing for a spell on bread and jam. He landed a job as a movie usher and a scholarship to study at the London School of Contemporary Dance, a bastion for the Martha Graham technique.

Long and lithe, Newson spent the first half of the decade as a member of Extemporary Dance Theatre, one of Britain's most prominent, middle-scale modern touring troupes. There his dance skills met with occasional resistance, particularly because by this time he'd opted for shaving his head and some spectators found it hard to reconcile this look (now a Newson trademark) with their notion of a standard romantic, neoclassical dancer. Ultimately it was Newson himself who was unable to reconcile himself to

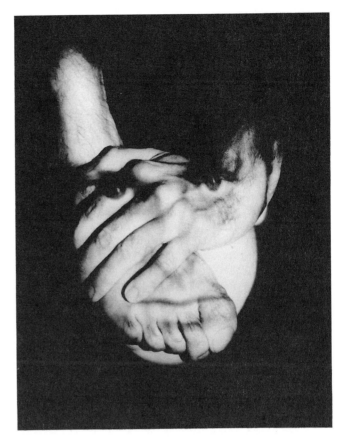

DV8 Physical Theatre: *Bound to Please.* Photograph by Thomas Gray.

Extemporary's aesthetics and hierarchy. He longed to do something more than initiate steps and assume attractive shapes. Though sometimes technically challenged, his personal politics remained unsatisfied.

Hence the formation of DV8 (the name both a pun and a reference to a video format). The company is composed of a shifting pool of dancers who work on a per-project basis, developing each piece through improvisation and experimentation. Newson guides them as they search out their own ways of working and moving. The source of the company's creative power is less the performers' technical proficiency than their ability and willingness to draw deep from the well of their own lives. The result has been a string of bold and unpredictable productions, their inherent purpose to lodge beneath one's skin and foster change, or at the very least a probing examination of attitudes.

My Sex, Our Dance, a duet for Newson and company co-founder Nigel Charnock, was built around issues of male trust, emotional and physical, apart from sex. Liz Ranken and Michelle Richecouer (another co-founder) joined them in *Deep End,* a dangerously intense barrage of sexual politics that had some feminists up in arms. Both pieces walked a tricky line between tenderness and brutality, each a confrontation on the battleground of human relationships. The concept was expanded in *My Body, Your Body* to include at least a dozen more dancers.

Dead Dreams of Monochrome Men was the company's critical breakthrough. Inspired by British serial killer Dennis Nilsen, this devastating, perceptive non-narrative charted the attempts of four men to overcome a gamut of conflicting feelings—including fear, desire, and loneliness—and establish connections within the sexually objectifying world of the (gay) disco. The piece was pervaded with frank eroticism, private ritual, and the shattering revelation of secret psychological spaces. As in all of DV8's work, virtually no formal dance conventions were observed, yet the body was used virtuosically as a vehicle for absolutely dynamic drama.

Strange Fish dealt with a woman (Wendy Houstoun, a DV8 stalwart) who reaches a crisis of faith through her desperate, even alienating efforts to connect with others. Houstoun was supported by six dancers and a singer who functioned as both Christ-figure and siren. *Bound to Please* posited dance as a metaphor for social conformity and complaisance by juxtaposing the experiences of two women, one a troubled, misfit dancer (Houstoun again) who wonders why she should march to the same drummer as everyone else, and the other a sexagenarian in physically and emotionally explicit involvement with a younger man. DV8's work is the kind that can yield greater riches at second viewing, as was the case with this superbly designed and layered piece. It was also the first time in the company's history that any movement as establishmentarian as an arabesque was executed in performance, but only in the context of some passages of pointedly generic, pseudoballetic contemporary dance.

Newson reverted to the male experience in both *MSM* and *Enter Achilles*. The first was, to all intents and purposes, a fragmentary but themed play culled from extensive interviews with men who "cottage," the practice of meeting other men for sex in public places. The latter, a physically daring study of the self-victimization inherent in British pub machismo, provided Newson with his biggest DV8 hit to date. Typical of the anticomplacent Newson, it, too, possessed a socio-philosophical resonance that stretched well beyond the confines of the dance world.

—Donald Hutera

NIGHTWANDERING

Choreography: Merce Cunningham
Music: Bo Nilsson
Set Design: Nicola Cernovich (Robert Rauschenberg, 1960)
First Production: Kungliche Teatern, Stockholm, Sweden, 5 October 1958
Original Dancers: Merce Cunningham, Carolyn Brown

Other productions include: Merce Cunningham and Dance Company, Hunter College Playhouse, New York, February 1965; 5 by 2 Plus with Jane Kosminsky and Bruce Becker, American Place Theatre, New York City, April 1978.

Publications

Beiswanger, George W., "No Dolt Can Do It: An Appraisal of Cunningham," *Dance News*, May 1965.
Horst, Louis, "13th American Dance Festival," *Dance Observer*, August-September 1960.
Hunt, Marilyn, "Reviews," *Dance Magazine*, August 1978.
Manchester, P. W., "Merce Cunningham and Dance Company, at Hunter College Playhouse," *Dance News*, March 1965.
Marks, Marcia, "Merce Cunningham and Dance Company, Hunter College," *Dance Magazine*, April 1965.
Stahle, Anna Greta, "Cunningham in Successful Debut in Stockholm," *Dance News*, November 1958.

* * *

Nightwandering is by its very existence a tribute to the genius and resourcefulness of its composer. Merce Cunningham created the work, sometimes called *Night Wandering*, with only three days' notice: on the third night, he and Carolyn Brown performed it at Stockholm's Kungliche Teatern.

Cunningham was visiting Scandinavia with Brown, one of his principal dancers and, by virtue of her ready adaptation to his experiments, a prized collaborator. When Cunningham, in Copenhagen at the time, was asked to compose a new dance using the music of Scandinavian composer Bo Nilsson, he came up with a piece that paid tribute both to the locale and to his partner. Don McDonagh, writing in *The Complete Guide to Modern Dance,* observed that "three days is an awfully short time to complete a dance, but undoubtedly the task was facilitated greatly by [Brown's] responsive intelligence."

The dance itself is clearly a metaphor for Cunningham's choreographic relationship with his leading talent, though its primal setting certainly reinforces the impression that it is simply about "man" and "woman." The players in this pas de deux are dressed in sleeveless, furry outfits that suggest animal skins, and the nature of their interaction implies that they are figures from prehistory, perhaps the Ice Age. (Some have interpreted the heavy costumes as an indication of a place, the Arctic, rather than a time; hence the note about a tribute to the Scandinavian locale.) Certainly this man and woman seem to exist in a rough physical world in which the woman is dependent on the superior strength of the male, but rather than lording it over her with his power, he shields and protects her. Their movements may pull them apart, but they usually pause with her resting on him; she rides his back, and at one point, she puts her feet on top of his while he walks her forward. But again, the dominant emotions are tenderness and gentleness, not domination or brute force, and this seems to be closely tied with Cunningham's own admiration for Brown. Perhaps for that reason, this very subtle composition has not enjoyed a long and varied life in its performance by others. Watching Jane Kosminsky and Bruce Becker stage *Nightwandering* nearly 20 years after its first production, Marilyn Hunt in *Dance Magazine* felt that something was amiss. In the two decades since Cunningham's and Brown's performance, the world had seen a sexual revolution and the rise of feminism: hence the male role required the utmost of deftness and precision to pull off, and it was doubtful that very many dancers could handle it. "What looks here like a failed Svengali aura," Hunt wrote, "presumably alluded with the original cast to the relationship of choreographer and favorite dancer."

—Judson Knight

NIKOLAIS, Alwin

American choreographer, composer, and scenic and costume designer

Born: 1910 in Southington, Connecticut. **Education:** Early training in piano; studied at Bennington College with Hanya Holm,

Martha Graham, Doris Humphrey, Charles Weidman, and Louis Horst. **Military Service:** U.S. Army, during World War II. **Career:** Created first ballet with Truda Kashmann, 1940; worked with Hanya Holm and became her assistant in New York and at Colorado College (where he met Murray Louis); named assistant director, Henry Street Playhouse, 1948; created Playhouse Dance Company (later known as Nikolais Dance Theatre); began collaboration with Louis, 1949; Nikolais Dance Theatre invited to the American Dance Festival, 1956; gained international acclaim during a season at the Théâtre des Champs-Elysées (Paris), 1968; formed the Centre Nationale de la Danse Contemporaine (Angers, France), 1978; formed Murray Louis and Nikolais Dance, 1989. **Awards:** John Simon Guggenheim fellowships; Andrew W. Mellon creativity grant; National Medal of Arts, bestowed by President Reagan at the Kennedy Center Honors, 1987; Grande Medaille de Vermeille de la Ville de Paris; Samuel H. Scripps American Dance Festival Award; Capezio Award; Circulo Criticios Award (Chile); Emmy Citation Award; *Dance Magazine* Award; Tiffany Award; American Dance Guild Award; knighted, France's Legion of Honor; Commander of the Order of Arts and Letters; special award from Mayor of New York City with Murray Louis; special medals from Mayors of Seville, Spain, and Athens, Greece; five honorary doctorates. **Died:** May 1993.

Works

1936	*Sabine Women,* Hartford, Connecticut
1937	*World We Live In,* Hartford, Connecticut
1939	*Eight Column Line* (mus. Krenek), Hartford
1940	*American Greetings* (mus. Horst), Hartford
	The Jazzy '20s (mus. MacLoughlin), Hartford
1941	*Opening Dance* (mus. MacLoughlin), Hartford
	American Folk Themes (mus. Guion), Hartford
	Pavanne (mus. Williamson), Hartford
	Evocation (mus. Reigger), Hartford
1942	*War Themes* (included *Rumor Monger, Complacent One, Defeatist,* and *Terrorist*), (mus. Prokofiev), Hartford
	Metamorphosis (mus. Osborne), Hartford
	Popular Theme (mus. Gershwin), Hartford
	Barber of Seville (opera; mus. Rossini), Hartford
1947	*Ten Maids and No Man* (opera; mus. Von Suppe), Hartford
	Fable of the Donkey (for children; mus. Miller), Colorado College, Colorado Springs
1948	*Romeo and Juliet* (mus. Gounod), Hartford
	Princess and the Vagabond (opera; mus. Freed), Hartford
	Dramatic Étude (mus. percussion), Colorado College, Colorado Springs
1949	*Extrados* (included *Focus Toward Faith, Submission to Faith,* and *Focus Towards Self*) (mus. Brooks/percussion), Henry Street Playhouse, New York City
	Lobster Quadrille (for children; mus. Miller), Henry Street Playhouse
	Shepherdess and Chimneysweep (for children; mus. Miller), Henry Street
1950	*Opening Suite* (mus. Waldron), Henry Street
1951	*Sokar and the Crocodile* (for children; mus. Miller), Henry Street
	Heritage of Cain (mus. Nicolait), Henry Street

	Invulnerables (mus. Waldron), Brooklyn Museum, Brooklyn
	Starbean Journey (for children; mus. Miller), Henry Street
	Indian Sun (for children; mus. percussion), Henry Street
1952	*Committee* (mus. Prokofiev), Columbia University, New York City
	Vortex (mus. recorded), Columbia University
	Merry-Go-Elsewhere (for children; mus. Miller), Henry Street
1953	*Masks, Props, and Mobiles* (included Aqueouscape, Noumenon Mobilus, and Forest of Three) (mus. Sibelius, percussion, Nikolais), Henry Street
	Farm Journal (mus. Moore), Sturbridge Village Theater, Sturbridge, Massachusetts
	Kaleidoscope (mus. Nikolais), Henry Street
	Devil and Daniel Webster (opera; mus. Moore), Sturbridge Village Theatre
	Tensile Involvement (mus. Nikolais)
1954	*Legend of the Winds* (mus. Chavez), Henry Street
1955	*Village of Whispers* (mus. arranged), Henry Street
1956	*Prism* (mus. arranged), Henry Street
1957	*The Bewitched* (mus. Partch), University of Illinois, Urbana
	Runic Canto (mus. Henry, Shaeffer, Phillipot, Nikolais), Connecticut College, New London
	Cantos (mus. Nikolais), Henry Street
1958	*Mirrors* (improvised; mus. Nikolais), Henry Street
1959	*Allegory* (mus. Nikolais), Henry Street
	Totem (mus. Nikolais), Henry Street
1961	*Stratus & Nimbus* (mus. Nikolais), Henry Street
	Illusions (mus. Nikolais), Comedia Canadienne, Montreal
1962	*Totem* (revised version; mus. Nikolais), Henry Street
1963	*Imago* (mus. Nikolais), West Hartford, Connecticut
1964	*Santum* (mus. Nikolais), Henry Street
1965	*Galaxy* (mus. Nikolais), Henry Street
	Vaudeville of the Elements (mus. Nikolais), Tyrone Guthrie Theater, Minneapolis
1967	*Somniloquoy* (mus. Nikolais), Guggenheim Museum, New York City
	Premiere (mus. Nikolais), George Abbott Theater, New York City
	Triptych (mus. Nikolais), Henry Street
1968	Costume and Environment Exhibit, Museum of Contemporary Arts and Crafts, New York City
	Tent (mus. Nikolais), University of South Florida, Tampa
1969	*Echo* (mus. Nikolais), New York City Center
1970	*Structures* (mus. Nikolais), New York City Center
1980	*Mechanical Organ* (mus. Darling and Nikolais)
	Schema, Paris Opera
1982	*Pond* (mus. Nikolais)
1986	*Velocities* (mus. Nikolais)
1987	*Blank on Blank* (mus. Nikolais)
1992	*Aurora*

Publications

By NIKOLAIS: articles—

"An Art of Magic: Interview with Dance and Dancers," *Dance and Dancers,* 1969.

"A New Method of Dance Notation," in *The Dance Experience: Readings in Dance Appreciation,* edited by Myron Howard Nadel and Constance Gwen Nadel, New York, 1970.

"What Is the Most Beautiful Dance," in *The Dance Has Many Faces,* edited by Walter Sorell, Cleveland and New York, 1951.

"Growth of a Theme," in *The Dance Has Many Faces*, second edition, edited by Walter Sorell, New York and London, 1966.

"The New Dimension of Dance," *Impulse*, 1958.

"No Man from Mars," in *The Modern Dance: Seven Statements of Belief,* edited by Selma Jeanne Cohen, Middletown, Connecticut, 1966.

On NIKOLAIS: books—

Cohen, Selma Jeanne, *The Modern Dance,* Connecticut, 1966.

Louis, Murray, *Inside Dance,* New York, 1980.

Mazo, Joseph, *Prime Movers: The Makers of Modern Dance in America,* New York, 1977.

McDonagh, Don, *The Rise and Fall and Rise of Modern Dance,* New York, 1970.

Rogosin, Elinor, *The Dance Makers: Conversations with American Choreographers,* New York, 1980.

On NIKOLAIS: articles—

Coleman, Martha, "On the Teaching of Choreography: An Interview with Alvin Nikolais," *Dance Observer*, 1950.

Copeland, Roger, "A Conversation with Alwin Nikolais," *Dance Scope,* Fall/Winter, 1973-74.

Lamhut, Phyllis, "Alwin Nikolais," *Ballet Review,* Fall 1993.

Louis, Murray, "The Contemporary Dance Theatre of Alwin Nikolais," *Dance Scope,* 1973-74.

"Nikolais, Alwin," in *Current Biography Yearbook 1968,* 1968.

Nickolich, Barbara Estelle, "The Nikolais Dance Theatre's Use of Light," *Drama Review,* June 1973.

Schonberg, Harold C., "Choreography, Music, Costumes, Sets, etc. etc., by Alwin Nikolais," *New York Times Magazine,* 6 December 1970.

Siegel, Marcia B. (ed.), "Nik: A Documentary," *Dance Perspectives,* Winter 1971.

Zupp, Nancy Thornhill, "An Analysis and Comparison of the Choreographic Process of Alwin Nikolais, Murray Louis, and Phyllis Lamhut," unpublished dissertation, University of North Carolina at Greensboro, 1978.

Films and Videotapes

Finials, Web, and *Kites* (all mus. Nikolais), NBC-TV, New York City, 1959; *Pavanne, Ritual, Seascape,* and *Paddles* (all mus. Nikolais), NBC-TV, Hollywood, 1959; *A Time to Dance* (mus. Nikolais), Ford Foundation Film Series, WGBH-TV, Boston, 1959; *Kaleidoscope* (revised for TV; mus. Nikolais), CBS-TV, Montreal, 1959; *Totem: The World of Alwin Nikolais* (film by Nikolais and Edmund Emschwiller; mus. Nikolais), 55th Street Playhouse, New York City, 1964; *Fusion* (film by Emschwiller; mus. Nikolais), Hilton Hotel, New York City, 1967; *Limbo* (mus. Nikolais), CBS-TV, New York City, 1968; *Nik and Murray* (documentary film by Christian Blackwood), PBS American Masters, 1987.

* * *

Alwin Nikolais was one of the most influential artists of modern dance; his performances are unforgettable. Nikolais cannot be thought of as just a choreographer—rather, he was a master of design, shape, color, motion, sound, and light, in other words, total theater. Although Nikolais studied dance during the mid-1930s, during the reign of notable, historic modern dancers such as Martha Graham, Louis Horst, Doris Humphrey, and Charles Weidman, Nikolais' choreography represented the new modern dance.

Nikolais was born in Connecticut in 1910. As a youngster, his mother would deposit Alwin, along with his brother, at the local theater's matinee show during her weekly shopping trips. The theater's venue was vaudeville, so Nikolais was exposed to a great variety of performances. As a young man, Nikolais was an accomplished pianist and was hired as an accompanist for a ballet and drama school and silent movie houses, and ran a marionette theater on the side. Nikolais was interested in the technical aspects of all these performances and found himself designing lighting and costumes. He started studying dance at the late age of 23, in Hartford, Connecticut, with Truda Kaschmann, and for several summers he went to the Bennington College to study with many prominent modern dancers, including Hanya Holm.

Nikolais' first choreographed pieces were composed while affiliated with the Federal Theater Project in Hartford. Though he was influenced by traditional modern dance, his work was out of the ordinary. One piece, *Sabine Women* (1936) featured a cast comprised of African Americans who were not trained dancers; another, *World We Live In* (1937), was a comedic piece based on insects—these and other works generally garnered favorable remarks from critics during Nikolais' early years as a choreographer in Connecticut.

His dance and choreography career was put on hold while Nikolais served in the U.S. Army during World War II, and in spare moments he developed a dance notation system he called "choroscript." After his discharge from the Army, Nikolais became the director of the Henry Street Playhouse located in the lower East side of New York in 1948, which he rehabilitated for dance. Nikolais and his dancers taught dance, developed a children's performing group, and gave performances at the theater. It was here that Murray Louis would join him, after the two met at Colorado College where Nikolais was assisting Hanya Holm.

During the early 1950s, perhaps as a reaction to the Cold War and the atomic age, Nikolais began to develop dances reflecting a philosophy that humankind must not dominate the universe. He also began to break away from the Freudian, "fetal-fertile-phallic" storytelling dances of his historic modern dance forebears. He relied on improvisation, a technique which allowed the use of the mind, psyche, and body's response to stimuli or the environment, to form his dances. Nikolais was concerned with illusion and imagery using all aspects of theater, and expressed his ideas through time, shape, motion, and space rather than through the use of psychodrama. Influenced by Holm's analysis of movement, Nikolais then added his own touches for a different approach to movement.

In contrast to classical dance, where the dancer's "center" is a rigidly erect torso, Nikolais "decentralized" the body. The spine and body became fluid and malleable, and the "center" could be anywhere in the body. Nikolais wanted his dancers to be able to isolate any part of their body and let it become the focal point. He made distinctions between movement and motion, perhaps akin to the distinction between quantity and quality. His works were abstract and proved an interesting addition to the American abstract art scene emerging at the time. While Nikolais received favorable comments from many critics, others thought that his creations were not dance at all. Further, he was criticized for dehumanizing dance—but what Nikolais really did was strip the dancers of their individual sexual stereotypes. Costumes were designed to minimize the

Alwin Nikolais with performers, 1984. Photograph © Johan Elbers.

differences between the dancers; or, the dancers dressed in gender-revealing, full-body tights, which in a sense made the dancer's bodies become essentially abstract. Males and females wore the same costumes, and they interchanged roles. Of course audiences were aware of the dancer's male or female physique, but viewers weren't concerned with gender because the dancers are metamorphosing, mobile pieces of sculpture. *Masks, Props, and Mobiles* (1953) was Nikolais' first "new" dance. In one part of the dance, three unidentifiable shapes are perched upon pedestals. The shapes slowly begin to move, the movement becomes bigger and more rhythmical, rocking the pedestals to and fro. Eventually, the shapes metamorphose into identifiable human figures.

Nikolais also experimented with new lighting techniques and used new, stretchy fabrics for his costumes. The invention of the tape recorder allowed endless editing possibilities—Nikolais was among the first choreographers to use prepared sound for dance accompaniment. *Forest of Three* and his well-known *Kaleidoscope* (both 1953) were his first dances set to prepared sound. Other well-known pieces that Nikolais created during the 1950s include *Prism, Cantos,* and *Allegory.* Although many of his performances would consist of only one work, the piece would take an entire evening to perform. As Nikolais' reputation continued to grow, so did his venues—in 1956 he was invited to the American Dance Festival for the first of many performances, and in 1959 Nikolais'

dance group appeared on the *Steve Allen Show.* His almost hallucinatory style of theater attracted increasingly large audiences, and Nikolais was soon experimenting further with the medium of television and choreographed several pieces, breaking even more new ground. His best-known dance using techniques unique to the television was *Limbo,* which aired on the Columbia Broadcasting System (CBS). Nikolais was also the first choreographer to break another taboo—to present nude dancers on television.

During the 1960s, he continued to choreograph similar works and created some of his most extraordinary pieces including *Totem, Imago, Sanctum,* and *Galaxy.* In a portion of *Sanctum,* paired dancers are dressed in leotards and tights. Each pair of dancers is enveloped in a stretchy loop of fabric, continually changing their overall, irregular shape—a triangle, a trapezoid, an oval, a pentagon. Again, the viewer is mainly concerned with the spatial relationship among the changing shapes and not the dancer's gender or costuming. In a part of *Imago,* from 1963, dancers wore segmented extensions on their arms and heads to give an unusual, overall effect of arthropods. Within a few years, Nikolais innovations in set, lighting, costume, and choreography attracted attention from abroad, and he was invited to the Théâtre de Champs-Elysées in Paris. After an extremely successful season in 1968, the Nikolais Dance Theatre was an international sensation invited to the top theatre venues around the world.

Although Nikolais broke away from traditional modern dance, his pieces are not without a story nor do they lack emotion. His pieces encompass a broad spectrum of human concerns, fears, joy, and sadness. Sometimes his message is harsh and other times, whimsical. Nikolais preferred large theaters to accommodate his large-scale pieces and production equipment. Perhaps his most unusual performance space was for a performance of *Tent*, a piece in which a large white tent has a life of its own. The performance took place in the desert, near a Roman ruin in Baalbeck, Lebanon, under a bright full moon on 20 July 1969—the day astronauts first landed on the moon.

In the 1970s, both Nikolais and Murray Louis thrived independently with their dance companies. Though there were frequent crossovers by Nikolais for music, design, or choreography, the two dance masters decided to officially combine their respective companies, in name at least, under the banner of Murray Louis and Nikolais Dance in 1978. The same year, Nikolais was invited by the French National Ministry of Culture to form a new dance center and company, which became the Centre Nationale de la Danse Contemporaine. In 1980, Nikolais created again for the French, with his 99th choreographic work, this one for the Paris Opera, called *Schema*. Declared "the most original exponent of American contemporary dance" by a French critic, Nikolais continued to tour and was deluged by commissions from throughout Europe, South America, and the Far East. Not one to slow down much, Nikolais' last choreographic endeavor was *Aurora*, in 1992, and he died in May of 1993. Upon Nikolais' death, Murray Louis assumed full directorship of Murray Louis and Nikolais Dance and has continued the extraordinary legacy begun by Nikolais.

—Christine Miner Minderovic

92nd STREET YM-YWHA

In New York City on 22 March 1874, a group of Jewish businessmen created an organization "to promote harmony and good fellowship among Hebrew young men." Formed "under the name and style of the Young Men's Hebrew Association," an organization first established in Baltimore two decades earlier, the New York YMHA had its first home on Lexington Avenue and 65th Street. By the turn of the century, its facilities overloaded, the Y moved to 92nd Street.

The establishment of what came to be called the 92nd Street Y was the result not so much of anti-Semitic discrimination—although that was certainly one factor—as it was an outgrowth of its founders' desire to preserve Jewish traditions. However, among Jewish traditions is an internationalist tendency, a desire "to provide a language of communication that unites people of various religious and ethnic backgrounds."

Those words came from the man who, more than any other individual, shaped the 92nd Street Y as it evolved into a significant cultural landmark during the 1930s and 1940s: William Kolodney. A rationalist and humanist, Kolodney maintained a cultural worldview at odds with that of the Y's governing powers, but they had the same ultimate aim: the betterment of their community. Faced with the 20th-century notion that God was dead, Kolodney sought the re-spiritualization of daily life through the arts, and dance was a cornerstone of his vision.

Thus a year after Kolodney became the social and educational director of the 92nd Street YMHA in 1934, his friend Doris Humphrey helped establish a Dance Center there. As a later director of the Dance Center, Joan Finkelstein, pointed out in a 1995 address before the Congress on Research in Dance, it was a critical juncture in the history of the art form. In 1934, the Bennington College summer program was established, as were the magazine *Dance Observer* and several modern dance programs at universities throughout the country.

In May 1935, Kolodney organized lectures and demonstrations at Theresa L. Kaufmann Auditorium (later renamed Kaufmann Concert Hall); through these, audiences were introduced to such figures as Martha Graham, Anna Sokolow, Hanya Holm, and Humphrey herself. A dance performance series established that fall brought in more notable innovators, including Elsa Findlay and Helen Tamiris.

Kolodney's democratic ideals, however, ensured that emerging talents got to share the stage of the Dance Theatre, established in 1937, along with more prominent names. Partly through the Audition Winners Concerts, inaugurated in 1942, some 500 artists had an opportunity to perform before the public, and thus the Y became a staging-ground for new generations of dancers and choreographers. Merce Cunningham, Daniel Nagrin, José Limón, Erick Hawkins, and other significant figures of the 1940s, 1950s, and 1960s all performed there. The Y also gave opportunities to African American artists, including Alvin Ailey, and to female choreographers, including Sophie Maslow, at a time when such opportunities were not abundant. Ailey, in fact, had his choreographic debut at the Y, as did Hawkins, Pearl Lang, Lester Horton, and Robert Joffrey.

In 1944, a year before the YMHA became the YM-YWHA in recognition of its large female membership, Humphrey became director of the Dance Center she had helped found. The next 14 years, until her death in 1958, are recognized as the golden age of dance at the Y. Her dance career finished due to advancing arthritis, Humphrey threw herself into teaching and the development of technique in legions of students who gained their training under her ultimate direction. Her legacy spread far and wide, in part through her concentration on children's programs under the immediate leadership of Bonnie Bird.

Humphrey established a number of other programs at the Y, and for a time she became the sole programming decision-maker. During her fruitful decade and a half, the Y saw the establishment of the Walter Terry Dance Laboratories, a series of lecture-demonstrations begun in 1947 and expanded in 1951 to include "open interviews" with such notable figures as George Balanchine, Jerome Robbins, Agnes de Mille, and others.

Thus the Y under Doris Humphrey and William Kolodney became, in modern dance terms, like Athens in its Golden Age: a place where events and people came together to create something almost mythical in its dimensions. Following Humphrey's death, the Kaufmann Concert Hall performance series dwindled, in part because the zeitgeist of dance, which the 92nd Street Y had largely defined at one time, had shifted elsewhere.

However, dance programs at the Y continued to flourish under the seven directors who succeeded Humphrey. Joan Finkelstein, who became director in 1992, danced with the Don Redlich Company when it took up residency at the Y during the 1980s. Under her leadership in 1997, the 92nd Street Y conducts nearly 100 classes a week for adults and children in styles that range from modern (mostly Hawkins, Limón, and Holm-oriented) to jazz, tap, ballet, Duncan, Afro-Caribbean, flamenco, ballroom—not to mention classes in Alexander technique, dance for mature adults, movement for people with Parkinson's disease, and a variety of other specialized programs. The professional workshops continue, as does teacher training. In 1993, the Y instituted its "Breaking Ground" series of interviews with choreographers, bringing in Cunningham, Twyla Tharp, Murray Louis, and other luminaries.

As exciting as all those activities are, there is something that surpassed them in the eyes of those who remember the golden age of the Y—or those who have imagined what it must have been like. Funding from the Harkness Foundations (the Dance Center is now the Harkness Dance Center) has allowed the Y to present fully produced dance performance again for the first time in 30 years. With programs at the nonunion Playhouse 91, it is quite possible that there may yet be another golden age to come.

Publications

Books—

Jackson, Naomi, *Converging Movements: Modern Dance and Jewish Culture at the 92nd Street Y, 1930-1960*, New York, 1998.
Stern, Alfred, ed., *Building Character for Seventy-Five Years*, New York, 1949.

Articles—

Finkelstein, Joan, "Doris Humphrey and the 92nd Street Y: A Dance Center for the People," *Congress on Research in Dance*, 1995.
Lanes, Doreen A., "The History of the 92nd Street YM-YWHA, 1934-1953," *Dance Research Collage*, 1979.

—Judson Knight

NOGUCHI, Isamu

Japanese-American sculptor and designer

Born: Isamu Gilmour 1904 in Los Angeles; son of American writer Leonie Gilmour and Japanese poet and art expert Yongiro (Yone) Noguchi; moved to Japan in 1906. **Education:** Apprentice to Japanese carpenter, 1913; sent to Interlaken School, Rolling Prairie, Indiana, 1918; graduated La Porte (Indiana) High School, 1922; served apprenticeship with Gutzon Borglum (Mt. Rushmore sculptor), 1922; entered premed program Columbia University, 1922; left Columbia for art school, 1924. **Career:** First exhibition and first studio in New York City, 1924; created first stage pieces, masks for Michio Ito's performance of Yeats' one-act play *At Hawk's Well*, 1925; went to Paris on Guggenheim Fellowship as assistant to abstract sculptor Constantin Brancusi and made stone and wood sculptures in Montparnasse studio, 1927; met Martha Graham in New York City and began portrait sculpture, 1929; made an image of dancer Ruth Page and designed costumes for her, 1932; created first set for Graham's *Frontier*, 1935 (continued to design Graham sets until 1966); designed set for Page's *The Bells*, 1946; designed set for *Stephen Acrobat* by Erick Hawkins and set and costumes for Merce Cunningham's *The Seasons*, 1947; designed sets and props for George Balanchine's *Orpheus*, 1948; created monumental sculp-

tures and sculpture gardens all over the world; established studio in Japan; opened the Isamu Noguchi Long Island City Garden Museum, 1985. **Awards:** John Simon Guggenheim fellowship, 1927; received National Medal of Arts, 1987. **Died:** 30 December 1988 in New York.

Works (designs for dance and theatre productions)

1925	Masks for *At the Hawk's Well* (Michio Ito)
1932	Costume for dancer Ruth Page
1935	Set, *Frontier* (Graham)
1936	Set, *Chronicle* (Graham)
1940	Set, *El Penitente* (Graham)
1944	Set, *Appalachan Spring* (Graham)
	Set, *Herodiade* (Graham)
	Set, *Imagined Wing* (Graham)
	Set, *The Bells* (Ruth Page)
1945	Set, *John Brown* (Graham and Erick Hawkins)
1946	Set, *Dark Meadow* (Graham)
	Set, *Cave of the Heart* (Graham)
1947	Set, *Errand into the Maze* (Graham)
	Set, *Night Journey* (Graham)
	Set, *Stephen Acrobat* (Hawkins)
	Set & costumes, *The Seasons* (Merce Cunningham)
1948	Set & costumes, *Orpheus* (George Balanchine)
	Set, *Diversion of Angels* (Graham)
	Set, *Tale of Seizure* (Yuriko Amemiya)
1950	Set, *Judith* (Graham)
1953	Set, *Voyage* (Graham)
1955	Set, *Seraphic Dialogue* (Graham)
	Set, *King Lear*, Royal Shakespeare Company starring John Gielgud
1958	Set, *Embattled Garden* (Graham)
	Set, *Clytemnestra* (Graham)
1960	Set, *Acrobats of God* (Graham)
	Set, *Alcestis* (Graham)
1962	Set, *Phaedra* (Graham)
1966	Set, *Cortege of Eagles* (Graham)

Publications

By NOGUCHI: books—

A Sculptor's World, New York, 1968.

On NOGUCHI: books—

Altshuler, Bruce, *Isamu Noguchi,* New York, 1995.
Balanchine, George and Francis Mason, *Balanchine's Complete Stories of the Great Ballets,* New York, 1977.
Croce, Arlene, *Sight Lines,* New York, 1987.
Denby, Edward, *Dance Writings,* New York, 1986.
Krokover, Roslyn, *The New Borzoi Book of Ballet,* New York, 1956.

On NOGUCHI: articles—

Brenson, Michael, "Isamu Noguchi, the Sculptor, Dies at 84," *New York Times,* 31 December 1988.
West, Martha Ullman, "Frontier of Design: Isamu Noguchi 1904-1988," *Dance Magazine,* May 1989.

Isamu Noguchi: Set for *Phaedra,* **1989. Photograph © Beatriz Schiller.**

Films and Videotapes

Noguchi—Stone and Paper, American Masters series, Public Broadcasting Service [PBS].

*   *   *

The fence for *Frontier,* the spiked metal "dress" for *Cave of the Heart,* the white rope and "breastbone" entry for *Errand into the Maze,* the off-kilter bed for *Night Journey,* and the abstract stained-glass window for *Seraphic Dialogue*—these sets by Isamu Noguchi, five out of the 20 he created for Martha Graham in a 30-year period, are as much a part of the dances as the dancing itself.

Theirs was a unique collaboration, one that changed the way dance was presented and perceived, and the first break from the traditional two-dimensional painted backdrops that had been the standard for scenic design in dance. The importance of Noguchi's contribution to 20th-century art, and Graham's work in particular, was eloquently expressed by the choreographer in the *New York Times* at the time of Noguchi's death in 1988: "So much of my life has been bound artistically with Isamu Noguchi. I feel the world has

lost an artist who, like a shaman, has translated [the] myths of all our lives into living memory. The works he created for my ballets brought to me a new vision, a new world of space and the utilization of space."

Born Isamu Gilmour in Los Angeles in 1904, the son of an Irish-American writer and a Japanese poet, Noguchi adopted his father's name at the time of his first exhibition of sculpture in 1924. While Noguchi received his training in art in the United States and in Europe, his childhood was spent in Japan where the arts are linked to each other and a part of everyone's life. Interaction with art was ordinary in ways that it never has been in the U.S., a young country with a culture still in the making. The sculptor, whose public art and sculpture gardens, as well as his designs for Akari lamps and furniture became as much a part of modern life as the mobiles of Alexander Calder was already interested in dance when he met Graham in New York in 1929, making a portrait bust of her the same year.

He had already done his first theatrical design in 1925, making masks for a Japanese Noh style production of W.B. Yeats' *At the Hawks Well.* It wasn't until 1935, however, when Noguchi made the spare, brilliant set for *Frontier* that his collaboration with Graham began. In his book, *A Sculptor's World* (1968) Noguchi described their process: "In our work together, it's Martha who comes to me with the idea, the theme, the myth upon which the piece is to be based. She will tell me if she has any special requirements—whether, for example, she wants a woman's place. The form then is my projection of those ideas. I always work with a scale model of the stage space in my studio. With Martha there is the wonder of her magic with props. She uses them as extensions of her own anatomy."

Writing of *Frontier*, a solo about a pioneer woman, Noguchi described his first scenic design as a point of departure for the rest—"space became a volume to be dealt with sculpturally," he said. This set, consisting of rope and wooden fence rails, was ambiguously simple and convertible to many uses. With some exceptions, in later years, Noguchi used materials that were light—papier-mâché, wire, and rope, making the set pieces portable and therefore easy to take on tour.

It was in the 1940s that the Graham-Noguchi collaboration was most fertile. Between 1940 and 1950 Noguchi designed the decor for nine highly memorable pieces, the 1944 *Appalachian Spring* with music by Aaron Copland, in Graham's biographer Don McDonagh's view, was a "collaboration occupying a special niche in the theatrical history of the country. Each contributed elements that meshed perfectly with the ideas and conceptions of the other." For this last piece in which Graham honored her American heritage, Noguchi designed a quite literal, if spare, set, including a rocking chair for the Pioneer Woman described by McDonagh as "of such slimness. . .it was almost like the profile of a chair rather than the actual thing."

As Graham moved toward the great mythic stories as the fodder for her dances, Noguchi, whose mother read the Greek myths with him during his Japanese childhood, turned out to be of like mind. *Cave of the Heart*, the story of Medea with the fiery dress, the heart turned on its side, and the red rope representing entrails, is, as Noguchi wrote, a work of transformation, like the Noh drama of Japan. With this piece, created in 1946, Graham and Noguchi were practicing cultural fusion long before the phrase was coined.

While the sculptor and the choreographer were usually of like minds, Graham did discard some of Noguchi's decor when she felt it was wrong. On one occasion, however, as McDonagh describes it, Noguchi produced a design of such beauty it made Graham reconceive the work. This was for *Seraphic Dialogue*, about Joan of Arc. "What Noguchi provided," McDonagh writes, "was a polished brass set that shone like gold. On the right were three seats upon which the dancers who portrayed aspects of Joan perched while one or another of them danced. To the left, opposite them, was an anchored stand on which hung a cross and a sword in the same polished brass. The rear. . .was a structure of circles, triangles, and rectangles resembling the tracery of a stained glass window."

Noguchi did most of his stage decor for Graham, although the *Seraphic* set was somewhat based on a 1944 set for *The Bells*, choreographed by Ruth Page. Closest to his heart, however, were the decor and costumes he designed for George Balanchine and Igor Stravinsky's 1948 *Orpheus*, a story he interpreted as about "the artist blinded by his vision." Describing the work as a controversial, avant-garde ballet, writer Rosalyn Krokover in the *New Borzoi Book of Ballet* (1956) said "[It] is a complicated design and it succeeds brilliantly in what its creators set out to accomplish."

Noguchi's last project with Graham was the 1966 *Cortege of Eagles*. The two were planning a new project, and to have an exhibition of their collaborations, at the time of his death on 30 December 1989. Commenting on the end of *Orpheus*, Noguchi might have been speaking of himself and his work when he said, "his art is not dead; his singing head has grown heroic as his spirit returns."

—Martha Ullman West

NORTH, Robert

American-born British dancer, choreographer, educator, and company director

Born: Robert Dodson, 1 June 1945, in Charleston, South Carolina. **Education:** Studied art at the Central School of Art, London; dance at the Royal Ballet School, London, 1965-67; with Kathleen Crofton; Graham-based dance at the London School of Contemporary Dance, 1966. **Career:** Founding member, London Contemporary Dance Theatre (LCDT), 1967; first public appearance in Paul Taylor's *Duet*, 1970; traveled to New York to work with Martha Graham and Merce Cunningham; first independent choreography for London Festival Ballet Workshop; performed and created works with the London Contemporary Dance Company, 1970s; became an associate choreographer of LCDT, 1975; created *Running Figures*, first of many works for Rambert Dance Company, 1975; choreographed first stage show, *Carte Blanche* (produced by Kenneth Tynan), London, 1975; taught modern dance at the Royal Ballet School in London, 1979-81; promoted to associate director with Robert Cohan of LCDT, 1980; took sole control of LCDT, 1981; created his last work for LCDT, *Song and Dances*, 1981; left LCDT to become artistic director of Ballet Rambert, working in an unofficial triumvirate with Richard Alston and Christopher Bruce, 1981; left Rambert to freelance as a choreographer and teacher, 1986; toured, choreographed and conducted dance workshops, 1989-90; ballet director of the Teatro Regio, in Turin, 1990-91; artistic director of the Goteborg Ballet of Sweden, 1991 to present. **Awards:** Won the Gold Prague Award and was nominated for an Emmy for *On the Overgrown Path*, a film for Danish Television, 1983.

Roles (with the LCDT, premiering in London, unless otherwise noted)

1969	*Sky* (Cohan)
	Cell (Cohan)
1970	*Duet* (Taylor)
	In the Playground of the Zodiac (Louther)
	Summer Games (Moreland)
	Nocturnal Dances (Moreland)
	Rainmakers (de Groot)
	Three Epitaphs (Taylor)
	Cantabile (Lapzeson)
1971	*X* (Cohan)
	The hero, *Stages* (Cohan)
	Nowhere Slowly (Alston)
	Dance Energies (O'Donell)
	Relay (Davies)
1973	*Tiger Balm* (Cohan)
	People (Cohan)
	Mass (Cohan)

The Sun, *Eclipse* (Cohan)
Blue Schubert Fragments (Alston)
1974   *Pilot* (Davies)
Waterless Method of Swimming Instruction (Cohan)
Orpheus, *No Man's Land* (Cohan)
Duet (Taylor)
Diversion of Angels (Graham)
Place of Change (Cohan)
Class (Cohan)
1976   Jacob, *Hunter of Angels* (Cohan)
The bandit, *Rashamon* (Seymour), Sadlers Wells Royal Ballet
Nympheus (Cohan)
When Summer's Breath
Songs, Lamentation and Praises (Cohan)
Cloven Kingdom (Taylor)
1980   *Something to Tell* (Davies), Siobhan Davies Dance Company
The sage, *The Rite of Spring* (Alston), Ballet Rambert
Ghost dancer, *Ghost Dances* (Bruce), Ballet Rambert
1982   God, *Mahogany* (Bruce), Ballet Rambert
"Great Hymn of Thanksgiving" from *Berlin Requiem* (Bruce), Ballet Rambert
Principal dancer, *Airs* (Taylor), Ballet Rambert
The father, *The Kitchen Table* (Cratty), Ballet Rambert, Bristol
1983   Principal dancer, *Chicago Brass* (Alston), Ballet Rambert, Birmingham
Principal dancer, *Fielding Sixes* (Cunningham), Ballet Rambert
Principal dancer, *Voices and Light Footsteps* (Alston), Ballet Rambert
1985   Principal dancer, *Mythologies* (Alston), Ballet Rambert
Principal dancer, *Java* (Alston), Ballet Rambert

Other roles include: Created roles in *Time of Snow, Plain of Prayer, Lady of the House of Sleep* and *Archaic Hours* with Martha Graham; danced in Graham's *Acrobats of God, Dark Meadow,* and as Paris in *Cortege of Eagles;* appeared on the British Granada Television production, *The Seven Deadly Sins,* 1984.

Works (premiered in London unless otherwise noted)

1967   *Death by Dimensions* (mus. Parsons), Ballet Rambert
Out of Doors (mus. Bartók), Festival Ballet Workshop
Pavane for a Dead Infanta (mus. Ravel), Balletmakers
1970   *Conversation Piece* (mus. Parsons), LCDT
1972   *Brian* (mus. Finnissy), solo, LCDT
One Was the Other w/Noemi Lapzeson (mus. Finnissy), LCDT
1974   *Dressed to Kill* (mus. Miller, Smith), LCDT, Southampton
Troy Game (mus. Batucadan, Downes), LCDT, Liverpool
1975   *Still Life* (mus. Downes), LCDT
David and Goliath w/Wayne Sleep (mus. Davis), LCDT
Running Figures (mus. Burgon), Ballet Rambert, Leeds
Gladly, Badly, Madly, Sadly w/Lynn Seymour (mus. Davis), LCDT
1976   *Reflections* (mus. Blake), Ballet Rambert, Horsham
Just a Moment (mus. Downes, Kool and the Gang), LCDT
1977   *Meeting and Parting* (mus. Blake), LCDT

Night Watch w/Micha Bergese, Robert Cohan and Siobhan Davies (mus. Blake), LCDT
1978   *Scriabin Preludes and Studies* (mus. Scriabin), LCDT
Dreams with Silences (mus. Brahms), LCDT
Macbeth (mus. Yamashta), Theatre Ballet of London
1979   *The Annunciation* (mus. Blake), LCDT
January to June (mus. Tchaikovsky), New London Ballet, Southsea
The Water's Edge (mus. Anderson, Palmer, Barre), Scottish Ballet, Glasgow
Reflections (reworked) (mus. Blake), LCDT
Five Circular Studies (Benstead), LCDT
Domestic Dances and Stories w/Janet Smith, Janet Smith and Dancers
1980   *Death and the Maiden* (mus. Schubert), LCDT, Exeter
Lonely Town, Lonely Street (mus. Withers), Janet Smith and Dancers, Leicester
1981   *Songs and Dances* (mus. Schubert), LCDT
1982   *Pribaoutki* (*A Telling*) (mus. Stravinsky), Ballet Rambert, Brighton
Electra (mus. Britten), Janet Smith and Dancers
1983   *Colour Moves* (mus. Benstead), Ballet Rambert, Edinburgh
For My Daughter (mus. Janácek), Royal Danish Ballet, for Danish National Television
On the Overgrown Path Danish National Television
1984   *Entre Dos Aguas* w/Hans van Manen (mus. Rogers, de Lucia), Ballet Rambert, Manchester
Miniatures (mus. Stravinsky), Janet Smith and Dancers, Leeds
1985   *Dances to Copland* (mus. Copland), Batsheva Dance Company, Israel
Singing on the Waters, Stuttgart Ballet, Germany
Changing Shapes (mus. Talking Heads), English Dance Theatre
Light and Shade (mus. Stravinsky), Ballet Rambert, Brighton
Einsame Reise (mus. Schubert), Stuttgart Ballet, Stuttgart
1986   *Fool's Day* (mus. Renaissance songs), Janet Smith and Dancers
Der Schlaf der Vernunft (mus. Shostakovich), Stuttgart Ballet, Stuttgart
1987   *Elvira Madigan* (mus. Benstead, Shostakovich, Sibelius, Neilsen), Royal Danish Ballet, Copenhagen
Whip it to a Jelly (mus. assorted blues excerpts), Janet Smith and Dancers, Leeds
Fabrications (mus. Rogers), LCDT
1988   *Sebastian* (mus. Menotti), Balletto di Toscana, Spoleto
1990   *Romeo and Juliet* (mus. Prokofiev), Ballet of the Grand Theatre, Geneva
Carmina Burana (mus. Orff), Goteborg Ballet, Goteborg
1991   *Living in America* (mus. Copland), Goteborg Ballet
Picasso and Matisse (mus. Stravinsky), Goteborg Ballet
The Heat (mus. Gabriel), Covent Garden Gala
1992   *A Stranger I Came* (mus. Schubert), English National Ballet, Cambridge
The Sidewinder (mus. Gabriel), Goteborg Ballet
Singing on the Water (mus. Schubert), Goteborg Ballet
1993   *Jungle* (mus. various rock), Ballet du Nord, France
1996   *Eva* (mus. Blake), Goteborg Ballet

Other works include: *Pilgrim,* for the Edinburgh Festival, 1975.

Publications

On NORTH: books—

Brinson, P. and C. Crisp, *The Pan Book of Ballet and Dance,* London, 1980.
Clarke, M. and C. Crisp, *London Contemporary Dance Theatre,* London, 1989.
Pritchard, Jane, *Rambert, a Celebration,* London, 1996.

On NORTH: articles—

Clarke, M., "Rambert at the Wells," *Dancing Times,* May 1984.
Constanti, S., "Ballet Rambert," *Dance Theatre Journal,* Summer 1985.
Cowan, J., "Rambert Rediscovered," *Dance and Dancers,* July 1982.
Dromgoole, N., "The Banished Star of British Dance," *Daily Telegraph* (London), 2 February 1991.
———, "Praising North and His Heavenly Host," *Sunday Telegraph* (London), 31 March 1996.
Goodwin, N., "Rambert at the Roundhouse," *Dance and Dancers,* June 1975.
Macauley, A., "The Rambertians," *Dancing Times,* May 1985.
Nugent, A., "Ballet Rambert's New Artistic Director," *Dance Gazette.*
Percival, J., "The Next Ten Years," *Dance and Dancers,* August 1976.
———, "Emotional Involvement," *Dance and Dancers,* May 1984.
Robertson, B., "The Thinking Man's Dancer," *Harpers and Queen* (London), March 1984.
Whitney, M., "Proud Export," *Ballet News,* October 1982.
Whyte, S., "A Season of Star-Crossed Lovers," *Dance and Dancers,* January 1991.
Williams, P., "A Golden Affair," *Dance and Dancers,* August 1976.

Films and Videotapes

Dancemakers, BBC2, 1986.
Slow Dancing in the Big City, choreography by North, dir. Avildsen, 1978.

*   *   *

Robert North's career as a performer and choreographer is inextricably linked with the histories of two of the United Kingdom's foremost contemporary dance companies. As a founding member, performer, and choreographer with London Contemporary Dance Theatre (LCDT) at The Place, his first choreography was born in a climate of experimentalism and discovery. As he moved on to the established Ballet Rambert to shape and influence the repertoire of this seminal company, his reputation as one of the great British movement makers was secured.

North was introduced to experimental, postmodern dance at London Contemporary Dance School, where he worked with many of the major dance artists of his generation. Involved in the dynamic early years of LCDT, he was quick to experiment with choreography, making his own work whilst performing in that of the other company members. A highly expressive dancer, North was quick to shape his ideas into movement, first for himself and then for others. North's first work for LCDT, *Brian,* was an obsessive solo, intensely focused upon inner emotional struggles. As he started to choreograph with other company members, such as Noemi Lapzeson, and as he grew in confidence, his work moved to a broader sphere. North began to incorporate influences from other dance styles, such as jazz, tap-dance, flamenco and disco, which were consistently to pattern his choreography.

North's training in art, and his interest and involvement with music, have continued to inform his movement vocabulary. Early experiments with film, song, and spoken word marked him as an artist with a wide vision, prepared to integrate dance with the other arts to find its fullest potential. In *Dressed to Kill,* made for LCDT in 1974, he paid humorous homage to the novels of Raymond Chandler, with a witty piece that was full of entertaining theatricality. After taking classes in the martial art of aikido, he created what is arguably his most popular work, *Troy Game.* With its muscular athleticism, vigorous posturing, and masculine good humour, this work was an immediate success for LCDT and soon entered into the repertoires of several international companies. In *Still Life,* made for the same company in 1975, North experimented with film and incorporated the designs of Peter Farmer into a complex hybrid production, self-conscious, dense, and somewhat ahead of its time. In 1983, North collaborated with visual artist Bridget Riley to animate her extraordinary graphic designs into *Colour Moves,* a visually arresting exposition of the dynamics of paint and the aesthetics of movement. Working with classical music, such as Brahms, in *Dreams and Silences,* Chopin, in *Scriabin Preludes,* and Schubert, in *Songs and Dances,* North has sought a profound relationship between the music and movement of his works. As he matured, North's movement vocabulary increased its classical content to support his developing explorations of the emotions of a group. North has worked closely with composer, Christopher Benstead (a musician also favoured by his wife, Janet Smith), to develop the musicality of his dance. As a teacher and company director, North has focused upon empowering his dancers by developing their musicality and broadening their awareness of other artistic expressions. North has often repeated his desire to project movement that combines the precision of an animal and the imagination of a highly intelligent human being. A profound dramatic sensibility is a quality he seeks to nurture in his dancers, and one which his increasingly emotive choreography demands. North's vision for Ballet Rambert was akin to that of the German Bauhaus, a meeting point for artists from all disciplines to gather and share ideas and inspirations. It was over this multivalent, broad vision that North was led to break with Ballet Rambert. Since leaving Rambert, North has moved around mainland Europe, restaging his ballets and creating new works for large, international companies.

—Sophie Hansen

NOVACK, Cynthia

American dancer, choreographer, and educator

Born: Cynthia Cohen, 6 September 1947 in Cincinnati, Ohio. **Education:** University of California, Berkeley, B.A.; Mills College, M.A.; Columbia University, M.A.; Columbia University, Ph.D. in anthropology; trained in dance, St. Louis, Missouri; studied Graham technique with David Wood, University of California, Berkeley; studied contact improvisation, Skinner releasing, and effort-shape notation. **Family:** Married Richard Bull. **Career:** Worked with Margaret Jenkins, Viola Farber, and Merce Cunningham; director, The Movable Feast, a West Coast dance collective; taught at SUNY, Brockport, 1970s; worked with Richard Bull, chairperson of the dance department at Brockport, 1970-78; co-founded (with Richard Bull and Peenzt Dubble) Improvisation Dance Ensemble (IDE); joined the Richard Bull Dance/Theatre, New York, 1978; assistant professor of dance, Wesleyan University, Middletown, Connecticut. **Died:** 27 September 1996.

Works

1975	*Brief Lives*
	Waiting
	Countdown
	Dance Concert
1976	*The Next Voice*
	The Longest Dance w/Richard Bull
	Bicentennial Vaudeville
	Transformations w/Susan Foster
1977	*Synchrony*
	One Week at a Time w/Susan Foster
	Déjà Vu
	Running Time w/Richard Bull and Bill Rowley
	Telepathic Duet w/Susan Foster
1978	*All in a Week* w/Susan Foster
	The Conspirators
	Crossovers, Improvisation Dance Ensemble (IDE), New York
	Story Dance, IDE, New York
	Making Contact, IDE, New York
1979	*Touch and Go* w/Peentz Dubble, IDE, New York
	Trilogy, IDE, New York
	Prologue, IDE, New York
	Slow Blues, IDE, New York
	Solo Set, IDE, New York
	Telltale, IDE, New York
	Cityscape, IDE, New York
1979	*Detective Story,* IDE, New York
	Elisions, IDE, New York
	Suite, IDE, New York
	La Parole, IDE, New York
	Groupdance, IDE, New York
1980	*Recursions,* IDE, New York
	Three Sets, IDE, New York
	Relay, IDE, New York
	Onagainoff, IDE, New York
	Soundings, IDE, New York
	My Story, IDE, New York

Publications

By NOVACK: book—

Sharing the Dance: Contact Improvisation and American Culture, Madison, Wisconsin, 1990.

On NOVACK: articles—

Dunning, Jennifer, Review of *Following Moves, New York Times,* 16 December 1984.

Jowitt, Deborah, Review of *Short Orders* and *The Dummy Dances, Village Voice,* 17 November 1992.

*   *   *

Cynthia Novack was born in Cincinnati, Ohio, in 1947. Her dance training took place in the mid-1960s and included study with such diverse teachers as Carmen Thomas True, David Wood, Marni Thomas, Margaret Jenkins, Viola Farber, and Merce Cunningham. She studied many different techniques and forms including improvisational dance, modern dance, ballet, tap, and West African dance, as well as popular and social dance. She also obtained a Ph.D. in anthropology from Columbia University. Novack taught dance at the State University of New York at Brockport, at Barnard College, and at Wesleyan University. While at Brockport she frequently presented concerts of her own choreography. These included the evening-length *Running Time,* a collaboration with filmmaker Bill Rowley. She also co-choreographed several duet concerts with dancer Susan Foster. It was also at Brockport that she met Richard Bull, director of the dance department from 1970 to 1978. Together with Peenzt Dubble, they formed a performing group called the Improvisation Dance Ensemble. In 1976 Novack and Richard Bull premiered *The Longest Dance* at Brockport. Novack stated in the press release for the 12-hour work, "We don't expect a lot of people to stay for the full 12 hours, though we're hoping that some of the audience will want to see the work in its entirety." *The Longest Dance* was performed by a 40-member cast many of whom danced throughout the afternoon and evening.

In 1978 the Brockport colleagues relocated to New York City and re-formed into a new group, eventually becoming the Richard Bull Dance/Theatre in 1983. Novack focused her efforts on what she called "choreographic performance improvisation." For several years the group had been performing structured improvisations in which the dancers took their cues from carefully plotted sound and lighting changes. In this way, the choreography was a work in progress.

In 1980 the trio of Bull, Novack, and Dubble gave performances of several pieces at the group's Warren Street Performance Loft in lower Manhattan. Included were *Strolling, Monkey Dance, Water Wheel, Didactic Dalliance,* and *Interactions.* Music was provided by Elliott Sharp and lighting by Lance Olson. When not performing, the dancers gave classes in modern technique and improvisation. When they appeared in 1984, performing *Following Moves* at their loft, dance critic Jennifer Dunning noted in the *New York Times* that the dancers exuded "an air of gentle camaraderie that is enhanced by the intimacy of the Warren Street Performance Loft. To watch them perform is a pleasant experience and their lively 'talk' pieces can be witty and provocative." Each of the women danced a solo in silence interrupted by an improvised score, performed to a computerized digital synthesizer. Yet the critic found that the piece, although smoothly performed and sometimes impish in its movements, could be lethargic and lacked risk-taking. In 1985 the Richard Bull Dance/Theatre appeared at the Bessie Schönberg Theater in New York City, performing *Invisible Cities, Making and Doing* (1970), and *Interactions* (1978).

In 1992 Novack appeared with the Richard Bull Dance/Theater at the Warren Street loft and was described by *Village Voice* dance critic Deborah Jowitt as "alert to the effect of shifts in dynamics, not committed to a particular style, and almost always lively without being arch." In *Short Orders,* Novack and fellow dancers Dubble, David Brick, Vicki Kurtz, and Peter Richards danced several small-scale sections in which solos turned into duets, and two duets were

Cynthia Novack (right) with Richard Bull and Peentz Dubble. Photograph © Johan Elbers.

performed at the same time against the same backdrop. On the same program was *The Dummy Dances,* an eerie duet for Cynthia and Richard in which they acted out puppet-master and robot-puppet. At first, Novack appeared to be the automaton manipulated by Richard Bull. Turned on as if she was an appliance, Novack danced a dance of elation. Jowitt admired the dancer's ability to convey a sexy, toy-like automaton one minute and then switch effortlessly into a flesh-and-blood woman the next. As the two dancers alternated the roles of manipulator and puppet, the dance took on a troubling tone but ended on a positive note, with the performers walking out together, as Jowitt put it, "still subtly jockeying for control, but fighting to quell that urge."

In 1990 Novack published *Sharing the Dance: Contact Improvisation and American Culture,* an anthropological analysis of contact improvisation, a mode of movement she defined as "momentum to move in concert with a partner's weight, rolling, suspending, lurching together" and which was initiated by dancer Steve Paxton in 1972. Since then, this form of dance has become a growing part of the modern dance movement both in the U.S. and abroad. Novack first became aware of contact improvisation in 1974 and began to study the form as an anthropologist in 1980, when she attended the annual conference of the American Dance Guild in Minneapolis.

Novack was tragically stricken with cancer in the early 1990s, forcing her to curtail her performing schedule. By late 1994 she was beginning to return to dancing and writing, starting work on a book with her husband, Richard Bull, entitled *Choreographic Improvisation: Adventures with the Richard Bull Dance/Theatre.* In September 1996, however, Cynthia Novack lost her battle with cancer. In June 1997 the Society of Dance History Scholars held a special memorial program in her honor during their conference in New York City. The written memorial was provided by Richard Bull.

—Adriane Ruggiero

NOWAK, Lisa

American dancer, choreographer, and company director

Born: 10 October 1939 in Detroit, Michigan. **Education:** Graduated from the Performing Arts Program of Cass Technical High

School, Detroit, 1957; attended Juilliard School, New York, as a dance major in the B.S. degree program, 1957-58; Adelphi University, Garden City, Long Island, New York, B.A. in dance, 1962; Sarah Lawrence College, Bronxville, New York, postgraduate training in dance and composition, 1962-63; modern dance training from José Limón, Betty Jones, Don Redlich, Viola Farber, Ethel Winter, and Mary Anthony; ballet training from Alfredo Corvino, Bunty Kelly, Meredith Baylis, and Norma Taynton; composition from Louis Horst, Ruth Currier, Ethel Winter, Don Redlich, and Bessie Schönberg; additional training at the Warsaw Ballet School in Poland, Robert Joffrey School, and the Martha Graham School; training in Ideokinesis at Laban Institute for Movement Studies. **Career:** Danced in *The Common Glory*, historical pageant in Willliamsburg, Virginia, choreographed by Myra Kinch, 1958; with Williamstown Summer Theatre as dance apprentice under the direction of Martha Meyers, 1959; with Charles Weidman Dance Company, New York, 1961; with The Dancers' Theatre Company, modern dance repertory company under the artistic direction of Beatrice Seckler and Martin Morginsky, New York, 1963-64; performed in concerts, the Jazz Jamboree (an international jazz festival sponsored by the Warsaw Philharmonic), and in two television specials featuring her choreography, Warsaw, Poland, 1964-66; guest instructor and choreographer-in-residence, Warsaw State Ballet School, 1964-66; founded Dance Department at the Detroit Community Music School (now the Dance Department at the Center for Creative Studies), 1966; director of department until 1976; instructor in modern dance and improvisation, University of Detroit Summer School of the Performing Arts, Detroit, 1970; founded Harbinger Dance Company, in Detroit, 1970; artistic director 1970-86. **Awards:** Honored by Michigan Legislature for contributions to dance and the quality of life in Michigan, 1985; Michigan Artist Award, Arts Foundation of Michigan. **Died:** 8 January 1997 of leukemia.

Works

1965   *American Suite* (mus. Duke Ellington), Jazz Jamboree, Warsaw, Poland

        Somnambulists (mus. Gracian Moncur), Jazz Jamboree, Warsaw, Poland

1969   *Amahl and the Night Visitors* (mus. Menotti), PBS-TV, Channel 56, Detroit

1970   *Solstice* (mus. Vivaldi), Harbinger

1982   *Three Japanese Dances* (mus. Bernard Rogers), Canton Ballet, Canton, Ohio

1983   *Syrinx* (mus. Yasukazu Amemiya), Ballet Michigan, Flint, Michigan

1986   *Cyrk* (mus. Andre Jolivet), Harbinger

1987   *Crossings* (mus. Steve Reich), Creighton University, Omaha

1988   *Ballare* (mus. Vivaldi), Alexandra Ballet, St. Louis

1989   *Half Wolf Dances Mad in Moonlight* (mus. Terry Riley), Michigan State University; performed at the American College Dance Festival, Ames, Iowa

1991   *Troubled Sleep* (mus. Ravel), Michigan State University; performed at American College Dance Festival, Central Michigan University

Other works include: *A-B-A* and *Arena*, two ballets commissioned by Polish State Television to music by Polish composers, filmed in Warsaw, 1965 and 1966; choreographed approximately 30 works for Harbinger, 1970-86, including a full production of *Carmina Burana* (mus. Orff), presented with orchestra and chorus, and an original dance/theater adaptation of Dickens' *Christmas Carol*, titled *Ebenezer*, performed with jazz ensemble, dancers and actors; dance sequences for *Michigan's 150 Spirited Years*, an original musical theater production created and produced by Actors Alliance Theatre in Detroit and funded by the State of Michigan, 1987.

Publications

On NOWAK: articles—

Anderson, Jack, review of *Night Dances*, *New York Times,* 11 November 1991.

Barron, John, interview with Nowak, *Detroit Monthly*, January 1987.

Hardy, Camille, review of Mid-States Regional Ballet Festival, *Dance Magazine,* October 1981.

———, Review of *Night Dances, Dance Magazine,* March 1992.

Films and Videotapes

Amahl and the Night Visitors, PBS Detroit, 1969.

*   *   *

The career of Detroit dancer Lisa Nowak and the history of Harbinger Dance Company, which she founded in 1970, in many ways epitomize the triumphs and the pitfalls experienced by many small regional dance companies. Nowak took pride in Harbinger's achievements during her 16 years as artistic director: it was Michigan's first professional modern dance company; it was in the National Endowment for the Arts touring program; it brought nationally known choreographers to work in Michigan and "contributed a great deal to the development of dance in Detroit and the state of Michigan," Nowak told John Barron in an interview with *Detroit Monthly* in January 1987. She was also proud that Harbinger was the first Michigan company to pay dancers a regular salary.

Despite its artistic successes, the company's financial base was always fragile. When federal and state funding declined, and corporate funding was not forthcoming, Nowak resigned in 1986, citing the inability of the Harbinger board to meet the company payroll and to raise the funds needed for artistic growth. Harbinger continued under three different artistic directors before suspending operations permanently in 1991. After leaving Harbinger, Nowak pursued a career of teaching and freelance choreography, working in Nebraska, Florida, Ohio, and Missouri, as well as in Michigan. Although suffering from leukemia during much of this period, she continued to teach, choreograph and rehearse her works until shortly before her death in 1997.

A native Detroiter, Nowak received much of her early dance training at Detroit's Cass Technical High School. She continued her studies in New York at the Juilliard School, Adelphi University, and Sarah Lawrence College. While in New York, she performed with the Charles Weidman Dance Company and the Dancers' Theatre Company before leaving in 1964 to study choreography in Poland. During two years in Warsaw, she directed an informal dance group and choreographed two works for Polish television.

Nowak returned to the United States during the unrest of the late 1960s, saying she wanted to be part of the social changes that were taking place at home. Back in Detroit, she founded the dance department of the Detroit Community Music School (now the Center for Creative Studies), and in the summer of 1970 she began developing a performance group with some of her students.

One of the dancers, Mitzi Carol, recalled how the class Nowak was teaching became a company—Harbinger Dance Company. The technical level of the dancers was not really high at the beginning but developed over time as they worked together, Carol said. An important turning point came in 1973, when "one night after dress rehearsal we were told we were going to start getting paid $50 a week. We were so excited, we cried." The company saw tremendous growth at that point, according to Carol. It joined the Regional Ballet Association. It hosted a Detroit Dance Festival at the newly reopened Music Hall for the Performing Arts. Eager to establish a repertory company, Nowak brought in such guest choreographers as Kathy Posin, Pauline Koner, and Ray Cook. Later, in the 1980s, Dan Wagoner and Bill Evans set works for Harbinger.

However, in 1976 the Detroit Community Music School, which had sponsored the company, withdrew its support. Nowak was unable to pay her dancers for two years. However, she persisted in locating space for classes and rehearsal and in establishing the company as a nonprofit corporation with a board of directors. By 1979, the company was able to move forward, collaborating with two city music organizations, Schola Cantorum and Orchestra Detroit in the city's first full production of *Carmina Burana* at Orchestra Hall. Nowak won praise for her innovative staging and her sensitivity to Orff's joyous score.

Nowak choreographed more than 30 works for Harbinger. She challenged her dancers; she was a perfectionist, former company member Gayle Stern Eubanks recalled. "One of her favorite expressions was 'One more time,'" Eubanks said. Although working in the modern idiom, Nowak was a classicist at heart, dedicated to making well-structured dances. Many reflected her lifelong concern with social issues. One of her earliest works, *Saigon Bride,* was a protest dance against the Vietnam war. A much later one, *Troubled Sleep,* was about women serving in the Persian Gulf War.

Describing her creative process in an interview with Frank P. Jarrell, Nowak said it was "mystifying how dances come into being. . . . I have to be truly inspired to make a good dance. Then I go to the studio and try to find the movement that expresses what I see happening in my mind. . . . Once I have a concept, I. . .tend to think in terms of the dancers I have, building on their specific abilities." Camille Hardy commented on this in her October 1981 *Dance Magazine* review of Harbinger at the Mid-States Ballet Association earlier that year:

> *Haze,* by Harbinger's artistic director Lisa Nowak, was the climax of the gala concert. Nowak's compositional and directorial skills make this a place that clearly distinguishes the difference between "doing" a dance and performing choreography specifically made for bodies that are accustomed to each other.... *Haze* contrasts the shapes and physical qualities of individuals as they appear alone or in groups that break up to redefine themselves in smaller clusters.... As the unhurried organic movement unfolds, it is punctuated by vivid surprises.

With free space at Oakland Community College in suburban Detroit, the company was able to have three Detroit seasons, plus a two-week upstate tour. Nevertheless, by September 1982, a $60,000 deficit forced Harbinger to suspend operations for a year. As a result, it lost its place in the NEA touring program, and Nowak freelanced during the company reorganization. Operations resumed in the fall of 1983, but the company was unable to get the touring dates and multiple Detroit engagements it had secured in the past. Its infrequent performances received glowing notices, but Nowak felt its shaky finances left too many needs unmet. She resigned in August 1986. Despite the loss she felt on leaving Harbinger and the onset of her illness, Nowak's last 10 years were amazingly productive. She was much in demand, both as a guest teacher and choreographer. In 1991, she was one of several choreographers represented on the Juilliard Dance Ensemble's Mozart Bicentennial concert. Colleague Dixie Durr of Michigan State University always liked to bring Nowak in to work with the MSU dance students because "they could see the structure" as they learned her dances. According to Professor Durr, Nowak "was wonderful about shaping movement."

—Kate O'Neill

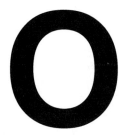

ODC/SAN FRANCISCO

American dance company

Founded in 1971 at Oberlin College as the Oberlin Dance Collective by a group of 18 performers, musicians, visual artists and choreographers; moved to San Francisco, 1976; bought and renovated their own building, 1979; established the New Performance Gallery as a separate entity, 1982 (in space co-owned with the Margaret Jenkins Dance Company until 1995) with a teaching studio and 250-seat theater; reorganized as ODC/San Francisco with Brenda Way as artistic director, 1982; repertoire includes some 90 works by four primary choreographers (Way, KT Nelson, Kimi Okada, and until 1984—Pam Quinn); has toured nationally and internationally (Australia and Southeast Asia, 1988; Soviet Union, 1989; Great Britain, 1997).

Works (from 1970 to 1976 performed at Oberlin College, and from 1977 to 1997 in San Francisco unless otherwise noted; choreographer's name in parentheses)

1970   *Myth Amerika* (Brenda Way)
     Renard (mus. Stravinksy), (Way)
     Tangerine: Parts I and II (Way)
1971   *9 Places for 30 People* (Way)
     Pas de Cinq (mus. Kagel) (Way)
     Maze (mus. Austen) (Way)
     Eidolon (mus. Pellegrino) (Way)
1972   *R & J Classic* (Way)
     Heliotrope Bouquet (mus. Joplin) (Way), Boston
     Beach Piece (Way), Martha's Vineyard
     Courtjest (Way)
     Format I (Way)
     And One (Kimi Okada)
1973   *Museum Piece* (Way)
     No Soap Radio w/Marc Beckerman (mus. Gay) (Way)
     Pieper's Parade (mus. Dylan) (Way)
     Niobe's Dream (mus. Israel) (Way)
1974   *A Natural History* w/Pam Quinn (Way), Boston
     Canon in D major (mus. Pachelbel) (Way), Boston
     Format V (Way)
     Deuce w/ Pam Quinn (mus. Faichney) (Way)
     Time and Again (Okada)
1976   *Format VI* (Way)
     Format III (Way)
     Ladies in Waiting (Way), Boston
     Hit or Miss (Okada)
1977   *'Til the Real Thing Comes Along* (mus. Mozart, Goodman) (Way)
     Red Shoes (mus. Skinner) (Way)

Domino (mus. and chor. Okada)
Looking Back and Walking Forward (mus. Rothenber) (KT Nelson)
Ad Infinitum (Pam Quinn)
1978   *A Matter of Degree* (Okada)
     Barelegged Americans (mus. Kottke) (Nelson)
     Formalities (Way)
     Format II (Way), Seattle
     Catching Up, Taking Notice and Gaining Perspective (Way), Seattle
     Entire FORMAT Series (mus. Coleman) (Way), Berkeley
     Keeping Things Whole (text and chor. Quinn)
1979   *A Formal Distraction* (Way), New York City
     Fall from Grace (mus. Dorsey) (Okada)
1980   *Wednesday's Child* (mus. Israel) (Way)
     Ohio Piece (mus. Jenks) (Way), Juneau, Alaska
     Designated Player (text Abbott & Costello) (Way), New York City
     Follow Suit (mus. and chor. Okada)
     Blunders (mus. Skinner) (Nelson)
1981   *Diminishing Returns* (mus. Christian) (Way)
     Beach (mus. Tenenbaum) (Nelson)
     Sleep Doesn't Come (mus. Lipson) (Quinn)
     Fast Forward (mus. Mendelsohn) (Quinn)
     Duets in Plaid (mus. Grisman) (Nelson)
1982   *The Course of Time* (mus. Mozart) (Way)
     The Plane of Change (mus. Nelson, Sweet Honey in the Rock) (Way)
     Second Wind (mus. Cooder) (Way), Berkeley
     In One Ear (Okada)
     Live Jive (Quinn)
     Ocean (mus. Tenenbaum) (Nelson)
     Split Decision (mus. Israel) (Okada)
1983   *Adam's Invisible Hand* (mus. Ballard) (Way)
     In a Manner of Speaking (Way), San Rafael, California
1984   *Entropics* (mus. Narell) (Way), Berkeley
1985   *Natural Causes* (mus. Rhiannon)
     Invisible Cities (mus. McNabb), Stanford
1986   *Tamina* (renamed *Prague and the Angels*/mus. Dresher) (Way)
     Constant Reminders (mus. Johnson) (Way), Berkeley
     The Tangle, "The Waltz Project" (mus. var.) (Way), Oakland
     Archipelago (mus. Hassell) (Okada)
1987   *Laundry Cycle: The Long and the Shorts* (mus. the Bobs) (Way)
     Sauce for the Goose (mus. various) (Okada)
1988   *Loose the Thread* (mus. Dresher) (Way)
1989   *The Yellow Wallpaper* (mus. Dresher) (Way)
     The Force of Circumstance (mus. Dresher) (Way)

ODC: *The Velveteen Rabbit,* 1992. Photograph © Johan Elbers.

Red Roads in Wyoming All Lead Home (mus. Sumera) (Nelson)

1990   *The Secret House* (mus. Dresher, Cloidt) (Way), Berkeley

Bold Sally (mus. Vivaldi) (Way)

The Velveteen Rabbit (mus. Britten) (Nelson)

1991   *Sweet William* (mus. Mozart) (Way)

1992   *Still Krazy/Kat* (adapted from 1990 version for San Franciso Ballet/mus. various) (Way)

1993   *John Somebody* (mus. Johnson) (Way)

River (mus. anc chor. Nelson)

Western Women (mus.Larsen, McFerrin) (Way)

I Wanna Be Bad (mus. var.) (Nelson)

1994   *Scout* (mus. Madsen) (Nelson)

Into the Inkwell (mus. Scott) (Okada)

Under the Jaguar Sun (mus. Santos, Wallace) (Way)

Part of a Longer Story (mus. Mozart) (Way)

Scissors Paper Stone (mus. various) (Way)

1995   *Angel's Doll* (mus. Penguin Café Orchestra) (Nelson)

Under the White Umbrella (mus. Pygmy Water Music) (Nelson)

1996   *Chapter and Verse* (mus. var.) (Way)

1997   *Frank* (mus. various) (Nelson)

Weird Weather (mus. various) (Nelson)

OutaWak (mus. Dresher) (Way)

Publications

On ODC: books—

Fridler Sharon E. and Susan B. Glazer, editors, *Dancing Female,* Harrowed Academic Publishers, 1997.

On ODC: articles—

Ross, Janice, "San Francisco's Oberlin Dance Collective," *Dance Magazine,* June 1984.

——, "ODC," *Dance Magazine,* April 1992.

Clipping files and archival material from the San Francisco Performing Arts Library and Museum.

*   *   *

Choreographer Brenda Way, artistic director of ODC/San Francisco, has said that "the greatest strength of American dance is that there are so many of us." She could have been talking about her own company. Unique among modern American dance companies, which commonly present the work of a single choreographer, ODC has managed to establish a distinct identity while integrating the multiple points of view of its choreographers Way, KT Nelson (now co-artistic director), Kimi Okada, and until 1984, Pam Quinn.

ODC started out as a collective and even though today it is more hierarchically structured, it still retains traces of its early idealism. "From the beginning in 1971," Way has said, "I wanted an institution that would, like an ideal family, provide the freedom for its members to grow up and thrive, to grow old even, that would provide opportunity, challenge and security." ODC has tried to live up to such loftiness. Shortly after its arrival in San Francisco, the company bought and renovated a building; established a teaching studio and community performance space which, until 1994, it shared with the Margaret Jenkins Dance Company. It committed to substantial home seasons, restricted touring, paid health benefits and put dancers on year-round salaries.

Early on, critic Deborah Jowitt described the then-Oberlin Dance Collective as "crisp and smart," still an accurate assessment, even though the company over the years has developed a richer more virtuosic style with increasing bows in the direction of theater and narrative. Whether in jazz shoes or sneakers, ODC embraces dance as communication with vigor, intelligence and wit. Easy grace and elegance is based on a strong athleticism which values understatement and implication over overt display. Emphasis is on expressivity through strong leg work, with relaxed upper body and arms allowing for fast changes in spatial orientation.

Interest in the nature of dance and the challenges of form and technique took the lead in ODC's plotless works of the 1970s. Procedures observed in the visual arts and music—permutation, retrograde, sequencing, overlapping, fragmentation, unison—were explored with an athletically robust vocabulary based on sports, vernacular movements and gestural language. Way created, among others, the five-part task-oriented *Format* series in which dancers' movements were compressed by time keepers, or they were asked to literally retrace their steps. In *Ladies in Waiting* she confined a quartet of women to a small square on the stage.

Okada choreographed a number of percussive, tap-influenced pieces (*Time Again, And One, One Ear, Hit or Miss*) in which she tried to make rhythm visible. Her work, including the 1994 comic-book inspired *Into the Inkwell*, has often leaned in the direction of humor.

In the 1980s Way emerged as the company's preeminent choreographer, creating substantial works which allowed her to explore narrative and her penchant for the complexities of nature and human behavior. Emotionally richer, her choreography now intrigued as much for its sensuous virtuosity as its intellectual challenges. *Entropics*, with a restricted movement vocabulary, was set as a languorous beach party; it examined instability and nature's tendency to revert from imposed order to chaos. In *The Tangle* she looked at courting styles—shy, flirtatious, sexy. *The Force of Circumstance* presented the icy constraints relationships can impose.

Inspiration during that time often came from literary or scientific sources. In the lyrical *Invisible Cities* (based on Italo Calvino's eponymous imaginary travelogue), Way paired live dancers with an interactive robot to look at the artifice/nature dichotomy and the power of the imagination. *Loose the Thread*, based on the tangled relationships among the Bloomsbury group, was the pretext for exploring concepts of shifting identity and loyalty. *The Yellow Wallpaper*, Way's first full-length solo (inspired by Charlotte Perkins Gilman's novel), traced a woman's haunting descent into madness. Allan Ulrich has described *Second Wind* as a study of isolation and partnering, signaling a new direction for Way as "she weaves sultry, long arabesques and diabolically speedy encounters." Of *Course of Time*, he has said that it is "a disturbing study in repetition and obsession and the narrow line between the two." On a much lighter note *Laundry Cycle: The Long and The Shorts* swung, tossed and blew its dancers much like mismatched piece of clothing in a washing machine.

The company's preeminent dancer, KT Nelson, started to choreograph consistently in the early 1990s. Her *Velveteen Rabbit*, based on Margery Williams' children's tale, has become the company's annual holiday offering. Using voice-over narration with movement, it tells its moral lessons with charm and restraint, featuring among others a twelve-foot-tall Nana and a splendid set of dancing animals and toys. In the *River* she contrasted and undercut concepts of strength and fragility in a quartet for burly men and slithering women. In the strongly narrative *Scout* (from Harper Lee's *To Kill a Mocking Bird*), the challenge was to communicate a twisting plot line from a child's nebulous perspective. The thrashing solo *I Wanna Be Bad* and *Angel's Doll* came out of Nelson's work with at-risk youth. The male trio *Frank* was a memorial to deceased ODC dancer Frank Everett.

As for Way, in 1993 she premiered an ambitious, evening-length trilogy *Western Women* in which she chronicled the history of American women in their westward migration. Using texts from actual diaries, the first part "Ghosts of an Old Ceremony" painted a genteel picture of the travails and sacrifices of pioneer women; Rosie the Riveter and Amelia Earhart became pioneers of a different sort in "Falling in Place;" "Dirt" expressed the aerobic energy and high spirited confidence of modern women. Way termed another full-length work, the two-act *OutaWak*, a "hipopera." Based on Norton Juster's *The Phantom Tollbooth*, it is a collage-like structure, much influenced by hiphop, in which narration, music, and dance attempted to exist on the same plane. She also continued her interest in partnerships with smaller-scale pieces, such as *Part of a Longer Story*; the companion duets *Bold Sally* and *Sweet William* and the trio *Scissor Paper Stone* which examined the tension between being involved in a"trio" and a "triangle."

—Rita Felciano

O'DONNELL, May

American dancer and choreographer

Born: 1909, in Sacramento. **Education:** Studied dance with Estelle Reed; studied Wigman technique in New York with Hanya Holm. **Family:** Married composer Ray Green. **Career:** Soloist, Martha Graham Company, 1932-38, 1944-52, creating roles in *Appalachian Spring, Dark Meadow, Herodiade,* and *Cave of the Heart,* and dancing principal roles in *Letter to the World, Deaths and Entrances, Punch and Judy, Every Soul Is a Circus,* and *Primitive Mysteries;* founded San Francisco Dance Theatre with Gertrude Shurr and Ray Green, 1939; toured with José Limón, 1941-43; instructor, High School of the Performing Arts and San Francisco Dance Theatre; first program of original works, 1945; formed her own company in 1949 and subsequently gave concerts of her own works.

Works

1937	*Of Pioneer Women*
1939	*Running Set*
1940	*So Proudly We Hail*
1941	*On American Themes*
	Dance Theme and Variations
1943	*Suspension*
1949	*Celtic Ritual*
	Forsaken Garden
	Horizon Song
	Jig for a Concert
1952	*Act of Renunciation*
	Dance Sonata No. 1
	Magic Ceremonies
	The Queen's Obsession
	Ritual of Transition
	Spell of Silence
1954	*Dance Concerto*
	Legendary Forest
1955	*Incredible Adventure*
1956	*Lilacs and Portals*
	Second Seven
	Dance Sonata No. 2
1958	*Dance Energies*
	Figure of the Individual
	Dance Sonatinas
1959	*The Haunted*
1961	*Sunday Sing Symphony*
1962	*Dance Scherzos*
1977	*The Pursuit of Happiness*
1978	*Vibrations*
1980	*Homage to Shiva*

Publications

On O'DONNELL: books—

Siegel, Marcia B., *The Shapes of Change,* Boston, 1979.

On O'DONNELL: articles—

Dunning, Jennifer, *New York Times,* 25 September 1994.
Tobias, Tobi, interview, *Ballet Review,* 1981.

*   *   *

May O'Donnell belongs to the generation of modern dance pioneers in the tradition of Martha Graham. Born in 1909 in Sacramento, California, she studied dance with Estelle Reed in San Francisco, and it was in Reed's company that she first performed. She later paid her own fare to Europe and spent a year based in Holland with Reed and four other members of the company, performing sporadically. In 1931 O'Donnell moved to New York to study the technique of German Expressionist choreographer Mary Wigman at a school directed by Hanya Holm. Disappointed in the Wigman classes, she later moved to the Martha Graham school and was a soloist in Graham's company from 1932 to 1938.

In 1939 O'Donnell founded the San Francisco Dance Theater with her husband, Ray Green and another graduate of the Graham school, Gertrude Shurr. The following year O'Donnell presented her first solo concert at the Veteran's Auditorium in San Francisco. Shortly thereafter, she joined the José Limón Company and toured with it for three years.

From 1944 to 1952, O'Donnell returned to the Graham Company as a guest artist, creating such roles as the Pioneer woman (*Appalachian Spring*), the attendant (*Herodiade*), She of the earth (*Dark Meadow*) and chorus (*Cave of the Heart*) as well as dancing many principal roles in the repertory.

O'Donnell worked with Graham when she was at the vanguard of the dramatic changes sweeping dance, and there is no doubt O'Donnell was influenced by Graham. She is described by Jennifer Dunning as "a member of the generation that carried the flame after the revolution." Moreover, in *The Shapes of Change*, Marcia B. Siegel writes, "May O'Donnell developed the rhythmic and bodily fragmentation of Graham, the irregularity and asymmetricality of form, to make mostly nonnarrative dances." At the same time, after leaving Graham's company, O'Donnell was an innovator in her own right, as illustrated by her well-known work, *Suspension*, first performed in San Francisco in 1943 and later forming part of her first New York program of original works at the YMHA in 1945. In *The Complete Guide to Modern Dance*, Don McDonagh writes of this work: "As one of the leading dancers of the Martha Graham company, O'Donnell was expected to reproduce works that bore the stamp of stressed drama, so familiar to Graham's work. Instead O'Donnell chose to design a serene piece that was calm and almost floating in its thrust."

Indeed, *Suspension*, which presents many dancers revolving through space in different patterns and phases, represented a departure because of its slow timing, unusual movement approach, and dreamlike quality. O'Donnell herself explained this piece with a quote from the poetry of T.S. Eliot: "at the still point of the turning world ... there the dance is ..." She elaborated on the work, which was written during World War II, in a conversation with Tobi Tobias for *Ballet Review* in 1981, stating, "I became intrigued with the idea of feeling slow and peaceful in space, of having an inner balance you could hang onto in the midst of the momentary terrors of war."

O'Donnell continued her innovative work, forming the May O'Donnell Dance Company in 1949. The company gave performances in New York and all over the United States until 1963. Interestingly, O'Donnell experienced something of a renaissance in the late 1970s. A former student asked her to remount *Suspension* for the Alvin Ailey company, she was invited to stage *Dance Energies* for the London Contemporary Dance Theatre, and the Houston Ballet requested a piece. So O'Donnell revived her dance company and performed at Jacob's Pillow, the 42nd Street Mall, the Delacorte Theater, and as part of the 1978 Umbrella Series.

Characteristic of O'Donnell's work is a sense of order, harmony, and craftsmanship. Lillie Rosen described the "May O'Donnell style," as "one concerned with the use of every last body part, with shifts of weight and balance and the most felicitous use of space and time." When putting a group together, O'Donnell generally didn't notice the individual dancers as much as the relationship of movement and lines. O'Donnell said, "mixing nondancers and dancers with different training and traditions is important to me. When people with different abilities do a step, you can see how the step is changed."

As a teacher, O'Donnell's goal has been to make the human body as "articulate" as possible and to make it free and "unmannered." She concerns herself with the movement of the body in space and the constant shifting of body weight and has emphasized the transfer of weight from body part to body part, the various kinds of expression in movement, and the endless interplay between weight, space, and time. After retiring from active performing, O'Donnell taught at a variety of schools, among them the School of Performing Arts, several special sessions at the University of California Extension Division, and master classes throughout the United States.

—Karen Zimmerman

OLLER, Ramón

Catalonian dancer, choreographer, educator, and company director

Born: 1 February 1962 in Esparraguera. **Education:** Trained in theater at the Institut de Teatre, Barcelona, 1980-81; studied ballet with Laura Tapias, Joan Tena, Ramón Solé, Martina Coll, and Dafna Rathause; studied modern dance at La Fábrica; also studied at The Place in London with Lydia Azzopardi and Gaye Andrews and in Paris with Claire Tallia and Yvonne Cartier (ballet), and Peter Gross and Jean-Marc Boler (modern dance); studied choreography and performance with Cesc Gelabert and participated in his first choreography workshop (with Toni Gelabert). **Career:** Began teaching, 1982; first independent choreography, 1983; joined the Ballet Contemporani de Barcelona, 1984; danced with Cesc Gelabert and Lydia Azzopardi, 1984-85; founded Metros Dance Company, 1985; choreographed for Spain's Compañía Nacional de Danza, 1994-95, New York's Ballet Hispánico, Cristina Hoyos Ballet Español, 1996, and the Ballet Nacional de España, 1998. **Awards:** Tórtola Valencia Second Prize, Barcelona, 1984; Creativity Award, Catalonia, 1985; Prize for Choreography, Spanish Association of Directors, 1993, 1997; National Dance Award, Spanish Ministry of Culture, 1994; Catalonian National Choreography Prize, 1994; Catalonian National Arts Award, 1996; City of Barcelona's Performing Arts Award, 1998.

Works

1984   *Dos dies i mig* (mus. David Burns), La Fábrica, Barcelona
1985   *La Parada* (mus. Keith Jarrett), Dansa a Catalunya, Teatre Condal, Barcelona
1986   *De metros i metros* (mus. Agustí Fernández), Dansa a Catalunya, Centre Cultural de la Caixa de Terrassa
1987   *Nofres* (mus. Agustí Fernández), Mercat de les Flors, Barcelona
1988   *Casi sola; Al fin sola; Perfectamente sola* (mus. Leo Mariño), La Fábrica, Barcelona
       Sols a soles (mus. René Aubry, Marlene Dietrich), Madrid en Danza
       Al borde (mus. René Aubry), La Fábrica, Barcelona

1989   *A tu vera* (mus. Paco de Lucía), Teatro Principal, Valencia
1990   *Qué pasó con las Magdalenas?* (mus. collage, Oscar Roig), Mercat de les Flors, Barcelona
1991   *Naranjas et citrons* w/Jean-Christophe Maillot (mus. Bertrand Maillot), Metros et Cie. Jean-Christophe Maillot, Eurodanse, Mulhouse, France
       Manolita (mus. René Aubry, Sara Montiel, Paco de Lucía), Teatro Albéniz, Madrid
1992   *Aquí no hi ha cap angel* (mus. Etienne Schwarz and traditional Catalonian), Sala Olimpia, Madrid en Danza
       Estem Divinament (mus. Oscar Roig, Mina), Mercat de les Flors, Barcelona
1993   *De aquí pa ya* w/Mari Carmen García (mus. Oscar Roig, popular), Théâtre Benodouze, Avignon
       Qién mató al niño Jesús? (mus. Michael Nyman, Fauré, popular Spanish), modern dance students of the Institut de Theatre, Longe Dans Festival, Rotterdam
1994   *Pral. 1* (mus. collage, Roig), Compañía Nacional de Danza, Teatro de Madrid
       Mentides de debó (mus. Marina Rossell), Festival Internacional de Sitges
       Cuartel de invierno (mus. Eduardo Rodríguez), duet with Nadine Astor, Itálica International Dance Festival, Teatro de la Maestranza, Seville
       Good Night Paradise (mus. Marina Rossell, Eduardo Rodríguez), Ballet Hispánico of New York, Joyce Theater, New York
1995   *T'odio amor meu* (mus. Cole Porter), Dagoll Dagom Theatre Company, Teatro Victoria, Barcelona
       Diwano (mus. collage, Roig), Compañía Nacional de Danza, Teatro de Madrid
       Retratos en la memoria (mus. José Antonio Rodríguez, collage of popular music), Centro Andaluz de Danza, Itálica International Dance Festival, Teatro Central, Seville
       Rigoletto (opera; mus. Verdi), Gran Teatre del Liceu, Teatro Victoria, Barcelona
       Tears for Violet (mus. popular Jewish, Roig), Ballet Hispánico of New York, Joyce Theater
       Duérmete ya (mus. Tchaikovsky, Meredith Monk, Roig), Mercat de les Flors, Barcelona
1996   *Romeo i Julieta: Barbacoa Pasional* (mus. Prokofiev), Teatre Grec, Barcelona
       Trocito Cielo (mus. Marina Rossell, Roig, Eduardo Rodríguez, Fito Paez), Auditorio de la Banca Nacional, Asunción, Paraguay
       Arsa y Toma w/Cristina Hoyos (mus. Flamenco), Opera d'Avignon
1997   *Romy and July* (mus. Prokofiev, Gounod, Berlioz), Teatre Polirama, Barcelona
       Pelo de tormenta (play by Francisco Nieva), Teatro María Guerrero, Madrid
       Azul añil (mus. Roig, Luis Carmona, Enrique Morente), Javier Barón Dance Company, Festival de Niebla, Huelva
       Poemas de problemas (mus. Armand Amar, Roig), Central Cultural de la Caixa de Terrassa
1998   *La Celestina* (mus. Carmelo Bernaola), Ballet Nacional de España, Teatro Real, Madrid

*   *   *

Ramón Oller, one of Spain's most respected and versatile dance artists, discovered dance while studying theater at Barcelona's well-known Institut de Teatre. After training with several independent ballet teachers in the city, he studied contemporary dance at La Fábrica for four years with Cesc Gelabert, Lydia Azzopardi, Alicia Pérez-Cabrero, and Montse Colomé. A focal point for contemporary dance in the 1980s, Oller began his teaching career and premiered many of his early choreographies there. Oller also studied abroad, attending classes at The Place in London and in Paris.

In 1984 his first choreography, *Dos dies I mig* was awarded the Tórtola Valencia second prize, given jointly by the region of Catalonia and greater metropolitan Barcelona. The following year he founded his company, Metros, and was invited to study at the Jacob's Pillow Dance Festival. In 1986 the ensemble premiered Oller's first full-length work, *De metros i metros,* a study of the contrast between daily motions and deeper emotion which uses the subway as a metaphor. *Nofres* (1987) explored the claustrophobic environment of a spa for convalescents.

Oller's next works mark a turning point in his creative focus. He began to draw on childhood memories and music that reflected on his own roots to create a nostalgic, emotionally intimate tone. *Sols a soles* (1988), a work "rooted in memory," showed us the world as seen through the eyes of a young child surrounded by a houseful of women.

In 1991 Jean-Christophe Maillot named Oller as choreographer in residence at the Centre Choréographique de Tours. He continued to create full-length works for Metros while receiving commissions to choreograph smaller pieces. Although he had often used popular Spanish and Flamenco music in his contemporary dance work, in 1993 he created *De aquí pa yá* with Mari Carmen García, thus initiating an ongoing collaboration with Spanish and Flamenco dance artists.

In 1994 Oller was awarded the Spanish Ministry of Culture's National Dance Prize, and his commissioned work increased. He became the first Spanish guest choreographer for Nacho Duato's Compañía Nacional de Danza, which retains two of his works in its repertoire. New York's Ballet Hispánico commissioned the first of two works, and Oller began an ongoing relationship with the Andalusian Cultural Council which included a full-length production, the very successful *Retratos en la memoria* (1995) for the regional dance ensemble. He has had an important influence on the development of contemporary dance in Andalusia through his workshops and the direction of an ongoing training program.

Oller branched out into choreography for musical theater and opera in 1995. He also created the full-length *Duérmete ya,* using Tchaikovsky's *Sleeping Beauty* to create a dream-world inspired by references to classical ballet and his own insomnia while exploring an expanded movement vocabulary.

The year 1996 brought another commission, *Romeo i Julieta: Barbacoa Pasional,* to Prokofiev's music, performed live out-of-doors at Barcelona's summer Grec Festival, with Oller and Nuria Moreno in the title roles. This "barbecue of the passions," adapted for the proscenium stage, became *Romi y July,* Oller's vision of Shakespeare's tragedy "as I would have like it told to me." The drama unfolds with wit, humor, and pathos in an anonymous urban environment complete with garbage containers and old tires. The Centro Dramático Nacional also called on Oller to set the choreography for a major work by Spanish playwright Francisco Nieva in 1997. In November the company presented *Poemas de problemas,* born of the artist's struggle to fashion something of beauty from an inchoate and solitary impulse.

Although Ramón Oller is firmly grounded in a dance tradition, his work maintains an intense emotional and theatrical content that reflects his early training in theater, in contrast to that of many of his contemporaries. He is often inspired by themes such as intimacy, the intricacy of love, the need for emotional communion, and the difficulty of maintaining it. His familiarity with Spanish popular culture, through his own upbringing in Catalonia and his mother's Andalusian roots, has served him well. The sensual and sensorial details of daily life, a richly shaded emotional palette, a certain nostalgia, tenderness, and humor (often kitsch) are present in Oller's work, as well as a complex and vigorous movement vocabulary. The ability to develop such universal themes with an essentially Spanish sense of poetry is one of the factors that has made Oller's dancing and choreography so attractive to an international audience.

—Laura Kumin

PAGE, Ruth

American dancer, choreographer, and company director

Born: 22 March 1900 in Indianapolis. **Education:** Began professional studies at age 12; studied with Jan Zalewski at Midway Gardens, Chicago, 1915; studied with Adolph Bolm and Enrico Cecchetti; studied with Harald Kreutzberg, 1932. **Family:** Married Thomas Hart Fisher, 1925; widowed, 1969; married artist Andre Delfau, 1983. **Career:** Appeared in Victor Herbert's revue *Miss 1917* with George Gershwin as rehearsal pianist, 1917; danced with Anna Pavlova on her South American tour, 1918-19; première danseuse, Adolph Bolm's Ballet Intime, 1920-22; Irving Berlin's *Music Box Revue,* 1922-24; Chicago Allied Arts, 1924-26; joined Diaghilev's Ballets Russes de Monte Carlo, 1925; commissioned *Polka Mélancolique* from George Balanchine, 1925; appeared as a guest artist and danced in command performance for Edward, Prince of Wales, Teatro Colon, Buenos Aires, Argentina, 1925; dancer/ballet director for Ravinia Opera, 1926-31; guest soloist, Metropolitan Opera, 1927; principal dancer, Adolph Bolm Ballet, 1927-28; guest artist, coronation ceremonies for Emperor Hirohito, Tokyo, Japan, 1928; appeared with Edwin Strawbridge, Tokyo and New York, 1928-29; toured Asia, Europe, and Cuba, 1928-29; guest artist, Sophil Society, Moscow, 1930; toured with Harald Kreutzberg, U.S. and Japan, 1933-36; guest artist and choreographer for Century of Progress, Chicago, 1933; began partnership with Bentley Stone, 1934; solo performances of new modern works, Cuba, 1932; throughout U.S., 1930-35; and in Scandinavia, 1937; dancer/ballet director of Chicago Opera, 1934-37; founder, dancer, and director, Ruth Page Ballet, 1934-38; dancer/co-director, Chicago Federal Theatre Project of the WPA, 1938-39; dancer/co-director, Page-Stone Ballet, 1940-49; dancer/ballet director, Chicago Opera Company, 1942-45; choreographed for Broadway musical *Music in My Heart,* 1947; artist-in-residence with Bentley Stone at Jacob's Pillow Dance Festival, 1948; co-director and principal dancer of Les Ballets Américains, Paris, 1950; choreographer/ballet director of Chicago Lyric Opera, 1954-70; choreographer/director, Ruth Page's Chicago Opera Ballet, 1955-66; featured Rudolf Nureyev in his U.S. stage debut at Brooklyn Academy of Music (BAM), 1962; choreographer and director Ruth Page's International Ballet, 1966-69; established the Ruth Page Foundation, 1970; toured with *Ruth Page's Invitation to the Dance,* 1970-72; founded the Ruth Page Foundation School of Dance, 1971; director of Chicago Ballet, 1972-78; restaged ballets, authored books, and lectured on dance, 1978-91. **Died:** 7 April 1991.

Roles

1919	Infanta, *Birthday of the Infanta*
1924	*Foyer de la Danse* (Bolm)
1925	*The Rivals, Polovetsian Dances, Mandragora, The Elopement,* and *Bal des Marionettes*
	Coq d'Or, Petrouchka, Lorelei, Teatro Colon, Buenos Aires
1926	*La Farce du Pont Neuf, Visual Mysticism,* and *Parnassus on Montmartre,* (Bolm)
1927	*The Bartered Bride,* Metropolitan Opera, New York
1928	Terpsichore, *Apollon Musagetes* (Bolm)
1931	Princess, *L'Histoire du Soldat*

Works

1921	*The Poisoned Flower* (mus. Hahn) solo, Apollo Theater, New York
1922	*Chopin Mazurka* (mus. Chopin) solo, Vassar College, Poughkeepsie, New York
1926	*Peter Pan and the Butterfly* (mus. Poldini) solo, Goodman Theater, Chicago
	Flapper and Quarterback w/Paul du Pont (mus. Loomis), Eighth Street Theater, Chicago
1927	*Creole Dances* (also known as *Bayou Ballads* and *Negro Dances of New Orleans*) w/Marcia Preble (mus. traditional), Central High School, Madison, Wisconsin
	The Snow Is Dancing w/Marcia Preble and Berenice Holmes (mus. Debussy), Hampden Theatre, New York
1928	*Barnum and Bailey* (also known as *Circus* and *Tightrope Walker*) w/Ann Sharkey (mus. Smetana), Ravinia Park, Chicago
	Coquette—1899 (mus. Joplin) solo, Ravinia Park, Chicago
	Moonlight Sailing w/Marguerite Stanton and Ann Sharkey (mus. Zeckwer), Ravinia Park, Chicago
	Blues (mus. Gershwin) solo, Ravinia Park, Chicago
	The Shadow of Death w/Edwin Strawbridge (mus. Mussorgsky), Imperial Theater, Tokyo
	Diana (mus. Mozart) solo, Imperial Theatre, Tokyo
	Ballet Scaffolding (mus. Prokofiev) solo, Imperial Theatre, Tokyo
1929	*Japanese Print* (mus. original themes arr. by Walter Goodell) solo, Ravinia Park, Chicago
	Oak Street Beach (also known as *Sun Worshippers*) w/Edwin Strawbridge and group (mus. Loomis), Ravinia Park, Chicago
	Two Balinese Rhapsodies (mus. original themes arr. by Horst) solo, Chicago Women's Club, Chicago
	St. Louis Blues (mus. Handy), Chicago Woman's Club, Chicago
	Étude op 10 No 3 (mus. Chopin) solo, Guild Theatre, New York
1930	*Iberian Monotone* (also known as *Bolero*) w/Blake Scott and Ravinia Opera Ballet (mus. Ravel), Ravinia Park, Chicago

Garçonette (mus. Poulenc) solo, Nashville

Incantation (mus. Albéniz) solo, Nashville

Modern Diana (mus. Hindemith) solo, Nashville

Pre-Raphaelite (mus. Mompou) solo, Nashville

1931 *Humoresque* (also know as *Three Humoresque*) (mus. Ibert and Casella) solo, Lewisburg, Kentucky

Cinderella (mus. Delannoy), Ravinia Park, Chicago

Pavane (mus. Ravel), Booth Theatre, New York

La Valse (also known as *Waltz* and *Choreographic Waltz*) (mus. Ravel), Booth Theatre, New York

1932 *Tropic* (mus. Scott) solo, Amalgamated Centre, Chicago

Cuban Night (mus. Casado) solo, State Normal University, Bloomington, Indiana

Lament (mus. Tcherepnine) solo, State Normal University, Bloomington, Indiana

Possessed (mus. Villa-Lobos) solo, State Normal University, Bloomington, Indiana

Vagabond (mus. Vaughan Williams) solo, Capen Auditorium, State Normal University, Bloomington, Indiana

Largo (mus. Vinci) solo, Festival Hall, Fargo, North Dakota

Expanding Universe (also known as *Figures in Space*) solo, (mus. Wolf), Fargo, North Dakota

1933 *Variations on Euclid* (mus. Mompou) solo, Loyola University, Chicago

Morning in Spring (mus. Vaughan Williams) solo, John Golden Theatre, New York

Country Dance w/Harald Kreutzberg (mus. Wilckens), Studebaker Theatre, Chicago

Promenade w/Harald Kreutzberg (mus. Poulenc), Studebaker Theatre, Chicago

La Guiablesse w/African American dance ensemble (mus. Grant Still), Auditorium Theatre, Chicago

Jungle (mus. Scott) solo, International House, Chicago

Mozart Waltzes (mus. Mozart) solo, International House, Chicago

My Sorrow Is My Song (mus. Milhaud) solo, International House, Chicago

Pendulum (mus. Mompou) solo, International House, Chicago

Resurgence (mus. Kodály) solo, International House, Chicago

Rustic Saint's Day (mus. Respighi) solo, International House, Chicago

Shadow Dance—Homage to Taglioni (mus. Mendelssohn) solo, International House, Chicago

Songs (mus. Gershwin, arr. by Robert Wolf) solo, International House, Chicago

1934 *Arabian Nights* w/Harald Kreutzberg (mus. Satie), Shrine Temple, Peoria, Illinois

Bacchanale w/Harald Kreutzberg (mus. Wilckens), Orchestra Hall, Chicago

Gold Standard (mus. Ibert), Chicago Opera Ballet, Chicago

Hear Ye! Hear Ye! (mus. Copland), Chicago Opera Ballet, Chicago

1935 *Body in Sunlight* (mus. Wolf) solo, Studebaker Theatre, Chicago

Fresh Fields (mus. Bartók) solo, Studebaker Theatre, Chicago

Night Melody (mus. Debussy) solo, Studebaker Theatre, Chicago

Valse Mondaine (mus. Castelnuovo-Tedesco) solo, Studebaker Theatre, Chicago

Fugitive Visions (mus. Prokofiev) solo, Carmel, New York

Love Song (mus. Schubert), Chicago Opera Ballet, Chicago

1936 *An American in Paris* (mus. Gershwin), Cincinnati Opera Company, Cincinnati, Ohio

Hicks at the Country Fair w/Bentley Stone (mus. Stravinsky), Woman's Club of Wisconsin

1937 *American Pattern* w/Bentley Stone (mus. Moross), Chicago City Opera Company, Chicago

1938 *Buenos Días Señorita* w/Bentley Stone (mus. Villa-Lobos), Mt. Vernon, Iowa

Gavotte w/Bentley Stone (mus. Bach), Mt. Vernon, Iowa

Delirious Delusion (mus. Mompou) solo, Rogers Park Woman's Club, Chicago

The Story of a Heart w/Bentley Stone and Walter Camryn (mus. Casella), Chicago

Frankie and Johnny w/Bentley Stone (mus. Moross), Federal Ballet, Chicago

1939 *Guns and Castanets* w/Bentley Stone (mus. Bizet, selected and adapted by Jerome Moross; songs from the poems of Lorca), Page-Stone Ballet, Chicago

Liebestod w/Bentley Stone (mus. Wagner), Civic Theatre, Chicago

Night of the Poor w/Bentley Stone (mus. Debussy), Civic Theatre, Chicago

Saudades w/Bentley Stone (mus. Villa-Lobos), Civic Theatre, Chicago

Three Shakespearean Heroines (mus. Schubert, Liszt, Wilckens and Beethoven, arr. by David Schienfield) solo, Chicago

Zephyr and Flora w/Bentley Stone (mus. Liszt), Civic Theatre, Chicago

1940 *Songs of Carl Sandburg* (mus. Carl Sandburg) solo, Chicago

Catarina; or The Daughter of the Bandit (mus. Drigo) solo, Sociedad Pro-Arte Musical, Havana, Cuba

1941 *Spanish Dance in Ballet Form* (mus. Albéniz) solo, Goodman Theatre, Chicago

Chopin in Our Time (mus. Chopin), Bentley Stone and company, Chicago

Les Incroyables w/Bentley Stone (mus. Wolf-Ferrari), Rainbow Room, New York

Park Avenue Odalisque (mus. Granados y Campra) solo, Rainbow Room, New York

1942 *Dances with Words and Music* (mus. Engel)

1943 *Death in Harlem* (mus. Garland, arr. by Engel with words by Langston Hughes) solo, Humphrey-Weidman Studio Theatre, New York

1946 *Les Petis Riens* (mus. Mozart), Ballet for America Company, Montreal

The Bells (mus. Milhaud), Ballet Russe de Monte Carlo, Chicago

Billy Sunday (mus. Gassman), Chicago Opera Ballet, Chicago

1948 *Harlequinade* w/Bentley Stone (mus. Casella), Maysville, Kentucky

1949 *Beauty and the Beast* (mus. Tchaikovsky), Chicago Grand Opera Ballet, Milwaukee

Dance of the Hours (mus. Ponchielli), Chicago Grand Opera Ballet, Milwaukee

1951   *Beethoven Sonata* (mus. Beethoven), Page-Stone-Camryn Ballet, Chicago

Impromptu Au Bois (mus. Ibert), Les Ballets des Champs-Élysées, Germany

Revenge (mus. Verdi, arr. by Van Grove), Les Ballets des Champs-Élysées, Paris

1952   *Daughter of Herodias* (also known as *Retribution*) duet, Evansville, Indiana

1953   *The Merry Widow* (also known as *Vilia*) (mus. Lehar, arr. by Van Grove), London Festival Ballet, Manchester

1954   *El Amor Brujo* (mus. De Falla), Ballet Guild of Chicago

Triumph of Chastity (mus. Ibert), Ballet Guild of Chicago

1956   *Susanna and the Barber* (mus. Rossini, arr. by Van Grove), Chicago Opera Ballet

1959   *Camille* (mus. Verdi), Chicago Opera Ballet, Columbia, Missouri

1960   *Carmen* (mus. Bizet, arr. by Van Grove), Ruth Page's Chicago Opera Ballet, Dubuque, Iowa

1961   *Concertino pour Trois* (mus. Constant), Rockford, Illinois

Die Fledermaus (mus. Strauss, arr. by Van Grove), Chicago Opera Ballet, Rockford, Illinois

1963   *Mephistofela* (mus. Gounod, Boito, Berlioz, arr. by Van Grove), Chicago Opera Ballet, Park Ridge, Illinois

Pygmalion (mus. Von Suppé), Chicago Opera Ballet, Park Ridge, Illinois

Combinations (mus. Van Grove), Ballet Guild of Chicago

1965   *Bullets and Bonbons* (also known as *All's Fair in Love and War*) (mus. Strauss), Chicago Opera Ballet, Springfield, Illinois

Carmina Burana w/Harald Kreutzberg (mus. Orff), Chicago Opera Ballet and Lyric Opera of Chicago

Nutcracker (mus. Tchaikovsky), Ruth Page's International Ballet, Chicago

1966   *The Jar* (mus. Casella), Chicago Opera Ballet

1968   *Bolero '69* (mus. Ravel), Ruth Page's International Ballet, LaCrosse, Wisconsin

1969   *Romeo and Juliet* (mus. Tchaikovsky), Ruth Page's International Ballet, Niles, Michigan

1970   *Alice in the Garden* (mus. various, arr. by Van Grove), Jacob's Pillow School of the Dance, Lee, Massachusetts

1973   *Catulli Carmina* (mus. Orff), Pittsburgh Ballet Theatre

Publications

By PAGE: books—

Class: Notes on Dance Classes Around the World, 1915-1980, Princeton, New Jersey, 1984.
Page by Page, Brooklyn, New York, 1978.

On PAGE: book—

Martin, John, *Ruth Page: An Intimate Biography,* New York, 1977.

On PAGE: articles—

Barzel, Ann, "Ruth Page: Chicago's Dance Legend," *Chicago Dance Coalition,* Fall 1991.

Wentink, Andrew Mark, "The Ruth Page Collection," *Bulletin of Research in the Humanities,* Spring 1980.
White, Thelma, "Who Is Ballet's Remarkable Ruth Page?" *Dance Teacher Now,* October 1990.

Films and Videotapes

Dance Macabre, film with appearance by Page, 1922.
Ruth Page: An American Original, Otter Productions, 1977.
Ruth Page: Once Upon A Dance, Thea Flaum Productions for WTTW-TV, 1988.
Ruth Page Video Archive, Thea Flaum Productions, 1990.

*   *   *

Dancer, choreographer, and company director, Ruth Page's contributions to modern dance are many. This Chicagoan, whose name is often connected with the ballet world, was an American dance pioneer who worked closely with many modern dancers and was instrumental in the development of the American themes, the dramatic expressions and styles, and the experimental movements that have characterized modern dance. She was also responsible for developing an international audience for this new dance form.

Page was born in Indianapolis, Indiana, in 1900. Her early training with Chicago-based Jan Zalewski, from the Anna Pavlova Company, led to further study with Pavlova's former partner and experimental choreographer, Adolph Bolm. Her early career included tours with Pavlova's company in South America and with Bolm throughout the U.S. and England. She studied with Enrico Cecchetti when he was teaching with Diaghilev's Ballets Russes de Monte Carlo. This resulted in her becoming the only American to join this prestigious company. While working with the company, she met a very young George Balanchine and asked him to choreograph one of his first works for her. These early associations with major innovators taught her well.

As early as 1926, Page began to choreograph dances with American themes. Her first Americana ballet, as they were called, was *The Flapper and the Quarterback.* It is an example of the kind of modern choreography she would carry into her later career. The most important of her works in this style is *Frankie and Johnny,* based on the lyrics of the popular American song. Created in conjunction with Bentley Stone for the WPA's Federal Theatre Project in 1938, this work remains a classic example of the Americana genre and is still performed today. Other works of this nature included *Creole Dances* (1927); *Blues* (1928), with music by George Gershwin; *Oak Street Beach* (1929); *St. Louis Blues* (1929), *Hear Ye! Hear Ye!* (1934), with the first commissioned dance score by Aaron Copland; *An American in Paris* (1936); *American Pattern* (1937), which is considered the first feminist dance work; and *Death in Harlem* (1943).

Page toured Asia, the Middle East, and South America as a young dancer. It was this extensive travel that developed her love for exotic, abstract, shocking, and highly dramatic presentations. Because of their stylized, primitive movements, her *Possessed* (1932) and *Tropic* (1932) were said to have shocked and delighted audiences whenever they were performed. Performed on the floor with a mask, *Tropic* was called a daring work when it was first introduced into her repertoire. Costumes, like the sticks and strings she wore in *Variations on Euclid* (1933), the sack in *Expanding Universe* (1932), the masks of *Fugitive Vision* (1935), and the huge Daliesque eye on her stomach in *Delirious Delusion* (1938), also contributed to the strikingly unusual look of her dances.

Some of the other titles in her repertoire that reflected these influences include *Flapper Goes Oriental* (1929), *Japanese Print* (1929), *Two Balinese Rhapsodies* (1929), *Jungle* (1933), *Songs* (1933), and *Body In Sunlight* (1935). Many of these works were performed by Page in a solo program called *New Dances* which she presented between 1933 and 1935 in the U.S. One such performance was part of a series called "Students' Dance Recitals" at Washington Irving High School in New York which also featured performances by Martha Graham, Doris Humphrey, and Charles Weidman. Page also toured with *New Dances,* traveling to Cuba in 1932 and to Scandinavia in 1937.

Poetry and the spoken word strongly influenced Page's dances. She led the way in creating pieces which were inspired by poems, performed to poetic rhythms, or in which the dancers spoke. Her *Songs of Carl Sandburg* (1940), in which she danced to a recording of Carl Sandburg, began this trend. This work was followed by *Chopin in Our Time* (1941), an offbeat treatment of Chopin's music accompanied by words. These creations culminated in a program of solo dances called *Dances with Words and Music* (1942-45) in which Page spoke and danced to the works of e.e. cummings, Archibald MacLeish, Mark Turbyfill, Dorothy Parker, Baudelaire, Ogden Nash, Eugene Field, Garcia Lorca, and Langston Hughes, to name a few. Page premiered a full evening of these works in the Humphrey-Weidman Studio Theatre in 1943. Her full-length "rowdy modern" ballet, *The Bells,* based on the Edgar Allan Poe poem of the same name, was created in 1946 for the Ballets Russes. The avant-garde *Billy Sunday,* which also opened in 1946, included a word-score as part of the dance.

In addition to her own contributions, Page had working relationships with many important modern dance pioneers. Her support of, and influence on, the careers of these early modern dance artists was considerable. In the mid-1920s modern dance pioneer Edwin Strawbridge joined her Ravinia Opera House company and danced with Page on tour in Japan. In the summer of 1932, Page studied with international modern dance great Harald Kreutzberg in Salzburg. The following year, she and Kreutzberg teamed up to develop a three-year partnership which gave joint recitals in the U.S., Canada, and Japan. She worked with him again in 1965 when he danced in her *Carmina Burana* at the Chicago Opera House. In November 1932 she premiered her *Expanding Universe* (sometimes called *Figures in Space*) which was danced inside the sack costume created by her close friend, and future Martha Graham designer, Japanese-American modern artist Isamu Noguchi. She collaborated with him again in 1946 when he did the costumes and set designs for *The Bells.*

Between 1932 and 1934, American modern dance composer Louis Horst played for her *New Dances* program. In 1934 renowned dance figure Katherine Dunham starred in Page's all-African American cast ballet, *La Guiablesse,* which was composed by William Grant Still. In 1946 she invited the famed anthropological modern dance artist, Pearl Primus, to play the witch doctor in the Chicago production of *The Emperor Jones.* In 1950 Page and her partner Bentley Stone collaborated with José Limón to create the controversial Les Ballets Américains, which was the first American modern dance company to appear in Paris after World War II. This company, which horrified Paris with its bold realism and candid humor, also included future modern dance choreographers Pauline Koner, Lucas Hoving, Betty Jones, and Talley Beatty.

As Page's career progressed, she became interested in creating more traditional opera ballets, choreographing more than a dozen such works in the latter part of her career. Her Chicago Opera Ballet, and later her International Ballet, became world-renowned. However, despite the classical nature of her later work, she still continued to be innovative, challenging her audiences with new ideas and styles of movement. In 1973 she founded the Chicago Ballet, with a repertoire ranging from classical ballet pieces to new and established modern dance works, including a reconstruction of Doris Humphrey's *Water Study.*

In 1970 Ruth Page established a foundation in Chicago to support all kinds of dance and dance related projects, as well as the rest of the performing arts. As part of this effort, in 1971 she founded a professional dance school which became one of the major training centers in the U.S. She used this school as a base for educating current and future dance audiences everywhere until her death in 1991.

When Ruth Page began dancing and choreographing, there were no modern dance audiences, companies, or training institutions. Her lifelong efforts changed all of this. Because she loved American themes, new and challenging ideas, and poetry, she incorporated them into her works which were seen worldwide, helping to promote and develop international modern dance audiences wherever she went. She not only created dances that showed open-mindedness, a willingness to explore, and the strength to withstand the controversy they created, but she also worked with and encouraged others in the dance world who were building the foundations of modern dance. Her collaborations with individual modern dance artists, composers, and designers, as well as her work with her own dance companies, are a testament to her far reaching influence. The creation of her own foundation and dance school would carry on the work she had begun; the trails blazed by Ruth Page helped modern dance to flourish and become what it is today.

—Paula Murphy

PALUCCA, Gret

German dancer, choreographer, and educator

Born: 8 January 1902 in Munich. **Education:** Studied ballet with Henrich Kröller, 1918; at the Munich State Opera, and with Mary Wigman, 1918-23. **Career:** Operated a dance school in Dresden, 1925-39; and again from 1945-93; founding member, Academy of Arts, Berlin, 1950; vice president, Academy of Arts, 1965-74. **Awards:** National Prize Second Class, 1960; Fatherland's Merit Order in Gold, 1972; Star of Friendship Among Nations in Gold, 1980; National Prize First Class, 1981. **Died:** 1993.

Works

1927   *Technical Improvisations*

Other works include: *Light Beginning, Bright Dances, Dark Force, Apassionata, Distant Swinging,* and *Two Fragments: Quiet Song, Driving Rhythm.*

Publications

By PALUCCA: articles—

"Gedanken und Erfahrungen," *Deutsche Tanzfestspiele* (Dresden), 1934.

"Ich Will Nicht Hübsch und Lieblich Tanzen," from *Palucca zum Fünfundachtzigsten*, Berlin, 1987.

On PALUCCA: books—

Anderson, Jack, *Art without Boundaries: The World of Modern Dance*, Iowa City, 1997.
Garske, Rolf, *Ballett: Chronik und Bilanz des Ballettjahres*, Zurich, 1985.

On PALUCCA: articles—

Arnheim, Rudolf, "Visiting Palucca," *Dance Scope*, Fall 1978.
Berghaus, Ruth, "In Memoriam Gret Palucca," *Ballett-Journal/Das Tanzarchiv* (Cologne), June 1993.
Bernard, Alain, "Zum 80: Geburtstag von Gret Palucca," *Tanz und Gymnastik* (Zurich), March 1982.
Bleier, Genia, "Ihrem Rhythmus Getreu: Zum 90. Geburtstag Von Gret Palucca," *Tanz und Gymnastik* (Zurich), 1992.
Garske, Rolf, "Learning to Think from an Early Age: Interview With Gret Palucca," *Ballett-International* (Cologne), December 1983.
Kramer, Klaus, "Gret Palucca—90 Jahre," *Tanzen* (Remscheid, Germany), 1992.
Oberzaucher-Schüller, Gunhild, "Gruss im Sprung: zum Tode von Gret Palucca," *Tanz Affiche* (Vienna), June/July 1993.
Peters, Kurt, "Deutscher Tanzpreis 1983: 'Bäume zum Blühen Bringen,' Laudationes für Tatjana Gsovsky und Gret Palucca," *Ballett-Journal/Das Tanzarchiv* (Cologne), June 1983.
———, "Mit der Jugend Jung Geblieben: Zum 85. Geburtstag Von Gret Palucca," *Ballett-Journal/Das Tanzarchiv* (Cologne), February 1987.
Rebling, Eberhard, "Dem Humanismus Verpflichtet: Gret Palucca Wurde 80 Jahre Alt," *Ballett-Journal/das Tanzarchiv* (Cologne), 1982.
Regitz, Hartmut, "Gret Palucca, 75," *Das Tanzarchiv* (Cologne), February 1977.

*   *   *

John Martin, visiting the July 1930 Third German Dance Congress in Munich, wrote somewhat critically of Mary Wigman's outstanding pupil Gret Palucca, by then already well-established as a dancer in her own right: "in spite of her many good points, [she] has fallen into mannerisms, physical and mental," and in "composition she is utterly unimaginative." And yet, Martin also wrote, "Her technique, however, is tremendous, and is not exhibited for its own sake at any time." Perhaps most significant was the contrast to the stereotypically "heavy" German style: "There is a charm of manner, a lightness of spirit, a lyrical lift, that make a rift in the heaviness of the Teutonic atmosphere."

Certainly Palucca's method as a dancer contrasted sharply with that of her teacher, Wigman. Just as Karl Marx—a man who would indirectly have a heavy effect on the latter part of Palucca's life—is said to have stood the philosophies of Hegel on their head, so Palucca reversed everything she learned from her mentor. Many have taken it as a credit to Wigman that her teaching allowed the pupil room in which to develop on her own, and Palucca certainly did, diverging widely from the dramatic, deeply emotional style of Wigman.

Palucca, who spent part of her childhood in California, returned to Germany as a young woman following World War I. Frustrated by the rigidity of ballet technique, she might have given up dance had Wigman not discovered her and brought her under her tutelage. In the *Mary Wigman Book,* Wigman described Palucca as a "narrow-hipped, boyish-looking girl with a pert face framed by reddish-blond hair." Yet this unlikely student, Wigman continued, had "an excellent temperament with a natural ability to jump such as I have never experienced." In 1925, when she was 23, Palucca formed her own school in Dresden, an institution she would operate—with the exception of the World War II years—continuously until her death nearly 70 years later. Palucca also began to perfect her style, which was classical in the purest sense of the term: economical, clean of line, unemotional, and abstract. "Choreographically," Jack Anderson has written, "Palucca concerned herself with movement qualities, rather than emotional evocations." Anderson notes the titles of her compositions, which suggest gradations of light or intensity rather than emotional states—e.g., *Bright Dances*, *Dark Force*.

One of her more well-known works was *Technical Improvisations* (1927), a sort of étude. Just as Chopin a century before turned finger-exercises on a piano into an art form of their own with his highly listenable études, Palucca built a dance on her morning warmup exercises. The movements she made when getting limbered up became, through the art of her own improvisation, "a systematic exploration of the anatomy" (in Rudolf Arnheim's words) which could evoke laughter from an audience. In a 1978 profile Arnheim, who had known Palucca for half a century, quoted approvingly Edgar Allan Poe's observation regarding Taglioni: "I should not say exactly that she dances, but that she laughs with her arms and legs."

In her dedication to precision, Palucca discovered a certain kinship with various visual artists. She kept a Mondrian on the wall above the piano in her studio, and Wassily Kandinsky professed admiration for her work: "What I want to stress here is the unusually precise structure," he wrote, "not only in the temporal development of her dances but first of all in the configuration of particular movements." Another admirer was Laszlo Moholy-Nagy of the Bauhaus school, who said she was "the newly found law of motion."

Whereas Palucca's work was formal, seldom engaging emotions beyond the sheer joy of doing or of a craft well-executed, her life took place against a perilous political landscape. While other artists escaped Germany after Hitler's accession to power in 1933, Palucca stayed on. She played a part not only in the Berlin Dance Festival of 1934, but in the pageantry that accompanied the staging of the infamous 1936 Berlin Olympics. Wigman, too, stayed on, and Anderson credits her inaction with harming Americans' view of German dance. At least Wigman got out of Dresden, unlike Palucca, who endured some of the worst bombing of the war. Perhaps even more disastrous to any further growth as an artist was the transfer of eastern Germany from the Nazis to the communist form of totalitarianism. Hitler's form of tyranny was so obviously evil that artists more political than Palucca were bound to speak out against it; but the half-century of repression that followed for East Germany did not evoke such reactions. Arnheim, for instance, visiting Palucca in Dresden in 1978, commented rather weakly about the influence of the Russian ballet, "which Palucca had fought as a child [but which] now added elements to the preparation of dancers for theater and opera."

In any case, Palucca's was not a style likely to develop or change even in a climate of much greater artistic freedom. It seems to have been fixed in place before the war, and by the time greater freedom came to her side of Germany, Palucca was almost 90. She would be remembered for her joyful style and her grace of movement, which Arnheim still glimpsed vividly when he visited her in her 77th year.

—Judson Knight

PARK Myung-sook

Korean dancer, choreographer, artistic director, and educator

Born: 5 August 1950 in Seoul. **Education:** Bachelor's and master's degrees, Ewha Women's University; Ph.D., Hanyang University; attended New York University's doctorate program, studying with Merce Cunningham, Alvin Ailey, and Martha Graham, 1980-88. **Career:** Mary Magdeline in Jesus Christ, Superstar (by Yook Wan-soon), 1975; formed Park Myung-sook Dance Company 1978; first performance abroad (*Invocation of the Dead Spirit*), Carnegie Hall, 1981; professor, Kyounghee University, 1981; changed company name to Park Myung-sook & Park Myung-sook Seoul Contemporary Dance Company, 1986; participated in Asian Games Cultural Celebration Arts Festival performance, 1986; the Olympic Festival performance of *The Light of the Beginning of the World*, 1988; Dance Expo, 1993; World Dramatic Art Festival, 1997; produced Park Myung-sook & Park Myung-sook Seoul Contemporary Dance Company on KBS-TV, 1995; founding member, Yaejang Rotary Club. **Awards:** Best acting, Dance Festival of Korea, 1981; Grand Prize in choreography, acting and music prizes, Seoul International Dance festival, 1991; Artist of the Year, Federation of Korean Artistic and Cultural Organizations, 1995.

Roles

1971	Lady in *The Origin of Dankun* (Yook Wan-soon), Orchesis Dance Company, Seoul
	Dessin II (Yook Wan-soon), Orchesis Dance Company, Seoul
	Self in *Forgotten Self* (Yook Wan-soon), Orchesis Dance Company, Seoul
1975	Mary Magdeline in *Jesus Christ Superstar* (Yook Wan-soon), Ewha Dance Company, Seoul, L.A., San Francisco, Chicago, Washington D.C., Atlantic City, Nashville, Rome, Cosenza
1976	Candle in *Oh! Candlelight* (Yook Wan-soon), Korea Contemporary Dance Company, Seoul
1980	*Salpuri '80* (Lee Jung-hee), Korea Contemporary Dance Company, Seoul
1981	*A Journey of 13th Month* (Kim Ki-in), Korea Dance Theater, New York
1982	*Hands from the Cauldron* (Barry Fisher), Barry Fisher Dance Theater, New York
1983	*About the Things that Pass On* (Kim Kyung-ock), Korea Contemporary Dance Company, Seoul
	Whale in *Whale Ride* (Throne Tyre), Korea Contemporary Dance Company, Seoul
1984	*Purple Color* (Kim Ki-in), Korea Contemporary Dance Company, Seoul
1985	Forsythia in *The Village of Forsythia* (Orita Gatzuko), Korea Modern Dance Company, Seoul

	The One Thing (Kim Ki-in), Korea Contemporary Dance Company, Seoul
1986	*Negro Spiritual* (Yook Wan-soon), Korea Contemporary Dance Company, Seoul
	Dove in *Only a Dove Flies* (Park In-sook), Korea Contemporary Dance Company, Seoul
1987	*Pac-Man* (Park In-sook), Korea Contemporary Dance Company, Seoul
1988	*Twirler-Theatre-Tambour* (Kim Ki-in), Korea Contemporary Dance Company, Seoul
1991	Chief Mourner in *Encounter* (Yook Wan-soon), Korea Dance Company, Moscow, Leningrad
1993	Mother Crane in *The Crane II* (Yook Wan-soon), Korea Contemporary Dance Company, Beijing, Seoul
1995	Lady in *Once Again, with the Beautiful Line of Vision* (Ahn Shin-hee), Korea Contemporary Dance Company, Seoul

Works

1976	*Mad Spirit* (mus. Jang Doug-sahn) solo, Academy House, Seoul
1977	*Paranoia* (mus. Jang Doug-sahn) solo, Academy House, Seoul
1978	*Everything Is Dance* (mus. Jang Doug-sahn), Korea Contemporary Dance Company, National Theatre of Korea, Seoul
	Appear and Disappear (mus. Jang Doug-sahn), Korea Contemporary Dance Company, National Theatre of Korea, Seoul
	The Melancholy Twilight (mus. Jang Doug-sahn) solo, Sejong Cultural Center, Seoul
1980	*Paper Flower* (mus. Jang Doug-sahn) solo, Space Theatre, Seoul
	To Greens (mus. Jang Doug-shan) solo, Space Theatre, Seoul
1981	*Cho-Hon* (mus. Kim Young-dong) solo, Carnegie Hall, New York
	Melody of Ka Na Da Ra (mus. Kim Jung-gil) solo, Carnegie Hall, New York
	Seung Mu (mus. Lee Young-jo) solo, Carnegie Hall, New York
	You've Come Secretly (mus. Lee Young-jo) solo, Carnegie Hall, New York
1982	*Some Silence* (mus. arranged Jang Doug-sahn), Park Myung-sook & Park Myung-sook Dance Company, Munye Theatre, Seoul
1983	*Phantansie* (mus. Kim Young-sik), Park Myung-sook & Park Myung-sook Dance Company, Catholic Center, Pusan
	Improvisation for Dancers (mus. Kim Young-sik), Park Myung-sook & Park Myung-sook Dance Company, Munye Theatre, Seoul
	Esquisse (mus. Kim Young-dong) solo, Munye Theatre, Seoul
1984	*Walking Man Who Is Sleeping, Walking Tree in Sleeping* (mus. various, arranged Jang Doug-sahn), Park Myung-sook & Park Myung-sook Dance Company, Munye Theatre, Seoul
	December (mus. various, arranged Jang Doug-sahn) solo, Munye Theatre, Seoul

1985   *A Human Being of Eden* (mus. arranged Jang, Doug-sahn), Korea Contemporary Dance Company, Hoam Art Hall, Seoul

Spring Spirit (mus. various, arranged Jang Doug-sahn), duet for Hong Seung-yub and Chang Ae-suk, NYU Dance Theatre, New York

Rain (mus. various, arranged Jang Doug-sahn) solo, Tokyo

Nine Clouds and Nine Dreams (mus. Lee Jong-eun), Korea Contemporary Dance Company, Hoam Art Hall, Seoul

1986   *Wedding and Funeral Ceremony* (mus. various, arranged Jang Doug-sahn), Park Myung-sook & Park Myung-sook Dance Company, Munye Theatre, Seoul

Illusion of Leaves of Grass (mus. Choi Dong-sun, arranged Lee Jong-eun), Korea Contemporary Dance Company, 10th Asian Games Dance Festival, National Theatre of Korea, Seoul

1987   *TIME* (mus. various, arranged Jang Doug-sahn), Park Myung-sook & Park Myung-sook Seoul Contemporary Dance Company, Munye Theatre, Seoul

Romeo 20 (mus. Jang Doug-sahn) for theater dir. Kim Sang-youl, Hyundai Theatre Company, Seoul

Oh Fellow, Give Me Your Hands (mus. Hong Yon-tack), Park Myung-sook & Park Myung-sook Seoul Contemporary Dance Company, National Theatre of Korea, Seoul

The House of Two Women (mus. Lee, Jong-eun) for film, dir. Kwak Ji-yoon, Seoul

Despite It's Being a Windy Day, the Flowers Bloom... (mus. Lee Jong-eun) for film, dir. Kim Jung-ock, Seoul

1988   *Light Silk Gown with White Hat* (mus. Lee Young-jo) solo, New Port Kangi Hogeng Hall, Tokyo

Light of the Beginning (mus. Kim Jung-gil), 24th Seoul Olympic Opening Ceremony, Chamsil Olympic Stadium, Seoul

Welcome (mus. Kim Jung-gil), 24th Seoul Olympic Ceremony, Chamsil Olympic Stadium, Seoul

The Rose Belongs to Nobody (mus.various, arranged Jang Doug-sahn), Park Myung-sook & Park Myung-sook Seoul Contemporary Dance Company, National Theatre of Korea, Seoul

1989   *A Tree Which Never Sleeps* (mus. various, arranged Jang Doug-sahn) for television, Park Myung-sook & Park Myung-sook Seoul Contemporary Dance Company, Munwha Broadcasting Corporation (MBC), Seoul

The Day of Dawn I (mus. Park Ill-kyu), Park Myung-sook & Park Myung-sook Seoul Contemporary Dance Company, Munye Theatre, Seoul

1990   *We Blew the Trumpet* (mus. Lee Jong-eun) for play, dir. Kim Sang-youl, Sinsi Theatre Company, Seoul

A Celebration of Wild Flowers (mus. various, arranged Park Ill-kyu), Park Myung-sook & Park Myung-sook Seoul Contemporary Dance Company, National Theatre of Korea, Seoul

The Torch of Koguryo (mus. Park Ill-kyu), Park Myung-sook & Park Myung-sook Seoul Contemporary Dance Company, Munye Theatre, Seoul

The Day of Dawn (mus. Park Ill-kyu), Park Myung-sook & Park Myung-sook Seoul Contemporary Dance Company, Symphony Space Inc., New York

1991   *Evaporated Desert* (mus. various, arranged Jang Doug-sahn), Park Myung-sook & Park Myung-sook Seoul Contemporary Dance Company, National Theatre of Korea, Seoul

Hwang Jo Ga (mus. Lee Dong-joon, arranged Park Ill-kyu), Park Myung-sook & Seoul Contemporary Dance Company, Munye Theatre, Seoul

1993   *The Morning Wakes Up Alone* (mus. various, arranged Cho Gap-joong), Park Myung-sook & Park Myung-sook Seoul Contemporary Dance Company, Munye Theatre, Seoul

Beyond Adversity/Toward the New Beginning (mus. Lee Bum-hee), Park Myung-sook & Seoul Contemporary Dance Company, Taejun EXPO '93

1994   *Soaring* (mus. Lee Bum-hee), Park Myung-sook & Park Myung-sook Seoul Contemporary Dance Company, Kyounghee University, Seoul

River (mus. Jang Dong-sahn), Park Myung-sook & Park Myung-sook Seoul Contemporary Dance Company, Sejong Cultural Center Open Stage, Seoul

Seoul Citizens (mus. Kim Jung-tack), Seoul Metropolitan Musical Company, Sejong Cultural Center, Seoul

1995   *Turn Round and Look Out* (mus. Lee Kun-young), Park Myung-sook & Park Myung-sook Seoul Contemporary Dance Company, Munye Theatre, Seoul

1996   *Ritual Dance* (mus. Kim Young-dong), Park Myung-sook & Park Myung-sook Seoul Contemporary Dance Company, Jangchung Stadium, Seoul

Dying Young (mus.various, arranged Jang Doug-sahn), Park Myung-sook & Park Myung-sook Seoul Contemporary Dance Company, Kyounghee University, Seoul

Total Eclipse (mus.various, arranged Jang Doug-sahn), Park Myung-sook & Park Myung-sook Seoul Contemporary Dance Company, 15th International Modern Dance Festival, Seoul Education Culture Center, Seoul

Invocation for the Dead Spirit (mus. Kim Young-dong), Park Myung-sook & Park Myung-sook Seoul Contemporary Dance Company, Barnsdall Gallery Theatre, Los Angeles

Emi (mus. Kim Tae-keun), Park Myung-sook & Park Myung-sook Seoul Contemporary Dance Company, Seoul Arts Center, Seoul

1997   *Dance of Ceremony, Celebrating!*(mus. Kim Young-dong), Park Myung-sook & Park Myung-sook Seoul Contemporary Dance Company, Jangchung Stadium, Seoul

Veils of Time and Tide (mus. Kim Tae-keun), Park Myung-sook & Park Myung-sook Seoul Contemporary Dance Company, ICHPER-SD 40th World Congress, Suwon Cultural Art Center, Suwon

Publications

By PARK: books—

The Use of Pure Vocal Sound in the Dance: Theatre Pieces of Meredith Monk, Seoul, 1991.

On PARK: articles—

Jang Kwang-ryul, "The Dancer Who Changed the Modern Dance Wave in Korea," *Magazine Auditorium* 11, January 1985.

Park Myung-sook performing *Invocation for the Dead Spirit*. Photograph by Kim Chan-bock.

Kim Kyung-ae, "Making Feminist Literature into a Dance," *Acclaim & Criticism* (Seoul), 1996.

Kim Tae-won, "Literary Themes of Dance Theater: Park Myung-sook's *Fireworks of Koguryo,*" in *The Vision of Culture and Dance,* Seoul, 1991.

————, "The Meaning of Thirty Years of Modern Dance," in *The Great Advent of Dance Art,* Seoul, 1997.

Kim Young-tae, "Finishing the Feeling, Gravity and the Oval," in *Brown Bodies: The Beautiful Umbrellas,* 1985.

————, "Meeting with Park Myung-sook," in *Can a View Be Danced?*, Seoul, 1996.

*   *   *

Generally, lyricism and deep emotion characterize the works of Park Myung-sook. Her dances express a range of inner emotions, from the most mild longing to terrible misery—sometimes bordering on the edge of emotional extravagance. Her early works are mostly pictures of the varied and delicate emotions of women's inner selves. Yet her focus does not always linger on the individual; beginning in the mid-1990s, her works focus simultaneously on women in society and the meaning of women's existence in history. For example, *Emi* reveals new facets of her long pursuit of the feminine spirit. In *Emi* (mother), a piece centering on an ex-comfort girl for Japanese soldiers who is now elderly and suffering from dementia, she handles such heavy subjects as women and society, women and history, the continuity and discontinuity of a generation, yet without burdening the audience.

Another of her important works dealing with women's issues is *Morning Wakes Up Alone*, based on the novel by Lee Kyung-ja, who is often regarded as a feminist writer. The piece deals with a woman who has turned inward for a long time and is faced with limitations when trying to reach out to others.

In addition to her emotional sensitivity, Park is recognized for successfully merging both Korean traditional dance and Western dance. *Cho-Hun* is a solo fused with ambivalent and contrasting inner emotions—a fusion which becomes Park's forte and appears in many of her later works. It verifies the fact that she, as a choreographer and a dancer, takes women's sensibility seriously, but this goes often goes beyond expressing one woman's feelings and becomes a tool for observing human nature in general.

Park Myung-sook's early sensibilities and lyricism were transformed in the late 1980s when Park began dealing with ancient Korean myths and history. Park Myung-sook's interest in the nation's ancient history made an early appearance in the work *Nine Clouds and Nine Dreams* (1985) based on an old Korean novel, but in works such as *Some Silence, Walking Man Who Is Sleeping,*

Walking Tree in Sleeping, A Human Being of Eden, Wedding and Funeral Ceremony, and *Time,* she begins to deal with a fuller range of human problems. These works try to express and solve the entanglements of human lives through poetic images and ancient Korean myths.

In view of the general trends in the Korean dance society, Park maintains a relatively good rapport with the artists and intellectuals in other fields, often leading to cooperative works. In particular, she had a close personal and artistic relationship with the late Choi Wuk-kyung. Her performance of *Wedding and Funeral Ceremony* was given in honor of and in tribute to Choi Wuk-kyung who had ceaselessly inspired her both intellectually and artistically.

An important aspect of Park's contribution to Korean dance is her role as an educator. Her devotion to teaching is well-known. About 30 of her students are with Park Myung-sook & Park Myung-sook Seoul Contemporary Dance Company, which she founded in 1986. Ten of them are also presently working as choreographers. The company's artistic and choreographic tendencies travel two paths: one dealing with lyrical works based on Korea's traditional aesthetics and values, and the other depicting the lives and dreams of the modern people. *Nostalgia,* a work in the former category, was co-choreographed by Jang Ae-suk and Ahn Jung-jun and is rich in Korean lyricism; it received special recognition at the Susan Della Competition in Israel. A work more representative of the latter, is *Cyber Odyssey Space,* choreographed by Choi Sung-ok, which won an award at the Seoul International Dance Festival.

—Lee Jong-ho

PARSONS, David

American dancer, choreographer, and company director

Born: 29 October 1959 in Rockford, Illinois; grew up in Kansas City, Missouri. **Education:** Active in sports during childhood, especially wrestling and gymnastics (specialty, trampoline); studied modern dance with Cliff Kirwin and Paul Chambers (disciples of Hanya Holm) at Camelot Academy Summer Arts Program, 1972; attended Hanya Holm's summer dance course at Colorado College, Colorado Springs, 1974; scholarship to Ailey school, 1977; studied Horton, Graham and ballet at Ailey, but left after eight months to pursue career in music recording engineering; invited to understudy at Paul Taylor Dance Company, 1978. **Career:** Joined Kirwin & Chambers dance company, Missouri Dance Theatre (MDT), 1972-76; choreographed first work at MDT, 1973; danced in Kansas City production of Bernstein's *Mass,* staged by Clive and Liz Thompson, 1975; lead dancer, Paul Taylor Dance Company, 1978-87; returned to Missouri to set piece on MDT, 1978; worked with Moses Pendleton and Momix, 1982-87; began choreographing at Dance Theatre Workshop, 1980; founder, Parsons Dance Company, 1987; with first U.S. tour, 1987; first European appearance at Spoleto/Italy, 1988; toured Japan, South America, and Australia; guest artist with White Oak Dance Project, 1992; Berlin Opera Ballet, 1982; New York City Ballet, 1988-91. **Awards:** National Endowment for the Arts choreography fellowships, 1988, 1989, 1995.

Roles (with the Paul Taylor Dance Company unless otherwise noted)

1978   *Airs* (mus. Handel), New York
       Diggity (mus. D. York), University of Massachusetts, Amherst
1979   *Nightshade* (mus. Scriabin), New York
1980   *Le Sacre du Printemps* (as Henchman/Police; mus. Stravinsky), Kennedy Center, Washington D.C.
1981   *Arden Court* (mus. Wm. Boyce), New York
       House of Cards (mus. Milhaud), Brooklyn Academy of Music
1982   *Lost, Found, Lost* (mus. Schubert), New York
       Mercuric Tidings (mus. Schubert), New York
1983   *Sunset* (mus. Elgar), New York
       Snow White (as Some Dwarfs; mus. York), New York
1985   *Last Look* (mus. York), New York
       Roses (mus. Wagner), New York
1986   *Ab Ovo Usque Ad Mala (Soup to Nuts)* (mus. PDQ Bach), New York
       A Musical Offering (mus. Bach), New York

Other roles include: *Insects and Heroes, Book of Beasts* (1971), *Byzantium, Cloven Kingdom* (1976), *Dust* (1977), and *Esplanade* (1975).

Works

1982   *Caught* (mus. Fripp), solo, Yonkers, New York
       Brothers w/Daniel Ezralow (mus. Stravinsky), Dance Theatre Workshop (DTW), New York
       Eyewitness (mus. various, text D. Greenspan), DTW, New York
1984   *Cedar* (mus. Kottke), Parsons & Pickup company, DTW, New York
1985   *Threshold* (mus. Britten), Parsons & Pickup company, DTW, New York
       Dream Against Day, Parsons & Pickup Company, DTW, New York
1986   *The Envelope* (mus. Rossini), Parsons & Pickup Company, New York
       The Uninvited (solo, mus. Gabriel)
       Walk This Way (duet, mus. Tchaikovsky), American Ballet Theatre, New York
       Around The Corner (mus. Raye), BalletMet, Columbus, Ohio
1987   *Inner Rhythm* (no mus.), Batsheva Dance Company, Tel Aviv, Israel
       Scrutiny (mus. Raye), PDC, Jacob's Pillow, Becket, Massachusetts
       Sleep Study (mus. Flim & the BBs), PDC, at DTW, New York
       Three Courtesies (mus. Bach), PDC, Jacob's Pillow, Becket, Massachusetts
       Tightwire (in silence), PDC, New York
       Edge (mus. Sculthorpe), PDC, New York
1988   *Linton* (mus. Linton), Bat Sheva Dance Company, Tel Aviv, Israel
       Elysian Fields (mus. Grieg), PDC, University of Illinois at Urbana
1990   *Incandescence* (mus. Stuck), PDC, University of Iowa, Iowa City

Nascimento (mus. M. Nascimento), PDC, University of Arizona, Tucson

Radio NYC (mus. live radio), PDC, New York

The Need (mus. Raye), National Ballet of Canada, Toronto

1991 *A Hairy Night on Bald Mountain* (mus. Moussorsky), Ballet Chicago

Reflections of Four (mus. Mozart), PDC, Jacob's Pillow, Becket, Massachusetts

Rise and Fall (mus. Turtle Island String Quartet), PDC, New York

Tower (solo; soundtrack: media excerpts), National Arts Center, Ottawa

Fine Dining (mus. Linton), PDC, Danmarks Radio production, Arhûs, Denmark

1993 *Ring Around the Rosie* (mus. Peaslee, lyrics Campbell), PDC, New York

Riff (mus. Scott), PDC, Clearwater, Florida

Union (mus. Corigliano), PDC, Metropolitan Opera House, New York

Destined (mus. L. Stuck), PDC, Milwaukee, Wisconsin

Bachiana (mus. Bach), PDC, Clearwater, Florida

1994 *Step Into My Dream* (mus. Taylor), PDC, Urbana, Illinois

Touched By Time (mus. Corigliano), PDC, Iowa City

Mood Swing (mus. M. Gould), PDC, Washington D.C.

1996 *Time Piece* (mus. Gorecki), Atlanta Ballet, Olympic Arts Festival, Georgia

The Almighty (mus. Powell), solo, David Parsons, Durham, North Carolina

Class Act (mus. Esquivel), PDC, Philadelphia

Touch (mus. Peaslee), New York City Ballet, New York

Pass the Oil, Please (pop songs), PDC, New York

The Rush (mus. Linton), PDC, National Arts Center, Ottawa, Ontario

Closure (mus. Powell), Repertory Dance Theatre, Salt Lake City, Utah

1997 *Channeling* (mus.M. Raye), PDC, George Mason University, Fairfax, Virginia

Films and Videotapes

Two Landmark Dances, Paul Taylor Dance Company, *Great Performances/Dance In America,* PBS, 1981.

Recent Dances, Paul Taylor Dance Company, *Great Performances/ Dance In America,* PBS, 1985).

Paul Taylor—Roses & Last Look, Paul Taylor Dance Company, *Great Performances/Dance In America,* PBS, 1987.

Caught, Parsons Dance Company for *Alive from Off-Center,* 1987.

Barber Violin Concertos, 1988.

Parsons Dance Company, prod. Thomas Grimm, Dansmark Radio Production, aired in U.S. on Bravo! Arts channel, 1992

Behind the Scenes, PBS, 1992.

Step Into My Dream, NETV, Lincoln, Nebraska, 1994.

*   *   *

At age 14, David Parsons choreographed his first work, a piece he performed on his childhood specialty, the trampoline. Ending the dance by bounding upward to grasp a light pole above the top of the proscenium, he made his exit "up and out" as the curtain closed. Members of that Kansas City audience were the first to glimpse what would become his hallmarks as performer and choreographer:

athleticism, an innate sense of showmanship, and the suggestion of something daring and audacious happening or about to occur. It was an auspicious beginning for a man who has since grown to become one of America's most fascinating dance artists.

Parsons is an inventive choreographer with a wide-ranging movement vocabulary who lists an impressive choreographic output (over 40 works to date). With frequent commissions, a strong international reputation, and solid federal and corporate funding, he maintains one of the most stable and well-organized professional dance companies around.

Growing up in the Midwest, Parsons, an athletic child, participated in several sports, his favorite being gymnastics, in which he excelled on the trampoline. The summer he was 12, his mother enrolled him in a performing arts camp with dance teachers Paul Chambers and Cliff Kirwin. Kirwin and Chambers, both schooled in the Hanya Holm tradition, subsequently invited young Parsons to join their professional company, Missouri Dance Theatre, where Parsons remained until 1976. Cast at age 16 in a local production of Leonard Bernstein's *Mass*, staged by Clive Thompson (principal dancer for the Alvin Ailey American Dance Theatre), brought Parsons more notice. Sensing tremendous talent and potential, Thompson arranged a work scholarship at the Ailey School. Parsons rushed to finish high school, and arrived in New York City at the age of seventeen.

Sadly, the Ailey atmosphere wasn't the right fit for him. After spending eight months studying ballet and Horton and Graham techniques, Parsons left. For the next several months, while pursuing a career in music recording engineering, he continued attending dance concerts, "looking for anything that was going to spark me." When he caught the Paul Taylor Dance Company's (PTDC) season at Brooklyn Academy of Music in 1978 (that evening's program included the great *Polaris* and *Esplanade*), Parsons knew he'd found where he belonged. Invited to understudy by Christopher Gillis, who remembered the strapping young dancer from an earlier master class, Parsons spent six months learning the company's repertory. A Taylor comapny dancer's injury became his big break—and Parsons was in—just in time for PTDC's 1978 Soviet Union tour.

At the time the youngest member of the company, Parsons soon attracted a great deal of attention. His large size and tremendous ease and speed echoed Taylor's style in performance. (In an interesting parallel, Parsons was invited by Peter Martins, choreographer and artistic director of New York City Ballet, to perform his *Barber Violin Concerto* with the company in 1988, the first modern dancer since Taylor to be so honored.) As dance critic Deborah Jowitt wrote in 1981: "How can men so big move so quickly and still look as carefree and springy as lions? Parsons' muscles have the resilience of warming taffy." Taylor created several stunning roles for Parsons during those years, most notably in *Arden Court,* and the contrasting roles in 1987's lyrical *Roses* and the frenetic *Last Look.*

During those years, Parsons continued to choreograph. At age 18 he had returned to Kansas City (while understudying at PTDC), to set a piece on Missouri Dance Theatre—and during the Taylor years, Parsons began experimenting with dance ideas, first on his own and then with fellow Taylor dance Daniel Ezralow, performing at Dance Theatre Workshop as a solo artist, then with Ezralwo's Pickup company, while continuing to dance for Taylor.

Also influencing Parsons' growing sense of artistic direction and independence were several years collaborating with Moses Pendleton, a founder of the Pilobolus and Momix dance companies. For several years during the 1980s, Parsons had ample opportunity

David Parsons (right) in *The Envelope*, 1986. Photograph © Lois Greenfield.

to hone an already strong sense of play, participating in what Pendleton calls, "our early Momix experiments." One such experiment found Parsons joining a field of sunflowers, standing at attention for hours; in another, he strapped flashlights to his head, looking "like a large bullfrog" joining other dances in an onstage improvisation.

Despite becoming a standout in a relatively "starless" company during his career with PTDC, by age 27, Parsons wanted more, "I got to the city when I was really young—I was living large in those days; I wanted to do it all." After a decade dancing for Taylor, he felt his real future was in creating his own dances. Distilling all he'd learned—from Taylor, the legitimacy of dance as career, the seriousness of craft, and from Pendleton the no-holds-barred exploration of the wild/child self, Parsons left Paul Taylor Dance Company at age 27 to found his own company. Parsons' fertile imagination and his sense of the outrageous crop up in both the comic—*Hairy Night on Bald Mountain* (1991), *Sleep Study* (1986), and *The Envelope* (1986), and the serious— *The Almighty* (1996), *Tower* (1991), *Ring Around the Rosie* (1993).

In 1982 at Dance Theatre Workshop, Parsons unveiled his brilliant signature work, *Caught*, which reflects a lifelong interest in photography combined with those early trampoline skills. *Caught* is the perfect synthesis of the two—which a lone dancer performs lit solely by strobe light. For nearly five minutes, the peak of each stag leap, straight-leg jump, and barrel turn is revealed in a flash of light, while all preparatory movement, all landings occur in blackout. The dancer appears to walk, run, float in air. Enormously popular, since its creation Parsons has included *Caught* on every program.

The experiments in photographing dancers in mid-air began with Parsons' friend, Kansas photographer Michael Manley, and were developed further through Parsons' long association with dance photographer Lois Greenfield. This collaboration led to signature work for both artists—photos of Parsons' airborne dances grace both his company's publicity materials and a good portion of Greenfield's commercial work. And Parsons' use of the body in flight appear and reappear throughout much of his choreographic work.

With eight dancers and himself, Parsons has amassed an ethnically and physically diverse group of men and women who easily dance as he does—they are supple, eager, springy, easily at home in the air. On them he has set works that early in his career were largely short and light, progressing to the longer and grittier—though his deeply inherent musicality continues to guide him, as in the sweeping, lyrical *Nascimento* (1990), 1997's dazzling *Closure*, and his beautifully layered *Elysian Fields* (1988).

Parsons remains the quintessential Midwesterner: direct, friendly, sensible, open, and down-to-earth, with a strong work ethic. In the early years of the Parsons Dance Company, he set a new trend, establishing unheard of remuneration for his dancers: salary 52 weeks a year, plus free medical and dental benefits. Parsons, who feels choreographers will "get the best dancers if they take care of them" sees this as the choreographers' and directors' responsibility to change. He frequently lectures on the business of running not-for-profit companies at Columbia University Business School and other organizations.

Despite his highly successful 20-year career, critics don't always go easy on Parsons; after a decade on his own, his choreography is still examined for the slightest hint of his mentor. In creating accessible work, Parsons is sometimes accused of being glib or commercial, of lacking "greatness." It is worthwhile recalling that Taylor's choreographic work wasn't heralded as such until he was past 50, while his early pieces managed to anger both modern dance's traditionalists and its avant-garde. Parsons, with his bold, intelligent choreography and his dynamic company of dancers, deserves to be judged on his own merits and given a similar amount of time to realize his fullest potential.

—Janine Gastineau

PAXTON, Steve

American postmodern dancer, choreographer, and educator

Born: 21 January 1939 in Tucson, Arizona. **Education:** Left gymnastics for dance after dance training with two former Graham students; studied in New York with José Limón, Merce Cunningham, Robert Dunn. **Career:** Dance, José Limón Dance Company, late 1950s; Merce Cunningham Dance Company, 1961-65; first choreography, 1962.

Works

1962	*Proxy*
	Transit
	English Word Words w/Yvonne Rainer
	Music for 'Word Words'
1963	*Left Hand, David Hays*
	Afternoon
1964	*Flat*
	Rialto
	First
	Title Lost Tokyo
	Jag Ville Gorna Telefonera (I Want a Telephone)
1965	*Section of a New Unfinished Work*
1966	*Section of a New Unfinished Work* (augmented)
	Deposits
	A.A.
	Earth Interior
	Physical Things
	Improvisation with Trisha Brown
1967	*Love Songs*
	Somebody Else
	Some Notes on Performance
	Walkin' There (AKA *Audience Performance #1*)
1968	*Satisfyin' Lover*
	The Sizes
	State
	Untitled Lecture
	Lecture on Performance (AKA *Beautiful Lecture*)
	Audience Performance #2
	The Atlantic
	Salt Lake City Deaths
1969	*Smiling*
	Lie Down
	Pre-history
	Intravenous Lecture
1970	*Untitled*
	Niagra Falls At
	With Rachel, Suzi, Jeff, Steve & Lincoln
	Roman Newspaper Phrase
1971	*St. Vincent's Hospital At*
	Collaboration with Wintersoldier
	Contact Improvisations (ongoing)
1972	*Magnesium*
	Benn Mutual w/Nita Little)
1973	*Dancing* (ongoing)
	Air
1974	*With David Moss* (ongoing)
	Roaming (Aroma)
1976	*Scribe*
1977	*Backwater: Twosome* w/David Moss (ongoing)
	Solos (ongoing)
1978	*The Reading*
1979	*Come to Pass*

Publications

On PAXTON: books—

Anderson, Jack, *The World of Modern Dance: Art without Boundaries,* Iowa City, 1997.

Steve Paxton performing *Backwater: Twosome*, 1977. Photograph © Johan Elbers.

Banes, Sally, *Terpsichore in Sneakers: Post-Modern Dance,* Boston, 1980.

Brown, Jean Morrison (ed.), *The Vision of Modern Dance*, Princeton, New Jersey, 1979.

Coe, Robert, *Dance in America*, New York, 1985.

McDonagh, Don, *The Rise and Fall and Rise of Modern Dance,* New York, 1970.

Robertson, Allen, and Donald Hutera, *The Dance Handbook*, Boston, 1988.

Wynne, Peter, *Judson Dance: An Annotated Bibliography of the Judson Dance Theater and of Five Major Choreographers— Trisha Brown, Lucinda Childs, Deborah Hay, Steve Paxton, and Yvonne Rainer,* Englewood, New Jersey, 1978.

On PAXTON: articles—

Banes, Sally, "Steve Paxton: Physical Things," *Dance Scope,* Winter/Spring 1979.

———, "Vital Signs: Steve Paxton's *Flat* in Perspective," *Dance Research Annual XVI,* 1987.

Laine, Barry, "In Search of Judson," *Dance Magazine,* September 1982.

Rainer, Yvonne, "Backwater: Twosome/Paxton and Moss," *Dance Scope,* Winter/Spring 1979.

*   *   *

Steve Paxton's revolutionary ideas about movement helped shape the postmodern period of modern dance. An accomplished dancer, Paxton chose to find inspiration in common movements, which could be performed without specialized training. He challenged ideas about the differentiation between audience and performer, at times used extreme elements of theatricality like inflatable tunnels and live animals, and developed "contact improvisation" as a new form of shared movement. Paxton's innovations in dance force audiences and performers to see dance and everyday actions in a new light.

Born in 1939 and raised in Arizona, Paxton began his study of dance to improve his skills as a gymnast. Under the instruction of two former students of Martha Graham, Paxton's ambitions soon turned from sports to dance. In 1958 Paxton moved to New York where he studied with José Limón and Merce Cunningham. He danced with the José Limón Dance Company in the late 1950s, including performances in *Missa Brevis* (1958) and *Tenebrae, 1914* (1959). Paxton toured with Merce Cunningham's company in the early 1960s and established his reputation as an outstanding performer.

Paxton has been described as one of modern dance's most gifted dancers. The fluidity of his movements and uncanny sense of balance help create an electrifying stage presence; the athleticism of his dance has him diving onto his hands, flipping on this back, and appearing to fall only to catch himself after the point at which one would assume it could not be done. Paxton has continued to perform in other's works after he began to choreograph. He appeared in Yvonne Rainer's *Terrain* (1963) and her remarkable *Trio A* (1966). He appeared in Deborah Hay's *Ten* (1968) and with Trisha Brown, among others.

When the YMHA rejected Paxton's first choreographic effort, *Proxy,* in 1962, he turned to avenues outside of the established dance community for a forum for his work. Several fellow students in Robert Dunn's composition class were also seeking a place where dancers and choreographers could see and analyze each other's work. Paxton and Yvonne Rainer approached the Judson Memorial Church in New York City with a request to use the church for weekly workshops and occasional concerts. In the summer of 1962, the Judson Dance Theater gave its first concert and during the remainder of the decade this cooperative of performers showcased diverse experiments in dance and also the visual arts, film, and music. Experimentation at the Judson Dance Theater stretched from pedestrian movement in dance to outlandish theatrical productions in multimedia. While many of the avant-garde ideas died away, others first explored at the Judson Dance Theater later became incorporated into established art forms.

The work at Judson marked the beginning of the postmodern movement in modern dance. Like Paxton, many of the Judson performers had been associated with Cunningham. While acknowledging their debt to his experimentation with the use of chance and nondance movement, most wanted to carry it further: they made the action of a dance paramount, as opposed to exhibiting character or attitude, and downplayed the technical abilities of dancers. Paxton developed the simple, but revolutionary concept that dance movements can be found in common, everyday actions which do not require any formal dance training at all.

Some of Paxton's performances at the Judson Dance Theater incorporated elaborate theatricality, including his work with inflatables beginning with 1963's *Music for 'Word Words'* to *Physical Things* in 1966. Paxton also included the audience in many of his works. In *Afternoon* (1963) he blurs the distance between performer and audience by having the audience wind its way through a park while watching dancers at a distance and among the observers. In Paxton's best-known creation, *Satisfyin' Lover* (1968), 22 to 42 people file across the performance space behind three chairs while other performers sit in chairs or watch the walkers. The energy of this work is created by the variations in how people walk, from the inhibited to the exhibitionist, and in the demonstration of how attention from the ones who watch affects the gait of the walker. As in many of Paxton's works, the experience created during the performance affects how one later looks at ordinary movements.

Paxton's score works, like *Jag Ville Gorna Telefonera* (1964), use a collage of pictures of dancers or sports players as inspiration for performers to discover movements and create a progression from one stance into another. Paxton's work with the Grand Union, an improvisational company of which he was a founding member, brought together many aspects of his ideas. In the early 1970s, he developed a new form of movement for two or more dancers who share support and movement which he named "contact improvisation," introduced in an ongoing dance of the same name in 1972. Jack Anderson says contact improvisation "in its most basic form involved two people who, in effect, have a dialogue in motion. They relate to each other. . .communicating by sensing the other's presence and though a constant give-and-take of weight and energy."

For the PBS television series *Dance in America*, Paxton described the essence of contact improvisation: "Both partners are surviving a dance moment and they have to be pretty open for almost anything to happen," he explains. "They can't preplan, they can't hold on to what they've just done, or consider it; they can't be too much in control, because the minute you start to try to control what you and someone else are doing, you've taken away from them their ability to interact with you." This extreme extension of nondisplay dancing can at times appear chaotic, but its liberating look at the spontaneity of dance has found its way into the heart of modern dance.

Paxton further developed his ideas of shared spontaneity in his work with percussionist David Moss. In ongoing performances beginning in the 1970s, Moss played the drums and bells surrounding him while Paxton danced. Each improvised independently in response to the shared experience.

Paxton has taught extensively to bring his revolutionary ideas about movement to others, both domestically and aboard, including stints in Amsterdam, Dartington College, Oberlin College, Bennington College, and others.

—Janette Goff Dixon

PENDLETON, Moses (Robb)

American dancer, choreographer, and company director

Born: 28 March 1949 in Lyndonville, Vermont. **Education:** B.A., Dartmouth College, 1971; studied with Alison Chase. **Family:** Married to Momix dancer Cynthia Quinn; one daughter. **Career:** Co-founder, Pilobolus Dance Theatre, 1971; dancer/collaborator, Pilobolus, 1971-80; five-week Broadway run for Pilobolus, 1977; toured Japan and South America with Pilobolus, sponsored by Pierre Cardin, 1977-78; sometime choreographer, Pilobolus, 1980 to present; created solo *Momix* (later the name of a touring duo with Alison Chase, then a five-member company), 1980; choreographed closing ceremonies, Lake Placid Winter Olympics, 1980; founder/artistic director, Momix Dance Theater (five-member troupe), 1984; toured Japan with Momix, sponsored by Dentsu Corporation, 1990; has taught and served artist-in-residence positions at universities throughout the U.S.; an accomplished photographer, has exhibited works both in the U.S. and abroad. **Awards:** Edinborough Fringe Festival Scotsman's Award, 1973; Berlin Critics Prize, 1975; National Endowment for the Arts grant, 1975; Guggenheim Fellowship, 1977; CINE Gold Eagle Award for *Moses Pendleton Presents Moses Pendleton*, 1982; International Emmy for *Pictures at an Exhibition*, 1991; Festival Choice Award at the Irish Life Dublin Theatre Festival, 1992; Gold Medal, Verona Festival, 1994.

Works

1971	*Pilobolus* w/Wolken and Johnson
	Walklydon w/Pilobolus
	Geode w/Pilobolus
1972	*Spyrogyra* w/Pilobolus
	Anaendrom w/Pilobolus
	Ocellus w/Robert Morgan Barnett, Michael Tracy, and Jonathan Wolken
1973	*Ciona* w/Pilobolus
	Aubade w/Pilobolus
	Syzygy w/Pilobolus
	Cameo w/Pilobolus
	Two Bits w/Pilobolus
	Pilobolus and Joan (film, starring the four original company members)
1974	*Pilea* w/Pilobolus
	Terra Cotta w/Pilobolus
	Pseudopodia w/Pilobolus

	Monkshood's Farewell w/Pilobolus
	Triptych w/Pilobolus
	Dispretzled w/Pilobolus
1975	*Ciona* (revised) w/Pilobolus
	Alrone w/Pilobolus
	Untitled w/Pilobolus
1976	*Lost and Found* w/Alison Chase
	Lost in Fauna w/Alison Chase
1977	*The Eve of Samhain* w/Pilobolus
1978	*Molly's Not Dead* w/Pilobolus
1979	*Bonsai,* performed by 5 x 2 Plus Company, then Pilobolus
	Intégrale Erik Satie, for the Paris Opera Ballet
	Shizen w/Chase
1980	*Momix,* solo
	The Detail of Phoebe Struchan
	Rélâche (revival of Picabia's work), for Joffrey Ballet
1981	*Day Two* for Pilobolus
	Kovanschina (mus. Mussorgsky), for La Scala Opera, Milan
	Homage à Picasso, performed by Pendleton, Fête de L'Humanité, Paris
1982	*Moses Pendleton Presents Moses Pendleton* (documentary)
	Tutuguri (based on Antonin Artaud's writings), for Deutsche Opera, Berlin
	Parsifal (mus. Wagner) for the Grand Théâtre de Genève
1985	*Stabat Mater* for Pilobolus
	Carmina Burana Side II for Pilobolus
	Tutuguri (revived), Berlin Opera
	Pulcinella, for the Ballet National of Nancy, France
1986	*Kiss of the Spiderwoman,* for Momix
	Spawning, for Momix
	Venus Envy, for Momix
	Medusa, for Momix
	Preface to Preview, for Momix
	Gifts from the Sea (excerpts; opera), for Spoleto Festival
1987	*Platee* (Rameau), for the Spoleto Festival USA
	Les Mariés de la Tour Eiffel (revival of Cocteau), for Alliance Française
	Platee, revived for Brooklyn Academy of Music (BAM)
1988	*Debut C,* for Pilobolus, Joyce Theater, New York
1989	*AccorDION,* Vorbuhne-Zurich Theatre
1991	*Baseball,* for Scottsdale Center for the Arts, Seattle
	Passion (mus. Peter Gabriel), for Momix
1993	*Carmen,* Munich State Opera
	Imagine (3-D film for IMAX theatres)
1994	*Baseball* (expanded), Momix, Joyce Theater, New York City
1997	*Sputnik,* for Momix, City Center, New York City

Publications

On Pendleton: books—

Anderson, Jack, *Ballet and Modern Dance: A Concise History,* Princeton, New Jersey, 1992.

Coe, Robert, *Dance in America,* New York, 1985.

Croce, Arlene, *Afterimages,* New York, 1977.

Jowitt, Deborah, *Time and the Dancing Image,* New York, 1988.

Robertson, Allen, and Donald Hutera, *The Dance Handbook,* Boston, 1988.

On Pendleton: articles—

Anderson, Jack, "Momix Merges Flesh and Spirit," *New York Times,* 19 December 1991.
———, "Pilobolus Dusts Off First Work," *New York Times,* 29 June 1996.
Dunning, Jennifer, "Moses Pendleton, Choreographer and Product of His Time," *New York Times,* 27 December 1989.
Kisselgoff, Anna, "Evolution as Spiritual Free-for-All," *New York Times*, 15 December 1994.
———, "The Boys and Girls of Summer In Another Field of Dreams," *New York Times*, 20 December 1994.
———, "When Confession Is All," *New York Times*, 3 October 1982.
"Moses Pendleton," in *Current Biography Yearbook 1989,* New York, 1990.
Raver, Anne, "On Fertile Ground with the Master of Momix," *New York Times*, 22 December 1996.
Rowes, Barbara, "From the Land of Steady Habits Springs an Antic Sprite, Avant-Garde Dancer Moses Pendleton," *People,* 20 July 1981.
Sulcas, Roslyn, "Momix," *Dance Magazine*, April 1997.

Films and Videotapes

Pilobolus and Joan, film by Ed Emshwiller, starring the four original company members, 1973.
Dance in America series, PBS, 1977 and 1980.
Moses Pendleton Presents Moses Pendleton, documentary for the ARTS cable network, 1982.
Too Late for Goodbyes, video by Julian Lennon, 1984.
Batdance, video by the artist formerly known as Princ, 1989.
Touch Me, video by Cathy Dennis, 1991.
Pictures at an Exhibition, Momix apprearance with Charles Dutoit and the Montreal Symphony, 1991.
Imagine, 3-D IMAX film, 1994.

*   *   *

Moses (formerly Robb) Pendleton is a co-founder of the modern dance group Pilobolus, known for its acrobatic virtuosity, and founder and artistic director of Momix, a company that employs multimedia and lighting, as well as gymnastic prowess, for visual effect. His influence, particularly his sense of humor and optimism, permeates the work of both groups.

Pendleton was born in 1949 in Lyndonville, Vermont. The joyousness and upbeat outlook that characterizes his choreography is a conscious reaction to a youth filled with misfortune. When Pendleton was 12, his father committed suicide after being burned in a fire. His mother, who suffered a nervous breakdown, died of cancer six years later. The choreographer's grandfather Moses, who founded American Woolen Mills (makers of Pendleton shirts), made a big impression on the younger Pendleton; the choreographer uses his grandfather's briefcase as a prop in one of his signature solos.

During his senior year at Dartmouth in 1971, Pendleton, along with classmate Jonathan Wolken, co-founded Pilobolus Dance Theater. While enrolled in a class taught by Alison Chase, the two students and Steve Johnson created *Pilobolus,* named after a fungus, as their first piece. The dance foreshadowed the future style of the eponymous company, in that it used the athletic dancers' interconnected bodies "at unlikely levels and angles, hinging and cantile-

vering in all directions in a kind of stream of consciousness sculptural grafitti," as described by Robert Coe.

Pendleton, Johnson and Wolken moved to Pendleton's family farm in Vermont the next summer to begin creating dances combining gymnastics, pantomime, broad humor, and sports. The three men, none of whom had formal dance training, are credited with introducing a new species of performance, popular with modern dance audiences yet not really dance. Soon afterward, Pendleton and Wolken were joined by Lee Harris and Robby Barnett in a performance at a Frank Zappa concert at Smith College. They were noticed by Murray Louis who, with Alwin Nikolais, sponsored the company's acclaimed first New York season. In 1973, Chase and Martha Clarke joined the group, and Harris left, replaced by Michael Tracy. The company lived communally, collaboratively creating dances that critic Deborah Jowitt likened to a series of "lyrical, slow-motion Rorschachs." Two of their best-known works are *Monkshod's Farewell* and *Untitled,* and while with Pilobolus, Pendleton co-choreographed an extensive roster of works, including *Alrone* (1975), *Lost in Fauna* (1976), *Shizen* (1977) and *The Eve of Samhain* (1977). Around 1980, Pendleton and the other original members of Pilobolus stopped performing with the group, but he continues to create choreography for them.

In 1979 Pendleton choreographed *Intégrale Erik Satie* for the Paris Opera Ballet, his first creative work outside Pilobolus. Pendleton and Chase, along with several ballet dancers, subsequently toured Europe with a program of modern dance and ballet. Afterward, Chase and Pendleton continued to tour with their own program, marking the beginning of a new troupe named after Pendleton's solo work, *Momix,* choreographed for the closing ceremonies of the 1980 Lake Placid Winter Olympics. By 1984 Momix Dance Theater became a five-member touring company with Pendleton as its artistic director, as position he still holds (Chase later stopped dancing during pregnancy). Momix's lineage as a Pilobolus spin-off is clear, but its early emphasis was more on solo and duet performances, until its reemergence as a five-dancer troupe. Pendleton also makes extensive use of props, lighting, and mixed media in his Momix works. Some of Momix's best-known works include Pendleton's *Passion* (1991) and *Baseball* (1994). One of Pendleton's latest creations for the troupe is *Sputnik* (1997).

Outside his contributions to Momix and Pilobolus, Pendleton choreographs for opera and ballet companies, as well as performing, sometimes with other Momix members. He revived Picabia's *Rélâche* for the Joffrey Ballet in 1980, and performed and choreographed *Homage à Picasso* at the Fête de l'Humanité in Paris in 1981. He created the dance sequences for *Khovanschina* at La Scala, also performing the role of the Fool, and choreographed *Tutuguri* for Berlin's Deutsche Oper, both in 1981. In 1992 he staged the dance sequences in *Parsifal* for the Grand Théâtre de Genève, and in 1985 did *Pulcinella* for the Ballet National de Nancy, France. In 1987, he created a new version of Rameau's *Platée* for the Spoleto Festival USA, and in 1988 created the mise-en-scène for *Les Mariés de la Tour Eiffel* in honor of the inauguration of the Florence Gould Hall at New York's Alliance Française. In 1989, he choreographed *AccorDION* for the Vorbuhne-Zurich Theatre, and in 1993 Lina Wertmuller's production of *Carmen* at the Munich State Opera. Pendleton has also been involved in choreographing for music videos by notable artists and creating works for television.

Pendleton's pieces are known for their overt sexuality, sense of hope and visual style, and incorporate a wide range of references, from classic music and literature to today's pop culture. Humor is one of the most characteristic elements of his work; Robert Joffrey has called him "the Charlie Chaplin of the dance world." Pendleton often uses slides projected on a scrim in front of the dancers to add meaning and visual appeal to his choreography, which contains acrobatics, gymnastics and mime, as well as dance movements. Despite his career-long emphasis on collaboration, Pendleton is considered an individualist, and his imaginative presence is evident in his entire body of creation.

Pendleton teaches, conducts workshops, and has taken artist-in-residence positions at universities throughout the United States. His awards, some earned with Pilobolus and Momix, include the Edinborough Fringe Festival Scotsman's Award, the Berlin Critics Prize, a National Endowment for the Arts grant and a Guggenheim Fellowship. Pendleton, who lives in Connecticut with his wife, Momix dancer Cynthia Quinn, and his daughter Quinn Elisabeth (who performs in some of his works), believes that his lifestyle and his work as a "visualist" and a "fantasist" are critically intertwined. He is also an accomplished photographer, exhibiting his work (much of it portraying his daughter) in London, Milan, Montreal, and Aspen.

—Karen Raugust

PEREZ, Rudy

American postmodern dancer, choreographer, and performance artist

Born: 24 November 1929 in New York City. **Education:** Graduated from High School of Music, 1948; began dance training, New Dance Group, 1950; also studied with Mary Anthony, Merce Cunningham, Martha Graham, and Erick Hawkins. **Career:** Joined Judson Dance Theater, 1962; first choreography, 1963; founder, Men's Coalition; founder/director, Rudy Perez Dance Theatre; founder, Classic Kitetails (young dancers); has taught at American University and George Washington University in Washington, D.C., Arizona State University, Brown University, Marymount College, New York University, Oberlin College, UCLA, University of Colorado at Boulder, University of Nevada at Las Vegas, and others. **Awards:** Grants, awards, and fellowships include National Endowment for the Arts (NEA), Brody Arts Fund, California Arts Council, Cultural Affairs Department of Los Angeles, Vanguard Award; Lester Horton Award for Outstanding Achievement, 1991, 1997; Los Angeles Music Center's Viva Artistas! award, 1992; honorary doctorate, Otis Institute of Art and Design, 1993.

Works

1963   *Take Your Alligator With You* (no music), Judson Memorial Church
1965   *Fieldgoal* (mus. collage), Mary Anthony Studio
1966   *Countdown* (mus. songs of the Auvergne), Mary Anthony Studio
        Monkey See, Monkey Wha? (mus. collage), The Bridge
        Bang Bang (sound: Julia Child "cooking asparagus"), Clark Center
1967   *Center Break* (mus. collage), Clark Center
1968   *Topload/Off Print* (mus. collage), Judson Memorial Church
        Loading Zone (mus. collage), Dance Theatre Workshop
        Re-Run Plus (mus. collage), Judson Memorial Church

1969   *Outline* (mus. collage), Dance Theatre Workshop
        Match (mus. collage), Cubiculo
        Arcade (mus. collage), Dance Theatre Workshop
1970   *Annual I & II* (mus. collage), WBAI Free Music Store
        Round-up (mus. collage), Barnard College
        Coverage (mus. collage), Cubiculo
1971   *Monumental Exchange* (mus. collage), Merce Cunningham Studio
        New Annual (mus. collage), Connecticut College
        Lot Piece (mus. collage), Marymount Manhattan College
1972   *Asparagus Beach* (mus. collage), Connecticut College
        Steeple People (mus. collage), Connecticut College
        Salute to the 25th (mus. collage), Connecticut College
1973   *Quadrangle* (mus. collage), Connecticut College
        Americana Plaid (mus. collage), Connecticut College
        Walla Walla (mus. collage), Connecticut College
        Running Board for a Narrative (mus. collage), Marymount Manhattan College
1974   *Pedestrian Mall* (mus. collage), Brooklyn Academy of Music
1975   *Parallax* (mus. Creshevsky), Marymount Manhattan College
        Colorado Ramble (mus. Reinholt), Marymount Manhattan College
1976   *System* (mus. collage), Marymount Manhattan College
        Update (mus. Creshevsky), Marymount Manhattan College
1977   *Rally,* (mus. collage), Barnard College
        . . .Just for the Sake of It (mus. collage), Riverside Church Theatre
1978   *According to What,* or *Is Dance Really About Dancing* (mus. Borden and Drews)
        Point of Departure (mus. Jarrett), Marymount Manhattan College
        Equinox—Run (mus. Drews), Marymount Manhattan College
1979   *Tribute* (mus. Bordon), solo, I.D.E.A. Studio, Santa Monica, California
        All Things Considered (mus. Drews), Pacific Design Center, Los Angeles
        Highway Parts 1 & 2 (mus. Howard), solo, Brand Library
        Men in Dance, Glendale, California
        Musdansic (mus. Howard), Garden Theatre Festival, Los Angeles
1980   *In Plain Sight* (mus. Rodgers), solo, Academy West Theatre, Santa Monica
        New Dance (mus. Jarrett), Dance Kaleidoscope, Los Angeles
1981   *Take Stock* (mus. Rodgers), solo, Royce Hall, UCLA (first performed as a site-specific work at Los Angeles Institute of Contemporary Art)
        Tracers (mus. Rodgers), Royce Hall, UCLA
        Flash Forward (mus. Rodgers), The House, Santa Monica
        Lessness w/Joseph DeMattia (mus. DNA, prose Samuel Beckett), Double "G" Gallery, Los Angeles
1982   *It Should Go Unsaid* (mus. Bryars), solo, Immanuel Presbyterian Church, Los Angeles
        Andromeda (mus. Durko), Immanuel Presbyterian Church, Los Angeles

Red Ice (mus. Rodgers & Cartesian Reunion Memorial Orchestra), Dance Kaleidoscope, Los Angeles

Choreographic Mix (mus. Rodgers), The House, Santa Monica

Meridian Pass (mus. Rodgers), large group work, Los Angeles Contemporary Exhibitions Gallery

1983   *Cheap Imitation* (mus. Brance), Santa Monica Arts Commission Outdoor Festival

Bette's Caper (mus. Rodgers & Cartesian Reunion Memorial Orchestra), Wadsworth Theatre, UCLA

Stations (mus. Bayer), Wadsworth Theater, UCLA

Sabrina Variations (mus. Glass), Los Angeles Pops Series, Pilot Theater

1984   *Urban Suite* (mus. Apple & Recchion), Academy West Theater, Santa Monica

Canopy at an Intersection (mus. Dunlap), David Geffen Museum

Triangles Red (mus. Rodgers), Double "G" Gallery, Los Angeles

1985   *Debut* (mus. sound collage), Academy West Theater, Santa Monica

Fall-Out (mus. Rodgers), Academy West Theater, Santa Monica

Urban Toys/Gallery Event (mus. O'Keefe), Eliot Gordon Gallery, Los Angeles

Where Angels Coast (mus. Byron), Dance Theatre Workshop

1986   *Cold Sweat* (mus. O'Keefe), Plaza de la Raza, Los Angeles

Celestial Ridge (mus. Bayer), Plaza de la Raza, Los Angeles

Equaltime (mus. Stone, O'Keefe, Byron, Dunlap, Recchion—alternating each performance), Academy West Theater

1987   *Whatwithall* (mus. Petrouchka/Stravinsky, performed live by the Los Angeles Philharmonic Orchestra), Symphonies for Youth, Dorothy Chandler Pavilion, Los Angeles

Coastal Acts (mus. Rodgers), Los Angeles Festival

Twice (mus. Byron), duet, Los Angeles Festival

Equaltime II (mus. Byron), Los Angeles Festival

Perpetual Acts (mus. Hilzik), Los Angeles Photography Center

Untitled (mus. Creshevsky), Los Angeles Photography Center

1988   *Toss-up* (mus. Hiltiz), El Camino College, Torrance, California

Celestial Acrobats (mus. Hiltiz), El Camino College, Torrance

1989   *Parallels* (mus. Cripe), retrospective, Los Angeles Contemporary Exhibitions

Racing Thoughts (mus. Hull-Goodman), Los Angeles Photography Center

1990   *One + 2 plus 1 = Mischief* (mus. Peltier), Dance Kaleidoscope, Los Angeles

Circadian Circle (mus. Keane), Keck Theater, Occidental College, Glendale

1991   *Red Wedge* (mus. sound tape/Jimenez), trio (site-specific), California Plaza, Los Angeles

One Potato, Two Potato (mus. Leahy), quartet (site-specific), California Plaza, Los Angeles

Spiritual Quest (mus. Hughes & Berg), Los Angeles Contemporary Exhibitions

Remain in Light (mus. Hughes & Berg), solo, Los Angeles Contemporary Exhibitions

Altered Vision (mus. Hughes & Berg), Los Angeles Contemporary Exhibitions

1992   *The Dance-Crazy Kid from New Jersey Meets Hofmannsthal* (homage to Ruth St. Denis), (mus. Bayer), w/an orchestra, singers, actors and dancers, Armory Center for the Arts, Pasadena

Losing the Light (mus. Stabat Mater/Pergolesi), solo, Dance Kaleidoscope, California State University

1993   *Crossover Acts* (mus. LULA), Pacific Dance Ensemble, Los Angeles Photography Center

Take 3: Dance With Moving Chairs (mus. arranged sounds), Los Angeles Festival

1994   *Crossover Acts 2* (mus. UNLV Percussion Ensemble), Faculty & Students, University of Nevada, Las Vegas

Take 4: Sign In, Please (mus. Beede), Los Angeles County High School for the Arts

Agenda (mus. Melnick), solo, Dance Without Borders, Los Angeles

1995   *Assorted Moves* (mus. Apple & Recchion), Los Angeles County High School for the Arts

Match (mus. Apple & Recchion), Dance Kaleidoscope, John Anson Ford Theater

Search The Inner Mirror/1000 Cranes (mus. Glass), Los Angeles County High School for the Arts

1996   *Laterals(s)* (mus. arranged), Los Angeles County High School for the Arts

1997   *Online* (mus. Glass), Los Angeles County High School for the Arts

Facismile (mus. Roper), solo with tuba player, Hot & Sticky, Los Angeles Contemporary Exhibitions

1998   *By George!* (mus. Lockwood), Los Angeles County High School for the Arts

Publications

On PEREZ—

Perlmutter, Donna, "Reviews: Rudy Perez Performance Ensemble," *Dance Magazine*, December 1992.

Siegel, Marcia B., *At the Vanishing Point: A Critic Looks at Dance*, New York, 1972.

Terry, Walter, *I Was There: Selected Dance Reviews and Articles, 1936-1976*, compiled and edited by Andrew Mark Wentink, New York, 1978.

Filma and Videotapes

District One, commissioned for *Dance for Camera,* WGBH-TV, 1975.

*   *   *

Born on 24 November 1929 in Manhattan, American choreographer and performance artist Rudy Perez entered the world of dance later than most people of his talent. The eldest of four sons of immigrant parents from Peru and Puerto Rico, Perez attended the High School of Music, graduating in 1948. He had always been

Rudy Perez performing *Countdown,* **1966. Photograph by Steve Sbarge.**

interested in social dancing, primarily as a diversion, and often danced in his home or in the homes of relatives for entertainment. Yet Perez did not have any formal dance training until he was 21, when he began studying at the New Dance Group. Thus, in his early twenties, Perez began a "double life," which lasted throughout the 1950s, of working as a computer operator/programmer by day and studying dance by night. Perez also studied with Martha Graham, Merce Cunningham, Erick Hawkins, and Mary Anthony; those of Graham seem to have had the most profound influence on his dancing and choreographic style in teaching Perez how to command an audience's attention, and unswervingly hold it. Yet after 10 years, Perez was still a student with no ties to an active dance company and set to change his circumstances from "professional" student to professional dancer.

During the 1960s Perez joined the Judson Dance Theater, among whose members were Trisha Brown, Lucinda Childs, Yvonne Rainer, Robert Rauschenberg, and others. At Judson, where the prevailing attitude was that almost "anything goes" Perez began choreographing. According to Don McDonagh in *The Rise and Fall and Rise of Modern Dance,* at Judson Perez learned "that technique was only one element in a dance presentation and only bore as much impor-

tance as the individual wanted to give it." This as McDonagh notes, was "a special revelation" to Perez and one that would characterize much of his work. *Take Your Alligator With You,* Perez's first choreographic work, was created at Judson in 1963 as a duet. It was a sly, witty indictment of fashion advertising into which Perez threw seemingly disparate elements like ordinary street clothing, spoken word, and unusual movements to convey his disdain for the fashion industry;s artifice. For a novice, Perez's performance was clean and strong, as McDonagh found, "Almost all of the elements that are found in his current choreography were present in some form or another in this first piece: meticulous workmanship, unusual juxtapositions of visual and aural material, and a weighty intensity."

Much of Perez's early choreography at Judson consisted of solos, including *Countdown, Fieldgoal, Monkey See, Monkey Wha?,* and *Bang Bang*. Not only did Perez dance and choreograph works, but educated himself in lighting, music, and other stage management, which he frequently put to work for others and later in his own productions. His next two works, 1965's *Countdown* and 1966's *Fieldgoal* were first performed at Mary Anthony's New York studio. The former piece was of intimate important to Perez, one McDonagh believes has become "a touchstone against which to measure his own choreographic progress," with Perez keeping it close to his heart and usually performing it annually. *Fieldgoal,* on the other hand, was a studied contrast in movement and music, something Perez would explore further with subsequent works.

Perez's use of sound has run the gamut from Julia Child's cooking instructions (*Bang Bang*) to dogs barking or street noises to silence, his use of this mix is calculated not on rhythmic response but to emotional expression.

Perez's ability to suspend time within his dances has become a trademark, just as his ability to inhabit the entire space around him, be that an indoor stage or outdoor plaza, has taken his work to another dramatic level. His deliberate use of time, space, and props have made Perez productions "a curious hybrid, almost as if they had been achieved by programming passion through a computer," says McDonagh, not a surprising comment given Perez's former work as a computer operator and programmer. Perez has been taking his craft into the classroom for many years, teaching and performing at UCLA, Brown University, Oberlin College, New York University, Arizona State University, the University of Colorado at Boulder, American University and George Washington University in Washington, D.C., University of Nevada at Las Vegas, and at Marymount College, where he was the resident artist-in-dance for nine years. During these years he produced many works with his students, some site-specific outdoor programs, like those he choreographed at the Los Angeles County High School for the Arts including 1994's *Take 4: Sign in, Please,* 1995's *Assorted Moves* and *Search for the Inner Mirror,* 1997's *Online,* and *By George!* in 1998.

Part of his training included work as a dance therapist at Bellevue Hospital as well as teaching dance at creative arts programs for children at Adelphi University and Friends Seminary in New York. While still on the East Coast, Perez was commissioned by WGBH-TV to create a work for its *Dance for Camera* program. His creation, *District One,* funded by the Ford Foundation, was broadcast in 1975. Before departing for the West Coast in the late 1970s, Perez formed an all-male group called the Men's Coalition. At that time he created *According to What* or *Is Dance Really About Dancing,* which was nominated for best choreography by the *Soho Arts News.*

Since arriving in Los Angeles in 1978 Perez has formed the Rudy Perez Dance Theatre, serving as choreographer, teacher, and director. He has been commissioned by LACE Gallery, MOCA/Mark Taper Forum, Pasadena Armory Center for the Arts, UCLA Center for the Performing Arts, Japan American Theater, and Visions Complex to create works, and many of these pieces have been performed nationally, globally, and locally by the Alvin Ailey American Dance Theatre, Ze'eva Cohen, Bonnie Oda Homsay, Ballet Repertory Theater (ABT II), Washington Ballet (D.C.), Tanzprojekt Munchen (Germany), Quebec et Danse (Montreal), DANCE/LA, and the Pacific Dance Ensemble.

Perez is a recipient of numerous state and national grants and awards from many organizations, including the NEA, Brody Arts Fund, California Arts Council, the National/State/County Partnership, and Cultural Affairs Department of Los Angeles. In 1991 Perez was recognized with the Lester Horton Award for Outstanding Achievement for a performance or solo; the next year he received the Los Angeles Music Center's Viva Artistas! Performing Arts award which honors distinguished Latino artists. In 1993 Perez received an honorary doctorate from the Otis Institute of Art and Design, and in 1997, Perez was again recognized with a Lester Horton Dance Award. This honor was twofold: first for Outstanding Teaching, and secondly for Outstanding Achievement for the

restaging, reconstruction or revival of a work, and Perez's *Equinox Run* (originally staged in 1978) took the honors.

Perez has been teaching dance since 1968 and is currently on the faculty of the Los Angeles County High School for the Arts and Westside Academy of Dance. Perez has co-founded Classic Kitetails, a dance company for young professionals. Perez says of his career, which includes over 40 works: "My choreography is a commentary, a nudge, an abstract message for the audience. I work tirelessly to ensure my choreography is thoughtful, singular, and communicative. . . I've been called 'the conscience of Los Angeles dance,'" he contends, because his pieces "come from deep within me and I work to refine and abstract my perception through movement until it takes its most condensed form. I cannot churn out a piece, though some come quickly. . .I grapple with a theme I cannot ignore: I explore what it feels like, what it looks like from different points of view, how I can most succinctly and directly express what I am exploring." Perez is also humble, thankful for his dancers and funding, "so that we may continue to work together to keep the art of dance awake and alive in Los Angeles." Rudy Perez is not only keeping dance in Los Angeles alive and well, but securing its future by sharing his talent with the young people who will in turn carry the torch.

—Sydonie Benet

PERRON, Wendy

American dancer, choreographer, educator, and writer

Born: 8 October 1947 in the Bronx. **Education:** Began dance studies at the New Milford School for Creative Dances (founded by her mother), 1952; studied ballet with Irine Fokine, the American School of Ballet, Martha Graham school, and Joffrey Ballet; attended Bennington College, 1965-69; spent summers at the American Dance Festival. **Career:** Danced with Jeff Duncan, Jack Moore, Rudy Perez, and Barbara Roan; joined Twyla Tharp's the Farm Club; sidelined by injuries, began writing about dance for *Soho Weekly News* and *The Drama Review;* first choreography, 1969; dancer, Trisha Brown Dance Company, 1975-78; taught at Bennington College, 1978-82; helped organize the Judson Project, a touring exhibit of Judson Dance Theater materials; founded Wendy Perron Dance Company, 1983; currently dance critic and director of the Jacob's Pillow extension program at Bennington College. **Awards:** National Endowment for the Arts choreographic fellowship, 1984; Deutscher Akademischer Austauschdienst award and residency, 1992.

Roles

1972	*The One of No Way* (Frances Alenikoff), solo
1973	*Gap* (Wlliam Dunas), solo
1974	Dancer/improvisor, *The Telaxic Synapsulator* (Kenneth King)
1975	Dancer/collaborator, *Dancing on View* (Sara Rudner)
	Dancer (cr), *Pyramid* (Trisha Brown)
1976	Dancer (cr), *Splang* (Trisha Brown)
1977	Dancer (cr), *Line-Up* (Trisha Brown)
1985	*Sons of Famous Men* (Susan Rethorst)

Other roles include: For the Rudy Perez Dance Company, 1970; *Resonances* by Jeff Duncan.

Works (from 1983 to 1994 performed by the Wendy Perron Dance Company unless otherwise noted)

1970	*A Piece of the Wind,* solo, New York
	Olympic for Three (mus. Noa Ain), trio, New York
1972	*Winter Pieces* (mus. Sounds of the Wolf, Del Vikings), solo, New York
	Dance in Shorts, duet, New York
1973	*Blueberry Rhyme* w/Rosalind Newman (mus. James P. Johnson), New York
	Oath (mus. African drumming and vocals), solo, New York
1974	*Flowering Bones* (mus. Schubert), trio, New York
	Thin Air (mus. piano by Michael Martin, harmonica by Duncan Smith), solo, New York
1975	*The Rise and Fear of October* (text by Perron), New York
	Head Ache (text by Perron), trio, Hartford, Connecticut
	Dancing on View w/Sara Rudner, Wendy Rogers and Risa Jaroslow, New York
	Sifting w/Stephanie Woodard and Peter Zummo (mus. Zummo), Hartford, Connecticut
	Sky Report w/Woodard & Zummo, New York
1976	*The Daily Mirror* (text: days of week), solo, New York
1977	*The Four-Way Daily Mirror,* New York
	Beads (mus. Zummo & Woodard)
1978	*Hands and Giants* w/Susan Rethorst, duet, New York
	Big Dog (mus. Plastic People of the Universe), duet
	Swan Dive (mus. Plastic People of the Universe), solo
	Quarters, New York
1979	*Series of Lies,* trio, New York
1980	*Three-Piece Suite,* quintet, New York
	Untitled Solo, solo, Aix-en-Provence, France
1981	*The Paris Sciences,* quintet, collaboration w/videographer Joan Blair, New York
	A Ststoryry: Impossible to Tell (text: Perron and Sophie Healy), New York
	Beach Piece w/Woodard (live music: Zummo), 16 dancers, New York
1982	*Dancing to Good Bands. . .As Revealing as Self Portraits* (mus. Craig Bromberg), quintet, New York
	Some Guests Complain (text: Perron), duet, New York
	The Vulcan in Its Day (found text), duet, New York
1983	*Blind Date,* solo, Basel, Switzerland
	Three Talking Duets (text: Perron), New York
	Child Judge/Party Crasher/Stiff Tricks (mus. Andy Blinx, Don Hunerberg), trio, New York
1984	*Standard Deviation,* collaboration w/videographer Cathy Weis (mus. Blinx, Hunerberg), 5 dancers plus three new people every night
	They Made Me Do It (mus. Miles Green), solo, New York
1986	*And Me with My X-Ray Eyes* (mus. Arto Lindsay & Peter Scherer)
	St. Cecilia or the Power of Music (mus. Peter Gordon), New York
	Divertissement w/David Van Tieghem (mus. Van Tieghem, found text), duet, New York

1987	*Down Like Rain* (mus. Schubert), New York
	Arena (mus. collage by Van Tieghem, set—22 live birds—by Komar & Melamid), Jacob's Pillow Dance Festival, Becket, Massachusetts
	Schumann Opus 102 (mus. Schumann), New York
	Second Skin (mus. Mimi Goese, Astor Piazzola), Repertory Dance Theatre, Salt Lake City, Utah
1988	*Don't Tell Us* (mus. Bosho), New York
1990	*Greetings* (mus. collage), Amsterdam, the Netherlands
	Ten Thoughts Slipping (mus. Beethoven), solo, New York
	Last Forever (mus. A. Leroy and Mimi Goese), New York
	Squall (mus. Jonathan Bepler), trio, New York
1991	*Interior with Six Figures* (mus. Philip Glass), New York
	Bartholomew and the Oobleck (text Dr. Seuss), New York
	You Don't Own Me (mus. Leslie Gore), solo for Valerie Levine of Ice Theatre of New York
1992	*Druckkammer (Compression Chamber),* (mus. Einstürzende Neubauten), Berlin
	Some Stand Some Fall (mus. collage), Berlin
1993	*Finding* (mus. Glass), solo for guest artist Peter Boal (New York City Ballet), New York
	Will I Rise (mus. traditional Irish arranged by A. Leroy), New York
	Squall Recycled (mus./costumes Gary Sojkowsky), trio, New York
1994	*One Thing Another Thing* (mus. David Hamburger), New York
	Thicket (mus. Zap Mama), New York
	Solos with Memories (mus. Elvis Presley, rooster sounds), New York
1995	*My Night Table Overflows,* solo w/readings, New York
1997	*Downtown Underground* (live music: 8 subway musicians), New York

Other works include: Commissions for new work by Jacob's Pillow Dance Festival (1987) and Lincoln Center Festival (1997).

Publications

By PERRON:

Editor, *Judson Dance Theater: 1962-1966,* Bennington College Judson Project catalogue, 1981.
"Containing Differences in Time," *Drama Review,* Summer 1985.
Guest editor, "The Legacy of Robert Dunn," *Movement Research Performance Journal #14.*

On PERRON: books—

Wynne, Peter, *Judson Dance: An Annotated Bibliography of the Judson Dance Theater and of Five Major Choreographers—Trisha Brown, Lucinda Childs, Deborah Hay, Steve Paxton, and Yvonne Rainer,* Englewood, New Jersey, 1978.

On PERRON: articles—

Deresiewicz, Bill, "Wendy Perron Dance Company," *Dance Magazine,* July 1993.
Jowitt, Deborah, "Dark Images," *Village Voice,* 22 November 1994.
———, "Masters of Risk," *Village Voice,* 2 May 1995.

Wendy Perron with David Van Tieghem performing *Divertissement,* 1986. Photograph © Beatriz Schiller.

Tobias, Tobi, "Postmodern Medley," *New York,* 8 May 1995.
———, "Significant Others," *New York,* 22 March 1993.
Underwood, Sharry Traver, "Wendy Perron: Unruly Element," *Dance Magazine*, March 1993.

Films and Videotapes

The Paris Sciences, a quintet and collaboration with videographer Joan Blair, New York, 1981.
Elevator, video by Burt Barr with performance by Perron, 1984.
Standard Deviation, collaboration with videographer Cathy Weis, 1984.

*   *   *

Dancing since the age of five, with her first performance for a community theater while in her teens, Wendy Perron is a noted dance critic, veteran postmodern performer, and choreographer with a lyrical, woman-centered technique characterized by use of accu-mulated movement and off-kilter stances. At the age of 37 she became the youngest choreographer to receive a three-year fellow-ship from the National Endowment for the Arts (NEA) and in the early 1990s the first choreographer from the United States to re-ceive the Deutscher Akademischer Austauschdienst fellowship resi-dency in Berlin.

Perron was born 8 October 1947 in the Bronx, New York. Her mother, Dorothy Wayne Perron studied with Martha Graham and danced for Jane Dudley. In 1952, when Perron was five, her mother founded the New Milford School of Creative Dance in their home in New Milford, New Jersey and Perron was able to receive early dance training from her mother. In her teens, Perron broke away from modern dance hoping to become a ballerina. She studied clas-sical ballet with Irine Fokine in Ridgewood, New Jersey, dancing the role of Louise in a community production of *Carousel.* During the summers she took classes at the School of American Ballet and the Martha Graham School of Contemporary Dance in New York City. At the age of 16 she added classes at the Joffrey School of Ballet hoping for an invitation to audition for the company. She never was invited and so enrolled in the dance program at Bennington College upon graduating from high school. "Bennington seemed like freedom to me," Perron told Sharry Traver Underwood in a interview for *Dance Magazine* in 1993. "The first year was a revelation of how mind and body could be connected." At Bennington she recaptured her interest in interpretive dance, though shedding her ballet vocabulary and mannerisms was hard work. She also began spending summers at the American Dance Festival.

After graduation she worked on various projects in New York City with Rudy Perez, Barbara Roan, Jeff Duncan, Jack Moore, and others. Twyla Tharp invited Perron to join her company, but Perron felt the movements to be awkward and declined. Later, she reconsidered after seeing a piece Tharp choreographed which struck her as incredibly inventive. Perron joined Tharp's adjunct company called the Farm Club. Shortly after joining, injuries to her back and ankle left her in debilitating pain. Perron, in her early 20s, found herself having to figure out movement for her own body to ease the pain and heal the injuries, which initiated a new phase of dancing. About this same time, Perron began writing about the *why* of dance as an art. She wrote features and reviews for *Soho Weekly News,* and *The Drama Review.* She continues to write in the late 1990s, currently a critic for *Dance Magazine, Village Voice,* and *Soho,* known for her keen interpretation and vision.

Perron began to choreograph at the age of 22, though the first piece she considers of significance was *Daily Mirror* composed at the age of 29 over a period of 100 days. Using accumulation, as most of her choreography does, she created a solo by recording one movement every day and adding it to the movements created on the previous days. This method allowed her to compose without worrying about where the piece was going or how it would end. She expanded on the piece a year later, creating *Four-Way Daily Mirror* in 1977. During the creation of these pieces she was with the Trisha Brown Dance Company, which she joined in 1975 and with which she remained until 1978. While with the Brown company, she collaborated on choreography with several other Brown members. In 1978 she left to teach at Bennington College, replacing Judith Dunn on the dance faculty. She remained there for four years with occasional trips to New York to work on various projects. During her appointment at Bennington College, she served as co-director of the Judson Project, organizing the exhibit, which traveled internationally, of photos and videotapes from the Judson Dance Theater. She is currently director of the Jacob's Pillow extension program at Bennington College.

Perron founded her own company in 1983; a year later she received her NEA fellowship and began to build her repertoire. In 10 years she created approximately 25 pieces. One of her first for the Wendy Perron Dance Company was *Standard Deviation.* Accumulated motions, segmented variations, creating repetitive, adjunct movements, and signaling ques have become standards of Perron's work—as are soft, off-kilter moves. Her pieces often reflect social issues and her philosophy about community involvement (everyone should find the time), and Perron lectures on the production of nuclear weapons as a public speaker for Physicians for Social Responsibility. One such work, *Last Forever,* about the longevity of plutonium was favorably reviewed by Deborah Jowitt in the *Village Voice,* who called it "profound and deeply mysterious."

One of Perron's more well-known pieces is *My Night Table Overflows.* Jowitt describes this work in a *Village Voice* review as winding back on itself "revealing the genesis of its gestures long after we first [see] them as a wildly dissimilar images strung together, stroked into compatibility." Similar praise came from a *New York* review

written by Tobi Tobias, who found the performance to be "the most focused work I've seen from [Perron]." Perron choreographed the solo for Peter Boal, a principal dancer with the New York City Ballet, and Tobias commented further that "Perron has enabled [Boal] to shed the noble classical look that is his most familiar image." In a *Dance Magazine* review, Bill Deresiewicz said *Finding* "mixes rapid, agitated gestures with fluid runs to suggest the story of a sensitive but troubled adolescent."

Postmodern dance, to Perron, says Underwood in her 1993 *Dance Magazine* article, "is choreography that expresses the conceptual by way of the kinetic. Her dance vocabulary draws from movements natural to her but characterized by broken lines, a sudden yielding in the joints, off-balance moves with a twisting recovery, and ironically, some classicism."

—Lisa A. Wroble

PETRONIO, Stephen

American dancer, choreographer, and company director

Born: 20 March 1956 in Newark, New Jersey. **Education:** Studied dance at Hampshire College, Amherst, Massachusetts (B.A 1978). **Career:** First male dancer in Trisha Brown Dance Company, 1979-86; founder, Stephen Petronio Company, 1984; first U.S. tour, 1985; first international tour, 1986; collaborated extensively with English dancer-choreographer Michael Clark, 1990-92. **Awards:** National Endowment for the Arts (NEA) choreography fellowships, 1985-88; New York Foundation for the Arts Choreographer's Fellowship, 1986; New York Dance and Performance Award ("Bessie"), 1986; American Choreographers Award, 1987; company grants from NEA and New York State Council on the Arts, 1987-97; John Simon Guggenheim Fellowship, 1988.

Roles

1975	*Locus* (Trishia Brown)
1976	*Line Up* (Trishia Brown)
1980	*Opal Loop* (cr) (Trishia Brown)
1981	*Son of Gone Fishin'* (cr) (Trishia Brown)
1981	*Set and Reset* (cr), (Trishia Brown)
1985	*Lateral Pass* (cr), (Trisha Brown)

Works

1975	*Wall Piece,* Stephen Petronio and student dancers, Hampshire College, Massachusetts
1978	*Pack Piece,* Stephen Petronio and student dancers, Hampshire College, Massachusetts
1980	*Micronesia* (mus. collage), Stephen Petronio, New York City
1980	*Splinter* (mus. collage), Stephen Petronio, Ottawa, Canada
1981	*City of Homes* (mus. collage), Stephen Petronio and Dancers, New York
	Wistful Vistas (mus. Orchestral Maneuvers in the Dark), Stephen Petronio and Dancers, New York
1982	*Deconstruction* (mus. Orchestral Maneuvers in the Dark; live circular saws), Stephen Petronio and Dancers, New York

1983　*Apollo Object* (mus. Rudd), Stephen Petronio and Dancers, New York

1984　*Adrift (with Clifford Arnell)* (mus. Pickett), Stephen Petronio Company, New York

1985　*The Sixth Heaven* (mus. Irwin), Stephen Petronio Company, New York

1986　*Walk-In* (mus. Linton), Stephen Petronio Company, New York

　　　#3 (mus. Pickett), Stephen Petronio Company, New York

1987　*Simulacrum Reels* (mus. Linton), Stephen Petronio Company, New York

1988　*Simulacrum Court* (mus. Linton), Frankfurt Ballet

　　　AnAmnesia (mus. Gordon), Stephen Petronio Company, New York

1989　*Surrender* (mus. Linton), Rotterdamse Dansgroep, Rotterdam

1990　Entr'acte in *Le Trouvère* (mus. Verdi), Tulsa Opera with Stephen Petronio Company, Tulsa, Oklahoma

　　　Surrender II (mus. Linton), Stephen Petronio Company, New York

　　　Close Your Eyes and Think of England (mus. Linton), Stephen Petronio Company, Glasgow

　　　MiddleSex Gorge (mus. Wire), Stephen Petronio Company, Lyon, France

　　　Bed Piece, Stephen Petronio and Michael Clark, London

1991　*Wrong Wrong* (mus. Stravinsky; co-choreographed with Michael Clark), Michael Clark Company and Stephen Petronio Company, Angers, France

　　　Laytext (mus. collage including Stravinsky, Wire, Madonna, voice of John F. Kennedy), Deutsche Oper, Berlin

1992　*Wet within Reason* (mus. Rodgers and Hammerstein; co-choreographed with Michael Clark) Michael Clark Company and Stephen Petronio Dance Company, Salzburg

　　　Cherry (mus. Linton), Annapolis Ballet, Annapolis, Maryland

　　　Half Wrong Plus Laytext (mus. Stravinsky with collage), Stephen Petronio Company, New York

　　　Half Wrong (mus. Stravinsky), Stephen Petronio Company, Dance Umbrella, London

　　　Full Half Wrong (mus. Stravinsky), Stephen Petronio Company, New York

1993　*She Says* (mus. Ono), Stephen Petronio Company, New York

　　　The King Is Dead (mus. Elvis Presley, Ravel), Stephen Petronio Company, New York

1995　*X-Obsessed* (mus. Debby Harry, The Buzzcocks), Stephen Petronio Company, Cannes

　　　Extravenous (mus. Linton), Lyon Opera Ballet, Lyon, France

　　　Lareigne (mus. The Stranglers, Linton), Stephen Petronio Company, New York

　　　A Midsummer Night's Dream (mus. Mendelssohn, Linton), Maggio Danza, Florence

1996　*#4* (mus. Galas), Stephen Petronio Company, New York

　　　Drawn That Way (mus. Suede, Tierstein), Stephen Petronio Company, New York

1997　*I Kneel Down before You* (mus. classical Armenian), Stephen Petronio Company, New York

　　　ReBourne (mus. The Beastie Boys, Sheila Chandra), Stephen Petronio Company, New York

Publications

On PETRONIO: Articles—

Ben-Itzak, Paul, "From India to the Beastie Boys in a Worldly Work," *New York Times,* 21 September 1997.

Kourlas, Gia, "Drawn to Structure," *Time Out New York,* 10-17 April 1996.

Linfield, Susie, "From One Mind to Many Bodies: A Dance Is Born," *New York Times,* 10 May 1992.

Mitchell, Jack, "Stephen Petronio: Mixing It Up," *Dance Magazine,* June 1994.

Tobias, Tobi, "Second Sight," *New York,* 20 February 1995.

Films and Videotapes

Retracing Steps, documentary, dir. Michael Blackwood.
The Kitchen Presents 2, for *Alive from Off-Center,* PBS, 1988.

*　　*　　*

Stephen Petronio was born to a lower middle-class family in New Jersey, and raised, he has said in interviews, with "no art, no music, no dance." Petronio credits performances by Rudolf Nureyev and improvisor Steve Paxton—two radically different models of masculine dancing—with inspiring him to begin dance classes in his first semester at Hampshire College, an experimental school in rural Massachusetts. He quickly dedicated himself to dance, studying improvisation and various modern techniques.

Moving to New York City after graduation, Petronio was soon hired by Trisha Brown as her company's first male dancer. Though he has said he never felt fluent in Brown's movement language, Petronio made an indelible impression, especially in a famous solo in *Set and Reset* (1981). By way of example and encouragement, Brown also became a generous mentor to his emergence as a choreographer.

Petronio began to choreograph while still a student and continued during his years with Brown's company. Though his earliest experiments used pedestrian movement to explore abstract structures with props in silence, his focus shifted rapidly. By the mid-1980s he was preoccupied with the development of an idiosyncratic, virtuosic vocabulary, and had begun to use his dancers as a resource in inventing variations on the movement he fashioned on his own body. *Walk-In,* premiered in 1986 at New York's Dance Theatre Workshop, was Petronio's breakthrough to wider recognition. His reputation has grown steadily since, with regular touring in the U.S. and Europe, including 11 tours to the United Kingdom, where he has been supported especially by Val Bourne, director of London's Dance Umbrella. Nancy Martino in San Francisco has been another major producer of his work.

Walk-In, like *Simulacrum Reels* (1987) and *AnAmnesia* (1988), already bears the hallmarks of Petronio's mature style. Dancers enter and exit constantly, with relentless speed, as though shot from the wings by offstage artillery, interrupting their traverses with drastic stops, like the instantaneous freezing of streams of molten metal. The movement texture ricochets between extremes of fluidity and constrained tension, pierced by peculiar suspended pauses. Signature Petronio motifs include turning stag leaps initiated by whiplash throws of the head; canted, off-balance sideways *chassées*; and slashing *grands ronds de jambes* that propel the body into falls, jumps, and turns. The onslaught of steps is punctu-

Stephen Petronio (center) performing *She Says*, 1993. Photograph © Beatriz Schiller.

ated by convulsive, crumbling, collapsing, or melting motions of spine or limbs.

While Petronio's dancers fill their performances with spontaneous energy, his choreography, even at its wildest, always looks controlled. Petronio initially sought to decompose familiar compositional devices, lending his late 1980s dances an air of calculated anarchy. His high-velocity juxtaposition of brief, discreet segments parallels the rapid-fire jump-cutting of 1980s cinema and, especially, popular music videos. Petronio's stylistic evolution since *Walk-In* has been steady and continuous, without abrupt changes. Petronio made a decisive advance in his approach to partnering with the empyrean erotic wrestling of *Surrender II* (1990), an extended duet with dancer Jeremy Nelson, whose characteristic movement style influenced Petronio considerably. The 1990s have seen a growing interest in patterning, especially in complex intersections of traveling groups. Since *Drawn That Way* (1996), Petronio has slightly deemphasized movement invention (one of his strengths) to concentrate on the unfolding of rigorously asymmetrical structures, both spatial and temporal.

Petronio's dances, he has said, originate in ideas, yet he is concerned to communicate not his ideas themselves but their effects on the body. Music typically comes last in his creative process. Petronio's only frequent musical collaborator is David Linton, from whom he has commissioned numerous assaultive electronic/percussion scores. Despite his preference for a heavy, driving beat, Petronio's choreography is inherently antimetrical (his dancers never count); he uses musical pulse as a source of energy, not rhythmic organization. The relationship between dance and music in most of his work is essentially arbitrary, except for a shared atmosphere of aggression.

From 1990 to 1992 Petronio formed an artistic (and romantic) partnership with British punk/ballet dancer Michael Clark, who appeared to extraordinary effect as a guest artist in a parallel duet with Petronio in *MiddleSex Gorge* (1990). Some critics have traced an enhanced balletic precision in leg movement and Petronio's increasingly provocative costuming to Clark's influence. More important is the lasting expansion of Petronio's musicality due to their collaborative work on Stravinsky's *The Rite of Spring*, called

Wrong Wrong, for which they amalgamated their companies during an extended residency in France in 1991. Petronio later evolved his own full-length version of the *Rite,* called *Full Half Wrong* (1992), one of his finest works. Stravinsky's bold, shifting rhythms forced Petronio to take greater account of musical phrase structure; the influence is visible in later pieces such as *Drawn That Way,* whose commissioned score, Andy Tierstein's *Rhapsody for Strings and Boy Soprano,* exerts a stronger force of gravity over the choreography than previously.

Petronio's dances leave many viewers with an impression of violence. Petronio said in a 1997 interview with Paul Ben-Itzak that his early work was "fueled by anger. . .a scream in the face of the void." Yet while Petronio's movement is violent in its dynamics, his dancers negotiate the complex shared-weight maneuvers of his partnering with tact and trust. The assault on the senses of late-20th-century life, not interpersonal aggression, is his theme. Similarly, critics have remarked constantly on the sexual provocativeness of Petronio's work; yet though his movement is palpably sensuous, the dancers address neither the audience nor each other in any literally erotic way. The sexual shock of Petronio's theatre lies almost entirely in his costuming: the men's upside-down-and-backwards pink corsets and buttock-baring flowered dance-belts in *MiddleSex Gorge* (by Clark, under the pseudonym H. Petal); the gaps at the inner thigh in Manolo's unitards for *Full Half Wrong*; and Manolo's pocket-fronted corsets for the men in *Lareigne* (1995)—push-up bras for the penis.

The dancer's body in the West has been an object of desire at least since the rise of the Romantic ballet. In a sense, Petronio applies to the male body the same fetishistic tropes of objectification attached in recent centuries to the female. In this, he is in tune with a prominent change in American visual culture in the 1980s and 1990s, namely, its saturation in homoerotic imagery, especially in fashion and advertising (significantly, most of Petronio's costumes have been created by fashion—not theatrical—designers). Furthermore, Petronio always treats male and female bodies as functional equals choreographically, and while his men often look vulnerable, his women—who, with Rebecca Hilton, Mia Lawrence, Susan Braham, and Petronio's longtime assistant director Kristen Borg, have included some of the finest downtown New York dancers of their generation—radiate power. The dancers' heroic effort and insistently unhistrionic deportment cloak them in a curious chastity. Petronio does not try to seduce the audience with his dancers' sexual beauty—he confronts us with it. Though Petronio's art is sensational—it aims to stimulate strong visual and visceral sensations in the viewer—it is not, finally, sensationalistic.

The aura of louche chic Petronio cultivates unfortunately distracts some viewers and critics from the depth of his project. For beneath his *mauvais garçon* veneer, Petronio is a profoundly serious artist. He has developed an unmistakable movement idiom (influential and much imitated) and subjected it to ruthless scrutiny, stretched the boundaries of nonballetic virtuosity, and produced a body of work that virtually defines its cultural moment. While Petronio's sexual politics are rooted in the particular self-consciousness instilled in gay American artists in the 1980s and 1990s, his aesthetic transcends his own experience. For Petronio, sexuality is an inalienable essence that permeates the body at a cellular level, a source of dignity, spiritual nourishment, and self-knowledge. As Petronio once said, only half in jest, to a British journalist who asked him to explain the title of his 1990 work

MiddleSex Gorge, "Sex is in the middle of everything, and it's gorgeous."

—Christopher Caines

PHILADANCO
American dance company

Founded by Joan Myers Brown as the Philadelphia Dance Company, 1970; conducts community outreach and education programs, and tours extensively; officially associated with the Philadelphia School of Dance Arts (founded by Brown in 1960); artistic director, Joan Myers Brown, from 1970.

Publications

Dacko, Karen, "National View: Philadanco," *Dance Magazine*, July 1997.

Dixon-Stowell, Brenda, "National Reviews: Philadelphia," *Dance Magazine*, January 1988.

Dunning, Jennifer, "Philadanco, Exuberant But Sleek," *New York Times*, 24 July 1996.

Fisher, Jennifer, "Energy and Attitude Drive Philadanco," *Los Angeles Times*, 7 October 1996.

Gottschild, Brenda Dixon, "Philadanco: Philadelphia's Multifaceted Moderns," *Dance Magazine*, April 1990.

———, "Philadelphia: Philadanco," *Dance Magazine*, September 1985.

Hering, Doris, "Philadanco's Kim Y. Bears: Molding Energy into Depth," *Dance Magazine*, April 1993.

———, "Philadanco: Silver Anniversary For 'Danco,'" *Dance Magazine*, June 1995.

———, "Reviews: Philadanco," *Dance Magazine*, August 1990.

Jowitt, Deborah, "Conversation Pieces," *Village Voice*, 2 June 1992

———, "Old Walt Freud," *Village Voice*, 1 May 1990

Kaufman, Sarah, "A Family Dance Threesome," *Washington Post*, 2 February 1996.

Lewis, Julinda, "Reviews: Philadanco," *Dance Magazine* (New York), September 1992.

Moore, Bill, "Philadanco Dances NYC Season with a Vengeance," *Attitude* (Brooklyn), Fall 1992.

Naude, Alice, "Reviews, New York City: Philadanco," *Dance Magazine*, October 1995.

Reardon, Christopher, "Philadanco Finds Ways to Make a Virtue of Flux," *New York Times,* 14 July 1996.

———, "Philadanco Smolders Quietly on the Edges of Dance Fame," *Christian Science Monitor*, 3 July 1995.

Sommers, Pamela, "The Dance Troupe of Motherly Love," *Washington Post*, 28 January 1996.

———, "Philadanco's Simple History Lesson," *Washington Post*, 6 February 1996.

Yaa Asantewaa, Eva, "La Machine: Philadanco," *Village Voice*, 11 May 1993.

*   *   *

Hallmarks of Philadanco's style are the energy of its performances and what critic Edward Denby referred to as an "angelic

Philadanco: *Surfacing II.*

unconcern toward emotion." These might seem contradictory, but they are united in the stoic yet dynamic character of founder Joan Myers Brown.

The Philadelphia Dance Company is often compared to other notable African-American ensembles such as the Alvin Ailey American Dance Theatre, the Dance Theatre of Harlem, and the Dayton Contemporary Dance Theatre. But one distinguishing characteristic of Philadanco—indeed, something that sets it apart from other dance companies, period—is its financial solvency. That is almost entirely thanks to Brown, who not only has managed to consistently balance the books, but has also been able to provide attractive perks such as housing and health care, which have proven a draw for talented dancers and choreographers.

Born Joan Belle Myers—she has been married and divorced three times—Brown came from an unusual background: "My grandmother was a German Jew; my grandfather was Ceylonese," she told *Dance Magazine* in 1995, on the occasion of Philadanco's 25th anniversary. "As for me, I'm darker than a paper bag. I guess you'd call me sweet-potato brown." Needless to say, opportunities were not abundant when she was growing up in the 1930s and 1940s. She went to work as a nightclub dancer, but Antony Tudor saw her potential to do much more. "With him," she said, "I didn't have to hide in the back line. I wasn't 'the black girl.'"

By 1960, she had founded the Philadelphia School of Dance Arts, which ultimately spawned Philadanco. In the years since, the company has won admiration not just for its performances, but for the way it is run. "More than just a company," *Village Voice* called it, "Philadanco is a sort of one-woman urban renewal project." Brown fixed up houses near the location of her studios, thus providing dancers a place to live. She also offered them free health care, and kept them employed year-round—itself an impressive feat. As a result, she has created a virtual showcase of African-American modern dance talent. Some of the leading figures include the assistant artistic director, Kim Y. Bears; choreographic director Milton Myers; renowned choreographer Talley Beatty; and many other dancers and choreographers, including Elisa Monte, Lynne Taylor-Corbett, Willie Hinton, and Hope Boykin.

Brown has managed to do this all with a budget that stays regularly in the black. She works closely with the Philadelphia business community—Philadanco has a spot on the city's Avenue of the Arts—and with leading community figures. Businesspeople admire Brown for her ability as a manager, but ironically her success has created a handicap. Too often, arts administrators see the company's balanced budget and assume that it doesn't need any help. But in the atmosphere of reduced public funding that emerged during the late 1990s, Philadanco promised to continue thriving.

Philadanco puts on shows in its native city, of course, and also performs regularly in the major cities of the East Coast. The company has appeared at Madison Square Garden, Lincoln Center, the Brooklyn Academy of Music, the Joyce and Delacorte theatres, Kennedy Center in Washington, and summer festivals at Wolf Trap and Jacob's Pillow. On its tours, it has gone to Atlanta, Kansas City, New Orleans, Pittsburgh, and other cities throughout the United States. It has also performed in Bermuda, the Virgin Islands, England, Germany, Turkey, and other parts of Europe and Asia. The Philadelphia Orchestra, the Louis Bellson Orchestra, the Duke Ellington Orchestra, and a number of pop celebrities have all performed with Philadanco.

Philadanco's signature style is a combination of vivid physical and rhythmic engagement on the part of the dancers, combined with a certain emotional detachment. It is almost as though the level of intensity created by the music and the movement—typically, the performances of Philadanco artists start off intensely and don't let up—will not permit anything other than that detachment. But there is also a lot of good humor to go around, as in the company's performance of *The Walkin, Talkin, Signifying Blues Hips, Sacred Hips, Lowdown Throwdown* (that's all one name!) by Jawole Willa Jo Zollar. That 1995 production celebrated the body parts named in the title—at least, the female versions thereof—and in it Hope Boykin and others satirized the movements of women "shaking their stuff." Also characteristic of Philadanco's repertoire is *Beauty Is Skin Deep, Ugly Is to the Bone* by Talley Beatty, with music by Quincy Jones and Earth, Wind and Fire.

More than just a dance company, Philadanco is richly engaged in the life of Philadelphia, and of African-Americans throughout the country. Focusing on members of the minority communities, it nonetheless reaches out to audiences across a wide range of ages and ethnic groups. And through the International Conference of Blacks in Dance and the International Association of Blacks in Dance, founded by Brown in 1988 and 1990 respectively, it helps to advance opportunities for African-Americans in the world of dance. Brown continues to work tirelessly for her company and her causes, including higher salaries for her dancers.

—Judson Knight

PHOTOGRAPHY AND MODERN DANCE

Modern dance and still photography are two art forms that have shared a natural connection since modern dance came into existence at the end of the last century. Although the idea of a still medium defining a moving one seems strange, dancers have always depended on photographers to capture some part of their elusive art, if only for a fleeting moment, in order to promote themselves or to document what they have created. The photographer, on the other hand, is interested in capturing the very essence of what the dancer does, or who the dancer is, and expressing it by using the camera and control of the light. Because they complement each other, and because both are primarily visual media, dance and photography have had a long and happy history together. Since both forms were profoundly influenced by the experimental art of the 20th century, modern dance and photography have had especially successful ties.

Some of the earliest and most significant modern dance images were created by photographers like Arnold Genthe and Edward Steichen, who both shot a series of portraits of Isadora Duncan. Genthe's soft, romantic photographs of her were made between 1915 and 1918 in New York. The famed Steichen, one of the leaders in developing the art of modern photography, studied Duncan while in Greece around 1920. He made one of the most memorable images of her at the portal of the Greek Parthenon. Both of these camerawork masters were said to have represented her true spirit through their work.

Many other photographers had similar success taking pictures of dancers in the early part of the century. Loie Fuller was photographed by Harry C. Ellis, Isaiah West Taber and Théodore Rivière.

Ruth St. Denis and Ted Shawn had the attention of Baron Adolphe de Meyer, E.O. Hoppé, George Hoyningen-Huene and Edward Weston, to name a few. Ted Shawn's All Male Dancers were studied by Edwin F. Townsend. Mary Wigman in Germany was the subject of expressive portraits by Hugo Erfurth and Lotte Jacobi as well as Charlotte Rudolph's documentary style. Imogen Cunningham found Adolph Bolm an interesting person to define with her lens. Without the camera work of these artists, these modern dance pioneers would only be oral histories to us. Likewise, without the stimulation of these avant-garde dancers, well-known photographers like Steichen, Weston, and Cunningham may have never followed their paths of developing abstraction and modernism in photography.

During the time that modern dance was becoming a solid and recognized art form, many photographers were there taking pictures. Soichi Sunami photographed such modern dance greats as Harald Kreutzberg, Doris Humphrey, and Martha Graham. Lotte Jacobi also worked with Kreutzberg and Wayne Albee with Doris Humphrey. Martha Graham had been photographed by Imogen Cunningham, Nicholas Muray, E.O. Hoppé and, most significantly of all, by Barbara Morgan.

Barbara Morgan has been the single most important photographer of modern dance. She began her work in the 1920s and, throughout the 1930s and 1940s, photographed modern dance innovators including Doris Humphrey, Charles Weidman, Erick Hawkins, Valerie Bettis, Pearl Primus, José Limón, Merce Cunningham, and many others. Her series of photographs of Martha Graham taken in the 1940s are the most famous images in dance photography, as well as being landmark photographs in the history of the medium as a whole. Morgan's work was the first to truly define the bridge between the two art forms. She was able to express what she called "life forces of rhythmic vitality" in her work. By capturing a magical moment in a dance movement, she breathed the life of the dancer into a still image. Morgan set the standard for all subsequent dance photography.

As the dance scene became a mixture of traditional and avant-garde works, American studio photographers and photojournalists like Maurice Seymour, Gordon Anthony, Fred Fehl, and George Platt Lynes worked along with Serge Lido in France, the Mydtskov family in Copenhagen, and Roger Wood, Baron, Houston Rogers, Roy Round, and Reg Wilson in England to continue the tradition of dance photography. The renowned Jack Mitchell, Martha Swope, Herbert Migdoll, and Anthony Crickmay all concentrate their efforts on both the ballet and modern dance worlds of today. Even other fine art photographers like Richard Avedon, Helmut Newton, and Robert Mapplethorpe have taken photographs of dancers. All of these artists' primary goal was to document the dancers through their unique viewfinders, but few compete with the artistry of Barbara Morgan.

In recent years there has been a new group of dance photographers that have sought a new way of looking at dance. This new generation is led by Lois Greenfield, who has worked closely with such dancers as David Parsons, Daniel Ezralow, Ashley Roland, Bill T. Jones. In Greenfield's studio dancers improvise and create new moments of movement. Instead of using choreography, they are free to discover what Greenfield calls their "kinesthetic personality," which she in turn translates into stimulating artistic expressions. This technique is also being used by Chicago dance photographer William Frederking, who works primarily with modern dancers, in trying to convey what dancers feel while they're executing a movement.

Currently Beatriz Schiller, Johan Elbers, Tom Brazil, Nan Melville, and Anja Hitzenberger are some of the newcomers to the New York dance photography scene. Cylla von Tiedemann works in Toronto, and Dieter Blum in Germany. All of them are exploring the world of movement though it is yet to be seen what will ultimately come of their journey.

Modern dance and photography are currently changing and working together. Technical advancements in photographic equipment have allowed pictures to be taken of movement that could never have been taken before; modern dancers are using photographs in their performances to enhance and convey their ideas. Film and video documentation of dance is also influenced by these two arts and they by it. Computer technology, too, has opened new doors for further exploration between the dancer and the photographer. This shared energy is a reflection of the artistic collaboration that has been evolving since the turn of the century. As modern dance and photography continue to support each others' mutual goals and work together in developing today's modern art, their combined future will undoubtedly continue down this fruitful path.

Publications

Books—

Ewing, William A., *Dance and Photography*, New York, 1987.

Articles—

Barnes, Clive, "Dance Photography," *Dance Magazine*, August 1991.
Barnes, Clive, "Jack Mitchell: Photographer to the Dance," *Dance Magazine,* January 1996.
Citron, Paula, "The View from Here: Toronto Moderns in the Camera's Eye," *Dance Magazine,* May 1990.
Kirschenbaum, Jill, "Women at Work: Lois Greenfield," *Ms.,* September 1989.
Mauro, Lucia, "Magic Moments," *Oak Leaves, Diversions,* 16 August 1995.
Patnaik, Deba P., "Barbara Morgan," *Contemporary Photographers.* New York, 1995.
———, "Barbara Morgan: Touched with Light," *Aperture,* Fall 1992.

—Paula Murphy

PILOBOLUS DANCE THEATER
American dance company

Of the modern dance companies which grew from the body-celebratory experiments of American college dance programs in the late 1960s, few achieved success on the level of Pilobolus Dance Theater. Founded in 1971 by a group of classmates at Ivy-League Dartmouth College, the company grew from a dance class taught by Alison Chase. As an assignment, Steve Johnson, Moses Pendleton, and Jonathan Wolken created a dance titled "Pilobolus," named for an intelligent, light-sensitive, single-celled phototropic fungus which flourishes in New England barnyards. Joined for an evening-length concert by Robby Barnett and Lee Harris, who replaced Johnson, the quartet received favorable audience response in their premiere at the New York studio of Murray Louis and Alwin Nikolais in December 1971. Critics immediately lauded their sculptural uses of the body, unself-conscious physicality, and playful kaleidoscopic transmogrifications, which suggested a utopian male community bound by the effort of weights and balances.

While the original company members had little or no formal dance background, Pilobolus added Martha Clarke and Allison Chase to its roster in 1973. Both women possessed extensive technical training, and their presence significantly altered the creative potential of the group's work. Pilobolus retained this six-member configuration of four men and two women through 1998.

Choreography by Pilobolus draws on acrobatics, pantomime, sculpture, and visual references to popular culture and literature. Their work typically exhibits a high theatricality, in either stylized lighting, which reveals only portions of the body at a time like in 1977's *Shizen*; fantastical costuming which transforms the shape of the body, as in *Untitled* (1975); or abstract stage settings, which provide synergistic backdrops for playful dances, like 1972's *Anaedrom*. The troupe also experiments successfully with nudity in some works. Most dances by Pilobolus, however, create visual effects from prolonged slow-motion movement, with measured foldings and unfoldings of limbs. Their hallmark use of the body to create sculptural illusion in improbable configurations set a high standard of physical control in modern dance. While early works exploited the acrobatic abilities of their performers, later works investigated psychological landscapes suggested by these oblique gestures and physical balances. Many of these ambiguous, imagis-

tic works convey narratives of metamorphosis and transformation. Their breakthrough work in this vein, *Untitled*, details a surreal encounter between two elongating women who give birth to a pair of nude men while being pursued by a pair of clothed suitors.

The creative method of Pilobolus is as remarkable as its prolific output. Working in an intensive, improvisatory manner, the company creates work collectively, with each dancer serving as one of several choreographers for group work. This distinctive method of collaborative creation diverges sharply from prevalent choreographic practice, as it provides its dancers a rare investment in movement patterns and theme. The eclectic tastes of the group are also reflected in its musical choices. While early work featured experiments with found instruments, later works celebrate classical compositions by a range of composers including Dimitri Shostakovich and John Harbison. Most works, however, are choreographed to electronic music created in collaboration with a regular roster of composers including Jon Appleton, Jane Ira Bloom, and Robert Dennis.

The unconventional idiom of the company garnered its share of detractors. While consistently popular with audiences, critics have periodically resisted writing about the group's defiantly accessible modes of performance as concert dance, preferring to term its work acrobatics or pantomime. Over the years, however, an infusion of trained dancers have altered the emotional range and accomplishment of the troupe. Several important dance personalities and choreographers have emerged from the group, including Jamey Hampton, Georgina Holmes, Rebecca Jung, Kent Lindemer, Trebien Pollard, Peter Pucci, Mark Santillano, and Michael Tracy. Although

Pilobolus: *Bonsai*, 1981. Photograph © Johan Elbers.

Pilobolus: Untitled, 1992. Photograph © Johan Elbers.

the troupe's founding members periodically formed offshoot groups, as when Pendleton and Chase formed Momix while Clarke and Barnett formed Crowsnest around 1980, its continued popularity builds on an active repertory of new work as well as revivals of dances from its earliest years.

Appearances by the company on Broadway in 1977 confirmed a broadly based, populist appeal of the company, especially among audiences not accustomed to attending dance events. Pilobolus has conducted several international tours sponsored by the U.S. State Department, beginning with a tour of India, Afghanistan, Sri Lanka, and Bangladesh in 1978.

Pilobolus laid the groundwork for a popular audience who attended dance events as they might the circus—to laugh at the clowning shenanigans of a man unable to walk upright; to marvel at the weightlessness of a body airborne, "flying" through space while supported by others; to meditate on the abstract shapes and balances accomplished by pretzeled dancers in unlikely positions. The company consistently performs to sold-out houses and an intergenerational, family audience. Still based in Washington, Connecticut, where the company owns a farm, Pilobolus continues to inspire dancers and audiences with its faith in communal creation.

Publications

Dunning, Jennifer, "Is Success Changing Pilobolus?" *New York Times,* 20 December 1981.
Fanger, Iris, "Pilobolus," *Dance Magazine*, July 1974.
Harris, William, "Pilobolus, Unruly as Ever, Pulls Together Anew," *New York Times*, 11 December 1988.

—Thomas DeFrantz

THE PLACE
British dance and choreography center

Headquarters for a panoply of educational and artistic services, The Place maintains its status as one of Britain's most important dance and choreography centres. Through its education, training, performance, and choreographic development programmes, it has become a mecca both for budding young students and seasoned professionals internationally.

The Place is governed by the Contemporary Dance Trust, a body founded in 1966 by arts philanthropist and Martha Graham devotee Robin Howard (1924-1989). Howard's pioneering vision provided the energy behind what today constitutes most of British modern dance. Working with former Graham dancer Robert Cohan, he initiated a series of peripatetic classes which grew into the London Contemporary Dance School, and from which was born the London Contemporary Dance Theatre (1967-1994). It wasn't until 1969 that either organization found a permanent home, settling at that point in a converted rifle and drill hall in central London's Bloomsbury area.

The school's early years were marked by the kind of creative anarchy wherein pupils (some experienced in such other disciplines as ballet, film, or the visual arts) might learn Cunningham, Limón and Nikolais techniques in addition to Graham, participate in workshops with musicians, actors, designers and theatre directors, and be encouraged to invent their own styles of choreography.

Within a decade the school's curriculum grew more rigid as its ethos of experimentation somewhat dissipated. Regardless, the LCDS was of inestimable value in expanding the boundaries of independent and contemporary British dance. Among the original students were Siobhan Davies and Richard Alston, just two from an enormous pool of artists whose varying aesthetics the school helped form. Today the LCDS offers one to three years of full-time, accredited vocational training to approximately 150 students, and operates its own touring performance group, dubbed 4D. More informally, The Place itself offers weekend and evening tuition in all dance forms to youth and adults.

The Place is of equal prestige as a theatrical venue. Dance artists from around the globe have made their London debut on its intimate stage. (The auditorium accommodates an audience of up to 300 viewers in steeply raked bleacher seats.) Lea Anderson, Matthew Bourne, Aletta Collins, Shobana Jeyasingh, Wayne McGregor, Lloyd Newson, and countless other British-based dancers and choreographers have boosted their careers at The Place, while for some it has also been an administrative home.

Alston, head of his own eponynmous dance company, came full circle via his 1994 appointment as The Place's overall artistic director. John Ashford, whose job title is theatre director, arrived eight years earlier to carve out a role for himself as the 'godfather' of new British dance. In his capacity as programmer he lent The Place a new lease on life, instituting a handful of annual themed seasons, including the now-defunct April in Paris (the best dance from France), Indian Summer (highlighting classical and folk traditions from the sub-continent), and the ongoing Re:Orient (contemporary dance from the Asian Pacific together with work by Asian-British dance artists). Of even greater ambition are Spring Loaded (a three-month celebration of the diversity of British dance), The Turning World (a month of the most innovative work from abroad, initally intended to be held yearly from 1990 to 2000), and Resolution! (a three-tiered platform for shorter works by emerging artists from the UK and Europe, lasting seven weeks). The Place has entered into co-productions with Sadler's Wells Theatre and the South Bank Centre, and regularly presents artists participating in the annual Dance Umbrella festival.

Besides nurturing resident choreographers, The Place extends clerical and artistic support to a handful of associate artists. The Place Dance Services, part of the network of National Dance Agencies, was established in 1991 to provide information and advice to members working within the independent dance sector both inside and outside of the UK. This includes access to the extensive archives of The Video Place and, since 1995, The Place Choreodrome, a summer programme which allows artists to use Place facilities to work on the creative process without the pressure to produce a performance.

—Donald Hutera

POMARE, Eleo
Columbian-born dancer, choreographer, and company director

Born: 22 October 1937 in Cartagena, Colombia; moved to New York, 1947. **Education:** Graduated from New York High School of Performing Arts, 1956; studied with José Limón, Louis Horst, Curtis James, Martha Graham, Geoffrey Holder, and Kurt Jooss.

Career: Co-founder with Dudley Williams, the Corbyantes; formed Eleo Pomare Dance Company, 1958; formed European company and toured Holland, 1962; taught at First International Ballet Seminar, Royal Danish Ballet; National Ballet of Holland; Scapino Ballet Company and School; Balletakademien, University of Stockholm; returned to U.S. and revived company, 1964; co-founder, Dancemobile performance series; toured South Africa as cultural ambassador for African Arts Fund, invited by President Nelson Mandela, 1992. **Awards:** John Hay Whitney Foundation fellowship, 1961; John Simon Guggenheim Foundation fellowship; American Dance Festival award; nominated for AUDELCO award for black theater; TOR Superior Artistry Award; honored with "Eleo Pomare Day" by New York Mayor David N. Dinkins, 7 January 1987; grants from the National Endowment for the Arts, New York State Council on the Arts, New York State Black and Puerto Rican Legislative Caucus/National Heritage Trust, New Voices of Harlem, and others.

Works

1958	*Cantos from a Monastery* (mus. Hovhaness), solo, Eleo Pomare Dance Company (EPDC), New York
1960	*En Rondeau* (mus. Rameau), EPDC
	Not Now (mus. Stravinsky), solo
	Rites (mus. Harrison), EPDC
1961	*Alienations* (mus. Bartók)
	Reflexes
	4 A.M. (mus. Krenek), solo
	The First Season (mus. Stravinsky), EPDC
1962	*Harlem Moods* (mus. Fuerstenau, Mingus, traditional), EPDC (an early version was subsequently revised and expanded into *Blues for the Jungle*)
	Gaucho (revised; mus. Katz), solo
1963	*Resonance* (mus. Bruynel), EPDC
	Impro (mus. Bruynel), solo
	Smiles and Tears (mus. Valjean), Scapino Ballet Company
	Blood Wedding (mus. Coltrane), Norwegian Television
1964	*Hex* (mus. Partch), solo
1965	*Odds and Ends* (mus. Southern), EPDC
	Missa Luba (mus. Congolese mass), EPDC
	Resonance
1966	*Serendipity* (mus. Handel), EPDC and Australian Dance Theatre
	Pavane for a Deadpan Minstrel (play, Paul Harrison), Actors Studio; subsequently revised and restaged for University of Buffalo
	Blues for the Jungle (mus. Brown, Belafonte, Mingus, traditional, collages by Levy), EPDC
	Gin. Woman. Distress (mus. Smith), solo, EPDC, Australian Dance Theatre
1967	*High Times* (mus. Jackson, Odetta, Smith), EPDC
	Las Desenamoradas (mus. Coltrane), EPDC
	At This Hour (J.H. Gresham), Nassau Community College
	Climb (mus. Kelemen), solo
	Up Tight (mus. Smith, Jackson, Jordan), EPDC (revised and expanded from *High Times*)
	Two Passing (mus. Yun), EPDC
1968	*Narcissus Rising* (sound collage by Levy), solo
	Over Here (mus. Reagan, spirituals, Hopi Indian, Franklin, U.S. Army Band), EPDC

	Benito Cereno, Nassau Community College
	Of Mice and Marigolds (mus. Hindemith, Poulenc, arr. by Levy), EPDC
	Beginsville (mus. Cunningham), for 1968 New York Upstate Summer Dancemobile
	Three Shades of Noon (mus. Veress), Australian Dance Theatre, Holland
	Passage (mus. Fellegara), solo, EPDC, Australian Dance Theatre, Philadelphia
1969	*Epitaph* (mus. collage by Levy), Clark Center for the Performing Arts Dance Workshop, New York
	Radiance of the Dark (mus. Edwin Hawkins Singers), EPDC
1970	*Movements for Two* (mus. Subotnick), duet, Brooklyn
1971	*Cleaver's Wife* (poetry by Last Poets), solo for Carole Johnson, ANTA Theatre, New York
	Sunday Afternoon in May (sound collage by Levy incl. Don Cherry, Malcolm X), solo for Frank Ashley, ANTA Theatre, New York
	Movements (incorporated *Movements for Two;* mus. Subotnick), ANTA Theatre, New York
	Burnt Ash (sound collage by Levy), EPDC, ANTA Theatre
	Torn (mus. Mingus), for New York City Dancemobile, Harlem Cultural Council
	'Nother Shade of Blue (mus. Flack, Collins, Nyro, traditional), EPDC, New York Dance Festival, Delacorte Theater, New York
1972	*Roots* (mus. Southern Folk Heritage, Holiday, Giovanni)
1974	*Hushed Voices* (mus. Coleman, Mingus, Thomas, Cherry, Chicago Art Ensemble)
	Transplant II (mus. Pointer Sisters, Graham, Central Station)
1975	*De La Tierra* (mus. Crumb, Carlos, Parten)
1976	*Sextet* (mus. Bach)
	The Queen's Chamber (mus. Bartók)
1978	*Henri Bendel's Window* (mus. Subotnick)
1979	*Orbweb* (mus. Rauchberg)
	Fallscape (mus. Coleman)
1980	*Sets* (mus. Coleman)
	Sombras (mus. Garbarek)
	Phoenix (mus. Reich)
	Broken Covenant (mus. Hovaness)
	Turns (mus. Coleman, Hiller)
	Sweet Deep Love (mus. Jones)
1981	*Resheet Hanekamah* (mus. Smith)
	Hopper (mus. Brown)
	No Score
	Third Degree (mus. Ellington)
1983	*Escola* (mus. Batucada)
	Local Stops on a Full Moon (mus. Leslee)
	Back to Bach (mus. Bach)
	Phoenix (mus. Reich)
1984	*Canaqua* (mus. Jarre)
1986	*Lord, Have Mercy* (mus. Perkinson)
	Morning Without Sunrise (mus. Roach)
1987	*Langston* (mus. Ellington)
	Grind Variations
1988	*Miles of Miles* (mus. Davis), solo, EPDC, New York
	Repeats (mus. Turley), EPDC, New York
	Black Breeze (mus. Roach)

1989   *Tabernacle* (mus. Reich)
1990   *Birds Want to Fly*
        T. 'N.' T. (mus. Johnson, Uptown String Quartet)
        Homemade Ice Cream (mus. traditional American)
        Folk Say (mus. White)
1991   *Epitasis* (mus. Adams)
        Esa Mujer (mus. Piazzola)
1992   *Angels of a Blind God* (mus. Coleman)
        Earth Cry (mus. Textureworks)
        Postcards From Soweto (mus. Makeba, Sedibe)
        Miles (mus. Davis)
1993   *Buffie Sings* (mus. St. Marie)
        River Dust Burial (mus. McIntyre)
        Plague (mus. Tract, Ono)
        Five (mus. McIntyre, Mighty Clouds of Joy)
1994   *A Horse Named Dancer* (mus. McIntyre), Adelaide Center for Performing Arts, Australia
1995   *Raft* (mus. Kabak, Echoes of Nature, Reich, Samite)

Other works include: *Construction in Green, Encounter, Wind and Quicksand, The Birthday of the Infanta,* among others.

Publications

On POMARE: articles—

Homzie, Hillary, "Pomare Travels to South Africa," *Dance Magazine*, August 1992.
Macher, Brigitte, "There's no Multiculturalism in Harlem," *ballett international tanz aktuel*, 1995.
Warren, Charmaine Patricia, "Eleo Pomare: Portrait of a Master Choreographer," *Black Masks*, January/February 1993.

Films and Videotapes

Performed and choreographed for Eurovision, including *Blood Wedding* (mus. Coltrane, Norwegian Television; as well as performances for Television of Holland, and German television.

*   *   *

Eleo Pomare eludes precise definition or classification. Born in Cartagena, Colombia, on 22 October 1937, he was raised in Panama. His maternal grandfather was a Frenchman who married a Haitian fugitive slave who bore 20 children of her own, then raised many of her grandchildren. In 1943, while crossing from the island of San Andrés to the mainland, the ship on which Pomare was traveling with his father was hit by a torpedo. Pomare survived; his father drowned. In 1947, at age 10, Pomare came to the U.S. and lived in Harlem where he observed and absorbed the culture while fiercely maintaining his own multicultural identity. Chronologically and artistically a contemporary of notable African-American choreographers Talley Beatty, Donald McKayle, Louis Johnson, and Alvin Ailey, Eleo Pomare formed his first company (the Corybantes, with fellow student Dudley Williams) while still attending the New York High School of Performing Arts, from which he graduated in 1956. After graduation, he continued his dance training with Martha Graham, José Limón, and others; some of these early influences are evident throughout the body of his work.

The Eleo Pomare Dance Company was formed in 1958, coincidentally the same year Ailey's American Dance Theatre was born.

Unlike his contemporaries, however, Pomare—a dancer, choreographer, painter, gourmet cook, and costume designer whose works are often narrative in form and are frequently inspired by literature, art, music, and literary themes—nonetheless earned the title "the angry young man of American modern dance" and "a man with a message." He has countered these labels by noting that many great modern dance works by American choreographers have grown out of protest, and furthermore that "anyone. . .angry for that long would have imploded." While it is undeniably true that many of Pomare's works are characterized by a hard-edged perhaps compulsive power, and mirror the conflicts and social issues of black America, from the upheavals of the Civil Rights movement to the Los Angeles riots of the 1990s, his creative juices are just as likely to be triggered by a European classical music score, a painting by an American artist, or by Latin literature. The stark and haunting 1967 work, *Las Desenamoradas*, is an adaptation of Federico Garcia Lorca's *The House of Bernarda Alba*; while Narcissus *Rising*, a solo Pomare created for himself in 1968, proved to be an erotic and enduringly shocking portrait of a black leather-clad, bad-boy biker. "If Eleo Pomare had chosen the literary field. . .instead of the dance world," wrote the late Bill Moore—a staunch supporter of Pomare—in *Crisis Magazine* in 1990, "he would have been a renowned figure in American arts. The literary world. . .would have welcomed and hailed Pomare's genius with a special space and reverence equal to that of [his friend James]Baldwin."

Pomare won a John Hay Whitney Fellowship in 1961 to study European approaches to modern dance and chose to study in Germany with Kurt Jooss. Pomare ended up spending three years touring Holland and Scandinavia with his own company, made up of an international cast. But his intellect, social consciousness, and curiosity drew him back to America in 1963 at the height of the Civil Rights movement for the Freedom March on Washington. He returned briefly to Europe, the adopted home of his friend James Baldwin, then revived his New York company in 1964 where he continued to work tirelessly for more than 30 years.

In 1966 Pomare's company premiered *Blues for the Jungle*, a signature work in the often controversially-debated genre of "black dance" that chronicles the latter part of the African diaspora, encompassing the life of blacks from slavery to Harlem. Set to a music collage including works by Harry Belafonte, Charles Mingus, and others, the work was immediately and sometimes unfavorably compared to Ailey's signature work, *Revelations*, choreographed in 1960. The latter presents a portrait of faith, triumph, and the black church. Noting that *Blues* was originally choreographed in Europe, as *Harlem Moods* (1962), Pomare dismisses comparisons, unfavorable or otherwise when he states, "We took the black experience into different directions. We all don't have a colonialistic mentality, and we all also don't have a street mentality."

Pomare is first and last a thinker, an intellectual. Ailey, McKayle, Beatty, and Johnson are numbered among his friends. His works, while they may reflect the times, his times, are themselves timeless and universal. His work, he says, "takes years to digest," yet despite a confluence of attitude, themes, and dynamics, it has never been analyzed or discussed in terms of a Pomare style or technique. And despite dancers such as the multitalented Loretta Abbott and Dyane Harvey, who emerged from his company a diva, name recognition has been fleeting and localized. Pomare himself eschews any taint of the commercial, leaving his work to stand on its own merits, and frequently declaring that he is not an entertainer. Yet in spite of the public image, Pomare is respected and sought after by his colleagues, as well as by a younger generation of African American

Eleo Pomare: *Postcards from Soweto.* **Photograph © Beatriz Schiller.**

choreographers and artistic directors who turn to him for advice, to commission new works from him, or reconstruct his older works for their own companies—Cleo Parker Robinson for her Denver-based company, the Alvin Ailey American Dance Theatre, the Maryland Ballet, the Dayton Contemporary Dance Company, and New York's Alpha Omega Theatrical Dance Company with whom Pomare and other small "sister" companies, in an effort to survive, formed an alliance called C.O.D.A. (Coalition of Dance Artists)/ New York to share space, performance venues, as well as dancers.

Among his contributions to history one must include his seminal role as co-founder, with Carol Johnson, of the Dancemobile series. A community-based organization, the Harlem Cultural Council, sponsored this traveling stage that each summer during the 1960s and into the 1970s, brought dance to Harlem, the inner city neighborhoods of New York City, and other underserved communities in New York State. Countless youths and their families were exposed to dance for the first time by the Dancemobile, which presented socially relevant works as well as lyrical ballets, African dance, and literary themes inspired by Langston Hughes and other writers and artists, by a diverse group of African American choreographers and artists. Paradoxically then, Pomare, who makes a distinction between "black dance" and "the arts of black people," found himself one of progenitors of the generation and genre that came to be known as "black dance."

In spite of a prolific body of work, his company never achieved the success and status of the Ailey company or the Dance Theatre of Harlem, yet by the 1980s and 1990s, Pomare saw many of his earlier works, which had earlier been declared angry or malformed, categorized as masterworks. In 1992 he traveled to South Africa at the invitation of South African president Nelson Mandela, part of a tour sponsored by the New York City-based African Arts Fund, an organization whose goal included developing the talent of black South African Artists. While there, he held workshops with Funda, a South African dance troupe, and made history again, not as an angry young man, but as a respected elder when white dancers, for the first time, traveled to the black township of Soweto to take part in Pomare's classes.

Three of Pomare's works have been reconstructed and documented in the series "The Black Tradition in American Modern Dance," for the American Dance Festival: *Las Desenamoradas*, *Blues for the Jungle*, and *Missa Luba*, which incorporates Catholic rituals and African images.

—Julinda Lewis-Ferguson

POSIN, Kathryn

American dancer, choreographer, and educator

Born: 23 March 1945 in Butte, Montana. **Education:** Bennington College with Jack Moore; studied with Anna Sokolow and at the Merce Cunningham studio, New York. **Career:** Member, Anna Sokolow Dance Company; member, Valerie Bettis Dance Company; founder, Kathryn Posin Dance Company, 1972; taught at Harvard Summer Dance Center, 1984; UCLA, 1986-88; workshop participant, Kinetics Dance Theatre (Ellicott City, Maryland), 1990; choreographer, National Dance Company of Taiwan, 1992; taught at California Institute of the Arts in Valencia, 1993; artist-in-residence, University of Wisconsin at Milwaukee, 1995. **Awards:** Sarasota Ballet Choreography Competition.

Works

1965	*Anecdote*
1967	*Call*
1968	*Block*
	The Closer She Gets...The Better She Looks
	40 Amp Mantis
	A: Arm, B: Yellow, Blue Leg
1969	*Guidesong*
1971	*Days*
	Three Countrysides
	Flight of the Baroque Airship
	The Black Dance
	Salvation (theater work)
1972	*Prism*
	Summer of '72
	The White Dance
	Subway
	Tunnel Lights
	A Dream Out of Time (theater work)
1973	*Grass*
	Ladies in the Arts
	Ghost Train
	Bach Pieces
	Port Authority
	Getting Off
1974	*Nuclear Energy I*
	Children of the Atomic Age
	Nuclear Energy II
1975	*Nuclear Energy III*
	Street Song
	The Waves (mus. Laurie Spiegel), for the American Dance Festival
1976	*Light Years—Four Plays for a Quarter*
	Tales from the Dark Wood
1977	*Soft Storm*
	Saks Fifth Avenue Suite
	The Cherry Orchard (theater work)
1978	*Clear Signals*
	Close Encounters of the Third Kind
1979	*Apache*
	Windowsill
	The Tempest (theater work)
1980	*Later that Day* (mus. Phillip Glass), Alvin Ailey American Dance Theatre
1981	*Galena Summit* (mus. Steve Reich's *Music for 19 Instruments*), Concert Dance Company
1983	*The Boys from Syracuse* (Alvin Epstein), Posin performed the stage choreography for this performance, Loeb Drama Center's American Repertory Theater, Boston, Massachussets
1984	*From the Hopi* (mus. Philip Glass, for the film *Koyaanisqatsiz*), commissioned by the University of Wisconsin at Milwaukee
	Hell Is Heaven, Harvard Summer Dance Center
1987	*Hurts Too Much to Stop*
1988	*Shock Crossing*
1990	*Of Rage and Remembrance* (mus. John Corigliano), Milwaukee Ballet
	Moebius (mus. Philip Glass), performed by the duo, Karen and Alvin

1991   *Shattered Sands*, Milwaukee Ballet
1995   *Hard Steps* (mus. The Cars), commissioned by the University of Wisconsin at Milwaukee
        Stepping Stones: A Ballet (collaboration w/composer Joan Tower)
1996   *Four World Songs*, Sarasota Ballet
1997   *A Poem without a Hero* (mus. monks at Zagorsk monastery in Russia), Cincinnati Ballet

Publications

On POSIN: articles—

Brown, Alan, "Kathryn Posin at Home in a Tropic 42nd Street," *Los Angeles Times*, 4 October 1987.

Buell, Richard, "Happy Union of Two Forms," *Boston Globe*, 13 April 1983.

Gladstone, Valerie, "Out of the Lofts...And Into the Spotlight," *Newsday*, 5 January 1997.

Harding, Cathryn, "Milwaukee Ballet's Twenty-Fifth Season," *Dance Magazine*, September 1994.

Horn, Laurie, "Modern Dance on the Lighter Side," *Miami Herald*, 22 May 1988.

Jackson, George, "Modern Jolt of Energy," *Washington Post*, 27 March 1990.

Pasles, Chris, "Culture Clash," *Los Angeles Times*, 28 July 1993.

Perlmutter, Donna, "UCLA Company at Royce Hall," *Los Angeles Times*, 7 March 1988.

Segal, Lewis, "At Wadsworth on Friday, A Limit on Spirit from Posin Dance," *Los Angeles Times*, 19 October 1987.

Smith, Sid, "*Of Rage* a Moving Commentary on AIDS Tragedy," *Chicago Tribune*, 11 November 1990.

Sommers, Pamela, "Experience Doesn't Hurt," *Washington Post*, 2 August 1991.

——, "Melding Arts into New Form," *Washington Post*, 23 March 1990.

Temin, Christine, "A Choreographer Simmers Down," *Boston Globe*, 5 July 1988.

——, "Eight Harvard Dance Teachers Toe the Creative Line," *Boston Globe*, 21 July 1984.

*   *   *

Kathryn Posin is a renowned choreographer, teacher, and dancer whose works combine traditional modern dance techniques with contemporary music and themes. She often choreographs to pop music, such as pieces by Brian Eno and the B-52s, and to composers favored by postmodernists, such as Steve Reich and Phillip Glass. Her works may focus on urban life in the 1990s, including social problems such as AIDS, but despite her often serious subject matter, many of her pieces are imbued with a humorous, even absurd quality.

Posin was trained by Anna Sokolow and Merce Cunningham, the latter of whom is counted among her major influences. She was a member of the companies of Sokolow and Valerie Bettis before forming her own New York-based modern dance troupe, comprised of a half-dozen members plus herself, in 1972. Her company has included, at various times, notable dancers such as Donald Byrd and Mark Morris. The Kathryn Posin Dance Company has earned critical acclaim; critic Arlene Croce called it one of the three or four best in the country in 1981.

Posin demands flexibility and accuracy from her dancers. Her works are known for incorporating difficult ballet techniques, such as demanding leg extensions, and she has choreographed several pieces for ballet companies as well as for modern dance troupes. Her choreography characteristically has an ensemble feel, and sometimes contains ritualistic images.

One of Posin's early works was *Waves*, created in 1975 for the American Dance Festival and set to a Laurie Spiegel score. In 1980 Posin choreographed *Later That Day* for the Alvin Ailey American Dance Theatre, in which the dancers wore 1920s-style play clothes, while performing to a futuristic score by Phillip Glass. The next year Concert Dance Company, among the leading modern dance troupe in Boston, commissioned *Galena Summit*, performed to Steve Reich's *Music for 19 Instruments*. The piece portrayed an intense struggle, as dancers strained to climb a mountain. Posin's roster of works illustrates her eclectic influences in terms of theme, music, costuming, and dance styles. *From the Hopi* (1984), is set to Glass' score for the film *Koyaanisqatsi*. Commissioned by the University of Wisconsin at Milwaukee (UMW), *From the Hopi* contains themes of suffering and isolation and, typical of Posin's choreography, makes strong demands on the dancers. In *Hard Steps* (1995), also commissioned by UWM as part of her company's 1995 residency there, dancers wore street-people clothing and perform to pop music by the Cars and other acts. *Hurts Too Much to Stop* (1987), is described by Posin as a satire, in part about bicoastalism and bisexualism, and is influenced by her work in both New York and Los Angeles.

Ethnic and international inspirations permeate several of Posin's works. In 1993, she premiered a work-in-progress at Ballet Pacifica's third annual summer choreographer's workshop. Set to an excerpt from Chinese composer Tan Dun's *Nine Songs for Ritual Opera*, which was inspired by the words of Chinese poet Qu Tuan (340-277 B.C.), the work is a surrealistic Chinese fable for four women and two men. The work developed out of Posin's work choreographing for the National Dance Company of Taiwan in 1992. International influences (including Posin's Russian heritage) also inspired *A Poem without a Hero* (1997), which was premiered by the Cincinnati Ballet and was set to medieval chants by the monks of the monastery at Zagorsk in Russia. *Four World Songs* (1996), which won the Sarasota Ballet's Choreography Competition and was premiered by that company, combines four styles: modern dance, hip-hop, African dance, and classical ballet.

Posin's attention to social issues is represented by *Of Rage and Remembrance,* premiered by the Milwaukee Ballet in 1990. The three-movement work, an AIDS requiem to a score by John Corigliano, features walk-throughs by 10 private citizens, who blend on stage with the dancers. It portrays anger and sadness as its characters die of AIDS, and counts the AIDS quilt as an inspiration. Critic Sid Smith of the *Chicago Tribune* commented in reviewing *Of Rage and Remembrance* that "For her part, Posin combines her style with hints of Agnes DeMille and a handful of social choreographers associated with Alvin Ailey. The result is a visceral elegy of undisguised lamentation and anger, a little indulgent, as such works tend to be, but undeniable in its fist-clenching tragedy and heartfelt embrace of the enduring bonds of remembered love and community." *Shattered Sands* (1991), an antiwar piece premiered in 1992 by the Milwaukee Ballet, also illustrates Posin's attention to social issues. Yet others from Posin display a fine sense of humor and border on performance art, like the whimsical *Shock Crossing* (1988).

Stepping Stones: A Ballet (1995) was a collaboration with composer Joan Tower and premiered with music for two pianos and synthetic percussion while performed on a set of raised platforms. Six men interact with six female dancers portraying the stages of a woman's life and six others depicting the woman's inner self. The dancers must, as is the rule with Posin choreography, perform difficult, athletic steps. The music is demarcated into five sections, called Introductions, Meeting, Alone, Interlude, and Love and Celebration. While much of Posin's work is performed by ballet companies, modern dance groups such as Karen and Alvin (Karen Bernstein and Alvin Mayes), a Washington D.C.-based duo, count Posin choreography among their repertoires. For example, Karen and Alvin performed her *Moebius,* set to Glass music, in 1990. Her own company also performs around the country, from the Joyce Theater in Manhattan to the Art of Dance series at the University of California at Los Angeles.

Posin has also tried her hand at stage choreography, creating tap-influenced dances for Alvin Epstein's 1983 production of *The Boys from Syracuse* at the Loeb Drama Center's American Repertory Theater in Boston. She has also devoted time to teaching. She taught at UCLA from 1986 to 1988, participated in modern dance workshops such as at the Kinetics Dance Theatre in Ellicott City, Maryland, in 1990, served as a member of the faculty of the Harvard Summer Dance Center in 1984 (where she premiered her *Hell Is Heaven*), and was an instructor at the California Institute of the Arts in Valencia for a year beginning in 1993.

Many of Posin's pieces portray strong emotions, ranging from rage to lamentation; yet the depth of emotional content in her choreography is well-balanced by healthy doses of humor and whimsy—as most would say, like real life.

—Karen Raugust

POSTMODERN DANCE

A handful of books on postmodern philosophy and culture written in the 1970s has been followed by hundreds published in the 1980s and 1990s, but among these no clear consensus has emerged about postmodernism. Modernism was an ideology of linear progress and a perennial critique of past and present practices that pinned its faith on working toward a better future. Postmodern sensibilities generally derive from a loss of faith in modernity and progress. The modernism of choreographers like Balanchine and Cunningham has been described as their contribution to the linear development of dance toward a purist goal of increasingly abstract dance, with each new generation of choreographers extending this development by superseding the achievements of their elders. Postmodern dance has broken with this linear tradition to encompass a plurality of different approaches. Pluralism is a postmodern buzz word, and postmodernism has evolved into many dance styles, including contact improvisation, the pedestrianism of the early 1960s, the minimalism of Lucinda Childs and Rosemary Butcher, and the very different minimalist repetition of Anne Teresa de Keersmaeker's early choreography.

Furthermore, in contrast to the high-minded seriousness of the pioneers of modern dance, postmodern choreographers often playfully and ironically recycle forms and genres that earlier modern dancers had rejected. Thus whereas modern dancers in both Europe and the United States saw their work as the antithesis of ballet and largely sought to distance themselves from dance as popular entertainment, postmodern choreographers were as likely to be inspired by the spectacle of postmodern mass media as they were by the "great" art of the past. Postmodern choreographers like Mark Morris and Jim Self have created works for ballet companies, while some, like Twyla Tharp and Lea Anderson, have turned to "raiding the image banks" of popular music, Hollywood cinema, or mass culture. Some, like Philippe Decouflé, have tried to reunite dance with popular entertainment, while others, like Meredith Monk, Robert Wilson, Lloyd Newson, and Pina Bausch, have blurred the boundaries between dance, film, theatre, and the other arts.

American dancer Yvonne Rainer is credited with first coining the phrase "postmodern dance." It was first used in print by Michael Kirby in 1975 in the "Post Modern Dance Issue" of the *Drama Review.* The term became much more widely used after Sally Banes gave the title *Terpsichore in Sneakers: Post Modern Dance* to her 1979 study of the work of Rainer, Trisha Brown, Steve Paxton, and others associated with the Judson Dance Theater in New York during the 1960s. These dancers initially attended a class that applied the compositional strategies of composers like John Cage to dance. This class was given by Robert Dunn at the Cunningham studio in 1961. The following year, at Dunn's suggestion, they performed at the Judson Church in Greenwich Village, a venue then being used by some visual artists who were developing "Happenings."

Probably the best known work performed at the Judson Dance Theater is Yvonne Rainer's *Trio A* of 1966. Personnel involved in Judson performances often included both dancers and painters, and what characterized the work of this group was their use of the concerns and strategies of the New York art world, including the use of ideas that had their origin in John Cage's work. The fact that some of the group, including Paxton, David Gordon, and Valda Setterfield, also danced in the Merce Cunningham Dance Company raises the question of Cunningham's relationship to postmodernism, given his own close association with Cage. Critic Jill Johnston, writing at the time in the *Village Voice,* observed that Cunningham, in pieces like *Story* (1963) and *Walk Around Time* (1968), used strategies similar to those of Rainer and Paxton to confound conventional expectations of dance just before the latter first employed them.

Although this experimental dance culture developed in New York during the 1960s, it was not until the 1970s and 1980s that dance artists in other countries began to carry out similar experiments. Whereas the Judson group was concerned primarily with aesthetic issues, elsewhere and later in America, feminist, African American, and other countercultural political concerns have informed the development of postmodern dance.

The "New Dance," which developed in Britain in the early 1970s, was strongly informed by feminist ideas, particularly in the work of Sally Potter and Jacky Lansley. Pina Bausch has always denied any direct connection between her work and feminism, but the Tanztheater that she and other German choreographers developed emerged in the 1970s when a younger generation engaged in developing a critique of West Germany's affluent authoritarianism and dared to ask uncomfortable questions about their parents' actions during the Nazi period.

As in Germany, much of the development of the "new wave" dance in France, Spain, Italy, Belgium, and Canada was inspired by visiting American dance companies, especially that of Merce Cunningham; but it also took the form of a reaction against the older

American modern dance of Graham and Humphrey and in some cases led to a rediscovery of early European modern dance concerns that had been abandoned in the aftermath of World War II. Postmodern choreographers like Lea Anderson and Angelin Preljocaj, who have made witty use of stereotypes of national identity, have thus rejected the universalizing, supposedly international nature of modern dance and modern ballet. In Japan Saburo Teshigawara's postmodernism similarly reacted against the Graham-like expressionism of the Butoh tradition. It was the end of the idea of a mainstream and with it an acknowledgment of the validity of pluralist traditions that has created a climate within which previously marginalized groups have been able to legitimate their experiences and identities within cultural forms. In New York performers like Carmelita Tropicana have used the strategies of postmodern dance to problematize and challenge stereotypes of Latino identity. Whereas gay and lesbian dancers were largely invisible in modern ballet and dance, postmodern artists like Lloyd Newson, Emilyn Claid, Joe Goode, Bill T. Jones, and Ishmael Houston Jones have made works that explore aspects of gay, black gay, and lesbian experience.

Publications

Books—(for additional books on Postmodern Dance, please see General Bibliography)

Goldberg, RoseLee, *Performance: Live Art 1909 to the Present,* London, 1979.
Johnston, Jill, *Marmalade Me,* New York, 1971.
Novack, Cynthia, *Sharing the Dance,* Madison, 1990.
Sayre, Henry M., *The Object of Performance: The American Avant-Garde Since 1970,* Chicago and London, 1992.

Articles—

Copeland, Roger, "Theatrical Dance: How Do We Know It When We See It If We Can't Define It?," *Performing Arts Journal,* vol. 26, no. 27, 1986.
Foster, Susan Leigh, "The Signifying Body," *Theatre Journal,* March 1985.
Kirby, Michael, "Introduction," *The Drama Review* (Post Modern Dance Issue), March 1975.

—Ramsay Burt

PRELJOCAJ, Angelin

French dancer, choreographer, and company director

Born: 19 January 1959 in Paris. **Education:** Studied modern dance at Schola Cantorum with Karin Waehner; in the U.S. with Zena Rommet, Merce Cunningham, 1980. **Career:** Dancer, with the companies of Quentin Rouiller, Viola Farber, Dominique Bagouet, 1981-84; founder, Preljocaj Company, 1984; guest choreographer, Lyon Opera Ballet, 1990; Paris Opera Ballet, 1994; founder, Preljocaj Ballet (permanent company of TNDI [National Theater of Dance and Pictures]), Chateauvallon, 1995; moved to Aix-en-Provence as National Center Preljocaj Ballet, January 1996. **Awards:** Bagnolet Prize for *Black Market,* 1985; Paribas Bank patronage, beginning 1990; Dance Prize of the Arts Ministry, 1992.

Works

1984	*Colonial Adventures*
1985	*Black Market*
	White Tears
	Blue Fears
1986	*To Our Heroes*
1987	*Hallali Romé*
1988	*Flesh Liqueurs*
	Caillebotte's Planemen (video-dance, produced by Cyril Collard)
1989	*Weddings*
1990	*Bitter America*
	Romeo and Juliet, for Lyon Opéra Ballet, set design by Enki Bilal
1992	*The World Skin*
1993	*Hommage to the Ballets Russes: Parade, The Spectre of the Rose*
1994	*The Park,* for Paris Opéra Ballet
1995	*Anoure* (mus. Cavanna)
1996	*Romeo and Juliet* (new version)
	Annunciation, for Paris Opéra Ballet Stars
1997	*Landscape after the Battle*
	The Stravaganza, for the 50th Anniversary of New York City Ballet

Publications

Bollack, J. et al, *Angelin Preljocaj,* Paris, 1992.
Brunet, Geneviève, and Elian Bachini, *Under the Skin,* Toulon, 1993.

*   *   *

Born in France of Albanian political exiles in 1959, Angelin Preljocaj first studied Expressionist dance in Paris with Karin Waehner and then moved on to modern. Living in the suburbs of Paris, where dance wasn't really considered an acceptable career choice for men, he was forced to spend his time pursuing more acceptable or "manly" sports such as boxing. Yet once he met and studied with Dominique Bagouet, Bagouet's rigorous teaching style gave the young Preljocaj a firm foundation for his future choreographic efforts. Preljocaj became a member of the Bagouet Company in 1982 and stayed for two years. In 1984, he founded the Preljocaj Company, and by the next year had already won a prestigious award—the 1985 Bagnolet Prize for *Black Market,* announcing that Angelin Preljocaj not only had real choreographic talent but had arrived. His first public success came with 1986's *To Our Heroes,* his first real group work (with seven dancers), which strove to break down the stereotypes surrounding heroes, who appeared in this work as victims.

Many of Preljocaj's works have challenged the links between dance and set designing, often shifting the emphasis of one or the other with each new creation. Mirroring the efforts of the legendary Diaghilev and his experiments in set design, Preljocaj has paid homage to the master by doing his own interpretations of such enduring classics as *Weddings* (originally choreographed by Nijinski), Massine's *Parade,* and Fokine's *The Spectre of the Rose.* Just as Diaghilev explored new avenues of dance through original and unique sets, inviting famous painters to design the decor and costumes, Preljocaj followed a similar path by working with famous artists, though with a twist. He made use of two different kinds of collaborations—in the first, painting accentuated the dance and inspired its development symbolically; Preljocaj's most famous work in this vein was a modernized version of *Romeo and Juliet* with a set designed and drawn by painter/comics author Enki Bilal. The set depicted lovers divided and disillusioned by a triumphant *perestroika*; the decor reminiscent of Orwell's *1984.* This work, commissioned by the Lyon Opera Ballet, has remained very popular and continues to be performed around the world, helped by the release in 1996 of a hip new movie version of *Romeo and Juliet,* starring Leonardo di Caprio and Claire Danes, and directed by Baz Luhrmann.

Preljocaj's second innovation in the collaboration of set and choreography focused on the creation of geometric patterns as a meeting place between dance and painting. *Caillebotte's Planemen* was just such an example in 1988—this video, taped by Cyrille Collard, was commissioned by the Orsay Museum of Paris, and sought to forge a bridge between the painter Caillebotte and the dancers. Preljocaj's choreography was a low "grounded" style of dance with elaborate contact between the dancers' bodies and the stage—the floor in contact with legs and chests, rolled up or twisted. The piece ended when dancers each found a pose corresponding to those of the set's paintings.

The World Skin, from 1992, also continued Preljocaj's research into the relationship between set and choreography. With its desert décor, this work was created by Preljocaj to present the themes of stillness and perpetual motion at the same time. The dual themes were symbolized by an incredible set, its floor resembling a desert hallucination, designed by plastics artist Thierry Leproust. Layered wooden strips offered the illusion of sand dunes, shaped by the wind, a stunning achievement with the roundness of the dunes contrasting with the obtuse angles of the dancers' legs and elbows.

Preljocaj has chosen to only work with what he classifies as "virtuoso" dancers, or professionals with great skills and technique, because of his creative methodology. Inspired by Merce Cunningham, he continues to change dance sequences until the last days of rehearsal. To keep up with Preljocaj's ever-evolving choreography, his dancers must be able to learn quickly and easily adapt to change.

In 1990, Preljocaj and his company were recognized for their contributions to dance through a Paris Bank patronage lasting five years, which brought subsidies for the creation of each new work. *Bitter America* was the first of these choreographic pieces, and has been followed by many others. The Paribas Foundation has also helped the company with both subsidies (10 percent of the company's budget) and logistical help such as organizing cocktail receptions, and planning press and public relations events around Preljocaj's performances. In addition, the Foundation published a book entitled *Under the Skin,* chronicling the creation of *The World Skin* in 1992. The book was a collaboration between writer Geneviève Brunet, photographer Elian Bachini, and Preljocaj, who explained his choreographic process, and was distributed to Parabas Foundation members as well as to audiences after performances.

Thanks to the contributions of Paris Bank and Parabas, Preljocaj is the most well-known and exported French choreographer and his company has been invited to perform around the globe, including stints in Sydney, Australia, in 1993, and in South America and Japan. Yet 1992 was one of Prejocaj's best years when he was given national recognition, the fruits of his labor earning him not only ongoing funds but the prestigious "Dance Prize" from the country's Arts Ministry in December of that year. The next year, 1993, Preljocaj was honored with a nomination to be director of the North Ballet Company of Lille, which came to an end in 1994 after a disagreement between the company's dancers and Preljocaj's wish to create more modern choreography. Soon after this incident, Preljocaj founded the Preljocaj Ballet, a ballet company with a distinct contemporary flavor which became the official ballet company of the TNDI theatre organization of Chateauvallon in southern France. Again, Preljocaj's stability was upended with the election of a new mayor running under the banner of nationalism and fascism in June 1995. Sensitive to his Albanian origins, Preljocaj refused to be subsidized by such a government and resigned.

Preljocaj's dance organization, the National Choreographic Center, was relocated to Aix-en-Provence in January 1996, with the monetary support of the French Arts Ministry. Preljocaj's company now operates with about 20 permanent dancers and he creates a new work each year in addition to works commissioned by others, like the Paris Opera Ballet, the Lyon Opera Ballet, and the New York City Ballet.

—Murielle Mathieu

PRESERVATION OF MODERN DANCE

Dance is, with little argument, the most difficult of the arts to document. A tradition handed down from generation to generation, teacher to student, dancer to dancer, the ephemeral art leaves few tangible records: prints and engravings of performances, some notations, reviews, still photographs, perhaps a film or video, or sketches of how performers looked.

Documenting dance has challenged both performers and historians alike; quite often, when the dancers leave the stage, the work is gone. As Marcia Siegal observed in her book, *The Shapes of Change,* "Continuity in dance must be worked at. Preservation—or the losing battle we fight with it—may be the basic issue of American dance. The immediacy and the ephemerality of dance are its most particular qualities."

Today, the purposes for which choreographers and dancers document dance are almost as varied as the types of documentation available. Those who create documentation include not only choreographers and performers, but also dance presenters, videographers, historians, critics and notators, as well as archivists and librarians in dance repositories.

Early modern dance was preserved principally in still photographs. Photographs of Nijinsky by Adolphe de Meyer, Isadora Duncan by Edward Steichen, and Doris Humphrey and Ruth St. Denis by Arnold Genthe were works of art themselves, capturing the dancers but not necessarily the choreography. Photographers were drawn to the art of Loie Fuller, Mary Wigman, and Denishawn. Throughout the century, still photographs have continued to preserve the dancing image, from Barbara Morgan's dramatic documentation of Martha Graham to George Platt Lynes' studies of Balanchine's choreography, to Lois Greenfield's art of capturing movement suspended in air.

Since its introduction, motion picture film has been used to preserve choreography as well as for theatrical presentations of dance. Some works from the 1930s and 1940s are preserved only in silent films taken by amateurs, while some choreographers, such as Massine, filmed their works to create a performance record for revivals. In the 1960s, the Dance Collection of the New York Public

Library began an effort to create as well as collect dance films. This program has resulted in the production of hundreds of films documenting contemporary choreography.

Dance notation preserves choreography by recording movement on paper. Although several systems for writing choreography—from stick figures to Feuillet notation—have been used for centuries, modern systems for notation were developed in the late 1920s utilizing abstract symbols to document dance. The system developed by Rudolf Laban, known as Labanotation, is a precise method used for both preservation and reconstruction of dances. The Benesh notation system, known as choreology, is popular throughout Europe. Both systems have training centers and libraries, the Dance Notation Bureau in New York and the Benesh Institute in London. Hanya Holm's choreography for *Kiss Me Kate*, recorded in Labanotation, was the first dance score to be accepted for copyright registration by the Library of Congress. Modern reconstructions from notation scores include many works by Doris Humphrey and the Joffrey Ballet's revival of Kurt Jooss' *The Green Table*.

The introduction of videotape provided what appeared to be a relatively affordable and sophisticated way to record and preserve dance; dancers and choreographers continue to use video for a wide range of purposes, from documenting rehearsals and performances to auditioning performers and supporting grant proposals. However, videotape proved to be an imperfect tool: half-inch reel-to-reel videotapes created in the 1970s disintegrated and cassette tapes were found to have a life span of 10 years or less. Numerous performances, rehearsals, television broadcasts and video histories thought to be preserved on tape were irrevocably lost to video dropout. Rapid changes in video technologies have rendered many formats obsolete and the equipment for playback all but nonexistent.

Numerous libraries and archives hold significant collections of dance materials; physical and intellectual preservation of these materials remain an ever-present challenge. A comprehensive directory of dance collections and archives, *Research in Dance: A Guide to Resources*, was compiled by Mary S. Bopp (now Strow) and published in 1994. A few dance companies have established in-house archival programs, notably the Cunningham Dance Foundation and the Dance Theatre of Harlem.

In the 1980s, dancers and dance companies became increasingly aware of the value of their historical materials. At this point, the dance community which had lost so many members to both age and AIDS, realized that documentation and preservation were imperative. Responding to this crisis, Preserve, Inc., a national service organization, was formed in 1987 to provide archival education to the dance community. In mid-1990, the Andrew W. Mellon Foundation and the Dance Program of the National Endowment for the Arts initiated a study of the national issues surrounding dance documentation and preservation. Entitled *Images of American Dance: Documenting and Preserving a Cultural Heritage*, the study's purpose was to learn what comprised the existing system of dance documentation and preservation, and to what extent the needs of the dance community were being met. The report concluded that "Creation in the absence of documentation and preservation only denies the future. It is the conveyance of a history, the continuity of an art form, and the preservation of works through which our own renaissance becomes more likely."

Subsequent to that report was the publication of Preserve's *Dance Archives: a practical manual for documenting and preserving the ephemeral art*, and the launch of *afterimages*, a quarterly newsletter on the subject. The Dance Heritage Coalition was formed by the heads of major repositoires and dance festivals (New York Public Library, Library of Congress, Harvard Theatre Collection, San Francisco Performing Arts Library and Museum, Lawrence and Lee Theatre Collection, American Dance Festival, and Jacob's Pillow) to address documentation and cataloging issues at the national level. Several other initiatives furthered the preservation of dance and dancers, including the Repertory Études Project of the American Dance Legacy Institute, archival documentaries created by the George Balanchine Foundation, and the Legacy Oral History Project.

Later, the Pew Charitable Trusts inaugurated the National Initiative to Preserve America's Dance (NIPAD), and the restructured National Endowment for the Arts (NEA) created a funding category for Heritage and Preservation. Both programs have provided funds for projects which preserve dance in all forms: ballet, modern, tap, jazz, baroque, court, folk and traditional dances.

At the close of the 20th century, new technologies are emerging to create, document, and preserve dance. Development of the software program *Lifeforms* and other movement-generation packages, allow choreographers to work at a computer instead of in a studio; programs such as *LabanWriter* give a new dimension to dance notation. Presently, new CD-ROMs are being developed, notably the Ohio State University Multimedia Dance Prototype (OSU-MDP), in which several digital technologies are integrated to create a composite picture of dancers and their work. New Internet technologies create universal on-line access to dance companies, library catalogs, and preservation resources.

Publications

afterimages: the newsletter of performing arts documentation and preservation, published quarterly by Preserve, Inc.

Bopp, Mary S., *Research in Dance: A Guide to Resources*, New York, 1994.

Ewing, William A., *The Fugitive Gesture: Masterpieces of Dance Photography*. London, 1987.

Hutchinson, Ann, *Labanotation, or Kinetography Laban: the System of Analyzing and Recording Movement*, 3rd edition, New York, 1977.

Keens, William, Leslie Hansen Kopp, and Mindy N. Levine, *Images of American Dance: Documenting and Preserving a Cultural Heritage*, report sponsored by the National Endowment for the Arts and the Andrew W. Mellon Foundation, Washington, DC, 1991.

Kopp, Leslie Hansen, *Dance Archives: A Practical Manual for Documenting and Preserving the Ephemeral Art*, Lee, MA, 1995.

Siegal, Marcia B., *The Shapes of Change: Images of American Dance*, Boston, 1979.

—Leslie Hansen Kopp

PRIMITIVE MYSTERIES

Choreography: Martha Graham
Music: Louis Horst
Lighting Design: Martha Graham
Costume Design: Martha Graham
First Performance: Craig Theatre, New York, 2 February 1931
Original Dancers: Martha Graham and Lillian Shapero, Dorothy Bird, Virginia Briton, Hortense Burkin, Grace Cornell, Louise

Creston, Ailes Gilmour, Georgia Graham, Pauline Nelson, Lillian Ray, Mary Rivoire, Ehtel Rudy, Bessie Schönberg, Gertrude Shurr, Anna Sokolow, Martha Todd, Ruth White, and Joane Woodruff

Other productions include: Martha Graham Dance Company, May 1944, May 1964, and June 1977.

Publications

Articles—

Jowitt, D., "A Conversation with Betty Schöenberg." *Ballet Review* 9(1), 1981.

Sears, D., "Graham Masterworks in Revival," *Ballet Review* 10(2), 1982.

*   *   *

Immediately hailed as a masterpiece at its premiere, *Primitive Mysteries* is Martha Graham's most important group work of the early 1930s. One source for the piece was a trip through New Mexico in 1930 with Louis Horst where they observed the Penitente Indians. This sect had originally been converted to Roman Catholicism by Spanish missionaries in the 17th century, but their harsh rituals included pre-Christian practices. Graham did not, however, borrow from or directly represent anything from the rituals she observed, but made an austere modernist piece in response to them. In 1930 Graham had also danced the role of the Chosen One in Massine's revival of his American version of *The Rite of Spring*. Both pieces represent rituals and contained circle dances.

Primitive Mysteries is danced by a chorus of 12 women and one solo dancer (initially danced by Graham herself) and has three parts: "Hymn to the Virgin," "Crucifixus," and "Hosanna." Before and after each section the dancers process on or off stage in silent formations flanking the soloist. In "Hymn to the Virgin," after the procession, the chorus divides into three groups; four dancers squat in a line across the rear of the stage and two groups of four settle midstage on either side. The soloist moves from one to the other of these two groups and poses in front of them while they make up angular patterns with their hands and arms or form little circle dances around her. The chorus seem to worship the soloist as if she were the Virgin Mary. Finally all 12 dancers form a circle around her which moves in an increasingly complicated, halting sequence—a few steps clockwise and back again—before the music unexpectedly stops. The dancers then reform in a stark rectangular formation with which the piece began and process in silence off the stage.

In the "Crucifixus," the soloist stands with head bowed while two women stand facing front either side of her, each holding one hand pointing upwards so that their arms frame her with a gothic arch. They are pointing to the invisible figure of Christ suffering on the cross behind the soloist's back. At the moment of Jesus' death the soloist stretches her arms out vertically to make the sign of the cross. This moment seems to be the high point of the ritual as a whole. The remaining 10 members of the chorus, who have formed a close group in front and to one side, each bend slightly forwards and raise one hand to their forehead with fingers pointing stiffly forward. One by one the dancers break out of the group into slow dragging leaps with their hands held behind their backs. They circle around the soloist and their dance gradually but painfully builds up speed. Again, as in the first section, the music stops, the dancers reform and process off in silence.

The mood of the final section—"Hosanna"—is more celebratory. The chorus of dancers skip lightly, though still in a slightly constrained way, while the soloist and an assistant enact the descent from the cross and the pietà. This too ends up with a circle of dancers while the soloist sits on the ground and her assistant kneels behind her in the middle, both making a cross with their arms. The attendant steps back, all the dancers form two rows and process off stage one last time.

Primitive Mysteries was one of the works photographed by Barbara Morgan in 1941. It was successfully revived (and filmed) with Yuriko Kikuchi in Graham's role in 1964. The 1977 revival was poorly received, the general consensus being that today's dancers were not sufficiently powerful for the roles. The themes of death and grieving in *Primitive Mysteries* occur in a number of Graham's best pieces. It was the cause of her laments in *Lamentation* (1930) and *Deep Song* (1937), while in *Night Journey* (1947), and *Clytemnestra* (1958), her heroines confronted their deaths. There is a death cart in *El Penitente* (1941) and *Eyes of the Goddess* (which was left unfinished when Graham died), was also about death.

—Ramsay Burt

PRIMUS, Pearl (E.)

Trinidad-born American dancer, choreographer, and educator

Born: 29 November 1919 in Trinidad, British West Indies; emigrated to New York in 1921. **Education:** Hunter College High School; Hunter College, New York, B.A. in biology and premed; graduate work at Columbia University; New York University, M.A. in educational sociology and anthropology; Ph.D. in anthropology, 1978. **Career:** Dancer, National Youth Association dance group, 1940; studied and taught at New Dance Group beginning in 1942; studied with Martha Graham, Doris Humphrey, and Charles Weidman; first concert at YMHA New York, subsequent to Audition Winners' Concert (shared with four other dancers), 1943; dancer, choreographer at Café Society and on Broadway with her company, 1944; independent concerts in New York and U.S. tours, 1944-45; choreographed and performed in touring revival of *Show Boat*, 1946; Command Performance for King George VI, London, England, as part of tour to Israel, France, and Italy, 1951; trip to Trinidad, 1953; director, Performing Arts Center of Liberia, Monrovia, Liberia, 1959-60; established African-Caribbean-American Institute of Dance, New York, 1963; established Pearl Primus Dance Language Institute in New Rochelle, New York, 1978; lectured at Hunter College, State University of New York (SUNY) at Buffalo, Smith College, and numerous guest residencies at other universities. **Awards:** Rosenwald Foundation Award, 1948; Monrovia, Liberia, Order of "Star of Africa," c. 1949; Scroll of Honor Award, National Council of Negro Women, c. 1951; Rebekah Harkness Foundation Award, 1962; National Culture through the Arts Award of New York Federation of Foreign Language Teachers, 1971; American Anthropological Association Distinguished Service Award, 1985; National Black Treasure Award, Hamilton Hills Arts Center; National Medal of Arts, United States, 1991; American Dance Festival Balasarawati/Joy Ann Dewey Beinecke Chair for Distinguished Teaching, 1991; National Endowment of the Arts Master Teachers/ Mentors Fellowship, 1994; Samuel H. Scripps/American Dance Festival Award, posthumously awarded 1995; honorary doctorates awarded by Spelman College, Hunter College, the California School of the Arts, New School for Social Research and the Boston Conservatory. **Died:** 29 October 1994.

Roles

1946   Lead dancer, *Show Boat* (Primus), New York
1947   Witch Doctor, *Emperor Jones* (Page), Chicago Opera Company, Chicago
         Caribbean Carnival, musical, New York

Works (premieres in New York City unless otherwise noted)

1943   *Te Moana* (solo, mus. traditional drums)
         Shouters of Sobo (solo, mus. traditional Trinidad chant)
         Strange Fruit (solo, mus. and words: Lewis Allen)
         Rock Daniel (solo, mus. Lucky Millinder)
         Hard Time Blues (solo, mus. Josh White)
         Jim Crow Train
         The Negro Speaks of Rivers (solo, mus. Sarah Malament, poem by Langston Hughes)
         Afro-Haitian Play Dance (solo, mus. traditional drums)
         Yanvaloo (mus. Afro-Haitian drums)
1944   *African Ceremonial* (mus: traditional drum), solo restaged for Pearl Primus and Company
         Study in Nothing (mus. Mary Lou Williams)
         Our Spring Will Come (solo, mus. John Cage)
         Slave Market (mus. traditional spirituals), Pearl Primus and Company
         Caribbean Conga
         Motherless Child (solo, mus. traditional spiritual)
         Mischievous Interlude (solo, mus. traditional spiritual)
1945   *Twinsome Twominds* (solo, mus. Williams)
         Just Born (solo, mus. Williams)
         Scorpio (solo, mus. Williams)
1946   *Dance of Beauty* (solo, mus. traditional drums)
         Myth (solo)
         Dance of Strength (solo, mus. traditional drums)
         War Dance (mus. traditional drums), Pearl Primus and New Dance Group members
         Great Gettin' Up Mornin' (solo, mus. traditional spiritual)
         Wade in the Water (solo, mus. traditional spiritual)
         Gonna Tell God All My Troubles (solo, mus. traditional spiritual)
         Chamber of Tears (solo, poem by Primus)
1947   *Santo* (solo, traditional Afro-Caribbean drums)
1948   *Caribbean Carnival* (musical), Boston
         Play Dances of the Caribbean (mus. traditional), Pearl Primus and Company
         Primitive Pastel (mus. Camilla De Leon), Pearl Primus and Company
         Another Man Done Gone (mus. traditional spiritual), Pearl Primus and Company
1949   *Fanga* (mus. Gio Ganga orchestra music), Monrovia, Liberia, U.S. premiere, New York
         Prayer of Thanksgiving (solo, mus. traditional Belgian drums)
         Go Down, Death (mus. traditional drums), Pearl Primus and Company
         Invocation (mus. traditional drums), Pearl Primus and Company

1950   *The Initiation* (mus. traditional drums), Pearl Primus and Company
         Everybody Loves Saturday Night, Pearl Primus and Company
         Fertility (solo, mus. traditional drums)
         Benis Woman's War Dance (solo, mus. traditional drums)
         Dance of the Fanti Fishermen (mus. traditional drums), Pearl Primus and Company
         Spirituals (solo, mus. traditional spirituals), including *Wade in the Water, Gonna Tell God All My Troubles, Great Gettin' Up Mornin'*, Lee, Massachusetts
1951   *Excerpts from an African Journey*, including *Egbo Esakpade* (mus. Charles Blackwell), and *Fanga* (solo, mus. traditional Liberian), Pearl Primus and Company,
         Royal Ishadi (mus. traditional spirituals, poem by James Weldon Johnson), Pearl Primus and Company
1952   *Impinyuza*, (mus. traditional drums), Pearl Primus and Company
1954   *La Jablesse* (mus. traditional drums), Pearl Primus and Company
1955   *Mister Johnson*, play directed by Robert Lewis
1958   *Temne*, Pearl Primus–Percival Borde Dance Company
         Yoruba Court Dance, Pearl Primus–Percival Borde Dance Company
         Ibo, Pearl Primus–Percival Borde Dance Company
         Earth Magician, Pearl Primus–Percival Borde Dance Company
         Engagement Dance, Pearl Primus–Percival Borde Dance Company
         Unesta, Pearl Primus–Percival Borde Dance Company
1959   *Ntimi*
1960   *Whispers*
         Story of a Chief
         Naffi Tombo
         Kwan
         Zo Zengai
1961   *The Wedding* (original title: *Congalese Wedding*; mus. traditional African and Solomon Ilori's Ishe Oliwa)
1963   *Mangbetu*
         Zebola
         Life Crises
1965   *Hi Life* (mus. traditional African), Pearl Primus–Percival Borde Dance Company
1974   *Fanga* and *The Wedding*, restaged for Alvin Ailey American Dance Theatre
1979   *Michael Row the Boat Ashore* (mus. traditional), Pearl Primus and Company
1988   *The Negro Speaks of Rivers, Hard Time Blues, Strange Fruit*, restaged at American Dance Festival, North Carolina, as part of "Black Tradition in American Modern Dance"
1990   *Impinyuza*, (mus. traditional African, adapted by Onwin S. Borde), restaged for Alvin Ailey American Dance Theatre

Publications

By PRIMUS: articles—

"Living Dance of Africa," *Dance Magazine*, June 1946.
"Primitive African Dance (and Its Influence on the Churches of the South)," *Dance Encyclopedia*, edited by Anatole Chujoy, New York, 1949.

Pearl Primus Dance Company, 1979. Photograph © Johan Elbers.

"Africa," *Dance Magazine,* March 1958.

"African Dance," *Presence Africaine 1961*, Special Edition, New York, 1963.

"Dreams and the Dance," *Monograph 8*: *Journal of the American Academy of Psychotherapists*, September 1964.

"Life Crises: Dance from Birth to Death," American Dance Therapy Association, *Proceedings of the Fourth Annual Conference of the American Dance Therapy Association*, 1969.

"African Dance," in *African Dance: An Artistic, Historical and Philosophical Inquiry*, edited by Kairamu Welsh Asante, Trenton, New Jersey, 1996.

On PRIMUS: books—

Emery, Lynne Fauley, *Black Dance from 1619 to Today*, 2nd edition, Princeton, 1988.

Lloyd, Margaret, *The Borzoi Book of Modern Dance*, 1949, New York, 1987.

Thorpe, Edward, *Black Dance*, New York, 1990.

On PRIMUS: articles—

Estrada, Ric, "Three Leading Negro Artists and How They Feel about Dance in the Community: Elo Pomare, Pearl Primus and Arthur Mitchell," *Dance Magazine*, November 1968.

Kisselgoff, Anna, "Pearl Primus Rejoices in the Black Tradition," *New York Times*, 19 June 1988.

*   *   *

Pearl Primus' place within dance history extends beyond revivals of her dances and memories of her breathtaking performances. Her legacy dates back to the early 1940s when she first exposed African Americans to their roots through dance and chipped away at racial stereotypes in the process. Her material was first and foremost the dancing body, particularly the African-American body, music and life experiences. Fostering understanding among people through dance, Primus journeyed to museums, labored alongside Southern sharecroppers in the fields, and danced in Caribbean and African villages. And as black Americans fought for their civil rights in the turbulent 1960s, Primus offered them a sense of identity, revealing in dance the dignity and grandeur of their ancestral roots.

Primus was brought to New York City from Trinidad at the age of two, and discriminatory practices absent in the West Indies became the topic of many of her dances. A graduate of Hunter College in New York, she was unable to find a job in her area of expertise, premedical studies, a situation that opened the door to dance in 1940. A brief stint at a National Youth Administration dance group turned Primus' athleticism from sports to dance. Within two years she was a scholarship student at the New Dance Group Studios. Under the tutelage of Jane Dudley and Sophie Maslow, the mixture of dance innovation, aesthetics, muscularity and social consciousness combined with Primus' personal ideals for dance and society. Praised for her contributions to black dance along with Katherine Dunham, Primus' adaptations of traditional dances were noted for maintaining authenticity while being grounded in American modern dance sensibilities. Strong choreographic structure came from studies with Martha Graham and Louis Horst, Doris Humphrey, and Charles Weidman. Critics John Martin, Edwin Denby and Margaret Lloyd quickly recognized and praised Primus' dances, commenting on her five-foot-high leaps, articulate, powerful torso, and rhythmic grace. Her talents transferred from the concert dance stage to Broadway, where she danced and choreographed at the Café Society and in a revival of the musical *Show Boat*.

A range of dances included those of social protest, inspiring other black dancers to look to their past for dance themes: Primus' *Hard Time Blues* was about sharecroppers; *Strange Fruit* embodied the terror of Southern lynchings; *The Negro Speaks of Rivers* was danced to Langston Hughes' poem about American ignorance of the black heritage; and *Michael Row Your Boat Ashore* was on the death of two girls in a Birmingham, Alabama, church bombing. Primus' movement was set to spirituals, traditional Caribbean and African drum rhythms and chants, and performed by a number of gifted musicians including Josh White, drummer Alphonse Cimber and her husband, Percival Borde.

Glimpses of a history of black oppression were countered by dances of joy and ritual. Research in museums and libraries led to *African Ceremonial* in 1943 with authenticity of movement and rhythms verified by African dancers and drummers. Later, Primus studied a wide variety of African traditional dances in their native environments. Her first African visit in 1948 was funded by a Julius Rosenwald Foundation grant, while the Rebekah Harkness Foundation sponsored her 1962 trip. Primus was honored by those whose lives and dances she studied, in such countries as the Belgian Congo, Sierra Leone, Nigeria, Liberia, and Senegal. She returned to Liberia in 1959 as director of the Liberian Performing Arts Center in Monrovia. Among the honors she received were the Liberian "Star of Africa," the titles "Omowale" meaning "child returned home" in Nigeria, "Jibundu" or "first among dancers," and honorary membership in royal families. The diversity of African rituals was highlighted by the dramatic head rolls of the Watsui royal dance *Iminyuza* (1951) and the exuberant Liberian welcome dance *Fanga* (1949), reconstructed for the Alvin Ailey American Dance Theatre.

Other trips led to the Caribbean and her Trinidad homeland in 1953, where Primus met Percival Borde—her drummer, fellow dancer, fellow teacher, and life partner. Between trips abroad, Primus co-founded studios, taught in universities, choreographed and performed with the Percival Borde Dance Company. In 1978, Primus received her doctorate in anthropology from New York University, only one aspect of a distinguished academic career in dance education, ethnic studies and anthropology. Among her students over the years were Donald McKayle and Garth Fagan.

In a 1968 magazine interview, Primus explained: "I dance not to entertain but to help people better understand each other. . . . Because through dance I have experienced the wordless joy of freedom, I seek it more fully now for my people and for all people everywhere." Receiving U.S. Department of Education funding in 1965, Primus shaped a program which used dance as a non-verbal means of fostering intercultural understanding among New York

City school children. Her dance concerts were fashioned into cohesive programs with such titles as *Dark Rhythms* (1952) and *Earth Theatre* (1964), with a narrator providing symbolic insight and contextualizing dances in their native sources.

Reviving works during numerous university residencies provided a new generation of dancers rare opportunities to study with Primus. An integral part of the reconstruction process included an education in the social environment which inspired the work. "It is not just a matter of lifting a leg, it's the why," as Primus explained to dance critic Anna Kisselgoff at the American Dance Festival in 1988. The intergenerational power of her work was honored by a U.S. National Medal of Arts in 1991.

Although well-known for dances of social protest, African and Caribbean themes, Primus' works also celebrated African-American contributions to the world of jazz, the blues and the jitterbug of legendary Harlem nightclubs. While entertainment was not her goal, sold-out shows and the masterpiece quality of dances restaged after as much as half a century attest to her artistry. As Primus explained in a 1968 interview, "I'm learning to deliberately reach beyond the color of the skin and go into people's souls and hearts and search out that part of them, black or white, which is common to all. Artists are the true militants." Primus' creative impulses as choreographer, performer, anthropologist and professor were born of African, American, and Caribbean experiences, yet transcended ethnic categories to reveal universal statements about humanity.

—Stacey Prickett

PROVISIONAL DANZA
Spanish dance company

Works

1988	*De momento. . . (At the moment)*
1989	*¿Tu que piensas ? (What do you think?)*
1990	*Una cuestión en la que no reparamos*
1991	*Del citoplasma y otros agentes reticulares*
1992	*Historia de unos colgados*
1993	*Pan de lágrimas (Bread of tears)*
1994	*Dos días para cinco (Two days for five)*
1995	*Sólo podría un huracán (Only a hurricane could)*
1996	*Coraje, escena 13 (Courage, scene 13)*
1997	*Rincón de lobos (Corner of wolves)*

Other works include: Several open-air pieces, including *Café de noite, Cuadro de una mujer fea (Picture of an ugly woman), Los hombres también mueven paredes (Men also move walls)*, and *Calle 4 (Street 4)*.

Films and Videotapes (featuring Provisional Danza)

Sombra de barro (Shadow of mud), 1993.
Z, 1994.
Como en el vacio (Like in the Emptiness), 1995.
Siete veces en una tarde (Seven times in the Afternoon), 1997.

*   *   *

When Provisional Danza was formed in 1987 by Carmen Werner, the company's name was a reflection of the instability of independent modern and contemporary dance companies in Madrid. Government financial support (private funding or sponsorship in Spain is extremely rare) was not meeting with the wealth of creativity coming from individual choreographers. Despite this state of affairs Werner launched her five-member company and financed her first three full-length productions with her own funds. Ten years later, Provisional Danza is now 10 dancers strong and recognized as one of Madrid's most stable and prolific contemporary dance companies.

Before creating her own company, Werner was not a prominent figure in the dance world. Whilst training in Madrid, London, and Barcelona, she came into contact with Christine Tanguay, Mathilde Monniers, Hans Züllig, and Anna Koren, amongst others, covering a wide scope of classical and modern dance techniques. However, what has most marked Werner's work as a dancer and particularly as a choreographer is her involvement in physical education. Licensed in physical education and sport at the Politechnical University of Madrid, she has managed to combine her work of teaching and training in schools with that of her company's demands. Her first body of dancers was from the same nondance background as herself; young talent she had handpicked from her classes, and whom she molded and nurtured herself. The rawness of Werner's dance was recognized as attractively honest, though it sometimes lacked integrity due to overused gesticulation and frantic movement that lacked weight and suspension. Werner constantly investigates the darker side of human nature, including restlessness and social and sexual incompatibility. Simple scenery of a prefab style has become paramount in demonstrating the extremes of temperament as bodies fight, hide, and abuse amongst these elements from daily life. Earlier works had an almost film-like narrative. With the 1995 production *Sólo podría un huracán (Only a hurricane could)*, dramatic content became less omnipresent and a matured style began to appear, rich in subtleties and a clearer defined dance vocabulary that allowed movement to be explored beyond narrative. This could be considered a natural process of development, but must also be attributed to the introduction of more experienced dancers to the company.

A breakthrough year in the history of Provisional Danza was 1991—they received local government funding for production. This enabled the company to set up its own modest dance base, "La Ventilla," in the north of the capital. Werner invited some of Madrid's best modern dance teachers such as Francesca Bravo—the Catalonian dancer, choreographer, and teacher in residence in Madrid—Teresa Nieto, and Christine Tanguay to give the company's daily open class. In 1994 they moved to a larger studio space in the same area which they henceforth shared with Madrid's other stable contemporary dance company, 10 & 10. La Ventilla soon became a dance forum of teaching, dance demonstrations and lectures. By 1991 Provisional Danza began to participate in official dance festivals throughout the country, but it would take another four years before the company was invited to perform beyond the Iberian peninsula.

Werner, as a choreographer, has worked with many theatre companies, including Deliciosa Royala, La farsa del Nuevo Teatro, and Matarile Teatro. In 1997 she took on a new venture collaborating with theatre director Javier Yagüe to produce a theatre dance production for children. Work with her own company has also included four dance videos, all of which have been premiered at Spain's most prestigious modern dance festival, Dansa Valencia. Nearly all her works have used original scores and texts in German that have given weight to dramatic intensity.

Los hombres tambien mueven paredes is probably the Werner work that has drawn the most attention in the public eye. This in due in part to its format, as an outdoor performance. In 1992 when Madrid was named the Cultural Capital of Europe, contemporary dance choreographers were commissioned by the Arts Ministry to create works for outdoor spaces with the idea of drawing a wider audience to dance. It has since become an annual highlight in the contemporary dance calendar in Madrid. *Los hombres* created in 1995 for this event is the company's most solicited work to date—and it encompasses the essence of Werner's work with the visual spectacular of abseiling.

The story of Provisional Danza is inseparable from that of Carmen Werner's story, one woman's struggle to establish a stronghold of dance in Madrid's whirlpool of creativity and artistic instability.

—Michelle Man

PUCCI, Peter
American dancer, choreographer, and company director

Born: 5 April 1954 in Baltimore, Maryland. **Education:** Active in all sports since childhood, played football, baseball, basketball, lacrosse in high school; began studying modern dance at Essex Community College (ECC) in Baltimore with Carol Drake, 1973-75; associate's degree in Physical Education, ECC, 1975; dance studies at Towson State University (Baltimore), 1975-77; full scholarship to Dallas Ballet Academy and Southern Methodist University (Dallas), 1977-78; attended North Carolina School of the Arts, 1978-80; B.F.A. in modern dance, NCSA, 1981. **Family:** Married Ellen Sirot (dancer with Peter Pucci Plus Dancers), 1993. **Career:** Created first choreographic work for ECC's Dimensional Dance Media, 1974; moved to New York, and joined Pilobolus Dance Theatre (PDT), 1980; began choreographing for PDT, 1981; stayed with PDT, until 1989; founder/dancer with Carol Parker, Parker/Pucci, 1983-86; founder/director Peter Pucci Plus Dancers (PP+D), 1986-present; first New York season, 1986; first U.S. tour, 1989; first European tour, 1991. **Awards:** Choo San Goh Award for choreography (with BalletMet), 1993; Absolut Joffrey Award for choreography, 1992; Samuel H. Scripps Humphrey/Weidman/Limón Fellowship from the American Dance Festival, 1990; Distinguished Alumni Award, Towson State Univeristy (Maryland), 1989.

Roles

Various roles for Pilobolus Dance Theater including *Alrune, Bonsai, Ciona, The Empty Suitor, Geode, Hot Pursuit, Land's Edge, Molly's Not Dead, Monkhood's Farewell, Ocellus, Pilobolus, Return to Maria La Baja, Tarleton's Resurrection, Untitled,* and *Walklyndon.*

Works

1981   *Day Two* (mus. Eno, Byrne, Talking Heads), Pilobolus Dance Theater (PDT), American Dance Festival, Durham, North Carolina

1982   *Elegy for the Moment* (mus. R. Dennis), PDT, New York

1983   *Mirage* (mus. Cherry, Walcott, Vasconcelos), PDT, New York

Can't Get Started w/Carol Parker (mus. Goodman, Dorsey, Molton), duet, Parker/Pucci, New York

Nonce w/Parker (mus. Kohlman), duet, Parker/Pucci, New York

Time Not in Motion w/Parker (mus. L. Anderson), duet, Parker/Pucci, New York

Scribble (mus. Sugihara), solo, Pucci, New York

1985 *Carmina Burana, Side II* (mus. Orff), PDT, New York

The Vacant Chair w/Parker (mus. Civil War-era songs), duet, Parker/Pucci, New York

1986 *Lure* (mus. mixed media score), solo, Pucci, Berkeley, California

Celina (mus. Kohlman), Peter Pucci Plus Dancers (PP+D), New York

Big City (mus. Sobatnik), PP+D, New York

1987 *I'm Left, You're Right, She's Gone* (mus. Presley), PDT, Clearwater, Florida

In The Garden (mus. Ives), duet for Pucci & Sirot, New York

Boomers (mus. Haydn), PP+D, New York

A Pui Tardi? (mus. Caruso), solo for Felix Blaska, New York

You Gotta Move (mus. J. Murads & the Harmonicats), solo, Pucci, New York

Mnemonsyne (mus. music-box), solo for Barbara France, New York

1988 *Debut C* (mus. Debussy), PDT, New York

Seeing the Elephant (mus. Kohlman), PP+D, New York

M-4 (live music performed by dancers), PP+D, New York

1989 *Mariachi* (mus. mariachi), Batsheva Dance Company, Tel Aviv

1990 *Heir of Civility* (mus. Gershwin), duet of Pucci & Jim Blanc, New York

13 x 13 (solo, mus. Shotts & Dykehead Pipe & Drum Corps), Pucci, New York

Something Pretty Fishy Goin' On in the Temporal Lobes (mus. Cosla & Campbell), PP+D, American Dance Festival, Durham, North Carolina

Pas de Fois Gras (mus. Poulenc), Pick of the Crop Music & Dance

1991 *Sylvan* (mus. A. Parsons), PP+D, New York

Broken Song (mus. Pärt), PP+D, New York

Rapt (mus. Mozart), solo, Pucci, New York

1992 *Hoop-La* (mus. Bach, Friedman, Moskowski, Palmgren, Rachmaninoff, Schumann), PP+D, New York

Love Duets (in silence), PP+D, New York

Then All Is Still Again (mus. Farre), trio, PP+D, New York

Blindsight (mus. Cherry), Avilez (in PP+D), New York

The Charnel House (mus. Dutilleux), PP+D, New York

Flick & Flack (mus. Hawaiian steel guitar), PP+D, New York

And I Know Not Where (mus. Goretski), Carlyle Project dancers, Carlyle, Pennsylvania

1993 *Moon of the Falling Leaves* (mus. Davids), Joffrey Ballet with guest artists Pucci and Miguel Avilez (dancer in PP+D), Minneapolis

Willing and Able from BILLBOARDS (mus. Prince), Joffrey Ballet, Iowa City

Two Rivers (mus. Barber), Chautauqua Ballet Co., Chautauqua, New York

The Elephant's Tricycle (mus. Simon & Garfunkel), cast of Off-Broadway play

1994 *Lifted by Love* (mus. k.d. lang), Alberta Ballet, Canada

Their Hearts Have Eyes (mus. Steiner), Pick of the Crop Music & Dance Ensemble, Buffalo, New York

a vesper (mus. Rachmaninoff), solo for Maureen Mansfield, New York

Ayego (mus. Simopoulos), PP+D, New York

Banner (mus. Hendrix), duet for Sirot & Yoav Kaddar, New York

Dither Dally (mus. Mozart), PP+D, New York

Joe (mus. Chopin), solo, Pucci, New York

Sing (mus. Scottish), solo, Pucci, New York

Foday (mus. F. Musa Suso), Tennessee Children's Dance Ensemble

1995 *Trio for the End of Time* (mus. Pärt), Ballet Arizona, Phoenix

Suite Mizike (mus. Zap Mama), BalletMet, Columbus, Ohio

Samson et Dalila, cast of Baltimore Opera, Maryland

As You Like It (mus. Gershwin, arr. D. Byrne), Juilliard School production cast, New York

1996 *Size Nine Spirit* (mus. Benny Goodman), Colorado Ballet, Denver

Thought through My Eyes (mus. Lutoslawski), Atlanta's Dance Force, Georgia

Down in Front (mus. F. Johnson), PP+D, New York

Each and All (mus. Simopoulos), PP+D, New York

Episode (mus. Stravinsky), Chautauqua Ballet Company, Chautauqua, New York

Beethoven Duet (mus. Beethoven), duet for Jennifer Cavanaugh & Barry Leone, Chautauqua Ballet Company, Chautauqua

1997 *River of Desire* (mus. Grieg) Pittsburgh Ballet Theatre

Eye Two I (mus. Vargas), duet for Sirot & Eric Dunlap, Arvada, Colorado

Films and Videotapes

Key Exchange, film featuring Pucci, 20th-Century Fox, 1985.

One Night Only, PP+D, 1990.

Peter Pucci: Curtain Time, KRMA-TV, Denver, 1994.

Willing and Able, performed by Joffrey Ballet on *Tonight Show* with Jay Leno, 1993, and aired nationally on PBS' *Great Performances: Dance In America*, 1994.

Size Nine Spirit, Colorado Ballet, KRMA-TV, Denver, 1997.

*   *   *

About dancer and choreographer Peter Pucci, noted dance critic Jennifer Dunning of the *New York Times* wrote in 1996, "It is hard to envision a choreographer with more personalities." Pucci's large appeal rests in these "personalities"—for he has created a body of work that has something in it for everyone. His innate irreverence, due in large part to his early career spent making and performing dances with Pilobolus Dance Theater, is realized in dances such as *Down in Front* (1996), *Heir of Civility* (1990), *Something Pretty Fishy Goin' On in the Temporal Lobes* (1990), and *Can't Get Started* (1983, choreographed with Carol Parker). A thoughtful thread runs through his *Love Duets* (1992), a series of all-things-equal tender couplings: man-man, man-woman, woman-woman. A tremulous

Peter Pucci performing *Rapt,* 1991. Photograph by Michael O'Neill.

hint of longing suffuses the "Sometimes I'm Happy" duet in 1996's big band piece *Size Nine Spirit.*

Pucci the performer always captivates—wearing a blustery streetwise charm that covers a core of vulnerability; tough but transparent. This dichotomy is revealed beautifully in his signature solo *Rapt* (1991), as one cool dude discovers he can groove to, of all things, Mozart. Pucci once described this character as "a combination of a hundred guys I grew up with, my brother included." His brave *13 x 13* slides through emotion after emotion, revealing Pucci's willingness to lay himself bare to get at the heart of things.

He arrived at a professional dance career via athletics. In high school, Pucci played football, baseball, basketball, and lacrosse and remembers his coach as being a strong influential force in is life. In college, working on his degree in physical education, he was drawn to dance before he finished. (No matter, the folks at Towson State—his alma mater—recently awarded him "Most Distinguished Alumni.")

His first taste of dance was through improvisation, taught in a modern dance class he took as a required course for his P.E. degree. This allowed, he said later, "a lot of moving freely before I learned technique." The class, taught by Carol Drake, was Pucci's first exposure to dance; she and other teachers Pucci studied with encouraged him to pursue dance further. Years of training followed, under full scholarship to the Dallas Ballet Academy, another to Southern Methodist University, and then to North Carolina School for the Arts. But thanks to the early dose of improvisation, Pucci has always retained a strong sense of fun and freedom within more formal dance structures, both as performer and choreographer. He is comfortable setting pieces on ballet companies, for example, though there is little that literally references ballet in his work; but it is there—in the men's "dance-off" in section five of *Size Nine Spirit* (1996), where several men toss off some fiendishly fast footwork and triple tours en l'air. Or the same ballet's finale—where reversés and pirouettes are performed alongside basic jazz and swing steps, with the occasional cartwheel thrown in for good measure. His "Willing and Able" duet from *Billboards* pokes fun at that hallowed ballet symbol—the woman's foot en pointe—when she briefly sticks it in her partner's mouth. When Pucci choreographs, any and all movement vocabularies are used seamlessly, and everything's up for grabs.

After attending North Carolina School of the Arts, Pucci moved to New York and began making the rounds. Within a month, he was hired by one of the most popular dance companies in the world—the innovative Pilobolus. At first enjoying the collaboratively creative process of the group, over time Pucci grew more eager to fully realize choreographic ideas of his own. Three years after joining, he was creating dances with Pilobolus member Carol Parker; as Parker/Pucci they frequently performed their work at various New York locations. By 1986 he had choreographed his second solo and decided to form a company to feature his work, while continuing to dance with Pilobolus to pay the bills.

But by 1989, the three-year grind of rehearsing and performing with two companies, not to mention the constant commute between New York City and Connecticut, left Pucci exhausted. He left Pilobolus to focus solely on his company, which has since appeared across the country and in Europe, as well as enjoying annual seasons in New York. With five dancers and himself, he has continued to create a body of work that reflects his overall personal eclecticism—in choice of music: classical, jazz, pop & rock, ethnic or world music; subject matter: abstract or narrative, humorous as well as serious; and his dance language: modern dance seamlessly infiltrated by concert, social, and folk dance. Like many modern choreographers in recent years, he is eager to test the waters of the professional theater world, and choreograph a musical.

Comfortable in any creative situation, Pucci's work crossed over into the commercial when in 1982 he choreographed several TV ads for businesses in Japan and Canada. In 1993 he returned to this arena, choreographing an industrial film for designer Laura Biagatti and a music video for country & western singer John Wesley Hardy. He's made several TV appearances himself, visiting the *Tonight Show* with Johnny Carson twice as a Pilobolus member, while his dances have appeared frequently on programs including on the *Tonight Show* with Jay Leno, PBS' *Great Performances: Dance in America*, and Denver's KRMA-TV.

As a performer, Pucci grows less eager these days to continue dancing with his company, although when that day arrives, it will be a sad occasion not to witness his effervescence and total commitment to every moment. The physically diverse, highly athletic dancers that make up his company will have to suffice: men and women either dark or blonde, tall or short, lean or compactly muscular—all of whom have been schooled in Pucci's deep sense of fun

and quiet expressiveness. It's just that he does this so well—and his dancing is a hard act to follow.

—Janine Gastineau

PULVERMACHER, Neta

Israeli-American dancer, choreographer, educator, and company director

Born: 1960 in Kibbutz Lehavot Habashan, Israel. **Education:** Studied dance with Ariela Peled; educated at Tel Hai Rodman Regional College, Haifa Dance Center, Bat Dor and Koldemama dance companies, 1972-80; scholarship student, Rina Schenfeld Dance Theater (Tel Aviv), 1979-82; Juilliard School, New York, 1982-85; studied with Bessie Schönberg at Dance Theatre Workshop's Choreographer's Lab, 1986; studied ballet with Kim Abel, Janet Paneta, Alfredo Corvino, and Cindi Green, 1985-96; B.A in English literature, writing, and photography, Empire State College, and Leach Fellow, 1993-98; studied writing and sociology at Columbia University, 1997—. **Family:** Married; son, born in 1982. **Career:** Has taught at Kibbutz Contemporary Dance Company School (Israel), Dance Space (Chicago), MoMing Dance and Arts Center and Chicago Repertory Dance Ensemble, Alaska Dance Theater, Juneau Dance Unlimited (Juneau, Alaska), Tel Hai School (Israel), Bikurei Haitim Dance Center and Tel Hai Regional College (Israel), 1992; Barnard College, Movement Research (New York), Lucy Moses School of Music & Dance (New York), Danspace Project and Peridance (New York); dancer, Glenn/Land Dance, Ze'eva Cohen & Dancers, Caitlin Cobb, Dance Collective; founder, dancer/choreographer, Neta Pulvermacher & Dancers, 1986—; choreographer-in-residence, The Yard, Martha's Vineyard, 1987; and American Dance Festival (North Carolina), 1987; the Field at Goddard College, Vermont, 1989 and others; commissions include American Dance Festival, Yellow Spring Institute, Ballet Arizona, Ohio Repertory Project, Ballet New England, Dance Theatre of Harlem School Ensemble, Colloquium Dance Company, and numerous colleges and universities. **Awards:** Getrude Kraus Choreographer's Competition, 1986; Bessie Schönberg Special Choreographer's Award, 1994; New York Foundation for the Arts choreography fellowship, 1994; National Endowment for the Arts choreographer's fellowship, 1995; scholarships from America Israel Cultural Foundation, Jewish Foundation for the Education of Women, Israeli Ministry of Education and Culture, and Performing Arts Foundation of International House, 1982-85; American Dance Festival's Commission for the Young Choreographers and Composers in Residence Program, 1987; Harkness Foundation for Dance, 1988; Space Grant at S.U.N.Y. Purchase, 1989; Joyce Mertz Gilmore Foundation grants, 1990-97; Mary Flagler Cary Charitable Trust, 1990-92, 1993, 1997; Mildred & George Weissman Philanthropic Fund, 1993-97 and others.

Works

1980	*Little Bird, Big Bird and Me* (solo), Tel Aviv, Israel
1981	*My Grandmother's Chair* (solo with a chair; mus. Mark Gustavson), Tel Aviv, Israel
1982	*Anna Magdalena* (solo; mus. Bach), Juilliard School, New York

Du Ao Da (mus. Phillip Glass), New York

Hell & Heaven (mus. Phillip Glass), Juilliard School, New York

1983 *Hops-Scotch* (mus. anonymous 17th-century Galliard), Juilliard School, New York

Roundabout (mus. Phillip Glass; slides by Nitzan Kimchi), New York

Virginia Slims (mus. Bach), New York

1984 *Flight Three, O. . .No* (mus. Laurie Anderson and original sounds collage), Juilliard School, New York

Three Variations on Ms. (mus. by Bach and improvised cello sounds), BACA, Brooklyn, New York

Loops (mus. collage from traditional Irish folk music and Indonesian Gamallan music; costumes and body painting by Pulvermacher), Juilliard School, New York

Terra (mus. collage from *Dido and Aeneas* by Henry Purcell), Juilliard School, New York

1985 *The Salad of Mr. Gray* (mus. Mark Gustavson), Toronto, Canada

1986 *Dust* (mus. ancient Hawaiian chant and John Adams), New York

Quintet (mus. Bach, *Violin Concerto in A Minor*), International House, New York

1987 *Better Days* (mus. popular Swing Era tunes), The Yard, Martha's Vineyard

The House (mus. Bach and Schumann), New York

A Minute a Day (mus. Robert Aldrige), American Dance Festival, Durham, North Carolina

1988 *Counting* (mus. Chopin), Columbia College, Chicago

The Great Big Orange (solo; mus. Schumann), MoMing, Chicago

Mystery (solo; mus. Le Mystere des Voix Bulgarian), MoMing, Chicago

Les Petite Rien (mus. Albinoni, *Concerto in B Flat Major*)

1989 *The Pioneers of the Swamp* (mus. 16th-century court and village dances), Juneau, Alaska

A Song (costumes by Neta Pulvermacher), Dia Center for the Arts, New York

The Window Project (mus. Arvo Part and traditional Tanzanian music), New York

World Premier (mus. Bach), Juneau, Alaska

1990 *Cintura* (solo; mus. George Crumb), St. Mark's Church, New York

Coffee (mus. Bach, *Coffee Cantata*), Dia Center for the Arts, New York

Nun & Naunet (mus. Anthony Coleman; set by Vesna Golubovic), Yellow Spring Institute, Pennsylvania

1991 *Bitter Land* (mus. Anthony Coleman; costumes by Pulvermacher), Dance Theatre of Harlem School Ensemble, New York

Matildas (mus. David Shea; costumes by Luigi Roncalli), Dia Center for the Arts, New York

1992 *Math Class* (mus. Chopin), AIS Alaska, Anchorage

May Day (solo; mus. international; costumes by Neta Pulvermacher), Danspace Project, New York

A Song (costumes by Neta Pulvermacher), Dia Center of the Arts, New York

1993 *Five Beds/Children of the Dream* (mus. Yuval Gabay), Danspace Project, New York

Hands (no music), Denmark

1994 *911* (mus. Richard Einhorn; costumes by Neta Pulvermacher), The Yard, Martha's Vineyard

Goodbye and Good Luck (mus. Anthony Coleman; costumes by Luigi Roncalli), Dance Theatre Workshop, New York

Long Story Short (mus. John Lurie and Pulvermacher; text from Samuel Beckett's *Cascando* and Pulvermacher; costumes by Pulvermacher), The Yard, Martha's Vineyard

She Must Be Seeing Things (mus. John Zorn and Masada; costumes by Pulvermacher), Miller Theater, New York

1995 *Dance on Wheels* (mus. Mozart; costumes by Pulvermacher), Dance Theatre Workshop, New York

Postcards (mus. and costumes by Pulvermacher), Dancing in the Streets, Wave Hill, Riverdale, New York

Young Green/Fresh Grass, Phoenix, Arizona (see also: *To Bite an Orange with Its Peel*)

1996 *Long Story Short 2* (mus. John Zorn; projections by Dona Ann McAdams), Danspace Project, New York

Ma Nishtana (mus. Pulvermacher), solo, Knitting Factory's Radical Passover Seder, New York

To Bite an Orange with Its Peel w/Jerry Gilmore (mus. Schumann; projections by Jerry Gilmore), Danspace Project, New York

1997 *Zaz* w/John Zorn (mus. John Zorn), Joyce Theater, Altogether Different Series, New York (also performed as a work-in-progress, The Radical New Jewish Culture Festival)

1998 *My Husband's Mole and Other Stories* (mus. Roy Nathanson and the Jazz Passengers; text David Cale), Neta Pulvermacher and Dancers, Playhouse 91st, New York

Publications

On PULVERMACHER: articles—

Anderson, Jack, "Goodbye and Good Luck," *New York Times,* 18 April 1994.

———, "Roots from Israel to Alaska," *New York Times,* 23 January 1997.

Ashdot, Dovik, "Dance," *Maariv America,* 25 March 1995.

"Dance," *New Yorker,* 27 January 1997.

Dunning, Jennifer, "The Allure of an Orange," *New York Times,* 21 February 1996.

Gelzer, Danit, "Neta Pulvermacher & Dancers," *Ma'ariv,* 5 March 1993.

Goldman, Phyllis, "Neta Pulvermacher & Dancers," *Back Stage,* 7-13 February 1997.

Hicks, Robert, "Film Provides a Frame for Choreography," in *The Villager,* 14 February 1996.

Josephs, Susan, "In Step with the Shapiros," *New York Jewish Week,* 25 July 1997.

Jowitt, Deborah, "Neta Pulvermacher," *Village Voice,* 6 April 1993.

———, "Two Plus," *Village Voice,* 5 March 1996.

———, "Under the Skin," *Village Voice,* 3 May 1994.

Kahn, Caroline, "Neta Pulvermacher and Dancers," *The New York Planet,* 21 April 1993.

Kisselgoff, Anna, "7 Contemporary. . .," *New York Times,* 31 October 1994.

Livingston, Lili Cockerille, "Ballet Arizona: Ballet Blossoms in the Desert," *Dance Magazine,* February 1996.

Neta Pulvermacher: *Zaz*, 1997, created in collaboration with composer John Zorn. Dancer: Maile Okamura. Photograph by David Hodgson.

Naude, Alice, "Neta Pulvermacher & Dancers," *Dance Magazine,*
   April 1997.
Nisbett, Susan Isaacs, "Guest Choreographer-Dancer Leads Reveal-
   ing Self-Drama," *Ann Arbor News,* 9 October 1995.
Norris, Carol, "Story of Growing Up in Kibbutz Energetic, But Often
   Troubling," *Cincinnati Enquirer,* 23 September 1995.
Ploebst, Helmut, "Where Uptown Meets Downtown," *Ballett In-
   ternational Tanz Aktuell,* March 1997.
Robinson, George, "Toward a 'Radical Jewish' Aesthetic," *New York
   Jewish Week,* 27 September 1996.
Schechter, Basya, "Israelis Dance Their Childhood Memories,"
   Forward, 19 March 1993.
Segal, Nancy, "Neta Pulvermacher," *Forward,* 10 January 1997.
Sloat, Susanna, "Neta Pulvermacher and Dancers: Good-bye and
   Good Luck," *Attitude,* Summer 1994.
Stanger, Amanda, "Neta Pulvermacher & Dancers," *Ann Arbor
   Observer,* October 1995.
Tobias, Tobi, "Been There, Done That," *New York,* 4 March 1996.

*   *   *

Neta Pulvermacher was born and raised in Kibbutz Lehavot
Habashan in Israel, where she began studying dance under the direction of Ariela Peled, also playing the violin and the flute and becoming involved in the Leftist Youth Movement. After being inducted
into the Army and stationed in Tel Aviv, Pulvermacher studied
dance at night under Juilliard graduate Rina Schenfeld at her Dance
Theater. This, combined with the friendship of another Juilliard
graduate, led Pulvermacher to a scholarship at Juilliard in 1982. She
moved to New York to pursue that avenue and graduated in 1985.
During her studies, she began presenting her own works, beginning
in such places as the International House and the BACA Downtown Cultural Center's Cubicolo Theater. She also performed works
by Ruby Shang and Peggy Lyman at the American Dance Festival
and danced with Glenn/Land Dance.

   After graduation she became a student of Bessie Schönberg at
Dance Theatre Workshop's Choreographer's Lab and began study-
ing ballet with such teachers as Kim Abel, Janet Paneta, Alfred
Corvino, and Cindi Green, something she continued through 1996.
She performed with Ze'eva Cohen & Dancers, Catlin Cobb, and the
NYC-TO Dance Collective and also presented her own works at
the Harkness Dance Center, and the Alternative Museum in New
York.

   Pulvermacher founded Neta Pulvermacher & Dancers in 1986
with the self-proclaimed interest of developing "a cinematic language in dance and theater that gives an expression to the human
experience and condition." The company's first performances were
at the 92nd Street YMHA, the Pineapple Studio, and International

House and at the Emelin Theater in Westchester, where they participated in the "New Generation of Dance" series. Although most of the troupe's performances have been in the cultural hubs of New York City and Chicago, Neta Pulvermacher & Dancers has toured the United States, Canada, and the world, including performances in cities such as San Diego, Atlanta, Phoenix, Cincinnati, Queens, Martha's Vineyard, DeKalb (Illinois), Durham (North Carolina) as well as the states of New Jersey, Pennsylvania, and Alaska and her homeland, Israel.

To the person on the street, Alaska conjures visions of frozen wastelands, icy steppes, white tundras, and penguins; certainly it is not a place one thinks of as a cultural gold mine. Pulvermacher thought different, taking her troupe to Juneau, Alaska, in their second season (1988) to perform as guest artists-in-residence at Juneau Dance Unlimited. It was the beginning of a long association with and love for that state. Neta Pulvermacher & Dancers returned to Juneau Dance Unlimited in 1989 and branched out to include residencies at Anchorage, Port Alexander, Whale Pass, and Pelican.

During her residencies in Alaska, Pulvermacher met with and interviewed native Alaskan elders, musicians, and dancers. As a result of these interviews and meetings, she created a piece called *A Song* (1990), an ironic name, since no one sings in this work. Inspired by the storytelling traditions of the Alaskan Tlingit people and incorporating folk elements from native Alaskan heritage and traditions, Pulvermacher created a movement language derived from the ancient Tlingit oral narratives described in the *Anchorage Times* as using "powerful, aggressive movements using the dancers' bodies to form shapes and ribbons of energy."

Critic Carolyn Kahn of the *New York Planet* contends that Pulvermacher "has mastered a style characterized by fragmentation, by shards of emotion and physicality fused in flight." Using discordant sounds and bursts of movement, mechanical gestures combined with fluidity, her works are described by writer Alice Naude in *Manhattan Spirit* as "a surrealist painting full of familiar images which have been mixed up or inventively skewed to present a vision of a distinctly different world." Whatever designation is used, Pulvermacher's distinctive repertory comes together when she and her ensemble of dancers collaborate with composers, visual artists, musicians, and costume designers to create "a total experience, one that engages all the senses."

Aside from picking up ideas from her travels, Pulvermacher relies heavily on her own Israeli/Jewish heritage to create "a primal, spontaneous prose-like landscape rich with rhythms and flavors" to explore "the process of memory and free association." Pulvermacher has said she tried for many years to deny her heritage before embracing it. Quoted in George Robinson's 1996 article in *New York Jewish Week,* Pulvermacher says, "I'm trying to make the connection between where I'm coming from and where I'm going." Among the works reflecting this heritage is the critically acclaimed *Five Beds/Children of the Dream,* a work dedicated to Pulvermacher's son, which is a telling of children growing up in a collective "children's house," separated from their parents for most of the day every day. Another "heritage" work is *Zaz,* a piece created with her regular collaborator, composer John Zorn and his band Masada. Inspired by "the vitality and ferocity of the Hebrew language" and combined with jazz, "the desert landscape of Masada," and the company's experimental and improvisational style, Neta Pulvermacher & Dancers performed the world premiere of this piece in 1997 at the Joyce Theater's "Altogether Different" series.

Seemingly never satisfied with anything resembling "status quo," Pulvermacher, in 1993, pursuing more education, began studying at Empire State College, where she will receive her B.A. as a Leach Fellow in English literature, writing, and photography in 1998. She is also studying writing and sociology at Columbia University. Pulvermacher's own dancing, choreographing, and setting and creating works for professional companies, colleges, and university dance departments—added to the troupe's full-company performances, lectures, demonstrations, workshops, and master classes in modern, ballet, composition, and improvisation, keep all concerned more than busy. With an explosive mix of raw movement, power, and sensual fluidity, and the recipient of countless awards, fellowships, and grants, Neta Pulvermacher & Dancers will continue to be a force in modern dance and ballet for years to come.

—Daryl F. Mallett

RABIN, Linda

Canadian dancer, choreographer, and educator

Born: 28 September 1946 in Montreal. **Education:** Studied dance in Montreal with Elsie Salomons, Séda Zaré and Birouté Nagys; Connecticut School of the Dance, 1963, 1965; Adelphi, 1964; classes with Zena Rommett; Martha Graham school, 1966-68; Juilliard School of Music, graduated 1967; theatre training with Richard Pochinko, Theatre Ressource Centre, Ottawa (mask workshops), and Ann Skinner (voice); somatic studies in Body Mind Centering for certification, also Alexander, Shiatsu, Kinesics, Pilates and Ideokinesis. **Career:** First choreographed work, 1972; performed in New York with Felix Fibich, 1966-68, Dance Uptown 1966-68, Contemporary Dance System 1967-68, Lia Schubert (Israel) 1969-70, and Daniel Léveillé in Montreal 1989 and 1991; rehearsal director for Batsheva Dance Company, 1971-73, and Ballet Rambert, 1973-74; teaching positions in Canada, Israel, England, and Guatemala, in professional studios and in universities; presently on the dance faculty of Université du Québéc a Montréal; founder of Triskelian Dance Foundation, and founder/director in 1981 of Les Ateliers de Danse Moderne de Montréal (LADMMI); jury member for the Canada Council, Quebec Arts Council.

Works

1972   *Three Out of Me* (mus. Ligeti, Handel), Batsheva Dance Company, Tel Aviv

1974   *Untitled* (mus. Arne Nordheim), Les Grands Ballets Canadiens Choreographic Workshop, Montreal

1975   *Solo for Susan* (mus. Warren Long, commissioned score), Vancouver Art Gallery Independent production

      A Moment Sitting (mus. Britten), Vancouver Art Gallery Independent production

      A Yesterday's Day (Souvenance) (mus. Ann Mortifee), Les Grands Ballets Canadiens

      Domino (mus. Frescobaldi, Bach), Winnipeg Contemporary Dancers

1976   *Kriza,* theater production directed by Nola Chelton, Municipal Theatre of Haifa

1977   *Borders, Boundaries, and Thresholds,* theater production directed by Eileen Thalenberg, Toronto

      The White Goddess (*La déesse blanche*) (mus. Sutherland, Rabin), independent production, Toronto

1978   *Women of the Tent* (mus. Michael J. Baker, commissioned score), Toronto Spring Festival

      Adieu Sylvia (mus. Schubert, Hahn), Simon Fraser University Dance Department, Vancouver

1979   *Premonition* (mus. Phillip Werren), Margie Gillis Dance Foundation, People's Republic of China

1980   *Ô Parade!* (mus. Vincent Dionne, commissioned score), Université de Quebec a Montreal Dance Department

1981   *Tellurian* (mus. Phillip Werren, commissioned score), Les Grands Ballets Canadiens, Guelph Spring Festival, Guelph, Ontario

1983   *Wands* (mus. Phillip Werren, commissioned score), Triskelian Dance Foundation, Montreal

1983   *Presto-Querelle* (mus. Bartók), Triskelian Dance Foundation Montreal

      In Twilight (mus. Bartók), Triskelian Dance, Montreal

      Avec Brahms (mus. Brahms), Triskelian Dance Foundation, Montreal

1984   *Ô Parade!* (mus. Vincent Dionne, commissioned score), Triskelian Dance Foundation, Montreal (reworked from 1980 version)

      Missa Brevis (mus. Britten), Triskelian Dance Foundation, Montreal

      Knot a Couple (mus. Brahams), Triskelian Dance Foundation, Montreal

1987   *Lehava* (mus. Pärt), Montreal Danse, Ontario National Arts Centre, Ottawa

      Stone Witness (mus. Phillip Werren, commissioned score), Les Grands Ballets Canadiens, Place des Arts, Montreal

      Dark Side of the Light (mus. Ligeti), Netherlands Dance Theatre 2, The Hague, Holland

1988   *Marching to Mozart* (mus. Mozart), Studios of LADMMI, Montreal

1992   *Ereshkigal,* w/Manon Levac (mus. indigenous from Mongolia and Tibet), solo for Levac, Danse Cité at Agora de la danse, Montreal

      Katabasis (mus. indigenous from Africa, Brazil, Yakut, Tuva, Mongolia, Tibet and Java), co-production by Linda Rabin, Montreal Danse, Danse Cité and the Canada Dance Festival, Agora de la danse, Montreal

1993   *In the Time of Waiting* w/Jacqueline Lemieux (solo for Lemieux), Agora de la danse, Montreal

      Sous un Brin d'Herbe (mus. live improvisation by the dancers), LADMMI, Montreal

      Adieulescence (mus. live improvixation by the dancers), Maison de la culture Frontenac, Montreal

*   *   *

Linda Rabin started dancing in her native Montreal with Elsie Salomons, Séda Zaré and Biroute Nagys, pioneer teachers of creative modern dance and ballet, then went on to train in the major contemporary dance schools of the United States. She graduated from Juilliard having had José Limón, Anna Sokolow, Martha Graham, and Daniel Lewis among her teachers. An artist of integrity, she was the first of her peers in Montreal to achieve an international career due to her mastery of various dance techniques. Though she has occasionally danced professionally, her main contribution is as an educator and a choreographer who has also mentored many Canadian dancers and/or choreographers such as Margie Gillis, Stephanie Ballard, Candace Loubert and Jacqueline Lemieux.

A highly respected master teacher, Rabin pioneered somatics training throughout Canada. Her classes are never static; they keep evolving, shifting their focus and refining themselves as they incorporate, but do not limit themselves, to Graham and Limón material, some ballet exercises and a floor barre. Her approach both as choreographer and master teacher is holistic and comes from her extensive training and research in somatics, body-mind awareness, and knowledge of kinesiology. Rabin manages to reconcile stylistic constraints with the developing and blossoming of the individual's personality both in her teaching and in the way she builds her works. Her instinctual musicalty helps make her movement phrases very organic and she at times provides her own drum accompaniment while teaching.

After many nomadic years spent studying and working abroad and guesting in different parts of Canada, Rabin returned to Montreal to settle permanently in 1980. Responding spontaneously to a need in the local dance community to have strong technical training for modern dancers she founded Les Ateliers de danse moderne de Montreal inc. (LADMMI) in 1981 together with Candace Loubert. This professional conservatory style programme holds a unique place in this city. In the early 1980s modern dance in Montreal was heavily theatrical and disrearded technique; meanwhile the impact of the two pioneer troupes Groupe Nouvelle Aire and Groupe de la Place Royale was waning: Groupe Nouvelle Aire would officially disband in 1982 while Groupe de la Place Royale had already moved to Ottawa in 1977. LADMMI filled a gap then, as it does to this day, since the new local dance companies that sprung subsequently in the city were not interested in having a school attached to their company and preferred hiring dancers who had trained elsewhere. As it is, in Montreal the only other modern dance training available is found within the university framework.

Rabin was discovered as a choreographer in Montreal in 1975 when Brian Macdonald, then artistic head of Les Grands Ballets Canadiens, brought her back from Israel to conduct a choreographic workshop. The result was *A Yesterday's Day (Souvenance)*, an intriguing group piece where dancers in unitards carted chairs from one spot to another. This piece subsequently entered the company's repertoire; in fact, Rabin's works are featured in many Canadian contemporary troupes as well as in the Nederlands Dans Theater. *The White Goddess,* a seminal group work created independently in 1977, incorporating theatre, ritual, dance, and chanting, took a full year to fine tune. This *in situ* ceremonial piece was the first evening-long one done in Montreal and required the spectators to move through three adjacent studios to view it. The performer/ audience relationship shifted from one room to another and the proximity of the dancers to the onlookers brought new insights and a participatory sense to this reenacted fertility ritual. Highly innovative at the time, *The White Goddess* set a trend of minimalism and slowed-up action in Montreal dancemaking. The work was inspired by ancient rites, a motif that often appears in her pieces as for example in *Katabasis, Women of the Tent, Ereshkigal, In the Time of Waiting* and *Tellurian.*

Another piece, the sparse and zen-like duet *A Moment Sitting,* displayed crystalline purity representative of the way Rabin builds universal, archetypal images simply but effectively. It also made use of a chair, one of her recurring props which she often handles by moving it around, thus contrasting the everyday reality of this piece of furniture with the symbolic images she conjures.

Other more abstract pieces have been created for Les Grands Ballets Canadiens, yet they still display the same breath and musical sensibility in their phrasing.

Rabin's impact as a Canadian dance educator must not be underestimated for she was the first to attempt to reconcile mind, body, emotions, dance techniques and the individual personality within dancemaking. As a choreographer she was able to develop a modern sensibility in dancers working in classical companies and at the same time bring a sense of form and method to those more contemporary trained. She stands alone in Montreal having created her own artistic space. Her steadfast integrity allows her to dismiss fads and not follow fashion by daring to go against the current trends and offer instead a timeless, universal vision.

—Iro Valaskakis Tembeck

RAINER, Yvonne
American dancer, choreographer, and filmmaker

Born: San Francisco, 1934. **Education:** Studied ballet with Nina Stroganova, Mia Slavenska, Barbara Fallis and others; dance with Edith Stephen, Syvilla Fort, Anna Halprin, Robert Dunn, and James Waring, and others; at the Graham school; at the Merce Cunningham Studio with Carolyn Brown, Judith Dunn, and Viola Farber. **Career:** Danced with Simone Forti, Lucinda Childs, Judith Dunn, the Grand Union, David Gordon, Steve Paxton, James Waring, and others; first choreography, 1960; has presented works throughout the world in the U.S., Germany, England, France, Scandinavia, and other countries; began integrating film into her works, 1968; *Lives of Performers* (first feature-length film), 1972; began teaching at the Independent Study Program, Whitney Museum, 1974; left dancing and choreographing entirely to make films, 1975; has taught at Connecticut College, George Washington University, Vancouver Art Gallery, University of California at Santa Cruz, Nova Scotia College of Art and Design, School of the Art Institute of Chicago, New York University and others. **Awards:** Harper's Bazaar "Woman of Accomplishment," 1967; Ingram-Merrill Foundation grant, 1968, 1971; Lena Robbins Foundation grant, 1969; John Simon Guggenheim Memorial Foundation fellowships, 1969, 1988; Foundation for Contemporary Arts grants, 1970; Experiments in Art and Technology award, 1971; National Endowment for the Arts, 1971; Creative Artists Public Service award, 1973, 1975; American Theater Laboratory, 1974; New York State Council on the Arts, 1975, 1976, 1979, 1983, 1987, 1995; Center for Advances Visual Studies, MIT, 1979-80; Special Achievement Award, Los Angeles Film Critics' Association for her film *Journeys from Berlin/1971* (co-produced with British Film Institute), 1980; Maya Deren Award (American Film Institute), 1988; Rockefeller Foundation, 1988, 1990, 1996; New York Foundation for the Arts, 1989, 1995; John D. and Catherine T. MacArthur Fellowship, 1990-95; Filmmaker's Trophy, Sundance Film Festival, and Geyer Werke Prize, International Documentary Film Festival (Munich) for *Privilege,* 1991; Dorothy Arzner/Women in Film award, 1992; Wexner Prize, 1995; American Film Institute award, 1995; Teddy Award, Berlin Film Festival for *MURDER and murder,* 1997; honorary doctorates from California Institute of the Arts, Massachusetts College of Art, School of the Art Institute of Chicago, Rhode Island School of Design.

Works

1961 *Three Satie Spoons,* Living Theatre, New York
      The Bells, Living Theatre
1962 *Satie for Two,* Maidman Playhouse, New York
      Three Seascapes, Maidman Playhouse
      Grass, Maidman Playhouse
      Dance for 3 People and 6 Arms, Master Theatre, New York
      Original Dance, Judson Church, New York
1963 *We Shall Run,* Judson Church
      Word Words w/Steve Paxton, Judson Church
      Terrain, Judson Church
      Person Dance (from *Dance for Fat Man, Dancer,* and *Person*), Pocket Theatre, New York
      Room Service w/Charles Ross, Judson Church
      Shorter End of a Small Peice, Judson Church
1964 *At My Body's House,* State University College, New Paltz, New York
      Dialogues, Surplus Dance Theatre, Stage 73, New York City
      Some Thoughts on Improvisation, Once Festival, Ann Arbor, Michigan
      Part of a Sextet, Judson Church
      Incidents w/Larry Loonin, Cafe Cino, New York City
      Part of a Sextet no.2 (Rope Deut), Kunstakademie, Düsseldorf
1965 *Parts of Some Sexets,* Wadsworth Atheneum, Hartford, Connecticut
      Partially Improvised New Untitled Solo with Pink T-Shirt, Blue Bloomers, Red Ball, Bach's Toccata, and Fugue in D Minor (later referred to as *United Solo*), Wadsworth Atheneum
1966 *The Mind Is a Muscle, Part 1* (later called *Trio A*), Judson Church
      The Mind Is a Muscle, (first version), Judson Church
      Carriage Discreteness (nine evenings), 69th Regiment Armory, New York City
1967 *Convalescent Dance,* Hunter College, New York City
1968 *Untitled Work for 40 people,* New York University Dance Department
      The Mind is A Muscle (final version), Anderson Theatre, New York
      Performance Demonstration no.1, Library for the Preforming Arts, New York
      North East Passing, Goddard College, Plainfield, Vermont
1969 *Rose Fractions,* Billy Rose Theater
      Performance Fractions for the West Coast, Vancouver Art Gallery
      Connecticut Composite, Connecticut College
1970 *Continuous Project—Altered Daily,* Whitney Museum of American Art
      WAR, Douglass College, New Brunswick, New Jersey
1971 *Grand Union Dreams,* Emmanuel Midtown YM-YWHA, New York
      Numerous Frames, Walker Art Center, Minneapolis
1972 *In the College,* Oberlin College, Ohio
      Performance, Hofstra University, Long Island
      Lives of Performers (film, cinematographer Babette Mangolte) screen at the Guggenheim Museum

1973 *This is the story of a woman who. . .,* Theater for the City, New York
      Kristina (for a. . .novella), Walker Art Center, Minneapolis

Publications

By RAINER: books—

Rainer, Yvonne, *Work 1961-73,* Halifax, Nova Scotia, and New York, 1974.

By RAINER: articles—

Article in *Tulane Drama Review,* Winter 1965.
"A Quasi Survey of Some 'Minimalist' Tendencies in the Quantitatively Minimal Dance Activity Midst the Plethora, or An Analysis of *Trio A,*" in *Minimal Art,* edited by Gregory Battcock, New York, 1968.
Interview in *Monthly Film Bulletin* (London), May 1977.
"More Kicking and Screaming from the Narrative Front/Backwater," *Wide Angle* (Athens, Ohio), vol. 7, no. 1/2, 1985.
Interview with Mitch Rosenbaum, in *Persistence of Vision* (Maspeth, New York), Summer 1988.
"Demystifying the Female Body," interview with Scott MacDonald, *Film Quarterly* (Berkeley), Fall 1991.
"A Legend Comes Out: Critically Acclaimed Filmmaker Yvonne Rainer," interview with Liz Kotz, *Advocate* (Los Angeles), 5 November 1991.
"Script of Privilege," in *Screen Writings: Scripts and Texts by Independent Filmmakers,* edited by Scott MacDonald, Berkeley, 1995.

On RAINER: books—

Anderson, Jack, *Choreography Observed,* Iowa City, 1987.
Cohen, Selma Jeanne, *Next Week, Swan Lake: Reflections on Dance and Dances,* Middletown, Connecticut, 1982.
Croce, Arlene, *Going to the Dance,* New York, 1982.
Jowitt, Deborah, *Time and the Dancing Image,* New York, 1988.
Robertson, Allen, and Donald Hutera, *The Dance Handbook,* Boston, 1988.

On RAINER: articles—

Borden, Lizzie, "Trisha Brown and Yvonne Rainer," in *Artforum* (New York), June 1973.
Klawans, Stuart, "Privilege," *The Nation,* 28 January 1991.
Koch, Stephen, "Performance: A Conversation," in *Artforum* (New York), December 1972.
Margolis, Harriet, "Radical Juxtaposition: The Films of Yvonne Rainer," *Film Quarterly,* Spring 1996.
Michelson, Annette, "Yvonne Rainer: The Dancer and the Dance," and "Yvonne Rainer: *Lives of Performers,*" in *Artforum* (New York), January and February 1974.
"Yvonne Rainer: An Introduction, in *Camera Obscura* (Berkeley), Fall 1976.
Rosenbaum, Jonathan, "The Ambiguities of Yvonne Rainer," in *American Film* (Washington, D.C.), March 1980.
Rich, B. Ruby, "Yvonne Rainer," in *Frauen und Film* (Berlin), October 1984.
Cook, Pam, "Love and Catastrophe—Yvonne Rainer," in *Monthly Film Bulletin* (London), August 1987.

Vincendeau, Ginette, and B. Reynaud, "Impossible Projections," in
  Screen (London), Autumn 1987.

Films and Videotapes (by Rainer)

Volleyball, 1967.
Hand Movie, 1968.
Line, 1969.
Lives of Performers, 1972.
Film about a Woman Who..., 1974.
Kristina Talking Pictures, 1976.
Journeys from Berlin/1971, 1980.
The Man Who Envied Women, 1985.
Privilege, 1990.
Murder and Murder, 1996.

*   *   *

Yvonne Rainer was one of the founding members of the influential Judson Dance Theater, which is credited with creating the postmodern dance movement. She was among its most prolific choreographers, but she grew disillusioned with dance and since the mid-1970s has concentrated on making films.

Born in San Francisco in 1934, Rainer moved to New York in 1956 after a short stint at Berkeley. She began her career as an aspiring actress, but switched to dance in 1957 after taking a class with Edith Stephens and witnessing a performance by Erick Hawkins. By 1959 she was studying at the Martha Graham school and elsewhere, attending as many as three classes a day that year. In 1960, she returned to California to participate in an experimental summer course at the Dancer's Workshop Company, led by Ann Halprin. This experience had a significant effect on Rainer's career as Halprin's ideas about creating dance using movements from everyday life were integral to Rainer's subsequent body of choreographic work.

After returning to New York that fall, Rainer started studying with the Merce Cunningham company, where she remained for seven years, until 1967. The study of a variety of dance forms remained important to Rainer, and throughout her career she took courses with Emile Faustin, Allan Wayne, Sevilla Fort, James Waring, Carolyn Brown, Judith Dunn, and Viola Farber, as well as ballet classes for seven years with many different instructors. In 1960, Rainer enrolled in a composition class led by Robert Dunn, along with several other dancers, including Steve Paxton, David Gordon, and Deborah Hay. Rainer's first choreographic work occurred during this period, starting with *Three Satie Spoons* (1961), and followed by *Satie for Two* (1962), *Ordinary Dance* (1962), and *Three Seascapes* (1962).

The members of Dunn's workshop gave their first performance on 6 July 6 1962 at Judson Memorial Church in Greenwich Village, which turned out to be one of the most significant experimental dance concerts of the 1960s. This concert became the first of many by what later became known as the Judson Dance Theater. The group members objected to the strict rules of ballet and modern dance and tried to change the way their audiences viewed the concept of performance. Rainer hoped to minimize the importance of technique and the need for perfection within dance.

The Judson days were Rainer's most prolific time as a choreographer, accounting for nearly half of her total works. These included *We Shall Run* (1963), which, characteristically, featured a variety of body types, little pattern or unity and no glamorous

costumes; *Word Words* (1963), a one-time performance by Rainer and Paxton; *At My Body's House* (1964); *Parts of Some Sextets* (1965), in which dancers flung themselves on mattresses; and *Carriage Discreteness* (1966), in which Rainer sat above the dancers and gave them instructions via walkie-talkie based on a list of predetermined movements.

Rainer experimented with various types of improvisational tools throughout her career. In 1966, she choreographed what is considered one of the most influential works in modern dance, called *Trio A: The Mind Is a Muscle*. *Trio A* was first presented as three simultaneous solos (one performed by Rainer, the others by David Gordon and Steve Paxton) under the title *The Mind Is a Muscle, Part I.* It contained a continuous flow of equally stressed movements, without a climax. The dancers, who retain a relaxed appearance and do not make eye contact with the audience, make no attempt to hide the difficulty of performing the dance. The piece includes as choreographic elements activities such as calisthenics, tumbling, sprinting, jumping, and galloping. Wooden laths dropped from a balcony serve as part of the accompaniment. As was suggested by *Trio A,* Rainer's theory is that dance should be perceived as simply what it is—a series of physical movements—and nothing more. She stripped down dance, eliminating symbolism, narrative, showiness, stage effects, emotion, and personality. Anyone, no matter what their physique or training, should be able to perform a dance, she believed. Rainer also felt that the choreographer was not supreme, but rather that the dancers should take part democratically and collaboratively in the creation of dance. In a 1968 program note for *The Mind Is a Muscle,* Rainer wrote: "If my rage at the impoverishment of ideas, narcissism, and disguised sexual exhibitionism of most dancing can be considered puritan moralizing, it is also true that I love the body—its actual weight, mass, and unenhanced physicality."

Rainer wanted the audience to observe the movement of the human body without sexual connotation or revulsion, and she tried to show this in one performance of *Rose Fractions* (1969), which contained monologues by Lenny Bruce. The dancers performed naked and were accompanied by pornographic recitations and films. Her philosophy was put forth in many written works, including a 1965 article in the *Tulane Drama Review*, in which she wrote: "NO to spectacle no to virtuosity no to transformations and magic and make-believe no to the glamour and transcendency of the star image. . .no to style no to camp no to moving or being moved."

Part of Rainer's technique was extensive use of props. Her works incorporate balls, guns, rope and string, books, stairs, bubble wrap, rubber matting, packages, white paper, white screens, mattresses and mats, food, wings, pillows, fake grass, large wooden boxes, suitcases, and other props, most of which are utilized in more than one of her dances. She often set her pieces to spoken words or unusual sound effects. In one piece, microphones were attached to the dancers' bodies, and the resultant bodily sounds were used as accompaniment.

In 1970, Rainer began work on *Continuous Project—Altered Daily,* for which she created new choreography before each performance as she tried to show that choreography and performance were interrelated, rather than separate, tasks. In *Grand Union Dreams* (1971), created for an improvisational troupe called Grand Union, which she had helped form, she started the choreographic process, but by the time the piece was performed, the dancers had much of the control over how the dance developed.

Rainer was frustrated by the lack of notice for her work, despite her frequent attempts to explain her work in writing. In fact, virtually the only performance that achieved public attention was a Robert Morris duet, *Waterman Switch,* which Rainer and Morris performed nude at the Albright-Knox Gallery in Buffalo and later at Judson Chuch. Rainer left the dance world in 1974 to become a noncommercial filmmaker.

—Karen Raugust

RAMBERT DANCE COMPANY
British dance company

Rambert Dance Company, Britain's oldest established dance company, has since its 1966 reformation embraced a wide-ranging repertory. It then developed from a medium-scale company (averaging 35 dancers) touring a mixture of the classics and original works to a more compact and creative group (16 to 20 dancers) which encouraged new dance works and thereby influenced the development of contemporary dance in Britain.

Rambert dates its existence from 1926 when Frederick Ashton choreographed *A Tragedy of Fashion* using pupils from Marie Rambert's studios. Marie Rambert's own background combined folk dancing learnt at school, admiration for Isadora Duncan, ballet training with Mme. Rat in Paris and Enrico Cecchetti in London, and three years with Emile Jaques-Dalcroze learning, teaching and demonstrating eurhythmics. She spent 10 months with Diaghilev's Ballets Russes, assisting Vaslav Nijinsky in his analysis of Stravinsky's score for *Le sacre du printemps* and coaching individual dancers in their roles. Marie Rambert was therefore exposed to a rich variety of dance. As a teacher she encouraged her pupils to investigate the wide horizons of dance and enabled them to appreciate a variety of theatrical presentations.

It was dancer-choreographer Norman Morrice who guided the 1966 Rambert reformation. He had been exposed to developments in American dance during a study trip to New York funded by a grant from the Ford Foundation; he had also worked with the Batsheva company in Israel. As a choreographer he had already given the company a new energy when he created his first work, *Two Brothers,* in 1958. He responded to the youth culture of the 1950s and 1960s using contemporary subjects as his narratives. Gradually (partly under the influence of an earlier Rambert choreographer, Antony Tudor) the specific stories became less significant and the productions became more concerned with general themes. In 1966, after much discussion about future options for Ballet Rambert, he was invited to become associate artistic director of the slimmer, more creative group. Marie Rambert remained titular director until her death in June of 1982 but the daily running of the company was the responsibility of a succession of co-directors: Morrice, then John Chesworth, and later Robert North.

Glen Tetley was the most important of the choreographers who worked with the new Rambert in the 1960s. With his personal experience of dancing with American Ballet Theatre and the Martha Graham Company and choreography which married both classical and contemporary dance techniques, Tetley's creations sat very effectively on the Rambert dancers, and works such as *Pierrot Lunaire* (first danced by Rambert in 1967) and *Embrace Tiger and Return to Mountain* (1968) continue to be performed by Rambert. It was really Tetley's choreography in productions designed by Nadine Baylis and lit by John B. Read which defined the visual image of the new Rambert. Yet Ballet Rambert was proud to have direct links with the American modern dance choreographers as well. Anna Sokolow, who had been invited to work with Rambert before the company's transformation, mounted her *Deserts* and *Opus '65;* works were also acquired from Lar Lubovitch, Louis Falco, Manuel Alum, and Cliff Keuter.

In addition, aspiring choreographers from within the ranks were encouraged to create ballets. Jonathan Taylor and Chesworth were among the first to produce works for the company in 1966 but the most important was Christopher Bruce, who choreographed his *George Frideric* in 1969. Other choreographers working in Britain were invited to choreograph, thus Robert North, who became the first artistic director from outside the organisation in 1981, contributed to Collaboration One in 1967 before choreographing a succession of works for the company. Siobhan Davies was well-established with London Contemporary Dance Theatre when she created *Celebration* in 1979, returning in 1988 to choreograph *Embarque* after which she became associate choreographer from 1989 to 1993; and Richard Alston was a respected freelance choreographer when after *Bell High* in 1980 he was invited to become resident choreographer.

Initially the company's contemporary work had a Graham orientation, but after Alston introduced Cunningham-based classes there was a marked shift of style. Under Alston (1986 to 1992) the company's orientation was more specific and the narrative/thematic aspect of productions diminished so that the focus was on the movement within the stage setting. Cunningham's works took a central position and other Americans who contributed to the repertory included Trisha Brown and Lucinda Childs, although British and European choreographers, including Michael Clark, Ashley Page, Mark Baldwin and Guido Severin were also significant.

Alston's narrow base for Britain's leading contemporary dance company made it less popular than funding bodies and the board hoped it would be, particularly at a time when, as costs rose, the larger touring companies seemed to be losing dates to independent organisations. Rambert Dance Company, however, has never been afraid to stop and reassess its work and, if necessary, take a different route. Bruce, who had stepped down as associate choreographer in 1987, was persuaded to return to Rambert in 1994 to form a new company. This was slightly larger and aimed to revitalise dance in Britain, bridging the gap between classical and contemporary choreography and, instead of having its own ensemble of musicians, calling on London Musici to provide accompaniment. The repertory was more oriented towards Europe than America with choreography by Jiri Kylian, Ohad Naharin, Per Jonsson, and Bruce himself, but it did not ignore the company's or the British contemporary dance heritage. Most of the post-1994 productions have a clear theme and the theatricality of the company is evident from the inclusion of Martha Clarke's *The Garden of Earthly Delights* in the company's relaunch tour and the revival of Bruce's own 1977 collaboration with Lindsay Kemp, *Cruel Garden,* in 1998.

Each time Rambert pauses to reconsider its development it looks back to its past, refocuses on its original twin purposes of tradition and experiment. Creativity and the encouragement of choreographers are placed alongside the opportunity to show internationally acclaimed masterworks. Without its own theatre Rambert constantly tours both in Britain and increasingly worldwide—its productions being performed by superb dancers who welcome the challenges such variety of repertory presents.

—Jane Pritchard

RANDAZZO, Peter

American-born dancer, choreographer, artistic director, and educator based in Canada

Born: 2 January 1942 in Brooklyn, New York. **Education:** Studied tap-dancing; studied modern dance with Martha Graham, Bertram Ross, Robert Cohan, Yuriko, and Helen McGehee at Martha Graham School of Contemporary Dance, New York, 1958-60; studied ballet with Anthony Tudor, Robert Joffrey, Leon Danelian and Madame Swoboda, New York. **Career:** Dancer, Martha Graham Dance Company, 1960-67; toured with José Limón Dance Company; appeared with Donald McKayle, Eleo Pomare, Aileen Passloff, and American Dance Theatre, 1960-67; first choreography, 1967; co-founder, Toronto Dance Theatre and School of Toronto Dance Theatre (with Patricia Beatty and David Earle), Toronto, 1968; co-artistic director, Toronto Dance Theatre (TDT), 1968-83; first solo concert of works, 1982; resident choreographer, TDT, 1983-96; taught at School of TDT and Martha Graham School of Contemporary Dance. Lives in Toronto, Ontario. **Awards:** Dance Ontario Award (with Patricia Beatty and David Earle), 1982; Toronto Arts Award for performing arts (with Patricia Beatty and David Earle), 1988; funding grants from Canada Council.

Roles   (all original cast roles)

1961   *One More Gaudy Night* (Graham), Martha Graham Dance Company, New York
1962   Bull Dancer, *Phaedra* (Graham), Martha Graham Dance Company, New York
       Secular Games (Graham), Martha Graham Dance Company, New York
       Legend of Judith (Graham), Martha Graham Dance Company, New York
1963   Goat, *Circe* (Graham), Martha Graham Dance Company, New York
1965   *The Witch of Endor* (Graham), Martha Graham Dance Company, New York
       Part Real—Part Dream (Graham), Martha Graham Dance Company, New York
1967   Astyanax, *Cortege of Eagles* (Graham), Martha Graham Dance Company, New York
       Dancing-Ground (Graham), Martha Graham Dance Company, New York
1969   *Lovers* (David Earle), Toronto Dance Theatre (TDT), Toronto
1970   *Hot and Cold Heroes* (Patricia Beatty), TDT
1972   *Boat River Moon* (David Earle), TDT
       Baroque Suite (includes *Mirrors, Lyrical Solo, Duet, Lament, Finale*) (David Earle), TDT
1973   *Ray Charles Suite* (David Earle), TDT
1974   *Bugs* (David Earle), TDT, Guelph Spring Festival, Guelph, Ontario

Other roles include: Performed roles in *Dark Meadow, Diversion of Angels, Clytemnestra, Alcestis, Acrobats of God,* and *A Look at Lightning,* with the Martha Graham Dance Company, New York, 1960-67; choreography by José Limón (José Limón Dance Company), Donald McKayle, Eleo Pomare, Aileen Passloff, 1960-67; ensemble, *The King and I,* City Centre, New York, 1963; solos in own works, 1967-87.

Works (for the TDT, premiering in Toronto, unless otherwise noted)

1967   *Fragments* (mus. Eugene Lester), New Dance Group of Canada, Toronto
1968   *Aftermath* (mus. Frank Martin), part of *Dance Concert* before TDT, Toronto
       Trapezoid (mus. Ann Southam, Donald Himes)
1969   *Imbroglio* (mus. Nadine Macdonald)
       Encounter (mus. Ann Southam)
       I Had Two Sons (mus. Stanley Sussman)
       Continuum (mus. Ann Southam)
1970   *Voyage for Four Male Dancers* (mus. Ann Southam)
       Untitled Solo (mus. Ann Southam; text Sean O'Huigin)
1971   *Dark of Moon* (mus. Robert Daigneault)
       Starscape (mus. Syrinx)
       Prospect Park (mus. Ann Southam)
       Visions for a Theatre of the Mind (mus. Ricardo Abreut), TDT, London, Ontario
1972   *The Amber Garden* (mus. Milton Barnes), TDT, St. Catharines, Ontario
       Three-Sided Room (mus. Milton Barnes)
       The Last Act (mus. Milton Barnes)
1973   *Figure in the Pit* (mus. Ann Southam), TDT, St. Catharines, Ontario
       A Flight of Spiral Stairs (mus. Milton Barnes), TDT, St. Catharines, Ontario
       A Walk in Time (mus. Robert Daigneault)
1974   *Mythic Journey* (mus. Ann Southam), TDT, Guelph, Ontario
       The Letter (mus. Michael Conway Baker)
1975   *L'Assassin menacé* (mus. Ann Southam, Mina, Love Unlimited), TDT, Detroit, Michigan
1976   *Nighthawks* (mus. Ann Southam, Tommy Dorsey)
1977   *Recital* (mus. Michael Conway Baker), TDT, St. John's, Newfoundland
       A Simple Melody (mus. collage), TDT, Ottawa, Ontario
1979   *The Light Brigade* (mus. collage)
1980   *Moving to Drumming* (mus. Steve Reich)
       Duet Untitled (mus. Michael Conway Baker)
1981   *Arc* (mus. Keith Jarrett)
       Last Dance (mus. Elgar)
       Octet (mus. Steve Reich)
       In Retrospect (mus. Poulenc)
1982   *Tango, So!* (mus. Gato Barbieri)
       Enter the Dawn (mus. Charlie Haden), solo
1985   *Rewind* (mus. Ann Southam)
1987   *Exit* w/Randy Glynn (mus. John Hammond, Jr.), Randy Glynn Dance Project, Toronto
1988   *The Sight of Silents* (mus. silent film scores), Anna Wyman Dance Theatre, Vancouver, British Columbia
       Vivaldi (mus. Vivaldi)
1990   *Outside in Time* (mus. Alexina Louis)
       Incantation (mus. Peter Gabriel), School of TDT
1992   *Summer Evening* (mus. Phillip Werren)
1995   *Phoenix* (mus. Geoff Bennett), solo, Michael Menegon and Friends, Toronto
       Concerto (mus. Vivaldi), trio, Michael Menegon and Friends, Toronto

Other works include: *Keeper of the Key,* Pavlychenko Studios, *Moving from Memory* (mus. Vangelis); collaborated with director

Blake Heathcote on *Coming Attractions, Trixie Truelove: Teenage Detective,* and *Restoration of Order*; works featured in television series *Three in One,* Canadian Broadcasting Corporation, 1972; *Music to See,* Canadian Broadcasting Corporation, 1977.

Publications

On RANDAZZO: books—

Macpherson, Susan, ed., *101 From the Encyclopedia of Theatre Dance in Canada,* Toronto, 1997.
Wyman, Max, *Dance Canada: An Illustrated History,* Vancouver, 1989.

On RANDAZZO: articles—

Citron, Paula, "A Step Back to Move Forward: Transition at Toronto Dance Theatre," *Performing Arts* (Toronto), Summer 1983.
———, "Four Choreographers Keep Dancer on Toes," *Toronto Star,* 16 January 1987.
———, "Peter Randazzo Breaks the Bottle," *Toronto Star,* 10 March 1990.
Kohl, Helen, "A Dance Manifesto," *Key to Toronto Magazine,* April 1982.
Littler, William, "Dancing a Hard Road," *Toronto Star,* 5 November 1988.

Films and Videotapes

Toronto Dance Theatre in England, Canadian Broadcasting Corporation, 1973.
L'Assassin menacé, dir. Robin Wall, chor. Randazzo, Television Ontario, 1988.
Originals in Art, Bravo! New Style Arts Channel, 1995.

*　　*　　*

The contribution to dance in Canada by Peter Randazzo and his fellow co-founders of Toronto Dance Theatre—Patricia Beatty and David Earle—cannot be overestimated. While experiments in contemporary dance had occurred previously in various Canadian cities, Toronto Dance Theatre (TDT) was the first professional dance company to plant the aesthetics of American modern dance in Canadian soil. The School of Toronto Dance Theatre—also founded by Randazzo, Beatty, and Earle—continues to be one of the most important training institutions for contemporary dance in the country, attracting students from across Canada and the world. Although the school uses a Graham-inspired syllabus, the three co-founders have not been creatively bound by the Graham technique but have gone on to establish their own individual choreographic style. Of the three, Randazzo has come closest to being a Graham purist, a feature of his career that has been both a strength and a bête noire.

Randazzo was born into a boisterous Sicilian family in Brooklyn, New York and, at an early age, became a champion tap-dancer. His modern dance epiphany occurred at the age of 16 when he accompanied a girlfriend to a class at Martha Graham's school. Randazzo became a full-time student himself, and by the age of 18 he was a member of the company. The most memorable role Graham created on Randazzo was the Goat in *Circe* (1963), which was perfectly suited to his satyr-like looks, slight frame, and lightning-fast, aggressive style of movement. He also appeared in eight other original company choreographies, as well as being one of Graham's favourite demonstrators in class. "Martha liked me because I stood up to her," Randazzo said in an interview with this author. During the Graham off-months, Randazzo did two tours with José Limón's company as well as appearing with a host of New York choreographers including Donald McKayle.

In 1967 Randazzo left the pressure cooker atmosphere of Graham's company to visit his Canadian friend and former Graham student, David Earle, who was working with Robert Cohan's London Contemporary Dance Theatre. It was in Liverpool, where the Cohan troupe was on tour, that the idea of starting a modern dance company called Toronto Dance Theatre was born. That same year, Randazzo and Earle paid a visit to Toronto and found that Patricia Beatty, also a former Graham student, had begun a modern dance school called New Dance Group of Canada two years earlier. Randazzo created his first choreography, *Fragments*—a trio for Beatty, Earle, and himself—for New Dance Group's first concert. Early in 1968, Earle and Randazzo mounted their own evening of work called *Dance Concert,* and, following discussions with Beatty, the three joined forces to create TDT later in the year.

Initially, Randazzo was the most prolific choreographer of the three, and his sophisticated, provocative works, set to hand-tailored, original scores by some of Canada's top composers, presented a unique viewpoint on stage. While committed to Graham's technique, his dances, individualized by his eccentric personality, were not derivative. Instead, Randazzo used Graham as a basis to make his own rules. Randazzo's choreography grew organically out of his own dancing, with his telltale, quirky physicality imbedded in the movement patterns. An instinctive choreographer, he was inspired by an image or mood of the moment, which then triggered a flood of physical ideas for Randazzo to play with. His choreography tended to be energetic, powerful, highly physical, and technically challenging, or, as one dancer described it, "murderously sadistic." He pushed his dancers to the limit to see how far they could go both physically and emotionally. His movement has been described as staccato, brittle, sharp, jagged, off-kilter, tight, unpredictable, and percussive, but it was also always clean, clear, and precise. His approach to themes, no matter how passionate and intense, was never sentimental. He could be, in turn, bizarre, hilarious, grotesque, or poetic. There was always an edge to his work that placed him outside the mainstream, yet he produced several pieces considered classics of Canadian dance.

Randazzo, a charismatic performer, constructed many of his dances to be theatrical tours de force for himself. Early dramatic works tended to centre on Randazzo surrounded by his favourite female dancers, radiating aspects of the dark sexual overtones, powerful primitivisms, and cosmic mysteries of his mentor Graham. Obscure themes challenged the audience to join Randazzo on his journey. For example, *Dark of Moon* (1971) with music by Robert Daigneault, pitted a male dancer against three women in a symbolic struggle of the individual against unnamed forces. Two years later, the Edgar Allan Poe-inspired *Figure in the Pit,* to a score by Ann Southam, had five women in elaborate eye makeup circling the prone body of the hero like devouring angels. In the mid 1970s, a cynical, humorous, noir, even anarchistic side of Randazzo became evident. The acclaimed *L'Assassin menacé* (1975) presented a dada-like romp. Randazzo played the Fantômas character trying to do in The Lady against a two-dimensional set that recreated the wit of French surreal artist René Magritte's original painting. *Recital* (1977) featured the revealing inner monologues of five neurotic people trapped at a piano concert, expressed both through tortured movement and spoken text. That same year, *A Simple Melody* trashed many aspects of culture with monks cavorting to Gregorian chants, dancers in gym clothes doing the breast stroke to the 1930s song "By a Waterfall," and a wild comic book parade of superheroes for a finale.

By the 1980s, Randazzo was flirting with pure movement in works such as *Moving to Drumming* (1980) and *Rewind* (1985), choreographed to minimalist scores by Steve Reich and Ann Southam respectively. Among Randazzo's most outstanding pieces is the trilogy based on paintings by American artist Edward Hopper set to both extant and original music. *Nighthawks* (1976) hauntingly recreated Hopper's all-night diner and the pathetic outcasts who frequent the place; *Enter the Dawn* (1982), a magnificent solo for Sarah Pettitt, was a moving portrayal of the frustration of a woman alone in her boudoir in the wee small hours of the morning; *Summer Evening* (1992) graphically exposed the tortured, romantic relationship of a couple while a young boy, concealed in the bushes, observed these intense, private moments.

By the late 1980s, Randazzo began to distance himself from both Toronto Dance Theatre and its school, disagreeing with the drift away from modern dance purity to a more generalized contemporary dance under new artistic director Christopher House and the school's administrators. His increasing marginalization was also caused by anger at the interference of funding councils who insisted Toronto Dance Theatre have a business manager and a single artistic director. "When the three of us were running the company and I did the books," he said, "we never had a deficit." For Randazzo, dance had somehow become about everything else instead of dance. He increasingly looked to outside choreographic commissions and his last official work for the company was 1992. Randazzo made a complete break with Toronto Dance Theatre in 1996 to pursue independent projects, including remounting a revival of *A Simple Melody* for the Danny Grossman Dance Company in 1998. Since a courageous, candid interview in 1990 with the *Toronto Star* about his struggle with alcoholism, he has also continued to work tirelessly on behalf of Alcoholics Anonymous.

—Paula Citron

RAUSCHENBERG, Robert

American painter, sculptor, set designer, dancer, and choreographer

Born: 22 October 1925 in Port Arthur, Texas. **Education:** Kansas City Art Institute, 1946-47; Académie Julian, Paris, 1947; Black Mountain College (North Carolina), 1948-50. **Family:** Married Susan Weil, 1950 (divorced, 1952), one son. **Military:** U.S. navy Reserve, 1942-45. **Career:** Professional artist, beginning 1950; first exhibition at the Betty Parsons Gallery, New York, 1951; taught at Black Mountain College and staged his first "Happening" with John Cage and others, 1952; collaboration with Merce Cunningham, began 1955; founded non-profit Experiment in Art and Technology, 1966; founded Change Inc., 1970; founded Rauschenberg Overseas Cultural Interchange (ROCI), 1973. **Awards:** Art Institute of Chicago prize, 1960; Ohara prize, National Museum of Modern Art (Tokyo), 1962; International Exhibition of Graphic Art (former

Yugoslavia), First prize, 1963, and Grand Prix d'Honneur, 1979; first prize, *Biennale* (Venice), 1964; Wm. A Clark Gold Medal and prize (*Corcoran Biennal Exhibition of Contemporary American Painters,* Washington, D.C.), 1965; Logan Award, Art Institute of Chicago, 1976; Mayor's Award of Honor in Arts and Culture (New York), 1977; Creative Arts Medal in Painting (Brandeis University), 1978; Chicago Arts Award, 1978; special award, *Graphic Arts Biennale* (Cracow, Poland), 1979; Skowhegan Medal for Painting (Maine), 1982; Grammy Award, 1984; Jerusalem Prize for Arts and Letters (Friends of Bezalel Academy), 1984; honorary D.H.L., Grinnell College (Iowa), 1967; D.F.A., University of South Florida (Tampa), 1976; Fellow, Rhode Island School of Design (Providence), 1978.

Works (for dance, selected)

1956	Collaboration w/Cage & Cunningham, *Suite for Five in Space and Time* (Cunningham), Merce Cunningham Dance Company
1957	*Epic* (lighting), Paul Taylor Dance Company
1959	*Summerspace* (set and costumes), Merce Cunningham Dance Company
	Antic Meet w/Cage & Cunningham, Merce Cunningham Dance Company
1960	*Three Epitaphs* (costumes), Paul Taylor Dance Company
1961	*Aeon* w/Cage & Cunningham, Merce Cunningham Dance Company
1963	*Pelican* w/Alex Hay and Carolyn Brown for the Washington Gallery of Modern Art as a performance piece
1984	*Set and Reset* (costumes), Trisha Brown

Publications

By RAUSCHENBERG: articles—

"A Collage Comment by Robert Rauschenberg in his Latest Suite of Prints," *Studio International,* December 1969.
"Carnal Clocks," *Art Now: New York,* May 1969.
"Robert Rauschenberg Talks to Maxime de la Falaise McKendry," *Interview,* May 1976.

On RAUSCHENBERG: books—

Klotsky, James, *Merce Cunningham,* New York, 1975.
McDonagh, Don, *The Rise and Fall and Rise of Modern Dance*, New York, 1970.
Retallack, Joan, editor, *Musicage,* Hanover, New Hampshire, 1996.
Siegel, Marcia, *The Shapes of Change,* Boston, 1979.
Sorrell, Walter, *The Dance through the Ages,* New York, 1967.
Tomkins, Calvin, *The Bride and the Bachelors: Five Masters of the Avant-Garde,* New York, 1974.
Tomkins, Calvin, *Off the Wall,* New York, 1980.
Wissman, Jürgen, *Rauschenberg: Black Market,* Stuttgart, 1970.

On RAUSCHENBERG: articles—

Hughes, Robert, "The Great Permitter," *Time,* 27 October 1997.
Sears, David, "A Trisha Brown-Robert Rauschenberg Collage," *Ballet Review,* Fall 1982.

Robert Rauschenberg: Sets for Merce Cunningham's *Travelogue,* 1977. Photograph © Johan Elbers.

Films and Videotapes

Canoe, film, New York, 1977.

*   *   *

Robert Rauschenberg is one of the most influential artists of the 20th century. He is a painter, sculptor, photographer, printmaker, set designer, dancer, and choreographer—perhaps he is best described as a multimedia artist. Rauschenberg's art has its roots in Abstract Expressionism but he is best known for his collages, assemblages, and his "Combines," and is the innovator of several contemporary art movements.

Rauschenberg received his early art training at the Kansas City Art Institute and School of Design through the GI Bill, and then studied for several months at the Académie Julian in Paris, where he met his future wife, Susan Weil. He returned to the U.S. to study with Joseph Albers at Black Mountain College, North Carolina, where he became acquainted with the artist Jasper Johns. While at Black Mountain College, he also met and became friends with painters Franz Kline and Cy Twombly, as well as composer John Cage

and choreographer Merce Cunningham. Rauschenberg and Cunningham were greatly influenced by Cage's artistic theory of "chance" and the three artists collaborated on several dance pieces over the course of many years. The farther Rauschenberg explored various media and broke down distinctions between art forms, the more eclectic his work became—eventually his work merged with his environment. Rauschenberg went from painting monochrome canvases to creating multimedia events.

Initially, Rauschenberg began adding bits of fabric and found objects to his canvases and then expanding upon the theme of added and found elements, to include items such as bottles, tires, and stuffed animals (*Monogram*, 1955), and a fully made-up bed (*The Bed*, 1955). Later, in addition to using discarded or "junk" objects, he used "working technology"—clocks, blinking lights, and sound. Rauschenberg's assemblages logically metamorphosed into environmental art, theater pieces and "Happenings." With this new art form, Rauschenberg eliminated the distinction between painting and sculpture, printmaking, photography, etc.—paintings became three-dimensional; they became the street, your living room, or a comingling of environments. Essentially, his art became complex assemblages with the added elements of time, movement, and sound.

663

Rauschenberg's works are full of metaphor, puns, and cryptic meanings—a plethora of images and messages—analogous to having several televisions or radios playing at the same time but tuned to different channels (á la John Cage).

Rauschenberg was closely associated with choreographer Merce Cunningham for many years. Through most of the 1950s Rauschenberg designed many of the Cunningham company's costumes. In 1961, he became the company's lighting director and stage manager for the duration of a world tour between 1961 and 1964. One well-known Cunningham piece for which Rauschenberg designed the costumes and set was *Summerspace* (1959), a piece exemplifying some of the crucial philosophical elements the two artists share. The stage floor, backdrop, and costumes are all painted in the same Impressionistic, pointillist pastels, creating a boundary-free environment. Dancers emerge out of and merge into their surroundings, appearing and disappearing; the dancers define the space. The dancers and the stage set are equally independent and dependent on one another, and there is no center or position of importance. Well-known pieces that the trio of Rauschenberg, Cage, and Cunningham collaborated on include *Suite for Five in Space And Time* (1956), *Antic Meet* (1959), and *Aeon* (1961).

Rauschenberg also collaborated with dancer and choreographer Paul Taylor who, as a dance student, worked as an assistant to Rauschenberg and Jasper Johns while the two artists were creating window displays. Rauschenberg designed the glittering black costumes for Taylor's popular piece *Three Epitaphs* (1960) and created the lighting for Taylor's *Epic* (1957). By the early 1960s, Rauschenberg was choreographing and performing his own pieces as well dancing for other choreographers such as Deborah Hay, Alex Hay, and Simone Forti. Similar to his multimedia paintings, his choreographed movement pieces were a combination of several elements. In the early 1960s an exhibition entitled "The Popular Image" was held at the Washington Gallery of Modern Art, in Washington, D.C. The exhibit included various live performances, and Rauschenberg created a movement piece called *Pelican* (1963) for this event. The performance space was an indoor roller skating rink, and the dance featured two men (Alex Hay and Rauschenberg) on skates, and a woman (Carolyn Brown) in toe shoes.

Rauschenberg's art is continuously evolving. Throughout his career, he has kept current with and explored available technologies, using electronic devices, computers, and lasers in his work. In 1966 Rauschenberg formed a non-profit foundation called Experiment in Art and Technology (EAT) with laser artist Billy Kluver with whom Rauschenberg has collaborated with on several projects. Some pieces Rauschenberg has created, such as *Oracle* (1965), *Revolvers*, and *Soundings* (1968) could be described as performance art but do not include dancers. Creating art is a form of social activism and like most artists, Rauschenberg uses his art to communicate his personal and political views. Civil rights, environmental protection, and pacifism are among some of the social themes portrayed in Rauschenberg's art—he even designed the first "Earth Day" poster. He also created a series of posters for the Apollo Space Program to promote peaceful exploration of space. In 1970 Rauschenberg formed Change, Inc. for destitute artists and in 1973 he founded the Rauschenberg Overseas Cultural Interchange (ROCI).

Rauschenberg began mounting retrospectives in the late 1970s and his works have been exhibited throughout the world. In 1997, his latest, aptly titled *Robert Rauschenberg: A Retrospective*, was sponsored by the Philip Morris Companies, Inc. and traveled to rave reviews from New York's Guggenheim museums—both uptown and SoHo—to Houston, then to Germany, Spain and other countries. Writing about Rauschenberg in *Time* magazine, Robert Hughes characterized the retrospective as a "Whitmanesque profusion" from the artist who, like Walt Whitman, is the "Great Permitter" and just might be "the artist of the American democracy, yearningly faithful to its clamor, its contradictions, its hope and its enormous demotic freedom, all of which find shape in his work." In other words, throughout Rauschenberg's career as an artist, he has aspired to communicate the interrelationship of all things, and has grandly succeeded.

—Christine Miner Minderovic

REDLICH, Don

American dancer, choreographer, and company director

Born: 17 August 1929 in Winona, Minnesota. **Education:** Studied at the University of Wisconsin with Margaret H'Doubler and Louise Kloepper, 1950-53; with Hanya Holm, Colorado College summer session, 1953; also studied at Holm's studio, and with Helen Tamiris and Doris Humphrey. **Career:** Danced in the companies of Holm, Tamiris, Humphrey, John Butler, Anna Sokolow, Murray Louis, Phyllis Lamhut, and Rod Alexander; taught at Holm's studio, and has had stints at Adelphi University, Colorado College, Sarah Lawrence College, New York University, Juilliard, and Rutgers University; conducted workshops at the University of Hawaii (Honolulu), University of Maryland (College Park), University of Wisconsin (Madison), and at the International Festival of Dance, New Delhi (India); founder, Don Redlich Dance Company (non-profit organization), 1966; selected to represent the Untied States at the International Festival of Dance in Paris, 1969; has toured with the company under the NEA's Arts Dance Touring Program and Artists in Schools program; restaged Holm's *Jocose* for Baryshnikov's White Oak Dance Project, 1993-94; choreographed Benjamin Britton's *Noah's Flood* for the Sante Fe Opera, 1996. **Awards:** National Endowment for the Arts (NEA) grants, 1968-80s; Professor Emeritus, Mason Gross School of the Arts, Rutgers University.

Works

1953	*Fall of the City*
1955	*Thieves' Carnival,* Off-Broadway production
1956	*Measure of a Moment*
1958	*Idyl*
	Three Figures of Delusion
	Electra and Orestes
	The Zanies
	The Visited Planet
	Flight
	Mark of Cain
1959	*Passin' Through*
	Eventide
1960	*Age of Anxiety,* Off-Broadway production
1963	*Earthling*
	Four Sonatas
	Tangents in Jazz
1964	*Cross-Currents*
	Salutations

	Duet
	Concertino de printemps
1965	*Forgetmenot*
	Eight + Three
	Oddities
1966	*Pococurante*
	Set of Five Dances
	Comedians
	Trumpet Concerto
	Alice and Henry
	Couplet
	Air Antique
1967	*Comedians II*
	Twosome
	Run-Through
	Reacher
	Struwwelper
	Cahoots
	Tyro
1968	*Tabloid*
	Slouching Toward Bethlehem
	Untitled
1969	*Jibe*
	Tristram and Isolt
1970	*Tristram, Isolt and Aida*
	Woyzeck, Broadway production
1971	*Stigmata*
	Tristan, Isolde, Aida, Hansel and Gretel
	Implex
	Estrange
1972	*The Ride Across Lake Constance,* Off-Broadway
	Harold
	Opero
	She Often Goes for a Walk Just after Sunset, American Dance Festival
1973	*Everybody's Doing It*
1974	*Three Bagatelles*
	Patina
	Ariadne auf Naxos, opera
1975	*Traces*
1978	*Finisterre*
1984	*Where Now, When Now?*
1987	*L'Histoire du Soldat*
1996	*Disposal III,* University of Wisconsin, Madison
	Noah's Flood (Benjamin Britten production), Sante Fe Opera

Publications

On REDLICH: books—

McDonagh, Don, *The Complete Guide to Modern Dance,* Garden City, New York, 1970.

Partsch-Bergsohn, Isa, *Modern Dance in Germany and the United States: Cross Currents and Differences,* Tucson, Arizona, 1994.

On REDLICH: articles—

"Critics' Picks," *Washington Post,* 28 April 1985.

"Critics' Picks," *Washington Post,* 25 March 1984.

"Notes on the Arts," *Philadelphia Inquirer,* June 15, 1988.

Siegel, Marcia B., ed., "Dancer's Notes," *Dance Persepctives,* Summer 1969.

Sommers, Pamela, "The Improvised and Otherwise," *Washington Post,* 30 March 1984.

*   *   *

Dancer, choreographer, and educator Don Redlich is known for his humor and light touch, and for his creative use of the often-nontraditional venues in which his dances are performed. His choreography is in the tradition of Mary Wigman and her student, Hanya Holm, with whom Redlich enjoyed a long association.

Born in 1929, Redlich was a student of Margaret H'Doubler at the University of Wisconsin. He first studied with Hanya Holm at a Colorado College summer session in 1953, and soon after began taking classes at her studio and dancing in her troupe in New York City. Redlich danced in the premieres of Holm's *Ionization* (1949), *Concertino da Camera* (1952), *Temperamental Behavior* (1953), *String Quartet No. 2* (1952), *Ozark Suite* (1957 and 1958), and *Imaginary Ballet* (1961) among others. He also performed in Holm's musical, *The Golden Apple,* began choreographing off-Broadway productions, including *Thieves' Carnival* and *Robber Bridegroom,* and even did some television work.

In addition to Holm, Redlich studied with other well-known modern dancers like Helen Tamiris and Doris Humphrey, then went on to acclaim dancing in their companies and those of Anna Sokolow, Murray Louis, John Butler, Phyllis Lamhut, and Rod Alexander. In 1966 Redlich formed his own group, the Don Redlich Dance Company, and started choreographing in earnest, producing *Idyl, Three Figures of Delusion, Electra and Orestes, The Zanies, The Visited Planet, Flight,* and *Mark of Cain*—all in 1958, and *Passin' Through* and *Eventide* in 1959. Throughout his career, he has concentrated on solos and small group works, and as a result his touring companies have been small and have included some well-known names like Gladys Bailin, Elina Mooney, Irene Feigenheimer, Lily Santangelo, Barbara Roan, Billy Siegenfeld, and Trish Casey. One of his most popular works is 1959's *Passin' Through,* a typically expressive solo about traveling salesmen in 19th-century America, which was first performed by Redlich at the 92nd Street YMHA in New York City.

As a choreographer, Redlich's decisions on props and themes are often primarily determined by which choice will allow the best possibilities for movement. For example, in *Reacher* (1967), created while he was artist-in-residence at the University of Wisconsin (his alma mater), dancers must climb up and down a large net on the stage, which creates choreography that is more pure movement than dance. The concept of searching is one of the themes, placing focus on the dancers' hands as they grab at the net. The physical, athletic quality of the dance is characteristic of Redlich's work, and is also evident in *Tangents in Jazz* and *Earthling* (both 1963). The athleticism of Redlich's choreography requires his dancers to be technically proficient, but doesn't overshadow the expressiveness of his dances.

Reacher also illustrates Redlich's interest in combining film and dance, an early experimentation in what has come to be know today as a "multimedia" production. His intent for the piece was to integrate film, movement, and sound by choreographing to an 11-minute film by Jackson Tiffany from the University of Wisconsin's photography department. The theme of the work, the smallness of man in his environment, was dictated by the perception of the human figure in miniature against the giant projection of the film. Sounds

Don Redlich Dance Company. Photograph by Tom Caravaglia.

incorporated into the piece characterized the noise of life—including gun shots, a roller coaster, voices, a calliope, clanging chains, a crying baby, and even the sound of breathing. Another of Redlich's multimedia works is *Dance for One Figure, Four Objects and Film Sequences,* which incorporated a filmed image of him dancing down long corridors, which was shown on screen as he was dancing in person on stage. The juxtaposition contrasted the confinement of the stage with the elongated space of the corridors in the film. Other of Redlich's works performed in unconventional spaces, such as the outdoors, includes *She Often Goes for a Walk Just after Sunset.* This particular work was performed at Connecticut College in New London as part of the American Dance Festival in 1972, and was specifically created for the outdoor setting of the campus.

Through the years, Redlich's ties with Holm remained strong, not just in terms of his sensibility but also in terms of their working relationship. In the 1970s Redlich taught at Holm's studio and choreographed some of her final productions. Holm's influence was in evidence throughout Redlich's career, in his own choreography as well as his later endeavors to keep Holm's works alive through new productions and restagings. Late in her career, Holm choreo-

graphed several pieces for the Don Redlich Dance Company, including *Jocose,* of which the first two parts were created in 1981 and the last in 1984. The piece illustrates the interactions among two men and three women, set to music by Ravel's *Sonata for Violin and Piano*, and takes a humorous look at some of the absurdities of male-female relationships. In turn, Redlich's preservation of Holm's works included recreations in diverse venues from a reconstructed *Jocose* for Mikhail Baryshnikov's White Oak Dance Project in 1993 and 1994, and Holm's *Ratatat* for the 70th anniversary of Lathrop Hall at the University of Wisconsin in 1996. Redlich also choreographed a new piece of his own, *Disposal III* (1996), which premiered at the event with 40 student and alumni performers from the school participating in the premiere.

Though Redlich is retired as a dancer and lives in New Mexico, he still teaches and choreographs. He has taught at Adelphi University, Sarah Lawrence College, New York University, Juilliard, and Rutgers University, where he is Professor Emeritus of the Mason Gross School of the Arts. Redlich has also directed productions of *Woyzeck* and *Volpone* for the National Theatre of the Deaf, and in 1996, in addition to a special performance at his alma mater in

Wisconsin, he also choreographed Benjamin Britten's *Noah's Flood* for the Sante Fe Opera.

Redlich's choreography is found in the repertoire's of several other modern dance companies across the United States and abroad. He has produced works for the Bat-Dor Dance Company of Israel, and stateside for the Nancy Hauser Dance Company of Minneapolis, Shirley Mordine's Mordine and Company of Chicago, the Portland Dance Company in Oregon, and the closer-to-home Albuquerque Dance Theatre. Another example, the Easy Moving Company, a troupe based in Raleigh, North Carolina, has performed Redlich's *Cahoots*, a humorous piece about the battle of the sexes; while Improvisations Unlimited, a resident troupe at the University of Maryland in College Park, commissioned and premiered Redlich's *Where Now, When Now?*, an expressionist piece about the chaos of contemporary living. Its movements include everyday tasks and actions, and the work incorporates a host of unusual props, such as cardboard boxes, crumpled newspapers, and balloons. Set to a theatrical score by Luciano Berio, the piece creates the impression of a mad world.

A unique contributor to modern dance influenced by Holm and in turn Mary Wigman, Redlich's work has run the gamut from Expressionist but not purely abstract, to occasional moody pieces, to inspired depictions of a world gone awry—though with humor as a frequent collaborator.

—Karen Raugust and Sydonie Benet

REITZ, Dana

American dancer, choreographer, artist, and educator

Born: c. 1948. **Education:** Studied oboe and piano, Rochester, New York; B.S. in dance education, University of Michigan, Ann Arbor, 1970; M.F.A./Research Fellow, Bennington College, Vermont, 1994; trained at the Merce Cunningham studio, studied ballet with Maggie Black and at the New York School of Ballet; also studied kinetic awareness with Elaine Summers, Kathakali, and anatomy for dancers with Andre Bernard. **Career:** Member, Twyla Tharp and Dancers, 1970-71; member, Laura Dean and Dance Company, 1971-72; original cast of *Einstein on the Beach,* by Robert Wilson and Philip Glass, 1976; collaborated with lighting designers Jennifer Tipton, Beverly Emmons, David Finn, and light/ space artist James Turrell; collaborated with filmmakers Dave Gearey and Phill Niblock, vocalist-composer Joan La Barbara, and violinist Malcolm Goldstein; taught at Bennington College, UCLA Department of World Arts and Cultures, Sydney Dance Project (Australia), residency at the Japanese Asia Dance Event (JADE), 1993; performer, Festival d'Automne (Paris), Avignon Festival, Brooklyn Academy of Music's Next Wave Festival, London Dance Umbrella, Kunsthalle (Switzerland), Spoleto Festival (South Carolina), the Kitchen Center (New York City), and Jacob's Pillow; created new solo work, *Unspoken Territory,* for Mikhail Baryshnikov, 1995; toured with Baryshnikov throughout the U.S. performing a program of solos with a duet, *Meeting Place,* 1996; choreographic drawings exhibited at the Pyramid Art Center (Rochester, New York), Walker Art Center (Minneapolis), Paula Cooper Gallery (New York), Franklin Furnace (New York), Art Gallery of Ontario (Toronto), and Les Musées de Marseille (France) as part of a European traveling exhibit. **Awards:** John Simon Guggenheim

Fellowship; National Endowment for the Arts (NEA) choreographer's fellowships; New York Dance and Performance Award ("Bessie") for *Severe Clear,* 1985; New York Dance and Performance Award ("Bessie") for *Circumstantial Evidence,* 1987; Creative Artists Public Service Program of New York; distinguished alumna-in-residence, University of Michigan, 1995.

Works

1973	*3 Piece Set*
1974	*Georgia*
	The Price of Sugar
	Brass Bells
	Grounded
1975	*Dances for Outdoor Space*
	Steps
1977	*Journey: Moves 1 through 7*
	Journey for Two Sides: A Solo Dance Duet
1978	*Phrase, Collection, Versions 1-12*
1979	*Steps*
	Between 2
1980	*4 Scores for Trio*
	Double Scores
	Single Score
1981	*Quintet Project*
	Changing Score
1983	*Field Papers*, collaboration w/Beverly Emmons
1984	*Solo from the Field Papers*
1985	*Severe Clear*, collaboration w/James Turrell
1986	*Movable Dwelling*
	Steps II
	Solo in Silence
1987	*Circumstantial Evidence*, collaboration w/Jennifer Tipton
1988	*Steps III*
1989	*Suspect Terrain* w/Tipton and Hans Peter Kuhn
1990	*White Plains*
1991	*Lichttontanz*
	Les Ondes Sur L'Etang
1992	*Re-Entry*
1993	*Necessary Weather* (costumes by Santo Loquasto)
1995	*Unspoken Territory,* solo for Mikhail Baryshnikov (cos. Loquasto)
	Private Collection
1996	*Meeting Place,* duet with Baryshnikov
	Shoreline

Films and Videotapes

A Collaboration in Vocal Sound & Movement, with vocalist Joan La Barbara, video by David Gearey and Phill Niblock, 1975.
Footage and Branches, with Gearey, 1975.
The Erotic Signal, film excerpt, Walter Gutman, 1978.
Two Sides: A Solo Dance Duet, video for two monitors with Eric Bogosian, 1978.
Mobile Homes, film excerpt, Rudy Burckhardt, 1979.
Severe Clear, documentation project, WGBH/Boston, produced by Susan Dowling, 1985.
Circumstantial Evidence, video, New York, Tom Bowes, 1987.
Suspect Terrain, video, New York, Michael Schwartz, 1989.
Lichttontanz, video, Hartmut Jahn, 1991.

Have You Seen a Moose? and *Wayward Women,* film excerpts, Rudy Burckhardt, 1991.
Airwaves, Once Again, and *3 Locations,* with Gearey, 1994.

Publications

On REITZ: articles—

Anderson, Jack, review, *New York Times,* 12 February 1983.
Clippings file of the Dance Research Collection of the New York Public Library at Lincoln Center.
Dalva, Nancy Vreeland, "Light Matters," *Dance Ink,* Summer 1994.
Dancing Times, London, May 1994.
de Marigny, Chris, *Dance Theatre Journal,* Winter 1993-94.
Dunning, Jennifer, review, *New York Times,* 30 April 1982.
Gopnik, Adam, "Climate of Thought," *Dance Ink,* Summer 1994.
Jowitt, Deborah, "Dana Reitz," *Drama Review,* December 1980.
———, review, *Village Voice,* 21 April 1987.
Schmidt, Jochen, review, *Ballett International,* June/July 1982.
Supree, Burt, interview, *Village Voice,* 15 February 1983.
———, review, *Village Voice,* 14 May 1979.

*   *   *

Dana Reitz is a leading choreographer and dancer of what she calls "performance landscapes." Many of Reitz's works are performed in silence; one of her aims in doing so is to reveal the musicality of the movement itself. She works with some of the dance world's leading performers and lighting directors to create theater pieces that disturb, mystify, and entrance. Her work is vibrantly cerebral without being desiccated. According to dance critic Susan Reiter, Reitz's choreography is characterized by meticulousness, sharpness, and clarity of detail. Reitz—a long-limbed, lithe dancer—works so smoothly that her dances "unfurl with serene logic." Her constant awareness of the place, the time, the aura of the evening, and her own state of mind is part of what makes Reitz's dancing so marvelous, according to Deborah Jowitt. Reitz's inspirations include the work of Merce Cunningham, John Cage, and the intensity of Mark Rothko's paintings. Reitz is artistic director of a not-for-profit organization, Field Papers, Inc.

As a youngster growing up in Rochester, New York, Reitz studied oboe and piano. She became an international exchange student to Japan, attended the University of Michigan at Ann Arbor from 1966-70 and earned a B.S. in dance education with a concentration in biology and theater. Her dance studies included sessions at the Connecticut College Summer School of Dance in New London, Connecticut, and the Long Beach Summer School of Dance, in Long Beach, California, from the middle to late 1960s. Reitz moved to New York City in the early 1970s to continue her dance studies. She was immediately drawn to the style and substance of Merce Cunningham. For ballet, she attended sessions with Barbara Fallis at the New York School of Ballet and with Maggie Black. She was also drawn to Tai Chi Chuan, a traditional Chinese movement regimen characterized by centered balance and fluidity. She began her dance career in earnest as a member of Twyla Tharp and Dancers and also toured with Laura Dean and Dance Company. After many years in the dance field, Reitz received an M.F.A. from Bennington College as a research fellow.

Reitz came to the attention of the dance world in the early 1970s. At that time, according to the late Chris de Marigny of *Dance Theatre Journal,* Reitz was a maverick choreographer and solo dancer on the edges of the postmodern dance movement. She soon became a special favorite among dance lovers. Reitz performed most of her works in total silence to create serene, meditative moods. No other choreographer has devoted herself so entirely to the exploration of silence as Reitz. She usually draws and paints to visualize movement phrasing during the process of creating the movement; and for the past 25 years has developed a highly refined personal technique. She develops intricate yet grounded movements. The plan of each Reitz piece may look minimal and spare, but within the frame of her style, the movements are highly evolved. Gestural details and timing are honed to a point of intense articulation. Some viewers call her style "virtuosic." Reitz's style involves an enormous amount of attentiveness. Jochen Schmidt, reviewing Reitz's performances at the 1981 Vienna Festival in *Ballett International,* found her work quiet, subtle, and femininely elegant. These qualities were pointed out by other critics, too. In her review of *Quintet Project* in the *New York Times,* Jennifer Dunning observed that Reitz's movements and gestures have "the delicacy of porcelain and the purposeful air of counting on fingers." In many of her works she often stays close to the same spot, while working in and around it determinedly.

Reitz works with developing movement from core ideas of action; at one time she described these core ideas as "blueprints" or maps for action. From these blueprints she evolves rhythmic and textural complexities, leaving the final solution or resolution of the choreography to each actual performance. Hence her work is both highly prepared and focused and yet spontaneous. In her dances she tries to find a steady, weighted center from which she can move as quickly or freely as she wants and to which she can return. She doesn't think of the way she moves as being related to any particular codified style of movement; it's a highly refined technique of warm-up and performance. As a dancer, Reitz uses her long and lean body in concentrated and rapid variations as a musician might play Mozart. According to reviewer Burt Supree, writing in the *Village Voice* in 1979, "The constant adjustments and articulations give a strong sense of inquiry to Reitz's dancing. It's as if she is trying the movement on for size. In the center of it all she remains composed and thoughtful. Her poise is perfect and her balance is never at risk. Sometimes what she does seems intensely comedic although this does not seem her intention. Her determination, control, and composure govern the dance."

Reitz has been delving into the nature of light and the mix of light with movement since the 1980s. She regards the use of light as a partner. At first she explored this theme on her own, then in 1983 she collaborated with lighting designer Beverly Emmons on *Field Papers.* Two years later she and light/space artist James Turrell collaborated on *Severe Clear.* Subsequent collaborations took place with well-known lighting designer Jennifer Tipton and in 1987 Reitz invited Tipton to fine-tune *Circumstantial Evidence,* a work Reitz had initially done on her own. The new version was a hit and won a New York Dance and Performance Award or "Bessie." *Suspect Terrain,* a work from 1989, was also a collaboration between Reitz and Tipton, along with audio designer Hans Peter Kuhn. Though what is considered the masterpiece in this vein is Reitz's 1993 *Necessary Weather,* an inquiry into the climates of movement and light—which resulted from a long, involved, exploratory process of over two years.

Reitz has described *Necessary Weather* as "a journey, in silence, along the edges of dream and real time." Two women in white, loose-fitting shirts and pants (designed by Santo Loquasto) move in silence under an even wash of light. As the work develops, the

Dana Reitz performing *Circumstantial Evidence*. **Photograph © Johan Elbers.**

light embodies a series of majestic shapes: a cone of light gives way to a light washing in from the sides of the space, which gives way to a central light. Each time, the light varies in its intensity but is always white. A straw hat, Reitz's trick, catches an intense downshaft of light. It pools in the hat and then shoots upward into the dancers' faces, a stunning creation according to Adam Gopnik of *Dance Ink*. The movement, while suggestive of dreaming, is fluid then jerky, but primarily seems to be about a dialogue. This feeling is sustained even when each dancer performs a solo. The power of Reitz's choreography, Gopnik suggests, rests in its "ability to create, just through light and movement, the rhythm of thought." As Reitz explains it, the dance and light are scored; the movement and light *together* form the "score" of the work and it's the performance that gives it life.

In her work for Mikhail Baryshnikov, *Unspoken Territory* (1995), Reitz worked from a base of core ideas that incorporated the dancer's timing, humor, and ability to create characters while allowing him many "possibilities." In all performances he has the latitude to alter the timing and phrasing of the movement. Clothed in Santo Loquasto's pale peach, short-skirted tunic, the dancer's movements sometimes evoke the hieratic poses of Egyptian statues in which the torso faces front while the head, arms, legs, and feet appear in profile. At other times, the dancer resembles photographs of Nijinsky in his famous *Spectre de la Rose* poses (arms wreathed around his head) or his angled-armed faun from *L'Aprés Midi d'un Faune*. As in previous works, Reitz created an integrated journey of movement, light, and decision-making in which the sense of time stretches—again in collaboration with Jennifer Tipton on the lighting.

In 1983 Reitz presented *Field Papers* at the Brooklyn Academy of Music. In this 70-minute work for four dancers (Sarah Skaggs, Maria Cutrona, Bebe Miller, and Reitz) and a violinist (Malcolm Goldstein), the choreographer investigated how each woman enters, one by one, and involves the performing space. Each dancer remained separate but gradually drew together, only to go their separate ways. Each dancer was given Reitz's signature of unbroken, unhurried twists, curls, and swings. As Jack Anderson observed in his 1983 *New York Times* review, the fact that the piece was performed in silence—except for a musical interlude in which Goldstein played music written for the event—emphasized its sense of immensity.

In 1990 Reitz was a master artist at the Atlantic Center for the Arts in New Smyrna Beach, Florida. Her work sessions investigated the influence of one's thought process and temperament on movement, as well as the influence of the external environment—changes of light, weather, and sound, for example—on one's movement and the influence of movement on the perception of the external environment. Sessions were held at different times of day, both indoors and outdoors.

Reitz believes that every audience and every space changes a piece of choreography; so does the attitude of the dancer. These are beliefs she has come to hold as a result of her 25-year career as a dancer-choreographer; in an interview with Burt Supree of the *Village Voice* in 1983 Reitz maintained that dancing isn't something you do on the outside of your life. As she stated, "There are no guarantees that anyone will like what you're doing. In a way, you meditate in space." Reitz noted that she often sleeps in the dancing space hours before the performance and starts to warm up slowly—turning her body into "liquid." The entire day becomes one vast preparation for the moment. Fully prepared, the dancer lives and is alive in the moment. As Reitz says, "You're ready to make masterful brush strokes; but you're never in charge. And therein lies the excitement."

—Adriane Ruggiero

REPERTORY DANCE THEATRE
American dance company

Resident company of the Capitol Theatre in Salt Lake City, Utah; inspired by Virginia Tanner and founded as a cooperative effort with the Salt Lake City community, University of Utah, and Rockefeller Foundation to help in the decentralization of dance in the U.S. and to preserve many historic American modern dance works, 1966; run initially as a collective with dancers selecting a "troika" of three company members to guide the artistic process, 1969; first summer workshop, 1971; Kennedy Center performance (first Utah company to perform at the Center), 1972; Rockefeller Foundation funds expire, 1974; Linda C. Smith and Kay Clark assume artistic directorship, 1977; first dance company to be featured on the cover of *Smithsonian* magazine, 1980; Smith becomes sole artistic director, 1983; recipient of the Utah Humanities Council Merit Award Project for production of *Separate Journeys,* 1990; featured image for the *International Tanz Festival* in Vienna, Austria, 1992; recipient, Distinguished Service Award, Western Alliance of Arts Administrators, 1992; left University of Utah facilities, 1992; moved to new studios at the Rose Wagner Performing Arts Center, 1997; well-known for its art residency programs in public schools, with projects focused on ecology, literature, history, cultural diversity; repertory includes works from Isadora Duncan, Ruth St. Denis, Ted Shawn, Doris Humphrey, Charles Weidman, Helen Tamiris, José Limón, Merce Cunningham, Laura Dean, and Lucinda Childs.

Works

In addition to 80 works choreographed by RDT dancers while in the company (Bill Evans, Christine Ollerton, Tim Wenger, Richard Rowsell, Kay Clark, Manzell Senters, Joan Moon, Kathleen McClintock, Ruth Post, Linda C. Smith, Martin Karvitz, Karen Steele, Ellen Bromberg, Ron Rubey, Robin Chmelar, Loa Mangelson,

Lynne Wimmer, and Dee Winterton), RDT has commissioned many new and restaged works. Until 1975, pieces premiered at Kingsbury Hall, University of Utah, Salt Lake City; after 1975, at the Capitol Theatre in Salt Lake City.

Newly commissioned works include:

1966	*Cakewalk* (Holder; mus. Holder)
	Summer Canticle (Ririe; mus. Rorem/Reynolds)
1967	*Danse Intime* (Keeler; mus. Stravinsky)
	Free Fall 22/43 (Tetley; mus. Schubel)
1968	*The Initiate* (Butler; mus. Bacewicz, Durko)
	Steps of Silence (Sokolow; mus. Vieru)
	Go Eleven (Woodbury; mus. Lamontaine)
	Recurrencies (Woodbury; mus. Rorem)
1969	*Encounters* (Butler; mus. Subotnick)
	Earth (Sanasardo; mus. Gerhardt)
1970	*Passengers* (Farber)
1971	*Age of Innocence* (Winter; mus. tradl.)
1972	*Five in the Morning* (Farber)
1973	*Opus Jazz Loves Bach* (Mattox; mus. Bach)
	Stationary Flying (Tetley; mus. Crumb)
1974	*Between Me and Other People Is a Table and a Few Empty Chairs* (Muller; mus. Alcantara)
1975	*Session* (Lubovitch)
1977	*Poe* (Sokolow)
1978	*Relief* (Dunn; mus. Driscoll)
1979	*Silent Film* (Diamond; mus. Dlugos/traditional)
	Arcs and Angels (Marks; mus. Bach)
1984	*City Songs* (Jenkins; mus. Rolnick)
1985	*Trappings* (Mangelson; mus. Gregory)
1986	*In the Beginning* (Evans, B.)
	Sacred Cow (Zane and Jones; mus. Nancarrow)
1987	*Peepstone* (Dunn; mus. Debussy, Dylan, Bartlet, Mozart, Gluck)
	Suite Benny (Evans, B.; mus. Goodman)
	Second Skin (Perron; mus. Leroy, Piazolla)
1989	*The Man Who Mistook His Life for a Hat* (Corning; mus. Monk)
	Avalon (Eisenberg; mus. Fowler/Clement)
1991	*Separate Journeys* (Wimmer; mus. Mitchel)
1993	*Erosion* (Gotheiner; mus. Killian)
1995	*Liquid Interior* (Jenkins; mus. Bimstein)
1996	*Watermark* (Evans, F.; mus. Nobis)
	Karyo (McLain; mus. Ruskin)
	Summit (Parsons; mus. Powell)
1997	*Der Mond* (Mead; mus. Orff)
	Turf (Shapiro & Smith; mus. Killian)
	Essence of Rose (Wimmer; mus. tradl.)

Works by local choreographers include:

1981	*Oh, Ghastly Glories of Saints* (Harris)
	The Egg and I (Wood)
1982	*Courtly Dances from Lindsy Gardens* (Harris)
1983	*Wedding* (Harris)
	Skirt Dance (Harris)
	The Foreigner (Wood)
1984	*Dust Bowl* (Debenham)
	Linton in the Next Room
	How We Die (Harris)

Repertory Dance Theater. Dancers: Todd Allen and Rebecca Keene Forde. Deseret News Photo, Kristan Jacobsen.

Dog Tango (Harris)

Green Jello (Harris)

Petrouchka (Harris)

1985   *Beach* (Harris)

Sundancedance (Harris)

1986   *Mont Blanc* (Harris)

1987   *Plurabelles* (Harris)

Bubble Gum and Grooming (Harris)

Still Life (Harris)

TV Dinner, Boys Chorus, A Fine Line (Wood)

1990   *I Will Sing Hallelujah* (White)

1993   *Through a Glass Darkly* (Bell)

Dying Swan (Harris)

Minute Waltz (Harris)

Blue Balls (Harris)

1996   *Bouquet* (Harris)

Charmeuse (Harris)

Publications

Articles—

Stowe, Dorothy, "Keeping Going: The Vision of Repertory Dance Theatre," *Dance Magazine,* April 1980.

Supree, Burt, "American Originals," *Village Voice,* August 1983.

Woodworth, Mark, "RDT—Democracy in Dance," *Dance Magazine,* March 1972.

*   *   *

Repertory Dance Theatre (RDT) of Salt Lake City has been hailed by the *New York Post* as "one of the liveliest and most imaginative modern dance troupes in the world" for its diversity, artistry, and ability to present works old and new—the great classics of American modern dance as well as newly commissioned works. The company's repertory includes many of the great 20th century works of American modern dance by artists such as Isadora Duncan, Ruth St. Denis, Ted Shawn, Doris Humphrey, and Helen Tamiris, as well as contemporary choreographers such as Charles Moulton, Wendy Perron, Shapiro & Smith, and Laura Dean.

Also known as one of the greatest continuing experiments in diversity and democracy in dance, RDT is a modern repertory company run as a collective in which responsibility for everything, including class instruction, touring schedules, repertory, and concert programs, is shared. The company was considered by Clive Barnes (March 1972) to have "the most interesting organizational concept in modern dance." Central to the self-governance of RDT at that time was its town meeting, called when decisions affecting the collective as a whole needed to be made.

In his 1972 *Dance Magazine* article, Mark Woodworth discussed previous experiments in establishing a modern repertory company that had failed, most notably, Helen Tamiris' 1930 Dance Repertory Theatre and José Limón's 1964 American Dance Theatre at Lincoln Center. But RDT's unique democratic character prevailed. Woodworth noted, "Not by trying to be all things to all people, but by exploring a style of working quietly together for the common good, and by fostering awareness of their art, past and present, does Repertory Dance Theatre serve the dance."

Central to obtaining the original Rockefeller funding for RDT was Virginia Tanner, longtime director of the nationally renowned Salt Lake City-based Children's Dance Theater. Tanner had thought of establishing a repertory company that would build a library of American modern dance classics for audiences west of New York City. Tanner had previously invited foundation-funded guest choreographers to Utah to work with the University of Utah Departments of Ballet and Modern Dance. Thus all the components were in place to help the Rockefeller Foundation meet its goals in establishing a new dance company that could serve as a repository for great works of American modern dance as well as new commissions—a site in the western U.S. with a sufficiently technical dance and music base to support a company, a major university offering year-round rehearsal and performance space, and dancers committed to self-governance.

In 1977 the organizational structure changed somewhat and Linda C. Smith and Kay Clark assumed the artistic directorship; in 1983, charter member Linda Smith was selected to direct the company. Even today dancers at RDT plan, administer, and manage the residencies, classes, and workshops so central to their work. Dancers are encouraged to collaborate and give individual input so they have the opportunity to develop their artistic vision and leadership.

In an unpublished manuscript (1990), Smith wrote, "RDT was created. . .as the realization of a dream. It began as an artistic experiment, an exploration of group artistic process, and a challenge." Addressing critics, she wrote, "Audiences seemed eager to accept the variety, but the marketing of such an event was problematic. On the one hand, RDT was praised for its courage and ingenuity, and, on the other, criticized for daring to present the work of artists who were not always on hand to rehearse and coach the Company."

The group has attempted to balance preservation of the heritage of dance with avoidance of exact duplication of classic modern works, which would seem to mimic or date the choreography. Says Smith, "It seems to us that the early dances are like old stories and legends that may change slightly in the telling, but that are filled with the original message and mystery. If we allow the memory of our dance heritage to die, we will suffer an unfathomable loss. Of all the arts, it is in dance most true that we must continue to know our past in order to know our present. . . . There are fewer and fewer dancers who carry the memory of the masters in their muscles. Those threads to the original works are precious beyond measure."

Together, company members develop their understanding about how dances are created, remembered, saved, and retrieved. "The terms 'revival' and 'reconstruction' do not adequately describe our project" Smith said in a 1996 interview. "We're celebrating a great era of expression, exploration, enthusiasm, and personal statement. There needs to be this dance thread, a dance literacy."

The participation required of the dancers, the exposure to many different styles, and the relative isolation of the company certainly influences the kinds of works RDT produces and performs. The company is seen as having a humanistic orientation, often dramatic, with an emphasis on exploration of content rather than experimentation with form.

The company tours extensively. According to former company manager Don Anderson, "Touring has always been a staple in RDT's activities. In addition to extensive tours throughout Utah and the West, the company continues to bring quality dance to communities large and small from Alaska to Florida. It was the first dance company to bring fully produced dance performances to the isolated communities of Alaska. . .with people traveling many miles from the surrounding wilderness to attend the performances."

Besides giving performances, RDT dancers also teach on tour. Their lecture-demonstrations are narrated programs, designed to inform the audience about the creative process and the connections between art, history, and the humanities. The company produces model programs and curriculum packages to educate and inspire children of all ages, building an audience for dance.

The company holds firm to the belief that modern dance is neither derivative nor imitative. "In the lexicon of modern dance, they're one of the most important companies we have—a repository for all of the major voices in the art form," stated Nolan Dennett, director of the dance program at Western Washington University. "Every significant choreographer in modern dance has set work on this company. The dances are simply beautiful in the way a harsh landscape can be beautiful, some have a mythic quality, others burst with the passion of youth."

—Gigi Berardi

REVELATIONS

Choreography: Alvin Ailey
Music: Traditional spirituals
First Production: Alvin Ailey American Dance Theatre, New York, 31 January 1960
Set Design: Laurence Maldonado
Lighting Design: Nicola Cernovich
Costume Design: Laurence Maldonado; later productions (after 1960), Ves Harper
Original Dancers: Joan Derby, Merle Derby, Jay Fletcher, Gene Hobgood, Nathaniel Horne, Herman Howell, Minnie Marshall, Nancy Redi, and Dorene Richardson

Publications

Articles—

Ailey, Alvin, "Roots of the Blues," *Dance and Dancers*, November 1961.
Harrold, Robert, "The Splendid Alvin Ailey," *Dancing Times*, May 1965.

*   *   *

Revelations tells a story of African-American faith and tenacity from slavery to freedom through a suite of dances set to religious music. Created by Alvin Ailey very early in his choreographic career, *Revelations* quickly became the signature work of the Alvin Ailey American Dance Theatre. It has been performed by that company on nearly every program since its premiere, and by 1995 had been seen by more people in the world than any other modern dance work.

Although explicitly concerned with the sacred music of African-American religion, the dance speaks to anyone who has ever felt oppression or channeled subjugation into religious faith. Ailey intended for the dance to be the second part of a larger, evening-length survey of African-American music which had been begun in 1958 with his work *Blues Suite*. While that plan was never fully realized, *Revelations* occupies a singular position as a dance of exquisite organization and infallible theatricality, at once unerringly simple and panoramic in its historical scope.

Revelations was created in bits and pieces. At its premiere, the dance had 15 selections, a live chorus of singers including two onstage soloists, and lasted over an hour. Sections later excised included a woman's solo and trio. Ailey did not dance in the world premiere, but as the early company personnel shifted, he performed some of its group sections as solos. An extensive tour of the Far East in 1962, sponsored by the U.S. State Department, forced Ailey to put the music for *Revelations* on tape, and the dance solidified into the three-part format familiar today. From its original scoring for guitar, percussion and voice, the piece is now also accompanied by gospel keyboards, drums and electric bass.

"Pilgrim of Sorrow," the opening Brown section, is devoted to the oldest and darkest spirituals, which Ailey described as "songs that yearn for deliverance, that speak of trouble, [and] of this world's trials and tribulations." The somber musical mood is reflected in muted lighting effects, brown and skin-toned costuming, and most profoundly, in movement terms, as the dancers perform abstract gestures with heads bowed and weighted bodies reaching powerfully upward. In "I've Been 'Buked," nine dancers work in hushed accord, performing a ritual of communal introspection. The "Fix Me, Jesus" duet of this section is a masterpiece of invention, as it conveys the strength of faith between a woman and her pastor through a subtle unfolding of leanings, balances, and leg extensions that speak of trust and the conviction of belief.

The second, White section, titled "Take Me to the Water," features an enactment of a ceremonial baptism. A large group of dancers clad in white sweep onto the stage as baptismal agents—a tree branch to sweep the earth, and a white cloth to cleanse the sky—lead a processional to the stream of purification. To the strains of "Wade in the Water," a devotional leader bearing a large umbrella baptizes a young couple at a river represented by yards of billowing blue silk stretched across the stage. The raucous ceremony is followed by the meditative solo "I Wanna Be Ready," which movingly communicates a devout man's preparations for death. Created by Ailey in collaboration with its original dancer James Truitte, the solo builds on exercises derived from the Horton technique.

"Move, Members, Move!" celebrates the liberating power of 20th-century gospel music. This part includes the Black section, the propulsive men's trio "Sinner Man," as well as the famous Yellow section, set in a southern Baptist rural church sanctuary. Eighteen dancers resplendent in yellow costumes enact a church service with simple props of fans and stools. Stretched across the stage with torsos proudly lifted, the dancers embody the joy of faith contained by complex stepping patterns performed in unison. A sense of humor and physical resiliency end the dance on a high note which rarely fails to bring the audience to its feet, clapping and cheering with the performers.

—Thomas DeFrantz

REYNA, Rosa
Mexican dancer, educator, choreographer, and researcher

Born: Rosa María Reyna y Salceda, 26 August 1924, in Mexico City. **Education:** Studied at the National Dance School (NDS) with Hipólito Zybin, 1932-34; studied with Anna Sokolow, Sergio Unger, Nelsy Dambre, Nini Theilade, Cynthia Richeliu, Adolf Bolm, Xavier Francis, Gene McDonald, Merce Cunningham, James Smith, Teodor Koslov, José Limón, Lucas Hoving, David Wood, Seki Sano,

Salvador Novo, Casilda Girard, Jesús Velasco, Jesús Durán, Mary Anthony, Alejandro Jorodowsky, Michael Lland, and Yuriko; awarded a grant to attend Connecticut College, 1952; took courses with Martha Graham, Louis Horst, Doris Humphrey, José Limón, Lucas Hoving, Sophie Maslow, Robert Cohan, Else Kresslinger, and Pauline Kohner; also attended New York–based schools of Martha Graham, Nikolais, Alvin Ailey and Luigi; Cuban methodology of teaching classical technique, 1975-76; music and body expression for drama with N. Lazariev, Bernard Aucouturier, Erik Nielsen and Heidi Weidlich, 1980; studied architecture at National Autonomous University of Mexico, 1939-43; graduate courses in art history; holds B.A. and M.A. degrees in artistic education and research. **Career:** Founder and dancer, the Blue Dove, first modern dance group in Mexico, directed by Anna Sokolow, 1939-40; dancer/choreographer for Mexican Dance Academy of the NIFA, under different names, 1948-62; dancer of Concert Ballet, 1953; dancer of Dance Concerts of Guillermo Keys, with works by Anna Sokolow, 1953; dancer and choreographer in the Quintet Ballet, 1954-55; dancer/choreographer and director/coordinator, Contemporary Mexico Ballet, 1963-66; dancer, Fine Arts Ballet, 1960-62; jury member, National Folklore Competition, NIFA, 1964, 1967; dance coordinator of International Culture Promotion Organization (OPIC), 1965-67; coordinator, 19th Olympic Games Organizing Committee (Mexico City), 1968; co-director/coordinator, technical consultant, choreographer and teacher of the Folkloric Ballet of Mexico, 1966-75; director/choreographer, first Folkloric Ballet of El Salvador and Central American Ballet, 1975; founder and technical consultant, Dance Council, 1976-78; artistic education programmer, National Education System, 1975-77, and 1980; vice-president, National Committee of the International Dance Board, 1979; artistic education programming, National Education System, 1980; programming, Culture House, NIFA, 1980-81; researcher, CENIDI-Danza "José Limón," NIFA, 1983—. **Awards:** Homage to her artistic value in Guadalajara, Jalisco, 1972; meritorious medal for teachings and a diploma for her educational work over 30 years, 1983; homage "A Life in Dance," NIFA, 1985.

Roles (performances in Mexico City unless otherwise noted)

1940   *Entre sombras anda el fuego* (*Fire Moves among Shadows*) (Sokolow), Mexican Group of Classic and Modern Dance

The baker, *La madrugada del panadero* (*The Baker's Dawn*) (Sokolow), Mexican Group of Classic and Modern Dance

A cat, *El renacuajo paseador* (*The Meandering Tadpole*) (Sokolow), Anna Sokolow with the Blue Dove

A sacerdotal arabesque, *Don Lindo de Almería* (Sokolow), Anna Sokolow with the Blue Dove

1945   *Preludios y mazurcas* (*Preludes and Mazurkas*) (Sokolow), Anna Sokolow and her ballet group

Danzas sobre temas rusos (*Russian Themes' Dances*) (Sokolow), Anna Sokolow and her ballet group

1949   The baker, *La madrugada del panadero* (*The Baker's Dawn*) (Sokolow), Mexican Dance Academy

Fecundidad (*Fertility*) (Keys), Mexican Dance Academy

1951   *Los cuatro soles* (*The Four Suns*) (Limón), Mexican Ballet, Mexican Academy of Dance

Mrs. Mouse, *El renacuajo paseador* (*The Meandering Tadpole*) (Sokolow), Mexican Ballet

Imaginerías (*Imagery*) (Francis), Mexican Ballet

Pasacalle (*Passacaglia*) (Humphrey), Mexican Ballet

Antígona (*Antigone*) (Limón), Mexican Ballet

A woman, *Redes* (*Nets*) (Limón), Mexican Ballet

1952   Mother Earth, *La balada mágica o Danza de las cuatro estaciones* (*The Magic Ballad, or Dance of Four Seasons*) (Arriaga), Mexican Ballet

La Valse (Gutiérrez), Mexican Ballet

Lucero and Sensemayá, *Sensemayá* (Bracho), Mexican Ballet

1953   *Suite italiana* (*Italian Suite*) (Jordán), Mexican Ballet

Al aire libre (*On the Open Air*) (Mérida), Mexican Ballet

1954   The nightingale, *Los pájaros* (*The Birds*) (Bracho), Mexican Ballet

A note, *El rincón de los niños* (*The Children's Corner*) (Peñalosa), Mexican Ballet

The dreams' seller, *Tienda de sueños* (*Dreams Shop*) (Keys), Mexican Ballet

A cloud and the moon, *La balada del venado y la luna* (*The Moon and the Deer Ballad*) (Mérida), Quintet Ballet

Corona de espinas (*Thorn Crown*) (Montoya), Quintet Ballet

Quinteto (*Quintet*) (Montoya), Quintet Ballet

Psique (*Psyque*) (Mérida), Mexican Ballet

1956   *Divertimiento* (*Divertissement*) (Bracho), Mexican Ballet

The general's wife, *Ballet 1910* (Martínez), Mexican Ballet

An angel, *Tonanzintla* (Limón), Mexican Ballet

1958   *El encuentro* (*The Meeting*) (Sakmari), Contemporary Ballet

Los payasos (*The Clowns*) (Sakmari), Contemporary Ballet

Ellas (*They*) (Sakmari), Contemporary Ballet

Quinteto (*Quintet*) (De Bernal), Contemporary Ballet

The moon, *El nacimiento de las Amazonas* (*The Birth of the Amazon*) (Gutiérrez), Contemporary Ballet

Huapango (Bracho), Contemporary Ballet

1959   *La culebra* (*The Snake*) (Benavides), Fine Arts Ballet

1960   *Orfeo* (*Orpheus*) (Sokolow), Fine Arts Ballet

She, *El hombre de barro* (*The Earth Man*) (Sakmari), Fine Arts Ballet

Opus 1960 (Sokolow), Fine Arts Ballet

Interludio (*Interlude*) (Lavalle), Fine Arts Ballet

Santa María 2 a.m. (*Saint Mary 2 a.m.*) (De Bernal), Fine Arts Ballet

1961   *MissaBrevis* (Limón), Fine Arts Ballet

Ofrenda musical (*Musical Offering*) (Sokolow), Fine Arts Ballet

Sueños (*Dreams*) (Sokolow), Fine Arts Ballet

1962   *La visita* (*The Visit*) (Bracho), Fine Arts Ballet

Intramuros (*Intramurally*) (Ortega), Fine Arts Ballet

The spider, *Fantasía* (*Fantasy*) (Sakmari), Fine Arts Ballet

Triángulo de silencios (*Triangle Silence*) (Mérida), Fine Arts Ballet

1966   *En el principio* (*At the Beginning*) (De Bernal), Contemporary Ballet of Mexico

Presencias (*Presences*) (Agüeria), Contemporary Ballet of Mexico

Todos somos extraños (*We Are All Strangers*) (Sakmari),
    Contemporary Ballet of Mexico
Movimientos de percusion (*Percussion Movements*)
    (Beristáin), Contemporary Ballet of Mexico

Works (performances in Mexico City unless otherwise noted)

1949   *Suite* (with Martha Bracho) (mus. Scarlatti-Casella),
        Mexican Dance Academy
1951   *La manda* (mus. Galindo), Mexican Ballet, Mexican Dance
        Academy
        Pastillita o La muñeca Pastillita (*Pastillita, or the Doll
        Pastillita*) (mus. Jiménez Mabarak), Mexican Dance
        Academy
1952   *La hija del Yori* (*The Daughter of Yori*) (mus. Galindo),
        Mexican Ballet
1953   *La Anunciación* (*The Annunciation*) (mus. Jiménez
        Mabarak), Mexican Ballet
1954   *Serenata* (*Serenade*) (mus. Mozart), Mexican Ballet
1956   *Gorgonio Esparza* (mus. Velázquez), Mexican Ballet
1957   *La Pascola* (mus. Galindo), Mexican Ballet
1958   *Movimiento perpetuo* (*Perpetual Movement*) (mus. Henry
        & Schaeffer), Fine Arts Ballet
1960   *Visiones fugitivas* (*Fugitive Visions*) (mus. Prokofieff-
        Adomian), Fine Arts Ballet
1962   *Presagios* (Owens) (mus. Chávez), Fine Arts Ballet
        La pausa de la risa (*The Laughter Pause*) (collective
        chor.), Fine Arts Ballet
1966   *Cinco de siete días* (*Five of Seven Days*) (mus. Albertine,
        El Dabband Abbit), Contemporary Ballet
1972   *Aquí* (*Here*) (poem by Octavio Paz)
1974   *Enlaces* (*Links*) (mus. anonymous, XII and XIII centu-
        ries)
1976   *Otoño de búsqueda* (*Searching Autumn*) (mus. Velázquez)
        Tiempos: ayer, hoy, quizá mañana (*Times: Yesterday, To-
        day, Maybe Tomorrow*) (mus. Henríquez)
1988   *Evocación* (*Evocation: Homage to José Limón*), Culiacán,
        Sinaloa, Culture Festival of Sinaloa

Other works include: Choreographer for mass spectacles, theater
works, films, television, and opera.

Publications

On REYNA: books—

50 años de danza en el Palacio de Bellas Artes, Mexico City, 1984.
Ramírez, Elisa, "Rosa Reyna," *Homenaje Una vida en la danza
    1985*, Mexico City, 1985.
Tortajada Margarita, *Mujeres de danza combativa*, Mexico City,
    1997.
Tortajada Quiroz, Margarita, *Danza y poder*, Mexico City, 1995.

Films and Videotapes

La Manda, filmed in Moscow, directed by Alexandrov, 1957.

*   *   *

The memory of Rosa Reyna as a dancer has been preserved over
the years. Many of her contemporaries concur that she was the
best Mexican dancer of the nationalist modern dance stage. The
criticism confirms this appraisal, as does the fact that she was
chosen by José Limón as his partner in *Antigone* (1951), and that
she was a favorite performer of numerous Mexican and foreign
choreographers who worked in that period (including Anna
Sokolow). This was not only due to her expressiveness and great
passion, but also to her versatile technique; she was capable of
moving the public and other dancers.

Besides being a fruitful choreographer, a devoted teacher, and a
demanding director, Reyna has become a leading authority on dance,
and her experience has led to her participation in several educational and research projects. As a child, Reyna entered the National
School of Dance, where she was instructed by the Russian teacher
Hipólito Zybin. When she left the school she continued to take
classes with this teacher until 1939, when she was introduced to
modern dance through Anna Sokolow. Despite the social prejudices
she confronted while pursuing dance (especially modern dance) as
a profession, Reyna fully solidified her commitment and became
one of the Sokolovas who have followed their teacher's principles
through the decades.

Sokolow showed Reyna a new panorama within the dance; she
taught her exigency and integrity. From then on, Reyna started to
believe in a dance which is born from the body's center and emphasizes content over form, yet at the same time demands a strict
discipline. At this time Reyna entered the group founded and directed by Sokolow, the Mexican Group of Classic and Modern
Dances, known afterwards as the Blue Dove, the name of the society which supported it. There she had the opportunity to work
with the North American choreographer, but also to make contact
with Mexican artists and the group of Spanish refugees consisting
of Rodolfo Halffter, José Bergamín, Antonio Ruiz, Ignacio Aguirre,
Silvestre Revueltas and Manuel Rodríguez Lozano, among others.

In 1940 Reyna made her professional debut as a part of the
original cast of the works Sokolow performed for the first time in
Mexico City: *Fire Moves among Shadows*, *The Baker's Dawn*, *The
Meandering Tadpole*, and *Don Lindo de Almería*. While Sokolow
did not maintain the objective of creating a nationalist dance, she
did inspire Reyna to develop in this sense. After a very difficult
period for modern dance, due to its marginal acceptance, a new
boom began in 1947. After a year, Sokolow returned to Mexico
City to work with the Mexican Dance Academy, and immediately
asked the Sokolovas, including Reyna, to join. The result of this
work was the staging of several very successful operas.

In 1949, the Academy entered a new dance season without the
presence of Sokolow, in which Reyna, together with Martha Bracho,
debuted her first choreography—*Suite*. Two years later, counting
on the presence of José Limón, Lucas Hoving, and Doris Humphrey,
a new dance season began under the aegis of the Mexican Ballet of
the Mexican Dance Academy. At these performances Reyna was
revealed as a great choreographer, presenting *La Manda*, which is
highly regarded as one of the most representative works of the
nationalist modern dance movement in Mexico. *La Manda*'s music
is an original score by Blas Galindo; the libretto was written by
José Durand (based on the story *Talpa*, by Juan Rulfo); the scenery
and costumes were designed by José Chávez Morado. Miguel
Covarrubias (chief of the Dance Department, NIFA and a leading
promoter of Mexican Ballet), referred to this Mexican work as
vigorous, original, and daring. Over the years many critics have
expressed their opinions, always agreeing on its well-understood
and authentic nationalism. In 1957 the Russian film director
Alexandrov (co-author, with Eisenstein of the film *Thunder Over*

México) filmed this work. That same year *La Manda* was applauded by audiences in Italy, Romania, and China, despite the fact that in China it was retired from the repertory after officials determined that its love triangle was unsuitable material for public viewing. *La Manda* was also included in the television series designed by the Educational Television Unit of the Public Education Secretary in 1984.

In addition to *La Manda*, Reyna danced many other choreographies of the Mexican Ballet's season in 1951 and 1952, including those by Limón and Humphrey. Among the most notable of these is her performance as *Antigone* in the ballet Limón created for her, dancing "Kreon" himself. This duet is renowned for their mutual understanding as expressive and passionate artists. As a result of her work, Reyna was awarded a grant in 1952 to study at Connecticut College. In addition to participating in the Mexican Ballet of the Mexican Dance Academy, Reyna was invited to several companies as a dancer: Concert Ballet, the Dance Concerts presented by Guillermo Keys, and Quintet Ballet, which gathered the five most prominent dancers of the era. However, the tour that proved to be the most important one for Mexican dance and for Reyna herself, was the one made by the Contemporary Ballet of México in 1957. Under Reyna's artistic direction, the Contemporary Ballet was invited to participate in the 7th Youth Festival in Moscow. There the company attracted the public's attention and were flattered by audiences and other dancers; nevertheless, the Russian authorities could not understand the nationalist modern dance. After the Festival, the Contemporary Ballet was invited to tour China, Romania, and Italy. With increased awareness of developments in international modern dance, the dancers initiated several new proposals upon their return to Mexico after six months of touring.

One of the most innovative and controversial of the new works was Reyna's *Perpetual Movement* (1958), to music by Henry and Schaeffer, with libretto by Emilio Carballido and scenery and costumes by José Cava. The critics were divided in their opinions; some of them praised the innovative approach, while others denied even the possibility of a different path for nationalist dance. However, Reyna succeeded in introducing a new type of choreographic creation. After drastic shifts in the state-sponsored dance and the disappearance of the Fine Arts Ballet, Reyna founded an independent, experimental company—the Contemporary México Ballet (1963)—which would become the last bastion of nationalist modern dance. However, it lacked funding and disappeared in 1966, despite the fact that it had performed throughout the country and had toured several U.S. universities.

From 1966 on, Reyna concentrated on teaching (an area in which she had been active since 1948), and worked as coordinator, consultant, and choreographer for several companies, including the Folkloric Ballet of México, the Folkloric Ballet of El Salvador and the Central American Ballet. Her participation has been fundamental in diverse educational institutions, where she has directed dance training: Artistic Education Centers, the Culture Houses, Artistic Area of the Educational Methods and Contents General Direction, Artistic Education of NIFA, and the National Educational System. Reyna is also founder and researcher (1983) of the Dance Research, Documentation and Information National Center "José Limón," where she has developed several research and promotional projects. Since 1994, she has been a member of the National System of Creators, artistic education at NIFA and Public Education system.

—Margarita Tortajada Quiroz
translated by Dolores Ponce Gutiérrez

RIRIE-WOODBURY DANCE COMPANY
American dance company

Formed as a collective of dancers, Choreodancers, 1953; established as Ririe-Woodbury Dance Company, 1964; invited to become part of the National Endowment for the Arts' Artists in Schools and Dance Touring programs, 1972; earned the distinction of the most National Endowment Artists in Schools bookings of any other company, from 1974-86; Bronze Award, 100 Best Public Service Advertising, 1987; Gold Star Award, Dance in Education, Dance on Camera, for *Teaching Beginning Dance Improvisation,* a videotape/workbook teaching package, 1989; Governor's Award in the Arts, Salt Lake City, 1990; Artists of the Year Award, Utah Alliance for the Arts and Humanities, 1992; chosen to be part of the Dance on Tour state-touring program from 1990 to 1994.

Works

Premieres at Kingsbury Hall, the University of Utah, in Salt Lake City from 1948 to 1985; after 1985, at the Capitol Theatre, unless otherwise noted.

1948	*Mister Chipmunk* (Ririe; solo; mus. Lindsay)
1949	*The Hill above the Mine* (Ririe; solo; mus. Bartók)
1950	*Ferdinand the Bull* (Ririe; mus. Dewsnup)
1951	*The High and the Low Place* (duet, Woodbury; mus. Haws), performed by Woodbury and Ruth Elew, University of Wisconsin dance studios, Madison
1952	*Allegro* (Woodbury; mus. Bartók)
	Feminine Gender (Woodbury; solo; mus. Mendum)
	Sing Sorrow (Ririe; solo; mus. Old English Ballad), YMHA, New York
1953	*Hoops* (Ririe; mus. Villa Lobos)
	On the Boards (Ririe and Woodbury; mus. Walton)
	Lord's Prayer (Ririe), students, Brigham Young University dance studios, Provo
	World Changers (Woodbury; mus. Dewsnup, Genther)
	Salem Episode (Woodbury; mus. Dewsnup)
1954	*Summer Interlude* (Ririe; mus. Kenton)
	Blood Wedding (Ririe and Woodbury; mus. Fowler)
	Haiku (Woodbury; solo; mus. Dalby)
	The Splendor Falls (Woodbury; mus. Britton)
1955	*Family Album* (Ririe; mus. Gould)
	The Sporting Scene (Woodbury; mus. Bowles)
1956	*Fads and Fancies* (Ririe; mus. Dello Joio)
	New York (Ririe; mus. Milhaud)
	Chow Wilie (Ririe; mus. Old English Ballad)
	Figure of the Moon (Woodbury; solo; mus. Kessler), Mary Wigman studios, Berlin
	Inside Myself (Woodbury; solo; mus. Kessler), Mary Wigman studios, Berlin
	Furucht (Woodbury; solo; mus. Kessler), Mary Wigman studios, Berlin
	Trio 1,2,3 (Woodbury; mus. Kessler), Mary Wigman studios, Berlin
1957	*Lonely Is the Heart* (Ririe; mus. Hovhaness)
	Haiku (Ririe; mus. Dalby)
	Screen Test (Ririe; mus. orig. percussion)
	Toccata for Percussion (Woodbury; mus. Carlos)
	Gopac (Woodbury; mus. Mussorgsky)

1958   *Duotoccata* (Ririe and Woodbury; duet; mus. Russon)
     Our Town (Ririe; mus. Copland)
     Monotony (Woodbury; solo; mus. Kenton)
     Love in the Dictionary (Woodbury; mus. Dougherty)

1959   *Antic Semantics* (Ririe; mus. sound collage)
     Rat Races and Other Ruts (Woodbury; mus. Fowler)

1960   *Allegro con Brio* (Woodbury; mus. Craig)

1961   *Seasonal Episodes* (Ririe; mus. Hatton)
     The Pearl (Woodbury; mus. Fowler)
     Vivance (Ririe; mus. Nussio)

1962   *Four Transparencies* (Ririe with Woodbury; mus. Nikolais)
     Flickers (Ririe; mus. Von Suppe and others)
     From Israel (Woodbury; mus. Israeli Folk music)
     Striped Celebrants (Totem) (Nikolais; mus. Bach)

1963   *Lochinvar* (Ririe)
     Absurd Concert (Ririe and Woodbury; mus. sound collage)
     Odes from Antigone (Woodbury; mus. Prigmore)

1964   *Exados* (Woodbury; mus. Rosenthal)
     Suite de Danse, Landscapes (Louis), RWDC

1965   *Life Song* (Ririe and Woodbury; mus. sound collage/live music)

1966   *Progressions* (Ririe and Woodbury; mus. Norem)
     Psychology of Cinema (Ririe and Woodbury; mus. sound collage), Orson Spencer Hall, University of Utah, Salt Lake City

1967   *Black Box* (Ririe and Woodbury), Pioneer Memorial Theatre, University of Utah
     Abe Feder Light Show (Ririe and Woodbury; mus. live rock music), outdoor performance, University of Utah, Salt Lake City
     Absurdities (Ririe and Woodbury; mus. sound collage), RWDC and students
     Sculpture Garden (Ririe and Woodbury; mus. Rorem)

1968   *Now* (Ririe; mus. Caulfield)

1969   *Light and Sound* (Ririe and Woodbury; mus. sound collage), Dance Department studios, University of Utah, Salt Lake City
     Fall Gently on the Head (Keuter), RWDC

1970   *Some Sounds* (Ririe; mus. Norem)
     Incantation (Woodbury; mus. LaMontaine)

1971   *Prisms* (Ririe; mus. Steiner)
     Everybody Can Dance (Ririe; mus. traditional and sound collage), RWDC, Capitol Theatre
     Affectionate Infirmities (Woodbury; mus. Mozart), Carleton College dance studios, RWDC, Carleton College, Northfield, Minnesota
     Flight Pay (Woodbury)

1972   *Line of Action* (Ririe; mus. sound collage), RWDC
     Bus Stop (solo; Woodbury; mus. sound collage), perf. by Ririe
     Games People Play (Winterton), RWDC
     Deeper and to the Right (Pelsmaeker), RWDC
     Charity (Renner), RWDC
     Walking Dance (Paxton), RWDC

1973   *Passing Change* (Ririe; mus. Goldberg, Steiner)
     Clouds (Ririe; mus. Byrd/Mascowitz), RWDC
     Coverings (Woodbury; mus. sound collage), RWDC

1974   *Paper Piece* (Ririe; mus. Steiner), RWDC, Northrup Hall, Minneapolis
     Who's in the Center Ring (Woodbury; mus. sound collage)
     Overlay (Clawson; mus. Gaburo), RWDC

1975   *Morning, Noon, Night* (Ririe; mus. Brunner)
     Fabrik (Woodbury; mus. Brunner)

1976   *Feet Feats* (Ririe; mus. Stravinsky)
     Boxes, etc. (Woodbury; mus. sound collage)

1977   *Collection* (Ririe; mus. Stravinsky)
     Physalia (Chase and Pendleton; mus. Dennis), RWDC, Capitol Theatre
     June, Where Are You? (Clawson; mus. Steiner), RWDC, Mesa, Arizona

1978   *Various Apparitions* (Ririe; solo; mus. Steiner), RWDC, Capitol Theatre
     No-Where Bird (Woodbury; mus. sound collage)
     Seven Easy Pieces (Woodbury; mus. classical, arr. for guitar)
     Vis-a-Vis (Bailin; mus. Vivaldi), RWDC, Capitol Theatre
     Forest Dreams (Beal; mus. Lande), RWDC, Capitol Theatre

1979   *Symmteria* (Ririe; mus. Crumb)
     Solo Concert (Ririe; solo; mus. Bach, Steiner, Ursula), University of Utah Museum of Art, Salt Lake City
     Traveling (Ririe; mus. live percussion), students, Jefferson High School, Portland, Oregon
     Diverse Creatures (Woodbury; mus. Scoville), Hayes-Christensen Theater, Alice Sheets Marriott Center for Dance
     Dummy Waltz (Woodbury; mus. Harmonica Gold), Hayes-Christensen Theater, Alice Sheets Marriott Center for Dance
     Proximities (Louis; mus. Brahms), RWDC, Capitol Theatre

1980   *Shy Hag's Magic Shadow Show* (Ririe, Keller, Woodbury, company; mus. Beach), RWDC, Capitol Theatre
     Jazz as Is (Ririe, Woodbury, company; mus. Jackstein), RWDC, Capitol Theatre
     Crowds-Collective Behavior (Ririe; mus. sound collage)
     Ha'Shoa (Ririe; mus. Penderecki)
     Sixteen Plus Two (Woodbury; mus. Siegel), students, University of West Virginia dance studios, Charleston
     Golden Oldies (Woodbury; mus. 1920s traditional), Hayes-Christensen Theater, Alice Sheets Marriott Center for Dance

1981   *Couples* (Ririe; mus. Cage, Stockhausen, Nobis)
     Poetics of Space (Woodbury; mus. Scoville and others)
     Glances (Louis; mus. Brubeck), RWDC, Capitol Theatre

1982   *Don't Kick Her One Minute & Swoon Over Her the Next* (Ririe; mus. Koplowitz), RWDC, Capitol Theatre
     Mattress, Mayhem, and Motorcycles (Ririe; mus. Koplowitz)
     Mixed Doubles (Woodbury; mus. Rovner)

1983   *Stromkarlen* (Ririe; mus. Lundsten), RWDC, Capitol Theatre
     White Solo (Ririe and Mangelson; mus. sound collage by Ririe and Russell), RWDC, Capitol Theatre
     Departures (Woodbury; mus. Crosby and Kranes)
     Musings (Woodbury; solo; mus. Debussy), performed by Renner, Snowbird Institute Plaza, Snowbird, Utah

1984   *It's the Rage* (Ririe; mus. Koplowitz)
     Imposures (Ririe; mus. Bley)
     Break Out (Ririe; mus. Bley)
     In Our Own Image (Pearson; mus. Penguin Cafe), RWDC, Capitol Theatre

Calligraph for Martyrs (Louis; mus. Nikolais), RWDC, Capitol Theatre

Future History (White; mus. Hassell, Eno), RWDC, Capitol Theatre, Salt Lake City

Encircled Embrace (Clawson; mus. Monk, Story), RWDC, Capitol Theatre

1985 *The Electronic Dance Transformer* (Ririe and Woodbury; mus. Jackman, Rouvner, Koplowitz), RWDC

Sheepherder's Saga (Ririe; mus. Poulenc, arr. by Banham)

Dominoes (Woodbury; mus. Gregory)

Three Day Guest (Woodbury; solo; mus. Brunner), performed by Phyllis Haskell, Speech and Drama Theater, University of Hawaii, Honolulu

Unaccompanied Achilles (Woodbury; mus. Lynch)

Kites (Woodbury; mus. Shadowfax)

Craps (Evans; mus. LaBarbera/Johnson), RWDC

Creation du Monde (Beal; mus. Milhaud), RWDC

Gracie (Beal; mus. Scoville), performed by Ririe

1986 *Mattress II* (Ririe; mus. Miklavcic), RWDC

ATHLETIKINETICS (Ririe; mus. Miklavcic), RWDC

Videovisions (Ririe), RWDC

Girls with Hair/Soft Camera (mus. Franke, Frosese, Schmoelling)

One-two-one Repression (mus. Franke, Frosese, Schmoelling)

Electronic Shuffle (mus. Holliday)

Plastic Solarization (mus. Markosian)

Quan and Quin Split (mus. Shkieve/Schulze)

In Stages (Woodbury; mus. Markosian), students, Kingsbury Hall

Craps (Evans; mus. Bill Evans Trio), RWDC

Talisman (Nikolais; mus. Nikolais), RWDC

A Woman's Influence (Smith; mus. Byrne, Eno), RWDC

1987 *Movie Moves* (Ririe; mus. Rota), RWDC

Day Watchers (Topovski; mus. Markosian), RWDC

Stonefields, Light Part II (Takei), RWDC

A Masque (White; mus. traditional medieval), RWDC

Cello Suites (Morgan; mus. Bach), RWDC

1988 *Windows* (Ririe; mus. Scoville, Miklavcic, Pond), students, Kingsbury Hall

Refusal to Dance (Woodbury, Todd Woodbury, VanDam; mus. Scoville), students and guest artists, Hayes-Christensen Theater, Alice Sheets Marriott Center for Dance

White (Mead; mus. Adams), RWDC

On a Walk (Nugent; mus. Oboe Lee), RWDC

Developing the Bunyip (Hampton; mus. Torque, Houppin), RWDC

No Pasaran (Hampton; mus. Jones), RWDC

Night Flight (Melrose; mus. Ashley, Maxfield)

Coffee Never Tasted So Good (Melrose; mus. Bach), RWDC

1989 *To Have and to Hold* (Shapiro & Smith; mus. Killian), RWDC

1990 *Banners of Freedom* (Ririe; mus. Beck), students, Kingsbury Hall

Madam X (Ririe; mus. DePonte), students, Kingsbury Hall

Circular Panning (Ririe; mus. Byrd), RWDC

Ladies, Ladies, Ladies (Woodbury, Saliva Sisters; mus. Saliva Sisters), RWDC

Episodes (Woodbury; mus. Wallace), students, Hayes-Christensen Theater, Alice Sheets Marriott Center for Dance

Unannounced Interruption (Johnson; mus. sound collage), RWDC

Blue Horses (Johnson; mus. Chopin), RWDC

1991 *Walls* (Ririe and Woodbury; mus. sound collage), RWDC, Opera House, Chemnitz, Germany

L'invasion (Woodbury, Cathey guitarists; mus. Gnatalli), students, Hayes-Christensen Theater, Alice Sheets Marriott Center for Dance

The Inky Deep (Nielsen; mus. Eric), RWDC

Wreck a Pair (Nielsen; mus. Scrambled, Tchaikovsky, Fink), RWDC

1992 *Three Aspects of the Moon* (Ririe; mus. Hulse), RWDC

GeBungee (Ririe; mus. Pond), RWDC

A Dancer and a Stool (Larson; mus. Poulenc), RWDC

Kitchen Table (Dennett; mus. Kronos String Quartet, Lurie, and others), RWDC

Hoopla! (Woodbury; mus. Scoville), RWDC

Mirage Blanc (Lamhut; mus. Helps, Moran, and others), RWDC

Rough Rising (Chase; mus. Suso, Tamasuza, Maraire), RWDC

1993 *Ball Passing* (Ririe; mus. Gonnawanaland), RWDC

Circle Cycle (Ririe and Woodbury; mus. Scoville, others), RWDC

Wanna Planet? (Skuba), RWDC

The Heisenberg Principle (Beal; mus. Scoville), RWDC

Balloons (Beal; mus. McFerrin, Yo-Yo Ma), RWDC

Ceremonial Rites (Mertz; mus. Glass), RWDC

1994 *Bathing* (Azcue and Nugent; mus. Feeney and Satoh), RWDC

Smashed Landscape (Varone; mus. Fugazi), RWDC

Tenmile (Dean; mus. Zeretzke), RWDC

The Catch (Moulton; mus. Leiber, Stoller, and others), RWDC

Short Stem Roses (Nielsen; mus. Vargas), RWDC

Long Story Short (Nielsen; mus. Rossini), RWDC

1995 *Threads of Dreams* (Woodbury; mus. Aubry), students, Hayes-Christensen Theater, Alice Sheets Marriott Center for Dance

Voices in the Wind (Host; mus. Robbie Robertson and Red Road Ensemble), RWDC

Ascension II (Creach & Koester; mus. Farrell), RWDC

1996 *Fifty Years* (Carlson), RWDC

Cowboy Poetry (Ririe and company; mus. BuckleBusters, Joe Turner Blues, and others), RWDC

Swirls, Splatters & Hiccups (White; mus. Scoville), RWDC

Night Story (Davidson; mus. Dale, Oboe Lee, and others), RWDC

Seated But Not Settled (Woodbury; mus. Scoville), students, Hayes-Christensen Theater, Alice Sheets Marriott Center for Dance

1997 *Travelling . . . There Are No Stars in My Sky* (Johnson; mus. Parte), RWDC

Bittersweet Chocolate (Rousseve; mus. Wagner), RWDC

Non-Sinatra Songs (Brenner; mus. vocals Sinatra), RWDC, middle school auditorium, Roosevelt, Utah

Figura (Louis; mus. Paul Winter Consort, Segovia, Lucuona), RWDC

Jill and Jack Went Up . . . (Mangelson-Clawson; mus. music collage), RWDC

Ririe-Woodbury Dance Company. Photograph by Brent Herridge and Associates.

Publications

Articles—

Forsberg, Helen, "Dancing to Allende," *The Salt Lake Tribune,* 27 October 1996.

Hayes, Elizabeth R., "An Interview with Joan Woodbury," *Design,* January/February 1982.

Jacobson, Dawn, "Ririe and Woodbury: Still Dancin' after All These Years," *Network,* March 1985.

Riley, T. Robin, "Communicating through Performance," *Communique,* 7(1), 1991.

Woodbury, Joan J., "Sharing the Gift of Dance," *Dance/USA Journal,* 1993.

*   *   *

An oft-quoted story about the early days of the prolific Ririe-Woodbury Dance Company (RWDC) characterizes its energetic and committed approach to performance and education. In 1968, while assisting Alwin Nikolais at the Tyrone Guthrie Theater in Minneapolis, Joan Woodbury accepted a Minnesota Arts Council invitation to present performances at four colleges. "Would the company be ready to perform within a week?" the Council asked.

Joan Woodbury and Shirley Ririe, together with Dee Winterton and Blaine Chambers, choreographed that Minnesota tour in the space of a week. Four years later, while performing at The Space in New York, the company was seen by representatives of the National Endowment for the Arts (NEA) and was accepted for the endowment's Artists in Schools and Dance Touring programs. For 12 years, the company had the most Artists in Schools bookings of any other company in the country.

It is no coincidence that the company devotes much of its time to community and school residencies, given the commitment to education of artistic co-directors Ririe and Woodbury. Woodbury has been a professor of modern dance at the University of Utah since

1951 and has taught workshops and master classes throughout the world. She was the first Fulbright scholar in dance, choosing to study with Mary Wigman in Germany. Ririe was a professor of modern dance at the University of Utah for almost 40 years. She has consulted for the NEA and serves on its National Advisory Committee for Young Audiences. She has produced two dance programs for the PBS Television Program "Arts Alive."

In an interview with Elizabeth Hayes, Woodbury noted, "I have found teaching dance to be most rewarding. I like working with young people who. . .constantly surprise me with the dances they create. I enjoy seeing students really dance in a class—seeing the transcendence in their faces. A lot of satisfaction comes from seeing people I taught years ago and finding that the experience we had together changed their lives and still affects them."

Ririe's work reflects many influences, including her studies with notable teachers such as Alwin Nikolais, Anna Halprin, Louis Horst, Elizabeth Hayes, Merce Cunningham, and Martha Graham. For Woodbury, the creative work of Mary Wigman, LaVeve Whetten, Alwin Nikolais, and Margaret H'Doubler guided her. H'Doubler was Woodbury's mentor at the University of Wisconsin, which she attended as an undergraduate. Other influential teachers were Louise Kloepper, Hanya Holm, Murray Louis, and Martha Graham.

A major component of the company's work is educational programs, particularly choreography and dance for school-age children. RWDC is one of the few professional modern dance companies in the U.S. that choreographs performances for young audiences. Programs include *Dance Is for Everybody, The Shy Hag's Magic Shadow Show, Electronic Dance Transformer,* and *Circle Cycle.* In this last piece, a narrator, with text provided by University of Utah Theatre professor Van Johnson, talks about all the wonderful teachers who have helped her understand the cyclical experiences of life.

Other educational programs include *Step Lively,* a statewide program designed to help teachers comply with the objectives of the state Fine Arts Core Curriculum, and *Teaching Dance Improvisation,* funded in part by the NEA Artists in Education program in recognition of its excellent work in the field of education.

Each year RWDC offers three seasons of performances at the Capitol Theatre in Salt Lake City, tours the U.S. for 14 to 18 weeks, gives six week-long residencies in Utah school districts, teaches a Summer Dance Workshop, and presents numerous other performances. The company has conducted residencies in more than half of Utah school districts. It has also pioneered the integration of dance and movement into school curricula throughout the country under the mantra, "dance is for everybody."

—Gigi Berardi

THE RITE OF SPRING
Le Sacre du printemps

Since the premiere of the ballet *Le Sacre du printemps* choreographed by Nijinsky for Diaghilev's Ballets Russes in 1913, Stravinsky's score has been used by more than 50 choreographers, many working with ballet companies but some working in the areas of modern and postmodern dance or *tanztheater.* In 1913 Stravinsky's music was considered too difficult for the dancers to understand, and Diaghilev hired Marie Rambert, at the time an expert in Dalcroze

eurythmics, to help the dancers with its complicated time signatures. Since then it is not just the popularity of the music in the repertoire of symphony orchestras but the sheer driving force of its complex, syncopated rhythms that has made *Sacre* attractive to choreographers, turning it, by the end of the century, into a cultural icon.

Although some critics at the time criticised Nijinsky's use of eurythmics—a form which contributed to the development of early German modern dance—Nijinsky's original version of *Sacre* was the work of a dancer trained in ballet and working with a ballet company. Nevertheless he used a shockingly unidealised conception of prehistoric Russia, presenting a springtime ritual leading to a human sacrifice, to deconstruct the highly valued vocabulary and syntax of classical ballet. While many of the ballet versions of *Sacre*—for example Béjart (1959), Neumeier (1972), and van Manen (1974)—have used *Sacre* to create modernist ballets, choreographers working outside the ballet world have used the score and libretto as a vehicle to explore ritual forms and ideologies of primitivism. Massine's 1930 ballet production of *Sacre* in Philadelphia and New York is important in this context for its casting of Martha Graham in the role of the Chosen One (the sacrificial victim who dances herself to death). It was only after this experience that Graham started to make pieces inspired by Native American subjects and rituals. The first of these, *Primitive Mysteries* (1931), contains circle dances and leaps that recall *Sacre.* The first American choreographer to create his own *Sacre* was the California-based modern dance pioneer Lester Horton. With an integrated cast that included Native American, African-American, Latino, and white dancers, Horton's *Rite of Spring* premiered at the Hollywood Bowl in 1937. Horton's primitivism proved scandalous. It divided its audience and provoked correspondence in the press between those passionately for and those against the production. In doing so it mirrored the more famous public reactions which had greeted the 1913 production.

As Susan Manning has noted in *Dance Chronicle,* many versions of *Sacre* have been produced in Germany, some in the 1950s, and most in the 1970s and 1980s. Mary Wigman achieved her biggest postwar success with her version of *Sacre* for the Berlin Festival in 1957. Working with some of her own dancers and with ballet dancers from the Berlin Stadtische Oper, she created a fusion of the expressive power of prewar German modern dance and the technical precision and clarity of ballet. This was against the trend of the time in Germany which rejected a nationally identified modern dance for the international language of ballet. Whereas Wigman's *Frühlingsweihe* (*Spring Ceremony*) distinguished between the corps and soloists, presenting Dore Hoyer as the Chosen One, Pina Bausch's *Frühlingsopfer* (*Spring Sacrifice*), choreographed 18 years later in 1975 and within a very different social and political climate, presented the dancers as an undifferentiated group; and while Wigman had focused on the nobility and heroism of the sacrifice, Bausch's production showed the women as a whole as victims of male violence. Male power over a victimised Chosen One was also the controversial theme of Martha Graham's *Rite of Spring* which she developed in 1984 at the age of 90. Here an all-powerful Shaman picks his victim almost at random. Unwilling and completely terrified, she is shown fighting all the way to her death from exhaustion.

There have been many more productions of *Sacre* than those mentioned above, ranging both geographically and conceptually from Paul Taylor's version in New York in 1980 which constituted a postmodern pastiche with "film noir" gangsters to Xing Liang's martial version in 1997 for the Guangdong Dance Company in

A 1984 Martha Graham Company performance of *The Rite of Spring.* **Photograph © Johan Elbers.**

China. Some choreographers have used Stravinsky's music as part of longer pieces. Saburo Teshigawara danced a solo to a piano version of *Sacre* in *dah-dah-sko-dah-dah* (1991), while Michael Clark's *Mmm* (1992)—initially titled *Modern Masterpiece*—created a provocative, "punk" version of *Sacre* with near nudity and his own 68-year-old mother appearing as the old sorceress. *Sacre* played a key role in the first half of the century not just in the ballet world but also in the development of modern dance. In the late 20th century it has become a vehicle for a variety of differing interpretations many of which have commented on previous productions and reinterpreted the idea of a spring sacrifice in the light of changing social circumstances.

Publications

Books—

Berg, Shelley C., *Le Sacre du printemps: Seven Productions from Nijinsky to Martha Graham,* Ann Arbor, Michigan, 1988.
Warren, Larry, *Lester Horton: Modern Dance Pioneer,* New York, 1977.

Articles—

Acocella, Joan and Lynn Garafola, "*Rites of Spring:* Catalogue Raisonné," *Ballet Review,* Summer 1992.
Helpern, Alice, "*The Rites of Spring,*" *Ballet Review,* 1984.
Manning, Susan, "German Rites: A History of *Le Sacre du printemps* on the German Stage," *Dance Chronicle,* 1991.

—Ramsay Burt

ROBINSON, Cleo Parker
American dancer, choreographer, and company director

Born: 1948; raised in Denver, Colorado. **Family:** Daughter of Jonathan (an actor, technical director and theater manager) and Martha Parker; married Tom Robinson (a dance company business manager). **Education:** Denver University (formerly Colorado

Women's College), B.S. in Dance Education Psychology. **Career:** Substitute dance teacher at Colorado University, age 15; taught dance as a high school student; mentors included Rita Berger (former Balanchine dancer) and Katherine Dunham; founded Cleo Parker Robinson Dance Ensemble, 1970; collaborated with filmmakers Gordon Parks, Sr. and Margie Soo Hoo Lee, poets Maya Angelou and Schyleen Qualls, and composer Jay Hoggard; has toured extensively, including Hawaii, New Mexico, U.S. Information Agency tour (Turkey, Bulgaria, Greece, Cyprus, and Germany), Second World Festival of Arts and Culture, American Dance Festival, New York City's Lincoln Center Out-of-Doors Festival, North Carolina's Dance On Tour Project, Dance Aspen, Olympic Arts Festival, Third Annual International Conference on Blacks in Dance, Black Choreographers Moving Towards the 21st Century; second vice-president of the International Association of Blacks in Dance, 1991—; longstanding member of the Board of Directors of the Denver Center for the Performing Arts. **Awards:** Thelma Hill Center for the Performing Arts Award for outstanding achievement in the world of dance, 1986; Colorado 100, 1992; Black in Colorado Hall of Fame, 1994; honorary doctorate of Fine Arts, University of Denver, 1991.

Works (for the Cleo Parker Robinson Dance Ensemble, unless otherwise noted)

1971	*To My Father's House*
	A Poem for Angela Davis
1972	*Four Women*
	Strange Fruit
1973	*Mournin' Sun*
	Flight
	Ytitendi
1974	*The Creators*
	Carmina
	Africa Suite
	Spiritual Suite (1974-89)
1976	*Run, Sister, Run*
1980	*With You I'm Born Again*
1983	*Lush Life*
1985	*Autumn Dance*
1987	*Blood River*
1988	*Scattin'*
1990	*Erotica*
1991	*Lunar Transformations*
1992	*Witness: Another Still Morning*
1994	*The Wisdom of the Baobab Tree*

Other works include: Choreography for musical theater, including: *Storyville, Sweeney Todd, Tinytypes, El Bravo, Working, Guys and Dolls, Jesus Christ Superstar, The Wiz, Tambourines to Glory, Don't Bother Me, I Can't Cope, Defiant Island, Shango De Ima, Pippin, Red White and Blue, Ti Jean and His Brothers,* and *Vev*; choreography for operatic works, including: *Verdi's Requiem Mass, Carmina Burana, Aida, Carmen,* and *Samson & Delilah.*

Publications

On ROBINSON: articles—

Oberdorfer, Kathryn, "Dance Is Just Life Out Loud," *Dance Teacher Now,* September 1996.

Films and Videotapes

African-Americans at Festac: Run, Sister, Run, Margie Soo Hoo Lee film with Gordon Parks, Sr., chor. by Robinson.
Black Women in the Arts, with Kim Fields and Stephanie Mills, 1986.
Borderline, Jeffrey Osborne music video, chor. by Robinson, 1986.

*   *   *

The Cleo Parker Robinson Dance Ensemble holds a unique place in the social milieu of American modern dance. A multicultural company under the leadership of a woman of mixed heritage, it is located in the heart of the Rocky Mountains in Denver, Colorado. Cleo Parker Robinson was born into an interracial family in 1948, and she and her four siblings were raised in Denver. Before she ever heard of dance, a number of events set the stage for Robinson's future. Her mother, Martha Parker, was fired when her employer became aware that her husband, Jonathan, was African-American. Robinson's early life was marked by instances of racism. When she was 10 years old, and the family was living in Dallas, Texas, Cleo suffered from a heart condition, but a local hospital refused to treat her. She also remembers being excluded from attending public schools, again because of her mixed racial heritage. Her parents embarked on a campaign to break down racial barriers by participating in sit-ins and marches and by walking picket lines.

At home, however, the Parker children were surrounded by music and theater. Martha Parker was a talented musician, and Jonathan Parker was active in theater, eventually making a name for himself as Denver's first prominent actor of color, becoming technical director for the theater at Colorado Women's College (Robinson's alma mater, and now part of the University of Denver), and manager of the Houston Fine Arts Center. The Parkers taught their children integrity, compassion, a love of the arts, and the importance of a good education, and these lessons were to have a profound effect on the kind of woman Cleo Parker Robinson would become and the kind of organization that she would lead.

As a child and adolescent, Robinson studied piano and began her dance training with Ernestine Smith at a neighborhood recreation center. At age 15 she studied dance with Rhoda Gerstein at the University of Colorado, and soon became a substitute for Gerstein. The teenage Robinson's desire to become a doctor gave way to a passion for the performing arts, and she entered Colorado Women's College as a psychology major, with a minor in dance. Former Balanchine dancer Rita Berger, a professor of dance at Colorado Women's College, encouraged her young prodigy to study in Denver and in New York with Alvin Ailey, Merce Cunningham, Murray Louis, José Limón, and Arthur Mitchell.

Robinson's company was started as a grass roots organization 1970, a part of the federally funded Model Cities Program. The group met first in a little room, then in an old loft. Her original technical and administrative staff included her parents and her husband, Tom Robinson, who is still the company's business manager. Most of Robinson's original dancers came to dance late in life and lacked training and technique, but they were committed, and Robinson was a master teacher. From the beginning, Robinson had a multicultural focus and a commitment to educational and community outreach. The group's first public performances were often at free outdoor festivals and area schools. Some of the young audience members were inspired to take classes, and the company was well on its way to gaining an identity and a name. In 1987 the Cleo Parker Robinson Dance Ensemble and school obtained a permanent home when the City and County of Denver donated a building, and the company and school are now located in the renovated Shorter AME Church in the Five Points community. The facility opened in 1989 and offers three dance studios, four classrooms, and a 300-seat theater. The year-round school offers dance, visual arts, music, drama, and martial arts for children and adults and since 1995 has hosted the International Summer Dance Institute.

The company was never merely a showcase for Robinson's own choreography but performs the works of a number of well-known contemporary and new choreographers, including Talley Beatty, Chuck Davis, Katherine Dunham, Kevin Jeff, Donald McKayle, Milton Myers, Eleo Pomare, Rod Rodgers, David Rousseve, and Paul Sansardo, among others. Many of the works reflect Robinson's interest in dance that reflects African American culture. As part of their ongoing series, "Traditions in American Modern Dance," the American Dance Festival commissioned Robinson's company to present works by Katherine Dunham and Donald McKayle. The reconstructed works in the company's repertoire now include Dunham's 1941 *Choros* and 1943 *Barrelhouse Blues* (a work in which Robinson makes one of her rare appearances as a performer, dancing the role Dunham originally created for herself) and several works by Donald McKayle, including *Saturday's Child* (1948) and *Nocturne* (1952). Dunham assisted in the restaging of her own works, which the company presented in 1995, along with McKayle's *Nocturne*. Also for the 1995 American Dance Festival, Dianne McIntyre restaged Helen Tamaris' 1937 *How Long Brethren*, a work by a pioneering white choreographer who was greatly concerned by the oppression of black Americans during the 1920s and 1930s that is based on Negro spirituals of that era. These reconstructions afforded a whole generation of dancers and audiences an introduction to seldom seen or legendary works by pioneering choreographers, and reflect Robinson's deep-seated commitment to history and community.

Considering her background, it is not surprising that much of Robinson's early choreography dealt with social issues. For the film *Run, Sister, Run*—a 1980 collaboration with photographer and filmmaker Gordon Parks—Robinson choreographed a ballet about activist Angela Davis. Her 1987 *Blood River* is about South Africa's apartheid system. More recently, her early experiences and education in the finer points of compassion resulted in Robinson's own *Witness: Another Still Morning*, a work inspired by the AIDS epidemic and the premiere by the company of Donald McKayle's *Ring-A-Levio*, a 1993 work that deals with gang violence. It is not surprising that Robinson would be drawn to the work of David Rousseve who, with his company REALITY, frequently uses movement, music, and text to explore his own Creole roots, as well as contemporary issues of gender, sexuality, and AIDS. His use of narrative, text, and live music merges traditional dance with the experimental and performance art. In 1993 Robinson and Rousseve collaborated on *Dry Each Other's Tears in the Stillness of the Night*. The work incorporates interviews with Jonathan Robinson and narration by Robinson and Rousseve in an attempt to use art to explore racial struggle and to suggest solutions to adversity.

Robinson received the Governor's Award in 1973, which motivated foundations and corporations to provide the financial support necessary to make Robinson's company one of the first full-time salaried dance organizations in the Rocky Mountain region. In 1995, Robinson obtained funding from the Center for Substance Abuse in Washington, D.C., to start a four-year model project offering the arts as an alternative to substance abuse and peer pres-

sure. Project Self Discovery, under the direction and guidance of Robinson and psychologist Harvey Milkman, targets at-risk youth who are involved with gangs or drug or alcohol abuse by using the arts to redirect their energy into positive activities. Robinson's school also includes the TraininGroup, an arts program for serious students ages 12 to 25 who take daily classes in jazz, improvisation, modern dance, choreography, theater, and voice. Internships and work-study opportunities in cooperation with such community groups as the Mayor's Program for Summer Youth and regional schools and colleges provide training and experience in technical assistance. New and future programs include the US West Alumni Project, aimed at reuniting and maintaining professional relationships with artists who have worked or trained with the company, and the Emerging Choreographers Program, which aims both to nurture and provide exposure to new choreographers and to bring diverse cultural influences to the region. Recalling the popular African proverb that it takes a village to raise a child, for Cleo Parker Robinson that village is dance.

—Julinda Lewis-Ferguson

ROBINSON, Jacqueline

English-born choreographer, educator, and writer based in France

Born: 26 October 1922 in London. **Education:** Studied music and rhythmic dance in both England and France; started dance classes with Brady; trained with Sigurd Leeder, London, 1945; took drama classes, Paris, 1947. **Career:** Dancer, Mila Cirul company, Paris, 1947; created a dance school in Nottingham (England), 1948; settled in France, 1949; co-founder with Jerome Andrews and Karin Waehner, Dance Companions Company, 1952; taught improvisation classes, 1949-55; founder with Pierre Tugal, the Dance Workshop, Paris, 1955; taught at the Wigman studio, Berlin, 1957; president, French Dance Federation, 1978-82.

Works (selected)

1943	*Hungarian Dance*, solo	
1945	*The Hooded Lover*, solo	
1954	*Hymn for the Earth* (mus. Semprun)	
1957	*The Thresholds* (mus. Semprun)	
1963	*Illuminations* (mus. Rimbaud, Britten)	
1965	*Nocturnos* (mus. Semprun), solo	
1968	*Exile World* (mus. Théodorakis)	
1974	*Lamento* (mus. Vivaldi), solo	
1986	*Passages*, solo	
1997	*Round Dance* (mus. Lesur)	

Publications

By ROBINSON: books—

My Child and Dance, Paris, 1975.
Elements of Choreographical Language, Paris, 1981.
Translator, *Dance Language* by Mary Wigman, Paris, 1986.
Children and Dance, Paris, 1988.

Introduction to Musical Language, Paris, 1989.
Adventures of Modern Dance in France (1920-1970), Paris, 1990.

*   *   *

Born in London in 1992 to an English father and a French mother, Jacqueline Robinson was fortunate to receive an artistic education from the best of both worlds—English and French. After studying music, Robinson became an accomplished pianist, and discovered dance during a move to Dublin during World War II. As an accompanist for dancer Erina Brady, Robinson was exposed to dance on a daily basis. She began taking classes in Expressionism with Brady, then trained with Sigurd Leeder in London. Robinson also took theater courses in 1947, at a well-known Parisian theater school, the E.P.J.D., which had given many future actors their start in the business. She received her first engagement as a dancer from choreographer Mila Cirul, a former student of Mary Wigman. Returning to England for a year, Robinson founded her first dance school in Nottingham in 1948, which became a stunning success when more than 300 students signed up for courses. Yet Robinson had decided to leave England and follow the man she loved to France, where she married and later had four children.

In the early 1950s, Robinson began attending Mary Wigman's summer workshops. This changed her life both artistically and professionally, for she was not only profoundly influenced by Wigman's style and technique—enough to change her entire outlook on dance—but also met several other dancer/choreographers who all became major forces in the development of French modern dance, Françoise and Dominique Dupuy, Jerome Andrews, and Karin Waehner. Along with Andrews and Waehner, Robinson helped create the Dance Companions Company in 1952, and danced in Andrews' works for three years. During the same time, she created her own first group works, like *Ritual Song* and *Hymn for the Earth,* both in 1953. *Ritual Song* was described as obsessive and powerful, and a work of "great distinction" by critic Marcelle Michel of *Dance Magazine.*

For Robinson, dance had to possess passion, reason, ritual, freedom, and harmony. Meticulous and with an acute sense of theater, Robinson radiated presence and strength in choreography, turning spacial limitations to symbolic and dramatic advantage, and freeing dance from the often excessive influence of music. The music didn't control the choreography, nor vice versa; according to French contemporary composer Pierre Daniel-Lesur, who created many musical compositions for her works, Robinson "is not a dancer who moves to music; she's a musician who dances music, who rediscovers its original [rhythms]."

Yet perhaps Robinson's biggest contribution to the history of French modern dance was her creation in 1955 of the Dance Workshop. The Dance Workshop was the anchor of the 1960s' French modernism, bringing a myriad of artists from around the world together to study dance and all its complexities. The Dance Workshop was the first school of its kind to not only have an complete course in modern dance, but had an overall program of studies that required three years to complete. It's students and teachers read like a who's-who of international artists, including choreographers Brigitte Garsky and Gilberto Motta; producers Jean-Pierre Brodier and Nikos Athanassiou; painters such as Basil Rakoczi and Maurice Lang; dancer/instructors Jerome Andrews, the Dupuys, Laura Sheleen, and Jacqueline Challet-Haas; and musicians Francisco Semprun, Ferdinand Pliesen, Michel Christodoulides, and others. The Dance Workshop be-

came known for its rigorous dance training and a keen observation for the development of its dancers. Robinson required each of her students to commit themselves completely to the Workshop's courses, both mentally and physically.

Robinson played a pivotal role in the birth of French modern dance, as a dance educator as well as a choreographer, but also as a writer and dance historian. She presided over the French Dance Federation from 1978 to 1982, helping to spread the praises of dance throughout France and beyond—and as a writer, she published many educational books, for amateurs and dance teachers. Her book, *Adventures of Modern Dance in France (1920-1970)* has become a seminal text about the history of French dance; telling the stories of its founders and taking an inventory of the styles and schools of the time. A genuine tribute to modern dance's founders, *Adventures* relates the ensuing difficulties of introducing this new form of dance in France, where ballet was beloved and well-established. Early reactions to modern dance by critics were negative, and the public even reacted violently to performances in the 1950s—like those of Mary Wigman in 1953, where critics cited the "ugliness" of her work in comparison to the "harmony and beauty" of ballet. Even Martha Graham's tour of Paris in 1957, and José Limón's in 1951 weren't really successful; the taste for classicism in a country dominated by ballet took nearly 20 years to evolve, due to the perseverance and thick skin of modern dance's earliest pioneers. Jacqueline Robinson, as an educator, writer, and historian, reminds us of the Herculean efforts of those few dancers and choreographers responsible for the position French modern dance holds today.

—Murielle Mathieu

RODGERS, Rod
American dancer, choreographer, and company director

Born: 1938. **Education:** Early dance training from his parents; studied with Mary Anthony, Erick Hawkins, Hanya Holm, and Charles Weidman in New York City. **Career:** Dancer, Erick Hawkins company; founder/director, Rod Rodgers Dance Company; founder, Association of Black Choreographers; co-founder, C.O.D.A. (Coalition of Dance Artists), New York; artist-in-residence, California State University at Long Beach, 1997. **Awards:** Fellowships and commissions from the John Hay Whitney Foundation (1965), the Beard fund, Creative Artists in Public Service, NEA, New State Council of the Arts, Rockefeller Foundation; Spirit of Detroit Creative Award; AUDELCO award.

Works

1964	*Inventions II*
1965	*Two Falling*
	Oscillating Figures
	Dance on a Line
	Intention in Three Parts
1966	*Discussion*
	Trajectories
	Folk Suite
	Quest

1967   *Percussion Suite* (Rhythmdances series), (mus. Rodgers)
1968   *Inventions*
        The Conjuring
        Tangents (Rhythmdances), (mus. Cage, Russell)
        Oscillating Figures
        Primitive Suite
        News. . .Recall
        Dance Poems . . .Black, Brown, Negro
1969   *Down in the Valley*
        Historical Tableau
        Trajectories
        Schism
        Sketches for Projected Space
        Early Dances
        Down in the Valley (theatre)
1970   *Harambee!*
        Now! Nigga
        Dances in Projected Space
        Black Cowboys (theatre)
1972   *Box*
        Shout
        In Hi-Rise Shadows
1973   *Rhythm Ritual* (Rhythmdances), (mus. Rodgers)
        Work Out
        Need to Help
        Vuca (Awaken)!
1974   *Intervals I*
        Prodigal Sister (theatre)
1975   *Intervals II*
1976   *Visions . . .of a New Blackness*
1978   *Jazz Fusions* (continuing inprovisations with musicians)
        Soft Days . . . Secret Dreams
        Freedom!, Fredome. . . (often included with Poets & Peacemakers series), (mus. Perkinson, Regan)
1981   *Langston Lives* (Poets & Peacemakers series; celebrating Langston Hughes), (mus. Pointer)
1984   *The Legacy* (Poets & Peacemakers; inspired by Martin Luther King, Jr.) (mus. Perkinson, Regan)
1986   *Against Great Odds* (Poets & Peacemakers; inspired by George Washington Carver)
1988   *Equinox Images* (mus. Winston)
1989   *Echoes of Ellington* (Poets & Peacemakers; inspired by Duke Ellington) (mus. Taylor)
        Victims
1990   *Keep On Goin'!* (Poets & Peacemakers; dedicated to heroic women of color), (mus. Regan, Chapman, Lateef)
1991   *In Hi-Rise Shadows* (mus. Lake)
1994   *Cameos of Women* (mus. Watson, Chapman)
1995   *Quest* (inspired by Malcolm X), (mus. Hakmaun)
1997   *Stance* (mus. Moore)

Publications

By RODGERS: articles—

"Men and Dance: Why Do We Question the Image?" *Dance Magazine*, 1966.
"For the Celebration of Our Blackness," *Dance Scope*, 1967.
"Is it Just for Jobs?" *Dance Magazine*, 1967.

*   *   *

Rod Rodgers, born in 1938, grew up in Detroit, Michigan, in a family of popular entertainers. His parents were his first dance teachers, teaching him tap styles at a young age. Early in his career he worked in Detroit with teachers and choreographers who had worked with or been influenced by prominent choreographers such as Katherine Dunham, Pearl Primus, and Hanya Holm. Rodgers moved to New York in 1963 to study and work with Mary Anthony, Erick Hawkins, Charles Weidman, and eventually, Holm. Rodgers' early development as a young performer and choreographer was due to his "being able to establish relationships. . .[with] musicians, designers, and some extraordinary dancers, who were also of substantial importance in determining the direction of my creative exploration."

Soon after his arrival in New York, Rodgers formed his own eponymous dance troupe with an expressed purpose to "maintain a tradition of being in the forefront of experimentation and innovation," while "celebrating positive black cultural images." Rodgers began making a name for himself and developed a series of what he characterizes as "Rhythmdances" with the dancers contributing to the music via handheld instruments incorporated into their dance. This seamless integration of percussion and movement has become a hallmark of many works, including the aptly named *Percussion Suite* from 1967, *Tangents* (1968), *Rhythm Ritual* (1973), and 1970's *Harambee!* (meaning "forward with unity"). These works are frequently performed outside the normal performance spaces, like in the streets; a style Rodgers has explored further with to test space limitations, both real and imaginary. Other examples include *Sketches for Projected Space* (1969) and the following year's *Dances in Projected Space*, which used photographic slides, and the later duet *Box* (1972), which portrays one dancer dancing in a real cage while another deals with psychic bonds.

Rodgers' divides his works into four categories, including the aforementioned Rhythmdances, along with dance drama tributes to black heroes called the "Poets & Peacemakers" series; jazz ballets using both tradition and experimental movement; and what he calls "sculptural movement landscapes," a recent example of which is *Stance,* with music by Cooper Moore and set design by Marhsall Williams, performed at Lincoln Center in March of 1997.

A substantial amount of Mr. Rodgers' work emphasizes, explores, and celebrates the black experience, especially his well-received Poets & Peacemakers series with works inspired by poet Langston Hughes (*Langston Lives*, 1981), Martin Luther King, Jr. (*The Legacy,* 1984), George Washington Carver (*Against Great Odds,* 1986), Duke Ellington (*Echoes of Ellington,* 1989), and 1990's *Keep On Goin'!* choreographed as a tribute to Harriet Tubman and other "heroic women of color." Other works, like 1978's *Freedom!, Fredome. . .,* which is often included with Poets & Peacemakers performances, and a more recent work, 1995's *Quest* (inspired by Malcolm X), give voice to Rodgers' respect for these historical figures and the need to keep them alive in the hearts and minds of audiences. Jennifer Dunning of the *New York Times* praised *Quest* finding that the "dancers' bodies might also be percussion instruments, so thoroughly is their movement informed by the rhythms of the music" as if the "bamboo sticks they beat are extensions of their arms."

In addition to his concert series, Rodgers has collaborated on projects with many prominent musicians and designers. These works include the choreography for the Syracuse Opera Company's production of *Aida*, directing and staging of his *Black Cowboys* (1972) for the Harlem Opera international tour, choreographing *A Study in Color* by Malcolm Boyd, *The Prodigal Sister* as an Off-Broadway

Rod Rodgers: Luis Martinez and Jerome Jamal Hardman in Rodgers' *The Legacy*. Photograph by Tom Caravaglia.

musical for Woody King, Jr., and both choreographing and performing the lead in the *Like it is TV* special. Rodgers also staged a reading of Ntozake Shanges' *Sassafras, Cypress & Indigo* produced by Joseph Papp for the Public Theatre in New York City, staged and directed productions for *Voices, Inc.,* and a touring production of a musical tribute to Martin Luther King later broadcast by CBS-TV.

Rodgers' contributions to the dance world have been recognized through favorable reviews as well as through funding including fellowships, commissions, and grants. Though he has received monetary assistance from organizations like the New York State Council of the Arts, the Rockefeller Foundation, and the NEA, the struggle for funding led Rodgers to co-found C.O.D.A. (Coalition of Dance Arts) in New York, as a non-profit collective to combat recent and ongoing arts cutbacks and "to bring the continuing creative expression of our artists to wider audiences." Each of C.O.D.A.'s four distinguished dance companies (Alpha Omega Theatrical Dance Company, Eleo Pomare Dance Company, Joan Miller's Dance Players, and Rodger's company) are directed by well-established African Americans who have united to promote both education and entertainment through varied approaches

to dance—traditional, contemporary, experimental, or a combination of these forms. In the future, C.O.D.A. may operate like a regional troupe, dividing the financial burdens of administration and space rental, while increasing funding possibilities.

The Rod Rodgers Dance Company has toured extensively at home and abroad; its performers have served as "cultural emissaries" through the U.S. Information Service (USIS) performing in Portugal, Syria, Senegal, Kenya, Zaire, Zambia, Nigeria, and Mexico. In addition to major concert circuits, colleges, and international festivals, the multiethnic dance ensemble has received awards of recognition for Outreach/Audience Development activities. The Company has also participated in community outreach programs, working with young audiences and taking its message to the streets, literally. Mobile theater units have taken Rodgers' works to underserved audiences, like C.O.D.A.'s 1967 Harlem Cultural Commission's Dancemobile project, which took dancing to the borough streets on the back of a flatbed truck.

Rodgers' company has created a uniquely varied repertoire collection, in many different stylistic directions. His *Echoes of Ellington*

(1989) with music by Billy Taylor, relied on what Rodgers' has called "an affectionately traditional approach to jazz," while *In Hi-Rise Shadows* (1991) with music by avant-garde artist Oliver Lake, is a sharp contemporary piece with only slight hints of a jazz. In addition to his choreography and fundraising efforts, Rodgers delivers his artistic message of unity and cultural respect through teaching at schools and major universities nationwide, collaborating with like-minded artists from several creative venues, and publishing articles in magazines and journals. His energetic, thought-provoking works are performed by not only his troupe, the Rod Rodgers Dance Company, but are in the repertories of companies across the country.

—Suzanne Neumayer and Sydonie Benet

ROSENTHAL, Jean

American lighting designer for dance, theater, and opera

Born: Eugenia Rosenthal, 16 March 1912 in New York City. **Education:** Manumit School, Pawling, New York; Friends Seminary, Manhattan; studied acting and dance with Martha Graham at Neighborhood Playhouse's School of the Theatre, 1929-30; studied theater history with George Pierce Baker, scene design with Donald Oenslager, costume design with Frank Bevin, and lighting with Stanley McCandless, Yale University, 1930-33. **Career:** Joined Works Project Administration Federal Theatre Project, 1933; technical assistant in Federal Theatre #891, working with John Houseman, Orson Welles, and designer Nat Carson, 1935; installed first lighting system for Leslie Howard's *Hamlet* in 1936 (which may have been first lighting credit); designed for Martha Graham Dance Company, 1939-69; designed lights for a Holiday Dance Festival, which began her relationship with George Balanchine and Lincoln Kirstein, 1939; opened Theatre Production Service, Inc., a theatrical supply house in New York, offering complete design and supply service for theatres and shows, 1940; designed for New York City Ballet, 1948-57; lighting designer and production director, the New York City Center Dance Theatre, designing for Charles Weidman, José Limón, and Dudley-Maslow-Bales Trio as well as Valerie Bettis, Nina Fonaroff, Eve Gentry, Katherine Litz, Iris Mabry, Merce Cunningham, and Peter Hamilton, 1949; lighting designer and production director, concert series presented by the Bethsabee De Rothschild Foundation at the Alvin Theatre, lighting work by Martha Graham, José Limón, Doris Humphrey, Merce Cunningham, Pearl Lang, May O'Donnell, and Nina Fonaroff, 1953; lighting director and production director, for a similar concert at the ANTA theater, 1955; established own theatrical consulting firm, Jean Rosenthal Associates, involved with architectural projects such as the Guthrie Theatre in Minneapolis, the American Shakespeare Festival in Stratford, Connecticut, the Juilliard School of Music in New York City, and the Los Angeles Music Center's Dorothy B. Chandler Pavilion, 1958; designed for American Ballet Theatre, 1960-68; designed lights for many Broadway musicals and plays, including *West Side Story* (1957), *The Sound of Music* (1959), *Barefoot in the Park* (1963), *Hello Dolly* (1964), *Fiddler on the Roof* (1964), John Gielgud's *Hamlet* starring Richard Burton (1964), *The Odd Couple* (1965), and *Cabaret* (1966). **Awards:** Henrietta Lord Memorial Award, Yale School of Drama, 1932; Outer Critics Circle Award for contribution to stage design, 1968-69 season. **Died:** New York, 1 May 1969.

Publications

By ROSENTHAL: books—

The Magic of Light, with Lael Wertenbacker, New York, 1972.

By ROSENTHAL: articles—

"Art and Language of Stage Lighting," *Theatre Arts,* 1961.
"Five Kings," *Theatre Arts,* 1961.
"General Technical Requirements for Summer Stock Operation," in Beckhard, Richard and Effrat, John, *Blueprint for Summer Theatres—1951 Supplement,* New York, 1951.
"Light for the Stage," *Opera News,* 1968.
"Lighting for the Theatre," *Musical America,* 1954.
"Native Son Backstage," *Theatre Arts,* 1941.
"Patterns of Light," *Impulse,* 1956.

On ROSENTHAL: books—

Lewis, Jerry, *A Description and Analysis of Some of the Lighting Designs of Jean Rosenthal,* unpublished MS thesis, University of Wisconsin, 1964.
Rubin, Joel E., and Watson, Leland H., *Theatrical Lighting Practice,* New York, 1954.

On ROSENTHAL: articles—

Goodman, Saul, "Meet Jean Rosenthal," *Dance Magazine,* 1962.
Obituary, *New York Times,* 2 May 1969.
Sargeant, Winthrop, "Please Darling, Bring Three to Seven . . . A Profile of Jean Rosenthal," *New Yorker,* 1956.
Skelton, Thomas, "Jean Rosenthal's Dance Lighting," *Theatre Crafts,* 1973.
Violett, Ellen, "Name in Lights," *Theatre Arts,* 1950.

*   *   *

The shaft of light referred to as Martha's Finger of God, the blue cycloramas associated with George Balanchine's pared down neoclassical ballets, light changes for dance keyed to both music and physical impulse, the meticulously graphed lighting plots (many of which are still in use) made without benefit of computers—these are part of the legacy of Jean Rosenthal, who wrote in her autobiography:

> I am a lighting designer. The profession is only as old as the years I have spent in it. This is astonishing when you consider the flexibility lighting by electricity had achieved before I was born. I think it simply never occurred to anyone until the 1930s that the lighting should be the exclusive concern of a craftsman, let alone under the artistic aegis of a specialist.

Rosenthal was born in 1912 in New York City, the daughter of two physicians with extremely progressive notions about education. As cultured people, they took full advantage of the city's offerings in the arts, especially in theatre, and their children were taken to see everything they could. At age 17, instead of going to college, Rosenthal enrolled at the Neighborhood Playhouse, although she had never wanted to act and hated to dance. "I loved props, scenery and lights," she remembered, in *The Magic of Light.*

At that time Martha Graham was teaching at the Neighborhood Playhouse, as was Louis Horst, with whom Rosenthal studied dance forms. The Graham Rosenthal knew in 1929 was, the lighting designer recalled, "a woman of imagination, of total purpose toward what she wished to achieve, and she was busy creating a new language in the dance. I was fortunate enough to grow up with her as it developed. My association with her was really the first I had in terms of lighting design." That association continued nearly four decades, to the moment of Rosenthal's death. Rosenthal designed the production for Graham's *Archaic Hours* on her hospital bed and attended the premiere in a wheelchair just 10 days before her death from cancer.

In 1930, Rosenthal, still extremely young, went to Yale University where she studied with Stanley McCandless, author of *A Method for Lighting,* a seminal textbook of the time, when the teaching of techniques demanded immersion in the entire stage environment as well as the historical context of the time. It was at Yale that Rosenthal learned that there must be a technique and a method for organizing the designer's ideas. Her disciplined, knowledgeable approach to lighting design stood her in very good stead when she began her professional career with the Mercury Theatre, three years later. Women, despite the considerable efforts of Loie Fuller in an earlier era, were far from welcome in the masculine atmosphere backstage but Rosenthal's soft-voiced courtesy and hard-headed practicality won her the respect of the lighting technicians so vital to the realization of her vision.

Some of her lighting plots for Graham were reproduced in *The Magic of Light* and showed the position of every light with the direction of every beam. Today such meticulousness seems obvious, but in the 1930s it was quite new.

Although Rosenthal designed lights for many theatrical productions (in 1966, just three years before her death, she had no less than 10 musicals and plays running on Broadway to her credit, including *Fiddler on the Roof, Cabaret, Hello Dolly,* and *Barefoot in the Park*) and in 1967 became the Metropolitan Opera's first resident lighting designer, her first love was the dance. She wrote in *The Magic of Light:*

> Light is quite tactile to me. It has shape and dimension. It has an edge. It has quality and has an entity. It is the one miracle of creation without which, to me, the others would be meaningless.... And always the most interesting aspect of lighting is that of the air and the space, the plastics of the stage, the sculptural values.

When Rosenthal began her career, lighting systems were highly inflexible in theaters, making them quite inappropriate for following and enhancing movement, which was fluid. She understood well the requirements for dance, as Walter Terry commented in a review: "[Rosenthal] created marvels and beauties: her lights do more than remove darkness from the stage and make the dancers visible. Rather does she make dance visible by stimulating light to perceive the stature of a human form, the mood of movement, the path of choreography."

Rosenthal, who designed lights for both ballet productions (New York City Ballet and its precursors, Ballet Caravan and Ballet Society, as well as American Ballet Theatre) and for modern choreographers (José Limón, Merce Cunningham, Anna Sokolow, and many others, as well as Martha Graham) made a clear distinction between the requirements of the two forms, but the purpose was always the same, "to underline the action and to make the movement visible in terms of mood. The method too is always the same," she wrote.

"As the dancer moves, so does the light." Classical and neoclassical ballet, however, demanded the illumination of form and movement: "for Balanchine it is lighting patterns in space; for Graham one is lighting the interior impulse."

Whether she was lighting dance, theater, musical comedy, or buildings—in 1958 she established Jean Rosenthal Associates, a theatrical consulting firm that led to her involvement in many architectural projects, including the Guthrie Theatre in Minneapolis, the Juilliard School of Music in New York City, and the Los Angeles Music Center's Dorothy B. Chandler Pavilion—Rosenthal was a thorough-going professional, able to tailor lighting to the individual requirements of her collaborators. "I am the Band-aid who holds things together," she said of her work in the theater (quoted in the *New York Times).* Many of her lighting plots are still in use, although the technology has changed enormously in the 30 years since her death.

Her fingerprints, too, are on the designs of many of her successors. Martha's Finger of God, that single key light coming from high up, creating, as she said, an angular pool of downlight that formed a diagonal that flows upstage, is used by many contemporary choreographers working with their own designers. "If I leave anything to posterity," Rosenthal predicted, "it will be, I think, most importantly in the field of dance lighting." About this and so many other aspects of her craft, she was right on the mark.

—Martha Ullman West

ROSS, Bertram

American dancer, educator, and choreographer

Born: 13 November 1920 in Brooklyn, New York. **Education:** Attended Oberlin College; studied painting at the Art Students' League in New York. **Career:** Dancer, Martha Graham Dance Company, 1948-73, dancing more than 35 leading roles; also served as Graham's main partner and co-director of the company; has choreographed since 1964 and presented his first recital at the 92nd Street Y in 1965; taught at Juilliard and the Graham school for many years following his departure from the Graham company in 1974; founder, Bertram Ross Dance Compnay, 1978; also taught at the Alvin Ailey Dance Center and at New York University School of the Arts.

Roles (with Martha Graham Company)

1955	*Seraphic Dialogue*
1958	*Embattled Garden*
	Clytemnestra
1960	*Acrobats of God*
	Alcestis
1961	*Samson Agonistes*
1962	*A Look at Lightning*
	Phaedra
	Legend of Judith
1963	*Circe*
1968	*Lady of the House of Sleep*
	A Time of Snow
1969	*The Archaic Hours*

Works

1964	*Untitled*
1965	*Triangle*
	Breakup
	Holy, Holy
1966	*If Only*
1968	*Reveal Me and Sing*
	Solo
	L'Histoire du Soldat
1970	*Oases*
	See You Around
	Trio
1971	*A Small Book of Poems*
	Still Life
1972	*New Math*
1978	*Nocturne*
	Rencounters
	How Fair How Fresh Were the Roses
	Theater Piece
	Totem
	Las Mujeres Sefardicas
1980	*Four Preludes*
	Threads
	Vanya: Three Poems
	Dear Friend and Gentle Heart

Publications

On ROSS: articles—

Dance Magazine, May 1960.
Dance Magazine, August 1976.

*   *   *

Bertram Ross was one of the most important dancers in the Martha Graham Dance Company. His imposing stage presence (he is over six feet tall) and strong technique made him an indispensable interpreter of Graham's imagination, especially in those works which tapped into Greek mythology. Ross was also Martha Graham's main partner during the 1950s. He had a firm mastery of Graham technique: the use of the center of the body, the creation of jagged and twisted shapes, and the earthbound quality so typical of all the Graham dance movement. The culminating masterpiece in Graham's mythological works, the full-length *Clytemnestra,* featured Bertram Ross in two roles: the husband Agamemnon and the son Orestes. Ross' devotion to Martha Graham and her company was profound. Although he danced in outside concerts, on television, and in a Broadway show, he stayed with the Graham company until 1974, even keeping it going when Graham was ill. With Ross' departure and a newly reconfigured Martha Graham company, the modern dance world lost one of its most experienced and dramatically gifted dancers. No one has been able to eclipse Bertram Ross in the roles Martha Graham created for him.

Bertram Ross' love of dance stemmed from his early introduction to the world of theater. His mother—a talented pianist and singer—introduced him to a nonstop infusion of all kinds of theater. Ross attended concerts, dance, and dramatic performances at the Brooklyn Academy of Music and also accompanied his mother on her far-flung trips to music and theater performances. Ross recalled

being "taken to see every show and every movie" during his young life. His mother, forbidden to go on the stage by her religious mother, poured her enthusiasm into her son. His father, a successful dentist, provided financial security. As Ross recalled in a 1976 *Dance Magazine* interview with Betty Jane Stein, the inculcation of so much theater, music, and art, left him over-stimulated. In fact, fantasy outweighed reality, "My theater memories are stronger than my living memories."

Ross studied piano at his mother's instigation but gravitated toward painting while in high school. During World War II, Ross and other young talented artists-to-be painted maps for the U.S. Coastal and Geodetic Survey. Soon Ross was called up to active service and was stationed in Germany. He helped prepare the map used by the Soviets at the historic meeting of the Soviet and American armies at the Elbe River. Upon returning home in 1947, Ross resumed his art studies at the Art Students' League. Dance was still a long way from his life, however.

While Ross performed skits as a child at summer camp, he never considered dance as a way of life until he got out of the army. He had seen the Graham company in Washington, D.C., while working for the government and saw them again in New York City in the 1950s. He was overwhelmed with the dancers' ability to portray anguish through dance movement. As a result, Ross saw every performance of the company during the New York engagement, and soon after he signed up for classes with them. His timing could not have been better: the Graham company needed a male dancer and the G.I. Bill of Rights was there to aid his studies. Within a year of joining the Graham company, Bertram Ross was on tour. He started almost immediately to get solo work; his first was Mad Tom in *Eye of Anguish* (based on the story of King Lear). In a very short time, he was partnering with Graham in many of her most famous roles. In 1954, during the Season of Modern Dance at New York's Alvin Theatre, Ross danced in many modern works for various choreographers. For Nina Fonaroff, he danced in *Lazarus,* for Pearl Lang, he appeared in *Legend* and also in *Rites.* And for Graham, he danced in some of her most memorable works: *Appalachian Spring, Diversion of Angels, Night Journey, Canticle for Innocent Comedians,* and *Voyage.*

The 1950s was a time of great productivity for Ross. He toured Europe, the Middle East, and Asia with the Graham company all the while adding more and more roles to his repertory. Ross' contribution to Graham's work went beyond being a dancer and partner. He had helped set the choreography for *Clytemnestra,* her masterpiece from 1958. In class, he demonstrated movements for her. When she began to limit her dancing as a result of advancing age, Ross tailored his own dancing to suit hers; he made sure she remained the star she was. When Graham stopped dancing and the company was pitched into a near-death dive, Ross (with fellow dancer Mary Hinkson and board member Lee Leatherman) kept the studio and the company going. When Graham returned from a serious illness accompanied by a new friend, Ron Protas (given the title of producer), Ross and the other loyal dancers were shunted aside. The company regrouped and Ross was without a job.

When Ross left the Martha Graham company in 1974 he guested with many other dance companies including the Joyce Trisler Dance Company and again with Pearl Lang. He appeared in Lang's *The Possessed* and also began teaching and choreographing at New York University, at the Toronto Dance Theatre, and at the Centre International de la Danse in Paris. He'd had some prior experience in choreographing and his version of *L'Histoire du soldat* from 1968 was an interesting attempt at setting dances to the difficult

Stravinsky score. He used a puppet booth and screens as scenery and employed James Cahill as the single narrator of the story of a young soldier who sells his soul to the devil.

In March 1978, Ross premiered his own dance company, and the following year the Bertram Ross Dance Company appeared at the Riverside Dance Festival with several new works. As a choreographer, Ross bore no resemblance to Martha Graham. His work tended to be linear and non-specific. He liked to explore such emotions as hostility, grief, and tenderness, for example. His stage pictures were sharp and continually shifting. Works such as *How Fair How Fresh Were the Roses* were frankly sentimental in tone. This work from 1978 is set in a dimly lit ballroom and explores the bittersweet quality of love: waltzing couples sweep around a solitary woman. Another work entitled *Theater Piece* featured Ross and others as they explored growing old, sexual identity, and morality. Some viewers found Ross' work exciting from the conceptual standpoint but limited in the way he expressed his ideas in dance.

In his later career Ross further explored acting. He used his strong stage presence and supple good looks to new advantage as he added monologues to dance pieces. These gave him the chance to utilize his resonant speaking voice. Over time, Ross gave solo dance performances in which he embodied diverse personalities. Ross never stopped studying. He took singing and tap lessons. In the late 1970s, he made his singing debut in a nightclub act in which he was accompanied by his close friend, the pianist and longtime cabaret performer, John Wallowitch. In 1983, Ross appeared as Prospero in the Riverside Shakespeare Company staging of *The Tempest*.

Ross had a long career as a teacher of Graham technique. He was most concerned with sincerity in performing. According to Ross, dancers who devote their lives to perfecting their technique are engaged in making a spiritual statement. Above all, Ross looked for students who had a strong theater sense in addition to dancing skills. As Ross stated in the 1976 *Dance Magazine* interview, the excitement of the Graham technique comes from the the pull of the earth, the shift of weight, of volume, rather than line. In his late seventies, Bertram Ross continues to dance, act, and sing.

—Adriane Ruggiero

ST. DENIS, Ruth

American pioneer of modern dance, choreographer, and educator

Born: Ruth Dennis 20 January 1879 in Sommerville, New Jersey. **Education:** Attended Sommerville High School, Dwight Moody School, Massachusetts, and the Packer-Collegiate Institute in Brooklyn. **Family:** Married Ted Shawn, 1914. **Career:** Began performing as a skirt dancer in dime museums, roof gardens, and in larger theater productions as well as on vaudeville, before choreographing and performing dances on tour in the U.S. and Europe; joined by Ted Shawn and founded Denishawn school and dance company, 1915; popularized modern dance to American audiences and gave Martha Graham, Doris Humphrey, and Charles Weidman their early training in dance. **Awards:** Capezio Award, 1961; Dance Teachers of America Award, 1964. **Died:** In California in 1968.

Roles

1894   Dancer, *The Passing Show* (Canary/Lederer), Casino Theatre, New York

1898   Dancer/Gloria, *The Ballet Girl* (Rice), Manhattan Theatre, New York

1899   Folly, the Carnival Dancer/Miss Creel, *A Runaway Girl* (Daly), U.S. tour

        Chorus Dancer, *Man in the Moon* (Marwig), U.S. tour

1900   Singer/Dancer, *Zaza* (Belasco), Garrick Theatre, London

        Adele, *Zaza* (Belasco), U.S. tour

1901   Mandy, *The Auctioneer* (Belasco), Bijou Theartre, New York

        Mlle. Le Grand, *Madame DuBarry* (Belasco), Criterion Theatre, New York

1902   Mlle. Le Grand, *Madame DuBarry* (Belasco), Belasco Theatre, New York

1905   Sanumati, *Sakuntala* (Progressive Stage Society), Madison Square Theatre, New York

Other roles include: Solos in own works from 1905-57, and solos and parts in works by Ted Shawn from 1914-32.

Works (selected)

1906   *Cobras* (mus. Delibes), solo, Hudson Theatre, New York

        Incense (mus. Loomis), solo, Hudson Theatre, New York

        Radha (mus. Delibes), solo, New York Theatre, New York

1908   *Nautch,* solo, Vienna

        A Shirabyoshi, solo, London

        The Yogi (mus. Meyrowitz), solo, Vienna

1910   *Egypta* (mus. Meyrowitz), solo, New Amsterdam Theatre, New York

        The Lotus Pond (mus. Meyrowitz), solo, Boston

1913   *Dance of Rosebuds,* solo, Ravinia Park, Chicago

        Bakawali (mus. Nevins), solo, Fulton Theatre, New York

        The Impromptu (mus. Herbert), solo, Ravinia, Chicago

        O-Mika (mus. Bowers), solo, Fulton Theatre, New York

1914   *Champagne Dance* (mus. Ilgenfritz), solo, Ravinia , Chicago

        Chitra Hunting (mus. Tchaikovsky), solo, Ravinia Park, Chicago

        Dance Impromptu, solo

        La Marquise (mus. Roth), solo, Ravinia Park, Chicago

        The Peacock (mus. Roth), solo, Ravinia Park, Chicago

        The Scherzo Waltz (mus. Ilgenfritz), solo, Kentucky

1915   *The Garden of Kama* w/Shawn (mus. Stoughton), St. Denis, Shawn and company, San Francisco

        A Lady of the Genvoko Period, solo, Mason Opera House, Los Angeles

        O-Mika Arranges Her Flowers and Starts for a Picnic (mus. Bowers), solo, Keith's Palace Theatre, New York

        The Spirit of the Sea (mus. MacDowell), solo, Mason Opera House, Los Angeles

1916   *Dance with Scarf,* solo, Sedalia, Kansas

        Review of Dance Pageant of India, Greece, and Egypt w/ Shawn (included *Tillers of the Soil* and other dances), (mus. Meyrowitz, DeLachau, Nevin), St. Denis, Shawn, and company

1918   *Dance from an Egyptian Frieze,* solo, Majestic Theatre, Dallas

        Dance of Tahoma, Margaret Loomis, Moore Theatre, Seattle

        Dance of Theodora (mus. Granados), solo, Orpheum Theatre, Denver

        Dance of the Royal Ballet of Siam (mus. Horst), St. Denis and company, Orpheum, Denver

        Danse Siamese, solo, Moore Theatre, Seattle

        Greek Scene (Pas de Trois, Greek Veil Plastique, Greek Dancer in Silhouette) (mus. Debussy, Glück), Orpheum Theatre, Denver

        An Indian Temple Girl, Loomis, Majestic Theatre, Fort Worth, Texas

        Jeptha's Daughter, solo, Majestic Theatre, Seattle

        Nautch (1918 version), Majestic Theatre, Dallas

        The Spirit of Democracy, St. Denis and company, Orpheum Theatre, Denver

        Syrian Sword Dance, Majestic Theatre, Fort Worth

        Rosamund (mus. Schubert), solo, Majestic Theatre, Fort Worth

1919   *At Evening* (mus. Schumann), Egan Little Theatre, Los Angeles

Dance of Devidassis, Proctor's Theatre, Newark
Coolan Dhu (mus. Leoni), Egan Little Theatre, Los Angeles
Dancer from the Court of King Ahasuerus (mus. Rudhyar), solo, Los Angeles
Danse (mus. Debussy), Egan Little Theatre, Los Angeles
First Arabesque (mus. Debussy), Egan Little Theatre
Egyptian Suite w/Ted Shawn
Floods of Spring (mus. Rachmaninoff), Egan Little Theatre
Gavotte (mus. Bach), Egan Little Theatre
Hungarian Dance No.6 (mus. Brahms), Egan Little Theatre
Impromptu (mus. Schubert), Egan Little Theatre
Intermezzo No. 1, Op.119 (mus. Brahms), Egan Little Theatre
Intermezzo No. 3 (mus. Brahms), Egan Little Theatre
J'ai pleuré rêve (mus. Hore), Los Angeles
Juggleress (mus. Moszkowski), Egan Little Theatre
Kuan Yin (mus. Satie), solo, Los Angeles
Little Banjo (mus. Hickman), Los Angeles
Orientale (mus. Amani), Los Angeles
Phryne (mus. Ganne), solo, Los Angeles
Polonaise (mus. Moszkowski), Egan Little Theatre
Prelude No.4 (mus. Chopin), Egan Little Theatre
Premiere Valse Oubliee (mus. Listz), solo, Los Angeles
Rigaudon (mus. MacDowell), Los Angeles
Romance (mus. Tschaikowsky), Egan Little Theatre
Schottische (mus. Chopin), Egan Little Theatre
Second Arabesque (mus. Debussy), Egan Little Theatre
Soaring (mus. Schumann), Egan Little Theatre
Sonata Pathetique (mus. Beethoven), Egan Little Theatre
The Spirit of the Rose (mus. Ganne), solo, Plantages Theatre, Portland
Street Nautch Dance (mus. Devi), solo, Egan Little Theatre
The Street of the Dancers, St. Denis and company, Pantages Theatre, Portland
Suite of Lyric Pieces (Waltz, Album Leaf, Skip Dance, March of the Dwarfs), (mus. Grieg), Egan Little Theatre
Three Ladies of the East (India, Burma, Algiers), Proctor's Theatre, Newark
Two Waltzes (mus. Jensen), Egan Little Theatre
Valse Brillante (mus. Mana-Zucca), Los Angeles
Vizione Veneziana (mus. Brogi), Los Angeles
Waltz No.15 (mus. Brahms), Egan Little Theatre
Why (mus. Schumann), Egan Little Theatre

1921 *The Beloved and the Sufi* (mus. Sadi), solo, San Diego
Hymn to the Sun, solo, San Diego
Impressions of a Japanese Tragedy, solo, San Diego
The Poet and the Dancer (mus. Hafiz), solo, San Diego
Poetess and the Thirteenth Century, solo, San Diego
The Salutation (mus. Foote), solo, San Diego
Sappho (mus. Bantock), solo, San Diego
When I Go Alone at Night. . . (mus. Devi, poetry Tagore), solo, San Diego

1922 *Liebestraum* (mus. Listz), solo, Academy of Music, Lynchburg, Tennessee
Street Nautch (mus. Cadman), Lynchburg
The Three Apsarases (mus. Crist), Lynchburg

Waltz, Op.33, No.15 (mus. Brahams), solo, Lynchburg
1923 *Dance, O Dance, Maidens Gay* (mus. Duarte), Town Hall, New York
Ishtar of the Seven Gates (mus. Griffes)
Sonata Tragica w/Humphrey (mus. MacDowell), Alantic City
The Spirit of the Sea (mus. Stoughton), Apollo Theatre, Atlantic City
1924 *Allegro Risoluto* (mus. Schutt), Academy of Music, Newburg, New York
Valse à la Loie (mus. Chopin), Newburg
Vision of the Aissoua w/Shawn (mus. Stoughton), Newburg
Waltz (mus. de Lauchau), Manhattan Opera House
Waltzes (mus. Schubert), solo, Newburg
1925 *Dance of the Volcano Goddess* (mus. Vaughan), solo, Imperial Theatre, Tokyo
Garland Plastique (mus. Schubert), Tokyo
Queen of Heaven (mus. Vaughan), solo, Tokyo
Love Crucified (no music), Imperial Theatre, Tokyo
1926 *A Burmese Yien Pwe* (mus. Vaughan), Victoria Theatre, Singapore
In the Bunnia Bazaar (mus. Vaughan, Anderson), Los Angeles
Invocation to the Buddha (mus. Vaughan), solo, Philharmonic Auditorium, Los Angeles
Javanese Court Dancer (mus. Vaughan), solo, Grand Opera House, Manilla
The Soul of India, solo, Los Angeles
Suite for Violin and Piano (mus. Schutt), Victoria Theatre, Singapore
White Jade (mus. Vaughan), solo, Los Angeles
A Yien Pwe w/Humphrey, Los Angeles
1927 *Dance of the Red and Gold Saree* (mus. Stoughton), solo, Fairbanks Theatre, Springfield, Ohio
1928 *The Batik Vender* (native music), Aurora Theatre, East Aurora, New York
Black and Gold Sari (mus. Stoughton), solo, Lewisohn Stadium, New York
The Lamp (mus. Liszt), Lewisohn Stadium
Three Coolie Girls (native music), Aurora Theatre
1929 *Burmese Dance* (mus. Vaughn), solo, Forrest Theatre, New York
Daughter of Desire (mus. Schenk), solo
Dojoji (mus. Bowers), solo, Figueroa Playhouse, Los Angeles
A Figure of Angkor Vat (mus. Bertge), solo, Figueroa Playhouse
Kwannon (mus. Satie), solo, Figueroa Playhouse
Prophet Bird (mus. Schumann), solo, Shubert Theater, New Haven, Connecticut
Scarf Dance (mus. Wachs), solo, Figueroa Playhouse
A Tagore Poem (mus. Moore-Koopmore), solo, Figueroa Playhouse
Waltz (mus. Rubinstein)
1930 *Angkor Vat* (mus. Sol Cohen), Lewisohn Stadium
A Buddhist Festival (mus. native airs), Lewisohn Stadium
Nautch Dance Ensemble (mus. Strickland-Scott), Washington Irving High School, New York
1931 *Dance Balinese* (mus. Hively), solo, Lewisohn Stadium
Modern Nautch (mus. Chadwick), solo, Lyric Theatre, Richmond, Virginia

The Prophetess (mus. Holst-Dyke), Lewisohn Stadium
Salome (mus. Strauss), solo, Lyric Theatre, Richmond
Unfinished Symphony w/Klarna Pinska (mus. Schubert),
    Lewisohn Stadium

1934   *Masque of Mary*
1946   *Color Study of the Madonna*
1950   *Gregorian Chant*
1951   *Three Poems in Rhythm*

Publications

By ST. DENIS: books—

Lotus Light, Cambridge, Massachusetts, 1932.
An Unfinished Life, New York, 1939.

By ST. DENIS: articles—

"The Secret of the Pharaoh's Favorite," *Atlanta Journal,* 26 February 1911.
"Does the Tango Need a Defender? If So Here She Is," *Chicago Sunday Tribune,* 15 June 1913.
"Ruth St. Denis' Ideas for the Dance Theatre," *Christian Science Monitor*, 23 October 1917.
"The Independent Art of Dance," *Theatre Arts*, June 1924.
"Music Visualization," *The Denishawn Magazine*, Spring 1925.
"Visualizing a Symphony—An Experiment in Musical Education," *Musical Courier*, 26 December 1931.
"The Dance as Life," *The Denishawn Magazine*, vol. 1, no. 1.

On ST. DENIS: books—

Schlundt, Christena L., *The Professional Appearances of Ruth St. Denis and Ted Shawn: A Chronology and Index of Dances 1906-1932,* New York, 1962.
Shawn, Ted, *Ruth St. Denis: Pioneer and Prophet*, San Francisco, 1920.
Shelton, Suzanne, *Divine Dancer: A Biography of Ruth St. Denis,* Garden City, New York, 1981.

On ST. DENIS: articles—

Martin, John, "The Neighborhood Playhouse," in *American Dancing: The Background and Personalities of the Modern Dance*, New York, 1936.
Ruyter, Nancy Lee Chalfa, "The American Way: Ruth St. Denis and Ted Shawn," in *Reformers and Visionaries: The Americanization of the Art of Dance,* New York, 1979.
Sherman, Jane, "Denishawn Revisited," *Ballet Review,* Spring 1981.
Sherman, Jane with Christina L. Schlundt, "Who is St. Denis? What Is She?" *Dance Chronicle*, 1987.

*   *   *

Ruth St. Denis was an important forerunner of modern dance in the United States along with Loie Fuller, Isadora Duncan, and Maud Allen. St. Denis' art and dance, however, had a more profound and lasting influence than the latter three. St. Denis was the first dancer to interpret Asian dance forms with imagination, integrity, and a spiritual seriousness which went far beyond the early and prurient scarf dancing and hootchy kootchy. In doing so, St. Denis explored the sources of movement in stillness and in the breath of ancient Asian practices like yoga. The other and more important influence came out of her partnership with Ted Shawn and their creation of the Denishawn Schools, the first of which opened in 1915 in California. Between 1922 and 1925, Denishawn schools were established in a dozen U.S. cities and these, along with the couple's ceaseless touring, popularized dance to an ever-widening and necessary audience.

St. Denis began performing in New York City as a skirt dancer in a dime museum offering a variety of entertainments and moved on to larger theater productions, most notably those of Augustin Daly and David Belasco. She learned a great deal about staging, design, and historical accuracy in detailing costumes and scenery during her tenure with Belasco's productions, knowledge she would later use to great effect in her Asian dances.

St. Denis's mother, Emily Dennis, introduced her daughter to Delsartian principles of movement and expression then popular in the States. When Ruth's talent for dancing became apparent, her mother worked steadily to get her auditions in New York, exhorting her to practice and working with her on choreography. Emily, who had completed a medical degree, was also an ardent dress reformer and admired the writings of Mary Baker Eddy which influenced St. Denis' philosophical and spiritual approach to dance. Reading American transcendentalists and European philosophers also shaded her thinking about the purpose of art in life. Even when on vaudeville, dance was a spiritual practice.

Other cultural influences converged in St. Denis' young experience before she produced her first original dances. She saw Genevieve Stebbins, a proponent of American Delsartian practice, when she was 13, and as Suzanne Shelton, author of *Divine Dancer: A Biography of Ruth St. Denis* (1981), has noted: "Ruthie experienced what she later called 'the real birth of my art life,' since Stebbins 'transformed a mechanical system of gesture into a dynamic art form.'" Parts of two of the dances St. Denis saw, *The Dance of Day* and *The Myth of Isis,* would later be transformed into her dance *Egypta*—inspired by an advertisement for Egyptian Deity Cigarettes.

While touring Europe with Belasco's production of *Zaza*, she immersed herself in European "orientalism" and went to the Paris Exhibition in 1900. While there, she saw ethnic dancers from Asia and the Middle East, as well as Sada Yacco, a Japanese actress who performed a Buddhist dance, and Loie Fuller, who performed her *Serpent Dance*. When St. Denis returned to the U.S. and was touring with the Belaso production of *Madame DuBarry*, she saw the now-legendary cigarette poster which was, as Suzanne Shelton points out "the catalyst in a long simmering process"—a catalyst which not only gave her an image around which to build her dance, but a larger artistic vision.

St. Denis choreographed, or at least sketched out enough of *Egypta* by 1905 to apply for a copyright; she would not stage it, however, for another five years. Instead she began work on what was to become *Radha* to sell on the vaudeville circuit to raise money for *Egypta*. *Radha* became one of her most popular compositions, and was championed in its early phase by wealthy New Yorkers in private performances. With these two dances, Ruth St. Denis began a pattern of trying to balance the popular and, hence money-making dances, with her more esoteric and serious dances—a tension she would feel her entire life.

In 1906, Henry Harris booked St. Denis into the Aldwych Theatre in London, and so began a highly successful three-year tour of Europe. Ruth found the warmest and most intellectual welcome in

Berlin, where she met and became friends with several artists including poet Hugo von Hofmannsthal and playwright Gerhart Hauptmann. At this time in the U.S., most artists working in any genre were compelled to go to Europe to make a name for themselves to be taken seriously back home. St. Denis returned with just such a European blessing after turning down an offer in Germany to build a school if she would stay for at least five years. On her return, she began a long series of tours crisscrossing the States, though because her troupe included several Indians she had met and worked with in New York, she did not venture across the Mason-Dixon line.

In 1914 in New York, Ted Shawn auditioned for classes and St. Denis took him on as dance partner immediately. They married within the year and began touring together and talked about beginning a school. They opened Denishawn in California and began accepting students for their fresh-air classes. Denishawn was largely the work of Shawn and his endless energy and idealism. St. Denis, as she said in her autobiography, was to "supply atmosphere" not to mention a well-known name. As early as 1936 in his book *American Dancing*, John Martin pointed to Denishawn as largely responsible for the establishment of dance in the United States, calling it the "parent organization of American Dance." For this to happen, according to Nancy Lee Chalfa Ruyter in *Reformers and Visionaries* (1979), "two things were necessary: to interest the American public in it and to overcome the moral prejudice against it." Dance not only had to be "attractive" and "nice" to gain support, but as Chalfa Ruyter contends "a cycle had to be initiated in which people would see dance and like it" and hopefully then "more would study it, and more would choose it as a career...." St. Denis and Shawn succeeded in initiating such a cycle from which modern dancers Martha Graham, Doris Humphrey, and Charles Weidman emerged—well-educated and well-supported in their artistic visions within the United States.

St. Denis and Shawn, though they remained married, lived separately from around 1928 on and only came together to perform for tours—though even these ended after Shawn began his all-male touring group. St. Denis remained an active performer after Deniswhan closed its doors in 1934. She worked largely on spiritual and liturgical dances, including *Color Study of the Madonna* with her Rhythmic Choir and usually performed at Jacob's Pillow after Shawn founded the annual dance festival on his Massachusetts farm. In later years, she received many awards, including the Capezio Award in 1961, confirming her contributions to early modern dance. St. Denis died in California in 1968 after almost seven decades of dancing.

—Glynis Benbow-Niemier

SANASARDO, Paul

American dancer, choreographer, educator, and company director

Born: 15 September 1928, in Chicago. **Education:** Studied painting and sculpture art, graduated from Art Institute of Chicago, 1950; studied under scholarship with Martha Graham; also studied with Antony Tudor, Mia Slavenska, Pearl Lang, and Erika Thimey. **Military Service:** Served in the U.S. Army, 1950-51. **Career:** Dancer, Erika Thimey Dance Troupe and partner of Thimey, 1952-53; dancer,

Anna Sokolow Company, with leading roles and as Sokolow's partner, 1953-57; *Red Roses for Me,* 1955; member, New York City Opera Ballet Company, 1956; guest artist with Pearl Lang, 1957-69; starred with Carmen Gutierrez in Shirley Clarke's award-winning dance film *A Moment of Love;* founder, Studio for Dance, 1958 (later renamed Modern Dance Artists Inc.); founder/director, Sanasardo Dance Company, 1958-86; company performed in Nassau, Bahamas as "The Nassau Civic Ballet," 1965; performed in Bermuda, 1966, and Puerto Rico, 1968; founder/artistic director, Theatre of Modern Dance Summer Dance Program, Saratoga Performing Arts Center, Saratoga Springs, New York, 1969-74; artistic director, Batsheva Dance Company, Tel Aviv, Israel, 1977-80; faculty, Whitman College Summer Dance Labs, 1982—. **Awards:** Guggenheim choreography fellowship, 1970; fellowships and grants from National Endowment for the Arts and New York State Council on the Arts.

Roles

1955   Original cast (cr), *Rooms* (Anna Sokolow), Anna Sokolow Company, New York
            Original cast, *Red Roses for Me* (Sean O'Casey), on Broadway

Other roles include: Original cast in *Lyric Suite* and *Poem,* Anna Sokolow Company; Father in *Rites,* Pluto in *Falls the Shadow Between,* Don Muerte (cr) in *Apasionada,* and original cast in *Shirah, And Joy Is My Witness,* and *Legend,* Pearl Lang Company.

Works

1956   *Three Dances of Death* (mus. Chopin; set des. David Lund)
1957   *Doctor Faustus Lights the Lights* (mus. Charles Wuorinen)
1958   *Because of Love* (mus. Villa-Lobos)
1959   *In View of God* w/Donya Feuer (mus. Ginastera & Blomdahl)
1960   *Laughter After All* w/Donya Feuer (mus. Varese)
1961   *Pictures in Our House* w/Feuer
            Excursions for Miracles, Part I (lighting by Nicola Cernovichc)
            Excursions for Miracles, Part II (lighting by Nicola Cernovichc)
1963   *Of Human Kindness* (mus. Edwin Finckel)
            Opulent Dream (mus. Scriabin)
            Two Movements for Strings (mus. Ginastera), also performed by Repertory Dancers of New Jersey in 1965
1964   *Metallics* (mus. Henry Cowell and Henk Badings; scenes/costumes by Sanasardo), 92nd Street YM-YWHA (later performed by Alvin Ailey American Dance Theatre, Bat-Dor Dance Company (Tel Aviv, Israel) and others
            Laughter After All (Revised) (mus. Varese)
1965   *Fatal Birds* (mus. Ginastera), also performed by Repertory Dancers of New Jersey, Utah Repertory Dance Theatre, and Dance Odyssey
1966   *An Earthly Distance* (mus. Henry)
            The Animal's Eye (mus. Schönberg)
            Excursions (mus. Eugene Lester and Jan Syrjala)
            Cut Flowers (mus. Kazimierz Serocki)
            Early Darkness (mus. Kodaly)

Paul Sanasardo, 1974. Photograph © Johan Elbers.

1967   *Three Dances* (mus. Paul Knopf)
1968   *The Descent* (mus. Maderna)
1969   *Pain* (mus. Witold Lutowski)
       Earth (commissioned by Repertory Dance Theatre; mus. Gerhard)
1970   *Footnotes* (mus. Eugene Lester)
1971   *The Myth*, First Chamber Dance Company
       Cyclometry
       Voices, Bat-Dor Dance Company, Tel Aviv
       Sightseeing
1972   *The Path*
       A Little Hell, Bat-Dor Dance Company, Tel Aviv
1973   *Small Prayers*
       Shadows, Bat-Dor Dance Company, Tel Aviv
       Carnival, Bat-Dor Dance Company, Tel Aviv
1974   *The Beggar's Ballroom*, Gulbenkian Ballet, Lisbon, Portugal
       A Sketch for Donna, American Ballet Company
       Disappearances, Detroit Dance

       The Platform
       The Amazing Graces
1975   *Sketches for Nostalgic Children*, Bat-Dor Dance Company, Tel Aviv
       Pearl River, Bat-Dor Dance Company, Tel Aviv
       A Consort for Dancers
       Memory Suite
       Saints and Lovers, Ballet Theatre Contemporain, Angers, France
1976   *Andantino Cantabile*, Lawrence Rhodes and Naomi Sorkin
       Abandoned Prayer
1977   *Triad*
       Romantic Realm, Dennis Wayne Dancers
       Ocean Beach, Atlanta Contemporary Dance Co.
       Step by Step with Haydn, Rondo Dance Theater; also performed by Batsheva Dance Company, Tel Aviv
       Providence, Rhode Island Dance Company
1978   *Lisztdelirium*, Batsheva Dance Company, Tel Aviv
       Meditations on an Open Stage, Galina Panov

1979   *Territories,* Joel Hall Dancers
1980   *Time No More,* Joan Lombardi Dancers
        Songs, Batsheva Dance Company, Tel Aviv
        The Stravinsky Rotating Dance Circus (mus. Israeli Phil-
            harmonic Orchestra), Batsheva Dance Company, Tel
            Aviv
        Babi-Yar, Batsheva Dance Company, Tel Aviv
1981   *Forget Me Not,* Cornish Dance Theater
        Solo from the Blue Window, Chicago Repertory Dance
            Ensemble
        Sunset-Sunrise, Cleo Parker Robinson Dance
1982   *Bagatelles,* Mid-America Dance Theatre
        The Abiding Void
        Miniatures
        The Blue Window
1983   *Premonitions*
1984   *Sunset-Sunrise (Revised)*
        The Wolf
1985   *Sleepless Nights*
        La Ronde des Femmes
        Children in the Mist
1986   *Mysteries*
        Scattered Clouds, Binghamtom Ballet Company
1987   *Etty,* Moving Feet Company
        Street Scene, Emma Willard Company
        Anyone Would Love You, Susquehannah School Dance
            Company

Other works include: Undated works *Because of Love* and *Poem;*
also choreographed for television shows including *Frontier, Lamp
unto My Feet, Directions,* and *Exploring.*

Publications

On SANASARDO: articles—

Anderson, Jack, "Sanasardo Dance Company," *Dance Magazine,*
    July 1973.
———, *"Void,* Other Dances by Sanasardo," *New York Times,* 26
    December 1982.
Barnes, Clive, "Dance View," *New York Times,* 15 June 1975.
———, *"Memory Suite,"* *New York Times,* 10 December 1975.
———, "Paul Sanasardo's Troupe Performs at Kaufman Hall," *New
    York Times,* 26 January 1967.
———, "Sanasardo Premiere in Marathon Finale," *New York Times,*
    November 1972.
Commanday, Robert, "Paul Sanasardo: Eloquent Dance View of
    Mankind," *San Francisco Chronicle,* 31 January 1972.
Gruen, T. "Close-Up: Paul Sanasardo," *Dance Magazine,* June 1975.
Hering, D. "A Darkening Pond," *Dance Magazine,* August 1971.
Jowitt, Deborah, review, *Village Voice,* 3 May 1973.
———, review, *Village Voice,* 6 June 1974.
———, review, *Village Voice,* 14 June 1994.
Kahn, Judy, "Paul Sanasardo Dance Company," *Dance Magazine,*
    October 1972.
Kisselgoff, Anna, "Sanasardo Group," *New York Times,* 28 April
    1973.
———, "Sanasardo Tour de Force," *New York Times,* 17 November
    1977.
———, "Sanasardo Troupe Opens a Season with *Consort,"* *New
    York Times,* 5 December 1975.
———, "Three Sanasardo Premieres," *New York Times,* 21 May
    1982.
Lewis, Jean Bailey, "Sanasardo at Lisner," *Washington Post,* 23
    January 1971.
McDonagh, Don, "Sanasardo's *Amazing Graces,"* *New York Times,*
    2 December 1974.
———, "Sanasardo's Blend of Dance and Poetry," *New York Times,*
    6 June 1975.
Pedro, Patricia F., "Impressive Start for Modern Dance Group,"
    Royal Gazette, 24 August 1966.
Peterson, Jackie, "Sanasardo: The Man Behind the Dance," *Sacra-
    mento Union,* 10 May 1978.
Reibstein, Janet, *"Pain,"* in *Dance Magazine,* July 1970.
Simpson, Herbert M., "Premiere of Paul Sanasardo's *Time No More,"*
    Dance Magazine, June 1980.
Stodelle, Ernestine, "Dance and Broken Lives," *New Haven Regis-
    ter,* 21 December 1975.
Temin, Christine, "The American Behind Israel's Ballet," *Boston
    Globe,* 19 May 1978.
Terry, Walter, "Sanasardo-Feuer," *New York Herald Tribune,* 16
    October 1961.
Tircuit, Heuwell, *"Consort for Dancers*: A Daring Attempt That
    Worked," *San Francisco Chronicle,* 29 October 1976.

Films and Videotapes

A Moment of Love, film starring Sanasardo and Carmen Gutierrez,
    dir. Shirley Clarke.
Cyclometry, choreographed by Sanasardo in 1971, has been televised
    repeatedly on PBS.

*   *   *

Paul Sanasardo has been a major force in the modern dance world
for more than four decades. He has choreographed more than 90
dance works for his own company and many of the leading dance
companies of the United States and Europe.

Sanasardo was born in 1928 in Chicago and grew up on the north
side of the city near the Art Institute of Chicago. He studied painting and sculpture there and graduated in 1950. At the University of
Chicago, he designed and built scenery for the "Tonight at 8:30"
group, under the direction of Paul Sills. While still in the U.S.
Army, stationed in Arlington, Virginia, in 1950 and 1951, Sanasardo
auditioned for Erika Thimey and the Washington Dance Theatre in
Washington, D.C.. Landing a part as a principal dancer, partially
because male dancers were in short supply at the time, Sanasardo
danced throughout the Washington, D.C., area and in the southern
United States in the evenings and on his weekends off from Army
duty.

In 1952 Sanasardo joined the Erika Thimey Dance Troupe, dancing lead roles and partnering with Thimey, who took Sanasardo to
New York where he thought he'd eventually outgrow dancing and
build the career he had studied for as a painter. But Thimey suggested he audition for Hanya Holm, who liked Sanasardo's style.
The two of them then suggested he audition for Martha Graham,
and Sanasardo was awarded a scholarship to study with Graham.
From there he built a stellar career as a dancer.

In 1953, Sanasardo joined the Anna Sokolow Dance Company in
New York City. He acknowledges that the work of Sokolow was a
direct influence on his own artistic development. Studying with
Sokolow, let alone Graham, put Sanasardo into a small group of

choreographers who can trace their dance "lineage" back to Denishawn (Ruth St. Denis and Ted Shawn), including colleagues Kei Takei and Kathryn Posin. From 1953 to 1956, he danced in leading roles in Sokolow company performances and created some of his own roles in some of her works. Sanasardo appeared at the 1955 American Dance Festival at the ANTA Theatre in New York in *Rooms* in the role he created, as well as *Lyric Suite* and *Poem,* and also performed on Broadway in Sean O'Casey's *Red Roses for Me.* The following year, Sanasardo became a performing member of the New York City Opera Ballet Company.

In 1957 Sanasardo performed as a guest artist with Pearl Lang's company and for an extended period (1957-69) danced leading roles for the Lang Company while partnering with Lang in concert. Some of his performances included playing the Father in *Rites* and Pluto in *Falls the Shadow Between.* He created the role of Don Muerte in *Apasionada* and also appeared in *Shirah, And Joy Is My Witness,* and *Legend.*

During his early years in New York, Sanasardo studied with the greats: aside from Graham, Sokolow, and Lang, he also worked with Antony Tudor and Mia Slavenska. In addition to dance, he starred with Carmen Gutierrez in Shirley Clarke's award-winning dance film, *A Moment of Love.* As both choreographer and dancer he appeared on national television programs such as *Frontier, Lamp Unto My Feet, Directions*, and *Exploring* and his piece *Cyclometry* was documented at the Schenectady Art Museum and has run repeatedly on PBS television.

In 1958 Sanasardo, with colleague Donya Feuer, established his own school, the Studio for Dance. The name was later changed to Modern Dance Artists Inc. and professional dancers from more than 30 countries have come to the States to study at the Modern Dance Artists School.

Sanasardo, again with Feuer, following in the tradition of creating a company based on the character and works of a single choreographer, formed the Paul Sanasardo Dance Company, with Pina Bausch as one of their principal members. Manuel Alum, who had previously danced with the Neville Black Company and who was a Martha Graham School of Contemporary Dance student, joined the company in the early 1960s, studying under Sanasardo and eventually becoming an assistant artistic director of the company.

In 1965 the Sanasardo Company performed in Nassau, the Bahamas, under the aegis of the Nassau Civic Ballet. The next year, the Bermuda Ballet Association sponsored a season for the Sanasardo Company in Bermuda under the patronage of His Excellency the Governor, the Right Honourable Lord Martonmere, making the company the first modern dance company to be so honored. In 1968 the company was invited by the Cultural Institute of Puerto Rico to perform in Rio Piedras, and again the company was acclaimed for its outstanding style and superb repertoire. In addition to running his own dance company, Sanasardo established the Theatre of Modern Dance at the Saratoga Performing Arts Center in Saratoga Springs, New York, in 1969, where he served as the artistic director during its five-year program.

Sanasardo received a Guggenheim Fellowship for Choreography in 1970 and went on to become a recipient of fellowships and grants from both the National Endowment for the Arts and New York State Council on the Arts. By the 1970s the Sanasardo Company was acclaimed as one of the unique artistic achievements in the modern dance industry, as one of the leading modern dance companies performing in the world. By the end of the decade 44 of Sanasardo's ballets had premiered in New York City during the company's annual New York seasons. A distinctive hallmark of Sanasardo's work is his total involvement with all aspects of his dances. A true auteur, Sanasardo is involved not only in choreography, but set design, costumes, and lighting, leading to an unusual fusion of theatre disciplines merged into one form. This approach has attracted prominent artists from other fields to supplement Sanasardo's vision with their own. Contemporary composers such as Charles Wuorinen, Steven Drew, and Eugene Lester have created original works for Sanasardo's dances. Robert Natkin and David Lund are but two artists who have worked on set design and decor with Sanasardo. Architect Robert Bayley designed the sets for Sanasardo's ballet *Pain.* This merging of diverse artistic disciplines caused the Schenectady Art Museum to allow Sanasardo to use their premises as a performing space in his innovative work *Cyclometry,* which was hailed by the museum world and documented by television stations WMHT-TV and WNET-TV and has since aired on PBS stations throughout the country.

In a rare move in the single choreographer tradition, Sanasardo allowed his company to provide as a crucible, a trial by fire for company members who wished to choreograph, performing 35 works by the late 1970s that had been choreographed by the company's principal dancers, which, in addition to Alum, included Diane Germaine, Willa Kahn, Judith Blackstone, Gerri Houlihan, Yon Martin, Martin Bland, and Joan Lombardi, who also eventually became an assistant artistic director. Some of Alum's repertoire included *Nightbloom* (1965, music by Serocki; set design by Robert Natkin), *Storm* (1965, music by Luciuk), *The Offering* (1966, music by Penderecki), *Fantasia* (1967, music by Hamilton), *The Cellar* (1967, music by Kilar), and *Palomas* (1968, commissioned by The Northern Westchester Dance Company, music by Oliveras). The company had by this time also served residencies at many major universities in the United States.

Hailed as one of the foremost of the successors of modern dance, by the mid-1970s Sanasardo had trained and worked with scores of dancers. Some of his more prominent students and performers by this time included Pina Bausch, Gus Solomons Jr., Laura Dean, Carla Maxwell, Sara Rudner, Cliff Keuter, Naomi Sorkin, Kenneth King, Miguel Godreau, and William Dunas. In addition, the list of former company members and guest artists who performed with the Sanasardo Company read like a veritable Who's Who of dancers, including Susan Bass, Art Bauman, Sally Bowden, Tony Catanzaro, Jay Fletcher, Cliff Keuter, Mark Franko, Renata Kuhn, Linda Sidon, Carl Woods, and Britt Swanson.

From November 1977 through 1980, Sanasardo was the artistic director of the Batsheva Dance Company of Tel Aviv, Israel. During his tenure there he created six ballets for Batsheva, one featuring Galina Panova. Three of the ballets were full-length for Israeli television—*The Stravinsky Rotating Dance Circus,* which was commissioned by the Israeli Philharmonic Orchestra, plus the highly acclaimed *Babi Yar* and *Songs.*

Recognized as one of the leading teachers and exponents of modern dance, Sanasardo's works have succeeded the retiring of his company in 1986, performed by companies such as Alvin Ailey American Dance Theatre, Utah Repertory Dance Theatre, and Detroit Dance. His works have been performed worldwide by such players as Le Ballet Theatre Contemporain in Angers, France, Gulbenkian Ballet in Lisbon, Portugal, Winnipeg Contemporary Dancers and Saskatchewan Dance Theater in Canada, and both Batsheva and Bat-Dor dance companies from Israel. Sanasardo himself has gone on to serve as a faculty member at the Summer Dance Lab of Whitman College, located in Walla Walla, Washington, and has been a guest teacher and lecturer at universities and colleges all over the U.S., continuing to teach today. He has also taken up painting again, though as a hobby, not as another career. Laughingly, he says, "One career was enough."

—Daryl F. Mallett

SARTORIO, Angiola

Italian-born dancer, choreographer, and educator based in the United States

Born: 30 September 1903 in Rome. **Education:** Studied modern dance with Sylvia Bodmer and Rudolf Laban; ballet with Lubov Egorova; as well as French acrobatics and character dancing. **Career:** Dancer and teacher with Kurt Jooss, Essen, 1925-29; choreographer, Rome Opera, 1932; choreographer, Musical May Festivals, Florence, 1933-38; founding director/choreographer, Ballet of the City of Florence, 1934-38; director, Professional Dancing School of the City of Florence, 1934-38; teacher, Katherine Dunham School of Dance and Theatre, New York, mid-1940s; teacher/choreographer, Jacob's Pillow, Lee, Massachusetts, 1945-46; founding director, teacher/choreographer, summer dance school and experimental company, Bar Harbor, Maine, 1947-54; teacher/choreographer, southern and central California, 1954-95. **Awards:** American Dance Guild Award of Artistry, 1994. **Died:** 26 May 1995 in Santa Barbara, California.

Roles

1929   Infanta (cr) in *Pavane on Death of the Infanta* (Jooss),
        Folkwang-Tanztheater, Essen

Works (some dates uncertain)

1932   Dances in *Macbeth,* Rome Opera
1933   Dances in *A Midsummer Night's Dream* (mus.
        Mendelssohn), Musical May Festival, Boboli Gardens,
        Florence
1934   *Intermezzo* (mus. Virgilio Mortari), Ballet of the City of
        Florence, Florence
        Don Quixote (mus. Mario Salerno), Ballet of the City of
        Florence
        The Mis-matched Lovers (mus. Mozart), Ballet of the
        City of Florence
1935   *Boudoir and Pantry* (mus. Sandro Levignani), Ballet of
        the City of Florence
        The Two Divas (mus. Sandro Levignani), Ballet of the
        City of Florence, Casino Municipale, San Remo
1936   *The Rage Over the Lost Penny* (mus. Beethoven), Ballet
        of the City of Florence
        Eternal Song (mus. J. Engel), Ballet of the City of Flo-
        rence
1937   *Barabau* (mus. Vittorio Rieti), Ballet of the City of Flo-
        rence
        The Turquoise Fish (mus. Mario Castelnuovo-Tedesco),
        Ballet of the City of Florence, May Festival
        La Primavera (mus. Vivaldi), Ballet of the City of Flo-
        rence, May Festival, Florence

1945   *Theme and Variations on Laban Scales,* Jacob's Pillow,
        Lee, Massachusetts
1953   *Four Studies* (mus. various piano selections), Choreogra-
        phers Workshop, YM-YWHA Dance Center, New
        York
1958   *St. Francis of Assisi,* Victor Moreno and Joyce Vanderveen,
        Dances of Faith, Los Angeles
1994   *Why Should I Fear?* (mus. Michael Mortilla), solo for
        Nina Watt, videotaped performance, Santa Barbara

Publications

By SARTORIO: articles—

"Eukinetics: The Science of Dance," *Dance News,* November 1945.
"Choreutics" and "Eukinetics," in *The Dance Encyclopedia,* Anatole
    Chujoy, editor, New York, 1949; revised, 1967.

On SARTORIO: articles—

Dionne, Alexandria, "Modern Dance Great Honored at Conference,"
    The Independent, 2 June 1994.
Reisel, Megan, "Angiola Sartorio in Conversation," *Laban Guild
    Movement and Dance Quarterly,* Fall 1995 and Winter 1995.

Films and Videotapes

A black-and-white short film of Sartorio demonstrating Laban scales at Jacob's Pillow, 1945 (by Carol Lynn), exists in the Dance Research Collection of the New York Public Library of the Performing Arts at Lincoln Center.

*   *   *

Though Angiola Sartorio founded what is commonly considered to have been the first modern dance company in Italy, she fled the fascist-controlled country in 1939 and chose, instead, to promulgate the ideas of her mentors Rudolf Laban and Kurt Jooss in the United States, where she choreographed and taught for almost 60 years.

Sartorio was born in Rome, but spent most of her youth in England and Sweden with her mother, who was separated from Sartorio's father, the celebrated Italian painter G. Aristide Sartorio. A well-schooled upper-class child, Sartorio was afforded lessons in painting and studied music with Émile Jaques-Dalcroze. She also studied modern dance in Frankfurt with Sylvia Bodmer, who was known as one of the finest interpreters of the work of the esteemed movement theorist Rudolf Laban. Sartorio, a short, strong dancer who exuded athletic power rather than sylph-like delicacy, later became one of Laban's prized pupils.

In 1925 Sartorio joined the Essen-based dance company and school of noted German Expressionist choreographer Kurt Jooss. A solo performer, Sartorio also taught classes in Laban movement theory at the school. For his 1929 work *Pavane on Death of the Infanta* Jooss created the role of the Infanta for Sartorio. Feeling the need to study ballet, which Jooss forbade, Sartorio then moved to Paris and studied with Lubov Egorova, a former ballerina from the Maryinsky company, and choreographed and performed solo dance recitals in Germany and France.

In 1932 she was asked to choreograph the dances for *Macbeth* at the Rome Opera, which led to an invitation to stage dances for reputed theatrical director Max Reinhardt's 1933 production of *A Midsummer Night's Dream* at the first Florentine Musical May Festival. Reinhardt was so impressed with Sartorio that he asked her to work with him on subsequent projects elsewhere. Sartorio chose, however, to remain in Florence to accept an invitation to form her own, and Italy's first, modern dance company.

In 1934 she founded the Ballet of the City of Florence and an affiliated, state-accredited school. Sartorio's company provided the dances for the annual May Festivals and operas and toured throughout Europe presenting her expressionistic, narrative works. By 1938, however, Sartorio had become disillusioned with the strict control Mussolini maintained over the arts in Italy and was deeply disturbed when her state-funded company had to do command performances for the Nazis.

Unable to abide Italy's political climate, in 1939 Sartorio moved to New York City, where she started her own school for professional dancers and organized a company of amateurs who wanted to study seriously and perform modern dance. She taught choreutics (an analysis of the relationships between dancers and space developed by Laban), eukinetics (a system of controlling the dynamics and expression of a dancer's body developed by Jooss), and dance composition. Sartorio also worked with physical trainer Joseph Pilates and taught at the Katherine Dunham School of Dance and Theatre in New York.

During the summers of 1945 and 1946 Sartorio taught and choreographed at Ted Shawn's summer dance festival at Jacob's Pillow in Lee, Massachusetts. A rare opportunity to see Sartorio at work was provided by photographer Carol Lynn, who filmed the choreographer demonstrating Laban scales at Jacob's Pillow in 1945. The 8.5-minute, silent, black-and-white film is housed in the Dance Collection of the New York Public Library of the Performing Arts at Lincoln Center.

From 1947 to 1954 Sartorio directed a summer dance school she founded in Bar Harbor, Maine. It was there, under Sartorio's tutelage, that the celebrated American modern choreographer Paul Taylor was first introduced to the study of dance. Recognized as an expert on the work of Laban and Jooss, Sartorio was asked to write articles on eukinetics and choreutics for *The Dance Encyclopedia* edited by Anatole Chujoy in 1949.

In 1953 her *Four Studies* was presented as part of the Choreographers' Workshop series at New York's 92nd Street YM-YWHA, an important venue for showcasing noteworthy new modern dance artists. Sartorio also choreographed operas at New York's City Center and was asked to choreograph for Ballet Theatre, but, concerned that the ballet company would not understand the modern sensibilities inherent in her work, she declined the offer—a decision she later regretted. The summer of 1954 she assisted choreographer Yurik Lazowski on the dances for the musical *Arabian Nights* presented at Jones Beach, Wantagh, New York. Soon after, Sartorio moved to California, where she continued to choreograph, direct modern dance groups, and teach, both privately and at local colleges and universities.

It was through her teaching that Sartorio may have had her most lasting influence on modern dance. Sartorio felt that as Laban's work was extended to nondance movement applications and his fame grew to rest largely on his written notation system, students began to lose sight of his artistic identity. She, therefore, stressed to her pupils that Laban's work was not simply a tool to analyze pedestrian movement, but a system of thinking about movement that was rooted in connections to emotional or dramatic expression. Sartorio's content-driven choreography was always expressive of human emotions and was never simply an exploration of the physical elements of dance. In addition, Sartorio inspired her students to approach dance intellectually. Nina Watt, a principal dancer with the Limón Company, studied with Sartorio as a child and recalled how her teacher continually presented her with intellectual challenges regarding the making of physical movements, often in an improvisational context.

A devout theosophist, in her later years Sartorio spent increasing amounts of her time and money supporting charities committed to environmental causes, Native Americans, and other groups suffering from poverty and/or discrimination. A self-effacing, modest person, Sartorio made no efforts to secure a place in modern dance history for herself and is, today, largely unrecognized. A year before she died, however, Sartorio received the 1994 American Dance Guild Award of Artistry, honoring her lifelong commitment to modern dance choreography and teaching.

—Lisa Jo Sagolla

SCHNEEMANN, Carolee
American performance artist, painter, filmmaker, and writer

Born: 12 October 1939 in Pennsylvania. **Education:** B.A., Bard College, 1960; M.F.A., University of Illinois, 1961; trained with Robert Dunn at Judson Memorial Church, New York. **Family:** Married to composer James Tenney. **Career:** Founder, Kinetic Theater, 1962; member, Judson Dance Theater, 1962-66; performance works, film showings throughout U.S. and Europe; performance installations include Palazzo Reale in Milan, and Art Institute of Chicago, 1980; performance tour *Fresh Blood—A Dream Morphology*, France, Belgium, Holland, 1981; retrospective exhibit, Max Hutchison Gallery, 1982; exhibitions Whitney Museum, 1984, 1985; U.S. traveling exhibition sculpture with video, 1986; retrospective, New Museum of Contemporary Art, New York, 1997; exhibitions at Frauen Museum, Bonn (Germany); the Kunstruam, Vienna; Centre Georges Pompidou, Paris; Museum of Contemporary Art, Los Angeles, 1997. **Awards:** Special Jury Selection, Cannes Film Festival, 1968, for *Fuses*; Creative Artists Public Service Program fellowship, 1978-79; New York State Council of the Arts grant, 1968; National Endowment for Arts (NEA) grants, 1974, 1977-78, 1983.

Works

1956	*Loving* w/James Tenney
	Cat's Cradle w/James Tenney
	White Eye w/Tenney
1960	*Labyrinths*
1962	*Glass Environment for Sound and Motion,* New York
	Mink Paws TURRET
1963	*Chromelodeon,* New York
	Lateral Splay, New York
	EYE BODY
	Newspaper Event, New York
1964	*Meat Joy,* Paris
	Music Box Music
1965	*"TV"*

The Queen's Dog, New York
Noise Bodies w/Tenney
Beast Event
1966   *Water Light/Water Needle,* New York and New Jersey
1967   *Snows,* New York
        Night Crawlers
        Ordeals
        Snug Harbor
        Round House, London
        Body Collage
1968   *Illinois Central,* Chicago
        Illinois Central Transposed
1969   *Nude Bride*
        Expansions
1970   *Chicago Festival of Life in London: Thames Crawling,*
        London
1971   *Electronic Activations*
        Schlaget-Auf (Ein Gestalt)
        Why We Run and Crawl
        Rainbow Blaze
1972   *Road Runners*
        Roller Moving Train Skating
1973   *Cooking With Apes,* Stockholm
1988   *Cycladic Imprints*
        Cat Scan
1989   *Cat Torture in the Liquid Gate*

Publications

By SCHNEEMANN: books—

Part of a Body House Book, London, 1972.
Cezanne, She Was a Great Painter, 1974.
More Than Meat Joy: Performance Works and Selected Writings,
    Kingston, New York, 1979, 1997.

On SCHNEEMANN: books—

Jowitt, Deborah, *Time and the Dancing Image,* New York, 1988.
McDonagh, Don, *The Complete Guide to Modern Dance,* Garden
    City, New York, 1976.
———, *Rise and Fall and Rise of Modern Dance,* New York, 1970.

On SCHNEEMAN: articles—

Castle, Ted, "The Woman Who Uses Her Body as Her Art," *Art
    Forum,* November 1980.

Films and Videotapes (by Schneemann)

Fuses, erotic film, 1968,
Kitch's Last Meal, video, 1973.
Up To and Including Her Limits, 1974-77.
Interior Scroll, 1975.
ABC-We Print Anything—In The Cards, 1976-77.
Homerunmuse, 1977.

*   *   *

An artist, poet, and author, Carolee Schneemann's choreography
falls into the category of performance art. Her first dance pieces

were part of the events known as "happenings" held at the Judson
Memorial Church in the 1960s. The happenings were spontaneous
collaborations of dancers, poets, musicians, and artists striving to
reach new levels of expression in the development of the postmodern
dance movement.

Schneemann was born 12 October 1939 in Pennsylvania and
grew up in Wisconsin. After receiving her B.A. from Bard College
in 1960, and an M.F.A. from the University of Illinois in 1961, she
moved to New York in 1962 with husband James Tenney, a composer. It was a marriage based on technicality—Tenney held a scholarship to Bennington College, but the ostensibly progressive
women's college would not allow their first male student to live
unmarried with a woman. Schneemann's first three works of choreography were collaborations with Tenney in the late 1950s.

Her first encounter with dance and choreography training was in
classes taught by Robert Dunn at the Judson Memorial Church in
Greenwich Village, New York. Choreographers including James
Waring, Robert Morris, John Cage, David Gordon, and Twyla Tharp,
among others developed the gatherings into the Judson Dance Theater. Schneemann was one of the first artists to work with the
Judson dancers. In a piece titled *Site,* choreographed by Bob Morris, her role was that of a statue "glued" to plywood. The dance's
prop, a painted box, was removed in pieces to reveal the naked
Schneemann.

Like her artwork, her other "performance" art pieces incorporated her naked body. In the solo performance art, not those works
she choreographed for a group, her nude body was painted and
adorned with tissue paper, moving about a room (usually her loft)
in which each piece of furniture was a part of the "living sculpture."
Site was an unusual addition to her creative credits. Schneemann
brought the philosophy behind her art to the performance arena.
She felt that any elements existing in the performance space be
utilized as part of the performance or be covered, for example,
heating radiators. At the same time she disfavored the thinking of
modern dance which had at it's inception been rebellious toward the
strict structure of ballet. "Her dances are a series of, in effect, mob
pieces," notes Don McDonagh in *The Rise and Fall and Rise of
Modern Dance,* "which are dedicated to the celebration of the fleshly
and the sensual. Schneemann does not concern herself with the finer
details of choreography so much as with the broad outlines of the
effects she wants to achieve."

As she became more involved with the happenings at the Judson
Church, she almost completely stopped painting. Photos of her
performed images are all that now remain of her art from this period. Though seeming chaotic, her performances were highly structured, often including scripts, yet leaving room for improvisation
between the performers. Her audiences, though enthusiastic, remained for the most part uncomprehending. "Since she was not a
dancer, she was not entirely welcomed in the hotly competitive
world of minimal modern dance where the women competed with
abstractions and mattresses while Carolee wanted to used naked-
ness, shards of glass, messes of paint, burned greasy underwear,
and vulgar music," commented Ted Castle in his November 1980
article in *Art Forum.* "She was," Castle contends, "to use a masculine analogy, Dionysius among the Apollonians."

Schneemann's most popular piece, *Meat Joy,* first performed in
1964, was also her first success as a "designer of human movement," according to McDonagh in 1976's *The Complete Guide to
Modern Dance.* It is an energetic piece focusing on the vivacity of
life and contrasting, through the use of whole chickens and fish that
are thrown about, limp flesh and flesh stimulated by life. In *Meat*

Joy, the cosmetic area, where the performers apply make-up and "prepare" for the dance is part of the stage setting. They soon move to the performance area acting out a series of casual encounters between males and females that escalate to overt sexual advances. Performers disrobe, crumble huge sheets of paper, and use the paint pots placed throughout the performing area to paint each other's bodies, mixing the paint by rubbing their bodies together. Fresh fish, chickens, and sausages are dumped on a pile of human "carcasses" and later used as props carried or dragged about during the performance. The outrageousness of the piece split both audiences and critics from its initial showing at an avant-garde festival in Paris through each subsequent showing in the United States and in London.

The Paris performance caused such uproar that she had to quickly leave France. In London she found a progressive church willing to take a chance on her and staged *Meat Joy* there in spring of 1964 where another twist of fate soon found the choreographer fleeing the country and police. Due to the paints and dyes used in the piece, the performers found a communal dressing arrangement beneficial, to aid in scrubbing dye off one another and making quick changes. The vicar's wife, however, entering what she thought was the women's dressing area was horrified. "The performers locked her into an elevator and sent her screaming up to another floor. The performances were concluded before the arrival of the police, and Schneemann returned home to stage *Meat Joy* at Judson Church," writes McDonagh in *The Rise and Fall and Rise of Modern Dance.*

Schneemann, ultimately a visual artist, begins creating her performances from drawings and continues to bring them to life through live animation—choreographed movement. Though she bears no formal dance technique, McDonagh describes her as "a performer of special talents. She is concerned with movement. It is difficult, critically speaking, to tell exactly why her pieces differ from 'happenings' but they do in their flow of energy." Describing her own choreography as kinetic theater, Schneemann is interested in combining movement with the elements of lighting, music, and dramatic bits, to speak to the audience in a way that paintings alone cannot. In performers she requires only for them to throw themselves into the piece, adding to it in a sort of improvisation, and once it is found to work is "scripted" for the future performance. "Of all the artists who have involved themselves in dance productions, Schneemann is probably the one who has come closest to the ecstatic feeling of moving in space. She has approached dance from its bodily rather than its conceptual component," writes McDonagh.

—Lisa A. Wroble

SCHÖNBERG, Bessie

German-born American dancer and educator

Born: 1906 in Hanover, Germany. **Education:** Studied at Jaques-Dalcroze school; University of Oregon (Eugene) with Martha Hill; B.A., Bennington College, 1934; also studied dance with Martha Graham and others at the Neighborhood Playhouse, New York. **Family:** Married Dimitri Varley, 1934 (died 1984). **Career:** Dancer, Martha Graham Dance Company, 1929-31; taught at Sarah Lawrence College, 1938-75; director of dance department, 1942-75; has also taught at Bennington College, Henry Street Settlement, International House, American Dance Festival, Dance Theater of Harlem, Dance Theatre Workshop, Jacob's Pillow Dance Festival, Juilliard, London Contemporary Dance School, New York University Tisch School of the Arts, and the Yard. **Awards:** New York Dance and Performance Award ("Bessie"—named after her) for lifetime achievement, 1988; New York State Governor's Arts Award, 1989; National Endowment for the Arts (NEA) first Master Teacher/Mentor fellowship, 1993; Dance/USA's "Ernie" Award, 1994; American Dance Festival's Balasaraswati/Joy Ann Dewey Beinecke Endowed Chair for Distinguished Teaching, 1997. **Died:** 14 May 1997.

Publications

By SCHÖNBERG: articles—

"A Lifetime of Dance," *Performing Arts Journal,* c.1979.

On SCHÖNBERG: articles—

Hering, Doris, "To Teach the Unteachable," *Dance Magazine,* August 1962.
Jowitt, Deborah, "A Conversation with Bessie Schönberg," *Ballet Review,* Spring 1981.
———, "Meet the Composer: The Original Bessie," *Dance Magazine,* September 1991.
Owen, Norton, "Bessie Schönberg, 1906-1997," *Dance Magazine,* August 1997.
Sachs, Curt, *World History of the Dance,* New York, 1937.
Tobias, Anne, "Bessie's Way," *Dance Ink,* Winter 1993/1994.

*   *   *

One of the great educators of modern dance, Bessie Schönberg influenced countless developing choreographers over the span of several generations. She was never interested in creating a distinct profile or identity as a choreographer herself. Instead, she turned her profound love of dance to enabling artists working in a wide spectrum of approaches to clarify their visions in ways that had lasting impact on the development of the field. Some of the artists she worked with include Lucinda Childs, Elizabeth Keen, and Meredith Monk.

Schönberg was born in Germany in 1906, and spent her childhood years in Dresden, briefly studying eurythmics at the Dalcroze School. When she was six, her mother, an American singer, left the family to pursue her opera career back in America. Schönberg yearned continually to dance as she grew up, and although her father took her to see many performances, he didn't allow her dance lessons. A locally displayed photograph of Mary Wigman became a continual focus of inspiration for her, as she struggled with feelings of being abandoned by her mother, and her dreams of expressing herself through the art of movement.

After the end of World War I, her mother, now on the faculty of the University of Oregon, unexpectedly sent for her. The 20-year-old Schönberg tore herself away from her cherished Dresden and enrolled in the university, where she was finally allowed to study dance, even though it was of a superficially lyric type that didn't appeal to someone who had been touched by Wigman's fiery expressionism. Soon, however, Martha Hill joined the faculty, and Schönberg fell in love with her clearly analytical approach to dance, influenced by Hill's recent studies with the young Martha Graham.

In 1929 Hill returned to New York to study further with Graham. Schönberg was not about to be left behind this time, and decided to go as well. Arriving in New York, she was awarded a scholarship at the Neighborhood Playhouse School of the Theatre, and was also soon accepted into Graham's company as a dancer. There she performed in some of Graham's seminal early works such as *Primitive Mysteries* and *Heretic*, at a time when being a Graham dancer also meant staying up late "sewing our costumes with Martha." A suddenly contracted knee injury tragically forced the end of her performing career within two years of its beginning.

Schönberg was devastated by feelings of disappointment at no longer being able to dance on stage. Hill managed to get her an assistant's teaching position at Bennington College, where, at the same time, Schönberg continued her own education, earning a B.A. in 1934. She turned the energy of her grief to immersion in the visual arts, studying most notably with stage designer Arch Lauterer, who was a great influence on her understanding of the power of space. From these studies she drew a strong sense of design, that would later define in part her understanding of the visual elements of dance.

In 1938 Schönberg began teaching at Sarah Lawrence College, and eventually became the director of the dance department in 1942. As her own knowledge and interests grew, she added a variety of courses for dance students, creating a full dance curriculum that included composition, improvisation, dance history, and music. She also staged and choreographed many plays and operas for the college. Over the years, her dance composition classes became legendary in their depth and rigor. Schönberg continued in her position until her retirement in 1975. Leaving Sarah Lawrence was hardly the end of her teaching activities though, and in the next 20 years she taught at a wide number of venues, including the Dance Theater of Harlem, the Juilliard School, New York University, Jacob's Pillow Dance Festival, Dance Theatre Workshop, the London Contemporary Dance School, and the American Dance Festival.

Schönberg's approach to choreography and its teaching was objective, analytical, and based on problem-solving. She was interested in how the physical facts of dance could be identified, manipulated, and consciously ordered to create meaning. The emphasis on looking deeply and clearly into a situation's potential informed many of her directions to students. One of her exercises was to ask the students to sit in front of a theater stage, and to focus meditatively on the empty space, allowing each to imagine any one of countless possibilities that could be brought to life within that space. She often insisted that young choreographers in her classes not dance in their own works, so that they could look at what they were making with a dispassionate outside eye. Her vision of dance was a whole one; she expected her dance students to be able to compose music, to fully account for the visual elements of their creations.

Schönberg directed choreographers to participate in discourse by speaking clearly about each other's work as fellow craftsmen, urging them to discussion based squarely on the singular intentions of the artist they were addressing. In her workshops there would often be a range of choreographic styles including jazz, experimental performance art, traditional ethnic styles, and ballet, with each participant becoming involved in critiquing work in a way that reached further than individual tastes and opinion. She compared her role to that of an archeologist or detective in helping artists dig deeply into their own impulses, to put the pieces together in a way that solved the mystery of their emerging visions. Her own taste was nonhierarchical; she was interested in seeing each new work of art strictly on its own terms. Her gift was in seeing the potential for truth inherent in a wide variety of interpretations and voices, continu-

ally searching for what was fresh and essential in each individual, and then finding an objective way to bring those qualities into light.

Schönberg continued to teach until four days before her death at the age of 90. The "Bessie" awards—the New York Dance and Performance Awards given annually by Dance Theatre Workshop since 1984—had been named after her, as well as theaters at Dance Theater Workshop and Sarah Lawrence. Her legacy remains with artists from every niche of modern dance, one that includes a demand for dedication and humility, for honoring through hard work and rigor the unique aspects of their own visions. In an interview with Anne Tobias in *Dance Ink*, Schönberg described her view of the choreographic process: "It comes without flurries or furbelows. It comes down to the energy, the capacity for work, diligence. Of course you do it again, of course you go there and do it again tomorrow, of course. How else?"

—Fiona Marcotty

SCHURMAN, Nona

Canadian-born dancer, choreographer, and educator

Born: 6 November 1909 in Oxford, Nova Scotia. **Education:** Macdonald School, Quebec; graduated from Westmount High School, 1927; studied cello, voice, French language, and literature, Les Fougères School in Lausanne, Switzerland, 1927-29; studied music theory, Lausanne Conservatory of Music; studied Dalcroze Eurythmics, Central Institute, Geneva, Switzerland, 1928; studied theatre at McGill University, Montreal, Canada, 1929-31; began dance training with Blanche Evans in Montreal, 1930; studied modern dance in New York City with Hanya Holm, 1934-36; began training with Doris Humphrey and Charles Weidman, 1936. **Career:** Member, Humphrey-Weidman Company, 1939-43; teacher, Humphrey-Weidman School, 1941-43; assistant to Humphrey and Weidman, New York University, 1942-43, and Bennington College School of Dance Summer Session, 1942; teacher of Humphrey/Weidman technique and dance composition, New Dance Group (NDG), 1939-67; director, Young Concert Dancers Lecture Demonstrations at NDG studio, 1956-64; modern dance director, Roxy Theatre, New York City, 1943-44; director/choreographer of *Evangeline,* opera by Otto Luening, Columbia University Opera Workshop, New York City, 1948; taught at 92nd Street YM-YWHA, 1946-68; Fieldston School, Ethical Culture Society, 1947; High School for Performing Arts, 1954; and Columbia University Teacher's College, 1961; director/founder of own school and company, the Center for Dance Study, 1954-68; board of directors, Dance Notation Bureau, 1958-68; Dance Film, Inc., 1956-68; assistant professor of Dance, SUNY-Geneseo, 1973-79; faculty at New York University, 1979; Cornish College (Seattle, Washington), 1980; Stephens College (Columbia, Missouri), 1983; and Ohio State University (Columbus, Ohio), 1994; director, film of Weidman Technique, 1985. **Awards:** Chancellor's Award for Excellence in Teaching, 1977.

Roles

1941   *Flickers* (Weidman)
1942   Clorinda in the Monteverdi opera, *Il Combatimento di Tancredi e Clorinda*

1945   *Up in Central Park* (Helen Tamiris), U.S.O. Camp Shows
        Shootin' Star (Lester Horton)

Other roles include: As a member of Humphrey-Weidman Company, 1939-43: *Song of the West, Danc"ings," The Shakers, Passacaglia in C Minor, New Dance, With My Red Fires, Partita, Life of the Bee,* and *Air for the G String* (all by Humphrey); in *And Daddy Was a Fireman* and *Lynchtown* (by Weidman).

Works

1943   *Tell Me of the Living,* 92nd Street YM-YWHA Dance
        Audition Winner, New York City
        This Earth, 92nd Street YM-YWHA Dance Audition
        Winner
        Running Together, 92nd Street YM-YWHA Dance Audition Winner
1948   *Evangeline,* Columbia University Opera Workshop, Columbia University Department of Music, New York City
1949   *Songs from the Hebrides,* 92nd Street YM-YWHA

Publications

By SCHURMAN: books—

With Sharon Leight Clark, *Modern Dance Fundamentals.*

By SCHURMAN: articles—

"Looking at Doris' Work Is Like Listening to Bach," *Journal of Health, Physical Education and Recreation,* February 1970.

On SCHURMAN: articles—

Finkelstein, Joan, "Doris Humphrey and the 92nd Street Y: A Dance Center for the People," *Dance Research Journal,* Fall 1996.
Hausler, Barbara, "In the Long Line," *Choreography and Dance,* 1997.
———, "Packaging Doris Humphrey or a Question of Form: Nona Schurman Shares Her Thoughts on Doris Humphrey's Choreography," *Dance Research Journal,* Fall 1996.

*   *   *

Nona Schurman's career as a dance educator began in the 1930s and has spanned six decades. Schurman is best known as a prominent authority on the techniques and styles of modern dance pioneers Doris Humphrey and Charles Weidman. Schurman's teaching style, although uniquely her own, is based on fall and recovery and breath-rhythm—the movement principles explored and developed by Doris Humphrey during her long and prolific career as a dancer and choreographer.

Schurman was born in Oxford, Nova Scotia, on 6 November 1909 and brought up in Ste. Anne de Bellevue, Quebec, a small French Canadian village near the confluence of the Ottawa and St. Lawrence rivers. According to Schurman, it is the constant flow of these impressive rivers that helped shape her character and serve as a metaphor for the "rush of time through space and the continuity of our ancient earthly heritage." Schurman sees modern dance as the only art form that can truly express this passage of time and sense of continuity—"because the instrument of modern dance is the physical body which progresses by means of an eternal fall and recovery from foot to foot through space."

Schurman began studying modern dance with Blanche Evans in Montreal in 1930, following a two-year excursion abroad where she traveled, studied music, language, and literature and completed a summer course in Dalcroze Eurythmics. A few years later Schurman moved to New York City, where she received a scholarship to study with Hanya Holm at the New York branch of the Mary Wigman school. Schurman trained with Holm from 1934 to 1936, eventually leaving to find an approach to modern dance she felt better suited her own temperament. It was in this period of searching that she saw the Humphrey-Weidman company perform. As she recalled in a 1996 *Dance Research Journal* article, after first seeing Humphrey's *New Dance,* "I thought 'philosophy in action! I have to work with this woman.'" Schurman began studying at the Humphrey-Weidman studio in 1936. She found the atmosphere at their studio wonderful and harmonious. In 1939 she joined the ranks of the Humphrey-Weidman company and by 1940 was serving as both a principal teacher at the school and an assistant to both Miss Humphrey and Mr. Weidman. Schurman performed with the Humphrey-Weidman company until 1943 when financial considerations and a prolonged illness prompted her to take a position as an exercise instructor at the Elizabeth Arden Studio. The new position, however, did not curb her performing and creative activity.

In 1943 Schurman's performances of her solos *Tell Me of the Living, This Earth,* and *Running Laughter* earned her the honor of Dance Auditions Winner at the 92nd Street YM-YWHA in New York. From 1943 to 1944 Schurman worked on the production staff at the Roxy Theatre in New York City, as the modern dance director. The following year she auditioned for the U.S.O and landed a part in the musical *Up In Central Park,* choreographed by Helen Tamiris, which toured Army bases in the European Theatre of Operations for six months just following V.E. day. When she returned to the U.S., she joined the cast of the musical *Shootin' Stars,* choreographed by Lester Horton. Miss Schurman began directing and choreographing for her own dance company in 1947. Her work, *Song of the Hebrides,* which premiered at the 92nd Street YM-YWHA in 1949, was recorded in Labanotation and was one of the first dance scores to receive a copyright from the Library of Congress in 1952.

Nona Schurman began teaching modern dance shortly after moving to New York in 1933. Her teaching philosophy is democratic—dance is for everybody and everybody should dance. She joined the staff of the New Dance Group studio in the late 1930s, where she led classes in Humphrey-Weidman technique, composition, percussion for teachers, and pedagogy until 1967. During her tenure at the New Dance Group she served as vice-president, chairman of the board, head of the school's Humphrey-Weidman department, and director of the Young Concert Dancers Lecture Demonstration program. In 1946 the Education Director, Dr. William Kolodney, asked Schurman to join the staff of the 92nd Street YM-YWHA dance department, where she taught modern dance technique and elementary and intermediate dance composition courses to adults until 1968. She also directed her own dance school in New York City—the Center for Dance Study—from 1954 to 1968. During the 1950s and 1960s, Schurman was invited to teach master classes at numerous colleges throughout the east coast. She also served on the dance faculty of the High School of Performing Arts, Teacher's College at Columbia University, and the High School for Music and Art and was an active member of the

Dance Notation Bureau, the Dance Teacher's Guild, and the Doris Humphrey Fund Committee.

Schurman's years of teaching experience at the New Dance Group, the 92nd Street YM-YWHA, and her own studio enabled her to test her teaching methods, experiment with the presentation of technical material, and thoroughly evaluate her ideas about dance in relation to educating students of all ages and ranges of experience. In 1968 she and co-author, Sharon Leigh Clark, began work on *Modern Dance Fundamentals,* a textbook of notated modern dance exercises based on the technical principles of Doris Humphrey and Charles Weidman.

In 1973, shortly after the book's publication, Schurman became an assistant professor of Dance at SUNY-Geneseo, where she reconstructed Humphrey's *Shakers* and Weidman's *Lynchtown.* She was awarded the Chancellor's Award for Excellence in Teaching in 1977 and retired from her post in 1979. In the early 1980s Schurman held guest teaching positions at New York University, Cornish College of the Arts, and Stephens College. In 1985 she directed a film of Weidman technique in New York City. Schurman's teaching activities decreased after she underwent hip replacement surgery in 1991, yet she continues to contribute to the field of dance education. She is currently working on a new book of modern dance technique with notated exercises.

—Elizabeth Cooper

SELF, Jim

American dancer, choreographer, and educator

Born: 6 March 1954 in Greenville, Alabama. **Education:** Studied in Chicago with Jackie Radis (1970-72), Shirley Mordine (1970-74), Nana Shineflug (1971-73), Tom Jaremba (1971), Richard Arve (1972-73), and at the Edward Parish Ballet Studio (1972-76); Merce Cunningham Dance Studio, 1973-79; Maggie Black, 1981-83; B.A. (summa cum laude), Cornell University, 1996. **Career:** Dancer/choreographer, Chicago Dance Troupe, 1972-74; co-founder, MoMing Dance and Art Center, 1974; founder/artistic director, Self Performing Arts Company, 1975-76; dancer, Merce Cunningham Dance Company, 1976-79; performer/choreographer, Robert Wilson's *The Civil Wars,* 1980-84; founder/artistic director, Jim Self and Dancers, 1980-88; has lectured or taught workshops at Centre Nationale de Danse Contemporaine, Columbia College (Chicago), University of Alabama, University of Iowa, University of Minnesota, State University of New York, Jacob's Pillow, Merce Cunningham Studio, Dance Umbrella, and others; senior dance lecturer, Cornell University, 1989 to present; American Ballet Theatre summer classes, beginning 1997. **Awards:** National Endowment for the Arts (NEA) choreographic fellowships, 1975, 1981, 1982, 1984, 1985, 1987; NEA film/video fellowships, 1982, 1985, 1987; New York Dance and Performance Award ("Bessie"), 1985; New York Foundation choreography fellowship, 1988; Alabama Arts Award, 1992.

Works

1973	*Miami Beach,* Columbia College, Chicago
1974	*Tuscaloosa,* MoMing, Chicago
	Transverse, Columbia College, Chicago
1975	*More of The Same in a Different Place 12 Times,* Self Performing Arts Studio, Chicago
	Self Studies 1-12, MoMing, Chicago
	Xanadu, MoMing, Chicago
	Friday Night at Moming, MoMing, Chicago
1976	*Scraping Bottoms,* Goodman Theater, Chicago
	White on White, Self Performing Arts Studio, Chicago
1977	*Up Roots,* Walker Art Center, Minneapolis
	Side Walks, Walker Art Center, Minneapolis
1980	*Les Égouts de Paris,* MoMing, Chicago
	A Domestic Interlude, Dance Theatre Workshop (DTW), New York
	Marking Time, Cunningham Studio, New York
	Silent Partner/Changing Hands w/Richard Elovich, Grey Art Gallery, New York
1981	*Architectural Stories,* DTW, New York
	Vocabulary Lessons, Part II, Performance Space 1 (P.S. 1), New York
	Blue Grotto w/Frank Moore, Jacob's Pillow, Massachusetts
	Goose on a Sidewalk, American Center, Paris
1982	*Ricochet,* Werkcentrum Dans, Leiden, Holland
	Perpetrator, American Dance Festival (ADF), Durham, North Carolina
	The Phoenix City Story, DTW, New York
	Lookout, DTW, New York
1983	*ex/stance,* SUNY Dance Corps, SUNY, Purchase
	The Harvest Dance/The Civil Wars, Rotterdam, Holland
	Heaven and Earth, The Kitchen, New York
	Beehive Flower Pas de Deux, The Kitchen, New York
1984	*No Memory,* MoMing, Chicago
	The Kachina Dance/The Civil Wars, Rome Opera Ballet, Italy
1985	*Beehive Film,* Public Theater, New York
	La Ruche des Abeilles, Centre National de Danse Contemporaine (CNDC), Angers, France
	New Zuyder Zee w/Richard Elovich, The Kitchen, New York
	Nuit Blanche, CNDC, Perros, France
1986	*Orpheus and Euridice,* Jacob's Pillow
	Between Lives, DTW, New York
	Pastorale, DTW, New York
	Urban Glance, DTW, New York
1987	*Beehive Ballet,* Boston Ballet, Boston
	Camellia, Bama Theater, Tuscaloosa, Alabama
	Miller's Wife, P.S. 1, New York
1988	*Surrender,* Mary Abrams, Minneapolis
	Crankhouse, DTW, New York
1989	*Monkey March,* Manhattanville College, New York
1990	*Getting Married,* New York
	Soap and Sin, Cornell University, Ithaca, New York
	Dreammaker/Heartbreaker, Cornell, Ithaca
1991	*Stairway to Paradise,* Cornell, Ithaca
1992	*The Dance,* Artists Space, New York
	Ramona's Transformation, Ohio Theater, New York
	I Dream of Genealogy and Jesus, Cornell, Ithaca
1993	*Ramona and the Wolfgang Work for a Cure,* Cornell
	Sanctuary, Danspace at St. Mark's Church, New York
1994	*Sweet Homecoming Chicago,* Link's Hall, Chicago
	Psyche Dreams: A Story of Love and Delight, Cornell

Jim Self. Photograph © Johan Elbers.

1995   *Chez Dada, Chez Moi—an Invocation*, solo, CORD Conference, Miami

        MC, JC, JJ, EF, LA, Dancing Iguana Consciousness, and a Bunch of Name-Dropping, Art-Barking Dummies, ACDFA, Cornell

        Merce Cunningham and the Shrine of the Dancing Iguana Consciousness: or the Life in John's Cage with Ella and Louis, Cornell

1996   *Suite: Dummy Dances for Love and Money*, Cornell

1997   *Terra Incognita*, American Ballet Theatre workshop, University of Alabama

        Rite Reverend Dada Channels Iguana Consciousness While Thinking Like a Squirrel, solo, Link's Hall, Chicago

1998   *Untitled Tribute to Duke Ellington*, Cornell

Films and Videotapes

Torse (1977) and *Locale* (1979) with the Merce Cunningham Dance Company; performed and choreographed Robert Wilson's *Stations* (1981); *Beehive,* directed by Frank Moore and Self (1984); *Jim Self Comes Home,* Alabama Public Television special (1986); *Retracing Steps* (Michael Blackwood production, 1988).

Publications

On SELF: articles—

Adams, Brooks, "Art Equals Life," *Interview*, January 1996.

Berman, Janice, "Summer Arts Preview," *Newsday*, 27 May 1990.

Goldman, Phyllis, "Megadance," *Back Stage*, 24 August 1990.

Smith, Sid, "Finding Its Niche, Unsung Link's Hall Studio Survives as a Small but Vital Performance Space," *Chicago Tribune*, 28 August 1994.

———, "Light on Their Feet," *Chicago Tribune*, 11 September 1994.

Temin, Christine, "Discovery Festival Results: One Big Hit and Numerous Problems," *Boston Globe*, 5 April 1987.

———, "Self's *Beehive* Better as Film," *Boston Globe*, 28 March 1987.

———, "A Tale of Two Cities," *Boston Globe*, 17 May 1987.

———, "The Year that Was. . .the Year to Come," *Boston Globe*, 27 December 1987.

Thom, Rose Anne, "Jim Self: Danspace Project at St. Mark's Church in-the-Bowery," *Dance Magazine*, April 1993.

*   *   *

Jim Self is an award-winning experimental postmodern dancer and choreographer whose work tends to border on performance art. His career started in Chicago, continued in New York, where he danced in the Merce Cunningham Dance Company before going out to perform his own choreographic works, and has since the criss-crossed the nation and world with one-of-a-kind performances.

Self was born in 1954 in Greenville, Alabama, and raised outside Chicago in Evanston, Illinois. His dance career began in Chicago in the early 1970s, where he studied at the Ruth Page Ballet School, the Chicago Dance Center, and the Columbia College Dance Center with a variety of educators including Shirley Mordine, Edward Parrish, Richard Arve, Nana Shineflug, and Tom Jaremba. The Columbia College Dance Center served as the venue for Self's earliest choreographic and performance work. In Chicago, Self also performed with various collectives specializing in experimental modern dance. He was with the Chicago Dance Troupe from 1972 to 1974, as well as with the performing group based at MoMing Dance and Art Center (of which he was a co-founder, along with Jackie Radis and Eric Trules) from 1974 to 1975. He also ran a studio and company called Self Performing Arts Company from 1975 to 1976 at Link's Hall, which was, along with MoMing, a center and performance space for dance in the city.

After moving to New York City, Self began studying with Merce Cunningham in 1973, and joined his company in 1976. During this period he also performed in the works of other area experimental choreographers, including Kenneth King, for whom he danced in *RadeoA.C.tiv(ID)ity,* about Marie Curie, in 1976. As a member of the Merce Cunningham Dance Company, Self performed in many of Cunningham's noted works, including *Torse, Exchange,* and *Locale,* as well as in Cunningham's "Events." He toured with the company in the U.S. and abroad. His co-members in the Cunningham troupe included Karole Armitage, Ellen Cornfield, Meg Harper, and Robert Kovich, among others. Self left the company in 1979 to pursue a career centering on his own choreography.

In the early 1980s, while creating his own works, Self continued his studies in New York with Maggie Black, honing his talent. He also teamed with Robert Wilson for *The Civil Wars,* which Self choreographed and performed in from 1980 to 1984, while also gaining a modest reputation as a soloist in his own works. Whether soloist or with small groups, Self performed his works in a wide variety of venues, particularly in New York and Chicago, but also in other cities. He frequently has staged dances in studios, such as Chicago's Cloud Hands Studio, and museums, such as the Walker Art Center in Minneapolis, and the downtown Whitney Museum in New York, in dance festivals like Jacob's Pillow and the American Dance Festival, as well as in theaters both domestic and international. He continued over the years to perform at his old haunts in Chicago, including Link's Hall and MoMing (which closed in 1990).

Self's choreography is representative of postmodern dance in its use of repetition and focused movement, with liberal doses of humor. Merce Cunningham's influence is felt in some of his work, such as *Perpetrator,* a work he created for the American Dance Festival in 1982 to an electronic score by Frankie Mann. Self's work tends to incorporate controversial elements, and is often considered more as performance art than as dance. For example, in his solo, *Scraping Bottoms,* Self becomes a "Chaplinesque" figure who pushes a telephone book, recites a monologue of non sequiturs, and spills coins on stage, all to a warped, wrong-speed rock record, after which he crawls off the stage. Self's dancers are trained in classical technique, and some of his movements are reminiscent of classical ballet. Yet the content of the pieces is abstract more than narrative. In *The Phoenix City Story,* for example, which is about his home town in Alabama, the people of the town change into trees and mate with bulls.

Self's life as a gay man and his connections to the art world inform many of his works. He has been involved with several artists, including Jasper Johns (who was a designer for Merce Cunningham), Richard Elovich, Mark Lancaster, and Robert Wilson. In 1990 Self created a performance art piece called *Getting Married* for a concert called "Megadance," part of Lincoln Center's Serious Fun Festival. The work was about the wedding of two men. Similarly, in *Sanctuary: Ramona and the Wolfgang Work for a Cure,* a 1993 piece, Self dances the role of a Shaman who dies and changes into a She-Wolf, Ramona, who becomes pregnant by the Wolf King and bears a child who learns the She-Wolf's dance. The second part of the piece centers on a ritualistic and erotic cleansing that is supposed to promote spiritual and physical healing in the age of AIDS, in which naked and nearly-naked men perform the healing massage on each other, while dancers around them improvise. The audience, meanwhile, learns how to breathe correctly. The intended significance of the work is explained by Self both verbally and in the program text. His connections with the art world are evident in works such as *Beehive,* which incorporates a film by artist Frank Moore, and in the lavish and colorful costuming that Self favors in many of his dances.

Self's performances often seem to confuse the critics, some of whom review him unfavorably and tend to find the pieces difficult to fathom. *Beehive* is one such example—a dance performance and film project created with Moore over eight years in the 1980s. The work was performed by Self's company in small spaces, as well as by the Boston Ballet in a production involving yellow-fake-fur-clad dancers portraying bees. Described by Moore as "kind of a *Honeymooners* for bees," the 50-minute dance involved dancer-bees, including drones, the queen, and an evil lady-in-waiting to the queen, plus various flowers and some weeds.

Despite the unusual and occasionally confusing elements in Self's works, they nonetheless entertain audiences with choreography that can be both witty and elegant. An example is *Urban Glance/ The Mozart Pieces,* set to Mozart's *Symphony No. 27 in G Major.* The movement includes scampering, shuffling, near-tapping, stomping, and gesturing majestically over a man who is apparently dead. This work also illustrates Self's deadpan demeanor, despite the humorous elements of the work. Throughout the years of choreographing and performing, Self has also found time to teach, including stints at Columbia College, the University of Alabama, University of Iowa, University of Minnesota at Minneapolis, the American Center in Paris, a long association with Cornell University in Ithaca, New York, from 1989 through today, where Self earned a B.A. (summa cum laude) in 1996.

—Karen Raugust

SET AND LIGHTING DESIGN

Modern dance took root in the West's two "modern," industrialized countries, Germany and the United States, neither of which had a history of formalized, classical dance. In spite of the modernist impulses that lay behind the creation of the Ballets Russes and its heir to the avant-garde tradition, the Ballets Suedois, their design remained mostly in the pictorial tradition of easel painting which allowed the dancers the greatest possible floor space to dance. Indeed as the productions gained in visual appeal, the impeccable style of dancing died out.

Duncan, with her politically charged, draped female body, Fuller with her blend of electricity and movement, and St. Denis with her exotica, all contributed to the design of modern dance, but it is Martha Graham who first integrates costume, scenery, and lighting and strikes an original and provocative approach to design's collaborative functions. Most famously, Isamu Noguchi created sculptural, iconic shapes in the dance space to provide design which intersected with the substance of her choreography. Arch Lauterer, the production director for the Bennington Festivals, designed for Graham (*Letter to the World, Penitente*, et al), Holm (*Trend, Namesake*), Humphrey (*Passacaglia, Fugue in C*), as well as for Cunningham and Hawkins. He was influenced by the writings of Appia and the work of the Bauhaus, and his work anticipated Noguchi's in its use of a minimal module in the center of the stage area, creating stage architecture rather than a pictorial expression. He created architectural structures of light, keeping a time relationship with the action of the dance, allowing light and movement to exist on the same terms, accentuating a continuous accompaniment of unfolding action. Nicola Cernovich also benefitted from a European influence, drawing on ideas of color theory from Josef Albers at Black Mountain College. Cernovich used color as a stimulant to the eye, continually raining fresh color on dancers to create and change space with light, most notably for Alvin Ailey in *Revelations*. He emigrated to Canada in 1973, continuing his work with Les Grandes Ballets Canadiens.

Jean Rosenthal banished the pictorial expressions of the Ballets Russes and the European avant-garde for Balanchine as her use of lighting on scrim created a "mood" for the dance. Her work for Graham blended the ideas of light with those of the dance, creating a parallel atmosphere of light for the emotional content of the dance. In contrast Thomas Skelton's lighting designs for Graham, Eliot Feld, and Paul Taylor used a sharp focus and intensity to pinpoint and heighten specific moments in the dance. He employed light to emphasize movement passages rather than rely on mood to help audiences through the dance. Skelton, like Lauterer, a poet of the theatre and an extraordinary teacher, believed that designers, far from being mere technicians, needed an "artistic predisposition." He was also a kind of anthropologist, working for many years assisting African dance companies on their design, staging, and lighting, allowing them to present authentic ethnic material to Western audiences. Designer John Pratt took the artifacts that his wife, anthropologist/dancer Katherine Dunham acquired in her journeys to Martinique, Jamaica, Trinidad, and Haiti and shaped and fashioned costumes and accessories for her dances.

By the late 1960s and early 1970s production values seemed to become equally as important as the dance itself. Robert Rauschenberg's startling designs reflected this as they developed from the tightly focused, isolated circles of light in Taylor's *Three Epitaphs* in the 1950s through the intersection of large pieces of fabric that combine and fan out in circles to create both scenery and movement in Cunningham's *Travelogue* and the projections in Trisha Brown's *Glacial Decoy* during the 1970s. He is the postmodern heir to Lauterer and Noguchi, moving the "icon," blending both movement and setting in pieces such as *Minutiae* and *Lateral Pass* for Cunningham and Brown. Jennifer Tipton is a former Graham student and pupil of Skelton. For Taylor and Tharp she created a strong sense of stage space by lighting with a strong point of view, employing sharp intensities and angles to reveal the closeness and collaboration between light and dance. Beverly Emmons began her career as a stage manager for Cunningham and was required to work with Cunningham in adapting to disparate touring venues. They developed a light for his pieces that looked like "normal daylight" and which remained independent of the dance with its own movement and variation. She helped to create both the gym and museum events in which she and Cunningham splintered pieces in nontraditional settings so the audience was surrounded with dance. Emmons would go on to collaborate with a diverse group of postmodernist choreographers such as Monk, Miller, Childs, and Dunn.

Alwin Nikolais, choreographer, designer, and subsequently, composer, with his fusion of color, architecture, and form might just be counted the supreme modernist. With his first work, *Lobster Quadrille*, he began to create a theatre of wonder in the artisan style of the Bauhaus, for he was the inheritor of the Wigman, Laban strain of modern dance. Starting in 1956 with *Prism*, Nikolais began to design his lighting as he choreographed. He utilized a variety of special lighting effects, including black light in *Galaxy*, adding internally lighted costumes controlled by dancers for *Vaudeville of the Elements*. His concern with the performance of the total body led him to the use of masks and headpieces, as well as projections which created not only scenery but costume patterning. Costumes and scenery are also the province of Santo Loquasto who has created witty and evocative designs for both Twyla Tharp (*Push Comes to Shove*) and precise slices of historical moments for Paul Taylor (*Company B*—complimented by Tipton's use of shadows—and *Offenbach Overtures*).

Alex Nichols employed distorting funhouse mirrors for Margaret Jenkins' *Steps Midway*. His design interacted with the dance, simultaneously concealing and revealing the nude, dancing body. Following in the iconic tradition of architectural structure, the dancers interact with a cage-like setting of four walls of gold beaded curtains in *Strange Attractions*. Nichols has also designed for the Ailey company and postmodern classicist Jacques D'Amboise. Adrienne Lobel and Jim Ingalls' scenery and lighting reflect the unpredictable and idiosyncratic movement style of Mark Morris' dances, while Elizabeth Streb's architectural structure for Streb/Ringside challenges dance to explore the cubic dimension of stage space while employing high-tech icons in the Lauterer/ Noguchi tradition.

—Louis Scheeder

SETTERFIELD, Valda

English-born dancer

Born: 1934 in Margate, England. **Education:** Ballet and theater classes, London, Italia Conti; studied ballet with Marie Rambert, Audrey de Vos, and Antony Tudor; studied modern dance with James Waring, Merce Cunningham, and José Limón; pantomime with Tamara Karsavina; acting with Michael Howard, New York. **Family:** Married choreographer David Gordon, 1962; one son. **Career:** Performer, Italian show revue; showgirl, Donald Saddler's American-style musicals, 1958; performer, pantos (traditional English pantomime Christmas concerts); dancer, James Waring's Living Theater Company, late 1950s; dancer, Judson Dance Theater,

1960s; dancer, Merce Cunningham Dance Company 1960-61, 1965-75; co-founder with David Gordon, Pick Up Company, 1974; dancer, Baryshnikov's White Oak Dance Project, 1992. actress, Guthrie Theater (Minneapolis), Playwrights Horizons (New York), American Repertory Theatre (Cambridge).

Roles

1959 *Crises* (Merce Cunningham)
1960 *Tableaux* (James Waring), Judson Dance Theater
   Peripatea (James Waring), Judson Dance Theater
1962 *Mama Goes Where Papa Goes* (David Gordon)
1963 *Aeon* (Merce Cunningham), La Comedie Canadienne, Montreal
   Random Breakfast (Trisha Brown), America on Wheels skating rink, Washington, D.C.
1965 *How to Pass, Kick, Fall and Run* (Cunningham), Harper Theater, Chicago
1966 *Place* (Cunningham), Fondation Maeght, Saint-Paul-de-Vence, France
1971 *Roof Piece* (Trisha Brown), performed in SoHo, New York City
1972 *One Part of the Matter* (David Gordon)
   Lives of Performers (Yvonne Rainer) (film)
1973 *Changing Steps* (Cunningham)
1974 *Chair* (Gordon)
1978 *What Happened* (Gordon)
   Not Necessarily Recognizable Objectives
1991 Marcel Duchamp, *The Mysteries* (Gordon)

Publications

On SETTERFIELD: articles—

Acocella, Joan, "All in the Family," *Art in America,* April 1995.
Croce, Arlene, "Making Work," *The New Yorker,* 29 November 1982.
Vaughan, David, "Born in UK, Made in USA: Valda Talks," *Dance Magazine,* February 1993.

* * *

Valda Setterfield is the English-born modern dancer who, together with choreographer-husband David Gordon, formed the Pick Up Company. James Waring and Merce Cunningham are among the influences who have helped Setterfield develop her technical skills and style, after training in ballet and work for an Italian show revue.

Valda Setterfield was born in England in 1934. She was raised in Margate on the southeast coast of Britain. Her interest and training in dance began at an early age; her first public performance was at the age of four at a garden fête. She was already learning about makeup, not eating while in costume, discipline, respect for the dance, and keeping quiet while others rehearsed. She had both ballet and theater classes at a professional studio in London, Italia Conti. By the age of 17 she was studying ballet with Marie Rambert and later with Audrey de Vos. At the Conti studio, personality was stressed in the musical comedy routines. Rambert stressed projecting to the audience. Later, when Setterfield worked with Merce Cunningham in the United States, she would learn to focus on amplifying energy.

Before emigrating to America in 1958, she toured in Italy as a showgirl in Donald Saddler's American-style musicals. She also studied pantomime with Tamara Karsavina and performed in "pantos," traditional English pantomimed Christmas concerts. In America David Vaughan introduced her to James Waring and she was soon working with the Judson Dance Theater. She studied composition with Waring and also took ballet classes with Antony Tudor at the Metropolitan Opera Ballet School. "[Waring] helped me to understand this strange thing called modern dance. Ballet dancers then didn't look at modern dance, nor did modern dancers look at ballet, but Jimmy looked at *dancing*, all of it, and he helped me to bring my previous training to bear on everything I was now doing," Setterfield said in a 1993 interview with Vaughn.

Her previous exposure to modern dance was during the auditions for the Italian musical revue. Those classes were "all about being sexy, except when taught by Richardena Jackson, who was a Katherine Dunham dancer. I was impressed by her economy and elegance—what she taught was all to do with the material," Setterfield said. She went on to appear in Waring's occasional concerts, including in 1960 his *Tableaux* and *Peripatea,* as well as his Living Theater productions, which emerged prior to the origination of the Judson Dance Theater. It was here that she met future husband David Gordon. They danced together in Waring compositions, as well as pieces Gordon created. One piece Gordon created called *Mama Goes Where Papa Goes* was performed in 1962. Setterfield, who was not technically strong, had a solo of successive jumps, all of different types and sizes. Gordon says of the demanding solo, "Valda was and is an incredibly musical and lyric dancer, and I, in some perverse way, needed to undo that."

At Waring's urging Setterfield also took classes with Merce Cunningham; her first opportunity to perform with the company came one short year after emigrating to America. Viola Farber was injured and Setterfield replaced her in *Crises.* She had little rehearsal and Cunningham did not provide her with much guidance, preferring to see what she would do with the piece instead. Cunningham would later work with Setterfield on her technique, showing her what parts to grab hold of to sustain her through technically difficult pieces of a routine.

Gordon and Setterfield married in 1962. When the first Judson Dance Theater performance was held in 1963, Setterfield was in the hospital giving birth to their son Ain. Though Gordon then performed his pieces solo, he and Setterfield later performed them together, both very strong dancers possessing perceptive wit. After the early years at Judson, Gordon quit choreographing for about five years to concentrate on technique and performing for other dance companies. Setterfield again joined the Merce Cunningham Dance Company where she remained for 10 years.

In 1974 Gordon and Setterfield started the Pick Up Company, for which Gordon choreographs and they "pick up" dancers as needed for performances. Their son Ain is a writer and director for theater pieces and has also worked as a member of the Pick Up Company. Ain's interest in theater has infected the family, with mother and father helping to direct and at times cast in parts. Since this family affair with the theater, Setterfield began studying acting with Michael Howard in New York. She has acted at the Guthrie in Minneapolis, at Playwrights Horizons in New York, and at American Repertory Theatre in Cambridge, mostly in Gordon productions. In 1991 she played Marcel Duchamp in David's *The Mysteries.* Setterfield says that acting is not a great leap for her since she has background in pantomine and that Gordon often includes speak-

Valda Setterfield performing *The Seasons*, 1986. Photograph © Johan Elbers.

ing parts in his compositions, as did Waring. To Setterfield acting is an extension of dancing—with her extensive performance experience the stage is a place she feels comfortable and is able to follow her instinct in knowing what to do next.

In the spring of 1992 she was invited to join Baryshnikov's White Oak Dance Project. The dance company is made up of mature performers and includes a very high level of expertise and professionalism. "Not since Rambert have I been in a company where the repertory comes from different sources," Setterfield told Vaughan of the Project. The variety of dance experience and the levels of dancers and range of choreographers she has worked with consolidates the star appeal with which she radiates. To have been worked with, and been influenced by, so many greats in the modern dance, postmodern dance, and theater scene has indeed been a great achievement.

In a 1981 *Dance Magazine* article about David Gordon, Setterfield sums up her own contribution and influence on postmodern dance. "I have always thought of myself as a very, very finely honed tool who will render other people's work faithfully and without distortion. I do not make work; I don't want to make work. I'm this kind of vessel through which this material is transmitted to a group of other people, visually. That is absolutely enough for me. I have no desire to invest it with my personality—I think that happens anyway."

—Lisa A. Wroble

THE SHAKERS

Choreography: Doris Humphrey
Music: Daniel Jahn
Costume Design: Pauline Lawrence
Recital premiere: Hunter College, New York, 30 November 1930
First Professional Production: Craig Theatre, New York, 1 February 1931
Original Dancers: Humphrey-Weidman Repertory Company

Publications

Arnold, Joseph, "Dance Events Reviewed: Charles Weidman, Doris Humphrey and Group, the Stadium Philharmonic Society Concerts, Lewissohn Stadium, August 10 and 11," *The American Dancer,* September 1933.

Mindlin, Naomi, "The Process of Dance Reconstruction," *Dance Notation Journal,* Spring 1984.

Sargeant, Winthrop, "Dance Reviews: Doris Humphrey and Charles Weidman," *Dance Observer,* May 1934.

Youngerman, Suzanne, "The translation of a culture into choreography: a study of Doris Humphrey's *The Shakers* based on Labananalysis," *Essays in Dance Research* (CORD Dance Research Annual 9), 1978.

Films and Videotapes

The Shakers, filmed by Helen Priest Rogers, Connecticut College, 1955; stored at the Dance Collection, New York Public Library at Lincoln Center.

The Shakers, notated by Ann Hutchinson, assisted by Els Grelinger (1948), checked by Lucy Venable, Connecticut College, 1955.

*   *   *

Doris Humphrey's *The Shakers* was first performed in 1930. Significant among the primary materials are Humphrey's word notes and diagrams of the choreography. A 15-minute black-and-white silent film was made by Thomas Bouchard in 1940 with dancers Humphrey, Charles Weidman and José Limón. *The Shakers* has continued to be staged by those who danced with Humphrey, and also by those who rely on Labanotation scores provided by Ann Hutchinson and Els Grelinger. Another black-and-white silent film, made with Humphrey's repertory class in 1955, was expressly for the purpose of aiding dance reconstruction. Among those who have restaged the dance are the American Dance Repertory Theatre, the Limón Company, the Louisville Ballet, the New York City Dance Theatre, the Repertory Theatre of Utah, and the University Dance Group of Ohio State University.

The Shakers is an approximately nine-minute dance to voice, drum, and harmonium for seven women and six men. The following synopsis of the choreography describes the version preserved in Humphrey's revival of the dance filmed in 1955 at Connecticut College. At the start of the dance, an equal number of men and women are grouped on the sides and front of the stage facing the Eldress with their backs to the audience. Humphrey choreographed for the dancers to struggle, fall, sway in a kneeling position, hands clasped in a gesture of prayer. With deliberate steps and what Humphrey characterized as "shaking" movements, the men and women face each other, form two parallel lines and side-step from stage front toward stage back. The men form a circling star figure on their side of the stage, and the women on their side form a similar figure. Sound and motion stop abruptly for the first "revelation."

The dancers' agitated movements resume, but again sound and motion abruptly stop. The corps will falls in response to the spoken words of the Eldress, who is now standing on the bench. "It hath been revealed, ye shall be free when ye are shaken clean of sin," she says, and falls first forward then back, as if overcome by the force of her words. Tension is felt between men and women on either side of an invisible center divide as they are in turn attracted toward and pull themselves away from each other with hands and bodies shaking. The wordless song resumes; the Eldress spins and further energizes the group. All tumble forward and back, moving upstage and finally the dancers fall to their knees in a semicircle and at the final amen (the only word in the otherwise wordless song), they present to the audience arms outstretched with hands clasped in a gesture of prayer.

Details of the dance were changed during its first years of performance. Humphrey's word notes describe a six-men, six-women version of the dance which is presumably earlier than the six-men, seven-women cast captured in the 1948 Labanotation score and the 1955 film. Winthrop Sargeant, in a 1934 *Dance Observer* review, wrote that in some initial performances, spoken lines were gibberish rather than English and that the curtain came down on a central dancer continuously jumping. Even though some reviewers of early 1930s Humphrey-Weidman Company performances faulted aspects of the choreography as too "synthetic" and too "theatrical," *The Shakers* seemed to have been popular even during its first years, given the number of times it appears on programs. *The Shakers* continues to be one of the most frequently staged of Humphrey's works due in part to the availability of reconstruction materials, the modest level of difficulty of the Labanotation score and technical ability required of the dancers, the brevity of the dance, and the fact that Humphrey allowed for women to dance the roles of men.

Background on the celibate Protestant sect has helped inform the choreography; in the dance, an Eldress leads a sort of impassioned prayer meeting where men and women are confined to separate halves of the meeting house stage. The Shakers were called "Shakers" initially after the shaking which some manifest in ecstasy or fear of God. However, as Humphrey explained in the recorded 1955 discussion, the dance was not intended to be representational but to convey a Shaker service in spirit.

Speculations found in some secondary literature about the origins of Humphrey's interest in the Shakers are dubious in light of the fact that Humphrey explained her interest explicitly in 1955: she admired the Shakers' positive outlook toward dance, an outlook that she felt was singular among Protestants. She wrote in a 1943 letter to John Martin that it "seems that the motivation behind all my dances, from the *Shakers* to the *Choral Preludes* (15 years) has been the same to the point of monotony—and can be epitomized in the Shaker faith that 'ye shall be saved, when ye are shaken free of sin'." Here she was quoting *The Shaker* Eldress, whose role she performed in the premiere.

—Judith Gelernter

SHANKAR, Uday

Indian dancer, choreographer, and company director

Born: Uday Shankar Chaudhry, 8 December 1900 in Udaipur, Rajasthan. **Family:** Married Amala Nandi, 1942; one son, one daughter. **Education:** Studied at Jhalawar, Rajasthan, and Nasrathpur and Ghazipur, India; J.J. School of Art, Bombay 1918-20; Royal College of Arts, to 1923; dancer in Anna Pavlova Company, 1923-24; formed Uday Shankar Company of Hindu Dances and Musicians, with patron Alice Boner, 1930; first performance, 1931; first U.S. tour, 1932; founded Uday Shankar India Culture Centre, Almora, United Provinces, India, 1939 (closed 1943); directed film *Kalpana,* 1948; opened Uday Shankar India Culture Centre in

Calcutta with wife Amala Shankar, 1965; Padma Vibhushan, 1971.
Awards: Honorary doctorate, Rabindra Bharati University, Calcutta,
1975. **Died:** 26 September 1977 in Calcutta.

Works

1923	*An Oriental Bride*
	Hindu Wedding
	Radha-Krishna
	Danse Hindoue
1924	*Danse du Sabre*
	Devil Dance
	Goddess Manasa Dance
	Nautch (Holi dance)
	Rajput Bride (Danse Nuptiale)
1925	*Indra*
1926	*Danse de Baiji*
	Danse des Bayaderes
	Danse du Chasseur
	Danse Kashmiri au Millieu des Fleurs
	Danse de Siva
	Danse du Temple Hindou (Devadasi)
	Danse Vaisya
	Fleurs et Fruits
	Gandarva et Apsara
	Manikarnika
	Melodie Hindou
	Melodie Oriental
	La Mort du Bhil
	La Mort du Pelerin
	Orientale
1929	*Danse du Poinard*
	Danse avec Chanson Bireha
	Gandharva (Gandarva et Apsara)
	Ganga Puja
	La Mort du Bucheron
1931	*Danse du printemps*
	Peasant Dance (La Danse Paysanne)
	Tandava Nrittya (Shiva)
1932	*Astra Puja*
	Beggars Dance
	Kama Dev (Five Arrows of Praddyuma)
	Rama Chandra (Festival Dance)
	Snanum
1933	*Dance of the Hunter*
	Dance of the Snake Charmer
	Kartikeyya
1935	*Deva Puja* (Devadasi)
	Basanta Nrittaya (Danse du Printemps)
	Harvest Dance
	Jamuna Tatha-Nrittya (Yamuna Tatha Nrittya)
	Mawari
	Mayoor Nrittya (Peacock Dance)
	Popular Dance (Peasant Dance)
	Udwega
1936	*Exorcism*
1937	*Chitra Sena*
	Lanka Dahana (Ramayana story)
	Mohini
	Nirasha
	Partha Kritartha

	Shiva Parvati (originally 1935, as *Nritya Dwanda*)
	Rasa Leela
	Rashik
	Varsha Mangala
	Vilasa
	Village Dance
	Young Father
1938	*Kalia Demon (Devil Dance)*
1939	*Kiratarjuna*
1940	*Patra Lipi*
1941	*Labour and Machinery*
	Ramayana Shadow Play
1949	*Bidai (farewell to a bride by her relations)*
	Eternal Melody
	Grass Cutters
	Manipuri Rasa
	Naga
	Pung Chalam
	Village Festival
1956	*Life of Lord Buddha* (originally conceived 1949)
1957	*Glimpses of India*
1962	*Brahmaputra*
	Panthadi
	Prakriti Ananda (modern ballet)
1971	*Shankarscope*

Publications

On SHANKAR: books—

Abrahams, Ruth K., *The Life and Art of Uday Shankar,* Ph.D. dissertation, New York University, 1986.
Khokar, Mohan, *His Dance, His Life: A Portrait of Uday Shankar,* New Delhi, 1983.

On SHANKAR: articles—

Banerjee, Projesh, "Uday Shankar—Father of Modern Ballet", in *Indian Ballet Dancing,* New Delhi, 1983.
Erdman, Joan L., "Performance as Translation: Uday Shankar in the West," in *Drama Review,* Spring 1987.
Sangeet Natak (Journal of the Sangeet Natak Akademi), April-June 1978, entire issue devoted to Uday Shankar.

*   *   *

On his way to becoming India's first modern dancer, Uday Shankar was enticed from a developing career as a painter into dance by prima ballerina Anna Pavlova. Later Shankar was known in Europe as an authentic exponent of the oriental dance, illustrating the difficulties inherent in cross-cultural categorization. In London in 1923 Pavlova asked the young Shankar to help her create two dances for her oriental suites. Choreographed by Shankar and based on Indian paintings and sculptures in London museum collections, these dances were *Hindu Wedding* and *Radha-Krishna*; Shankar partnered Pavlova in the latter.

Prior to coming to London in 1920, Shankar, eldest of seven sons of Bengali Brahmin parents, spent his childhood in India. He lived mainly in Jhalawar, a princely state where his father was in the service of the Maharaj Rana and eventually became Prime Minister, and in Nasrathpur, his mother's natal village near Banares. Shankar was an unruly student who eventually found a mentor in a teacher who taught him art, photography, music and technical skills. His father, Shyam Shankar Chaudhry, often abroad in London with the Jhalawar ruler, eventually brought Uday there in 1920 from Bombay where he was studying art at the J.J. School of Art. He wanted Uday to help him produce Indian shows in support of Indian soldiers injured in the first world war. Uday Shankar was enrolled in the Royal College of Arts, and nominated for the Prix de Rome, when Pavlova discovered him in 1923.

In 1930 Shankar created his first company, co-owned by a Swiss sculptor, Alice Boner, who admired Shankar's dance. It was composed initially of family members, including his youngest brother Rabindra (now known as sitar virtuoso Pandit Ravi Shankar). Based in Paris, the company toured Europe, the United States, the Middle East, Asia and India, playing more than 880 shows in 30 countries in seven years between 1931 and 1938. Their repertoire, which is described in elegant programs, included both short dances (based on Indian themes and folk dances), and ballets, narrating stories from Hindu culture in Shankar's style. Live musicians, playing exotic Indian instruments, and featured on stage and in the intervals, included music directors Timir Baran, Vishnudass Shirali, and for one year, India's renowned Ustad Alauddin Khan, who later became Ravi Shankar's teacher.

In 1939, after a brief break in Bali, Shankar founded the Uday Shankar India Culture Centre at Almora in the foothills of the Himalayas. Conceived to include dance, music, arts, and other cultural studies, the centre engaged dance students in a planned five-year course, as well as special courses for summer students. In addition to Uday Shankar who taught creative dance, there were gurus for three styles of classical dance—bharata natyam taught by Guru Kundappa Pillai, Manipur taught by Guru Amobi Singh, and Kathakali taught by Guru Shankaran Namboodiri, as well as music with Ustad Alauddin Khan.

The troupe, which toured India every winter when the season was too cold at Almora for residence, included former and new members. At Almora, Shankar, with the help of Zohra Mumtaz (later Segal) who had obtained a diploma in dance pedagogy from Mary Wigman's School in Dresden in 1930, codified his movements and developed a practical method for teaching Shankarstyle dance. His main disciples were Narendra Sharma, Sachin Shankar (a cousin of Uday), Shanti Bardhan, Devilal Samar, and the troupe included Zohra, Simkie (Simone Barbier, who had been his partner since the late 1920s in Paris), Amala Nandi (whom Shankar married in 1942), his brothers Rajendra and Debendra who had been with him in Paris and on tour, and later Narendra Sharma, Kameshwar Segal, Prabhat Ganguli, and other students. At Almora Uday Shankar and Zohra taught the modern classes, and Shankar and others created new choreography, including *Rhythm of Life*, and *Labour and Machinery*, and the *Ramayana Shadow Play* performed with live dancers. These dances brought more modern themes to his choreography, incorporating allegory and parody to critique princely selfishness, colonial rule, and heartless industrialization.

In 1942, Shankar decided to close the Almora Centre in order to make his feature film, *Kalpana* (*Imagination*) which was eventually produced at Gemini Studios in Madras. This film, presumed autobiographical by the public but denied as such by Uday and Amala Shankar, continued Shankar's critique of colonial India and the privileges of the princes. The movie integrated dance scenes choreographed especially for the screen with a narrative about a dancer and two women who vied for his affections and his success. According to India's famed filmmaker and Academy Award-winner

Satyajit Ray, the dance scenes were filmed in such a creative manner that they were viewed by all who came after as a model. Released in 1948, the film was a success with audiences but a commercial failure. Shankar returned to Madras and continued to tour with his dance company, sometimes sponsored by the new Government of India. In 1954 he and Amala moved with their son Ananda to Calcutta, where his daughter Mamata was born. In 1965 Amala and Uday Shankar opened the Uday Shankar India Culture Centre in Calcutta, which continues to this day. Their son Ananda has become a well-known composer, and with his wife Tanusree who was trained by Amala Shankar at the Centre, runs both a school and a popular dance company in Calcutta. After Shankar's death in 1977, Amala Shankar continued the Centre company and school, where Calcutta's children are trained in Shankar style. The company periodically presents programs of Shankar's choreography, in India and abroad, and in 1984 appeared at the American Dance Festival in Durham, North Carolina.

Shankar's main contribution to India's modern dance is his movements and choreography where he created a style that is distinctively Indian, yet not the specific movements of any indigenous form, either folk or classical. Integrating gestures learned from observing sculptures, paintings, classical and folk dances, as well as everyday kinetics in India, and creating music especially for his dances, Shankar inaugurated an all-India dance for modern India, which transcended regionality and gave Indians a national identity in the arts. While some of his later choreography from Calcutta had a distinctively Bengali flavor, his themes and messages remained for all Indians everywhere recognizably products of their own culture. Shankar's legacy continues today in India with Shankar-style choreography, with creative dance based on all-India and contemporary themes, and with innovative combinations of traditional and modern movements in ballets and modern short pieces.

—Joan L. Erdman

SHARIR, Yacov

Israeli-American dancer, choreographer, educator, and company director

Born: 22 August 1940, of Jewish parents in Casablanca, Morocco. **Education:** Raised and educated in Israeli kibbutzim; early dance training under Hasia Levi and Gertrude Kraus at the Rubin Academy of Music and Dance, Jerusalem; entered Bat-Sheva Dance Company School, 1965-67; additional training at Ballet Theatre Contemporaine in Paris, Stuttgart Ballet, Ballet de Flanders, and with Don Farnworth, New York City; graduated from Jerusalem Bezalel Academy of Fine Arts with degree in sculpture and ceramics, 1966. **Career:** Dancer, Bat-Sheva Dance Company, 1966-74; founder/artistic director, Koldemama/Moshe Efrati Dance Company, Tel Aviv, 1974-76; founder/artistic director, American Deaf Dance Company, Austin, Texas, 1977-82; dance faculty member, University of Texas at Austin, 1978-present; founder/artistic director, Sharir Dance Company, Austin, 1982-present; created first full-length work, *Homage to Jerome Robbins*, for Israeli Ballet Company, Tel Aviv, 1976; *The Great Variation* for Bat-Sheva Dance Company, 1977; *Percussion Concerto* for Hartford Ballet, 1979; first Sharir Dance Company international tour, 1994; first major new technology work, *Dancing with the Virtual Dervish/Virtual*

Bodies, 1994. **Awards:** National Endowment for the Arts Choreographic Fellowships, 1979, 1981; Meet the Composer/Choreographer Grant with Pauline Oliveros, 1989, 1990; University of Texas College of Fine Arts Teaching Excellence Award, 1991; National Endowment for the Arts Advancement Grant, 1988-94 and 1995-98; Banff Centre for the Arts Fellowship in Arts and Virtual Environments, 1992-94; New Work Award, Rencontres Choregraphiques Internationales de Bagnolet, 1994; Honorary Award, Suzanne Dellal International Choreography Competition, 1994; National Foundation for Advancement in the Arts Award, 1995-96.

Works

1976	*Three Variations*, Kibbutz Dance Company, Tel Aviv
	Homage to Jerome Robbins, Israeli Ballet Company, Tel Aviv
1977	*Mechanical Doll*, Dallas Ballet, Dallas
	Interaction I, II, III, American Deaf Dance Company, Austin
	The Great Variation, Bat-Sheva Dance Company, Tel Aviv
1979	*Continuation in Silence*, American Deaf Dance Company, Austin
	Right to Left, American Deaf Dance Company, Austin
	Quadroped, w/Dee McCandless, Austin
	Percussion Concerto, Hartford Ballet Company, Hartford, Connecticut
1980	*Shapes*, American Deaf Dance Company, Austin
	Rotations, Kibbutz Dance Company, Tel Aviv
	Circles, American Deaf Dance Company, Austin
	Percussion Concerto II, Austin Civic Ballet, Austin
1981	*Thirteen Haiku*, Austin Repertory Dancers, Austin
	Giant Steps, Bat-Sheva Dance Company, Tel Aviv
	Variations, American Deaf Dance Company, Austin
	Jazz Blanche, San Antonio Ballet, San Antonio
1982	*Haiku*, American Deaf Dance Company, Austin
	Dimension II, Kibbutz Dance Company, Tel Aviv
1983	*Landscape*, Kibbutz Dance Company, Tel Aviv
	Collage, Sharir Dance Company, Austin
1984	*Four Legs*, Sharir Dance Company, Austin
	Parade, Hartford Ballet, Hartford, Connecticut
	Seven Little Dances, Sharir Dance Company, Austin
1985	*Isamu Noguchi's Garden Dance*, University of Texas Dance Repertory Theatre, Austin
	Gestures, Sharir Dance Company, Austin
	Twelve Legs, Sharir Dance Company, Austin
1986	*Bach*, w/Dee McCandless, Austin
	Shapes, Sharir Dance Company (restaged from the 1980 original version), Austin
	Mona Lisa, w/José Luis Bustamante and Diana Prechter, Austin
	Trilogy I, Sharir Dance Company, Austin
1987	*Inside the Square/Sideshow*, Sharir Dance Company, Austin
	What, Why, How?, Sharir Dance Company, Austin
	Impressions on West Texas, University of Texas Dance Repertory Theatre, Austin
	The @#$%&?!! Ballet w/José Luis Bustamante, Sharir Dance Company, Austin
	Homage to Arnie Zane, Sharir Dance Company, Austin
1988	*Trilogy II*, Sharir Dance Company, Austin
	Four Love Studies w/José Luis Bustamante, Sharir Dance Company, Austin
	Trilogy III, Sharir Dance Company, Austin
1989	*Love Studies*, Sharir Dance Company, Austin
	Trio, Sharir Dance Company, Austin
	Conversations, Sharir Dance Company, Austin
	Dissonance and Harmony, University of Texas Dance Repertory Theatre, Austin
	Mezzaluna w/José Luis Bustamante, Sharir Dance Company, Austin
	de la nuit. . .le jour w/José Luis Bustamante, Sharir Dance Company, Austin
	Percussion Concerto III, Sharir Dance Company, Austin
	Four Love Studies w/José Luis Bustamante, Sharir Dance Company, Austin
	Trilogy III, Sharir Dance Company, Austin
1990	*The Blind Man* w/José Luis Bustamante, Sharir Dance Company, Austin
	Deep Listening, Sharir Dance Company, Austin
	My White Cow, Sharir Dance Company, Austin
1991	*Tell Me the Moon*, Sharir Dance Company, Austin
	Sheltered Body, Heywood McGriff, Austin
	Dissonance II and Harmony, Sharir Dance Company, Austin
	A Cart with Apples II, Sharir Dance Company, Austin
	Uomo Nella Luna, Sharir Dance Company, Austin
1992	*The Egg*, Sharir Dance Company, Austin
	Hats, Sharir Dance Company, Austin
	Yet Untitled, Tnuatron, Tel Aviv
1993	*Cecilia's Filaments*, Sharir Dance Company, Austin
	Frictions, Inbal Dance Theatre, Jerusalem
	Margo's World, Sharir Dance Company, Austin
	Dogs, Sharir Dance Company, Austin
	Love Studies, Utah's Repertory Dance Theatre, Salt Lake City
	The Egg, Utah's Repertory Dance Theatre, Salt Lake City
1994	*SINE*, Sharir Dance Company, Austin
	Homage to. . ., Rina Schenfeld Dance Theatre, Tel Aviv
	CU See Me, Sharir Dance Company, Austin
	Dancing with the Virtual Dervish/Virtual Bodies, Sharir Dance Company, Austin/Banff
1995	*Hollow Ground I*, Sharir Dance Company, Austin
	Earth Verses w/Andrea Beckham, Austin
1996	*Untitled*, University of Texas Dance Repertory Theatre, Austin
	Sine II, Sharir Dance Company, Austin
	Hollow Ground II, Sharir Dance Company, Austin
1997	*Sine*, Utah Repertory Dance Theatre, Salt Lake City
	Margo's World, Sharir Dance Company, Austin
	2 x 5 +, Sharir Dance Company, Austin

Publications

By SHARIR: articles—

"Virtual Bodies, Dances Within," with Diane Gromala, *Movement Research*, New York, 1993.

"Dancing with the Virtual Dervish," with Diane Gromala, *4th Biennial Symposium on Arts and Technology Proceedings*, New London, Connecticut, 1993.

"Blurring Boundaries," *5th Biennial Symposium on the Arts and Technology Proceedings,* New London, Connecticut, 1995.

"Dancing with the Virtual Dervish/Virtual Bodies," in *Immersed in Technology, Art, and Virtual Environments,* edited by Mary Anne Moser, Cambridge, Massachusetts, 1995.

"Transcending Boundaries," *The International Dance and Technology III Proceedings,* Toronto, 1995.

"Zero Gravity: Dancing in Virtual Spaces/Environments," *Israel Dance Magazine,* Tel Aviv, 1996.

"World Dance & Technology," *Ballet International/ACTUELL Tanz,* Berlin, 1997.

*   *   *

From his early dance years with the Bat-Sheva Dance Company to his present research into new technologies and dance, Yacov Sharir has contributed to modern dance for more than three decades as performer, choreographer, artistic director, teacher, and researcher. Sharir spent his childhood in an Israeli kibbutz. After his compulsory military duty, he graduated from the Bezalel Academy of Art with a degree in sculpture and ceramics. Sharir began his formal dance training in college, where he first studied modern dance at the Rubin Academy of Music and Dance in Jerusalem. He entered the Bat-Sheva Dance Company School in Tel Aviv in 1965, where he studied under Martha Graham, Linda Hodes, Pearl Lang, José Limón, and Anna Sokolow. In 1966 Sharir joined the Bat-Sheva Dance Company, eventually performing leading roles in works by Graham, Limón, Sokolow, Jerome Robbins, John Cranko, Donald McKayle, Glenn Tetley, John Butler, and others.

Throughout his career with Bat-Sheva, Sharir continued studying ballet and modern dance, primarily in Stuttgart, Paris, and New York City. His studies of various ballet and modern dance forms later helped him develop his own hybrid choreographic style. He began teaching modern dance early in his professional career and used his classes as a choreographic laboratory for new ideas. He joined the teaching staff of the Bat-Sheva Dance Company School in 1966 and also taught modern technique classes for the Israeli Ballet and the Kibbutz Contemporary Dance Company.

To fulfill his public service obligations in Israel, Sharir began working with deaf dance students in the early 1970s. As a result of his success teaching deaf dancers, he was awarded a U.S. National Endowment for the Arts grant to work with deaf dancers in Texas. Sharir arrived in Austin, Texas, in 1977 and founded the American Deaf Dance Company, the first professional company for deaf dancers in the U.S. Under Sharir's artistic direction, the company completed three national tours, along with numerous regional and statewide tours from 1977 to 1982.

Sharir's groundbreaking work with the American Deaf Dance Company proved that deaf and hearing-impaired individuals could successfully compete with hearing dancers on a professional level. Many of the company's original members settled throughout the U.S. to continue training of other deaf performers and choreographers.

In 1982 Sharir decided to incorporate a company for hearing dancers and founded the Sharir Dance Company, a professional avant-garde dance company in residence at the University of Texas at Austin College of Fine Arts. Composed primarily of graduates from the university's department of theatre and dance, where he was teaching, the company soon developed into the leading modern dance troupe in the southern United States. The company now tours nationally and internationally.

Sharir's initial goal in creating his company was to educate audiences about new dance. In the troupe's early years, Sharir often showcased works by up-and-coming modern choreographers as well as offering joint performances with established troupes. Under his direction, Sharir Dance Company has produced, presented, and collaborated with groups such as the Merce Cunningham Dance Foundation, the Trisha Brown Dance Company, Bella Lewitzky Dance Company, and many others. By creating an audience for modern dance in a politically conservative area of the U.S., and one primarily noted for regional ballet only, Sharir secured his own company's reputation while simultaneously paving the way for other modern dance choreographers. He made modern dance acceptable and accessible.

Sharir has created more than 30 works for Sharir Dance Company and choreographed for companies in the U.S., Europe, and the Middle East. He has received several NEA company grants, awards, and choreographic fellowships. In 1994 his company won an honorary award at the Suzanne Dellal International Choreography Competition in Tel Aviv for performing his work *The Egg.* The same year, the company won a New Works' Award at the Rencontres Choreographiques Internationales de Bagnolet in Paris.

Although he trained and performed primarily in Graham technique, Sharir's choreographic style shows no Graham influence. His choreography has incorporated elements of contact improvisation, a fluid upper body and spine, and highly complex, rhythmic footwork. He hires dancers who are skilled, versatile technicians with extensive training in both ballet and modern dance.

Sharir's company and choreography have been grounded in a firm technical base, yet he has experimented over the years with nontraditional elements such as use of text, minimalism, multimedia works, and, more recently, computer-aided choreography and dance for virtual reality environments.

Sharir's most important contributions to the field of modern dance lay not only in his bringing a new level of sophistication to modern dance in the southern and southwestern U.S., but also in his breakthough research in computer technology and art. Sharir is internationally recognized as a pioneer in new technology and dance and as one of the United States' leading authorities on computer-aided choreography.

In 1992 Sharir was awarded a two-year fellowship from the Banff Centre for the Arts in Alberta, Canada, to develop *Dancing with the Virtual Dervish/Virtual Bodies,* a multidisciplinary project in virtual environments and cyberspace involving his collaborator, visual artist Diane Gromala. *Dancing with the Virtual Dervish/Virtual Bodies* was a seminal work for Sharir, combining an interactive, networked virtual environment with dance and video. Working with software engineers at Banff's computer research facility, Sharir helped design new computer programming to facilitate choreographing in virtual environments and upgrades for existing computer choreography software. The project culminated with performances in May 1994, in Austin and in Banff.

Sharir is a frequent speaker at arts and technology conferences and symposia in the U.S. and abroad. He has contributed to several international publications, journals, and books regarding dance/art and technology. In addition to teaching modern dance and choreography at the University of Texas, Sharir teaches multidisciplinary art and technology courses, including computer-aided choreography in virtual reality. Sharir has served on the National Endowment for the Arts Choreographic Fellowship Dance Panel, the Texas Commission on the Arts Dance Panel, the Mid-America Dance on Tour Panel, and on international arts councils in Israel, Spain, and France.

—Sondra Lomax

SHAWN, Ted

American pioneer of modern dance, choreographer, and educator

Born: Ted Edwin Myers Shawn, 21 October 1891 in Kansas City, Missouri. **Education:** Began dancing as therapy for partial paralysis and became the first American professional male dancer. **Family:** Married Ruth St. Denis, 1914. **Career:** Co-founded Denishawn school and dance company with St. Denis, 1915; company toured extensively in the U.S., Europe, and Asia; founded, published, and wrote for *Denishawn Magazine;* Denishawn school disbanded, 1932; founded a "University of the Dance" on his farm, Jacob's Pillow; created Ted Shawn and His Men Dancers, 1933; toured the States and Europe promoting dance and breaking down stereotypes against male dancers, 1933-40; director, Jacob's Pillow, until 1972. **Awards:** Honorary degree, Springfield College (M.A.); Capezio Award, 1957; Cross of Knight Dannebrog by King of Denmark. **Died:** 1972.

Selected Works

1914   *Grecian Suite* (*Humoresque, Dance of the Harvester, Classic Waltz, Diana and Endymion*) Shawn, Norma Gould, Adelaide Munn, Santa Fe Reading Room tour

National Suite (*A Hungarian Mazurka, A French Love Waltz, A German Peasant Dance, A Slavic Sword Dance*) Shawn, Gould, Munn, and Otis Williams, Sante Fe Reading Room tour

Oriental Suite (*Scarf Dance, Cymbal Dance, Zuleika, Poem of Love*) Shawn, Gould, and Munn, Sante Fe Reading Room tour

Dagger Dance (mus. Herbert), solo, Kentucky Theatre, Paducah

Pipes of Pan (mus. Delibes), Hilda Beyer, Kentucky Theatre, Paducah

Earth Cycle, Shawn, Hilda Beyer, Evan Burrows Fontaine, Shubert Theatre, Kansas City

Arabic Suite (mus. Rubinstein-Herbert), Shawn and St. Denis, Ravinia Park, Chicago

1915   *Japanese Sword Dance* (mus. arr Horst), solo, Mason Opera House, Los Angeles

St. Denis Mazurka, Shawn and St. Denis, Mason Opera House

1916   *Pyrrhic Dance*, Shawn and Karl Heberlein, Chatterton Theatre, Bloomington, Illinois

1919   *Julnar of the Sea*, Lillian Powel and company, Pantages Theater, Los Angeles

1920   *Les Mysteres Dionysiaques* (mus. Massenet) Shawn and company, Greek Theater Berkeley

1921   *Japanese Spear Dance* (mus. Horst), solo, Hotel Coronado, San Diego

Invocation to the Thunderbird (mus. Sousa), solo, Egan Little Theatre, Los Angeles

Spanish Suite I (*Valse Aragonaise, Tango, Malaguena*) (mus. Thome, Jonas, Moszkowski), Shawn and Martha Graham, Egan Little Theatre, Los Angeles

Street Nautch (mus. Michaelis), Dorothea Bowen, Egan Little Theatre, Los Angeles

Xochitl (mus. Grunn), Martha Graham and company, Long Beach

1922   *Spanish Suite II* (*Danza, Tango, Malaguena*) (mus. Granados), Shawn and St. Denis, Temple Theatre, Lewiston

1923   *Cuadro Flamenco* (mus. Horst), Shawn, St. Denis and company, Apollo Thearte, Atlantic City

The Feather of Dawn (mus. Cadman), Shawn, Louise Brooks, Pauline Lawrence and company, Apollo Theatre, Atlantic City

1924   *Adagio Pathetique/Death of Adonis* (mus. Godard), solo, Academy of Music, Newburg, New York

1925   *Spanish Suite III* (*Shawl Plastique [Danza Espagnol], Tango, Allegrias, Malaguena*), (mus. Valverde), Shawn and St. Denis, Lewisohn Stadium, New York

Valse Denishawn (mus. Wenk), Shawn and St. Denis, Imperial Theatre, Tokyo

1926   *Danse Sacree* and *Danse Profane* (mus. Debussy), St. Denis and Shawn, Victoria Theatre, Singapore

General Wu's Farewell to his Wife (mus. Vaughan), Weidman, Douglas, Day, Steares, Sherman, Lawrence, Howry, and Graham, Victoria Theatre, Singapore

Spanish Suite IV (*Shawl Plastique [Danza Espagnol], Flamenco Dances*, and *Danza de Quatro*) (mus. MSS), Shawn, St. Denis, Weidman, Day, and Graham, Philharmonic Auditorium, Los Angeles

1928   *Orpheus* (mus. Liszt), solo, Lewisohn Stadium, New York

1929   *Mevlevi Dervish* (mus. Fuleihan), solo, Carnegie Hall, New York

Shawl Dance, Estelle Dennis, Joan Keena, Klarna, Casino Hall, Atlantic City

Prometheus Bound (mus. Scriabin), solo, Lewisohn Stadium

1930   *Group Dance for Male Ensemble* (mus. W.F. Bach), Shawn and company, Lewisohn Stadium

Orpheus Dionysus w/Margarete Wallmann (mus. Glück), Shawn, Wallman, and German dance group, National Theater, Munich

1931   *The Divine Idiot* (mus. Scriabin), solo, Washington Irving High School, New York

O Brother Sun and Sister Moon (mus. Respighi), solo, Chapin Hall, Williamstown

Two Music Visualizations: Intermezzo and *Rhapsody* (mus. Brahms), Shawn and company, Chapin Hall, Williamstown

Zuni Ghost Dance (mus. Troyer), solo, Chapin Hall, Williamstown

1933   *Fetish* (mus. Meeker), Ted Shawn and His Men Dancers (TSMD), Barton Mumaw, Strong Theatre, Burlington, Vermont

Negro Spirituals I (includes *Go Down Moses* and other dances), TSMD, Repertory Theatre, Boston

Negro Spirituals II (includes *Nobody Knows de Trouble I've Seen, Swing Low, Sweet Chariot*, and other dances) (mus. arr Meeker), TSMD, Strong Theatre, Burlington

1934   *Hopi Indian Eagle Dance* (mus. Meeker), solo, Hawley Armory, Storrs, Connecticut

Hound of Heaven (mus. Meeker), solo, Hawley Armory, Storrs

Labor Symphony (*Labor of the Fields, Labor of the Forests, Labor of the Seas, Mechanized Labor*) (mus. Meeker), TSMD, Hawley Armory, Storrs

Maori War Haka (mus. Meeker), TSMD, Hawley Armory, Storrs

Pioneers' Dance (mus. Powell), TSMD, Hawley Armory, Storrs

1935   *Gothic* (mus. Satie), Fred Hearn, Foster Fitz-Simons and Ned Coupland, Clark School, Goshen, New York

Kinetic Molpai (mus. Meeker), TSMD, Clark School, Goshen

1936   *New World Symphony* (mus. Dvorak), TSMD, Robin Hood Dell, Philadelphia

1937   *O, Libertad!* (mus. Meeker), TSMD, Connecticut State College, Storrs

1938   *Dance of the Ages* (mus. Meeker), TSMD, Massachusetts State College, Amherst, Massachusetts

1940   *The Dome* (mus. Bach), TSMD, Temple Theatre, Miami

Jacob's Pillow Concert (choreographed with company members/mus. Meeker), TSMD, Temple Theatre, Miami

Toccata and Fugue in D Minor (mus. Bach), TSMD, Temple Theatre, Miami

1949   *Dreams of Jacob*

1951   *Song of Songs*

1964   *Siddhas of the Upper Air* w/St. Denis (mus. Meeker), Shawn and St. Denis, Jacob's Pillow

Publications

By SHAWN: books—

Ruth St. Denis: Pioneer and Prophet, San Francisco, 1920.
Gods Who Dance, New York, 1929.
Fundamentals of Dance Education, Girard, Kansas, 1937.
Dance We Must, Pittsfield, Massachusetts, 1950.
with Grey Poole, *One Thousand and One Night Stands*, Garden City, New York, 1960.
Every Little Movement: A Book About François Delsarte, Pittsfield, Massachusetts, 1963.

By SHAWN: articles—

Series of 27 articles, published three per week for nine weeks, *Boston Herald*, 1936.

On SHAWN: books—

Dreier, Katherine S., *Shawn: The Dancer*, New York, 1933.
Schlundt Christina L., *The Professional Appearances of Ruth St. Denis and Ted Shawn: A Chronology and Index of Dances 1906-1932*, New York, 1962.
———, *The Professional Appearances of Ted Shawn and His Men Dancers: A Chronology and Index of Dances 1933-1940,* New York, 1967.
Terry, Walter, *Ted Shawn: Father of American Dance*, New York, 1976.

*   *   *

Ted Shawn began studying ballet at the age of 18 to regain strength and coordination after contracting diptheria and being partially paralyzed. Instead of returning to his interrupted divinity studies at the University of Denver, he decided to become a dancer. He faced opposition from some of his classmates who felt dancing could not be a serious occupation for a man, but he was determined and later worked hard to counter prejudice against professional male dancers. Shawn studied with Hazel Wallach, who had trained and danced with the Metropolitan Opera Ballet, and then went to southern California to broaden his dance training. He met Norma Gould, a ballet instructor, and taking advantage of the ballroom dancing craze in the United States, they began performing *the dansant* or "tango teas" to make money.

Shawn was a dynamo whose zeal for the dance was akin to a preacher's for the pulpit. He was constantly making plans for dance projects. While in Los Angeles, he made a film, *Dance Through the Ages,* using the new medium of film to showcase dance. He and Gould proposed a tour of dance entertainments for the reading rooms along the Santa Fe railroad. Together, with a small touring company, they performed in exchange for round-trip tickets to New York. At the end of the tour, Shawn disbanded the company and studied Delsartian movement with Mrs. (Mary) Perry King. He performed and taught classes in New York City. Through an acquaintance, Shawn arranged to audition for Ruth St. Denis whom he greatly admired and had seen three years earlier, in 1911, in Denver. When St. Denis saw Shawn perform she immediately asked him to dance with her company.

The partnership was advantageous for both: St. Denis had an established name and reputation, and Shawn, according to Nancy Lee Chalfa Ruyter in *Reformers and Visionaries* (1979): "brought a comprehensive knowledge of the types of dance available in America at the time, experience in teaching dance and organizing programs, [and] a well-built body" to the team. Shawn widened the scope of the dance program St. Denis offered and brought a new vigor to their choreography. After joining St. Denis in 1914, they and a small troupe toured the U.S. and within the year, Shawn had persuaded St. Denis not only to marry him—beginning a lifelong partnership if not traditional marriage—but to open a school as well.

Ever practical, Shawn was the driving force behind the school, because, as Don McDonagh has noted in *The Complete Guide to Modern Dance*, the school supplied "dancers, an assured income, and a base where they could create new productions and store scenery and props." Denishawn opened its doors in Los Angeles in 1915. One of the young dancers taking classes that first season was Martha Graham, who became Shawn's protégé and for whom he choreographed the successful *Xochitl*, in 1921. Graham stayed with Denishawn long enough to help Shawn establish a New York school and for the first vaudeville tour of 1922, then left to establish a trailblazing career of her own.

Concurrent with the opening of Denishawn in California, St. Denis was asked to appear at the Greek Theatre in Berkeley—the first-ever such invitation extended to a dancer. Shawn helped her plan a large pageant, including a dance foreshadowing his future direction as choreographer. In his memoir, *One Thousand and One Night Stands* (1960), Shawn remembered "Sixteen men dancers, leaping and jumping with power, muscles, and virile strength, created an impact that thrilled the pageant's audiences and won paragraphs of newspaper praise. Many years elapsed before I formed my own group of men dancers but after the reception of *Pyrrhic Dance* I always had in the back of my mind plans, choreographies, and dance themes suitable for men dancers."

The vaudeville tours from 1922 to 1925, organized by Daniel Mayer (an important impresario of the time), represented the height of Denishawn's box office drawing power, and as Shawn pointed out in his memoir they "were the first truly American dance group" to perform for 28 consecutive weeks during three successive years. After the Mayer tours, Denishawn toured Asia and returned triumphant.

While touring Asia, Shawn went to great lengths to see and photograph indigenous dance and costumes. While both he and St. Denis claimed not to choreograph authentic ethnic dances but to interpret them, they both felt it was important to see and know the real thing and to preserve it for others. Many of the materials they collected, including the only extant copy of the *Bugaku* costume volume from the Japanese Imperial household, are housed in the New York Public Library's Denishawn Collection. But Shawn's interest in international dance went beyond documentation; it was an important part of his work. Early on Shawn established an eclectic study of dance, seeking out its different forms wherever he traveled—studying flamenco and Spanish dancing in Spain, searching for authentic "ouled nail" dancers in North Africa, studying at the Wigman school in Germany. He was the first to bring an authorized Wigman teacher (Margarete Wallmann) to the U.S.; in later years, through Jacob's Pillow, his dance school and festival, Shawn was instrumental in introducing international dance companies like Ballet Rambert and the Royal Danish Ballet to Americans.

From 1928 on, Shawn and St. Denis increasingly lived and worked separately, though they never divorced. Shawn took his first solo tour to Europe in 1930 where he was well-received and was invited to perform in Margarete Wallmann's *Orpheus Dionysos* during the Third German Dance Congress in Munich. The same year, he bought a farm called Jacob's Pillow in Massachusetts and began teaching there. In 1933, after having taught dance to male students at Springfield College, he began his all-male troupe. For the next seven years until 1940, Ted Shawn and His Men Dancers toured the U.S. and Europe. The tours did much to change public opinion about men dancing professionally which, as Shawn said, "was considered to be effeminate, trivial, and an unworthy occupation for the strapping and well-muscled male. I knew this to be utterly false. . . I was sure that when people saw young American athletes going through masculine dances, prejudice would be overcome and dancing as a career would take its place with other legitimate professions."

In the last decades of his life, Shawn traveled extensively looking for dance companies and dancers to come to Jacob's Pillow, which today is one of the largest dance festivals in the world. In recognition of his work on behalf of dance in the U.S., Shawn was given the Capezio Award in 1957. Among the many other awards he prized was the Cross of Knight of Dannebrog from his Majesty Frederick IX, King of Denmark, for his diligent work promoting international dance. Shawn died in 1972, still active at Jacob's Pillow to the last.

—Glynis Benbow-Niemier

SIMONS, Ton

Dutch dancer, choreographer, educator, and company director

Born: 29 March 1961 in Beesel, the Netherlands. **Education:** Briefly attended Jooss Academy of Art and the Margriet Franken ballet studio in Breda; studied at the Dans Academy, Rotterdam; studied with Lucas Hoving in New York, 1970-73; studied as scholarship student at the Merce Cunningham Studio and Joffrey School, New York, 1974. **Career:** Dancer/choreographer, Werkcentrum Dans (now De Rotterdamse Dansgroep) led by former Nederlands

Dans Theater soloist Käthy Gosschalk, the Netherlands, 1975-78; dancer, with choreographers Jim Self, Robert Kovich, and Karole Armitage, New York; founder, Ton Simons and Dancers, group projects, 1981-present; worked with the Colorado Repertory Dance Company, Washington Ballet, Pacific Northwest Ballet, Reflex, Karin Post Comany, and Conservatory in the Czech capital Prague; tours to the Netherlands (Holland Dance Festival), France (Festival d'Automne Paris), Germany, and Japan; choreographer, Rotterdamse Dansgroep, the Netherlands; collaborated with Ellen van Schuylenbruch (Holland) and Brenda Daniels (USA), Käthy Gosschalk (Rotterdamse Dansgroep), Dutch musicians Hans Dulfer, Horst Rickels, and Michel Waisvisz, British group Test Dept., Michael Brown (USA), the Ordinaires (USA), visual artists Roe Aldarada, Charles Atlas, Simon Costin, David Feldman, William Katz, Brös Knegjes, Mark Lancaster, and Andrew Lord; taught numerous international residencies, master classes, technique, repertory, and composition workshops. **Awards:** National Choreography Prize of the Netherlands for *Grace,* 1990; Individual Artist's Fellowship, National Endowment for the Arts, 1991; two-year choreographer's fellowship, NEA, 1992-93; nominated, National Choreography Prize of the Netherlands for *The Idea of Order,* 1993; company funding for Ton Simons and Dancers from the NEA 1994; Sonia Gaskell Prize for *Song,* the Netherlands, 1997.

Roles

Danced mainly solos and duets in own choreographies, 1973-95; danced regular season repertoire of Werkcentrum Dans (now Rotterdamse Dansgroep), including works by Nils Christe, Amy Gale, Robert North, Hans Tuerlings, and Lenny Westerdijk, 1975-78; danced his last role, in *Q* (Simons), Birmingham, Alabama, 1995.

Works

1973   *Chantal Meteor* (duet; mus. Simons), Amsterdam Summer Academy, Stadsschouwburg, Amsterdam; later performed with Valerie Bettis, New York

1975   *31 Simple Steps* (mus. Lord), Werkcentrum Dans (now Rotterdamse Dansgroep), Lantaren, Rotterdam

1976   *Two Evenings I* (mus. Dulfer), Werkcentrum Dans, Lantaren, Rotterdam

1977   *Throw Wood at Green* (mus. Mozart), Werkcentrum Dans, Lantaren, Rotterdam

        Two Evenings II/Video (later also called *Credo in Us;* mus. Cage), Werkcentrum Dans, Lantaren, Rotterdam

1978   *Jumble* (mus. Cage), Werkcentrum Dans, Lantaren, Rotterdam

        Two Evenings III/Icon (mus. Toebosch, Waisvisz), Werkcentrum Dans, Lantaren, Rotterdam

1979   *Kameubel/Kamengelmoes,* an entertainment for children (mus. Waisvisz), Werkcentrum Dans, Theater Zuidplein, Rotterdam

        Two Evenings IV/Field Piece (mus. from four radio stations), Werkcentrum Dans, Theater Bellevue, Amsterdam

        Sleeve (duet), Ton Simons and Dancers, Paula Cooper Gallery, New York

1980   *Commonplace Quintet* (mus. Waisvisz), Werkcentrum Dans, Lantaren, Rotterdam

Countermix, Ton Simons and Dancers, Cunningham Studio, New York

1981   *Echo* (mus. Dylan), The Yard, Riverside Church, New York

Tally (mus. Lancaster), Ton Simons and Dancers, Centre Pompidou, Paris

1982   *Spread* (mus. Lord), Ton Simons and Dancers, The Kitchen, New York

The Knife Sharpener, a tableau (mus. Busby), Ton Simons and Dancers, The Kitchen, New York

Echo II (mus. Dylan), Werkcentrum Dans, Lantaren, Rotterdam

Ball (mus. Brown), Ton Simons and Dancers, Tanzproject, München

Slow Rose (mus. Waisvisz), The Yard, Riverside Church, New York

1984   *Rondo* (mus. Waisvisz), Werkcentrum Dans, Theater Zuidplein, Rotterdam

1985   *Suite Ordinaire* (mus. the Ordinaires), Ton Simons and Dancers, Pineapple Dance Center, New York

Visions from a Witch's Cauldron (mus. Waisvisz), Werkcentrum Dans, Theater Zuidplein, Rotterdam

1986   *Disconnected Dances* (mus. the Ordinaires), Ton Simons and Dancers, Whitney Museum of American Art, New York

The Chara Trio (mus. the Ordinaires), Ton Simons and Dancers, Suntory Hall, Tokyo

1987   *Discreet Quantities* (mus. the Ordinaires), Stephens College Dance Department, Columbia, Missouri

The Palace at 4 a.m./Spinoza Variations (first version; mus. the Ordinaires), Ton Simons and Dancers & Reflex, Holland Festival, Doelen Theater, Amsterdam

Local Color (mus. Test Dept.), Stephens College Dance Department, Perry-Mansfield Theater, Steamboat Springs, Colorado

Moonlight (mus. Test Dept.), Rotterdamse Dansgroep, Conservatorium, the Hague

Palace Variations (mus. the Ordinaires), Reflex, Stadsschouwburg, Groningen

1988   *The Nairobi Trio* (mus. the Foretunetellers), Ton Simons and Dancers, Leo Castelli Gallery, New York

Materia Prima (mus. Test Dept.), Rotterdamse Dansgroep, Schouwburg, Rotterdam

The Palace at 4 a.m./Spinoza Variations (new version; mus. the Ordinaires), Ton Simons and Dancers, R.A.P.P. Theater, New York

Solitude/Im Auge Gottes (mus. Mozart, Einstürzende Neubauten), Rotterdamse Dansgroep, Schouwburg, Rotterdam

Grace (mus. Mozart), Rotterdamse Dansgroep, Stadsschouwburg, Eindhoven

1989   *Solitude Duet* (mus. Mozart), duet, Ton Simons and Dancers, Whitney Museum at Equitable Center, New York

In the Studio/Shapes (in 1992 restaged as *In the Studio/Shapes I;* mus. Brown), Ton Simons and Dancers, Whitney Museum at Equitable Center, New York

1990   *Duet with Falling Figure* (mus. the Ordinaires), Stephens College Dance Department, Columbia, Missouri

Shape Septet (mus. Brown), Stephens College Dance Department, Perry-Mansfield Theater

Still Life One (mus. Morrison), Stephens College Dance Department, Perry-Mansfield College

Still Life Two (mus. Morrison), Stephens College Dance Department, Perry-Mansfield Theater

1991   *Sleepless Nights* (mus. Spector, Branca), Rotterdamse Dansgroep, Schouwburg, Rotterdam

Grace (restaged; mus. Mozart), Ton Simons and Dancers, National Theater Nova Scena, Prague

Incarnatus Variation (mus. Mozart), Stephens College Dance Department, Perry-Mansfield Theater

Still Life III (trio; mus. Morrison), Ton Simons and Dancers, Holland Dance Festival, Koninklijke Schouwburg, the Hague

In the Studio (*Shapes*) *II* (mus. Morrison), Ton Simons and Dancers, Holland Dance Festival, Koninklijke Schouwburg, the Hague

Private Debates/Public Exhibition (mus. Mozart), Ton Simons and Dancers, Holland Dance Festival, Koninklijke Schouwburg, the Hague

1992   *Pantheon Pace* (mus. Mozart), Rotterdamse Dansgroep, Schouwburg, Rotterdam

Allegro from Private Debates for 8 Dancers (mus. Mozart), Stephens College Dance Department, Perry-Mansfield Theater

Still Life IV (mus. Morrison), Ton Simons and Dancers, Dampfzentrale, Bern

Black Mirror (mus. Velvet Underground), Ton Simons and Dancers, Dampfzentrale, Bern

In the Studio (*Shapes*) *I* (restaged version; mus. Brown), part of programme *Twine,* Karin Post Company, Toneelschuur Haarlem

1993   *The Idea of Order* (mus. Velvet Underground, Mozart, Oliveros), Rotterdamse Dansgroep, Schouwburg, Rotterdam

Still Life VI & III (mus. Morrison), Colorado Repertory Dance Company, Aurora Fox Theater, Denver

Divertimento K.563 (mus. Mozart), Ton Simons and Dancers, Joyce Theater, New York

Sextet (mus. Velvet Underground), Ton Simons and Dancers, Joyce Theater, New York

10 Formulations (*"In the room the women come and go, talking of Michelangelo"*) (mus. Hendrix, Mozart, Velvet Underground, traditional), Perry-Mansfield Summer Company, Perry Mansfield Theater

Tally 1993 (mus. Lancaster), Rotterdamse Dansgroep, Spui Theater, the Hague

Commonplace Quintet 1993 (revised; mus. Waisvisz), Rotterdamse Dansgroep, Spui Theater, the Hague

Clay (mus. Mozart), Rotterdamse Dansgroep, Schouwburg, Rotterdam

1994   *Dance Diagram* (mus. Cage), Stephens College Dance Department, Columbia, Missouri

Colorado Variations (mus. Cage), Perry-Mansfield Summer Company, Steamboat Springs, Colorado

GOD/DOG Variations (mus. 14 composers), Rotterdamse Dansgroep, Schouwburg, Rotterdam

1995   *Q* (mus. live and variable), Ton Simons and Dancers, Danspace, St. Mark's Church, New York

Perilous Night (mus. Mozart), Pacific Northwest Ballet, Off-Stage Project, Studio Theater, Seattle

Composition for Dancers and Color (mus. Rickels), Rotterdamse Dansgroep, Nederlands Dans Theater, the Hague

1996   *Violin Concerto no. 1* (mus. Mozart), Ton Simons and
        Dancers, Cunningham Studio, New York
        Ration (mus. Hindemith), Ton Simons and Dancers,
        Cunningham Studio, New York
        Violin Voice (solo; mus. Mozart), Rotterdamse Dansgroep,
        Schouwburg, Rotterdam
        The Tenderness of Patient Minds (mus. Mozart), Pacific
        Northwest Ballet, City Center Theater, New York
        Song (mus. Mozart), Rotterdamse Dansgroep,
        Schouwburg, Rotterdam
1997   *Clay II & I* (mus. Mozart), Rotterdamse Dansgroep,
        Schouwburg, Rotterdam
        Through the Wall (mus. Shipp), Rotterdamse Dansgroep,
        Schouwburg, Rotterdam

Publications

On SIMONS: articles—

Gosschalk, Käthy, "Ton Simons—Nederlander in New York,"
    Dansjaarboek 92/93, Amsterdam, 1993.
Hunt, Marilyn, *Dancemagazine,* New York, 1997.
Lartigue, Pierre, "Ton Simons et Ellen van Schuylenburch. Le bel
    auhourd'hui," *Festival d'Automne a Paris 1972-1982,* Paris, 1982.

*   *   *

A schoolboy dreaming over an old scrapbook full of romantic
ballet pictures does not always get into a career in modern dance.
But this actually did happen in the case of Ton Simons, who
grew up in a small Dutch village with no dance companies around.
He practiced drawing and painting and built spatial creations,
but had never seen any dance. An accidentally found scrapbook
with Maria Tallchief as the "black swan" opened his eyes and
gave direction to his slumbering talent for movement and space.

In a relatively short time he encountered four very important
people for his career. His ballet teacher for two years, Margriet
Franken discovered his real abilities. He then attended the
Rotterdam Dance Academy where the inspiring Lucas Hoving
taught him not only professionalism and truthfulness, but sent
him to the Cunningham Studio in New York. Merce Cunningham
taught Ton Simons, with his strong urge to create things, how to
handle this urgency by giving him the tools of time, space, and
energy with which to work. With these simple but proper tools
Simons could articulate his creative impulses. Käthy Gosschalk
(Dutch dancer, actress, choreographer, and director) invited
Simons in 1975 to dance in her new company, Werkcentrum
Dans (now Rotterdamse Dansgroep), where he stayed as an
ensemble member for three years. She also gave him the opportunity to choreograph at least one piece a year in Rotterdam,
from his first year as starting artist until the present day, while
having New York as his residence.

The combination of dancer and choreographer had its limits;
Simons was never a technical virtuoso, though he had strong
points like keeping prolonged balances in unusual positions. He
could portray a character well, but could from time to time not
resist demonstrating a rebellious attitude toward discipline. All
in all, he could give the impression of a clear-cut performance.
These dancing qualities are, in a way, preserved in his pieces.
Knowing his own technical limitations, he soon decided to perform only in his own work. In spite of the "black swan" from

the scrapbook, the obvious narrative or romantic style never
was his cup of tea. Ton Simons has always focused on dance
more resembling the abstract movements of Cunningham. Right
after his studies with Cunningham in New York, Simons made
rather rigid conceptual pieces in the style of his model-teacher.
After some years he grew away from the rigidity and found the
freedom to make dance with a style of his own, also gradually
adding more emotional expression to his dance pieces. His choreographies are best defined as a combination of visual and moving art.

Traveling between New York and Rotterdam kept a constancy
in Simons' career: from New York, where it was a constant
struggle to keep a fledgling dance company alive; to Rotterdam,
where the well-organised and funded Rotterdamse Dansgroep
awaited his return. In Rotterdam, Simons was spoiled during his
years there as choreographer, though the alternation seems to
have been good for his work. Contrasts, anyway, have played
their part. This is obvious in his choice of music—the elegant
classical Mozart and mercilessly loud industrial sounds. These
antipodes are very confrontational when combined in the piece
Solitude, with pleasing, enchanting Mozart and disturbing, loud
Glenn Branca. Both have meaning for Simons: "The use of
contrasts helps to make the [dissention] of those antipodes clear.
It has to do with my view on the world—I think of the world as
full of contrasts, and my own position in that world."

Since 1985 his work developed an emphatically stronger ripening quality. Living in New York, experiencing the many aspects of that world capital of dance, had a maturing effect. In
contrast with the Ton Simons in his younger years he could
show a new attitude, more serious with his dance and more
involved with his profession. Distortions in formerly clean movements changed the appearance of his work. These distorted
phrasings, an interesting addition to the formerly academic look,
can also be regarded as expressing the pain of big-city life. With
this quality the Dutch-born Simons can be connected to the
rather serious Dutch dance tradition, where there is hardly any
room for frivolity. Notable in recent years, the dancers in these
pieces increasingly express an awareness and communication
that considerably enrich the performances.

This is all part of Simons' signature as a mature choreographer, a signature frequently recognised by his peers. He receives
awards regularly; in general, he has been the recipient of grants,
and, more specifically, in the Netherlands, his solo work has
also been awarded. In 1997, Simon's choreography for *Song,*
with its impressive silence and slow movements, was lauded by
jurors for the Sonia Gaskill prize as "distinguished by eloquence
of the motion on itself, joined with a great sense for music,
bizarre ideas, and strong feeling for theatrical shaping. Nowhere
is the dance only illustrating the sentiment in the music or just
following the musical structure." Further, the judges found
Simons' "integrity, his sense of responsibility for the art form,
his craftmanship and choreographic talent, in combination with
his searching and remarkable twisting spirit, make us look forward to his next 72 pieces."

Simons, at the time of the prize consideration, was working
on *Through the Wall,* a "jazz piece" to music by Matthew Shipp
for the Rotterdamse Dansgroep. He thanked the jurors, and stated
simply that in creating dance, "There is only one way: the thinking and creating is in just doing it."

—Jan Baart

SKAGGS, Sarah

American dancer, choreographer, and company director

Born: 11 October 1957 in St. Louis, Missouri. **Education:** Sweet
Briar College, Virginia, B.A. in Theatre Arts, 1979; studied with
Eija Celli at Sweet Briar, also at Cunningham Studio, and in the
techniques of Erick Hawkins and José Limón; studied ideokinesis
with Andre Benard, Bartinieff with Risa Friedman, Effort/Shape at
the Laban Center, and improvisation and composition with Lisa
Kraus. **Career:** Dancer, Dana Reitz, 1981-85; premiered solo concert at Kiva Dance Studios, New York City, 1983; creator of participatory "dance events" outside New York modern dance circuit.
Awards: National Endowment of the Arts (NEA) choreography
fellowships, 1986-94; New York Foundation for the Arts fellowship, 1986, 1990; grants from Creative Time Citywide, 1993; U.S.
Information Agency, 1994; and Trust for Mutual Understanding to
Prague, 1994.

Works

1983   *Satie in Five Movements,* Kiva Studios, New York
1984   *Cross Cultural Studies,* P.S. 122, New York
1986   *Noh Body,* Danspace, St. Mark's Church, New York
1987   *Force of Circumstance,* The Kitchen, New York
         Primary Anticipation, The Kitchen, New York
         Wholly Holy, The Kitchen, New York
1988   *(blue),* Lincoln Center, "Serious Fun" Festival, New York
1989   *Callas,* P.S. 122, New York
1990   *Divine Interventions,* American Dance Festival, Durham,
         North Carolina
         Prelude to Salomé, Danspace, St. Mark's Church, New
         York
         Berlin, Danspace, St. Mark's Church, New York
1991   *Deep Song (remix),* Dance Theatre Workshop, New York
1993   *Higher Ground,* St. Patrick's Youth Center, New York
1994   *Folked Up,* Prague Old Time Square, Hong Kong
1995   *Reeling,* Joyce Theater, Altogether Different series, New
         York
1996   *Twister Mixer,* Art Awareness, Catskills, New York
1997   *Paradise,* Manhattan Ballroom, New York

*   *   *

Considering her work analogous to an independent film rather
than a mainstream Hollywood production, Sarah Skaggs's choreography defies the traditional dance performance model. In her recent
work, with performances in gymnasiums, community centers,
schools, and clubs, rather than on the proscenium stage, Skaggs
focuses on the accessibility of her art to her audience viewers.
Concerned with the way, and to the degree in which audiences
receive dance, Skaggs's work is at the cutting edge of transformation within the modern dance performance paradigm.

With childhood training in ballet, Skaggs happened on modern
dance as a way of fulfilling a physical education requirement at
Sweet Briar College in Virginia. She was a theatre arts major, with a
minor in art history, and graduated with distinction in theatre in
1979. It was in college that Skaggs worked with modern dance
teacher Eija Celli, who continues to be her mentor. Celli connected
dance to architecture, painting, and other art forms, and improvisa-

tion was valued much more than purely technical exercises. Studying dance and choreography as derivatives of improvisation influenced Skaggs by providing her with insight into her own preferred
creative process.

During her years at Sweet Briar, Skaggs spent winter residencies
in New York studying technique at major dance studios, such as
those of Cunningham and Limón. She learned the atmosphere and
hierarchy of the New York dance scene, but when she finally arrived in New York in 1980 she was prepared to abandon the traditional structure of dance technique training, performance and
proscenium-biased choreography. Discouraged with auditioning for
choreographers whose work held no interest to her, Skaggs sought
body therapies to de-program her body of the codified dance techniques she had been studying at the major studios. She wanted to
find her own movement style. She studied Bartinieff fundamentals
and effort/shape at the Laban Center and the Mabel Todd/Lulu
Sweigard model of ideokinesis with Andre Benard. One type of
dance technique that did resonate well with her was Hawkins technique, which she had studied with Nancy Meehan.

Skaggs danced with Dana Reitz and toured with the company
from 1981 through 1985. The travel opportunities that Skaggs had
while touring with Reitz provided her with ethnological inspirations that informed her own future creative work. During the time
Skaggs was working with Reitz and discovering her own movement
proclivities through extensive body therapy study, Skaggs produced her first solo dance concert titled *Satie Dance in Five Movements* (1983). With this choreography, Skaggs wanted to investigate the way her body moved. The bodywork she was exploring
provided her with information and clarity about her own movement
style. It was not until 1984, however, when Skaggs premiered *Cross
Cultural Studies* at P.S. 122 in New York City, that she began to
take her work as a choreographer seriously. She did not expect
critical reviews of the concert, but surmising from the favorable
responses to the work, Skaggs realized that she could have some
interesting creativity to explore in choreography.

In 1986 Skaggs received her first NEA Grant and produced *Noh
Body* at the Danspace Project at St. Mark's Church in New York
City. Here Skaggs began to notice that the ethnological information
that captured her attention during her travels was informing her
creative work. Not only did the aesthetics of other cultures affect
her creative choices, but the interweaving of traditional dance and
modern dance became a model with which Skaggs worked. Through
Dance Theatre Workshop's Suitcase Fund, Skaggs was invited to
teach in Hong Kong, Taipei, and Prague. With the earnings she made
from her teaching, Skaggs went to Bali. This was a pivotal time for
Skaggs because she was impressed with the integration of the sacred and the secular in Balinese culture. All aspects of Balinese
life—art, religion, recreation, and so on—seemed integrated rather
than compartmentalized or disparate as in American culture. She
stayed with Balinese families and learned some traditional Balinese
dance. As a participant in this culture, Skaggs was struck by the
fact that dance was not "taught" per se, but rather transmitted from
teacher to student. This idea of transmission intrigued her in relation to her own work.

Returning from Bali, Skaggs was inspired to "create a transcendent experience within an everyday setting." She wanted to abandon the elitist model of the traditional proscenium dance concert by
producing a dance concert outside the modern dance circuit in New
York City. Skaggs acquired lighting designer/photographer Mary
Gearhart as a primary collaborator for the work ahead. With a
mission to reintegrate dance into American culture, Skaggs sought a

Sarah Skaggs. Photograph © Lois Greenfield.

community environment as a new performance space. With the declaration, "dance is the most public art form there is," written in crayon on a grant application, Skaggs secured a gymnasium in Little Italy, New York, as well as equipment to produce a show. *Higher Ground* was in the works. Dancers were auditioned, a local Disc Jockey was hired, and community members collaborated with Mary Gearhart to create a hybrid set design of local decoration and theatrical instruments. With its premiere in 1993 at the St. Patrick's Youth Center Gymnasium, *Higher Ground* showed every Saturday in January. As part of this "evening of dance" *Higher Ground*

audiences are invited into the performance space to share the kinetic thrill of dance with the performers. In this case, concert art dance merges with the social and participatory club dance atmosphere.

Skaggs is concerned with "shifting how audiences receive and participate in dance." By using traditional, social, and familiar as well as more crafted/developed modern dance movements, Skaggs creates ecstatic, energetic pieces that transmit the joy of kineticism to the audience. Skaggs is interested in developing formal craftsmanship of choreography in the three-dimensional format that is suited to her dance performance events. Feeling that modern dance evolved as a more "humanistic" art form than ballet, she is puzzled that contemporary dance fails to communicate to broader audiences. She desires the removal of esotericism from modern dance by returning to a more ancient, communal format where social dance is knitted to performance. To Skaggs, dance is a calling, and her response is to transmit dance at every level by bringing it more into public arenas. By providing experiential performances, Skaggs hopes to change the way Americans receive and participate in American contemporary dance.

—Diana Stanton

SMITH, Janet

English dancer, choreographer, and artistic director

Born: Leeds, Yorkshire. **Education:** Studied dance and drama at Dartington College of Arts, Devon; trained professionally with Dan Wagoner, Viola Farber, Merce Cunningham, and teachers at the Erick Hawkins and Joffrey schools, New York, 1972-74. **Family:** Married to choreographer Robert North. **Career:** First performance of two solo programmes, 1975; formed Janet Smith and Dancers, touring nationally and internationally throughout Europe and the Middle East, 1976; company performed at the London Festival of Contemporary Dance, and ADMA, 1977; joined London Contemporary Dance Theatre as a guest performer, 1980-81; danced as a soloist with Robert North and Dancers, 1980; first independent choreography (with composer-performer-musician Gordon Jones), 1974; first work for own company, 1982; first full-evening production, 1984; retired from performing and made her first work for a foreign company, 1989; directed 4D, a one-year performance course for graduate students at London Contemporary Dance School, 1989-90; lecturer in dance at University College, Bretton Hall, Yorkshire, 1993-96; Janet Smith and Dancers joined Smith as company-in-residence at Bretton Hall, 1996; choreographed for theatre and opera companies including the Playhouse Company (Durban), the Royal Shakespeare Company (London), Opera Northern (Ireland); succeeded Neville Campbell as artistic director of Scottish Dance Theatre (formerly Dundee Rep Dance Company), 1997; guest choreographer for Batsheva Dance Company, Werkcentrum Dans, Balletto di Roma, Cisne Negra Dance Company, Feigberger Dans Theater, Dance Theatre of Ireland, London Festival Ballet, and Scottish Ballet; taught at Royal Ballet School, Laban Centre, Rambert Academy, London Contemporary Dance School, London Contemporary Dance Company, and in Rome, Sicily, and Sardinia.

Works

1975   *Dances* w/Gordon Jones, solo
        Down to Earth w/Gordon Jones, solo
1978   *Domestic Dances* w/Robert North
        The Man who Painted the Sun (mus. Glandfield), Janet
            Smith and Dancers
        Fence, Janet Smith and Dancers
1980   *Studies in Solitude,* Janet Smith and Dancers
1982   *Another Man Drowning* (mus. Benstead), Janet Smith
            and Dancers

1983   *Enchanted Places* (mus. Benstead), Janet Smith and Dancers, Hexham
1984   *Bells,* Janet Smith and Dancers, ADMA Festival, London
        Ghosts, Janet Smith and Dancers, ADMA Festival, London
        Street Scenes (mus. Benstead), Janet Smith and Dancers, ADMA Festival, London
        Young and Foolish, Janet Smith and Dancers, ADMA Festival, London
        Feet Behind a Sheet, Janet Smith and Dancers, ADMA Festival, London
        Cranes in their Nest (mus. Yamaguchi), Janet Smith and Dancers, ADMA Festival, London
        Con Spirito, Janet Smith and Dancers
1986   *Out into the Night* (mus. Shostakovich), Janet Smith and Dancers, Leeds
        Still no Word from Anton (mus. Benstead), Janet Smith and Dancers, Leeds
1987   *Five Preludes and A Study in the Art of Drooping* (mus. Kok), Janet Smith and Dancers, Leeds
1989   *The World Outside my Window* (mus. Benstead), Janet Smith and Dancers, London
        Dividing, Feigberger Dans Theater, Germany
        The Dance of the Bungaloo (mus. Benstead), London Festival Ballet
1990   *To Keep Out the Dark,* Scottish Ballet, Glasgow
1991   *Some Secret Superstitions* (mus. Ganberg), Janet Smith and Dancers, London
1993   *The First Time I Met the Blues* (mus. blues and rock montage), Uppercut Dans, Denmark
        Turquoise is Tender (mus. Ganberg), Dundee Rep Dance Company
1994   *Intimate Strangers* (mus. Benstead and Ganberg), Janet Smith and Dancers, Leeds
        Muddy (mus. Muddy Waters), Balletto di Roma, Italy
1995   *Dixit Dominus* (mus. Handel), community performance project for Yorkshire Movement and Dance
1996   *Touching Zulu* (mus. Ganberg and Russell), Janet Smith and Dancers, Leeds
        Chiaroscuro (mus. Ganberg and Russell), Janet Smith and Dancers, Leeds
1997   *Chiaroscuro* (mus. Ganberg and Russell), Scottish Dance Theatre

Other works include: Choreographed works for theatre including *Give and Take,* Playhouse Theatre Company, Durban, 1994; *The Broken Heart,* Royal Shakespeare Company, London, 1994; *The Cunning Little Vixen* (Janacek opera), Opera Northern Ireland, Belfast, 1995; *Much Ado about Nothing,* Royal Shakespeare Company, London, 1996; filmed works include *Intimate Strangers.*

Publications

On SMITH: books—

Howard, T. and J. Smith, *NRCD Resource Pack,* Guildford, England, 1992.

On SMITH: articles—

Kane, N., "Touching the Moon," *Animated* (London), summer 1997.

Levene, L., "Down the Ladder and off the Wall, Profile of Janet Smith," *Independent on Sunday* (London), June 1991.
Meredith, J., "Janet Smith," *Dancing Times,* March 1994.
Percival, J., Profile of Janet Smith, *Dance and Dancers,* July 1991.

*   *   *

Janet Smith is a household name for contemporary dance lovers in the U.K. She has been involved in the teaching of an entire generation of dancers through the extensive education work carried out by her company, Janet Smith and Dancers, as well as through her solo teaching of courses across the country and the inclusion of several of her works on educational curricula. This breadth of involvement is characteristic of Smith's approach to dance as an accessible art form, open to the widest possible range of audiences and participants. Over its chequered history, her company was to suffer the financial instability typical to all those operating at this scale in the U.K., yet Smith has continued to direct a changing body of dancers under this name since 1976. Smith has been a prolific choreographer and has made many works for her own dancers, as well as for other companies. Her style is instantly recognisable, and the pressure of commissions continues to confirm her status as one of the U.K.'s most distinctive movement makers.

Smith's early training in dance and drama at Dartington College of the Arts was broad and liberating. Her love of improvisation sprung from this period of inventiveness and experimentation when, as she explained in an interview with Nina Kane for *Animated* in 1997, "dance didn't have to justify itself by being academic." Her early exposure to theatre, music, and the visual arts impressed upon Smith the richness of the many elements of theatrical expression available to the dancemaker. Smith's stay in the U.S. further broadened her vision, as she studied the Cunningham-based dramatic movement styles of Dan Wagoner and Eric Hawkins. Wagoner remains a strong influence upon Smith, who admires his humour and passion. Moving away from the angst and intensity of her earliest training in Graham, and the technicality of her further studies in Cunningham, Smith began to build her own movement language in solos and duets with her husband and fellow choreographer, Robert North. By seeking to draw from her limbs a full spectrum of emotions, Smith aimed to create expansive, porous movement, conveying a multiplicity of messages. Smith's credo is that every movement embodies a meaning, and her resourceful acquisition of new influences and inspirations demonstrates her confidence in the ability of dance to convey the meaning inherent in all forms of expression.

The early performances of Janet Smith and Dancers at key events, such as the ADMA festival in London, were characterised by their use of popular music, wit, and a recognisably everyday gestural language. In *Fence,* which was performed at ADMA in 1978, the dancers literally constructed a fence with their bodies, animating it with a surprisingly inventive and entertaining range of movement, relished by contemporary audiences but not altogether popular with critics. This split in the reception of Smith's work continued throughout her career, as her stated aim of accessibility was interpreted by many as a disregard for high artistic standards. Unfashionably singular, her work remained focused throughout the development of contemporary dance in the U.K. As Eurocrash introduced dynamic, bruising choreography to English stages, Smith continued to work with subtle movement, investigating intricacy and tenderness in her quietly reflective works of this period. The lyrical dancing in *The World Outside my Window,* based on the poetry of Sally Smith and inspired by the illness of Janet Smith's sister, demonstrated the softness and compassion of her approach.

Early works such as *Another Man Drowning,* based on the paintings of L.S. Lowry, were influenced by Smith's northern roots and her desire to speak directly to her audiences. The spiky lines of movement in this work, combined with the sense of community developed by her groupings, animated images which held important local cultural resonances. Praise for the "Englishness" of her work, typified by the cricketing movement vocabulary of *Square Leg,* did not prevent Smith from exploring other cultural influences, such as the language of the African landscapes she observed while travelling and interpreted in *Touching Zulu.* American culture has infiltrated her work in the form of the Edward Hopper paintings that inspired *Intimate Strangers* and the soap operas that drove the many dramas of *Still no Word from Anton.*

Smith continued to innovate and develop her movement by building strong collaborative partnerships. Her strong relationship with Christopher Benstead, which began with his idiosyncratic compositions and performance in *Another Man Drowning* in 1982, led the following year to the creation of her first full-evening piece, *Enchanted Places,* a ballet based on A.A. Milne's Winnie the Pooh stories. Benstead has created the score for most of Smith's major works, both for Smith's own company and for commissions for others. Benstead has also worked with another Smith favourite, Barry Ganberg, collaborating to create the music for *Some Secret Superstitions* and *Intimate Strangers.* These creative partnerships exemplify Smith's respect for the many forms of expression operating within a dance performance. Her interest in lighting developed during her residency periods at organisations such as Bretton Hall and was manifest in *Chiaroscuro,* in which she explored the interplay of darkness and light in movement through space. By using filmic techniques of foregrounding certain actions and erasing others through lighting, Smith was aiming to edit and distort the narrative, a device which is characteristic of her works.

Currently privileged by her position as director of Scottish Dance Theatre, a large touring company and major organisation for dance networking in Scotland, Smith sees her future role as a developer of choreographic talent in that country. She aims to bring artists from far afield to Scotland, so that they may work with local dancers and choreographers and thereby enrich the dance culture of the nation as a whole.

—Sophie Hansen

SOKOLOW, Anna

American dancer, choreographer, educator, and company director

Born: 9 February 1910 in Hartford, Connecticut. **Education:** Studied dance with Martha Graham, choreography with Louis Horst at the Neighborhood Playhouse. *Career:* Dancer, Graham's first company, 1929-37; assisted Horst for several years; formed her own company, Theater Union Dancers, 1933; worked extensively in Mexico and Israel, forming the first professional dance companies in both countries; has choreographed for Broadway including *Street Scene, Regina, Candide, Hair,* and stage play *Camino Real;* first achieved national recognition for *Lyric Suite* (1954) and *Rooms* (1955); has taught dance and staged her works for colleges and

Anna Sokolow's Players Project performing *Kurt Weil.* **Photograph © Johan Elbers.**

universities in the U.S. and in Sweden, Holland, Switzerland, Germany, and Japan; founder, Players' Project, 1981. **Awards:** Bennington College choreographic fellowship, 1937; American Dancer Award, Best Solo, 1938; *Dance Magazine* Award, 1961; Senior Fulbright to Japan, 1966; Brandeis University Creative Arts Medal, 1974; America-Israel Cultural Foundation Tarbut Medal, 1974; Senior Fulbright Scholar, 1975; 92nd Street YM-YWHA award, "For her great and prolonged record of service to the world of dance," 1975; Maryland Dance Theater Performance tribute, Kennedy Center, 1982; Ballet Independiente performance in her honor, Mexico City, 1982; 30th anniversary celebration for her work in Tel Aviv, 1983; gala performance in her honor, Joyce Theater, 1986; Encomienda, Aztec Eagle Honor (the highest civilian honor awarded in Mexico to a foreigner), Mexico City, 1988; 80th birthday tribute at 92nd Street "Y" 1991; Samuel E. Scripps Lifetime Achievement Award, 1991; I.S.T.P.A.A. Tiffany Award, 1991; honorary member, American Academy of Arts and Letters, 1993; 15 February 1985 declared Anna Sokolow Day by the mayor of Manhattan, Ruth W. Messinger; honorary doctorates from the Boston Conservatory and Ohio State University; inducted into the American Dance Hall of Fame, National Museum of Dance, 1998.

Works (selected; premiered in New York City unless otherwise noted)

1933	*Anti-War Trilogy* (mus. North), group
	Folk Motifs (mus. Bartók, Miaskovksy), solo
	Homage to Lenin (mus. Miaskovsky), solo
1934	*Two Pioneer Marches* (mus. Prokofiev)
	Death of a Tradition (mus. Lapatnikoff), Sokolow and group
1935	*Strange American Funeral* (mus. Seigmeister), group
	American Dance Hall (mus. North), solo
1936	*Ballad* (in a Popular Style), (mus. North), solo
	Inquisition '36 (mus. North), solo
1937	*Case History No.—* (mus. Riegger), solo
	Excerpts from a War Poem (mus. North), Sokolow and group
1938	*Dance of All Nations* (pageant for 14th anniversary of Lenin's death)
1939	*The Exile* (mus. traditional Palestinian, poem by Funaroff)
	Sing for Your Supper-The Last Waltz (musical; mus. North), group
1940	*Don Lindo de Almeria* (mus. Hallfter), group, Mexico

	Sinfonia de Antigona (mus. Chávez), group, Mexico
1941	*Homage to García Lorca* (includes solo *Lament for the Death of a Bullfighter*; mus. Revueltas), Sokolow and group
	Mama Beautiful (mus. North), solo
1943	*Revelations* (mus. North, Neuman), group, Montreal
1945	*Danzas Sobre Temas Rusas* (mus. Tchaikovsky), group, Mexico
	Kaddish (mus. Ravel), solo
1946	*The Bride* (mus. traditional Jewish folk), solo
	Images from the Old Testament (mus. Hemsi, Engle, and folk), solo
	Street Scene (musical; mus. Weill, lyrics Langston Hughes)
1947	*Life Is a Fandango* (mus. traditional Mexican folk), solo
1949	*Regina* (musical; mus. Blitzstein), group
1951	*The Dybbuk* (based on play by Ansky; mus. Landau), solo
1952	*Purim Festival* (mus. Secunda), group
1953	*Camino Real* (stage play by Tennessee Williams), group
1954	*Lyric Suite* (mus. Berg), group
1955	*Rooms* (mus. Hopkins), group
1956	*Poem* (mus. Scriabin), group
	Candide (musical based on Voltaire; mus. Bernstein)
1957	*Metamorphosis* (mus. Hopkins, Walberg), group
	Le Grand Spectacle (mus. Macero), group
1958	*Opus Jazz* (mus. Macero), group
1960	*Opus '60* (mus. Macero) Group—Israel
1961	*Dreams* (mus. Macero; later versions Bach added), group
1963	*Opus '63* (mus. Macero), group
1964	*Odes* (mus. Boscovitch), group, Israel
	The Question (mus. Webern), group
1966	*Time + 6* (mus. Macero), group, Boston
	Night (mus. Berio), group
1967	*Deserts* (mus. Varèse), group
	Seven Deadly Sins (mus. Weill; libretto Brecht), Holland
1968	*Bananas* (stage play; directed by Sokolow)
1970	*Magritte, Magritte* (mus. Lizst, Scriabin, Thome, French songs), group
1973	*Homage to Federico García Lorca* (mus. Revueltas), group, Mexico
	Ride the Culture Loop (mus. Macero), group
1976	*Ellis Island* (mus. Ives), group
1977	*Untitled* (later *Poe*; mus. Druckman, Chopin, Harrison), group
1978	*Asi es la Vida en Mexico* (mus. Revueltas), group
1979	*Wings* (mus. Kopytman), group, Israel
1980	*For Langston* (Hughes), (mus. Macero), group
1981	*Los Conversos (The Converted)*, (mus. Neumann), group
1982	*Everything Must Go* (mus. Macero), group
	Les Noces (mus. Stravinsky), group, Israel
1984	*Homenaje a David Alfaro Siqueiros* (mus. Corea, Elizondo, Revueltas), group, Mexico
1987	*Golda Meir: Ideals and Dreams* (dance drama; mus. Thome; libretto Eden), group, Miami
	Poems of Scriabin (mus. Scriabin), group, Miami
1988	*The Stations of the Cross* (mus. Dupre), group
1989	*Three Songs* (mus. Mahler, Bloch), group
1995	*September Sonnet* (mus. composite), Lorry and Jim May
1997	*Frida* (tribute to Frida Kohler; mus. composite), Lorry May

Publications

On SOKOLOW: books—

Cohen, Selma Jeanne, editor, *The Modern Dance: Seven Statements of Belief,* Middletown, Connecticut, 1966.
Lloyd, Margaret, *The Borzoi Book of Modern Dance,* New York, 1949, 1974.
Mazo, Joseph H., *Prime Movers: The Makers of Modern Dance in America,* New York, 1977.
Warren, Larry, *Anna Sokolow: The Rebellious Spirit,* Princeton, New Jersey, 1991.

On SOKOLOW: articles—

Church, Marjorie, *Dance Observer,* March 1937.
Hering, Doris, *Dance Magazine,* May 1951.
Kraus, Gertrud, *Jerusalem Post,* 4 July 1962.
Martin, John, *New York Times,* 21 January 1934.

*　　*　　*

Anna Sokolow's extraordinary career has spanned over six decades, and has had a profound effect on the course of modern dance in the United States, Mexico, Israel, and other countries as well. She has been a pioneer in the creation of dances that explore the innermost feelings of men and women in reaction to the social and psychological pressure of contemporary life. Recognized as one of the most forceful and uncompromising of contemporary choreographers, Anna has had a distinguished career in teaching as well. In her classes for both dancers and actors, she insists students transcend their technical accomplishments to give, through movement, the deepest expression of what they have garnered in their lives concerning the specific subject at hand, be it love, hate, fear, anger, or loneliness.

Anna Sokolow's calling to dance first came when, at the age of 10, she wandered into a dance class in a community center in mid-Manhattan and was fascinated by what she saw. The next day she enrolled in the class and within a few weeks she began to wonder why classes were not taught more often; dance was becoming the center of her life. By her mid-teens she started to take classes at the Neighborhood Playhouse where Martha Graham was exploring, developing, and testing many of her new ideas. Anna watched, listened, and learned a great deal.

Anna also studied at the Playhouse with Louis Horst, Graham's musical director, who was the first teacher of modern dance choreography in the U.S., framing the study in the context of pre-classic dance forms. She excelled in this work and in a short time became Horst's assistant. In 1929, at the age of 19, Anna accepted an invitation from Martha Graham to join her first professional company. She danced for Graham for eight years, appearing in the premieres of such landmark works as *Primitive Mysteries* and *Celebration.*

In 1933 Sokolow decided she had some of her own things to say in dance, and, without leaving Graham, she started her own company. It was the time of the Depression, and for her new Theatre Dance Group Anna choreographed many works focused on the social and economic issues of the time. (There were also lighter pieces in her repertoire ranging from pre-classic dances to jazz.) A few years later, in reaction to the growth of fascism in Spain, Italy, and Germany, she created several powerful indictments of the racism, lust for power, and drive for expansion by military conquest in those countries. Even with works dealing with such explosive subjects, Anna managed to be more the artist than the agitator. In her choreographic works she was making an impassioned statement of how she felt about these horrendous happenings; giving form to her feelings, but not proposing solutions. This was unique for her time, when "flag waving" and calls to action through movement for "the cause" were not uncommon.

Anna's composer for most of these works was Alex North, a gifted musician at the Juilliard School, whom she met in 1932 and became closely associated with for several years. North shared with Anna an acute responsiveness to the social issues of the time, and working together they were able to make a powerful statement of those feelings in the theater. In 1934 Alex was able to arrange for performances in Soviet Russia, where, regardless of the revolution, classical ballet traditions were being carefully preserved.

Although they were well-received by many of their audiences, the ballet hierarchy was not happy with what they saw; dances of protest were of no interest. They did, however, admire Anna's strength and beauty as a performer, and offered her a scholarship if she would stay and study classical ballet. She politely refused.

In 1937 Anna received one of the first fellowships awarded to gifted young choreographers by Bennington College in Vermont. She was given room and board, studio space and dancers needed for the works which would be performed in the Bennington Festival. Here she created *Facade—Esposizione Italiana,* a powerful condemnation of fascism in Italy, with music by North. Her dynamic performance in the final solo of the work came to a dazzling climax when she literally ran up the wall.

In 1939 Anna was invited to perform with her company (now called Dance Unit) in Mexico City. The 23 performances to nearly sold-out houses led to an invitation, which she accepted, to stay and help form a company. For many years afterward she returned regularly to teach and choreograph.

In the early 1950s Anna was asked to go to Israel and assist in the development of Inbal, a young Yemenite dance company. With her help and encouragement, Inbal grew in stature as it was being readied for international touring. As in Mexico, her unique talents were clearly recognized, and in the early 1960s she was asked to be a guiding light in the formation of a professional modern dance company in Israel. In 1962 Lyric Theater was born, largely as the result of Anna's teaching, choreographing, and writing of formal proposals to the government. This fine company led to the development of several other modern dance groups in Israel, most of which have had Sokolow works in their repertoire. In her early fifties, in addition to the growing recognition of her fine talents in the United States, Anna was recognized both in Israel and Mexico as the founder of modern dance in their countries.

Anna's distinguished work for the Broadway stage included the choreography, in 1947, for Elmer Rice's 1929 Pulitzer Prize-winning play, *Street Scene,* which was turned into a musical with music by Kurt Weill. In the steamy duet, "Moon-Faced and Starry Eyed," Anna broke fresh ground for the musical stage, using the vernacular-jitterbug to express the passionate feelings of the protagonists. This unique approach could easily have been the inspiration for Jerome Robbins' handling of his epoch-making *West Side Story,* with a brilliant score by Leonard Bernstein. Anna's other significant groundbreaking work on Broadway was for the 1967 premiere production of the non-narrative tribal love rock musical *Hair,* about hippies, love children, the Vietnam war, and racism. As it had in *Street Scene,* her choreography emanated from a full consciousness

of the environment. *Hair* was followed by a number of rock musicals influenced by Anna's work. Once again, she was in the forefront; this time it was the forefront of what came to be known as "alienated youth ballets."

Anna's timeless 1955 work, *Rooms,* with a jazz score by Kenyon Hopkins, deals with the devastating aloneness that can grip people who cannot make contact with others except on the most superficial level. There are no heroes, no central characters. The work portrays not so much how these people act in their isolated worlds, but how they feel being there. The central characters could be any one of us. By touching on the universality of human isolation in so direct and visceral a manner, Anna created one of the enduring masterpieces of 20th-century dance. Her use of a jazz score for so intense a work is yet another groundbreaking credit for Anna. Soon after the work was premiered, the practice started to become commonplace, and still is. *Rooms* has been performed (and is still being performed), by dance companies throughout the United States, as well as abroad.

After the popular and critical success of *Rooms,* Anna began to expand on the theme of detachment and alienation. Her creative focus went from lost individuals to a lost society made up of people who could no longer deal with their pain in isolation. Now they stood as an angry group with an aggressive statement. They were the "beat generation," a generation that stressed nonconformity. In these works, starting with *Session '58,* the dancers expressed their feelings about the times with youthful rebelliousness. In later versions, after terrifying images of war there was an affirmative coming together, a spiritual linking of arms. Then the performers came to the front of the stage and sat at the edge accusing and challenging "the establishment."

Although best-known for her dances of social significance (from the protest works of the 1930s to the beat generation dances of the 1960s), from her earliest days as a choreographer, Sokolow has resisted any temptation to limit herself to any one area of expression. In her stunning 1954 *Lyric Suite,* she integrated vignettes of a wide range of human emotion with sections that soar lyrically; some that are thoughtfully serene. Her 1961 *Dreams* touches on the inner torment of victims of the Nazi Holocaust; their desperation, helplessness, and irretrievable losses. Outstanding among her delightful satires is *The Evolution of Ragtime,* a 1952 work in which the scholarly narrator of a lecture-demonstration is so preoccupied with himself that he is unaware that the dancers illustrating his points are doing so with a mock seriousness.

An exceptional teacher with a style of her own, Anna's intensity in the classroom is legend. Her primary focus is not on technical skills, but rather on movement as a language—always demanding more passion, more commitment, greater clarity of intent. The demand for inner motivation is constant. She is looking for a direct flow from emotion to physical expression, and in the process, helping her students and company members to find the confidence to move in ways they initially felt were not in their capacities. In a letter to the author (7 March 1989) dancer/choreographer Linda Tarnay wrote, "Anna taught me, both by her example and exhortation, that a dramatic idea or feeling calls up its own specific movement. The imagination must be allowed to enter the flesh and move the body. Since working with her, I have had to dig deeper for a new movement vocabulary for each piece. When, out of fatigue or desperation, I resort to a generalized vocabulary, I am painfully, guiltily aware of it."

—Larry Warren

SOLOMONS, Gus, jr.

American dancer, choreographer, educator, and writer

Born: 27 August 1940 in Boston. **Education:** Boston Conservatory of Music, 1956-59; Massachusetts Institute of technology, bachelors degree in architecture, 1961; Martha Graham School, 1961-66. **Career:** Dancer, Donald McKayle Compnay, 1961-64, Martha Graham Company, 1964-65, Merce Cunningham Company, 1965-68; founder and artistic director, Solomons Dance Company, from 1972; numerous teaching posts and residencies; faculty member, Tisch School of the Arts, since 1994; numerous television appearances; writer and contributor to *Dance Magazine,* the *Village Voice,* and other publications.

Roles

1961   Role (cr), *Legendary Landscape* (McKayle), Donald McKayle Dance Company, New York

1964   Role (cr), *Winterbranch* (Cunningham), Merce Cunningham Dance Company, Hartford, Connecticut

1965   Role (cr), *The Witch of Endor* (Graham), Martha Graham Company, New York

Role (cr), *How to Pass, Kick, Fall, and Run* (Cunningham), Merce Cunningham Dance Company, New York

Variations V (Cunningham), Merce Cunningham Dance Company, New York

1966   *Place* (Cunningham), Merce Cunningham Dance Company, St. Paul de Vence, France

1968   *Rainforest* (Cunningham), Merce Cunningham Dance Company, Buffalo

Other roles include: Additional performances with Merce Cunningham, Joyce Trisler, Pearl Lang, and Paul Sanasardo.

Works

1959   *Construction II*
1960   *Etching of Man*
1962   *Fogrum*
        Match
        Rag Caprices
1963   *Fast*
        Kinesia for Women and a Man
1964   *Four Field of Six*
        The Ground Is Warm and Cool
        Construction II & 1/2
1966   *Simply This Fondness*
1967   *Ecce Homo*
        Kinesia for Five
        Neon
        Notebook
1968   *City-Motion-Space-Game*
        Two Reeler
1969   *Christmas Piece*
        Draft Alteration
        Obligato 69
        Phreaque
        We don't know only how much time we have. . .
1970   *cat. #CCS70-10/13 NSSR-GSJ9M*
        A Dance in Report Form/A Report in Dance Form

        Quad
        Warm-Up Piece
1971   *On Par*
        Patrol
        Pyrothronium
        Title Meet
        Urban Recreation/The Ultimate Pastoral
1972   *Beetcan Conservatives*
        Grandular Dilemma and a Vision
        The Gut-Stomp Lottery Kill
        Masse
        Pocketcard Process No. 2
        The Son of Cookie Monster
1973   *Brill-o*
        Decimal Banana
        Par/Tournament
        Yesterday
1974   *Chapter One*
        Molehill
        A Shred of Prior Note
        Stoneflesh
1975   *Statements of Nameless Root: Part I, Observation*
        Steady Work
1976   *Ad Hoc Transit*
        Conversation
        Forty
        Statements of Nameless Root: Part II, Conclusions
1977   *All but One*
        Bone Jam
        Boogie
1978   *Acrylic-Flake Diagram*
        Psycho Motor Works
        Signals
        Wide Wide World of Sports and Dance
1979   *make me no boxes to put me in*
        Dance Is a 5-Letter Word
        Stepchart
1980   *Steps—Progressive Pieces*
        NOZ
1993   *Red Squalls* (mus. Toby Twining), Lincoln Center Out of Doors Festival, New York
1994   *Air*
        Boomershine's Coil
        Private Parts
1995   *Fatstick*
1997   *Red Squalls II* (mus. Walter Thompson), Lincoln Center Out of Doors Festival, New York

Publications

On SOLOMONS: books—

Kaplan, Peggy Jarrell, *Portraits of Choreographers,* New York, 1988.
Long, Richard, *The Black Tradition in American Dance,* New York, 1989.

On SOLOMONS: articles—

Anderson, Jack, "Performers Who Keep their Secrets," *New York Times,* 25 June 1994.
Jowitt, Deborah, "Worth the Climb," *Village Voice,* 26 July 1994.

Gus Solomons jr., 1988. Photograph © Johan Elbers.

————, "Body Tales," *Village Voice,* 20 June 1995.
Simpson, Herbert M., "Gus Solomons: Make No Boxes to Put Me In," *Dance Magazine,* September 1987.

*   *   *

Gus Solomons jr.'s dancing and dances are marked by precision and clarity and the use of space, not surprising for a dancer and choreographer who began a dance career as he simultaneously completed the requirements for a degree in architecture at the Massachusetts Institute of Technology.

Born 27 August 1940 in Boston, Solomons studied jazz and tap as a child, but had no further training until he was a sophomore at MIT. He attended classes at the Boston Conservatory of Music, where Jan Veen directed the dance program. It was from Veen, a student of Mary Wigman, that Solomons got his Expressionist dance training. Solomons also took ballet classes with E. Virginia Williams, the founder of the Boston Ballet Company. With apparent boundless energy, Solomons once rehearsed in nine different dances or plays simultaneously.

Solomons joined the Boston modern dance company Dance Makers in 1960, where he danced in the works of others and created dances for himself. From the start, Solomons seemed to effortlessly assemble rather formal dances set to conventional music. The quartet *Fogrum* (1962) was set to Baroque music. The dance featured two couples who approached each other in a serious of elaborate greetings, which grew more and more ridiculous; one of their greetings was performed with the two women dancers seated on the men's shoulders as the men bowed to each other. The game aspect of this dance would be seen in much of Solomon's future work.

In 1962 Solomons moved to New York. Over the next few years he danced with several modern dance companies, including those of Martha Graham, Pearl Lang, Donald McKayle, Joyce Trisler, Paul Sanasardo and Flower Hujer. He joined Merce Cunningham in 1965; and relished this extended opportunity to watch the creation of dances, rather than simply dancing ready-made products. He was particularly fascinated with the interplay of the dancers in Cunningham's company. He credits Cunningham with giving him the freedom to create dances based on movement alone, rather than on narrative.

Solomons created roles in many of Cunningham's important works, including *Winterbranch* (1964), *Variations V* (1965), *How to Pass, Kick, Fall and Run* (1965), *Place* (1966) and *Rainforest* (1968). His long muscular body emphasized his grace and quickness. His light movement over the dance floor led him to be compared to a dragonfly skimming over the surface of water. This period ended abruptly due to a degenerative spinal disc condition. Solomons knew that if he continued to perform such a vigorous schedule he would only be able to dance for a few more years. He chose to extend his dancing career by leaving the company and spending more time on choreography, founding the Gus Solomons Dance Company in 1969. He has remained in his position as artistic director ever since. By 1969 Solomons was already uncomfortable with labels, and would have preferred to not have his works labeled "dances." However, their construction and their dependence on expert technical dance skills made the label stick, despite his avant-garde innovations.

His intellectual playfulness and adherence to rules of logic have been viewed by some as difficult and cerebral. Solomons has also battled the label of being a Cunningham "clone" because of his close association with Cunningham and his formal preoccupations and rationality. In creating a solo, Solomons might conceive of a dancer as the center of an imaginary cube of space. He has said he sees dance as "fluid architecture" and a dance may be created through the solving of formal problems. In the 1969 work *Obligato*, he satisfied his desire to combine tap with the unrelated idea of the body laid bare—thus for the first half of the dance he moved about the stage, fully clothed, doing a casual tap routine accompanied by melodramatic radio broadcasts from the 1930s and 1940s, which then shifted into an undistinguished, watered-down jazz. Solomons, however, seemed unaware of any sound at all until strains of the first bits from the original black sources could be heard. Suddenly, he stopped, and then began methodically disrobing as the lights grew dimmer and dimmer, until finally he stood in the near dark wearing only his dance belt.

The genesis of another dance might be a game in which the logic of the movement is defined by the game's rules. In *Private Parts* (1994) the game has five players. The program notes that each dancer invented a scenario to explain their choreographic actions. Because the dancers keep their scenarios secret, they must keep a close eye on each other as they interact. While some of the actions are preset, others are randomly shaped by what the cast members read on slips of paper drawn randomly; on the slips are printed three verbs which loosely suggest the next direction. The dancers play off each other, copying and borrowing movements drawn from Solomon's overall scheme. Obviously, the dance will never be the same twice, but because the operative variables are predetermined, the dance retains its structural integrity. As usual, Solomons aims for being deeply interesting rather than conventionally dramatic. Strong rhythms and fast pacing in conjunction with the element of randomness afford an exhilarating sense of risk to the performances.

Similarly, *Fatstick* (1995), a collaboration with the Walter Thompson Jazz Ensemble, also combines set choreography with improvisational material in a game-like structure, with the additional interaction between live musicians and dancers. Speech and synthesized music have also been essential ingredients in some of his compositions; like other postmodern choreographers, Solomons has experimented in site-specific work. In 1993, the Lincoln Center for the Performing Arts commissioned a work for their Lincoln Center Out of Doors Festival. The results was *Red Squalls*, created in collaboration with composer Toby Twining and architects Scott DeVere and Philip Tefft, and performed around Lincoln Center's North Plaza.

Rather than be restricted to the limits of works that cannot easily be recreated, Solomons more typically has invented dances that travel well, which he takes on the road in the form of nationwide residencies, for Solomons is widely sought after as a visiting artist. *Fatstick,* for example, is not only constantly evolving, with sections being added or revised, but is adaptable to a wide range of available performance venues, from theaters to museums to public parks.

Well into the third decade of his dance career, Solomons still receives kudos for his compelling performances. In addition to his choreography, guest performing, teaching and directing, his reviews and articles appear regularly in the *Village Voice* and *Dance Magazine.*

—Valerie Vogrin

SPARLING, Peter

American dancer, choreographer, company director, and educator

Born: 4 June 1951 in Detroit. **Education:** Graduated from Interlochen Arts Academy, 1969; Juilliard School, B.F.A. 1973. **Career:** Dancer, companies of Elizabeth Keen, Saeko Ichinohe, Toronto Dance Theater, Los Angeles Dance Theater, Contemporary Dance System, Connecticut Dance Theater, Rhode Island Dance Repertory Theater, Lincoln Center Student Program, Miracle Players of Glastonbury, England, Dance Mobile, 1969-75, José Limón Dance Company, 1971-73, Martha Graham Dance Company, 1973-87, Affiliate Artists, Inc., 1981-85; dancer and choreographer for various productions and for Ann Arbor Dance Works, Ann Arbor, Michigan, since 1984; artistic director, Peter Sparling Dance Company, 1978-84; director, University of Michigan Dance Company, 1988-95; instructor, Martha Graham School of Contemporary Dance, 1975-79, Juilliard School, 1980-87, London Contemporary Dance Theatre, 1983-84, University of Michigan, from 1984 (currently professor, department of dance); founder and artistic director, Dance Gallery/Peter Sparling & Co., from 1993; numerous teaching residencies throughout the world; appeared in PBS television specials *Dance in America, Live from Wolftrap,* and *The Met Celebrates 100 Years with the Martha Graham Dance Company.* **Awards:** NEA choreographers fellowships, 1971, 1979, 1983; Louis Horst Memorial Scholarship, Juilliard School, 1972; Michigan Dance Association Choreographer's Festival Adjudication, 1988; Artist's Award, Arts Foundation of Michigan, 1989 and 1993; Faculty Recognition Award, University of Michigan, 1991; Washtenaw Council for the Arts "Annie" Award for Dance Performance, 1993; fellow, University of Michigan Institute for the Humanities.

Works

1969	*Streetsong* (mus. tape collage)
	Environments I & II (mus. Epstein)
1970	*Sitting Harlequin* (mus. tape collage)
	Suicide Remarks (mus. tape collage)
1971	*December Prose* (mus. tape collage)

The Bather and the Lady (mus. Webern)
Six Bagatelles (mus. Webern)
1972   *Blue Granite Mappings* (mus. Epstein)
As Quiet As ... (mus. Colgrass)
Field and Stream (mus. Carter)
1974   *Little Incarnations* (mus. Fahey)
1975   *Divining Rod* (mus. Epstein)
1977   *Three Farewells* (mus. Beethoven)
Architecture for a Swoon (mus. Beethoven)
Once in a Blue Moon (mus. Epstein)
1978   *A Thief's Progress* (mus. Lester)
Nocturnes for Euridyce (mus. Martin)
Suite to Sleep (mus. Corea)
1979   *In Stride!* (mus. James P. Johnson)
Heralds' Round (mus. Bach)
This Place (mus. Ives)
1980   *Hard Rock* (mus. Shapey)
Orion (mus. Ginastera)
The Tempest (A Fantasia) (mus. Rzewski)
What She Forgot He Remembered (mus. Brahms)
1981   *Popular Songs* (mus. Epstein)
A Fearful Symmetry (mus. Hindemith)
1982   *From Out the Clearing* (mus. Vaughn Williams)
Swing Serenade (mus. 1940s medley)
1983   *Viola Songs* (mus. Brahms)
Round Dance (retitled *Reel*) (mus. Peter "Madcat" Ruth, Epstein)
1984   *Bright Bowed River* (mus. David Gregory)
Nocturnes (mus. Chopin)
Etude Perdue et Trouvee (no mus.)
1985   *Tableaux* (mus. F. Rzewski)
1986   *Nocturne* (mus. Chopin)
Requiem for a Swimmer (mus. Mozart)
Modern Life (mus. David Gregory)
Prime Time (mus. Tim Sparling)
1987   *Rondo* (mus. David Gregory)
L'Histoire du Soldat (mus. Stravinsky)
Alibi (mus. Scott Johnson)
Forest through the Trees (mus. Joe Lucasik)
1988   *Sancerre* (mus. Mozart)
Aria degli Angeli della Terra (mus. Bellini)
Scenes from Petrouschka (mus. Stravinsky)
Wings (mus. Joan Tower)
Ode (mus. Ralph Shapey)
Heart's Crossing (mus. Brahms)
Zappa! (mus. Frank Zappa)
1989   *Winteranze II* (mus. Pärt)
Rounding the Square (mus. traditional Scottish fiddle)
De Profundis (mus. Pärt)
Petrushka (mus. Stravinsky)
1990   *Orion* (mus. Christopher Thall)
Zigzag (mus. Peter "Madcat" Ruth)
Intermezzo (mus. Brahms)
Three Etudes (mus. Todd Levin)
Witness (mus. Vincent Persichetti; Pärt)
1991   *Don't Worry 'Bout Me* (mus. Billie Holiday; Bloom)
Passion Play (mus. Pergolesi)
Double Exposure (mus. Information Society)
Miranda on the Veranda (mus. Carlos Paredes)
Second Thoughts Blues (mus. Matt Levy/Prism)
The Boy Who Played with Dolls (mus. Alfred Schnittke)

1992   *Bride of Grand Prairie* (mus. Tim Sparling)
Jealousy (mus. Alfred Schnittke)
Gates of Eden (no mus.)
1993   *Local Color* (mus. pop collage)
Johnny Angel (mus. Todd Levin)
Mas Fuerte (mus. Stephen Rush)
1994   *Travelogue* (mus. Frank Pahl)
1995   *The Four Seasons* (mus. Vivaldi)
The Pursuit of Happiness (mus. Esquivel)
1996   *Seven Enigmas* (mus. Daniel Roumain)
Sonata (mus. Jean-Marie Leclair)
Popular Songs (mus. James Brown, k.d. lang, Rickie Lee Jones, Dick Siegel, Talking Heads, Bach)
New Bach (mus. Bach)
1997   *Berliner Mass* (mus. Pärt)
Unfinished (mus. Schubert)

*   *   *

Peter Sparling, a Detroiter, joined first the José Limón Dance Company and then the Martha Graham Dance Company early in his career, but subsequently returned to Michigan in 1984 to join the dance faculty at the University of Michigan. As a dancer, teacher, and choreographer and the artistic director of a small regional dance company, Sparling has brought the legacy of two dance pioneers to students and audiences in the Midwest. A prolific choreographer for most of his life, his work reflects his interests in many disciplines and his wide-ranging experiences as an artist who has lived and traveled all over the world.

The child of two musicians, Sparling was a serious violin student from the age of nine (although he had briefly taken a dance class when he was eight). Planning to become a concert violinist, Sparling left the Detroit public schools after ninth grade to study violin on scholarship at Interlochen Arts Academy, a private arts high school in northern Michigan. During his first year at Interlochen, Sparling took an introduction to dance class to fulfill a physical education requirement. He soon decided that "this was what I really want to do: dance gave me access to my imagination as classical music did not."

When he graduated from Interlochen in 1969 with a double major in violin and dance, Sparling and two of his classmates, Janet Eilber and Diana Hart, were advised by their teacher William Hug to continue their training at the Juilliard School. A few years later, all three were dancing in the Martha Graham Dance Company.

Looking back on his early career, Sparling believes he was exceptionally fortunate to have two giants of modern dance—Graham and Limón—as mentors. As a member of the Limón company during his last two years at Juilliard, Sparling had "learned men's roles, created by a man." After Limón died in 1973, Sparling was asked to join the Graham company, which was resuming activity after a hiatus of several years. "It was an extraordinary experience," he recalled. "The company was catching the crest of the NEA touring program. I was dancing all over the globe." In six years, Sparling rose from the corps to dance in new works that Graham was creating on him: *Scarlet Letter, Holy Jungle, Shadows, Flute of Pan, Song* (from *Song of Songs*), and *Frescoes*. At first, Graham "trusted me with a lot of her new pieces, but not with the old ones—her big classics," Sparling told John Gruen in a *Dance Magazine* interview in April 1987. "She would speak to me about dancing too much in my mind. She said I had to physicalize the dancing....She wanted us to come alive at every moment through

Peter Sparling performing *A Fearful Symmetry.* **Photograph © Johan Elbers.**

absolute commitment in our bodies so that our musicality and spirituality would just flow out." And Sparling says, "After years and years, I learned the lesson, but it was a struggle."

At the same time Sparling was refining his Graham roles, he was also establishing himself as a choreographer, giving solo concerts in New York during periods when the Graham company was off. His "major interest was always to make dances," he said. When he choreographed his first student compositions at Interlochen, he had been inspired by Merce Cunningham's technique and philosophy although he noted, "I hadn't seen him [then]; I had just read about him." But at Juilliard, studying with members of the Graham and Limón companies, Sparling was soon immersed in the techniques and aesthetic of those choreographers.

After viewing one of his early solo programs at the Riverside Dance Festival in October 1979, Anna Kisselgoff wrote in the *New York Times*: "There was a consistent suggestion that Mr. Sparling was consciously breaking out of the ramrod correctness of the Graham roles, and yet it was clear he was also naturally suited to them. . . . [His] most fascinating choreographic signature, however, is an ability to incorporate the most disparate movements into a single unbroken phrase." In addition, Kisselgoff commented that Sparling's "use of the Graham vocabulary was discreet and original."

By 1979 Sparling was ready to leave Graham to form his own company, while continuing solo performances as well. Among his solo works, his dance portrayal of the life of Vincent Van Gogh received high praise from a number of New York critics. "Few young modern-dance makers" could bring it off, Jennifer Dunning wrote in her *New York Times* review, "Peter Sparling did."

"I wanted to make my own mistakes," Sparling said about his departure from the Graham company to form the Peter Sparling Dance Company. "I learned all about setting up a nonprofit corporation, fund-raising, PR—the whole bit," he maintained, yet exhausted by these multiple responsibilities, he gave up his company after five years and returned to Graham, where he felt "free to soar onstage," he told Gruen. Then he left to teach for the London Contemporary Dance Theater, and the need to choreograph soon reasserted itself.

Sparling decided to take a permanent position with the dance department at the University of Michigan in Ann Arbor, where he had twice been an guest instructor. With dance faculty members Gay Delanghe, Bill DeYoung, and Jessica Fogel, he founded Ann Arbor Dance Works, a resident faculty company, which provided an outlet for both choreography and performing. His contract with the university also allowed him to continue to dance with Graham during the company's New York seasons. At Michigan, Sparling supervised reconstructions of numerous works by Graham, Limón, Doris Humphrey, Lucas Hoving, and Murray Louis for the student dance company. He was also the chief consultant for the University's Martha Graham Centenary Festival.

In 1993 Sparling had the opportunity to take over the artistic directorship of a small local company, now known as Dance Gallery/Peter Sparling and Company. With several local performances annually, and tours in Michigan and Indiana, it has become a showcase for Sparling's choreography. In 1996 Sparling added Graham's *El Penitente* to the repertoire, by special arrangement with the Graham company.

In 1997 Sparling's widespread interests led him to co-direct The Enigmas Project, a multidisciplinary collaboration for film, set design, music, dance, brain and space research. "I love overlaying different media," he said. "But I'll always be making more traditional dances that depend on movement and music. I feel close to the Mark Morrises of the world. We are all repressed musicians, and we have to make music with our bones."

—Kate O'Neill

SPINK, Ian

Australian dancer, choreographer, and company director

Born: 1947 in Australia. **Education:** Moorabbin West, Highett High School Dance Training, Victorian Ballet Guild, 1963-66; Australian Ballet School, 1967-68. **Career:** Dancer, Australian Ballet, 1969-74; dancer, Australian Dance Theatre, 1973; dancer, Dance Company of New South Wales, 1975-77; Richard Alston and Dancers, 1978-79; Basic Space Dance Theatre, 1978-79; independent choreographer, 1974-present; Artistic Director, Ian Spink Group, 1978-81; Artistic Director, Second Stride, 1982 to present. **Awards:** Australian National Choreographic Competition winner, 1973; Australian National Choreographic Competition winner, 1977; Best Fringe Event Award, Adelaide Arts Festival, 1980; Laurence Olivier Award Nomination, *Weighing the Heart*, 1988; Digital Dance Awards, 1989, 1991.

Works

1971	*Starship* (mus. MC5), Australian Ballet Workshop, Melbourne
1972	*Waltzes* (mus. Brahms), Australian Ballet Workshop, Melbourne
1973	*Four Explorations* (mus. Prokofiev), Australian Ballet Workshop, Melbourne
	Landscape (mus. Peter Sculthorpe), assembled group for Australian National Choreographic Competition, Sydney
1974	*Came* (mus.Stravinsky), Dance Company of New South Wales, Sydney
	Aspects (mus. H.W. Henze), Queensland Ballet, Sydney
	Couple (mus. H.W. Henze), Australian Ballet Workshop, Canberra
1976	*Players* (mus Romano Crevicki), State Dance Theatre of Victoria, Castlemaine
	New Work I (mus. Elhay), Dance Company of New South Wales, New South Wales
	New Work II (mus. Xenakis), Dance Company of New South Wales, Sydney
	Cut Lunge (mus. Vine/Fontana), Sydney
1977	*Slow Turn* (mus. Cameron Allan), assembled for Australian National Choreographic Competition, Sydney
	Two Numbers (mus. Allan/McMahon), Dance Company of New South Wales, Sydney
	Work in Progress, Lamford/Smith/Spink, London
	Low Budget Dances (mus. Lamford/Wilson), Gregory/Smith/Spink, London
1978	*Conspectus I* (mus. Srawley), Gregory/St. Clair/Smith/Spink, London
	Duet, Basic Space Dance Theatre, Dundee, Scotland

Trio (mus. Beethoven), Basic Space Dance Theatre, Aberdeen, Scotland

Elly's Arm, Ian Spink Group, London

Goanna (mus. J Spink), Ian Spink Group, London

26 Solos, Brickhill/Gregory/Smith, London

Autumn Walk (mus. BBC sound effects), Dancers Dances, Tolworth, Surrey

1979 *Nude Banana* (improvised text), Craig Givens, London

Low Budget Dances II, Ian Spink Group, London

Standing Swing, Maedée Duprés, London

Tropical Flashes (mus. Carl Vine), Basic Space Dance Theatre, Edinburgh

Three Dances (mus. Cage), Ian Spink Group, Aldershot

Cloud Cover (mus. Brian Eno), Werkcentrum Dans, Holland

1980 *Elly's Arm II,* Spink Inc., Sydney

Return (mus. Carl Vine), Australian Dance Theatre, Melbourne

Solo (mus. Zimmerman), Australian Dance Theatre, Adelaide

Solo with Sheep (mus. Takahashi), Spink Inc., Sydney

Scene Shift (mus. Vine), Spink Inc., Sydney

Three Poems (mus. Takahashi), Spink Inc., Sydney

When Soft (mus. Alan Holley), Spink Inc., Sydney

Dead Flight (mus. Brian Eno), Ian Spink Group, London

Ice Cube (mus. Vine), Ian Spink Group, London

Kondalilla (mus. Vine/de Haan), Ian Spink Group, London

1981 *(Two Untitled Solos)* (mus. Nyman/the Flying Lizards), Belinda Neave, Aberystwyth

Madrigal for Donna (mus. Vine), Ian Spink Group, Coventry

Some Fugues (mus. Bach), Ian Spink Group, London

Blue Table (mus. Jane Wells), Ian Spink Group, London

Being British (mus. mixed British), Cycles Dance Company, Leamington Spa

Coolhaven (mus. Bach), Werkcentrum Dans, Rotterdam

De Gas (mus. Wells), Ian Spink Group, York

Canta (mus. David Cunningham), Ian Spink Group, York

Canta II (mus. David Cunningham), Ian Spink Group, London

1982 *Vesalii Icones* (mus. Maxwell Davies), Mark Wraith, London

There Is No Other Woman (mus. Stravinsky), Second Stride, Oxford

Threeway (mus. Wells; written by Michael Birch), Intermedia, London

New Tactics w/director Tim Albery (mus. Orlando Gough), Second Stride, Leeds

1984 *Lean, Don't Lean, Jasper* (mus. David Owen), P6, Bristol

Work in Progress (improvised text), P6, Bristol

Coco Loco (mus. Owen), Extemporary Dance Theatre, Basildon

Further and Further into Night (mus. Gough), Second Stride, Brighton

1985 *Slow Down* (mus. Man Jumping), Transitions Dance Company, London

Solo, Simon Limbrick, London

1986 *Bösendorfer Waltzes* (mus. Gough), Second Stride, Bristol

Mercure (mus. Satie; arr. Birtwistle), Ballet Rambert, London

1987 *Weighing the Heart* (mus. Gough), Second Stride, Brighton

1988 *Left-handed Woman* (mus. John Thorne), Belinda Neave, Cardiff

Dancing and Shouting (mus. Evelyn Ficarra), Second Stride, Basildon

1989 *Heaven Ablaze in his Breast* (mus. Judith Weir), Second Stride, Basildon

1991 *Lives of the Great Poisoners* (mus. Gough; written by Caryl Churchill), Second Stride, Bristol

1992 *4 MARYS* w/dir. Martin Duncan (mus. Peter Salem), Second Stride, Bristol

Why Things Happen (written by Marty Cruikshank; mus. Bach/Weir), Second Stride, Grantham

5 Dances, 5 Floors (with Hans Peter Kuhn), Lambert/Von Schulenberg, London

1993 *Escape at Sea* w/McDonald (mus. Gough), Second Stride, Salisbury

1994 *That Ship* w/David Cunningham, Intoto Dance Group, London

1995 *The Hour We Knew Nothing of Each Other* w/Pete Brooks; written by Peter Handke; mus. Evelyn Ficarra), National Youth Dance Company, London

Badenheim (mus. Gough; written by Sian Evans), Second Stride, Newcastle

1997 *Hotel: 8 Rooms/2 Nights* (mus. Gough; written by Caryl Churchill), Second Stride, Hanover

Other works include: Theatre: *War Crimes* (1981), *Secret Gardens* (1983), *Under Western Eyes* (1983), *The Winter's Tale* (1984, 1987), *The Crucible* (1984), *A Mouthful of Birds* (1986), *For the Love of the Nightingale* (1988), *Pelican* (1992), *Antony and Cleopatra* (1992), and *Henry V* (1994); opera productions: *Death in Venice* (1980, 1992), *Mazeppa* (1984), *Orlando* (1985, 1992), *The Midsummer Marriage* (1985), *The Marriage of Figaro* (1986), *The Trojans (Fall of Troy)* (1987), *The Trojans (Trojans in Carthage)* (1987), *Tannhäuser* (1987), *Carmen* (1987), *Macbeth* (1990), *Clarissa* (1990), *The Vanishing Bridegroom* (1990), *Mary Stuart* (1990), and *Rigoletto* (1995).

Films and Videotapes

Three untitled pieces for *Dance-lines*, dir. Terry Braun, Dance-lines Productions, Channel 4, 1987.

Fugue, dir. Spink, written by Churchill, Channel 4, 1988.

Heaven Ablaze in His Breast, dir. Peter Mumford; Dance-lines Productions, BBC2, 1991.

Much Ado about Knitting, fashion show, London, 1991.

Publications

On SPINK: books—

Jordan, Stephanie, *Striding Out: Aspects of Contemporary and New Dance in Britain.* London, 1992.

On SPINK: articles—

Jordan, Stephanie, "Second Stride; The First Six Years," *Dance Theatre Journal,* 1988.

Macauley, Alastair, "Second Stride Second Year," *Dance Theatre Journal,* 1983.

Rubidge, Sarah, "Ian Spink," *Dance Theatre Journal,* 1985.
———, "Weighing Spink's Heart," *Dance Theatre Journal,* 1987.
———, "The Spink-Gough Collaboration," *Choreography & Dance,* 1992.

*   *   *

Ian Spink arrived in Britain from Australia in 1977. Within a year of his arrival he was dancing with Richard Alston and Dancers and had formed his own company, the Ian Spink Group. He was adopted rapidly as a "British" choreographer. As far back as 1978 Spink's work for the Ian Spink Group was already beginning to reveal the choreographic tendencies that were to become his hallmark, the marriage of modern dance and experimental theatre practices. *26 Solos* and *Dead Flight* both made theatrical devices and contexts integral to the work. At this time dance-theatre had yet to make its mark as an artistic genre in Britain, much of the work from British independent dance artists being derived from the formalist aesthetic associated with Merce Cunningham. While Spink never fully abandoned the rigour of formalism, it was clear even then that he was moving into new directions of dance practice. His dance work made its final move into theatricality in 1984 with *New Tactics* (Albery directing). Since then his work has been firmly based in theatre practice. Although Spink's influences include Merce Cunningham and Pina Bausch, it is with Robert Wilson that his early dance theatre work is most closely aligned, particularly in its precision of movement, clarity of stage image, restrained mode of performance, and rigour of form. All this remains in his later work, although the latter is often injected with a more vigorous performance quality.

A major step in Spink's career occurred in 1982 when the Ian Spink Group and Siobhan Davies and Dancers joined forces to form Second Stride Dance Company. It is with Second Stride that Spink has been able to develop his unique artistic voice and working practices over the years. Few of the pieces he has made since 1983 can be credited solely to Spink. Rather, he consistently works in collaboration with a team of artists (performers, directors, designers, playwrights, composers) whose collective minds produce the multilayered works that have become the hallmark of his oeuvre. Many of Spink's main collaborators have been with him for several years—Gough and McDonald, with whom he has made seven major works for Second Stride, and Caryl Churchill and composer Judith Weir being the most prominent.

A major feature of Spink's dance-theatre work is that its multiple sources frequently lie outside of the world of dance. This gives it the kind of richness of reference one associates more readily with theatre and opera. References to mythology and classical literature, to science and world history, to literature and opera, and classical ballet and music are not uncommon. *New Tactics* drew from Oliver Sachs' book *Awakenings* for its subject matter and material, *Further and Further into Night* from Hitchcock's film *Notorious, Weighing the Heart* from the *Egyptian Book of the Dead, Escape at Sea* from Chekov's *The Seagull.* Even when Spink draws on dance-historical themes the lateral thinking he and his collaborators apply to them take the audience into realms they had not previously imagined as relevant to the source work. *Bösendorfer Waltzes,* which has its source in Fokine's *The Firebird,* features characters from the surrealist and dadaist movements (Diaghilev's *Ballets Russes* coincided with these artistic movements historically). A multitude of other images jostled against each other. The *Golden Apple Dance* from *The Firebird* is performed by the Bösendorfer family around an elegantly laid Chekovian dinner table, and the wedding took place on a stage strewn with apples under an iconic hammer and sickle. *Heaven Ablaze in His Heart* took as its starting point the Romantic ballet *Coppelia,* but turned to the original source of that ballet, E. T. A. Hoffman's story "The Sandman" for its substance, resulting in a dark work that bore little resemblance to the ballet from which it emanated. Psychoanalysis, references to Freud, who had analysed the original story, and Kokoschka, who made a doll to replace his absent lover, and scientific experiments all found their way into the performance text.

At the same time as he was developing his career as an independent choreographer Spink was pursuing a parallel career in theatre and opera. By 1981 he had become part of a group of emerging theatre artists who included director Tim Albery, designer Antony McDonald, composer Orlando Gough, and designer/director Tom Cairns. He choreographed Albery's *War Crimes* in 1981 and co-directed *Secret Gardens* in 1983. From 1984 onward he regularly choreographed for opera companies, including English National Opera, Opera North, the Welsh National Opera, The Royal Opera, and Scottish Opera. He also made inroads into directing, Judith Weir's *The Vanishing Bridegroom* being his directorial debut in opera. Spink's unique approach to choreographing opera can be credited with extending conventional directorial perceptions of what the role of dance in opera could be. At the same time Spink worked with the Royal Shakespeare Company, the Royal Court Theatre, and The National Theatre and, in 1994, directed Strindberg's *The Pelican* for the Citizens Theatre in Glasgow, Scotland. Just as Second Stride's work fed into his work in mainstream theatre and opera, so his work in opera and theatre fed back into his work with Second Stride.

Multilayered, multidisciplinary, and deliberately ambiguous and polysemic—in short, postmodernist—Spink's work has consistently challenged dance audiences and critics alike. In 1991, with the funding climate becoming increasingly conservative in Britain, Spink, it seems, challenged the dance establishment once too often and Second Stride's grant was rescinded. The respect with which Spink's experimental work was held in the other performing arts in Britain, however, came unexpectedly to light through the letters of support for the company sent to the Arts Council by the directors of Britain's major theatre and opera companies, including the Royal Shakespeare Company, the Royal National Theatre, and the English National Opera, Scottish Opera, and Welsh Opera. Spink's work with Second Stride, unbeknownst to the dance establishment, had been feeding directly into mainstream theatre and opera practice through his work as choreographer and director in these companion theatrical disciplines.

Spink has consistently served as an important figure in Britain's theatre dance culture since the early 1980s. In refusing to accept artificial distinctions between the theatrical genres, Spink has spawned new approaches to dance practice, both directly and indirectly, and has helped to give dance the kind of status in the eyes of the mainstream performing arts that it has not enjoyed for several decades.

—Sarah Rubidge

STILL/HERE

Choreography and Direction: Bill T. Jones
Music: Kenneth Frazelle (*Still*), sung by Odetta, played by the

Still/Here. **Photograph © Johan Elbers.**

Lark String Quartet with Bill Finizio, percussion; Vernon Reid (*Here*)
Visual Concept and Media Environment: Gretchen Bender
Costume Design: Liz Prince
Lighting: Robert Wierzel
Spoken Text: "Denial" monologue by Lawrence Goldhuber
First Production: Bill T. Jones/Arnie Zane Dance Company, TNP Villeurbanne, Lyon, 14 September 1994; first New York performance at Next Wave Festival, BAM Opera House, 30 November 1994

Publications

Croce, Arlene, "A Critic at Bay: Discussing the Undiscussable," *New Yorker*, 26 December 1994-2 January 1995.

Croce, Arlene, "In the Mail: Who's the Victim? Dissenting Voices Answer Arlene Croce's Critique of Victim Art," *New Yorker*, 30 January 1995.

Dacko, Karen, "Victim Art Tops Agenda at Critics Conference," *Dance Magazine*, October 1995.

Dekle, Nicole, "Griot Lyons," *Dance Magazine*, February 1995.

Duffy, Martha, "Push Comes to Shove: Decrying a Choreographer for Making 'Victim Art,'" *Time*, 6 February 1995.

Garafola, Lynn, "Black Dance: Revelations," *Nation*, 17 April 1995 (also see the exchange of letters between Croce and Garafola in the 12 June 1995 issue, titled "Balletomane Poisoning."

Gates, Henry Louis, "Onward and Upward with the Arts: The Body Politic," *New Yorker*, 28 November 1994.

Goldstein, Richard, "The Croce Criterion," *Village Voice*, 3 January 1995.

Jones, Bill T, "*Still/Here*" in *Last Night on Earth*, New York, 1995.

Jowitt, Deborah, "Critic as Victim," *Village Voice*, 10 January 1995.

Kriegsman, Allen M., "Bill T. Jones, on Matters of Life and Death," *Washington Post*, 21 November 1994.

Tobias, Tobi, "Heaven Can Wait," *Dance Magazine*, October 1995.

Shapiro, Laura, "The Art of Victimization," *Newsweek*, 6 February 1995.

Sims, Caitlin, "Jones' Race a Factor in Croce's *New Yorker* 'Victim Art' Article," *Dance Magazine*, February 1996.

Films and Videotapes

Still/Here for the *Alive TV* series (condensed), produced by Catherine Tatge, KTCA, Independent Television Service and La Sept-Arte, Amaya Distribution, 1995; complete 111-minute documentary video of the 1994 performance at BAM available at the Dance Collection of the New York Public Library for the Performing Arts at Lincoln Center.

*   *   *

Choreographer Bill T. Jones derived source material for *Still/Here* from 11 "Survival Workshops" (advertised as "Talking and Moving about Life and Death") hosted by community organizations in cities around the United States from November 1992 to

April 1994. In these sessions Jones led 84 people living with terminal illnesses (mostly AIDS and cancer) through exercises in movement, visualization, and storytelling. Jones and his dancers culled the workshop videotapes for movement; composer Kenneth Frazelle used participants' words to write the lyrics for the song cycle accompanying *Still,* the evening-length work's first half, while Vernon Reid constructed his score for *Here* partly from digital samples of speech and ambient noises from the video soundtracks; and videographer Gretchen Bender manipulated shots of the participants speaking and moving to create the intermittent large-scale projections that dominate the work's visual design. The video also incorporates rapid-fire montage sequences of anatomical images (mainly created with medical diagnostic imaging techniques) and, in *Here,* huge pumping hearts.

The dance idiom of *Still/Here* is a synthesis of athletic, post-Cunningham modern dance and pedestrian locomotor steps—simply patterned walking and frantic running—with expressive gestures found in the workshop videos. Jones also embeds quotations from such sources as capoeira, karate, hiphop, and hopscotch (again, related to experiences of workshop members). The most important reiterated motif involves a falling or off-kilter dancer's being rescued, buoyed, or held by another dancer or dancers, even by the whole group—an obvious metaphor for one of the work's central themes, the sustaining power of community.

Though the evening's two halves share the same movement vocabulary, they differ in mood. Costumed in white and lit in cool washes (based on "video blue," the hue of a blank monitor screen), *Still* is quieter, suggesting an internal realm of private contemplation, its score's hushed string textures and sustained vocal lines punctuated only rarely by eruptions of strident anguish. *Here* is costumed and lit in blood red, and evokes a public arena riven by conflict and aggression; *Here*'s harsh electronic-rock music, busy video, and more chaotic stage action replace *Still*'s ritualistic wholeness with a palpable sense of fragmentation. In the finale, the dancers recapitulate all the work's gestural phrases (in silhouette or downspots) while one dancer wheels a video monitor around the stage, on which Jones appears, guiding one of the Survival Workshop groups—and by extension, his dancers, and the audience—through a visualization of our own death.

Given the way Jones thus situates his audience as members of his workshops, placing us in an extended community that includes the healthy with the sick, and given the emphasis on the workshops in *Still/Here*'s publicity campaign, it is finally impossible to consider the work separately from the process by which it was created. It is equally impossible to discuss *Still/Here* apart from the controversy that surrounded its American premiere.

When, instead of reviewing *Still/Here, New Yorker* dance critic Arlene Croce published an essay in which she declared her refusal to see the work, denouncing it as an archetype of "victim art," she detonated the fiercest controversy since Louis Horst's infamous blank column in his *Dance Observer* review of Paul Taylor's *Seven New Dances* in 1957. Whereas the brouhaha surrounding Horst's snub of Taylor remained within the cloister of the dance world, Croce touched off an avalanche of commentary that swept through journals in the U.S., Canada, England, France, Germany, and Australia, even rolling down to reach the official level of popular culture represented by *Time* and *Newsweek.* The swiftness and vehemence of the response proved that Croce had stabbed a nerve already exposed. While the issue of "victim art"—a term Croce did not invent, but which she succeeded, albeit briefly, in engraving in the American national lexicon—thus received a thorough airing, many

of the rejoinders to Croce's article evaded or misconstrued her arguments; Croce herself was partly responsible for this, since she used Jones' work as a launching pad for a scattershot salvo aimed at an array of targets, in a broad indictment of American culture from the 1960s onward.

Croce's core argument is worth recalling: she dismissed Jones' Survival Workshops as a "messianic traveling medicine show," and the stage work that resulted from them as "intolerably voyeuristic" and "unintelligible as theater." By "working dying people into his act," wrote Croce, Jones "crossed the line between theater and reality" putting himself "beyond the reach of criticism." She saw Jones as an exemplary "extreme case among the distressingly many now representing themselves to the public not as artists but as victims or martyrs," narcissists who think that "victimhood in and of itself is sufficient to the creation of an art spectacle." Croce decried victimhood as a "mass delusion," and victim art as "a politicized version of blackmail" that, ironically, victimizes both audience and critics.

Croce's essay was in part an impassioned *cri de coeur* from a critic feeling legitimately beleaguered by the implicit special pleading that accompanied much self-consciously political performance in the 1980s and 1990s. Yet Croce's argument contained an element of bad faith, for if it is true that *Still/Here* is guilty of coercing its audience, it is equally true that no critic can rightfully attack a piece she has never seen. Moreover, Croce was incorrect in asserting that *Still/Here*'s incorporation of dying people on video set the work beyond the reach of criticism. The piece raises problems common to all biographical or autobiographical artworks, problems perhaps more familiar in literature and the visual arts. Jones is finally no more "undiscussable" than Anne Sexton or Frieda Kahlo.

Still/Here was in fact criticized on many counts: as often happens in dances that use projections, the video tends to dominate the dancers and distract attention from them. Although Jones explicitly intended his dancers to signify the indomitable spirits of the workshop participants, and not their suffering bodies, the piece nonetheless labors, as do works that address similarly drastic subjects such as war or the Holocaust, under the contradiction of representing the afflicted by young, healthy, beautiful dancers. Despite the direness of its theme, many viewers were struck above all by the work's tidy structures, its easy good taste, which made some parts, such as *Still*'s "Slash, Burn, Poison" section (its lyric based on blackly ironic vernacular terms for surgery, radiation, and chemotherapy) seem overwrought, even melodramatic. To some, including critic Lynn Garafola, Jones' use of his workshop members' testimonials was cavalier—certainly his recorded questioning of them heard in the score sounded almost like interrogation. Perhaps the work's limitations were chiefly due to its creative method, which confined the collaborators to the selection and rearrangement of their source materials, and neglected some transformative act of imagination that could relieve biographical fact of its responsibility for guaranteeing the work's value.

Croce's piece, which had without question a tonic effect on public discourse, depended on her not having seen *Still/Here*—had she seen it, she couldn't have written as she did. For in the end, "victimhood" never emerges as the work's theme; the interview subjects as they appear in the projected video are free of self-pity. *Still/Here*'s real theme is, rather, struggle, survival, heroism, and above all, hope. For this, as much as for the controversy it triggered, *Still/Here* is a quintessential work of its era.

—Christopher Caines

STRANGE FRUIT

Choreography: Pearl Primus
First Production: 92nd St. YMHA, New York City, 14 February, 1943
Sound: narrated poem, "Strange Fruit," by Lewis Allan
Lighting Design: Doris S. Einstein (1945 & 1946)
Costume Design: Edyth Gilfond
Original Dancer: Pearl Primus
Other productions include: Reconstruction by the Philadelphia-based Philadanco, performed by Kim Bears for the 1988 ADF; 1994 performance by Michele Simmons at a commemorative concert for Pearl Primus by the Los Angeles Dance Theater

Publications:

Barber, Beverly Hillsman, "Pearl Primus: Rebuilding America's Cultural Infrastructure," *African American Genius in Modern Dance,* Durham, North Carolina, 1993.

Denby, Edwin, *Dance Writings,* New York, 1986.

Emery, Lynne Fauley, *Black Dance: From 1619 to Today,* Princeton, NJ, 1988.

Lloyd, Margaret, *The Borzoi Book of Modern Dance,* Brooklyn, 1949.

Long, Richard, *The Black Tradition in American Dance,* New York, 1989.

Simmons, Michele, "Experiencing and Performing the Choreography of Pearl Primus," *Talking Drums,* January 1995.

* * *

When Pearl Primus performed *Strange Fruit* in 1943 it was one of three solos performed by Primus. Black dance historian Lynne Emery has identified it as the first time Primus appeared as professional dancer. However, various sources suggest that other presentations of the work may have occurred in less formal settings before the 1943 YMHA production. Emery has stated that *Strange Fruit* represented one of a series of Primus' "dances of protest" or "message dances."

Primus composed *Strange Fruit* to document the injustices inflicted upon African Americans in the south during the pre-Civil Rights era. The work was based on a poem by Lewis Allan by the same title. Its powerful and graphic imagery described the lynching of a black man: "Southern trees bear strange fruit. . . Black bodies swinging in the southern breeze. Strange fruit hanging from the poplar trees." Initially, Primus performed the work while the poem was recited by Vinnette Carroll. Although, as dance critic Margaret Lloyd noted, Primus did not follow the verse nor its rhythm. Rather, she chose to use the intensity of its content to fuel her choreography. Later, Primus deleted the text altogether, deciding the piece worked better without it.

There are three striking features of *Strange Fruit.* The first is that Primus chose to choreograph the piece from the perspective of a woman who is a member of the lynch mob. Initially seduced by the frenzy of the mob's vicious sentiments, the woman, obviously white, realizes the atrocity that has just been committed and succumbs to total grief and remorse. The second was Primus' interpretation of this heinous crime. Performed in the absence of music, Primus' powerful execution of movements was made audible, the energy more visible, the reaction more viceral, and subsequently,

the message clearer to audiences. Lloyd provided rich documentation of Primus' performance of *Strange Fruit* and a glimpse of the work's original spirit and intensity in the following description:

> With no sound but the brush of her garment, the swish and thud of her bare feet and fists, the dancer hugs the earth, beating it, flinging herself upon it, groveling in it, twisting her sinuous body into fantastic shapes across it, now fleeing, now facing in timid fascination the invisible sacrificial tree which is the focus of the dance.

The third striking feature of *Strange Fruit* is that with this work Primus can be considered the first African American dance artist to fuse black themes with modern dance technique, as dance educator and historian Beverly Barber has recounted. Unlike Katherine Dunham, whose technique was derived from the blending of Afro-Haitian dance forms and ballet, Primus trained with many of the modern dance pillars of her time. Her artistry was rooted in a solid understanding of modern dance technique coupled with her own African American movement vocabulary.

After viewing *Strange Fruit* in its debut concert at the YMHA, *New York Times* dance critic John Martin encouraged Primus to pursue dance seriously. *Strange Fruit* launched Primus' artistic career and remains one of her most enduring contributions to American modern dance. Moreover, the work helped facilitate discussion of the racial divisions in the United States during the mid-20th century, fulfilling one of Primus' most cherished humanitarian goals.

—Julie A. Kerr-Berry

STRATE, Grant
Canadian dancer, choreographer, and educator

Born: 7 December 1927 in Cardston, Alberta. **Education:** University of Alberta at Edmonton, B.A. 1949, LL.B. 1950. Studied modern dance with Laine Metz. **Career:** Charter member, National Ballet of Canada, 1951; character dancer with the company and assistant to the artistic director, 1951-70; created first choreography in 1956 and was named resident choreographer in 1963, creating 17 works (including three for the Stratford Music Festival and one for the National Ballet School) during his tenure to 1970; teacher and choreographer, Juilliard School of Music and Dance, New York, 1962-63; traveled extensively as emissary for the National Ballet of Canada to London, Copenhagen, Stuttgart, Munich, Florence, Paris and New York; founding chairman, dance department, faculty of fine arts, York University, Ontario, 1970-76; acting chairman of the department, 1977-78; appointed director of the Centre for the Arts, Simon Fraser University, Burnaby, B.C., 1980-89; served as coordinator of the dance program, 1991-92 and as director of the Contemporary Arts Summer Institute, 1989-94; organized and administered choreographic seminars at York University, 1978, Banff, 1980, and Simon Fraser University, 1985 and 1991; founding chairman and board member, Dance in Canada Association, 1973-78; board member, Vancouver Dance Centre, 1985-95 (chairman: 1985-91); chairman, World Dance Alliance Americas Center Third Assembly, 1997; has served on numerous national, provincial and municipal arts councils and organizations and on juries of both national and provincial granting agencies. **Awards:** Centennial Medal,

1967; Queen's Silver Jubilee Medal, 1978; Dance Ontario Award, 1979; Dance in Canada Award, 1984; Canada Dance Award, 1988; Jean R. Chalmers Award for Creativity in Dance, 1993; Order of Canada (C.M.), 1994; Governor General's Performing Arts Award, 1996.

Roles (for the National Ballet of Canada, Toronto)

1951	Dr. Coppelius, *Coppelia,* (Franca after Saint-Leon)
	John the Baptist (cr), *Salomé* (Franca)
1952	Hilarion, *Giselle* (Franca after Coralli)
	Faun (cr), *L'Après-midi d'une faune* (Franca)
	Old Man (cr), *Le Pommier* (Franca)
	Louis XIV (cr), *Ballet Behind Us* (Adams)
1953	Benno, *Swan Lake* (Franca after Petipa)
·1955	Third Song, *Dark Elegies* (Tudor)
1957	Eusebius, Florestan, *Le Carnaval* (Fokine)
1963	Friar Lawrence, Duke of Verona, *Romeo and Juliet* (Cranko)

Works

1956	*Jeune pas de deux* (mus. Massenet), National Ballet of Canada, Toronto
	The Fisherman and his Soul (mus. Somers), National Ballet of Canada, Toronto
1957	*The Willow* (mus. Foote), National Ballet of Canada, Toronto
1958	*Ballad* (mus. Somers), National Ballet of Canada, Toronto
1960	*Antic Spring* (mus. Ibert), National Ballet of Canada, Toronto
1962	*Time Cycle* (mus. Foss); produced for the Stratford Music Festival, National Ballet of Canada
	Sequel (mus. Webern); produced for the Stratford Music Festival, National Ballet of Canada
1964	*House of Atreus* (mus. Sowers); National Ballet of Canada, Toronto; first version (mus. Ginastera) produced for the Juilliard Dance Ensemble, New York
1963	*Electre* (mus. Pousseur); produced for the Stratford Music Festival, Natioanl Ballet of Canada
1965	*Triptych* (mus. Mozart), National Ballet of Canada, Toronto
	Pulcinella (mus. Stravinsky), National Ballet of Canada, Toronto
1966	*The Arena* (mus. Britten), National Ballet of Canada
	Cycles (mus. Welffens), Studio Ballet, Antwerp, revised 1968
1967	*Studies in White* (mus. Telemann), National Ballet of Canada
	Old Airs for Young Dancers (Mus. Respighi), Studio Ballet, Antwerp
	Phases (mus. Satie), National Ballet of Canada, Toronto
	Bird Life (mus. Debussy), Studio Ballet, Antwerp
	Le Pretendent (mus. various), Studio Ballet, Antwerp
1968	*Game* (mus. Couture), Royal Swedish Ballet, Stockholm
1975	*Ricercare* (mus. Webern), York University Dance Program
1976	*Encounter* (mus. Freedman), York University Dance Program
	Watching Once More (mus. Lutoslawski), Dancemakers, Toronto

1977	*Trackings* (mus. Byron), York University Dance Program
1978	*Foot Paths* (mus. Bald), York University Dance Program
	Sandsteps (mus. Shostakovich), Dancemakers, Toronto
1979	*Islands* (mus. Hovhaness), Mountain Dance Theatre, Vancouver
1983	*Offrande* (mus. Bach, arr. Garrant), Danse Partout, Montreal
	Choreograms (mus. various), Simon Fraser University Dance
1984	*Dances in Solus* (film, dir. Hauka; mus. Gotfrit, Newby and Raine-Reusch)
1985	*Lyric Dance* (mus. Beethoven), Regina Modern Dance Works
	They Who Seek (mus. Ives), Regina Modern Dance Works
1986	*New Crossings* (mus. Bald), Laban Centre, London
	Past Zero (mus. Ligeti), Laban Centre, London
	Interregnum (mus. Ferrari), Repertory Dance Theatre of Canada, Vancouver
	The Place Between (mus. Sobotnik), Repertory Dance Theate of Canada, Vancouver
	Divertimento: Three Duets (mus. Stravinsky), Dance Gallery, Vancouver
	Sextet & Vivaldi (mus. Vivaldi), Dance Gallery, Vancouver
	Beginnings (mus. Bach), Dance Gallery, Vancouver
	Tango (mus. Piazzolla), Dance Gallery, Vancouver
	The Time After (mus. Rosen), Mauryne Allan Dance Theatre, Vancouver
1988	*Quatros Pasos* (mus. Barroso), Olympics Arts Festival, Calgary
1990	*Continuous Voyage* (mus. Adams), Beijing Dance Academy
1991	*The Electra Project* (mus. Macnulty), Simon Fraser University Dance Program
1992	*Dances in The Soldier's Tale* (mus. Stravinsky), Simon Fraser University Dance Program
1993	*Other Voices, Parts I-II* (mus. Tenney), Simon Fraser University Dance Program
1994	*Triptych* (mus. Niemans), Ricketts Dance Company, Copenhagen
1995	*Escalator* (mus. Underhill), Simon Fraser University Dance Program
1997	*Street* (mus. Gorecki), Ricketts Dance Company, Copenhagen

Publications

By STRATE: articles—

"Canadian Dance in Progress: A Personal View," *Canadian Dance Studies* 1 (North York, Ontario), 1994.
"The Open Eye: Understanding Dance," *Dance in Canada* (Toronto), Spring 1979.
"Public Image and Private Reality: Homosexuality and the Male Dancer," *Dance in Canada* (Toronto), Fall 1981.
"The Thinking Foot: Teaching Dance Literacy in School," *Dance in Canada* (Toronto), Fall 1983.

By STRATE: books—

China Dance Diary, Toronto, Dance Collection Danse, 1997.

On STRATE: articles—

Crabb, Michael, "Prime Mover Number One: Grant Strate and Dance in Canada," *Dance in Canada,* Winter 1983-84.

On STRATE: books—

The National Ballet of Canada: A Celebration; with Photographs by Ken Bell and a Memoir by Celia Franca, Toronto, 1978.
Neufeld, James, *Power to Rise: The Story of the National Ballet of Canada,* Toronto, 1996.
Whittaker, Herbert, *Canada's National Ballet,* Toronto, 1967.
Wyman, Max, *Dance Canada: An Illustrated History,* Vancouver, 1989.

*   *   *

Arguably the prime mover in the development of a contemporary dance establishment in Canada, Grant Strate began his career at age 23 as the result of a fateful meeting in 1951 with Celia Franca. Franca, who had been imported from England to organize and direct a ballet company with national aspirations headquartered in Toronto, was making an auditions tour to the Western provinces, recruiting ballet-trained dancers en route. Strate had only recently graduated with a degree in law and was articling for an Edmonton firm. His only dance education consisted of tap dance lessons in childhood and during his undergraduate years some recreational training in the classes of Laine Metz, an Estonian who advocated a Wigman-style of European modern dance encouraging a free creative and interpretive approach. Franca saw some of his dances and found them promising. She also saw in him intelligence, a disciplined mind, and a strong potential for leadership—talents which would be developed over the first five years of his tenure at the National Ballet of Canada.

The only recruit thus exempted from the ballet audition, Strate did his first plie in class as a charter member of the company. Franca felt it essential that he master the classical ballet discipline before attempting any creative activity, an approach that Strate agreed to with some reluctance. Consequently from 1951 to 1956 his desire to express his real interest—choreography—was thwarted as he took on assignments in the ensembles of the standard ballet classics, the Fokine repertoire, and new creations by Franca herself, ultimately becoming an accomplished character dancer. Her version in 1952 of *L'Après-midi d'une faune* offered Strate the only stellar role in the years of his apprenticeship. His accomplishments in gaining an understanding of ballet, however, gave him another dimension of achievement which he continued to enjoy over the years as a sought-after teacher of ballet. Strate served as special assistant to Franca in both artistic and business affairs and conducted the company's summer study programs. In the second decade of his tenure he was effective as an emissary for the company as he took on assignments in New York and Europe to negotiate the acquisition for the National of ballets by such esteemed choreographers as George Balanchine and John Cranko. He also taught extensively in ballet studios abroad during his travels.

Strate's works during his tenure as the National's resident choreographer generally ran the gamut of genres and styles characteristic of the fare enjoyed by ballet audiences of the era. His three works commissioned for the Stratford Festival—*Electre, Sequel,* and *Time Cycle* were by contrast more experimental in intention. His epic *House of Atreus,* originally composed to music by Ginastera for performance at New York's Juilliard School, lost stature in its transfer to the National Ballet, due to what New York Times critic Allen Hughes deplored as "Harold Town's rash costumes, masks, headdresses, wigs and whatnot," a musical score of less stature by Harry Somers and "the balletic cliches which have crept into what was terse, expressive dancing."

A Canada Council Senior Arts Fellowship in 1962 had permitted Strate to work at Juilliard at the invitation of Antony Tudor, and he found himself in heady company, creating *House of Atreus* on a program which included works by Anna Sokolow, Doris Humphrey, José Limón and two by Tudor himself. The experience in such a vital setting clarified his own direction, and in the following year when he visited ballet establishments in Great Britain, he articulated his position in a letter sent home to the National Ballet:

> We must no longer look back to mother England for supplemental dancers and artistic inspiration. There is nothing here which could possibly set a new trend and we must not be content to follow anymore. New York should be our communication line. . . . British ballet can sink into the ocean for all of me. Saccharine romance and pretty dancing still seems to be the standard.

During his last year at the National Ballet, Strate was assigned the task of setting up an academic dance program at York University in Ontario, and in 1970 he assumed the position of founding chairman. And while the curriculum included traditional education in dance history and criticism, notation and the principles of dance therapy, New York had indeed served as a diversified model for his scheme; at York he brought under one roof all the training possibilities existing in the mainstream city, giving Canadian dancers the full range of modern techniques. The focus of the program was to train and produce dancers and choreographers fully equipped to survive as professionals, and over the next decade a generation of new companies evolved from the York experience.

In 1978 he initiated at York the first Choreographic Seminar, an intensive study session which allowed dancers, choreographers and musicians to work together in the achievement of a common production. The project was again offered in 1980 at Banff, at which time Strate moved to British Columbia to head Simon Fraser University's Centre for the Arts, where his expertise at York was invaluable in the evolution of its youthful dance program, one with fewer academic preoccupations but with a strong dedication to performance and creativity. Additional sessions of the Choreographic Seminar were realized at S.F.U. in 1985 and 1991.

Strate has choreographed extensively for students at both Canadian universities where he was officially employed and has created dances and taught both classical ballet and modern techniques in academic studios and company classrooms all over the world. In his work as an independent choreographer he tends to eschew narrative forms, preferring taut, well-structured and focused studies; sometimes he deals with topical material, conveying issues of human emotion and experience. He creates to both established music and to specially composed scores. Four trips to teach in China, 1986 to 1996, have been particularly fruitful in helping a nation achieve its own identity in the development of a contemporary dance style. His dedication to dance is demonstrated by ongoing involvements in both his immediate environment and the world community: largely through his efforts the actuality of a Dance Centre in Vancouver is being achieved, one which will offer rehearsal and administrative space to dance companies and individual artists, and his involvement as Planning Chairman of the Americas Chapter of the World Dance Alliance for the 1997 congress in Vancouver reflects his belief in the necessity for acknowledging any creative community as part of a global scheme.

—Leland Windreich

SULLIVAN, Françoise

Canadian dancer, choreographer, and visual artist

Born: Montreal, Quebec. **Education:** Studied painting at L'École des Beaux-Arts, Montreal; studied ballet with Gerald Crevier, Montreal; modern dance with Mary Anthony, Martha Graham, La Meri, Pearl Primus, and Louis Horst, New York, 1945-46; also studied with Franziska Boas (whom she favored). **Family:** Married visual artist Paterson Ewen; four sons. **Career:** Dancer, several recitals by Crevier; met painter Paul-Émile Borduas, 1942; began teaching, 1947; began dancing and choreographing with Jeanne Renaud, 1947-48; signed the Automatist Manifesto *Refus Global*, contributing "Le Danse et L'Espoir" (Dance and Hope) essay, 1948; began producing for her own company, 1949; choreographed for television until 1956; concentrated on visual arts, designing sets for Jeanne Renaud, Le Groupe de la Place Royale, 1960, 1965, 1967; returned to dance occasionally, 1970—; lecturer in dance, Concordia University, 1979-81. **Awards:** Prix Maurice Cullen (for painting), 1943; Prix du Québec (for sculpture), 1963; Martin Lynch Staunton Award, 1984; Prix du Québec Paul-Émile Borduas, 1987; member of the Royal Academy, 1991—.

Works

1945	*Revue Bleu et Or*, University of Montreal
1946	*Dualité* (mus. Mercure)
1947	*Black and Tan Fantasy* (mus. Ellington)
	Déploration sur la mort (mus. Binchois)
	Moi, je suis de cette race rouge et épaisse w/Jeanne Renaud, to a poem by Thérèse Renaud
1948	*Dédales*
	Crédo (mus. Bach)
	Gothique (mus. Prévert)
	Lucrèce (mus. Mercure)
	Femme Archâque (mus. Mercure)
	Berceuse (accompanied by percussion)
	Deux danses à midi (mus. percussion)
1950	*Le Combat de Tancrède et de Clorinde* (mus. from Monteverdi's *L'Opéra Minute*)
1953	*Rose Latulipe* (mus. Blackburn)
1954	*Danses sacrés et profanes* (mus. Debussy)
	Concerto pour trompettes (mus. Haydn)
	Les Indes Galantes (mus. Rameau)
	Le Tombeau de Couperin (mus. Ravel)
1970	*Walk from one museum to the other, and back*
1973	*Droit debout* (text Sullivan), for Le Groupe de la Place Royale
1976	*Journée chorégraphique* (reconstruction of *Dédales* and improvisation), Le Groupe Nouvelle Aire
	Walk, meeting Apollo (conceptual)

	Walk among the oil refineries (conceptual)
1977	*Dédales* (remounted and danced by Ginette Laurin)
1978	*Hiérophanie* for Le Groupe Nouvelle Aire (mus. Vincent Dionne)
	Walk around Temple of Diana, Delphy (conceptual)
	Meeting my Shadow, small amphitheatre, Delphy (conceptual)
	Blocking and unblocking doors or windows, Santori, Greece, and Blasket Island, Ireland (conceptual)
1979	*Accumulation I*, in an art gallery
	Accumulation II, in a forest
	Accumulation III, in Victoria subway station, unfinished as stopped by police
	Accumulation IV, Palazzo dei Diamanti, Ferrara, Italy
	Choreography for Five Cars and Six Dancers, in a parking lot
1981	*Et la nuit a la nuit* (mus. Ràcine)
	Labyrinthe
1982	*A tout prendre* (mus. Ràcine)
1987	*Cycle* (mus. Smith), for Montreal Dance Company
1988	*Récital de danse* (by Jeanne Renaud, reconstruction from 1948), Musée d'art contemporain de Montréal
1992	*Ginette Boutin danse Françoise Sullivan Théâtre*
	Elles (mus. Paganini)
1993	*En face de moi* (mus. Bouliane)

Publications

On SULLIVAN: books—

Ellenwood, Ray (translator), *Total Refusal: The Complete 1948 Manifesto of the Montreal Automatists,* Toronto, 1985.
Françoise Sullivan: Rétrospective, compiled by Ministere des Affaires Culturelles, Québec, 1981.

On SULLIVAN: articles—

Stanworth, Karen, "Re-Placing Performance: The Inter-Media Practice of Françoise Sullivan," in Selma Odom and Mary Jane Warner, eds. *Canadian Dance Studies 1,* North York, 1994.
Tembeck, Iro, "Dancing in Montreal: Seeds of a Choreographic History," *Journal of the Society of Dance History Scholars*, Fall 1994.

*   *   *

In the early 1940s five young students at the École des Beaux-Arts in Montreal began to discuss among themselves their dissatisfaction with the narrow academic teaching in the school. They soon met artist and École de Meuble teacher Paul-Émile Borduas, who invited them to meet at his studio. When they left, well after 3 a.m., the young artists were spellbound, in awe of Borduas' art and ideas. The group continued to meet discussing everything from children's art to surrealism, art history, society, and the oppressive, patriarchal Duplessis government in Quebec. With a great sense of urgency they produced a manifesto called *Refus Global* (*Total Refusal*), signed by 15 visual artists, poets, and dancers, including Françoise Sullivan. The publication shook the sociocultural foundations of Quebec; some of the people who signed it lost their jobs, most of them left Quebec for New York City or Paris.

As a contributor to *Refus Global,* Sullivan wrote "La Danse et l'Espoir" (*Dance and Hope*), the first known philosophical text on dance written by a French-Canadian. In the essay, Sullivan states the collective unconscious is a part of dance, that a dancer can go "beyond the individual towards the universal," and that the body is a storehouse of cosmic energy. Sullivan felt her movement symbolized the collective psyche. Like other Automatists she believed spontaneity was essential, as "dance is a reflex, a spontaneous expression of intense emotion." Further, she denounced the obsolete training practices in dance, stating "Academic dance, the kind we still see most often today, is out-of-date. The pleasure it offers the spectator is purely visual, depending on exceptionally skillful leg movements and ignoring the rest of the body as it strives to break the laws of gravity."

Ironically, Sullivan was in fact quite an accomplished ballerina. She studied ballet for several years with Gerald Crevier performing in several of his recitals, but gradually turned away from classical ballet and became a pioneer in experimental dance in Quebec. She was among the first students to gather around Borduas and the future Automatists who often met in Montreal or Mont St. Hilaire studios to discuss their revolutionary ideas. In the mid-1940s, Sullivan traveled to New York City and began studying with Franziska Boas, and developed her skills as a choreographer.

When Sullivan returned to Montreal in 1947, she lectured on dance and this was when she contributed to *Refus Global*. She also produced a modern dance recital with Jeanne Renaud. Among her choreography in this period is *Black and Tan Fantasy* (1947) which drew inspiration from jazz with movement echoing Duke Ellington's teasing, sensual music. It was performed in a daring costume created for Sullivan by fellow Automatist Jean-Paul Rousseau. In 1948, *Gothique* was inspired by the stance of medieval statues; *Crédo* was a lyrical piece built on the principles of the fugue and set to music by Bach; *Femme Archâque* looked at female archetypes, ritual, and magic and was set to a commissioned score by Pierre Mercure; and *Dédales* was a solo piece exploring the movement gesture swing. Performed in silence, the latter dance placed emphasis on the sound of the dancer's breath.

Shortly after the recital with Renaud, Sullivan married visual artist Paterson Ewen. As her family grew in size, Sullivan gradually turned her attention to raising her four sons and to creating visual art. Meanwhile, about half the Automatistes had scattered outside the country. For awhile Sullivan continued to dance and choreograph, often for television productions such as *L'heure du Concert* and other programs. For the inauguration of the Montreal/Toronto television network she created *Rose Latulipe*, a dance for 12 dancers based on a Quebec folk legend. In 1950, the Opéra Minute commissioned her choreography (in which she danced) for *Le Combat de Tancrède et Clorinde* by Monteverdi, and it was repeated on television in 1956. During those years she also choreographed some classical works for Les Ballet Chiriaeff (later Les Grands Ballets Canadiens).

Though some of these pieces can boast some sort of invention, Sullivan feels this temporary return to classical forms was an effect of the dark period experienced in the 1950s when all support had vanished. She says that similar returns from the boldness of earlier works occurred with European artists such as Picasso and Braque who, after the heroic period of cubism, returned to less adventurous forms. Sullivan states, in retrospect, after choreographing *Dédales*, she should have continued in that direction, but hindsight is always clearer and her time had been filled with domestic responsibilities. She says that even at the best of times, "to take one step into the unknown remains a remarkable thing."

With motherhood, Sullivan turned her focus to other passions, the visual arts and sculpture in particular. She returned to dance in the 1970s when Paul-André Fortier, then a student at the Nouvelle Aire studio, organized a series of days with a choreographer from the past. Sullivan remounted *Dédales* for student Fernande Paquet, and it was also performed later by Ginette Laurin. With Le Groupe Nouvelle Aire, Sullivan choreographed a series of dance experiments called *Accumulations* which were performed in art galleries, Mount Royal Park, public parking lots, and the Palazzo dei Diamenti in Ferraro, Italy.

A notable figure of the Montreal School in the visual arts, Sullivan continues to paint and exhibits internationally. Her work in the various media of choreography, sculpture, documented actions, and painting indicate her continuing pursuit of a reflective inner necessity. Informed by occurring and changing sensibilities, Sullivan confronted some of the burning issues of our time and her contribution to the cultural field in Quebec is exceptional. Her choreography from 50 years ago is as fresh and innovative as if it had been created yesterday. Timeless, spontaneous, innovative, risky—each of these words can describe the vast body of dance and art Sullivan has created.

—Amy Bowring

SYDNEY DANCE COMPANY
Australian dance company

Sydney Dance Company is Australia's leading contemporary dance group. Its performing base is the Sydney Opera House in Sydney, New South Wales, where it has premiered commissioned works since 1977. Sydney Dance Company (SDC) was founded as an educational group—simply known as the Dance Company in New South Wales—in 1965 by Suzanne Musitz, a dancer with the Australian Ballet. The company did not become fully professional until 1971 and changed its name eight years later to the Sydney Dance Company. The company serves a huge area and delivers a wide variety of styles to audiences worldwide; in 1997 the company reflected the multinational personality of Australia's largest city with dancers coming from Australia, England, Japan, Sweden, China, South Africa, and Canada.

Innovation has been the key element in the performing profile of SDC from its earliest years. Its policy of commissioning new works from young choreographers has provided a creative environment unequaled in the world of contemporary dance. The Dutch dancer and choreographer Jaap Flier led the company from 1975 to 1976 and concentrated on a contemporary repertoire. In 1976, Graeme Murphy, a former dancer with the Australian Ballet, Britain's Royal Ballet, and Ballets Felix Blaska in Grenoble, France, took over as artistic director and resident choreographer, positions he still occupies. Janet Verson is the current associate artistic director.

Sydney Dance Company has developed an extensive repertory of original works which blend classical and modern styles and range over a wide spectrum of sources from Fred Astaire and Ginger Rogers movies to Greek mythology. Over 40 of these works have been created by Murphy; 20 have been full-length productions. Murphy's first successful piece for the SDC was *Poppy*, a 1978 multimedia work based on the life and art of Jean Cocteau. Murphy described *Poppy* as "a Cocteau-esque poem. . .with Cocteau style and tableaux and decor. . ." The work was important for several reasons: first, *Poppy* featured choreography, music, and decor by

Sydney Dance Company in Graeme Murphy's *Free Radicals*, 1996. Photograph © Lois Greenfield.

Australians: music by Carl Vine, visuals and set design created by George Gittoes and Gabrielle Dalton, and puppets fashioned by Joe Gladwin; second, *Poppy* represented a substantial risk for Murphy and the SDC because of its length. Previously, the company had done short works, repertory pieces, and a great deal of outside choreography. But Murphy was determined to move the company in a new direction—and his daring and his ability to push the company in different ways paid off. *Poppy* was received with great critical acclaim both at home and abroad. Other full-length works by Murphy soon followed, including *Rumours, Sheherazade,*

Daphnis and Chloe, The Protecting Veil, Kraanerg, After Venice, King Roger, Beauty and the Beast, Synergy with Synergy, Some Rooms, and *Berlin.*

Rumours was the second full-length work performed by Sydney Dance Company and followed *Poppy* by a year. It was created in two stages—with the first part, *Rumours I*, made in 1978 for the Ballet 78 Festival at the Sydney Opera House. This original work was then expanded with *Rumours II* and *Rumours III* in 1979. The all-inclusive *Rumours* appeared in its trilogy version in March 1979 at the Sydney Opera House with music by composer Barry

Conyngham and sets by designer Alan Oldfield. The story was simple enough—about "Sydneysiders"—or residents of Sydney, and took the audience through several stages of Sydney life, shedding light on those who live in big cities near oceans, who love the sea and the sky, and who grow from youth to old age in this setting. The work's divisions include pure dance dealing with images one associates with Sydney—the harbor, sails, images of sea birds; a beach scene; and a depiction of the lives of the old in an outdoor, youth-oriented culture.

Graeme Murphy's overall choreographic approach is to come to the studio without formed steps or patterns. He is guided by an image he wants to express combined with a witty theatricality. His energetic and athletic dancers are completely comfortable in conveying his approach. This is not to say that the choreography lacks subtlety. According to Jill Sykes, writing in *Dance Magazine* in 1981, "the Sydney Dance Company doesn't fit into any ordinary category of dance. . . .Murphy and his dancers have a background of classical training but that is only the starting point of the Murphy style." Murphy once explained that modern dance was a style out of the "past" and that his style was inspired from everything and anything. After all, as Murphy has pointed out "dance is dance."

Equality of the sexes and a frank sexuality are often evident in the SDC's style. Men dance with men, women with women, as well as with each other. Bodies are boldly displayed either clad in imaginative costumes or dressed in costumes simulated to appear nude. Murphy is also unafraid of having fun with classic stories. In his version of *Daphnis and Chloe* (1981), Cupid appears on a skateboard and the Three Nymphs cavort on roller skates.

In 1994, Murphy debuted a work which moved away from his customary spectacle approach. *The Protecting Veil*, performed to the music of the same name by British composer John Tavener, was described by reviewer Patricia Laughlin for *Dance Magazine* in May 1994 as an "enigmatic" work which shows off the choreographer's inventiveness. *The Protecting Veil* consists of duets, trios, quartets, and ensembles; each complements the solo dancing of a mysterious woman in purple (danced by longtime Murphy colleague Janet Vernon) whose appearances during the dance are described as "crossings." Brief at first, these crossings become longer as the work progresses. The leader of the dance is a man (Alfred Taahi) who both draws the group together and separates them. The purple-clad female dances a pas de deux with her partner (Carl Plaisted) even as they are separated by a thin curtain. The female is attracted to another male, however, and fixes him with a hypnotic gaze after which she leads him away.

Some critics have found Graeme Murphy's choreography and theatrical approach lacking. Writer Marilyn Hunt, reviewing SDC's appearances in New York City in 1985, noted an inconsistency in the work of the choreographer. She felt that while he was boldly imaginative and gifted with a strong visual sense, some of his works simply did not succeed. Overly extended partnering (such as in the work *Homelands*), according to Hunt, often loses its point. *Some Rooms* and *After Venice* are full-length works given a cinematic treatment; critic Hunt found the latter a vulgarization of Thomas Mann's *Death in Venice* but found much to laud in *Some Rooms*— a multimedia work about the maturation of a boy (danced by Paul Mercurio).

Murphy has used Australia's history and culture as the jumping-off point for an amazing number of dances. Generally, his themes are universal and his approach of dramatic power through move-

ment alone echoes Kurt Jooss. In 1997, the company performed *Free Radicals* in New York City's Joyce Theater during a tour of the United States. In this work (first performed in 1996 at the Sydney Opera House) for 16 dancers and three percussionists, Murphy and his designer Matthew Serventy devised a stage area draped in dark blue curtains and decorated with blue-shaded, industrial-style lamps. Three large "Sputnik"-like structures were suspended from the ceiling, and pools of light were created by John Rayment. *Free Radicals* is comprised of group dances, solos, trios, and quartets. According to the choreographer, the work stemmed from his fascination with the fusion of dance and live percussion. Each element was generated by the artists during the working process. Dancers responded to the music of Michael Askill, Alison Eddington, and Alison Low Choy. In turn, the musicians challenged the dancers with a wide variety of rhythms. *Free Radicals* is initiated by a caller who yells out counts to the gyrating dancers. Vigorous stamps, jumps, tapping, banging, skips, throws, and leaps follow as the work unfolds. The dance is a highly segmented work in which dancers and percussionists take turns holding the stage or collaborate with one another. At turns playful, slapstick, or eerie, *Free Radicals* exhibited the well-known vigor and attractiveness of the company. In one section, a female dancer plays with a globe of light controlled by a stage hand. The light playfully bounces off her body and breaks up into two, then three lights. The globes of light take on a life of their own as the woman is transfixed. In another section, two men manipulate a woman in supported lifts. Daring as some of these lifts are, the woman is never in danger. She exhibits her own strength and power as well by supporting a man on her back. In other sections, a common motif emerges—a man rolls across the floor while moving the body of woman which rests on top of him. Props also figure into the work; the dancers dance with tall torch lights and use these to support themselves. They also slap their bodies and clap their hands as they become percussion instruments and "play" themselves. The least successful elements of this one-hour piece are those involving the playing of cymbals in a large tub of water.

The Sydney Dance Company tours often. Its first appeared in the U.S. was in 1981 and SDC has toured throughout the world since then. Appearances have included performances at the New York City Center, Charleston/Spoleto Festival, San Antonio Festival, and the Wolftrap Farm Park for the Performing Arts. In 1997 the company performed in 10 cities within the States as well as appearing in New Zealand and Germany.

Publications

Sykes, Jill, "The Sydney Dance Company," *Dance Magazine*, May 1981.

Hunt, Marilyn, "Sydney Dance Company Triggers Mixed Reactions," *Dance Magazine*, July 1985.

Clippings file on the Sydney Dance Company in the Dance Research Collection of the New York Public Library at Lincoln Center.

Cargher, John, "The Spice of Life: Graeme Murphy's Sydney Dance Company comes to the U.S.," *Ballet News*, May 1981.

De Berg, Hazel, "Growing in Australian Soil: An Interview with Graeme Murphy," *Brolga, An Australian Journal about Dance*, December 1994.

—Adriane Ruggiero

TAIAO DANCE THEATRE
New Zealand dance company

Taiao Dance Theatre (1988-94) was a unique but highly derivative form of modern dance that mixed culture, politics, histories, and personal experiences with theatre performance. Taiao's artistic direction insisted that there be a cultural base and shared kaupapa (wisdom, understanding) of the nature of the work of the group, rather than pursuit of dancing or creativity for creativity's sake. The word "kaupapa" entails spirituality, politics, aesthetics and traditions, and gives the reason to dance as well as giving the dance meaning.

Taiao was formed in 1988 by core members of Te Kanikani o te Rangatahi (The Dance of the Youth), a group active from 1985 to 1987 which had grown out of the Tamaki Maori Creative Arts Scheme. This project, established in Auckland in 1984 to educate and empower Maori youth through the arts, was funded as a government work scheme. The programme was holistic and all participated as a whanau (family) in dance classes, rehearsals, te reo me ona tikanga (language and protocol), arts hui (gatherings) and productions.

The dances of Te Kanikani o te Rangatahi were based on the life experiences of its members, a wide-ranging and culturally diverse group of individuals. Te Kanikani believed it was relevant to perform the daily routines and conventions that living in an urban

Taiao Dance Theatre: *Whakaoho.*

context presented. Their multidisciplinary work *Concrete Tent* (1986), which examined the impact of the city on the young people who live within its boundaries, is the work most remembered from this period. The members of the company were multiracial, of varying backgrounds and dance abilities. Stephen Bradshaw led, taught and choreographed, but other members, including Rozanne Worthington, Pita Te Tau and Brigitte Te Whiti, also contributed choreographies.

In 1987, after long, gruelling regional and national tours, financial difficulties, and growing independence artistically and culturally, Te Kanikani o te Rangatahi's members decided to pursue various individual directions. Late in 1987, core Maori members Gail Richards, Pita Te Tau and Dorothy Waetford, with Stephen Bradshaw as artistic director, committed themselves to the formation of the first Maori professional contemporary dance theatre of Aotearoa. The name given to the new company was Taiao.

The company embraced Maori traditions, values and philosophy. The dancers had to be multi-skilled with training in both modern dance and in traditional Maori culture. They were selected for their ability to perform from the heart and to communicate issues of importance to them. Their "continuum dance" approach acknowledged the double spiral of time seen from the Maori perspective, the belief that we move backward into our future bringing with us our cultural traditions and knowledge, along paths laid down by our ancestors.

The development of new work was prioritised. Taiao enlisted the support of Maori theatre director Roma Potiki to jointly devise a work about colonised Maori youth. *Whakaoho (Awakening)* (1988) was a dance-theatre work that endorsed Maori language, protocols, marae (ancestral houses) and whakapapa (genealogy). In the following years, Maori choreographers were invited to make works with the company within an established and supportive environment, and these works were showcased. There were also times when a single choreographer was able to present an evening length work. Charles Koroneho presented *Waimarirangi* (1991) and Stephen Bradshaw, *Te Ao Turoa* (1990) and *Tama i te Ao Marama* (1994).

Taiao toured extensively throughout the country presenting performances, educational residencies, classes and workshops in a wide range of settings. Every time they performed, the performance space or theatre became a marae (meeting house) for them and the audience. They fostered the development of Maori modern dance and music through both experimental and main bill programmes, and received critical acclaim for their multimedia productions. Many of the now-prominent Maori choreographers, performers, musicians and artists worked on Taiao productions over the years. Merenia Gray continues to choreograph, most notably for Footnote Dance Company with *Poutokomanawa* (1993) and *Rough Fusion* (1997). Charles Koroneho has expanded his craft to include sculpture and performance art, and in 1997 presented *Te Toko Haruru: The Resounding Adze* to great critical acclaim. Others, such as Norman Potts, continue their work in traditional Maori cultural performance.

The work of Taiao has contributed to dance history in Aotearoa and has left a legacy of cultural affirmation, creativity and politics that provides guidelines for dances in this genre. Taiao has provided an alternative to ballet, modern dance and Maori competitive kapa kaka (traditional) dance for Maori performers, and has contributed a kaupapa within an evolving tradition of Maori theatre that is enduring beyond the company itself.

—Stephen Bradshaw

TAIWAN

Modern dance in Taiwan was first introduced during the Japanese occupation from 1895 to 1945, by touring Japanese dance companies, which had come under the influence of German and American modern dance of the West As early as the 1930s, Japanese modern dance pioneer Ishii Baku led his company to Taiwan, inspiring two young Taiwanese teenage girls, Tsai Ryueh and Lee Tsai-er, to travel to Tokyo to study with him. These two eventually joined Baku's company and performed in various countries in Southeast Asia around World War II. However, both Tsai and Lee returned to Taiwan after the war and pioneered the teaching and performing of modern dance, based on their studies of ballet, eurythmics, and other improvisational dance techniques known as "creative dance," with Lee teaching in the southern city of Kaoshiung, and Tsai up in Taipei.

Nevertheless, after the Nationalist government led by Chiang Kai-shek retreated to Taiwan after the Chinese Civil War in 1949, only dances that promoted politically-correct Chinese culture was encouraged. With the annual Chinese folk dance competitions sponsored by the Ministry of Defense after 1952, ballet and the surging styles of modern dance were left out. Private dance studios literally invented what they thought to be Chinese folk dance by appropriating movements from the Peking Opera, Taiwanese Opera, and other forms of Chinese performing arts. Only few dance educators such as Liu Feng-shueh could resist being drawn into this whirlpool, for modern dance and ballet were discouraged based on their foreign origins—in other words, the political climate in the 1950s delayed the prosperity of modern dance in Taiwan.

It was not until the 1960s, when closer ties with the United States were formed, that various American modern dance companies visited Taiwan as cultural ambassadors. Alvin Ailey, Paul Taylor, and José Limón were among the few creating a major impact on the local audience. Eventually, Chinese-American Al Chung-liang Huang came to Taiwan in 1966 to conduct modern dance workshops at the China Dance Arts Institute founded by Tsai Ryueh. This event drew interested aspiring dancers such as Henry Yu, Lin Hwai-min, H.T. Chen, and many others, who eventually left for the U.S. in the late 1960s to study firsthand with modern dance pioneers of the West. Ren-lu Wang, another Chinese-American who studied at the Martha Graham School also visited Taiwan in 1967 and introduced the Graham technique to Taiwan for the first time. A few years later, with the return of dancers and choreographers such as Lin, who founded the highly- influential Cloud Gate Dance Theatre in 1973, and Yu, who had became the first Chinese dancer to enter the Martha Graham company in 1974 and returned to Taiwan to found Henry Yu Dance Company in 1983, the emotionally-intense Graham technique became the stepping stone for this generation of modern dance in Taiwan.

Although Liu Feng-shueh had begun the Modern Dance Centre in 1967, promoting her own style of Chinese modern dance, based on her training of largely German-influenced modern dance taught indirectly through Japanese instructors and her own study of traditional Chinese dance, Cloud Gate remained the only professional dance company in Taiwan for 15 years until 1988. During this period, Lin addressed his social concerns through his choreography. His signature piece *Legacy* (1979) remains unsurpassed in terms of the number of people who have seen or heard of it. Premiered during the politically-sensitive time when the U.S. switched allegiance to the Communist regime of mainland China, it represented the nationalistic fervor of the people of Taiwan during that decade.

With the rising affluence of Taiwan by the 1980s, more attention was given to the arts both by the public and private sectors. The Council for Cultural Affairs was formed in 1981 and the influential New Aspects Arts Centre, a private arts management company run by composer/impresario Hsu Po-yun and musician wife Fan Man-nung, invited many top-rated international performing artists to tour Taiwan. More importantly, the rising social unrest which led to the lifting of martial law in 1987, 38 years since its implementation in 1949, enabled more freedom of expression, heralding the next generation of independent choreographers, many of whom formed their own companies around the same time Cloud Gate folded, in 1989. Ex-Cloud Gate dancers who have branched out on their own include Liou Shaw-lu who, in 1984, founded Taipei Dance Circle with his dancer-wife Yang Wan-rung; Lin Hsiu-wei, who founded Tai-Gu Tales Dance Theatre in 1988 with her husband, Peking opera actor Wu Hsing-kuo; as well as Cheng Su-chi, Wu Shu-chun, Yeh Tai-chu, and Lo Man-fei (also a former dancer with Liu Feng-Shueh), who co-founded the Taipei Crossover Dance Company in 1994.

Two other companies founded in 1989 with no direct lineage to Cloud Gate include Taipei Dance Forum, the second professional modern dance company founded by director Ping Heng, and Taos Dance Theatre, founded by anthropology-trained Tao Fu-lann. Earlier in 1983, another choreographer, Hsiao Ching-wen, a former student of Tsai Ryueh who later studied at the Merce Cunningham studio, founded a company bearing her name, and ran it with her sister Hsiao Wo-ting, Tsai's daughter-in-law. Other choreographers who got their start around 1990 include Ku Ming-shen and Yang Kuei-chuan, the former now known for her efforts in advocating contact improvisation in Taiwan, and the latter for her interest in adapting the art of Chinese calligraphy with modern dance, among others.

By 1991, the two major companies, Cloud Gate Dance Theatre and the Neo-Classic Dance Company (founded by Liu Feng-shueh in 1976 but temporarily inactive in the late 1980s when she left for England to pursue a Ph.D. in dance), were back and active. There is now a third generation of Taiwanese dancers, including Ho Hsiao-mei, Liu Shu-ying, Cho Ting-chu, and Su An-li, proving the field of modern dance is indeed rich in individualistic styles. Two prominent camps have arisen. The first, the Oriental body aesthetics camp, mostly refers to Lin Hsiu-wei, Liou Shaw-lu, and Tao Fu-lann, who base their work on meditation, tai-chi, yoga, and other Eastern methods of bodily training, in order to form a unique dance aesthetic different from the West. The other major camp belongs to choreographers such as Lo Man-fei and Sunny Pang (artistic director of the Taipei Dance Forum, brought in from Hong Kong), who feel quite at ease in making dances from Western techniques with multimedia applications, while combining contemporary urban experiences into their dances. Furthermore, various choreographers have drawn their inspiration from the indigenous cultures in Taiwan, as well as other local rituals. Yet the third or "X"generation choreographers are less burdened with such issues of cultural identity. Their works most often focus on interpersonal relationships (e.g. Cho Ting-Chu' s *Absent Partner [Oh-chueh]*), or even dances incorporating newborn babies on stage (e.g. Ho Hsiao-mei' s 1997 work *Dancing Cradles*).

The development of modern dance in Taiwan is full of possibilities. Through influences from the West (mainly the United States), Manila, and China, as well as Japan and its colonial past, individual choreographers search for identity, whether through native culture or personal experiences, and these provide them with material rich enough to not only produce interesting works, but ones that have won recognition in the international community of modern dance.

—Yatin C. Lin

TAKEI, Kei

Japanese-American dancer, choreographer, and company director

Born: Takei Keiko in Tokyo, c. 1947. **Education:** Early training included lessons at Sakaki Bara Children's Dance School (Japanese folk dance, etc.) and Kaitani Ballet school; *nihon buyo* (Japanese classical dance) with Fujima Kiyoe, 1965-67; creative dance with Kenji Hinoki; attended Juilliard School as a Fulbright scholar, 1967-69; also studied in New York at the Merce Cunningham Studio, Martha Graham School, Alwin Nikolais School, and with Alfredo Corvino (ballet), Trisha Brown, and Anna Halprin. **Family:** Married Laz Brezer, 1980. **Career:** Solo debut in New Choreographers Series at the Clark Center for the Performing Arts, 1967; first group work and premiere of first section of *Light* at Dance Theatre Workshop, 1969; formally founded dance-theater company, Moving Earth, 1975; first marathon performance, "*Light, Parts 1-9*" (7 hours), Brooklyn Academy of Music (BAM), 1975; subsequent marathons include "*Light, Parts 1-15*" (11 hours), touring U.S. and Europe, 1981; and "24 Hours of *Light* " (Walker Arts Center, Minneapolis, Minnesota, 1991); with funding from Japan-United States Friendship Commission, toured Japan for seven weeks of performances, demonstrations, workshops, and study, 1985; television appearances include *Beyond the Mainstream* for the *Dance in America* series (WNET-TV, New York), 1979; moved to Tokyo, 1992; renamed company Moving Earth Orient Sphere, 1992. Has created commissioned works for Nederlands Dans Theater, Improvisations Unlimited, Inbal Dance Theatre (Israel), Shaliko Theater Company (New York), Reinhild Hoffmann Tanztheater (Bochum, Germany), Shinkinkai Theater Company (Tokyo), and Work Media Theatre Company (Japan). **Awards:** Fulbright scholarship to study at Juilliard, 1967-68; numerous grants from the National Endowment for the Arts (NEA) and the New York State Council on the Arts; John Simon Guggenheim Foundation fellowships in choreography, 1978, 1988; Japanese Dance Critics Association Award for Most Oustanding Performance of the Year, 1979.

Works (premiered in New York City unless otherwise noted)

1967	*The Path*, Takei
	Search, Takei
1968	*Voix/ko-e*, Takei and John Wilson
	Unaddressed Letter, Takei
1969	*Light*, Part 1, Takei and dancers
	Mushihuzi, Takei and dancers
1970	*Light*, Part 2, (mus. Geki Koyama), Takei and dancers
	Lunch, Kei Takei and dancers
	Light, Part 3, (mus. Lloyd Ritter), Takei and dancers
	Light, Part 4, (mus. Lloyd Ritter), Takei and dancers
1971	*Light*, Part 5, (mus. Marcus Parsons), Takei and dancers

Light, Part 6, (mus. Jacques Coursil and Marcus Parsons III), Takei and dancers

Playing This Everyday Life, Takei and dancers

1972   *Rainbow Dances,* Takei and dancers

Talking Desert Blues, Takei and dancers

Once Upon a Time: A Journey, Takei and dancers

1973   *Light,* Part 7, ("Diary of the Field"), (mus. Spanish folk song, performed by Maldwyn Pate and Lloyd Ritter), Takei and dancers

1974   *Light,* Part 8, (mus. Japanese Buddhist chant; revised 1991, mus. by Yukio Tsuji), Takei and dancers

1975   *After Lunch,* Moving Earth

Light, Part 9, Moving Earth

Light, Part 10, ("The Stone Field"), (mus. Takei, [stone percussion performed by dancers]), Moving Earth

1976   *Light,* Part 12, ("The Stone Field"), (mus. Takei, [stone percussion performed by dancers]), Moving Earth, Graz, Austria

1978   *Variable Landscape,* Moving Earth, Minneapolis

Light, Part 11, ("The Stone Field"), (mus. Takei, [stone percussion performed by dancers]), Nederlands Dans Theatre, the Hague

1979   *Light,* Part 13, ("The Stone Field"), (mus. Takei, [stone percussion performed by dancers]), Moving Earth, Tokyo

Light, Part 14, ("Pinecone Field"), (mus. Takei [vocal], performed by dancers), Moving Earth, Johnson, Vermont

1980   *Light,* Part 15 ("The Second Windfield"), (mus. Japanese folk song, recorded wind), Moving Earth, Durham, North Carolina

1982   *The Dreamcatchers,* Improvisations Unlimited, Maryland, College Park, Maryland

Light, Part 16 ("Vegetable Fields: The First Daikon Field Solo"), (mus. Buddhist chant), Moving Earth

Light, Part 17 ("Dreamcatcher's Diary"), Moving Earth

Whirlwind Field (S'dei, Ma'Arbolet), Inbal Dance Theatre, Tel Aviv

Light, Part 18 ("Wheat Field"), (mus. David Moss), Moving Earth

Light, Part 16 ("Vegetable Fields: The Second Daikon Field Solo"), Moving Earth, Durham, North Carolina

1984   *Light,* Part 19 ("Dreamcatcher's Diary II"), Moving Earth

1985   *Light,* Part 20, ("The Diary of the Dream"), Moving Earth, Los Angeles

Evocations, Moving Earth

1986   *Light,* Part 21, ("The Diary of the Dream"), (mus. David Moss), Moving Earth

Light, Part 22, (mus. Japanese folk song), Concert Dance Company, Boston

Flower Field, Improvisations Unlimited, College Park, Maryland

Light, Part 23, ("Pilgrimage, Section I"), (mus. Michael de Roo), Moving Earth, Purchase, New York

Light, Part 23, ("Pilgrimage, Section III"), (mus. traditional Japanese drumming), Nederlands Dans Theater, the Hague

1987   *Light,* Part 23, ("Pilgrimage, Section II"), (mus. Yukio Tsuji), Moving Earth, Jerusalem

Light, Part 23, ("Pilgrimage, Sections IV & V"), Moving Earth, Jerusalem

Light, Part 24, ("Chanting Hills"), Juilliard Dance Ensemble

1988   *One Woman's Pilgrimage,* (*Light,* Part 25), Moving Earth, Cambridge, Massachusetts

One Woman's Death, (*Light,* Part 26), (mus. Yukio Tsuji), Moving Earth

1989   *The Last Rice Field,* (*Light,* Part 27), (mus. Yukio Tsuji), Moving Earth

Wild Grass River Festival, (mus. Yukio Tsuji), Moving Earth

1991   *Okome O Arau Onna (The Rice Washer),* (*Light,* Part 28) (mus. Yukio Tsuji), Moving Earth, Iwaki, Japan

Light, Part 29, (mus. Elena Chernin; revised 1992, mus. David Moss), Reinhild Hoffmann Tanztheater, Bochum, Germany

One Man's Pilgrimage, (*Light,* Part 30), (mus. Yukio Tsuji and David Moss), Moving Earth, Minneapolis, Minnesota

1994   *Nakaniwa (Time Diary),* (mus. Yukio Tsuji), Moving Earth Orient Sphere, Tokyo

1995   *Zenryoku Shiso (The Neverending Path),* (mus. Yukio Tsuji), Moving Earth Orient Sphere, Tokyo

1996   *Empyrean Passage* (*Light,* Part 31), (mus. Yukio Tsuji), Moving Earth Orient Sphere

1998   *Mahoroba no Tamago,* (mus. Taro Shinjo), Moving Earth Orient Sphere, Nagano, Japan

Publications

On TAKEI: articles—

Acocella, Joan Ross, "Reviews, New York City," *Dance Magazine,* January 1983.

Kriegsman, Alan M., "Heavenly *Earth,*" *Washington Post,* 18 March 1980.

Wagner, Ursula, "To Cross Borders," (interview with Kei Takei), *tanzAKTUELL,* December 1990.

Films and Videotapes

There are more than 80 documentary videotapes of Kei Takei's performances, covering her entire career, in the Dance Collection of the New York Public Library for the Performing Arts at Lincoln Center.

*   *   *

Kei Takei studied many forms of dance from an early age, and as a teenager found a mentor in Kenji Hinoki, one of the pioneers of experimental dance in Japan. Anna Sokolow discovered Takei during a trip to Tokyo, and recommended her for a Fulbright fellowship, which brought Takei to New York to study at the Juilliard School in 1967. Just as she had felt both tradition-bound Japanese classical dance theater and the emerging school of *but h* to be equally restrictive, Takei never felt accomplished or at home in ballet or in any of the conventional modern techniques she studied, and she struck out on her own within months of her arrival in the United States.

After making her solo debut in 1967, Takei began to work with a small group of colleagues from classes at the Henry Street Settlement House, and in 1969 premiered her first group work, simply

Kei Takei in *Empyrean Passage,* **Butoh, 1996. Photograph © Johan Elbers.**

titled *Light.* Prophetically, the dance showed four women laden with bundles struggling to begin a journey, while another squats, rocking ominously. This modest piece became the first chapter in an epic work that would by 1998 include some 31 self-contained sections—many constitute substantial pieces in themselves—a life-long artistic odyssey without precedent or peer in American dance.

The small group of friends who performed Takei's early works evolved into her company, Moving Earth, in 1975, the year of her first retrospective performance, of *Light*'s first nine sections, at the Brooklyn Academy of Music. Other important milestones in the company's history include a tour of *Light* Parts 1 through 15 in 1981, and "24 Hours of *Light,*" an uninterrupted daylong marathon of most of the work's sections, first performed in 1991. Through-out Takei's American years, Moving Earth remained a somewhat loosely organized group, with frequently changing personnel. The company, which usually numbered 10 to 14 dancers, and expanded to more than 20 for some sections of *Light,* has included actors and untrained performers as well as professional dancers. Key figures in Moving Earth have included Maldwyn Pate, Elsi Miranda, and Takei's husband (since 1980) and co-director, Laz Brezer. The company has toured to some 70 cities in the U.S. and 17 countries overseas. Since 1978 Takei has created dances, including some sections of *Light,* on companies other than her own. She has also made several pieces that aren't officially part of *Light,* though all Takei's works are stylistically akin, and comprise a single, evolving, organic whole. In 1991 Takei returned to Tokyo, and founded a new company (all Japanese actor-dancers, with the exception of Brezer), naming the group Moving Earth Orient Sphere.

Light could be described as an unfolding anthropological documentary of an imaginary archetypal human tribe, a small band migrating through a vast terrain of time and space. Many parts of the work begin with a ceremonial processional entrance, as if the dancers have trekked onstage from the last-seen section; the pieces often end the same way, with the clan marching off to *Light*'s next scene—whether a theatrical audience happens to be watching or not, the tribe's voyage continues. *Light* proceeds in a suspended, timeless realm in the ancient past, at the farthest shores of collective memory; at the same time, some of the work's sections seem to encompass entire epochs of human cultural evolution. The journey proceeds through a sequence of "fields"—fields of wind, stones, wheat, rice, vegetables, dreams—each new terrain is a symbolic space as much as landscape. Along the way *Light* encompasses an enormous wealth of mysterious ritual, as we watch the tribe play, make magic, couple, make war, mourn, worship. In the group sections, the emphasis is always on the whole community, though men and women, as in many tribal societies, frequently dance separately, witnessed by the other sex. While individual dancers at times adopt archetypal roles—shaman, seer, leader, warrior, youth, maiden, mother, crone—Takei presents neither defined characters as such nor linear story. Nonetheless, there is always a narrative pressure, a sense of mythic tale, of unfolding revelation. *Light* seems to be not so much made as remembered.

Clad almost always in simple garments of unbleached cotton, their faces and clothes occasionally marked with black paint, Takei's dancers often carry knapsacks or bulky bundles, which represent not only the material burdens necessary to sustain human life, but the weight of cultural history, memory, destiny, even time itself. The natural world within and against which they struggle is neither benevolent nor hostile, but simply implacable. Early parts of *Light,* including the several "stone fields," feature game-like competitive structures that suggest battle, as well as building, hunting, and gath-

ering. Parts 14 through 22 mainly evoke agricultural communities, often engaged in seasonal rites of planting and harvest. The pilgrimages of later sections often seem more explicitly spiritual—travels through psychic landscapes. Some darker episodes suggest descents to the underworld, or journeys through a time-warp to a devastated future. Part 31 represents a new departure: a journey through the heavens, a walk on the clouds, perhaps travel to distant planets.

Takei's movement vocabulary makes little overt use of conventional dance technique, but demands bold physicality and forthright presence, exceptional focus, concentration, and stamina, and above all a rooted imagination and radical authenticity of gesture. The typical stance is grounded, with relaxed feet kept parallel or in positions related to Asian martial arts. Takei's dancers learn her choreography as much through sequences of images as sequences of steps—unity of impulse matters more than identity of contour in unison material. Takei uses no mime; the effort in her style is always real. Her performers appear not so much to dance as to *work,* laboring at predestined tasks. In a 1990 interview with Ursula Wagner, Takei described her method "to build up the energy...of an animal and to concentrate its wildness on an issue. The body finds then its way of expression."

Takei favors an improvisational working process in which music and dance evolve together in the studio (though she uses no improvisation in performance). Her most frequent composers have been David Moss and Yukio Tsuji, and her scores typically feature drums, gongs, and other percussion, with flutes, voices, or natural sounds of wind and water. Many pieces use only silence, or sounds created by the dancers themselves—clacking stones, pounding feet, songs, shouts, cries, keens, calls. Takei's many collaborations with set and prop designer Tetsu Maeda have been widely celebrated. Most of *Light*'s components are structured in discrete blocks of tasklike activity with abrupt internal transitions. Takei often juxtaposes stillness and enigmatic slow motion with passages of blunt, driving rhythm. Though there is a recognizable "Japaneseness" in Takei's aesthetic—its blend of roughness and refinement, its decorative pictorial quality—her work transcends her cultural background, and the elements of Zen or Shinto many commentators detect are implicit, not sought for.

Though interest in the primitive dates back to the beginnings of modernism, few artists, especially in theater, have succeeded as Takei has in evoking the primeval without sanctimony or phoniness. Her elemental kinesthesia, her humor, and her gift for creating images that are vivid and specific, pregnant with symbolic resonance yet never literal, make Takei unique.

—Christopher Caines

TAMBUTTI, Susana
Argentine choreographer

Born: 4 October 1947 in Bueno Aires. **Education:** University of Buenos Aires, degree in architecture 1972; studied dance at the London School of Contemporary Dance and Martha Graham school; also studied ballet with Fergus Early and choreography with Carolyn Carlson. **Family:** Divorced; has chidren. **Career:** Co-founder and co-artistic director of Nucleodanza, beginning 1974. **Awards:** National Choreography Award for the Arts and Sciences, 1983; Estrella de Mar Award, 1990; Venice Festival Critics Award for choreography in the film *Tangos: El exilio de gardel,* 1995; Fulbright 50th Anniversary Distinguished Fellowship, 1996.

Works (selected)

1980	*Espejismos* (mus. Ethiopian folk), Nucleodanza, Buenos Aires
1981	*Pasos Perdidos* (mus. popular songs from the 1960s), Nucleodanza, Buenos Aires
1982	*Como de costumbre* (mus. Rodolfo Mederos, Astor Piazzolla), Nucleodanza, Buenos Aires
1983	*Living-Room* (mus. Edgardo Rudnitzky), Nucleodanza, Buenos Aires
1984	*Los de al lado* (mus. Edgardo Rudnitzky), Ballet Contemporáneo del Teatro Municipal General San Martín, Buenos Aires
1985	*Tangos: El exilio de Gardel* (film; dir. Pino Solanas)
1986	*La Puñalada (The Stab)* (mus. compilation by Tambutti and Anibal Zorilla), Nucleodanza, Montevideo, Uruguay
1987	*La Espera* (mus. Fisher Tull), Nucleodanza, Lisbon
1989	*Jugar con fuego (Playing with Fire)* (mus. compilation by Rudnitzky), American Dance Festival, Raleigh, North Carolina
	Patagonia Trio (mus. compilation by Runitzky), Nucleodanza, Salvado do Bahia, Brazil
1990	*Misteriosamente esto no pasa (The Mourning Kiss)* (mus. Rudnitzky), American Dance Festival, Raleigh, North Carolina
1992	*Como un pulpo (Like an Octopus)* (mus. Carla Bley, Rudnitzky), American Dance Festival, Raleigh, North Carolina
1994	*Lava* (mus. Rudnitzky), Zenon Company, Minneapolis
1995	*Ketiak* (mus. Akira Nishimura), Zenon Company, Minneapolis
1996	*Round Up the Usual Suspects* (mus. Adam, Bizet, Verdi, Stravinsky), American Dance Festival, Raleigh, North Carolina
1997	*A Certain Death* (based on *Round Up the Usual Suspects;* mus. idem), Zenon Company, Minneapolis

Publications

By TAMBUTTI: books—

Closing in on the Study of the History of Western Dance, Buenos Aires, 1995.

*   *   *

The only daughter of an immigrant mother and an Argentine father, Tambutti was born in a fashionable middle-class neighborhood in Buenos Aires during the final years of the Peronist decade of the 1940s. Educated in church schools, she studied 10 years to fulfill the humble bourgeois dream of attending the university, where, in keeping with her family's plans, she graduated in architecture. During this period, the only contact she had with dance were the classes in Argentine folklore which she took in her childhood, as did all well-educated young girls of the time.

After becoming an architect and at the suggestion of a friend on the faculty, she started taking classes in modern dance with Ana Kamien, a prestigious choreographer who worked in the revolutionary Instituto DiTella. Soon, however, what had begun as a hobby transformed into her passion. She abandoned architecture forever and dedicated herself completely to dance.

Tambutti's early pieces were interpretations of famous works of Argentine choreographers such as Oscar Araiz, Liz Jelin, Ana Kamien, and Ana Maria Stekelman, among others. In 1974, she founded with Margarita Bali the group Nucleodanza, which, considering the economic problems which Argentina suffered and suffers still, has miraculously survived until today, becoming the longest-lasting, independent contemporary dance company in the country.

Towards the end of the 1970s, during Argentina's military regime, Tambutti continued to study dance out of the country. She relocated to London and studied at the London School of Contemporary Dance. Then she moved to the United States, where she studied in Martha Graham's school.

Returning to her country at the beginning of the 1980s, she began her choreographic career. Her first works were for her own company, Nucleodanza. To this era belong works such as *Cubocubo, Espejismos,* and *Pasos perdidos,* all of an experimental nature. Tambutti received good reviews and her name began to carry weight in the dance world. In 1983, she won first prize for choreography in the Primer Concurso Nacional a las Artes y Ciencias with the work *Living Room.* This was her first work with the music of Edgardo Rudnitzky, which would accompany her through nearly all of her productions. The prize opened the door to the Ballet Contemporáneo del Teatro Municipal General San Martín, the only official modern dance company in the country, which staged the work *Los de al lado.*

Toward the end of the decade, Nucleodanza began touring various parts of the world, including France, Belgium, Germany, Austria, the Netherlands, Spain, Portugal, Hungary, Australia, Korea, and especially the United States, where Tambutti established strong ties with the American Dance Festival. This allowed her to perform many of her works in the festival and in other U.S. companies. Her most famous work, the solo *La Puñalada (The Stab),* a classic in Argentina, was danced by prestigious foreign dancers such as Carol Parker (formerly of Pilobolus) and Janet Eilber (a soloist with Martha Graham's company). This work was revived at the Kennedy Center on the same program as Martha Graham's *Lamentation* and Mary Wigman's *The Witch.*

Since 1987, Tambutti has been a professor at the University of Buenos Aires, teaching general dance theory. At the same time, she also began publishing books and articles. She is truly one of Argentina's most outstanding choreographers. Her work is marked by the permanent search of the internal conflict of the work, in whichever domain this is to be found: movement, emotion, or narrative.

—Marcelo Isse Moyano
translated by Rita Velazquez

TAMIRIS, Helen

American dancer, choreographer, and company director

Born: Helen Becker, 1905. **Education:** Studied both ballet and modern in many venues, including the Neighborhood Playhouse, Metropolitan Opera, Michel Fokine's studio, and others. **Family:**

Married to Daniel Nagrin. **Career:** Dancer, Metropolitan Opera Ballet; soloist, Bracale Opera Company, 1923; first solo performance (changing her name to Tamiris), 1927; created School of American Dance, 1929; founded Dance Repertory Theater with Graham, Humphrey, and Weidman (Agnes de Mille joined the next season), 1930; choreographer, Federal Dance Theater, 1936-39; founder/director, Tamiris' Studio Theatre, 1940-44; choreographed for Broadway, 1945-57; co-founder/director, Tamiris-Nagrin Dance Company, 1960-63. **Died:** August 1966.

Works

1927	*Florentine*
	Melancholia
	Portrait of a Lady
	Circus Sketches
	The Queen Walks in the Garden
	Three Kisses
	Two Poems
	Impressions of the Bull Ring
	Tropic
	Amazon
	Subconscious
	1927
1928	*Gayety*
	Perpetual Movement
	Country Holiday
	Hypocrisy
	Harmony in Athletics
	Negro Spirituals: Nobody Knows the Trouble I See
	Negro Spirituals: Joshua Fit de Battle ob Jericho
	Twentieth-Century Bacchante
	Prize Fight Studies
	Peasant Rhythms
1929	*American Serenade I*
	American Serenade II
	Popular Rhythms
	Dance of the City
	Negro Spirituals: Swing Low Sweet Chariot
	Revolutionary March
	Fiesta (play)
1930	*Sentimental Dance*
	Play Dance
	Romantic
	Dirge
	Triangle Dance
1931	*Woodblock Dance*
	Olympus Americanus: A 20th-Century Ballet
	Mirage
	South American Dance
	Dance of Exhuberance
	Transition
	Mourning Ceremonial
	Eroica
	Maenad
	Dance for a Holiday
	Negro Spirituals: Crucifixion
1932	*Composition for Group*
	Negro Spirituals: Git on Board, Li'l Chillun
	Negro Spirituals: Go Down, Moses
	Gris-Gris Ceremonial

1933	*Cymbal Dance*
1934	*Walt Whitman Suite*
	Toward the Light
	Group Dance
	Gold Eagle Guy (p)
1935	*Cycle of Unrest*
	Mass Study
	Dance of Escape
	Flight
	Harvest 1935
1936	*Momentum*
1937	*How Long, Brethren*
1938	*Trojan Incident (p)*
1939	*Adelante*
1940	*These Yearnings, Why Are They?*
	Floor Show
1941	*Negro Spirituals: When the Saints Go Marchin' In*
	As in a Dream
	Song of Today
	Liberty Song
1942	*Bayou Ballads*
	Negro Spirituals: Little David, Play Your Harp
	Negro Spirituals: No Hidin' Place
1943	*Porterhouse Lucy*
1944	*Marianne (musical comedy)*
	Stovepipe Hat (musical comedy)
1945	*Up in Central Park (musical comedy)*
1946	*Show Boat (musical comedy)*
	Annie Get Your Gun (musical comedy)
	Park Avenue (musical comedy)
1947	*The Great Campaign (musical comedy)*
	The Promised Valley (musical comedy)
1948	*Inside U.S.A. (musical comedy)*
1949	*Touch and Go (musical comedy)*
1950	*Great to Be Alive (musical comedy)*
	Bless You All (musical comedy)
1951	*Flahooley (musical comedy)*
1953	*Carnival in Flanders (musical comedy)*
1954	*Fanny (musical comedy)*
	By the Beautiful Sea (musical comedy)
1955	*Plain and Fancy (musical comedy)*
1957	*Memoir*
1958	*Dance for Walt Whitman*
	The Vine or the Tree
1960	*Women's Song*
1961	*Once Upon a Time. . .*
1963	*Arrows of Desire*
	Rituals
	. . .Versus. . .

Publications

Brown, Lorraine, and John O'Connor, editors, *Free, Adult, Uncensored: The Living History of the Federal Theatre Project,* Washington, DC, 1978.

*   *   *

Helen Tamiris was an exciting and original dancer, but her most enduring contribution was as a popularizer of modern dance via her evolutionary Broadway choreography that integrated dance into a musical's plot. Although peers like Martha Graham, Doris Humphrey, and Charles Weidman each did more to ensure modern dance's survival on the concert stage, Tamiris did at least as much, however, by reaching the general public through a more inclusive, accessible style of dance. Thanks in large part to Tamiris, the very idea of a Broadway musical without dance now seems absurd.

Throughout her long career, Tamiris embodied 20th-century American modernity. She was free of rigid doctrine, optimistically responsive to the demands of her environment and artistically versatile when called upon to carry the banner for modern dance. Even her stage name reflected confidence. It allegedly came from a poem about a Persian queen: "Thou art Tamiris, the ruthless queen who banishes all obstacles." If anything, Tamiris' warm vibrancy now seems too ephemeral and dependent upon the climate of her times, especially when judged against Graham's and Humphrey's cool asceticism.

From an early age, Tamiris was drawn to dance, learning both ballet and modern dance technique. Unlike other modern dance pioneers, she was successful in ballet, even touring Brazil as a second soloist with the Bracale Opera Company in 1923. By the time of her first solo performance in 1927, she was wholly committed to the crusade to reform dance. For her second solo concert, in 1928, she set forth this manifesto: "Dancing is simply movement with a personal conception of rhythm.... The dance of today must have a dynamic tempo and be vital, precise, spontaneous, free, normal, natural, and human."

This performance included two of the many Negro spirituals that were ultimately among her most enduring dances. Their success as individual works eventually led Tamiris to devise a complete suite, "Negro Spirituals" (1942). Their highly emotional content was perfect for her sweeping, dramatic style and enabled her to use dance as a persuasive tool for social change. She was the first choreographer of any race to select the spiritual for concert dance production and later became one of the first to hire dancers based on artistic needs, not their race.

Between 1927-29, Tamiris danced 27 solo dances in seven concerts, including three in Europe. She rejected traditional theatricality in favor of a more contemporary American sensibility, using jazz and music by George Gershwin. Her activist leanings were apparent even then: "No artist can achieve full maturity unless he recognizes his role as a citizen, taking responsibility, not only to think, but to act," she wrote.

Ironically, Tamiris' administrative and promotional skills and cooperative nature more than once led her to promote modern dance while her own career suffered. During 1930-31, she formed the collaborative Dance Repertory Theater with Graham, Humphrey, Weidman, and (in the second season) Agnes de Mille. Although the pooled resources of the group kept them afloat, artistic differences prevailed and each set out again on their own, more solvent than when they had started—except Tamiris.

By 1934, Tamiris was back on her feet financially, and formed her own group. During the next two years, she produced several artistic highlights, of which the lyrical *Walt Whitman Suite* (1934) was the most significant. During this time, Tamiris' philosophical differences from the new mainstream became increasingly apparent. Her work never achieved "significant form" in the eyes of the Bennington group (Graham, Humphrey, Weidman, and Hanya Holm). It was equally distant from the revolutionary dancers like Anna Sokolow, who used dance as an overtly political tool.

In 1936, however, Tamiris was recruited as a choreographer by the Federal Dance Theater of the Works Progress Administration

and, again, pledged herself to keep dancers dancing and audiences attending, arguably at the expense of her own career. There were several artistic successes nonetheless, as she later made clear: "In the 1920s, there were many times when I doubted that modern dance would ever reach a large audience. But. . .when Charles Weidman's *Candide* (1936) and my *How Long, Brethren?* (1937) and *Adelante* (1939) were presented to cheering audiences that had never seen a dance recital, I knew that the modern dance was not an esoteric passing phase of dance to be enjoyed only the cognoscenti, but one that could reach large audiences."

Following World War II, Tamiris achieved her greatest fame as a Broadway choreographer. She considered this to be a logical progression: she could choreograph, collaborate artistically, and, most importantly, promote the cause of dance by introducing it to the general public. Despite her obvious skill, Tamiris' Broadway work dimmed her luster in the eyes of those devoted solely to the concert stage. Whereas she perceived it to be an expansion of horizons, many in the dance establishment thought this new effort lacked an appropriate seriousness. The noted critic John Martin wrote in Tamiris' defense, though: "By carrying over the tenets of the modern dance, she has introduced into the musical a wonderfully frank and honest expressiveness that is quite novel."

Tamiris' premise, preceded only by Agnes de Mille in *Oklahoma* (1943) was that dance could advance the plot when used appropriately. She was an eager collaborator and thought she has much to bring to the creative process: "Too few writers really understand how much the dance can speak for them, that it can sometimes carry a plot forward with more intensity and theatricality and, in its proper place, be more eloquent than speech," she wrote. "Just as the choreographers must respect and not abuse the script, so also must the authors not degrade the dance by using it as an inane, relaxing interlude in the progress of the story."

In all, Tamiris choreographed 18 musicals between 1945-57, paving the way for Jerome Robbins' choreographic pinnacle, *West Side Story* (1957). Her first success was *Up in Central Park* (1945), which was notable for its Currier & Ives-like ballet, followed by *Annie, Get Your Gun* (1946). *Touch and Go* (1948) and *Plain and Fancy* (1955) were also well-received.

Concert work and teaching occupied her in the late 1950s. She and her husband, dancer Daniel Nagrin, led the Tamiris-Nagrin Dance Company from 1960-63. Because her style of dance was so personal and she always encouraged her students to search within themselves, not emulate her, there is no "Tamiris style." Her most identifiable legacy is indeed found on the Broadway stage. Tamiris died in August 1966, leaving modern dance much more firmly entrenched in the artistic pantheon than when she found it 40 years earlier.

—Darcy Lewis

TANGENTE
Canadian dance organization

The Tangente dance organization was founded by a group of artists in 1980 during the thick of a North American arts movement which, in Canada, was termed the "artist-run space network." The 1980s also marked the onset of a vibrant postmodern dance movement in Montreal choreography, locally called *nouvelle danse,* which today holds a prominent place on international stages. From its informal beginnings in a warehouse loft to its permanent site in a university heritage building, this energetic small-scale dance institution remains an essential catalyst and support for the development of contemporary choreography and its audiences in Montreal.

Within its structure Tangente has developed an international resource center and Quebec archive for contemporary dance, and a 100-seat laboratory performance space, Espace Tangente, in which 35 weeks of programming are presented between September and June. Complementary to its artistic functions in the community, Tangente acts as an information clearinghouse and consulting service to the dance milieu, and also serves as a dance educator to hundreds of school children invited into its theatre each year. It is this commitment to fostering an understanding of contemporary experimental dance in the wider community that links Tangente to a dozen other dance presenters across Canada in the CanDance Network (similar to National Performance Network members in the United States, kin to the regional Dance Agencies in England) of which it is a founding member.

In 1980 a two-story loft space on lower boulevard St-Laurent was transformed into a performance loft/rehearsal space, art gallery, resource center, and offices. The four founding members (Howard Abrams, Dena Davida, Louis Guillemette, Silvy Panet-Raymond) undertook to provide the burgeoning arts community with a central meeting place for dancers and Montreal's first public dance performance space. A first season of performances and workshops was launched in January 1981 with artists from Canada, the U.S. and even France; although biased towards choreography and movement-based work, programming was (and remained) interdisciplinary, and included composers, performance artists and theatre groups. In the early years, many of the performers came from outside of Quebec, but as local choreography and experimental performance flourished, the programming grew in both quantity and in local content.

Throughout the first decade, Tangente was kept moving from one space to another by uncomprehending city inspectors and landlords: rue Ste-Catherine in the center of downtown (1983-84); a third-floor loft on upper St-Laurent in the Latin Quarter (1984-86). With no permanent site from 1986 to 1991, shorter performance series were organized in several local institutions with whom Tangente created long-term associations: the Musée d'art contemporain, the Theatre Experimental des Femmes, the Maison de Culture city network. The city of Montreal finally situated Tangente in the basement of the Bibliothèque National in the French Quarter on rue St-Denis, where a last season was presented before moving to its permanent present-day quarters at 840 Cherrier, the Pavillon Latourelle of the University of Quebec and also now called Agora de la danse (literally meaning "public meeting place for dance"). The creation of this first provincial dance building in 1991 was a partnership forged through heated debate and delicate diplomacy by Tangente, the University of Quebec's dance department, and the choreographer's committee of the local dancers' association.

Over the years, Tangente's programming outlook has remained decidedly contemporary and eclectic. Performances include work from all artistic generations, tendencies, and disciplines. Each season is composed of a multitude of special projects with local and international institutions (museums, performance spaces, festivals, and artists' companies). The Moment'Homme series of men's choreographies, in November 1984, marked the first of many thematic events which later included Le Corps Politique (political dances), SaGeste (women's dances), Mue-danse (visual arts/dance fusions), Chorégraphies d'artistes (visual artists making dance), Ascendance

(culture as form and content), Drôles de danse (irony and strangeness in dance), Le Corps Electronique (electronic media in performance), Danse Incorporée (collective-made dances). Also, in this period, Tangente initiated artist exchanges with other small-scale and like-minded presenting organizations, beginning with the seminal Danséchange New York/Montreal with Performance Space 122, soon followed by exchanges with Théâtre de la Bastille in Paris, Dance Plus in Belgium, Teatro Pradillo in Madrid, DanceWorks in Toronto, and Dance Umbrella in Boston. This international activity culminated in the establishment of two permanent artist exchange and touring projects with Europe (Les Bancs d'essai internationaux and Les Repérages de Danse à Lille), and ongoing projects with the United States and Mexico (Libre-échange).

Within the larger world of 20th-century contemporary dance, Tangente can be seen as part of a collective, grass roots undertaking among artists to gain control of the production and dissemination of their work. An extensive international network of artist-run organizations has sprung up in North America, parts of Europe and South America, particularly flourishing since the 1960s, which function as community institutions to support and foster choreographic experimentation and its audiences.

—Dena Davida

TANKARD, Meryl
Australian dancer, choreographer, and company director

Born: 8 September 1955 in Darwin. **Education:** Attended Australia Ballet School. **Career:** Dancer, Australian Ballet, mid-1970s, rising to the rank of corpyhee; choreographed first work, *Birds Behind Bars,* 1977, for the Australian Ballet; member, Pina Bausch's Tanztheater Wuppertal; 1977-83; director, Meryl Tankard Company, Canberra, 1989-92; director, Meryl Tankard Australian Dance Theatre, Adelaide, from 1993 to present. **Awards:** Grant from the state of South Australia, 1996.

Works

1977	*Birds Behind Bars*
1984	*Echo Point,* independent project, Sydney
1986	*Travelling Light,* independent project, ICA, London and Edinburgh
1988	*Two Feet,* solo, World Expo on Stage, Brisbane
1989	*Banshee,* Meryl Tankard Company, Australian National Gallery, Canberra
	VX18504, Meryl Tankard Company, Canberra Theatre Center, Canberra
1990	*Kikimora,* Meryl Tankard Company, Rovereto Dance Festival, Sicily and Rome
	Nuti, Meryl Tankard Dance Company, Rovereto Dance Festival, Sicily and Rome
	Court of Flora, Meryl Tankard Company, Floriade, Canberra
1991	*Chants de mariage I & II,* Meryl Tankard Company, National Festival of Australian Theatre, Canberra
1993	*Songs with Mara,* Meryl Tankard Company, Meryl Tankard Studios, Canberra

Furioso, Meryl Tankard Australian Dance Theatre, Playhouse Festival Centre, Adelaide

Orphee et Eurydice, Meryl Tankard Australian Dance Theatre, Sydney Opera House

1994   *Aurora,* Meryl Tankard Australian Dance Theatre, Playhouse Festival Centre, Adelaide

O Let Me Weep, Meryl Tankard Australian Dance Theatre, International Barossa Music Festivsl, Barossa Valley

1995   *Possessed,* Meryl Tankard Australian Dance Theatre, International Barossa Music Festival, Barossa Valley

Rasa, Meryl Tankard Australian Dance Theatre, Adelaide Festival

1996   *The Deep End,* Australian Ballet, Melbourne

1997   *Inuk,* Meryl Tankard Australian Dance Theatre, Adelaide

Seulle, Meryl Tankard Australian Dance Theatre, International Barossa Music Festival, Barossa Valley

Publications

On TANKARD: articles—

Dance and Dancers, October 1986.
Dance and Dancers, November 1986.
Dance Australia, April/May 1996.
Dance Australia, September/November 1996.
Dance Australia, June/July 1997.
Newman, Barbara, "Speaking of Dance: Meryl Tankard," *Dancing Times,* October 1986.

*   *   *

Meryl Tankard is one of the leaders of contemporary dance in Australia in the l990s. She heads the Australian Dance Theatre, a position she took over in 1993. Prior to that she was the artistic director of the Meryl Tankard Company in Canberra from 1989 to 1992.

Tankard was born in Darwin, Australia, and grew up in Melbourne, Penang, and Newcastle. Her father was in the Air Force and young Meryl often moved as a result of her father's work. Like many military children she grew up alone even though she had two older sisters. Dance was something she felt she could hold onto as her family tranferred from one posting to another. Tankard began taking ballet classes and enjoyed the discipline of the routine. Her teachers were stern and demanding and Tankard met their requirements with a drive to succeed. It wasn't until many years later that she realized it was possible to enjoy the ballet.

Tankard's hard work paid off when she was accepted into the Australian Ballet School and later graduated into the Australian Ballet in 1974. The rigidity of classical ballet training and the purely classical repertory of the Australian Ballet left Tankard searching for more, however. Early encouragement came from Anne Wooliams, the director of the Australian Ballet from 1976 to 1977. Wooliams thought Tankard could be a choreographer. Tankard's first work, for the Australian Ballet, was entitled *Birds Behind Bars* and featured three women on pointe doing the cha-cha. The music was from Soweto, South Africa. Tankard received a grant from the company to travel to Europe to look at other dance companies. Using the grant money and her own funds, Tankard traveled to Rome, London, France, Holland, and Germany. At the time her intention was

to observe ballet companies and study. A friend from Australia suggested she take a look at German choreographer Pina Bausch's company. Tankard attended some performances and liked what she saw. Bausch's approach seemed to epitomize theater to the young Tankard, who auditioned for the company and was accepted. Tankard subsequently became one of Pina Bausch's performers.

Tankard enjoyed the improvisational approach employed by Bausch and the contribution each dancer made to the creation of a work. What appeared to be game-playing was in fact very hard work, Tankard explained, as Bausch urged her dancers to dig deeper and deeper for something new to express. In the long run Tankard found the work regimen of the Bausch company grueling and the lenghty running times of its performances even more demanding than the double Wednesday and Saturday bills of the Australian Ballet. The violent emotions dancers were required to transmit was also draining, Tankard later noted.

Tankard made her way back to Australia in 1982 with the Pina Bausch company when it appeared at the Adelaide Festival. Given a grant to choreograph a work of her own, Tankard decided to leave Bausch and stay in Australia to pursue her own choreography. Her first work upon returning home was *Echo Point* (1984). It deals with growing up within Australia's beach culture. *Two Feet* (1988) grew from Tankard's experiences as a ballet student. Another early work, *Travelling Light* (1986) was billed as a "dance theater cabaret" and involved Tankard and four males traveling around Australia as they explored the concept of being "en voyage." The work featured a mixture of song and dance, movement and talking. According to critic Robert Shaw in *Dance and Dancers,* "the dance did not amount to much but formed part of a lively, individual and likeable show." Tankard initially appeared in her works but soon decided she cared more for directing than dancing.

Tankard had a prolific period in Canberra as head of her own company beginning in 1989. Most of her work from this time was heavily based on images, as evidenced in her collaborations with Regis Lansac, a French born photographer and painter. These pieces introduced the effect of photographic images projected onto still and moving bodies.

Bausch's influence can be seen in Tankard's work in that her individual style of dance-movement does not fit any generally recognized category. In fact, Tankard's choreography often does not resemble dance in any conventional sense. Like Bausch's work, Tankard's choreography is made up of gestures that range from the banal to the sublime. The resulting work "bombards the senses and besieges the emotions."

Since moving to Adelaide in 1993, Tankard has experimented with a more strongly based dance movement. In *Furioso,* she tried to extend the range of movement of her dancers through the use of ropes. The dancers are suspended from ropes and are airborne for long stretches of the work. Tankard's choice of topics also ranges far and wide. In *Aurora* (1994), Tankard set the story of Sleeping Beauty, one of the most famous stories in classical ballet, in a postmodernist version.

Despite the fact that Tankard's movements look simple and easy to do, only well-trained dancers can execute her choreography. Her movements require supreme control and the ability to repeat tiny details from performance to performance. She has also called upon her dancers to speak, sing, and sometimes scream during the course of a piece. A memorable Tankard work was her 1990 piece, *Nuti.* It was inspired by images of daily life as depicted in ancient Egyptian friezes. The 40-minute work takes its name from the name the ancient Egyptians gave to the active power which breathed life into the dead. Tankard used her dancers to bring the friezes—Lansac's slides of Egyptian sculpture and paintings projected on the floor, back and sides of the stage—to life. The dancers, with upper bodies plastered in white makeup and lower bodies covered in skirts, entered the dancing space slowly and in profile. The lighting gave their bodies the appearance of stone. Sometimes the dancers' slow, intensely controlled movements broke into frenzied motions. At times, the women came forward and let out a chorus of long screams, like the cats the Egyptians worshipped. At the end, the dancers—who had no physical contact with one another—retreated toward the projected friezes. They waved and blew breaths to the audience as they departed. The music was provided by flutes, gongs, stringed instruments, and resonating bowls.

Kikimora, another work from 1990, developed from dancers' stories about their childhood as told during rehearsals. Tankard used the grotesque black-and-white makeup devised by Mikhail Larionov for a Russian folk character in Massine's *Contes Russes* (1917). In her work, Tankard recalled the *Kikimora* of Russian folktales, a wicked, evil, charming, and troublemaking figure. Sometimes she was as small as a thumb, while at other times she could be invisible. Tankard tried to make her dancers look small by having them walk on bent legs on the outer soles of their feet. They wore white face makeup with harsh red lipstick. A projection on the back of the stage showed hundreds of dolls staring emptily at the audience. A Nanny figure—on platform shoes—accompanied them. She wore the grotesque *Kikimora* makeup. All the costumes were in shades of black, grey, or white. The children played games which combined innocence and wickedness. Cruelty is never far from the children's rope-jumping or skipping games. The audience was led to believe that the children, like the gruesome-looking Nanny, are *Kikimora,* too. In the words of reviewer Patricia Laughlin *Kikimora* "is both amusing and entertaining but with a black undercurrent to the humor."

In 1993, Tankard choreographed *Songs with Mara,* a theater/dance work to 15 songs of Mara Kiek, an Australian musician who specializes in the folk music of Bulgaria. The images of women's hair—wet, dry, plastered on the face, or swinging free—made this work unique. Much of the choreography derived from real experiences developed during rehearsals with Tankard's dancers. While men beat drums and sing, six women improvise dances in which they rock and sway, advance, retreat, and glance at the audience.

In *The Deep End,* a work choreographed for the Australian Ballet in 1996, Tankard set her dance in and around a swimming pool. The music varied from the cha-cha to a string quartet by Michael Nyman. The dancers moved across a bridge that traverses high up under the arch of the stage until one of them falls into the "pool" which is the stage. Harnesses and ropes attached to the dancers send them hurtling into the void. Several themes unfolded: a drowning girl drifts in deep water. Her boyfriend tries to save her but she floats away leaving him grieving. A solo of rippling floor movements and yearning jumps registers his emotion. The work closes in a dance for three girls attached to ropes manipulated from the ground by their male partners.

Tankard quickly realized that her style of movement posed problems for many viewers both in Australia and abroad. According to Tankard, her style is just another way of dancing. The trouble with people, in Tankard's view, is that they want to be able to label something as ballet, or cabaret, or a send-up. Getting inspiration from life, from what you see in the streets, is what appeals to Tankard.

—Adriane Ruggiero

TANZTHEATER

The most universal definition that the term Tanztheater ("dance theater") brings to mind is: the union of genuine dance and theatrical methods of stage performance, creating a new, unique dance form (especially in Germany), which, in contrast to classical ballet, distinguishes itself through an intended reference to reality.

The term had already been used by members of the German expressive dance movement of the 1910s and 1920s who wished to distance themselves from the traditions of classical ballet. Rudolf von Laban, the most important theorist of expressive dance, used the term for the dance culture he was to create. Through dance, he hoped to unite all art media and achieve an all-embracing, radical change in humankind. According to Laban, dance theater, which he understood to be an interdisciplinary total art form, should allow one to be drawn into an inherent eurythmic harmony which is then expressed on stage.

Dance should primarily be an expression of inner emotion and a certain spiritual perspective, yet must in the process advance to an intimately personal level. Through his dance-theater concept, Laban freed dance from the rigidity history had imposed upon it, at the same time creating a new image of mankind. Just as classical ballet, which arose from royal tradition, mainly focused on the harmonious representation of fairy-tale-like themes, Laban re-opened to dance the entire spectrum of movement and a broad palette of expressive possibilities. The idea of a flexible torso as the central origin of movement established an autonomic individual free of all external constraints. This means man is free, only committed to his own experience, which the dance artist should formulate in intimately personal works.

Rudolf von Laban's dance concept became the springboard of modern dance, and his influence would be felt far beyond German borders and reach even the young dance choreographers of the late 1960s and early 1970s. Laban's pupil Kurt Jooss functioned as the principal connecting link between generations. Just as Laban was mainly the guiding theorist, Jooss proved himself as a practitioner of the new dance theater. While basing his choreography on Laban's analysis of movement, he also incorporated elements of ballroom dance as well as classical ballet, which he considered to be one of the traditional dance forms. Jooss developed a narrative form of dance theater, not based on fairy tales, but invariably on real people in real-life situations. In his pieces, he began with everyday human behavior and attempted to work it out via dance. For Jooss, every movement could become a dance movement, without belonging to a predetermined set of rules such as those imposed by classical dance.

In 1927, Kurt Jooss became the head of the dance department at the Essen Folkwang Academy, but Hitler's seizure of power forced him to emigrate to England in 1933. He returned to Germany in 1949 and immediately began to rebuild his company and the Folkwang Academy. He continued teaching until 1968, establishing in Essen one of the most significant German schools of contemporary dance, which would produce important pioneers of the new dance generation (such as Pina Bausch, Reinhild Hoffmann and Susanne Linke).

The forerunners of the new dance theater also felt indebted to Rudolf von Laban's teachings, but they utilized the system's flexibility to develop a completely new and different style. The integration of everyday movements remained important, the processing of social issues, as well as the rejection of toe dance. New elements included the use of speech and song. However, the doors to theater were primarily opened as the result of a resuscitation of trivial dance tradition (such as revue, vaudeville, and music hall) and the collage technique, the most important style characteristic of the entire modern age. With these methods, which were linked to create freely associated imagery chains and movement sequences, a new generation of choreography once again began to confront the problems of the real world. In the words of Pina Bausch, they were no longer mainly interested in *how* people move, but *what* moves them.

One of the first to experiment with the new form was Austrian-born Johann Kresnik. Inspired by the student protests of the late 1960s, he sought expressive forms for a politically engaged dance theater. In 1968, he became the director of the Bremen Ballet, initially writing aggressive political revues for them, bringing together widely diverse styles and techniques, among others, jazz dance, which was still new at that time. Using an analytical social critique as a starting point, as in *"Pigasus"* (1970), depicting an America under Richard Nixon, he sought to discuss the latest political events, which he knew how to intensify provocatively. Traditional ballet classics were at most used for ironic titles, such as *Schwanensee AG (Swan Lake Inc.)* (1971). Fairies and fantasy tales were replaced by a preoccupation with current events, often in the agitprop tradition of the Weimar Republic. Via Heidelberg, a revisit to Bremen, and a new venture at the Berlin People's Stage, Kresnik developed his own version of what he termed choreographic theater. The reoccurring topics were the principal grievances of the student movement: the confrontation of the National Socialist past ("family dialogue") and capitalism ("sellout"). In addition, Kresknik was repeatedly involved with artist biographies, which he portrayed either as social victims (*Sylvai Plath, Pasolini*), or aggressors *(Ernst Jünger, Leni Riefenstahl).* In his pieces, he often combined actors and dancers, a collage that produced entertaining yet provoking revues that sought to confront the audience and initiate political engagement.

Gerhard Bohner developed another variety of dance theater. Especially in his solos, he devoted himself to intricate movement studies, following the movement logic of a theme and its variations, closely adhering to the theories of Rudolf von Laban. Although often conflicting with stage designers and composers, Bohner found a sober form of self-reassurance in which the individual relates himself to space and thus to the world, quite in contrast to the emotion generally evident in dance theater.

It was Folkwang graduate Pina Bausch who helped the new German dance theater become firmly established and find international recognition. Directress of the Dance Theater Wuppertal since 1973, she has executed the most radial break with conventional ballet and given dance a new form of expression by linking the most diverse scenic themes and eliminating disciplinary boundaries. In accordance with Laban's dictum, in which any movement can be dance, Pina Bausch jarred the conventional comprehension of dance as few before her had done. Often reduced to minimalistic motions, carried out in a sitting or kneeing position, dance was liberated from all vanity and superficiality and once again became an expression of inner emotion, as the expressive dancers had previously done in an entirely different manner.

Similar to Pina Bausch, the Folkwang graduate Reinhild Hoffmann also used the specifically female experience as a starting point for her choreographic works. Later, however, she integrated conventional dance into her productions. After making her breakthrough with *Solo mit (with) Sofa* (1977) and an appointment to head the Bremen Ballet (1978-86, thereafter in Bochum), she developed a style distinguished by extremely picturesque tableaux that repeat-

edly flow into choreographed solo and group scenes. In her earlier works, such as *Hochzeit (Wedding), Unkrautgarten (Weed Garden),* or *Callas,* a psychological symbolism dominates, particularly emphasizing the limitations of female fantasy and lifestyle. Reinhild Hoffmann further developed the theme in later pieces, expanding it into a social panorama. A binding corset, similar to the one used in Kurt Jooss' *Pavane auf den Tod einer Infantin (Pavane to the Death of an Infanta),* represents rigid formal behavior. In contrast to Pina Bausch's continuous struggle to overcome communication breakdown, Hoffmann depicts the freezing and atrophy of human warmth and affection under the dictatorship of inadequate or archaic social rules. Since 1995, she has been living and choreographing in Berlin, once again concentrating on solo work. An earlier characteristic of her work, the examination of materials (a sofa, paper dresses, stones, boards), gains importance once more. Similar to Gerhard Bohner in his later solos, Reinhild Hoffmann pursues a meticulously detailed study of movement, reduced to a minimum and carried out with the utmost concentration.

For Susanne Linke, the third dance-theater pioneer from the Folkwang Academy, the feminine standpoint again plays an important role. The central themes of her choreography are the uneven distribution of power between the sexes and the meaningless repetition of a woman's daily routine, which she expresses predominantly through dance. However, Susanne Linke has thus far found international recognition as a soloist.

Since the mid-1960s, the new dance theater movement in Germany has led to the founding of numerous independent companies, now totaling more than 200. Alternative stages such as Berlin's Hebbel Theater, the Frankfurt Mouson Tower, or the Hamburg Kampnagel Factory have developed into centers for a new contemporary dance. Additional choreographers have sprung from the Essen Folkwang Academy, now firmly established in theaters: Urs Dietrich, Joachim Schloemer (first in Ulm, later in Weimar, now in Basel) and Daniel Goldin (in Muenster). Former dancers of the Wuppertal Dance Theater founded ensembles in their native countries, such as the now internationally recognized Meryl Tankard of Australia. In the 1970s and 1980s, dance theater influenced and formed international development by representing a new aesthetic and realistic form of contemporary dance. The immense variety of styles in dance theater, movement theater, choreographic and physical theater can be traced back to the stimulus provided by the pioneers of the new German dance theater. For the second time, it marks a caesura in international dance development, after the expressive dance of the early decades of this century. It marks the return to the body, not as a mere medium, but as the source of one's own story.

—Norbert Servos

TAYLOR, Paul

American dancer, choreographer, and company director

Born: 29 July 1930 in Englewood, Pennsylvania. **Education:** Attended Syracuse University; left to study dance, first at the American Dance Festival (New London, Connecticut); studied in New York at Juilliard, Metropolitan Opera Ballet School, Martha Graham School of Contemporary Dance. **Career:** Dancer, Merce Cunningham Dance Company, 1953-54; also danced with the companies of Pearl Lang and Anna Sokolow; founded the Paul Taylor Dance Company, first choreography, 1954; dancer, Martha Graham Dance Company, 1955-62; guest artist, New York City Ballet, *Episodes* (Balanchine and Graham), 1959; published his memoirs, *Private Domain,* 1987; formed Taylor 2, 1993; continues to teach and choreograph. **Awards:** Guggenheim choreographic fellowships, 1961, 1966, 1983; Théâtre des Nations Dance Festival (Paris), best choreographer, 1962; named "Dancer of the Year" by London's *Dance and Dancers,* 1965; Critic's Art Circle of Chile award, 1965; Capezio Award, 1967; Brandeis University Creative Arts Award, 1978; *Dance Magazine* Award, 1980; Samuel H. Scripps/American Dance Festival Award, 1983; Officer, Order of Arts and Letters (France), 1984; MacArthur Foundation "Genius Award,"1985; New York State Governor's Arts Award, 1987; autobiography, *Private Domain,* nominated by National Book Critics Circle as the most distinguished biography, 1987; New York City Mayor's Award, 1989; member, American Academy and Institute of Arts and Letters, 1989; Commander, Order of Arts and Letters (France), 1990; Emmy award for *Speaking in Tongues,* 1992; Kennedy Center Honors, Washington, D.C., 1992; National Medal of Arts, awarded by President Clinton, 1993; Algur H. Meadows Award for Excellence in the Arts, 1995; honored for outstanding achievement, Library of Congress' Scholarly Programs and Marquis Who's Who, 1995; Certificate of Appreciation, signed by New York Mayor Guiliani, 1997; honorary degrees from Connecticut College, Duke University, and several others. **Company website:** http://www.ptdc.org.

Works

1954	*Jack and the Beanstalk* (mus. Gubernick), New York
1955	*Circus Polka* (later retitled *Little Circus*; mus. Stravinsky), solo, New York
1956	*The Least Flycatcher* (mus. Rauschenberg), New York
	3 Epitaphs (mus. New Orleans jazz, Laneville-Johnson Union Brass Band), New York
	Untitled Duet (no music), New York
	Tropes (mus. taped folk), New York
	Obertura Republicana w/Remy Charlip, Marian Sarach, David Vaughan, James Waring (mus. Chavez), New York
1957	*The Tower* (mus. Cooper), New York
	Seven New Dances, New York
	Epic (mus. telephone signal)
	Events I (mus. wind sounds)
	Resemblance (mus. Cage)
	Panorama (mus. heartbeats)
	Duet (mus. Cage)
	Events II (mus. rain sounds)
	Opportunity (accompaniment—noise)
1958	*Rebus* (mus. Hollister), Brunswick, New Jersey
	Images and Reflections (mus. Feldman), New York
1960	*Option* (mus. Maxfield), New York
	Images and Reflections (mus. Feldman), duet, New York
	Meridian (mus. Boulez, ensemble, Feldman), trio, Spoleto
	Tablet (mus. Hollister), duet, Spoleto
	The White Salamander for Netherlands Ballet (mus. Stockermans), Amsterdam
1961	*Fibers* (mus. Schönberg), New York
	Insects and Heroes (mus. McDowell), New London, Connecticut
	Junction (mus. Bach), New York

1962	*Tracer* (mus. Tenny), Paris
	Aureole (mus. Handel), New London, Connecticut
	Piece Period (mus. Vivaldi, Telemann, Haydn, and others), New York
1963	*La Negra* (mus. Mexican folk), Mexico City
	Poetry in Motion w/Katherine Litz (mus. Leopold Mozart), New York
	Scudorama (mus. Jackson), New London, Connecticut
	Party Mix (mus. Haieff), New York
1964	*The Red Room* (mus. Schuller), Spoleto
	Duet (mus. Haydn), Minneapolis
1965	*9 Dances with Music by Corelli* (mus. Corelli), New York
	Post Meridian (new version of *The Red Room*; mus. Lohoeffer de Boeck), New York
	From Sea to Shining Sea (mus. Ives, later McDowell), New York
1966	*Orbs* (in two acts; mus. Beethoven), the Hague
1967	*Agathe's Tale* (mus. Surinach), New London
	Lento (mus. Haydn), New London
1968	*Public Domain* (mus. McDowell), New York
1969	*Private Domain* (mus. Xenakis), New York
	Duets (mus. medieval), New London
	Churchyard (mus. Savage), New York
1970	*Foreign Exchange* (mus. Subotnick), Washington, D.C.
	Big Bertha (mus. St. Louis Melody Museum collection of band machines; arr. McDowell), Detroit
1971	*Book of Beasts* (mus. various), New London
	Fêtes (mus. Debussy), Burnaby, British Columbia
1972	*Guests of May* (mus. Debussy), Worchester, Massachusetts
1973	*American Genesis,* Boston
	The Creation (mus. Bach)
	Before Eden (mus. Haydn)
	So Long Eden (mus. Fahey)
	West of Eden (mus. Martinu)
	Noah's Minstrels (mus. Gottschalk)
1974	*Sports and Follies* (Company; mus. Satie), Lake Placid, New York
	Untitled Quartet (mus. Stravinsky), Brockport, New York
1975	*Esplanade* (mus. Bach), Washington, D.C.
	Runes (mus. Busby), Lake Placid, New York
1976	*Cloven Kingdom* (mus. various arr. McDowell), New York
	Polaris (mus. York), Newport, Rhode Island
1977	*Images* (mus. Debussy), New York
	Dust (mus. Poulenc), New York
	Aphrodisiamania (mus. *Golden Oldies of the Renaissance,* York), New York
1978	*Airs* (mus. Handel), New York
	Diggity (mus. York), Amherst, Massachusetts
1979	*Nightshade* (mus. Scriabin), New York
	Profiles (mus. Radzynski), Durham, North Carolina
1980	*Le Sacre du Printemps (The Rehearsal),* (mus. Stravinsky), New York
1981	*Arden Court* (mus. Boyce), New York
	House of Cards (mus. Milhaud), New York
1982	*Lost, Found and Lost* (mus. wallpaper music orchestrated by Donald York), New York
	Mercuric Tidings (mus. Shubert), New York

Paul Taylor Dance Company: *Equinox.* **Photograph © Beatriz Schiller.**

1983	*Musette* (mus. Handel), New York
	Sunset (mus. Elgar), New York
	Snow White (mus. York), New York
	Equinox (mus. Brahms), Washington, D.C.
1984	*... Byzantium* (mus. Varèse), New York
1985	*Roses* (mus. Wagner), New York
	Last Look (mus. York), New York
1986	*Ab Ovo Usque Ad Mala (From Soup to Nuts),* (mus. P.D.Q. Bach), New York
	A Musical Offering (mus. Bach), New York
	solo from *Episodes* (Balanchine, reconstructed by Taylor for Peter Frame, New York City Ballet)
1987	*Kith and Kin* (mus. Mozart), New York
	Syzygy (mus. York), New York
1988	*Brandenburgs* (mus. Bach), New York
	Counterswarm (mus. Ligeti), New York
	Danbury Mix for New York City Ballet (mus. Ives), New York
	Speaking in Tongues (mus. Matthew Patton), Philadelphia

1989	*Minikin Fair* (mus. Koblitz, Wieselman, Spae), New York
	The Sorcerer's Sofa (mus. Dukas), Washington, D.C.
1990	*Of Bright and Blue Birds and the Gala Sun* (mus. York), New York
1991	*Fact and Fancy* (mus. jazz, reggae), Durham, North Carolina
	Company B (mus. Andrews Sisters), Houston Ballet, Washington, D.C.
1992	*Oz* for White Oak Dance Project (mus. Horvitz)
1993	*A Field of Grass* (mus. Harry Nilsson), New York
	Spindrift (Company; mus. Schönberg), Durham, North Carolina
1994	*Funny Papers* (mus. novelty tunes), New York
	Moonbine (mus. Debussy), New York
1995	*Offenbach Overtures* (mus. Offenbach), New York
1997	*Eventide* (mus. Ralph Vaughan Williams), New York
	Prime Numbers (mus. Israel), New Delhi, India
	Piazzolla Caldera (Company; mus. Piazzolla), Durham, North Carolina

Publications

By TAYLOR: book—

Private Domain, New York, 1987.

By TAYLOR: article—

"Portrait of the Artist as Two Young Men," *Dance Magazine,* January 1993.

On TAYLOR: books—

Anderson, Jack, *The World of Modern Dance: Art Without Boundaries,* Iowa City, 1997.
Coe, Robert. *Dance in America,* New York, 1985.
Cohen, Selma Jeanne (ed.), *The Modern Dance: Seven Statements of Belief,* Middletown, CT., 1966.
Hodgson, Moira, *Quintet: Five American Dance Companies,* New York, 1976.
Lyle, Cynthia, *Dancers on Dancing,* New York and London, 1977.
Mazo, Joseph H., *Prime Movers: The Makers of Modern Dance in America,* New York, 1977.
McDonagh, Don, *The Rise and Fall and Rise of Modern Dance,* New York, 1970.

On TAYLOR: articles—

Anderson, Jack, "Paul Taylor: Surface and Substance," *Ballet Review,* 1977-78.
Barnes, Clive, "Paul Taylor," *Ballet Review,* 1967.
McDonagh, Don, "Paul Taylor in Orbit," *Dance Scope,* Fall 1966.
Rosen, Lillie F., "Talking with Paul Taylor," *Dance Scope,* Winter/Spring, 1979.

*   *   *

The career of dancer and choreographer Paul Taylor is characterized by an impressive diversity of artistic expression. Beginning as the darling of the avant-garde in the 1950s, then moving into more traditional modern forms, Taylor has spent his career stretching his expressive range and striking a balance that is uniquely his own. It's this wide scope of his choreographic career that makes Taylor such an interesting artist, one whose work continues to resonate with balletomanes and modern dance enthusiasts alike.

Paul Taylor was born in 1930 in Edgewood, Pennsylvania, and grew up in and around Washington, D.C. Originally interested in visual art, Taylor attended Syracuse University where he studied painting and supported himself through an athletic scholarship in swimming. After observing dance classes and engaging in some student work during his junior year, Taylor decided to become a dancer. Though he was 22 years old at the time and virtually untrained, he followed his intuition and left the University at the end of the year, abandoning both scholarship and degree to pursue a career in dance. Before making his way to New York, Taylor spent the summer in New London, Connecticut, at the American Dance Festival, where he made the acquaintance of Martha Graham and had his first true experience on stage in a student performance of two Doris Humphrey works.

That Taylor's training, performing, and choreographing all began within the same few years testifies to his faith and determination to become a dancer. Upon his arrival in New York in 1952, Taylor secured scholarships from the Juilliard School, the Metropolitan Opera Ballet School, and the Martha Graham School of Contemporary Dance. His early training was in Graham technique and in Cecchetti-style ballet taught by Alfred Corvino, Margaret Craske, and Antony Tudor. Taylor began his professional career in 1953, when he joined the fledgling Merce Cunningham Company; he went on to dance in the companies of Pearl Lang, Anna Sokolow, and then as a soloist with the Martha Graham Dance Company from 1955 to 1962, creating and performing some of the most important roles in Graham's repertory.

Taylor received round praise for his dancing; critics especially noted that this powerfully-built dancer exhibited a muscular command and control on stage yet moved with lyricism and grace. These qualities caught the eye of George Balanchine, who in 1959 featured Taylor as a soloist in *Episodes,* a rare collaborative effort between dance greats Graham and Balanchine. Aside from the Webern score, the only thing both choreographers had in common was dancer Paul Taylor, who was featured in both sections. This was the first collaboration of its kind, and Taylor was under pressure to make a good showing for modern dance; that he was so well-received was a feather in his cap.

Taylor's career as a choreographer began in these same few years, though critics did not greet his first endeavors with the same hearty response they did his dancing. In 1954, Taylor left Cunningham's company to form his own group, the Paul Taylor Dance Company. The company's first performances were in the shared concerts organized by James Waring's Dance Associates. Taylor's initial process was reminiscent of Graham's beginnings in the 1920s— both artists stripped away the elaborations of the modern style in order to find something basic from which to work. But where Graham had used breath and pelvic tension as her basic tenets, Taylor found his muse in pedestrian movement. He was very much influenced at the time by the developments in the visual arts, namely the avant-garde. Artist Robert Rauschenberg, Taylor's acquaintance and collaborator for years to come, was experimenting in the mid-1950s with landscaped plots of earth as a kind of "found" painting. Taylor's approach to dance was similar in that he used movements found in everyday urban life—standing, sitting, or waiting for the bus. This line of development, now known as his radical experimentalist phase, culminated in Taylor's first legitimate concert, his famous 1957 performance at the 92nd Street YM-YWHA entitled *Seven New Dances.*

What Taylor presented in his concert completely baffled the traditionalists. In one piece, Taylor stood in a business suit making small gestural changes to the accompaniment of a telephone. A dog was introduced to the stage in *Resemblance,* and one piece was an exercise in complete stillness. It was an experiment Taylor felt compelled to carry out, though it won him little praise. Critic Walter Terry headlined his response "Experiment? Joke? War of Nerves?" and accused Taylor of trying to drive him insane. A few weeks later, Louis Horst published his now famous review in the *Dance Observer*: four inches of blank space with Horst's initials at the bottom.

Taylor admits in a 1993 article in *Dance Magazine,* "I had . . . assumed, perhaps wrongly, that I had earned the right to throw technical brilliance out the window. I had not learned that, as sublime as simplicity may be, it can produce snores." Taylor not only learned the importance of audience but increased his awareness of the communicability of dance by discerning the inherent drama of gesture. The discovery of theatrical possibilities in "found"

Paul Taylor Dance Company: *Sunset.* **Photograph © Beatriz Schiller.**

movement was one he would return to again and again throughout his career.

In 1962 Taylor did an apparent about-face with *Aureole*, a light, lyrical piece set to music by Handel and so classical in temperament it has been likened to the classical "ballet blanc." Those who had connected with Taylor as an experimental felt alienated and the more traditional moderns felt it was now safe to call him their own. Yet Taylor never remained in one genre long enough to warrant categorization. The vast scope of his choreographic work reveals Taylor as an unpredictable artist of many voices. His work ranges from lyrical to grotesque, narrative to abstract, and like many of his generation, Taylor's pieces explore community and social interaction, in his case with an astute and ironic eye toward our animal nature. Don McDonagh, in his *The Rise and Fall and Rise of Modern Dance,* describes *Insects and Heroes* (1961) as "a dance focused on the balance point where the human and not-so-human meet." In *Scudorama* (1963), Taylor's dancers are reduced to sub-human figures, scuttling and slithering across the ground. Most amusing, perhaps, is the duet of human posturing in *Speaking in Tongues* (1988), where Taylor drives home his point with a musical score containing barnyard noises. Taylor's work can be serious too, but unlike the stormy psychological terrain of Graham's work, Taylor handles his serious subjects with a light touch. Then there's his interest in the vernacular, coupled with his theatrical sensibil-

ity; his dancers may show off their grace and virtuosity only to land downstage right, standing in profile and tapping their feet, humans waiting impatiently for the bathroom.

For all the diversity in his work, Taylor's choreography speaks with a clear and distinctive voice. His innate musicality gives to his dances a naturalness and organic unity as evident in his pieces set to Bach as in his compositions to John Cage (and his musical range is that broad). His movement vocabulary, which draws its material from ballet, modern, and pedestrian movement, is executed with a weightedness that is unmistakably Taylor. The company style has been influenced, too, by Taylor's own movement preferences; he has infused his dancers with the same qualities he himself exhibited on stage: athleticism, strength, lyricism, and exuberance. Many of the Taylor dancers stand out as renowned performers, among them Bettie de Jong, Christopher Gillis, and Kate Johnson. Others have gone on to become distinguished choreographers in their own right: Twyla Tharp, Dan Wagoner, Senta Driver, Laura Dean, and David Parsons, to name a few.

Taylor's sweeping choreographic career proves confusing to some, but on the first page of his autobiography *Private Domain* (1987), Taylor tells us he is, "proud to be a plurality—ambivalent and inexplicable maybe, yet definitely a group—a whole band of criss-crossing travelers unto myself." He even has a named alter ego, Dr. George Tacet, with whom he not only credits numerous costume designs but has ongoing conversations and disagreements. This ability to give expression to the different parts of his person parallels his artistic path and reveals the internal synthesis of Taylor's many-voiced artistry.

Well into its fourth decade, the Paul Taylor Dance Company remains one of the most well-liked and highly respected modern dance companies, both in the U.S. and abroad. The company continues to do extensive touring and has, to date, completed more than 50 overseas tours. With the formation of Taylor 2 in 1993, the artist's works have reached an even greater audience. As one component in a project to preserve Taylor's works, the smaller company not only gives performances and lecture/demonstrations, but also restages earlier works and performs pieces not in the current repertory. In 1994 Taylor 2 performed in six African nations and the 1996-97 season found the company in Estonia, Latvia, and Lithuania. Numerous works can be found in the repertories of over 50 companies worldwide, among them the Royal Danish Ballet, American Ballet Theatre, and London Contemporary Dance Theatre.

Taylor remains today a prolific choreographer and his catalogue of works numbers well over 100. Widely recognized as a formative voice in contemporary art and culture, Taylor is the recipient of many prestigious awards including three Guggenheim fellowships and an Emmy award. But of all his accomplishments, perhaps most impressive is Taylor's ability to follow his own intuition. He succeeds again and again in doing what so many of us long to do, express the many parts of ourselves in the space of one lifetime. That his career has enjoyed such variety of expression—and that he's made a cohesive synthesis out of his many artistic voices—makes Paul Taylor a formidable, likable, accessible, and human figure in the world of modern dance.

—Siobhán Scarry

TECHNOLOGY AND MODERN DANCE

"Dance and Technology" is a term used to describe the hybrid forms that occur when dance in the kinesthetic form is mediated by contemporary technologies such as video, midi interfaces, interactivity, and computer-controlled environments. One of the most well-known applications of technology to dance and specifically choreography, is the *Lifeforms* three-dimensional human animation software program developed by Tom Calvert of Simon Fraser University in Vancouver, British Columbia. Though limited in its applications, *Lifeforms* has gained notoriety due in part to Merce Cunningham's use of the program to choreograph a number of dances for the stage including *Trackers* and others. Cunningham's contribution to dance and technology is lifelong; he began experimenting with film and video in the early 1960s, first with Charles Atlas and later with Elliot Caplan, and has created some of the most important work in the field.

In 1968 Cunningham predicted in his book, *Changes: Notes on Choreography,* that technology would provide artist with a mechanism for visualizing dance. In *Trackers,* his first piece using the *Lifeforms* program, dancers move in ways one wouldn't expect. According to Anne Pierce, in her book *Merce Cunningham's Living*

Notebook, "A basic walk turns into a collaboration of limbs; the dancers combine primitive images and complex, independent rhythms, all overlaid onto a simple traveling motion. They pace around to one rhythm; their arms move to another. . . . Each arc, swivel, and wave is so distinctive, it's as if fragments of the gesture were plotted and timed completely independently, then applied inside the structure of a phrase." This peculiar movement vocabulary is a product of the choreographer working not on the body, but instead on a computer representation of the body, one without the rigors of gravity or physicality.

There is a long history of experiments in dance and technology including very early photographic work from 1890 to 1898 by Eadward Muybridge and dance films by Thomas Edison from 1904, including *Annabelle the Dancer.* As technology is a relative term, it is prudent to contextualize it within a given historical period; as Muybridge and Edison were inventing ways of fixing images within a photographic environment, others were inventing ways of using newly invented audio recording and playback devices to augment performance. As early as 1913 the Futurist Russolo was performing "noise music" in Milan using specially constructed boxes that produced various industrial noises such as explosions, train sounds, and shouting crowds. The Futurists embraced the machine age and all of its permutations, laying the groundwork for future generations of artists to further explore the marriage of art and technology. Oscar Schlemmer placed his Bauhaus "dances" from 1925 to 1927 in a mathematical environment, which also tacitly acknowledged the body as machine—while other Bauhaus artists combined movement with technology in various ways including the "Mechanical Ballets" of Manda Von Kreibig (*Slat Dance,* 1927) and Carla Grosch (*Glass Dance,* 1929). In 1924 Kurt Schmidt created a Mechanical Ballet called *Man and Machine* which exploited the mechanical nature of movement and extended the Futurists' ideas about machines as well.

Dance has had an especially contingent relationship with technology throughout modern history. In its earliest modern incarnation, dance relied on film as its method of documentation, then later video, and also on audio recording technology to provide music when live orchestras weren't possible. For many years, technology merely served as a way to archive and record dance for the sake of history. While archiving is still an important application of technology to dance, especially now that video has improved dramatically and digital storage is possible, artists persist in finding new and experimental applications for technology as well.

In 1965 John Cage presented a work called *Variations V* at the Philharmonic Hall in New York. The piece was a collaboration with choreographer Merce Cunningham, David Tudor, Gordon Mumma and Barbara Lloyd. The stage itself was fitted with photoelectric sensors by which the dancers' movements triggered sound and lighting effects. This model of interactivity is still prevalent today in dance and technology collaborations, and has become a genre in itself supported by research at Arizona State University's Institute for Studies in the Arts and at the University of Wisconsin at Madison's Dance and Interarts and Technology program and others.

The same year Cage debuted *Variations V,* physicist Billy Kluver began working with a group of American artists on a series of art and technology projects. It was during this time frame that John Cage, David Tudor, and a number of choreographers who had worked at the Judson Memorial Church began to collaborate on events combining technology with performance. In 1966 Kluver and Robert Rauschenberg collaborated on a project which brought together 30 engineers with artists to produce an event called *Nine Evenings: Theater and Engineering. Nine Evenings* was not the success the collaborators had hoped for—the engineers weren't used to working within theatrical confines and the artists weren't accustomed to the very precise, costly and time-consuming nature of working with technology. However, this interaction was nonetheless useful in beginning a dialogue between artists and technicians, and set the stage for future collaborations.

Rauschenberg has continued his relationship with dance and technology through his collaborations with choreographer Trisha Brown including the work, *Astral Convertible* (1989), in which the dancers' movements triggered sound and lights via on-stage towers. *Astral Convertible* was a successful marriage of dance and technology wherein there is no hierarchy of disciplines, i.e. dance is not privileged over the scenic and interactive stage elements, but rather what is presented on stage is a synergistic hybrid. Trisha Brown's choreography maintains its integrity while engaging the technology that Rauschenberg used in his stage design, and the piece itself functions as an integrated work of art.

In contemporary times dance and technology has moved into the digital domain with the advent of CD-ROMs, digital and nonlinear video, laser discs, multimedia applications and the Internet. There are numerous websites devoted entirely to dance as well as online courses such as Pegge Vissacaro's "Cross-Cultural Dance Perspectives," an internet course taught at Arizona State University. The Internet course allows students from around the world to participate and receive credit through Arizona State University. Ms. Vissicaro has recently initiated a new project called "Multi-Ethnic Dance Access" (MEDA), intended to be a global network and database service devoted to promoting online resources of multiethnic dance.

An institutional pioneer in interactive dance and the support of digitally mediated dance performance, the Institute for Studies in the Arts of the University of Arizona in Tempe is the home of the "Intelligent Stage" which operates through the use of video to analyze movement within predefined areas. The stage can respond to what is perceived, and react in accordance with the design of the composer, choreographer, or director. These responses can include changes in environmental elements such as lighting, sound, and video, or actually effect the structure of the environment itself. The flexibility of the Intelligent Stage allows artists to tailor its many elements: where sensors are located, what kind of actions the sensors are sensitive to, and what responses occur when actions are recognized. For instance, a dancer's movement may trigger a laser disc of video images or a previously stored clip of dialogue, or it may be programmed to trigger a number of events simultaneously. The Intelligent Stage is a media-controlled space providing innovative tools and paradigms in which artists can create a new generation of technologically based performance works.

Diane Gromala and Yacov Sharir, frequent collaborators in dance and technology projects, have sought "to explore questions related to how virtual reality, cyberspace, telepresence and emergent electronic technologies may influence the artistic processes and experiences of the body in the visual arts and dance." Creating dance that is contingent on emerging technologies allows the makers to dematerialize the body in such a way as to cease its reliance on real time/ space presence. It has become increasingly possible to create danceworks in the digital realm which in fact require no "dancers" at all in the traditional sense. Using virtual space as the stage for

these digital dances, choreographers such as Sharir, Cunningham, and others are questioning the very nature of dance in the postmodern/electronic era. As such they are part of a continuum of artists who often engage technology in ways vastly different from its original or intended usage.

—Douglas Rosenberg

TENT

Choreography: Alwin Nikolais
Music: Alwin Nikolais
Set & Lighting Design: Alwin Nikolais
First Production: University of South Florida, Tampa, June 1968
Original Dancers: Murray Louis, Phyllis Lamhut, Carolyn Carlson, Michael Ballard, Emery Hermans, Gale Ormiston, Wanda Pruska, Sara Shelton, Robert Soloman, Batya Zamir

Other productions include: Murray Louis, Phyllis Lamhut, and Carolyn Carlson with members of the Nikolais Dance Theatre: Michael Ballard, Emery Hermans, Gale Ormiston, Wanda Pruska, Sara Shelton, Robert Solomon, and Jeanette Stoner at Bavaria Film Studio, Munich, September 1969 (telecast WNET-TV, New York, 10 May 1972 on the *Vibrations* series); Nikolais/Louis Foundation for Dance, with Simonetta Bucci, Karen Safrit, Stephanie Scopelitis, Donna Scro, Joelle van Sickle, Kay Andersen, Clarence Brooks, Alberto del Saz, Eric Dunlap, and Peter Kyle, Tribeca Performing Arts Center, New York, 1996.

Publications

Barnes, Clive, "Alwin Nikolais Company Opens in Brooklyn: Presents a Triple Bill at Academy Festival," *New York Times,* 28 November 1968.
Dowlin, John, "Alwin Nikolais Dance Company," *Dance Magazine,* January 1969.
Manchester, P. W., "Alwin Nikolais Dance Company," *Dance News,* January 1969.
Mazo, Joseph H., "Nik Knacks," *Village Voice,* 3 November 1992.
———, "The Nik of Time," *Dance Magazine,* July 1993.
Nickolich, Barbara E., "The Nikolais Dance Theatre's Uses of Light," *Drama Review,* June 1973.
Regner, Otto Friedrich, *Reclams Ballettführer,* Stuttgart, 1972.
Tobias, Tobi, "Clout on a Limb," *New York,* 9 August 1993.

*   *   *

When Alwin Nikolais died in 1993, a number of critics had interesting things to say about his uses of technology and props in general and his implementation of these in specific ways for *Tent,* which premiered in 1968. For some dances, props are merely that; with *Tent,* however, the eponymous prop is the central figure. A group of dancers marches onto the stage carrying a folded white cloth with a hole in the center and then let it settle onto the floor. Ultimately, the cloth will swallow up the men and women who so confidently brought it onto the stage a few minutes before.

First, a series of wires with clips is lowered from the ceiling and the dancers attach the wires to the cloth, which soon becomes their covering. For a few moments the dancers move gracefully beneath the tent, yet soon the tent—more graceful than they are—descends on them and stops their motion. A man rises through the circular opening, and others follow, but their movements are more disturbed now. It is clear that the tent has had some sort of disruptive effect on their primitive assemblage, rather like the appearance of the monolith among the proto-humans at the beginning of Stanley Kubrick's *2001: A Space Odyssey*, a film released the same year as *Tent*. The tent rises again, but its dominance is now established and the wires make it seem to move of its own volition. Eventually, it covers the dancers again, until their legs and arms come up, bearing facial masks, an image that Don McDonagh compared to a many-headed hydra. Once more the tent comes up and seems to toy with the dancers, moving rapidly up and down while they move uncertainly beneath it. And then, finally, it falls and does not rise again.

Without a doubt, this is pessimistic stuff, and Tobi Tobias—in a review of a 1993 production honoring the recently deceased artist—compared the tent to "a fiery cloud," among other things. "Mushroom cloud" might be another image, because *Tent* appears to be about the Frankenstein quality of technology, which eventually comes to dominate its erstwhile master. "Use material as a weapon," Joseph Mazo wrote in his review of *Tent*, "it backfires; make it into a god and be eaten alive."

It is ironic, then, that one of the outstanding qualities of Nikolais as a choreographer was his very use of technology, the dangerous creation. It is hard to imagine that a work such as *Tent* once would have been considered high-tech. As Mazo wrote after Nikolais's death, however, that was not only because technology has progressed, but because Nikolais himself brought so many innovations to the world of modern dance. Hence Tobias could compare "Nik's stage" (Nikolais was often referred to by that "nickname") to "a lush, sophisticated screen saver," a deliberately anachronistic reference to his advanced use of mechanics and electronics.

In the 1960s, in fact, the technological aspects of Nikolais's work often seemed to overwhelm the other elements. It was, after all, an era when James Bond movies thrilled audiences with such far-fetched gadgets as a little box attached to Bond's belt that would beep when someone called him and a phone in his car by which he could return the call. By the 1990s, just as Bond movies were no longer even attempting to outpace the reality of technological innovation, viewers of Nikolais's pieces were able to see the brilliance, rather than the technical wizardry, at the heart of his work. In Mazo's words, "the metaphors finally strike home."

That metaphor is clearly a cautionary note on technology, and the irony of this fact obscures another, equally noteworthy, contradiction. The figures in *Tent* are far from individuals; whatever hope of individuality they have is swallowed by the tent itself. The choreographer said that his work was meant to illustrate "man in a whole world, not man in a little personal world." Yet Nikolais himself was a powerful individual presence. As Tobias noted, "The credit line running under the titles of his works. . .indicates the multifaceted nature of his gift: 'Choreography, Costume Design, Lighting Design and Sound Scores by Alwin Nikolais.'" He was unquestionably a revolutionary, and in the end the effects of his revolution in modern dance were so pervasive that people often failed to realize the origins of those innovations.

—Judson Knight

TESHIGAWARA, Saburo

Japanese dancer, choreographer, and company director

Born: 1953 in Tokyo. **Education:** Studied the sculpture and creation of plastic models, 1972; studied at a local ballet school, 1976. **Career:** First independent choreography and solo concert, 1981; co-founder Company KARAS (with Kei Miyata), Tokyo, 1985; first Paris concert, 1986; first American concert, Dance Umbrella Festival, Boston, 1989; has appeared on television and in films, as well as directed; has held art exhibitions, including *Ao (Blue)*, his private collection, Kirin Plaza Osaka, 1991; installation *Dance of Air* exhibited as part of a group exhibition and tour for *Kyokaisen no Bijutsu (Art on the Borderline)*, Saison Museum of Modern Art, 1991-92. **Awards:** Second and Special prizes, Concours Choreographique International de Bagnolet, France, 1986; Award of Dance Critics Society of Japan, Tokyo, 1988; Prix du Public, Festival International de Nouvelle Danse (FIND), Montreal, 1989, 1991; Award of Dance Critics Society, Munich, Germany, 1991; Japan Cultural Design Award, Tokyo, 1994; Culture and Arts Award, Grand Prix, Tokyo, 1994.

Works

1981	*Tsuki no Gin no Ringo (Moon's Silver Apple)*, Tokyo
1982	*Kuu (To Eat)*, Yokohama
	Anma (Japanese massage), Yokohama
1983	*Kanashiki Gangu (Sad Toy)*, Tokyo
1984	*Aozora (Blue Sky)*, Tokyo
	Seruroido no Oji (Celluloid Prince), Tokyo
1985	*Kaze no Sentan—Obaku Kibun (The Point of the Wind, the Odd Hearsay of Ohbaku)*, Tokyo
	Gekko Kiso (Strange Thought in the Moonlight), Tokyo
1986	*L'Enfant Pale*, Company KARAS, Tokyo
	The Point of the Wind, Concours Choreographique International de Bagnolet, Bagnolet, France
	Constellation, Company KARAS, Bordeau, France
1987	*The Arm of the Blue Sky*, Company KARAS, Tokyo
	Blue Meteorite, Company KARAS, Tokyo
	The Enemy of Electricity, Teshigawara and workshop students, Tokyo
	The Moon Is Quicksilver, Company KARAS, Tokyo
	Station, Company KARAS, Tokyo
1988	*A Thought in the Night*, Company KARAS, Tokyo
	Saburo Fragment, Company KARAS, Yokohama
	Saracens, Company KARAS, Tokyo
	Ishi-No-Hana, Company KARAS, Aix-en Provence, France
1989	*The Wisdom of the Buttons*, Company KARAS, Tokyo
	Melancholia, Company KARAS, Tokyo
	Karada-no-Yume, Company KARAS, Tokyo
1990	*Kitai*, Company KARAS, Osaka
	Montage, Company KARAS, Tokyo
	Marmalade, Star Dancers Ballet, Tokyo
1991	*DAH-DAH-SKO-DAH-DAH*, Company KARAS
	Bones in Pages (solo by Teshigawara), Frankfurt
1992	*Noiject*, Company KARAS, Yokohama
1993	*Season of Burns*, Company KARAS, Tokyo
1994	*White Clouds under the Heels*, Part 1 (mus. collage), Frankfurt Ballet

1995   *Here to Here*, Teshigawara and Kei Miyata, Frankfurt
        White Clouds Under the Heels, Part 2 (mus. collage),
           Frankfurt Ballet
1996   *I was Real—Documents*, Company KARAS, Frankfurt
        In: Edit, Company KARAS, Newcastle, U.K.
        Vacuum, Company KARAS, Fujisawa, Kanagawa, Japan
1997   *Q*, Company KARAS, Tokyo
        Petrouchka (mus. Stravinsky), Company KARAS, Tokyo
        Invisible Room, Teshigawara Education Project (STEP)
           Workshop students, London
        Morning Glory, KARAS workshop students, Tokyo

Publications

By TESHIGAWARA: books—

Aoi Inseki (Blue Meteorite), photos by Nobuyoshi Araki, text and
   illustrations by Teshigawara), Kyuryu Do Publishers, Tokyo,
   1989.
Hone to Kuki (Bones and Air), Hakusui Sha Publishers, Tokyo, 1994.

*   *   *

The modernity of modern art is transient; when modern dance germinated in Japan in the 1910s, to many it appeared as just another Occidental dancing form. Over the years, modern dance practitioners faithfully absorbed and have been influenced by the dance of pioneers like Wigman, Dalcroze, and Graham. Saburo Teshigawara, however, didn't follow anyone's modern style, and his works don't fit easily into any of those associated with conventional modern dance. His choreography is not a restatement of modern dance's heritage; his is a unique, redefining of dance.

Born and raised in Tokyo, Teshigawara studied plastic arts in the early 1970s and his interest soon expanded beyond plastics when he began taking classes in classical ballet in 1976. He began to choreograph independently in 1981; his early works were mostly solos, although they are barely documented. After founding his company, KARAS, in 1985, Teshigawara began creating group works and his company entered the Concours Choreographique International de Bagnolet in 1986, France. *The Point of the Wind*, created for the occasion, earned the second and special prizes. Following KARAS' appearance and awards at Bagnolet, invitations poured in from theaters and festivals in Europe, the United States, and Japan. To date, Teshigawara has enjoyed unprecedented success as a Japanese modern dancer and choreographer in the international dance circuit—as a direct result of his unconventional creative style.

Set design constitutes a significant feature of Teshogawara's works. As a proponent of plastic arts, he assigns the same importance to scenography as to dancing. Set design isn't a mere background to dancing; both are created equal in Teshigawara's eyes. Similar to Merce Cunningham's use of design, Teshigawara takes it a step further, with his scenography more actively integrated into the dancing.

Teshigawara uses specific materials to deliver the dominant theme of each work: sheet glass, for example, is used in *Blue Meteorite* and *The Moon Is Quicksilver*, both from 1987. The floor is covered with sheet glass, where Teshigawara stands, stomps, and kneels down, smashing and cracking the glass, which in turn creates dazzling effects with the stage lighting. Glass, here, is synonymous with plurality; a solid matter like glass instantly turns into shapeless wonder, it makes noise, and reflects light. Such plurality—the transience or uncertainty of solid existence—is a recurring theme in Teshigawara's work. He manipulates a variety of materials as if experimenting with chemical change.

Transparent acrylic boards are another material of choice, used in *Montage*, from 1990. Though transparent, boxes become visible and gain solid shape as smoke filters into the performance area. Another innovation appeared in *Noiject* (1992), where Teshigawara fused noise and steel, using metal boards and sound speakers; in *Bones in Pages*, 1991, he danced in front of a huge wall of old books and a crow (the company name "Karas" means crow in Japanese), as his nod to the connotation of time in both the past and the present. If compared to such diverse materials and sets incorporates into his works, Teshigawara's movement appears a little short on variety. Yet his movement vocabulary is idiosyncratic, projecting a refreshingly different modern dance technique; with Graham, Cunningham, and Butoh all thrown together. His movements are unpredictable, their shape, speed, and tone changing abruptly—sometimes he moves the dancers so quickly that their bodies appear blurred. Other noted characteristics are quirky movements accented with swift change of directions and center of gravity, sometimes likened to clockwork. Also used to much advantage were the falls used during the 1980s, where dancers suddenly collapse and bang to the floor (his dancers developed calluses).

Techigawara was a late bloomer who took his first ballet lessons in his twenties and was not thoroughly exposed to modern dance training. Such a background prevented him from being a classical virtuoso; yet he is a natural dancer endowed with innate lightness, clarity, and sharpness. Kei Miyata, co-founder of KARAS, and Shun Ito and Koichi Ienaga, the company's dancers since the 1980s, embody much of the same quality as Teshigawara.

In 1990, the Tokyo-based Star Dancers Ballet commissioned Teshigawara to create a new piece. It was a rare offer for him, because Japanese ballet companies favor established, overseas ballet choreographers rather than modern dance choreographers, especially those who are Japanese. *Marmalade*, premiered by three female dancers, marked the first work Teshigawara choreographed for dancers other than his company's. From this period onward, Teshigawara began to work with larger groups, including classically trained dancers. This led to a commission from William Forsythe of the Frankfurt Ballet, and in 1994 the first part of *White Clouds under the Heels* premiered by Frankfurt Ballet, with the second part following in 1995.

Teshigawara's career, as one of the most sought after choreographers in Japan and abroad, has now spanned over a decade. "I can only say that my dance derives from 'the present,'" he wrote in a program note for performances in 1994. Instead of following the retrospective modern dance prototype, Teshigawara proceeds and succeeds as a choreographer and artist in his own light.

—Sako Ueno

TETLEY, Glen
American dancer, choreographer, and company director

Born: Glenford Andrew Tetley, Jr., 3 February 1926 in Cleveland, Ohio. **Education:** Franklin and Marshall College, 1944-46; New

York University (B.S.), 1946-48; studied ballet with Margaret Craske and Antony Tudor, and at the School of American Ballet; studied modern dance with Hanya Holm and Martha Graham. **Military Service:** U.S. Navy, 1944-46. **Career:** Dancer and director's assistant, Hanya Holm Company, 1946-51; danced with the New York City Opera, 1952-54; member, John Butler Dance Company, 1953-55; principal dancer, Joffrey Ballet, 1956-57; member, Martha Graham Dance Company, 1958; principal dancer, American Ballet Theatre and Jerome Robbins Ballets USA, 1960-61; founder and director, Glen Tetley Dance Company, 1962-69; dancer/choreographer, Nederlans Dans Theater, 1962-71; then co-director, 1969-71; succeeded John Cranko as director of Stuttgart Ballet, 1974-76; artistic associate, National Ballet of Canada, Toronto, 1987-89; guest choreographer, the Royal Ballet (Covent Garden), American Ballet Theatre, National Ballet of Canada, Houston Ballet, Norwegian National Ballet, La Scala, Australian Ballet, English National Ballet, and most major world ballet companies, 1990s. **Awards:** Die Feder German Critics Award, 1969; Queen Elizabeth II Coronation Award, Royal Academy of Dancing, 1981; Prix-Italia Rai Prize, 1982; Tennant-Caledonian Award, Edinburgh Festival, 1983; Ohioana Career Medal, 1986; New York University Achievement Award, 1988; knighted by King Harold of Norway, Order of Merit, 1997.

Roles

1946   A Sailor, *On the Town* (Robbins), Adelphi Theatre, New York

Dancer (cr), *Walt Whitman Suite, Windows* (Holm), Hanya Holm Company, Colorado Springs, Colorado

1947   Barber (cr), *The Great Campaign* (Sokolow), Princess Theatre, New York

Dancer (cr), *The Insect Comedy* (Holm), Hanya Holm Company, Colorado Springs, Colorado

1948   Xochipili (cr), *Ozark Suite* (Holm), Hanya Holm Company, Colorado Springs

Harlequin (cr), *Kiss Me Kate* (Holm), Century Theater, New York

1949   Principal dancer (cr), *Baroque Concerto* (Pauline Koner), Pauline Koner Company, New York

Principal dancer, *Atavisms* (Weidman), Charles Weidman Company, New York

1950   Adonis (cr), *Out of This World* (Holm), Century Theater, New York

1951   Dancer, *Gentlemen Prefer Blondes* (Agnes de Mille) Ziegfeld Theater, New York

Dancer (cr), *Amahl and the Night Visitors* (opera), New York City Opera, NBC-TV

1952   Principal dancer (cr), *Rites* (Lang), Pearl Lang Company, New York

Principal dancer (cr), *And Joy Is My Witness* (Lang), Pearl Lang Company, New York

1953   Principal dancer (cr), *Malocchio* (Butler), John Butler Dance Company, New York

Principal dancer (cr), *Masque of the Wild Man* (Butler), John Butler Dance Company, New York

Principal dancer (cr), *Three Promenades with the Lord* (Butler), John Butler Dance Company, New York

1954   Principal dancer (cr), *Brass World* (Butler), John Butler Dance Company, New York

Principal dancer, *Long-Legged Jig* (Butler), John Butler Dance Company, New York

Principal dancer, *Triad* (Butler), John Butler Dance Company, New York

1956   Principal dancer, *Pas des Deésses* (Joffrey), Robert Joffrey Ballet, New York

1957   Principal dancer, *Passacaglia* (Humphrey), Doris Humphrey Company, New London, Connecticut

1958   Iago, *The Moor's Pavane* (Limón), José Limón Company, New York

Preacher, *The Glory Folk* (John Butler), John Butler Dance Company, Festival of Two Worlds, Spoleto, Italy

The Stranger (cr), *Embattled Garden* (Graham), Martha Graham Company, New York

Apollo (cr), *Clytemnestra* (Graham), Martha Graham Company, New York

1959   Slip-Jig, *Juno* (de Mille), Ziegfeld Theater, New York

Principal dancer (cr), *Carmina Burana* (Butler), New York City Opera, New York

Principal dancer (cr), *Serenade for Seven Dancers* (H. Ross), Spoleto Festival, Charleston, South Carolina

Principal dancer (cr), *The Sybil* (Butler), Spoleto Festival, Charleston, South Carolina

1960   The Friend, *Pillar of Fire* (Tudor), American Ballet Theatre, New York

The Lover, *Jardin aux Lilas* (Tudor), American Ballet Theatre, New York

Jean, *Miss Julie* (Cullberg), American Ballet Theatre, New York

Title role, *Bluebeard* (Fokine), American Ballet Theatre, New York

Wangel, *Lady from the Sea* (Cullberg), American Ballet Theatre, New York

The Sailor, *Lady from the Sea* (Cullberg), American Ballet Theatre, New York

Alias, *Billy the Kid* (Loring), American Ballet Theatre, New York

1961   Principal dancer, *Afternoon of a Faun* (Robbins), Ballets: USA, European tour

Husband, *The Concert* (Robbins), Ballets: USA, European tour

The Intruder, *The Cage* (Robbins), Ballets: USA, European tour

Principal dancer (cr), *Events* (Robbins), Ballets: USA, Spoleto Festival, Italy

Pas de deux, *Moves* (Robbins), Ballets: USA, European tour

1962   Title role (cr), *Pierrot Lunaire* (Tetley), Glen Tetley and Dancers, New York

Works

1946   *Richard Cory* (text by E.A. Robinson), Colorado College Summer Dance, Colorado College

1948   *The Canary* (mus. Berg), Cherry Lane Theater, New York

Triptych (mus. Wilson), Humphrey-Weidman Studio Theater, New York

1951   *Daylight's Dauphin* (mus. Debussy), Brooklyn High School Concert Series, Brooklyn, New York

Hootin' Blues (mus. Reilly), Brooklyn High School Concert Series, Brooklyn, New York

Western Wall (mus. Ravel), Brooklyn High School Concert Series, Brooklyn

1959   *Mountain Way Chant* (mus. Chavez), Alvin Ailey American Dance Theatre, New York

1961   *Ballet Ballads: The Eccentricities of Davy Crockett* (mus. Moss), East 74th Street Theater, New York

1962   *Birds of Sorrow* (mus. Hartman), Glen Tetley and Company, New York

       Gleams in the Bone House (mus. Shapero), Glen Tetley and Company, New York

       How Many Miles to Babylon? (mus. Surinach), Glen Tetley and Company, New York

       Pierrot Lunaire (mus. Schönberg), Glen Tetley and Company, New York

1963   *Harpsichord Concerto* (mus. de Falla), Glen Tetley and Company, Jacob's Pillow Dance Festival, Lee, Massachusetts

1964   *The Anatomy Lesson* (mus. Landowski), Nederlands Dans Theater, the Hague

       Sargasso (mus. Krenek), Nederlands Dans Theater, the Hague

1965   *Fieldmass* (mus. Martinu), Nederlands Dans Theater, Amsterdam

       The Game of Noah (mus. Stravinsky), Nederlands Dance Theater, the Hague

       Mythical Hunters (mus. Partos-Hezionot), Batsheva Dance Company, Tel-Aviv

1966   *Chronochromie* (mus. Messiaen), Glen Tetley Dance Company, Jacob's Pillow Dance Festival, Lee, Massachusetts

       Lovers (mus. Rorem), Glen Tetley and Company, New York

       Psalms (mus. Partos-Tehilim), Batsheva Dance Company, Tel-Aviv

       Ricercare (mus. Seter), American Ballet Theatre, New York

1967   *Dithyramb* (mus. Henzel), Glen Tetley and Company, New York

       Freefall (mus. Schubel), Repertory Dance Theatre, University of Utah, Salt Lake City

       The Seven Deadly Sins (mus. Weill), Glen Tetley Dance Company, Vancouver

       Ziggurat (mus. Stockhausen), Ballet Rambert, London

1968   *Circles* (mus. Berio), Nederlands Dans Theater, the Hague

       Embrace Tiger and Return to Mountain (mus. Subotnick), Ballet Rambert, London

1969   *Arena* (mus. Subotnick), Nederlands Dans Theater, the Hague

1970   *The Field Figures* (mus. Stockhausen), Royal Ballet, Nottingham

       Imaginary Film (mus. Schönberg), Nederlands Dans Theater, Scheveningen

       Mutations (mus. Stockhausen), Nederlands Dans Theater, Scheveningen

1971   *Rag Dances* (mus. Hymas), Ballet Rambert, London

1972   *Laborintus* (mus. Berio), Royal Ballet, London

       Small Parades (mus. Varèse), Nederlands Dans Theater, the Hague

       Strophe-Antistrophe (mus. Bussotti), Batsheva Dance Company, Tel-Aviv

       Threshold (mus. Berg), Hamburg State Opera Ballet, Hamburg

1973   *Gemini* (mus. Henze), Australian Ballet, Sydney

       Moveable Garden (mus. Foss), Tanz Forum, Cologne

       Rite of Spring (mus. Stravinsky), Bavarian State Opera Ballet, Munich

       Stationary Flying (mus. Crumb), Utah Repertory Dance Theater, University of Utah, Salt Lake City

       Voluntaries (mus. Poulenc), Stuttgart Ballet

1975   *Alegrias* (mus. Chavez), Stuttgart Ballet

       Daphnis und Chloe (mus. Ravel), Stuttgart Ballet

       Greening (mus. Nordheim), Stuttgart Ballet

       Strender (mus. Nordheim), Norwegian National Ballet, Oslo

       Tristan (mus. Henze), Paris Opéra Ballet

1977   *Poème Nocturne* (mus. Scriabin), Spoleto Festival, Charleston, South Carolina

       Sphinx (mus. Martinú), American Ballet Theatre, Washington, D.C.

1978   *Praeludium* (mus. Webern), Ballet Rambert, Manchester

1979   *Contredances* (mus. Webern), American Ballet Theatre, New York

       The Tempest (mus. Nordheim), Ballet Rambert, Schwetzingen

1980   *Dances of Albion* (mus. Britten), Royal Ballet, London

       Summer's End (mus. Dutilleux), Nederlands Dans Theater, the Hague

1981   *The Firebird* (mus. Stravinsky), Royal Danish Ballet, Copenhagen

1983   *Murderer Hope of Women* (mus. percussion, arranged Tyrrell), Ballet Rambert, Edinburgh

       Odalisque (mus. Satie), National Ballet School Gala, Toronto

1984   *Pulcinella* (mus. Stravinsky), London Festival Ballet, London

       Revelation and Fall (mus. Maxwell), Australian Dance Theatre, Adelaide

1985   *Dream Walk of the Shaman* (mus. Krenek), Aterballetto, Reggio Emilia, Italy

1986   *Alice* (mus. del Tredici), National Ballet of Canada, Toronto

1987   *Orpheus* (mus. Stravinsky), Australian Ballet, Melbourne

       La Ronde (mus. Korngold), National Ballet of Canada, Toronto

1989   *Tagore* (mus. Zemlinsky), National Ballet of Canada, Toronto

Publications

By TETLEY: articles—

"American Dancer," *Dance Magazine*, February 1963.

"Pierrot in Two Worlds," *Dance and Dancers* (London), December 1967.

"Tai-chi and the Dance," *Dance and Dancers* (London), November 1968.

"Dutch Mutations," *Dance Magazine*, February 1971.

On TETLEY: books—

Anawalt, Sasha, *The Joffrey Ballet: Robert Joffrey and the Making of an American Dance Company,* New York, 1996.

Buckle, Richard, *Buckle at the Ballet,* New York, 1980.

Gruen, John, *The Private World of Ballet*, New York, 1975.

Neufeld, James, *Power to Rise,* Toronto, 1996.

Rogosin, Elinor, *The Dance Makers: Conversations with American Choreographers*, New York, 1980.

Webb, Peter, *The Erotic Arts,* New York, 1975.

On TETLEY: articles—

Anderson, Jack, "A Gallery of American Ballet Theatre Choreographers," *Dance Magazine*, January 1966.

Brown, Ismene, "Dance Master and the Woman He Adores," *Daily Telegraph,* April 1997.

Crabb, Michael, "Tetley Makes La Ronde Go 'Round," *Dance Magazine*, 1988.

Citron, Paula, "Ballet Responding to the Tetley Touch," *Toronto Star,* 6 November 1987.

Christofis, Lee, "Mystery at Work with Dancing's Deepest Roots," *The Australian,* 29 August 1997.

Davies, Richard, "After the Tempest," *Classical Music,* 1 March 1980.

Duncan, Donald, "One Dancer, Many Faces," *Dance Magazine*, October 1960.

Garske, Rolf, "Creativity or Craft," *Das Ballett und die Künste,* (Cologne), 1972.

Goldman, Phyllis, "Choreographer Glen Tetley Comments on the American Ballet Scene," *Backstage,* 15 July 1988.

Harkavy, Benjamin, "Tetley/Schönberg *Pierrot Lunaire* Enriches Juilliard's Inter Arts Offering," *Juilliard Journal*, December 1996/January 1997.

Kelly, Dierdre, "The Shadowy Glen Tetley is Happily Going in Circles," *Globe and Mail,* 10 November 1987.

Laughlin, Patricia, "Talking to Tetley," *Dance Australia,* July/August 1984.

Parry, Jan, "Wonderland's Choreographer," *The Observer,* 28 June 1987.

Percival, John, "Tetley All the Way," *Dance and Dancers*, September 1969.

———, "Glen Tetley," *Experimental Dance*, (London), 1971.

Robertson, Allen, "Talking with Tetley," *Dance Magazine*, October 1971

———, "Tetley's Thrist," *Time Out,* 7 June 1984.

Stevens, David, "When Freelancer Weds Ballet Company," *International Herald Tribune,* 17 January 1975.

"Glen Tetley," *Tanzblätter* (Vienna), March 1980.

Thorpe, Edward, "Full Circle: Glen Tetley Returns to Greatness with *La Ronde*," *Dance Gazette,* February 1988.

Films and Videotapes

In Search of Lovers: The Birth of a Dance, prod. Jac Venza and Virginia Kessel for National Educational Television, 1966.

Glen Tetley: Choreographer at Work, dir. Bob Lockyer, BBC and RM Productions, 1979.

Pierrot Lunaire, performed by Ballet Rambert, dir. Colin Nears, BBC and RM Productions, c. 1979.

Septet extra, Voluntaries, performed by the Royal Danish Ballet, prod. Thomas Grimm, Denmark, 1980.

Greening, prod./dir. Thomas Grimm, Dansmark Radio and Zweites Deutsches Fernsehen, 1981.

Firebird, performed by the Royal Danish Ballet, prod./dir. Thomas Grimm, Dansmark Radio and RM Arts, 1982.

Alice, performed by the National Ballet of Canada, dir. Norman Campbell, Primedia Production for CBC, 1987.

La Ronde, performed by the National Ballet of Canada, dir. Norman Campbell, Primedia Production for CBC, 1987.

Glen Tetley, for *Eye on Dance*, WNYC-TV, 1991.

Glen Tetley: A Profile, Michael Blackwood Productions, 1995.

*　　*　　*

American dancer, choreographer, and company director Glen Tetley was born Glenford Andrew Tetley, Jr., in Cleveland, Ohio, on 3 February 1926. His father was a businessman who became vice president of Lumbermen's Mutual Insurance Company, and when Tetley was six, the family moved to Pittsburgh. Tetley's childhood activities were limited by a nine-year bout with a tumor, which temporarily paralyzed his left arm. At age 16 Tetley performed as an extra with the American Ballet Theatre (ABT) in the company's Pittsburgh performances of *Aurora's Wedding* and *Sorochinsk.* According to an interview with Ian Woodward, dance critic for the *Christian Science Monitor*, it was in the ABT's peformance of Tudor's *Romeo and Juliet* that Tetley found the first thing that had ever made sense to him.

Tetley enlisted in the Navy's V-12 program in 1944, entering Franklin and Marshall College in Lancaster, Pennsylvania as a premedical student. In 1946, after finishing his premed training, he moved to New York and enrolled in Columbia's College of Physicians and Surgeons. Later transferring to New York University, he gave up his medical pursuits and received a B.S. degree in 1948 and then decided he wanted to be a dancer. Tetley had no financial support, and was soon out of money. Needing cash, he went to borrow from a friend who was performing in the Broadway play *On the Town*; choreographer Jerome Robbins thought Tetley was there to audition for the play and asked Tetley to try out. Tetley's first attempt at tap dance wasn't good, but Robbins gave him another assignment and Tetley remained in the show for six months. Robbins recommended Tetley to his own dance instructor, Helen Platova, and soon thereafter Tetley discovered Hanya Holm.

Tetley studied modern dance with Holm from 1946 to 1951. Still having no money, he cleaned Holm's dance studio in Greenwich Village to pay for his room and board, which was actually the men's dressing room. Holm's style was a perfect match to Tetley's medical training. Tetley later reflected in an interview with John Gruen, "The beauty of Hanya's technique was its absolutely sound basis, anatomically, physiologically, and every way to psychologically." Determined to accelerate a late start in dance, Tetley enrolled in the Metropolitan Opera Ballet School, studying classic ballet under Margaret Craske and Antony Tudor. Soon Tetley became Holm's assistant and served as a guest choreographer for her summer dance sessions at Colorado College from 1946 to 1949 and at the Yale Dramatic Workshop in 1947 and '48. With Holm, Tetley gained a strict technical discipline and an understanding of the purpose and meaning of movement—both trademarks of Holm's tutelage.

Just two years after his first dance lesson, in 1948, Tetley appeared as a featured dancer in *The Eccentricities of Davy Crockett* at the Experimental Theatre. In 1950 he danced in *Kiss Me Kate* and *Out of This World*, all choreographed by Holm. On the NBC Opera, Tetley danced in the world premiere of Gian Carlo Menotti's *Amahl and the Night Visitors*. Tetley's performance in these roles gained him a spot as soloist with the New York City Opera from 1952 to 1954. In 1958, along with Carmen de Lavallade and Buzz Miller, Tetley danced at the first Festival of Two Worlds in Spoleto, Italy. When he returned from Italy, Agnes de Mille asked him to be in the musical *Juno.* She had created a special dance for him called a "Slip-

Jig," which came at the end of the first act and stopped the show. Glen Tetley was an overnight sensation. After this, Martha Graham asked Tetley to join her company, which he did from 1957 to 1959. Graham's influence can be seen in much of Tetley's early work; in particular, her use of three-dimensional structures.

In 1959 Tetley danced in John Butler's production of Carl Orff's *Carmina Burana*. As a principal dancer in Butler's company, Tetley toured Europe and appeared in several televised works. His first professional acknowledgment came from critic Walter Terry who claimed in a New York *Herald Tribune* review (1955) that Tetley was "one of the top male dancers in America" based on his role in Butler's stage production *Three Promenades With the Lord* and as a classical dancer in Kate Forbes' *Classical Garden*. In 1960 Tetley joined the ABT, in which he danced Tudor's *Lilac Garden* and *Pillar of Fire* and performed roles such as Jean in Birgit Cullberg's *Miss Julie* and the Husband in Cullberg's *Lady from the Sea*. Tetley was asked by Robbins to join his year-old company Ballets USA. After a year, Robbins and Tetley had a falling-out over billing, so Tetley decided to leave the company and take a year off. He refused many offers to perform, and instead thought of choreographing original works.

Tetley commissioned three composers to write original scores, and within a year his work was ready for the public. On 5 May 1962, he rented the auditorium of New York's Fashion Institute of Technology and presented "An Evening of Theater Dance"—his first choreography. Four original one-act ballets were performed by his own company—*Gleams in the Bone House* (Harold Shapero), *Birds of Sorrow* (Peter Hartman), *How Many Miles to Babylon?* (Carlos Surinach), and *Pierrot Lunaire* (Arnold Schönberg). The last work was a choreographic interpretation of the traditional *commedia dell'arte* contest between innocence and experience. Tetley's interpretation inspired critic John Martin to note "the presence of a work of subtle, imaginative and wholly enchanting art" in May 1962 review in the *New York Times*. In Martin's opinion, the combination of the visual and aural elements produced a stunning theatrical piece. *Pierrot Lunaire* launched Tetley's choreographic career.

For his work on *Pierrot Lunaire*, Tetley was asked to join the Netherlands Dance Theatre (formed in 1959) as a guest artist. He composed several new ballets for the Dutch company, his first being *The Anatomy Lesson*, based on Rembrandt's one-act allegory of life and death. His innovative choreography in works such as *Sargasso* (Ernst Krenek) in 1964, *Field Figures* (Karl Stockhausen) in 1965, and *Circles* (Luciano Berio) in 1969 accelerated the development of the Nederlands Dans Theater and in turn, Tetley's choreographic stature was elevated. In 1967 Marie Rambert invited him to join her company, Ballet Rambert, which she was reorganizing with Norman Morrice. Tetley, in his staging of *Pierrot Lunaire* and *Ricercare* (Mordecai Seter) and his creation of the works *Embrace Tiger and Return to Mountain* (Morton Subotnick) and *Ziggurat* (Karl Stockhausen), was a major influence on Ballet Rambert as a contemporary dance company

In 1969 Tetley returned to New York to restart his own company. With a grant from the National Endowment for the Arts, he put together a company of 12 dancers and began touring America and Europe. During one European tour, Tetley was approached by Nederlands Dans Theater to be its co-director. Tetley accepted and began to reshape the company. In 1970 he choreographed *Mutations* (Stockhausen) with film sequences by Hans van Manen. The ballet was controversial because of its nudity and was a study on aggression and liberation. However, critics hotly contested the use

of nudity. In his *Newsweek* review (April 1972), Hubert Saal complained that "the less the dancers wore the less they danced." Also in 1970, came one of Tetley's most important works, *Field Figures*, first created for the Royal Ballet and in a revolutionary contemporary style. The next year, after a falling-out with Nederlands Dans Theatre management over policy, Tetley resigned as co-director and departed.

In 1974 Tetley became director of the Stuttgart Ballet and created one of the company's most significant works, *Voluntaries* (Francis Poulenc). In the following two years Tetley created and staged an astounding 10 of his works for the company. He next worked closely with ABT, staging for *Voluntaries, The Rite of Spring,* and *Sargasso* and creating *Sphinx* in 1977 and *Contredances* in 1979. Tetley's choreography for dancers such as Makarova and Baryshnikov was their first experience in bridging classical technique with modern dance. In 1986 Tetley choreographed *Alice* for the National Ballet of Canada, hailed by Anna Kisselgoff in the *New York Times* as "a rare and beautiful ballet." The popularity of this work led the company to ask Tetley to be an artistic associate and he continued to choreograph with the Canadian company through the 1990s. He continues to work as a freelance choreographer for nearly every major Western ballet company.

Glen Tetley's career has been unusually diverse. An appealing and passionate dancer, he was one of the first soloists to work in the various areas of the dance world. He holds a unique place in dance history, being one of the first choreographers to try to blend modern dance with classical ballet. Both as a choreographer and a dancer, he worked in these two areas and it was his synthesis of these dance forms that has characterized his choreographic work. According to Allen Robertson and Donald Hutera of *The Dance Handbook*, Tetley's "pioneering works have a fervid intensity and nonstop propulsion coupled with a voluptuous physicality and an open sensuality."

Throughout his career, Tetley has sought new sources of movement to supplement his dance vocabulary. His work, both in the U.S. and aboard has enabled him to mold choreographic policy and repertory. He is credited with introducing modern dance to many classically-trained companies, opening up new ways of thinking about choreography. Internationally, Tetley has been an important influence on choreography—by breaking down barriers, and opening attitudes to movement, music, and design. In his seventies, Glen Tetley is still influencing the dance world.

—Barbara Long

THARP, Twyla
American dancer, choreographer and company director

Born: 1 July 1941 in Portland, Indiana; grew up in Rialto, California. **Education:** Studied ballet, tap, flamenco, baton twirling, acrobatics, and several musical instruments as a child; attended Pomona College; B.A. in art history, Barnard College, 1963; studied dance with John Butler, Carmen de Lavallade, Barbara Fallis, Martha Graham, Merce Cunningham, Luigi, Margaret Craske, Alwin Nikolais, Paul Taylor and others. **Family:** Married Peter Young, (divorced); married Robert Huot, (divorced); one child. **Career:** Dancer, Paul Taylor Dance Company, 1963-65; founded/directed own company, 1965-88; artistic associate, American Ballet Theatre, 1988-90; toured new works and repertoire with pickup companies including *Cutting Up* with Mikhail Baryshnikov, 1991-94; formed new company, Tharp!, 1996; freelance choreography includes works for American Ballet Theatre, Australian Ballet, Boston Ballet, Hubbard Street Dance Chicago, Joffrey Ballet, New York City Ballet, Paris Opera Ballet, Royal Ballet, and has reset repertory on other companies; two works for Olympic ice skater John Curry; directed and choreographed Broadway production of *Singin' in the Rain.* **Awards:** Numerous grants and awards, including Creative Arts Award (Brandeis University), 1972; *Dance Magazine* Award, 1981; two Emmy Awards for *Baryshnikov by Tharp*, 1985; MacArthur Foundation fellowship, 1992.

Works (premiered in New York City unless otherwise noted)

1965   *Tank Dive*, Hunter College Art Department, New York
       Stage Show, New York World's Fair
       Stride (film)
       Cede Blue Lake, Hunter College
       Unprocessed, Hunter College
1966   *Re-Moves*, Judson Memorial Church
       Yancey Dance, Judson Memorial Church
1967   *One Two Three*, Kunstverein Museum, Stuttgart
       Jam, Stedelijk Museum, Amsterdam
       Disperse, Richmond Professional Institute, Richmond, Virginia
       Three Page Sonata for Four, SUNY, Potsdam, New York
       Forevermore, Midsummer Inc., Southampton, New York
1968   *Generation*, Wagner College Gymnasium, Staten Island, New York
       One Way, Wagner College Gymnasium, Staten Island, New York
       Excess, Idle, Surplus, Notre Dame University, South Bend, Indiana
1969   *After "Suite,"* Billy Rose Theatre, New York
       Group Activities, Brooklyn Academy of Music (BAM)
       Medley, American Dance Festival, Connecticut College, New London, Connecticut
       Dancing in the Streets of London and Paris, Continued in Stockholm and Sometimes Madrid, Wadsworth Atheneum, Hartford, Connecticut
1970   *Pymffyppmfynm Ypf*, Sullins College, Bristol, Virginia
       The Fugue, University of Massachusetts, Amherst
       Rose's Cross Country, University of Massachusetts
       The One Hundreds, University of Massachusetts
1971   *The History of Up and Down, I and II,* Oberlin College, Oberlin, Ohio
       Eight Jelly Rolls (mus. Jelly Roll Morton, Red Hot Chili Peppers), Oberlin College; revised, New York Shakespeare Dance Festival
       The Willie Smith Series (videotape), New Berlin, New York
       Mozart Sonata, K.545, The Mall, Washington, D.C.
       Torelli (mus. Guiseppe Trelli), Sunrise, Fort Tryon Park, New York
       The Bix Pieces (mus. Bix Beiderbecke, Paul Whiteman's Orchestra, *Abide with Me* by Thelonious Monk), International Festival of Dance, Paris
1972   *The Raggedy Dances* (mus. Scott Joplin, Mozart), a portion set separately as *The Rags Suite*, St. Paul, Minnesota, 1975

1973   *Deuce Coupe* (mus. Beach Boys), Joffrey Ballet and Tharp Dancers, Chicago; revised as *Deuce Coupe II,* St. Louis, Missouri, 1975
       As Time Goes By (mus. Haydn), Joffrey Ballet
1974   *In the Beginnings* (mus. Jeffrey Moss), Minneapolis
       All about Eggs (television; mus. Bach) for WGBH, Boston
       The Bach Duet (mus. Bach), New York Shakespeare Dance Festival
1975   *Sue's Leg* (mus. Fats Waller), St. Paul, Minnesota
       The Double Cross (mus. various), St. Paul, Minnesota
       Ocean's Motion (mus. Chuck Berry), Spoleto Festival, Italy
1976   *Push Comes to Shove* (mus. Haydn, Joseph Lamb), American Ballet Theatre (ABT)
       Give and Take (mus. Werner, Sousa, Franko, Meacham, Ronell), BAM
       Once More, Frank (mus. Sinatra), Tharp and Baryshnikov for ABT
       Country Dances (mus. Peaslee), Edinburgh Festival, Scotland
       Happily Ever After (mus. Peaslee), Joffrey Ballet
       After All (mus. Tomaso Albinoni), for gold-medal figure skater John Curry
1977   *Mud* (mus. Mozart), BAM
       Simon Medley (mus. Paul Simon), BAM
       Making Television Dance (television; mus. "Snuffy Jenkins, "Pappy" Sherill, and the Hired Hands), PBS
       Cacklin' Hen (mus. Peaslee), BAM
1979   *Hair* (film), choreography by Tharp
       1903 (mus. Randy Newman), BAM
       Chapters & Verses (mus. various), BAM
       Baker's Dozen (mus. Willie "The Lion" Smith), BAM
1980   *Three Fanfares*, performed by John Curry, Closing Ceremonies, 1980 Winter Olympics
       Brahms' Paganini (mus. Brahms)
       When We Were Very Young (mus. John Simon)
       Assorted Quartets (mus. fiddle reels), Saratoga, New York
       Short Stories (mus. Supertramp, Bruce Springsteen), Ghent, Belgium
       Third Suite (mus. Bach), Paris
1981   *Uncle Edgar Dyed His Hair Red* (mus. Dick Sebouh), Elmira, New York
       The Catherine Wheel (mus. David Byrne); *The Golden Section* reset as a separate work, University of Texas, Austin, 1983
       Confessions of a Cornermaker (television), featuring *Baker's Dozen, Short Stories,* and *Duet* from the *Third Suite,* CBS
1982   *Nine Sinatra Songs* (mus. Sinatra), Vancouver, British Columbia
       Bad Smells (mus. Glenn Branca), Vancouver, British Columbia
1983   *Fait Accompli* (mus. David Van Tieghem), University of Texas, Austin
       Telemann (mus. Telemann), University of Texas
       Bach Partita (mus. Bach), ABT, Washington, D.C.
       Sinatra Suite (mus. Sinatra), ABT, Washington, D.C.
1984   *The Little Ballet* (mus. Alexander Glazunov), ABT, Minneapolis
       Brahms/Handel w/Jerome Robbins (mus. Brahms), New York City Ballet

Twyla Tharp: *Nine Sinatra Songs*. **Photograph © Beatriz Schiller.**

Sorrow Floats (mus. George Bizet), American Dance Festival, Durham, North Carolina

1985 *Singin' in the Rain* (Broadway musical), choreographed and directed by Tharp, New York

1986 *In the Upper Room* (mus. Glass), Ravinia Festival, Highland Park, Illinois

Ballare (mus. Mozart), Ravinia Festival, Highland Park, Illinois

1988 *Four Down Under* (mus. Bruce Smeaton), Melbourne, Australia

1989 *Quartet* (mus. Terry Riley), ABT, Miami Beach

Bum's Rush (mus. Dick Hyman), ABT, Chicago

Rules of the Game (mus. Bach), Paris Opéra Ballet, Paris

Everlast (mus. Jerome Kern), ABT, San Francisco

1990 *Brief Fling* (mus. Percy Grainger, Michel Colombier), ABT, San Francisco

1991 *Grand Pas: Rhythm of Saints* (mus. Paul Simon), Paris Opéra Ballet, Paris

The Men's Piece (mus. George Gershwin, Tammy Wynette), Ohio State University, Columbus

Octet (mus. Edgar Meyer), Ohio State University, Columbus

1992 *Sextet* (mus. Bob Telson, Peter Melnick)

Cutting Up (mus. various, Giovanni Battista Pergolesi), University of Texas

1993 *Demeter and Persephone* (mus. various, klezmer), Martha Graham Company

Pergolesi (mus. Pergolesi), revision of duet from *Cutting Up* for Mikhail Baryshnikov, White Oak Dance Project

Brahms Paganini-Book II (mus. Brahms), Milan, Italy

1994 *Waterbaby Bagatelles* (mus. various), Boston Ballet

Red, White and Blues (mus. mixed, including Bartók), Washington, D.C.

1995 *How Near Heaven* (mus. Britten), ABT, Washington, D.C.

Americans We (mus. Donald Hunsberger), ABT

1996   *Jump Start* (mus. Wynton Marsalis), ABT
     Mr. Worldly Wise (mus. Rossini), Royal Ballet, London
1996   *I Remember Clifford* (mus. various), Hubbard Street Dance
     Chicago, Chicago
     The Elements (mus. Jean-Fery Rebel), ABT
     Sweet Fields (mus. William Billings, others), University
     of California, Berkeley
     66 (mus. various), University of California, Berkeley
     Heroes (mus. Glass), University of California, Berkeley
1997   *The Storyteller* (mus. Kiyong Kim), Australian Ballet,
     Melbourne Festival, Australia
     Roy's Joys (mus. Roy Eldridge, others)
1998   *Yemayá* (mus. Enrique Jorrín, others), Miami

Publications

By THARP: books—

Push Comes to Shove, New York, 1992.

On THARP: books—

Copeland, Roger, and Marshall Cohen, *What Is Dance?,* New York, 1983.

Croce, Arlene, *Afterimages,* New York, 1978.

———, *Going to the Dance,* New York, 1982.

———, *Sight Lines,* New York, 1987.

Foster, Susan Leigh, *Reading Dancing: Bodies and Subjects in Contemporary American Dance,* Berkeley, 1986.

Siegel, Marcia B., *Watching the Dance Go By,* Boston, 1977.

———, *The Shapes of Change: Images of American Dance,* Boston, 1979.

———, *The Tail of the Dragon: New Dance, 1976-1982,* Durham, North Carolina, 1991.

Switzer, Ellen, *Dancers! Horizons in American Dance,* New York, 1982.

Robertson, Allen, and Donald Hutera, *The Dance Handbook,* Boston, 1990.

Rogosin, Elinor, *The Dance Makers: Conversations with American Choreographers,* New York, 1980.

On THARP: articles—

Acocella, Joan, "Balancing Act," *Dance Magazine,* October 1990.

Albert, Steven, "Utopia Lost—and Found? A Look at Tharp's Way," *Ballet Review,* Spring 1986.

Denison, D.C., "The Interview: Twyla Tharp," *Boston Globe Magazine,* 30 May 1993.

Dooley, Meg, "The World According to Tharp," *Columbia,* November 1986.

Macaulay, Alistair, "Twyla Tharp Dance," *Dancing Times,* February 1984.

Vaughan, David, "Twyla Tharp: Launching a New American Classicism," *Dance Magazine,* May 1984.

Twyla Tharp Archive, Jerome Lawrence and Robert E. Lee Theatre Research Institute, Ohio State University.

Films and Videotapes

Film credits: *Hair, Ragtime, Amadeus, White Nights,* and *I'll Do Anything; Dance Is a Man's Sport Too* for Peter Martins and football player Lynn Swann; *All about Eggs* (made-for-televi-

sion), adaptations of stage works including *Scrapbook Tape* and *Baryshnikov by Tharp; Eight Jelly Rolls,* produced for television, London Weekend Televison, London, 1974; *The Bix Pieces,* produced for CBS Camera Three, 1973; *Sue's Leg, Remembering the Thirties,* produced for PBS' *Dance in America* series, 1976; *The Catherine Wheel,* produced for BBC and PBS, for *Dance in America* series; *Confessions of a Cornermaker,* featuring *Baker's Dozen, Short Stories,* and *Duet* from the *Third Suite,* CBS cable, 1981; *Scrapbook Tape,* video anthology of Tharp's works since 1965, directed by Tharp, PBS, 1982; produced for television in *Twyla Tharp: Oppositions, Dance in America* series, PBS, 1996.

*   *   *

As one of the most eclectic choreographers of the 20th century, Twyla Tharp defies easy classification. Beginning with the Judson Dance-influenced minimalism of her early work through the charming, yet powerful *Baker's Dozen,* to angry dances such as *Bad Smells,* to the virtuosic *In the Upper Room* and the uplifting *Sweet Fields,* Tharp has proven herself to be creative, innovative, and highly skilled.

From a childhood filled with instruction through college years during which she studied with many great modern and ballet teachers, Tharp assimilated physical material that has contributed to her signature style: a deceptively loose-limbed, seemingly spontaneous but totally controlled movement with off-centered ease, torquing bodies, unusual lifts and turns, big, breathtaking physicality as well as throwaway squiggles, performed without visible preparation. She has incorporated and manipulated many forms including pedestrian movement, folk and social dance, and the theatrical and concert forms she studied, to create works ranging from abstract to issue-filled, neutral to witty, ironic, or angry. From her background in music studies and art history, Tharp derived a deep understanding of structure and contrapuntal techniques that have remained important elements of her work.

In 1965, Tharp premiered her first work, *Tank Dive,* and also began her company with Margaret Jenkins, soon adding Sara Rudner. Others joined including ballet dancer Rose Marie Wright in 1968, Kenneth Rinker, the first man in the company in 1971, and Shelley Washington, now ballet mistress for Tharp, in 1975. Each of Tharp's dancers brought a different physicality, technique, and ability, and many stayed with the company for a number of years. Tharp has always acknowledged the contributions her dancers have made to her art.

Tharp's early works were based on music composition techniques and mathematical principles and were performed with a neutral facial expression. In the few reviews of the company in the early years, critics often called the work cold, yet most found Tharp's work as a dancer beautiful, and her work as a choreographer promising. The company performed without music in a variety of nontraditional settings including outdoors, gymnasiums, and art museums, but rarely on a proscenium stage. For example, *Rose's Cross Country* was performed by Wright dancing across campus.

For Tharp, *The Fugue,* 20 variations on a movement theme, was the pinnacle of her contrapuntal work. Critics also felt she had found something with this work—perhaps the "quintessential Tharp dance" according to Arlene Croce. Originally for three women, Tharp re-set *The Fugue* for three men, a change Marcia Siegel noted as "redefin[ing] male dancing." *The Fugue* remains in the Tharp repertory today.

Having reached an understanding of the innate musicality of movement without music, Tharp embarked on a new direction with *Eight*

Twyla Tharp: *Fait Accompli,* 1984. Photograph by Tom Caravaglia.

Jelly Rolls, to music by Jelly Roll Morton and the Red Hot Chili Peppers. Subsequently she has used a variety of music by popular musicians, from ethnic and country traditions, by composers of classical and art music, and new and commissioned works by composers including Philip Glass, David Byrne, David Van Tieghem, and Edgar Meyer.

The Bix Pieces was an early experiment in the use of narrative, performed as a lecture-demonstration with narrator and dancers, a format Tharp has continued to use in discussing her work with audiences. In *When We Were Very Young,* with a script by playwright Thomas Babe, and *The Catherine Wheel,* Tharp expanded her work in the use of narrative, with critical reaction to both works mixed. Learning from these experiences, Tharp moved away from their intensely personal scenarios, but has continued to explore use of narrative, recent examples of which are *Demeter and Persephone,* and *Mr. Worldly Wise.*

Tharp has explored the dance configuration of the couple in such works as *Nine Sinatra Songs* and *The Men's Piece. Nine Sinatra Songs,* to tunes sung by Frank Sinatra and costumed by Oscar de la

Renta, is an excursion into romance, and sometimes conflict, between a man and a woman set in a Tharp-expanded ballroom form in which men and women are equal.

Tharp has used videotape for documentation and as a creative medium for years. Works include such made-for-television works as *All about Eggs,* adaptations of stage works including *Scrapbook Tape* and *Baryshnikov by Tharp,* and the video camera onstage as in *Bad Smells.*

In 1973 Tharp expanded her horizons by creating *Deuce Coupe* for the Joffrey Ballet and her own company, mixing not only modern dance and ballet on the stage, but setting the work to music by the Beach Boys with a scenic backdrop by graffiti artists. In *Watching the Dance Go By,* Marcia Siegel found the work an "innovative ballet" that "demand[ed] that the audience overhaul its habitual way of looking at ballet." Tharp established herself firmly in the ballet world with *Push Comes to Shove* for Mikhail Baryshnikov at American Ballet Theatre. Many of her works since the late 1980s, including ballets from her tenure as artistic associate at American Ballet Theatre, have been for ballet companies.

While the Tharp company did not take curtain calls in the early years, Tharp was nonetheless quite aware of the audience and its perceptions as in *Re-Moves*, of which the audience progressively saw less until they only heard the dancers, and *Dancing in the Streets. . .* where dancers mingled with often unsuspecting museumgoers. In *Sue's Leg*, Tharp approached the problem of the frequent incomprehensibility of modern dance by opening rehearsals during development of the work. Tharp's ongoing commitment to demystifying dance has resulted in dances of depth that can be appreciated on many levels.

Artistic collaborations have been important to Tharp, beginning with Jennifer Tipton's lighting and Robert Huot's costumes for *Tank Dive*. Tipton continues to light most of Tharp's works. Longtime Tharp associate Santo Loquasto has designed costumes as well as sets including the backdrops and metal structure for *The Catherine Wheel*. Other designers have included Kermit Love, Ralph Lauren, Norma Kamali, Oscar de la Renta, William Ivey Long, Isaac Mizrahi, and Gianni Versace.

—Nena Couch

THOMPSON, Clive

Jamaican-American dancer, artistic director, educator, and choreographer

Born: 20 October 1940, Kingston. **Education:** Studied with Ivy Baxter, Jamaica, 1950s; studied at Martha Graham School of Contemporary Dance, New York. **Career:** Dancer, Martha Graham Company, 1960s; dancer, Alvin Ailey American Dance Theatre, 1970s; founder, Clive Thompson Dancecenter, Staten Island, 1980; founder, Clive Thompson DanceCompany, Staten Island, 1981; National Dance Theatre Company/School of Dance, Kingston, Jamaica, beginning 1988.

Roles

1961	*One More Gaudy Night* (Graham)
1962	*Secular Games* (Graham)
1963	*Circe* (Graham)
	Life of a Tree (Yuirko)
	Flowers with Me
1965	*Part Real-Part Dream* (Graham)
	Wind Drum
1967	*Night Fantasy*
	Wanderers
1968	*Strange Landscape*
1971	*Myth* (Ailey)
	Choral Dances (Ailey)
1972	*The Lark Ascending* (Ailey)
1973	*Hidden Rites* (Ailey)
	Blues Suite (Ailey)
1974	*Revelations* (Ailey)
1976	*Black, Brown and Beige* (Ailey)
	Three Black Kings (Ailey)
1980	*Threepenny Pieces* (Elizabeth Keen)
1987	*The Moor's Pavane* (Limón)

Other roles include: *Carmina Burana* (Butler); *Shirah* (Lang); *Missa Brevis* (Limón); *The Wedding* (Primus); *Kinetic Molpai* (Shawn).

Works

1990	*Phases of the Three Moons* (mus. Villa-Lobos, Ives), National Dance Theatre Company, Kingston
1993	*Journeys Beyond Survival*, National Dance Theatre Company, Kingston

Other works include: Thompson has choreographed a number of works performed by the New York-based Clive Thompson Dance Company in the 1980s and the National Dance Theatre Company of Jamaica in the 1990s.

Publications

On THOMPSON: articles—

Cox, Dan, "Going Back to Jamaica," *Dance Magazine*, February 1988.

Cunningham, Katharine, "Jacob's Pillow Fiftieth Anniversary Season," *Dance News*, October 1982.

Gladstone, Valerie, "Clive Thompson in Paradise," *Dance Magazine*, July 1993.

Lewis, Julinda, review, *Dance Magazine*, January 1985.

———, reviews, *Attitude*, August 1984.

Livingston, Lili Cockerille, "Tulsa: The Clive Thompson Dance Company," *Dance Magazine*, March 1986.

Stoop, Norma McLain, "All the World's a Stage, for Clive Thompson of the Alvin Ailey American Dance Theatre," *Dance Magazine*, October 1978.

Stoop, Norma McLain, "Jacob's Pillow Dance Festival," *Dance Magazine*, January 1983.

*   *   *

In the 1990s Clive Thompson, who had long before returned to his homeland of Jamaica, was living a life many would envy. As *Dance Magazine* reported in 1993, the former dancer had a house high in the hills above Kingston, the Caribbean island's capital, surrounded by flowers, a farm, and even a miniature zoo. He and his wife Liz, executive director of Jacob's Pillow, had a swimming pool as well as separate quarters for Thompson's mother. Working as a choreographer and instructor with the National Dance Theatre, Thompson also made money as a massage therapist and by raising chickens, bees, and exotic plants and birds. And just in case he got tired of life in paradise, he made regular trips back to New York, where he maintained directorship of his Clive Thompson Dance Company/Center. "When I go to New York," he said, "I spend all my time at the theater and opera, but I don't miss it otherwise."

Thompson's experience is proof that a person can live many lives over a span of years. In his career he has experienced dance from a number of perspectives: as a performer, choreographer, artistic director, and instructor. Thompson has been blessed with youthful looks, and he is reticent about his age. (Though his birthday is October 20, the year of 1940 is not a certainty.) But if one considers that he danced in the premiere of Martha Graham's *Part Real-Part Dream* on 3 November 1965, for instance, it is easy to gain some sense of the great breadth of his career.

Moving to New York in 1960 after having studied with Ivy Baxter in Jamaica, Thompson became part of the Martha Graham School of Contemporary Dance. During two decades with Graham's and later Alvin Ailey's dance companies, he performed in numerous roles. Even later, when he formed his own dance company and school at the age of 40, he continued to perform. *Dance Magazine* reported on his final performance, in José Limón's *Moor's Pavane* in December 1987, when Thompson was just three years away from his 50th birthday.

But long before that putative last performance, Thompson had begun to experience the behind-the-scenes aspects of dance—not just choreography, which he enjoyed, but the logistics of management, which he didn't. He has expressed disgust at the situation of "professional begging" into which many artistic directors are forced. "Modern dance is suffering," he told *Dance Magazine.* "Most presenters would rather spend megabucks for mega-companies than take a chance on a small company."

And the Clive Thompson DanceCompany was certainly a small, intimate one. Though Thompson is Afro-Caribbean by birth, the company and its school were not distinguished so much by a particular cultural or ethnic perspective as by Thompson's own exuberance for dance, for art, for life. "I was coming over the Verrazano Bridge one day," he recalled, "and I said to myself, 'I want Staten Island to dance.'" So he founded the Dancecenter in 1980 and the DanceCompany in 1981, by which time he had more prospective students than he had open slots in the school. For Thompson, who said he wanted his own company because he was tired of "having my life choreographed four years down the road," it was a chance to experiment with works by a variety of choreographers—including Clive Thompson.

His own work, as one might expect, is energetic and—given his multicultural perspective—eclectic. His *Journeys Beyond Survival,* for instance, illustrates the lives of four men whose careers showed numerous similarities but as many differences, not least of which was their nationality: the Jamaican Marcus Garvey, the Indian Mahatma Gandhi, the American Martin Luther King, and the South African Nelson Mandela. *Phases of the Three Moons* is divided into three sections that display, in turn, the experiences of awe, erotic attraction, and love. (As it turns out, reports of Thompson's retirement from dance itself were premature; in 1993 the fifty-something artist was performing opposite Melanie Graham in the "love" section, displaying what *Dance Magazine* called "a Chaplinesque talent his New York admirers rarely saw.")

It appears that Thompson as choreographer did not blossom—an appropriate metaphor, given his horticultural talent—until he went back to Jamaica. Just as he had once founded his dance company to get away from the rat race of performance, in 1988 he made the move from Staten Island to Kingston to get even further away from it all. Leaving the company and school under the artistic directorship of former rehearsal director Robert Bisbee, he dedicated his talents to the National Dance Theatre Company (NDTC), founded in 1962 by Rex Nettleford, who remained as director in the 1990s.

The NDTC has been enormously popular with the Jamaican people, though it has existed without government support, and lack of funding has meant that many dancers miss rehearsals because of having to hold down other jobs. This doesn't seem to bother Thompson, however, and he has often taken on several roles in practice sessions to make up for the missing people. Clearly, funding problems in Kingston have not been the same headache as funding problems in Staten Island, and if one were to ask Thompson, he would undoubtedly say that a bad day in Jamaica still beats a great one in New York.

—Judson Knight

TIPTON, Jennifer
American lighting designer for dance, theater, and opera

Born: 11 September 1937 in Columbus, Ohio. **Education:** At age 15, briefly studied dance with Martha Graham and José Limón; B.A. in English (after shifting from physics), Cornell University, 1958. **Career:** Became rehearsal director of Merry-Go-Rounders, a New York City company that performed for high school students, 1958; participated in stage lighting workshop with Thomas Skelton at the American Dance Festival at Connecticut College, 1963; became Skelton's assistant, then took his place as resident lighting designer with the Paul Taylor Dance Company, 1965; went on tour with company and lit much of Taylor's work for the next three decades (including *Orbs* in 1996); designed the lights for Twyla Tharp's first ballet in 1965 and all of her work until 1984, collaborating since then with Tharp on a number of projects; designed lights for Robert Joffrey Ballet and worked as Joffrey's production assistant for three years; designed lights for the Feld Ballet, the Limón Dance Company, and a number of Mikhail Baryshnikov's works for American Ballet Theatre; began designing lights for New York Shakespeare Festival in 1973 (first production, *The Tempest*), after designing lights for Jerome Robbins's ballet *Celebration;* began working with modern choreographer Dana Reitz, 1987; began collaborating with the Wooster Group, a New York-based avant garde theater company, early 1990s; associate professor of lighting, Yale School of Drama; directorial debut, Guthrie Theater production of *The Tempest,* Minneapolis, Minnesota, 1991; collaborated with Reitz and modern choreographer Sara Rudner on *Necessary Weather* (with the lights as full partner in the work), 1994; associate professor of lighting, Yale School of Drama; designed lights for Guthrie Theater production of *As You Like It,* Minneapolis, Minnesota, 1995; worked in Europe as well as the U.S. in 1997, with Baryshnikov's White Oak Project, Taylor, Tharp, Robbins, Dan Wagoner, Jiri Kylian of Nederlands Dans Theater, and theater directors Robert Wilson, JoAnne Akalaitis, and Mike Nichols. **Member:** The Builders Association (a theater group). **Awards:** Creative Arts Award in Dance, Brandeis University, 1982; *Dance Magazine* award, 1991.

Publications

By TIPTON: articles—

"Some Thoughts about Lighting Dance," *Lighting Dimensions,* New York, May/June 1978.

On TIPTON: articles—

Copeland, Roger, "She Casts Ballet Dancers in the Proper Light," *Dance Scrapbook,* London, 3 July 1997.
Dalva, Nancy, "Light Matters," *Dance Ink,* Summer 1994.
Gopnik, Adam, "Climate of Thought," *Dance Ink,* Summer 1994.

Gussow, Mel, profile, *New York Times,* 11 January 1995.

Kisselgoff, Anna, "Necessary Weather" (review), *New York Times,* 9 March 1994.

———, "Playing Fate's Game in a Twisted World" (review), *New York Times,* 13 October 1994.

Ostlere, Hilary, "Jennifer Tipton: Leading Lighter," *Dance Magazine,* April 1990.

Reynolds, Nancy, interview, *Connoisseur Magazine,* February 1985.

Robertson, Nan, profile, *New York Times,* 11 February 1984.

Films and Videotapes

Critical Looks at Dance Trends, interview for *Eye on Dance* series, NYETV, 1988.

Sharing Visions of Poet, Choreographer and Lighting Designer, interview for *Eye on Dance,* NYETV, 1988.

*   *   *

Jennifer Tipton, like Loie Fuller before her, melds scientific curiosity with artistic creativity. She has been a lighting designer for dance since 1965, when she began working with contemporary choreographers Paul Taylor and Twyla Tharp. In her more than three decades at the light board she has become one of the most innovative and skilled masters of the craft, spanning its short history. In 1997, as she approached her 60th birthday, Tipton was so much in demand as a lighting designer for theater as well as dance, both in Europe and the United States, that her schedule was planned at least a year in advance.

Tipton also taught lighting at the Yale School of Drama, although, as she said to Hilary Ostlere in a 1990 interview published in *Dance Magazine,* "You can't really teach design. What it really is is consciousness raising, and you raise your own consciousness as well as your students'."

Born in Columbus, Ohio, the daughter of a physicist mother and a zoologist/biologist father, she entered Cornell University intending to become an astrophysicist and, as she once commented, wanting to be one of the first to land on the moon. Instead, she fell in love with the art of the dance and graduated from Cornell with a major in English. In 1963, after becoming rehearsal director for the Merry-Go-Rounders, a group engaged in what we now call outreach to high school students, Tipton took a course taught by the late and still highly acclaimed Thomas Skelton at Connecticut College. Hooked by the master on lighting design, Tipton became both his apprentice and his secretary, in the former capacity reproducing both his and other designers' lighting for countless performances and, like a 19th-century student of painting, copying masterpieces in museums and refining her own technical skills.

Two years later in 1965, when Skelton took on a Broadway assignment, Tipton's long association with Paul Taylor began when she created the lights for his *Orbs.* According to Hilery Ostlere, in the course of the work's European tryouts, Tipton refined her design, changing things as they went along in a hands-on process that taught her a great deal. Traveling with Taylor's company, Tipton became closely acquainted with Tharp, then a member of the company and occasionally Tipton's roommate. In the subsequent years, she designed the lighting for much of Tharp's groundbreaking work, including *Fait Accompli,* for which she created what writer Joseph Mazo deemed the "memorable curtain of light," and the "mist" for the same choreographer's relentlessly paced 1987 ballet, *In the Upper Room.*

In 1988 Tipton appeared on television's "Eye on Dance" and discussed the changes in her work over a period of 20 years. "The more I look," she said, "the more I see, and feel. I become more and more sensitive. I'm helped by my dance background to see rhythm and dynamics and how light changes the floor, the color and the space." Tipton's ability to explore, learn, and keep her eyes open at all times, translating what she sees into lighting terms that make work intelligible to the audience, have garnered her rave reviews for both her theatrical and her dance designs. Speaking of Tipton's lights for *In the Upper Room,* Nancy Dalva wrote in an article for *Dance Ink* published in 1994, "Without [her], dancers wouldn't appear, disappear, and reappear out of the mist. . . .They wouldn't be there, and then not there. We would see the transitions." Dalva continued, stating "What of Taylor, that man of opposites whose every work has its own peculiar season? . . .[Both] would be seen differently." The same article explained Tipton's working process, developed in the nearly three decades since she first lit Taylor's work: she began with the choreographer's specific requirements for the work—the placement of the dancers, the decor and what it may demand or inhibit, the colors used for both decor and costumes— then Tipton would go home and think about it.

Tipton the English major is revealed in what she says about lighting design in a 1988 "Eye on Dance" interview: "You speak a different language for each production that you do. You establish the words that you're going to use, and then you begin to use sentences and begin speaking the language. The light supports the work." The light, as well as various stage effects, can also create a certain mood, as is more than evident in Tipton's design for Taylor's seemingly lighthearted work, the 1991 *Company B,* for which the precise implementation of her lighting plot is crucial. The work is in the repertoires of a number of ballet companies, as well as Taylor's own. The World War II Andrews Sisters score is not ominous in itself, but with Tipton's lights, as well as Taylor's choreography, it suggests that many of the soldier boys do not come home again. When the lights are wrong and the silhouettes of figures with guns or fallen soldiers are not so visible, the piece loses the strong anti-war sentiment that has been its impetus.

In 1992, Tipton became a less silent collaborator when she received well-deserved equal billing for a piece titled *Necessary Weather, A Choreography of Light and Movement,* choreographed and danced by Sara Rudner and Dana Reitz, with whom Tipton had worked for as many years as with Taylor, Tharp, and Dan Wagoner. Deemed a major work by no less a standard-setter than *New Yorker* dance critic Arlene Croce, it had the ability "to create, just through light and movement, the rhythm of thought. [It] moved the way thought moves, lightly, with a direction rather than a drama and a purpose rather than a plot." Tipton's ballet credits include the Royal Ballet's *Giselle;* Agnes de Mille's *The Informer,* for which she gave the stage the grainy atmosphere of the black-and-white film on which it is based; Jerome Robbins' *Dances at a Gathering;* and many other works in American Ballet Theatre's repertoire. She has also designed lights for Mikhail Baryshnikov's White Oak Project, Trisha Brown, and Jiri Kylian.

Like her predecessor, Jean Rosenthal, Tipton designs lights for theatrical productions and opera as well as modern dance and classical ballet, winning numerous awards for both, including the *Dance Magazine* award in 1991 and in 1982 the Creative Arts Award in Dance from Brandeis University. She received a Guggenheim Fellowship for the 1986-87 season as well as a grant in the National Theatre Artist Residency Program fund by the Pew Charitable Trusts.

—Martha Ullman West

TORONTO DANCE THEATRE
Canadian dance company

Founded by three choreographers, Toronto natives Patricia Beatty and David Earle and New Yorker Peter Randazzo. Initially Graham-based, TDT's creators became renowned for innovative, original choreography. The company gave its first performances, December 1968; Earle began the Professional Training Program of the School of the Toronto Dance Theatre in 1979; Christopher House became resident choreographer, 1981; Kenny Pearl was artistic director, 1983-87; Earle became artistic director, 1987-94; House named artistic director, from 1994; has toured extensively in Canada, the U.S., Europe, Mexico, and Asia.

Publications

Books—

101 from the Encyclopedia of Theatre Dance in Canada, Toronto, 1997.
Wyman, Max, *Dance Canada,* Vancouver, 1989.

Articles—

Anderson, Jack, "Devotees at the Altar of Movement," *New York Times,* 9 November 1995.
————, "Troupe from Canada Needs No Treaty to Bring Innovation Across the Border," *New York Times,* 2 December 1993.
Citron, Paula, "Toronto Dance Theatre: Where the Past and Future Meet," *Dance Magazine,* March 1996.
Crabb, Michael, "Reshaping a Vision," *Vandance International,* Fall 1992.
Kisselgoff, Anna, "Some Heavy Artillery from Toronto," *New York Times,* 14 November 1991.
Kelly, Deirdre, "Startling Messianic Images," *The Globe and Mail,* 12 December 1996.
————, "Balancing Disparate Forms of Expression," *The Globe and Mail,* 28 March 1996.
Littler, William, "Dance Moves in Mysterious Ways," *Toronto Star,* 22 November 1995.
Mason, Francis, "A Conversation with Christopher House," *Canadian Dance Studies 2, 1997,* Graduate Programme in Dance, York University, Selma Odom, Mary Jane Warner, editors, 1997.

*   *   *

Over the 30 years of Toronto Dance Theatre's existence the company has dominated and paled, soared and fallen, and risen out of debt and artistic exhaustion to declare its new vitality. The company and the affiliated School of the Toronto Dance Theatre today are a foundation of contemporary dance in Canada, an influential centre of creation and training.

In 1968 Torontonian Patricia Beatty joined forces with David Earle, another Toronto native, and Peter Randazzo, to create the Toronto Dance Theatre (TDT). Beatty, daughter of a well-connected Toronto family, completed a dance degree at Bennington College and went to New York. She danced with Pearl Lang and Sophie Maslow, and studied at the Graham School for five years. There she encountered David Earle, who had danced with the

Toronto Children's Players and with one of Toronto's first modernist movers, Yone Kvietys, before setting out for the evolved modern dance scene in New York City. Earle studied at the Graham School, and was also drawn to the sweep and humanism of Limón's work. He danced with the Limón company before embarking for London, where philanthropist Robin Howard was inviting talented Commonwealth artists to be part of the birth of a new London dance company. Earle was active in the early days of London Contemporary Dance Theatre, acting as Robert Cohan's assistant director for the company's first London season in 1968. Peter Randazzo, the third of the TDT founders, has claimed that Toronto Dance Theatre was born in a casual conversation on the top of a doubledecker bus in Manchester. Whatever its origins, the time was ripe; earlier Toronto companies had faded away, tied to the energies of their pioneering founders.

Patricia Beatty returned from the U.S. to found the New Dance Group of Canada in 1967. Beatty's group, with guests Randazzo and Earle, gave its inaugural performance in December 1967, at the Ryerson Institute Theatre. To the Toronto audience, unacquainted with their way of moving, the dancers were amazing creatures, seemingly half-animal and half-spirit. They danced a work by Beatty, titled *Momentum,* set to music by Couperin, Rameau, and Ann Southam, based on the story of *Macbeth.* Beatty, Earle, and Randazzo danced Randazzo's first choreographic work, titled *Fragments.* After the performances Earle returned to London and Randazzo to New York, but both were dissatisfied. They determined to start a Toronto company, and were about to finalize an agreement with John Sime, founder of the Three Schools, a Toronto haven for artists during the 1960s. Instead they joined forces with Beatty, and the Toronto Dance Theatre was born. The company gave its first performances in December 1968 at the Toronto Workshop Productions Theatre.

The creative personalities of the three founders were distinctive from the beginning. A commanding, womanly presence as a dancer, the essence of Patricia Beatty's work is chiseled, complex, a highly serious ideal of dance informing her choreographic choices. Randazzo has loved to provoke, to push; his dances represent a giant scope of aspiration, while Earle's choreography mines a vein of passionate humanism—a majority of his more than 100 works have been created for TDT though he has also produced works for other dance companies, festivals, opera, and television. For the first 12 years of TDT's existence these three creators shared the stage—somehow the programs always encompassed the woman's mind revealed in Beatty's works; the lush, musical impasto of Earle's work; and the sly, expert challenges of Randazzo's send-ups and dramas. The seriousness of the company's work at times distanced them from developing a warm audience following, but they persevered and the company shifted shape following the changes in their prolific creative output. In 1988 the three shared the prestigious Toronto Arts Award for changing the face of dance in Toronto.

At TDT the art of dancing has always run parallel in respect, importance, and attention to the art of choreography. Many of its extraordinary dancers have gone on to important careers as directors, dancers, teachers and choreographers. Among these are Amelia Itcush, one whom it was impossible to tell what she was, exactly, whether she was woman or man, flesh or spirit. She danced the young Mary Magdalene in Earle's *A Thread of Sand* (1969), moving like a wraith, a vapor trail, a memory. Others include Barry Smith (long, ascetic, and seemingly consumed by the passion of dancing), Susan Macpherson (gloriously dramatic and tall), Keith Urban (handsome, dramatic, moved with flow and forceful physi-

Toronto Dance Theatre: *Pingo Slink.* **Photograph by Cylla von Tiedemann.**

cality), Helen Jones (exquisite plasticity gave a maddening cool edge to her extraordinary beauty), Peggy Baker (passionate, intelligent, marvelously gifted, now an icon of Canadian dance), and later Grace Miyagawa (goddess qualities in her strong, mysterious dancing), Karen DuPlessis (whose presence was piquant as a lemon tart, swift, a sharp-eyed seabird, soaring and darting), Robert Desrosiers (unmistakably virtuostic, another legend), Benoit Lachambre's dancing resonates, possessed and transcendently physical, Claudia Moore (an intense spirit, muse, and inspiration). And then there was Christopher House.

Christopher House, initially aiming for a career in the diplomatic corps, changed course after studies with Elizabeth Langley at the University of Ottawa and went on to graduate from York University's dance program. By the time he went downtown to dance with TDT in 1978, it was clear that he was a spectacularly talented dancer and he quickly developed as a choreographer. From the first, his musicality and searchingly innovative movement dazzled. *Toss Quintet* (1980) marked a choreographic watershed. He became resident choreographer at TDT in 1981 and

has been the recipient of all of Canada's major choreographic awards.

Toronto Dance Theatre has been involved in a long arc of change. By 1982 the three founding choreographers were fatigued, their creative output low. The company was staggering under the accumulated debt-load of their $1.2 million investment in St. Enoch's Church, the large building which houses the company, school, and Winchester Street Theatre. The company was on the verge of severe cuts from its funding agencies, and considered anachronistic by some dance observers. At David Earle's suggestion, in 1983 the company came under the directorship of Kenny Pearl, a former dancer with Alvin Ailey. Pearl, the first person in TDT's history to be titled "artistic director," was determined to give the company a fresh look. He nurtured the talents of the company's dancers, and programmed work by all four resident choreographers, but focusing on the vivid talents of Christopher House. The company's image was quickly reinvigorated by the lightning complexity and expertise of House's formidable creative output. Pearl's four-year directorship was stormy, as the three founders struggled to maintain their creative priorities in a shifting mandate.

Pearl was replaced by Earle as artistic director in 1987. Under Earle's directorship the company found stability and continuing growth, embracing a broader perspective in its programming than in earlier days. The company enjoyed great acclaim in New York in 1991 with a program including James Kudelka's *Fifteen Heterosexual Duets* (1991). Earle led the company on a return engagement to the Joyce Theater and on tour in Europe and Asia. Earle resigned as artistic director in 1994, following TDT's 25th anniversary, and at that time House became the company's artistic director.

Its reputation for excellence enhanced by critical acclaim in New York and elsewhere, TDT has continued to broaden its touring base, traveling to Tokyo, Mexico City, widely in Europe and increasingly in Asia. While he is firmly committed to movement as his expressive medium, rather than a blend of theatre and other influences, House has a keen interest in the dynamic challenges of performing to live music. Collaboration is key to his vision, as in the projects the company has undertaken with the respected Toronto new music ensemble ArrayMusic. In a 1995 version of Terry Riley's *Cactus Rosary*, the dancers and musicians were truly integrated. The companies, with solo artist Peggy Baker, joined in an ambitious 1997 venture titled *MusicDanceArray*. In 1997 House was collaborating with radical Korean artist Kim Soo-Ja and composer Kung Chi Shing on *Bottari*, part of the company's Asian touring repertory in January-February 1998. Also in '97, Chandralekha, the visionary Indian choreographer, was asked to create a work with TDT.

House is interested in the cultivation of the superb dancers in the fourteen-member company. Some of these are also promising choreographers, among them Coralee McLaren, Michael Trent, and Laurence Lemieux. House is devoted to TDT enduring and continuing its strengths, "committed to exploring new ideas in choreographic expression while embracing the fresh and vital aspects of inherited traditions."

—Carol Anderson

TREND

Choreography: Hanya Holm
Music: Wallingford Riegger and Edward Varese
Costumes: Betty Joiner
Set Design: Arch Lauterer
Lighting: Gerard Gentire
First Production: Bennington Festival of 1937, the Workshop Production of the Bennington School of the Dance, Bennington College, 13 August 1937; first New York performance, Mecca Auditorium (the present-day City Center), 28 December 1937 with Lauterer doing both lights and sets
Dancers: Hanya Holm with Louise Kloepper, Keith Coppage, Carolyn Durand, Henrietta Greenwood, Marva Jaffay, Miriam Kagan, Ruth Ledoux, Lydia Tarnower, Bernice Van Gelder, Elizabeth Waters, and Lucretia Wilson as the Concert Group; with an additional 22 dancers as members of the Workshop Group

Publications

Lloyd, Margaret, *The Borzoi Book of Modern Dance*, New York, Alfred A. Knopf, 1949.

Magazine of Art, March 1938.
Sorell, Walter, *Hanya Holm: The Biography of an Artist,* Middletown, Connecticut, 1969.

*   *   *

Hanya Holm, the German-American dancer, teacher, and choreographer, premiered *Trend,* a dramatic dance epic, in 1937. It was her first major composition and was performed by her own company, Hanya Holm and Group, and an ensemble of 30. Along with Holm's *Metropolitan Diary* (1938) and *Tragic Exodus* (1939), *Trend* commented on the state of society in a world about to be consumed by war. The work was considered revolutionary in 1937. The program note described the work in the following terms: "*Trend* is a picture of man's survival when the usages of living have lost their meaning and he has fallen into routine patterns of conformity. Though in this direction of decadence lie only catastrophe and ultimate annihilation, there emerges out of the ordeal. . .a recognition of the common purposes of men and the conscious unity of life." Despite this rather pessimistic view of the state of society, Holm was not without hope. She firmly believed in timeless creative forces that could never be destroyed. At the conclusion of *Trend,* these forces rise up again in a renewed sense of affirmation. Holm choreographed and danced a slow solo for herself.

Trend was a hugely ambitious work reflecting Holm's profound sense of space and direction. It was composed of six sections performed to an original score for flute, oboe, bassoon, trumpet, piano, and percussion by Riegger. A mechanical reproduction (performed on electrical equipment by Mirko Paneyko) of Edward Varese's *Ionization* was used for the final section. When the work was performed for the first time in New York City, a new finale was added to Varese's *Octandre.*

There was no traditional stage setting for *Trend;* instead, Holm's designer Arch Lauterer used inclined planes, ramps, and steps to convey a sense of monumentality. At the premiere performance, the orchestra level of the Moorish-inspired Mecca Theater was closed off for use by the dancers. The audience looked down on the action from the balconies. The stage's rear wall was left exposed to create a sense of loneliness. The principal soloists in the first performance included Louise Kloepper, Lucretia Wilson, Elizabeth Waters, and Henrietta Greenhood. Valerie Bettis was one of the dancers in the "augmented" group. Holm arranged her dancers on Lauterer's ramps, steps, and planes in either balanced groupings or in counterpoint to one another. John Martin of the *New York Times* praised Holm's use of space in his review of 26 February 1938. He went so far as to call *Trend* the season's most important work. Not all observers were equally impressed. The dance's length and unconventional staging left some confused and impatient.

Trend consisted of solos and group dances. The main emphasis was on the group as a whole, however. "Mask Motions, Our Daily Bread" consisted of a group of regimented workers droning emptily in their workaday lives; "Satiety" depicted the boredom of the idle rich while the drive to get money was depicted in "Money Madness." A series of solos focused on the general humdrum tenor of life: with Louise Kloepper's neurotic solo called "The Effete" and religious fanaticism captured in "From Heaven, Ltd." as a solo for Lucretia Wilson. The search for release from suffering in the use of drugs, drink, and empty pleasures was captured in another solo, "Lest We Remember," performed by Elizabeth Waters while Henrietta Greenhood danced in "He, the Great," a commentary on hero worship. Finally, the entire group joined together in "Cataclysm" to dance out the forces and emotions dividing the world. In "The Gates Are Desolate" the dancers perform a dance of awakening, while a mass stirring of hope is depicted in "Resurgence," followed by "Assurance," in which the world is made whole again.

Well-known photographs from performances of *Trend* showed Holm leading a quartet of women, arranged in profile on several levels. The dancers, costumed in long, white jersey dresses, bent backwards as they gently curved one arm around their heads. The other arm was held behind their backs. Other photographs showed Holm's arrangement of dancers on the famous ramps. *Trend* was notable for its continual use of flowing, ebbing movement and the massing of groups of dancers in powerful designs. Margaret Lloyd described it as unfolding "like a colossal panorama."

—Adriane Ruggiero

TRISLER, Joyce

American dancer, choreographer, educator, and company director

Born: 21 August 1934 in Los Angeles. **Family:** Married to Charles Woodford; one son, Jonathan. **Education:** Washington High School, Los Angeles; attended University of California at Los Angeles. Studied dance with Lester Horton, Carmelita Maracci, Antony Tudor, Hanya Holm, Robert Joffrey, and Edward Caton; studied at the Juilliard School where Tudor was one of her teachers. **Career:** Danced with the Lester Horton Dance Theater, 1951-54; after Horton's death in 1953, was brought to New York City by Doris Humphrey and became the leading performer of the Juilliard Dance Theatre throughout its five-year existence; freelance performer from the mid-1950s through the 1960s, performing with the companies of John Wilson and Alvin Ailey; principal dancer with Alvin Ailey, until 1964; appeared in concerts at the 92nd Street YMHA, dancing with James Truitte in *Bagatelle* (1960) and *Variegations* (1958); dancer, Valerie Bettis group's concerts of the American Dance Theatre, 1965; founder, Danscompany, which grew directly out of *Rite of Spring*, which she choreographed in 1974; choreographer for opera, plays, and musicals; set dances on the New York City Opera, San Francisco Opera, and Boston Opera; choreographer, New York Shakespeare Festival's productions in Central Park, 1967-71; a leading teacher of Horton technique, revived his work on several companies; supervised the reconstruction of *The Beloved* for the Alvin Ailey American Dance Theatre; revived works of Ruth St. Denis and Ted Shawn; Danscompany frequently performed the Denishawn repertory for entire seasons in New York and on tour. **Died:** 13 October 1979 in New York City, of a heart attack.

Roles

1952	*Seven Scenes with Ballabilli* (Horton)
	Prado de Pena (Horton)
	Dedication in Our Times (Horton)
1955	*The Rock and the Spring* (Humphrey)
1956	*Descent into the Dream* (Humphrey)
	Dawn in New York (Humphrey)
1958	*Out of the Chrysalis* (McKayle)
1964	*The Beloved* (Horton), Alvin Ailey American Dance Theatre

Works

1956	*Playthings of the Wind*
1958	*Journey*
	The Pearl
	Place of Panic
	Everyman Today (theatre)
1959	*Bewitched*
	Theater Piece
1960	*Bergamesca*
	Dance for Percussion
	Nite Life
	Primera Cancion
1961	*Dance for Percussion*, 92nd Street YMHA
	Eccosaises
1964	*Ballroom*
1965	*Perilous Times*, solo for Earle Sieveling, Boston Ballet
1967	*Titus Andronicus* (theatre)
1968	*Henry IV* (theatre)
	Romeo and Juliet (theatre)
	King Arthur (opera)
1969	*Bronx Zoo Cantata*
	Peer Gynt (theatre)
	Dance for Six (mus. Vivaldi)
	La Strada (theatre)
1970	*Look to the Lillies* (theatre)
	Journey, solo
1971	*Timon of Athens* (theatre)
	Great Scot! (theatre)
1972	*Ambassador* (theatre)
1973	*Beatrix Cenci* (opera)
1974	*Rite of Spring*
	Soliloquy of a Bhiksuni
1975	*Four Temperaments*
	Death in Venice (opera)
	Little Red Riding Hood
1976	*Four Against the Gods*, Theatre of Riverside Church
	Little Red Riding Hood, Theatre of Riverside Church
	The Good Soldier Schweik (opera)
1978	*Fantasies and Fugues*
1979	*By Dawn's Early Light*
	Concerto in E

Publications

On TRISLER: articles—

Dunning, Jennifer, *New York Times,* 23 December 1979.
Clippings File on Joyce Trisler, the Dance Collection of the Performing Arts Research Center in the New York Public Library at Lincoln Center.

*   *   *

Known for her outspokenness and breezy, wisecracking sense of humor, Joyce Trisler worked with some of the leading modern dance luminaries of the 20th century as well as forming and appearing with a number of companies small and large. Trisler was a leading authority on the technique of Lester Horton, the California-based innovator of modern dance. She was also a member of the Juilliard Dance Theatre from 1955 to 1959, during which time she

Joyce Trisler's Danscompany. Photograph © Beatriz Schiller.

worked closely with Doris Humphrey, the pioneering American modern dance choreographer and the company's founder. While in New York, Trisler danced with Alvin Ailey, another Lester Horton protégé, during Ailey's first European tour in 1964. Her own company, Danscompany, was best remembered for its program *The Spirit of Denishawn,* an evening of dances by Ruth St. Denis and Ted Shawn, revived by Klarna Plinska, a former St. Denis dancer. Above all, Trisler was a woman of the theater who once said "the theater is in my blood." Yet Trisler knew the tremendous struggle required to work in modern dance. She supported herself by teaching for three years at Sarah Lawrence College in Bronxville, New York, and by choreographing for Broadway shows, plays, and operas.

Trisler was born in Los Angeles, California, and had a year of dance training. Then she left the classroom behind. As Trisler told Jennifer Dunning in a 1978 interview, she didn't always want to dance, but dance lured her back. During high school she appeared in plays given by Geller's Theatre Workshop and acted in a weekly dramatic show on the radio station of the University of Southern California. She also performed in educational short films. Trisler developed an interest in social dancing, and after winning several contests decided to study modern dance. She began classes at Lester Horton's school and progressed rapidly under Horton's direction. During her first year at Horton, she was invited to join his dance group but only after an ultimatum was delivered: "I was the big Shakespearean actress in California. I walked in late to rehearsal one day. . .and Lester said to me, 'You're either going to be Ophelia or you're going to be in this company.' I couldn't make up my mind. He threw me out twice but after awhile I realized that actors are 10 times more boring than dancers." Trisler spent five years with the Lester Horton group and gained great experience in dancing as well as in theater design, costuming, and lighting.

In the summer of 1954, Trisler traveled to New York City to audition for Doris Humphrey at the Connecticut College Summer School of Dance. Since Humphrey was also teaching at Juilliard, Trisler enrolled there for the three-year course in dance and academics. She also became a member of the newly-formed Juilliard Dance Theatre, where Trisler's dramatic intensity was used to fine advantage in the revival of Humphrey's *Life of the Bee.* Her lyricism earned her a leading role in the Humphrey work *Dawn in New York.* Her decision to hook up with Humphrey was a turning point in her career. Being brought up at Juilliard and educated by Tudor, Graham, and Limón gave Trisler one of the best educations in dance then available. In addition, Trisler served as the assistant to the ill Humphrey while at the Juilliard Dance Theater.

Trisler started setting dances from the time she arrived in New York. Her works are in the repertories of the Alvin Ailey American Dance Theatre and the Boston Ballet. She taught modern dance in New York for many years and was a member of the teaching staffs of the New Dance Group Studio and the Alvin Ailey American Dance Center.

With Ailey, Trisler helped keep the Lester Horton technique alive. She worked in a no-nonsense style and demanded that students perform the quick falls and rises and fast-paced small steps called for by Horton. She passed along the Horton look: a sustained long line, high-stretching extensions and strong, rounded arms, supple backs and "controlled freedom." Despite the physical demands of Horton technique, Trisler found young dance students of the 1970s willing to embrace it. Growing up in a tight, middle-class environment on the West Coast, Trisler recalled that Horton's technique freed her. However, she found contemporary young dancers had a more expansive sense of themselves. As Trisler once stated, "they're dancing for joy."

In 1961 Trisler presented several new dances at the 92nd Street YMHA. Among them was *Dance for Percussion,* which was characterized by feet pounding into the floor and powerful percussive leaps. Trisler was joined by James Truitte in a duet. Trisler never allowed her dance phrases to be merely a bridge from symbol to symbol. Instead the symbols were incidental posts along a dramatic way. Trisler made headlines as a dancer with the Alvin Ailey company in the 1960s. Viewers who saw the five-foot, eight-inch, slender, dark-haired Trisler and James Truitte in Horton's *The Beloved* as staged by Ailey were thunderstruck. Upon seeing the Ailey company on tour, English dance critics called Trisler and Truitte "two of the best modern dancers ever to visit London: fluent, mobile, sensitive, and consistently rewarding in their movements." No other two dancers have come close to creating the duet between a dogmatic husband and servile wife. Gradually as they dance, all of the husband's religious fanaticism and bigotry becomes apparent until he finally strangles his wife. Some reviewers saw this as a continuation in the lives of the young New England couple who built a house in Graham's *Appalachian Spring.* It is considered a remarkable short modern dance work.

Far from looking askance at ballet, Trisler maintained that ballet dancers could do anything. In 1965 she set a modern dance work on the Boston Ballet. Entitled *Perilous Times,* the solo for Earle Sieveling explored the theme of the lone dreamer blindly opposed and finally crushed by the crowd. Trisler danced the mother image who first consoles, then mourns. Sieveling achieved the demands of Trisler's choreography in his first modern dance role. Trisler left the world of dance for 10 years and bought a farm in Pennsylvania. She supported herself doing shows for La Mama and for Joseph Papp's Public Theater. Pulled back into choreographing for herself in 1969, Trisler scored a great success with *Dance for Six* to a score by Vivaldi. It was a choreographic work for three couples. A work of substantial energy and smooth flow, filled with caressing diagonal sweeps and clusters of dancers, *Dance for Six* was the culmination of her years as a choreographer.

Gradually she was drawn further into the modern dance world. Trisler's approach to making dances began with listening to all types of music hoping for that moment when a piece became "visual," and a dance started to take shape in her mind. Watching a Trisler ballet reveals dancers trained in both modern dance and ballet technique. Her work is highly athletic and seeks total use and freedom of space. She continually sought dances with dramatic moods and meanings. Her dancers move uninterruptedly from the floor to the air. Above all, she demonstrated an affection for what she has called the "almost insane joy that comes back from the audience when you feel they want to get up and dance with you."

Her 1970 solo piece *Journey* set to Charles Ives' *The Unanswered Question* is a somber but lyrical dance. The theme—journeying, searching—was danced by Trisler in slow, sustained movements. In one movement she repeats a step in which the dancer places her weight on an outstretched front foot and raised her other foot high behind her in a kind of knee-down attitude. Trisler danced her solo superbly with her long arms and legs achieving the subtle, elegant purity of line demanded by her theme. As one reviewer pointed out, "nobody but a woman could have created it, nobody but a woman could have danced it. Possibly more than any modern dance work—either for groups or soloists—this dance shows the flowing possibilities of modern dance movement—it ripples like delicate seaweed on an ebb tide."

In *Rite of Spring* (1974), Trisler set her dancers running, leaping, and tumbling across the stage in jagged diagonals. They eddy at the center with flexed feet and spread their fingers suggesting ritual. According to Jennifer Dunning in the *New York Times,* "*Rite* achieves its savagery and moments of mystery in terms of dance and music alone." This is a demanding dance with such Trisler hallmarks as skewed lifts and high-energy flow. In 1976, Trisler presented her Danscompany at the Theatre of the Riverside Church. In *Four Against the Gods,* Trisler depicted four women who shaped modern dance—Isadora Duncan, Ruth St. Denis, Doris Humphrey, and Martha Graham. It was as one critic pointed out, "more than a fascinating sketch of the possibilities." Several hard fast unison passages jar the singularity and dignity of the subjects. It is only when the four interact that the dance finds a form of communication. Yet the same reviewer hoped Trisler would continue to explore the rich and important material the work presented. On the same program, *Little Red Riding Hood* (the fable transferred to New York City) is popular art at its best. While reviewers found the story banal, the dancing had flow, colorful characterization, and fine, unaffected performances. Yet the public responded to Trisler's choreography with mixed reactions.

Trisler's work as a teacher in New York City was important to many young dancers. In addition, her associations with Horton and Humphrey helped keep the work of these two dance legends alive. Her revivals of the work of Denishawn were extremely important to the dance world, too, not only to celebrate the achievements of these early pioneers, but to reintroduce them to newer, receptive audiences. As a teacher, dancer, and choreographer she touched with spirit deeply. At the time of her death in 1979 she was reconstructing her 1974 piece *Rite of Spring.* Alvin Ailey later dedicated a new dance, *Memoria,* to the "joy, beauty, creativity and wild spirit" of Joyce Trisler.

—Adriane Ruggiero

TRUITTE, James
American dancer, choreographer, and educator

Born: 1925 in Chicago. **Education:** Attended UCLA, premed; pursued dance instead studying with Frances Allis, Janet Collins, Carmalita Maracci, and Archie Savage; began training with Lester Horton, 1948. **Career:** Toured with *Carmen Jones,* 1945-47; dancer, Lester Horton Dancers, beginning 1950; dancer and associate artistic director, Alvin Ailey American Dance Theatre, 1960-68; taught at Cincinnati College Conservatory of Music, becoming associate professor, 1973. **Awards:** John Hay Whitney Foundation fellowship. **Died:** August 1995.

Works

1955	*Introduction to the Dance*
	Miss Salomé
	Mirror, Mirror
1958	*With Timbrel and Dance Praise His Name,* Los Angeles
	Two Spirituals
	The Duke's Bard
	Variegations
1960	*Bagatelles*
1971	*Guernica* (mus. Carmon de Leone), for Cincinnati Ballet Company
1975	*With Timbrel and Dance Praise His Name* (revised and expanded; mus. de Leone)
1979	*Variegations* (restaged; mus. de Leone) for Cincinnati Ballet

Films and Videotapes

Major motion pictures include: *Carmen Jones* (1954), *The Mole People* (1956), *South Pacific* (1959), and *The Sins of Rachel Cade* (1961).

*   *   *

James Truitte is known more for his efforts to educate other dancers and to keep the methodology of Lester Horton alive than for his own pursuits in the dance world as a performer. But that does not in any way diminish his talent as a dancer, a teacher and a choreographer.

Truitte had aspirations of becoming a doctor in his hometown of Chicago, Illinois. After he went away to college at the University of California in Los Angeles, he discovered dance. Archie Savage, Janet Collins, Frances Allis and Carmalita Maracci were among the initial dance teachers who shaped his skills. His professional career began with a national tour of the musical *Carmen Jones* from 1945 to 1947, and in 1948, after encouragement from Collins, he began serious dance training with Lester Horton in Los Angeles. By 1950 he was a member of the Lester Horton Dancers, where he advanced to a principal soloist and danced with another company member and aspiring choreographer, Alvin Ailey. Upon the death of Horton in 1953, Truitte became the company's principal teacher and choreographer. The next year, 1954, he reprised his *Carmen Jones* role for the silver screen, and went on to appear in *South Pacific* in 1959.

Alvin Ailey, meanwhile, had departed the West Coast for New York City and had formed his own company, the Alvin Ailey American Dance Theatre (AAADT). Truitte came to New York and in 1960 joined AAADT as a principal soloist and associate artistic director. While with Ailey, he danced in many of the company's signature works, including *The Twelve Gates* in 1964, a duet for him and Carmen de Lavallade, performed at the Jacob's Pillow dance festival in Lee, Massachusetts.

As a dancer, Truitte explored movement, joyously imparting a contagious enthusiasm. His technique and dynamic transitions made him extremely versatile. Whether as a principal soloist with the Lester Horton Dancers on the West Coast or with the Alvin Ailey American Dance Theatre on the East Coast, he was a dancer with a style and class all his own. As a teacher, Truitte was equally gifted. Using humor and gentle prodding he was able to allow his students to be themselves by giving them the freedom to open up. It was impossible for Truitte's attitude not to pour into even the most difficult of exercises and make them enjoyable.

As a choreographer, James Truitte melded technique and artistry into a chorus of power. This is evidenced most in 1971's *Guernica*, an original choreographic work created for the Cincinnati Ballet. The piece was inspired by the Picasso painting of the same name, detailing the aftermath of Nazi bombers on the Basque town in Spain. Though choreographically based on a movement study of Lester Horton's, Truitte punctuated the piece with fleeting jetés and dancers plunging to their knees as if shot down. In 1975's *With Timbrel and Dance Praise His Name*, Truitte used vocal soloists, an orchestra and a chorus to celebrate rituals of devotion and joy. Whether in solos or group dances, Truitte choreographed with fluid transitions while he advanced the piece artistically through a range of emotions. An earlier work, 1958's *Variegations,* is an artistic journey through the progression of the deep floor exercises of Lester Horton. Here Truitte employed his theatricality to infuse classroom exercises with tension and drama such as gravity-defying off-balances and converting simple hollowing stretches with contractions to convey anguish and terror. *Variegations* was restaged in 1979, with original music by Carmon de Leone, for the Cincinnati Ballet.

Truitte went on to become an associate professor in 1973 at the Cincinnati College's Conservatory of Music, where he brought national recognition to the school for performing the works of Lester Horton. The world of modern dance rarely applauds those that follow; rather it lauds those who depart from the path and follow an inner guide—and this is exactly what James Truitte managed to do. He knew the value of the Horton technique and chose to follow his own inner guidance to teach and preserve it. He was a dancer who cared about the future by preserving the past—a great gift for the many who may never have come into contact with Horton—and his devotion became Truitte's own contribution to modern dance.

—Cynthia Roses-Thema and Sydonie Benet

TUERLINGS, Hans
Dutch dancer, choreographer, and company director

Born: 31 May 1951 in Tilburg, the Netherlands. **Education:** Dance Dept., Brabants Conservatory, Tilburg, 1970-73; Rotterdam Conservatory, Rotterdam, 1973-74. **Career:** Dancer, Penta Theater, Rotterdam, 1974-75; choreographer, since 1975, first mainly for Werkcentrum Dans (now Rotterdamse Dansgroep) led by former

Nederlands Dans Theater soloist Käthy Gosschalk and for Scapino Ballet, Jiri Kylian's Nederlands Dans Theater, and Intro Dans, all in the Netherlands; choreographer, Yehudit Arnon's Kibbutz Contemporary Dance Company, Israel; teacher of composition, Scapino Dance Department and Dance Expression Department, Amsterdam, 1981-85; columnist, Dutch dance magazines *Dansbulletin* and *Notes,* 1982-90; choreographer, children's productions and amateur productions, from 1985-present; choreographer for own groups, TUERLINGS (formerly Sodemieter Op) and from 1990 on, for Raz.

Works

1975   *Koffie voor vijf* (mus. Vivaldi), ad hoc project, Stadsschouwburg, Amsterdam

1976   *Nobody Cares about the Railroad Anymore* (also called *Trein;* mus. 1930s boogie-woogie), Werkcentrum Dans (now Rotterdamse Dansgroep), Pakhus 13, Kopenhagen

    Twee Avonden (half of a two-part program; mus. Chopin/De Haas), Werkcentrum Dans, Lantaren, Rotterdam

    Om los te lopen (mus. hit parade Italia), Werkcentrum Dans, Lantaren, Rotterdam

    Koffie voor vijf (restaged; mus. Vivaldi), Scapino Ballet, Stadsschouwburg, Amsterdam

1977   *Harem* (mus. Nilsson), Werkcentrum Dans, Lantaren, Rotterdam

    Populaire Klassieken (mus. collage march music), Werkcentrum Dans, Lantaren, Rotterdam

    Een aardigheidje (mus. Prokofiev), Werkcentrum Dans, Lantaren, Rotterdam

    Masquerade (mus. Katchaturian), Scapino Ballet, Stadsschouwburg, Amsterdam

1978   *Tutto Liscio* (solo; mus. trad./Van Beurden), Johan Meyer, Nederlands Dans Theater, Hot Theater, the Hague

    Drie liefdes (mus. Prokofiev), Werkcentrum Dans, Lantaren, Rotterdam

    Scorza i Banana, (mus. diverse), Werkcentrum Dans, Lantaren, Rotterdam

    Suske en Wiske (mus. Alkema), Werkcentrum Dans, Lantaren, Rotterdam

1979   *De truc met de kist* (mus. Carpenter), Nederlands Dans Theater, Hot Theater, the Hague

    Tutto Liscio (restaged; mus. trad./Van Beurden), Werkcentrum Dans, Lantaren, Rotterdam

    Chris (mus. Nilsson), Werkcentrum Dans & Bodybuilders, Holland Festival, Theater Bellevue, Amsterdam

1980   *Wasteland* (with director Franz Marijnen), RO Theater & Werkcentrum Dans, Schouwburg, Rotterdam

    Waltzing Mathilda (mus. Reed), Scapino Ballet, Stadsschouwburg, Amsterdam

    Quaquaraqua (mus. Italian film music), Werkcentrum Dans, Lantaren, Rotterdam

    Om los te lopen (restaged; mus. hit parade Italia), Kibbutz Contemporary Dance Compagny, studio kibbutz Gaaton, Israel

    ETC (mus. diverse), Kibbutz Contemporary Dance Company, studio kibbutz Gaaton, Israel

1981   *Zweth* (mus. Landry), Introdans, Schouwburg, Arnhem

    Tutto Liscio (mus. trad./Van Beurden), restaged as duet, Scapino Ballet, Holland

    UHM UHM (mus. collage), Werkcentrum Dans, Lantaren, Rotterdam

    De Slungels w/director Lodewijk de Boer (mus. Waisvisz), Theater Bellevue, Amsterdam

1982   *P.M.* (mus. Van Domselaer, Jarrett, D.A.F.), Werkcentrum Dans & RO Theater, Holland Festival, Schouwburg, Rotterdam

1983   *Scassapagghiara* (mus. Italian film music), Introdans, Schouwburg, Arnhem

    Wie vermoordde Richard Wagner, STIFT, Lak Theater, Leiden

    Vertchou (mus. diverse), Werkcentrum Dans, Lantaren, Rotterdam

1984   *Boulevard* (mus. Jarreth), Multi Media/Bart Stuyf, Toneelschuur, Haarlem

    Sirenetta, of de kleine zeemeermin (mus. Tchaikovsky), Introdans, Schouwburg, Arnhem

1985   *Sodemieter op, Wat!* (mus. Antheil), De Engelenbak, Amsterdam

    Keetje Baba en de tijdrovers (mus. collage), Cees Brandt, Schouwburg, Rotterdam

1986   *Piet Hutten* (mus. Alkema), Sodemieter op, De Engelenbak, Amsterdam

    Romeo & Julia w/Rufus Collins (mus. Klein, Kuiper), De Engelenbak, Amsterdam

    Om los te lopen (restaged; mus. hit parade Italia), Werkcentrum Dans, Holland Dance Festival, Spui Theater, the Hague

    Nessune o tutti (mus. Kleijn, Kuiper), Reflex, Stadsschouwburg, Groningen

    Acte sans paroles, part 1 (play by Beckett; dir. Cees Brandt), Toneelschuur, Haarlem

1987   *Puntenland (Toen puntje bij paaltje kwam)* (mus. collage), Cees Brandt, Shaffy Theater (now Felix Meritis), Amsterdam

    Twee Dingen (mus. Beethoven), Dansend Hart, Stadsschouwburg, Utrecht

    De Kinderen Hutten w/Patrizia Tuerlings (mus. Alkema), Sodemieter op, De Engelenbak, Amsterdam

1988   *A Noeud Coulant!* (mus. Kleijn, Kuiper), duet, Reflex, Stadschouwburg, Groningen

    The Mandarina Day (mus. Birnbach), Rotterdamse Dansgroep, Theater Zuidplein, Rotterdam

1989   *I Am a Hotel* (mus. Kleijn, Kuiper), Reflex, Stadsschouwburg, Groningen

    Bedrog (play by Pinter; mus. Kleijn, Kuiper), De Voorziening, Studio De Voorziening, Groningen

    BAM w/Patrizia Tuerlings; mus. trad. Russian, Pirchner), Dansgroep Tuerlings, Holland Festival, De Krakeling, Amsterdam

    De Plicht (mus. diverse), De Salon, Frascati, Amsterdam

1990   *Vue perspective intérieure coloriée* (mus. Frith), Nationaal Fonds, Felix Meritis, Amsterdam

    Duet for *Kataloog* (concept programme Piet Rogie; mus. Davis), duet, Compagnie Peter Bulcaen, Lantaren, Rotterdam

    Hangen in karton (mus. Andriessen), Reflex, Stadsschouwburg, Groningen

    Razbliuto of een serieuze studie in hedendaagse verwarring (mus. Frith, Schnittke, a.o.), Raz, Stadsschouwburg, Breda

1991   *Le sacre du printemps* (mus. Stravinsky/Bon), coproduction Raz & Reflex, Akademie Theater, Utrecht

100.000 CC (mus. Frith), duet, for children, coproduction Raz & Eindhoven Festival, Stadsschouwburg, Eindhoven

1992   *Tutto Liscio* (mus. trad./Van Beurden), restaged back to solo, Reflex, Stadsschouwburg, Groningen

de Reis (mus. Kleijn, Kuiper), Raz, Stadsschouwburg, Tilburg

Spel zonder woorden (mus. Van Vliet), for children, Raz, Stadsschouwburg, Tilburg

PM de voorstelling (mus. Van Vliet), coproduction Faculteit der Kunsten Tilburg & Raz, Stadsschouwburg Concordia, Breda

1993   *de Reis 3* (mus. Kleijn, Kuiper), Raz, Schouwburg, Casino Den Bosch

1994   *You see what you wanna see you hear what you wanna hear did you see new delhi? and I said no!* w/Patrizia Tuerlings (mus. Frith, Zorn, Waisvisz), coproduction Raz & Reflex, Grand Theater, Groningen

Mooi & Lelijk of ik haal liever nog even adem (mus. Van Vliet), coproduction Raz & Nationaal Fonds, Akademie Theater, Utrecht

Daniel and the Dancers (mus. Steinbachek), coproduction Raz, Remote Control, Theater am Turm, Dansens Hus, Nes-theaters & Lantaren/Venster, Stadsschouwburg, Tilburg

1995   *de Reis 2, sans peau et sans arêtes* (mus. Van Vliet), Raz, Akademie Theater, Utrecht

Achterland (mus. Van Vliet), living room project *Seul,* Bis producties, a living room, Den Bosch

1996   *Ik ga zei zij waarheen zei hij* (mus. Van Vliet), a piece for children, coproduction Raz & Springdance 1996, Stadsschouwburg, Utrecht

de Reis 4 ça va pas. . . (mus. Gainsbourg, Van Vliet), Raz, Stadsschouwburg, Tilburg

1997   *Bla bla cha cha* (mus. De Clercq), "Bal moderne," Springdance 1997, Winkel van Sinkel, Utrecht

Planet Lulu (mus. Steinbachek), coproduction Raz, Remote Control, Kulturhus Århus, Theater am Turm, Hebbel Theater, Monty, Dansens Hus and Two Moon, Stadsschouwburg, Utrecht

Rewind/Play (mus. Van Vliet), living room project *Seul,* Produktiehuis Brabant, a living room, Den Bosch

Bagno blu (casa del sogno) (mus. Van Vliet), Raz, Schouwburg, Tilburg

*   *   *

Participating in an operetta performance, where he was asked to act as a dancing partner for a lady, opened Hans Tuerlings' eyes to dance. He quit his study of biochemistry at the university and went to the dance department in Tilburg, where he was the only male student. He received a strict classical education from Hans van der Togt (formerly of the Nederlands Dans Theater) and Simon André (formerly of Het Nationale Ballet). After a switch to Rotterdam he was fortunate in finding American Lucas Hoving. Hoving was an understanding teacher, who was driven to stimulate his students to get into choreography. This nudge was what Tuerlings needed. Through reading many books, watching films, sitting in pubs, and wandering around, mostly in Italy, came the beginning of a slow process that later burst out in a explosion

of energy to choreograph. As a novice, Tuerlings was impressed by the theatrical work of choreographer Louis Falco, and especially Polish creator Tomaszewski, in whose work he saw not just dance but a rich form of theatre without words. Tuerlings then knew: "This is what I want." In the famous Dutch choreographer Hans van Manen's very stylized aesthetics, though very different in appearance from Tuerlings' style, the younger choreographer felt something for which he himself also strived.

His first piece, *Koffie voor vijf,* was a result of a workshop in 1975, commissioned by the Ministry of Culture. After this he worked professionally as a choreographer—in the beginning primarily for Werkcentrum Dans (now Rotterdamse Dansgroep) led by former Nederlands Dans Theater soloist Käthy Gosschalk, later for the Scapino Ballet, Nederlands Dans Theater, Intro Dans, and, more recently for the former company Reflex, all in the Netherlands. He went abroad to create for the Kibbutz Contemporary Dance Company in Israel, and also began to choreograph for children and amateur productions. On all of these occasions the working process, in Tuerlings' view, differed very little; he made the usual 20-minute pieces and noticed that it was not always easy to find the right dancers and opportunities for what he had in mind. So he concentrated in those cases more on experimenting with the dance instead of his own theatrical ideas. Still, for years, he created pieces in which the atmosphere, images, and music surrounded the dancers as a theatrical cloud. The dancers were not there merely to share that atmosphere; they came on stage to fill in roles inspired by a book or movie, or even when no one could even trace such a connection.

In addition to his creative work, Tuerlings was teaching composition at both the Scapino Dance Department and Dance Expression Department in Amsterdam during the 1980s. His cynical and often offending columns in the Dutch dance magazines *Dansbulletin* and *Notes* became notorious, in sharp contrast to the private, friendly and easygoing person. It became very clear in the 1990s, since Tuerlings had been working with his own group since 1986, that things were changing a great deal and for the better. He was working as choreographer with his contracted, self-chosen dancers and for a longer time; his dancers each had a special "role" in his work; and this enabled him not only to develop his theatrical ideas, with those particular "roles," in the Raz studio in Tilburg, but also to create pieces over several years in a series. An important example is the series inspired by the French writer Louis-Ferdinand Céline, *De Reis,* in four separate parts. Tuerlings gave different views in each of the four parts on Céline's book *Voyage au bout de la nuit.* Intelligence and irony was still an important part in his work and even grew to a more biting cynical tone, but at the same time more romantic and elegant details were added in the movement. The scene was bare and open, sometimes like one of his dancers alone on stage. Traditional dance elements were often exchanged for everyday motions, referring more to the postmodern school of thought than to academic modern dance.

Tuerlings' ambiguous dance theatre of the 1990s, disenchanting in effect and undeniably with his signature, is not always easy to understand. There is much implicit detail, and it demands knowledge and imagination to recognize that it's all about the phenomenon of being human, and all the emotions this entails. In the end, there is also more than a hint about the development of dance and its evolution until now. In 1997, Tuerlings began another new journey—this time with *Bagno blu (casa del sogno)* a series of 16 different productions, reflecting his view on the literature and landscape of Italy, the country of his dreams. Appropriately, Tuerlings is writing the credits for his new pieces in Italian.

—Jan Baart

UNITED STATES

Modern dance in the United States for much of its history has been almost as contrary as its practitioners—feisty, mystic, free-wheeling loners who longed for communal values and new ways of expressing themselves in movement. Their goal was to project what is globally human and what is uniquely American. They discerned in the American character a pluralistic society's complexity and tried to make this mesh with getting back to basics. Perhaps what most strongly links the diverse dancers and choreographers of the U.S. is the Seabees' motto from World War II: "can do." (For an aesthetic overview of modern dance in America and elsewhere, see the Introduction by Don McDonagh).

Where does American modern dance begin—in the 19th century with the disciples of François Delsarte and their ideas from Europe, or at the bridge from the 19th to the 20th centuries with Loie Fuller dancing on a platform of glass, setting herself "on fire" with lights projected onto silk in motion? Where does American modern dance end—with the Judson Church and the postmodernists of the 1960s or was that just a new beginning in an evolving art form?

Like modern dancers elsewhere, Americans, if pressed, chose truth over beauty, freedom before discipline, education rather than entertainment, and discovery instead of tradition. Europeans tended to study modern dance in order to live the modern life; Asians did so to prepare for the next one; pragmatic Americans studied in order to dance. Giving dance "concerts" was the chief goal for Americans who for many years avoided the term "performance" because it smacked of artifice, theatricality, and the ballet. Fuller early on rebelled against the narrative content of ballet and may have been the first American to make abstract pieces with a plastic, not musical, base. At the end of the 20th century, sculptural form and spatial dimensions still determine the character of American modern dance more than aural or temporal influences and at mid-century—Alwin Nikolais, with his Bauhaus-influenced stage effects and costuming placed himself in the continuum of non-narrative dance spectacle that Fuller began.

While the early American moderns—Fuller, Isadora Duncan, Ruth St. Denis, and Ted Shawn—didn't emphasize technique, the second generation—Doris Humphrey, Martha Graham, José Limón et al—not only stressed technique but created it. This was in marked contrast to some of their European contemporaries who proudly declared "we have no technique, we improvise." In America, dance methodology became so important that at times choreography was seen only as an example of a particular technique. This meant that the body remained primary, whereas in Europe the modern dancer's anatomy was seen by some simply as a vector to mark space. Interestingly, it was Germany's Mary Wigman who remarked on America's great distances and the influence of such landscapes on her American pupils who "sooner or later danced a dance of spreading out into space."

It is also worth noting that while New York on the East Coast is the mecca for American dance of all kinds, many modern dancers came from the West at a time when the spaces there were truly wide open: Duncan, Graham (although Pennsylvania-born) and José Limón all grew up in California; then Merce Cunningham, and later Trisha Brown and Mark Morris came from the Pacific Northwest. And Denishawn, America's first center for dance, was established by Ruth St. Denis and Ted Shawn in Los Angeles in 1915.

Colleges and universities, not just dance schools and performing arts conservatories, became centers of modern dance in America, first with individual teachers placed in physical education departments, and, beginning in 1962 at the University of California in Los Angeles, with entire dance departments in which ballet, if represented at all, was strictly a minor. Elsewhere in the world, this professionalization of modern dance was practically unheard of until the end of the century. The academic atmosphere on American campuses was hospitable to the codifying of dance techniques, the presenting of concerts, and the institutionalization of such scholarly endeavors as dance notation, history and criticism and, recently, historical dance and reconstruction.

Compared to ballet, the audience for modern dance in the United States has seldom been large, with the exception of the very theatrical Martha Graham at the peak of her popularity in the 1960s and 1970s when ballet superstars Margot Fonteyn and Rudolf Nureyev appeared as guest artists with her company, and in the 1990s when another ballet superstar, Mikhail Baryshnikov, founded the White Oak Dance Project, a modern dance repertory project. However, modern dance artists increasingly have been choreographing for ballet companies—postmodern Twyla Tharp actually became a resident choreographer at American Ballet Theatre for a time and more and more ballet technique is currently being taught in modern dance studios. In this respect, America has lagged behind Europe where the fusion of the once opposed forms began to gather pace following World War I. Valerie Bettis was the first modern dancer in America to choreograph for a classical company, the Ballets Russes de Monte Carlo in 1947. While at one time there was a perceptible difference in the anatomies of modern and ballet dancers, at the end of the century many dancers of both persuasions seem to have the long-limbed, streamlined look of the ballet.

The contours and course of modern dance in the U.S. have been buffeted by many forces. Ethnic diversity (African, Asian and Southeast Asian, Hispanic, Irish, Jewish, Native American, Slavic, etc.) has enriched modern dance in America and also reflected the late century's emphasis on separating the ingredients of the melting pot: on the rosters of the new Vietnamese-American dance companies dancers of Asian extraction predominate; the Alvin Ailey American Dance Company is primarily African-American.

Political and social issues have also informed modern dance in America; in the 1930s and 1940s it was usually left-wing points of view, then from the 1970s on questions of gender and sexual identity—although Duncan was certainly a feminist and Graham's pieces about heroic women, from the pioneers in *Appalachian Spring* to *Joan of Arc* and *Clytemnestra* are arguably feminist statements. The tragedy of AIDS has had considerable impact on modern dance artists and particularly in the American West, choreographers are very much concerned with our relationship to nature.

The influx of European modern dancers fleeing the post-World War I inflation, the rise of the Nazis and World War II had a variable influence on American modern dance. There was always some trans-atlantic interchange. Fuller and Duncan danced more in Europe than at home: St. Denis and Shawn toured Europe and such Europeans as Rita Sacchetto, the Wiesenthal sisters and Ronny Johansson performed and/or taught in America. Johansson was particularly important in this regard, demonstrating floor exercises at Denishawn in the 1920s when Graham, Doris Humphrey, and Charles Weidman were there. Hanya Holm, who came to conquer America for Wigman after one of her tours in the early 1930s, acclimated successfully but Valeska Gert, a refugee from Hitler, remained isolated from American modern dance, influencing American avant-garde theater instead.

Following World War II, American modern dance was dominant in Europe. The Germans were the first to take back the art form, especially with Tanztheater. But a revolution had occurred in America as well when the choreographers who made up the Judson Dance Theater and the Grand Union in New York rebelled against the "old" academic modern, with its set values and codified tech-nique. Their way had been paved by a third generation of American modern dancers, however, among them two former members of Graham's company: Merce Cunningham with his distillation of movement and fracturing of form, and Paul Taylor, with his storytelling skill and susceptibility to music.

Also in the 1960s and 1970s American modern dancers culti-vated an athletic look in the same way the early moderns had allied themselves with the physical culture movement. Terpsichore, as critic and historian Sally Banes points out, no longer had bare feet but wore sneakers. Further, in the 1970s, East Asian forms such as Butoh have influenced and been influenced by American modern and postmodern dance, and there are fusions most notably by Kei Takei, and Eiko and Koma. With the penchant Americans have for finding socially redeeming qualities in art, a trend begun by Anna Halprin in the 1970s, and continued in the late 1990s by Liz Lerman and others, is to make dance pieces and hold workshops in which movement melds with therapy. Bill T. Jones' *Still/Here* was the most famous and controversial example of this genre in the early 1990s.

The rise and fall and rise of American modern dance described by McDonagh seems to be ongoing. The latest fall may be due less to aesthetic reasons than to political assaults which have caused drastic funding cuts at the National Endowment for the Arts. Puritanism, aroused when Duncan bared her breast in Bos-ton, again harasses the arts, especially dance. Yet as Jack Ander-son has seen, writing in *Ballet and Modern Dance: A Concise History*, "modern dance represents one way of channeling the energy for which Americans are famous." Will the next rise of modern dance happen soon?

A caution! Looking for national character or generational traits in modern dance and its practitioners can obscure qualities that have nothing to do with where or when they first appeared. Sybil Shearer (American, peak activity 1940s and 1950s) attending a concert by Susanne Linke (German, peaking in 1970s and 1980s), beheld her younger self. Linke, when she learned to dance Shearer's old solos, felt as if they were her own dances.

Publications (see also General Bibliography)

Anderson, Jack, *Ballet & Modern Dance: A Concise History,* Princeton, New Jersey, 1992.
———, *The World of Modern Dance: Art without Boundaries,* Iowa City, Iowa, 1997.
Banes, Sally, *Terpsichore in Sneakers: Post-Modern Dance,* Boston, 1987.
Conner, Lynn, *Spreading the Gospel of Modern Dance,* Pittsburgh, Pennsylvania, 1997.
Denby, Edwin, *Dance Writings,* New York, 1986.
Duncan, Isadora, *My Life,* New York, 1955.
Fuller, Loie, *Fifteen Years of a Dancer's Life,* New York, 1975.
Mazo, Joseph, *Prime Movers: The Makers of Modern Dance in America,* New York, 1977.
McDonagh, Don, *The Rise and Fall and Rise of Modern Dance,* Chicago, 1990.
Siegel, Marcia B., *The Shapes of Change,* Boston, 1979.

—Martha Ulmann West and George Jackson

URIS, Victoria

American dancer, choreographer, artistic director, and educator

Born: 28 November 1949. **Education:** B.F.A., New York Univer-sity; studied with Nanette Charisse, May O'Donnell, Viola Farber, Stuart Hodes, and Rachel Lampert; M.F.A., Ohio State University, 1989. **Career:** Dancer, New York Dance Collective; danced with Norman Walker, Sandra Neels, Bowyer and Bruggeman, and Rosalind Newman companies; guest performer with Connecticut Ballet and Annabelle Gamson; dancer, Paul Taylor Dance Company, 1975-81; choreographer, beginning in 1981; choreographed 13 works for Uris/Bahr & Dancers with Jill Bahr, 1982-86; co-artistic director, 5 Minds, Inc., 1991-97; associate professor, Ohio State University School for the Performing Arts, 1990s. **Awards:** Choreographic Commission, Wexner Center for the Arts, 1995-96; Ohio Art Council Individual Artist Fellowship, 1995-96; other grants and awards include those from Hazelbaker Foundation, the Center for New Television, and Randolf Street Gallery.

Roles

1975   *Esplanade* (Taylor), Washington, D.C.
1976   *Cloven Kingdom* (Taylor), New York
1977   *Images* (Taylor), New York
        Dust (Taylor), New York
        Aphrodisiamania (Taylor), New York
1978   *Airs* (Taylor), New York
1979   *Nightshade* (Taylor), New York

Other roles include: *Big Bertha* and *From Sea to Shining Sea* by Paul Taylor, and various roles in works by Debra Wanner, Clarice Marshall, Rachel Lampert, Livia Drapkin, and Polly Sherer.

Works

1982   *Sea Dreams* (mus. Harold Budd), Schimmel Center, Pace University
        Delta, Schimmel Center, Pace University
        Three on a Match, Schimmel Center, Pace University

1996   *9 Scenes with Interviews,* Wexner Center for the Arts

Other works include: Uris and Jill Bahr collaborated on 13 works performed by Uris/Bahr and Dancers, 1982-86; since 1981, Uris has choreographed more than 50 works for American Ballet Theatre II, Connecticut Ballet Company, Phoenix Repertory Dance Theatre, Maryland Dance Theatre, Contemporary Dance Works, and Dayton Contemporary Dance Company.

Publications

By URIS: articles—

With Joel Lobenthal, "Victoria Uris: Dancing for Paul Taylor," *Ballet Review,* Spring 1987.

On URIS: articles—

Onoda, Karen, "New York City Reviews," *Dance Magazine,* October 1986.
Smith, Amanda, "Victoria Uris and Susan Marshall," *Dance Magazine,* September 1982.
Tobias, Tobi, "Bright Young Things," *New York,* 12 April 1982.

                          *   *   *

In 1987, after more than four years as a choreographer working on collaborative projects with Jill Bahr through their Uris/Bahr & Dancers company, Victoria Uris went back to school to earn her M.F.A. in dance at Ohio State University. Six years before, she had retired from dance itself after six physically exhausting years with Paul Taylor. On the eve of her return to college, Uris worked with Joel Lobenthal on a lengthy profile for *Ballet Review* in which she recalled, with self-effacing good humor, her formative experiences under Taylor's demanding tutelage.

Uris spoke of having been born at an ideal time—10 years old in 1960 and 20 by 1970—and fondly remembered "schmoozing around Greenwich Village with the likes of Janis Joplin and Donovan, experimenting with drugs, and not saying 'no' to anything." She was already studying dance at New York University, but in an age when discipline was unpopular and distractions abounded, her ambition might have foundered for years had she and Taylor not crossed paths.

When she was just 16, Uris had awakened one day (as she described it) and said, "I'm going to be a dancer." She had honed her talent by studying under Norman Walker and May O'Donnell; then in 1970, while a student taking part in a protest of the Kent State University shootings, she was part of a crowd that thronged the lobby of the ANTA Theater, where Taylor's troupe was putting on a performance. They waited till intermission to do the protest, though, "watch[ing] politely for the first half of the concert."

It would be another five years before Uris joined the Paul Taylor Company, by which time she was 25, "but a very young 25." She was eager to be challenged, and Taylor's style of motivation and teaching certainly offered challenge, as she would find out. Taylor and Uris shared certain physical characteristics that made her particularly congenial to his choreographic style—loose shoulder and ankle joints, for instance—and after initially telling the large-boned dancer to lose some weight, Taylor in 1975 hired her with the promise (in Uris' paraphrase): "You are a gold-mine of a dancer. I'm dyin' to work with you, just so long as you don't blow up like a balloon."

As she began working with Taylor, Uris discovered that she had a pro-ballet prejudice, but soon she became enamored with his style of upward movement, wrapped arms, and "total body/soul involvement." His method, which she felt suited her more than anything else she had ever tried, required "being iron from the hips down and willow from the waist up"—terms that well describe Uris's style as a dancer. Taylor favored fast, natural movements, and observed in Uris a propensity for jumping, which he would put to use in numerous roles for her.

Uris learned various techniques from co-performers such as Eileen Cropley, who she called "Queen of the Gesture," but her principal teacher was always Taylor, who pushed her to her physical limits. While the troupe was putting on *Esplanade,* for instance, a role in which she slid onto the stage and rapidly turned on her side, pushing with her arms, she was often in pain. "About once a month," she recalled, "my left arm would come right out of the socket—you'd hear a *rriipp!*" One day during rehearsals for *Images,* when Taylor was instructing her alone, he began giving her rapid-fire instructions, and the faster he barked orders, the faster she moved. Rehearsals were even harder for *Airs,* a role that called on the full extent of her jumping abilities, and she remembered feeling "as if I were in orbit." But even Uris had her limits. For her role in *Airs,* as a figure like the prophetess Cassandra from Greek mythology, Taylor and designer Gene Moore pictured her topless. With characteristically self-deprecating wit, Uris recalled how she told Taylor, "it's been nice knowing you" and even showed her breasts to a fellow dancer who agreed with her that she should keep her top on. Eventually Moore designed a less revealing costume. On the other hand, she played her role as an erotic snake-charmer in *Aphrodisiamania* with aplomb. (Originally the performance required her to say, with a straight face, the line, "Virginity is like a bubble that vanishes with the first prick.")

Uris, who has expressed the idea that choreographers above all require dancers who allow them complete freedom to experiment creatively, obviously enjoyed working with Taylor. But her body could no longer stand the beating it regularly took, and in 1981 she began a second career as a choreographer. In works such as *Sea Dreams* in 1982, she made use of the sinuous movements that had characterized her earlier snake-charmer role, creating gentle waves of movement out of languid arms and legs. And then at the age of 37 Uris went back to school, and a decade later she remained a member of the faculty of her alma mater, Ohio State. As an associate professor, she taught modern, improvisation, composition, repertory, and videodance. She made regular use of multimedia, and she and colleague John Giffin produced a show called *An Evening with Igor,* presenting choreographic works to the music of Stravinsky. But teaching seems to have become the focal point for Uris, who is such a draw for Ohio State that the university markets a CD-ROM about her career and techniques. It seems fitting that Uris, who has so strongly retained the imprint of her own teacher, should be passing on that learning to new generations of dancers.

                                                          —Judson Knight

VALENCIA, Tórtola

Spanish dancer and choreographer

Born: Carmen Tórtola Valencia 18 June 1882 in Seville, Spain.
Education: Attended London and Paris boarding schools; self-

taught dancer. **Career:** First professional appearance as a Spanish dancer in the musical *Havana*, produced by George Edwards in London, 1908; appeared on the same program as Loie Fuller at the Folies Bergère, 1908; toured European music halls as a solo dancer 1908-1914; first professional appearance in Spain at Madrid's Romea Theatre, 1911; arranged dances for Roshanara in the Oscar Asche and Lily Brayton production of *Kismet*, 1911; performed and arranged ensemble dances in Max Reinhardt's theatre productions of *Sumurûn* in Paris, 1912; *Sumurûn* revival in London, 1913; performed and arranged dances for Reinhardt's German productions of *Kismet* and *Orpheus in the Underworld*, 1912; professor of aesthetics at the Munich Art Theatre 1912-14; first dancer to perform in *el Ateneo*, Madrid's aristocratic academy of arts and letters, 1913; first woman to be elected a member of Madrid's *el Ateneo*, 1913; appeared on same program with Ellen Tels at the Werkbund-Theater, Cologne, 1914; performed in second act of Delibes' opera *Lakmé* at a benefit for soprano María Barrientos (Barcelona), 1915; starred in two silent films by Condal (Barcelona), *Pasionara* (directed by José Mariá Codina) and *Pacto de Lágrimas*, 1915; debuted in North America in *Maja Dance* as part of *Miss 1917*, produced by Charles Dillingham and Florenz Ziegfeld, Jr. in New York, 1917; performed a solo matinee concert of Oriental, Classic, Spanish repertoire produced by Dillingham and Ziegfeld, Jr. in New York, 1917; retired in Sarrià, suburb of Barcelona, 1930. **Awards:** The provincial government in Catalonia established the annual *Tórtola Valencia Premio*, a juried award for best new choreographic creation of the year, 1985. **Died:** 13 February 1955 of a heart attack in Barcelona, Spain.

Works (selected; more than 70 works were produced between 1908-1930)

1908-12	*Danza Arabe* (mus. Tchaikowsky)
	Danza del Incienso (mus. Buccalossi)
	La Naütche (mus. Delibes)
	La Serpiente (mus. Delibes)
	Romance (mus. Rubenstein)
	Danza (mus. Chopin)
	Muerte de Aase (mus. Grieg)
	Danza de los Gnomos (mus. Grieg)
	Canción de Solveig (mus. Grieg)
	Claro de Luna (mus. Beethoven)
	La Bayadera (mus. Delibes)
	La Gitana de los Pies Desnudos (mus. Sant -Saëns)
	Lakmé (mus. Delibes)
	El Cisne (a.k.a. *La Muerte del Cisne*) (mus. Saint-Saens)
	Vals Capricho (mus. Rubinstein)
	Danza de Anitra (mus. Grieg)
1913	*La Rosa Moribunda* (mus. Chopin)
	Tirana (renamed *La Maja*) (mus. Aroca)
	La Juventud (mus. Rubinstein)
	La Noche (mus. Delibes)
1915	*La Maja* (mus. Aroca)
	Baile Gitano (mus. Granados)
	Bacanal (mus. Rubenstein)
1916	*Capricho Valenciano* (mus. Tárrega)
	Juego de Pelota (antigua danza griega) (mus. Rubinstein)
	Marcha Fúnebre (mus. Chopin)
	Momento Musicale (mus. Schubert)
1917	*Danza India* (mus. Luigini)

1918	*Salomé* (mus. Strauss)
	La Rektah (mus. Luigini)
	Serenata Española (mus. Albéniz)
	La Muñeca de Porcelana de Porcelana (mus. Drigo)
	La Cicana (mus. Granados)
	Capricho Arabe (mus. Tárrega)
	Baile Hawaii (mus. Yaka Hickey Hula Dula)
	Minuet (mus. Paderewsky)
	Canción de Noche (Schumann)
1919	*Gavotta* (mus. Lïncke)
	Vals VII "Gainsborough" (mus. Chopin)
	Nocturno II (mus. Chopin)
	Las Mariposas, danced by Tórtola Valencia and Rosita Corma (mus. Chopin)
	El Ave Negra (mus. Rubinstein)
	Vals Danubio Azul (mus. Strauss)
	Danza Mora (mus. Chapi)
	Serenata (mus. Drigo)
1921	*Tehuana* (Danza Mexicana) (mus. Santos)
	Danza Hindú (mus. Valverde/Bantock)
	Cisne de Tounela (mus. Sibelius)
	Turkish March (mus. Beethoven)
	Sombra das Follias (mus. Thomé)
	Capricho Oriental (mus. Bernier)
	Egyptian Dance 1, 2, 4 (Luigini)
1922	*Danza China* (mus. Katalkasky)
	Danza Arabesca (mus. Burull)
	Guajiras (mus. Burull)
	Recuerdos de Versailles (mus. Gabriel-Marie)
	Serenata de Pierrot (changed to *Penas de Pierrot*) (mus. Toselli)
	Recuerdos Ibéricos (mus. Dotras Vila)
	Gitana y Arabe (mus. Barrachina)
	Domadora de Serpientos (mus. Bantock)
1925	*Danza Guerrera Arcaíca del Perú* (Mus. trad.)
	Danza Tortolesca (mus. Dotras Vila)

Other works include: Additional dances were created between 1925-30 (e.g. *Danza Africana*).

Publications

On VALENCIA: books—

Fontbona, Frances and Luis Antonio de Vellena, *Una Aproximación al Arte Frívolo: Tórtola Valencia/José de Zamora*, exposition catalog, coordinated by Andrés Peláez y Femanda Anclura, Comunidad de Madrid/Consejería de Cultura, 1988-89.
Peypoch, Irene, *Tórtola Valencia*, Barcelona, 1984.
Solrac, Odelot, *Tórtola Valencia and Her Times*, New York, 1982.

On VALENCIA: articles—

Garland, Iris, "Early Modern Dance in Spain: Tórtola Valencia, Dancer of the Historical Intuition," *Dance Research Journal*, Fall 1997.
———, "Modernist Values and Historical Neglect: The Case of Tórtola Valencia," *Proceedings of the Fifth Study of Dance Conference*, Border Tensions: Dance and Discourse, University of Surrey, Guildford, England, 1995.
María de Baranbano, Kosme, "Tórtola Valencia: Umzu tanzen, muss ich zuerst die Musik spuren," *Ballett-Journal* (Cologne), Koln, June 1986.

Murias Vila, Carlos, "Tórtola Valencia: La Sphynge Espagnole," *Pour la Dansa*, November 1989.

————,"La magicienne aux yeux d'abime: mystere et legende de Tórtola Valencia,"*Danser* (Paris), September 1992.

Toledo, Carlos, "El Arte Inolvidable de Tórtola Valencia" *Razon* (Havana), May 1955.

*   *   *

Tórtola Valencia was one of the last great dancers of the *belle époque*, that period at the beginning of the 20th century until World War I, which indulged in the extravagance of the senses as an antidote to an increasingly rational and technological society. Breaking with the traditions and sterility of the classical ballet, Isadora Duncan, Ruth St. Denis, and Maud Allan delved into the past for inspiration, and found remote cultures, such as Greece and the Orient, a fertile ground for recreating a natural, instinctual, and a sense-oriented approach to the dance. Diaghilev debuted his Ballet Russes in Paris in 1909 with the exotic and colorful ballets of Michel Fokine. Tórtola Valencia debuted in London in 1908, and there is little doubt that she was influenced by all of them. Nevertheless, her strong personal style distinguished her art from her contemporaries, and in her time she was considered by critics as an equal, and on occasion superior, to the best known dancers of her era. She was often categorized and compared with Isadora Duncan and Anna Pavlova. Similar to other early modern dancers, Valencia had no formal dance training in any style, researched her themes in libraries and museums, appeared first in the European music-hall circuit before establishing herself as a solo concert artist, and interpreted the music of the great classical composers. Her repertory of dances encompassed oriental, classical, and Spanish impressions, and she was considered more eclectic in her themes than Duncan, Allan, or Pavlova.

At the beginning of her career Valencia specialized in Oriental dances, for example, *Dansa del Incienso, Dansa Arabe, La Bayadera, La Serpiente,* but many critics later in her career attributed her transformation into different characters, times, and places as a hallmark of her success. Whereas St. Denis was mystical in her approach to the Orient, Valencia was earthy and passionate. Her style was vigorous, and according to Carlos Toledo in a 1955 article for *Razon,* "gave the impression at times, of something supernatural, as a mysterious force of nature unleashed, and taking its course."

Tórtola Valencia's true origins and background are uncertain. Even Valencia's closest friends doubted the authenticity of her birth certificate, which stated the place of her birth as Seville. Valencia, who was notorious for self-invention and imaginative stories to the press, claimed her mother was a gypsy and her father was a Spanish nobleman. She allegedly was raised in London by a foster family, and well-educated in London and Paris. Noted for her beauty, intelligence, wit, and flamboyance, Tórtola Valencia received critical acclaim on the stages of the European music halls as an Oriental dancer from 1908 to 1914. During and after World War I, Valencia performed exclusively in Hispanic countries.

Valencia's debut in Spain in December 1911 at Madrid's Romea Theater, a Spanish-style music hall, was a watermark in her career. A group of young Spanish intellectuals, writers, and artists known as *modernistas* including Federico García Sanchiz, Jacinto Benavente, Pompeyo Gener, Hermen Anglada Camarasa, Eduardo Chicharro, Ricardo and Pío Baroja, Anselmo Miguel Nieto, Ignacio Zuloaga, Valentín Zubiaurre, José Zamora, and Beltrán Massés considered her the embodiment of their own artistic visions. Several critics,

who were well-respected writers, claimed her dances could be understood and appreciated only by an educated, cultivated audience. Portraits of Tórtola Valencia were painted by many famous Spanish artists, including Zuloaga, Zubiaurre, Nieto, Penagos, and Zamora. Valencia became known as the "Muse of the Poets," including Ramón Valle-Inclán. Her tours throughout Spain received enthusiastic press coverage, and she attracted cultivated, elite audiences in every place she performed.

In 1916 Valencia performed in South America: Argentina, Venezuela, and Chile. Initially her reception was cool, but critics and audiences in each city increased their appreciation for her work during the course of her season. Valencia's North American debut occurred in New York in 1917, as a featured Spanish dancer in the Dillingham and Ziegfeld, Jr. production of *Miss 1917*. This was perhaps the least successful engagement of Tórtola Valencia's career. In the midst of Broadway chorus girls and American vaudeville headliners, she did not make the impact expected by the producers. During a special matinee concert of Valencia's oriental, classical, and Spanish repertory at the Century Theatre, American critics compared her favorably to Duncan, St. Denis, and the Diaghilev's Ballet Russes.

Valencia debuted *Salomé*, one of her most acclaimed works, in Mexico in April 1918. During her Latin America tour from 1921 to 1925, Valencia performed in almost every country in South and Central America with great critical success. A highlight of this tour was her creation and debut in Lima, Peru, in 1925, of *Danza Guerrera Arcaíca del Perú* based on her research of the Incas. This work was a triumph in Lima, and the performance was attended by the President of Peru, and the diplomatic corps. A last tour to South America in 1930 was Tórtola Valencia's farewell before her retirement. New dancers had caught the public's fancy, and Valencia was declining in her physical prowess as a dancer. Her last performance was in Guayaquil, Ecuador, on 28 November 1930.

Tórtola Valencia remained a solo dancer throughout her career. She never took a partner, formed a dance company, or started a school. Her legacy is not a style, a school, or a technique, but rather an affirmation of that uncodifiable power of an individual dance artist to create poetry in movement, which transports the audience beyond the quotidian into another realm.

—Iris Garland

VALGEIRSDÓTTIR, Sigríður

Icelandic dancer, choreographer, educator, and historian

Born: 16 November 1919 in Reykjavík, Iceland. **Education:** Started dancing at the age of eight mostly doing Icelandic folk dancing and ballroom dancing; studied gymnastics along with education as a teacher of physical education; graduated from the College of Physical Education and Sport, Iceland, 1942; University of California, Berkeley, department of health, physical education and recreation, teachers credentials and M.A., 1947; postgraduate work at New York State University of Buffalo, M.Ed., 1968; Ph.D. in educational psychology (thesis on psychometrics), 1974. **Career:** Orchesis dance group from 1944 and student of Ms. Lucille Czarmowski; principal dancer and choreographer of *The Story of the Soldier* with Orchesis, 1947; attended dance and choreography workshops with Martha Graham, Doris Humphrey, Charles

Weidman, Antony Tudor, Merce Cunningham, José Limón, and Rudolph Laban; teacher at the College of Physical Education and Sport, Iceland, 1949-51; founder of the Folk Dance Society of Reykjavík, 1951; professor of Educational Psychology at the Teachers College of Iceland and director of the Institute of Educational Research of Iceland, 1982-91. **Awards**: The Icelandic Sport Union Golden Pin, 1950; honored by the Gymnastic Society of Reykjavík (IR), 1956; cultural awards for choreography in Germany, 1969; honored by the Folk Dance Society of Reykjavík, 1976; Order of the Falcon from the President of Iceland, 1990.

Works

1945	*The Juggler from Notre-Dame,* (mus. Orchesis musician), Orchesis, Modern Dance Society of University of California Berkeley
1946	*The Women of Vík,* (mus. Orchesis musician), Orchesis, Modern Dance Society of University of California, Berkeley
1947	Dances in *The Story of the Soldier* (mus. Stravinsky), music and drama departments of University of California, Berkeley
1949	*Spring, Ice and Hot Springs* (mus. Jórunn Viðar), gymnastic and modern group, Iceland and Sweden
1957	*±10* (mus. Jórunn Viðar), Íþróttafélag Reykjavíkur (IR), Iceland and London

Other works include: Choreography and reconstruction of Icelandic folk dances from the Middle Ages, and a director of numerous performances, the Folk Dance Society of Reykjavík, Iceland, Sweden, Canada, Norway, 1951-94; choreography for several plays for the National Theater of Iceland, 1954-67.

Publications

By VALGEIRSDÓTTIR: books—

Leikir (Games), Leiftur, Reykjavík, 1958.
Þjóðdansar I (Folk Dances), Menntamálaráðuneytið, Reykjavík, 1959.
Gömlu dansarnir (Old-Time Dances in Iceland), Leiftur, Reykjavík, 1986.

*   *   *

The practice of modern dance in Iceland owes much to Sigríður Valgeirsdóttir who was the first to bring the emerging tradition to the island. Valgeirsdóttir studied modern dance at the University of California, Berkeley, and returned to her home country enthusiastic to spread what she had learned from the pioneers of modern dance. Well aware of the popularity of modern dance in the U.S., Valgeirsdóttir wanted to establish a modern dance company in Iceland. Shortly after her return to Iceland she put out a call for youngsters who wanted to dance. She was about to choose the future dancers of her company when she realized there was a problem—the girls who attended her first class were surprised and disappointed when they found out that they were to dance barefoot instead of in pointe shoes. Valgeirsdóttir realized the girls were expecting to train to become prima ballerinas, clearly revealing how

new modern dance was to them. Valgeirsdóttir realized that Icelanders, who had only recently become familiar with classical ballet, weren't prepared to accept a new form in modern dance. Realistic but not discouraged, Valgeirsdóttir, with her training as a physical education teacher, managed to incorporate modern dance technique into the gymnastic classes of the Icelandic College of Physical Education and Sport. For 20 years she taught and choreographed pure modern dance technique there and at the Teachers College of Iceland, although the classes were always called "gymnastic-modern." In time Valgeirsdóttir was able to put together a group of dancers who were skilled enough for public performance, thereby attaining her goal of an Icelandic modern dance company, although the style continued to be referred to as gymnastic-modern. She toured with the group in Iceland, Sweden, and England and received very positive reviews. Modern dance was as new to the Scandinavian countries as it was to Iceland and Valgeirsdóttir's troupe became modern dance pioneers in all of Scandinavia. In addition to training and running her dance group, Valgeirsdóttir was employed as a freelance choreographer and teacher for many years, working for such organizations as the National Theater of Iceland, where she choreographed dances for many plays, and teaching at the Icelandic School of Acting.

When Valgeirsdóttir realized how oblivious the Icelandic nation was to its own dance history, she decided to collect what recollections remained of traditional Icelandic dance among the elderly of the society. She has spent over 30 years collecting Icelandic dances through interviews, Labanotation (by Mínerva Jónsdóttir) and observations in which descriptions of dances had been written down or taped. The second part of her archival work has been the reconstruction of dances from the Middle Ages in Iceland through the study of Icelandic manuscripts and European literature on the history of dance. Through her work, Valgeirsdóttir has preserved the dance heritage of Iceland and brought a new awareness of dance to the Icelandic nation.

—Ragna Sara Jónsdóttir

VANDEKEYBUS, Wim
Belgian actor, dancer, choreographer, filmmaker, and company director

Born: 1964 in Herentals, Flanders. **Education:** Studied psychology, University of Leuven, before concentrating on film, video, and theater. **Career:** Extensive work with theater director Jan Fabre; founder, Ultima Vez, 1985; first choreography *What the Body Does Not Remember,* 1987; artist-in-residence, Royal Flemish Theatre (KVS), Brussels, 1993; choreographed *Exhaustion from Dreamt Love* for Batsheva Dance Company (Israel), 1996; considered the "Cultural Ambassador of Flanders." **Awards:** New York Dance and Performance Award ("Bessie"), 1987, 1988; London Dance and Performance Award (1988); Prague d'Or and Dance Screen Award, 1991; IMZ, Frankfurt, 1991; Special Jury Prize at the Brussels International Film Festival, 1994.

Works

| 1987 | *What the Body Does Not Remember* (mus. de Mey, Vermeersch), Brussels |

1989	*Les porteuses de mauvaises nouvelles* (mus. de Mey), Paris
1990	*The Weight of a Hand* (mus. de Mey and Vermeersch), Paris
1991	*Immer das Selbe gelogen* (mus. Vermeersch, Calvo, Wegener), Brussels
1993	*Her Body Doesn't Fit Her Soul* (mus. Vermeerch), Munich
1994	*Mountains Made of Barking* (mus. Vermeersch, van Dam, Calvo), Brussels
1995	*Alle Groessen decken sich zu* (theater), (mus. various, words Verano), Brussels
1996	*Bereft of a Blissful Union* (mus. Vermeeersch, van Dam), Brussels
	Exhaustion from Dreamt Love, for Batsheva Dance Company, Tel Aviv
1997	*7 for a Secret Never to Be Told* (mus. various), Barcelona

Films and Videotapes

Roseland, video, 1990.
La Mentira, video, 1992.
Elba and Federico, film, 1993.

Publications

Steele, Mike, Review, *Minneapolis Star-Tribune,* 14 October 1989.

*   *   *

Wim Vandekeybus, the son of a veterinarian, grew up in Flanders as an expert horseback rider and athlete, but with no dance training. His interest in dance and movement appears to have come from two major sources. As a child he was impressed with the self-protective mechanisms of animals to keep out of harm's way; a horse, he has said, will instinctively move to the side in order not to stumble into a hole; a bird knows how to curl its feet around a branch. Human beings, Vandekeybus believes, have a similar preconscious level of decision-making which connects them to the external world without any interference of volition or choice. Secondly, in his work with theater artist Jan Fabre, Vandekeybus (who trained as an acrobat) explored a physical theater which exploded existing boundaries and sought to synthesize many artistic disciplines. All of Vandekeybus' theatrical work is concerned with digging underneath the skin-deep layer of civilization which separates human beings from the instinctual part of themselves and through that with nature at large.

In a Vandekeybus work dancers throw themselves at full-force and top-speed into movement that is acrobatic, athletic, and dangerous. They launch themselves likes missiles, crashing to the floor, only to leap up again, flinging themselves at a partner who is toppled by the impact. Such is their explosive energy that they often appear on the point of self-destruction. The only reason they don't break their necks is that they are extremely well-trained with impeccable timing and a finely honed trust in themselves and each other. Yet there is no aggression involved in such extreme physical maneuvers, as Mike Steele, writing in the *Minneapolis Star-Tribune* in 1989 has pointed out: "With Vandekeybus, the aggressors aren't the other dancers but the fundamental components of dance: balance, gravity and weight, the reality of the physical world. Instead of denying them, Vandekeybus' dancers confront them, acknowledge them and hurtle their bodies against them."

What makes the work so appealing is that Vandekeybus infuses his high impact choreography with a light touch and a cheeky sense of humor. The works are non-narrative and imagistic, abounding with references to sports and games. His dancers playfully compete with each other; juggling objects, they duck darts, bricks, and eggs thrown at them or plummet to the floor when supporting ropes are cut. "I want people to stop believing in their own security," Vandekeybus has said. Life is full of risks; danger lurks everywhere, he seems to say, but if you stay alert and respond instinctively, you will survive. Some of these confrontations may be dangerous, but they are also fun. It's part of participating in the game of life.

In Vandekeybus' *What the Body Does Not Remember* and *Les porteuses de mauvaises nouvelles* he evokes the small mishaps that can throw ordinary lives into chaos. In *What the Body Does Not Remember,* a friendly roll on the floor suddenly escalates into mortal combat; people casually get stripped of their clothes, i.e. dignity; daily activities are threatened by flying bricks coming out of nowhere. In *Les porteuses de mauvaises nouvelles,* the metaphor is one of the ground being pulled out from under one's feet. A floor made up of wooden pallets is dismantled and reassembled into fluctuating staircases and towers on which the dancers try to gain a foothold. What is needed to survive is nimble feet and even nimbler minds.

In 1988 Vandekeybus encountered Carlo Wegener (a.k.a. Carlo Verano), an 89-year-old German who had survived life's vicissitudes with remarkable dignity. Though now partly living in a dream world of his own making, he had retained an acute taste for life. *Immer das Selbe gelogen,* the film *La Mentira,* and the theater piece *Alle Groessen decken sich zu* are based on Vandekeybus' friendship with the old man. In *Immer das Selbe gelogen,* there are filmed conversations and images of Carlo along with girls wildly swinging in hammocks and men running a gauntlet of trying to safeguard dozens of eggs—metaphors of the fragility of life. The film *La Mentira* intersperses filmed sequences of interviews with Carlo with dance sequences.

Her Body Doesn't Fit Her Soul (which includes a film about an alienated couple, *Elba and Federico*) and *Mountains Made of Barking* are companion pieces in the way they explore perception. Two of the performers in the former work are blind, and the piece's imagistic physicality is so structured to highlight different forms of apprehending such as listening, feeling, touching, talking, and imagining. Included is a cinema verité film about how the reality of work schedules keeps two people from communicating. *Mountains* is focused on the nightmarish world of the blind Third World-performer Said Gharbi in which nothing is as it appears. The dancers perform in rough animal costumes, as if their skins had been turned inside out. Here Vandekeybus projects a violent, cruel physicality that is unpredictable and hostile, a world in which the head is literally removed from the body, in which a gesture of endearment becomes one of enslavement. *Mountains Made of Barking* is considered Vandekeybus' darkest piece so far.

—Rita Felciano

VAN DYKE, Jan

American dancer, choreographer, and educator

Born: 15 April 1941 in Washington, D.C. **Education:** Began studying dance in Germany where her father, a State Department official, was stationed after World War II; returned to the United States at the age of nine; studied dance in the Washington, D.C., area in the late 1950s and 1960, with Heidi Pope, Ethel Butler, and with teachers at the Washington School of Ballet; University of Wisconsin, B.A. in dance 1963; George Washington University, M.A. in dance education 1966; later studied at Martha Graham and Merce Cunningham studios; also studied with Alwin Nikolais. **Career:** Professional debut at the Charlotte Summer Theater, Charlotte, North Carolina, June 1964; dancer, Washington Dance Repertory Company, 1966-68, Georgetown Workshop, 1967-69, Ethel Butler Company, 1968, Dance Theatre Workshop, New York, 1969-71, Elizabeth Keen Company, New York, 1971-72; began to choreograph while serving as an administrator for arts festivals in the Washington-Baltimore area; founder and director of the Dance Project, a school and performance space and home for her company, Jan Van Dyke & Dancers, 1973; co-director of the Gamble/Van Dyke Dance Company; held teaching positions at Ohio University, Long Beach Summer School of Dance, University of Maryland, George Washington University, University of Hawaii, and University of North Carolina, Greensboro. **Awards:** National Endowment for the Arts grant, 1973; Fulbright grant.

Works

1965	*Diversion*
1966	*Canto*
1967	*Six Sections of Orange*
	Dream Forcing
	Solitude's Dance
1968	*Rose Garden*
	Camp Lilies
	Sisters
	Jungle Perches
	Hot Sleep
1969	*I Am Waiting*
	One Potato, Two...
	Backwater
1970	*3 Ringling*
	Park Dance
	Going On
	Two
1971	*Duet I*
	Duet II
	Benches On & Off
	Bird
	Ready
1973	*Big Show*
	Waltz
	Park Dance II
1974	*U.S. Lions*
	Ceremony I in Six Acts
1975	*Ella*
	Paradise Castle
1976	*Ceremony II with Roses*
	Silence
	Elly's Dance
	The Story of Twilight
1977	*Fleetwood Mac Suite*
	No Name
1978	*A Dance Parade*

	The Passenger
	Variations on a Theme
1979	*A Dance in Two Spaces*
	Two Dances in One Space
1980	*Looping the Circle* (also known as *Circling*)
	Stamping Dance
	Untitled Duet
	Double Times

Publications

By VAN DYKE: articles—

"An American Choreographer in Portugal," *Dance Teacher Now,* November/December 1994.

*　　*　　*

Jan Van Dyke's career as a modern dancer, choreographer, teacher, and arts administrator has taken her into nearly every aspect of dance. Van Dyke was a major dance personality in Washington, D.C., during the 1960s and 1970s and was one of the main forces behind the attempt to establish a modern-dance presence in the nation's capital. Her dances combine clarity of conception with a calm, deadpan manner, according to Jean Norhaus in the *Washington Review of the Arts.*

Van Dyke began dancing while a child in Germany, where her father was stationed after World War II. When he returned to the States, Jan continued her dance studies in Alexandria, Virginia, and built up several years' experience performing and teaching while in high school. She went on to earn two degrees in dance: one a B.S. from the University of Wisconsin-Madison and a M.A. from George Washington University. A meeting with Merce Cunningham at a Connecticut College summer program strengthened her desire to dance. After college, she went to New York with the intention of studying with Cunningham, but he was away and she signed up for classes with Alwin Nikolais instead. She also studied with Martha Graham but not happily. As Van Dyke pointed out in an interview with the Washington *Daily Rag* : "[Graham's] technique is so regimented that it has become like a ballet class. Her exercises can be harmful for certain body types; especially for men. It is a very female technique. Graham works with so much unnecessary tension. It can work against you." Cunningham's technique was more comfortable for Van Dyke. She found his technique improved her balance while allowing her to be loose at the top of her body. He seemed to synthesize the very best of ballet and Graham.

Van Dyke began to create her own pieces in 1965. For several years she performed solo pieces devised by herself and collaborated with other dancers in the Washington area. Critics were appreciative of her work; they saw in her a cool, "neat" dancer whose movement had a balanced, understated quality. These qualities inspired her choreography which was noted for both detachment and whimsy. Even when she works against the music or chooses not to use any, her dances show off a quiet lyricism and great visual delicacy. Hers is, according to Jean Norhaus, cool dance with a mischievous facade and an irrational, demonic undercurrent.

Van Dyke's work is often introspective: her well-known solo *Waltz* (1978) was characterized by a daring stillness in which the dancer stood for a long time with her back to the audience while the strains of Johann Strauss' *Blue Danube Waltz* washed over the scene. Slowly, she raised her arms and turned around in what was

Jan Van Dyke: *Woof.* Photograph © Kenton Robertson.

the first of a series of slow gestures. The movement wound and unwound back into itself in a unbroken flow of movement. She seemed to be stretching time itself. Details usually overlooked—such as the way a foot is placed on the floor—took on huge importance. While Van Dyke never actually waltzed she seemed to be remembering a waltz as she dipped and revolved in a slow-motion soliloquy. She continued moving after the music stopped. In *U.S. Lions* and *Big Show* (1973) Van Dyke poked fun at American culture. *Lions* spoofed football jocks and their adoring mob of cheerleaders. In *Big Show* she strutted, circled, bounced, and generally showed off as she evoked the artificial grimaces of the bigtop or any American spectacle. Reviewing both works in *Dance Magazine,* Victoria Huckenpahler praised Van Dyke's ability to hit a familiar chord in her choice of movement. However, the reviewer found both works lacking in precise definition. Lewis Segal of the *Los Angeles Times* found her less interested in expressing her own identity and emotions than in exhibiting dances through which viewers might renew their perception of the familiar.

Van Dyke has also experimented with the relationship between the content of dances and the spaces they are performed in. She has set her dances in sacred spaces such as the Washington Cathedral or in public art galleries such as the Corcoran Gallery. In the Corcoran she worked the doors, walkways, columns, and stairs into the choreography. As the dancers moved from room to room, the audience followed. Occasionally she has performed in silence.

Alan Kriegsman of the *Washington Post* found Van Dyke's choreography in *Self-Portraits: Rites of Passage* (1976) to be richly

suggestive in imagery but often reliant on too many repetitive, vacuous passages. On the positive side, he admired the way Van Dyke combined surrealism with wit, irony, and self-mockery. As Kriegsman pointed out in his review of 15 May 1976, "the content [of *Self-Portraits*] is sometimes heavy but the touch is almost invariably light. Don McDonagh, writing in the *New York Times* noted how Van Dyke used her strong, evenly proportioned body as the base for her performing force, deployed with casual elegance. In his review of *Waltz*, McDonagh found it to be an "exquisite miniature that conveys the spirit of the waltz while retaining the feeling of a classroom exercise."

One of her most characteristic and ambitious works was *Circling.* This 30-minute piece for eight dancers was first performed in 1980 at the Dance Project in Washington. According to the program note prepared by Van Dyke, it is a palindrome, concerned with emphatic, vigorous movement and rhythms generated by the dancers' physical actions. It also presents a formidable physical and mental challenge to the performers. At midpoint, the entire sequence of the dance is repeated backwards, both the order and direction of the movements reversed.

In the early 1980s, Van Dyke began to experiment with rhythm. The manipulation of meter became a favorite exercise and brought a precision, focus, and understated passion to her work according to one reviewer. In *Untitled Duet* Van Dyke set a dance on two women to the music of Bach. They work against the music as they support each other and gesture with their hands. The dancers alternately place their palms together as in prayer or fling imaginary water droplets. Jerry Stein, writing in the *Cincinnati Post*, found the counterpoint between the dance and the sound created a fascinating tension. In *Double Times*, a solo performed by Van Dyke, she doubles and triples a complex movement pattern while taking unexpected falls and clenching her fists. In *Stamping Dance* four women tap and jump with rhythmic bounty.

Van Dyke was one of the leaders of the free dance movement in the nation's capital. She organized the Heat Festival in the summer of 1973 and the Free Dance Festival in 1974. She received funding from the D.C. Commission on the Arts and the Meyer Foundation to pay her dancers and theater people who would not otherwise have had an outlet for their talents. She was continually busy searching for funding sources to establish a professional company and to be able to tour outside of Washington. She has also enjoyed a long and distinguished teaching career, holding posts at universities throught the U.S. and visiting numerous other countries.

—Adriane Ruggiero

VAN TUYL, Marian
American educator, choreographer, writer, and filmmaker

Born: 16 October 1907 in Wascousta, Michigan. **Education:** University of Michigan, degree in dance, 1928; additional training, University of Chicago. **Family:** Married psychiatrist Dr. Douglas Gordon Campbell; three children. **Career:** Teacher, ten years, University of Chicago; launched the Marian Van Tuyl Dancers; guest teacher, Mills College, Oakland, California, 1938; teacher, creator of dance department in fine arts division, Mills College, 1939 (built one of first, most innovative dance departments in U.S. and developed educational approach of rigorous and wide-ranging dance education); supported collaboration with composers Darius Mihaud and Henry Cowell and designer Arch Lauterer; one of first to understand importance of film as collaborative medium in dance and made two seminal dance films, *Clinic of Stumble* and *Horror Dream;* published and edited scholarly dance journal *Impulse, An Annual Journal of Contemporary Dance* (launched at the Halprin/Lathrop studio in San Francisco in 1947), 1951-70; founder, San Francisco Dance League, the Congress on the Research in Dance (CORD), and CORD News; published *Modern Dance Forms in Relation to the Other Modern Arts* by Louis Horst and Carroll Russell, 1961; *Anthology of Impulse, 1951-66* published by Dance Horizons, 1969; president, American Dance Festival, 1973-75. **Awards:** John D. Rockefeller Award from the American Dance Guild, 1971; inducted into Isadora Duncan Hall of Fame, 1984. **Died:** 10 November 1987 in San Francisco.

Works

1934   *Dido and Aeneas* (mus. Purcell), Chicago
        Handel's Xerxes (mus. Handel), Chicago
1935   *Handel's Suite* (mus. Handel), University of Chicago students, Chicago
1936   *In the Clearing* (mus. Tucker), Chicago
        Two Archaic Dances: Triumphant Figure and Epilogue to Victory (mus. Esther Williamson and Williams, composed under Louis Horst's tutelage, Bennington), Chicago

1937   *Schwanda Fugue from Schwanda the Bagpipe Player* (mus. Weinberger), Chicago
        Directions: Flight, Indecision, Redirection (mus. Lopatnikoff)
        Apprehension 1938 (mus. Achron), Chicago
1938   *Out of One Happening: Final Dance* (mus. Tucker), Mills College
1939   *Chaconne (Fanfare)* (mus. Cowell), Mills College
        Ritual of Wonder (mus. Cowell and Harrison), Mills College
        Opening Dance (mus. Harrison), Mills College
        Uneasy Rapture (mus. Harrison), Mills College
1940   *Fads and Fancies in the Academy—A Gentle Satire on Progressive Education* (mus. Cage), Mills College
        The Trojan Women, Treasure Island, San Francisco
1942   *Cortege* (mus. Berger)
        Entertainment Piece (mus. Berger), Mills College
1944   *Down with Drink: A Sequence of American Temperance Songs* (mus. Jones), Mills College
1947   *In Time of Waiting: Entrance into Limbo; Transition Ritual; Immediate Destiny* (mus. Schönberg), San Francisco
        In the Clearing #2 (mus. Tucker), Mills College
        Horror Dream (film), Museum of Modern Art, San Francisco
1948   *Clinic of Stumble* (film), Museum of Modern Art, San Francisco

Publications

Archives of Marian Van Tuyl, private library of Joanna Gewertz Harris, Berkeley, California.
Obituary, *Mills Quarterly,* 1987.
Obituary, *Oakland Tribune,* 12 November 1987.
Obituary, *San Francisco Examiner,* 13 November 1987.

Filma and Videotapes

All works, except *The Trojan Women* and *Cortege,* exist on film, most in the collection of the New York Public Library for the Performing Arts Dance Collection at Lincoln Center.

*   *   *

When Marian Van Tuyl was five, she began dancing in her hometown of Wascousta, Michigan, near Ann Arbor. At eight she assisted classes; by the time she was 15 she was choreographing everything that needed dance in high school. Her early and indefatigable energy augured a future in which she was to be a source of constant intellectual invention, leading her to Mills College, where she was given carte blanche to create one of the first and most innovative dance departments in the country. Subsequently, she edited and published a pioneering dance journal, *Impulse, An Annual of Contemporary Dance,* which discussed dance from myriad and impassioned points of view.

Van Tuyl was an intellectual and experimentalist, who dedicated herself to the improvement of dance education and tirelessly proselytized on its behalf. This was part of a grander quest to ensure that dance both in its practice and scholarship was an equal of the other art forms. Among her greatest achievements was her success in moving the dance department at Mills College from the physical education department into the Division of Fine Arts. This not only vitalized dance education at the college and made it an exemplar for other institutions, but forged a tradition of collaboration there between dance, avant-garde music, and theater, which remains the model for many institutions and artists.

In 1928, a time when few pursued dance seriously, let alone received university training in the art, Van Tuyl graduated from the University of Michigan with a degree in dance. From there she moved on to the University of Chicago to study teaching and, for 10 years, to be one of the university's dance instructors. She also ran her own private studio and occasionally taught at the University of Indiana and Milwaukee State Teacher's College.

Even though it was a period in which many modern dancers eschewed all other dance, Van Tuyl ignored convention and studied and incorporated into her choreography various dance genres, including folk forms and ballet. It was also during this time that she met her future husband, Dr. Douglas Gordon Campbell, a prominent psychiatrist whose friends included Buckminster Fuller. Fuller built his legendary car in the Campbells' basement.

Van Tuyl launched the Marian Van Tuyl Dancers while in Chicago and set out to tour the West, traveling what she called the "gymnasium circuit," since the only available performing space on the road was often a college or high school gymnasium. According to Van Tuyl, this hardship forced on these young pioneers, including John Cage, Merce Cunningham, and Lou Harrison, a need for invention in these large undefined spaces. Her pioneering spirit also took the company to visit northern New Mexico in the dead of winter in 1940 and made them the first modern dancers ever to perform at Zuni and Navajo reservations.

In 1938 Van Tuyl was invited to be a visiting professor at Mills College, and in announcing her first concert on the Pacific Coast the school described her as "one of the leading younger dancers in the field of modern dance." The college was so impressed by her that President Aurelia Reinhardt set out to lure her permanently to Oakland. Van Tuyl returned to Chicago and confronted the president of the university with the news that Mills College was willing to give her freedom to reinvent its dance training and to double her salary. She, in turn, would spice the bargain by bringing along her prized student, Eleanor Lauer. Chicago was unmoved, so Van Tuyl and Lauer headed west and, before long, Mills was rivaling Bennington College in its exciting experimentalism in dance.

Van Tuyl was the first Bennington fellow from outside the New York dance world and for many summers worked with Martha Graham, Hanya Holm, Louis Horst, and Doris Humphrey. In the summer of 1939 the Bennington Summer School was held on the campus of Mills College. It was that summer that Martha Graham first spotted Merce Cunningham and invited him to join her company in New York.

Van Tuyl's arrival at Mills coincided with that of French refugee Darius Milhaud, who taught on the Oakland campus from 1940 until 1971. Avant-garde composers Lou Harrison and Henry Cowell also taught and shaped the music department, and over the years Van Tuyl and her student dancers collaborated extensively with them, carrying on the spirit of musical collaboration instituted by Louis Horst during the Bennington summers. She also collaborated extensively with stage and scenic designer Arch Lauterer, brought from Bennington College to head the Theater Department at Mills, and together they effected the redesign of the campus theater, which in turn influenced the construction of the cutting-edge dance space, Haas Pavilion.

Before most others, Van Tuyl recognized the importance of film to dance beyond the realm of the documentary. Her two cinematic works, *Horror Dream* (1948), set to an original score by John Cage, and *Clinic of Stumble* (1947), were filmed by filmmaker Sidney Peterson as experiments in cinematographic choreography for Art in Cinema at the Museum of Modern Art in San Francisco.

In addition to her unceasing activities as a college professor, Van Tuyl tended the public dance realm. She was a founding member of the San Francisco Dance League in the 1940s and subsequently of the now-defunct service organization, the San Francisco Bay Area Dance Coalition. During her first period of retirement from Mills, beginning in 1947, Van Tuyl, Anna Halprin, and students at the Halprin/Lathrop dance studio in San Francisco launched *Impulse,* one of the first scholarly journals dedicated solely to dance. From 1951 to 1970, Van Tuyl took over as editor and publisher, which she produced from her home. Brainy and freewheeling, *Impulse* dedicated each issue to an aspect of dance, with experts covering such subjects as dance and education, dance and related arts, dance theory, and dance therapy.

In 1961 Van Tuyl published *Modern Dance Forms in Relation to the Other Modern Arts* by Louis Horst and Carroll Russell, and in 1969 the *Anthology of Impulse, 1951-66* was published by Dance Horizons. Van Tuyl was one of the founders of the Congress on the Research in Dance (CORD) and the CORD News.

Van Tuyl, who had three children, returned to Mills in 1963, where she remained until 1970, when Eleanor Lauer succeeded her. In 1971 she received a John D. Rockefeller Award from the American Dance Guild, and from 1973 to 1975 she was the president of the American Dance Festival. She was inducted into the Isadora Duncan Hall of Fame in 1984. During her second retirement, Van Tuyl nursed her ailing husband, who had suffered a debilitating back injury and was confined to a wheelchair. To support her family Van Tuyl became a practitioner of Japanese healing arts from her San Francisco home until just a month before her death in 1987 at the age of 80.

—Ann Murphy

VARONE, Doug
American dancer, choreographer, and artistic director

Born: 5 November 1956 in New York City. **Education:** Studied tap dance; attended SUNY at Purchase, studied with Carole Fried, Kazuko Hirabayashi, Mel Wong, Royes Fernandez, Will Glassman, and Roseanne Servalli; studied ballet technique with Maggie Black and Zena Rommett. **Career:** Dancer, José Limón troupe, early 1970s; dancer, Lar Lubovitch troupe, late 1970s; founder/director, Doug Varone and Dancers, beginning 1980s.

Roles

1976 *Marimba* (Lubovitch)
1978 *Figura* (M. Louis)
1979 *Carlotta* (Limón)
1980 *Cavalcade* (Lubovitch)
1986 *Nine Person Precision Ball Passing* (Moulton)

Other roles include: *Diversion of Angels* (Graham), *The Shakers* (Humphrey), *Passacaglia and Fugue* (Humphrey), all as a student

Doug Varone: *Rise.* **Photograph © Beatriz Schiller.**

at SUNY; as a dancer of the Limón company, performed in *Passacaglia and Fugue in C Minor* (Humphrey), *Choreographic Offering* (Limón), *There Is a Time* (Limón), *The Traitor* (Limón), and *The Green Table* (Jooss). Also *Points and Plots, Surface, Hot Peppers,* and *Jazz Babies and Creoles.*

Works

1978	*Mendet,* Clark Center for Performing Arts
1980	*Fortress,* Clark Center for Performing Arts
	Parallels, Clark Center for Performing Arts
	Ain't Nothing That Keeps Us Here, Clark Center for Performing Arts
1987	*Cantata 78* (mus. Bach), Performance Space 122, New York
	Nocturne in D Flat Major (mus. Chopin; Varone as solo performer)
1990	*Force Majeure*
1991	*Home*
1992	*Barcarolle and Nocturne,* Joyce Theater, New York
	Stranded Landfish, Joyce Theater, New York
	A Momentary Order, Bates Dance Festival, Lewiston, Maine
1993	*Rise* (mus. John Adams)
1994	*Planets* (with Lubovitch; mus. Holtz)
1995	*Possession* (mus. Philip Glass)
	Strict Love
1996	*In Thine Eyes* (mus. Michael Nyman), Dance Umbrella Concert Series, London
	Let's Dance (Riffs on Seven Vernaculars)

Publications

On VARONE: books—

Carbonneau, Suzanne, *A Momentary Order: An Arts-Community Partnership,* Bates Dance Festival, Lewiston, Maine, 1994.

On VARONE: articles—

Anderson, Jack, "New York Newsletter," *Dancing Times*, April 1996.

———, "New York Newsletter," *Dancing Times*, February 1995.

Jackson, Paul, "Umbrella Music," *Dance Now*, Winter 1996-97.

Jowitt, Deborah, "Angst: 1991," *Village Voice*, 30 April 1991.

———, "Critic as Victim," *Village Voice*, 10 January 1995.

———, "Doug Varone and Dancers," *Village Voice*, 20 February 1996.

———, "Not Very Alike," *Village Voice*, 28 January 1992.

———, "Perilous Worlds," *Village Voice*, 19 January 1993.

———, "Some Women," *Village Voice*, 29 October 1991.

———, "Ties That Bind," *Village Voice*, 16 February 1988.

———, "Too Much!" *Village Voice*, 23 January 1990.

Poesio, Giannandrea, "Been Here Before," *Spectator*, 16 November 1996.

Reynolds, Nancy, review, *Dance Magazine*, May 1990.

Stenn, Rebecca, "Doug Varone Goes for Abstract *In Thine Eyes*," *Dance Magazine*, January 1996.

Stuart, Otis, "Eye on Performance: New York," *Dance Magazine*, May 1988.

Sulcas, Roslyn, "French Connection," *Dance International*, Summer 1995.

Supree, Burt, "Personal Best," *Village Voice*, 30 May 1989.

Thom, Rose Anne, "Reviews: Altogether Different," *Dance Magazine*, May 1992.

Tobias, Anne, "Doug Varone and Dancers, at Playhouse 91, New York, Dec. 14-18, 1994," *Dance Magazine*, May 1995.

Tobias, Tobi, "Good Time," *Village Voice*, 14 January 1997.

Zimmer, Elizabeth, "New World Chaos," *Village Voice*, 1 February 1994.

*   *   *

At first glance, attempts at classifying Doug Varone's work appear problematic. A notice of an upcoming performance by Doug Varone and Dancers in 1997, for instance, quoted the *New York Times* as praising him for being "that rare choreographer with a gift for expressing emotion through dance" and characterized his company as "profoundly human superhumans who dance on a dime, wheeling, darting, and slicing the air at lethal-looking speeds." Yet Deborah Jowitt, writing in the *Village Voice* in 1995, described Varone's style as a vocabulary of uncertainty. Referring to choreographers who "make a point of undercutting dancerly prowess" by "creat[ing] blurry or distorted movement to suggest indecision," Jowitt identified Varone as a member of a "school of unease." These two sets of descriptions hardly seem to square with one another; nor do the comments of other critics, some of whom see Varone as constantly inventing new movements, others of whom criticize his penchant for repetition.

In fact there is not so much a contradiction at work between the critics, or even within Varone himself; rather, the apparent conflict of ideas come from the frenetic energy—sometimes boundlessly confident, sometimes halting and uncertain—inherent in Varone's style. In a 1992 review of a performance by Varone's company along with other newcomers in the Altogether Different Festival at the Joyce Theater, Rose Ann Thom identified Varone's "choreographic concerns" as "uncertain gesturing. . .contrasted with spurts of dynamic, full-bodied, lyrical phases." It was a style that understandably seemed to suit Varone's solo performance in *Nocturne* more than it did the entire group in *Stranded Landfish*. But Varone, who was only 36 but already had 14 years' experience as a choreographer at the time, was always open to fresh approaches. Hence the latter work used the music of Luis Pauta, a saxophonist who Varone first heard on the subway.

Jowitt in 1995 identified a possible source of the apparently contradictory use of uncertain movements and others that are "too ripe, too beautiful." Gwen Welliver, dancing a solo in *Rise*, cut into a graceful leap by slashing at the air, "throwing away [rather] than gathering in." The sharp gestures of the dancer's arms on one plane seemed to undermine the smooth lines of her movement in another. Observing a performance by Doug Varone and Dancers at Playhouse 91 around the same time as Jowitt's article, Anne Tobias wrote that Varone "even looks a little crazy" and that a viewing of works such as *Rise* and *Possession* together revealed an oppressive monotony of forms. Yet even she could not deny that "Varone still displays episodes of inspiration."

He has likewise shown a talent for invention and reinvention, exploration and the acceptance of new challenges. With *In Thine Eyes* in 1996, he set a new benchmark for himself by designing the work around "two beings, without defining who they are." The duet, inspired to some degree by Shakespeare's *The Tempest*, explored the uses of the spine and pushed the limits of abstraction. Deborah Jowitt, calling *In Thine Eyes* "one of Varone's most disturbing works," described the pair of beings (which she interpreted as a man and a woman) as a "hapless Adam and Eve [who looked] like God's rejected test models for humanity." Nancy Coenen, one of the two performers on the night Jowitt attended, looked like "a heroic statue attempting to crack into motion," sending "infinitesimal aftershocks" into her fellow performer, David Neumann.

Yet in the same program, Varone premiered his *Let's Dance*, as lighthearted as the other composition was heavy. In contrast to Anne Tobias's observation that Varone only had a few moves that he repeated over and over, Jowitt praised the fact that "Varone can spool out one movement after another with never a hint of repetition." In a review of his company's first London performance, *The Spectator* likewise cited how "each dance explored diverse forms of movement, thus encompassing a dazzling, wide range of choreography."

As for *Let's Dance*, it was a joyful, potentially participatory experience. (Writing about it in the *Village Voice* in early 1997, Tobi Tobias noted that "the spectators declined the company's invitation to dance with them after the choreographed show.") Nonetheless, the aspect of audience participation prevailed in the setting, in this instance a school auditorium, transformed by the company into a dimly lit club complete with candles under chintzy red glass on every table. The music came from the favorites of the two generations preceding Varone's: "A Fine Romance," "Sentimental Journey," and other hits of the interwar and World War II eras.

Tobias noted that Varone's use of tap added an edge to the evening's performance and may offer one clue to his impressive range. He learned tap as a young man growing up on Long Island, and then attended SUNY-Purchase, where he studied under a wide range of dance instructors that included Mel Wong, Royes Fernandez, and Carole Fried. As a student he danced in Graham and Humphrey revivals, and he later went to work with the Limón company. Hence when he founded his own company, after a stint with the Lar Lubovitch troupe, Varone had a wide vocabulary from which to draw. His work in the 1990s suggests that he has plenty more to offer.

—Judson Knight

WAGONER, Dan

American dancer, choreographer, and company director

Born: Robert Dan Wagoner, 13 July 1932 in Springfield, West Virginia. **Education:** B.S. in pharmacy, West Virginia University, 1954; began dance training with Ethel Butler and Doris Humphrey, 1950s; scholarship to American Dance Festival, 1956; classes with Martha Graham, José Limón, and Louis Horst. **Military Service:** U.S. Army Medical Corps, Fort Meade, Maryland, 1954-56. **Family:** Companion from 1958, poet and art curator George H. Montgomery (died 7 April 1997). **Career:** Member, Doris Humphrey Repertory Group, Connecticut College, 1956; principal dancer, Martha Graham Dance Company, 1957-62; dancer, Merce Cunningham Dance Company, 1958-59; principal dancer, Paul Taylor Dance Company, 1960-68; artistic director/choreographer, Dan Wagoner Dance Company, 1969-94; artistic director, London Contemporary Dance Theatre, 1988-90; has choreographed over 70 dances since 1969 for his own company and others including the London Contemporary Dance Theatre, Ballet Rambert, Winnipeg Contemporary Dancers, Concert Dance Company of Boston, and New Dance Ensemble of Minneapolis; visiting faculty member at various colleges and universities including Bates College, Harvard University, and UCLA (1994-96); professor, Connecticut College, 1995 to present. **Awards:** Numerous grants from the National Endowment for the Arts, New York State Council on the Arts, the New York Foundation for the Arts, Meet the Composer, the Robert Sterling Clark Foundation, Philip Morris Companies Inc., and many other arts and dance supporters.

Roles

1958   *Clytemnestra* (Graham)
1961   *Junction* (Taylor)
       Insects and Heroes (Taylor)
1962   *Piece Period* (Taylor)
       Aureole (Taylor)
1963   *Scudorama* (Taylor)
1966   *Orbs* (Taylor)

Other roles include: Various principal roles with Martha Graham's company, including the young Samson in *Samson Agonistes*, as well as others performances with the Paul Taylor Dance Company.

Works (most with lighting design by Jennifer Tipton and music selected by George Montgomery)

1968   *Dan's Run Penny Supper*
1969   *Brambles*
       Duet (Dido's Lament)

1972   *Changing Your Mind*
       Broken-Hearted Rag
1973   *Yonker Dingle Variations*
1975   *A Dance for Grace and Elwood*
1977   *Songs*
1980   *A Play, with Images and Walls*
       Lila's Garden Ox
1981   *Stop Stars*
       Spiked Sonata
1982   *'Round This World, Baby Mine*
       Otjibwa Ango (retitled *Amara* in 1984)
1984   *Magnolia,* Joyce Theater, New York
1985   *Two Trios,* Columbia College, South Carolina
1986   *Flee as a Bird*
       Evening Star
1988   *To Comfort Ghosts,* Joyce Theater, New York
1989   *Fata Morgana (A Ritual for George),* Joyce Theater
1990   *Turtles All the Way Down,* London
1991   *White Heat,* London
       Songs to Dance, Joyce Theater
       Dolly Sods: After the Flood, Joyce Theater

Publications

On WAGONER: books—

Kreemer, Connie, *Further Steps: Fifteen Choreographers on Modern Dance,* New York, 1987.
Taylor, Paul, *Private Domain,* New York, 1987.

On WAGONER: articles—

Dunning, Jennifer, "A Dark Pastorale by a One-Time Cherub," *New York Times,* 10 October 1991.
Farmer, Ann, "Profile: Dan Wagoner," *Movement Research Performance Journal #16,* Spring 1998.
Jowitt, Deborah, "How to Fly in Ten Directions at Once and Stay in One Place," *Village Voice,* 27 November 1984.
Kisselgoff, Anna, "A Hermetic Poem by Dan Wagoner," *New York Times,* 5 May 1988.
Supree, Burt, "Coming Home," *Village Voice,* 15 May 1984.
———, "Rough Hewn," *Ballet News: The Magazine of Dance,* November 1984.
Tobias, Tobi, "Swan Song," *New York Magazine,* 29 May 1989.
Vaughan, David, "Images and Walls: About Dan Wagoner," *Dance Magazine,* November 1984.

Films and Videotapes

Dances broadcast on PBS' *Dance in America, Alive from Off-Center,* and *Eye on Dance* series; feature-length interviews produced for broadcast by WGBH in Boston (including the made-for-video dance, *George's House*) and SCE-TV in Columbia.

*   *   *

In West Virginia's Allegheny mountains, Dan Wagoner's farming family lived with country things in a simple style echoing a pioneer life. The youngest of 10 children, Wagoner knew from an early age that he wanted to dance. "There was no precedent for that in Springfield, West Virginia," he says. "I didn't even know for a long time that you could do it as a profession." Contenting himself with performing in family entertainments and dancing at church socials, Wagoner eventually attended college on a scholarship and, after completing a degree in pharmacy, joined the U.S. Army Medical Corps stationed at Fort Meade, Maryland. There he began to study modern dance with Ethel Butler, "one of the original fall-down-and-get-up-in-one-count women," and ballet with Lisa Gardiner and Mary Day in Washington, D.C.

His professional career began while attending the American Dance Festival as a scholarship student, where he came to Martha Graham's attention. Upon his release from the Army, he went to New York, was given a scholarship to Martha Graham's school and soon was dancing in her company. In the summer of 1959, at the American Dance Festival at Connecticut College, Remy Charlip introduced Wagoner to Merce Cunningham, who asked him to join his company's tour that year. Then, in 1960, Wagoner divided his time between Paul Taylor's newly formed company and Graham's—but in 1962 he left the Graham company to dance with Taylor's full-time. He remained there until 1968, solidifying his reputation as a riveting performer and creating lead roles in many of Taylor's classic works, when he left to form his own company and pursue his emerging choreographic vision.

Dan Wagoner and Dancers made its debut in 1969 with a concert at New York City's historic Judson Memorial Church. Over its 25-year history, the company performed to wide critical acclaim in hundreds of U.S. cities and on four continents, and appeared at the Holland Festival, the Edinburgh International Festival, and Jacob's Pillow. In 1984 the company was selected by the South Carolina Arts Commission to maintain a "second home" in their state, marking the first such dual residency for a modern dance company, which lasted for four successful years.

Although he began his choreographic career at the Judson Memorial Church, Wagoner did not pursue the more intellectual stream of postmodernism that subsequently flourished there. Instead, he developed the more kinetic possibilities of that historic school and remains located squarely in the modern tradition. Wagoner's dances rely on speed and style shifts, sudden reversals of direction, stops and starts and, perhaps most of all, an uncanny sense of weight and balance. Writing in *Ballet News* in 1984, Burt Supree articulated key elements of Wagoner's aesthetic:

> The dances have a straightforward sculptural vividness and a clean force no matter how abrupt and contrary and full of non sequiturs the movement frequently may be, or how changeable and giddy. The dances' contradictions are solidly welded, they flow together directly and broadly without submerging each other. Wagoner designs big open movements, upper body contractions, bold, busy thrusts of the arms that are wedded to the dramatic or quizzical gestural elements and hard, rhythmic accents that give his dances high color. Often eccentric in context, spiking the move-

ment like exclamatory utterances or urgent communications, those gestures usually seem both mysterious and apt.

Some of Wagoner's dances have a strong, particular flavor of a post-pioneering, just-settled America. But even when his dances are abstract. . .they often convey a kind of sociable gaiety and companionableness, a gracious formality and affection, with the emotions contained behind a modest demeanor. Openhearted and upright are the qualities of his dances. And they are ideal American qualities.

Also describing Wagoner's style, Deborah Jowitt wrote in the *Village Voice* that he "not only tolerates but celebrates oddities of style, eccentricity of behavior, differences between dancers, and wry dance statements that don't point to the next statement, but light up where they are and then disappear, like fireflies on a summer night." In the *New York Times*, Jennifer Dunning wrote that his "dance spills across the stage in clear, cantilevered, pivoting shapes that hug the ground as the dancers bound playfully across it, informed by the whimsical good manners of another time and another place." In addition, Mike Steele has noted in the *Minneapolis Tribune* that "Wagoner will begin a movement in utter elegance and suddenly have a delicately pointed toe flex up, an elongated pose droop into a heap, quicksilver steps across the floor drop into a waddle with the feet thumping the stage. He will flood the stage with movement so there's almost too much to take in, with a slow trio winding into an organic blob at one side while a group cavorts through a flurry of quick moves on the other."

Wagoner's music or sound accompaniment choices are integral to his choreographic process. The music ranges from classical symphonic and operatic music to traditional banjo, ragtime, country and western hits, and turn-of-the-century parlor songs. Some experimental approaches have included recordings of summer rain and thunderstorms, whale songs, poetry recitation, reading from the daily newspaper, and silence. For some time, Wagoner had been interested in using words as an element in dance structure—he and Frank O'Hara had talked about making a piece together before the poet's untimely death in 1966. His collaboration on performances with George Montgomery dates from the late 1960s when, in the dance *Brambles*, Montgomery described the actions of Wagoner's (imaginary) partner and describes the paintings that supposedly form the setting for the dance. Wagoner has commissioned original music for several pieces, including the 1989 piece *Songs to Dance*, set to arrangements of Montgomery's poems by Pulitzer Prize-winning composer William Bolcom and sung by concert soprano Joan Morris.

Wagoner made his first dance, *Dan's Run Penny Supper*, in 1968, naming it for a popular church fundraiser from his West Virginia childhood. He choreographed the piece for himself and a dozen female dance students from Adelphi University. The dance's centerpiece, an angular, sharp solo full of ritual intensity, is set to a hammer dulcimer version of *Amazing Grace*. Burt Supree again noted that another early piece, *Duet*, set to Purcell's *Dido's Lament*, is "full of moments of strong yet modest inner feeling, amplified with leans and bends, contrasting stiffness and curling in, with much close movement belly to back and occasional hard, urgent flutters or scrawls of a hand or foot. The dance is almost stately, for all its tenderness," and heralded the emotional sincerity and modest strength that would inform Wagoner's developing choreographic style.

'Round This World, Baby Mine became a signature dance among what one critic called Wagoner's "hillbilly works." Set to a suite of

Dan Wagoner Dance Company: *To Comfort Ghosts,* **1988. Photograph © Johan Elbers.**

bluegrass and country and western songs, the dance for seven was Wagoner's first in which he did not perform. During the company's 20th anniversary season in 1988 at New York's Joyce Theater, Wagoner premiered *To Comfort Ghosts,* which is generally regarded as his most important work to date. *New York Times* critic Anna Kisselgoff called the piece "easily the best premier of the 1988 dance season. . .[which] reconfirms the profundity that lies at the base of Mr. Wagoner's imagination." She noted that the dance "has the hallmark of a new maturity. Keeping his usual bursts of movement surprises and bizarre shapes, Mr. Wagoner now channels his personal style into something much deeper. Within [lighting designer Jennifer] Tipton's superbly dramatic chiaroscuro effect, the dancers' limbs appear sculptural and molded as the dancers emerge like shadows in a moving frieze." Further, Kisselgoff lauded the "naturalness with which one floor pattern flows into another creates an air of true inevitability about *To Comfort Ghosts.* It is a major work."

Wagoner disbanded his company in 1994, owing to the decline of funding for dance in the U.S. and the demands of caring for his partner of 40 years, George Montgomery, who was suffering from Huntington's disease. After more than 30 years of creating dances in his Greenwich Village studios, Wagoner accepted a two-year post as director of the London Contemporary Dance Theatre. Since 1995, he has lived in New London, Connecticut, and taught dance at Connecticut College, while continuing to choreograph for compa-

nies around the world, including recent commissions by the Chinese International Dance Festival. "We all carry our geography and history in our bodies," Wagoner says. "Our faces tell about the journey we've made and what we think of ourselves. Any time I go to move, I think barefooted 'mountain-ness' in me comes out, and I love it."

—Rhonda Shary

WALDEEN
American dancer and choreographer

Born: Waldeen von Falkenstein, 1 February 1913 in Dallas, moved to Los Angeles in 1918. **Education:** Studied ballet with Theodore Kosloff, Vera Fredova, and Alexandra Baldina-Kosloff at Kosloff's School of Imperial Russian Ballet in Los Angeles, 1918-28; soloist for the Los Angeles Opera and Kosloff's Ballet, by age 13; quit ballet and studied with Benjamin Zemach and Harald Kreutzberg; joined Michio Ito's company, touring the United States, Canada, Japan, and Mexico, 1931; performed in Mexico for six months as a soloist, 1934; returned to the U.S. to tour and teach, performing a solo concert at the Guild Theatre, New York, 1938; created School of Modern Dance, 1939; became the director of the Ballet of the National Fine Arts Institute, Mexico City, and premiered *La Coronela* (based on the Mexican Revolution with music composed by Mexican composer Silvestre Revueltas) which was considered the beginning of the Mexican national modern dance movement, 1940; became part of the Theatre of the Arts, working intermittently, 1940-60; under the auspices of the Mexican government and Rockefeller's Inter-American Affairs Committee, toured the U.S. with her Fine Arts Academy company, 1941; directed modern group Ballet Waldeen and created first mass ballet, *Siembra* (cast of 2,000 dancers), 1942-45; choreographed Sir Thomas Beecham's Mozart Festival in Mexico City, 1944; returned to New York, taught and choreographed at the Hunter College Choreographers Workshop, the New School for Social Research (dir. Erwin Piscator), the Nicholas Roerich Museum, and the 100th Anniversary Celebration of the Communist Party in Madison Square Garden, 1946; returned to Mexico, creating the Ballet Moderno (Modern Ballet) under the patronage of the Corn Commission of the Secretary of Public Education, 1948; translated segments of Pablo Neruda's *Canto General* published and adapted several times, 1950-54; became a Mexican citizen and again named director of the Ballet of the National Fine Arts Institute, 1958; formed Ballet Waldeen of Mexico and toured Mexico, southern U.S. and Central America, 1960; invited to direct Cuba's National School of Modern Dance concurrently with the Cuban School of Dance for Art Instructors, 1962; returned to Mexico, 1966; received the Mexican Music and Theatre Critics' Award for Best Choreographer, 1969; filmed *The History of Dance Is the History of Humanity,* 1972; created *Al filo del alba* (At the Break of Dawn) for the First International Congress of Third World Educators using professional dancers (alumnus of the National Academy of Dance) and children from the Mexico City homeless shelters, 1975; directed and choreographed for the Mexican Contemporary Dance Company, 1976-81; created a seminar on prehispanic arts entitled *el Taller Ometeotl* (the Ometeotl workshop) for the Coordinator General of Artistic Education of the National Institute of Art, and helped develop the judging criteria for Mexico's National Dance Prize, 1980; published anthology, *Dance: An Image of Continuous Creation,* 1982; continued to teach, choreograph and write until her death. **Died:** 19 August 1993 in Cuernavaca, Morelios, Mexico.

Works

1938   *Dance for Regeneration* (mus. Jones), New York
        Epigrams: Fragments of Old Spain (mus. Arvey), New York
        Three Negro Spirituals (mus. Forsythe), New York
        Juba (mus. Morris), New York
        Prelude (mus. Harris), New York
        Nocturne, New York
1939   *Salutación y Reafirmación del romance (Greetings and Reaffirmations)* (mus. Beethoven), Mexico City
        Rondes d' enfants (Children's Rounds) (mus. Turina), Mexico City
        Credo (Creed) (mus. Bach), Mexico City
        Dos variaciones de Goldberg (Two Goldberg Variations) (mus. Bach), Mexico City
1940   *La Coronela (The Lady Colonel)* (mus. Revueltas), Mexico City
        Seis danzas clásicas (Six Classical Dances) (mus. Bach), Mexico City

Procesional (mus. Moncada), Mexico City
Danza de las fuerzas nuevas (Dances of the New Forces), Mexico City
1945   *Elena la traicionera (The Traitor, Elena)* (mus. Halffter) Mexico City
        En la boda (In the Wedding) (mus. Galindo), Mexico City
        Siembra (Seed Time) (mus. Galindo), Mexico City
        Suite de danzas (Suite of Dances) (mus. Couperin), Mexico City
        Cinco danzas en ritmo búlgaro (Five Dances in Bulgarian Rhythm) (mus. Bartók), Mexico City
        Allegreto de la 5a. Sinfonía (Allegretto of the Fifth Symphony) (mus. Shostakovich), Mexico City
        Valses (Waltzes) (mus. Brahms), Mexico City
        Sonatas españolas (Spanish Sonatas) (mus. Soler), Mexico City
        Tres preludios (Three Preludes) (mus. Chavez), Mexico City
        Sinfonía concertante por violín y viola (Harmonic Symphony for Violin and Viola) (mus. Mozart), Mexico City
1949   *Homenaje a García Lorca (Tribute to Garcia Lorca)* (mus. Revueltas)
        Tres ventanas a la vida patria (Three Windows Onto Native Life) (mus. Revueltas), Mexico City
1950   *Preludio y Fuga (Prelude and Fugue)* (mus. Bach), Mexico City
1952   *Divertimento* (mus. Mozart), Mexico city
        Contra la muerta (Against Death) (mus. Bartók), Mexico City
1954   *Coro de primavera (Spring chorus)* (mus. Revueltas, Mexico city
1959   *Horas de junio (The Hours of June)* (mus. Revueltas), Mexico
        La rama dorada (The Golden Bough) (mus. Bartók), Mexico
        Caprichos (Caprices) (mus. Scarlatti and Soler), Mexico
        Sombras de la ciudad (Shadows of the City) (mus. Revueltas), Mexico
        Concierto de Brandenburgo No. 2 (Brandenburg Concerto No. 2) (mus. Bach), Mexico
1960   *El hombre es hecho de maíz (Man Is Made of Corn)* (mus. Revueltas), Mexico
1962   *La zafra (The Sugar Crop)* (mass ballet), Cuba
        Solidaridad (Solidarity) (mass ballet), Cuba
1969   *Tiempo entre dos tiempos (Time Between Two Times)* (mus. Bach and Schönberg), Mexico City
        El espacio y el tiempo (Space and Time) (mus. Bartók), Mexico
1973   *Al filo del alba (The Break of Dawn)* (mass ballet of 500), Mexico
1976   *Tres danzas para un mundo nuevo (Three Dances for a New World)* (mus. Velázquez), Mexico City
1984   *Tres rostros de Carmen Serdán (The Three Faces of Carmen Serdán)* (mus. Ponce), Mexico

Publications

By WALDEEN: book—

La danza: Imagen de creación continua (The Dance: An Image of Continuous Creation), Mexico, 1982.

Waldeen during her 1931 tour of Japan.

By WALDEEN: articles—

"Social Influences and Emotional Motivation," *The Dance Has Many Faces*, ed. Walter Sorrell, 1951.

"Images and Aphorisms on the Dance," *Magazine of the National University of Mexico*, 1964.

"Teoría general de la danza (General Theory of Dance)," *INBA Conference*, August 1979.

"La Mujer artista en la historía humana (The Female Artist in Human History)," *Boletin CID DANZA* (Mexico), July-September 1987.

"El expresionismo dentro de mi participación en la danza moderno méxicana (Expressionism within My Work in Mexican Modern Dance)," *La Revista: Plural* (Mexico City).

On WALDEEN: books—

Dallal, Alberto, *La danza contra la muerte (Dance Counters Death)*, Mexico, 1979.

———, *La Danza en Situación*, Mexico City, 1984.

50 Anos de danza (50 Years of Dance), National Institute of Fine Arts, Mexico, 1986.

National Institute of Fine Arts, *Waldeen. . . su universo (Waldeen. . .Her Universe)*, 24th International Dance Festival, San Luis Potosi, Mexico, 10 July - 7 August 1997.

On WALDEEN: articles—

Arriaga, Guillermo, "Waldeen," *Cuadernos del CID DANZA* 17 (Mexico City), 1987.

Cohen, Johnathan, "Waldeen and the Americas: The Dance has Many Faces," *The American Voice*, Fall 1989.

Lavalle, Josefina, "'Lo Nacional' en el nacimiento de la danza moderna mexicana y su creadora: Waldeen ('Nationalism' and the Birth of Mexican Modern Dance and Its Creator: Waldeen)," *Lineas y arte en espacios* 1 No. 3, 1992.

Rivera, Diego, "A Tribute to Waldeen," *Novedades: Sunday Supplement*, 8 July 1956.

* * *

Waldeen's entire life was dedicated to the dance. Initially a ballet protégé invited to study with Pavlova, she became disenchanted with a lifestyle she saw as tawdry and confining. Inspired by her own drive to move in ways not allowed within the ballet discipline, and backed up by Isadora Duncan's *My Life,* she left the ballet at age 15, never to return. Within five years she had developed a body of work and was teaching in Los Angeles and touring women's clubs throughout California and Canada. Within 12 years she was to become the hub around which Mexican nationalistic sentiments about dance would coalesce.

Waldeen was born Waldeen von Falkenstein in Dallas, Texas. Her parents moved to Los Angeles when Waldeen was five so that, amongst other reasons, she might study at Theodore Kosloff's School of the Imperial Russian Ballet. She was clearly a gifted dancer, performing as a soloist for Kosloff and the Los Angeles Opera at the age of 13. During her time with Kosloff, Waldeen was granted an audition with Pavlova and was invited to go to England to live and study with the great ballerina. However, due to her family's financial situation, she never was able to make this dream materialize.

Leaving the ballet, she studied with Benjamin Zumach and Harald Kreutzberg, taught in a rented studio to earn her living, and worked ceaseless hours developing her own dance vocabulary. She toured in both California and Canada, finding a ready audience in the women's clubs of the era. In 1931 she joined Michio Ito's company, an auspicious move as it was while on tour with Ito that she went to Mexico for the first time. Completing the company tour in Mexico, Waldeen remained in the country for another six months performing to audiences who gave her five and six standing ovations a night.

Upon returning to the U.S., Waldeen continued to dance and teach, as well as perform in Hollywood musicals, so she might earn enough money to present her own concert in New York City. Performing in Hollywood extravaganzas was to galvanize her budding humanism. She tells of one shoot where she and many other dancers were made to work "en pointe" (on pointe in ballet toe shoes) for two hours in the hot southern California sun. She was so furious she went up and took the megaphone from the director and told all the dancers to go home. Immediately after this she helped organize the dancers under the Screen Actors Guild.

Her New York debut was in the form of a solo concert at the Guild Theatre on 13 February 1938. The next day in the New York *Herald*, dance critic Jerome Bohm wrote, "Waldeen's style is essentially lyric [and]. . .all of her offerings were set forth with the certainty of one who has taken the pains to acquire a thorough grounding in the principles of her calling." On the same day in the New York *Times*, John Martin stated, "The impression is a distinctly favorable one. She brings to her work a quite apparent background of experience, and has poise and authority." However, the New York City modern dance scene in 1938 was not much to Waldeen's liking, as she much preferred the lyricism of Duncan to the mechanistic angst-ridden movements of Graham. Of her time in New York, she stated, "in 1938 I was. . .an 'outsider' with my 'old hat' humanism in both technique and my constant search for a dynamic emotional style."

Yet her "humanism" was to find welcoming arms in the form of the Mexican Nationalist Movement. December 1938 found her with an invitation from the Mexican Secretary General of Education to come back to Mexico to perform and perhaps remain to found a national school of modern dance under the auspices of the National Institute of Fine Arts. Waldeen had been very taken with Mexico on her first visit, and so without hesitation left New York for Mexico.

Arriving in Mexico, she presented a series of solo concerts at the Palace of Fine Arts and began to build a Mexican modern company. Of her philosophy, she stated:

> Humanism has meant revolution in Mexico; reform has meant humanism. Its people in the multiplicity of their contradictions and inheritance provide an intricate, illimitable tapestry whose weaving never ceases, whether its woof be threaded with the dark blood-colored strands of her history's battles for freedom, or its warf [sic] gleam with lunar splendor, where the music, dance, poetry and painting of her people have impregnated all that is created. What contemporary Mexican art-form can ignore these powerful images and motivations?

Further, she maintained that she "mine(d) the fertile earth of Mexico's great heritage, digging these precious metals for dance creations" and "listened to the underground murmuring of buried gods and goddesses, watched their progeny walk firmly down the paths of their fields and along the streets of the cities (all) to discover *their* rhythm and step, *their* turn of head and hand; so as not to impose other world forms on this world's specific, powerfully native shape."

That she was successful is clearly documented by Mexican critics and writers. Following her solo concerts of 1939, the then-director of the Palace of Fine Arts, Celestino Gorostiza, requested Waldeen direct the newly formed Ballet of Fine Arts, a company which had briefly had Anna Sokolow as a previous director. At this same time there was a group of mostly Mexican (Waldeen, Theatre director Seki Sano, and Bauhaus director Hannes Meyer being the exceptions) artists and intellectuals who, with the sponsorship of the Mexican Electrician's Union, united to create the Teatro de las Artes. Composer Silvestre Revueltas, muralists Xavier Guerrero and David Alfaro Siguieras, and painter and set designer Gabriel Fernández Ledesma were also members of this group. Amidst discussions of what this new movement was and what form it would take, came the invitation from Gorostiza, and, as the Theatre of the Arts was still under construction, Waldeen invited her colleagues to collaborate with her on the difficult task of creating a Mexican dance company. The result of the collaboration was the 1940 premiere of *La Coronela*, a full-length work based on the Mexican Revolution. The work was an instant success and Waldeen and the company flourished until a change in the administration of the Ministry of Education left Waldeen unemployed and almost penniless. Throughout her life, this was to become a pattern; directing a national company, and the money and sponsorship that this entailed would be contingent on who was in the administration. That which Waldeen so fervently wished for her adopted country, that its art be purely its own, was the reason she fell in and out of favor, and the nationalistic fervor of Mexico frequently led to her exclusion precisely because she was not of Mexican blood.

Whether Waldeen was in or out of favor, she produced prolifically, begging bed, food, and rehearsal space from friends when she had to in order to continue creating. By 1958 Mexican nationalism was at a fever pitch, and fearing she would be deported—thus separated from her young son (she had by then married a Mexican, Rudolfo de Valencia), Waldeen renounced her U.S. citizenship to become a Mexican citizen. Then in 1960 she was invited by Castro to come to Cuba and found his National School of Dance while her husband developed Cuban theatre. The three remained in Cuba for three years, returning to Mexico after putting Cuban theatre and modern dance well on its feet. Coming back to Mexico was a bittersweet affair as it put Waldeen back into the vicious cycle of Mexican politics, something she hadn't had to contend with under the stability of Castro's dictatorship. Additionally, where in past lean times she'd been able to journey to the U.S. to visit friends, teach, and work, having given up her U.S. citizenship and then having lived in Cuba, she had become a persona non-grata in her native country, and was repeatedly turned down when requesting visas.

Yet, as she had always done, Waldeen continued to write, choreograph, and teach, and by the time of her death in 1993 was able to see many of her longtime adversaries acknowledge her contributions to the world of Mexican dance. In his book, *La danza en situación (The Dance in Place)* (1984), Alberto Dallel, Mexico's premiere dance writer, stated that Waldeen "was the basic element in a movement intimately connected with muralism and nationalistic music in Mexico. . . . She discovered something hidden in the body, the temperament, the space, the art and culture of the country. . .creating choreographies which directly conveyed these awarenesses (to her public.)"

Waldeen's works continue to be reset, and the first generation of dancers she fostered in Mexico (Amalia Hernández, Guilleramina Bravo, Josefina Lavalle, Guillermo Arriaga and Ana Merida) have contributed substantially to the wealth of Mexican dance, as has her Cuban protégé, Manuel Vazquez, to Cuba. Yet these early dancers were not her only beneficiaries, as a whole generation of younger dancers and writers also see her as their spiritual mother.

—Deborah Smith

WALKER, Norman

American dancer, choreographer, and educator

Born: 21 June 1934 in New York City. **Education:** Studied drama at the New York School of Performing Arts; graduated from City College; studied modern dance with May O'Donnell, Gertrude Shurr, and at the Martha Graham School; studied ballet with Valentina Pereyaslavec and Robert Joffrey. **Military Service:** U.S. Army, 1957-59. **Career:** Dancer, May O'Donnell Company, debut 1953, became lead male dancer, 1955; performer in and director of his own company, 1960-71, frequently partnering with Cora Cahan; resident choreographer for Harkness Ballet, 1974; has staged choreography for the stage and television; teacher at the High School of Performing Arts, Adelphi University, and other institutions.

Works

1956	*Four Cantos from a Sacred Will*
1960	*Baroque Concerto*
	Variations from Day to Day
	Terrestrial Figure
1961	*Cowboy in Black*
	Prussian Blue
	Splendors and Obscurities
	Crossed Encounter
	In Praise of. . .
1962	*Clear Songs after Rain*
1963	*Enchanted Threshold*
	Reflections
1964	*Meditations of Orpheus*
	Ritual and Dance
	The Testament of Cain
	Trionfo di Afrodite
	Figures and Masks
1965	*The Night Chanter*
1966	*A Certain Slant of Light*
	Night Song
1967	*Baroque Concerto No. 3*
	A Broken Twig
	Eloges
	Passage of Angels
1968	*Illuminations*
1969	*L'Enfant et les sortilèges*
	Baroque Concerto No. 4
	Illusive Image
	Kleediscopic
1970	*Spatial Variations on a Theme by Benjamin Britten*

1971   *Baroque Concerto No. 6*
1972   *Mahler's Fifth Symphony*
1973   *Three Psalms*
        Lazarus
1974   *Ceremonials*
        Ballade
1990   *In the Mountain Forest*

Publications

Cunningham, Katherine, "A Romantic Poet—A Sculptor in Space," *Dance Magazine,* December 1969.

Fineman, Mark, "Chinese Ballet Tiptoeing Around Politics," *Los Angeles Times,* 19 January 1990.

Goodman, Saul, "Brief Biographies: Norman Walker," *Dance Magazine,* July 1961.

"Norman Walker to Head Jacob's Pillow Festival," *Dance Magazine,* February 1975.

Terry, Walter, "O, Brother Sun and Sister Moon," *Saturday Review,* 29 July 1967.

———, "The Pas de Deux, Martial Style," *Saturday Review,* 5 August 1967.

*   *   *

Internationally known modern dancer and choreographer Norman Walker has created many works for his own company and others; he has also taught extensively throughout the United States and around the world. A graduate of the High School for Performing Arts (HSPA) and the City College of New York, Walker studied drama until a "movement for actors" class took him to the Gertrude Shurr-May O'Donnell studio. There he was converted to dance. Walker trained extensively in ballet under Robert Joffrey and Valentina Pereyaslavec, and in modern dance under O'Donnell and Shurr, as well as at the Martha Graham School.

Walker made his dance debut with the May O'Donnell Company in 1953 and became the company's leading male dancer in 1955. He also performed with the companies of Pearl Lang and Yuriko. A teaching position at his alma mater, the High School for Performing Arts, allowed Walker to pursue his interest in choreography. Indeed, his first dance work, *Four Cantos* (1956) set to the music of Vivaldi, was for a student performance. In 1961, he staged this same work in New Jersey for the Garden State Ballet. At HSPA, he continued to choreograph for student recitals and later for the Dance Department's annual spring performances. Hoping to dance and choreograph more frequently, Walker formed his own company in 1960, maintaining it until 1971. The company debuted at the YM-YWHA in New York with Walker and Cora Cahan in the leading roles. The following summer, the company was invited to perform at Jacob's Pillow, marking the beginning of Walker's many years of involvement with the summer dance festival. During his tenure at Jacob's Pillow, Walker performed, choreographed, and taught modern dance; in 1975, he was invited to direct the program. The Jacob's Pillow performances led to Walker's first solo concert in New York. His company then began to secure out-of-town engagements, including a residency at Utah State for four summers.

An examination of the early years of Walker's career reveals several defining aspects of his work. First, music is an essential element in Walker's choreography; he learns the music thoroughly and absorbs it before creating a step. Moreover, his choice of music can be eclectic. In a 1969 article in *Dance Magazine,* Katharine

Cunningham notes that in a summer at Jacob's Pillow, Walker choreographed to Bartók, Boulez, Mayazumi, Penderecki, and Stoelzel. For student performances, he employed rock music, automobile sounds, a fugue, a Finnish folk dance, and a modern Swedish piece.

When he choreographs, Walker also wants to know his performers well, so that their qualities enter into the dance. For this reason, he does not plan out his work completely; instead, he wants the dancers' reactions to be part of the dance. Walker is also known for his lyricism in modern dance, especially in the many duets he created for himself and partner, Cora Cahan. *Meditations of Orpheus* (1964) exemplifies his ability to express intense emotion in dance and is described by Don McDonagh in *The Complete Guide to Modern Dance* as follows: "Walker's talent for the sinuous duet reached a peak in this piece. . .It had both an exquisite lyricism and a tense dramatic sense that made the fate of the doomed couple poignantly real." Cahan herself said of Walker, "Norman has a tremendous feeling for sculpting in space—he has a romantic vision of life and beauty and truth that is most rare." She is, indeed, qualified to comment on Walker's work. In 1969, Cunningham wrote of the Walker-Cahan partnership, "[it] is virtually unique in modern dance. They have an empathy and a non-verbal communication that they both admit is very rare."

Besides choreographing for his own company, Walker has created works primarily for ballet companies, among them the Boston Ballet, the Batsheva Dance Company of Israel, which he directed for several years, and the Harkness Ballet. He is well-known for being able to perform and choreograph in both ballet and modern techniques.

Among Walker's recent projects have been several cultural exchanges; he worked on contract with Ballet Philippines, and in early 1990 conducted an intensive four-week workshop with the Central Ballet of China. For this project, the first cultural exchange between America and China since the crackdown on pro-democracy demonstrators of Tiananmen Square, he worked with 22 of the finest ballet dancers in the People's Republic of China, blending classical and contemporary ballet and Western and Chinese dance. In a 1990 interview, Walker noted that the project was more a "recombination" than a groundbreaking experience and theorized that pioneers of modern dance adopted many styles from traditional Chinese folk dance during forays to the Far East in the 1920s.

Walker is a popular teacher; he has traveled extensively around the country and in Germany, Sweden, and Finland as an artist-in-residence. In his classes, his movement studies are based on those he learned from Gertrude Shurr, but he added sequences in movement with male dancers in mind. In the early 1990s he continued to teach as a professor in the Performing Arts Department at Adelphi College.

—Karen Zimmerman

WALLMANN, Margarethe
Austrian dancer and choreographer

First name also rendered as Margarete, Margarita, Margherita. **Born:** 22 June 1904 (or 22 July 1901) in Berlin (or Vienna). Wallmann's year and place of birth are difficult to determine because the artist does not provide clear information, and biographical sources (including her contract with the Vienna State Opera) include conflicting data. **Education:** She may have studied at the Berlin Royal Opera's Ballet School. It is certain that her teachers were Eugenia Eduardowa, in Berlin, and later Heinrich Kröll and Anna Ornelli in Munich. In 1923, she started studying with Mary Wigman in Dresden, also joining her teacher's legendary touring company, whose members also included Hanya Holm and Gret Pallucca. **Career:** Held a lecture series in New York on the Wigman technique as well as the essence of expressive dance, 1928; assumed the directorship of the Wigman School in Berlin, 1929; founded the "Dancers' Collective," 1930; productions include *Orpheus Dionysos* (Munich, 1930), with Wallmann and Ted Shawn in the principal roles; invited to the Salzburg Festival; choreographed a series of theater and opera productions for the Salzburg Festival; choreographer and ballet director, Vienna State Opera, 1933-38; founded the Teatro Colon Ballet in Buenos Aires, Argentina, in 1939, remained until 1948; moved to Milan, Italy, 1949, and worked as an opera director with great success; returned to the Salzburg Festival, 1954; she directed *Tosca* at the Vienna State Opera, 1958; worked as an opera director for the most prominent opera companies until the 1970s. **Awards:** First Prize, Third Dancers' Congress in Munich, for *Orpheus Dionysos,* 1930. **Died:** 2 May 1992 in Monte Carlo.

Works (selected)

1930	*Orpheus Dionysos* (mus. Gluck), Munich
1931	*The Last Judgment* (mus. Händel), Salzburg Festival
1933	*Orpheus and Eurydice* (also director; mus. Gluck), Salzburg Festival
1934	*Fanny Essler* (mus. Nádor), Vienna State Opera
	Austrian Peasant Wedding (mus. Salmhofer), Vienna State Opera
1936	*Der liebe Augustin* (mus. Steinbrecher), Vienna State Opera
1937	*The Birds* and *Ancient Dances and Airs* (mus. Respighi), La Scala, Milan
1948	*Joan of Arc at the Stake* (also director; mus. Honegger)

Publications

By WALLMANN: books—

Les balcons du ciel, Paris, 1976.

*   *   *

Margarethe Wallmann's work as a choreographer exemplifies the transition from stormy Expressionism to a more polished, stylized form of the dance drama, which relied on classical ballet literature for sources (as traditional as *The Sleeping Beauty* at the Scala). Soon after she began her education as a dancer, she started following in Mary Wigman's footsteps, subsequently assuming the leadership of Wigman's school in Berlin. In 1930, when she founded her own ensemble, named, significantly, "Dancers' Collective," she was already interested in the plurality of dance styles. Her group, which in 1931 had 37 dancers, included not only people of various national origin, but dancers of different stylistic orientations, including Andrei Jerschik, Ted Shawn, and Mila Cirul. It was Shawn who in 1931 invited Wallmann to teach Wigman technique at the Denishawn School in Los Angeles. During this period, large productions were staged in an effort to fight Berlin's growing unem-

ployment. In 1933, when Wallmann, after her 1930 success as choreographer of *Orpheus Dionysos* in Munich, was engaged by the Salzburg Festival, the leading conductor Bruno Walter looked forward to working with one of the great choreographers of that time. In *The Last Judgment,* which was described as a ballet-mystery play, Wallmann combined all the accomplishments of modern expression dance (from Delsarte's naturalness and Dalcroze's rhythm to Laban's space) to create a harmonious whole. The production was remarkable for the expressive performance by the soloists and the chorus. Still oriented toward the moralizing themes of *Ausdruckstanz,* she turned to the Vienna State Opera, where she hoped, as dance director, to realize her aesthetical ideas. The strengths of an ensemble trained in the classical academic tradition had to be taken into consideration; Wallmann's main accomplishments at Vienna were three large choreographies for works with specifically Austrian themes: *Fanny Elssler, An Austrian Peasant Wedding,* and *Der liebe Augustin.* In 1935, the American film company Metro-Goldwyn-Mayer wanted to produce a film version of the ballet *Fanny Elssler,* but the project fell through. However, that year, Wallmann was involved in a film about Johann Strauss. In Vienna, Wallmann was criticized by the defenders of classical ballet for her work methods, and for a tendency to plan repertoires based exclusively on her own works. In 1933, when Jews were forbidden by law to work in Germany, Wallmann moved to Austria. However, in 1938, following Hitler's invasion of Austria, her contract with the Vienna State Opera was cancelled, in the wake of a "cleansing operation." However, Wallmann, who had worked in Milan the previous year, moved to Buenos Aires, where she formed the Ballet Ensemble at the Teatro Colon. Following her engagement with the Salzburg Festival, which lasted until 1937, Wallman worked increasingly, and with great success, as an opera director.

—Andrea Amort; translated by Zoran Minderovic

WARING, James
American dancer, choreographer, and artist

Born: 1 November 1922 in Alameda, California. **Education:** Early influence by Jaques-Dalcroze and Isadora Duncan; studied with Raoul Pausé, Gertrude Shurr, Ann (later Anna) Halprin, Welland Lathrop, and at the San Francisco Ballet School; then in New York at the School of American Ballet with Muriel Stuart, Anatole Vilzak, Merce Cunningham, John Cage, and others. **Military Serivce:** Served during World War II. **Career:** Co-founder, Dance Associates, 1951; formed his own company; involved with Judson Dance Theater, early 1960s; taught summers at Indian Hill camp (Massachusetts); artistic director, New England Dinosaur (formerly New England Dance Theater), 1974-75. **Died:** 2 December 1975 in New York.

Works (first performed in New York City unless otherwise noted)

1956	*Adagietto* (mus. John Herbert McDowell)
	Pieces and Interludes (mus. John Cooper)
	Fantasy and Fugue in C Major (mus. Mozart)
	Suite (mus. Mozart)
	Obertura Republicana (mus. Chavez)
	Phrases (mus. Satie)

1957   *Humoresque* (mus. tape collage)
        Poeta Nascitur (mus. improvised by audience)
        Ornaments (mus. Couperin, MacRae Cook, Maria Alba)
        Dances before the Wall (mus. various), Henry Street Playhouse

1958   *Octandre* (mus. varese), Master Theater

1959   *In the Mist* (mus. Hy Gubernick), Master Theater
        Pyrrhic (mus. Stockhausen), Living Theater
        Corner Piece (mus. Philip Corner), Living Theater
        Extravaganza (mus. John herbert McDowell), Living Theater

1960   *Peripateia* (mus. Richard Maxfield), New York Institute of Fashion
        Tableaux (mus. Terry Jennings), New York Institute of Fashion
        Gossoon (mus. George Brecht), Living Theater
        Landscape (mus. John Herbert McDowell), Princeton University
        Lunamble (mus. Richard Maxfield), Living Theater
        A Swarm of Butterflies Encountered on the Ocean (mus. Richard Maxfield), Master Theater

1961   *Dromenon* (mus. Richard Maxfield), La Comedie Canadienne, Montreal
        Little Kootch piece, No. 2 (mus. Richard Maxfield), Living Theater

1962   *Two More Moon Dances* (mus. Richard Maxfield), Henry Street Playhouse
        Dithyramb (mus. George Brecht), Henry Street Playhouse
        Exercise (mus. Richard Maxfield), Maidman Playhouse
        Bacchanale (mus. Richard Maxfield), Hunter College Playhouse
        At the Hallelujah Gardens (mus. Richard Maxfield), Hunter College Playhouse

1963   *Divertimento* (mus. Mozart), Judson Memorial Church
        Poet's Vaudeville (mus. John Herbert McDowell, texts by Diane DiPrima), Judson Memorial Church

1964   *Double Concerto* (mus. Bach, events by George Brecht), Judson Memorial Church
        Stanzas in Meditation, four-part work: *Painted Lace* (mus. Malcolm Goldstein); *Curtain Dream* (mus. John Herbert McDowell); *Glazed Glitter* (mus. Philip Corner); *Stanzas in Meditation* (mus. Albert Fine), Judson Memorial Church
        Rondo in A Minor and Fugue in C Major (mus. Mozart), Indian Hill Theater, Stockbridge, Massachusetts

1965   *Three Symphonies* (mus. Richard Maxfield), Judson Memorial Church
        Musical Moments, ten-part work: *Panacea* (mus. John Herbert McDowell); *Tomato Expose* (mus. Gliere); *Les Batons Rouges* (mus. McDowell); *The Vamp* (mus. Byron Gay); *William Tell Overture* (mus. Rossini); *Manhattan Serenade* (mus. Louis Alter); *Pas des Fleurs* (mus. Delibes); *Tambourine Dance* (mus. traditional Spanish); *The Love Parade* (mus. Victor Schertzinger); *Life of Washington* (illustrated slide lecture by George Brecht); Judson Memorial Church
        In Old Madrid (mus. traditional Spanish, Ravel), YMHA, Newark
        Adante Amoroso and Adagietto (mus. Mahler), YMHA, Newark

        Minuete, Gigue, and Finale (mus. Mozart), Indian Hill Theater, Stockbridge, Massachusetts
        Three Dances from the Triumph of Night: Scenes for a Masque (mus. Liszt), Indian Hill Theater, Stockbridge, Massachusetts
        La Serenata in Maschera (mus. Mozart), Cambridge, Massachusetts

1966   *March: To Johann Joachim Kandler* (mus. Mozart), Kaufmann Concert Hall
        The Phantom of the Opera (mus. John Herbert McDowell), Sterling Forest Summer Theater, Tuxedo, New York
        Mazurkas for Pavlova (mus. Chopin), Judson Memorial Church, revised 1969
        Northern Lights (mus. Schönberg), Theater 80, St. Marks Place
        Good Times at the Cloud Academy (mus. John Herbert McDowell), Indian Hill Theater, Stockbridge, Massachusetts

1967   *Arena* (mus. Stravinsky), Theater 80, St. Mark's Place
        Salute (mus. Berlioz), Judson Memorial Church

1968   *Spell* (mus. Debussy), Harkness Festival, Delacorte Theater
        Winter Circus (mus. Debussy), Judson Memorial Church
        Amethyst Path (mus. Liszt), Judson Memorial Church
        A Waltz for Moonlight Comedians (mus. Tchaikovsky), Judson Memorial Church
        At the Cafe Fleurette (mus. Herbert), Judson Memorial Church
        An Oriental Ballet (mus. Griffes), Judson Memorial Church
        Seven Poems by Wallace Stevens (mus. Griffes), Judson Memorial Church
        Polkas and Interludes (mus. Smetana, S. Hartke), Judson Memorial Church

1969   *Dance Scene, Interlude, and Finale* (mus. Schönberg), Judson Memorial Church
        Spookride (mus. Chopin, Ezra Simms), Boston
        Beyond the Ghost Spectrum (mus. R. Lecly), Tanglewood, Massachusetts
        Purple Moment (mus. Bach and popular songs of the 1920s and 1930s), Boston
        Pumpernickel and Circumstance (mus. C. Turner), Indian Hill Theater, Stockbridge, Massachusetts
        Amoretti (mus. Schubert), Jacob's Pillow, Massachusetts

1970   *Spookride Version II* (mus. Chopin, E. Simms), Pennsylvania Ballet, Philadelphia

Publications

By WARING: articles—

"Five Essays on Dancing," *Ballet Review,* 1967.
"My Work," *Ballet Review,* 1975-76.

On WARING: articles—

Anderson, Jack, "The Paradoxes of James Waring," *Dance Magazine,* November 1968.
Chin, Daryl, "Remembering James Waring," *Dance Scope,* Spring 1976.
Tobias, Tobi, "The Next Step," *New York,* 18 November 1985.
———, "Taking Stock," *New York,* 26 November 1990.

Vaughan, David, "Remembering James Waring," *Ballet Review,* 1975-76.

*   *   *

A modern dance experimentalist, James Waring was a prolific choreographer who blended ballet and modern dance techniques, helping to bring unity to the two teachings once held in such aversion to each other. He was also an accomplished collagist, an element reflected in his choreography and the force behind his designing and making many of the costumes for his pieces. His interest in painting, literature, and music is also evident in his compositions. Before his death at the age of 53, he choreographed over 135 works and helped establish the Judson Dance Theater and in doing so set the stage for the postmodern movement. Says Daryl Chin, "With the exception of Merce Cunningham, no choreographer did more for what's now called the New Dance. And in the beginning (1959-63), maybe Waring did more."

Waring was born in 1922 in Alameda, California, and raised in the San Francisco Bay area. In Oakland he studied ballet and "plastique," an early form of interpretive dance derived from ethnic dancing and influenced by Isadora Duncan. During a time when modern dance and ballet were seen as contradictory, Waring had received academic ballet training in addition to contemporary technique. He continued his ballet studies at the San Francisco Ballet School, and his modern dance study in Welland Lathrop's composition workshops, as well as with Gertrude Shurr, and Ann (later Anna) Halprin.

After returning from service in the army during World War II, he went to New York and studied at the School of American Ballet with Muriel Stuart and Anatole Vilzak. He also studied modern dance with Merce Cunningham and John Cage, who were also teaching there. In an essay published after his death in *Ballet Review,* Waring says of his early work that it was "not necessarily a synthesis of styles but at least a kind of accommodation in which I felt at liberty to work with whatever materials seemed right to me at the moment." His earliest pieces were created for and produced by Choreographer's Workshop, which dissolved. In 1952, Waring started a choreographer's cooperative with David Vaughan, Alec Rubin, Paul Taylor, and other young choreographers, called Dance Associates, to take up where the Choreographer's Workshop had left off. Later he directed his own company, yet only on a part-time basis, so he could earn money teaching dance in order to stage performances.

Early works, such as the *Wanderers* (1951) and *Prisoners* (1952) were loose narrations of a scenario of Waring's creation. They were abstract, built upon Waring's interest at the time in primitive art. After working with Cunningham, Waring was encouraged to rethink the relationship between music and dance and to explore rhythm and phrase-making. As he developed his ability, his range of style and choice of subject matter broadened. "Some dances by Waring are raucous avant-garde hellzapoppins. Some are evocations of Romantic ballet as fragile as a Victorian pressed flower. Others are curiously grim comedies. . .Still others are meticulous reconstructions of the musical comedy styles of the 1920s and 1930s," writes Jack Anderson. Waring was especially fond of the reconstructions, spending much time researching the costuming of the exact date he was undertaking, and choreographing the nuances of poise and gesture he noticed in movies or films of those time periods to authenticate the performance.

When not in a narrative form, Waring's dances often reflected the art of collage, bringing disparate pieces together into one composition. His work was also characterized as moving from the serious to the light-hearted with the smoothness of a pendulum. Another type of work Waring choreographed was the "celebration" or "jubilee." These were large works intended for large casts with many different segments taking place at the same time to resemble a choreographic carnival. Their result was to "exhilarate some spectators and bewilder others. What the 'celebrations' celebrate is the diversity of existence itself," commented Anderson. *At the Hallelujah Gardens* (1963) was one celebration Waring collaborated on with seven other choreographers including George Brecht and Al Hansen in which two or more things were going on at any given moment.

It has been noted that Waring had a liking for collaboration and has worked with a wide range of other artists, including David Vaughan, Paul Taylor, John Herbert McDowell, Julian Beck, Diane Di Prima, and Phil Corner, as well as carefully mining student talent. Aileen Passloff, Arlene Rothlein, Valda Setterfield, David Gordon, and Lucinda Childs are a few of the students he worked with; in teaching and creating dances for many of these students, Waring set the stage for the formation of the Judson Dance Theater which he helped to direct in his later years.

For many summers, Waring taught at the Indian Hill camp in Stockbridge, Massachusetts, creating dances especially for these students. "One of Jimmy's extraordinary gifts was that he could take children—or adults, for that matter—who had little or no training, put them on stage and make them look as though they belonged there," wrote David Vaughan in a 1976 article in *Ballet Review.* "It was at Indian Hill that he did what may well have been the first ballet set to music by Scott Joplin, *Ragtime Dances.*"

Waring claimed he worked intuitively, and continued to learn by thinking about his work after he had finished creating. In a manuscript written in 1965 and found after his death in December 1975, he says: "I have evolved no theories or rules about choreography. I don't believe that mine is the only way, especially since my way keeps changing. (I try to work through serenity and love and trust.) I think it's good to know as much as you can but not to depend on any of it."

—Lisa A. Wroble

WARREN, Leigh

British-born Australian dancer, choreographer, and artistic director

Born: 1952 in Birmingham, England. **Education:** Attended James Cook Memorial High School in Sydney (New South Wales) and Australian Ballet School; studied at Juilliard in New York. **Career:** Dancer, Australian Ballet, Ballet Rambert, and Nederlands Dans Theater; taught at Victorian College for the Arts, Melbourne; artistic director, Australian Dance Theatre, Adelaide (South Australia); founder/artistic director, Leigh Warren and Dancers, 1993.

Works

1993   *Petrouchka,* National Gallery of Australia, Canberra
        Bindies, National Gallery of Australia, Canberra
        Front Lawn, National Gallery of Australia, Canberra

Fast Yarns, Norwood Concert Hall, Adelaide

Helix, Norwood Concert Hall, Adelaide

Andy's Arranging Flowers (mus. Graham Fitkin and Stewart Copeland)

1994   *Klinghoffer*, Norwood Concert Hall, Adelaide

Blue, Playhouse, Perth

1995   *Hooked: Lure and Bait* (mus. Ingram Marshall), Street Theatre, Canberra

1998   *Quiver*, Norwood Concert Hall, Adelaide

Publications

On WARREN: articles—

Brissenden, Alan, "Reviews: Contrasts Figure," *Dance Australia*, February/March 1996.

———, "Powerful Music-Theatre," *Dance Australia,* August/September 1994.

———, "Fast and Fluid," *Dance Australia*, October/November 1993.

———, "Footloose and Rent-Free," *Dance Australia,* August/September 1993.

Christofis, Lee, "From the Ashes," *Dance Australia*, December 1992/January 1993.

Donaldson, Anita, "Up and Dancing," *Dance Australia*, February/March 1994.

Laughlin, Patricia Jean, "Hot Dreams: Hooked," *Dance Australia*, April-May 1997

Murray, Jan, "Dutch Deductions: Dutch Delights," *Dance Theatre Journal*, Winter 1993/94.

Potter, Michelle, "Tempting Dance," *Dance Australia*, October/November 1995.

———, "Reviews: Exhilarating Debut," *Dance Australia,* August/September 1993.

Van Ulzen, Karen, "The Changing of Leigh Warren," *Dance Australia,* April/May 1991.

Whitford, Susan, "Forsythe Fulcrum," *Dance Australia*, October/November 1994.

*   *   *

Leigh Warren is one of Australia's leading choreographers and the founder of Leigh Warren and Dancers, based in Adelaide. Founded in 1993, the company is dedicated to the presentation of "original and innovative work," often bringing in a combination of various disciplines, including film and choral works. It tours nationally and internationally, with a 1998 itinerary that includes Australia, Singapore, Japan, Korea, Taiwan, and Holland.

Warren trained with the Australian Ballet and at the Juilliard School in New York before performing with Ballet Rambert in London, and as a soloist for the Nederlands Dans Theater. In the late 1980s he began teaching at he Victorian College of the Arts in Melbourne, then became the artistic director of the Australian Dance Theatre (ADT) of Adelaide, South Australia. Due to creative disagreements over the company's direction, Warren left ADT and Meryl Tankard took over, and the company was eventually renamed the Meryl Tankard Australian Dance Theatre.

Warren acts as both choreographer and artistic director for Leigh Warren and Dancers, overseeing a troupe of six part-time dancers, most former members of the ADT. An administrator, publicist, and finance manager, as well as an eight-member board, are part of the business end of the company. The infrastructure of the company is minuscule, as is often the case in the world of modern dance: an artistic staff of one, along with one part-time production staff person and three part-time administrative staff workers. The company's offices are in Adelaide's Lion Arts Centre, and its home theater is the Norwood Concert Hall.

Leigh Warren and Dancers has a mission statement containing a number of listed aims. On an artistic level, the company seeks "to be a leader in contemporary dance" and "to collaborate with and commission work from other artists, particularly visual artists and composers." Along with this idea of reaching out to other artists are related notions: "to be sensitive to the environment in which the company lives and to endeavor to be of service to other dance organizations (performance and educational) within the state, as well as encouraging community interaction with the company; to sustain international contacts and repertoire, in such proportion as enhances a program of dominantly Australian choreographers." In terms of its audience, aims include the following: "to present quality dance to as broad a cross-section of the public as possible; to have a company style which is physically skilled and intellectually challenging, yet accessible and appealing to people of all ages."

On an operational level, goals of Leigh Warren and Dancers include being "a compact, versatile and flexible touring dance company." The mission statement puts a value on several business-related areas: "to be original, innovative and economical in all areas of operation; to consult with major investors on how best to achieve the most viable company possible." In the political realm, the statement concludes with a stated desire "to not only be a leader in equal opportunity for women, but to reflect throughout [the company's] personnel the multicultural composition of the society for which the company performs and creates."

Among Warren's choreographic works is *Quiver*, which the company presents in 1998 in conjunction with the Australian String Quartet and Pablo Percusso. Costume and set design is by Mary Moore, who has worked closely with Warren on other productions such as *Hooked*, for which her design was inspired by the paintings of Mondrian. First presented in 1995, the latter is a frank and upfront look at romantic games between people. Another production was *The Ethereal Eye*, presented at their home theatre of Norwood Concert Hall. Choreographed by Nanette Hassall with music by Jonathan Mills, *Eye* was inspired by the work of American architects Walter and Marion Burley Griffin, who designed the planned Australian capital at Canberra.

The story behind the Burley Griffins is one of "Frustrated idealism, bureaucratic obstruction, parochial jealousy, even a Royal Commission." These words are taken from promotional material for the Adelaide Festival '96, but they could just as easily describe the vagaries of running a small modern dance company. In 1997, Leigh Warren and Dancers received several grants from various arts councils (figures are in Australian dollars.) The South Australia Ministry for the Arts announced that it would increase the Warren company budget by $20,000 to $140,000 to fund new work and a tour as part of a locally sponsored program called "Made to Move." In May of that year, the company also received a grant of $35,771 to tour with *Hooked* and teach workshops throughout South Australia and the Northern Territory.

Earlier, in October 1996, Warren took part in something called the "Australian Performing Arts Market," an event in Canberra in which members of the arts community quite literally seek to sell themselves to people with funds. Jon Ashford from The Place in London invited Warren to visit England, and was so impressed by the company that he travelled to Adelaide from Canberra to see them in their home setting.

—Judson Knight

WATER STUDY

Choreography: Doris Humphrey
Music: Performed in silence, originally with gong accompaniment
Costume Design: Pauline Lawrence
First Production: Humphrey-Weidman Company, Civic Repertory Theater, New York City, 28 October 1928.
Original Dancers: Cleo Atheneos, Justine Douglas, Evelyn Fields, Margaret Gardner, Georgia Graham, Eleanor King, Virginia Landreth, Dorothy Lathrop, Katherine Manning, Sylvia Manning, Jean Nathan, Celia Rausch, Jane Sherman, Gertrude Shurr and Rose Yasgour

Other productions include: In J.P. McEvoy's *Americana,* with the addition of blue cellophane floor, walls, and front panel, 1931; "Gymnasium Circuit" tour, 1935; in *Decade* (a retrospective of the Humphrey-Weidman partnership), Bennington Festival, 1941; The José Limón Dance Company, 1946-57; the Juilliard Dance Theatre, 1955-59; and in the form of hundreds of reconstructions after Humphrey's death in 1958.

Publications

Books—

Adair, Christy, *Women and Dance: Sylphs and Sirens,* New York, 1992.
Cohen, Selma Jean, *Dance as a Theatre Art: Source Readings in Dance History from 1581 to the Present,* New York, 1975.
———, *Doris Humphrey: An Artist First,* Wesleyan University Press, 1972.
Dance Notation Bureau, *Doris Humphrey: The Collected Works, Vol. I,* New York: Dance Notation Bureau Press, 1978.
Holmes, Olive, editor, *Motion Arrested: Dance Reviews of H.T. Parker,* Wesleyan University Press, 1982.
Stodelle, Ernestine, *The Dance Technique of Doris Humphrey and Its Creative Potential,* Princeton, New Jersey, 1978.

Articles—

Downes, Olin, "Grace Cordell Makes Debut in Dances Ably Aided by Frank Parker, Doris Humphrey and Charles Weidman Please," *New York Times,* 29 October 29 1928.

Films and Videotapes

Water Study, performed by Washington Dance Repertory Company, Washington, D.C., 1966.

*   *   *

As the story goes, after seeing Pavlova perform in 1913 Doris Humphrey decided to become a dancer because she wanted to get to the root of the state of being human. From 1920 to 1927 she performed with and choreographed for the Denishawn Dancers (directed by Ruth St. Denis and Ted Shawn). Humphrey first consciously formulated her movement ideas while reading Nietzsche's *Birth of Tragedy,* which introduced her to concepts of duality: Apollonian/Dionysian, rest/activity, security/risk, etc. Humphrey eventually created a dance technique characterized by the principles of fall/recovery and "the arc between those two deaths."

Humphrey choreographed *Water Study* while she and partner Charles Weidman were in charge of the New York Denishawn School. *Water Study* began as an experiment in natural movement, which led to the identification of three natural rhythms: motor, pulse, and breath. It also started, Humphrey later told dance critic Margaret Lloyd, "with human feeling—the body movement and its momentum in relation to the psyche and to gravity. As it developed the movements took on the form and tempo of moving water." *Water Study* was the first modern dance created out of a "breath language," a novelty within the context of the stylized, ornamental dances that dance audiences had come to expect from Ruth St. Denis.

The dance begins with 16 dancers evenly spaced around the stage, each tightly curved into a ball, resting on her knees. One by one, starting stage left, a ripple passes across the stage as the dancers rise slightly with a breath impulse initiated in the pelvis and sink back down. The ripple is repeated four times, with more lengthening of the trunk each time. Eventually, the dancers are arching, running, jumping, falling, somersaulting, spiraling, and flinging, both individually and in groups. Finally, the momentum subsides, the tempo slows, and when all the dancers are prone, *Water Study* is over. In the original production, the dancers wore flesh-colored leotards that, says Lloyd, "under blue lights and seen from a distance gave the impression of modest nudity."

Critic Mary Watkins observed that the dance had "the authentic feeling of the sea casting itself relentlessly in torpid or in stormy mood, against the wall of some New England shore." Watkins added, "Real genius has gone into the creating of this." The *New York Times* music critic Olin Downes covered the 1928 premiere of *Water Study* with the following glowing review:

> At the Civic Repertory Theatre, Doris Humphrey, Charles Weidman, and their student concert group made their first appearance of the season in a brilliant repertoire of solos and ensembles. In the latter medium Miss Humphrey demonstrated anew her mastery of the handling of mass movement in *Water Study,* which found itself on the program along with *Color Harmony* and the Grieg concerto. That it is an even more notable composition than these lies in the fact that it is performed without music and eschews as far as may be all musical rhythm. [Also on the program: *Sarabande, Ringside, Pavane, Minstrels, Air for the G String,* a "Japanese Dance"]. A large and distinguished audience received them with enthusiasm.

H.T. Parker, who reviewed *Water Study* for the *Boston Evening Transcript* (8 March, 1930), offered another perspective: "Unfortunately, human bodies, though dance-schooled, are not as fluid as the waters. Unfortunately, there are stream-like and wave-like motions that, however transfused into a more stubborn medium, do try the sense of humor.

Water Study is one of 11 dances choreographed by Doris Humphrey (out of 97 concert dances) that has been labanotated, and the Labanotation Bureau in New York owns the license for

Water Study. Although three versions exist, the Bureau reconstructs the Ruth Currier version, notated in 1966, aided by notes from Barbara Hoenig and Sally Fan Hangar, who danced in the 1954 revival of *Water Study* at Connecticut College School of Dance, and by Currier's memory of dancing the work while a member of the José Limón Dance Company. Ernestine Stodelle and Letitia Ide's (dancers with Humphrey) versions are on file at the Bureau for study purposes only. According to Leslie Rotman, Director of Reconstructions at the Bureau, *Water Study* has been performed "hundreds and hundreds" of times since Doris Humphrey's death in 1958. Rotman says small modern dance companies and universities request it the most. Since 1995 alone, *Water Study* has been reconstructed by Bureau-approved notators for the University of Washington's Chamber Dance Company, the Utah Repertory Dance Theater, Western Oregon State College, York University (Toronto), Agnes Scott College (Georgia), and Momentum Dance Company (Boston).

When *Water Study* is reconstructed, dancers are told to pay special attention to "successions, movement impulses that travel through the entire body like the life force itself." A sense of weight is also of primary concern. Currier says a dancer in *Water Study* should feel "as if she had 50 pounds in weights evenly distributed over her body." As well, the dance should be performed with a detached, impersonal gaze, and leg rotation not more than 45-55 degrees in side-to-side movement. *Water Study* is not counted, but should be felt, as though the dancers were one single breathing organism.

Dance critic and historian Marcia Siegel singles *Water Study* out as "one of the most extraordinary works in American dance—a masterpiece of the choreographer's art. It is an example—perhaps a very extreme one because it is so well-fulfilled—of what the modern dance theorists were proposing when the fires of idealism burned strongest in them."

—Lodi McClellan

WEBB, Brian

Canadian dancer, choreographer, educator, and company director

---

Born: 25 May 1951 in Unity, Saskatchewan. **Education:** B.F.A. in drama, University of Alberta, Edmonton, 1973; M.F.A. in choreography, California Institute of the Arts, Valencia, 1986; studied at Erick Hawkins School of Dance, 1973-77; studied at Carol Conway School of Dance, 1974-77; studied at Martha Graham School of Dance, 1982. **Career:** Choreographer, National Choreographic Seminar directed by Robert Cohan, Banff, Alberta, 1981; solo artist, Le Groupe de la Place Royale Laboratory, 1992; dancer and teacher, Erick Hawkins Dance Company, 1973-74; dancer/choreographer, and teacher, Carol Conway Dance Company, 1973-77; founder, Brian Webb Dance Company, Edmonton, Alberta, 1979; co-producer of *Acts,* a series of dance/visual art collaborations from across Canada for *The Works: A Visual Arts Celebration;* presenter of numerous dance artists and companies in Edmonton, Alberta, 1991-97; member, Canadian CanDance Network; chair, Dance Program at Grant MacEwan Community College, Edmonton, Alberta, 1993-97. **Awards:** In collaboration with Blair Brennan, sculptor, received interdisciplinary Work and Performance Art "B" grant, Canada Council, 1992; numerous project grants, Alberta Foundation for the Arts, 1991-94; Syncrude Award for Artistic Direction, 1995; Interdisciplinary Long Term Award, Canada Council, 1996.

Works

1986   *Biography* (performance art), commissioned by the Latitude 53 Society of Artists, Edmonton, Alberta
1987   *Public/Private* (solo dances), Edmonton and Toronto
1989   *The Light Watering Studio* (multimedia collaboration w/ writer Scott Taylor), commissioned by Grant MacEwan Community College
1990   *Wrestling* w/sculptor Blair Brennan
        Bone White Time w/sculptor Blair Brennan, a part of *Acts, The Works: A Visual Arts Celebration,* Edmonton
        What the Thunder Said, a part of *Acts, The Works: A Visual Arts Celebration,* Edmonton
        Bohater (mus. George Arasimowicz), 17th International Festival of Electronic Music, Oberlin Conservatory of Music, Oberlin, Ohio
1991   *Sam* (interdisciplinary performance with scripts by Samuel Beckett), premiered at the Edmonton Fringe Festival
        Victories Over Us/Defeat at Our Hands w/Brennan, *FACTS, The Works: A Visual Arts Celebration,* a series of installation performances, Edmonton (later performed in Montreal and Vancouver)
        Crowns, Thorns, and Pillows w/Brennan, Dancing on the Edge Festival, Vancouver
1992   *The Dreams of Odysseus* w/visual artist Carol Johnston (mus. Poitr Grella), Edmonton Fringe Festival (later performed in Vancouver)
        The New: Dance and Music Made in Edmonton (mus. Poitr Grella), solo dances, Made in Canada Festival, Edmonton
        (if I wanted to know) The Exact Dimensions of Heaven w/ Brennan, site specific for Locations with Latitude 53 Gallery, Edmonton
1993   *the first february/the last january,* Dancing on the Edge Festival, Vancouver
        Magic/Magick/Miracles, commissioned by Gallery 101, Ottawa
1995   *Qualities of Darkness,* Edmonton
1996   *Stabat Mater/a minor feast,* Edmonton
1997   *Project Desire/the mountains and the plains* w/Jeff McMahon, premiered in Edmonton
        Cycles, commissioned by the Edmonton Symphony Orchestra with dancers from the Alberta Ballet Company, Edmonton

Publications

On WEBB: articles—

Anthony, Pamela, "A Collaborative Recasting of Heaven with New Angels," *Edmonton Journal,* 7 July 1997.
———, "Exploring Rites and Religion," *Edmonton Journal,* 19 October 1994.
———, "Rituals Riveting in Magical Show," *Edmonton Journal,* 22 October 1994.

Laviolette, Mary-Beth, "Brian Webb: Two Views," by Thom Heyd and an interview with Heather Elton, *Artichoke,* Spring 1993.

Philpott, Wendeline, and Andrew Houston, "Brian Webb Dance Company/Latitude 53," *Dance Connection,* February/March, 1993.

Thiessen, Vern, "Edmonton Fringe Festival," *Dance Connection,* November/December/January 1993.

* * *

Brian Webb's work crosses the borders between performance art and dance. Webb's earliest experiences with dance were as a theatre student in movement for actors courses at the University of Alberta. His professional dance training and experience began in New York with Erick Hawkins and Carol Conway. He premiered many of his first choreographic works with the Carol Conway Dance Company. In 1979 Webb founded the Brian Webb Dance Company in Edmonton, Alberta. His experiences in the MFA Program in choreography at the California Institute of the Arts (1986) in Valencia, California marked a shift toward interdisciplinary collaboration with visual artists, writers, composers, and performance artists. After 1986 Webb's work focused on a series of self-portraits in collaboration with interdisciplinary artists, including sculptor Blair Brennan composers Piotr Grella-Mozdjko and Jamie Philp, and writer Scott Taylor. His work has been described as autobiographical, and confronts provocative sociopolitical issues in contemporary society: for example, homosexuality in *The Dreams of Odysseus;* AIDS in *Magic/Magick/Miracles;* resistance to patriarchal power structures in *Crowns, Thorns and Pillows;* and current Canadian attitudes toward indigenous First Nations people in *(I wanted to know) the Exact Dimensions of Heaven.* For this reason Webb's work is of interest to other groups aside from dance audiences, as evidenced by his performance of *Crowns, Thorns and Pillows* at the Freedom Within the Margins/The Politics of Exclusion Conference, University of Calgary in 1992.

Webb also performs in traditional theatre venues, and his work is occasionally performed by other professional dance companies—such as *Cycles,* commissioned by the Edmonton Symphony Orchestra in 1997, with the Alberta Ballet Company. His collaborative interdisciplinary works, however, are often performed as site specific installations and in contemporary art galleries.

Webb influences, and is influenced by, his collaborators. For example, sculptor Blair Brennan and Webb have developed a common interest in the interface between religion, ritual, and art. Brennan's sculpture is characterized by repetition of images, utilizing Christian symbols such as crucifixes and the lighting of candles, intertwined with pagan rites. Webb's approach to performance is through a series of events aimed at being experienced as ritual by both the audience and the performer, according to Pamela Anthony, writing in the *Edmonton Journal* in 1994. Mary-Beth Laviolette and Thom Heyd found Webb also uses repetitive symbols in his work: dirt, flaming oil drums, trucks, steel crowns, and blood samples, with which he interacts in a stylized pedestrian manner, while maintaining a physicality and formality in the structure of the work.

While critics have found Webb's dance art challenges audiences and, at times, is disturbing and alienating, it is postmodern in the sense that Webb addresses current social political issues and invites the audience to participate in an experience outside the conventions of any single art form.

—Iris Garland

WEBER, Carmela

American dancer, choreographer, and company director

Born: Suffern, New York, 16 February 1966. **Education:** Studied ballet and modern dance at the North Carolina School of the Arts, 1984-87; scholarship student at American Dance Festival, 1987, and Colorado Dance Festival, 1990; University of Colorado at Boulder, B.F.A. in dance 1990. **Career:** Dancer, Claudia Murphey Dance Company, Fairfax, Virginia, 1987-88, Full Circle, Washington, D.C., 1988-89, Desperate Figures Dance Theater, Wiesbaden, Germany, 1992, Hannah Kahn Dance Company, Denver, from 1991; founder and director, Carmela Weber Vertical Dance, Boulder, from 1991; guest artist, Cleo Parker Robinson School, 1994, Cleo Parker Robinson Dance Ensemble, 1995, University of Colorado, Boulder, 1996; New World School of the Arts Residency, Hannah Kahn Dance Company, 1995; choreographic resident, Glenwood Springs Dance Festival, 1995, 1997; member of scholarship committee, 1995, and treasurer of board of directors, 1996, Colorado Dance Festival; panel member, Arts Innovation Reward, 1995. **Awards:** University Dance awards, University of Colorado, 1990-91; Arts Innovation Award and fellowship, Colorado Federation for the Arts, 1993; COVisions Recognition Award, Colorado Council on the Arts, 1995.

Works

1990	*Alluding to Purpose* (mus. Beth Quist), Irey Theater, Boulder
1991	*Elsewhere* (mus. Farrell Lowe), Space for Dance, Boulder
1992	*Belonging* (mus. Stewart Lewis), Space for Dance, Boulder
1993	*Hang* (mus. Stewart Lewis), Space for Dance, Boulder
1994	*Maintain! Climbing the Walls* (mus. Jesse Manno), Auditorium Theater, Denver Performing Arts Complex
1995	*No Re-Entry Eastbound* (mus. Jesse Manno), Macky Auditorium, University of Colorado, Boulder
1996	*An Unbalanced Load* (mus. Jesse Manno), Main Stage Theater, University of Colorado, Boulder

* * *

Carmela Weber's innovative blend of athletic rock climbing and fluid choreography reflect a current experimental trend in modern dance. Without sacrificing craftsmanship for the novelty of vertical choreography, Weber is essentially an innovator of a new form of dance. The dramatic climbing walls in Weber's pieces exist not only as a vehicle for the unusual vertical direction of dance movement, but also as important visual and thematic elements of set design in her often polemic sociopolitical choreography. Weber's unique fusion of sport and dance is certain to influence the future contemporary dance scene.

Weber began movement training as a serious competitive gymnast. She attended the North Carolina School of the Arts and received quite regimented training in ballet and modern dance. A scholarship to the American Dance Festival in 1987 introduced Weber to Sharon Wyrrick, whom Weber found to be inspirational because of her emotionally raw dance and theatre work. Weber left school and joined Wyrrick's company in Washington, D.C., and danced with the company from 1988 to 1989. Weber spent summers rock climbing in New Hampshire, but city life in D.C. was not agreeable to her so she moved to Boulder, Colorado.

With a prevalent rock climbing scene in Boulder, Weber decided to finish her education in dance at the University of Colorado where she received her B.F.A. As her degree project, Weber choreographed her first vertical dance piece, which ended up being an evening-length concert. The atmosphere at the University of Colorado was supportive and creatively fruitful, and after this experience, Weber embraced the idea of becoming a choreographer.

As Weber began to develop her own creative ideas, she was also dancing professionally with Hannah Kahn in Denver and the Desperate Figures Dance Theatre in Wiesbaden, Germany. While in Germany, Weber saw Pina Bausch and was extremely moved by the fact that Bausch could create a simple gesture that communicated a common denominator of humanity. Weber appreciated the poignancy of simplicity in Bausch's work.

Development of her own work has manifested in numerous local performances and teaching residencies. Knowing that her innovative form walks a careful line of spectacle, Weber conscientiously avoids this tendency. The form of her work is derived from the thematic content she wishes to express. Though classically trained, Weber seeks a sense of adventure in her work, and humor often balances out profound subject material. Because the thematic content of her work is vital to its creation, Weber recognizes her need to step away from choreography at times in order to exist as a human in society, rather than only existing in the enclave of an artist in the arts. In order for audiences to find something in her work that moves them, Weber feels she must stay in touch with the world outside the arts. She also uses her dancers and their frames of reference, to inform and develop her work.

Weber's unique sensitivity to contemporary sociological trends is often reflected in her work in humorous ways. The proscenium canvas she creates gives the stage a sense of environment; the climbing walls often seem to be metaphors for various manifestations of the human condition. Yet, movement invention and choreographic craftsmanship are equally important partners to Weber's creations. Although spectacular, the vertical choreography is not exploited as gimmick, but rather, used as another dimension in which to craft movement. Weber's innovative form is cutting-edge modern dance.

—Diana Stanton

WEIDMAN, Charles

American dancer and choregrapher

Born: 22 July 1901 in Lincoln, Nebraska. **Education:** Studied with Eleanor Frampton in Lincoln; with Theodore Kosloff, and with Denishawn. **Career:** Member of Denishawn company, 1921-27; founder and director, Humphrey-Weidman Company, 1928-45; choreographed and directed Broadway productions; instructor, Experimental Unit of the Federal Dance Theater during the 1930s; founder, Theatre Dance Company, 1948; later became known as Charles Weidman Dance Company; taught primarily on the West Coast throughout the 1950s; founded Expression of Two Arts Theatre with Mikhail Santaro in New York in the early 1960s; continued choreographing and performing until his death. **Died:** 15 July 1975 in New York.

Roles

1921	The King, *Xochitl* (Shawn), Denishawn
	Pierrot Forlorn, Denishawn
1922	*Egyptian Ballet,* Denishawn
1924	*Five American Sketches,* Denishawn
	Crapshooter, Denishawn
1926	*General Wu's Farewell to His Wife,* Denishawn
	Seneghalese Devil Dance, Denishawn
	Momijii Gari, Denishawn
	Whims (Humphrey), Denishawn
1929	*Ein Heldenleben,* Neighborhood Playhouse, New York
1930	The Stranger, *Die Glückliche Hand,* Philadephia Opera House
	Le Sacre du Printemps (Massine), Philadelphia Opera House
1933	Dancing Master, *A School for Husbands,* Theatre Guild, New York

Works

1928	*A Japanese Actor,* Denishawn, New York
	Minstrels, trio, Denishawn, New York
	Ringside, Denishawn, New York
	Cathédrale Engloutie (Submerged Cathedral), solo, Denishawn, New York
1929	*On the Steppes of Central Asia*
	Passion and Compassion (mus. Bach), Humphrey-Weidman, New York
	Five Studies (mus. Honneger), Humphrey-Weidman, New York
	Americanisms
	Leprechaun
	Rhythmic Patterns of Java, Humphrey-Weidman, New York
	Seneghalese Drum Recital (mus. traditional drums), solo, Humphrey-Weidman, New York
	Rumanian Rhapsody
	Scherzo
	Marionette Show (mus. Prokofiev), Humphrey-Weidman, New York
	Preludes (mus. Gershwin), Humphrey-Weidman, New York
1930	*The Tumbler of Our Lady,* Dance Repertory Theatre, New York
	Three Studies, Dance Repertory Theatre, New York
	The Conspirator (no. mus.), Dance Repertory Theatre, New York
	Lysistrata w/ Humphrey (bacchanale section of play)
	Two Studies w/Humphrey
	Commedia (mus. Coppola), Humphrey-Weidman, Philadelphia
	Danse Profane (mus. Debussy), Humphrey-Weidman, Philadelphia
1931	*Music of the Troubadors* w/Blanche Talmud
	The Happy Hypocrite (mus. Herbert Elwell), Dance Repertory Theatre, New York
	Steel and Stone, Dance Repertory Theatre, New York
	Piccoli Soldati and *Notturno* (mus. Pick-Mangiagalli), Humphrey-Weidman, Westport, Connecticut
	Gymnopédies (mus. Satie), Humphrey-Weidman, Westport, Connecticut

Puerto del Vino (mus. Debussy), Humphrey-Weidman, New York

1932 *Dance of Work, Dance of Sport* w/Limón and William Matons, Humphrey-Weidman, New York

Studies in Conflict, Humphrey-Weidman, New York

Carmen w/Humphrey (opera)

Aida w/Humphrey (opera)

1933 *Candide* (mus. Genevieve Pitot), Humphrey-Weidman, New York

As Thousands Cheer (for Broadway)

Cotillion, Humphrey-Weidman, Palais Royal, New York

1934 *Life Begins at 8:40* (musical revue), New York

Kinetic Pantomime, solo, Humphrey-Weidman, New York

Alcina Suite (mus. Handel), Humphrey-Weidman, New York

Memorials, Humphrey-Weidman, New York

1935 *Duo-Drama,* duet with Humphrey, New York

Affirmations (mus. Vivian Fine), solo, New York

Iphigenia at Aulis w/Humphrey (opera), Philadelphia

American Saga

1936 *Quest*

Atavisms (mus. Lehman Engel), Humphrey-Weidman, New York

Promenade

I'd Rather Be Right (for Broadway)

1937 *A Cult Ballad*

1938 *Air Raid Blues*

This Passion

Studies in Technique for Men

Opus 51 (mus. Vivian Fine), Weidman/Humphrey Compnay, Bennington, Vermont

1940 *On My Mother's Side*

Flickers (mus. Lionel Nowak), Humphrey-Weidman Company, New York

1941 *And Daddy Was a Fireman* (mus. Herbert Haufrecht), Humphrey-Weidman Company, New York

War Dance for Wooden Indians

The Happy Farmer w/Peter Hamilton

Portraits of Famous Dancers

1942 *Theatrical Dances* w/Lee Sherman

1943 *Star Dust* (for Broadway)

Spoon River Anthology (for Broadway)

Rhumba to the Moon

La Comparsa

Park Avenue Intrigue

Promenade

Imitations and Satires

1944 *Sing Out, Sweet Land* (for Broadway)

The New Moon (for Broadway)

The Heart Remembers

Dialogue

1945 *Three Antique Dances*

A House Divided (mus. Nowak), Charles Weidman Dance Company, New York

David and Goliath

1946 *If the Shoe Fits* (for Broadway)

1948 *Fables for Our Time* (mus. Freda Miller), Charles Weidman Dance Company, Jacob's Pillow

1949 *Rose of Sharon*

1950 *The Barrier* (for Broadway)

1955 *The Littlest Revue* (for Broadway)

1956 *Waiting for Godot* (play)

1958 *Portofino* w/Ray Harrison (play)

1959 *The War between Men and Women,* Charles Weidman Dance Company, New York

1960 *Is Sex Necessary?*, Charles Weidman Dance Company, New York

1961 *A Song for You*

1963 *King David*

Danse Russe

Saints, Sinners, and Scriabin

1964 *Jacob's Wedding*

1971 *Brahms Waltzes, Op. 39* (mus. Brahms), New York

1972 *Easter Oratorio*

Diabelli Variations

1973 *Bach's St. Matthew Passion* (mus. Bach)

In the Beginning

1974 *Visualizations, or, From a Farm in New Jersey*

Publications

On WEIDMAN: books—

Palmer, Winthrop, *Theatrical Dancing in America*, New York: A.S. Barnes & Co., 1978.

On WEIDMAN: articles—

Barnes, Clive, "An Appraisal," *New York Times*, 17 July 1975.

Kisselgoff, Anna, "A Tribute to Charles Weidman," *New York Times*, 7 October 1975.

Lloyd, Margaret, "Creative Revolutionist: Humphrey & Weidman," in *The Borzoi Book of Modern Dance*, New York: Alfred A. Knopf, 1949.

Obituary, *New York Times*, 16 July 1975.

Wynne, David W., "Three Years with Charles Weidman," *Dance Perspectives* 50, Winter 1974.

Films and Videotapes

Dance: Four Pioneers, NET, 1966.

Charles Weidman, On His Own, Dance Horizons Video, 1990.

*   *   *

Charles Weidman's career as a performer and choreographer spanned 50 years; he last performed in his studio just a week before his death at age 73. It was a career noteworthy for his celebrated partnership with Doris Humphrey, for their company passed many milestones over the course of its history—it was the first company to include male and female dancers from its inception, the first to present a full-length work, and the first to make an extended tour. As an individual dancer and choreographer he was known as a consummate comedian, and in an art form that often seemed marked by earnestness and was frequently dedicated to the tragic, Weidman's steadfast refusal to take himself or dance seriously was utterly unique.

As a child in Lincoln, Nebraska, Weidman had aspirations of being a cartoonist, but was later distracted and inspired by pictures of Isadora Duncan and Ruth St. Denis. Before leaving home he staged elaborate dance recitals and studied with Eleanor Frampton. His career began in earnest in Los Angeles where he studied ballet

Charles Weidman with Doris Humphrey in *New Dance.* **Photograph by Alfred A. Cohn.**

with Theodore Kosloff and enrolled in the Denishawn school of Ruth St. Denis and Ted Shawn. He began dancing roles in their various companies almost immediately, successfully creating roles in Shawn's repertory works, including *Pierrot Forlorn* (1921), *Crapshooter* (1924) and sections from *Five American Sketches* (1924). He also met and studied with Doris Humphrey, with whom he left for New York in 1927. Weidman and Humphrey moved to New York to help establish a new Denishawn School; however, they soon moved off to open their own studio, the Humphrey-Weidman Group and school, where they worked together for the next 16 years as dancers, teachers, and collaborators.

Following the lead of Ted Shawn, Weidman made significant strides in creating and expanding a place for male dancers in modern dance, getting men involved to begin with, developing an exceptionally successful system of technical exercises, and then creating some of his best roles for them. An oft-told story relates his ingenious 1928 solution to the lack of male students. The school began offering free classes to the male relatives of female pupils. The classes were free, but absenteeism cost $2 a lesson. Though no prodigies emerged,

classes dedicated solely to men were no longer unheard of. Over the years he would train many male dancers in virile, dynamic movement and have many gifted students such as Bob Fosse, José Limón and Tony Charmoli.

In 1935 the Humphrey-Weidman Group began an extensive tour, traveling through southern and western United States and Canada, performing as well as holding master classes and technique demonstrations along the way. As members of the faculty at Bennington in the late 1930s, their work received additional exposure. After years of struggle in New York and on the road, by 1940 they had firmly established themselves as one of the great pioneer dance companies. That year they opened the Studio Theater and the next five years, before Doris retired from the stage, were wonderfully productive ones in their new home.

Comparing the two as choreographers, Weidman was generally regarded as less talented and more limited; Humphrey was seen as the serious one. Perhaps he was responsible for putting on a good show, as he longed to entertain. He often spent time working on costumes himself or coming up with some inventive prop to help get the audience in the proper spirit. It should also be noted that Weidman created several memorable dances with somber themes, such as *Lynchtown* (1936), a frightening study of mob mentality, and *A House Divided* (1945), which dealt with the Civil War and Abraham Lincoln's character. His relative lightheartedness can be seen as a preference rather than a lack of ability as Weidman was a joyous and gifted comedic dancer. Somewhat Chaplinesque, his forceful, intuitive gifts as a performer set him wholly apart. He had the tall, thin body of a jester and made use of his whole body to make jokes, literally from his fingers to his toes. He had the mobile, subtle mouth of a clown, which Margaret Lloyd, author of the *Borzoi Book of Modern Dance,* called "a cave of comedy in itself."

Weidman was also a fantastic mimic onstage and off. He incorporated his own brand of mime into his dances, what John Martin of the *New York Times* called "kinetic pantomime." Weidman assented to this appellation, explaining that his mime wasn't aimed at being representational, but was concerned with the rhythmic properties of gestures people used to express their feelings. His choreography followed the trajectory of a gesture, with various movements being linked kinetically rather than by meaning. Abrupt changes in tempo or rhythm were common and comedy was often the result of the ensuing incongruities and surprises.

Hilarious as these dances could be in their physical humor, they were also quite often characterized by the poignant humor of insight into the human condition. Weidman wasn't nearly as interested as his contemporaries in the theme of man the individual; he was concerned with man in society, and he's been noted as modern dance's first satirist.

A Bennington creation and premiere, the rollicking *Opus 51* (1938), poked fun at seemingly everything, from camp meetings to Bennington itself. The dancing defied the eye, with so many gags running into each other that the audience couldn't tell where one ended and another began. A woman piously working her prayer beads would pull each bead firmly down as she ended a prayer, while nearby a man would tug upward on an imaginary fishing pole to balance the rhythm of her gesture. *Flickers* (1940) is another Weidman classic. Jerky movements and large cardboard cutouts serve to nostalgically recreate the feel of silent movies even as their formulaic stories are gently ridiculed. Several of his works take on his own family tree. *On My Mother's Side* (1940) begins with the story of his great-grandfather, an ambitious Midwestern pioneer, and ends with himself in the form of the character Sonny. "Today a fellow likes to dance / No one knows why." *And Daddy was a Fireman* (1943) describes the travails of his father's bumpy career.

Weidman received perhaps the most recognition for the work he did based on the short stories of James Thurber. *Fables for Our Time* (1948), which he completed with the assistance of a Guggenheim fellowship, was the feature of a very complimentary article in *Life* magazine. Several of the vignettes concerned the battle of the sexes, including "The Shrike and the Chipmunks," in which Weidman's played one of his best-known roles, that of a lazy, henpecked chipmunk. In "The Owl Who Was God" a solemn, old owl is mistaken for the divine by some easily impressed and none-to-bright creatures; the owl ends up leading his devoted followers in an outlandish march right over the edge of a cliff. Again in 1959, Weidman turned to Thurber for inspiration for *The War Between Men and Women.* This affinity is quite understandable, for he shared with Thurber a highly developed sense of the absurd. Both also comprehended the serious side of comedy.

Humphrey and Weidman worked briefly together on Broadway in the early 1930s, but she apparently didn't have much of an appetite for it. Weidman was a natural for the theater, however, and it was a world that appreciated his talents. Though some critics chided this aspect of his career, accusing him of selling out for the money, it was clear he thrived there, staging dances for popular shows such as *Americana* (1932), *Life Begins at 8:40* (1934), *Sing Out, Sweet Land* (1944) and *The Littlest Revue* (1955). He was instrumental in opening theater and opera to modern dancers.

During his time as dance director of the New York City Opera Company, entire operas became movement dramas in which it was impossible to differentiate the dance sequences from the rest of the movement and the singing. Perhaps Weidman loved opera because as he put it, opera was a distorted form, not unlike the dances he created, with their pantomime and over-the-top expressiveness.

After his association with Humphrey ended in 1945, Weidman formed his own company, the Theater Dance Company, for which he continued to create new works. In the early 1950s the studio fell apart, and he struggled for a time, financially and with alcoholism. He taught for a while on the West Coast, eventually returning to New York. He set up a new studio there in 1960, which became the Expression of Two Arts Theatre, in which he shared programs with sculptor Mikhail Santaro. The studio was small, with none of the fanfare of the heyday Humphrey-Weidman years, yet he was able to continue teaching, performing and choreographing until his death.

—Valerie Vogrin

WHITE OAK DANCE PROJECT
American dance company

Founded by Mikhail Baryshnikov, Florida, 1990; named for late philanthropist Howard Gilman's White Oak Plantation on the Florida/Georgia border; premiere in Boston featuring an all Mark Morris program, October 1990; toured worldwide with a range of modern American works.

Works (choreographer in parentheses)

1990	*Going Away Party* (Morris)
	Motorcade (Morris)
	Pas de Poisson (Morris)
	Ten Suggestions (Morris)
1991	*Canonic 3/4 Studies* (Morris)
	Deck of Cards (Morris)
	A Lake (Morris)
	El Penitente (Graham)
	Nocturne (Clarke)
	Waiting for Sunrise (Lubovitch)
	Harmonica Breakdown (Dudley)
1992	*Break* (Monk)
	Duet from Concerto Six Twenty-Two (Lubovitch)
	Oz (Taylor)
	Punch & Judy (Gordon)
	Three Preludes (Morris)
	Variations Opus 30 from Episodes (Balanchine)
	Farewell (Gillis)
	Solo from Equinox (Taylor)

1993	*Jocose* (Holm)
	Mosaic and United (Morris)
	Pergolesi (Tharp)
	Quartet for IV (O'Day)
1994	*Signals* (Cunningham)
	A Suite of Dances (Robbins)
	Behind White Lilies (Schlömer)
	Blue Heron (Schlömer)
	The Good Army (O'Day)
1995	*Tongue & Groove* (Feld)
	Greta in the Ditch (O'Conner)
	Chickens (Moulton)
	Three Russian Preludes (Morris)
	Flys (Patterson)
	make like a tree (Patterson)
	Unspoken Territory (Reitz)
1996	*Stille Nacht* (Schlömer)
	Septet (Cunningham)
	What a Beauty! (Patterson)
	A Cloud in Trousers (O'Day)
	Chaconne (Limón)
	Embodied (Murphy)
	Quiet As It's Kept... (Salomons)
	Layers (Scott)
1997	*Journey of a Poet* (Hawkins)
	Remote (Stuart)
	Piano Bar (Béjart)
	Tryst (Patterson)
	Heartbeat: mb (Janney/Rudner)

Publications

Articles—

Dalva, Nancy Vreeland, "Misha and Mark: Out on a Limb," *Dance Magazine,* January 1991.

Fanger, Iris, "In Concert: Close-Up on Baryshnikov, Morris and the White Oak Dance Project," *Vandance,* Winter 1990-91.

Garafola, Lynn, "White Oak Dance Project (Brooklyn Academy of Music Opera House, New York, New York)," *Dance Magazine,* July 1997.

Gold, Sylviane, "Mikhail Baryshnikov, American: The White Oak Dance Project Returns to New York, and Its Leading Figure Is Thoroughly at Home," *Newsday,* 25 March 1997.

Hluchy, Patricia, "Thoroughly Modern Misha," *Maclean's,* 18 September 1995.

Jowitt, Deborah, "Modern Dance Junkie: Baryshnikov Grooms Eclectic Repertory for BAM," *Village Voice,* 25 March 1997.

Kourlas, Gia, "Misha Accomplished: Age and Injury Have Not Diminished Baryshnikov—As a Dancer or Director," *Time Out New York,* 27 March 1997.

Lobenthal, J., "New York: Mikhail Baryshnikov and the White Oak Dance Project at the Brooklyn Academy of Music," *Ballet Review,* Summer 1997.

Macaulay, Alastair, "Surpassing Perfection," *Times Literary Supplement,* 13 September 1996.

Ostlere, Hilary, "White Oak Dance Project: Baryshnikov Hits a New Personal Best," *Dance Magazine,* March 1994.

Reiter, Susan, "Baryshnikov's Personal Project," *Dance Australia,* February/March 1995.

Shapiro, Laura, "Just Follow the Feet," *Newsweek,* 28 February 1994.

Tobias, Tobi, "The Loveliness of the Long-Distance Dancer," *New York,* 21 March 1994.

Trucco, Terry, "Baryshnikov & Co.: We Don't Do Ballet," *New York Times,* 27 February 1994.

Versteeg, Coos, "Michail Baryshnikov: A Unique Commitment to Dance," *Ballett international/Tanz aktuell* [English ed.], November 1995.

*   *   *

The White Oak Dance Project encompasses about 25 members, including dancers, musicians, technicians, and administrators. Because of financial constraints, membership has decreased during the years since the group's 1990 founding, with the original 14 dancers having shrunk to nine, and the 15-piece orchestra becoming a quintet of four strings and piano. Most of the original members had substantial previous experience dancing with other companies. Mikhail Baryshnikov and John Gardner had danced with the American Ballet Theater (ABT), Keith Sabado with Mark Morris, Rob Besserer and Nancy Colahan with Lar Lubovitch, Kate Johnson with Paul Taylor, Jamie Bishton with Twyla Tharp, and Patricia Lent with Merce Cunningham.

The dancers rehearse on the expansive White Oak Plantation-turned-nature preserve, on the northern border of Florida, which was owned by Baryshnikov's longtime friend and arts patron, the late Howard Gilman. Lodgings were built for the dancers and provisions furnished. An existing shed on the grounds was remodeled into an exceptional dance studio. The site is removed from everyday distractions to make it easy to focus on dance; the group has been known to rehearse seven days a week. Beyond Gilman's generosity, the troupe supports itself through ticket sales from tours. In 1996 alone, White Oak gave over 100 performances worldwide, and performances routinely sell out. The White Oak Dance Project could last as long as performances continue to sell tickets, or as long as the troupe wishes to continue dancing. They make no long-term contracts, so that if they wish, they could disband tomorrow.

The dancers ranged in age from 30 into the 40s when the group started, and their general maturity meant that Baryshnikov has been surrounded by peers. They use their experience to coach one another, and those who are not in a piece do not leave the rehearsal but, rather, stay to watch and comment. Contrary to comments often seen in literature, advancing age and a knee injury did not force Baryshnikov's shift from ballet to the contemporary choreography that is White Oak's focus. In fact, Baryshnikov was interested in seeing modern dance as soon as he arrived in North America in the 1970s. He believes that dancing with Martha Graham opened his mind in new directions, and in 1976, when Twyla Tharp worked with him on *Push Comes to Shove,* Tharp showed him that he could use his ballet training in new ways. Now he prefers modern choreography to classical, and declared in an interview with Terry Trucco in 1994, "Modern is less mannered, more human, in a way more pedestrian, more grounded and more direct."

The White Oak Dance Project has commissioned new works from established choreographers such as Mark Morris, Twyla Tharp, Paul Taylor, Jerome Robbins, and Kevin O'Day, as well as from first-time choreographers Kraig Patterson, Vernon Scott, and Ruthlyn Salomons. It has also presented revivals of works by Martha Graham, Hanya Holm, and José Limón. White Oak has adopted works made for others, such as *Ten Suggestions,* which Mark Morris created for himself, and *Septet,* which Merce Cunningham created for his Merce Cunningham Dance Company. Other works have been adapted for White Oak. For example, Baryshnikov expanded *Journey of a Poet* for the troupe, a work Erick Hawkins had created before his death in 1994. Twyla Tharp also refashioned *Pergolesi*, originally created as a duet for herself and Baryshnikov, into a solo for Baryshnikov. Still other works, such as Jerome Robbins' *A Suite of Dances,* have been newly created for Baryshnikov. A choreographer's only limitation in creating for White Oak is that any accompaniment must be played by the White Oak Chamber Ensemble.

The troupe mostly dances different works in each performance circuit rather than relying on a set repertoire because it is what Baryshnikov prefers; he feels it's best to perform works by different choreographers so that the relationship with the choreographer does not become worn. Seeking out works and commissions is among the White Oak activities he enjoys the most. With its varied performance palette, the material is constantly challenging and stimulating to the dancers, who must learn the distinctive style of each choreographer. Baryshnikov remarked in a 1995 interview with Susan Reiter: "There's no hidden message in our presentations. Good dancing—that's what we're good for."

The factors that make the White Oak Dance Project unique—the maturity of its dancers, the choreographic variety of its repertoire, its democratic organization, dancers working with musicians, its self-supporting financial structure, and temporary troupe status as a "project"—become clear in light of the career of its de facto director. Baryshnikov came to White Oak after performing with the Kirov for six years, performing as principal dancer for American Ballet Theater (ABT) for one year, with Ballanchine at the New York City Ballet for a year, and as both dancer and director of ABT for 10 years. By 1990 he had earned an international reputation, so it isn't surprising that with his experience dancing and directing, he would wish to form his own troupe, and that he would want his fellow dancers to be comparable to him in experience. His growing boredom with the classical repertoire and his having to re-dance ballets such as *Giselle,* led to his turning toward contemporary dance in order to avoid the set repertoire that can become a dancer's burden. His ultimate disaffection with the ABT directorship explains his structuring White Oak as a democracy. The troupe's democratic structure relieves him of sole responsibility for every decision, while reserving for him the right to make creative choices as to what the troupe will dance. In fact, his name is listed alphabetically among the dancers on White Oak programs. The troupe consistently takes on new works because of Baryshnikov's joy of learning. By choosing new choreographers as well as new works, he also ensures that the dancers retain their independent spirit.

The White Oak Dance Project has been criticized for what some see as a lack of distinct artistic identity. But White Oak is only partially about the art of dance. Baryshnikov's reputation is a powerful attraction. Recognizing this, he remarked to Patricia Hluchy in 1995: "I don't really care what brings people to the theater. I care about what they feel after the show." Besides, Baryshnikov's dancing in his late forties confirms his reputation for brilliance. Even though he performs fewer virtuosic feats, his dancing remains musical, precise, and intelligent. He received the 1997 New York Dance and Performance Award, the "Bessie," for his contributions to modern dance.

It is unlikely that other troupes will be founded on the model of the White Oak Dance Project because the circumstances that underlie its continuing box-office success—namely, the international reputation of Mikhail Baryshnikov—are in themselves unique. Unless the modern imagination elevates another dancer/director to the status of superstar, economics will probably prevent the repetition of the White Oak story.

—Judith Gelernter

WIESENTHAL, Grete
Austrian dancer and choreographer

Born: Margarete Wiesenthal, 9 December 1885 in Vienna. **Education:** School of Ballet at the Royal and Imperial Opera, Vienna, from 1895 to 1901. **Career:** Chorus member at the Royal and Imperial Ballet from 1901; from 1902 to 1907, expert advisor at the Royal and Imperial Ballet; after that, free-lance dancer and choreographer; formed an independent dance ensemble with her sisters Elsa and Bertha, 1908; between 1908 and 1910, Wiesenthal was active, with her sisters, predominantly as a choreographer and performer of waltzes; after 1910, performed exclusively in roles that she created for herself; active founding dance schools in Vienna between 1919 and 1927; started teaching in dance department of the Academy for Music and Drama in Vienna, 1934, serving as department head from 1945-52; founded the Vienna Chamber Dance Ensemble during World War II; last public performance 1938 at the Hofburg theater in Vienna; the "Grete Wiesenthal Ensemble," which she founded in 1945, was active till 1956; worked at the Salzburg Festival as a choreographer, 1930-59, (from 1952 to 1959, she was in charge of the choreography of *Everyman*); in 1977, 1984, and 1986, Wiesanthal choreographies were restaged by Vilma Kostka and Erika Kniza, former dancers and students of the "Wiesenthal Ensemble," for the Ballet of the Vienna State Opera. **Died:** 22 June 1970, Vienna.

Works

1907	*La Muette de Portici* (mus. F. Aubert), Royal and Imperial Opera, Vienna.
	Die Tänzerin und die Marionette (*The Dancer and the Marionette*) (mus. Rudolf) Vienna
1908	Waltzes by Lanner and Schubert, Vienna
	Beethoven Allegreto (mus. Beethoven), Vienna
	Danube Waltz (mus. Strauss), Vienna
	Roses from the South (mus. Strauss), Vienna
1908	*Birthday of the Infanta* w/Elsa (mus. Schreker), Vienna; revised by Grete, 1954
1909	*Voices of Spring* (mus. Strauss), Vienna
1910	*Sumurûn* w/Bertha
1911	*Amor and Psyche* (also director), Berlin
	The Foreign Maiden (also director), Berlin
1912	*Le Bourgeois gentilhomme* (also director), performed with Richard Strauss' opera *Ariadne auf Naxos,* Stuttgart
1916	*The Bee* (also director; mus. Clemens von Franckenstein), Darmstadt
1918	*Rosenkavalier Waltz* (mus. Strauss), Vienna
1922	*Wine, Women, and Song* (mus. Strauss), Vienna
1928	*The Lovers* (mus. *Viennese Blood,* Strauss), duet with Toni Birkmeyer
	The Good-for-Nothing in Vienna (mus. F. Salmhofer; also director and principal role), commissioned for the Vienna State Opera Ballet

1933   *Death and the Maiden* (mus. Schubert), duet with Willy
        Fränz, New York
1934   *The Interrupted Rendez-vous* (mus. Strauss, overture to
        Die Fledermaus), Vienna
1936   *Heaven's Meadows* (mus. Schubert), Vienna
1945   *The Impertinent Dance Teacher* (mus. J. Lanner), Vienna

Publications

On WIESENTHAL: books—

Amort, Andrea, "Ausdruckstanz in Österreich bis 1938," in
    Ausdruckstanz, Wilhemlhaven, 1992.
Caffin, Caroline, and Charles H., *Dancers and Dancing of Today,*
    1912, reprint 1978.
Fiedler, Leonhard M. and Martin Lang, *Grete Wiesenthal: Die
    Schönheit der Sprache des Körpers im Tanz,* Salzburg and Vienna,
    1985.
Prenner, Ingeborg, *Grete Wiesenthal,* dissertation, University of
    Vienna, 1950.

Films and Videotapes

The Foreign Maiden, film, Stockholm, 1913.

According to Ingeborg Prenner, "If you have ever seen Wiesenthal
dance, you have seen Vienna itself—the best, noblest, the Vienna
that lives apart from its many flatterers and falsifiers, the Vienna of
dreams, of the soul." Indeed, Wiesenthal essentially embodies, despite the fact she is considered part of the Expressionist movement,
the Impressionist variant of free dance in Austria. Born into an
artistic family, she was aware of the movement for women's rights.
Therefore, influenced by Isadora Duncan, whose first performance
in Vienna was in 1902, Wiesenthal decided, at the age of 22, to leave
the Vienna Royal Opera Ballet. "To skip, measure after measure,
without feeling and expressing the essence of the music," this had
become off-putting to her. Subsequently, in 1908, in an act of bold
rebellion, the young woman and her sisters Elsa and Bertha made
their debut as a free dance ensemble at the Fledermaus Cabaret, in
the heart of the city of Vienna. The Cabaret belonged to Fritz
Wärndorfer, founder of the Vienna Workshop. The trio's program
mostly consisted of waltz performances. Significantly, these dances
had nothing to do with kitsch or sentimentalism, allowing, transforming the music (mostly the music of Johann Strauss) into swinging movement. In the following years, Wiesenthal worked on developing a special technique for swings, leaps, and spins. Although
this technique stemmed from the foundations of classical ballet, it
aimed to relax the body of the rigidly trained classical dancers.
Wiesenthal emphasized the interrelations between physical, spiritual, and psychological forces. Prenner has noted: "Grete delighted
in using all kinds of turns to fully awaken the potential of the
dancer's swinging body; to her, intuition was crucial, not the number of executed turns." Wiesenthal's novel method, which the artist
described in her lecture "Sphärischer Tanz," emphasized rhythm,
dynamics, as well as a representation of weightlessness, which was
created by special balancing exercises. From the very beginning
(1908), Wiesenthal insisted on adapting the body's slanted position, as well as the natural curvature of the dancer's back, to the
dance. Hardly any dancer could execute the characteristic high leaps,
her knees drawn, as masterfully as Wiesenthal herself. The
Wiesenthal method was taught at the Vienna Academy for Music

and Drama until 1973, and is currently part of the training program
for ballet dancers at the Austrian State Theater.

This joyful expression of music through dance made the Wiesenthal
sisters famous overnight. They subsequently received encouragement from artistic circles, particularly those connected with the
Secession movement and the Vienna Workshop. Wiesenthal immediately terminated her partnerships with her sisters when she started
working for the celebrated director Max Reinhardt as a director and
choreographer of musical pantomimes (in collaboration with the
famous poet Hugo von Hofmannsthal). Theater circle in Central
Europe expected this new genre to galvanize musical theater. Her
career as a solo dancer and choreographer took off. Her dance style
reflected her world view—that of a knowledgeable and emanci-
pated woman; on stage, it was her inner light that constantly radiated. The principal figures of drama and musical drama (Max
Reinhardt, Richard Strauss) demanded that she be "the ambassadress of waltz": she traveled as far as New York (her first visit was
in 1912). In 1912, a no lesser figure than Serge Diaghilev offered a
one-month contract for 1913. Vaclav Nijinski revered her. She was
unable, for health reasons, to accept Diaghilev's offer. Wiesenthal's
wholesome aesthetic world view was strongly influenced by the
ecstatic abandon of *Jugendstil.* The 1922 solo, based on Johann
Strauss's "Wine, Woman, and Song," which was filmed by Margot
Fonteyne and the Viennese dancer Susanne Kirnbauer exemplifies
this world view: it is a cheerfully provocative and thoroughly erotic
dance, replete with swings and turn. The dancer, clad in a long
dress, is holding a fan and tipping a glass of champagne. Wiesenthal's
proverbial smile was constantly on her lips. All of her work is
characterized by this cheerfulness and lightheartedness. While her
waltz choreographies (preserved through restagings by Wiesenthal's
above-mentioned students) remain, even decades later, convincing,
owing to their ecstatic nature, some of her restaged pantomimes
from the turn of the century now seem strangely cloying.

In her prime (during the 1920s), Wiesenthal was the supremely
successful soloist who brought her inimitable style to the world,
traveling to London and New York. During and after World War II,
she led her own dance ensemble and was regarded as an institution
among Vienna's artists, dancers, and literary figures. Not only is her
dancing style, the Wiesenthal method, still taught, but it is regarded
as the hallmark of Vienna State Opera's School of Ballet.

—Andrea Amort
translated by Zoran Minderovic

WIGMAN, Mary

German modern dance pioneer, choreographer, and educator

Born: 13 November 1886 in Hanover, Germany. **Education:** Boarding school in England (hence her command of English); studied in
Switzerland and Holland, before attending Dalcroze school, Hellerau,
Germany; studied with Rudolf Laban, 1913-20. **Career:** Began
performing her own choreography, 1914; left Laban and opened her
own school in Dresden, in operation until World War II; taught at
the Academy of Performing Arts, Leipzig; opened another school,
West Berlin, 1949; toured as a soloist in the United States, 1930-
33; stopped dancing, 1942; continued to teach and choreograph
(including opera, such as Glück's *Orpheus and Eurydice,* 1947, and
Stravinsky's *Le Sacre du Printemps,* 1957. **Died:** 1973.

Works (selected)

1914   *Witch Dance I,* solo
         Lento, solo
         A Day of Elves, solo
1918   *Ecstatic Dances (Prayer, Sacrifice, Idolatry,* and *Temple Dance)* solo
1920   *Dance Suite (Prelude, Play, Waltz,* and *Allegro con brio)* (mus. Dvorak) solo
         Dances of the Night: Shadow and *Dream,* solo
         The Spook, solo
         Vision, solo
1920   *Dance Rhythms I: Triste* and *The Call,* solo
         Dance Rhythms II: Song of the Sword, Lament, and *Zamacueca,* solo
         Two Dances of Silence, solo
1921   *The Seven Dances of Life* (mus. Pringsheim; poem Wigman), Wigman and company, Opera House, Frankfurt/Main
1924   *Dances in the Evenings (Three Elegies),* solo
1925   *Vision I—Ceremonial Figure,* solo
         Vision II—Masked Figure, solo
         Vision III—Spectre, solo
1926   *Two Monotonies: Restrained* and *Turning,* solo
         Vision IV—Witch Dance (mask dance), solo
         Dance of Death (mus. Hastings) Wigman and company, Konigsberg
         Hymns in Space (Festive Prelude, Swinging Row, The Ray, Rhythm) Wigman and company
1927   *Bright Oscillations: With a Big Verve, Tender Flowing,* and *Playful,* solo
         Vision V—Dream Figure, solo
         Vision VI—Ceremonial Figure, solo
         Vision VII—Ghostly Figure, solo
1928   *Vision VIII—Space Study,* solo
         Celebration (final version), Wigman and company
1929   *Shifting Landscape* (cycle: *Invocation, Seraphic Song, Faces of Night, Pastoral, Festive Rhythm, Dance of Summer,* and *Storm Song)* solo
1930   *Totenmal* (mus. and poem Albert Talhoff), Munich
1931   *Sacrifice* (cycle: *Song of Sword, Dance for the Sun, Death Call, Dance for the Earth, Lament,* and *Dance into Death)* solo
1934   *Women's Dances* (cycle: *Wedding Dance, Maternal Dance, Lament for the Dead, Dance of Silent Joy, Prophetess, Witch Dance)* Wigman and company
1935   *Song of Fate,* solo
1936   *Lament for the Dead* (mus. large chorus), Olympic Stadium, Berlin
1937   *Autumnal Dances* (cycle: *Dance of Remembrance, Blessing, Windswept, Hunting Song,* and *Dance in Stillness)* solo
1942   *Be Calm, My Heart,* solo
1946   *Three Choric Studies of the Misery of Time (Escape, Those Seeking, In Loving Memory),* students of Wigman School, Leipzig
1947   *Orpheus and Eurydice* (mus. Glück), Municipal Opera, Leipzig
1952   *Choric Studies (Those Waiting, The Homeless, Grievance and Accusation)* Students of Wigman, Berlin
1957   *Le Sacre du Printemps* (mus. Stravinsky), Municipal Opera, Berlin Festivals

1958   *Alcestis* (mus. Glück) National Theatre, Mannheim

Publications

By WIGMAN: books—

The Language of Dance, translated by Walter Sorrel, Middletown, Connecticut, 1974.
The Mary Wigman Book, edited and translated by Walter Sorrel, Middletown, Connecticut, 1975.

By WIGMAN: article—

"The New German Dance," in *Modern Dance,* New York, 1935.

On WIGMAN: book—

Manning, Susan Allene, *Ecstasy and the Demon: Feminism and Nationalism in the Dances of Mary Wigman,* Berkeley, Los Angeles, London, 1993.

On WIGMAN: articles—

Howe, Dianne Sheldon, "The Notion of Mysticism in the Philosophy and Choreography of Mary Wigman 1914-1931," *Dance Research Journal,* Summer 1987.
———, "Parallel Visions: Mary Wigman and the German Expressionists," in *Dance: Current Selected Research, Volume 1,* Eds. Lynnette Y. Overby and James H. Humphrey, New York, 1989.
Manning, Susan Allene, "From Modernism to Fascism: The Evolution of Wigman's Choreography," *Ballet Review,* Winter 1987.
Muller, Hedwig, "Wigman and National Socialism," *Ballet Review,* Spring 1987.
Odom, Maggie, "Mary Wigman: The Early Years, 1913-1925," *The Drama Review,* December 1980.
Toepfer, Karl, "Speech and Sexual Difference in Mary Wigman's Dance Aesthetic," in Laurence Selnick's *Gender in Performance: The Presentation of Difference in the Performing Arts,"* Hanover, New Hampshire & London, 1992.

                    *   *   *

Mary Wigman, born Marie Wigmann in November 1886, was one of the most important dance innovators and proponents of modern dance or *Ausdruckstanz* in Germany, and her influence, though muted after World War II, was felt in the United States as well.

As a young girl, Wigman was sent to boarding school in England where she learned English and developed her taste for adventure: she remembered taking a small hammer and tapping on the stones in the local cathedral looking for a rumored secret passage. She did not want to become a "hausfrau" as was suggested to her by a teacher, and so after completing school, she was, as she has said in her memoirs "still searching." She began to travel: "I adventured in other lands, traveling to Switzerland, to Holland. . . I adventured in the arts, studying music and singing." In 1910 after having seen the Weisenthal sisters' lilting dance performances to waltz music and hearing of Jacque-Dalcroze's method of coordinating musical and body rhythm, Wigman decided to go Hellerau to study at his school.

In 1913, at the suggestion of the Expressionist painter, and friend, Émile Nolde, she spent a summer in Ascona, in the Swiss Alps, to take a course with Rudolf Laban, who Nolde told her "moves as you do and he dances as you do—with no music." While in Ascona, Wigman received a letter offering her the position of director of the Dalcroze school in Berlin. Wigman felt torn between the untraveled path she glimpsed from her work with Laban and the secure position and living provided by Dalcroze. In a much quoted story, Wigman credits Laban with helping her decide: "I can only congratulate you. . .what a pity! Actually you are a dancer who ought to be on the stage." She did not sign the contract and prepared to spend the next summer with Laban. As the second summer of studies got under way, however, World War I broke out and most the students left for service or for home. Wigman stayed on to help Laban with work on his theory, the "Harmony of Movement," (based on tension and relaxation of the body) by repeatedly demonstrating movement combinations for him. Wigman later claimed "the foundation of my career as a dancer as well as a pedagogue were laid in those few weeks."

Her first public appearance was on the program of another of Laban's dancers. She danced early versions of *Lento* and *Witch Dance*. This first performance was well-received though this would not always be the case. Even after Wigman was a well-established doyenne of German *Ausdruckstanz*, she would have strong critics. Dance critic André Levinson felt her dancing barbaric and full of hubris. In the collection of his essays, *André Levinson on the Dance* (1991), he describes her performance of *Rites* at the Essen Conference in 1928 as "insufferably tedious, rotten with intellectual vainglory, vitiated in its humanity by the inflation of feeling." He felt her dances to be motivated by "instinct" as opposed to reason, and was horrified by what he called an "expression of terpsichorean barbarism." But to someone like John Martin, as Jack Anderson has pointed out in 1997's *The World of Modern Dance: Art Without Boundaries*, Wigman "was amazing" because he thought her choreography and performance placed dance at the center of attention, stripped of narrative, pantomime, and even music. Martin said her dancing was " a revelation of the principles upon which [modern dance] may enlarge its borders and deepen its awareness."

Wigman's dance did appeal to instinct and emotion and should be seen in the context of German Expressionism within which it first flourished. Wigman knew many visual artists who were part of the Dada movement and who were, like Émile Nolde, considered Expressionists. According to H.H. Arnason in *The History of Modern Art*, German Expressionism grew out of work at the turn of the century exploring theories of empathy and the relation of science and art. One of these theorists, philosopher Conrad Fiedler, felt "the form of the work grew out of the content, the idea was indistinguishable from it" and that "the work of art was essentially the result of the artist's unique, visual perception, given free form by his powers of selection." These statements sound very close to Wigman's own statements about her art and its sources: "Therefore the dancer-choreographer must turn his inner feelings and perceptions into visible expression, he must clarify and give expression to his personal life experiences through the medium of dance."

Dance or movement was for Wigman the entire medium of expression. Though she worked with accompanists (including Hanns Hastings from 1928 through 1941), she often used no music, or only percussion instruments to highlight the dancers' rhythms. Writing about her theories of dance, Wigman states, "It is the rhythm of dance which releases and engenders the musical rhythm. The musical accompaniment ought to arise from the dance composition.

Of course, any music thus created can never claim to be an independent work of art." She composed many solo and ensemble dances in cycles or series, the most well-known being her *Vision* series, including *Shifting Landscapes* (solo), *Sacrifice* (solo), *The Seven Dances of Life* (group), *Scenes from a Dance Drama* (group), and *Women's Dances* (group).

Wigman spent seven years studying with Laban and became his assistant in Zurich. In 1919 she moved to Dresden where she opened a school with the financial help of Berthe (Bibi) Trumpi who was her student and assistant. Many of the most important dancers in Germany walked through the doors of the Dresden school, including Harald Kreutzberg, Gret Palucca, Yvonne Georgi, Margarete Wallmann, and Hanya Holm, who would be the first to open a Wigman school in New York in 1931. Wigman toured the United States successfully three times between 1930 and 1933. But the rise of the National Socialist Party (Nazi) in Germany and the advent of World War II changed many things. In 1936, because of strong anti-German sentiment in the United States, Hanya Holm changed the name of the Wigman school (with Wigman's approval) to the Hanya Holm Studio. Wigman was criticized for staying in Germany, and Jack Anderson has surmised that "more than any other person's action or decision, Wigman's refusal to leave Germany helped destroy the reputation of German dance in America." The Nazi party appropriated certain aspects of *Ausdruckstanz* for its own ends including the strong nationalist element of some German dance, and the emotionally compelling, dramatic choric dances; because of this Wigman and other dancers who stayed enjoyed a certain amount of support from the Nazis at first, but were soon enough under suspicion of being degenerate artists and were eventually "silenced" as Anderson puts it. When the funding for her school was drastically reduced, Wigman closed it and moved to Leipzig to teach.

Wigman's influence as a choreographer (she stopped dancing in 1942) never regained its prewar status even in Germany. In the eyes of many, *Ausdruckstanz* was tainted by its association with the Nazis and younger dancers were looking elsewhere for inspiration. Ironically, classical ballet became the new site for innovation in Germany after the war, where its historical absence had led to such a vigorous modern dance. Wigman moved to West Berlin in 1949 and continued teaching and choreographing group dances for her students and for the opera including Glück's *Orpheus and Eurydice,* and a critically acclaimed production of Stravinsky's *Le Sacre du Printemps* in 1957. In poor health the last years of her life, Wigman died in 1973.

—Glynis Benbow-Niemier

WILLIAMS, Dudley

American dancer

Born: August 1938 in New York City. **Education:** Graduate of New York's High School of Performing Arts; studied tap, jazz, modern, and ballet (with Antony Tudor at the Metropolitan Opera Ballet School, and Juilliard). **Career:** Co-founder, the Corybantes, with Eleo Pomare; performed with the companies of May O'Donnell, Hava Kohav, and Donald McKayle; dancer, Martha Graham Dance Company, 1961-68; dancer, Alvin Ailey Dance Theatre, beginning 1963; assistant ballet master, beginning 1974. **Awards:** *Dance Magazine* Award, 1997.

Roles

1956	*Theme and Variation* (May O'Donnell)
1960	*Congo Tango Palace* (Talley Beatty)
1962	*Reflections in D* (Ailey)
1963	*To Broadway with Love* (Donald Saddler)
1966	*Circe* (Graham)
	Clytemnestra (Graham)
	Legend of Judith (Graham)
	Acrobats of God (Graham)
	Diversion of Angels (Graham)
	Embattled Garden (Graham)
	Part Real—Part Dream (Graham)
	Pot Luck (musical review)
1967	*Cortege of Eagles* (Graham)
	Dancing—Ground (Graham)
	Black New World (McKayle)
1968	*A Time of Snow* (Graham)
	Lady of the House of Sleep (Graham)
1970	*Streams* (Ailey)
1971	*Choral Dances* (Ailey)
	Mary Lou's Mass (Ailey)
1972	*A Song for You* (Ailey)
	Love Songs (Ailey)
1974	*Nocturnes* (John Jones)
1975	*Night Creature* (Ailey)
1976	*Three Black Kings* (Ailey)
1980	*Later That Day* (Kathryn Posin)
	Phases (Ailey)
1986	*Survivors* (Ailey)
1988	*Opus McShann* (Ailey)

Other roles include: Productions of *Blues Suite, Roots of the Blues, Revelations,* and *Hermit Songs* (all Ailey); *District Storyville* and *Road of the Phoebe Snow* (Beatty), *Caravan* (Falco), *Rainbow 'Round My Shoulder* (McKayle), and *Do Not Go Gentle into That Good Night* (Pomare).

Publications

On WILLIAMS: books—

Dunning, Jennifer, *Alvin Ailey: A Life in Dance*, New York, 1996.
Robertson, Allen, and Donald Hutera, *The Dance Handbook*, Boston, 1990.

On WILLIAMS: articles—

Goodman, Saul, "Brief Biographies: Dudley Williams," *Dance Magazine*, March 1967.
Tracy, Robert, "Dudley Wiliams: Love Songs to Alvin," *Dance Magazine,* December 1997.

*   *   *

Dudley Williams is an energetic and expressive American dancer who has performed as a member of two prominent modern dance troupes: the Martha Graham Dance Company and the Alvin Ailey American Dance Theatre (AAADT). His performance career began while he was still a student at the New York's Performing Arts high school and through one of his mentors, Alvin Ailey, Williams' was able to explore his gift and be molded into the dynamic dancer he is today.

Williams was born in August 1938 in New York City. His earliest introduction to dance was short-lived: at the age of six he took tap lessons which was a tear-filled experience. He pursued piano instead, an interest he continued through high school. Accompanying a relative to voice lessons, he was able to observe dance lessons conducted in the same building. The 12-year-old Dudley again expressed interest in dance and was soon taking weekly ballet and modern dance lessons. The reputation of New York's School for the Performing Arts prompted Williams to apply. He missed the deadline for music, but qualified for and was accepted into the dance program. His mother insisted he also pursue his music, so he reapplied for the music program six months later and passed the entrance exam. By now he was quite involved in dance and though his studies involved both the disciplines of music and dance, his heart placed dance first.

With his schoolmate Eleo Pomare, Williams created a fledgling dance company called the Corybantes, and they performed locally in New York, mostly at community centers. While still a student at the Performing Arts school, he received scholarships for additional ballet study with Karel Shook and later with George Caffee. When modern dance dominated his interest, he applied for and received a scholarship to study with May O'Donnell. In 1956 he danced in O'Donnell's *Theme and Variation*. Two years later, he graduated from the School of Performing Arts in 1958.

Williams' dance training was just beginning, however, as the young dancer continued to perform and receive scholarships and opportunities for further study. Back when he was still a high school student, Alvin Ailey saw him perform one of the Corybantes pieces. Ailey then cast the young Williams in the balletic *Sonera* as part of a choreographers' competition at the City Center. Williams inquired at that time about joining the Alvin Ailey American Dance Theatre but Ailey thought of Williams as predominately a ballet dancer and did not extend an invitation.

The summer after graduating Williams accompanied a group of Performing Arts graduates in a tour of the West, where the young adults participated in the summer dance program at Utah State University, appearing in concerts directed by May O'Donnell. Williams returned home in early August for his first professional engagement as a replacement in the musical *Showboat* at Jones Beach Stadium. In the fall he continued to study modern dance with O'Donnell, appearing in her local concerts. He also received a scholarship to the Juilliard School and another for classes with Antony Tudor at the Metropolitan Opera Ballet School.

During the summer of 1960 Williams was fortunate enough to travel to Spoleto, Italy, where he performed pieces choreographed by Donald McKayle, Paul Taylor, and Karel Shook. He returned to New York for another semester at Juilliard before receiving a scholarship to the Martha Graham School for six months of intensive study. Although still attracted to Ailey's eclectic repertoire and the company's appeal to a broad audience with energy-charged dances celebrating black America, Williams was, however, not invited to audition and instead joined the Martha Graham Dance Company in 1961. His first performances with the company were in late 1962 during a three-month tour of Israel and Western Europe. Lulls in the performance schedule allowed him to dance in McKayle concerts, as well as in pieces choreographed by Talley Beatty, Louis Falco, Kathryn Posin, and John Jones.

Disillusioned with the Graham Company, Williams was prepared to sail for Greece and seek dance opportunities there when he

Dudley Williams with Judith Jamison in *Blood Memories,* **1976. Photograph © Johan Elbers.**

received a call from Ailey in 1963. The company needed a replacement dancer for a European tour two weeks away. Williams' mother talked him into attending a rehearsal before making the decision to leave for Greece. He stayed to join the Ailey company. In her book *Alvin Ailey: A Life in Dance*, Jennifer Dunning writes that Williams had found the Ailey environment very "different," than at Graham's company, and although Graham "had been kind to him. . .the atmosphere could be forbidding in her studio." Finally realizing his dream to be with Ailey, Dunning writes, "Williams was soon dancing with the company at the Delacorte, where not so long ago he had seen and fallen in love with Alvin's work. But he was in for a shock in Paris, when, out of the blue, Alvin told the young dancer that he was to replace him in *Reflections in D.*"

Ailey taught the solo to Williams that morning. Not until Williams had the routine down did Ailey inform Williams he would be performing it that very afternoon. With Ailey's encouragement that Williams could do anything if he believed enough in himself, Williams was able to get through the performance, and in the following years to make the solo distinctively his own. According to Dunning, fellow Ailey company star James Truitte complimented the young Williams, saying: "To this day I don't feel that any dancer of great talent, even after being taught by Dudley, will ever bring to *Reflections in D* the supreme serenity, sophistication, elegance and musicality that he brought to that choreography. Dudley is one of those rare dancers born with those qualities."

Williams continued to dance for both the Graham and Ailey companies until 1968. He then left the Graham company to focus on performances and teaching with Ailey, and in 1974 he became assistant ballet master.

Ailey's choreography used a blend of rhythms with Graham-style contractions, and many of Ailey's dancers had completed rigorous training at the Graham school. Williams added an expressive energy and lyricism to the creation of his roles for the company, which helped him attain the status of one of the memorable great dancers of his time. One of the most popular works in the AAADT repertoire is Williams' male solo *Love Songs*, first performed in 1972, though Williams went on to dance in many of Ailey's landmark works including *Revelations, Blues Suite,* and others.

—Lisa A. Wroble

WINNIPEG CONTEMPORARY DANCERS
Canadian dance company

Founded in 1964 by Rachel Browne, a U.S.-born ballet dancer, WCD is Canada's senior modern dance company, based in Winnipeg, Manitoba; Browne resigned as director, 1983; Bill Evans directed for one year; Tedd Senmon Robinson, a WCD alumnus, named director, 1984-90; during Robinson's tenure, company was briefly known as Contemporary Dancers Canada; Robinson started the Festival of Canadian Modern Dance and was the festival's artistic director, 1985-90; Charles Moulton named artistic director of WCD, 1990-91; Tom Stroud, 1991; the School of Contemporary Dancers, started by Browne, is affiliated with the WCD and celebrated its 25th anniversary in 1997.

Publications

Forzley, Richard, "Telling the Dancer from the Dance: Rachel Browne and Contemporary Dancers, Canada," *Border Crossings*, Fall 1985.
McCracken, Melinda, "A 30th Anniversary in Winnipeg," *The News 36,* Danse Collection Danse, 1994.
Wyman, Max, *Dance Canada,* Vancouver, 1989.

*   *   *

Winnipeg Contemporary Dancers (WCD) is Canada's oldest modern dance company, dating its official beginning from 1964. The company has had a rough ride at times, but out of financial and artistic struggle have come new creative directions. A radical redefinition of what is essential, endemic to the character of the entity itself, is a legacy of its tenacious founder Rachel Browne. The company, with its current artistic director Tom Stroud, has succeeded in weathering change and reinventing itself for new times.

Rachel Browne was at the helm of Contemporary Dancers for 19 years. Browne came to Canada to dance with the Royal Winnipeg Ballet (RWB) in 1957 and stayed until 1961, when she left to raise a family. Becoming restless, and wanting to teach and choreograph, she founded Winnipeg Contemporary Dancers and it soon became a flourishing amateur group, affiliated with the University of Manitoba at Winnipeg, where it gave its first performances. The company was in demand for school and concert appearances, and began to undertake small tours in Manitoba and other prairie provinces.

Browne's professional experience in the New York-based Ryder-Frankel company and with the Royal Winnipeg Ballet had taken her out on the road on long, grueling tours which became the model for her new company. As it grew, Browne remained committed to the idea of directing a "people's company." It agreed with her politics and her dance background to tour an accessible repertory. Initially Browne was the company's chief dancer, teacher, tour-booker, and fund-raiser; somehow she also managed to choreograph. The early artistic history of the company is tied to Browne's burgeoning identity as a modern dancer and choreographer; though WCD wasn't funded by the Canada Council, Browne herself was, acknowledged for the quality of her dancing. As she deepened her knowledge, Browne shared it with the dancers she trained in her young company. By 1970, WCD was a full-time professional entity with a grant from the Canada Council for annual operations and by 1972 the School of Contemporary Dancers, which Browne has formed, was full-fledged. It is esteemed as one of Canada's small number of fine training centres for modern dance. A high percentage of its graduates are working dancers.

Given WCD's schedule of touring small communities, Browne stuck to her belief that "repertory which reflected a variety of dance styles by various choreographers was the best way of reaching unsophisticated audiences." She mounted work by U.S. choreographers, among them Cliff Keuter, Paul Sanasardo, Dan Wagoner, Bill Evans and Robert Moulton, and Fred Mathews and Gary Masters. For the 1972-73 season James Waring created an original work, *Happy Endings,* as well as a solo for Rachel Browne, *Rune to a Green Star.* Lynn Taylor-Corbett, working with Winnipeg composer Judith Lander, created *Spy, Where We Are Now,* and *Diary,* a significant work in the company's repertory. Norman Morrice was another important contributor to the company's repertory. As a guest artist, Ze'eva Cohen enriched the Winnipeg community, as did Annabelle Gamson, who in 1978 brought works by Isadora Duncan and Mary Wigman to life in Winnipeg performances. As well, WCD undertook to recreate classic modern dance works by José Limón (*Exiles*, in 1983) and Doris Humphrey (*Two Ecstatic Themes,* in 1982).

Many of the company's landmark creations have been Canadian. During the 1970s the company was an important breeding ground for developing Canadian choreographers. Karen Jamieson (*Snakes and Ladders*), Judith Marcuse (*Re-entry*), Linda Rabin (*Domino*), Paula Ravitz (*Inside Out*), and Jennifer Mascall (*The Light at the End of the Tunnel May Be a Train*), all worked with the company to create original works. Anna Blewchamp contributed *Baggage* and *Homage* to WCD, while others including Brian Macdonald (*Tryst*), former RWB dancer Nenad Lhotka (*First Century Garden*), David Earle (*Angelic Visitation* and *Baroque Suite)* and Norbert Vesak (*Gift to be Simple)* all graced the company with their contributions.

Winnepeg Contemporary Dancers has had a significant role in nurturing talent within the company as well. Award-winning choreographer Stephanie Ballard was a company member from 1972 to 1977, when she began choreographing for the company, and became associate director from 1980 to 1983. She refined her skills in choreographic workshops which were started in 1977, initially in partnership with RWB. She created *Prairie Song* (1980) and *Time Out* (1982) for WCD; she also choreographed *Christmas Carol* (1981), and *The Snow Goose*, a full-length production for children. As well, company member Tedd Robinson got his choreographic start in these workshops, as did Conrad Alexandrowicz, Odette Heyn-Penner, Gaile Petursson-Hiley and Ruth Cansfield. In 1989 Petursson-Hiley and Cansfield, as co-directors, formed Winnipeg's Dance Collective, a forum for their talents. The Collective, an active entity, also showcased three evenings by Stephanie Ballard and Dancers, including *Continuum* (1990), which brought together Rachel Browne, Peggy Baker, Linda Rabin and Margie Gillis. Tedd Senmon Robinson, after a sojourn at Le Groupe de la Place Royale, launched a successful career as an independent choreographer, creating work based in the Buddhist philosophy of which he is a disciple. Heyn-Penner and Faye Thompson, both nurtured by Browne, became the directors of the School of Contemporary Dancers, which currently has more than 200 full-time students. The School, largely because of efforts by Faye Thompson, enjoys an accreditation link with the University of Manitoba, as well as with the local CEGEP, the Francophone college. The School celebrated its 25th anniversary in 1997.

Winnipeg Contemporary Dancers had recurrent difficulties with conflicting expectations of management and artistic staff. By 1981 discontent was stirring among dancers and board members at WCD. The climate across the country had changed. Montreal's risky, innovative dance-theatre was taking audiences by storm. Creators and dance audiences across Canada had acquired a sophisticated, cosmopolitan literacy. Rachel Browne's sincere modernist offerings, her aspirations for the company, did not seem priorities in this new national picture. The assault on Browne's directorship grew serious. Late in 1983 Browne, after a coup by the board, resigned. Released from her responsibilities as WCD's artistic director, Browne has since started a second career as an independent choreographer, and has found a new expressive voice. In 1983, however, she insisted on maintaining ties to the company she had birthed and nurtured, offering to assist in the search for a new artistic director. Bill Evans, her suggestion, was director for one year (1983-84), after which Tedd Robinson became the company's artistic director (1984-1990). Robinson enjoyed great popular success with his

theatrical, metaphoric work such as *Lepidoptera,* a co-production with the National Arts Centre, and *Camping Out.* In 1985 Robinson launched the Festival of Canadian Modern Dance, of which he was artistic director from 1985-90. This annual event on the national dance calendar, gave a strong focus to the innovative work Canadian companies were offering by the mid-1980s.

Following Robinson's departure, New York-based Charles Moulton was hired as the company's artistic director in 1990. His was a very brief stay; there was dissatisfaction with many artistic choices Moulton made. When Tom Stroud was hired as artistic director in 1991, he inherited a massive $208,000 debt, an empty building and a damaged company reputation. Stroud was faced with a tremendous challenge. There was widespread doubt about Contemporary Dancers having a future. But Stroud is an earnest, honest negotiator. He worked without salary for a time, taking heart from the integrity which had characterized the company. He looked to a sense of continuity from the company's beginnings, back to the passion which had driven Rachel Browne to tour endless prairie roads in an old school bus, drawn on by her determination and her enduring love of dance and creation.

In 1993 Winnipeg's Contemporary Dancers, revitalized by the efforts of Stroud and the company's management executive Alanna Keefe, celebrated its 30th anniversary. The gala celebrated all the key figures of the company's history; works by Browne included her first choreography *Odetta's Songs and Dances* (1964). Since 1983 Browne has been the recipient of prestigious choreographic and artistic leadership awards; in 1997 her artistic and pioneering contributions were recognized by the Order of Canada.

Tom Stroud is a creator with a strong theatrical background. An early work, *Under the Table Wrestling with Dad* (1984), is a direct, sincere, physical look at the emotional charge of a father-son competition. Stroud danced with Karen Jamieson, Toronto Independent Dance Enterprise and Jean-Pierre Perreault. His work shows a commitment to experimentation and a love of collaboration, as in *R and J*, a telling of the Romeo and Juliet story. Stroud organized a touring production of Jean-Pierre Perreault's milestone work *Joe* in 1994, with WCD, Dancemakers and Fondation Jean-Pierre Perreault. In 1998 Winnipeg Contemporary Dancers marked its 35th anniversary, celebrating the impulses of experimentation and love of dance which lie at the root of the company's existence.

—Carol Anderson

WINTER, Ethel
American dancer, choreographer, and educator

Born: 1924 in Wrentham, Massachusetts. **Education:** B.A., M.A., Bennington College, 1945; studied with Martha Hill and Martha Graham. **Career:** Dancer, Martha Graham Dance Company, 1944-69; began teaching at Juilliard, 1953 to present; choreographed for her own company, 1962-68; director, Graham School of Contemporary Dance, 1973-74; faculty, Graham school, until 1995; guest teacher and artist worldwide, including for the Adelphi University, American Dance Festival, Batsheva Dance Company, Bennington College, International Ballet Competition, Neighborhood Playhouse, New York High School of Performing Arts, Repertory Dance Theater, University of Hawaii, and others.

Roles (for the Martha Graham Dance Company, choreographed by
Graham, unless otherwise noted)

1945	Follower, *Appalachian Spring*
1946	*Dark Meadow*
1947	*Night Journey*
1948	*Salem Shore* (reconstructed 1995)
	Diversion of Angels
1954	*Lyric Suite* (Anna Sokolow)
1955	Joan of Arc, *Seraphic Dialogue*
1958	Helen of Troy, *Clytemnestra*
1959	*Episodes: Part I*
1960	*Alcestis*
	The Bride, *The Ghost* (Yuriko)
1961	*One More Gaudy Night*
1962	Aphrodite, *Phaedra*
1963	*Herodiade*
1964	*Frontier*
1967	*Cortege of Eagles*

Other roles include: *Sea Bourne* (William Bales), *The Dybbuk*
(Sophie Maslow), and numerous other productions of Graham
works.

Works

1955	*Drift wood*
1964	*En Dolor*
	Suite of Three
	Night Forest
	The Magic Mirror
	Fun and Fancy
1969	*Tempi Variations*
	Two Shadows Passed
1970	*An Age of Innocence*
1971	*Promise*
1972	*In Praise of Music*

Publications

On WINTER: books—

Denby, Edwin, *Dance Writings*, New York, 1986.
Leatherman, LeRoy, *Martha Graham: Portrait of the Lady as an
    Artist*, New York, 1966.
Sorell, Walter, ed., *The Dance Has Many Faces*, New York, 1966.

*   *   *

Ethel Winter is a gifted dancer and was a soloist in many important modern dance performances; she also performed and choreographed for her own company. Through her extensive teaching
career, Winter has shared her understanding of dance with students
and audiences worldwide.

Winter was born in Wrentham, Massachusetts, in 1924. She
attended Bennington College in Vermont, studying dance with
Martha Hill, and graduated in 1945 with a B.A. and M.A. Winter
first studied and danced with Martha Graham while a student at
Bennington. She then moved to New York to join Graham's company, where she was a member from 1944 to 1969. Her talents as
a dancer and her deep understanding of Graham's technique made

Winter an invaluable contributor to Graham's ability to create works
for her company. Her first major performance with Graham's company was as the "Follower" in the 1945 premiere of Graham's
Appalachian Spring. The expressiveness and depth of characterization Winter brought to her roles established her as a prominent
modern dancer. In *The Dance Has Many Faces*, Walter Sorell describes Ethel Winter as "one of the most gifted dancers of our time,
[who] represents continuity of the expressionistic modern dance in
terms of Graham technique and personal style."

Winter's versatility and range of characterization is evident in the
breadth of her many acclaimed roles. She portrayed Helen of Troy
in *Clytemnestra* (1958) with a sweetness and candor which provided a stark contrast for Graham's tormented Clytemnestra. As
Aphrodite in *Phaedra* (1962), Winter was thoroughly vulgar and
vicious, the essence of venomous spite; yet as Joan of Arc in *Seraphic Dialogue* (1955), she was beautiful and heartbreaking. On at
least one occasion, Winter captivatingly danced both of these widely
diverging roles in the same performance.

In his book *Martha Graham: Portrait of the Lady as an Artist*
published in 1966, LeRoy Leatherman describes Winter's metamorphosis as a dancer: "For a long time, her great patrician beauty
and her way of moving had an aura of poignance; she was like a
princess. . .whose end was by no means certain to be happy, and
she still perfectly projects this quality when, playing the part of
Helen of Troy, she paces the battlements, looking down upon the rape
of the town." Additionally, Leatherman noted, "there seems to be no
limit to her range." Just such a range was portrayed in her numerous
Graham company roles, including *Dark Meadow* (1946), *Night Journey* (1947), *Episodes, Part I* (1959), *Alcestis* (1960), *Cortege of Eagles*
(1967), *One More Gaudy Night* (1961), and *Diversion of Angels* (1948).

As testament to Winter's abilities, Graham selected her to assume roles which she had created for and performed herself. During
the 1948 New York season, Graham first relinquished two roles:
the first, her solo in *Salem Shore*, a work Winter later helped reconstruct for a 1992 performance by the Martha Graham Dance Company. Winter also assumed Graham's roles in *Herodiade* in 1963
and in *Night Journey*. She performed the solo in *Frontier* in the
1964 Louis Horst Memorial Program at the American Dance Festival, New London, and the next year she replaced Graham as "The
Bride" in *Appalachian Spring*.

Winter was director of the Martha Graham School of Contemporary Dance in 1973 and 1974 and served on its faculty until 1995. In
addition to performing with Graham's company, Winter appeared
in other companies, Broadway productions, television, and summer stock. She was a featured soloist with the New York City
Opera. In 1954 she danced in Anna Sokolow's *Lyric Suite* at its
premiere at the 92nd Street YM-YWHA in New York. She was
"The Bride" in *The Ghost* (1960), choreographed by Yuriko, a fellow former Graham company member, as well as performing with
Sophie Maslow, also from Graham's company, in Maslow's *The
Dybbuk* and in the annual Hanukkah festivals staged by Maslow
beginning in the mid-1950s. With the Dudley-Maslow-Bales Trio,
Winter played the woman in love in William Bales' *Sea Bourne*.

Winter directed and choreographed for her own company from
1962 to 1968. Winter's choreography reflected Graham's strong
influence. The company toured the U.S. and was known for its
superb dancing, and its works included sensitive drama, satire, and
Americana humor.

Winter also choreographed and taught for Israel's Batsheva Dance
Company in 1964 and at several schools in London in 1965. Winter's
contributions as an educator in schools worldwide is extensive—

she was a guest teacher and lecturer for ballet seminars in Ilkley, England, in 1983 and for the International Ballet Competition in Jackson, Mississippi, in 1986. She was also a guest artist for the English Dance Theater in 1984 and 1985. She has served on the faculty at Bennington College, Adelphi University, the Neighborhood Playhouse School of Theater, and the Repertory Dance Theater of Utah. She has been a guest artist and teacher at Point Park College in Pittsburgh, Rosary Hill in Buffalo, University of California at Long Beach, University of Hawaii, Hood College, and the American Dance Festival at Duke University. She currently is on the faculty at the Juilliard School, with which she has been affiliated since 1953. She continues her guest teaching during the winter months at the New World School of the Arts in Miami.

—Janette Goff Dixon

WINTERBRANCH

Choreography: Merce Cunningham
Music: La Monte Young (*2 Sounds*, composed April 1960)
Set Design: Robert Rauschenberg
First Production: Wadsworth Atheneum, Hartford, Connecticut, 21 March 1964
Principal Dancers: Merce Cunningham, Carolyn Brown, Viola Farber, Barbara Lloyd, Albert Reid, Gus Solomons Jr.
Other productions include: New York premiere, New York State Theatre, 4 March 1965; Boston Ballet, 1974; Brooklyn Academy of Music.

Publications

Articles—

Dell, Cecily, "*Winterbranch* . . . and Hundreds of Years," *Dance Scope*, Spring 1965.
Goldner, Nancy, review, *Dance News,* January 1975.
Hughes, Allen, "Spotlight on Dance," *New York Times*, 21 March 1965.
Manchester, P. W., review, *Dance News,* April 1965.
Marks, Marcia, review, *Dance Magazine*, April 1965.
———, review, *Dance Magazine,* June 1966.
———, "Scenes from an Unreachable World," *Dance Magazine,* March 1970.
McDonagh, Don, "Cunningham Dances at New London Fete," *New York Times*, 7 August 1967.
Mueller, John E., "Films: Cunningham on Camera Three and Elsewhere," *Dance Magazine*, July 1975.
Potter, Michelle, "'A License to Do Anything': Robert Rauschenberg and the Merce Cunningham Dance Company," *Dance Chronicle*, 1993.
Siegel, Marcia B., "Bostonsnatch: Boston Ballet Does Summerspace and *Winterbranch*," *Dance Magazine,* January 1975.

*   *   *

On the occasion of a *Winterbranch* revival in Boston in 1974, Marcia B. Siegel in *Dance Magazine* made an apt comparison. The debut of Merce Cunningham's composition 10 years before, she wrote, was like the pivotal first production of Stravinsky's *Le Sacre du printemps* (*Rite of Spring*) much earlier. As *Rite of Spring* caused a riot of sorts with its wild, discordant music, so *Winterbranch* evoked violent reactions. "At one performance," Don McDonagh wrote, "an outraged man seated near me shouted angrily that he wanted the lights turned out, which were shining across the audience and momentarily dazzling some."

The music, too, had the power to irritate, even infuriate: people routinely complained it was too loud, and Joseph H. Mazo described it as "a bit like trying to listen to a friend playing Bach while a jackhammer breaks up the sidewalk outside your cage." Yet, as Mazo conceded, John Cage—whose compositions accompanied much of Merce Cunningham's work—would not have minded the comparison.

Nor, one imagines, would Cunningham himself. The term "music," in fact, is charitable, because the aural backdrop by La Monte Young is quite literally what its title suggests: *2 Sounds*, one high-pitched and one low in tone. It is a fitting accompaniment to a dance which has no plot and seems to take place in no particular setting. Some have suggested it is symbolic of the devastation following a nuclear war, or a concentration camp, or simply the hell of the human soul. In any case, it is quite modern, striking an appropriately nihilistic tone.

The dancers' movements seem fraught with the force of entropy. Dressed in black, with smudges of black beneath their eyes like football players, they take a long time to fall and a long time to rise; then, perversely, they will move with quick, jerky motions. There is no sense of progress in the movement of the six bodies on stage: one dancer may help another rise from the floor, but in the process the second cancels out the action by dragging the first dancer down. Toward the end—which is the end only in a temporal sense, because there is absolutely no dramatic resolution or really any drama to resolve—a strange contraption moves across the stage, looking like a robot from a futuristic film.

From the title to Rauschenberg's stage design to the "music," the composition is one unrelenting tableau of bleakness, with dancers writhing around in the middle of it. Not surprisingly, then, audiences have not been particularly responsive—at least in any positive way—to this piece. Siegel seemed astounded by the provinciality of the unappreciative Boston audience, who "chattered and giggled, held loud sarcastic conversations, took their time about getting up and leaving."

Certainly the rudeness to the performers themselves was inexcusable, but Siegel's conclusion that they were refusing to receive an important message, and her suggestion that the audience was complacent like people in Hitlerian Germany, seems excessive. *Winterbranch* is difficult after all. Cunningham himself offered few clues as to what he meant by it all, except to say that it was about the "fact" of falling.

—Judson Knight

WONG, Mel
American dancer, choreographer, and artistic director

Born: 2 December 1938 in Oakland, California. **Education:** Studied with Ann (later Anna) Halprin of the San Francisco Dancers'

Workshop, and Harold Christensen of the San Francisco Ballet; also studied at American Ballet Center, New York School of Ballet, School of American Ballet, and Merce Cunningham studio. **Family:** Married to author Connie Kreemer. **Career:** Dancer, Merce Cunningham Dance Company, 1968-72; appeared in the film *Ghiradelli Square;* independent choreographer, beginning 1970; formed Mel Wong Dance Company, 1975; taught at the State University of New York (SUNY), Purchase, 1970s-80s; lectured at Hong Kong Academy for Performing Arts, 1985-88; artistic director, dance division, University of Colorado, Boulder, 1988. **Awards:** John Simon Guggenheim Foundation fellowship, 1983.

Roles

Many performances as a member of the Merce Cunningham Dance Company from 1968-72, including *Tread.*

Works

1970	*Dance for One Mile*
	Subway Piece
1971	*Continuous Dance Project*
	Water Walk
	Wax Walk
	Ramp Walk
1972	*Zip Code*, Washington Square Methodist Church, New York
1973	*Catalogue 34*
1974	*Four or Five Hours with Her*
	Watertown
1975	*Rocktown*
	A Town in Three Parts
	Bath
1976	*Wells*
	Breath
	C-10-20-W
	Glass (mus. Skip La Plante), American Theater Laboratory, New York
1977	*Quick Run*
	Envelope (mus. La Plante), Cunningham Studio, New York
	Trees
	I Was Flying the Other Day
1978	*Winds*
	Harbor
	The Organization, Performed by the Organization: We Are Looking for the Letter
	You See It All Started Like This. . . (mus. Bach, Rob Kaplan, La Plante), Dance Umbrella, New York
	Door 1, Door 2, Door 3
1979	*Epoxy*
	Salt (mus. Kaplan), Cunningham Studio
	Windows
	Peaks (mus. Kaplan)
1980	*Phones*
	Streams
	Wings-Arc
	Untitled
	Bouncing
	Kiezelstenen
	Imprint

1981	*Palms*
1982	*Desert Ghosts* (mus. Kaplan, La Plante), Theatre of the Riverside Church
	Telegram (mus. Kaplan, La Plante), Riverside Church
1985	*Buddha Meets Einstein at the Great Wall*, Asia Society, New York
1996	*Bolero* (mus. Ravel), Dance Theatre Workshop

Other works include: A number of works from the mid-1980s onward, including *Luminary Come Light.*

Publications

On WONG: books—

Kreemer, Connie, *Further Steps: Fifteen Choreographers on Modern Dance*, New York, 1987.

On WONG: articles—

Banes, Sally, "Return of the Ritual," *Dance Magazine*, September 1977.
———, "Mel Wong Dance Company," *Dance Magazine*, March 1979.
Hering, Doris, "Kenneth Rinker, Jan Van Dyke, Mel Wong. . .," *Dance Magazine*, December 1971.
Kahn, Judy, "Mel Wong's *Zip Code*," *Dance Magazine*, August 1972.
Lewis, Julinda, "Mel Wong Dance Company," *Dance Magazine*, February 1980.
———, "New York Performances," *Dance Magazine*, April 1983.
———, "Mel Wong Dance Company," *Dance Magazine*, August 1985.
Onoda, Karen, "New York Briefs," *Dance Magazine*, August 1984.
Pikula, Joan, "Dancing from Inside: Mel Wong, Katherine Liepe, Anne Sahl and David Varney; Ithaca Dancemakers," *Dance Magazine*, March 1977.
Ries, Daryl, "Mel Wong: East Meets West Via Modern Dance," *Dance Magazine*, December 1988.
Rosen, Lillie F., "Mel Wong, American Theater Laboratory," *Dance News*, April 1977.
———, "Reviews," *Attitude*, August 1984.
Zimmer, Elizabeth, "Mel Wong Dance Company," *Dance Magazine*, November 1982.

*   *   *

In the world of modern dance, where Martha Graham—still avant-garde by anyone else's standards—is practically considered a traditionalist, and Merce Cunningham's compositions to music by John Cage are viewed as standard fare, Mel Wong still manages to baffle. In a September 1977 *Dance Magazine* review of Wong's *Envelope*, Sally Banes wrote memorably of "four musicians, chanting lists of cities and zip codes, banging gongs and xylophones, slapping knees and popping puffed cheeks but somehow sounding like a cross between a Catholic Mass and a Zen Buddhist sitting." What is one to make of this? Not much, in the estimation of Banes, who concluded that *Envelope* was "too many ideas and not enough magic."

Other critics have been similarly harsh. Joan Pikula, writing in the same publication half a year earlier, saw much of interest in Wong's *Glass*, but concluded it "was such a mixture of dazzling movement and quiet serenity that I kept getting the feeling somebody was playing with my mind and my senses. Messing up my head. I'm not sure I like that." Julinda Lewis, watching *Peaks* two years later, tried to get caught up in action that included "everyone jogging in unison" while "eight dancers performed a ritualistic sequence of mundane movements, then each picked up a box and left." But in the end, it was too much to keep up with, and she "felt cheated of the revelation implied by the sustained mystery of it all." Still two years later, in 1982, Elizabeth Zimmer was nonplussed by the "sometimes amusing, sometimes inaccurate incantation of names" in *Telegram*, asking "who is 'Julia Childs'?"

No wonder, then, that Wong, who was born and raised in the United States, found himself more at home in Hong Kong. He had traveled there, as well as to China, on a prestigious Guggenheim fellowship in 1983, and when the Hong Kong Academy for Performing Arts invited him to return as senior modern dance lecturer, he accepted. Seeing a need for an infusion of art into the daily life of that busy, frenetic city, he said: "The academy is like a microcosm of [Hong Kong] itself. There's a lot of hard work and energy, but a shortage of emotional contact. Art is still a very separate matter from living."

Trained in ballet, Wong had performed with the Cunningham company starting in 1968, when he was 30 years old. He began choreographing in 1970, and left Cunningham in 1972. Three years later, he started the Mel Wong Dance Company, and engaged in experimentation that won him plenty of admirers as well as detractors. His first two compositions made creative use of the urban landscape: *Dance for One Mile* was written to be performed on the streets, and his *Subway Piece* was intended as just that. His work was highly cerebral, even if viewers didn't always get it: several Wong productions, called "booklet dances," required audiences to make reference to a detailed set of printed instructions. Thus Wong could be seen as a sort of James Joyce of modern dance, weaving a multilayered *Finnegan's Wake*-ish spell over the stage. He made great use of multimedia, including slides and film, as well as props such as melting ice. In Hong Kong, he was inspired in a direction that made sense, given his cultural background, fusing Eastern and Western styles as he did in 1985's *Buddha Meets Einstein at the Great Wall*. But his time in the East only proved that Wong was truly a Westerner, because while he was interested in learning elements of traditional Chinese dance, the Chinese were mad to learn about modern styles. In his teaching at the Hong Kong Academy, therefore, he sought a blend of Chinese discipline and Western individuality.

Before going to Hong Kong, Wong had worked at the State University of New York at Purchase, and with his dance company. He gave up both to make his journey to the East, but by 1988 he had returned to the U.S. with new perspective. He took a position at the University of Colorado in Boulder, the "New Age Athens," teaching at the dance division where wife Connie Kreemer was academic director. In his choreography, Wong continued to experiment with taking old or familiar things and making them new; hence he managed to impress one of the toughest critics, Tobi Tobias, who lauded his reinterpretation of Ravel's *Bolero* in the July 1996 *Village Voice*. The composition, long stereotyped for its erotic undertones, had seemed to defy attempts to make it fresh, but under Wong's hand—with Sylvia Martins performing solo—it became "a portrait of a complex, fascinating, contemporary woman." Divorced from props and complicated stage business, Wong's art had a clean and simple power.

—Judson Knight

WOOD, Donna
American dancer

Born: 1954 in New York City. **Education:** Began ballet as a child with Josephine Schwarz of the Dayton Ballet Company (Ohio); scholarship to Dance Theatre of Harlem. **Career:** Joined Dayton Contemporary Dance Company, 1963; joined Dayton Ballet Company, 1966; dancer, Alvin Ailey American Dance Theatre, 1972-85; director of marketing and public relations, Alvin Ailey American Dance Theatre, 1986-87; founder/president, Donna Wood Foundation (for young dancers); dancer on the television show *Fame*. **Awards:** Honorary degree in fine arts, Wheaton College, 1984; Candace Award from the National Coalition of 100 Black Women, 1988.

Roles

1971	*Gazelle* (Faison)
1972	*The Time Before the Time After (After the Time Before)* (Lubovitch)
1974	*Suite Otis* (Faison)
1976	*Pas de Duke* (Ailey)
1979	*Memoria* (Ailey)
1980	*Joseph's Legende* (Neumeier)
	Mass (Bernstein)
1984	*The Still Point* (Bolender)
1988	*Zorba the Greek* (ballet)

Other roles include: Many Ailey classics, including *Blues Suite, Masekela Language, Cry, Revelations;* Talley Beatty's *The Road of the Phoebe Snow,* John Butler's *Seven Journeys,* Ulysses Dove's *Inside,* Louis Falco's *Caravan,* Judith Jamison's *Divining,* Lar Lubovitch's *Les Noces,* Donald McKayle's *Rainbow 'Round My Shoulder* and *District Storyville,* and others.

Publications

On WOOD: books—

Anderson, Jack, *Choreography Observed*, Iowa City, Iowa, 1987.
Jamison, Judith, and Howard Kaplan, *Dancing Spirit: An Autobiography,* New York, 1993.
Mitchell, Jack, *Alvin Ailey American Dance Theatre: Jack Mitchell Photographs*, Kansas City, 1993.
Willis, J., editor, *Dance World*, New York, 1966, 1979.

On WOOD: articles—

"Donna Wood: Staying Fit for the Stage," *Ebony*, July 1984.
"Donna Wood Tribute," *New York Times*, 20 December 1985.
Gruen, John, "Donna Wood—'Alvin Ailey Taught Me to be Myself,'" *New York Times*, 14 December 1980.
Levy, Suzanne, "Ailey's Fine Finale," *Washington Post*, 20 April 1985.
"Raising Culture," *Philadelphia Inquirer*, 9 January 1983.
Temin, Christine, "Lives in the Arts: Ups and Downs of a Dancer," *Boston Globe*, 18 March 1981.

Films and Videotapes

The Eleventh Hour, performance by Wood, televised special in honor of Alvin Ailey's death, 1989.

*   *   *

Donna Wood (right) in Alvin Ailey's *District Storyville*, 1988. Photograph © Johan Elbers.

Donna Wood is best known for her more than a decade as a lead dancer and soloist with the Alvin Ailey American Dance Theatre. Well versed in both ballet and modern dance, she has also frequently been featured in operas, ballets, and theatrical productions staged by other companies.

Wood was born in 1954 in New York City, but moved to Dayton, Ohio, as a child. She began dancing at age five, taking ballet classes with Josephine Schwarz, head of the Dayton Ballet Company, in Dayton. At age nine, she joined the Dayton Contemporary Dance Company and, at age 12, began performing with the Dayton Ballet Company. She remained with the Dayton groups, performing both in that city and around the country, until graduating from high school in 1972. That year, she moved to New York to pursue her career further.

After studying for a summer on a scholarship at the Dance Theatre of Harlem (DTH), headed by Arthur Mitchell, she auditioned for and won a spot in the Ailey in 1972, declining an invitation to join DTH. She danced with the Ailey for 13 years, becoming a lead dancer/soloist and performing in most of the repertory, including both the works of Alvin Ailey and those of other choreographers. In fact, Wood assumed many of the roles created for Ailey's protégé, Judith Jamison, after Jamison left to join the Broadway show *Sophisticated Ladies*. Among the many classic Ailey-choreographed pieces in which Wood danced were *Revelations, Blues Suite, Masekela Language, Memoria, Pas de Duke* (to the music of Duke Ellington, which she performed with Patrick Dupond), and the solo *Cry*, a 20-minute piece created for Jamison intended as a tribute to black women.

The Ailey company is known for performing works by a wealth of other choreographers in addition to Ailey, and Wood danced a myriad of roles in notable pieces, including Lar Lubovitch's *Les Noces* and *The Time Before the Time After (After the Time Before),* in which she was originally partnered with Ulysses Dove; Louis Falco's *Caravan*; George Faison's *Gazelle* and *Suite Otis*; John Butler's *Seven Journeys*; Jamison's *Divining;* Dove's *Inside*; Donald McKayle's *Rainbow 'Round My Shoulder* and *District Storyville*, in which Wood danced the role of the Madam; and Talley Beatty's *The Road of the Phoebe Snow*.

Wood was a versatile performer, critic Jack Anderson noted that the tall dancer had the ability to change the quality of her movement unexpectedly, transforming suddenly from a classical ballerina "into a squabbling harridan." In 1984, when Wood danced the role created for Melissa Hayden in a 31-year-old work, Todd Bolender's *The Still Point*, the *Washington Post*'s Suzanne Levy said, "That Donna Wood can dance the role originated by Hayden with complete strength and conviction is a testament to her place in today's pantheon of dancers." In addition to Dove, Dupond, and Jamison, Wood danced with a wide variety of acclaimed modern dancers during her tenure with the Ailey. They include Dudley Williams, Sarita Allen, Michihiko Oka, Peter Woodin, Sara Yarborough, and many others. She also helped teach the repertory, notably the solo *Cry*, to newer dancers. In appreciation of her contributions to the company, Wood was honored in a tribute by the Ailey company after her retirement in 1985, during which she reprised her performance in *Cry*.

Wood, who studied jazz and Graham technique in addition to ballet, was known for being equally at home both in the ballet and modern dance styles. In addition to her work with the Ailey, Wood frequently performed as a guest artist with ballet and modern dance companies alike. She often returned to the Dayton Contemporary Dance Company and its ballet counterpart as a guest performer,

primarily in pieces from the Ailey repertoire. She was also featured with the Vienna State Opera Ballet, where her performances included John Neumeier's *Joseph's Legende* and Leonard Bernstein's *Mass* (which she spent two months performing there in 1980), as well as with the Hamburg Ballet. She also made guest appearances at the Capitol Ballet Company in Washington, D.C., and the Royal Danish Ballet, where she performed two of Ailey's works, *Cry* and *Memoria*. She danced with regional companies around the U.S. and in Canada, and appeared in fundraisers and other special programs, such as in a benefit for the Filene Center at Wolf Trap National Park for the Performing Arts in 1983.

In a 1980 article in the *New York Times*, Wood was quoted as saying, "There's a whole wide world out there and one day I'd like to get to know other fields, other disciplines. Just to dance is kind of limited, and being limited is something I don't believe in." Her career after the Ailey follows this philosophy: from 1984 to 1986, Wood taught in Los Angeles at the California Institute of the Arts, while also studying acting and voice as she prepared for a dramatic career; subsequently, she starred in a U.S.-Soviet Union production of Duke Ellington's *Sophisticated Ladies*, which toured for two months in Moscow, Leningrad, and Tblisi in the then-Soviet Union, as well as in Japan and Washington, D.C. In 1988 she starred in a ballet production of *Zorba the Greek* in Verona, Italy, along with Vladimir Vassiliev of the Bolshoi Ballet and Jorge Iancu of La Scala. The next year Wood danced at Alvin Ailey's funeral, which was filmed and featured as a television special, *The Eleventh Hour*. She also appeared on the television series *Fame* in a dance role.

Since 1989, Wood has focused on a career in arts administration, starting with a position as a manager of external affairs at the Philip Morris company, where she remained until 1986. She subsequently returned to the Alvin Ailey American Dance Theatre in an administrative position, serving as director of marketing and public relations from 1986 to 1987. She is also the president of the Donna Wood Foundation, which assists teenaged professional dancers, encouraging them in their education and skill development. Wood received an honorary degree in fine arts from Wheaton College in 1984 and received the Candace Award from the National Coalition of 100 Black Women in 1988.

—Karen Raugust

WU Xiao-bang

Chinese dancer, choreographer, and educator

Born: 18 December 1906, in Taicang County, Jiangsu Province. **Education:** Attached High School to Dongwu University class in Suzhou; worked as an apprentice at the Jiangsu Provincial Bank while studying English, algebra, geometry, etc. at an evening school; took banking courses at an American international correspondence school; resumed education at the Attached High School to Hujiang University in Shanghai; attended Chizhi University, 1926, and later the Central Military & Political School which forced him to leave China for Japan several times betweeen 1929-37; studied violin 1929-32, classical ballet at the Dance Institute of Masao Takada, 1929-34, and German modern dance at the Modern Dance Workshop of Takaya Eguchi & Misako Miya. **Career:** Established Xiaobang Dance School, Shanghai, the first theatrical and ballet-based dance school in China, 1931; opened Xiao-bang Dance Institute,

1935; gave his first recital of balletic solos choreographed and danced by himself, 1935; joined the "Anti-Enemy" Theater Team and the Battlefield Service Company of the New Fourth Army when the War of Resistance against Japan broke out in 1937; choreographed and danced many dances to express his patriotism; taught modern dance at the Children's Team of the Red Army, Shanghai, 1937; Sino-France Theatre School and Workers' Club, Shanghai, 1938; Xin'an Touring Company, Shanghai, 1939-40; Guangdong Provincial Arts Center, Qujiang, Guangdong Province, 1940; Dance Program at Yucai School, Chongqing, Sichuan Province, 1941; School of National Experimental Theater (later Opera School), Chongqing, 1941; National Theater School, Jiang'an, Sichuan, 1942; Guangdong Provincial Arts School, Qujiang, Guangdong, 1942-1943; Children's Arts Program at Xi'an Nursery School, Xi'an, Shanxi Province, 1944; Luxun Literary & Arts Academy in Yan'an, 1945; Institute of Literature & Arts under the Northern China Allied University in Zhangjiakou, 1945-46; Arts Troupe of Inner Mongolia, 1946; Dance Team of Propaganda Troupe under the Northeastern Allied Army of Democracy and Luxun Literary & Arts Academy in Shenyang, 1948; created dances both based on the local ethnic styles and the Chinese soldiers' life; came to Beijing, took part in the First All-China Conference of Literary & Arts Workers' Representatives and was elected vice chairman of China National Dance Artists Association (CNDAA); went to Wuhan and opened a workshop at the Arts School and Dance Company under the Fourth Field Army, 1949; appointed founding director of the Dance Company of China Youth Art Theater; published the first modern dance book on both theory and practice in China; took charge of education and teaching at the Training Workshop for Dance Movement Cadres under the Central Academy of Drama, 1951-52; founding director of Arts Troupe under the Central Institute for Nationalities, 1952-54; director of the preparatory committee of Beijing Dance School, 1953-54; founding chairman of China Dance Art Research Society, 1954-57; founded his own experimental modern dance company, Heavenly Horse Dance Studio, 1957, and closed it for political reasons, 1960; stayed at home for eighteen years with no chance to choreograph or dance, and started to practise calligraphy and Taiji, 1960-79; elected chairman of CNDAA, 1979; appointed founding director of Dance Research Institute under China National Arts Academy, 1980, and began concentrating on writing more theoretical books and giving lectures and workshops all over China, spreading the concepts and methodology of his Chinese New Dance tradition, his adaptation and development of the Western modern dance.

Awards: In 1985, 1990 and 1995, CNDAA and several regional dance associations held symposia on his New Dance Art as well as his life-long contributions; *March of the Volunteers* was selected nominee for the "Masterpiece of Chinese Dance in the 20th Century," 1994; *The Song of the Guerrillas* and *Hungry Fire* were named "Masterpieces of Chinese Dance in the 20th Century" in 1994. **Died:** Beijing, 8 July 1995.

Works

1933 *Puppet* (solo; mus. percussion), Tokyo
      Restless Motion (solo; mus. percussion), Tokyo
1934 *Washing Yarn Dance, Dance for Two and Sword Dance* (three dances choreographed for the film *Xi Shi*), Shanghai
      Tambourine Dancey (for the drama *Nora*), Shanghai
      Remaking (solo, mus. percussion), Cardan Theater, Shanghai

      Tired of Life (solo, mus. R. Schuman), Cardan Theater, Shanghai
      The Year of 1925: The Great Revolution (solo, mus. Tchaikovsky), Cardan Theater, Shanghai
      Desire (solo, mus. Chen Ge-xin), Cardan Theater, Shanghai
1935 *Taking Part in a Funeral Procession* (solo, mus. Chopin), Cardan Theatre, Shanghai
      By the Huangpu River (solo, mus. Chopin), Cardan Theater, Shanghai
      Peace Illusion (solo, mus. Rakhmaninov), Cardan Theater, Shanghai
      A Minstrel (solo, mus. Joseph J. Raff), Cardan Theater, Shanghai
      Sorrow of Love (solo, mus. Kraisel), Cardan Theater, Shanghai
      Clown (solo, mus. Tchaikovsky), Cardan Theater, Shanghai
1937 *Emotion of an Eclectic* (solo, mus. Joseph J. Raff), Shanghai
      Relieving the Annoyance (solo, no mus.), Shanghai
      Longing for Peace (solo, mus. Rakhmaninov), Shanghai
      Hero (solo, mus. Saint-Saens), Shanghai
      Money Worship (solo, mus. Stravinsky), Shanghai
      Liberation (solo, mus. Chopin), Shanghai
      Magic Dream (solo, mus. percussion), Shanghai
      A Panic-Stricken Period (solo, mus. Beethoven's Pathetic Sonata: Movement III), Shanghai
      Broadsword Dance (solo, mus. anti-Japanese invaders song), in the countryside
      To Beat and Kill the Traitors (group dance, mus. anti-Japanese invaders song), in the countryside
      March of the Volunteers (solo, mus. Nie Er), Wuxi, Jiangsu Province
1938 *The Song of the Guerrillas* (solo, later pas de trois and pas de six, mus. He Lu-ting), Chenjialing, Nanchang, Jiangxi Province
1939 *A Messenger* (solo, no mus.), Shanghai
      Three Persons with Different Psychological States, in three parts—A: Hesitation (solo, mus. Chen Ge-xin), *B: Hope* (solo, mus. Chen Ge-xin), and *C: Making a Firm Effort* (solo, no mus.), Shanghai
      An Ugly Traitor (solo, mus. Chen Ge-xin), Shanghai
      March of Broadsword (solo, mus. anti-Japanese invaders song), Shanghai
      Fragrance of a Hundred Flowers in Spring (solo, mus. He Lu-ting, for the film At the Crossroad), Shanghai
      Internationale (solo, mus. Eugene Pottier), Shanghai
      United to Fight Against Invaders (group dance, mus. anti-Japanese invaders song), Shanghai
      Poppy Flower (dance drama of six scenes, with Sheng Jie, Hu Feng, Yang Fan, Lu Ji in the major roles, mus. Chen Ge-xin), Shanghai
      Aspiration (solo, mus. Beethoven), Shanghai
      Friendship (pas de deux, mus. unidentified), Shanghai
1940 *Love in Man's World* (dance drama of one act, four scenes, mus. Chen Ge-xin), restaged on the students of Dance Program under Guangdong Provincial Arts School in 1942, Qujiang, Guangdong Province
      The News of Spring (song-and-dance drama of three scenes with Yue Rong-lie, Chen Ming, Zhang Tian-hong in the major roles, mus. Chen Ge-xin), Xin'an Touring Company, Guilin, Guangxi Province

Happy Dance of Farmers (group dance, mus. Chen Ge-xin), Guilin, Guangxi Province

Rattle Stick Dance (group dance, mus. folk music), Guilin, Guangxi Province

Remembering the Past Times (group dance, mus. Beethoven), Guilin, Guangxi Province

Harvest Dance (group dance, mus. Xian Xing-hai), Guilin, Guangxi Province

Joy of Love (solo, mus. F. Kreisler), Guilin, Guangxi Province

In Front of the Martyr's Statue (solo, mus. unidentified), Guilin, Guangxi Province

Anti-Japanese Invaders Suite (group dance, mus. Huang You-di, He Lu-ting & Nie Er), Guilin, Guangxi Province

Master Tiger (dance drama of four acts, mus. Liu Shi-xin), Guilin, Guangxi Province

1941   *A Debt of Blood* (solo, mus. unidentified), Hall of Anti-Japanese-Invaders & Constructing China, Chongqing, Sichuan Province

March of Red Flag (pas de deux with Dai Ai-lian, mus. unidentified), Hall of Anti-Japanese-Invaders & Constructing China, Chongqing, Sichuan Province

Going out to Battle (pas de deux with Sheng Jie, mus. unidentified), Hall of Anti-Japanese-Invaders & Constructing China, Chongqing, Sichuan Province

Joining Efforts (pas de trois with Dai Ai-lian and Sheng Jie, mus. unidentified), Hall of Anti-Japanese-Invaders & Constructing China, Chongqing, Sichuan Province

Exile Trilogy (solo, mus. Liu Xue-an), Hall of Anti-Japanese-Invaders & Constructing China, Chongqing, Sichuan Province

The Death Knell Sounds for the Fascists (song and dance drama, mus. unidentified), Chongqing Children's Troupe

1942   *Three Hungry People* (pas de trois, mus. percussion of night-watcher's clapper), Qujiang, Guangdong Province

Pagoda Gateway (dance drama of three acts, mus. Chen Bei-xun), students of Dance Program under Guangdong Provincial Arts School in 1942, Qujiang

Lamentation of Life (solo, mus. Chopin), Qujiang, Guangdong Province

1943   *Hungry Fire* (solo, percussion of night-watcher's clapper), Qujiang, Guangdong Province

Man in Net (solo, mus. percussion), Qujiang, Guangdong Province

Welcoming Spring (solo, mus. Huang You-di), Qujiang, Guangdong Province

Longing for the Mortal World (solo, mus. Huang You-di), Qujiang, Guangdong Province

Singing of the Spring Buffalo (solo, mus. folk music), Qujiang, Guangdong Province

Moonlight Sonata (group dance, mus. Beethoven), Qujiang, Guangdong Province

Song of Flowers (pas de deux, mus. Lang Yi-ge), Qujiang, Guangdong Province

To Alice (solo, mus. Beethoven), Qujiang, Guangdong Province

Dance of the Sea (group dance, mus. percussion), Qujiang, Guangdong Province

Serenade (solo, mus. Chopin), Qujiang, Guangdong Province

On an Endless Road (group dance, mus. Tchaikovsky), Qujiang, Guangdong Province

Meditation (solo, mus. Tayse), Qujiang, Guangdong Province

1944   *Waltz of Recalling* (pas de deux, mus. Mangia), Nanhong, Chengdu, Sichuan Province

To Die a Martyr's Death (solo, mus. Saint-Saens), Nanhong, Chengdu, Sichuan Province

Autumn Resentment (solo, mus. Saint-Saens), Nanhong, Chengdu, Sichuan Province

Affestion at Farewell (pas de deux, mus. Ataert-Jun Smoui), Nanhong, Chengdu, Sichuan Province

March of Joy (solo, mus. Conta), Nanhong, Chengdu, Sichuan Province

1946   *The Mongolian Dance* (solo, mus. Mongolian folk song), Chinese Inner Mongolia

Hope (pas de deux, mus. Mongolian folk song), Chinese Inner Mongolia

Trilogy of the Inner Mongolian People (dance drama, mus. unidentified), Chinese Inner Mongolia

1948   *Troop Training Dance* (group dance, mus. Yan Ke), Harbin, Heilongjiang Province

Marching Dance (group dance, mus. Yan Ke), Harbin, Heilongjiang Province

1950   *Angry Flame* (dance drama, mus. arranged by the Xin'an Touring Company), Shanghai

1957   *Dance of a Green Phoenix* (solo, mus. ancient music of the Tao), Chongqing, Sichuan Province

Cutting into a Mountain (solo, mus. Nuo dance music of Jiangxi Province), Chongqing, Sichuan Province

Textile Women (solo, mus. Nuo dance music of Guangxi Province), Chongqing, Sichuan Province

Peace Dance (pas de deux, mus. traditional music of the Kunqu Opera), Chongqing, Sichuan Province

Flute and Feather Dance (group dance, mus. ritualistic music at the Confucius Temple), Chongqing, Sichuan Province

Fisherman's Joy (solo, mus. Taoist song: Happy Drunken Immortal), Chongqing, Sichuan Province

1958   *Two Cats Playing with a Ball* (pas de deux, folk music of Chaozhou), Guangzhou

Wild Geese Wheeling in the Sky (pas de deux, mus. traditional), Guangzhou

The Spring Snow (solo, mus. ancient music of Pipa), Guangzhou

Landscape in the Northern China (solo, mus. traditional), Fuzhou, Fujian Province

General Cleaning (group dance, mus. self arranged), Xiamen, Fujian Province

1959   *A Lazy Butterfly* (dance drama, mus. traditional tunes from the Anhui Floral Lantern Dance), Hefei, Anhui Province

Better than Southern China (group dance, mus. traditional music from Anhui and percussion), Hefei, Anhui Province

Back from Fishing (group dance, mus. traditional tune of Chaozhou), Nanning

The Winter Sweet Exercises (group dance, mus. Da Qu traditional), Auditorium of China Federation of Literary and Art Circles (ACFLAC), Beijing

Beside a River on a Moonlit Spring Night (pas de quatre, mus. ancient Chinese song: By the Xunyang River), ACFLAC, Beijing

A Branch of Spring (Shepherd Boy Learning to Read) (solo, folk tune of Chaozhou), ACFLAC, Beijing

Ambush in Ten Directions (group dance, mus. ancient music of Pipa), ACFLAC, Beijing

An Old Man Growing Chrysanthemum (solo, mus. Pipa traditional), ACFLAC, Beijing

Singing of Our Motherland (group dance, mus. Wang Xin), ACFLAC, Beijing

The Winter Sweet Theme & Three Variations (pas de deux, mus. Guqin), ACFLAC, Beijing

Football Dance (group dance, mus. folk music), ACFLAC, Beijing

Dance with Strings of Beads (group dance, mus. folk), ACFLAC, Beijing

Publications

By WU (in Chinese):

Introduction to the New Dance Art, Shanghai, 1950; revised edition, Beijing, 1982.

My Career of Dance Art, Hong Kong, 1981; revised edition, Beijing, 1982.

New Theory on Dance, Shanghai, 1985.

Anthology of Dance Theory, Chengdu, 1985.

Dancology Studies, Beijing, 1988.

Wu Xiao-bang on Dance & Art, Beijing, 1988.

New Anthology of Dance Theory, Beijing, 1989.

Editor, *The Collection of the Chinese National Folk Dances,* 30 volumes, Beijing, 1988—.

Editor, *The Chinese Encyclopaedia: Music & Dance Volume,* Beijing and Shanghai, 1989.

Editor, *Contemporary China: Dance Volume,* Beijing, 1993.

On WU (in English):

Ou, Jian-ping, "Dance Scholarship in China: Yesterday, Today and Tomorrow," in *Documentation—Beyond Performance: Dance Scholarship Today,* Susan Au and Frank-Manuel Peter, eds., Essen, 1989.

———, "From 'Beast' to 'Flowers': Modern Dance in China," in *East Meets West in Dance: Voices in Cross Cultural Dialogues, Choreography and Dance Studies Vol. 9,* Ruth Solomon and John Solomon, eds., Chur, Switzerland, 1995.

Ou, Jian-ping, translator, *Brief Biographies of the Contemporary Chinese Dance Celebrities,* Beijing, 1995.

*   *   *

Wu is considered the father of Chinese modern dance. Initially influenced by traditional Western ballet, he later developed his own dance style based on the ideas of German Expressionism and those of Isadora Duncan. In addition, stimulated by the "May 4th New Culture Movement" (started in 1919, its dual aims to thwart foreign invasion and Chinese feudalistic domination and to hold high the two flags of democracy and science), and influenced by Marxism and Sun Yat-sen's democratic, nationalist ideals, Wu took an active part in the patriotic and progressive movements which rocked Chinese culture in the 1930s and 1940s. Indeed, he chose his very name—Xiao-bang—as a homonym for "Chopin" to express solidarity with and respect for the exiled Polish patriot.

Wu was born into a peasant family in Jiangsu Province but was adopted by a wealthy man at the age of 10 months. After a varied education which included training in business as well as the arts, he opened a dance studio in 1931, planning to bring Western ballet to Chinese audiences. However, his performances were all but ignored—his first recital in 1935 was attended only by one Polish woman. Realizing that in a climate of poverty, political corruption, and social unrest, the Chinese people were hardly in a frame of mind to appreciate his Western, ballet-based works, which obviously belonged to an illusory other world, Wu was forced to give up his dream of bringing classical ballet and classical music to the Chinese stage.

Wu subsequently developed his New Chinese Dance style based on the ideas of American Isadora Duncan and the German Expressionist dancers, initially horrifying audiences by appearing in his bare feet, a monstrous and absurd behavior in Old China. The Japanese invasion of 1931 provided compelling subject matter for many of these early works, and they eventually became an important cultural rallying cry for Chinese troops and civilian resisters alike. Out of his repertoire of 102 dances and dance dramas, most of which exposed the cruelty of the Japanese invaders and extolled the dauntless heroism of the Chinese soldiers and civilians, his most famous and best representative choreography is *March of the Volunteers,* the music of which became the national anthem when the People's Republic of China was founded in 1949. Wu performed the piece five times at the frontlines of the war at the request of the Chinese soldiers. As a result of choreographing and performing such provocative dances, Wu was regarded as an "artist dancing to the pulse of his times," which is the nature of Western modern dance.

After New China was born in 1949, Wu purposely changed his focus from social criticism to a more romantic spirit by choreographing more of his New Dances to traditional Chinese music. His modern dance company, the Heavenly Horse Dance Studio, extolled the new life of the Chinese people in a more aesthetic but indirect way, eschewing clumsy and superficial eulogy of its achievements, and he thus paved the way for the "fever of rejuvenating the ancient Chinese dance" started in 1980.

As the "father of Chinese theater dance," Wu inexhaustibly trained and educated five generations of Chinese theater dancers, both professional and amateur, and even Chinese dramatic actresses and actors, either on a short or long term over the course of his 60-year teaching career. In addition to teaching at dozens of institutions, he established the first and second Masters in Dance degree program in China (Beijing, 1982-88). Wu set a great example for the younger generations to follow in combining both theory and practice, dancing, choreographing, teaching, writing and organizing, with not only 102 choreographies, but also seven books to his credit, an unrivaled achievement in Chinese dance history.

In summary, what Western modern dance provided Wu was not only a physical form for his ideas and an artistic expression, but also a vital power to fill his life, and a spiritual encouragement to face all the challenges on his way to his ideals. His achievements stemmed from his desire to answer the questions "Why should we dance and how should we live?"

—Ou Jian-ping

WYMAN, Anna

Canadian dancer, choreographer, and educator

Born: Anna Margaret Fladnitzer in Graz, Austria, 29 April 1928. **Education:** Keplerschule in Graz; from the age of five, Graz Opera Ballet School; also studied the movement theories of Rudolf von Laban in London in the early 1950s. **Family:** Married (and divorced) Max Wyman; children: Trevor and Gabrielle. **Career:** Danced on stage in several operas from an early age; by mid-teens was a principal dancer with the Graz Opera Ballet, touring Europe; also performed with the Schonemann Ballet. Founder, Anna Wyman Dancers, 1970 (name later changed to Anna Wyman Dance Theatre or AWDT); became artistic director and choreographer, the Anna Wyman School of Dance Arts, West Vancouver, 1970. Appeared with AWDT in *Gala*, a 1982 National Film Board of Canada (NFB) documentary of the May 1981 appearance of eight of the country's leading dance companies at Ottawa's National Arts Centre; AWDT featured in *For the Love of Dance*, directed by Norman Campbell, NFB, 1981; *Anna Wyman Dance Theatre*, a KCTS-9 Public Broadcasting Service (PBS) documentary, made in 1985. **Awards:** Woman of Distinction Award Arts & Culture, 1984; Vancouver Sweney Award Excellence in Arts, 1985.

Works (all created for Anna Wyman Dance Theatre)

1970	*Reverberations* (mus. William Kraft), West Vancouver
1971	*Lines in Simplicity* (mus. Weber), North Vancouver
	The Wedding Dance (mus. Mozart), Bowen Island, B.C.
	Zyklus (later, *Cycles*) (mus. Stockhausen), West Vancouver
1972	*Planes* (mus. Iannis Xenakis), North Vancouver
	Depths (mus. Kazimierz Serocki), North Vancouver
	Gabi (solo; mus. Tchaikowsky), North Vancouver
	Springspell (mus. Vivaldi), North Vancouver
	The Pay-Phone Piece (no mus.), North Vancouver
	The Five Senses (based on improv; no mus.), first performed at the Vancouver Art Gallery, later modified for stage as *The Two Senses (Hearing and Taste)*
	Here at the Eye of the Hurricane (mus. Stockhausen), Victoria, B.C.
	The Incredible Unfolding Universe (no mus.), Vancouver Art Gallery
	Boxes (later the end of *Number One*; no mus.), Vancouver Art Gallery
	Citysight (mus. Xenakis), Vancouver Art Gallery
	Tree (improv; no mus.), Vancouver Art Gallery
	Amnios (later Part II of *Peacemaker*; mus. Xenakis), Vancouver Art Gallery
1973	*Peacemaker - Part I (Coloured Piece)* (mus. Ligeti); *Part II (Amnios)* (mus. Xenakis); *Part III (The Hand)* (mus. Witold Lutoslawsky), Vancouver
	Dance Is... (no mus.), Vancouver
1974	*Radetzky March* (mus. Liszt), performed once with the Vancouver Symphony Orchestra for a Sun Family Pops Concert at the Queen Elizabeth Theatre, Vancouver
	Tales from the Vienna Woods and *The Blue Danube Waltz* (mus. Strauss), both performed once with the Vancouver Symphony Orchestra, Queen Elizabeth Theatre, Vancouver

1975	*Number One* (mus. Rolling Stones, Ricardo Abreut, and Tchaikovsky), Thunder Bay, Ontario
	Undercurrents (mus. R. Murray Schafer), Vancouver
1976	*Klee Wyck: A Ballet for Emily* (mus. Anne Mortifee), commissioned by the Vancouver Art Gallery in recognition of International Women's Year, premiering at the VAG
	Quicksilver (mus. *Tangerine Dream* by Franke/Froese/Bauman), Vancouver
	Deflection (mus. commissioned from John Mills-Cockell), Vancouver
1977	*Sixes and Sevens* (mus. Webster and Fain, *Love Is a Many Splendored Thing*), Vancouver
	Tremolo (mus. Keith Jarrett), Vancouver
	Two People (mus. Handel and Sean O. Raida's *Women of Ireland*), Vancouver
1979	*Surya Savitar* (mus. Keith Jarrett), North Vancouver
	Hamartia (mus. Penderecki), North Vancouver
	Scribouillage (mus. Ramsay Lewis, Janacek), North Vancouver
1980	*A Dancer's Circus* (mus. various), Duncan, B.C.
1986	*City Piece* (mus. Edgar Froese), Vancouver
1987	*The Stand* (mus. Frederic Mette), Vancouver
1988	*Maskerade* (mus. various), Vancouver
	Universal Rhythm (mus. John McDowell), Vancouver
1990	*Walls* (mus. John Adams), Vancouver

*   *   *

Several modern dance companies were formed in Canada during the dance boom of the late 1960s and early 1970s; one of the longer lasting and most professional of these was the Anna Wyman Dance Theatre in Vancouver. Modern dance was still fairly new to the city when Wyman emigrated there from Austria, via London, in 1968. She came to the growing West Coast city with a rich European background, having been a principal dancer with the Graz Opera Ballet where she was required to dance using several techniques such as those for classical ballet as well as various national styles. Later, in England, Wyman was able to put that aside to take on the pure, unstylized movement of Rudolf von Laban. She would also put aside her own career as a performer soon after forming her own company.

Wyman opened the Anna Wyman School of Dance Arts only two years after her arrival in Vancouver, and her dancers were initially drawn from among the advanced students. From the beginning, Wyman was committed to developing real dance technique in the company; over time this did happen, even among the male dancers, who were particularly difficult to find in those years. As the dancers grew in sophistication, so did Wyman's choreography.

From the first semi-improvised performance at the Vancouver Art Gallery, Anna Wyman Dance Theatre (AWDT), which numbered from 8 to 12 dancers, grew over its almost 20 years of existence into a polished and technically proficient troupe. The company began modestly, with a series of noon-hour shows called *Process and Product* performed at the Vancouver Art Gallery. With the move to proper theatrical spaces, however, the product became the focus. Wyman began to create her own contemporary style of choreography, in which the initial abstract explorations of shapes and lines were eventually filled in with an almost romantic shading. In May of 1973 the company made its first appearance at the mid-sized Queen Elizabeth Playhouse, premiering *Peacemaker*, with projected film and two dancers sharing a long, fabric tube. The commitment to appearing in the community, however, was always strong and there were numerous citywide performances over the years at outdoor or other public venues.

In 1973, only two years after its professional debut, AWDT was invited by the Canadian External Affairs Department to attend the International Young Choreographer's Competition in Cologne, Germany, where Wyman's *Here at the Eye of the Hurricane* was chosen as one of three most outstanding entries. For the company's American debut in January 1975 it was awarded a grant by the Washington State government. It made its first tour across Canada the same year, becoming the first modern dance company to undertake a national tour. In December 1980 AWDT was the first modern dance company invited to tour China, and three years later was the first Canadian troupe to tour India.

AWDT's New York debut at Brooklyn College's Whitman Hall in 1985 was disrupted when dancer Christopher Neil Wortley was struck by a bus and had to be replaced; nonetheless, Anna Kisselgoff's review was mostly favorable, finding the "real cue to Miss Wyman's approach to dance. . .in the credits given in the program. All the works were choreographed by her yet each title said simply 'Visual concept by Anna Wyman.'" Though Kisselgoff found the kinesthetic element not as strong as it might have been, Wyman's focus on theatricality (she was often compared with Alwin Nikolais) was more often perceived as part of the uniqueness of her work.

Wyman was the sole choreographer for her company until 1987, when a dry artistic period led her to relax this restriction. For AWDT's October 1987 performances at the North Vancouver Centennial Theatre, Reid Anderson choreographed *Three Visions and a Hymn.* Also on the bill was *Everyday a Sunday* by Tsutomu Ben Iida of Swiss Dance Theatre, and Wyman's own *The Stand,* which contained a brilliant and sensual woman's solo.

The company was the first from British Columbia to receive Canada Council funding, which continued generously over the years until the Council cut its contributions by 25 percent in 1986 and it was finally cut off completely in 1990. A serious reduction in provincial subsidies in the same year led to the company's folding. Yet it was enormously popular over the years, especially in Vancouver, and the local press coverage in the city's two dailies (*The Vancouver Sun* and *The Province*) showed an avid and proprietorial interest in the company and its artistic director.

—Kaija Pepper

Y-Z

YOOK Wan-soon

Korean dancer, choreographer, writer, artistic director, and educator

Born: 16 June 1933 in Ch'ungju, South Korea. **Education:** B.A. (1956) and M.A. (1961), Ewha Women's University; studied at the University of Illinois; attended Martha Graham School of Contemporary Dance, American Dance Festival, Connecticut Summer Dance School, 1961-63; University of California Summer Dance Program (Long Beach), 1971; first dancer in Korea to attain Ph.D. from Hanyang University, 1986. **Career:** Lecturer, Ewha Women's University, Kyounghee University, Sookmyoung Women's University, Hanyang University, and Sangmyoung University, 1959-91; first performance, Seoul, 1963; formed Orchesis Dance Company, 1963; first solo concert at Carnegie Hall, 1972; participated in international conferences abroad and teaching workshops, 1972; international dance tours to New York, Paris, London, Vancouver, Russia, from 1975-96; founder/director, Korea Contemporary Dance Company, beginning 1975; founder, Modern Dance Company 'Duljje' (now TAM) 1980; established Modern Dance Association of Korea, 1980; formed Modern Dance Promotion of Korea, 1985; directed/choreographed, Seoul Olympics, 1988; choreographer of opening ceremony for the '93 Taejun EXPO; choreographer for the opening of the 50th Anniversary of Independence Celebration Ceremony, 1995; directed/choreographed, Muju Winter Universiad closing ceremony, 1997; hosted American Dance Festival in Seoul, beginning 1990; staged Environmental Arts Festival with Jung Myoung-hoon, 1996; 1st Seoul International Children & Youth Dance Festival, 1997. **Awards:** Seoul Cultural Award, 1981; Republic of Korea Social Educator's Award, 1982; Christian Cultural Award, 1987; Choreography Award, 1988 Seoul Olympics; Republic of Korea Award for Artistic Achievement, 1989; Appreciation Award, Mayor of Los Angeles, 1993.

Roles

1955   *A Rose in a Bunch of Roses* (Park Woe-sun), Ewha Dance Company, Seoul
        Love in Nocturne (Park Woe-sun), Ewha Dance Company, Seoul
        Pioneer in Progress (Ji Kyung-won), Ewha Dance Company, Seoul
1956   *An Elder in Retrospection* (Kwun You-sung), Kwun You-sung Dance Company, Seoul
1961   *Girl in Tracing* (Stockman), Stockman Company, Urbana, Illinois

Works

1963   *Nongae* (mus. Ahn Ick-tae), solo, Orchesis Dance Company, National Theatre, Seoul

Basic Movement (mus. various, arranged Yook Wan-soon), Orchesis Dance Company, National Theatre, Seoul
Impression of America (mus. various, arranged Yook Wan-soon), solo, Orchesis Dance Company, National Theatre, Seoul
Negro Spiritual (mus. Negro Spiritual Melody, arranged Yook Wan-soon), Orchesis Dance Company, National Theatre, Seoul
Fear (mus. various, arranged Yook Wan-soon), solo, National Theatre, Seoul
Wave of Mind (mus. Vivaldi), Orchesis Dance Company, National Theatre, Seoul
1965   *The Resurrection* (mus. various, arranged Yook Wan-soon) solo, Orchesis Dance Company, National Theatre, Seoul
        Endless Movement (mus. Park Jae-youl), Orchesis Dance Company, National Theatre, Seoul
        Invocation for a Dead Spirit (poem by Kim So-wol), solo, National Theatre, Seoul
        Harmony of Spring (mus. Brahams), Orchesis Dance Company, National Theatre, Seoul
1966   *Toward Milkyway* (mus. various, arranged Lee Kyung-hwan), Orchesis Dance Company, National Theatre, Seoul
        Unforgettable (mus. traditional British Melody, arranged Yook Wan-soon), Orchesis Dance Company, National Theatre, Seoul
        The Image of Mankind (dialogue) Orchesis Dance Company, National Theatre, Seoul
1969   *Wasteland* (mus. various, arranged Lee Kyung-hwan) solo, Orchesis Dance Company, National Theatre, Seoul
        Dessin (mus. Various, arranged Lee Kyung-hwan) solo, Orchesis Dance Company, National Theatre, Seoul
        The Forest (mus. Hwang Byoung-ki), Orchesis Dance Company, National Theatre, Seoul
1971   *The Origin of Dankun* (mus. Park Young-hee), Orchesis Dance Company, National Theatre, Seoul
        Dessin (mus. Vivaldi), Orchesis Dance Company, National Theatre, Seoul
        Forgotten Self (mus. Pommy James), Orchesis Dance Company, National Theatre, Seoul
1972   *The Forest* (mus. Hwang Byoung-ki) solo, Carnegie Recital Hall, New York
        Desire to Become Human (mus. Park Young-hee) solo, Carnegie Recital Hall, New York
        The Love of the Heavens and the Earth (mus. Park Young-hee), Carnegie Recital Hall, New York
1973   *Jesus Christ Superstar* (mus. Weber) solo, Ewha Dance Company, Ewha University, Seoul
1974   *Time Being* (mus. percussion), Ewha Dance Company, Ewha University, Seoul

1975   *Monologue* (mus. Cho Oak-hyun), Korea Contemporary Dance Company, Christian Academy House, Seoul

Ave maria (mus. Schubert), Korea Contemporary Dance Company, Ewha University, Seoul

1976   *Shaman Dance* (mus. Park Bum-hun), Korea Contemporary Dance Company, National Theatre, Seoul

Oh! Candlelight (poem by Kim Nam-jo), Korea Contemporary Dance Company, National Theatre, Seoul

Suite Champetre (mus. Vittorio Rieri) solo, Korea Contemporary Dance Company, National Theatre, Seoul

1977   *Agony of Jesus* (mus. sacred song) solo, Korea Contemporary Dance Company, Yonsei University, Seoul

Mutt (mus. Korean traditional Sanjo, arranged Yook Wan-soon) Pretoria, Republic of South Africa

1978   *Coming into Being* (mus. percussion, arranged Cho Bok-sung), Ewha Dance Company, Ewha University, Seoul

1979   *Rhythmic Streams* (mus. Korean traditional Kayakeum, arranged Yook Wan-soon), Marshall Theatre, Duluth, Minnesota

1980   *Chorus of Angels* (mus. Beethoven), Yook Wan-soon Dance Company, Daesin Church, Seoul

1981   *Legend* (mus. Hwang Byoung-ki), Yook Wan-soon Dance Company, Manila, Philippines

1982   *Ryu Kwan Soon* (mus. Kim Young-dong) solo, Yook Wan-soon Dance Company, Commonwealth Institute Theatre, London

Transgression (mus. Korean traditional Danso & Sungmu, arranged Yook Wan-soon) solo, Yook Wan-soon Dance Company, Paris

1983   *The Light* (mus. Ha Jae-eun), Yook Wan-soon Dance Company, Munye Theatre, Seoul

Shalom (mus. various, arranged Yook Wan soon), Yook Wan-soon Dance Company, Kongduck Church, Seoul

1984   *The Crane* (mus. Hwang Byoung-ki, arranged Yook Wan-soon), Yook Wan-soon Dance Company, Wingate University, Wingate, Israel

The Shamanist (mus. Park Bum-hun), Yook Wan-soon Dance Company, Wingate University, Wingate, Israel

Amazing Grace (mus. Arranged E.O. Excell), Korea Contemporary Dance Company, Kongduck Hall, Seoul

The Sound of Bipa (mus. Vivaldi), Korea Contemporary Dance Company, National Theatre of Korea, Seoul

1985   *Pray* (mus. Ha Jae-eun), Korea Contemporary Dance Company, London

Salpuri (mus. Korean festival folk melody), Korea Contemporary Dance Company, NYU Theater, New York

Psalm 57 (mus. Ha Jae-eun), Korea Contemporary Dance Company, NYU Theater, New York

1986   *Han-Du-Re* (mus. Kim Young-dong), Korea Modern Dance Company, National Theatre of Korea, Seoul

Light from the East (mus. Kim Jung-gil), Korea Modern Dance Company, Sejong Cultural Center, Seoul

1987   *The Silk Road* (mus. Hwang Byoung-ki), Korea Contemporary Dance Company, U.B.C. Theatre, Vancouver

Solo with Him (mus. various, arranged Yook Wan soon), KBS TV, Seoul

1988   *Light of the Beginning* (mus. Choi Dong-sun), Korea Modern Dance Company, Olympic Stadium, Seoul

Welcome (mus. Choi Dong-sun), Korea Modern Dance Company, Olympic Stadium, Seoul

The Crest of Waters (mus. Park Jae-eun), Korea Modern Dance Company, National Theatre of Korea, Seoul

1989   *Eternal Echo* (mus. Kim Young-dong), Isadora Duncan Center, Athene

1990   *Ecstasy* (with Kook Soo-ho; mus. Korean folk music, arranged Kook Soo-ho), Korea Contemporary Dance Company, Shivenik, Yugoslavia

1991   *Encounter Manga* (mus. Park Bung-chon), Korea Contemporary Dance Company, Russia Theatre, Moscow

1993   *The Crane* (mus. Kim Ji-wuk), Korea Contemporary Dance Company, Segi Theatre, Beijing

Four Seasons of Civilization (mus. Kim Jung-gil, Kim Bul-re), Seoul Performing Arts Company, Korea Contemporary Dance Company, Taejun

1994   *The Sound of Bipa* (mus. Vivaldi), Korea Contemporary Dance Company, Munye Theatre, Seoul

Triumph (mus. Zamfir), Korea Contemporary Dance Company, Yonsei University, Seoul

1995   *Unendurable Nostalgia* (poem, Kim So-yeub), Korea Contemporary Dance Company, Yonsei University, Seoul

Fantasy of Unity of Korea (mus. Kim Jung-tack), Korea Modern Dance Company, Kwanghwamun, Seoul

Joy of Birth (mus. Kim Jung-gil), Korea Contemporary Dance Company, Myungsung Main Chapel, Seoul

Le Carnival des animaux (mus. Saint-Saens), Korea Contemporary Dance Company, Boys & Girl Dance Company, Se Jong Cutural Center, Seoul

1996   *Penitence* (poem, Kim So-yeub), Korea Contemporary Dance Company, Yonsei University, Seoul

Psalm 23 (mus. Na Un-young), Korea Contemporary Dance Company, Korea Methodist Divinity University, Seoul

Festival (mus. Boccherini), Korea Contemporary Dance Company, Changchun Hall, Seoul

Glory (mus. Kim Jung-gil), Korea Contemporary Dance Company, Sejong Cultural Center Open Stage, Seoul

1997   *Arirang* (mus. Whang Sung-ho), Korea Modern Dance Company, Ski Field, Muju

Your Triumph (poem, Kim So-yeub), Korea Contemporary Dance Company, Yonsei University, Seoul

Where to (mus. Kim Jung-gil), Korea Contemporary Dance Company, Myungsung Main Chapel, Seoul

Happy Overpass (poem, Kim So-yeub), Myungsung Main Chapel, Somang Hall, Konjiam, Korea

Publications

By YOOK: books—

Modern Dance, Seoul, 1979.
Modern Dance Techniques, Seoul, 1981.
Dance Improvisation, Seoul, 1983.
Choreography, Seoul, 1984.
Martha Graham, translator, Seoul, 1984.
History of Western Dance, translator, Seoul, 1986.
Letters on Dancing and Ballets, translator, Seoul, 1987.
Isadora & Esenin, translator with Ha Jung-ae, Park Myung-sook, Kwun Yoon-bang, Seoul, 1988.
Curriculum in Dance Education, with Lee Hee-sun Seoul, 1992.

Yook Wan-soon performing *Ryu Kwan Soon*, **1982. Photograph © Kim Chan-Bock.**

On YOOK: articles—

Kim Tchae-hyoen, "The Chance of an Inspired New Wave for
   Modern Dance," *Dance & Image* 2, Seoul, 1990.
Kim Tea-won, "ADF Instruction in Seoul and the Need for Synthetic
   Dance Education," *Dance & Image* 2, Seoul, 1990.
———, "The Meaning of 30 years of Modern Dance of Korea,"
   CHOOM 215, Seoul, January 1994.

*   *   *

Yook Wan-soon is an important pioneer of modern dance in
Korea. She trained under Martha Graham and José Limón in the
United States and introduced American modern dance to Korea for
the first time in 1963, when she staged her first performance at the
National Theatre in Seoul. Dance critic Park Yong-ku referred to
Yook Wan-soon as the beginning of the "new generation of dance."
He felt *Negro Spiritual* and other dances in her repertoire were
works that were well worth recording in the history of Korean
modern dance. She has formed several dance troupes, including
Orchesis Dance Company (1963-74), Korea Contemporary Dance
Company (1975), and Modern Dance Company Duljje (presently
called TAM) in 1980. She also established the Modern Dance Association of Korea in 1980 and Modern Dance Promotion of Korea
in 1985.

Of the companies Yook Wan-soon founded or co-founded, Korea
Contemporary Dance Company has been the most important. Its
progressive dance spirit was a quiet revolution in the dance world
of Korea. The opening performance was in December of 1975, and
the group has acted as the leader of Korean contemporary dance to
the present time and has produced many new works. Yook founded
the company along with Lee Chung-ja, Lee Jung-hee, Kim Ok-
kyoo, Kim Bock-hee, Kim Wha-suk, Park Myung-sook, Park In-
sook, and Yang Jung-soo, and was the first artistic director. She,
along with the successive acting heads of the company have helped
to promote Korean contemporary dance both in and outside of the
country. Since 1982, the company has played a leading role in the
International Modern Dance Festival, and the company has won
various prizes in the Dance Festival of Korea.

Yook's works, such as *Han-Du-Re* (1986) and *The Crest of Waters* (1988), show a certain emotional feeling that is uniquely Korean. Yook's *Han-Du-Re* was a grand-scale performance featuring
50 performers. Kim Young-dong was the conductor for this piece
and presented the audience with a mixed sound of synthesizer and
traditional Korean instruments which was quite new and notable.
In the fourth act a bridge is placed between the people to resolve
their differences, and the dancers come down and take the hands of
audience members—and suddenly the audience is drawn into the
performance as well. Yook's belief in the power of dance to unite is
clearly seen here in the choreography of *Han-Du-Re*.

In *The Silk Road* and *The Forest,* she collaborated with Hwang
Byoung-ki and Yook's choreographic pattern of expressing an inner
Asian sensibility in a western way was recognized internationally.
Performed at a special performance commemorating the Korean-
Chinese cultural relationship in Beijing, *The Crane* had a unique
Korean theme that illustrates the proud crane's grace and elegance.
The technique and the harmony of costumes were noted as the
archetype of modern Korean dance. In 1993, Contemporary Dance
Company received an invitation from the St. Petersburg National
Ballet and held a joint performance in St. Petersburg, Russia. Boris
Epeman, the director of St. Petersburg National Ballet said of the

work *Encounter* "watching this performance, I had been given a
chance to look into the soul of the Korean people. It was a very
impressive performance. The group's technique and acting is brilliant. Their sets and stage props are also excellent. There was nothing to find fault with." He also noted, "Because this is a rarely seen
form of modern dance in the Soviet Union, the crowd seemed to feel
a different sense of enthusiasm."

Some of her other works which have been exceptionally well-
received overseas are *Transgression* (London, 1982), *Ryu Kwan
Soon* (Paris, 1982), *Legend* (Philippines, 1981), *Salpuri* (New York,
1985), *The Silk Road* (Vancouver, 1987), *The Crane,* (Israel, 1984
and Beijing, 1993), *Pray* (London, 1985), *Eternal Echo* (Greece,
1989), and *Encounter,* (Russia, 1991).

To celebrate 30 years of Korean modern dance, Yook's representative works, from the premiere piece *Basic Movement* to *The Crane*,
were staged. She was recognized for her originality, fluidity, and
expression. Valerie Warm noted that Yook chose a modern composition for a classical Korean instrument (the Kayakeum) in one
dance and that "this dynamic combination suggested a creative
synthesis that the dancer hopefully will pursue in future works."

In 1996, Yook held the first Seoul International Children & Youth
Dance Festival with a theme of "Children, Peace and Dance." It
was an educational event where children from all over the world
became friends. Also in 1996, she worked on the Environmental
Arts Festival with Maestro Jung Myoung-hoon. She is presently
introducing new Korean choreographers to the Rencontres
Internationales Choregraphiques de Seine-St.-Denis.

Yook Wan-soon tilled the ground and planted the seeds for Korean
modern dance. It can be said that the seeds she planted have now
bloomed. She is a larger-than-life personality and truly the godmother
of Korean modern dance. As a dancer and choreographer, she has left
a legacy of many valuable works; as a leader of modern dance, she has
brought Korean modern dance to international stages.

—Kim Young-Tae

YORK, Lila
American dancer, choreographer, and educator

Born: In the late 1940s near Albany, New York. **Education:** Trained
in ballet with Gertrude Hallenbeck; graduated with a degree in literature from Skidmore College, Saratoga Springs, New York; won a
scholarship to study in New York City with Paul Sanasardo; took
classes at the Martha Graham School and with Alvin Ailey; granted
a scholarship to study at the American Dance Center. **Family:**
Married to composer and pianist Donald York. **Career:** Worked in
regional theater in upstate New York; member of the Paul Taylor
Dance Company, 1973-85; toured throughout the U.S. and 53 nations, dancing in more than 60 works; created roles in many of
Taylor's most well-known dances including *Cloven Kingdom, Esplanade, Mercuric Tidings, Images, Diggity, Nightshade,* and *Lost,
Found and Lost*; appeared in four of PBS' *Dance in America* programs; appeared in *Vienna: Lusthaus* and *The Garden of Earthly
Delights* by Martha Clarke; freelance choreographer, since mid-
1980s; staged the works of Paul Taylor for the San Francisco Ballet,
Pittsburgh Ballet Theatre, and American Ballet Theatre; director,
the Pacific Northwest Ballet Offstage, a showcase for emerging
choreographers, 1990; taught at New York University and the

Juilliard School; choreographed works on Atlanta Ballet, Boston Ballet, Connecticut Ballet Theatre, and Pacific Northwest Ballet; appeared in the film *Desperately Seeking Susan.*

Roles (with the Paul Taylor Dance Company unless otherwise noted)

1974	*Sports and Follies* (mus. Satie)
1975	*Esplanade* (mus. Bach)
1976	*Cloven Kingdom* (mus. Corelli, Cowell, Miller, arranged by John Herbert McDowell)
	Polaris (mus. York)
1977	*Images* (mus. Debussy)
	Dust (mus. Poulenc)
	Aphrodisiamania (mus. "golden oldies of the Renaissance")
1978	*Airs* (mus. Handel)
1979	*Diggity* (mus. York)
1980	*Le Sacre du Printemps (The Rehearsal)* (mus. Stravinsky)
1981	*Arden Court* (mus. Boyce)
1982	*Mercuric Tidings* (mus. Schubert)
	Lost, Found and Lost (mus. "wallpaper music" orchestrated by Donald York)
1983	*Sunset* (mus. Elgar)
1984	*Big Bertha* (mus. St. Louis Melody Museum montage)
1986	*Vienna: Lusthaus* (Martha Clarke)

Works

York has worked mainly with ballet companies since the 1980s, some of her works include *Roses* (1989), *Strays, Rapture* (1995), *Windhover* (1995), *Celts* (mus. the Chieftains, Moving Hearts, and Bill Ruyle, 1996), and *The American Variations* (1996).

Publications

By YORK: articles—

Interview with Elizabeth Zimmer, *Dance Magazine,* July 1996.

On YORK: articles—

Garafola, Lynn, review of *Rapture,* performed by the Juilliard Dance Ensemble, *Dance Magazine,* June 1995.
Lila York Programs File and Paul Taylor Clippings and Programs File, Dance Research Collection of the New York Public Library at Lincoln Center, New York.

*   *   *

Lila York was a member of the Paul Taylor Dance Company from 1973 to 1985. During this 12-year period, York created numerous roles and appeared in many of Paul Taylor's most important works. In 1976 alone, a vintage year for Taylor, York appeared in such critically acclaimed works as *Runes, Cloven Kingdom,* and *Polaris.* She also toured extensively with the company visiting innumerable cities in the U.S. and abroad. In her career with the Paul Taylor Dance Company, York appeared in such diverse venues as the New World Festival in Miami, Florida; the American Dance Festival in Durham, North Carolina; Jacob's Pillow Dance Festival in Lee, Massachusetts; with the Israeli

Philharmonic Orchestra in Tel Aviv, Israel; at the Nervi Festival in Italy; and at the Athens Festival in Greece. After leaving the Taylor company in 1985, York staged Taylor's works on other companies. In 1989 she staged *Roses* on the dancers of the Pacific Northwest Ballet in Seattle, Washington. It proved to be a happy experience which opened up other possibilities for York. In 1990 York became the director of Pacific Northwest Ballet Offstage and premiered works by Llory Wilson, Hugh Bigney, and Lisa de Ribere at a small theater in Seattle's Opera House. Ballet Offstage presents both ballet and modern works by up-and-coming choreographers and mature choreographers who work out of the mainstream. The works are set on the dancers of the Pacific Northwest Ballet. There are no restrictions on the work of the choreographers. In 1995 York presented works by herself, Ton Sinons, and Victoria Morgan. "Out of all the things I do, I think I'm proudest of this service in the dance field," York stated in an interview with Martha Ullman West in May 1995.

The five-foot-tall, auburn-haired York made her way to a career in professional dance after graduating from college. Born in upstate New York, York began her dance training at age 13 with Gertrude Hallenbeck. The focus of these early lessons was ballet, a discipline York continued to study into her twenties. While attending Skidmore College in Saratoga Springs, York, a literature major, encountered the modern dancer, teacher, and choreographer Paul Sanasardo who headed the School of Modern Dance in Saratoga. After graduating from college, York moved to New York City where she continued to study dance with Sanasardo and to take lessons at the Martha Graham and Alvin Ailey schools. In between dance classes, York supported herself by waiting tables and by working as an editorial assistant at a publishing house. In 1970 it was possible for young dancers to survive in New York City, York recounted in a 1996 interview with Elizabeth Zimmer in *Dance Magazine.* Rents were affordable and food was relatively cheap.

York was hired by Paul Taylor in 1972 as an understudy dancer. Her small stature did deter Taylor, who looks for dancers with assertive personalities and unusual physiques. The diminutive York has always been identified as a short dancer, but she never danced small. Taylor recognized York's ability to draw the eye of the observer. With his uncanny ability to find out what makes dancers tick, Taylor used York to great advantage by showcasing her wit, energy, and breathtaking, ground-skimming allegro work. Her abandon in jumps, falls, and runs was also impressive. Taylor's masterpiece, *Esplanade* (1975), saw York engaged in the choreographer's walking, running, skipping, and hopping steps to a Bach score. Other memorable roles included that of the accomplice to Elie Chaib's gangleader in Taylor's droll 1980 work, *Le Sacre du Printemps (The Rehearsal);* a witty performance as the pint-sized General Havoc in Taylor and Charles Ludlum's *Aphrodisiamania;* and a milkmaid who had to fuss with several milk pails—one of which emerged from beneath her costume—in a revival of *Piece Period.* While dancing with the Taylor company, York was married to composer and pianist Donald York who became the musical director of the Paul Taylor Dance Company.

York left the Paul Taylor company in 1985. She appeared in Martha Clarke's dance-theater works *Vienna: Lusthaus* and *The Garden of Earthly Delights.* These performances provided York with a transition from full-time dancing to choreography. When York began to choreograph in earnest, she set her dances on ballet groups rather than modern dance companies. There were several reasons for this, York explained to Zimmer: ballet companies are better established than modern dance companies, and their audiences are larger. They also tend to have more dancers. York also likes to experiment with how ballet dancers use their pointe shoes in rendering modern dance movements. Most of her works are danced

845

Lila York performing *Diggety,* 1979. Photograph © Johan Elbers.

in soft shoes, however. Setting dances on university students has also resulted in happy experiences for York. She appreciates the students' lack of ego and their willingness to try anything. Time is also a factor. York feels that the flexible scheduling that comes from working within a school environment is beneficial to creativity.

York is regarded by many in the dance field as one of America's most promising choreographers. In February 1995 she premiered *Rapture,* a work for twenty student dancers of the Juilliard Dance Ensemble. Reviewing *Rapture* for *Dance Magazine* in 1995, Lynn Garafola stated that the work was "ambitious and large in scale. It is also thrilling, with rushes of movement that animate every corner of the stage and huge, expansive diagonals that infuse it with visual drama." As shown in *Rapture,* York draws on ballet jumps and turns while using the falls and free swinging arms so deeply associated with Paul Taylor's style. She skillfully blends classical ballet's stretched, taut lines with fearless falls and adds backbends, spins, and arabesques to create a seamless, exhilarating whole. Critic Garafola praised York's use of the youthful ensemble and her ability to make use of space in shifting the dancers around in varying patterns. Dance critics were deeply impressed by York's assured, powerful style.

As a choreographer, York delights in moving dancers across space and being emotionally moved. "Dance . . . is not about thinking—it's a visceral response," exclaimed York. She has set dances to music by Prokofiev and Shostakovich. *Celts,* a work to music by the Chieftains and Moving Hearts, was choreographed for the Boston Ballet in March 1996. The music—a combination of bagpipes, whistles, drums, and a percussion section written for the work by Bill Ruyle—was inspired by York's love of Irish culture. On a recent visit to Ireland, York, of Scottish-Irish heritage herself, was stunned by the beauty of the Irish countryside and was touched by the warmth of the people and their strong feelings for the land. She tried to incorporate these sentiments into *Celts.* It will be interesting to see where her talents lead her next.

—Adriane Ruggiero

YURIKO

American dancer and choreographer

Born: Yuriko Kikuchi, 2 February 1920 in San Jose, California; raised in Japan. **Education:** Studied with Konami Ishil in Tokyo. **Career:** Dancer, Konami Ishii Dance Company, 1930-37; Dorothy Lyndall's Junior Dance Company, Los Angeles, 1937-41; interned in Arizona during World War II; dancer, 1944-67, and guest artist since 1967, Martha Graham Company, New York; formed her own dance company, 1960; performed the role of Eliza in the Broadway production of *The King and I,* 1951-54, and in the 1956 film; also appeared in the musical *Flower Drum Song,* 1958.

Roles (selected; with Martha Graham Graham Dance Company)

1944	*Appalachian Spring*
	Imagined Wing
1946	*Cave of the Heart*
1948	*Diversion of Angels*
1952	*Canticle for Innocent Comedians*
1954	*Ardent Song*
1958	*Clytemnestra*
	Embattled Garden

1967	*Cortege of Eagles*
1978	*Equatorial*

Works

1944	*Stubborn*
	Earth Primative
	Troubled Hour
1945	*Images*
	Thin Cry
	The Gift
1946	*Young Memories*
	Shut Not Your Doors
1947	*Tale of Seizure*
1949	*Perpetual Notions*
	Incident
	Servant at the Pillars
	Suite
1954	*Four Windows*
	. . . where the roads . . .
1960	*Shochikubai*
	A Fool's Tale
	In the Glory
	The Ghost
1963	*The Cry*
	Three Dances
	Flowers for Me
	Life of a Tree
	Colors of the Heart
1964	*Conversations*
	The Trapped
	Remembrance
	. . . and the Wind
1965	*Wind Drum*
	Forgotten One
	Wanderers
	Three Dances
1966	*Tragic Memory*
	Celebrations
1967	*Five Characters*
1968	*Strange Landscape*
	Dances for Dancers
	Moss Garden
	Shadowed
	Night Fantasy
1970	*Spirit of the Ink*
	Events I
1971	*Quintet*
	Events II
1972	*Events III*
1978	*Moments*
	City Square
	Epitaphim

Publications

On YURIKO: articles—

Aloff, Mindy, "Family Values: The Legacy of Martha Graham Dwindles," *New Republic,* 11 September 1995.

Gruen, John, "Dance Return to Broadway: Lar Lubovitch, Onto the Stage," *Dance Magazine*, April 1996.

Horosko, Marian, "Dancers Over 40," *Dance Magazine*, January 1996.

Tucker, Marilyn, "What's Ahead for Graham Dancers," *San Francisco Chronicle*, 4 March 1992.

*   *   *

Yuriko Kikuchi, known professionally as Yuriko, is best known for her 50-year association with the Martha Graham Dance Company as a dancer, teacher, coach, and producer of revivals. She is also an independent choreographer and performer, staging concerts with her own company and starring on Broadway.

Born in San Jose, California, in 1920, Yuriko was raised in Japan. She studied dance with Konami Ishii starting at age six, and then toured throughout Asia with the Konami Ishii Dance Company for seven years starting in 1930 at age 10. In 1937 Yuriko returned to the United States, joining Dorothy Lyndall's Junior Dance Company in Los Angeles and performing with the UCLA Dance Group until 1941. During World War II, Yuriko was placed in an internment camp outside of Phoenix, Arizona, where she taught dance. After her release she moved to New York and began studying at the Martha Graham School.

Yuriko joined Graham's company in 1944, where she remained, with a few breaks, until 1994. She soon became a soloist, dancing her first leading role as the Princess in *Serpent Heart*, later known as *Cave of the Heart*, in 1946. She created a number of roles in works from Graham's choreographic peak, including the Moon in *Canticle for Innocent Comedians* (1952), Iphigenia in *Clytemnestra* (1958), and Eve in *The Embattled Garden* (1958). She also danced in the premieres of *Appalachian Spring* (1944) as one of the Followers, *Imagined Wing* (1944), *Dark Meadow* (1946), as one of they who dance together, *Diversion of Angels* (1948), *Ardent Song* (1954), *Cortege of Eagles* (1967), and *Equatorial* (1978). She was also featured in a pas de deux with Bertram Ross in a film about Graham, called *A Dancer's World*. All told, Yuriko danced in the bulk of Graham's repertoire from the mid-1940s through the 1970s.

In her performing days with the Graham company, Yuriko worked with many of the leading modern dancers of the period, including Helen McGehee, Ethel Winter, Bertram Ross, Paul Taylor, Erick Hawkins, Merce Cunningham, Nina Fonaroff, Pearl Lang, May O'Donnell, Stuart Hodes, Mark Ryder, and many others. Like her female Graham colleagues, Yuriko was a strong, lyrical dancer whose individual personality shone through in her performances. Small and compact, her dance style was quick, physical, and with an air of independence. Many of the roles created for her by Graham were of a childlike nature, but she also successfully assumed several roles created by Graham for herself, such as in revivals of *Primitive Mysteries* (1931) and *Dark Meadow* (1946).

Yuriko also had a long career as a choreographer and performer outside of her association with Graham. During leaves from the Graham company, she performed on Broadway, most notably creating the role of Eliza in Jerome Robbins' *The King and I* (1951). She has become closely associated with that musical, dancing the role in the 1956 film, and recreating the choreography for many revivals of the show in the U.S. and Europe. She received solo choreography credit for the 1977 Broadway revival. (Her daughter, Susan Kikuchi, danced the role in the *King and I* for many years after Yuriko retired from it, and teaches Yuriko's choreography to

the casts of newer productions, such as Lar Lubovitch's Broadway staging in 1996.) Yuriko was also featured as a dancer in Carol Haney's *Flower Drum Song*, and choreographed for the play *The Emperor's Nightingale*, both in 1958.

In 1946 Yuriko began her solo concert career, winning the annual dance audition at New York's 92nd Street YMHA and presenting a concert there. In 1960 she staged her first major dance program with her newly formed company at New York City's Phoenix Theatre. She frequently performed in New York and elsewhere thereafter, both in solos and with her company.

Yuriko's choreography has often contained themes focusing on relationships or solitude. Her works were influenced both by Graham and Japanese theater.

Although Yuriko effectively retired from performing in the 1970s, changing her focus to teaching and staging revivals, she remained an important member of Graham's company as a coach and choreographer. Graham had always liked her choreography, and incorporated it into some of her own works, such as *Embattled Garden*, where a duet by Adam and Eve was based on some of Yuriko's work. Yuriko also founded the Martha Graham Ensemble, a junior company composed of apprentices and students from the Martha Graham School, in the early 1980s. They performed works by Graham and by Yuriko.

Yuriko is among the most respected instructors of Graham technique, which she has taught at the Martha Graham School, Rochester University, and Brooklyn College, as well as in seminars in New York and other venues. She has coached guest performers in Graham's works, such as Mikhail Baryshnikov in a revival of *El Penitente*. During the 1980s, Yuriko also staged many acclaimed revivals of Graham pieces, especially from the 1930s and 1940s, including *Primitive Mysteries, Heretic, Steps in the Street* from *Chronicle, Panorama,* and *Celebration* (the latter with other surviving cast members).

Yuriko eventually became associate artistic director of the Martha Graham Dance Company, working under co-directors Ron Protas and Linda Hodes after Graham's death in 1991. In 1994 she left the company because of philosophical differences with Protas, a non-dancer and heir to Martha Graham. After leaving, Yuriko remained active in dance, taking body conditioning sessions with Robert Fitzgerald and joining Dancers Over 40, a performance group for aging professional dancers and choreographers.

—Karen Raugust

ZAMIR, Batya
American dancer and choreographer

Born: Brooklyn, New York. **Education:** Studied with Alwin Nikolais, Gladys Bailin, Phyllis Lamhut, and Murray Louis. **Family:** Married to Richard Van Buren. **Career:** Member, Alwin Nikolais Dance Theatre, 1960s; toured the U.S., Europe, and India with Alwin Nikolais Dance Theatre and Murray Louis Dance Company; began choreographing her own works, 1969; taught at various institutions including New York University, Yale University, Amherst College, Trinity College, Oberlin College, and the School of Visual Arts. **Awards:** Grants from New York State Council on the Arts, the National Endowment of the Arts, and from the Australia Council Visual Art Board.

Works (premiered in New York City unless otherwise noted)

1967	*Tea Ceremony*, Henry Street Playhouse
	One on One, Spencer Memorial Church, Brooklyn
1968	*Attached*, Henry Street Playhouse
	Silence, Henry Street Playhouse
1969	*Releases*, Sensory Overload Studio (SOS)
	Carrys, SOS
	Prances, SOS
	Crawls, SOS
	Releases (duets), SOS
	Shadow Slot Follows, Emanu-El Midtown YMHA
	Slot Changes, Emanu-El YMHA
	Laying Down Rolls, Emanu-El YMHA
	Gravity Falls, Emanu-El YMHA
	Trio Release, Emanu-El YMHA
	Trio Exchange, Emanu-El YMHA
	Direction Changes, Emanu-El YMHA
1970	*Solos and Duets I*, 29 Wooster Street Studio
1971	*Performers For Peace*, Spring Street Gallery
	Solos, School of Visual Arts
	Alicia, Cubicolo Theatre
	Thom Hen, Cubicolo Theatre
	Angel Nel, Cubicolo Theatre
	Kenfish, Cubicolo Theatre
	All Loving, Cubicolo Theatre
	Head Turns, Cubicolo Theatre
	Duo, Cubicolo Theatre
	RSC, Cubicolo Theatre
1972	*Solos and Duets II*, Paula Cooper Gallery
	Two Solo Dances, 22 Green Street Gallery
1973	*Solos* (untitled), West Broadway Dance Studio
	Solos (untitled), Yale University, New Haven, Connecticut
	Sculptural Move, 112 Green Street Gallery
1974	*Botticelli's Revenge*, The Kitchen
	On and Off the Wall and Between the Columns, West Broadway Dance Studio
	Prelude to Botticelli's Revenge or Scar Baby and Two Dicks
	Saturday Morning on Sunday Afternoon, West Broadway Dance Studio
1975	*Collaborations*, Paula Cooper Gallery
	Botticelli's Revenge Revisited, School of Visual Arts
1976	*Doors*, Commissioned by University of Delaware, Wilmington, Delaware
	Wall Work, Commissioned by University of Delaware
	Floor Improv, Commissioned by University of Delaware
	Batons, Commissioned by University of Delaware
	Back Balance, Commissioned by University of Delaware
	Turn Ball, Commissioned by University of Delaware
	Flip Offs, Commissioned by University of Delaware
	Rebound, West Broadway Dance Studio
1977	*Sweet Sensation of Oberlin*, Oberlin College, Oberlin, Ohio
	Red Dance for Betsey Johnson, P.S. 1 (Institute for Art and Urban Resources), Queens
	Horizontals, P.S. 1
	Vertical Climb, P.S. 1
	Air Line Duet, P.S. 1
	Double Loop Swing, P.S. 1

1978	*Air-Lines for Adelaide*, Adelaide Festival, Adelaide, Australia
	Air-Lines for Sydney, Sydney, Australia
	Out of the Blue for New Mexico, The University of New Mexico, Albuquerque
	Out of the Blue for St. Clements, St. Clements Theatre
1979	*Halloween Hang*, Studio 54
1980	*Valentine Loop Swing*, Studio 54
	Coming and Going, Tenth Avenue Dance Studio
	Mat Dance, Tenth Avenue Dance Studio
	Air Lines for Kids, Tenth Avenue Dance Studio
	Air Line Solo, Tenth Avenue Dance Studio
1981	*Outdoors*, Bronx Zoo, Bronx
1982	*Line-Up*, Teatro Spaziozero, Rome, Italy
	Air-Ways, Festival Di Milano, Italy
	Outdoor Excursions, Festival Di Milano, Italy
1983	*Up and Down Column Walk*, P.S. 122
	For My Whole Life I Have Been Folding Clothes, P.S. 122
	Take a Walk in My Shoes, P.S. 122
	Put Your Foot in Your Hand and on Your Knee, P.S. 122
	Up My Sleeve, P.S. 122
1984	*Solo Swivel*, Kamikaze
	Paint Movement, Maryland Art Institute College of Art, Baltimore
1986	*Drawing Field*, Lexington
1987	*Wet Paint*, Art in General Gallery
	Swivel II, Far Rockaway High School
1988	*Memorial Dance for Ronald Bladen*, St. Peter's Lutheran Church
1989	*Air Muse with Dharma Bums*, The Limelight
	I Walk, William Cullen Bryant High School, Long Island
	There Is a River, William Cullen Bryant High School
1990	*Dara Factor I*, William Cullen Bryant High School
	Dara Factor II, William Cullen Bryant High School
	Time of My Life, William Cullen Bryant High School
	Gymnopodies, Pier 41, Brooklyn
	Inspiration, Pier 41, Brooklyn
1991	*Air Lines*, Brooklyn Friends School
	Swivel, Brooklyn Friends School
1992	*Walking on Air*, Brooklyn Children's Museum
1993	*Air Lines*, Henry Street Settlement Playhouse Centennial Celebration

Other works include: *Individual Turns, Circles to Turns, Circle Exchange, Slot Exchanges, Dancing Solo, Off the Wall, Dance-Music Concert.*

Publications

On ZAMIR: books—

McDonagh, Don, *The Rise and Fall and Rise of Modern Dance*, Chicago, 1990.
Willis, J., editor, *Dance World*, New York, 1966 and 1979.

On ZAMIR: articles—

Anderson, Jack, "Batya Zamir in *Coming and Going*," *New York Times*, 23 June 1980.
"Batya Zamir," in *Biographical Dictionary of Modern Dance*, by Barbara Naomi Cohen-Stratyner, New York, 1982.

"Batya Zamir," in *The Complete Guide to Modern Dance* by Don McDonagh, New York, 1976.

Carroll, Noël, "Air Dancing," *Tulane Drama Review*, March 1975.

*   *   *

Dancer and choreographer Batya Zamir has focused on two primary elements in her work: first, she is concerned with dancing as an everyday activity that anyone can do—many of her dances are created for adults and children without formal dance training; and second, she is known for her aerial dances, performed sometimes on trapeze-like hanging ropes designed by the sculptor Richard Van Buren and sometimes on architectural features.

Zamir was born in Brooklyn, New York. She studied dance at the Alwin Nikolais school, as well as with Gladys Bailin, Phyllis Lamhut, Murray Louis, Mimi Garrard, Rachel Fibish, and Joy Boutilier. She joined the Alwin Nikolais Dance Theatre in the 1960s, where she remained for five years, touring with his and Murray Louis' companies throughout the U.S., Europe, and India. Zamir's own choreography has been influenced by Alwin Nikolais in that both create works that are entertaining as well as abstract.

Zamir began staging her own works in 1969. She became interested in creating dances to be performed by people who were not dancers, and who were of a variety of sizes, shapes and ages. She was married to the sculptor Richard Van Buren, and began to teach dance movements to people in their social circle who were primarily artists rather than dancers. She then featured these students in performances, which were presented at nontraditional spaces such as gymnasiums. Her choreography includes simple movements such as carrying, tumbling, jumping and follow-the-leader (where the other performers try to disrupt the leader). She avoids the concept of dance as "art," but rather sets up movement exercises that are akin to games, which are performed improvisationally during the piece.

Her performers wear street clothing and are of all physical types, with some performing gracefully and others vigorously. They are characterized by their energy and humor, and have been described by critic Don McDonagh as always "tinglingly alive." Men and women perform the same steps, with the only differentiation occurring as a result of varying size and strength. Her works' unstructured quality makes them sometimes seem like practice or a game among friends rather than a performance.

One of her works, *Carrys* (1969), is typical of her early choreography in many ways. It was performed in a gym by men and women of various sizes. The men and women pick each other up, with everyone picking each other up at least once. The contrast between the ease with which a large man picks up a small woman and the awkwardness of the reverse situation characterizes the piece. The intent is not to look professional or even practiced. Another focus of Zamir's body of work is air dancing. These are sequences performed by herself or other performers—some trained and some not, and including both adults and children—on suspended soft sculptures designed by Van Buren, that serve as trapezes. The dancers hang from them and perform movements akin to gymnastics, using the sculptures to frame their bodies. The sculptures have been constructed from ropes, rubber cords, wires, or a combination of these materials. Unlike other aerial dancers, Zamir does not mind if the audience reacts as they would at a circus. The theatricality inherent in trapeze work is part of the experience.

Zamir frequently combines air dancing with floor dancing (often using a wall or scaffolding as a support, or even as a sort of partner) within the same dance. In fact, her pieces can be performed on the façades of buildings, on ceilings, doors, windows and columns; each dance is designed for the space in which it is performed. Her works, particularly the air dancing portions, are referred to as antiillusionist, meaning that, rather than trying to portray beautiful movements while making it look easy, she wants the audience to focus on the difficulty of what she is doing and on how her body and the materials she relies on interact with one another. One of Zamir's objectives is to place the audience's attention on the coordination, strength, and endurance required to perform the movements. She wants viewers to recognize that her actions test the limits of the human body. Viewers focus on each muscle and how difficult it has to work in order for the element to succeed. Zamir's movements are precise, and her facility at working with her environment is one of the main sources of interest in her pieces. Her works are not intellectual, but concerned with the physical mechanics of movement. She often contrasts certain actions with others so that audiences can perceive the different muscles required for each, and focuses on non-natural movements that emphasize the body's abilities. Zamir sometimes removes articles of clothing during her pieces, until she is completely nude, which allows each muscle in the body to be clearly seen. As the muscles tremble and bulge, the audience's perception of how the body works is heightened. Her work is often improvised; she rehearses a group of movements appropriate to the specific environment, but does not choreograph the order in which they occur.

Coming and Going, staged in 1980, is typical of her combined air and floor works. It involved the use of eight children and two adults (including Zamir and Rodney Clark). The children have mats strapped to their backs, and perform gymnastics and trapeze work on Van Buren-designed cords. Zamir completes a duet with Clark as well as a solo against a wall and one on the ropes. Held in a gymnasium, the piece is informal, with the dancers applauding each other's efforts. Some of her many works, which have been performed both indoors and outdoors throughout the U.S. and in Italy and Australia, include *Releases, Prances,* and *Crawls* (all 1969); *Individual Turns, Circles to Turns* and *Directional Changes* (all 1971); *Dancing Solo* (1973); *Prelude to Botticelli's Revenge or Scar Baby and the Two Dicks, Saturday Morning on Sunday Afternoon* and *Prelude* (all 1974); *Gymnopodies* (1990); and *Air Lines* (1993). Zamir has also taught dance at various institutions, including New York University, Yale, Amherst, Trinity, Oberlin and the School of Visual Arts. She has received grants from the New York State Council on the Arts, the National Endowment for the Arts and the Australia Council Visual Art Board.

—Karen Raugust

ZOLLAR, Jawole Willa Jo

American dancer, choreographer, educator, and company director

Born: Willa Jo Zollar, 21 December 1950 in Kansas City, Missouri. **Education:** Early dance training in Kansas City with Katherine Dunham student Joseph Stevenson; B.A. in dance, University of Missouri, Kansas City, 1975; M.F.A. in dance, Florida State University, Tallahassee, 1979; studied with Dianne McIntyre, New York, 1980. **Career:** Dancer, Dianne McIntyre's Sounds in

Urban Bush Women: *Nyabinghi Dreamtime*. Photograph © Johan Elbers.

Motion, New York City, 1980-83; founder/artistic director, dance/ theater company Urban Bush Woman (UBW), 1984—; UBW performed in New York area and Washington, D.C., 1984; toured the U.S., 1985-86; began international touring, 1986; professor of dance, Florida State University, Tallahassee, Florida, 1996—; keynote speaker at meetings of the following organizations: Dance Critics Association Annual Meeting, 1990; New England Presenters Conference, 1994; Association of Performing Arts Presenters, 1995; California Arts Council, Governor's Conference on the Arts, 1997.

Awards: National Endowment for the Arts choreography fellowships, 1988-90; New York Foundation for the Arts fellowship, 1984; New York Dance and Performance Award ("Bessie"), 1992; *Worlds of Thought* Resident Scholar, Mankato State University, Minnesota, 1993-94; Capezio Foundation Dance Award, 1994; Who's Who in America, 1995; Regent Lecturer, Department of World Arts and Culture, University of California, Los Angeles, 1995-96.

Works (all choreography by Jawole Willa Jo Zollar in collaboration with company members of Urban Bush Women)

1984 *River Songs* (mus. live a cappella vocalizations), Ethnic Folk Arts Center, New York City

 Life Dance . . . The Fool's Journey (mus. Carl Riley), Aaron Davis Hall, Bronx, New York

1985 *Working for Free* (no mus.), New Heritage Theater, New York City

1986 *Anarchy, Wild Women and Dinah* (mus. South Eastern Coastal Islands; traditional African American; Tiye Giraud), Clark Center Summer Dance Festival

 Girlfriends, an adaptation from *Anarchy, Wild Women and Dinah* (no mus.), Clark Summer Dance Festival, New York City

 Madness (text from *Vibration Cooking* by Verta Mae Smart-Grosevenor), Clark Center Summer Dance Festival, New York City

 LifeDance I . . . The Magician (The Return of She) (mus. Tiye Giraud and Edwina Lee Tyler) P.S.1, Institute for Art and Urban Resources, Long Island City, New York

1987 *Bitter Tongue* (mus. Junior "Gabu" Wedderburn), The Yard, Chilmark, Massachusetts

1988 *Heat* (mus. Craig Harris), Montpellier Danse '88, Montpellier, France

 Lipstick, an adaptation from *Heat* (text ThoughtMusic: Laurie Carlos, Jessica Hagedorn, and Robbie McCauley), Montpellier Danse '88, Montpellier, France

Shelter, an adaptation from *Heat* (mus. Junior "Gabu" Wedderburn; text Hattie Gossett and Laurie Carlos), Montpellier Danse '88, Montpellier, France

LifeDance II . . . The Papess (mus. Tiye Giraud and Edwina Lee Tyler), The Kitchen, New York

1989   *I Don't Know, But I Been Told, If You Keep on Dancin' You Never Grow Old* (mus. David Pleasant), American Festival at Cornell University, Ithaca, New York

1990   *Praise House* w/Pat Hall-Smith (mus. Carl Riley; mus. dir. Tiye Giraud; text Angelyn DeBord), Spoleto Festival U.S.A., Charleston, South Carolina

1992   *LifeDance III . . . The Empress (Womb Wars)* (text Zollar), Eisenhower Theater at Penn State University, State College, Pennsylvania

1994   *Nyabinghi Dreamtime* (mus. Junior "Gabu" Wedderburn, the company and the Revival, Kumina, and Rastafarian traditional music), Joyce Theater, New York

Vocal Attack (mus. company vocalizations), Krannert Center, Urbana, Illinois

1995   *Batty Moves* (mus. concept Zollar; percussion, Junior "Gabu" Wedderburn), DanceAfrica, Miami, Florida

BONES AND ASH: A Gilda Story (mus. Toshi Reagon), Hancher Auditorium, Iowa City, Iowa

1996   *Transitions* (mus. Michael Wimberly; text Zollar), Kentucky Center for the Arts, Louisville, Kentucky

1997   *Self Portrait* (text Carl Hancock Rux), Krannert Center for the Arts, Urbana, Illinois

Publications

On ZOLLAR: books—

Black Dance, Woodstock, New York, 1989.

Banes, Sally, *Writing Dancing in the Age of Postmodernism,* Hanover, New Hampshire, 1994.

Gere, David, et al, eds., *LOOKING OUT, Perspectives on Dance and Criticism in a Multicultural World,* Schirmer Books, 1995.

O'Brien, Mark, and Little, Craig, eds., *Reimaging America: The Arts of Social Change,* New Society Publishers, 1990.

On ZOLLAR: articles—

Adler, Andrew, "Troupe Is a Whirlwind of Motion, Drumming," *Courier-Journal* (Louisville Kentucky), 12 January 1997.

Dunning, Jennifer, "Things Just Go from Hot to Hotter," *New York Times,* 16 December 1995.

Gladstone, Valerie, "Finding New Life Amid the Vampires," *New York Times,* 10 November 1996.

Greaves, McLean, "Urban Bush Women: Poetry in Motion," *Essence,* July 1995.

Patrick, K. C., "Capezio Award to Urban Bush Women," *Dance Teacher Now,* May/June 1994.

Shange, Ntozake, "Urban Bush Women: Dances for the Voiceless," *New York Times,* 8 September 1991.

Sunder, Madhavi, "Urban Bush Women: Dancing Their Politics," *Ms. Magazine,* March/April 1994.

Films and Videotapes

Praise House (dir. Julie Dash), KTCA-TV's *Alive from Off-Center,* 1991.

*   *   *

Jawole Willa Jo Zollar is one of a generation of so-called postmodern or new dance choreographers who emerged in the United States during the 1980s and one of a distinguished group of African American choreographers who have made major contributions to 20th century concert dance. Zollar is in the lineage of, among others, choreographer and anthropologist Katherine Dunham. From ages seven to 17 Zollar studied with Dunham's disciple Joseph Stevenson. After receiving B.A. and M.F.A. degrees in dance she spent the next three years, from 1980 to 1983, working and performing with Dianne McIntyre's Sounds in Motion in New York. In 1984 Zollar founded Urban Bush Women, the first major dance company consisting of all African American women dancers.

Zollar's work explores African American sacred and secular life and is a synthesis of numerous influences: modern dance (including Dunham, Graham, Cunningham, and Limón techniques), Afro-Cuban, Haitian, and Congolese traditions, among others. She has been referred to as an anthropologist for her astute observations of African American and Caribbean life. As much as she transforms ordinary activities into art Zollar also masterfully illuminates the art of the everyday. In Zollar's choreography, double-Dutch jump ropers, cheerleaders, and gossiping girlfriends are featured for their lack of self-conscious artistry. Playwright and poet Ntozake Shange wrote in the *New York Times* in 1991, "Chants of Carolinian drill teams or worshipers of the Yoruba deity Yemaya, the fancy footwork of double-Dutch jumpers or lindy hoppers, the attitudes of a biker's gal or your grandmother strolling the porch—any one of these specters may jump out during a performance of Urban Bush Women."

Zollar's artistic direction had firmly taken hold by the time she began Urban Bush Women. Weaving vocalizations, a cappella song, story telling, and social commentary together in a dance-theater that is as new and contemporary as it is familiar, Urban Bush Women defy strict categorization. The work often draws inspiration from the experiences of women of color living in the United States. Even when the work isn't about women's issues per se, the company of women of color tells a powerful and poetic story. Zollar encourages her dancers' individuality in collective dance-making. Her pieces are often creative collaborations with company members who bring their diverse experiences, emotions, humor, songs, and movement styles to the work.

Zollar wanted to create a dance company that showed African-American culture in a way that resembled how blacks express themselves "when not in the presence of whites . . . I wanted to lift the veil." To that end, according to an article in 1994 in *Ms.* magazine, she adapted "the structures that come out of the African American community: church testifying, emotional energy shaping the form, and the rawness of that form, like you have in jazz." In addition, Zollar's humor, musicality, and extraordinary sense of timing are evident in her solos and structured improvisations. In Sally Banes' 1994 *Writing Dancing in the Age of Postmodernism,* Zollar called improvisation "a spiritual philosophy as well as a movement tool" that includes "the Marxist concept of collectivity, the African notion of cooperative tribal action, [and] the Native American council."

Girlfriends (1986) is a youthful, exuberant piece. The work portrays a group of giggling, gossiping girls whose spontaneity and lack of self-consciousness fill the theater with contagious giddiness and laughter even though the entire piece is performed in silence. *Shelter* (1988) effectively communicates the human and political issues surrounding homelessness. With text by poets Laurie Carlos, Hattie Gossett, and Carl Hancock Rux, the piece works as both dance-theater and harrowing social commentary. After spending

Jawole Willa Jo Zollar. Photograph © Lois Greenfield.

time in Jamaica, Zollar and the company created *Nyabinghi Dreamtime* (1994), a dramatization of a traditional Kumina ritual. *Batty Moves* (1995) is another Jamaican-inspired piece. "*Batty* is Jamaican slang for *buttocks,* and in one section of the piece, the dancers moved in unison with their backs to the audience, while the body parts in question twitched and rolled in flirtatious harmony with the beat of percussionist Michael Wimberly's live drumming," wrote Tresca Weinstein in the *Albany Times Union* in 1997.

The members of UBW have been pioneers in community arts activism, striving to encourage grass-roots development of artistic and critical tools on the premise that the arts are a catalyst for social change. Their long-term residencies are one aspect of a socially and culturally conscious aesthetic that has become a hallmark of many dance companies and performing artists in the last decade. Zollar and UBW live and work in various communities for several weeks at a time teaching dance, improvisation, and conducting community workshops such as "Survival through Cultural Traditions." In July 1997 UBW started a new project, the Summer Dance Institute: *A New Dancer for a New Society—Developing a Critical Understanding of Social Context and Cultural Traditions as an Integral Part of Dance Training.* Based in Tallahassee, Florida, the Summer Dance Institute is a natural outgrowth of UBW's community work over the past decade. Through it they hope to foster recognition of personal cultural and historical contexts and to show how performance can address personal and social issues.

Since 1984 Zollar has created 21 works, including three important evening-length works: *Song of Lawino* (1988), a collaboration with composer Edwina Lee Tyler and director Valeria Vasileski and based on the poem by Ugandan writer Okot p'Bitek; *Praise House* (1990), with co-choreographer Pat Hall-Smith, composer Carl Riley, and writer Angelyn DeBord; and *BONES AND ASH: A Gilda Story* (1995), adapted by Jewelle Gomez from her book and co-directed by Steve Kent with original music by composer/lyricist Toshi Reagon. An adaption of *Praise House,* directed by filmmaker Julie Dash, was aired in 1991 as part of KTCA-TV's *Alive from Off-Center.* Zollar recently choreographed Anna Deveare Smith's new theater work *HOUSE ARREST: First Edition* (1997).

—J. Hussie-Taylor

ZÜLLIG, Hans
Swiss dancer, choreographer, and educator

Born: Rorschach, Switzerland, 1 February 1914. **Education:** Attended college for two years; began professional dance studies in 1931 at the Folkwangschule in Essen, Germany, with Kurt Jooss and Sigurd Leeder; studied Spanish dance with Juan Martinez in Paris. **Career:** Dancer, Ballet Jooss, 1935-47, Sadler's Wells Theatre Ballet, 1948-49, Jooss' Folkwang Tanztheater, 1949-52; Zurich Ballet; 1953-54; teacher, Essen Folkwangschule, 1954-56; also served as ballet master (with Jooss) at the Dusseldorf Ballet; teacher, choreographer, and dancer at Chilean University, Santiago, 1956-61; rejoined the teaching department of the Folkwangschule, 1961; appointed the director of its dance department, 1969; served in this post until his retirement in 1983; continued to give master classes until he fell ill in the summer of 1992. **Died:** Essen, Germany, 8 November 1992.

Roles

1935	The Young Man, *The Big City* (debut)
	The Young Soldier, *The Green Table*
	Marquis, *Ballade*
	Her admirer, *A Ball in Old Vienna*
	Johann Strauss, Tonight!
1939	Prince, *A Spring Tale*
	Mysterious companion, *Prodigal Son*
	Philippe, *Chronica*
1943	Armando, *Company at the Manor*
1948	Poet, *Selina*
1949	*Sea Change*
	Les Sylphides
	Le Carnaval
	The Gods-Go-a-Begging

Works

1945	*Le Bosquet*
1951	*Fantasie*
1958	*Cupid and the Loves of the Ballet Master*

Publications

On ZÜLLIG: books—

Coton, A. V., *The New Ballet: Kurt Jooss and His Work,* London, 1946.

On ZÜLLIG: articles—

Ballet International, February 1993.
Dance and Dancers, March 1993.
The Dancing Times, December 1933.
The Dancing Times, May 1935.
The Dancing Times, January, 1993.

*   *   *

Hans Züllig's long career spanned dance styles, countries, and continents. An expressive, handsome and versatile dancer, he was one of the most important interpreters of the work of the German choreographer and social commentator Kurt Jooss, whose work successfully melded classical and modern dance in theatrical ballets with striking contemporary ideas. Züllig's breadth of performing style was vast. Züllig could be convincing as a gentle soldier in one ballet and starkly contrast this with a portrayal of an insidious war profiteer in another. He could be a romantic Elizabethan nobleman in yet another work. So great was his impact on stage that Peggy van Praagh (a dancer and one-time ballet mistress of the Sadler's Wells Theatre Ballet), once remarked on seeing Züllig dance, "I would rather see one gesture of Hans' than all the virtuosity in the world." Züllig was also an important teacher. Peter Wright, former director of the Birmingham Royal Ballet and a student of Kurt Jooss, recalled how Züllig "knew how to pass on to others amazing control, breadth of movement, expression, light and shade and dynamic energy."

Born in neutral Switzerland just before the outbreak of World War I, Züllig came of age just as Europe was to become embroiled in another bloody conflict. In 1931 he was in Essen, a city in the Ruhr district of Germany, studying with Jooss, then head of the Folkwang Tanztheater-Studio. Jooss' dance style was rooted in the space-movement theories of Rudolf von Laban which promoted a kind of movement free from artificial conventions. Between 1929 and 1934 Jooss choreographed numerous ballets for his dance group. Jooss' ballets were presented against black backcloths with a minimum of costumes and scenery but with the use of dramatic lighting. The emphasis was on the emotional feeling of the characters. The culminating work of the company was the 1932 masterpiece, *The Green Table*. A bitter, satiric ballet, this is Jooss' finest work; its antiwar message remains powerful more than six decades after its premiere. *The Green Table* was given its first performance at the International Dance Competition in Paris and won first prize. Züllig was in the original 1932 company although only as a member of the ensemble.

When Jooss and his partner, Sigurd Leeder, emigrated to England in 1934 (out of fear for the fate of Jewish company members), Züllig went with them. He performed as a soloist and later as principal dancer with the Folkwang Tanzbuhne (renamed Ballet Jooss) from 1935 to 1947 during its residence in Devonshire, England, and later in Cambridge. Züllig made his professional debut with the Ballet Jooss in September 1935 in London. His dancing was noted for its power and drama and also its elegance. When Jooss set up operations in Devonshire, England, operating as a cooperative, Züllig was one of the student-dancers who took part in collaborative classes. In these sessions, students worked with their teachers in devising movements according to a theme. Jooss' approach was to take advantage of a dancer's personality in constructing a part around him or her. Züllig was a beneficiary of this approach as were other dancers of the company. Züllig made a heartbreaking Young Soldier in *The Green Table* but also had great impact as the Profiteer in the same ballet. Züllig is most remembered for another role from this period: the Young Man who loses his girlfriend to a rich libertine in Jooss' ballet, *The Big City. The Big City* is reputed to be the first ballet with a socially critical point of view, depicting the loneliness of urban people. Züllig's melancholy force (he had striking, intense eyes), in this work was unforgettable.

In 1945 Züllig created his own work for Ballet Jooss. It was entitled *Le Bosquet* and was a ballet in one act to music by Jean Philippe Rameau. Noelle de Mosa and Züllig danced the leading roles. In this work, the heroine calls up memories of a lost lover.

Six years later he followed this work with another ballet entitled *Fantasie.* As a choreographer, Züllig's work was criticized for being formless and reliant more on charm than structure. When Jooss disbanded his troupe (due to financial troubles) in 1947, Züllig had to find other engagements. He joined the Sadler's Wells Theatre Ballet (the precursor of the Royal Ballet) as a principal dancer and danced with that company from 1948 to 1949. During this time he appeared in the company revivals of the Michel Fokine ballets *Les Sylphides* and *Le Carnaval,* in Ninette De Valois' *The Gods Go a-Begging,* and Andree Howard's *Selina* (1948). He also danced in John Cranko's first major work for SWTB, *Sea Change* (1949). Although his stay with SWTB was brief, Züllig was a valuable and versatile member of the company. His ability to change himself into each character left viewers spellbound.

In 1949 Züllig returned to Germany with Jooss, who started to reorganize his company. It was now called Folkwang Tanztheater. The company did not last long, however. It toured postwar Germany and then appeared in London at the Sadler's Wells Theater before disbanding in 1953. Züllig was busy as both a dancer and teacher during these hectic years. From 1949 to 1952 he danced with the Folkwang Tanztheater in Essen and from 1953 to 1954 with the Zurich Ballet in his native Switzerland. He took up simultaneous positions in Germany in the 1950s: teaching at the Essen Folkwangschule from 1954 to 1956 and also acting as ballet master (with Jooss) at the Dusseldorf State Opera Ballet. From 1956 to 1961, Züllig taught Jooss-Leeder technique in Santiago, Chile, where former Jooss dancer Ernst Uthoff had settled and started a dance school as part of the University of Chile. This school eventually became the Chilean National Ballet. Züllig returned to Essen and the Folkwangschule in 1961. During the 1960s he and other Jooss dancers and students from the masterclasses of the Folkwangschule occasionally gave performances. *The Green Table,* Jooss' trademark ballet, was their most often performed work. In 1969 Züllig succeeded Jooss as the head of the dance department of the Folkwangschule. Reinhild Hoffman and Pina Bausch were among his pupils. He remained in this post until his retirement in 1983. On his death in 1992, one writer described him as "the poet of the dance."

—Adriane Ruggiero

BIBLIOGRAPHY

Abeele, Maarten Vanden. *Pina Bausch.* Edition Plume, 1996.

Adair, Christy. *Women and Dance: Sylphs and Sirens.* New York: New York University Press, 1992.

Adshead-Lansdale, Janet and June Layson, editors. *Dance History: An Introduction.* Revised and updated 2nd edition, London and New York: Routledge, 1994.

Ailey, Alvin, with A. Peter Bailey. *Revelations: The Autobiography of Alvin Ailey.* New York: Birch Lane Press, 1995.

Anderson, Jack. *The American Dance Festival.* Durham, North Carolina: Duke University Press, 1987.

———. *Ballet and Modern Dance: A Concise History.* Pennington, New Jersey, 1992.

———. *Choreography Observed.* Iowa City, Iowa: University of Iowa Press, 1987.

———. *Dance.* New York: Newsweek Books, 1974.

———. *The World of Modern Dance: Art without Boundaries.* Iowa City, Iowa: University of Iowa Press, 1997.

Armitage, Merle. *Dance Memoranda,* edited by Edwin Corle. New York: Duell, Sloan and Pearce, 1949.

———. *Martha Graham.* Los Angeles: privately printed, 1937, reprinted Brooklyn: Dance Horizons, 1966.

Au, Susan. *Ballet and Modern Dance.* London: Thames & Hudson, 1988.

Bach, Rudolf. *Das Mary Wigman-Werk.* Dresden, 1933.

Banes, Sally. *Democracy's Body: Judson Dance Theater 1962-64.* Durham, North Carolina: Duke University Press, 1995.

———. *Terpsichore in Sneakers: Post-Modern Dance.* Boston: Houghton-Mifflin, 1980.

Birringer, Johannes. *Theatre, Theory, Postmodernism.* Bloomington and Indianapolis: Indiana University Press, 1991.

Blom, Lynne Anne, and L. Tarin Chaplin. *The Intimate Act of Choreography.* Pittsburgh, 1982.

Boaz, Franziska. *The Function of Dance in Human Society.* New York: Boaz School, 1944.

Bodenwiser, Gertrud. *The New Dance.* Vaucluse, Australia: Rondo Studios/M. Cuckson, n.d.

Bopp, Mary S. *Research in Dance: A Guide to Resources.* New York and Toronto: G.K. Hall and Company, 1993.

Brandenburg, Hans. *Der moderne Tanz.* Munich, 1921.

Brown, Jean Morrison, editor, *The Vision of Modern Dance.* Princeton, New Jersey: Princeton Book Company, 1979.

Cage, John. *Silence.* Middletown, Conneticut: Wesleyan University Press, 1961.

Cass, Joan. *Dancing through History.* Englewood Cliffs, New Jersey: Prentice Hall, 1993.

Chujoy, Anatole. *Dance Encyclopedia.* New York: A.S. Barnes and Co., Inc., 1949, revised and enlarged by Anatole Chujoy and P.W. Manchester, New York: Simon and Schuster, 1967.

Clarke, Mary, and Clement Crisp. *The History of Dance.* New York, Crown, 1981.

———. *London Contemporary Dance Theatre.* London: Dance Books, 1989.

Clarke, Mary, and David Vaughan, editors, *The Encyclopedia of Dance and Ballet.* New York: G.P. Putnam's Sons, 1977.

Coe, Robert. *Dance in America.* New York, 1985.

Cohen, Selma Jeanne. *Dance as a Theatre Art: Source Readings in Dance History from 1581 to the Present.* New York: Dodd, Mead & Co., 1974.

———. *Doris Humphrey: An Artist First.* Middletown, Conneticut: Wesleyan University Press, 1972.

———. *Next Week, Swan Lake: Reflections on Dance and Dances.* Middletown, Conneticut: Wesleyan University Press, 1982.

Cohen, Selma Jeanne, editor, *The International Encyclopedia of Dance.* Six volumes, New York: Oxford University Press, 1998.

———, editor, *The Modern Dance: Seven Statements of Belief.* Middletown, Conneticut: Wesleyan University Press, 1966.

Cohen-Stratyner, Barbara Naomi. *Biographical Dictionary of Dance.* New York: Schirmer Books, 1982.

Copeland, Roger and Marshall Cohen, editors. *What Is Dance?* New York: Oxford University Press, 1983.

Croce, Arlene. *Afterimages.* New York: Alfred A. Knopf, 1978.

———. *Going to the Dance.* New York: Alfred A. Knopf, 1982.

———. *Sight Lines.* New York, 1987.

Cunningham, Merce. *Changes: Notes on Choreography.* New York: Something Else Press, 1968.

Cunningham, Merce, and Jacqueline Lesschaeve. *The Dancer and the Dance.* New York and London, 1980, reprinted 1985.

Dance Notation Bureau. *Doris Humphrey: The Collected Works, Vol. I.* New York: Dance Notation Bureau Press, 1978.

de Mille, Agnes. *America Dances.* New York: Macmillan Company, 1980.

———. *The Book of the Dance.* New York: Golden Press, 1963.

———. *The Life and Work of Martha Graham.* New York, 1991.

Denby, Edwin. *Dance Writings.* New York, 1986

———. *Dancers, Buildings and People in the Street.* New York: Popular Library, 1965.

———. *Looking at the Dance.* New York: Horizon Press, 1949.

Desti, Mary. *The Untold Story: The Life of Isadora Duncan 1921-1927.* New York: Horace Liveright, 1929.

Dreier, Katherine Sophie. *Shawn the Dancer.* London: J.M. Dent & Son, Ltd., 1933.

Duncan, Irma. *Duncan Dancer.* Middletown, Conneticut: Wesleyan University Press, 1966.

———. *Isadora Duncan: Pioneer in the Art of Dance.* New York: New York Public Library, 1958.

———. *The Technique of Isadora Duncan.* New York: Kamin Publishers, 1937, reprinted Brooklyn: Dance Horizons, 1970.

Duncan, Isadora. *The Art of the Dance.* New York: Theatre Arts Books, 1928, reprinted 1970.

———. *My Life.* New York: Boni & Liveright, 1927, reprinted 1955.

Dunning, Jennifer. *Alvin Ailey: A Life in Dance.* New York: Addison Wesley, 1996.

Durkin, Kathleen, and Paul Levesque, editors. *Catalog of Dance Films,* compiled by Susan Braun and Dorothy H. Currie. New York: Dance Films Association, Inc., 1974.

Ellfeldt, Lois V. *A Primer for Choreographers.* Palo Alto, California: National Press Books, 1967.

Ellis, Havelock. *Dance of Life.* Boston, Houghton Mifflin, 1923.

Emery, Lynne Fauley. *Black Dance in the United States from 1619 to 1970.* Palo Alto, California: National Press Books, 1972.

Forti, Simone. *Handbook in Motion.* Halifax, Nova Scotia: Press of Nova Scotia College of Art and Design, 1973.

Foster, Susan Leigh. *Reading Dancing: Bodies and Subjects in Contemporary American Dance.* Berkeley, Los Angeles, and London, 1986.

Fuller, Loie. *Fifteen Years of a Dancer's Life.* Boston: Small, Maynard & Co., 1913, reprinted Brooklyn: Dance Horizons, 1976.

Getz, Leslie. *Dancers and Choreographers: A Selected Bibliography.* Wakfield, Rhode Island and London: Asphodel Press, 1995.

Goldberg, RoseLee. *Performance: Live Art 1909 to the Present.* London: Thames & Hudson, 1979.

Gopal, Ram. *Indian Dancing.* London: Phoenix House, 1951.

Graham, Martha. *The Notebooks of Martha Graham,* introduction by Nancy Wilson Ross. New York: Harcourt, Brace, Jovanovich, 1973.

Grayburn, Patricia, editor. *Gertrud Bodenwieser: A Celebratory Monograph on the 100th Anniversary of Her Birth.* Guildford, Surrey, England: University of Surrey Press, 1990.

Gruen, John. *People Who Dance: 22 Dancers Tell Their Own Stories.* Princeton, New Jersey: Princeton Book Company, 1988.

H'Doubler, Margaret. *Dance: A Creative Art Experience.* New York: Appleton-Century-Crofts, 1940, reprinted Madison: University of Wisconsin Press, 1959, and 1966.

Hering, Doris. *Twenty-Five Years of American Dance.* New York, Orthwine, 1951.

Highwater, Jamake. *Dance: Rituals of Experience.* New York: A. & W. Publishers, 1978.

Hodgson, Moira. *Quintet: Five American Dance Companies.* New York: William Morrow, 1976.

Horst, Louis, and Carol Russell. *Modern Forms in Relation to the Other Arts.* San Francisco: Impulse Publications, 1961, reprinted 1963.

———. *Pre-Classic Forms.* New York: Kamin Dance Publishers, 1953, reprinted Brooklyn: Dance Horizons, 1968.

Humphrey, Doris. *The Art of Making Dances,* edited by Barbara Pollack. New York and Toronto: Rinehart & Company, 1959, reprinted Grove Press, 1962.

Jamison, Judith, and Howard Kaplan. *Dancing Spirit: An Autobiography.* New York: Doubleday, 1993.

Johnston, Jill. *Marmalade Me.* New York: E.P. Dutton, 1971.

Jordan, Stephanie. *Striding Out: Aspects of Contemporary and New Dance in Britain.* London: Dance Books, 1992.

Jowitt, Deborah. *Dance Beat: Selected Views and Reviews 1967-1976.* New York: Marcel Dekker, Inc., 1977.

———. *The Dance in Mind.* Boston, 1985.

———. *Time and the Dancing Image.* New York: William Morrow, 1988.

Kaprelian, Mary H., editor, *Aesthetics for Dancers: A Selected Annotated Bibliography.* Washington, D.C.: American Alliance for Health, Physical Education and Recreation, 1976.

Kendall, Elizabeth. *Where She Danced.* New York: Knopf, 1979.

Klosty, James, editor. *Merce Cunningham.* New York: Saturday Review Press, E.P. Dutton, 1975.

Koner, Pauline. *Solitary Song.* Durham, North Carolina and London: Duke University Press, 1989.

Kostelanetz, Richard, editor. *Merce Cunningham: Dancing in Space and Time: Essays 1944-1992.* Pennington, New Jersey, 1992.

Kraus, Richard. *History of the Dance.* Englewood Cliffs, New Jersey: Prentice-Hall, Inc., 1969.

Kreemer, Connie. *Further Steps: Fifteen Choreographers on Modern Dance.* New York: Harper & Row, 1987.

Kriegsman, Sali Ann. *Modern Dance in America: The Bennington Years.* Boston: G.K. Hall, 1981.

Laban, Rudolf. *Choreutics,* edited by Lisa Ullman. London: MacDonald & Evans, 1966.

———. *A Life for Dance.* New York: Theatre Arts Books, 1975.

———. *The Mastery of Movement.* London: MacDonald & Evans, 1960.

———. *Principles of Dance and Movement Notation.* London: MacDonald & Evans, 1956.

———. *Gymnastik und Tanz.* Oldenburg, 1926.

Lämmel, Rudolf. *Der moderne Tanz.* Berlin, 1928.

Leatherman, Leroy. *Martha Graham: Portrait of the Lady as an Artist.* New York: Alfred A. Knopf, 1966.

Lewis, Daniel. *The Illustrated Dance Technique of José Limón.* New York: Harper & Row, 1984.

Limón, José. *José Limón: An Unfinished Memoir,* edited by Lynn Garafola. Middletown, Conneticut: Wesleyan University Press, 1998.

Livet, Anne, editor. *Contemporary Dance.* New York: Abbeville Press, 1978.

Lloyd, Margaret. *The Borzoi Book of Modern Dance.* New York: Alfred A. Knopf, 1949, reprinted Brooklyn: Dance Horizons, 1970.

Long, Richard. *The Black Tradition in American Dance.* New York: Rizzoli International Publications Inc., 1989.

Louis, Murray. *Inside Dance.* New York: St. Martin's Press, 1980.

Lyle, Cynthia. *Dancers on Dancing.* New York and London: Drake Publishers, 1977.

MacDougall, Allan Ross. *Isadora: A Revolutionary in Art and Love.* New York: Thomas Nelson & Sons, 1960.

MacTavish, Shona Dunlop. *An Ecstasy of Purpose: The Life and Art of Gertrud Bodenwieser.* Dunedin, New Zealand: Shona Dunlop MacTavish, Les Humphrey and Associates, 1987.

Manning, Susan A. *Ecstasy and the Demon: Feminism and Nationalism in the Dances of Mary Wigman.* Berkeley, 1993.

Mitchell, Jack. *Alvin Ailey American Dance Theater: Jack Mitchell Photographs.* Kansas City, Andrews & McMeel, 1993.

Magriel, Paul David. *A Bibliography of Dancing.* New York: M.W. Wilson, 1936, reprinted Benjamin, 1966.

Magriel, Paul David, editor. *Chronicles of the American Dance.* New York: Henry Holt & Co., 1948, reprinted Da Capo Press, 1978.

———, editor. *Isadora Duncan.* New York: Henry Holt & Co., 1947.

Martin, John. *America Dancing: The Background and Personalities of the Modern Dance.* New York: Dodge Publishing, 1936, reprinted Brooklyn: Dance Horizons, 1966.

———. *The Dance.* New York: Tudor Publishing Co., 1946.

———. *Introduction to the Dance.* New York: A.S. Barnes, 1933, reprinted Brooklyn: Dance Horizons, 1965.

———. *John Martin's Book of the Dance.* New York: Tudor Publishing Co., 1963.

———. *The Modern Dance.* New York: A.S. Barnes, 1933, reprinted Brooklyn: Dance Horizons, 1965.

———. *Ruth Page: An Intimate Biography.* New York: Marcel Dekker, 1977.

Matson, Tim. *Pilobolus.* New York: Random House, 1978.

Maynard, Olga. *American Modern Dancers: The Pioneers.* Boston and Toronto: Little, Brown and Co., 1965.

Mazo, Joseph H. *Prime Movers: The Makers of Modern Dance in America.* New York: William Morrow, 1977.

McDonagh, Don. *The Complete Guide to Modern Dance.* Garden City, New York: Doubleday, 1976, reprinted Popular Library, 1977.

———. *Martha Graham: A Biography.* New York: Praeger, 1974.

———. *The Rise and Fall and Rise of Modern Dance.* New York: Outerbridge and Dienstfrey, 1970, reprinted New American Library, 1971.

Morgan, Barbara. *Martha Graham: Sixteen Dances in Photographs.* New York: Duell, Sloan, and Pearce, 1941.

Müller, Hedwig. *Mary Wigman. Leben und Werk der grossen Tänzerin.* Berlin, 1986.

Müller, John. *Dance Film Directory: An Annotated and Evaluative Guide to Films on Ballet and Modern Dance.* Princeton, New Jersey: Princeton Book Company, Publishers, 1979.

Nadel, Myron Howard, and Nadel, Constance Gwen. editors, *The Dance Experience: Readings in Dance Appreciation.* New York: Praeger Publishers, 1970.

New York Public Library. *Dictionary Catalog: New York Public Library Dance Collection,* 10 volumes. New York: New York Public Library, Astor, Lenox, and Tilden Foundation, distributed by G. K. Hall, Boston, 1974, supplemental issues 1975, reprinted 1976 and 1977.

Novack, Cynthia. *Sharing the Dance.* Madison: University of Wisconsin, 1990.

Oberzaucher-Schüller, Gunhild, editor. *Ausdruckstanz.* Wilhelmshaven, 1992.

Partsch-Bergsohn, Isa. *Modern Dance in Germany and the United States: Cross Currents and Differences.* Tucson: University of Arizona, 1994.

Percival, John. *Experimental Dance.* New York: Universe Books, 1971.

Peter, Frank-Manuel, editor. *Dore Hoyer.* Berlin, 1992.

Plett, Nicole, editor, *Eleanor King: Sixty Years in American Dance.* Santa Cruz, New Mexico, 1988.

Pollack, Barbara, and Charles Humphrey Woodford. *Dance Is a Moment: A Portrait of José Limón in Words and Pictures.* Pennington, New Jersey: Princeton Book Company, 1993.

Preston-Dunlop, Valerie, and Susanne Lahusen, editors. *Schrifttanz.* London: Dance Books, 1990.

Prevots, Naima. *Dancing in the Sun: Hollywood Choreographers, 1915-1937.* Ann Arbor, Michigan, and London: UMI Research Press, 1987.

Rainer, Yvonne. *Work, 1961-73.* Halifax: Press of Nova Scotia College of Art and Design and New York: New York University Press, 1974.

Robertson, Allen, and Donald Hutera. *The Dance Handbook.* Boston: G.K. Hall & Co., 1990.

Rochlein, Harvey. *Notes on Contemporary American Dance 1964.* Baltimore: University Extension Press, 1964.

Rogosin, Elinor. *The Dance Makers: Conversations with American Choreographers.* New York: Walker and Company, 1980.

Ruyter, Nancy Lee Chalfa. *Reformers and Visionaries: The Americanization of the Art of Dance.* New York: Dance Horizons, 1979.

Sachs, Curt. *World History of the Dance.* New York: W.W. Norton, 1965.

St. Denis, Ruth. *An Unfinished Life.* New York and London: Harper & Bros., 1939, reprinted Brooklyn: Dance Horizons, 1969.

Sayre, Henry M. *The Object of Performance: The American Avant-Garde Since 1970.* Chicago and London: Chicago University Press, 1992.

Schlicher, Susanne. *Tanztheater: Tradionen und Freiheiten.* Rowohlt Taschenbuch Verlag GmbH, Reinbek bei Hamburg, 1987.

Schlundt, Christena. *The Professional Appearances of Ruth St. Denis and Ted Shawn: A Chronology and an Index of Dances, 1906-1932.* New York: New York Public Library, 1962.

———. *The Professional Appearances of Ted Shawn and His Men Dancers: A Chronology and an Index of Dances 1933-1940.* New York: New York Public Library, 1967.

———. *Tamiris: A Chronicle of Her Dance Career.* New York: New York Public Library, 1972.

Schmidt, Jochen. *Tanztheater in Deutschland.* Propyläen Verlag, Frankfurt am Main, 1992.

Schneider, Ilya Ilyich. *Isadora Duncan: The Russian Years,* translated by David Magershack. London: MacDonald, 1968.

Seroff, Victor. *The Real Isadora.* London: Hutchinson, 1972.

Servos, Norbert. *Pina Bausch Wuppertal Dance Theater: Or the Art of Training a Goldfish—Excursions into Dance,* translated by Patricia Stadié. Cologne: Ballet-Bühnen Verlag, 1984.

Shawn, Ted. *Dance We Must.* Pittsfield, Masschussetts: Eagle Printing and Binding Co., 1940, reprinted 1950 and 1963.

———. *Denishawn: The Enduring Influence.* Boston: Twayne Publishers, 1983.

———. *Fundamentals of Dance Education.* Girard, Kansas: Haldeman-Julius Publications, 1937.

Shawn, Ted, with Gray Poole. *One Thousand and One Night Stands.* New York: Doubleday, 1960, reprinted Da Capo Press, 1979.

Sheets, Maxine. *The Phenomenology of Dance.* Madison: University of Wisconsin Press, 1966.

Shelton, Suzanne. *Divine Dancer: A Biography of Ruth St. Denis.* Garden City, New York: Doubleday, 1981.

Sherman, Jan. *The Drama of Denishawn Dance.* Middletown, Conneticut: Wesleyan University Press, 1979.

Siegel, Marcia B. *At the Vanishing Point: A Critic Looks at Dance.* New York: Saturday Review Press, 1972.

———. *Days on Earth: The Dance of Doris Humphrey.* New Haven: Yale University Press, 1987.

———. *The Shapes of Change: Images of American Dance.* Boston: Houghton-Mifflin, 1979.

———. *The Tail of the Dragon: New Dance, 1976-1982.* Durham, North Carolina, 1991.

———. *Watching the Dance Go By.* Boston: Houghton-Mifflin, 1977.

Sorell, Walter. *Dance in Its Time: The Emergence of an Art Form.* Garden City, New York: Anchor Press/Doubleday, 1981.

———. *The Dance through the Ages.* New York: Grosset and Dunlap, 1967.

———. *The Dancer's Image: Points and Counterpoints.* New York: Columbia University Press, 1971.

———. *Hanya Holm: Biography of an Artist.* Middletown, Conneticut: Wesleyan University Press, 1969.

———, editor, *The Dance Has Many Faces.* Cleveland and New York: World Publishing Co., 1951, 2nd revised edition, New York and London: Columbia University Press, 1966.

Stebbins, Genevieve. *The Delsarte System of Expression.* Brooklyn: Dance Horizons, 1978.

Steegmuller, Francis, editor, *Your Isadora: The Love Story of Isadora Duncan and Gordon Craig.* New York, 1974.

Steinberg, Cobbett, editor. *The Dance Anthology.* New York: New American Library, 1980.

Stewart, Virginia, and Merle Armitage, editors, *The Modern Dance.* New York: E. Weyhe, 1935, reprinted Brooklyn: Dance Horizons, 1970.

Stodelle, Ernestine. *The Dance Technique of Doris Humphrey and Its Creative Potential.* Princeton, New Jersey: Princeton Book Company, 1978.

———. *Deep Song: The Dance Story of Martha Graham.* New York, 1984.

Taylor, Paul. *Private Domain.* New York: Alfred A. Knopf, 1987.

Terry, Walter. *The Dance in America.* New York: Harper and Bros., 1956, revised Harper and Row, 1971.

———. *Frontiers of Life: The Life of Martha Graham.* New York: Thomas Y. Crowell, 1975.

———. *Isadora Duncan: Her Life, Her Art, Her Legacy.* New York: Dodd, Mead & Co., 1963.

———. *I Was There: Selected Dance Reviews and Articles, 1936-1976,* compiled and edited by Andrew Mark Wentink. New York: Marcel Dekker Press, 1978.

———. *Miss Ruth: The More Living Life of Ruth St. Denis.* New York: Dodd, Mead & Co., 1969.

———. *Ted Shawn: Father of American Dance.* New York: Dial Press, 1977.

Tharp, Twyla. *Push Comes to Shove: An Autobiography.* New York: Bantam Books, 1992.

Toepfer, Carl. *Empire of Ecstasy: Nudity, Movement, and German Body Culture, 1910-1935.* Berkeley, 1997.

Trowbridge, Charlotte. *Dance Drawings of Martha Graham,* forward by Martha Graham. New York: Dancer Observer, 1945.

Turner, Margery J., with Ruth Grauert and Arlene Zallman. *New Dance: Approaches to Nonliteral Choreography.* Pittsburgh: University of Pittsburgh Press, 1971.

Van Tuyl, Marian, editor, *Anthology of Impulse.* Brooklyn: Dance Horizons, 1970.

Waldeen. *La Danza: Imagen de creacion continua.* Mexico City: National University of Mexico, 1982.

Warner, Mary Jane. *Toronto Dance Teachers 1825-1925.* Toronto: Dance Collection Danse Press/es, 1995.

Warren, Larry. *Anna Sokolow: The Rebellious Spirit.* Princeton, New Jersey: Princeton Book Company, 1991.

———. *Lester Horton: Modern Dance Pioneer.* New York: Marcel Dekker Press, 1977, reprinted Princeton Book Company, 1991.

Wigman, Mary. *The Language of Dance,* translated by Walter Sorell. Middletown, Conneticut: Wesleyan University Press, 1966.

———. *The Mary Wigman Book,* edited and translated by Walter Sorell. Middletown, Conneticut: Wesleyan University Press, 1975.

Willis, J., editor, *Dance World.* New York: Crown Publishers, 1966, reprinted 1979.

Wyman, Max. *Dance Canada: An Illustrated History.* Vancouver: Douglas & McIntyre, 1989.

Wynne, Peter. *Judson Dance: An Annotated Bibliography of the Judson Dance Theater and of Five Major Choreographers—Trisha Brown, Lucinda Childs, Deborah Hay, Steve Paxton, and Yvonne Rainer.* Englewood, New Jersey, 1978.

NATIONALITY INDEX

American

Alvin Ailey
Alaska Dance Theatre
Maud Allan
Alvin Ailey American Dance Theatre
Jerome Andrews
Mary Anthony
William Bales
Art Bauman
Talley Beatty
Valerie Bettis
Bonnie Bird
Ellen Bromberg
Carolyn Brown
Ronald K. Brown
Trisha Brown
Rachel Browne
Susan Buirge
Richard Bull
John Butler
Donald Byrd
John Cage
Terese Capucilli
Ann Carlson
Remy Charlip
Lucinda Childs
Ping Chong
Martha Clarke
Robert Cohan
Jane Comfort
Blondell Cummings
Merce Cunningham
Ruth Currier
Christine Dakin
Nora Daniel
Chuck Davis
Carmen de Lavallade
Laura Dean
Mark Dendy
David Dorfman
Ulysses Dove
Paul Draper
Senta Driver
Jane Dudley
Isadora Duncan
Jeff Duncan
Katherine Dunham
Douglas Dunn
Eiko & Koma
Janet Eilber
Angna Enters
Jean Erdman
Jan Erkert
Bill Evans
Daniel Ezralow
Garth Fagan
George Faison
Louis Falco
Viola Farber
Molissa Fenley
Nina Fonaroff

Laura Foreman
Simone Forti
Loie Fuller
Annabelle Gamson
Midi Garth
Joe Goode
David Gordon
Lotte Goslar
Hellmut Gottschild
Grace Graff
Martha Graham
The Grand Union
Harriette Ann Gray
Neil Greenberg
Danny Grossman
Anna Halprin
Meg Harper
Nancy Hauser
Erick Hawkins
Deborah Hay
Margaret H'Doubler
Martha Hill
Mary Hinkson
Linda Hodes
Louis Horst
Lester Horton
Hubbard Street Dance Chicago
Doris Humphrey
Bill James
Judith Jamison
Margaret Jenkins
Betty Jones
Bill T. Jones and Arnie Zane
Paula Josa-Jones
Maggie Kast
Elizabeth Keen
Cliff Keuter
Eleanor King
Kenneth King
Demetrius Klein
Chris Komar
Pauline Koner
Phyllis Lamhut
Rachel Lampert
Pearl Lang
Ralph Lemon
Liz Lerman
Bella Lewitzky
Li Chiao-Ping
José Limón
Gertrude Lippincott
Katherine Litz
Murray Louis
William Louther
Lar Lubovitch
Iris Mabry
Terrill Maguire
Sara Shelton Mann
Susan Marshall
Sophie Maslow
Helen McGehee

Donald McKayle
Nancy Meehan
Annelise Mertz
Barbara Mettler
Bebe Miller
Momix
Meredith Monk
Elisa Monte
Claudia Moore
Jack Moore
Mark Morris
Robert Morris
Jennifer Muller
Barton Mumaw
Daniel Nagrin
Phoebe Neville
New Dance Group
Alwin Nikolais
Isamu Noguchi
Robert North
Cynthia Novack
Lisa Nowak
ODC/San Francisco
May O'Donnell
Ruth Page
David Parsons
Steve Paxton
Moses Pendleton
Rudy Perez
Wendy Perron
Stephen Petronio
Philadanco
Pilobolus Dance Theater
Eleo Pomare
Kathryn Posin
Pearl Primus
Neta Pulvermacher
Yvonne Rainer
Peter Randazzo
Robert Rauschenberg
Don Redlich
Dana Reitz
Repertory Dance Theatre
Ririe-Woodbury Dance Company
Cleo Parker Robinson
Rod Rodgers
Jean Rosenthal
Bertram Ross
Ruth St. Denis
Paul Sanasardo
Angiola Sartorio
Carolee Schneemann
Bessie Schönberg
Jim Self
Yacov Sharir
Ted Shawn
Sarah Skaggs
Gus Solomons jr.
Peter Sparling
Kei Takei
Helen Tamiris

Paul Taylor
Glen Tetley
Twyla Tharp
Clive Thompson
Jennifer Tipton
Joyce Trisler
James Truitte
Victoria Uris
Jan Van Dyke
Marian Van Tuyl
Doug Varone
Dan Wagoner
Waldeen
Norman Walker
James Waring
Carmela Weber
Charles Weidman
White Oak Dance Project
Dudley Williams
Ethel Winter
Mel Wong
Donna Wood
Lila York
Yuriko
Batya Zamir
Jawole Willa Jo Zollar

Argentine
Alejandro Cervera
Daniel Goldin
Susana Tambutti

Australian
Gertrud Bodenwieser
Elizabeth Cameron Dalman
Meryl Tankard Australian Dance Theatre
Graeme Murphy
Lloyd Newson
Ian Spink
Sydney Dance Company
Meryl Tankard
Leigh Warren

Austrian
Gertrud Bodenwieser
Rosalia Chladek
Kurt Graff
Emile Jaques-Dalcroze
Gertrud Kraus
Margarethe Wallmann
Grete Wiesenthal

Belgian
Anne Teresa de Keersmaeker
Wim Vandekeybus

British
Richard Alston
Lea Anderson
Mark Baldwin
Anna Blewchamp

Matthew Bourne
Elaine Bowman
Jonathan Burrows
Rosemary Butcher
Chisenhale Dance Space
Michael Clark
Robert Cohan
Siobhan Davies
Shobana Jeyasingh
Lloyd Newson
Robert North
The Place
Rambert Dance Company
Jacqueline Robinson
Valda Setterfield
Janet Smith
Leigh Warren

Canadian

Carol Anderson
Peggy Baker
Patricia Beatty
Serge Bennathan
Anna Blewchamp
Elaine Bowman
Rachel Browne
Marie Chouinard
James Cunningham
Dancemakers
Robert Desrosiers
William Douglas
David Earle
EDAM Performing Arts Society
Paul-André Fortier
Patricia Fraser
Fringe Festival of Independent Dance (FFIDA)
Margie Gillis
Danny Grossman
Groupe de la Place Royale
Groupe Nouvelle Aire
Christopher House
Karen Jamieson
Judy Jarvis
Edouard Lock
Terrill Maguire
Judith Marcuse
Jennifer Mascall
Claudia Moore
Linda Rabin
Peter Randazzo
Nona Schurman
Grant Strate
François Sullivan
Tangente
Toronto Dance Theatre
Brian Webb
Winnipeg Contemporary Dancers
Anna Wyman

Catalonian

Ramón Oller

Chinese

Dai Ai-lian
Guangdong Modern Dance Company
Wu Xiao-bang

Colombian

Eleo Pomare

Dutch

Krisztina de Châtel
Bettie de Jong
Lucas Hoving
Leine & Roebana
Ton Simons
Hans Tuerlings

Fijian

Mark Baldwin

French

Dominique Bagouet
Serge Bennathan
Claude Brumachon
Susan Buirge
Compagnie Beau-geste
François Delsarte
Maguy Marin
Josef Nadj
Angelin Preljocaj
Jacqueline Robinson

German

Pina Bausch
Gerhard Bohner
Viola Farber
Folkwang Hochschule
Yvonne Georgi
Lotte Goslar
Hellmut Gottschild
Hanya Holm
Rui Horta
Dore Hoyer
Kurt Jooss
Harald Kreutzberg
Sigurd Leeder
Susanne Linke
Annelise Mertz
Gret Palucca
Bessie Schönberg
Mary Wigman

Hungarian

Krisztina de Châtel
Rudolf Laban

Icelandic

Sigríður Valgeirsdóttir

Indian

Chandralekha
Shobana Jeyasingh

Uday Shankar

Israeli
Bat-Dor Dance Company
Batsheva Dance Company
Ze'eva Cohen
Itzik Galili
Inbal Dance Theatre
Kibbutz Contemporary Dance Company
Koldemama Dance Company
Liat Dror & Nir Ben-Gal Dance Company
Neta Pulvermacher
Yacov Sharir

Italian
Simone Forti
Angiola Sartorio

Jamaican
Garth Fagan
Clive Thompson

Japanese
Eiko & Koma
Isamu Noguchi
Kei Takei
Saburo Teshigawara

Korean
Ahn Ae-soon
Choi Chung-ja
Jeon Mi-sook
Kim Wha-suk
Nam Jeong-ho
Park Myung-sook
Yook Wan-soon

Mexican
Guillermo Arriaga
Guillermina Bravo
Nellie and Gloria Campobello
Luis Fandiño
Raúl Flores Canelo
Sergio Franco
Josefina Lavalle
José Limón
Rosa Reyna

Moroccan
Edouard Lock

New Zealander
Commotion Company
Douglas Wright Dance Company
Shona Dunlop
Footnote Dance Company
Impulse Dance Theatre
Jordan & Present Company
Limbs Dance Company
Taiao Dance Theatre

Portuguese
Rui Horta

Puerto Rican
Manuel Alum

Slavic
Josef Nadj

South African
Sylvia Glasser
Jazzart Dance Theatre
Vincent Sekwati Mantsoe
Moving into Dance Performance Company

Spanish
Compañia Nacional de Danza
Nacho Duato
Mal Pelo
Provisional Danza
Tórtola Valencia

Swedish
Ronny Johansson

Swiss
Urs Dietrich
Hans Züllig

Taiwanese
Lin Hwai-min

Trinidadian
Pearl Primus

SUBJECT INDEX

Associations & Governmental Organizations

Federal Dance Theatre
Gendai Buyo Kyokai
José Limón Dance Foundation
Tangente

Choreographers

Ahn Ae-soon
Alvin Ailey
Maud Allan
Richard Alston
Manuel Alum
Carol Anderson
Lea Anderson
Jerome Andrews
Mary Anthony
Guillermo Arriaga
Dominique Bagouet
Peggy Baker
Mark Baldwin
William Bales
Art Bauman
Pina Bausch
Patricia Beatty
Talley Beatty
Serge Bennathan
Valerie Bettis
Anna Blewchamp
Gertrud Bodenwieser
Gerhard Bohner
Matthew Bourne
Elaine Bowman
Guillermina Bravo
Ellen Bromberg
Carolyn Brown
Ronald K. Brown
Trisha Brown
Rachel Browne
Claude Brumachon
Susan Buirge
Richard Bull
Jonathan Burrows
Rosemary Butcher
John Butler
Donald Byrd
Nellie and Gloria Campobello
Ann Carlson
Alejandro Cervera
Chandralekha
Remy Charlip
Lucinda Childs
Rosalia Chladek
Choi Chung-ja
Ping Chong
Marie Chouinard
Michael Clark
Martha Clarke
Robert Cohan
Ze'eva Cohen
Jane Comfort

Blondell Cummings
James Cunningham
Merce Cunningham
Ruth Currier
Dai Ai-lian
Christine Dakin
Elizabeth Cameron Dalman
Nora Daniel
Siobhan Davies
Chuck Davis
Krisztina de Châtel
Carmen de Lavallade
Anne Teresa de Keersmaeker
Laura Dean
Mark Dendy
Robert Desrosiers
Urs Dietrich
David Dorfman
William Douglas
Ulysses Dove
Paul Draper
Senta Driver
Nacho Duato
Jane Dudley
Isadora Duncan
Jeff Duncan
Katherine Dunham
Shona Dunlop
Douglas Dunn
David Earle
Eiko & Koma
Janet Eilber
Angna Enters
Jean Erdman
Jan Erkert
Bill Evans
Daniel Ezralow
Garth Fagan
George Faison
Louis Falco
Luis Fandiño
Viola Farber
Molissa Fenley
Raúl Flores Canelo
Nina Fonaroff
Laura Foreman
Simone Forti
Paul-André Fortier
Sergio Franco
Patricia Fraser
Loie Fuller
Itzik Galili
Annabelle Gamson
Midi Garth
Yvonne Georgi
Margie Gillis
Sylvia Glasser
Daniel Goldin
Joe Goode
David Gordon
Lotte Goslar

Angiola Sartorio
Nona Schurman
Jim Self
Uday Shankar
Yacov Sharir
Ted Shawn
Ton Simons
Sarah Skaggs
Janet Smith
Gus Solomons jr.
Peter Sparling
Ian Spink
Grant Strate
François Sullivan
Kei Takei
Susana Tambutti
Helen Tamiris
Meryl Tankard
Paul Taylor
Saburo Teshigawara
Glen Tetley
Twyla Tharp
Clive Thompson
Joyce Trisler
James Truitte
Hans Tuerlings
Victoria Uris
Tórtola Valencia
Sigríður Valgeirsdóttir
Jan Van Dyke
Marian Van Tuyl
Wim Vandekeybus
Doug Varone
Dan Wagoner
Waldeen
Norman Walker
Margarethe Wallmann
James Waring
Leigh Warren
Brian Webb
Carmela Weber
Charles Weidman
Grete Wiesenthal
Mary Wigman
Ethel Winter
Mel Wong
Wu Xiao-bang
Anna Wyman
Yook Wan-soon
Lila York
Yuriko
Batya Zamir
Jawole Willa Jo Zollar
Hans Züllig

Companies
Alaska Dance Theatre
Alvin Ailey American Dance Theatre
Bat-Dor Dance Company
Batsheva Dance Company
Commotion Company

Compagnie Beau-Geste
Compañia Nacional de Danza
Dancemakers
Douglas Wright Dance Company
EDAM Performing Arts Society
15 Dance Laboratorium
Footnote Dance Company
The Grand Union
Le Groupe Nouvelle Aire
Le Groupe de la Place Royale
Guangdong Modern Dance Company
Hubbard Street Dance Chicago
Impulse Dance Theatre
Inbal Dance Theatre
Jazzart Dance Theatre
Jordan & Present Company
Judson Dance Theater
Kibbutz Contemporary Dance Company
Koldemama Dance Company
Leine & Roebana
Liat Dror & Nir Ben-Gal Dance Company
Limbs Dance Company
London Contemporary Dance Theatre
Mal Pelo
Meryl Tankard Australian Dance Theatre
Momix
Moving into Dance Performance Company
New Dance Group
ODC/San Francisco
Philadanco
Pilobolus Dance Theater
Provisional Danza
Rambert Dance Company
Repertory Dance Theatre
Ririe-Woodbury Dance Company
Sydney Dance Company
Taiao Dance Theatre
Toronto Dance Theatre
White Oak Dance Project
Winnipeg Contemporary Dancers

Company Directors
Alvin Ailey
Richard Alston
Manuel Alum
Lea Anderson
Guillermo Arriaga
Dominique Bagouet
Peggy Baker
Mark Baldwin
William Bales
Pina Bausch
Talley Beatty
Serge Bennathan
Valerie Bettis
Anna Blewchamp
Matthew Bourne
Elaine Bowman
Guillermina Bravo
Ronald K. Brown
Rachel Browne

Claude Brumachon
Susan Buirge
Richard Bull
Jonathan Burrows
Rosemary Butcher
Choi Chung-ja
Ping Chong
Marie Chouinard
Michael Clark
Robert Cohan
Jane Comfort
Merce Cunningham
Dai Ai-lian
Elizabeth Cameron Dalman
Siobhan Davies
Chuck Davis
Krisztina de Châtel
Anne Teresa de Keersmaeker
Laura Dean
Robert Desrosiers
David Dorfman
William Douglas
Nacho Duato
Jane Dudley
Katherine Dunham
Shona Dunlop
Douglas Dunn
Janet Eilber
Jean Erdman
Bill Evans
Garth Fagan
George Faison
Luis Fandiño
Molissa Fenley
Raúl Flores Canelo
Nina Fonaroff
Laura Foreman
Paul-André Fortier
Sergio Franco
Patricia Fraser
Itzik Galili
Margie Gillis
Sylvia Glasser
Daniel Goldin
Joe Goode
Lotte Goslar
Martha Graham
Neil Greenberg
Danny Grossman
Anna Halprin
Nancy Hauser
Erick Hawkins
Hanya Holm
Rui Horta
Lester Horton
Doris Humphrey
Bill James
Karen Jamieson
Judith Jamison
Judy Jarvis
Shobana Jeyasingh

Bill T. Jones and Arnie Zane
Kurt Jooss
Paula Josa-Jones
Maggie Kast
Elizabeth Keen
Cliff Keuter
Kim Wha-suk
Eleanor King
Demetrius Klein
Rudolf Laban
Rachel Lampert
Pearl Lang
Josefina Lavalle
Ralph Lemon
Liz Lerman
Li Chiao-Ping
Lin Hwai-min
Susanne Linke
Edouard Lock
Murray Louis
William Louther
Lar Lubovitch
Judith Marcuse
Maguy Marin
Susan Marshall
Donald McKayle
Nancy Meehan
Annelise Mertz
Bebe Miller
Meredith Monk
Mark Morris
Jennifer Muller
Graeme Murphy
Josef Nadj
Phoebe Neville
Lloyd Newson
Robert North
Lisa Nowak
May O'Donnell
Ramón Oller
Ruth Page
Park Myung-sook
David Parsons
Moses Pendleton
Rudy Perez
Wendy Perron
Stephen Petronio
Eleo Pomare
Angelin Preljocaj
Peter Pucci
Neta Pulvermacher
Peter Randazzo
Don Redlich
Rosa Reyna
Cleo Parker Robinson
Rod Rodgers
Paul Sanasardo
Jim Self
Uday Shankar
Yacov Sharir
Ton Simons

Helen McGehee
Donald McKayle
Nancy Meehan
Annelise Mertz
Barbara Mettler
Bebe Miller
Meredith Monk
Elisa Monte
Claudia Moore
Jack Moore
Mark Morris
Robert Morris
Jennifer Muller
Barton Mumaw
Graeme Murphy
Josef Nadj
Daniel Nagrin
Nam Jeong-ho
Phoebe Neville
Lloyd Newson
Robert North
Cynthia Novack
Lisa Nowak
May O'Donnell
Ramón Oller
Ruth Page
Gret Palucca
Park Myung-sook
David Parsons
Steve Paxton
Moses Pendleton
Rudy Perez
Wendy Perron
Stephen Petronio
Eleo Pomare
Kathryn Posin
Angelin Preljocaj
Pearl Primus
Peter Pucci
Neta Pulvermacher
Linda Rabin
Yvonne Rainer
Peter Randazzo
Robert Rauschenberg
Don Redlich
Dana Reitz
Rosa Reyna
Cleo Parker Robinson
Rod Rodgers
Bertram Ross
Ruth St. Denis
Paul Sanasardo
Angiola Sartorio
Bessie Schönberg
Nona Schurman
Jim Self
Valda Setterfield
Uday Shankar
Yacov Sharir
Ted Shawn
Ton Simons

Sarah Skaggs
Janet Smith
Gus Solomons jr.
Peter Sparling
Ian Spink
Grant Strate
François Sullivan
Kei Takei
Helen Tamiris
Meryl Tankard
Paul Taylor
Saburo Teshigawara
Glen Tetley
Twyla Tharp
Clive Thompson
Joyce Trisler
James Truitte
Hans Tuerlings
Victoria Uris
Tórtola Valencia
Sigríður Valgeirsdóttir
Jan Van Dyke
Wim Vandekeybus
Doug Varone
Dan Wagoner
Waldeen
Norman Walker
Margarethe Wallmann
James Waring
Leigh Warren
Brian Webb
Carmela Weber
Charles Weidman
Grete Wiesenthal
Mary Wigman
Dudley Williams
Ethel Winter
Mel Wong
Donna Wood
Wu Xiao-bang
Anna Wyman
Yook Wan-soon
Lila York
Yuriko
Batya Zamir
Jawole Willa Jo Zollar
Hans Züllig

Dances
Air for the G String
Appalachian Spring
The Beloved
Catherine Wheel
Clytemnestra
Congo Tango Palace
Cry
Deaths and Entrances
Dreams
Einstein on the Beach
Esplanade
Fables for Our Time

Frontier
Games
Griot New York
La Malinche
Lamentation
Lynchtown
The Moor's Pavane
New Dance Trilogy: Theatre Piece, With My Red Fires, and New Dance
Nightwandering
Primitive Mysteries
Revelations
The Rite of Spring
The Shakers
Still/Here
Strange Fruit
Tent
Trend
Water Study
Winterbranch

Educators
Richard Alston
Carol Anderson
Mary Anthony
Guillermo Arriaga
Peggy Baker
Patricia Beatty
Talley Beatty
Valerie Bettis
Bonnie Bird
Anna Blewchamp
Gertrud Bodenwieser
Elaine Bowman
Guillermina Bravo
Carolyn Brown
Rachel Browne
Susan Buirge
Rosemary Butcher
Donald Byrd
Nellie and Gloria Campobello
Rosalia Chladek
Ze'eva Cohen
Blondell Cummings
James Cunningham
Ruth Currier
Dai Ai-lian
Christine Dakin
Elizabeth Cameron Dalman
Nora Daniel
Carmen de Lavallade
William Douglas
Jane Dudley
Isadora Duncan
Katherine Dunham
David Earle
Jean Erdman
Bill Evans
Luis Fandiño
Raúl Flores Canelo
Nina Fonaroff

Paul-André Fortier
Patricia Fraser
Sylvia Glasser
Harriette Ann Gray
Neil Greenberg
Anna Halprin
Nancy Hauser
Margaret H'Doubler
Martha Hill
Linda Hodes
Hanya Holm
Lester Horton
Christopher House
Lucas Hoving
Dore Hoyer
Doris Humphrey
Bill James
Karen Jamieson
Judy Jarvis
Jeon Mi-sook
Ronny Johansson
Betty Jones
Kurt Jooss
Paula Josa-Jones
Elizabeth Keen
Cliff Keuter
Kim Wha-suk
Eleanor King
Chris Komar
Pauline Koner
Gertrud Kraus
Pearl Lang
Josefina Lavalle
Sigurd Leeder
Bella Lewitzky
José Limón
Gertrude Lippincott
Iris Mabry
Terrill Maguire
Sara Shelton Mann
Vincent Sekwati Mantsoe
Judith Marcuse
Sophie Maslow
Helen McGehee
Nancy Meehan
Annelise Mertz
Barbara Mettler
Claudia Moore
Jennifer Muller
Barton Mumaw
Daniel Nagrin
Nam Jeong-ho
Robert North
Cynthia Novack
May O'Donnell
Ramón Oller
Gret Palucca
Park Myung-sook
Steve Paxton
Wendy Perron
Kathryn Posin

Margaret H'Doubler
Rudolf Laban
Josefina Lavalle
Ralph Lemon
Lin Hwai-min
Gertrude Lippincott
Donald McKayle
Barbara Mettler
Daniel Nagrin
Ruth Page
Wendy Perron
Jacqueline Robinson
Carolee Schneemann
Gus Solomons jr.
Paul Taylor
Marian Van Tuyl

NOTES ON
ADVISERS AND CONTRIBUTORS

ALTER, Judith B. Ed.D. and M.A. in teaching from Harvard Graduate School of Education, and an M.A. in dance from Mills College. Studied dance with members of Humphrey-Weidman, Graham, Wigman, and Horton dance companies; has choreographed solos and group works for 22 years. Author of *Surviving Exercise*, 1983, 1990, *Stretch and Strengthen*, 1986 1990, *Dance-Based Dance Theory*, 1991, and *Dancing and Mixed Media*, 1994; also author of articles on dance philosophy, education, history, and the creative potential of performing art. **Essays:** H'Doubler; Mettler.

AMORT, Andrea. Dance scholar. **Essays:** Chladek; Wallmann; Wiesenthal.

ANDERSON, Carol. See entry. **Essays:** Bowman; Browne; Canada; Fraser; Jarvis; Toronto Dance Theatre; Winnipeg Contemporary Dancers.

BAART, Jan. Attended classical and jazz dance classes; studied architecture and Dutch literature; organized music festivals. Member of the Arts Council for Music and Dance. Head of the Dutch Association of Theater Critics. Received Lifetime Achievement Award from Gus Giordano and the Jazz Dance World Congress, 1997. Author of book on mime in Holland and a catalogue of dance in Holland, as well as numerous dance-related articles for newspapers and magazines. **Essays:** Simons; Tuerlings.

BARBOUR, Karen. M.A. in philosophy and diploma in contemporary dance from UNITEC School of Performing and Screen Arts. Dancer, choreographer, and freelance writer. Co-director of Curve, a female dance company. Contributor to *DANZ Magazine* and *Dance Net.* **Essay:** Limbs Dance Company.

BARNES, Clive. Born in London. Dance and/or drama critic, London *Times, New York Times,* 1965-77, and *New York Post,* since 1977. Senior editor, *Dance Magazine.* Author of numerous books; contributor of many articles to periodicals.

BARZEL, Ann. Graduate of University of Chicago; studied dance with Adolph Bolm, Michel Fokine, Doris Humphrey, and at the School of American Ballet. Dance critic for *Chicago American* and historian. Dancer of opera ballet and with experimental ballet group; teacher of dance. Currently assisting in establishing a dance collection for Newberry Library, Chicago. Senior editor and contributor of special articles and reviews, *Dance Magazine.* **Essays:** Graff; Kast.

BELANS, Linda. Host of weekly public radio program covering public, political, and cultural issues, "The State of Things"; also host of "Talk about Dance!," a lively, pre-performance interview and discussion series for local and national dance events. Directs domestic and international dance critics conferences. Former board member, Dance Critics Association. Dance writer, *Raleigh News and Observer* and *Nando* online where she has an award-winning site (http://www.nando.net/events/dance). **Essay:** Dendy.

BENBOW-NIEMIER, Glynis. Ph.D. in education from New York University; teaches writing workshops for the Institute for Writing and Thinking, Bard College. Poet and freelance writer with a long-held interest in dance. **Essays:** Delsarte & Jaques-Dalcroze; Shawn; St. Denis; Wigman.

BENET, Sydonie. Freelance editor, writer, and consultant living in the Chicago area. **Essays:** Bodenwieser; Byrd; Charlip; Koner; Lampert; Mertz; Perez; Redlich; Rodgers; Truitte.

BERARDI, Gigi. Fulbright scholar with a graduate degree in dance from University of California, Los Angeles. Dance writer and editor currently residing in Bellingham, Washington. Board member, Dance Critics Association. Author of *Finding Balance: Fitness and Training for a Lifetime in Dance;* correspondent for *Dance Magazine.* Author of features and of dance column published in *The Olympian;* also contributor to newspapers, magazines and journals, including *Anchorage Daily News, Los Angeles Times, LA Style,* and *Dance Research Journal.* Former editor of *Kinesiology and Medicine for Dance.* Book review editor, *Dance Medicine and Science.* **Essays:** Alaska Dance Theatre; Li Chiao-Ping; Repertory Dance Theatre; Ririe-Woodbury Dance Company.

BERG, Peggy. Attended University of Wisconsin-Madison; B.A. in dance, Bennington College. Currently in the process of earning an M.A. in dance/movement therapy, Naropa Institute, Boulder, Colorado. Has taught, choreographed, and performed around the world, including residencies in France, China, and Taiwan. Professor of dance, Colorado College. Former member of faculty, Washington University in St. Louis, Missouri. **Essays:** Comfort; Dorfman; Josa-Jones.

BOWRING, Amy. B.A. in fine arts, York University, and M.A. in journalism, University of Western Ontario. Archivist and administrator, Canadian Children's Dance Theatre, Toronto, Canada. Guest teacher of Canadian dance history, York University, Cawthra Park Secondary School's Dance Department, and Canadian Children's Dance Theatre. Assists with various projects at the archive and publishing house, Dance Collection Danse; currently conducting research on Canadian dance festivals. Contributor of historical essays and articles, *Canadian Dance Studies, Dance Collection Danse News,* and *Canadian Encyclopedia,* 1998 edition. **Essays:** 15 Dance Laboratorium; Anderson, Carol; Blewchamp; Canadian Festivals; Dancemakers; Grossman; House; Maguire; Sullivan.

BRADSHAW, Stephen. Of Ngati Maru (Maru Tribe) decent. Currently completing postgraduate study. Formal dance training with Limbs and NZ School of Dance. Tutor, artistic director, choreographer, and performer with Te Kanikani o te Rangatahi and Taiao. Freelance choreographer. Lecturer in dance, Northland Polytech School of Applied Arts. **Essay:** Taiao Dance Theatre.

BROILLI, Susan. Has covered dance and the American Dance Festival for 15 years, as a reporter and arts and entertainment editor for Herald Company, Inc., and for the past five years for *Dance Magazine.* Currently covers crime, the arts and features for Herald Company's *The Chapel Hill Herald.* Writing awards include first place award for dance criticism, North Carolina Press Association first place award for dance criticism, and Durham Arts Council Emerging Artist Award in literature. Author of fiction, poetry, and journal writing. **Essay:** American Dance Festival.

BURNS, Diane Hubbard. Bachelor of fine arts in dance and bachelor of arts in mass communication, University of South Florida, Tampa. Contributor on dance and theater, *The Palm Beach Post* and *The Fort Lauderdale Sun-Sentinel;* dance critic for *The Orlando Sentinel.* **Essays:** Hawkins, Erick; Klein, Demetrius; Lubovitch, Lar.

BURT, Ramsay. Senior research fellow in dance, DeMontfort University, Leicester. Author of *The Male Dancer: Bodies, Spectacle, Sexualities,* 1995, and *Alien Bodies: Representations of Modernity, "Race," and Nation in Early Modern Dance,* 1998. **Essays:** *Air for the G String; Moor's Pavane; New Dance Trilogy;* Postmodern Dance; *Primitive Mysteries; Rite of Spring.*

CAINES, Christopher. A.B. in literature, Harvard University, 1986. Lives in New York City, working as a performer, choreographer, composer for dance and theater, and writer. Contributor and editor, DanceOnline. Contributor to *The International Encyclopedia of Dance,* 1998, and *The American National Biography,* forthcoming, both for Oxford University Press. **Essays:** *Einstein on the Beach; Fables for Our Time;* Morris, Mark; Petronio; *Still/Here;* Takei.

CHAIKLIN, Sharon. Dance therapist for over 30 years working in psychiatric hospitals and private practice. Teacher, writer, and organizationally active. **Essay:** Lerman.

CHEESMAN, Sue. Born in New Zealand; worked for 13 years in England. M.A., University of Surrey in Guildford. Lecturer in dance and drama, Auckland College of Education; former lecturer in dance for four years, University of Otago, Dunedin. Choreographer, performer, teacher, and researcher in dance. Recipient of several Arts Council choreographic awards; current research concerns attack the issues of representation. **Essay:** Dunlop.

CITRON, Paula. Toronto-based dance and opera reviewer for radio station, Classical 96-FM, and reviewer of opera recordings for station's "Sunday Night at the Opera." Programmer and scriptwriter for "Regards to Broadway," a weekly program devoted to music theatre. Freelance arts writer and broadcaster specializing in dance, classical music, and theatre. Contributor to various Canadian and international periodicals, including *Dance Magazine, Dance International,* and *Opera Canada;* also contributor of dance reviews to Toronto's *Globe and Mail.* **Essays:** Baker; Beatty, Patricia; Bennathan; Desrosiers; Earle; Fringe Festival; James; Moore, Claudia; Randazzo.

COLOMÉ, Delfin. Spanish dance critic, composer, and writer. Career diplomat, currently Spain's ambassador to the Philippines. Professor of dance aesthetics, Madrid Autonomous University. Author of *The Indiscreet Charm of Dance* and *Isadora's Daughters.* Contributor of more than 200 articles and reviews to *Diario 16,* and other periodicals.

CONNOR, Lynne. Ph.D. in theater history and performance studies. Dance critic for WQED-FM, Pittsburgh, Pennsylvania. Author of *Spreading the Gospel of the Modern Dance: Newspaper Dance Criticism in the United States, 1850-1934;* contributor of numerous articles and reviews of the dance field. **Essay:** Criticism, American.

COOPER, Elizabeth. Degree in archeological studies, Yale University, 1987, and M.F.A. in dance, University of Washington. Professional dancer since 1980. Teacher of dance technique, Washington, D.C. Contributor to *Dance Research Journal.* Currently doing research on the Federal Dance Project. **Essays:** Federal Dance Theatre; Schurman.

CORNELL, Katherine. Masters degree in dance from York University, Toronto, Ontario. Archivist for many companies, including Toronto Dance Theatre and the National Ballet of Canada. Currently co-authoring a book on the history of Toronto Dance Theatre. **Essay:** Jamieson.

COUCH, Nena. Curator and associate professor, Jerome Lawrence and Robert E. Lee Theatre Research Institute, Ohio State University. Founding member of Les Menus Plaisirs, a Baroque dance troupe, and with Karen Woods, she recently created a baroque-style dance adaptation of Alexander Pope's poem *The Rape of the Lock.* Co-editor, *The Humanities and the Library,* second edition; co-author of performing arts chapter, "Dance Libraries" in *Managing Performing Arts Collections;* editor and author of introduction, *Sidney Kingsley: Five Prizewinning Plays.* **Essays:** *Catherine Wheel;* Tharp.

CRAIG, Jenifer. Ph.D., University of Southern California. Associate professor and chair of the department of dance, University of Oregon. Director and teacher in the dance program Dougherty Dance Theatre, University of Oregon. Associated with the Bella Lewitzky Dance Foundation, 1976. Editor, *The Dance Gallery Newsletter;* has worked in public relations and personnel for the Lewitzky Dance Foundation from 1977-88. Second-term member of board of directors, Society of Dance History Scholars; member of editorial board of the Congress on Research in Dance. **Essay:** Lewitzky.

CRISTOFORI, Marilyn. Professor emeritus, California State University, Chico; invited to lecture in dance history and dance theory at University of California, Santa Cruz and University of Hawaii, Manoa. Former professional dance artist; performed in ballet and modern dance companies in London, San Francisco, New York, and Rhode Island; dance/movement specialist for the National Endowment for the Arts, Artists-in-Schools program. Currently executive director for the Hawaii Alliance for Arts Education (HAAE). Executive producer of the award-winning documentary, *Hanya: Portrait of a Pioneer,* nationally broadcast on public television stations. Contributor of several articles on Hanya Holm; served as the issue editor for *Choreography and Dance, An International Journal's Hanya Holm: A Pioneer in American Dance,* 1992. **Essay:** Holm.

DAVIDA, Dena. American-born dancer living in Quebec since 1977; teacher and performer in the Nikolais tradition; veteran contact inprovisor as well as founder and programmer of an international dance festival and laboratory performance space. Currently doing doctoral research to create an ethnography of Montreal *nouvelle danse.* **Essays:** Douglas, FIND, Tangente.

DeFRANTZ, Thomas. Book editor, Dance Critics Association newsletter; serves on editorial board, Society of Dance History Scholars. Organizes the dance history course at the Alvin Ailey American Dance Center, New York City; member of the theater arts faculty, Massachusetts Institute of Technology, Cambridge. Contributor to *Encyclopedia of African American Culture and History* and *Village Voice.* **Essays:** Ailey; Alvin Ailey American Dance Theatre; Louther; Pilobolus Dance Theater; *Revelations.*

DIOUDONNAT, Edwige. Masters' degrees in philosophy and international cultural exchanges; currently working on her Ph.D in flamenco and kathak dances. Lecturer in ethnology and sociology, University of Nice, Sophia-Antipolis, France. Contributor of articles on dance. **Essays:** Brumachon; Compagnie Beau-Geste.

DIXON, Janette Goff. Freelance writer. **Essays:** Allan; Charlip; Currier; Dudley; Duncan, Jeff; Keen; Keuter; Maslow; Paxton; Winter.

DIXON, Melanye White. Dancer, educator, and historian. Ed.D.; studied dance with Dance Theatre of Harlem; merit scholar at Alvin Ailey American Dance Center. Associate professor of dance, Ohio State University. Taught and performed in the United States and abroad. Temple University Alumni fellow, 1991; received several research grants. Contributor to *Dance Research Journal, SAGE: A Scholarly Journal on Black Women, International Encyclopedia of Dance,* and *Black Women in America.* **Essay:** Jamison.

DONALDSON, Anita. Dean of performing arts, University of Adelaide, South Australia. Taught in tertiary dance programs since 1970, specializing in history, criticism, and choreological studies. Author and critic. Her 1993 Ph.D. dissertation from the Laban Centre, *The Choreutic Parameter: A Key Determinant of Choreographic Structural Style,* was the first study of its type, and has formed the basis for subsequent research projects. Contributor of occasional pieces to a variety of publications in the field. **Essays:** Dalman; Meryl Tankard Australian Dance Theatre; Murphy.

ELLISON, Teren Damato. Ballet and jazz dance performer and teacher. Trained in classical ballet at an early age, spent her youth performing with the San Diego Civic Youth Ballet in numerous featured roles; worked in local summer stock productions; featured dancer with California Ballet Company for two years. Master's degree in dance history and criticism, 1995; studied jazz, tap and pantomime in Los Angeles; worked in stage, film, and television with choreographers Roland Dupree and Ron Field, among others. Taught extensively in the Los Angeles area, and at the University of New Mexico. Currently writing a book on the multicultural legacy of jazz dance technique. **Essays:** Beatty, Talley; *Congo Tango Palace.*

ERDMAN, Joan. Professor of anthropology at Columbia College, Chicago, and research associate in the Committee on South Asian Studies at the University of Chicago. Author of the book *Stages: The Art and Adventures of Zohra Segal.* **Essays:** India; Shankar.

FELCIANO, Rita. Dance critic, *San Francisco Bay Guardian;* correspondent for *Dance Magazine* and *Dance View Magazine.* Contributor to periodicals, including *Ballet Review, Los Angeles Times, San Francisco Chronicle, San Francisco Examiner, Dance Now, Dance International, Dance USA/Journal,* and *Dance Connection;*

also contributor of the entry on Romeo and Juliet in *Encyclopedia of Dance,* Oxford Unversity Press. **Essays:** Bausch; *Cry;* de Keersmaeker; *Games;* Linke; Marin; ODC/San Francisco; Vandekeybus.

GARLAND, Iris. Independent choreographer; currently engaged in applications of telelearning to the university dance curriculum. Professor of dance and founder of the dance program, Simon Fraser University, Burnaby, British Columbia. Research about Tórtola Valencia has been presented at conferences of the Society for Dance History Scholars, Toronto, 1995, and Congress on Research in Dance, Miami, 1995. Author of *Border Tensions: Dance and Discourse,* University of Surrey, 1995; also author of "Early Modern Dance in Spain: Tórtola Valencia, Dancer of the Historical Intuition," *Dance Research Journal,* Fall 1997. **Essays:** Valencia; Webb.

GASTINEAU, Janine. Freelance writer. **Essays:** Parsons; Pucci.

GELERNTER, Judith. Librarian and archivist, Dance Notation Bureau, New York City from 1995-97. Library director and art curator for the Union Club, New York City. Writes about contemporary and historical dance; reviewer, *Dance Research Journal.* Editor, *Channels,* the World Dance Alliance Americas Center Newsletter, 1995-96. **Essays:** *The Shakers;* White Oak Dance Project.

GIERSDORF, Jens Richard. Currently writing dissertation in dance history and theory, University of California, Riverside. Research focuses on the creation of an ideal socialist body and the citizens' resistance to the state's surveillance and disciplining. Received Magister in theater theory, dance theory, and music theater theory, College of Performing Arts "Hans Otto," Leipzig, Germany. Contributor of performance reviews, interviews, and articles to *Tanz Aktuell, Morgenpost,* and *DAZ.* **Essay:** Hoyer.

GOLDBERG, RoseLee. Graduate, Courtauld Institute of Art. Pioneered the study of performance art. Director, Royal College of Art Gallery, London; curator of the Kitchen Center for Video, Music and Performance, New York. In 1990, organized "Six Evenings of Performance" as part of New York Museum of Modern Art's exhibition *High and Low: Modern Art and Popular Culture.* Teaches at New York University. Author of *Performance Art from Futurism to the Present,* 1979. Frequent contributor to *Artforum* and other journals. **Essay:** Fenley.

HÀGER, Bengt. Head of the Carina Ari Library. Founder, Stockholm Dance Museum; president of UNESCO's International Dance Council; appointed general secretary, Archives Internationales de la Danse, Paris, 1947. Organized tours for dance companies throughout Scandinavia and other European countries. Founder with Marcel Marceau of a French-Swedish school of mime; administrative director, Cullberg Ballet Company, Sweden's leading modern dance theatre. For 25 years was dance critic and wrote a weekly dance column for the Swedish government's daily paper. Author of several books and scholarly articles. **Essay:** Johansson.

HANSEN, Sophie. Scottish writer, working in administration with contemporary dance companies in London. Worked with dance companies in the Netherlands and Melbourne, Australia. Received the Chris de Marigny Dance Writer's Award, 1997. Writer and reviewer of dance in London. **Essays:** North; Smith, Janet.

HARRIS, Holly Parke. Graduate student, University of New Mexico. Scholarly preferences are criticism and aesthetic analysis, movement preference is improvisation. **Essay:** Gordon.

HARRIS, Joanna Gewertz. Ph.D.; dancer, choreographer, teacher, therapist, dance historian, and dance critic. Taught at University of California, Berkeley, Santa Cruz, California State University, Hayward, and Sonoma State; currently member of faculty, Center for Psychological Studies, Albany, Modern Dance Center, Berkeley. Adviser, Isadora Duncan Awards Committee (the "Izzies"), San Francisco. Contributor and editor of *IMPULSE* magazine and *American Journal of Dance Therapy.* **Essay:** New Dance Group.

HARRIS, Kristin M. M.A. in dance history and ethnology, York University, 1997; currently pursuing Ph.D. in folklore, Memorial University of Newfoundland. Current research interests include Bournonville, liturgical dance, feminism in the arts, and the integration of folklore and dance. **Essays:** *Frontier;* Music for Modern Dance.

HATHAWAY, Dawn. Currently undertaking an M.A. in aesthetics at Sussex University, where she is pursuing a philosophical enquiry into the nature of the visual arts, specifically dance performance. Freelance dance writer based in London. Regular contributor, *Ballet International.* **Essay:** Baldwin.

HOWE-BECK, Linda. Career journalist following the development of Montreal dance for 25 years; dance critic, *The Gazette,* Montreal; contributor of articles on dance and general topics for various international periodicals. **Essays:** Gillis; Lock.

HUSSIE-TAYLOR, J. Freelance writer, journalist, and curator living in Boulder, Colorado. Former artistic director, Colorado Dance Festival; currently artistic director, Theater at the Boulder Museum of Contemporary Art. Currently writing book entitled, *Women of the Wild Isle: Contemporary Irish Women Artists.* **Essay:** Zollar.

HUTERA, Donald. Writer about the arts and travel since 1977. Co-author, with Allen Robertson, of *The Dance Handbook,* Dance Books, London, 1998. Contributor to numerous periodicals in the U.S. and U.K., including *New York Times, Los Angeles Times, Times, Time Out Magazine* (London)*, The Scotsman, Dance Now,* and *Dance Europe.* **Essays:** Anderson, Lea; Bournew; Chisenhale Dance Space; Clark, Michael; Newson; The Place.

INGBER, Judith Brin. Member of faculty, University of Minnesota's Department of Theatre Arts and Dance. Member of New York staff as assistant to editors, Lydia Joel and Doris Hering, *Dance Magazine.* Author of the *Dance Perspectives* monograph, "Shorashim: Roots of Israel Folk Dance." Contributor of articles on Gertrud Kraus, dance in Israel, and dance in Minnesota to *Dance Magazine,* and of articles to *International Encyclopedia of Dance,* Oxford University Press. **Essays:** Cohen; Lippincott.

JACKSON, George. Lecturer, writer, and scholar of dance, publishing articles in the *Washington Post, Dance Magazine,* and *Ballet Review.* Member of board of directors, Dance Critics Association. **Essay:** United States.

JACKSON, Naomi. B.A., McGill University, M.A., University of Surrey in England; completed Ph.D. in performance studies,

New York University, 1997. Assistant professor of dance, Arizona State University. Presented papers at numerous conferences since 1990; contributor to *Dance Research Journal, Dance Connection,* and *Dance Research.* Currently writing a book on the history of dance at the 92nd Street Y in New York. Specializations include dance history, theory notation, and Jewish studies. **Essay:** *The Beloved.*

JONES, Chris. Freelance dance editor and researcher currently based in England. **Essays:** Burrows; Butcher.

JÓNSDÓTTIR, Ragna Sara. Icelandic dancer and freelance writer. Trained as an anthropologist; has researched dance in different cultures. Writes about dance occasionally for *Dance Europe* (Britain) and regularly for *Morgunblaoio* (Iceland). **Essays:** Iceland; Valgeirsdóttir.

JORDAN, Susan. Has had an extensive career in dance with first professional engagements as a child. Initially trained in ballet and performed professionally with the New Zealand Ballet Company; retrained in modern dance. In 1981 received Arts Council support to study at American University Washington, D.C., graduating with M.A. in dance in 1982. Professional career as a choreographer commenced in 1976; received numerous project grants for choreography for her own company and as a freelance artist. Currently head of the dance programme at the University of Auckland. **Essays:** Footnote Dance Company; Impulse Dance Theatre; New Zealand.

KEEFE, Maura. M.F.A. in dance from Smith College; currently working on her PhD. in dance history and theory at University of California, Riverside. Dissertation research explores the strategies contemporary U.S. choreographers employ when working with spoken text in their work. Dancer and choreographer in Riverside. Member of audience enrichment staff as a scholar-in-residence at Jacob's Pillow. Contributor of interview with Mark Morris to *Salmagundi,* Winter 1994/95. **Essay:** Mumaw.

KERR-BERRY, Julie A. Associate professor of dance, coordinator of the dance program, and artistic director of the Mankato State University Dance Ensemble, Mankato State University, Mankato, Minnesota. Scholarly interests focus on African American dance history, dance ethnology, performance studies, world dance, and cross-cultural aesthetics. **Essay:** *Strange Fruit.*

KHAN, Naseem. Trained in South Indian classical dance. Freelance journalist and critic; arts administrator. Co-director of London's Academy of Indian Dance and Theatre. Editor of magazine, *Time Out.* Senior policy officer for cultural diversity responsible for reshaping national policy, Arts Council of England. **Essay:** Chandralekha.

KIM Kyong-ae. Korean dance critic. Producer, National Theatre of Korea, 1984. Chief editor, monthly magazine, *Korean Drama,* 1981; editor, *CHOOM,* since 1986. Contributor of reviews, *Joining and Looking On,* Yureum Publishing, 1990, *Confrontation and Cooperation,* Seoul Scope Publishing, 1996, and *Acclaim and Criticism,* Seoul Scope Publishing, 1996. Author of series "Dancers's Graves of the World," for *CHOOM,* since 1994. **Essay:** Korea.

KLOOSS, Helma. Producer, Danskaravan, a multicultural dance festival. Dance critic, *Haagsche Courant;* Dutch correspondent, *Dance Magazine.* **Essays:** de Châtel; Galili; Leine & Roebana.

KNIGHT, Judson. Freelance writer in Atlanta; ghostwriter and editor of number of books. Operates, with wife, the Knight Agency, a firm specializing in literary sales and marketing. **Essays:** 92nd Street YM-YWHA; *Deaths and Entrances*; Driver; Hauser; Horta; *Lynchtown*; Mertz; Nagrin; *Nightwandering*; Palucca; Philadanco; *Tent*; Thompson; Uris; Varone; Warren; *Winterbranch*; Wong.

KOPP, Leslie Hansen. Executive director of Preserve, Inc., and editor/publisher of *afterimages*, the quarterly journal of performing arts documentation and preservation; author of *Dance Archives: A Practical Manual for Documenting and Preserving the Ephemeral Art*, which received the 1996 Arline Custer Award from the Mid-Atlantic Regional Archives Conference. Also serves as archives preservation consultant to numerous organizations and was specialist researcher for the study "Images of American Dance," sponsored by the National Endowment for the Arts and the Andrew W. Mellon Foundation. **Essay:** Preservation of Modern Dance.

KOURLAS, Gia. Dance editor weekly magazine, *Time Out New York.* Contributor to *Dance Magazine, Vogue, New York, Allure,* and *New York Times.* **Essays:** Brown, Ronald K.; Ping Chong; de Jong.

KOWAL, Rebekah. Ph.D. candidate in American studies, New York University; dissertation, *Insect and Heroes: Modern Dance, New York, and the Cold War,* examines the counter-narrative turn in dance during the 1950s and early 1960s. Dancer. **Essays:** Dunn; Greenberg.

KRAUT, Anthea. B.A., Carleton College; currently pursuing a Ph.D. in theatre and drama, Northwestern University. **Essays:** Brown, Carolyn; Clarke; Erkert; Hubbard Street Dance Chicago.

KUMIN, Laura. Master's degree in arts administration, Complutense University, 1996. Arts administrator, producer, writer, and dance teacher; former dancer. Founding director of dance department, Madrid Regional Arts Council, 1989-95; co-founder and director, Certamen Coreográfico de Madrid, a platform for new work in Spanish contemporary dance, since 1987. **Essay:** Oller.

KURTZ, Sandra. Teacher of and writer on dance history in Seattle, Washington. **Essay:** Modern Dance and Classical Ballet.

LEWIS, Darcy. Accomplished violist and architectural historian, with abiding interest in the arts in all their forms. Award-winning freelance writer based in Riverside, Illinois. Contributor to a variety of magazines and newspapers, including *Chicago Tribune* and *Strings Magazine.* **Essay:** Tamiris.

LEWIS-FERGUSON, Julinda. Dance critic and writer, for twenty years. Elementary school teacher, dancer, and choreographer with the Ayinde Dance Ensemble of St. Paul's Baptist Church. Member of panel, New York State Council on the Arts, National Endowment for the Arts, and Arts Midwest, Minneapolis. Author of *Alvin Ailey: A Life in Dance;* editor of *Black Choreographers Moving: A National Dialogue.* Contributor to *Dance Magazine,* and various New York City publications. **Essays:** Fagan; Pomare; Robinson.

LIN, Yatin Christina. M.F.A. in dance from York University, Toronto; graduate student from Taiwan currently pursuing Ph.D. in

dance history and theory, University of California, Riverside. Dance editor, *Performing Arts Review Monthly,* published by National Theatre and Concert Hall, Taipei, Taiwan, 1994-97. **Essays:** Lin Hwai-min; Taiwan.

LIZENBERY, Gregg. Principal dancer with the original Utah Repertory Dance Theater appearing in choreography by José Limón, Anna Sokolow, Donald McKayle, John Butler, Glen Tetley, Matt Mattox, Violas Farber, Ethel Winter, Doris Humphrey, and Jennifer Muller. Co-founder and principal dancer with the Bill Evans Dance Company until 1981. Solo concert tour, *Men Dancing,* a retrospective of men in dance from the 1930s through 1980s. Currently creating an hour-long documentary about Donald McKayle. Associate professor and director and graduate chair of dance program, University of Hawaii at Manoa. **Essay:** McKayle.

LOMAX, Sondra. M.F.A. in dance history/criticism, York University, Toronto. Member of dance faculty teaching ballet technique, University of Texas at Austin, since 1984. Served for six years on the board of directors for Society of Dance History Scholars. Writer on dance for *Austin American Statesman* newspaper and *Dance Magazine.* **Essay:** Sharir.

MALLETT, Daryl F. Freelance writer, editor, actor, and founder/owner of Angel Enterprises, Jacob's Ladder Books, and Dustbunny Productions. Author of and contributor to numerous publications, including "Tongue-Tied: Bubo's Tale," in *Star Wars: Tales from Jabba's Palace,* Bantam Books, 1996, and the storyline from the two-part *Star Trek: The Next Generation* episode "Birthright" (with Barbara Wallace, Arthur Loy Holcomb, and George Brozak). Currently working on numerous projects; forthcoming books include *Reginald's Science Fiction and Fantasy Awards, Fourth Edition,* Borgo Press, and *Pilgrims and Pioneers: The History and Speeches of the Science Fiction Research Association Award Winners,* SFRA Press. **Essays:** Bodenwieser; Byrd; Ezralow; Gottschild; *Griot New York;* Pulvermacher; Sanasardo.

MAN, Michelle. Freelance writer; contributor of numerous articles on dance to various periodicals. **Essays:** Mal Pelo; Provisional Danza.

MANN, Lisa Anderson. Writer in northern California, specializing in articles and advertising copywriting. **Essays:** Forti; Hodes.

MANOR, Giora. Member of kibbutz Mishmar Haemek. Studied theater in London. Producer of plays for the stage, television, and radio. Israeli correspondent of *Ballett international/tanz aktuell* in Berlin. Dance critic and editor-in-chief of *Israel Dance Quarterly,* since 1970. Author of several books about dance. **Essays:** Bat-Dor Dance Company; Batsheva Dance Company; Inbal Dance Theatre; Israel; Kibbutz Contemporary Dance Company; Koldemama Dance Company; Kraus; Liat Dror & Nir Ben-Gal Dance Company.

MARCOTTY, Fiona. Independent New York-based choreographer, and international and national performer. Director of aesthetic development programs, the Field, an arts service organization for independent artists in Manhattan. **Essays:** Childs; Schönberg.

MATHIEU, Murielle. M.S., INSA LYON, France, B.A. in dance, Pierre Mendes-France University of Grenoble, and M.A., Dauphine University, Paris. Choreographer, Rainbow Company. Awarded second prize, European Art Festival of Dijon, France, 1991. Member of transdisciplinary team conducting research on European symbolism and culture. **Essays:** Andrews; Bagouet; Buirge; Nadj; Preljocaj; Robinson.

McCLELLAN, Lodi. B.A. in dance, Mt. Holyoke College, and M.F.A. in dance, University of Washington. Taught ballet and modern technique at numerous colleges, universities, and at many private studios on both coasts. Member of faculty, American Dance Institute and Cornish College of Performing Arts. Artist-in-residence, Massachusetts Institute of Technology, for three years. Freelance dance writer, *Seattle Weekly, Eastside Week,* and *Dance International*; contributing editor, *DanceNet*. **Essays:** Carlson; *Dreams*; Komar; *Water Study*.

McDONAGH, Don. Author of *The Complete Guide to Modern Dance* and *Martha Graham: A Biography.* Author of dance column, *Dance Magazine.* Currently co-authoring a collection of interviews with people who knew and worked with Martha Graham.

McMANUS, Donald. Ph.D. in theatre studies, University of Michigan. Actor, director, and clown. **Essay:** Goslar.

MILLER, Judi. Studied dance at Julliard School of Music and with Martha Graham Company. Author of several books. **Essay:** Duncan, Isadora.

MINDEROVIC, Christine Miner. Studied various forms of dance for several years. Performer and teacher of dance in Detroit area; freelance writer. **Essays:** Alum; Bauman; Cage; Cunningham, Merce; Dance Theatre Workshop; Dunham; Garth; Louis; Nikolais; Rauschenberg.

MOYANO, Marcelo Isse. M.A. from University of Buenos Aires. Associate professor in dance theory, dance delegate to Argentine Center of the International Theater Institute, and director of the Dance Project of the Research Institute of the Performing Arts, University of Buenos Aires. Author of three books; contributor of articles. **Essays:** Cervera; Tambutti.

MURPHY, Ann. Former dancer; dance critic and writer for *East Bay Express, Oakland Tribune,* and *Dance Magazine.* Contributor to national and international publications. **Essays:** Hoving; Mann; Van Tuyl.

MURPHY, Paula. Librarian and researcher, Dominican University; archivist, Doris Humphrey Society and Ruth Page Foundation. Member of American Library Association, especially active in its ACRL arts section. **Essays:** Page; Photography and Modern Dance.

ODOM, Selma. Teacher of dance and women's studies, York University, Toronto. Research focuses on dance, music, education, and gender in the 19th and 20th centuries.

O'NEILL, Kate. Writer on dance and theater, *Lansing State Journal,* Lansing, Michigan; Michigan correspondent, *Dance Magazine.* Editor, *Dance Education in Michigan; Recollections of Three Pioneers: Grade Ryan, Ruth Murray and Fannie Aronson.* **Essays:** Nowak; Sparling.

OU Jian-ping. Professor of dance; director of foreign dance studies, Dance Research Institute, China National Arts Academy. Committee member of All-China Youth Federation. China correspondent for *Dance Magazine;* advisor to *International Encyclopedia of Dance,* Oxford University Press. **Essays:** Dai Ai-lian; Guangdong Modern Dance Company; Wu Xiao-bang.

OWEN, Norton. Institute director, José Limón Foundation; director of preservation, Jacob's Pillow Dance Festival. Curator of many exhibitions, National Museum of Dance, Saratoga Springs, New York. Author of *A Certain Place: The Jacob's Pillow Story;* contributor of numerous articles to *Dance Magazine, Performing Arts Resources,* and other periodicals. **Essays:** Jacob's Pillow Dance Festival; José Limón Dance Foundation.

PEPPER, Kaija. B.A. in communication arts, magna cum laude, Concordia University; currently completing masters program in liberal studies, Simon Fraser University. Writer of quarterly, "View from Vancouver" *Dance International;* editor, Vancouver Dance Centre's monthly newsletter, a forum for the exchange of news, ideas, and personal storytelling from the province's dance community. **Essays:** EDAM Performing Arts Society; Mascall; Wyman.

PEREZ, Guillermo. Native of Cuba, grew up in Miami; Ph.D. specializing in Latin American theater, University of Florida. Currently teaches dance criticism at the New World School of the Arts in Miami. South Florida correspondent, *Dance Magazine,* since 1989; reviewer of dance, Fort Lauderdale *Sun Sentinel.* Contributor to other publications. **Essay:** Contact Improvisation.

PERRON, Wendy. Dancer, choreographer, teacher, writer, and researcher; see entry. **Essay:** Judson Dance Theater.

PONCE GUTIERREZ, Dolores. Bachelor's degree in sociology, National Autonomous University of Mexico, master's degree in social science, and Ph.D. in modern literature, Iberoamerican University. Mexican social science and dance researcher. Researcher and translator, Dance Research, Documentation and Information National Center "José Limón" of the National Institute of Fine Arts. Social science analyst; author of many books and articles on art and social sciences. **Essays:** (as translator) Arriaga; Bravo; Campobello; Fandiño; Flores Canelo; Franco; Lavalle; Mexico; Reyna.

PONZIO, Barbejoy A. Master's degree in theatre and dance with a major emphasis in dance history and criticism, University of New Mexico. Teacher of dance appreciation courses, University of New Mexico, Paradise Valley Community College, Phoenix State University, and Arizona State University, Tempe, Arizona. Initiated and implemented dance programs into the physical education departments at five secondary schools in the United States, American School in Kinshasa, Zaire, and the Fine and Performing Arts Department, Cairo American College, Cairo, Egypt. **Essays:** Daniel; Fusion in Modern Dance.

PREDOCK-LINNELL, Jennifer. Ph.D. and professor of dance, University of New Mexico. Awarded NEA choreographic fellowships and research and new creative works grants, University of New Mexico and the State of New Mexico. Dance works have been performed in the United States, Australia, France, Israel, and New Zealand. Current research includes contemporary dance in Mexico and educational theories of the creative process. Contributor of article, "Standing Aside and Making Space: Mentoring Student Choreographers," *Impulse,* July 1996; also contributor of articles to *50 Contemporary Choreographers,* and *Dance: Current Selected Research,* volume 5. **Essays:** Goode; Marshall.

PRESTON-DUNLOP, Valerie. Dip. Ed., M.A., and Ph.D. Advisor for postgraduate studies and research, Laban Centre for Movement and Dance, London, with responsibility for doctoral supervision. Internationally known practitioner, especially on choreological perspectives for choreographers. Writer on dance, especially on the life and work of Rudolf Laban, on methods of dance analysis, and on education in dance. **Essays:** Choreological Studies; Laban.

PRICKETT, Stacey. M.A. and Ph.D. with dissertations on the American revolutionary dance movement of the 1920s and 1930s, Laban Centre for Movement and Dance, London, England. Guest lecturer, University of California, Berkeley; part-time lecturer on dance, Sonoma State University, California. Contributor of chapter, *Dance in the City,* edited by Helen Thomas; also contributor of reviews and articles to *Studies in Dance History, Dance Research, Dance Theatre Journal,* and *Dance View.* **Essay:** Primus.

PRITCHARD, Jane. Archivist for Rambert Dance Company, English National Ballet, and the Place, home to the London School of Contemporary Dance and formerly to the London Contemporary Dance Theatre Group. **Essays:** Cohan; London Contemporary Dance Theatre; Rambert Dance Company.

RAUGUST, Karen. Minneapolis-based freelance writer and consultant specializing in entertainment, business, and the arts. Author of several nonfiction books and reports. Contributor to variety of trade and consumer magazines. **Essays:** Anthony; Bales; Bromberg; Butler; Davis, Chuck; Dean; Dove; Draper; Eiko & Koma; Eilber; Falco; Foreman; Gamson; Georgi; The Grand Union; Harper; Jenkins; Jooss; King, Kenneth; King, Eleanor; Kreutzberg; Lamhut; McGehee; MoMing Dance & Arts Center; Momix; Monte; Moore; Morris, Robert; Pendleton; Posin; Rainer; Redlich; Self; Wood; Yuriko; Zamir.

ROHMAN, Carrie. Currently doctoral student in English, Indiana University, where her research investigates the discourse of animality in British modernist fiction. Performer, choreographer, and teacher of modern dance, University of Dayton Dance Ensemble; member of Windfall Dancers, a small performing company in Bloomington, Indiana. **Essays:** *Appalachian Spring; Clytemnestra.*

ROSENBERG, Douglas. Assistant professor at the University of Wisconsin-Madison. Has worked in field of dance/video since early 1980s; director of Video Archival Program, American Dance Festival, since 1987. Independent producer/director and scholar of dance for the camera, working with numerous choreographers and dance companies including, Pilobolus, Erick Hawkins, Bill T. Jones/Arnie Zane Co., Eiko and Koma, Molissa Fenley, Li Chiao-Ping, and others. Awarded numerous grants and awards, including Southeast Media fellowship, Izzie Award, and Independent Production Fund Video Project grant. Currently writing a book on dance for the camera. **Essays:** Film, Video, and Dance; Technology and Modern Dance.

ROSES-THEMA, Cynthia. B.F.A. in dance, University of Cincinnati. Professional dancer since age 17; principal ballerina with the Chicago and Cincinnati Ballet Companies creating over 50 roles for stage and screen. Artistic director of the Studio Center for Excellence in Dance and Photography and the Nokomis Dance Ensemble. Dance writer/critic, *Sarasota Herald-Tribune* and *Dance Answer Wizard* on AOL's Culturefinder website. Contributor of articles and critiques, *Dance Magazine* and *Dance Teacher Now.* **Essays:** Brown, Trisha; Butoh; Koner; Truitte.

ROY, Sanjoy. Director of Dance Books; freelance writer and critic on contemporary dance. Co-editor, *Dance Now.* **Essays:** Davies; Jeyasingh.

RUBIDGE, Sarah. Lecturer and writer on dance based in the United Kingdom. Former head of M.A. in dance studies, Laban Centre. Works with British contemporary choreographers and contributes to the dissemination of their work through writings since the early 1980s. **Essays:** Alston; Spink.

RUGGIERO, Adriane. Freelance editor and writer, specializing in nonfiction; areas of interest include history, biography, and international affairs. Author of *The Baltic Countries: Estonia, Latvia, and Lithuania,* 1997. **Essays:** Bull; Capucilli; Costume Design; Cummings; Cunningham, James; de Lavallade; Erdman; *Esplanade*; Jones, Betty; *La Malinche*; Lang; Leeder; Litz; Mabry; Meehan; Novack; Reitz; Ross; Sydney Dance Company; Tankard; *Trend*; Trisler; Van Dyke; York; Züllig.

SAGOLOA, Lisa Jo. Ed.D.; teacher of dance, Columbia University, Marymount Manhattan College, and Dance Theatre of Harlem. Choreographer of more than 75 productions of Off-Broadway, regional, summer stock, and university theatres. Author of dance criticism for *Backstage;* currently writing a biography of the dancer-actress Joan McCracken. Contributor of articles to journals and encyclopedia entries on dance and musical theatre as well as curriculum and assessment reports on the arts in education. **Essay:** Sartorio.

SCARRY, Siobhán. Former dancer, freelance editor, and writer based in San Francisco. **Essays:** Graham; *Lamentation*; Taylor.

SCHEEDER, Louis. Teacher, director, and founder of Classical Studio, New York University. **Essay:** Set and Lighting Design for Modern Dance.

SCHNEIDER, Katja. M.A. and Ph.D.; studied modern German literature, theatre science, and philosophy. Freelance dance critic. **Essay:** Goldin.

SERVOS, Norbert. Free-lance writer and choreographer since 1983. Artistic director, TanzLabor Berlin, Academy of Arts, Berlin. Former guest teacher and choreographer in Germany and abroad. Co-founder and member of editorial board, *Ballett International.* Author of several books on Pina Bausch; also author of poetry. **Essays:** Bohner; Tanztheater.

SHARY, Rhonda. Writer and development consultant for the arts, environment, and education, living in Brooklyn, New York. Administrator, Dan Wagoner Dance Foundation/Dan Wagoner and Dancers, 1984-89. **Essay:** Wagoner.

SICHEL, Adrienne. B.A. in speech and drama, University of Natal, Durban. South-African born journalist specialising in dance and theatre. Writer, *Tonight,* a daily entertainment supplement of *The Star* newspaper in Johannesburg, since 1983. **Essay:** Jazzart Dance Theatre.

SIMPSON, Herbert L. Ph.D. in English from University of Maryland and Ph.D. in theater arts from Carnegie-Mellon University. Associate professor of English, State University of New York at Geneseo. Member of Dance Critics Association and American Theater Critics Association. Contributor of articles and reviews to a variety of publications. **Essay:** Bettis.

SIMPSON, Michael Wade. M.F.A., Smith College, 1994. Covered Jacob's Pillow for Boston newspapers while in graduate school. Dancer in New York and Boston; founder of community-based dance company, Newburyport, Massachusetts. Currently lives in San Francisco and is working on his second novel. **Essay:** Jones and Zane.

SMITH, Deborah Lothrop Breen. M.F.A., University of California, Irvine; B.A. in Spanish literature, Stanford University. Authorized biographer, Waldeen von Falkenstein; executive director and former soloist, Wing & A Prayer Dance Company, an intergenerational contemporary dance company, Reno, Nevada. Former assistant director and soloist, International Folkloric Ballet. **Essay:** Waldeen.

SOARES, Janet Mansfield. B.S., Julliard School; M.A. and Ed.D. from Columbia University. Chair of dance department, Barnard College. Author of *Louis Horst: Musician in a Dancer's World,* 1992. **Essay:** Fonaroff.

STANTON, Diana. M.F.A. in dance, University of Colorado, Boulder, 1997. Dance teacher, choreographer, and bodyworker. **Essays:** Lemon; Skaggs; Weber.

STÒCKEMANN, Patricia. Ph.D.; educated as a dance pedagogue; studied musicology and theatre science. Lecturer of dance history and dance theory at Folkwang-Hochschule, Essen, and University of Hamburg. Editor, *Tanzdrama.* Writer on modern dance. **Essays:** Dietrich; Folkwang Hochschule.

STROW, Mary. B.S. and M.S. in dance. Librarian for reference services, Undergraduate Library, Indiana University at Bloomington. Teacher of modern dance, university level, for 14 years. Author of *Research in Dance: A Guide to Resources,* 1995. **Essay:** Gray.

SZPORER, Philip. Dance writer, broadcaster, and lecturer based in Montreal. Author of dance column, *HOUR,* Montreal; contributor to numerous periodicals, including *Dance Connection, Montreal Gazette, Village Voice,* and *Globe and Mail.* **Essays:** Canada Dance Festival; Chouinard; Fortier.

TARR, Patricia. Member of board, Cunningham Dance Foundation; president, Dance Ink Foundation. Editor of *Dance Ink Photographs,* 1997.

TEMBECK, Iro Valaskakis. Ph.D. and former dancer, teacher, and choreographer with several Montreal-based companies. Professor and historian in the dance department and head of the masters' programme, Universite du Quebec a Montreal. Author of *Danser a Montreal: Germination d'une histoire choregraphique,* 1991, translated as *Dancing in Montreal: Seeds of a Choreographic History.* Awarded CORD award for Outstanding Publication, 1996, for *Dancing in Montreal.* **Essays:** Groupe de la Place Royale; Groupe Nouvelle Aire; Rabin.

THOMAS-CLARKE, Kristen. B.A. from Haverford College; master's degree in political science from University of Wisconsin at Madison; master's degree in library science from Rutgers University. Reference librarian, Immaculata College, Pennsylvania. **Essays:** Hay; Hill.

TOEPFER, Karl. Professor of theatre arts, San José State University. Author of *The Voice of Rapture,* 1991, *Theatre, Aristocracy, and Pornocracy,* 1991, and *Empire of Ecstasy: Nudity and Movement in German Body Culture, 1910-1935,* 1997. Contributor of over twenty articles in scholarly performance journals. Currently, working on a book on ancient Roman dance culture, *Idolized Bodies.* **Essay:** Germany.

TORTAJADA QUIROZ, Margarita. Bachelor's degree in political science, Politics and Social Science Faculty, National Autonomous University of Mexico; master's degree in artistic education and research, National Institute of Fine Arts; and Ph.D. in social sciences, Metropolitan Autonomous University. Studied dance at Mexican Dance Academy, 1969. Dance researcher and Mexican dancer. Research coordinator, Dance Research, Documentation, and Information National Center "José Limón" of the National Institute of Fine Arts. Member of various contemporary dance groups. Author of *Danza y poder,* 1995, and *Mujeres de danza combativa,* 1997; also contributor of many articles on dance. **Essays:** Arriaga; Bravo; Campobello; Fandiño; Flores Canelo; Franco; Lavalle; Mexico; Reyna.

UENO, Sako. Instructor in dance history, Meiji University, Tokyo. Freelance dance critic in Tokyo; regular contributor to *Dance Magazine* and *Asahi Evening News,* an English-language daily paper published in Tokyo. **Essays:** Gendai Buyo Kyokai; Japan; Teshigawara.

VACHON, Ann. Performer with José Limón Dance Company, 1958-75; reconstructed several historic Limón and Humphrey works for her Philadelphia-based company, Dance Conduit. Member of dance faculty, Temple University, since 1978. Currently producing a documentary film on the life and work of José Limón. **Essay:** Limón.

VOGRIN, Valerie. Freelance writer living and working in Olympia, Washington. **Essays:** Bennington School of Dance; Bird; Evans; Horst; Monk; Neville; Solomons; Weidman.

WARREN, Larry. Professor emeritus, Department of Dance, University of Maryland at College Park. Co-founder and director, Maryland Dance Theater. Author of *Lester Horton: Modern Dance Pioneer,* and *Anna Sokolow: The Rebellious Spirit.* **Essay:** Horton.

WATERMAN, Jill. B.A. in speech and drama, and post graduate dance studies diploma, Laban Center for Movement and Dance, London. Lecturer and teacher in the dance studies program, School of Performance and Media Studies, University of Witwatersrand. Teacher of dance history working on the new learning program for vocational training in dance, National School of the Arts. Dance consultant, Moving into Dance, and at times publicist for its performance. **Essays:** Glasser; Mantsoe; Moving into Dance.

WEST, Martha Ullman. Arts writer based in Portland, Oregon with a special concentration in dance. Contributor to *Dance Magazine* as Oregon correspondent, reviewer, and feature writer, since 1980; also writer on dance for *Oregonian,* the state's newspaper of record, 1988-97, and for a number of Pacific Northwest publications, including *Dance Chronicle.* **Essays:** Fuller; Futurism; Miller; Noguchi; Rosenthal; Tipton; United States.

WHYTE, Raewyn. M.A. in dance criticism, Simon Fraser University, Burnaby, B.C., Canada. New Zealand dance writer and educator. Teacher of dance studies, UNITEC School of Performing and Screen Arts and University of Auckland. Host of website "A dance is worth 10,000 words" at <http://url.co.nz/arts/dance.html>. Writer on dance, since 1980; editor of *Dance News,* a national quarterly journal, 1981-86. Contributor to newspapers, magazines, and dance journals in New Zealand, Canada, and Australia; also contributor of column "Dancing on the Web" to periodicals published in New Zealand, Australia, Paraguay, and United States. **Essays:** Commotion Company; Douglas Wright Dance Company; Footnote Dance Company; Jordan & Present Company; Limbs Dance Company.

WINDREICH, Leland. Born in San Francisco and emigrated to Canada in 1961. Introduced to dance through the tours of the Ballet Russes companies in the 1940s; researcher of the careers of Canadian dancers. Writer on dance performances, dance book reviews, critical studies, monographs, profiles, and promotional articles for English-language dance periodicals in the United States, Canada, and the United Kingdom. **Essays:** Marcuse; Strate.

WOODFORD, Charles Humphrey. Publisher, Princeton Book Company, New Jersey. Son of Doris Humphrey. **Essay:** Humphrey.

WROBLE, Lisa A. Freelance writer from Plymouth, Michigan dividing time between employment at the Redford Township District Library and writing nonfiction for children and adults. Member of Society of Children's Book Writers and Illustrators. Author of "Kids throughout History" series for elementary readers. Contributor to *Native American Tribes, Dictionary of Hispanic Biography, Law in Society, Notable Native Americans, Twentieth Century Young Adult Writers,* and *Dictionary of Literary Biography: British Children's Writers.* Contributor, *The ALAN Review.* **Essays:** Dakin; Farber; Hinkson; Lampert; Perron; Schneemann; Setterfield; Waring; Williams.

ZIMMERMAN, Karen. Writing teacher and freelance writer living in Germantown, Maryland. **Essays:** Enters; Faison; Halprin; O'Donnell; Walker.

3M